Webster's
New Young
American
Dictionary

Created in Cooperation with the Editors of
MERRIAM-WEBSTER

SMITHMARK
REFERENCE

This edition published in 1995 by SMITHMARK Publishers, a division of
U.S. Media Holdings, Inc., 16 East 32nd Street, New York, NY 10016.

SMITHMARK books are available for bulk purchase for sales promotion and
premium use. For details write or call the manager of special sales,
SMITHMARK Publishers, 16 East 32nd Street, New York, NY 10016.

Library of Congress Cataloging-in-Publication Data

Webster's new young American dictionary.
    p. cm.
    Updated ed. of: Merriam-Webster's elementary dictionary, © 1994.
    ISBN 0-8317-9166-7
    1. English language—Dictionaries, Juvenile.   I. Merriam-Webster,
Inc.   II. Merriam-Webster's elementary dictionary.
PE1628.5.W56378   1995
423—dc20   95-2040
                                               CIP
                                               AC

Printed in the United States of America

10 9 8 7 6 5 4 3 2

CONTENTS

PREFACE

Webster's New Young American Dictionary is written especially for young students. This dictionary is more advanced than the simple picture dictionaries meant for children who are not in school yet. The definitions are in plain language, yet the dictionary has many of the features of larger dictionaries designed for adults.

Webster's New Young American Dictionary contains the meanings and uses of more than 32,000 words and phrases. In addition, many other kinds of information appear in the dictionary, including common abbreviations, presidents and vice presidents of the United States, Branches of Government, and Geographical names.

Because there are so many different kinds of information and so little space to put it in, the dictionary relies upon different type styles and a number of abbreviations, special words, and symbols, each of which has a special meaning. To get the most from your dictionary, you should carefully read the next section, Using Your Dictionary.

Webster's New Young American Dictionary was created in cooperation with the editors of Merriam-Webster Inc., a company that has been publishing dictionaries for nearly 150 years.

USING YOUR DICTIONARY

1. Main Entry Words

When you open your dictionary to any page, you will find a list of words down the left-hand side of each column printed in heavy black type called **boldface**. Each of these is followed by information that explains or tells something about the word. The boldface word or phrase together with the explanation is a **dictionary entry,** and the boldface word itself is the **entry word** or **main entry.**

s \'es\ *n, pl* **s's** *or* **ss** \'es-əz\ *often cap* **1** : the nineteenth letter of the English alphabet **2** : a grade rating a student's work as satisfactory

²**-s** *vb suffix* — used to form the third person singular present of most verbs that do not end in *s, z, sh, ch,* or *y* following a consonant ⟨fall*s*⟩ ⟨take*s*⟩ ⟨play*s*⟩

sa·ber–toothed tiger \ˌsā-bər-ˌtütht-\ *n* : a very large prehistoric cat with long sharp curved eyeteeth

²**safe** *n* : a metal chest for keeping something (as money) safe

¹**safe·guard** \'sāf-ˌgärd\ *n* : something that protects and gives safety

safety pin *n* : a pin that is bent back on itself to form a spring and has a guard that covers the point

The main entry may take many forms. It may be a single letter like **s** or a single word like **safe.** It may also be a compound made up of two or more words written together (**safeguard**) or as separate words (**safety pin**) or with a hyphen (**saber–toothed tiger**). Sometimes an entry will be made up of all capital letters (**IOU** or **TV**) or of a letter and number (**A1**) or even of a letter and a word (**T–shirt**).

Finally some entries are only parts of words. The entry **-s** is one of these, and the entries **bi-** and **-graph,** shown below, are two more examples. Such entries all begin or end with a hyphen. They are the building blocks of our language, for they are used to create many new words.

bi- *prefix* **1** : two **2** : coming or occurring every two **3** : into two parts ⟨*bi*sect⟩ **4** : twice : doubly : on both sides

-graph \ˌgraf\ *n suffix* **1** : something written **2** : instrument for making or sending records ⟨tele*graph*⟩

For example, **bi-** ("two") when combined with **cycle** gives us **bicycle** (literally "two wheels"). The word part **-graph** ("something written") combines with other word parts to give us such words as **autograph** and **paragraph.** The hyphen with the entry word is only there to show you where the word part is attached to other word parts. The entry **bi-** goes at the beginning of a word and is called a **prefix.** The entry **-graph** goes at the end of a word and is called a **suffix.**

All of the words in this dictionary are arranged in alphabetical order. To find a word, you simply look it up by the way it is spelled.

Now when we arrange words in alphabetical order, we do not count spaces or hyphens between words. The words are arranged just as if the space or hyphen were not there. So you will find these words that begin **doub-** arranged in the dictionary in just the order you see them here.

⁴**double** *vb* . . .
dou·ble bass \ˌdəb-əl-'bās\ *n* . . .
dou·ble–cross \ˌdəb-əl-'kròs\ *vb* . . .
dou·ble·head·er \ˌdəb-əl-'hed-ər\ *n* . . .

Some of the main entries in this dictionary are groups of letters that are not pronounced like ordinary words. But these entries, such as **DDT** and **TV,** are used like words, and they are arranged among the other words using the same rule of alphabetical order. Thus you will find **TV** between **tutor** and **twaddle.**

Whenever the main entry has a number in it, like **A1,** it is arranged as if the number were spelled out. You will find **A1** between the words **anywise** and **aorta** as if it were spelled **A one.**

2. End-of-Line Divisions

Most of the entry words in the dictionary are shown with dots at different places in the word. These dots are there to show you where you can put a hyphen if you have to break up a word because there is room for only part of it at the end of a line.

sat·is·fac·tion \ˌsat-əs-ˈfak-shən\ *n* **1** : the act of satisfying : the condition of being satisfied **2** : something that satisfies

In the example shown above, the word is normally written **satisfaction,** but if you have to divide it at the end of a line, the dots show you three places where you can put a hyphen.

sat-
isfaction

satis-
faction

satisfac-
tion

Words should not be divided so that only one letter comes at the end of a line or at the beginning of the next line.

End-of-line divisions do not always separate the syllables of a word. Syllables are shown only in the pronunciation, explained in the next section.

When two or more main entries have the same spelling and the same end-of-line divisions, the dots are shown only in the first of these entries.

3. Pronunciation Symbols

In order to show the pronunciations of words in this book, we use special **pronunciation symbols.** Each pronunciation symbol stands for one sound in English. Most of the symbols look like letters of the regular alphabet. However, do not think of pronunciation symbols as letters. Learn the sound each symbol stands for. When you see a symbol, think of its sound. Pronunciation symbols are always written between slant lines \ˌlīk-ˈthis\ so you will know that they are not regular letters. To see how a pronunciation is given in an actual entry, look at the example **saunter** here.

saun·ter \ˈsȯnt-ər\ *vb* : to walk in a slow relaxed way : STROLL

A list of all the pronunciation symbols is printed in the front of this dictionary. A shorter list is printed at the bottom of the right-hand column of every right-hand page in the dictionary. In both lists the symbols are followed by words containing the sound of each symbol. The boldface letters in these words stand for the same sound as the symbol. If you say the sample word in your regular voice, you will hear the sound that the symbol stands for.

We use hyphens with the pronunciation symbols to show the syllables of a word, as in these examples.

beast \ˈbēst\ *n* . . .
  (1 syllable)
bed·side \ˈbed-ˌsīd\ *n* . . .
  (2 syllables)
¹cast·away \ˈkas-tə-ˌwā\ *adj* . . .
  (3 syllables)
op·ti·mism \ˈäp-tə-ˌmiz-əm\ *n* . . .
  (4 syllables)

Notice in the last two examples given above, **castaway** and **optimism,** that the number and position of the hyphens are not the same as the number and position of the dots in the entry words. These dots are meant to show where you can put a hyphen if you have to break a word at the end of a line. They are not meant to show the syllables in the word.

Some syllables of a word are spoken with greater force, or **stress,** than others. Two kinds of stress are marked in this dictionary. **Primary stress,** or **strong stress,** is shown by a high mark \ˈ\ placed *before* the syllable of a word that is spoken with the greatest force. **Secondary stress,** or **medium stress,** is shown by a low mark \ˌ\ before a syllable. Syllables that have no marks are spoken with weak stress. Each of these kinds of stress is shown in the pronunciation for **penmanship.**

pen·man·ship \ˈpen-mən-ˌship\ *n* ...

The first syllable has primary stress. The second syllable has weak stress. The third syllable has secondary stress. If you say the word to yourself, you will hear each kind of stress.

Many words are pronounced in two, three, or even more differnt ways. Two or more pronunciations for an entry are separated by commas. Look at the example **ration.**

¹ra·tion \ˈrash-ən, ˈrā-shən\ *n* ...

The order in which different pronunciations are given does not mean that the pronunciation placed first is somehow better or more correct than the others. All the pronunciations that are shown in your dictionary are used by large numbers of educated people, and you will be correct whichever one you use.

Sometimes when a second or third pronunciation is shown, only the part of the pronunciation that changes will be shown. To get the full second or third pronunciation of a word, just add the part that changes to the part that does not change.

greasy \ˈgrē-sē, -zē\ *adj* ...
pa·ja·mas \pə-ˈjäm-əz, -ˈjam-əz\ *n pl* ...

The second pronunciation of **greasy** is \ˈgrē-zē\ and the second pronunciation of **pajamas** is \pə-ˈjam-əz\.

If two or more entries are spelled the same and have the same pronunciation and end-of-line division, we show the pronunciation only for the first of these entries. Many compound entries are made up of two or three separate words. If we do not show a pronunciation for all or part of such an entry, the missing pronunciation is the same as that for the individual word or words.

When a boldface word appears without a definition at the end of a main entry, sometimes we show only part of the pronunciation. This means the rest of the word is pronounced the same as the main entry.

post·pone \pōst-ˈpōn\ *vb* ... — **post-pone·ment** \-mənt\ *n*

In the example **postpone** the complete pronunciation of **postponement** is \pōst-ˈpōn-mənt\ . Some of these entries will show no pronunciation at all. In these cases the pronunciation of the compound is the same as the pronunciation of the main entry plus the pronunciation of the word ending, which is found at its own alphabetical place in the dictionary.

re·mote \ri-ˈmōt\ *adj* ... — **re·mote·ly** *adv* — **re·mote·ness** *n*

In the example **remote,** the entry **remotely** is pronounced \ri-ˈmōt-lē\ and **remoteness** is pronounced \ri-ˈmōt-nəs\ . The pronunciations \lē\ and \nəs\ are found at the entries for the suffixes **-ly** and **-ness.**

4. Variant Spellings

After the main entry word you may see a second or third spelling, also in boldface type. Aditional spellings are called **variant spellings** or simply **variants.** Sometimes the variant spellings are very similar (**scepter** *or* **sceptre**) and sometimes they are quite different (**catsup** *or* **ketchup**).

scep·ter *or* **scep·tre** \ˈsep-tər\ *n* : a rod carried by a ruler as a sign of authority
cat·sup \ˈkech-əp, ˈkach-əp, ˈkat-səp\ *or* **ketch·up** \ˈkech-əp, ˈkach-\ *n* ...

Variant spellings are usually separated by *or.* The *or* tells you that both spellings are common in good usage. One appears about as often as the other.

Usually we show variants in alphabetical order when one form is not used much more often than another. This is the case with the entries **scepter** *or* **sceptre** and **catsup** *or* **ketchup.** If, however, one form does seem to be preferred, we show that one first. This sometimes means that variants will be out of alphabetical order.

Gyp·sy *or* **Gip·sy** \\'jip-sē\ *n* . . .

In the example **Gypsy** *or* **Gipsy** this is the case, since in strict alphabetical order the **Gipsy** spelling would come first. The order of the variants tells you that the spelling **Gypsy** is used a little more often than **Gipsy.**

Keep in mind that all of the variants shown in this dictionary are correct. However, you should pick one form to use in all of your writing.

Occasionally you will see a variant spelling shown after the word *also.* Look at the example **pea.**

pea \\'pē\ *n, pl* **peas** *also* **pease** . . .

The *also* tells you that the next spelling is much less common in ordinary usage than the first, although it is still a correct spelling.

When variant spellings are shown at the beginning of the entry, all of the variants are used in all meanings. If one variant form is shown at a particular definition, however, that spelling is more common for that meaning.

disk *or* **disc** \\'disk\ *n* **1 :** something that is or appears to be flat and round **2** *usually disc* : a phonograph record — **disk·like** \-ˌlīk\ *adj*

The information at the entry for **disk** *or* **disc** tells you that both spellings are used for both meanings. The form **disk** is more often used for meaning **1** (remember that when variants are not in alphabetical order you know the first one is used more often). The label *usually disc* at meaning **2** tells you that **disc** is more common than **disk** for meaning **2.**

5. Functional Labels

Words are used in many different ways in a sentence. You know, for example, that if a word is used as the name of something (**car, house, rainbow**), it is called a **noun.** If it describes some action or state of being (**run, stand, live**), the word is a **verb.** Words that show a quality of something (**tall, short, fast**) are **adjectives,** and words that tell how, when, or where something happens (**quickly, very, yesterday, here**) are **adverbs. Pronouns (them, you, that)** are words which substitute for nouns, and **conjunctions (and, but, yet)** join two words or groups of words. **Prepositions (to, for, by)** combine with nouns and pronouns to form phrases that answer such questions as where?, how?, and which?, and **interjections (hi, adios, ouch)** stand alone and often show a feeling or a reaction to something rather than a meaning.

To show you how the various entry words are used, or how they function in a sentence, we use **functional labels** before the definitions. These labels are usually abbreviations in slanting type called *italic,* and they come right after the pronunciation—when one is shown—or immediately after the entry word.

sea·coast \\'sē-ˌkōst\ *n* **:** the shore of the sea

The eight most common functions, known as **parts of speech,** are shown in the examples below.

²**cereal** *n* . . .
²**fish** *vb* . . .
hos·tile \\'häst-l\ *adj* . . .
²**just** *adv* . . .
¹**none** \\'nən\ *pron* . . .
³**since** *conj* . . .
²**under** *prep* . . .
⁴**why** \wī, hwī\ *interj* . . .

In addition to these parts of speech, a few other special functional labels are used in this book. The words **the, a,** and **an** are used before nouns to show that a certain one or any one of a certain group is being talked about. Because the word **the** points out a certain one, it is called a **definite article.** The words **a** and **an,** which refer to any one of many, are called **indefinite articles.**

The prefixes and suffixes are also indicated by a functional label. Often it will be combined with a part-of-speech label when the suffix or prefix always makes one kind of word.

-g·ra·phy \g-rə-fē\ *n suffix*

In the example, **-graphy** always combines with other words or word parts to form nouns (**photography, biography**), so its functional label is *noun suffix.*

There are a few special verbs that sometimes are used to help other verbs, such as **may** in a question like "May I go with you?" These special verbs are shown with the italic functional label *helping verb.*

may \mā\ *helping verb, past* **might** \mīt\ *present sing & pl* **may** . . .

6. Homographs

Often you will find two, three, or more main entries that come one after another and are spelled exactly alike.

¹**seal** \'sēl\ *n* **1** : a sea mammal that swims with flippers, lives mostly in cold regions, mates and bears young on land, eats flesh, and is hunted for fur, hides, or oil **2** : the soft dense fur of a northern seal

²**seal** *n* **1** : something (as a pledge) that makes safe or secure **2** : a device with a cut or raised design or figure that can be stamped or pressed into wax or paper **3** : a piece of wax stamped with a design and used to seal a letter or package **4** : a stamp that may be used to close a letter or package ⟨Christmas *seals*⟩ **5** : something that closes tightly **6** : a closing that is tight and perfect

³**seal** *vb* **1** : to mark with a seal **2** : to close or make fast with or as if with a seal — **seal·er** *n*

Although these words look alike, they are different words because they have different functions in a sentence or because they come from different sources and so have different meanings.

These similar entries are called **homographs** (from **homo-** "the same" and **-graph** "something written"—in this case "words written in the same way"). Each homograph has a small raised number before it. This number is used only in the dictionary entry to show you that these are different words. The number is not used when you write the word.

Let's look closely at the homographs for **seal** to see just why they are different. The first entry, a noun, is defined as "a sea mammal." The second **seal** entry is also a noun, but this meaning, "something (as a pledge) that makes safe or secure," is completely different from the meaning of the first entry. The third homograph of **seal** is certainly related to the second, but ³**seal** is a verb, and since it has a different use in the sentence, we show it as a different entry word.

7. Inflected Forms

Whenever we talk about more than one of something, we have to use a special form of a noun. If we want to say that an action is taking place now or has happened already, we need a different form of the verb for each meaning. To say that this is bigger, smaller, or quicker than that, we have to use a special form of an adjective or adverb. These special forms usually involve a change in spelling. These forms are called **inflected forms** or **inflections** of the words.

¹**shade** \'shād\ *n* **1** : partial darkness ⟨the trees cast *shade*⟩ **2** : space sheltered from light or heat and especially from the sun ⟨sit in the *shade* of a tree⟩ **3** **shades** *pl* : the shadows that gather as darkness falls ⟨the *shades* of night⟩ **4** : GHOST, SPIRIT **5** : something that blocks off or cuts down light ⟨a lamp *shade*⟩ ⟨a window *shade*⟩ **6** : the darkening of some objects in a painting or drawing to suggest that they are in shade **7** : the darkness or lightness of a color ⟨four *shades* of brown⟩ **8** : a very small difference or amount ⟨just a *shade* taller⟩ ⟨*shades* of meaning⟩

²**shade** *vb* **shad·ed; shad·ing 1** : to shelter from light or heat **2** : to mark with shades of light or color ⟨*shade* a drawing⟩ **3** : to show or begin to have slight differences of color, value, or meaning **shady** \'shād-ē\ *adj* **shad·i·er; shad·i·est 1** : sheltered from the sun's rays **2** : not right or honest ⟨*shady* business deals⟩ — **shad·i·ness** *n*

Nouns show more than one by means of **plural** forms—"the *shades* of night." Verbs can be made to show that something is happening now by the use of the **present participle** form—"that tree is *shading* our flowers"—or that something happened before but is not happening now by use of the **past tense** or the **past participle** forms—"I *shaded* my eyes; we have *shaded* parts of the drawing to show shadows." Adjectives and adverbs show how one thing is compared with another or with all others of the same kind by **comparative** and **superlative** forms—"this spot is *shadier* than that, but over there is the *shadiest* spot in the garden."

For most words inflected forms are made in a regular way. That is, plurals usually are formed simply by adding **-s** or **-es** to the base word *(shade → shades; box → boxes)*; verb inflections are formed by adding **-ed** for the past tense and past participle *(walk → walked)*, **-ing** for the present participle *(walk → walking)*, and **-s** or **-es** for the third person singular present tense form *(walk → walks; wash → washes)*. Comparative and superlative forms of adjectives and adverbs are considered regular if they are formed by adding **-er** and **-est** to the base word or if the words *more* and *most* are used *(high → higher, highest; natural → more natural, most natural)*.

We do not show most regular inflections in this dictionary since they should give you no problems in spelling. We do show inflections, however, when they are formed in any way other than by simply adding a suffix. If the base word is changed in any way when the suffix is added or if there are variant inflected forms, these forms are shown.

> **proph•e•cy** \'präf-ə-sē\ *n, pl* **proph•e•cies** ...
> ²**model** *vb* **mod•eled** *or* **mod•elled; mod•el•ing** *or* **mod•el•ling** ...

We also show inflections for a word when no suffix is added

> **deer** \'diər\ *n, pl* **deer** ...

and for any words that have regular inflections when we think you might have questions about how they are formed.

> **chim•ney** \'chim-nē\ *n, pl* **chim•neys** ...

For verb inflections only the past tense (the **-ed** form) and the present participle (the **-ing** form) are normally shown. The past participle is shown only when it is different from the past tense form. When it is shown, it comes between the past tense and present participle.

The third person singular present tense form (he *likes,* she *knows,* it *seems*) is the most regular of the verb inflections. For most verbs it is formed simply by adding **-s** or **-es** to the base word—even for verbs whose other inflections are not regular. We show this inflection only when we think its spelling or pronunciation might present a problem. When it is shown, this form comes after the present participle form.

> **go** \'gō\ *vb* **went** \'went\; **gone** \'gȯn\; **go•ing** \'gō-ing\; **goes** ...

Nouns are usually entered in this dictionary in the singular form, that is, in the form that means only one of something. And these words can either be used as a singular or be made into plural nouns. However, there are some entries that are used only in the plural. These are shown by the special label *n pl.*

> **aus•pic•es** \'ȯ-spə-səz\ *n pl* : support and guidance of a sponsor ⟨a concert given under the *auspices* of the school⟩

Some words that end in an **-s,** like **gymnastics,** may be thought of as singular in some uses and as plural in others.

> **gym•nas•tics** \jim-'nas-tiks\ *n sing or pl* : physical exercises for developing skill, strength, and control in the use of the body or a sport in which such exercises are performed

If you use this word for the sport, for example, you might think of it as singular, like this—"gymnastics is a sport in the Olympic Games." But if you think of the various exercises themselves, you might think of the word as a plural and use a plural verb, like this—"I think gymnastics are very hard to do." The *n sing or pl* label at such entries tells you that sometimes the word is used as a singular and sometimes as a plural.

There are a few entries in this dictionary that have unusual plural uses at individual meanings.

> ¹**dart** \'därt\ *n* **1** : a small pointed object that is meant to be thrown **2 darts** *pl* : a game in which darts are thrown at a

target **3** : a quick sudden movement **4** : a stitched fold in a garment

These special uses we show by a *pl* label at the individual definitions. In the **dart** example, the *pl* label at meaning **2** tells you that the spelling is **darts** and it is plural in use. If the plural form has already been shown in boldface at the beginning of the entry, we show it in italic type before the individual definition.

Sometimes a noun entry will show variant plural forms, but only one of these variants is used in a particular meaning. To show this situation, we place the plural form after the *pl* label at the individual meaning.

¹hose \'hōz\ *n, pl* **hose** *or* **hos•es** **1** *pl* *hose* : STOCKING, SOCK **2** : a flexible tube for carrying fluid

This is shown in the example **hose,** where the *pl hose* label tells you that the plural form for this meaning is **hose** but the use is usually singular.

Occasionally you will see a noun entry where you think an inflected form should be shown but it is not. Words like **diplomacy** are not used as plurals, so no plural form is shown.

8. Usage Labels

In addition to functional labels at individual entries we use another kind of italic label to give you information about how a word is used. These **usage labels** come after the functional labels or, if they apply only to a particular meaning, just before the beginning of the definition.

¹sire \'sīr\ *n* **1** *often cap* : ¹FATHER **1** **2** : ANCESTOR **3** : the male parent of an animal

One of the things the usage label may tell you is whether or not a particular word is sometimes written with a capital letter. Whenever a word is always or usually written with a capital letter, is has a capital letter in the main entry.

Thurs•day \'thərz-dē\ *n* : the fifth day of the week

But some words are written with a small letter or a capital letter about equally often. These entries have an italic label *often cap*. Other words are written with a capital letter in some meanings and not in others. These words are usually shown in the dictionary with a small first letter. The italic label tells you when the word is always spelled with a capital letter *(cap)* or very frequently spelled with a capital letter *(often cap)*.

³host *n, often cap* : the bread used in Christian Communion

dip•per \'dip-ər\ *n* **1** : one that dips **2** : a ladle or scoop for dipping **3** *cap* : a group of seven stars in the northern sky arranged in a form like a dipper with the two stars that form the outer edge of the cup pointing to the North Star **4** *cap* : a group of seven stars in the northern sky similar to the Dipper but with the North Star forming the outer end of the handle

french fry *n, often cap 1st F* : a strip of potato fried in deep fat ⟨steak and *french fries*⟩

In the example **³host,** the label tells you that sometimes the word is spelled with a capital letter and sometimes not. In the example **dipper,** the word is normally written with a capital letter (notice the *cap* label) when the meaning is **3** or **4** but with a small letter when the meaning is **1** or **2.**

The label at the entry **french fry** means that you can expect to see the word sometimes spelled **French fry**.

Another thing the usage labels can tell you is whether a word or a particular meaning is limited in use. One kind of word with limited use is one that is not used much anymore although is was quite common a long time ago.

thou \thaú\ *pron, archaic* : the one these words are spoken or written to

The *archaic* label at the sample entry **thou** tells you that **thou** is such a word. It is shown in this book because you may sometimes see it in very old writings, for example, in the Bible.

The last kind of usage label tells you a certain word or meaning is most commonly used in a limited area of the English-speaking world.

²lift *n* **1** : the amount that may be lifted at

one time : LOAD **2** : the action or an instance of lifting **3** : help especially in the form of a ride ⟨give a person a *lift*⟩ **4** *chiefly British* : ELEVATOR 2 **5** : an upward force (as on an airplane wing) that opposes the pull of gravity

In the sample entry **lift** you will see that meaning 4 is labeled *chiefly British*. This means that the word in this meaning is used more often in Great Britain than in the United States.

9. Definitions

skim \'skim\ *vb* **skimmed; skim·ming 1** : to clean a liquid of scum or floating substance : remove (as cream or film) from the top part of a liquid **2** : to read or examine quickly and not thoroughly **3** : to throw so as to skip along the surface of water **4** : to pass swiftly or lightly over

The definitions are what many people consider the most important part of the dictionary, because meanings are what people usually think of when they think of a dictionary.

All of the definitions in this dictionary start with a boldface colon that sets them off from other information included in the entry. The colon is used for each definition, even when there are two or more definitions for one meaning. (Look at meaning 1 of **skim.**) Most of the words entered in this book have more than one meaning and therefore they have more than one definition. These separate meanings are shown by boldface numbers placed in front of the colons. **Skim** has four numbered meanings.

We have arranged the definitions in your dictionary in historical order. The oldest meaning is shown as meaning number 1 and the next oldest meaning is shown as meaning number 2, and so on. The meanings that have most recently come into use are at the end. This allows you to see, just by reading the entry, how a word has grown in use from the first meaning to the last.

Let's look at meaning number 1 of **skim.** This meaning first came into use in English many centuries ago, and through the years it gained a more specific use,

that of taking the cream off milk. This specific use is shown as the second definition at meaning **1.** The second definition does not change the original meaning. It only adds a little.

Meaning **2** of **skim** seems to have come into use as a figure of speech. If you think of a spoon barely touching the surface of water or milk or going just under the surface to scoop off something, you realize that the scoop is only taking off what can be seen on the surface. Most of the liquid remains behind. By first applying the word **skim** to reading or examining something and only getting what could be seen "on the surface" without going more deeply into the work, someone was using **skim** as a figure of speech. As more and more people used the word in this way, it came to have a set meaning.

Meaning **3,** which developed after meanings **1** and **2,** seems to have come from the first meaning in a similar way. This time, though, the idea of "just touching" a surface was the one that carried over to the act of causing rocks or other objects to bounce along the surface of a lake.

Can you guess at how meaning **4** came into use? Here it seems the meaning moved one more step away, from the idea of "just touching the surface" to that of "just missing the surface."

With the entry **skim,** you can see just how the word grew from one meaning to four. And the arrangement of the four meanings in historical order lets you follow that growth.

There may be times when you will look up a word and not be sure which of several meanings is the right one for the use you are checking. The way to tell which is the right definition is to substitute each definition in place of your word in the sentence until you find the one that is right.

Suppose you were reading the sentence "I just skimmed the book" and you were not certain what *skim* meant. By reading the definitions of **skim** in the sentence you would be able to find the right meaning by substitution. You know that "I just removed cream from the top of the book" certainly is not correct, and it is most unlikely that the writer was "throwing a book so that it skipped across the surface of water" or "passing swiftly over the book." But when you substitute meaning **2** in the sentence, you get a sentence that makes sense. "I was just reading or examining the book quickly and not thoroughly." This is using the method of substitution to find the right meaning.

10. Synonyms and Cross-references

slav·ery \'slā-və-rē, 'slāv-rē\ *n* **1** : hard tiring labor : DRUDGERY **2** : the state of being a slave : BONDAGE **3** : the custom or practice of owning slaves

In the entry **slavery** meanings **1** and **2** both have two definitions, each one beginning with a colon. The second definition in each case is a single word that means the same thing as the entry word **slavery** for that particular use. These words with the same meaning as the entry word are called **synonyms.** All synonyms in this dictionary are written in small capital letters. Any word in small capital letters is a **cross-reference,** referring you to another place in the book. In the case of these synonyms, the small capitals tell you to look at the entry for that word for a full explanation of the meaning or use.

You can see that **drudgery** is a synonym of the first meaning of **slavery** ("hard tiring labor") and **bondage** is a synonym of the second meaning ("the state of being a slave"). If you turn to the entry for **drudgery,** for example, you will find a definition that matches the definition for meaning **1** of **slavery.**

When using synonymous cross-references, we have always put the full definition at the most common of the synonyms.

Sometimes you will see a number used as part of the cross-reference, as in the first meaning given for **host.**

¹host \'hōst\ *n* **1** : ARMY 1 **2** : MULTITUDE

The cross-reference to : ARMY 1 tells you to look at meaning number **1** of the entry

army for a definition that fits this meaning of **host.**

Because the definition of the synonym must also be a good definition of the entry word, both the entry word and the synonym will always have the same part of speech. Thus, if the synonym of a verb is an entry with two or more homographs, you will always know that the right entry will be the homograph that is a verb. Nevertheless, your dictionary helps you by showing the proper homograph number at the cross-reference when necessary.

dint \'dint\ *n* **1** : ¹POWER 6, FORCE . . .

The cross-reference printed in small capital letters is also used at certain entries that are variants or inflected forms of another entry.

caught *past of* CATCH
cauldron *variant of* CALDRON

In the examples **caught** and **cauldron** the cross-reference tells you that you will find a definition or explanation at the entry shown in small capital letters.

11. Verbal Illustrations

¹snap \'snap\ *vb* **snapped; snap·ping 1** : to grasp or grasp at something suddenly with the mouth or teeth ⟨fish *snapping* at the bait⟩ **2** : to grasp at something eagerly ⟨*snapped* at the chance to go⟩ **3** : to get, take, or buy at once ⟨*snap* up a bargain⟩ **4** : to speak or utter sharply or irritably ⟨*snap* out a command⟩ . . .

At times you may look up a word in your dictionary and understand the definition but still not be sure about the right way to use the word. Sometimes the several meanings are similar but the ways in which the word is actually used in a sentence are quite different. To help you better understand these more difficult words and usages, we have given along with some definitions a brief phrase or sentence called a **verbal illustration.** It shows you a typical use of the word. Most of the definitions at **snap** have verbal illustrations to show how the word is used in each of those meanings. A verbal illustration is always placed after the definition, it is enclosed in pointed brackets, and it has the entry word, or an inflection of it, printed in italic type.

12. Run-in Entries

Sometimes you will see boldface words in the middle of a definition. These are called **run-in entries.** Run-in entries are themselves defined by part of the main definition.

> **sol•stice** \'säl-stəs, 'sōl-, 'sȯl-\ *n* : the time of the year when the sun is farthest north (**summer solstice,** about June 22) or south (**winter solstice,** about December 22) of the equator

Within the main entry **solstice** the run-in entry **summer solstice** is being defined as "the time of the year when the sun is farthest north of the equator," and **winter solstice** is being defined as "the time of the year when the sun is farthest south of the equator."

13. Usage Notes

The italic usage labels that come before definitions are one way we give you information on the usage of the entry word, and the verbal illustrations after the definitions are another way. In this dictionary we give information on usage in still another way—**usage notes** that follow definitions. Usage notes are short phrases that are separated from the definition by a dash. They tell you how or when the entry word is used.

> **son•ny** \'sən-ē\ *n, pl* **son•nies** : a young boy — used mostly to address a stranger

The example **sonny** shows you one kind of usage note The following examples show some other kinds of information found in these notes.

> **cas•ta•net** \ˌkas-tə-'net\ *n* : a rhythm instrument that consists of two small ivory, wooden, or plastic shells fastened to the thumb and clicked by the fingers in time

to dancing and music — usually used in pl.

> **²cheer** *vb* . . . **4** : to grow or be cheerful — usually used with *up*

The note at **castanet** tells you that the word is usually used as a plural, **castanets,** although it is defined as a singular. This information is different from what would be given if the word had been entered as **castanets** or shown as **castanets** *pl* just before the definition. In both of those cases, you would be told that the word is defined as plural and is always plural in this use. Do you see how the note "usually used in pl." is different? It tells you that the word is singular—it is defined as a singular and may sometimes be used as singular—but is most often used in the plural form and with a plural verb.

Usage notes like the one at **cheer** tell you what words are usually used with the entry word in a sentence. In this case, the expression is usually *cheer up*.

In a few entries we use a usage note in place of a definition. This is done when the way the word is used is more important than what the word means.

> **³both** *conj* — used before two words or phrases connected with *and* to stress that each is included ⟨*both* New York and London⟩
>
> **amen** \'ā-'men, 'ä-\ *interj* — used to express agreement (as after a prayer or a statement of opinion)

14. Undefined Run-on Entries

> **¹sour** \'saȯr\ *adj* **1** : having an acid taste **2** : having become acid through spoiling ⟨*sour* milk⟩ **3** : suggesting decay ⟨a *sour* smell⟩ **4** : not pleasant or friendly ⟨a *sour* look⟩ **5** : acid in reaction ⟨*sour* soil⟩ — **sour•ish** \-ish\ *adj* — **sour•ly** *adv* — **sour•ness** *n*

The boldface words at the end of the entry **sour** are **undefined run-on entries.** Each of these run-on entries is shown without a definition. You can easily discover the meaning of any of these words by simply combining the meaning of the base word (the main entry) and that of the suffix. For example, **sourish** is simply **sour** plus **-ish** ("somewhat") and so means "somewhat sour"; **sourly** is simply **sour** plus **-ly** ("in a specified manner") and so means "in a sour manner"; and **sourness** is **sour** plus **-ness** ("state : condition") and so means "the state or condition of being sour."

We have run on only words whose meanings you should have no trouble figuring out. Whenever a word derived from a main entry has a meaning that is not easily understandable from the meanings of the two parts, we have entered and defined it at its own alphabetical place.

15. Synonym Paragraphs

At the end of certain entries, you will see a special kind of cross-reference like the one at **sparkle.**

¹**spar·kle** \'spär-kəl\ *vb* **spar·kled; spar·kling 1 :** to throw off sparks **2 :** to give off small flashes of light ⟨the diamond *sparkled*⟩ **3 :** to be lively or active ⟨the conversation *sparkled*⟩ **synonyms** see GLEAM

The direction "**synonyms** see GLEAM" means "for a discussion of synonyms that includes **sparkle,** see the entry **gleam.**"

At several entries in this dictionary like **gleam** and **splendid,** shown here, there are short discussions of the differences between certain synonyms.

splen·did \'splen-dəd\ *adj* **1 :** having or showing splendor : BRILLIANT **2 :** impressive in beauty, excellence, or magnificence ⟨did a *splendid* job⟩ ⟨a *splendid* palace⟩ **3 :** GRAND **4 — splen·did·ly** *adv*

synonyms SPLENDID, GLORIOUS, and SUPERB mean very impressive. SPLENDID suggests that something is far above the ordinary in excellence or magnificence ⟨what a *splendid* idea⟩ ⟨a *splendid* jewel⟩ GLORIOUS suggests that something is radiant with light or beauty ⟨a *glorious* sunset⟩ SUPERB suggests the highest possible point of magnificence or excellence ⟨a *superb* museum⟩ ⟨the food was *superb*⟩

These discussions are called **synonym paragraphs.** Synonyms can often be substituted freely for one another in a sentence because they mean basically the same thing. But some words that are synonyms because they mean nearly the same thing cannot always be substituted for one another. They may differ slightly in what they suggest to the reader—in the image they call to mind. These suggested meanings are what make one synonym a better choice than another in certain situations. In the synonym paragraphs we indicate these little differences between synonyms.

16. Defined Run-on Phrases

The last kind of boldface entry you will find in your dictionary is the **defined run-on phrase.** These phrases are groups of words that, when used together, have a special meaning that is more than just the sum of the ordinary meanings of each word.

¹**stand** \'stand\ *vb* **stood** \'stůd\; **standing 1 :** to be in or take a vertical position on one's feet **2 :** to take up or stay in a specified position or condition ⟨*stands* first in the class⟩ ⟨*stands* accused⟩ ⟨machines *standing* idle⟩ **3 :** to have an opinion ⟨how do you *stand* on taxes?⟩ **4 :** to rest, remain, or set in a usually vertical position ⟨*stand* the box in the corner⟩ **5 :** to be in a specified place ⟨the house *stands* on the hill⟩ **6 :** to stay in effect ⟨the order still *stands*⟩ **7 :** to put up with : ENDURE ⟨can't *stand* pain⟩ **8 :** UNDERGO ⟨*stand* trial⟩ **9 :** to perform the duty of ⟨*stand* guard⟩ — **stand by :** to be or remain loyal or true to ⟨*stand by* a promise⟩ — **stand for 1 :** to be a symbol for : REPRESENT **2 :** to put up with : PERMIT ⟨won't *stand for* any nonsense⟩

The **defined run-on phrases** are placed at the end of the entry that is the first major word of the phrase. Normally this will be the first noun or verb rather than an adjective or preposition. The phrases run on at **stand** all begin with the entry word **stand.** But some run-on phrases will not have the major word at the beginning. Keep in mind that the phrase will be entered at the first major word in the phrase. This word is usually a noun or a verb. Thus the phrase **do away with** will be found at the entry word **do**, the phrase **in the doghouse** will be found at **doghouse**, and **on fire** will be found at **fire**.

The phrase **read between the lines** contains both a verb (**read**) and a noun (**lines**). But if you remember that the phrase will be entered at the *first* major word, in this case the verb **read,** you should have no trouble finding the phrases entered in this dictionary.

17. Word History Paragraphs

sur·ly \\'sər-lē\ *adj* **sur·li·er; sur·li·est**
: having a mean rude disposition : UN-
FRIENDLY

Word History The word *surly* comes from the word *sir*. Long ago, some Englishmen who had the title *Sir* became too proud of it. Such men were called *sirly,* a word that meant "overbearing" and "arrogant." Over the years the spelling changed to *surly* and came to be used of anyone who is rude and unfriendly.

One of the important jobs of people who study words and write dictionaries is finding out where the words we use every day in English came from. Some of our words are made up by people using the language today. For instance, a new chemical element is often named by the scientist who discovers it.

But most of the words in the English language have a long history. Some words can be traced back to the earliest stages of English. Other words came into English a long time ago from other languages such as ancient Greek or Latin. The study of the origins of words can be fascinating, for many of our words have very interesting stories behind them.

In this dictionary, we share with you some of the interesting stories of word origins and trace the development of meanings in special short **word history paragraphs.**

Guide Words

To save you from having to search up and down page after page looking for the word you want, we have printed a pair of entry words in large type at the top of each page—one on each side. The paired words are called **guide words,** and they guide you to the right page for finding your entry word. They are usually the alphabetically first and last main entry words on the page, and they let you know at a glance what words are on each page. By looking at the guide words and thinking about whether the word you are hunting will fit in alphabetically between them, you can quickly move from page to page until you find the right one.

Say, for example, you are looking up the word *anonymous* and you have already turned to the section of words that begin with the letter **a.** You next would look at the guide words at the top of the pages. On page 21 you will see this:

ancient   21   **anguished**

Since the guide words are **ancient** and **anguished,** you can see that **anonymous** comes after the last guide word on the page and must be farther along in the book.

If you look at the top of page 23 you find:

answerable   23   **anticipating**

You can see that your word, **anonymous**, comes before the first guide word **answerable**.

A look at the top of page 22 confirms that **anonymous** should be on that page, since it falls between the guide words alphabetically:

angular   22   **answer**

Now we said that the guide words are *usually* the first and last main entries on each page. But not always. You see, the guide words show you the alphabetically first and alphabetically last entry words on the page, and this includes every boldface entry. A guide word may be a main entry or a variant spelling, an inflected form, an undefined run-on entry, a defined run-on phrase, or even a run-in entry.

If you look again at page 23 you will find:

answerable   23   anticipating

(first main entry on the page:)

an·swer·able \'an-sə-rə-bəl\ *adj* **1** : RE-SPONSIBLE **1** ⟨*answerable* for . . .

(last main entry on the page:)

an·tic·i·pate \an-'tis-ə-pāt\ *vb* **an·tic·i·pat·ed; an·tic·i·pat·ing 1:** to foresee and deal with . . .

Notice that **answerable**, the first guide word is also the first main entry, but **anticipating**, the last guide word, is an inflected form of the last main entry **anticipate**. Since **anticipating** comes alphabetically later than **anticipate**, it is chosen as the last guide word here.

Like the main entries in this dictionary, the guide words throughout the book are always in alphabetical order from page to page. Sometimes that presents a problem if a word that might normally be used as a guide word on one page is actually later in alphabetical order than the first guide word on the next page.

Look at this example.

bank   45   bare

(first main entry on the page:)

²bank *vb* **1** : to raise a bank around **2** : to . . .

(last main entry on the page:)

¹bare \'baər, 'beər\ *adj* **bar·er; bar·est 1** : having no covering : NAKED . . .

Note that the alphabetically last entry on this page is **baring**, the present participle of **¹bare**. Yet it is not used as the last guide word in this case because it would be out of alphabetical order with the first guide word on page 46, which is **bare**— the first main entry on page 46 is **²bare**. If you happen to be looking for **baring** and do not find it on the page where you expect it, just remember that we always keep guide words in alphabetical order, and this rule will help you find the right page.

Abbreviations Used in This Dictionary

adj	adjective	*interj*	interjection	*prep*	preposition
adv	adverb	*n*	noun	*pron*	pronoun
cap	capitalized	*n pl*	noun plural	*sing*	singular
conj	conjunction	*pl*	plural	*vb*	verb

PRONUNCIATION SYMBOLS

ə ...... (called *schwa* \'shwä\) banana, collide, abut; in stressed syllables as in humdrum, mother, abut

ər ..... further, learner

a ..... mat, mad, gag

ā ..... day, fade, mate, vacation

ä ..... bother, cot, cart

à ..... father as pronounced by those who do not rhyme it with *bother*. (Not everyone uses this sound.)

aủ .... now, loud, out

b ..... baby, rib

ch .... chin, match, nature \'nā-chər\

d ..... did, ladder

e ..... bed, pet

ē ..... beat, easy, me, carefree

f ...... fifty, cuff, phone

g ..... go, dig, bigger

h ..... hat, ahead

hw .... whale as pronounced by those who do not pronounce *whale* and *wail* the same

i ...... bid, tip, banish, active

ī ...... side, site, buy

j ...... job, gem, judge

k ..... kick, cook, ache

l ...... lily, pool, cold, battle, metal

m ..... murmur, dim, lamp

n ..... no, own, cotton, maiden

ng .... sing \'sing\, singer \'sing-ər\, finger \'fing-gər\, ink \'ingk\

ō ..... bone, know, soap

ò ..... saw, all, moth, taut

òi ..... coin, destroy

p ..... pepper, lip

r ...... red, rarity, rhyme, car

s ..... source, less

sh .... shy,. mission, machine, special

t ...... tie, attack, hot, water

th .... thin, ether

t͟h .... this, either

ü ..... rule, youth, few \'fyü\, union \'yün-yən\

ủ ... pull, wood, foot, cure \'kyủr\

v ..... give, vivid

w ..... we, away

y ..... yet, you, cue \'kyü, union \'yün-yən\

yü .... youth, union, cue, few, music

yủ .... cure, fury

z ...... zone, raise

zh .... vision, azure \'azh-ər\

\ \ ... slant lines used to mark the beginning and end of a pronunciation: \'pen\

' ...... mark at the beginning of a syllable with primary (strongest) stress: \'pen-mən\

ˌ ...... mark at the beginning of a syllable with secondary (next-strongest) stress: \'pen-mən-ˌship\

- ...... a hyphen separates syllables in pronunciations

, ... a comma separates pronunciation variants: \'rüm, 'rủm\

¹a \'ā\ *n, pl* **a's** *or* **as** \'āz\ *often cap* **1** : the first letter of the English alphabet **2** : a grade that shows a student's work is excellent

²a \ə, ā\ *indefinite article* **1** : some one not identified or known ⟨there's *a* dog in the yard⟩ **2** : the same ⟨two of *a* kind⟩ **3** : ¹ANY 1 ⟨it's hard for *a* person to bear⟩ **4** : for or from each ⟨an apple *a* day⟩ ⟨charges ten dollars *a* person⟩

a- \ə\ *prefix* **1** : on : in : at ⟨*a*bed⟩ **2** : in (such) a state, condition, or manner ⟨*a*fire⟩ ⟨*a*loud⟩ **3** : in the act or process of ⟨gone *a*-hunting⟩

aard·vark \'ärd-,värk\ *n* : an African animal with a long snout and a long sticky tongue that feeds mostly on ants and termites and is active at night

aardvark

ab- *prefix* : from : differing from ⟨*ab*normal⟩

aback \ə-'bak\ *adv* : by surprise ⟨taken *aback* by the change in plan⟩

aba·cus \'ab-ə-kəs\ *n, pl* **aba·ci** \'ab-ə-,sī\ *or* **aba·cus·es** : an instrument for doing arithmetic by sliding counters along rods or in grooves

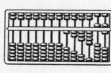

abacus

abaft \ə-'baft\ *adv* : toward or at the back part of a ship

ab·a·lo·ne \,ab-ə-'lō-nē\ *n* : a large sea snail that has a flattened shell with a pearly lining

¹aban·don \ə-'ban-dən\ *vb* **1** : to give up

completely : FORSAKE ⟨*abandon* a sinking ship⟩ **2** : to give (oneself) up to a feeling or emotion — **aban·don·ment** \-mənt\ *n*

synonyms ABANDON, DESERT, and FORSAKE mean to give up completely. ABANDON suggests that one has no interest in what happens to the person or thing one has given up ⟨*abandoned* the wrecked car on the side of the road⟩ DESERT suggests leaving something to which one has a duty or responsibility ⟨*desert* one's family and job⟩ FORSAKE suggests that one is leaving someone or something for which one once had affection ⟨don't *forsake* old friends in times of trouble⟩

²abandon *n* : a complete yielding to feelings or wishes ⟨drove with reckless *abandon*⟩

aban·doned \ə-'ban-dənd\ *adj* : given up : left empty or unused ⟨*abandoned* houses⟩

abash \ə-'bash\ *vb* : to destroy the self-confidence of

abate \ə-'bāt\ *vb* **abat·ed; abat·ing** : to make or become less ⟨the flood *abated* slowly⟩

ab·bess \'ab-əs\ *n* : the head of an abbey for women

ab·bey \'ab-ē\ *n, pl* **ab·beys** **1** : MONASTERY, CONVENT **2** : a church that once belonged to an abbey ⟨Westminster *Abbey*⟩

ab·bot \'ab-ət\ *n* : the head of an abbey for men

ab·bre·vi·ate \ə-'brē-vē-,āt\ *vb* **ab·bre·vi·at·ed; ab·bre·vi·at·ing** : to make briefer : SHORTEN

ab·bre·vi·a·tion \ə-,brē-vē-'ā-shən\ *n* **1** : a making shorter **2** : a shortened form of a word or phrase

ab·di·cate \'ab-di-,kāt\ *vb* **ab·di·cat·ed; ab·di·cat·ing** : to give up a position of power or authority ⟨the ruler was forced to *abdicate*⟩

ab·di·ca·tion \,ab-di-'kā-shən\ *n* : the giving up of a position of power or authority

ab·do·men \'ab-də-mən, ab-'dō-\ *n* **1** : the part of the body between the chest and the

\ə\ **abut**	\au̇\ **out**	\i\ **tip**	\ȯ\ **saw**	\u̇\ **foot**	
\ər\ **further**	\ch\ **chin**	\ī\ **life**	\ȯi\ **coin**	\y\ **yet**	
\a\ **mat**	\e\ **pet**	\j\ **job**	\th\ **thin**	\yü\ **few**	
\ā\ **take**	\ē\ **easy**	\ng\ **sing**	\th\ **this**	\yu̇\ **cure**	
\ä\ **cot, cart**	\g\ **go**	\ō\ **bone**	\u̇\ **food**	\zh\ **vision**	

hips including the cavity in which the chief digestive organs lie **2** : the hind part of the body of an arthropod (as an insect)

ab·dom·i·nal \ab-'däm-ən-l\ *adj* : of, relating to, or located in the abdomen

ab·duct \ab-'dəkt\ *vb* : to take a person away by force : KIDNAP

abeam \ə-'bēm\ *adv or adj* : on a line at right angles to a ship's keel

abed \ə-'bed\ *adv or adj* : in bed

ab·er·ra·tion \,ab-ə-'rā-shən\ *n* : a differing from what is normal or usual

ab·hor \ab-'hȯr\ *vb* **ab·horred; ab·hor·ring** : to shrink from in disgust : LOATHE

ab·hor·rent \ab-'hȯr-ənt\ *adj* : causing or deserving strong dislike

abide \ə-'bīd\ *vb* **abode** \-'bōd\ *or* **abided; abid·ing** **1** : to bear patiently : TOLERATE **2** : ENDURE 1 **3** : to live in a place : DWELL — **abide by** : to accept the terms of : OBEY

abil·i·ty \ə-'bil-ət-ē\ *n, pl* **abil·i·ties** **1** : power to do something **2** : natural talent or acquired skill

> **synonyms** ABILITY and TALENT mean bodily or mental power to do or accomplish something. ABILITY may suggest an inborn power to do something especially well ⟨the athlete's *ability* to run very fast⟩ TALENT suggests an unusual ability to create things ⟨you should develop your *talent* for writing short stories⟩

-abil·i·ty *also* **-ibil·i·ty** \ə-'bil-ət-ē\ *n suffix, pl* **-abil·i·ties** *also* **-ibil·i·ties** : ability, fitness, or likeliness to act or be acted upon in (such) a way

ab·ject \'ab-,jekt\ *adj* : low in spirit or hope ⟨an *abject* coward⟩ — **ab·ject·ly** *adv* — **ab·ject·ness** *n*

ablaze \ə-'blāz\ *adj* **1** : being on fire **2** : bright with light or color

able \'ā-bəl\ *adj* **abler** \-blər\; **ablest** \-bləst\ **1** : having enough power or skill to do something ⟨*able* to swim⟩ **2** : having or showing much of skill

> **synonyms** ABLE and CAPABLE mean having the power to do or accomplish. ABLE may suggest that one has exceptional skill and has done well in the past ⟨an *able* surgeon with years of experience⟩ CAPABLE stresses that one has the characteristics that make one suitable for a particular kind of work ⟨a very *capable* soldier⟩

-able *also* **-ible** \ə-bəl\ *adj suffix* **1** : capable of, fit for, or worthy of being ⟨lov*able*⟩ **2** : tending or likely to ⟨perish*able*⟩ — **-ably** *also* **-ibly** \ ə-blē\ *adv suffix*

ably \'ā-blē\ *adv* : in an able way

ab·nor·mal \ab-'nȯr-məl\ *adj* : differing from the normal usually in a noticeable way ⟨an *abnormal* growth⟩ — **ab·nor·mal·ly** *adv*

¹aboard \ə-'bōrd\ *adv* : on, onto, or within a ship, train, bus, or airplane

²aboard *prep* : on or into especially for passage ⟨go *aboard* ship⟩

¹abode \ə-'bōd\ *past of* ABIDE

²abode *n* : the place where one stays or lives

abol·ish \ə-'bäl-ish\ *vb* : to do away with : put an end to ⟨*abolish* discrimination⟩

ab·o·li·tion \,ab-ə-'lish-ən\ *n* : a complete doing away with ⟨the *abolition* of war⟩

A–bomb \'ā-,bäm\ *n* : ATOM BOMB

abom·i·na·ble \ə-'bäm-ə-nə-bəl\ *adj* **1** : deserving or causing disgust **2** : very disagreeable or unpleasant ⟨an *abominable* odor⟩ — **abom·i·na·bly** \-blē\ *adv*

abom·i·na·tion \ə-,bäm-ə-'nā-shən\ *n* : something abominable

ab·o·rig·i·ne \,ab-ə-'rij-ə-nē\ *n, pl* **ab·o·rig·i·nes** : a member of the original race to live in a region : NATIVE

abound \ə-'baund\ *vb* **1** : to be plentiful : TEEM **2** : to be fully supplied ⟨the book *abounds* with pictures⟩

¹about \ə-'baut\ *adv* **1** : on all sides : AROUND **2** : ALMOST, nearly ⟨*about* an hour ago⟩ **3** : one after another ⟨turn *about* is fair play⟩ **4** : in the opposite direction ⟨the ship came *about*⟩

²about *prep* **1** : on every side of : AROUND ⟨trees *about* the house⟩ **2** : on the point of ⟨we're *about* to leave⟩ **3** : having to do with ⟨a story *about* dogs⟩

¹above \ə-'bəv\ *adv* : in or to a higher place

²above *prep* **1** : higher than : OVER ⟨*above* the clouds⟩ **2** : too good for ⟨thought myself *above* that kind of work⟩ **3** : more than ⟨won't pay *above* ten dollars⟩

³above *adj* : said or written earlier

¹above·board \ə-'bəv-,bōrd\ *adv* : in an honest open way

²aboveboard *adj* : free from tricks and secrecy

abrade \ə-'brād\ *vb* **abrad·ed; abrad·ing** : to wear away by rubbing

¹abra·sive \ə-'brā-siv\ *adj* : having the effect of or like that of abrading ⟨an *abrasive* voice⟩

²abrasive *n* : a substance for grinding, smoothing, or polishing

abreast \ə-'brest\ *adv or adj* **1** : side by side **2** : up to a certain level of knowledge ⟨keep *abreast* of the news⟩

abridge \ə-'brij\ *vb* **abridged; abridg·ing** : to shorten by leaving out some parts ⟨*abridge* a dictionary⟩

abridg·ment *or* **abridge·ment** \ə-'brij-mənt\ *n* : a shortened form of a written work

abroad \ə-'bröd\ *adv or adj* **1** : over a wide area **2** : in the open : OUTDOORS **3** : in or to a foreign country **4** : known to many people ⟨the rumor soon got *abroad*⟩

abrupt \ə-'brəpt\ *adj* **1** : happening without warning : SUDDEN **2** : ¹STEEP 1 ⟨an *abrupt* drop⟩ — **abrupt·ly** *adv* — **abrupt·ness** *n*

ab·scess \'ab-ˌses\ *n* : a collection of pus with swollen and red tissue around it — **ab·scessed** \-ˌsest\ *adj*

ab·sence \'ab-səns\ *n* **1** : a being away **2** : ²LACK 1, WANT

¹ab·sent \'ab-sənt\ *adj* **1** : not present **2** : not existing **3** : showing that one is not paying attention ⟨an *absent* stare⟩

²ab·sent \ab-'sent\ *vb* : to keep (oneself) away

ab·sen·tee \ˌab-sən-'tē\ *n* : a person who is absent

ab·sent·mind·ed \ˌab-sənt-'mīn-dəd\ *adj* : not paying attention to what is going on or to what one is doing — **ab·sent·mind·ed·ly** *adv* — **ab·sent·mind·ed·ness** *n*

ab·so·lute \'ab-sə-ˌlüt\ *adj* **1** : free from imperfection : PERFECT, COMPLETE **2** : free from control or conditions ⟨*absolute* power⟩ **3** : free from doubt : CERTAIN ⟨*absolute* proof⟩ — **ab·so·lute·ly** *adv* — **ab·so·lute·ness** *n*

ab·so·lu·tion \ˌab-sə-'lü-shən\ *n* : a forgiving of sins

ab·solve \əb-'zälv, -'sälv\ *vb* **ab·solved; ab·solv·ing** : to set free from a duty or from blame

ab·sorb \əb-'sȯrb, -'zȯrb\ *vb* **1** : to take in or swallow up ⟨a sponge *absorbs* water⟩ **2** : to hold all of one's interest **3** : to receive without giving back ⟨a surface that *absorbs* sound⟩

ab·sorb·en·cy \əb-'sȯr-bən-sē, -'zȯr-\ *n* : the quality or state of being absorbent

ab·sorb·ent \əb-'sȯr-bənt, -'zȯr-\ *adj* : able to absorb ⟨*absorbent* cotton⟩

ab·sorp·tion \əb-'sȯrp-shən, -'zȯrp-\ *n* **1** : the process of absorbing or being absorbed ⟨the *absorption* of water by soil⟩ **2** : complete attention

ab·stain \əb-'stān\ *vb* : to keep oneself from doing something ⟨*abstain* from voting⟩ — **ab·stain·er** *n*

ab·sti·nence \'ab-stə-nəns\ *n* : an avoiding by choice especially of certain foods or of liquor

¹ab·stract \'ab-ˌstrakt\ *adj* **1** : expressing a quality apart from an actual person or thing that posseses it ⟨"honesty" is an *abstract* word⟩ **2** : hard to understand — **ab·stract·ly** *adv* — **ab·stract·ness** *n*

²ab·stract \'ab-ˌstrakt\ *n* : ²SUMMARY

³ab·stract \ab-'strakt\ *vb* **1** : to take away : SEPARATE **2** : SUMMARIZE

ab·strac·tion \ab-'strak-shən\ *n* **1** : the act of abstracting : the state of being abstracted **2** : an abstract idea

ab·struse \ab-'strüs\ *adj* : hard to understand — **ab·struse·ly** *adv* — **ab·struse·ness** *n*

ab·surd \əb-'sərd, -'zərd\ *adj* : completely unreasonable or untrue : RIDICULOUS — **ab·surd·ly** *adv*

synonyms ABSURD, FOOLISH, and SILLY mean not showing good sense. ABSURD suggests that something is not in keeping with common sense, good reasoning, or accepted ideas ⟨the *absurd* notion that horses can talk⟩ FOOLISH suggests that something is not thought of by others as wise or sensible ⟨you made a *foolish* investment of your money⟩ SILLY suggests that something makes no sense and has no purpose ⟨a *silly* argument over who ate the most⟩

ab·sur·di·ty \əb-'sərd-ət-ē, -'zərd-\ *n, pl* **ab·sur·di·ties** **1** : the fact of being absurd **2** : something that is absurd

abun·dance \ə-'bən-dəns\ *n* : a large quantity : PLENTY

abun·dant \ə-'bən-dənt\ *adj* : more than enough : PLENTIFUL — **abun·dant·ly** *adv*

¹abuse \ə-'byüz\ *vb* **abused; abus·ing** **1** : to blame or scold rudely **2** : to use wrongly : MISUSE ⟨*abuse* privileges⟩ **3** : to treat cruelly : MISTREAT ⟨*abuse* a horse by overworking it⟩

²abuse \ə-'byüs\ *n* **1** : a dishonest practice ⟨election *abuses*⟩ **2** : wrong or unfair treatment or use ⟨drug *abuse*⟩ **3** : harsh insulting language

abu·sive \ə-'byü-siv, -ziv\ *adj* : using or characterized by abuse — **abu·sive·ly** *adv* — **abu·sive·ness** *n*

abut \ə-'bət\ *vb* **abut·ted; abut·ting** : to touch along a border or with a part that sticks out

abut·ment \ə-'bət-mənt\ *n* : something

\ə\ **abut**	\au̇\ **out**	\i\ **tip**	\o̅\ **saw**	\u̇\ **foot**
\ər\ **further**	\ch\ **chin**	\ī\ **life**	\o̅i\ **coin**	\y\ **yet**
\a\ **mat**	\e\ **pet**	\j\ **job**	\th\ **thin**	\yü\ **few**
\ā\ **take**	\ē\ **easy**	\ng\ **sing**	\t̲h̲\ **this**	\yu̇\ **cure**
\ä\ **cot, cart**	\g\ **go**	\o̅\ **bone**	\ü\ **food**	\zh\ **vision**

against which another thing rests its weight or pushes with force

abyss \ə-'bis\ *n* : a gulf so deep or space so great that it cannot be measured

ac·a·dem·ic \,ak-ə-'dem-ik\ *adj* **1** : of or relating to schools or colleges **2** : having no practical importance 〈an *academic* question〉 — **ac·a·dem·i·cal·ly** \-i-kə-lē\ *adv*

acad·e·my \ə-'kad-ə-mē\ *n*, *pl* **acad·e·mies** **1** : a private high school **2** : a high school or college where special subjects are taught 〈a military *academy*〉 **3** : a society of learned persons

Word History In ancient Greece, a wise man named Plato started a school at a gymnasium. The gymnasium was named for a hero of Greek mythology. The English word *academy* came from the name of the hero for whom Plato's school was named.

ac·cede \ak-'sēd\ *vb* **ac·ced·ed; ac·ced·ing** : to agree to

ac·cel·er·ate \ak-'sel-ə-,rāt\ *vb* **ac·cel·er·at·ed; ac·cel·er·at·ing** **1** : to bring about earlier : HASTEN **2** : to move or cause to move faster

ac·cel·er·a·tion \ak-,sel-ə-'rā-shən\ *n* : a speeding up

ac·cel·er·a·tor \ak-'sel-ə-,rāt-ər\ *n* : a pedal in an automobile for controlling the speed of the motor

¹ac·cent \'ak-,sent\ *n* **1** : a way of talking shared by a group (as the residents of a country) **2** : greater stress or force given to a syllable of a word in speaking or to a beat in music **3** : a mark (as ' or ˌ) used in writing or printing to show the place of greater stress on a syllable

²ac·cent \'ak-,sent, ak-'sent\ *vb* **1** : to give a greater force or stress **2** : to mark with a written or printed accent

ac·cen·tu·ate \ak-'sen-chə-,wāt\ *vb* **ac·cen·tu·at·ed; ac·cen·tu·at·ing** **1** : ²ACCENT **2** : EMPHASIZE

ac·cept \ik-'sept, ak-\ *vb* **1** : to receive or take willingly 〈*accept* a gift〉 **2** : to agree to

ac·cept·able \ik-'sep-tə-bəl, ak-\ *adj* **1** : worthy of being accepted 〈an *acceptable* excuse〉 **2** : ADEQUATE 〈plays an *acceptable* game of tennis〉 — **ac·cept·able·ness** *n* — **ac·cept·ably** \-blē\ *adv*

ac·cept·ance \ik-'sep-təns, ak-\ *n* **1** : the act of accepting **2** : the quality or state of being accepted or acceptable

ac·cess \'ak-,ses\ *n* **1** : the right or ability to approach, enter, or use 〈*access* to secret information〉 **2** : a way or means of approach 〈*access* to the sea〉

ac·ces·si·ble \ak-'ses-ə-bəl\ *adj* **1** : capable of being reached 〈a resort *accessible* by train or bus〉 **2** : OBTAINABLE 〈the book is *accessible* in your school library〉 — **ac·ces·si·bly** \-blē\ *adv*

ac·ces·sion \ak-'sesh-ən\ *n* : a coming to a position of power

¹ac·ces·so·ry \ik-'ses-ə-rē, ak-\ *n*, *pl* **ac·ces·so·ries** **1** : an object or device not necessary in itself but adding to the beauty or usefulness of something else 〈clothing *accessories*〉 **2** : a person who helps another in doing wrong 〈an *accessory* to murder〉

²accessory *adj* : adding to or helping in a secondary way : SUPPLEMENTARY

ac·ci·dent \'ak-səd-ənt, -sə-,dent\ *n* **1** : something that happens by chance or from unknown causes : MISHAP 〈automobile *accident*〉 **2** : lack of intention or necessity : CHANCE

ac·ci·den·tal \,ak-sə-'dent-l\ *adj* **1** : happening by chance or unexpectedly 〈an *accidental* discovery of oil〉 **2** : not happening or done on purpose 〈an *accidental* shooting〉 — **ac·ci·den·tal·ly** *adv*

¹ac·claim \ə-'klām\ *vb* : ¹PRAISE **1** 〈a book *acclaimed* by the critics〉

²acclaim *n* : ²PRAISE 1, APPLAUSE

ac·cli·mate \ə-'klī-mət, 'ak-lə-,māt\ *vb* **ac·cli·mat·ed; ac·cli·mat·ing** : to change to fit a new climate or new surroundings

ac·cli·ma·tize \ə-'klī-mə-,tīz\ *vb* **ac·cli·ma·tized; ac·cli·ma·tiz·ing** : ACCLIMATE

ac·com·mo·date \ə-'käm-ə-,dāt\ *vb* **ac·com·mo·dat·ed; ac·com·mo·dat·ing** **1** : to provide with a place to stay or sleep **2** : to provide with something needed : help out **3** : to have room for 〈the bus *accommodates* forty people〉

ac·com·mo·dat·ing \ə-'käm-ə-,dāt-ing\ *adj* : ready to help — **ac·com·mo·dat·ing·ly** *adv*

ac·com·mo·da·tion \ə-,käm-ə-'dā-shən\ *n* **1** : something supplied that is useful or handy **2** **accommodations** *pl* : lodging and meals or traveling space and related services 〈overnight *accommodations*〉

ac·com·pa·ni·ment \ə-'kəm-pə-nē-mənt\ *n* : music played along with a solo part to enrich it

ac·com·pa·ny \ə-'kəm-pə-nē\ *vb* **ac·com·pa·nied; ac·com·pa·ny·ing** **1** : to go with as a companion **2** : to play a musical accompaniment for **3** : to happen at the same time as

ac·com·plice \ə-'käm-pləs\ *n* : a partner in wrongdoing

ac·com·plish \ə-'käm-plish\ *vb* : to succeed in doing : manage to do

ac·com·plished \ə-'käm-plisht\ *adj*
: skilled through practice or training : EX-
PERT ⟨an *accomplished* dancer⟩

ac·com·plish·ment \ə-'käm-plish-mənt\
n **1** : the act of accomplishing : COMPLE-
TION **2** : something accomplished **3** : an
acquired excellence or skill

¹ac·cord \ə-'kȯrd\ *vb* **1** : ¹GIVE 6 ⟨*accord*
them special privileges⟩ **2** : to be in harmony : AGREE ⟨your story of the accident
accords with theirs⟩

²accord *n* **1** : AGREEMENT 1, HARMONY
⟨acted in *accord* with their parents'
wishes⟩ **2** : willingness to act or to do
something ⟨went of their own *accord*⟩

ac·cor·dance \ə-'kȯrd-ns\ *n* : AGREE-
MENT 1

ac·cord·ing·ly \ə-'kȯrd-ing-lē\ *adv* **1** : in
the necessary way : in the way called for **2**
: as a result : CONSEQUENTLY, SO

ac·cord·ing to *prep* **1** : in agreement with
⟨everything was done *according to* the
rules⟩ **2** : as stated by ⟨*according to* the
experts⟩

¹ac·cor·di·on \ə-'kȯrd-ē-ən\ *n* : a portable keyboard musical instrument played
by forcing air from a bellows past metal
reeds

accordion

²accordion *adj* : folding or creased or
hinged to fold like an accordion ⟨a skirt
with *accordion* pleats⟩

ac·cost \ə-'kȯst\ *vb* : to approach and
speak first to

¹ac·count \ə-'kaunt\ *n* **1** : a record of
money received and money paid out **2** : a
statement of explanation or of reasons or
causes **3** : a statement of facts or events
: REPORT **4** : ²WORTH 1, IMPORTANCE — **on
account of** : for the sake of : BECAUSE OF
— **on no account** : not ever or for any
reason

²account *vb* **1** : to think of as : CONSIDER
⟨*account* them lucky⟩ **2** : to give an explanation ⟨try to *account* for what you did⟩ **3**
: to be the only or chief reason ⟨heavy
rains *accounted* for the flood⟩

ac·coun·tant \ə-'kaunt-nt\ *n* : a person
whose job is accounting

ac·count·ing \ə-'kaunt-ing\ *n* : the work of
keeping track of how much money is
made and spent in a business

ac·cu·mu·late \ə-'kyü-myə-ˌlāt\ *vb* **ac·cu·
mu·lat·ed; ac·cu·mu·lat·ing** **1** : COLLECT
1, GATHER ⟨*accumulated* several swimming trophies⟩ **2** : to increase in quantity
or number

ac·cu·mu·la·tion \ə-ˌkyü-myə-'lā-shən\ *n*
1 : a collecting together ⟨a steady *accumulation* of snow⟩ **2** : something accumulated : COLLECTION ⟨an *accumulation*
of junk⟩

ac·cu·ra·cy \'ak-yə-rə-sē\ *n* : freedom from
mistakes

ac·cu·rate \'ak-yə-rət\ *adj* : free from mistakes : RIGHT ⟨an *accurate* answer⟩ **synonyms** see CORRECT — **ac·cu·rate·ly**
adv — **ac·cu·rate·ness** *n*

ac·cu·sa·tion \ˌak-yə-'zā-shən\ *n* : a claim
that someone has done something bad or
illegal

ac·cuse \ə-'kyüz\ *vb* **ac·cused; ac·cus·
ing** : to blame a fault, wrong, or crime on
(a person) — **ac·cus·er** *n*

ac·cus·tom \ə-'kəs-təm\ *vb* : to cause
(someone) to get used to something

ac·cus·tomed \ə-'kəs-təmd\ *adj* **1** : CUS-
TOMARY 2, USUAL ⟨their *accustomed* lunch
hour⟩ **2** : familiar with : USED ⟨*accustomed* to hard luck⟩

¹ace \'ās\ *n* **1** : a playing card with one
large figure in its center **2** : a person who
is expert at something

Word History An Old French word referring to the side of a dice with a single spot
came from a Latin word that meant "a unit"
or "a single thing." The English word *ace*
came from the Old French word. At first *ace*
meant "the side of a dice that has a single
spot." Later, however, the word *ace* came
to be used for a playing card with a single
mark in its center. Other meanings of *ace*
have come from this meaning.

²ace *adj* : of the very best kind

¹ache \'āk\ *vb* **ached; ach·ing** **1** : to suffer
a dull continuous pain **2** : YEARN

\ə\ abut	\au\ out	\i\ tip	\ȯ\ saw	\u\ foot
\ər\ further	\ch\ chin	\ī\ life	\ȯi\ coin	\y\ yet
\a\ mat	\e\ pet	\j\ job	\th\ thin	\yü\ few
\ā\ take	\ē\ easy	\ng\ sing	\th\ this	\yu\ cure
\ä\ cot, cart	\g\ go	\ō\ bone	\ü\ food	\zh\ vision

²ache *n* : a dull continuous pain

achieve \ə-'chēv\ *vb* **achieved; achiev-ing 1** : to bring about : ACCOMPLISH **2** : to get by means of one's own efforts : WIN
synonyms see REACH

achieve·ment \ə-'chēv-mənt\ *n* **1** : the act of achieving **2** : something achieved es-pecially by great effort

¹ac·id \'as-əd\ *adj* **1** : having a taste that is sour, bitter, or stinging **2** : sour in temper : CROSS ⟨*acid* remarks⟩ **3** : of, relating to, or like an acid — **ac·id·ly** *adv*

²acid *n* : a chemical compound that tastes sour and forms a water solution which turns blue litmus paper red

acid·i·ty \ə-'sid-ət-ē\ *n, pl* **acid·i·ties** : the quality, state, or degree of being acid

ac·knowl·edge \ik-'näl-ij, ak-\ *vb* **ac-knowl·edged; ac·knowl·edg·ing 1** : to admit the truth or existence of ⟨*ac-knowledged* their mistake⟩ **2** : to recog-nize the rights or authority of **3** : to make known that something has been received or noticed

ac·knowl·edged \ik-'näl-ijd, ak-\ *adj* : generally accepted ⟨the *acknowledged* leader⟩

ac·knowl·edg·ment *or* **ac·knowl·edge-ment** \ik-'näl-ij-mənt, ak-\ *n* **1** : an act of acknowledging some deed or achieve-ment **2** : something done or given in return for something done or received

ac·ne \'ak-nē\ *n* : a skin condition in which pimples and blackheads are present

acorn \'ā-ˌkȯrn, -kərn\ *n* : the nut of the oak tree

acous·tic \ə-'kü-stik\ *or* **acous·ti·cal** \-sti-kəl\ *adj* **1** : of or relating to hear-ing or sound **2** : deadening sound ⟨*acoustical* tile⟩

acorns

acous·tics \ə-'kü-stiks\ *n sing or pl* **1** : a science dealing with sound **2** : the qualities in a room or hall that make it easy or hard for a person in it to hear clearly

ac·quaint \ə-'kwānt\ *vb* **1** : to cause to know personally ⟨became *acquainted* at school⟩ **2** : to make familiar : INFORM ⟨*acquaint* them with their duties⟩

ac·quain·tance \ə-'kwānt-ns\ *n* **1** : per-sonal knowledge **2** : a person one knows slightly

ac·qui·esce \ˌak-wē-'es\ *vb* **ac·qui-esced; ac·qui·esc·ing** : to accept, agree, or give consent by keeping silent or by not making objections

ac·qui·es·cence \ˌak-wē-'es-ns\ *n* : the act of acquiescing

ac·quire \ə-'kwīr\ *vb* **ac·quired; ac·quir-ing** : to get especially by one's own efforts : GAIN

ac·quire·ment \ə-'kwīr-mənt\ *n* **1** : the act of acquiring **2** : ACCOMPLISHMENT 3

ac·qui·si·tion \ˌak-wə-'zish-ən\ *n* **1** : the act of acquiring **2** : something acquired

ac·quis·i·tive \ə-'kwiz-ət-iv\ *adj* : GREEDY 2 — **ac·quis·i·tive·ly** *adv* — **ac·quis·i-tive·ness** *n*

ac·quit \ə-'kwit\ *vb* **ac·quit·ted; ac·quit-ting 1** : to declare innocent of a crime or of wrongdoing **2** : to conduct (oneself) in a certain way

ac·quit·tal \ə-'kwit-l\ *n* : the act of acquit-ting someone

acre \'ā-kər\ *n* : a measure of land area equal to 43,560 square feet (about 4047 square meters)

acre·age \'ā-kə-rij, 'ā-krij\ *n* : area in acres

ac·rid \'ak-rəd\ *adj* **1** : sharp or bitter in taste or odor **2** : very harsh or unpleasant ⟨an *acrid* manner⟩

ac·ro·bat \'ak-rə-ˌbat\ *n* : a person (as a circus performer) who is very good at stunts like jumping, balancing, tumbling, and swinging from things

ac·ro·bat·ic \ˌak-rə-'bat-ik\ *adj* : of or relat-ing to acrobats or acrobatics

ac·ro·bat·ics \ˌak-rə-'bat-iks\ *n sing or pl* **1** : the art or performance of an acrobat **2** : stunts of or like those of an acrobat

acrop·o·lis \ə-'kräp-ə-ləs\ *n* : the upper fortified part of an ancient Greek city

¹across \ə-'krȯs\ *adv* : from one side to the other ⟨boards sawed *across*⟩

²across *prep* **1** : to or on the opposite side of ⟨ran *across* the street⟩ **2** : so as to pass, go over, or intersect at an angle ⟨lay one stick *across* another⟩

¹act \'akt\ *n* **1** : something that is done : DEED **2** : the doing of something ⟨caught in the *act* of stealing⟩ **3** : a law made by a governing body **4** : a main division of a play

²act *vb* **1** : to perform (a part) on the stage ⟨*act* the hero in a play⟩ **2** : to behave oneself in a certain way ⟨*acts* like a cow-ard⟩ **3** : to do something : MOVE ⟨*act* quickly in an emergency⟩ **4** : to have a result : make something happen : WORK ⟨the medicine *acts* on the heart⟩ **syn-onyms** see IMPERSONATE

act·ing \'ak-ting\ *adj* : serving for a short time only or in place of another

ac·tion \'ak-shən\ *n* **1** : the working of one thing on another so as to produce a change **2** : the doing of something **3** : something done **4** : the way something runs or works **5** : combat in war ⟨was killed in *action*⟩

ac·ti·vate \'ak-tə-ˌvāt\ *vb* **ac·ti·vat·ed; ac·ti·vat·ing** : to make active or more active

ac·tive \'ak-tiv\ *adj* **1** : producing or involving action or movement **2** : showing that the subject of a sentence is the doer of the action represented by the verb ⟨"hit" in "they hit the ball" is *active*⟩ **3** : quick in physical movement : LIVELY ⟨an *active* child⟩ **4** : taking part in an action or activity — **ac·tive·ly** *adv*

ac·tiv·i·ty \ak-'tiv-ət-ē\ *n, pl* **ac·tiv·i·ties 1** : energetic action **2** : something done especially for relaxation or fun

ac·tor \'ak-tər\ *n* : a person who acts especially in a play or movie

ac·tress \'ak-trəs\ *n* : a woman or girl who acts especially in a play or movie

ac·tu·al \'ak-chə-wəl\ *adj* : really existing or happening : not false **synonyms** see REAL

ac·tu·al·ly \'ak-chə-wə-lē\ *adv* : in fact : REALLY

acute \ə-'kyüt\ *adj* **acut·er; acut·est 1** : measuring less than a right angle ⟨*acute* angles⟩ **2** : mentally sharp **3** : SEVERE ⟨*acute* distress⟩ **4** : developing quickly and lasting only a short time ⟨*acute* illness⟩ **5** : CRITICAL 4, urgent ⟨an *acute* need for help⟩ — **acute·ly** *adv* — **acute·ness** *n*

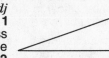

acute angle

ad \'ad\ *n* : ADVERTISEMENT

ad·age \'ad-ij\ *n* : an old familiar saying : PROVERB

ad·a·mant \'ad-ə-mənt\ *adj* : not giving in

Ad·am's apple \ˌad-əmz-\ *n* : the lump formed in the front of a person's neck by cartilage in the throat

adapt \ə-'dapt\ *vb* : to make or become suitable or able to function — **adapt·er** *n*

adapt·abil·i·ty \ə-ˌdap-tə-'bil-ət-ē\ *n* : the quality or state of being adaptable

adapt·able \ə-'dap-tə-bəl\ *adj* : capable of adapting or being adapted

ad·ap·ta·tion \ˌad-ˌap-'tā-shən\ *n* **1** : the act or process of adapting **2** : something adapted or helping to adapt ⟨lungs are an *adaptation* to breathing air⟩

add \'ad\ *vb* **1** : to join or unite to something ⟨*add* a wing to the house⟩ **2** : to say something more ⟨the teacher *added*, "It's not only wrong, it's foolish"⟩ **3** : to combine numbers into a single sum

ad·dend \'ad-ˌend\ *n* : a number that is to be added to another number

ad·den·dum \ə-'den-dəm\ *n, pl* **ad·den-**

da \ə-'den-də\ : something added (as to a book)

ad·der \'ad-ər\ *n* **1** : any of several poisonous snakes of Europe or Africa **2** : any of several harmless North American snakes (as the **puff adder**)

adder

¹ad·dict \ə-'dikt\ *vb* : to cause to have a need for something ⟨*addicted* to drugs⟩

²ad·dict \'ad-ˌikt\ *n* : a person who is addicted (as to a drug)

ad·dic·tion \ə-'dik-shən\ *n* : the state of being addicted (as to the use of harmful drugs)

ad·di·tion \ə-'dish-ən\ *n* **1** : the adding of numbers to obtain their sum **2** : something added ⟨an *addition* to a house⟩ — **in addition** : ¹BESIDES, ALSO — **in addition to** : over and above : ²BESIDES

ad·di·tion·al \ə-'dish-ən-l\ *adj* : ¹EXTRA ⟨we needed *additional* time to finish⟩ — **ad·di·tion·al·ly** \-ē\ *adv*

¹ad·di·tive \'ad-ət-iv\ *adj* : relating to or produced by addition

²additive *n* : a substance added to another in small amounts ⟨a gasoline *additive* to improve engine performance⟩

ad·dle \'ad-l\ *vb* **ad·dled; ad·dling** : to make confused

¹ad·dress \ə-'dres\ *vb* **1** : to apply (oneself) to something ⟨*addressed* themselves to the problem⟩ **2** : to speak or write to **3** : to put directions for delivery on ⟨*address* a letter⟩

²ad·dress \ə-'dres, 'ad-ˌres\ *n* **1** : a rehearsed speech : LECTURE **2** : the place where a person can usually be reached ⟨a business *address*⟩ **3** : the directions for delivery placed on mail

ad·dress·ee \ˌad-ˌres-'ē\ *n* : the person to whom something is addressed

ad·e·noids \'ad-n-ˌoidz\ *n pl* : fleshy growths near the opening of the nose into the throat

adept \ə-'dept\ *adj* : very good at something ⟨*adept* at swimming⟩ — **adept·ly** *adv* — **adept·ness** *n*

Word History A long time ago people claimed to have found the trick of turning

\ə\ **abut**	\au̇\ **out**	\i\ **tip**	\ȯ\ **saw**	\u̇\ **foot**
\ər\ **further**	\ch\ **chin**	\ī\ **life**	\ȯi\ **coin**	\y\ **yet**
\a\ **mat**	\e\ **pet**	\j\ **job**	\th\ **thin**	\yü\ **few**
\ā\ **take**	\ē\ **easy**	\ng\ **sing**	\th\ **this**	\yu̇\ **cure**
\ä\ **cot, cart**	\g\ **go**	\ō\ **bone**	\ü\ **food**	\zh\ **vision**

common metals to gold. No one could really do this. There was even a Latin word used to describe a person who could make gold from other metals. The English word *adept*, which means "highly skilled," came from this Latin word. Certainly, a person who could make gold in this way would have to be highly skilled.

ad·e·quate \'ad-i-kwət\ *adj* **1** : ¹ENOUGH ⟨the meal was not *adequate* to feed six people⟩ **2** : good enough ⟨your grades are barely *adequate*⟩ — **ad·e·quate·ly** *adv* — **ad·e·quate·ness** *n*

ad·here \ad-'hiər\ *vb* **ad·hered; ad·her·ing** **1** : to stay loyal (as to a promise) **2** : to stick tight : CLING

ad·her·ence \ad-'hir-əns\ *n* : steady or faithful attachment ⟨*adherence* to the truth⟩

ad·her·ent \ad-'hir-ənt\ *n* : a person who adheres to a belief, an organization, or a leader

ad·he·sion \ad-'hē-zhən\ *n* : the act or state of adhering

¹ad·he·sive \ad-'hē-siv, -ziv\ *adj* : tending to stick : STICKY — **ad·he·sive·ly** *adv* — **ad·he·sive·ness** *n*

²adhesive *n* : an adhesive substance

adi·os \ˌad-ē-'ōs, ˌäd-\ *interj* — used instead of goodbye

ad·ja·cent \ə-'jās-nt\ *adj* : next or near to something — **ad·ja·cent·ly** *adv*

ad·jec·ti·val \ˌaj-ik-'tī-vəl\ *adj* : of, relating to, or functioning as an adjective ⟨an *adjectival* phrase⟩ — **ad·jec·ti·val·ly** *adv*

ad·jec·tive \'aj-ik-tiv\ *n* : a word that says something about a noun or pronoun ⟨"good" in "good people," "someone good," "it's good to be here," and "they seem very good" is an *adjective*⟩

ad·join \ə-'join\ *vb* : to be next to or in contact with

ad·journ \ə-'jərn\ *vb* : to bring or come to a close for a period of time ⟨*adjourn* a meeting⟩ — **ad·journ·ment** \-mənt\ *n*

ad·junct \'aj-ˌəngkt\ *n* : something joined or added to something else but not a necessary part of it

ad·just \ə-'jəst\ *vb* **1** : to settle or fix by agreement ⟨*adjust* conflicts⟩ **2** : to move the parts of an instrument or a machine to make them work better ⟨*adjust* the brakes on a car⟩ **3** : to become used to ⟨*adjust* to a new school⟩ — **ad·just·er** *n*

ad·just·able \ə-'jəs-tə-bəl\ *adj* : possible to adjust ⟨an *adjustable* wrench⟩

ad·just·ment \ə-'jəst-mənt\ *n* **1** : the act or process of adjusting : the state of being adjusted **2** : a deciding about and paying

of a claim or debt **3** : something that is used to adjust one part to another

ad·ju·tant \'aj-ət-ənt\ *n* : an officer who assists a commanding officer

ad–lib \'ad-'lib\ *vb* **ad–libbed; ad–lib·bing** : to improvise something and especially music or spoken lines

ad·min·is·ter \əd-'min-əs-tər\ *vb* **1** : to be in charge of : MANAGE ⟨*administer* an athletic program⟩ **2** : to give out as deserved ⟨*administer* justice⟩ **3** : to give or supply as treatment ⟨*administer* a dose of medicine⟩

ad·min·is·tra·tion \əd-ˌmin-ə-'strā-shən\ *n* **1** : the act or process of administering **2** : the work involved in managing something **3** : the persons who direct the business of something (as a city or school)

ad·min·is·tra·tive \əd-'min-ə-ˌstrāt-iv\ *adj* : of or relating to administration

ad·mi·ra·ble \'ad-mə-rə-bəl, 'ad-mrə-bəl\ *adj* : deserving to be admired — **ad·mi·ra·bly** \-blē\ *adv*

ad·mi·ral \'ad-mə-rəl, -mrəl\ *n* : a commissioned officer in the Navy or Coast Guard ranking above a vice admiral

Word History The word *admiral* looks a lot like the word *admire*. The two words, though, are not related. *Admire* came from a Latin verb that meant "to marvel at." *Admiral* came from an Arabic title that meant "commander of the." It was part of a phrase that meant "commander of the sea."

ad·mi·ral·ty \'ad-mə-rəl-tē, -mrəl-\ *adj* : of or relating to conduct on the sea ⟨*admiralty* law⟩

ad·mi·ra·tion \ˌad-mə-'rā-shən\ *n* : great and delighted approval

ad·mire \əd-'mīr\ *vb* **ad·mired; ad·mir·ing** : to feel admiration for : think very highly of — **ad·mir·er** *n*

ad·mis·si·ble \əd-'mis-ə-bəl\ *adj* : deserving to be admitted or allowed : ALLOWABLE

ad·mis·sion \əd-'mish-ən\ *n* **1** : an admitting of something that has not been proved ⟨an *admission* of guilt⟩ **2** : the act of admitting **3** : the right or permission to enter ⟨*admission* to college⟩ **4** : the price of entrance

ad·mit \əd-'mit\ *vb* **ad·mit·ted; ad·mit·ting** **1** : ¹PERMIT **2**, ALLOW ⟨this law *admits* no exceptions⟩ **2** : to allow to enter : let in **3** : to make known usually with some unwillingness ⟨*admitted* that they really didn't know⟩

ad·mit·tance \əd-'mit-ns\ *n* : permission to enter

ad·mon·ish \ad-'män-ish\ *vb* **1** : to criticize or warn gently but seriously ⟨*admonish* a student for talking⟩ **2** : to give friendly advice or encouragement

ad·mo·ni·tion \,ad-mə-'nish-ən\ *n* : a gentle or friendly criticism or warning

ado \ə-'dü\ *n* : fussy excitement or hurrying about

ado·be \ə-'dō-bē\ *n* **1** : brick made of earth or clay dried in the sun **2** : a building made of adobe

ad·o·les·cence \,ad-l-'es-ns\ *n* : the period of life between childhood and adulthood

ad·o·les·cent \,ad-l-'es-nt\ *n* : a person who is no longer a child but not yet adult

adopt \ə-'däpt\ *vb* **1** : to take (a child of other parents) as one's own **2** : to take up and practice as one's own **3** : to accept and put into action — **adopt·er** *n*

adop·tion \ə-'däp-shən\ *n* : the act of adopting : the state of being adopted

ador·able \ə-'dōr-ə-bəl\ *adj* : CHARMING, LOVELY — **ador·able·ness** *n* — **ador·ably** \-blē\ *adv*

ad·o·ra·tion \,ad-ə-'rā-shən\ *n* : deep love

adore \ə-'dōr\ *vb* **adored; ador·ing** **1** : ²WORSHIP 1 **2** : to be very fond of — **adorer** *n*

adorn \ə-'dȯrn\ *vb* : to try to make prettier by adding decorations

adorn·ment \ə-'dȯrn-mənt\ *n* **1** : DECORATION 1 **2** : ¹ORNAMENT 1

adrift \ə-'drift\ *adv or adj* : in a drifting state ⟨a ship *adrift* in the storm⟩

adroit \ə-'drȯit\ *adj* : having or showing great skill or cleverness⟨an *adroit* leader⟩⟨*adroit* at handling problems⟩ — **adroit·ly** *adv* — **adroit·ness** *n*

ad·u·la·tion \,aj-ə-'lā-shən\ *n* : very great admiration

¹adult \ə-'dəlt, 'ad-,əlt\ *adj* : fully developed and mature

²adult *n* : an adult person or thing

adul·ter·ate \ə-'dəl-tə-,rāt\ *vb* **adul·ter·at·ed; adul·ter·at·ing** : to make impure or weaker by adding something different or of poorer quality

adult·hood \ə-'dəlt-,hu̇d\ *n* : the period of being an adult

¹ad·vance \əd-'vans\ *vb* **ad·vanced; ad·vanc·ing** **1** : to move forward **2** : to help the progress of ⟨laws that *advance* freedom⟩ **3** : to raise to a higher rank **4** : to give ahead of time ⟨*advanced* me five dollars from my wages⟩ **5** : PROPOSE 1 ⟨*advance* a new plan⟩

²advance *n* **1** : a forward movement **2** : IMPROVEMENT 1 **3** : a rise in price, value, or amount **4** : a first step or approach ⟨an

unfriendly look discourages *advances*⟩ **5** : a giving (as of money) ahead of time ⟨asked for an *advance* on my salary⟩ — **in advance** : ¹BEFORE 1 — **in advance of** : ahead of

ad·vanced \əd-'vanst\ *adj* **1** : being far along in years or progress ⟨an *advanced* civilization⟩ **2** : being beyond the elementary or introductory level ⟨*advanced* mathematics⟩

ad·vance·ment \əd-'van-smənt\ *n* **1** : the action of advancing : the state of being advanced **2** : a raising or being raised to a higher rank or position

ad·van·tage \əd-'vant-ij\ *n* **1** : the fact of being in a better position or condition **2** : personal benefit or gain ⟨it's to your own *advantage*⟩ **3** : something that benefits the one it belongs to ⟨speed is an *advantage* in sports⟩

ad·van·ta·geous \,ad-vən-'tā-jəs, -,van-\ *adj* : giving an advantage : HELPFUL — **ad·van·ta·geous·ly** *adv*

ad·vent \'ad-,vent\ *n* : the arrival or coming of something ⟨the *advent* of spring⟩

¹ad·ven·ture \əd-'ven-chər\ *n* **1** : an action that involves unknown dangers and risks **2** : an unusual experience

²adventure *vb* **ad·ven·tured; ad·ven·tur·ing** : to expose to or go on in spite of danger or risk — **ad·ven·tur·er** \əd-'ven-chər-ər\ *n*

ad·ven·ture·some \əd-'ven-chər-səm\ *adj* : likely to take risks : DARING

ad·ven·tur·ous \əd-'ven-chə-rəs\ *adj* **1** : ready to take risks or to deal with new or unexpected problems ⟨*adventurous* explorers⟩ **2** : DANGEROUS 1, RISKY ⟨an *adventurous* voyage⟩ — **ad·ven·tur·ous·ly** *adv* — **ad·ven·tur·ous·ness** *n*

synonyms ADVENTUROUS, VENTURESOME, and DARING mean taking risks that are not required by duty or courage. ADVENTUROUS suggests that one goes in search of adventure in spite of the possible dangers ⟨*adventurous* youngsters on a hike through the forest⟩ VENTURESOME suggests that one is willing to take many chances ⟨*venturesome* explorers searching for lost treasure⟩ DARING suggests that one is fearless and willing to take unnecessary risks ⟨the early airplane pilots were especially *daring*⟩

ad·verb \'ad-,vərb\ *n* : a word used to

\ə\ **abut**	\au̇\ **out**	\i\ **tip**	\ȯ\ **saw**	\u̇\ **foot**
\ər\ **further**	\ch\ **chin**	\ī\ **life**	\ȯi\ **coin**	\y\ **yet**
\a\ **mat**	\e\ **pet**	\j\ **job**	\th\ **thin**	\yü\ **few**
\ā\ **take**	\ē\ **easy**	\ng\ **sing**	\th\ **this**	\yu̇\ **cure**
\ä\ **cot, cart**	\g\ **go**	\ō\ **bone**	\ü\ **food**	\zh\ **vision**

modify a verb, an adjective, or another adverb and often used to show degree, manner, place, or time ⟨"almost" and "very" in "at almost three o'clock on a very hot day" are *adverbs*⟩

ad·ver·bi·al \ad-'vər-bē-əl\ *adj* : of, relating to, or used an an adverb — **ad·ver·bi·al·ly** *adv*

ad·ver·sary \'ad-vər-ˌser-ē\ *n, pl* **ad·ver·sar·ies** : OPPONENT, enemy

ad·verse \ad-'vərs\ *adj* **1** : acting against or in an opposite direction ⟨*adverse* winds⟩ **2** : not helping or favoring ⟨*adverse* circumstances⟩ — **ad·verse·ly** *adv* — **ad·verse·ness** *n*

ad·ver·si·ty \ad-'vər-sət-ē\ *n, pl* **ad·ver·si·ties** : hard times : MISFORTUNE

ad·ver·tise \'ad-vər-ˌtīz\ *vb* **ad·ver·tised; ad·ver·tis·ing** **1** : to announce publicly ⟨*advertise* a coming event⟩ **2** : to call to public attention to persuade to buy **3** : to put out a public notice or request ⟨*advertise* for a lost dog⟩ **synonyms** see DE-CLARE — **ad·ver·tis·er** *n*

ad·ver·tise·ment \ˌad-vər-'tīz-mənt, ad-'vərt-əz-\ *n* : a notice or short film advertising something

ad·ver·tis·ing \'ad-vər-ˌtī-zing\ *n* **1** : speech, writing, pictures, or films meant to persuade people to buy something **2** : the business of preparing advertisements

ad·vice \əd-'vīs\ *n* : suggestions about a decision or action ⟨took their *advice* on buying a new car⟩

ad·vis·able \əd-'vī-zə-bəl\ *adj* : reasonable or proper to do : DISCREET ⟨it is not *advisable* to swim after a meal⟩ — **ad·vis·ably** \-blē\ *adv*

ad·vise \əd-'vīz\ *vb* **ad·vised; ad·vis·ing** **1** : to give advice to : COUNSEL **2** : to give information about something ⟨were *advised* of bad flying conditions⟩ — **ad·vis·er** *or* **ad·vi·sor** \ -'vī-zər\ *n*

ad·vi·so·ry \əd-'vī-zə-rē, -'vīz-rē\ *adj* **1** : having the power or right to advise **2** : containing advice

¹**ad·vo·cate** \'ad-və-kət, -ˌkāt\ *n* **1** : a person who argues for another in court **2** : a person who argues for or supports an idea or plan

²**ad·vo·cate** \'ad-və-ˌkāt\ *vb* **ad·vo·cat·ed; ad·vo·cat·ing** : to argue for

adz *or* **adze** \'adz\ *n* : a cutting tool that has a thin curved

adz

blade at right angles to the handle and is used for shaping wood

-aemia — see -EMIA

ae·on *or* **eon** \'ē-ən, 'ē-ˌän\ *n* : a very long period of time : AGE

aer- *or* **aero-** *prefix* : air : atmosphere : gas ⟨*aer*ate⟩ ⟨*aero*sol⟩ ⟨*aero*space⟩

aer·ate \'aər-ˌāt, 'eər-\ *vb* **aer·at·ed; aer·at·ing** **1** : to supply (blood) with oxygen by breathing **2** : to supply or cause to be filled with air **3** : to combine or fill with gas — **aer·at·or** \-ər\ *n*

aer·a·tion \aər-'ā-shən, eər-\ *n* : the process of aerating

¹**ae·ri·al** \'ar-ē-əl, ā-'ir-ē-əl\ *adj* **1** : of, relating to, or occurring in the air **2** : running on cables or rails that are raised above the ground ⟨an *aerial* railway⟩ **3** : of or relating to aircraft ⟨*aerial* navigation⟩ **4** : taken from or used in or against aircraft ⟨*aerial* camera⟩ ⟨*aerial* warfare⟩ — **ae·ri·al·ly** *adv*

²**aer·i·al** \'ar-ē-əl, 'er-\ *n* : a radio or television antenna

ae·rie \'aər-ē, 'eər-, 'iər-, 'ā-ə-rē\ *or* **ey·rie** \'ir-ē *or like* AERIE\ *n* : the nest of a bird (as an eagle) high on a rock

aero·nau·ti·cal \ˌar-ə-'nȯt-i-kəl\ *or* **aero·nau·tic** \-ik\ *adj* : of or relating to aeronautics ⟨*aeronautical* engineer⟩

aero·nau·tics \ˌar-ə-'nȯt-iks\ *n* : a science dealing with the building and flying of aircraft

aero·sol \'ar-ə-ˌsäl, 'er-, -ˌsȯl\ *n* : a substance that is made up of tiny solid or liquid particles in gas

aero·space \'ar-ō-ˌspās, 'er-\ *n* **1** : the earth's atmosphere and the space beyond **2** : a science dealing with aerospace

aes·thet·ic *or* **es·thet·ic** \es-'thet-ik\ *adj* : of or relating to beauty and what is beautiful — **aes·thet·i·cal·ly** \-i-kə-lē\ *adv*

¹**afar** \ə-'fär\ *adv* : from, at, or to a great distance

²**afar** *n* : a long way off ⟨there came a voice from *afar*⟩

af·fa·ble \'af-ə-bəl\ *adj* : polite and friendly in talking to others — **af·fa·bly** \-blē\ *adv*

af·fair \ə-'faər, -'feər\ *n* **1 affairs** *pl* : BUSINESS **1** ⟨government *affairs*⟩ **2** : something that relates to or involves one ⟨that's no *affair* of mine⟩ **3** : an action or occasion only partly specified ⟨the *affair* of the year⟩

¹**af·fect** \ə-'fekt\ *vb* **1** : to be fond of using or wearing ⟨*affect* bright colors⟩ **2** : AS-SUME **3**

²**affect** *vb* **1** : to attack or act on as a disease does **2** : to have an effect on

af·fect·ed \ə-'fek-təd\ *adj* : not natural or genuine ⟨*affected* manners⟩ — **af·fect·ed·ly** *adv*

af·fect·ing \ə-'fek-ting\ *adj* : causing pity or sadness ⟨an *affecting* story⟩

af·fec·tion \ə-'fek-shən\ *n* : a feeling of attachment : liking for someone

af·fec·tion·ate \ə-'fek-shə-nət\ *adj* : feeling or showing a great liking for a person or thing : LOVING — **af·fec·tion·ate·ly** *adv*

af·fi·da·vit \,af-ə-'dā-vət\ *n* : a sworn statement in writing

af·fil·i·ate \ə-'fil-ē-,āt\ *vb* **af·fil·i·at·ed; af·fil·i·at·ing** : to associate as a member or branch

af·fin·i·ty \ə-'fin-ət-ē\ *n, pl* **af·fin·i·ties** : a strong liking for or attraction to someone or something

af·firm \ə-'fərm\ *vb* **1** : to declare to be true **2** : to say with confidence : ASSERT

af·fir·ma·tion \,af-ər-'mā-shən\ *n* : an act of affirming

¹af·fir·ma·tive \ə-'fər-mət-iv\ *adj* **1** : declaring that the fact is so **2** : being positive or helpful

²affirmative *n* **1** : an expression (as the word *yes*) of agreement **2** : the affirmative side in a debate or vote

¹af·fix \ə-'fiks\ *vb* : FASTEN 1, 2, ATTACH

²af·fix \'af-,iks\ *n* : a letter or group of letters that comes at the beginning or end of a word and has a meaning of its own

af·flict \ə-'flikt\ *vb* : to cause pain or unhappiness to

af·flic·tion \ə-'flik-shən\ *n* **1** : the state of being afflicted **2** : something that causes pain or unhappiness

af·flu·ence \'af-,lü-əns\ *n* : the state of having much money or property

af·flu·ent \'af-,lü-ənt\ *adj* : having plenty of money and things that money can buy

af·ford \ə-'fōrd\ *vb* **1** : to be able to do or bear without serious harm ⟨one cannot *afford* to waste one's strength⟩ **2** : to be able to pay for ⟨can't *afford* a new coat this winter⟩ **3** : to supply one with ⟨tennis *affords* good exercise⟩

¹af·front \ə-'frənt\ *vb* : to insult openly

²affront *n* : ²INSULT

afield \ə-'fēld\ *adv* **1** : to, in, or into the countryside **2** : away from home **3** : outside of one's usual circle or way of doing **4** : ASTRAY 2

afire \ə-'fir\ *adj* : being on fire

aflame \ə-'flām\ *adj* : burning with flames

afloat \ə-'flōt\ *adv or adj* : carried on or as if on water

aflut·ter \ə-'flət-ər\ *adj* **1** : flapping quickly **2** : very excited and nervous

afoot \ə-'fut\ *adv or adj* **1** : on foot ⟨traveled *afoot*⟩ **2** : happening now : going on

afore·men·tioned \ə-'fōr-,men-chənd\ *adj* : mentioned before

afore·said \ə-'fōr-,sed\ *adj* : named before ⟨the *aforesaid* persons⟩

afraid \ə-'frād\ *adj* : filled with fear

afresh \ə-'fresh\ *adv* : again from the beginning : from a new beginning

¹Af·ri·can \'af-ri-kən\ *adj* : of or relating to Africa or the Africans

²African *n* : a person born or living in Africa

African violet *n* : a tropical African plant grown often for its showy white, pink, or purple flowers and its velvety leaves

Af·ro–Amer·i·can \,af-rō-ə-'mer-ə-kən\ *adj* : of or relating to Americans having African and especially black ancestors

aft \'aft\ *adv* : toward or at the back part of a ship or the tail of an aircraft

¹af·ter \'af-tər\ *adv* : following in time or place

²after *prep* **1** : behind in time or place ⟨got there *after* me⟩ **2** : for the reason of catching, seizing, or getting ⟨run *after* the ball⟩ ⟨go *after* the championship⟩

³after *conj* : following the time when

⁴after *adj* **1** : later in time ⟨in *after* years⟩ **2** : located toward the back part

af·ter·ef·fect \'af-tər-ə-,fekt\ *n* : an effect that follows its cause after some time has passed

af·ter·glow \'af-tər-,glō\ *n* : a glow remaining (as in the sky after sunset) where a light has disappeared

af·ter·life \'af-tər-,līf\ *n* : an existence after death

af·ter·math \'af-tər-,math\ *n* : a usually bad result

af·ter·noon \,af-tər-'nün\ *n* : the part of the day between noon and evening

af·ter·thought \'af-tər-,thȯt\ *n* : a later thought about something one has done or said

af·ter·ward \'af-tər-wərd\ *or* **af·ter·wards** \-wərdz\ *adv* : at a later time

again \ə-'gen\ *adv* **1** : once more : ANEW ⟨did it *again*⟩ **2** : on the other hand ⟨but then *again*, you might not⟩ **3** : in addition ⟨half as much *again*⟩

against *prep* **1** : opposed to ⟨war *against* disease⟩ **2** : as protection from ⟨a shield *against* aggression⟩ **3** : in or into contact with ⟨bounced *against* the wall⟩

\ə\ **abut**	\au̇\ **out**	\i\ **tip**	\ȯ\ **saw**	\u̇\ **foot**
\ər\ **further**	\ch\ **chin**	\ī\ **life**	\ȯi\ **coin**	\y\ **yet**
\a\ **mat**	\e\ **pet**	\j\ **job**	\th\ **thin**	\yü\ **few**
\ā\ **take**	\ē\ **easy**	\ng\ **sing**	\th\ **this**	\yu̇\ **cure**
\ä\ **cot, cart**	\g\ **go**	\ō\ **bone**	\ü\ **food**	\zh\ **vision**

agape \ə-'gāp\ *adj* : wide open ⟨with mouth *agape*⟩

ag·ate \'ag-ət\ *n* **1** : a mineral that is a quartz with colors arranged in stripes, cloudy masses, or mossy forms **2** : a child's marble of agate or of glass that looks like agate

aga·ve \ə-'gäv-ē\ *n* : a plant that has sword-shaped leaves with spiny edges and is sometimes grown for its large stalks of flowers

agave

¹age \'āj\ *n* **1** : the time from birth to a specified date ⟨a child six years of *age*⟩ **2** : the time of life when a person receives full legal rights ⟨one comes of *age* at eighteen⟩ **3** : the later part of life ⟨a mind as active in *age* as in youth⟩ **4** : normal lifetime **5** : a period of time associated with a special person or feature ⟨the machine *age*⟩ **6** : a long period of time **synonyms** see PERIOD

²age *vb* **aged** \'ājd\; **ag·ing** *or* **age·ing** **1** : to grow old or cause to grow old **2** : to become or cause to become fit for use : MATURE ⟨*age* cheese in a cave⟩

-age \ij\ *n suffix* **1** : collection **2** : action : process ⟨cover*age*⟩ **3** : result of **4** : rate of ⟨shrink*age*⟩ **5** : house or place of ⟨orphan*age*⟩ **6** : state : rank **7** : fee : charge ⟨post*age*⟩

aged \'ā-jəd *for 1*, 'ājd *for 2*\ *adj* **1** : very old ⟨an *aged* oak⟩ **2** : of age ⟨a child *aged* ten⟩

age·less \'āj-ləs\ *adj* : not growing old or showing the effects of age — **age·less·ly** *adv*

agen·cy \'ā-jən-sē\ *n, pl* **agen·cies** **1** : a person or thing through which power is used or something is achieved **2** : the office or function of an agent **3** : an establishment doing business for another ⟨automobile *agency*⟩ **4** : a part of a government that runs projects in a certain area ⟨a health *agency*⟩

agen·da \ə-'jen-də\ *n* : a list of things to be done or talked about

agent \'ā-jənt\ *n* **1** : something that produces an effect ⟨cleansing *agents*⟩ **2** : a person who acts or does business for another

ag·gra·vate \'ag-rə-ˌvāt\ *vb* **ag·gra·vat·ed; ag·gra·vat·ing** **1** : to make worse or more serious ⟨*aggravate* an injury⟩ **2**

: to make angry by bothering again and again

ag·gra·va·tion \ˌag-rə-'vā-shən\ *n* **1** : an act or the result of aggravating **2** : something that aggravates

¹ag·gre·gate \'ag-ri-gət\ *adj* : formed by the collection of units or particles into one mass or sum

²ag·gre·gate \'ag-ri-ˌgāt\ *vb* **ag·gre·gat·ed; ag·gre·gat·ing** : to collect or gather into a mass or whole

³ag·gre·gate \'ag-ri-gət\ *n* **1** : a mass or body of units or parts **2** : the whole sum or amount

ag·gre·ga·tion \ˌag-ri-'gā-shən\ *n* **1** : the collecting of units or parts into a mass or whole **2** : a group, body, or mass composed of many distinct parts

ag·gres·sion \ə-'gresh-ən\ *n* : an attack made without reasonable cause

ag·gres·sive \ə-'gres-iv\ *adj* **1** : showing a readiness to attack others ⟨an *aggressive* dog⟩ **2** : practicing aggression ⟨an *aggressive* nation⟩ **3** : being forceful and sometimes pushy — **ag·gres·sive·ly** *adv* — **ag·gres·sive·ness** *n*

ag·gres·sor \ə-'gres-ər\ *n* : a person or a country that attacks without reasonable cause

ag·grieved \ə-'grēvd\ *adj* **1** : having a troubled or unhappy mind **2** : having cause for complaint

aghast \ə-'gast\ *adj* : struck with terror or amazement

ag·ile \'aj-əl\ *adj* **1** : able to move quickly and easily **2** : having a quick mind — **ag·ile·ly** *adv*

agil·i·ty \ə-'jil-ət-ē\ *n* : the ability to move quickly and easily

aging *present participle of* AGE

ag·i·tate \'aj-ə-ˌtāt\ *vb* **ag·i·tat·ed; ag·i·tat·ing** **1** : to move with an irregular rapid motion ⟨water *agitated* by wind⟩ **2** : to stir up : EXCITE ⟨*agitated* by bad news⟩ **3** : to try to stir up public feeling ⟨*agitate* for civil rights⟩ — **ag·i·ta·tor** \-ər\ *n*

ag·i·ta·tion \ˌaj-ə-'tā-shən\ *n* : the act of agitating : the state of being agitated

agleam \ə-'glēm\ *adj* : giving off gleams of light

aglow \ə-'glō\ *adj* : glowing with light or color

ago \ə-'gō\ *adv* : before this time ⟨a week *ago*⟩

agog \ə-'gäg\ *adj* : full of excitement

ag·o·nize \'ag-ə-ˌnīz\ *vb* **ag·o·nized; ag·o·niz·ing** : to suffer greatly in body or mind

ag·o·ny \'ag-ə-nē\ *n, pl* **ag·o·nies** : great pain of body or mind

agree \ə-'grē\ *vb* **agreed; agree·ing** **1** : to

give one's approval or permission **2** : to have the same opinion **3** : ADMIT 3 ⟨*agreed* that I was right⟩ **4** : to be alike ⟨their stories don't *agree*⟩ **5** : to come to an understanding ⟨*agree* on a price⟩ **6** : to be fitting or healthful ⟨the climate *agrees* with you⟩

agree·able \ə-ˈgrē-ə-bəl\ *adj* **1** : pleasing to the mind or senses ⟨an *agreeable* taste⟩ **2** : willing to agree ⟨*agreeable* to my suggestion⟩ — **agree·able·ness** *n* — **agree·ably** \-blē\ *adv*

agree·ment \ə-ˈgrē-mənt\ *n* **1** : the act or fact of agreeing **2** : an arrangement made about action to be taken

ag·ri·cul·tur·al \ˌag-ri-ˈkəl-chə-rəl, -ˈkəlch-rəl\ *adj* : of, relating to, or used in agriculture

ag·ri·cul·ture \ˈag-ri-ˌkəl-chər\ *n* : the cultivating of the soil, producing of crops, and raising of livestock

aground \ə-ˈgraund\ *adv or adj* : on or onto the shore or the bottom of a body of water

ah \ˈä\ *interj* — used to express delight, relief, disappointment, or scorn

aha \ä-ˈhä\ *interj* — used to express surprise, triumph, or scorn

ahead \ə-ˈhed\ *adv or adj* **1** : in or toward the front **2** : into or for the future

ahead of *prep* **1** : in front of ⟨stood *ahead of* me in line⟩ **2** : earlier than

ahoy \ə-ˈhȯi\ *interj* — used in calling out to a passing ship or boat ⟨ship *ahoy!*⟩

¹aid \ˈād\ *vb* : ¹HELP 1, ASSIST

²aid *n* **1** : the act of helping **2** : help given **3** : someone or something that is of help or assistance

aide \ˈād\ *n* : a person who acts as an assistant

AIDS \ˈādz\ *n* : a serious disease of the human immune system in which large numbers of the cells that help fight infection are destroyed by a virus carried in the blood and other fluids of the body

ail \ˈāl\ *vb* **1** : to be wrong with ⟨what *ails* you?⟩ **2** : to suffer especially with ill health ⟨has been *ailing* for years⟩

ai·le·ron \ˈā-lə-ˌrän\ *n* : a movable part of an airplane wing that is used to steer it to one side or the other

ail·ment \ˈāl-mənt\ *n* : SICKNESS 2

¹aim \ˈām\ *vb* **1** : to point a weapon toward an object **2** : INTEND ⟨we *aim* to

aileron

please⟩ **3** : to direct to or toward a specified object or goal

> **Word History** Both *aim* and *estimate* come from a Latin word that meant "to estimate." An early French word, meaning "to guess" and "to aim" as well as "to estimate," came from this Latin word. The English word *aim* came from this French word. The English word *estimate* came directly from the Latin word that meant "to estimate."

²aim *n* **1** : the directing of a weapon or a missile at a mark **2** : ¹PURPOSE

aim·less \ˈām-ləs\ *adj* : lacking purpose — **aim·less·ly** *adv* — **aim·less·ness** *n*

¹air \ˈaər, ˈeər\ *n* **1** : the invisible mixture of odorless tasteless gases that surrounds the earth **2** : air that is compressed ⟨a drill run by *air*⟩ **3** : AIRCRAFT ⟨travel by *air*⟩ **4** : AVIATION ⟨*air* safety⟩ **5** : a radio or television system ⟨gave a speech on the *air*⟩ **6** : outward appearance ⟨an *air* of mystery⟩ **7 airs** *pl* : an artificial way of acting ⟨put on *airs*⟩

²air *vb* **1** : to place in the air for cooling, freshening, or cleaning ⟨*air* blankets⟩ **2** : to make known in public ⟨*air* one's opinions⟩

air base *n* : a base of operations for military aircraft

air–con·di·tion \ˌaər-kən-ˈdish-ən, ˌeər-\ *vb* : to equip with a device for cleaning air and controlling its humidity and temperature — **air conditioner** *n* — **air–con·di·tion·ing** *n*

air·craft \ˈaər-ˌkraft, ˈeər-\ *n, pl* **aircraft** : a vehicle (as a balloon, airplane, or helicopter) that can travel through the air and that is supported either by its own lightness or by the action of the air against its surfaces

air·drome \ˈaər-ˌdrōm, ˈeər-\ *n* : AIRPORT

air·field \ˈaər-ˌfēld, ˈeər-\ *n* **1** : the landing field of an airport **2** : AIRPORT

air force *n* : the military organization of a nation for air warfare

air lane *n* : AIRWAY 2

air·lift \ˈaər-ˌlift, ˈeər-\ *n* : a system of moving people or cargo by aircraft usually to or from an area that cannot be reached otherwise

air·line \ˈaər-ˌlīn, ˈeər-\ *n* : a system of transportation by aircraft including its routes, equipment, and workers

\ə\ abut	\au̇\ out	\i\ tip	\ȯ\ saw	\u̇\ foot
\ər\ further	\ch\ chin	\ī\ life	\ȯi\ coin	\y\ yet
\a\ mat	\e\ pet	\j\ job	\th\ thin	\yü\ few
\ā\ take	\ē\ easy	\ng\ sing	\th\ this	\yu̇\ cure
\ä\ cot, cart	\g\ go	\ō\ bone	\ü\ food	\zh\ vision

air·lin·er \'aər-ˌlī-nər, 'eər-\ *n* : a large passenger airplane flown by an airline

airliner

¹**air·mail** \'aər-'māl, 'eər-\ *n* **1** : the system of carrying mail by airplanes **2** : mail carried by airplanes

²**airmail** *vb* : to send by airmail

air·man \'aər-mən, 'eər-\ *n, pl* **air·men** \-mən\ **1** : an enlisted person in the Air Force in one of the ranks below sergeant **2** : AVIATOR

airman basic *n* : an enlisted person of the lowest rank in the Air Force

airman first class *n* : an enlisted person in the Air Force ranking above an airman second class

airman second class *n* : an enlisted person in the Air Force ranking above an airman basic

air·plane \'aər-ˌplān, 'eər-\ *n* : an aircraft with a fixed wing that is heavier than air, driven by a propeller or jet engine, and supported by the action of the air against its wings

air·port \'aər-ˌpōrt, 'eər-\ *n* : a place either on land or water that is kept for the landing and takeoff of aircraft and for receiving and sending off passengers and cargo

air·ship \'aər-ˌship, 'eər-\ *n* : an aircraft lighter than air that is kept in the air by a container filled with gas and has an engine, propeller, and rudder

airship

air·sick \'aər-ˌsik, 'eər-\ *adj* : sick to one's stomach while riding in an airplane because of its motion — **air·sick·ness** *n*

air·strip \'aər-ˌstrip, 'eər-\ *n* : a runway without places (as hangars) for the repair of aircraft or shelter of passengers or cargo

air·tight \'aər-'tīt, 'eər-\ *adj* : so tight that no air can get in or out — **air·tight·ness** *n*

air·wave \'aər-ˌwāv, 'eər-\ *n* : the radio waves used in radio and television transmission — usually used in pl.

air·way \'aər-ˌwā, 'eər-\ *n* **1** : a place for a current of air to pass through **2** : a regular route for aircraft **3** : AIRLINE

airy \'aər-ē, 'eər-ē\ *adj* **air·i·er; air·i·est 1** : of, relating to, or living in the air **2** : open to the air : BREEZY ⟨an *airy* room⟩ **3** : like air in lightness and delicacy

aisle \'īl\ *n* : a passage between sections of seats (as in a church or theater)

ajar \ə-'jär\ *adv or adj* : slightly open

akim·bo \ə-'kim-bō\ *adv or adj* : with hands on hips

akin \ə-'kin\ *adj* **1** : related by blood **2** : SIMILAR

¹**-al** \əl, l\ *adj suffix* : of, relating to, or showing ⟨fiction*al*⟩

²**-al** *n suffix* : action : process ⟨rehears*al*⟩

al·a·bas·ter \'al-ə-ˌbas-tər\ *n* : a smooth usually white stone used for carving

a la carte \ˌal-ə-'kärt, ˌä-lə-\ *adv or adj* : with a separate price for each item on the menu

alac·ri·ty \ə-'lak-rət-ē\ *n* : a cheerful readiness to do something

¹**alarm** \ə-'lärm\ *n* **1** : a warning of danger **2** : a device (as a bell) that warns or signals people **3** : the fear caused by sudden danger ⟨filled with *alarm* at the thought of flying⟩

²**alarm** *vb* : to cause a sense of danger in : FRIGHTEN

alas \ə-'las\ *interj* — used to express unhappiness, pity, or worry

al·ba·tross \'al-bə-ˌtrós\ *n* : a very large seabird with webbed feet

al·bi·no \al-'bī-nō\ *n, pl* **al·bi·nos 1** : a person or an animal that has little or no coloring matter in skin, hair, and eyes **2** : a plant with little or no coloring matter

albatross

al·bum \'al-bəm\ *n* **1** : a book with blank pages in which to put a collection (as of photographs, stamps, or autographs) **2** : one or more phonograph records or tape recordings carrying a major musical work or a group of related pieces

al·bu·men \al-'byü-mən\ *n* **1** : the white of an egg **2** : ALBUMIN

al·bu·min \al-'byü-mən\ *n* : any of various proteins that are soluble in water and occur in plant and animal tissues

al·co·hol \'al-kə-ˌhȯl\ *n* **1** : a colorless flammable liquid that in one form is the substance in fermented and distilled liquors (as beer, wine, or whiskey) that can make one drunk **2** : a drink (as beer, wine, or whiskey) containing alcohol

¹al·co·hol·ic \ˌal-kə-'hȯl-ik, -'häl-\ *adj* **1** : of, relating to, or containing alcohol ⟨*alcoholic* drinks⟩ **2** : affected with alcoholism

²alcoholic *n* : a person affected with alcoholism

al·co·hol·ism \'al-kə-ˌhȯl-ˌiz-əm\ *n* : a sickness of body and mind caused by too much use of alcoholic drinks

al·cove \'al-ˌkōv\ *n* : a small part of a room set back from the rest of it

al·der \'ȯl-dər\ *n* : a tree or shrub related to the birches that has toothed leaves and grows in moist soil

alder

ale \'āl\ *n* : an alcoholic drink made from malt and flavored with hops that is usually more bitter than beer

¹alert \ə-'lərt\ *adj* **1** : watchful and ready to meet danger **2** : quick to understand and act **3** : ACTIVE 3, brisk — **alert·ly** *adv* — **alert·ness** *n*

²alert *n* **1** : a signal (as an alarm) of danger **2** : the period during which an alert is in effect — **on the alert** : watchful against danger

³alert *vb* : to call to a state of readiness : WARN

al·fal·fa \al-'fal-fə\ *n* : a plant with purple flowers that is related to the clovers and is grown as a food for horses and cattle

al·ga \'al-gə\ *n, pl* **al·gae** \'al-ˌjē\ : any of a large group of simple plants that contain chlorophyll, are not divisible into roots, stems, and leaves, do not produce seeds, and include the seaweeds and related freshwater and land plants

al·ge·bra \'al-jə-brə\ *n* : a branch of mathematics in which symbols (as letters and numbers) are combined according to the rules of arithmetic

¹ali·as \'ā-lē-əs\ *adv* : otherwise known as

²alias *n* : a false name

¹al·i·bi \'al-ə-ˌbī\ *n, pl* **al·i·bis** **1** : the explanation given by a person accused of a crime that he or she was somewhere else when the crime was committed **2** : ²EXCUSE 2

²alibi *vb* **al·i·bied; al·i·bi·ing** **1** : to offer an excuse **2** : to make an excuse for

¹alien \'ā-lē-ən, 'āl-yən\ *adj* : FOREIGN 2

²alien *n* : a resident who was born elsewhere and is not a citizen of the country in which he or she now lives

alien·ate \'ā-lē-ə,nāt, 'āl-yə-\ *vb* **alien·at·ed; alien·at·ing** : to cause (one who used to be friendly or loyal) to become unfriendly or disloyal

¹alight \ə-'līt\ *vb* **alight·ed** *also* **alit** \ə-'lit\; **alight·ing** **1** : to get down : DISMOUNT **2** : to come down from the air and settle ⟨ducks *alighting* on a pond⟩

²alight *adj* : full of light : lighted up

align \ə-'līn\ *vb* : to bring into line ⟨*align* the wheels of an automobile⟩ — **align·er** *n* — **align·ment** \-mənt\ *n*

¹alike \ə-'līk\ *adj* : being like each other — **alike·ness** *n*

²alike *adv* : in the same way

al·i·men·ta·ry \ˌal-ə-'ment-ə-rē, -'men-trē\ *adj* : of or relating to food and nourishment

alimentary canal *n* : a long tube made up of the esophagus, stomach, and intestine into which food is taken and digested and from which wastes are passed out

al·i·mo·ny \'al-ə-ˌmō-nē\ *n* : money for living expenses paid regularly by one spouse to another after their legal separation or divorce

alit *past of* ALIGHT

alive \ə-'līv\ *adj* **1** : having life : not dead **2** : being in force, existence, or operation ⟨it kept our hopes *alive*⟩ **3** : aware of the existence of ⟨was *alive* to the danger⟩ — **alive·ness** *n*

al·ka·li \'al-kə-ˌlī\ *n, pl* **al·ka·lies** *or* **al·ka·lis** **1** : any of numerous substances that have a bitter taste and react with an acid to form a salt **2** : a salt or a mixture of salts sometimes found in large amounts in the soil of dry regions

al·ka·line \'al-kə-ˌlīn, -lən\ *adj* : of or relating to an alkali

¹all \'ȯl\ *adj* **1** : the whole of ⟨sat up *all* night⟩ **2** : the greatest possible ⟨told in *all* seriousness⟩ **3** : every one of ⟨*all* students can go⟩

\ə\ abut	\au̇\ out	\i\ tip	\ȯ\ saw	\u̇\ foot
\ər\ further	\ch\ chin	\ī\ life	\ȯi\ coin	\y\ yet
\a\ mat	\e\ pet	\j\ job	\th\ thin	\yü\ few
\ā\ take	\ē\ easy	\ng\ sing	\th\ this	\yu̇\ cure
\ä\ cot, cart	\g\ go	\ō\ bone	\ü\ food	\zh\ vision

²**all** *adv* **1** : COMPLETELY ⟨sat *all* alone⟩ **2** : so much ⟨is *all* the better for it⟩ **3** : for each side ⟨the score is two *all*⟩

³**all** *pron* **1** : the whole number or amount ⟨*all* of us⟩ ⟨ate *all* of the candy⟩ **2** : EVERYTHING ⟨*all* is lost⟩

Al·lah \'al-ə, ä-'lä\ *n* : the Supreme Being of the Muslims

all-around \ˌȯl-ə-'raúnd\ *adj* **1** : having ability in many areas **2** : useful in many ways

al·lay \ə-'lā\ *vb* **1** : to make less severe ⟨*allay* pain⟩ **2** : to put to rest ⟨*allay* fears⟩

al·lege \ə-'lej\ *vb* **al·leged; al·leg·ing** : to state as fact but without proof ⟨*allege* a person's guilt⟩

al·le·giance \ə-'lē-jəns\ *n* : loyalty and service to a group, country, or idea **synonyms** see LOYALTY

al·le·lu·ia \ˌal-ə-'lü-yə\ *interj* : HALLELUJAH

al·ler·gic \ə-'lər-jik\ *adj* : of, relating to, or causing allergy

al·ler·gy \'al-ər-jē\ *n, pl* **al·ler·gies** : a condition in which a person is made sick by something that is harmless to most people

al·le·vi·ate \ə-'lē-vē-ˌāt\ *vb* **al·le·vi·at·ed; al·le·vi·at·ing** : to make easier to put up with

al·ley \'al-ē\ *n, pl* **al·leys** **1** : a narrow passageway between buildings **2** : a special narrow wooden floor on which balls are rolled in bowling

al·li·ance \ə-'lī-əns\ *n* **1** : connection between families, groups, or individuals **2** : an association formed by two or more nations for assistance and protection **3** : a treaty of alliance

al·lied \ə-'līd, 'al-ˌīd\ *adj* **1** : being connected or related in some way ⟨chemistry and *allied* subjects⟩ **2** : joined in alliance ⟨*allied* nations⟩

al·li·ga·tor \'al-ə-ˌgāt-ər\ *n* : a large four-footed water animal related to the snakes and lizards

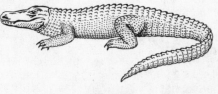

alligator

al·lot \ə-'lät\ *vb* **al·lot·ted; al·lot·ting** : to give out as a share or portion

al·lot·ment \ə-'lät-mənt\ *n* **1** : the act of allotting **2** : something that is allotted

al·low \ə-'laú\ *vb* **1** : to assign as a share or suitable amount (as of time or money) **2** : to take into account **3** : to accept as true : CONCEDE **4** : to give permission to **5** : to fail to prevent ⟨*allow* the dog to roam⟩ **6** : to make allowance ⟨*allow* for growth⟩

al·low·able \ə-'laú-ə-bəl\ *adj* : not forbidden — **al·low·ably** \-blē\ *adv*

al·low·ance \ə-'laú-əns\ *n* **1** : a share given out **2** : a sum given as repayment or for expenses ⟨a weekly *allowance*⟩ **3** : affect a result

al·loy \'al-ˌȯi, ə-'lȯi\ *n* : a substance made of two or more metals melted together ⟨brass is an *alloy* of copper and zinc⟩

all right *adj or adv* **1** : satisfactory in quality or condition **2** : very well

all–round \'ȯl-'raúnd\ *adj* : ALL-AROUND

al·lude \ə-'lüd\ *vb* **al·lud·ed; al·lud·ing** : to talk about or hint at without mentioning directly

al·lure \ə-'lúr\ *vb* **al·lured; al·lur·ing** : to try to influence by offering what seems to be a benefit or pleasure

al·lu·sion \ə-'lü-zhən\ *n* : an act of alluding or of hinting at something

¹**al·ly** \ə-'lī, 'al-ˌī\ *vb* **al·lied; al·ly·ing** : to form a connection between : join in an alliance

²**al·ly** \'al-ˌī, ə-'lī\ *n, pl* **al·lies** : one (as a person or a nation) associated or united with another in a common purpose

al·ma·nac \'ȯl-mə-ˌnak, 'al-\ *n* : a book containing a calendar of days, weeks, and months and usually facts about the rising and setting of the sun and moon, changes in the tides, and information of general interest

al·mighty \ȯl-'mīt-ē\ *adj, often cap* : having absolute power over all ⟨*Almighty* God⟩

al·mond \'ä-mənd, 'am-ənd\ *n* : a nut that is the edible kernel of a small tree related to the peach

al·most \'ȯl-ˌmōst\ *adv* : only a little less than : very nearly

alms \'ämz, 'älmz\ *n, pl* **alms** : something and especially money given to help the poor : CHARITY

aloft \ə-'lȯft\ *adv or adj* **1** : at or to a great height **2** : in the air and especially in flight **3** : at, on, or to the top of the mast or the higher rigging of a ship

¹**alone** \ə-'lōn\ *adj* **1** : separated from others **2** : not including anyone or anything else ⟨food *alone* is not enough for health⟩

synonyms ALONE, SOLITARY, and LONELY mean separated from others. ALONE stresses that one is entirely by oneself ⟨I was left *alone* in the room⟩ SOLITARY may emphasize the fact of being alone ⟨an old tree with a *solitary* apple⟩ but often it stresses the pleasure this gives ⟨*solitary* people who choose peace and quiet⟩ LONELY suggests that one longs for company ⟨felt *lonely* after my friends left⟩

²alone *adv* **1** : and nothing or no one else ⟨did it for money *alone*⟩ ⟨you *alone* are responsible⟩ **2** : without company or help ⟨we thought we could do it *alone*⟩

¹along \ə-'lȯng\ *prep* **1** : on or near in a lengthwise direction ⟨walk *along* the trail⟩ **2** : at a point on ⟨stopped *along* the way⟩

²along *adv* **1** : farther forward or on ⟨move *along*⟩ **2** : as a companion or associate ⟨brought a friend *along*⟩ **3** : throughout the time ⟨knew it all *along*⟩

along·shore \ə-'lȯng-,shōr\ *adv or adj* : along the shore or coast

¹along·side \ə-'lȯng-,sīd\ *adv* : along or by the side

²alongside *prep* : parallel to ⟨boats *alongside* the dock⟩

¹aloof \ə-'lüf\ *adv* : at a distance ⟨stood *aloof*⟩

²aloof *adj* : RESERVED 1 ⟨a shy *aloof* manner⟩ — **aloof·ly** *adv* — **aloof·ness** *n*

aloud \ə-'laȯd\ *adv* : using the voice so as to be clearly heard ⟨read *aloud*⟩

al·paca \al-'pak-ə\ *n* : a South American animal related to the camel and llama that is raised for its long woolly hair which is woven into warm strong cloth

alpaca

al·pha·bet \'al-fə-,bet\ *n* : the letters used in writing a language arranged in their regular order

al·pha·bet·i·cal \,al-fə-'bet-i-kəl\ *or* **al·pha·bet·ic** \-ik\ *adj* : arranged in the order of the letters of the alphabet — **al·pha·bet·i·cal·ly** *adv*

al·pha·bet·ize \'al-fə-bə-,tīz\ *vb* **al·pha·bet·ized; al·pha·bet·iz·ing** : to arrange in alphabetical order

al·ready \ȯl-'red-ē\ *adv* : before a certain time : by this time ⟨I had *already* left when you called⟩

al·so \'ȯl-sō\ *adv* : in addition : TOO

al·tar \'ȯl-tər\ *n* **1** : a usually raised place on which sacrifices are offered **2** : a platform or table used as a center of worship

al·ter \'ȯl-tər\ *vb* : to change partly but not completely ⟨*alter* old clothes⟩ **synonyms** SEE CHANGE

al·ter·ation \,ȯl-tə-'rā-shən\ *n* **1** : a making or becoming different in some respects **2** : the result of altering : MODIFICATION

¹al·ter·nate \'ȯl-tər-nət\ *adj* **1** : occurring or following by turns ⟨*alternate* sunshine and rain⟩ **2** : arranged one above, beside, or next to another ⟨*alternate* layers of cake and filling⟩ **3** : every other : every second ⟨we have meat on *alternate* days⟩ — **al·ter·nate·ly** *adv*

²al·ter·nate \'ȯl-tər-,nāt\ *vb* **al·ter·nat·ed; al·ter·nat·ing** : to take place or cause to take place by turns

³al·ter·nate \'ȯl-tər-nət\ *n* : a person named to take the place of another whenever necessary ⟨*alternates* to a convention⟩

alternating current *n* : an electric current that reverses its direction of flow regularly many times per second

al·ter·na·tion \,ȯl-tər-'nā-shən\ *n* : the act, process, or result of alternating

¹al·ter·na·tive \ȯl-'tər-nət-iv\ *adj* : offering or expressing a choice ⟨*alternative* plans⟩ — **al·ter·na·tive·ly** *adv*

²alternative *n* **1** : a chance to choose between two things **2** : one of the things between which a choice is to be made

al·though \ȯl-'thō\ *conj* : in spite of the fact that ⟨*although* you say it, you don't mean it⟩

al·ti·tude \'al-tə-,tüd, -,tyüd\ *n* **1** : height above a certain level and especially above sea level **2** : the perpendicular distance from the base of a geometric figure to the vertex or to the side parallel to the base **synonyms** SEE HEIGHT

al·to \'al-tō\ *n, pl* **al·tos 1** : the lowest

\ə\ **abut**	\aȯ\ **out**	\i\ **tip**	\ȯ\ **saw**	\ȯ\ **foot**
\ər\ **further**	\ch\ **chin**	\ī\ **life**	\ȯi\ **coin**	\y\ **yet**
\a\ **mat**	\e\ **pet**	\j\ **job**	\th\ **thin**	\yü\ **few**
\ā\ **take**	\ē\ **easy**	\ng\ **sing**	\th\ **this**	\yu\ **cure**
\ä\ **cot, cart**	\g\ **go**	\ō\ **bone**	\ü\ **food**	\zh\ **vision**

female singing voice **2** : the second highest part in four-part harmony **3** : a singer or an instrument having an alto range or part

al·to·geth·er \ˌȯl-tə-ˈgeth-ər\ adv **1** : COMPLETELY ⟨I'm not altogether sure⟩ **2** : on the whole ⟨altogether our school is one of the best⟩

al·tru·ism \ˈal-trü-ˌiz-əm\ n : unselfish interest in others

al·um \ˈal-əm\ n : either of two aluminum compounds that have a sweetish-sourish taste and puckering effect on the mouth and are used in medicine (as to stop bleeding)

alu·mi·num \ə-ˈlü-mə-nəm\ n : a silver-white light metallic chemical element that is easily worked, conducts electricity well, resists weathering, and is the most plentiful metal in the earth's crust

alum·na \ə-ˈləm-nə\ n, pl **alum·nae** \-ˌnē\ : a girl or woman who has attended or has graduated from a school, college, or university

alum·nus \ə-ˈləm-nəs\ n, pl **alum·ni** \-ˌnī\ : one who has attended or has graduated from a school, college, or university

al·ways \ˈȯl-wēz, -wəz, -wāz\ adv **1** : at all times ⟨always knows the answer⟩ **2** : throughout all time : FOREVER

am \əm, am\ present 1st sing of BE

amal·ga·ma·tion \ə-ˌmal-gə-ˈmā-shən\ n : the combining of different elements into a single body

amass \ə-ˈmas\ vb : to collect or gather together ⟨amass a fortune⟩

¹am·a·teur \ˈam-ə-ˌtər, -ət-ər\ n **1** : a person who takes part in sports or occupations for pleasure and not for pay **2** : a person who takes part in something without having experience or skill in it — **am·a·teur·ish** \ˌam-ə-ˈtər-ish\ adj

Word History The English word amateur came from a French word which in turn came from a Latin word that meant "lover." In English, amateurs are so called because they do something for the love of doing it and not for pay.

²amateur adj : of, relating to, or done by amateurs : not professional

amaze \ə-ˈmāz\ vb **amazed; amaz·ing** : to surprise or puzzle very much **synonyms** see SURPRISE

amaze·ment \ə-ˈmāz-mənt\ n : great surprise

am·bas·sa·dor \am-ˈbas-ə-dər\ n : a person sent as the chief representative of his or her government in another country — **am·bas·sa·dor·ship** \-ˌship\ n

am·ber \ˈam-bər\ n **1** : a hard yellowish to brownish clear substance that is a fossil resin from trees long dead, takes a polish, and is used for ornamental objects (as beads) **2** : a dark orange yellow

ambi- prefix : both

am·bi·dex·trous \ˌam-bi-ˈdek-strəs\ adj : using both hands with equal ease — **am·bi·dex·trous·ly** adv

am·bi·gu·ity \ˌam-bə-ˈgyü-ət-ē\ n, pl **am·bi·gu·ities** : the fact or state of being ambiguous

am·big·u·ous \am-ˈbig-yə-wəs\ adj : able to be understood in more than one way ⟨an ambiguous answer⟩ — **am·big·u·ous·ly** adv

am·bi·tion \am-ˈbish-ən\ n **1** : a desire for success, honor, or power **2** : the aim or object one tries for ⟨my ambition is to become a jet pilot⟩

Word History Like the candidates of today, some men ran for public office in ancient Rome by going around and asking people to vote for them. The Latin word for this practice meant "a going around." Since looking for votes showed "a desire for power or honor," the Latin word took on that meaning. The English word ambition came from the Latin word that once meant "a going around."

am·bi·tious \am-ˈbish-əs\ adj **1** : possessing ambition ⟨ambitious to be president of the class⟩ **2** : showing ambition ⟨an ambitious plan⟩ — **am·bi·tious·ly** adv

¹am·ble \ˈam-bəl\ vb **am·bled; am·bling** : to go at an amble

²amble n : a slow easy way of walking

am·bu·lance \ˈam-byə-ləns\ n : a vehicle meant to carry sick or injured persons

¹am·bush \ˈam-ˌbush\ vb : to attack from an ambush

²ambush n : a hidden place from which a surprise attack can be made

ameba variant of AMOEBA

amen \ˈā-ˈmen, ˈä-\ interj — used to express agreement (as after a prayer or a statement of opinion)

ame·na·ble \ə-ˈmē-nə-bəl, -ˈmen-ə-\ adj : readily giving in or agreeing ⟨amenable to our wishes⟩

amend \ə-ˈmend\ vb **1** : to change for the better : IMPROVE **2** : to change the wording or meaning of : ALTER ⟨amend a law in congress⟩

amend·ment \ə-ˈmend-mənt\ n : a change in wording or meaning especially in a law, bill, or motion

amends \ə-ˈmendz\ n sing or pl : something done or given by a person to make up for a loss or injury he or she has caused ⟨make *amends*⟩

ame·ni·ty \ə-'men-ət-ē, -'mē-nət-\ *n, pl* **ame·ni·ties** **1** : the quality of being pleasant or agreeable **2** *amenities pl* : something (as good manners or household appliances) that makes life easier or more pleasant

¹Amer·i·can \ə-'mer-ə-kən\ *n* **1** : a person born or living in North or South America **2** : a citizen of the United States

²American *adj* **1** : of or relating to North or South America or their residents **2** : of or relating to the United States or its citizens

American Indian *n* : ¹INDIAN 2

am·e·thyst \'am-ə-thəst\ *n* : a clear purple or bluish violet quartz used as a gem

Word History People once believed that amethysts could cure drunkenness. The ancient Greeks gave the stone a name that reflected this belief. This name was formed from a prefix that meant "not" and a verb that meant "to be drunk." This verb came from a Greek word that meant "wine." The English word *amethyst* came from the Greek name for the stone.

ami·a·ble \'ā-mē-ə-bəl\ *adj* : having a friendly and pleasant manner — **ami·a·bly** \-blē\ *adv*

am·i·ca·ble \'am-i-kə-bəl\ *adj* : showing kindness or goodwill — **am·i·ca·bly** \-blē\ *adv*

amid \ə-'mid\ *or* **amidst** \-'midst\ *prep* : in or into the middle of ⟨advanced *amid* cheering crowds⟩

amid·ships \ə-'mid-,ships\ *adv* : in or near the middle of a ship

ami·no acid \ə-'mē-nō-\ *n* : any of numerous acids that contain carbon and nitrogen, include some which are the building blocks of protein, and are made by living plant or animal cells or obtained from the diet

¹amiss \ə-'mis\ *adv* : in the wrong way ⟨now, don't take this remark *amiss*⟩

²amiss *adj* : not right : WRONG ⟨something is *amiss* here⟩

am·i·ty \'am-ət-ē\ *n, pl* **am·i·ties** : FRIENDSHIP ⟨there is *amity* between our country and Canada⟩

am·me·ter \'am-,ēt-ər\ *n* : an instrument for measuring electric current in amperes

am·mo·nia \ə-'mō-nyə\ *n* **1** : a colorless gas that is a compound of nitrogen and hydrogen, has a sharp smell and taste, can be easily made liquid by cold and pressure, and is used in making ice, fertilizers, and explosives **2** : a solution of ammonia and water

am·mu·ni·tion \,am-yə-'nish-ən\ *n* **1** : objects (as bullets) fired from guns **2** : explosive objects (as bombs) used in war

am·ne·sia \am-'nē-zhə\ *n* : an abnormal and usually complete loss of one's memory

amoe·ba \ə-'mē-bə\ *n, pl* **amoe·bas** *or* **amoe·bae** \-bē\ : a tiny water animal that is a single cell which flows about and takes in food

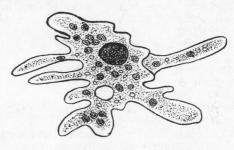

amoeba

among \ə-'məng\ *also* **amongst** \-'məngst\ *prep* **1** : in or through the middle of ⟨*among* the crowd⟩ **2** : in the presence of : WITH ⟨you're *among* friends⟩ **3** : through all or most of ⟨discontent *among* the poor⟩ **4** : in shares to each of ⟨candy divided *among* friends⟩ **synonyms** see BETWEEN

¹amount \ə-'maunt\ *vb* **1** : to add up ⟨the bill *amounted* to ten dollars⟩ **2** : to be the same in meaning or effect ⟨acts that *amount* to treason⟩

²amount *n* : the total number or quantity

am·pere \'am-,piər\ *n* : a unit for measuring the strength of an electric current

am·per·sand \'am-pər-,sand\ *n* : a character & standing for the word *and*

am·phet·amine \am-'fet-ə-,mēn, -mən\ *n* : a drug that causes the nervous system to become more active

am·phib·i·an \am-'fib-ē-ən\ *n* **1** : an amphibious animal **2** : any of a group of cold-blooded animals with smooth skins including the frogs, toads, and salamanders **3** : an airplane meant to take off from and land on either land or water

am·phib·i·ous \am-'fib-ē-əs\ *adj* **1** : able to live both on land and in water ⟨*amphibious* animals⟩ **2** : meant to be used on

\ə\ abut	\aú\ out	\i\ tip	\ó\ saw	\ú\ foot
\ər\ further	\ch\ chin	\ī\ life	\ói\ coin	\y\ yet
\a\ mat	\e\ pet	\j\ job	\th\ thin	\yü\ few
\ā\ take	\ē\ easy	\ng\ sing	\th\ this	\yú\ cure
\ä\ cot, cart	\g\ go	\ō\ bone	\ü\ food	\zh\ vision

both land and water 〈*amphibious* vehicles〉 **3** : made by land, sea, and air forces acting together 〈*amphibious* attack〉 — **am·phib·i·ous·ly** *adv* — **am·phib·i·ous·ness** *n*

am·phi·the·a·ter \'am-fə-ˌthē-ət-ər\ *n* : an arena with seats rising in curved rows around an open space

am·ple \'am-pəl\ *adj* : more than enough in amount or size 〈an *ample* fireplace〉 〈an *ample* supply of food〉 — **am·ply** \-plē\ *adv*

am·pli·fy \'am-plə-ˌfi\ *vb* **am·pli·fied; am·pli·fy·ing** **1** : to add to 〈*amplify* a statement〉 **2** : to make louder or greater 〈*amplify* the voice by using a megaphone〉 — **am·pli·fi·er** *n*

am·pu·tate \'am-pyə-ˌtāt\ *vb* **am·pu·tat·ed; am·pu·tat·ing** : to cut off 〈*amputate* a leg〉

am·u·let \'am-yə-lət\ *n* : a small object worn as a charm against evil

amuse \ə-'myüz\ *vb* **amused; amus·ing** **1** : to entertain with something pleasant 〈*amuse* oneself with a book〉 **2** : to please the sense of humor of 〈the joke *amused* everyone〉

synonyms AMUSE and ENTERTAIN mean to cause the time to pass in an agreeable way. AMUSE suggests simply keeping one interested in anything that is pleasant or humorous 〈the toy *amused* the child for hours〉 ENTERTAIN suggests providing amusement for someone by preparing or doing something special 〈the school put on a show to *entertain* the parents〉

amuse·ment \ə-'myüz-mənt\ *n* **1** : something that amuses or entertains 〈what are your favorite *amusements*〉 **2** : the condition of being amused

an \ən, an\ *indefinite article* : ²A — used before words beginning with a vowel sound 〈*an* oak〉〈*an* hour〉

¹-an \ən\ *or* **-ian** *also* **-ean** \ē-ən, yən, ən\ *n suffix* **1** : one that belongs to 〈American〉 **2** : one skilled in or specializing in 〈magician〉

²-an *or* **-ian** *also* **-ean** *adj suffix* **1** : of or relating to 〈American〉 **2** : like : resembling

an·a·con·da \ˌan-ə-'kän-də\ *n* : a large South American snake of the boa family

anal·y·sis \ə-'nal-ə-səs\ *n, pl* **anal·y·ses** \-ə-ˌsēz\ : an examination of something to find out how it is made or works or what it is

an·a·lyst \'an-l-əst\ *n* : a person who analyzes or is skilled in analysis

an·a·lyt·ic \ˌan-l-'it-ik\ *or* **an·a·lyt·i·cal** \ˌan-l-'it-i-kəl\ *adj* : of, relating to, or skilled in analysis — **an·a·lyt·i·cal·ly** *adv*

an·a·lyze \'an-l-ˌīz\ *vb* **an·a·lyzed; an·a·lyz·ing** : to examine something to find out what it is or what makes it work

an·ar·chist \'an-ər-kəst\ *n* : a person who believes in or practices anarchy

an·ar·chy \'an-ər-kē\ *n* **1** : the condition of a country where there is no government or law and order **2** : a state of confused disorder or lawlessness

anaconda

an·a·tom·i·cal \ˌan-ə-'täm-i-kəl\ *or* **an·a·tom·ic** \-'täm-ik\ *adj* : of or relating to anatomy

anat·o·my \ə-'nat-ə-mē\ *n, pl* **anat·o·mies** **1** : a science that has to do with the structure of the body **2** : the structural makeup especially of a person or animal 〈the *anatomy* of the cat〉

-ance \əns\ *n suffix* **1** : action or process 〈perform*ance*〉 **2** : quality or state 〈resembl*ance*〉 **3** : amount or degree

an·ces·tor \'an-ˌses-tər\ *n* : one from whom an individual is descended

an·ces·tral \an-'ses-trəl\ *adj* : of, relating to, or coming from an ancestor 〈their *ancestral* home〉

an·ces·try \'an-ˌses-trē\ *n, pl* **an·ces·tries** : one's ancestors

¹an·chor \'ang-kər\ *n* **1** : a heavy iron or steel device attached to a ship by a cable or chain and so made that when thrown overboard it digs into the bottom and holds the ship in place **2** : something that keeps something else fastened or steady

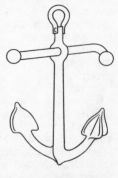
anchor 1

²anchor *vb* **1** : to hold or become held in place with an anchor 〈*anchor* a ship〉 **2** : to fasten tightly 〈*anchor* the cables of a bridge〉

an·chor·age \'ang-kə-rij\ *n* : a place where boats can be anchored

¹**an·cient** \'ān-shənt, -chənt\ *adj* **1** : very old ⟨*ancient* customs⟩ **2** : of or relating to a time long past or to those living in such a time

²**ancient** *n* **1** : a very old person **2 ancients** *pl* : the civilized peoples of ancient times and especially of Greece and Rome

-an·cy \ən-sē, -n-sē\ *n suffix, pl* **-an·cies** : quality or state ⟨buoy*ancy*⟩

and \ənd, and\ *conj* **1** : added to ⟨2 *and* 2 make 4⟩ **2** : AS WELL AS, ALSO ⟨ice cream *and* cake⟩⟨strong *and* healthy⟩ — **and so forth** : and others or more of the same kind — **and so on** : AND SO FORTH

and·iron \'an-ˌdī-ərn\ *n* : one of a pair of metal supports for firewood in a fireplace

an·ec·dote \'an-ik-ˌdōt\ *n* : a short story about something interesting or funny in a person's life

ane·mia \ə-'nē-mē-ə\ *n* : a sickness in which there is too little blood or too few red blood cells or too little hemoglobin in the blood

an·e·mom·e·ter \ˌan-ə-'mäm-ət-ər\ *n* : an instrument for measuring the speed of the wind

anem·o·ne \ə-'nem-ə-nē\ *n* : a plant related to the buttercup that blooms in spring and is often grown for its large white or colored flowers

anemone

an·es·the·sia \ˌan-əs-'thē-zhə\ *n* : loss of feeling or consciousness

¹**an·es·thet·ic** \ˌan-əs-'thet-ik\ *adj* : of, relating to, or capable of producing anesthesia

²**anesthetic** *n* : something that produces anesthesia

anew \ə-'nü, -'nyü\ *adv* **1** : over again ⟨begin *anew*⟩ **2** : in a new or different form ⟨tear down and build *anew*⟩

an·gel \'ān-jəl\ *n* **1** : a spiritual being serving God especially as a messenger **2** : a person thought to be like an angel (as in goodness or beauty)

¹**an·ger** \'ang-gər\ *n* : a strong feeling of displeasure and often of active opposition to an insult, injury, or injustice

synonyms ANGER, RAGE, and FURY mean excitement of the feelings brought about by great displeasure. ANGER can be used of either a strong or a mild feeling ⟨I was able to hide my *anger*⟩ RAGE suggests such strong, violent feeling that one cannot control oneself ⟨screaming with *rage*⟩ FURY suggests an overwhelming rage that is almost like madness and may cause one to destroy things ⟨in their *fury* the people smashed windows and turned over cars⟩

²**anger** *vb* : to make angry

¹**an·gle** \'ang-gəl\ *n* **1** : the figure formed by two lines meeting at a point **2** : a sharp corner **3** : POINT OF VIEW ⟨consider a problem from a new *angle*⟩

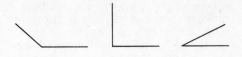
angles

²**angle** *vb* **an·gled; an·gling** : to turn, move, or direct at an angle

³**angle** *vb* **an·gled; an·gling 1** : to fish with hook and line **2** : to try to get what one wants in a sly way ⟨*angle* for a compliment⟩

an·gler \'ang-glər\ *n* : a person who fishes with hook and line especially for pleasure

an·gle·worm \'ang-gəl-ˌwərm\ *n* : EARTH-WORM

an·gling \'ang-gling\ *n* : fishing with hook and line for pleasure

An·glo- \'ang-glō\ *prefix* **1** : English **2** : English and

¹**An·glo–Sax·on** \ˌang-glō-'sak-sən\ *n* **1** : a member of the German people who conquered England in the fifth century A.D. **2** : a person whose ancestors were English

²**Anglo–Saxon** *adj* : of or relating to the Anglo-Saxons

an·go·ra \ang-'gōr-ə\ *n* : cloth or yarn made from the soft silky hair of a special usually white domestic rabbit (**Angora rabbit**) or from the long shiny wool of a goat (**Angora goat**)

an·gry \'ang-grē\ *adj* **an·gri·er; an·gri·est** : feeling or showing anger — **an·gri·ly** \-grə-lē\ *adv*

an·guish \'ang-gwish\ *n* : great pain or trouble of body or mind

an·guished \'ang-gwisht\ *adj* : full of anguish ⟨an *anguished* cry⟩

\ə\ abut	\au̇\ out	\i\ tip	\ȯ\ saw	\u̇\ foot
\ər\ further	\ch\ chin	\ī\ life	\ȯi\ coin	\y\ yet
\a\ mat	\e\ pet	\j\ job	\th\ thin	\yü\ few
\ā\ take	\ē\ easy	\ng\ sing	\th\ this	\yu̇\ cure
\ä\ cot, cart	\g\ go	\ō\ bone	\ü\ food	\zh\ vision

an·gu·lar \'ang-gyə-lər\ *adj* **1** : having angles or sharp corners **2** : being lean and bony ⟨an *angular* face⟩

an·i·mal \'an-ə-məl\ *n* **1** : any of the great group of living beings (as jellyfishes, crabs, birds, and people) that differ from plants typically in being able to move about, in not having cell walls made of cellulose, and in depending on plants and other animals as sources of food **2** : any of the animals lower than humans in the natural order **3** : MAMMAL

¹an·i·mate \'an-ə-mət\ *adj* : having life

²an·i·mate \'an-ə-ˌmāt\ *vb* **an·i·mat·ed; an·i·mat·ing** **1** : to give life or energy to : make alive or lively **2** : to make appear to move ⟨*animate* a cartoon⟩

an·i·mat·ed \'an-ə-ˌmāt-əd\ *adj* **1** : full of life and energy : LIVELY **2** : appearing to be alive or moving

an·i·mos·i·ty \ˌan-ə-'mäs-ət-ē\ *n, pl* **an·i·mos·i·ties** : ²DISLIKE, HATRED

an·kle \'ang-kəl\ *n* **1** : the joint between the foot and the leg **2** : the area containing the ankle joint

an·klet \'ang-klət\ *n* : a sock reaching slightly above the ankle

an·nals \'an-lz\ *n pl* **1** : a record of events arranged in yearly sequence **2** : historical records : HISTORY

an·neal \ə-'nēl\ *vb* : to heat (as glass or steel) and then cool so as to toughen and make less brittle

¹an·nex \ə-'neks, 'an-ˌeks\ *vb* : to add (something) to something else usually so as to become a part of it ⟨*annex* a postscript to a letter⟩ ⟨the United States *annexed* Texas and it became our twenty-eighth state⟩

²an·nex \'an-ˌeks\ *n* : something (as a wing of a building) added on

an·nex·ation \ˌan-ˌek-'sā-shən\ *n* : an annexing especially of new territory

an·ni·hi·late \ə-'nī-ə-ˌlāt\ *vb* **an·ni·hi·lat·ed; an·ni·hi·lat·ing** : to destroy entirely : put completely out of existence

an·ni·ver·sa·ry \ˌan-ə-'vərs-ə-rē, -'vərs-rē\ *n, pl* **an·ni·ver·sa·ries** : the return every year of the date when something special (as a wedding) happened

an·nounce \ə-'naůns\ *vb* **an·nounced; an·nounc·ing** **1** : to make known publicly **2** : to give notice of the arrival, presence, or readiness of ⟨*announce* dinner⟩ **synonyms** see DECLARE

an·nounce·ment \ə-'naůn-smənt\ *n* **1** : the act of announcing **2** : a public notice announcing something

an·nounc·er \ə-'naůn-sər\ *n* : a person who introduces radio or television pro-

grams, makes announcements, and gives the news and station identification

an·noy \ə-'nòi\ *vb* : to disturb or irritate especially by repeated disagreeable acts

synonyms ANNOY, PESTER, and TEASE mean to disturb and upset a person. ANNOY suggests bothering someone to the point of anger ⟨I am *annoyed* by your bad behavior⟩ PESTER suggests bothering someone over and over ⟨stop *pestering* me for more money⟩ TEASE often suggests continually tormenting someone until that person is provoked or upset ⟨they *teased* the child to the point of tears⟩

an·noy·ance \ə-'nòi-əns\ *n* **1** : the act of annoying **2** : the feeling of being annoyed **3** : a source or cause of being annoyed ⟨the dog's barking was a constant *annoyance*⟩

an·noy·ing \ə-'nòi-ing\ *adj* : causing annoyance ⟨an *annoying* habit⟩ — **an·noy·ing·ly** *adv*

¹an·nu·al \'an-yə-wəl\ *adj* **1** : coming, happening, done, made, or given once a year **2** : completing the life cycle in one growing season ⟨*annual* plants⟩ — **an·nu·al·ly** *adv*

²annual *n* : an annual plant

an·nu·ity \ə-'nü-ət-ē, -'nyü-\ *n, pl* **an·nu·ities** : a sum of money paid at regular intervals

an·nul \ə-'nəl\ *vb* **an·nulled; an·nul·ling** : to bring to an end : to make null ⟨*annul* a marriage⟩ — **an·nul·ment** \-mənt\ *n*

an·ode \'an-ˌōd\ *n* **1** : the positive electrode of an electrolytic cell **2** : the negative end of a battery that is delivering electric current **3** : the electron-collecting electrode of an electron tube

anoint \ə-'nòint\ *vb* **1** : to rub or cover with oil or grease **2** : to put oil on as part of a religious ceremony

anon·y·mous \ə-'nän-ə-məs\ *adj* **1** : not named or identified ⟨an *anonymous* caller⟩ **2** : made or done by someone unknown ⟨an *anonymous* phone call⟩ — **anon·y·mous·ly** *adv*

¹an·oth·er \ə-'nəth-ər\ *adj* **1** : some other ⟨choose *another* day⟩ **2** : one more ⟨bring *another* cup⟩

²another *pron* **1** : one more ⟨hit one homer in the first game and *another* in the second⟩ **2** : someone or something different ⟨horseplay is one thing, but vandalism is *another*⟩

¹an·swer \'an-sər\ *n* **1** : something said or written in reply (as to a question) **2** : a solution of a problem

²answer *vb* **1** : to speak or write in reply

to **2** : to take responsibility ⟨*answered* for the children's safety⟩ **3** : ¹SERVE 5, DO

an·swer·able \'an-sə-rə-bəl\ *adj* **1** : RESPONSIBLE 1 ⟨*answerable* for your actions⟩ **2** : possible to answer ⟨an *answerable* argument⟩

ant \'ant\ *n* : a small insect related to the bees and wasps that lives in colonies and forms nests in the ground or in wood in which it stores food and raises its young

ant- *see* ANTI-

¹-ant \ənt\ *n suffix* **1** : one that does or causes a certain thing ⟨deodor*ant*⟩ **2** : thing that is acted upon in a certain way

²-ant *adj suffix* **1** : doing a certain thing or being a certain way **2** : causing a certain action

an·tag·o·nism \an-'tag-ə-ˌniz-əm\ *n* : a state of not liking and being against something

an·tag·o·nist \an-'tag-ə-nəst\ *n* : a person who is against something or someone else : OPPONENT

an·tag·o·nis·tic \an-ˌtag-ə-'nis-tik\ *adj* : being against something or someone : HOSTILE, UNFRIENDLY — **an·tag·o·nis·ti·cal·ly** \-ti-kə-lē\ *adv*

an·tag·o·nize \an-'tag-ə-ˌnīz\ *vb* **an·tag·o·nized; an·tag·o·niz·ing** : to stir up dislike or anger in ⟨parents who *antagonize* their children⟩

ant·arc·tic \ant-'ärk-tik, -'ärt-ik\ *adj, often cap* : of or relating to the south pole or to the region around it⟨*antarctic* explorers⟩

an·te- \'ant-i\ *prefix* **1** : before in time : earlier ⟨*ante*date⟩ **2** : in front of ⟨*ante*room⟩

ant·eat·er \'ant-ˌēt-ər\ *n* : any of several animals that have long noses and long sticky tongues and feed chiefly on ants

an·te·cham·ber \'ant-i-ˌchām-bər\ *n* : ANTEROOM

an·te·lope \'ant-l-ˌōp\ *n* : any of a group of cud-chewing animals that have horns that extend upward and backward

an·ten·na \an-'ten-ə\ *n* **1** *pl* **an·ten·nae** \'ten-ē\ : one of two or four threadlike movable feelers on the heads of insects or crustaceans (as lobsters) **2** *pl* **an·ten·nas** : a metallic device (as a rod or wire) for sending or receiving radio waves

Word History Long ago, a wise man in Greece wrote about insects. His name was Aristotle. Aristotle used a Greek word that meant "horn" to refer to the insects' feelers. The Greek word for "horn" had another meaning —"sail yard." (A sail yard supports and spreads the sails on a sailing ship.) When Aristotle's book was translated into Latin, the Latin word for "sail yard" was used instead of the Latin word for "horn." That is how the Latin word that meant "sail yard" came to mean "feeler" as well. The English word *antenna* came from this Latin word.

an·te·room \'ant-i-ˌrüm, -ˌrum\ *n* : a room used as an entrance to another

an·them \'an-thəm\ *n* **1** : a sacred song usually sung by a church choir **2** : a patriotic song of praise and love for one's country

an·ther \'an-thər\ *n* : the enlargement at the tip of a flower's stamen that contains pollen

anther

ant·hill \'ant-ˌhil\ *n* : a mound of dirt thrown up by ants in digging their nest

an·thol·o·gy \an-'thäl-ə-jē\ *n, pl* **an·thol·o·gies** : a collection of writings (as stories and poems)

an·thra·cite \'an-thrə-ˌsīt\ *n* : a hard glossy coal that burns without much smoke

an·thrax \'an-ˌthraks\ *n* : a dangerous bacterial disease of warm-blooded animals that can affect humans

an·thro·poid \'an-thrə-ˌpȯid\ *adj* : looking somewhat like humans ⟨the *anthropoid* apes⟩

an·thro·pol·o·gy \ˌan-thrə-'päl-ə-jē\ *n* : a science that studies people and especially their history, development, distribution and culture

an·ti- \'ant-i, 'an-ˌtī\ *or* **ant-** \ant\ *prefix* **1** : opposite in kind, position, or action ⟨*anti*cyclone⟩ **2** : hostile toward ⟨*anti*social⟩

an·ti·bi·ot·ic \ˌant-i-bī-'ät-ik\ *n* : a substance produced by living things and especially by bacteria and fungi that is used to kill or prevent the growth of harmful germs

an·ti·body \'ant-i-ˌbäd-ē\ *n, pl* **an·ti·bod·ies** : a substance produced by the body that counteracts the effects of a disease germ or its poisons

an·tic \'ant-ik\ *n* : a wildly playful or funny act or action

an·tic·i·pate \an-'tis-ə-ˌpāt\ *vb* **an·tic·i·pat·ed; an·tic·i·pat·ing** **1** : to foresee and deal with or provide for beforehand

\ə\ abut	\au̇\ out	\i\ tip	\ȯ\ saw	\u̇\ foot
\ər\ further	\ch\ chin	\ī\ life	\ȯi\ coin	\y\ yet
\a\ mat	\e\ pet	\j\ job	\th\ thin	\yü\ few
\ā\ take	\ē\ easy	\ng\ sing	\th\ this	\yu̇\ cure
\ä\ cot, cart	\g\ go	\ō\ bone	\ü\ food	\zh\ vision

⟨*anticipated* my objections⟩ ⟨*anticipate* your every wish⟩ **2** : to look forward to ⟨*anticipating* their visit⟩

an·tic·i·pa·tion \an-ˌtis-ə-'pā-shən\ *n* **1** : an action that takes into account and deals with or prevents a later action **2** : pleasurable expectation **3** : a picturing beforehand of a future event or state

an·ti·cy·clone \ˌant-i-'sī-ˌklōn\ *n* : a system of winds that whirls clockwise about a center of high atmospheric pressure

an·ti·dote \'ant-i-ˌdōt\ *n* : something used to reverse or prevent the action of a poison

an·ti·freeze \'ant-i-ˌfrēz\ *n* : a substance added to the liquid in an automobile radiator to prevent its freezing

an·ti·mo·ny \'ant-ə-ˌmō-nē\ *n* : a silvery white metallic chemical element

an·tip·a·thy \an-'tip-ə-thē\ *n, pl* **an·tip·a·thies** : a strong feeling of dislike

an·ti·quat·ed \'ant-ə-ˌkwāt-əd\ *adj* : OLD-FASHIONED 1, OBSOLETE

¹an·tique \an-'tēk\ *adj* : belonging to or like a former style or fashion ⟨*antique* lamps⟩

²antique *n* : an object (as a piece of furniture) made at an earlier time

an·tiq·ui·ty \an-'tik-wət-ē\ *n* **1** : ancient times **2** : very great age ⟨a castle of great *antiquity*⟩

¹an·ti·sep·tic \ˌant-ə-'sep-tik\ *adj* : killing or making harmless the germs that cause decay or sickness ⟨iodine is *antiseptic*⟩

²antiseptic *n* : an antiseptic substance

an·ti·so·cial \ˌant-i-'sō-shəl, ˌan-ˌtī-\ *adj* **1** : being against or bad for society ⟨*antisocial* acts of the criminal⟩ **2** : UNFRIENDLY

an·tith·e·sis \an-'tith-ə-səs\ *n, pl* **an·tith·e·ses** \-ə-ˌsēz\ : the exact opposite

an·ti·tox·in \ˌant-i-'täk-sən\ *n* : a substance that is formed in the blood of one exposed to a disease and that prevents or acts against that disease

ant·ler \'ant-lər\ *n* : the entire horn or a branch of the horn of an animal of the deer family — **ant·lered** \-lərd\ *adj*

ant lion *n* : an insect larva with long jaws that digs a hole shaped like a cone in which it waits to catch insects (as ants) on which it feeds

an·to·nym \'an-tə-ˌnim\ *n* : a word of opposite meaning ⟨"hot" and "cold" are *antonyms*⟩

an·vil \'an-vəl\ *n* : an iron block on which pieces of metal are hammered into shape

anx·i·ety \ang-'zī-ət-ē\ *n, pl* **anx·i·eties** : fear or nervousness about what might happen

anx·ious \'angk-shəs\ *adj* **1** : afraid or nervous about what may happen ⟨*anxious* about the child's health⟩ **2** : wanting very much : EAGER ⟨*anxious* to make good⟩ **synonyms** see EAGER — **anx·ious·ly** *adv*

¹any \'en-ē\ *adj* **1** : whatever kind of ⟨*any* person you meet⟩ **2** : of whatever number or amount ⟨need *any* help I can get⟩

²any *pron* **1** : any individuals ⟨are *any* of you ready⟩ **2** : any amount ⟨is there *any* left⟩

³any *adv* : to the least amount or degree ⟨can't get it *any* cleaner⟩ ⟨was never *any* good⟩

any·body \'en-ē-ˌbäd-ē, -ˌbad-ē\ *pron* : ANYONE

any·how \'en-ē-ˌhaú\ *adv* **1** : in any way, manner, or order **2** : at any rate : in any case

any·more \ˌen-ē-'mōr\ *adv* : NOWADAYS ⟨we never see them *anymore*⟩

any·one \'en-ē-ˌwən\ *pron* : any person ⟨*anyone* may come to the party⟩

any·place \'en-ē-ˌplās\ *adv* : in any place

any·thing \'en-ē-ˌthing\ *pron* : a thing of any kind ⟨didn't do *anything* all day⟩

any·way \'en-ē-ˌwā\ *adv* : ANYHOW

any·where \'en-ē-ˌhwear, -ˌwear, -ˌhwaər, -ˌwaər\ *adv* : in, at, or to any place

any·wise \'en-ē-ˌwīz\ *adv* : in any way whatever

A1 \'ā-'wən\ *adj* : of the very best kind

aor·ta \ā-'ȯrt-ə\ *n* : the main artery that carries blood from the heart for distribution to all parts of the body

apace \ə-'pās\ *adv* : at a quick pace : FAST

apart \ə-'pärt\ *adv* **1** : away from each other ⟨towns many miles *apart*⟩ **2** : as

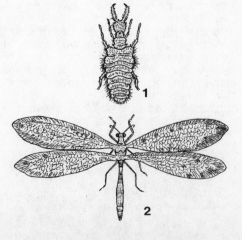

ant lion: 1 larva, 2 adult

something separated : SEPARATELY ⟨considered *apart* from other points⟩ **3** : into parts : to pieces ⟨took the clock *apart*⟩ **4** : one from another ⟨could not tell the twins *apart*⟩

apart·ment \ə-'pärt-mənt\ *n* **1** : a room or set of rooms used as a home **2** : a building divided into individual apartments

ap·a·thet·ic \,ap-ə-'thet-ik\ *adj* : having or showing little or no feeling or interest — **ap·a·thet·i·cal·ly** \-i-kə-lē\ *adv*

ap·a·thy \'ap-ə-thē\ *n* : lack of feeling or of interest : INDIFFERENCE

apato·sau·rus \ə-,pat-ə-'sȯr-əs\ *n* : BRONTOSAURUS

¹ape \'āp\ *n* **1** : a usually large and tailless monkey **2** : ²MIMIC

²ape *vb* **aped; ap·ing** : to imitate (someone) awkwardly

ap·er·ture \'ap-ər-,chùr\ *n* : an opening or open space : HOLE

apex \'ā-,peks\ *n, pl* **apex·es** *or* **api·ces** \'ā-pə-,sēz\ : the highest point : PEAK

aphid \'ā-fəd\ *n* : PLANT LOUSE

apiece \ə-'pēs\ *adv* : for each one

aplomb \ə-'pläm\ *n* : complete freedom from nervousness or uncertainty

apol·o·get·ic \ə-,päl-ə-'jet-ik\ *adj* : sorry for having done something wrong ⟨they were most *apologetic* about the mistake⟩ — **apol·o·get·i·cal·ly** \-i-kə-lē\ *adv*

apol·o·gize \ə-'päl-ə-,jīz\ *vb* **apol·o·gized; apol·o·giz·ing** : to make an apology

apol·o·gy \ə-päl-ə-jē\ *n, pl* **apol·o·gies** : an expression of regret (as for a mistake or a rude remark)

apos·tle \ə-'päs-əl\ *n* **1** : one of the twelve close followers of Jesus sent out to teach the gospel **2** : the first Christian missionary to a region **3** : the person who first puts forward an important belief or starts a great reform — **apos·tle·ship** \-,ship\ *n*

apos·tro·phe \ə-'päs-trə-fē\ *n* : a mark ' used to show that letters or figures are missing (as in "can't" for "cannot" or "'76" for "1776") or to show the possessive case (as in "James's") or the plural of letters or figures (as in "cross your t's")

apoth·e·cary \ə-'päth-ə-,ker-ē\ *n, pl* **apoth·e·car·ies** : DRUGGIST

ap·pall \ə-'pȯl\ *vb* : to shock or overcome with horror

ap·pall·ing *adj* : being shocking and terrible

ap·pa·ra·tus \,ap-ə-'rat-əs, -'rāt-\ *n, pl* **apparatus** *or* **ap·pa·ra·tus·es** : the equipment or material for a particular use or job ⟨gymnasium *apparatus*⟩ ⟨laboratory *apparatus*⟩

ap·par·el \ə-'par-əl\ *n* : things that are worn : WEAR **2** ⟨summer *apparel*⟩

ap·par·ent \ə-'par-ənt, -'per-\ *adj* **1** : open to view : VISIBLE ⟨a night in which many stars are *apparent*⟩ **2** : clear to the understanding : EVIDENT ⟨it was *apparent* that we could not win⟩ **3** : appearing to be real or true ⟨the *apparent* meaning of the speech⟩ — **ap·par·ent·ly** *adv* — **ap·par·ent·ness** *n*

ap·pa·ri·tion \,ap-ə-'rish-ən\ *n* **1** : an unusual or unexpected sight **2** : GHOST

¹ap·peal \ə-'pēl\ *n* **1** : a legal action by which a case is brought to a higher court for review **2** : an asking for something badly needed or wanted : PLEA ⟨an *appeal* for funds⟩ **3** : the power to cause enjoyment : ATTRACTION ⟨the *appeal* of music⟩

²appeal *vb* **1** : to take action to have a case or decision reviewed by a higher court **2** : to ask for something badly needed or wanted **3** : to be pleasing or attractive

ap·pear \ə-'piər\ *vb* **1** : to come into sight **2** : to present oneself ⟨*appear* in court⟩ **3** : SEEM 1 ⟨*appears* to be tired⟩ **4** : to come before the public ⟨the book *appeared* last year⟩ **5** : to come into existence

ap·pear·ance \ə-'pir-əns\ *n* **1** : the act or an instance of appearing ⟨a movie star's personal *appearance*⟩ **2** : way of looking ⟨the room has a cool *appearance*⟩

ap·pease \ə-'pēz\ *vb* **ap·peased; ap·peas·ing 1** : to make calm or quiet ⟨*appease* their anger⟩ **2** : to give in to — **ap·pease·ment** \-mənt\ *n* — **ap·peas·er** *n*

ap·pend \ə-'pend\ *vb* : to add as something extra ⟨*append* a postscript⟩

ap·pend·age \ə-'pen-dij\ *n* : something (as a leg) attached to a larger or more important thing

ap·pen·di·ci·tis \ə-,pen-də-'sīt-əs\ *n* : inflammation of the intestinal appendix

ap·pen·dix \ə-'pen-diks\ *n, pl* **ap·pen·dix·es** *or* **ap·pen·di·ces** \-də-,sēz\ **1** : a part of a book giving added and helpful information (as notes or tables) **2** : a small tubelike part growing out from the intestine

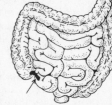

appendix

ap·pe·tite \'ap-ə-,tīt\ *n* **1** : a natural desire

especially for food **2** : ²TASTE 4 ⟨an *appetite* for adventure⟩

ap·pe·tiz·er \'ap-ə-ˌtī-zər\ *n* : a food or drink usually served before a meal to make one hungrier

ap·pe·tiz·ing \'ap-ə-ˌtī-zing\ *adj* : pleasing to the appetite ⟨an *appetizing* smell⟩

ap·plaud \ə-'plȯd\ *vb* **1** : ¹PRAISE 1 **2** : to show approval especially by clapping the hands

ap·plause \ə-'plȯz\ *n* : approval shown especially by clapping the hands

ap·ple \'ap-əl\ *n* : the round or oval fruit with red, yellow, or green skin of a spreading tree (**apple tree**) that is related to the rose

ap·pli·ance \ə-'plī-əns\ *n* **1** : a device designed for a certain use **2** : a piece of household or office equipment that runs on gas or electricity

ap·pli·ca·ble \'ap-li-kə-bəl\ *adj* : capable of being put to use or put into practice

ap·pli·cant \'ap-li-kənt\ *n* : a person who applies for something (as a job)

ap·pli·ca·tion \ˌap-lə-'kā-shən\ *n* **1** : the act or an instance of applying ⟨the *application* of paint to a house⟩ **2** : something put or spread on a surface ⟨cold *applications* on a sprained ankle⟩ **3** : ¹REQUEST 1 ⟨an *application* for a job⟩ **4** : ability to be put to practical use

ap·pli·ca·tor \'ap-lə-ˌkāt-ər\ *n* : a device for applying a substance (as medicine or polish)

ap·ply \ə-'plī\ *vb* **ap·plied; ap·ply·ing 1** : to put to use ⟨*applied* my knowledge⟩ **2** : to lay or spread on ⟨*apply* a coat of paint⟩ **3** : to place in contact ⟨*apply* heat⟩ **4** : to give one's full attention ⟨*applied* myself to my work⟩ **5** : to have relation or a connection ⟨this law *applies* to everyone⟩ **6** : to request especially in writing ⟨*apply* for a job⟩

ap·point \ə-'pȯint\ *vb* **1** : to decide on usually from a position of authority ⟨the teacher *appointed* a time for our meeting⟩ **2** : to choose for some duty, job, or office ⟨I was *appointed* to wash the dishes⟩ ⟨the school board *appointed* three new teachers⟩ ⟨the president *appoints* the cabinet⟩

ap·poin·tee \ə-ˌpȯin-'tē\ *n* : a person appointed to an office or position

ap·point·ment \ə-'pȯint-mənt\ *n* **1** : the act or an instance of appointing ⟨holds office by *appointment*⟩ **2** : a position or office to which a person is named **3** : an agreement to meet at a fixed time ⟨an eight-o'clock *appointment*⟩ **4 appointments** *pl* : FURNISHINGS

ap·po·si·tion \ˌap-ə-'zish-ən\ *n* : a grammatical construction in which a noun is followed by another that explains it ⟨in "my friend the doctor," the word "doctor" is in *apposition* with "friend"⟩

ap·pos·i·tive \ə-'päz-ət-iv\ *n* : the second of a pair of nouns in apposition ⟨in "my friend the doctor," the word "doctor" is an *appositive*⟩

ap·prais·al \ə-'prā-zəl\ *n* : an act or instance of appraising

ap·praise \ə-'prāz\ *vb* **ap·praised; ap·prais·ing** : to set a value on

ap·pre·cia·ble \ə-'prē-shə-bəl\ *adj* : large enough to be noticed or measured — **ap·pre·cia·bly** \-blē\ *adv*

ap·pre·ci·ate \ə-'prē-shē-ˌāt\ *vb* **ap·pre·ci·at·ed; ap·pre·ci·at·ing 1** : to admire greatly and with understanding ⟨*appreciates* poetry⟩ **2** : to be fully aware of ⟨I *appreciate* how important this is⟩ **3** : to be grateful for ⟨we *appreciate* your help⟩ **4** : to increase in number or value

synonyms APPRECIATE, TREASURE, and CHERISH mean to think very much of something. APPRECIATE suggests that one understands and enjoys the true worth of something ⟨I can *appreciate* good music⟩ TREASURE is often used of something of great sentimental value that one thinks of as precious and keeps in a safe place ⟨parents *treasure* gifts that their children make⟩ CHERISH suggests that one loves and cares for something very much and often for a long time ⟨*cherished* their friendship for many years⟩

ap·pre·ci·a·tion \ə-ˌprē-shē-'ā-shən\ *n* **1** : the act of appreciating **2** : awareness or understanding of worth or value **3** : a rise in value

ap·pre·cia·tive \ə-'prē-shət-iv\ *adj* : having or showing appreciation ⟨an *appreciative* smile⟩ — **ap·pre·cia·tive·ly** *adv*

ap·pre·hend \ˌap-ri-'hend\ *vb* **1** : ¹ARREST 2 ⟨*apprehend* a burglar⟩ **2** : to look forward to with fear and uncertainty **3** : UNDERSTAND 1

ap·pre·hen·sion \ˌap-ri-'hen-chən\ *n* **1** : ²ARREST **2** : an understanding of something **3** : fear of or uncertainty about what may be coming

ap·pre·hen·sive \ˌap-ri-'hen-siv\ *adj* : fearful of what may be coming — **ap·pre·hen·sive·ly** *adv* — **ap·pre·hen·sive·ness** *n*

¹ap·pren·tice \ə-'prent-əs\ *n* : a person who is learning a trade or art by experience under a skilled worker

²apprentice *vb* **ap·pren·ticed; ap·pren·tic·ing** : to set at work as an apprentice

ap·pren·tice·ship \ə-'prent-əs-ˌship\ *n* **1** : service as an apprentice **2** : the period during which a person serves as an apprentice

¹ap·proach \ə-'prōch\ *vb* **1** : to come near or nearer : draw close **2** : to begin to deal with ⟨*approach* a problem⟩

²approach *n* **1** : an act or instance of approaching **2** : a beginning step **3** : a way (as a path or road) to get to some place

ap·proach·able \ə-'prō-chə-bəl\ *adj* : easy to meet or deal with

¹ap·pro·pri·ate \ə-'prō-prē-ˌāt\ *vb* **ap·pro·pri·at·ed; ap·pro·pri·at·ing** **1** : to take possession of **2** : to set apart for a certain purpose or use

²ap·pro·pri·ate \ə-'prō-prē-ət\ *adj* : especially suitable — **ap·pro·pri·ate·ly** *adv* — **ap·pro·pri·ate·ness** *n*

ap·pro·pri·a·tion \ə-ˌprō-prē-'ā-shən\ *n* **1** : an act or instance of appropriating **2** : a sum of money appropriated for a specific use

ap·prov·al \ə-'prü-vəl\ *n* : an act or instance of approving

ap·prove \ə-'prüv\ *vb* **ap·proved; ap·prov·ing** **1** : to think well of **2** : to accept as satisfactory

¹ap·prox·i·mate \ə-'präk-sə-mət\ *adj* : nearly correct or exact ⟨the *approximate* cost⟩ — **ap·prox·i·mate·ly** *adv*

²ap·prox·i·mate \ə-'präk-sə-ˌmāt\ *vb* **ap·prox·i·mat·ed; ap·prox·i·mat·ing** **1** : to bring near or close **2** : to come near : APPROACH

ap·prox·i·ma·tion \ə-ˌpräk-sə-'mā-shən\ *n* **1** : a coming near or close (as in value) **2** : an estimate or figure that is almost exact

apri·cot \'ap-rə-ˌkät, 'ā-prə-\ *n* : a small oval orange-colored fruit that looks like the related peach and plum

April \'ā-prəl\ *n* : the fourth month of the year

Word History English *April* came from the Latin name of the month. We are not at all certain where the Latin name of the month came from. It may have been derived from the name of an ancient goddess.

apron \'ā-prən\ *n* **1** : a piece of cloth worn on the front of the body to keep the clothing from getting dirty **2** : a paved area for parking or handling airplanes

apt \'apt\ *adj* **1** : just right : SUITABLE ⟨an *apt* reply⟩ **2** : having a tendency : LIKELY ⟨is *apt* to become angry over small things⟩ **3** : quick to learn ⟨a pupil *apt* in arithmetic⟩ — **apt·ly** *adv* — **apt·ness** *n*

ap·ti·tude \'ap-tə-ˌtüd, -ˌtyüd\ *n* **1** : ability to learn **2** : natural ability : TALENT

aqua \'ak-wə, 'äk-\ *n* : a light greenish blue

aqua·ma·rine \ˌak-wə-mə-'rēn, ˌäk-\ *n* : a transparent gem that is blue, blue-green, or green

aqua·naut \'ak-wə-ˌnȯt, 'äk-\ *n* : a person who lives for a long while in an underwater shelter used as a base for research

aquar·i·um \ə-'kwer-ē-əm\ *n* **1** : a container (as a tank or bowl) in which living water animals or water plants are kept **2** : a building in which water animals or water plants are exhibited

Aquar·i·us \ə-'kwar-ē-əs, -'kwer-\ *n* **1** : a constellation between Capricorn and Pisces imagined as a man pouring water **2** : the eleventh sign of the zodiac or a person born under this sign

aquat·ic \ə-'kwät-ik, -'kwat-\ *adj* : growing, living, or done in water ⟨*aquatic* animals⟩

aq·ue·duct \'ak-wə-ˌdəkt\ *n* : an artificial channel (as a structure that takes the water of a canal across a river or hollow) for carrying flowing water from one place to another

aqueduct

aque·ous \'ā-kwē-əs, 'ak-wē-\ *adj* **1** : of, relating to, or like water **2** : made of, by, or with water ⟨an *aqueous* solution⟩

-ar \ər\ *adj suffix* : of or relating to ⟨molecul*ar*⟩

¹Ar·ab \'ar-əb\ *n* **1** : a person born or living in the Arabian Peninsula **2** : a member of a people that speaks Arabic

²Arab *adj* : of or relating to the Arabs : ARABIAN

¹A·ra·bi·an \ə-'rā-bē-ən\ *adj* : of or relating to the Arabian Peninsula or Arabians

²Arabian *n* : ¹ARAB 1

¹Ar·a·bic \'ar-ə-bik\ *adj* **1** : of or relating to Arabia, the Arabs, or Arabic **2** : expressed in or making use of Arabic numerals ⟨21 is an *Arabic* number⟩

²Arabic *n* : a language spoken in the

\ə\ abut	\au̇\ out	\i\ tip	\ȯ\ saw	\u̇\ foot
\ər\ further	\ch\ chin	\ī\ life	\ȯi\ coin	\y\ yet
\a\ mat	\e\ pet	\j\ job	\th\ thin	\yü\ few
\ā\ take	\ē\ easy	\ng\ sing	\th\ this	\yu̇\ cure
\ä\ cot, cart	\g\ go	\ō\ bone	\ü\ food	\zh\ vision

Arabian Peninsula, Iraq, Jordan, Lebanon, Syria, Egypt, and parts of northern Africa

Arabic numeral *n* : one of the number symbols 1, 2, 3, 4, 5, 6, 7, 8, 9, and 0

ar·a·ble \'ar-ə-bəl\ *adj* : fit for or cultivated by plowing : suitable for producing crops

Arap·a·ho *or* **Arap·a·hoe** \ə-'rap-ə-,hō\ *n, pl* **Arapaho** *or* **Arapahos** *or* **Arapahoe** *or* **Arapahoes** : a member of an Indian people of the plains region of the United States and Canada

ar·bi·ter \'är-bət-ər\ *n* **1** : ARBITRATOR **2** : a person having the power to decide what is right or proper

ar·bi·trary \'är-bə-,trer-ē\ *adj* **1** : coming from or given to free exercise of the will without thought of fairness or right ⟨*arbitrary* decisions⟩ ⟨an *arbitrary* ruler⟩ **2** : chosen by chance ⟨punctuation marks are *arbitrary* symbols⟩ — **ar·bi·trari·ly** \,är-bə-'trer-ə-lē\ *adv* — **ar·bi·trari·ness** \'är-bə-,trer-ē-nəs\ *n*

ar·bi·trate \'är-bə-,trāt\ *vb* **ar·bi·trat·ed; ar·bi·trat·ing** **1** : to settle a disagreement after hearing the arguments of both sides **2** : to refer a dispute to others for settlement

ar·bi·tra·tion \,är-bə-'trā-shən\ *n* : the settling of a disagreement in which both sides present their arguments to a third person or group for decision

ar·bi·tra·tor \'är-bə-,trāt-ər\ *n* : a person chosen to settle differences in a disagreement

ar·bor \'är-bər\ *n* : a shelter of vines or branches or of a frame covered with growing vines

ar·bo·re·al \är-'bōr-ē-əl\ *adj* **1** : of or relating to a tree **2** : living in or often found in trees

ar·bo·re·tum \,är-bə-'rēt-əm\ *n, pl* **ar·bo·re·tums** *or* **ar·bo·re·ta** \-'rēt-ə\ : a place where trees and plants are grown to be studied

arbor

ar·bor·vi·tae \,är-bər-'vīt-ē\ *n* : any of several evergreen trees with tiny scalelike leaves on flat branches shaped like fans

ar·bu·tus \är-'byüt-əs\ *n* : a plant that spreads along the ground and in the spring has bunches of small fragrant flowers with five white or pink petals

arc \'ärk\ *n* **1** : a glowing light across a gap in an electric circuit or between electrodes **2** : a part of a curved line between any two points on it

ar·cade \är-'kād\ *n* **1** : a row of arches with the columns that support them **2** : an arched or covered passageway often between two rows of shops

¹arch \'ärch\ *n* **1** : a usually curved part of a structure that is over an opening and serves as a support (as for the wall above the opening) **2** : something suggesting an arch ⟨the *arch* of the foot⟩ — **arched** \'ärcht\ *adj*

arch 1: four types of arches

²arch *vb* **1** : to cover with an arch **2** : to form or shape into an arch

³arch *adj* **1** : ²CHIEF 1, PRINCIPAL ⟨*arch*-villain⟩ **2** : being clever and mischievous ⟨an *arch* look⟩ — **arch·ly** *adv* — **arch·ness** *n*

ar·chae·ol·o·gy *or* **ar·che·ol·o·gy** \,är-kē-'äl-ə-jē\ *n* : a science that deals with past human life and activities as shown by fossils and the monuments and tools left by ancient peoples

ar·cha·ic \är-'kā-ik\ *adj* **1** : of or relating to an earlier time **2** : surviving from an earlier period

arch·an·gel \'är-,kān-jəl\ *n* : a chief angel

arch·bish·op \'ärch-'bish-əp\ *n* : the bishop of highest rank in a group of dioceses

ar·cher \'är-chər\ *n* : a person who shoots with a bow and arrow

ar·chery \'är-chə-rē, 'ärch-rē\ *n* : the sport or practice of shooting with bow and arrows

ar·chi·pel·a·go \,är-kə-'pel-ə-,gō, ,är-chə-\ *n, pl* **ar·chi·pel·a·goes** *or* **ar·chi·pel·a·gos** **1** : a body of water (as a sea) with many islands **2** : a group of islands in an archipelago

ar·chi·tect \'är-kə-,tekt\ *n* : a person who designs buildings

ar·chi·tec·tur·al \,är-kə-'tek-chə-rəl\ *adj* : of or relating to architecture — **ar·chi·tec·tur·al·ly** *adv*

ar·chi·tec·ture \'är-kə-,tek-chər\ *n* **1** : the art of making plans for buildings **2** : a style of building ⟨a church of modern *architecture*⟩

ar·chive \'är-,kīv\ *n* : a place in which public records or historical papers are saved

arch·way \'ärch-,wā\ *n* **1** : a passage under an arch **2** : an arch over a passage

-archy \,är-kē, *in a few words also* ər-kē\ *n suffix, pl* **-archies** : rule : government ⟨mon*archy*⟩

arc·tic \\'ärk-tik, 'ärt-ik\\ *adj* **1** *often cap* : of or relating to the north pole or to the region around it 〈*arctic* explorers〉 **2** : very cold

Word History The Big Dipper is a group of stars in the northern sky. It looks like a dipper to us, but ancient people thought it looked like a large bear. The ancient Greeks gave it a name that meant "bear." The English word *arctic* came from the Greek name for the Big Dipper. If we look at the Big Dipper we are looking toward the north pole. The word *arctic* refers to the region around the north pole.

ar·dent \\'ärd-nt\\ *adj* : showing or having warmth of feeling : PASSIONATE — **ar·dent·ly** *adv*

ar·dor \\'ärd-ər\\ *n* **1** : warmth of feeling **2** : great eagerness : ZEAL

ar·du·ous \\'är-jə-wəs\\ *adj* : DIFFICULT **1** 〈climbing the mountain was more *arduous* than we thought it would be〉— **ar·du·ous·ly** *adv* — **ar·du·ous·ness** *n*

are \\ər, är\\ *present 2d sing or present pl of* BE

ar·ea \\'ar-ē-ə, er-\\ *n* **1** : a flat surface or space **2** : the amount of surface included within limits 〈the *area* of a triangle〉 **3** : REGION 1 〈a farming *area*〉 **4** : a field of activity or study

are·na \\ə-'rē-nə\\ *n* **1** : an enclosed area used for public entertainment **2** : a building containing an arena **3** : a field of activity 〈the political *arena*〉

Word History In ancient Rome gladiators fought in big outdoor theaters. These theaters had a large open space in the middle covered with sand. The Latin word for this space meant "sand." The English word *arena* came from this Latin word.

aren't \\ärnt, 'är-ənt\\ : are not

ar·gue \\'är-gyü\\ *vb* **ar·gued; ar·gu·ing 1** : to give reasons for or against something 〈*argue* in favor of lower taxes〉 **2** : to discuss some matter usually with different points of view 〈*argue* about politics〉 **3** : to persuade by giving reasons 〈could not *argue* my parents into getting a new car〉 **synonyms** see DISCUSS — **ar·gu·er** *n*

ar·gu·ment \\'är-gyə-mənt\\ *n* **1** : a reason for or against something **2** : a discussion in which reasons for and against something are given **3** : an angry disagreement : QUARREL

ar·id \\'ar-əd\\ *adj* **1** : not having enough rainfall to support agriculture **2** : UNINTERESTING, DULL 〈an *arid* lecture〉

Ar·ies \\'ar-ēz, 'ar-ē-ēz, 'er-\\ *n* **1** : a constellation between Pisces and Taurus imagined as a ram **2** : the first sign of the zodiac or a person born under this sign

aright \\ə-'rīt\\ *adv* : in a correct way

arise \\ə-'rīz\\ *vb* **arose** \\-'rōz\\; **aris·en** \\-'riz-n\\; **aris·ing** \\-'rī-zing\\ **1** : to move upward 〈mist *arose* from the valley〉 **2** : to get up from sleep or after lying down **3** : to come into existence 〈a dispute *arose*〉

ar·is·toc·ra·cy \\,ar-ə-'stäk-rə-sē\\ *n*, *pl* **ar·is·toc·ra·cies 1** : a government that is run by a small class of people **2** : an upper class that is usually based on birth and is richer and more powerful than the rest of a society **3** : persons thought of as being better than the rest of the community

aris·to·crat \\ə-'ris-tə-,krat, 'ar-ə-stə-\\ *n* : a member of an aristocracy

aris·to·crat·ic \\ə-,ris-tə-'krat-ik, ,ar-ə-stə-\\ *adj* : of or relating to the aristocracy or aristocrats — **aris·to·crat·i·cal·ly** \\-i-kə-lē\\ *adv*

¹**arith·me·tic** \\ə-'rith-mə-,tik\\ *n* **1** : a science that deals with the addition, subtraction, multiplication, and division of numbers **2** : an act or method of adding, subtracting, multiplying, or dividing

²**ar·ith·met·ic** \\,ar-ith-'met-ik\\ *or* **ar·ith·met·i·cal** \\-i-kəl\\ *adj* : of or relating to arithmetic

ar·ith·met·ic mean \\,ar-ith-,met-ik-\\ *n* : a quantity formed by adding quantities together and dividing by their number 〈the *arithmetic mean* of 6, 4, and 5 is 5〉

ark \\'ärk\\ *n* **1** : the ship in which an ancient Hebrew of the Bible named Noah and his family were saved from a great flood that God sent down on the world because of its wickedness **2** : a sacred chest in which the ancient Hebrews kept the two tablets of the Law **3** : a closet in a synagogue for the scrolls of the Law

¹**arm** \\'ärm\\ *n* **1** : a human upper limb especially between the shoulder and wrist **2** : something like an arm in shape or position 〈an *arm* of the sea〉 〈the *arm* of a chair〉 **3** : ¹POWER 1 〈the long *arm* of the law〉 **4** : a foreleg of a four-footed animal — **armed** \\'ärmd\\ *adj*

²**arm** *vb* **1** : to provide with weapons **2** : to provide with a way of defense 〈*armed* with facts〉

³**arm** *n* **1** : WEAPON, FIREARM **2** : a branch

\ə\ abut	\au̇\ out	\i\ tip	\ȯ\ saw	\u̇\ foot
\ər\ further	\ch\ chin	\ī\ life	\ȯi\ coin	\y\ yet
\a\ mat	\e\ pet	\j\ job	\th\ thin	\yü\ few
\ā\ take	\ē\ easy	\ng\ sing	\th\ this	\yu̇\ cure
\ä\ cot, cart	\g\ go	\ō\ bone	\ü\ food	\zh\ vision

of an army or of the military forces **3 arms** *pl* : the designs on a shield or flag of a family or government **4 arms** *pl* : actual fighting : WARFARE ⟨a call to *arms*⟩

ar·ma·da \är-'mäd-ə, -'mäd-\ *n* **1** : a large fleet of warships **2** : a large number of moving things (as planes)

ar·ma·dil·lo \,är-mə-'dil-ō\ *n, pl* **ar·ma·dil·los** : a small burrowing animal of Latin America and Texas whose head and body are protected by a hard bony armor

armadillo

ar·ma·ment \'är-mə-mənt\ *n* **1** : the military strength and equipment of a nation **2** : the supply of materials for war **3** : the process of preparing for war

ar·ma·ture \'är-mə-chər\ *n* : the part of an electric motor or generator that turns in a magnetic field

arm·chair \'ärm-,cheər, -,chaər\ *n* : a chair with arms

arm·ful \'ärm-,fùl\ *n, pl* **arm·fuls** \-,fùlz\ *or* **arms·ful** \'ärmz-,fùl\ : as much as a person's arm can hold

ar·mi·stice \'är-mə-stəs\ *n* : a pause in fighting brought about by agreement between the two sides

ar·mor \'är-mər\ *n* **1** : a covering (as of metal) to protect the body in battle **2** : something that protects like metal armor ⟨safe in the *armor* of prosperity⟩ **3** : armored forces and vehicles (as tanks)

armor 1

ar·mored \'är-mərd\ *adj* : protected by or equipped with armor

ar·mo·ry \'är-mə-rē\ *n, pl* **ar·mo·ries** **1** : a supply of arms **2** : a place where arms are kept and where soldiers are often trained **3** : a place where arms are made

arm·pit \'ärm-,pit\ *n* : the hollow under a person's arm where the arm joins the shoulder

arm·rest \'ärm-,rest\ *n* : a support for the arm

ar·my \'är-mē\ *n, pl* **ar·mies** **1** : a large body of men and women trained for land warfare **2** *often cap* : the complete military organization of a nation for land warfare **3** : a great number of people or things **4** : a body of persons organized to advance an idea

aro·ma \ə-'rō-mə\ *n* : a noticeable and pleasant smell ⟨the *aroma* of coffee⟩

ar·o·mat·ic \,ar-ə-'mat-ik\ *adj* : of, relating to, or having an aroma

arose *past of* ARISE

¹around \ə-'raùnd\ *adv* **1** : in circumference ⟨a tree five feet *around*⟩ **2** : in or along a curving course **3** : on all sides ⟨papers lying *around*⟩ **4** : NEARBY ⟨stay *around* a while⟩ **5** : here and there in various places ⟨travel *around* from state to state⟩ **6** : to each in turn ⟨pass the candy *around*⟩ **7** : in an opposite direction ⟨turn *around*⟩ **8** : in the neighborhood of : APPROXIMATELY ⟨a price of *around* five dollars⟩

²around *prep* **1** : in a curving path along the outside boundary of ⟨walked *around* the house and peeked in the windows⟩ **2** : on every side of **3** : here and there in ⟨travel *around* the country⟩ **4** : near in number or amount ⟨they left *around* three o'clock⟩

arouse \ə-'raùz\ *vb* **aroused; arous·ing** **1** : to awaken from sleep **2** : to excite to action

ar·range \ə-'rānj\ *vb* **ar·ranged; ar·rang·ing** **1** : to put in order and especially a particular order **2** : to make plans for ⟨*arrange* a program⟩ **3** : to come to an agreement about : SETTLE ⟨*arrange* a truce⟩ **4** : to make a musical arrangement of — **ar·rang·er** *n*

ar·range·ment \ə-'rānj-mənt\ *n* **1** : a putting in order : the order in which things are put ⟨the *arrangement* of furniture in a room⟩ **2** : preparation or planning done in advance ⟨make *arrangements* for a trip⟩ **3** : something made by arranging ⟨a flower *arrangement*⟩ **4** : a changing of a piece of music to suit voices or instruments for which it was not first written

¹ar·ray \ə-'rā\ *vb* **1** : to set in order : DRAW

up ⟨soldiers *arrayed* for review⟩ **2** : to dress especially in fine or beautiful clothing

²array *n* **1** : regular order or arrangement **2** : a group of persons (as soldiers) drawn up in regular order **3** : fine or beautiful clothing **4** : an impressive group **5** : a group of mathematical elements (as numbers or letters) arranged in rows and columns

ar·rears \ə-'riərz\ *n pl* **1** : the state of being behind in paying debts ⟨two months in *arrears*⟩ **2** : unpaid and overdue debts

¹ar·rest \ə-'rest\ *vb* **1** : to stop the progress or movement of : CHECK ⟨*arrest* a disease⟩ **2** : to take or keep in one's control by authority of law ⟨*arrest* someone on suspicion of robbery⟩ **3** : to attract and hold the attention of

²arrest *n* : the act of taking or holding in one's control by authority of law

ar·riv·al \ə-'rī-vəl\ *n* **1** : the act of arriving **2** : a person or thing that has arrived

ar·rive \ə-'rīv\ *vb* **ar·rived; ar·riv·ing 1** : to reach the place one started out for ⟨*arrive* home at six o'clock⟩ **2** : to gain a goal or object ⟨*arrive* at a decision⟩ **3** : COME 2 ⟨the time to leave finally *arrived*⟩ **4** : to gain success

ar·ro·gance \'ar-ə-gəns\ *n* : a sense of one's own importance that shows itself in a proud and insulting way

ar·ro·gant \'ar-ə-gənt\ *adj* : overly proud of oneself or of one's own opinions — **ar·ro·gant·ly** *adv*

ar·row \'ar-ō\ *n* **1** : a weapon that is made to be shot from a bow and is usually a stick with a point at one end and feathers at the other **2** : a mark to show direction

ar·row·head \'ar-ō-ˌhed\ *n* : the pointed end of an arrow

arrowheads

ar·row·root \'ar-ō-ˌrüt, -ˌrüt\ *n* : a starch obtained from the roots of a tropical plant

ar·se·nal \'ärs-nəl, -n-əl\ *n* : a place where military equipment is made and stored

ar·se·nic \'ärs-nik, -n-ik\ *n* : a solid poisonous chemical element that is usually steel gray and snaps easily

ar·son \'ärs-n\ *n* : the illegal burning of a building or other property

art \'ärt\ *n* **1** : skill that comes through experience or study ⟨the *art* of making friends⟩ **2** : an activity that requires skill ⟨cooking is an *art*⟩ **3** : an activity (as painting, music, or writing) whose purpose is making things that are beautiful to look at, listen to, or read **4** : works (as pictures, poems, or songs) made by artists

ar·tery \'ärt-ə-rē\ *n, pl* **ar·ter·ies 1** : one of the branching tubes that carry blood from the heart to all parts of the body **2** : a main road or waterway

ar·te·sian well \är-ˌtē-zhən-\ *n* **1** : a bored well from which water flows up like a fountain **2** : a deep bored well

art·ful \'ärt-fəl\ *adj* **1** : done with or showing art or skill **2** : clever at taking advantage — **art·ful·ly** \-fə-lē\ *adv* — **art·ful·ness** *n*

ar·thri·tis \är-'thrīt-əs\ *n* : a condition in which the joints are painful and swollen

ar·thro·pod \'är-thrə-ˌpäd\ *n* : any of a large group of animals (as crabs, insects, and spiders) with jointed limbs and a body made up of segments

ar·ti·choke \'ärt-ə-ˌchōk\ *n* : a tall plant of the aster family with a flower head cooked and eaten as a vegetable

ar·ti·cle \'ärt-i-kəl\ *n* **1** : a separate part of a document ⟨the third *article* of the constitution of the United States⟩ **2** : a piece of writing other than fiction or poetry that forms a separate part of a

artichoke

publication (as a magazine) **3** : a word (as *a*, *an*, or *the*) used with a noun to limit it or make it clearer **4** : one of a class of things ⟨*articles* of clothing⟩

¹ar·tic·u·late \är-'tik-yə-lət\ *adj* **1** : clearly understandable **2** : able to express oneself clearly and well — **ar·tic·u·late·ly** *adv* — **ar·tic·u·late·ness** *n*

²ar·tic·u·late \är-'tik-yə-ˌlāt\ *vb* **ar·tic·u·lat·ed; ar·tic·u·lat·ing** : to speak clearly

ar·tic·u·la·tion \är-ˌtik-yə-'lā-shən\ *n* : the making of articulate sounds (as in speaking)

\ə\ abut	\au̇\ out	\i\ tip	\o̅\ saw	\u̇\ foot
\ər\ further	\ch\ chin	\ī\ life	\oi\ coin	\y\ yet
\a\ mat	\e\ pet	\j\ job	\th\ thin	\yü\ few
\ā\ take	\e̅\ easy	\ng\ sing	\th\ this	\yu̇\ cure
\ä\ cot, cart	\g\ go	\ō\ bone	\ü\ food	\zh\ vision

ar·ti·fice \'ärt-ə-fəs\ *n* **1** : a clever trick or device ⟨used every *artifice* to avoid work⟩ **2** : clever skill ⟨a vase made with much *artifice*⟩

ar·ti·fi·cial \,ärt-ə-'fish-əl\ *adj* **1** : made by humans ⟨an *artificial* lake⟩ **2** : not natural in quality ⟨an *artificial* smile⟩ **3** : made to look like something natural ⟨*artificial* flowers⟩ — **ar·ti·fi·cial·ly** *adv*

artificial respiration *n* : the forcing of air into and out of the lungs of a person whose breathing has stopped

ar·til·lery \är-'til-ə-rē\ *n* **1** : large firearms (as cannon or rockets) **2** : a branch of an army armed with artillery

ar·ti·san \'ärt-ə-zən\ *n* : a person (as a carpenter) who works at a trade requiring skill with the hands

art·ist \'ärt-əst\ *n* **1** : a person skilled in one of the arts (as painting, sculpture, music, or writing) **2** : a person who has much ability in a job requiring skill

ar·tis·tic \är-'tis-tik\ *adj* **1** : relating to art or artists **2** : showing skill and imagination — **ar·tis·ti·cal·ly** \-ti-kə-lē\ *adv*

¹-ary \,er-ē, ə-rē\ *n suffix, pl* **-aries** : thing or person belonging to or connected with ⟨bound*ary*⟩

²-ary *adj suffix* : of, relating to, or connected with ⟨legend*ary*⟩

¹as \əz, az\ *conj* **1** : in equal amount or degree with ⟨cold *as* ice⟩ **2** : in the same way that ⟨do *as* I say⟩ **3** : at the time that ⟨sang *as* they marched⟩ **4** : BECAUSE, SINCE ⟨stayed home, *as* I had no car⟩

²as *adv* **1** : to the same degree or amount ⟨*as* deaf as a post⟩ **2** : for example

³as *pron* **1** : THAT, WHO, WHICH ⟨had the same name *as* my cousin⟩ **2** : a fact that ⟨you are happy, *as* we all know⟩ ⟨*as* I said before, you must leave⟩

⁴as *prep* **1** : ⁴LIKE 1 ⟨came dressed *as* a clown⟩ **2** : in the position or role of ⟨works *as* an editor⟩

as·bes·tos \as-'bes-təs, az-\ *n* : a grayish mineral that separates easily into long flexible fibers and is used in making fireproof materials

as·cend \ə-'send\ *vb* : to go up : RISE

as·cen·sion \ə-'sen-chən\ *n* : the act or process of ascending

as·cent \ə-'sent\ *n* **1** : the act of rising or climbing upward **2** : an upward slope : RISE

as·cer·tain \,as-ər-'tān\ *vb* : to find out with certainty ⟨*ascertain* the date of the game⟩

as·cribe \ə-'skrīb\ *vb* **as·cribed; as·crib·ing** : to think of as coming from a specified cause, source, or author

asex·u·al \'ā-'sek-shə-wəl\ *adj* : of, relating to, or being a process of reproduction (as the dividing of one cell into two cells) that does not involve the combining of male and female germ cells — **asex·u·al·ly** \-wə-lē\ *adv*

¹ash \'ash\ *n* : a common shade tree or timber tree that has winged seeds and bark with grooves

ash

²ash *n* **1** : the solid matter left when something is completely burned **2 ashes** *pl* : the last remains of the dead human body

ashamed \ə-'shāmd\ *adj* **1** : feeling shame, guilt, or disgrace ⟨*ashamed* of my behavior⟩ **2** : kept back by fear of shame ⟨*ashamed* to beg⟩

ash·en \'ash-ən\ *adj* **1** : of the color of ashes **2** : very pale

ashore \ə-'shōr\ *adv* : on or to the shore

ash·tray \'ash-ˌtrā\ *n* : a container for tobacco ashes and cigarette and cigar butts

Ash Wednesday *n* : the first day of Lent

ashy \'ash-ē\ *adj* **ash·i·er; ash·i·est** **1** : of or relating to ashes **2** : very pale

¹Asian \'ā-zhən\ *adj* : of or relating to Asia or the Asians

²Asian *n* : a person born or living in Asia

aside \ə-'sīd\ *adv* **1** : to or toward the side ⟨stepped *aside*⟩ **2** : out of the way : AWAY **3** : away from one's thought ⟨joking *aside*⟩

aside from *prep* : with the exception of

synonyms ASCEND, MOUNT, and CLIMB mean to move upward or toward the top. ASCEND may suggest a gradual upward movement ⟨slowly *ascended* the staircase⟩ MOUNT suggests reaching the very top of something ⟨*mounted* the hill and placed a flag there⟩ CLIMB suggests effort and often the use of the hands and feet in moving up something ⟨*climbed* the rugged mountain⟩

⟨*aside from* a few pieces of bread, the food is gone⟩

as if *conj* **1** : the way it would be if ⟨it's *as if* we'd never left⟩ **2** : the way one would if ⟨acted *as if* they'd never heard of me⟩ **3** : ³THAT **1** ⟨seems *as if* it never changes⟩

ask \'ask\ *vb* **1** : to seek information **2** : to make a request ⟨*ask* for help⟩ **3** : to set as a price ⟨*ask* ten dollars an hour⟩ **4** : INVITE 2 **5** : to behave as if looking ⟨you're *asking* for trouble⟩

askance \ə-'skans\ *adv* **1** : with a side glance **2** : with distrust or disapproval

askew \ə-'skyü\ *adv or adj* : out of line

aslant \ə-'slant\ *adv or adj* : in a slanting direction

¹asleep \ə-'slēp\ *adj* **1** : being in a state of sleep **2** : having no feeling ⟨my foot was *asleep*⟩

²asleep *adv* : into a state of sleep

as of *prep* : ¹ON 5, AT ⟨we begin work *as of* Tuesday⟩⟨*as of* the moment, we are fine⟩

as·par·a·gus \ə-'spar-ə-gəs\ *n* : a vegetable that is the thick young shoots of a garden plant that is related to the lilies and lives for many years

as·pect \'as-ˌpekt\ *n* **1** : a position facing a certain direction **2** : a certain way in which something appears or may be thought of **3** : the appearance of an individual : LOOK

as·pen \'as-pən\ *n* : a poplar tree whose leaves move easily in the breeze

as·phalt \'as-ˌfȯlt\ *n* **1** : a dark-colored substance obtained from natural beds or from petroleum **2** : any of various materials that are used for pavements and as a waterproof cement

aspen

as·phyx·i·ate \as-'fik-sē-ˌāt\ *vb* **as·phyx·i·at·ed; as·phyx·i·at·ing** : to cause (as a person) to become unconscious or die by cutting off the normal taking in of oxygen whether by blocking breathing or by replacing the oxygen of the air with another gas

as·pi·rant \'as-pə-rənt, ə-'spī-\ *n* : a person who aspires ⟨an *aspirant* to the presidency⟩

as·pi·ra·tion \ˌas-pə-'rā-shən\ *n* : a strong desire to achieve something high or great

as·pire \ə-'spīr\ *vb* **as·pired; as·pir·ing** : to very much want something and especially something high or fine ⟨*aspire* to greatness⟩

as·pi·rin \'as-prən, 'as-pə-rən\ *n* : a white drug used to relieve pain and fever

ass \'as\ *n* **1** : an animal that looks like but is smaller than the related horse and has shorter hair in mane and tail and longer ears : DONKEY **2** : a dull stupid person

as·sail \ə-'sāl\ *vb* : to attack violently with blows or words

as·sail·ant \ə-'sā-lənt\ *n* : a person who attacks

as·sas·sin \ə-'sas-n\ *n* : one who kills another person either for pay or from loyalty to a cause

Word History Long ago a secret Muslim group thought it was their religious duty to murder their enemies. Before they killed, the members of this group took a drug called "hashish." Because of this they became known in Arabic by a word that meant "a user of hashish." A Latin word was formed from this Arabic word. The English word *assassin* came from the Latin word.

as·sas·si·nate \ə-'sas-n-ˌāt\ *vb* **as·sas·si·nat·ed; as·sas·si·nat·ing** : to murder a usually important person by a surprise or secret attack **synonyms** see KILL

as·sas·si·na·tion \ə-ˌsas-n-'ā-shən\ *n* : the act of assassinating

¹as·sault \ə-'sȯlt\ *n* **1** : a violent or sudden attack **2** : an unlawful attempt or threat to harm someone

²assault *vb* : to make an assault on

¹as·say \'as-ˌā, a-'sā\ *n* : an analyzing (as of an ore or drug) to determine the presence, absence, or amount of one or more substances

²as·say \a-'sā, 'as-ˌā\ *vb* : to analyze (as an ore) for one or more valuable substances

as·sem·blage \ə-'sem-blij\ *n* : a collection of persons or things

as·sem·ble \ə-'sem-bəl\ *vb* **as·sem·bled; as·sem·bling** **1** : to collect in one place or group **2** : to fit (parts) together ⟨*assemble* a toy⟩ **3** : to meet together ⟨the class *assembled*⟩ **synonyms** see GATHER — **as·sem·bler** *n*

as·sem·bly \ə-'sem-blē\ *n, pl* **as·sem·blies** **1** : a gathering of persons : MEETING ⟨a school *assembly*⟩ **2** *cap* : a lawmaking body **3** : the act of assembling : the state of being assembled **4** : a collection of parts that make up a complete unit

\ə\ abut	\au̇\ out	\i\ tip	\ȯ\ saw	\u̇\ foot
\ər\ further	\ch\ chin	\ī\ life	\ȯi\ coin	\y\ yet
\a\ mat	\e\ pet	\j\ job	\th\ thin	\yü\ few
\ā\ take	\ē\ easy	\ng\ sing	\th\ this	\yu̇\ cure
\ä\ cot, cart	\g\ go	\ō\ bone	\ü\ food	\zh\ vision

¹**as·sent** \ə-'sent\ *vb* : to agree to something

²**assent** *n* : an act of assenting : AGREEMENT

as·sert \ə-'sərt\ *vb* **1** : to state clearly and strongly ⟨*assert* an opinion loudly⟩ **2** : to show the existence of ⟨*assert* your independence⟩ — **assert oneself** : to insist strongly that others respect one's rights

as·ser·tion \ə-'sər-shən\ *n* **1** : the act of asserting **2** : a positive statement

as·sess \ə-'ses\ *vb* **1** : to decide on the rate or amount of ⟨the jury *assessed* damages of $5000⟩ **2** : to assign a value to for purposes of taxation **3** : to put a charge or tax on — **as·ses·sor** \-ər\ *n*

as·set \'as,et\ *n* **1 assets** *pl* : all the property belonging to a person or an organization **2** : ADVANTAGE **3** ⟨your sense of humor is an *asset*⟩

as·sid·u·ous \ə-'sij-ə-wəs\ *adj* : DILIGENT — **as·sid·u·ous·ly** *adv* — **as·sid·u·ous·ness** *n*

as·sign \ə-'sīn\ *vb* **1** : to appoint to a post or duty **2** : to give out with authority ⟨*assign* a lesson⟩ **3** : to decide on definitely ⟨*assigned* a date for the trip⟩

as·sign·ment \ə-'sīn-mənt\ *n* **1** : the act of assigning ⟨the *assignment* of seats⟩ **2** : something assigned ⟨an *assignment* in arithmetic⟩

as·sim·i·late \ə-'sim-ə-,lāt\ *vb* **as·sim·i·lat·ed; as·sim·i·lat·ing** : to take something in and make it part of the thing it has joined

as·sim·i·la·tion \ə-,sim-ə-'lā-shən\ *n* : the act or process of assimilating

¹**as·sist** \ə-'sist\ *vb* : to give aid : HELP

²**assist** *n* : an act of assisting

as·sis·tance \ə-'sis-təns\ *n* **1** : the act of helping **2** : the help given

¹**as·sis·tant** \ə-'sis-tənt\ *adj* : acting as a helper to another ⟨an *assistant* manager⟩

²**assistant** *n* : a person who assists another

¹**as·so·ci·ate** \ə-'sō-shē-,āt\ *vb* **as·so·ci·at·ed; as·so·ci·at·ing** **1** : to join or come together as partners, friends, or companions **2** : to connect in thought ⟨*associate* soldiers with war⟩

²**as·so·ci·ate** \ə-'sō-shē-ət, -shət\ *adj* **1** : closely joined with another (as in duties or responsibility) **2** : having some but not all rights and privileges ⟨an *associate* member of the club⟩

³**as·so·ci·ate** \ə-'sō-shē-ət, -shət\ *n* **1** : a fellow worker : PARTNER **2** : a person who is one's friend or companion

as·so·ci·a·tion \ə-,sō-sē-'ā-shən, -shē-\ *n* **1** : the act of associating : the state of being associated **2** : an organization of persons having a common interest ⟨an athletic *association*⟩ **3** : a feeling, memory, or thought connected with a person, place, or thing

as·so·cia·tive \ə-'sō-shē-,āt-iv, -shət-iv\ *adj* **1** : serving to associate ⟨*associative* nerve cells⟩ **2** : being a property of a mathematical operation (as addition or multiplication) in which the result is independent of the original grouping of the elements

as·sort \ə-'sort\ *vb* : to sort into groups

as·sort·ed \ə-'sort-əd\ *adj* **1** : made up of various kinds ⟨*assorted* chocolates⟩ **2** : suited to one another ⟨a well *assorted* pair⟩

as·sort·ment \ə-'sort-mənt\ *n* **1** : the act of assorting : the state of being assorted **2** : a collection of assorted things or persons

as·sume \ə-'süm\ *vb* **as·sumed; as·sum·ing** **1** : to take upon oneself : UNDERTAKE ⟨*assume* new duties⟩ **2** : to take over usually by force ⟨the dictator *assumed* power⟩ **3** : to pretend to have or be ⟨*assumed* a look of happiness⟩ **4** : to accept as true ⟨I *assume* you're right⟩

as·sump·tion \ə-'səmp-shən\ *n* **1** : the act of assuming ⟨the *assumption* of power by a new ruler⟩ **2** : something accepted as true ⟨the *assumption* that you will be here⟩

as·sur·ance \ə-'shur-əns\ *n* **1** : the act of assuring **2** : the state of being certain **3** : a being sure and safe : SECURITY **4** : confidence in one's own self

as·sure \ə-'shur\ *vb* **as·sured; as·sur·ing** **1** : to make safe : INSURE **2** : to give confidence to **3** : to make sure or certain ⟨*assure* the success of the plan⟩ **4** : to inform positively

as·sured \ə-'shurd\ *adj* **1** : made sure or certain **2** : very confident — **as·sur·ed·ly** \-'shur-əd-lē\ *adv* — **as·sur·ed·ness** \-'shur-əd-nəs\ *n*

as·ter \'as-tər\ *n* : any of various herbs related to the daisies that have leafy stems and white, pink, purple, or yellow flower heads which bloom in the fall

aster

as·ter·isk \'as-tə-,risk\ *n* : a character * used in printing or in writing as a reference mark or to show that letters or words have been left out

astern \ə-'stərn\ *adv* **1** : behind a ship or airplane **2** : at or toward the stern **3** : ¹BACKWARD 1 ⟨full speed *astern*⟩

as·ter·oid \'as-tə-ˌrȯid\ *n* : one of thousands of small planets that move in orbits mostly between those of Mars and Jupiter and have diameters from a fraction of a kilometer to nearly 800 kilometers

asth·ma \'az-mə\ *n* : an ailment of which difficult breathing, wheezing, and coughing are symptoms

astir \ə-'stər\ *adj* **1** : showing activity **2** : being out of bed : UP

as to *prep* **1** : with respect to : ABOUT ⟨confused *as to* what happened⟩ **2** : ACCORDING TO 1 ⟨graded *as to* size and color⟩

as·ton·ish \ə-'stän-ish\ *vb* : to strike with sudden wonder or surprise **synonyms** see SURPRISE

as·ton·ish·ment \ə-'stän-ish-mənt\ *n* : great surprise : AMAZEMENT

as·tound \ə-'staund\ *vb* : to fill with puzzled wonder

astray \ə-'strā\ *adv or adj* **1** : off the right path or route **2** : in or into error

¹astride \ə-'strīd\ *adv* : with one leg on each side

²astride *prep* : with one leg on each side of

as·trin·gent \ə-'strin-jənt\ *adj* : able or tending to shrink body tissues ⟨an *astringent* lotion⟩ — **as·trin·gent·ly** *adv*

as·tro- \'as-trə, -ˌtrō\ *prefix* : star : heavens : astronomical

as·trol·o·gy \ə-'sträl-ə-jē\ *n* : the telling of fortunes by the stars

as·tro·naut \'as-trə-ˌnȯt\ *n* : a traveler in a spacecraft

as·tro·nau·tics \ˌas-trə-'nȯt-iks\ *n* : the science of the construction and operation of spacecraft

as·tron·o·mer \ə-'strän-ə-mər\ *n* : a person who is skilled in astronomy

as·tro·nom·i·cal \ˌas-trə-'näm-i-kəl\ *or* **as·tro·nom·ic** \-ik\ *adj* **1** : of or relating to astronomy **2** : extremely or unbelievably large ⟨the cost was *astronomical*⟩ — **as·tro·nom·i·cal·ly** *adv*

as·tron·o·my \ə-'strän-ə-mē\ *n* : the science of celestial bodies and of their motions and makeup

as·tute \ə-'stüt, -'styüt\ *adj* : very alert and aware : CLEVER ⟨an *astute* observer⟩ — **as·tute·ly** *adv* — **as·tute·ness** *n*

asun·der \ə-'sən-dər\ *adv or adj* **1** : into parts ⟨torn *asunder*⟩ **2** : apart from each other in position ⟨their views of the problem were far *asunder*⟩

as well as *prep or conj* : in addition to : and also ⟨the cat is pretty *as well as* smart⟩

asy·lum \ə-'sī-ləm\ *n* **1** : a place of protection and shelter **2** : protection given especially to political refugees **3** : a place for the care of the poor or sick and especially of the insane

at \ət, at\ *prep* **1** — used to indicate a particular place or time ⟨they're *at* the door⟩ ⟨be here *at* six⟩ **2** — used to indicate a goal ⟨swing *at* the ball⟩ ⟨laughed *at* me⟩ **3** — used to indicate position or condition⟨*at* rest⟩ **4** — used to tell how or why something is done ⟨sold *at* auction⟩

ate *past of* EAT

¹-ate \ət, ˌāt\ *n suffix* : one acted upon in such a way

²-ate *n suffix* : office : rank : group of persons holding such an office or rank

³-ate *adj suffix* : marked by having

⁴-ate \ˌāt\ *vb suffix* : cause to be changed or influenced by : cause to become ⟨acti-*vate*⟩ : furnish with ⟨aer*ate*⟩

athe·ist \'ā-thē-əst\ *n* : a person who believes there is no God

ath·lete \'ath-ˌlēt\ *n* : a person who is trained in or good at games and exercises that require physical skill, endurance, and strength

athlete's foot *n* : a fungus infection of the foot marked by blisters, itching, and cracks between and under the toes

ath·let·ic \ath-'let-ik\ *adj* **1** : of, relating to, or characteristic of athletes or athletics **2** : vigorously active **3** : STURDY 2

ath·let·ics \ath-'let-iks\ *n sing or pl* : games, sports, and exercises requiring strength, endurance, and skill

-a·tion \'ā-shən\ *n suffix* : action or process ⟨comput*ation*⟩ : something connected with an action or process ⟨discolor*ation*⟩

-a·tive \ət-iv, ˌāt-\ *adj suffix* **1** : of, relating to, or connected with ⟨authorit*ative*⟩ **2** : tending to ⟨talk*ative*⟩

at·las \'at-ləs\ *n* : a book of maps

at·mo·sphere \'at-mə-ˌsfiər\ *n* **1** : the gas surrounding a celestial body : AIR **2** : the air in a particular place ⟨the stuffy *atmosphere* of this room⟩ **3** : a surrounding influence or set of conditions ⟨the home *atmosphere*⟩

at·mo·spher·ic \ˌat-mə-'sfiər-ik, -'sfer-\ *adj* : of or relating to the atmosphere

\ə\ abut	\au̇\ out	\i\ tip	\ȯ\ saw	\u̇\ foot
\ər\ further	\ch\ chin	\ī\ life	\ȯi\ coin	\y\ yet
\a\ mat	\e\ pet	\j\ job	\th\ thin	\yü\ few
\ā\ take	\ē\ easy	\ng\ sing	\t̲h̲\ this	\yu̇\ cure
\ä\ cot, cart	\g\ go	\ō\ bone	\ü\ food	\zh\ vision

atoll \'a-ˌtȯl, -ˌtäl\ *n* : a ring-shaped coral island or string of islands consisting of a coral reef surrounding a lagoon

atoll

at·om \'at-əm\ *n* **1** : a tiny particle : BIT **2** : the smallest particle of an element that can exist alone or in combination

Word History The English word *atom* came from a Greek word that meant "not able to be divided." People believed that if something were divided into its smallest parts those parts would be atoms. The atoms themselves, however, could not be divided. This is how the atom got its name.

atom bomb *or* **atomic bomb** *n* : a bomb whose great power is due to the sudden release of the energy in the atomic nucleus

atom·ic \ə-'täm-ik\ *adj* : of, relating to, or concerned with atoms, atomic energy, or atom bombs

atomic energy *n* : energy that can be freed by changes in the nucleus of an atom (as by splitting of a heavy nucleus or fusion of light nuclei into heavier ones)

at·om·iz·er \'at-ə-ˌmī-zər\ *n* : a device for spraying a liquid (as a perfume or disinfectant)

atone \ə-'tōn\ *vb* **atoned; aton·ing** : to do something to make up for a wrong that has been done

atone·ment \ə-'tōn-mənt\ *n* : a making up for an offense or injury

atop \ə-'täp\ *prep* : on top of

atro·cious \ə-'trō-shəs\ *adj* **1** : savagely brutal, cruel, or wicked **2** : very bad ⟨*atrocious* weather⟩ — **atro·cious·ly** *adv* — **atro·cious·ness** *n*

atroc·i·ty \ə-'träs-ət-ē\ *n, pl* **atroc·i·ties** : an atrocious act, object, or situation

at·tach \ə-'tach\ *vb* **1** : to take (money or property) legally in order to obtain payment of a debt ⟨*attach* a person's salary⟩ **2** : to fasten one thing to another ⟨*attach* a bell to a bicycle⟩ **3** : to bind by feelings of affection ⟨the children were *attached* to their dog⟩ **4** : to assign by authority ⟨*attach* an officer to headquarters⟩ **5** : to think of as belonging to something ⟨*attach* no importance to it⟩

at·tach·ment \ə-'tach-mənt\ *n* **1** : connection by feelings of affection or regard **2** : a device that can be attached to a machine or tool **3** : a connection by which one thing is joined to another

¹**at·tack** \ə-'tak\ *vb* **1** : to take strong action against : ASSAULT ⟨the dog *attacked* a skunk⟩ **2** : to use unfriendly or bitter words against ⟨*attack* the mayor on the radio⟩ **3** : to begin to affect or to act upon harmfully ⟨the camp was *attacked* by fever⟩ **4** : to start to work on ⟨*attacked* my homework⟩ — **at·tack·er** *n*

²**attack** *n* **1** : the act of attacking **2** : beginning to work **3** : a spell of sickness

at·tain \ə-'tān\ *vb* **1** : to reach as a desired goal ⟨*attain* an ambition⟩ **2** : to come into possession of **3** : to arrive at ⟨*attain* the top of the hill⟩ — **at·tain·able** \ə-'tā-nə-bəl\ *adj*

at·tain·ment \ə-'tān-mənt\ *n* **1** : the act of attaining : the state of being attained **2** : ACCOMPLISHMENT **3** ⟨a school famous for scientific *attainments*⟩

at·tar \'at-ər\ *n* : a sweet-smelling oil from flowers

¹**at·tempt** \ə-'tempt\ *vb* **1** : to try to do or perform ⟨*attempt* an escape⟩ **2** : to try to do something ⟨*attempt* to solve a problem⟩

²**attempt** *n* : the act or an instance of attempting

at·tend \ə-'tend\ *vb* **1** : to pay attention to ⟨*attend* to what I say⟩ **2** : to go with especially as a servant or companion ⟨a ruler *attended* by the court⟩ **3** : to care for ⟨nurses *attend* the sick⟩ **4** : to go to or be present at ⟨*attend* school⟩ ⟨*attend* a party⟩ **5** : to take charge ⟨*attend* to taking out the rubbish⟩

at·ten·dance \ə-'ten-dəns\ *n* **1** : the act of attending **2** : the number of persons present

¹**at·ten·dant** \ə-'ten-dənt\ *adj* : coming with or following closely as a result ⟨*attendant* circumstances⟩

²**attendant** *n* : a person who attends something or someone

at·ten·tion \ə-'ten-chən\ *n* **1** : the act or the power of fixing one's mind on something : careful listening or watching ⟨pay *attention*⟩ **2** : a state of being aware ⟨attract *attention*⟩ **3** : careful thinking about something so as to be able to take action on it ⟨a matter requiring *attention*⟩ **4** : an act of kindness or politeness **5** : a military posture with body stiff and straight, heels together, and arms at the sides

at·ten·tive \ə-'tent-iv\ *adj* **1** : paying attention ⟨an *attentive* listener⟩ **2** : being thoughtful and polite ⟨*attentive* to their parents⟩ — **at·ten·tive·ly** *adv* — **at·ten·tive·ness** *n*

at·test \ə-'test\ *vb* : to give proof of

at·tic \'at-ik\ *n* : a room or a space just under the roof of a building

¹at·tire \ə-'tīr\ *vb* **at·tired; at·tir·ing** : to put clothes and especially fine clothes on

²attire *n* : clothing meant for a particular occasion ⟨formal *attire*⟩

at·ti·tude \'at-ə-,tüd, -,tyüd\ *n* **1** : the position of the body, or of the parts of the body, or of an object **2** : a feeling or opinion about a certain fact or situation

at·tor·ney \ə-'tər-nē\ *n*, *pl* **at·tor·neys** : a person who acts as agent for another in dealing with business or legal matters

at·tract \ə-'trakt\ *vb* **1** : to draw to or toward oneself ⟨a magnet *attracts* iron⟩ **2** : to draw by appealing to interest or feeling ⟨*attract* attention⟩

at·trac·tion \ə-'trak-shən\ *n* **1** : the act or power of attracting **2** : something that attracts or pleases ⟨the *attractions* of a city⟩

at·trac·tive \ə-'trak-tiv\ *adj* : having the power or quality of attracting : PLEASING — **at·trac·tive·ly** *adv* — **at·trac·tive·ness** *n*

¹at·tri·bute \'at-rə-,byüt\ *n* **1** : a quality belonging to a particular person or thing **2** : a word (as an adjective) indicating a quality

²at·trib·ute \ə-'trib-yət\ *vb* **at·trib·ut·ed; at·trib·ut·ing** **1** : to explain as the cause of ⟨we *attribute* their success to hard work⟩ **2** : to think of as likely to be a quality of a person or thing ⟨*attribute* stubbornness to mules⟩

at·tri·bu·tion \,at-rə-'byü-shən\ *n* : the act of attributing

at·tune \ə-'tün, -'tyün\ *vb* **at·tuned; at·tun·ing** : to bring into harmony : TUNE

atyp·i·cal \'ā-'tip-i-kəl\ *adj* : not typical — **atyp·i·cal·ly** *adv*

au·burn \'ȯ-bərn\ *adj* : of a reddish brown color ⟨*auburn* hair⟩

¹auc·tion \'ȯk-shən\ *n* : a public sale at which things are sold to those who offer to pay the most

²auction *vb* : to sell at auction

auc·tion·eer \,ȯk-shə-'niər\ *n* : a person in charge of auctions

au·da·cious \ȯ-'dā-shəs\ *adj* **1** : very bold and daring : FEARLESS **2** : very rude : INSOLENT — **au·da·cious·ly** *adv* — **au·da·cious·ness** *n*

au·dac·i·ty \ȯ-'das-ət-ē\ *n*, *pl* **au·dac·i·ties** : the fact or an instance of being audacious

au·di·ble \'ȯd-ə-bəl\ *adj* : loud enough to be heard — **au·di·bly** \-blē\ *adv*

au·di·ence \'ȯd-ē-əns\ *n* **1** : a group that listens or watches (as at a play or concert) **2** : a chance to talk with a person of very high rank **3** : those of the general public who give attention to something said, done, or written

¹au·dio \'ȯd-ē-,ō\ *adj* **1** : of or relating to sound or its reproduction **2** : relating to or used in the transmitting or receiving of sound (as in radio or television)

²audio *n* **1** : the transmitting, receiving, or reproducing of sound **2** : the section of television equipment that deals with sound

¹au·dit \'ȯd-ət\ *n* : a thorough check of business accounts

²audit *vb* : to make an audit of

¹au·di·tion \ȯ-'dish-ən\ *n* : a short performance to test the talents of a singer, dancer, or actor

²audition *vb* : to test or try out in an audition

au·di·tor \'ȯd-ət-ər\ *n* **1** : a person who listens especially as a member of a radio or TV audience **2** : a person who audits business accounts

au·di·to·ri·um \,ȯd-ə-'tȯr-ē-əm\ *n* **1** : the part of a public building where an audience sits **2** : a hall used for public gatherings

au·di·to·ry \'ȯd-ə-,tȯr-ē\ *adj* : of or relating to hearing

au·ger \'ȯ-gər\ *n* : a tool used for boring holes

aught \'ȯt\ *n* : ZERO 1

aug·ment \ȯg-'ment\ *vb* : to increase in size, amount, or degree

au·gust \ȯ-'gəst\ *adj* : being grand and noble : MAJESTIC — **au·gust·ly** *adv* — **au·gust·ness** *n*

Au·gust \'ȯ-gəst\ *n* : the eighth month of the year

auger

Word History The first Roman calendar began the year with March. The sixth

\ə\ abut	\au̇\ out	\i\ tip	\ȯ\ saw	\u̇\ foot
\ər\ further	\ch\ chin	\ī\ life	\ȯi\ coin	\y\ yet
\a\ mat	\e\ pet	\j\ job	\th\ thin	\yü\ few
\ā\ take	\ē\ easy	\ng\ sing	\t̲h̲\ this	\yu̇\ cure
\ä\ cot, cart	\g\ go	\ō\ bone	\ü\ food	\zh\ vision

month was the one we now know as August. The first Latin name given to this month came from a Latin word that meant "sixth." Then the emperor Augustus decided that he wanted to have a month named after him. The sixth month was given his name. The English word *August* came from the emperor's Latin name.

auk \'ȯk\ *n* : a diving seabird of cold parts of the northern hemisphere with a heavy body and small wings

aunt \'ant, 'ȧnt\ *n* **1** : a sister of one's parent **2** : the wife of one's uncle

au·ra \'ȯr-ə\ *n* : a feeling that seems to be given off by a person or thing ⟨an *aura* of mystery⟩

auk

au·ral \'ȯr-əl\ *adj* : of or relating to the ear or sense of hearing — **au·ral·ly** *adv*

au·ri·cle \'ȯr-i-kəl\ *n* : the part of the heart that receives blood from the veins

au·ro·ra bo·re·al·is \ə-,rōr-ə-,bōr-ē-'al-əs\ *n* : broad bands of light that have a magnetic and electrical source and that appear in the sky at night especially in the arctic regions

aus·pic·es \'ȯ-spə-səz\ *n pl* : support and guidance of a sponsor ⟨a concert given under the *auspices* of the school⟩

aus·pi·cious \ȯ-'spish-əs\ *adj* **1** : promising success ⟨an *auspicious* beginning⟩ **2** : PROSPEROUS 1⟨the team had a very *auspicious* season⟩ — **aus·pi·cious·ly** *adv*

aus·tere \ȯ-'stiər\ *adj* **1** : seeming or acting harsh and stern **2** : ¹PLAIN 1 ⟨an *austere* room⟩ — **aus·tere·ly** *adv*

aus·ter·i·ty \ȯ-'ster-ət-ē\ *n, pl* **aus·ter·i·ties** **1** : an austere act or manner **2** : lack of all luxury

¹Aus·tra·lian \ȯ-'strāl-yən\ *n* : a person born or living in Australia

²Australian *adj* : of or relating to Australia or the Australians

aut- \ȯt\ *or* **au·to-** \'ȯt-ə, 'ȯt-ō\ *prefix* **1** : self : same one ⟨*auto*biography⟩ **2** : automatic

au·then·tic \ə-'thent-ik, ȯ-\ *adj* **1** : being really what it seems to be : GENUINE ⟨an *authentic* signature⟩ **2** : being correct or true ⟨a report *authentic* in every detail⟩ — **au·then·ti·cal·ly** \-i-kə-lē\ *adv*

au·thor \'ȯ-thər\ *n* **1** : a person who writes something (as a novel) **2** : one that starts or creates ⟨the *author* of a new tax system⟩

au·thor·i·ta·tive \ə-'thȯr-ə-,tāt-iv\ *adj* : having or coming from authority ⟨an *authoritative* order⟩ — **au·thor·i·ta·tive·ly** *adv* — **au·thor·i·ta·tive·ness** *n*

au·thor·i·ty \ə-'thȯr-ət-ē\ *n, pl* **au·thor·i·ties** **1** : a fact or statement used to support a position **2** : a person looked to as an expert **3** : power to influence the behavior of others **4** : persons having powers of government ⟨state *authorities*⟩

au·tho·rize \'ȯ-thə-,rīz\ *vb* **au·tho·rized; au·tho·riz·ing** **1** : to give authority to : EMPOWER ⟨*authorized* to act for them⟩ **2** : to give legal or official approval to

au·thor·ship \'ȯ-thər-,ship\ *n* : the profession of writing

au·to \'ȯt-ō\ *n, pl* **au·tos** : AUTOMOBILE

auto- — see AUT-

au·to·bi·og·ra·phy \,ȯt-ə-bī-'äg-rə-fē\ *n, pl* **au·to·bi·og·ra·phies** : the biography of a person written by that person

¹au·to·graph \'ȯt-ə-,graf\ *n* : a person's signature written by hand

²autograph *vb* : to write one's signature in or on (as a book)

au·to·mate \'ȯt-ə-,māt\ *vb* **au·to·mat·ed; au·to·mat·ing** : to make automatic ⟨*automate* a factory⟩

¹au·to·mat·ic \,ȯt-ə-'mat-ik\ *adj* **1** : INVOLUNTARY ⟨*automatic* blinking of eyelids⟩ **2** : being a machine or device that acts by or regulates itself ⟨an *automatic* washer⟩ — **au·to·mat·i·cal·ly** \-i-kə-lē\ *adv*

²automatic *n* **1** : an automatic machine or device **2** : an automatic firearm

au·to·ma·tion \,ȯt-ə-'mā-shən\ *n* **1** : the method of making a machine, a process, or a system work automatically **2** : automatic working of a machine, process, or system by mechanical or electronic devices that take the place of humans

¹au·to·mo·bile \,ȯt-ə-mō-'bēl, 'ȯt-ə-mō-,bēl\ *adj* : AUTOMOTIVE

²automobile *n* : a usually four-wheeled vehicle that runs on its own power and is designed to carry passengers

au·to·mo·tive \,ȯt-ə-'mōt-iv\ *adj* : SELF-PROPELLED

au·tumn \'ȯt-əm\ *n* : the season between summer and winter that in the northern hemisphere is usually the months of September, October, and November

au·tum·nal \ȯ-'təm-nəl\ *adj* : of or relating to autumn

¹aux·il·ia·ry \ȯg-'zil-yə-rē, -'zil-ə-rē, -'zil-rē\ *adj* : available to provide something extra ⟨a sailboat with an *auxiliary* engine⟩

²**auxiliary** *n, pl* **aux·il·ia·ries 1** : an auxiliary person, group, or device **2** : HELPING VERB

¹**avail** \ə-'vāl\ *vb* : to be of use or help

²**avail** *n* : help toward reaching a goal : USE ⟨our work was of little *avail*⟩

avail·able \ə-'vā-lə-bəl\ *adj* **1** : SUITABLE, USABLE ⟨used every *available* excuse to get out of work⟩ **2** : possible to get : OBTAINABLE ⟨*available* supplies⟩

av·a·lanche \'av-ə-ˌlanch\ *n* : a large mass of snow and ice or of earth or rock sliding down a mountainside or over a cliff

av·a·rice \'av-ə-rəs, 'av-rəs\ *n* : strong desire for riches : GREED

av·a·ri·cious \ˌav-ə-'rish-əs\ *adj* : greedy for riches — **av·a·ri·cious·ly** *adv* — **av·a·ri·cious·ness** *n*

avenge \ə-'venj\ *vb* **avenged; aveng·ing** : to take revenge for — **aveng·er** *n*

av·e·nue \'av-ə-ˌnü, -ˌnyü\ *n* **1** : a way of reaching a goal ⟨saw the job as an *avenue* to success⟩ **2** : a usually wide street

¹**av·er·age** \'av-ə-rij, 'av-rij\ *n* **1** : ARITHMETIC MEAN **2** : something usual in a group, class, or series

²**average** *adj* **1** : equaling or coming close to an average ⟨the *average* age of the class is eleven⟩ **2** : being ordinary or usual ⟨the *average* person⟩

³**average** *vb* **av·er·aged; av·er·ag·ing 1** : to amount to usually **2** : to find the average of

averse \ə-'vərs\ *adj* : having a feeling of dislike ⟨*averse* to exercise⟩

aver·sion \ə-'vər-zhən\ *n* **1** : a strong dislike **2** : something strongly disliked

avert \ə-'vərt\ *vb* **1** : to turn away ⟨*avert* one's eyes⟩ **2** : to keep from happening ⟨*avert* disaster⟩

avi·ary \'ā-vē-ˌer-ē\ *n, pl* **avi·ar·ies** : a place (as a large cage) where birds are kept

avi·a·tion \ˌā-vē-'ā-shən\ *n* **1** : the flying of aircraft **2** : the designing and making of aircraft

avi·a·tor \'ā-vē-ˌāt-ər\ *n* : the pilot of an aircraft

av·id \'av-əd\ *adj* : very eager ⟨an *avid* football fan⟩ — **av·id·ly** *adv*

av·o·ca·do \ˌav-ə-'käd-ō, ˌäv-\ *n, pl* **av·o·ca·dos** : a usually green fruit that is shaped like a pear or an egg, grows on a tropical American tree, and has a rich oily flesh

av·o·ca·tion \ˌav-ə-'kā-shən\ *n* : an interest or activity that is not one's regular job : HOBBY

avoid \ə-'vȯid\ *vb* : to keep away from

avoid·ance \ə-'vȯid-ns\ *n* : a keeping away from something ⟨*avoidance* of trouble⟩

avocado

avow \ə-'vaủ\ *vb* : to declare openly and frankly

avow·al \ə-'vaủ-əl\ *n* : an open declaration

await \ə-'wāt\ *vb* **1** : to wait for ⟨*await* a train⟩ **2** : to be ready or waiting for ⟨dinner was *awaiting* them on their arrival⟩

¹**awake** \ə-'wāk\ *vb* **awoke** \-'wōk\ *also* **awaked; awak·ing 1** : to arouse from sleep : wake up **2** : to become conscious or aware of something ⟨*awoke* to their danger⟩

²**awake** *adj* : not asleep

awak·en \ə-'wā-kən\ *vb* : ¹AWAKE 1 — **awak·en·er** *n*

¹**award** \ə-'wȯrd\ *vb* **1** : to give by judicial decision ⟨*award* damages⟩ **2** : to give or grant as deserved or needed ⟨*award* a medal⟩ ⟨*award* a pension⟩

²**award** *n* : something (as a prize) that is awarded

aware \ə-'waər, -'weər\ *adj* : having or showing understanding or knowledge : CONSCIOUS ⟨*aware* of what's happening⟩ — **aware·ness** *n*

awash \ə-'wȯsh, -'wäsh\ *adv or adj* **1** : washed by waves or tide **2** : floating about **3** : flooded or covered with water

¹**away** \ə-'wā\ *adv* **1** : from this or that place ⟨go *away*⟩ **2** : in another place or direction ⟨turn *away*⟩ **3** : out of existence ⟨the echo died *away*⟩ **4** : from one's possession ⟨gave *away* a fortune⟩ **5** : without stopping or slowing down ⟨talk *away*⟩ **6** : at or to a great distance in space or time : FAR ⟨*away* back in 1910⟩

²**away** *adj* **1** : ¹ABSENT 1 ⟨be *away* from home⟩ **2** : DISTANT 1 ⟨a lake ten kilometers *away*⟩

¹**awe** \'ȯ\ *n* : a feeling of mixed fear, respect, and wonder

\ə\ abut	\aủ\ out	\i\ tip	\ȯ\ saw	\ủ\ foot
\ər\ further	\ch\ chin	\ī\ life	\ȯi\ coin	\y\ yet
\a\ mat	\e\ pet	\j\ job	\th\ thin	\yü\ few
\ā\ take	\ē\ easy	\ng\ sing	\th\ this	\yủ\ cure
\ä\ cot, cart	\g\ go	\ō\ bone	\ü\ food	\zh\ vision

²awe *vb* **awed; aw·ing :** to fill with awe

awe·some \'ȯ-səm\ *adj* : causing a feeling of awe

aw·ful \'ȯ-fəl\ *adj* **1 :** causing fear or terror ⟨an *awful* disaster⟩ **2 :** very disagreeable or unpleasant ⟨an *awful* cold⟩ **3 :** very great ⟨an *awful* lot⟩

aw·ful·ly \'ȯ-flē, *especially for 1* -fə-lē\ *adv* **1 :** in a disagreeable or unpleasant manner **2 :** to a very great degree ⟨was *awfully* tired⟩

awhile \ə-'hwīl, ə-'wīl\ *adv* : for a while : for a short time ⟨sit down and rest *awhile*⟩

awk·ward \'ȯ-kwərd\ *adj* **1 :** not graceful : CLUMSY **2 :** likely to embarrass ⟨an *awkward* question⟩ **3 :** difficult to use or handle ⟨*awkward* tools⟩ — **awk·ward·ly** *adv* — **awk·ward·ness** *n*

awl \'ȯl\ *n* : a pointed tool for making small holes (as in leather or wood)

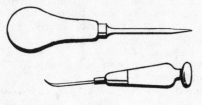

awl

aw·ning \'ȯ-ning\ *n* : a cover (as of canvas) that shades or shelters like a roof

awoke *past of* AWAKE

awry \ə-'rī\ *adv or adj* **1 :** turned or twisted to one side : ASKEW **2 :** out of the right course : AMISS ⟨the plans had gone *awry*⟩

ax *or* **axe** \'aks\ *n* : a tool that has a heavy head with a sharp edge fixed to a handle and is used for chopping and splitting wood

ax·i·om \'ak-sē-əm\ *n* **1 :** MAXIM **2 :** a statement thought to be clearly true

ax·is \'ak-səs\ *n, pl* **ax·es** \'ak-ˌsēz\ : a straight line about which a body or a geometric figure rotates or may be supposed to rotate ⟨the earth's *axis*⟩

ax·le \'ak-səl\ *n* : a pin or shaft on or with which a wheel or pair of wheels turns

ax·on \'ak-ˌsän\ *n* : a long fiber that carries impulses away from a nerve cell

¹aye \'ī\ *adv* : **¹**YES 1 ⟨*aye, aye,* sir⟩

²aye \'ī\ *n* : an affirmative vote or voter ⟨the *ayes* have it⟩

aza·lea \ə-'zāl-yə\ *n* : a usually small rhododendron that sheds its leaves in the fall and has flowers of many colors which are shaped like funnels

azalea

azure \'azh-ər\ *n* : the blue color of the clear daytime sky

b \'bē\ *n, pl* **b's** *or* **bs** \'bēz\ *often cap* **1 :** the second letter of the English alphabet **2 :** a grade that shows a student's work is good

¹baa \'ba, 'bä\ *n* : the cry of a sheep

²baa *vb* : to make the cry of a sheep

¹bab·ble \'bab-əl\ *vb* **bab·bled; bab·bling** \'bab-ə-ling, 'bab-ling\ **1 :** to make meaningless sounds **2 :** to talk foolishly **3 :** to make the sound of a brook — **bab·bler** \'bab-ə-lər, 'bab-lər\ *n*

²babble *n* **1 :** talk that is not clear **2 :** the sound of a brook

babe \'bāb\ *n* : **¹**BABY 1 ⟨a *babe* in arms⟩

ba·boon \ba-'bün\ *n* : a large monkey of Africa and Asia with a doglike face

baboon

¹**ba·by** \'bā-bē\ *n, pl* **ba·bies 1** : a very young child **2** : the youngest of a group **3** : an older person who acts like a baby

²**baby** *adj* : ¹YOUNG 1 ⟨a *baby* deer⟩

³**baby** *vb* **ba·bied; ba·by·ing** : to treat as a baby

ba·by·hood \'bā-bē-,hùd\ *n* **1** : the time in a person's life when he or she is a baby **2** : the state of being a baby

ba·by·ish \'bā-bē-ish\ *adj* : like a baby

ba·by–sit \'bā-bē-,sit\ *vb* **ba·by–sat** \-,sat\; **ba·by–sit·ting** : to care for children usually during a short absence of the parents

ba·by–sit·ter \'bā-bē-,sit-ər\ *n* : a person who baby-sits

bach·e·lor \'bach-ə-lər, 'bach-lər\ : a man who has not married

ba·cil·lus \bə-'sil-əs\ *n, pl* **ba·cil·li** \-'sil-,ī\ **1** : a rod-shaped bacterium that forms internal spores **2** : a bacterium that causes disease : GERM, MICROBE

¹**back** \'bak\ *n* **1** : the rear part of the human body from the neck to the end of the spine : the upper part of the body of an animal **2** : the part of something that is opposite or away from the front part **3** : a player in a team game who plays behind the forward line of players — **backed** \'bakt\ *adj*

²**back** *adv* **1** : to, toward, or at the rear ⟨the crowd moved *back*⟩ **2** : in or to a former time, state, or place ⟨some years *back*⟩ ⟨went *back* home⟩ **3** : under control ⟨kept *back* my anger⟩ **4** : in return or reply ⟨talk *back*⟩ — **back and forth** : backward and forward : from one place to another

³**back** *adj* **1** : located at the back ⟨the *back* door⟩ **2** : not yet paid : OVERDUE ⟨*back* rent⟩ **3** : no longer current ⟨*back* issues of a magazine⟩

⁴**back** *vb* **1** : to give support or help to : UPHOLD **2** : to move back — **back·er** *n*

back·bone \'bak-,bōn\ *n* **1** : the column of bones in the back : SPINAL COLUMN **2** : the strongest part of something **3** : firmness of character

¹**back·fire** \'bak-,fīr\ *n* **1** : a fire that is set to check the spread of a forest fire or a grass fire by burning off a strip of land ahead of it **2** : a loud engine noise that happens when fuel ignites with a valve open

²**backfire** *vb* **back·fired; back·fir·ing 1** : to make a backfire **2** : to have a result opposite to what was planned ⟨the joke *backfired*⟩

back·ground \'bak-,graùnd\ *n* **1** : the scenery or ground that is behind a main figure or object ⟨the curtains had red flowers printed on a gray *background*⟩ **2** : a position that attracts little attention ⟨tried to keep in the *background*⟩ **3** : the total of a person's experience, knowledge, and education

¹**back·hand** \'bak-,hand\ *n* **1** : a stroke made with the back of the hand turned in the direction in which the hand is moving **2** : handwriting in which the letters slant to the left

backhand 1

²**backhand** *adv or adj* : with a backhand ⟨struck *backhand* at the ball⟩

back·hand·ed \'bak-,han-dəd\ *adj* **1** : ²BACKHAND ⟨a *backhanded* blow⟩ **2** : not sincere ⟨*backhanded* praise⟩

back of *prep* : ²BEHIND 1

back·stage \'bak-'stāj\ *adv or adj* : in or to the area behind the stage

back·track \'bak-,trak\ *vb* : to go back over a course or a path

¹**back·ward** \'bak-wərd\ *or* **back·wards** \-wərdz\ *adv* **1** : toward the back ⟨look *backward*⟩ **2** : with the back first ⟨ride *backward*⟩ **3** : opposite to the usual way ⟨count *backward*⟩

²**backward** *adj* **1** : turned toward the back ⟨a *backward* glance⟩ **2** : BASHFUL **3** : slow in learning or development ⟨a *backward* child⟩

back·wa·ter \'bak-,wòt-ər, -,wät-\ *n* **1** : water held or turned back from its course **2** : a backward place or condition

back·woods \'bak-'wùdz\ *n pl* **1** : wooded

\ə\ abut	\aù\ out	\i\ tip	\ò\ saw	\ù\ foot
\ər\ further	\ch\ chin	\ī\ life	\òi\ coin	\y\ yet
\a\ mat	\e\ pet	\j\ job	\th\ thin	\yü\ few
\ā\ take	\ē\ easy	\ng\ sing	\th\ this	\yù\ cure
\ä\ cot, cart	\g\ go	\ō\ bone	\ü\ food	\zh\ vision

or partly cleared areas away from cities **2** : a place that is backward in culture

ba·con \'bā-kən\ *n* : salted and smoked meat from the sides and the back of a pig

bac·te·ri·um \bak-'tir-ē-əm\ *n*, *pl* **bac·te·ri·a** \-ē-ə\ : any of numerous microscopic plants that are single cells and are important to humans because of their chemical activities and as causes of disease

bad \'bad\ *adj* **worse** \'wərs\; **worst** \'wərst\ **1** : not good : POOR ⟨*bad* weather⟩ **2** : not favorable ⟨a *bad* impression⟩ **3** : not fresh or sound ⟨*bad* fish⟩ **4** : not good or right : morally evil ⟨a *bad* person⟩ ⟨*bad* behavior⟩ **5** : not enough ⟨*bad* lighting⟩ **6** : UNPLEASANT ⟨*bad* news⟩ **7** : HARMFUL ⟨*bad* for the health⟩ **8** : SEVERE 4 ⟨a *bad* cold⟩ **9** : not correct ⟨*bad* spelling⟩ **10** : ¹ILL 4, SICK ⟨a cold that made me feel *bad*⟩ **11** : SORRY 1 ⟨felt *bad* about my mistake⟩ — **bad·ness** *n*

synonyms BAD, EVIL, WICKED, and NAUGHTY mean not doing or being what is right. BAD is used of anyone or anything that is objectionable ⟨you're a bad dog for chewing on the furniture⟩ ⟨had to stay after school for *bad* behavior⟩ EVIL is a more powerful word than *bad* and often suggests something threatening ⟨criminals planning *evil* deeds⟩ WICKED is used of someone or something that is truly and deliberately bad ⟨a very *wicked* ruler who put many people to death⟩ NAUGHTY is usually used of children or of unimportant wrongdoing ⟨a *naughty* child knocked over the milk⟩

bade *past of* BID

badge \'baj\ *n* : something worn to show that a person belongs to a certain group or rank

¹**bad·ger** \'baj-ər\ *n* : a furry burrowing animal with short thick legs and long claws on the front feet

badger

²**badger** *vb* : to annoy again and again

bad·ly \'bad-lē\ *adv* **worse** \'wərs\; **worst** \'wərst\ **1** : in a bad manner **2** : very much ⟨wanted the toy *badly*⟩

bad·min·ton \'bad-,mint-n\ *n* : a game in which a shuttlecock is hit back and forth over a net by players using light rackets

baf·fle \'baf-əl\ *vb* **baf·fled**; **baf·fling** \'baf-ə-ling, 'baf-ling\ : to defeat or check by confusing

¹**bag** \'bag\ *n* **1** : a container made of flexible material (as paper or plastic) **2** : ¹PURSE 1, HANDBAG **3** : SUITCASE

²**bag** *vb* **bagged**; **bag·ging 1** : to swell out **2** : to put into a bag **3** : to kill or capture in hunting

ba·gel \'bā-gəl\ *n* : a hard roll shaped like a doughnut

bag·gage \'bag-ij\ *n* : the trunks, suitcases, and personal belongings of travelers

bag·gy \'bag-ē\ *adj* **bag·gi·er**; **bag·gi·est** : hanging loosely or puffed out like a bag ⟨*baggy* pants⟩

bag·pipe \'bag-,pīp\ *n* : a musical instrument played especially in Scotland that consists of a tube, a bag for air, and pipes from which the sound comes

¹**bail** \'bāl\ *n* : a promise or a deposit of money needed to free a prisoner until his or her trial

²**bail** *vb* : to get the release of (a prisoner) by giving bail

³**bail** *vb* : to dip and throw out water from a boat

bagpipe

bail out *vb* : to jump out of an airplane with a parachute

¹**bait** \'bāt\ *vb* **1** : to torment by repeated attacks ⟨*baited* the speaker by whistling and shouting⟩ **2** : to put bait on or in ⟨*bait* a trap⟩

²**bait** *n* : something and especially food used to attract animals to a hook or into a trap

bake \'bāk\ *vb* **baked**; **bak·ing 1** : to cook or become cooked in a dry heat especially in an oven **2** : to dry or harden by heat

bak·er \'bā-kər\ *n* : a person who bakes and sells bread, cakes, or pastry

baker's dozen *n* : THIRTEEN

bak·ery \'bā-kə-rē, 'bā-krē\ *n*, *pl* **bak·er·ies** : a place where bread, cakes, and pastry are made or sold

baking powder *n* : a powder used in baking cakes and biscuits to make the dough rise

baking soda *n* : SODIUM BICARBONATE

¹bal·ance \'bal-əns\ *n* **1** : an instrument for weighing **2** : a steady position or condition ⟨kept my *balance*⟩ **3** : equal total sums on the two sides of a bookkeeping account **4** : something left over : REMAINDER **5** : the amount by which one side of an account is greater than the other ⟨a *balance* of ten dollars on the credit side⟩

Word History The first meaning of the word *balance* was "an instrument used to weigh things." (Other meanings have come from this one.) Some weighing instruments have two scales. The English word *balance* came from a Latin word that meant "having two scales." This Latin word was a compound. It was formed from a Latin prefix that meant "two" and a Latin noun that meant "plate" or "scale."

²balance *vb* **bal·anced; bal·anc·ing 1** : to make the two sides of (an account) add up to the same total **2** : to make equal in weight or number **3** : to weigh against one another : COMPARE **4** : to put in or as if in balance

bal·co·ny \'bal-kə-nē\ *n, pl* **bal·co·nies 1** : a platform enclosed by a low wall or a railing built out from the side of a building **2** : a platform inside a building extending out over part of a main floor (as of a theater)

bald \'bȯld\ *adj* **1** : lacking a natural covering (as of hair) **2** : ¹PLAIN **3** ⟨the *bald* facts⟩ — **bald·ness** *n*

bald eagle *n* : the common North American eagle that when full-grown has white head and neck feathers

bald eagle

¹bale \'bāl\ *n* : a large bundle of goods tightly tied for storing or shipping ⟨a *bale* of cotton⟩

²bale *vb* **baled; bal·ing** : to make up into a bale — **bal·er** *n*

¹balk \'bȯk\ *n* : HINDRANCE

²balk *vb* **1** : to keep from happening or succeeding ⟨rain *balked* our plans for a hike⟩ **2** : to stop short and refuse to go

balky \'bȯ-kē\ *adj* **balk·i·er; balk·i·est** : likely to balk ⟨a *balky* engine⟩

¹ball \'bȯl\ *n* **1** : something round or roundish ⟨a *ball* of twine⟩ **2** : a usually round object used in a game or sport **3** : a game or sport (as baseball) played with a ball **4** : a solid usually round shot for a gun **5** : the rounded bulge at the base of the thumb or big toe ⟨the *ball* of the foot⟩ **6** : a pitched baseball that is not hit and is not a strike

²ball *vb* : to make or come together into a ball

³ball *n* : a large formal party for dancing

bal·lad \'bal-əd\ *n* **1** : a simple song **2** : a short poem suitable for singing that tells a story in simple language

ball–and–socket joint *n* : a joint (as in the shoulder) in which a rounded part can move in many directions in a socket

bal·last \'bal-əst\ *n* **1** : heavy material used to make a ship steady or to control the rising of a balloon **2** : gravel, cinders, or crushed stone used in making a roadbed ⟨*ballast* for railroad tracks⟩

ball bearing *n* **1** : a bearing in which the revolving part turns on metal balls that roll easily in a groove **2** : one of the balls in a ball bearing

bal·le·ri·na \,bal-ə-'rē-nə\ *n* : a female ballet dancer

bal·let \'ba-,lā, ba-'lā\ *n* **1** : a stage dance that tells a story in movement and pantomime **2** : a group that performs ballets

¹bal·loon \bə-'lün\ *n* **1** : a bag that rises and floats above the ground when filled with heated air or with a gas that is lighter than air **2** : a toy consisting of a rubber bag that can be blown up with air or gas **3** : an outline containing words spoken or thought by a character (as in a cartoon)

²balloon *vb* : to swell or puff out like a balloon

¹bal·lot \'bal-ət\ *n* **1** : an object and especially a printed sheet of paper used in voting **2** : the action or a system of voting **3**

\ə\ **abut**	\au̇\ **out**	\i\ **tip**	\ȯ\ **saw**	\u̇\ **foot**
\ər\ **further**	\ch\ **chin**	\ī\ **life**	\ȯi\ **coin**	\y\ **yet**
\a\ **mat**	\e\ **pet**	\j\ **job**	\th\ **thin**	\yü\ **few**
\ā\ **take**	\ē\ **easy**	\ng\ **sing**	\th\ **this**	\yu̇\ **cure**
\ä\ **cot, cart**	\g\ **go**	\ō\ **bone**	\ü\ **food**	\zh\ **vision**

: the right to vote **4** : the number of votes cast

²**ballot** *vb* : to vote or decide by ballot

ball·point pen \,bȯl-,pȯint-\ *n* : a pen whose writing point is a small metal ball that inks itself from an inner supply

ball·room \'bȯl-,rüm, -,ru̇m\ *n* : a large room for dances

balmy \'bäm-ē, 'bäl-mē\ *adj* **balm·i·er; balm·i·est** : gently soothing ⟨a *balmy* breeze⟩

bal·sa \'bȯl-sə\ *n* : the very light but strong wood of a tropical American tree

bal·sam \'bȯl-səm\ *n* **1** : a material with a strong pleasant smell that oozes from some plants **2** : a plant (as the evergreen **balsam fir** often used as a Christmas tree) that yields balsam

bal·us·ter \'bal-əs-tər\ *n* : a short post that supports the upper part of a railing

bal·us·trade \'bal-əs-,trād\ *n* : a row of balusters topped by a rail to serve as an open fence (as along the edge of a terrace or a balcony)

bam·boo \bam-'bü\ *n* : a tall treelike tropical grass with a hard jointed stem that is used in making furniture and in building

bamboo

¹**ban** \'ban\ *vb* **banned; ban·ning** : to forbid especially by law or social pressure

²**ban** *n* : an official order forbidding something ⟨a *ban* on the sale of a book⟩

ba·nana \bə-'nan-ə\ *n* : a yellow or red fruit that is shaped somewhat like a fin-

banana

ger and grows in bunches on a large tree-like tropical plant (**banana plant** or **ba·nana tree**) with very large leaves

¹**band** \'band\ *n* **1** : something that holds together or goes around something else **2** : a strip of material around or across something ⟨a hat *band*⟩ **3** : a range of frequencies (as of radio waves)

²**band** *vb* **1** : to put a band on : tie together with a band **2** : to unite in a group ⟨*banded* together for protection⟩

³**band** *n* **1** : a group of persons or animals **2** : a group of musicians performing together

¹**ban·dage** \'ban-dij\ *n* : a strip of material used especially to dress and bind up wounds

²**bandage** *vb* **ban·daged; ban·dag·ing** : to bind or cover with a bandage

ban·dan·na *or* **ban·dana** \ban-'dan-ə\ *n* : a large handkerchief usually with a colorful design printed on it

ban·dit \'ban-dət\ *n* : a lawless person : one who lives outside the law

band·stand \'band-,stand\ *n* : an outdoor platform used for band concerts

band·wag·on \'ban-,dwag-ən\ *n* **1** : a wagon carrying musicians in a parade **2** : a candidate, side, or movement that attracts growing support

¹**bang** \'bang\ *vb* : to beat, strike, or shut with a loud noise

²**bang** *n* **1** : a violent blow **2** : a sudden loud noise **3** : ²THRILL 1 ⟨I got a *bang* out of it⟩

³**bang** *n* : hair cut short across the forehead

⁴**bang** *vb* : to cut (hair) short and squarely across

ban·ish \'ban-ish\ *vb* **1** : to force to leave a country **2** : to drive away : DISMISS ⟨*banish* fears⟩

ban·ish·ment \'ban-ish-mənt\ *n* : a banishing from a country

ban·is·ter \'ban-ə-stər\ *n* **1** : one of the slender posts used to support the handrail of a staircase **2 banisters** *pl* : a stair rail and its supporting posts **3** : the handrail of a staircase

ban·jo \'ban-jō\ *n, pl* **ban·jos** : a musical instrument with four or five strings and a fretted neck

banjo

¹**bank** \'bangk\ *n* **1** : a mound or ridge especially of earth **2** : something shaped like a mound ⟨a *bank* of clouds⟩ **3** : an

undersea elevation : SHOAL ⟨the *banks* of Newfoundland⟩ **4** : the rising ground at the edge of a river, lake, or sea ⟨the *banks* of the Hudson⟩

²**bank** *vb* **1** : to raise a bank around **2** : to heap up in a bank ⟨*banked* the snow against the door⟩ **3** : to build (a curve) with the road or track sloping upward from the inside edge **4** : to cover with fuel or ashes so as to reduce the speed of burning ⟨*bank* a fire⟩ **5** : to tilt an airplane to one side when turning

³**bank** *n* : a group or series of objects arranged near together in a row ⟨a *bank* of seats⟩

⁴**bank** *n* **1** : a place of business that lends, exchanges, takes care of, or issues money **2** : a small closed container in which money may be saved **3** : a storage place for a reserve supply ⟨blood *bank*⟩

⁵**bank** *vb* **1** : to have an account in a bank ⟨we *bank* locally⟩ **2** : to deposit in a bank ⟨*bank* ten dollars⟩

bank·er \'bang-kər\ *n* : a person who is engaged in the business of a bank

bank·ing \'bang-king\ *n* : the business of a bank or banker

¹**bank·rupt** \'bang-ˌkrəpt\ *n* : a person who becomes unable to pay his or her debts and whose property is by court order divided among the creditors

²**bankrupt** *vb* : to make bankrupt

³**bankrupt** *adj* : unable to pay one's debts

bank·rupt·cy \'bang-ˌkrəpt-sē\ *n, pl* **bank·rupt·cies** : the state of being bankrupt

¹**ban·ner** \'ban-ər\ *n* **1** : ¹FLAG **2** : a piece of cloth with a design, a picture, or some writing on it

²**banner** *adj* : unusually good or satisfactory ⟨a *banner* year for apples⟩

ban·quet \'bang-kwət\ *n* : a formal dinner for many people often in honor of someone

ban·tam \'bant-əm\ *n* : a very small domestic hen or rooster

¹**ban·ter** \'bant-ər\ *vb* : to speak to in a friendly but teasing way

²**banter** *n* : good-natured teasing and joking

bap·tism \'bap-ˌtiz-əm\ *n* : the act or ceremony of baptizing

bap·tize \bap-'tīz, 'bap-ˌtīz\ *vb* **bap·tized; bap·tiz·ing** **1** : to dip in water or sprinkle water on as a part of the ceremony of receiving into the Christian church **2** : to give a name to as in the ceremony of baptism : CHRISTEN

¹**bar** \'bär\ *n* **1** : a usually slender rigid piece (as of wood or metal) that has many uses (as for a lever or barrier) **2** : a usually

rectangular solid piece or block of something ⟨a *bar* of soap⟩ **3** : something that blocks the way **4** : a submerged or partly submerged bank along a shore or in a river **5** : a court of law **6** : the profession of law **7** : a straight stripe, band, or line longer than it is wide **8** : a counter on which liquor is served **9** : a place of business for the sale of alcoholic drinks **10** : a vertical line across a musical staff marking equal measures of time **11** : ¹MEASURE 6

bar 10

²**bar** *vb* **barred; bar·ring** **1** : to fasten with a bar ⟨*bar* the doors⟩ **2** : to block off ⟨*barred* by a chain across the road⟩ **3** : to shut out

³**bar** *prep* : with the exception of

barb \'bärb\ *n* : a sharp point that sticks out and backward (as from the tip of an arrow or fishhook) — **barbed** \'bärbd\ *adj*

bar·bar·ian \bär-'ber-ē-ən, -'bar-\ *n* : an uncivilized person

bar·bar·ic \bär-'bar-ik\ *adj* : of, relating to, or characteristic of barbarians

bar·ba·rous \'bär-bə-rəs, -brəs\ *adj* **1** : not civilized ⟨a *barbarous* tribe⟩ **2** : CRUEL 2, HARSH ⟨*barbarous* treatment of captives⟩ — **bar·ba·rous·ly** *adv*

¹**bar·be·cue** \'bär-bi-ˌkyü\ *n* **1** : a large animal roasted whole **2** : an outdoor social gathering at which food is barbecued and eaten

²**barbecue** *vb* **bar·be·cued; bar·be·cu·ing** **1** : to cook over or before an open source of heat **2** : to cook in a highly seasoned sauce

bar·ber \'bär-bər\ *n* : a person whose business is cutting and dressing hair and shaving beards

bard \'bärd\ *n* **1** : a person in ancient societies skilled at composing and singing songs about heroes **2** : POET

¹**bare** \'baər, 'beər\ *adj* **bar·er; bar·est** **1** : having no covering : NAKED ⟨trees *bare*

\ə\ **abut**	\au̇\ **out**	\i\ **tip**	\ȯ\ **saw**	\u̇\ **foot**
\ər\ **further**	\ch\ **chin**	\ī\ **life**	\ȯi\ **coin**	\y\ **yet**
\a\ **mat**	\e\ **pet**	\j\ **job**	\th\ **thin**	\yü\ **few**
\ā\ **take**	\ē\ **easy**	\ng\ **sing**	\th\ **this**	\yu̇\ **cure**
\ä\ **cot, cart**	\g\ **go**	\ō\ **bone**	\ü\ **food**	\zh\ **vision**

of leaves⟩ **2** : ¹EMPTY 1 ⟨the cupboard was *bare*⟩ **3** : having nothing left over or added : MERE **4** : ¹PLAIN 3 ⟨the *bare* facts⟩ **synonyms** see NAKED

²bare *vb* **bared; bar·ing** : UNCOVER 1, 2

bare·back \'baər-ˌbak, 'beər-\ *adv or adj* : on the bare back of a horse : without a saddle

bare·foot \'baər-ˌfu̇t, 'beər-\ *adv or adj* : with the feet bare

bare·head·ed \'baər-'hed-əd, 'beər-\ *adv or adj* : with the head bare : without a hat

bare·ly \'baər-lē, 'beər-\ *adv* : with nothing to spare ⟨*barely* enough to eat⟩ ⟨*barely* passed the test⟩

¹bar·gain \'bär-gən\ *n* **1** : an agreement between persons settling what each is to give and receive in a business deal ⟨make a *bargain* to mow a neighbor's lawn for five dollars⟩ **2** : something bought or offered for sale at a desirable price

²bargain *vb* : to talk over the terms of a purchase or agreement

barge \'bärj\ *n* : a broad boat with a flat bottom used chiefly in harbors and on rivers and canals ⟨a coal *barge*⟩

bar graph *n* : a chart that uses parallel bars whose lengths are in proportion to the numbers represented

bari·tone \'bar-ə-ˌtōn\ *n* **1** : a male singing voice between bass and tenor in range **2** : a singer having a baritone voice **3** : a horn used in bands that is lower than the trumpet but higher than the tuba

¹bark \'bärk\ *vb* **1** : to make the short loud cry of a dog **2** : to shout or speak sharply ⟨*bark* out a command⟩

²bark *n* : the sound made by a barking dog

³bark *n* : the outside covering of the trunk, branches, and roots of a tree

⁴bark *vb* : to rub or scrape the skin off

⁵bark *or* **barque** \'bärk\ *n* **1** : a small sailing boat **2** : a three-masted ship with foremast and mainmast square-rigged

bark·er \'bär-kər\ *n* : a person who stands at the entrance to a show or a store and tries to attract people to it

bar·ley \'bär-lē\ *n* : a cereal grass with flowers in dense heads that is grown for its grain which is used mostly to feed farm animals or make malt

barn \'bärn\ *n* : a building used for storing grain and hay and for housing farm animals

bar·na·cle \'bär-ni-kəl\ *n* : a small saltwater shellfish that fastens itself on rocks or on wharves and the bottoms of ships

barn·yard \'bärn-ˌyärd\ *n* : a usually fenced area next to a barn

ba·rom·e·ter \bə-'räm-ət-ər\ *n* : an instrument that measures air pressure and is used to forecast changes in the weather

bar·on \'bar-ən\ *n* : a member of the lowest rank of the British nobility

bar·on·ess \'bar-ə-nəs\ *n* **1** : the wife or widow of a baron **2** : a woman who holds the rank of a baron in her own right

bar·on·et \'bar-ə-nət\ *n* : the holder of a rank of honor below a baron but above a knight

ba·ro·ni·al \bə-'rō-nē-əl\ *adj* : of, relating to, or suitable for a baron

barque *variant of* BARK

bar·racks \'bar-əks, -iks\ *n sing or pl* : a building or group of buildings in which soldiers live

bar·rage \bə-'räzh\ *n* : a barrier formed by continuous artillery or machine-gun fire directed upon a narrow strip of ground

¹bar·rel \'bar-əl\ *n* **1** : a round bulging container that is longer than it is wide and has flat ends **2** : the amount contained in a full barrel **3** : something shaped like a cylinder ⟨the *barrel* of a gun⟩

²barrel *vb* **bar·reled** *or* **bar·relled; barrel·ing** *or* **bar·rel·ling** : to move at a high speed

¹bar·ren \'bar-ən\ *adj* **1** : unable to produce seed, fruit, or young ⟨*barren* plants⟩ **2** : growing only poor or few plants ⟨*barren* soil⟩

²barren *n* : an area of barren land

bar·rette \bä-'ret, bə-\ *n* : a clasp or bar used to hold a woman's hair in place

¹bar·ri·cade \'bar-ə-ˌkād\ *vb* **bar·ri·cad·ed; bar·ri·cad·ing** : to block off with a barricade

²barricade *n* : a barrier made in a hurry for protection against attack or for blocking the way

bar·ri·er \'bar-ē-ər\ *n* **1** : something (as a fence) that blocks the way **2** : something that keeps apart or makes progress difficult

bar·ring *prep* : aside from the possibility of

¹bar·row \'bar-ō\ *n* : a castrated male hog

²barrow *n* **1** : WHEELBARROW **2** : PUSHCART

¹bar·ter \'bärt-ər\ *vb* : to trade by exchanging one thing for another without the use of money

²barter *n* : the exchange of goods without the use of money

¹base \'bās\ *n* **1** : a thing or a part on which something rests : BOTTOM, FOUNDATION ⟨the *base* of a statue⟩ **2** : a line or surface of a geometric figure upon which an altitude is or is thought to be constructed ⟨*base* of a triangle⟩ **3** : the main substance in a mixture **4** : a supporting or carrying substance (as in a medicine or paint) **5** : a place where a military force keeps its supplies or from which it starts its operations ⟨an air force *base*⟩ **6** : a number with reference to which a system of numbers is constructed **7** : a starting place or goal in various games **8** : any of the four stations a runner in baseball must touch in order to score **9** : a chemical substance (as lime or ammonia) that reacts with an acid to form a salt and turns red litmus paper blue

²base *vb* **based; bas·ing** : to provide with a base or basis

³base *adj* **bas·er; bas·est** **1** : of low value and not very good in some ways ⟨*base* metals⟩ **2** : not honorable : MEAN ⟨*base* conduct⟩ — **base·ness** *n*

base·ball \'bās-ˌbȯl\ *n* **1** : a game played with a bat and ball by two teams of nine players on a field with four bases that mark the course a runner must take to score **2** : the ball used in baseball

base·board \'bās-ˌbȯrd\ *n* : a line of boards or molding extending around the walls of a room and touching the floor

base·ment \'bā-smənt\ *n* : the part of a building that is partly or entirely below ground level

bash \'bash\ *vb* : to hit very hard

bash·ful \'bash-fəl\ *adj* : uneasy in the presence of others **synonyms** see SHY

ba·sic \'bā-sik\ *adj* **1** : of, relating to, or forming the base of something ⟨the *basic* facts⟩ **2** : relating to or characteristic of a chemical base — **ba·si·cal·ly** \-si-kə-lē\ *adv*

ba·sil \'baz-əl, 'bāz-\ *n* : a fragrant mint used in cooking

ba·sin \'bās-n\ *n* **1** : a wide shallow usually round dish or bowl for holding liquids **2** : the amount that a basin holds **3** : a natural or artificial hollow or enclosure containing water ⟨a *basin* for anchoring ships⟩ **4** : the land drained by a river and its branches

ba·sis \'bā-səs\ *n, pl* **ba·ses** \-ˌsēz\ : FOUNDATION 2, BASE ⟨a story with a *basis* in fact⟩

bask \'bask\ *vb* : to lie or relax in pleasantly warm surroundings ⟨*bask* in the sun⟩

bas·ket \'bas-kət\ *n* **1** : a container made by weaving together materials (as reeds, straw, or strips of wood) **2** : the contents of a basket ⟨berries for sale at a dollar a *basket*⟩ **3** : something that is like a basket in shape or use **4** : a goal in basketball — **bas·ket·like** \-ˌlīk\ *adj*

bas·ket·ball \'bas-kət-ˌbȯl\ *n* **1** : a game in which each of two teams tries to throw a round inflated ball through a raised basketlike goal **2** : the ball used in basketball

bas·ket·ry \'bas-kə-trē\ *n* **1** : the making of objects (as baskets) by weaving or braiding long slender pieces (as of reed or wood) **2** : objects made of interwoven twigs or reeds

bas-re·lief \ˌbä-ri-'lēf\ *n* : a sculpture in which the design is raised very slightly from the background

bas-relief

¹bass \'bas\ *n, pl* **bass** *or* **bass·es** : any of numerous freshwater and sea fishes that are caught for sport and food

²bass \'bās\ *n* **1** : a tone of low pitch **2** : the lowest part in harmony that has four parts **3** : the lower half of the musical pitch range **4** : the lowest male singing voice **5** : a singer or an instrument having a bass range or part

bass drum \'bās-\ *n* : a large drum with two heads that produces a low booming sound when played

bas·soon \bə-'sün, ba-\ *n* : a wind instrument of low pitch having a long double wooden tube with finger holes and keys

Word History The bassoon, the English horn, and the oboe belong to the same group of wind instruments. The bassoon has the lowest pitch of the three. The English word *bassoon* comes from the French name for the instrument which in turn comes from the Italian name. This

\ə\ **abut**	\aù\ **out**	\i\ **tip**	\ȯ\ **saw**	\ù\ **foot**	
\ər\ **further**	\ch\ **chin**	\ī\ **life**	\ȯi\ **coin**	\y\ **yet**	
\a\ **mat**	\e\ **pet**	\j\ **job**	\th\ **thin**	\yü\ **few**	
\ā\ **take**	\ē\ **easy**	\ng\ **sing**	\th\ **this**	\yù\ **cure**	
\ä\ **cot, cart**	\g\ **go**	\ō\ **bone**	\ü\ **food**	\zh\ **vision**	

name in Italian was formed from an Italian word that means "low" or "bass."

bassoon

bass viol \'bās-\ *n* : DOUBLE BASS

bass·wood \'bas-ˌwu̇d\ *n* : a pale wood with straight grain from the linden or a related tree

¹**baste** \'bāst\ *vb* **bast·ed; bast·ing** : to sew with long loose stitches so as to hold the work temporarily in place

²**baste** *vb* **bast·ed; bast·ing** : to moisten (as with melted fat or juices) while roasting

¹**bat** \'bat\ *n* **1** : a stout solid stick ⟨a baseball *bat*⟩ **2** : a sharp blow or slap

²**bat** *vb* **bat·ted; bat·ting** : to strike with or as if with a bat

³**bat** *n* : a small furry animal that has a mouselike body and long front limbs covered with skin so as to form wings

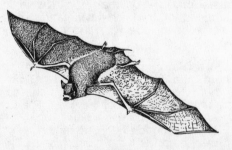

bat

batch \'bach\ *n* **1** : a quantity of something baked at one time ⟨a *batch* of cookies⟩ **2** : a quantity of material for use at one time

or produced at one operation **3** : a group of persons or things ⟨a *batch* of letters⟩

bath \'bath, 'bȧth\ *n, pl* **baths** \'ba*thz*, 'bȧ*thz*\ **1** : a washing of the body **2** : water for bathing ⟨draw a *bath*⟩ **3** : a place, room, or building where persons may bathe **4** : BATHTUB **5** : a liquid in which objects are placed so that it can act upon them

bathe \'bāth\ *vb* **bathed; bath·ing 1** : to take a bath **2** : to go into a body of water (as the sea or a river) for pleasure : go swimming **3** : to give a bath to ⟨*bathe* the baby⟩ **4** : to apply a liquid to ⟨*bathe* the eyes⟩ **5** : to cover with or as if with a liquid ⟨a scene *bathed* by moonlight⟩ — **bath·er** *n*

bath·room \'bath-ˌru̇m, 'bȧth-, -ˌru̇m\ *n* : a room containing a bathtub or shower and usually a washbowl and toilet

bath·tub \'bath-ˌtəb, 'bȧth-\ *n* : a tub in which to take a bath

ba·ton \bə-'tän, ba-\ *n* **1** : a stick with which a leader directs an orchestra or band **2** : a rod with a ball on one end carried by a drum major or drum majorette

bat·tal·ion \bə-'tal-yən\ *n* **1** : a part of an army consisting of two or more companies **2** : a large body of persons organized to act together ⟨labor *battalions*⟩

¹**bat·ter** \'bat-ər\ *vb* **1** : to beat with repeated violent blows ⟨a shore *battered* by waves⟩ **2** : to wear down or injure by hard use ⟨wore a *battered* old hat⟩

²**batter** *n* : a thin mixture made chiefly of flour and a liquid beaten together and used in making cakes and biscuits

bat·ter·ing ram \'bat-ə-ring-\ *n* **1** : an ancient military machine that consisted of a heavy beam with an iron tip mounted in a frame and swung back and forth in order to batter down walls **2** : a beam or bar with handles used to batter down doors or walls

bat·tery \'bat-ə-rē\ *n, pl* **bat·ter·ies 1** : two or more big military guns that are controlled as a unit **2** : an electric cell for providing electric current or a group of such cells ⟨a flashlight *battery*⟩ **3** : a number of machines or devices grouped together ⟨a *battery* of lights⟩

bat·ting \'bat-ing\ *n* : cotton or wool in sheets used mostly for stuffing quilts or packaging goods

¹**bat·tle** \'bat-l\ *n* **1** : a fight between armies, warships, or airplanes **2** : a fight between two persons or animals **3** : a long or hard struggle or contest ⟨the *battle* against hunger⟩ **4** : WARFARE

²battle *vb* **bat·tled; bat·tling** : to engage in battle

bat·tle-ax *or* **bat·tle–axe** \'bat-l-ˌaks\ *n* : an ax with a broad blade formerly used as a weapon

bat·tle·field \'bat-l-ˌfēld\ *n* : a place where a battle is fought or was once fought

bat·tle·ground \'bat-l-ˌgraùnd\ *n* : BATTLEFIELD

bat·tle·ment \'bat-l-mənt\ *n* : a low wall (as at the top of a castle or tower) with openings to shoot through

bat·tle·ship \'bat-l-ˌship\ *n* : a large warship with heavy armor and large guns

¹bawl \'bòl\ *vb* **1** : to shout or cry loudly ⟨*bawl* a command⟩ **2** : to weep noisily

²bawl *n* : a loud cry

bawl out *vb* : to scold severely

¹bay \'bā\ *vb* : to bark with long deep tones

²bay *n* **1** : the baying of dogs **2** : the position of an animal or a person forced to face pursuers when it is impossible to escape ⟨brought to *bay*⟩ **3** : the position of pursuers who are held off ⟨kept the hounds at *bay*⟩

³bay *n* **1** : a bay-colored horse **2** : a reddish brown

⁴bay *n* : a part of a large body of water extending into the land

⁵bay *n* : the laurel or a related tree or shrub

bay·ber·ry \'bā-ˌber-ē\ *n, pl* **bay·ber·ries** : a shrub with leathery leaves and small bluish white waxy berries used in making candles

¹bay·o·net \'bā-ə-nət, ˌbā-ə-'net\ *n* : a weapon like a dagger made to fit on the end of a rifle

²bayonet *vb* **bay·o·net·ted; bay·o·net·ting** : to stab with a bayonet

bay·ou \'bī-ō, -ü\ *n* : a creek that flows slowly through marshy land

bay window \'bā-\ *n* : a window or a set of windows that sticks out from the wall of a building

ba·zaar \bə-'zär\ *n* **1** : an oriental marketplace containing rows of small shops **2** : a large building where many kinds of goods are sold **3** : a fair for the sale of goods especially for charity

ba·zoo·ka \bə-'zü-kə\ *n* : a portable shoulder gun consisting of a tube open at both ends that shoots an explosive rocket able to pierce armor

be \bē\ *vb, past 1st & 3d sing* **was** \wəz, 'wəz, wäz\; *2d sing* **were** \wər, 'wər\; *pl* **were**; *past subjunctive* **were**; *past participle* **been** \bin\; *present participle* **being** \'bē-ing\; *present 1st sing* **am** \əm, am\; *2d sing* **are** \ər, är\; *3d sing* **is** \iz, əz\; *pl* **are**; *present subjunctive* **be 1** : to equal in meaning or identity ⟨that teacher *is* my neighbor⟩ **2** : to have a specified character or quality ⟨the leaves *are* green⟩ **3** : to belong to the class of ⟨apes *are* mammals⟩ **4** : EXIST 1, LIVE ⟨once there *was* a knight⟩ **5** — used as a helping verb with other verbs ⟨*was* walking along⟩ ⟨the ball *was* thrown⟩

be- *prefix* **1** : on : around : over **2** : provide with or cover with : dress up with ⟨*be*whiskered⟩ **3** : about : to : upon ⟨*be*moan⟩ **4** : make : cause to be ⟨*be*little⟩ ⟨*be*friend⟩

¹beach \'bēch\ *n* : a sandy or gravelly part of the shore of the sea or of a lake

²beach *vb* : to run or drive ashore ⟨*beach* a boat⟩

beach·head \'bēch-ˌhed\ *n* : an area on an enemy shore held by an advance force of an invading army to protect the later landing of troops or supplies

bea·con \'bē-kən\ *n* **1** : a guiding or warning light or fire on a high place **2** : a radio station that sends out signals to guide aircraft

¹bead \'bēd\ *n* **1** : a small piece of solid material with a hole through it by which it can be strung on a thread **2** : a small round mass ⟨a *bead* of sweat⟩ **3** : a small knob on a gun used in taking aim

Word History In early English the word *bead* meant "a prayer." Then, as now, people sometimes used strings of little round balls to keep track of their prayers. Each little ball stood for a prayer. In time the word that meant "prayer" came to be used for the little balls themselves. Now any small object that can be strung on a string is called a *bead*.

bazooka

\ə\ **abut**	\aú\ **out**	\i\ **tip**	\ò\ **saw**	\ú\ **foot**
\ər\ **further**	\ch\ **chin**	\ī\ **life**	\òi\ **coin**	\y\ **yet**
\a\ **mat**	\e\ **pet**	\j\ **job**	\th\ **thin**	\yü\ **few**
\ā\ **take**	\ē\ **easy**	\ng\ **sing**	\th\ **this**	\yù\ **cure**
\ä\ **cot, cart**	\g\ **go**	\ō\ **bone**	\ü\ **food**	\zh\ **vision**

(caption for battle-ax illustration) **battle-ax**

²**bead** *vb* **1** : to cover with beads **2** : to string together like beads

beady \'bēd-ē\ *adj* **bead·i·er; bead·i·est** : like a bead especially in being small, round, and shiny ⟨*beady* eyes⟩

bea·gle \'bē-gəl\ *n* : a small hound with short legs and a smooth coat

beagle

beak \'bēk\ *n* **1** : the bill of a bird ⟨an eagle's *beak*⟩ **2** : a part shaped like a beak — **beaked** \'bēkt\ *adj*

bea·ker \'bē-kər\ *n* : a deep cup or glass with a wide mouth and usually a lip for pouring

¹**beam** \'bēm\ *n* **1** : a long heavy piece of timber or metal used as a main horizontal support of a building or a ship **2** : a ray of light **3** : a constant radio wave sent out from an airport to guide pilots along a course

²**beam** *vb* **1** : to send out beams of light **2** : to smile with joy **3** : to aim a radio broadcast by use of a special antenna

bean \'bēn\ *n* **1** : the edible seed or pod of a bushy or climbing garden plant related to the peas and clovers **2** : a seed or fruit like a bean ⟨coffee *beans*⟩

¹**bear** \'baər, 'beər\ *n, pl* **bears** **1** *or pl* **bear** : a large heavy mammal with long shaggy hair and a very short tail **2** : a grumpy or glum person

²**bear** *vb* **bore** \'bōr\; **borne** \'bōrn\; **bear·ing** **1** : ¹SUPPORT 4 ⟨*bear* a burden⟩ **2** : to have as a feature or characteristic ⟨*bear* marks of suffering⟩ **3** : to bring forth : give birth to ⟨*bear* fruit⟩ ⟨*bear* children⟩ **4** : to put up with ⟨could not *bear* pain⟩ **5** : ²PRESS 1 ⟨*bear* down hard on your crayon⟩ **6** : to have a relation to the matter at hand ⟨facts *bearing* on the question⟩

bear·able \'bar-ə-bəl, 'ber-\ *adj* : possible to bear

beard \'biərd\ *n* **1** : the hair on the face of a man **2** : a hairy growth or tuft

bear·er \'bar-ər, 'ber-\ *n* **1** : someone or something that bears, supports, or carries **2** : a person holding a check or an order for payment

bear·ing \'baər-ing, 'beər-\ *n* **1** : the manner in which one carries or conducts oneself ⟨has the *bearing* of a soldier⟩ **2** : a part of a machine in which another part turns **3** : the position or direction of one point with respect to another or to the compass **4 bearings** *pl* : understanding of one's position or situation ⟨lost my *bearings*⟩ **5** : CONNECTION 2 ⟨personal feelings had no *bearing* on our decision⟩

beast \'bēst\ *n* **1** : a mammal with four feet (as a bear, deer, or rabbit) ⟨*beasts* of the field and fowls of the air⟩ **2** : a farm animal especially when kept for work ⟨oxen and horses used as *beasts* of burden⟩ **3** : a mean or horrid person

¹**beat** \'bēt\ *vb* **beat; beat·en** \'bēt-n\ *or* **beat; beat·ing** **1** : to strike again and again ⟨*beat* a drum⟩ **2** : ¹THROB 2, PULSATE ⟨heart still *beating*⟩ **3** : to flap against ⟨wings *beating* the air⟩ **4** : to mix by stirring rapidly ⟨*beat* two eggs⟩ **5** : to win against ⟨*beat* the enemy⟩ **6** : to measure or mark off by strokes ⟨*beat* time to the music⟩ — **beat·er** *n*

²**beat** *n* **1** : a blow or a stroke made again and again ⟨the *beat* of drums⟩ **2** : a single pulse (as of the heart) **3** : a measurement of time or accent in music **4** : an area or place regularly visited or traveled through ⟨a police officer's *beat*⟩

³**beat** *adj* **1** : being very tired **2** : having lost one's morale

beat·en \'bēt-n\ *adj* : worn smooth by passing feet ⟨a *beaten* path⟩

be·at·i·tude \bē-'at-ə-,tüd, -,tyüd\ *n* : one of the statements made in the Sermon on the Mount (Matthew 5: 3-12) beginning "Blessed are"

beau \'bō\ *n, pl* **beaux** \'bōz\ *or* **beaus** \'bōz\ : BOYFRIEND

beau·te·ous \'byüt-ē-əs\ *adj* : BEAUTIFUL

beau·ti·cian \byü-'tish-ən\ *n* : a person who gives beauty treatments (as to skin and hair)

beau·ti·ful \'byüt-i-fəl\ *adj* : having qualities of beauty : giving pleasure to the mind or senses — **beau·ti·ful·ly** *adv*

synonyms BEAUTIFUL, PRETTY, and HANDSOME mean pleasing or delightful in some way. BEAUTIFUL is used of whatever is most pleasing to the senses or the mind ⟨a *beautiful* sunset⟩ ⟨a *beautiful* poem⟩ PRETTY is usually used of something that is small or dainty ⟨a *pretty* little doll⟩ HANDSOME is used of something that is well formed and therefore pleasing to look at ⟨a *handsome* desk⟩

beau·ti·fy \ˈbyüt-ə-ˌfī\ *vb* **beau·ti·fied; beau·ti·fy·ing** : to make beautiful ⟨*beautified* the room with flowers⟩

beau·ty \ˈbyüt-ē\ *n, pl* **beau·ties 1** : the qualities of a person or a thing that give pleasure to the senses or to the mind ⟨the *beauty* of the landscape⟩ ⟨a poem of great *beauty*⟩ **2** : a beautiful person or thing

beauty shop *n* : a place of business for the care of customers' hair, skin, and nails

bea·ver \ˈbē-vər\ *n* : an animal related to the rats and mice that has webbed hind feet and a broad flat tail, builds dams and houses of sticks and mud in water, and is prized for its soft but strong fur

beaver

be·calm \bi-ˈkäm, -ˈkälm\ *vb* : to bring to a stop because of lack of wind ⟨a ship *becalmed*⟩

became *past of* BECOME

be·cause \bi-ˈkȯz, bi-kəz\ *conj* : for the reason that ⟨I ran *because* I was scared⟩

because of *prep* : as a result of ⟨the game was canceled *because of* rain⟩

beck \ˈbek\ *n* : a beckoning motion

beck·on \ˈbek-ən\ *vb* : to call or signal by a motion (as a wave or nod) ⟨they *beckoned* to us to come over⟩

be·come \bi-ˈkəm\ *vb* **be·came** \-ˈkām\; **become; be·com·ing 1** : to come or grow to be ⟨a tadpole *becomes* a frog⟩ ⟨days *become* shorter as summer ends⟩ **2** : to be suitable to : SUIT ⟨look for clothes that *become* you⟩ — **become of** : to happen to ⟨what has *become of* my friend⟩

be·com·ing \bi-ˈkəm-ing\ *adj* : having a pleasing effect ⟨*becoming* clothes⟩ — **be·com·ing·ly** *adv*

¹bed \ˈbed\ *n* **1** : a piece of furniture on which one may sleep or rest **2** : a place for sleeping or resting ⟨make a *bed* in the grass⟩ **3** : a level piece of ground prepared for growing plants **4** : the bottom of something ⟨the *bed* of a river⟩ **5** : LAYER 2 ⟨a thick *bed* of rock⟩

²bed *vb* **bed·ded; bed·ding 1** : to put or go to bed **2** : to plant in beds

bed·bug \ˈbed-ˌbəg\ *n* : a small wingless insect that sucks blood and is sometimes found in houses and especially in beds

bed·clothes \ˈbed-ˌklōz, -ˌklōthz\ *n pl* : coverings (as sheets and pillowcases) for a bed

bed·ding \ˈbed-ing\ *n* **1** : BEDCLOTHES **2** : material for a bed ⟨straw for the cows' *bedding*⟩

be·dev·il \bi-ˈdev-əl\ *vb* : to trouble or annoy again and again : PESTER, HARASS

bed·lam \ˈbed-ləm\ *n* : a place or scene of uproar and confusion

Word History *Bedlam,* an old form of *Bethlehem,* was the popular name for the *Hospital of Saint Mary of Bethlehem.* This hospital served as an insane asylum in London. The word *bedlam* came to be used for any place of uproar and confusion.

be·drag·gled \bi-ˈdrag-əld\ *adj* : soiled from or as if from being dragged in dust or mud ⟨*bedraggled* clothes⟩

bed·rid·den \ˈbed-ˌrid-n\ *adj* : forced to stay in bed by sickness or weakness

bed·rock \ˈbed-ˈräk\ *n* : the solid rock found under surface materials (as soil)

bed·room \ˈbed-ˌrüm, -ˌrùm\ *n* : a room to sleep in

bed·side \ˈbed-ˌsīd\ *n* : the place beside a bed

bed·spread \ˈbed-ˌspred\ *n* : a decorative top covering for a bed

bed·stead \ˈbed-ˌsted\ *n* : the framework of a bed

bed·time \ˈbed-ˌtīm\ *n* : time to go to bed

bee \ˈbē\ *n* **1** : an insect with four wings that is related to the wasps, gathers pollen and nectar from flowers from which it makes beebread and honey for food, and usually lives in large colonies **2** : a gathering of people to do something together ⟨a sewing *bee*⟩

bee·bread \ˈbē-ˌbred\ *n* : a bitter yellowish brown food material prepared by bees from pollen and stored in their honeycomb

\ə\ abut	\aù\ out	\i\ tip	\ȯ\ saw	\ù\ foot
\ər\ further	\ch\ chin	\ī\ life	\òi\ coin	\y\ yet
\a\ mat	\e\ pet	\j\ job	\th\ thin	\yü\ few
\ā\ take	\ē\ easy	\ng\ sing	\th\ this	\yù\ cure
\ä\ cot, cart	\g\ go	\ō\ bone	\ü\ food	\zh\ vision

beech \'bēch\ *n* : a tree with smooth gray bark, deep green leaves, and small triangular nuts

beef \'bēf\ *n, pl* **beefs** \'bēfs\ *or* **beeves** \'bēvz\ **1** : the flesh of a steer, cow, or bull **2** : a steer, cow, or bull especially when fattened for food — **beef·like** \'bē-,flīk\ *adj*

beech

beef·steak \'bēf-,stāk\ *n* : a slice of beef suitable for broiling or frying

bee·hive \'bē-,hīv\ *n* : HIVE 1

bee·line \'bē-,līn\ *n* : a straight direct course

been *past participle of* BE

beer \'biər\ *n* : an alcoholic drink made from malt and flavored with hops

bees·wax \'bēz-,waks\ *n* : wax made by bees and used by them in building honeycomb

beet \'bēt\ *n* : a leafy plant with a thick juicy root that is used as a vegetable or as a source of sugar

bee·tle \'bēt-l\ *n* **1** : any of a group of insects with four wings the outer pair of which are stiff cases that cover the others when folded **2** : an insect (as a bug) that looks like a beetle

beetle

beeves *pl of* BEEF

be·fall \bi-'fol\ *vb* **be·fell** \-'fel\; **be·fall·en** \-'fo-lən\; **be·fall·ing** **1** : to take place : HAPPEN **2** : to happen to

be·fit \bi-'fit\ *vb* **be·fit·ted; be·fit·ting** : to be suitable to or proper for

¹**be·fore** \bi-'fōr\ *adv* **1** : in front : AHEAD ⟨go on *before*⟩ **2** : in the past ⟨have been here *before*⟩ **3** : at an earlier time ⟨come at six o'clock, not *before*⟩

²**before** *prep* **1** : in front of ⟨stand *before* a mirror⟩ **2** : in the presence of ⟨spoke *before* the legislature⟩ **3** : earlier than ⟨got there *before* me⟩

³**before** *conj* **1** : ahead of the time when ⟨wash *before* you eat⟩ **2** : more willingly than ⟨I'd starve *before* I'd steal⟩

be·fore·hand \bi-'fōr-,hand\ *adv* : ¹BE-FORE 1 : ahead of time

be·friend \bi-'frend\ *vb* : to act as a friend to : help in a friendly way

beg \'beg\ *vb* **begged; beg·ging** **1** : to ask for money, food, or help as a charity ⟨*beg* in the streets⟩ **2** : to ask as a favor in an earnest or polite way ⟨*beg* to be taken to the circus⟩ ⟨*beg* pardon⟩

beg·gar \'beg-ər\ *n* **1** : one who lives by begging **2** : PAUPER

be·gin \bi-'gin\ *vb* **be·gan** \-'gan\; **be·gun** \-'gən\; **be·gin·ning** **1** : to do the first part of an action ⟨*begin* your homework⟩ **2** : to come into existence

be·gin·ner \bi-'gin-ər\ *n* : a young or inexperienced person

be·gin·ning \bi-'gin-ing\ *n* **1** : the point at which something begins ⟨the *beginning* of the war⟩ **2** : first part ⟨the *beginning* of the song⟩

be·gone \bi-'gon\ *vb* : to go away : DEPART — used especially in the imperative mood ⟨*begone*, you rascal⟩

be·go·nia \bi-'gōn-yə\ *n* : a plant with a juicy stem, ornamental leaves, and bright waxy flowers

be·grudge \bi-'grəj\ *vb* **be·grudged; be·grudg·ing** : to give or do reluctantly ⟨*begrudge* a person a favor⟩

begun *past of* BEGIN

be·half \bi-'haf, -'håf\ *n* : one's interest or support ⟨argued in my *behalf*⟩

be·have \bi-'hāv\ *vb* **be·haved; be·hav·ing** **1** : to conduct oneself ⟨the children *behaved* well at the party⟩ **2** : to conduct oneself properly ⟨tell them to *behave*⟩ **3** : to act or function in a particular way ⟨the car *behaves* well on icy roads⟩

be·hav·ior \bi-'hāv-yər\ *n* **1** : the way in which one conducts oneself **2** : the whole activity of something and especially a living being

be·head \bi-'hed\ *vb* : to cut off the head of

¹**be·hind** \bi-'hīnd\ *adv* **1** : in a place that is being or has been departed from ⟨leave your books *behind*⟩ ⟨stay *behind*⟩ **2** : at, to, or toward the back ⟨look *behind*⟩ ⟨fall *behind*⟩ **3** : not up to the general level ⟨*behind* in school⟩

²**behind** *prep* **1** : at or to the back of ⟨*behind* the door⟩ **2** : not up to the level of ⟨*behind* the rest of the class⟩

be·hold \bi-'hōld\ *vb* **be·held** \-'held\; **be·hold·ing** : to look upon : SEE — **be·hold·er** *n*

beige \'bāzh\ *n* : a yellowish brown

be·ing \'bē-ing\ *n* **1** : the state of having life or existence **2** : one that exists in fact or thought **3** : a living thing

be·la·bor \bi-'lā-bər\ *vb* : to keep working on to excess ⟨*belabor* the argument⟩

be·lat·ed \bi-'lāt-əd\ *adj* : delayed beyond the usual or expected time

¹**belch** \'belch\ *vb* **1** : to force out gas suddenly from the stomach through the mouth **2** : to throw out or be thrown out violently ⟨smoke *belched* from the chimney⟩

²**belch** *n* : a belching of gas

bel·fry \'bel-frē\ *n, pl* **bel·fries** : a tower or room in a tower for a bell or set of bells

Word History The words *bell* and *belfry* sound similar. Belfries even have bells in them. These facts might make you think the two words must be related, but they are not. The word *bell* came from an Old English word meaning "bell." The word *belfry*, on the other hand, came from a Greek phrase meaning "a movable war tower."

¹**Bel·gian** \'bel-jən\ *adj* : of or relating to Belgium or the Belgians

²**Belgian** *n* : a person born or living in Belgium

be·lief \bə-'lēf\ *n* **1** : a feeling sure that a person or thing exists or is true or trustworthy ⟨*belief* in Santa Claus⟩ ⟨*belief* in democracy⟩ **2** : religious faith : CREED **3** : something that one thinks is true ⟨it's my *belief* that our team really won⟩

synonyms BELIEF and FAITH mean agreement with the truth of something. BELIEF suggests that there is some kind of evidence for believing even though the believer is not always sure of the truth ⟨my *belief* in ghosts⟩ FAITH suggests that the believer is certain even if there is no evidence or proof ⟨even after the robbery, I kept my *faith* in the goodness of people⟩ **synonyms** see in addition OPINION

be·liev·able \bə-'lē-və-bəl\ *adj* : possible to believe ⟨a *believable* excuse⟩

be·lieve \bə-'lēv\ *vb* **be·lieved; be·liev·ing 1** : to have faith or confidence in the existence or worth of ⟨*believe* in ghosts⟩ ⟨*believes* in daily exercise⟩ **2** : to accept as true ⟨*believe* the report⟩ **3** : to accept the word of ⟨they didn't *believe* me⟩ **4** : THINK 2

be·liev·er \bə-'lē-vər\ *n* : one who has faith (as in a religion)

be·lit·tle \bi-'lit-l\ *vb* **be·lit·tled; be·lit·tling** : to make (a person or a thing) seem small or unimportant

bell \'bel\ *n* **1** : a hollow metallic device that is shaped somewhat like a cup and makes a ringing sound when struck

⟨church *bells*⟩ **2** : the stroke or sound of a bell that tells the hour **3** : the time indicated by the stroke of a bell **4** : a half-hour period of watch on shipboard **5** : something shaped like a bell ⟨the *bell* of a trumpet⟩

bell·boy \'bel-,bȯi\ *n* : BELLHOP

bell·hop \'bel-,häp\ *n* : a hotel or club employee who answers calls for service by bell or telephone and assists guests with luggage

¹**bel·lig·er·ent** \bə-'lij-ə-rənt\ *adj* **1** : carrying on war **2** : eager to fight

²**belligerent** *n* **1** : a nation at war **2** : a person taking part in a fight

bell jar *n* : a usually glass vessel shaped like a bell and used to cover objects or to contain gases or a vacuum

¹**bel·low** \'bel-ō\ *vb* : to give a loud deep roar like that of a bull

²**bellow** *n* : a loud deep roar

bel·lows \'bel-ōz, -əz\ *n sing or pl* **1** : a device that produces a strong current of air when its sides are pressed together **2** : the folding part of some cameras

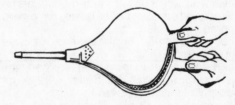

bellows 1

¹**bel·ly** \'bel-ē\ *n, pl* **bel·lies 1** : ABDOMEN 1 **2** : the under part of an animal's body **3** : STOMACH 1 **4** : an internal cavity (as of the human body) **5** : the thick part of a muscle

²**belly** *vb* **bel·lied; bel·ly·ing** : to swell out

be·long \bə-'lȯng\ *vb* **1** : to be in a proper place ⟨this book *belongs* on the top shelf⟩ **2** : to be the property of a person or group of persons ⟨the watch *belongs* to me⟩ **3** : to be a part of : be connected with : go with ⟨the tools that *belong* to the vacuum cleaner⟩

be·long·ings \bə-'lȯng-ingz\ *n pl* : the things that belong to a person

be·lov·ed \bə-'ləv-əd, -'ləvd\ *adj* : greatly loved : very dear

\ə\ abut	\aú\ out	\i\ tip	\ȯ\ saw	\ú\ foot
\ər\ further	\ch\ chin	\ī\ life	\ȯi\ coin	\y\ yet
\a\ mat	\e\ pet	\j\ job	\th\ thin	\yü\ few
\ā\ take	\ē\ easy	\ng\ sing	\th\ this	\yú\ cure
\ä\ cot, cart	\g\ go	\ō\ bone	\ü\ food	\zh\ vision

¹be·low \bə-'lō\ *adv* : in or to a lower place

²below *prep* : lower than : BENEATH

¹belt \'belt\ *n* **1** : a strip of flexible material (as leather or cloth) worn around a person's body for holding in or supporting clothing or weapons or for ornament **2** : something like a belt : BAND, CIRCLE ⟨a *belt* of trees⟩ **3** : a flexible endless band running around wheels or pulleys and used for moving or carrying something ⟨a fan *belt* on a car⟩ **4** : a region suited to or producing something or having some special feature ⟨the cotton *belt*⟩ — **belt·ed** \'bel-təd\ *adj*

²belt *vb* **1** : to put a belt on or around **2** : to strike hard

be·moan \bi-'mōn\ *vb* : to express grief over

bench \'bench\ *n* **1** : a long seat for two or more persons **2** : a long table for holding work and tools ⟨a carpenter's *bench*⟩ **3** : the position or rank of a judge

¹bend *vb* **bent** \'bent\; **bend·ing** **1** : to make, be, or become curved or angular rather than straight or flat **2** : to move out of a straight line or position : STOOP ⟨*bend* over and pick it up⟩ **3** : to turn in a certain direction : DIRECT ⟨*bent* their steps toward home⟩

²bend *n* : something that is bent : CURVE

¹be·neath \bi-'nēth\ *adv* : in a lower place

²beneath *prep* **1** : lower than : UNDER ⟨the sun sank *beneath* the horizon⟩ **2** : not worthy of ⟨work *beneath* my dignity⟩

bene·dic·tion \,ben-ə-'dik-shən\ *n* **1** : an expression of approval **2** : a short blessing by a minister or priest at the end of a religious service

bene·fac·tor \'ben-ə-,fak-tər\ *n* : one who helps another especially by giving money

ben·e·fi·cial \,ben-ə-'fish-əl\ *adj* : producing good results : HELPFUL — **ben·e·fi·cial·ly** *adv*

ben·e·fi·cia·ry \,ben-ə-'fish-ē-,er-ē\ *n, pl* **ben·e·fi·cia·ries** : a person who benefits or is expected to benefit from something

¹ben·e·fit \'ben-ə-,fit\ *n* **1** : something that does good to a person or thing ⟨the *benefits* of sunshine⟩ **2** : money paid in time of death, sickness, or unemployment or in old age (as by an insurance company)

²benefit *vb* **ben·e·fit·ed** *or* **ben·e·fit·ted**; **ben·e·fit·ing** *or* **ben·e·fit·ting** **1** : to be useful or profitable to **2** : to receive benefit

be·nev·o·lence \bə-'nev-ə-ləns\ *n* : KINDNESS, GENEROSITY

be·nev·o·lent \bə-'nev-ə-lənt\ *adj* : having a desire to do good : KINDLY, CHARITABLE

be·nign \bi-'nīn\ *adj* **1** : of a gentle disposition **2** : likely to bring about a good outcome — **be·nign·ly** *adv*

¹bent \'bent\ *adj* **1** : changed by bending : CROOKED ⟨a *bent* pin⟩ **2** : strongly favorable to : quite determined ⟨I am *bent* on going anyway⟩

²bent *n* : a strong or natural liking ⟨children with a *bent* for study⟩

be·queath \bi-'kwēth, -'kwēth\ *vb* **1** : to give or leave by means of a will ⟨my parents *bequeathed* me some money⟩ **2** : to hand down ⟨knowledge *bequeathed* to later times⟩

be·quest \bi-'kwest\ *n* **1** : the act of bequeathing **2** : something given or left by a will

¹be·reaved \bi-'rēvd\ *adj* : suffering the death of a loved one ⟨*bereaved* parents⟩

²bereaved *n, pl* **bereaved** : a bereaved person

be·reft \bi-'reft\ *adj* **1** : not having something needed, wanted, or expected **2** : ¹BEREAVED

be·ret \bə-'rā\ *n* : a soft round flat cap without a visor

berg \'bərg\ *n* : ICEBERG

beri·beri \,ber-ē-'ber-ē\ *n* : a disease caused by lack of a vitamin in which there is weakness, wasting, and damage to nerves

¹ber·ry \'ber-ē\ *n, pl* **ber·ries** **1** : a small pulpy fruit (as a strawberry) **2** : a simple fruit (as a grape or tomato) in which the ripened ovary wall is fleshy **3** : a dry seed (as of the coffee tree)

beret

²berry *vb* **ber·ried; ber·ry·ing** : to gather berries

berth \'bərth\ *n* **1** : a place where a ship lies at anchor or at a wharf **2** : a bed on a ship, train, or airplane

be·seech \bi-'sēch\ *vb* **be·sought** \-'sȯt\ *or* **be·seeched; be·seech·ing** : to ask earnestly

be·set \bi-'set\ *vb* **be·set; be·set·ting** **1** : to attack from all sides **2** : SURROUND

be·side \bi-'sīd\ *prep* **1** : by the side of : NEXT TO ⟨sit *beside* me⟩ **2** : compared with ⟨looks small *beside* you⟩ **3** : ²BESIDES ⟨expect no one *beside* you⟩ **4** : away from : wide of ⟨that remark is *beside* the point⟩ — **beside oneself** : very upset ⟨*beside myself* with worry⟩

¹be·sides \bi-'sīdz\ *adv* : in addition : ALSO ⟨had ice cream and cake and candy *besides*⟩

²besides *prep* **1** : in addition to ⟨*besides* cookies they also baked a cake⟩ **2** : other than ⟨no one here *besides* me⟩

be·siege \bi-'sēj\ *vb* **be·sieged; be·sieg·ing** **1** : to surround with armed forces for the purpose of capturing **2** : to crowd around — **be·sieg·er** *n*

besought *past of* BESEECH

¹best \'best\ *adj, superlative of* GOOD : good or useful in the highest degree : most excellent — **best part** : ³MOST ⟨spent the *best part* of the day at school⟩

²best *adv, superlative of* WELL **1** : in the best way **2** : ²MOST 1 ⟨*best* able to do the work⟩

³best *n* **1** : a person or thing or part of a thing that is best **2** : one's greatest effort

⁴best *vb* : to get the better of

be·stir \bi-'stər\ *vb* **be·stirred; be·stir·ring** : to stir up : rouse to action

be·stow \bi-'stō\ *vb* : to present as a gift

¹bet \'bet\ *n* **1** : an agreement requiring the person who guesses wrong about the result of a contest or the outcome of an event to give something to the person who guesses right **2** : the money or thing risked in a bet

²bet *vb* **bet** *or* **bet·ted; bet·ting** **1** : to risk in a bet ⟨*bet* a dollar⟩ **2** : to be sure enough to make a bet ⟨*bet* it will rain⟩

be·tray \bi-'trā\ *vb* **1** : to give over to an enemy by treason or fraud ⟨*betray* a fort⟩ **2** : to be unfaithful to ⟨*betray* a friend⟩ **3** : REVEAL 2, SHOW ⟨*betrayed* fear⟩

be·troth \bi-'träth, -'tróth, -'trōth, *or with* th\ *vb* : to promise to marry or give in marriage

be·troth·al \bi-'trōth-əl, -'tróth-, -'trōth-\ *n* : an engagement to be married

¹bet·ter \'bet-ər\ *adj, comparative of* GOOD **1** : more satisfactory than another thing **2** : improved in health — **better part** : more than half ⟨waited the *better part* of an hour⟩

²better *adv, comparative of* WELL : in a superior or more excellent way

³better *n* **1** : a better person or thing ⟨a change for the *better*⟩ **2** : ADVANTAGE 1, VICTORY ⟨got the *better* of the argument⟩

⁴better *vb* : to make or become better — **bet·terment** \-mənt\ *n*

bet·tor *or* **bet·ter** \'bet-ər\ *n* : one that bets

¹be·tween \bi-'twēn\ *prep* **1** : by the efforts of each of ⟨*between* us we can get the job done⟩ **2** : in or into the interval separating ⟨*between* sundown and sunup⟩ ⟨*between*

the two desks⟩ **3** : functioning to separate or tell apart ⟨the differences *between* soccer and football⟩ **4** : by comparing ⟨choose *between* two things⟩ **5** : shared by ⟨a strong bond *between* parent and child⟩ **6** : in shares to each of ⟨divided the money *between* the two children⟩

synonyms BETWEEN and AMONG are both used to show the relationship of things in terms of their position or distribution. BETWEEN is always used of two objects ⟨divided the work *between* my brother and me⟩ ⟨competition *between* their school and ours⟩ AMONG is usually used of more than two objects ⟨divided the work *among* all of us⟩ ⟨competition *among* the three schools⟩

²between *adv* : in a position between others

¹bev·el \'bev-əl\ *n* : a slant or slope of one surface or line against another

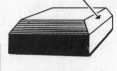

bevel

Word History At first the word *bevel* was used for a certain kind of angle. This was the angle formed by two surfaces that are not at right angles. Look at the opening of such an angle. You may be able to imagine that it looks like an open mouth. The English word *bevel* came from an Old French word that meant "with open mouth." This word was formed from an Old French word that meant "to yawn."

²bevel *vb* **bev·eled** *or* **bev·elled; bev·el·ing** *or* **bev·el·ling** : to cut or shape (an edge or surface) so as to form a bevel

bev·er·age \'bev-ə-rij, 'bev-rij\ *n* : a liquid that is drunk for food or pleasure

be·ware \bi-'waər, -'wear\ *vb* : to be cautious or careful

be·whis·kered \bi-'hwis-kərd, -'wis-\ *adj* : having whiskers

be·wil·der \bi-'wil-dər\ *vb* : to fill with uncertainty : CONFUSE — **be·wil·der·ment** \-mənt\ *n*

be·witch \bi-'wich\ *vb* **1** : to gain an influence over by means of magic or witchcraft **2** : to attract or delight as if by magic — **be·witch·ment** \-mənt\ *n*

¹be·yond \bē-'änd\ *adv* : on or to the farther side

\ə\ **abut**	\aú\ **out**	\i\ **tip**	\ò\ **saw**	\ú\ **foot**
\ər\ **further**	\ch\ **chin**	\ī\ **life**	\ói\ **coin**	\y\ **yet**
\a\ **mat**	\e\ **pet**	\j\ **job**	\th\ **thin**	\yü\ **few**
\ā\ **take**	\ē\ **easy**	\ng\ **sing**	\th\ **this**	\yú\ **cure**
\ä\ **cot, cart**	\g\ **go**	\ō\ **bone**	\ü\ **food**	\zh\ **vision**

²beyond *prep* **1** : on the other side of ⟨*beyond* the sea⟩ **2** : out of the reach or sphere of ⟨*beyond* help⟩

bi- *prefix* **1** : two **2** : coming or occurring every two **3** : into two parts ⟨*bisect*⟩ **4** : twice : doubly : on both sides

¹bi·as \'bī-əs\ *n* **1** : a seam, cut, or stitching running in a slant across cloth **2** : a favoring of one way of feeling or acting over another : PREJUDICE

²bias *vb* **bi·ased** *or* **bi·assed; bi·as·ing** *or* **bi·as·sing** : to give a bias to

bib \'bib\ *n* **1** : a cloth or plastic shield tied under a child's chin to protect the clothes **2** : the upper part of an apron or of overalls

Bi·ble \'bī-bəl\ *n* **1** : the book made up of the writings accepted by Christians as coming from God **2** : a book containing the sacred writings of a religion

bib·li·cal \'bib-li-kəl\ *adj* : relating to, taken from, or found in the Bible

bib·li·og·ra·phy \,bib-lē-'äg-rə-fē\ *n, pl* **bib·li·og·ra·phies** : a list of writings about an author or a subject

bi·car·bon·ate of soda \bī-'kär-bə-nət-, -,nāt-\ : SODIUM BICARBONATE

bi·ceps \'bī-,seps\ *n, pl* **biceps** *also* **bi·ceps·es** : a large muscle of the upper arm

bick·er \'bik-ər\ *vb* : to quarrel in a cross or silly way ⟨*bickered* over who would pay⟩

bi·cus·pid \bī-'kəs-pəd\ *n* : either of the two teeth with double points on each side of each jaw of a person

¹bi·cy·cle \'bī-,sik-əl\ *n* : a light vehicle having two wheels one behind the other, a saddle seat, and pedals by which it is made to move

²bicycle *vb* **bi·cy·cled; bi·cy·cling** \'bī-,sik-ə-ling, -,sik-ling\ : to ride a bicycle

bi·cy·clist \'bī-,sik-ləst\ *n* : a person who rides a bicycle

¹bid \'bid\ *vb* **bade** \'bad\ *or* **bid; bid·den** \'bid-n\ *or* **bid; bid·ding** **1** : ²ORDER 2, COMMAND ⟨do as I *bid* you⟩ **2** : to express ⟨*bade* our guests good-bye⟩ **3** : to make an offer for something (as at an auction) — **bid·der** *n*

²bid *n* **1** : an offer to pay a certain sum for something or to do certain work at a stated fee **2** : INVITATION 2

bide \'bīd\ *vb* **bode** \'bōd\ *or* **bid·ed** \'bīd-əd\; **bid·ed; bid·ing** : to wait or wait for ⟨*bide* a while⟩ ⟨*bide* one's time⟩

¹bi·en·ni·al \bī-'en-ē-əl\ *adj* **1** : occurring every two years **2** : growing stalks and leaves one year and flowers and fruit the next before dying — **bi·en·ni·al·ly** \-ē-ə-lē\ *adv*

²biennial *n* : a biennial plant

bier \'biər\ *n* : a stand on which a corpse or coffin is placed

big \'big\ *adj* **big·ger; big·gest** **1** : large in size **2** : IMPORTANT 1 — **big·ness** *n*

Big Dipper *n* : DIPPER 3

big·horn \'big-,hȯrn\ *n* : a grayish brown wild sheep of mountainous western North America

bighorn

big tree *n* : a very large California sequoia with light soft brittle wood

bike \'bīk\ *n* **1** : BICYCLE **2** : MOTORCYCLE

bile \'bīl\ *n* : a thick bitter yellow or greenish fluid supplied by the liver to aid in digestion

bi·lin·gual \,bī-'ling-gwəl, -gyə-wəl\ *adj* : of, expressed in, or using two languages ⟨a *bilingual* dictionary⟩ ⟨*bilingual* signs⟩

¹bill \'bil\ *n* **1** : the jaws of a bird together with their horny covering **2** : a part of an animal (as a turtle) that suggests the bill of a bird — **billed** \'bild\ *adj*

²bill *n* **1** : a draft of a law presented to a legislature for consideration ⟨the representative introduced a *bill* in Congress⟩ **2** : a record of goods sold, services performed, or work done with the cost involved ⟨a telephone *bill*⟩ **3** : a sign or poster advertising something **4** : a piece of paper money ⟨a dollar *bill*⟩

³bill *vb* : to send a bill to

bill·board \'bil-,bōrd\ *n* : a flat surface on which outdoor advertisements are displayed

bill·fold \'bil-,fōld\ *n* : a folding pocketbook especially for paper money : WALLET

bil·liards \'bil-yərdz\ *n* : a game played by driving solid balls with a cue into each other or into pockets on a large rectangular table

bil·lion \'bil-yən\ *n* **1** : a thousand millions **2** : a very large number ⟨*billions* of dollars⟩

¹bil·lionth \'bil-yənth\ *adj* : being last in a series of a billion

²billionth *n* : number 1,000,000,000 in a series

¹bil·low \'bil-ō\ *n* : a great wave

²billow *vb* **1** : to roll in great waves ⟨the *billowing* ocean⟩ **2** : to swell out ⟨sails *billowing* in the breeze⟩

bil·ly club \'bil-ē-\ *n* : a heavy club (as of wood) carried by a police officer

bil·ly goat \'bil-ē-\ *n* : a male goat

bin \'bin\ *n* : a box or enclosed place used for storage ⟨a coal *bin*⟩

bind \'bīnd\ *vb* **bound** \'baund\; **bind·ing** **1** : to fasten by tying **2** : to hold or restrict by force or obligation **3** : ²BANDAGE **4** : to finish or decorate with a binding ⟨*bind* the hem of a skirt⟩ **5** : to fasten together and enclose in a cover ⟨*bind* a book⟩

bind·er \'bīn-dər\ *n* **1** : a person who binds books **2** : a cover for holding together loose sheets of paper **3** : a machine that cuts grain and ties it into bundles

bind·ing \'bīn-ding\ *n* **1** : the cover and the fastenings of a book **2** : a narrow strip of fabric used along the edge of an article of clothing

bin·go \'bing-gō\ *n* : a game of chance played by covering a numbered space on a card when the number is matched by one drawn at random and won by the first player to cover five spaces in a row

bin·oc·u·lar \bī-'näk-yə-lər, bə-\ *adj* : of, using, or suited for the use of both eyes

bin·oc·u·lars \bə-'näk-yə-lərz, bī-\ *n pl* : a hand-held instrument for seeing at a distance that is made up of two telescopes usually having prisms

bio- *prefix* : living matter

bio·de·grad·able \,bī-ō-di-'grād-ə-bəl\ *adj* : possible to break down and make harmless by the action of living things (as bacteria)

bio·di·ver·si·ty \,bī-ō-də-'vər-sə-tē, -dī-\ *n* : biological variety in an environment as shown by numbers of different kinds of plants and animals

bio·graph·i·cal \,bī-ə-'graf-i-kəl\ *adj* : of or relating to the history of people's lives

bi·og·ra·phy \bī-'äg-rə-fē\ *n, pl* **bi·og·ra·phies** : a written history of a person's life

bi·o·log·i·cal \,bī-ə-'läj-i-kəl\ *adj* : of or relating to biology

bi·ol·o·gist \bī-'äl-ə-jəst\ *n* : a specialist in biology

bi·ol·o·gy \bī-'äl-ə-jē\ *n* : a science that deals with living things and their relationships, distribution, and behavior

bio·tech·nol·o·gy \,bī-ō-tek-'näl-a-jē\ *n* : the use of techniques from genetics to combine inherited characteristics selected from different kinds of organisms into one organism in order to produce useful products (as drugs)

bi·ped \'bī-,ped\ *n* : an animal (as a person) that has only two feet

bi·plane \'bī-,plān\ *n* : an airplane with two wings on each side of the body usually placed one above the other

biplane

birch \'bərch\ *n* : a tree with hard wood and a smooth bark that can be peeled off in thin layers

bird \'bərd\ *n* : an animal that lays eggs and has wings and a body covered with feathers

bird·bath \'bərd-,bath, -,bath\ *n* : a basin for birds to bathe in

bird dog *n* : a dog trained to hunt or bring in game birds

bird·house \'bərd-,haus\ *n* **1** : an artificial nesting place for birds **2** : AVIARY

bird of prey : a bird (as an eagle or owl) that feeds almost entirely on meat taken by hunting

bird·seed \'bərd-,sēd\ *n* : a mixture of small seeds used chiefly for feeding wild or caged birds

bird's—eye \'bərd-,zī\ *adj* : seen from above as if by a flying bird ⟨a *bird's-eye* view⟩

birth \'bərth\ *n* **1** : the coming of a new individual from the body of its parent **2** : the act of bringing into life **3**

\ə\ abut	\au̇\ out	\i\ tip	\ȯ\ saw	\u̇\ foot	
\ər\ further	\ch\ chin	\ī\ life	\ȯi\ coin	\y\ yet	
\a\ mat	\e\ pet	\j\ job	\th\ thin	\yü\ few	
\ā\ take	\ē\ easy	\ng\ sing	\t̶h\ this	\yu̇\ cure	
\ä\ cot, cart	\g\ go	\ō\ bone	\ü\ food	\zh\ vision	

: LINEAGE 1 ⟨a person of noble *birth*⟩ 4 : ORIGIN 2

birth·day \'bərth-ˌdā\ *n* **1** : the day on which a person is born **2** : a day of beginning ⟨July 4, 1776 is sometimes called the *birthday* of our country⟩ **3** : the return each year of the date on which a person was born or something began

birth·place \'bərth-ˌplās\ *n* : the place where a person was born or where something began ⟨the *birthplace* of freedom⟩

birth·right \'bərth-ˌrīt\ *n* : a right belonging to a person because of his or her birth

bis·cuit \'bis-kət\ *n* **1** : a crisp flat cake : CRACKER **2** : a small cake of raised dough baked in an oven

bi·sect \'bī-ˌsekt\ *vb* **1** : to divide into two usually equal parts **2** : INTERSECT

Word History When you bisect something you are cutting it in two. The word *bisect* itself will tell you that if you know Latin. The word was formed in English, but it came from two Latin elements. The *bi-* came from a Latin prefix meaning "two." The *-sect* came from a Latin word meaning "to cut."

bish·op \'bish-əp\ *n* **1** : a member of the clergy of high rank **2** : a piece in the game of chess

Word History The main duty of a bishop is to watch over the members of a church as a shepherd watches over a flock. The English word *bishop* came from a Greek word. This Greek word meant "overseer" or "bishop." It was formed from two Greek words. The first meant "on" or "over," and the second meant "watcher."

bis·muth \'biz-məth\ *n* : a heavy grayish white metallic chemical element that is used in alloys and in medicine

bi·son \'bīs-n, 'bīz-\ *n, pl* **bison** : a large animal with short horns and a shaggy mane that is related to the cows and oxen

¹bit \'bit\ *n* **1** : a part of a bridle that is put in the horse's mouth **2** : the cutting or boring edge or part of a tool

²bit *n* **1** : a small piece or quantity ⟨a *bit* of food⟩ **2** : a short time ⟨rest a *bit*⟩ **3** : ¹SOMEWHAT ⟨a *bit* of a fool⟩

bitch \'bich\ *n* : a female dog

¹bite \'bīt\ *vb* **bit** \'bit\; **bit·ten** \'bit-n\; **bit·ing** \'bīt-ing\ **1** : to seize, grip, or cut into with or as if with teeth ⟨*bite* an apple⟩ **2** : to wound or sting usually with a stinger or fang **3** : to cause to sting ⟨pepper *bites* the mouth⟩ **4** : to take a bait ⟨the fish are *biting*⟩

²bite *n* **1** : a seizing of something with the teeth or the mouth **2** : a wound made by biting : STING ⟨a mosquito *bite*⟩ **3** : the amount of food taken at a bite **4** : a sharp or biting sensation

bit·ing \'bīt-ing\ *adj* : producing bodily or mental distress : SHARP

bit·ter \'bit-ər\ *adj* **1** : sharp, biting, and unpleasant to the taste **2** : hard to put up with ⟨a *bitter* disappointment⟩ **3** : very harsh or sharp : BITING ⟨a *bitter* wind⟩ **4** : caused by anger, distress, or sorrow ⟨*bitter* tears⟩ — **bit·ter·ly** *adv* — **bit·ter·ness** *n*

bit·tern \'bit-ərn\ *n* : a brownish marsh bird which has a loud booming cry

bit·ter·sweet \'bit-ər-ˌswēt\ *n* **1** : a poisonous vine with purple flowers and red berries **2** : a woody climbing plant with orange seedcases that open and show the red-coated seeds

bi·tu·mi·nous coal \bə-ˌtü-mə-nəs-, -ˌtyü-\ *n* : a soft coal that gives much smoke when burned

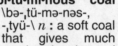

bittersweet 2

bi·zarre \bə-'zär\ *adj* : very strange or odd

blab \'blab\ *vb* **blabbed; blab·bing** : to talk too much

¹black \'blak\ *adj* **1** : of the color black **2** : very dark ⟨a *black* night⟩ **3** : of or relating to any peoples having dark skin and especially any of the original peoples of Africa south of the Sahara **4** *often cap* : of or relating to Americans having ancestors from Africa south of the Sahara ⟨*black* studies⟩ **5** : WICKED ⟨a *black* deed⟩ **6** : very sad or gloomy ⟨a *black* mood⟩ **7** : UNFRIENDLY ⟨a *black* look⟩ — **black·ness** *n*

²black *n* **1** : a black pigment or dye **2** : the color of coal : the opposite of white **3** : black clothing ⟨dressed in *black*⟩ **4** : a person belonging to a people having dark skin and especially a black African **5** *often cap* : an American having black ancestors

³black *vb* : BLACKEN 1

black–and–blue \ˌblak-ən-'blü\ *adj* : darkly discolored (as from a bruise)

black·ber·ry \'blak-ˌber-ē\ *n, pl* **black·ber·ries** : the black or dark purple sweet juicy berry of a prickly plant related to the raspberry

black·bird \'blak-ˌbərd\ *n* : any of several birds of which the males are mostly black

black·board \'blak-ˌbōrd\ *n* : CHALKBOARD

black·en \'blak-ən\ *vb* **1** : to make or become black **2** : ²SPOIL 2 ⟨*blacken* an enemy's reputation⟩

black-eyed Su·san \ˌblak-ˌīd-'süz-n\ *n* : a daisy with yellow or orange petals and a dark center

black·head \'blak-ˌhed\ *n* : a dark oily plug of hardened material blocking the opening of a skin gland

black·ish \'blak-ish\ *adj* : somewhat black

¹black·mail \'blak-ˌmāl\ *n* **1** : the forcing of someone to pay money by threatening to reveal a secret that might bring disgrace on him or her **2** : money paid under threat of blackmail

black-eyed Susan

²blackmail *vb* : to threaten with the revealing of a secret unless money is paid — **black·mail·er** *n*

black·out \'blak-ˌaut\ *n* **1** : a period of darkness observed as a protection against airplane raids in time of war **2** : a temporary loss of vision or consciousness

black out *vb* : to lose consciousness or the ability to see for a short time

black·smith \'blak-ˌsmith\ *n* : a person who makes things out of iron by heating and hammering it

black·snake \'blak-ˌsnāk\ *n* : either of two harmless snakes of the United States with blackish skins

black·top \'blak-ˌtäp\ *n* : a black material used to pave highways, parking lots, and play areas

black widow *n* : a poisonous spider having a black female with a red mark on the abdomen

blad·der \'blad-ər\ *n* **1** : a pouch into which urine passes from the kidneys **2** : a container that can be filled with air or gas

blade \'blād\ *n* **1** : a leaf of a plant and especially of a grass **2** : the broad flat part of a leaf **3** : something that widens out like the blade of a leaf ⟨a shoulder *blade*⟩ ⟨the

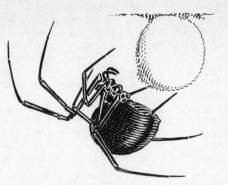

black widow

blade of a propeller⟩ ⟨the *blade* of a fan⟩ **4** : the cutting part of a tool or machine ⟨a knife *blade*⟩ **5** : SWORD **6** : the runner of an ice skate — **blad·ed** \'blād-əd\ *adj*

¹blame \'blām\ *vb* **blamed; blam·ing** **1** : to find fault with **2** : to hold responsible ⟨*blamed* me for everything⟩ **3** : to place responsibility for ⟨don't *blame* it on us⟩

²blame *n* **1** : expression of disapproval ⟨receive both praise and *blame*⟩ **2** : responsibility for something that fails ⟨took the *blame* for the defeat⟩ — **blame·less** \'blām-ləs\ *adj*

blame·wor·thy \'blām-ˌwər-_thē_\ *adj* : deserving blame

blanch \'blanch\ *vb* **1** : ¹BLEACH, WHITEN **2** : to scald so as to remove the skin from ⟨*blanch* almonds⟩ **3** : to turn pale

¹blank \'blangk\ *adj* **1** : seeming to be confused ⟨a *blank* look⟩ **2** : not having any writing or marks ⟨a *blank* sheet of paper⟩ **3** : having empty spaces to be filled in ⟨a *blank* form⟩

²blank *n* **1** : an empty space in a line of writing or printing **2** : a paper with empty spaces to be filled in ⟨an application *blank*⟩ **3** : a cartridge loaded with powder but no bullet

¹blan·ket \'blang-kət\ *n* **1** : a heavy woven covering used for beds **2** : a covering layer ⟨a *blanket* of snow⟩

²blanket *vb* : to cover with a blanket

¹blare \'blaər, 'bleər\ *vb* **blared; blar·ing** **1** : to sound loud and harsh ⟨heard the trumpet *blare*⟩ **2** : to present in a harsh noisy manner ⟨loudspeakers *blaring* advertisements⟩

\ə\ abut	\aú\ out	\i\ tip	\ò\ saw	\ú\ foot
\ər\ further	\ch\ chin	\ī\ life	\òi\ coin	\y\ yet
\a\ mat	\e\ pet	\j\ job	\th\ thin	\yú\ few
\ā\ take	\ē\ easy	\ng\ sing	\th\ this	\yü\ cure
\ä\ cot, cart	\g\ go	\ō\ bone	\ü\ food	\zh\ vision

B b b b b b b b b b b b b b b b b b b b

²**blare** *n* : a harsh loud noise

¹**blast** \'blast\ *n* **1** : a strong gust of wind ⟨the icy *blasts* of winter⟩ **2** : a stream of air or gas forced through an opening **3** : the sound made by a wind instrument ⟨the *blast* of a whistle⟩ **4** : EXPLOSION 1

²**blast** *vb* **1** : ²BLIGHT **2** : to break to pieces by an explosion : SHATTER

blast–off \'blas-ˌtòf\ *n* : an instance of blasting off (as of a rocket)

blast off \blas-'tòf\ *vb* : to take off — used of vehicles using rockets for power

¹**blaze** \'blāz\ *n* **1** : a bright hot flame **2** : great brightness and heat ⟨the *blaze* of the sun⟩ **3** : OUTBURST 1 ⟨a *blaze* of anger⟩ **4** : a bright display ⟨a *blaze* of color⟩

²**blaze** *vb* **blazed; blaz•ing 1** : to burn brightly **2** : to shine as if on fire

³**blaze** *n* : a mark made on a tree by chipping off a piece of the bark

⁴**blaze** *vb* **blazed; blaz•ing 1** : to make a blaze on **2** : to mark by blazing trees ⟨*blaze* a trail⟩

¹**bleach** \'blēch\ *vb* : to make white by removing the color or stains from

²**bleach** *n* : a preparation used for bleaching

bleach•er \'blē-chər\ *n* : open seats for people to watch from (as at a game) usually arranged like steps — usually used in pl.

bleak \'blēk\ *adj* **1** : open to wind or weather ⟨a *bleak* coast⟩ **2** : being cold and cutting ⟨a *bleak* wind⟩ **3** : not hopeful or encouraging ⟨the future looks *bleak*⟩ — **bleak•ly** *adv* — **bleak•ness** *n*

¹**bleat** \'blēt\ *vb* : to make the cry of a sheep, goat, or calf

²**bleat** *n* : the sound of bleating

bleed \'blēd\ *vb* **bled** \'bled\; **bleed•ing 1** : to lose or shed blood ⟨a cut finger *bleeds*⟩ **2** : to feel pain or pity ⟨my heart *bleeds* for you⟩ **3** : to draw fluid from ⟨*bleed* a tire⟩

¹**blem•ish** \'blem-ish\ *vb* : to spoil by or as if by an ugly mark

²**blemish** *n* : a mark that makes something imperfect : FLAW

¹**blend** \'blend\ *vb* **1** : to mix so completely that the separate things mixed cannot be told apart **2** : to shade into each other : HARMONIZE ⟨soft colors that *blend* well⟩ **synonyms** see MIX

²**blend** *n* **1** : a complete mixture : a product made by blending **2** : a word formed by combining parts of two or more other words so that they overlap ⟨"smog" is a *blend* of "smoke" and "fog"⟩ **3** : a group of two or more consonants (as *gr-* in green) beginning a syllable without a vowel between

bless \'bles\ *vb* **blessed** \'blest\ *or* **blest; bless•ing 1** : to make holy by a religious ceremony or words ⟨*bless* an altar⟩ **2** : to ask the favor or protection of God for ⟨*bless* a congregation in church⟩ **3** : to praise or honor as holy ⟨*bless* the Lord⟩ **4** : to give happiness or good fortune to ⟨*blessed* with good health⟩

Word History The Christian religion reached England a long time ago. It is likely that blood was used in some early Christian ceremonies. For example, it may have been used to bless altars. The word *bless* reflects this religious use of blood. It came from an Old English word that meant "blood."

bless•ed \'bles-əd, 'blest\ *adj* **1** : HOLY 1 **2** : enjoying happiness — **bless•ed•ness** \'bles-əd-nəs\ *n*

bless•ing \'bles-ing\ *n* **1** : the act of one who blesses **2** : APPROVAL ⟨gave their *blessing* to the plan⟩ **3** : something that makes one happy or content ⟨the *blessings* of peace⟩

blew *past of* BLOW

¹**blight** \'blīt\ *n* **1** : a plant disease marked by drying up without rotting **2** : an organism (as a germ or insect) that causes a plant blight

²**blight** *vb* : to injure or destroy by or as if by a blight

blimp \'blimp\ *n* : an airship filled with gas like a balloon

¹**blind** \'blīnd\ *adj* **1** : unable or nearly unable to see **2** : lacking in judgment or understanding **3** : closed at one end ⟨a *blind* alley⟩ **4** : using only the instruments within an airplane and not landmarks as a guide ⟨*blind* flying⟩ — **blind•ly** *adv* — **blind•ness** *n*

²**blind** *vb* **1** : to make blind **2** : to make it impossible to see well : DAZZLE ⟨*blinded* by the lights of an approaching car⟩

³**blind** *n* **1** : a device to reduce sight or keep out light ⟨window *blinds*⟩ **2** : a place of hiding ⟨shot the birds from a *blind*⟩

⁴**blind** *adv* : with only instruments as guidance ⟨fly *blind*⟩

¹**blind•fold** \'blīnd-ˌfōld\ *vb* : to shut light out of the eyes of with or as if with a bandage

²**blindfold** *n* : a covering over the eyes

blind•man's buff \ˌblīnd-ˌmanz-'bəf\ *n* : a game in which a blindfolded player tries to catch and identify one of the other players

blink \'blingk\ *vb* **1** : to look with partly shut eyes **2** : to shut and open the eyes quickly **3** : to shine with a light that goes or seems to go on and off ⟨lights *blink-ing*⟩

blink·er \'bling-kər\ *n* : a light that blinks

bliss \'blis\ *n* : great happiness : JOY — **bliss·ful** \-fəl\ *adj* — **bliss·ful·ly** \-fə-lē\ *adv*

¹**blis·ter** \'blis-tər\ *n* **1** : a small raised area of the skin filled with a watery liquid **2** : a swelling (as in paint) that looks like a blister

²**blister** *vb* **1** : to develop a blister : rise in blisters ⟨my heel *blistered* on the hike⟩ ⟨*blistering* paint⟩ **2** : to cause blisters on ⟨tight shoes can *blister* your feet⟩

blithe \'blīth, 'blīth\ *adj* **blith·er; blith·est** : free from worry : MERRY, CHEERFUL — **blithe·ly** *adv*

bliz·zard \'bliz-ərd\ *n* : a long heavy snowstorm

bloat \'blōt\ *vb* : to make swollen with or as if with fluid

blob \'bläb\ *n* : a small lump or drop of something thick ⟨a *blob* of paint⟩

¹**block** \'bläk\ *n* **1** : a solid piece of some material (as stone or wood) usually with one or more flat sides ⟨building *blocks*⟩ **2** : something that stops or makes passage or progress difficult : OBSTRUCTION ⟨a traffic *block*⟩ **3** : a case enclosing one or more pulleys **4** : a number of things thought of as forming a group or unit ⟨a *block* of seats⟩ **5** : a large building divided into separate houses or shops ⟨an apartment *block*⟩ **6** : a space enclosed by streets **7** : the length of one side of a block ⟨ran three *blocks*⟩

²**block** *vb* **1** : to stop or make passage through difficult : OBSTRUCT ⟨*block* the doorway with a bicycle⟩ **2** : to stop or make the passage of difficult ⟨*block* a bill in Congress⟩ **3** : to make an opponent's movement (as in football) difficult **4** : to mark the chief lines of ⟨*block* out a plan⟩

¹**block·ade** \blä-'kād\ *n* : the shutting off of a place (as by warships) to prevent the coming in or going out of persons or supplies

²**blockade** *vb* **block·ad·ed; block·ad·ing** : to close off by a blockade

block·house \'bläk-,haus\ *n* : a building (as of heavy timbers or of concrete) built with holes in its sides through which persons inside may fire out at an enemy

¹**blond** \'bländ\ *adj* **1** : of a light color ⟨*blond* hair⟩ **2** : having light hair and skin

²**blond** *or* **blonde** \'bländ\ *n* : someone who is blond

blood \'bləd\ *n* **1** : the red fluid that circu-

blockhouse

lates in the heart, arteries, capillaries, and veins of persons and animals **2** : relationship through a common ancestor : KINSHIP ⟨ties of *blood*⟩ — **blood·ed** \'bləd-əd\ *adj*

blood bank *n* : blood stored for emergency use in transfusion

blood·hound \'bləd-,haund\ *n* : a large hound with long drooping ears, a wrinkled face, and a very good sense of smell

bloodhound

blood pressure *n* : pressure of the blood on the walls of blood vessels and especially arteries

blood·shed \'bləd-,shed\ *n* : ¹MURDER, SLAUGHTER

blood·shot \'bləd-,shät\ *adj* : being red and sore ⟨*bloodshot* eyes⟩

blood·stream \'bləd-,strēm\ *n* : the circulating blood in the living body

blood·suck·er \'bləd-,sək-ər\ *n* : an animal that sucks blood — **blood·suck·ing** \-,sək-ing\ *adj*

blood·thirsty \'bləd-,thərs-tē\ *adj* : eager to kill or hurt — **blood·thirst·i·ly** \-tə-lē\ *adv* — **blood·thirst·i·ness** \-tē-nəs\ *n*

\ə\ abut	\au\ out	\i\ tip	\o\ saw	\u\ foot
\ər\ further	\ch\ chin	\ī\ life	\oi\ coin	\y\ yet
\a\ mat	\e\ pet	\j\ job	\th\ thin	\yu\ few
\ā\ take	\ē\ easy	\ng\ sing	\th\ this	\yu\ cure
\ä\ cot, cart	\g\ go	\ō\ bone	\u\ food	\zh\ vision

blood vessel *n* : an artery, vein, or capillary of the body

bloody \'bləd-ē\ *adj* **blood·i·er; blood·i·est 1** : smeared or stained with blood **2** : causing or accompanied by bloodshed

¹**bloom** \'blüm\ *n* **1** : ¹FLOWER **1 2** : the period or state of blooming **3** : a condition or time of beauty, freshness, and strength ⟨the *bloom* of youth⟩ **4** : the rosy color of the cheek **5** : the delicate powdery coating on some fruits and leaves

²**bloom** *vb* **1** : to produce blooms : FLOWER **2** : to be in a state of youthful beauty and freshness

¹**blos·som** \'bläs-əm\ *n* **1** : ¹FLOWER **1 2** : ¹BLOOM **2**

²**blossom** *vb* **1** : ²BLOOM **2** : to unfold like a blossom

¹**blot** \'blät\ *n* **1** : a spot or stain of dirt or ink **2** : STIGMA **1**, REPROACH ⟨the lie was a bad *blot* on my record⟩

²**blot** *vb* **blot·ted; blot·ting 1** : ²SPOT **1 2** : to hide completely ⟨the fog *blotted* out the lighthouse⟩ **3** : to dry with a blotter

blotch \'bläch\ *n* **1** : a blemish on the skin **2** : a large irregular spot of color or ink — **blotched** \'blächt\ *adj*

blot·ter \'blät-ər\ *n* : a piece of blotting paper

blot·ting paper \'blät-ing-\ *n* : a soft spongy paper used to absorb wet ink

blouse \'blaus\ *n* **1** : a loose outer garment like a smock **2** : the jacket of a uniform **3** : a loose garment for women and children covering the body from the neck to the waist

¹**blow** \'blō\ *vb* **blew** \'blü\; **blown** \'blōn\; **blow·ing 1** : to move or be moved usually with speed and force ⟨wind *blowing* from the north⟩ **2** : to move in or with the wind ⟨dust *blew* through the cracks⟩ **3** : to send forth a strong stream of air from the mouth or from a bellows ⟨*blow* on your hands⟩ **4** : to make a sound or cause to sound by blowing ⟨the whistle *blows*⟩ ⟨*blow* a horn⟩ **5** : to clear by forcing air through ⟨*blow* your nose⟩ **6** : to shape by forcing air into ⟨*blow* glass⟩ — **blow·er** \'blō-ər\ *n*

²**blow** *n* : a blowing of wind : GALE

³**blow** *n* **1** : an act of hitting (as with the fist or a weapon) **2** : a sudden act **3** : a sudden happening that causes suffering or loss ⟨the dog's death was a severe *blow*⟩

blow·gun \'blō-ɡən\ *n* : a tube from which a dart may be shot by the force of the breath

blow·out \'blō-aut\ *n* : a bursting of a container (as an automobile tire) by pressure of the contents on a weak spot

blow·pipe \'blō-pīp\ *n* **1** : a small round tube for blowing air or gas into a flame so as to make it hotter **2** : BLOWGUN

blow·torch \'blō-torch\ *n* : a small portable burner in which the flame is made hotter by a blast of air or oxygen

blow up *vb* **1** : EXPLODE **1 2** : to fill with a gas (as air) ⟨*blow* the balloon *up*⟩

¹**blub·ber** \'bləb-ər\ *n* : the fat of various sea mammals (as whales) from which oil can be obtained

²**blubber** *vb* : to weep noisily

¹**blue** \'blü\ *adj* **blu·er; blu·est 1** : of the color blue **2** : low in spirits : MELANCHOLY

²**blue** *n* **1** : the color in the rainbow between green and violet : the color of the clear daytime sky **2** : something blue in color — **out of the blue** : suddenly and unexpectedly

blue·bell \'blü-bel\ *n* : a plant with blue flowers shaped like bells

blue·ber·ry \'blü-ber-ē\ *n, pl* **blue·ber·ries** : a sweet blue berry that has small seeds and grows on a bush related to the huckleberry

blue·bird \'blü-bərd\ *n* : any of several small North American songbirds more or less blue above

bluebell

blue·bot·tle \'blü-bät-l\ *n* : a large blue hairy fly

blue cheese *n* : cheese ripened by and full of greenish blue mold

blue·fish \'blü-fish\ *n* : a bluish saltwater food fish of the eastern coast of the United States

blue·grass \'blü-gras\ *n* : a grass with bluish green stems

blueing *variant of* BLUING

blue jay \'blü-jā\ *n* : any of several crested and mostly blue American birds related to the crows

blue jeans *n pl* : pants or overalls made of blue denim

¹**blue·print** \'blü-print\ *n* **1** : a photographic print made with white lines on a blue background and used for copying maps and building plans **2** : a detailed plan of something to be done

²**blueprint** *vb* : to make a blueprint of

blues \'blüz\ *n pl* **1** : low spirits ⟨overcome by the *blues*⟩ **2** : a sad song in a style that was first used by American blacks

blue whale *n* : a very large whale that is probably the largest living animal

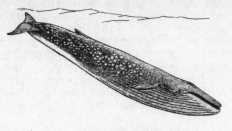

blue whale

¹bluff \'bləf\ *adj* **1** : rising steeply with a broad front **2** : frank and outspoken in a rough but good-natured way — **bluff·ly** *adv* — **bluff·ness** *n*

²bluff *n* : a high steep bank : CLIFF

³bluff *vb* : to deceive or frighten by pretending to have more strength or confidence than one really has — **bluff·er** *n*

⁴bluff *n* **1** : an act or instance of bluffing **2** : a person who bluffs

blu·ing *or* **blue·ing** \'blü-ing\ *n* : something made with blue or violet dyes that is added to the water when washing clothes to prevent yellowing of white fabrics

blu·ish \'blü-ish\ *adj* : somewhat blue

¹blun·der \'blən-dər\ *vb* **1** : to move in a clumsy way **2** : to make a mistake — **blun·der·er** *n*

²blunder *n* : a bad or stupid mistake **synonyms** see ERROR

blun·der·buss \'blən-dər-ˌbəs\ *n* : a short gun that has a barrel which is larger at the end and that was used long ago for shooting at close range without taking exact aim

blunderbuss

¹blunt \'blənt\ *adj* **1** : having a thick edge or point : DULL **2** : speaking or spoken in plain language without thought for other people's feelings — **blunt·ly** *adv*

²blunt *vb* : to make or become blunt

¹blur \'blər\ *n* : something that cannot be seen clearly ⟨could see only a *blur*⟩

²blur *vb* **blurred; blur·ring** **1** : to make hard to see or read by smearing **2** : to make or become smeared or confused

blurt \'blərt\ *vb* : to say or tell suddenly and without thinking ⟨*blurt* out a secret⟩

¹blush \'bləsh\ *vb* **1** : to become red in the face from shame, confusion, or embarrassment **2** : to feel ashamed or embarrassed

²blush *n* **1** : a reddening of the face from shame, confusion, or embarrassment **2** : a rosy color

¹blus·ter \'bləs-tər\ *vb* **1** : to blow hard and noisily **2** : to talk or act in a noisy boastful way

²bluster *n* : noisy violent action or speech

boa \'bō-ə\ *n* : a large snake (as a python) that coils around and crushes its prey

boar \'bōr\ *n* **1** : a male pig **2** : a wild pig

¹board \'bōrd\ *n* **1** : a sawed piece of lumber that is much broader and longer than it is thick **2** : a dining table **3** : meals given at set times for a price ⟨room and *board*⟩ **4** : a number of persons having authority to manage or direct something ⟨the school *board*⟩ **5** : a usually rectangular piece of rigid material used for some special purpose ⟨a diving *board*⟩ ⟨a game *board*⟩ — **on board** : ABOARD

²board *vb* **1** : to go aboard ⟨*boarded* the plane in New York⟩ **2** : to cover with boards ⟨the windows were *boarded* up⟩ **3** : to give or get meals at set times for a price

board·er \'bōrd-ər\ *n* : a person who pays for meals or for meals and lodging at another's house

board·ing·house \'bōrd-ing-ˌhaůs\ *n* : a house at which people are given meals and often lodging

boarding school *n* : a school at which most of the students live during the school year

board·walk \'bōrd-ˌwȯk\ *n* : a walk made of planks especially along a beach

¹boast \'bōst\ *n* **1** : an act of boasting **2** : a cause for boasting or pride

²boast *vb* **1** : to praise what one has or has done ⟨*boasted* of their strength⟩ **2** : to have and be proud of having

boast·ful \'bōst-fəl\ *adj* **1** : having the habit of boasting **2** : full of boasts — **boast·ful·ly** \-fə-lē\ *adv* — **boast·ful·ness** *n*

¹boat \'bōt\ *n* **1** : a small vessel driven on the water by oars, paddles, sails, or a motor **2** : ¹SHIP 1

²boat *vb* : to use a boat — **boat·er** *n*

boat·house \'bōt-ˌhaůs\ *n* : a house or shelter for boats

\ə\ abut	\aů\ out	\i\ tip	\ȯ\ saw	\ů\ foot
\ər\ further	\ch\ chin	\ī\ life	\ȯi\ coin	\y\ yet
\a\ mat	\e\ pet	\j\ job	\th\ thin	\yü\ few
\ā\ take	\ē\ easy	\ng\ sing	\th\ this	\yů\ cure
\ä\ cot, cart	\g\ go	\ō\ bone	\ü\ food	\zh\ vision

boat·man \'bōt-mən\ *n, pl* **boat·men** \-mən\ : a person who works on or deals in boats

boat·swain \'bōs-n\ *n* : a warrant officer on a warship or a petty officer on a commercial ship who has charge of the hull, anchors, boats, and rigging

¹**bob** \'bäb\ *vb* **bobbed; bob·bing 1 :** to move or cause to move with a short jerky motion **2 :** to appear suddenly ⟨they may *bob* up anywhere⟩ **3 :** to try to seize something with the teeth ⟨*bob* for apples⟩

²**bob** *n* : a short jerky up-and-down motion

³**bob** *n* **1 :** a float used to buoy up the baited end of a fishing line **2 :** a woman's or child's short haircut

⁴**bob** *vb* **bobbed; bob·bing :** to cut in the style of a bob ⟨had my hair *bobbed*⟩

bob·by pin \'bäb-ē-\ *n* : a flat metal hairpin with the two ends pressed close together

bob·cat \'bäb-ˌkat\ *n* : an American wildcat that is a small rusty brown variety of the lynx

bob·o·link \'bäb-ə-ˌlingk\ *n* : an American songbird related to the blackbirds

bob·sled \'bäb-ˌsled\ *n* : a racing sled made with two sets of runners, a hand brake, and often a steering wheel

bob·tail \'bäb-ˌtāl\ *n* **1 :** a short tail : a tail cut short **2 :** an animal with a short tail

bob·white \bäb-'hwīt, -'wīt\ *n* : an American quail with gray, white, and reddish coloring

bode *past of* BIDE

bod·ice \'bäd-əs\ *n* : the upper part of a dress

bod·i·ly \'bäd-l-ē\ *adj* : of or relating to the body ⟨*bodily* comfort⟩

body \'bäd-ē\ *n, pl* **bod·ies 1 :** the material whole of a live or dead person or animal **2 :** the main part of a person, animal, or plant **3 :** the main or central part ⟨the *body* of a letter⟩ **4 :** a group of persons or things united for some purpose ⟨a *body* of troops⟩ **5 :** a mass or portion of something distinct from other masses ⟨a *body* of water⟩ ⟨a *body* of cold air⟩ — **bod·ied** \'bäd-ēd\ *adj*

body·guard \'bäd-ē-ˌgärd\ *n* : a person or a group of persons whose duty it is to protect someone

¹**bog** \'bäg, 'bȯg\ *n* : wet spongy ground that is usually acid and found next to a body of water (as a pond)

²**bog** *vb* **bogged; bog·ging :** to sink or stick fast in or as if in a bog ⟨the car *bogged* down⟩

bo·gey *or* **bo·gy** *or* **bo·gie** *n, pl* **bo·geys** *or* **bo·gies 1** \'bùg-ē, 'bō-gē\ : GHOST, goblin **2** \'bō-gē, 'bùg-ē\ : something one is afraid of without reason

¹**boil** \'bȯil\ *n* : a hot red painful lump in the skin that contains pus and is caused by infection

²**boil** *vb* **1 :** to heat or become heated to the temperature (**boiling point**) at which bubbles rise and break at the surface ⟨*boil* water⟩ **2 :** to cook or become cooked in boiling water ⟨*boil* eggs⟩ ⟨let the stew *boil* slowly⟩ **3 :** to become angry or upset

³**boil** *n* : the state of something that is boiling

boil·er \'bȯi-lər\ *n* **1 :** a container in which something is boiled **2 :** a tank heating and holding water **3 :** a strong metal container used in making steam (as to heat buildings)

bois·ter·ous \'bȯi-stə-rəs, -strəs\ *adj* : being rough and noisy — **bois·ter·ous·ly** *adv* — **bois·ter·ous·ness** *n*

bold \'bōld\ *adj* **1 :** willing to meet danger or take risks : DARING **2 :** not polite and modest : FRESH **3 :** showing or calling for courage or daring ⟨a *bold* plan⟩ **synonyms** see BRAVE — **bold·ly** *adv* — **boldness** *n*

bold·face \'bōld-ˌfās\ *n* : a heavy black type — **bold–faced** \-ˌfāst\ *adj*

bo·le·ro \bə-'leər-ō\ *n, pl* **bo·le·ros 1 :** a Spanish dance or the music for it **2 :** a loose short jacket open at the front

boll \'bōl\ *n* : the seedpod of a plant (as cotton)

boll weevil *n* : a grayish insect that lays its eggs in cotton bolls

¹**bol·ster** \'bōl-stər\ *n* : a long pillow or cushion sometimes used to support bed pillows

²**bolster** *vb* : to support with or as if with a bolster ⟨help to *bolster* up their courage⟩

¹**bolt** \'bōlt\ *n* **1 :** a stroke of lightning : THUNDERBOLT **2 :** a sliding bar used to fasten a door **3 :** the part of a lock worked by a key **4 :** a metal pin or rod usually with a head at one end and a screw thread at the other that is used to hold something in place **5 :** a roll of cloth or wallpaper

²**bolt** *vb* **1 :** to move suddenly and rapidly ⟨*bolted* from the room⟩ **2 :** to run away ⟨the horse shied and *bolted*⟩ **3 :** to fasten with a bolt ⟨be sure to *bolt* the door⟩ **4 :** to swallow hastily or without chewing ⟨don't *bolt* your food⟩

¹**bomb** \'bäm\ *n* **1 :** a hollow case or shell filled with explosive material and made to be dropped from an airplane, thrown by hand, or set off by a fuse **2 :** a container in which something (as an insecticide) is

stored under pressure and from which it is released in a fine spray

²bomb *vb* : to attack with bombs

bom·bard \bäm-'bärd\ *vb* **1** : to attack with heavy fire from big guns : SHELL ⟨*bombard* a fort⟩ **2** : to attack again and again ⟨*bombard* a person with questions⟩

bomb·er \'bäm-ər\ *n* : an airplane specially made for dropping bombs

bon·bon \'bän-,bän\ *n* : a candy with a soft coating and a creamy center

¹bond \'bänd\ *n* **1** : something that binds **2** : a force or influence that brings or holds together ⟨a *bond* of friendship⟩ **3** : a legal agreement in which a person agrees to pay a sum of money if he or she fails to do a certain thing **4** : a government or business certificate promising to pay a certain sum by a certain day

²bond *vb* : to stick or cause to stick together

bond·age \'bän-dij\ *n* : SLAVERY

¹bone \'bōn\ *n* **1** : the hard material of which the skeleton of most animals is formed **2** : any of the pieces into which the bone of the skeleton is naturally divided ⟨break a *bone* in one's arm⟩ — **bone·less** \-ləs\ *adj*

²bone *vb* **boned; bon·ing** : to remove the bones from ⟨*bone* a fish⟩

bon·fire \'bän-,fir\ *n* : a large fire built outdoors

bong \'bäng, 'bòng\ *n* : a deep sound like that of a large bell

bon·go \'bäng-gō, 'bòng-gō\ *n, pl* **bongos** *also* **bongoes** : either of a pair of small drums of different sizes fitted together and played with the fingers

bon·net \'bän-ət\ *n* : a child's or woman's hat usually tied under the chin by ribbons or strings

bon·ny *or* **bon·nie** \'bän-ē\ *adj* **bon·ni·er; bon·ni·est** *chiefly British* : HANDSOME 3, BEAUTIFUL

bo·nus \'bō-nəs\ *n* : something given to somebody (as a worker) in addition to what is usual or owed

bony \'bō-nē\ *adj* **bon·i·er; bon·i·est** **1** : of or relating to bone ⟨a *bony* skeleton⟩ **2** : like bone especially in hardness ⟨*bony* material⟩ **3** : having bones and especially large or noticeable bones ⟨a *bony* fish⟩

¹boo \'bü\ *interj* — used to express disapproval or to startle or frighten

²boo *n, pl* **boos** : a cry expressing disapproval

³boo *vb* : to express disapproval of with boos

boo·by \'bü-bē\ *n, pl* **boo·bies** : an awkward foolish person

¹book \'bùk\ *n* **1** : a set of sheets of paper bound together **2** : a long written work ⟨a *book* about birds⟩ **3** : a large division of a written work ⟨the *books* of the Bible⟩ **4** : a pack of small items bound together ⟨a *book* of matches⟩

Word History The word *book* is related to *beech*, the name of a tree. The ancestors of the early English people did not write on paper. They carved inscriptions on stone and wood. It is likely that the use of beech wood for this carved writing gave us the word *book*.

²book *vb* : to reserve for future use ⟨*book* rooms at the hotel⟩

book·case \'bùk-,kās\ *n* : a set of shelves to hold books

book·end \'bùk-,end\ *n* : a support at the end of a row of books to keep them standing up

book·keep·er \'bùk-,kē-pər\ *n* : a person who keeps accounts for a business

book·keep·ing \'bùk-,kē-ping\ *n* : the work of keeping business accounts

book·let \'bùk-lət\ *n* : a little book usually having paper covers and few pages

book·mark \'bùk-,märk\ *n* : something placed in a book to show the page one wants to return to later

book·mo·bile \'bùk-mō-,bēl\ *n* : a truck with shelves of books that is a traveling library

¹boom \'büm\ *n* **1** : a long pole used especially to stretch the bottom of a sail **2** : a long beam sticking out from the mast of a derrick to support or guide something that is being lifted

boom 1

²boom *vb* **1** : to make a deep hollow rumbling sound ⟨the cannon *boomed*⟩ **2** : to increase or develop rapidly ⟨business *boomed* during the war⟩

³boom *n* **1** : a booming sound **2** : a rapid increase in activity or popularity

boom box *n* : a large portable radio and often tape player with two attached speakers

\ə\ **abut**	\aù\ **out**	\i\ **tip**	\ò\ **saw**	\ù\ **foot**	
\ər\ **further**	\ch\ **chin**	\ī\ **life**	\òi\ **coin**	\y\ **yet**	
\a\ **mat**	\e\ **pet**	\j\ **job**	\th\ **thin**	\yü\ **few**	
\ā\ **take**	\ē\ **easy**	\ng\ **sing**	\th\ **this**	\yù\ **cure**	
\ä\ **cot, cart**	\g\ **go**	\ō\ **bone**	\ü\ **food**	\zh\ **vision**	

boo·mer·ang \'bü-mə-ˌrang\ *n* : a curved club that can be thrown so as to return to the thrower

boon \'bün\ *n* **1** : something asked or granted as a favor **2** : something pleasant or helpful that comes at just the right time ⟨the rain was a *boon* to the farmers⟩

¹**boost** \'büst\ *vb* **1** : to raise or push up from below ⟨*boosted* me through the window⟩ **2** : to make bigger or greater ⟨*boost* production⟩ — **boost·er** *n*

²**boost** *n* : an act of boosting : a push up ⟨give me a *boost*⟩

¹**boot** \'büt\ *n* : a covering usually of leather or rubber for the foot and part of the leg

²**boot** *vb* : ¹KICK 1

boot·ee *or* **boot·ie** \'büt-ē\ *n* : an infant's knitted sock

booth \'büth\ *n, pl* **booths** \'bü<u>th</u>z\ **1** : a covered stall for selling or displaying goods (as at a fair or exhibition) **2** : a small enclosure giving privacy for one person ⟨a telephone *booth*⟩ **3** : a section of a restaurant consisting of a table between two backed benches

boo·ty \'büt-ē\ *n* : goods seized from an enemy in war : PLUNDER

bo·rax \'bōr-ˌaks\ *n* : a compound of boron used as a cleansing agent and water softener

¹**bor·der** \'bȯrd-ər\ *n* **1** : the outer edge of something ⟨the *border* of a lake⟩ **2** : a boundary especially of a country or state **3** : an ornamental strip on or near the edge of a flat object

synonyms BORDER, EDGE, and RIM mean a line or narrow space that marks the limit of something. BORDER is used of the area on or right next to the boundary line ⟨built several forts along the *border*⟩ EDGE is used of the line formed by two surfaces that meet ⟨a knife with a sharp *edge*⟩ RIM is used of the edge of something that is round or curving ⟨the *rim* of a bowl⟩

²**border** *vb* **1** : to put a border on ⟨*border* the garden with flowers⟩ **2** : to be close or next to ⟨the United States *borders* on Canada⟩

bor·der·line \'bȯrd-ər-ˌlīn\ *adj* : not quite average, standard, or normal

¹**bore** \'bōr\ *vb* **bored**; **bor·ing** **1** : to make a hole in especially with a drill ⟨*bore* a piece of wood⟩ **2** : to make by piercing or drilling ⟨*bore* a hole⟩ ⟨*bore* a well⟩ — **bor·er** *n*

²**bore** *n* **1** : a hole made by boring **2** : a cavity (as in a gun barrel) shaped like a cylinder **3** : the diameter of a hole or cylinder

³**bore** *past of* BEAR

⁴**bore** *n* : an uninteresting person or thing

⁵**bore** *vb* **bored**; **bor·ing** : to make weary and restless by being uninteresting ⟨this long-winded story *bores* me⟩

bore·dom \'bōrd-əm\ *n* : the state of being bored

bo·ric acid \ˌbōr-ik-\ *n* : a weak acid containing boron used to kill germs

born \'bȯrn\ *adj* **1** : brought into life by birth : brought forth **2** : having a certain characteristic from or as if from birth ⟨a *born* loser⟩ ⟨a *born* leader⟩

borne *past participle of* BEAR

bo·ron \'bōr-ˌän\ *n* : a powdery or hard solid chemical element that melts at a very high temperature and is found in nature only in combination

bor·ough \'bər-ō\ *n* **1** : a self-governing town or village in some states **2** : one of the five political divisions of New York City

bor·row \'bär-ō\ *vb* **1** : to take or receive something with the promise of returning it **2** : to take for one's own use something begun or thought up by another : ADOPT ⟨*borrow* an idea⟩ — **bor·row·er** \'bär-ə-wər\ *n*

¹**bos·om** \'bu̇z-əm\ *n* : the front of the human chest : the breasts of a woman

²**bosom** *adj* : ³CLOSE 8, INTIMATE ⟨*bosom* friends⟩

¹**boss** \'bȯs\ *n* **1** : the person (as an employer or foreman) who tells workers what to do **2** : the head of a group (as a political organization)

²**boss** *vb* **1** : to be in charge of ⟨*boss* a job⟩ **2** : to give orders to ⟨don't *boss* me around⟩

bossy \'bȯ-sē\ *adj* **boss·i·er**; **boss·i·est** : liking to order people around

bo·tan·i·cal \bə-'tan-i-kəl\ *adj* : of or relating to botany

bot·a·nist \'bät-n-əst\ *n* : a specialist in botany

bot·a·ny \'bät-n-ē, 'bät-nē\ *n* : a branch of biology dealing with plants

botch \'bäch\ *vb* : to do clumsily and unskillfully : SPOIL, BUNGLE

¹**both** \'bōth\ *adj* : the two ⟨*both* books are mine⟩

²**both** *pron* : the one and the other : the two ⟨*both* of us⟩

³**both** *conj* — used before two words or phrases connected with *and* to stress that each is included ⟨*both* New York and London⟩

¹both·er \'bä<u>th</u>-ər\ *vb* **1** : to trouble (someone) in body or mind : DISTRACT, ANNOY ⟨*bothered* by flies⟩ **2** : to cause to worry ⟨your illness *bothers* me⟩ **3** : to take the time or trouble ⟨don't *bother* to dress up⟩

²bother *n* **1** : someone or something that bothers in a small way ⟨what a *bother* a cold can be⟩ **2** : COMMOTION **3** : the condition of being bothered

¹bot·tle \'bät-l\ *n* **1** : a container (as of glass or plastic) usually having a narrow neck and mouth and no handle **2** : the quantity held by a bottle

²bottle *vb* **bot·tled; bot·tling 1** : to put into a bottle **2** : to shut up as if in a bottle ⟨*bottle* up your feelings⟩

bot·tle·neck \'bät-l-ˌnek\ *n* : a place or condition where improvement or movement is held up

bot·tom \'bät-əm\ *n* **1** : the under surface of something ⟨the *bottom* of a shelf⟩ **2** : a supporting surface or part : BASE ⟨chair *bottoms*⟩ **3** : the bed of a body of water ⟨the lake *bottom*⟩ **4** : the lowest part of something ⟨*bottom* of the heap⟩ **5** : low land along a river ⟨Mississippi river *bottoms*⟩

bot·tom·less \'bät-əm-ləs\ *adj* **1** : having no bottom **2** : very deep ⟨a *bottomless* pit⟩

bough \'bau̇\ *n* : a usually large or main branch of a tree

bought *past of* BUY

bouil·lon \'bü-ˌyän, 'bu̇l-ˌyän, 'bu̇l-yən\ *n* : a clear soup made from meat (as beef or chicken)

boul·der \'bōl-dər\ *n* : a large detached and rounded or very worn mass of rock

bou·le·vard \'bu̇l-ə-ˌvärd\ *n* : a wide avenue often having grass strips with trees along its center or sides

Word History The French made a word from a Dutch word that meant "bulwark." At first this French word meant "bulwark," but later it came to mean "boulevard" as well. The first boulevards were laid out where the city fortifications, or bulwarks, had been torn down. The English word *boulevard* came from the French word that meant "bulwark" or "boulevard."

¹bounce \'bau̇ns\ *vb* **bounced; bouncing 1** : to spring back or up after hitting a surface ⟨the ball *bounced* into the street⟩ **2** : to leap suddenly **3** : to cause to bounce ⟨*bounce* a ball⟩

²bounce *n* **1** : a sudden leap **2** : ²REBOUND 1

¹bound \'bau̇nd\ *adj* : going or intending to go ⟨homeward *bound*⟩

²bound *vb* : to form the boundary of ⟨a farm *bounded* by a river on one side⟩

³bound *past of* BIND

⁴bound *adj* **1** : tied or fastened with or as if with bands **2** : required by law or duty **3** : covered with binding ⟨a *bound* book⟩ **4** : firmly determined ⟨we were *bound* we would succeed⟩ **5** : very likely to do something : CERTAIN, SURE ⟨it is *bound* to rain⟩

⁵bound *n* : a fast easy leap

⁶bound *vb* : to make a bound or move in bounds

bound·ary \'bau̇n-də-rē, 'bau̇n-drē\ *n, pl* **bound·aries** : something that points out or shows a limit or end : a dividing line

bound·less \'bau̇nd-ləs\ *adj* : having no limits ⟨*boundless* energy⟩

bounds \'bau̇ndz\ *n pl* : a point or a line beyond which a person or thing cannot go ⟨out of *bounds*⟩

boun·te·ous \'bau̇nt-ē-əs\ *adj* **1** : LIBERAL 1 **2** : ABUNDANT ⟨a *bounteous* harvest⟩

boun·ti·ful \'bau̇nt-i-fəl\ *adj* **1** : giving freely or generously ⟨a *bountiful* host⟩ **2** : PLENTIFUL 2 ⟨a *bountiful* feast⟩ — **boun·ti·ful·ly** \-fə-lē\ *adv*

boun·ty \'bau̇nt-ē\ *n, pl* **boun·ties 1** : GENEROSITY 1 **2** : generous gifts **3** : money given as a reward for killing certain harmful animals

bou·quet \bō-'kā, bü-\ *n* : a bunch of flowers

bout \'bau̇t\ *n* **1** : a contest of skill or strength between two persons ⟨a wrestling *bout*⟩ **2** : ²ATTACK **3** ⟨a bad *bout* of flu⟩

¹bow \'bau̇\ *vb* **1** : ¹YIELD 8 ⟨*bow* to the authority of the king⟩ **2** : to lower the head or bend the body in greeting or respect or in giving in

²bow *n* : a bending of the head or body to express respect or greeting

³bow \'bō\ *n* **1** : a weapon used for shooting arrows and usually made of a strip of wood bent by a cord connecting the two ends **2** : something shaped

bow 1

\ə\ **abut**	\au̇\ **out**	\i\ **tip**	\ȯ\ **saw**	\u̇\ **foot**
\ər\ **further**	\ch\ **chin**	\ī\ **life**	\ȯi\ **coin**	\y\ **yet**
\a\ **mat**	\e\ **pet**	\j\ **job**	\th\ **thin**	\yü\ **few**
\ā\ **take**	\ē\ **easy**	\ng\ **sing**	\<u>th</u>\ **this**	\yu̇\ **cure**
\ä\ **cot, cart**	\g\ **go**	\ō\ **bone**	\ü\ **food**	\zh\ **vision**

in a curve like a bow **3** : a rod with horse-hairs stretched from end to end used for playing a stringed instrument (as a violin) **4** : a knot made with one or more loops ⟨tie the ribbon in a *bow*⟩

⁴**bow** \ˈbō\ *vb* **1** : to bend into a bow **2** : to play with a bow ⟨*bowed* two strings at once⟩

⁵**bow** \ˈbaů\ *n* : the forward part of a ship

bow·el \ˈbaů-əl\ *n* **1** : INTESTINE — usually used in pl. **2** : a part of the intestine ⟨the large *bowel*⟩

bow·er \ˈbaů-ər\ *n* : a shelter in a garden made of boughs of trees or vines

¹**bowl** \ˈbōl\ *n* **1** : a round hollow dish without handles **2** : the contents of a bowl ⟨eat a *bowl* of cereal⟩ **3** : something in the shape of a bowl (as part of a spoon or pipe)

²**bowl** *n* : a rolling of a ball in bowling

³**bowl** *vb* **1** : to roll a ball in bowling **2** : to move rapidly and smoothly as if rolling **3** : to hit with or as if with something rolled ⟨was *bowled* over by surprise⟩

bow·leg·ged \ˈbō-ˈleg-əd, -ˈlegd\ *adj* : having the legs bowed outward

bow·line \ˈbō-lən\ *n* : a knot used for making a loop that will not slip

bowl·ing \ˈbō-ling\ *n* : a game in which balls are rolled so as to knock down pins

bow·man \ˈbō-mən\ *n, pl* **bow·men** \-mən\ : ARCHER

bow·sprit \ˈbaů-ˌsprit, ˈbō-\ *n* : a large spar sticking out forward from the bow of a ship

bow·string \ˈbō-ˌstring\ *n* : the cord connecting the two ends of a bow

bowline

¹**box** \ˈbäks\ *n* : an evergreen shrub or small tree used for hedges

²**box** *n* **1** : a container usually having four sides, a bottom, and a cover **2** : the contents of a box ⟨eat a whole *box* of candy⟩ **3** : an enclosed place for one or more persons ⟨a sentry *box*⟩ ⟨a *box* in a theater⟩

³**box** *vb* : to enclose in or as if in a box

⁴**box** *vb* : to engage in boxing

box·car \ˈbäks-ˌskär\ *n* : a roofed freight car usually having sliding doors in the sides

box elder *n* : an American maple with leaves divided into several leaflets

¹**box·er** \ˈbäk-sər\ *n* : a person who boxes

²**boxer** *n* : a compact dog of German origin that is of medium size with a square build and has a short and often tan coat with a black mask

box·ing \ˈbäk-sing\ *n* : the sport of fighting with the fists

box office *n* : a place where tickets to public entertainments (as sports or theatrical events) are sold

boy \ˈbȯi\ *n* **1** : a male child from birth to young manhood **2** : a male servant

¹**boy·cott** \ˈbȯi-ˌkät\ *vb* : to join with others in refusing to deal with someone (as a person, organization, or country) usually to show disapproval or to force acceptance of terms

²**boycott** *n* : the process or an instance of boycotting

boy·friend \ˈbȯi-ˌfrend\ *n* : a regular male companion of a girl or woman

boy·hood \ˈbȯi-ˌhůd\ *n* : the time or condition of being a boy

boy·ish \ˈbȯi-ish\ *adj* : of, relating to, or having qualities often felt to be typical of boys — **boy·ish·ly** *adv* — **boy·ish·ness** *n*

Boy Scout *n* : a member of a scouting program (as the Boy Scouts of America)

bra \ˈbrä\ *n* : a woman's undergarment for breast support

¹**brace** \ˈbrās\ *n* **1** : two of a kind ⟨a *brace* of quail⟩ **2** : a tool with a U-shaped bend that is used to turn wood-boring bits **3** : something that braces ⟨a *brace* for a fence post⟩ ⟨a *brace* for a crippled leg⟩ **4** : a usually wire device worn on the teeth for changing faulty position **5** : a mark { or } used to connect words or items to be considered together

²**brace** *vb* **braced; brac·ing** : to make strong, firm, or steady

brace·let \ˈbrā-slət\ *n* : a decorative band or chain usually worn on the wrist or arm

brack·en \ˈbrak-ən\ *n* : a large coarse branching fern

¹**brack·et** \ˈbrak-ət\ *n* **1** : a support for a weight (as a shelf) that is usually attached to a wall **2** : one of a pair of marks [ ] (**square brackets**) used to enclose letters or numbers or in mathematics to enclose items to be treated together **3** : one of a pair of marks < > (**angle brackets**) used to enclose letters or numbers

²**bracket** *vb* **1** : to place within brackets **2** : to put into the same class : GROUP

brack·ish \ˈbrak-ish\ *adj* : somewhat salty

brad \\'brad\ *n* : a slender wire nail with a small longish but rounded head

brag \\'brag\ *vb* **bragged; brag·ging** : ²BOAST 1

brag·gart \\'brag-ərt\ *n* : a person who brags a lot

¹braid \\'brād\ *vb* : to weave together into a braid ⟨*braided* rugs⟩

²braid *n* : a length of cord, ribbon, or hair formed of three or more strands woven together

braille \\'brāl\ *n, often cap* : a system of printing for the blind in which the letters are represented by raised dots

braille alphabet

Word History More than a hundred years ago, Louis Braille was a teacher in France. He taught blind people and was himself blind. He invented the system of printing for the blind called *braille,* which is named after him.

¹brain \\'brān\ *n* **1** : the part of the nervous system that is inside the skull, consists of grayish nerve cells and whitish nerve fibers, and is the organ of thought and the central control point for the nervous system **2 brains** *pl* : a good mind : INTELLIGENCE **3** : someone who is very smart

²brain *vb* : to hurt or kill by a blow on the head ⟨*brained* by a falling tree⟩

brain·storm \\'brān-ˌstȯrm\ *n* : a sudden inspiration or idea

brainy \\'brā-nē\ *adj* **brain·i·er; brain·i·est** : very smart

¹brake \\'brāk\ *n* : a thick growth of shrubs, small trees, or canes

²brake *n* : a device for slowing or stopping motion (as of a wheel) usually by friction

³brake *vb* **braked; brak·ing** : to slow or stop by using a brake

brake·man \\'brāk-mən\ *n, pl* **brake·men** \-mən\ : a crew member on a train whose duties include inspecting the train and helping the conductor

bram·ble \\'bram-bəl\ *n* : any of a group of woody plants with prickly stems that include the raspberries and blackberries and are related to the roses

bran \\'bran\ *n* : the broken coat of the seed of cereal grain separated (as by sifting) from the flour or meal

¹branch \\'branch\ *n* **1** : a part of a tree that grows out from the trunk or from a large bough **2** : something extending from a main line or body like a branch ⟨a *branch* of a railroad⟩ **3** : a division or subordinate part of something ⟨the bank opened a new *branch*⟩ — **branched** \\'brancht\ *adj*

²branch *vb* : to send out a branch : spread or divide into branches

¹brand \\'brand\ *n* **1** : a mark of disgrace (as one formerly put on criminals with a hot iron) **2** : a mark made by burning (as on cattle) or by stamping or printing (as on manufactured goods) to show ownership, maker, or quality **3** : TRADEMARK **4** : a class of goods identified by a name as the product of a certain maker

²brand *vb* **1** : to mark with a brand **2** : to show or claim (something) to be bad or wrong ⟨opponents *branded* the test a failure⟩

bran·dish \\'bran-dish\ *vb* : to wave or shake in a threatening manner ⟨*brandishing* their swords⟩

brand—new \\'bran-'nü, -'nyü\ *adj* : completely new and unused

bran·dy \\'bran-dē\ *n, pl* **bran·dies** : an alcoholic liquor made from wine or fruit juice

brass \\'bras\ *n* **1** : an alloy made by combining copper and zinc **2** : the musical instruments of an orchestra or band that are usually made of brass and include the cornets, trumpets, trombones, French horns, and tubas

brat \\'brat\ *n* : a naughty annoying child

¹brave \\'brāv\ *adj* **brav·er; brav·est** : feeling or showing no fear — **brave·ly** *adv*

synonyms BRAVE, COURAGEOUS, and BOLD mean showing no fear. BRAVE suggests that one has or shows no fear when faced with danger or difficulty ⟨the *brave* crew tried to save the ship⟩ COURAGEOUS suggests that one is always prepared to meet danger or difficulty ⟨the early pioneers were *courageous* people ready to put up with great hardships⟩ BOLD suggests that one welcomes dangerous situations ⟨*bold* explorers in search of adventure⟩

\ə\ **abut**	\aů\ **out**	\i\ **tip**	\ȯ\ **saw**	\ů\ **foot**
\ər\ **further**	\ch\ **chin**	\ī\ **life**	\ȯi\ **coin**	\y\ **yet**
\a\ **mat**	\e\ **pet**	\j\ **job**	\th\ **thin**	\yü\ **few**
\ā\ **take**	\ē\ **easy**	\ng\ **sing**	\th\ **this**	\yů\ **cure**
\ä\ **cot, cart**	\g\ **go**	\ō\ **bone**	\ü\ **food**	\zh\ **vision**

²brave *n* : an American Indian warrior

³brave *vb* **braved; brav·ing** : to face or take bravely ⟨*braved* the raging storm⟩

brav·ery \'brā-və-rē, 'brāv-rē\ *n* : COURAGE

¹brawl \'brȯl\ *vb* : to quarrel or fight noisily

²brawl *n* : a noisy quarrel or fight

brawn \'brȯn\ *n* : muscular strength

brawny \'brȯ-nē\ *adj* **brawn·i·er; brawn·i·est** : having large strong muscles

¹bray \'brā\ *vb* : to make the loud harsh cry of a donkey

²bray *n* : a sound of braying

bra·zen \'brāz-n\ *adj* **1** : made of brass **2** : sounding harsh and loud ⟨*brazen* voices⟩ **3** : not ashamed of or embarrassed by one's bad behavior : IMPUDENT

Bra·zil nut \brə-,zil-\ *n* : a dark three-sided nut with a white kernel

¹breach \'brēch\ *n* **1** : a breaking of a law : a failure to do what one should **2** : an opening made by breaking

²breach *vb* : to make a break in

Brazil nut

¹bread \'bred\ *n* **1** : a baked food made from flour or meal **2** : FOOD 1 ⟨our daily *bread*⟩

²bread *vb* : to cover with bread crumbs

breadth \'bredth\ *n* **1** : distance measured from side to side **2** : SCOPE 2

¹break \'brāk\ *vb* **broke** \'brōk\; **bro·ken** \'brō-kən\; **break·ing 1** : to separate into parts suddenly or forcibly ⟨*break* a stick⟩ ⟨glass *breaks* easily⟩ **2** : to fail to keep ⟨*broke* the law⟩ **3** : to force a way ⟨*break* into a house⟩ ⟨*broke* out of jail⟩ **4** : ²TAME 1 ⟨*break* a wild horse⟩ **5** : to reduce the force of ⟨*break* one's fall⟩ **6** : to do better than ⟨*broke* the school record⟩ **7** : to interrupt or put an end to : STOP ⟨a shout *broke* the silence⟩ ⟨let's *break* for lunch⟩ **8** : to develop or burst out suddenly ⟨day is *breaking*⟩ ⟨*broke* into laughter⟩ **9** : to make known ⟨*broke* the news⟩ **10** : SOLVE ⟨*break* a code⟩ **11** : ¹CHANGE 4 ⟨*break* a ten-dollar bill⟩

²break *n* **1** : an act of breaking ⟨make a *break* for freedom⟩ ⟨at *break* of day⟩ **2** : something produced by breaking ⟨a bad *break* in the leg⟩ **3** : an accidental event ⟨a lucky *break*⟩

break·down \'brāk-,daún\ *n* : bodily or mental collapse : FAILURE 6

break·er \'brā-kər\ *n* **1** : a person or thing that breaks something ⟨a circuit *breaker*⟩ **2** : a wave that breaks on shore

¹break·fast \'brek-fəst\ *n* : the first meal of the day

²breakfast *vb* : to eat breakfast

break·neck \'brāk-,nek\ *adj* : very fast or dangerous ⟨*breakneck* speed⟩

break out *vb* **1** : to develop a skin rash **2** : to start up suddenly ⟨a fight *broke* out⟩

break·through \'brāk-,thrü\ *n* : a sudden advance or successful development ⟨a *breakthrough* in cancer research⟩

break up *vb* **1** : to separate into parts **2** : to bring or come to an end ⟨the fighting *broke up* the meeting⟩ **3** : to end a romance **4** : to go into a fit of laughter

break·wa·ter \'brā-,kwȯt-ər, -,kwät-\ *n* : an offshore wall to protect a beach or a harbor from the sea

¹breast \'brest\ *n* **1** : a gland that produces milk **2** : the front part of the body between the neck and the abdomen — **breast·ed** \'bres-təd\ *adj*

²breast *vb* : to face or oppose bravely

breast·bone \'brest-'bōn\ *n* : the bony plate at the front and center of the breast

breast–feed \'brest-'fēd\ *vb* **breast–fed** \-'fed\; **breast–feed·ing** : to feed (a baby) from a mother's breast

breast·plate \'brest-,plāt\ *n* : a piece of armor for covering the breast

breast·work \'bres-,twərk\ *n* : a wall thrown together to serve as a defense in battle

breath \'breth\ *n* **1** : a slight breeze ⟨not a *breath* of air⟩ **2** : ability to breathe : ease of breathing ⟨lost my *breath* for a moment⟩ **3** : air taken in or sent out by the lungs — **out of breath** : breathing very rapidly as a result of hard exercise

breathe \'brēth\ *vb* **breathed; breath·ing 1** : to draw air into and expel it from the lungs **2** : ¹LIVE 1 **3** : ¹SAY 1, UTTER ⟨don't *breathe* a word of this⟩

breath·er \'brē-thər\ *n* : a pause for rest

breath·less \'breth-ləs\ *adj* **1** : panting from exertion **2** : holding one's breath from excitement or fear — **breath·less·ly** *adv*

breath·tak·ing \'breth-,tā-king\ *adj* : very exciting

breech·es \'brich-əz\ *n pl* **1** : short pants fastening below the knee **2** : PANTS

¹breed \'brēd\ *vb* **bred** \'bred\; **breed·ing 1** : to produce or increase (plants or animals) by sexual reproduction ⟨*breed* cattle for market⟩ **2** : to produce offspring by sexual reproduction **3** : to bring up : TRAIN ⟨born and *bred* in this town⟩ **4** : to bring about : CAUSE ⟨familiarity *breeds* contempt⟩ — **breed·er** *n*

²breed *n* **1** : a kind of plant or animal that is found only under human care and is different from related kinds ⟨a beef *breed* of cattle⟩ **2 :** ¹CLASS 6, KIND

breed·ing \'brēd-ing\ *n* **:** training especially in manners **:** UPBRINGING ⟨your behavior shows good *breeding*⟩

breeze \'brēz\ *n* **:** a gentle wind

breezy \'brē-zē\ *adj* **breez·i·er; breez·i·est 1 :** somewhat windy **2 :** lively and somewhat carefree ⟨a *breezy* reply⟩ — **breez·i·ly** \-zə-lē\ *adv* — **breez·i·ness** \-zē-nəs\ *n*

brethren *pl of* BROTHER — used chiefly in formal or solemn address

breve \'brēv, 'brev\ *n* **:** a mark ˘ placed over a vowel to show that the vowel is short

brev·i·ty \'brev-ət-ē\ *n* **:** the condition of being short or brief

¹brew \'brü\ *vb* **1 :** to make (beer) from water, malt, and hops **2 :** to prepare by soaking in hot water ⟨*brew* the tea⟩ **3 :** ²PLAN 2 ⟨*brewing* mischief⟩ **4 :** to start to form ⟨a storm is *brewing*⟩ — **brew·er** *n*

²brew *n* **:** a brewed beverage

brew·ery \'brü-ə-rē\ *n, pl* **brew·er·ies :** a place where malt liquors are brewed

briar *variant of* BRIER

¹bribe \'brīb\ *n* **:** something given or promised to a person in order to influence a decision or action dishonestly

²bribe *vb* **bribed; brib·ing :** to influence or try to influence by a bribe

brib·ery \'brī-bə-rē\ *n, pl* **brib·er·ies :** the act of giving or taking a bribe

¹brick \'brik\ *n* **1 :** a building or paving material made from clay molded into blocks and baked **2 :** a block made of brick

²brick *vb* **:** to close, face, or pave with bricks

brick·lay·er \'brik-,lā-ər\ *n* **:** a person who builds or paves with bricks

brid·al \'brīd-l\ *adj* **:** of or relating to a bride or a wedding

bride \'brīd\ *n* **:** a woman just married or about to be married

bride·groom \'brīd-,grüm\ *n* **:** a man just married or about to be married

brides·maid \'brīdz-,mād\ *n* **:** a woman who attends a bride at her wedding

¹bridge \'brij\ *n* **1 :** a structure built over something (as water, a low place, or a railroad) so people can cross **2 :** a platform above and across the deck of a ship for the captain or officer in charge **3 :** something like a bridge ⟨the *bridge* of the nose⟩

²bridge *vb* **bridged; bridg·ing :** to make a bridge over or across ⟨*bridge* a gap⟩

³bridge *n* **:** a card game for four players in two teams

¹bri·dle \'brīd-l\ *n* **:** a device for controlling a horse made up of a set of straps enclosing the head, a bit, and a pair of reins

²bridle *vb* **bri·dled; bri·dling** \'brīd-ling, -l-ing\ **1 :** to put a bridle on **2 :** RESTRAIN **2** ⟨*bridle* one's anger⟩ **3 :** to hold the head high and draw in the chin as an expression of resentment ⟨*bridle* at criticism⟩

bridle

¹brief \'brēf\ *adj* **:** not very long **:** SHORT — **brief·ly** *adv*

²brief *vb* **:** to give information or instructions to

brief·case \'brēf-,kās\ *n* **:** a flat case for carrying papers or books

briefs \'brēfs\ *n pl* **:** short snug underpants

bri·er *or* **bri·ar** \'brī-ər\ *n* **:** a plant (as the rose or blackberry) with a thorny or prickly woody stem

brig \'brig\ *n* **:** a square-rigged sailing ship with two masts

brig

bri·gade \bri-'gād\ *n* **1 :** a body of soldiers consisting of two or more regiments **2 :** a group of persons organized for acting together ⟨a fire *brigade*⟩

brig·a·dier general \,brig-ə-,diər-\ *n* **:** a commissioned officer in the Army, Air Force, or Marine Corps ranking above a colonel

\ə\ abut	\aú\ out	\i\ tip	\ó\ saw	\ú\ foot
\ər\ further	\ch\ chin	\ī\ life	\òi\ coin	\y\ yet
\a\ mat	\e\ pet	\j\ job	\th\ thin	\yü\ few
\ā\ take	\ē\ easy	\ng\ sing	\th\ this	\yù\ cure
\ä\ cot, cart	\g\ go	\ō\ bone	\ü\ food	\zh\ vision

bright \'brīt\ *adj* **1** : giving off or filled with much light ⟨a *bright* fire⟩ ⟨a *bright* day⟩ **2** : very clear or vivid in color ⟨a *bright* red⟩ **3** : INTELLIGENT, CLEVER ⟨a *bright* child⟩ **4** : CHEERFUL — **bright·ly** *adv* — **bright·ness** *n*

synonyms BRIGHT, RADIANT, and BRILLIANT mean shining or glowing with light. BRIGHT can be used either of something that reflects a great amount of light ⟨a *bright* full moon⟩ or of something that produces much light ⟨*bright* stars⟩ RADIANT is more often used of something that sends forth its own light ⟨the sun is a *radiant* body⟩ BRILLIANT is used of something that shines with a sparkling or flashing light ⟨*brilliant* diamonds⟩

bright·en \'brīt-n\ *vb* : to make or become bright or brighter

bril·liance \'bril-yəns\ *n* : great brightness

bril·liant \'bril-yənt\ *adj* **1** : flashing with light : very bright ⟨*brilliant* jewels⟩ **2** : very impressive ⟨a *brilliant* career⟩ **3** : very smart or clever ⟨a *brilliant* student⟩ **synonyms** see BRIGHT, INTELLIGENT — **bril·liant·ly** *adv*

¹**brim** \'brim\ *n* **1** : the edge or rim of something hollow ⟨a cup filled to the *brim*⟩ **2** : the part of a hat that sticks out around the lower edge

²**brim** *vb* **brimmed**; **brim·ming** : to be or become full to overflowing ⟨*brimming* with happiness⟩

brin·dled \'brin-dld\ *adj* : having dark streaks or spots on a gray or brownish background

brine \'brīn\ *n* **1** : water containing a great deal of salt **2** : OCEAN

bring \'bring\ *vb* **brought** \'brȯt\; **bring·ing** **1** : to cause to come with oneself by carrying or leading : take along ⟨told to *bring* lunches⟩ ⟨*bring* your friend⟩ **2** : to cause to reach a certain state or take a certain action ⟨*bring* water to a boil⟩ ⟨couldn't *bring* myself to say it⟩ **3** : to cause to arrive or exist ⟨the storm *brought* snow and ice⟩ **4** : to sell for ⟨the cow *brought* a high price⟩ — **bring·er** *n*

bring about *vb* : to cause to happen : EFFECT

bring forth *vb* : to give birth to : PRODUCE

bring out *vb* : to produce and offer for sale ⟨*brought out* a new book⟩

bring to *vb* : to bring back from unconsciousness : REVIVE

bring up *vb* : to bring to maturity through care and education ⟨*bring up* a child⟩

brink \'bringk\ *n* **1** : the edge at the top of a steep place **2** : a point of beginning ⟨*brink* of crisis⟩

briny \'brī-nē\ *adj* **brin·i·er**; **brin·i·est** : of or like salt water : SALTY

brisk \'brisk\ *adj* **1** : very active : LIVELY **2** : very refreshing ⟨*brisk* fall weather⟩ — **brisk·ly** *adv* — **brisk·ness** *n*

¹**bris·tle** \'bris-əl\ *n* **1** : a short stiff hair ⟨a hog's *bristle*⟩ **2** : a stiff hair or something like a hair fastened in a brush

²**bristle** *vb* **bris·tled**; **bris·tling** **1** : to rise up and stiffen like bristles ⟨makes your hair *bristle*⟩ **2** : to show signs of anger ⟨*bristled* at the insult⟩

bris·tly \'bris-lē\ *adj* **bris·tli·er**; **bris·tli·est** : of, like, or having many bristles

britch·es \'brich-əz\ *n pl* : BREECHES

¹**Brit·ish** \'brit-ish\ *adj* : of or relating to Great Britain or the British

²**British** *n pl* : the people of Great Britain

brit·tle \'brit-l\ *adj* **brit·tler**; **brit·tlest** : hard but easily broken ⟨*brittle* glass⟩ — **brit·tle·ness** *n*

synonyms BRITTLE, CRISP, and FRAGILE mean easily broken. BRITTLE suggests that something is hard and dry ⟨*brittle* twigs snapping under our feet⟩ CRISP suggests that something is hard and dry but also fresh ⟨crackers no longer *crisp*⟩ FRAGILE is used of anything so delicate that it may be broken easily ⟨a piece of *fragile* china⟩

broach \'brōch\ *vb* : to bring up as a subject for discussion ⟨*broach* a question⟩

broad \'brȯd\ *adj* **1** : not narrow : WIDE ⟨a *broad* stripe⟩ **2** : extending far and wide : SPACIOUS ⟨*broad* prairies⟩ **3** : ¹COMPLETE 1, FULL ⟨*broad* daylight⟩ **4** : not limited ⟨a *broad* choice of subjects⟩ **5** : not covering fine points : GENERAL ⟨gave a *broad* outline of the problem⟩ — **broad·ly** *adv*

¹**broad·cast** \'brȯd-ˌkast\ *vb* **broadcast**; **broadcast·ing** **1** : to scatter far and wide ⟨*broadcast* seed⟩ **2** : to make widely known **3** : to send out by radio or television from a transmitting station ⟨the speech will be *broadcast*⟩ — **broad·cast·er** *n*

²**broadcast** *adv* : so as to spread far and wide

³**broadcast** *n* **1** : an act of broadcasting **2** : the material broadcast by radio or television : a radio or television program

broad·cloth \'brȯd-ˌklȯth\ *n* : a fine cloth with a firm smooth surface

broad·en \'brȯd-n\ *vb* : to make or become broad or broader : WIDEN

broad—mind·ed \'brȯd-ˈmīn-dəd\ *adj*

: willing to consider opinions, beliefs, and practices that are unusual or different from one's own — **broad–mind·ed·ly** *adv* — **broad–mind·ed·ness** *n*

¹**broad·side** \'bród-ˌsīd\ *n* **1** : the part of a ship's side above the waterline **2** : a firing of all of the guns that are on the same side of a ship ⟨fire a *broadside*⟩

²**broadside** *adv* **1** : with one side forward ⟨turned *broadside*⟩ **2** : from the side ⟨hit the other car *broadside*⟩

broad·sword \'bród-ˌsōrd\ *n* : a sword having a broad blade

bro·cade \brō-'kād\ *n* : a cloth with a raised design woven into it

broc·co·li \'bräk-ə-lē, 'bräk-lē\ *n* : an open branching form of cauliflower whose green stalks and clustered flower buds are used as a vegetable

broil \'bróil\ *vb* **1** : to cook or be cooked directly over or under a heat source (as a fire or flame) **2** : to make or be extremely hot ⟨a *broiling* sun⟩

broil·er \'brói-lər\ *n* : a young chicken suitable for broiling

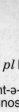

broadsword

¹**broke** \'brōk\ *adj* : having no money

²**broke** *past of* BREAK

bro·ken \'brō-kən\ *adj* **1** : shattered into pieces ⟨*broken* glass⟩ **2** : having gaps or breaks ⟨a *broken* line⟩ **3** : not kept ⟨a *broken* promise⟩ **4** : imperfectly spoken ⟨*broken* English⟩

bro·ken·heart·ed \ˌbrō-kən-'härt-əd\ *adj* : overwhelmed by grief : very sad

bro·ker \'brō-kər\ *n* : a person who acts as an agent for others in the buying or selling of property

bro·mine \'brō-ˌmēn\ *n* : a chemical element that is a deep red liquid giving off an irritating vapor of disagreeable odor

bron·chi·al \'bräng-kē-əl\ *adj* : relating to the branches (**bronchial tubes**) of the windpipe

bron·chi·tis \brän-'kīt-əs\ *n* : a sore raw state of the bronchial tubes

bron·co \'bräng-kō\ *n*, *pl* **bron·cos** : MUSTANG

bron·to·sau·rus \ˌbränt-ə-'sòr-əs\ *n* : any of several very large dinosaurs that probably ate plants

¹**bronze** \'bränz\ *n* **1** : an alloy of copper and tin and sometimes other elements **2** : a yellowish brown color

²**bronze** *vb* **bronzed; bronz·ing** : to make bronze in color

brooch \'brōch, 'brüch\ *n* : an ornamental pin or clasp for the clothing

brooch

¹**brood** \'brüd\ *n* **1** : the young of birds hatched at the same time ⟨a *brood* of chicks⟩ **2** : a group of young children or animals having the same mother

²**brood** *vb* **1** : to sit on eggs to hatch them **2** : to think long and anxiously about something ⟨*brooded* over the mistake⟩

brood·er \'brüd-ər\ *n* **1** : one that broods **2** : a building or a compartment that can be heated and is used for raising young fowl

brook \'brük\ *n* : a small stream — **brook·let** \-lət\ *n*

broom \'brüm, 'brùm\ *n* **1** : a woody plant of the pea family with long slender branches along which grow many drooping yellow flowers **2** : a brush with a long handle used for sweeping

broom·stick \'brüm-ˌstik, 'brùm-\ *n* : the handle of a broom

broth \'bróth\ *n* : the liquid in which a meat, fish, or vegetable has been boiled

broth·er \'brəth-ər\ *n*, *pl* **broth·ers** *also* **breth·ren** \'breth-rən\ **1** : a boy or man related to another person by having the same parents **2** : a fellow member of an organization

broth·er·hood \'brəth-ər-ˌhùd\ *n* **1** : the state of being a brother **2** : an association of people for a particular purpose **3** : those who are engaged in the same business or profession

broth·er–in–law \'brəth-ər-ən-ˌlò\ *n*, *pl* **broth·ers–in–law 1** : the brother of one's husband or wife **2** : the husband of one's sister

broth·er·ly \'brəth-ər-lē\ *adj* **1** : of or relating to brothers **2** : ¹KINDLY 2, AFFECTIONATE

\ə\ abut	\aù\ out	\i\ tip	\ò\ saw	\ù\ foot
\ər\ further	\ch\ chin	\ī\ life	\òi\ coin	\y\ yet
\a\ mat	\e\ pet	\j\ job	\th\ thin	\yü\ few
\ā\ take	\ē\ easy	\ng\ sing	\th\ this	\yù\ cure
\ä\ cot, cart	\g\ go	\ō\ bone	\ü\ food	\zh\ vision

brought *past of* BRING

brow \'braủ\ *n* **1** : EYEBROW **2** : FOREHEAD **3** : the upper edge of a steep slope

¹**brown** \'braủn\ *adj* **1** : of the color brown **2** : having a dark or tanned complexion

²**brown** *n* : a color like that of coffee or chocolate

³**brown** *vb* : to make or become brown

brown·ie \'braủ-nē\ *n* **1** : a cheerful elf believed to perform helpful services at night **2** *cap* : a member of a program of the Girl Scouts for girls in the first through third grades in school **3** : a small rectangle of chewy chocolate cake

brown·ish \'braủ-nish\ *adj* : somewhat brown

browse \'braủz\ *vb* **browsed; brows·ing 1** : to nibble young shoots and foliage ⟨*browsing* cattle⟩ **2** : to read or look over something (as in a book or a store) in a light or careless way

bru·in \'brü-ən\ *n* : ¹BEAR 1

¹**bruise** \'brüz\ *vb* **bruised; bruis·ing** : to injure the flesh (as by a blow) without breaking the skin

²**bruise** *n* : a black-and-blue spot on the body or a dark spot on fruit caused by bruising (as from a blow)

¹**bru·net** *or* **bru·nette** \brü-'net\ *adj* : having dark brown or black hair and dark eyes

²**brunet** *or* **brunette** *n* : someone who is brunet

brunt \'brənt\ *n* : the main force or stress (as of an attack) ⟨the *brunt* of a storm⟩

¹**brush** \'brəsh\ *n* : BRUSHWOOD

²**brush** *n* **1** : a tool made of bristles set in a back or a handle and used for cleaning, smoothing, or painting **2** : a bushy tail ⟨a fox's *brush*⟩ **3** : an act of brushing **4** : a light stroke ⟨a *brush* of the hand⟩

³**brush** *vb* **1** : to scrub or smooth with a brush ⟨*brush* your hair⟩ **2** : to remove with or as if with a brush ⟨*brush* up the dirt⟩ **3** : to pass lightly across ⟨a twig *brushed* my cheek⟩

⁴**brush** *n* : a brief fight or quarrel

brush·wood \'brəsh-,wůd\ *n* **1** : branches and twigs cut from trees **2** : a heavy growth of small trees and bushes

brus·sels sprouts \,brəs-əlz-\ *n pl, often cap B* : green heads like tiny cabbages growing thickly on the stem

brussels sprouts

of a plant of the cabbage family and used as a vegetable

bru·tal \'brüt-l\ *adj* : being cruel and inhuman — **bru·tal·ly** *adv*

bru·tal·i·ty \brü-'tal-ət-ē\ *n, pl* **bru·tal·i·ties 1** : the quality of being brutal **2** : a brutal act or course of action

¹**brute** \'brüt\ *adj* **1** : of or relating to beasts **2** : typical of beasts : like that of a beast ⟨*brute* force⟩

²**brute** *n* **1** : a four-footed animal especially when wild **2** : a brutal person

brut·ish \'brüt-ish\ *adj* : being unfeeling and stupid

¹**bub·ble** \'bəb-əl\ *vb* **bub·bled; bub·bling 1** : to form or produce bubbles **2** : to flow with a gurgle ⟨a *bubbling* brook⟩

²**bubble** *n* **1** : a tiny round body of air or gas in a liquid ⟨*bubbles* in boiling water⟩ **2** : a round body of air within a solid ⟨a *bubble* in glass⟩ **3** : a thin film of liquid filled with air or gas ⟨soap *bubbles*⟩

bu·bon·ic plague \bü-,bän-ik-, byü-\ *n* : a dangerous disease which is spread by rats and in which fever, weakness, and swollen lymph glands are present

buc·ca·neer \,bək-ə-'niər\ *n* : PIRATE

¹**buck** \'bək\ *n* : a male deer or antelope or a male goat, hare, rabbit, or rat

²**buck** *vb* **1** : to spring or jump upward with head down and back arched ⟨a bronco *bucking*⟩ **2** : to charge or push against ⟨*bucking* the waves⟩ **3** : to act in opposition to : OPPOSE ⟨*bucking* the system⟩

buck·board \'bək-,bōrd\ *n* : a lightweight carriage with four wheels that has a seat supported by a springy platform

buckboard

buck·et \'bək-ət\ *n* **1** : PAIL 1 **2** : a container in which something is collected and carried ⟨a coal *bucket*⟩ **3** : the amount a bucket holds

buck·eye \'bək-,ī\ *n* : a horse chestnut or a closely related tree or shrub

¹**buck·le** \'bək-əl\ *n* : a fastening device which is attached to one end of a belt or strap and through which the other end is passed and held

²buckle *vb* **buck·led; buck·ling 1 :** to fasten with a buckle **2 :** to apply oneself earnestly ⟨*buckle* down to business⟩ **3** : to bend, crumple, or give way ⟨the pavement *buckled* in the heat⟩

buck·shot \'bək-ˌshät\ *n* **:** coarse lead shot

buck·skin \'bək-ˌskin\ *n* **:** a soft flexible leather usually having a suede finish

buck·wheat \'bək-ˌhwēt, -ˌwēt\ *n* **:** a plant with pinkish white flowers that is grown for its dark triangular seeds which are used as a cereal grain

¹bud \'bəd\ *n* **1 :** a small growth at the tip or on the side of a stem that later develops into a flower or branch **2 :** a flower that has not fully opened **3 :** a part that grows out from the body of an organism and develops into a new organism ⟨a *bud* on a yeast plant⟩ **4 :** an early stage of development

²bud *vb* **bud·ded; bud·ding 1 :** to form or put forth buds **2 :** to grow or reproduce by buds

bud·dy \'bəd-ē\ *n, pl* **bud·dies :** ¹CHUM

budge \'bəj\ *vb* **budged; budg·ing :** to move or cause to move from one position to another

¹budg·et \'bəj-ət\ *n* **1 :** a statement of estimated income and expenses for a period of time ⟨the government *budget*⟩ **2** : a plan for using money ⟨work out a *budget* so we can buy a car⟩

²budget *vb* **1 :** to include in a budget ⟨*budget* money for food⟩ **2 :** to plan as in a budget ⟨*budget* your time wisely⟩

¹buff \'bəf\ *n* **1 :** an orange yellow **2** : a stick or wheel with a soft surface for applying polishing material

Word History The French made a word from an Italian word that means "buffalo" or "wild ox." The English word *buff* came from this French word and at first meant "buffalo." Later *buff* came to mean "buffalo leather." It was also used to refer to the orange yellow color which is the color of buffalo leather. Still later a stick covered with buffalo leather and used for polishing was also called a *buff*.

²buff *vb* **:** to polish with or as if with a buff

buf·fa·lo \'bəf-ə-ˌlō\ *n, pl* **buffalo** *or* **buf·fa·loes :** any of several wild oxen and especially the American bison

Word History The ancient Greeks had a name for an African gazelle. This name came from the Greek word that meant "a bull or cow." The ancient Romans made a Latin word from the Greek name of the ga-

zelle. This Latin word meant "wild ox." The Spanish made a word that meant "wild ox" from this Latin word, and the Italians did, too. The English word *buffalo* came from these Spanish and Italian words.

buffalo

1buf·fet \'bəf-ət\ *vb* **:** to pound repeatedly : BATTER

²buf·fet \ˌbə-'fā, bü-\ *n* **1 :** a cabinet or set of shelves for the display of dishes and silver : SIDEBOARD **2 :** a meal set out on a buffet or table from which people may serve themselves

bug \'bəg\ *n* **1 :** an insect or other small creeping or crawling animal **2 :** any of a large group of insects that have four wings, suck liquid food (as plant juices or blood), and have young which resemble the adults but lack wings **3 :** FLAW ⟨try to get the *bugs* out of the TV set⟩ **4 :** a person who is enthusiastic about something ⟨I'm a camera *bug*⟩

bug·a·boo \'bəg-ə-ˌbü\ *n, pl* **bug·a·boos :** BUGBEAR

bug·bear \'bəg-ˌbaər, -ˌbeər\ *n* **1 :** an imaginary creature used to frighten children **2 :** something one is afraid of

bug·gy \'bəg-ē\ *n, pl* **bug·gies :** a light carriage with a single seat that is usually drawn by one horse

bu·gle \'byü-gəl\ *n* **:** an instrument like a simple trumpet used chiefly for giving military signals

Word History In early English *bugle* meant "a buffalo." It also meant "a musical instrument made from buffalo horn." The word *bugle* came from an Old French word that had these same meanings. This French word came from a Latin word that meant "a young steer."

\ə\ abut	\aú\ out	\i\ tip	\ȯ\ saw	\ú\ foot
\ər\ further	\ch\ chin	\ī\ life	\ȯi\ coin	\y\ yet
\a\ mat	\e\ pet	\j\ job	\th\ thin	\yü\ few
\ā\ take	\ē\ easy	\ng\ sing	\th\ this	\yú\ cure
\ä\ cot, cart	\g\ go	\ō\ bone	\ü\ food	\zh\ vision

bu·gler \'byü-glər\ *n* : a person who plays a bugle

¹**build** \'bild\ *vb* **built** \'bilt\; **build·ing** **1** : to make by putting together parts or materials **2** : to produce or create gradually by effort ⟨*build* a winning team⟩ **3** : to move toward a peak ⟨excitement was *building* up⟩

synonyms BUILD, CONSTRUCT, and ERECT mean to make a structure. BUILD suggests putting together several parts or materials to form something ⟨*build* a house⟩ CONSTRUCT stresses the designing of something and the process of fitting its parts together ⟨*constructing* a system of dams across the river⟩ ERECT stresses the idea of building something that stands up ⟨*erected* a high tower⟩

²**build** *n* : form or kind of structure : PHYSIQUE

build·er \'bil-dər\ *n* : a person whose business is the construction of buildings

build·ing \'bil-ding\ *n* **1** : a permanent structure built as a dwelling, shelter, or place for human activities or for storage ⟨an office *building*⟩ **2** : the art, work, or business of assembling materials into a structure

built–in \'bil-'tin\ *adj* : forming a permanent part of a structure ⟨*built-in* bookcases⟩

bulb \'bəlb\ *n* **1** : an underground resting form of a plant which consists of a short stem with one or more buds surrounded by thick leaves and from which a new plant can grow **2** : a plant structure (as a corm or tuber) that is somewhat like a bulb **3** : a rounded object or part shaped more or less like a bulb ⟨a lamp *bulb*⟩

**bulb 1: bulbs of (clockwise from top left)
hyacinth, onion, tulip, lily**

bulb·ous \'bəl-bəs\ *adj* **1** : having a bulb **2** : like a bulb in being round and swollen

¹**bulge** \'bəlj\ *n* : a swelling part : a part that sticks out

²**bulge** *vb* **bulged; bulg·ing** : to swell or curve outward ⟨*bulging* muscles⟩

bulk \'bəlk\ *n* **1** : greatness of size or volume ⟨hard to handle because of its *bulk*⟩ **2** : the largest or chief part

bulk·head \'bəlk-,hed\ *n* : a wall separating sections in a ship

bulky \'bəl-kē\ *adj* **bulk·i·er; bulk·i·est 1** : having bulk **2** : being large and awkward to handle

bull \'bul\ *n* : the male of an animal of the ox and cow family and of certain other large animals (as the elephant and the whale)

¹**bull·dog** \'bul-,dog\ *n* : a dog of English origin with short hair and a stocky powerful build

bulldog

²**bulldog** *vb* **bull·dogged; bull·dog·ging** : to throw by seizing the horns and twisting the neck ⟨*bulldog* a steer⟩

bull·doz·er \'bul-,dō-zər\ *n* : a motor vehicle with beltlike tracks that has a broad blade for pushing (as in clearing land of trees)

bul·let \'bul-ət\ *n* : a shaped piece of metal made to be shot from a firearm — **bul·let·proof** \,bul-ət-'prüf\ *adj*

bul·le·tin \'bul-ət-n\ *n* : a short public notice usually coming from an informed or official source

bulletin board *n* : a board for posting bulletins and announcements

bull·fight \'bul-,fit\ *n* : a public entertainment in which people excite bulls, display daring in escaping their charges, and finally kill them — **bull·fight·er** *n*

bull·finch \'bùl-,finch\ *n* : a European songbird that has a thick bill and a red breast and is often kept in a cage

bull·frog \'bùl-,fròg, -,fräg\ *n* : a large heavy frog that makes a booming or bellowing sound

bull·head \'bùl-,hed\ *n* : any of various fishes with large heads

bul·lion \'bùl-yən\ *n* : gold or silver metal in bars or blocks

bull·ock \'bùl-ək\ *n* **1** : a young bull **2** : ¹STEER, OX

bull's—eye \'bùl-,zī\ *n* **1** : the center of a target **2** : a shot that hits the center of a target

¹bul·ly \'bùl-ē\ *n, pl* **bul·lies** : a person who teases, hurts, or threatens smaller or weaker persons

²bully *vb* **bul·lied; bul·ly·ing** : to act like a bully toward

bul·rush \'bùl-,rəsh\ *n* : any of several large rushes or sedges that grow in wet places

bul·wark \'bùl-wərk\ *n* **1** : a solid structure like a wall built for defense against an enemy **2** : something that defends or protects

bum \'bəm\ *n* **1** : a person who avoids work and tries to live off others **2** : ²TRAMP 1, HOBO

bum·ble·bee \'bəm-bəl-,bē\ *n* : a large hairy bee that makes a loud humming sound

¹bump \'bəmp\ *vb* **1** : to strike or knock against something ⟨*bump* into a door⟩ **2** : to move along unevenly : JOLT

²bump *n* **1** : a sudden heavy blow or shock **2** : a rounded swelling of flesh as from a blow **3** : an unevenness in a road surface

¹bump·er \'bəm-pər\ *n* : a bar across the front or back of a motor vehicle intended to lessen the shock or damage from collision

²bumper *adj* : larger or finer than usual

bun \'bən\ *n* : a sweetened roll or biscuit

¹bunch \'bənch\ *n* **1** : a number of things of the same kind growing together ⟨a *bunch* of grapes⟩ **2** : ¹GROUP ⟨a *bunch* of children⟩

²bunch *vb* : to gather in a bunch

¹bun·dle \'bən-dl\ *n* : a number of things fastened or wrapped together : PACKAGE

²bundle *vb* **bun·dled; bun·dling** : to make into a bundle : WRAP

bung \'bəng\ *n* **1** : the stopper in the bunghole of a barrel **2** : BUNGHOLE

bun·ga·low \'bəng-gə-,lō\ *n* : a house with a single story

bung·hole \'bəng-,hōl\ *n* : a hole for emptying or filling a barrel

bun·gle \'bəng-gəl\ *vb* **bun·gled; bun·gling** : to act, do, make, or work badly ⟨*bungled* the job⟩ — **bun·gler** *n*

bun·ion \'bən-yən\ *n* : a sore reddened swelling of the first joint of a big toe

¹bunk \'bəngk\ *n* **1** : a built-in bed **2** : a sleeping place

²bunk *vb* : to share or sleep in a bunk

bun·ny \'bən-ē\ *n, pl* **bun·nies** : RABBIT

¹bunt \'bənt\ *vb* : to strike or push with the horns or head : BUTT

²bunt *n* : ²BUTT, PUSH

¹bun·ting \'bənt-ing\ *n* : any of various birds that are similar to sparrows in size and habits but have stout bills

²bunting *n* **1** : a thin cloth used chiefly for making flags and patriotic decorations **2** : flags or decorations made of bunting

¹buoy \'bü-ē, 'bòi\ *n* **1** : a floating object anchored in a body of water so as to mark a channel or to warn of danger **2** : LIFE BUOY

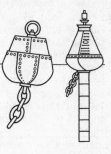

buoy 1

²buoy *vb* **1** : to keep from sinking : keep afloat **2** : to brighten the mood of ⟨*buoyed* by the hope of success⟩

buoy·an·cy \'bòi-ən-sē, 'bü-yən-\ *n* **1** : the power of rising and floating (as on water or in air) ⟨the *buoyancy* of cork in water⟩ **2** : the power of a liquid to hold up a floating body ⟨the *buoyancy* of seawater⟩

buoy·ant \'bòi-ənt, 'bü-yənt\ *adj* **1** : able to rise and float in the air or on the top of a liquid ⟨*buoyant* cork⟩ **2** : able to keep a body afloat **3** : LIGHT-HEARTED, CHEERFUL

bur *or* **burr** \'bər\ *n* **1** : a rough or prickly covering or shell of a seed or fruit **2** : something that is like a bur (as in sticking)

¹bur·den \'bərd-n\ *n* **1** : something carried : LOAD **2** : something that is hard to take ⟨a heavy *burden* of sorrow⟩ **3** : the carrying of loads ⟨beast of *burden*⟩ **4** : the capacity of a ship for carrying cargo

²burden *vb* : to put a burden on

bur·den·some \'bərd-n-səm\ *adj* : so heavy or hard to take as to be a burden

\ə\ **abut**	\aù\ **out**	\i\ **tip**	\ò\ **saw**	\ú\ **foot**	
\ər\ **further**	\ch\ **chin**	\ī\ **life**	\òi\ **coin**	\y\ **yet**	
\a\ **mat**	\e\ **pet**	\j\ **job**	\th\ **thin**	\yü\ **few**	
\ā\ **take**	\ē\ **easy**	\ng\ **sing**	\<u>th</u>\ **this**	\yù\ **cure**	
\ä\ **cot, cart**	\g\ **go**	\ō\ **bone**	\ü\ **food**	\zh\ **vision**	

bur·dock \'bər-ˌdäk\ *n* : a tall coarse weed related to the thistles that has prickly purplish heads of flowers

bu·reau \'byu̇r-ō\ *n* **1** : a low chest of drawers with a mirror for use in a bedroom **2** : a division of a government department ⟨the Weather *Bureau*⟩ **3** : a business office that provides services ⟨a travel *bureau*⟩

bur·glar \'bər-glər\ *n* : a person who is guilty of burglary

bur·glary \'bər-glə-rē\ *n, pl* **bur·glar·ies** : the act of breaking into a building to steal

buri·al \'ber-ē-əl\ *n* : the placing of a dead body in a grave or tomb

bur·lap \'bər-ˌlap\ *n* : a rough cloth made usually from jute or hemp and used mostly for bags and wrappings

bur·ly \'bər-lē\ *adj* **bur·li·er; bur·li·est** : strongly and heavily built — **bur·li·ness** *n*

¹burn \'bərn\ *vb* **burned** \'bərnd\ *or* **burnt** \'bərnt\; **burn·ing 1** : to be on fire or to set on fire **2** : to destroy or be destroyed by fire or heat ⟨*burn* the trash⟩ ⟨a house that *burned* to the ground⟩ **3** : to make or produce by fire or heat ⟨*burn* a hole in a coat⟩ **4** : to give light ⟨a light *burning*⟩ **5** : to injure or affect by or as if by fire or heat ⟨*burned* my finger⟩ **6** : to feel or cause to feel as if on fire ⟨*burn* with anger⟩

²burn *n* : an injury produced by burning

burn·er \'bər-nər\ *n* : the part of a stove or furnace where the flame or heat is produced

bur·nish \'bər-nish\ *vb* : to make shiny

burr *variant of* BUR

bur·ro \'bər-ō\ *n, pl* **bur·ros** : a small donkey often used as a pack animal

¹bur·row \'bər-ō\ *n* : a hole in the ground made by an animal (as a rabbit or fox) for shelter or protection

²burrow *vb* **1** : to hide in or as if in a burrow **2** : to make a burrow **3** : to make one's way by or as if by digging

¹burst \'bərst\ *vb* **burst; burst·ing 1** : to break open or in pieces (as by an explosion from within) ⟨bombs *bursting* in air⟩ ⟨buds *bursting* open⟩ **2** : to suddenly show one's feelings ⟨*burst* into tears⟩ **3** : to come or go suddenly ⟨*burst* into the room⟩ **4** : to be filled to the breaking point ⟨*bursting* with energy⟩

²burst *n* : a sudden release or effort ⟨a *burst* of laughter⟩ ⟨a *burst* of energy⟩

bury \'ber-ē\ *vb* **bur·ied; bury·ing 1** : to put (a dead body) in a grave or tomb **2** : to place in the ground and cover over for concealment ⟨*buried* treasure⟩ **3** : to cover up : HIDE ⟨*buried* my face in my hands⟩

bus \'bəs\ *n, pl* **bus·es** *or* **bus·ses** : a large motor vehicle for carrying passengers

bush \'bu̇sh\ *n* **1** : a usually low shrub with many branches **2** : a stretch of uncleared or lightly settled country

bush·el \'bu̇sh-əl\ *n* **1** : a unit of dry capacity equal to four pecks or thirty-two quarts (about thirty-five liters) **2** : a container holding a bushel

bushy \'bu̇sh-ē\ *adj* **bush·i·er; bush·i·est 1** : overgrown with bushes **2** : being thick and spreading ⟨a *bushy* beard⟩

busi·ness \'biz-nəs\ *n* **1** : the normal activity of a person or group ⟨learning is the *business* of a student⟩ **2** : a commercial enterprise ⟨opened a new *business*⟩ **3** : the making, buying, and selling of goods or services **4** : personal concerns ⟨none of your *business*⟩ **synonyms** see TRADE

busi·ness·man \'biz-nəs-ˌman\ *n, pl* **busi·ness·men** \-ˌmen\ : a man in business especially as an owner or a manager

busi·ness·wom·an \'biz-nə-ˌswu̇m-ən\ *n, pl* **busi·ness·wom·en** \-ˌswim-ən\ : a woman in business especially as an owner or a manager

¹bust \'bəst\ *n* **1** : a piece of sculpture representing the upper part of the human figure including the head and neck **2** : a woman's bosom

²bust *vb* **1** : to hit with the fist **2** : ¹BREAK 1

¹bus·tle \'bəs-əl\ *vb* **bus·tled; bus·tling** : to move about in a fussy or noisy way

²bustle *n* : fussy or noisy activity

¹busy \'biz-ē\ *adj* **busi·er; busi·est 1** : actively at work **2** : being used ⟨the line is *busy*⟩ **3** : full of activity ⟨a *busy* day⟩ — **busi·ly** \'biz-ə-lē\ *adv*

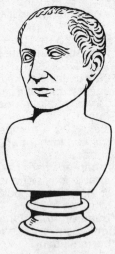

bust 1

²busy *vb* **bus·ied; busy·ing** : to make busy ⟨*busy* oneself with chores⟩

busy·body \'biz-ē-ˌbäd-ē\ *n, pl* **busy·bod·ies** : a person who meddles in the affairs of others

¹but \bət\ *conj* **1** : except that : UNLESS ⟨never rains *but* it pours⟩ **2** : while just the opposite ⟨I ski *but* you don't⟩ **3** : yet nevertheless ⟨fell *but* wasn't hurt⟩

²but *prep* : other than : EXCEPT ⟨everyone *but* you⟩

³but *adv* : ²ONLY 1 ⟨we have *but* one choice⟩

¹butch·er \'bùch-ər\ *n* 1 : one whose business is killing animals for sale as food 2 : a dealer in meat 3 : a person who kills in large numbers or in a brutal manner

²butcher *vb* 1 : to kill and dress (an animal) for food 2 : ¹MASSACRE 3 : to make a mess of : BOTCH

but·ler \'bət-lər\ *n* : the chief male servant of a household

¹butt \'bət\ *vb* : to strike or thrust with the head or horns

²butt *n* : a blow or thrust with the head or horns

³butt *n* : a person who is treated badly or made fun of ⟨made the *butt* of the joke⟩

⁴butt *n* 1 : the thicker or bottom end of something ⟨the *butt* of a rifle⟩ 2 : an unused remainder ⟨a cigarette *butt*⟩

butte \'byüt\ *n* : an isolated hill with steep sides

¹but·ter \'bət-ər\ *n* 1 : a solid yellowish fatty food obtained from cream or milk by churning 2 : a substance that is like butter in texture and use ⟨apple *butter*⟩⟨peanut *butter*⟩

²butter *vb* : to spread with or as if with butter

but·ter·cup \'bət-ər-ˌkəp\ *n* : a common wild flower with bright yellow blossoms

buttercup

but·ter·fat \'bət-ər-ˌfat\ *n* : the natural fat of milk that is the chief ingredient of butter

but·ter·fly \'bət-ər-ˌflī\ *n, pl* **but·ter·flies** : an insect that has a slender body and large colored wings covered with tiny overlapping scales and that flies mostly in the day-time

butterfly

but·ter·milk \'bət-ər-ˌmilk\ *n* : the liquid left after churning butter from milk or cream

but·ter·nut \'bət-ər-ˌnət\ *n* : an oily nut produced by an American tree related to the walnuts

but·ter·scotch \'bət-ər-ˌskäch\ *n* : a candy made from sugar, corn syrup, and water

but·tock \'bət-ək\ *n* 1 : the back of the hip which forms one of the rounded parts on which a person sits 2 **buttocks** *pl* : RUMP 1

¹but·ton \'bət-n\ *n* 1 : a small ball or disk used for holding parts of a garment together or as an ornament 2 : something that suggests a button ⟨push the light *button*⟩

²button *vb* : to close or fasten with buttons

but·ton·hole \'bət-n-ˌhōl\ *n* : a slit or loop for fastening a button

but·ton·wood \'bət-n-ˌwùd\ *n* : SYCAMORE 2

¹but·tress \'bə-trəs\ *n* 1 : a structure built against a wall or building to give support and strength 2 : something that supports, props, or strengthens

²buttress *vb* : to support with or as if with a buttress

buttress 1

bux·om \'bək-səm\ *adj* : having a healthy plump form

¹buy \'bī\ *vb* **bought** \'bòt\; **buy·ing** : to get by paying for : PURCHASE — **buy·er** *n*

²buy *n* : ¹BARGAIN 2

¹buzz \'bəz\ *vb* 1 : to make a low humming sound like that of bees 2 : to be filled with a low hum or murmur ⟨a room that *buzzed* with excitement⟩ 3 : to fly an airplane low over

²buzz *n* : a sound of buzzing

buz·zard \'bəz-ərd\ *n* : a usually large bird of prey that flies slowly

buzz·er \'bəz-ər\ *n* : an electric signaling device that makes a buzzing sound

¹by \'bī\ *prep* 1 : close to : NEAR ⟨stood *by* the door⟩ 2 : so as to go on ⟨went *by* the back road⟩⟨travel *by* bus⟩ 3 : so as to go through ⟨left *by* the back window⟩ 4 : so as to pass ⟨drove *by* the house⟩ 5 : AT 1, DURING ⟨travel *by* night⟩ 6 : no later than ⟨leave *by* noon⟩ 7 : with the use or help of ⟨won *by* cheating⟩ 8 : through the action of ⟨was seen *by* the others⟩ 9 : ACCORDING TO ⟨play *by* the rules⟩ 10 : with respect to ⟨a lawyer *by* profession⟩⟨a Canadian *by* birth⟩ 11 : to the amount of ⟨won *by* a mile⟩ 12 — used to join two or more measurements ⟨a room 4 meters wide *by* 6 meters long⟩ or to join the numbers in a

\ə\ **abut**	\aù\ **out**	\i\ **tip**	\ò\ **saw**	\ù\ **foot**
\ər\ **further**	\ch\ **chin**	\ī\ **life**	\òi\ **coin**	\y\ **yet**
\a\ **mat**	\e\ **pet**	\j\ **job**	\th\ **thin**	\yü\ **few**
\ā\ **take**	\ē\ **easy**	\ng\ **sing**	\th\ **this**	\yù\ **cure**
\ä\ **cot, cart**	\g\ **go**	\ō\ **bone**	\ü\ **food**	\zh\ **vision**

statement of multiplication or division ⟨divide 8 *by* 4⟩

²by *adv* **1** : near at hand ⟨stand *by*⟩ **2** : ⁴PAST ⟨walk *by*⟩ ⟨in days gone *by*⟩

by–and–by \ˌbī-ən-'bī\ *n* : a future time

by and by \ˌbī-ən-'bī\ *adv* : after a while

by•gone \'bī-ˌgȯn\ *adj* : gone by : PAST

by•gones \'bī-ˌgȯnz\ *n pl* : events that are over and done with ⟨let *bygones* be *bygones*⟩

¹by•pass \'bī-ˌpas\ *n* **1** : a way for passing to one side **2** : a road serving as a substitute route around a crowded area

²bypass *vb* : to make a detour around

by–prod•uct \'bī-ˌpräd-əkt\ *n* : something produced (as in manufacturing) in addition to the main product

by•stand•er \'bī-ˌstan-dər\ *n* : a person present or standing near but taking no part in what is going on

by•way \'bī-ˌwā\ *n* : a less traveled road off a main highway

c \'sē\ *n*, *pl* **c's** *or* **cs** \'sēz\ *often cap* **1** : the third letter of the English alphabet **2** : 100 in Roman numerals **3** : a grade that shows a student's work is fair

cab \'kab\ *n* **1** : a light closed carriage pulled by a horse **2** : TAXICAB **3** : the covered compartment for the engineer and the controls of a locomotive or for the operator of a truck, tractor, or crane

ca•bana \kə-'ban-ə, -yə\ *n* : a shelter usually with an open side facing the sea or a swimming pool

cab•bage \'kab-ij\ *n* : a garden plant related to the turnips that has a firm head of leaves used as a vegetable

cab•in \'kab-ən\ *n* **1** : a private room on a ship **2** : a place below deck on a small boat for passengers or crew **3** : a part of an airplane for cargo, crew, or passengers **4** : a small simple dwelling usually having only one story

cab•i•net \'kab-ə-nət, 'kab-nət\ *n* **1** : a case or cupboard with shelves or drawers for keeping or displaying articles ⟨filing *cabinet*⟩ **2** : a group of persons who act as advisers (as to the head of a country) ⟨a meeting of the president and the *cabinet*⟩

¹ca•ble \'kā-bəl\ *n* **1** : a very strong rope, wire, or chain **2** : a bundle of wires to carry electric current **3** : CABLEGRAM

²cable *vb* **ca•bled; ca•bling** : to telegraph by underwater cable

ca•ble•gram \'kā-bəl-ˌgram\ *n* : a message sent by underwater cable

ca•boose \kə-'büs\ *n* : a car usually at the rear of a freight train for the use of the train crew and railroad workers

ca•cao \kə-'kau̇, kə-'kā-ō\ *n*, *pl* **ca•caos** : a South American tree with fleshy yellow pods that contain fatty seeds from which chocolate is made

¹cache \'kash\ *n* **1** : a place for hiding, storing, or preserving treasure or supplies **2** : something hidden or stored in a cache

²cache *vb* **cached; cach•ing** : to place, hide, or store in a cache

¹cack•le \'kak-əl\ *vb* **cack•led; cack•ling** **1** : to make the sharp broken noise or cry a hen makes especially after laying an egg **2** : to laugh or chatter noisily

²cackle *n* : a cackling sound

cac•tus \'kak-təs\ *n*, *pl* **cac•tus•es** *or* **cac•ti** \-ˌtī, -tē\ : any of a large group of flowering plants of dry regions that have thick juicy stems and branches with scales or prickles

¹cad•die *or* **cad•dy** \'kad-ē\ *n*, *pl* **cad•dies** : a person who carries a golfer's clubs

²caddie *or* **caddy** *vb* **cad•died; cad•dy•ing** : to work as a caddie

cad•dis fly \'kad-əs-\ *n* : an insect that has four wings and a larva (**caddisworm** *or* **caddis**) which lives in water in a silk case covered with bits of wood or gravel and is often used for fish bait

ca•dence \'kād-ns\ *n* : the beat of rhythmic motion or sound (as of marching) : RHYTHM

ca•det \kə-'det\ *n* : a student in a military school or college

ca•fé *also* **ca•fe** \ka-'fā, kə-\ *n* **1** : ¹BAR 9 **2** : RESTAURANT **3** : NIGHTCLUB

caf•e•te•ria \ˌkaf-ə-'tir-ē-ə\ *n* : a restaurant where the customers serve themselves or are served at a counter but carry their own food to their tables

caf·feine \ka-'fēn, 'ka-ˌfēn\ *n* : a stimulating substance in coffee and tea

¹cage \'kāj\ *n* **1** : a box or enclosure that has large openings covered usually with wire net or bars and is used to confine or carry birds or animals **2** : an enclosure like a cage in shape or purpose

²cage *vb* **caged; cag·ing** : to put or keep in or as if in a cage

ca·gey \'kā-jē\ *adj* **ca·gi·er; ca·gi·est** : hard to trap or trick

cais·son \'kā-ˌsän\ *n* **1** : a chest for ammunition usually set on two wheels **2** : a watertight box or chamber used for doing construction work under water or used as a foundation

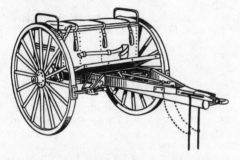

caisson 1

ca·jole \kə-'jōl\ *vb* **ca·joled; ca·jol·ing** : to coax or persuade especially by flattery or false promises : WHEEDLE

Word History The English word *cajole* came from a French word meaning "to chatter like a bird in a cage." This modern French word came in turn from an earlier French word that meant "bird cage." The French word that means "bird cage" came from a Latin word that meant "little cage." The English word *cave* is also related to this Latin word.

¹cake \'kāk\ *n* **1** : a small piece of food (as dough or batter, meat, or fish) that is baked or fried **2** : a baked food made from a sweet batter or dough **3** : a substance hardened or molded into a solid piece ⟨a *cake* of soap⟩

²cake *vb* **caked; cak·ing 1** : ENCRUST **2** : to form or harden into a cake

ca·lam·i·ty \kə-'lam-ət-ē\ *n, pl* **ca·lam·i·ties 1** : great distress or misfortune **2** : an event that causes great harm

cal·ci·um \'kal-sē-əm\ *n* : a silvery soft metallic chemical element that is an essential for most plants and animals

calcium carbonate *n* : a solid substance that is found as limestone and marble and in plant ashes, bones, and shells

cal·cu·late \'kal-kyə-ˌlāt\ *vb* **cal·cu·lat·ed; cal·cu·lat·ing 1** : to find by adding, subtracting, multiplying, or dividing : COMPUTE **2** : ¹ESTIMATE 1 **3** : to plan by careful thought

Word History The English word *calculate* came from a Latin word that meant "to figure" or "to compute." Long ago pebbles were sometimes used in figuring. The Latin word that meant "to figure" came from another Latin word that meant "pebble."

cal·cu·la·tion \ˌkal-kyə-'lā-shən\ *n* **1** : the process or an act of calculating **2** : the result obtained by calculating

cal·cu·la·tor \'kal-kyə-ˌlāt-ər\ *n* **1** : a person who calculates **2** : a usually small electronic device for solving mathematical problems

cal·cu·lus \'kal-kyə-ləs\ *n* : TARTAR 2

cal·dron *also* **caul·dron** \'kȯl-drən\ *n* : a large kettle

cal·en·dar \'kal-ən-dər\ *n* **1** : a chart showing the days, weeks, and months of the year **2** : a schedule of coming events ⟨a church *calendar*⟩

¹calf \'kaf, 'kȧf\ *n, pl* **calves** \'kavz, 'kȧvz\ **1** : the young of the cow **2** : the young of various large animals (as the elephant, moose, or whale) **3** *pl* **calfs** : CALFSKIN

²calf *n, pl* **calves** : the muscular back part of the leg below the knee

calf·skin \'kaf-ˌskin, 'kȧf-\ *n* : the skin of a calf or the leather made from it

cal·i·ber *or* **cal·i·bre** \'kal-ə-bər\ *n* **1** : the diameter of a bullet **2** : the diameter of the hole in the barrel of a gun

¹cal·i·co \'kal-i-ˌkō\ *n, pl* **cal·i·coes** *or* **cal·i·cos** : cotton cloth especially with a colored pattern printed on one side

²calico *adj* : marked with blotches of color ⟨a *calico* cat⟩

cal·i·per *or* **cal·li·per** \'kal-ə-pər\ *n* : an instrument with two adjustable legs used to measure the thickness of objects or the distance between surfaces — usually used in pl. ⟨a pair of *calipers*⟩

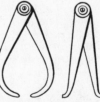

caliper

\ə\ abut	\au̇\ out	\i\ tip	\ȯ\ saw	\u̇\ foot
\ər\ further	\ch\ chin	\ī\ life	\ȯi\ coin	\y\ yet
\a\ mat	\e\ pet	\j\ job	\th\ thin	\yü\ few
\ā\ take	\ē\ easy	\ng\ sing	\th\ this	\yu̇\ cure
\ä\ cot, cart	\g\ go	\ō\ bone	\ü\ food	\zh\ vision

ca·liph *or* **ca·lif** \ˈkā-ləf\ *n* : an important official in some Arab countries

cal·is·then·ics \ˌkal-əs-ˈthen-iks\ *n sing or pl* : exercise to develop strength and grace that is done without special equipment

¹calk \ˈkȯk\ *variant of* CAULK

²calk *or* **caulk** *n* : a tapered piece extending downward from a shoe (as of a horse) to prevent slipping

³calk *or* **caulk** *vb* : to provide with calks

¹call \ˈkȯl\ *vb* **1** : to speak in a loud clear voice so as to be heard at a distance : SHOUT ⟨*call* for help⟩ **2** : to say in a loud clear voice ⟨*call* an order to a worker⟩ **3** : ⟨*call* a halt⟩ **4** : SUMMON 1, 2 ⟨*call* children from play⟩ **5** : to bring into action or discussion ⟨*call* up reserves⟩ **6** : to make a request or demand ⟨*call* for an investigation⟩ **7** : to get in touch with by telephone **8** : to make a short visit ⟨*call* on a neighbor⟩ **9** : ²NAME 1 ⟨*called* the cat "Patches"⟩ **10** : to estimate as ⟨*call* it an even dollar⟩ — **call for** : to require as necessary or suitable ⟨we'll do whatever is *called for*⟩

²call *n* **1** : a loud shout or cry **2** : a cry of an animal **3** : a request or command to come or assemble **4** : ¹DEMAND 1, CLAIM **5** : ¹REQUEST 1 ⟨many *calls* for mystery books⟩ **6** : a short visit ⟨a neighborly *call*⟩ **7** : a name or thing called **8** : the act of calling on the telephone

call down *vb* : ²REPRIMAND

call·er \ˈkȯ-lər\ *n* : one who calls **synonyms** see VISITOR

call·ing \ˈkȯ-ling\ *n* : OCCUPATION 1, PROFESSION

cal·li·o·pe \kə-ˈlī-ə-pē\ *n* : a keyboard musical instrument consisting of a set of steam whistles

calliper *variant of* CALIPER

cal·lous \ˈkal-əs\ *adj* **1** : having a callus **2** : feeling no sympathy for others

cal·lus \ˈkal-əs\ *n* : a hard thickened spot (as of skin)

¹calm \ˈkäm, ˈkälm\ *n* **1** : a period or condition of freedom from storm, wind, or rough water **2** : a peaceful state : QUIET

²calm *adj* **1** : not stormy or windy : STILL ⟨a *calm* night⟩ **2** : not excited or angry ⟨a *calm* reply⟩ — **calm·ly** *adv* — **calm·ness** *n*

synonyms CALM, PEACEFUL, and TRANQUIL mean quiet and free from disturbance. CALM suggests that one is free from disturbance even when there is cause for excitement ⟨stayed *calm* even during the fire⟩ PEACEFUL suggests that one has reached a quiet state after some period of disturbance ⟨the storm is over and the lake is *peaceful* again⟩ TRANQUIL suggests a total or lasting state of rest ⟨a *tranquil* village in the mountains⟩

³calm *vb* : to make or become calm

cal·o·rie \ˈkal-ə-rē, ˈkal-rē\ *n* **1** : a unit for measuring heat equal to the heat required to raise the temperature of one gram of water one degree Celsius **2** : a unit equal to 1000 calories — used especially to indicate the value of foods for producing heat and energy in the human body

calve \ˈkav, ˈkàv\ *vb* **calved; calv·ing** : to give birth to a calf

calves *pl of* CALF

ca·lyp·so \kə-ˈlip-sō\ *n, pl* **ca·lyp·sos** : a folk song or style of singing of the West Indies

ca·lyx \ˈkā-liks\ *n, pl* **ca·lyx·es** *or* **ca·ly·ces** \-lə-ˌsēz\ : the outer usually green or leafy part of a flower

cam \ˈkam\ *n* : a device (as a tooth on a wheel) by which circular motion is changed to back-and-forth motion

cam·bi·um \ˈkam-bē-əm\ *n, pl* **cam·bi·ums** *or* **cam·bia** \-bē-ə\ : soft tissue in woody plants from which new wood and bark grow

came *past of* COME

cam·el \ˈkam-əl\ *n* : a large hoofed animal that chews the cud and is used in the deserts of Asia and Africa for carrying burdens and for riding

camel

cam·era \ˈkam-ə-rə, ˈkam-rə\ *n* **1** : a box that has a lens on one side to let the light in and is used for taking pictures **2** : the part of a television sending device in which the image to be sent out is formed

¹cam·ou·flage \ˈkam-ə-ˌfläzh, -ˌfläj\ *n* **1** : the hiding or disguising of something by covering it up or changing the way it looks

2 : the material (as paint or branches) used for camouflage

²camouflage *vb* **cam·ou·flaged; cam·ou·flag·ing** : to hide or disguise by camouflage

¹camp \'kamp\ *n* **1** : a place where temporary shelters are erected **2** : a place usually in the country for recreation or instruction during the summer **3** : a group of people in a camp

²camp *vb* **1** : to make or occupy a camp **2** : to live in a camp or outdoors — **camp·er** *n*

¹cam·paign \kam-'pān\ *n* **1** : a series of military operations in a certain area or for a certain purpose ⟨the Italian *campaign*⟩ **2** : a series of activities meant to get a certain thing done ⟨the election *campaign*⟩

²campaign *vb* : to take part in a campaign — **campaign·er** *n*

Camp Fire Girl *n* : a member of a national organization for girls from seven to eighteen

cam·phor \'kam-fər\ *n* : a white fragrant solid that comes from the wood and bark of a tall Asian tree (**camphor tree**) and is used mostly in medicine and in making plastics

cam·pus \'kam-pəs\ *n* : the grounds and buildings of a university, college, or school

¹can \kən, kan\ *helping verb, past* **could** \kəd, kud\; *present sing & pl* **can 1** : know how to ⟨we *can* read⟩ **2** : be able to ⟨I *can* hear you⟩ **3** : be permitted by conscience to ⟨they *can* hardly blame me⟩ **4** : have permission to : MAY ⟨you *can* go now⟩

²can \'kan\ *n* **1** : a usually cylindrical metal container ⟨garbage *can*⟩ **2** : the contents of a can ⟨a *can* of tomatoes⟩

³can \'kan\ *vb* **canned; can·ning** : to keep fit for later use by sealing (as in an airtight jar) ⟨*can* peaches for winter⟩

¹Ca·na·di·an \kə-'nād-ē-ən\ *adj* : of or relating to Canada or the Canadians

²Canadian *n* : a person born or living in Canada

ca·nal \kə-'nal\ *n* **1** : an artificial waterway for boats or for irrigation of land **2** : a tubelike passage in the body

ca·nary \kə-'neər-ē\ *n, pl* **ca·nar·ies** : a small usually yellow songbird often kept in a cage

Word History Long ago explorers from Africa went to a group of islands off the northern coast. On the islands they found great numbers of very large dogs. The Romans read about the dogs and gave the islands a Latin name that meant "dog islands." The English name *Canary Islands* came from the Latin name. In the sixteenth century small birds from the Canary Islands were sold in Europe. In England they were called *canary birds*. Later the name for these ancestors of our canaries was shortened to *canary*.

can·cel \'kan-səl\ *vb* **can·celed** *or* **cancelled; can·cel·ing** *or* **can·cel·ling 1** : to cross out or strike out with a line : DELETE ⟨*cancel* what has been written⟩ **2** : to take back : WITHDRAW ⟨*canceled* the invitation⟩ **3** : to equal in force or effect : OFFSET **4** : to remove (a common divisor) from numerator and denominator : remove (equivalents) on opposite sides of an equation or account **5** : to mark (as a postage stamp) so as to make impossible to use again

can·cel·la·tion \ˌkan-sə-'lā-shən\ *n* **1** : an act of canceling ⟨*cancellation* of a game⟩ **2** : a mark made to cancel something

can·cer \'kan-sər\ *n* **1** : a harmful growth on or in the body that may keep spreading and be fatal if not treated **2** : a condition of the body characterized by a cancer or cancers

can·de·la·bra \ˌkan-də-'lä-brə, -'lab-rə\ *n* : CANDELABRUM

can·de·la·brum \ˌkan-də-'lä-brəm, -'lab-rəm\ *n, pl* **can·de·la·bra** \-'lä-brə, -'lab-rə\ *also* **can·de·la·brums** : a candlestick that has several branches for holding candles

can·did \'kan-dəd\ *adj* **1** : FRANK, STRAIGHTFORWARD **2** : relating to photography of people acting naturally without being posed — **can·did·ly** *adv* — **can·did·ness** *n*

candelabrum

can·di·da·cy \'kan-də-də-sē\ *n, pl* **can·di·da·cies** : the state of being a candidate

can·di·date \'kan-də-ˌdāt\ *n* : a person who runs for or is nominated by others for an office or honor

Word History Men who ran for public office in ancient Rome wore white togas.

\ə\ abut	\aú\ out	\i\ tip	\ȯ\ saw	\ú\ foot
\ər\ further	\ch\ chin	\ī\ life	\ȯi\ coin	\y\ yet
\a\ mat	\e\ pet	\j\ job	\th\ thin	\yü\ few
\ā\ take	\ē\ easy	\ng\ sing	\th\ this	\yu̇\ cure
\ä\ cot, cart	\g\ go	\ō\ bone	\ü\ food	\zh\ vision

The Latin word for such a man meant "one dressed in white" and came from another Latin word that meant "white." The English word *candidate* came from the Latin word meaning "one dressed in white."

can·died \'kan-dēd\ *adj* : preserved in or coated with sugar ⟨*candied* ginger⟩

¹can·dle \'kan-dl\ *n* : a stick of tallow or wax containing a wick and burned to give light

²candle *vb* **can·dled; can·dling** : to examine (as eggs) by holding between the eye and a light — **can·dler** *n*

can·dle·light \'kan-dl-ˌlīt\ *n* **1** : the light of a candle **2** : a soft artificial light

can·dle·stick \'kan-dl-ˌstik\ *n* : a holder for a candle

can·dor \'kan-dər\ *n* : sincere and honest expression

¹can·dy \'kan-dē\ *n, pl* **can·dies** : a sweet made of sugar often with flavoring and filling

²candy *vb* **can·died; can·dy·ing** **1** : to coat or become coated with sugar often by cooking **2** : to crystallize into sugar

¹cane \'kān\ *n* **1** : an often hollow, slender, and somewhat flexible plant stem **2** : a tall woody grass or reed (as sugarcane) **3** : WALKING STICK 1 **4** : a rod for beating

²cane *vb* **caned; can·ing** **1** : to beat with a cane **2** : to make or repair with cane ⟨*cane* a chair seat⟩

¹ca·nine \'kā-ˌnīn\ *adj* **1** : of or relating to the dogs or to the group of animals (as wolves) to which the dog belongs **2** : like or typical of a dog

²canine *n* **1** : a pointed tooth next to the incisors **2** : a canine animal

can·is·ter \'kan-əs-tər\ *n* : a small box or can for holding a dry product

can·nery \'kan-ə-rē\ *n, pl* **can·ner·ies** : a factory where foods are canned

can·ni·bal \'kan-ə-bəl\ *n* **1** : a human being who eats human flesh **2** : an animal that eats other animals of its own kind

can·non \'kan-ən\ *n, pl* **can·nons** *or* **cannon** **1** : a heavy gun mounted on a carriage **2** : an automatic gun of heavy caliber on an airplane

can·non·ball \'kan-ən-ˌbȯl\ *n* : a usually round solid missile for firing from a cannon

can·not \'kan-ˌät, kə-ˈnät\ : can not

can·ny \'kan-ē\ *adj* **can·ni·er; can·ni·est** : watchful of one's own interest — **can·ni·ly** \'kan-l-ē\ *adv*

¹ca·noe \kə-ˈnü\ *n* : a long light narrow boat with sharp ends and curved sides usually driven by paddles

²canoe *vb* **ca·noed; ca·noe·ing** : to

canoe

travel or carry in a canoe — **ca·noe·ist** \-ˈnü-əst\ *n*

can·on \'kan-ən\ *n* **1** : a rule or law of a church **2** : an accepted rule ⟨the *canons* of good taste⟩

can·o·py \'kan-ə-pē\ *n, pl* **can·o·pies** **1** : a covering fixed over a bed or throne or carried on poles (as over a person of high rank) **2** : something that hangs over and shades or shelters something else

can't \kant, kȧnt, känt, kānt\ : can not

can·ta·loupe \'kant-l-ˌōp\ *n* : a muskmelon usually with a hard ridged or rough skin and reddish orange flesh

canopy

can·tan·ker·ous \kan-ˈtang-kə-rəs\ *adj* : QUARRELSOME

can·ta·ta \kən-ˈtät-ə\ *n* : a poem or story set to music to be sung by a chorus and soloists

can·teen \kan-ˈtēn\ *n* **1** : a store (as in a camp or factory) in which food, drinks, and small supplies are sold **2** : a place of recreation for people in military service **3** : a small container for carrying liquid (as drinking water)

can·ter \'kant-ər\ *n* : a horse's gait like but slower than the gallop

can·ti·le·ver \'kant-l-ˌē-vər, -ˌev-ər\ *n* **1** : a beam or similar structure fastened (as by being built into a wall) only at one end **2** : either of two structures that extend from piers toward each other and when joined form a span in a bridge (**cantilever bridge**)

can·to \'kan-ˌtō\ *n, pl* **can·tos** : one of the major divisions of a long poem

can·ton \'kant-n, 'kan-ˌtän\ *n* : a division of a country (as Switzerland)

can·tor \'kant-ər\ *n* : a synagogue official

who sings religious music and leads the congregation in prayer

can·vas \'kan-vəs\ *n* **1** : a strong cloth of hemp, flax, or cotton that is used sometimes for making tents and sails and as the material on which oil paintings are made **2** : something made of canvas or on canvas

can·vas·back \'kan-vəs-ˌbak\ *n* : a North American wild duck with reddish head and grayish back

¹**can·vass** \'kan-vəs\ *vb* : to go through (a district) or go to (people) to ask for votes, contributions, or orders for goods or to determine public opinion — **can·vass·er** *n*

²**canvass** *n* : an act of canvassing

can·yon \'kan-yən\ *n* : a deep valley with high steep slopes

¹**cap** \'kap\ *n* **1** : a head covering that has a visor and no brim **2** : something that serves as a cover or protection for something ⟨a bottle *cap*⟩ **3** : a paper or metal container holding an explosive charge ⟨a toy pistol for shooting *caps*⟩

²**cap** *vb* **capped; cap·ping 1** : to cover or provide with a cap ⟨*cap* a bottle⟩ **2** : to match with something equal or better

ca·pa·bil·i·ty \ˌkā-pə-'bil-ət-ē\ *n*, *pl* **ca·pa·bil·i·ties** : the quality or state of being capable

ca·pa·ble \'kā-pə-bəl\ *adj* **1** : having the qualities (as ability, power, or strength) needed to do or accomplish something ⟨you are *capable* of better work⟩ **2** : able to do one's job well : EFFICIENT ⟨a very *capable* teacher⟩ **synonyms** see ABLE — **ca·pa·bly** \-blē\ *adv*

ca·pa·cious \kə-'pā-shəs\ *adj* : able to hold a great deal ⟨a *capacious* pocket⟩

ca·pac·i·ty \kə-'pas-ət-ē\ *n*, *pl* **ca·pac·i·ties 1** : ability to contain or deal with something ⟨the seating *capacity* of a room⟩ ⟨factories working to the limit of their *capacity*⟩ **2** : mental or physical power ⟨you have the *capacity* to do better⟩ **3** : VOLUME 3 ⟨a tank of twenty-gallon *capacity*⟩ **4** : ROLE 1, STATUS ⟨in your *capacity* of student⟩

¹**ca·par·i·son** \kə-'par-ə-sən\ *n* **1** : an ornamental covering for a horse **2** : rich clothing and ornaments worn by a person

²**caparison** *vb* : to adorn with rich and beautiful clothing

¹**cape** \'kāp\ *n* : a point of land that juts out into the sea or into a lake

²**cape** *n* : a sleeveless garment worn so as to hang over the shoulders, arms, and back

¹**ca·per** \'kā-pər\ *vb* : to leap about in a lively way

²**caper** *n* **1** : a gay bounding leap or spring **2** : a playful or mischievous trick **3** : an illegal or questionable act

¹**cap·il·lary** \'kap-ə-ˌler-ē\ *adj* **1** : having a long slender form and a small inner diameter ⟨a *capillary* tube⟩ **2** : being the action by which the surface of a liquid where it is in contact with a solid (as in a capillary tube) is raised or lowered **3** : or or relating to a capillary

²**capillary** *n*, *pl* **cap·il·lar·ies** : one of the slender hairlike tubes that are the smallest blood vessels and connect arteries with veins

¹**cap·i·tal** \'kap-ət-l, 'kap-tl\ *adj* **1** : punishable by or resulting in death ⟨a *capital* crime⟩ ⟨*capital* punishment⟩ **2** : being like the letters A, B, C, etc. rather than a, b, c, etc. ⟨*capital* letters⟩ **3** : being the location of a government ⟨the *capital* city of a state⟩ **4** : of or relating to capital **5** : EXCELLENT ⟨a *capital* idea⟩

²**capital** *n* **1** : accumulated wealth especially as used to produce more wealth **2** : persons holding capital **3** : profitable use ⟨they made *capital* out of my weakness⟩ **4** : a capital letter ⟨begin each sentence with a *capital*⟩ **5** : a capital city ⟨name the *capital* of North Dakota⟩

³**capital** *n* : the top part of an architectural column

capital

cap·i·tal·ism \'kap-ət-l-ˌiz-əm\ *n* : a system under which the ownership of land and wealth is for the most part in the hands of private individuals

¹**cap·i·tal·ist** \'kap-ət-l-əst\ *n* **1** : a person who has capital and especially business capital **2** : a person who favors capitalism

²**capitalist** *adj* **1** : owning capital **2** : CAPITALISTIC

cap·i·tal·is·tic \ˌkap-ət-l-'is-tik\ *adj* **1** : practicing or favoring capitalism **2** : of or

\ə\ abut	\aů\ out	\i\ tip	\ȯ\ saw	\ů\ foot
\ər\ further	\ch\ chin	\ī\ life	\ȯi\ coin	\y\ yet
\a\ mat	\e\ pet	\j\ job	\th\ thin	\yü\ few
\ā\ take	\ē\ easy	\ng\ sing	\th\ this	\yů\ cure
\ä\ cot, cart	\g\ go	\ō\ bone	\ü\ food	\zh\ vision

relating to capitalism or capitalists — **cap·i·tal·is·ti·cal·ly** \-ti-kə-lē\ *adv*

cap·i·tal·iza·tion \ˌkap-ət-l-ə-ˈzā-shən\ *n* **1** : the act or process of capitalizing **2** : the amount of money used as capital in business

cap·i·tal·ize \ˈkap-ət-l-ˌīz\ *vb* **cap·i·tal·ized; cap·i·tal·iz·ing** **1** : to write with a beginning capital letter or in capital letters **2** : to use as capital (as in a business) : furnish capital for (a business) **3** : to gain by turning something to advantage ⟨*capitalize* on another's mistakes⟩

cap·i·tol \ˈkap-ət-l, ˈkap-tl\ *n* **1** : the building in which a state legislature meets **2** *cap* : the building in Washington in which the United States Congress meets

ca·po \ˈkā-pō\ *n, pl* **ca·pos** : a bar that can be fitted on the fingerboard especially of a guitar to raise the pitch of all the strings

ca·pon \ˈkā-ˌpän\ *n* : a castrated male chicken

ca·price \kə-ˈprēs\ *n* : a sudden change in feeling, opinion, or action : WHIM

Word History The English word *caprice* came from an Italian word which at first meant "a shiver of fear." It was formed from two Italian words. One meant "head," and the other meant "hedgehog." Try to picture very frightened people with their hair standing on end. They might look a bit like hedgehogs covered with spines. In time the meaning of the Italian word that meant "a shiver of fear" changed to "a sudden whim." This is the meaning of our English word *caprice*.

ca·pri·cious \kə-ˈprish-əs\ *adj* : moved or controlled by caprice : likely to change suddenly — **ca·pri·cious·ly** *adv* — **ca·pri·cious·ness** *n*

cap·size \ˈkap-ˌsīz\ *vb* **cap·sized; cap·siz·ing** : to turn over : UPSET ⟨*capsize* a canoe⟩

cap·stan \ˈkap-stən\ *n* : a device that consists of a drum to which a rope is fastened and that is used especially on ships for moving or raising weights

capstan

cap·sule \ˈkap-səl\ *n* **1** : a case enclosing the seeds or spores of a plant **2** : a small case of material that contains medicine to be swallowed **3** : a closed compartment for travel in space

¹cap·tain \ˈkap-tən\ *n* **1** : a leader of a group : one in command ⟨the *captain* of a football team⟩ **2** : a commissioned officer in the Navy or Coast Guard ranking above a commander **3** : a commissioned officer in the Army, Air Force, or Marine Corps ranking above a first lieutenant **4** : the commanding officer of a ship

²captain *vb* : to be captain of

cap·tion \ˈkap-shən\ *n* **1** : the heading especially of an article or document **2** : a comment or title that goes with a picture (as in a book)

cap·ti·vate \ˈkap-tə-ˌvāt\ *vb* **cap·ti·vat·ed; cap·ti·vat·ing** : to fascinate by some special charm

¹cap·tive \ˈkap-tiv\ *adj* **1** : taken and held prisoner especially in war **2** : kept within bounds or under control ⟨a *captive* balloon⟩ **3** : of or relating to captivity

²captive *n* : one that is captive : PRISONER

cap·tiv·i·ty \kap-ˈtiv-ət-ē\ *n* : the state of being a captive

cap·tor \ˈkap-tər\ *n* : one that has captured a person or thing

¹cap·ture \ˈkap-chər\ *n* : the act of capturing

²capture *vb* **cap·tured; cap·tur·ing** **1** : to take and hold especially by force ⟨*capture* a city⟩ **2** : to put into a lasting form ⟨*captured* the scene in a photo⟩ **synonyms** see CATCH

car \ˈkär\ *n* **1** : a vehicle (as an automobile) that moves on wheels **2** : the compartment of an elevator

ca·rafe \kə-ˈraf\ *n* : a bottle that has a lip and is used to hold water or beverages

car·a·mel \ˈkar-ə-məl, ˈkär-məl\ *n* **1** : burnt sugar used for coloring and flavoring **2** : a firm chewy candy

car·at \ˈkar-ət\ *n* : a unit of weight for precious stones equal to 200 milligrams

car·a·van \ˈkar-ə-ˌvan\ *n* **1** : a group (as of merchants or pilgrims) traveling together on a long journey through desert or in dangerous places **2** : a group of vehicles traveling together one behind the other

car·a·vel \ˈkar-ə-ˌvel\ *n* : a small sailing ship of the fifteenth and sixteenth centuries with a broad bow and high stern and three or four masts

car·a·way \ˈkar-ə-ˌwā\ *n* : an herb related to the carrots that is grown for its seeds used especially as a seasoning

car·bine \ˈkär-ˌbēn, -ˌbīn\ *n* : a short light rifle

car·bo·hy·drate \ˌkär-bō-ˈhī-ˌdrāt\ *n* : a nutrient that is rich in energy and is made up of carbon, hydrogen, and oxygen

car·bol·ic acid \,kär-,bäl-ik-\ *n* : a poison present in coal tar and wood tar that is diluted and used as an antiseptic

car·bon \'kär-bən\ *n* : a chemical element occurring as diamond and graphite, in coal and petroleum, and in plant and animal bodies

carbon di·ox·ide \-dī-'äk-,sīd\ *n* : a heavy colorless gas that is formed by burning fuels and by decay and that is the simple raw material from which plants build up compounds for their nourishment

carbon mon·ox·ide \-mə-'näk-,sīd\ *n* : a colorless odorless very poisonous gas formed by incomplete burning of carbon

carbon tet·ra·chlo·ride \-,tet-rə-'klōr-,īd\ *n* : a colorless poisonous liquid that does not burn and is used for dissolving grease

car·bu·re·tor \'kär-bə-,rāt-ər\ *n* : the part of an engine in which liquid fuel (as gasoline) is mixed with air to make it burn easily

car·cass \'kär-kəs\ *n* : the body of an animal prepared for use as meat

¹card \'kärd\ *vb* : to clean and untangle fibers and especially wool by combing with a card — **card·er** *n*

²card *n* : an instrument usually with bent wire teeth that is used to clean and untangle fibers (as wool)

³card *n* **1** : PLAYING CARD **2 cards** *pl* : a game played with playing cards **3** : a flat stiff piece of paper or thin pasteboard that can be written on or that contains printed information ⟨lost my library *card*⟩

card·board \'kärd-,bōrd\ *n* : a stiff material made of wood pulp that has been pressed and dried

car·di·ac \'kärd-ē-,ak\ *adj* : of, relating to, or affecting the heart

¹car·di·nal \'kärd-nəl, -n-əl\ *adj* : of first importance : MAIN, PRINCIPAL ⟨a *cardinal* rule⟩

²cardinal *n* **1** : a high official of the Roman Catholic Church ranking next below the pope **2** : a bright red songbird with a crest and a whistling call

cardinal flower *n* : the bright red flower of a North American plant that blooms in late summer

cardinal 2

car·di·nal·i·ty \,kärd-n-'al-ət-ē\ *n*, *pl* **car·di·nal·i·ties** : the number of elements in a given mathematical set

cardinal number *n* : a number (as 1, 5, 22) that is used in simple counting and answers the question "how many?"

cardinal point *n* : one of the four chief points of the compass which are north, south, east, west

¹care \'keər, 'kaər\ *n* **1** : a heavy sense of responsibility **2** : serious attention ⟨take *care* in crossing streets⟩ **3** : PROTECTION 1, SUPERVISION ⟨under a doctor's *care*⟩ **4** : an object of one's care

²care *vb* **cared; car·ing** **1** : to feel interest or concern ⟨we *care* what happens⟩ **2** : to give care ⟨*care* for the sick⟩ **3** : to have a liking or desire ⟨do you *care* for more tea⟩

ca·reer \kə-'riər\ *n* **1** : the course followed or progress made in one's job or life's work **2** : a job followed as a life's work

care·free \'keər-,frē, 'kaər-\ *adj* : free from care

care·ful \'keər-fəl, 'kaər-\ *adj* **1** : using care ⟨a *careful* driver⟩ **2** : made, done, or said with care ⟨gave a *careful* answer⟩ — **care·ful·ly** \-fə-lē\ *adv* — **care·ful·ness** *n*

synonyms CAREFUL and CAUTIOUS mean taking care to avoid trouble. CAREFUL sug-

caravel

\ə\ **abut**	\au̇\ **out**	\i\ **tip**	\ȯ\ **saw**	\u̇\ **foot**
\ər\ **further**	\ch\ **chin**	\ī\ **life**	\ȯi\ **coin**	\y\ **yet**
\a\ **mat**	\e\ **pet**	\j\ **job**	\th\ **thin**	\yü\ **few**
\ā\ **take**	\ē\ **easy**	\ng\ **sing**	\th\ **this**	\yu̇\ **cure**
\ä\ **cot, cart**	\g\ **go**	\ō\ **bone**	\ü\ **food**	\zh\ **vision**

gests that one is alert and thus able to prevent mistakes or accidents ⟨be *careful* when you paint the fence⟩ CAUTIOUS suggests that one takes care to avoid further problems or difficulties ⟨a *cautious* driver will drive slowly in bad weather⟩

care·less \'keər-ləs, 'kaər-\ *adj* **1** : CARE-FREE **2** : not taking proper care ⟨a *careless* worker⟩ **3** : done, made, or said without being careful — **care·less·ly** *adv* — **care·less·ness** *n*

¹ca·ress \kə-'res\ *n* : a tender or loving touch or hug

²caress *vb* : to touch in a tender or loving way

care·tak·er \'keər-ˌtā-kər, 'kaər-\ *n* : a person who takes care of property for another person

car·fare \'kär-ˌfaər, -ˌfeər\ *n* : the fare charged for carrying a passenger (as on a bus)

car·go \'kär-gō\ *n, pl* **car·goes** *or* **car·gos** : the goods carried by a ship, airplane, or vehicle

car·i·bou \'kar-ə-ˌbü\ *n* : a large deer of northern and arctic North America that is closely related to the Old World reindeer

car·ies \'kaər-ēz, 'keər-\ *n, pl* **caries** : a decayed condition of a tooth or teeth

car·il·lon \'kar-ə-ˌlän, -lən\ *n* : a set of bells sounded by hammers controlled by a keyboard

car·nage \'kär-nij\ *n* : ¹SLAUGHTER 3

car·na·tion \kär-'nā-shən\ *n* : a fragrant usually white, pink, or red garden or greenhouse flower that is related to the pinks

car·ne·lian \kär-'nēl-yən\ *n* : a hard reddish quartz used as a gem

car·ni·val \'kär-nə-vəl\ *n* **1** : a season or festival of merrymaking just before Lent **2** : a noisy merrymaking **3** : a traveling group that puts on a variety of amusements **4** : a program of entertainment ⟨a church fair and *carnival*⟩

Word History Just before Lent many cities hold a time of merrymaking called a "carnival." This practice started in Rome, Italy, and was intended to make up for the fasting and penance during Lent. The English word *carnival* came from an Italian word that meant "carnival." The Italian word was formed from two words. One meant "flesh." The other meant "to remove." The practice of not eating meat in Lent inspired the Italian word for "carnival."

car·ni·vore \'kär-nə-ˌvōr\ *n* : an animal that feeds on meat

car·niv·o·rous \kär-'niv-ə-rəs\ *adj* **1** : feeding on animal flesh **2** : of or relating to carnivores

¹car·ol \'kar-əl\ *n* : a usually religious song of joy

²carol *vb* **car·oled** *or* **car·olled; car·ol·ing** *or* **car·ol·ling** **1** : to sing in a joyful manner **2** : to sing carols and especially Christmas carols — **car·ol·er** *or* **car·ol·ler** *n*

¹car·om \'kar-əm\ *n* : a bouncing back especially at an angle

²carom *vb* : to hit and bounce back at an angle

¹carp \'kärp\ *vb* : to find fault

²carp *n* : a freshwater fish that lives a long time and may weigh as much as eighteen kilograms

car·pel \'kär-pəl\ *n* : one of the ring of parts that form the ovary of a flower

car·pen·ter \'kär-pən-tər\ *n* : a worker who builds or repairs things made of wood

car·pen·try \'kär-pən-trē\ *n* : the work or trade of a carpenter

¹car·pet \'kär-pət\ *n* **1** : a heavy woven fabric used especially as a floor covering **2** : a covering like a carpet ⟨a *carpet* of grass⟩

²carpet *vb* : to cover with or as if with a carpet

car·riage \'kar-ij\ *n* **1** : the manner of holding the body : POSTURE **2** : a vehicle with wheels used for carrying persons **3** : a support with wheels used for carrying a load ⟨a gun *carriage*⟩ **4** : a movable part of a machine that carries or supports some other moving part

car·ri·er \'kar-ē-ər\ *n* **1** : a person or thing that carries ⟨mail *carrier*⟩ **2** : a person or business that transports passengers or goods **3** : one that carries disease germs and passes them on to others

car·ri·on \'kar-ē-ən\ *n* : dead and decaying flesh

car·rot \'kar-ət\ *n* : the long orange edible root of a garden plant (**carrot plant**)

car·ry \'kar-ē\ *vb* **car·ried; car·ry·ing** **1** : to take or transfer from one place to another ⟨*carry* a package⟩ ⟨*carry* a number in addition⟩ **2** : ¹SUPPORT 4, BEAR ⟨pillars that *carry* an arch⟩ **3** : WIN 4 ⟨*carry* an election⟩ **4** : to contain and direct the course of ⟨a pipe *carrying* water⟩ **5** : to wear or have on one's person or have within one ⟨*carry* a gun⟩ ⟨*carrying* an unborn child⟩ **6** : to have as an element, quality, or part ⟨*carry* a guarantee⟩ **7** : to hold or bear the body or some part of it ⟨*carry* your head high⟩ **8** : to sing in correct pitch ⟨*carry* a tune⟩ **9** : to have for sale ⟨the market *carries* fresh fish⟩ **10** : PUBLISH 2 ⟨the paper *carries* weather reports⟩ **11** : to go over or travel a distance ⟨your voice *carries* well⟩

car·ry·all \'kar-ē-ˌȯl\ *n* : a large bag or carrying case

carry away *vb* : to cause strong feeling in ⟨*carried away* by the music⟩

carry on *vb* **1** : MANAGE 1 ⟨*carry on* a business⟩ **2** : to behave badly **3** : to continue in spite of difficulties

carry out *vb* : to put into action or effect

¹cart \'kärt\ *n* **1** : a heavy vehicle with two wheels usually drawn by horses and used for hauling **2** : a light vehicle pushed or pulled by hand

²cart *vb* : to carry in a cart — **cart·er** *n*

car·ti·lage \'kärt-l-ij\ *n* : an elastic tissue that makes up most of the skeleton of very young animals and is later mostly changed into bone

car·ti·lag·i·nous \ˌkärt-l-'aj-ə-nəs\ *adj* : of, relating to, or made of cartilage

car·ton \'kärt-n\ *n* : a cardboard container

car·toon \kär-'tün\ *n* **1** : a drawing (as in a newspaper) making people or objects look funny or foolish **2** : COMIC STRIP **3** : a movie composed of cartoons

car·toon·ist \kär-'tü-nəst\ *n* : a person who draws cartoons

car·tridge \'kär-trij\ *n* **1** : a case or shell containing gunpowder and shot or a bullet for use in a firearm **2** : a case containing an explosive for blasting **3** : a container like a cartridge

cart·wheel \'kärt-ˌhwēl, -ˌwēl\ *n* : a handspring made to the side with arms and legs sticking out

carve \'kärv\ *vb* **carved; carv·ing** **1** : to cut with care ⟨*carve* ivory⟩ **2** : to make or get by cutting ⟨*carve* a figure⟩ **3** : to slice and serve (meat) ⟨*carve* the turkey⟩ — **carv·er** *n*

cas·cade \kas-'kād\ *n* : a steep usually small waterfall

cas·cara \ka-'skar-ə\ *n* : the dried bark of a western North American shrub used as a laxative

¹case \'kās\ *n* **1** : a particular instance, situation, or example ⟨a *case* of injustice⟩ **2** : a situation or an object that calls for investigation or action (as by the police) **3** : a question to be settled in a court of law **4** : a form of a noun, pronoun, or adjective showing its grammatical relation to other words **5** : the actual situation ⟨such is the *case*⟩ **6** : a convincing argument **7** : an instance of disease or injury ⟨a *case* of measles⟩ **8** : ²PATIENT

²case *n* **1** : a container (as a box) for hold-

ing something **2** : a box and its contents ⟨a *case* of books⟩ **3** : an outer covering **4** : the frame of a door or window

ca·sein \kā-'sēn\ *n* : a whitish to yellowish material made from milk especially by the action of acid and used in making paints and plastics

case·ment \'kā-smənt\ *n* **1** : a window sash opening on hinges **2** : a window with a casement

¹cash \'kash\ *n* **1** : money in the form of coins or bills **2** : money or its equivalent (as a check) paid for goods at the time of purchase or delivery

²cash *vb* : to pay or obtain cash for

cash·ew \'kash-ü\ *n* : an edible nut that is shaped like a kidney and comes from a tropical American tree

¹ca·shier \ka-'shiər\ *vb* : to dismiss from service especially in disgrace

²cash·ier \ka-'shiər\ *n* : a person who is responsible for money (as in a bank or business)

cash·mere \'kazh-ˌmiər, 'kash-\ *n* : a soft yarn or fabric once made from the fine wool of an Indian goat but now often from sheep's wool

cashew

cas·ing \'kā-sing\ *n* : something that covers or encloses ⟨sausage *casings*⟩

cask \'kask\ *n* **1** : a container that is shaped like a barrel and is usually used for liquids **2** : the amount contained in a cask

cas·ket \'kas-kət\ *n* **1** : a small box for storage or safekeeping (as for jewels) **2** : COFFIN

cas·se·role \'kas-ə-ˌrōl\ *n* **1** : a deep dish in which food can be baked and served **2** : the food cooked and served in a casserole

cas·sette \kə-'set\ *n* **1** : a container holding photographic film or plates that can be easily loaded into a camera **2** : a container holding magnetic tape with the tape on one reel passing to the other

¹cast \'kast\ *vb* **cast; cast·ing** **1** : ¹THROW 1 ⟨*cast* a stone⟩ ⟨*cast* a fishing line⟩ **2** : to

\ə\ abut	\aů\ out	\i\ tip	\ȯ\ saw	\ů\ foot
\ər\ further	\ch\ chin	\ī\ life	\ȯi\ coin	\y\ yet
\a\ mat	\e\ pet	\j\ job	\th\ thin	\yü\ few
\ā\ take	\ē\ easy	\ng\ sing	\th\ this	\yů\ cure
\ä\ cot, cart	\g\ go	\ō\ bone	\ü\ food	\zh\ vision

throw out, off, or away : SHED ⟨snakes *cast* their skins⟩ **3** : to direct to or toward something or someone ⟨*cast* a glance⟩ **4** : to put on record ⟨*cast* a vote for class president⟩ **5** : to assign parts to as actors for a play ⟨I was *cast* as the hero⟩ **6** : to give shape to liquid material by pouring it into a mold and letting it harden ⟨*cast* a statue in bronze⟩ ⟨*cast* steel⟩ **7** : to make by looping or catching up ⟨*cast* on fifty stitches⟩ — **cast lots** : to take or receive an object at random in order to decide something by chance ⟨*cast lots* to see who goes first⟩

²cast *n* **1** : an act of casting : THROW, FLING **2** : the form in which a thing is made **3** : the characters or the people acting in a play or story **4** : the distance to which a thing can be thrown **5** : something formed by casting in a mold or form ⟨a bronze *cast* of a statue⟩ **6** : a stiff surgical dressing of plaster hardened around a part of the body ⟨had a *cast* on my broken leg⟩ **7** : a hint of color ⟨a bluish *cast*⟩ **8** : ²SHAPE 1 ⟨a face with a rugged *cast*⟩ **9** : something (as the skin of an insect) thrown out or off

cas·ta·net \ˌkas-tə-'net\ *n* : a rhythm instrument that consists of two small ivory, wooden, or plastic shells fastened to the thumb and clicked by the fingers in time to dancing and music — usually used in pl.

castanet

¹cast·away \'kas-tə-ˌwā\ *adj* **1** : thrown away **2** : cast adrift or ashore

²castaway *n* **1** : something that has been thrown away **2** : a shipwrecked person

caste \'kast\ *n* **1** : one of the classes into which the people of India were formerly divided **2** : a division or class of society based on wealth, rank, or occupation **3** : social rank : PRESTIGE

cast·er \'kas-tər\ *n* **1** : one that casts **2** : a small container (as for salt or pepper) with holes in the top **3** *or* **cas·tor** \'kas-tər\ : a small wheel that turns freely and is used for supporting furniture

cas·ti·gate \'kas-tə-ˌgāt\ *vb* **cas·ti·gat·ed; cas·ti·gat·ing** : to punish or correct with words or blows

cast·ing \'kas-ting\ *n* **1** : the act or action of one that casts **2** : something that is cast in a mold ⟨a bronze *casting*⟩ **3** : some-

thing (as skin or feathers) that is cast out or off

cast iron *n* : a hard and brittle alloy of iron, carbon, and silicon shaped by being poured into a mold while melted

cas·tle \'kas-əl\ *n* **1** : a large building or group of buildings usually having high walls with towers and a surrounding moat for protection **2** : a large or impressive house

cast·off *n* : a cast-off person or thing

cast–off \'kas-ˌtof\ *adj* : thrown away or aside

cas·tor oil \'kas-tər-\ *n* : a thick yellowish liquid that comes from the seeds (**castor beans**) of a tropical herb and is used as a lubricant and as a strong laxative

cas·trate \'kas-ˌtrāt\ *vb* **cas·trat·ed; cas·trat·ing** : to remove the sex glands of

ca·su·al \'kazh-ə-wəl, 'kazh-wəl, 'kazh-əl\ *adj* **1** : happening unexpectedly or by chance : not planned or foreseen ⟨a *casual* meeting⟩ **2** : occurring without regularity : OCCASIONAL **3** : showing or feeling little concern : NONCHALANT **4** : meant for informal use — **ca·su·al·ly** *adv*

ca·su·al·ty \'kazh-əl-tē\ *n, pl* **ca·su·al·ties** **1** : a serious or fatal accident : DISASTER **2** : a military person lost (as by death) during warfare **3** : a person or thing injured, lost, or destroyed

cat \'kat\ *n* **1** : a common furry flesh-eating animal kept as a pet or for catching mice and rats **2** : any of the group of mammals (as lions, tigers, and wildcats) to which the domestic cat belongs

¹cat·a·log *or* **cat·a·logue** \'kat-l-ˌog\ *n* **1** : a list of names, titles, or articles arranged by some system **2** : a book or file containing a catalog

²catalog *or* **catalogue** *vb* **cat·a·loged** *or* **cat·a·logued; cat·a·log·ing** *or* **cat·a·logu·ing** **1** : to make a catalog of **2** : to enter in a catalog — **cat·a·log·er** *or* **cat·a·logu·er** *n*

ca·tal·pa \kə-'tal-pə\ *n* : a tree of America and Asia with broad leaves, bright flowers, and long pods

¹cat·a·pult \'kat-ə-ˌpəlt\ *n* **1** : an ancient military machine for hurling stones and arrows **2** : a device for launching an airplane from the deck of a ship

²catapult *vb* **1** : to throw or launch by or as if by a catapult **2** : to become catapulted

ca·tarrh \kə-'tär\ *n* : a red sore state of mucous membrane especially when chronic

ca·tas·tro·phe \kə-'tas-trə-fē\ *n* **1** : a sudden disaster **2** : complete failure : FIASCO

cat·bird \'kat-ˌbərd\ n : a dark gray songbird that has a call like a cat's mewing

cat·boat \'kat-ˌbōt\ n : a sailboat with a single mast set far forward and a single large sail with a long boom

cat·call \'kat-ˌkȯl\ n : a sound like the cry of a cat or a noise expressing disapproval (as at a sports event)

¹**catch** \'kach, 'kech\ vb **caught** \'kȯt\; **catch·ing** 1 : to capture or seize something in flight or motion 2 : to discover unexpectedly ⟨*caught* them in the act⟩ 3 : to check suddenly 4 : to take hold of 5 : to get tangled ⟨*catch* a sleeve on a nail⟩ 6 : to hold firmly : FASTEN ⟨a lock that will not *catch*⟩ 7 : to become affected by ⟨*catch* fire⟩⟨*catch* a cold⟩ 8 : to take or get briefly or quickly ⟨*catch* a glimpse of a friend⟩ 9 : to be in time for ⟨*catch* the next bus⟩ 10 : to grasp by the senses or the mind 11 : to play catcher on a baseball team

synonyms CATCH, CAPTURE, and TRAP mean to get into one's possession or under one's control by or as if by seizing. CATCH suggests that what one is trying to seize is moving or hiding ⟨*catch* that dog⟩ CAPTURE suggests a struggle or some other kind of difficulty ⟨*captured* the robbers as they tried to flee⟩ TRAP suggests the use of a device that catches and holds the prey ⟨made a living by *trapping* beavers⟩

²**catch** n 1 : something caught : the amount caught at one time ⟨a large *catch* of fish⟩ 2 : the act of catching 3 : a pastime in which a ball is thrown and caught 4 : something that checks, fastens, or holds immovable ⟨a *catch* on a door⟩ 5 : a hidden difficulty

catch·er \'kach-ər, 'kech-\ n 1 : one that catches 2 : a baseball player who plays behind home plate

catch·ing \'kach-ing, 'kech-\ adj 1 : INFECTIOUS 1, CONTAGIOUS 2 : likely to spread as if infectious ⟨the laughter was *catching*⟩

catchy \'kach-ē, 'kech-\ adj **catch·i·er; catch·i·est** 1 : likely to attract ⟨*catchy* music⟩ 2 : TRICKY 2

cat·e·chism \'kat-ə-ˌkiz-əm\ n 1 : a series of questions and answers used in giving instruction and especially religious instruction 2 : a set of formal questions

cat·e·go·ry \'kat-ə-ˌgȯr-ē\ n, pl **cat·e·go·ries** : a class or division of things : KIND

ca·ter \'kāt-ər\ vb 1 : to provide a supply of food ⟨*cater* for parties⟩ 2 : to supply what is needed or wanted — **ca·ter·er** n

cat·er·pil·lar \'kat-ər-ˌpil-ər, 'kat-ə-ˌpil-\ n : a wormlike often hairy larva of an insect (as a moth or butterfly)

Word History The English word *caterpillar* came from an early French word that meant "caterpillar." The literal meaning of this French word was "hairy cat." It was formed from two French words. The first of these words meant "female cat." The second meant "hairy."

cat·fish \'kat-ˌfish\ n : any of a group of fishes with large heads and feelers about the mouth

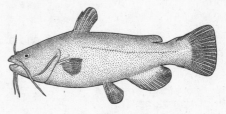

catfish

cat·gut \'kat-ˌgət\ n : a tough cord made from intestines of animals (as sheep) and used for strings of musical instruments and rackets and for sewing in surgery

ca·the·dral \kə-'thē-drəl\ n : the principal church of a district headed by a bishop

cath·o·lic \'kath-ə-lik, 'kath-lik\ adj 1 : broad in range ⟨a person of *catholic*

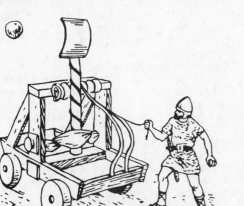

catapult 1

\ə\ abut	\au\ out	\i\ tip	\ȯ\ saw	\ù\ foot
\ər\ further	\ch\ chin	\ī\ life	\ȯi\ coin	\y\ yet
\a\ mat	\e\ pet	\j\ job	\th\ thin	\yü\ few
\ā\ take	\ē\ easy	\ng\ sing	\th\ this	\yù\ cure
\ä\ cot, cart	\g\ go	\ō\ bone	\ü\ food	\zh\ vision

interests⟩ **2** *cap* : of or relating to the Roman Catholic Church

Catholic *n* **1** : a member of a Christian church tracing its history back to the apostles **2** : a member of the Roman Catholic Church

cat·kin \'kat-kən\ *n* : a flower cluster (as of the willow and birch) in which the flowers grow in close circular rows along a slender stalk

cat·like \'kat-,līk\ *adj* : like a cat (as in grace or slyness)

cat·nap \'kat-,nap\ *n* : a very short light nap

cat·nip \'kat-,nip\ *n* : a plant of the mint family enjoyed by cats

cat–o'–nine–tails \,kat-ə-'nīn-,tālz\ *n, pl* **cat–o'–nine–tails** : a whip made of nine knotted cords fastened to a handle

cat·sup \'kech-əp, 'kach-əp, 'kat-səp\ *or* **ketch·up** \'kech-əp, 'kach-\ *n* : a seasoned sauce (as for meat) usually made of tomatoes

cattails

cat·tail \'kat-,tāl\ *n* : a tall plant with long flat leaves and tall furry stalks that grows in marshy areas

cat·tle \'kat-l\ *n, pl* **cattle** : domestic animals with four feet and especially cows, bulls, and calves

cat·walk \'kat-,wȯk\ *n* : a narrow walk or way (as along a bridge)

caught *past of* CATCH

cauldron *variant of* CALDRON

cau·li·flow·er \'kȯ-li-,flaù-ər, 'käl-i-\ *n* : a vegetable closely related to the cabbage that is grown for its white head of undeveloped flowers

cauliflower

¹caulk *or* **calk** \'kȯk\ *vb* : to fill up a crack, seam, or joint so as to make it watertight

²caulk *variant of* CALK

¹cause \'kȯz\ *n* **1** : a person or thing that brings about a result ⟨carelessness is the cause of many accidents⟩ **2** : a good or good enough reason for something ⟨a cause for rejoicing⟩ **3** : something (as a question) to be decided **4** : something supported or deserving support ⟨a worthy cause⟩

²cause *vb* **caused; caus·ing** : to be the cause of

cause·way \'kȯz-,wā\ *n* : a raised road or way across wet ground or water

caus·tic \'kȯ-stik\ *adj* **1** : capable of eating away by chemical action : CORROSIVE **2** : ¹SHARP 8, BITING ⟨*caustic* remarks⟩

¹cau·tion \'kȯ-shən\ *n* **1** : ADMONITION **2** : carefulness in regard to danger : PRECAUTION

²caution *vb* : to advise caution to : WARN

cau·tious \'kȯ-shəs\ *adj* : showing or using caution **synonyms** see CAREFUL — **cau·tious·ly** *adv*

cav·al·cade \,kav-əl-'kād\ *n* **1** : a procession especially of riders or carriages **2** : a dramatic series (as of related events)

¹cav·a·lier \,kav-ə-'liər\ *n* **1** : a mounted soldier **2** : a brave and courteous gentleman

²cavalier *adj* **1** : easy and lighthearted in manner **2** : tending to disregard the rights or feelings of others : ARROGANT

cav·al·ry \'kav-əl-rē\ *n, pl* **cav·al·ries** : troops mounted on horseback or moving in motor vehicles

cav·al·ry·man \'kav-əl-rē-mən\ *n, pl* **cav·al·ry·men** \-mən\ : a cavalry soldier

¹cave \'kāv\ *n* : a hollow underground place with an opening on the surface

²cave *vb* **caved; cav·ing** : to fall or cause to fall in or down : COLLAPSE ⟨the mine *caved* in⟩

cave·man \'kāv-,man\ *n, pl* **cave·men** \-,men\ : a person living in a cave especially during the Stone Age

cav·ern \'kav-ərn\ *n* : a cave often of large or unknown size

cav·ern·ous \'kav-ər-nəs\ *adj* **1** : having caverns or hollow places **2** : like a cavern because large and hollow ⟨a *cavernous* cellar⟩

cav·i·ty \'kav-ət-ē\ *n, pl* **cav·i·ties** : a hollow place ⟨a *cavity* in a tooth⟩

ca·vort \kə-'vȯrt\ *vb* : to move or hop about in a lively way

¹caw \'kȯ\ *vb* : to make a caw

²caw *n* : the cry of a crow or a raven

cay·enne pepper \,kī-'en-, ,kā-,en-\ *n* : dried ripe hot peppers ground and used to add flavor to food

cease \'sēs\ *vb* **ceased; ceas·ing** : to come or bring to an end : STOP

cease·less \'sēs-ləs\ *adj* : CONSTANT 3

ce·cro·pia moth \si-ˌkrō-pē-ə-\ *n* : a silkworm moth that is the largest moth of the eastern United States

cecropia moth

ce·dar \'sēd-ər\ *n* : any of a number of trees having cones and a strong wood with a pleasant smell

cede \'sēd\ *vb* **ced·ed; ced·ing** : to give up especially by treaty ⟨territory *ceded* by one country to another⟩

ceil·ing \'sē-ling\ *n* **1** : the overhead inside surface of a room **2** : the greatest height at which an airplane can fly properly **3** : the height above the ground of the bottom of the lowest layer of clouds **4** : an upper limit ⟨a *ceiling* on prices⟩

cel·e·brate \'sel-ə-ˌbrāt\ *vb* **cel·e·brat·ed; cel·e·brat·ing 1** : to perform publicly and according to certain rules ⟨*celebrate* Mass⟩ **2** : to observe in some special way (as by merrymaking or by staying away from business) **3** : ¹PRAISE 1

cel·e·brat·ed \'sel-ə-ˌbrāt-əd\ *adj* : widely known and talked about

cel·e·bra·tion \ˌsel-ə-'brā-shən\ *n* **1** : the act of celebrating **2** : the activities or ceremonies for celebrating a special occasion

ce·leb·ri·ty \sə-'leb-rət-ē\ *n, pl* **ce·leb·ri·ties 1** : FAME **2** : a celebrated person

cel·ery \'sel-ə-rē, 'sel-rē\ *n* : a plant related to the carrots whose crisp leafstalks are used for food

ce·les·ta \sə-'les-tə\ *n* : a keyboard instrument with hammers that strike steel plates to make ringing sounds

ce·les·tial \sə-'les-chəl\ *adj* **1** : of, relating to, or suggesting heaven **2** : of or relating to the sky

cell \'sel\ *n* **1** : a very small room (as in a prison or a monastery) **2** : a small enclosed part or division (as in a honey-comb) **3** : a small mass of living matter that is made of protoplasm, includes a nucleus, is enclosed in a membrane, and is the basic unit of which all plants and animals are made up **4** : a container with substances which can produce an electric current by chemical action — **celled** \'seld\ *adj*

cel·lar \'sel-ər\ *n* : a room or set of rooms below the surface of the ground : BASEMENT

cel·lo \'chel-ō\ *n, pl* **cel·los** : a large stringed instrument of the violin family that plays the bass part

cel·lo·phane \'sel-ə-ˌfān\ *n* : a thin clear material made from cellulose and used as a wrapping

cel·lu·lar \'sel-yə-lər\ *adj* **1** : of, relating to, or made up of cells ⟨*cellular* tissue⟩ **2** : of, relating to, or being a telephone that connects to others by radio and is part of a system of in which a geographic area is divided into small sections each served by a transmitter of limited range

cel·lu·lose \'sel-yə-ˌlōs\ *n* : a substance that is the chief part of the cell walls of plants and is used in making various products (as paper and rayon)

cell wall *n* : the firm outer nonliving boundary of a plant cell

Cel·si·us \'sel-sē-əs\ *adj* : relating to or having a thermometer scale on which the interval between the freezing point and the boiling point of water is divided into 100 degrees with 0 representing the freezing point and 100 the boiling point

¹ce·ment \si-'ment\ *n* **1** : a powder that is made mainly from compounds of aluminum, calcium, silicon, and iron heated together and then ground, that combines with water and hardens into a mass, and that is used in mortar and concrete **2** : ²CONCRETE, MORTAR **3** : a substance that by hardening sticks things together firmly

²cement *vb* **1** : to join together with or as if with cement **2** : to cover with concrete

ce·men·tum \si-'ment-əm\ *n* : a thin bony layer covering the part of a tooth inside the gum

cem·e·tery \'sem-ə-ˌter-ē\ *n, pl* **cem·e·ter·ies** : a place where dead people are buried : GRAVEYARD

Ce·no·zo·ic \ˌsē-nə-'zō-ik, ˌsen-ə-\ *n* : an era of geological history lasting from seventy million years ago to the present time

\ə\ abut	\aů\ out	\i\ tip	\ò\ saw	\ů\ foot
\ər\ further	\ch\ chin	\ī\ life	\òi\ coin	\y\ yet
\a\ mat	\e\ pet	\j\ job	\th\ thin	\yü\ few
\ā\ take	\ē\ easy	\ng\ sing	\th\ this	\yů\ cure
\ä\ cot, cart	\g\ go	\ō\ bone	\ü\ food	\zh\ vision

in which there has been a rapid evolution of mammals and birds and of flowering plants

¹cen·sor \'sen-sər\ *n* : an official who checks writings or movies to take out things thought to be objectionable

²censor *vb* : to examine (as a book) to take out things thought to be objectionable

¹cen·sure \'sen-chər\ *n* **1** : the act of finding fault with or blaming **2** : an official criticism

²censure *vb* **cen·sured; cen·sur·ing** : to find fault with especially publicly

cen·sus \'sen-səs\ *n* : a count of the number of people in a country, city, or town

cent \'sent\ *n* **1** : a hundredth part of the unit of the money system in a number of different countries ⟨in the United States 100 *cents* equal one dollar⟩ **2** : a coin, token, or note representing one cent

Word History The English word for the hundredth part of a dollar came from a Latin word. This Latin word meant "hundred."

cen·taur \'sen-,tor\ *n* : a creature in Greek mythology that is part man and part horse

centaur

cen·te·nar·i·an \,sent-n-'er-ē-ən\ *n* : a person 100 or more years old

¹cen·ten·ni·al \sen-'ten-ē-əl\ *n* : a 100th anniversary or a celebration of this event

²centennial *adj* : relating to a period of 100 years

¹cen·ter \'sent-ər\ *n* **1** : the middle point of a circle or a sphere equally distant from every point on the circumference or surface **2** : one (as a person or area) that is very important to some activity or concern ⟨a shopping *center*⟩ **3** : the middle part of something ⟨the *center* of the room⟩ **4** : a

player occupying a middle position on a team

²center *vb* **1** : to place or fix at or around a center or central area **2** : to collect at or around one point

center of gravity : the point at which the entire weight of a body may be thought of as centered so that if supported at this point the body would balance perfectly

cen·ter·piece \'sent-ər-,pēs\ *n* : a piece put in the center of something and especially a decoration (as flowers) for a table

centi- *prefix* : hundredth part ⟨*centi*meter⟩ — used in terms of the metric system

cen·ti·grade \'sent-ə-,grād\ *adj* : CELSIUS

cen·ti·gram \'sent-ə-,gram\ *n* : a unit of weight equal to 1/100 gram

cen·ti·li·ter \'sent-ə-,lēt-ər\ *n* : a unit of liquid capacity equal to 1/100 liter

cen·ti·me·ter \'sent-ə-,mēt-ər\ *n* : a unit of length equal to 1/100 meter

cen·ti·pede \'sent-ə-,pēd\ *n* : a small animal that has a long body and many legs and is related to the insects

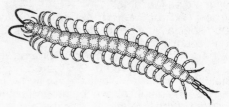

cen·tral \'sen-trəl\ *adj* **1** : containing or being the center **2** : most important : CHIEF ⟨the *central* person in a story⟩ **3** : placed at, in, or near the center — **cen·tral·ly** *adv*

¹Central American *adj* : of or relating to Central America or the Central Americans

²Central American *n* : a person born or living in Central America

central angle *n* : an angle with its vertex at the center of a circle and with sides that are radii of the circle

cen·tral·ize \'sen-trə-,līz\ *vb* **cen·tral·ized; cen·tral·iz·ing** : to bring to a central point or under a single control

cen·trif·u·gal force \sen-,trif-yə-gəl-\ *n* : the force that tends to cause a thing or parts of a thing to go outward from a center of rotation

cen·tu·ry \'sen-chə-rē, 'sench-rē\ *n, pl* **cen·tu·ries** : a period of 100 years

ce·ram·ic \sə-'ram-ik\ *n* **1 ceramics** *pl* : the art of making things (as pottery or tiles) of baked clay **2** : a product made by ceramics

¹ce·re·al \'sir-ē-əl\ *adj* **1** : relating to grain or the plants that it comes from **2** : made of grain

Word History In Roman mythology Ceres was the goddess of agriculture. A Latin word meaning "of the goddess of agriculture" was formed from her name. Since Ceres was in charge of grain and grain plants, the word formed from her name came to mean "of grain" as well. The English word *cereal* came from this Latin word.

²cereal *n* **1** : a plant (as a grass) that yields grain for food **2** : a food prepared from grain

cer·e·bel·lum \ˌser-ə-'bel-əm\ *n, pl* **cer·e·bel·lums** *or* **cer·e·bel·la** \-'bel-ə\ : a part of the brain concerned especially with the coordination of muscles and with keeping the body in proper balance

ce·re·bral \sə-'rē-brəl, 'ser-ə-brəl\ *adj* **1** : of or relating to the brain or mind **2** : of, relating to, or affecting the cerebrum

ce·re·brum \sə-'rē-brəm, 'ser-ə-brəm\ *n, pl* **ce·re·brums** *or* **ce·re·bra** \-brə\ : the enlarged front and upper part of the brain that is the center of thinking

¹cer·e·mo·ni·al \ˌser-ə-'mō-nē-əl\ *adj* : of, relating to, or being a ceremony

²ceremonial *n* : a ceremonial act, action, or system

cer·e·mo·ni·ous \ˌser-ə-'mō-nē-əs\ *adj* **1** : ¹CEREMONIAL **2** : given to ceremony : FORMAL — **cer·e·mo·ni·ous·ly** *adv*

cer·e·mo·ny \'ser-ə-ˌmō-nē\ *n, pl* **cer·e·mo·nies** **1** : an act or series of acts performed in some regular way according to fixed rules **2** : very polite behavior : FORMALITY

¹cer·tain \'sərt-n\ *adj* **1** : being fixed or settled ⟨a *certain* percentage of the profit⟩ **2** : known but not named ⟨a *certain* person told me⟩ **3** : sure to have an effect ⟨a *certain* cure⟩ **4** : known to be true ⟨it's *certain* that they were here⟩ **5** : bound by the way things are ⟨*certain* to succeed⟩ **6** : assured in thought or action

²certain *pron* : certain ones ⟨*certain* of the students could work harder⟩

cer·tain·ly \'sərt-n-lē\ *adv* **1** : with certainty : without fail ⟨I will *certainly* see to it⟩ **2** : without doubt ⟨it is *certainly* cool this evening⟩

cer·tain·ty \'sərt-n-tē\ *n, pl* **cer·tain·ties** **1** : something that is certain **2** : the quality or state of being certain ⟨answered with *certainty*⟩

cer·tif·i·cate \sər-'tif-i-kət\ *n* **1** : a written or printed statement that is proof of some

fact ⟨a vaccination *certificate*⟩ **2** : a paper showing that a person has met certain requirements (as of a school) **3** : a paper showing ownership

cer·ti·fy \'sərt-ə-ˌfi\ *vb* **cer·ti·fied; cer·ti·fy·ing** **1** : to show to be true or as claimed by a formal or official statement ⟨*certify* a student's record⟩ **2** : to guarantee the quality, fitness, or value of officially ⟨*certified* milk⟩ ⟨*certify* a check⟩ **3** : to show to have met certain requirements ⟨*certify* a student for graduation⟩

ce·ru·le·an \sə-'rü-lē-ən\ *adj* : somewhat like the blue of the sky

ces·sa·tion \se-'sā-shən\ *n* : a coming to a stop

chafe \'chāf\ *vb* **chafed; chaf·ing** **1** : IRRITATE 1, VEX **2** : to be bothered : FRET **3** : to warm by rubbing ⟨*chafed* my hands⟩ **4** : to rub so as to wear away or make sore

¹chaff \'chaf\ *n* **1** : the husks of grains and grasses separated from the seed in threshing **2** : something worthless

²chaff *vb* : to tease in a friendly way

cha·grin \shə-'grin\ *n* : a feeling of being annoyed by failure or disappointment

¹chain \'chān\ *n* **1** : a series of links or rings usually of metal **2** : something that restricts or binds : BOND **3** : a series of things joined together as if by links ⟨a *chain* of mountains⟩ ⟨a *chain* of events⟩

²chain *vb* : to fasten, bind, or connect with or as if with a chain

chair \'cheər, 'chaər\ *n* **1** : a seat with legs and a back for use by one person **2** : an official seat or a seat of authority or honor ⟨take the *chair* at a meeting⟩ **3** : an office or position of authority or honor **4** : an official who conducts a meeting

chair·man \'cheər-mən, 'chaər-\ *n, pl* **chair·men** \-mən\ : CHAIR 4 — **chair·man·ship** \-ˌship\ *n*

chair·per·son \'cheər-ˌpərs-n, 'chaər-\ *n* : CHAIR 4

chair·wom·an \'cheər-ˌwùm-ən, 'chaər-\ *n, pl* **chair·wom·en** \-ˌwim-ən\ : a woman who conducts a meeting

chaise longue \'shāz-'lȯng\ *n* : a long chair somewhat like a couch

chaise lounge \'shāz-'laùnj, 'chās-\ *n* : CHAISE LONGUE

cha·let \sha-'lā\ *n* **1** : a herdsman's hut in the Alps away from a town or village **2** : a Swiss dwelling with a roof that sticks far

\ə\ abut	\aù\ out	\i\ tip	\ȯ\ saw	\ú\ foot
\ər\ further	\ch\ chin	\ī\ life	\ȯi\ coin	\y\ yet
\a\ mat	\e\ pet	\j\ job	\th\ thin	\yü\ few
\ā\ take	\ē\ easy	\ng\ sing	\th\ this	\yú\ cure
\ä\ cot, cart	\g\ go	\ō\ bone	\ü\ food	\zh\ vision

out past the walls **3** : a cottage built to look like a chalet

chalet 2

chal·ice \'chal-əs\ *n* : a drinking cup : GOBLET

¹chalk \'chȯk\ *n* **1** : a soft white, gray, or buff limestone made up mainly of very small seashells **2** : a material like chalk especially when used in the form of a crayon

²chalk *vb* **1** : to rub, mark, write, or draw with chalk **2** : to record or add up with or as if with chalk

chalk·board \'chȯk-ˌbȯrd\ *n* : a dark smooth surface (as of slate) used for writing or drawing on with chalk

chalky \'chȯ-kē\ *adj* **chalk·i·er; chalk·i·est** **1** : made of or like chalk **2** : easily crumbled **3** : very pale ⟨*chalky* from fright⟩

¹chal·lenge \'chal-ənj\ *vb* **chal·lenged; chal·leng·ing** **1** : to halt and demand a password from **2** : to object to as bad or incorrect : DISPUTE **3** : to demand proof that something is right or legal ⟨*challenge* a vote⟩ **4** : to invite or dare to take part in a contest ⟨*challenge* us to race⟩ — **chal·leng·er** *n*

²challenge *n* **1** : an objection to something as not being true, genuine, correct, or proper or to a person (as a juror) as not being qualified or approved : PROTEST **2** : a sentry's command to halt and prove identity **3** : a demand that someone take part in a duel **4** : a call or dare for someone to compete in a contest or sport

cham·ber \'chām-bər\ *n* **1** : a room in a house and especially a bedroom **2** : an enclosed space, cavity, or compartment (as in a gun) **3** : a meeting hall of a government body (as an assembly) **4** : a room where a judge conducts business out of court **5** : a group of people organized into a lawmaking body **6** : a board or council of volunteers (as businessmen) — **cham·bered** \-bərd\ *adj*

cham·ber·lain \'chām-bər-lən\ *n* **1** : a chief officer in the household of a ruler or noble **2** : TREASURER ⟨city *chamberlain*⟩

cham·ber·maid \'chām-bər-ˌmād\ *n* : a maid who takes care of bedrooms (as in a hotel)

chamber music *n* : instrumental music to be performed in a room or small hall

cha·me·leon \kə-'mēl-yən\ *n* : a lizard that has the ability to change the color of its skin

Word History Many of the lizards of the Old World must have looked quite startling. They may even have reminded the ancients of small lions. The Greeks gave these strange-looking lizards a name made up of two Greek words. The first meant "on the ground," and the second meant "lion." The English word *chameleon* came from the Greek name of the lizards.

cham·ois \'sham-ē\ *n, pl* **cham·ois** \-ē, -ēz\ **1** : a small antelope living on the highest mountains of Europe and Asia **2** : a soft yellowish leather made from the skin of the chamois or from sheepskin

chamois

¹champ \'champ\ *vb* : to bite and chew noisily ⟨a horse *champing* its bit⟩

²champ *n* : ¹CHAMPION 2, 3

¹cham·pi·on \'cham-pē-ən\ *n* **1** : a person who fights or speaks for another person or in favor of a cause **2** : a person accepted as better than all others in a sport or in a game of skill **3** : the winner of first place in a competition

²champion *vb* : to protect or fight for as a champion

cham·pi·on·ship \'cham-pē-ən-,ship\ *n* **1** : the act of defending as a champion **2** : the position or title of champion **3** : a contest held to find a champion

¹chance \'chans\ *n* **1** : the uncertain course of events ⟨they met by *chance*⟩ **2** : OPPORTUNITY 1 ⟨had a *chance* to travel⟩ **3** : ¹RISK, GAMBLE ⟨take *chances*⟩ **4** : PROBABILITY 1 ⟨a slight *chance* of rain⟩ **5** : a ticket in a raffle

²chance *vb* **chanced; chanc·ing** **1** : to take place by chance **2** : to come unexpectedly ⟨*chanced* on a bargain⟩ **3** : to leave to chance : RISK

³chance *adj* : happening by chance ⟨a *chance* meeting⟩

chan·cel·lor \'chan-sə-lər, 'chan-slər\ *n* **1** : a high state official (as in Germany) **2** : a high officer of some universities **3** : a chief judge in some courts — **chan·cel·lor·ship** \-,ship\ *n*

chan·de·lier \,shan-də-'liər\ *n* : a lighting fixture with several branches that usually hangs from the ceiling

¹change \'chānj\ *vb* **changed; chang·ing** **1** : to make or become different : ALTER ⟨*change* the looks of a room⟩ ⟨*changing* autumn leaves⟩ **2** : to give a different position, course, or direction to ⟨*change* one's plans⟩ **3** : to put one thing in the place of another : SWITCH, EXCHANGE ⟨*change* places⟩ **4** : to give or receive an equal amount of money in usually smaller units of value or in the money of another country ⟨*change* a ten-dollar bill⟩ **5** : to put fresh clothes or covering on ⟨*change* a bed⟩ **6** : to put on different clothes ⟨we always *change* for dinner⟩

synonyms CHANGE, ALTER, and VARY mean to make or become different. CHANGE may suggest making such a basic difference in a thing that it becomes something else ⟨they've *changed* the house into a restaurant⟩ or it may apply to substituting one thing for another ⟨*change* that shirt for a clean one⟩ ALTER suggests making a small difference in something ⟨*altered* the skirt by making it a bit shorter⟩ VARY suggests making a difference in order to break away from a routine ⟨*vary* the tasks given to each worker⟩

²change *n* **1** : the act, process, or result of changing ⟨*change* of seasons⟩ **2** : a fresh

set of clothes ⟨take several *changes* on your vacation⟩ **3** : money in small units of value received in exchange for an equal amount in larger units ⟨*change* for a ten-dollar bill⟩ **4** : money returned when a payment is more than the amount due ⟨wait for your *change*⟩ **5** : money in coins

change·able \'chān-jə-bəl\ *adj* : able or likely to change

¹chan·nel \'chan-l\ *n* **1** : the bed of a stream **2** : the deeper part of a waterway (as a river or harbor) **3** : a strait or a narrow sea ⟨the English *Channel*⟩ **4** : a closed course (as a tube) through which something flows **5** : a long groove **6** : a means by which something is passed or carried **7** : a range of frequencies used by a single radio or television station in broadcasting

²channel *vb* **chan·neled** *or* **chan·nelled; chan·nel·ing** *or* **chan·nel·ling** **1** : to form a channel in **2** : to direct into or through a channel

¹chant \'chant\ *vb* **1** : to sing especially in the way a chant is sung **2** : to recite or speak with no change in tone

²chant *n* **1** : a melody in which several words or syllables are sung on one tone **2** : something spoken in the style of a chant

cha·os \'kā-,äs\ *n* : complete confusion and disorder

cha·ot·ic \kā-'ät-ik\ *adj* : being in a state of chaos

¹chap \'chap\ *n* : ¹FELLOW 4

²chap *vb* **chapped; chap·ping** : to open in slits : CRACK ⟨lips *chapped* by wind and cold⟩

chap·el \'chap-əl\ *n* **1** : a building or a room or place for prayer or special religious services **2** : a religious service or assembly held in a school or college

¹chap·er·on *or* **chap·er·one** \'shap-ə-,rōn\ *n* : an older person who goes with and is responsible for a young woman or a group of young people (as at a dance)

²chaperon *or* **chaperone** *vb* **chap·er·oned; chap·er·on·ing** : to act as a chaperon

chap·lain \'chap-lən\ *n* **1** : a member of the clergy officially attached to a special group (as the army) **2** : a person chosen to conduct religious services (as for a club)

\ə\ abut	\au̇\ out	\i\ tip	\ȯ\ saw	\u̇\ foot
\ər\ further	\ch\ chin	\ī\ life	\ȯi\ coin	\y\ yet
\a\ mat	\e\ pet	\j\ job	\th\ thin	\yü\ few
\ā\ take	\ē\ easy	\ng\ sing	\th\ this	\yu̇\ cure
\ä\ cot, cart	\g\ go	\ō\ bone	\ü\ food	\zh\ vision

chaps \'shaps, 'chaps\ *n pl* : a set of leather coverings for the legs used especially by western ranch workers

chap·ter \'chap-tər\ *n* **1** : a main division of a book or story **2** : a local branch of a club or organization

char \'chär\ *vb* **charred; char·ring 1** : to change to charcoal by burning **2** : to burn slightly : SCORCH

char·ac·ter \'kar-ək-tər\ *n* **1** : a mark, sign, or symbol (as a letter or figure) used in writing or printing **2** : ²CHARACTERISTIC **3** : the group of qualities that make a person, group, or thing different from others **4** : a person who is unusual or peculiar **5** : a person in a story or play **6** : REPUTATION 1 **7** : moral excellence ⟨a person of *character*⟩

¹**char·ac·ter·is·tic** \,kar-ək-tə-'ris-tik\ *adj* : serving to stress some special quality of an individual or a group : TYPICAL ⟨replied with *characteristic* carelessness⟩

²**characteristic** *n* : a special quality or appearance that makes an individual or a group different from others

char·ac·ter·is·ti·cal·ly \,kar-ək-tə-'ris-ti-kə-lē\ *adv* : in a characteristic way

char·ac·ter·ize \'kar-ək-tə-,rīz\ *vb* **charac·ter·ized; char·ac·ter·iz·ing 1** : to point out the character of an individual or a group : DESCRIBE **2** : to be characteristic of

char·coal \'chär-,kōl\ *n* : a black or dark absorbent carbon made by heating animal or vegetable material in the absence of air

¹**charge** \'chärj\ *vb* **charged; charg·ing 1** : ¹FILL 1 ⟨*charge* a furnace with coal⟩ **2** : to give an electric charge to **3** : to restore the active materials in a storage battery by passage of an electric current through it **4** : to give a task, duty, or responsibility to **5** : ¹COMMAND 1 **6** : to accuse formally ⟨*charged* with speeding⟩ **7** : to rush against : ASSAULT **8** : to take payment from or make responsible for payment ⟨you *charged* me too much⟩ **9** : to enter as a debt or responsibility on a record ⟨*charge* a purchase to one's account⟩ ⟨*charge* books on a library card⟩ **10** : to ask or set as a price ⟨they *charge* too much for everything⟩ ⟨*charged* $100 for repairs⟩

²**charge** *n* **1** : the amount (as of ammunition or fuel) needed to load or fill something **2** : an amount of electricity available **3** : a task, duty, or order given to a person

: OBLIGATION **4** : the work or duty of managing ⟨has *charge* of the building⟩ **5** : a person or thing given to a person to look after **6** : ²COMMAND 2 ⟨a judge's *charge* to a jury⟩ **7** : the price demanded especially for a service ⟨storage *charges*⟩ **8** : an amount listed as a debt on an account **9** : ACCUSATION **10** : a rushing attack **synonyms** see PRICE

charg·er \'chär-jər\ *n* : a cavalry horse

char·i·ot \'char-ē-ət\ *n* : a vehicle of ancient times that had two wheels, was pulled by horses, and was used in war and in races and parades

chariot

char·i·ta·ble \'char-ət-ə-bəl\ *adj* **1** : freely giving money or help to needy persons : GENEROUS **2** : given for the needy : of service to the needy **3** : kindly in judging other people

char·i·ty \'char-ət-ē\ *n, pl* **char·i·ties 1** : love for others **2** : kindliness in judging others **3** : the giving of aid to the poor and suffering **4** : public aid for the poor **5** : an institution or fund for helping the needy

char·ley horse \'chär-lē-,hòrs\ *n* : pain and stiffness in a muscle (as in a leg)

¹**charm** \'chärm\ *n* **1** : a word, action, or thing believed to have magic powers **2** : something worn or carried to keep away evil and bring good luck **3** : a small decorative object worn on a chain or bracelet **4** : a quality that attracts and pleases

²**charm** *vb* **1** : to affect or influence by or as if by a magic spell ⟨*charm* a snake⟩ **2** : FASCINATE, DELIGHT ⟨sounds that *charm* the ear⟩ **3** : to protect by or as if by a charm ⟨leads a *charmed* life⟩ **4** : to attract by grace or beauty

charm·ing \'chär-ming\ *adj* : very pleasing

¹**chart** \'chärt\ *n* **1** : ¹MAP **2** : a map showing coasts, reefs, currents, and depths of water **3** : a sheet giving information in a table or lists or by means of diagrams

²**chart** *vb* **1** : to make a map or chart of ⟨*chart* the seas⟩ **2** : to lay out a plan for

chaps

¹char·ter \'chärt-ər\ *n* **1 :** an official document granting, guaranteeing, or showing the limits of the rights and duties of the group to which it is given **2 :** a contract by which the owners of a ship lease it to others

²charter *vb* **1 :** to grant a charter to **2 :** to hire (as a bus or an aircraft) for temporary use

¹chase \'chās\ *vb* **chased; chas·ing 1 :** to follow in order to catch up with or capture ⟨*chase* a thief⟩ ⟨*chase* a bus⟩ **2 :** ¹HUNT 1 ⟨*chase* the fox⟩ **3 :** to drive away or out

synonyms CHASE, PURSUE, and FOLLOW mean to go after someone or something. CHASE suggests that one moves swiftly in order to catch up with something ⟨*chased* the cat all over the yard⟩ PURSUE suggests a long, continual chase ⟨they *pursued* the bear for miles⟩ FOLLOW does not suggest speed or a desire to actually catch up with something ⟨*follow* the children and find out where their hideout is⟩

²chase *n* **1 :** the act of chasing : PURSUIT **2 :** the hunting of wild animals **3 :** something pursued

chasm \'kaz-əm\ *n* : a deep split or gap in the earth

chas·sis \'shas-ē, 'chas-\ *n, pl* **chas·sis** \-ēz\ : a structure that supports the body (as of an automobile or airplane) or the parts (as of a television set)

chaste \'chāst\ *adj* **chast·er; chast·est 1** : pure in thought and act : MODEST **2** : simple or plain in design

chas·ten \'chās-n\ *vb* : to correct by punishment or suffering : DISCIPLINE

chas·tise \chas-'tīz\ *vb* **chas·tised; chas·tis·ing** : to punish severely (as by whipping)

chas·ti·ty \'chas-tət-ē\ *n* : the quality or state of being chaste

¹chat \'chat\ *vb* **chat·ted; chat·ting** : to talk in a friendly manner of things that are not serious

²chat *n* : a light friendly conversation

¹chat·ter \'chat-ər\ *vb* **1 :** to make quick sounds that suggest speech but lack meaning ⟨monkeys *chattering* in the trees⟩ **2 :** to speak rapidly, without thinking, or so as to be hard to hear or understand : JABBER **3 :** to click again and again and without control ⟨teeth *chattering* from the cold⟩ — **chat·ter·er** *n*

²chatter *n* : the act or sound of chattering

chat·ter·box \'chat-ər-ˌbäks\ *n* : a person who talks all the time

chat·ty \'chat-ē\ *adj* **chat·ti·er; chat·ti·est 1 :** TALKATIVE **2 :** having the style and manner of friendly conversation ⟨a *chatty* letter⟩

chauf·feur \'shō-fər, shō-'fər\ *n* : a person hired to drive people around in a car

¹cheap \'chēp\ *adj* **1 :** not costing much ⟨a *cheap* watch⟩ **2 :** worth little : not very good **3 :** gained without much effort ⟨a *cheap* victory⟩ **4 :** lowered in one's own opinion ⟨feel *cheap*⟩ **5 :** charging low prices ⟨a *cheap* hotel⟩ — **cheap·ly** *adv*

²cheap *adv* : at low cost

cheap·en \'chē-pən\ *vb* : to make or become cheap or cheaper

¹cheat \'chēt\ *n* **1 :** an act of cheating : DECEPTION, FRAUD **2 :** a dishonest person

²cheat *vb* **1 :** to take something away from or keep from having something by dishonest tricks : DEFRAUD **2 :** to use unfair or dishonest methods to gain an advantage ⟨*cheat* on a test⟩ ⟨*cheat* at cards⟩

¹check \'chek\ *n* **1 :** a sudden stopping of progress : PAUSE **2 :** something that delays, stops, or holds back : RESTRAINT **3** : a standard or guide for testing and studying something **4 :** EXAMINATION 1, INVESTIGATION **5 :** a written order telling a bank to pay out money from a person's account to the one named on the order ⟨pay a bill by *check*⟩ **6 :** a ticket or token showing a person's ownership, identity, or claim to something ⟨a baggage *check*⟩ **7 :** a slip of paper showing the amount due : BILL ⟨who will pay the *check* at dinner⟩ **8 :** a pattern in squares **9 :** material with a design in squares **10 :** a mark typically ✓ placed beside a written or printed item to show that something has been specially noted

²check *vb* **1 :** to bring to a sudden stop **2** : to keep from expressing ⟨*check* one's temper⟩ **3 :** to make sure that something is correct or satisfactory : VERIFY **4 :** to mark with a check ⟨*check* the correct answer⟩ **5 :** to mark with squares ⟨a *checked* suit⟩ **6 :** to leave or accept for safekeeping or for shipment ⟨*check* baggage⟩ **7 :** to be the same on every point : TALLY

check·er·board \'chek-ər-ˌbōrd\ *n* : a board marked with sixty-four squares in two colors and used for games (as checkers)

check·ers \'chek-ərz\ *n* : a game played on a checkerboard by two players each having twelve pieces

\ə\ **abut**	\aù\ **out**	\i\ **tip**	\ò\ **saw**	\ù\ **foot**
\ər\ **further**	\ch\ **chin**	\ī\ **life**	\òi\ **coin**	\y\ **yet**
\a\ **mat**	\e\ **pet**	\j\ **job**	\th\ **thin**	\yü\ **few**
\ā\ **take**	\ē\ **easy**	\ng\ **sing**	\th\ **this**	\yù\ **cure**
\ä\ **cot, cart**	\g\ **go**	\ō\ **bone**	\ü\ **food**	\zh\ **vision**

check·up \'chek-,əp\ *n* **1** : INSPECTION, EXAMINATION **2** : a physical examination

cheek \'chēk\ *n* **1** : the side of the face below the eye and above and beside the mouth **2** : IMPUDENCE

¹**cheep** \'chēp\ *vb* : ¹PEEP, CHIRP

²**cheep** *n* : ¹CHIRP

¹**cheer** \'chiər\ *n* **1** : state of mind or heart : SPIRIT ⟨be of good *cheer*⟩ **2** : good spirits ⟨full of *cheer*⟩ **3** : something that gladdens ⟨words of *cheer*⟩ **4** : a shout of praise or encouragement ⟨three *cheers* for the team⟩

²**cheer** *vb* **1** : to give hope to : make happier : COMFORT ⟨*cheer* the sick⟩ **2** : to urge on especially with shouts or cheers ⟨*cheer* a team to victory⟩ **3** : to shout with joy, approval, or enthusiasm **4** : to grow or be cheerful — usually used with *up*

cheer·ful \'chiər-fəl\ *adj* : full of good spirits : PLEASANT — **cheer·ful·ly** \-fə-lē\ *adv* — **cheer·ful·ness** *n*

cheer·less \'chiər-ləs\ *adj* : offering no cheer : GLOOMY ⟨a *cheerless* room⟩

cheery \'chiər-ē\ *adj* **cheer·i·er; cheer·i·est** : merry and bright in manner or effect : CHEERFUL — **cheer·i·ly** \-ə-lē\ *adv* — **cheer·i·ness** \-ē-nəs\ *n*

cheese \'chēz\ *n* : the curd of milk pressed for use as food

cheese·cloth \'chēz-,klȯth\ *n* : a thin loosely woven cotton cloth

cheesy \'chē-zē\ *adj* **chees·i·er; chees·i·est** : like or suggesting cheese

chef \'shef\ *n* **1** : a chief cook **2** : ¹COOK

¹**chem·i·cal** \'kem-i-kəl\ *adj* : of or relating to chemistry or chemicals — **chem·i·cal·ly** *adv*

²**chemical** *n* : a substance (as an acid) that is formed when two or more other substances act upon one another or that is used to produce a change in another substance (as in making plastics)

chem·ist \'kem-əst\ *n* : a person trained or engaged in chemistry

chem·is·try \'kem-əs-trē\ *n* **1** : a science that deals with the composition and properties of substances and of the changes they undergo **2** : chemical composition and properties ⟨the *chemistry* of food⟩

cher·ish \'cher-ish\ *vb* **1** : to hold dear ⟨*cherish* a friend⟩ **2** : to keep deeply in mind : cling to ⟨*cherish* a belief⟩ **synonyms** see APPRECIATE

Cher·o·kee \'cher-ə-kē\ *n, pl* **Cherokee** *or* **Cherokees** : a member of an Indian people originally from the southern Appalachian mountains

cher·ry \'cher-ē\ *n, pl* **cher·ries** **1** : the round red or yellow fruit of a tree (**cherry tree**) that is related to the plum **2** : a medium red

cher·ub \'cher-əb\ *n* **1** : a painting or drawing of a beautiful child usually with wings **2** : a chubby rosy child

chess \'ches\ *n* : a game of capture played on a board by two players each using sixteen pieces that have set moves

chest \'chest\ *n* **1** : a container (as a box or case) for storing, safekeeping, or shipping ⟨tool *chest*⟩ ⟨linen *chest*⟩ **2** : a public fund ⟨community *chest*⟩ **3** : the part of the body enclosed by the ribs and breastbone — **chest·ed** \'ches-təd\ *adj*

chest·nut \'ches-nət\ *n* **1** : a sweet edible nut that grows in burs on a tree (**chestnut tree**) related to the beech **2** : a reddish brown

chev·ron \'shev-rən\ *n* : a sleeve badge of one or more bars or stripes usually in the shape of an upside down V indicating the wearer's rank (as in the armed forces)

¹**chew** \'chü\ *vb* : to crush or grind with the teeth

²**chew** *n* **1** : the act of chewing **2** : something for chewing ⟨a *chew* of tobacco⟩

chew·ing gum \'chü-ing-\ *n* : gum usually of sweetened and flavored chicle prepared for chewing

chewy \'chü-ē\ *adj* **chew·i·er; chew·i·est** : requiring chewing ⟨*chewy* candy⟩

¹**chic** \'shēk\ *n* : fashionable style

²**chic** *adj* : STYLISH, SMART ⟨*chic* clothes⟩

¹**Chi·ca·no** \chi-'kän-ō\ *n, pl* **Chicanos** : an American of Mexican ancestry

²**Chicano** *adj* : of or relating to Chicanos

chick \'chik\ *n* **1** : a young chicken **2** : CHILD 2

chick·a·dee \'chik-ə-dē\ *n* : a small bird with fluffy grayish feathers and usually a black cap

chickadee

¹**chick·en** \'chik-ən\ *n* **1** : the common domestic fowl especially when young : a young hen or rooster **2** : the flesh of a chicken for use as food

²**chicken** *adj* : CHICKENHEARTED

chick·en·heart·ed \,chik-ən-'härt-əd\ *adj* : COWARDLY, TIMID

chicken pox *n* : a contagious disease especially of children in which there is fever and the skin breaks out in watery blisters

chick·weed \'chik,wēd\ *n* : a weedy

plant related to the pinks that has small pointed leaves and whitish flowers

chi·cle \'chik-əl, -lē\ *n* : a gum obtained from the sap of a tropical American tree and used in making chewing gum

chide \'chīd\ *vb* **chid** \'chid\ *or* **chid·ed** \'chīd-əd\; **chid** *or* **chid·den** \'chid-n\ *or* **chided; chiding** : to find fault with : SCOLD

chickweed

¹**chief** \'chēf\ *n* : the head or a group : LEADER ⟨the *chief* of police⟩ — **in chief** : in the chief position or place ⟨editor *in chief*⟩

²**chief** *adj* **1** : highest in rank or authority ⟨*chief* executive⟩ **2** : most important : MAIN ⟨the *chief* streets are kept clean⟩

chief·ly \'chē-flē\ *adv* **1** : above all **2** : for the most part

chief master sergeant *n* : a noncommissioned officer in the Air Force ranking above a senior master sergeant

chief petty officer *n* : a petty officer in the Navy or Coast Guard ranking above a petty officer first class

chief·tain \'chēf-tən\ *n* : a chief especially of a band, tribe, or clan

chief warrant officer *n* : a warrant officer in any of the three top grades

chig·ger \'chig-ər\ *n* : the larva of some mites that has six legs, clings to the skin, and causes itching

chil·blain \'chil-ˌblān\ *n* : a red swollen itchy condition caused by cold that occurs especially on the hands or feet

child \'chīld\ *n*, *pl* **chil·dren** \'chil-drən\ **1** : an unborn or recently born person **2** : a young person of either sex between infancy and youth **3** : one's son or daughter of any age

child·birth \'chīld-ˌbərth\ *n* : the act or process of giving birth to a child

child·hood \'chīld-ˌhùd\ *n* : the period of life between infancy and youth

child·ish \'chīl-dish\ *adj* **1** : of, like, or thought to be suitable to children ⟨*childish* laughter⟩ **2** : showing the less pleasing qualities (as silliness) often thought to be those of children

child·like \'chīld-ˌlīk\ *adj* **1** : of or relating to a child or childhood **2** : showing the more pleasing qualities (as innocence and trustfulness) often thought to be those of children

chili *or* **chile** \'chil-ē\ *n*, *pl* **chil·ies** *or* **chil·es** **1** : a plant whose small red fruits are hot peppers **2** : a dish made of hot peppers and meat

¹**chill** \'chil\ *vb* **1** : to make or become cold or chilly **2** : to make cool especially without freezing ⟨*chill* pudding for dessert⟩ **3** : to harden the surface of (as metal) by sudden cooling

²**chill** *adj* **1** : unpleasantly cold : RAW ⟨a *chill* wind⟩ **2** : not friendly ⟨a *chill* greeting⟩

³**chill** *n* **1** : a feeling of coldness accompanied by shivering ⟨suffering from a *chill*⟩ **2** : unpleasant coldness ⟨a *chill* in the air⟩

chilly \'chil-ē\ *adj* **chill·i·er; chill·i·est** : noticeably cold — **chill·i·ness** *n*

¹**chime** \'chīm\ *n* **1** : a set of bells tuned to play music **2** : the music from a set of bells — usually used in pl. **3** : a musical sound suggesting bells

²**chime** *vb* **chimed; chim·ing 1** : to make sounds like a bell : ring chimes **2** : to call or indicate by chiming ⟨the clock *chimed* midnight⟩

chime in *vb* : to break into or join in a discussion

chim·ney \'chim-nē\ *n*, *pl* **chim·neys 1** : a passage for smoke especially in the form of a vertical structure of brick or stone that reaches above the roof of a building **2** : a glass tube around a lamp flame

chimney sweep *n* : a person who cleans soot from chimneys

chimney swift *n* : a small dark gray bird with long narrow wings that often attaches its nest to chimneys

chimp \'chimp\ *n* : CHIMPANZEE

chim·pan·zee \ˌchim-ˌpan-'zē, chim-'pan-zē\ *n* : an African ape that lives mostly in trees and is smaller than the related gorilla

¹**chin** \'chin\ *n* : the part of the face below the mouth and including the point of the lower jaw

²**chin** *vb* **chinned; chin·ning** : to raise oneself while hang-

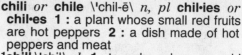
chimpanzee

\ə\ abut	\aù\ out	\i\ tip	\ȯ\ saw	\ù\ foot
\ər\ further	\ch\ chin	\ī\ life	\òi\ coin	\y\ yet
\a\ mat	\e\ pet	\j\ job	\th\ thin	\yü\ few
\ā\ take	\ē\ easy	\ng\ sing	\t̲h̲\ this	\yu̇\ cure
\ä\ cot, cart	\g\ go	\ō\ bone	\ü\ food	\zh\ vision

ing by the hands until the chin is level with the support

chi·na \'chī-nə\ *n* **1** : porcelain ware **2** : pottery (as dishes) for use in one's home

chin·chil·la \chin-'chil-ə\ *n* : a South American animal that is somewhat like a squirrel and is hunted or raised for its soft silvery gray fur

chinchilla

¹Chi·nese \chī-'nēz\ *adj* : of or relating to China, the Chinese people, or Chinese

²Chinese *n, pl* **Chinese 1** : a person born or living in China **2** : a group of related languages used in China

chink \'chink\ *n* : a narrow slit or crack (as in a wall)

chi·no \'chē-nō, 'shē-\ *n, pl* **chinos 1** : a usually khaki cotton fabric **2** *pl* : clothing made of chino

¹chip \'chip\ *n* **1** : a small piece (as of wood, stone, or glass) cut or broken off **2** : a small thin slice of food **3** : a flaw left after a small piece has been broken off

²chip *vb* **chipped; chip·ping 1** : to cut or break chips from **2** : to break off in small pieces

chip·munk \'chip-,məngk\ *n* : a small striped animal related to the squirrels

chipmunk

chip·ping sparrow \'chip-ing-\ *n* : a small North American sparrow that often nests about houses and has a weak chirp as a call

¹chirp \'chərp\ *n* : the short sharp sound made by crickets and some small birds

²chirp *vb* : to make a chirp

¹chis·el \'chiz-əl\ *n* : a metal tool with a sharp edge at the end of a usually flat piece used to chip away stone, wood, or metal

²chisel *vb* **chis·eled** *or* **chis·elled; chis·el·ing** *or* **chis·el·ling** : to cut or shape with a chisel

chiv·al·rous \'shiv-əl-rəs\ *adj* **1** : of or relating to chivalry **2** : having or showing honor, generosity, and courtesy **3** : showing special courtesy and regard to women

chiv·al·ry \'shiv-əl-rē\ *n* **1** : a body of knights **2** : the system, spirit, ways, or customs of knighthood **3** : chivalrous conduct

Word History The French word for a knight came from a Latin word meaning "horseman." Knights are taught to be brave, loyal, and kind, and the French had a word for this way of acting. It was made from the French word for a knight. Our word *chivalry* comes from the French word for the knight's behavior.

chlo·rine \'klōr-,ēn, -ən\ *n* : a chemical element that is a greenish yellow irritating gas of strong odor used as a bleach and as a disinfectant to purify water

¹chlo·ro·form \'klōr-ə-,fórm\ *n* : a colorless heavy liquid used especially to dissolve fatty substances and in the past in medicine to deaden the pain of operations but now mostly replaced by less poisonous substances

²chloroform *vb* : to make unconscious or kill with chloroform

chlo·ro·phyll \'klōr-ə-,fil\ *n* : the green coloring matter by means of which green plants produce carbohydrates from cabon dioxide and water

chlo·ro·plast \'klōr-ə-,plast\ *n* : one of the tiny bodies in which chlorophyll is found

chock–full \'chäk-'fùl\ *or* **chuck–full** \'chək-\ *adj* : full to the limit

choc·o·late \'chäk-ə-lət, 'chäk-lət, 'chók-\ *n* **1** : a food prepared from ground roasted cacao beans **2** : a beverage of chocolate in water or milk **3** : a candy made or coated with chocolate

¹choice \'chȯis\ *n* **1** : the act of choosing : SELECTION **2** : the power of choosing : OPTION **3** : a person or thing chosen **4** : the best part **5** : a large enough number and variety to choose among

²choice *adj* **choic·er; choic·est** : of very good quality

choir \'kwīr\ *n* **1** : an organized group of singers especially in a church **2** : the part of a church set aside for the singers

¹choke \'chōk\ *vb* **choked; chok·ing 1** : to keep from breathing in a normal way by cutting off the supply of air ⟨*choked* by thick smoke⟩ **2** : to have the windpipe blocked entirely or partly ⟨*choke* on a bone⟩ **3** : to slow or prevent the growth or action of ⟨flowers *choked* by weeds⟩ **4** : to block by clogging ⟨leaves *choked* the sewer⟩

²choke *n* **1** : the act or sound of choking **2** : something that chokes

choke·cher·ry \'chōk-₁cher-ē\ *n, pl* **choke-cher·ries** : a wild cherry tree with long clusters of reddish black fruits that pucker the mouth

chokecherry

chol·era \'käl-ə-rə\ *n* : a dangerous infectious disease of Asian origin in which violent vomiting and dysentery are present

choose \'chüz\ *vb* **chose** \'chōz\; **cho·sen** \'chōz-n\; **choos·ing 1** : to select freely and after careful thought ⟨*choose* a leader⟩ **2** : DECIDE 3 ⟨we *chose* to leave⟩ **3** : to see fit ⟨do as you *choose*⟩

synonyms CHOOSE, ELECT, and SELECT mean to decide upon one from among several. CHOOSE suggests that one does some thinking and makes a careful judgment before deciding ⟨*chose* to follow the right course⟩ ELECT may suggest that of two things one is deliberately picked and the other rejected ⟨*elect* one candidate for president⟩ SELECT suggests that there are many things from which to choose ⟨customers may *select* from a great variety of goods⟩

choosy \'chü-zē\ *adj* **choos·i·er; choos·i·est** : careful in making choices

¹chop \'chäp\ *vb* **chopped; chop·ping 1** : to cut by striking especially over and over with something sharp ⟨*chop* down a tree⟩ **2** : to cut into small pieces : MINCE ⟨*chop* meat⟩ **3** : to strike quickly or again and again

²chop *n* **1** : a sharp downward blow or stroke (as with an ax) **2** : a small cut of meat often including a part of a rib ⟨a lamb *chop*⟩ **3** : a short quick motion (as of a wave)

chop·per \'chäp-ər\ *n* **1** : someone or something that chops **2** : HELICOPTER

¹chop·py \'chäp-ē\ *adj* **chop·pi·er; chop·pi·est** : frequently changing direction ⟨a *choppy* wind⟩

²choppy *adj* **chop·pi·er; chop·pi·est 1** : rough with small waves **2** : JERKY

chops \'chäps\ *n pl* : the fleshy covering of the jaws

chop·stick \'chäp-₁stik\ *n* : one of two thin sticks used chiefly in oriental countries to lift food to the mouth

chopstick

cho·ral \'kōr-əl\ *adj* : of, relating to, or sung or recited by a chorus or choir or in chorus

cho·rale \kə-'ral\ *n* **1** : a hymn sung by the choir or congregation at a church service **2** : CHORUS 1

¹chord \'kȯrd\ *n* : a group of tones sounded together to form harmony

²chord *n* : a straight line joining two points on a curve

chore \'chōr\ *n* **1 chores** *pl* : the regular light work about a home or farm **2** : an ordinary task **3** : a dull, unpleasant, or difficult task

cho·re·og·ra·phy \₁kōr-ē-'äg-rə-fē\ *n* : the art of dancing or of arranging dances and especially ballets — **cho·re·og·ra·pher** \-fər\ *n*

cho·ris·ter \'kōr-ə-stər\ *n* : a singer in a choir

chor·tle \'chȯrt-l\ *vb* **chor·tled; chor·tling** : to chuckle especially in satisfaction

¹cho·rus \'kōr-əs\ *n* **1** : a group of singers : CHOIR **2** : a group of dancers and singers (as in a musical comedy) **3** : a part of a song or hymn that is repeated every so often : REFRAIN **4** : a song meant to be sung by a group : group singing **5** : sounds uttered by a group of persons or animals together

²chorus *vb* : to speak, sing, or sound at the same time or together

chose *past of* CHOOSE

\ə\ abut	\au̇\ out	\i\ tip	\ȯ\ saw	\u̇\ foot
\ər\ further	\ch\ chin	\ī\ life	\ȯi\ coin	\y\ yet
\a\ mat	\e\ pet	\j\ job	\th\ thin	\yü\ few
\ā\ take	\ē\ easy	\ng\ sing	\th\ this	\yu̇\ cure
\ä\ cot, cart	\g\ go	\ō\ bone	\ü\ food	\zh\ vision

cho·sen \'chōz-n\ *adj* **1** : picked to be given favor or special privilege ⟨a *chosen* few⟩ **2** : picked by God for special protection ⟨a *chosen* people⟩

chow \'chaù\ *n* : a muscular dog with a blue-black tongue, a short tail curled close to the back, straight legs, and a thick coat

chow·der \'chaùd-ər\ *n* : a soup or stew made of fish, clams, or a vegetable usually simmered in milk

Christ \'krīst\ *n* : JESUS

chris·ten \'kris-n\ *vb* **1** : BAPTIZE 1 **2** : to give a name to at baptism ⟨*christened* the baby Robin⟩ **3** : to name or dedicate (as a ship) in a ceremony like that of baptism

Chris·ten·dom \'kris-n-dəm\ *n* **1** : the entire body of Christians **2** : the part of the world in which Christianity is most common

chris·ten·ing \'kris-ning, 'kris-n-ing\ *n* : BAPTISM

¹Chris·tian \'kris-chən\ *n* **1** : a person who believes in Jesus and follows his teachings **2** : a member of a Christian church

²Christian *adj* **1** : of or relating to Jesus or the religion based on his teachings **2** : of or relating to Christians ⟨a *Christian* nation⟩ **3** : being what a Christian should be or do ⟨*Christian* behavior toward others⟩

Chris·tian·i·ty \,kris-chē-'an-ət-ē\ *n* **1** : CHRISTENDOM 1 **2** : the religion of Christians

Christian name *n* : the personal name given to a person at birth or christening

Christ·mas \'kris-məs\ *n* : December 25 celebrated in honor of the birth of Christ

Christ·mas·tide \'kris-mə-,stīd\ *n* : the season of Christmas

Christmas tree *n* : a usually evergreen tree decorated at Christmas

chro·mat·ic scale \krō-,mat-ik-\ *n* : a musical scale that has all half steps

chrome \'krōm\ *n* **1** : CHROMIUM **2** : something plated with an alloy of chromium

chro·mi·um \'krō-mē-əm\ *n* : a bluish white metallic chemical element used especially in alloys

chro·mo·some \'krō-mə-,sōm\ *n* : one of the rodlike bodies of a cell nucleus that contain genes and divide when the cell divides

chron·ic \'krän-ik\ *adj* **1** : continuing for a long time or returning often ⟨a *chronic* disease⟩ **2** : HABITUAL 2 ⟨a *chronic* complainer⟩ — **chron·i·cal·ly** \-i-kə-lē\ *adv*

¹chron·i·cle \'krän-i-kəl\ *n* : an account of events in the order of their happening : HISTORY

²chronicle *vb* **chron·i·cled; chron·i·cling** : to record in or as if in a chronicle

chron·o·log·i·cal \,krän-l-'äj-i-kəl\ *adj* : arranged in or according to the order of time ⟨*chronological* tables of American history⟩ — **chron·o·log·i·cal·ly** *adv*

chrys·a·lis \'kris-ə-ləs\ *n* : a moth or butterfly pupa that is enclosed in a firm protective case

chry·san·the·mum \kri-'san-thə-məm\ *n* : a plant related to the daisies that has deeply notched leaves and brightly colored often double flower heads

chub·by \'chəb-ē\ *adj* **chub·bi·er; chub·bi·est** : ³PLUMP ⟨a *chubby* baby⟩

¹chuck \'chək\ *vb* **1** : to give a pat or tap to ⟨*chucked* me under the chin⟩ **2** : ¹TOSS 2 ⟨*chuck* a ball back and forth⟩

²chuck *n* **1** : a pat or nudge under the chin **2** : ²TOSS

chuck–full *variant of* CHOCK-FULL

¹chuck·le \'chək-əl\ *vb* **chuck·led; chuck·ling** : to laugh in a quiet way

²chuckle *n* : a low quiet laugh

chuck wagon \'chək-\ *n* : a wagon carrying a stove and food for cooking

¹chug \'chəg\ *n* : a dull explosive sound

²chug *vb* **chugged; chug·ging** : to move with chugs ⟨an old car *chugging* along⟩

¹chum \'chəm\ *n* : a close friend : PAL

²chum *vb* **chummed; chum·ming** : to be chums

chum·my \'chəm-ē\ *adj* **chum·mi·er; chum·mi·est** : being on close friendly terms : SOCIABLE

chunk \'chəngk\ *n* : a short thick piece (as of ice)

chunky \'chəng-kē\ *adj* **chunk·i·er; chunk·i·est** : STOCKY

church \'chərch\ *n* **1** : a building for public worship and especially Christian worship **2** : an organized body of religious believers **3** : public worship

church·yard \'chərch-,yärd\ *n* : a yard that belongs to a church and is often used as a burial ground

¹churn \'chərn\ *n* : a container in which milk or cream is stirred or shaken in making butter

²churn *vb* **1** : to stir or shake in a churn (as in making butter) **2** : to stir or shake violently

chute \'shüt\ *n* **1** : a sloping plane, trough, or passage down or through which things are slid or dropped **2** : ¹PARACHUTE

ci·ca·da \sə-'kād-ə\ *n* : an insect that has transparent wings and a stout body and is related to the true bugs

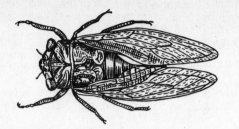

cicada

-cide \ˌsīd\ *n suffix* **1** : killer ⟨insecti*cide*⟩ **2** : killing

ci·der \ˈsīd-ər\ *n* : the juice pressed out of fruit (as apples) and used especially as a drink and in making vinegar

ci·gar \si-ˈgär\ *n* : a small roll of tobacco leaf for smoking

cig·a·rette \ˌsig-ə-ˈret\ *n* : a small roll of cut tobacco wrapped in paper for smoking

cil·i·um \ˈsil-ē-əm\ *n, pl* **cil·ia** \ˈsil-ē-ə\ : any of the structures on the surface of some cells that look like tiny flexible eyelashes

¹cinch \ˈsinch\ *n* **1** : GIRTH 1 **2** : a sure or an easy thing

²cinch *vb* **1** : to fasten or tighten a girth on ⟨*cinch* up a horse⟩ **2** : to fasten with or as if with a girth ⟨*cinch* a saddle⟩ in place

cin·cho·na \sing-ˈkō-nə\ *n* : a South American tree whose bark yields quinine

cin·der \ˈsin-dər\ *n* **1** : SLAG **2** : a piece of partly burned coal or wood that is not burning **3** : EMBER **4** **cinders** *pl* : ²ASH 1

cin·e·ma \ˈsin-ə-mə\ *n* **1** : a movie theater **2** : the movie industry

cin·na·mon \ˈsin-ə-mən\ *n* : a spice made from the fragrant bark of tropical trees related to the Old World laurel

¹ci·pher \ˈsī-fər\ *n* **1** : ZERO 1 **2** : an unimportant or worthless person : NONENTITY **3** : a method of secret writing or the alphabet or letters and symbols used in such writing **4** : a message in code

²cipher *vb* : to use figures in doing a problem in arithmetic : CALCULATE

¹cir·cle \ˈsər-kəl\ *n* **1** : a closed curve every point of which is equally distant from a central point within it : the space inside such a closed curve **2** : something in the form of a circle or part of a circle **3** : ¹CYCLE 2, ROUND ⟨the wheel has

come full *circle*⟩ **4** : a group of people sharing a common interest

²circle *vb* **cir·cled**; **cir·cling** **1** : to enclose in or as if in a circle **2** : to move or revolve around **3** : to move in or as if in a circle

cir·cuit \ˈsər-kət\ *n* **1** : a boundary line around an area **2** : an enclosed space **3** : a moving around (as in a circle) ⟨the *circuit* of the earth around the sun⟩ **4** : a traveling from place to place in an area (as by a judge) so as to stop in each place at a certain time : a course so traveled **5** : a chain of theaters at which stage shows are shown in turn **6** : the complete path of an electric current

cir·cu·itous \ˌsər-ˈkyü-ət-əs\ *adj* **1** : having a circular or winding course **2** : not saying what one means in simple and sincere language

¹cir·cu·lar \ˈsər-kyə-lər\ *adj* **1** : having the form of a circle : ROUND ⟨a *circular* track⟩ **2** : passing or going around in a circle ⟨*circular* motion⟩ **3** : CIRCUITOUS 2 **4** : sent around to a number of persons ⟨a *circular* letter⟩

²circular *n* : a printed notice or advertisement given or sent to many people

cir·cu·late \ˈsər-kyə-ˌlāt\ *vb* **cir·cu·lat·ed**; **cir·cu·lat·ing** **1** : to move around in a course ⟨blood *circulates* in the body⟩ **2** : to pass or be passed from place to place or from person to person ⟨money *circulates*⟩ ⟨*circulate* a rumor⟩

cir·cu·la·tion \ˌsər-kyə-ˈlā-shən\ *n* **1** : motion around in a course ⟨the *circulation* of air in a room⟩ **2** : passage from place to place or person to person ⟨coins in *circulation*⟩ **3** : the average number of copies (as of a newspaper) sold in a given period

cir·cu·la·to·ry \ˈsər-kyə-lə-ˌtōr-ē\ *adj* : of or relating to circulation (as of the blood)

circum- *prefix* : around : about ⟨*circum*polar⟩

cir·cum·fer·ence \sər-ˈkəm-fə-rəns, -fərns\ *n* **1** : the line that goes around a circle **2** : a boundary line or circuit enclosing an area **3** : the distance around something

cir·cum·nav·i·gate \ˌsər-kəm-ˈnav-ə-ˌgāt\ *vb* **cir·cum·nav·i·gat·ed**; **cir·cum·nav·i·gat·ing** : to go completely around (as the earth) especially by water

cir·cum·po·lar \ˌsər-kəm-ˈpō-lər\ *adj* **1** : continually visible above the horizon ⟨a

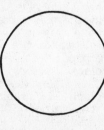

circle 1

\ə\ abut	\au̇\ out	\i\ tip	\ȯ\ saw	\u̇\ foot
\ər\ further	\ch\ chin	\ī\ life	\ȯi\ coin	\y\ yet
\a\ mat	\e\ pet	\j\ job	\th\ thin	\yü\ few
\ā\ take	\ē\ easy	\ng\ sing	\th\ this	\yu̇\ cure
\ä\ cot, cart	\g\ go	\ō\ bone	\ü\ food	\zh\ vision

circumpolar star⟩ **2 :** surrounding or found near the north pole or south pole

cir·cum·stance \'sər-kəm-ˌstans\ *n* **1 :** a fact or event that must be considered along with another fact or event **2 circumstances** *pl* **:** conditions at a certain time or place ⟨under the *circumstances* I must leave home⟩ **3 circumstances** *pl* **:** situation with regard to wealth ⟨in easy *circumstances*⟩ **4 :** ¹CHANCE 1, FATE ⟨an unfortunate victim of *circumstance*⟩

cir·cum·vent \ˌsər-kəm-'vent\ *vb* **1 :** to go around **:** BYPASS **2 :** to get the better of or avoid the force or effect of especially by trickery ⟨*circumvented* the tax laws⟩

cir·cus \'sər-kəs\ *n* **1 :** a show that usually travels from place to place and that has a variety of exhibitions including riding, acrobatic feats, wild animal displays, and the performances of jugglers and clowns **2 :** a circus performance **3 :** the performers and equipment of a circus

cir·rus \'sir-əs\ *n, pl* **cir·ri** \'sir-ī\ **:** a thin white cloud of tiny ice crystals that forms at a very high altitude

cis·tern \'sis-tərn\ *n* **:** an artificial reservoir or tank for storing water usually underground

cit·a·del \'sit-əd-l, -ə-ˌdel\ *n* **1 :** a fortress that sits high above a city **2 :** a strong fortress

ci·ta·tion \sī-'tā-shən\ *n* **1 :** an act or instance of quoting **2 :** QUOTATION 1 **3 :** a formal statement of what a person did to be chosen to receive an award

cite \'sīt\ *vb* **cit·ed; cit·ing** **1 :** to quote as an example, authority, or proof **2 :** to refer to especially in praise

cit·i·zen \'sit-ə-zən\ *n* **1 :** a person who lives in a city or town **2 :** a person who owes loyalty to a government and is protected by it

cit·i·zen·ry \'sit-ə-zən-rē\ *n* **:** the whole body of citizens

cit·i·zen·ship \'sit-ə-zən-ˌship\ *n* **:** the state of being a citizen

cit·ron \'si-trən\ *n* **1 :** a citrus fruit like the smaller lemon and having a thick rind that is preserved for use in cakes and puddings **2 :** a small hard watermelon used especially in pickles and preserves

cit·rus \'si-trəs\ *adj* **:** of or relating to a group of often

citron 1

thorny trees and shrubs of warm regions whose fruits include the lemon, lime, orange, and grapefruit

city \'sit-ē\ *n, pl* **cit·ies** **1 :** a place in which people live that is larger or more important than a town **2 :** the people of a city

civ·ic \'siv-ik\ *adj* **:** of or relating to a citizen, a city, or citizenship ⟨*civic* pride⟩ ⟨*civic* duty⟩

civ·ics \'siv-iks\ *n* **:** a study of the rights and duties of citizens

civ·il \'siv-əl\ *adj* **1 :** of or relating to citizens ⟨*civil* liberties⟩ **2 :** of or relating to the state **3 :** of or relating to ordinary or government affairs rather than to those of the military or the church **4 :** polite without being friendly ⟨gave a *civil* answer⟩ **5 :** relating to court action between individuals having to do with private rights rather than criminal action

synonyms CIVIL, POLITE, and COURTEOUS mean obeying the rules of good behavior. CIVIL suggests showing only enough proper behavior to avoid being actually rude ⟨that bank teller is barely *civil*⟩ POLITE suggests good manners and thoughtfulness ⟨the host was *polite* and made us feel at home⟩ COURTEOUS may suggest a politeness that is somewhat dignified ⟨the servants were taught to be *courteous* always⟩

¹ci·vil·ian \sə-'vil-yən\ *n* **:** a person not on active duty in a military, police, or firefighting force

²civilian *adj* **:** of or relating to a civilian

ci·vil·i·ty \sə-'vil-ət-ē\ *n, pl* **ci·vil·i·ties** **1 :** civil behavior **2 :** COURTESY 1

civ·i·li·za·tion \ˌsiv-ə-lə-'zā-shən\ *n* **1 :** an advanced stage (as in art, science, and government) of social development **2 :** the way of life of a people ⟨Greek *civilization*⟩

civ·i·lize \'siv-ə-ˌlīz\ *vb* **civ·i·lized; civ·i·liz·ing** **:** to cause to develop out of a primitive state

civil service *n* **:** the branch of a government that takes care of the business of running a state but that does not include the lawmaking branch, the military, or the court system

civil war *n* **:** a war between opposing groups of citizens of the same country

¹clack \'klak\ *vb* **1 :** PRATTLE **2 :** to make or cause to make a clatter

²clack *n* **1 :** rapid continous talk **:** CHATTER **2 :** a sound of clacking ⟨the *clack* of a typewriter⟩

clad \'klad\ *adj* **:** being covered **:** wearing clothes

¹claim \'klām\ *vb* **1** : to ask for as rightfully belonging to oneself **2** : to call for : REQUIRE ⟨business that *claims* attention⟩ **3** : to state as a fact : MAINTAIN **4** : to make a claim ⟨*claims* to know nothing about it⟩

²claim *n* **1** : a demand for something due or believed to be due ⟨an insurance *claim*⟩ **2** : a right to something **3** : a statement that may be doubted **4** : something (as an area of land) claimed as one's own ⟨a prospector's *claim*⟩

¹clam \'klam\ *n* : a shellfish with a soft body and a hinged double shell

²clam *vb* **clammed; clam·ming** : to dig or gather clams

clam·bake \'klam-ˌbāk\ *n* : an outing where food is cooked usually on heated rocks covered by seaweed

clam [caption]

clam·ber \'klam-bər\ *vb* : to climb in an awkward way (as by scrambling)

clam·my \'klam-ē\ *adj* **clam·mi·er; clam·mi·est** : unpleasantly damp, soft, sticky, and usually cool — **clam·mi·ly** \'klam-ə-lē\ *adv* — **clam·mi·ness** \'klam-ē-nəs\ *n*

¹clam·or \'klam-ər\ *n* **1** : a noisy shouting **2** : a loud continous noise **3** : strong and active protest or demand ⟨public *clamor* for a tax cut⟩

²clamor *vb* : to make a clamor

clam·or·ous \'klam-ə-rəs\ *adj* : full of clamor : very noisy

¹clamp \'klamp\ *n* : a device that holds or presses parts together firmly

²clamp *vb* : to fasten or to hold together with or as if with a clamp

clan \'klan\ *n* **1** : a group (as in the Scottish Highlands) made up of households whose heads claim to have a common ancestor **2** : a group of persons united by some common interest

¹clang \'klang\ *vb* : to make or cause to make a loud ringing sound

²clang *n* : a loud ringing sound like that made by pieces of metal striking together

¹clank \'klangk\ *vb* **1** : to make or cause to make a clank or series of clanks ⟨the radiator hissed and *clanked*⟩ **2** : to move with a clank

²clank *n* : a sharp short ringing sound

¹clap \'klap\ *vb* **clapped; clap·ping 1** : to strike noisily : SLAM, BANG ⟨*clap* two boards together⟩ ⟨the door *clapped* shut⟩ **2** : to strike (one's hands) together again and again in applause **3** : to strike with the open hand ⟨*clap* a friend on the

shoulder⟩ **4** : to put or place quickly or with force

²clap *n* **1** : a loud noisy crash made by or as if by the striking together of two hard surfaces **2** : a hard or a friendly slap

clap·board \'klab-ərd, -ˌōrd\ *n* : a narrow board thicker at one edge than at the other used as siding for a building

clap·per \'klap-ər\ *n* : one (as the tongue of a bell) that makes a clapping sound

clar·i·fy \'klar-ə-ˌfi\ *vb* **clar·i·fied; clar·i·fy·ing 1** : to make or to become pure or clear ⟨*clarify* a liquid⟩ **2** : to make or become more easily understood ⟨*clarify* a statement⟩

clar·i·net \ˌklar-ə-'net\ *n* : a woodwind instrument in the form of a tube with finger holes and keys

clar·i·on \'klar-ē-ən\ *adj* : being loud and clear

clar·i·ty \'klar-ət-ē\ *n* : clear quality or state ⟨the *clarity* of the explanation⟩

¹clash \'klash\ *vb* **1** : to make or cause to make a clash ⟨*clashing* cymbals⟩ **2** : to come into conflict ⟨pickets *clashed* with the police⟩ **3** : to not match well ⟨our ideas *clashed*⟩ ⟨the colors *clashed*⟩

clarinet [caption]

²clash *n* **1** : a loud sharp sound usually of metal striking metal ⟨the *clash* of swords⟩ **2** : a struggle or strong disagreement

¹clasp \'klasp\ *n* **1** : a device for holding together objects or parts of something **2** : ²GRASP 1, GRIP **3** : ²EMBRACE

²clasp *vb* **1** : to fasten with or as if with a clasp **2** : ¹EMBRACE 1 **3** : ²GRASP 1

¹class \'klas\ *n* **1** : a group of pupils meeting at set times for study or instruction **2** : the period during which a study group meets **3** : a course of instruction ⟨a *class* in science⟩ **4** : a body of students who are to graduate at the same time **5** : a group or rank of society ⟨the working *class*⟩ **6** : a group of persons or things of the same kind ⟨birds form a *class* of animals⟩ **7** : a

\ə\ **abut**	\au̇\ **out**	\i\ **tip**	\ȯ\ **saw**	\u̇\ **foot**
\ər\ **further**	\ch\ **chin**	\ī\ **life**	\ȯi\ **coin**	\y\ **yet**
\a\ **mat**	\e\ **pet**	\j\ **job**	\th\ **thin**	\yü\ **few**
\ā\ **take**	\ē\ **easy**	\ng\ **sing**	\th\ **this**	\yu̇\ **cure**
\ä\ **cot, cart**	\g\ **go**	\ō\ **bone**	\ü\ **food**	\zh\ **vision**

grouping or standing (as of goods or services) based on quality

²class *vb* : CLASSIFY

¹clas·sic \'klas-ik\ *adj* **1** : serving as a standard of excellence **2** : fashionable year after year ⟨a *classic* style⟩ **3** : of or relating to the ancient Greeks and Romans or their culture **4** : being very good or typical of its kind ⟨a *classic* example of good writing⟩

²classic *n* **1** : a written work or author of ancient Greece or Rome **2** : a great work of art **3** : something regarded as outstanding of its kind

clas·si·cal \'klas-i-kəl\ *adj* **1** : of or relating to the classics of literature or art and especially to the ancient Greek and Roman classics **2** : of or relating to serious music in the European tradition **3** : concerned with a general study of the arts and sciences

clas·si·fi·ca·tion \,klas-ə-fə-'kā-shən\ *n* **1** : the act of classifying or arranging in classes **2** : an arrangement in classes ⟨a *classification* of plants⟩

clas·si·fy \'klas-ə-,fī\ *vb* **clas·si·fied; clas·si·fy·ing** : to group in classes

class·mate \'klas-,māt\ *n* : a member of the same class in a school or college

class·room \'klas-,rüm, -,rüm\ *n* : a room in a school or college in which classes meet

¹clat·ter \'klat-ər\ *vb* **1** : to make or cause to make a rattling sound ⟨dishes *clattering* in the kitchen⟩ **2** : to move or go with a clatter ⟨the cart *clattered* down the road⟩

²clatter *n* **1** : a rattling sound (as of hard objects striking together) ⟨the *clatter* of pots and pans⟩ **2** : COMMOTION

clause \'klóz\ *n* **1** : a separate part of a document (as a will) **2** : a group of words having its own subject and predicate but forming only part of a complete sentence ⟨"when it rained" in "when it rained they went inside" is a *clause*⟩

clav·i·cle \'klav-i-kəl\ *n* : COLLARBONE

¹claw \'kló\ *n* **1** : a sharp usually thin and curved nail on the finger or toe of an animal (as a cat or bird) **2** : the end of a limb of a lower animal (as an insect, scorpion, or lobster) that is pointed or like pincers **3** : something like a claw in shape or use

²claw *vb* : to scratch, seize, or dig with claws

clay \'klā\ *n* **1** : an earthy material that is sticky and easily molded when wet and hard when baked **2** : a plastic substance used like clay for modeling

¹clean \'klēn\ *adj* **1** : free of dirt or evil ⟨put on a *clean* shirt⟩ ⟨the candidate has a *clean* record⟩ **2** : free of objectionable behavior or language ⟨led a *clean* life⟩ ⟨a *clean* joke⟩ **3** : THOROUGH 1, COMPLETE ⟨a *clean* sweep⟩ **4** : having a simple graceful form : TRIM ⟨a ship with *clean* lines⟩ **5** : ¹SMOOTH 1 ⟨the knife made a *clean* cut⟩

²clean *adv* **1** : so as to clean ⟨a new broom sweeps *clean*⟩ **2** : in a clean way ⟨fight *clean*⟩ **3** : all the way ⟨went *clean* through⟩

³clean *vb* : to make or become clean ⟨*clean* a room⟩ ⟨*clean* up for supper⟩ — **clean·er** *n*

clean·li·ness \'klen-lē-nəs\ *n* : the condition of being clean : the habit of keeping clean

¹clean·ly \'klen-lē\ *adj* **clean·li·er; clean·li·est** **1** : careful to keep clean ⟨a *cleanly* animal⟩ **2** : kept clean ⟨*cleanly* surroundings⟩

²clean·ly \'klēn-lē\ *adv* : in a clean way

cleanse \'klenz\ *vb* **cleansed; cleans·ing** : to make clean

cleans·er \'klen-zər\ *n* : a substance (as a scouring powder) used for cleaning

¹clear \'kliər\ *adj* **1** : BRIGHT 1, LUMINOUS ⟨*clear* sunlight⟩ **2** : free of clouds, haze, or mist ⟨a *clear* day⟩ **3** : UNTROUBLED ⟨a *clear* gaze⟩ **4** : free of blemishes ⟨*clear* skin⟩ **5** : easily seen through ⟨glass is *clear*⟩ ⟨*clear* water⟩ **6** : easily heard, seen, or understood ⟨a *clear* voice⟩ ⟨the meaning is *clear*⟩ **7** : free from doubt : SURE **8** : INNOCENT ⟨a *clear* conscience⟩ **9** : not blocked or limited ⟨a *clear* path⟩ — **clear·ly** *adv* — **clear·ness** *n*

²clear *adv* **1** : in a clear manner **2** : all the way ⟨the hole goes *clear* through⟩

³clear *vb* **1** : to make or become clear ⟨the sky *cleared*⟩ **2** : to go away : DISPERSE ⟨the clouds *cleared* away⟩ **3** : to free from blame ⟨*cleared* my name⟩ **4** : to approve or be approved by ⟨*cleared* for secret work⟩ ⟨the proposal *cleared* the committee⟩ **5** : EXPLAIN 1 ⟨*clear* the matter up⟩ **6** : to free of things blocking ⟨*clear* land of timber⟩ **7** : to get rid of : REMOVE ⟨*clear* the dishes from the table⟩ **8** : ⁴NET **9** : to go over or by without touching ⟨the hit ball *cleared* the fence⟩

⁴clear *n* : a clear space or part — **in the clear** : free from guilt or suspicion

clear·ance \'klir-əns\ *n* **1** : the act or process of clearing **2** : the distance by which one object avoids hitting or touching another

clear·ing \'kliər-ing\ *n* : an area of land from which trees and bushes have all been removed

cleat \'klēt\ *n* **1** : a wooden or metal device used to fasten a line or a rope **2** : a strip or projection fastened on or across something to give strength or a place to hold or to prevent slipping 〈the *cleats* on football shoes〉

cleav·age \'klē-vij\ *n* **1** : the tendency of a rock or mineral to split readily in one or more directions **2** : the action of cleaving **3** : the state of being cleft

¹cleave \'klēv\ *vb* **cleaved** *or* **clove** \'klōv\; **cleav·ing** : to cling to a person or thing closely

²cleave *vb* **cleaved** *or* **cleft** \'kleft\ *or* **clove** \'klōv\; **cleaved** *or* **cleft** *or* **clo·ven** \'klō-vən\; **cleav·ing** : to divide by or as if by a cutting blow : SPLIT

cleav·er \'klē-vər\ *n* : a heavy knife used for cutting up meat

cleaver

clef \'klef\ *n* : a sign placed on the staff in writing music to show what pitch is represented by each line and space

¹cleft \'kleft\ *n* **1** : a space or opening made by splitting or cracking : CREVICE **2** : ¹NOTCH 1

²cleft *adj* : partly split or divided

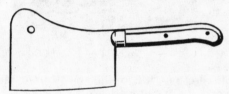

clem·en·cy \'klem-ən-sē\ *n, pl* **clemen·cies 1** : MERCY 1 **2** : an act of mercy

clench \'klench\ *vb* **1** : to hold tightly : CLUTCH **2** : to set or close tightly 〈*clench* your teeth〉

clefs

cler·gy \'klər-jē\ *n, pl* **cler·gies** : the group of religious officials (as priests, ministers, and rabbis) specially prepared and authorized to lead religious services

cler·gy·man \'klər-ji-mən\ *n, pl* **cler·gy·men** \-mən\ : a member of the clergy

cler·i·cal \'kler-i-kəl\ *adj* **1** : of or relating to the clergy **2** : of or relating to a clerk or office worker

¹clerk \'klərk\ *n* **1** : a person whose job is to keep records or accounts 〈city *clerk*〉 **2** : a salesperson in a store

²clerk *vb* : to act or work as a clerk

clev·er \'klev-ər\ *adj* **1** : showing skill especially in using one's hands **2** : having a quick inventive mind 〈a *clever* designer〉 **3** : showing wit or imagination 〈a *clever* joke〉 **synonyms** see INTELLIGENT — **clev·er·ly** *adv* — **clev·er·ness** *n*

¹click \'klik\ *n* : a slight sharp noise

²click *vb* **1** : to make or cause to make a click 〈*click* your tongue〉 **2** : to fit in or work together smoothly 〈by the middle of the season the team *clicked*〉

cli·ent \'klī-ənt\ *n* : a person who uses the professional advice or services of another 〈a lawyer's *client*〉

cli·en·tele \,klī-ən-'tel\ *n* : a group of clients

cliff \'klif\ *n* : a high steep surface of rock

cli·mate \'klī-mət\ *n* : the average weather conditions of a place over a period of years

cli·max \'klī-,maks\ *n* : the time or part of something that is of greatest interest, excitement, or importance

¹climb \'klīm\ *vb* **1** : to rise little by little to a higher point 〈smoke *climbing* in the air〉 **2** : to go up or down often with the help of the hands in holding or pulling **3** : to go upward in growing (as by winding around something) 〈a *climbing* vine〉 **synonyms** see ASCEND — **climb·er** \'klī-mər\ *n*

²climb *n* **1** : a place where climbing is necessary **2** : the act of climbing

clime \'klīm\ *n* : CLIMATE

¹clinch \'klinch\ *vb* **1** : to turn over or flatten the end of (as a nail sticking out of a board) **2** : to fasten by clinching **3** : to show to be certain or true 〈facts that *clinched* the argument〉

²clinch *n* : a fastening with a clinched nail, bolt, or rivet : the clinched part of a nail, bolt, or rivet

cling \'kling\ *vb* **clung** \'kləng\; **cling·ing 1** : to hold fast or stick closely to a surface **2** : to hold fast by grasping or winding around 〈*cling* to a ladder〉 **3** : to remain close 〈*clings* to the family〉

clin·ic \'klin-ik\ *n* **1** : a group meeting for teaching a certain skill and working on individual problems 〈a reading

\ə\ abut	\aú\ out	\i\ tip	\ó\ saw	\ù\ foot
\ər\ further	\ch\ chin	\ī\ life	\oi\ coin	\y\ yet
\a\ mat	\e\ pet	\j\ job	\th\ thin	\yü\ few
\ā\ take	\ē\ easy	\ng\ sing	\t̲h̲\ this	\yú\ cure
\ä\ cot, cart	\g\ go	\ō\ bone	\ü\ food	\zh\ vision

clinic⟩ **2** : a place where people can receive medical examinations and usually treatment for minor ailments ⟨outpatient *clinic*⟩

¹**clink** \'klingk\ *vb* : to make or cause to make a slight short sound like that of metal being struck

²**clink** *n* : a clinking sound

¹**clip** \'klip\ *vb* **clipped; clip·ping** : to fasten with a clip ⟨*clip* the papers together⟩

²**clip** *n* : a device that holds or hooks

³**clip** *vb* **clipped; clip·ping 1** : to shorten or remove by cutting (as with shears or scissors) ⟨*clip* a hedge⟩ ⟨*clip* out a news item⟩ **2** : to cut off or trim the hair or wool of ⟨have a dog *clipped*⟩

⁴**clip** *n* **1** : an instrument with two blades for cutting the nails **2** : a sharp blow **3** : a rapid pace ⟨moved along at a good *clip*⟩

clip·board \'klip-ˌbōrd\ *n* : a small board with a clip at the top for holding papers

clip·per \'klip-ər\ *n* **1** : a person who clips **2 clippers** *pl* : a device used for clipping especially hair or nails **3** : a fast sailing ship with usually three tall masts and large square sails

clip·ping \'klip-ing\ *n* : something cut out or off ⟨grass *clippings*⟩ ⟨a newspaper *clipping*⟩

clique \'klēk, 'klik\ *n* : a small group of people that keep out outsiders

¹**cloak** \'klōk\ *n* **1** : a long loose outer garment **2** : something that hides or covers ⟨a *cloak* of secrecy surrounded the talks⟩

²**cloak** *vb* : to cover or hide with a cloak

cloak·room \'klō-ˌkrüm, -ˌkrům\ *n* : a room (as in a school) in which coats and hats may be kept

¹**clock** \'kläk\ *n* : a device for measuring or telling the time and especially one not meant to be worn or carried by a person

²**clock** *vb* **1** : to time (as a person or a piece of work) by a timing device **2** : to show (as time or speed) on a recording device

clock·wise \'kläk-ˌwīz\ *adv or adj* : in the direction in which the hands of a clock turn

clock·work \'kläk-ˌwərk\ *n* : machinery (as in mechanical toys) like that which makes clocks go

clod \'kläd\ *n* **1** : a lump or mass especially of earth or clay **2** : a clumsy or stupid person

¹**clog** \'kläg\ *n* **1** : something that hinders or holds back **2** : a shoe having a thick usually wooden sole

²**clog** *vb* **clogged; clog·ging** : to make passage through difficult or prevent passage through ⟨snow *clogged* the roads⟩ ⟨a toy fell down the drain and *clogged* it up⟩

¹**clois·ter** \'klȯi-stər\ *n* **1** : MONASTERY, CONVENT **2** : a covered usually arched passage along or around the walls of a court

cloister 2

²**cloister** *vb* **1** : to shut away from the world **2** : to surround with a cloister

clop \'kläp\ *n* : a sound like that of a hoof against pavement

¹**close** \'klōz\ *vb* **closed; clos·ing 1** : to stop up : prevent passage through ⟨*close* a gap⟩ ⟨the street was *closed*⟩ **2** : to fill or cause to fill an opening ⟨the door *closed* softly⟩ **3** : to bring or come to an end ⟨*close* an account⟩ ⟨then the meeting *closed*⟩ **4** : to end the operation of ⟨*closed* the school⟩ **5** : to bring the parts or edges of together ⟨*closed* a book⟩ **6** : ¹APPROACH 1 ⟨night *closed* in⟩

²**close** \'klōz\ *n* : the point at which something ends

³**close** \'klōs\ *adj* **clos·er; clos·est 1** : having little space in which to move ⟨a *close* prisoner⟩ ⟨in *close* quarters⟩ **2** : SECRETIVE **3** : lacking fresh or moving air ⟨a *close* room⟩ **4** : not generous ⟨*close* with money⟩ **5** : not far apart in space, time, degree, or effect ⟨*close* neighbors⟩ ⟨it's *close* to nine o'clock⟩ **6** : ¹SHORT 1 ⟨a *close* haircut⟩ **7** : very like ⟨the material is a *close* match with the curtains⟩ **8** : having a strong liking each one for the other ⟨*close* friends⟩ **9** : strict and careful in attention to details ⟨*close* examination⟩ **10** : decided by a narrow margin ⟨a *close* election⟩ — **close·ly** *adv* — **close·ness** *n*

⁴**close** \'klōs\ *adv* : ¹NEAR 1

close call \'klōs-\ *n* : a barely successful escape from a difficult or dangerous situation

closed \'klōzd\ *adj* **1** : not open ⟨a *closed* door⟩ **2** : having mathematical elements that when subjected to an operation produce only elements of the same set ⟨whole numbers are *closed* under addition and multiplication⟩

¹clos·et \'kläz-ət\ *n* **1** : a small room for privacy **2** : a small room for clothing or for supplies for the house ⟨clothes *closet*⟩

²closet *vb* **1** : to shut up in or as if in a closet **2** : to take into a private room for an interview

close–up \'klō-ˌsəp\ *n* : a photograph taken at close range

clo·sure \'klō-zhər\ *n* **1** : an act of closing **2** : the condition of being closed

¹clot \'klät\ *n* : a lump made by some substance getting thicker and sticking together ⟨a blood *clot*⟩

²clot *vb* **clot·ted; clot·ting** : to thicken into a clot

cloth \'klȯth\ *n, pl* **cloths** \'klȯthz, 'klȯths\ **1** : a woven or knitted material (as of cotton or nylon) **2** : a piece of cloth for a certain use ⟨a polishing *cloth*⟩ **3** : TABLECLOTH

clothe \'klōth\ *vb* **clothed** *or* **clad** \'klad\; **cloth·ing** **1** : to cover with or as if with clothing : DRESS **2** : to provide with clothes ⟨fed and *clothed* my family⟩ **3** : to express in a certain way ⟨*clothed* their ideas in badly chosen words⟩

clothes \'klōz, 'klōthz\ *n pl* : CLOTHING 1

clothes moth *n* : a small yellowish moth whose larvae feed on wool, fur, and feathers

clothes·pin \'klōz-ˌpin, 'klōthz-\ *n* : a peg (as of wood) with the lower part slit or a clamp for holding clothes in place on a line

cloth·ing \'klō-thing\ *n* **1** : covering for the human body **2** : COVERING

¹cloud \'klaúd\ *n* **1** : a visible mass of tiny bits of water or ice hanging in the air usually high above the earth **2** : a visible mass of small particles in the air ⟨a *cloud* of dust⟩ **3** : something thought to be like a cloud ⟨a *cloud* of mosquitoes⟩ — **cloud·less** \-ləs\ *adj*

²cloud *vb* **1** : to make or become cloudy **2** : to darken or hide as if by a cloud

cloud·burst \'klaúd-ˌbərst\ *n* : a sudden heavy rainfall

cloudy \'klaúd-ē\ *adj* **cloud·i·er; cloud·i·est** **1** : overspread with clouds ⟨a *cloudy* sky⟩ **2** : showing confusion ⟨*cloudy* thinking⟩ **3** : not clear ⟨a *cloudy* liquid⟩ — **cloud·i·ness** *n*

¹clout \'klaút\ *n* : a blow especially with the hand

²clout *vb* : to hit hard

¹clove \'klōv\ *n* : the dried flower bud of a tropical tree used as a spice

²clove *past of* CLEAVE

cloven *past participle of* ²CLEAVE

clo·ven hoof \ˌklō-vən-\ *n* : a hoof (as of a cow) with the front part divided into two sections

clo·ver \'klō-vər\ *n* : any of various plants grown for hay and pasture that have leaves with three leaflets and usually roundish red, white, yellow, or purple flower heads

¹clown \'klaún\ *n* **1** : a rude and often stupid person **2** : a performer (as in a play or circus) who entertains by playing tricks and who usually wears comical clothes and makeup

²clown *vb* : to act like a clown : SHOW OFF

¹club \'kləb\ *n* **1** : a heavy usually wooden stick used as a weapon **2** : a stick or bat used to hit a ball in various games ⟨golf *club*⟩ **3** : a group of people associated because of a shared interest **4** : the meeting place of a club

²club *vb* **clubbed; club·bing** : to beat or strike with or as if with a club

club·house \'kləb-ˌhaús\ *n* **1** : a house used by a club **2** : locker rooms used by an athletic team

club moss *n* : a low often trailing evergreen plant that forms spores instead of seeds

¹cluck \'klək\ *vb* : to make or call with a cluck

²cluck *n* : the call of a hen especially to her chicks

clue \'klü\ *n* : something that helps a person to find something or to solve a mystery

¹clump \'kləmp\ *n* **1** : a group of things clustered together ⟨a *clump* of bushes⟩ **2** : a cluster or lump of something **3** : a heavy tramping sound

²clump *vb* **1** : to walk clumsily and noisily **2** : to form or cause to form clumps

clum·sy \'kləm-zē\ *adj* **clum·si·er; clum·si·est** **1** : lacking skill or grace in movement ⟨*clumsy* fingers⟩ **2** : not knowing how to get along with others **3** : badly or awkwardly made or done — **clum·si·ly** \-zə-lē\ *adv* — **clum·si·ness** \-zē-nəs\ *n*

clung *past of* CLING

¹clus·ter \'kləs-tər\ *n* : a number of similar things growing, collected, or grouped

\ə\ **abut**	\aú\ **out**	\i\ **tip**	\ȯ\ **saw**	\ú\ **foot**
\ər\ **further**	\ch\ **chin**	\ī\ **life**	\ȯi\ **coin**	\y\ **yet**
\a\ **mat**	\e\ **pet**	\j\ **job**	\th\ **thin**	\yü\ **few**
\ā\ **take**	\ē\ **easy**	\ng\ **sing**	\th\ **this**	\yú\ **cure**
\ä\ **cot, cart**	\g\ **go**	\ō\ **bone**	\ü\ **food**	\zh\ **vision**

closely together : BUNCH ⟨a *cluster* of houses⟩

²cluster *vb* : to grow, collect, or assemble in a cluster

¹clutch \'kləch\ *vb* **1** : to grasp or hold tightly with or as if with the hands or claws **2** : to make a grab ⟨*clutching* at the falling child⟩

²clutch *n* **1** : the state of being clutched **2** : a device for gripping an object **3** : a coupling for connecting and disconnecting a driving and a driven part in machinery **4** : a lever or pedal operating a clutch

¹clut·ter \'klət-ər\ *vb* : to throw into disorder : fill or cover with scattered things

²clutter *n* : a crowded or confused collection : DISORDER

co- *prefix* **1** : with : together : joint : jointly **2** : in or to the same degree **3** : fellow : partner ⟨*coauthor*⟩

¹coach \'kōch\ *n* **1** : a large carriage that has four wheels and a raised seat outside in front for the driver and is drawn by horses **2** : a railroad passenger car without berths **3** : a class of passenger transportation in an airplane at a lower fare than first class **4** : a person who teaches students individually **5** : a person who instructs or trains a performer or team

coach 1

²coach *vb* : to act as coach

coach·man \'kōch-mən\ *n, pl* **coach·men** \-mən\ : a person whose business is driving a coach or carriage

co·ag·u·late \kō-'ag-yə-ˌlāt\ *vb* **co·ag·u·lat·ed; co·ag·u·lat·ing** : to gather into a thick compact mass : CLOT

coal \'kōl\ *n* **1** : a piece of glowing or charred wood : EMBER **2** : a black solid mineral substance that is formed by the partial decay of vegetable matter under the influence of moisture and often increased pressure and temperature within the earth and is mined for use as a fuel

coarse \'kōrs\ *adj* **1** : of poor or ordinary quality **2** : made up of large particles ⟨*coarse* sand⟩ **3** : being harsh or rough

⟨*coarse* dry skin⟩ ⟨a *coarse* fabric⟩ **4** : crude in taste, manners, or language — **coarse·ly** *adv* — **coarse·ness** *n*

coars·en \'kōrs-n\ *vb* : to make or become coarse ⟨hands *coarsened* by hard labor⟩

¹coast \'kōst\ *n* : the land near a shore

²coast *vb* **1** : to slide downhill by the force of gravity over snow or ice **2** : to move along (as on a bicycle when not pedaling) without applying power

coast·al \'kōst-l\ *adj* : of, relating to, or located on, near, or along a coast ⟨*coastal* trade⟩

coast·er \'kō-stər\ *n* **1** : someone or something that coasts **2** : a sled or small wagon used in coasting

coast guard *n* : a military force that guards a coast

¹coat \'kōt\ *n* **1** : an outer garment that differs in length and style according to fashion or use **2** : the outer covering (as fur or feathers) of an animal **3** : a layer of material covering a surface ⟨a *coat* of paint⟩ — **coat·ed** \-əd\ *adj*

²coat *vb* : to cover with a coat or covering

coat·ing \'kōt-ing\ *n* : ¹COAT 3, COVERING ⟨a thin *coating* of ice⟩

coat of arms : the heraldic arms belonging to a person, family, or group or a representation of these (as on a shield)

coat of mail : a garment of metal scales or rings worn long ago as armor

co·au·thor \'kō-'ȯ-thər\ *n* : an author who works with another author

coax \'kōks\ *vb* **1** : to influence by gentle urging, special attention, or flattering **2** : to get or win by means of gentle urging or flattery ⟨*coaxed* a raise from the boss⟩

cob \'käb\ *n* : CORNCOB

co·balt \'kō-ˌbȯlt\ *n* : a tough shiny silvery white metallic chemical element found with iron and nickel

cob·bled \'käb-əld\ *adj* : paved or covered with cobblestones

cob·bler \'käb-lər\ *n* **1** : a person who mends or makes shoes **2** : a fruit pie with a thick upper crust and no bottom crust that is baked in a deep dish

cob·ble·stone \'käb-əl-ˌstōn\ *n* : a naturally rounded stone larger than a pebble and smaller than a boulder once used in paving streets

co·bra \'kō-brə\ *n* : a very poisonous snake of Asia and Africa that puffs out the skin around its neck into a hood when excited

cob·web \'käb-ˌweb\ *n* **1** : the fine network spread by a spider **2** : something like or suggesting a spider's web

co·caine \kō-'kān\ *n* : a habit-forming drug

cobra

obtained from the leaves of a South American shrub and sometimes used as a medicine to deaden pain

coc·cus \'käk-əs\ *n*, *pl* **coc·ci** \'käk-ˌsī, -ˌī, -ˌsē, -ˌē\ : a bacterium shaped like a ball

¹**cock** \'käk\ *n* **1** : a male bird : ROOSTER **2** : a faucet or valve for controlling the flow of a liquid or a gas **3** : a cocked position of the hammer of a gun ⟨a rifle at half *cock*⟩

²**cock** *vb* **1** : to draw back the hammer of (a gun) in readiness for firing ⟨*cock* a pistol⟩ **2** : to set or draw back in readiness for some action ⟨*cock* your arm to throw⟩ **3** : to turn or tip upward or to one side

³**cock** *n* : the act of tipping at an angle : TILT

cock·a·too \'käk-ə-ˌtü\ *n*, *pl* **cock·a·toos** : any of several large, noisy, and usually brightly colored crested parrots mostly of Australia

cockatoo

cock·eyed \'käk-'īd\ *adj* **1** : tilted to one side **2** : FOOLISH ⟨a *cockeyed* plan⟩

cock·le \'käk-əl\ *n* : an edible shellfish with a shell that has two parts and is shaped like a heart

cock·le·bur \'käk-əl-ˌbər, 'kək-\ *n* : a plant with prickly fruit that is related to the thistles

cockleshell

cock·le·shell \'käk-əl-ˌshel\ *n* : a shell of a cockle

cock·pit \'käk-ˌpit\ *n* **1** : an open space in the deck from which a small boat (as a yacht) is steered **2** : a space in an airplane for the pilot or pilot and passengers or pilot and crew

cock·roach \'käk-ˌrōch\ *n* : a troublesome insect found in houses and ships and active chiefly at night

cocky \'käk-ē\ *adj* **cock·i·er; cock·i·est** : very sure of oneself : boldly self-confident

co·coa \'kō-kō\ *n* **1** : chocolate ground to a powder after some of its fat is removed **2** : a drink made from cocoa powder

co·co·nut \'kō-kə-nət, -ˌnət\ *n* : a large nutlike fruit that has a thick husk and grows on a tall tropical palm (**coconut palm**)

co·coon \kə-'kün\ *n* : the silky covering which caterpillars make around themselves and in which they are protected while changing into butterflies or moths

cod \'käd\ *n*, *pl* **cod** : a large food fish found in the deep colder parts of the northern Atlantic ocean

cod·dle \'käd-l\ *vb* **cod·dled; cod·dling** **1** : to cook slowly in water below the boiling point ⟨*coddle* eggs⟩ **2** : to treat with very much and usually too much care : PAMPER

¹**code** \'kōd\ *n* **1** : a collection of laws arranged in some orderly way ⟨criminal *code*⟩ **2** : a system of rules or principles ⟨moral *code*⟩ **3** : a system of signals or letters and symbols with special meanings used for sending messages **4** : GENETIC CODE

²**code** *vb* **cod·ed; cod·ing** : to put in the form of a code

cod·fish \'käd-ˌfish\ *n*, *pl* **codfish** *or* **cod·fish·es** : COD

cod·ger \'käj-ər\ *n* : an odd or cranky man

co·erce \kō-'ərs\ *vb* **co·erced; co·erc·ing** : ²FORCE 1, COMPEL

cof·fee \'kò-fē\ *n* **1** : a drink made from the roasted and ground seeds of a tropical plant **2** : the seeds of the coffee plant

cof·fee·pot \'kò-fē-ˌpät\ *n* : a covered utensil for preparing or serving coffee

coffee table *n* : a low table usually placed in front of a sofa

cof·fer \'kò-fər\ *n* : a box used especially for holding money and valuables

cof·fin \'kò-fən\ *n* : a box or case to hold a dead body

\ə\ **abut**	\aù\ **out**	\i\ **tip**	\ò\ **saw**	\ù\ **foot**
\ər\ **further**	\ch\ **chin**	\ī\ **life**	\òi\ **coin**	\y\ **yet**
\a\ **mat**	\e\ **pet**	\j\ **job**	\th\ **thin**	\yü\ **few**
\ā\ **take**	\ē\ **easy**	\ng\ **sing**	\th\ **this**	\yù\ **cure**
\ä\ **cot, cart**	\g\ **go**	\ō\ **bone**	\ü\ **food**	\zh\ **vision**

cog \'käg\ *n* : a tooth on the rim of a wheel or gear

cog·i·tate \'käj-ə-ˌtāt\ *vb* **cog·i·tat·ed; cog·i·tat·ing** : to think over : PONDER

cog·i·ta·tion \ˌkäj-ə-'tā-shən\ *n* : MEDITATION

cog·wheel \'käg-ˌhwēl, -ˌwēl\ *n* : a wheel with cogs on the rim

co·he·sion \kō-'hē-zhən\ *n* **1** : the action of sticking together **2** : the force of attraction between the molecules in a mass

cogwheel

¹coil \'kȯil\ *vb* **1** : to wind into rings or a spiral ⟨*coil* a rope⟩ **2** : to form or lie in a coil

²coil *n* **1** : a circle, a series of circles, or a spiral made by coiling **2** : something coiled

¹coin \'kȯin\ *n* **1** : a piece of metal put out by government authority as money **2** : metal money ⟨change these bills for *coin*⟩

²coin *vb* **1** : to make coins especially by stamping pieces of metal : MINT **2** : to make metal (as gold or silver) into coins **3** : to make up (a new word or phrase)

coin·age \'kȯi-nij\ *n* **1** : the act or process of coining **2** : something coined

co·in·cide \ˌkō-ən-'sīd\ *vb* **co·in·cid·ed; co·in·cid·ing** **1** : to occupy the same space **2** : to happen at the same time **3** : to agree exactly

co·in·ci·dence \kō-'in-sə-dəns\ *n* **1** : a coinciding in space or time **2** : two things that happen at the same time by accident but seem to have some connection

coke \'kōk\ *n* : gray lumps of fuel made by heating soft coal in a closed chamber until some of its gases have passed off

col- — see COM-

col·an·der \'kəl-ən-dər, 'käl-\ *n* : a utensil with small holes for draining foods

colander

¹cold \'kōld\ *adj* **1** : having a low temperature or one much below normal ⟨a *cold* day⟩ **2** : lacking warmth of feeling : UNFRIENDLY **3** : suffering from lack of warmth ⟨feel *cold*⟩ — **cold·ly** *adv* — **cold·ness** *n*

²cold *n* **1** : a condition of low temperature : cold weather **2** : the bodily feeling produced by lack of warmth : CHILL **3** : COMMON COLD

cold–blood·ed \'kōld-'bləd-əd\ *adj* **1** : lacking or showing a lack of normal human feelings ⟨a *cold-blooded* criminal⟩ **2** : having a body temperature that varies with the temperature of the environment ⟨frogs are *cold-blooded* animals⟩ **3** : sensitive to cold

co·le·us \'kō-lē-əs\ *n* : a plant of the mint family grown for its many-colored leaves

col·ic \'käl-ik\ *n* : sharp pain in the bowels — **col·ick·y** \'käl-ə-kē\ *adj*

col·i·se·um \ˌkäl-ə-'sē-əm\ *n* : a large structure (as a stadium) for athletic contests or public entertainment

col·lab·o·rate \kə-'lab-ə-ˌrāt\ *vb* **col·lab·o·rat·ed; col·lab·o·rat·ing** **1** : to work with others (as in writing a book) **2** : to cooperate with an enemy force that has taken over one's country

col·lage \kə-'läzh\ *n* : a work of art made by gluing pieces of different materials to a flat surface

¹col·lapse \kə-'laps\ *vb* **col·lapsed; col·laps·ing** **1** : to break down completely : fall in **2** : to shrink together suddenly **3** : to suffer a physical or mental breakdown **4** : to fold together ⟨the umbrella *collapses* to pocket size⟩

²collapse *n* : the act or an instance of collapsing : BREAKDOWN

col·laps·ible \kə-'lap-sə-bəl\ *adj* : capable of collapsing or possible to collapse

¹col·lar \'käl-ər\ *n* **1** : a band, strap, or chain worn around the neck or the neckline of a garment **2** : a part of the harness of draft animals fitted over the shoulders **3** : something (as a ring to hold a pipe in place) that is like a collar — **col·lar·less** \-ləs\ *adj*

²collar *vb* **1** : to seize by or as if by the collar : CAPTURE, GRAB **2** : to put a collar on

col·lar·bone \'käl-ər-ˌbōn\ *n* : a bone of the shoulder joined to the breastbone and the shoulder blade

col·league \'käl-ˌēg\ *n* : an associate in a profession : a fellow worker

col·lect \kə-'lekt\ *vb* **1** : to bring or come together into one body or place **2** : to gather from a number of sources ⟨*collect* stamps⟩ ⟨*collect* taxes⟩ **3** : to gain or regain control of ⟨*collected* my thoughts⟩ **4** : to receive payment for ⟨*collect* a bill⟩ **synonyms** see GATHER

col·lect·ed \kə-'lek-təd\ *adj* : ²CALM 2

col·lec·tion \kə-'lek-shən\ *n* **1** : the act or process of gathering together ⟨the *collec-*

tion of mail by the letter carrier⟩ **2** : something collected and especially a group of objects gathered for study or exhibition **3** : a gathering of money (as for charitable purposes)

col·lec·tive \kə-'lek-tiv\ *adj* **1** : having to do with a number of persons or things thought of as a whole ⟨*collective* nouns⟩ **2** : done or shared by a number of persons as a group ⟨made a *collective* effort⟩ — **col·lec·tive·ly** *adj*

col·lec·tor \kə-'lek-tər\ *n* **1** : a person or thing that collects ⟨stamp *collector*⟩ **2** : a person whose business it is to collect money ⟨a bill *collector*⟩

col·lege \'käl-ij\ *n* : a school higher than a high school

col·le·giate \kə-'lē-jət\ *adj* **1** : having to do with a college ⟨*collegiate* studies⟩ **2** : of, relating to, or characteristic of college students ⟨*collegiate* clothes⟩ ⟨*collegiate* humor⟩

col·lide \kə-'līd\ *vb* **col·lid·ed; col·lid·ing** **1** : to strike against each other **2** : ¹CLASH 2

col·lie \'käl-ē\ *n* : a large usually long-coated dog of a Scottish breed used to herd sheep

collie

col·li·sion \kə-'lizh-ən\ *n* : an act or instance of colliding

col·lo·qui·al \kə-'lō-kwē-əl\ *adj* : used in or suited to familiar and informal conversation

col·lo·qui·al·ism \kə-'lō-kwē-ə-,liz-əm\ *n* : a colloquial word or expression

co·logne \kə-'lōn\ *n* : a perfumed liquid made up of alcohol and fragrant oils

¹co·lon \'kō-lən\ *n* : the main part of the large intestine

²colon *n* : a punctuation mark : used mostly to call attention to what follows (as a list, explanation, or quotation)

col·o·nel \'kərn-l\ *n* : a commissioned offi-

cer in the Army, Air Force, or Marine Corps ranking above a lieutenant colonel

¹co·lo·ni·al \kə-'lō-nē-əl\ *adj* **1** : of, relating to, or characteristic of a colony **2** *often cap* : of or relating to the original thirteen colonies that formed the United States

²colonial *n* : a member of or a person living in a colony

col·o·nist \'käl-ə-nəst\ *n* **1** : a person living in a colony **2** : a person who helps to found a colony

col·o·nize \'käl-ə-,nīz\ *vb* **col·o·nized; col·o·niz·ing** **1** : to establish a colony in or on **2** : to settle in a colony

col·on·nade \,käl-ə-'nād\ *n* : a row of columns usually supporting the base of a roof structure

col·o·ny \'käl-ə-nē\ *n, pl* **col·o·nies** **1** : a group of people sent out by a state to a new territory : the territory in which these people settle **2** : a distant territory belonging to or under the control of a nation **3** : a group of living things of one kind living together ⟨a *colony* of ants⟩ **4** : a group of people with common qualities or interests located in close association ⟨an art *colony*⟩

¹col·or \'kəl-ər\ *n* **1** : the appearance of a thing apart from size and shape when light strikes it ⟨red is the *color* of blood⟩ **2** : a hue other than black, white, or gray ⟨dressed in bright *colors*⟩ **3** : outward show : APPEARANCE **4** : the normal rosy tint of skin **5** : ²BLUSH **6** **colors** *pl* : an identifying flag **7** **colors** *pl* : military service **8** : ¹INTEREST 6 **9** : the quality of sound in music ⟨the *color* and richness of an instrument⟩

²color *vb* **1** : to give color to **2** : to change the color of **3** : MISREPRESENT ⟨*color* the truth⟩ **4** : to take on or change color : BLUSH

col·or·ation \,kəl-ə-'rā-shən\ *n* : use or arrangement of colors or shades : COLORING

color–blind \'kəl-ər-,blīnd\ *adj* : unable to tell some colors apart

col·ored \'kəl-ərd\ *adj* **1** : having color ⟨*colored* glass⟩ **2** : of a race other than the white

col·or·ful \'kəl-ər-fəl\ *adj* **1** : having bright colors **2** : full of variety or interest

col·or·ing \'kəl-ə-ring\ *n* **1** : the act of applying colors **2** : something that produces color ⟨vegetable *coloring*⟩ **3** : the effect

\ə\ abut	\aú\ out	\i\ tip	\ò\ saw	\ú\ foot
\ər\ further	\ch\ chin	\ī\ life	\òi\ coin	\y\ yet
\a\ mat	\e\ pet	\j\ job	\th\ thin	\yü\ few
\ā\ take	\ē\ easy	\ng\ sing	\th\ this	\yu̇\ cure
\ä\ cot, cart	\g\ go	\ō\ bone	\ü\ food	\zh\ vision

produced by the use of color **4** : natural color : COMPLEXION ⟨a person of delicate *coloring*⟩

col·or·less \'kəl-ər-ləs\ *adj* **1** : having no color **2** : WAN, PALE **3** : [1]DULL 8

co·los·sal \kə-'läs-əl\ *adj* : very large : HUGE

colt \'kōlt\ *n* **1** : FOAL **2** : a young male horse

col·um·bine \'käl-əm-ˌbīn\ *n* : a plant related to the butter-cups that has leaves with three parts and showy flowers usually with five petals ending in spurs

col·umn \'käl-əm\ *n* **1** : one of two or more vertical sections of a printed page ⟨the left *col-umn* of the page⟩ **2**

columbine

: a special regular feature in a newspaper or magazine ⟨a sports *column*⟩ **3** : a pillar supporting a roof or gallery **4** : something like a column in shape, position, or use ⟨the spinal *col-umn*⟩ ⟨a *column* of water⟩ ⟨a *column* of figures⟩ **5** : a long straight row (as of sol-diers)

col·um·nist \'käl-əm-nəst, -ə-məst\ *n* : a writer of a column in a newspaper or mag-azine

com- *or* **col-** *or* **con-** *prefix* : with : to-gether : jointly usually *com-* before *b*, *p*, or *m*, *col-* before *l* and *con-* before other sounds

co·ma \'kō-mə\ *n* : a deep sleeplike state caused by sickness or injury

[1]**comb** \'kōm\ *n* **1** : a toothed implement used to smooth and arrange the hair or worn in the hair to hold it in place **2** : a toothed instrument used for separating fi-bers (as of wool or flax) **3** : a fleshy crest often with points suggesting teeth on the head of a fowl and some related birds **4** : [1]HONEYCOMB 1

comb 3

[2]**comb** *vb* **1** : to smooth, arrange, or un-tangle with a comb **2** : to search over or through carefully ⟨police *combed* the building⟩

[1]**com·bat** \kəm-'bat, 'käm-ˌbat\ *vb* **com-bat·ed** *or* **com·bat·ted; com·bat·ing** *or* **com·bat·ting** : to fight with : fight against : OPPOSE ⟨*combat* disease⟩

[2]**com·bat** \'käm-ˌbat\ *n* **1** : a fight or con-test between individuals or groups **2** : [1]CONFLICT 2 **3** : active military fighting ⟨soldiers lost in *combat*⟩

[1]**com·bat·ant** \kəm-'bat-nt, 'käm-bət-ənt\ *n* : a person who takes part in a combat

[2]**combatant** *adj* : engaging in or ready to engage in combat

com·bi·na·tion \ˌkäm-bə-'nā-shən\ *n* **1** : a result or product of combining or being combined **2** : a union of persons or groups for a purpose **3** : a series of letters or numbers which when dialed by a disk on a lock will operate or open the lock **4** : a union of different things

[1]**com·bine** \käm-'bīn\ *vb* **com·bined; com·bin·ing** : to join together so as to make or to seem one thing : UNITE, MIX

[2]**com·bine** \'käm-ˌbīn\ *n* **1** : a union of persons or groups of persons espe-cially for business or political benefits **2** : a machine that harvests and threshes grain

com·bus·ti·ble \kəm-'bəs-tə-bəl\ *adj* **1** : possible to burn **2** : catching fire or burn-ing easily

com·bus·tion \kəm-'bəs-chən\ *n* : the pro-cess of burning

come \'kəm, kəm\ *vb* **came** \'kām\; **come; com·ing** \'kəm-ing\ **1** : to move toward : APPROACH ⟨*come* here⟩ **2** : to reach the point of being or becoming ⟨the water *came* to a boil⟩ ⟨the rope *came* untied⟩ **3** : to add up : AMOUNT ⟨the bill *comes* to ten dollars⟩ **4** : to take place ⟨the holiday *comes* on Tuesday⟩ **5** : ORIGINATE 2, ARISE ⟨they *come* from a good family⟩ **6** : to be available ⟨these books *come* in four bind-ings⟩ **7** : [1]REACH 3 ⟨the water *came* to our knees⟩

co·me·di·an \kə-'mēd-ē-ən\ *n* **1** : an actor who plays comic roles **2** : an amusing person

com·e·dy \'käm-ə-dē\ *n*, *pl* **com·e·dies 1** : an amusing play that has a happy end-ing **2** : an amusing and often ridiculous event

come·ly \'kəm-lē\ *adj* **come·li·er; come-li·est** : pleasing to the sight : good-looking

com·et \'käm-ət\ *n* : a bright celestial body that develops a cloudy tail as it moves in an orbit around the sun

Word History The tail of a comet looks rather like long hair streaming behind the head. The ancient Greeks gave comets a name that meant "long-haired." This Greek name was formed from a Greek word meaning "hair." The English word *comet* came from the Greek name for comets.

come to *vb* : to become conscious again

¹**com·fort** \'kəm-fərt\ *n* **1** : acts or words that comfort **2** : the feeling of the one that is comforted **3** : something that makes a person comfortable ⟨the *comforts* of home⟩

²**comfort** *vb* **1** : to give hope and strength to : CHEER **2** : to ease the grief or trouble of

com·fort·able \'kəm-fərt-ə-bəl, 'kəmf-tər-bəl\ *adj* **1** : giving comfort and especially physical ease ⟨a *comfortable* chair⟩ **2** : more than what is needed ⟨a *comfortable* income⟩ **3** : physically at ease — **comfort·ably** \-blē\ *adj*

com·fort·er \'kəm-fərt-ər\ *n* **1** : one that gives comfort **2** : ¹QUILT

com·ic \'käm-ik\ *adj* **1** : of, relating to, or characteristic of comedy **2** : FUNNY 1

com·i·cal \'käm-kəl\ *adj* : FUNNY 1, RIDICULOUS ⟨a *comical* sight⟩ — **com·i·cal·ly** *adv*

comic book *n* : a magazine made up of a series of comic strips

comic strip *n* : a series of cartoons that tell a story or part of a story

com·ma \'käm-ə\ *n* : a punctuation mark , used chiefly to show separation of words or word groups within a sentence

¹**com·mand** \kə-'mand\ *vb* **1** : to order with authority **2** : to have power or control over : be commander of **3** : to have for one's use **4** : to demand as right or due : EXACT ⟨*commands* a high fee⟩ **5** : to survey from a good position

²**command** *n* **1** : the act of commanding **2** : an order given ⟨obey a *command*⟩ **3** : the ability to control and use : MASTERY ⟨a good *command* of the language⟩ **4** : the authority, right, or power to command : CONTROL **5** : the people, area, or unit (as of soldiers and weapons) under a commander **6** : a position from which military operations are directed

com·man·dant \'käm-ən-,dant, -,dänt\ *n* : a commanding officer

com·mand·er \kə-'man-dər\ *n* : a commissioned officer in the Navy or Coast Guard ranking above a lieutenant commander

commander in chief : a person who holds supreme command of the armed forces of a nation

com·mand·ment \kə-'mand-mənt\ *n* : something given as a command and especially one of the Ten Commandments in the Bible

com·man·do \kə-'man-dō\ *n, pl* **com·man·dos** *or* **com·man·does** **1** : a band or unit of troops trained for making surprise raids into enemy territory **2** : a member of a commando unit

command sergeant major *n* : a noncommissioned officer in the Army ranking above a first sergeant

com·mem·o·rate \kə-'mem-ə-,rāt\ *vb* **com·mem·o·rat·ed; com·mem·o·rat·ing** **1** : to call or recall to mind **2** : to observe with a ceremony **3** : to serve as a memorial of

com·mem·o·ra·tion \kə-,mem-ə-'rā-shən\ *n* **1** : the act of commemorating **2** : something (as a ceremony) that commemorates

com·mence \kə-'mens\ *vb* **com·menced; com·menc·ing** : BEGIN, START

com·mence·ment \kə-'mens-mənt\ *n* **1** : the act or the time of commencing : BEGINNING **2** : graduation exercises

com·mend \kə-'mend\ *vb* **1** : to give into another's care : ENTRUST **2** : to speak of with approval : PRAISE

com·men·da·tion \,käm-ən-'dā-shən\ *n* : ²PRAISE 1, APPROVAL

¹**com·ment** \'käm-,ent\ *n* **1** : an expression of opinion either in speech or writing **2** : mention of something that deserves notice

²**comment** *vb* : to make a comment : REMARK

com·men·ta·tor \'käm-ən-,tāt-ər\ *n* **1** : a person who makes comments **2** : a person who reports and discusses news events (as over radio)

com·merce \'käm-ərs, -,ərs\ *n* : the buying and selling of goods especially on a large scale and between different places : TRADE

¹**com·mer·cial** \kə-'mər-shəl\ *adj* **1** : having to do with commerce **2** : having financial profit as the chief goal — **com·mer·cial·ly** *adv*

²**commercial** *n* : an advertisement broadcast on radio or television

com·mer·cial·ize \kə-'mər-shə-,līz\ *vb* **com·mer·cial·ized; com·mer·cial·iz·ing**

\ə\ abut	\au̇\ out	\i\ tip	\o̅\ saw	\u̇\ foot
\ər\ further	\ch\ chin	\ī\ life	\o̅i\ coin	\y\ yet
\a\ mat	\e\ pet	\j\ job	\th\ thin	\yü\ few
\ā\ take	\ē\ easy	\ng\ sing	\th\ this	\yu̇\ cure
\ä\ cot, cart	\g\ go	\ō\ bone	\ü\ food	\zh\ vision

: to manage with the idea of making a profit

¹com·mis·sion \kə-'mish-ən\ n **1** : an order or instruction granting the power to perform various acts or duties : the right or duty in question **2** : a certificate that gives military or naval rank and authority : the rank and authority given **3** : authority to act as agent for another : a task or piece of business entrusted to an agent **4** : a group of persons given orders and authority to perform specified duties ⟨a park *commission*⟩ **5** : an act of doing something wrong ⟨the *commission* of a crime⟩ **6** : a fee paid to an agent for taking care of a piece of business

²commission vb **1** : to give a commission to **2** : to put (a ship) into service

commissioned officer \kə-,mish-ənd-\ n : an officer in the armed forces who ranks above the enlisted persons or warrant officers and who is appointed by a commission from the president

com·mis·sion·er \kə-'mish-ə-nər, -'mish-nər\ n **1** : a member of a commission **2** : an official who is the head of a government department

com·mit \kə-'mit\ vb **com·mit·ted; com·mit·ting 1** : to make secure or put in safekeeping : ENTRUST **2** : to place in or send to a prison or mental institution **3** : to bring about : PERFORM ⟨*commit* a crime⟩ **4** : to pledge or assign to a certain course or use — **com·mit·ment** \-mənt\ n

com·mit·tee \kə-'mit-ē\ n : a group of persons appointed or elected to consider some subject of interest or to perform some duty

com·mod·i·ty \kə-'mäd-ət-ē\ n, pl **com·mod·i·ties** : something produced by agriculture, mining, or manufacture

com·mo·dore \'käm-ə-,dōr\ n **1** : a former wartime commissioned officer rank in the Navy and Coast Guard between the ranks of captain and rear admiral **2** : the chief officer of a yacht club **3** : the senior captain of a line of merchant ships

¹com·mon \'käm-ən\ adj **1** : having to do with, belonging to, or used by everybody : PUBLIC **2** : belonging to or shared by two or more individuals or by the members of a family or group ⟨a *common* ancestor⟩ **3** : ¹GENERAL 1 ⟨facts of *common* knowledge⟩ **4** : occurring or appearing frequently **5** : not above the average in rank, excellence, or social position ⟨a *common* soldier⟩ **6** : falling below ordinary standards (as in quality or manners) : INFERIOR **7** : COARSE 4, VULGAR

synonyms COMMON, ORDINARY, and FAMILIAR mean occurring often. COMMON suggests that something is of the everyday sort and frequently occurs ⟨fishing boats are a *common* sight around here⟩ ORDINARY suggests that something is of the usual standard ⟨an *ordinary* TV show⟩ FAMILIAR suggests that something is well-known and easily recognized ⟨a *familiar* song⟩

²common n : land (as a park) owned and used by a community — **in common** : shared together

common cold n : a contagious disease which causes the lining of the nose and throat to be sore, swollen, and red and in which there is usually much mucus and coughing and sneezing

common denominator n : a common multiple of the denominators of a number of fractions

com·mon·er \'käm-ə-nər\ n : one of the common people

common multiple n : a multiple of each of two or more numbers

common noun n : a noun that names a class of persons or things or any individuals of a class ⟨"child," "city," and "day" are *common nouns*⟩

¹com·mon·place \'käm-ən-,plās\ n : something that is often seen or met with

²commonplace adj : often seen or met with : ORDINARY

common sense n : ordinary good sense and judgment

com·mon·wealth \'käm-ən-,welth\ n **1** : a political unit (as a nation or state) **2** : a state of the United States and especially Kentucky, Massachusetts, Pennsylvania, or Virginia

com·mo·tion \kə-'mō-shən\ n : noisy excitement and confusion : TURMOIL

¹com·mune \kə-'myün\ vb **com·muned; com·mun·ing** : to be in close accord or communication with someone or something

²com·mune \'käm-,yün\ n : a community in which individuals have close personal ties to each other and share property and duties

com·mu·ni·ca·ble \kə-'myü-ni-kə-bəl\ adj : possible to communicate ⟨a *communicable* disease⟩

com·mu·ni·cate \kə-'myü-nə-,kāt\ vb **com·mu·ni·cat·ed; com·mu·ni·cat·ing 1** : to make known **2** : to pass (as a disease) from one to another : SPREAD **3** : to get in touch (as by telephone)

com·mu·ni·ca·tion \kə-,myü-nə-'kā-shən\

n **1** : the exchange (as by speech or letter) of information between persons **2** : information communicated **3 communications** *pl* : a system of sending messages (as by telephone) **4 communications** *pl* : a system of routes for moving troops, supplies, and vehicles

com·mu·nion \kə-'myü-nyən\ *n* **1** : an act or example of sharing **2** : a religious ceremony commemorating with bread and wine the last supper of Jesus **3** : the act of receiving the sacrament **4** : friendly communication **5** : a body of Christians having a common faith and discipline

com·mu·nism \'käm-yə-ˌniz-əm\ *n* **1** : a social system in which property and goods are held in common **2** : a theory that supports communism

com·mu·nist \'käm-yə-nəst\ *n* **1** : a person who believes in communism **2** *cap* : a member or follower of a Communist party or plan for change

com·mu·ni·ty \kə-'myü-nət-ē\ *n, pl* **com·mu·ni·ties 1** : the people living in a certain place (as a village or city) : the area itself **2** : a natural group (as of kinds of plants and animals) living together and depending on one another for various necessities of life **3** : a group of people with common interests living together 〈a *community* of artists〉 **4** : people in general : PUBLIC **5** : common ownership or participation

com·mu·ta·tive \'käm-yə-ˌtāt-iv\ *adj* : being a property of a mathematical operation (as addition or multiplication) in which the result of combining elements is independent of the order in which they are taken

com·mute \kə-'myüt\ *vb* **com·mut·ed; com·mut·ing 1** : to change (as a penalty) to something less severe **2** : to travel back and forth regularly — **com·mut·er** *n*

¹com·pact \kəm-'pakt, 'käm-ˌpakt\ *adj* **1** : closely united or packed **2** : arranged so as to save space 〈a *compact* house〉 **3** : not wordy : BRIEF **synonyms** see DENSE — **com·pact·ly** *adv* — **com·pact·ness** *n*

²com·pact \'käm-ˌpakt\ *n* **1** : a small case for cosmetics **2** : a somewhat small automobile

³com·pact \'käm-ˌpakt\ *n* : AGREEMENT 2

com·pan·ion \kəm-'pan-yən\ *n* **1** : a person or thing that accompanies another **2** : one of a pair of matching things **3** : a person employed to live with and serve another

Word History The word *companion* came from a Latin word that meant "comrade." Comrades can be thought of as people who share bread or eat together.

The Latin word meaning "comrade" was made up of two parts. The first was a Latin prefix that meant "together." The second was a Latin word that meant "bread."

com·pan·ion·ship \kəm-'pan-yən-ˌship\ *n* : FELLOWSHIP 1, COMPANY

com·pan·ion·way \kəm-'pan-yən-ˌwā\ *n* : a ship's stairway from one deck to another

com·pa·ny \'käm-pə-nē, 'kəmp-nē\ *n, pl* **com·pa·nies 1** : FELLOWSHIP 1 **2** : a person's companions or associates 〈known by the *company* you keep〉 **3** : guests or visitors especially at one's home 〈we have *company*〉 **4** : a group of persons or things **5** : a body of soldiers and especially an infantry unit normally led by a captain **6** : a band of musical or dramatic performers 〈opera *company*〉 **7** : the officers and crew of a ship **8** : an association of persons carrying on a business

com·pa·ra·ble \'käm-pə-rə-bəl, -prə-bəl\ *adj* : being similar or about the same

¹com·par·a·tive \kəm-'par-ət-iv\ *adj* **1** : of, relating to, or being the form of an adjective or adverb that shows a degree of comparison that is greater or less than its positive degree **2** : measured by comparisons : RELATIVE — **com·par·a·tive·ly** *adv*

²comparative *n* : the comparative degree or a comparative form in a language 〈"taller" is the *comparative* of "tall"〉

com·pare \kəm-'paər\ *vb* **com·pared; com·par·ing 1** : to point out as similar : LIKEN 〈*compare* an anthill to a town〉 **2** : to examine for likenesses or differences 〈*compare* two bicycles〉 **3** : to appear in comparison to others 〈*compares* well with the rest of the class〉 **4** : to state the positive, comparative, and superlative forms of an adjective or adverb

synonyms COMPARE and CONTRAST mean to set side by side in order to show likenesses and differences. COMPARE stresses showing the likenesses between two or more things 〈*compare* these sofas for size and comfort〉 CONTRAST stresses showing the differences and especially the characteristics which are opposite 〈*contrast* country and city life〉

com·par·i·son \kəm-'par-ə-sən\ *n* **1** : the act of comparing : the condition of being compared **2** : an examination of two or more objects to find the likenesses and differences between them **3** : change in

\ə\ **abut**	\aú\ **out**	\i\ **tip**	\ó\ **saw**	\ú\ **foot**
\ər\ **further**	\ch\ **chin**	\ī\ **life**	\ói\ **coin**	\y\ **yet**
\a\ **mat**	\e\ **pet**	\j\ **job**	\th\ **thin**	\yü\ **few**
\ā\ **take**	\ē\ **easy**	\ng\ **sing**	\th\ **this**	\yú\ **cure**
\ä\ **cot, cart**	\g\ **go**	\ō\ **bone**	\ü\ **food**	\zh\ **vision**

the form and meaning of an adjective or an adverb (as by adding *-er* or *-est* to the word or by adding *more* or *most* before the word) to show different levels of quality, quantity, or relation

com·part·ment \kəm-'pärt-mənt\ *n* **1** : one of the parts into which a closed space is divided **2** : a separate division or section

com·pass \'kəm-pəs\ *n* **1** : BOUNDARY, CIRCUMFERENCE **2** : a closed-in space **3** : ¹RANGE 6, SCOPE ⟨ within the *compass* of my voice⟩ **4** : a device having a magnetic needle that indicates direction on the earth's surface by pointing toward the north **5** : a device that indicates direction by means other than a magnetic needle **6** : an instrument for drawing circles or marking measurements consisting of two pointed legs joined at the top by a pivot — usually used in pl.

com·pas·sion \kəm-'pash-ən\ *n* : pity for and a desire to help another

com·pas·sion·ate \kəm-'pash-ə-nət\ *adj* : having or showing compassion

com·pat·i·ble \kəm-'pat-ə-bəl\ *adj* : capable of existing together in harmony

com·pa·tri·ot \kəm-'pā-trē-ət\ *n* : a person from one's own country

com·pel \kəm-'pel\ *vb* **com·pelled; com·pel·ling** : to make (as a person) do something by the use of physical, moral, or mental pressure : FORCE ⟨lameness *compels* me to use a cane⟩ ⟨felt *compelled* to tell the truth⟩

com·pen·sate \'käm-pən-ˌsāt\ *vb* **com·pen·sat·ed; com·pen·sat·ing** **1** : to make up for ⟨care can *compensate* for lack of experience⟩ **2** : ¹RECOMPENSE, PAY ⟨*compensate* an injured worker⟩

com·pen·sa·tion \ˌkäm-pən-'sā-shən\ *n* **1** : something that makes up for or is given to make up for something else **2** : money paid regularly

com·pete \kəm-'pēt\ *vb* **com·pet·ed; com·pet·ing** : to strive for something (as a prize or a reward) for which another is also striving

com·pe·tence \'käm-pət-əns\ *n* : the quality or state of being competent

com·pe·tent \'käm-pət-ənt\ *adj* : CAPABLE 1, EFFICIENT ⟨a *competent* teacher⟩

com·pe·ti·tion \ˌkäm-pə-'tish-ən\ *n* **1** : the act or process of competing **2** : a contest in which all who take part compete for the same thing

com·pet·i·tive \kəm-'pet-ət-iv\ *adj* : relating to, characterized by, or based on competition

com·pet·i·tor \kəm-'pet-ət-ər\ *n* : some-

one or something that competes especially in the selling of goods or services : RIVAL

com·pile \kəm-'pīl\ *vb* **com·piled; com·pil·ing** **1** : to collect into a volume or list **2** : to collect information from books or documents and arrange it in a new form

com·pla·cence \kəm-'plās-ns\ *n* : calm or satisfied feeling about one's self or one's position

com·pla·cen·cy \kəm-'plās-n-sē\ *n* : COMPLACENCE

com·pla·cent \kəm-'plās-nt\ *adj* : feeling or showing complacence

com·plain \kəm-'plān\ *vb* **1** : to express grief, pain, or discontent : find fault **2** : to accuse someone of wrongdoing — **com·plain·er** *n*

com·plaint \kəm-'plānt\ *n* **1** : expression of grief, pain, or discontent **2** : a cause or reason for complaining ⟨the noise is my biggest *complaint*⟩ **3** : a sickness or disease of the body **4** : a charge of wrongdoing against a person

¹com·ple·ment \'käm-plə-mənt\ *n* : something that completes or fills : the number required to complete or make perfect

²com·ple·ment \'käm-plə-ˌment\ *vb* : to form or serve as a complement to ⟨a hat that *complements* the costume⟩

com·ple·men·ta·ry \ˌkäm-plə-'ment-ə-rē\ *adj* : serving as a complement

¹com·plete \kəm-'plēt\ *adj* **1** : having no part lacking : ENTIRE ⟨a *complete* set of books⟩ **2** : brought to an end **3** : THOROUGH — **com·plete·ness** *n*

²complete *vb* **com·plet·ed; com·plet·ing** **1** : to bring to an end : FINISH ⟨*complete* a job⟩ **2** : to make whole or perfect

com·plete·ly \kəm-'plēt-lē\ *adv* : as much as possible : in every way or detail

com·ple·tion \kəm-'plē-shən\ *n* : the act or process of completing : the condition of being complete

com·plex \käm-'pleks, kəm-'pleks, 'käm-ˌpleks\ *adj* **1** : made up of two or more parts **2** : not simple

complex fraction *n* : a fraction with a fraction or mixed number in the numerator or denominator or both ⟨5/1¾ is a *complex fraction*⟩

com·plex·ion \kəm-'plek-shən\ *n* **1** : the color or appearance of the skin and especially of the face **2** : general appearance or impression

com·plex·i·ty \kəm-'plek-sət-ē\ *n, pl* **com·plex·i·ties** **1** : the quality or condition of being complex ⟨the *complexity* of a problem⟩ **2** : something complex ⟨the *complexities* of business⟩

com·pli·cate \'käm-plə-ˌkāt\ *vb* **com·pli·cat·ed; com·pli·cat·ing** : to make or become complex or difficult

com·pli·ca·tion \ˌkäm-plə-'kā-shən\ *n* **1** : a confused situation **2** : something that makes a situation more difficult

¹com·pli·ment \'käm-plə-mənt\ *n* **1** : an act or expression of praise, approval, respect, or admiration **2 compliments** *pl* : best wishes

²com·pli·ment \'käm-plə-ˌment\ *vb* : to pay a compliment to

synonyms COMPLIMENT, PRAISE, and FLATTER mean to express approval or admiration to someone personally. COMPLIMENT suggests a courteous or pleasant statement of admiration ⟨*complimented* the students on their neat work⟩ PRAISE may suggest that the statement of approval comes from a person in authority ⟨the boss *praised* us for doing a good job⟩ FLATTER suggests complimenting a person too much and especially when one is not sincere ⟨we *flattered* the teacher in the hope of getting better grades⟩

com·pli·men·ta·ry \ˌkäm-plə-'ment-ə-rē, -'men-trē\ *adj* **1** : expressing or containing a compliment **2** : given free as a courtesy or favor ⟨*complimentary* tickets⟩

com·ply \kəm-'plī\ *vb* **com·plied; com·ply·ing** : to act in agreement with another's wishes or in obedience to a rule

com·pose \kəm-'pōz\ *vb* **com·posed; com·pos·ing** **1** : to form by putting together ⟨*compose* a song⟩ **2** : to be the parts or materials of ⟨cloth *composed* of silk and wool⟩ **3** : to put in order : SETTLE ⟨*compose* one's mind⟩

com·posed \kəm-'pōzd\ *adj* : being calm and in control of oneself ⟨sat *composed* during the whole interview⟩

com·pos·er \kəm-'pō-zər\ *n* **1** : a person who composes **2** : a writer of music

com·pos·ite \kəm-'päz-ət\ *adj* : made up of different parts or elements

composite number *n* : an integer that is a product of two or more whole numbers each greater than 1

com·po·si·tion \ˌkäm-pə-'zish-ən\ *n* **1** : the act of composing (as by writing) **2** : the manner in which the parts of a thing are put together **3** : MAKEUP 1, CONSTITUTION ⟨the *composition* of rubber⟩ **4** : a literary, musical, or artistic production **5** : a short piece of writing done as a school exercise

com·post \'käm-ˌpōst\ *n* : decayed organic material used to improve soil for growing crops

com·po·sure \kəm-'pō-zhər\ *n* : calmness especially of mind, manner, or appearance

¹com·pound \käm-'paund\ *vb* **1** : to mix or unite together into a whole **2** : to form by combining separate things ⟨*compound* a medicine⟩

²com·pound \'käm-ˌpaund\ *adj* : made of or by the union of two or more parts

³com·pound \'käm-ˌpaund\ *n* **1** : a word made up of parts that are themselves words ⟨"rowboat" and "hide-and-seek" are *compounds*⟩ **2** : something (as a chemical) that is formed by combining two or more parts or elements

⁴com·pound \'käm-ˌpaund\ *n* : an enclosed area containing a group of buildings

compound fracture *n* : a breaking of a bone in which bone fragments stick out through the flesh

com·pre·hend \ˌkäm-pri-'hend\ *vb* **1** : to understand fully **2** : to take in : INCLUDE

com·pre·hen·sion \ˌkäm-pri-'hen-chən\ *n* : ability to understand

com·pre·hen·sive \ˌkäm-pri-'hen-siv\ *adj* : including much : INCLUSIVE ⟨a *comprehensive* course of study⟩ ⟨a *comprehensive* description⟩ — **com·pre·hen·sive·ness** *n*

¹com·press \kəm-'pres\ *vb* **1** : to press or squeeze together **2** : to reduce the volume of by pressure ⟨a pump for *compressing* air⟩

²com·press \'käm-ˌpres\ *n* : a pad (as of folded cloth) applied firmly to a part of the body (as to check bleeding)

com·pres·sion \kəm-'presh-ən\ *n* : the process of compressing : the state of being compressed

com·pres·sor \kəm-'pres-ər\ *n* **1** : one that compresses **2** : a machine for compressing something (as air)

com·prise \kəm-'prīz\ *vb* **com·prised; com·pris·ing** **1** : to be made up of : consist of **2** : ²FORM 3

¹com·pro·mise \'käm-prə-ˌmīz\ *n* **1** : an agreement over a dispute reached by each side changing or giving up some demands **2** : the thing agreed upon as a result of a compromise

²compromise *vb* **com·pro·mised; com·pro·mis·ing** **1** : to settle by compromise **2** : to expose to risk, suspicion, or disgrace ⟨*compromise* national security⟩

\ə\ **abut**	\au\ **out**	\i\ **tip**	\ȯ\ **saw**	\u̇\ **foot**
\ər\ **further**	\ch\ **chin**	\ī\ **life**	\ȯi\ **coin**	\y\ **yet**
\a\ **mat**	\e\ **pet**	\j\ **job**	\th\ **thin**	\yü\ **few**
\ā\ **take**	\ē\ **easy**	\ng\ **sing**	\th\ **this**	\yu̇\ **cure**
\ä\ **cot, cart**	\g\ **go**	\ō\ **bone**	\ü\ **food**	\zh\ **vision**

com·pul·sion \kəm-'pəl-shən\ *n* **1** : an act of compelling : the state of being compelled **2** : a force that compels **3** : a very strong urge to do something

com·pul·so·ry \kəm-'pəls-ə-rē, -'pəls-rē\ *adj* **1** : required by or as if by law ⟨*compulsory* education⟩ **2** : having the power of forcing someone to do something ⟨a *compulsory* law⟩

com·pu·ta·tion \ˌkäm-pyə-'tā-shən\ *n* **1** : the act or action of computing **2** : a result obtained by computing

com·pute \kəm-'pyüt\ *vb* **com·put·ed; com·put·ing** : to find out by using mathematics

com·put·er \kəm-'pyüt-ər\ *n* : an automatic electronic machine that can store, recall, and process data

com·rade \'käm-ˌrad, -rəd\ *n* : COMPANION 1

¹con \'kän\ *adv* : on the negative side ⟨argue pro and *con*⟩

²con *n* : an opposing argument, person, or position ⟨the pros and *cons* of the question⟩

con- — see COM-

con·cave \kän-'kāv\ *adj* : hollow or rounded inward like the inside of a bowl

con·ceal \kən-'sēl\ *vb* **1** : to hide from sight ⟨a *concealed* weapon⟩ **2** : to keep secret

con·ceal·ment \kən-'sēl-mənt\ *n* **1** : the act of hiding : the state of being hidden **2** : a hiding place

con·cede \kən-'sēd\ *vb* **con·ced·ed; con·ced·ing** **1** : to grant as a right or privilege **2** : to admit to be true ⟨*concede* defeat⟩

con·ceit \kən-'sēt\ *n* : too much pride in oneself or one's ability

con·ceit·ed \kən-'sēt-əd\ *adj* : VAIN 2

con·ceiv·able \kən-'sē-və-bəl\ *adj* : possible to conceive, imagine, or understand

con·ceive \kən-'sēv\ *vb* **con·ceived; con·ceiv·ing** **1** : to form an idea of : IMAGINE ⟨unable to *conceive* how it happened⟩ **2** : THINK 2

con·cen·trate \'kän-sən-ˌtrāt\ *vb* **con·cen·trat·ed; con·cen·trat·ing** **1** : to bring or come to or direct toward a common center **2** : to make stronger or thicker by removing something (as water) ⟨*concentrated* orange juice⟩ **3** : to fix one's powers, efforts, or attentions on one thing

con·cen·tra·tion \ˌkän-sən-'trā-shən\ *n* **1** : the act or process of concentrating : the state of being concentrated **2** : close mental attention to a subject

con·cept \'kän-ˌsept\ *n* **1** : ²THOUGHT 4 **2** : a general idea

¹con·cern \kən-'sərn\ *vb* **1** : to relate to : be about **2** : to be of interest or importance to : AFFECT **3** : to be a care, trouble, or distress to ⟨an illness that *concerned* my parents⟩ **4** : ENGAGE 3, OCCUPY

²concern *n* **1** : something that relates to or involves a person : AFFAIR **2** : a state of interest and uncertainty **3** : a business organization ⟨a banking *concern*⟩

con·cerned \kən-'sərnd\ *adj* : being worried and disturbed ⟨*concerned* parents⟩

con·cern·ing \kən-'sər-ning\ *prep* : relating to : ABOUT ⟨a notice *concerning* poor attendance⟩

con·cert \'kän-sərt, -ˌsərt\ *n* **1** : AGREEMENT 1 ⟨working in *concert* to finish the job⟩ **2** : a musical performance by several voices or instruments or by both

con·cer·ti·na \ˌkän-sər-'tē-nə\ *n* : a small musical instrument like an accordion

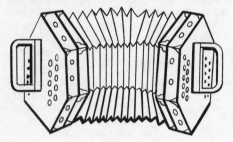

concertina

con·cer·to \kən-'chert-ō\ *n, pl* **con·cer·tos** : a musical composition usually in three parts for orchestra with one or more principal instruments

con·ces·sion \kən-'sesh-ən\ *n* **1** : the act or an instance of granting something **2** : something granted **3** : a special right or privilege given by an authority ⟨a *concession* to sell souvenirs on the beach⟩ ⟨a mining *concession*⟩

conch \'kängk, 'känch, 'kȯngk\ *n, pl* **conchs** \'kängks, 'kȯngks\ *or* **conch·es** \'kän-chəz\ : a very large sea snail with a tall thick spiral shell

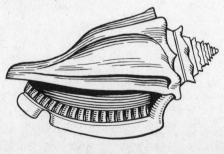

conch shell

con·cil·i·ate \kən-'sil-ē-ˌāt\ *vb* **con·cil·i·at·ed; con·cil·i·at·ing** **1** : to bring into agreement : RECONCILE ⟨it is hard to *conciliate* the true stories of what happened⟩ **2** : to gain or regain the goodwill or favor of ⟨*conciliate* an angry friend by an apology⟩

con·cise \kən-'sīs\ *adj* : expressing much in few words

con·clude \kən-'klüd\ *vb* **con·clud·ed; con·clud·ing** **1** : to bring or come to an end : FINISH ⟨*conclude* a speech⟩ **2** : to form an opinion ⟨I *conclude* that I was wrong⟩ **3** : to bring about as a result ⟨*conclude* an agreement⟩

con·clu·sion \kən-'klü-zhən\ *n* **1** : final decision reached by reasoning **2** : the last part of something **3** : a final settlement

con·clu·sive \kən-'klü-siv\ *adj* : DECISIVE 1 ⟨*conclusive* evidence⟩ — **con·clu·sive·ly** *adv*

con·coct \kən-'käkt, kän-\ *vb* **1** : to prepare (as food) by putting several different things together **2** : to make up : DEVISE ⟨*concoct* a plan⟩

con·cord \'kän-ˌkȯrd\ *n* : a state of agreement

con·course \'kän-ˌkōrs\ *n* **1** : a flocking, moving, or flowing together (as of persons or streams) : GATHERING **2** : a place where roads meet or people may pass or gather

¹con·crete \kän-'krēt\ *adj* **1** : ¹MATERIAL 1, REAL **2** : made of or relating to concrete

²con·crete \'kän-ˌkrēt\ *n* : a hardened mixture of cement, sand, and water with gravel or broken stone used in construction (as of pavements and buildings)

con·cur \kən-'kər\ *vb* **con·curred; con·cur·ring** **1** : to act or happen together **2** : to be in agreement (as in action or opinion) : ACCORD

con·cus·sion \kən-'kəsh-ən\ *n* **1** : a sharp hard blow or the effect of this **2** : injury to the brain by jarring (as from a blow)

con·demn \kən-'dem\ *vb* **1** : to declare to be wrong **2** : to declare guilty **3** : ²SENTENCE **4** : to declare to be unfit for use

con·dem·na·tion \ˌkän-ˌdem-'nā-shən, -dəm-\ *n* **1** : ¹CENSURE 1, BLAME **2** : the act of judicially condemning **3** : the state of being condemned

con·den·sa·tion \ˌkän-ˌden-'sā-shən, -dən-\ *n* **1** : the act or process of condensing **2** : something that has been condensed

con·dense \kən-'dens\ *vb* **con·densed; con·dens·ing** : to make or become more compact, more concise, closer, or denser : CONCENTRATE

con·de·scend \ˌkän-di-'send\ *vb* **1** : to stoop to a level considered lower than

one's own **2** : to grant favors with a show of being better than others

¹con·di·tion \kən-'dish-ən\ *n* **1** : something agreed upon or necessary if some other thing is to take place **2** **conditions** *pl* : state of affairs **3** : state of being ⟨water in a frozen *condition*⟩ **4** : situation in life ⟨people of humble *condition*⟩ **5** : state of health or fitness

²condition *vb* **1** : to put into the proper or desired condition **2** : to change the habits of usually by training

con·di·tion·al \kən-'dish-ən-l\ *adj* : depending on a condition ⟨a *conditional* promise⟩

con·dor \'kän-dər\ *n* : a very large American vulture having a bare head and neck and a frill of white feathers on the neck

condor

¹con·duct \'kän-ˌdəkt\ *n* **1** : the act or way of carrying something on ⟨the *conduct* of foreign trade⟩ **2** : personal behavior

²con·duct \kən-'dəkt\ *vb* **1** : ²GUIDE 1 **2** : to

\ə\ **abut**	\aú\ **out**	\i\ **tip**	\ȯ\ **saw**	\ú\ **foot**	
\ər\ **further**	\ch\ **chin**	\ī\ **life**	\ȯi\ **coin**	\y\ **yet**	
\a\ **mat**	\e\ **pet**	\j\ **job**	\th\ **thin**	\yü\ **few**	
\ā\ **take**	\ē\ **easy**	\ng\ **sing**	\th\ **this**	\yu̇\ **cure**	
\ä\ **cot, cart**	\g\ **go**	\ō\ **bone**	\ü\ **food**	\zh\ **vision**	

carry on or out from a position of command : LEAD ⟨*conduct* a business⟩ **3** : BEHAVE **1** ⟨*conduct* oneself well at a party⟩ **4** : to have the quality of transmitting light, heat, sound, or electricity

synonyms CONDUCT, DIRECT, and MANAGE mean to provide the leadership or guidance for something. CONDUCT suggests leading something in person ⟨*conduct* an orchestra⟩ DIRECT suggests guiding something that needs constant attention ⟨*directed* the building of a new school⟩ MANAGE suggests the handling of the small items of something (as a business) or the careful guiding of something to a goal ⟨*manage* a political campaign⟩

con·duc·tion \kən-'dək-shən\ *n* **1** : the act of transporting something ⟨pipes for the *conduction* of water⟩ **2** : transmission through a conductor

con·duc·tor \kən-'dək-tər\ *n* **1** : a person in charge of a public means of transportation (as a train) **2** : a person or thing that directs or leads ⟨the *conductor* of our school orchestra⟩ **3** : a substance or body capable of transmitting light, electricity, heat, or sound

cone \'kōn\ *n* **1** : the scaly fruit of certain trees (as the pine or fir) **2** : a solid body tapering evenly to a point from a circular base **3** : something resembling a cone in shape **4** : an ice-cream holder **5** : a cell of the retina of the eye that is sensitive to colored light

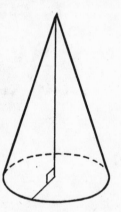

cone 2

con·fec·tion \kən-'fek-shən\ *n* : a fancy dish or sweet : DELICACY, CANDY

con·fec·tion·er \kən-'fek-shə-nər\ *n* : a maker of or dealer in confections (as candies)

con·fec·tion·ery \kən-'fek-shə-,ner-ē\ *n*, *pl* **con·fec·tion·er·ies** **1** : sweet things to eat (as candy) **2** : a confectioner's business or place of business

con·fed·er·a·cy \kən-'fed-ə-rə-sē\ *n*, *pl* **con·fed·er·a·cies** **1** : a league of persons, parties, or states **2** *cap* : the eleven southern states that seceded from the United States in 1860 and 1861

¹con·fed·er·ate \kən-'fed-ə-rət\ *adj* **1** : united in a league **2** *cap* : of or relating to the Confederacy

²confederate *n* **1** : a member of a confederacy **2** : ACCOMPLICE **3** *cap* : a soldier of or a person who sided with the Confederacy

³con·fed·er·ate \kən-'fed-ə-,rāt\ *vb* **con·fed·er·at·ed; con·fed·er·at·ing** : to unite in an alliance or confederacy

con·fer \kən-'fər\ *vb* **con·ferred; con·fer·ring** **1** : BESTOW, PRESENT **2** : to compare views especially in studying a problem

con·fer·ence \'kän-fə-rəns, -frəns\ *n* : a meeting for discussion or exchange of opinions

con·fess \kən-'fes\ *vb* **1** : to tell of or make known (as something private or damaging to oneself) **2** : to make known one's sins to God or to a priest

con·fes·sion \kən-'fesh-ən\ *n* **1** : an act of confessing **2** : an admission of guilt **3** : a formal statement of religious beliefs

con·fide \kən-'fid\ *vb* **con·fid·ed; con·fid·ing** **1** : to have or show faith **2** : to show confidence by telling secrets ⟨*confide* in a friend⟩ **3** : to tell in confidence ⟨*confided* the secret to a pal⟩ **4** : ENTRUST 2

con·fi·dence \'kän-fə-dəns\ *n* **1** : a feeling of trust or belief ⟨have *confidence* in a person⟩ **2** : SELF-CONFIDENCE **3** : reliance on another's secrecy or loyalty **4** : ²SECRET

con·fi·dent \'kän-fə-dənt\ *adj* : having or showing confidence — **con·fi·dent·ly** *adv*

con·fi·den·tial \,kän-fə-'den-chəl\ *adj* **1** : ¹SECRET 1 ⟨*confidential* information⟩ **2** : ²INTIMATE 2 **3** : trusted with secret matters ⟨a *confidential* clerk⟩ — **con·fi·den·tial·ly** *adv*

con·fine \kən-'fin\ *vb* **con·fined; con·fin·ing** **1** : to keep within limits ⟨*confined* the message to twenty words⟩ **2** : to shut up : IMPRISON **3** : to keep indoors ⟨*confined* by sickness⟩ — **con·fine·ment** \-mənt\ *n*

con·fines \'kän-,finz\ *n pl* : the boundary or limits of something

con·firm \kən-'fərm\ *vb* **1** : to make firm or firmer (as in a habit, in faith, or in intention) : STRENGTHEN **2** : APPROVE 2, ACCEPT ⟨the senate *confirmed* the treaty⟩ **3** : to administer the rite of confirmation to **4** : to make sure of the truth of ⟨*confirm* a suspicion⟩

con·fir·ma·tion \,kän-fər-'mā-shən\ *n* **1** : an act of confirming **2** : a religious ceremony admitting a person to full privileges in a church or synagogue **3** : something that confirms

con·firmed \kən-'fərmd\ *adj* **1** : being firmly established ⟨*confirmed* distrust of anything new⟩ **2** : unlikely to change ⟨a *confirmed* drunkard⟩

con·fis·cate \'kän-fə-ˌskāt\ *vb* **con·fis·cat·ed; con·fis·cat·ing** : to seize by or as if by public authority

con·fla·gra·tion \ˌkän-flə-'grā-shən\ *n* : a large destructive fire

¹con·flict \'kän-ˌflikt\ *n* **1** : an extended struggle : BATTLE **2** : a clashing disagreement (as between ideas or interests)

²con·flict \kən-'flikt\ *vb* : to be in opposition

con·form \kən-'fȯrm\ *vb* **1** : to make or be like : AGREE, ACCORD **2** : COMPLY ⟨*conform* to school customs⟩

con·for·mi·ty \kən-'fȯr-mət-ē\ *n, pl* **con·for·mi·ties** **1** : agreement in form, manner, or character **2** : action in accordance with some standard or authority

con·found \kən-'faúnd, kän-\ *vb* : to throw into disorder : mix up : CONFUSE

con·front \kən-'frənt\ *vb* **1** : to face especially in challenge : OPPOSE ⟨*confront* an enemy⟩ **2** : to cause to face or meet ⟨*confronted* us with the evidence⟩

con·fuse \kən-'fyüz\ *vb* **con·fused; con·fus·ing** **1** : to make mentally foggy or uncertain : PERPLEX **2** : to make embarrassed **3** : to fail to tell apart ⟨teachers always *confused* the twins⟩

con·fu·sion \kən-'fyü-zhən\ *n* **1** : an act or instance of confusing **2** : the state of being confused

con·geal \kən-'jēl\ *vb* **1** : to change from a fluid to a solid state by or as if by cold : FREEZE **2** : to make or become hard, stiff, or thick

con·ge·nial \kən-'jē-nyəl\ *adj* **1** : alike or sympathetic in nature, disposition, or tastes **2** : existing together in harmony **3** : tending to please or satisfy ⟨*congenial* work⟩

con·gest \kən-'jest\ *vb* : to make too crowded or full : CLOG ⟨a *congested* neighborhood⟩

¹con·glom·er·ate \kən-'gläm-ə-rət\ *adj* : made up of parts from various sources or of various kinds

²conglomerate *n* : a mass (as a rock) formed of fragments from various sources

con·grat·u·late \kən-'grach-ə-ˌlāt\ *vb* **con·grat·u·lat·ed; con·grat·u·lat·ing** : to express pleasure on account of success or good fortune ⟨*congratulate* the winner⟩

con·grat·u·la·tion \kən-ˌgrach-ə-'lāshən\ *n* **1** : the act of congratulating **2** : an expression of joy or pleasure at another's success or good fortune — usually used in pl.

con·gre·gate \'käng-gri-ˌgāt\ *vb* **con·gre·gat·ed; con·gre·gat·ing** : to collect or gather into a crowd or group : ASSEMBLE

con·gre·ga·tion \ˌkäng-gri-'gā-shən\ *n* **1** : a gathering or collection of persons or things **2** : an assembly of persons gathered especially for religious worship **3** : the membership of a church or synagogue

con·gress \'käng-grəs\ *n* **1** : a formal meeting of delegates for discussion and action : CONFERENCE **2** : the chief lawmaking body of a nation and especially of a republic that in the United States is made up of separate houses of senators and representatives

con·gress·man \'käng-grə-smən\ *n, pl* **con·gress·men** \-smən\ : a member of a congress and especially of the United States House of Representatives

con·gress·wom·an \'käng-grə-ˌswúm-ən\ *n, pl* **con·gress·wom·en** \-grə-ˌswim-ən\ : a woman member of a congress and especially of the United States House of Representatives

con·gru·ent \kən-'grü-ənt, 'käng-grə-wənt\ *adj* : having the same size and shape ⟨*congruent* triangles⟩

con·ic \'kän-ik\ *adj* **1** : CONICAL **2** : of or relating to a cone

con·i·cal \'kän-i-kəl\ *adj* : shaped like a cone

con·i·fer \'kän-ə-fər, 'kō-nə-\ *n* : any of a group of mostly evergreen trees and shrubs (as pines) that produce cones — **co·nif·er·ous** \kō-'nif-ə-rəs,kə-\ *adj*

¹con·jec·ture \kən-'jek-chər\ *n* : **²GUESS**

²conjecture *vb* **con·jec·tured; con·jec·tur·ing** : **¹GUESS 1, SURMISE**

con·junc·tion \kən-'jəngk-shən\ *n* **1** : a joining together : UNION **2** : a word or expression that joins together sentences, clauses, phrases, or words

con·jure \'kän-jər, 'kən-jər; *in sense 1* kən-'júr\ *vb* **con·jured; con·jur·ing** **1** : to beg earnestly or solemnly : BESEECH **2** : to practice magical arts **3** : IMAGINE 1 ⟨*conjure* up an image⟩

con·nect \kə-'nekt\ *vb* **1** : to join or link together ⟨*connect* two wires⟩ **2** : to attach by close personal relationship ⟨*connected* by marriage⟩ **3** : to bring together in thought ⟨*connect* the smell of burning leaves with childhood⟩ — **con·nec·tor** \-'nek-tər\ *n*

\ə\ abut	\aú\ out	\i\ tip	\ȯ\ saw	\ú\ foot
\ər\ further	\ch\ chin	\ī\ life	\ȯi\ coin	\y\ yet
\a\ mat	\e\ pet	\j\ job	\th\ thin	\yü\ few
\ā\ take	\ē\ easy	\ng\ sing	\th\ this	\yú\ cure
\ä\ cot, cart	\g\ go	\ō\ bone	\ü\ food	\zh\ vision

con•nec•tion \kə-'nek-shən\ *n* **1** : the act of connecting **2** : the fact or condition of being connected : RELATIONSHIP **3** : a thing that connects : BOND, LINK **4** : a person connected with others (as by kinship) **5** : a social, professional, or commercial relationship **6** : the act or the means of continuing a journey by transferring (as to another train)

con•nois•seur \ˌkän-ə-'sər\ *n* : a person qualified to act as a judge in matters involving taste and appreciation

con•quer \'käng-kər\ *vb* **1** : to get or gain by force : win by fighting **2** : OVERCOME 1

con•quer•or \'käng-kər-ər\ *n* : one that conquers : VICTOR

con•quest \'kän-ˌkwest\ *n* **1** : the act or process of conquering : VICTORY **2** : something that is conquered **synonyms** see VICTORY

con•quis•ta•dor \kȯng-'kēs-tə-ˌdȯr\ *n, pl* **con•quis•ta•do•res** \-ˌkēs-tə-'dȯr-ēz\ *or* **con•quis•ta•dors** : a leader in the Spanish conquest especially of Mexico and Peru in the sixteenth century

con•science \'kän-chəns\ *n* : knowledge of right and wrong and a feeling that one should do what is right

con•sci•en•tious \ˌkän-chē-'en-chs\ *adj* **1** : guided by or agreeing with one's conscience **2** : using or done with careful attention

con•scious \'kän-chəs\ *adj* **1** : aware of facts or feelings ⟨*conscious* of the cold⟩ **2** : known or felt by one's inner self ⟨*conscious* guilt⟩ **3** : mentally awake or active **4** : INTENTIONAL — **con•scious•ly** *adv*

con•scious•ness \'kän-chəs-nəs\ *n* **1** : the condition of being conscious **2** : the upper level of mental life involving conscious thought and the will

con•se•crate \'kän-sə-ˌkrāt\ *vb* **con•se•crat•ed; con•se•crat•ing 1** : to declare to be sacred or holy : set apart for the service of God ⟨*consecrate* a church⟩ **2** : to dedicate to a particular purpose

con•sec•u•tive \kən-'sek-yət-iv\ *adj* : following one another in order without gaps

¹con•sent \kən-'sent\ *vb* : to express willingness or approval : AGREE ⟨*consented* to speak at the banquet⟩

²consent *n* : approval of or agreement with what is done or suggested by another person

con•se•quence \'kän-sə-ˌkwens\ *n* **1** : something produced by a cause or following from a condition **2** : real importance ⟨a person of *consequence*⟩

con•se•quent \'kän-si-kwənt\ *adj* : following as a result or effect

con•se•quent•ly \'kän-sə-ˌkwent-lē\ *adv* : as a result

con•ser•va•tion \ˌkän-sər-'vā-shən\ *n* **1** : PROTECTION 1, PRESERVATION **2** : planned management of natural resources (as timber) to prevent waste, destruction, or neglect

¹con•ser•va•tive \kən-'sər-vət-iv\ *adj* **1** : favoring a policy of keeping things as they are : opposed to change **2** : favoring established styles and standards ⟨*conservative* in dress⟩ — **con•ser•va•tive•ly** *adv*

²conservative *n* : a person who holds conservative views : a cautious person

con•ser•va•to•ry \kən-'sər-və-ˌtōr-ē\ *n, pl* **con•ser•va•to•ries 1** : GREENHOUSE **2** : a place of instruction in some special study (as music)

¹con•serve \kən-'sərv\ *vb* **con•served; con•serv•ing** : to keep in a safe condition : SAVE

²con•serve \'kän-ˌsərv\ *n* **1** : a candied fruit **2** : a rich fruit preserve

con•sid•er \kən-'sid-ər\ *vb* **1** : to think over carefully : PONDER, REFLECT **2** : to treat in a kind or thoughtful way ⟨you never *consider* my feelings⟩ **3** : to think of in a certain way : BELIEVE

con•sid•er•able \kən-'sid-ə-rə-bəl\ *adj* : rather large in extent, amount, or size ⟨a *considerable* estate⟩ ⟨was in *considerable* pain⟩ — **con•sid•er•ably** \-blē\ *adv*

con•sid•er•ate \kən-'sid-ə-rət\ *adj* : thoughtful of the rights and feelings of others

con•sid•er•ation \kən-ˌsid-ə-rā-shən\ *n* **1** : careful thought : DELIBERATION **2** : thoughtfulness for other people **3** : something that needs to be considered before deciding or acting **4** : a payment made in return for something

con•sign \kən-'sīn\ *vb* **1** : ENTRUST 2 **2** : to give, transfer, or deliver to another **3** : to send (as goods) to an agent to be sold or cared for — **con•sign•ment** \-mənt\ *n*

con•sist \kən-'sist\ *vb* : to be made up or composed ⟨coal *consists* mostly of carbon⟩

con•sis•ten•cy \kən-'sis-tən-sē\ *n, pl* **con•sis•ten•cies 1** : degree of compactness, firmness, or stickiness ⟨dough of the right *consistency*⟩ **2** : agreement or harmony between parts or elements **3** : a sticking with one way of thinking or acting

con•sis•tent \kən-'sis-tənt\ *adj* : showing consistency ⟨*consistent* behavior⟩ — **con•sis•tent•ly** *adv*

con•so•la•tion \ˌkän-sə-'lā-shən\ *n* **1** : the act of consoling : the state of being con-soled **2** : something that lessens disappointment, misery, or grief

¹con·sole \kən-'sōl\ *vb* **con·soled; con·sol·ing** : to comfort in a time of grief or distress

²con·sole \'kän-ˌsōl\ *n* **1** : the part of an organ at which the organist sits and which contains the keyboard and controls **2** : a panel or cabinet on which are dials and switches for controlling an electronic or mechanical device **3** : a radio, phonograph, or television cabinet that stands on the floor

con·sol·i·date \kən-'säl-ə-ˌdāt\ *vb* **con·sol·i·dat·ed; con·sol·i·dat·ing 1** : to join together into one whole : UNITE **2** : STRENGTHEN

con·so·nant \'kän-sə-nənt\ *n* **1** : a speech sound (as \p\, \n\, or \s\) produced by narrowing or closing the breath channel at one or more points **2** : a letter in the English alphabet other than *a, e, i, o,* or *u*

¹con·sort \'kän-ˌsòrt\ *n* : a wife or husband especially of a king or queen

²con·sort \kən-'sòrt\ *vb* : to go together as companions : ASSOCIATE

con·spic·u·ous \kən-'spik-yə-wəs\ *adj* **1** : easily seen **2** : attracting attention : PROMINENT

con·spir·a·cy \kən-'spir-ə-sē\ *n, pl* **con·spir·a·cies 1** : the act of conspiring or plotting **2** : an agreement among conspirators **3** : a group of conspirators

con·spir·a·tor \kən-'spir-ət-ər\ *n* : a person who conspires

con·spire \kən-'spīr\ *vb* **con·spired; con·spir·ing 1** : to make an agreement especially in secret to do an unlawful act : PLOT **2** : to act together ⟨measles and the weather *conspired* to spoil our holiday⟩

con·sta·ble \'kän-stə-bəl, 'kən-\ *n* : a police officer usually of a village or small town

con·stan·cy \'kän-stən-sē\ *n* : firmness and loyalty in one's beliefs or personal relationships

con·stant \'kän-stənt\ *adj* **1** : always faithful and true ⟨*constant* friends⟩ **2** : remaining steady and unchanged ⟨a *constant* temperature⟩ **3** : occurring over and over again ⟨*constant* headaches⟩ — **con·stant·ly** *adv*

con·stel·la·tion \ˌkän-stə-'lā-shən\ *n* : any of eighty-eight groups of stars forming patterns

con·ster·na·tion \ˌkän-stər-'nā-shən\ *n* : amazement, alarm, or disappointment that makes one feel helpless or confused

con·sti·pate \'kän-stə-ˌpāt\ *vb* **con·sti·**

pat·ed; con·sti·pat·ing : to cause constipation in

con·sti·pa·tion \ˌkän-stə-'pā-shən\ *n* : difficult or infrequent passage of dry hard material from the bowels

¹con·stit·u·ent \kən-'stich-ə-wənt\ *n* **1** : one of the parts or materials of which something is made : ELEMENT, INGREDIENT **2** : any of the voters who elect a person to represent them

²constituent *adj* **1** : serving to form or make up a unit or whole **2** : having power to elect or appoint or to make or change a constitution ⟨a *constituent* assembly⟩

con·sti·tute \'kän-stə-ˌtüt, -ˌtyüt\ *vb* **con·sti·tut·ed; con·sti·tut·ing 1** : to appoint to an office or duty ⟨the *constituted* authorities⟩ **2** : SET UP 2 ⟨a fund *constituted* to help needy students⟩ **3** : to make up : FORM ⟨twelve months *constitute* a year⟩

con·sti·tu·tion \ˌkän-stə-'tü-shən, -'tyü-\ *n* **1** : the bodily makeup of an individual **2** : the basic structure of something **3** : the basic beliefs and laws of a nation, state, or social group by which the powers and duties of the government are established and certain rights are guaranteed to the people

¹con·sti·tu·tion·al \ˌkän-stə-'tü-shən-l, -'tyü-\ *adj* **1** : having to do with a person's bodily or mental makeup **2** : of, relating to, or in agreement with a constitution (as of a nation)

²constitutional *n* : an exercise (as a walk) taken for one's health

con·strain \kən-'strān\ *vb* : COMPEL, FORCE ⟨*constrained* to retire by ill health⟩

con·straint \kən-'strānt\ *n* **1** : COMPULSION 1, 2 ⟨act under *constraint*⟩ **2** : a keeping back of one's natural feelings ⟨the *constraint* between former friends⟩

con·strict \kən-'strikt\ *vb* : to make narrower or smaller by drawing together : SQUEEZE

con·stric·tion \kən-'strik-shən\ *n* : an act or instance of constricting

con·stric·tor \kən-'strik-tər\ *n* : a snake (as a boa) that kills prey by crushing in its coils

con·struct \kən-'strəkt\ *vb* : to make or form by combining parts **synonyms** see BUILD

con·struc·tion \kən-'strək-shən\ *n* **1** : the arrangement of words and the relationship between words in a sentence **2** : the

\ə\ abut	\aů\ out	\i\ tip	\ò\ saw	\ů\ foot
\ər\ further	\ch\ chin	\ī\ life	\òi\ coin	\y\ yet
\a\ mat	\e\ pet	\j\ job	\th\ thin	\yü\ few
\ā\ take	\ē\ easy	\ng\ sing	\th\ this	\yů\ cure
\ä\ cot, cart	\g\ go	\ō\ bone	\ü\ food	\zh\ vision

process, art, or manner of constructing **3** : something built or put together : STRUC-TURE ⟨a flimsy *construction*⟩ **4** : INTER-PRETATION ⟨believes in the strict *construction* of the constitution⟩

construction paper *n* : a thick paper available in many colors for school art work

con·struc·tive \kən-'strək-tiv\ *adj* : helping to develop or improve something ⟨*constructive* criticism⟩

con·strue \kən-'strü\ *vb* **con·strued; con·stru·ing** : to understand or explain the sense or intention of

con·sul \kän-səl\ *n* : an official appointed by a government to live in a foreign country in order to look after the commercial interests of citizens of the appointing country

con·sult \kən-'səlt\ *vb* **1** : to seek the opinion or advice of ⟨*consult* a doctor⟩ **2** : to seek information from ⟨*consult* a dictionary⟩ **3** : to talk something over ⟨will have to *consult* with my lawyer⟩

con·sul·ta·tion \ˌkän-səl-'tā-shən\ *n* **1** : a discussion between doctors on a case or its treatment **2** : the act of consulting

con·sume \kən-'süm\ *vb* **con·sumed; con·sum·ing 1** : to destroy by or as if by fire **2** : to use up : SPEND **3** : to eat or drink up **4** : to take up the interest or attention of ⟨*consumed* with curiosity⟩

con·sum·er \kən-'sü-mər\ *n* **1** : one that consumes **2** : a person who buys and uses up goods

con·sump·tion \kən-'səmp-shən\ *n* **1** : the act or process of consuming and especially of using up something (as food or coal) **2** : a wasting away of the body especially from tuberculosis of the lungs

¹con·tact \'kän-ˌtakt\ *n* **1** : a meeting or touching of persons or things **2** : a person one knows who has influence especially in the business or political world

²contact *vb* **1** : to come or bring into contact **2** : to get in touch or communication with

con·tact lens \ˌkän-ˌtakt-\ *n* : a thin lens used to correct bad eyesight and worn right over the cornea of the eye

con·ta·gion \kən-'tā-jən\ *n* **1** : the passing of a disease from one individual to another as a result of some contact between them **2** : a contagious disease

con·ta·gious \kən-'tā-jəs\ *adj* : spreading by contagion ⟨a *contagious* disease⟩

con·tain \kən-'tān\ *vb* **1** : to keep within limits : RESTRAIN, CHECK ⟨tried to *contain* my anger⟩ **2** : to have within : HOLD ⟨the box *contained* some old books⟩ **3** : to

consist of or include ⟨the building *contains* classrooms⟩

con·tain·er \kən-'tā-nər\ *n* : something into which other things can be put (as for storage)

con·tam·i·nate \kən-'tam-ə-ˌnāt\ *vb* **con·tam·i·nat·ed; con·tam·i·nat·ing 1** : to soil, stain, or infect by contact or association **2** : to make unfit for use by adding something harmful or unpleasant

con·tem·plate \'känt-əm-ˌplāt\ *vb* **con·tem·plat·ed; con·tem·plat·ing 1** : to view with careful and thoughtful attention **2** : to have in mind : plan on ⟨*contemplate* a trip to Europe⟩

con·tem·pla·tion \ˌkänt-əm-'plā-shən\ *n* **1** : the act of thinking about spiritual things : MEDITATION **2** : the act of looking at or thinking about something for some time **3** : a looking ahead to some future event

¹con·tem·po·rary \kən-'tem-pə-ˌrer-ē\ *adj* **1** : living or occurring at the same period of time **2** : MODERN 1 ⟨our *contemporary* writers⟩

²contemporary *n, pl* **con·tem·po·rar·ies** : a person who lives at the same time or is of about the same age as another

con·tempt \kən-'tempt\ *n* **1** : the act of despising : the state of mind of one who despises **2** : the state of being despised

con·tempt·ible \kən-'temp-tə-bəl\ *adj* : deserving contempt ⟨a *contemptible* lie⟩

con·temp·tu·ous \kən-'temp-chə-wəs\ *adj* : feeling or showing contempt : SCORNFUL

con·tend \kən-'tend\ *vb* **1** : COMPETE ⟨*contend* for a prize⟩ **2** : to try hard to deal with ⟨many problems to *contend* with⟩ **3** : to argue or state earnestly

¹con·tent \kən-'tent\ *adj* : pleased and satisfied with what one has or is

²content *vb* : to make content : SATISFY

³content *n* : freedom from care or discomfort

⁴con·tent \'kän-ˌtent\ *n* **1** : something contained — usually used in pl. ⟨the *contents* of a room⟩ **2** : the subject or topic treated (as in a book) — usually used in pl. ⟨a table of *contents*⟩ **3** : the important part or meaning (as of a book) **4** : the amount contained or possible to contain ⟨oil with a high *content* of sulfur⟩⟨the jug has a *content* of one liter⟩

con·tent·ed \kən-'tent-əd\ *adj* : satisfied or showing satisfaction with one's possessions or one's situation in life ⟨a *contented* smile⟩

con·ten·tion \kən-'ten-chən\ *n* **1** : an act or instance of contending **2** : an idea or point for which a person argues (as in a debate or argument) **3** : COMPETITION 2

con·tent·ment \kən-'tent-mənt\ *n* : freedom from worry or restlessness : peaceful satisfaction

¹con·test \kən-'test\ *vb* : to make (something) a cause of dispute or fighting ⟨*contest* a claim⟩

²con·test \'kän-ˌtest\ *n* : a struggle for victory : COMPETITION ⟨a *contest* for a prize⟩

con·tes·tant \kən-'tes-tənt\ *n* : one who takes part in a contest ⟨a *contestant* on a quiz program⟩

con·ti·nent \'känt-n-ənt\ *n* **1** : one of the great divisions of land on the globe (as Africa, Antarctica, Asia, Australia, Europe, North America, or South America) **2** *cap* : the continent of Europe

con·ti·nen·tal \ˌkänt-n-'ent-l\ *adj* : of or relating to a continent

con·tin·gent \kən-'tin-jənt\ *adj* : depending on something else that may or may not exist or occur ⟨our trip is *contingent* on our being able to get tickets⟩

con·tin·u·al \kən-'tin-yə-wəl\ *adj* **1** : going on without stopping **2** : occurring again and again at short intervals — **con·tin·u·al·ly** *adv*

con·tin·u·ance \kən-'tin-yə-wəns\ *n* **1** : the act of continuing **2** : the quality of being continual

con·tin·u·a·tion \kən-ˌtin-yə-'wā-shən\ *n* **1** : the making longer of a state or activity **2** : a going on after stopping **3** : a thing or part by which something is continued

con·tin·ue \kən-'tin-yü\ *vb* **con·tin·ued; con·tin·u·ing 1** : to do or cause to do the same thing without changing or stopping ⟨I *continued* to work hard⟩ ⟨the weather *continued* hot and sunny⟩ **2** : to begin again after stopping ⟨to be *continued* next week⟩

con·ti·nu·ity \ˌkänt-n-'ü-ət-ē, -'yü-\ *n, pl* **con·ti·nu·ities** : the quality or state of being continuous

con·tin·u·ous \kən-'tin-yə-wəs\ *adj* : continuing without a stop — **con·tin·u·ous·ly** *adv*

con·tort \kən-'tòrt\ *vb* : to give an unusual appearance or unnatural shape to by twisting

con·tor·tion \kən-'tòr-shən\ *n* **1** : a twisting or a being twisted out of shape **2** : a contorted shape or thing

con·tour \'kän-ˌtùr\ *n* **1** : the outline of a figure, body, or surface **2** : a line or a drawing showing an outline

contra- *prefix* **1** : against : contrary : contrasting **2** : pitched below normal bass

con·tra·band \'kän-trə-ˌband\ *n* **1** : goods forbidden by law to be owned or to be brought into or out of a country **2** : smuggled goods

¹con·tract \'kän-ˌtrakt\ *n* **1** : an agreement that the law can force one to keep **2** : a writing made to show the terms and conditions of a contract

²contract \kən-'trakt, *1 is also* 'kän-ˌtrakt\ *vb* **1** : to agree by contract ⟨*contracted* to build a house⟩ **2** : to become sick with : CATCH ⟨*contract* pneumonia⟩ **3** : to draw together and make shorter and broader ⟨*contract* one's muscles⟩ **4** : to make or become smaller : SHRINK ⟨cold metal *contracts*⟩ **5** : to make (as a word) shorter by dropping sounds or letters

con·trac·tion \kən-'trak-shən\ *n* **1** : the act or process of contracting : the state of being contracted **2** : a shortening of a word or word group by leaving out a sound or letter **3** : a form (as *don't* or *they've*) produced by contraction

con·tra·dict \ˌkän-trə-'dikt\ *vb* **1** : to deny the truth of a statement : say the opposite of what someone else has said **2** : to be opposed to ⟨your actions *contradict* your words⟩

con·tra·dic·tion \ˌkän-trə-'dik-shən\ *n* : something (as a statement) that contradicts something else

con·tra·dic·to·ry \ˌkän-trə-'dik-tə-rē\ *adj* : involving, causing, or being a contradiction ⟨*contradictory* reports⟩

con·tral·to \kən-'tral-tō\ *n, pl* **con·tral·tos 1** : the lowest female singing voice : ALTO **2** : a singer with a contralto voice

con·trap·tion \kən-'trap-shən\ *n* : GADGET

¹con·trary \'kän-ˌtrer-ē\ *n, pl* **con·trar·ies** : something opposite or contrary — **on the contrary** : just the opposite : NO

²con·trary \'kän-ˌtrer-ē, *4 is often* kən-'treər-ē\ *adj* **1** : exactly opposite : altogether different ⟨we hold *contrary* opinions about that⟩ **2** : being against or opposed to ⟨actions *contrary* to the law⟩ **3** : not favorable ⟨*contrary* winds delayed the ship⟩ **4** : unwilling to obey or behave well ⟨*contrary* children⟩

¹con·trast \'kän-ˌtrast\ *n* **1** : a person or thing that shows differences when compared to another **2** : difference or unlikeness (as in color or brightness) between related things especially when very plain

²con·trast \kən-'trast\ *vb* **1** : to show noticeable differences **2** : to compare two

\ə\ abut	\aú\ out	\i\ tip	\ò\ saw	\ú\ foot
\ər\ further	\ch\ chin	\ī\ life	\òi\ coin	\y\ yet
\a\ mat	\e\ pet	\j\ job	\th\ thin	\yü\ few
\ā\ take	\ē\ easy	\ng\ sing	\th\ this	\yù\ cure
\ä\ cot, cart	\g\ go	\ō\ bone	\ü\ food	\zh\ vision

persons or things so as to show the differences between them **synonyms** see COMPARE

con·trib·ute \kən-'trib-yət\ vb **con·trib·ut·ed; con·trib·ut·ing 1** : to give along with others **2** : to have a share in something ⟨you all *contributed* to the success of the plan⟩ **3** : to supply (as an article) for publication especially in a magazine — **con·trib·u·tor** \kən-'trib-yət-ər\ n

con·tri·bu·tion \ˌkän-trə-'byü-shən\ n **1** : the act of contributing **2** : the sum or thing contributed

con·trite \'kän-ˌtrīt, kən-'trīt\ adj : feeling or showing sorrow for some wrong that one has done : REPENTANT

con·triv·ance \kən-'trī-vəns\ n : something (as a scheme or a mechanical device) produced with skill and cleverness

con·trive \kən-'trīv\ **con·trived; con·triv·ing 1** : ²PLAN 1, PLOT ⟨*contrive* a way to escape⟩ **2** : to form or make in some skillful or clever way **3** : to manage to bring about or do

¹con·trol \kən-'trōl\ vb **con·trolled; con·trol·ling 1** : to keep within bounds : RESTRAIN ⟨learn to *control* your temper⟩ ⟨*control* a horse⟩ **2** : to have power over

²control n **1** : the power or authority to control or command **2** : ability to control ⟨anger that is out of *control*⟩ ⟨lose *control* of an automobile⟩ **3** : SELF-RESTRAINT **4** : REGULATION ⟨price *controls*⟩ **5** : a device used to start, stop, or change the operation of a machine or system ⟨a radio *control*⟩ **6** : something used in an experiment or study to provide a check on results

con·tro·ver·sial \ˌkän-trə-'vər-shəl\ adj : relating to or causing controversy ⟨a *controversial* law⟩

con·tro·ver·sy \'kän-trə-ˌvər-sē\ n, pl **con·tro·ver·sies 1** : an often long or heated discussion of something about which there is great difference of opinion **2** : ¹QUARREL 2

co·nun·drum \kə-'nən-drəm\ n : ¹RIDDLE

con·va·lesce \ˌkän-və-'les\ vb **con·va·lesced; con·va·lesc·ing** : to regain health and strength gradually after sickness or injury

con·va·les·cence \ˌkän-və-'les-ns\ n : the period or process of convalescing

¹con·va·les·cent \ˌkän-və-'les-nt\ adj : passing through convalescence

²convalescent n : a person who is convalescent

con·vec·tion \kən-'vek-shən\ n : motion in a gas (as air) or a liquid in which the warmer portions rise and the colder portions sink ⟨heat transferred by *convection*⟩

con·vene \kən-'vēn\ vb **con·vened; con·ven·ing 1** : ASSEMBLE 3 ⟨the legislature *convened* on Tuesday⟩ **2** : to cause to assemble

con·ve·nience \kən-'vē-nyəns\ n **1** : the quality or state of being convenient **2** : personal comfort ⟨thought only of my own *convenience*⟩ **3** : OPPORTUNITY 1 ⟨come at your earliest *convenience*⟩ **4** : something that gives comfort or advantage ⟨a house with modern *conveniences*⟩

con·ve·nient \kən-'vē-nyənt\ adj **1** : suited to a person's comfort or ease ⟨a *convenient* time⟩ ⟨a *convenient* house⟩ **2** : suited to a certain use ⟨*convenient* tools⟩ **3** : easy to get to ⟨several *convenient* stores⟩ — **con·ve·nient·ly** adv

con·vent \'kän-vənt, -ˌvent\ n **1** : a group of nuns living together **2** : a house or a set of buildings occupied by a community of nuns

con·ven·tion \kən-'ven-chən\ n **1** : AGREEMENT 2 ⟨a *convention* among nations⟩ **2** : a custom or a way of acting and doing things that is widely accepted and followed **3** : a meeting of persons gathered together for a common purpose ⟨a teachers' *convention*⟩

con·ven·tion·al \kən-'ven-chən-l\ adj **1** : behaving according to convention ⟨very *conventional* people⟩ **2** : used or accepted through convention ⟨*conventional* signs and symbols⟩

con·ver·sa·tion \ˌkän-vər-'sā-shən\ n : talking or a talk between two or more people

con·verse \kən-'vərs\ vb **con·versed; con·vers·ing** : to have a conversation **synonyms** see SPEAK

con·ver·sion \kən-'vər-zhən\ n **1** : the act of converting : the state of being converted **2** : a change in the nature or form of a thing **3** : a change of religion

¹con·vert \kən-'vərt\ vb **1** : to change from one belief, religion, view, or party to another **2** : to change from one form to another **3** : to exchange for an equivalent ⟨*convert* francs into dollars⟩

²con·vert \'kän-ˌvərt\ n : a person who has been converted

¹con·vert·ible \kən-'vərt-ə-bəl\ adj : possible to change in form or use

²convertible n **1** : something that is convertible **2** : an automobile with a top that can be raised, lowered, or removed

con·vex \kän-'veks, 'kän-ˌveks\ adj : rounded like the outside of a ball or circle

con·vey \kən-'vā\ vb **con·veyed; con·vey·ing 1 :** to carry from one place to another : TRANSPORT **2 :** to serve as a way of carrying ⟨pipes *convey* water⟩ **3 :** IMPART 2, COMMUNICATE ⟨we use words to *convey* our thoughts⟩

con·vey·ance \kən-'vā-əns\ n **1 :** the act of conveying **2 :** something used to carry goods or passengers

¹con·vict \kən-'vikt\ vb : to prove or find guilty

²con·vict \'kän-,vikt\ n : a person serving a prison sentence usually for a long time

con·vic·tion \kən-'vik-shən\ n **1 :** the act of convicting : the state of being convicted **2 :** the state of mind of a person who is sure that what he or she believes or says is true **3 :** a strong belief or opinion

con·vince \kən-'vins\ vb **con·vinced; con·vinc·ing :** to argue so as to make a person agree or believe ⟨*convinced* them to go along⟩ ⟨*convinced* me it was true⟩

con·vinc·ing \kən-'vin-sing\ adj : causing one to believe or agree : PERSUASIVE — **con·vinc·ing·ly** adv

con·vulse \kən-'vəls\ vb **con·vulsed; con·vuls·ing :** to shake violently or with jerky motions ⟨*convulsed* with laughter⟩

con·vul·sion \kən-'vəl-shən\ n **1 :** an attack of violent involuntary muscular contractions : FIT **2 :** a violent disturbance : UPHEAVAL

con·vul·sive \kən-'vəl-siv\ adj : being or producing a convulsion — **con·vul·sive·ly** adv

¹coo \'kü\ vb **cooed; coo·ing 1 :** to make the soft sound made by doves and pigeons or one like it **2 :** to talk fondly or lovingly

²coo n, pl **coos** : the sound made in cooing

¹cook \'kuk\ n : a person who prepares food for eating

²cook vb **1 :** to prepare food for eating by the use of heat **2 :** to go through the process of being cooked

cook·book \'kuk-,buk\ n : a book of cooking recipes and directions

cook·ie or **cooky** \'kuk-ē\ n, pl **cook·ies** : a small sweet cake

cook·out \'kuk-,aut\ n : an outing at which a meal is cooked and served outdoors

cook up vb : to think up : DEVISE ⟨*cook up* a scheme⟩

¹cool \'kül\ adj **1 :** somewhat cold : not warm ⟨a *cool* day⟩ ⟨a *cool* room⟩ **2 :** not letting or keeping in heat ⟨*cool* clothes⟩ **3 :** ²CALM 2 **4 :** not friendly or interested : INDIFFERENT — **cool·ly** adv

²cool vb : to make or become cool

³cool n : a cool time or place

cool·er \'kü-lər\ n : a container for keeping food or drink cool

coon \'kün\ n : RACCOON

¹coop \'küp, 'kup\ n : a building for housing poultry

²coop vb : to restrict to a small space ⟨children *cooped* up by bad weather⟩

coo·per \'kü-pər, 'kup-ər\ n : a worker who makes or repairs wooden casks, tubs, or barrels

co·op·er·ate \kō-'äp-ə-,rāt\ vb **co·op·er·at·ed; co·op·er·at·ing :** to act or work together so as to get something done

co·op·er·a·tion \kō-,äp-ə-'rā-shən\ n : the act or process of cooperating

¹co·op·er·a·tive \kō-'äp-ə-rət-iv\ adj **1 :** willing to cooperate or work with others **2 :** of, relating to, or organized as a cooperative ⟨a *cooperative* store⟩

²cooperative n : an association formed to enable its members to buy or sell to better advantage

¹co·or·di·nate \kō-'ord-n-ət\ adj : equal in rank or importance

²co·or·di·nate \kō-'ord-n-,āt\ vb **co·or·di·nat·ed; co·or·di·nat·ing :** to work or cause to work together smoothly

co·or·di·na·tion \kō-,ord-n-'ā-shən\ n : smooth working together (as of parts) ⟨good muscular *coordination*⟩

cop \'käp\ n : POLICE OFFICER

cope \'kōp\ vb **coped; cop·ing :** to struggle or try to manage especially with some success ⟨*cope* with a tough problem⟩

cop·i·er \'käp-ē-ər\ n **1 :** a person who copies **2 :** a machine for making copies (as of letters or drawings)

co·pi·lot \'kō-,pī-lət\ n : an assistant airplane pilot

co·pi·ous \'kō-pē-əs\ adj : very plentiful : ABUNDANT — **co·pi·ous·ly** adv

cop·per \'käp-ər\ n **1 :** a tough reddish metallic chemical element that is one of the best conductors of heat and electricity **2 :** a copper or bronze coin

cop·per·head \'käp-ər-,hed\ n : a mottled reddish brown poisonous snake of the eastern United States

cop·pice \'käp-əs\ n : a thicket, grove, or growth of small trees

co·pra \'kō-prə\ n : dried coconut meat

copse \'käps\ n : COPPICE

¹copy \'käp-ē\ n, pl **cop·ies 1 :** something that is made to look exactly like something

\ə\ abut	\aú\ out	\i\ tip	\ò\ saw	\ú\ foot
\ər\ further	\ch\ chin	\ī\ life	\òi\ coin	\y\ yet
\a\ mat	\e\ pet	\j\ job	\th\ thin	\yü\ few
\ā\ take	\ē\ easy	\ng\ sing	\th\ this	\yú\ cure
\ä\ cot, cart	\g\ go	\ō\ bone	\ü\ food	\zh\ vision

else : DUPLICATE ⟨a *copy* of a letter⟩ ⟨a *copy* of a painting⟩ **2** : one of the total number of books, magazines, or papers printed at one time **3** : written or printed material to be set in type

²**copy** *vb* **cop·ied; copy·ing 1** : to make a copy of : DUPLICATE **2** : IMITATE 1, 3

synonyms COPY, IMITATE, and MIMIC mean to make something so that it resembles something else. COPY suggests trying to duplicate a thing as much as possible ⟨*copy* this drawing exactly⟩ IMITATE suggests that one uses something as an example but does not try to make an exact copy ⟨*imitated* the actions of their parents⟩ MIMIC suggests carefully copying something (as a person's voice) often for the purpose of making fun of it ⟨the comedian *mimicked* a popular singer⟩

¹**copy·right** \'käp-ē-ˌrīt\ *n* : the legal right to be the only one to reproduce, publish, and sell the contents and form of a literary or artistic work

²**copyright** *vb* : to get a copyright on

¹**cor·al** \'kȯr-əl\ *n* **1** : a stony or horny material consisting of the skeletons of tiny colonial sea animals related to the jellyfishes and including one kind that is red and used in jewelry **2** : one or a colony of the animals that form coral **3** : a dark pink

²**coral** *adj* **1** : made of coral ⟨a *coral* reef⟩ **2** : of the color of coral

coral snake *n* : a small poisonous American snake brightly ringed with red, black, and yellow or white

cord \'kȯrd\ *n* **1** : material like a small thin rope that is used mostly for tying things **2** : something like a cord **3** : an amount of firewood equal to a pile of wood eight feet long, four feet high, and four feet wide or 128 cubic feet (about 3.6 cubic meters) **4** : a rib or ridge woven into cloth **5** : a ribbed fabric **6** : a small insulated cable used to connect an electrical appliance with an outlet

cord·ed \'kȯrd-əd\ *adj* : having or drawn into ridges or cords

cor·dial \'kȯr-jəl\ *adj* : being warm and friendly ⟨a *cordial* welcome⟩ — **cor·dial·ly** *adv*

cor·dial·i·ty \ˌkȯr-jē-'al-ət-ē, kȯr-'jal-\ *n* : sincere affection and kindness

cor·du·roy \'kȯrd-ə-ˌrȯi\ *n* **1** : a heavy ribbed usually cotton cloth **2 corduroys** *pl* : trousers made of corduroy **3** : a road built of logs laid crosswise side by side (as across a swampy place)

¹**core** \'kōr\ *n* **1** : the central part of some fruits (as pineapples or pears) **2** : a central or innermost part of something ⟨the *core* of a problem⟩

²**core** *vb* **cored; cor·ing** : to remove the core from ⟨*core* an apple⟩

¹**cork** \'kȯrk\ *n* **1** : the light but tough material that is the outer layer of bark of a tree (**cork oak**) and is used especially for stoppers and insulation **2** : a usually cork stopper for a bottle or jug

²**cork** *vb* : to stop with a cork ⟨*cork* a bottle⟩

¹**cork·screw** \'kȯrk-ˌskrü\ *n* : a pointed spiral piece of metal with a handle that is screwed into corks to draw them from bottles

²**corkscrew** *adj* : like a corkscrew

cor·mo·rant \'kȯr-mə-rənt\ *n* : a large black seabird with a long neck and a slender hooked beak

cormorant

¹**corn** \'kȯrn\ *n* **1** : the seeds or grain of a cereal plant (as wheat or oats) **2** : INDIAN CORN **3** : a plant whose seeds are corn

²**corn** *vb* : to preserve by packing with salt or by soaking in salty water ⟨*corned* beef⟩

³**corn** *n* : a hardening and thickening of the skin (as on a person's toe)

corn·cob \'kȯrn-ˌkäb\ *n* : the woody core on which grains of Indian corn grow

cor·nea \'kȯr-nē-ə\ *n* : the transparent outer layer of the front of the eye covering the pupil and iris

¹**cor·ner** \'kȯr-nər\ *n* **1** : the point or place where edges or sides meet **2** : the place where two streets or roads meet **3** : a piece used to mark, form, or protect a corner (as of a book) **4** : a place away from ordinary life or business ⟨a quiet *corner* of a big city⟩ **5** : a position from which

escape or retreat is difficult or impossible ⟨talked themselves into a *corner*⟩ — **cornered** \-nərd\ *adj*

²**corner** *vb* **1** : to drive into a corner ⟨*corner* a rat⟩ **2** : to put in a difficult position

³**corner** *adj* **1** : located at a corner ⟨a *corner* store⟩ **2** : used or usable in or on a corner

cor·net \kȯr-'net\ *n* : a brass musical instrument similar to but shorter than a trumpet

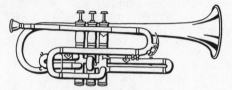

cornet

corn·flow·er \'kȯrn-ˌflaú-ər\ *n* : a European plant related to the daisies that is often grown for its bright heads of blue, pink, or white flowers

cor·nice \'kȯr-nəs\ *n* **1** : an ornamental piece that forms the top edge of the front of a building or pillar **2** : an ornamental molding placed where the walls meet the ceiling of a room

corn·meal \'kȯrn-'mēl\ *n* : meal ground from corn

corn·stalk \'kȯrn-ˌstȯk\ *n* : a stalk of Indian corn

corn·starch \'kȯrn-ˌstärch\ *n* : a fine starch made from Indian corn and used as a thickening agent in cooking

corn syrup *n* : a syrup made from cornstarch and used chiefly in baked goods and candy

cor·nu·co·pia \ˌkor-nə-'kō-pē-ə, -nyə-\ *n* : a container in the shape of a horn overflowing with fruits and flowers used as a symbol of plenty

cornucopia

corny \'kȯr-nē\ *adj* **corn·i·er; corn·i·est** : so simple, sentimental, or old-fashioned as to be annoying ⟨*corny* music⟩

co·rol·la \kə-'räl-ə\ *n* : the part of a flower that is formed by the petals

cor·o·nary \'kȯr-ə-ˌner-ē\ *adj* : of or relating to the heart or its blood vessels

cor·o·na·tion \ˌkȯr-ə-'nā-shən\ *n* : the act or ceremony of crowning a king or queen

cor·o·net \ˌkȯr-ə-'net\ *n* **1** : a small crown worn by a person of noble but less than royal rank ⟨a duke's *coronet*⟩ **2** : an ornamental wreath or band worn around the head

¹**cor·po·ral** \'kȯr-pə-rəl, 'kȯr-prəl\ *adj* : of or relating to the body : BODILY ⟨*corporal* punishment⟩

²**corporal** *n* : a noncommissioned officer ranking above a private in the Army or above a lance corporal in the Marine Corps

cor·po·ra·tion \ˌkȯr-pə-'rā-shən\ *n* : a group authorized by law to carry on an activity (as a business) with the rights and duties of a single person

cor·po·re·al \kȯr-'pōr-ē-əl\ *adj* : having, consisting of, or relating to a physical body

corps \'kōr\ *n, pl* **corps** \'kōrz\ **1** : an organized branch of a country's military forces ⟨Marine *Corps*⟩ **2** : a group of persons acting under one authority ⟨diplomatic *corps*⟩

corpse \'kȯrps\ *n* : a dead body

cor·pu·lent \'kȯr-pyə-lənt\ *adj* : very stout and heavy : extremely fat

cor·pus·cle \'kȯr-ˌpəs-əl\ *n* : one of the very small cells that float freely in the blood

¹**cor·ral** \kə-'ral\ *n* : an enclosure for keeping or capturing animals

²**corral** *vb* **cor·ralled; cor·ral·ling** **1** : to confine in or as if in a corral **2** : to get hold of or control over

¹**cor·rect** \kə-'rekt\ *vb* **1** : to make or set right ⟨*correct* a misspelled word⟩ **2** : to change or adjust so as to bring to some standard or to a required condition **3** : to punish in order to improve ⟨*correct* a child for bad manners⟩ **4** : to show how a thing can be improved or made right ⟨*correct* the students' papers⟩

²**correct** *adj* **1** : meeting or agreeing with some standard : APPROPRIATE ⟨*correct* behavior⟩ ⟨*correct* dress for a picnic⟩ **2** : free from mistakes : ACCURATE — **cor·rect·ly** *adv* — **cor·rect·ness** *n*

\ə\ **abut**	\aú\ **out**	\i\ **tip**	\ȯ\ **saw**	\ú\ **foot**
\ər\ **further**	\ch\ **chin**	\ī\ **life**	\ȯi\ **coin**	\y\ **yet**
\a\ **mat**	\e\ **pet**	\j\ **job**	\th\ **thin**	\yü\ **few**
\ā\ **take**	\ē\ **easy**	\ng\ **sing**	\th\ **this**	\yú\ **cure**
\ä\ **cot, cart**	\g\ **go**	\ō\ **bone**	\ü\ **food**	\zh\ **vision**

synonyms CORRECT, EXACT, and ACCURATE mean agreeing with a fact, truth, or standard. CORRECT stresses that something contains no error ⟨a *correct* answer⟩ EXACT stresses that something agrees very closely with fact or truth ⟨the *exact* measurements of the room⟩ ACCURATE stresses that great care has been taken to make sure that something agrees with the facts ⟨an *accurate* description of the battle⟩

cor·rec·tion \kə-'rek-shən\ *n* **1** : the act of correcting **2** : a change that makes something right **3** : PUNISHMENT 1

cor·re·spond \ˌkȯr-ə-'spänd\ *vb* **1** : to be alike : AGREE ⟨what one gets seldom *corresponds* with what one hopes for⟩ **2** : to be equivalent ⟨"give" and "donate" *correspond* closely in meaning⟩ **3** : to communicate with a person by exchange of letters

cor·re·spon·dence \ˌkȯr-ə-'spän-dəns\ *n* **1** : agreement between certain things **2** : communication by means of letters : the letters exchanged

cor·re·spon·dent \ˌkȯr-ə-'spän-dənt\ *n* **1** : a person with whom another person communicates by letter **2** : a person who sends news stories or comment to a newspaper, magazine, or broadcasting company especially from a distant place

cor·ri·dor \'kȯr-ə-dər\ *n* : a passage into which rooms open

cor·rode \kə-'rōd\ *vb* **cor·rod·ed; cor·rod·ing** : to wear away little by little (as by rust or acid)

cor·ro·sion \kə-'rō-zhən\ *n* : the process or effect of corroding

cor·ro·sive \kə-'rō-siv, -ziv\ *adj* : tending or able to corrode

cor·ru·gate \'kȯr-ə-ˌgāt\ *vb* **cor·ru·gat·ed; cor·ru·gat·ing** : to make wrinkles in or shape into wavy folds ⟨*corrugated* paper⟩

¹cor·rupt \kə-'rəpt\ *vb* **1** : to change (as in morals, manners, or actions) from good to bad **2** : to influence a public official in an improper way (as by a bribe)

²corrupt *adj* **1** : morally bad : EVIL **2** : behaving in a bad or improper way : doing wrong ⟨*corrupt* judges who accept bribes⟩ — **cor·rupt·ly** *adv* — **cor·rupt·ness** *n*

cor·rup·tion \kə-'rəp-shən\ *n* **1** : physical decay or rotting **2** : lack of honesty **3** : the causing of someone else to do something wrong **4** : a being changed for the worse ⟨*corruption* of art forms⟩

cor·sage \kȯr-'säzh\ *n* : a bouquet of flowers usually worn on the shoulder

corse·let *or* **cors·let** \'kȯr-slət\ *n* : the body armor worn by a knight especially on the upper part of the body

cor·set \'kȯr-sət\ *n* : a tight undergarment worn to support or give shape to waist and hips

cos·met·ic \käz-'met-ik\ *n* : material (as a cream, lotion, or powder) used to beautify especially the complexion

cos·mic \'käz-mik\ *adj* : of or relating to the whole universe

cosmic ray *n* : a stream of very penetrating particles that enter the earth's atmosphere from outer space at high speed

cos·mo·naut \'käz-mə-ˌnȯt\ *n* : a Soviet astronaut

cos·mos \'käz-məs\ *n* **1** : the orderly universe **2** : a tall garden plant related to the daisies that has showy white, pink, or rose-colored flower heads

¹cost \'kȯst\ *n* **1** : the amount paid or charged for something : PRICE ⟨at a *cost* of eight dollars per book⟩ **2** : loss or penalty involved in gaining something ⟨the greatest *cost* of war⟩ **synonyms** SEE PRICE

cosmos 2

²cost *vb* **cost; cost·ing** **1** : to have a price of ⟨a ticket *costing* one dollar⟩ **2** : to cause one to pay, spend, or lose ⟨it *cost* me my job⟩

cost·ly \'kȯst-lē\ *adj* **cost·li·er; cost·li·est** **1** : of great cost or value : EXPENSIVE, DEAR **2** : made at great expense or sacrifice

¹cos·tume \'käs-ˌtüm, -ˌtyüm\ *n* **1** : style of clothing, ornaments, and hair used especially during a certain period, in a certain region, or by a certain class or group ⟨ancient Roman *costume*⟩ ⟨peasant *costume*⟩ **2** : special or fancy dress (as for wear on the stage or at a masquerade) **3** : a person's outer garments

²costume *vb* **cos·tumed; cos·tum·ing** **1** : to provide with a costume **2** : to design costumes for ⟨*costume* a play⟩

¹cot \'kät\ *n* : a small house : COTTAGE, HUT

²cot *n* : a narrow bed often made to fold up

cot·tage \'kät-ij\ *n* **1** : a small usually frame house for one family **2** : a small house for vacation use

cottage cheese *n* : a very soft cheese made from soured skim milk

¹cot·ton \'kät-n\ *n* **1** : a soft fluffy material made up of twisted hairs that surrounds the seeds of a tall plant (**cotton plant**) related to the mallows and that is spun into yarn **2** : thread, yarn, or cloth made from cotton

cotton 1

²cotton *adj* : made of cotton

cotton gin *n* : a machine for removing seeds from cotton

cot·ton·mouth \'kät-n-ˌmaùth\ *n* : MOCCASIN 2

cot·ton·seed \'kät-n-ˌsēd\ *n* : the seed of the cotton plant from which comes a meal rich in protein and an oil used especially in cooking

cot·ton·tail \'kät-n-ˌtāl\ *n* : a small rabbit with a white tail

cot·ton·wood \'kät-n-ˌwùd\ *n* : any of several poplar trees that have seeds with bunches of hairs suggesting cotton and that include some which grow rapidly

couch \'kaùch\ *n* : a piece of furniture (as a bed or sofa) that one can sit or lie on

cou·gar \'kü-gər\ *n* : a large yellowish brown North American wild animal related to the domestic cat

cougar

Word History The word *cougar* came from a word in the language of a group of Indians in Brazil. Their word for a cougar meant "false deer." A modern Latin word was formed from this Indian word. The French changed the Latin word and made a French word of it. The English word *cougar* came from this French word.

¹cough \'kòf\ *vb* **1** : to force air from the lungs with a sharp short noise or series of noises **2** : to get rid of by coughing ⟨*cough* up mucus⟩

²cough *n* **1** : a condition in which there is severe or frequent coughing **2** : an act or sound of coughing

could \kəd, kùd\ *past of* CAN **1** — used as a helping verb in the past ⟨*could* read at the age of five⟩ **2** — used as a polite form instead of *can* ⟨*could* you help me⟩

couldn't \'kùd-nt\ : could not

coun·cil \'kaùn-səl\ *n* : a group of persons appointed or elected to make laws or give advice ⟨a city *council*⟩

coun·cil·or *or* **coun·cil·lor** \'kaùn-sə-lər\ *n* : a member of a council ⟨a town *councilor*⟩

¹coun·sel \'kaùn-səl\ *n* **1** : advice given ⟨a parent's *counsel* to a child⟩ **2** : the discussion of reasons for or against a thing : an exchange of opinions ⟨take *counsel* with friends⟩ **3** *pl* **counsel** : a lawyer engaged in the trial and management of a case in court

²counsel *vb* **coun·seled** *or* **coun·selled; coun·sel·ing** *or* **coun·sel·ling 1** : to give counsel : ADVISE ⟨*counsel* a student⟩ **2** : to seek counsel ⟨*counsel* with a teacher⟩

coun·sel·or *or* **coun·sel·lor** \'kaùn-sə-lər\ *n* **1** : a person who gives counsel **2** : LAWYER **3** : a supervisor of campers or activities at a summer camp

¹count \'kaùnt\ *vb* **1** : to add one by one in order to find the total number in a collection ⟨*count* the apples in a box⟩ **2** : to name the numerals in order up to a particular point ⟨*count* ten⟩ **3** : to name the numbers one by one or by groups ⟨*count* to 100 by fives⟩ **4** : to include in counting or thinking about ⟨don't *count* Sunday as a work day⟩ **5** : to consider or judge to be ⟨*count* myself lucky⟩ **6** : to include or leave out by or as if by counting ⟨*counted* ourselves out⟩ **7** : RELY, DEPEND ⟨you can *count* on them⟩ **8** : ²PLAN 1 ⟨*count* on our coming⟩ **9** : to have value, force, or importance ⟨the people who really *count*⟩

²count *n* **1** : the act or process of counting **2** : a total arrived at by counting ⟨a *count* of ten⟩ **3** : any one charge in a legal declaration or indictment ⟨guilty on all *counts*⟩

³count *n* : a European nobleman whose rank is like that of a British earl

count·down \'kaùnt-ˌdaùn\ *n* : a counting

\ə\ abut	\aù\ out	\i\ tip	\ò\ saw	\ù\ foot
\ər\ further	\ch\ chin	\ī\ life	\òi\ coin	\y\ yet
\a\ mat	\e\ pet	\j\ job	\th\ thin	\yü\ few
\ā\ take	\ē\ easy	\ng\ sing	\th\ this	\yù\ cure
\ä\ cot, cart	\g\ go	\ō\ bone	\ü\ food	\zh\ vision

off of the time remaining before an event (as the launching of a rocket)

¹coun·te·nance \'kaúnt-n-əns\ *n* : the human face or its expression ⟨a kind *countenance*⟩

²countenance *vb* **coun·te·nanced; coun·te·nanc·ing** : to give approval or tolerance to

¹count·er \'kaúnt-ər\ *n* **1** : a piece (as of plastic or ivory) used in counting or in games **2** : a level surface usually higher than a table that is used for selling, serving food, displaying things, or working on

²count·er *n* **1** : one that counts **2** : a device for showing a number or amount

³coun·ter \'kaúnt-ər\ *vb* **1** : to act in opposition to : OPPOSE **2** : RETALIATE

⁴coun·ter *adv* : in another or opposite direction ⟨go *counter* to advice⟩

⁵coun·ter *n* : an answering or opposing force or blow

⁶coun·ter *adj* : moving or acting in an opposite way : CONTRARY ⟨a *counter* tide⟩ ⟨made a *counter* offer⟩

coun·ter- *prefix* **1** : opposite ⟨*counter*clockwise⟩ **2** : opposing **3** : like : matching ⟨*counter*part⟩ **4** : duplicate : substitute

coun·ter·act \‚kaúnt-ər-'akt\ *vb* : to act against so as to prevent something from acting in its own way

coun·ter·clock·wise \‚kaúnt-ər-'kläk-‚wīz\ *adv or adj* : in a direction opposite to that in which the hands of a clock move

¹coun·ter·feit \'kaúnt-ər-‚fit\ *vb* **1** : PRETEND **2** ⟨*counterfeit* enthusiasm⟩ **2** : to imitate or copy especially in order to deceive ⟨*counterfeiting* money⟩ — **coun·ter·feit·er** *n*

²counterfeit *adj* **1** : made in exact imitation of something genuine and meant to be taken as genuine ⟨*counterfeit* money⟩ **2** : not sincere ⟨*counterfeit* sympathy⟩

³counterfeit *n* : something made to imitate another thing with the desire to deceive

coun·ter·part \'kaúnt-ər-‚pärt\ *n* : a person or thing that is very like or corresponds to another person or thing

coun·ter·point \'kaúnt-ər-‚póint\ *n* : one or more independent melodies added above or below and in harmony with a given melody

coun·ter·sign \'kaúnt-ər-‚sīn\ *n* : a secret signal that must be given by a person wishing to pass a guard : PASSWORD

count·ess \'kaúnt-əs\ *n* **1** : the wife or widow of a count or an earl **2** : a woman who holds the rank of a count or an earl in her own right

counting number *n* : NATURAL NUMBER

count·less \'kaúnt-ləs\ *adj* : too many to be counted ⟨*countless* grains of sand⟩

coun·try \'kən-trē\ *n, pl* **coun·tries 1** : REGION 1, DISTRICT ⟨good farming *country*⟩ **2** : a land lived in by a people with a common government **3** : the people of a nation ⟨a whole *country* in revolt⟩ **4** : open rural land away from big towns and cities ⟨take a ride in the *country*⟩

country and western *n* : music coming from or imitating the folk music of the southern United States or the Western cowboy

coun·try·man \'kən-trē-mən\ *n, pl* **coun·try·men** \-mən\ **1** : a person born in the same country as another : a fellow citizen **2** : a person living or raised in the country

coun·try·side \'kən-trē-‚sīd\ *n* : a rural area or its people

coun·ty \'kaúnt-ē\ *n, pl* **coun·ties** : a division of a state or country for local government

coupe \kü-'pā, 2 *is often* 'küp\ *n* **1** : a carriage with four wheels and an enclosed body seating two persons and with an outside seat for the driver in front **2** : an enclosed two-door automobile for usually two persons

¹cou·ple \'kəp-əl\ *vb* **cou·pled; cou·pling 1** : to join or link together : CONNECT ⟨*coupled* freight cars⟩ **2** : to join in pairs

²couple *n* **1** : two persons who are paired together or closely associated **2** : two things of the same kind that are connected or that are thought of together

cou·plet \'kəp-lət\ *n* : two rhyming lines of verse one after another ⟨"The butcher, the baker,/ The candlestick maker" is an example of a *couplet*⟩

cou·pling \'kəp-ling\ *n* **1** : the act of bringing or coming together **2** : something that joins or connects two parts or things ⟨a pipe *coupling*⟩

cou·pon \'kü-‚pän, 'kyü-\ *n* **1** : a ticket or form that allows the holder to receive some service, payment, or discount **2** : a part of an advertisement meant to be cut out for use as an order blank

cour·age \'kər-ij\ *n* : the strength of mind that makes one able to meet danger and difficulties with firmness

cou·ra·geous \kə-'rā-jəs\ *adj* : having or showing courage **synonyms** *see* BRAVE — **cou·ra·geous·ly** *adv*

¹course \'kōrs\ *n* **1** : motion from one point to another : progress in space or time ⟨the stars in their *course* through the sky⟩ ⟨during the *course* of a year⟩ **2** : the path over which something moves **3** : direction of motion ⟨the *course* of a ship⟩ **4** : a natural channel for water ⟨followed the river's *course*⟩ **5** : way of doing something ⟨choose a *course* of action⟩ **6** : a series of acts or proceedings arranged in regular order ⟨a *course* of lectures⟩ **7** : a series of studies leading to a diploma or a degree ⟨a four-year *course* in law⟩ **8** : a part of a meal served at one time ⟨finished the meat *course*⟩ **9** : a continuous level range of brick or masonry throughout a wall — **of course** : as might be expected

²course *vb* **coursed; cours·ing** **1** : to run through or over **2** : to move rapidly : RACE

¹court \'kōrt\ *n* **1** : the home of a ruler **2** : a ruler's assembly of advisers and officers as a governing power **3** : the family and people who follow a ruler **4** : an open space completely or partly surrounded by buildings **5** : a short street **6** : a space arranged for playing a certain game ⟨tennis *court*⟩ ⟨basketball *court*⟩ **7** : an official meeting led by a judge for settling legal questions or the place where it is held **8** : respect meant to win favor ⟨pay *court* to the king⟩

²court *vb* **1** : to try to gain or get the support of : SEEK ⟨*courting* favor with the authorities⟩ ⟨*court* the new voters⟩ **2** : to seem to be asking for : TEMPT ⟨*court* disaster⟩ **3** : to seek the liking of

cour·te·ous \'kərt-ē-əs\ *adj* : showing respect and consideration for others : POLITE **synonyms** see CIVIL — **cour·te·ous·ly** *adv* — **cour·te·ous·ness** *n*

cour·te·sy \'kərt-ə-sē\ *n, pl* **cour·te·sies** **1** : the quality or state of being courteous **2** : a courteous act or expression **3** : something that is a favor and not a right

court·house \'kōrt-ˌhaus\ *n* **1** : a building in which courts of law are held **2** : a building in which county offices are housed

court·i·er \'kōrt-ē-ər\ *n* : a member of a royal court

court·ly \'kōrt-lē\ *adj* **court·li·er; court·li·est** : suitable to a royal court : ELEGANT, POLITE ⟨*courtly* manners⟩

court·ship \'kōrt-ˌship\ *n* : the act or process of courting or seeking the liking of someone

court·yard \'kōrt-ˌyärd\ *n* : ¹COURT 4

cous·in \'kəz-n\ *n* : a child of one's uncle or aunt

cove \'kōv\ *n* : a small sheltered inlet or bay

cov·e·nant \'kəv-ə-nənt\ *n* : a formal or solemn agreement ⟨a *covenant* between nations⟩

¹cov·er \'kəv-ər\ *vb* **1** : to provide protection to or against ⟨*covered* the landing with artillery⟩ **2** : to maintain a check on especially by patrolling ⟨police *cover* the highways⟩ **3** : to hide from sight or knowledge ⟨*covered* my embarrassment⟩ **4** : to place or spread something over ⟨*cover* the rolls with a cloth⟩ **5** : to dot thickly ⟨*covered* with freckles⟩ **6** : to form a cover or covering over ⟨snow *covered* the ground⟩ **7** : to take into account ⟨a review *covering* the term's work⟩ **8** : to have as one's field of activity or interest ⟨a reporter *covering* the courthouse⟩ **9** : to pass over or through ⟨*cover* a country in one week⟩

²cover *n* **1** : something that protects, shelters, or hides **2** : something that is placed over or about another thing : LID, TOP **3** : a binding or a protecting case **4** : a covering (as a blanket) used on a bed **5** : an envelope or wrapper for mail

cov·er·age \'kəv-ə-rij, 'kəv-rij\ *n* **1** : insurance against something ⟨fire *coverage*⟩ **2** : the value or amount of insurance ⟨a thousand dollars' *coverage*⟩

cov·er·all \'kəv-ə-ˌrȯl\ *n* : an outer garment that combines shirt and pants and is worn to protect one's regular clothes — usually used in pl.

covered wagon *n* : a large long wagon with a curving canvas top

covered wagon

cov·er·ing \'kəv-ə-ring, 'kəv-ring\ *n* : something (as a roof or an envelope) that covers or conceals

cov·er·let \'kəv-ər-lət\ *n* : BEDSPREAD

¹co·vert \'kəv-ərt, 'kō-vərt\ *adj* : made or done secretly ⟨a *covert* glance⟩ ⟨*covert* military operations⟩ — **co·vert·ly** *adv* — **co·vert·ness** *n*

\ə\ abut	\au\ out	\i\ tip	\o\ saw	\u\ foot
\ər\ further	\ch\ chin	\ī\ life	\oi\ coin	\y\ yet
\a\ mat	\e\ pet	\j\ job	\th\ thin	\yü\ few
\ā\ take	\ē\ easy	\ng\ sing	\th\ this	\yu\ cure
\ä\ cot, cart	\g\ go	\ō\ bone	\ü\ food	\zh\ vision

²covert *n* **1** : a hiding place (as a thicket that gives shelter to game animals) **2** : one of the small feathers around the bottom of the quills on the wings and tail of a bird

cov·et \'kəv-ət\ *vb* : to wish for greatly or with envy ⟨*covet* success⟩ ⟨*covet* a friend's happiness⟩

cov·et·ous \'kəv-ət-əs\ *adj* : having or showing too much desire for wealth or possessions or for something belonging to another person

cov·ey \'kəv-ē\ *n, pl* **cov·eys 1** : a small flock (as of quail) **2** : ¹GROUP ⟨a *covey* of airplanes⟩

¹cow \'kau̇\ *n* : the mature female of cattle or of an animal (as the moose) of which the male is called *bull*

²cow *vb* : to lower the spirits or courage of : make afraid ⟨*cowed* by threats⟩

cow·ard \'kau̇-ərd\ *n* : a person who shows dishonorable fear

cow·ard·ice \'kau̇-ərd-əs\ *n* : dishonorable fear

cow·ard·ly \'kau̇-ərd-lē\ *adj* : being or behaving like a coward — **cow·ard·li·ness** *n*

cow·bell \'kau̇-ˌbel\ *n* : a bell hung around the neck of a cow to tell where it is

cow·bird \'kau̇-ˌbərd\ *n* : a small American blackbird that lays its eggs in the nests of other birds

cow·boy \'kau̇-ˌbȯi\ *n* : a man or boy who works on a ranch or performs at a rodeo

cow·catch·er \'kau̇-ˌkach-ər\ *n* : a strong frame on the front of a railroad engine for moving things blocking the track

cow·er \'kau̇-ər\ *vb* : to shrink away or crouch down shivering (as from fear)

cow·girl \'kau̇-ˌgərl\ *n* : a girl or woman who works on a ranch or performs at a rodeo

cow·hand \'kau̇-ˌhand\ *n* : a person who works on a cattle ranch

cow·herd \'kau̇-ˌhərd\ *n* : a person who tends cows

cow·hide \'kau̇-ˌhīd\ *n* **1** : the hide of cattle or leather made from it **2** : a whip of rawhide or braided leather

cowl

cowl \'kau̇l\ *n* : a hood or long hooded cloak especially of a monk

cow·lick \'kau̇-ˌlik\ *n* : a small bunch of hair that sticks out and will not lie flat

cow·pox \'kau̇-ˌpäks\ *n* : a disease of cattle that when given to humans (as by vaccination) protects from smallpox

cow·punch·er \'kau̇-ˌpən-chər\ *n* : COWBOY

cow·slip \'kau̇-ˌslip\ *n* **1** : a common Old World primrose with yellow or purple flowers **2** : MARSH MARIGOLD

cox·swain \'käk-sən, -ˌswān\ *n* : the person who steers a boat

coy \'kȯi\ *adj* : falsely shy or modest

Word History In earlier English *coy* meant "quiet" as well as "shy." The English word *coy* came from an early French word that meant "calm." This French word came from a Latin word that meant "quiet." The English word *quiet* also came from this Latin word.

coy·ote \'kī-ˌōt, kī-'ōt-ē\ *n* : a small wolf chiefly of western North America

coyote

¹co·zy \'kō-zē\ *adj* **co·zi·er; co·zi·est** : enjoying or providing warmth and comfort — **co·zi·ly** \-zə-lē\ *adv* — **co·zi·ness** \-zē-nəs\ *n*

²cozy *n, pl* **co·zies** : a padded covering for a container (as a teapot) to keep the contents hot

¹crab \'krab\ *n* : a sea animal related to the lobsters but having a flat shell and a small abdomen pressed against the underside of the body

crab

²crab *vb* **crabbed; crab·bing :** to find fault **:** COMPLAIN

³crab *n* **:** a person who is usually cross

crab apple *n* **1 :** a small wild sour apple **2 :** a cultivated apple with small usually brightly colored acid fruit

crab·bed \'krab-əd\ *adj* **:** CRABBY

crab·by \'krab-ē\ *adj* **crab·bi·er; crab·bi·est :** being cross and irritable

crab·grass \'krab-ˌgras\ *n* **:** a weedy grass with coarse stems that root at the joints

¹crack \'krak\ *vb* **1 :** to break or cause to break with a sudden sharp sound **2 :** to make or cause to make a sound of cracking as if breaking ⟨*crack* a whip⟩ **3 :** to break often without completely separating into parts ⟨the ice *cracked* in several places⟩ **4 :** to tell (a joke) especially in a clever way **5 :** to lose self-control **:** break down ⟨*cracked* under the strain of battle⟩ **6 :** to change in tone quality ⟨my voice *cracked* from emotion⟩ **7 :** to strike or receive a sharp blow

²crack *n* **1 :** a sudden sharp noise **2 :** a sharp clever remark **3 :** a narrow break or opening ⟨a *crack* in the glass⟩ **4 :** a broken tone of the voice **5 :** the beginning moment ⟨at the *crack* of dawn⟩ **6 :** a sharp blow **7 :** ²ATTEMPT ⟨my first *crack* at writing⟩

³crack *adj* **:** of high quality or ability ⟨*crack* troops⟩

crack·er \'krak-ər\ *n* **:** a dry thin baked food made of flour and water

¹crack·le \'krak-əl\ *vb* **crack·led; crack·ling 1 :** to make many small sharp noises **2 :** to form little cracks in a surface

²crackle *n* **:** the noise of repeated small cracks (as of burning wood)

crack–up \'krak-ˌəp\ *n* **1 :** BREAKDOWN **2 :** ²CRASH **3,** WRECK ⟨*crack-up* of an airplane⟩

crack up \'krak-'əp\ *vb* **:** to cause or have a crack-up ⟨*crack up* a car⟩ ⟨you will *crack up* if you don't rest⟩

¹cra·dle \'krād-l\ *n* **1 :** a baby's bed or cot usually on rockers **2 :** place of beginning ⟨the *cradle* of civilization⟩ **3 :** a framework or support resembling a baby's cradle in appearance or use **4 :** a rocking device used in panning gold **5 :** a support for a telephone receiver

²cradle *vb* **cra·dled; cra·dling 1 :** to hold or support in or as if in a cradle ⟨*cradled* my head in my arms⟩ **2 :** to wash (as earth or sand) in a miner's cradle

craft \'kraft\ *n* **1 :** skill in making things especially with the hands **2 :** an occupation or trade requiring skill with the hands

or as an artist ⟨carpentry is a *craft*⟩ **3 :** skill in deceiving for a bad purpose **:** CUNNING **4 :** the members of a trade or a trade group **5** *pl usually* **craft :** a boat especially when of small size **6** *pl usually* **craft :** AIRCRAFT

crafts·man \'kraft-smən\ *n, pl* **crafts·men** \-smən\ **1 :** a person who works at a trade or handicraft **2 :** a highly skilled worker in any field

crafty \'kraf-tē\ *adj* **craft·i·er; craft·i·est :** skillful at deceiving others **:** CUNNING — **craft·i·ly** \'kraf-tə-lē\ *adv* — **craft·i·ness** \-tē-nəs\ *n*

crag \'krag\ *n* **:** a steep rock or cliff

crag·gy \'krag-ē\ *adj* **crag·gi·er; crag·gi·est :** having many crags

cram \'kram\ *vb* **crammed; cram·ming 1 :** to stuff or pack tightly ⟨*cram* clothes into a bag⟩ **2 :** to fill full ⟨barns *crammed* with hay⟩ **3 :** to study hard just before a test **synonyms** see PACK

¹cramp \'kramp\ *n* **1 :** a sudden painful involuntary tightening of a muscle **2 :** sharp pain in the abdomen — usually used in pl.

²cramp *vb* **1 :** to cause cramp in ⟨the cold water *cramped* the swimmer⟩ **2 :** to hold back from free action or expression **:** HAMPER

cran·ber·ry \'kran-ˌber-ē\ *n, pl* **cran·ber·ries :** a sour bright red berry that is eaten in sauces and jelly and is the fruit of an evergreen swamp plant related to the blueberries

¹crane \'krān\ *n* **1 :** a tall wading bird that looks like a heron but is related to the rails **2 :** a machine with a swinging arm for lifting and carrying heavy weights **3 :** a mechanical arm that swings freely from a center and is used to support or carry a weight

²crane *vb* **craned; cran·ing :** to stretch one's neck to see better ⟨*craned* out the window to see the parade⟩

cra·ni·al \'krā-nē-əl\ *adj* **:** of or relating to the cranium

cra·ni·um \'krā-nē-əm\ *n, pl* **cra·ni·ums** *or* **cra·nia** \-nē-ə\ **1 :** SKULL **2 :** the part of the skull enclosing the brain

¹crank \'krangk\ *n* **1 :** a bent armlike part with a handle that is turned to start or run machinery **2 :** a person with strange ideas **3 :** a cross or irritable person

²crank *vb* **:** to start or run by turning a crank

\ə\ **abut**	\au̇\ **out**	\i\ **tip**	\ȯ\ **saw**	\u̇\ **foot**	
\ər\ **further**	\ch\ **chin**	\ī\ **life**	\ȯi\ **coin**	\y\ **yet**	
\a\ **mat**	\e\ **pet**	\j\ **job**	\th\ **thin**	\yü\ **few**	
\ā\ **take**	\ē\ **easy**	\ng\ **sing**	\th\ **this**	\yu̇\ **cure**	
\ä\ **cot, cart**	\g\ **go**	\ō\ **bone**	\ü\ **food**	\zh\ **vision**	

crane 1

cranky \'krang-kē\ *adj* **crank·i·er; crank·i·est** : easily angered or irritated — **crank·i·ness** *n*

cran·ny \'kran-ē\ *n, pl* **cran·nies** : a small break or slit (as in a cliff)

crap·pie \'kräp-ē\ *n* : either of two sunfishes native to the Great Lakes and Mississippi valley of which the larger and darker one (**black crappie**) is an important sport fish and the other (**white crappie**) is used as a table fish

¹crash \'krash\ *vb* **1** : to break or go to pieces with or as if with violence and noise : SMASH **2** : to fall or strike something with noise and damage ⟨the plane *crashed* in the storm⟩ ⟨the lamp *crashed* to the floor⟩ **3** : to hit or cause to hit something with force and noise ⟨the car *crashed* into a tree⟩ **4** : to make or cause to make a loud noise ⟨thunder *crashed* overhead⟩ **5** : to move or force a way roughly and noisily ⟨the door *crashed* shut⟩ ⟨we *crashed* the brush out of our path⟩

²crash *n* **1** : a loud sound (as of things smashing) **2** : a breaking to pieces by or as if by hitting something : SMASH, COLLISION **3** : the crashing of something ⟨was injured in the *crash*⟩ **4** : a sudden weakening or failure (as of a business or prices)

¹crate \'krāt\ *n* : a box or frame of wooden slats or boards for holding and protecting something in shipment

²crate *vb* **crat·ed; crat·ing** : to pack in a crate ⟨*crate* furniture for shipping⟩

cra·ter \'krāt-ər\ *n* **1** : a hollow in the shape of a bowl around the opening of a volcano or geyser **2** : a hole (as in the surface of the earth or moon) formed by an impact (as of a meteorite)

cra·vat \krə-'vat\ *n* : NECKTIE

crave \'krāv\ *vb* **craved; crav·ing** **1** : to ask for earnestly ⟨*crave* one's pardon⟩ **2** : to want greatly : long for ⟨*craves* candy⟩ ⟨*craving* affection⟩ **synonyms** see DESIRE

cra·ven \'krā-vən\ *adj* : COWARDLY

crav·ing \'krā-ving\ *n* : a great desire or longing

craw \'krȯ\ *n* **1** : ¹CROP 2 **2** : the stomach of an animal

craw·fish \'krȯ-ˌfish\ *n, pl* **crawfish** : CRAYFISH

¹crawl \'krȯl\ *vb* **1** : to move slowly with the body close to the ground : move on hands and knees **2** : to go very slowly or carefully **3** : to be covered with or have the feeling of being covered with creeping things ⟨the food was *crawling* with flies⟩

²crawl *n* **1** : the act or motion of crawling **2** : a swimming stroke that looks a little like crawling

cray·fish \'krā-ˌfish\ *n, pl* **crayfish** **1** : a freshwater shellfish that looks like the related lobster but is much smaller **2** : a spiny saltwater shellfish that looks like the related lobster but lacks very large claws

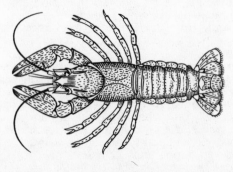

crayfish 1

¹cray·on \'krā-ˌän, -ən\ *n* : a stick of white or colored chalk or of colored wax used for writing or drawing

²crayon *vb* : to draw or color with a crayon

craze \'krāz\ *n* : something that is very popular for a short while

cra·zy \'krā-zē\ *adj* **cra·zi·er; cra·zi·est 1** : having a diseased or abnormal mind : INSANE **2** : not sensible or logical ⟨a *crazy* idea⟩ **3** : very excited or pleased ⟨*crazy* about their new house⟩ — **cra·zi·ly** \'krā-zə-lē\ *adv* — **cra·zi·ness** \-zē-nəs\ *n*

¹creak \'krēk\ *vb* : to make a long scraping or squeaking sound

²creak *n* : a long squeaking or scraping noise

creaky \'krē-kē\ *adj* **creak·i·er; creak·i·est** : making or likely to make a creaking sound — **creak·i·ly** \'krē-kə-lē\ *adv*

¹cream \'krēm\ *n* **1** : the oily yellowish part of milk **2** : a food prepared with cream **3** : something having the smoothness and thickness of cream ⟨face *cream*⟩ **4** : the best part ⟨the *cream* of the crop⟩ **5** : a pale yellow

²cream *vb* **1** : to furnish, prepare, or treat with cream ⟨*cream* one's face⟩ **2** : to rub or beat (as butter) until creamy

cream·ery \'krē-mə-rē, 'krēm-rē\ *n, pl* **cream·er·ies** : DAIRY 1, 3

creamy \'krē-mē\ *adj* **cream·i·er; cream·i·est 1** : full of or containing cream **2** : like cream in appearance, color, or taste — **cream·i·ness** *n*

¹crease \'krēs\ *n* : a line or mark usually made by folding or wrinkling

²crease *vb* **creased; creas·ing 1** : to make a crease in or on **2** : to become creased

cre·ate \krē-'āt\ *vb* **cre·at·ed; cre·at·ing** : to cause to exist : bring into existence : PRODUCE **synonyms** see INVENT

cre·a·tion \krē-'ā-shən\ *n* **1** : the act of creating : the bringing of the world into existence out of nothing **2** : something created **3** : all created things

cre·a·tive \krē-'āt-iv\ *adj* : able to create especially new and original things — **cre·a·tive·ly** *adv* — **cre·a·tive·ness** *n*

cre·a·tor \krē-'āt-ər\ *n* **1** : one that creates or produces : MAKER **2** *cap* : GOD 1

crea·ture \'krē-chər\ *n* **1** : a living being **2** : a lower animal **3** : PERSON 1

cred·i·ble \'kred-ə-bəl\ *adj* : possible to believe : deserving belief — **cred·i·bly** \-blē\ *adv*

¹cred·it \'kred-ət\ *n* **1** : the balance in an account in a person's favor **2** : trust given to a customer for future payment for goods purchased ⟨buy on *credit*⟩ **3** : time given for payment ⟨extended them 30 days' *credit*⟩ **4** : belief or trust in the truth of something ⟨rumors that deserve no *credit*⟩ **5** : good reputation especially for honesty : high standing **6** : a source of

honor or pride ⟨you are a *credit* to your school⟩ **7** : recognition or honor received for some quality or work ⟨was given *credit* for the discovery⟩ **8** : a unit of schoolwork ⟨took two *credits* in math⟩

²credit *vb* **1** : BELIEVE **2** ⟨*credit* a statement⟩ **2** : to place something in a person's favor on (a business account) ⟨*credit* your account with ten dollars⟩ **3** : to give credit or honor to for something ⟨*credited* them with discovering a new vaccine⟩

cred·it·able \'kred-ət-ə-bəl\ *adj* : good enough to deserve praise ⟨a *creditable* attempt⟩

cred·i·tor \'kred-ət-ər\ *n* : a person to whom a debt is owed

cred·u·lous \'krej-ə-ləs\ *adj* : quick to believe especially without very good reasons

creed \'krēd\ *n* **1** : a statement of the basic beliefs of a religious faith **2** : a set of guiding rules or beliefs

creek \'krēk, 'krik\ *n* : a stream of water usually larger than a brook and smaller than a river

creel \'krēl\ *n* : a basket for holding a catch of fish

¹creep \'krēp\ *vb* **crept** \'krept\; **creep·ing 1** : to move along with the body close to the ground or floor : move slowly on hands and knees : CRAWL **2** : to move or advance slowly, timidly, or quietly ⟨the tide *crept* up the beach⟩ **3** : to grow or spread along the ground or along a surface ⟨ivy *creeping* up a wall⟩

²creep *n* **1** : a creeping movement **2** : a feeling as of insects crawling over one's skin : a feeling of horror — usually used in pl.

creep·er \'krē-pər\ *n* **1** : one that creeps **2** : a small bird that creeps about trees and bushes in search of insects **3** : a plant (as ivy) that grows by spreading over a surface

creepy \'krē-pē\ *adj* **creep·i·er; creep·i·est 1** : having or causing a feeling as of insects creeping on the skin **2** : causing fear : SCARY ⟨a *creepy* story⟩ — **creep·i·ness** *n*

cre·mate \'krē-,māt\ *vb* **cre·mat·ed; cre·mat·ing** : to burn (as a dead body) to ashes

cre·ma·tion \kri-'mā-shən\ *n* : the act or practice of cremating

crepe \'krāp\ *n* : a thin crinkled fabric (as of silk or wool)

\ə\ **abut**	\au̇\ **out**	\i\ **tip**	\ȯ\ **saw**	\u̇\ **foot**
\ər\ **further**	\ch\ **chin**	\ī\ **life**	\ȯi\ **coin**	\y\ **yet**
\a\ **mat**	\e\ **pet**	\j\ **job**	\th\ **thin**	\yü\ **few**
\ā\ **take**	\ē\ **easy**	\ng\ **sing**	\th\ **this**	\yu̇\ **cure**
\ä\ **cot, cart**	\g\ **go**	\ō\ **bone**	\ü\ **food**	\zh\ **vision**

crepe paper *n* : paper with a crinkled or puckered look and feel

crept *past of* CREEP

cre·scen·do \kri-'shen-dō\ *n, pl* **cre·scen·dos** *or* **cre·scen·does** : a gradual increase in the loudness of music

¹**cres·cent** \'kres-nt\ *n* **1** : the shape of the visible moon during about the first week after new moon or the last week before the next new moon **2** : something shaped like a crescent moon

²**crescent** *adj* : shaped like the new moon

cress \'kres\ *n* : any of several salad plants of the mustard group

crescent 1

crest \'krest\ *n* **1** : a showy growth (as of flesh or feathers) on the head of an animal **2** : an emblem or design on a helmet (as of a knight) or over a coat of arms **3** : something forming the top of something else ⟨the *crest* of the wave⟩ ⟨the *crest* of a hill⟩ — **crest·ed** \'kres-təd\ *adj*

crest·fall·en \'krest-ˌfȯ-lən\ *adj* : greatly distressed or disappointed

crev·ice \'krev-əs\ *n* : a narrow opening (as in the earth) caused by cracking or splitting : FISSURE

crew \'krü\ *n* **1** : a gathering of people ⟨a happy *crew* on a picnic⟩ **2** : a group of people working together ⟨the kitchen *crew*⟩ **3** : the group of people who operate a ship, train, or airplane

crib \'krib\ *n* **1** : a manger for feeding animals **2** : a small bed frame with high sides for a child **3** : a building or bin for storing ⟨corn *crib*⟩

¹**crick·et** \'krik-ət\ *n* : a small leaping insect noted for the chirping notes of the males

²**cricket** *n* : a game played on a large field with bats, ball, and wickets by two teams of eleven players each

cricket

cri·er \'krī-ər\ *n* : one who calls out orders or announcements ⟨the town *crier*⟩

crime \'krīm\ *n* **1** : the doing of an act forbidden by law : the failure to do an act required by law **2** : an act that is sinful, foolish, or disgraceful ⟨it's a *crime* to waste food⟩

¹**crim·i·nal** \'krim-ən-l\ *adj* **1** : being or guilty of crime ⟨a *criminal* act⟩ **2** : relating to crime or its punishment ⟨*criminal* law⟩ — **crim·i·nal·ly** \-ən-l-ē\ *adv*

²**criminal** *n* : a person who has committed a crime

crim·son \'krim-zən\ *n* : a deep purplish red

cringe \'krinj\ *vb* **cringed; cring·ing** **1** : to shrink in fear : COWER **2** : to behave in a very humble way : FAWN

crin·kle \'kring-kəl\ *vb* **crin·kled; crin·kling** **1** : to form or cause little waves or wrinkles on the surface : WRINKLE **2** : ¹RUSTLE 1

crin·kly \'kring-klē\ *adj* **crin·kli·er; crin·kli·est** : full of small wrinkles

¹**crip·ple** \'krip-əl\ *n* : a lame or disabled person

²**cripple** *vb* **crip·pled; crip·pling** **1** : to cause to become a cripple ⟨*crippled* by rheumatism⟩ **2** : to make useless or imperfect

cri·sis \'krī-səs\ *n, pl* **cri·ses** \'krī-ˌsēz\ **1** : a turning point for better or worse in a disease **2** : an unstable or critical time or state of affairs

¹**crisp** \'krisp\ *adj* **1** : being thin and hard and easily crumbled ⟨*crisp* potato chips⟩ **2** : pleasantly firm and fresh ⟨*crisp* celery⟩ **3** : having a sharp distinct outline ⟨*crisp* drawings⟩ **4** : being clear and brief ⟨a *crisp* reply⟩ **5** : pleasantly cool and invigorating : BRISK ⟨a *crisp* autumn day⟩ **synonyms** see BRITTLE

²**crisp** *vb* : to make or become crisp

criss·cross \'kris-ˌkrȯs\ *vb* **1** : to mark with or make lines that cross one another **2** : to go or pass back and forth

crit·ic \'krit-ik\ *n* **1** : a person who makes or gives a judgment of the value, worth, beauty, or quality of something **2** : a person given to finding fault or complaining

crit·i·cal \'krit-i-kəl\ *adj* **1** : inclined to criticize especially in an unfavorable way **2** : consisting of or involving criticism or the judgment of critics ⟨*critical* writings⟩ **3** : using or involving careful judgment ⟨a *critical* examination of a patient⟩ **4** : of, relating to, or being a turning point or crisis ⟨the *critical* stage of a fever⟩ — **crit·i·cal·ly** *adv*

crit·i·cism \'krit-ə-ˌsiz-əm\ *n* **1** : the act of criticizing and especially of finding fault **2** : a critical remark or comment **3** : a careful judgment or review especially by a critic

crit·i·cize \'krit-ə-ˌsīz\ *vb* **crit·i·cized; crit·i·ciz·ing 1 :** to examine and judge as a critic **2 :** to find fault with

¹croak \'krōk\ *vb* **1 :** to make a deep harsh sound ⟨frogs *croaked*⟩ **2 :** to speak in a hoarse throaty voice

²croak *n* **:** a hoarse harsh sound or cry

¹cro·chet \krō-'shā\ *n* **:** work done or a fabric formed by crocheting

²crochet *vb* **:** to make (something) or create a fabric with a hooked needle by forming and interlacing loops in a thread

crock \'kräk\ *n* **:** a thick pot or jar of baked clay

crock·ery \'kräk-ə-rē\ *n* **:** EARTHENWARE

croc·o·dile \'kräk-ə-ˌdīl\ *n* **:** a very large animal related to the alligator that crawls on short legs about tropical marshes and rivers

crocodile

cro·cus \'krō-kəs\ *n* **:** a plant related to the irises that has grasslike leaves and is often planted for its white, yellow, or purple spring flowers

cro·ny \'krō-nē\ *n, pl* **cro·nies :** a close companion **:** CHUM

¹crook \'kru̇k\ *n* **1 :** a shepherd's staff with one end curved into a hook **2 :** a dishonest person (as a thief or swindler) **3 :** a curved or hooked part of a thing **:** bend

²crook *vb* **:** ²BEND 2, CURVE ⟨*crook* your finger⟩

crook·ed \'kru̇k-əd\ *adj* **1 :** having bends and curves ⟨a *crooked* path⟩ **2 :** not set or placed straight ⟨the picture is *crooked*⟩ **3 :** DISHONEST ⟨a *crooked* card game⟩ — **crook·ed·ly** *adv* — **crook·ed·ness** *n*

croon \'krün\ *vb* **:** to hum or sing in a low soft voice ⟨*croon* a lullaby⟩

¹crop \'kräp\ *n* **1 :** a short riding whip **2 :** an enlargement just above the stomach of a bird or insect in which food is stored for a while **3 :** the amount gathered or harvested **:** HARVEST ⟨a *crop* of wheat⟩ **4 :** BATCH 3, LOT

²crop *vb* **cropped; crop·ping 1 :** to remove (as by cutting or biting) the upper or outer parts of **:** TRIM ⟨sheep *cropping* clo-

ver⟩ **2 :** to grow or yield a crop (as of grain) **:** cause (land) to bear a crop **3 :** to come or appear when not expected ⟨problems *crop* up daily⟩

crop rotation *n* **:** the practice of growing first one crop and then another on the same land especially to preserve the ability of the soil to produce crops

cro·quet \krō-'kā\ *n* **:** a game in which players drive wooden balls with mallets through a series of wickets set out on a lawn

cro·quette \krō-'ket\ *n* **:** a roll or ball of hashed meat, fish, or vegetables fried in deep fat

¹cross \'krȯs\ *n* **1 :** a structure consisting of one bar crossing another at right angles **2** *often cap* **:** the structure on which Jesus was crucified used as a symbol of Christianity and of the Christian religion **3 :** sorrow or suffering as test of patience or virtue ⟨had their *crosses* to bear⟩ **4 :** an object or mark shaped like a cross ⟨a stone *cross*⟩ ⟨put a *cross* next to the name⟩ **5 :** a mixing of breeds, races, or kinds **:** the product of such a mixing

²cross *vb* **1 :** to lie or be situated across **2 :** to divide by passing through or across (a line or area) **:** INTERSECT **3 :** to move, pass, or extend across or past ⟨*cross* the street⟩ **4 :** to make the sign of the cross upon or over (as in prayer) **5 :** to cancel by marking crosses on or by drawing a line through ⟨*cross* out a word⟩ **6 :** to place one over the other ⟨*cross* your legs⟩ **7 :** to act against **:** OPPOSE ⟨*crossed* my parent's wishes⟩ **8 :** to draw a line across ⟨*cross* your *t*'s⟩ **9 :** to cause (an animal or plant) to breed with one of another kind **:** produce hybrids **10 :** to pass going in opposite directions ⟨their letters *crossed* in the mail⟩

³cross *adj* **1 :** lying, falling, or passing across ⟨a *cross* street⟩ **2 :** ²CONTRARY 1 ⟨at *cross* purposes⟩ **3 :** hard to get along with **:** IRRITABLE — **cross·ly** *adv* — **cross·ness** *n*

cross·bar \'krȯs-ˌbär\ *n* **:** a bar, piece, or stripe placed crosswise or across something

cross·bones \'krȯs-ˌbōnz\ *n pl* **:** two leg or arm bones placed or pictured as lying across each other ⟨a skull and *crossbones*⟩

\ə\ **abut**	\au̇\ **out**	\i\ **tip**	\ȯ\ **saw**	\u̇\ **foot**
\ər\ **further**	\ch\ **chin**	\ī\ **life**	\ȯi\ **coin**	\y\ **yet**
\a\ **mat**	\e\ **pet**	\j\ **job**	\th\ **thin**	\yü\ **few**
\ā\ **take**	\ē\ **easy**	\ng\ **sing**	\th\ **this**	\yu̇\ **cure**
\ä\ **cot, cart**	\g\ **go**	\ō\ **bone**	\ü\ **food**	\zh\ **vision**

cross·bow \'krȯs-ˌbō\ *n* : a short bow mounted crosswise near the end of a wooden stock that shoots short arrows

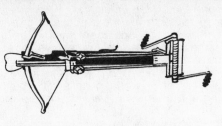

crossbow

cross–ex·am·ine \ˌkrȯ-sig-ˈzam-ən\ *vb* **cross–ex·am·ined; cross–ex·am·in·ing** : to question (a person) in an effort to show that statements or answers given earlier were false — **cross–ex·am·in·er** *n*

cross–eyed \'krȯ-ˈsīd\ *adj* : having one or both eyes turned toward the nose

cross·ing \'krȯ-sing\ *n* **1** : a point where two lines, tracks, or streets cross each other **2** : a place provided for going across a street, railroad tracks, or a stream **3** : a voyage across a body of water

cross·piece \'krȯ-ˌspēs\ *n* : something placed so as to cross something else

cross–ref·er·ence \'krȯs-ˈref-ə-rəns, -ˈref-rəns\ *n* : a reference made from one place to another (as in a dictionary)

cross·roads \'krȯs-ˌrōdz\ *n sing or pl* : a place where roads cross

cross section *n* **1** : a cutting made across something (as a log or an apple) **2** : a representation of a cross section ⟨a *cross section* of a wire⟩ **3** : a number of persons or things selected from a group to stand for the whole

cross·walk \'krȯ-ˌswȯk\ *n* : a specially paved or marked path for people walking across a street or road

cross·wise \'krȯ-ˌswīz\ *adv* : so as to cross something : ACROSS

cross·word puzzle \ˌkrȯ-ˌswərd-\ *n* : a puzzle in which words are filled into a pattern of numbered squares in answer to clues so that they read across and down

crotch \'kräch\ *n* : an angle formed by the spreading apart of two legs or branches or of a limb from its trunk ⟨the *crotch* of a tree⟩

¹crouch \'kraùch\ *vb* : to stoop or bend low with the arms and legs close to the body

²crouch *n* : the position of crouching

¹crow \'krō\ *n* : a glossy black bird that has a harsh cry

²crow *vb* **1** : to make the loud shrill sound that a rooster makes **2** : to make sounds of delight **3** : ²BOAST 1 ⟨*crowed* over our victory⟩

³crow *n* **1** : the cry of a rooster **2** : a cry of triumph

crow·bar \'krō-ˌbär\ *n* : a metal bar used as a lever (as for prying things apart)

¹crowd \'kraùd\ *vb* **1** : to press or push forward ⟨*crowd* into an elevator⟩ **2** : to press close ⟨the players *crowded* around the coach⟩ **3** : to collect in numbers : THRONG **4** : to fill or pack by pressing together ⟨cars *crowded* the roads⟩

²crowd *n* **1** : a large number of persons collected together : THRONG **2** : the population as a whole : ordinary people ⟨books that appeal to the *crowd*⟩ **3** : a group of people having a common interest ⟨running around with the wrong *crowd*⟩

¹crown \'kraùn\ *n* **1** : a wreath or band especially as a mark of victory or honor **2** : a royal headdress **3** : the highest part (as of a tree or mountain) **4** : the top of the head **5** : the top part of a hat **6** : the part of a tooth outside of the gum **7** : something suggesting a crown **8** *cap* : royal power or authority or one having such power **9** : any of various coins (as a British coin worth five shillings) — **crowned** \'kraùnd\ *adj*

²crown *vb* **1** : to place a crown on : make sovereign **2** : to declare officially to be ⟨was *crowned* champion⟩ **3** : to give something as a mark of honor or reward **4** : ²TOP 2 ⟨snow *crowned* the mountain⟩ **5** : to bring to a successful conclusion : COMPLETE, PERFECT **6** : to put an artificial crown on a damaged tooth **7** : to hit on the head

crow's nest *n* : a partly enclosed place to stand high on the mast of a ship for use as a lookout

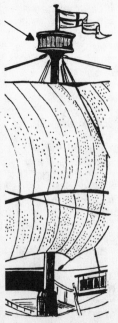

cru·cial \'krü-shəl\ *adj* **1** : being a final or very important test or decision : DECISIVE ⟨a *crucial* battle⟩ **2** : very important : SIGNIFICANT ⟨water is a *crucial* element in our weather⟩

crow's nest

cru·ci·ble \'krü-sə-bəl\ *n* : a pot made of a substance not easily damaged by fire that is used for holding something to be treated under great heat

cru·ci·fix \'krü-sə-ˌfiks\ *n* : a cross with a figure of Christ crucified on it

cru·ci·fix·ion \ˌkrü-sə-'fik-shən\ *n* **1** : an act of crucifying **2** *cap* : the crucifying of Christ on the cross

cru·ci·fy \'krü-sə-ˌfi\ *vb* **cru·ci·fied; cru·ci·fy·ing 1** : to put to death by nailing or binding the hands and feet to a cross **2** : to treat cruelly : TORTURE, PERSECUTE ⟨were *crucified* in the newspapers⟩

crude \'krüd\ *adj* **crud·er; crud·est 1** : in a natural state and not changed by special treatment : RAW ⟨*crude* oil⟩ ⟨*crude* sugar⟩ **2** : not having or showing good manners : VULGAR **3** : planned or done in a rough or unskilled way ⟨a *crude* drawing⟩ — **crude·ly** *adv* — **crude·ness** *n*

cru·el \'krü-əl\ *adj* **cru·el·er** *or* **cru·el·ler; cru·el·est** *or* **cru·el·lest 1** : ready to hurt others ⟨a *cruel* master⟩ **2** : causing or helping to cause suffering ⟨*cruel* punishment⟩ — **cru·el·ly** *adv*

cru·el·ty \'krü-əl-tē\ *n, pl* **cru·el·ties 1** : the quality or state of being cruel **2** : cruel treatment

cru·et \'krü-ət\ *n* : a bottle for holding vinegar, oil, or sauce for table use

cruet

¹cruise \'krüz\ *vb* **cruised; cruis·ing 1** : to travel by ship often stopping at a series of ports ⟨*cruise* along the coast⟩ **2** : to travel for pleasure **3** : to travel at the best operating speed

²cruise *n* : an act or instance of cruising

cruis·er \'krü-zər\ *n* **1** : a warship that is smaller than a battleship **2** : a police car used for patrolling streets and equipped with radio for communicating with headquarters **3** : a motorboat equipped for living aboard

crul·ler \'krəl-ər\ *n* : a small sweet cake made of egg batter usually cut in strips or twists and fried in deep fat

¹crumb \'krəm\ *n* **1** : a small piece especially of bread **2** : a little bit

²crumb *vb* : to break into crumbs : CRUMBLE

crum·ble \'krəm-bəl\ *vb* **crum·bled;**

crum·bling 1 : to break into small pieces ⟨*crumble* bread⟩ **2** : to fall to pieces : fall into ruin

crum·bly \'krəm-blē\ *adj* **crum·bli·er; crum·bli·est** : easily crumbled

crum·ple \'krəm-pəl\ *vb* **crum·pled; crum·pling 1** : to press or crush out of shape : RUMPLE ⟨*crumple* paper⟩ **2** : to become crumpled **3** : ¹COLLAPSE 1

¹crunch \'krənch\ *vb* **1** : to chew or grind with a crushing noise ⟨*crunching* on hard candy⟩ **2** : to make the sound of being crushed or squeezed ⟨the snow *crunching* underfoot⟩

²crunch *n* : an act or sound of crunching

¹cru·sade \krü-'sād\ *n* **1** *cap* : one of the military expeditions made by Christian countries in the eleventh, twelfth, and thirteenth centuries to recover the Holy Land from the Muslims **2** : a campaign to get things changed for the better

²crusade *vb* **cru·sad·ed; cru·sad·ing** : to take part in a crusade

cru·sad·er \krü-'sād-ər\ *n* : a person who takes part in a crusade

¹crush \'krəsh\ *vb* **1** : to squeeze together so as to change or destroy the natural shape or condition ⟨*crush* grapes⟩ **2** : ¹HUG 1 **3** : to break into fine pieces by pressure ⟨*crush* stone⟩ **4** : OVERWHELM 2 ⟨*crush* an enemy⟩ **5** : OPPRESS 1

²crush *n* **1** : an act of crushing **2** : a tightly packed crowd **3** : a foolish or very strong liking : INFATUATION ⟨have a *crush* on someone⟩

crust \'krəst\ *n* **1** : the hardened outside surface of bread **2** : a hard dry piece of bread **3** : the pastry cover of a pie **4** : a hard outer covering or surface layer ⟨a *crust* of snow⟩ **5** : the outer part of the earth

crus·ta·cean \ˌkrəs-'tā-shən\ *n* : any of a large group of mostly water animals (as crabs, lobsters, and shrimps) with a body made of segments, a firm outer shell, two pairs of antennae, and limbs that are jointed

crusty \'krəs-tē\ *adj* **crust·i·er; crust·i·est 1** : having or being a crust **2** : ³CROSS 3 ⟨a *crusty* reply⟩

crutch \'krəch\ *n* **1** : a support usually made with a piece at the top to fit under the armpit that is used by a lame person as an aid in walking **2** : something (as a prop or support) like a crutch in shape or use

\ə\ abut	\au̇\ out	\i\ tip	\ȯ\ saw	\u̇\ foot
\ər\ further	\ch\ chin	\ī\ life	\ȯi\ coin	\y\ yet
\a\ mat	\e\ pet	\j\ job	\th\ thin	\yü\ few
\ā\ take	\ē\ easy	\ng\ sing	\th\ this	\yu̇\ cure
\ä\ cot, cart	\g\ go	\ō\ bone	\ü\ food	\zh\ vision

¹cry \'krī\ *vb* **cried; cry·ing 1 :** to make a loud call or cry : SHOUT, EXCLAIM **2 :** to shed tears : WEEP **3 :** to utter a special sound or call **4 :** to make known to the public : call out

Word History The English word *cry* came from an Old French word. This Old French word meant "to shout" or "to cry." It came from a Latin word meaning "to shout out" or "to scream." The literal meaning of the Latin word was "to cry out for help from a citizen." It was formed from a Latin word meaning "Roman citizen."

²cry *n, pl* **cries 1 :** a loud call or shout (as of pain, fear, or joy) **2 :** ¹APPEAL 2 ⟨*cries* of the poor⟩ **3 :** a fit of weeping ⟨had a good *cry*⟩ **4 :** the special sound made by an animal

cry·ba·by \'krī-,bā-bē\ *n, pl* **cry·ba·bies :** a person who cries easily or who complains often

¹crys·tal \'krist-l\ *n* **1 :** quartz that is colorless and transparent or nearly so **2 :** something transparent like crystal **3 :** a body formed by a substance hardening so that it has flat surfaces in an even arrangement ⟨an ice *crystal*⟩ ⟨a salt *crystal*⟩ **4 :** a clear colorless glass of very good quality **5 :** the transparent cover over a clock or watch dial

²crystal *adj* **:** made of or being like crystal : CLEAR

crys·tal·line \'kris-tə-lən\ *adj* **1 :** made of crystal or composed of crystals **2 :** like crystal : TRANSPARENT

crys·tal·lize \'kris-tə-,līz\ *vb* **crys·tal·lized; crys·tal·liz·ing 1 :** to form or cause to form crystals or grains **2 :** to take or cause to take definite form ⟨the plan *crystallized* slowly⟩

cub \'kəb\ *n* **1 :** the young of various animals (as the bear, fox, or lion) **2 :** CUB SCOUT

cub·by·hole \'kəb-ē-,hōl\ *n* **:** a snug place (as for storing things)

¹cube \'kyüb\ *n* **1 :** a solid body having six equal square sides **2 :** the product obtained by multiplying the square of a number by the number itself ⟨27 is the *cube* of 3⟩

²cube *vb* **cubed; cub·ing 1 :** to take (a number) as a factor three times ⟨3 *cubed* is 27⟩ **2 :** to form into a cube or divide into cubes

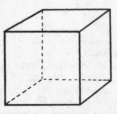

cube 1

cu·bic \'kyü-bik\ *adj* **:** being the volume of a cube whose edge is a specified unit ⟨a *cubic* centimeter⟩

cu·bi·cal \'kyü-bi-kəl\ *adj* **1 :** having the form of a cube **2 :** relating to volume

cu·bit \'kyü-bət\ *n* **:** a unit of length usually equal to about forty-six centimeters

cub scout *n* **:** a member of the Boy Scouts of America program for boys of the age range eight to ten

cuck·oo \'kük-ü, 'kúk-\ *n, pl* **cuck·oos 1 :** any of several related birds (as a grayish brown European bird) that mostly lay their eggs in the nests of other birds for them to hatch **2 :** the call of the European cuckoo

cu·cum·ber \'kyü-,kəm-bər\ *n* **:** a long usually green-skinned vegetable that is used in salads and as pickles and is the fruit of a vine related to the melons and gourds

cud \'kəd\ *n* **:** a portion of food brought up from the first stomach of some animals (as the cow and sheep) to be chewed again

cud·dle \'kəd-l\ *vb* **cud·dled; cud·dling 1 :** to hold close for warmth or comfort or in affection **2 :** to lie close : NESTLE, SNUGGLE

¹cud·gel \'kəj-əl\ *n* **:** a short heavy club

²cudgel *vb* **cud·geled** *or* **cud·gelled; cud·gel·ing** *or* **cud·gel·ling :** to beat with or as if with a cudgel

¹cue \'kyü\ *n* **1 :** a word, phrase, or action in a play serving as a signal for the next actor to speak or to do something **2 :** something serving as a signal or suggestion : HINT

²cue *n* **:** a straight tapering stick used in playing billiards and pool

¹cuff \'kəf\ *n* **1 :** a band or turned-over piece at the end of a sleeve **2 :** the turned-back hem of a trouser leg

²cuff *vb* **:** to strike especially with or as if with the palm of the hand : SLAP

³cuff *n* **:** ¹SLAP 1

¹cull \'kəl\ *vb* **1 :** to select from a group **2 :** to identify and remove the culls from

²cull *n* **:** something rejected from a group or lot as not as good as the rest

cul·mi·nate \'kəl-mə-,nāt\ *vb* **cul·mi·nat·ed; cul·mi·nat·ing :** to reach the highest point

cul·pa·ble \'kəl-pə-bəl\ *adj* **:** deserving blame

cul·prit \'kəl-prət\ *n* **1 :** one accused of or charged with a crime or fault **2 :** one guilty of a crime or fault

cul·ti·vate \'kəl-tə-,vāt\ *vb* **cul·ti·vat·ed; cul·ti·vat·ing 1 :** to prepare land for the raising of crops **2 :** to raise or assist the growth of crops by tilling or by labor and care **3 :** to improve or develop by careful attention, training, or study : devote time and thought to **4** : to seek the company and friendship of

cul·ti·vat·ed \'kəl-tə-ˌvāt-əd\ *adj* **1** : raised or produced under cultivation ⟨*cultivated* fruits⟩ **2** : having or showing good education and proper manners

cul·ti·va·tion \ˌkəl-tə-'vā-shən\ *n* **1** : the act or process of cultivating especially the soil **2** : REFINEMENT 2

cul·ti·va·tor \'kəl-tə-ˌvāt-ər\ *n* **1** : one (as a farmer) that cultivates something **2** : a tool or machine for loosening the soil and killing weeds between rows of a crop

cul·tur·al \'kəl-chə-rəl\ *adj* : of or relating to culture — **cul·tur·al·ly** *adv*

cul·ture \'kəl-chər\ *n* **1** : CULTIVATION 1 **2** : the raising or development (as of a crop or product) by careful attention ⟨grape *culture*⟩ **3** : the improvement of the mind, tastes, and manners through careful training **4** : a certain stage, form, or kind of civilization ⟨Greek *culture*⟩

cul·tured \'kəl-chərd\ *adj* **1** : having or showing refinement in taste, speech, or manners **2** : produced under artificial conditions ⟨*cultured* pearls⟩

cul·vert \'kəl-vərt\ *n* : a drain or waterway crossing under a road or railroad

cum·ber·some \'kəm-bər-səm\ *adj* : hard to handle or manage because of size or weight

cu·mu·la·tive \'kyü-myə-lət-iv, -ˌlāt-\ *adj* : increasing (as in force, strength, or amount) by one addition after another ⟨a *cumulative* effect⟩

cu·mu·lus \'kyü-myə-ləs\ *n, pl* **cu·mu·li** \-ˌlī, -ˌlē\ : a massive cloud form having a flat base and rounded outlines often piled up like a mountain

¹**cu·ne·i·form** \kyü-'nē-ə-ˌform\ *adj* **1** : shaped like a wedge **2** : made up of or written with marks or letters shaped like wedges

²**cuneiform** *n* : cuneiform writing

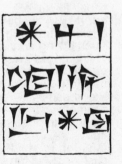

cuneiform

¹**cun·ning** \'kən-ing\ *adj* **1** : SKILLFUL 1, INVENTIVE **2** : using clever ways to deceive : TRICKY ⟨a *cunning* thief⟩ **3** : CUTE, PRETTY ⟨a *cunning* baby⟩ **synonyms** see SLY

²**cunning** *n* **1** : SKILL 1, DEXTERITY **2** : cleverness in getting what one wants often by tricks or deceiving

¹**cup** \'kəp\ *n* **1** : something to drink out of in the shape of a small bowl usually with a handle **2** : the contents of a cup : CUPFUL ⟨drink a *cup* of tea⟩ **3** : a trophy in the shape of a cup with two handles **4** : something like a cup in shape or use

²**cup** *vb* **cupped; cup·ping** : to curve into the shape of a cup

cup·board \'kəb-ərd\ *n* : a closet usually with shelves for dishes or food

cup·cake \'kəp-ˌkāk\ *n* : a small cake baked in a mold shaped like a cup

cup·ful \'kəp-ˌful\ *n, pl* **cup·fuls** \-ˌfulz\ *or* **cups·ful** \'kəps-ˌful\ **1** : the amount held by a cup **2** : a half pint : eight ounces (about 236 milliliters)

cu·pid \'kyü-pəd\ *n* : a picture or statue of Cupid the Roman god of love often as a winged child with a bow and arrow

cu·pid·i·ty \kyü-'pid-ət-ē\ *n* : excessive desire for wealth : GREED

cu·po·la \'kyü-pə-lə, -ˌlō\ *n* **1** : a rounded roof or ceiling : DOME **2** : a small structure built on top of a roof

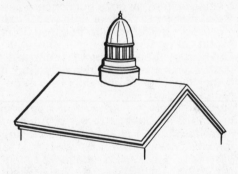

cupola

cur \'kər\ *n* : a worthless or mongrel dog

cur·able \'kyur-ə-bəl\ *adj* : possible to cure

cu·rate \'kyur-ət\ *n* : a member of the clergy who assists the rector or vicar of a church

¹**curb** \'kərb\ *n* **1** : a chain or strap on a horse's bit used to check the horse by pressing against the lower jaw **2** : ¹CHECK 2 ⟨a *curb* on rising prices⟩ **3** : an enclosing border (as of stone or concrete) often along the edge of a street

²**curb** *vb* : to control by or furnish with a curb

curb·ing \'kər-bing\ *n* **1** : material for making a curb **2** : ¹CURB 3

curd \'kərd\ *n* : the thickened or solid part of sour or partly digested milk

cur·dle \'kərd-l\ *vb* **cur·dled; cur·dling** : to change into curd : COAGULATE

¹cure \'kyur\ *n* **1** : a method or period of medical treatment **2** : recovery or relief from a disease **3** : ¹REMEDY 1 ⟨a *cure* for colds⟩

²cure *vb* **cured; cur·ing 1** : to make or become healthy or sound again **2** : to prepare by a chemical or physical process for use or storage ⟨*cure* pork in brine⟩ **3** : to undergo a curing process

cur·few \'kər-ˌfyü\ *n* **1** : a rule requiring certain or all people to be off the streets or at home at a stated time **2** : a signal (as the ringing of a bell) formerly given to announce the beginning of a curfew **3** : the time when a curfew is sounded

cu·rio \'kyur-ē-ˌō\ *n, pl* **cu·ri·os** : a rare or unusual article : CURIOSITY

cu·ri·os·i·ty \ˌkyur-ē-'äs-ət-ē\ *n, pl* **cu·ri·os·i·ties 1** : an eager desire to learn and often to learn what does not concern one **2** : something strange or unusual **3** : an object or article valued because it is strange or rare

cu·ri·ous \'kyur-ē-əs\ *adj* **1** : eager to learn : INQUISITIVE **2** : attracting attention by being strange or unusual : ODD — **cu·ri·ous·ly** *adv*

¹curl \'kərl\ *vb* **1** : to twist or form into ringlets **2** : to take or move in a curved form ⟨*curl* up in a chair⟩ ⟨smoke *curling* from the chimney⟩

²curl *n* **1** : a lock of hair that coils : RINGLET **2** : something having a spiral or winding form : COIL ⟨a *curl* of smoke⟩ **3** : the action of curling : the state of being curled

curly \'kər-lē\ *adj* **curl·i·er; curl·i·est 1** : tending to curl **2** : having curls

cur·rant \'kər-ənt\ *n* **1** : a small seedless raisin used in baking and cooking **2** : a sour red or white edible berry produced by a low spreading shrub related to the gooseberry

cur·ren·cy \'kər-ən-sē\ *n, pl* **cur·ren·cies 1** : common use or acceptance ⟨a rumor that had wide *currency*⟩ **2** : money in circulation

¹cur·rent \'kər-ənt\ *adj* **1** : now passing ⟨the *current* month⟩ **2** : occurring in or belonging to the present time ⟨*current* events⟩ **3** : generally and widely accepted, used, or practiced ⟨*current* customs⟩

²current *n* **1** : a body of fluid moving in a specified direction **2** : the swiftest part of a stream **3** : the general course : TREND ⟨the *current* of public opinion⟩ **4** : a flow of charges of electricity

cur·ric·u·lum \kə-'rik-yə-ləm\ *n, pl* **cur·ric·u·la** \-lə\ *or* **cur·ric·u·lums** : all the courses of study offered by a school

cur·ry \'kər-ē\ *vb* **cur·ried; cur·ry·ing** : to rub and clean the coat of ⟨*curry* a horse⟩

¹curse \'kərs\ *n* **1** : a calling for harm or injury to come to someone **2** : a word or an expression used in cursing or swearing **3** : evil or misfortune that comes as if in answer to a curse **4** : a cause of great harm or evil

²curse *vb* **cursed; curs·ing 1** : to call upon divine power to send harm or evil upon **2** : SWEAR 5 **3** : to bring unhappiness or evil upon : AFFLICT

curt \'kərt\ *adj* : rudely brief in language

cur·tail \ˌkər-'tāl\ *vb* : to shorten or reduce by cutting off the end or a part of ⟨had to *curtail* my speech⟩

¹cur·tain \'kərt-n\ *n* **1** : a piece of material (as cloth) hung up to darken, hide, divide, or decorate **2** : something that covers, hides, or separates like a curtain ⟨a *curtain* of secrecy⟩

²curtain *vb* **1** : to furnish with curtains **2** : to hide or shut off with a curtain

¹curt·sy *or* **curt·sey** \'kərt-sē\ *n, pl* **curt·sies** *or* **curt·seys** : a bow made especially by women as a sign of respect that consists of a slight lowering of the body and bending of the knees

²curtsy *or* **curtsey** *vb* **curt·sied** *or* **curt·seyed; curt·sy·ing** *or* **curt·sey·ing** : to make a curtsy

cur·va·ture \'kər-və-ˌchur\ *n* **1** : a curving or bending **2** : the state of being curved

¹curve \'kərv\ *vb* **curved; curv·ing 1** : to turn or change from a straight line or course ⟨the road *curved* to the left⟩ **2** : to cause to curve

²curve *n* **1** : a bending or turning without angles : BEND ⟨a *curve* in the road⟩ **2** : something curved **3** : a ball thrown so that it moves away from a straight course

¹cush·ion \'kush-ən\ *n* **1** : a soft pillow or pad to rest on or against **2** : something like a cushion in use, shape, or softness **3** : something that serves to soften or lessen the effects of something bad or unpleasant

²cushion *vb* **1** : to place on or as if on a cushion **2** : to furnish with a cushion **3** : to soften or lessen the force or shock of

cusp \'kəsp\ *n* : a point or pointed end (as on the crown of a tooth)

cus·pid \'kəs-pəd\ *n* : ²CANINE 1

cuss \'kəs\ *vb* : SWEAR 5

cus·tard \'kəs-tərd\ *n* : a sweetened mixture of milk and eggs baked, boiled, or frozen

cus·to·di·an \ˌkəs-'tōd-ē-ən\ *n* : one that guards and protects or takes care of ⟨the school *custodian*⟩

cus·to·dy \'kəs-tə-dē\ *n* **1** : direct responsibility for care and control **2** : the state of being arrested or held by police

¹cus·tom \'kəs-təm\ *n* **1** : the usual way of doing things : the usual practice **2** **customs** *pl* : duties or taxes paid on imports or exports **3** : support given to a business by its customers

²custom *adj* **1** : made or done to personal order **2** : specializing in custom work

cus·tom·ary \'kəs-tə-ˌmer-ē\ *adj* **1** : based on or existing by custom **2** : commonly done or observed

cus·tom·er \'kəs-tə-mər\ *n* : a person who buys from or uses the services of a company especially regularly

¹cut \'kət\ *vb* **cut**; **cut·ting** **1** : to penetrate or divide with or as if with an edged tool : GASH, CLEAVE ⟨*cut* a finger⟩ ⟨*cut* the cake into neat wedges⟩ **2** : to be possible to shape or penetrate with an edged tool ⟨cheese *cuts* easily⟩ **3** : to experience the growth of through the gum ⟨the baby is *cutting* teeth⟩ **4** : to hurt someone's feelings ⟨that remark really *cut*⟩ **5** : to strike sharply or at an angle ⟨the wind *cut* our faces⟩ **6** : to make less ⟨*cut* costs⟩ **7** : ²CROSS 2, INTERSECT ⟨the lines *cut* each other⟩ **8** : ¹SWERVE ⟨*cut* to avoid a hole in the road⟩ **9** : to go by a short or direct path or course ⟨we *cut* across the lawn⟩ **10** : to divide into parts ⟨*cut* a deck of cards⟩ **11** : to stop or cause to stop ⟨*cut* the motor⟩ ⟨*cut* that whispering⟩ **12** : ¹SNUB ⟨*cut* a former friend⟩

²cut *n* **1** : something cut or cut off ⟨a *cut* of pie⟩ ⟨a *cut* of beef⟩ **2** : ¹SHARE 1 ⟨took their *cut* of the winnings⟩ **3** : something (as a gash or wound) produced by or as if by cutting **4** : a passage made by digging or cutting ⟨a railroad *cut*⟩ **5** : a pictorial illustration (as in a book) **6** : something that is done or said that hurts the feelings ⟨an unkind *cut*⟩ **7** : a straight path or course **8** : a cutting stroke or blow **9** : the way in which a thing is cut, formed, or made **10** : REDUCTION 1 ⟨a *cut* in pay⟩

cute \'kyüt\ *adj* **cut·er**; **cut·est** **1** : KEEN 4, SHREWD **2** : attractive especially in looks or actions

cu·ti·cle \'kyüt-i-kəl\ *n* **1** : an outer layer (as of skin or a leaf) often produced by the cells beneath **2** : a dead or horny layer of skin especially around a fingernail

cut·lass \'kət-ləs\ *n* : a short heavy curved sword

cut·lery \'kət-lə-rē\ *n* **1** : cutting tools (as knives and scissors) **2** : utensils used in cutting, serving, and eating food

cut·let \'kət-lət\ *n* **1** : a small slice of meat cut for broiling or frying **2** : a piece of food shaped like a cutlet

cut·out \'kət-ˌaut\ *n* : something cut out or intended to be cut out from something else ⟨a page of animal *cutouts*⟩

cutlass

cut out \ˌkət-'aut\ *vb* : to form by cutting ⟨*cut out* a pattern⟩

cut·ter \'kət-ər\ *n* **1** : someone or something that cuts ⟨a diamond *cutter*⟩ ⟨a cookie *cutter*⟩ **2** : a boat used by warships for carrying passengers and stores to and from the shore **3** : a small sailing boat with one mast **4** : a small armed boat used by the Coast Guard

cut·ting \'kət-ing\ *n* : a part (as a shoot) of a plant able to grow into a whole new plant

cut·tle·fish \'kət-l-ˌfish\ *n* : a sea animal with ten arms that is related to the squid and octopus

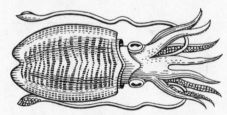

cuttlefish

cut·up \'kət-ˌəp\ *n* : a person who clowns or acts in a noisy manner

cut·worm \'kət-ˌwərm\ *n* : a moth caterpillar that has a smooth body and feeds on the stems of plants at night

-cy \sē\ *n suffix, pl* **-cies** **1** : action : practice **2** : rank : office **3** : body : class **4** : state : quality ⟨accura*cy*⟩ ⟨bankrupt*cy*⟩

cy·a·nide \'sī-ə-ˌnīd\ *n* : any of several compounds containing carbon and nitrogen and including two very poisonous substances

cy·cad \'sī-kəd\ *n* : a tropical tree like a palm but related to the conifers

\ə\ **abut**	\au̇\ **out**	\i\ **tip**	\o̅\ **saw**	\u̇\ **foot**
\ər\ **further**	\ch\ **chin**	\ī\ **life**	\oi\ **coin**	\y\ **yet**
\a\ **mat**	\e\ **pet**	\j\ **job**	\th\ **thin**	\yü\ **few**
\ā\ **take**	\ē\ **easy**	\ng\ **sing**	\th\ **this**	\yu̇\ **cure**
\ä\ **cot, cart**	\g\ **go**	\ō\ **bone**	\ü\ **food**	\zh\ **vision**

¹**cy·cle** \'sī-kəl\ *n* **1** : a period of time taken up by a series of events or actions that repeat themselves again and again in the same order ⟨the *cycle* of the seasons⟩ **2** : a complete round or series **3** : a long period of time : AGE **4** : BICYCLE **5** : TRI-CYCLE **6** : MOTOR-CYCLE

²**cycle** *vb* **cy·cled; cy·cling** : to ride a cycle

cy·clist \'sī-kləst\ *n* : a person who rides a cycle and especially a bicycle

cy·clone \'sī-ˌklōn\ *n* **1** : a storm or system of winds that rotates about a center of low air pressure, moves at a speed of thirty to fifty kilometers an hour, and often brings lots of rain **2** : TORNADO

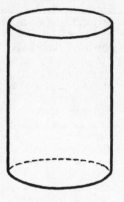
cylinder

cy·clops \'sī-ˌkläps\ *n, pl* **cyclops** : WATER FLEA

cyl·in·der \'sil-ən-dər\ *n* : a long round body whether hollow or solid

cy·lin·dri·cal \sə-'lin-dri-kəl\ *adj* : having the shape of a cylinder

cym·bal \'sim-bəl\ *n* : either of a pair of brass plates that are clashed together to make a sharp ringing sound and that together form a musical percussion instrument

cy·press \'sī-prəs\ *n* : any of various evergreen trees that are related to the pines, bear cones, and have strong reddish wood which is not easily damaged by moisture

cyst \'sist\ *n* **1** : an abnormal sac in a living body **2** : a covering like a cyst or a body (as a spore) with such a covering

cy·to·plasm \'sīt-ə-ˌplaz-əm\ *n* : the protoplasm of a cell except for the nucleus

czar \'zär\ *n* : the ruler of Russia until the 1917 revolution

cza·ri·na \zä-'rē-nə\ *n* **1** : the wife of a czar **2** : a woman who has the rank of czar

d \'dē\ *n, pl* **d's** *or* **ds** \'dēz\ *often cap* **1** : the fourth letter of the English alphabet **2** : 500 in Roman numerals **3** : a grade that shows a student's work is poor

¹**dab** \'dab\ *n* **1** : a sudden poke **2** : a light quick touch

²**dab** *vb* **dabbed; dab·bing** **1** : to strike or touch lightly **2** : to apply with light or uneven strokes ⟨*dab* on paint⟩ — **dab·ber** *n*

³**dab** *n* : a small amount ⟨a *dab* of butter⟩

dab·ble \'dab-əl\ *vb* **dab·bled; dab·bling** **1** : to wet by splashing : SPATTER **2** : to paddle in or as if in water **3** : to work without real interest or effort — **dab·bler** \'dab-lər\ *n*

dace \'dās\ *n, pl* **dace** : any of several small fishes related to the carps

dachs·hund \'däks-ˌhunt, 'däk-sənt\ *n* : a small hound with a long body, very short legs, and long drooping ears

dachshund

Word History The Germans developed a dog with short legs and a long body. These dogs were used to hunt burrowing animals such as badgers. Such a dog could follow a badger right down its hole.

The Germans gave these dogs a name that meant "badger dog." The English word *dachshund* came from this German name.

dad \'dad\ *n*, *often cap* : ¹FATHER 1

dad·dy \'dad-ē\ *n*, *pl* **dad·dies** *often cap* : ¹FATHER 1

dad·dy long·legs \ˌdad-ē-'lȯng-ˌlegz\ *n*, *pl* **daddy longlegs** **1** : an insect like a spider but with a small rounded body and long slender legs **2** : a slender two-winged fly with long legs

daf·fo·dil \'daf-ə-ˌdil\ *n* : a plant that grows from a bulb and has long slender leaves and yellow, white, or pinkish flowers suggesting trumpets and having a scalloped edge and leaflike parts at the base

daffodil

daft \'daft\ *adj* : FOOLISH, CRAZY — **daft·ly** *adv* — **daft·ness** *n*

dag·ger \'dag-ər\ *n* : a short knife used for stabbing

dahl·ia \'dal-yə, 'däl-\ *n* : a tall plant related to the daisies and widely grown for its bright flowers

¹**dai·ly** \'dā-lē\ *adj* **1** : occurring, done, produced, or issued every day or every weekday **2** : given or paid for one day ⟨a *daily* wage⟩

²**daily** *n*, *pl* **dai·lies** : a newspaper published every weekday

³**daily** *adv* : every day ⟨jogs three miles *daily*⟩

¹**dain·ty** \'dānt-ē\ *n*, *pl* **dain·ties** : DELICACY 1

²**dainty** *adj* **dain·ti·er**; **dain·ti·est** **1** : tasting good **2** : pretty in a delicate way **3** : having or showing delicate taste — **dain·ti·ly** \'dānt-l-ē\ *adv* — **dain·ti·ness** \'dānt-ē-nəs\ *n*

dairy \'deər-ē, 'daər-ē\ *n*, *pl* **dair·ies** **1** : a place where milk is stored or is made into butter and cheese **2** : a farm that produces milk **3** : a company or a store that sells milk products

Word History *Dairy* came from an Old English word that meant "kneader of dough." The modern English word *dough* is a relative of this word. In time the word that meant "kneader of dough" came to mean "maid." The word was also used for a special kind of maid, a dairymaid. A new word was formed later on by adding an ending meaning "place" to the word meaning "dairymaid." The new word then was used for the place where the dairymaid worked. The modern English word *dairy* came from this earlier English word. The ending can still be seen in the last two letters of the modern word.

dairy·ing \'der-ē-ing\ *n* : the business of producing milk or milk products

dairy·maid \'deər-ē-ˌmād\ *n* : a woman or girl who works in a dairy

dairy·man \'deər-ē-mən\ *n*, *pl* **dairy·men** \-mən\ : a man who operates a dairy farm or works in a dairy

da·is \'dā-əs, 'dī-\ *n* : a raised platform (as in a hall)

dai·sy \'dā-zē\ *n*, *pl* **dai·sies** : any of a large group of plants with flower heads consisting of one or more rows of white or colored flowers like petals around a central disk of tiny often yellow flowers closely packed together

Word History The modern English word *daisy* came from an Old English word that meant "daisy." The literal meaning of this Old English word was "day's eye." The yellow center of a daisy looks a bit like the sun. The sun may be thought of as the bright eye of the day.

dale \'dāl\ *n* : VALLEY

dal·ly \'dal-ē\ *vb* **dal·lied**; **dal·ly·ing** **1** : to act playfully **2** : to waste time **3** : LINGER, DAWDLE

dal·ma·tian \dal-'mā-shən\ *n*, *often cap*

dalmatian

\ə\ abut	\aů\ out	\i\ tip	\ȯ\ saw	\ů\ foot
\ər\ further	\ch\ chin	\ī\ life	\ȯi\ coin	\y\ yet
\a\ mat	\e\ pet	\j\ job	\th\ thin	\yü\ few
\ā\ take	\ē\ easy	\ng\ sing	\th\ this	\yů\ cure
\ä\ cot, cart	\g\ go	\ō\ bone	\ü\ food	\zh\ vision

: a large dog having a short white coat with black or brown spots

¹dam \'dam\ *n* : a female parent — used especially of a domestic animal

²dam *n* : a barrier (as across a stream) to hold back a flow of water

³dam *vb* **dammed; dam·ming** : to hold back or block with or as if with a dam

¹dam·age \'dam-ij\ *n* **1** : loss or harm due to injury **2 damages** *pl* : money demanded or paid according to law for injury or damage **synonyms** see HARM

²damage *vb* **dam·aged; dam·ag·ing** : to cause damage to

dam·ask \'dam-əsk\ *n* : a fancy cloth used especially for household linen

dame \'dām\ *n* : a woman of high rank or social position

¹damn \'dam\ *vb* **1** : to condemn to everlasting punishment especially in hell **2** : to declare to be bad or a failure **3** : to swear at : CURSE

²damn *n* : the word *damn* used as a curse

dam·na·ble \'dam-nə-bəl\ *adj* : very bad : OUTRAGEOUS — **dam·na·bly** \-blē\ *adv*

¹damned \'damd\ *adj* **damned·er** \'dam-dər\; **damned·est** \-dəst\ **1** : DAMNABLE ⟨a *damned* nuisance⟩ **2** : REMARKABLE ⟨the *damnedest* sight⟩

²damned *adv* : to a high degree : VERY

¹damp \'damp\ *n* **1** : a harmful gas found especially in coal mines **2** : MOISTURE

²damp *vb* : DAMPEN

³damp *adj* : slightly wet : MOIST — **damp·ly** *adv* — **damp·ness** *n*

damp·en \'dam-pən\ *vb* **1** : to make dull or less active ⟨rain *dampened* our enthusiasm for a picnic⟩ **2** : to make or become damp — **damp·en·er** *n*

damp·er \'dam-pər\ *n* **1** : something that checks, discourages, or deadens **2** : a valve or movable plate for controlling a flow of air

dam·sel \'dam-zəl\ *n* : GIRL 1, MAIDEN

¹dance \'dans\ *vb* **danced; danc·ing** **1** : to glide, step, or move through a series of movements usually in time to music **2** : to move about or up and down quickly and lightly **3** : to perform or take part in as a dancer — **danc·er** *n*

²dance *n* **1** : an act of dancing **2** : a social gathering for dancing **3** : a set of movements or steps for dancing usually in time to special music **4** : the art of dancing

dan·de·li·on \'dan-dl-ˌī-ən\ *n* : a weedy plant related to the daisies that has a ring of long deeply toothed leaves often eaten as cooked greens or in salad and bright yellow flowers with hollow stems

dan·druff \'dan-drəf\ *n* : thin dry whitish flakes that form on the scalp and come off freely

¹dan·dy \'dan-dē\ *n*, *pl* **dan·dies** **1** : a man who pays a great deal of attention to his clothes **2** : an excellent or unusual example

²dandy *adj* **dan·di·er; dan·di·est** : very good

Dane \'dān\ *n* : a person born or living in Denmark

dan·ger \'dān-jər\ *n* **1** : the state of not being protected from harm or evil : PERIL **2** : something that may cause injury or harm

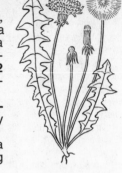

dandelion

---

synonyms DANGER, HAZARD, and RISK mean a threat of loss, injury, or death. DANGER suggests possible harm that may or may not be avoided ⟨the *danger* of a new war starting⟩ HAZARD suggests danger from something beyond one's control ⟨the *hazards* of mining for coal⟩ RISK suggests danger that may result from a chance voluntarily taken ⟨willing to take the *risks* that come with flying a plane⟩

---

dan·ger·ous \'dān-jə-rəs, 'dānj-rəs\ *adj* **1** : full of danger ⟨*dangerous* work⟩ **2** : able or likely to injure ⟨a *dangerous* tool⟩ — **dan·ger·ous·ly** *adv*

dan·gle \'dang-gəl\ *vb* **dan·gled; dan·gling** **1** : to hang loosely especially with a swinging or jerking motion **2** : to depend on something else **3** : to cause to dangle

¹Dan·ish \'dā-nish\ *adj* : of or relating to Denmark, the Danes, or Danish

²Danish *n* : the language of the Danes

dank \'dangk\ *adj* : unpleasantly wet or moist — **dank·ly** *adv* — **dank·ness** *n*

dap·per \'dap-ər\ *adj* : neat and trim in dress or appearance

dap·ple \'dap-əl\ *vb* **dap·pled; dap·pling** : to mark or become marked with rounded spots of color ⟨*dappled* horse⟩

¹dare \'daər, 'deər\ *vb* **dared; dar·ing** **1** : to have courage enough for some purpose : be bold enough ⟨they *dared* to try something new⟩ — sometimes used as a helping verb ⟨we *dare* not say a word⟩ **2** : to challenge to do something especially as a proof of courage ⟨I *dare* you to jump⟩

²dare *n* : a demand that one do something difficult or dangerous as proof of courage

dare·dev·il \'daər-ˌdev-əl, 'deər-\ *n* : a person so bold as to be reckless

¹dar·ing \'daər-ing, 'deər-\ *adj* : ready to take risks : BOLD, VENTURESOME **syn·onyms** see ADVENTUROUS — **dar·ing·ly** *adv*

²daring *n* : bold fearlessness : readiness to take chances

¹dark \'därk\ *adj* **1** : being without light or without much light **2** : not light in color **3** : not bright and cheerful : GLOOMY **4** : being without knowledge and culture ⟨the *Dark* Ages⟩ — **dark·ish** \'där-kish\ *adj* — **dark·ly** *adv* — **dark·ness** *n*

²dark *n* **1** : absence of light **2** : a place or time of little or no light ⟨got home before *dark*⟩

dark·en \'där-kən\ *vb* **1** : to make or grow dark or darker **2** : to make or become gloomy — **dark·en·er** *n*

dark·room \'där-ˌkrüm, -ˌkrum\ *n* : a usually small lightproof room used in developing photographic plates and film

¹dar·ling \'där-ling\ *n* **1** : a dearly loved person **2** : ¹FAVORITE ⟨the *darling* of the crowd⟩

²darling *adj* **1** : dearly loved **2** : very pleasing : HARMING

¹darn \'därn\ *vb* : to mend by interlacing threads ⟨*darn* socks⟩

²darn *n* : a place that has been darned

³darn *n* : ²DAMN

darning needle *n* : DRAGONFLY

¹dart \'därt\ *n* **1** : a small pointed object that is meant to be thrown **2 darts** *pl* : a game in which darts are thrown at a target **3** : a quick sudden movement **4** : a stitched fold in a garment

²dart *vb* : to move or shoot out suddenly and quickly ⟨a toad *darted* out its tongue⟩

¹dash \'dash\ *vb* **1** : to knock, hurl, or shove violently **2** : ¹SMASH 1 ⟨*dash* the plate to pieces on the floor⟩ **3** : ¹SPLASH 2 ⟨clothes *dashed* with mud⟩ **4** : DESTROY 1 ⟨their hopes were *dashed*⟩ **5** : to complete or do hastily ⟨*dash* off a note⟩ **6** : to move with sudden speed

²dash *n* **1** : a sudden burst or splash ⟨a *dash* of cold water⟩ **2** : a punctuation mark — that is used most often to show a break in the thought or structure of a sentence **3** : a small amount : TOUCH **4** : liveliness in style and action **5** : a sudden rush or attempt ⟨a *dash* for the goal⟩ **6** : a short fast race ⟨100-yard *dash*⟩ **7** : a long click or buzz forming a letter or part of a letter (as in telegraphy) **8** : DASH-BOARD

dash·board \'dash-ˌbȯrd\ *n* : a panel across an automobile or aircraft below the windshield usually containing dials and controls

dash·ing \'dash-ing\ *adj* : having clothes or manners that are very fancy and stylish

das·tard \'das-tərd\ *n* : a mean and sneaky coward

das·tard·ly \'das-tərd-lē\ *adj* : of or like a dastard — **das·tard·li·ness** *n*

da·ta \'dāt-ə, 'dat-ə, 'dät-ə\ *n sing or pl* **1** : facts about something that can be used in calculating, reasoning, or planning **2** : DATUM

¹date \'dāt\ *n* : the sweet brownish fruit of an Old World palm (**date palm**)

Word History The English word for the fruit of the date palm came from a Greek word. The first meaning of this Greek word was "finger," but it was also used for the fruit. A cluster of dates on a palm tree must have looked to someone rather like the cluster of fingers on a hand.

²date *n* **1** : the day, month, or year of a happening **2** : a statement of time on something (as a coin, letter, book, or building) **3** : APPOINTMENT 3 **4** : a person with whom one has a social engagement

Word History Long ago the Romans wrote on their letters the place and date of sending. For example a Roman might use a Latin phrase that meant "given at Rome on the first of April." The first word of this phrase, which meant "given," came to be used to mean "date." The English word *date* came from this Latin word.

³date *vb* **dat·ed; dat·ing** **1** : to find or show the date of **2** : to write the date on ⟨*date* a letter⟩ **3** : to make or have a date with **4** : to belong to or have survived from a time ⟨my house *dates* from the war of 1812⟩ **5** : to show to be old-fashioned or belonging to a past time ⟨their slang *dates* them⟩

da·tum \'dāt-əm, 'dat-, 'dät-\ *n, pl* **da·ta** \-ə\ *or* **da·tums** : a single piece of information : FACT

¹daub \'dȯb\ *vb* **1** : to cover with something soft and sticky ⟨*daubed* with mud⟩ **2** : to paint or color carelessly or badly — **daub·er** *n*

²daub *n* : something daubed on : SMEAR

daugh·ter \'dȯt-ər\ *n* **1** : a female child or offspring **2** : a woman or girl associated with or thought of as a child of something

\ə\ abut	\au̇\ out	\i\ tip	\ȯ\ saw	\u̇\ foot
\ər\ further	\ch\ chin	\ī\ life	\ȯi\ coin	\y\ yet
\a\ mat	\e\ pet	\j\ job	\th\ thin	\yü\ few
\ā\ take	\ē\ easy	\ng\ sing	\th\ this	\yu̇\ cure
\ä\ cot, cart	\g\ go	\ō\ bone	\ü\ food	\zh\ vision

(as a country, race, or religion) ⟨the *daughters* of Africa⟩ — **daugh·ter·ly** *adj*

daugh·ter–in–law \ˈdȯt-ər-ən-ˌlȯ\ *n, pl* **daugh·ters–in–law** : the wife of one's son

daunt \ˈdȯnt\ *vb* : DISCOURAGE 1, INTIMIDATE ⟨dangers to *daunt* the bravest⟩

daunt·less \ˈdȯnt-ləs\ *adj* : bravely determined — **daunt·less·ly** *adv* — **daunt·less·ness** *n*

dau·phin \ˈdȯ-fən\ *n* : the oldest son of a king of France

dav·en·port \ˈdav-ən-ˌpōrt\ *n* : a large sofa

da·vit \ˈdā-vət, ˈdav-ət\ *n* : one of a pair of posts fitted with ropes and pulleys and used for supporting and lowering a ship's boat

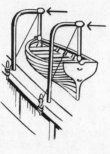

davit

daw·dle \ˈdȯd-l\ *vb* **daw·dled; daw·dling** **1** : to spend time wastefully : DALLY **2** : to move slowly and without purpose — **daw·dler** \ˈdȯd-lər\ *n*

¹dawn \ˈdȯn\ *vb* **1** : to begin to grow light as the sun rises **2** : to start becoming plain or clear ⟨it *dawned* on us that we were lost⟩

²dawn *n* **1** : the time when the sun comes up in the morning **2** : a first appearance : BEGINNING

day \ˈdā\ *n* **1** : the time between sunrise and sunset : DAYLIGHT **2** : the time the earth takes to make one turn on its axis **3** : a period of twenty-four hours beginning at midnight **4** : a specified day or date ⟨election *day*⟩ **5** : a specified period : AGE ⟨in your grandparent's *day*⟩ **6** : the time set apart by custom or law for work

day·bed \ˈdā-ˌbed\ *n* : a couch with low head and foot pieces

day·break \ˈdā-ˌbrāk\ *n* : ²DAWN 1

¹day·dream \ˈdā-ˌdrēm\ *n* : a happy or pleasant imagining about oneself or one's future

²daydream *vb* : to have a daydream — **day·dream·er** *n*

day·light \ˈdā-ˌlīt\ *n* **1** : the light of day **2** : DAYTIME **3** : ²DAWN 1 ⟨from *daylight* to dark⟩

daylight saving time *n* : time usually one hour ahead of standard time

day·time \ˈdā-ˌtīm\ *n* : the period of daylight

¹daze \ˈdāz\ *vb* **dazed; daz·ing** : to stun especially by a blow

²daze *n* : a dazed state

daz·zle \ˈdaz-əl\ *vb* **daz·zled; daz·zling** **1** : to confuse or be confused by too much light or by moving lights **2** : to confuse, surprise, or delight by being or doing something special and unusual — **daz·zler** \ˈdaz-lər\ *n* — **daz·zling·ly** \ˈdaz-ling-lē\ *adv*

DDT \ˌdē-ˌdē-ˈtē\ *n* : a chemical formerly used as an insecticide but found to damage the environment

de- *prefix* **1** : do the opposite of ⟨decode⟩ **2** : reverse of **3** : remove or remove from a specified thing ⟨deforest⟩ **4** : reduce **5** : get off of

dea·con \ˈdē-kən\ *n* **1** : an official in some Christian churches ranking just below a priest **2** : a church member who has special duties (as helping a minister)

¹dead \ˈded\ *adj* **1** : no longer living : LIFELESS **2** : having the look of death ⟨a *dead* faint⟩ **3** : ¹NUMB 1 **4** : very tired **5** : never having lived : INANIMATE ⟨dead matter⟩ **6** : lacking motion, activity, energy, or power to function ⟨a *dead* battery⟩ **7** : no longer in use : OBSOLETE ⟨dead languages⟩ **8** : lacking warmth, vigor, or liveliness ⟨a *dead* fire⟩ **9** : ACCURATE, PRECISE ⟨a *dead* shot⟩ **10** : being sudden and complete ⟨a *dead* stop⟩ **11** : ¹COMPLETE 1, TOTAL ⟨dead silence⟩

²dead *n, pl* **dead** **1** *dead pl* : those that are dead ⟨the living and the *dead*⟩ **2** : the time of greatest quiet ⟨the *dead* of night⟩

³dead *adv* **1** : in a whole or complete manner ⟨dead right⟩ **2** : suddenly and completely ⟨stopped *dead*⟩ **3** : ²STRAIGHT ⟨dead ahead⟩

dead·en \ˈded-n\ *vb* : to take away some of the force of : make less ⟨deaden pain⟩

dead end *n* : an end (as of a street) with no way out

dead heat *n* : a contest that ends in a tie

dead letter *n* : a letter that cannot be delivered by the post office or returned to the sender

dead·line \ˈded-ˌlīn\ *n* : a date or time by which something must be done

¹dead·lock \ˈded-ˌläk\ *n* : a stopping of action because both sides in a struggle are equally strong and neither will give in

²deadlock *vb* : to bring or come to a deadlock

¹dead·ly \ˈded-lē\ *adj* **dead·li·er; dead·li·est** **1** : causing or capable of causing death ⟨deadly weapons⟩ **2** : meaning or hoping to kill or destroy ⟨deadly enemies⟩ **3** : very accurate ⟨deadly aim⟩ **4** : causing spiritual death **5** : suggestive of death **6** : ¹EXTREME 1 ⟨*deadly* serious-ness⟩ — **dead·li·ness** *n*

synonyms DEADLY, MORTAL, and FATAL mean causing or capable of causing death. DEADLY is used of something that is certain or very likely to cause death ⟨a *deadly* poison⟩ MORTAL is used of something that already has caused death or is about to cause death ⟨received a *mortal* wound in battle⟩ FATAL stresses the certainty of death, even though there may be a period of time coming between the time death is caused (as by injury) and the time of death itself ⟨the wounds proved to be *fatal*, and death occurred three days later⟩

²**deadly** *adv* **1** : in a way suggestive of death ⟨*deadly* pale⟩ **2** : to an extreme degree ⟨*deadly* dull⟩

deaf \'def\ *adj* **1** : wholly or partly unable to hear **2** : unwilling to hear or listen — **deaf·ness** *n*

deaf·en \'def-ən\ *vb* **1** : to make deaf **2** : to stun with noise

deaf–mute \'def-ˌmyüt\ *n* : a person who can neither hear nor speak

¹**deal** \'dēl\ *n* **1** : an indefinite amount ⟨means a great *deal*⟩ **2** : one's turn to deal the cards in a card game

²**deal** *vb* **dealt** \'delt\; **deal·ing** \'dē-ling\ **1** : to give out one or a few at a time **2** : ¹GIVE 5, ADMINISTER ⟨*dealt* the dog a blow⟩ **3** : to have to do ⟨a book that *deals* with airplanes⟩ **4** : to take action ⟨*deal* harshly with lawbreakers⟩ **5** : to buy and sell regularly : TRADE — **deal·er** \'dē-lər\ *n*

³**deal** *n* **1** : an agreement to do business **2** : treatment received ⟨got a bad *deal*⟩ **3** : a secret agreement **4** : ¹BARGAIN 2

deal·ing \'dē-ling\ *n* **1** : ³DEAL 1 **2** : a way of acting or doing business ⟨fair *dealing*⟩

dean \'dēn\ *n* **1** : a church official in charge of a cathedral **2** : the head of a section (as a college) of a university ⟨the *dean* of medicine⟩ **3** : an official in charge of students or studies in a school or college ⟨the *dean* of women⟩ — **dean·ship** \-ˌship\ *n*

¹**dear** \'diər\ *adj* **1** : greatly loved or cared about ⟨liberty is *dear* to our hearts⟩ **2** — used as form of address especially in letters ⟨*Dear* Sir⟩ **3** : high-priced **4** : deeply felt : EARNEST ⟨my *dearest* wish⟩ — **dear·ly** *adv* — **dear·ness** *n*

²**dear** *adv* : at a high price ⟨buy cheap and sell *dear*⟩

³**dear** *n* : a loved one : DARLING

dearth \'dərth\ *n* : SCARCITY, LACK

death \'deth\ *n* **1** : the end or ending of life

⟨sudden *death*⟩ **2** : the cause of loss of life **3** : the state of being dead **4** : DESTRUCTION 2 ⟨the *death* of all hope⟩ — **death·less** \-ləs\ *adj* — **death·like** \-ˌlīk\ *adj*

death·bed \'deth-ˌbed\ *n* **1** : the bed a person dies in **2** : the last hours of life

death·blow \'deth-ˌblō\ *n* : a fatal or crushing blow or event

¹**death·ly** \'deth-lē\ *adj* : of, relating to, or suggesting death ⟨a *deathly* silence⟩

²**deathly** *adv* : in a way suggesting death ⟨*deathly* pale⟩

de·bar \di-'bär\ *vb* **de·barred; de·bar·ring** : to keep from having or doing something

de·base \di-'bās\ *vb* **de·based; de·bas·ing** : to make less good or valuable than before — **de·base·ment** \-mənt\ *n*

de·bat·able \di-'bāt-ə-bəl\ *adj* : possible to question or argue about

¹**de·bate** \di-'bāt\ *n* **1** : a discussion or argument carried on between two teams **2** : DISCUSSION

²**debate** *vb* **de·bat·ed; de·bat·ing** **1** : to discuss a question by giving arguments on both sides : take part in a debate **2** : to consider reasons for and against **synonyms** see DISCUSS — **de·bat·er** *n*

de·bil·i·tate \di-'bil-ə-ˌtāt\ *vb* **de·bil·i·tat·ed; de·bil·i·tat·ing** : to make feeble : WEAKEN

de·bil·i·ty \di-'bil-ət-ē\ *n, pl* **de·bil·i·ties** : a weakened state especially of health

¹**deb·it** \'deb-ət\ *n* : a business record showing money paid out or owed

²**debit** *vb* : to record as a debit

deb·o·nair \ˌdeb-ə-'naər, -'neər\ *adj* : gaily and gracefully charming ⟨a *debonair* manner⟩ — **deb·o·nair·ly** *adv* — **deb·o·nair·ness** *n*

de·bris \də-'brē\ *n, pl* **de·bris** \-'brēz\ : the junk or pieces left from something broken down or destroyed

debt \'det\ *n* **1** : ¹SIN **2** : something owed to another **3** : the condition of owing money

debt·or \'det-ər\ *n* : a person who owes a debt

de·but \'dā-ˌbyü, dā-'byü\ *n* **1** : a first public appearance ⟨a singer's *debut*⟩ **2** : the formal entrance of a young woman into society

deb·u·tante \'deb-yu̇-ˌtänt\ *n* : a young woman making her debut

deca- *or* **dec-** *or* **deka-** *or* **dek-** *prefix* : ten ⟨*deca*gon⟩

\ə\ abut	\aú\ out	\i\ tip	\ò\ saw	\ú\ foot
\ər\ further	\ch\ chin	\ī\ life	\òi\ coin	\y\ yet
\a\ mat	\e\ pet	\j\ job	\th\ thin	\yü\ few
\ā\ take	\ē\ easy	\ng\ sing	\th\ this	\yú\ cure
\ä\ cot, cart	\g\ go	\ō\ bone	\ü\ food	\zh\ vision

de·cade \'dek-,ād, de-'kād\ *n* : a period of ten years

deca·gon \'dek-ə-,gän\ *n* : a closed figure having ten angles and ten sides

de·cal \'dē-,kal\ *n* : a design made to be transferred (as to glass) from specially prepared paper

deca·logue \'dek-ə-,lòg\ *n*, *often cap* : the ten commandments of God given to Moses on Mount Sinai

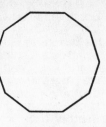

decagon

de·camp \di-'kamp\ *vb* : to go away suddenly and usually secretly : run away

de·cant·er \di-'kant-ər\ *n* : an ornamental glass bottle used especially for serving wine

de·cap·i·tate \di-'kap-ə-,tāt\ *vb* **de·cap·i·tat·ed**; **de·cap·i·tat·ing** : to cut off the head of : BEHEAD

¹de·cay \di-'kā\ *vb* : to weaken in health or soundness (as by aging or rotting)

²decay *n* **1** : the state of something that is decayed or decaying : a spoiled or rotting condition **2** : a gradual getting worse or failing ⟨the *decay* of civilization⟩ **3** : a natural change of a radioactive element into another form of the same element or into a different element

¹de·cease \di-'sēs\ *n* : DEATH 1

²decease *vb* **de·ceased**; **de·ceas·ing** : ¹DIE 1

de·ce·dent \di-'sēd-nt\ *n* : a dead person

de·ceit \di-'sēt\ *n* **1** : the act or practice of deceiving : DECEPTION **2** : a statement or act that misleads a person or causes him or her to believe what is false : TRICK

de·ceit·ful \di-'sēt-fəl\ *adj* : full of deceit : not honest — **de·ceit·ful·ly** \-fə-lē\ *adv* — **de·ceit·ful·ness** *n*

de·ceive \di-'sēv\ *vb* **de·ceived**; **de·ceiv·ing** **1** : to cause to believe what is not true : MISLEAD **2** : to be dishonest and misleading — **de·ceiv·er** *n*

de·cel·er·ate \dē-'sel-ə-,rāt\ *vb* **de·cel·er·at·ed**; **de·cel·er·at·ing** : to slow down

De·cem·ber \di-'sem-bər\ *n* : the twelfth month of the year

Word History The first Roman calendar started the year with the month of March. The tenth month was December. The Latin name for this month came from the Latin word that meant "ten." The English name *December* came from the Latin name for the tenth month in the Roman calendar.

de·cen·cy \'dēs-n-sē\ *n*, *pl* **de·cen·cies** **1** : a being decent : modest or proper behavior **2** : something that is right and proper

de·cent \'dēs-nt\ *adj* **1** : meeting an accepted standard of good taste (as in speech, dress, or behavior) **2** : being moral and good : not dirty ⟨*decent* literature⟩ **3** : fairly good ⟨a *decent* salary⟩ — **de·cent·ly** *adv*

de·cep·tion \di-'sep-shən\ *n* **1** : the act of deceiving **2** : ¹TRICK 1

de·cep·tive \di-'sep-tiv\ *adj* : tending or able to deceive — **de·cep·tive·ly** *adv*

deci- *prefix* : tenth part ⟨*deci*meter⟩

deci·bel \'des-ə-,bel, -bəl\ *n* : a unit for measuring the relative loudness of sounds

de·cide \di-'sīd\ *vb* **de·cid·ed**; **de·cid·ing** **1** : to make a judgment on ⟨the judge *decided* the case⟩ **2** : to bring to an end ⟨one blow *decided* the fight⟩ **3** : to make or cause to make a choice

de·cid·ed \di-'sīd-əd\ *adj* **1** : UNMISTAKABLE ⟨had a *decided* advantage⟩ **2** : free from doubt ⟨a *decided* manner⟩ — **de·cid·ed·ly** *adv*

de·cid·u·ous \di-'sij-ə-wəs\ *adj* : made up of or having a part that falls off at the end of a period of growth and use ⟨*deciduous* trees⟩

¹dec·i·mal \'des-ə-məl, 'des-məl\ *adj* **1** : based on the number 10 : numbered or counting by tens **2** : expressed in or including a decimal

²decimal *n* : a proper fraction in which the denominator is 10 or 10 multiplied one or more times by itself and is indicated by a point (**decimal point**) placed at the left of the numerator ⟨the *decimal* .2=²⁄₁₀, the *decimal* .25=25/100, the *decimal* .025=25/1000⟩

dec·i·me·ter \'des-ə-,mēt-ər\ *n* : a unit of length equal to one tenth meter

de·ci·pher \dē-'sī-fər\ *vb* **1** : to translate from secret writing : DECODE **2** : to make out the meaning of something not clear ⟨*decipher* a blurred postmark⟩

de·ci·sion \di-'sizh-ən\ *n* **1** : the act or result of deciding **2** : promptness and firmness in deciding

de·ci·sive \di-'sī-siv\ *adj* **1** : deciding or able to decide a question or dispute ⟨*decisive* proof⟩ **2** : RESOLUTE ⟨*decisive* minds⟩ **3** : ¹CLEAR 7, UNMISTAKABLE ⟨a *decisive* victory⟩ — **de·ci·sive·ly** *adv* — **de·ci·sive·ness** *n*

¹deck \'dek\ *n* **1** : a floor that goes from one side of a ship to the other **2** : something like the deck of a ship **3** : a pack of playing cards

²deck *vb* : to dress or decorate especially in a showy way

dec·la·ra·tion \,dek-lə-'rā-shən\ *n* **1** : an act of declaring **2** : something declared or a document containing such a declaration ⟨the *Declaration* of Independence⟩

de·clar·a·tive \di-'klar-ət-iv, -'kler-\ *adj* : making a statement ⟨a *declarative* sentence⟩

de·clare \di-'klaər, -'kleər\ *vb* **de·clared; de·clar·ing 1** : to make known in a clear or formal way ⟨*declare* war⟩ **2** : to state as if certain

synonyms DECLARE, ANNOUNCE, and AD-VERTISE mean to make known to the public. DECLARE suggests that something is said very clearly and often in a formal manner ⟨the governor *declared* that all must pay the tax⟩ ANNOUNCE suggests that something of interest is declared for the first time ⟨*announced* the discovery of a new planet⟩ ADVERTISE suggests repeating a statement over and over and all around ⟨they *advertised* all over the neighborhood that they were getting a pony⟩

¹de·cline \di-'klīn\ *vb* **de·clined; de·clin·ing 1** : to bend or slope downward **2** : to pass toward a lower, worse, or weaker state ⟨prices *declined*⟩ ⟨*decline* in health⟩ **3** : to refuse to accept, do, or agree ⟨*decline* an invitation⟩ ⟨*decline* to leave⟩

²decline *n* **1** : a gradual weakening in body or mind **2** : a change to a lower state or level ⟨a business *decline*⟩ **3** : the time when something is nearing its end

de·code \dē-'kōd\ *vb* **de·cod·ed; de·cod·ing** : to change a message in code into ordinary language

de·com·pose \,dē-kəm-'pōz\ *vb* **de·com·posed; de·com·pos·ing 1** : to separate a thing into its parts or into simpler compounds **2** : to break down in decaying — **de·com·pos·er** *n*

de·com·po·si·tion \,dē-,käm-pə-'zish-ən\ *n* **1** : the process of decomposing **2** : the state of being decomposed

dec·o·rate \'dek-ə-,rāt\ *vb* **dec·o·rat·ed; dec·o·rat·ing 1** : to make more attractive by adding something nice looking ⟨*decorate* one's room⟩ **2** : to award a decoration of honor to ⟨*decorate* a soldier for bravery⟩

dec·o·ra·tion \,dek-ə-'rā-shən\ *n* **1** : the act of decorating **2** : ¹ORNAMENT 1 **3** : a badge of honor

dec·o·ra·tive \'dek-ə-rət-iv, 'dek-rət-\ *adj* : serving to decorate : ORNAMENTAL

dec·o·ra·tor \'dek-ə-,rāt-ər\ *n* : a person who decorates especially the rooms of houses

de·co·rum \di-'kōr-əm\ *n* : proper behavior

¹de·coy \di-'kȯi, 'dē-,kȯi\ *n* : a person or thing (as an artificial bird) used to lead or lure into a trap or snare

²decoy *vb* : to lure by or as if by a decoy

¹de·crease \di-'krēs\ *vb* **de·creased; de·creas·ing** : to grow less or cause to grow less

²de·crease \'dē-,krēs\ *n* **1** : the process of decreasing **2** : REDUCTION 2

¹de·cree \di-'krē\ *n* : an order or decision given by a person or group in authority

²decree *vb* **de·creed; de·cree·ing** : to order by a decree

de·crep·it \di-'krep-ət\ *adj* : worn out or weakened by age or use

de·cre·scen·do \,dā-krə-'shen-dō\ *n* : a gradual decrease in the loudness of music

ded·i·cate \'ded-i-,kāt\ *vb* **ded·i·cat·ed; ded·i·cat·ing 1** : to set apart for some purpose and especially for a sacred or serious purpose : DEVOTE **2** : to address or write something in (as a book) as a compliment to someone

ded·i·ca·tion \,ded-i-'kā-shən\ *n* **1** : an act of dedicating **2** : something written in dedicating a book **3** : devotion to the point of giving up what one needs or loves

de·duct \di-'dəkt\ *vb* : to take away an amount of something : SUBTRACT

de·duc·tion \di-'dək-shən\ *n* **1** : SUBTRAC-TION **2** : an amount deducted

¹deed \'dēd\ *n* **1** : a usually fine or brave act or action : FEAT **2** : a legal document containing the record of an agreement or especially of a transfer of real estate

²deed *vb* : to transfer by a deed

deem \'dēm\ *vb* : to hold as an opinion ⟨*deem* it wise to wait⟩

¹deep \'dēp\ *adj* **1** : reaching down far below the surface ⟨*deep* roots⟩ ⟨*deep* snow⟩ **2** : reaching far back from the front or outer part ⟨a *deep* forest⟩ **3** : hard to understand ⟨a *deep* book⟩ **4** : located well below the surface or well within the boundaries of ⟨*deep* in the ground⟩ **5** : fully developed : PROFOUND ⟨a *deep* sleep⟩ ⟨took *deep* pleasure in the gift⟩ **6** : dark and rich in color ⟨a *deep* red⟩ **7** : low in tone ⟨a *deep* voice⟩ **8** : completely busy ⟨*deep* in study⟩ — **deep·ly** *adv*

\ə\ **abut**	\au̇\ **out**	\i\ **tip**	\ȯ\ **saw**	\u̇\ **foot**
\ər\ **further**	\ch\ **chin**	\ī\ **life**	\ȯi\ **coin**	\y\ **yet**
\a\ **mat**	\e\ **pet**	\j\ **job**	\th\ **thin**	\yü\ **few**
\ā\ **take**	\ē\ **easy**	\ng\ **sing**	\th\ **this**	\yu̇\ **cure**
\ä\ **cot, cart**	\g\ **go**	\ō\ **bone**	\ü\ **food**	\zh\ **vision**

²**deep** *adv* : to a great depth : DEEPLY ⟨drink *deep*⟩

³**deep** *n* **1** : a very deep place or part ⟨the ocean *deeps*⟩ **2** : OCEAN 1 ⟨the briny *deep*⟩

deep·en \'dē-pən\ *vb* : to make or become deep or deeper

deer \'diər\ *n, pl* **deer** : any of a group of mammals that chew the cud and have cloven hoofs and in the male antlers which are often branched

deer·skin \'diər-ˌskin\ *n* : leather made from the skin of a deer or a garment made of such leather

de·face \di-'fās\ *vb* **de·faced; de·fac·ing** : to destroy or mar the face or surface of — **de·face·ment** \-mənt\ *n* — **de·fac·er** *n*

¹**de·fault** \di-'fȯlt\ *n* : failure to do something required by law or duty

²**default** *vb* : to fail to do one's duty — **de·fault·er** *n*

¹**de·feat** \di-'fēt\ *vb* **1** : to bring to nothing ⟨*defeat* a hope⟩ **2** : to win victory over

²**defeat** *n* : loss of a contest or battle

de·fect \'dē-ˌfekt, di-'fekt\ *n* : a lack of something necessary for completeness or perfection

de·fec·tive \di-'fek-tiv\ *adj* : lacking something necessary : FAULTY ⟨a *defective* plan⟩

de·fend \di-'fend\ *vb* **1** : to protect from danger or attack **2** : to act or speak in favor of when others are opposed — **de·fend·er** *n*

synonyms DEFEND, PROTECT, and SAFEGUARD mean to keep secure. DEFEND suggests that danger or attack is actual or threatening ⟨*defended* the fort against enemy troops⟩ PROTECT stresses the use of some kind of shield to prevent possible attack or injury ⟨*protect* your eyes with dark glasses⟩ SAFEGUARD suggests the taking of a course of action to protect against merely possible danger ⟨public health rules that *safeguard* the city from epidemics⟩

de·fense *or* **de·fence** \di-'fens\ *n* **1** : the act of defending **2** : something that defends or protects **3** : a defensive team — **de·fense·less** \-ləs\ *adj*

¹**de·fen·sive** \di-'fen-siv\ *adj* **1** : serving or meant to defend or protect **2** : of or relating to the attempt to keep an opponent from scoring (as in a game) — **de·fen·sive·ly** *adv*

²**defensive** *n* : a defensive position or attitude

¹**de·fer** \di-'fər\ *vb* **de·ferred; de·fer·ring** : to put off to a future time — **de·fer·ment** \mənt\ *n*

²**defer** *vb* **de·ferred; de·fer·ring** : to yield to the opinion or wishes of another

def·er·ence \'def-ə-rəns, 'def-rəns\ *n* : respect and consideration for the wishes of another

de·fi·ance \di-'fi-əns\ *n* **1** : an act of defying **2** : a willingness to resist

de·fi·ant \di-'fi-ənt\ *adj* : showing defiance — **de·fi·ant·ly** *adv*

de·fi·cien·cy \di-'fish-ən-sē\ *n, pl* **de·fi·cien·cies** : the state of being without something necessary and especially something required for health

de·fi·cient \di-'fish-ənt\ *adj* : lacking something necessary for completeness or health

def·i·cit \'def-ə-sət\ *n* : a shortage especially in money needed

de·file \di-'fīl\ *vb* **de·filed; de·fil·ing** **1** : to make filthy **2** : ¹CORRUPT 1 **3** : ²DISHONOR — **de·file·ment** \-mənt\ *n*

de·fine \di-'fīn\ *vb* **de·fined; de·fin·ing** **1** : to set or mark the limits of **2** : to make distinct in outline **3** : to find out and explain the meaning of ⟨*define* a word⟩ — **de·fin·er** *n*

def·i·nite \'def-ə-nət\ *adj* **1** : having certain or distinct limits ⟨a *definite* period of time⟩ **2** : clear in meaning ⟨a *definite* answer⟩ **3** : UNQUESTIONABLE ⟨a *definite* improvement⟩ — **def·i·nite·ly** *adv* — **def·i·nite·ness** *n*

definite article *n* : the article *the* used to show that the following noun refers to one or more specific persons or things

def·i·ni·tion \ˌdef-ə-'nish-ən\ *n* **1** : an act of defining **2** : a statement of the meaning of a word or a word group **3** : clearness of outline or detail

de·flate \di-'flāt\ *vb* **de·flated; de·flat·ing** **1** : to let the air or gas out of something that has been blown up **2** : to reduce in size or importance

de·flect \di-'flekt\ *vb* : to turn aside

de·for·est \dē-'fȯr-əst\ *vb* : to clear of forests

de·form \di-'fȯrm\ *vb* : to spoil the form or the natural appearance of

de·for·mi·ty \di-'fȯr-mət-ē\ *n, pl* **de·for·mi·ties** **1** : the condition of being deformed **2** : a flaw or blemish in something and especially in the body of a person or animal

de·fraud \di-'frȯd\ *vb* : to take or keep something from by deceit : CHEAT

de·frost \di-'frȯst\ *vb* **1** : to thaw out **2** : to remove ice from — **de·frost·er** *n*

deft \'deft\ *adj* : quick and neat in action : SKILLFUL — **deft·ly** *adv* — **deft·ness** *n*

de·fy \di-'fī\ *vb* **de·fied; de·fy·ing** **1** : to

challenge to do something thought to be impossible : DARE **2** : to refuse boldly to obey or yield to **3** : to resist the effects of or attempts at ⟨beauty that *defies* age⟩

deg·ra·da·tion \,deg-rə-'dā-shən\ *n* **1** : an act of degrading **2** : the state of being degraded

de·grade \di-'grād\ *vb* **de·grad·ed; de·grad·ing 1** : to reduce from a higher to a lower rank or degree **2** : to bring to a low state : DEBASE, CORRUPT

de·gree \di-'grē\ *n* **1** : a step in a series ⟨advanced by *degrees*⟩ **2** : amount of something as measured by a series of steps ⟨a high *degree* of progress⟩ **3** : one of the three forms an adjective or adverb may have when it is compared **4** : a title given (as to students) by a college or university ⟨a *degree* of doctor of medicine⟩ **5** : one of the divisions marked on a measuring instrument (as a thermometer) **6** : a 360th part of the circumference of a circle **7** : a line or space of the staff in music or the difference in pitch between two notes

de·hu·mid·i·fy \,dē-hyü-'mid-ə-,fī\ *vb* **de·hu·mid·i·fied; de·hu·mid·i·fy·ing** : to take moisture from (as the air) — **de·hu·mid·i·fi·er** *n*

de·hy·drate \dē-'hī-,drāt\ *vb* **de·hy·drat·ed; de·hy·drat·ing 1** : to take water from (as foods) **2** : to lose water or body fluids

de·ice \dē-'īs\ *vb* **de·iced; de·ic·ing** : to free or keep free of ice ⟨*deice* an airplane⟩ — **de·ic·er** *n*

de·i·fy \'dē-ə-,fī\ *vb* **de·i·fied; de·i·fy·ing** : to make a god of

deign \'dān\ *vb* : CONDESCEND 1

de·i·ty \'dē-ət-ē, 'dā-\ *n, pl* **de·i·ties 1** *cap* : GOD 1 **2** : GOD 2, GODDESS ⟨Roman *de·ities*⟩

de·ject·ed \di-'jek-təd\ *adj* : low in spirits ⟨we were *dejected* at losing the game⟩ — **de·ject·ed·ly** *adv*

de·jec·tion \di-'jek-shən\ *n* : a dejected state

deka- *or* **dek-** — see DECA-

¹de·lay \di-'lā\ *n* **1** : a putting off of something **2** : the time during which something is delayed

²delay *vb* **1** : to put off **2** : to stop or prevent for a time **3** : to move or act slowly

¹del·e·gate \'del-i-gət\ *n* : a person sent with power to act for another or others ⟨was a *delegate* at the convention⟩

²del·e·gate \'del-ə-,gāt\ *vb* **del·e·gat·ed; del·e·gat·ing 1** : to entrust to another ⟨the voters *delegate* power to their congressmen⟩ **2** : to make responsible for getting something done ⟨we were *delegated* to clean up the yard⟩

del·e·ga·tion \,del-ə-'gā-shən\ *n* **1** : the act of delegating **2** : one or more persons chosen to represent others

de·lete \di-'lēt\ *vb* **de·let·ed; de·let·ing** : to take out from something written especially by erasing, crossing out, or cutting

de·le·tion \di-'lē-shən\ *n* **1** : an act of deleting **2** : something deleted

¹de·lib·er·ate \di-'lib-ə-rət, -'lib-rət\ *adj* **1** : showing careful thought ⟨a *deliberate* decision⟩ **2** : done or said on purpose ⟨a *deliberate* lie⟩ **3** : slow in action : not hurried **synonyms** see VOLUNTARY — **de·lib·er·ate·ly** *adv* — **de·lib·er·ate·ness** *n*

²de·lib·er·ate \di-'lib-ə-,rāt\ *vb* **de·lib·er·at·ed; de·lib·er·at·ing** : to think about carefully

de·lib·er·a·tion \di-,lib-ə-'rā-shən\ *n* **1** : careful thought : CONSIDERATION **2** : a being deliberate

del·i·ca·cy \'del-i-kə-sē\ *n, pl* **del·i·ca·cies 1** : something pleasing to eat that is rare or a luxury **2** : fineness of structure ⟨lace of great *delicacy*⟩ **3** : weakness of body : FRAILTY **4** : a situation needing careful handling **5** : consideration for the feelings of others

del·i·cate \'del-i-kət\ *adj* **1** : pleasing because of fineness or mildness ⟨a *delicate* flavor⟩ ⟨*delicate* blossoms⟩ **2** : able to sense very small differences ⟨a *delicate* instrument⟩ **3** : calling for skill and careful treatment ⟨a *delicate* operation⟩ **4** : easily damaged **5** : SICKLY 1 ⟨a *delicate* child⟩ **6** : requiring tact — **del·i·cate·ly** *adv*

del·i·ca·tes·sen \,del-i-kə-'tes-n\ *n* : a store where prepared foods (as salads and cooked meats) are sold

de·li·cious \di-'lish-əs\ *adj* : giving great pleasure especially to the taste or smell — **de·li·cious·ly** *adv* — **de·li·cious·ness** *n*

¹de·light \di-'līt\ *n* **1** : great pleasure or satisfaction : JOY **2** : something that gives great pleasure

²delight *vb* **1** : to take great pleasure **2** : to give joy or satisfaction to

de·light·ed \di-'līt-əd\ *adj* : very pleased

de·light·ful \di-'līt-fəl\ *adj* : giving delight : very pleasing — **de·light·ful·ly** \-fə-lē\ *adv*

de·lir·i·ous \di-'lir-ē-əs\ *adj* **1** : suffering delirium **2** : wildly excited — **de·lir·i·ous·ly** *adv*

de·lir·i·um \di-'lir-ē-əm\ *n* **1** : a condition of

\ə\ **abut**	\aů\ **out**	\i\ **tip**	\ȯ\ **saw**	\ů\ **foot**
\ər\ **further**	\ch\ **chin**	\ī\ **life**	\ȯi\ **coin**	\y\ **yet**
\a\ **mat**	\e\ **pet**	\j\ **job**	\th\ **thin**	\yü\ **few**
\ā\ **take**	\ē\ **easy**	\ng\ **sing**	\<u>th</u>\ **this**	\yů\ **cure**
\ä\ **cot, cart**	\g\ **go**	\ō\ **bone**	\ü\ **food**	\zh\ **vision**

mind in which thought and speech are confused and which often goes along with a high fever **2** : wild excitement

de·liv·er \di-'liv-ər\ *vb* **1** : to set free : RESCUE ⟨*deliver* us from evil⟩ **2** : ¹TRANSFER 2 ⟨*deliver* a letter⟩ ⟨this store *delivers*⟩ **3** : to help in childbirth **4** : ²UTTER 2 ⟨*deliver* a speech⟩ **5** : to send to an intended target — **de·liv·er·er** *n*

de·liv·er·ance \di-'liv-ə-rəns, -'liv-rəns\ *n* : an act of delivering or the state of being delivered : a setting free

de·liv·ery \di-'liv-ə-rē, -'liv-rē\ *n, pl* **de·liv·er·ies** **1** : a setting free (as from something that hampers or holds one back) **2** : the transfer of something from one place or person to another **3** : the act of giving birth **4** : speaking or manner of speaking (as of a formal speech) **5** : the act or way of throwing ⟨an underhand *delivery*⟩

dell \'del\ *n* : a small valley usually covered with trees

del·phin·i·um \del-'fin-ē-əm\ *n* : a tall plant related to the buttercups and often grown for its large stalks of showy flowers

del·ta \'del-tə\ *n* : a piece of land in the shape of a triangle or fan made by deposits of mud and sand at the mouth of a river

de·lude \di-'lüd\ *vb* **de·lud·ed; de·lud·ing** : DECEIVE, MISLEAD

¹del·uge \'del-yüj\ *n* **1** : a flooding of land by water : FLOOD **2** : a drenching rain **3** : a sudden huge stream of something ⟨a *deluge* of mail⟩

²deluge *vb* **del·uged; del·ug·ing** **1** : ²FLOOD 1 **2** : to overwhelm as if with a deluge

delphinium

de·lu·sion \di-'lü-zhən\ *n* **1** : an act of deluding or the state of being deluded **2** : a false belief that continues in spite of the facts

de·luxe \di-'lùks, -'ləks\ *adj* : very fine or luxurious

delve \'delv\ *vb* **delved; delv·ing** **1** : DIG **2** : to work hard looking for information in written records — **delv·er** *n*

¹de·mand \di-'mand\ *n* **1** : an act of demanding ⟨payable on *demand*⟩ **2** : an expressed desire to own or use something ⟨the *demand* for new cars⟩ **3** : a seeking or being sought after ⟨good teachers are in great *demand*⟩

²demand *vb* **1** : to claim as one's right ⟨*demand* an apology⟩ **2** : to ask earnestly or in the manner of a command ⟨the sentry *demanded* the password⟩ **3** : to call for : REQUIRE ⟨the situation *demands* attention⟩ — **de·mand·er** *n*

de·mean \di-'mēn\ *vb* **de·meaned; de·mean·ing** : to behave or conduct (oneself) usually in a proper way

de·mean·or \di-'mē-nər\ *n* : outward manner or behavior

de·ment·ed \di-'ment-əd\ *adj* : INSANE 1, MAD — **de·ment·ed·ly** *adv*

de·mer·it \dē-'mer-ət\ *n* : a mark placed against a person's record for doing something wrong

demi- *prefix* **1** : half **2** : one that partly belongs to a specified type or class ⟨*demi*god⟩

demi·god \'dem-ē-,gäd\ *n* : one who is partly divine and partly human

de·mo·bi·lize \di-'mō-bə-,līz\ *vb* **de·mo·bi·lized; de·mo·bi·liz·ing** : to let go from military service ⟨*demobilized* soldiers⟩

de·moc·ra·cy \di-'mäk-rə-sē\ *n, pl* **de·moc·ra·cies** **1** : government by the people : majority rule **2** : government in which the highest power is held by the people and is usually used through representatives **3** : a political unit (as a nation) governed by the people **4** : belief in or practice of the idea that all people are socially equal

dem·o·crat \'dem-ə-,krat\ *n* : one who believes in or practices democracy

dem·o·crat·ic \,dem-ə-'krat-ik\ *adj* **1** : of, relating to, or favoring political democracy **2** : believing in or practicing the idea that people are socially equal — **dem·o·crat·i·cal·ly** \-i-kə-lē\ *adv*

de·mol·ish \di-'mäl-ish\ *vb* **1** : to destroy by breaking apart ⟨*demolish* a building⟩ **2** : to ruin completely : SHATTER

de·mon \'dē-mən\ *n* **1** : an evil spirit : DEVIL **2** : a person of great energy or skill

dem·on·strate \'dem-ən-,strāt\ *vb* **dem·on·strat·ed; dem·on·strat·ing** **1** : to show clearly **2** : to prove or make clear by reasoning **3** : to explain (as in teaching) by use of examples or experiments **4** : to show to people the good qualities of an article or a product ⟨*demonstrate* a new car⟩ **5** : to make a public display (as of feelings or military force)

dem·on·stra·tion \\,dem-ən-'strā-shən\\ *n*
1 : an outward expression (as a show of feelings) **2** : an act or a means of demonstrating ⟨a cooking *demonstration*⟩ **3** : a showing or using of an article for sale to display its good points **4** : a parade or a gathering to show public feeling

de·mon·stra·tive \\di-'män-strət-iv\\ *adj* **1** : pointing out the one referred to and showing that it differs from others ⟨in "this is my dog" and "that is their dog," "this" and "that" are *demonstrative* pronouns⟩ **2** : showing feeling freely ⟨a very *demonstrative* person⟩

dem·on·stra·tor \\'dem-ən-,strāt-ər\\ *n* **1** : a person who makes or takes part in a demonstration **2** : a manufactured article used for demonstration

de·mor·al·ize \\di-'mȯr-ə-,līz\\ *vb* **de·mor·al·ized; de·mor·al·iz·ing** : to weaken the discipline or spirit of

de·mote \\di-'mōt\\ *vb* **de·mot·ed; de·mot·ing** : to reduce to a lower grade or rank

de·mure \\di-'myu̇r\\ *adj* **1** : MODEST 3 **2** : pretending to be modest : COY — **de·mure·ly** *adv* — **de·mure·ness** *n*

den \\'den\\ *n* **1** : the shelter or resting place of a wild animal **2** : a quiet or private room in a home **3** : a hiding place (as for thieves)

de·na·ture \\dē-'nā-chər\\ *vb* **de·na·tured; de·na·tur·ing** : to make alcohol unfit for humans to drink

den·drite \\'den-,drīt\\ *n* : any of the usually branched fibers that carry nerve impulses toward a nerve cell body

de·ni·al \\di-'nī-əl\\ *n* **1** : a refusal to give or agree to something asked for **2** : a refusal to admit the truth of a statement **3** : a refusal to accept or believe in someone or something **4** : a cutting down or limiting ⟨a *denial* of one's appetite⟩

den·im \\'den-əm\\ *n* **1** : a firm often coarse cotton cloth **2 denims** *pl* : overalls or pants of usually blue denim

Word History The word *denim* came from a French phrase that meant "serge of Nimes." Serge is a kind of sturdy cloth. Nimes is a city in the southern part of France. Making cloth is a big industry there even today. When the English borrowed the French phrase that meant "serge of Nimes" they made it *serge denim.* Later this phrase was shortened to *denim.*

de·nom·i·na·tion \\di-,näm-ə-'nā-shən\\ *n* **1** : a name especially for a class of things **2** : a religious body made up of a number of congregations having the same beliefs

3 : a value in a series of values (as of money)

de·nom·i·na·tor \\di-'näm-ə-,nāt-ər\\ *n* : the part of a fraction that is below the line ⟨5 is the *denominator* of the fraction ⅗⟩

de·note \\di-'nōt\\ *vb* **de·not·ed; de·not·ing** **1** : to serve as a mark or indication of ⟨the hands of a clock *denote* the time⟩ **2** : to have the meaning of : MEAN

de·nounce \\di-'nau̇ns\\ *vb* **de·nounced; de·nounc·ing** **1** : to point out as wrong or evil : CONDEMN **2** : to inform against : ACCUSE — **de·nounce·ment** \\-mənt\\ *n* — **de·nounc·er** *n*

dense \\'dens\\ *adj* **dens·er; dens·est** **1** : having its parts crowded together : THICK ⟨*dense* fog⟩ **2** : STUPID 1 — **dense·ly** *adv* — **dense·ness** *n*

synonyms DENSE, THICK, and COMPACT mean having parts that are gathered tightly together. DENSE is used of something in which the parts are very close together ⟨a *dense* forest⟩ THICK is used of something that has many small parts that form a single mass ⟨a *thick* head of hair⟩ COMPACT is used of something that has a close and firm gathering of parts, especially within a small area ⟨a *compact* town where everything is within walking distance⟩

den·si·ty \\'den-sət-ē\\ *n, pl* **den·si·ties** **1** : the state of being dense **2** : the amount of something in a specified volume or area

¹**dent** \\'dent\\ *n* : a notch or hollow made in a surface by a blow or by pressure

²**dent** *vb* **1** : to make a dent in or on **2** : to become marked by a dent

den·tal \\'dent-l\\ *adj* : of or relating to the teeth or dentistry — **den·tal·ly** *adv*

dental floss *n* : flat thread used for cleaning between teeth

den·ti·frice \\'dent-ə-frəs\\ *n* : a powder, paste, or liquid used in cleaning the teeth

den·tin \\'dent-n\\ *or* **den·tine** \\'den-,tēn\\ *n* : a hard bony material that makes up the main part of a tooth

den·tist \\'dent-əst\\ *n* : a person whose profession is the care, treatment, and repair of the teeth

den·tist·ry \\'dent-ə-strē\\ *n* : the profession or practice of a dentist

den·ture \\'den-chər\\ *n* : a set of false teeth

de·nude \\di-'nüd, -'nyüd\\ *vb* **de·nud·ed;**

\\ə\\ abut	\\au̇\\ out	\\i\\ tip	\\ȯ\\ saw	\\u̇\\ foot
\\ər\\ further	\\ch\\ chin	\\ī\\ life	\\ȯi\\ coin	\\y\\ yet
\\a\\ mat	\\e\\ pet	\\j\\ job	\\th\\ thin	\\yü\\ few
\\ā\\ take	\\ē\\ easy	\\ng\\ sing	\\th\\ this	\\yu̇\\ cure
\\ä\\ cot, cart	\\g\\ go	\\ō\\ bone	\\ü\\ food	\\zh\\ vision

de·nud·ing : to strip of covering : make bare

de·ny \di-'nī\ *vb* **de·nied; de·ny·ing 1** : to declare not to be true ⟨*deny* a report⟩ **2** : to refuse to grant ⟨*deny* a request⟩ **3** : DISOWN, REPUDIATE ⟨*deny* one's religion⟩

de·odor·ant \dē-'ōd-ə-rənt\ *n* : something used to remove or hide unpleasant odors

de·odor·ize \dē-'ōd-ə-,rīz\ *vb* **de·odor·ized; de·odor·iz·ing** : to remove odor and especially a bad smell from

de·part \di-'pärt\ *vb* **1** : to go away or go away from : LEAVE **2** : ¹DIE 1 **3** : to turn aside

de·part·ment \di-'pärt-mənt\ *n* : a special part or division of an organization (as a government or college)

department store *n* : a store having individual departments for different kinds of goods

de·par·ture \di-'pär-chər\ *n* **1** : a going away **2** : a setting out (as on a new course) **3** : a turning away or aside (as from a way of doing things)

de·pend \di-'pend\ *vb* **1** : to rely for support ⟨children *depend* on their parents⟩ **2** : to be determined by or based on some action or condition ⟨success *depends* on hard work⟩ **3** : ²TRUST 1, RELY

de·pend·able \di-'pen-də-bəl\ *adj* : TRUST-WORTHY, RELIABLE — **de·pend·ably** \-blē\ *adv*

de·pen·dence \di-'pen-dəns\ *n* **1** : a condition of being influenced and caused by something else **2** : a state of being dependent on someone or something **3** : ¹TRUST 1, RELIANCE

¹de·pen·dent \di-'pen-dənt\ *adj* **1** : CONTINGENT ⟨our plans are *dependent* on the weather⟩ **2** : relying on someone else for support **3** : requiring something (as a drug) to feel or act normally

²dependent *n* : a person who depends upon another for support

de·pict \di-'pikt\ *vb* **1** : to represent by a picture **2** : to describe in words

de·plete \di-'plēt\ *vb* **de·plet·ed; de·plet·ing** : to reduce in amount by using up

de·plor·able \di-'plōr-ə-bəl\ *adj* **1** : deserving to be deplored : REGRETTABLE **2** : very bad : WRETCHED — **de·plor·ably** \-blē\ *adv*

de·plore \di-'plōr\ *vb* **de·plored; de·plor·ing 1** : to regret strongly **2** : to consider deserving of disapproval

de·port \di-'pōrt\ *vb* **1** : BEHAVE 1, CONDUCT **2** : to force (a person who is not a citizen) to leave a country

de·port·ment \di-'pōrt-mənt\ *n* : BEHAVIOR 1

de·pose \di-'pōz\ *vb* **de·posed; de·pos-** ing : to remove from a high office ⟨*depose* a king⟩

¹de·pos·it \di-'päz-ət\ *vb* **1** : to place for or as if for safekeeping **2** : to put money in a bank **3** : to give as a pledge that a purchase will be made or a service used ⟨*deposit* ten dollars on a new bicycle⟩ **4** : to lay down : PUT **5** : to let fall or sink

²deposit *n* **1** : the state of being deposited ⟨money on *deposit*⟩ **2** : money that is deposited in a bank **3** : something given as a pledge or as part payment ⟨a *deposit* of ten dollars on a new bicycle⟩ **4** : something laid or thrown down **5** : mineral matter built up in nature ⟨a coal *deposit*⟩

de·pos·i·tor \di-'päz-ət-ər\ *n* : a person who makes a deposit especially of money in a bank

de·pot *usually* 'dep-,ō *for 1 & 2,* 'dē-,pō *for 3*\ *n* **1** : a place where military supplies are kept **2** : STOREHOUSE 1 **3** : a railroad or bus station

de·pre·ci·ate \di-'prē-shē-,āt\ *vb* **de·pre·ci·at·ed; de·pre·ci·at·ing 1** : to lower the price or value of **2** : BELITTLE **3** : to lose value

de·press \di-'pres\ *vb* **1** : to press down ⟨*depress* a lever⟩ **2** : to lessen the activity or strength of ⟨bad weather had *depressed* sales⟩ **3** : to lower the spirits of : make sad and dull

de·pres·sant \di-'pres-nt\ *adj or n* : SEDATIVE

de·pres·sion \di-'presh-ən\ *n* **1** : an act of depressing : a state of being depressed **2** : a hollow place or part ⟨a *depression* in a road⟩ **3** : low spirits **4** : a period of low activity in business with much unemployment

de·pri·va·tion \,dep-rə-'vā-shən, ,dē-,prī-\ *n* **1** : an act or instance of depriving **2** : the state of being deprived

de·prive \di-'prīv\ *vb* **de·prived; de·priv·ing** : to take something away from or keep from having or doing something ⟨*deprive* a ruler of power⟩ ⟨the noise *deprived* me of sleep⟩

depth \'depth\ *n* **1** : a deep place in a body of water (as a sea or a lake) **2** : measurement from top to bottom or from front to back ⟨*depth* of a cupboard⟩ **3** : the innermost part of something : MIDDLE, MIDST ⟨in the *depth* of winter⟩ **4** : ABUNDANCE, COMPLETENESS ⟨*depth* of knowledge⟩ **5** : the quality of being deep

depth charge *n* : an explosive for use underwater especially against submarines

dep·u·tize \'dep-yə-,tīz\ *vb* **dep·u·tized; dep·u·tiz·ing** : to appoint as deputy

dep·u·ty \'dep-yət-ē\ *n, pl* **dep·u·ties**

: a person appointed to act for or in place of another

de·rail \di-'rāl\ *vb* : to cause to leave the rails ⟨*derail* a train⟩ — **de·rail·ment** \-mənt\ *n*

de·range \di-'rānj\ *vb* **de·ranged; de·rang·ing** **1** : to put out of order : DIS-ARRANGE **2** : to make insane — **de·range-ment** \-mənt\ *n*

der·by \'dər-bē\ *n, pl* **der·bies** **1** : a horse race for three-year-olds usually held every year **2** : a stiff felt hat with a narrow brim and a rounded top

derby 2

de·ride \di-'rīd\ *vb* **de·rid·ed; de·rid-ing** : to laugh at in scorn : make fun of : RIDICULE

der·i·va·tion \ˌder-ə-'vā-shən\ *n* **1** : the formation of a word from an earlier word or root **2** : ETYMOLOGY **3** : ORIGIN 3, SOURCE **4** : an act or process of deriving

¹de·riv·a·tive \di-'riv-ət-iv\ *adj* : derived from something else — **de·riv·a·tive·ly** *adv*

²derivative *n* **1** : a word formed by deriva-tion **2** : something derived

de·rive \di-'rīv\ *vb* **de·rived; de·riv·ing** **1** : to receive or obtain from a source ⟨*de-rive* new ideas from reading⟩ **2** : to trace the derivation of **3** : to come from a certain source

der·mal \'dər-məl\ *adj* : of or relating to skin

der·mis \'dər-məs\ *n* : the inner sensitive layer of the skin

de·rog·a·to·ry \di-'räg-ə-ˌtōr-ē\ *adj* : intended to hurt the reputation of a per-son or thing ⟨a *de-rogatory* remark⟩

der·rick \'der-ik\ *n* **1** : a machine for mov-ing or lifting heavy weights by means of a long beam fitted with ropes and pul-leys **2** : a framework or tower over an oil well for supporting machinery

derrick 2

Word History Once there was in London a hangman named *Derick*. The people of London called his gallows by his name. *Derick*, or *derrick*, was soon used as a term for any gallows. Later a machine for lifting came to be called *derrick* as well. This was because the machine looked a bit like a gallows.

de·scend \di-'send\ *vb* **1** : to come or go down from a higher place or level to a lower one ⟨*descend* a hill⟩ **2** : to come down in sudden attack ⟨locusts *de-scended* on the crops⟩ **3** : to come down from an earlier time ⟨a custom *descended* from ancient times⟩ **4** : to come down from a source : DERIVE ⟨*descended* from an ancient family⟩ **5** : to be handed down to an heir ⟨the property will *descend* to the children⟩ **6** : to sink in a social or moral scale : STOOP ⟨never thought they would *descend* to cheating⟩

de·scen·dant \di-'sen-dənt\ *n* : one that is descended from a particular ancestor or family

de·scent \di-'sent\ *n* **1** : a coming or going down **2** : one's line of ancestors **3** : a downward slope ⟨a steep *descent*⟩ **4** : a sudden attack

de·scribe \di-'skrīb\ *vb* **de·scribed; de·scrib·ing** **1** : to write or tell about : give an account of ⟨*describe* a football game⟩ **2** : to draw the outline of ⟨*describe* a circle⟩ **synonyms** SEE REPORT — **de·scrib·er** *n*

de·scrip·tion \di-'skrip-shən\ *n* **1** : an ac-count of something especially of a kind that presents a picture to a person who reads or hears it **2** : ¹SORT 1, KIND ⟨people of every *description*⟩

de·scrip·tive \di-'skrip-tiv\ *adj* : serving to describe — **de·scrip·tive·ly** *adv*

des·e·crate \'des-i-ˌkrāt\ *vb* **des·e·crat-ed; des·e·crat·ing** : to treat a sacred place or sacred object shamefully or with great disrespect

de·seg·re·gate \dē-'seg-ri-ˌgāt\ *vb* **de·seg·re·gat·ed; de·seg·re·gat·ing** : to end segregation in : free of any law or practice setting apart members of a certain race

de·seg·re·ga·tion \dē-ˌseg-ri-'gā-shən\ *n* : the act or process or an instance of de-segregating

¹des·ert \'dez-ərt\ *n* : a dry barren region where only a few special kinds of plants can grow without an artificial water supply

\ə\ **abut**	\au̇\ **out**	\i\ **tip**	\ȯ\ **saw**	\u̇\ **foot**	
\ər\ **further**	\ch\ **chin**	\ī\ **life**	\ȯi\ **coin**	\y\ **yet**	
\a\ **mat**	\e\ **pet**	\j\ **job**	\th\ **thin**	\yü\ **few**	
\ā\ **take**	\ē\ **easy**	\ng\ **sing**	\th\ **this**	\yu̇\ **cure**	
\ä\ **cot, cart**	\g\ **go**	\ō\ **bone**	\ü\ **food**	\zh\ **vision**	

²**desert** *adj* : of, relating to, or being a desert

³**de·sert** \di-'zərt\ *n* **1** : worthiness of reward or punishment ⟨rewarded according to their *deserts*⟩ **2** : a just reward or punishment

⁴**de·sert** \di-'zərt\ *vb* **1** : to leave usually without intending to return **2** : to leave a person or a thing that one should stay with **3** : to fail in time of need ⟨my courage *deserted* me⟩ **synonyms** see ABANDON — **de·sert·er** *n*

de·serve \di-'zərv\ *vb* **de·served; de·serv·ing** : to be worthy of : MERIT

synonyms DESERVE, MERIT, and EARN mean to be worthy of something. DESERVE suggests that one should rightly receive something good or bad because of what one has done or what one is ⟨a naughty child *deserves* to be punished⟩ MERIT stresses the fact that someone or something is especially worthy of reward, punishment, or consideration ⟨students who *merit* special praise⟩ EARN suggests that one has spent time and effort and that one actually gets what one deserves ⟨you've *earned* a long vacation⟩

de·serv·ed·ly \di-'zər-vəd-lē, -'zərv-dlē\ *adv* : as one deserves ⟨*deservedly* punished⟩

de·serv·ing \di-'zər-ving\ *adj* : WORTHY

¹**de·sign** \di-'zīn\ *vb* **1** : to think up and plan out in the mind **2** : to set apart for or have as a special purpose : INTEND ⟨purchases *designed* to be used as gifts⟩ **3** : to make a pattern or sketch of — **de·sign·er** *n*

²**design** *n* **1** : ¹PLAN 2, SCHEME **2** : a planned intention ⟨had ambitious *designs* for their children⟩ **3** : a secret purpose : PLOT **4** : a preliminary sketch, model, or plan **5** : an arrangement of parts in a structure or a work of art **6** : a decorative pattern

des·ig·nate \'dez-ig-ˌnāt\ *vb* **des·ig·nat·ed; des·ig·nat·ing** **1** : to mark or point out : INDICATE **2** : to appoint or choose for a special purpose : NAME ⟨*designate* a leader⟩ **3** : to call by a name or title

des·ig·na·tion \ˌdez-ig-'nā-shən\ *n* **1** : an act of designating **2** : a name, sign, or title that identifies something

de·sign·ing \di-'zī-ning\ *adj* : CRAFTY

de·sir·able \di-'zī-rə-bəl\ *adj* **1** : having pleasing qualities : ATTRACTIVE **2** : worth having or seeking — **de·sir·ably** \-blē\ *adv*

¹**de·sire** \di-'zīr\ *vb* **de·sired; de·sir·ing** **1** : to long for : wish for in earnest ⟨*desire*

peace⟩ **2** : to express a wish for : REQUEST

synonyms DESIRE, WISH, and CRAVE mean to want something very much. DESIRE stresses great feeling and actual striving to get what one wants ⟨the immigrants *desired* a better life⟩ WISH may suggest wanting something that one has little or no chance of getting ⟨sat around and *wished* for wealth⟩ CRAVE suggests the force of bodily or mental needs (as hunger or love) ⟨*craving* for food⟩

²**desire** *n* **1** : a strong wish : LONGING **2** : a wish made known : REQUEST **3** : something desired

de·sist \di-'zist, -'sist\ *vb* : to stop something one is doing

desk \'desk\ *n* : a piece of furniture with a flat or sloping surface for use in writing or reading

¹**des·o·late** \'des-ə-lət\ *adj* **1** : ABANDONED ⟨a *desolate* ghost town⟩ **2** : having no comfort or companionship : LONELY **3** : left neglected or in ruins **4** : CHEERLESS, GLOOMY ⟨a *desolate* wasteland⟩

²**des·o·late** \'des-ə-ˌlāt\ *vb* **des·o·lat·ed; des·o·lat·ing** : to make or leave desolate

des·o·la·tion \ˌdes-ə-'lā-shən\ *n* **1** : the state of being desolated : RUIN **2** : sadness resulting from grief or loneliness

¹**de·spair** \di-'spaər, -'speər\ *vb* : to give up or lose all hope or confidence

²**despair** *n* **1** : loss of hope : a feeling of complete hopelessness **2** : a cause of hopelessness

despatch *variant of* DISPATCH

des·per·ate \'des-pə-rət, -prət\ *adj* **1** : being beyond or almost beyond hope : causing despair **2** : reckless because of despair : RASH — **des·per·ate·ly** *adv* — **des·per·ate·ness** *n*

des·per·a·tion \ˌdes-pə-'rā-shən\ *n* : a state of hopeless despair leading to recklessness

de·spi·ca·ble \di-'spik-ə-bəl, 'des-pik-\ *adj* : deserving to be despised — **de·spi·ca·bly** \-blē\ *adv*

de·spise \di-'spīz\ *vb* **de·spised; de·spis·ing** : to consider as beneath one's notice or respect : feel scorn and dislike for

synonyms DESPISE and SCORN mean to consider a person or thing as not worthy of one's notice or interest. DESPISE may be used of feeling ranging from strong dislike to true hatred ⟨I *despise* liars⟩ SCORN is used of a deep and ready feeling of angry disgust for anything that one considers beneath oneself ⟨*scorned* the soldiers who were lazy or cowardly⟩

de·spite \di-'spīt\ *prep* : in spite of

de·spoil \di-'spȯil\ *vb* : to rob of possessions or belongings : PLUNDER — **de·spoil·er** *n*

de·spon·den·cy \di-'spän-dən-sē\ *n* : MELANCHOLY, DEJECTION

de·spon·dent \di-'spän-dənt\ *adj* : feeling quite discouraged or depressed : being in very low spirits — **de·spon·dent·ly** *adv*

des·pot \'des-pət\ *n* : a ruler having absolute power and authority and especially one who rules cruelly

des·sert \di-'zərt\ *n* : a course of sweet food, fruit, or cheese served at the end of a meal

des·ti·na·tion \,des-tə-'nā-shən\ *n* : a place that one starts out for or that something is sent to

des·tine \'des-tən\ *vb* **des·tined; des·tin·ing 1** : to decide in advance on the future condition, use, or action of ⟨soldiers *destined* to lead the attack received extra training⟩ **2** : to set aside for a special purpose ⟨money *destined* for a new car⟩

des·ti·ny \'des-tə-nē\ *n, pl* **des·ti·nies 1** : the fate or lot to which a person or thing is destined **2** : the course of events held to be arranged by a superhuman power

des·ti·tute \'des-tə-,tüt, -,tyüt\ *adj* **1** : lacking something needed or desirable ⟨a room *destitute* of comforts⟩ **2** : very poor

de·stroy \di-'strȯi\ *vb* **1** : to put an end to : do away with **2** : ¹KILL 1

de·stroy·er \di-'strȯi-ər\ *n* **1** : one that destroys **2** : a small fast warship armed with guns, depth charges, torpedoes, and sometimes missiles

de·struc·ti·ble \di-'strək-tə-bəl\ *adj* : possible to destroy

de·struc·tion \di-'strək-shən\ *n* **1** : the act or process of destroying something **2** : the state or fact of being destroyed : RUIN **3** : something that destroys

de·struc·tive \di-'strək-tiv\ *adj* **1** : causing destruction ⟨a *destructive* storm⟩ **2** : not positive or helpful ⟨*destructive* criticism⟩ — **de·struc·tive·ly** *adv* — **de·struc·tive·ness** *n*

de·tach \di-'tach\ *vb* : to separate from something else or from others especially for a certain purpose — **de·tach·able** \-ə-bəl\ *adj*

de·tached \di-'tacht\ *adj* **1** : not joined or connected : SEPARATE **2** : not taking sides or being influenced by others ⟨a *detached* attitude⟩ — **de·tached·ly** \-'tach-əd-lē, -'tach-tlē\ *adv*

de·tach·ment \di-'tach-mənt\ *n* **1** : SEPARATION 1 **2** : a body of troops or ships sent on special duty **3** : a keeping apart : lack of interest in worldly concerns **4** : IMPARTIALITY

¹de·tail \di-'tāl, 'dē-,tāl\ *n* **1** : a dealing with something item by item ⟨go into *detail*⟩ **2** : a small part : ITEM **3** : a soldier or group of soldiers picked for special duty

²detail *vb* **1** : to report in detail : give the details of **2** : to select for some special duty

de·tailed \di-'tāld, 'dē-,tāld\ *adj* : including many details ⟨a *detailed* report⟩

de·tain \di-'tān\ *vb* **1** : to hold or keep in or as if in prison **2** : to stop especially from going on : DELAY ⟨*detained* by an accident⟩ — **de·tain·ment** \-mənt\ *n*

de·tect \di-'tekt\ *vb* : to learn of the existence, presence, or fact of ⟨*detect* an odor of escaping gas⟩

de·tec·tion \di-'tek-shən\ *n* : the act of detecting : the state or fact of being detected : DISCOVERY

¹de·tec·tive \di-'tek-tiv\ *adj* **1** : able to detect or used in detecting something ⟨a *detective* device⟩ **2** : of or relating to detectives or their work

²detective *n* : a person (as a police officer) whose business is solving crimes and catching criminals or gathering information that is not easy to get

de·ten·tion \di-'ten-chən\ *n* **1** : the act of detaining : the state of being detained : CONFINEMENT **2** : a forced delay

de·ter \di-'tər\ *vb* **de·terred; de·ter·ring** : to discourage or prevent from doing something

¹de·ter·gent \di-'tər-jənt\ *adj* : able to clean : used in cleaning

²detergent *n* : a substance that is like soap in its ability to clean

de·te·ri·o·rate \di-'tir-ē-ə-,rāt\ *vb* **de·te·ri·o·rat·ed; de·te·ri·o·rat·ing** : to make or become worse or of less value

de·ter·mi·na·tion \di-,tər-mə-'nā-shən\ *n* **1** : a coming to a decision or the decision reached **2** : a settling or making sure of the position, size, or nature of something **3** : firm or fixed intention

de·ter·mine \di-'tər-mən\ *vb* **de·ter·mined; de·ter·min·ing 1** : to fix exactly and with certainty **2** : to come to a decision **3** : to learn or find out exactly **4** : to be the cause of or reason for

\ə\ abut	\au̇\ out	\i\ tip	\ȯ\ saw	\u̇\ foot	
\ər\ further	\ch\ chin	\ī\ life	\ȯi\ coin	\y\ yet	
\a\ mat	\e\ pet	\j\ job	\th\ thin	\yü\ few	
\ā\ take	\ē\ easy	\ng\ sing	\th\ this	\yu̇\ cure	
\ä\ cot, cart	\g\ go	\ō\ bone	\ü\ food	\zh\ vision	

de·ter·mined \di-'tər-mənd\ *adj* **1** : free from doubt **2** : not weak or uncertain : FIRM ⟨a very *determined* opponent⟩ — **de·ter·mined·ly** *adv*

de·ter·min·er \di-'tər-mə-nər\ *n* : a word belonging to a group of noun modifiers that can occur before descriptive adjectives modifying the same noun ⟨"the" in "the red house" is a *determiner*⟩

de·test \di-'test\ *vb* : to dislike very much

de·test·able \di-'tes-tə-bəl\ *adj* : causing or deserving strong dislike — **de·test·ably** \-blē\ *adv*

de·throne \di-'thrōn\ *vb* **de·throned; de·thron·ing** : to drive from a throne : DEPOSE — **de·throne·ment** \-mənt\ *n*

¹de·tour \'dē-ˌtůr\ *n* : a roundabout way that temporarily replaces part of a regular route

²detour *vb* : to use or follow a detour

de·tract \di-'trakt\ *vb* : to take away (as from value or importance)

det·ri·ment \'de-trə-mənt\ *n* : injury or damage or its cause : HARM

dev·as·tate \'dev-ə-ˌstāt\ *vb* **dev·as·tat·ed; dev·as·tat·ing** : to reduce to ruin : lay waste

dev·as·ta·tion \ˌdev-ə-'stā-shən\ *n* : the action of devastating : the state of being devastated

de·vel·op \di-'vel-əp\ *vb* **1** : to make or become plain little by little : UNFOLD ⟨as the story *develops*⟩ **2** : to apply chemicals to exposed photographic material (as a film) in order to bring out the picture **3** : to bring out the possibilities of : IMPROVE **4** : to make more available or usable ⟨*develop* land⟩ **5** : to gain gradually ⟨*develop* a taste for reading⟩ **6** : to grow toward maturity — **de·vel·op·er** *n*

de·vel·oped \di-'vel-əpt\ *adj* : having many large industries and a complex economic system ⟨*developed* nations⟩

de·vel·op·ment \di-'vel-əp-mənt\ *n* **1** : the act or process of developing : a result of developing **2** : the state of being developed

de·vi·ate \'dē-vē-ˌāt\ *vb* **de·vi·at·ed; de·vi·at·ing** : to turn aside from a course, principle, standard, or topic

de·vice \di-'vīs\ *n* **1** : a scheme to deceive : TRICK **2** : a piece of equipment or mechanism for a special purpose **3** : ²DESIRE 2, WILL ⟨left to our own *devices*⟩

¹dev·il \'dev-əl\ *n* **1** *often cap* : the personal supreme spirit of evil **2** : an evil spirit : DEMON, FIEND **3** : a wicked or cruel person **4** : a reckless or dashing person **5** : a mischievous person **6** : a person to be pitied ⟨poor *devils*⟩

²devil *vb* **dev·iled** *or* **dev·illed; dev·il·ing** *or* **dev·il·ling** **1** : to chop fine and season highly ⟨*deviled* eggs⟩ **2** : ¹TEASE, ANNOY

dev·il·ment \'dev-əl-mənt\ *n* : reckless mischief

de·vise \di-'vīz\ *vb* **de·vised; de·vis·ing** : to think up : PLAN, INVENT — **de·vis·er** *n*

de·void \di-'vȯid\ *adj* : entirely lacking

de·vote \di-'vōt\ *vb* **de·vot·ed; de·vot·ing** **1** : to set apart for a special purpose **2** : to give up to entirely or in part ⟨*devote* oneself to reading⟩

de·vot·ed \di-'vōt-əd\ *adj* **1** : completely loyal ⟨*devoted* supporters and admirers⟩ **2** : AFFECTIONATE, LOVING — **de·vot·ed·ly** *adv*

de·vo·tion \di-'vō-shən\ *n* **1** : a religious exercise or practice (as prayers) especially for use in private worship **2** : an act of devoting : the quality of being devoted ⟨felt a real *devotion* to music⟩ **3** : deep love or affection

de·vour \di-'vaůr\ *vb* **1** : to eat up greedily **2** : CONSUME 1 ⟨buildings *devoured* by flames⟩ **3** : to take in eagerly by the senses or mind

de·vout \di-'vaůt\ *adj* **1** : devoted to religion **2** : warmly sincere and earnest ⟨*devout* thanks⟩ — **de·vout·ly** *adv* — **de·vout·ness** *n*

dew \'dü, 'dyü\ *n* : moisture condensed on cool surfaces at night

dew·ber·ry \'dü-ˌber-ē, 'dyü-\ *n, pl* **dew·ber·ries** : a sweet edible berry that grows on a prickly vine and is related to the blackberries

dew·lap \'dü-ˌlap, 'dyü-\ *n* : a hanging fold of skin under the neck of some animals

dewlap

dew point *n* : the temperature at which the moisture in the air begins to turn to dew

dewy \'dü-ē, 'dyü-\ *adj* **dew·i·er; dew·i·est** : moist with or as if with dew — **dew·i·ly** \-ə-lē\ *adv* — **dew·i·ness** \-ē-nəs\ *n*

dex·ter·i·ty \dek-'ster-ət-ē\ *n, pl* **dex·ter-**

i·ties 1 : skill and ease in bodily activity **2** : mental skill or quickness

dex·ter·ous *or* **dex·trous** \'dek-stə-rəs, -strəs\ *adj* **1** : skillful with the hands **2** : mentally skillful and clever **3** : done with skill — **dex·ter·ous·ly** *adv* — **dex·ter·ous·ness** *n*

di·a·be·tes \ˌdī-ə-'bēt-ēz, -'bēt-əs\ *n* : a disease in which too little insulin is produced and the body cannot use sugar and starch in the normal way

di·a·bet·ic \ˌdī-ə-'bet-ik\ *n* : a person with diabetes

di·a·crit·i·cal mark \ˌdī-ə-ˌkrit-i-kəl-\ *n* : a mark used with a letter or group of letters to show a pronunciation different from that given a letter or group of letters not marked or marked in a different way

di·a·dem \'dī-ə-ˌdem\ *n* : a band for the head worn especially by monarchs

di·ag·nose \'dī-əg-ˌnōs\ *vb* **di·ag·nosed; di·ag·nos·ing** : to recognize (as a disease) by signs and symptoms

di·ag·no·sis \ˌdī-əg-'nō-səs\ *n, pl* **di·ag·no·ses** \-ˌsēz\ : the art or act of recognizing a disease from its signs and symptoms

¹di·ag·o·nal \dī-'ag-ən-l, -'ag-nəl\ *adj* **1** : running from one corner to the opposite corner of a figure with four sides **2** : running in a slanting direction ⟨*diagonal* stripes⟩ — **di·ag·o·nal·ly** \-ē\ *adv*

²diagonal *n* : a diagonal line, direction, or pattern

¹di·a·gram \'dī-ə-ˌgram\ *n* : a drawing, sketch, plan, or chart that makes something clearer or easier to understand

²diagram *vb* **di·a·gramed** \'dī-ə-ˌgramd\ *or* **di·a·grammed; di·a·gram·ing** \-ˌgram-ing\ *or* **di·a·gram·ming** : to put in the form of a diagram

¹di·al \'dī-əl\ *n* **1** : the face of a watch or clock **2** : SUNDIAL **3** : a face or series of marks on which some measurement or other number is shown usually by means of a pointer ⟨the *dial* of a pressure gauge⟩ **4** : a disk usually with a knob or holes that may be turned to operate something (as a telephone)

²dial *vb* **di·aled** *or* **di·alled; di·al·ing** *or* **di·al·ling** : to use a dial so as to operate, select, or call

di·a·lect \'dī-ə-ˌlekt\ *n* **1** : a form of a language belonging to a certain region **2** : a form of a language used by the members of a certain occupation or class

di·a·logue *or* **di·a·log** \'dī-ə-ˌlòg\ *n* **1** : a conversation between two or more persons **2** : conversation given in a written story or a play

di·am·e·ter \dī-'am-ət-ər\ *n* **1** : a straight line that joins two points of a figure or body and passes through the center **2** : the distance through the center of an object from one side to the other : THICKNESS ⟨the *diameter* of a tree trunk⟩

diameter 1

di·a·mond \'dī-ə-mənd, 'dī-mənd\ *n* **1** : a very hard mineral that is a form of carbon, is usually nearly colorless, and is used especially in jewelry **2** : a flat figure ◇ like one of the surfaces of certain cut diamonds **3** : INFIELD 1

di·a·per \'dī-ə-pər, 'dī-pər\ *n* : a piece of absorbent material drawn up between the legs of a baby and fastened about the waist

di·a·phragm \'dī-ə-ˌfram\ *n* **1** : a muscular wall separating the chest from the abdomen **2** : a thin circular plate (as in a microphone) that vibrates when sound strikes it

di·ar·rhea \ˌdī-ə-'rē-ə\ *n* : abnormally frequent and watery bowel movements

di·a·ry \'dī-ə-rē, 'dī-rē\ *n, pl* **di·a·ries 1** : a daily record especially of personal experiences and thoughts **2** : a book for keeping a diary

¹dice \'dīs\ *n, pl* **dice** : a small cube marked on each face with one to six spots and used usually in pairs in games

²dice *vb* **diced; dic·ing** : to cut into small cubes ⟨*dice* carrots⟩

dick·er \'dik-ər\ *vb* : ²BARGAIN, HAGGLE

¹dic·tate \'dik-ˌtāt\ *vb* **dic·tat·ed; dic·tat·ing 1** : to speak or read for someone else to write down or for a machine to record ⟨*dictate* a letter⟩ **2** : to say or state with authority : ORDER

²dictate *n* : a statement made or direction given with authority : COMMAND

dic·ta·tion \dik-'tā-shən\ *n* **1** : the giving of orders often without thought of whether they are reasonable or fair **2** : the dictating of words **3** : something dictated or taken down from dictation

dic·ta·tor \'dik-ˌtāt-ər\ *n* **1** : a person who rules with total authority and often in a cruel or brutal manner **2** : a person who dictates — **dic·ta·tor·ship** \dik-'tāt-ər-ˌship\ *n*

\ə\ abut	\aù\ out	\i\ tip	\ò\ saw	\ù\ foot
\ər\ further	\ch\ chin	\ī\ life	\òi\ coin	\y\ yet
\a\ mat	\e\ pet	-\j\ job	\th\ thin	\y\ few
\ā\ take	\ē\ easy	\ng\ sing	\th\ this	\yù\ cure
\ä\ cot, cart	\g\ go	\ō\ bone	\ü\ food	\zh\ vision

dic·ta·to·ri·al \,dik-tə-'tōr-ē-əl\ *adj* : of, relating to, or like a dictator or a dictatorship

dic·tion \'dik-shən\ *n* 1 : choice of words especially with regard to correctness, clearness, and effectiveness 2 : ENUNCIATION

dic·tio·nary \'dik-shə-,ner-ē\ *n, pl* **dic·tio·nar·ies** 1 : a book giving the meaning and usually the pronunciation of words listed in alphabetical order 2 : an alphabetical reference book explaining words and phrases of a field of knowledge ⟨a medical *dictionary*⟩ ⟨biographical *dictionary*⟩ 3 : a book listing words of one language in alphabetical order with definitions in another language

did *past of* DO

didn't \'did-nt\ : did not

¹**die** \'dī\ *vb* **died; dy·ing** 1 : to stop living 2 : to pass out of existence ⟨a *dying* race of people⟩ 3 : to disappear little by little ⟨the wind *died* down⟩ 4 : to wish eagerly ⟨*dying* to go⟩ 5 : ¹STOP 4 ⟨the motor *died*⟩

²**die** *n* 1 *pl* **dice** \'dīs\ : ¹DICE 2 *pl* **dies** \'dīz\ : a device for forming or cutting material by pressure

die·sel \'dē-zəl, -səl\ *n* 1 : DIESEL ENGINE 2 : a vehicle driven by a diesel engine

diesel engine *n* : an engine in which the mixture of air and fuel is compressed until enough heat is created to ignite the mixture

¹**di·et** \'dī-ət\ *n* 1 : the food and drink that a person or animal usually takes 2 : the kind and amount of food selected or allowed in certain circumstances (as ill health)

²**diet** *vb* : to eat or cause to eat less or according to certain rules — **di·et·er** *n*

³**diet** *adj* : reduced in calories ⟨a *diet* soft drink⟩

di·e·tary \'dī-ə-,ter-ē\ *adj* : of or relating to a diet or to rules of diet

di·e·ti·tian *or* **di·e·ti·cian** \,dī-ə-'tish-ən\ *n* : a person trained to apply the principles of nutrition to the planning of food and meals

dif·fer \'dif-ər\ *vb* 1 : to be not the same : be unlike 2 : DISAGREE 2

dif·fer·ence \'dif-ə-rens, 'dif-rəns\ *n* 1 : what makes two or more persons or things different 2 : a disagreement about something 3 : REMAINDER 2

dif·fer·ent \'dif-ə-rənt, 'dif-rənt\ *adj* 1 : not of the same kind 2 : not the same ⟨went to *different* schools⟩ — **dif·fer·ent·ly** *adv*

dif·fer·en·ti·ate \,dif-ə-'ren-chē-,āt\ *vb* **dif·fer·en·ti·at·ed; dif·fer·en·ti·at·ing** 1 : to make or become different 2 : to recognize or state the difference between ⟨*differentiate* two colors⟩

dif·fer·en·ti·a·tion \,dif-ə-,ren-chē-'ā-shən\ *n* : the process of change by which immature living structures develop to maturity

dif·fi·cult \'dif-i-,kəlt\ *adj* 1 : hard to do or make ⟨a *difficult* climb⟩ 2 : hard to deal with ⟨a *difficult* child⟩ 3 : hard to understand

dif·fi·cul·ty \'dif-i-,kəl-tē\ *n, pl* **dif·fi·cul·ties** 1 : the state of being difficult ⟨the *difficulty* of a task⟩ 2 : great effort 3 : OBSTACLE 4 : a difficult situation : TROUBLE ⟨in financial *difficulties*⟩

dif·fi·dent \'dif-əd-ənt\ *adj* 1 : lacking confidence 2 : RESERVED 1 — **dif·fi·dent·ly** *adv*

dif·fuse \dif-'yüz\ *vb* **dif·fused; dif·fus·ing** : to undergo diffusion

dif·fu·sion \dif-'yü-zhən\ *n* : the mixing of particles of liquids or gases so that they move from a region of high concentration to one of lower concentration

¹**dig** \'dig\ *vb* **dug** \'dəg\; **dig·ging** 1 : to turn up, loosen, or remove the soil 2 : to form by removing earth ⟨*dig* a hole⟩ ⟨*dig* a cellar⟩ 3 : to uncover or search by or as if by turning up earth ⟨*dig* potatoes⟩ ⟨*dig* for gold⟩ 4 : DISCOVER, UNCOVER ⟨*dig* up information⟩ 5 : ¹PROD 1, POKE ⟨*dug* me in the ribs⟩ 6 : to work hard — **dig·ger** *n*

²**dig** *n* 1 : ²POKE, THRUST 2 : a nasty remark

¹**di·gest** \'dī-,jest\ *n* : information in shortened form

²**di·gest** \dī-'jest, də-\ *vb* 1 : to think over and get straight in the mind ⟨*digest* a lesson⟩ 2 : to change (food) into simpler forms that can be taken in and used by the body 3 : to become digested

di·gest·ible \dī-'jes-tə-bəl, də-\ *adj* : possible to digest

di·ges·tion \dī-'jes-chən, də-\ *n* : the process or power of digesting something (as food)

di·ges·tive \dī-'jes-tiv, də-\ *adj* : of, relating to, or functioning in digestion

dig·it \'dij-ət\ *n* 1 : any of the numerals 1 to 9 and the symbol 0 2 : ¹FINGER 1, ¹TOE 1

dig·ni·fied \'dig-nə-,fīd\ *adj* : having or showing dignity

dig·ni·fy \'dig-nə-,fī\ *vb* **dig·ni·fied; dig·ni·fy·ing** : to give dignity or importance to

dig·ni·tary \'dig-nə-,ter-ē\ *n, pl* **dig·ni·tar·ies** : a person of high position or honor

dig·ni·ty \'dig-nət-ē\ *n, pl* **dig·ni·ties** 1 : the quality or state of being worthy of honor and respect 2 : high rank or office 3 : a dignified look or way of behaving

dike *or* **dyke** \'dīk\ *n* : a bank of earth thrown up from a ditch or heaped up to form a boundary or to control water

di·lap·i·dat·ed \də-'lap-ə-ˌdāt-əd\ *adj*
: partly fallen apart or ruined from age or from lack of care

di·late \dī-'lāt\ *vb* **di·lat·ed; di·lat·ing** : to make or grow larger or wider

di·lem·ma \də-'lem-ə\ *n* : a situation in which a person has to choose between things that are all bad or unsatisfactory

dil·i·gence \'dil-ə-jəns\ *n* : careful and continued work

dil·i·gent \'dil-ə-jənt\ *adj* : showing steady and earnest care and effort ⟨a *diligent* search⟩ — **dil·i·gent·ly** *adv*

dill \'dil\ *n* : an herb related to the carrot with fragrant leaves and seeds used mostly in flavoring pickles

dil·ly·dal·ly \'dil-ē-ˌdal-ē\ *vb* **dil·ly·dal·lied; dil·ly·dal·ly·ing** : to waste time : DAWDLE

di·lute \dī-'lüt, də-\ *vb* **di·lut·ed; di·lut·ing** : to make thinner or more liquid

di·lu·tion \dī-'lü-shən, də-\ *n* **1** : the act of diluting : the state of being diluted **2** : something (as a solution) that is diluted

¹dim \'dim\ *adj* **dim·mer; dim·mest 1** : not bright or distinct : FAINT **2** : not seeing or understanding clearly — **dim·ly** *adv* — **dim·ness** *n*

²dim *vb* **dimmed; dim·ming 1** : to make or become dim **2** : to reduce the light from

dime \'dīm\ *n* : a United States coin worth ten cents

Word History Our name for the coin that is worth a tenth of a dollar came from an early French word. This early French word meant "tenth part." It came from a Latin word meaning "tenth," which in turn came from a Latin word meaning "ten."

di·men·sion \də-'men-chən\ *n* : the length, width, or height of something

di·min·ish \də-'min-ish\ *vb* **1** : to make less or cause to seem less **2** : BELITTLE **3** : DWINDLE — **di·min·ish·ment** \-mənt\ *n*

di·min·u·en·do \də-ˌmin-yə-'wen-dō\ *n, pl* **di·min·u·en·dos** *or* **di·min·u·en·does** : DECRESCENDO

di·min·u·tive \də-'min-yət-iv\ *adj* : very small : TINY ⟨a *diminutive* tree⟩

dim·mer \'dim-ər\ *n* : a device for regulating the brightness of an electric lighting unit (as the lights in a room)

¹dim·ple \'dim-pəl\ *n* : a slight hollow spot especially in the cheek or chin

²dimple *vb* **dim·pled; dim·pling** : to mark with or form dimples

¹din \'din\ *n* : loud confused noise

²din *vb* **dinned; din·ning 1** : to make a din **2** : to repeat again and again in order to impress on someone's mind

dine \'dīn\ *vb* **dined; din·ing 1** : to eat dinner ⟨*dine* out⟩ **2** : to give a dinner to

din·er \'dī-nər\ *n* **1** : a person eating dinner **2** : a railroad dining car or a restaurant in the shape of one

di·nette \dī-'net\ *n* : a separate area or small room used for dining

ding·dong \'ding-ˌdȯng\ *n* : the sound of a bell ringing

din·ghy \'ding-ē, 'ding-gē, 'ding-kē\ *n, pl* **din·ghies 1** : a small light rowboat **2** : a rubber life raft

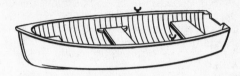

dinghy 1

din·gle \'ding-gəl\ *n* : a small narrow wooded valley

din·gy \'din-jē\ *adj* **din·gi·er; din·gi·est** : rather dark and dirty ⟨a *dingy* room⟩ — **din·gi·ness** *n*

din·ner \'din-ər\ *n* **1** : the main meal of the day **2** : BANQUET

di·no·saur \'dī-nə-ˌsȯr\ *n* : a member of a group of huge reptiles that lived on the earth millions of years ago

dint \'dint\ *n* **1** : ¹POWER 6, FORCE ⟨succeeded by *dint* of hard work⟩ **2** : ¹DENT

di·o·cese \'dī-ə-səs, -ˌsēz\ *n* : the district over which a bishop has authority

¹dip \'dip\ *vb* **dipped; dip·ping 1** : to sink or push briefly into a liquid ⟨*dip* a cloth into water⟩ **2** : to take out with or as if with a ladle **3** : to lower and quickly raise again : drop or sink and quickly rise again ⟨*dip* a flag⟩ **4** : to sink out of sight ⟨the sun *dipped* below the horizon⟩ **5** : to slope downward

²dip *n* **1** : a plunge into water for fun or exercise : a short swim **2** : a downward slope **3** : something obtained by or used in dipping ⟨a *dip* of ice cream⟩ **4** : a tasty sauce into which solid food may be dipped

diph·the·ria \dif-'thir-ē-ə, dip-\ *n* : a contagious disease in which the air passages become coated with a membrane that often makes breathing difficult

diph·thong \'dif-ˌthȯng, 'dip-\ *n* : two vowel sounds joined in one syllable to

\ə\ **abut**	\aú\ **out**	\i\ **tip**	\ȯ\ **saw**	\ú\ **foot**	
\ər\ **further**	\ch\ **chin**	\ī\ **life**	\ȯi\ **coin**	\y\ **yet**	
\a\ **mat**	\e\ **pet**	\j\ **job**	\th\ **thin**	\yü\ **few**	
\ā\ **take**	\ē\ **easy**	\ng\ **sing**	\th\ **this**	\yú\ **cure**	
\ä\ **cot, cart**	\g\ **go**	\ō\ **bone**	\ü\ **food**	\zh\ **vision**	

form one speech sound ⟨the sounds of "ou" in "out" and of "oy" in "boy" are *diphthongs*⟩

di·plo·ma \də-'plō-mə\ *n* : a certificate that shows a person has finished a course or graduated from a school

di·plo·ma·cy \də-'plō-mə-sē\ *n* 1 : the work of keeping up relations between the governments of different countries 2 : skill in dealing with others

dip·lo·mat \'dip-lə-ˌmat\ *n* 1 : a person whose work is diplomacy 2 : a person who is good at not saying or doing things that hurt or make people angry

dip·lo·mat·ic \ˌdip-lə-'mat-ik\ *adj* 1 : of or relating to diplomats and their work 2 : TACTFUL — **dip·lo·mat·i·cal·ly** \-i-kə-lē\ *adv*

dip·per \'dip-ər\ *n* 1 : one that dips 2 : a ladle or scoop for dipping 3 *cap* : a group of seven stars in the northern sky arranged in a form like a dipper with the two stars that form the outer edge of the cup pointing to the North Star 4 *cap* : a group of seven stars in the northern sky similar to the Dipper but with the North Star forming the outer end of the handle

dire \'dīr\ *adj* 1 : causing horror or terror : DREADFUL 2 : very great ⟨in *dire* need⟩ — **dire·ly** *adv* — **dire·ness** *n*

¹di·rect \də-'rekt, dī-\ *vb* 1 : to put an address on (as a letter) 2 : ¹AIM 3, TURN 3 : to show or tell the way 4 : to guide the production of ⟨*direct* a play⟩ 5 : ²ORDER 2, COMMAND **synonyms** see CONDUCT

²direct *adj* 1 : going from one point to another without turning or stopping : STRAIGHT 2 : going straight to the point ⟨a *direct* answer⟩ 3 : being in an unbroken family line ⟨a *direct* ancestor⟩ — **di·rect·ness** *n*

³direct *adv* : DIRECTLY 1

direct current *n* : an electric current flowing in one direction only

di·rec·tion \də-'rek-shən, dī-\ *n* 1 : SUPERVISION, MANAGEMENT 2 : an order or instruction to be followed 3 : the path along which something moves, lies, or points

di·rect·ly \də-'rekt-lē, dī-\ *adv* 1 : in a direct course or way ⟨the road runs *directly* north⟩ 2 : right away : IMMEDIATELY

direct object *n* : a word that represents the main goal or the result of the action of a verb ⟨"me" in "you hit me" is a *direct object*⟩

di·rec·tor \də-'rek-tər, dī-\ *n* : a person who directs something

di·rec·to·ry \də-'rek-tə-rē, dī-\ *n, pl* **di·rec·to·ries** : a book containing an alphabetical list of names and addresses

dirge \'dərj\ *n* : a song or hymn of grief

dir·i·gi·ble \'dir-ə-jə-bəl, də-'rij-ə-\ *n* : AIRSHIP

dirk \'dərk\ *n* : a long dagger with a straight blade

dirt \'dərt\ *n* 1 : a filthy or soiling substance (as mud or dust) 2 : ²SOIL ⟨packed *dirt* around the plant⟩

¹dirty \'dərt-ē\ *adj* **dirt·i·er; dirt·i·est** 1 : soiled or polluted by dirt or impurities ⟨*dirty* clothes⟩ ⟨*dirty* air⟩ 2 : UNFAIR, MEAN ⟨a *dirty* trick⟩ 3 : INDECENT, VULGAR ⟨*dirty* talk⟩ 4 : not clear in color ⟨a *dirty* red⟩ 5 : showing dislike or anger ⟨gave me a *dirty* look⟩ — **dirt·i·ness** *n*

²dirty *vb* **dirt·ied; dirty·ing** : to make or become dirty

dis- *prefix* 1 : do the opposite of ⟨*dis*own⟩ 2 : deprive of ⟨*dis*able⟩ 3 : expel from ⟨*dis*bar⟩ 4 : opposite or absence of ⟨*dis*approval⟩ 5 : not ⟨*dis*agreeable⟩

dis·abil·i·ty \ˌdis-ə-'bil-ət-ē\ *n, pl* **dis·abil·i·ties** 1 : the state of being disabled : lack of power to do something 2 : something that disables

dis·able \dis-'ā-bəl\ *vb* **dis·abled; dis·abling** : to make unable or incapable : CRIPPLE — **dis·able·ment** \-bəl-mənt\ *n*

dis·ad·van·tage \ˌdis-əd-'vant-ij\ *n* : something that makes it hard for a person to succeed or do something

dis·ad·van·ta·geous \ˌdis-ˌad-ˌvan-'tā-jəs\ *adj* : making it harder for a person to succeed or do something — **dis·ad·van·ta·geous·ly** *adv* — **dis·ad·van·ta·geous·ness** *n*

dis·agree \ˌdis-ə-'grē\ *vb* **dis·agreed; dis·agree·ing** 1 : to be unlike each other : be different 2 : to have unlike ideas or opinions ⟨*disagreed* over the price⟩ 3 : QUARREL 4 : to have an unpleasant effect ⟨fried foods *disagree* with me⟩

dis·agree·able \ˌdis-ə-'grē-ə-bəl\ *adj* 1 : UNPLEASANT ⟨a *disagreeable* taste⟩ 2 : having a bad disposition : PEEVISH ⟨a *disagreeable* child⟩ — **dis·agree·ably** \-blē\ *adv*

dis·agree·ment \ˌdis-ə-'grē-mənt\ *n* 1 : the act or fact of disagreeing 2 : the condition of being different 3 : a difference of opinion

dis·ap·pear \ˌdis-ə-'piər\ *vb* 1 : to stop being visible : pass out of sight 2 : to stop existing ⟨dinosaurs *disappeared* long ago⟩

dis·ap·pear·ance \ˌdis-ə-'pir-əns\ *n* : the act or fact of disappearing

dis·ap·point \ˌdis-ə-'point\ *vb* : to fail to satisfy the hope or expectation of

dis·ap·point·ment \ˌdis-ə-'point-mənt\ *n* 1 : the act of disappointing 2 : the condition or feeling of being disappointed **3** : one that disappoints

dis·ap·prov·al \,dis-ə-'prü-vəl\ *n* : the feeling of not liking or agreeing with something or someone

dis·ap·prove \,dis-ə-'prüv\ *vb* **dis·ap·proved; dis·ap·prov·ing** : to dislike or be against something

dis·arm \dis-'ärm\ *vb* **1** : to take weapons from ⟨*disarm* a prisoner⟩ **2** : to reduce the size and strength of the armed forces of a country **3** : to make harmless ⟨*disarm* a bomb⟩ **4** : to remove any feelings of doubt, mistrust, or unfriendliness : win over ⟨a *disarming* smile⟩ — **dis·ar·ma·ment** \-'är-mə-mənt\ *n*

dis·ar·range \,dis-ə-'rānj\ *vb* **dis·ar·ranged; dis·ar·rang·ing** : to make all mussed up or mixed up — **dis·ar·range·ment** \-mənt\ *n*

di·sas·ter \diz-'as-tər, dis-\ *n* : something (as a flood or a tornado) that happens suddenly and causes much suffering or loss : CALAMITY

Word History The word *disaster* came from an old Italian word. This Italian word was used in astrology. It was the term for a bad influence due to the positions of stars and planets. This Italian word was made up of two parts. The first was a negative prefix. The second was a word that meant "star."

di·sas·trous \diz-'as-trəs\ *adj* : being or resulting in a disaster — **di·sas·trous·ly** *adv*

dis·band \dis-'band\ *vb* : to break up and stop being a group — **dis·band·ment** \-mənt\ *n*

dis·bar \dis-'bär\ *vb* **dis·barred; dis·bar·ring** : to deprive (a lawyer) of the rights of membership in the legal profession — **dis·bar·ment** \-mənt\ *n*

dis·be·lief \,dis-bə-'lēf\ *n* : refusal or inability to believe

dis·be·lieve \,dis-bə-'lēv\ *vb* **dis·be·lieved; dis·be·liev·ing** : to think not to be true or real — **dis·be·liev·er** *n*

dis·burse \dis-'bərs\ *vb* **dis·bursed; dis·burs·ing** : to pay out — **dis·burse·ment** \-mənt\ *n*

disc *variant of* DISK

¹**dis·card** \dis-'kärd\ *vb* **1** : to throw down an unwanted playing card from one's hand **2** : to get rid of as useless or unwanted

²**dis·card** \'dis-,kärd\ *n* **1** : the act of discarding **2** : something discarded

dis·cern \dis-'ərn, diz-\ *vb* : to see, recognize, or understand something

¹**dis·charge** \dis-'chärj\ *vb* **dis·charged; dis·charg·ing** **1** : to relieve of a load or burden : UNLOAD **2** : SHOOT 1, 2, FIRE ⟨*discharge* a gun⟩ **3** : to set free ⟨*discharge* a prisoner⟩ **4** : to dismiss from service ⟨*discharge* a worker⟩ **5** : to let go or let off **6** : to give forth the contents (as a fluid) **7** : to get rid of by paying or doing ⟨*discharge* a debt⟩

²**dis·charge** \'dis-,chärj\ *n* **1** : the act of discharging, unloading, or releasing **2** : a certificate of release or payment **3** : a firing off **4** : a flowing out (as of blood or pus) **5** : a firing of a person from a job **6** : complete separation from military service

dis·ci·ple \di-'sī-pəl\ *n* **1** : a person who accepts and helps to spread the teachings of another **2** : APOSTLE 1

¹**dis·ci·pline** \'dis-ə-plən\ *n* **1** : strict training that corrects or strengthens **2** : PUNISHMENT 1 **3** : habits and ways of acting that are gotten through practice **4** : a system of rules

²**discipline** *vb* **dis·ci·plined; dis·ci·plin·ing** **1** : to punish for the sake of discipline **2** : to train in self-control or obedience **3** : to bring under control ⟨*discipline* troops⟩
synonyms *see* PUNISH

disc jockey *n* : a radio announcer who plays records

dis·claim \dis-'klām\ *vb* : to deny being part of or responsible for

dis·close \dis-'klōz\ *vb* **dis·closed; dis·clos·ing** : to make known : REVEAL

dis·clo·sure \dis-'klō-zhər\ *n* **1** : an act of disclosing **2** : something disclosed

dis·col·or \dis-'kəl-ər\ *vb* : to change in color especially for the worse

dis·col·or·a·tion \dis-,kəl-ə-'rā-shən\ *n* **1** : change of color **2** : a discolored spot

dis·com·fort \dis-'kəm-fərt\ *n* : the condition of being uncomfortable

dis·con·cert \,dis-kən-'sərt\ *vb* : to make confused and a little upset

dis·con·nect \,dis-kə-'nekt\ *vb* : to undo the connection of ⟨*disconnect* a hose⟩

dis·con·nect·ed \,dis-kə-'nek-təd\ *adj* : INCOHERENT ⟨a *disconnected* speech⟩ — **dis·con·nect·ed·ly** *adv*

dis·con·so·late \dis-'kän-sə-lət\ *adj* : too sad to be cheered up — **dis·con·so·late·ly** *adv*

¹**dis·con·tent** \,dis-kən-'tent\ *vb* : to make dissatisfied

\ə\ abut	\au̇\ out	\i\ tip	\ȯ\ saw	\u̇\ foot
\ər\ further	\ch\ chin	\ī\ life	\ȯi\ coin	\y\ yet
\a\ mat	\e\ pet	\j\ job	\th\ thin	\yü\ few
\ā\ take	\ē\ easy	\ng\ sing	\th\ this	\yu̇\ cure
\ä\ cot, cart	\g\ go	\ō\ bone	\ü\ food	\zh\ vision

²dis·con·tent *n* : the condition of being dissatisfied

dis·con·tent·ed \,dis-kən-'tent-əd\ *adj* : not contented — **dis·con·tent·ed·ly** *adv*

dis·con·tin·ue \,dis-kən-'tin-yü\ *vb* **dis·con·tin·ued; dis·con·tin·u·ing** : to bring to an end : STOP

dis·cord \'dis-,kȯrd\ *n* : lack of agreement or harmony

dis·cord·ant \dis-'kȯrd-nt\ *adj* : being in disagreement : not being in harmony

¹dis·count \'dis-,kaủnt\ *n* : an amount taken off a regular price

²discount \'dis-,kaủnt, dis-'kaủnt\ *vb* **1** : to lower the amount of a bill, debt, or charge usually in return for cash or quick payment **2** : to believe only partly ⟨*discount* a rumor⟩

dis·cour·age \dis-'kər-ij\ *vb* **dis·cour·aged; dis·cour·ag·ing 1** : to make less determined, hopeful, or sure of oneself ⟨*discouraged* by past failure⟩ **2** : DETER ⟨tried to *discourage* the idea⟩ **3** : to try to persuade not to do something — **dis·cour·age·ment** \-mənt\ *n*

¹dis·course \'dis-,kōrs\ *n* **1** : CONVERSATION **2** : a long talk or composition about a subject

²dis·course \dis-'kōrs\ *vb* **dis·coursed; dis·cours·ing** : to talk especially for a long time

dis·cour·te·ous \dis-'kərt-ē-əs\ *adj* : not polite : RUDE — **dis·cour·te·ous·ly** *adv*

dis·cour·te·sy \dis-'kərt-ə-sē\ *n, pl* **dis·cour·te·sies 1** : rude behavior **2** : a rude act

dis·cov·er \dis-'kəv-ər\ *vb* : to find out, see, or learn of especially for the first time : FIND **synonyms** see INVENT — **dis·cov·er·er** *n*

dis·cov·ery \dis-'kəv-ə-rē, -'kəv-rē\ *n, pl* **dis·cov·er·ies 1** : an act of discovering **2** : something discovered

¹dis·cred·it \dis-'kred-ət\ *vb* **1** : to refuse to accept as true **2** : to cause to seem dishonest or untrue

²discredit *n* : loss of good name or respect ⟨brought *discredit* on the family⟩

dis·creet \dis-'krēt\ *adj* : having or showing good judgment especially in conduct or speech — **dis·creet·ly** *adv*

dis·cre·tion \dis-'kresh-ən\ *n* **1** : good sense in making decisions **2** : the power of deciding for oneself ⟨I'll leave it to your *discretion*⟩

dis·crim·i·nate \dis-'krim-ə-,nāt\ *vb* **dis·crim·i·nat·ed; dis·crim·i·nat·ing 1** : to be able to tell the difference between things **2** : to treat some people better than others without any fair or proper reason

dis·crim·i·na·tion \dis-,krim-ə-'nā-shən\ *n* **1** : the act of discriminating **2** : the ability to see differences **3** : the treating of some people better than others without any fair or proper reason

dis·crim·i·na·to·ry \dis-'krim-ə-nə-,tōr-ē\ *adj* : showing discrimination : being unfair

dis·cus \'dis-kəs\ *n, pl* **dis·cus·es** : an object that is shaped like a disk and hurled for distance in a track-and-field event

discus

dis·cuss \dis-'kəs\ *vb* **1** : to argue or consider fully and openly **2** : to talk about

synonyms DISCUSS, ARGUE, and DEBATE mean to talk about something in order to reach a decision or to convince someone of a point of view. DISCUSS suggests that there is an exchange of ideas and that statements both for and against something are made ⟨we will *discuss* plans for the school picnic⟩ ARGUE suggests the giving of evidence or reasons for something ⟨*argued* for the need for more hospitals⟩ DEBATE suggests an argument between opposing persons or groups according to rules and often before an audience ⟨the candidates will *debate* on TV⟩

dis·cus·sion \dis-'kəsh-ən\ *n* : conversation or debate for the purpose of understanding a question or subject

¹dis·dain \dis-'dān\ *n* : a feeling of scorn for something considered beneath oneself — **dis·dain·ful** *adj* — **dis·dain·ful·ly** \-fə-lē\ *adv*

²disdain *vb* **1** : to think oneself far too good for something or someone ⟨*disdained* the younger children⟩ **2** : to refuse because of scorn ⟨*disdained* to answer⟩

dis·ease \diz-'ēz\ *n* **1** : a change in a living body (as of a person or plant) that interferes with its normal functioning : ILLNESS **2** : an instance or a kind of disease ⟨heart *disease*⟩ — **dis·eased** \-'ēzd\ *adj*

dis·em·bark \ˌdis-əm-'bärk\ *vb* : to go or put ashore from a ship

dis·en·tan·gle \ˌdis-n-'tang-gəl\ *vb* **dis·en·tan·gled; dis·en·tan·gling** : to straighten out : UNTANGLE — **dis·en·tan·gle·ment** \-gəl-mənt\ *n*

dis·fa·vor \dis-'fā-vər\ *n* **1** : DISAPPROVAL **2** : the state of being disliked

dis·fig·ure \dis-'fig-yər\ *vb* **dis·fig·ured; dis·fig·ur·ing** : to spoil the looks of — **dis·fig·ure·ment** \-mənt\ *n*

dis·fran·chise \dis-'fran-ˌchīz\ *vb* **dis·fran·chised; dis·fran·chis·ing** : to take away the right to vote — **dis·fran·chise·ment** \-ˌchīz-mənt, -chəz-\ *n*

¹dis·grace \dis-'grās\ *vb* **dis·graced; dis·grac·ing** : to bring shame to — **dis·grac·er** *n*

²disgrace *n* **1** : the condition of being looked down on : loss of respect **2** : ¹DISHONOR 1 **3** : a cause of shame ⟨you are a *disgrace* to your profession⟩

dis·grace·ful \dis-'grās-fəl\ *adj* : bringing or deserving disgrace — **dis·grace·ful·ly** \-fə-lē\ *adv* — **dis·grace·ful·ness** *n*

dis·grun·tle \dis-'grənt-l\ *vb* **dis·grun·tled; dis·grun·tling** : to make grouchy or cross

¹dis·guise \dis-'gīz\ *vb* **dis·guised; dis·guis·ing** **1** : to change the looks of so as to conceal identity **2** : to keep from revealing ⟨*disguise* one's motive⟩

²disguise *n* **1** : clothing put on to hide one's true identity or to imitate another's **2** : an outward appearance that hides what something really is ⟨a blessing in *disguise*⟩

¹dis·gust \dis-'gəst\ *n* : the strong dislike one feels for something nasty and sickening

²disgust *vb* : to cause to feel disgust — **dis·gust·ed·ly** *adv*

dis·gust·ing \dis-'gəs-ting\ *adj* : causing disgust — **dis·gust·ing·ly** *adv*

¹dish \'dish\ *n* **1** : a hollowed out vessel for serving food at table **2** : the contents of a dish ⟨a *dish* of strawberries⟩

²dish *vb* : to put into a dish : SERVE

dis·heart·en \dis-'härt-n\ *vb* : DISCOURAGE 1 — **dis·heart·en·ing·ly** *adv*

di·shev·eled *or* **di·shev·elled** \di-'shev-əld\ *adj* : mussed up : UNTIDY

dis·hon·est \dis-'än-əst\ *adj* : not honest or trustworthy — **dis·hon·est·ly** *adv*

dis·hon·es·ty \dis-'än-ə-stē\ *n* : lack of honesty : the quality of being dishonest

¹dis·hon·or \dis-'än-ər\ *n* **1** : loss of honor or good name **2** : a cause of disgrace

²dishonor *vb* : to bring shame on : DISGRACE

dis·hon·or·able \dis-'än-ə-rə-bəl\ *adj* : not honorable : SHAMEFUL — **dis·hon·or·ably** \-blē\ *adv*

dis·il·lu·sion \ˌdis-ə-'lü-zhən\ *vb* : to free from mistaken beliefs or foolish hopes — **dis·il·lu·sion·ment** \-mənt\ *n*

dis·in·fect \ˌdis-n-'fekt\ *vb* : to free from germs that might cause disease

¹dis·in·fec·tant \ˌdis-n-'fek-tənt\ *n* : something that frees from germs

²disinfectant *adj* : serving to disinfect

dis·in·her·it \ˌdis-n-'her-ət\ *vb* : to deprive (an heir) of the right to inherit

dis·in·te·grate \dis-'int-ə-ˌgrāt\ *vb* **dis·in·te·grat·ed; dis·in·te·grat·ing** : to separate or break up into small parts or pieces

dis·in·te·gra·tion \dis-ˌint-ə-'grā-shən\ *n* : the act or process of disintegrating : the state of being disintegrated

dis·in·ter·est·ed \dis-'in-trəs-təd, -'int-ə-rəs-\ *adj* **1** : not interested **2** : free of selfish interest — **dis·in·ter·est·ed·ly** *adv* — **dis·in·ter·est·ed·ness** *n*

dis·joint·ed \dis-'jȯint-əd\ *adj* : not clear and orderly ⟨*disjointed* speech⟩ — **dis·joint·ed·ly** *adv*

disk *or* **disc** \'disk\ *n* **1** : something that is or appears to be flat and round **2** *usually* **disc** : a phonograph record — **disk·like** \-ˌlīk\ *adj*

¹dis·like \dis-'līk\ *vb* **dis·liked; dis·lik·ing** : to feel dislike for

²dislike *n* : a strong feeling of not liking or approving

dis·lo·cate \'dis-lō-ˌkāt, dis-'lō-\ *vb* **dis·lo·cat·ed; dis·lo·cat·ing** : to displace a bone from its normal connections with another bone

dis·lo·ca·tion \ˌdis-lō-'kā-shən\ *n* : the state of being dislocated

dis·lodge \dis-'läj\ *vb* **dis·lodged; dis·lodg·ing** : to force out of a resting place or a place of hiding or defense

dis·loy·al \dis-'lȯi-əl\ *adj* : not loyal **synonyms** see FAITHLESS — **dis·loy·al·ly** *adv*

dis·loy·al·ty \dis-'lȯi-əl-tē\ *n, pl* **dis·loy·al·ties** **1** : lack of loyalty **2** : a disloyal act

dis·mal \'diz-məl\ *adj* : very gloomy and depressing

\ə\ abut	\au̇\ out	\i\ tip	\ȯ\ saw	\u̇\ foot
\ər\ further	\ch\ chin	\ī\ life	\ȯi\ coin	\y\ yet
\a\ mat	\e\ pet	\j\ job	\th\ thin	\yü\ few
\ā\ take	\ē\ easy	\ng\ sing	\th\ this	\yu̇\ cure
\ä\ cot, cart	\g\ go	\ō\ bone	\ü\ food	\zh\ vision

Word History A long time ago people thought that two days in each month were unlucky, making twenty-four unlucky days a year in all. These unlucky days were given a Latin name that meant "evil days" and were marked on calendars. The English name for the twenty-four unlucky days was *dismal*. This noun came from the Latin name that meant "evil days." The adjective *dismal* came from the noun *dismal*. We no longer use the noun.

dis·man·tle \dis-'mant-l\ *vb* **dis·man·tled; dis·man·tling 1** : to strip of furniture or equipment **2** : to take completely apart (as for storing or repair) — **dis·man·tle·ment** \-'mant-l-mənt\ *n*

¹dis·may \dis-'mā\ *vb* : to cause to be unable to act because of surprise, fear, or confusion

²dismay *n* **1** : sudden loss of courage or determination because of fear **2** : a feeling of fear or disappointment

dis·miss \dis-'mis\ *vb* **1** : to send away **2** : to discharge from an office or job **3** : to decide not to think about

dis·miss·al \dis-'mis-əl\ *n* : the act of dismissing : the state or fact of being dismissed

dis·mount \dis-'maunt\ *vb* **1** : to get down from something (as a horse or bicycle) **2** : to cause to fall off or get off **3** : to take (as a cannon) off a support **4** : to take apart (as a machine)

dis·obe·di·ence \,dis-ə-'bēd-ē-əns\ *n* : an act or the fact of disobeying

dis·obe·di·ent \,dis-ə-'bēd-ē-ənt\ *adj* : not obeying — **dis·obe·di·ent·ly** *adv*

dis·obey \,dis-ə-'bā\ *vb* **dis·obeyed; dis·obey·ing** : to refuse, neglect, or fail to obey

¹dis·or·der \dis-'ord-ər\ *vb* **1** : to disturb the order of **2** : to disturb the regular or normal functioning of

²disorder *n* **1** : lack of order or of orderly arrangement : CONFUSION **2** : an abnormal state of body or mind : SICKNESS

dis·or·der·ly \dis-'ord-ər-lē\ *adj* **1** : not behaving quietly or well : UNRULY **2** : not neat or orderly — **dis·or·der·li·ness** *n*

dis·or·ga·nize \dis-'or-gə-,nīz\ *vb* **dis·or·ga·nized; dis·or·ga·niz·ing** : to break up the regular arrangement or system of

dis·own \dis-'ōn\ *vb* : to refuse to accept any longer as one's own

dis·par·age \dis-'par-ij\ *vb* **dis·par·aged; dis·par·ag·ing** : to speak of as unimportant or not much good : BELITTLE — **dis·par·age·ment** \-mənt\ *n*

dis·pas·sion·ate \dis-'pash-ə-nət\ *adj* : not influenced by strong feeling : CALM, IMPARTIAL — **dis·pas·sion·ate·ly** *adv*

¹dis·patch *or* **des·patch** \dis-'pach\ *vb* **1** : to send away quickly to a certain place or for a certain reason **2** : ¹KILL 1 ⟨*dispatch* a sick animal⟩ — **dis·patch·er** *n*

²dispatch *or* **despatch** *n* **1** : MESSAGE **2** : a news story sent in to a newspaper **3** : SPEED 1 ⟨act with *dispatch*⟩

dis·pel \dis-'pel\ *vb* **dis·pelled; dis·pel·ling** : to drive away

dis·pense \dis-'pens\ *vb* **dis·pensed; dis·pens·ing 1** : to give out in shares : DISTRIBUTE ⟨*dispense* charity⟩ **2** : ADMINISTER 2 ⟨*dispense* justice⟩ **3** : to put up or prepare medicine in a form ready for use — **dispense with** : to do or get along without

dis·pens·er \dis-'pen-sər\ *n* : a container that gives out something one at a time or a little at a time

dis·perse \dis-'pərs\ *vb* **dis·persed; dis·pers·ing** : to break up and scatter ⟨the clouds *dispersed*⟩ ⟨police *dispersed* the crowd⟩

dis·pir·it \dis-'pir-ət\ *vb* : to take away the cheerfulness or enthusiasm of

dis·place \dis-'plās\ *vb* **dis·placed; dis·plac·ing 1** : to remove from the usual or proper place **2** : to remove from office : DISCHARGE **3** : to take the place of : REPLACE — **dis·place·ment** \-mənt\ *n*

¹dis·play \dis-'plā\ *vb* **1** : to put (something) in plain sight ⟨*display* toys in a store window⟩ **2** : to make clear the existence or presence of : show plainly ⟨*display* anger⟩ ⟨*displayed* a gift for acting⟩

²display *n* : a showing of something ⟨a *display* of bad manners⟩

dis·please \dis-'plēz\ *vb* **dis·pleased; dis·pleas·ing** : to be or do something that makes (a person) cross or not pleased or satisfied

dis·plea·sure \dis-'plezh-ər\ *n* : a feeling of dislike and irritation : DISSATISFACTION

dis·pos·able \dis-'pō-zə-bəl\ *adj* : made to be thrown away after use ⟨*disposable* diapers⟩

dis·pos·al \dis-'pō-zəl\ *n* **1** : ARRANGEMENT 1 **2** : a getting rid of ⟨trash *disposal*⟩ **3** : right or power to use : CONTROL ⟨money at my *disposal*⟩

dis·pose \dis-'pōz\ *vb* **dis·posed; dis·pos·ing 1** : to put in place : ARRANGE **2** : to make ready and willing ⟨was *disposed* to help⟩ — **dis·pos·er** *n* — **dispose of 1** : to finish with **2** : to get rid of

dis·po·si·tion \,dis-pə-'zish-ən\ *n* **1** : ARRANGEMENT 1 **2** : one's usual attitude or mood ⟨has a nasty *disposition*⟩ **3** : TEN-DENCY 2, LIKING

dis·pro·por·tion \,dis-prə-'pōr-shən\ *n* : lack of normal or usual proportions

dis·prove \dis-'prüv\ *vb* **dis·proved; dis·prov·ing** : to show to be false

dis·put·able \dis-'pyüt-ə-bəl, 'dis-pyət-\ *adj* : not yet proved : DEBATABLE — **dis·put·ably** \-blē\ *adv*

¹**dis·pute** \dis-'pyüt\ *vb* **dis·put·ed; dis·put·ing 1** : ARGUE 2 **2** : to question or deny the truth or rightness of ⟨*dispute* a state-ment⟩ **3** : to fight over ⟨the two nations *disputed* the territory⟩ — **dis·put·er** *n*

²**dispute** *n* **1** : ARGUMENT 2, DEBATE **2** : ¹QUARREL 2

dis·qual·i·fy \dis-'kwäl-ə-,fī\ *vb* **dis·qual·i·fied; dis·qual·i·fy·ing** : to make or de-clare unfit or not qualified

¹**dis·qui·et** \dis-'kwī-ət\ *vb* : to make un-easy or worried : DISTURB

²**disquiet** *n* : an uneasy feeling

dis·qui·et·ing \dis-'kwī-ət-ing\ *adj* : caus-ing worry or uneasiness — **dis·qui·et·ing·ly** *adv*

¹**dis·re·gard** \,dis-ri-'gärd\ *vb* : to pay no attention to **synonyms** see NEGLECT

²**disregard** *n* : the act of disregarding : the state of being disregarded

dis·re·pair \,dis-ri-'pȧər, -'peər\ *n* : the condition of needing repair

dis·rep·u·ta·ble \dis-'rep-yət-ə-bəl\ *adj* : not respectable — **dis·rep·u·ta·bly** \-blē\ *adv*

dis·re·spect \,dis-ri-'spekt\ *n* : LACK OF RE-SPECT : DISCOURTESY — **dis·re·spect·ful** *adj* — **dis·re·spect·ful·ly** \-fə-lē\ *adv*

dis·robe \dis-'rōb\ *vb* **dis·robed; dis·rob·ing** : UNDRESS

dis·rupt \dis-'rəpt\ *vb* : to throw into disor-der : BREAK UP ⟨*disrupted* the class⟩ ⟨*disrupt* a friendship⟩

dis·sat·is·fac·tion \di-,sat-əs-'fak-shən\ *n* : a being dissatisfied

dis·sat·is·fy \di-'sat-əs-,fī\ *vb* **dis·sat·is·fied; dis·sat·is·fy·ing** : to fail to satisfy : DISPLEASE

dis·sect \di-'sekt\ *vb* : to cut or take apart especially for examination

dis·sen·sion \di-'sen-chən\ *n* : disagree-ment in opinion : DISCORD

¹**dis·sent** \di-'sent\ *vb* : DISAGREE 2 — **dis·sent·er** *n*

²**dissent** *n* : difference of opinion

dis·ser·vice \di-'sər-vəs\ *n* : a harmful, un-fair, or unjust act

dis·sim·i·lar \di-'sim-ə-lər\ *adj* : not similar : DIFFERENT

dis·si·pate \'dis-ə-,pāt\ *vb* **dis·si·pat·ed; dis·si·pat·ing 1** : to break up and drive off

: DISPERSE ⟨the sun *dissipated* the fog⟩ **2** : to scatter or waste foolishly : SQUANDER

dis·si·pat·ed \'dis-ə-,pāt-əd\ *adj* : en-joying bad, foolish, or harmful activities

dis·si·pa·tion \,dis-ə-'pā-shən\ *n* **1** : the act of dissipating or the state of being dis-sipated **2** : a dissipated way of life

dis·so·lute \'dis-ə-,lüt\ *adj* : having or showing bad morals or behavior — **dis·so·lute·ly** *adv* — **dis·so·lute·ness** *n*

dis·solve \di-'zälv\ *vb* **dis·solved; dis·solv·ing 1** : to mix or cause to mix with a liquid so that the result is a liquid that is the same throughout ⟨sugar *dissolves* in wa-ter⟩ **2** : to bring to an end : TERMINATE ⟨*dissolved* their partnership⟩ **3** : to fade away as if by melting or breaking up

dis·so·nance \'dis-ə-nəns\ *n* : an unpleas-ant combination of musical sounds

dis·suade \di-'swād\ *vb* **dis·suad·ed; dis·suad·ing** : to persuade or advise not to do something

dis·tance \'dis-təns\ *n* **1** : how far from each other two points or places are **2** : the quality or state of not being friendly : RE-SERVE **3** : a distant point or region

dis·tant \'dis-tənt\ *adj* **1** : separated in space or time ⟨two miles *distant* from the house⟩ **2** : REMOTE 1 ⟨a *distant* spot⟩ **3** : not closely related ⟨*distant* cousins⟩ **4** : ¹COLD 2, UNFRIENDLY — **dis·tant·ly** *adv*

dis·taste \dis-'tāst\ *n* : ²DISLIKE

dis·taste·ful \dis-'tāst-fəl\ *adj* : UNPLEAS-ANT

dis·tend \dis-'tend\ *vb* : EXPAND 2, SWELL

dis·till *also* **dis·til** \dis-'til\ *vb* **dis·tilled; dis·till·ing** : to obtain or purify by distilla-tion ⟨*distill* water⟩ — **dis·till·er** *n*

dis·til·la·tion \,dis-tə-'lā-shən\ *n* : the pro-cess of heating a liquid or solid until it sends off a gas or vapor and then cooling the gas or vapor until it becomes liquid

dis·tinct \dis-'tingkt\ *adj* **1** : real and dif-ferent from each other ⟨guilty of three *dis-tinct* crimes⟩ **2** : easy to see, hear, or understand ⟨a *distinct* sound⟩ — **dis·tinct·ly** *adv* — **dis·tinct·ness** *n*

dis·tinc·tion \dis-'tingk-shən\ *n* **1** : the seeing or pointing out of a difference **2** : DIFFERENCE 1 ⟨the *distinction* between good and evil⟩ **3** : great worth : EXCEL-LENCE ⟨a writer of *distinction*⟩ **4** : some-thing that makes a person or thing special or different ⟨has the *distinction* of being the oldest building in the state⟩

\ə\ **abut**	\au̇\ **out**	\i\ **tip**	\ȯ\ **saw**	\u̇\ **foot**	
\ər\ **further**	\ch\ **chin**	\ī\ **life**	\ȯi\ **coin**	\y\ **yet**	
\a\ **mat**	\e\ **pet**	\j\ **job**	\th\ **thin**	\yü\ **few**	
\ā\ **take**	\ē\ **easy**	\ng\ **sing**	\t̲h̲\ **this**	\yu̇\ **cure**	
\ä\ **cot, cart**	\g\ **go**	\ō\ **bone**	\ü\ **food**	\zh\ **vision**	

dis·tinc·tive \dis-'tingk-tiv\ *adj* **1** : clearly marking a person or a thing as different from others ⟨a *distinctive* walk⟩ **2** : having or giving a special look or way ⟨*distinctive* clothes⟩ — **dis·tinc·tive·ly** *adv* — **dis·tinc·tive·ness** *n*

dis·tin·guish \dis-'ting-gwish\ *vb* **1** : to recognize by some mark or quality ⟨*distinguish* the sound of the piano in the orchestra⟩ **2** : to know the difference ⟨*distinguish* between right and wrong⟩ **3** : to set apart as different or special ⟨*distinguished* themselves by heroic actions⟩

dis·tin·guish·able \dis-'ting-gwish-ə-bəl\ *adj* : possible to recognize or tell apart from others

dis·tin·guished \dis-'ting-gwisht\ *adj* : widely known and admired

dis·tort \dis-'tort\ *vb* **1** : to tell in a way that is misleading : MISREPRESENT ⟨*distorted* the facts⟩ **2** : to twist out of shape — **dis·tort·er** *n*

dis·tor·tion \dis-'tor-shən\ *n* : the act of distorting : the state or fact of being distorted

dis·tract \dis-'trakt\ *vb* **1** : to draw the mind or attention to something else **2** : to upset or trouble in mind to the point of confusion

dis·trac·tion \dis-'trak-shən\ *n* **1** : the act of distracting : the state of being distracted **2** : complete confusion of mind **3** : something that makes it hard to pay attention

¹dis·tress \dis-'tres\ *n* **1** : suffering or pain of body or mind **2** : DANGER 1 ⟨a ship in *distress*⟩ — **dis·tress·ful** *adj*

²distress *vb* : to cause distress to — **dis·tress·ing·ly** *adv*

dis·trib·ute \dis-'trib-yət\ *vb* **dis·trib·ut·ed; dis·trib·ut·ing** **1** : to divide among several or many **2** : to spread out so as to cover something **3** : to divide or separate especially into classes : SORT — **dis·trib·u·tor** \dis-'trib-yət-ər\ *n*

dis·tri·bu·tion \,dis-trə-'byü-shən\ *n* **1** : the act of distributing **2** : the way things are distributed **3** : something distributed

dis·trib·u·tive \dis-'trib-yət-iv\ *adj* **1** : of or relating to distribution **2** : producing the same answer when operating on the sum of several numbers as when operating on each and collecting the results ⟨multiplication is *distributive*⟩ — **dis·trib·u·tive·ly** *adv*

dis·trict \'dis-,trikt\ *n* **1** : an area or section (as of a city or nation) set apart for some purpose ⟨our school *district*⟩ **2** : an area or region with some special feature ⟨lived in a coal-mining *district*⟩

¹dis·trust \dis-'trəst\ *vb* : to have no trust or confidence in

²distrust *n* : a lack of trust or confidence : SUSPICION — **dis·trust·ful** *adj* — **dis·trust·ful·ly** \-fə-lē\ *adv*

dis·turb \dis-'tərb\ *vb* **1** : to interfere with : INTERRUPT ⟨the bad weather *disturbed* our plans⟩ **2** : to change the arrangements of : move from its place ⟨don't *disturb* the flowers⟩ **3** : to trouble the mind of : UPSET ⟨I am very *disturbed* by your behavior⟩ **4** : to make confused or disordered ⟨*disturb* the peace⟩

dis·tur·bance \dis-'tər-bəns\ *n* **1** : the act of disturbing : the state of being disturbed **2** : ²DISORDER 1, COMMOTION

dis·use \dis-'yüs\ *n* : lack of use

dis·used \dis-'yüzd\ *adj* : not used any more

¹ditch \'dich\ *n* : a long narrow channel or trench dug in the earth

²ditch *vb* **1** : to dig a ditch in or around (as for drainage) **2** : to get rid of : DISCARD **3** : to make a forced landing in an airplane on water

dith·er \'di<u>th</u>-ər\ *n* : a very nervous or excited state

dit·ty \'dit-ē\ *n, pl* **dit·ties** : a short simple song

di·van \'dī-,van\ *n* : a large couch often with no back or arms

¹dive \'dīv\ *vb* **dived** *or* **dove** \'dōv\; **div·ing** **1** : to plunge into water headfirst **2** : SUBMERGE 1 ⟨the submarine *dived*⟩ **3** : to fall fast **4** : to descend in an airplane at a steep angle **5** : to shove suddenly into or at something ⟨we *dived* for cover⟩ — **div·er** *n*

²dive *n* **1** : an act of diving **2** : a quick drop (as of prices)

di·verse \dī-'vərs, də-\ *adj* : different from each other : UNLIKE — **di·verse·ly** *adv* — **di·verse·ness** *n*

di·ver·sion \də-'vər-zhən, dī-\ *n* **1** : an act or instance of diverting or turning aside **2** : something that relaxes, amuses, or entertains

di·ver·si·ty \də-'vər-sət-ē, dī-\ *n, pl* **di·ver·si·ties** : the condition or fact of being different

di·vert \də-'vərt, dī-\ *vb* **1** : to turn aside : turn from one course or use to another **2** : to turn the attention away : DISTRACT **3** : to give pleasure to : AMUSE

¹di·vide \də-'vīd\ *vb* **di·vid·ed; di·vid·ing** **1** : to separate into two or more parts or pieces **2** : to give out in shares ⟨*divide* the candy among friends⟩ **3** : to be or make different in opinion or interest ⟨the country was *divided* over the issue⟩ **4** : to subject to mathematical division ⟨*divide* 10 by 2⟩ **5** : to branch off : FORK ⟨the road *divides* here⟩ **synonyms** see SEPARATE — **di·vid·er** \də-'vīd-ər\ *n*

²divide *n* : WATERSHED 1

div·i·dend \'div-ə-ˌdend\ *n* **1** : a sum to be divided and given out **2** : a number to be divided by another number

¹di·vine \də-'vīn\ *adj* **1** : of or relating to God or a god ⟨*divine* will⟩ **2** : being in praise of God : RELIGIOUS, HOLY ⟨*divine* services⟩ **3** : GODLIKE — **di·vine·ly** *adv*

²divine *n* : a member of the clergy

di·vin·i·ty \də-'vin-ət-ē\ *n, pl* **di·vin·i·ties 1** : the quality or state of being divine **2** : DEITY **3** : the study of religion

di·vis·i·ble \də-'viz-ə-bəl\ *adj* : possible to divide or separate

di·vi·sion \də-'vizh-ən\ *n* **1** : the act or process of dividing : the state of being divided **2** : a part or portion of a whole **3** : a large military unit **4** : something that divides, separates, or marks off **5** : the finding out of how many times one number is contained in another

di·vi·sor \də-'vī-zər\ *n* : the number by which a dividend is divided

¹di·vorce \də-'vōrs\ *n* **1** : a complete legal ending of a marriage **2** : complete separation

²divorce *vb* **di·vorced; di·vorc·ing 1** : to make or keep separate ⟨our constitution *divorces* church and state⟩ **2** : to end one's marriage legally : get a divorce

di·vulge \də-'vəlj, dī-\ *vb* **di·vulged; di·vulg·ing** : to make public : REVEAL, DISCLOSE

dix·ie·land \'dik-sē-ˌland\ *n* : lively jazz music in a style developed in New Orleans

diz·zy \'diz-ē\ *adj* **diz·zi·er; diz·zi·est 1** : having the feeling of whirling **2** : confused or unsteady in mind **3** : causing a dizzy feeling ⟨*dizzy* heights⟩ — **diz·zi·ly** \'diz-ə-lē\ *adv* — **diz·zi·ness** \'diz-ē-nəs\ *n*

DNA \ˌdē-ˌen-'ā\ *n* : a complicated organic acid that carries genetic information in the chromosomes

¹do \'dü\ *vb* **did** \'did\; **done** \'dən\; **do·ing** \'dü-ing\; **does** \'dəz, dəz\ **1** : to cause (as an act or action) to happen : CARRY OUT, PERFORM ⟨tell me what to *do*⟩ ⟨*do* me a favor⟩ **2** : ²ACT 2, BEHAVE ⟨*do* as I say, not as I *do*⟩ **3** : to work at ⟨what one *does* for a living⟩ **4** : to make progress ⟨*doing* well in school⟩ **5** : to work on, prepare, or put in order ⟨*do* the dishes⟩ ⟨*do* your home-

work⟩ **6** : ¹FINISH 1 ⟨the work is nearly *done*⟩ **7** : to put forth : EXERT ⟨*do* your best⟩ **8** : to serve the purpose : SUIT ⟨this will *do* very well⟩ **9** — used as a helping verb (1) before the subject in a question ⟨I *do* you work⟩, (2) in a negative statement ⟨I *do* not know⟩, (3) for emphasis ⟨you *do* know⟩, and (4) as a substitute for a preceding predicate ⟨you work harder than I *do*⟩ — **do away with 1** : to get rid of **2** : ¹KILL 1

²do \'dō\ *n* : the first note of the musical scale

doc·ile \'däs-əl\ *adj* : easily taught, led, or managed — **doc·ile·ly** *adv*

¹dock \'däk\ *n* : the solid part of an animal's tail

²dock *vb* **1** : to cut off the end of **2** : to take away a part of ⟨*dock* your wages⟩

³dock *n* **1** : an artificial basin for ships that has gates to keep the water in or out **2** : a waterway usually between two piers to receive ships **3** : a wharf or platform for loading or unloading materials

⁴dock *vb* **1** : to haul or guide into a dock **2** : to come or go into a dock **3** : to join (as two spacecraft) mechanically while in space

⁵dock *n* : the place in a court where a prisoner stands or sits during trial

¹doc·tor \'däk-tər\ *n* : a person (as a physician or veterinarian) skilled and specializing in the art of healing

²doctor *vb* **1** : to use remedies on or for ⟨*doctor* a boil⟩ **2** : to practice medicine

doc·trine \'däk-trən\ *n* : something (as a rule or principle) that is taught, believed in, or considered to be true

doc·u·ment \'däk-yə-mənt\ *n* : a written or printed paper that gives information about or proof of something

¹dodge \'däj\ *vb* **dodged; dodg·ing 1** : to move suddenly aside or to and fro ⟨*dodged* through the crowd⟩ **2** : to avoid by moving quickly ⟨*dodge* a blow⟩ **3** : EVADE ⟨*dodged* the question⟩ — **dodg·er** *n*

²dodge *n* : a sudden movement to one side

dodge ball *n* : a game in which players stand in a circle and try to hit a player inside the circle by throwing a large inflated ball

\ə\ abut	\aů\ out	\i\ tip	\ȯ\ saw	\u̇\ foot
\ər\ further	\ch\ chin	\ī\ life	\ȯi\ coin	\y\ yet
\a\ mat	\e\ pet	\j\ job	\th\ thin	\yü\ few
\ā\ take	\ē\ easy	\ng\ sing	\t͟h\ this	\yů\ cure
\ä\ cot, cart	\g\ go	\ō\ bone	\ü\ food	\zh\ vision

do·do \'dōd-ō\ *n, pl*
do·does *or* **do·dos**
: a large heavy bird
unable to fly that
once lived on some
of the islands of the
Indian ocean

doe \'dō\ *n* : the female of an animal
(as a deer) the male
of which is called
buck

dodo

do·er \'dü-ər\ *n* : one
that does ⟨you are more a thinker than a
doer⟩

does *present third sing of* DO

does·n't \'dəz-nt\ : does not

doff \'däf, 'dȯf\ *vb* : to take off (as one's
hat as an act of politeness)

¹dog \'dȯg\ *n* **1** : a domestic animal that
eats meat and is related to the wolves and
foxes **2** : a device (as a metal bar with a
hook at the end) for holding, gripping, or
fastening something — **dog·like**
\'dȯ-ˌglīk\ *adj*

²dog *vb* **dogged; dog·ging** : to hunt,
track, or follow like a hound

dog·cart \'dȯg-ˌkärt\ *n* **1** : a cart pulled by
dogs **2** : a light one-horse carriage with
two seats back to back

dog·catch·er \'dȯg-ˌkach-ər\ *n* : an official
paid to catch and get rid of stray dogs

dog days *n pl* : the hot period between
early July and early September

Word History The Latin name for a certain group of stars in the summer sky
meant "the greater dog." The ancient Romans gave the brightest star in this group
a name that meant "small dog." Some
very hot days were associated with the
rising of this star. The Latin name for these
days meant "days of the small dog." In
English *dog days* is a translation of this
Latin name.

dog-eared \'dȯ-ˌgiərd\ *adj* : having a lot of
pages with corners turned over ⟨a *dog-
eared* book⟩

dog·fish \'dȯg-ˌfish\ *n* : any of several small sharks often seen near
shore

dog·ged \'dȯ-gəd\ *adj* : stubbornly determined — **dog·ged·ly** *adv* — **dog·ged-
ness** *n*

dog·gy *or* **dog·gie** \'dȯ-gē\ *n, pl* **dog·gies**
: a usually small or young dog

dog·house \'dȯg-ˌhaus\ *n* : a shelter for a
dog — **in the doghouse** : in trouble over
some wrongdoing

dog·ma \'dȯg-mə\ *n* **1** : something firmly

believed **2** : a belief or set of beliefs taught
by a church

dog·mat·ic \dȯg-'mat-ik\ *adj* **1** : of or relating to dogma **2** : seeming or sounding
absolutely certain about something —
dog·mat·i·cal·ly \-i-kə-lē\ *adv*

¹dog·trot \'dȯg-ˌträt\ *n* : a slow trot

²dogtrot *vb* **dog·trot·ted; dog·trot·ting**
: to move at a dogtrot

dog·wood \'dȯg-ˌwud\ *n* : any of several
shrubs and small trees with clusters of
small flowers often surrounded by four
showy leaves that look like petals

doi·ly \'dȯi-lē\ *n, pl* **doi·lies** : a small often
ornamental mat used on a table

do·ings \'dü-ingz\ *n pl* : things that are
done or that go on

dol·drums \'dōl-drəmz, 'däl-, 'dȯl-\ *n pl* **1**
: a spell of low spirits **2** : a part of the ocean
near the equator known for its calms

¹dole \'dōl\ *n* **1** : a giving out especially of
food, clothing, or money to the needy **2**
: something given out as charity

²dole *vb* **doled; dol·ing** **1** : to give out as
charity **2** : to give in small portions

dole·ful \'dōl-fəl\ *adj* : full of grief : SAD —
dole·ful·ly \-fə-lē\ *adv* — **dole·ful·ness** *n*

doll \'däl\ *n* : a small figure of a human
being used especially as a child's plaything

dol·lar \'däl-ər\ *n* : any of various coins or
pieces of paper money (as of the United
States or Canada) equal to 100 cents

Word History Many years ago there was
a silver mine near a town in Bohemia. In
German this town was called *Sankt Joachimsthal* and meant "Saint Joachim's
valley." The German word for the silver
coins made at Sankt Joachimsthal was
formed from the name of the town. This
word was *joachimstaler*, and in time it
was shortened to *taler*. The English word
dollar came from the German word *taler*.

dolly \'däl-ē\ *n, pl* **doll·ies** **1** : DOLL **2**
: a platform on a roller or on wheels for
moving heavy things

dol·phin \'däl-fən, 'dȯl-\ *n* **1** : a small whale with teeth and a long nose **2** : either of two large food fishes of the sea

dolphin 1

dolt \'dōlt\ *n* : a stupid person — **dolt·ish** \'dōl-tish\ *adj* — **dolt·ish·ly** *adv* — **dolt·ish·ness** *n*

-dom \dəm\ *n suffix* **1** : dignity : office **2** : realm : jurisdiction ⟨king*dom*⟩ **3** : state or fact of being ⟨free*dom*⟩ **4** : those having a certain office, occupation, interest, or character

do·main \dō-'mān\ *n* **1** : land under the control of a ruler or a government **2** : a field of knowledge or activity

dome \'dōm\ *n* : a bulge or a rounded top or roof that looks like half of a ball — **domed** \'dōmd\ *adj*

¹do·mes·tic \də-'mes-tik\ *adj* **1** : of or relating to a household or a family ⟨*domestic* life⟩ **2** : of, relating to, made in, or done in one's own country **3** : living with or under the care of human beings : TAME — **do·mes·ti·cal·ly** \-ti-kə-lē\ *adv*

dome

²domestic *n* : a household servant

do·mes·ti·cate \də-'mes-ti-ˌkāt\ *vb* **do·mes·ti·cat·ed; do·mes·ti·cat·ing** : to bring under the control of and make usable by humans

dom·i·cile \'däm-ə-ˌsīl\ *n* : a dwelling place

dom·i·nance \'däm-ə-nəns\ *n* : the state or fact of being dominant

dom·i·nant \'däm-ə-nənt\ *adj* : controlling or being over all others — **dom·i·nant·ly** *adv*

dom·i·nate \'däm-ə-ˌnāt\ *vb* **dom·i·nat·ed; dom·i·nat·ing** : to have a commanding position or controlling power over

dom·i·neer \ˌdäm-ə-'niər\ *vb* : to rule or behave in a bossy way

do·min·ion \də-'min-yən\ *n* **1** : ruling or controlling power : SOVEREIGNTY **2** : a territory under the control of a ruler : DOMAIN

dom·i·no \'däm-ə-ˌnō\ *n, pl* **dom·i·noes** *or* **dom·i·nos** : one of a set of flat oblong dotted pieces used in playing a game (**dominoes**)

don \'dän\ *vb* **donned; don·ning** : to put on

do·nate \'dō-ˌnāt\ *vb* **do·nat·ed; do·nat·ing** : to make a gift of : CONTRIBUTE **synonyms** see GIVE — **dona·tor** \'dō-ˌnāt-ər, dō-'nāt-\ *n*

do·na·tion \dō-'nā-shən\ *n* : a giving of something without charge : the thing given (as to charity)

done *past participle of* DO

don·key \'däng-kē, 'dəng-, 'dȯng-\ *n, pl* **don·keys** **1** : an animal related to but smaller than the horse that has short hair in mane and tail and very large ears **2** : a silly or stupid person

do·nor \'dō-nər\ *n* : one who gives, donates, or presents — **do·nor·ship** \-ˌship\ *n*

don't \dōnt\ : do not

¹doo·dle \'düd-l\ *vb* **doo·dled; doo·dling** : to make a doodle — **doo·dler** \'düd-lər\ *n*

²doodle *n* : a scribble, design, or sketch done while thinking about something else

doo·dle·bug \'düd-l-ˌbəg\ *n* : ANT LION

¹doom \'düm\ *n* **1** : a decision made by a court : SENTENCE **2** : a usually unhappy end : FATE

²doom *vb* **1** : to give judgment against : CONDEMN **2** : to make sure that something bad will happen ⟨the plan was *doomed* to failure⟩

dooms·day \'dümz-ˌdā\ *n* : the day of final judgment : the end of the world

door \'dōr\ *n* **1** : a usually swinging or sliding frame or barrier by which an entrance (as into a house) is closed and opened **2** : a part of a piece of furniture like a house's door **3** : DOORWAY

door·man \'dōr-ˌman, -mən\ *n, pl* **door·men** \-ˌmen\ : a person who tends a door of a building

door·step \'dōr-ˌstep\ *n* : a step or a series of steps before an outer door

door·way \'dōr-ˌwā\ *n* : the opening or passage that a door closes

door·yard \'dōr-ˌyärd\ *n* : a yard outside the door of a house

\ə\ abut	\au̇\ out	\i\ tip	\ȯ\ saw	\u̇\ foot
\ər\ further	\ch\ chin	\ī\ life	\ȯi\ coin	\y\ yet
\a\ mat	\e\ pet	\j\ job	\th\ thin	\yü\ few
\ā\ take	\ē\ easy	\ng\ sing	\th\ this	\yu̇\ cure
\ä\ cot, cart	\g\ go	\ō\ bone	\ü\ food	\zh\ vision

dope \'dōp\ *n* **1** : a thick sticky material (as one used to make pipe joints tight) **2** : a narcotic substance **3** : a stupid person **4** : INFORMATION 2

dop·ey \'dō-pē\ *adj* **dop·i·er; dop·i·est 1** : lacking alertness and activity : SLUGGISH **2** : STUPID 2 ⟨a *dopey* remark⟩

dorm \'dȯrm\ *n* : DORMITORY

dor·mant \'dȯr-mənt\ *adj* : being in an inactive state for the time being

dor·mer \'dȯr-mər\ *n*
1 : a window placed upright in a sloping roof **2** : the structure containing a dormer window

dor·mi·to·ry \'dȯr-mə-ˌtōr-ē\ *n, pl* **dor·mi·to·ries 1** : a sleeping room especially for several people **2** : a residence hall having many sleeping rooms

dormer 2

dor·mouse \'dȯr-ˌmaús\ *n, pl* **dor·mice** \-ˌmīs\ : a small European animal that is like a squirrel, lives in trees, and feeds on nuts

dormouse

dor·sal \'dȯr-səl\ *adj* : of, relating to, or being on or near the surface of the body that in humans is the back but in most animals is the upper surface ⟨a fish's *dorsal* fin⟩ — **dor·sal·ly** *adv*

do·ry \'dōr-ē\ *n, pl* **do·ries** : a boat with a flat bottom, high sides that curve upward and outward, and a sharp bow

¹**dose** \'dōs\ *n* : a measured amount (as of a medicine) to be used at one time

²**dose** *vb* **dosed; dos·ing** : to give medicine to

¹**dot** \'dät\ *n* **1** : a small point, mark, or spot **2** : a certain point in time **3** : a short click forming a letter or part of a letter (as in telegraphy)

²**dot** *vb* **dot·ted; dot·ting** : to mark with or as if with dots ⟨*dotted* my i's⟩

dote \'dōt\ *vb* **dot·ed; dot·ing** : to be foolishly fond ⟨*doted* on their grandchild⟩ — **dot·er** *n* — **dot·ing·ly** *adv*

¹**dou·ble** \'dəb-əl\ *adj* **1** : having a twofold relation or character : DUAL **2** : made up of two parts or members **3** : being twice as great or as many **4** : folded in two **5** : having more than the usual number of petals ⟨*double* roses⟩

²**double** *n* **1** : something that is twice another **2** : a hit in baseball that enables the batter to reach second base **3** : one that is very like another

³**double** *adv* **1** : DOUBLY **2** : two together

⁴**double** *vb* **dou·bled; dou·bling 1** : to make or become twice as great or as many : multiply by two **2** : to make of two thicknesses **3** : CLENCH 2 ⟨*doubled* my fist⟩ **4** : to become bent or folded usually in the middle **5** : to take the place of another **6** : to turn sharply and go back over the same course

dou·ble bass \ˌdəb-əl-'bās\ *n* : an instrument of the violin family that is the largest member and has the deepest tone

dou·ble–cross \ˌdəb-əl-'krȯs\ *vb* : BETRAY 2

dou·ble·head·er \ˌdəb-əl-'hed-ər\ *n* : two games played one right after the other on the same day

dou·ble–joint·ed \ˌdəb-əl-'jȯint-əd\ *adj* : having a joint that permits unusual freedom of movement of the parts that are joined

double play *n* : a play in baseball by which two base runners are put out

dou·blet \'dəb-lət\ *n*
: a close-fitting jacket worn by men in Europe especially in the sixteenth century

dou·ble–talk \'dəb-əl-ˌtȯk\ *n* : language that seems to make sense but is actually a mixture of sense and nonsense

dou·bloon \ˌdəb-'lün\ *n* : an old gold coin of Spain and Spanish America

doublet

dou·bly \'dəb-lē\ *adv* : to twice the amount or degree

¹**doubt** \'daút\ *vb* **1** : to be uncertain about **2** : to lack confidence in : DISTRUST **3** : to consider unlikely — **doubt·er** *n* — **doubt·ing·ly** *adv*

²doubt *n* **1** : uncertainty of belief or opinion **2** : the condition of being undecided **3** : a lack of confidence : DISTRUST

doubt·ful \'daút-fəl\ *adj* **1** : not clear or certain as to fact ⟨a *doubtful* claim⟩ **2** : of a questionable kind ⟨*doubtful* intentions⟩ **3** : undecided in opinion **4** : not certain in outcome — **doubt·ful·ly** \-fə-lē\ *adv*

doubt·less \'daút-ləs\ *adv* **1** : without doubt **2** : in all probability

dough \'dō\ *n* **1** : a soft mass of moistened flour or meal thick enough to knead or roll **2** : MONEY 1, 2

dough·nut \'dō-,nət\ *n* : a small ring of sweet dough fried in fat

dough·ty \'daút-ē\ *adj* **dough·ti·er; dough·ti·est** : very strong and brave — **dough·ti·ly** \'daút-l-ē\ *adv* — **dough·ti·ness** \'daút-ē-nəs\ *n*

dour \'daúr, 'dúr\ *adj* : looking or being stern or sullen — **dour·ly** *adv* — **dour·ness** *n*

douse \'daús\ *vb* **doused; dous·ing 1** : to stick into water **2** : to throw a liquid on **3** : to put out : EXTINGUISH ⟨*douse* a light⟩

¹dove \'dəv\ *n* : any of various mostly small pigeons

²dove \'dōv\ *past of* DIVE

dowdy \'daúd-ē\ *adj* **dowd·i·er; dowd·i·est 1** : not neatly or well dressed or cared for **2** : not stylish — **dowd·i·ly** \'daúd-l-ē\ *adv* — **dowd·i·ness** \'daúd-ē-nəs\ *n*

dow·el \'daú-əl\ *n* : a pin or peg used for fastening together two pieces of wood

¹down \'daún\ *n* : a rolling grassy upland — usually used in pl.

²down *adv* **1** : toward or in a lower position **2** : to a lying or sitting position **3** : toward or to the ground, floor, or bottom **4** : in cash ⟨paid five dollars *down*⟩ **5** : in a direction opposite to up **6** : to or in a lower or worse condition **7** : from a past time ⟨heirlooms handed *down*⟩ **8** : to or in a state of less activity ⟨quiet *down*⟩

³down *adj* **1** : being in a low position **2** : directed or going downward ⟨the *down* escalator⟩ **3** : being at a lower level ⟨sales were *down*⟩ **4** : low in spirits : DOWNCAST

⁴down *prep* : down in : down along : down on : down through ⟨fell *down* a hole⟩ ⟨walked *down* the road⟩

⁵down *n* : a low or falling period ⟨the ups and *downs* of life⟩

⁶down *vb* : to go or cause to go or come down

⁷down *n* **1** : soft fluffy feathers (as of young birds) **2** : something soft and fluffy like down — **down·like** \-,līk\ *adj*

down·beat \'daún-,bēt\ *n* : the first beat of a measure of music

down·cast \'daún-,kast\ *adj* **1** : low in spirit : SAD **2** : directed down ⟨*downcast* eyes⟩

down·fall \'daún-,fόl\ *n* : a sudden fall (as from power, happiness, or a high position) or the cause of such a fall — **down·fall·en** \-,fόl-ən\ *adj*

¹down·grade \'daún-,grād\ *n* : a downward slope (as of a road) ⟨lost my brakes on the *downgrade*⟩

²downgrade *vb* **down·grad·ed; down·grad·ing** : to lower in grade, rank, position, or standing

down·heart·ed \'daún-'härt-əd\ *adj* : DOWNCAST 1 — **down·heart·ed·ly** *adv* — **down·heart·ed·ness** *n*

¹down·hill \'daún-'hil\ *adv* : ¹DOWNWARD 1

²down·hill \'daún-,hil\ *adj* : sloping downhill

down payment *n* : a part of a price paid when something is bought or delivered leaving a balance to be paid later

down·pour \'daún-,pōr\ *n* : a heavy rain

¹down·right \'daún-,rīt\ *adv* : REALLY, VERY ⟨that was *downright* stupid⟩

²downright *adj* : ²OUTRIGHT 1, ABSOLUTE ⟨a *downright* lie⟩

down·stage \'daún-'stāj\ *adv or adj* : toward or at the front of a theatrical stage

¹down·stairs \'daún-'staərz, -'steərz\ *adv* : down the stairs : on or to a lower floor

²down·stairs \'daún-,staərz, -,steərz\ *adj* : situated on a lower floor or on the main or first floor

³down·stairs \'daún-'staərz, -'steərz\ *n sing or pl* : the lower floor of a building

down·stream \'daún-'strēm\ *adv* : in the direction a stream is flowing

down·town \'daún-'taún\ *adv or adj* : to, toward, or in the main business district ⟨walked *downtown*⟩ ⟨the *downtown* stores⟩

¹down·ward \'daún-wərd\ *or* **down·wards** \-wərdz\ *adv* **1** : from a higher place or condition to a lower one **2** : from an earlier time

²downward *adj* : going or moving down

down·wind \'daún-'wind\ *adv or adj* : in the direction the wind is blowing

downy \'daú-nē\ *adj* **down·i·er; down·i·est 1** : like down **2** : covered with down

dow·ry \'daú-rē\ *n, pl* **dow·ries** : the property that a woman brings to her husband in marriage

\ə\ abut	\aú\ out	\i\ tip	\ό\ saw	\ú\ foot
\ər\ further	\ch\ chin	\ī\ life	\όi\ coin	\y\ yet
\a\ mat	\e\ pet	\j\ job	\th\ thin	\yü\ few
\ā\ take	\ē\ easy	\ng\ sing	\th\ this	\yú\ cure
\ä\ cot, cart	\g\ go	\ō\ bone	\ü\ food	\zh\ vision

¹doze \'dōz\ *vb* **dozed; doz·ing** : to sleep lightly — **doz·er** *n*

²doze *n* : a light sleep

doz·en \'dəz-n\ *n, pl* **doz·ens** *or* **dozen** : a group of twelve

¹drab \'drab\ *n* : a light olive brown

²drab *adj* **drab·ber; drab·best** **1** : of the color drab **2** : lacking change and interest : DULL ⟨a *drab* life⟩ — **drab·ly** *adv* — **drab·ness** *n*

¹draft \'draft, 'dráft\ *n* **1** : the act of pulling or hauling : the thing or amount pulled **2** : the act or an instance of drinking or inhaling : the portion drunk or inhaled at one time **3** : a medicine prepared for drinking **4** : something represented in words or lines : DESIGN, PLAN **5** : a quick sketch or outline from which a final work is produced **6** : the act of drawing out liquid (as from a cask) : a portion of liquid drawn out **7** : the depth of water a ship needs in order to float **8** : a picking of persons for required military service **9** : an order made by one party to another to pay money to a third party ⟨a bank *draft*⟩ **10** : a current of air **11** : a device to regulate an air supply (as in a stove)

²draft *adj* **1** : used for pulling loads ⟨a *draft* animal⟩ **2** : TENTATIVE ⟨a *draft* treaty⟩ **3** : ready to be drawn from a container ⟨*draft* beer⟩

³draft *vb* **1** : to pick especially for required military service **2** : to make a draft of : OUTLINE ⟨*draft* a speech for the boss⟩ **3** : COMPOSE 1, PREPARE ⟨quickly *drafted* an answer to the telegram⟩ — **draft·er** *n*

drafts·man \'drafts-mən, 'dráfts-\ *n, pl* **drafts·men** \-mən\ : a person who draws plans (as for machinery) — **drafts·man·ship** \-,ship\ *n*

drafty \'draf-tē, 'dráf-\ *adj* **draft·i·er; draft·i·est** : exposed to a draft or current of air ⟨a *drafty* hall⟩ — **draft·i·ness** *n*

¹drag \'drag\ *n* **1** : something without wheels (as a sledge for carrying heavy loads) that is dragged, pulled, or drawn along or over a surface **2** : something used for dragging (as a device used underwater to catch something) **3** : something that stops or holds back progress **4** : a dull event, person, or thing ⟨the party was a *drag*⟩

²drag *vb* **dragged; drag·ging** **1** : to haul slowly or heavily ⟨*drag* a trunk across a room⟩ **2** : to move with distressing slowness or difficulty **3** : to pass or cause to pass slowly ⟨the hot day *dragged* on⟩ **4** : to hang or lag behind **5** : to trail along on the ground **6** : to search or fish with a drag

drag·gle \'drag-əl\ *vb* **drag·gled; drag-**gling **1** : to make or become wet and dirty by dragging **2** : to follow slowly : STRAGGLE

drag·net \'drag-,net\ *n* **1** : a net to be drawn along in order to catch something **2** : a network of planned actions for going after and catching a criminal

drag·on \'drag-ən\ *n* : an imaginary animal usually pictured as a huge serpent or lizard with wings and large claws

drag·on·fly \'drag-ən-,flī\ *n, pl* **drag·on·flies** : a large insect with a long slender body and four wings

dragonfly

dra·goon \drə-'gün\ *n* : a soldier on horseback

drag race *n* : a race for two vehicles at a time from a standstill to a point a quarter mile away

¹drain \'drān\ *vb* **1** : to draw off or flow off gradually or completely ⟨*drain* water from a tank⟩ **2** : to make or become dry or empty a little at a time ⟨*drain* a swamp⟩ **3** : to let out surface or surplus water **4** : ¹EXHAUST 3

²drain *n* **1** : a means of draining (as a pipe, channel, or sewer) **2** : the act of draining **3** : a using up a little at a time

drain·age \'drā-nij\ *n* **1** : an act of draining **2** : something that is drained off **3** : a method of draining : system of drains

drain·pipe \'drān-,pīp\ *n* : a pipe for drainage

drake \'drāk\ *n* : a male duck

dra·ma \'dräm-ə, 'dram-ə\ *n* **1** : a written work that tells a story through action and speech and is meant to be acted out on a stage **2** : dramatic art, literature, or affairs

dra·mat·ic \drə-'mat-ik\ *adj* **1** : of or relating to the drama **2** : like that of the drama : VIVID — **dra·mat·i·cal·ly** \-i-kə-lē\ *adv*

dram·a·tist \'dram-ət-əst, 'dräm-\ *n* : PLAYWRIGHT

dram·a·tize \'dram-ə-,tīz, 'dräm-\ *vb* **dram·a·tized; dram·a·tiz·ing** **1** : to make into a drama **2** : to present or represent in a dramatic manner — **dra·ma·ti·za·tion** \,dram-ət-ə-'zā-shən, ,dräm-\ *n*

drank *past of* DRINK

¹**drape** \'drāp\ *vb* **draped; drap·ing 1 :** to decorate or cover with or as if with folds of cloth **2 :** to arrange or hang in flowing lines

²**drape** *n* **1 drapes** *pl* : DRAPERY 2 **2** : arrangement in or of folds **3** : the cut or hang of clothing

drap·ery \'drā-pə-rē, 'drā-prē\ *n, pl* **drap·er·ies 1 :** a decorative fabric hung in loose folds **2 :** curtains of heavy fabric often used over thinner curtains

dras·tic \'dras-tik\ *adj* **1 :** acting rapidly and strongly **2 :** severe in effect : HARSH — **dras·ti·cal·ly** \-ti-kə-lē\ *adv*

draught \'draft, 'dràft\ *chiefly Brit variant of* DRAFT

¹**draw** \'dró\ *vb* **drew** \'drü\; **drawn** \'drón\; **draw·ing 1 :** to cause to move by pulling : cause to follow **2 :** to move or go usually steadily or a little at a time ⟨day was *drawing* to a close⟩ **3 :** ATTRACT 1 ⟨*draw* a crowd⟩ **4 :** to call forth : PROVOKE ⟨*draw* enemy fire⟩ **5 :** INHALE ⟨*draw* a deep breath⟩ **6 :** to bring or pull out ⟨the dentist *drew* the tooth⟩ ⟨*draw* a sword⟩ **7 :** to bring or get from a source ⟨*draw* a pail of water⟩ **8 :** to need (a certain depth) to float in ⟨the boat *draws* three feet of water⟩ **9 :** to take or receive at random ⟨*draw* lots⟩ ⟨*drew* the winning number⟩ **10 :** to bend (a bow) by pulling back the string **11 :** to cause to shrink or pucker : WRINKLE **12 :** to leave (a contest) undecided : TIE **13 :** to produce a likeness of by making lines on a surface : SKETCH **14 :** to write out in proper form ⟨*draw* a check⟩ — often used with *up* ⟨*draw* up a deed⟩ **15 :** FORMULATE ⟨*draw* a conclusion from facts⟩ **16 :** to produce or make use of a current of air ⟨the furnace *draws* well⟩

²**draw** *n* **1 :** the act or result of drawing **2 :** a tie game or contest **3 :** something that draws attention **4 :** a gully shallower than a ravine

draw·back \'dró-ˌbak\ *n* : ¹HANDICAP 3

draw·bridge \'dró-ˌbrij\ *n* : a bridge made to be drawn up, down, or aside to permit or prevent passage

draw·er \'dró-ər, 'dròr\ *n* **1 :** one that draws **2 :** a sliding boxlike compartment (as in a desk) **3 drawers** *pl* : an undergarment for the lower part of the body

draw·ing \'dró-ing\ *n* **1 :** an act or instance of drawing lots **2 :** the act or art of making a figure, plan, or sketch by means of lines **3 :** a picture made by drawing

drawing room *n* : a formal room for entertaining company

¹**drawl** \'dról\ *vb* : to speak slowly with vowel sounds drawn out beyond their usual length

drawl *n* : a drawling way of speaking

draw on *vb* : to come closer : APPROACH ⟨as night *drew on*⟩

draw out *vb* : to cause or encourage to speak freely ⟨tried to *draw* the frightened child *out*⟩

draw·string \'dró-ˌstring\ *n* : a string, cord, or tape used to close a bag, control fullness in clothes, or open or close curtains

draw up *vb* **1 :** to arrange (as a body of troops) in order **2 :** to straighten (oneself) to an erect posture **3 :** to bring or come to a stop

dray \'drā\ *n* : a strong low cart or wagon without sides for hauling heavy loads

¹**dread** \'dred\ *vb* **1 :** to fear greatly **2 :** to be very unwilling to meet or face

²**dread** *n* : great fear especially of harm to come

³**dread** *adj* : causing great fear or anxiety

dread·ful \'dred-fəl\ *adj* **1 :** causing a feeling of dread **2 :** very disagreeable, unpleasant, or shocking ⟨had a *dreadful* cold⟩ ⟨such *dreadful* manners⟩ — **dread·ful·ly** \-fə-le\ *adv* — **dread·ful·ness** *n*

drawbridge

dread·nought \'dred-ˌnòt\ *n* : a very large battleship

¹**dream** \'drēm\ *n* **1 :** a series of thoughts, pictures, or feelings occurring during sleep **2 :** a dreamlike creation of the imag-

ination : DAYDREAM **3** : something notable for its pleasing quality **4** : a goal that is longed for : IDEAL — **dream·like** \-ˌlīk\ *adj*

²dream *vb* **dreamed** \'dremt, 'drēmd\ *or* **dreamt** \'dremt\; **dream·ing** \'drē-ming\ **1** : to have a dream or dreams **2** : to spend time having daydreams **3** : to think of as happening or possible — **dream·er** \'drē-mər\ *n*

dream·land \'drēm-ˌland\ *n* : an unreal delightful country existing only in imagination or in dreams

dream·less \'drēm-ləs\ *adj* : having no dreams ⟨a *dreamless* sleep⟩ — **dream·less·ly** *adv* — **dream·less·ness** *n*

dreamy \'drē-mē\ *adj* **dream·i·er; dream·i·est 1** : tending to spend time dreaming **2** : having the quality of a dream **3** : being quiet and soothing ⟨*dreamy* music⟩ **4** : SUPERB — **dream·i·ly** \-mə-lē\ *adv* — **dream·i·ness** \-mē-nəs\ *n*

drea·ry \'driər-ē\ *adj* **drea·ri·er; drea·ri·est** : DISMAL, GLOOMY — **drea·ri·ly** \'drir-ə-lē\ *adv* — **drea·ri·ness** \'drir-ē-nəs\ *n*

¹dredge \'drej\ *n* **1** : a heavy iron fame with a net attached to be dragged (as for gathering oysters) over the sea bottom **2** : a machine for scooping up or removing earth usually by buckets on an endless chain or by a suction tube **3** : a barge used in dredging

²dredge *vb* **dredged; dredg·ing** : to dig or gather with or as if with a dredge — **dredg·er** *n*

dregs \'dregz\ *n pl* **1** : solids that settle out of a liquid **2** : the worst or most useless part

drench \'drench\ *vb* : to wet thoroughly

¹dress \'dres\ *vb* **1** : to make or set straight (as soldiers on parade) **2** : to put clothes on : CLOTHE **3** : to wear formal or fancy clothes **4** : to trim or decorate for display ⟨*dress* a store window⟩ **5** : to treat with remedies and bandage ⟨*dress* a wound⟩ **6** : to arrange by combing, brushing, or curling ⟨*dress* hair⟩ **7** : to prepare (a meat animal) for food **8** : to apply fertilizer to

²dress *n* **1** : CLOTHING 1, APPAREL **2** : an outer garment with a skirt for a woman or child

¹dress·er \'dres-ər\ *n* : a piece of furniture (as a chest or a bureau) with a mirror

²dresser *n* : a person who dresses in a certain way ⟨a sloppy *dresser*⟩ ⟨a stylish *dresser*⟩

dress·ing \'dres-ing\ *n* **1** : the act or process of one who dresses **2** : a sauce added to a food (as a salad) **3** : a sea-

soned mixture used as a stuffing (as for a turkey) **4** : material used to cover an injury **5** : something used as a fertilizer

dress·mak·er \'dres-ˌmā-kər\ *n* : a person who makes dresses

dress·mak·ing \'dres-ˌmā-king\ *n* : the process or occupation of making dresses

dress up *vb* **1** : to put on one's best or formal clothes **2** : to put on strange or fancy clothes ⟨*dress up* for Halloween⟩

dressy \'dres-ē\ *adj* **dress·i·er; dress·i·est 1** : showy in dress **2** : suitable for formal occasions

drew *past of* DRAW

¹drib·ble \'drib-əl\ *vb* **drib·bled; drib·bling 1** : to fall or let fall in small drops : TRICKLE **2** : ¹SLOBBER, DROOL **3** : to move forward by bouncing, tapping, or kicking ⟨*dribble* a basketball⟩

²dribble *n* **1** : a trickling flow **2** : the act of dribbling a ball

drib·let \'drib-lət\ *n* **1** : a small amount **2** : a falling drop

dri·er *or* **dry·er** \'drī-ər\ *n* **1** : something that removes or absorbs moisture **2** : a substance that speeds up the drying of oils, paints, and inks **3** *usually* **dryer** : a device for drying ⟨a clothes *dryer*⟩

¹drift \'drift\ *n* **1** : the motion or course of something drifting **2** : a mass of matter (as snow or sand) piled in a heap by the wind **3** : a course something appears to be taking ⟨the *drift* of the conversation⟩ **4** : the meaning of something said or implied ⟨I don't get your *drift*⟩

²drift *vb* **1** : to float or to be driven along by winds, waves, or currents **2** : to move along without effort or purpose ⟨*drift* through life⟩ **3** : to pile up in drifts — **drift·er** *n*

drift·wood \'drift-ˌwu̇d\ *n* : wood drifted or floated by water

¹drill \'dril\ *vb* **1** : to bore with a drill **2** : to teach by means of repeated practice — **drill·er** *n*

²drill *n* **1** : a tool for making holes in hard substances **2** : the training of soldiers (as in marching) **3** : regular strict training and instruction in a subject

³drill *n* : a farming implement for making holes or furrows and planting seeds in them

⁴drill *vb* : to sow seeds with or as if with a drill

drily *variant of* DRYLY

¹drink \'dringk\ *vb* **drank** \'drangk\; **drunk** \'drəngk\; **drink·ing 1** : to swallow liquid **2** : to absorb a liquid ⟨plants *drink* up water⟩ **3** : to take in through the senses

⟨*drank* in the beautiful scenery⟩ **4** : to drink alcoholic liquor — **drink·er** *n*

²**drink** *n* **1** : BEVERAGE **2** : alcoholic liquor

drink·able \'dring-kə-bəl\ *adj* : suitable or safe for drinking

¹**drip** \'drip\ *vb* **dripped; drip·ping 1** : to fall or let fall in or as if in drops **2** : to let fall drops of liquid ⟨a *dripping* faucet⟩

²**drip** *n* **1** : a falling in drops **2** : dripping liquid **3** : the sound made by falling drops

¹**drive** \'drīv\ *vb* **drove** \'drōv\; **driv·en** \'driv-ən\; **driv·ing** \'drī-ving\ **1** : to push or force onward **2** : to direct the movement or course of ⟨*drive* a car⟩ **3** : to go or carry in a vehicle under one's own control ⟨*drive* into town⟩ **4** : to set or keep in motion or operation ⟨machines *driven* by electricity⟩ **5** : to carry through : CONCLUDE ⟨*drive* a bargain⟩ **6** : to force to work or to act ⟨*driven* by hunger to steal⟩ **7** : to bring into a specified condition ⟨the noise *drove* me crazy⟩ — **driv·er** \'drī-vər\ *n*

²**drive** *n* **1** : a trip in a carriage or automobile **2** : a collecting and driving together of animals **3** : DRIVEWAY **4** : an often scenic public road **5** : an organized usually thorough effort to carry out a purpose **6** : the means for giving motion to a machine or machine part

drive–in \'drī-,vin\ *adj* : designed and equipped to serve customers while they remain in their automobiles ⟨a *drive-in* bank⟩

drive·way \'drīv-,wā\ *n* : a private road leading from the street to a house or garage

¹**driz·zle** \'driz-əl\ *vb* **driz·zled; driz·zling** : to rain in very small drops

²**drizzle** *n* : a fine misty rain

droll \'drōl\ *adj* : having an odd or amusing quality ⟨a *droll* expression⟩ — **droll·ness** *n* — **drol·ly** \'drōl-lē\ *adv*

drom·e·dary \'dräm-ə-,der-ē\ *n, pl* **drom·e·dar·ies 1** : a speedy camel trained for riding **2** : the camel of western Asia and northern Africa that has only one hump

¹**drone** \'drōn\ *n* **1** : a male bee **2** : a lazy person : one who lives on the labor of others

²**drone** *vb* **droned; dron·ing** : to make or to speak with a low dull monotonous hum

³**drone** *n* : a droning sound

drool \'drül\ *vb* : to let liquid flow from the mouth : SLOBBER

¹**droop** \'drüp\ *vb* **1** : to sink, bend, or hang down ⟨flowers *drooping* in the hot sun⟩ **2** : to become sad or weak ⟨my spirits *drooped*⟩

²**droop** *n* : the condition or appearance of drooping

¹**drop** \'dräp\ *n* **1** : the amount of liquid that falls naturally in one rounded mass **2 drops** *pl* : a dose of medicine measured by drops **3** : something (as a small round candy) that is shaped like a liquid drop **4** : an instance of dropping **5** : the distance of a fall **6** : a slot into which something may be dropped

²**drop** *vb* **dropped; drop·ping 1** : to fall or let fall in drops **2** : to let fall ⟨*drop* a book⟩ **3** : to lower in pitch and volume ⟨my voice *dropped*⟩ **4** : SEND 1 ⟨*drop* me a note about it⟩ **5** : to let go : DISMISS ⟨*drop* a subject⟩ **6** : to knock down : cause to fall **7** : to go lower ⟨the temperature *dropped*⟩ **8** : to make a brief visit ⟨*drop* in on a friend⟩ **9** : to pass into a less active state ⟨*drop* off to sleep⟩ **10** : to withdraw from membership or from taking part ⟨*drop* out of school⟩ **11** : LOSE 4

drop·let \'dräp-lət\ *n* : a tiny drop

drop·out \'dräp-,aut\ *n* : one that drops out especially from school or a training program

drop·per \'dräp-ər\ *n* **1** : one that drops **2** : a short glass tube with a rubber bulb used to measure out liquids by drops

drought *or* **drouth** \'draut, 'drauth\ *n* **1** : lack of rain or water **2** : a long period of dry weather

¹**drove** \'drōv\ *n* **1** : a group of animals being driven or moving in a body **2** : a crowd of people moving or acting together

²**drove** *past of* DRIVE

drov·er \'drō-vər\ *n* : a worker who drives cattle or sheep

drown \'draun\ *vb* **1** : to suffocate in a liquid and especially in water **2** : to cover with water : FLOOD **3** : to overpower especially with noise ⟨*drowned* the speaker out with boos⟩

¹**drowse** \'drauz\ *vb* **drowsed; drows·ing** : to be half asleep : sleep lightly

²**drowse** *n* : a light sleep : DOZE

drowsy \'drau-zē\ *adj* **drows·i·er; drows·i·est 1** : ready to fall asleep **2** : making one sleepy ⟨the *drowsy* buzz of bees⟩ — **drows·i·ly** \-zə-lē\ *adv* — **drows·i·ness** \-zē-nəs\ *n*

drub \'drəb\ *vb* **drubbed; drub·bing 1** : to beat severely **2** : to defeat completely

\ə\ **abut**	\au̇\ **out**	\i\ **tip**	\ȯ\ **saw**	\u̇\ **foot**
\ər\ **further**	\ch\ **chin**	\ī\ **life**	\ȯi\ **coin**	\y\ **yet**
\a\ **mat**	\e\ **pet**	\j\ **job**	\th\ **thin**	\yü\ **few**
\ā\ **take**	\ē\ **easy**	\ng\ **sing**	\th\ **this**	\yu̇\ **cure**
\ä\ **cot, cart**	\g\ **go**	\ō\ **bone**	\ü\ **food**	\zh\ **vision**

drudge \'drəj\ *n* : a person who does hard or dull work

drudg•ery \'drəj-ə-rē\ *n, pl* **drudg•er•ies** : hard or dull work

¹drug \'drəg\ *n* **1** : a substance used as a medicine or in making medicines **2** : medicine used to deaden pain or bring sleep **3** : a substance that may harm or make an addict of a person who uses it

²drug *vb* **drugged; drug•ging** **1** : to poison with or as if with a drug ⟨the wine was *drugged*⟩ **2** : to dull a person's senses with drugs

drug•gist \'drəg-əst\ *n* : a seller of drugs and medicines : PHARMACIST

drug•store \'drəg-ˌstōr\ *n* : a retail store where medicines and often other things are sold : PHARMACY

¹drum \'drəm\ *n* **1** : a percussion instrument usually consisting of a metal or wooden cylinder with flat ends covered by tightly stretched skin **2** : a sound of or like a drum **3** : an object shaped like a drum ⟨oil *drum*⟩

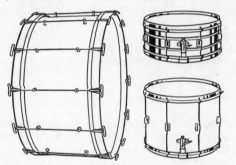

drum 1

²drum *vb* **drummed; drum•ming** **1** : to beat a drum **2** : to beat or sound like a drum **3** : to gather together by or as if by beating a drum ⟨*drum* up customers⟩ **4** : to drive or force by steady or repeated effort ⟨*drummed* the lesson into their heads⟩ **5** : to beat or tap in a rhythmic way

drum major *n* : the marching leader of a band or drum corps

drum ma•jor•ette \ˌdrəm-ˌmā-jə-'ret\ *n* : a girl who is a drum major

drum•mer \'drəm-ər\ *n* **1** : a person who plays a drum **2** : a traveling salesman

drum•stick \'drəm-ˌstik\ *n* **1** : a stick for beating a drum **2** : the lower section of the leg of a fowl

¹drunk \'drəngk\ *past participle of* DRINK

²drunk *adj* **1** : being so much under the influence of alcohol that normal thinking and acting become difficult or impossible **2** : controlled by some feeling as if under the influence of alcohol ⟨*drunk* with power⟩

³drunk *n* **1** : a period of drinking too much alcoholic liquor **2** : a drunken person

drunk•ard \'drəng-kərd\ *n* : a person who is often drunk

drunk•en \'drəng-kən\ *adj* **1** : ²DRUNK 1 **2** : resulting from being drunk ⟨a *drunken* sleep⟩ — **drunk•en•ly** *adv* — **drunk•en•ness** *n*

¹dry \'drī\ *adj* **dri•er; dri•est** **1** : free or freed from water or liquid : not wet or moist **2** : having little or no rain ⟨a *dry* climate⟩ **3** : lacking freshness : STALE **4** : not being in or under water ⟨*dry* land⟩ **5** : THIRSTY 1, 2 **6** : no longer liquid or sticky ⟨the paint is *dry*⟩ **7** : containing no liquid ⟨a *dry* creek⟩ **8** : not giving milk ⟨a *dry* cow⟩ **9** : not producing phlegm ⟨a *dry* cough⟩ **10** : amusing in a sharp or acid way ⟨*dry* humor⟩ **11** : UNINTERESTING ⟨a *dry* lecture⟩ **12** : not sweet ⟨*dry* wines⟩ — **dry•ly** *adv* — **dry•ness** *n*

²dry *vb* **dried; dry•ing** : to make or become dry

dry cell *n* : a small cell producing electricity by means of chemicals in a sealed container

dry–clean \'drī-ˌklēn\ *vb* : to clean (fabrics) with chemical solvents — **dry clean•er** -ˌklē-nər *n* — **dry clean•ing** -ˌklē-ning *n*

dryer *variant of* DRIER

dry goods \'drī-ˌgůdz\ *n pl* : cloth goods (as fabrics, lace, and ribbon)

dry ice *n* : solidified carbon dioxide used chiefly to keep something very cold

du•al \'dü-əl, 'dyü-\ *adj* : consisting of two parts : having two like parts : DOUBLE ⟨a car with *dual* controls⟩ — **du•al•ly** *adv*

¹dub \'dəb\ *vb* **dubbed; dub•bing** **1** : to make a knight of by a light tapping on the shoulder with a sword **2** : ²NAME 1, NICKNAME

²dub *vb* **dubbed; dub•bing** : to add (sound effects) to a film or broadcast

du•bi•ous \'dü-bē-əs, 'dyü-\ *adj* **1** : causing doubt : UNCERTAIN **2** : feeling doubt **3** : QUESTIONABLE 1 — **du•bi•ous•ly** *adv*

duch•ess \'dəch-əs\ *n* **1** : the wife or widow of a duke **2** : a woman who holds the rank of a duke in her own right

¹duck \'dək\ *n* : any of a group of swimming birds that have broad flat bills and are smaller than the related geese and swans

²duck *vb* **1** : to push or pull under water for a moment **2** : to lower the head or body suddenly **3** : ¹DODGE 1, 2 ⟨*duck* a blow⟩ **4** : to avoid a duty, question, or responsibility

³duck *n* **1** : a coarse usually cotton fabric rather like canvas **2 ducks** *pl* : clothes (as trousers) made of duck

duck·bill \'dək-,bil\ *n* : a small mammal of Australia that lays eggs and has webbed feet and a bill like that of a duck

duckbill

duck·ling \'dək-ling\ *n* : a young duck

duck·weed \'dək-,wēd\ *n* : a very small stemless plant that floats in fresh water

duct \'dəkt\ *n* : a pipe, tube, or vessel that carries something (as a bodily secretion, water, or hot air) — **duct·less** \-ləs\ *adj*

ductless gland *n* : ENDOCRINE GLAND

dud \'dəd\ *n* **1 duds** *pl* : CLOTHING **2** : a complete failure **3** : a missile that fails to explode

dude \'düd, 'dyüd\ *n* : a man who pays too much attention to his clothes

¹due \'dü, 'dyü\ *adj* **1** : owed or owing as a debt or a right **2** : SUITABLE ⟨treat one's teacher with *due* respect⟩ **3** : being a result — used with *to* ⟨accidents *due* to carelessness⟩ **4** : required or expected to happen ⟨*due* to arrive soon⟩

²due *n* **1** : something owed : DEBT ⟨give the devil his *due*⟩ **2 dues** *pl* : a regular or legal charge or fee

³due *adv* : DIRECTLY 1 ⟨*due* north⟩

¹du·el \'dü-əl, 'dyü-\ *n* **1** : a combat between two persons fought with deadly weapons by agreement and in the presence of witnesses **2** : a contest between two opponents

²duel *vb* **du·eled** *or* **du·elled; du·el·ing** *or* **du·el·ling** : to fight in a duel — **du·el·ist** \'dü-ə-ləst, 'dyü-\ *n*

du·et \dü-'et, dyü-\ *n* **1** : a musical composition for two performers **2** : two performers playing or singing together

due to *prep* : because of

dug *past of* DIG

dug·out \'dəg-,aut\ *n* **1** : a boat made by hollowing out a log **2** : a shelter dug in a

hillside or in the ground **3** : a low shelter facing a baseball diamond and containing the players' bench

duke \'dük, 'dyük\ *n* : a member of the highest rank of the British nobility

¹dull \'dəl\ *adj* **1** : mentally slow : STUPID **2** : LISTLESS ⟨was feeling *dull* **3** : slow in action : SLUGGISH ⟨business was *dull*⟩ **4** : not sharp in edge or point : BLUNT **5** : lacking brightness or luster ⟨a *dull* finish⟩ **6** : not clear and ringing ⟨a *dull* sound⟩ **7** : CLOUDY 1, OVERCAST **8** : not interesting : TEDIOUS **9** : slightly grayish ⟨a *dull* red⟩ — **dull·ness** *or* **dul·ness** *n* — **dul·ly** *adv*

²dull *vb* : to make or become dull

du·ly \'dü-lē, 'dyü-\ *adv* : in a due or suitable manner, time, or degree

dumb \'dəm\ *adj* **1** : lacking the normal power of speech ⟨deaf and *dumb* persons⟩ **2** : normally unable to speak ⟨*dumb* animals⟩ **3** : not willing to speak : SILENT **4** : STUPID 1, FOOLISH — **dumb·ly** *adv* — **dumb·ness** *n*

dumb·bell \'dəm-,bel\ *n* **1** : a short bar with two weighted balls or disks at the ends usually used in pairs for strengthening the arms **2** : a stupid person

dumbbell 1

dumb·found *or* **dum·found** \,dəm-'faund\ *vb* : to cause to become speechless with astonishment : AMAZE

dumb·wait·er \'dəm-'wāt-ər\ *n* : a small elevator for carrying food and dishes or other small items from one floor to another

dum·my \'dəm-ē\ *n, pl* **dum·mies 1** : a person who does not have or seems not to have the power of speech **2** : a stupid person **3** : an imitation used as a substitute for something ⟨*dummies* in a store window⟩

¹dump \'dəmp\ *vb* : to let fall in a heap : get rid of

²dump *n* **1** : a place for dumping something (as trash) **2** : a place for storage of military materials or the materials stored **3** : a messy or shabby place ⟨the *dump* we lived in then⟩

dump·ling \'dəmp-ling\ *n* : a small mass of dough cooked by boiling or steaming

dumps \'dəmps\ *n pl* : low spirits

dumpy \'dəm-pē\ *adj* **dump·i·er; dump-**

\ə\ **abut**	\au̇\ **out**	\i\ **tip**	\o̅\ **saw**	\u̇\ **foot**
\ər\ **further**	\ch\ **chin**	\ī\ **life**	\oi\ **coin**	\y\ **yet**
\a\ **mat**	\e\ **pet**	\j\ **job**	\th\ **thin**	\yü\ **few**
\ā\ **take**	\ē\ **easy**	\ng\ **sing**	\th\ **this**	\yu̇\ **cure**
\ä\ **cot, cart**	\g\ **go**	\o̅\ **bone**	\ü\ **food**	\zh\ **vision**

i·est : short and thick in build — **dump·i·ness** n

¹**dun** \'dən\ n : a slightly brownish dark gray

²**dun** vb **dunned; dun·ning** : to make repeated demands upon for payment

dunce \'dəns\ n : a stupid person

dune \'dün, 'dyün\ n : a hill or ridge of sand piled up by the wind

dung \'dəng\ n : FECES

dun·ga·ree \,dəng-gə-'rē\ n **1** : a heavy cotton cloth **2 dungarees** pl : pants or work clothes made of dungaree

dun·geon \'dən-jən\ n : a dark usually underground prison

dung·hill \'dəng-,hil\ n : a pile of manure

dunk \'dəngk\ vb : to dip (as a doughnut) into liquid (as coffee)

duo \'dü-ō, 'dyü-\ n, pl **du·os 1** : a duet especially for two performers at two pianos **2** : ¹PAIR 1

¹**dupe** \'düp, 'dyüp\ n : a person who has been or is easily deceived or cheated

²**dupe** vb **duped; dup·ing** : to make a dupe of : TRICK

du·plex \'dü-,pleks, 'dyü-\ adj : ¹DOUBLE 2

¹**du·pli·cate** \'dü-pli-kət, 'dyü-\ adj **1** : having two parts exactly the same or alike **2** : being the same as another

²**duplicate** n : a thing that is exactly like another

³**du·pli·cate** \'dü-pli-,kāt, 'dyü-\ vb **du·pli·cat·ed; du·pli·cat·ing 1** : to make double **2** : to make an exact copy of

du·pli·ca·tion \,dü-pli-'kā-shən, ,dyü-\ n **1** : the act or process of duplicating **2** : the state of being duplicated

du·ra·bil·i·ty \,dur-ə-'bil-ət-ē, ,dyur-\ n : ability to last or to stand hard or continued use

du·ra·ble \'dur-ə-bəl, 'dyur-\ adj : able to last a long time — **du·ra·ble·ness** n — **du·ra·bly** \-blē\ adv

du·ra·tion \du-'rā-shən, dyu-\ n : the time during which something exists or lasts

dur·ing \,dur-ing, ,dyur-\ prep **1** : throughout the course of 〈swims every day *during* the summer〉 **2** : at some point in the course of 〈you may phone me *during* the day〉

dusk \'dəsk\ n **1** : the darker part of twilight especially at night **2** : partial darkness

dusky \'dəs-kē\ adj **dusk·i·er; dusk·i·est 1** : somewhat dark in color **2** : somewhat dark : DIM 〈a *dusky* room〉 — **dusk·i·ness** n

¹**dust** \'dəst\ n **1** : fine dry powdery particles (as of earth) : a fine powder **2** : the powdery remains of bodies once alive **3**

: something worthless **4** : the surface of the ground — **dust·less** \-ləs\ adj

²**dust** vb **1** : to make free of dust : brush or wipe away dust **2** : to sprinkle with or as if with fine particles — **dust·er** \'dəs-tər\ n

dust·pan \'dəst-,pan\ n : a pan shaped like a shovel and used for sweepings

dust storm n : a violent wind carrying dust across a dry region

dusty \'dəs-tē\ adj **dust·i·er; dust·i·est 1** : filled or covered with dust **2** : like dust

¹**Dutch** \'dəch\ adj : of or relating to the Netherlands, its people, or the Dutch language

²**Dutch** n **1 Dutch** pl : the people of the Netherlands **2** : the language of the Dutch

Dutch door n : a door divided so that the lower part can be shut while the upper part remains open

Dutch door

Dutch treat n : a treat for which each person pays his or her own way

du·ti·ful \'düt-i-fəl, 'dyüt-\ adj : having or showing a sense of duty 〈a *dutiful* child〉 — **du·ti·ful·ly** \-fə-lē\ adv — **du·ti·ful·ness** n

du·ty \'düt-ē, 'dyüt-\ n, pl **du·ties 1** : conduct owed to parents and those in authority **2** : the action required by one's position or occupation **3** : something a person feels he or she ought to do **4** : a tax especially on imports into a country **synonyms** see TASK

¹dwarf \'dwȯrf\ *n, pl* **dwarfs** \'dwȯrfs\ *also* **dwarves** \'dwȯrvz\ **1** : a person, animal, or plant much below normal size **2** : a small legendary being usually pictured as a deformed and ugly person

²dwarf *vb* **1** : to prevent from growing to natural size : STUNT ⟨*dwarf* a tree⟩ **2** : to cause to appear smaller

³dwarf *adj* : of less than the usual size

dwell \'dwel\ *vb* **dwelt** \'dwelt\ *or* **dwelled** \'dweld\; **dwell·ing** **1** : to stay for a while **2** : to live in a place : RESIDE **3** : to keep the attention directed ⟨*dwelt* on their mistakes⟩ — **dwell·er** *n*

dwell·ing \'dwel-ing\ *n* : RESIDENCE 2, 3

dwin·dle \'dwin-dəl\ *vb* **dwin·dled; dwin·dling** : to make or become less ⟨*dwin-dling* fuel resources⟩

¹dye \'dī\ *n* **1** : a color produced by dyeing **2** : a material used for dyeing

²dye *vb* **dyed; dye·ing** **1** : to give a new color to especially by treating with a dye **2** : to take up color from dyeing — **dy·er** *n*

dye·stuff \'dī-ˌstəf\ *n* : material used for dyeing

dying *present participle of* DIE

dyke *variant of* DIKE

dy·nam·ic \dī-'nam-ik\ *adj* : full of energy : ACTIVE, FORCEFUL

¹dy·na·mite \'dī-nə-ˌmīt\ *n* : an explosive used in blasting

²dynamite *vb* **dy·na·mit·ed; dy·na·mit·ing** : to blow up with dynamite — **dy·na·mit·er** *n*

dy·na·mo \'dī-nə-ˌmō\ *n, pl* **dy·na·mos** : a machine for producing electric current

dy·nas·ty \'dī-nə-stē\ *n, pl* **dy·nas·ties** : a series of rulers of the same family

dys·en·tery \'dis-n-ˌter-ē\ *n* : a disease in which much watery material mixed with mucus and blood is passed from the bowels

e \'ē\ *n, pl* **e's** *or* **es** \'ēz\ *often cap* **1** : the fifth letter of the English alphabet **2** : a grade that shows a student's work is failing

¹each \'ēch\ *adj* : being one of two or more individuals

²each *pron* : each one

³each *adv* : to or for each : APIECE

each other *pron* : each of two or more in a shared action or relationship ⟨greeted *each other*⟩

ea·ger \'ē-gər\ *adj* : desiring very much : IMPATIENT — **ea·ger·ly** *adv* — **ea·ger·ness** *n*

> **synonyms** EAGER, ANXIOUS, and KEEN mean having or showing a strong desire or interest. EAGER suggests much enthusiasm and often impatience ⟨*eager* passengers waiting for the tour to start⟩ ANXIOUS suggests fear of failure or disappointment ⟨*anxious* to learn who won⟩ KEEN suggests great interest and readiness to act ⟨the new scouts are *keen* and willing to learn⟩

ea·gle \'ē-gəl\ *n* : any of several large birds of prey noted for keen sight and powerful flight

ea·glet \'ē-glət\ *n* : a young eagle

-ean — SEE -AN

¹ear \'iər\ *n* **1** : the organ of hearing **2** : the sense of hearing ⟨a good *ear* for music⟩ **3** : willing or sympathetic attention ⟨give *ear* to a request⟩ **4** : something like an ear in shape or position — **eared** \'iərd\ *adj*

²ear *n* : the seed-bearing head of a cereal grass

ear·ache \'iər-ˌāk\ *n* : an ache or pain in the ear

ear·drum \'iər-ˌdrəm\ *n* : the membrane that separates the outer and middle parts of the ear and vibrates when sound waves strike it

earl \'ərl\ *n* : a member of the British nobility ranking below a marquess and above a viscount

¹ear·ly \'ər-lē\ *adv* **ear·li·er; ear·li·est** **1** : at or near the beginning of a period of time or a series **2** : before the usual time

²early *adj* **ear·li·er; ear·li·est** : occurring near the beginning or before the usual time

\ə\ **abut**	\au̇\ **out**	\i\ **tip**	\ȯ\ **saw**	\u̇\ **foot**
\ər\ **further**	\ch\ **chin**	\ī\ **life**	\ȯi\ **coin**	\y\ **yet**
\a\ **mat**	\e\ **pet**	\j\ **job**	\th\ **thin**	\yü\ **few**
\ā\ **take**	\ē\ **easy**	\ng\ **sing**	\th\ **this**	\yu̇\ **cure**
\ä\ **cot, cart**	\g\ **go**	\ō\ **bone**	\ü\ **food**	\zh\ **vision**

ear·muff \'iər-,məf\ *n* : one of a pair of coverings joined by a flexible band and worn to protect the ears from cold or noise

earn \'ərn\ *vb* **1** : to get for services given ⟨*earn* a good wage⟩ **2** : to deserve especially as a reward or punishment **synonyms** see DESERVE

ear·nest \'ər-nəst\ *adj* : not light or playful **synonyms** see SERIOUS — **ear·nest·ly** *adv* — **ear·nest·ness** *n*

earn·ings \'ər-ningz\ *n pl* : money received as wages or gained as profit

ear·phone \'iər-,fōn\ *n* : a device that converts electrical energy into sound and is worn over the opening of the ear or inserted into it

ear·ring \'iər-,ring\ *n* : an ornament worn on the ear lobe

ear·shot \'iər-,shät\ *n* : the range within which an unaided human voice can be heard

earth \'ərth\ *n* **1** : ²SOIL 1 **2** : areas of land as distinguished from the sea and the air **3** *often cap* : the planet that we live on

earth·en \'ər-thən\ *adj* : made of earth

earth·en·ware \'ər-thən-,waər, -,weər\ *n* : things (as dishes) made of baked clay

earth·ly \'ərth-lē\ *adj* **1** : having to do with or belonging to the earth : not heavenly ⟨*earthly* joys⟩ **2** : IMAGINABLE, POSSIBLE ⟨of no *earthly* use⟩

earth·quake \'ərth-,kwāk\ *n* : a shaking or trembling of a portion of the earth

earth·worm \'ərth-,wərm\ *n* : a worm that has a long body made up of similar segments and lives in damp soil

earthy \'ər-thē\ *adj* **earth·i·er**; **earth·i·est** **1** : consisting of or like earth **2** : PRACTICAL 4 **3** : not polite : CRUDE ⟨*earthy* humor⟩

ear·wig \'iər-,wig\ *n* : an insect with long slender feelers and a large forcepslike organ at the end of its abdomen

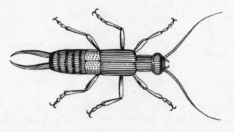

earwig

Word History The modern English word *earwig* came from an Old English word that meant "earwig." This word was a compound of two Old English words. The first meant "ear." The second meant "in-sect." The earwig probably owes its name to an old belief that these insects crawl into human ears.

¹ease \'ēz\ *n* **1** : freedom from pain or trouble : comfort of body or mind ⟨a life of *ease*⟩ **2** : freedom from any feeling of difficulty or embarrassment

²ease *vb* **eased; eas·ing** **1** : to free from discomfort or worry : RELIEVE **2** : to make less tight : LOOSEN **3** : to move very carefully

ea·sel \'ē-zəl\ *n* : a frame for holding a flat surface in an upright position

Word History The English word *easel* came from a Dutch word. The basic meaning of this Dutch word was "ass" or "donkey." Like a beast of burden, an easel is used to hold things. This must have been why the Dutch word that meant "ass" developed the meaning "easel."

eas·i·ly \'ē-zə-lē, 'ēz-lē\ *adv* **1** : in an easy manner : without difficulty ⟨won the race *easily*⟩ **2** : without doubt or question ⟨*easily* the best person for the job⟩

¹east \'ēst\ *adv* : to or toward the east

²east *adj* : placed toward, facing, or coming from the east

³east *n* **1** : the direction of sunrise : the compass point opposite to west **2** *cap* : regions or countries east of a certain point

Eas·ter \'ē-stər\ *n* : a Christian church festival observed in memory of the Resurrection

Easter lily *n* : a white garden lily that blooms in spring

east·er·ly \'ē-stər-lē\ *adv or adj* **1** : toward the east **2** : from the east ⟨an *easterly* wind⟩

east·ern \'ē-stərn\ *adj* **1** *often cap* : of, relating to, or like that of the East **2** : lying toward or coming from the east

¹east·ward \'ēs-twərd\ *adv or adj* : toward the east

²eastward *n* : an eastward direction or part

easy \'ē-zē\ *adj* **eas·i·er**; **eas·i·est** **1** : not hard to do or get : not difficult ⟨an *easy* lesson⟩ **2** : not hard to please ⟨an *easy* teacher⟩ **3** : free from pain, trouble, or worry ⟨an *easy* mind⟩ **4** : COMFORTABLE ⟨an *easy* chair⟩ **5** : showing ease : NATURAL ⟨an *easy* manner⟩

eat \'ēt\ *vb* **ate** \'āt\; **eat·en** \'ēt-n\; **eat·ing** **1** : to chew and swallow food **2** : to take a meal or meals ⟨*eat* at home⟩ **3** : to destroy as if by eating : CORRODE — **eat·er** *n*

eat·able \'ēt-ə-bəl\ *adj* : fit to be eaten

eaves \'ēvz\ *n sing or pl* : the lower edge of a roof that sticks out past the wall

eaves·drop \'ēvz-ˌdräp\ *vb* **eaves-dropped; eaves-drop·ping** : to listen secretly to private conversation

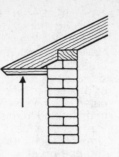

eaves

Word History An early English noun *eavesdrop* was used to refer to the water that falls in drops from the eaves of a house. The ground on which water fell from the eaves was called *eavesdrop*, too. A person might stand on this ground listening to what was going on inside a house. Such a person was called an *eavesdropper*. The verb *eavesdrop* probably came from this word.

¹**ebb** \'eb\ *n* **1** : the flowing out of the tide **2** : a passing from a high to a low point or the time of this

²**ebb** *vb* **1** : to flow out or away : RECEDE **2** : ¹DECLINE 2, WEAKEN

¹**eb·o·ny** \'eb-ə-nē\ *n, pl* **eb·o·nies** : a hard heavy wood that wears well and comes from tropical trees related to the persimmon

²**ebony** *adj* **1** : made of or like ebony **2** : ¹BLACK 1

¹**ec·cen·tric** \ik-'sen-trik, ek-\ *adj* **1** : acting or thinking in a strange way ⟨an *eccentric* person⟩ **2** : not of the usual or normal kind ⟨*eccentric* behavior⟩

²**eccentric** *n* : an eccentric person

ec·cle·si·as·ti·cal \i-ˌklē-zē-'as-ti-kəl\ *adj* : of or relating to the church or its affairs

¹**echo** \'ek-ō\ *n, pl* **ech·oes** : the repeating of a sound caused by the reflection of sound waves

²**echo** *vb* **ech·oed; echo·ing 1** : to send back or repeat a sound **2** : to say what someone else has already said

éclair \ā-'klaər, ā-'kleər\ *n* : an oblong pastry with whipped cream or custard filling

Word History The English word *éclair* came from a French word, whose first meaning was "lightning" or "a flash of lightning." We are not sure why the éclair was named after lightning. Some say it was because it is so light a pastry. Others say that the éclair got its name because it is likely to be eaten in a flash.

¹**eclipse** \i-'klips\ *n* **1** : a complete or partial hiding of the sun caused by the moon's passing between the sun and the earth **2** : a darkening of the moon caused by the moon's entering the shadow of the earth **3** : the hiding of any celestial body by another **4** : a falling into disgrace or out of use or public favor

²**eclipse** *vb* **eclipsed; eclips·ing 1** : to cause an eclipse of **2** : to be or do much better than : OUTSHINE

ecol·o·gist \i-'käl-ə-jəst\ *n* : a specialist in ecology

ecol·o·gy \i-'käl-ə-jē\ *n* : a branch of science dealing with the relation of living things to their environment — **e·co·log·i·cal** \ˌē-kə-'läj-i-dəl, ˌek-ə-\ *adj*

eco·nom·ic \ˌek-ə-'näm-ik, ˌē-kə-\ *adj* **1** : of or relating to economics **2** : of, relating to, or based on the making, selling, and using of goods and services

eco·nom·i·cal \ˌek-ə-'näm-i-kəl, ˌē-kə-\ *adj* **1** : using what one has carefully and without waste : FRUGAL **2** : operating with little waste or at a saving ⟨an *economical* car⟩ — **eco·nom·i·cal·ly** *adv*

synonyms ECONOMICAL, THRIFTY, and SPARING mean careful in the use of money or goods. ECONOMICAL suggests that one makes the most of what one has, using things in the best possible way and not wasting anything ⟨an *economical* cook who feeds us well⟩ THRIFTY suggests that one manages things well and is industrious ⟨the *thrifty* shopkeeper was able to save much money⟩ SPARING suggests that one spends or uses as little as possible ⟨very *sparing* in giving money to charity⟩

eco·nom·ics \ˌek-ə-'näm-iks, ˌē-kə-\ *n* : the science that studies and explains facts about the making, selling, and using of goods and services

econ·o·mize \i-'kän-ə-ˌmīz\ *vb* **econ·o·mized; econ·o·miz·ing 1** : to practice economy : be thrifty **2** : to reduce expenses : SAVE

econ·o·my \i-'kän-ə-mē\ *n, pl* **econ·o·mies 1** : the careful use of money and goods : THRIFT **2** : the way an economic system (as of a country or a period in history) is organized

eco·sys·tem \'ē-kō-ˌsis-təm, 'ek-ō-\ *n* : the whole group of living and nonliving things that make up an environment and affect each other

\ə\ **abut**	\aú\ **out**	\i\ **tip**	\ȯ\ **saw**	\ú\ **foot**
\ər\ **further**	\ch\ **chin**	\ī\ **life**	\ȯi\ **coin**	\y\ **yet**
\a\ **mat**	\e\ **pet**	\j\ **job**	\th\ **thin**	\yü\ **few**
\ā\ **take**	\ē\ **easy**	\ng\ **sing**	\th\ **this**	\yú\ **cure**
\ä\ **cot, cart**	\g\ **go**	\ō\ **bone**	\ü\ **food**	\zh\ **vision**

ec·sta·sy \'ek-stə-sē\ *n, pl* **ec·sta·sies** : very great happiness : extreme delight

ec·stat·ic \ek-'stat-ik\ *adj* : of, relating to, or showing ecstasy

ec·ze·ma \ig-'zē-mə, 'eg-zə-mə, 'ek-sə-mə\ *n* : a disease in which the skin is red, itchy, and marred by scaly or crusted spots

¹**-ed** \d *after a vowel or* b, g, j, l, m, n, ng, r, th, v, z, zh; əd, id *after* d, t; t *after other sounds*\ *vb suffix or adj suffix* **1** — used to form the past participle of verbs ⟨end*ed*⟩ ⟨fad*ed*⟩ ⟨tried⟩ ⟨patt*ed*⟩ **2** : having : showing ⟨cultur*ed*⟩ **3** : having the characteristics of ⟨dogg*ed*⟩

²**-ed** *vb suffix* — used to form the past tense of verbs ⟨judg*ed*⟩ ⟨deni*ed*⟩ ⟨dropp*ed*⟩

¹**ed·dy** \'ed-ē\ *n, pl* **ed·dies** : a current of air or water running against the main current or in a circle

²**eddy** *vb* **ed·died; ed·dy·ing** : to move in an eddy

¹**edge** \'ej\ *n* **1** : the cutting side of a blade **2** : the line where a surface ends : MARGIN, BORDER **synonyms** *see* BORDER — **edged** \'ejd\ *adj* — **on edge** : NERVOUS 3, TENSE

²**edge** *vb* **edged; edg·ing** **1** : to give an edge to **2** : to move slowly and little by little

edge·ways \'ej-,wāz\ *or* **edge·wise** \-,wīz\ *adv* : with the edge in front : SIDEWAYS

ed·i·ble \'ed-ə-bəl\ *adj* : fit or safe to eat

edict \'ē-,dikt\ *n* : a command or law given or made by an authority (as a ruler)

ed·i·fice \'ed-ə-fəs\ *n* : a large or impressive building (as a church)

ed·it \'ed-ət\ *vb* **1** : to correct, revise, and get ready for publication : collect and arrange material to be printed ⟨*edit* a book of poems⟩ **2** : to be in charge of the publication of something (as an encyclopedia or a newspaper) that is the work of many writers

edi·tion \i-'dish-ən\ *n* **1** : the form in which a book is published ⟨an illustrated *edition*⟩ **2** : the whole number of copies of a book, magazine, or newspaper published at one time **3** : one of several issues of a newspaper for a single day ⟨the evening *edition*⟩

ed·i·tor \'ed-ət-ər\ *n* **1** : a person who edits **2** : a person who writes editorials

¹**ed·i·to·ri·al** \,ed-ə-'tōr-ē-əl\ *adj* **1** : of or relating to an editor ⟨an *editorial* office⟩ **2** : being or like an editorial ⟨an *editorial* statement⟩

²**editorial** *n* : a newspaper or magazine article that gives the opinions of its editors or publishers

ed·u·cate \'ej-ə-,kāt\ *vb* **ed·u·cat·ed; ed·u·cat·ing** **1** : to provide schooling for **2** : to develop the mind and morals of especially by formal instruction : TRAIN — **ed·u·ca·tor** \'ej-ə-,kāt-ər\ *n*

ed·u·ca·tion \,ej-ə-'kā-shən\ *n* **1** : the act or process of educating or of being educated **2** : knowledge, skill, and development gained from study or training **3** : the study or science of the methods and problems of teaching

ed·u·ca·tion·al \,ej-ə-'kā-shən-l\ *adj* **1** : having to do with education **2** : offering information or something of value in learning ⟨an *educational* film⟩ — **ed·u·ca·tion·al·ly** *adv*

¹**-ee** \'ē, ,ē\ *n suffix* **1** : person who receives or benefits from a specified thing or action ⟨appoint*ee*⟩ **2** : person who does a specified thing

²**-ee** *n suffix* **1** : a certain and especially a small kind of ⟨boot*ee*⟩ **2** : one like or suggesting ⟨goat*ee*⟩

eel \'ēl\ *n* : a long snakelike fish with a smooth slimy skin

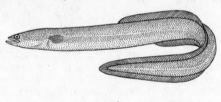

eel

e'en \ēn\ *adv* : EVEN

-eer \'iər\ *n suffix* : person who is concerned with or conducts or produces as a profession ⟨auction*eer*⟩

e'er \eər, aər\ *adv* : EVER

ee·rie *also* **ee·ry** \'iər-ē\ *adj* **ee·ri·er; ee·ri·est** : causing fear and uneasiness : STRANGE

ef·face \i-'fās\ *vb* **ef·faced; ef·fac·ing** : to erase or blot out completely

¹**ef·fect** \i-'fekt\ *n* **1** : an event, condition, or state of affairs that is produced by a cause **2** : EXECUTION 1, OPERATION ⟨the law went into *effect* today⟩ **3** : REALITY 1, FACT ⟨the hint was in *effect* an order⟩ **4** : the act of making a certain impression ⟨tears that were only for *effect*⟩ **5** : ¹INFLUENCE 1 ⟨the *effect* of climate on growth⟩ **6 effects** *pl* : personal property or possessions ⟨household *effects*⟩

²**effect** *vb* : BRING ABOUT

ef·fec·tive \i-'fek-tiv\ *adj* **1** : producing or able to produce a desired effect ⟨*effective* measures to reduce traffic accidents⟩ **2** : IMPRESSIVE ⟨an *effective* speech⟩ **3**

: being in actual operation ⟨the law will become *effective* next year⟩ — **ef·fec·tive·ly** *adv* — **ef·fec·tive·ness** *n*

ef·fec·tu·al \i-'fek-chə-wəl\ *adj* : producing or able to produce a desired effect

ef·fi·ca·cy \'ef-i-kə-sē\ *n, pl* **ef·fi·ca·cies** : power to produce effects : efficient action

ef·fi·cien·cy \i-'fish-ən-sē\ *n, pl* **ef·fi·cien·cies** : the quality or degree of being efficient

ef·fi·cient \i-'fish-ənt\ *adj* : capable of bringing about a desired result with little waste (as of time or energy) — **ef·fi·cient·ly** *adv*

ef·fort \'ef-ərt\ *n* **1** : hard work of mind or body : EXERTION **2** : a serious attempt : TRY

ef·fort·less \'ef-ərt-ləs\ *adj* : showing or needing little or no effort — **ef·fort·less·ly** *adv*

¹egg \'eg, 'āg\ *vb* : INCITE, URGE ⟨we *egged* them on to fight it out⟩

²egg *n* **1** : a shelled oval or rounded body by which some animals (as birds or snakes) reproduce and from which the young hatches out **2** : an egg cell usually together with its protective coverings

egg cell *n* : a cell produced by an ovary that when fertilized by a sperm cell can develop into an embryo and finally a new mature being

egg·nog \'eg-,näg, 'āg-\ *n* : a drink made of eggs beaten with sugar, milk or cream, and often alcoholic liquor

egg·plant \'eg-,plant, 'āg-\ *n* : an oval vegetable with a usually glossy purplish skin and white flesh that is the fruit of a plant related to the tomato

eggplant

egg·shell \'eg-,shel, 'āg-\ *n* : the shell of an egg

egret \'ē-grət, i-'gret\ *n* : any of various herons that have long plumes during the breeding season

egret

¹Egyp·tian \i-'jip-shən\ *adj* : of or relating to Egypt or the Egyptians

²Egyptian *n* **1** : a person who is born or lives in Egypt **2** : the language of the ancient Egyptians

ei·der \'īd-ər\ *n* : a large northern sea duck that is mostly white above and black below and has very soft down

ei·der·down \'īd-ər-,daun\ *n* **1** : the down of the eider used for filling quilts and pillows **2** : a quilt filled with down

¹eight \'āt\ *adj* : being one more than seven

²eight *n* : one more than seven : two times four : 8

¹eigh·teen \ā-'tēn, āt-\ *adj* : being one more than seventeen

²eighteen *n* : one more than seventeen : three times six : 18

¹eigh·teenth \ā-'tēnth, āt-\ *adj* : coming right after seventeenth

²eighteenth *n* : number eighteen in a series

¹eighth \'āth\ *adj* : coming right after seventh

²eighth *n* **1** : number eight in a series **2** : one of eight equal parts

¹eight·i·eth \'āt-ē-əth\ *adj* : coming right after seventy-ninth

²eightieth *n* : number eighty in a series

¹eighty \'āt-ē\ *adj* : being eight times ten

²eighty *n* : eight times ten : 80

¹ei·ther \'ē-thər, 'ī-\ *adj* **1** : ¹EACH ⟨flowers on *either* side of the road⟩ **2** : being one or the other ⟨take *either* road⟩

²either *pron* : the one or the other

³either *conj* — used before words or phrases the last of which follows "or" to

\ə\ **abut**	\aú\ **out**	\i\ **tip**	\ȯ\ **saw**	\ú\ **foot**	
\ər\ **further**	\ch\ **chin**	\ī\ **life**	\ȯi\ **coin**	\y\ **yet**	
\a\ **mat**	\e\ **pet**	\j\ **job**	\th\ **thin**	\yü\ **few**	
\ā\ **take**	\ē\ **easy**	\ng\ **sing**	\th\ **this**	\yú\ **cure**	
\ä\ **cot, cart**	\g\ **go**	\ō\ **bone**	\ü\ **food**	\zh\ **vision**	

show that they are choices or possibilities ⟨you can *either* go or stay⟩

ejac•u•late \i-'jak-yə-ˌlāt\ *vb* **ejac•u•lat•ed; ejac•u•lat•ing** : EXCLAIM

eject \i-'jekt\ *vb* : to drive out or throw off or out ⟨was *ejected* from the meeting⟩

eke out \'ēk-'aut\ *vb* **eked out; ek•ing out 1** : to add to bit by bit ⟨*eked out* a pension with odd jobs⟩ **2** : to get with great effort ⟨*eke out* a living⟩

¹**elab•o•rate** \i-'lab-ə-rət, -'lab-rət\ *adj* : worked out with great care or with much detail ⟨an *elaborate* plot⟩ — **elab•o•rate•ly** *adv*

²**elab•o•rate** \i-'lab-ə-ˌrāt\ *vb* **elab•o•rat•ed; elab•o•rat•ing** : to work out in detail

elapse \i-'laps\ *vb* **elapsed; elaps•ing** : to slip past without being noticed : go by ⟨nearly a year *elapsed*⟩

¹**elas•tic** \i-'las-tik\ *adj* : capable of returning to original shape or size after being stretched, pressed, or squeezed together

²**elastic** *n* **1** : an elastic fabric made of yarns containing rubber **2** : a rubber band

elas•tic•i•ty \i-ˌlas-'tis-ət-ē\ *n* : the quality or state of being elastic

elate \i-'lāt\ *vb* **elat•ed; elat•ing** : to fill with joy or pride

ela•tion \i-'lā-shən\ *n* : the quality or state of being elated

¹**el•bow** \'el-ˌbō\ *n* **1** : the joint of the arm or of the same part of an animal's forelimb **2** : a part (as of a pipe) bent like an elbow

²**elbow** *vb* : to push or force a way through with the elbows

¹**el•der** \'el-dər\ *n* : a shrub or small tree related to the honeysuckles that has flat clusters of white flowers followed by fruits like berries

²**elder** *adj* : OLDER ⟨an *elder* cousin⟩

³**elder** *n* **1** : one who is older **2** : a person having authority because of age and experience ⟨*elders* of the village⟩ **3** : an official in some churches

el•der•ber•ry \'el-dər-ˌber-ē\ *n, pl* **el•der•ber•ries** : the juicy black or red fruit of the elder

el•der•ly \'el-dər-lē\ *adj* : somewhat old : past middle age

el•dest \'el-dəst\ *adj* : OLDEST ⟨the *eldest* child⟩

¹**elect** \i-'lekt\ *adj* : chosen for office but not yet holding office ⟨the president-*elect*⟩

²**elect** *vb* **1** : to select by vote ⟨*elect* a senator⟩ **2** : to make a choice ⟨the home team *elected* to kick off⟩ **synonyms** see CHOOSE

elec•tion \i-'lek-shən\ *n* : an electing or being elected especially by vote

elec•tive \i-'lek-tiv\ *adj* : chosen or filled by election

elec•tor \i-'lek-tər\ *n* : a person qualified or having the right to vote in an election

electr- *or* **electro-** *prefix* **1** : electricity **2** : electric **3** : electric and **4** : electrically

elec•tric \i-'lek-trik\ *or* **elec•tri•cal** \-tri-kəl\ *adj* **1** : of or relating to electricity or its use ⟨an *electric* current⟩ ⟨*electrical* engineering⟩ **2** : heated, moved, made, or run by electricity ⟨an *electric* iron⟩ ⟨an *electric* locomotive⟩ **3** : having a thrilling effect **4** : giving off sounds through an electronic amplifier ⟨an *electric* guitar⟩ — **elec•tri•cal•ly** *adv*

Word History A man in ancient Greece found that if he rubbed a piece of amber it would attract light things like straws and small feathers. In other words, the rubbing gave the amber an electric charge. We owe the English word *electric* to this property of amber. Our word came from a Greek word that meant "amber."

elec•tri•cian \i-ˌlek-'trish-ən\ *n* : a person who installs, operates, or repairs electrical equipment

elec•tric•i•ty \i-ˌlek-'tris-ət-ē\ *n* **1** : an important form of energy that is found in nature but that can be artificially produced by rubbing together two unlike things (as glass and silk), by the action of chemicals, or by means of a generator **2** : electric current

elec•tri•fy \i-'lek-trə-ˌfī\ *vb* **elec•tri•fied; elec•tri•fy•ing 1** : to charge with electricity **2** : to equip for use of electric power **3** : to supply with electric power **4** : to excite suddenly and sharply : THRILL

elec•tro•cute \i-'lek-trə-ˌkyüt\ *vb* **elec•tro•cut•ed; elec•tro•cut•ing** : to kill by an electric shock

elec•trode \i-'lek-ˌtrōd\ *n* : a conductor (as a metal or carbon) used to make electrical contact with a part of an electrical circuit that is not metallic

elec•trol•y•sis \i-ˌlek-'träl-ə-səs\ *n* : the producing of chemical changes by passage of an electric current through a liquid

elec•tro•lyte \i-'lek-trə-ˌlīt\ *n* : a substance (as an acid or salt) that when dissolved (as in water) conducts an electric current

elec•tro•lyt•ic \i-ˌlek-trə-'lit-ik\ *adj* : of or relating to electrolysis or an electrolyte

elec•tro•mag•net \i-ˌlek-trō-'mag-nət\ *n* : a

piece of iron encircled by a coil of wire through which an electric current is passed to magnetize the iron

elec·tro·mag·net·ic wave \i-ˌlek-trō-mag-ˌnet-ik\ *n* : a wave (as a radio wave or wave of light) that travels at the speed of light and consists of a combined electric and magnetic effect

elec·tron \i-ˈlek-ˌträn\ *n* : a very small particle that has a negative charge of electricity and travels around the nucleus of an atom

elec·tron·ic \i-ˌlek-ˈträn-ik\ *adj* **1** : of, relating to, or using the principles of electronics ⟨an *electronic* device⟩ **2** : operating by means of or using an electronic device (as a computer) ⟨an *electronic* typewriter⟩⟨*electronic* banking⟩ — **elec·tron·i·cal·ly** *adv*

electronic mail *n* : messages sent and received electronically (as between computer terminals linked by telephone lines)

elec·tron·ics \i-ˌlek-ˈträn-iks\ *n* : a science that deals with the giving off, action, and effects of electrons in vacuums, gases, and semiconductors and with devices using such electrons

electron tube *n* : a device in which conduction of electricity by electrons takes place through a vacuum or a gas within a sealed container and which has various uses (as in radio and television)

elec·tro·scope \i-ˈlek-trə-ˌskōp\ *n* : an instrument for discovering the presence of an electric charge on a body and for finding out whether the charge is positive or negative

el·e·gance \ˈel-i-gəns\ *n* **1** : refined gracefulness **2** : decoration that is rich but in good taste

el·e·gant \ˈel-i-gənt\ *adj* : showing good taste (as in dress or manners) : having or showing beauty and refinement — **el·e·gant·ly** *adv*

el·e·gy \ˈel-ə-jē\ *n, pl* **el·e·gies** : a sad or mournful poem usually expressing sorrow for one who is dead

el·e·ment \ˈel-ə-mənt\ *n* **1** : one of the parts of which something is made up **2** : something that must be learned before one can advance ⟨the *elements* of arithmetic⟩ **3** : a member of a mathematical set **4** : any of more than 100 substances that cannot by ordinary chemical means be separated into different substances ⟨gold and carbon are *elements*⟩

el·e·men·ta·ry \ˌel-ə-ˈment-ə-rē, -ˈmen-trē\ *adj* : of or relating to the beginnings or first

principles of a subject ⟨*elementary* arithmetic⟩

el·e·phant \ˈel-ə-fənt\ *n* : a huge thickset mammal with the nose drawn out into a long trunk and two large curved tusks

elephants

el·e·vate \ˈel-ə-ˌvāt\ *vb* **el·e·vat·ed; el·e·vat·ing** : to lift up : RAISE

el·e·va·tion \ˌel-ə-ˈvā-shən\ *n* **1** : height especially above sea level : ALTITUDE ⟨a hill with an *elevation* of 1500 feet⟩ **2** : a raised place (as a hill) **3** : the act of elevating : the condition of being elevated **synonyms** see HEIGHT

el·e·va·tor \ˈel-ə-ˌvāt-ər\ *n* **1** : a device (as an endless belt) for raising material **2** : a floor or little room that can be raised or lowered for carrying persons or goods from one level to another **3** : a building for storing grain **4** : a winglike device on an airplane to produce motion up or down

¹**elev·en** \i-ˈlev-ən\ *adj* : being one more than ten

²**eleven** *n* : one more than ten : 11

¹**elev·enth** \i-ˈlev-ənth\ *adj* : coming right after tenth

²**eleventh** *n* : number eleven in a series

elf \ˈelf\ *n, pl* **elves** \ˈelvz\ : an often mischievous fairy

elf·in \ˈel-fən\ *adj* **1** : of or relating to elves **2** : having a strange beauty or charm

el·i·gi·ble \ˈel-i-jə-bəl\ *adj* : worthy or qualified to be chosen

elim·i·nate \i-ˈlim-ə-ˌnāt\ *vb* **elim·i·nat·ed; elim·i·nat·ing** : to get rid of : do away with

elim·i·na·tion \i-ˌlim-ə-ˈnā-shən\ *n* : a getting rid especially of waste from the body

\ə\ **abut**	\aů\ **out**	\i\ **tip**	\ȯ\ **saw**	\ů\ **foot**
\ər\ **further**	\ch\ **chin**	\ī\ **life**	\ȯi\ **coin**	\y\ **yet**
\a\ **mat**	\e\ **pet**	\j\ **job**	\th\ **thin**	\yü\ **few**
\ā\ **take**	\ē\ **easy**	\ng\ **sing**	\th\ **this**	\yů\ **cure**
\ä\ **cot, cart**	\g\ **go**	\ō\ **bone**	\ü\ **food**	\zh\ **vision**

elk \'elk\ *n* **1 :** a large deer of Europe and Asia with broad spreading antlers like those of a moose **2 :** a large North American deer with curved antlers having many branches

elk 2

el·lipse \i-'lips\ *n* **:** a closed curve that looks like a circle pulled out on opposite sides
el·lip·tic \i-'lip-tik\ *or* **el·lip·ti·cal** \-ti-kəl\ *adj* **:** of or like an ellipse
elm \'elm\ *n* **:** a tall shade tree with a broad rather flat top and spreading branches

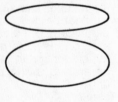

ellipse

el·o·cu·tion \,el-ə-'kyü-shən\ *n* **:** the art of reading or speaking well in public
elo·dea \i-'lōd-ē-ə\ *n* **:** a common floating water plant with small green leaves
elon·gate \i-'lòng-,gāt\ *vb* **elon·gat·ed; elon·gat·ing :** to make or grow longer
elope \i-'lōp\ *vb* **eloped; elop·ing :** to run away to be married — **elope·ment** \-mənt\ *n*
el·o·quence \'el-ə-kwəns\ *n* **1 :** speaking or writing that is forceful and able to persuade **2 :** the art or power of speaking or writing with force and in a way to persuade
el·o·quent \'el-ə-kwənt\ *adj* **1 :** expressing oneself or expressed clearly and with force ⟨an *eloquent* speaker⟩ **2 :** clearly showing some feeling or meaning ⟨an *eloquent* look⟩ — **el·o·quent·ly** *adv*
¹else \'els\ *adv* **1 :** in a different way or place or at a different time ⟨nowhere *else* to go⟩ **2 :** if the facts are or were different **:** if not

²else *adj* **1 :** being other and different ⟨ask someone *else*⟩ **2 :** being in addition ⟨what *else* can you bring⟩
else·where \'els-,hwear, -,hwaər, -,wear, -,waər\ *adv* **:** in or to another place
elude \i-'lüd\ *vb* **elud·ed; elud·ing :** to avoid or escape by being quick, skillful, or tricky
elu·sive \i-'lü-siv\ *adj* **1 :** clever in eluding **2 :** hard to understand or define
elves *pl of* ELF
em- — see EN-
E–mail \'ē-,māl\ *n* **:** ELECTRONIC MAIL
eman·ci·pate \i-'man-sə-,pāt\ *vb* **eman·ci·pat·ed; eman·ci·pat·ing :** to set free from control or slavery **:** LIBERATE
eman·ci·pa·tion \i-,man-sə-'pā-shən\ *n* **:** a setting free ⟨the *emancipation* of slaves⟩
em·balm \im-'bäm, -'bälm\ *vb* **:** to treat a dead body so as to preserve it from decay — **em·balm·er** *n*
em·bank·ment \im-'bangk-mənt\ *n* **:** a raised bank or wall to carry a roadway, prevent floods, or hold back water
em·bar·go \im-'bär-gō\ *n, pl* **em·bar·goes :** an order of a government prohibiting commercial shipping from leaving its ports
em·bark \im-'bärk\ *vb* **1 :** to go on or put on board a ship or an airplane **2 :** to begin some project or task
em·bar·rass \im-'bar-əs\ *vb* **1 :** to involve in financial difficulties **2 :** to cause to feel confused and distressed **:** FLUSTER
em·bas·sy \'em-bə-sē\ *n, pl* **em·bas·sies 1 :** an ambassador and his assistants **2 :** the residence or office of an ambassador
em·bed *or* **im·bed** \im-'bed\ *vb* **em·bed·ded** *or* **im·bed·ded; em·bed·ding** *or* **im·bed·ding :** to set solidly in or as if in a bed ⟨*embed* a post in concrete⟩
em·bel·lish \im-'bel-ish\ *vb* **:** to add ornamental details to — **em·bel·lish·ment** \-mənt\ *n*
em·ber \'em-bər\ *n* **:** a glowing piece of coal or wood in the ashes from a fire
em·bez·zle \im-'bez-əl\ *vb* **em·bez·zled; em·bez·zling :** to take (property entrusted to one's care) dishonestly for one's own use
em·bit·ter \im-'bit-ər\ *vb* **:** to make bitter **:** stir bitter feeling in
em·blem \'em-bləm\ *n* **:** an object or a likeness of an object used to suggest a thing that cannot be pictured **:** SYMBOL

synonyms EMBLEM, SYMBOL, and TOKEN mean a visible thing that stands for something that cannot be pictured. EMBLEM is usually used of an object or a picture that represents a group such as a family, an organization, or a nation ⟨the eagle is one of our national *emblems*⟩ SYMBOL may be used of anything that serves as an outward sign for something else and especially for something ideal or spiritual ⟨the lion is the *symbol* of courage⟩ TOKEN is used of an object or act that gives evidence of the existence of something else ⟨this gift is a *token* of our love⟩

em·body \im-'bäd-ē\ *vb* **em·bod·ied; em·body·ing** 1 : to bring together so as to form a body or system ⟨the basic law of the United States is *embodied* in its constitution⟩ 2 : to make a part of a body or system ⟨*embody* a new rule in a state constitution⟩ 3 : to represent in visible form

em·boss \im-'bäs, -'bòs\ *vb* : to ornament with a raised pattern or design

¹**em·brace** \im-'brās\ *vb* **em·braced; em·brac·ing** 1 : to clasp in the arms 2 : to enclose on all sides ⟨low hills *embraced* the valley⟩ 3 : to take up readily or gladly ⟨*embrace* an opportunity⟩ 4 : TAKE IN 5, INCLUDE ⟨mathematics *embraces* arithmetic, algebra, and geometry⟩

²**embrace** *n* : an encircling with the arms : HUG

em·broi·der \im-'broid-ər\ *vb* 1 : to make or fill in a design with needlework ⟨*embroider* a flower on a towel⟩ 2 : to decorate with needlework 3 : to add to the interest of (as a story) with details far beyond the truth

em·broi·dery \im-'broid-ə-rē\ *n, pl* **em·broi·der·ies** 1 : needlework done to decorate cloth 2 : the act or art of embroidering

em·bryo \'em-brē-ō\ *n, pl* **em·bry·os** 1 : an animal in the earliest stages of growth when its basic structures are being formed 2 : a tiny young plant inside a seed

¹**em·er·ald** \'em-ə-rəld, 'em-rəld\ *n* : a precious stone of a rich green color

²**emerald** *adj* : brightly or richly green

emerge \i-'mərj\ *vb* **emerged; emerg·ing** 1 : to come out or into view (as from water or a hole) 2 : to become known especially as a result of study or questioning

emer·gen·cy \i-'mər-jən-sē\ *n, pl* **emer·gen·cies** : an unexpected situation calling for prompt action

em·ery \'em-ə-rē, 'em-rē\ *n, pl* **em·er·ies** : a mineral used in the form of powder or grains for polishing and grinding

-emia *or* **-ae·mia** \'ē-mē-ə\ *n suffix* : condition of having a specified disorder of the blood

em·i·grant \'em-i-grənt\ *n* : a person who emigrates

em·i·grate \'em-ə-,grāt\ *vb* **em·i·grat·ed; em·i·grat·ing** : to leave a country or region to settle somewhere else

em·i·gra·tion \,em-ə-'grā-shən\ *n* : a going away from one region or country to live in another

em·i·nence \'em-ə-nəns\ *n* 1 : the condition of being eminent 2 : a piece of high ground : HILL

em·i·nent \'em-ə-nənt\ *adj* : standing above others in rank, merit, or worth

em·is·sary \'em-ə-,ser-ē\ *n, pl* **em·is·sar·ies** : a person sent on a mission to represent another

emit \ē-'mit\ *vb* **emit·ted; emit·ting** : to give out : send forth ⟨*emit* light⟩ ⟨*emit* a shriek⟩

emo·tion \i-'mō-shən\ *n* 1 : strong feeling ⟨speak with *emotion*⟩ 2 : a mental and bodily reaction (as anger or fear) accompanied by strong feeling

emo·tion·al \i-'mō-shən-l\ *adj* 1 : of or relating to the emotions ⟨an *emotional* upset⟩ 2 : likely to show or express emotion 3 : expressing emotion ⟨an *emotional* speech⟩ — **emo·tion·al·ly** *adv*

em·per·or \'em-pər-ər\ *n* : the supreme ruler of an empire

em·pha·sis \'em-fə-səs\ *n, pl* **em·pha·ses** \-,sēz\ 1 : a forcefulness of expression that gives special importance to something 2 : special force given to one or more words or syllables in speaking or reading 3 : special importance given to something

em·pha·size \'em-fə-,sīz\ *vb* **em·pha·sized; em·pha·siz·ing** : to give emphasis to

em·phat·ic \im-'fat-ik\ *adj* : showing or spoken with emphasis ⟨an *emphatic* refusal⟩

em·phy·se·ma \,em-fə-'zē-mə, -'sē-mə\ *n* : a disease in which the lungs become stretched and inefficient

em·pire \'em-,pīr\ *n* 1 : a group of territories or peoples under one ruler ⟨the Roman *empire*⟩ 2 : a country whose ruler is called an emperor 3 : the power or rule of an emperor

¹**em·ploy** \im-'plòi\ *vb* 1 : to make use of ⟨*employ* bricks in building⟩ 2 : to use the services of : hire for wages or salary

²**employ** *n* : the state of being employed

\ə\ abut	\aú\ out	\i\ tip	\ò\ saw	\ú\ foot
\ər\ further	\ch\ chin	\ī\ life	\òi\ coin	\y\ yet
\a\ mat	\e\ pet	\j\ job	\th\ thin	\yü\ few
\ā\ take	\ē\ easy	\ng\ sing	\th\ this	\yù\ cure
\ä\ cot, cart	\g\ go	\ō\ bone	\ü\ food	\zh\ vision

em·ploy·ee or **em·ploye** \im-ˌplȯi-'ē\ n : a person who works for pay in the service of an employer

em·ploy·er \im-'plȯi-ər\ n : one that employs others

em·ploy·ment \im-'plȯi-mənt\ n **1** : OCCUPATION 1, ACTIVITY **2** : the act of employing : the state of being employed

em·pow·er \im-'paủ-ər\ vb : to give authority or legal power to

em·press \'em-prəs\ n **1** : the wife of an emperor **2** : a woman who is the ruler of an empire in her own right

¹emp·ty \'emp-tē\ adj **emp·ti·er; emp·ti·est** **1** : containing nothing **2** : not occupied or lived in : VACANT ⟨an empty house⟩ — **emp·ti·ness** n

synonyms EMPTY and VACANT mean lacking contents which could or should be present. EMPTY is a general term and often the opposite of *full*. It then suggests that a thing has nothing in it at all ⟨an *empty* milk bottle⟩ or it may replace *vacant* ⟨the company left and the room is *empty*⟩ VACANT is the opposite of *occupied* and is used of something that is not occupied usually only for a while ⟨that apartment is *vacant* right now⟩

²empty vb **emp·tied; emp·ty·ing** **1** : to make empty : remove the contents of ⟨*empty* a barrel⟩ **2** : to transfer by emptying a container ⟨*empty* the flour into the bin⟩ **3** : to become empty **4** : ¹DISCHARGE 6 ⟨the river *empties* into the gulf⟩

emp·ty–hand·ed \ˌemp-tē-'han-dəd\ adj **1** : having nothing in the hands **2** : having gotten or gained nothing ⟨walked away from the contest *empty-handed*⟩

emp·ty–head·ed \ˌemp-tē-'hed-əd\ adj : having a merry silly nature

emu \'ē-ˌmyü\ n : an Australian bird that is like but smaller than the related ostrich and runs very fast

em·u·late \'em-yə-ˌlāt\ vb **em·u·lat·ed; em·u·lat·ing** : to try hard to equal or do better than ⟨*emulate* great people⟩

em·u·la·tion \ˌem-yə-'lā-shən\ n : ambition or effort to equal or do better than others

emul·si·fy \i-'məl-sə-ˌfi\ vb **emul·si·fied; emul·si·fy·ing** : to make an emulsion of

emul·sion \i-'məl-shən\ n : a material consisting of a mixture of liquids so that fine drops of one liquid are scattered throughout the other ⟨an *emulsion* of oil in water⟩

en- also **em-** prefix **1** : put into or on to ⟨*en*case⟩ ⟨*en*throne⟩ : go into or on to **2** : cause to be ⟨*en*slave⟩ **3** : provide with ⟨*em*power⟩ — in all senses usually *em-* before *b, m,* or *p*

¹-en \ən, -n\ also **-n** \n\ adj suffix : made of : consisting of ⟨earth*en*⟩ ⟨wool*en*⟩

²-en vb suffix **1** : become or cause to be ⟨sharp*en*⟩ **2** : cause or come to have ⟨length*en*⟩

en·able \in-'ā-bəl\ vb **en·abled; en·abling** : to give strength, power, or ability to : make able

en·act \in-'akt\ vb **1** : to make into law **2** : to act the part of (as in a play) — **en·act·ment** \-mənt\ n

¹enam·el \i-'nam-əl\ vb **enam·eled** or **enam·elled; enam·el·ing** or **enam·el·ling** : to cover with or as if with enamel

²enamel n **1** : a glassy substance used for coating the surface of metal, glass, and pottery **2** : the hard outer surface of the teeth **3** : a paint that forms a hard glossy coat

en·camp \in-'kamp\ vb : to set up and occupy a camp

en·camp·ment \in-'kamp-mənt\ n **1** : the act of making a camp **2** : CAMP

en·case \in-'kās\ vb **en·cased; en·cas·ing** : to enclose in or as if in a case

-ence \əns, -ns\ n suffix : action or process ⟨refer*ence*⟩

en·chant \in-'chant\ vb **1** : to put under a spell by or as if by charms or magic **2** : to please greatly — **en·chant·er** n — **en·chant·ment** \-mənt\ n

en·chant·ing \in-'chant-ing\ adj : very attractive : CHARMING

en·chant·ress \in-'chan-trəs\ n : a woman who enchants : WITCH, SORCERESS

en·cir·cle \in-'sər-kəl\ vb **en·cir·cled; en-**

emu

cir·cling 1 : to form a circle around : SURROUND **2 :** to pass completely around

en·close *or* **in·close** \in-'klōz\ *vb* **en·closed** *or* **in·closed**; **en·clos·ing** *or* **in·clos·ing 1 :** to close in all around : SURROUND ⟨a porch *enclosed* with glass⟩ **2 :** to put in the same parcel or envelope with something else ⟨*enclose* a snapshot with a letter⟩

synonyms ENCLOSE, ENVELOP, and FENCE mean to surround something and in this way close it off. ENCLOSE suggests putting up barriers (as walls) or a cover around something so as to give it protection or privacy ⟨a high hedge *encloses* the garden⟩ ENVELOP suggests something is completely surrounded by some kind of soft layer or covering that serves to screen or protect ⟨clouds *enveloped* the peaks of the mountains⟩ FENCE suggests that something is enclosed with or as if with a fence so that nothing may freely enter or leave ⟨a stone wall *fences* in the yard⟩

en·clo·sure *or* **in·clo·sure** \in-'klō-zhər\ *n* **1 :** the act of enclosing **2 :** an enclosed space **3 :** something (as a fence) that encloses **4 :** something enclosed (as in a letter)

en·com·pass \in-'kəm-pəs\ *vb* **1 :** ENCIRCLE 1 **2 :** INCLUDE

¹en·core \'än-,kōr\ *n* **1 :** a demand for the repeating of something on a program made by applause from an audience **2 :** a further appearance or performance given in response to applause

²encore *vb* **en·cored**; **en·cor·ing :** to call for an encore

¹en·coun·ter \in-'kaùnt-ər\ *vb* **1 :** to meet as an enemy : FIGHT **2 :** to meet face-to-face or unexpectedly ⟨*encounter* a friend⟩

²encounter *n* **1 :** a meeting with an enemy : COMBAT **2 :** a meeting face-to-face and often by chance

en·cour·age \in-'kər-ij\ *vb* **en·cour·aged**; **en·cour·ag·ing 1 :** to give courage, spirit, or hope to : HEARTEN **2 :** to give help to : AID

en·cour·age·ment \in-'kər-ij-mənt\ *n* **1 :** the act of encouraging : the state of being encouraged **2 :** something that encourages

en·croach \in-'krōch\ *vb* **1 :** to take over the rights or possessions of another little by little or in secret **2 :** to go beyond the usual or proper limits

en·crust *also* **in·crust** \in-'krəst\ *vb* **:** to cover with or as if with a crust

en·cum·ber \in-'kəm-bər\ *vb* **1 :** to weigh down : BURDEN **2 :** HINDER, HAMPER

-en·cy \ən-sē, -n-sē\ *n suffix, pl* **-en·cies :** quality or state ⟨despond*ency*⟩

en·cy·clo·pe·dia \in-,sī-klə-'pēd-ē-ə\ *n* **:** a book or a set of books containing information on all branches of learning in articles arranged alphabetically by subject

¹end \'end\ *n* **1 :** the part near the boundary of an area ⟨the south *end* of a town⟩ **2 :** the point (as of time or space) where something ceases to exist ⟨the *end* of vacation⟩ **3 :** the first or last part of a thing ⟨the front *end* of the car⟩ ⟨knotted the *end* of the rope⟩ **4 :** DEATH 1, DESTRUCTION ⟨a ship met its *end* in the storm⟩ **5 :** ¹PURPOSE, GOAL

²end *vb* **:** to bring or come to an end : STOP

en·dan·ger \in-'dān-jər\ *vb* **:** ²RISK 1

en·dear \in-'diər\ *vb* **:** to make dear or beloved ⟨their humor *endeared* them to the public⟩

en·dear·ment \in-'diər-mənt\ *n* **:** a word or an act that shows love or affection

¹en·deav·or \in-'dev-ər\ *vb* **:** to make an effort : TRY

²endeavor *n* **:** a serious determined effort

end·ing \'en-ding\ *n* **:** the final part : END

en·dive \'en-,dīv\ *n* **:** either of two plants related to the daisies and often used in salads

end·less \'end-ləs\ *adj* **1 :** having or seeming to have no end **2 :** joined at the ends ⟨an *endless* belt⟩ **— end·less·ly** *adv* **— end·less·ness** *n*

en·do·crine gland \,en-də-krən-, -,krīn-\ *n* **:** any of several glands of which the product passes into the blood rather than being discharged through ducts

en·dorse *or* **in·dorse** \in-'dòrs\ *vb* **en·dorsed** *or* **in·dorsed**; **en·dors·ing** *or* **in·dors·ing 1 :** to sign one's name on the back of (a check) to obtain payment **2 :** to give one's support to openly ⟨*endorse* a candidate⟩ **— en·dorse·ment** \-mənt\ *n*

en·dow \in-'daù\ *vb* **1 :** to provide with money for support ⟨*endow* a hospital⟩ **2 :** to provide with something freely or naturally ⟨humans are *endowed* with reason⟩

en·dow·ment \in-'daù-mənt\ *n* **:** the providing of a permanent fund for support or the fund provided

end·point \'end-,pòint\ *n* **:** either of two points that mark the ends of a line segment or a point that marks the end of a ray

en·dur·ance \in-'dùr-əns, -'dyùr-\ *n* **:** the

\ə\ abut	\aù\ out	\i\ tip	\ò\ saw	\ù\ foot
\ər\ further	\ch\ chin	\ī\ life	\òi\ coin	\y\ yet
\a\ mat	\e\ pet	\j\ job	\th\ thin	\yü\ few
\ā\ take	\ē\ easy	\ng\ sing	\th\ this	\yù\ cure
\ä\ cot, cart	\g\ go	\ō\ bone	\ü\ food	\zh\ vision

ability to put up with strain, suffering, or hardship

en·dure \in-'du̇r, -'dyu̇r\ *vb* **en·dured; en·dur·ing 1** : to continue in existence : LAST ⟨a civilization that has *endured* for centuries⟩ **2** : to put up with (as pain) patiently or firmly

end·ways \'en-ˌdwāz\ *adv or adj* **1** : on end **2** : with the end forward **3** : ¹LENGTHWISE

en·e·ma \'en-ə-mə\ *n* : the injection of liquid into the bowel or the liquid injected

en·e·my \'en-ə-mē\ *n, pl* **en·e·mies 1** : one that hates another : one that attacks or tries to harm another **2** : something that harms or threatens **3** : a nation with which one's own country is at war or a person belonging to such a nation

en·er·get·ic \ˌen-ər-'jet-ik\ *adj* : having or showing energy : ACTIVE, VIGOROUS — **en·er·get·i·cal·ly** \-i-kə-lē\ *adv*

en·er·gy \'en-ər-jē\ *n, pl* **en·er·gies 1** : ability to be active : strength of body or mind to do things or to work **2** : usable power or the resources (as oil) for producing such power **synonyms** see POWER

en·fold \in-'fōld\ *vb* **1** : to wrap up : cover with or as if with folds **2** : ¹EMBRACE 1

en·force \in-'fōrs\ *vb* **en·forced; en·forc·ing 1** : to demand and see that one gets ⟨*enforce* obedience to school rules⟩ **2** : to put into force ⟨*enforce* a law⟩ — **en·force·ment** \mənt\ *n*

en·gage \in-'gāj\ *vb* **en·gaged; en·gag·ing 1** : to pledge (as oneself) to do something : PROMISE **2** : to catch and hold fast (as the attention) ⟨the story *engaged* my interest⟩ **3** : to take part in something ⟨*engage* in a sport⟩ **4** : to enter into contest or battle with ⟨*engage* the enemy⟩ **5** : to arrange for the services or use of : HIRE ⟨*engage* a plumber⟩ ⟨*engage* a room at the hotel⟩ **6** : to put or become in gear : MESH

en·gaged \in-'gājd\ *adj* **1** : busy with some activity ⟨I am *engaged* just now⟩ **2** : pledged to be married ⟨an *engaged* couple⟩

en·gage·ment \in-'gāj-mənt\ *n* **1** : the act of engaging : the state of being engaged **2** : EMPLOYMENT 2 ⟨a week's *engagement* at the theater⟩ **3** : an appointment at a certain time and place **4** : a fight between armed forces

en·gag·ing \in-'gā-jing\ *adj* : ATTRACTIVE ⟨an *engaging* smile⟩

en·gen·der \in-'jen-dər\ *vb* : to cause to be or develop : PRODUCE

en·gine \'en-jən\ *n* **1** : a mechanical tool or device ⟨tanks, planes, and other *engines* of war⟩ **2** : a machine for driving or operating something especially by using the energy of steam, gasoline, or oil **3** : ¹LOCOMOTIVE

Word History The English word *engine* came from a Latin word that meant "natural talent." At first the word *engine* meant "skill" or "cleverness." In time the word came to be used for things that are products of human skills—tools and machines, for example.

¹en·gi·neer \ˌen-jə-'niər\ *n* **1** : a member of a military group devoted to engineering work **2** : a person who specializes in engineering ⟨an electrical *engineer*⟩ ⟨a mining *engineer*⟩ **3** : a person who runs or has charge of an engine or of machinery or technical equipment

²engineer *vb* **1** : to plan, build, or manage as an engineer **2** : to plan out : CONTRIVE

en·gi·neer·ing \ˌen-jə-'niər-ing\ *n* : a science by which the properties of matter and the sources of energy in nature are made useful to man in structures (as roads and dams), machines (as automobiles and computers), and products (as plastics and radios)

¹En·glish \'ing-glish\ *adj* : of or relating to England, its people, or the English language

²English *n* **1** : the language of England, the United States, and some other countries now or at one time under British rule **2 English** *pl* : the people of England

English horn *n* : a woodwind instrument that is similar to an oboe but is longer and has a deeper tone

English horn

en·grave \in-'grāv\ *vb* **en·graved; en·grav·ing 1** : to cut or carve (as letters or designs) on a hard surface **2** : to cut lines, letters, figures, or designs on or into (a hard surface) often for use in printing **3** : to print from a cut surface ⟨an *engraved* invitation⟩ — **en·grav·er** *n*

en·grav·ing \in-'grā-ving\ *n* **1** : the art of cutting something especially into the surface of wood, stone, or metal **2** : a print made from an engraved surface

en·gross \in-'grōs\ *vb* : to take up the whole interest of ⟨be *engrossed* in a puzzle⟩

en·gulf \in-'gəlf\ *vb* : to flow over and

swallow up ⟨the town was *engulfed* by the flood⟩ ⟨a person *engulfed* by fear⟩

en·hance \in-'hans\ *vb* **en·hanced; en·hanc·ing** : to make greater or better

enig·ma \i-'nig-mə\ *n* : something hard to understand

en·joy \in-'jȯi\ *vb* **1** : to take pleasure or satisfaction in ⟨*enjoy* camping⟩ **2** : to have for one's use or benefit ⟨*enjoy* good health⟩

en·joy·able \in-'jȯi-ə-bəl\ *adj* : being a source of pleasure

en·joy·ment \in-'jȯi-mənt\ *n* **1** : the action or condition of enjoying something **2** : something that gives pleasure **synonyms** see PLEASURE

en·large \in-'lärj\ *vb* **en·larged; en·larg·ing** : to make or grow larger : EXPAND

en·large·ment \in-'lärj-mənt\ *n* **1** : an act of enlarging **2** : the state of being enlarged **3** : a photographic print made larger than the negative

en·light·en \in-'līt-n\ *vb* : to give knowledge to

en·list \in-'list\ *vb* **1** : to join the armed forces as a volunteer **2** : to obtain the help of ⟨*enlist* friends in painting the house⟩ — **en·list·ment** \-mənt\ *n*

en·list·ed man \in-'lis-təd-\ *n* : a man or woman serving in the armed forces who ranks below a commissioned officer or warrant officer

en·liv·en \in-'lī-vən\ *vb* : to put life or spirit into : make active or cheerful

en·mi·ty \'en-mət-ē\ *n, pl* **en·mi·ties** : hatred especially when shared : ILL WILL

enor·mous \i-'nȯr-məs\ *adj* : unusually large : HUGE — **enor·mous·ly** *adv*

¹**enough** \i-'nəf\ *adj* : equal to the needs or demands ⟨there was just *enough* food⟩

²**enough** *adv* : in sufficient amount or degree ⟨are you warm *enough*⟩

³**enough** *pron* : a sufficient number or amount ⟨we have *enough* to meet our needs⟩

en·rage \in-'rāj\ *vb* **en·raged; en·rag·ing** : to fill with rage : ANGER

en·rich \in-'rich\ *vb* **1** : to make rich or richer **2** : to improve the quality of food by adding vitamins and minerals **3** : to make more fertile ⟨*enrich* soil with fertilizer⟩

en·roll *or* **en·rol** \in-'rōl\ *vb* **en·rolled; en·roll·ing** : to include (as a name) on a roll or list

en·roll·ment *or* **en·rol·ment** \in-'rōl-mənt\ *n* **1** : the act of enrolling or being enrolled **2** : the number of persons enrolled

en route \än-'rüt\ *adv* : on or along the way

en·sem·ble \än-'säm-bəl\ *n* : a group of musicians or dancers performing together

en·shrine \in-'shrīn\ *vb* **en·shrined; en·shrin·ing** : to cherish as if sacred

en·sign \'en-sən, *1 is also* -ˌsīn\ *n* **1** : a flag flown as the symbol of nationality **2** : a commissioned officer of the lowest rank in the Navy or Coast Guard

en·slave \in-'slāv\ *vb* **en·slaved; en·slav·ing** : to make a slave of

en·sue \in-'sü\ *vb* **en·sued; en·su·ing** : to come after in time or as a result : FOLLOW

en·sure \in-'shu̇r\ *vb* **en·sured; en·sur·ing** : to make sure, certain, or safe : GUARANTEE

en·tan·gle \in-'tang-gəl\ *vb* **en·tan·gled; en·tan·gling** **1** : to make tangled or confused **2** : to catch in a tangle — **en·tan·gle·ment** \-gəl-mənt\ *n*

en·ter \'ent-ər\ *vb* **1** : to come or go in or into ⟨you may *enter* now⟩ ⟨*enter* a room⟩ **2** : to put into a list : write down **3** : to become a member or a member of : JOIN **4** : to become a party to or take an interest in something ⟨*enter* into a treaty⟩ **5** : PENETRATE 1, PIERCE ⟨the thorn *entered* my thumb⟩ **6** : to cause to be admitted (as to a school) ⟨*enter* students in college⟩

en·ter·prise \'ent-ər-ˌprīz\ *n* **1** : an undertaking requiring courage and energy **2** : willingness to engage in daring or difficult action **3** : a business organization or activity

en·ter·pris·ing \'ent-ər-ˌprī-zing\ *adj* : bold and energetic in trying or experimenting

en·ter·tain \ˌent-ər-'tān\ *vb* **1** : to greet in a friendly way and provide for especially in one's home : have as a guest ⟨*entertain* friends over the weekend⟩ **2** : to have in mind ⟨*entertain* kind thoughts⟩ **3** : to provide amusement for **synonyms** see AMUSE

en·ter·tain·er \ˌent-ər-'tā-nər\ *n* : a person who performs for public entertainment

en·ter·tain·ment \ˌent-ər-'tān-mənt\ *n* **1** : the act of entertaining or amusing **2** : something (as a show) that is a form of amusement or recreation

en·thrall *or* **en·thral** \in-'thrȯl\ *vb* **en·thralled; en·thrall·ing** : to hold the attention of completely : CHARM

en·throne \in-'thrōn\ *vb* **en·throned; en·thron·ing** **1** : to seat on a throne **2** : to place in a high position

\ə\ **abut**	\au̇\ **out**	\i\ **tip**	\ȯ\ **saw**	\u̇\ **foot**
\ər\ **further**	\ch\ **chin**	\ī\ **life**	\ȯi\ **coin**	\y\ **yet**
\a\ **mat**	\e\ **pet**	\j\ **job**	\th\ **thin**	\yü\ **few**
\ā\ **take**	\ē\ **easy**	\ng\ **sing**	\th\ **this**	\yu̇\ **cure**
\ä\ **cot, cart**	\g\ **go**	\ō\ **bone**	\ü\ **food**	\zh\ **vision**

en·thu·si·asm \in-'thü-zē-,az-əm, -'thyü-\ *n* : strong feeling in favor of something ⟨their *enthusiasm* for sports⟩

en·thu·si·ast \in-'thü-zē-,ast, -'thyü-\ *n* : a person filled with enthusiasm

en·thu·si·as·tic \in-,thü-zē-'as-tik, -,thyü-\ *adj* : full of enthusiasm : EAGER

en·thu·si·as·ti·cal·ly \in-,thü-zē-'as-ti-kə-lē, -,thyü-\ *adv* : with enthusiasm

en·tice \in-'tīs\ *vb* **en·ticed; en·tic·ing** : to attract by raising hope or desire : TEMPT

en·tire \in-'tīr\ *adj* : complete in all parts or respects ⟨the *entire* day⟩ ⟨was in *entire* control⟩ — **en·tire·ly** *adv*

en·tire·ty \in-'tī-rət-ē, -'tīr-tē\ *n, pl* **en·tire·ties 1** : a state of completeness **2** : ²WHOLE 2

en·ti·tle \in-'tīt-l\ *vb* **en·ti·tled; en·ti·tling 1** : to give a title to **2** : to give a right or claim to ⟨buying a ticket *entitles* you to a seat⟩

en·trails \'en-trəlz, -,trālz\ *n pl* : the internal parts of an animal

¹en·trance \'en-trəns\ *n* **1** : the act of entering **2** : a door, gate, or way for entering **3** : permission to enter : ADMISSION ⟨apply for *entrance* to college⟩

²en·trance \in-'trans\ *vb* **en·tranced; en·tranc·ing 1** : to put into a trance **2** : to fill with delight and wonder

en·trap \in-'trap\ *vb* **en·trapped; en·trap·ping** : to catch in or as if in a trap

en·treat \in-'trēt\ *vb* : to ask in an earnest way : BEG

en·treaty \in-'trēt-ē\ *n, pl* **en·treat·ies** : an act of entreating : PLEA

en·trust *or* **in·trust** \in-'trəst\ *vb* **1** : to give care of something to as a trust ⟨*entrusted* me with their money⟩ **2** : to give to another with confidence ⟨I'll *entrust* the job to you⟩

en·try \'en-trē\ *n, pl* **en·tries 1** : the act of entering : ENTRANCE **2** : a place (as a hall or door) through which entrance is made **3** : the act of making (as in a book or a list) a written record of something **4** : something entered in a list or a record ⟨dictionary *entries*⟩ **5** : a person or thing entered in a contest

en·twine \in-'twīn\ *vb* **en·twined; en·twin·ing** : to twist or twine together or around

enu·mer·ate \i-'nü-mə-,rāt, -'nyü-\ *vb* **enu·mer·at·ed; enu·mer·at·ing 1** : ¹COUNT 1 **2** : to name one after another : LIST

enun·ci·ate \ē-'nən-sē-,āt\ *vb* **enun·ci·at·ed; enun·ci·at·ing 1** : ANNOUNCE 1 **2** : to pronounce words or parts of words

enun·ci·a·tion \ē-,nən-sē-'ā-shən\ *n* : clearness of pronunciation

en·vel·op \in-'vel-əp\ *vb* : to put a covering completely around : wrap up or in **synonyms** see ENCLOSE

en·ve·lope \'en-və-,lōp, 'än-\ *n* : an enclosing cover or wrapper (as for a letter)

en·vi·ous \'en-vē-əs\ *adj* : feeling or showing envy — **en·vi·ous·ly** *adv* — **en·vi·ous·ness** *n*

en·vi·ron·ment \in-'vī-rən-mənt, -'vī-ərn-mənt\ *n* : the conditions or influences that affect growth and development (as of a child or a plant)

en·voy \'en-,vói, 'än-\ *n* **1** : a representative sent by one government to another **2** : MESSENGER

¹en·vy \'en-vē\ *n, pl* **en·vies 1** : a feeling of discontent at another's good fortune together with a desire to have the same good fortune oneself ⟨filled with *envy* on seeing their playmate's presents⟩ **2** : a person or a thing that is envied ⟨the *envy* of all my friends⟩

²envy *vb* **en·vied; en·vy·ing** : to feel envy toward or because of

en·zyme \'en-,zīm\ *n* : one of the substances produced by body cells that help bodily chemical activities (as digestion) to take place but are not destroyed in so doing

eon *variant of* AEON

¹ep·ic \'ep-ik\ *adj* : of, relating to, or characteristic of an epic

²epic *n* : a long poem that tells the story of a hero's deeds

¹ep·i·dem·ic \,ep-ə-'dem-ik\ *adj* : spreading widely and affecting large numbers of people at the same time ⟨an *epidemic* disease⟩

²epidemic *n* **1** : a rapidly spreading outbreak of disease **2** : something that spreads or develops rapidly like an epidemic disease

ep·i·der·mis \,ep-ə-'dər-məs\ *n* **1** : a thin outer layer of skin covering the dermis **2** : any of various thin outer layers of plants or animals

ep·i·sode \'ep-ə-,sōd\ *n* : an event or one of a series of events that stands out clearly in one's life, in history, or in a story

epis·tle \i-'pis-əl\ *n* : ¹LETTER 2

ep·i·taph \'ep-ə-,taf\ *n* : a brief statement on a tombstone in memory of a dead person

ep·och \'ep-ək\ *n* : a period marked by unusual or important events

¹equal \'ē-kwəl\ *adj* **1** : exactly the same in number, amount, degree, rank, or quality ⟨an *equal* number of apples and oranges⟩ ⟨of *equal* rank⟩ **2** : evenly balanced ⟨an *equal* contest⟩ **3** : having enough strength, ability, or means : ADEQUATE ⟨*equal* to the task⟩ **synonyms** see SAME — **equal·ly** \'ē-kwə-lē\ *adv*

²equal *n* : one that is equal to another

³equal *vb* **equaled** *or* **equalled; equaling** *or* **equal·ling** : to be equal to

equal·i·ty \i-'kwäl-ət-ē\ *n, pl* **equal·i·ties** : the condition or state of being equal

equal·ize \'ē-kwə-,līz\ *vb* **equal·ized; equal·iz·ing** : to make equal or even

equa·tion \i-'kwā-zhən\ *n* **1** : a statement of the equality of two mathematical expressions **2** : an expression representing a chemical reaction by means of chemical symbols

equa·tor \i-'kwāt-ər\ *n* : an imaginary circle around the earth everywhere equally distant from the north pole and the south pole

equa·to·ri·al \,ē-kwə-'tōr-ē-əl, ,ek-wə-\ *adj* **1** : of, relating to, or lying near the equator **2** : of, coming from, or suggesting the region at or near the equator

eques·tri·an \i-'kwes-trē-ən\ *adj* : of or relating to horses or to the riding or riders of horses

equi·lat·er·al \,ē-kwə-'lat-ə-rəl, ,ek-wə-\ *adj* : having all sides of equal length ⟨an *equilateral* triangle⟩

equi·lib·ri·um \,ē-kwə-'lib-rē-əm, ,ek-wə-\ *n* **1** : a state of balance between opposing weights, forces, or influences **2** : the normal bodily adjustment of a person or animal in relation to its environment

equi·nox \'ē-kwə-,näks, 'ek-wə-\ *n* : either of the two times each year when the sun's center crosses the equator and day and night (as on March 21 and September 23) are everywhere of equal length

equip \i-'kwip\ *vb* **equipped; equip·ping** : to make ready for a purpose by supplying what is necessary

equip·ment \i-'kwip-mənt\ *n* **1** : an act of equipping **2** : supplies and tools needed for a special purpose

¹equiv·a·lent \i-'kwiv-ə-lənt\ *adj* : alike or equal in number, value, or meaning

²equivalent *n* : something equivalent

¹-er \ər\ *adj suffix or adv suffix* — used to form the comparative degree of adjectives and adverbs of one syllable ⟨hott*er*⟩ ⟨dri*er*⟩ and of some adjectives and adverbs of two or more syllables ⟨complet*er*⟩ ⟨earli*er*⟩

²-er \ər\ *also* **-ier** \ē-ər, yər\ *or* **-yer** \yər\ *n suffix* **1** : a person whose work or business is connected with ⟨hatt*er*⟩ ⟨furri*er*⟩ ⟨law*yer*⟩ **2** : a person or thing belonging

to or associated with ⟨old-tim*er*⟩ **3** : a native of : resident of ⟨New York*er*⟩ **4** : one that has **5** : one that produces **6** : one that does or performs a specified action ⟨report*er*⟩ **7** : one that is a suitable object of a specified action **8** : one that is ⟨foreign*er*⟩

era \'ir-ə, 'er-ə\ *n* **1** : a period of time starting from some special date or event ⟨the Christian *era*⟩ **2** : an important period of history ⟨the colonial *era*⟩

erad·i·cate \i-'rad-ə-,kāt\ *vb* **erad·i·cat·ed; erad·i·cat·ing** : to remove by or as if by tearing up by the roots : destroy completely

erase \i-'rās\ *vb* **erased; eras·ing** : to cause to disappear by rubbing or scraping ⟨*erase* a chalk mark⟩

eras·er \i-'rā-sər\ *n* : something (as a piece of rubber or a felt pad) for erasing marks

era·sure \i-'rā-shər\ *n* **1** : an act of erasing **2** : something erased

¹ere \eər, aər\ *prep* : ²BEFORE 3

²ere *conj* : ³BEFORE 2

¹erect \i-'rekt\ *adj* : being straight up and down — **erect·ly** *adv* — **erect·ness** *n*

²erect *vb* **1** : to put up by fitting together materials or parts **2** : to set straight up **synonyms** see BUILD — **erector** \i-'rek-tər\ *n*

er·mine \'ər-mən\ *n* : a weasel of northern regions that is valued for its winter coat of white fur with a tail tipped in black

ermine

erode \i-'rōd\ *vb* **erod·ed; erod·ing** : to eat into : wear away : destroy by wearing away ⟨a shore *eroded* by the sea⟩

ero·sion \i-'rō-zhən\ *n* : the act of eroding : the state of being eroded

err \'eər, 'ər\ *vb* **1** : to make a mistake **2** : to do wrong : SIN

er·rand \'er-ənd\ *n* **1** : a short trip made to take care of some business **2** : the business done on an errand

\ə\ **abut**	\aů\ **out**	\i\ **tip**	\ȯ\ **saw**	\ů\ **foot**
\ər\ **further**	\ch\ **chin**	\ī\ **life**	\ȯi\ **coin**	\y\ **yet**
\a\ **mat**	\e\ **pet**	\j\ **job**	\th\ **thin**	\yü\ **few**
\ā\ **take**	\ē\ **easy**	\ng\ **sing**	\th\ **this**	\yů\ **cure**
\ä\ **cot, cart**	\g\ **go**	\ō\ **bone**	\ü\ **food**	\zh\ **vision**

er·rant \'er-ənt\ *adj* **1** : wandering in search of adventure ⟨an *errant* knight⟩ **2** : straying from a proper course

er·rat·ic \i-'rat-ik\ *adj* : not following the usual or expected course

er·ro·ne·ous \i-'rō-nē-əs\ *adj* : INCORRECT 1

er·ror \'er-ər\ *n* : a failure to be correct or accurate : MISTAKE ⟨an *error* in adding figures⟩

synonyms ERROR, MISTAKE, and BLUNDER mean an act or statement that is not right or true or proper. ERROR suggests that one fails to follow a model correctly ⟨an *error* in addition⟩ MISTAKE suggests that one misunderstands something or does not intend to do wrong ⟨took someone else's coat by *mistake*⟩ BLUNDER suggests a really bad mistake made because of a lack of knowledge, intelligence, caution, or care ⟨the actors made several *blunders* during the play⟩

erupt \i-'rəpt\ *vb* **1** : to burst forth or cause to burst forth ⟨lava *erupting* from a volcano⟩ **2** : to break through a surface **3** : to break out (as with a skin rash)

erup·tion \i-'rəp-shən\ *n* **1** : a bursting forth ⟨*eruption* of lava from a volcano⟩ **2** : a breaking out (as of a skin rash) or the resulting rash

-ery \ə-rē, rē\ *n suffix, pl* **-er·ies** **1** : qualities considered as a group : character : -NESS **2** : art : practice **3** : place of doing, keeping, producing, or selling ⟨fish*ery*⟩ ⟨bak*ery*⟩ **4** : collection : aggregate ⟨fin*ery*⟩ **5** : state or condition ⟨slav*ery*⟩

1-es \əz, iz *after s, z, sh, ch; z after v or a vowel*\ *n pl suffix* **1** — used to form the plural of most nouns that end in *s* ⟨glass*es*⟩, *z* ⟨buzz*es*⟩, *sh* ⟨bush*es*⟩, *ch* ⟨peach*es*⟩, or a final *y* that changes to *i* ⟨dad*ies*⟩ and of some nouns ending in *f* ⟨loav*es*⟩ **2** : 1-s 2

2-es *vb suffix* — used to form the third person singular present of most verbs that end in *s* ⟨bless*es*⟩, *z* ⟨fizz*es*⟩, *sh* ⟨hush*es*⟩, *ch* ⟨catch*es*⟩, or a final *y* that changes to *i* ⟨def*ies*⟩

es·ca·la·tor \'es-kə-ˌlāt-ər\ *n* : a moving stairway arranged like an endless belt

es·ca·pade \'es-kə-ˌpād\ *n* : a daring or reckless adventure

1es·cape \is-'kāp\ *vb* **es·caped; es·cap·ing** **1** : to get away : get free or clear ⟨*escape* from a burning building⟩ **2** : to keep free of : AVOID ⟨managed to *escape* injury⟩ **3** : to fail to be noticed or remembered by ⟨the name *escapes* me⟩ **4** : to leak out from some enclosed place

Word History Picture a person who is held fast by a cape or cloak. The person being held may be able to slip out of the garment and so escape from the captor. The word *escape* is based on such a picture. The English word *escape* came from an Old French word that came from two Latin words. The first of these Latin words meant "out of" and the second meant "cloak."

2escape *n* **1** : the act of escaping **2** : a way of escaping

1es·cort \'es-ˌkort\ *n* **1** : one (as a person or group) that accompanies another to give protection or show courtesy **2** : the man who goes on a date with a woman

2es·cort \is-'kort\ *vb* : to accompany as an escort

1-ese \'ēz\ *adj suffix* : of, relating to, or coming from a certain place or country ⟨Japan*ese*⟩

2-ese *n suffix, pl* **-ese** **1** : native or resident of a specified place or country ⟨Chin*ese*⟩ **2** : language of a particular place, country, or nationality **3** : speech or literary style of a specified place, person, or group

Es·ki·mo \'es-kə-ˌmō\ *n, pl* **Es·ki·mos** : a member of a group of peoples of Alaska, northern Canada, Greenland, and northeastern Siberia

Eskimo dog *n* : a sled dog of northern North America

esoph·a·gus \i-'säf-ə-gəs\ *n, pl* **esoph·a·gi** \-ˌgī, -ˌjī\ : the tube that leads from the mouth through the throat to the stomach

es·pe·cial \is-'pesh-əl\ *adj* : SPECIAL — **es·pe·cial·ly** *adv*

es·pi·o·nage \'es-pē-ə-ˌnäzh\ *n* : the practice of spying : the use of spies

es·py \is-'pī\ *vb* **es·pied; es·py·ing** : to catch sight of

-ess \əs\ *n suffix* : female ⟨godd*ess*⟩

1es·say \e-'sā, 'es-ˌā\ *vb* : 1TRY 6

2es·say \'es-ˌā, 1 also e-'sā\ *n* **1** : 2ATTEMPT **2** : a usually short piece of writing dealing with a subject from a personal point of view

es·say·ist \'es-ˌā-əst\ *n* : a writer of essays

es·sence \'es-ns\ *n* **1** : the basic part of something ⟨freedom is the *essence* of democracy⟩ **2** : a substance made from a plant or drug and having its special qualities **3** : 1PERFUME 2

1es·sen·tial \i-'sen-chəl\ *adj* **1** : forming or belonging to the basic part of something ⟨free speech is an *essential* right of citizenship⟩ **2** : important in the highest degree ⟨it is *essential* that we all meet here⟩ — **es·sen·tial·ly** *adv*

²**essential** *n* : something that is essential

-est \əst\ *adj suffix or adv suffix* — used to form the superlative degree of adjectives and adverbs of one syllable ⟨fatt*est*⟩ ⟨lat*est*⟩ and of some adjectives and adverbs of two or more syllables ⟨lucki*est*⟩ ⟨often*est*⟩

es·tab·lish \is-'tab-lish\ *vb* **1** : to bring into being : FOUND ⟨*establish* a colony⟩ **2** : to put beyond doubt : PROVE

es·tab·lish·ment \is-'tab-lish-mənt\ *n* **1** : the act of establishing **2** : a place for residence or for business

es·tate \is-'tāt\ *n* **1** : ¹STATE 1 ⟨the low *estate* of the poor⟩ **2** : the property of all kinds that a person leaves at death **3** : a fine country house on a large piece of land

¹**es·teem** \is-'tēm\ *n* : high regard

²**esteem** *vb* : to think well or highly of

esthetic *variant of* AESTHETIC

¹**es·ti·mate** \'es-tə-ˌmāt\ *vb* **es·ti·mat·ed; es·ti·mat·ing** **1** : to give or form a general idea of (as the value, size, or cost of something) ⟨*estimate* the height of a friend⟩ **2** : to form an opinion ⟨I *estimate* our team will win⟩

²**es·ti·mate** \'es-tə-mət\ *n* **1** : an opinion or judgment especially of the value or quality of something **2** : an approximation of the size or cost of something

es·ti·ma·tion \ˌes-tə-'mā-shən\ *n* **1** : the making of an estimate : JUDGMENT **2** : an estimate formed : OPINION

et cet·era \et-'set-ə-rə, -'se-trə\ : and others of the same kind : and so forth : and so on

etch \'ech\ *vb* : to produce designs or figures on metal or glass by lines eaten into the substance by acid

etch·ing \'ech-ing\ *n* **1** : the art or process of producing drawings or pictures by printing from etched plates **2** : a picture made from an etched plate

eter·nal \i-'tərn-l\ *adj* **1** : lasting forever : having no beginning and no end **2** : continuing without interruption

eter·ni·ty \i-'tər-nət-ē\ *n, pl* **eter·ni·ties** **1** : time without end **2** : the state after death **3** : a period of time that seems to be endless

-eth — see -TH

ether \'ē-thər\ *n* **1** : the clear upper part of the sky **2** : a light flammable liquid used to dissolve fats and as an anesthetic

ethe·re·al \i-'thir-ē-əl\ *adj* **1** : HEAVENLY 1 **2** : very delicate : AIRY

eth·i·cal \'eth-i-kəl\ *adj* **1** : of or relating to

ethics **2** : following accepted rules of behavior ⟨an *ethical* doctor⟩

eth·ics \'eth-iks\ *n sing or pl* **1** : a branch of philosophy dealing with moral duty and with questions of what is good and bad **2** : the rules of moral behavior governing an individual or a group

eth·nic \'eth-nik\ *adj* : of or relating to races or large groups of people classed according to common characteristics and customs — **eth·ni·cal·ly** \-ni-kə-lē\ *adv*

et·i·quette \'et-i-kət, -ˌket\ *n* : the rules governing the proper way to behave or to do something

-ette \'et\ *n suffix* **1** : little one ⟨kitchen-*ette*⟩ **2** : female **3** : imitation

et·y·mol·o·gy \ˌet-ə-'mäl-ə-jē\ *n, pl* **et·y·mol·o·gies** : the history of a word shown by tracing it or its parts back to the earliest known forms and meanings both in its own language and any other language from which it may have been taken

Word History We can trace the English word *etymology* back to a Greek word. This Greek word meant "the true meaning of a word based on its origin." This word came in turn from a Greek word which meant "true."

eu·ca·lyp·tus \ˌyü-kə-'lip-təs\ *n, pl* **eu·ca·lyp·ti** \-ˌtī\ *or* **eu·ca·lyp·tus·es** : a tree of a kind native mainly to western Australia and widely grown for shade, timber, gum, and oil

Eu·cha·rist \'yü-kə-rəst\ *n* : COMMUNION 2

eu·gle·na \yü-'glē-nə\ *n* : any of numerous tiny green plants that are single cells which swim about with long flagella

¹**Eu·ro·pe·an** \ˌyùr-ə-'pē-ən\ *adj* : of or relating to Europe or the Europeans

²**European** *n* : a native or resident of Europe

evac·u·ate \i-'vak-yə-ˌwāt\ *vb* **evac·u·at·ed; evac·u·at·ing** **1** : to make empty : empty out **2** : to discharge waste matter from the body **3** : to remove troops or people from a place of danger ⟨*evacuate* a city⟩

evade \i-'vād\ *vb* **evad·ed; evad·ing** : to get away from or avoid meeting directly ⟨*evade* a question⟩

eval·u·ate \i-'val-yə-ˌwāt\ *vb* **eval·u·at·ed; eval·u·at·ing** : to find or estimate the value of

\ə\ abut	\aù\ out	\i\ tip	\ó\ saw	\ù\ foot
\ər\ further	\ch\ chin	\ī\ life	\ói\ coin	\y\ yet
\a\ mat	\e\ pet	\j\ job	\th\ thin	\yü\ few
\ā\ take	\ē\ easy	\ng\ sing	\th\ this	\yù\ cure
\ä\ cot, cart	\g\ go	\ō\ bone	\ü\ food	\zh\ vision

eval·u·a·tion \i-ˌval-yə-'wā-shən\ *n* : the act or result of evaluating

evan·ge·list \i-'van-jə-ləst\ *n* : a Christian preacher who goes about from place to place trying to change or increase people's religious feelings

evap·o·rate \i-'vap-ə-ˌrāt\ *vb* **evap·o·rat·ed; evap·o·rat·ing** **1** : to change into vapor ⟨a liquid that *evaporates* quickly⟩ **2** : to disappear without being seen to go **3** : to remove some of the water from something (as by heating)

evap·o·ra·tion \i-ˌvap-ə-'rā-shən\ *n* : the process of evaporating

eve \'ēv\ *n* **1** : EVENING **2** : the evening or day before a special day ⟨Christmas *eve*⟩ **3** : the period just before an important event

¹even \'ē-vən\ *adj* **1** : being without breaks or bumps ⟨*even* ground⟩ **2** : staying the same over a period of time ⟨*even* breathing⟩ **3** : being on the same line or level ⟨water *even* with the rim of a glass⟩ **4** : equal in size, number, or amount ⟨bread cut in *even* slices⟩ **5** : ¹EQUAL 2, FAIR ⟨an *even* trade⟩ **6** : possible to divide by two ⟨*even* numbers⟩ **synonyms** see LEVEL — **even·ly** *adv* — **even·ness** *n*

²even *adv* **1** : at the very time : JUST ⟨*even* as the clock struck⟩ **2** : INDEED ⟨we were willing, *even* eager, to help⟩ **3** — used to stress an extreme or highly unlikely condition or instance ⟨so simple *even* a child can do it⟩ **4** : to a greater extent or degree : STILL ⟨*even* better⟩ **5** : so much as ⟨didn't *even* offer to help⟩

³even *vb* : to make or become even

eve·ning \'ēv-ning\ *n* : the final part of the day and early part of the night

evening star *n* : a bright planet (as Venus) seen in the western sky after sunset

event \i-'vent\ *n* **1** : something usually of importance that happens **2** : a social occasion (as a party) **3** : the fact of happening ⟨in the *event* of rain⟩ **4** : a contest in a program of sports **synonyms** see INCIDENT

event·ful \i-'vent-fəl\ *adj* **1** : filled with events **2** : very important

even·tide \'ē-vən-ˌtīd\ *n* : EVENING

even·tu·al \i-'ven-chə-wəl\ *adj* : coming at some later time ⟨*eventual* success⟩ — **even·tu·al·ly** *adv*

ev·er \'ev-ər\ *adv* **1** : at all times : ALWAYS ⟨*ever* faithful⟩ **2** : at any time ⟨has this *ever* been done before⟩ **3** : in any way ⟨how can I *ever* thank you⟩

ev·er·glade \'ev-ər-ˌglād\ *n* : a swampy grassland

¹ev·er·green \'ev-ər-ˌgrēn\ *adj* : having leaves that stay green through more than one growing season

²evergreen *n* **1** : an evergreen plant (as a pine or a laurel) **2** **evergreens** *pl* : branches and leaves of evergreens used for decorations

ev·er·last·ing \ˌev-ər-'las-ting\ *adj* **1** : lasting forever : ETERNAL ⟨*everlasting* fame⟩ **2** : going on for a long time or for too long a time ⟨stop that *everlasting* noise⟩ — **ev·er·last·ing·ly** *adv*

ev·er·more \ˌev-ər-'mōr\ *adj* : FOREVER 1

ev·ery \'ev-rē\ *adj* : being each of a group or series without leaving out any ⟨heard *every* word you said⟩

ev·ery·body \'ev-ri-ˌbäd-ē, -bəd-ē\ *pron* : every person

ev·ery·day \ˌev-rē-'dā\ *adj* : used or suitable for every day : ORDINARY

ev·ery·one \'ev-rē-wən, -ˌwən\ *pron* : every person

ev·ery·thing \'ev-rē-ˌthing\ *pron* : every thing : ALL

ev·ery·where \'ev-rē-ˌhweər, -ˌhwaər, -ˌweər, -ˌwaər\ *adv* : in or to every place or part

evict \i-'vikt\ *vb* : to put out from property by legal action

ev·i·dence \'ev-ə-dəns\ *n* **1** : an outward sign : INDICATION ⟨find *evidence* of a robbery⟩ **2** : material presented to a court to help find the truth in a matter

ev·i·dent \'ev-ə-dənt\ *adj* : clear to the sight or to the mind : PLAIN — **ev·i·dent·ly** \-dənt-lē, -ˌdent-\ *adv*

¹evil \'ē-vəl\ *adj* **1** : morally bad : WICKED ⟨*evil* deeds⟩ **2** : causing harm : tending to injure **synonyms** see BAD

²evil *n* **1** : something that brings sorrow, trouble, or destruction ⟨the *evils* of poverty⟩ **2** : the fact of suffering or wrongdoing

evoke \i-'vōk\ *vb* **evoked; evok·ing** : to call forth or up : SUMMON

evo·lu·tion \ˌev-ə-'lü-shən, ˌē-və-\ *n* **1** : the process of development of an animal or a plant **2** : the theory that the various kinds of existing animals and plants have come from kinds that existed in the past

evolve \i-'välv\ *vb* **evolved; evolv·ing** : to grow or develop out of something

ewe \'yü\ *n* : a female sheep

ex- \'eks\ *prefix* **1** : out of : outside **2** : former

¹ex·act \ig-'zakt\ *vb* : to demand and get by force or threat

²exact *adj* : showing close agreement with fact : ACCURATE **synonyms** see CORRECT — **ex·act·ly** *adv* — **ex·act·ness** *n*

ex·act·ing \ig-'zak-ting\ *adj* : making

many or difficult demands upon a person : TRYING

ex•ag•ger•ate \ig-'zaj-ə-,rāt\ *vb* **ex•ag•ger•at•ed; ex•ag•ger•at•ing** : to enlarge a fact or statement beyond what is true

ex•ag•ger•a•tion \ig-,zaj-ə-'rā-shən\ *n* **1** : the act of exaggerating **2** : an exaggerated statement

ex•alt \ig-'zólt\ *vb* **1** : to raise in rank or power **2** : to praise highly

ex•am \ig-'zam\ *n* : EXAMINATION

ex•am•i•na•tion \ig-,zam-ə-'nā-shən\ *n* **1** : the act of examining or state of being examined 〈go to the doctor for a physical *examination*〉 **2** : a test given to determine progress, fitness, or knowledge 〈a college entrance *examination*〉

ex•am•ine \ig-'zam-ən\ *vb* **ex•am•ined; ex•am•in•ing** **1** : to look at or check carefully **2** : to question closely

ex•am•ple \ig-'zam-pəl\ *n* **1** : a sample of something taken to show what the whole is like : INSTANCE **2** : something to be imitated : MODEL 〈set a good *example*〉 **3** : something that is a warning to others **4** : a problem to be solved to show how a rule works 〈an *example* in arithmetic〉 **synonyms** see MODEL

ex•as•per•ate \ig-'zas-pə-,rāt\ *vb* **ex•as•per•at•ed; ex•as•per•at•ing** : to make angry

ex•as•per•a•tion \ig-,zas-pə-'rā-shən\ *n* **1** : extreme annoyance : ANGER **2** : a source of annoyance or anger

ex•ca•vate \'eks-kə-,vāt\ *vb* **ex•ca•vat•ed; ex•ca•vat•ing** **1** : to hollow out : form a hole in 〈*excavate* the side of a hill〉 **2** : to make by hollowing out **3** : to dig out

ex•ca•va•tion \,eks-kə-'vā-shən\ *n* **1** : the act of excavating **2** : a hollow place formed by excavating

ex•ceed \ik-'sēd\ *vb* **1** : to go or be beyond the limit of 〈*exceed* the speed limit〉 **2** : to be greater than 〈the cost must not *exceed* your allowance〉

ex•ceed•ing•ly \ik-'sēd-ing-lē\ *adv* : to a very great degree

ex•cel \ik-'sel\ *vb* **ex•celled; ex•cel•ling** : to do better than others : SURPASS

ex•cel•lence \'ek-sə-ləns\ *n* **1** : high quality **2** : an excellent quality : VIRTUE

ex•cel•lent \'ek-sə-lənt\ *adj* : very good of its kind — **ex•cel•lent•ly** *adv*

¹ex•cept \ik-'sept\ *vb* : to leave out from a number or a whole : EXCLUDE

²except *prep* **1** : not including 〈daily *except* Sundays〉 **2** : other than : BUT 〈take no orders *except* from me〉

³except *conj* : if it were not for the fact that : ONLY 〈I'd go, *except* it's too far〉

ex•cep•tion \ik-'sep-shən\ *n* **1** : the act of leaving out **2** : a case to which a rule does not apply **3** : an objection or a reason for objecting

ex•cep•tion•al \ik-'sep-shən-l\ *adj* **1** : forming an exception 〈an *exceptional* amount of rain〉 **2** : better than average : SUPERIOR — **ex•cep•tion•al•ly** *adv*

¹ex•cess \ik-'ses, 'ek-,ses\ *n* **1** : a state of being more than enough 〈eat to *excess*〉 **2** : the amount by which something is more than what is needed or allowed

²excess *adj* : more than is usual or acceptable

ex•ces•sive \ik-'ses-iv\ *adj* : showing excess — **ex•ces•sive•ly** *adv*

¹ex•change \iks-'chānj\ *n* **1** : a giving or taking of one thing in return for another : TRADE 〈a fair *exchange*〉 **2** : the act of substituting one thing for another **3** : the act of giving and receiving between two groups 〈an *exchange* of students between two countries〉 **4** : a place where goods or services are exchanged

²exchange *vb* **ex•changed; ex•chang•ing** : to give in exchange : TRADE, SWAP

ex•cit•able \ik-'sīt-ə-bəl\ *adj* : easily excited

ex•cite \ik-'sīt\ *vb* **ex•cit•ed; ex•cit•ing** **1** : to increase the activity of **2** : to stir up feeling in : ROUSE

ex•cite•ment \ik-'sīt-mənt\ *n* **1** : the state of being excited : AGITATION **2** : something that excites or stirs up

ex•cit•ing \ik-'sīt-ing\ *adj* : producing excitement

ex•claim \iks-'klām\ *vb* : to cry out or speak out suddenly or with strong feeling

ex•cla•ma•tion \,eks-klə-'mā-shən\ *n* **1** : a sharp or sudden cry of strong feeling **2** : strong expression of anger or complaint

exclamation point *n* : a punctuation mark ! used mostly to show a forceful way of speaking or strong feeling

ex•clam•a•to•ry \iks-'klam-ə-,tōr-ē\ *adj* : containing or using exclamation

ex•clude \iks-'klüd\ *vb* **ex•clud•ed; ex•clud•ing** : to shut out : keep out

ex•clu•sion \iks-'klü-zhən\ *n* : the act of excluding : the state of being excluded

ex•clu•sive \iks-'klü-siv, -ziv\ *adj* **1** : excluding or trying to exclude others 〈an *exclusive* neighborhood〉 **2** : ⁴SOLE 2 〈that family has *exclusive* use of a bathing beach〉 **3** : ENTIRE, COMPLETE 〈give me

\ə\ **abut**	\aú\ **out**	\i\ **tip**	\ó\ **saw**	\ú\ **foot**
\ər\ **further**	\ch\ **chin**	\ī\ **life**	\ói\ **coin**	\y\ **yet**
\a\ **mat**	\e\ **pet**	\j\ **job**	\th\ **thin**	\yü\ **few**
\ā\ **take**	\ē\ **easy**	\ng\ **sing**	\th\ **this**	\yú\ **cure**
\ä\ **cot, cart**	\g\ **go**	\ō\ **bone**	\ü\ **food**	\zh\ **vision**

your *exclusive* attention⟩ **4** : not including ⟨on weekdays, *exclusive* of Saturdays⟩ — **ex·clu·sive·ly** *adv*

ex·crete \ik-'skrēt\ *vb* **ex·cret·ed; ex·cret·ing** : to separate and give off waste matter from the body usually as urine or sweat

ex·cre·tion \ik-'skrē-shən\ *n* **1** : the process of excreting **2** : waste material excreted

ex·cre·to·ry \'ek-skrə-ˌtōr-ē\ *adj* : of or relating to excretion : used in excreting

ex·cur·sion \ik-'skər-zhən\ *n* **1** : a brief pleasure trip **2** : a trip at special reduced rates

ex·cus·able \ik-'skyü-zə-bəl\ *adj* : possible to excuse

¹ex·cuse \ik-'skyüz\ *vb* **ex·cused; ex·cus·ing** **1** : to make apology for ⟨*excuse* yourself for being late⟩ **2** : to overlook or pardon as of little importance ⟨please *excuse* my clumsiness⟩ **3** : let off from doing something ⟨the class was *excused* from homework because of the holidays⟩ **4** : to be an acceptable reason for ⟨nothing *excuses* bad manners⟩

²ex·cuse \ik-'skyüs\ *n* **1** : the act of excusing **2** : something offered as a reason for being excused **3** : something that excuses or is a reason for excusing

ex·e·cute \'ek-sə-ˌkyüt\ *vb* **ex·e·cut·ed; ex·e·cut·ing** **1** : to put into effect : CARRY OUT, PERFORM ⟨*execute* a plan⟩ **2** : to put to death according to a legal order **3** : to make according to a plan or design

ex·e·cu·tion \ˌek-sə-'kyü-shən\ *n* **1** : the act or process of executing : a carrying through of something to its finish **2** : a putting to death as a legal penalty

¹ex·ec·u·tive \ig-'zek-yət-iv\ *adj* **1** : fitted for or relating to the carrying of things to completion ⟨*executive* skills⟩ **2** : concerned with or relating to the carrying out of the law and the conduct of public affairs ⟨the *executive* branch of our government⟩

²executive *n* **1** : the executive branch of a government **2** : a person who manages or directs ⟨a sales *executive*⟩

ex·em·pli·fy \ig-'zem-plə-ˌfī\ *vb* **ex·em·pli·fied; ex·em·pli·fy·ing** : to show by example

¹ex·empt \ig-'zempt\ *adj* : free or released from some condition or requirement that other persons must meet or deal with

²exempt *vb* : to make exempt

ex·emp·tion \ig-'zemp-shən\ *n* **1** : the act of exempting : the state of being exempt **2** : something that is exempted

¹ex·er·cise \'ek-sər-ˌsīz\ *n* **1** : the act of

putting into use, action, or practice ⟨the *exercise* of patience⟩ **2** : bodily activity for the sake of health ⟨go walking for *exercise*⟩ **3** : a school lesson or other task performed to develop skill : practice work : DRILL ⟨finger *exercises*⟩ **4 exercises** *pl* : a program of songs, speeches, and announcing of awards and honors ⟨graduation *exercises*⟩

²exercise *vb* **ex·er·cised; ex·er·cis·ing** **1** : to put into use : EXERT ⟨*exercise* authority⟩ **2** : to use again and again to train or develop ⟨*exercise* a muscle⟩ **3** : to take part in bodily activity for the sake of health or training

ex·ert \ig-'zərt\ *vb* **1** : to put forth (as strength) : bring into play **2** : to put (oneself) into action or to tiring effort

ex·er·tion \ig-'zər-shən\ *n* **1** : the act of exerting ⟨they won by the *exertion* of great effort⟩ **2** : use of strength or ability

ex·hale \eks-'hāl\ *vb* **ex·haled; ex·hal·ing** **1** : to breathe out **2** : to send forth : give off

¹ex·haust \ig-'zȯst\ *vb* **1** : to draw out or let out completely ⟨*exhaust* the water from a tank⟩ **2** : to use up completely ⟨*exhausted* our supplies on the camping trip⟩ **3** : to tire out : FATIGUE

²exhaust *n* **1** : the gas that escapes from an engine **2** : a system of pipes through which exhaust escapes

ex·haus·tion \ig-'zȯs-chən\ *n* **1** : the act of exhausting **2** : the condition of being exhausted

¹ex·hib·it \ig-'zib-ət\ *vb* **1** : to show by outward signs : REVEAL ⟨*exhibit* interest in something⟩ **2** : to put on display ⟨*exhibit* a collection of paintings⟩ **synonyms** see SHOW

²exhibit *n* **1** : an article or collection shown in an exhibition **2** : an article presented as evidence in a law court

ex·hi·bi·tion \ˌek-sə-'bish-ən\ *n* **1** : the act of exhibiting **2** : a public showing (as of athletic skill or works of art)

ex·hil·a·rate \ig-'zil-ə-ˌrāt\ *vb* **ex·hil·a·rat·ed; ex·hil·a·rat·ing** : to make cheerful or lively

ex·hort \ig-'zȯrt\ *vb* : to try to influence by words or advice : urge strongly

¹ex·ile \'eg-ˌzīl, 'ek-ˌsīl\ *n* **1** : the sending or forcing of a person away from his or her own country or the situation of a person who is sent away **2** : a person who is expelled from his or her own country

²exile *vb* **ex·iled; ex·il·ing** : to force to leave one's own country

ex·ist \ig-'zist\ *vb* **1** : to have actual being : be real ⟨wonder if other worlds than ours *exist⟩ **2** : to continue to live **3** : to be found : OCCUR

ex·ist·ence \ig-'zis-təns\ *n* **1** : the fact or the condition of being or of being real ⟨the largest animal in *existence*⟩ **2** : the state of being alive : LIFE ⟨owe one's *existence* to medical skill⟩

¹ex·it \'eg-zət, 'ek-sət\ *n* **1** : the act of going out of or away from a place : DEPARTURE **2** : a way of getting out of a place

²exit *vb* : to go out : LEAVE, DEPART

ex·o·dus \'ek-sə-dəs\ *n* : the going out or away of a large number of people

ex·or·bi·tant \ig-'zor-bət-ənt\ *adj* : going beyond the limits of what is fair, reasonable, or expected ⟨*exorbitant* prices⟩

exo·sphere \'ek-sō-,sfiər\ *n* : the outer fringe region of the atmosphere

ex·ot·ic \ig-'zät-ik\ *adj* : introduced from a foreign country ⟨an *exotic* flower⟩

ex·pand \ik-'spand\ *vb* **1** : to open wide : UNFOLD **2** : to take up or cause to take up more space ⟨metals *expand* under heat⟩ **3** : to work out in greater detail ⟨*expand* a plan⟩

ex·panse \ik-'spans\ *n* : a wide area or stretch ⟨a vast *expanse* of desert⟩

ex·pan·sion \ik-'span-chən\ *n* : the act of expanding or the state of being expanded : ENLARGEMENT

ex·pect \ik-'spekt\ *vb* **1** : to look for or look forward to something that ought to or probably will happen ⟨*expect* rain⟩ ⟨*expects* to go to town tomorrow⟩ **2** : to consider to be obliged ⟨*expected* you to pay your debts⟩

ex·pec·tant \ik-'spek-tənt\ *adj* : looking forward to or waiting for something

ex·pec·ta·tion \,ek-,spek-'tā-shən\ *n* : a looking forward to or waiting for something

ex·pe·di·ent \ik-'spēd-ē-ənt\ *adj* : suitable for bringing about a desired result often without regard to what is fair or right — **ex·pe·di·ent·ly** *adv*

ex·pe·di·tion \,ek-spə-'dish-ən\ *n* **1** : a journey for a particular purpose (as for exploring) **2** : the people making an expedition

ex·pel \ik-'spel\ *vb* **ex·pelled; ex·pel·ling 1** : to force out **2** : to drive away

ex·pend \ik-'spend\ *vb* **1** : to pay out : SPEND **2** : to use up

ex·pen·di·ture \ik-'spen-di-chər\ *n* **1** : the act of spending (as money, time, or energy) **2** : something that is spent

ex·pense \ik-'spens\ *n* **1** : something spent or required to be spent : COST ⟨*expenses* of a trip⟩ **2** : a cause for spending ⟨a car can be a great *expense*⟩

ex·pen·sive \ik-'spen-siv\ *adj* : COSTLY 1 — **ex·pen·sive·ly** *adv*

¹ex·pe·ri·ence \ik-'spir-ē-əns\ *n* **1** : the actual living through an event or events ⟨learn by *experience*⟩ **2** : the skill or knowledge gained by actually doing a thing ⟨a job that requires someone with *experience*⟩ **3** : something that one has actually done or lived through ⟨a soldier's *experiences* in war⟩

²experience *vb* **ex·pe·ri·enced; ex·pe·ri·enc·ing** : to have experience of : UNDERGO

ex·pe·ri·enced \ik-'spir-ē-ənst\ *adj* : made skillful or wise through experience

¹ex·per·i·ment \ik-'sper-ə-mənt\ *n* : a trial or test made to find out about something

²ex·per·i·ment \ik-'sper-ə-,ment\ *vb* : to make experiments ⟨*experiment* with a new hair style⟩

ex·per·i·men·tal \ik-,sper-ə-'ment-l\ *adj* : of, relating to, or based on experiment ⟨an *experimental* science⟩

¹ex·pert \'ek-,spərt, ik-'spərt\ *adj* : showing special skill or knowledge gained from experience or training **synonyms** see SKILLFUL — **ex·pert·ly** *adv* — **ex·pert·ness** *n*

²ex·pert \'ek-,spərt\ *n* : a person with special skill or knowledge of a subject

ex·pi·ra·tion \,ek-spə-'rā-shən\ *n* : an act or instance of expiring

ex·pire \ik-'spīr\ *vb* **ex·pired; ex·pir·ing 1** : ¹DIE 1 **2** : to come to an end ⟨when your insurance *expires*⟩ **3** : to breathe out : EXHALE

ex·plain \ik-'splān\ *vb* **1** : to make clear : CLARIFY 2 **2** : to give the reasons for or cause of — **ex·plain·able** \-'splā-nə-bəl\ *adj*

ex·pla·na·tion \,ek-splə-'nā-shən\ *n* **1** : the act or process of explaining **2** : a statement that makes something clear

ex·plan·a·to·ry \ik-'splan-ə-,tōr-ē\ *adj* : giving explanation : helping to explain

ex·plic·it \ik-'splis-ət\ *adj* : so clear in statement that there is no doubt about the meaning

ex·plode \ik-'splōd\ *vb* **ex·plod·ed; ex·plod·ing 1** : to burst or cause to burst with violence and noise ⟨*explode* a bomb⟩ **2** : to burst forth ⟨*exploded* with anger⟩

¹ex·ploit \'ek-,sploit\ *n* : a brave or daring act

²ex·ploit \ik-'sploit\ *vb* **1** : to get the value

\ə\ **abut**	\au̇\ **out**	\i\ **tip**	\ȯ\ **saw**	\u̇\ **foot**
\ər\ **further**	\ch\ **chin**	\ī\ **life**	\ȯi\ **coin**	\y\ **yet**
\a\ **mat**	\e\ **pet**	\j\ **job**	\th\ **thin**	\yü\ **few**
\ā\ **take**	\ē\ **easy**	\ng\ **sing**	\th\ **this**	\yu̇\ **cure**
\ä\ **cot, cart**	\g\ **go**	\ō\ **bone**	\ü\ **food**	\zh\ **vision**

or use out of ⟨*exploit* a coal mine⟩ **2** : to make use of unfairly for one's own benefit

ex·plo·ra·tion \‚ek-splə-'rā-shən\ *n* : the act or an instance of exploring

ex·plore \ik-'splōr\ *vb* **ex·plored; ex·plor·ing 1** : to search through or into : examine closely ⟨*explore* old writings⟩ **2** : to go into or through for purposes of discovery ⟨*explore* a cave⟩

ex·plor·er \ik-'splōr-ər\ *n* : a person (as a traveler seeking new geographical or scientific information) who explores something

ex·plo·sion \ik-'splō-zhən\ *n* **1** : the act of exploding : a sudden and noisy bursting (as of a bomb) **2** : a sudden outburst of feeling

1ex·plo·sive \ik-'splō-siv, -ziv\ *adj* **1** : able to cause explosion ⟨the *explosive* power of gunpowder⟩ **2** : likely to explode ⟨an *explosive* temper⟩ — **ex·plo·sive·ly** *adv*

2explosive *n* : an explosive substance

ex·po·nent \ik-'spō-nənt\ *n* : a numeral written above and to the right of a number to show how many times the number is to be used as a factor ⟨the *exponent* 3 in 10^3 indicates $10 \times 10 \times 10$⟩

1ex·port \ek-'spōrt\ *vb* : to send or carry abroad especially for sale in foreign countries

2ex·port \'ek-‚spōrt\ *n* **1** : something that is exported **2** : the act of exporting

ex·pose \ik-'spōz\ *vb* **ex·posed; ex·pos·ing 1** : to leave without protection, shelter, or care **2** : to let light strike the photographic film or plate in taking a picture **3** : to put on exhibition : display for sale **4** : to make known ⟨*expose* a dishonest scheme⟩

ex·po·si·tion \‚ek-spə-'zish-ən\ *n* **1** : an explaining of something **2** : a public exhibition

ex·po·sure \ik-'spō-zhər\ *n* **1** : an act of making something public ⟨the *exposure* of a plot⟩ **2** : the condition of being exposed ⟨suffer from *exposure* to the cold⟩ **3** : the act of letting light strike a photographic film or the time during which a film is exposed **4** : a section of a roll of film for one picture **5** : position with respect to direction ⟨a room with a southern *exposure*⟩

ex·pound \ik-'spaùnd\ *vb* : EXPLAIN 1, INTERPRET

1ex·press \ik-'spres\ *adj* **1** : clearly stated ⟨an *express* order⟩ **2** : of a certain sort ⟨came for an *express* purpose⟩ **3** : sent or traveling at high speed ⟨*express* mail⟩

2express *n* **1** : a system for the special transportation of goods ⟨send a package

by *express*⟩ **2** : a vehicle (as a train or elevator) run at special speed with few or no stops

3express *vb* **1** : to make known especially in words ⟨*express* disapproval⟩ **2** : to represent by a sign or symbol **3** : to send by express

ex·pres·sion \ik-'spresh-ən\ *n* **1** : the act or process of expressing especially in words **2** : a meaningful word or saying ⟨an odd *expression*⟩ **3** : a way of speaking, singing, or playing that shows mood or feeling ⟨read with *expression*⟩ **4** : the look on one's face ⟨a pleased *expression*⟩ — **ex·pres·sion·less** \-ləs\ *adj*

ex·pres·sive \ik-'spres-iv\ *adj* : expressing something : full of expression — **ex·pres·sive·ly** *adv* — **ex·pres·sive·ness** *n*

ex·press·way \ik-'spres-‚wā\ *n* : a divided highway for rapid traffic

ex·pul·sion \ik-'spəl-shən\ *n* : the act of expelling : the state of being expelled

ex·quis·ite \ek-'skwiz-ət, 'ek-skwiz-\ *adj* **1** : finely made or done ⟨*exquisite* workmanship⟩ **2** : very pleasing (as through beauty or fitness) ⟨*exquisite* flowers⟩ **3** : very severe : INTENSE ⟨*exquisite* pain⟩

ex·tend \ik-'stend\ *vb* **1** : 1STRETCH 2 ⟨*extend* a sail⟩ **2** : to hold out ⟨*extend* a hand⟩ **3** : to make longer ⟨*extend* a visit⟩ **4** : ENLARGE ⟨*extend* the meaning of a word⟩ **5** : to stretch out or across something ⟨flood water *extended* to the door⟩ ⟨a bridge *extends* across the stream⟩

ex·ten·sion \ik-'sten-chən\ *n* **1** : a stretching out : an increase in length or time **2** : a part forming an addition or enlargement

ex·ten·sive \ik-'sten-siv\ *adj* : having wide extent : BROAD

ex·tent \ik-'stent\ *n* **1** : the distance or range over which something extends **2** : the point, degree, or limit to which something extends

1ex·te·ri·or \ek-'stir-ē-ər\ *adj* : EXTERNAL

2exterior *n* : an exterior part or surface

ex·ter·mi·nate \ik-'stər-mə-‚nāt\ *vb* **ex·ter·mi·nat·ed; ex·ter·mi·nat·ing** : to get rid of completely : wipe out ⟨*exterminate* rats⟩

1ex·ter·nal \ek-'stərn-l\ *adj* : situated on or relating to the outside : OUTSIDE

2external *n* : something that is external

ex·tinct \ik-'stingkt\ *adj* **1** : no longer active ⟨an *extinct* volcano⟩ **2** : no longer existing

ex·tinc·tion \ik-'stingk-shən\ *n* **1** : an act of extinguishing or an instance of being extinguished **2** : the state of being extinct

ex·tin·guish \ik-'sting-gwish\ *vb* **1** : to

cause to stop burning **2** : to cause to die out : DESTROY — **ex·tin·guish·er** *n*

ex·tol \ik-'stōl\ *vb* **ex·tolled; ex·tol·ling** : to praise highly : GLORIFY

¹ex·tra \'ek-strə\ *adj* : being more than what is usual, expected, or due

²extra *n* **1** : something extra **2** : an added charge **3** : a special edition of a newspaper **4** : a person hired for a group scene (as in a movie)

³extra *adv* : beyond the usual size, amount, or degree ⟨*extra* large eggs⟩

extra- *prefix* : outside : beyond

¹ex·tract \ik-'strakt\ *vb* **1** : to remove by pulling ⟨*extract* a tooth⟩ **2** : to get out by pressing, distilling, or by a chemical process ⟨*extract* juice from apples⟩ **3** : to choose and take out for separate use ⟨*extract* a few lines from a poem⟩

²ex·tract \'ek-ˌstrakt\ *n* **1** : a selection from a writing **2** : a product obtained by extraction

ex·trac·tion \ik-'strak-shən\ *n* **1** : an act of extracting ⟨the *extraction* of a tooth⟩ **2** : ORIGIN 1, DESCENT ⟨of French *extraction*⟩

ex·tra·cur·ric·u·lar \ˌek-strə-kə-'rik-yə-lər\ *adj* : of or relating to those activities (as athletics) that are offered by a school but are not part of the course of study

ex·traor·di·nary \ik-'strȯrd-n-ˌer-ē, ˌek-strə-'ȯrd-\ *adj* : so unusual as to be remarkable — **ex·traor·di·nar·i·ly** \ik-ˌstrȯrd-n-'er-ə-lē, ˌek-strə-ˌȯrd-n-'er-\ *adv*

ex·trav·a·gance \ik-'strav-ə-gəns\ *n* **1** : the wasteful or careless spending of money **2** : something that is extravagant **3** : the quality or fact of being extravagant

ex·trav·a·gant \ik-'strav-ə-gənt\ *adj* **1** : going beyond what is reasonable or suitable ⟨*extravagant* praise⟩ **2** : wasteful especially of money — **ex·trav·a·gant·ly** *adv*

¹ex·treme \ik-'strēm\ *adj* **1** : existing to a very great degree ⟨*extreme* heat⟩ ⟨*extreme* poverty⟩ **2** : farthest from a center ⟨the *extreme* edge⟩ — **ex·treme·ly** *adv*

²extreme *n* **1** : something as far as possible from a center or from its opposite ⟨*extremes* of heat and cold⟩ **2** : the greatest possible degree : MAXIMUM

ex·trem·i·ty \ik-'strem-ət-ē\ *n, pl* **ex·trem·i·ties** **1** : the farthest limit, point, or part ⟨the *extremity* of the island⟩ **2** : an end part of a limb of the body (as a foot) **3** : an extreme degree (as of emotion or distress)

ex·tri·cate \'ek-strə-ˌkāt\ *vb* **ex·tri·cat·ed; ex·tri·cat·ing** : to free from entanglement or difficulty

ex·ult \ig-'zəlt\ *vb* : to be in high spirits : REJOICE

Word History When we exult we feel like jumping for joy though we may not really move at all. At first the English word *exult* meant "to jump for joy." *Exult* came from a Latin word meaning "to jump up." This Latin word was formed from a prefix meaning "out" and a verb meaning "to jump."

ex·ult·ant \ig-'zəlt-nt\ *adj* : full of or expressing joy or triumph — **ex·ult·ant·ly** *adv*

-ey — see -Y

¹eye \'ī\ *n* **1** : the organ of seeing **2** : the ability to see **3** : the ability to recognize ⟨a keen *eye* for a bargain⟩ **4** : GLANCE ⟨caught my *eye*⟩ **5** : close attention : WATCH ⟨keep an *eye* on the dinner⟩ **6** : JUDGMENT 1 ⟨guilty in the *eyes* of the law⟩ **7** : something like or suggesting an eye ⟨the *eye* of a needle⟩ **8** : the center of something ⟨the *eye* of a hurricane⟩ — **eyed** \'īd\ *adj* — **eye·less** \'ī-ləs\ *adj*

²eye *vb* **eyed; eye·ing** *or* **ey·ing** : to look at : watch closely

eye·ball \'ī-ˌbȯl\ *n* : the whole eye

eye·brow \'ī-ˌbraù\ *n* : the arch or ridge over the eye : the hair on the ridge over the eye

eye·drop·per \'ī-ˌdräp-ər\ *n* : DROPPER 2

eye·glass \'ī-ˌglas\ *n* **1** : a glass lens used to help one to see clearly **2 eyeglasses** *pl* : a pair of glass lenses set in a frame and used to help one to see clearly

eye·lash \'ī-ˌlash\ *n* : a single hair of the fringe on the eyelid

eye·let \'ī-lət\ *n* **1** : a small hole (as in cloth or leather) for a lace or rope **2** : GROMMET

eye·lid \'ī-ˌlid\ *n* : the thin movable cover of an eye

eye·piece \'ī-ˌpēs\ *n* : the lens or combination of lenses at the eye end of an optical instrument (as a microscope or telescope)

eye·sight \'ī-ˌsīt\ *n* : ¹SIGHT 4, VISION

eye·sore \'ī-ˌsōr\ *n* : something displeasing to the sight ⟨that old building is an *eyesore*⟩

eye·strain \'ī-ˌstrān\ *n* : a tired or irritated state of the eyes (as from too much use)

eye·tooth \'ī-'tüth\ *n, pl* **eye·teeth** \-'tēth\ : a canine tooth of the upper jaw

eyrie *variant of* AERIE

\ə\ **abut**	\aù\ **out**	\i\ **tip**	\ȯ\ **saw**	\ù\ **foot**	
\ər\ **further**	\ch\ **chin**	\ī\ **life**	\ȯi\ **coin**	\y\ **yet**	
\a\ **mat**	\e\ **pet**	\j\ **job**	\th\ **thin**	\yü\ **few**	
\ā\ **take**	\ē\ **easy**	\ng\ **sing**	\th\ **this**	\yù\ **cure**	
\ä\ **cot, cart**	\g\ **go**	\ō\ **bone**	\ü\ **food**	\zh\ **vision**	

F

f \ˈef\ *n, pl* **f's** *or* **fs** \ˈefs\ *often cap* **1** : the sixth letter of the English alphabet **2** : a grade that shows a student's work is failing

fa \ˈfä\ *n* : the fourth note of the musical scale

fa·ble \ˈfā-bəl\ *n* **1** : a story that is not true **2** : a story in which animals speak and act like people and which is usually meant to teach a lesson

fab·ric \ˈfab-rik\ *n* **1** : the basic structure ⟨the *fabric* of society⟩ **2** : CLOTH 1 **3** : a structural plan or material

fab·u·lous \ˈfab-yə-ləs\ *adj* **1** : told in or based on fable **2** : like a fable especially in being marvelous or beyond belief ⟨*fabulous* wealth⟩

fa·cade \fə-ˈsäd\ *n* : the face or front of a building

¹face \ˈfās\ *n* **1** : the front part of the head **2** : an expression of the face ⟨put on a sad *face*⟩ **3** : outward appearance ⟨looks easy on the *face* of it⟩ **4** : GRIMACE ⟨made a *face*⟩ **5** : DIGNITY 1, PRESTIGE ⟨afraid of losing *face*⟩ **6** : a front, upper, or outer surface **7** : one of the flat surfaces that bound a solid ⟨a *face* of a prism⟩

facade

²face *vb* **faced; fac·ing 1** : to cover the front or surface of ⟨a building *faced* with marble⟩ **2** : to have the front or face toward ⟨the house *faces* east⟩ ⟨*face* the class⟩ **3** : to oppose firmly ⟨*face* danger⟩

fac·et \ˈfas-ət\ *n* : one of the small surfaces of a cut gem

fa·ce·tious \fə-ˈsē-shəs\ *adj* : intended or trying to be funny

face–to–face \ˌfās-tə-ˈfās\ *adv or adj* : in person ⟨met *face-to-face*⟩

fa·cial \ˈfā-shəl\ *adj* : of or relating to the face — **fa·cial·ly** *adv*

fa·cil·i·tate \fə-ˈsil-ə-ˌtāt\ *vb* **fa·cil·i·tat·ed; fa·cil·i·tat·ing** : to make easier

fa·cil·i·ty \fə-ˈsil-ət-ē\ *n, pl* **fa·cil·i·ties 1** : freedom from difficulty **2** : ease in doing something : APTITUDE ⟨shows *facility* in reading⟩ **3** : something that makes an action, operation, or activity easier ⟨cooking *facilities*⟩

fac·sim·i·le \fak-ˈsim-ə-lē\ *n* **1** : an exact copy ⟨a *facsimile* of a document⟩ **2** : a system of transmitting and reproducing printed matter or pictures by mean of signals sent over telephone lines

fact \ˈfakt\ *n* **1** : something (as an event or an act) that really exists or has occurred ⟨life and death are *facts*⟩ **2** : physical reality or actual experience ⟨this is a matter of *fact*, not fiction⟩

¹fac·tor \ˈfak-tər\ *n* **1** : something that helps produce a result **2** : any of the numbers that when multiplied together form a product

²factor *vb* : to find the factors of a number

fac·to·ry \ˈfak-tə-rē, ˈfak-trē\ *n, pl* **fac·to·ries** : a place where goods are manufactured

fac·tu·al \ˈfak-chə-wəl\ *adj* : of, relating to, or based on facts — **fac·tu·al·ly** *adv*

fac·ul·ty \ˈfak-əl-tē\ *n, pl* **fac·ul·ties 1** : ability to do something : TALENT ⟨a *faculty* for making friends⟩ **2** : one of the powers of the mind or body ⟨the *faculty* of hearing⟩ **3** : the teachers in a school or college

fad \ˈfad\ *n* : a way of doing or an interest widely followed for a time **synonyms** see FASHION

fade \ˈfād\ *vb* **fad·ed; fad·ing 1** : to dry up : WITHER ⟨a *faded* flower⟩ **2** : to lose or cause to lose brightness of color **3** : to grow dim or faint ⟨the path *faded* out⟩

Fahr·en·heit \ˈfar-ən-ˌhīt\ *adj* : relating to or having a temperature scale on which the boiling point of water is at 212 degrees above the zero of the scale and the freezing point is at 32 degrees above zero

¹fail \ˈfāl\ *vb* **1** : to lose strength : WEAKEN ⟨*failing* in health⟩ **2** : to die away **3** : to stop functioning ⟨the engine *failed*⟩ **4** : to fall short ⟨their try *failed* of success⟩ **5** : to be or become absent or not enough ⟨the water supply *failed*⟩ **6** : to be unsuccessful ⟨*failed* the test⟩ ⟨*failed* in the new job⟩ **7** : to become bankrupt ⟨the business *failed*⟩ **8** : DISAPPOINT, DESERT ⟨*fail* a friend in need⟩ **9** : ¹NEGLECT **2** ⟨*fail* to answer the phone⟩

²fail *n* : FAILURE 1 ⟨promised to go without *fail*⟩

fail·ing \'fā-ling\ *n* : a slight moral weakness or flaw

fail·ure \'fāl-yər\ *n* **1** : a failing to do or perform ⟨*failure* to keep a promise⟩ **2** : a state of being unable to work in a normal way ⟨heart *failure*⟩ **3** : a lack of success ⟨*failure* in a test⟩ **4** : BANKRUPTCY **5** : a falling short ⟨crop *failure*⟩ **6** : a breaking down ⟨a *failure* of memory⟩ **7** : a person or thing that has failed

¹faint \'fānt\ *adj* **1** : lacking courage : COWARDLY **2** : being weak or dizzy and likely to collapse ⟨feel *faint*⟩ **3** : lacking strength : FEEBLE ⟨a *faint* attempt⟩ **4** : not clear or plain : DIM — **faint·ly** *adv* — **faint·ness** *n*

²faint *vb* : to lose consciousness

³faint *n* : an act or condition of fainting

faint·heart·ed \'fānt-'härt-əd\ *adj* : TIMID

¹fair \'faər, 'feər\ *adj* **1** : attractive in appearance : BEAUTIFUL ⟨our *fair* city⟩ **2** : not stormy or cloudy ⟨*fair* weather⟩ **3** : not favoring one over another ⟨received *fair* treatment⟩ **4** : observing the rules ⟨*fair* play⟩ **5** : being within the foul lines ⟨*fair* ball⟩ **6** : not dark : BLOND ⟨*fair* hair⟩ **7** : neither good nor bad ⟨a *fair* grade in spelling⟩ — **fair·ness** *n*

²fair *adv* : in a fair manner ⟨play *fair*⟩

³fair *n* **1** : a gathering of buyers and sellers at a certain time and place for trade **2** : an exhibition (as of livestock or farm products) usually along with entertainment and amusements ⟨county *fair*⟩ **3** : a sale of articles for a charitable purpose ⟨a church *fair*⟩

fair·ground \'faər-,graund, 'feər-\ *n* : an area set aside for fairs, circuses, or exhibitions

fair·ly \'faər-lē, 'feər-\ *adv* **1** : in a manner of speaking : QUITE ⟨*fairly* bursting with pride⟩ **2** : in a fair manner : JUSTLY ⟨treated *fairly*⟩ **3** : for the most part : RATHER ⟨a *fairly* easy job⟩

¹fairy \'faər-ē, 'feər-ē\ *n, pl* **fair·ies** : an imaginary being who has the form of a very tiny human being and has magic powers

Word History The English word *fairy* was derived from an Old French word that meant "fairy." This Old French word came from the Latin name of the Roman goddess of fate, who got her name from a Latin word that meant "fate." The English word *fate* came from this same Latin word.

²fairy *adj* : of, relating to, or like a fairy

fairy·land \'faər-ē-,land, 'feər-\ *n* **1** : the land of fairies **2** : a place of delicate beauty or magical charm

fairy tale *n* **1** : a story about fairies **2** : a small lie : FIB

faith \'fāth\ *n* **1** : loyalty to duty or to a person **2** : belief in God **3** : firm belief even in the absence of proof **4** : a system of religious beliefs : RELIGION **synonyms** see BELIEF

faith·ful \'fāth-fəl\ *adj* **1** : RELIABLE ⟨a *faithful* worker⟩ **2** : firm in devotion or support ⟨a *faithful* friend⟩ **3** : true to the facts : ACCURATE — **faith·ful·ly** \-fə-lē\ *adv* — **faith·ful·ness** *n*

synonyms FAITHFUL, LOYAL, and TRUE mean firm in one's allegiance to something. FAITHFUL suggests that one has a firm and constant allegiance to something to which one is united by or as if by a promise or pledge ⟨always be *faithful* to your duty⟩ LOYAL suggests that one firmly refuses to desert or betray ⟨citizens who are *loyal* to their country⟩ TRUE stresses that one is personally devoted to someone or something ⟨a *true* friend who was ready to help in time of need⟩

faith·less \'fāth-ləs\ *adj* : not true to allegiance or duty — **faith·less·ly** *adv* — **faith·less·ness** *n*

synonyms FAITHLESS, DISLOYAL, and TRAITOROUS mean not being true to something that has a right to one's allegiance. FAITHLESS suggests breaking a promise or pledge to remain loyal to someone or something ⟨our *faithless* friends left us at the first sign of trouble⟩ DISLOYAL suggests that one is unfaithful to someone or something that has the right to expect loyalty ⟨*disloyal* citizens will be punished⟩ TRAITOROUS suggests either actual treason or a betrayal of trust ⟨the *traitorous* soldier was giving secrets to the enemy⟩

¹fake \'fāk\ *vb* **faked; fak·ing 1** : to change or treat in a way that gives a false effect **2** : ¹COUNTERFEIT 2 ⟨*fake* a signature⟩ **3** : PRETEND 1 ⟨*fake* surprise⟩

²fake *n* : a person or thing that is not really what is pretended

³fake *adj* : ²COUNTERFEIT

fal·con \'fal-kən, 'föl-\ *n* **1** : a hawk trained for use in hunting small game **2** : any of

\ə\ abut	\au\ out	\i\ tip	\ȯ\ saw	\u̇\ foot
\ər\ further	\ch\ chin	\ī\ life	\ȯi\ coin	\y\ yet
\a\ mat	\e\ pet	\j\ job	\th\ thin	\yü\ few
\ā\ take	\ē\ easy	\ng\ sing	\th\ this	\yu̇\ cure
\ä\ cot, cart	\g\ go	\ō\ bone	\ü\ food	\zh\ vision

several small hawks with long wings and swift flight

fal·con·ry \'fal-kən-rē, 'fȯl-\ *n* : the art or sport of hunting with a falcon

¹fall \'fȯl\ *vb* **fell** \'fel\; **fall·en** \'fȯl-ən\; **fall·ing 1** : to come or go down freely by the force of gravity ⟨an apple *fell* from the tree⟩ **2** : to come as if by falling ⟨night *fell*⟩ **3** : to become lower (as in degree or value) ⟨the temperature *fell* ten degrees⟩ **4** : to topple from an upright position ⟨the tree *fell*⟩ **5** : to collapse wounded or dead ⟨*fall* in battle⟩ **6** : to become captured ⟨the city *fell* to the enemy⟩ **7** : to occur at a certain time ⟨*falls* on the first Monday in September⟩ **8** : to pass from one condition of body or mind to another ⟨*fall* asleep⟩ ⟨*fall* ill⟩ — **fall short** : be lacking in something

²fall *n* **1** : the act or an instance of falling ⟨a *fall* from a horse⟩ **2** : AUTUMN **3** : a thing or quantity that falls ⟨a heavy *fall* of snow⟩ **4** : a loss of greatness : DOWNFALL ⟨the *fall* of Rome⟩ **5** : WATERFALL — usually used in pl. ⟨Niagara *Falls*⟩ **6** : a decrease in size, amount, or value ⟨a *fall* in prices⟩ **7** : the distance something falls

fal·la·cy \'fal-ə-sē\ *n, pl* **fal·la·cies 1** : a false or mistaken idea **2** : false reasoning

fall back *vb* : ²RETREAT

fall·out \'fȯ-ˌlau̇t\ *n* : the usually radioactive particles falling through the atmosphere as a result of the explosion of an atom bomb

fall out \fȯ-'lau̇t\ *vb* : ²QUARREL 2

¹fal·low \'fal-ō\ *n* : land for crops that lies idle

²fallow *vb* : to till without planting a crop

³fallow *adj* : not tilled or planted

fallow deer *n* : a small European deer with broad antlers and a pale yellowish coat spotted with white in summer

¹false \'fȯls\ *adj* **fals·er; fals·est 1** : not true, genuine, or honest ⟨*false* testimony⟩ ⟨*false* documents⟩ ⟨*false* teeth⟩ **2** : not faithful or loyal ⟨*false* friends⟩ **3** : not based on facts or sound judgment ⟨a *false* feeling of security⟩ — **false·ly** *adv* — **false·ness** *n*

²false *adv* : in a false or misleading manner

false·hood \'fȯls-ˌhu̇d\ *n* **1** : ³LIE **2** : the habit of lying ⟨given to *falsehood*⟩

fal·si·fy \'fȯl-sə-ˌfī\ *vb* **fal·si·fied; fal·si·fy·ing** : to make false ⟨*falsified* the accounts to cover up a theft⟩

fal·si·ty \'fȯl-sət-ē\ *n, pl* **fal·si·ties 1** : something false **2** : the quality or state of being false

fal·ter \'fȯl-tər\ *vb* **1** : to move unsteadily : WAVER **2** : to hesitate in speech **3** : to hesitate in purpose or action

fame \'fām\ *n* : the fact or condition of being known to and usually thought well of by the public : RENOWN

famed \'fāmd\ *adj* : known widely and well : FAMOUS

fa·mil·ial \fə-'mil-yəl\ *adj* : of, relating to, or typical of a family

fa·mil·iar \fə-'mil-yər\ *adj* **1** : closely acquainted : INTIMATE ⟨*familiar* friends⟩ **2** : INFORMAL 1 ⟨spoke in a *familiar* way⟩ **3** : too friendly or bold **4** : often seen or experienced **5** : having a good knowledge of ⟨parents should be *familiar* with their children's schools⟩ **synonyms** see COMMON

fa·mil·iar·i·ty \fə-ˌmil-'yar-ət-ē, -ˌmil-ē-'ar-\ *n, pl* **fa·mil·iar·i·ties 1** : close friendship : INTIMACY **2** : good knowledge of something **3** : INFORMALITY 1

fa·mil·iar·ize \fə-'mil-yə-ˌrīz\ *vb* **fa·mil·iar·ized; fa·mil·iar·iz·ing** : to make familiar ⟨*familiarized* students with the library⟩

fam·i·ly \'fam-ə-lē, 'fam-lē\ *n, pl* **fam·i·lies 1** : a group of persons who come from the same ancestor **2** : a group of persons living under one roof or one head **3** : a group of things sharing certain characteristics ⟨a *family* of languages⟩ **4** : a

fallow deer

social group made up of parents and their children **5** : a group of related kinds of plants or animals ⟨peaches, apples, and roses all belong to one *family*⟩

fam·ine \'fam-ən\ *n* **1** : a very great and general lack of food **2** : a great shortage

fam·ish \'fam-ish\ *vb* : to suffer from hunger : STARVE

fam·ished \'fam-isht\ *adj* : very hungry

fa·mous \'fā-məs\ *adj* : very well-known

fa·mous·ly \'fā-məs-lē\ *adv* : very well

¹fan \'fan\ *n* **1** : something (as a hand-waved semicircular device or a mechanism with rotating blades) for producing a current of air **2** : something like a fan — **fan·like** \-,līk\ *adj*

fan 1

²fan *vb* **fanned; fan·ning** **1** : to move air with a fan **2** : to direct a current of air upon with a fan

³fan *n* : an enthusiastic follower or admirer

¹fa·nat·ic \fə-'nat-ik\ *adj* : too enthusiastic or devoted

Word History The word *fanatic* can be traced back to a Latin noun that meant "temple." A Latin adjective was formed from this noun. At first the adjective meant "of a temple," but later it was used to refer to people who were thought to be inspired by the gods. Since insane people were believed to be possessed by gods, the adjective later came to mean "frantic" or "insane." Our English word *fanatic* came from this Latin adjective, and at first it too meant "insane" or "frantic."

²fanatic *n* : a fanatic person

fan·ci·ful \'fan-si-fəl\ *adj* **1** : showing free use of the imagination ⟨a *fanciful* tale⟩ **2** : coming from fancy rather than reason ⟨a *fanciful* scheme for getting rich⟩ — **fan·ci·ful·ly** \-fə-lē\ *adv* — **fan·ci·ful·ness** *n*

¹fan·cy \'fan-sē\ *n, pl* **fan·cies** **1** : the power of the mind to think of things that are not present or real : IMAGINATION **2** : LIKING ⟨took a *fancy* to them⟩ **3** : IDEA 2, NOTION

²fancy *vb* **fan·cied; fan·cy·ing** **1** : ¹LIKE 1, ENJOY ⟨*fancies* candied apples⟩ **2** : IMAGINE 1 ⟨well, *fancy* that⟩

³fancy *adj* **fan·ci·er; fan·ci·est** **1** : not plain or ordinary ⟨a *fancy* dress⟩ **2** : being above the average (as in quality or price) ⟨*fancy* fruits⟩ **3** : done with great skill and grace ⟨*fancy* diving⟩ — **fan·ci·ly** \'fan-sə-lē\ *adv* — **fan·ci·ness** \-sē-nəs\ *n*

fang \'fang\ *n* **1** : a long sharp tooth by which animals seize and hold their prey **2** : one of the usually two long hollow or grooved teeth by which a poisonous snake injects its poison — **fanged** \'fangd\ *adj*

fan·tas·tic \fan-'tas-tik\ *adj* **1** : produced by or like something produced by the fancy ⟨a *fantastic* scheme⟩ **2** : barely believable — **fan·tas·ti·cal·ly** \-ti-kə-lē\ *adv*

fan·ta·sy *or* **phan·ta·sy** \'fant-ə-sē, -zē\ *n, pl* **fan·ta·sies** *or* **phan·ta·sies** **1** : IMAGINATION 1 **2** : something produced by the imagination

¹far \'fär\ *adv* **far·ther** \'fär-thər\ *or* **fur·ther** \'fər-\; **far·thest** \'fär-thəst\ *or* **fur·thest** \'fər-\ **1** : at or to a great distance in space or time ⟨*far* from home⟩ ⟨read *far* into the night⟩ **2** : to a great extent : MUCH ⟨*far* better⟩ **3** : to or at a definite distance or point ⟨as *far* as I know⟩ **4** : to an advanced point ⟨a smart student can go *far*⟩

²far *adj* **far·ther** *or* **fur·ther; far·thest** *or* **fur·thest** **1** : very distant in space or time ⟨a *far* country⟩ **2** : LONG **3** ⟨a *far* journey⟩ **3** : the more distant of two ⟨on the *far* side of the stream⟩

far·away \,fär-ə-,wā\ *adj* **1** : REMOTE 1, DISTANT ⟨*faraway* lands⟩ **2** : PREOCCUPIED ⟨a *faraway* look⟩

¹fare \'faər, 'feər\ *vb* **fared; far·ing** : to get along : SUCCEED

²fare *n* **1** : the money a person pays to travel (as on a bus) **2** : a person paying a fare **3** : FOOD 1

¹fare·well \faər-'wel, feər-\ *n* : an expression of good wishes at parting — often used as an interjection

²fare·well \,faər-,wel, ,feər-\ *adj* : of or relating to a time or act of leaving : FINAL ⟨a *farewell* speech⟩

far·fetched \'fär-'fecht\ *adj* : not likely to be true

¹farm \'färm\ *n* **1** : a piece of land used for raising crops or animals **2** : an area

\ə\ abut	\au̇\ out	\i\ tip	\o̅\ saw	\u̇\ foot
\ər\ further	\ch\ chin	\ī\ life	\o̅i\ coin	\y\ yet
\a\ mat	\e\ pet	\j\ job	\th\ thin	\yü\ few
\ā\ take	\ē\ easy	\ng\ sing	\th\ this	\yu̇\ cure
\ä\ cot, cart	\g\ go	\o̅\ bone	\ü\ food	\zh\ vision

of water where fish or shellfish are grown

²**farm** *vb* : to work on or run a farm — **farm·er** *n*

farm·hand \'färm-,hand\ *n* : a farm laborer

farm·house \'färm-,haus\ *n* : the dwelling house of a farm

farm·yard \'färm-,yärd\ *n* : the yard around or enclosed by farm buildings

far–off \'fär-'of\ *adj* : distant in time or space

far–reach·ing \'fär-'rē-ching\ *adj* : EXTEN-SIVE

far·sight·ed \'fär-'sīt-əd\ *adj* **1** : able to see distant things more clearly than near ones **2** : able to judge how something will work out in the future — **far·sight·ed·ness** *n*

¹**far·ther** \'fär-<u>th</u>ər\ *adv* **1** : at or to a greater distance or more advanced point **2** : ¹BESIDES

²**farther** *adj* : more distant

¹**far·thest** \'fär-<u>th</u>əst\ *adj* : most distant

²**farthest** *adv* **1** : to or at the greatest distance in space or time **2** : to the most advanced point

fas·ci·nate \'fas-n-,āt\ *vb* **fas·ci·nat·ed; fas·ci·nat·ing 1** : to seize and hold the attention of **2** : to attract greatly

fas·ci·na·tion \,fas-n-'ā-shən\ *n* : the state of being fascinated

fas·cism \'fash-,iz-əm\ *n* : a political system headed by a dictator in which the government controls business and labor and opposition is not permitted

fas·cist \'fash-əst\ *n, often cap* : one who approves of or practices fascism

¹**fash·ion** \'fash-ən\ *n* **1** : the make or form of something **2** : MANNER 2, WAY **3** : the popular style of a thing at a certain time

synonyms FASHION, STYLE, and FAD mean the way that up-to-date people do things. FASHION is used of any custom (as a way of dressing or behaving) that is widely accepted at any one time or place ⟨it was once the *fashion* for everyone to wear hats⟩ STYLE may suggest a fashion that is approved of by people with money and taste ⟨the house was decorated in the latest *style*⟩ FAD suggests something (as a way of dressing) that is very popular and often only for a short time ⟨running as a popular sport may be just a *fad*⟩

²**fashion** *vb* : to give shape or form to : MOLD

fash·ion·able \'fash-ə-nə-bəl, 'fash-nə-\ *adj* : following the fashion or established style — **fash·ion·ably** \-blē\ *adv*

¹**fast** \'fast\ *adj* **1** : firmly placed ⟨tent pegs *fast* in the ground⟩ **2** : totally loyal ⟨*fast* friends⟩ **3** : moving, operating, or acting quickly ⟨a *fast* train⟩ ⟨a *fast* thinker⟩ **4** : taking a short time ⟨a *fast* trip⟩ **5** : indicating ahead of the correct time ⟨the clock is *fast*⟩ **6** : not likely to fade ⟨*fast* colors⟩

synonyms FAST, RAPID, and SWIFT mean moving, proceeding, or acting with great speed. FAST is used of the thing that moves ⟨a *fast* horse⟩ RAPID is used of the movement itself ⟨the horse moved at a *rapid* pace⟩ SWIFT suggests ease of movement along with great speed ⟨the *swift* horse easily jumped the high fence⟩

²**fast** *adv* **1** : in a fast or fixed way ⟨stuck *fast* in the mud⟩ **2** : to the full extent : SOUND ⟨*fast* asleep⟩ **3** : with great speed ⟨run *faster* than a rabbit⟩

³**fast** *vb* **1** : to go without eating **2** : to eat in small amounts or only certain foods

⁴**fast** *n* **1** : the act of fasting **2** : a period of fasting

fas·ten \'fas-n\ *vb* **1** : to attach or join by or as if by pinning, tying, or nailing ⟨*fasten* clothes on a line⟩ **2** : to fix firmly **3** : to become fixed or joined — **fas·ten·er** *n*

fas·ten·ing \'fas-n-ing\ *n* : something that holds another thing shut or in the right position

fas·tid·i·ous \fas-'tid-ē-əs\ *adj* : hard to please : very particular

¹**fat** \'fat\ *adj* **fat·ter; fat·test 1** : having much body fat ⟨*fat* people⟩ **2** : ¹THICK 1 ⟨a *fat* book of poems⟩ **3** : richly rewarding or profitable ⟨signed a *fat* contract⟩ **4** : swollen up ⟨got a *fat* lip in the fight⟩ — **fat·ness** *n*

synonyms FAT, STOUT, and PLUMP mean having much flesh. FAT suggests that there is too much soft fatty tissue ⟨*fat* flabby people gasping for breath⟩ STOUT suggests a thick figure with a large amount of flesh that is usually more muscular ⟨many wrestlers are *stout*⟩ PLUMP suggests a soft, pleasing, full figure ⟨people just love *plump* little babies⟩

²**fat** *n* **1** : animal or plant tissue containing much greasy or oily material **2** : any of numerous compounds of carbon, hydrogen, and oxygen that make up most of animal or plant fat and that are important to nutrition as sources of energy **3** : a solid fat as distinguished from an oil **4** : the best or richest part ⟨the *fat* of the land⟩

fa·tal \'fāt-l\ *adj* **1** : FATEFUL ⟨on that *fatal* day⟩ **2** : causing death : MORTAL ⟨received a *fatal* blow from a falling tree⟩ **syno-nyms** see DEADLY — **fa·tal·ly** *adv*

fa·tal·i·ty \fā-'tal-ət-ē\ *n, pl* **fa·tal·i·ties** : a death resulting from a disaster or accident

fate \'fāt\ *n* **1** : a power beyond human control that is held to determine what happens : DESTINY ⟨blamed their failure on *fate*⟩ **2** : something that happens as though determined by fate : FORTUNE **3** : final outcome

fate·ful \'fāt-fəl\ *adj* : having serious results ⟨a *fateful* decision⟩ ⟨that *fateful* day⟩ — **fate·ful·ly** \-fə-lē\ *adv* — **fate·ful·ness** *n*

1fa·ther \'fä<u>th</u>-ər, 'fä<u>th</u>-\ *n* **1** *often cap* : a male parent **2** *cap* : GOD 1 **3** : ANCESTOR **4** : one who cares for another as a father might **5** : one deserving the respect and love given to a father **6** : a person who invents or begins something ⟨the *father* of modern science⟩ **7** : PRIEST — used especially as a title — **fa·ther·hood** \-,hu̇d\ *n* — **fa·ther·less** \-ləs\ *adj*

2father *vb* **1** : to become the father of **2** : to care for as a father

fa·ther–in–law \'fä<u>th</u>-ər-ən-,lȯ, 'fä<u>th</u>-\ *n, pl* **fa·thers–in–law** : the father of one's husband or wife

fa·ther·land \'fä<u>th</u>-ər-,land, 'fä<u>th</u>-\ *n* : one's native land

fa·ther·ly \'fä<u>th</u>-ər-lē, 'fä<u>th</u>-\ *adj* **1** : of or like a father **2** : showing the affection or concern of a father

1fath·om \'fa<u>th</u>-əm\ *n* : a unit of length equal to six feet (about 1.8 meters) used chiefly in measuring the depth of water

2fathom *vb* **1** : to measure the depth of water by means of a special line **2** : to see into and come to understand ⟨can't *fathom* their reasons⟩

1fa·tigue \fə-'tēg\ *n* : a state of being very tired

2fatigue *vb* **fa·tigued; fa·tigu·ing** : to tire by work or exertion

fat·ten \'fat-n\ *vb* : to make or become fat

fat·ty \'fat-ē\ *adj* **fat·ti·er; fat·ti·est** : containing or like fat

fau·cet \'fȯ-sət\ *n* : a fixture for controlling the flow of a liquid (as from a pipe or cask)

Word History The English word *faucet* can be traced back to a Latin adjective that meant "false." A Latin verb meaning "to falsify" was formed from this adjective. A French verb came from this Latin verb. But in French the verb meant "to hurt or break" as well as "to falsify." A French noun for the stopper that is used to plug a cask was formed from the French verb. If you think about it, a stopper does look as though it might be breaking into the cask. Our English word *faucet* came from the French word for stopper. *Faucet* is now used not only for a stopper but for any fixture used to get liquid from a cask or pipe.

fault \'fȯlt\ *n* **1** : a weakness in character **2** : FLAW, IMPERFECTION ⟨a *fault* in the weaving of the cloth⟩ **3** : ERROR ⟨found a *fault* in the text⟩ **4** : responsibility for something wrong ⟨your own *fault*⟩ **5** : a crack in the earth's crust along which movement occurs — **at fault** : BLAMEWORTHY

fault·less \'fȯlt-ləs\ *adj* : free from fault : PERFECT — **fault·less·ly** *adv* — **fault·less·ness** *n*

faulty \'fȯl-tē\ *adj* **fault·i·er; fault·i·est** : having a fault or blemish : IMPERFECT — **fault·i·ly** \-tə-lē\ *adv* — **fault·i·ness** \-tē-nəs\ *n*

faun \'fȯn\ *n* : a Roman god of country life represented as part goat and part man

fau·na \'fȯ-nə\ *n* : the animal life typical of a region, period, or special environment

1fa·vor \'fā-vər\ *n* **1** : APPROVAL, LIKING ⟨look with *favor* on a plan⟩ **2** : a preferring of one side over another : PARTIALITY **3** : an act of kindness ⟨do me a *favor*⟩ **4** : a small gift or decorative item ⟨party *favors*⟩

2favor *vb* **1** : to regard with favor ⟨*favors* a bill to cut taxes⟩ **2** : OBLIGE **3** **3** : to prefer especially unfairly **4** : to make possible or easier ⟨the weather *favored* our plan for a picnic⟩ **5** : to look like

fa·vor·able \'fā-və-rə-bəl, 'fāv-rə-\ *adj* **1** : showing favor ⟨a *favorable* opinion⟩ **2** : PROMISING ⟨*favorable* weather⟩ — **fa·vor·able·ness** *n* — **fa·vor·ably** \-blē\ *adv*

1fa·vor·ite \'fā-və-rət, 'fāv-rət\ *n* : a person or a thing that is favored above others

2favorite *adj* : being a favorite ⟨our *favorite* food⟩

1fawn \'fȯn\ *vb* **1** : to show affection — used especially of a dog **2** : to try to win favor by behavior that shows lack of self-respect

2fawn *n* **1** : a young deer **2** : a light grayish brown

1fax \'faks\ *n* **1** : FACSIMILE **2** : a machine used to send or receive material by facsimile **3** : something sent or received by facsimile

2fax *vb* : to send material by facsimile

\ə\ **abut**	\au̇\ **out**	\i\ **tip**	\ȯ\ **saw**	\u̇\ **foot**
\ər\ **further**	\ch\ **chin**	\ī\ **life**	\ȯi\ **coin**	\y\ **yet**
\a\ **mat**	\e\ **pet**	\j\ **job**	\th\ **thin**	\yü\ **few**
\ā\ **take**	\ē\ **easy**	\ng\ **sing**	\<u>th</u>\ **this**	\yu̇\ **cure**
\ä\ **cot, cart**	\g\ **go**	\ō\ **bone**	\ü\ **food**	\zh\ **vision**

faze \\'fāz\\ *vb* **fazed; faz·ing :** DAUNT

¹fear \\'fiər\\ *n* : a strong unpleasant feeling caused by being aware of danger or expecting something bad to happen

²fear *vb* : to be afraid of : feel fear

fear·ful \\'fiər-fəl\\ *adj* **1** : causing fear ⟨the *fearful* roar of a lion⟩ **2** : filled with fear ⟨*fearful* of danger⟩ **3** : showing or caused by fear — **fear·ful·ly** \\-fə-lē\\ *adv* — **fear·ful·ness** *n*

fear·less \\'fiər-ləs\\ *adj* : free from fear : BRAVE — **fear·less·ly** *adv* — **fear·less·ness** *n*

fear·some \\'fiər-səm\\ *adj* : causing fear

fea·si·ble \\'fē-zə-bəl\\ *adj* : possible to do or carry out ⟨a *feasible* plan⟩

¹feast \\'fēst\\ *n* **1** : a fancy meal **2** : a religious festival

²feast *vb* **1** : to eat well **2** : ²DELIGHT 1

feat \\'fēt\\ *n* : an act showing courage, strength, or skill

¹feath·er \\'feth-ər\\ *n* **1** : one of the light horny growths that make up the outer covering of a bird **2** : VARIETY 3, SORT ⟨people of that *feather*⟩ — **feath·ered** \\-ərd\\ *adj* — **feath·er·less** \\-ər-ləs\\ *adj*

²feather *vb* : to grow or form feathers

feather bed *n* **1** : a mattress filled with feathers **2** : a bed with a feather mattress

feath·ery \\'feth-ə-rē\\ *adj* **1** : like a feather or tuft of feathers **2** : covered with feathers

¹fea·ture \\'fē-chər\\ *n* **1** : a single part (as the nose or the mouth) of the face **2** : something especially noticeable **3** : a main attraction **4** : a special story in a newspaper or magazine

²feature *vb* **fea·tured; fea·tur·ing** : to stand out or cause to stand out ⟨health care *features* in the new law⟩ ⟨*featured* a new singer⟩

Feb·ru·ary \\'feb-yə-ˌwer-ē, 'feb-rə-, 'feb-ə-\\ *n* : the second month of the year

Word History In ancient Rome a feast of purification, or cleansing, was held each year. It took place in the middle of the second month. The Latin name for this month was formed from the name of the feast. English *February* came from the Latin name of the month.

fe·ces \\'fē-ˌsēz\\ *n pl* : body waste that passes out from the intestine

fed·er·al \\'fed-ə-rəl, 'fed-rəl\\ *adj* : of or relating to a nation formed by the union of several states or nations

fee \\'fē\\ *n* **1** : a fixed charge ⟨admission *fees*⟩ **2** : a charge for services ⟨a doctor's *fee*⟩

fee·ble \\'fē-bəl\\ *adj* **fee·bler** \\-blər\\; **fee·blest** \\-bləst\\ **1** : lacking in strength or endurance **2** : not loud ⟨a *feeble* cry⟩ **synonyms** see WEAK — **fee·ble·ness** \\-bəl-nəs\\ *n* — **fee·bly** \\-blē\\ *adv*

¹feed \\'fēd\\ *vb* **fed** \\'fed\\; **feed·ing 1** : to give food to or give as food ⟨*fed* the baby⟩ ⟨*fed* cereal to the baby⟩ **2** : to take food into the body : EAT ⟨cattle *feeding* on hay⟩ **3** : to supply with something necessary (as to growth or operation) ⟨*fed* plants with fertilizer⟩ — **feed·er** *n*

²feed *n* : food especially for livestock

¹feel \\'fēl\\ *vb* **felt** \\'felt\\ **feel·ing 1** : to be aware of through physical contact ⟨*feel* cold⟩ **2** : to examine or test by touching **3** : to be conscious of ⟨*felt* a fear of the dark⟩ **4** : to seem especially to the touch ⟨*feels* like silk⟩ **5** : to sense oneself to be ⟨*felt* sick⟩

²feel *n* **1** : SENSATION 2, FEELING **2** : the quality of something as learned through or as if through touch

feel·er \\'fē-lər\\ *n* **1** : a long flexible structure (as an insect's antenna) that is an organ of touch **2** : a suggestion or remark made to find out the views of other people

feel·ing \\'fē-ling\\ *n* **1** : the sense by which a person knows whether things are hard or soft, hot or cold, heavy or light **2** : a sensation of temperature or pressure ⟨a *feeling* of cold⟩ ⟨a *feeling* of pain⟩ **3** : a state of mind ⟨a *feeling* of joy⟩ **4 feelings** *pl* the state of a person's emotions ⟨hurt my *feelings*⟩ **5** : the condition of being aware **6** : IMPRESSION 4

feet *pl of* FOOT

feign \\'fān\\ *vb* : PRETEND 2

¹feint \\'fānt\\ *n* : a pretended blow or attack at one point or in one direction to take attention away from the point or direction one really intends to attack

²feint *vb* : to make a feint

¹fe·line \\'fē-ˌlīn\\ *adj* **1** : of or relating to cats or the cat family **2** : like or like that of a cat

²feline *n* : a feline animal : CAT

¹fell \\'fel\\ *vb* : to cut or knock down

²fell *past of* FALL

¹fel·low \\'fel-ō\\ *n* **1** : COMPANION 1, COMRADE **2** : an equal in rank, power, or character **3** : one of a pair : MATE **4** : a male person

²fellow *adj* : being a companion, mate, or equal

fel·low·man \\ˌfel-ō-'man\\ *n, pl* **fel·low·men** \\-'men\\ : a fellow human being

fel·low·ship \\'fel-ō-ˌship\\ *n* **1** : friendly relationship existing among persons **2** : a group with similar interests

fel·on \\'fel-ən\\ *n* : ²CRIMINAL

fel·o·ny \'fel-ə-nē\ *n, pl* **fel·o·nies** : a very serious crime

¹felt \'felt\ *n* : a heavy material made by rolling and pressing fibers together

²felt *past of* FEEL

¹fe·male \'fē-ˌmāl\ *n* : a female being

²female *adj* **1** : of, relating to, or being the sex that bears young or lays eggs **2** : having a pistil but no stamens **3** : of, relating to, or characteristic of females — **fe·male·ness** *n*

fem·i·nine \'fem-ə-nən\ *adj* : ²FEMALE 1, 3

fen \'fen\ *n* : low land covered by water

¹fence \'fens\ *n* : a barrier (as of wood or wire) to prevent escape or entry or to mark a boundary

²fence *vb* **fenced; fenc·ing** **1** : to enclose with a fence **2** : to practice fencing **synonyms** see ENCLOSE — **fenc·er** *n*

fenc·ing \'fen-sing\ *n* : the sport of having a pretended fight with blunted swords

fend \'fend\ *vb* **1** : REPEL 1 ⟨*fend* off an attack⟩ **2** : to try to get along without help ⟨*fend* for oneself⟩

fend·er \'fen-dər\ *n* **1** : a frame on the lower front of a locomotive or streetcar to catch or throw off anything that is hit **2** : a guard over an automobile or cycle wheel

¹fer·ment \fər-'ment\ *vb* : to undergo or cause to undergo fermentation

²fer·ment \'fər-ˌment\ *n* **1** : something (as yeast) that causes fermentation **2** : a state of excitement

fer·men·ta·tion \ˌfər-mən-'tā-shən\ *n* : a chemical breaking down of an organic material that is controlled by an enzyme and usually does not require oxygen

fern \'fern\ *n* : a plant that produces no flowers and has leaves divided into many parts — **fern·like** \-ˌlīk\ *adj*

fe·ro·cious \fə-'rō-shəs\ *adj* : FIERCE 1, SAVAGE — **fe·ro·cious·ly** *adv* — **fe·ro·cious·ness** *n*

fe·roc·i·ty \fə-'räs-ət-ē\ *n, pl* **fe·roc·i·ties** : the quality or state of being ferocious

¹fer·ret \'fer-ət\ *n* : a partly domesticated European polecat of a pale color sometimes kept for hunting vermin (as rats)

²ferret *vb* **1** : to hunt with a ferret **2** : to find by eager searching ⟨*ferret* out the answer⟩

Fer·ris wheel \'fer-əs-\ *n* : an amusement device consisting of a large vertical wheel that is driven by a motor and has seats around its rim

¹fer·ry \'fer-ē\ *vb* **fer·ried; fer·ry·ing** **1** : to carry by boat over a body of water **2** : to

cross by a ferry **3** : to deliver an airplane under its own power **4** : to transport in an airplane

²ferry *n, pl* **fer·ries** **1** : a place where persons or things are ferried **2** : FERRY-BOAT

fer·ry·boat \'fer-ē-ˌbōt\ *n* : a boat used to ferry passengers, vehicles, or goods

fer·tile \'fərt-l\ *adj* **1** : producing much vegetation or large crops **2** : capable of developing and growing ⟨a *fertile* egg⟩

fer·til·i·ty \ˌfər-'til-ət-ē\ *n* : the condition of being fertile

fer·til·iza·tion \ˌfərt-l-ə-'zā-shən\ *n* **1** : an act or process of making fertile **2** : the joining of an egg cell and a sperm cell to form the first stage of an embryo

fer·til·ize \'fərt-l-ˌīz\ *vb* **fer·til·ized; fer·til·iz·ing** : to make fertile or more fertile

fer·til·iz·er \'fərt-l-ˌī-zər\ *n* : material added to soil to make it more fertile

fer·vent \'fər-vənt\ *adj* : very warm in feeling : ARDENT — **fer·vent·ly** *adv*

fer·vor \'fər-vər\ *n* : strong feeling or expression

fes·ter \'fes-tər\ *vb* : to become painfully red and sore and usually full of pus

fes·ti·val \'fes-tə-vəl\ *n* **1** : a time of celebration ⟨a harvest *festival*⟩ **2** : a program of cultural events or entertainment

fes·tive \'fes-tiv\ *adj* **1** : having to do with a feast or festival **2** : very merry and joyful ⟨a *festive* party⟩

fes·tiv·i·ty \fes-'tiv-ət-ē\ *n, pl* **fes·tiv·i·ties** **1** : a festive state **2** : festive activity : MERRYMAKING

ferret

\ə\ **abut**	\au̇\ **out**	\i\ **tip**	\ȯ\ **saw**	\u̇\ **foot**
\ər\ **further**	\ch\ **chin**	\ī\ **life**	\ȯi\ **coin**	\y\ **yet**
\a\ **mat**	\e\ **pet**	\j\ **job**	\th\ **thin**	\yü\ **few**
\ā\ **take**	\ē\ **easy**	\ng\ **sing**	\th\ **this**	\yu̇\ **cure**
\ä\ **cot, cart**	\g\ **go**	\ō\ **bone**	\ü\ **food**	\zh\ **vision**

¹fes·toon \fes-'tün\ *n*
: an ornament (as a
chain) hanging be-
tween two points

²festoon *vb* : to hang
or form festoons on

fetch \'fech\ *vb* **1**
: to go after and
bring back **2** : to
bring as a price : sell
for

festoon

fetch·ing \'fech-ing\ *adj* : very attractive
— **fetch·ing·ly** *adv*

¹fet·ter \'fet-ər\ *n* **1** : a shackle for the feet
2 : something that holds back : RESTRAINT

²fetter *vb* **1** : to put fetters on **2** : to keep
from moving or acting freely

fe·tus \'fēt-əs\ *n* : an animal not yet born or
hatched but more developed than an em-
bryo

¹feud \'fyüd\ *n* : a long bitter quarrel carried on especially between families or
clans and usually having acts of violence
and revenge

²feud *vb* : to carry on a feud

feu·dal \'fyüd-l\ *adj* : of or relating to feu-
dalism

feu·dal·ism \'fyüd-l-,iz-əm\ *n* : a system of
social organization existing in medi-
eval Europe in which a vassal served a
lord and received protection and land in
return

fe·ver \'fē-vər\ *n* **1** : a rise of body temperature above normal **2** : a disease in
which fever is present

fe·ver·ish \'fē-və-rish\ *adj* **1** : having a fever **2** : of, relating to, or being fever **3**
: showing great emotion or activity : HEC-
TIC — **fe·ver·ish·ly** *adv* — **fe·ver·ish·
ness** *n*

¹few \'fyü\ *pron* : not many : a small number

²few *adj* : not many but some ⟨caught a
few fish⟩ ⟨they had *few* pleasures⟩

³few *n* : a small
number of individ-
uals ⟨a *few* of the
students⟩

fez \'fez\ *n, pl* **fez-
zes** : a round red felt
hat that usually has
a tassel but no brim

fi·as·co \fē-'as-kō\ *n,
pl* **fi·as·coes** : a
complete failure

¹fib \'fib\ *n* : an unimportant lie

²fib *vb* **fibbed; fib-
bing** : to tell a fib —
fib·ber *n*

fez

fi·ber *or* **fi·bre** \'fī-bər\ *n* : a long slender
threadlike structure

fi·brous \'fī-brəs\ *adj* : containing, consisting of, or like fibers ⟨*fibrous* roots⟩

-fi·ca·tion \fə-'kā-shən\ *n suffix* : the act
or process of or the result of ⟨ampli*fica-
tion*⟩

fick·le \'fik-əl\ *adj* : INCONSTANT ⟨*fickle*
friends⟩ ⟨*fickle* weather⟩ — **fick·le·ness** *n*

fic·tion \'fik-shən\ *n* **1** : something told or
written that is not fact **2** : a made-up story

fic·tion·al \-shən-l\ *adj* : of, relating to, or
suggesting fiction — **fic·tion·al·ly** \-l-ē\
adv

fic·ti·tious \fik-'tish-əs\ *adj* : not real

¹fid·dle \'fid-l\ *n* : VIOLIN

²fiddle *vb* **fid·dled; fid·dling 1** : to play
on a fiddle **2** : to move the hands or
fingers restlessly ⟨kept *fiddling* with a
ring⟩ **3** : to spend time in aimless activity
⟨*fiddled* around and did nothing⟩ **4** : TAM-
PER ⟨*fiddled* with the lock⟩ — **fid·dler**
\'fid-lər\ *n*

fid·dle·sticks \'fid-l-,stiks\ *n* : NONSENSE **1**
— used as an interjection

fi·del·i·ty \fə-'del-ət-ē, fī-\ *n* **1** : LOYALTY **2**
: ACCURACY

fidg·et \'fij-ət\ *vb* : to move in a restless or
nervous way

fidg·ets \'fij-əts\ *n pl* : uneasy restlessness shown by nervous movements

fidg·ety \'fij-ət-ē\ *adj* : tending to fidget

fief \'fēf\ *n* : an estate given to a vassal by
a feudal lord

¹field \'fēld\ *n* **1** : a piece of open, cleared,
or cultivated land **2** : a piece of land put to
a special use or giving a special product
⟨a ball *field*⟩ ⟨an oil *field*⟩ **3** : an open
space **4** : an area of activity or influence
⟨the *field* of science⟩ **5** : a background on
which something is drawn, painted, or
mounted

²field *vb* : to catch or stop and throw a ball

³field *adj* : of or relating to a field

field·er \'fēl-dər\ *n* : a baseball player
other than the pitcher or catcher on the
team that is not at bat

field glasses *n pl* : a hand-held instrument for seeing at a distance that is made
up of two telescopes usually without
prisms

field goal *n* : a score in football made by
kicking the ball through the goal during
ordinary play

fiend \'fēnd\ *n* **1** : DEMON 1, DEVIL **2** : a
very wicked or cruel person — **fiend·ish**
\'fēn-dish\ *adj*

fierce \'fiərs\ *adj* **fierc·er; fierc·est 1**
: likely to attack ⟨a *fierce* animal⟩ **2** : having or showing very great energy or enthu-

siasm **3** : wild or threatening in appearance — **fierce·ly** *adv* — **fierceness** *n*

fi·ery \'fi-ə-rē, 'fir-ē\ *adj* **fi·er·i·er; fi·er·i·est 1** : being on fire **2** : hot like a fire **3** : full of spirit

fi·es·ta \fē-'es-tə\ *n* : FESTIVAL 1, CELEBRATION

fife \'fif\ *n* : a small musical instrument like a flute that produces a shrill sound

¹fif·teen \fif-'tēn\ *adj* : being one more than fourteen

²fifteen *n* : one more than fourteen : three times five : 15

¹fif·teenth \fif-'tēnth\ *adj* : coming right after fourteenth

²fifteenth *n* : number fifteen in a series

¹fifth \'fifth\ *adj* : coming right after fourth

²fifth *n* **1** : number five in a series **2** : one of five equal parts

¹fif·ti·eth \'fif-tē-əth\ *adj* : coming right after forty-ninth

²fiftieth *n* : number fifty in a series

¹fif·ty \'fif-tē\ *adj* : being five times ten

²fifty *n* : five times ten : 50

fig \'fig\ *n* : an edible fruit that is oblong or shaped like a pear and that grows on a tree related to the mulberry

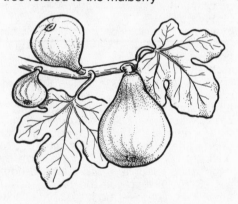

fig

¹fight \'fit\ *vb* **fought** \'fot\; **fight·ing 1** : to take part in a fight : COMBAT **2** : to try hard **3** : to struggle against ⟨*fight* discrimination⟩ — **fight·er** *n*

²fight *n* **1** : a meeting in battle or in physical combat **2** : ¹QUARREL 2 **3** : strength or desire for fighting ⟨full of *fight*⟩

¹fig·ure \'fig-yər\ *n* **1** : a symbol (as 1, 2, 3) that stands for a number : NUMERAL **2 figures** *pl* : ARITHMETIC 2 ⟨has a good head for *figures*⟩ **3** : value or price expressed in figures ⟨sold for a high *figure*⟩ **4** : the shape or outline of something **5** : the shape of the body especially of a person

⟨a slender *figure*⟩ **6** : an illustration in a printed text **7** : ¹PATTERN 3 ⟨cloth with red *figures*⟩ **8** : a series of movements in a dance **9** : an outline traced by a series of movements (as by an ice skater) **10** : a well-known or important person

²figure *vb* **fig·ured; fig·ur·ing 1** : to decorate with a pattern **2** : CALCULATE 1 ⟨*figure* the cost⟩

fig·ure·head \'fig-yər-,hed\ *n* : a figure, statue, or bust on the bow of a ship

figurehead

figure of speech : an expression (as a simile or a metaphor) that uses words in other than a plain or literal way

figure out *vb* : to work out in the mind ⟨*figure out* the answer⟩

fil·a·ment \'fil-ə-mənt\ *n* : a fine thread : a slender threadlike object (as the fine wire in an electric light bulb) — **fil·a·men·tous** \,fil-ə-'ment-əs\ *adj*

fil·bert \'fil-bərt\ *n* : the hazel or its nut

Word History Hazels are common in England. Their nuts are picked in late summer. The feast day of a certain saint (Saint Philbert) falls about the time that people pick hazelnuts. *Filbert*, a word for hazelnuts, came from the name of this saint.

filch \'filch\ *vb* : PILFER

¹file \'fil\ *n* : a steel tool with sharp ridges or teeth for smoothing or rubbing down hard substances

²file *vb* **filed; fil·ing** : to rub, smooth, or cut away with a file

\ə\ **abut**	\aù\ **out**	\i\ **tip**	\o\ **saw**	\ù\ **foot**	
\ər\ **further**	\ch\ **chin**	\ī\ **life**	\oi\ **coin**	\y\ **yet**	
\a\ **mat**	\e\ **pet**	\j\ **job**	\th\ **thin**	\yü\ **few**	
\ā\ **take**	\ē\ **easy**	\ng\ **sing**	\th\ **this**	\yù\ **cure**	
\ä\ **cot, cart**	\g\ **go**	\ō\ **bone**	\ü\ **food**	\zh\ **vision**	

³file *vb* **filed; fil•ing 1** : to arrange in order ⟨*filed* the cards in alphabetical order⟩ **2** : to enter or record officially ⟨*file* a claim⟩

⁴file *n* **1** : a device for keeping papers or records **2** : a collection of papers or records kept in a file

⁵file *n* : a row of persons or things arranged one behind the other ⟨walk in single *file*⟩

⁶file *vb* **filed; fil•ing** : to move in a file ⟨*file* out of the building⟩

fil•ial \'fil-ē-əl, 'fil-yəl\ *adj* **1** : of, relating to, or suitable for a son or daughter ⟨*filial* obedience⟩ **2** : being or having the relation of offspring

¹fill \'fil\ *vb* **1** : to make or become full ⟨*fill* a pail⟩ ⟨the pail *filled* slowly⟩ **2** : to occupy fully ⟨cars *filled* the street⟩ **3** : to spread through ⟨laughter *filled* the room⟩ **4** : to stop up : PLUG ⟨*fill* a tooth⟩ **5** : to write information on or in : COMPLETE ⟨*fill* in the blanks⟩ ⟨*fill* out a form⟩ **6** : to do the duties of ⟨*fill* the office of president⟩ **7** : to supply according to directions ⟨*fill* a prescription⟩

²fill *n* **1** : an amount that satisfies ⟨ate my *fill*⟩ **2** : material for filling something

fill•er \'fil-ər\ *n* **1** : one that fills **2** : a material used for filling

fil•let \'fil-ət, fi-'lā\ *n* : a piece of lean boneless meat or fish

fill•ing \'fil-ing\ *n* : a substance used to fill something else ⟨a *filling* for a tooth⟩

filling station *n* : SERVICE STATION

fil•ly \'fil-ē\ *n, pl* **fil•lies** : a female foal : a young female horse

¹film \'film\ *n* **1** : a thin coating or layer ⟨a *film* of ice⟩ **2** : a roll of material prepared for taking pictures **3** : MOVIE

²film *vb* **1** : to cover or become covered with film **2** : to photograph on a film **3** : to make a movie

film•strip \'film-ˌstrip\ *n* : a strip of film for projecting still pictures on a screen

filmy \'fil-mē\ *adj* **film•i•er; film•i•est** : of, like, or made of film

¹fil•ter \'fil-tər\ *n* **1** : a device or a mass of material (as sand) with tiny openings through which a gas or liquid is passed to separate out something which it contains ⟨a *filter* for removing dust from the air⟩ **2** : a transparent material that absorbs light of some colors and is used for changing light (as in photography)

²filter *vb* **1** : to pass through a filter ⟨*filter* water⟩ **2** : to remove by means of a filter

filth \'filth\ *n* : disgusting dirt

filthy \'fil-thē\ *adj* **filth•i•er; filth•i•est** : disgustingly dirty — **filth•i•ness** *n*

fil•tra•tion \fil-'trā-shən\ *n* : the process of filtering

fin \'fin\ *n* **1** : any of the thin parts that stick out from the body of a water animal and especially a fish and are used in moving or guiding the body through the water **2** : something shaped like a fin

¹fi•nal \'fin-l\ *adj* **1** : not to be changed : CONCLUSIVE ⟨the decision of the judges is *final*⟩ **2** : coming or happening at the end ⟨*final* examinations⟩ **synonyms** *see* LAST — **fi•nal•ly** *adv*

²final *n* **1** : the last match or game of a tournament **2** : a final examination in a course

fi•na•le \fə-'nal-ē\ *n* : the close or end of something (as a musical work)

fi•nal•i•ty \fi-'nal-ət-ē\ *n* : the condition of being final

¹fi•nance \fə-'nans, 'fi-ˌnans\ *n* **1 finances** *pl* : money available to a government, business, or individual **2** : the system that includes the circulation of money, the providing of banks and credit, and the making of investments

²finance *vb* **fi•nanced; fi•nanc•ing** : to provide money for ⟨*finance* a trip⟩

fi•nan•cial \fə-'nan-chəl, fi-\ *adj* : having to do with finance or with finances — **fi•nan•cial•ly** *adv*

fin•an•cier \ˌfin-ən-'siər\ *n* : a specialist in finance and especially in the financing of businesses

finch \'finch\ *n* : a small songbird (as a sparrow, bunting, or canary) that eats seeds

¹find \'find\ *vb* **found** \'faúnd\; **find•ing 1** : to come upon by chance ⟨*found* a dime⟩ **2** : to come upon by searching, study, or effort ⟨finally *found* the answer⟩ **3** : to decide on ⟨*find* a verdict⟩ **4** : to know by experience ⟨people *found* the child honest⟩ **5** : to gain or regain the use of ⟨*found* my voice again⟩ — **find fault** : to criticize in an unfavorable way

²find *n* : something found

find•er \'fin-dər\ *n* **1** : one that finds **2** : a device on a camera that shows the view being photographed

find out *vb* : to learn by studying or watching : DISCOVER

¹fine \'fin\ *n* : a sum of money to be paid as a punishment

²fine *vb* **fined; fin•ing** : to punish by a fine

³fine *adj* **fin•er; fin•est 1** : very small or thin ⟨*fine* print⟩ **2** : not coarse ⟨*fine* sand⟩ **3** : very good in quality or appearance ⟨a *fine* person⟩ — **fine•ly** *adv* — **fine•ness** *n*

⁴fine *adv* : very well ⟨doing *fine*⟩

fin•ery \'fi-nə-rē\ *n, pl* **fin•er•ies** : stylish or showy clothes and jewelry

¹fin•ger \'fing-gər\ *n* **1** : one of the five divisions of the end of the hand including the thumb **2** : something that is like or does the work of a finger **3** : the part of a glove into which a finger goes — **fin•ger-like** \-,līk\ *adj*

²finger *vb* : to touch with the fingers : HANDLE

fin•ger•board \'fing-gər-,bōrd\ *n* : a strip on the neck of a stringed instrument (as a guitar) against which the fingers press the strings to change the pitch

finger hole *n* : any of a group of holes in a wind instrument that may be covered with a finger to change the pitch

fin•ger•ling \'fing-gər-ling\ *n* : a young fish

fin•ger•nail \'fing-gər-,nāl\ *n* : the hard covering at the end of a finger

¹fin•ger•print \'fing-gər-,print\ *n* : the pattern of marks made by pressing a finger on a surface especially when the pattern is made in ink in order to identify a person

²fingerprint *vb* : to take the fingerprints of

fingerprints

fin•icky \'fin-i-kē\ *adj* : very hard to please : FUSSY — **fin•ick•i-ness** *n*

¹fin•ish \'fin-ish\ *vb* **1** : to bring or come to an end : COMPLETE, TERMINATE **2** : to put a final coat or surface on

²finish *n* **1** : ¹END 2, CONCLUSION ⟨a close *finish* in a race⟩ **2** : the final treatment or coating of a surface or the appearance given by finishing

fi•nite \'fi-,nīt\ *adj* : having certain limits

Finn \'fin\ *n* : a person born or living in Finland

finned \'find\ *adj* : having fins

¹Finn•ish \'fin-ish\ *adj* : of or relating to Finland, its people, or the Finnish language

²Finnish *n* : the language of the Finns

fiord *variant of* FJORD

fir \'fər\ *n* : a tall evergreen tree related to the pine that yields useful lumber

¹fire \'fīr\ *n* **1** : the light and heat and especially the flame produced by burning **2** : fuel that is burning (as in a fireplace or stove) **3** : the destructive burning of something (as a building or a forest) **4** : a being lively : ENTHUSIASM **5** : the shooting of firearms ⟨rifle *fire*⟩ — **on fire** : actively burning — **under fire 1** : exposed to the firing of enemy guns **2** : under attack

²fire *vb* **fired; fir•ing 1** : to set on fire ⟨vandals *fired* the barn⟩ **2** : EXCITE 2, STIR ⟨a story to *fire* the imagination⟩ **3** : to dismiss from employment **4** : to set off : EXPLODE ⟨*fire* a firecracker⟩ **5** : ¹SHOOT 2 ⟨*fire* a gun⟩ **6** : to subject to great heat ⟨*fire* pottery⟩

fire•arm \'fīr-,ärm\ *n* : a small weapon from which shot or a bullet is driven by the explosion of gunpowder

fire•bug \'fīr-,bəg\ *n* : a person who sets destructive fires on purpose

fire•crack•er \'fīr-,krak-ər\ *n* : a paper tube containing an explosive to be set off for amusement

fire engine *n* : a truck equipped to fight fires

fire escape *n* : a stairway that provides a way of escape from a building in case of fire

fire extinguisher *n* : something (as a metal container filled with chemicals) that is used to put out a fire

fire fighter *n* : a person whose job is to put out fires

fire•fly \'fīr-,flī\ *n, pl* **fire•flies** : a small beetle producing a soft light

fire•house \'fīr-,haus\ *n* : FIRE STATION

fire•man \'fīr-mən\ *n, pl* **fire•men** \-mən\ **1** : FIRE FIGHTER **2** : a person who tends a fire (as in a large furnace)

fire•place \'fīr-,plās\ *n* : a structure with a hearth on which an open fire can be built for heating or especially outdoors for cooking

fire•plug \'fīr-,pləg\ *n* : HYDRANT

fire•proof \'fīr-'prüf\ *adj* : not easily burned : made safe against fire

fire•side \'fīr-,sīd\ *n* **1** : a place near the hearth **2** : ¹HOME 1

fire station *n* : a building housing fire engines and usually fire fighters

fire•wood \'fīr-,wůd\ *n* : wood cut for fuel

fire•work \'fīr-,wərk\ *n* **1** : a device that makes a display of light or noise by the burning of explosive or flammable materials **2 fireworks** *pl* : a display of fireworks

¹firm \'fərm\ *adj* **1** : STRONG 1, VIGOROUS ⟨had a *firm* grip on the wheel⟩ **2** : having a solid compact texture ⟨*firm* ground⟩ **3** : not likely to be changed ⟨a *firm* price⟩ **4** : not easily moved or shaken : FAITHFUL ⟨a *firm* believer⟩ ⟨*firm* friends⟩ **5** : showing

\ə\ **abut**	\au̇\ **out**	\i\ **tip**	\ȯ\ **saw**	\u̇\ **foot**
\ər\ **further**	\ch\ **chin**	\ī\ **life**	\ȯi\ **coin**	\y\ **yet**
\a\ **mat**	\e\ **pet**	\j\ **job**	\th\ **thin**	\yü\ **few**
\ā\ **take**	\ē\ **easy**	\ng\ **sing**	\th\ **this**	\yu̇\ **cure**
\ä\ **cot, cart**	\g\ **go**	\ō\ **bone**	\ü\ **food**	\zh\ **vision**

no weakness **synonyms** see HARD — **firm·ly** *adv* — **firm·ness** *n*

²firm *n* : BUSINESS 2

fir·ma·ment \'fər-mə-mənt\ *n* : the arch of the sky

¹first \'fərst\ *adj* **1** : being number one ⟨the *first* day of the week⟩ **2** : coming before all others

²first *adv* **1** : before any other ⟨reached the goal *first*⟩ **2** : for the first time ⟨we *first* met at a party⟩

³first *n* **1** : number one in a series **2** : something or someone that is first

first aid *n* : care or treatment given to an ill or injured person before regular medical help can be gotten

first·hand \'fərst-'hand\ *adj or adv* : coming right from the original source

first lieutenant *n* : a commissioned officer in the Army, Air Force, or Marine Corps ranking above a second lieutenant

first–rate \'fər-'strāt\ *adj* : EXCELLENT

first sergeant *n* **1** : a noncommissioned officer serving as the chief assistant to a military commander **2** : a noncommissioned officer ranking above a sergeant first class in the Army or above a gunnery sergeant in the Marine Corps

firth \'fərth\ *n* : a narrow arm of the sea

¹fish \'fish\ *n, pl* **fish** *or* **fish·es** **1** : an animal that lives in water — usually used in combination ⟨star*fish*⟩ **2** : any of a large group of vertebrate animals that live in water, breathe with gills, and usually have fins and scales — **fish·like** \-,līk\ *adj*

²fish *vb* **1** : to attempt to catch fish **2** : to try to find or to find out something by groping

fish·er·man \'fish-ər-mən\ *n, pl* **fish·er·men** \-mən\ : a person who fishes

fish·ery \'fish-ə-rē\ *n, pl* **fish·er·ies** **1** : the business of catching fish **2** : a place for catching fish

fish·hook \'fish-,hùk\ *n* : a hook used for catching fish

fishy \'fish-ē\ *adj* **fish·i·er; fish·i·est** **1** : of or like fish ⟨a *fishy* odor⟩ **2** : QUESTIONABLE ⟨the story sounds *fishy* to me⟩

fis·sion \'fish-ən\ *n* **1** : a splitting or breaking into parts **2** : a method of reproduction in which a living cell or body divides into two or more parts each of which grows into a whole new individual **3** : the splitting of an atomic nucleus with the release of large amounts of energy

fis·sure \'fish-ər\ *n* : a narrow opening or crack ⟨a *fissure* in rock⟩

fist \'fist\ *n* : the hand with the fingers doubled tight into the palm

¹fit \'fit\ *n* : a sudden attack or outburst

²fit *adj* **fit·ter; fit·test** **1** : good enough ⟨*fit* to eat⟩ **2** : healthy in mind and body ⟨feel *fit*⟩ — **fit·ness** *n*

³fit *vb* **fit·ted; fit·ting** **1** : to be suitable for or to ⟨dressed to *fit* the occasion⟩ **2** : to be the right shape or size ⟨this shirt doesn't *fit*⟩ **3** : to bring to the right shape or size ⟨have a suit *fitted*⟩ **4** : EQUIP ⟨*fitted* the ship with new engines⟩

⁴fit *n* **1** : the way something fits **2** : a piece of clothing that fits

fit·ful \'fit-fəl\ *adj* : IRREGULAR 4 ⟨*fitful* sleep⟩

¹fit·ting \'fit-ing\ *adj* : ²APPROPRIATE, SUITABLE — **fit·ting·ly** *adv*

²fitting *n* : a small accessory part ⟨a pipe *fitting*⟩

¹five \'fiv\ *adj* : being one more than four

²five *n* **1** : one more than four : 5 **2** : the fifth in a set or series

¹fix \'fiks\ *vb* **1** : to make firm or secure ⟨*fix* a machine in place⟩ **2** : to cause to combine chemically ⟨bacteria that *fix* nitrogen⟩ **3** : to set definitely : ESTABLISH ⟨*fix* the date of a meeting⟩ **4** : to get ready : PREPARE ⟨*fix* dinner⟩ **5** : ¹REPAIR 1, MEND — **fix·er** \'fik-sər\ *n*

²fix *n* : an unpleasant or difficult position

fixed \'fikst\ *adj* **1** : not changing : SET ⟨living on a *fixed* income⟩ **2** : not moving : INTENT ⟨a *fixed* stare⟩ — **fix·ed·ly** \'fik-səd-lē\ *adv*

fixed star *n* : a star so distant that its motion can be measured only by very careful observations over long periods

fix·ture \'fiks-chər\ *n* : something attached as a permanent part ⟨bathroom *fixtures*⟩

¹fizz \'fiz\ *vb* : to make a hissing or sputtering sound

²fizz *n* **1** : a hissing or sputtering sound **2** : a bubbling drink

¹fiz·zle \'fiz-əl\ *vb* **fiz·zled; fiz·zling** : to fail after a good start

²fizzle *n* : FAILURE 3

fjord *or* **fiord** \fē-'ȯrd\ *n* : a narrow inlet of the sea between cliffs or steep slopes

flab·by \'flab-ē\ *adj* **flab·bi·er; flab·bi·est** : not hard and firm : SOFT — **flab·bi·ness** *n*

¹flag \'flag\ *n* : a piece of cloth with a special design or color that is used as a symbol (as of a nation) or as a signal

²flag *vb* **flagged; flag·ging** : to signal with or as if with a flag

³flag *vb* **flagged; flag·ging** : to become weak

fla·gel·lum \flə-'jel-əm\ *n, pl* **fla·gel·la** \-'jel-ə\ : a long whiplike structure by which some tiny plants and animals move

flag·man \'flag-mən\ *n, pl* **flag·men** \-mən\ : a person who signals with a flag

flag·on \'flag-ən\ *n*
: a container for liquids usually having a handle, spout, and lid

flag·pole \'flag-ˌpōl\ *n* : a pole from which a flag flies

fla·grant \'flā-grənt\ *adj* : so bad as to be impossible to overlook ⟨a *flagrant* violation of the rules⟩ — **fla·grant·ly** *adv*

flag·ship \'flag-ˌship\ *n* : the ship carrying the commander of a group of ships and flying a flag that tells the commander's rank

flagon

flag·staff \'flag-ˌstaf\ *n, pl* **flag·staffs** : FLAGPOLE

flag·stone \'flag-ˌstōn\ *n* : a piece of hard flat rock used for paving

¹**flail** \'flāl\ *n* : a tool for threshing grain by hand

²**flail** *vb* : to hit with or as if with a flail

flair \'flaər, 'fleər\ *n* : natural ability

¹**flake** \'flāk\ *n* : a small thin flat piece

²**flake** *vb* **flaked; flak·ing** : to form or separate into flakes

flaky \'flā-kē\ *adj* **flak·i·er; flak·i·est** : tending to flake ⟨a *flaky* pie crust⟩ — **flak·i·ness** *n*

flam·boy·ant \flam-'bȯi-ənt\ *adj* : liking or making a dashing show — **flam·boy·ant·ly** *adv*

¹**flame** \'flām\ *n* **1** : the glowing gas that makes up part of a fire ⟨the *flame* of a candle⟩ **2** : a condition or appearance suggesting a flame

²**flame** *vb* **flamed; flam·ing** : to burn with or as if with a flame

flame·throw·er \'flām-ˌthrō-ər\ *n* : a device that shoots a burning stream of fuel

fla·min·go \flə-'ming-go\ *n, pl* **fla·min·gos** *or* **fla·min·goes** : a water bird with very long neck and legs, scarlet wings, and a broad bill bent downward at the end

flamingo

Word History The English word *flamingo* came from the bird's Spanish name. It is likely that this Spanish word was taken from a language of southern France. The word for a flamingo in this language came from a Latin word. This Latin word meant "flame." When a flamingo takes flight there is a sudden bright flash of its scarlet wing feathers. This looks a bit like a burst of flame.

flam·ma·ble \'flam-ə-bəl\ *adj* : capable of being easily set on fire and of burning quickly ⟨a *flammable* liquid⟩

¹**flank** \'flangk\ *n* **1** : the fleshy part of the side between the ribs and the hip **2** : ¹SIDE 3 **3** : the right or left side of a formation (as of soldiers)

²**flank** *vb* **1** : to pass around the flank of **2** : to be located at the side of : BORDER

flank·er \'flang-kər\ *n* : a football player stationed wide of the formation

fjord

\ə\ **abut**	\au̇\ **out**	\i\ **tip**	\ȯ\ **saw**	\u̇\ **foot**
\ər\ **further**	\ch\ **chin**	\ī\ **life**	\ȯi\ **coin**	\y\ **yet**
\a\ **mat**	\e\ **pet**	\j\ **job**	\th\ **thin**	\yü\ **few**
\ā\ **take**	\ē\ **easy**	\ng\ **sing**	\th\ **this**	\yu̇\ **cure**
\ä\ **cot, cart**	\g\ **go**	\ō\ **bone**	\ü\ **food**	\zh\ **vision**

flan·nel \'flan-l\ *n* : a soft cloth made of wool or cotton

¹flap \'flap\ *n* **1** : something broad and flat or limber that hangs loose **2** : the motion made by something broad and limber (as a sail or wing) moving back and forth or the sound produced

²flap *vb* **flapped; flap·ping 1** : to give a quick light blow **2** : to move with a beating or fluttering motion ⟨birds *flapping* their wings⟩

flap·jack \'flap-,jak\ *n* : PANCAKE

¹flare \'flaər, 'fleər\ *vb* **flared; flar·ing 1** : to burn with an unsteady flame **2** : to shine with great or sudden light **3** : to become angry ⟨*flared* up at the remarks⟩ **4** : to spread outward

²flare *n* **1** : a sudden blaze of light **2** : a blaze of light used to signal, light up something, or attract attention **3** : a device or material used to produce a flare **4** : a sudden outburst (as of sound or anger) **5** : a spreading outward : a part that spreads outward

¹flash \'flash\ *vb* **1** : to shine in or like a sudden flame ⟨lightning *flashed*⟩ **2** : to send out in or as if in flashes ⟨*flash* a message⟩ **3** : to come or pass very suddenly ⟨a car *flashed* by⟩ **4** : to make a sudden display (as of feeling)

²flash *n* **1** : a sudden burst of or as if of light ⟨a *flash* of wit⟩ **2** : a very short time

³flash *adj* : beginning suddenly and lasting only a short time ⟨*flash* floods⟩

flash·light \'flash-,līt\ *n* : a small portable electric light that runs on batteries

flashy \'flash-ē\ *adj* **flash·i·er; flash·i·est** : GAUDY ⟨*flashy* clothes⟩

flask \'flask\ *n* : a container like a bottle with a flat or rounded body

¹flat \'flat\ *adj* **flat·ter; flat·test 1** : having a smooth level surface ⟨a *flat* rock⟩ **2** : spread out on or along a surface ⟨*flat* on the ground⟩ **3** : having a broad smooth surface and little thickness ⟨a phonograph record is *flat*⟩ **4** : ²OUTRIGHT 1, POSITIVE ⟨a *flat* refusal⟩ **5** : FIXED 1 ⟨charge a *flat* rate⟩ **6** : having nothing lacking or left over : EXACT ⟨got there in two minutes *flat*⟩ **7** : INSIPID ⟨a *flat* story⟩ ⟨the stew is too *flat*⟩ **8** : having lost air pressure ⟨a *flat* tire⟩ **9** : lower than the true musical pitch **10** : lower by a half step in music **11** : free from gloss ⟨*flat* paint⟩ **synonyms** see LEVEL — **flat·ly** *adv* — **flat·ness** *n*

²flat *n* **1** : a level place : PLAIN **2** : a flat part or surface **3** : a note or tone that is a half step lower than the note named **4** : a sign ♭ meaning that the pitch of a musical note

is to be lower by a half step **5** : a deflated tire

³flat *adv* **1** : on or against a flat surface ⟨lie *flat*⟩ **2** : below the true musical pitch ⟨sang *flat*⟩

⁴flat *n* : an apartment on one floor

flat·boat \'flat-,bōt\ *n* : a large boat with a flat bottom and square ends

flat·fish \'flat-,fish\ *n* : a fish (as the flounder) that swims on its side and has both eyes on the upper side

flat·iron \'flat-,ī-ərn\ *n* : ¹IRON

flat·ten \'flat-n\ *vb* : to make or become flat

flat·ter \'flat-ər\ *vb* **1** : to praise but not sincerely **2** : to show too favorably ⟨a picture that *flatters* me⟩ **synonyms** see COMPLIMENT — **flat·ter·er** *n* — **flat·ter·ing·ly** *adv*

flat·tery \'flat-ə-rē\ *n, pl* **flat·ter·ies** : praise that is not deserved or meant

flaunt \'flȯnt\ *vb* **1** : to wave or flutter in a showy way **2** : to make too much show of : PARADE

¹fla·vor \'flā-vər\ *n* **1** : the quality of something that affects the sense of taste **2** : a substance added to food to give it a desired taste — **fla·vored** \-vərd\ *adj*

²flavor *vb* : to give or add a flavor to

fla·vor·ing \'flā-və-ring, 'flāv-ring\ *n* : ¹FLAVOR 2

flaw \'flȯ\ *n* : a small often hidden fault

flax \'flaks\ *n* : a plant with blue flowers that is grown for its fiber from which linen is made and for its seed from which oil and livestock feed are obtained

flax·en \'flak-sən\ *adj* **1** : made of flax **2** : having a light straw color ⟨*flaxen* hair⟩

flax·seed \'flak-,sēd\ *n* : the seed of flax from which linseed oil comes and which is used in medicine

flay \'flā\ *vb* **1** : ²SKIN **2** : to scold severely

flea \'flē\ *n* : a small bloodsucking insect that has no wings and a hard body

¹fleck \'flek\ *vb* : to mark with small streaks or spots ⟨bananas *flecked* with brown⟩

²fleck *n* **1** : ¹SPOT 2, MARK **2** : ¹FLAKE, PARTICLE

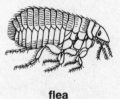

flea

fledg·ling \'flej-ling\ *n* : a young bird that has just grown the feathers needed to fly

flee \'flē\ *vb* **fled** \'fled\; **flee·ing** : to run away or away from : FLY

¹fleece \'flēs\ *n* : the woolly coat of an animal and especially a sheep

²**fleece** *vb* **fleeced; fleec·ing :** to take money or property from by trickery

fleecy \'flē-sē\ *adj* **fleec·i·er; fleec·i·est :** covered with, made of, or like fleece

¹**fleet** \'flēt\ *n* **1 :** a group of warships under one command **2 :** a country's navy **3 :** a group of ships or vehicles that move together or are under one management ⟨a fishing *fleet*⟩ ⟨a *fleet* of taxis⟩

²**fleet** *adj* **:** very swift ⟨*fleet* of foot⟩ — **fleet·ly** *adv* — **fleet·ness** *n*

Fleet Admiral *n* **:** the highest ranking commissioned officer in the Navy ranking above an admiral

flesh \'flesh\ *n* **1 :** the soft and especially the edible muscular parts of an animal's body **2 :** a fleshy edible plant part (as the pulp of a fruit) — **fleshed** \'flesht\ *adj*

fleshy \'flesh-ē\ *adj* **flesh·i·er; flesh·i·est 1 :** like or consisting of flesh **2 :** rather stout

flew *past of* FLY

flex \'fleks\ *vb* **:** to bend often again and again

flex·i·bil·i·ty \ˌflek-sə-'bil-ət-ē\ *n* **:** the quality or state of being flexible

flex·i·ble \'flek-sə-bəl\ *adj* **1 :** possible to bend or flex **2 :** able or suitable to meet new situations ⟨a *flexible* mind⟩ — **flex·i·bly** \'flek-sə-blē\ *adv*

¹**flick** \'flik\ *n* **:** a light snapping stroke

²**flick** *vb* **:** to strike or move with a quick motion

¹**flick·er** \'flik-ər\ *vb* **:** to burn unsteadily ⟨a *flickering* candle⟩

²**flicker** *n* **1 :** a quick small movement ⟨a *flicker* of the eyelids⟩ **2 :** a flickering light

³**flicker** *n* **:** a large North American woodpecker

fli·er *or* **fly·er** \'flī-ər\ *n* **1 :** one that flies **2 :** AVIATOR

¹**flight** \'flīt\ *n* **1 :** an act or instance of passing through the air by the use of wings **2 :** a passing through the air or space ⟨a balloon *flight*⟩ ⟨the *flight* of a rocket to the moon⟩ **3 :** the distance covered in a flight **4 :** a scheduled trip by an airplane ⟨a four o'clock *flight*⟩ **5 :** a group of similar things flying through the air together ⟨a *flight* of ducks⟩ ⟨a *flight* of bombers⟩ **6 :** a passing above or beyond ordinary limits ⟨a *flight* of imagination⟩ **7 :** a continuous series of stairs

²**flight** *n* **:** the act of running away

flight·less \'flīt-ləs\ *adj* **:** unable to fly

flighty \'flīt-ē\ *adj* **flight·i·er; flight·i·est 1 :** easily excited : SKITTISH ⟨a *flighty* horse⟩ **2 :** not wise or sober : FRIVOLOUS

flim·sy \'flim-zē\ *adj* **flim·si·er; flim·si·est :** not strong or solid ⟨a *flimsy* cardboard suitcase⟩ ⟨a *flimsy* excuse⟩ — **flim·si·ly** \-zə-lē\ *adv* — **flim·si·ness** \-zē-nəs\ *n*

flinch \'flinch\ *vb* **:** to draw back from or as if from pain ⟨*flinch* at a loud noise⟩

¹**fling** \'fliŋ\ *vb* **flung** \'fləŋ\; **fling·ing 1 :** to move suddenly **2 :** to throw hard or without care ⟨*flung* the junk out the window⟩

²**fling** *n* **1 :** an act of flinging **2 :** a time of freedom for pleasure

flint \'flint\ *n* **:** a very hard stone that produces a spark when struck by steel

flint·lock \'flint-ˌläk\ *n* **:** an old-fashioned firearm using a flint for striking a spark to fire the charge

¹**flip** \'flip\ *vb* **flipped; flip·ping :** to move or turn by or as if by tossing ⟨*flip* a coin⟩ ⟨*flip* a switch⟩

²**flip** *n* **:** an act of flipping : TOSS

flip·pant \'flip-ənt\ *adj* **:** not respectful : SAUCY — **flip·pant·ly** *adv*

flip·per \'flip-ər\ *n* **:** a broad flat limb (as of a seal) specialized for swimming

¹**flirt** \'flərt\ *vb* **:** to show a liking for someone of the opposite sex just for the fun of it

²**flirt** *n* **:** a person who flirts a lot

flit \'flit\ *vb* **flit·ted; flit·ting :** to move by darting about

¹**float** \'flōt\ *n* **1 :** something that floats in or on the surface of a liquid **2 :** a cork or bob that holds up the baited end of a fishing line **3 :** a floating platform anchored near a shore for the use of swimmers or boats **4 :** a hollow ball that controls the flow or level of the liquid it floats on (as in a tank) **5 :** a vehicle with a platform used to carry an exhibit in a parade

²**float** *vb* **1 :** to rest on the surface of a liquid ⟨cork will *float*⟩ **2 :** to drift on or through or as if on or through a fluid ⟨dust *floating* through the air⟩ **3 :** to cause to float — **float·er** *n*

¹**flock** \'fläk\ *n* **1 :** a group of animals (as geese or sheep) living or kept together **2 :** a group someone (as a minister) watches over

²**flock** *vb* **:** to gather or move in a crowd

floe \'flō\ *n* **:** a sheet or mass of floating ice

flog \'fläg\ *vb* **flogged; flog·ging :** to beat severely with a rod or whip

¹**flood** \'fləd\ *n* **1 :** a huge flow of water that rises and spreads over the land **2 :** the flowing in of the tide **3 :** a very large number or amount ⟨a *flood* of requests⟩

\ə\ **abut**	\au̇\ **out**	\i\ **tip**	\ȯ\ **saw**	\u̇\ **foot**
\ər\ **further**	\ch\ **chin**	\ī\ **life**	\ȯi\ **coin**	\y\ **yet**
\a\ **mat**	\e\ **pet**	\j\ **job**	\th\ **thin**	\yü\ **few**
\ā\ **take**	\ē\ **easy**	\ng\ **sing**	\t͟h\ **this**	\yu̇\ **cure**
\ä\ **cot, cart**	\g\ **go**	\ō\ **bone**	\ü\ **food**	\zh\ **vision**

²flood *vb* **1** : to cover or become filled with water **2** : to fill as if with a flood

flood·light \'fləd-,līt\ *n* : a lamp that gives a bright broad beam of light

flood·plain \'fləd-,plān\ *n* : low flat land along a stream that is flooded when the steam overflows

flood·wa·ter \'fləd-,wȯt-ər, -,wät-\ *n* : the water of a flood

¹floor \'flōr\ *n* **1** : the part of a room on which one stands **2** : the lower inside surface of a hollow structure ⟨the *floor* of a car⟩ **3** : a ground surface ⟨the ocean *floor*⟩ **4** : a story of a building

²floor *vb* **1** : to cover or provide with a floor ⟨*floor* a garage with concrete⟩ **2** : to knock down

floor·ing \'flōr-ing\ *n* **1** : ¹FLOOR 1 **2** : material for floors

¹flop \'fläp\ *vb* **flopped; flop·ping** **1** : to flap about ⟨a fish *flopping* on the deck⟩ **2** : to drop or fall limply ⟨*flopped* into the chair⟩ **3** : ¹FAIL 6

²flop *n* **1** : the act or sound of flopping **2** : FAILURE 3

flop·py \'fläp-ē\ *adj* **flop·pi·er; flop·pi·est** : being soft and flexible

flo·ra \'flōr-ə\ *n* : the plant life typical of a region, period, or special environment

flo·ral \'flōr-əl\ *adj* : of or relating to flowers

flo·ret \'flōr-ət\ *n* : a small flower

flo·rist \'flōr-əst\ *n* : a person who sells flowers and ornamental plants

¹floss \'fläs, 'flȯs\ *n* **1** : soft thread used in embroidery **2** : fluffy material full of fibers

²floss *vb* : to use dental floss on (one's teeth)

flo·til·la \flō-'til-ə\ *n* : a fleet of usually small ships

¹flounce \'flaúns\ *vb* **flounced; flounc·ing** : to move with exaggerated jerky motions

²flounce *n* : a strip of fabric attached by its upper edge ⟨a *flounce* on a skirt⟩

¹floun·der \'flaún-dər\ *n* : a flatfish used for food

²flounder *vb* **1** : to struggle to move or get footing ⟨*floundering* in the mud⟩ **2** : to behave or do something in a clumsy way ⟨*floundered* through the speech⟩

flour \'flaúr\ *n* : the finely ground meal of a cereal grain and especially of wheat

¹flour·ish \'flər-ish\ *vb* **1** : to grow well : THRIVE ⟨plants *flourish* in this rich soil⟩ **2** : to do well : PROSPER **3** : to make sweeping movements with ⟨*flourish* a sword⟩

²flourish *n* **1** : a fancy bit of decoration added to something (as handwriting) **2** : a sweeping motion

flout \'flaút\ *vb* : to show lack of respect for : DISREGARD ⟨*flouted* their parents' advice⟩

¹flow \'flō\ *vb* **1** : to move in a stream **2** : to glide along smoothly **3** : to hang loose and waving

²flow *n* **1** : an act of flowing **2** : the flowing in of the tide **3** : a smooth even movement **4** : ¹STREAM 2, 3

¹flow·er \'flaú-ər\ *n* **1** : a plant part that produces seed **2** : a plant grown chiefly for its showy flowers **3** : the state of bearing flowers ⟨in full *flower*⟩ **4** : the best part or example — **flow·ered** \-ərd\ *adj* — **flow·er·less** \-ər-ləs\ *adj*

²flower *vb* : to produce flowers

flow·er·ing plant \'flaú-ə-ring-\ *n* : a seed plant whose seeds are produced in the ovary of a flower

flow·er·pot \'flaú-ər-,pät\ *n* : a pot in which to grow plants

flow·ery \'flaú-ə-rē\ *adj* **1** : having many flowers **2** : full of fine words ⟨*flowery* language⟩ — **flow·er·i·ness** *n*

flown *past participle of* FLY

flu \'flü\ *n* **1** : INFLUENZA **2** : any of several virus diseases something like a cold

fluc·tu·ate \'flək-chə-,wāt\ *vb* **fluc·tu·at·ed; fluc·tu·at·ing** : to change continually and especially up and down ⟨the temperature *fluctuated*⟩

flue \'flü\ *n* : an enclosed passage (as in a chimney) for smoke or air

flu·en·cy \'flü-ən-sē\ *n* : the ability to speak easily and well

flu·ent \'flü-ənt\ *adj* **1** : able to speak easily and well ⟨was *fluent* in Spanish⟩ **2** : that is smooth and correct : GOOD ⟨speaks *fluent* German⟩ — **flu·ent·ly** \-ənt-lē\ *adv*

¹fluff \'fləf\ *n* : ⁷DOWN, NAP

²fluff *vb* : to make or become fluffy

fluffy \'fləf-ē\ *adj* **fluff·i·er; fluff·i·est** : having, covered with, or like down ⟨a *fluffy* little chick⟩

¹flu·id \'flü-əd\ *adj* **1** : capable of flowing like a liquid or gas **2** : being smooth and easy — **flu·id·ly** *adv*

²fluid *n* : something that tends to flow and take the shape of its container

flung *past of* FLING

flunk \'fləngk\ *vb* : ¹FAIL 6 ⟨*flunk* a test⟩

flu·o·res·cent lamp \,flú-ə-,res-nt-\ *n* : an electric lamp in the form of a tube in which light is produced through the action of ultraviolet radiation on the inside coating

flu·o·ri·date \'flúr-ə-,dāt, 'flȯr-\ *vb* **flu·o·ri·dat·ed; flu·o·ri·dat·ing** : to add a fluorine compound to (as drinking water)

flu·o·ri·da·tion \ˌflu̇r-ə-ˈdā-shən, ˌflȯr-\ *n* : the act of fluoridating

flu·o·rine \ˈflu̇r-ˌēn, -ən\ *n* : a yellowish flammable irritating gaseous chemical element

¹flur·ry \ˈflər-ē\ *n, pl* **flur·ries** **1** : a gust of wind **2** : a brief light snowfall **3** : a brief outburst (as of activity)

²flurry *vb* **flur·ried; flur·ry·ing** : ¹FLUSTER, EXCITE

¹flush \ˈfləsh\ *vb* : to begin or cause to begin flight suddenly ⟨a hunting dog *flushing* quail⟩

²flush *n* **1** : an act of flushing **2** : ²BLUSH 1

³flush *vb* **1** : ¹BLUSH ⟨*flushed* with pleasure⟩ **2** : to pour water over or through

⁴flush *adj* : having one edge or surface even with the next ⟨*flush* paneling⟩ ⟨a *flush* joint⟩

⁵flush *adv* : so as to be flush

¹flus·ter \ˈfləs-tər\ *vb* : to make nervous and confused : UPSET

²fluster *n* : a state of nervous confusion

¹flute \ˈflüt\ *n* : a woodwind instrument in the form of a hollow slender tube open at only one end that is played by blowing across a hole near the closed end

flute

²flute *vb* **flut·ed; flut·ing** : to make a sound like that of a flute

¹flut·ter \ˈflət-ər\ *vb* **1** : to move the wings rapidly without flying or in making short flights ⟨butterflies *flutter*⟩ **2** : to move with a quick flapping motion ⟨flags *fluttered* in the wind⟩ **3** : to move about busily without getting much done

²flutter *n* : an act of fluttering

¹fly \ˈflī\ *vb* **flew** \ˈflü\; **flown** \ˈflōn\; **fly·ing** **1** : to move in or pass through the air with wings ⟨birds *fly*⟩ **2** : to move through the air or before the wind ⟨paper *flying* in all directions⟩ **3** : to float or cause to float, wave, or soar in the wind ⟨*fly* a kite⟩ ⟨*fly* a flag⟩ **4** : to run away : FLEE **5** : to move or pass swiftly ⟨how time does *fly*⟩ **6** : to operate or travel in an aircraft

²fly *n, pl* **flies** **1** : a flap of material to cover a fastening in a garment **2** : the outer canvas of a tent that has a double top **3** : a baseball hit high in the air

³fly *n, pl* **flies** **1** : a winged insect **2** : any of a large group of mostly stout-bodied two-winged insects (as the common housefly) **3** : a fishhook made to look like an insect

fly·catch·er \ˈflī-ˌkach-ər\ *n* : a small bird that eats flying insects

flyer *variant of* FLIER

fly·ing boat \ˈflī-ing-\ *n* : a seaplane with a hull designed to support it on the water

flying fish *n* : a fish with large fins that let it jump from the water and move for a distance through the air

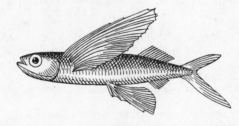

flying fish

fly·pa·per \ˈflī-ˌpā-pər\ *n* : sticky paper to catch and kill flies

fly·speck \ˈflī-ˌspek\ *n* : a spot of feces left by a fly on a surface

fly·way \ˈflī-ˌwā\ *n* : a route regularly followed by migratory birds

¹foal \ˈfōl\ *n* : a young animal of the horse family especially while less than one year old

²foal *vb* : to give birth to a foal

¹foam \ˈfōm\ *n* : a mass of tiny bubbles that forms in or on the surface of liquids or in the mouths or on the skins of animals

²foam *vb* : to produce or form foam

foamy \ˈfō-mē\ *adj* **foam·i·er; foam·i·est** : covered with or looking like foam ⟨the *foamy* tops of the waves⟩ — **foam·i·ness** *n*

fo·cal \ˈfō-kəl\ *adj* : of, relating to, or having a focus

¹fo·cus \ˈfō-kəs\ *n, pl* **fo·cus·es** *or* **fo·ci** \ˈfō-ˌsī\ **1** : a point at which rays (as of light, heat, or sound) meet after being reflected or bent : the point at which an image is formed **2** : the distance from a lens or

\ə\ abut	\au̇\ out	\i\ tip	\ȯ\ saw	\u̇\ foot
\ər\ further	\ch\ chin	\ī\ life	\ȯi\ coin	\y\ yet
\a\ mat	\e\ pet	\j\ job	\th\ thin	\yü\ few
\ā\ take	\ē\ easy	\ng\ sing	\t͟h\ this	\yu̇\ cure
\ä\ cot, cart	\g\ go	\ō\ bone	\ü\ food	\zh\ vision

mirror to a focus **3 :** an adjustment (as of a person's eyes or glasses) that gives clear vision ⟨bring into *focus*⟩ **4 :** a center of activity or interest

²focus *vb* **fo·cused** *or* **fo·cussed; fo·cus·ing** *or* **fo·cus·sing 1 :** to bring or come to a focus ⟨*focus* rays of light⟩ **2 :** to adjust the focus of ⟨*focus* the eyes⟩

fod·der \'fäd-ər\ *n* **:** coarse dry food (as stalks of corn) for livestock

foe \'fō\ *n* **:** an enemy especially in war

¹fog \'fȯg, 'fäg\ *n* **1 :** fine particles of water floating in the air at or near the ground **2 :** a confused state of mind ⟨this problem has me in a *fog*⟩

²fog *vb* **fogged; fog·ging :** to cover or become covered with fog

fog·gy \'fȯg-ē, 'fäg-\ *adj* **fog·gi·er; fog·gi·est 1 :** filled with fog **2 :** confused as if by fog — **fog·gi·ness** *n*

fog·horn \'fȯg-,hȯrn, 'fäg-\ *n* **:** a loud horn sounded in a fog to give warning

fo·gy \'fō-gē\ *n, pl* **fo·gies :** a person with old-fashioned ideas

foi·ble \'fȯi-bəl\ *n* **:** an unimportant weakness or failing

¹foil \'fȯil\ *vb* **:** to keep from succeeding or from reaching a goal

²foil *n* **:** a fencing weapon having a light flexible blade with a blunt point

³foil *n* **1 :** a very thin sheet of metal ⟨aluminum *foil*⟩ **2 :** something that makes another thing more noticeable by being very different from it

¹fold \'fōld\ *n* **:** an enclosure or shelter for sheep

²fold *vb* **:** to pen up (sheep) in a fold

³fold *vb* **1 :** to double something over itself ⟨*fold* a blanket⟩ **2 :** to clasp together ⟨*fold* your hands⟩ **3 :** ¹EMBRACE 1, 2, CLASP ⟨*folded* the child in my arms⟩

⁴fold *n* **1 :** a doubling of something over on itself **2 :** a part doubled or laid over another part : BEND ⟨a *fold* in a rock⟩

-fold \,fōld\ *suffix* **1 :** multiplied by a specified number : times — in adjectives ⟨a twelve*fold* increase⟩ and adverbs ⟨repay you ten*fold*⟩ **2 :** having so many parts ⟨a three*fold* problem⟩

fold·er \'fōl-dər\ *n* **1 :** one that folds **2 :** a folded printed sheet ⟨a travel *folder*⟩ **3 :** a folded cover or large envelope for loose papers

fo·li·age \'fō-lē-ij\ *n* **:** the leaves of a plant (as a tree) — **fo·li·aged** \-ijd\ *adj*

¹folk \'fōk\ *or* **folks** *n pl* **1 :** persons of a certain class, kind, or group ⟨the old *folk*⟩ ⟨rich *folks*⟩ **2 folks** *pl* **:** people in general ⟨most *folks* agree⟩ **3 folks** *pl* **:** the members of one's family : one's relatives

²folk *adj* **:** created by the common people ⟨a *folk* dance⟩ ⟨*folk* music⟩

folk·lore \'fō-,klōr\ *n* **:** customs, beliefs, stories, and sayings of a people handed down from generation to generation

folk·sing·er \'fōk-,sing-ər\ *n* **:** a person who sings songs (**folk songs**) created by and long sung among the common people

folk·tale \'fōk-,tāl\ *n* **:** a story made up and handed down by the common people

fol·low \'fäl-ō\ *vb* **1 :** to go or come after or behind ⟨the dog *followed* the children⟩ **2 :** to be led or guided by : OBEY ⟨*follow* instructions⟩ **3 :** to proceed along ⟨*follow* a path⟩ **4 :** to work in or at something as a way of life ⟨*follow* the sea⟩ **5 :** to come after in time or place ⟨spring *follows* winter⟩ **6 :** to result from ⟨panic *followed* the fire⟩ **7 :** to keep one's eyes or attention on ⟨*follow* the bouncing ball⟩ **synonyms** see CHASE — **fol·low·er** \'fäl-ə-wər\ *n* —

follow suit 1 : to play a card that belongs to the same group (as hearts or spades) as the one led **2 :** to do the same thing someone else has just done

¹fol·low·ing \'fäl-ə-wing\ *adj* **:** coming just after

²following *n* **:** a group of followers

follow through *vb* **:** to complete an action

follow up *vb* **:** to show continued interest in or take further action regarding

fol·ly \'fäl-ē\ *n, pl* **fol·lies 1 :** lack of good sense **2 :** a foolish act or idea

fond \'fänd\ *adj* **1 :** having a liking or love ⟨*fond* of candy⟩ **2 :** AFFECTIONATE, LOVING ⟨a *fond* farewell⟩ — **fond·ly** *adv* — **fond·ness** *n*

fon·dle \'fän-dl\ *vb* **fon·dled; fon·dling :** to touch or handle in a tender or loving manner

font \'fänt\ *n* **:** a basin to hold water for baptism

food \'füd\ *n* **1 :** material containing carbohydrates, fats, proteins, and supplements (as minerals and vitamins) that is taken in by and used in the living body for growth and repair and as a source of energy for activities **2 :** inorganic substances taken in by green plants and used to build organic nutrients **3 :** organic materials formed by

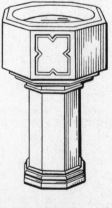

font

plants and used in their growth and activities **4** : solid food as distinguished from drink

food chain *n* : a sequence of organisms in which each depends on the next and usually lower member as a source of food

food·stuff \'füd-,stəf\ *n* : a substance with food value

¹fool \'fül\ *n* **1** : a person without good sense or judgment **2** : JESTER 1

Word History In Latin there was a word that meant "bellows" or "bag." This word came to be used to refer to fools, whose heads seem, like bellows or bags, to be empty of all but air. The English word *fool* came from this Latin word.

²fool *vb* **1** : to spend time idly ⟨just *fooling* around⟩ **2** : to meddle or tamper with something ⟨don't *fool* with that gun⟩ **3** : to speak or act in a playful way or in fun : JOKE ⟨we were only *fooling*⟩ **4** : ²TRICK

fool·har·dy \'fül-,härd-ē\ *adj* **fool·har·di·er; fool·har·di·est** : foolishly adventurous or bold

fool·ish \'fü-lish\ *adj* : showing or resulting from lack of good sense : SENSELESS **synonyms** see ABSURD — **fool·ish·ly** *adv* — **fool·ish·ness** *n*

fool·proof \'fül-'prüf\ *adj* : done, made, or planned so well that nothing can go wrong

¹foot \'füt\ *n, pl* **feet** \'fēt\ **1** : the end part of the leg of an animal or person : the part of an animal on which it stands or moves **2** : a unit of length equal to twelve inches (about .3 meter) **3** : something like a foot in position or use ⟨*foot* of a hill⟩ ⟨*foot* of the bed⟩ — **on foot** : by walking

²foot *vb* **1** : to go on foot **2** : ¹PAY 2 ⟨*foot* the bill⟩

foot·ball \'füt-,bȯl\ *n* **1** : a game played with a blown up oval ball on a large field by two teams of eleven players that move the ball by kicking, passing, or running with it **2** : the ball used in football

foot·ed \'füt-əd\ *adj* **1** : having a foot or feet ⟨a *footed* goblet⟩ **2** : having such or so many feet ⟨four-*footed* animals⟩

foot·fall \'füt-,fȯl\ *n* : the sound of a footstep

foot·hill \'füt-,hil\ *n* : a hill at the foot of higher hills

foot·hold \'füt-,hōld\ *n* : a place where the foot may be put (as for climbing)

foot·ing \'füt-ing\ *n* **1** : a firm position or placing of the feet ⟨lost my *footing*⟩ **2** : FOOTHOLD **3** : position in relation to others ⟨we all started on the same *footing*⟩ **4** : social relationship ⟨on good *footing* with the neighbors⟩

foot·lights \'füt-,līts\ *n pl* : a row of lights set across the front of a stage floor

foot·man \'füt-mən\ *n, pl* **foot·men** \-mən\ : a male servant who lets visitors in and waits on table

foot·note \'füt-,nōt\ *n* : a note at the bottom of a page

foot·path \'füt-,path, -,páth\ *n* : a path for walkers

foot·print \'füt-,print\ *n* : a track left by a foot

foot·sore \'füt-,sōr\ *adj* : having sore feet from walking a lot

foot·step \'füt-,step\ *n* **1** : a step of the foot **2** : the distance covered by a step **3** : FOOTPRINT

foot·stool \'füt-,stül\ *n* : a low stool to support the feet

foot·work \'füt-,wərk\ *n* : the skill with which the feet are moved (as in boxing)

¹for \fər, fȯr\ *prep* **1** : by way of getting ready ⟨wash up *for* supper⟩ **2** : toward the goal of ⟨saved *for* a new bike⟩ **3** : in order to reach ⟨left *for* home⟩ **4** : as being ⟨took me *for* a fool⟩ **5** : because of ⟨cried *for* joy⟩ **6** — used to show who or what is to receive something ⟨a letter *for* you⟩ **7** : in order to help or defend ⟨fought *for* their country⟩ **8** : directed at : AGAINST ⟨a cure *for* cancer⟩ **9** : in exchange as equal to ⟨pay ten dollars *for* a hat⟩ **10** : with regard to : CONCERNING ⟨a talent *for* music⟩ **11** : taking into account ⟨tall *for* your age⟩ **12** : through the period of ⟨slept *for* ten hours⟩

²for *conj* : BECAUSE ⟨I know we won, *for* I heard the cheers⟩

¹for·age \'fȯr-ij\ *n* : food (as pasture) for browsing or grazing animals

²forage *vb* **for·aged; for·ag·ing** : ¹SEARCH 1

for·ay \'fȯr-,ā\ *n* : ¹RAID

for·bear \fȯr-'baər, -'beər\ *vb* **for·bore** \-'bōr\; **for·borne** \-'bōrn\; **for·bear·ing** **1** : to hold back ⟨*forbore* from striking the bully⟩ **2** : to control oneself when provoked

for·bid \fər-'bid\ *vb* **for·bade** \-'bad\ *or* **for·bad; for·bid·den** \-'bid-n\; **for·bid·ding** : to order not to do something

for·bid·ding \fər-'bid-ing\ *adj* : tending to frighten or discourage

¹force \'fōrs\ *n* **1** : POWER 4 ⟨the *force* of the wind⟩ **2** : the state of existing and being enforced : EFFECT ⟨that law is still in *force*⟩ **3** : a group of persons gathered

\ə\ abut	\aú\ out	\i\ tip	\ȯ\ saw	\ú\ foot
\ər\ further	\ch\ chin	\ī\ life	\ȯi\ coin	\y\ yet
\a\ mat	\e\ pet	\j\ job	\th\ thin	\yü\ few
\ā\ take	\ē\ easy	\ng\ sing	\th\ this	\yú\ cure
\ä\ cot, cart	\g\ go	\ō\ bone	\ü\ food	\zh\ vision

together and trained for action ⟨a police *force*⟩ **4** : power or violence used on a person or thing ⟨opened the door by *force*⟩ **5** : an influence (as a push or pull) that tends to produce a change in the speed or direction of motion of something ⟨the *force* of gravity⟩

²force *vb* **forced; forc·ing 1** : to make (as a person) do something ⟨*forced* them to work⟩ **2** : to get or make by using force ⟨*forced* their way into the room⟩ **3** : to break open by force ⟨*forced* the door⟩ **4** : to speed up the development of

force·ful \'fōrs-fəl\ *adj* : having much force : VIGOROUS ⟨*forceful* action⟩ ⟨a *forceful* speech⟩ — **force·ful·ly** \-fə-lē\ *adv* — **force·ful·ness** *n*

for·ceps \'fōr-səps\ *n, pl* **forceps** : an instrument for grasping, holding, or pulling on things especially in delicate operations (as by a jeweler or surgeon)

forceps

forc·ible \'fōr-sə-bəl\ *adj* **1** : got, made, or done by force or violence ⟨a *forcible* entrance⟩ **2** : showing a lot of force or energy — **forc·ibly** \-blē\ *adv*

¹ford \'fōrd\ *n* : a shallow place in a body of water where one can wade across

²ford *vb* : to cross by wading

¹fore \'fōr\ *adv* : in or toward the front

²fore *adj* : being or coming before in time, place, or order

³fore *n* : ¹FRONT 2 ⟨came to the *fore*⟩

⁴fore *interj* — used by a golfer to warn someone within range of a hit ball

fore- *prefix* **1** : earlier : beforehand ⟨*fore*see⟩ **2** : at the front : in front ⟨*fore*leg⟩ **3** : front part of something specified ⟨*fore*arm⟩

fore–and–aft \,fōr-ə-'naft\ *adj* : being in line with the length of a ship ⟨*fore-and-aft* sails⟩

fore·arm \'fōr-,ärm\ *n* : the part of the arm between the elbow and the wrist

fore·bear \'fōr-,baər, -,beər\ *n* : ANCESTOR

fore·bod·ing \fōr-'bōd-ing\ *n* : a feeling that something bad is going to happen

¹fore·cast \'fōr-,kast\ *vb* **forecast** *or* **fore·cast·ed; fore·cast·ing** : to predict often after thought and study of available evidence **synonyms** see FORETELL — **fore·cast·er** *n*

²forecast *n* : a prediction of something in the future ⟨a weather *forecast*⟩

fore·cas·tle \'fōk-səl\ *n* **1** : the forward

part of the upper deck of a ship **2** : quarters for the crew in the forward part of a ship

fore·fa·ther \'fōr-,fäth-ər, -,fath-\ *n* : ANCESTOR

fore·fin·ger \'fōr-,fing-gər\ *n* : INDEX FINGER

fore·foot \'fōr-,fút\ *n, pl* **fore·feet** \-,fēt\ : one of the front feet of an animal with four feet

fore·front \'fōr-,frənt\ *n* : the very front : VANGUARD

forego *variant of* FORGO

fore·go·ing \fōr-'gō-ing\ *adj* : being before in time or place

fore·gone conclusion \,fōr-,gȯn-\ *n* : something felt to be sure to happen

fore·ground \'fōr-,graùnd\ *n* : the part of a picture or scene that seems to be nearest to and in front of the person looking at it

fore·hand \'fōr-,hand\ *n* : a stroke (as in tennis) made with the palm of the hand turned in the direction in which the hand is moving

forehand

fore·head \'fōr-əd, 'fōr-,hed\ *n* : the part of the face above the eyes

for·eign \'fȯr-ən\ *adj* **1** : located outside of a place or country and especially outside of one's country ⟨a *foreign* nation⟩ **2** : belonging to a place or country other than the one under consideration ⟨many Danes speak *foreign* languages⟩ **3** : relating to or having to do with other nations ⟨*foreign* trade⟩ ⟨*foreign* affairs⟩ **4** : not normal or wanted ⟨*foreign* material in food⟩

for·eign·er \'fȯr-ə-nər\ *n* : a person who is from a foreign country

fore·leg \'fōr-,leg\ *n* : a front leg

fore·limb \'fōr-,lim\ *n* : an arm, fin, wing, or leg that is or occupies the position of a foreleg

fore·man \'fōr-mən\ *n, pl* **fore·men** \-mən\ : the leader of a group of workers

fore·mast \'fōr-ˌmast, -məst\ *n* : the mast nearest the bow of the ship

¹fore·most \'fōr-ˌmōst\ *adj* : first in time, place, or order : most important

²foremost *adv* : in the first place

fore·noon \'fōr-ˌnün\ *n* : MORNING

fore·quar·ter \'fōr-ˌkwòrt-ər\ *n* : the front half of a side of the body or carcass of an animal with four feet ⟨a *forequarter* of beef⟩

fore·run·ner \'fōr-ˌrən-ər\ *n* : one that comes before especially as a sign of the coming of another

fore·see \fōr-'sē\ *vb* **fore·saw** \-'sò\; **fore·seen** \-'sēn\; **fore·see·ing** : to see or know about beforehand

fore·sight \'fōr-ˌsīt\ *n* **1** : the act or power of foreseeing **2** : care for the future : PRU-DENCE

for·est \'fòr-əst\ *n* : a growth of trees and underbrush covering a large area — **for·est·ed** \-əs-təd\ *adj*

fore·stall \fōr-'stòl\ *vb* : to keep out, interfere with, or prevent by steps taken in advance

for·est·ry \'fòr-ə-strē\ *n* : the science and practice of caring for forests — **for·est·er** \-stər\ *n*

fore·tell \fōr-'tel\ *vb* **fore·told** \-'tōld\; **fore·tell·ing** : to tell of a thing before it happens

synonyms FORETELL, PREDICT, and FORE-CAST mean to tell about or announce something before it happens. FORETELL may suggest the use of extraordinary powers to reveal the future ⟨the wizards *foretold* a great war⟩ PREDICT may suggest a fairly exact statement that is the result of the gathering of information and the use of scientific methods ⟨scientists can sometimes *predict* earthquakes⟩ FORECAST often suggests that one has weighed evidence and is telling what is most likely to happen ⟨*forecasted* that it would snow⟩

fore·thought \'fōr-ˌthòt\ *n* : a thinking or planning for the future

for·ev·er \fə-'rev-ər\ *adv* **1** : for a limitless time ⟨will last *forever*⟩ **2** : at all times ⟨is *forever* bothering the teacher⟩

for·ev·er·more \fə-ˌrev-ər-'mōr\ *adv* : FOR-EVER 1

fore·word \'fōr-ˌwərd\ *n* : PREFACE

¹for·feit \'fòr-fət\ *n* : something forfeited

²forfeit *vb* : to lose or lose the right to something through a fault, error, or crime

¹forge \'fōrj\ *n* : a furnace or a place with a furnace where metal is shaped and worked by heating and hammering

²forge *vb* **forged; forg·ing** **1** : to shape and work metal by heating and hammering **2** : to produce something that is not genuine : COUNTERFEIT ⟨*forge* a check⟩ — **forg·er** *n*

³forge *vb* **forged; forg·ing** : to move forward slowly but steadily ⟨*forged* ahead through the blizzard⟩

forg·ery \'fōr-jə-rē\ *n, pl* **forg·er·ies** **1** : the crime of falsely making or changing a written paper or signing someone else's name **2** : something that has been forged

for·get \fər-'get\ *vb* **for·got** \-'gät\; **for·got·ten** \-'gät-n\ *or* **for·got; for·get·ting** **1** : to be unable to think of or recall ⟨*forget* a name⟩ **2** : to fail by accident to do (something) : OVERLOOK ⟨*forgot* to pay the bill⟩

for·get·ful \fər-'get-fəl\ *adj* : forgetting easily — **for·get·ful·ly** \-fə-lē\ *adv* — **for·get·ful·ness** *n*

for·get—me—not \fər-'get-mē-ˌnät\ *n* : a small low plant with bright blue flowers

for·give \fər-'giv\ *vb* **for·gave** \-'gāv\; **for·giv·en** \-'giv-ən\; **for·giv·ing** : to stop feeling angry at or hurt by

for·give·ness \fər-'giv-nəs\ *n* : the act of forgiving or the state of being forgiven

for·go *or* **fore·go** \fòr-'gō, fōr-\ *vb* **for·went** *or* **fore·went** \-'went\; **for·gone** *or* **fore·gone** \-'gòn\; **for·go·ing** *or* **fore·go·ing** : to hold oneself back from : GIVE UP ⟨*forgo* an opportunity⟩

¹fork \'fòrk\ *n* **1** : an implement having a handle and two or more prongs for taking up (as in eating), pitching, or digging **2** : something like a fork in shape **3** : the place where something divides or branches ⟨a *fork* in the road⟩ **4** : one of the parts into which something divides or branches ⟨the left *fork*⟩ — **forked** \'fòrkt, 'fòr-kəd\ *adj*

²fork *vb* **1** : to divide into branches **2** : to pitch or lift with a fork

for·lorn \fər-'lòrn\ *adj* : sad from being left alone — **for·lorn·ly** *adv*

¹form \'fòrm\ *n* **1** : the shape and structure of something **2** : an established way of doing something ⟨different *forms* of worship⟩ **3** : a printed sheet with blank spaces for information ⟨fill out a *form*⟩ **4** : a mold in which concrete is placed to set **5** : ¹SORT 1, KIND ⟨early *forms* of plant life⟩ ⟨coal is one *form* of carbon⟩ **6** : a plan of

\ə\ abut	\aú\ out	\i\ tip	\ò\ saw	\ú\ foot
\ər\ further	\ch\ chin	\ī\ life	\òi\ coin	\y\ yet
\a\ mat	\e\ pet	\j\ job	\th\ thin	\yü\ few
\ā\ take	\ē\ easy	\ng\ sing	\th\ this	\yú\ cure
\ä\ cot, cart	\g\ go	\ō\ bone	\ü\ food	\zh\ vision

arrangement or design (as for a work of art) **7** : one of the different pronunciations, spellings, or inflections a word may have

²**form** *vb* **1** : to give form or shape to **2** : DEVELOP 5 **3** : to come or bring together in making **4** : to take form : come into being ⟨clouds will *form*⟩ **synonyms** see MAKE

¹**for·mal** \'fȯr-məl\ *adj* : following established form, custom, or rule — **for·mal·ly** *adv*

²**formal** *n* : something (as a dress) formal in character

for·mal·i·ty \fȯr-'mal-ət-ē\ *n, pl* **for·mal·i·ties 1** : the quality or state of being formal **2** : an established way of doing something

for·ma·tion \fȯr-'mā-shən\ *n* **1** : a forming of something ⟨the *formation* of good habits⟩ **2** : something that is formed ⟨a cloud *formation*⟩ **3** : an arrangement of something (as persons or ships) ⟨battle *formation*⟩ ⟨punt *formation*⟩

for·mer \'fȯr-mər\ *adj* : coming before in time ⟨a *former* president⟩

for·mer·ly \'fȯr-mər-lē\ *adv* : at an earlier time

for·mi·da·ble \'fȯr-mə-də-bəl\ *adj* **1** : exciting fear or awe ⟨a *formidable* problem⟩ **2** : offering serious difficulties

form·less \'fȯrm-ləs\ *adj* : having no regular form or shape — **form·less·ly** *adv* — **form·less·ness** *n*

for·mu·la \'fȯr-myə-lə\ *n* **1** : a direction giving amounts of the substances for the preparation of something (as a medicine) **2** : a milk mixture or substitute for feeding a baby **3** : a general fact or rule expressed in symbols ⟨a *formula* for finding the size of an angle⟩ **4** : an expression in symbols giving the makeup of a substance ⟨the *formula* for water is H_2O⟩ **5** : an established form or method

for·mu·late \'fȯr-myə-ˌlāt\ *vb* **for·mu·lat·ed; for·mu·lat·ing** : to state definitely and clearly

for·sake \fər-'sāk\ *vb* **for·sook** \-'su̇k\; **for·sak·en** \-'sā-kən\; **for·sak·ing** : to give up or leave entirely **synonyms** see ABANDON

for·syth·ia \fər-'sith-ē-ə\ *n* : a bush often grown for its bright yellow flowers that appear in early spring

fort \'fȯrt\ *n* : a strong

forsythia

or fortified place especially when held by soldiers

forth \'fōrth\ *adv* **1** : onward in time, place, or order ⟨from that time *forth*⟩ **2** : out into view

forth·com·ing \fōrth-'kəm-ing\ *adj* **1** : being about to appear **2** : ready or available when needed

forth·right \'fōr-ˌthrīt\ *adj* : going straight to the point clearly and firmly ⟨a *forthright* answer⟩ — **forth·right·ly** *adv*

forth·with \fōrth-'with, -'with\ *adv* : without delay : IMMEDIATELY

¹**for·ti·eth** \'fȯrt-ē-əth\ *adj* : coming right after thirty-ninth

²**fortieth** *n* : number forty in a series

for·ti·fi·ca·tion \ˌfȯrt-ə-fə-'kā-shən\ *n* **1** : the act of fortifying **2** : something that strengthens or protects

for·ti·fy \'fȯrt-ə-ˌfī\ *vb* **for·ti·fied; for·ti·fy·ing 1** : to make strong (as by building defenses) **2** : ENRICH 2, 3 ⟨*fortify* food with vitamins⟩

for·ti·tude \'fȯrt-ə-ˌtüd, -ˌtyüd\ *n* : strength of mind that lets a person meet and put up with trouble

fort·night \'fȯrt-ˌnīt\ *n* : two weeks

for·tress \'fȯr-trəs\ *n* : a fortified place

for·tu·nate \'fȯr-chə-nət\ *adj* **1** : bringing some unexpected good **2** : receiving some unexpected good : LUCKY — **for·tu·nate·ly** *adv*

for·tune \'fȯr-chən\ *n* **1** : favorable results that come partly by chance **2** : what happens to a person : good or bad luck **3** : what is to happen to one in the future ⟨had my *fortune* told⟩ **4** : WEALTH

for·tune—tell·er \'fȯr-chən-ˌtel-ər\ *n* : a person who claims to foretell future events

¹**for·ty** \'fȯrt-ē\ *adj* : being four times ten

²**forty** *n* : four times ten : 40

for·ty—nin·er \ˌfȯrt-ē-'nī-nər\ *n* : a person in the California gold rush of 1849

fo·rum \'fōr-əm\ *n* **1** : the marketplace or public place of an ancient Roman city serving as the center for public business **2** : a program of open discussion

¹**for·ward** \'fȯr-wərd\ *adj* **1** : near, at, or belonging to the front part ⟨a ship's *forward* gun⟩ **2** : lacking proper modesty or reserve **3** : moving, tending, or leading to a position in front

²**forward** *adv* : to or toward what is in front

³**forward** *n* : a player at or near the front of his or her team or near the opponent's goal

⁴**forward** *vb* **1** : to help onward : ADVANCE **2** : to send on or ahead ⟨*forward* a letter⟩

for·wards \'fȯr-wərdz\ *adv* : ²FORWARD

fos·sil \'fäs-əl\ *n* : a trace or print or the

remains of a plant or animal of a past age preserved in earth or rock

¹fos·ter \'fòs-tər\ *adj* : giving, receiving, or sharing parental care even though not related by blood or legal ties ⟨a *foster* parent⟩

²foster *vb* **1** : to give parental care to **2** : to help the growth and development of

fought *past of* FIGHT

¹foul \'faůl\ *adj* **1** : disgusting in looks, taste, or smell ⟨a *foul* sewer⟩ **2** : full of or covered with dirt **3** : being vulgar or insulting ⟨*foul* language⟩ **4** : being wet and stormy ⟨*foul* weather⟩ **5** : very unfair ⟨would use fair means or *foul*⟩ **6** : breaking a rule in a game or sport ⟨a *foul* blow in boxing⟩ **7** : being outside the foul lines ⟨hit a *foul* ball⟩ — **foul·ly** \'faůl-lē\ *adv* — **foul·ness** *n*

²foul *n* **1** : a breaking of the rules in a game or sport **2** : a foul ball in baseball

³foul *vb* **1** : to make or become foul or filthy ⟨*foul* the air⟩ ⟨*foul* a stream⟩ **2** : to make a foul **3** : to become or cause to become entangled

foul line *n* : either of two straight lines running from the rear corner of home plate through first and third base to the boundary of a baseball field

foul play *n* : VIOLENCE 1

¹found \'faůnd\ *past of* FIND

²found *vb* : ESTABLISH 1 ⟨*found* a college⟩

foun·da·tion \faůn-'dā-shən\ *n* **1** : the act of founding **2** : the support upon which something rests ⟨the *foundation* of a building⟩

¹found·er \'faůn-dər\ *n* : a person who founds something

²foun·der \'faůn-dər\ *vb* : ¹SINK 1

found·ling \'faůnd-ling\ *n* : an infant found after being abandoned by unknown parents

found·ry \'faůn-drē\ *n, pl* **found·ries** : a building or factory where metals are cast

foun·tain \'faůnt-n\ *n* **1** : a spring of water **2** : SOURCE 2 **3** : an artificial stream or spray of water (as for drinking or ornament) or the device from which it comes

fountain pen *n* : a pen with ink inside that is fed as needed to the writing point

¹four \'fōr\ *adj* : being one more than three

²four *n* **1** : one more than three : two times two : 4 **2** : the fourth in a set or series

four·fold \'fōr-ˌfōld\ *adj* : being four times as great or as many

four·score \'fōr-ˌskōr\ *adj* : ¹EIGHTY

four·some \'fōr-səm\ *adj* : a group of four persons or things

¹four·teen \fōr-'tēn, fōrt-\ *adj* : being one more than thirteen

²fourteen *n* : one more than thirteen : two times seven : 14

¹four·teenth \fōr-'tēnth, fōrt-\ *adj* : coming right after thirteen

²fourteenth *n* : number fourteen in a series

¹fourth \'fōrth\ *adj* : coming right after third

²fourth *n* **1** : number four in a series **2** : one of four equal parts

fowl \'faůl\ *n, pl* **fowl** *or* **fowls** **1** : BIRD ⟨wild *fowls*⟩ **2** : a common domestic rooster or hen **3** : the flesh of a mature domestic fowl for use as food

fox \'fäks\ *n* : a wild animal closely related to the dog that has a sharp snout, pointed ears, and a long bushy tail

fox

foxy \'fäk-sē\ *adj* **fox·i·er; fox·i·est** : cunning and careful in planning and action — **fox·i·ly** \-sə-lē\ *adv* — **fox·i·ness** \-sē-nəs\ *n*

foy·er \'fòi-ər, 'fòi-ˌā\ *n* **1** : a lobby especially in a theater **2** : an entrance hall

fra·cas \'frāk-əs, 'frak-\ *n* : a noisy quarrel : BRAWL

frac·tion \'frak-shən\ *n* **1** : a part of a whole : FRAGMENT **2** : a number (as ½, ⅔, 17/100) that indicates one or more equal parts of a whole or group and that may be considered as indicating also division of the number above the line by the number below the line

frac·tion·al \'frak-shən-l\ *adj* **1** : of, relating to, or being a fraction **2** : fairly small

¹frac·ture \'frak-chər\ *n* **1** : a breaking or being broken (as of a bone) **2** : damage or an injury caused by breaking

²fracture *vb* **frac·tured; frac·tur·ing** : to cause a fracture in : BREAK

frag·ile \'fraj-əl\ *adj* : easily broken : DELICATE **synonyms** *see* BRITTLE

frag·ment \'frag-mənt\ *n* : a part broken off or incomplete

frag·men·tary \\'frag-mən-,ter-ē\\ *adj*
: made up of fragments : INCOMPLETE

fra·grance \\'frā-grəns\\ *n* : a sweet or
pleasant smell

fra·grant \\'frā-grənt\\ *adj* : sweet or pleasant in smell — **fra·grant·ly** *adv*

frail \\'frāl\\ *adj* : very delicate or weak in
structure or being **synonyms** see WEAK

frail·ty \\'frāl-tē\\ *n, pl* **frail·ties 1** : the quality or state of being weak **2** : a weakness
of character

¹frame \\'frām\\ *vb* **framed; fram·ing 1**
: ²FORM 1, CONSTRUCT **2** : to enclose in a
frame

²frame *n* **1** : the structure of an animal and
especially a human body : PHYSIQUE **2**
: an arrangement of parts that give form or
support to something ⟨the *frame* of a
house⟩ **3** : an open case or structure for
holding or enclosing something ⟨window
frame⟩ ⟨picture *frame*⟩ **4** : a particular
state or mood ⟨in a pleasant *frame* of
mind⟩

³frame *adj* : having a wooden frame ⟨a
two-story *frame* house⟩

frame·work \\'frām-,wərk\\ *n* : a basic supporting part or structure ⟨the *framework*
of an argument⟩

franc \\'frangk\\ *n* **1** : a French coin or bill **2**
: any of various coins or bills used in countries where French is widely spoken

Fran·co- \\'frang-kō\\ *prefix* **1** : French
and **2** : French

frank \\'frangk\\ *adj* : free in speaking one's
feelings and opinions — **frank·ly** *adv* —
frank·ness *n*

Word History The word *frank* came from
the name of a group of people, the Franks,
who controlled France a long time ago.
When the Franks were in power, they
were the only people in the country who
had complete freedom. A Latin word that
meant "free" was formed from the Latin
word that meant "a Frank." The English
word *frank* came from the Latin word that
meant "free." At first English *frank* meant
"free," but now it has a more specific
meaning.

frank·furt·er \\'frangk-fərt-ər\\ *n* : a cooked
sausage (as of beef or beef and pork)

frank·in·cense \\'frang-kən-,sens\\ *n* : a
fragrant gum that is burned for its sweet
smell

fran·tic \\'frant-ik\\ *adj* : wildly excited

fran·ti·cal·ly \\'frant-i-kə-lē\\ *adv* : in a frantic way

fra·ter·nal \\frə-'tərn-l\\ *adj* **1** : having to do
with brothers **2** : made up of members
banded together like brothers

fra·ter·ni·ty \\frə-'tər-nət-ē\\ *n, pl* **fra·ter·ni·-
ties** : a society of boys or men (as in a
college)

fraud \\'frȯd\\ *n* **1** : TRICKERY, DECEIT **2** : an
act of deceiving : TRICK **3** : a person who
pretends to be what he or she is not

fraud·u·lent \\'frȯ-jə-lənt\\ *adj* : based on or
done by fraud — **fraud·u·lent·ly** *adv*

fraught \\'frȯt\\ *adj* : full of some quality ⟨a
situation *fraught* with danger⟩

¹fray \\'frā\\ *n* : ²FIGHT 1, BRAWL

²fray *vb* : to wear into shreds

fraz·zle \\'fraz-əl\\ *n* : a tired or nervous
condition ⟨worn to a *frazzle*⟩

¹freak \\'frēk\\ *n* : a strange, abnormal, or
unusual person, thing, or event ⟨circus
freaks⟩

²freak *adj* : being or suggesting a freak
: IMPROBABLE ⟨a *freak* accident⟩

¹freck·le \\'frek-əl\\ *n* : a small brownish
spot on the skin

²freckle *vb* **freck·led; freck·ling** : to mark
or become marked with freckles ⟨a *freck-
led* face⟩

¹free \\'frē\\ *adj* **fre·er** \\'frē-ər\\; **fre·est**
\\'frē-əst\\ **1** : having liberty : not being a
slave ⟨*free* citizens⟩ **2** : not controlled by
others ⟨a *free* country⟩ **3** : released or not
suffering from something unpleasant or
painful ⟨*free* from worry⟩ **4** : given without
charge ⟨a *free* ticket⟩ **5** : not held back by
fear or distrust : OPEN ⟨a *free* expression
of opinion⟩ **6** : not blocked : CLEAR **7** : not
combined ⟨*free* oxygen⟩ — **free·ly** *adv*

²free *adv* **1** : FREELY **2** : without charge

³free *vb* **freed; free·ing** : to make or set
free

freed·man \\'frēd-mən\\ *n, pl* **freed·men**
\\-mən\\ : a person freed from slavery

free·dom \\'frēd-əm\\ *n* **1** : the condition of
being free : LIBERTY, INDEPENDENCE **2**
: ability to move or act freely **3** : the quality
of being very frank : CANDOR **4** : free and
unlimited use

free·hand \\'frē-,hand\\ *adj or adv* : done
without mechanical aids ⟨a *freehand*
drawing⟩

free·man \\'frē-mən\\ *n, pl* **free·men** \\-mən\\
: a free person : one who is not a slave

free·stand·ing \\'frē-'stan-ding\\ *adj*
: standing alone or on its own foundation
free of attachment or support

free·way \\'frē-,wā\\ *n* : an expressway that
can be used without paying tolls

¹freeze \\'frēz\\ *vb* **froze** \\'frōz\\; **fro·zen**
\\'frōz-n\\; **freez·ing 1** : to harden into or be
hardened into a solid (as ice) by loss of
heat ⟨the river *froze* over⟩ ⟨*freeze* cream⟩
2 : to be or become uncomfortably cold **3**
: to damage by cold ⟨plants *frozen* by

heavy frost〉 **4** : to clog or become clogged by ice 〈water pipes *frozen* overnight〉 **5** : to become fixed or motionless 〈*freeze* in your tracks〉

²**freeze** *n* **1** : a period of freezing weather : cold weather **2** : an act or instance of freezing **3** : the state of being frozen

freez·er \'frē-zər\ *n* : a compartment or room used to freeze food or keep it frozen

freezing point *n* : the temperature at which a liquid becomes solid

¹**freight** \'frāt\ *n* **1** : the amount paid (as to a shipping company) for carrying goods **2** : goods or cargo carried by a ship, train, truck, or airplane **3** : the carrying (as by truck) of goods from one place to another **4** : a train that carries freight

²**freight** *vb* : to send by freight

freight·er \'frāt-ər\ *n* : a ship or airplane used to carry freight

¹**French** \'french\ *adj* : of or relating to France, its people, or the French language

²**French** *n* **1 French** *pl* : the people of France **2** : the language of the French

french fry *n, often cap 1st F* : a strip of potato fried in deep fat 〈steak and *french fries*〉

French horn *n* : a circular brass musical instrument with a large opening at one end and a mouthpiece shaped like a small funnel

French horn

fren·zied \'fren-zēd\ *adj* : very excited and upset

fren·zy \'fren-zē\ *n, pl* **fren·zies** : great and often wild or disorderly activity

fre·quen·cy \'frē-kwən-sē\ *n, pl* **fre·quen·cies** **1** : frequent repetition **2** : rate of repetition

¹**fre·quent** \'frē-kwənt\ *adj* : happening often 〈*frequent* trips to town〉 — **fre·quent·ly** *adv*

²**fre·quent** \frē-'kwent\ *vb* : to visit often 〈we *frequented* the beach during the summer〉

fresh \'fresh\ *adj* **1** : not salt 〈*fresh* water〉 **2** : PURE 1, BRISK 〈*fresh* air〉 〈a *fresh* breeze〉 **3** : not frozen, canned, or pickled 〈*fresh* vegetables〉 **4** : not stale, sour, or spoiled 〈*fresh* bread〉 〈meat kept *fresh* in the refrigerator〉 **5** : not dirty or rumpled 〈a *fresh* shirt〉 **6** : NEW 6 〈make a *fresh* start〉 **7** : newly made or received 〈a *fresh* wound〉 〈*fresh* news〉 **8** : IMPUDENT 〈*fresh* talk〉 — **fresh·ly** *adv* — **fresh·ness** *n*

fresh·en \'fresh-ən\ *vb* : to make or become fresh 〈took a shower to *freshen* up〉 〈the wind *freshened*〉

fresh·et \'fresh-ət\ *n* : a sudden overflowing of a stream

fresh·man \'fresh-mən\ *n, pl* **fresh·men** \-mən\ : a first year student (as in college)

fresh·wa·ter \,fresh-'wȯt-ər, -'wät-\ *adj* : of, relating to, or living in fresh water

¹**fret** \'fret\ *vb* **fret·ted; fret·ting** : to make or become worried 〈*fret* over a problem〉

²**fret** *n* : an irritated or worried state

³**fret** *n* : a design of short lines or bars

⁴**fret** *n* : one of a series of ridges fixed across the fingerboard of a stringed musical instrument — **fret·ted** *adj*

fret

fret·ful \'fret-fəl\ *adj* : likely to fret : IRRITABLE 〈a *fretful* baby〉 — **fret·ful·ly** \-fə-lē\ *adv* — **fret·ful·ness** *n*

fri·ar \'frī-ər\ *n* : a member of a Roman Catholic religious order for men

fric·tion \'frik-shən\ *n* **1** : the rubbing of one thing against another **2** : resistance to motion between bodies in contact 〈the *friction* of a box sliding along the floor〉 **3** : disagreement among persons or groups

Fri·day \'frīd-ē\ *n* : the sixth day of the week

friend \'frend\ *n* **1** : a person who has a strong liking for and trust in another person **2** : a person who is not an enemy 〈*friend* or foe〉 **3** : a person who aids or favors something 〈was a *friend* to good causes〉 — **friend·less** \-ləs\ *adj*

friend·ly \'frend-lē\ *adj* **friend·li·er; friend·li·est** **1** : showing friendship **2** : being other than an enemy — **friend·li·ness** *n*

friend·ship \'frend-,ship\ *n* : the state of being friends

frieze \'frēz\ *n* : a band or stripe (as around a building) used as a decoration

frig·ate \'frig-ət\ *n* : a square-rigged warship

fright \'frīt\ *n* **1** : sudden terror : great fear **2** : something that frightens or is ugly or shocking

fright·en \'frīt-n\ *vb* : to make afraid : TERRIFY — **fright·en·ing·ly** *adv*

fright·ful \'frīt-fəl\ *adj* **1** : causing fear or alarm 〈a *frightful* scream〉 **2** : SHOCKING, OUTRAGEOUS 〈the *frightful* cost of war〉

\ə\ **abut**	\aů\ **out**	\i\ **tip**	\ȯ\ **saw**	\ů\ **foot**
\ər\ **further**	\ch\ **chin**	\ī\ **life**	\ȯi\ **coin**	\y\ **yet**
\a\ **mat**	\e\ **pet**	\j\ **job**	\th\ **thin**	\yü\ **few**
\ā\ **take**	\ē\ **easy**	\ng\ **sing**	\<u>th</u>\ **this**	\yů\ **cure**
\ä\ **cot, cart**	\g\ **go**	\ō\ **bone**	\ü\ **food**	\zh\ **vision**

— **fright·ful·ly** \-fə-lē\ *adv* — **fright·ful-ness** *n*

frig·id \'frij-əd\ *adj* **1** : freezing cold **2** : not friendly — **frig·id·ly** *adv* — **frig·id·ness** *n*

frill \'fril\ *n* **1** : ²RUFFLE **2** : something added mostly for show

frilly \'fril-ē\ *adj* **frill·i·er; frill·i·est** : having frills ⟨*frilly* clothes⟩

¹**fringe** \'frinj\ *n* **1** : a border or trimming made by or made to look like the loose ends of the cloth **2** : something suggesting a fringe

²**fringe** *vb* **fringed; fring·ing 1** : to decorate with a fringe **2** : to serve as a fringe for

frisk \'frisk\ *vb* : to move around in a lively or playful way ⟨dogs *frisking* about⟩

frisky \'fris-kē\ *adj* **frisk·i·er; frisk·i·est** : tending to frisk : PLAYFUL, LIVELY

¹**frit·ter** \'frit-ər\ *n* : a small amount of fried batter often containing fruit or meat

²**fritter** *vb* : to waste on unimportant things

friv·o·lous \'friv-ə-ləs\ *adj* **1** : of little importance : TRIVIAL ⟨a *frivolous* matter⟩ **2** : lacking in seriousness : PLAYFUL

frizzy \'friz-ē\ *adj* **frizz·i·er; frizz·i·est** : very curly ⟨*frizzy* hair⟩

fro \'frō\ *adv* : in a direction away ⟨nervously walking to and *fro*⟩

frock \'fräk\ *n* : a woman's or girl's dress

frog \'frȯg, 'fräg\ *n* **1** : a tailless animal with smooth skin and webbed feet that spends more of its time in water than the related toad **2** : an ornamental fastening for a garment — **frog in one's throat** : HOARSENESS

frog 2

frog·man \'frȯg-,man, 'fräg-\ *n, pl* **frog·men** \-,men\ : a swimmer equipped to work underwater for long periods of time

¹**frol·ic** \'fräl-ik\ *vb* **frol·icked; frol·ick·ing** : to play about happily : ROMP ⟨the dog *frolicked* in the snow⟩

²**frolic** *n* : FUN 1, GAIETY

frol·ic·some \'fräl-ik-səm\ *adj* : given to frolic : PLAYFUL

from \frəm, 'frəm, 'främ\ *prep* **1** — used to show a starting point ⟨a letter *from* home⟩ **2** — used to show a point of separation ⟨the boat tore loose *from* its moorings⟩ **3** — used to show a material, source, or cause ⟨a doll made *from* rags⟩ ⟨read *from* a book⟩ ⟨suffering *from* the cold⟩

frond \'fränd\ *n* : a large leaf (as of a palm or fern) with many divisions or something like such a leaf

¹**front** \'frənt\ *n* **1** : a region in which active warfare is taking place **2** : the forward part or surface **3** : the boundary between bodies of air at different temperatures ⟨a cold *front*⟩

²**front** *vb* : ²FACE 2 ⟨the cottage *fronts* on the lake⟩

³**front** *adj* : of, relating to, or situated at the front

front·al \'frənt-l\ *adj* : of, relating to, or directed at the front ⟨a *frontal* attack⟩

fron·tier \,frən-'tiər\ *n* **1** : a border between two countries **2** : the edge of the settled part of a country

fron·tiers·man \,frən-'tiərz-mən\ *n, pl* **fron·tiers·men** \-mən\ : a person living on the frontier

¹**frost** \'frȯst\ *n* **1** : temperature cold enough to cause freezing **2** : a covering of tiny ice crystals on a cold surface formed from the water vapor in the air

²**frost** *vb* : to cover with frost or with something suggesting frost ⟨*frost* a cake⟩

frost·bite \'frȯst-,bīt\ *n* : slight freezing of a part of the body or the effect of this

frost·ing \'frȯs-ting\ *n* **1** : ICING **2** : a dull finish on glass

frosty \'frȯ-stē\ *adj* **frost·i·er; frost·i·est 1** : cold enough to produce frost ⟨a *frosty* evening⟩ **2** : covered with or appearing to be covered with frost ⟨a *frosty* glass⟩ — **frost·i·ly** \-stə-lē\ *adv* — **frost·i·ness** \-stē-nəs\ *n*

¹**froth** \'frȯth\ *n* : bubbles formed in or on liquids

²**froth** *vb* : to produce or form froth

frothy \'frȯ-thē, -thē\ *adj* **froth·i·er; froth·i·est** : full of or made up of froth — **froth·i·ness** *n*

¹**frown** \'fraún\ *vb* **1** : to wrinkle the forehead (as in anger or thought) **2** : to look with disapproval

²**frown** *n* : a wrinkling of the brow

froze *past of* FREEZE

frozen *past participle of* FREEZE

fru·gal \'frü-gəl\ *adj* : careful in spending or using resources — **fru·gal·ly** *adv*

¹**fruit** \'früt\ *n* **1** : a pulpy or juicy plant part (as rhubarb or a strawberry) that is often eaten as a dessert and is distinguished from a vegetable **2** : a reproductive body of a seed plant that consists of the ripened ovary of a flower with its included seeds **3** : ²RESULT 1, PRODUCT ⟨the *fruits* of your labors⟩ — **fruit·ed** \-əd\ *adj*

²**fruit** *vb* : to bear or cause to bear fruit

fruit·cake \'früt-,kāk\ *n* : a rich cake containing nuts, dried or candied fruits, and spices

fruit·ful \'früt-fəl\ *adj* **1** : very productive ⟨a *fruitful* soil⟩ **2** : bringing results ⟨a *fruitful* idea⟩ — **fruit·ful·ly** \-fə-lē\ *adv* — **fruit·ful·ness** *n*

fruit·less \'früt-ləs\ *adj* **1** : not bearing fruit **2** : UNSUCCESSFUL — **fruit·less·ly** *adv* — **fruit·less·ness** *n*

fruity \'früt-ē\ *adj* **fruit·i·er; fruit·i·est** : relating to or suggesting fruit ⟨a *fruity* smell⟩

frus·trate \'frəs-ˌtrāt\ *vb* **frus·trat·ed; frus·trat·ing 1** : to prevent from carrying out a purpose **2** : ¹DEFEAT 1 **3** : DISCOURAGE 1

frus·tra·tion \ˌfrəs-'trā-shən\ *n* : DISAPPOINTMENT 2, DEFEAT

¹**fry** \'frī\ *vb* **fried; fry·ing** : to cook in fat

²**fry** *n, pl* **fry 1** : recently hatched or very young fishes **2** : persons of a particular group ⟨small *fry*⟩

fudge \'fəj\ *n* : a soft creamy candy often containing nuts

¹**fu·el** \'fyü-əl\ *n* : a substance (as oil) that can be burned to produce heat or power

²**fuel** *vb* **fu·eled** *or* **fu·elled; fu·el·ing** *or* **fu·el·ling** : to supply with or take on fuel

¹**fu·gi·tive** \'fyü-jət-iv\ *adj* : running away or trying to escape ⟨a *fugitive* slave⟩

²**fugitive** *n* : a person who is running away

¹**-ful** \fəl\ *adj suffix* **1** : full of ⟨event*ful*⟩ **2** : characterized by ⟨peace*ful*⟩ **3** : having the qualities of ⟨master*ful*⟩ **4** : -ABLE ⟨mourn*ful*⟩

²**-ful** \ˌfül\ *n suffix* : number or quantity that fills or would fill ⟨spoon*ful*⟩

ful·crum \'fül-krəm, 'fəl-\ *n, pl* **ful·crums** *or* **ful·cra** \-krə\ : the support on which a lever turns in lifting something

F **fulcrum**

ful·fill *or* **ful·fil** \fül-'fil\ *vb* **ful·filled; ful·fill·ing 1** : ACCOMPLISH ⟨*fulfill* a plan⟩ **2** : SATISFY 1 ⟨*fulfill* a requirement⟩ — **ful·fill·ment** \-mənt\ *n*

¹**full** \'fül\ *adj* **1** : containing as much as possible or normal ⟨a *full* glass⟩ **2** : ¹COMPLETE 1 ⟨waited a *full* year⟩ **3** : plump and rounded in outline ⟨a *full* face⟩ **4** : having much material ⟨a *full* skirt⟩ — **full·ness** *n*

²**full** *adv* **1** : ²VERY 1 **2** : COMPLETELY ⟨fill the glass *full*⟩

³**full** *n* **1** : the highest state, extent, or degree **2** : the complete amount ⟨paid in *full*⟩

full moon *n* : the moon with its whole disk lighted

ful·ly \'fül-ē\ *adv* **1** : COMPLETELY **2** : at least ⟨*fully* half of them⟩

¹**fum·ble** \'fəm-bəl\ *vb* **fum·bled; fum·bling** : to feel about for or handle something clumsily

²**fumble** *n* : an act of fumbling

¹**fume** \'fyüm\ *n* : a disagreeable smoke, vapor, or gas — usually used in pl.

²**fume** *vb* **fumed; fum·ing 1** : to give off fumes **2** : to show bad temper : be angry

fu·mi·gate \'fyü-mə-ˌgāt\ *vb* **fu·mi·gat·ed; fu·mi·gat·ing** : to disinfect by exposing to smoke, vapor, or gas

fun \'fən\ *n* **1** : something that provides amusement or enjoyment **2** : AMUSEMENT

¹**func·tion** \'fəngk-shən\ *n* **1** : the action or purpose for which a thing exists or is used **2** : a large important ceremony or social affair

²**function** *vb* : to serve a certain purpose : WORK ⟨the new machine *functions* well⟩

fund \'fənd\ *n* **1** : ¹STOCK 5, SUPPLY ⟨a *fund* of jokes⟩ **2** : a sum of money for a special purpose ⟨a book *fund*⟩ **3 funds** *pl* : available money ⟨out of *funds*⟩

¹**fun·da·men·tal** \ˌfən-də-'ment-l\ *adj* : being or forming a foundation : BASIC, ESSENTIAL ⟨a discovery *fundamental* to modern science⟩ ⟨our *fundamental* rights⟩ — **fun·da·men·tal·ly** *adv*

²**fundamental** *n* : a basic part ⟨the *fundamentals* of arithmetic⟩

fu·ner·al \'fyü-nə-rəl, 'fyün-rəl\ *n* : the ceremonies held for a dead person (as before burial)

fun·gi·cide \'fən-jə-ˌsīd\ *n* : a substance used to kill fungi — **fun·gi·cid·al** \ˌfən-jə-'sīd-l\ *adj*

fun·gous \'fəng-gəs\ *or* **fun·gal** \-gəl\ *adj* : of, relating to, or caused by fungi

fun·gus \'fəng-gəs\ *n, pl* **fun·gi** \'fən-ˌjī, -ˌgī\ *also* **fun·gus·es** : any of a large group of plants (as mushrooms, molds, and rusts) that have no chlorophyll and must live on other plants or animals or on decaying material

\ə\ **abut**	\au̇\ **out**	\i\ **tip**	\ȯ\ **saw**	\u̇\ **foot**
\ər\ **further**	\ch\ **chin**	\ī\ **life**	\ȯi\ **coin**	\y\ **yet**
\a\ **mat**	\e\ **pet**	\j\ **job**	\th\ **thin**	\yü\ **few**
\ā\ **take**	\ē\ **easy**	\ng\ **sing**	\th\ **this**	\yu̇\ **cure**
\ä\ **cot, cart**	\g\ **go**	\ō\ **bone**	\ü\ **food**	\zh\ **vision**

fun•nel \\'fən-l\ *n* **1** : a utensil usually shaped like a hollow cone with a tube extending from the point and used to catch and direct a downward flow (as of liquid) **2** : a large pipe for the escape of smoke or for ventilation (as on a ship)

funnel

fun•nies \\'fən-ēz\ *n pl* : the comic strips or a section containing comic strips (as in a newspaper)

fun•ny \\'fən-ē\ *adj* **fun•ni•er; fun•ni•est 1** : causing laughter **2** : STRANGE 2 ⟨a *funny* noise⟩

fur \\'fər\ *n* **1** : a piece of the pelt of an animal **2** : an article of clothing made with fur **3** : the hairy coat of a mammal especially when fine, soft, and thick — **furred** \\'fərd\ *adj*

Word History At first the pelt of an animal was called *fur* only when it was part of a person's garment. The English noun *fur* came from an earlier verb *fur*. This verb meant "to line or trim with fur." The English verb *fur* came from an early French verb. This early French verb came from an early French noun that meant "sheath." Lining or trimming a garment with fur was likened to putting a knife in a sheath.

fu•ri•ous \\'fyur-ē-əs\ *adj* **1** : very angry **2** : very active : VIOLENT ⟨a *furious* storm⟩ — **fu•ri•ous•ly** *adv*

furl \\'fərl\ *vb* : to wrap or roll close to or around something ⟨*furl* a flag⟩

fur•long \\'fər-ˌlong\ *n* : a unit of length equal to 220 yards (about 201 meters)

fur•lough \\'fər-lō\ *n* : a leave of absence from duty ⟨a soldier's *furlough*⟩

fur•nace \\'fər-nəs\ *n* : an enclosed structure in which heat is produced (as for heating a house or for melting metals)

fur•nish \\'fər-nish\ *vb* **1** : to provide with what is needed ⟨the cave *furnished* us with shelter⟩ **2** : to supply to someone or something ⟨*furnish* food to the guests⟩

fur•nish•ings \\'fər-nish-ingz\ *n pl* : articles of furniture for a room or building

fur•ni•ture \\'fər-ni-chər\ *n* : movable articles used to furnish a room

fur•ri•er \\'fər-ē-ər\ *n* : a dealer in furs

¹fur•row \\'fər-ō\ *n* **1** : a trench made by or as if by a plow **2** : a narrow groove : WRINKLE

²furrow *vb* : to make furrows in

fur•ry \\'fər-ē\ *adj* **fur•ri•er; fur•ri•est 1** : like fur **2** : covered with fur

¹fur•ther \\'fər-thər\ *adv* **1** : ¹FARTHER 1 **2** : ¹BESIDES, ALSO **3** : to a greater degree or extent

²further *adj* **1** : ²FARTHER **2** : going or extending beyond : ADDITIONAL ⟨*further* study⟩

³further *vb* : to help forward : PROMOTE

fur•ther•more \\'fər-thər-ˌmōr\ *adv* : MOREOVER ⟨they came, *furthermore* they came on time⟩

fur•ther•most \\'fər-thər-ˌmōst\ *adj* : most distant : FARTHEST

fur•thest \\'fər-thəst\ *adv or adj* : FARTHEST

fur•tive \\'fərt-iv\ *adj* : done in a sneaky or sly manner — **fur•tive•ly** *adv* — **fur•tive•ness** *n*

fu•ry \\'fyur-ē\ *n, pl* **fu•ries 1** : violent anger : RAGE **2** : wild and dangerous force ⟨the *fury* of the storm⟩ **synonyms** see ANGER

¹fuse \\'fyüz\ *n* **1** : a cord that is set afire to ignite an explosive by carrying fire to it **2** *usually* **fuze** : a device for setting off a bomb or torpedo

²fuse *vb* **fused; fus•ing 1** : to change into a liquid or to a plastic state by heat **2** : to unite by or as if by melting together

³fuse *n* : a device having a metal wire or strip that melts and interrupts an electrical circuit when the current becomes too strong

fu•se•lage \\'fyü-sə-ˌläzh, -zə-\ *n* : the central body part of an airplane that holds the crew, passengers, and cargo

fu•sion \\'fyü-zhən\ *n* **1** : a fusing or melting together **2** : union by or as if by melting **3** : union of atomic nuclei to form heavier nuclei resulting in the release of enormous quantities of energy

¹fuss \\'fəs\ *n* **1** : unnecessary activity or excitement often over something unimportant **2** : ¹PROTEST 2 **3** : a great show of interest ⟨made a *fuss* over the baby⟩

²fuss *vb* : to make a fuss

fussy \\'fəs-ē\ *adj* **fuss•i•er; fuss•i•est 1** : inclined to complain or whine ⟨a *fussy* child⟩ **2** : needing much attention to details ⟨a *fussy* job⟩ **3** : hard to please ⟨*fussy* about food⟩

fu•tile \\'fyüt-l\ *adj* : having no result or effect : USELESS ⟨their efforts to win were *futile*⟩ — **fu•tile•ly** *adv* — **fu•tile•ness** *n*

fu•til•i•ty \\fyü-'til-ət-ē\ *n* : the quality or state of being futile

¹fu•ture \\'fyü-chər\ *adj* : coming after the present ⟨*future* events⟩

²future *n* **1** : future time **2** : the chance of future success ⟨you've a bright *future*⟩

fuze *variant of* FUSE

fuzz \\'fəz\\ *n* : fine light particles or fibers

fuzzy \\'fəz-ē\\ *adj* **fuzz·i·er; fuzz·i·est 1** : covered with or looking like fuzz **2** : not clear — **fuzz·i·ly** \\'fəz-ə-lē\\ *adv* — **fuzz·i·ness** \\'fəz-ē-nəs\\ *n*

-fy \\ˌfī\\ *vb suffix* **-fied; -fy·ing 1** : make : form into ⟨solid*fy*⟩ **2** : make similar to ⟨beauti*fy*⟩

g \\'jē\\ *n, pl* **g's** *or* **gs** \\'jēz\\ *often cap* **1** : the seventh letter of the English alphabet **2** : a unit of force equal to the weight of a body on which the force acts ⟨an astronaut during takeoff of the rocket vehicle may experience ten *G*'s⟩

¹gab \\'gab\\ *vb* **gabbed; gab·bing** : to talk in an idle way

²gab *n* : idle talk : CHATTER

gab·ar·dine \\'gab-ər-ˌdēn\\ *n* : a firm cloth with diagonal ribs and a hard smooth finish

¹gab·ble \\'gab-əl\\ *vb* **gab·bled; gab·bling** : ¹CHATTER 2

²gabble *n* : loud or fast talk that has no meaning

gab·by \\'gab-ē\\ *adj* **gab·bi·er; gab·bi·est** : given to talking a lot : TALKATIVE

ga·ble \\'gā-bəl\\ *n* : the triangular part of an outside wall of a building formed by the sides of the roof sloping down from the ridgepole to the eaves

gable

gad \\'gad\\ *vb* **gad·ded; gad·ding** : to roam about : WANDER

gad·about \\'gad-ə-ˌbaut\\ *n* : a person who goes from place to place without much reason

gad·fly \\'gad-ˌflī\\ *n, pl* **gad·flies 1** : a large biting fly **2** : a person who is an annoying pest

gad·get \\'gaj-ət\\ *n* : an interesting, unfamiliar, or unusual device

gaff \\'gaf\\ *n* **1** : an iron hook with a handle **2** : something hard to take ⟨couldn't stand the *gaff*⟩

¹gag \\'gag\\ *vb* **gagged; gag·ging 1** : to keep from speaking or crying out by or as if by stopping up the mouth **2** : to cause to feel like vomiting : RETCH

²gag *n* **1** : something that gags **2** : ¹JOKE 1, 2

gage *variant of* GAUGE

gai·ety \\'gā-ət-ē\\ *n, pl* **gai·eties 1** : MERRYMAKING 1 **2** : bright spirits or manner

gai·ly \\'gā-lē\\ *adv* **1** : in a merry or lively way **2** : in a bright or showy way ⟨*gaily* dressed crowds⟩

¹gain \\'gān\\ *n* **1** : advantage gained or increased : PROFIT ⟨financial *gains*⟩ **2** : an increase in amount, size, or degree ⟨a *gain* in weight⟩

²gain *vb* **1** : to get hold of often by effort or with difficulty : WIN ⟨*gain* knowledge by study⟩ ⟨*gain* strength by exercise⟩ ⟨*gained* a great victory⟩ **2** : to get to : REACH ⟨the swimmer *gained* the shore⟩ **3** : to get advantage : PROFIT ⟨we all *gained* from the lesson⟩ **synonyms** *see* REACH — **gain·er** *n*

gain·ful \\'gān-fəl\\ *adj* : producing gain

gait \\'gāt\\ *n* : way of walking or running

¹ga·la \\'gā-lə, 'gal-ə, 'gäl-ə\\ *n* : a gay celebration : FESTIVITY

²gala *adj* : suitable for festivities : FESTIVE

ga·lac·tic \\gə-'lak-tik\\ *adj* : of or relating to a galaxy ⟨*galactic* light⟩

gal·axy \\'gal-ək-sē\\ *n, pl* **gal·ax·ies 1** : MILKY WAY GALAXY **2** : one of billions of collections of stars, gas, and dust that make up the universe

Word History A band of light in the night sky is caused by many faint stars. We call

\\ə\\ abut	\\au̇\\ out	\\i\\ tip	\\ȯ\\ saw	\\u̇\\ foot
\\ər\\ further	\\ch\\ chin	\\ī\\ life	\\ȯi\\ coin	\\y\\ yet
\\a\\ mat	\\e\\ pet	\\j\\ job	\\th\\ thin	\\yü\\ few
\\ā\\ take	\\ē\\ easy	\\ng\\ sing	\\th\\ this	\\yu̇\\ cure
\\ä\\ cot, cart	\\g\\ go	\\ō\\ bone	\\ü\\ food	\\zh\\ vision

f F f g G g g g g g g g g g g g g g g g g g g g g g g g g g g g g g this band the *Milky Way* because it looks a bit like a stream of milk. The stars of the Milky Way belong to our galaxy, the Milky Way galaxy. The idea that the Milky Way looks like milk is much older than the English language. The ancient Greek name for this star system was formed from the Greek word for milk. The English word *galaxy* came from the Greek name for the Milky Way.

gale \'gāl\ *n* **1** : a strong wind **2** : a wind of from about fourteen to twenty-four meters per second **3** : OUTBURST 1 ⟨*gales* of laughter⟩

ga·le·na \gə-'lē-nə\ *n* : a bluish gray mineral that is the main ore of lead

¹gall \'gȯl\ *n* **1** : bile especially when stored in a small sac (**gall bladder**) attached to the liver **2** : IMPUDENCE

²gall *n* : a sore spot (as on a horse's back) caused by rubbing

³gall *vb* **1** : to make sore by rubbing **2** : IRRITATE 1

⁴gall *n* : a swelling or growth on a twig or leaf

gal·lant \'gal-ənt\ *adj* **1** : showing no fear : BRAVE **2** : CHIVALROUS 2, NOBLE **3** \gə-'lant, -'länt\ : very polite to women

gal·lant·ry \'gal-ən-trē\ *n* **1** : polite attention shown to women **2** : COURAGE, BRAVERY

gal·le·on \'gal-ē-ən\ *n* : a large sailing ship of the time of Columbus and later

galleon

gal·lery \'gal-ə-rē, 'gal-rē\ *n, pl* **gal·ler·ies** **1** : a long narrow room or hall usually with windows along one side **2** : an indoor structure (as in a theater or church) built out from one or more walls **3** : a room or hall used for a special purpose (as showing pictures)

gal·ley \'gal-ē\ *n, pl* **gal·leys** **1** : a large low ship of olden times moved by oars and sails **2** : the kitchen of a ship

galley slave *n* : a person forced to row on a galley

gal·li·vant \'gal-ə-ˌvant\ *vb* : GAD

gal·lon \'gal-ən\ *n* : a unit of liquid capacity equal to four quarts (about 3.8 liters)

¹gal·lop \'gal-əp\ *n* **1** : a fast springing way of running of an animal with four feet and especially a horse **2** : a ride or run at a gallop

²gallop *vb* : to go or cause to go at a gallop

gal·lows \'gal-ōz\ *n, pl* **gallows** *or* **gal·lows·es** : a structure from which criminals are hanged

ga·losh \gə-'läsh\ *n* : an overshoe worn in snow or wet weather

gal·va·nize \'gal-və-ˌnīz\ *vb* **gal·va·nized; gal·va·niz·ing** **1** : to excite or stir by or as if by an electric shock **2** : to coat with zinc for protection

¹gam·ble \'gam-bəl\ *vb* **gam·bled; gam·bling** **1** : to play a game in which something (as money) is risked : BET **2** : to take risks on the chance of gain : take a chance ⟨we *gambled* on not being seen⟩

²gamble *n* : something that is risky to do

gam·bler \'gam-blər\ *n* : a person who gambles

gam·bol \'gam-bəl\ *vb* **gam·boled** *or* **gam·bolled; gam·bol·ing** *or* **gam·bol·ling** : to run or skip about playfully : FROLIC

¹game \'gām\ *n* **1** : AMUSEMENT, PLAY ⟨children happy at their *games*⟩ **2** : a contest carried on according to rules with players in direct opposition to each other **3** : animals hunted for sport or for food **4** : the meat from game animals

²game *adj* **gam·er; gam·est** **1** : full of spirit or eagerness **2** : of or relating to animals that are hunted ⟨the *game* laws⟩

game·cock \'gām-ˌkäk\ *n* : a rooster trained for fighting

game·keep·er \'gām-ˌkē-pər\ *n* : a person in charge of the breeding and protection of game animals or birds on private land

game·ly \'gām-lē\ *adv* : with spirit and courage

game·ness \'gām-nəs\ *n* : the quality or state of being spirited and courageous

game show *n* : a television program on which contestants compete for prizes in a game (as a quiz)

game warden *n* : a person who sees that fishing and hunting laws are obeyed

gam·ing \'gā-miŋ\ *n* : the practice of gambling

gam·ma rays \'gam-ə-\ *n pl* : very penetrating rays like X rays but of shorter wave length

gamy \'gā-mē\ *adj* **gam·i·er; gam·i·est**

: having the flavor of wild game especially when slightly spoiled

gan·der \'gan-dər\ *n* : a male goose

gang \'gang\ *n* **1** : a group of persons working or going about together **2** : a group of persons acting together to do something illegal

gan·gli·on \'gang-glē-ən\ *n*, *pl* **gan·glia** \-glē-ə\ : a mass of nerve cells especially outside the brain or spinal cord

gang·plank \'gang-,plangk\ *n* : a movable bridge from a ship to the shore

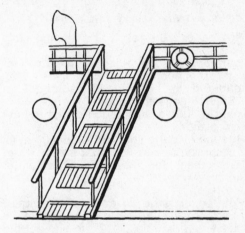

gangplank

gan·grene \'gang-,grēn\ *n* : death of body tissue when the blood supply is cut off

gang·ster \'gang-stər\ *n* : a member of a gang of criminals

gang·way \'gang-,wā\ *n* **1** : a way into, through, or out of an enclosed space **2** : GANGPLANK

gan·net \'gan-ət\ *n* : a large bird that eats fish and spends much time far from land

gan·try \'gan-trē\ *n*, *pl* **gan·tries** **1** : a structure over railroad tracks for holding signals **2** : a movable structure for preparing a rocket for launching

gap \'gap\ *n* **1** : an opening made by a break or a coming apart **2** : an opening between mountains **3** : a hole or space where something is missing

¹**gape** \'gāp\ *vb* **gaped**; **gap·ing** **1** : to open the mouth wide **2** : to stare with open mouth **3** : to open or part widely

²**gape** *n* : an act or instance of gaping

¹**ga·rage** \gə-'räzh, -'räj\ *n* : a building where automobiles or trucks are repaired or kept when not in use

²**garage** *vb* **ga·raged**; **ga·rag·ing** : to keep or put in a garage

¹**garb** \'gärb\ *n* : style or kind of clothing

²**garb** *vb* : CLOTHE 1

gar·bage \'gär-bij\ *n* : waste food especially from a kitchen

gar·ble \'gär-bəl\ *vb* **gar·bled**; **gar·bling** : to change or twist the meaning or sound of

Word History At first the word *garble* meant "to sift" or "to sort or pick out." If you pick out a few misleading parts of a message and report only those parts, you distort the message. *Garble* came to mean "to distort." It is the meaning "sift," however, that reflects the origin of *garble*. The English word *garble* came from an old Italian word that meant "to sift." This word came in turn from an Arabic word that meant "sieve." The Arabs took this word from a Latin word that meant "sieve."

¹**gar·den** \'gärd-n\ *n* **1** : a piece of ground in which fruits, flowers, or vegetables are grown **2** : an enclosure for the public showing of plants or animals ⟨a botanical *garden*⟩

²**garden** *vb* : to make or work in a garden

gar·den·er \'gärd-nər, -n-ər\ *n* : a person who gardens especially for pay

gar·de·nia \gär-'dē-nyə\ *n* : a large white or yellowish flower with a fragrant smell

¹**gar·gle** \'gär-gəl\ *vb* **gar·gled**; **gar·gling** : to rinse the throat with a liquid kept in motion by air forced through it from the lungs

²**gargle** *n* **1** : a liquid used in gargling **2** : a gargling sound

gar·goyle \'gär-,goil\ *n* : a waterspout in the form of a strange or frightening human or animal figure sticking out at the roof or eaves of a building

gargoyle

gar·ish \'gaər-ish, 'geər-\ *adj* : too bright or showy : GAUDY ⟨dressed in *garish* colors⟩

¹**gar·land** \'gär-lənd\ *n* : a wreath or rope of leaves or flowers

²**garland** *vb* : to form into or decorate with a garland

gar·lic \'gär-lik\ *n* : a plant related to the onion and grown for its bulbs that have a

\ə\ abut	\aů\ out	\i\ tip	\ò\ saw	\ů\ foot
\ər\ further	\ch\ chin	\ī\ life	\òi\ coin	\y\ yet
\a\ mat	\e\ pet	\j\ job	\th\ thin	\yü\ few
\ā\ take	\ē\ easy	\ng\ sing	\th\ this	\yů\ cure
\ä\ cot, cart	\g\ go	\ō\ bone	\ü\ food	\zh\ vision

strong smell and taste and are used to flavor foods

gar·ment \'gär-mənt\ *n* : an article of clothing

gar·ner \'gär-nər\ *vb* : to gather in and store

gar·net \'gär-nət\ *n* : a deep red mineral used as a gem

¹gar·nish \'gär-nish\ *vb* : to add decorations or seasoning (as to food)

²garnish *n* : something used in garnishing

gar·ret \'gar-ət\ *n* : a room or unfinished part of a house just under the roof

¹gar·ri·son \'gar-ə-sən\ *n* : a place in which troops are regularly stationed

²garrison *vb* **1** : to station troops in **2** : to send (troops) to a garrison

gar·ter \'gärt-ər\ *n* : a band worn to hold up a stocking or sock

garter snake *n* : any of numerous harmless American snakes with stripes along the back

¹gas \'gas\ *n, pl* **gas·es** **1** : a substance (as oxygen or hydrogen) having no fixed shape and tending to expand without limit **2** : a gas or a mixture of gases used as a fuel or to make one unconscious (as for an operation) **3** : a fluid that poisons the air or makes breathing difficult **4** : GASOLINE

²gas *vb* **gassed; gas·sing; gas·ses** **1** : to treat with gas **2** : to poison with gas **3** : to supply with gas

gas·eous \'gas-ē-əs, 'gash-əs\ *adj* : of or relating to gas

¹gash \'gash\ *vb* : to make a long deep cut in

²gash *n* : a long deep cut

gas mask *n* : a covering for the face that is connected to a device for purifying air and used to protect the face and lungs against poisonous gas

gas·o·line \'gas-ə-,lēn, ,gas-ə-'lēn\ *n* : a flammable liquid made especially from gas found in the earth and from petroleum and used mostly as an automobile fuel

¹gasp \'gasp\ *vb* **1** : to breathe with difficulty : PANT ⟨*gasping* after a race⟩ **2** : to utter with quick difficult breaths

²gasp *n* **1** : the act of gasping **2** : something gasped ⟨a *gasp* of surprise⟩

gas station *n* : SERVICE STATION

gas·tric juice \'gas-trik-\ *n* : an acid liquid made by the stomach that helps to digest food

gate \'gāt\ *n* **1** : an opening in a wall or fence often with a movable frame or door for closing it **2** : a part of a barrier (as a fence) that opens and closes like a door

¹gath·er \'gath-ər\ *vb* **1** : to bring or come together **2** : to pick out and collect

⟨*gather* fruit⟩ **3** : to gain little by little ⟨*gather* speed⟩ **4** : to get an idea : CONCLUDE **5** : to draw together in folds

synonyms GATHER, COLLECT, and ASSEMBLE mean to come or bring together. GATHER may suggest the coming or bringing together of different kinds of things ⟨*gathered* all the goods in the house and sold them⟩ COLLECT may suggest a careful or orderly gathering of things that are often of one kind ⟨it's fun to *collect* coins⟩ ASSEMBLE suggests a gathering of units into an orderly whole ⟨the choir *assembled* and started to sing⟩

²gather *n* : the result of gathering cloth : PUCKER

gath·er·ing \'gath-ə-ring\ *n* : a coming together of people : MEETING

gau·cho \'gaù-chō\ *n, pl* **gau·chos** : a South American cowboy

gaudy \'gȯd-ē\ *adj* **gaud·i·er; gaud·i·est** : too showy

¹gauge *or* **gage** \'gāj\ *n* **1** : measurement according to a standard **2** : SIZE 2 **3** : an instrument for measuring, testing, or registering ⟨a rain *gauge*⟩ ⟨a steam *gauge*⟩

²gauge *or* **gage** *vb* **gauged** *or* **gaged; gaug·ing** *or* **gag·ing** **1** : to measure exactly ⟨*gauge* rainfall⟩ **2** : to find out the capacity or contents of **3** : ¹ESTIMATE 1, JUDGE

gaunt \'gȯnt\ *adj* : very thin and bony (as from illness or starvation)

¹gaunt·let \'gȯnt-lət\ *n* **1** : a glove made of small metal plates and worn with a suit of armor **2** : a glove with a wide cuff that covers and protects the wrist and part of the arm

gauntlet 1

²gauntlet *n* : a double file of persons who beat someone forced to run between them

gauze \'gȯz\ *n* : a thin transparent fabric

gauzy \'gȯ-zē\ *adj* **gauz·i·er; gauz·i·est** : thin and transparent like gauze

gave *past of* GIVE

gav·el \'gav-əl\ *n* : a mallet with which the person in charge raps to call a meeting or court to order

gavel

gawk \'gȯk\ *vb* : to stare stupidly

gawky \'gȯ-kē\ *adj* **gawk·i·er; gawk·i·est** : AWKWARD 1, CLUMSY — **gawk·i·ly** \-kə-lē\ *adv* — **gawk·i·ness** \-kē-nəs\ *n*

gay \'gā\ *adj* **gay·er; gay·est** **1** : MERRY **2** : brightly colored

¹gaze \'gāz\ *vb* **gazed; gaz·ing** : to fix the eyes in a long steady look

> **synonyms** GAZE, STARE, and GLARE mean to look at with concentration. GAZE suggests a long and fixed look ⟨stood *gazing* at the sunset⟩ STARE suggests a wide-eyed often curious, rude, or absent-minded gaze ⟨*stared* in surprise at the strange creature⟩ GLARE suggests an angry stare ⟨*glared* at the naughty children until they behaved themselves⟩

²gaze *n* : a long steady look

ga·zelle \gə-'zel\ *n* : a swift graceful antelope with large bright eyes

gazelle

ga·zette \gə-'zet\ *n* **1** : NEWSPAPER **2** : a journal giving official information

gaz·et·teer \ˌgaz-ə-'tiər\ *n* : a geographical dictionary

¹gear \'giər\ *n* **1** : EQUIPMENT 2 **2** : a group of parts that has a specific function in a machine ⟨steering *gear*⟩ **3** : a toothed wheel : COGWHEEL **4** : the position the gears of a machine are in when they are ready to work ⟨in *gear*⟩ **5** : one of the adjustments in a motor vehicle that determine the direction of travel and the relative speed between the engine and the motion of the vehicle ⟨second *gear*⟩⟨reverse *gear*⟩

²gear *vb* **1** : to make ready for operation ⟨*gear* up for production⟩ **2** : to make suitable ⟨a book *geared* to children⟩

gear·shift \'giər-ˌshift\ *n* : a mechanism by which gears are connected and disconnected

gee \'jē\ *interj* — used to show surprise or enthusiasm

geese *pl of* GOOSE

Gei·ger counter \ˌgī-gər-\ *n* : an instrument for detecting the presence of cosmic rays or radioactive substances

gel·a·tin \'jel-ət-n\ *n* **1** : a protein obtained by boiling animal tissues and used especially as food **2** : an edible jelly formed with gelatin

gem \'jem\ *n* : a usually valuable stone cut and polished for jewelry

Gem·i·ni \'jem-ə-nē, -ˌnī\ *n* **1** : a constellation between Taurus and Cancer imagined as twins **2** : the third sign of the zodiac or a person born under this sign

gen·der \'jen-dər\ *n* : SEX 1

gene \'jēn\ *n* : a unit of DNA that controls the development of a single characteristic in an individual

genera *pl of* GENUS

¹gen·er·al \'jen-ə-rəl, 'jen-rəl\ *adj* **1** : having to do with the whole ⟨a matter of *general* interest⟩ **2** : not specific or detailed **3** : not specialized ⟨a *general* store⟩

²general *n* : a commissioned officer in the Army, Air Force, or Marine Corps ranking above a lieutenant general

gen·er·al·iza·tion \ˌjen-ə-rə-lə-'zā-shən\ *n* **1** : the act of generalizing **2** : a general statement

gen·er·al·ize \'jen-ə-rə-ˌlīz, 'jen-rə-\ *vb* **gen·er·al·ized; gen·er·al·iz·ing** : to put in the form of a general rule : draw or state a general conclusion from a number of different items or instances

gen·er·al·ly \'jen-ə-rə-lē, 'jen-rə-\ *adv* : as a rule : USUALLY

General of the Air Force : the highest ranking commissioned officer in the Air Force ranking above a general

General of the Army : the highest ranking commissioned officer in the Army ranking above a general

gen·er·ate \'jen-ə-ˌrāt\ *vb* **gen·er·at·ed; gen·er·at·ing** : to cause to come into being

gen·er·a·tion \ˌjen-ə-'rā-shən\ *n* **1** : those having the same parents and being a step in a line from one ancestor ⟨a family that has lived in the same house for four *generations*⟩ **2** : a group of individuals born about the same time ⟨the younger *generation*⟩ **3** : the act of generating something

gen·er·a·tor \'jen-ə-ˌrāt-ər\ *n* : DYNAMO

\ə\ abut	\au̇\ out	\i\ tip	\ȯ\ saw	\u̇\ foot
\ər\ further	\ch\ chin	\ī\ life	\ȯi\ coin	\y\ yet
\a\ mat	\e\ pet	\j\ job	\th\ thin	\yü\ few
\ā\ take	\ē\ easy	\ng\ sing	\th\ this	\yu̇\ cure
\ä\ cot, cart	\g\ go	\ō\ bone	\ü\ food	\zh\ vision

gen•er•os•i•ty \,jen-ə-'räs-ət-ē\ *n, pl* **gen-er•os•i•ties** **1** : willingness to give or to share **2** : a generous act

gen•er•ous \'jen-ə-rəs, 'jen-rəs\ *adj* **1** : free in giving or sharing **2** : ABUNDANT ⟨a *generous* supply⟩ — **gen•er•ous•ly** *adv*

gen•e•sis \'jen-ə-səs\ *n, pl* **gen•e•ses** \-,sēz\ : a coming into being

ge•net•ic \jə-'net-ik\ *adj* : of or relating to genetics

genetic code *n* : the arrangement of chemical groups within the genes by which genetic information is passed on

ge•net•i•cist \jə-'net-ə-səst\ *n* : a specialist in genetics

ge•net•ics \jə-'net-iks\ *n* : a science dealing with heredity and the way living things vary

ge•nial \'jēn-yəl\ *adj* : pleasantly cheerful — **ge•nial•ly** \'jēn-yə-lē\ *adv*

ge•nie \'jē-nē\ *n* : a magic spirit believed to take human form and serve the person who calls it

gen•i•tal \'jen-ə-tl\ *adj* : of or relating to reproduction or sex

ge•nius \'jēn-yəs\ *n* **1** : great natural ability ⟨a person of *genius*⟩ **2** : a very gifted person

gen•tian \'jen-chən\ *n* : an herb with smooth opposite leaves and usually blue flowers

gentian

¹gen•tile \'jen-,tīl\ *n, often cap* : a person who is not Jewish

²gentile *adj, often cap* : of or relating to people not Jewish

gen•til•i•ty \jen-'til-ət-ē\ *n* **1** : good birth and family **2** : the qualities of a well-bred person **3** : good manners

gen•tle \'jent-l\ *adj* **gen•tler; gen•tlest 1** : easily handled : not wild **2** : not harsh or stern : MILD **3** : ¹MODERATE 1 ⟨a *gentle* slope⟩ — **gen•tle•ness** \'jent-l-nəs\ *n*

gen•tle•folk \'jent-l-,fōk\ *n pl* : GENTRY 1

gen•tle•man \'jent-l-mən\ *n, pl* **gen•tle-men** \-mən\ **1** : a man or good birth and position **2** : a man of good education and social position **3** : a man with very good manners **4** : MAN — used in the plural when speaking to a group of men — **gen-tle•man•ly** *adj*

gen•tle•wom•an \'jent-l-,wùm-ən\ *n, pl* **gen•tle•wom•en** \-,wim-ən\ **1** : a woman of good birth and position **2** : a woman with very good manners : LADY 2

gen•tly \'jent-lē\ *adv* : in a gentle manner

gen•try \'jen-trē\ *n* **1** : people of good birth, breeding, and education **2** : people of a certain class

gen•u•flect \'jen-yə-,flekt\ *vb* : to kneel on one knee and rise again as an act of deep respect

gen•u•ine \'jen-yə-wən\ *adj* **1** : being just what it seems to be : REAL ⟨*genuine* gold⟩ **2** : HONEST 1, SINCERE ⟨*genuine* interest⟩ — **gen•u•ine•ly** *adv* — **gen•u-ine•ness** *n*

ge•nus \'jē-nəs\ *n, pl* **gen•era** \'jen-ə-rə\ : a group of plants or animals related in structure and heredity that can be further divided into species

geo- *prefix* **1** : earth ⟨*geo*chemistry⟩ **2** : geographical

geo•chem•is•try \,jē-ō-'kem-ə-strē\ *n* : chemistry that deals with the earth's crust

geo•de•sic \,jē-ə-'des-ik, -'dēs-\ *n* : the shortest line between two points on a surface

geo•graph•ic \,jē-ə-'graf-ik\ *or* **geo-graph•i•cal** \-i-kəl\ *adj* : of or relating to geography

ge•og•ra•phy \jē-'äg-rə-fē\ *n* **1** : a science that deals with the location of living and nonliving things on earth and the way they affect one another **2** : the natural features of an area

geo•log•ic \,jē-ə-'läj-ik\ *or* **geo•log•i•cal** \-i-kəl\ *adj* : of or relating to geology

ge•ol•o•gist \jē-'äl-ə-jəst\ *n* : a specialist in geology

ge•ol•o•gy \jē-'äl-ə-jē\ *n* **1** : a science that deals with the history of the earth and its life especially as recorded in rocks **2** : the geologic features (as mountains or plains) of an area

geo·mag·net·ic \ˌjē-ō-mag-'net-ik\ *adj* : of or relating to the magnetism of the earth

geo·met·ric \ˌjē-ə-'met-rik\ *adj* : of or relating to geometry

ge·om·e·try \jē-'äm-ə-trē\ *n* : a branch of mathematics that deals with points, lines, angles, surfaces, and solids

ge·ra·ni·um \jə-'rā-nē-əm\ *n* : an herb often grown for its bright flowers

Word History Many of the plants of the geranium family have long, thin, pointed fruits. These fruits look a bit like the bill of a bird. The ancient Greeks thought that the fruit of the wild geranium looked like the bill of a crane. They gave the plant a name that meant "little crane." The English word *geranium* came from this Greek name.

ger·bil \'jər-bəl\ *n* : a small Old World leaping desert rodent

germ \'jərm\ *n* **1** : a bit of living matter capable of forming a new individual **2** : a source from which something develops ⟨the *germ* of an idea⟩ **3** : a microbe that causes disease

¹Ger·man \'jər-mən\ *n* **1** : a person born or living in Germany, East Germany, or West Germany **2** : the language of the Germans

²German *adj* : of or relating to Germany, East Germany, West Germany, the German people, or their language

ger·ma·ni·um \jər-'mā-nē-əm\ *n* : a white hard brittle element used as a semiconductor

germ cell *n* : a reproductive cell (as an egg or sperm cell)

ger·mi·cide \'jər-mə-ˌsīd\ *n* : a substance that destroys germs

ger·mi·nate \'jər-mə-ˌnāt\ *vb* **ger·mi·nat·ed; ger·mi·nat·ing** : ¹SPROUT

ger·mi·na·tion \ˌjər-mə-'nā-shən\ *n* : a beginning of development (as of a seed)

ges·tic·u·late \jes-'tik-yə-ˌlāt\ *vb* **ges·tic·u·lat·ed; ges·tic·u·lat·ing** : to make gestures especially when speaking

¹ges·ture \'jes-chər\ *n* **1** : a motion of the limbs or body that expresses an idea or a feeling **2** : something said or done that shows one's feelings ⟨a *gesture* of friendship⟩

²gesture *vb* **ges·tured; ges·tur·ing** : to make or direct with a gesture

get \get\ *vb* **got** \gät\; **got** *or* **got·ten** \'gät-n\; **get·ting** \'get-ing\ **1** : to gain possession of (as by receiving, earning, buying, or winning) ⟨*get* a present⟩ ⟨*got* new clothes⟩ **2** : ARRIVE **1** ⟨*get* home early⟩ **3** : GO **1**, MOVE ⟨*get* out⟩ ⟨*get* about on crutches⟩ **4** : BECOME **1** ⟨*get* angry⟩ **5** : ¹CATCH **7** ⟨*get* pneumonia⟩ **6** : to cause to be ⟨*get* your hair cut⟩ **7** : UNDERSTAND **1** ⟨now I've *got* it⟩ **8** : PERSUADE ⟨*get* them to lower the price⟩ — **get ahead** : to achieve success (as in business) — **get around 1** : to get the better of **2** : EVADE ⟨*get around* a tax law⟩ — **get at 1** : to reach with or as if with the hand ⟨can't *get at* the switch⟩ **2** : to turn one's attention to **3** : to try to prove or make clear ⟨what are you *getting at*?⟩ — **get away with** : to do (as something wrong) without being caught — **get back at** : to get even with — **get even** : to get revenge — **get even with** : to pay back for a real or imagined injury — **get one's goat** : to make one angry or annoyed — **get over** : to recover from — **get together 1** : to bring or come together **2** : to reach agreement — **get wind of** : to become aware of : hear about

get along *vb* **1** : to approach old age **2** : to meet one's needs ⟨*getting along* on a small income⟩ **3** : to stay friendly ⟨we *get along* well⟩

get by *vb* **1** : GET ALONG **2** **2** : to succeed with the least possible effort or accomplishment ⟨barely *got by* on the test⟩

get off *vb* **1** : START ⟨*got off* on their trip to Europe⟩ **2** : to escape punishment or harm ⟨*got off* with just a warning⟩

get out *vb* **1** : ESCAPE ⟨might not *get out* alive⟩ **2** : to become known ⟨their secret *got out*⟩

get–to·geth·er \'get-tə-ˌgeth-ər\ *n* : an informal social gathering

get up *vb* **1** : to arise from bed **2** : to rise to one's feet **3** : PREPARE, ORGANIZE ⟨*get up* a new club⟩ **4** : DRESS ⟨was *got up* as a pirate⟩

gey·ser \'gī-zər\ *n* : a spring that now and then shoots up hot water and steam

ghast·ly \'gast-lē\ *adj* **ghast·li·er; ghast·li·est 1** : HORRIBLE, SHOCKING ⟨a *ghastly* crime⟩ **2** : like a ghost : PALE ⟨a *ghastly* face⟩

ghet·to \'get-ō\ *n, pl* **ghet·tos** *or* **ghet·toes** : a part of a city in which members of a minority group live because of social, legal, or economic pressure

ghost \'gōst\ *n* : the spirit of a dead person thought of as living in an unseen world or as appearing to living people

\ə\ abut	\aú\ out	\i\ tip	\ò\ saw	\ú\ foot
\ər\ further	\ch\ chin	\ī\ life	\òi\ coin	\y\ yet
\a\ mat	\e\ pet	\j\ job	\th\ thin	\yü\ few
\ā\ take	\ē\ easy	\ng\ sing	\th\ this	\yú\ cure
\ä\ cot, cart	\g\ go	\ō\ bone	\ü\ food	\zh\ vision

ghost·ly \'gōst-lē\ *adj* **ghost·li·er; ghost-li·est** : of, relating to, or like a ghost

ghost town *n* : a town deserted because some nearby natural resource has been used up

ghoul \'gül\ *n* **1** : an evil being of legend that robs graves and feeds on corpses **2** : someone whose activities suggest those of a ghoul

¹gi·ant \'jī-ənt\ *n* **1** : an imaginary person of great size and strength **2** : a person or thing that is very large or powerful

²giant *adj* : much larger than ordinary : HUGE

gib·ber·ish \'jib-ə-rish\ *n* : confused meaningless talk

gib·bon \'gib-ən\ *n* : an ape of southeastern Asia and the East Indies that can stand on two feet and looks a little like a person

gibbon

¹gibe *or* **jibe** \'jīb\ *vb* **gibed; gib·ing** : ¹JEER

²gibe *or* **jibe** *n* : ²JEER

gib·let \'jib-lət\ *n* : an edible inner organ (as the heart or liver) of a fowl ⟨*giblet* gravy⟩

gid·dy \'gid-ē\ *adj* **gid·di·er; gid·di·est** **1** : having a feeling of whirling or spinning about : DIZZY **2** : causing dizziness ⟨a *giddy* height⟩ **3** : SILLY 3 — **gid·di·ness** *n*

gift \'gift\ *n* **1** : a special ability : TALENT ⟨a *gift* for music⟩ **2** : something given : PRESENT

gift·ed \'gif-təd\ *adj* : having great ability ⟨a *gifted* child⟩

gig \'gig\ *n* **1** : a long light boat for a ship's captain **2** : a light carriage having two wheels and pulled by a horse

gi·gan·tic \jī-'gant-ik\ *adj* : like a giant (as in size, weight, or strength)

gig·gle \'gig-əl\ *vb* **gig·gled; gig·gling** : to laugh with repeated short high sounds

Gi·la monster \ˌhē-lə-\ *n* : a large black and orange poisonous lizard of the southwestern United States

Gila monster

gild \'gild\ *vb* **gild·ed** *or* **gilt** \'gilt\; **gilding** : to cover with a thin coating of gold

¹gill \'jil\ *n* : a unit of liquid capacity equal to a quarter of a pint (about 120 milliliters)

²gill \'gil\ *n* : an organ (as of a fish) for taking oxygen from water

¹gilt \'gilt\ *n* : gold or something like gold applied to a surface

²gilt *n* : a young female hog

gim·let \'gim-lət\ *n* : a small tool for boring

¹gin \'jin\ *n* : a machine to separate seeds from cotton

²gin *vb* **ginned; gin·ning** : to separate seeds from cotton in a gin

³gin *n* : a strong alcoholic liquor flavored with juniper berries

gin·ger \'jin-jər\ *n* : a hot spice obtained from the root of a tropical plant and used to season foods (as cookies) or in medicine

ginger ale *n* : a soft drink flavored with ginger

gin·ger·bread \'jin-jər-ˌbred\ *n* : a dark cake flavored with ginger and molasses

gin·ger·ly \'jin-jər-lē\ *adv* : with great caution or care

gin·ger·snap \'jin-jər-ˌsnap\ *n* : a thin brittle cookie flavored with ginger

ging·ham \'ging-əm\ *n* : a cotton cloth in plain weave

gipsy *variant of* GYPSY

gi·raffe \jə-'raf\ *n* : a spotted mammal of Africa that has a long neck and chews the cud

giraffe

gird \'gərd\ *vb* **gird·ed** *or* **girt** \'gərt\; **gird·ing** : to encircle or fasten with or as if with a belt or cord

gird·er \'gərd-ər\ *n* : a horizontal main supporting beam ⟨a *girder* of a bridge⟩

¹**gir·dle** \'gərd-l\ *n* **1** : something (as a belt or sash) that encircles or binds **2** : a light corset worn below the waist

²**girdle** *vb* **gir·dled; gir·dling 1** : to bind with or as if with a girdle, belt, or sash : ENCIRCLE **2** : to strip a ring of bark from a tree trunk

girl \'gərl\ *n* **1** : a female child or young woman **2** : a female servant **3** : GIRL FRIEND

girl·friend *n* \'gərl-ˌfrend\ **1** : a female friend **2** : a regular female companion of a boy or man

girl·hood \'gərl-ˌhůd\ *n* : the state or time of being a girl

girl·ish \'gər-lish\ *adj* : of, relating to, or having qualities often felt to be typical of a girl — **girl·ish·ly** *adv* — **girl·ish·ness** *n*

Girl Scout *n* : a member of the Girl Scouts of the United States of America

girth \'gərth\ *n* **1** : a band put around the body of an animal to hold something (as a saddle) on its back **2** : the measure or distance around something ⟨a person of huge *girth*⟩ ⟨a tree's *girth*⟩

gist \'jist\ *n* : the main point of a matter

¹**give** \'giv\ *vb* **gave** \'gāv\; **giv·ing 1** : to hand over to be kept : PRESENT ⟨*give* a friend a present⟩ **2** : ¹PAY **1 3** : ²UTTER ⟨*give* a yell⟩ ⟨*give* a speech⟩ **4** : FURNISH, PROVIDE ⟨a candle that *gives* light⟩ **5** : to cause to have ⟨*give* someone a lot of trouble⟩ **6** : to let someone or something have ⟨*give* permission⟩ **7** : to yield slightly ⟨the mattress *gave* under our weight⟩ **8** : to yield as a product : PRODUCE ⟨2 plus 2 *gives* 4⟩

synonyms GIVE, PRESENT, and DONATE mean to hand over to someone without looking for a return. GIVE can be used of anything that is delivered in any way ⟨*give* me your coat⟩ ⟨*give* a friend a gift⟩ PRESENT suggests that something is given with some ceremony ⟨*presented* a trophy to the winner⟩ DONATE suggests giving to a charity ⟨some kind person *donated* the toys⟩

— **give way 1** : to yield oneself without control ⟨*give way* to tears⟩ **2** : to break down : COLLAPSE ⟨the bridge *gave way*⟩

²**give** *n* : the quality of being able to bend under pressure

give in *vb* **1** : ¹OFFER 2 **2** : ¹SURRENDER 1, YIELD

giv·en \'giv-ən\ *adj* **1** : being likely to have or do something ⟨*given* to quarreling⟩ **2** : decided on beforehand ⟨at a *given* time⟩

given name *n* : a first name

give up *vb* **1** : to let go : ABANDON ⟨*give up* a plan⟩ **2** : to stop trying : QUIT ⟨refused to *give up*⟩

giz·zard \'giz-ərd\ *n* : a large muscular part of the digestive tube (as of a bird) in which food is churned and ground small

gla·cial \'glā-shəl\ *adj* **1** : very cold **2** : of or relating to glaciers

gla·cier \'glā-shər\ *n* : a large body of ice moving slowly down a slope or over a wide area of land

glad \'glad\ *adj* **glad·der; glad·dest 1** : being happy and joyful **2** : bringing or causing joy ⟨*glad* news⟩ **3** : very willing ⟨I'd be *glad* to help⟩ — **glad·ly** *adv* — **glad·ness** *n*

glad·den \'glad-n\ *vb* : to make glad

glade \'glād\ *n* : a grassy open space in a forest

glad·i·a·tor \'glad-ē-ˌāt-ər\ *n* : a person taking part in a fight to the death as public entertainment for the ancient Romans

glad·i·o·lus \ˌglad-ē-'ō-ləs\ *n*, *pl* **glad·i·o·li**

gladiolus

\ə\ abut	\aů\ out	\i\ tip	\ȯ\ saw	\ů\ foot
\ər\ further	\ch\ chin	\ī\ life	\ȯi\ coin	\y\ yet
\a\ mat	\e\ pet	\j\ job	\th\ thin	\yü\ few
\ā\ take	\ē\ easy	\ng\ sing	\th\ this	\yů\ cure
\ä\ cot, cart	\g\ go	\ō\ bone	\ü\ food	\zh\ vision

\-lē, -,lī\ *or* **gladiolus** *or* **glad·i·o·lus·es** : a plant with long stiff pointed leaves and stalks of brightly colored flowers

glad·some \'glad-səm\ *adj* : giving or showing joy

glam·or·ize \'glam-ə-rīz\ *vb* **glam·or·ized; glam·or·iz·ing 1** : to make glamorous **2** : to cause to seem glamorous

glam·or·ous \'glam-ə-rəs\ *adj* : full of glamour

glam·our *or* **glam·or** \'glam-ər\ *n* **1** : appeal or attractiveness especially when it is misleading **2** : tempting or fascinating personal attraction

Word History A long time ago, back when the spelling of English was not fixed as it is for most words now, *glamour* was just another way to spell *grammar*. In those days *grammar* could mean not only the study of how language is used but also any kind of learning or study. Latin was the language used by learned people then, and the common people who did not understand Latin were often afraid of those who spoke it. For all they knew students of grammar might be wicked magicians or enchanters. In time *grammar* and *glamour* came to mean "a magic spell." After a while, as people learned to feel less fear of scholars, *grammar* lost this sense completely and *glamour* just meant "a mysterious attraction" without any real suggestion of magic. Even today, though, someone who has *glamour* may seem to cast a spell over us.

¹glance \'glans\ *vb* **glanced; glanc·ing 1** : to strike at an angle and fly off to one side **2** : to give a quick look

²glance *n* : a quick look

gland \'gland\ *n* : an organ in the body that prepares a substance to be used by the body or given off from it ⟨a saliva *gland*⟩

glan·du·lar \'glan-jə-lər\ *adj* : of or relating to glands

¹glare \'glaər, 'gleər\ *vb* **glared; glar·ing 1** : to shine with a harsh bright light **2** : to look fiercely or angrily **synonyms** see GAZE

²glare *n* **1** : a harsh bright light **2** : a fierce or angry look

glar·ing \'glaər-ing, 'gleər-\ *adj* **1** : so bright as to be harsh ⟨*glaring* sunlight⟩ **2** : ANGRY, FIERCE ⟨a *glaring* look⟩ **3** : very noticeable : OBVIOUS ⟨a *glaring* error⟩

¹glass \'glas\ *n* **1** : a hard brittle usually transparent substance commonly made from sand heated with chemicals **2** : something made of glass **3 glasses** *pl* : EYEGLASS **2 4** : the contents of a glass

²glass *vb* : to fit or protect with glass ⟨*glass* in a porch⟩

glass·blow·ing \'glas-,blō-ing\ *n* : the art of shaping a mass of melted glass by blowing air into it through a tube

glass·ful \'glas-,fül\ *n* : the amount a glass will hold

glass·ware \'glas-,waər, -,weər\ *n* : articles of glass

glassy \'glas-ē\ *adj* **glass·i·er; glass·i·est 1** : like glass (as in smoothness) **2** : not shiny or bright : DULL ⟨*glassy* eyes⟩

¹glaze \'glāz\ *vb* **glazed; glaz·ing 1** : to set glass in ⟨*glaze* a window⟩ **2** : to cover with a glassy surface ⟨*glaze* pottery⟩ **3** : to become shiny or glassy in appearance

²glaze *n* : a glassy surface or coating

gla·zier \'glā-zhər\ *n* : a person who sets glass in window frames

¹gleam \'glēm\ *n* **1** : a faint, soft, or reflected light ⟨the first *gleam* of dawn⟩ **2** : a small bright light **3** : a short or slight appearance ⟨a *gleam* of hope⟩

²gleam *vb* **1** : to shine with a soft light **2** : to give out gleams of light

synonyms GLEAM, SPARKLE, and GLITTER mean to send forth light. GLEAM is likely to suggest that the light shines through something else or is reflected or shines against a dark background ⟨the lighthouse *gleamed* through the fog⟩ SPARKLE suggests that something has several changing points of light ⟨the water *sparkled* in the sunlight⟩ GLITTER suggests a very cold sort of sparkling ⟨the jewels *glittered* brightly⟩

glean \'glēn\ *vb* **1** : to gather from a field what is left by the harvesters **2** : to gather (as information) little by little with patient effort

glee \'glē\ *n* : great joy : DELIGHT

glee club *n* : a singing group organized especially as a social activity in a school or college

glee·ful \'glē-fəl\ *adj* : full of glee

glen \'glen\ *n* : a narrow hidden valley

glib \'glib\ *adj* **glib·ber; glib·best** : speaking or spoken with careless ease and often with little regard for the truth — **glib·ly** *adv* — **glib·ness** *n*

¹glide \'glīd\ *vb* **glid·ed; glid·ing** : to move with a smooth silent motion

²glide *n* : the act or action of gliding

glid·er \'glīd-ər\ *n* **1** : an aircraft without an engine that glides on air currents **2** : a porch seat hung from a frame (as by chains)

¹glim·mer \'glim-ər\ *vb* : to shine faintly and unsteadily

²glimmer *n* : a faint unsteady light

¹glimpse \'glimps\ *vb* **glimpsed; glimps-ing** : to catch a quick view of

²glimpse *n* : a short hurried look

¹glint \'glint\ *vb* : to shine with tiny bright flashes

²glint *n* : a brief flash

glis·ten \'glis-n\ *vb* : to shine with a soft reflected light

¹glit·ter \'glit-ər\ *vb* **1** : to sparkle brightly **2** : to sparkle with light that is harsh and cold **3** : to be very bright and showy **synonyms** see GLEAM

²glitter *n* : sparkling brightness

gloat \'glōt\ *vb* : to gaze at or think about something with great satisfaction and often with mean or selfish satisfaction

glob·al \'glō-bəl\ *adj* **1** : shaped like a globe **2** : having to do with the whole earth

globe \'glōb\ *n* **1** : a round object : BALL, SPHERE **2** : EARTH 3 **3** : a round model of the earth or heavens

globe–trot·ter \'glōb-ˌträt-ər\ *n* : a person who travels widely

glob·u·lar \'gläb-yə-lər\ *adj* : shaped like a globe : SPHERICAL

glob·ule \'gläb-yül\ *n* : a small round mass ⟨fat *globules*⟩

glock·en·spiel \'gläk-ən-ˌspēl\ *n* : a porta-ble musical instru-ment consisting of a series of metal bars played with ham-mers

gloom \'glüm\ *n* **1** : partial or complete darkness **2** : a sad mood

gloomy \'glü-mē\ *adj* **gloom·i·er; gloom-i·est 1** : partly or completely dark **2** : SAD 1, BLUE **3** : causing lowness of spirits ⟨a *gloomy* story⟩ **4** : not hopeful : PESSIMISTIC ⟨the future looks *gloomy*⟩

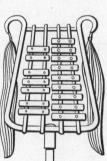

glockenspiel

glo·ri·fi·ca·tion \ˌglōr-ə-fə-'kā-shən\ *n* : the act of glorifying : the state of being glorified

glo·ri·fy \'glōr-ə-ˌfi\ *vb* **glo·ri·fied; glo·ri-fy·ing 1** : to honor or praise as divine : WORSHIP ⟨*glorify* God⟩ **2** : to give honor and praise to ⟨*glorify* a hero⟩ **3** : to show in a way that looks good ⟨*glorify* war⟩

glo·ri·ous \'glōr-ē-əs\ *adj* **1** : having or deserving glory ⟨*glorious* deeds⟩ **2** : hav-ing great beauty or splendor **3** : DELIGHT-FUL **synonyms** see SPLENDID

¹glo·ry \'glōr-ē\ *n, pl* **glo·ries 1** : praise, honor, and admiration given to a person by others **2** : something that brings honor, praise, or fame ⟨the *glories* of ancient Greece⟩ **3** : BRILLIANCE, SPLENDOR **4** : HEAVEN 2

²glory *vb* **glo·ried; glo·ry·ing** : to rejoice proudly : be proud or boastful

¹gloss \'gläs, 'glòs\ *n* **1** : brightness from a smooth surface : LUSTER, SHEEN **2** : a falsely attractive surface appearance

²gloss *vb* **1** : to give a gloss to **2** : to smooth over : explain away ⟨*gloss* over a mistake⟩

glos·sa·ry \'gläs-ə-rē, 'glòs-\ *n, pl* **glos-sa·ries** : a list of the hard or unusual words used in a book given with their meanings

glossy \'gläs-ē, 'glòs-ē\ *adj* **gloss·i·er; gloss·i·est** : smooth and shining on the surface

glove \'gləv\ *n* : a covering for the hand having a separate section for each finger

¹glow \'glō\ *vb* **1** : to shine with or as if with great heat **2** : to show strong bright color **3** : to be or to look warm and flushed (as with exercise)

²glow *n* **1** : light such as comes from something that is very hot but not flaming **2** : brightness or warmth of color ⟨a rosy *glow* in the sky⟩ **3** : a feeling of physical warmth (as from exercise) **4** : warmth of feeling

glow·er \'glaů-ər\ *vb* : to stare angrily : SCOWL

glow·worm \'glō-ˌwərm\ *n* : an insect or insect larva that gives off light

glu·cose \'glü-ˌkōs\ *n* : a sugar in plant saps and fruits that is the usual form in which carbohydrate is taken in by the ani-mal body

¹glue \'glü\ *n* : a substance used to stick things tightly together

²glue *vb* **glued; glu·ing** : to stick with or as if with glue

glu·ey \'glü-ē\ *adj* **glu·i·er; glu·i·est 1** : sticky like glue **2** : covered with glue

glum \'gləm\ *adj* **glum·mer; glum-mest 1** : ¹SULKY **2** : seeming gloomy and sad — **glum·ly** *adv* — **glum-ness** *n*

¹glut \'glət\ *vb* **glut·ted; glut·ting 1** : to make quite full : fill completely **2** : to flood with goods so that supply is greater than demand

²glut *n* : too much of something

\ə\ **abut**	\aů\ **out**	\i\ **tip**	\ò\ **saw**	\ů\ **foot**
\ər\ **further**	\ch\ **chin**	\ī\ **life**	\òi\ **coin**	\y\ **yet**
\a\ **mat**	\e\ **pet**	\j\ **job**	\th\ **thin**	\yü\ **few**
\ā\ **take**	\ē\ **easy**	\ng\ **sing**	\th\ **this**	\yů\ **cure**
\ä\ **cot, cart**	\g\ **go**	\ō\ **bone**	\ü\ **food**	\zh\ **vision**

glu·ti·nous \'glüt-n-əs\ *adj* : like glue : STICKY — **glu·ti·nous·ly** *adv*

glut·ton \'glət-n\ *n* : a person or animal that overeats — **glut·ton·ous** \'glət-n-əs\ *adj* — **glut·ton·ous·ly** *adv*

glut·tony \'glət-n-ē\ *n, pl* **glut·ton·ies** : the act or habit of eating or drinking too much

glyc·er·in *or* **glyc·er·ine** \'glis-ə-rən\ *n* : a sweet thick liquid that is found in various oils and fats and is used to moisten or dissolve things

gly·co·gen \'glī-kə-jən\ *n* : a white tasteless starchy substance that is the chief stored carbohydrate of animals

G–man \'jē-,man\ *n, pl* **G–men** \-,men\ : a special agent of the Federal Bureau of Investigation

gnarled \'närld\ *adj* : being full of knots, twisted, and rugged ⟨a *gnarled* old oak⟩

gnash \'nash\ *vb* : to strike or grind (the teeth) together (as in anger)

gnat \'nat\ *n* : a very small two-winged fly

gnaw \'nȯ\ *vb* **gnawed; gnaw·ing** : to bite so as to wear away little by little : bite or chew upon ⟨the dog *gnawed* the bone⟩

gnome \'nōm\ *n* : one of an imaginary race of dwarfs believed to live inside the earth and guard treasure

gnu \'nü, 'nyü\ *n, pl* **gnu** *or* **gnus** : a large African antelope with a head like that of an ox, curving horns, a short mane, and a tail somewhat like that of a horse

gnu

go \'gō\ *vb* **went** \'went\; **gone** \'gȯn\; **go·ing** \'gō-ing\; **goes** **1** : to pass from one place to or toward another ⟨we *went* home⟩ **2** : to move away : LEAVE ⟨the crowd has *gone*⟩ **3** : to become lost, used, or spent ⟨our money was all *gone*⟩ **4** : to continue its course or action : RUN ⟨some machines *go* by electricity⟩ **5** : to make its own special sound ⟨a kitten *goes*

like this⟩ **6** : to be suitable : MATCH ⟨the scarf *goes* with the coat⟩ **7** : to reach some state ⟨*go* to sleep⟩ ⟨the tire *went* flat⟩

¹goad \'gōd\ *n* **1** : a pointed rod used to keep an animal moving **2** : something that stirs one to action

²goad *vb* : to drive or stir with a goad

goal \'gōl, 2 also 'gül\ *n* **1** : the point at which a race or journey is to end **2** : an area to be reached safely in certain games **3** : ¹PURPOSE ⟨one's *goal* in life⟩ **4** : an object into which a ball or puck must be driven in various games in order to score **5** : a scoring of one or more points by driving a ball or puck into a goal

goal·ie \'gō-lē\ *n* : GOALKEEPER

goal·keep·er \'gōl-,kē-pər\ *n* : a player who defends a goal

goal·tend·er \'gōl-,ten-dər\ *n* : GOALKEEPER

goat \'gōt\ *n* : a horned animal that chews the cud and is related to but more lively than the sheep — **goat·like** \-,līk\ *adj*

goa·tee \gō-'tē\ *n* : a small beard trimmed to a point

goat·herd \'gōt-,hərd\ *n* : a person who tends goats

goat·skin \'gōt-,skin\ *n* : the skin of a goat or leather made from it

gob \'gäb\ *n* : ¹LUMP ⟨a *gob* of mud⟩

¹gob·ble \'gäb-əl\ *vb* **gob·bled; gob·bling** : to eat fast or greedily

²gobble *vb* **gob·bled; gob·bling** : to make the call of a turkey or a similar sound

³gobble *n* : the loud harsh call of a turkey

goatee

go–be·tween \'gō-bə-,twēn\ *n* : a person who acts as a messenger or peacemaker

gob·let \'gäb-lət\ *n* : a drinking glass with a foot and stem

gob·lin \'gäb-lən\ *n* : an ugly imaginary creature with evil or sly ways

god \'gäd\ *n* **1** *cap* : the Being considered the holy and ruling power who made and sustains all things of the universe **2** : a being believed to have more than human powers ⟨ancient peoples worshiped many *gods*⟩ **3** : a natural or artificial object worshiped as divine **4** : something believed to be the most important thing in existence ⟨money is their *god*⟩

god·child \'gäd-,chīld\ *n, pl* **god·chil-**

dren \-,chil-drən\ : a person for whom another person is sponsor at baptism

god·dess \'gäd-əs\ *n* : a female god

god·fa·ther \'gäd-,fäth-ər, -,fåth-\ *n* : a boy or man who is sponsor for a child at its baptism

god·less \'gäd-ləs\ *adj* **1** : not believing in God or a god **2** : WICKED 1, EVIL — **god·less·ness** *n*

god·like \'gäd-,līk\ *adj* : like or suitable for God or a god

god·ly \'gäd-lē\ *adj* **god·li·er; god·li·est** : DEVOUT 1, PIOUS — **god·li·ness** *n*

god·moth·er \'gäd-,məth-ər\ *n* : a girl or woman who is sponsor for a child at its baptism

god·par·ent \'gäd-,par-ənt, -,per-\ *n* : a sponsor at baptism

god·send \'gäd-,send\ *n* : some badly needed thing that comes unexpectedly

goes *present 3d sing of* GO

go–get·ter \'gō-,get-ər\ *n* : a very active and aggressive person

gog·gle \'gäg-əl\ *vb* **gog·gled; gog·gling 1** : to roll the eyes **2** : to stare with bulging or rolling eyes

gog·gle–eyed \,gäg-ə-'līd\ *adj* : having bulging or rolling eyes

gog·gles \'gäg-əlz\ *n pl* : eyeglasses worn to protect the eyes (as from dust, sun, or wind)

go·ings–on \,gō-ing-'zȯn, -'zän\ *n pl* : things that happen

goi·ter \'gȯit-ər\ *n* : a swelling on the front of the neck caused by enlargement of the thyroid gland

gold \'gōld\ *n* **1** : a soft yellow metallic chemical element used especially in coins and jewelry **2** : gold coins **3** : MONEY 3 **4** : a deep yellow

gold·en \'gōl-dən\ *adj* **1** : like, made of, or containing gold **2** : of the color of gold **3** : very good or desirable ⟨a *golden* opportunity⟩ **4** : being prosperous and happy ⟨a *golden* age⟩

gold·en·rod \'gōl-dən-,räd\ *n* : a plant with tall stiff stems topped with rows of tiny yellow flower heads on slender branches

goldenrod

golden rule *n* : a rule that one should treat others as one would want others to treat oneself

gold·finch \'gōld-,finch\ *n* **1** : a European finch with a yellow patch on each wing **2** : an American finch that looks like the canary

gold·fish \'gōld-,fish\ *n* : a small usually golden yellow or orange carp often kept in aquariums

gold·smith \'gōld-,smith\ *n* : a person who makes or deals in articles of gold

golf \'gälf, 'gȯlf\ *n* : a game played by driving a small ball (**golf ball**) with one of a set of clubs (**golf clubs**) around an outdoor course (**golf course**) and into various holes in as few strokes as possible

golf·er \'gäl-fər, 'gȯl-\ *n* : a person who plays golf

gol·ly \'gäl-ē\ *interj* — used to express surprise or annoyance

gon·do·la \'gän-də-lə, 2 and 3 also gän-'dō-lə\ *n* **1** : a long narrow boat used in the canals of Venice **2** : a freight car with no top **3** : an enclosure that hangs from a balloon and carries passengers or instruments

GONDOLA 1

gone \'gȯn\ *adj* **1** : ADVANCED 1 ⟨far *gone* in crime⟩ **2** : INFATUATED ⟨*gone* on each other⟩ **3** : ¹DEAD 1 **4** : WEAK 1, LIMP ⟨had a *gone* feeling⟩

gon·er \'gȯ-nər\ *n* : one whose case is hopeless

gong \'gäng, 'gȯng\ *n* : a metallic disk that produces a harsh ringing tone when struck

¹good \'gu̇d\ *adj* **bet·ter** \'bet-ər\; **best** \'best\ **1** : suitable for a use : SATISFACTORY ⟨a *good* light for reading⟩ **2** : being at least the amount mentioned ⟨it takes a *good* hour to get there⟩ **3** : CONSIDERABLE ⟨a *good* bit of trouble⟩ **4** : DESIRABLE, ATTRACTIVE ⟨looking for a *good* job⟩ **5** : HELPFUL, KIND ⟨how *good* of you to wait⟩ **6** : behaving well ⟨a *good* child⟩ **7** : being honest and upright **8** : ¹SOUND 5, 6, RELI-

\ə\ **abut**	\au̇\ **out**	\i\ **tip**	\ȯ\ **saw**	\u̇\ **foot**
\ər\ **further**	\ch\ **chin**	\ī\ **life**	\ȯi\ **coin**	\y\ **yet**
\a\ **mat**	\e\ **pet**	\j\ **job**	\th\ **thin**	\yu̇\ **few**
\ā\ **take**	\ē\ **easy**	\ng\ **sing**	\th\ **this**	\yü\ **cure**
\ä\ **cot, cart**	\g\ **go**	\ō\ **bone**	\ü\ **food**	\zh\ **vision**

ABLE ⟨*good* advice⟩ **9** : better than average ⟨*good* work⟩

²good *n* **1** : something good **2** : WELFARE 1, BENEFIT ⟨for your own *good*⟩ **3 goods** *pl* : WARE 2 ⟨canned *goods*⟩ **4 goods** *pl* : personal property **5 goods** *pl* : a length of cloth

¹good–bye *or* **good–by** \gud-'bī\ *interj* — used as a farewell remark

²good–bye *or* **good–by** *n* : a farewell remark ⟨said our *good-byes*⟩

Good Friday *n* : the Friday before Easter observed as the anniversary of the crucifixion of Christ

good–heart·ed \'gud-'härt-əd\ *adj* : having a kindly generous disposition — **good–heart·ed·ly** *adv* — **good–heart·ed·ness** *n*

good–hu·mored \'gud-'hyü-mərd, -'yü-\ *adj* : GOOD-NATURED — **good–hu·mored·ly** *adv* — **good–hu·mored·ness** *n*

good·ly \'gud-lē\ *adj* **good·li·er; good·li·est 1** : of pleasing appearance ⟨a *goodly* person⟩ **2** : LARGE, CONSIDERABLE ⟨a *goodly* number⟩

good–na·tured \'gud-'nā-chərd\ *adj* : having or showing a pleasant disposition — **good–na·tured·ly** *adv*

good·ness \'gud-nəs\ *n* **1** : the quality or state of being good **2** : excellence of morals and behavior

good–tem·pered \'gud-'tem-pərd\ *adj* : not easily angered or upset

good·will \'gud-'wil\ *n* **1** : kindly feelings **2** : the value of the trade a business has built up

goody \'gud-ē\ *n, pl* **good·ies** : something especially good to eat

¹goof \'güf\ *n* **1** : a stupid or silly person **2** : ²BLUNDER

²goof *vb* : to make a blunder

goofy \'gü-fē\ *adj* **goof·i·er; goof·i·est** : SILLY 1

goose \'güs\ *n, pl* **geese** \'gēs\ **1** : a water bird with webbed feet that is related to the smaller duck and the larger swan **2** : a female goose **3** : the flesh of a goose used as food **4** : a silly person

goose·ber·ry \'güs-,ber-ē, 'güz-\ *n, pl* **goose·ber·ries** : the sour berry of a thorny bush related to the currant

goose·flesh \'güs-,flesh\ *n* : a roughening of a person's skin caused by cold or fear

goose pimples *n pl* : GOOSEFLESH

go·pher \'gō-fər\ *n* **1** : a burrowing animal that is about the size of a rat and has strong claws on the forefeet and very large outside cheek pouches **2** : a striped ground squirrel of the prairies **3** : a burrowing American land tortoise

¹gore \'gōr\ *n* : shed or clotted blood

²gore *vb* **gored; gor·ing** : to pierce or wound with a horn or tusk

¹gorge \'gòrj\ *n* : a narrow passage (as between two mountains)

²gorge *vb* **gorged; gorg·ing** : to eat greedily

gor·geous \'gòr-jəs\ *adj* : very beautiful — **gor·geous·ly** *adv* — **gor·geous·ness** *n*

Word History We can trace the word *gorgeous* back to an early French word that meant "throat." A long time ago women wore a kind of headdress that surrounded the neck and head. Only the face was not covered. The French word for such a headdress was formed from the French word that meant "throat." An elegant headdress was the mark of a lady of fashion. The French word for the headdress came to mean "elegant." The English word *gorgeous* came from this French word.

go·ril·la \gə-'ril-ə\ *n* : an African ape that can stand on two feet and is the largest of the apes that look a little like people

gory \'gōr-ē\ *adj* **gor·i·er; gor·i·est** : covered with gore

gos·ling \'gäz-ling\ *n* : a young goose

gos·pel \'gäs-pəl\ *n* **1** *often cap* : the teachings of Christ and the apostls **2** : something told or accepted as being absolutely true

gos·sa·mer \'gäs-ə-mər, 'gäz-\ *adj* : very light and flimsy

¹gos·sip \'gäs-əp\ *n* **1** : a person who repeats stories about other people **2** : talk or rumors having no worth

Word History At first the word *gossip* meant "godparent." Later it came to mean "close friend" as well. Close friends, of course, share secrets. *Gossip* has come to refer to anyone, close friend

gopher 1

gorilla

or not, who is eager to share the secrets of others.

²gos·sip *vb* : to spread gossip

got *past of* GET

got·ten *past participle of* GET

¹gouge \'gaúj\ *n* **1** : a chisel with a curved blade for scooping or cutting holes **2** : a hole or groove made with or as if with a gouge

²gouge *vb* **gouged; goug·ing** : to dig out with or as if with a gouge

gou·lash \'gü-,läsh\ *n* : a beef stew made with vegetables and paprika

gourd \'górd\ *n* : the fruit of a vine (**gourd vine**) related to the pumpkin and melon

gour·met \'gúr-,mā\ *n* : a person who appreciates fine food and drink

gov·ern \'gəv-ərn\ *vb* **1** : ²RULE **2 2** : to influence the actions and conduct of : CONTROL

gov·ern·able \'gəv-ər-nə-bəl\ *adj* : possible to govern

gourds

gov·ern·ess \'gəv-ər-nəs\ *n* : a woman who teaches and trains a child especially in a private home

gov·ern·ment \'gəv-ərn-mənt, -ər-mənt\ *n* **1** : control and direction of public business (as of a city or a nation) **2** : a system of control : an established form of political rule ⟨a democratic *government*⟩ **3** : the persons making up a governing body

gov·ern·men·tal \,gəv-ərn-'ment-l, -ər-'ment-l\ *adj* : of or relating to government or the government

gov·er·nor \'gəv-ə-nər, 'gəv-ə-nər\ *n* **1** : a person who governs and especially the elected head of a state of the United States **2** : a device attached to an engine for controlling its speed

gov·er·nor·ship \'gəv-ər-nər-,ship, 'gəv-ə-nər-\ *n* **1** : the office or position of governor **2** : the term of office of a governor

gown \'gaún\ *n* **1** : a woman's dress ⟨an evening *gown*⟩ **2** : a loose robe

¹grab \'grab\ *vb* **grabbed; grab·bing** : ¹SNATCH

²grab *n* : the act or an instance of grabbing

¹grace \'grās\ *n* **1** : GOODWILL 1, FAVOR ⟨saved by the *grace* of God⟩ **2** : a short prayer at a meal **3** : pleasing and attractive behavior or quality ⟨social *graces*⟩ **4** : the condition of being in favor ⟨in their good *graces*⟩ **5** : a sense of what is proper ⟨accept criticism with good *grace*⟩ **6** : an extra note or notes in music (as a trill) added for ornamentation **7** : beauty and ease of movement

²grace *vb* **graced; grac·ing** **1** : to do credit to : HONOR **2** : to make more attractive : ADORN

grace·ful \'grās-fəl\ *adj* : showing grace or beauty in form or action — **grace·ful·ly** \-fə-lē\ *adv* — **grace·ful·ness** *n*

grace·less \'grās-ləs\ *adj* : lacking grace — **grace·less·ly** *adv* — **grace·less·ness** *n*

gra·cious \'grā-shəs\ *adj* **1** : being kind and courteous **2** : GRACEFUL — **gra·cious·ly** *adv* — **gra·cious·ness** *n*

grack·le \'grak-əl\ *n* : a large blackbird with shiny feathers that show changeable green, purple, and bronze colors

¹grade \'grād\ *n* **1** : a position in a scale of rank, quality, or order ⟨a high *grade* in the army⟩ ⟨leather of the poorer *grades*⟩ **2** : a class of things that are of the same rank, quality, or order **3** : a division of a school course representing a year's work ⟨start the fourth *grade*⟩ **4** : the group of pupils in

\ə\ abut	\aú\ out	\i\ tip	\ó\ saw	\ú\ foot
\ər\ further	\ch\ chin	\ī\ life	\ói\ coin	\y\ yet
\a\ mat	\e\ pet	\j\ job	\th\ thin	\yü\ few
\ā\ take	\ē\ easy	\ng\ sing	\th\ this	\yú\ cure
\ä\ cot, cart	\g\ go	\ō\ bone	\ü\ food	\zh\ vision

a school grade **5 grades** *pl* : the elementary school system ⟨teach in the *grades*⟩ **6** : a mark or rating especially in school ⟨a *grade* of ninety on a test⟩ **7** : the degree of slope (as of a road or railroad track) : SLOPE

²grade *vb* **grad·ed; grad·ing 1** : to arrange in grades : SORT ⟨*grade* apples⟩ **2** : to make level or evenly sloping ⟨*grade* a highway⟩ **3** : to give a grade to **4** : to assign to a grade

grade school *n* : a school including the first six or the first eight grades

grad·u·al \'graj-ə-wəl\ *adj* : moving or happening by steps or degrees — **grad·u·al·ly** *adv*

¹grad·u·ate \'graj-ə-wət\ *n* : a person who has completed the required course of study in a college or school

²grad·u·ate \'graj-ə-ˌwāt\ *vb* **grad·u·at·ed; grad·u·at·ing** : to become a graduate : finish a course of study

grad·u·a·tion \ˌgraj-ə-'wā-shən\ *n* **1** : the act or process of graduating **2** : COMMENCEMENT 2

Graeco- — see GRECO-

¹graft \'graft\ *vb* **1** : to insert a twig or bud from one plant into another plant so they are joined and grow together **2** : to join one thing to another as if by grafting ⟨*graft* skin or bone⟩ **3** : to gain money or advantage in a dishonest way — **graft·er** *n*

²graft *n* **1** : a grafted plant **2** : the act of grafting **3** : something (as skin or a bud) used in grafting **4** : something (as money or advantage) gotten in a dishonest way and especially by betraying a public trust

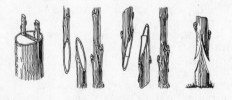

graft 1

grain \'grān\ *n* **1** : the edible seed or seedlike fruit of some grasses (as wheat or oats) or a few other plants (as buckwheat) **2** : plants that produce grain **3** : a small hard particle ⟨a *grain* of sand⟩ **4** : a tiny amount : BIT ⟨a *grain* of sense in what they were saying⟩ **5** : a unit of weight equal to 0.0648 gram **6** : the arrangement of fibers in wood — **grained** \'grānd\ *adj*

gram *or* **gramme** \'gram\ *n* : a unit of mass in the metric system equal to ¹⁄₁₀₀₀ kilogram

-gram \ˌgram\ *n suffix* : drawing : writing : record ⟨tele*gram*⟩

gram·mar \'gram-ər\ *n* **1** : the study of the classes of words and their uses and relations in sentences **2** : the study of what is good and bad to use in speaking and writing **3** : speech or writing judged according to the rules of grammar

gram·mat·i·cal \grə-'mat-i-kəl\ *adj* : of, relating to, or following the rules of grammar — **gram·mat·i·cal·ly** *adv*

gra·na·ry \'grā-nə-rē, 'gran-ə-\ *n, pl* **gra·na·ries** : a storehouse for grain

grand \'grand\ *adj* **1** : higher in rank than others : FOREMOST ⟨the *grand* prize⟩ **2** : great in size ⟨a *grand* mountain⟩ **3** : COMPREHENSIVE, INCLUSIVE ⟨a *grand* total⟩ **4** : showing wealth or high social standing **5** : IMPRESSIVE ⟨a *grand* view⟩ **6** : very good ⟨*grand* weather⟩ — **grand·ly** *adv* — **grand·ness** *n*

grand·aunt \'grand-'ant, -'ànt\ *n* : GREAT-AUNT

grand·child \'grand-ˌchīld, 'gran-\ *n, pl* **grand·chil·dren** \-ˌchil-drən\ : a child of one's son or daughter

grand·daugh·ter \'gran-ˌdòt-ər\ *n* : a daughter of one's son or daughter

gran·dee \gran-'dē\ *n* : a man of high rank especially in Spain or Portugal

gran·deur \'gran-jər\ *n* : impressive greatness (as of power or nature) ⟨the *grandeur* of these ideas⟩

grand·fa·ther \'grand-ˌfäth-ər, 'gran-, -ˌfäth-\ *n* **1** : the father of one's father or mother **2** : ANCESTOR — **grand·fa·ther·ly** *adj*

grandfather clock *n* : a tall clock standing directly on the floor

grand·ma \'gram-ˌò, 'gram-ˌä, 'gran-ˌmò, 'gran-ˌmä\ *n* : GRANDMOTHER 1

grand·moth·er \'grand-ˌməth-ər, 'gran-\ *n* **1** : the mother of one's father or mother **2** : a female ancestor — **grand·moth·er·ly** *adj*

grand·neph·ew \'grand-'nef-yü, 'gran-\ *n* : a grandson of one's brother or sister

grand·niece \'grand-'nēs, 'gran-\ *n* : a granddaughter of one's brother or sister

grandfather clock

grand·pa \'gram-ˌpȯ, 'gram-ˌpä, 'gran-\ *n* : GRANDFATHER 1

grand·par·ent \'grand-ˌpar-ənt, 'gran-, -ˌper-\ *n* : a parent of one's father or mother

grand·son \'grand-ˌsən, 'gran-\ *n* : a son of one's son or daughter

grand·stand \'grand-ˌstand, 'gran-\ *n* : the main stand (as on an athletic field) for spectators

grand·un·cle \'gran-'dəng-kəl\ *n* : GREAT-UNCLE

gran·ite \'gran-ət\ *n* : a very hard rock that is used for building and for monuments

gran·ny \'gran-ē\ *n, pl* **gran·nies** : GRANDMOTHER 1

granny knot *n* : a knot that is not very firm and is often made instead of a square knot

granny knot

gra·no·la \grə-'nō-lə\ *n* : a mixture of oats and other ingredients (as brown sugar, raisins, coconut, or nuts) that is eaten especially for breakfast

¹grant \'grant\ *vb* **1** : to agree to ⟨*grant* a request⟩ **2** : to give as a favor or right **3** : to admit (something not yet proved) to be true

²grant *n* **1** : the act of granting **2** : GIFT 2

grape \'grāp\ *n* : a juicy berry that has a smooth green or whitish to deep red, purple, or black skin and grows in clusters on a woody vine (**grapevine**)

grape·fruit \'grāp-ˌfrüt\ *n* : a large fruit with a yellow skin that is related to the orange and lemon

graph \'graf\ *n* : a diagram that by means of dots and lines shows a system of relationships between things ⟨a *graph* showing the rise and fall in temperature during a period of time⟩

-graph \ˌgraf\ *n suffix* **1** : something written **2** : instrument for making or sending records ⟨tele*graph*⟩

graph·ic \'graf-ik\ *adj* **1** : being written, drawn, printed, or engraved **2** : told or described in a clear exciting way ⟨a *graphic* account of an accident⟩ **3** : of or relating to the pictorial arts or to printing **4** : relating to or being in the form of a graph ⟨a *graphic* record of the weather⟩ — **graph·i·cal·ly** \-i-kə-lē\ *adv*

graph·ite \'graf-ˌīt\ *n* : a soft black carbon used in making lead pencils and as a lubricant

-g·ra·phy \g-rə-fē\ *n suffix, pl* **-g·ra·phies** : writing or picturing in a special way, by a special means, or of a special thing

grap·nel \'grap-nl\ *n* : a small anchor with several claws that can be used to anchor a boat or to take and keep a hold on an object (as another boat or something under water)

¹grap·ple \'grap-əl\ *n* **1** : the act of grappling or seizing **2** : a device for grappling

²grapple *vb* **grap·pled; grap·pling 1** : to seize or hold with an instrument (as a hook) **2** : to seize and struggle with another

¹grasp \'grasp\ *vb* **1** : to seize and hold with or as if with the hand : GRIP ⟨*grasp* a bat⟩ **2** : to make the motion of seizing : CLUTCH **3** : UNDERSTAND 1, COMPREHEND **synonyms** see TAKE

²grasp *n* **1** : the act of grasping : a grip of the hand **2** : ²CONTROL 1, HOLD ⟨a land in the *grasp* of a tyrant⟩ **3** : the power of seizing and holding : REACH **4** : ¹UNDERSTANDING 1, COMPREHENSION ⟨have a *grasp* of a subject⟩

grasp·ing \'gras-ping\ *adj* : GREEDY 2

grass \'gras\ *n* **1** : herbs suitable for or eaten by grazing animals **2** : any of a large natural group of green plants with jointed stems, long slender leaves, and stalks of clustered flowers **3** : GRASSLAND — **grass·like** \-ˌlīk\ *adj*

grass·hop·per \'gras-ˌhäp-ər\ *n* : a common leaping insect that feeds on plants

grasshopper

grass·land \'gras-ˌland\ *n* : land covered with herbs (as grass and clover) rather than shrubs and trees

grassy \'gras-ē\ *adj* **grass·i·er; grass·i·est** : of, like, or covered with grass

¹grate \'grāt\ *n* **1** : a frame containing parallel or crossed bars (as in a window) **2** : a frame of iron bars for holding burning fuel

²grate *vb* **grat·ed; grat·ing 1** : to break into small pieces by rubbing against something rough **2** : to grind or rub against something with a scratching noise **3** : to have a harsh effect ⟨a *grating* sound⟩

\ə\ abut	\aú\ out	\i\ tip	\ȯ\ saw	\ú\ foot
\ər\ further	\ch\ chin	\ī\ life	\ȯi\ coin	\y\ yet
\a\ mat	\e\ pet	\j\ job	\th\ thin	\yü\ few
\ā\ take	\ē\ easy	\ng\ sing	\th\ this	\yú\ cure
\ä\ cot, cart	\g\ go	\ō\ bone	\ü\ food	\zh\ vision

grate·ful \'grāt-fəl\ *adj* **1** : feeling or showing thanks **2** : providing pleasure or comfort — **grate·ful·ly** \-fə-lē\ *adv* — **grate·ful·ness** *n*

grat·er \'grāt-ər\ *n* : a device with a rough surface for grating

grat·i·fi·ca·tion \,grat-ə-fə-'kā-shən\ *n* **1** : the act of gratifying : the state of being gratified **2** : something that gratifies

grat·i·fy \'grat-ə-,fi\ *vb* **grat·i·fied; grat·i·fy·ing** : to give pleasure or satisfaction to

grat·ing \'grāt-ing\ *n* : ¹GRATE 1

grat·i·tude \'grat-ə-,tüd, -,tyüd\ *n* : the state of being grateful

¹grave \'grāv\ *n* : a hole in the ground for burying a dead body

²grave *adj* **grav·er; grav·est 1** : deserving serious thought : IMPORTANT **2** : having a serious look or way of acting — **grave·ly** *adv* — **grave·ness** *n*

grav·el \'grav-əl\ *n* : small pieces of rock and pebbles larger than grains of sand

grav·el·ly \'grav-ə-lē\ *adj* **1** : containing or made up of gravel **2** : sounding harsh or scratchy ⟨a *gravelly* voice⟩

grave·stone \'grāv-,stōn\ *n* : a monument on a grave

grave·yard \'grāv-,yärd\ *n* : CEMETERY

grav·i·tate \'grav-ə-,tāt\ *vb* **grav·i·tat·ed; grav·i·tat·ing** : to move or be drawn toward something

grav·i·ta·tion \,grav-ə-'tā-shən\ *n* **1** : a force of attraction that tends to draw particles or bodies together **2** : the act or process of gravitating

grav·i·ty \'grav-ət-ē\ *n, pl* **grav·i·ties 1** : the condition of being grave **2** : the attraction of bodies by gravitation toward the center of the earth **3** : GRAVITATION 1

gra·vy \'grā-vē\ *n, pl* **gra·vies** : a sauce made from the juice of cooked meat

¹gray *or* **grey** \'grā\ *adj* **1** : of the color gray **2** : having gray hair **3** : lacking cheer or brightness ⟨a *gray* day⟩ — **gray·ness** *n*

²gray *or* **grey** *n* **1** : something gray in color **2** : a color that is a blend of black and white

³gray *or* **grey** *vb* : to make or become gray

gray·ish \'grā-ish\ *adj* : somewhat gray

¹graze \'grāz\ *vb* **grazed; graz·ing 1** : to eat grass **2** : to supply with grass or pasture

²graze *vb* **grazed; graz·ing 1** : to rub lightly in passing : barely touch **2** : to scrape by rubbing against something

³graze *n* : a scrape or mark caused by grazing

¹grease \'grēs\ *n* **1** : a more or less solid substance obtained from animal fat by

melting **2** : oily material **3** : a thick lubricant

²grease \'grēs, 'grēz\ *vb* **greased; greas·ing 1** : to smear with grease **2** : to lubricate with grease

grease·paint \'grēs-,pānt\ *n* : actors' makeup

greasy \'grē-sē, -zē\ *adj* **greas·i·er; greas·i·est 1** : smeared with grease **2** : like or full of grease

great \'grāt\ *adj* **1** : very large in size : HUGE **2** : large in number : NUMEROUS ⟨a *great* crowd⟩ **3** : long continued ⟨a *great* while⟩ **4** : much beyond the average or ordinary ⟨a *great* weight⟩ **5** : IMPORTANT 1, DISTINGUISHED ⟨a *great* artist⟩ **6** : remarkable in knowledge or skill ⟨*great* at diving⟩ **7** : GRAND 6 — **great·ly** *adv*

great–aunt \'grāt-'ant, -'änt\ *n* : an aunt of one's father or mother

great–grand·child \'grāt-'grand-,chīld, -'gran-\ *n, pl* **great–grand·chil·dren** \-,chil-drən\ : a grandson (**great–grandson**) or granddaughter (**great–granddaughter**) of one's son or daughter

great–grand·par·ent \'grāt-'grand-,par-ənt, -'gran-, -,per-\ *n* : a grandfather (**great–grandfather**) or grandmother (**great–grandmother**) of one's father or mother

great–un·cle \'grāt-'əng-kəl\ *n* : an uncle of one's father or mother

grebe \'grēb\ *n* : any of a group of swimming and diving birds related to the loons

Gre·cian \'grē-shən\ *adj* : ²GREEK

Gre·co- *or* **Grae·co-** \'grē-kō\ *prefix* **1** : Greece : Greeks **2** : Greek and

greed \'grēd\ *n* : greedy desire (as for money or food)

greedy \'grēd-ē\ *adj* **greed·i·er; greed·i·est 1** : having a strong appetite for food or drink : very hungry **2** : trying to grab more than one needs or more than one's share — **greed·i·ly** \'grēd-l-ē\ *adv* — **greed·i·ness** \'grēd-ē-nəs\ *n*

¹Greek \'grēk\ *n* **1** : a person born or living in Greece **2** : the language of the Greeks

²Greek *adj* : of or relating to Greece, its people, or the Greek language

¹green \'grēn\ *adj* **1** : of the color green **2** : covered with green vegetation ⟨*green* fields⟩ **3** : made of green plants or of the leafy parts of plants ⟨a *green* salad⟩ **4** : not ripe ⟨*green* bananas⟩ **5** : not fully processed, treated, or seasoned ⟨*green* lumber⟩ **6** : lacking training or experience ⟨*green* troops⟩ — **green·ly** *adv* — **green·ness** *n*

²green *n* **1** : a color that ranges between blue and yellow **2 greens** *pl* : leafy parts of plants used for decoration or food **3** : a grassy plain or plot

green·ery \'grē-nə-rē\ *n, pl* **green·er·ies** : green plants or foliage

green·horn \'grēn-ˌhȯrn\ *n* : a person who is new at something

green·house \'grēn-ˌhaŭs\ *n* : a building with glass walls and roof for growing plants

greenhouse effect *n* : warming of the lower atmosphere of the earth that occurs when radiation from the sun is absorbed by the earth and then given off again and absorbed by carbon dioxide and water vapor in the atmosphere

green·ish \'grē-nish\ *adj* : somewhat green

green·ling \'grēn-ling\ *n* : any of a group of food and sport fishes of the Pacific coast

green manure *n* : a leafy crop (as of clover) plowed under to improve the soil

green thumb *n* : an unusual ability to make plants grow

green·wood \'grēn-ˌwŭd\ *n* : a forest green with leaves

greet \'grēt\ *vb* **1** : to speak to in a friendly polite way upon arrival or meeting **2** : to receive or react to in a certain way ⟨*greeted* the speech with boos⟩ **3** : to present itself to ⟨a pretty scene *greeted* them⟩ — **greet·er** *n*

greet·ing \'grēt-ing\ *n* **1** : an expression of pleasure on meeting someone **2** : SALUTATION **3** : an expression of good wishes ⟨holiday *greetings*⟩

gre·gar·i·ous \gri-'gar-ē-əs\ *adj* : tending to live together with or associate with others of one's own kind ⟨*gregarious* insects⟩ — **gre·gar·i·ous·ly** *adv* — **gre·gar·i·ous·ness** *n*

gre·nade \grə-'nād\ *n* : a small bomb designed to be thrown by hand or fired (as by a rifle)

gren·a·dier \ˌgren-ə-'diər\ *n* : a member of a European regiment formerly armed with grenades

grew *past of* GROW

grey *variant of* GRAY

grey·hound \'grā-ˌhaŭnd\ *n* : a tall swift dog with a smooth coat and good eyesight

grid \'grid\ *n* **1** : a group of electrical conductors that form a network **2** : a network of horizontal and perpendicular lines (as for locating places on a map)

grid·dle \'grid-l\ *n* : a flat surface or pan on which food is cooked

griddle cake *n* : PANCAKE

grid·iron \'grid-ˌī-ərn\ *n* **1** : a grate with parallel bars for broiling food **2** : a football field

grief \'grēf\ *n* **1** : very deep sorrow **2** : a cause of sorrow **3** : MISHAP **synonyms** see SORROW

griev·ance \'grē-vəns\ *n* **1** : a cause of uneasiness or annoyance **2** : a formal complaint

grieve \'grēv\ *vb* **grieved; griev·ing 1** : to cause grief to **2** : to feel or show grief

griev·ous \'grē-vəs\ *adj* **1** : causing suffering **2** : SERIOUS 5, GRAVE ⟨a *grievous* error⟩

¹grill \'gril\ *vb* **1** : to broil on a grill **2** : to distress with continued questioning

²grill *n* **1** : a grate on which food is broiled **2** : a dish of broiled food **3** : a simple restaurant

grille *or* **grill** \'gril\ *n* : an often ornamental arrangement of bars (as of metal) forming a barrier or screen

grim \'grim\ *adj* **grim·mer; grim·mest 1** : ¹SAVAGE 2, CRUEL **2** : harsh in appearance : STERN ⟨a *grim* look⟩ **3** : UNYIELDING 2 ⟨*grim* determination⟩ **4** : FRIGHTFUL 1 ⟨a *grim* tale⟩ — **grim·ly** *adv* — **grim·ness** *n*

¹gri·mace \'grim-əs, gri-'mās\ *n* : a twisting of the face (as in disgust)

²grim·ace *vb* **grim·aced; grim·ac·ing** : to make a grimace

grime \'grīm\ *n* : dirt rubbed into a surface

grimy \'grī-mē\ *adj* **grim·i·er; grim·i·est** : full of grime : DIRTY

¹grin \'grin\ *vb* **grinned; grin·ning** : to draw back the lips and show the teeth

²grin *n* : an act of grinning

¹grind \'grīnd\ *vb* **ground** \'graŭnd\;

greyhound

grind·ing **1** : to make or be made into meal or powder by rubbing **2** : to wear down, polish, or sharpen by friction ⟨*grind* an ax⟩ **3** : to rub together with a scraping noise ⟨*grind* the teeth⟩ **4** : to operate or produce by or as if by turning a crank

²**grind** *n* **1** : an act of grinding **2** : steady hard work

grind·stone \'grīnd-ˌstōn\ *n* : a flat round stone that turns on an axle and is used for sharpening tools and for shaping and smoothing

¹**grip** \'grip\ *vb* **gripped; grip·ping 1** : to grasp firmly **2** : to hold the interest of

²**grip** *n* **1** : a strong grasp **2** : a special handshake used by some secret societies **3** : strength in holding : POWER ⟨the *grip* of a disease⟩ **4** : ¹HANDLE **5** : a small suitcase

grippe \'grip\ *n* : a disease like or the same as influenza

gris·ly \'griz-lē\ *adj* **gris·li·er; gris·li·est** : HORRIBLE, GHASTLY ⟨a *grisly* murder⟩

grist \'grist\ *n* : grain to be ground or that is already ground

gris·tle \'gris-əl\ *n* : CARTILAGE — **gris·tli·ness** \'gris-lē-nəs\ *n* — **gris·tly** \'gris-lē\ *adj*

grist·mill \'grist-ˌmil\ *n* : a mill for grinding grain

¹**grit** \'grit\ *n* **1** : rough hard bits especially of sand **2** : strength of mind or spirit

²**grit** *vb* **grit·ted; grit·ting** : ¹GRIND 3, GRATE

grits \'grits\ *n pl* : coarsely ground hulled grain

grit·ty \'grit-ē\ *adj* **grit·ti·er; grit·ti·est 1** : containing or like grit **2** : bravely refusing to yield : PLUCKY — **grit·ti·ness** *n*

griz·zled \'griz-əld\ *adj* : streaked or mixed with gray

griz·zly \'griz-lē\ *adj* **griz·zli·er; griz·zli·est** : GRIZZLED, GRAYISH

grizzly bear *n* : a large powerful usually brownish yellow bear of western North America

¹**groan** \'grōn\ *vb* **1** : to make or express with a deep moaning sound **2** : to creak under a strain

²**groan** *n* : a low moaning sound

gro·cer \'grō-sər\ *n* : a dealer in food

gro·cery \'grōs-ə-rē, 'grōs-rē\ *n, pl* **gro·cer·ies 1 groceries** *pl* : the goods sold by a grocer **2** : a grocer's store

grog·gy \'gräg-ē\ *adj* **grog·gi·er; grog·gi·est** : weak and confused and unsteady on one's feet — **grog·gi·ly** \'gräg-ə-lē\ *adv* — **grog·gi·ness** \'gräg-ē-nəs\ *n*

Word History Once there was an English admiral who was nicknamed "Old Grog." He gave his sailors a daily ration of rum mixed with water. The sailors called this rum *grog*, after Old Grog. In time the word *grog* came to be used for any liquor. Now a person who acts weak and confused as if drunk is called *groggy*.

groin \'groin\ *n* : the fold or area where the abdomen joins the thigh

grom·met \'gräm-ət\ *n* : an eyelet of firm material to strengthen or protect an opening

¹**groom** \'grüm\ *n* **1** : a servant especially in charge of horses **2** : BRIDEGROOM

²**groom** *vb* **1** : to make neat and attractive (as by cleaning and brushing) ⟨*groom* a dog⟩ **2** : to make fit or ready ⟨*groom* a candidate for office⟩

¹**groove** \'grüv\ *n* **1** : a narrow channel made in a surface (as by cutting) **2** : ¹ROUTINE

²**groove** *vb* **grooved; groov·ing** : to form a groove in

groovy \'grü-vē\ *adj* **groov·i·er; groov·i·est** : very good : EXCELLENT

grope \'grōp\ *vb* **groped; grop·ing 1** : to feel one's way ⟨*groping* along the dark hallway⟩ **2** : to seek by or as if by feeling around ⟨*groping* for the light switch⟩ ⟨*grope* for an answer⟩

gros·beak \'grōs-ˌbēk\ *n* : a finch with a strong conical bill

¹**gross** \'grōs\ *adj* **1** : GLARING 3 ⟨a *gross* error⟩ **2** : BIG **3** : ¹THICK 3 **4** : consisting of a whole before anything is deducted ⟨*gross* earnings⟩ **5** : COARSE 4, VULGAR ⟨*gross* words⟩

²**gross** *n* : the whole before anything is deducted

³**gross** *n, pl* **gross** : twelve dozen

grosbeak

gro·tesque \grō-'tesk\ *adj* : very strange and unexpected : FANTASTIC

grot·to \'grät-ō\ *n, pl* **grot·toes 1** : ¹CAVE, CAVERN **2** : an artificial structure like a cave

¹**grouch** \'graùch\ *n* **1** : a fit of bad temper **2** : a person with a bad disposition

²**grouch** *vb* : ¹GRUMBLE 1, COMPLAIN

grouchy \'graù-chē\ *adj* **grouch·i·er; grouch·i·est** : having a bad disposition

: CANTANKEROUS — **grouch·i·ly** \-chə-lē\ *adv* — **grouch·i·ness** \-chē-nəs\ *n*

¹ground \'graund\ *n* **1** : the bottom of a body of water ⟨the boat struck *ground*⟩ **2 grounds** *pl* : SEDIMENT **1** ⟨coffee *grounds*⟩ **3** : a reason for a belief, action, or argument ⟨*ground* for complaint⟩ **4** : the surface or material upon which something is made or displayed or against which it appears **5** : the surface of the earth : SOIL **6** : an area used for some purpose ⟨a hunting *ground*⟩ **7 grounds** *pl* : the land around and belonging to a building ⟨the capitol *grounds*⟩ **8** : an area to be won or defended as if in a battle ⟨gain *ground*⟩

²ground *vb* **1** : to instruct in basic knowledge or understanding **2** : to run or cause to run aground **3** : to connect electrically with the ground **4** : to prevent (a plane or pilot) from flying

³ground *past of* GRIND

ground crew *n* : the mechanics and technicians who take care of an airplane

ground·hog \'graund-ˌhȯg, -ˌhäg\ *n* : WOODCHUCK

ground·less \'graun-dləs\ *adj* : being without foundation or reason ⟨*groundless* fears⟩

ground swell *n* : a broad deep ocean swell caused by a distant storm or earthquake

ground·work \'graun-ˌdwərk\ *n* : FOUNDATION 2

¹group \'grüp\ *n* : a number of persons or things that form one whole

²group *vb* : to arrange in or put into a group

¹grouse \'graus\ *n, pl* **grouse** : a game bird that is much like the domestic fowl

grouse

²grouse *vb* **groused; grous·ing** : ¹GRUMBLE 1, GROUCH

grove \'grōv\ *n* : a small wood or a planting of trees

grov·el \'gräv-əl, 'grəv-\ *vb* **grov·eled** *or* **grov·elled; grov·el·ing** *or* **grov·el·ling 1** : to creep or lie face down on the ground (as in fear) **2** : CRINGE — **grov·el·er** *or* **grov·el·ler** *n*

grow \'grō\ *vb* **grew** \'grü\; **grown** \'grōn\; **grow·ing 1** : to spring up and develop to maturity ⟨the wheat is *growing* well⟩ **2** : to be able to live and develop ⟨most algae *grow* in water⟩ ⟨oranges *grow* in the tropics⟩ **3** : to be related in some way by reason of growing ⟨tree branches *grown* together⟩ **4** : ¹INCREASE, EXPAND ⟨the city is *growing* rapidly⟩ **5** : BECOME 1 ⟨*grow* old⟩ **6** : to cause to grow : RAISE — **grow·er** *n*

¹growl \'graul\ *vb* **1** : to make a rumbling noise **2** : to make a growl ⟨the dog *growled*⟩ **3** : ¹GRUMBLE 1

²growl *n* **1** : a deep threatening sound (as of a dog) **2** : a grumbling or muttered complaint

grown \'grōn\ *adj* : having reached full growth : MATURE ⟨a *grown* person⟩

¹grown–up \'grō-ˌnəp\ *adj* : ¹ADULT

²grown–up *n* : an adult person

growth \'grōth\ *n* **1** : a stage or condition in growing ⟨reach one's full *growth*⟩ **2** : a process of growing ⟨*growth* of a crystal⟩ **3** : a gradual increase ⟨the *growth* of wealth⟩ **4** : something (as a covering of plants) produced by growing

grow up *vb* : to become adult

¹grub \'grəb\ *vb* **grubbed; grub·bing 1** : to root out by digging : DIG ⟨*grub* out potatoes⟩ **2** : to work hard

²grub *n* **1** : a soft thick wormlike larva (as of a beetle) **2** : FOOD 1

grub·by \'grəb-ē\ *adj* **grub·bi·er; grub·bi·est** : ¹DIRTY 1 — **grub·bi·ly** \'grəb-ə-lē\ *adv* — **grub·bi·ness** \'grəb-ē-nəs\ *n*

¹grub·stake \'grəb-ˌstāk\ *n* : supplies or funds given to a prospector in return for a promise of a share in the finds

²grubstake *vb* **grub·staked; grub·stak·ing** : to provide with a grubstake

¹grudge \'grəj\ *vb* **grudged; grudg·ing** : BEGRUDGE

²grudge *n* : a feeling of sullen dislike that lasts a long time

gru·el \'grü-əl\ *n* : a thin porridge

\ə\ abut	\au̇\ out	\i\ tip	\ȯ\ saw	\u̇\ foot
\ər\ further	\ch\ chin	\ī\ life	\ȯi\ coin	\y\ yet
\a\ mat	\e\ pet	\j\ job	\th\ thin	\yü\ few
\ā\ take	\ē\ easy	\ng\ sing	\th\ this	\yu̇\ cure
\ä\ cot, cart	\g\ go	\ō\ bone	\ü\ food	\zh\ vision

gru·el·ing or **gru·el·ling** \'grü-ə-ling\ adj : calling for much effort ⟨a grueling run⟩

grue·some \'grü-səm\ adj : HORRIBLE, GHASTLY — **grue·some·ly** adv — **grue·some·ness** n

gruff \'grəf\ adj : rough in speech or manner : HARSH — **gruff·ly** adv — **gruff·ness** n

¹**grum·ble** \'grəm-bəl\ vb **grum·bled; grum·bling** 1 : to complain or mutter in discontent 2 : ¹RUMBLE

²**grumble** n 1 : the act of grumbling 2 : ²RUMBLE

grumpy \'grəm-pē\ adj **grump·i·er; grump·i·est** : GROUCHY, CROSS — **grump·i·ly** \-pə-lē\ adv — **grump·i·ness** \-pē-nəs\ n

¹**grunt** \'grənt\ n : a deep short sound (as of a hog)

²**grunt** vb : to make a grunt — **grunt·er** n

¹**guar·an·tee** \ˌgar-ən-'tē, ˌgär-\ n 1 : GUARANTOR 2 : the act of guaranteeing 3 : a promise that something will work the way it should 4 : SECURITY 2

²**guarantee** vb **guar·an·teed; guar·an·tee·ing** 1 : to promise to answer for the debt or duty of another person ⟨guarantee that a loan will be repaid⟩ 2 : to give a guarantee on or about ⟨guarantee a car for one year⟩

guar·an·tor \ˌgar-ən-'tòr, ˌgär-\ n : a person who gives a guarantee

¹**guard** \'gärd\ n 1 : the act or duty of keeping watch 2 : a person or a body of persons that guards against injury or danger 3 : a device giving protection

²**guard** vb 1 : to protect from danger : DEFEND 2 : to watch over so as to prevent escape 3 : to keep careful watch ⟨guard against mistakes⟩

guard·ed \'gärd-əd\ adj : CAUTIOUS ⟨a guarded answer⟩

guard·house \'gärd-ˌhaús\ n 1 : a building used as a headquarters by soldiers on guard duty 2 : a military jail

guard·ian \'gärd-ē-ən\ n 1 : a person who guards or looks after something : CUSTODIAN 2 : a person who legally has the care of another person or of that person's property — **guard·ian·ship** \-ˌship\ n

guard·room \'gärd-ˌrüm, -ˌrùm\ n : a room used by a military guard while on duty

guards·man \'gärdz-mən\ n, pl **guards·men** \-mən\ : a member of a military guard

gu·ber·na·to·ri·al \ˌgü-bər-nə-'tōr-ē-əl, ˌgyü-\ adj : of or relating to a governor

gud·geon \'gəj-ən\ n : any of several small fishes

guer·ril·la or **gue·ril·la** \gə-'ril-ə\ n : a member of a band of persons carrying on warfare but not part of a regular army

¹**guess** \'ges\ vb 1 : to judge without sure knowledge ⟨guess at a person's weight⟩ 2 : to solve correctly ⟨guess a riddle⟩ 3 : THINK 2, BELIEVE — **guess·er** n

²**guess** n : an opinion formed by guessing

guess·work \'ges-ˌwərk\ n : work done or results gotten by guessing

guest \'gest\ n 1 : a person entertained in one's house or at one's table 2 : a person using a hotel, motel, inn, or restaurant **synonyms** see VISITOR

¹**guf·faw** \ˌgə-'fò\ n : a burst of loud laughter

²**guffaw** vb : to laugh noisily

guid·ance \'gīd-ns\ n : the act or process of guiding or being guided : DIRECTION

¹**guide** \'gīd\ n : someone or something (as a book) that leads, directs, or shows the right way

²**guide** vb **guid·ed; guid·ing** 1 : to show the way to ⟨guide a group on a tour⟩ 2 : DIRECT, INSTRUCT ⟨guide foreign students in English⟩

guide·book \'gīd-ˌbúk\ n : a book of information for travelers

guide·post \'gīd-ˌpōst\ n : a post with signs giving directions for travelers

guide word n : either of the terms at the head of a page of an alphabetical reference work (as a dictionary) usually showing the first and last entries on the page

guild \'gild\ n : an association of persons with similar aims or common interests

guile \'gīl\ n : sly trickery — **guile·ful** \'gīl-fəl\ adj — **guile·ful·ly** \-fə-lē\ adv

¹**guil·lo·tine** \'gil-ə-ˌtēn\ n : a machine for cutting off a person's head with a heavy blade that slides down two grooved posts

²**guillotine** vb **guil·lo·tined; guil·lo·tin·ing** : to cut off a person's head with a guillotine

guillotine

guilt \'gilt\ n 1 : the fact of having done something wrong and especially something punishable by law 2 : conduct that causes one to feel shame or regret or the feeling experienced — **guilt·less** \-ləs\ adj

guilty \'gil-tē\ *adj* **guilt·i·er; guilt·i·est 1** : having done wrong **2** : aware of, suffering from, or showing guilt ⟨feel *guilty*⟩ ⟨had a *guilty* look⟩ — **guilt·i·ly** \-tə-lē\ *adv* — **guilt·i·ness** \-tē-nəs\ *n*

guin·ea \'gin-ē\ *n* : an old British gold coin

guinea fowl *n* : an African bird related to the pheasants that has a bare head and neck and usually dark gray feathers with white speckles and is sometimes raised for food

guinea fowl

guinea pig *n* : a stocky rodent with short ears and a very short tail

guise \'gīz\ *n* **1** : a style of dress **2** : outward appearance

gui·tar \gə-'tär\ *n* : a musical instrument with six strings played by plucking or strumming

gulch \'gəlch\ *n* : RAVINE

gulf \'gəlf\ *n* **1** : a part of an ocean or sea extending into the land ⟨the *Gulf* of Mexico⟩ **2** : CHASM, ABYSS **3** : a wide separation (as in age)

gull \'gəl\ *n* : a water bird with webbed feet that is usually blue-gray or whitish in color and has a thick strong bill

gull

gul·let \'gəl-ət\ *n* : THROAT 2, ESOPHAGUS

gull·ible \'gəl-ə-bəl\ *adj* : easily tricked or misled

gul·ly \'gəl-ē\ *n, pl* **gul·lies** : a trench worn in the earth by running water

¹gulp \'gəlp\ *vb* **1** : to swallow eagerly or in large amounts at a time **2** : to keep back as if by swallowing ⟨*gulp* down a sob⟩ **3** : to catch the breath as if after a long drink

²gulp *n* **1** : the act of gulping **2** : a large swallow

¹gum \'gəm\ *n* : the flesh along the jaws at the roots of the teeth

²gum *n* **1** : a sticky substance obtained from plants that hardens on drying **2** : a substance like a plant gum (as in stickiness) **3** : CHEWING GUM

³gum *vb* **gummed; gum·ming** : to smear, stick together, or clog with or as if with gum

gum·bo \'gəm-,bō\ *n, pl* **gum·bos** : a rich soup thickened with okra pods

gum·drop \'gəm-,dräp\ *n* : a candy usually made from corn syrup and gelatin

gum·my \'gəm-ē\ *adj* **gum·mi·er; gum·mi·est 1** : consisting of, containing, or covered with gum **2** : GLUEY, STICKY

gump·tion \'gəmp-shən\ *n* : ¹SPIRIT 5, COURAGE

¹gun \'gən\ *n* **1** : CANNON 1 **2** : a portable firearm (as a rifle, shotgun, or pistol) **3** : something like a gun in shape or function **4** : a discharge of a gun (as in a salute)

²gun *vb* **gunned; gun·ning 1** : to hunt with a gun **2** : to open the throttle of quickly so as to increase speed ⟨*gun* the engine⟩

gun·boat \'gən-,bōt\ *n* : a small armed ship for use in coastal waters

gun·fire \'gən-,fir\ *n* : the firing of guns

gung ho \'gəng-'ho\ *adj* : extremely enthusiastic

Word History Many years ago a commander of a Marine Corps battalion wanted to give his troops something that would make them more cooperative and effective in working together. He knew of a Chinese organization that was referred to as "gung ho," and he decided that his troops' motto should be "gung ho." He said this means "work together" in Chinese. Actually the Chinese name is a

\ə\ abut	\aů\ out	\i\ tip	\ȯ\ saw	\ů\ foot
\ər\ further	\ch\ chin	\ī\ life	\ȯi\ coin	\y\ yet
\a\ mat	\e\ pet	\j\ job	\th\ thin	\yü\ few
\ā\ take	\ē\ easy	\ng\ sing	\th\ this	\yů\ cure
\ä\ cot, cart	\g\ go	\ō\ bone	\ü\ food	\zh\ vision

shortened form of the full name of the organization, part of which means "cooperative." The motto apparently worked for the troops, and the expression soon took on the added idea of being "enthusiastic."

gun·man \'gən-mən\ *n, pl* **gun·men** \-mən\ : a criminal armed with a gun

gun·ner \'gən-ər\ *n* : a person who operates a gun

gun·nery \'gən-ə-rē\ *n* : the use of guns

gunnery sergeant *n* : a noncommissioned officer in the Marine Corps ranking above a staff sergeant

gun·ny \'gən-ē\ *n, pl* **gun·nies** **1** : coarse jute sacking **2** : BURLAP

gun·pow·der \'gən-,paủd-ər\ *n* : an explosive powder used in guns and blasting

gun·shot \'gən-,shät\ *n* **1** : a shot from a gun **2** : the effective range of a gun

gun·wale \'gən-l\ *n* : the upper edge of a ship's side

gup·py \'gəp-ē\ *n, pl* **gup·pies** : a small tropical minnow often kept as an aquarium fish

¹gur·gle \'gər-gəl\ *vb* **gur·gled; gur·gling** **1** : to flow in a broken uneven noisy current **2** : to sound like a liquid flowing with a gurgle

²gurgle *n* : a sound of or like gurgling liquid

¹gush \'gəsh\ *vb* **1** : ¹SPOUT 1, 3 **2** : to be too affectionate or enthusiastic

²gush *n* : a sudden free pouring out

gush·er \'gəsh-ər\ *n* : an oil well with a large natural flow

gust \'gəst\ *n* **1** : a sudden brief rush of wind **2** : a sudden outburst (as of emotion)

gusty \'gəs-tē\ *adj* **gust·i·er; gust·i·est** : WINDY

¹gut \'gət\ *n* **1** : ENTRAILS — usually used in pl. **2** : the digestive tube or a part of this ⟨the small *gut*⟩ **3** : CATGUT **4** **guts** *pl* : COURAGE

²gut *vb* **gut·ted; gut·ting** **1** : to remove the entrails from **2** : to destroy the inside of ⟨fire *gutted* the building⟩

¹gut·ter \'gət-ər\ *n* **1** : a trough along the eaves of a house to catch and carry off water **2** : a low area (as at the side of a road) to carry off surface water

²gutter *vb* **1** : to flow in small streams **2**

: to have wax flowing down the sides after melting through the rim ⟨a *guttering* candle⟩

¹guy \'gī\ *n* : a rope, chain, rod, or wire (**guy wire**) attached to something to steady it

²guy *n* : PERSON 1, FELLOW

Word History Once a group of men made a plot to blow up the Houses of Parliament in London on November 5. The plot was foiled. One of the plotters, a man named Guy Fawkes, was put to death. November 5 is now celebrated in England as Guy Fawkes Day. Figures made of old clothes stuffed with straw or rags are burned. These figures are called *guys*, for Guy Fawkes. In the United States *guy* came to be used as a general term for a person.

gym \'jim\ *n* : GYMNASIUM

gym·na·si·um \jim-'nā-zē-əm\ *n* : a room or building for sports events or gymnastics

gym·nast \'jim-,nast, -nəst\ *n* : a person who is skilled in gymnastics

gym·nas·tic \jim-'nas-tik\ *adj* : of or relating to gymnastics

gym·nas·tics \jim-'nas-tiks\ *n sing or pl* : physical exercises for developing skill, strength, and control in the use of the body or a sport in which such exercises are performed

Gyp·sy *or* **Gip·sy** \'jip-sē\ *n, pl* **Gyp·sies** *or* **Gip·sies** : a member of a group of people coming from India to Europe long ago and living a wandering way of life

Word History Gypsies first came to England about four hundred years ago. The English thought that these strangers had come from Egypt. They gave them the name *Egyptian*. In time this name was shortened and altered to *Gypsy*.

gypsy moth *n* : a moth whose caterpillar has a spotty grayish look and does great damage to trees by eating the leaves

gy·rate \'jī-,rāt\ *vb* **gy·rat·ed; gy·rat·ing** : to move in a circle around a center : SPIN ⟨the child set the top *gyrating*⟩

gy·ro·scope \'jī-rə-,skōp\ *n* : a wheel mounted to spin rapidly so that its axis is free to turn in various directions

gy·ro·scop·ic \,jī-rə-'skäp-ik\ *adj* : of or relating to a gyroscope

h \'āch\ *n, pl* **h's** *or* **hs** \'ā-chəz\ *often cap*
: the eighth letter of the English alphabet
ha \'hä\ *interj* — used to show surprise or
joy
hab·it \'hab-ət\ *n* **1** : clothing worn for a
special purpose ⟨a riding *habit*⟩ **2** : usual
way of behaving ⟨the *habits* of a wild ani-
mal⟩ **3** : a way of acting or doing that has
become fixed by being repeated often **4**
: characteristic way of growing ⟨trees of
spreading *habit*⟩
hab·it·able \'hab-ət-ə-bəl\ *adj* : suitable or
fit to live in ⟨a *habitable* house⟩
hab·i·tat \'hab-ə-ˌtat\ *n* : the place where a
plant or animal grows or lives in nature
hab·i·ta·tion \ˌhab-ə-'tā-shən\ *n* **1** : the act
of living in a place **2** : a place to live
ha·bit·u·al \hə-'bich-ə-wəl\ *adj* **1** : being
or done by habit ⟨*habitual* kindness⟩ **2**
: doing or acting by force of habit ⟨*habitual* criminals⟩ **3** : ¹REGULAR — **ha·bit·u·**
al·ly \-wə-lē\ *adv* — **ha·bit·u·al·ness** *n*
ha·ci·en·da \ˌhä-sē-'en-də\ *n* **1** : a large
estate especially in a Spanish-speaking
country **2** : the main house of a hacienda
¹hack \'hak\ *vb* **1** : to cut with repeated
chopping blows **2** : to cough in a short
broken way
²hack *n* : a short broken cough
³hack *n* **1** : a horse let out for hire or used
for varied work **2** : a person who works for
pay at a routine writing job **3** : a writer who
is not very good
hack·les \'hak-əlz\ *n pl* : hairs (as on the
neck of a dog) that can be made to stand
up
hack·ney \'hak-nē\ *n, pl* **hack·neys** : a
horse for ordinary riding or driving
hack·saw \'hak-ˌsȯ\ *n* : a saw used for
cutting hard materials (as metal) that consists of a frame and a blade with small
teeth
had *past of* HAVE
had·dock \'had-ək\ *n, pl* **haddock** *or*
had·docks : a food fish related to but
smaller than the cod
hadn't \'had-nt\ : had not
haf·ni·um \'haf-nē-əm\ *n* : a gray metallic
chemical element
hag \'hag\ *n* **1** : WITCH 1 **2** : an ugly old
woman
hag·gard \'hag-ərd\ *adj* : having a hungry,
tired, or worried look

hag·gle \'hag-əl\ *vb* **hag·gled; hag·gling**
: to argue especially over a price — **hag·**
gler \'hag-lər\ *n*
ha–ha \hä-'hä\ *interj* — used to show
amusement or scorn
hai·ku \'hī-ˌkü\ *n, pl* **haiku** **1** : a Japanese
verse form without rhyme having three
lines with the first and last lines having five
syllables and the middle having seven **2**
: a poem written in this form
¹hail \'hāl\ *n* **1** : small lumps of ice and
snow that fall from the clouds sometimes
during thunderstorms **2** : ¹VOLLEY 1 ⟨a
hail of bullets⟩
²hail *vb* **1** : to fall as hail **2** : to pour down
like hail
³hail *interj* — used to show enthusiastic
approval
⁴hail *vb* **1** : GREET 1, WELCOME **2** : to call
out to ⟨*hail* a taxi⟩ — **hail from** : to come
from ⟨*hails from* Oklahoma⟩
⁵hail *n* : an exclamation of greeting, approval, or praise
hail·stone \'hāl-ˌstōn\ *n* : a lump of hail
hail·storm \'hāl-ˌstȯrm\ *n* : a storm that
brings hail
hair \'haər, 'heər\ *n* **1** : a threadlike growth
from the skin of a person or lower animal **2**
: a covering or growth of hairs (as on one's
head) **3** : something (as a growth on a
leaf) like an animal hair — **haired** \'haərd,
'heərd\ *adj* — **hair·less** \'haər-ləs, 'heər-\
adj — **hair·like** \-ˌlīk\ *adj*
hair·brush \'haər-ˌbrəsh, 'heər-\ *n* : a
brush for the hair
hair·cut \'haər-ˌkət, 'heər-\ *n* : the act, process, or result of cutting the hair
hair·do \'haər-ˌdü, 'heər-\ *n, pl* **hair·dos**
: a way of arranging a person's hair
hair·dress·er \'haər-ˌdres-ər, 'heər-\ *n*
: one who dresses or cuts hair — **hair·**
dress·ing *n*
hair·pin \'haər-ˌpin, 'heər-\ *n* : a pin in
the shape of a U for holding the hair in
place
hair–rais·ing \'haər-ˌrā-zing, 'heər-\ *adj*
: causing terror, excitement, or great surprise

\ə\ **abut**	\au̇\ **out**	\i\ **tip**	\ȯ\ **saw**	\u̇\ **foot**
\ər\ **further**	\ch\ **chin**	\ī\ **life**	\ȯi\ **coin**	\y\ **yet**
\a\ **mat**	\e\ **pet**	\j\ **job**	\th\ **thin**	\yü\ **few**
\ā\ **take**	\ē\ **easy**	\ng\ **sing**	\th\ **this**	\yu̇\ **cure**
\ä\ **cot, cart**	\g\ **go**	\ō\ **bone**	\ü\ **food**	\zh\ **vision**

hairy \'haər-ē, 'heər-ē\ *adj* **hair·i·er; hair·i·est** : covered with hair — **hair·i·ness** *n*

¹hale \'hāl\ *adj* : being strong and healthy

²hale *vb* **haled; hal·ing** : to force to go ⟨*haled* them into court⟩

¹half \'haf, 'háf\ *n, pl* **halves** \'havz, 'hávz\ **1** : one of two equal parts into which something can be divided **2** : a part of something that is about equal to the remainder ⟨*half* the distance⟩ **3** : one of a pair

²half *adj* **1** : being one of two equal parts ⟨a *half* liter of oil⟩ **2** : amounting to about a half : PARTIAL ⟨a *half* success⟩

³half *adv* **1** : to the extent of half ⟨*half* full⟩ **2** : not completely ⟨*half* persuaded⟩

half–breed \'haf-ˌbrēd, 'háf-\ *n* : a person whose parents are of different races

half brother *n* : a brother by one parent only

half·heart·ed \'haf-'härt-əd, 'háf-\ *adj* : lacking spirit or interest — **half·heart·ed·ly** *adv* — **half·heart·ed·ness** *n*

half–knot \'haf-ˌnät, 'háf-\ *n* : a knot in which two rope ends are wrapped once around each other and which is used to start other knots

half–life \'haf-ˌlīf, 'háf-\ *n, pl* **half–lives** \-ˌlīvz\ : the time required for half of the atoms of a radioactive substance to change composition

half sister *n* : a sister by one parent only

¹half·way \'haf-'wā, 'háf-\ *adv* : at or to half the distance ⟨open the door *halfway*⟩

²halfway *adj* **1** : midway between two points **2** : PARTIAL **3** ⟨*halfway* measures⟩

half–wit \'haf-ˌwit, 'háf-\ *n* : a very stupid person — **half–wit·ted** \-'wit-əd\ *adj*

hal·i·but \'hal-ə-bət\ *n, pl* **halibut** *or* **hal·i·buts** : a very large flatfish much used for food

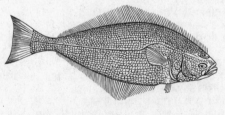

halibut

hall \'hol\ *n* **1** : a large building used for public purposes ⟨city *hall*⟩ **2** : a building (as of a college) set apart for a special purpose ⟨Science *Hall*⟩ **3** : an entrance room **4** : CORRIDOR **5** : AUDITORIUM

hal·le·lu·jah \ˌhal-ə-'lü-yə\ *interj* — used to express praise, joy, or thanks

hal·low \'hal-ō\ *vb* : to set apart for holy purposes : treat as sacred

Hal·low·een \ˌhal-ə-'wēn, ˌhäl-\ *n* : October 31 observed with parties and with the playing of tricks by children during the evening

Word History The first of November is All Saints' Day in the Christian calendar. It is celebrated in honor of all the saints in heaven. An old name for this day was *All Hallow Day*. (*Hallow* was an old word that meant "saint.") The day before *All Hallow Day* was called *All Hallow Eve* or *All Hallow Even*. (*Even* was an old word for "evening.") This name has been contracted to *Halloween*.

hal·lu·ci·na·tion \hə-ˌlüs-n-'ā-shən\ *n* : the seeing of objects or the experiencing of feelings that are not real but are usually the result of mental disorder or the effect of a drug

hal·lu·ci·no·gen \hə-'lüs-n-ə-jən\ *n* : a drug that causes hallucinations — **hal·lu·ci·no·gen·ic** \hə-ˌlüs-n-ə-'jen-ik\ *adj*

hall·way \'hol-ˌwā\ *n* : CORRIDOR

ha·lo \'hā-lō\ *n, pl* **ha·los** *or* **ha·loes 1** : a circle of light around the sun or moon caused by tiny ice crystals in the air **2** : a circle drawn or painted around the head of a person in a picture as a symbol of holiness

halo 2

¹halt \'holt\ *vb* : HESITATE 1

²halt *n* : ¹END **2** ⟨call a *halt*⟩

³halt *vb* **1** : to stop or cause to stop marching or traveling **2** : ²END ⟨*halt* work⟩

hal·ter \'hol-tər\ *n* **1** : a rope or strap for leading or tying an animal **2** : a headstall to which a halter may be attached **3** : a brief blouse usually without a back and fastened by straps around the neck

halter 2

halve \'hav, 'háv\ *vb* **halved; halv·ing 1** : to divide into halves ⟨*halve* an apple⟩ **2** : to reduce to one half ⟨*halve* a recipe⟩

halves *pl of* HALF

hal·yard \'hal-yərd\ *n* : a rope for raising or lowering a sail

ham \'ham\ *n* **1** : a buttock with the connected thigh **2** : a cut of meat consisting of a thigh usually of pork **3** : an operator of an amateur radio station

ham·burg·er \'ham-,bər-gər\ *or* **ham·burg** \-,bərg\ *n* **1** : ground beef **2** : a sandwich made of a patty of ground beef in a split bun

ham·let \'ham-lət\ *n* : a small village

¹**ham·mer** \'ham-ər\ *n* **1** : a tool consisting of a head fastened to a handle and used for pounding (as in driving nails) **2** : something like a hammer in shape or action **3** : a heavy metal ball with a flexible handle thrown for distance in a track-and-field contest (**hammer throw**)

²**hammer** *vb* **1** : to strike with a hammer **2** : to fasten (as by nailing) with a hammer **3** : to produce by or as if by means of repeated blows ⟨*hammer* out an agreement⟩

ham·mock \'ham-ək\ *n* : a swinging cot usually made of canvas or netting

¹**ham·per** \'ham-pər\ *vb* : to keep from moving or acting freely ⟨*hampered* by heavy fog⟩

²**hamper** *n* : a large basket usually with a cover ⟨a clothes *hamper*⟩

ham·ster \'ham-stər\ *n* : a stocky rodent with a short tail and large cheek pouches

hamster

¹**hand** \'hand\ *n* **1** : the end part of the arm fitted (as in humans) for handling, grasping, and holding **2** : a bodily structure (as the hind foot of an ape) like the human hand in function or form **3** : something like a hand ⟨*hands* of a clock⟩ **4** : ²CONTROL 1 ⟨in the *hands* of the enemy⟩ **5** : on one side of a problem ⟨on the one *hand* . . . on the other *hand*⟩ **6** : a pledge especially of marriage **7** : HANDWRITING **8** : ABILITY 1 ⟨tried my *hand* at painting⟩ **9** : a unit of measure equal to about ten centimeters ⟨a horse fifteen *hands* high⟩ **10** : ²HELP 1, ASSISTANCE ⟨lend a *hand*⟩ **11** : a part or share in doing something ⟨had a *hand* in the crime⟩ **12** : an outburst of applause ⟨give them a *hand*⟩ **13** : the cards held by a player in a card game **14** : a hired worker : LABORER — **at hand** : near in time or place — **by hand** : with the hands — **in hand 1** : in one's possession or control **2** : in preparation — **off one's hands** : out of one's care — **on hand 1** : in present possession **2** : ³PRESENT 1 — **out of hand** : out of control

²**hand** *vb* : to give or pass with the hand

hand·bag \'hand-,bag\ *n* : a bag used for carrying money and small personal articles

hand·ball \'hand-,bȯl\ *n* : a game played by hitting a small rubber ball against a wall or board with the hand

hand·bill \'hand-,bil\ *n* : a printed sheet (as of advertising) distributed by hand

hand·book \'hand-,bu̇k\ *n* : a book of facts usually about one subject

hand·car \'hand-,kär\ *n* : a small railroad car that is made to move by hand or by a small motor

hand·cart \'hand-,kärt\ *n* : a cart drawn or pushed by hand

¹**hand·cuff** \'hand-,kəf\ *vb* : to put handcuffs on

²**handcuff** *n* : a metal fastening that can be locked around a person's wrist

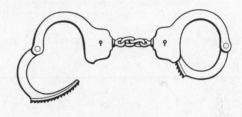

handcuffs

hand·ed \'han-dəd\ *adj* : having such or so many hands ⟨a right-*handed* child⟩

hand·ful \'hand-,fu̇l\ *n, pl* **hand·fuls** \-,fu̇lz\ *or* **hands·ful** \'handz-,fu̇l\ **1** : as much or as many as the hand will grasp **2** : a small amount or number

¹**hand·i·cap** \'han-di-,kap\ *n* **1** : a contest in which one more skilled is given a disadvantage and one less skilled is given an advantage **2** : the disadvantage or advantage given in a contest **3** : a disadvantage that makes progress or success difficult

²**handicap** *vb* **hand·i·capped; hand·i·cap·ping 1** : to give a handicap to **2** : to put at a disadvantage

hand·i·craft \'han-di-,kraft\ *n* **1** : an occupation (as weaving or pottery making) that

\ə\ **abut**	\au̇\ **out**	\i\ **tip**	\ȯ\ **saw**	\u̇\ **foot**
\ər\ **further**	\ch\ **chin**	\ī\ **life**	\ȯi\ **coin**	\y\ **yet**
\a\ **mat**	\e\ **pet**	\j\ **job**	\th\ **thin**	\yü\ **few**
\ā\ **take**	\ē\ **easy**	\ng\ **sing**	\th̲\ **this**	\yu̇\ **cure**
\ä\ **cot, cart**	\g\ **go**	\ō\ **bone**	\ü\ **food**	\zh\ **vision**

requires skill with the hands **2** : articles made by one working at handicraft

hand·i·ly \'han-də-lē\ *adv* : in a handy manner : EASILY ⟨won *handily*⟩

hand·i·work \'han-di-,wərk\ *n* : work done by the hands

hand·ker·chief \'hang-kər-chif\ *n*, *pl* **hand·ker·chiefs** \-chifs, -,chēvz\ : a small usually square piece of cloth used for wiping the face, nose, or eyes

¹**han·dle** \'han-dəl\ *n* : the part by which something (as a dish or tool) is picked up or held — **han·dled** \-dəld\ *adj*

²**handle** *vb* **han·dled; han·dling 1** : to touch, feel, hold, or move with the hand **2** : to manage with the hands **3** : to deal with (as in writing or speaking) **4** : MANAGE 1, DIRECT **5** : to deal with or act on **6** : to deal or trade in — **han·dler** \-dlər\ *n*

han·dle·bars \'han-dəl-,bärz\ *n pl* : a bar (as on a bicycle) that has a handle at each end and is used for steering

hand·made \'hand-'mād\ *adj* : made by hand rather than by machine

hand–me–downs \'hand-mē-,daunz\ *n pl* : used clothes

hand organ *n* : a small musical instrument cranked by hand

hand·out \'han-,daut\ *n* : something (as food) given to a beggar

hand·rail \'han-,drāl\ *n* : a rail to be grasped by the hand for support

hands down \'handz-'daun\ *adv* : without question : EASILY ⟨won the race *hands down*⟩

hand·shake \'hand-,shāk\ *n* : a clasping of hands by two people (as in greeting)

hand·some \'han-səm\ *adj* **hand·som·er; hand·som·est 1** : CONSIDERABLE ⟨a *handsome* sum⟩ **2** : more than enough ⟨a *handsome* tip⟩ **3** : having a pleasing and impressive appearance **synonyms** see BEAUTIFUL

hand·spring \'hand-,spring\ *n* : a feat of tumbling in which the body turns forward or backward in a full circle from a standing position and lands first on the hands and then on the feet

hand·stand \'hand-,stand\ *n* : a stunt in which a person balances the body in the air upside down supported on the hands

hand–to–hand \,han-tə-'hand\ *adj* : involving bodily contact ⟨*hand-to-hand* combat⟩

hand·work \'han-,dwərk\ *n* : work done by hand and not by machine

hand·writ·ing \'hand-,drīt-ing\ *n* : writing done by hand

handy \'han-dē\ *adj* **hand·i·er; hand·i·est 1** : within easy reach **2** : easy to use

or manage **3** : VERSATILE 2 **4** : DEXTEROUS 1 ⟨*handy* at small jobs⟩

¹**hang** \'hang\ *vb* **hung** \'həng\ *also* **hanged; hang·ing 1** : to fasten or be fastened to something without support from below : SUSPEND ⟨*hang* curtains⟩ **2** : to kill or be killed by suspending (as from a gallows) by a rope tied around the neck **3** : to fasten so as to allow free motion forward and backward ⟨*hang* a door⟩ **4** : to cause to droop ⟨*hang* one's head⟩ — **hang on to** : to hold or keep with determination

²**hang** *n* **1** : the way in which a thing hangs **2** : MEANING 1 **3** : KNACK 1 ⟨soon got the *hang* of it⟩

hang·ar \'hang-ər\ *n* : a shelter for housing and repairing aircraft

hang·er \'hang-ər\ *n* : a device on which something hangs

hang·man \'hang-mən\ *n*, *pl* **hang·men** \-mən\ : one who hangs criminals

hang·nail \'hang-,nāl\ *n* : a bit of skin hanging loose about a fingernail

hang·out \'hang-,aut\ *n* : a place where a person spends much idle time or goes often

hang·over \'hang-,ō-vər\ *n* **1** : something (as a surviving custom) that remains from what is past **2** : a sick uncomfortable state that comes from drinking too much liquor

han·ker \'hang-kər\ *vb* : to have a great desire ⟨*hankering* for candy⟩

han·som \'han-səm\ *n* : a light covered carriage that has two wheels and a driver's seat elevated at the rear

hansom

Ha·nuk·kah \'hän-ə-kə\ *n* : a Jewish holiday lasting eight days and celebrating the cleansing and second dedication of the Temple after the Syrians were driven out of Jerusalem in 165 B.C.

hap·haz·ard \hap-'haz-ərd\ *adj* : marked

by lack of plan, order, or direction — **hap·haz·ard·ly** *adv* — **hap·haz·ard·ness** *n*

hap·less \'hap-ləs\ *adj* : ¹UNFORTUNATE 1

hap·pen \'hap-ən\ *vb* **1** : to occur or come about by chance **2** : to take place **3** : to have opportunity : CHANCE ⟨I *happened* to overhear this⟩ **4** : to come especially by way of injury or harm ⟨nothing will *happen* to you⟩

hap·pen·ing \'hap-ə-ning, 'hap-ning\ *n* : something that happens

hap·py \'hap-ē\ *adj* **hap·pi·er; hap·pi·est** **1** : FORTUNATE 1, LUCKY **2** : being suitable for something ⟨a *happy* choice⟩ **3** : enjoying one's condition : CONTENT **4** : JOYFUL **5** : feeling or showing pleasure : GLAD — **hap·pi·ly** \'hap-ə-lē\ *adv* — **hap·pi·ness** \'hap-ē-nəs\ *n*

hap·py–go–lucky \ˌhap-ē-gō-'lək-ē\ *adj* : free from care

ha·rangue \hə-'rang\ *n* : a scolding speech or writing

ha·rass \hə-'ras, 'har-əs\ *vb* **1** : to worry and hinder by repeated attacks **2** : to annoy again and again — **ha·rass·ment** \-mənt\ *n*

Word History The English word *harass* came from a French word. This French word came from an earlier French word that meant "to set a dog on." The earlier word was formed from a cry used long ago by French hunters to urge their dogs to chase game.

¹har·bor \'här-bər\ *n* **1** : a place of safety and comfort : REFUGE **2** : a part of a body of water (as a sea or lake) so protected as to be a place of safety for ships : PORT

²harbor *vb* **1** : to give shelter to **2** : to have or hold in the mind ⟨*harbor* a belief⟩

¹hard \'härd\ *adj* **1** : not easily cut, pierced, or divided : not soft **2** : high in alcoholic content **3** : containing substances that prevent lathering with soap **4** : difficult to put up with : SEVERE ⟨*hard* words⟩ ⟨a *hard* winter⟩ **5** : UNFEELING 2 **6** : carried on with steady and earnest effort ⟨hours of *hard* study⟩ **7** : DILIGENT, ENERGETIC ⟨a *hard* worker⟩ **8** : sounding as in *cold* and *geese* — used of *c* and *g* **9** : difficult to do or to understand ⟨a *hard* job⟩ ⟨a *hard* book⟩

synonyms HARD, FIRM, and SOLID mean having a structure that can stand up against pressure. HARD is used of something that does not easily bend, stretch, or dent ⟨steel is *hard*⟩ FIRM is used of something that is flexible but also tough or compact ⟨*firm* muscles⟩ SOLID is used of

something that has a fixed structure and is heavy and compact all the way through ⟨a *solid* wall of bricks⟩

²hard *adv* **1** : with great effort or energy **2** : in a violent way ⟨the wind blew *hard*⟩ **3** : with pain, bitterness, or resentment ⟨took the defeat *hard*⟩

hard·en \'härd-n\ *vb* **1** : to make or become hard or harder **2** : to make or become hardy or strong **3** : to make or become stubborn or unfeeling ⟨*harden* your heart⟩ — **hard·en·er** *n*

hard·head·ed \'härd-'hed-əd\ *adj* **1** : STUBBORN 1 **2** : using or showing good judgment — **hard·head·ed·ly** *adv* — **hard·head·ed·ness** *n*

hard·heart·ed \'härd-'härt-əd\ *adj* : showing or feeling no pity : UNFEELING — **hard·heart·ed·ly** *adv* — **hard·heart·ed·ness** *n*

hard·ly \'härd-lē\ *adv* : only just : BARELY

hard·ness \'härd-nəs\ *n* : the quality or state of being hard

hard palate *n* : the bony front part of the roof of the mouth

hard·ship \'härd-ˌship\ *n* : something (as a loss or injury) that is hard to put up with

hard·tack \'härd-ˌtak\ *n* : a hard biscuit made of flour and water without salt

hard·ware \'här-ˌdwaər, -ˌdweər\ *n* : things (as utensils and tools) made of metal

¹hard·wood \'här-ˌdwúd\ *n* : the usually hard wood of a tree belonging to the group bearing broad leaves as distinguished from the wood of a tree (as a pine) with leaves that are needles

²hardwood *adj* : having or made of hardwood ⟨*hardwood* trees⟩ ⟨*hardwood* floors⟩

har·dy \'härd-ē\ *adj* **har·di·er; har·di·est** **1** : BOLD 1, BRAVE **2** : able to stand weariness, hardship, or severe weather — **hardi·ness** \'härd-ē-nəs\ *n*

hare \'haər, 'heər\ *n* : a timid animal like the related rabbit but having young that are born with the eyes open and a furry coat

hare

hare·brained \'haər-'brānd, 'heər-\ *adj* : FOOLISH

hark \'härk\ *vb* : LISTEN

¹harm \'härm\ *n* **1** : physical or mental damage : INJURY ⟨the storm did little *harm* to the sheltered beach⟩ **2** : MISCHIEF 1 ⟨meant no *harm*⟩

synonyms HARM, INJURY, and DAMAGE mean an act that causes loss or pain. HARM can be used of anything that causes suffering or loss ⟨the frost did great *harm* to the crops⟩ ⟨received no *harm* in the fight⟩ INJURY is likely to be used of something that has as a result the loss of health or success ⟨an *injury* to the eyes⟩ DAMAGE stresses the idea of loss (as of value or fitness) ⟨the fire caused much *damage* to the furniture⟩

²harm *vb* : to cause harm to : HURT

harm·ful \'härm-fəl\ *adj* : causing harm : INJURIOUS — **harm·ful·ly** \-fə-lē\ *adv* — **harm·ful·ness** *n*

harm·less \'härm-ləs\ *adj* : not harmful — **harm·less·ly** *adv* — **harm·less·ness** *n*

har·mon·ic \här-'män-ik\ *adj* : of or relating to musical harmony rather than melody or rhythm — **har·mon·i·cal·ly** \-i-kə-lē\ *adv*

har·mon·i·ca \här-'män-i-kə\ *n* : a small musical instrument held in the hand and played by the mouth : MOUTH ORGAN

har·mo·ni·ous \här-'mō-nē-əs\ *adj* **1** : having a pleasant sound : MELODIOUS **2** : combining so as to produce a pleasing result ⟨*harmonious* colors⟩ **3** : showing harmony in action or feeling — **har·mo·ni·ous·ly** *adv* — **har·mo·ni·ousness** *n*

har·mo·nize \'här-mə-ˌnīz\ *vb* **har·mo·nized; har·mo·niz·ing** **1** : to play or sing in harmony **2** : to be in harmony — **har·mo·niz·er** *n*

har·mo·ny \'här-mə-nē\ *n, pl* **har·mo·nies** **1** : the playing of musical tones together in chords **2** : a pleasing arrangement of parts **3** : AGREEMENT 1, AC-CORD

¹har·ness \'här-nəs\ *n* : an arrangement of straps and fastenings placed on an animal so as to control it or prepare it to pull a load

²harness *vb* **1** : to put a harness on **2** : to put to work : UTILIZE ⟨*harness* a waterfall⟩

¹harp \'härp\ *n* : a musical instrument

harp

consisting of a triangular frame set with strings that are plucked by the fingers

²harp *vb* : to call attention to something over and over again

¹har·poon \här-'pün\ *n* : a barbed spear used especially for hunting whales and large fish

²harpoon *vb* : to strike with a harpoon

harp·si·chord \'härp-si-ˌkord\ *n* : a keyboard instrument similar to a piano with strings that are plucked

¹har·row \'har-ō\ *n* : a heavy frame set with metal teeth or disks used in farming for breaking up and smoothing soil

²harrow *vb* **1** : to drag a harrow over (plowed ground) **2** : ²DISTRESS

har·ry \'har-ē\ *vb* **har·ried; har·ry·ing** : HARASS

harsh \'härsh\ *adj* **1** : having a coarse surface : rough to the touch **2** : disagreeable to any of the senses ⟨a *harsh* taste⟩ **3** : causing physical discomfort ⟨a *harsh* wind⟩ **4** : SEVERE 2 ⟨*harsh* punishment⟩ — **harsh·ly** *adv* — **harsh·ness** *n*

synonyms HARSH, ROUGH, and RUGGED mean not smooth or even. HARSH suggests that something has a surface or texture that is unpleasant to the touch ⟨used a *harsh* sandpaper on the floor⟩ ROUGH suggests a surface with points or ridges ⟨a *rough* piece of wood⟩ RUGGED is used of a surface on land that is very uneven ⟨a *rugged* road up the mountain⟩

¹har·vest \'här-vəst\ *n* **1** : the season when crops are gathered **2** : the gathering of a crop **3** : a ripe crop (as of grain)

²harvest *vb* : to gather in a crop

har·vest·er \'här-və-stər\ *n* **1** : one that gathers by or as if by harvesting **2** : a machine for harvesting field crops

has *present 3d sing of* HAVE

¹hash \'hash\ *vb* : to chop into small pieces

²hash *n* **1** : cooked meat and vegetables chopped together and browned **2** : ²JUMBLE

hash·ish \'hash-ˌēsh\ *n* : a drug from the hemp plant that causes hallucinations

hash over *vb* : to talk about : DISCUSS

hasn't \'haz-nt\ : has not

hasp \'hasp\ *n* : a fastener (as for a door) consisting of a hinged metal strap that fits over a staple and is held by a pin or padlock

hasp

has·sle \'has-əl\ *n* **1** : a loud angry argument **2** : a brief fight **3** : something that annoys or bothers

has·sock \\'has-ək\\ *n* : a firm stuffed cushion used as a seat or leg rest

haste \\'hāst\\ *n* **1** : quickness of motion or action : SPEED **2** : hasty action ⟨*haste* makes waste⟩

has·ten \\'hās-n\\ *vb* : to move or act fast : HURRY

hasty \\'hā-stē\\ *adj* **hast·i·er; hast·i·est 1** : done or made in a hurry ⟨a *hasty* trip⟩ **2** : made, done, or decided without proper care and thought ⟨a *hasty* decision⟩ — **hast·i·ly** \\-stə-lē\\ *adv*

hat \\'hat\\ *n* : a covering for the head having a crown and usually a brim

¹**hatch** \\'hach\\ *n* **1** : an opening in the deck of a ship or in the floor or roof of a building **2** : a small door or opening (as in an airplane) ⟨escape *hatch*⟩ **3** : the cover for a hatch

²**hatch** *vb* **1** : to produce from eggs **2** : to come forth from an egg **3** : to develop usually in secret ⟨*hatch* a plan⟩

hatch·ery \\'hach-ə-rē\\ *n, pl* **hatch·er·ies** : a place for hatching eggs ⟨a chick *hatchery*⟩

hatch·et \\'hach-ət\\ *n* : a small ax with a short handle

hatch·way \\'hach-,wā\\ *n* : a hatch usually having a ladder or stairs

¹**hate** \\'hāt\\ *n* : deep and bitter dislike

²**hate** *vb* **hat·ed; hat·ing** : to feel great dislike toward

hate·ful \\'hāt-fəl\\ *adj* **1** : full of hate **2** : causing or deserving hate ⟨a *hateful* crime⟩ — **hate·ful·ly** \\-fə-lē\\ *adv* — **hate·ful·ness** *n*

ha·tred \\'hā-trəd\\ *n* : ¹HATE

hat·ter \\'hat-ər\\ *n* : a person who makes, sells, or cleans and repairs hats

haugh·ty \\'hòt-ē\\ *adj* **haugh·ti·er; haugh·ti·est** : acting as if other people are not as good as oneself — **haugh·ti·ly** \\'hòt-l-ē\\ *adv* — **haugh·ti·ness** \\'hòt-ē-nəs\\ *n*

¹**haul** \\'hòl\\ *vb* **1** : to pull or drag with effort **2** : to transport in a vehicle

²**haul** *n* **1** : the act of hauling **2** : an amount collected ⟨a burglar's *haul*⟩ **3** : the distance or route over which a load is moved ⟨a long *haul*⟩

haunch \\'hònch\\ *n* **1** : HIP **2** : HINDQUARTER

¹**haunt** \\'hònt\\ *vb* **1** : to visit often **2** : to come to mind frequently ⟨the song *haunts* me⟩ **3** : to visit or live in as a ghost

²**haunt** *n* : a place often visited

have \\hav, həv, əv, *in sense 3 before "to" usually* 'haf\\ *vb, past & past participle* **had** \\had, həd, əd\\; *present participle* **hav·ing** \\'hav-ing\\; *present 3d sing* **has**

\\has, həz, əz\\ **1** : to hold for one's use or as property ⟨*have* the tickets⟩ **2** : to consist of ⟨April *has* 30 days⟩ **3** : to be forced or feel obliged ⟨*have* to stay⟩ **4** : to stand in some relationship to ⟨a bad person to *have* as an enemy⟩ **5** : OBTAIN, GAIN, GET ⟨the best car to be *had*⟩ **6** : to possess as a characteristic ⟨*has* red hair⟩ **7** : ²EXERCISE 1 ⟨*have* mercy⟩ **8** : to be affected by ⟨*have* a cold⟩ **9** : to be in : CARRY ON ⟨*had* a fight⟩ **10** : to hold in the mind ⟨*have* doubts⟩ **11** : to cause to be ⟨*have* your hair cut⟩ **12** : to cause to ⟨I'll *have* them call you⟩ **13** : ¹PERMIT 1 ⟨we'll *have* none of that⟩ **14** : ²TRICK ⟨we've been *had*⟩ **15** : to give birth to ⟨*had* twins⟩ **16** : to partake of ⟨*have* dinner⟩ **17** — used as a helping verb with the past participle of another verb ⟨*has* gone home⟩

ha·ven \\'hā-vən\\ *n* : a safe place

haven't \\'hav-ənt\\ : have not

hav·er·sack \\'hav-ər-,sak\\ *n* : a bag worn over one shoulder for carrying supplies

Word History The English word *haversack* came from a French word. This French word came in turn from a German word that meant "a bag for oats." This German word was a compound of a word that meant "oats" and another that meant "bag, sack."

hav·oc \\'hav-ək\\ *n* **1** : wide destruction **2** : great confusion and lack of order

Ha·wai·ian \\hə-'wä-yən\\ *n* **1** : a person born or living in Hawaii **2** : the language of the Hawaiians

¹**hawk** \\'hòk\\ *n* : a bird of prey that has a strong hooked bill and sharp curved claws and is smaller than most eagles

²**hawk** *vb* : to offer for sale by calling out in the street ⟨*hawk* fruit⟩ — **hawk·er** *n*

³**hawk** *vb* : to make a harsh coughing sound in clearing the throat

haw·ser \\'hò-zər\\ *n* : a large rope for towing or tying up a ship

haw·thorn \\'hò-,thòrn\\ *n* : any of several thorny shrubs or small trees with shiny leaves, white, pink, or red flowers, and small red fruits

hawthorn

¹**hay** \\'hā\\ *n* : any of

\\ə\\ **abut**	\\aù\\ **out**	\\i\\ **tip**	\\ò\\ **saw**	\\ù\\ **foot**
\\ər\\ **further**	\\ch\\ **chin**	\\ī\\ **life**	\\òi\\ **coin**	\\y\\ **yet**
\\a\\ **mat**	\\e\\ **pet**	\\j\\ **job**	\\th\\ **thin**	\\yü\\ **few**
\\ā\\ **take**	\\ē\\ **easy**	\\ng\\ **sing**	\\<u>th</u>\\ **this**	\\yù\\ **cure**
\\ä\\ **cot, cart**	\\g\\ **go**	\\ō\\ **bone**	\\ü\\ **food**	\\zh\\ **vision**

various herbs (as grasses) cut and dried for use as fodder

²hay *vb* : to cut plants for hay

hay fever *n* : a sickness like a cold usually affecting people sensitive to plant pollen

hay·loft \'hā-,lòft\ *n* : a loft in a barn or stable for storing hay

hay·mow \'hā-,mau\ *n* : HAYLOFT

hay·stack \'hā-,stak\ *n* : a large pile of hay stored outdoors

hay·wire \'hā-,wīr\ *adj* **1** : working badly or in an odd way ⟨the TV went *haywire*⟩ **2** : CRAZY 1, WILD

¹haz·ard \'haz-ərd\ *n* : a source of danger ⟨a fire *hazard*⟩ **synonyms** see DANGER

Word History English *hazard* was originally the name of a game of chance played with dice. The English word was taken from an early French word for this game. This French word came in turn from an Arabic word that meant "the die" (that is, "one of the dice").

²hazard *vb* : to risk something : take a chance

haz·ard·ous \'haz-ərd-əs\ *adj* : DANGEROUS — **haz·ard·ous·ly** *adv* — **haz·ard·ous·ness** *n*

¹haze \'hāz\ *vb* **hazed; haz·ing** : to make or become hazy or cloudy

²haze *n* : fine dust, smoke, or fine particles of water in the air

ha·zel \'hā-zəl\ *n* **1** : a shrub or small tree that bears an edible nut **2** : a light brown

ha·zel·nut \'hā-zəl-,nət\ *n* : the nut of a hazel

hazy \'hā-zē\ *adj* **haz·i·er; haz·i·est 1** : partly hidden by haze **2** : not clear in thought or meaning : VAGUE — **haz·i·ly** \-zə-lē\ *adv* — **haz·i·ness** \-zē-nəs\ *n*

H–bomb \'āch-,bäm\ *n* : HYDROGEN BOMB

he \hē, ē\ *pron* **1** : that male one **2** : a or the person : ²ONE 2 ⟨*he* who hesitates is lost⟩

¹head \'hed\ *n* **1** : the part of the body containing the brain, eyes, ears, nose, and mouth **2** : ¹MIND 2 ⟨a good *head* for figures⟩ **3** : control of the mind or feelings ⟨kept a level *head* in time of danger⟩ **4** : the side of a coin or medal usually thought of as the front **5** : each person among a number ⟨count *heads*⟩ **6** *pl* **head** : a unit of number ⟨thirty *head* of cattle⟩ **7** : something like a head in position or use ⟨the *head* of a bed⟩ **8** : the place a stream begins **9** : a skin stretched across one or both ends of a drum **10** : DIRECTOR, LEADER **11** : a compact mass of plant parts (as leaves or flowers) ⟨a *head* of cabbage⟩ **12**

: a part of a machine, tool, or weapon that performs the main work ⟨*head* of a spear⟩ ⟨shower *head*⟩ **13** : a place of leadership or honor ⟨*head* of one's class⟩ **14** : CLIMAX, CRISIS ⟨events came to a *head*⟩ — **out of one's head** : DELIRIOUS 1 — **over one's head** : beyond one's understanding

²head *adj* **1** : ²CHIEF 1 **2** : located at the head **3** : coming from in front ⟨*head* wind⟩

³head *vb* **1** : to provide with or form a head ⟨this cabbage *heads* early⟩ **2** : to be or put oneself at the head of ⟨*head* a revolt⟩ **3** : to be or get in front of ⟨*head* off the runaway⟩ ⟨*head* the list⟩ **4** : to go or cause to go in a certain direction ⟨let's *head* for home⟩

head·ache \'hed-,āk\ *n* **1** : pain in the head **2** : something that annoys or confuses

head·band \'hed-,band\ *n* : a band worn on or around the head

head·dress \'hed-,dres\ *n* : a covering or ornament for the head

HEADDRESS

head·ed \'hed-əd\ *adj* : having such a head or so many heads ⟨curly-*headed*⟩ ⟨a gold-*headed* cane⟩

head·first \'hed-'fərst\ *adv* : with the head in front ⟨fell *headfirst* down the stairs⟩

head·gear \'hed-,giər\ *n* : something worn on the head

head·ing \'hed-ing\ *n* : something (as a title or an address) at the top or beginning (as of a letter)

head·land \'hed-lənd\ *n* : a point of high land sticking out into the sea

head·light \'hed-,līt\ *n* : a light at the front of a vehicle

¹head·line \'hed-,līn\ *n* : a title over an article in a newspaper

²headline *vb* **head·lined; head·lin·ing** : to provide with a headline

¹head·long \'hed-'lòng\ *adv* **1** : HEADFIRST **2** : without waiting to think things through

²headlong \'hed-,lòng\ *adj* **1** : ¹RASH, IMpulsive **2** : plunging headfirst ⟨a *head-long* dive⟩

head·mas·ter \'hed-ˌmas-tər\ *n* : a man who heads the staff of a private school

head·mis·tress \'hed-ˌmis-trəs\ *n* : a woman who heads the staff of a private school

head—on \'hed-'ȯn, -'än\ *adv or adj* : with the front hitting or facing an object ⟨struck the tree *head-on*⟩

head·phone \'hed-ˌfōn\ *n* : an earphone held over the ear by a band worn on the head

head·quar·ters \'hed-ˌkwȯrt-ərz\ *n sing or pl* : a place where a leader gives out orders

head·stall \'hed-ˌstȯl\ *n* : an arrangement of straps or rope that fits around the head of an animal and forms part of a bridle or halter

head start *n* : an advantage given at the beginning (as to a school child or a runner)

head·stone \'hed-ˌstōn\ *n* : a stone at the head of a grave

head·strong \'hed-ˌstrȯng\ *adj* : always wanting one's own way

head·wait·er \'hed-'wāt-ər\ *n* : the head of the staff of a restaurant or of the dining room of a hotel

head·wa·ters \'hed-ˌwȯt-ərz, -ˌwät-\ *n pl* : the beginning and upper part of a stream

head·way \'hed-ˌwā\ *n* **1** : movement in a forward direction (as of a ship) **2** : ¹PROGRESS 2

heal \'hēl\ *vb* **1** : ²CURE 1 **2** : to return to a sound or healthy condition — **heal·er** *n*

health \'helth\ *n* **1** : the condition of being free from illness or disease **2** : the overall condition of the body ⟨in poor *health*⟩

health·ful \'helth-fəl\ *adj* : good for the health — **health·ful·ly** *adv* — **health·ful·ness** *n*

healthy \'hel-thē\ *adj* **health·i·er; health·i·est** **1** : being sound and well : not sick **2** : showing good health **3** : aiding or building up health ⟨*healthy* exercise⟩ — **health·i·ly** \-thə-lē\ *adv* — **health·i·ness** \-thē-nəs\ *n*

¹heap \'hēp\ *n* **1** : things or material piled together ⟨a rubbish *heap*⟩ ⟨a *heap* of earth⟩ **2** : a large number or amount ⟨*heaps* of fun⟩

²heap *vb* **1** : to throw or lay in a heap : make into a pile **2** : to provide in large amounts ⟨*heaped* scorn on our efforts⟩ **3** : to fill to capacity ⟨*heap* a plate with food⟩

hear \'hiər\ *vb* **heard** \'hərd\; **hear·ing** \'hiər-ing\ **1** : to take in through the ear : have the power of hearing **2** : to gain

knowledge of by hearing **3** : to listen to with care and attention ⟨*hear* both sides of a story⟩ — **hear·er** \'hir-ər\ *n*

hear·ing \'hiər-ing\ *n* **1** : the act or power of taking in sound through the ear : the sense by which a person hears **2** : EARSHOT **3** : a chance to be heard or known ⟨give both sides a fair *hearing*⟩

hearing aid *n* : an electronic device used by a partly deaf person to make sounds louder

hear·ken \'här-kən\ *vb* : LISTEN

hear·say \'hiər-ˌsā\ *n* : something heard from another : RUMOR

hearse \'hərs\ *n* : a vehicle for carrying the dead to the grave

heart \'härt\ *n* **1** : a hollow organ of the body that expands and contracts to move blood through the arteries and veins **2** : something shaped like a heart **3** : the part nearest the center **4** : the most essential part **5** : human feelings ⟨speak from the *heart*⟩ **6** : COURAGE — **BY HEART** : so as to be able to repeat from memory ⟨learn a song *by heart*⟩

heart·ache \'härt-ˌāk\ *n* : ¹SORROW 1, 2

heart·beat \'härt-ˌbēt\ *n* : a single contracting and expanding of the heart

heart·break \'härt-ˌbrāk\ *n* : very great or deep grief

heart·break·ing \'härt-ˌbrā-king\ *adj* : causing great sorrow

heart·bro·ken \'härt-ˌbrō-kən\ *adj* : overcome by sorrow

heart·en \'härt-n\ *vb* : to give new hope or courage to

heart·felt \'härt-ˌfelt\ *adj* : deeply felt : SINCERE

hearth \'härth\ *n* **1** : an area (as of brick) in front of a fireplace **2** : the floor of a fireplace **3** : ¹HOME 1

hearth·stone \'härth-ˌstōn\ *n* : a stone forming a hearth

heart·i·ly \'härt-l-ē\ *adv* **1** : with sincerity or enthusiasm ⟨I agree *heartily*⟩ **2** : COMPLETELY ⟨I am *heartily* sick of this arguing⟩

heart·less \'härt-ləs\ *adj* : UNFEELING 2, CRUEL — **heart·less·ly** *adv* — **heart·less·ness** *n*

heart·sick \'härt-ˌsik\ *adj* : DESPONDENT

heart·wood \'härt-ˌwủd\ *n* : the usually dark wood in the center of a tree

hearty \'härt-ē\ *adj* **heart·i·er; heart·i·est** **1** : friendly and enthusiastic ⟨a *hearty* wel-

\ə\ abut	\aủ\ out	\i\ tip	\ȯ\ saw	\ủ\ foot
\ər\ further	\ch\ chin	\ī\ life	\ȯi\ coin	\y\ yet
\a\ mat	\e\ pet	\j\ job	\th\ thin	\yü\ few
\ā\ take	\ē\ easy	\ng\ sing	\th\ this	\yủ\ cure
\ä\ cot, cart	\g\ go	\ō\ bone	\ü\ food	\zh\ vision

come⟩ **2** : strong, healthy, and active **3** : having a good appetite **4** : AMPLE ⟨a *hearty* meal⟩ — **heart·i·ness** *n*

¹heat \'hēt\ *vb* : to make or become warm or hot

²heat *n* **1** : a condition of being hot : WARMTH **2** : high temperature **3** : a form of energy that causes a body to rise in temperature **4** : strength of feeling or force of action **5** : a single race in a contest that includes two or more races

heat·ed \'hēt-əd\ *adj* **1** : HOT 1 **2** : ANGRY ⟨*heated* words⟩ — **heat·ed·ly** *adv*

heat·er \'hēt-ər\ *n* : a device for heating

heath \'hēth\ *n* **1** : any of a group of low, woody, and often evergreen plants that grow on poor sour wet soil **2** : a usually open level area of land on which heaths can grow

¹hea·then \'hē-thən\ *adj* **1** : of or relating to the heathen **2** : UNCIVILIZED 1

²heathen *n, pl* **hea·thens** *or* **hea·then 1** : a person who does not know about and worship the God of the Bible : PAGAN **2** : an uncivilized person

heath·er \'heth-ər\ *n* : an evergreen heath of northern and mountainous areas with pink flowers and needlelike leaves

¹heave \'hēv\ *vb* **heaved** *or* **hove** \'hōv\; **heav·ing 1** : to raise with an effort ⟨*heave* a trunk onto a truck⟩ **2** : HURL, THROW ⟨*heave* a rock⟩ **3** : to utter with an effort ⟨*heave* a sigh⟩ **4** : to rise and fall again and again ⟨the runner's chest was *heaving*⟩ **5** : to be thrown or raised up

²heave *n* **1** : an effort to lift or raise **2** : a forceful throw **3** : an upward motion (as of the chest in breathing)

heav·en \'hev-ən\ *n* **1** : SKY 1 — usually used in pl. **2** *often cap* : the dwelling place of God and of the blessed dead **3** *cap* : GOD 1 **4** : a place or condition of complete happiness

heav·en·ly \'hev-ən-lē\ *adj* **1** : of or relating to heaven or the heavens ⟨*heavenly* bodies such as the sun, moon, and stars⟩ **2** : of or relating to the Heaven of God and the blessed dead ⟨*heavenly* angels⟩ **3** : entirely delightful ⟨a *heavenly* day⟩

heav·i·ly \'hev-ə-lē\ *adv* **1** : with or as if with weight ⟨bear down *heavily*⟩ **2** : in a slow and difficult way ⟨breathing *heavily*⟩ **3** : very much ⟨*heavily* damaged⟩

heavy \'hev-ē\ *adj* **heav·i·er; heav·i·est 1** : having great weight **2** : hard to put up with ⟨a *heavy* sorrow⟩ **3** : burdened by something important or troubling ⟨a *heavy* heart⟩ **4** : having little strength or energy **5** : unusually great in amount, force, or

effect ⟨*heavy* rain⟩ ⟨*heavy* sleep⟩ — **heav·i·ness** *n*

¹He·brew \'hē-brü\ *adj* : of or relating to the Hebrew peoples or Hebrew

²Hebrew *n* **1** : a member of any of a group of peoples including the ancient Jews **2** : JEW **3** : the language of the Hebrews

hec·tic \'hek-tik\ *adj* : filled with excitement, activity, or confusion ⟨a *hectic* day of shopping⟩

hecto- *prefix* : hundred ⟨*hecto*meter⟩

hec·to·me·ter \'hek-tə-,mēt-ər\ *n* : a unit of length in the metric system equal to 100 meters

he'd \hēd, ēd\ : he had : he would

¹hedge \'hej\ *n* : a fence or boundary made up of a thick growth of shrubs or low trees

²hedge *vb* **hedged; hedg·ing 1** : to surround or protect with a hedge **2** : to avoid giving a direct or exact answer or promise

hedge·hog \'hej-,hȯg, -,häg\ *n* **1** : a European mammal that eats insects, has sharp spines mixed with the hair on its back, and is able to roll itself up into a ball **2** : PORCUPINE

hedgehog 1

hedge·row \'hej-,rō\ *n* : a hedge of shrubs or trees around a field

¹heed \'hēd\ *vb* : to pay attention to : MIND

²heed *n* : ATTENTION 1 ⟨pay *heed* to a warning⟩ — **heed·ful** *adj* — **heed·ful·ly** \-fə-lē\ *adv*

heed·less \'hēd-ləs\ *adj* : not taking heed : CARELESS — **heed·less·ly** *adv* — **heed·less·ness** *n*

¹heel \'hēl\ *n* **1** : the back part of the human foot behind the arch and below the ankle **2** : the part of an animal's limb corresponding to a person's heel **3** : one of the crusty ends of a loaf of bread **4** : a part (as of a stocking) that covers the human heel **5** : the solid part of a shoe that supports the heel **6** : a rear, low, or bottom part **7** : a mean selfish person — **heel·less** \'hēl-ləs\ *adj*

²**heel** \'heel\ *vb* : to lean to one side 〈a boat *heeling* in the wind〉

heft \'heft\ *vb* : to test the weight of by lifting

hefty \'hef-tē\ *adj* **heft·i·er; heft·i·est** : HEAVY 1

heif·er \'hef-ər\ *n* : a young cow

height \'hīt\ *n* **1** : the highest point or greatest degree 〈the *height* of stupidity〉 **2** : the distance from the bottom to the top of something standing upright **3** : distance upward

> **synonyms** HEIGHT, ALTITUDE, and ELEVATION mean distance upward. HEIGHT may be used in measuring something from bottom to top 〈a wall that is ten feet in *height*〉 ALTITUDE is used in measuring the distance above a fixed level 〈a plane flying at a low *altitude*〉 ELEVATION is used in measuring the height to which something is raised 〈the *elevation* of the tower is 300 feet〉

height·en \'hīt-n\ *vb* **1** : to make greater : INCREASE 〈*heightened* their interest〉 **2** : to make or become high or higher

heir \'aər, 'eər\ *n* **1** : a person who inherits or has the right to inherit property after the death of its owner **2** : a person who has legal claim to a title or a throne when the person holding it dies

heir·ess \'ar-əs, 'er-\ *n* : a female heir

heir·loom \'aər-ˌlüm, 'eər-\ *n* : a piece of personal property handed down in a family from one generation to another

held *past of* HOLD

he·li·cop·ter \'hel-ə-ˌkäp-tər, 'hē-lə-\ *n* : an aircraft supported in the air by horizontal propellers

he·li·port \'hel-ə-ˌpōrt, 'hē-lə-\ *n* : a place for a helicopter to land and take off

he·li·um \'hē-lē-əm\ *n* : a very light gaseous chemical element that is found in various natural gases, will not burn, and is used in balloons

hell \'hel\ *n* **1** : a place where souls are believed to survive after death **2** : a place or state of punishment for the wicked after death : the home of evil spirits **3** : a place or state of misery or wickedness — **hell·ish** \-ish\ *adj*

he'll \hēl, ēl\ : he shall : he will

hell·ben·der \'hel-ˌben-dər\ *n* : a

large American salamander that lives in water

hel·lo \hə-'lō, he-\ *interj* — used as a greeting or to express surprise

helm \'helm\ *n* **1** : a lever or wheel for steering a ship **2** : a position of control

hel·met \'hel-mət\ *n* : a protective covering for the head

¹**help** \'help\ *vb* **1** : to provide with what is useful in achieving an end : AID, ASSIST **2** : to give relief from pain or disease 〈rest *helps* a cold〉 **3** : PREVENT 1 〈a mistake that could not be *helped*〉 **4** : ¹SERVE 9 〈*help* yourself to candy〉

²**help** *n* **1** : an act or instance of helping : AID **2** : the state of being helped 〈we are beyond *help*〉 **3** : a person or a thing that helps 〈you've been a real *help*〉 **4** : a body of hired helpers

help·er \'hel-pər\ *n* **1** : one that helps **2** : a less skilled person who helps a skilled worker

help·ful \'help-fəl\ *adj* : providing help 〈a *helpful* idea〉 — **help·ful·ly** \-fə-lē\ *adv* — **help·ful·ness** *n*

help·ing \'hel-ping\ *n* : a serving of food

helping verb *n* : a verb (as *am, may*, or *will*) that is used with another verb to express person, number, mood, or tense

help·less \'help-ləs\ *adj* : not able to help or protect oneself — **help·less·ly** *adv* — **help·less·ness** *n*

hel·ter–skel·ter \ˌhel-tər-'skel-tər\ *adv* : in great disorder

¹**hem** \'hem\ *n* : a border of a cloth article made by folding back an edge and sewing it down

²**hem** *vb* **hemmed; hem·ming** **1** : to finish with or make a hem **2** : SURROUND 〈a village *hemmed* in by mountains〉

hemi- *prefix* : half 〈*hemi*sphere〉

hemi·sphere \'hem-ə-ˌsfiər\ *n* **1** : one of the halves of the earth as divided by the equator into northern and southern parts (**northern hemisphere, southern hemisphere**) or by a meridian into two parts so that one half (**eastern hemisphere**) to the east of the Atlantic ocean includes Europe, Asia, and Africa and the half (**western hemisphere**) to the west includes North and South America and surrounding waters **2** : a half of a sphere **3** : either the left or the right half of the cerebrum

hemi·spher·ic \ˌhem-ə-'sfiər-ik, -'sfer-\ *or*

hellbender

\ə\ abut	\aú\ out	\i\ tip	\ò\ saw	\ú\ foot
\ər\ further	\ch\ chin	\ī\ life	\òi\ coin	\y\ yet
\a\ mat	\e\ pet	\j\ job	\th\ thin	\yü\ few
\ā\ take	\ē\ easy	\ng\ sing	\th\ this	\yü\ cure
\ä\ cot, cart	\g\ go	\ō\ bone	\ü\ food	\zh\ vision

hemi·spher·i·cal \-'sfir-i-kəl, -'sfer-\ *adj* : of or relating to a hemisphere

hem·lock \'hem-ˌläk\ *n* **1** : a poisonous plant of the carrot family **2** : an evergreen tree of the pine family

he·mo·glo·bin \'hē-mə-ˌglō-bən\ *n* : the coloring material of the red blood cells that carry oxygen from the lungs to the tissues

hem·or·rhage \'hem-ə-rij\ *n* : great loss of blood by bleeding

hemp \'hemp\ *n* : a tall plant grown for its tough woody fiber that is used in making rope and for its flowers and leaves that yield drugs (as marijuana)

hen \'hen\ *n* **1** : a female domestic fowl **2** : a female bird

hence \'hens\ *adv* **1** : from this place **2** : from this time **3** : as a result : THEREFORE

hence·forth \'hens-ˌfōrth\ *adv* : from this time on

hench·man \'hench-mən\ *n, pl* **hench·men** \-mən\ : a trusted follower or supporter

hep·a·ti·tis \ˌhep-ə-'tīt-əs\ *n* : a disease which is caused by a virus and in which the liver is damaged and there is yellowing of the skin and fever

hepta- *or* **hept-** *prefix* : seven

hep·ta·gon \'hep-tə-ˌgän\ *n* : a closed figure having seven angles and seven sides

¹her \hər, ər\ *adj* : of or relating to her or herself ⟨*her* book⟩ ⟨*her* illness⟩

²her \ər, hər, 'hər\ *pron objective case of* SHE

¹her·ald \'her-əld\ *n* **1** : an official messenger **2** : a person who brings news or announces something

²herald *vb* : to give notice of : ANNOUNCE

he·ral·dic \he-'ral-dik\ *adj* : of or relating to heralds or heraldry

her·ald·ry \'her-əl-drē\ *n* : the art or science of tracing a person's ancestors and determining what coat of arms his or her family has the right to

herb \'ərb, 'hərb\ *n* **1** : a plant with soft stems that die down at the end of the growing season **2** : a plant or plant part used in medicine or in seasoning foods

her·biv·o·rous \ˌhər-'biv-ə-rəs, ˌər-'biv-\ *adj* : eating or living on plants

¹herd \'hərd\ *n* : a number of animals of one kind kept or living together ⟨a *herd* of cows⟩

²herd *vb* **1** : to gather or join in a herd **2** : to form into or move as a herd ⟨*herd* cattle⟩ — **herd·er** \'hərd-ər\ *n*

herds·man \'hərdz-mən\ *n, pl* **herds·men** \-mən\ : one who owns or tends a flock or herd

¹here \'hiər\ *adv* **1** : in or at this place ⟨stand *here*⟩ **2** : ¹NOW **1** ⟨*here* it is Monday again⟩ **3** : to or into this place : HITHER ⟨come *here*⟩

²here *n* : this place ⟨get away from *here*⟩

here·abouts \'hiər-ə-ˌbaůts\ *or* **here·about** \-ˌbaůt\ *adv* : near or around this place

¹here·af·ter \hiər-'af-tər\ *adv* **1** : after this **2** : in some future time or state

²hereafter *n* **1** : ²FUTURE **1** **2** : life after death

here·by \hiər-'bī\ *adv* : by means of this

he·red·i·tary \hə-'red-ə-ˌter-ē\ *adj* **1** : capable of being passed from parent to offspring ⟨*hereditary* disease⟩ **2** : received or passing from an ancestor to an heir

he·red·i·ty \hə-'red-ət-ē\ *n, pl* **he·red·i·ties** : the passing on of characteristics (as looks or ability) from parents to offspring

here·in \hiər-'in\ *adv* : in this

here·of \hiər-'əv, -'äv\ *adv* : of this

here·on \hiər-'ón, -'än\ *adv* : on this

her·e·sy \'her-ə-sē\ *n, pl* **her·e·sies** **1** : the holding of religious beliefs opposed to church doctrine : such a belief **2** : an opinion opposed to a generally accepted belief

her·e·tic \'her-ə-ˌtik\ *n* : a person who believes or teaches something opposed to accepted beliefs (as of a church)

he·ret·i·cal \hə-'ret-i-kəl\ *adj* : of, relating to, or being heresy

here·to·fore \'hiər-tə-ˌfōr\ *adv* : HITHERTO

here·up·on \'hiər-ə-ˌpón, -ˌpän\ *adv* : right after this

here·with \hiər-'with, -'with\ *adv* : with this

her·i·tage \'her-ət-ij\ *n* : something that comes to one from one's ancestors

her·mit \'hər-mət\ *n* : one who lives apart from others especially for religious reasons

he·ro \'hē-rō, 'hiər-ō\ *n, pl* **he·roes** **1** : a person admired for great deeds or fine qualities ⟨*heroes* of a nation's history⟩ **2** : one who shows great courage **3** : the chief male character in a story, play, or poem

he·ro·ic \hi-'rō-ik\ *adj* **1** : of, relating to, or like heroes **2** : COURAGEOUS, DARING ⟨a *heroic* rescue⟩ — **he·ro·i·cal·ly** \-i-kə-lē\ *adv*

her·o·in \'her-ə-wən\ *n* : a very harmful drug that comes from morphine

her·o·ine \'her-ə-wən\ *n* **1** : a woman admired for great deeds or fine qualities **2** : the chief female character in a story, poem, or play

her·o·ism \'her-ə-ˌwiz-əm\ *n* **1** : great courage especially for a noble purpose **2** : the qualities of a hero

her·on \'her-ən\ *n* : a wading bird that has long legs and a long neck and feeds on frogs, lizards, and small fish

her·ring \'her-ing\ *n* : a widely used food fish of the north Atlantic ocean

hers \'hərz\ *pron* : that which belongs to her ⟨this book is *hers*⟩ ⟨these books are *hers*⟩

her·self \hər-'self, ər-\ *pron* : her own self ⟨she hurt *herself*⟩ ⟨she *herself* did it⟩

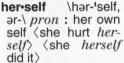

heron

he's \hēz, ēz\ : he is : he has

hes·i·tan·cy \'hez-ə-tən-sē\ *n* : the quality or state of being hesitant

hes·i·tant \'hez-ə-tənt\ *adj* : feeling or showing hesitation — **hes·i·tant·ly** *adv*

hes·i·tate \'hez-ə-,tāt\ *vb* **hes·i·tat·ed; hes·i·tat·ing** **1** : to pause because of forgetfulness or uncertainty **2** : to speak or say in a weak or broken way

hes·i·ta·tion \,hez-ə-'tā-shən\ *n* : an act or instance of hesitating

hew \'hyü\ *vb* **hewed** *or* **hewn** \'hyün\; **hew·ing** **1** : to chop down **2** : to shape by cutting with an ax

hex \'heks\ *n* : a harmful spell : JINX

hexa- *or* **hex-** *prefix* : six

hex·a·gon \'hek-sə-,gän\ *n* : a closed figure having six angles and six sides

hex·ag·o·nal \hek-'sag-ən-l\ *adj* : having six sides — **hex·ag·o·nal·ly** *adv*

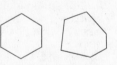

hexagons

hey \'hā\ *interj* — used to call attention or to express surprise or joy

hey·day \'hā-,dā\ *n* : the time of greatest strength, energy, or success

hi \'hī\ *interj* — used especially as a greeting

hi·ber·nate \'hī-bər-,nāt\ *vb* **hi·ber·nat·ed; hi·ber·nat·ing** : to pass the winter in a resting state — **hi·ber·na·tor** \-,nāt-ər\ *n*

hi·ber·na·tion \,hī-bər-'nā-shən\ *n* : the state of one that hibernates

¹hic·cup \'hik-,əp\ *n* : a gulping sound caused by sudden movements of muscles active in breathing

²hiccup *vb* **hic·cuped** *also* **hic·cupped;**

hic·cup·ing *also* **hic·cup·ping** : to make a hiccup

hick·o·ry \'hik-ə-rē, 'hik-rē\ *n, pl* **hick·o·ries** : a tall tree related to the walnuts that has strong tough elastic wood and bears an edible nut (**hickory nut**) in a hard shell

¹hide \'hīd\ *vb* **hid** \'hid\; **hid·den** \'hid-n\ *or* **hid; hid·ing** \'hīd-ing\ **1** : to put or stay out of sight **2** : to keep secret **3** : to screen from view ⟨clouds *hiding* the sun⟩

²hide *n* : the skin of an animal whether fresh or prepared for use

hide–and–go–seek \,hīd-n-gō-'sēk\ *n* : HIDE-AND-SEEK

hide–and–seek \,hīd-n-'sēk\ *n* : a game in which one player covers his or her eyes and after giving the others time to hide goes looking for them

hide·away \'hīd-ə-,wā\ *n* : ¹RETREAT 3, HIDEOUT

hid·eous \'hid-ē-əs\ *adj* : very ugly or disgusting : FRIGHTFUL — **hid·eous·ly** *adv* — **hid·eous·ness** *n*

hide·out \'hī-,daùt\ *n* : a secret place for hiding (as from the police)

hi·ero·glyph·ic \,hī-ə-rə-'glif-ik\ *n* : any of the symbols in the picture writing of ancient Egypt

hieroglyphic

hi–fi \'hī-'fī\ *n* **1** : HIGH FIDELITY **2** : equipment for reproduction of sound with high fidelity

hig·gle·dy–pig·gle·dy \,hig-əl-dē-'pig-əl-dē\ *adv or adj* : in confusion : TOPSY-TURVY

¹high \'hī\ *adj* **1** : extending to a great distance above the ground **2** : having a specified elevation : TALL **3** : of greater degree, size, amount, or cost than average **4** : of more than usual importance ⟨*high* crimes⟩ **5** : having great force ⟨*high* winds⟩ **6** : pitched or sounding above some other sound

synonyms HIGH, TALL, and LOFTY mean above the usual level in height. HIGH is used of height that is measured from the ground or some other standard ⟨a *high* hill⟩ TALL is used of something that is con-

\ə\ abut	\aù\ out	\i\ tip	\ȯ\ saw	\ù\ foot
\ər\ further	\ch\ chin	\ī\ life	\ȯi\ coin	\y\ yet
\a\ mat	\e\ pet	\j\ job	\th\ thin	\yü\ few
\ā\ take	\ē\ easy	\ng\ sing	\th\ this	\yù\ cure
\ä\ cot, cart	\g\ go	\ō\ bone	\ü\ food	\zh\ vision

sidered high when compared to others of the same kind ⟨a *tall* youngster for that age⟩ LOFTY is used of something that rises to a grand or impressive height ⟨*lofty* mountains⟩

²high *adv* : at or to a high place or degree
³high *n* **1** : the space overhead : SKY ⟨watched the birds on *high*⟩ **2** : a region of high barometric pressure **3** : a high point or level ⟨prices reached a new *high*⟩ **4** : the arrangement of gears in an automobile giving the highest speed of travel
high·brow \'hī-ˌbrau̇\ *n* : a person of great learning or culture
high fidelity *n* : the reproduction of sound with a high degree of accuracy
high·land \'hī-lənd\ *n* : high or hilly country
¹high·light \'hī-ˌlīt\ *n* : a very interesting event or detail ⟨*highlights* of the trip⟩
²highlight *vb* **high·light·ed; high·light·ing 1** : EMPHASIZE ⟨the speech *highlighted* the problems⟩ **2** : to be a highlight of ⟨a band concert *highlighted* the program⟩
high·ly \'hī-lē\ *adv* **1** : to a high degree : very much **2** : with much approval
high·ness \'hī-Nəs\ *n* **1** : the quality or state or being high **2** — used as a title for a person of very high rank ⟨Your Royal *Highness*⟩
high school *n* : a school usually including the ninth to twelfth or tenth to twelfth grades
high seas *n pl* : the open part of a sea or ocean
high–spir·it·ed \'hī-'spir-ət-əd\ *adj* : LIVELY 1
high–strung \'hī-'strəng\ *adj* : very sensitive or nervous ⟨a *high-strung* horse⟩
high tide *n* : the tide when the water is at its greatest height
high·way \'hī-ˌwā\ *n* : a main road
high·way·man \'hī-ˌwā-mən\ *n, pl* **high·way·men** \-mən\ : a person who robs travelers on a road
¹hike \'hīk\ *vb* **hiked; hik·ing** : to take a long walk — **hik·er** *n*
²hike *n* : a long walk especially for pleasure or exercise
hi·lar·i·ous \hil-'ar-ē-əs, -'er-\ *adj* : enjoying or causing hilarity : MERRY — **hi·lar·i·ous·ly** *adv* — **hi·lar·i·ous·ness** *n*
hi·lar·i·ty \hil-'ar-ət-ē, -'er-\ *n* : noisy fun
¹hill \'hil\ *n* **1** : a usually rounded elevation of land lower than a mountain **2** : a little heap or mound of earth **3** : several seeds or plants planted in a group rather than a row

²hill *vb* **1** : to form into a heap **2** : to draw earth around the roots or base of ⟨*hill* corn⟩
hill·bil·ly \'hil-ˌbil-ē\ *n, pl* **hill·bil·lies** : a person from a backwoods area
hill·ock \'hil-ək\ *n* : a small hill
hill·side \'hil-ˌsīd\ *n* : the part of a hill between the top and the foot
hill·top \'hil-ˌtäp\ *n* : the highest part of a hill
hilly \'hil-ē\ *adj* **hill·i·er; hill·i·est** : having many hills ⟨a *hilly* city⟩
hilt \'hilt\ *n* : a handle especially of a sword or dagger
him \him, im\ *pron objective case of* HE
him·self \him-'self, im-\ *pron* : his own self ⟨he hurt *himself*⟩ ⟨he *himself* did it⟩
hind \'hīnd\ *adj* : being at the end or back : REAR
hin·der \'hin-dər\ *vb* : to make slow or difficult ⟨snow and high winds *hindered* our trip⟩
hind·quar·ter \'hīnd-ˌkwȯrt-ər\ *n* : the back half of a complete side of a four-footed animal or carcass
hin·drance \'hin-drəns\ *n* : something that hinders : OBSTACLE
hind·sight \'hīnd-ˌsīt\ *n* : understanding of something only after it has happened
¹hinge \'hinj\ *n* : a jointed piece on which a door, gate, or lid turns or swings
²hinge *vb* **hinged; hing·ing 1** : to attach by or provide with hinges **2** : DEPEND 2
¹hint \'hint\ *n* **1** : information that helps one guess an answer or do something more easily **2** : a small amount : TRACE ⟨a *hint* of spring in the air⟩
²hint *vb* : to suggest something without plainly asking or saying it ⟨*hint* for some help⟩
hin·ter·land \'hint-ər-ˌland\ *n* : a region far from cities
hip \'hip\ *n* : the part of the body that curves out below the waist on each side
hip·pie *or* **hip·py** \'hip-ē\ *n, pl* **hippies** : a young person who acts and dresses differently from other people and often uses drugs
hip·po \'hip-ō\ *n, pl* **hip·pos** : HIPPOPOTAMUS
hip·po·pot·a·mus \ˌhip-ə-'pät-ə-məs\ *n, pl* **hip·po·pot·a·mus·es** *or* **hip·po·pot·a·mi** \-ˌmī\ : a large hoglike animal with thick hairless skin that eats plants and lives in African rivers

Word History The English word *hippopotamus* came from the Greek name for the animal. The ancient Greeks made up a good name for a beast that spends most of its time in rivers. This Greek name was a compound of two Greek words. The first meant "horse," and the second meant "river."

hire \'hīr\ *vb* **hired; hir·ing 1 :** ¹EMPLOY 2 **2 :** to get the temporary use of in return for pay ⟨*hire* a hall⟩ **3 :** to take a job ⟨*hired* out as a cook⟩

synonyms HIRE, LET, and RENT mean to use or to let another use something for a price. HIRE more often suggests that one pays to use something ⟨*hire* a machine to clean the carpet⟩ LET usually suggests that one receives money for the use of something ⟨the family has a spare room to *let*⟩ RENT stresses the payment of money in exchange for the use of property ⟨*rented* a car for 50 dollars⟩

¹his \hiz, iz\ *adj* **:** of or relating to him or himself ⟨*his* desk⟩ ⟨*his* turn⟩
²his \'hiz\ *pron* **:** that which belongs to him ⟨the book is *his*⟩ ⟨the books are *his*⟩
¹His·pan·ic \his-'pan-ik\ *adj* **:** of or relating to people of Latin American origin
²Hispanic *n* **:** a person of Latin American origin
¹hiss \'his\ *vb* **1 :** to make a hiss **2 :** to show dislike by hissing
²hiss *n* **:** a sound like a long \s\ sometimes used as a sign of dislike ⟨the *hiss* of steam⟩
his·to·ri·an \his-'tōr-ē-ən\ *n* **:** a person who studies or writes about history
his·tor·ic \his-'tȯr-ik\ *adj* **:** famous in history
his·tor·i·cal \his-'tȯr-i-kəl\ *adj* **1 :** of, relating to, or based on history ⟨*historical* writings⟩ **2 :** known to be true ⟨*historical* fact⟩ — **his·tor·i·cal·ly** *adv*
his·to·ry \'his-tə-rē\ *n, pl* **his·to·ries 1 :** a telling of events **:** STORY **2 :** a written report of past events **3 :** a branch of knowledge that records and explains past events

hippopotamus

¹hit \'hit\ *vb* **hit; hit·ting 1 :** to touch or cause to touch with force **2 :** to strike or cause to strike something aimed at ⟨the arrow *hit* the target⟩ **3 :** to affect as if by a blow ⟨*hit* hard by the loss⟩ **4 :** OCCUR 2 ⟨the storm *hit* without warning⟩ **5 :** to happen to get **:** come upon ⟨*hit* upon the right answer⟩ **6 :** to arrive at ⟨prices *hit* a new high⟩ — **hit·ter** *n*
²hit *n* **1 :** a blow striking an object aimed at ⟨score a *hit*⟩ **2 :** COLLISION **3 :** something very successful **4 :** a batted baseball that enables the batter to reach base safely
hit–and–run \,hit-n-'rən\ *adj* **:** being or involving a driver who does not stop after being in an automobile accident
¹hitch \'hich\ *vb* **1 :** to move by jerks **2 :** to fasten by or as if by a hook or knot **3 :** HITCHHIKE
²hitch *n* **1 :** a jerky movement or pull ⟨give one's pants a *hitch*⟩ **2 :** an unexpected stop or obstacle **3 :** a knot used for a temporary fastening
hitch·hike \'hich-,hīk\ *vb* **hitch·hiked; hitch·hik·ing :** to travel by getting free rides in passing vehicles — **hitch·hik·er** *n*
hith·er \'hith-ər\ *adv* **:** to this place
hith·er·to \'hith-ər-,tü\ *adv* **:** up to this time

hitch 3

HIV \,āch-,ī-'vē\ *n* **:** a virus that causes AIDS by destroying large numbers of cells that help the human body fight infection
hive \'hīv\ *n* **1 :** a container for housing honeybees **2 :** a colony of bees **3 :** a place swarming with busy people
hives \'hīvz\ *n pl* **:** an allergic condition in which the skin breaks out in large red itching patches
ho \'hō\ *interj* — used especially to attract attention
¹hoard \'hōrd\ *n* **:** a supply usually of something of value stored away or hidden
²hoard *vb* **:** to gather and store away ⟨*hoard* food during war⟩ — **hoard·er** *n*
hoar·frost \'hōr-,frȯst\ *n* **:** ¹FROST 2

\ə\ abut	\au̇\ out	\i\ tip	\ȯ\ saw	\u̇\ foot
\ər\ further	\ch\ chin	\ī\ life	\ȯi\ coin	\y\ yet
\a\ mat	\e\ pet	\j\ job	\th\ thin	\yü\ few
\ā\ take	\ē\ easy	\ng\ sing	\th\ this	\yu̇\ cure
\ä\ cot, cart	\g\ go	\ō\ bone	\ü\ food	\zh\ vision

hoarse \'hōrs\ *adj* **hoars·er; hoars·est 1** : harsh in sound **2** : having a rough voice — **hoarse·ly** *adv* — **hoarse·ness** *n*

hoary \'hōr-ē\ *adj* **hoar·i·er; hoar·i·est** : gray or white with age

¹hoax \'hōks\ *vb* : to trick into thinking something is true or real when it isn't

²hoax *n* **1** : an act meant to fool or deceive **2** : something false passed off as real

¹hob·ble \'häb-əl\ *vb* **hob·bled; hob·bling 1** : to walk with difficulty : LIMP **2** : to tie the legs of to make movement difficult

²hobble *n* **1** : a limping walk **2** : something used to hobble an animal

hob·by \'häb-ē\ *n, pl* **hob·bies** : an interest or activity engaged in for pleasure

hob·by·horse \'häb-ē-,hòrs\ *n* **1** : a stick with a horse's head on which children pretend to ride **2** : ROCKING HORSE

hob·gob·lin \'häb-,gäb-lən\ *n* **1** : a mischievous elf **2** : BOGEY 2

hob·nail \'häb-,nāl\ *n* : a short nail with a large head driven into soles of heavy shoes to protect against wear — **hob·nailed** \-,nāld\ *adj*

ho·bo \'hō-bō\ *n, pl* **ho·boes** : ¹VAGRANT

hock·ey \'häk-ē\ *n* : a game played on ice or in a field by two teams who try to drive a puck or ball through a goal by hitting it with a stick

hod 1

hod \'häd\ *n* **1** : a wooden tray or trough that has a long handle and is used to carry mortar or bricks **2** : a bucket for holding or carrying coal

hodge·podge \'häj-,päj\ *n* : a disorderly mixture

¹hoe \'hō\ *n* : a tool with a long handle and a thin flat blade used for weeding and cultivating

²hoe *vb* **hoed; hoe·ing** : to weed or loosen the soil around plants with a hoe

¹hog \'hòg, 'häg\ *n* **1** : an adult domestic swine **2** : a greedy or dirty person

²hog *vb* **hogged; hog·ging** : to take more than one's share

ho·gan \'hō-,gän\ *n* : a dwelling of some American Indians made of logs or sticks covered with earth

hog·gish \'hòg-ish, 'häg-\ *adj* : very self-ish or greedy — **hog·gish·ly** *adv* — **hog·gish·ness** *n*

hogs·head \'hògz-,hed, 'hägz-\ *n* **1** : a very large cask **2** : a unit of liquid measure equal to sixty-three gallons (about 238 liters)

¹hoist \'hòist\ *vb* : to lift up especially with a pulley **synonyms** see LIFT

²hoist *n* **1** : an act of hoisting **2** : a device used for lifting heavy loads

¹hold \'hōld\ *vb* **held** \'held\; **hold·ing 1** : to have or keep in one's possession or under one's control ⟨*hold* a fort⟩ ⟨*hold* territory⟩ **2** : to limit the movement or activity of : RESTRAIN ⟨the nut *held* the bolt⟩ ⟨*hold* the dogs⟩ **3** : to make accept a legal or moral duty ⟨they *held* me to my promise⟩ **4** : to have or keep in one's grasp ⟨*hold* a book⟩ **5** : ¹SUPPORT 4 ⟨a floor that will *hold* ten tons⟩ **6** : to take in and have within : CONTAIN ⟨a jar that *holds* a quart⟩ **7** : to have in mind ⟨*hold* opposing opinions⟩ **8** : CONSIDER 3, REGARD **9** : to carry on by group action ⟨*hold* a meeting⟩ **10** : to continue in the same way or state : LAST ⟨believes the good weather will *hold*⟩ **11** : to remain fast or fastened ⟨the lock *held*⟩ **12** : to bear or carry oneself

²hold *n* **1** : the act or way of holding : GRIP **2** : ¹INFLUENCE 1 ⟨the *hold* of the school on our minds⟩ **3** : a note or rest in music kept up longer than usual

³hold *n* **1** : the part of a ship below the decks in which cargo is stored **2** : the cargo compartment of an airplane

hold·er \'hōl-dər\ *n* : one that holds

hold out *vb* : to refuse to yield or agree ⟨*held out* until help arrived⟩

hold·up \'hōl-,dəp\ *n* **1** : robbery by an armed robber **2** : ¹DELAY

hold up \hōl-'dəp\ *vb* **1** : ²DELAY 2 **2** : to rob while threatening with a weapon

hogan

hole \'hōl\ *n* **1** : an opening into or through something **2** : CAVITY **3** : DEN 1, BURROW

hol·i·day \'häl-ə-ˌdā\ *n* **1** : a day of freedom from work especially when celebrating some event **2** : VACATION

ho·li·ness \'hō-lē-nəs\ *n* **1** : the quality or state of being holy **2** — used as a title for persons of high religious position ⟨His *Holiness* the Pope⟩

¹hol·ler \'häl-ər\ *vb* : to cry out : SHOUT

²holler *n* : ²SHOUT, CRY

¹hol·low \'häl-ō\ *adj* **1** : curved inward : SUNKEN **2** : having a space inside : not solid **3** : suggesting a sound made in an empty place ⟨a *hollow* roar⟩ **4** : not sincere — **hol·low·ly** *adv* — **hol·low·ness** *n*

²hollow *vb* : to make or become hollow

³hollow *n* **1** : a low spot in a surface ⟨the *hollow* of the land⟩ **2** : VALLEY **3** : CAVITY

holly

hol·ly \'häl-ē\ *n, pl* **hol·lies** : an evergreen tree or shrub that has shiny leaves with prickly edges and red berries much used for Christmas decorations

hol·ly·hock \'häl-ē-ˌhäk\ *n* : a plant with large rounded leaves and tall stalks of bright showy flowers

ho·lo·caust \'häl-ə-ˌkȯst, 'hō-lə-\ *n* : a complete destruction especially by fire

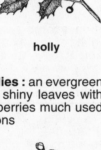

hollyhock

Word History At first the English word *holocaust* meant "a burnt sacrifice." This English word came from a Greek word that meant "burnt whole." This Greek word was a compound of a word that meant "whole" and another that meant "burnt."

ho·lo·gram \'hō-lə-ˌgram, 'häl-ə-\ *n* : a three-dimensional picture made by laser light reflected onto photographic film without the use of a camera

hol·stein \'hōl-ˌstēn, -ˌstīn\ *n* : any of a breed of large black-and-white dairy cattle giving large quantities of milk

hol·ster \'hōl-stər\ *n* : a usually leather case in which a pistol is carried or worn

ho·ly \'hō-lē\ *adj* **ho·li·er; ho·li·est** **1** : set apart for the service of God or of a divine being : SACRED ⟨a *holy* temple⟩ **2** : having a right to expect complete devotion ⟨the *holy* Lord God⟩ **3** : pure in spirit

Holy Ghost *n* : HOLY SPIRIT

Holy Grail \'hō-lē-ˌgrāl, -ˌgrāəl\ *n* : the cup that according to legend was used by Christ and was sought after by knights during the Middle Ages

Holy Spirit *n* : the third person of the Trinity

hom- *or* **homo-** *prefix* : one and the same : similar : alike ⟨*homograph*⟩

hom·age \'häm-ij, 'äm-\ *n* **1** : a feudal ceremony in which a person pledges loyalty to a lord and becomes a vassal **2** : ¹RESPECT 2

¹home \'hōm\ *n* **1** : the house in which one or one's family lives **2** : the place where one was born or grew up **3** : HABITAT **4** : a place for the care of persons unable to care for themselves **5** : the social unit formed by a family living together **6** : ¹HOUSE 1 ⟨new *homes* for sale⟩ **7** : the goal or point to be reached in some games — **home·less** \-ləs\ *adj*

²home *adv* **1** : to or at home **2** : to the final place or limit ⟨drive a nail *home*⟩

home economics *n* : the study of the care and maintenance of a household

home·land \'hōm-ˌland\ *n* : native land

home·like \'hōm-ˌlīk\ *adj* : like a home (as in comfort and kindly warmth) ⟨a *homelike* atmosphere⟩

home·ly \'hōm-lē\ *adj* **home·li·er; home·li·est** **1** : suggesting home life ⟨*homely* comfort⟩ **2** : not handsome

home·made \'hōm-'mād\ *adj* : made in the home ⟨*homemade* bread⟩

home·mak·er \'hōm-ˌmā-kər\ *n* : a person who manages a household especially as a wife and mother — **home·mak·ing** \-ˌmā-king\ *n or adj*

home plate *n* : the base that a baseball runner must touch to score

hom·er \'hō-mər\ *n* : HOME RUN

home·room \'hōm-ˌrüm, -ˌrùm\ *n* : a

\ə\ **abut**	\aú\ **out**	\i\ **tip**	\ȯ\ **saw**	\ù\ **foot**
\ər\ **further**	\ch\ **chin**	\ī\ **life**	\ȯi\ **coin**	\y\ **yet**
\a\ **mat**	\e\ **pet**	\j\ **job**	\th\ **thin**	\yü\ **few**
\ā\ **take**	\ē\ **easy**	\ng\ **sing**	\th\ **this**	\yù\ **cure**
\ä\ **cot, cart**	\g\ **go**	\ō\ **bone**	\ü\ **food**	\zh\ **vision**

schoolroom where pupils of the same class report at the start of each day

home run *n* : a hit in baseball that enables the batter to go around all the bases and score

home·sick \'hōm-ˌsik\ *adj* : longing for home and family — **home·sick·ness** *n*

¹home·spun \'hōm-ˌspən\ *adj* **1** : spun or made at home **2** : made of homespun **3** : not fancy : SIMPLE ⟨*homespun* humor⟩

²homespun *n* : a loosely woven usually woolen or linen fabric originally made from homespun yarn

¹home·stead \'hōm-ˌsted\ *n* **1** : a home and the land around it **2** : a piece of land gained from United States public lands by living on and farming it

²homestead *vb* : to acquire or settle on public land for use as a homestead — **home·stead·er** \'hōm-ˌsted-ər\ *n*

home·ward \'hōm-wərd\ *or* **home·wards** \-wərdz\ *adv or adj* : toward home

home·work \'hōm-ˌwərk\ *n* : work (as school lessons) to be done at home

hom·ey \'hō-mē\ *adj* **hom·i·er; hom·i·est** : HOMELIKE — **hom·ey·ness** *or* **hom·i·ness** *n*

ho·mi·cid·al \ˌhäm-ə-ˈsīd-l, ˌhō-mə-\ *n* : having a nature that suggests one is likely to kill another person — **ho·mi·cid·al·ly** \-ˈsīd-l-ē\ *adv*

ho·mi·cide \'häm-ə-ˌsīd, 'hō-mə-\ *n* : a killing of one human being by another

hom·ing pigeon \ˌhō-ming-\ *n* : a racing pigeon trained to return home

hom·i·ny \'häm-ə-nē\ *n* : hulled corn with the germ removed

homo- — see HOM-

ho·mog·e·nize \hō-ˈmäj-ə-ˌnīz, hə-\ *vb* **ho·mog·e·nized; ho·mog·e·niz·ing** : to reduce the particles in (as milk or paint) to the same size and spread them evenly in the liquid

ho·mo·graph \'häm-ə-ˌgraf, 'hō-mə-\ *n* : one of two or more words spelled alike but different in meaning or origin or pronunciation ⟨the noun "conduct" and the verb "conduct" are *homographs*⟩

hom·onym \'häm-ə-ˌnim, 'hō-mə-\ *n* **1** : HOMOPHONE **2** : HOMOGRAPH **3** : one of two or more words spelled and pronounced alike but different in meaning ⟨the noun "bear" and the verb "bear" are *homonyms*⟩

ho·mo·phone \'häm-ə-ˌfōn, 'hō-mə-\ *n* : one of two or more words pronounced alike but different in meaning or origin or spelling ⟨"to," "too," and "two" are *homophones*⟩

hone \'hōn\ *vb* **honed; hon·ing** : to sharpen with or as if with a fine abrasive stone

hon·est \'än-əst\ *adj* **1** : free from fraud or trickery : STRAIGHTFORWARD ⟨an *honest* answer⟩ **2** : not given to cheating, stealing, or lying : UPRIGHT, TRUSTWORTHY **3** : being just what is indicated : REAL, GENUINE ⟨put in a day's *honest* work⟩ **synonyms** see UPRIGHT

hon·es·ty \'än-ə-stē\ *n* : the quality or state of being honest

hon·ey \'hən-ē\ *n* **1** : a sweet sticky fluid made by bees from the liquid drawn from flowers **2** : an outstanding example ⟨a *honey* of a fight⟩

hon·ey·bee \'hən-ē-ˌbē\ *n* : a bee whose honey is used by people as food

honeybee

¹hon·ey·comb \'hən-ē-ˌkōm\ *n* **1** : a mass of wax cells built by honeybees in their nest to contain young bees and stores of honey **2** : something like a honeycomb in structure or appearance

²honeycomb *vb* : to make or become full of holes like a honeycomb

hon·ey·dew melon \ˌhən-ē-ˌdü-, -ˌdyü-\ *n* : a pale muskmelon with greenish sweet flesh and smooth skin

¹hon·ey·moon \'hən-ē-ˌmün\ *n* **1** : a holiday taken by a recently married couple **2** : a period of harmony especially just after marriage

²honeymoon *vb* : to have a honeymoon — **hon·ey·moon·er** *n*

hon·ey·suck·le \'hən-ē-ˌsək-əl\ *n* : a climbing vine or a bush with fragrant white, yellow, or red flowers

honeysuckle

¹honk \'hängk, 'hȯngk\ *n* **1** : the cry of a goose **2** : a sound like the cry of a goose ⟨the *honk* of a horn⟩

²honk *vb* : to make a honk

¹hon·or \'än-ər\ *n* **1** : public admiration

: REPUTATION **2** : outward respect : RECOGNITION ⟨a dinner in *honor* of a new coach⟩ **3** : PRIVILEGE ⟨you will have the *honor* of leading the parade⟩ **4** — used especially as a title for an official of high rank (as a judge) ⟨if Your *Honor* please⟩ **5** : a person whose worth brings respect or fame ⟨an *honor* to your profession⟩ **6** : evidence or a symbol of great respect ⟨a writer who has won many national *honors*⟩ **7** : high moral standards of behavior

²honor *vb* **1** : ²RESPECT ⟨*honor* your parents⟩ **2** : to give an honor to

hon·or·able \'än-ə-rə-bəl, 'än-rə-bəl\ *adj* **1** : bringing about or deserving honor ⟨an *honorable* achievement⟩ **2** : observing ideas of honor or reputation ⟨seeking an *honorable* peace⟩ **3** : having high moral standards of behavior : ETHICAL, UPRIGHT ⟨too *honorable* to stoop to scheming⟩

hon·or·ary \'än-ə-‚rer-ē\ *adj* : given or done as an honor ⟨an *honorary* degree⟩

¹hood \'hu̇d\ *n* **1** : a covering for the head and neck and sometimes the face **2** : something like a hood **3** : the movable covering for an automobile engine — **hood·ed** \'hu̇d-əd\ *adj*

²hood *vb* : to cover with or as if with a hood

-hood \‚hu̇d\ *n suffix* **1** : state : condition : quality : nature ⟨child*hood*⟩ ⟨hardi*hood*⟩ **2** : instance of a specified state or quality ⟨false*hood*⟩ **3** : individuals sharing a specified state or character

hood·lum \'hu̇d-ləm, 'hu̇d-\ *n* : a brutal ruffian : THUG

hood·wink \'hu̇d-‚wiŋk\ *vb* : to mislead by trickery

hoof \'hu̇f, 'hüf\ *n, pl* **hooves** \'hu̇vz, 'hüvz\ *or* **hoofs** **1** : a covering of horn that protects the ends of the toes of some animals (as horses, oxen, or swine) **2** : a hoofed foot (as of a horse) — **hoofed** \'hu̇ft, 'hüft\ *adj*

¹hook \'hu̇k\ *n* **1** : a curved device (as a piece of bent metal) for catching, holding, or pulling something **2** : something curved or bent like a hook — **by hook or by crook** : in any way : fairly or unfairly

²hook *vb* **1** : to bend in the shape of a hook **2** : to catch or fasten with a hook ⟨*hook* a fish⟩

hook·worm \'hu̇k-‚wərm\ *n* : a small worm that lives in the intestines and makes people sick by sucking their blood

hoop \'hu̇p, 'hüp\ *n* **1** : a circular band used for holding together the strips that make up the sides of a barrel or tub **2** : a circular figure or object ⟨embroidery *hoops*⟩ **3** : a circle or series of circles of flexible material (as wire) used for holding a woman's skirt out from the body

hooray *variant of* HURRAH

¹hoot \'hüt\ *vb* **1** : to utter a loud shout usually to show disapproval **2** : to make the noise of an owl or a similar cry **3** : to express by hoots ⟨*hooted* disapproval⟩

²hoot *n* **1** : a sound of hooting **2** : the least bit ⟨doesn't care a *hoot*⟩

¹hop \'häp\ *vb* **hopped**; **hop·ping** **1** : to move by short quick jumps **2** : to jump on one foot **3** : to jump over ⟨*hop* a puddle⟩ **4** : to get aboard by or as if by hopping ⟨*hop* a bus⟩ **5** : to make a quick trip especially by air

²hop *n* **1** : a short quick jump especially on one leg **2** : ²DANCE 2 **3** : a short trip especially by air

³hop *n* **1** : a twining vine whose greenish flowers look like cones **2 hops** *pl* : the dried flowers of the hop plant used chiefly in making beer and ale and in medicine

hop

¹hope \'hōp\ *vb* **hoped**; **hop·ing** : to desire especially with expectation that the wish will be granted

²hope *n* **1** : ¹TRUST 1 **2** : desire together with the expectation of getting what is wanted **3** : a cause for hope **4** : something hoped for

hope·ful \'hōp-fəl\ *adj* **1** : full of hope **2** : giving hope : PROMISING ⟨a *hopeful* sign⟩ — **hope·ful·ly** \-fə-lē\ *adv* — **hope·ful·ness** *n*

hope·less \'hō-pləs\ *adj* **1** : having no hope ⟨*hopeless* about the future⟩ **2** : offering no hope ⟨the situation looks *hopeless*⟩ — **hope·less·ly** *adv* — **hope·less·ness** *n*

hop·per \'häp-ər\ *n* **1** : one that hops **2** : an insect that moves by leaping **3** : a container usually shaped like a funnel for delivering material (as grain or coal) into a machine or a bin **4** : a tank holding liquid and having a device for releasing its contents through a pipe

hop·scotch \'häp-‚skäch\ *n* : a game in

\ə\ abut	\au̇\ out	\i\ tip	\o̅\ saw	\u̇\ foot
\ər\ further	\ch\ chin	\ī\ life	\oi\ coin	\y\ yet
\a\ mat	\e\ pet	\j\ job	\th\ thin	\yü\ few
\ā\ take	\ē\ easy	\ng\ sing	\th\ this	\yu̇\ cure
\ä\ cot, cart	\g\ go	\ō\ bone	\ü\ food	\zh\ vision

which a player tosses a stone into sections of a figure drawn on the ground and hops through the figure and back to pick up the stone

horde \'hōrd\ *n* : MULTITUDE, SWARM ⟨a *horde* of ants⟩

ho·ri·zon \hə-'rīz-n\ *n* **1** : the line where the earth or sea seems to meet the sky **2** : the limit of a person's outlook or experience

¹hor·i·zon·tal \ˌhòr-ə-'zänt-l\ *adj* : level with the horizon — **hor·i·zon·tal·ly** *adv*

²horizontal *n* : something (as a line or plane) that is horizontal

hor·mone \'hòr-ˌmōn\ *n* : a secretion of an endocrine gland

horn \'hòrn\ *n* **1** : one of the hard bony growths on the head of many hoofed animals (as cattle, goats, or sheep) **2** : the material of which horns are composed or a similar material ⟨a knife with a *horn* handle⟩ **3** : something made from a horn ⟨each soldier carried a *horn* of powder⟩ **4** : something shaped like a horn **5** : a musical or signaling instrument made from an animal's horn **6** : a brass musical instrument (as a trumpet or French horn) **7** : a usually electrical device that makes a noise like that of a horn — **horned** \'hòrnd\ *adj* — **horn·less** \'hòrn-ləs\ *adj* — **horn·like** \-ˌlīk\ *adj*

horned toad *n* : a small harmless lizard with scales and hard pointed growths on the skin

hor·net \'hòr-nət\ *n* : a large wasp that can give a severe sting

horn of plenty : CORNUCOPIA

horny \'hòr-nē\ *adj* **horn·i·er; horn·i·est** : like or made of horn

hor·ri·ble \'hòr-ə-bəl\ *adj* : causing horror : TERRIBLE — **hor·ri·bly** \-blē\ *adv*

hor·rid \'hòr-əd\ *adj* **1** : HORRIBLE **2** : very unpleasant : DISGUSTING — **hor·rid·ly** *adv*

hor·ri·fy \'hòr-ə-ˌfī\ *vb* **hor·ri·fied; hor·ri·fy·ing** : to cause to feel horror

hor·ror \'hòr-ər\ *n* **1** : great and painful fear, dread, or shock **2** : great dislike **3** : a quality or thing that causes horror

horse \'hòrs\ *n* **1** : a large hoofed animal that feeds on grasses and is used

horse 3

as a work animal and for riding **2** : a frame that supports something (as wood while being cut) **3** : a piece of gymnasium equipment used for vaulting exercises —

horse·less \'hòr-sləs\ *adj* — **from the horse's mouth** : from the original source

¹horse·back \'hòrs-ˌbak\ *n* : the back of a horse

²horseback *adv* : on horseback

horse·car \'hòr-ˌskär\ *n* **1** : a streetcar drawn by horses **2** : a car for transporting horses

horse chestnut *n* : a shiny brown nut that is unfit to eat and is the fruit of a tall tree with leaves divided into fingerlike parts and large flower clusters shaped like cones

horse·fly \'hòrs-ˌflī\ *n, pl* **horse·flies** : a large swift two-winged fly the females of which suck blood from animals

horse·hair \'hòrs-ˌhaər, -ˌheər\ *n* **1** : the hair of a horse especially from the mane or tail **2** : cloth made from horsehair

horse latitudes *n pl* : either of two regions in the neighborhoods of 30° north and 30° south of the equator marked by calms and light changeable winds

horse·man \'hòrs-smən\ *n, pl* **horse·men** \-smən\ **1** : a horseback rider **2** : a person skilled in handling horses — **horse·man·ship** \-ˌship\ *n*

horse opera *n* : a movie or a radio or television play about cowboys

horse·play \'hòr-ˌsplā\ *n* : rough play

horse·pow·er \'hòr-ˌspaù-ər\ *n* : a unit of power that equals the work done in raising 550 pounds one foot in one second

horse·rad·ish \'hòrs-ˌrad-ish\ *n* : a hot relish made from the root of an herb of the mustard family

horse·shoe \'hòrs-ˌshü\ *n* **1** : a protective iron plate that is nailed to the rim of a horse's hoof **2** : something shaped like a horseshoe **3 horseshoes** *pl* : a game in which horseshoes are tossed at a stake in the ground

horse·tail \'hòr-ˌstāl\ *n* : any of a group of primitive plants that produce spores and have hollow stems with joints and leaves reduced to sheaths about the joints

horse·whip \'hòr-ˌswip, 'hòrs-ˌhwip\ *vb* **horse·whipped; horse·whip·ping** : to beat severely with a whip made to be used on a horse

horse·wom·an \'hòr-ˌswùm-ən\ *n, pl* **horse·wom·en** \-ˌswim-ən\ : a woman skilled in riding on horseback or in handling horses

hors·ey *or* **horsy** \'hòr-sē\ *adj* **hors·i·er;**

hors·i·est : of or relating to horses or horsemen and horsewomen

ho·san·na \hō-'zan-ə\ *interj* — used as a cry of approval, praise, or love

¹hose \'hōz\ *n, pl* **hose** *or* **hos·es 1** *pl* hose : STOCKING, SOCK **2** : a flexible tube for carrying fluid

²hose *vb* **hosed; hos·ing** : to spray, water, or wash with a hose

ho·siery \'hō-zhə-rē\ *n* : stockings or socks in general

hos·pi·ta·ble \hä-'spit-ə-bəl, 'häs-pit-\ *adj* **1** : friendly and generous in entertaining guests **2** : willing to deal with something new — **hos·pi·ta·bly** \-blē\ *adv*

hos·pi·tal \'häs-,pit-l\ *n* : a place where the sick and injured are cared for

hos·pi·tal·i·ty \,häs-pə-'tal-ət-ē\ *n* : friendly and generous treatment of guests

hos·pi·tal·ize \'häs-,pit-l-,īz\ *vb* **hos·pi·tal·ized; hos·pi·tal·iz·ing** : to place in a hospital for care and treatment — **hos·pi·tal·iza·tion** \,häs-,pit-l-ə-'zā-shən\ *n*

¹host \'hōst\ *n* **1** : ARMY 1 **2** : MULTITUDE

²host *n* : one who receives or entertains guests

³host *n, often cap* : the bread used in Christian Communion

hos·tage \'häs-tij\ *n* : a person given or held to make certain that promises will be kept

hos·tel \'häst-l\ *n* : a place providing inexpensive lodging for use by young travelers

host·ess \'hō-stəs\ *n* : a woman who receives or entertains guests

hos·tile \'häst-l\ *adj* **1** : of or relating to an enemy ⟨in *hostile* territory⟩ **2** : UN-FRIENDLY

hos·til·i·ty \hä-'stil-ət-ē\ *n, pl* **hos·til·i·ties 1** : a hostile state, attitude, or action **2** *hostilities pl* : acts of warfare

hot \'hät\ *adj* **hot·ter; hot·test 1** : having a high temperature ⟨a *hot* stove⟩ ⟨a *hot* day⟩ **2** : easily excited ⟨a *hot* temper⟩ **3** : having or causing the sensation of an uncomfortable degree of body heat **4** : recently made or received ⟨*hot* news⟩ **5** : close to something sought ⟨keep looking, you're getting *hot*⟩ **6** : PUNGENT ⟨*hot* mustard⟩ **7** : RADIOACTIVE **8** : recently stolen ⟨*hot* jewels⟩ — **hot·ly** *adv* — **hot·ness** *n*

hot·bed \'hät-,bed\ *n* : a bed of heated earth covered by glass for growing tender plants early in the season

hot dog \'hät-,dȯg\ *n* : a frankfurter and especially a cooked one served in a long split roll

ho·tel \hō-'tel\ *n* : a place that provides lodging and meals for the public : INN

hot·head \'hät-,hed\ *n* : a person who is easily excited or angered — **hot·head·ed** \-'hed-əd\ *adj*

hot·house \'hät-,haús\ *n* : a heated building enclosed by glass for growing plants

hot plate \'hät-,plāt\ *n* : a small portable appliance for heating or cooking

hot rod *n* : an automobile rebuilt for high speed and fast acceleration

hot water *n* : a difficult or distressing situation : TROUBLE

¹hound \'haúnd\ *n* : a dog with drooping ears and deep bark that is used in hunting and follows game by the sense of smell

²hound *vb* : to hunt, chase, or annoy without ceasing

hour \'aúr\ *n* **1** : one of the twenty-four divisions of a day : sixty minutes **2** : the time of day **3** : a fixed or particular time **4** : a measure of distance figured by the amount of time it takes to cover it ⟨it's two *hours* by car⟩

hour·glass \'aúr-,glas\ *n* : a device for measuring time in which sand runs from the upper into the lower part of a glass in an hour

¹hour·ly \'aúr-lē\ *adv* : at or during every hour ⟨planes leaving *hourly*⟩

²hourly *adj* **1** : occurring every hour **2** : figured by the hour ⟨an *hourly* wage⟩

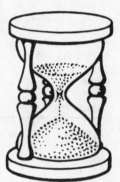

hourglass

¹house \'haús\ *n, pl* **hous·es** \'haú-zəz\ **1** : a place built for people to live in **2** : something (as a nest or den) used by an animal for shelter **3** : a building in which something is stored ⟨*tool* house⟩ **4** : ¹HOUSEHOLD **5** : FAMILY 1 ⟨the *house* of Windsor⟩ **6** : a body of persons assembled to make the laws for a country ⟨the two *houses* of the United States Congress⟩ **7** : a business firm ⟨a publishing *house*⟩ **8** : the audience in a theater or concert hall — **on the house** : free of charge

²house \'haúz\ *vb* **1** : to provide with living quarters or shelter **2** : CONTAIN 3

house·boat \'haús-,bōt\ *n* : a roomy pleasure boat fitted for use as a place to live

\ə\ **abut**	\aú\ **out**	\i\ **tip**	\ȯ\ **saw**	\ú\ **foot**
\ər\ **further**	\ch\ **chin**	\ī\ **life**	\ȯi\ **coin**	\y\ **yet**
\a\ **mat**	\e\ **pet**	\j\ **job**	\th\ **thin**	\yü\ **few**
\ā\ **take**	\ē\ **easy**	\ng\ **sing**	\th\ **this**	\yú\ **cure**
\ä\ **cot, cart**	\g\ **go**	\ō\ **bone**	\ü\ **food**	\zh\ **vision**

house·boy \'haus-ˌbȯi\ *n* : a boy or man hired to do housework

house·fly \'haus-ˌflī\ *n*, *pl* **house·flies** : a two-winged fly that is common about houses and often carries disease germs

¹house·hold \'haus-ˌhōld\ *n* : all the persons who live as a family in one house

²household *adj* **1** : of or relating to a household **2** : FAMILIAR

house·hold·er \'haus-ˌhōl-dər\ *n* : one who lives in a dwelling alone or as the head of a household

house·keep·er \'hau-ˌskē-pər\ *n* : a person employed to take care of a house

house·keep·ing \'hau-ˌskē-ping\ *n* : the care and management of a house

house·maid \'hau-ˌsmād\ *n* : a woman or girl hired to do housework

house·moth·er \'hau-ˌsmᵗh-ər\ *n* : a woman who acts as hostess, supervisor, and often housekeeper in a residence for young people

house·plant \'hau-ˌsplant\ *n* : a plant grown or kept indoors

house·top \'hau-ˌstäp\ *n* : ¹ROOF 1

house·warm·ing \'hau-ˌswȯr-ming\ *n* : a party to celebrate moving into a new home

house·wife \'hau-ˌswīf\ *n*, *pl* **house-wives** \-ˌswīvz\ : a married woman in charge of a household

house·work \'hau-ˌswərk\ *n* : the actual labor involved in housekeeping

hous·ing \'hau-zing\ *n* **1** : dwellings provided for a number of people ⟨*housing* for the aged⟩ **2** : something that covers or protects

hove *past of* HEAVE

hov·el \'həv-əl, 'häv-\ *n* : a small poorly built usually dirty house

hov·er \'həv-ər, 'häv-\ *vb* **1** : to hang fluttering in the air or on the wing **2** : to move to and fro near a place ⟨waiters *hovered* about⟩

¹how \'hau\ *adv* **1** : in what way : by what means ⟨*how* do you work this thing⟩ ⟨*how* did they get here⟩ **2** : for what reason ⟨*how* can you treat me so⟩ **3** : to what degree, number, or amount ⟨*how* cold is it⟩ **4** : in what state or condition ⟨*how* are you⟩ — **how about** : what do you say to or think of ⟨*how about* a soda⟩ — **how come** : ¹WHY — **how do you do** : HELLO

²how *conj* : in what manner or condition ⟨study *how* plants grow⟩ ⟨asked them *how* they were⟩

how·ev·er \hau-'ev-ər\ *adv* **1** : to whatever degree or extent ⟨*however* long it takes⟩ **2** : in whatever way ⟨*however* you want to do it⟩ **3** : in spite of that ⟨*however*, we did try to help⟩

¹howl \'haul\ *vb* **1** : to make a loud long mournful sound like that of a dog ⟨wind *howling* through the trees⟩ **2** : to cry out loudly (as with pain)

²howl *n* **1** : a loud long mournful sound made by dogs **2** : a long loud cry (as of distress, disappointment, or rage) **3** : COMPLAINT 1 ⟨set up a *howl* over taxes⟩ **4** : something that causes laughter

hub \'həb\ *n* **1** : the center of a wheel, propeller, or fan **2** : a center of activity

hub·bub \'həb-ˌəb\ *n* : UPROAR

huck·le·ber·ry \'hək-əl-ˌber-ē\ *n*, *pl* **huck·le·ber·ries** : a dark edible berry with bony seeds that is related to the blueberry

huck·ster \'hək-stər\ *n* **1** : PEDDLER, HAWKER **2** : a writer of advertising

¹hud·dle \'həd-l\ *vb* **hud·dled; hud·dling** **1** : to crowd, push, or pile together ⟨people *huddled* in a doorway⟩ **2** : to get together to talk something over **3** : to curl up ⟨*huddled* under a blanket⟩

²huddle *n* **1** : a closely packed group **2** : a private meeting or conference

hue \'hyü\ *n* **1** : ¹COLOR 1 ⟨flowers of every *hue*⟩ **2** : a shade of a color

¹huff \'həf\ *vb* : to give off puffs (as of air or steam)

²huff *n* : a fit of anger or temper

huffy \'həf-ē\ *adj* **huff·i·er; huff·i·est** **1** : easily offended : PETULANT **2** : ¹SULKY — **huff·i·ly** \'həf-ə-lē\ *adv* — **huff·i·ness** \'həf-ē-nəs\ *n*

¹hug \'həg\ *vb* **hugged; hug·ging** **1** : to clasp in the arms : EMBRACE **2** : to keep close to

²hug *n* : ²EMBRACE

huge \'hyüj, 'yüj\ *adj* **hug·er; hug·est** : very large : VAST

hulk \'həlk\ *n* **1** : a person or thing that is bulky or clumsy **2** : the remains of an old or wrecked ship

hulk·ing \'həl-king\ *adj* : very large and strong : MASSIVE

¹hull \'həl\ *n* **1** : the outside covering of a fruit or seed **2** : the frame or body of a ship, flying boat, or airship

²hull *vb* : to remove the hulls of — **hull·er** *n*

hul·la·ba·loo \'həl-ə-bə-ˌlü\ *n*, *pl* **hul·la·ba·loos** : a confused noise : HUBBUB, COMMOTION

¹hum \'həm\ *vb* **hummed; hum·ming** **1** : to utter a sound like a long \m\ **2** : to make the buzzing noise of a flying insect **3** : to sing with closed lips **4** : to give forth a low murmur of sounds ⟨a street *humming* with activity⟩ **5** : to be very busy or active

²hum *n* : the act or an instance of humming : the sound produced by humming

¹hu·man \'hyü-mən, 'yü-\ *adj* **1** : of, relating to, being, or characteristic of people as distinct from lower animals **2** : having human form or characteristics

²**human** *n* : a human being — **hu·man·like** \'hyü-mən-ˌlīk, 'yü-\ *adj*

hu·mane \hyü-'mān, yü-\ *adj* : having sympathy and consideration for others — **hu·mane·ly** *adv* — **hu·mane·ness** *n*

¹**hu·man·i·tar·i·an** \hyü-ˌman-ə-'ter-ē-ən, yü-\ *n* : a person devoted to and working for the health and happiness of other people

²**humanitarian** *adj* : of, relating to, or characteristic of humanitarians

hu·man·i·ty \hyü-'man-ət-ē, yü-\ *n, pl* **hu·man·i·ties 1** : KINDNESS 2, SYMPATHY **2** : the quality or state of being human **3** *humanities pl* : studies (as literature, history, and art) concerned primarily with human culture **4** : the human race

hu·man·ly \'hyü-mən-lē, 'yü-\ *adv* : within the range of human ability ⟨a task not *humanly* possible⟩

¹**hum·ble** \'həm-bəl, 'əm-\ *adj* **hum·bler; hum·blest 1** : not bold or proud : MODEST **2** : expressing a spirit of respect for the wishes of another ⟨*humble* apologies⟩ **3** : low in rank or condition ⟨people of *humble* origin⟩ — **hum·bly** \-blē\ *adv*

²**humble** *vb* **hum·bled; hum·bling 1** : to make humble **2** : to destroy the power of

¹**hum·bug** \'həm-ˌbəg\ *n* **1** : FRAUD 3 **2** : NONSENSE 1

²**humbug** *vb* **hum·bugged; hum·bug·ging** : DECEIVE 1

hum·ding·er \'həm-'ding-ər\ *n* : something striking or extraordinary

hum·drum \'həm-ˌdrəm\ *adj* : MONOTONOUS

hu·mid \'hyü-məd, 'yü-\ *adj* : MOIST ⟨*humid* day⟩

hu·mid·i·fy \hyü-'mid-ə-ˌfī, yü-\ *vb* **hu·mid·i·fied; hu·mid·i·fy·ing** : to make (as the air of a room) more moist — **hu·mid·i·fi·er** *n*

hu·mid·i·ty \hyü-'mid-ət-ē, yü-\ *n, pl* **hu·mid·i·ties** : the degree of wetness especially of the atmosphere : MOISTURE

hu·mil·i·ate \hyü-'mil-ē-ˌāt, yü-\ *vb* **hu·mil·i·at·ed; hu·mil·i·at·ing** : to lower the pride or self-respect of

hu·mil·i·a·tion \hyü-ˌmil-ē-'ā-shən, yü-\ *n* **1** : the state of being humiliated **2** : an instance of being humiliated

hu·mil·i·ty \hyü-'mil-ət-ē, yü-\ *n* : the quality of being humble

hum·ming·bird \'həm-ing-ˌbərd\ *n* : a tiny brightly colored American bird whose wings make a humming sound in flight

hum·mock \'həm-ək\ *n* **1** : a rounded mound of earth : KNOLL **2** : a ridge or pile of ice

¹**hu·mor** \'hyü-mər, 'yü-\ *n* **1** : state of mind : MOOD ⟨in a bad *humor*⟩ **2** : the amusing quality of something ⟨the *humor* of a situation⟩ **3** : the ability to see or report the amusing quality of things

²**humor** *vb* : to give in to the wishes of

hu·mor·ist \'hyü-mə-rəst, 'yü-\ *n* : a person who writes or talks in a humorous way

hu·mor·ous \'hyü-mə-rəs, 'yü-\ *adj* : full of humor : FUNNY — **hu·mor·ous·ly** *adv*

hump \'həmp\ *n* **1** : a rounded bulge or lump (as on the back of a camel) **2** : a difficult part (as of a task) — **humped** \'həmpt\ *adj*

hump·back \'həmp-ˌbak\ *n* **1** : a humped back **2** : HUNCHBACK 2 — **hump·backed** \-'bakt\ *adj*

hu·mus \'hyü-məs, 'yü-\ *n* : the dark rich part of earth formed from decaying material

¹**hunch** \'hənch\ *vb* **1** : to bend one's body into an arch or hump ⟨don't *hunch* over when you walk⟩ **2** : to draw up close together or into an arch ⟨*hunch* one's shoulders⟩ ⟨the cat *hunched* its back⟩

²**hunch** *n* **1** : HUMP 1 **2** : a strong feeling about what will happen

hunch·back \'hənch-ˌbak\ *n* **1** : HUMPBACK 1 **2** : a person with a humped or crooked back

¹**hun·dred** \'hən-drəd\ *n* **1** : ten times ten : 100 **2** : a very large number ⟨*hundreds* of times⟩

²**hundred** *adj* : being 100

¹**hun·dredth** \'hən-drədth\ *adj* : coming right after ninety-ninth

²**hundredth** *n* : number 100 in a series

hung *past of* HANG

¹**hun·ger** \'həng-gər\ *n* **1** : a desire or a need for food **2** : a strong desire

²**hunger** *vb* **1** : to feel hunger **2** : to have a strong desire

hun·gry \'həng-grē\ *adj* **hun·gri·er; hun·gri·est 1** : feeling or showing hunger **2** : having a strong desire — **hun·gri·ly** \-grə-lē\ *adv*

hunk \'həngk\ *n* : a large lump or piece

¹**hunt** \'hənt\ *vb* **1** : to follow after in order to capture or kill ⟨*hunt* deer⟩ **2** : to try to find **synonyms** see SEEK

²**hunt** *n* : an instance or the practice of hunting

hunt·er \'hənt-ər\ *n* **1** : a person who hunts

\ə\ **abut**	\aů\ **out**	\i\ **tip**	\ȯ\ **saw**	\ů\ **foot**
\ər\ **further**	\ch\ **chin**	\ī\ **life**	\ȯi\ **coin**	\y\ **yet**
\a\ **mat**	\e\ **pet**	\j\ **job**	\th\ **thin**	\yů\ **few**
\ā\ **take**	\ē\ **easy**	\ng\ **sing**	\th\ **this**	\yü\ **cure**
\ä\ **cot, cart**	\g\ **go**	\ō\ **bone**	\ü\ **food**	\zh\ **vision**

game **2** : a dog or horse used or trained for hunting **3** : a person who searches for something 〈a bargain *hunter*〉

hunts·man \'hənt-smən\ *n, pl* **hunts·men** \-smən\ : HUNTER 1

¹hur·dle \'hərd-l\ *n* **1** : a barrier to be jumped in a race (**hur·dles**) **2** : OBSTACLE

hurdle 1

²hurdle *vb* **hur·dled; hur·dling** **1** : to leap over while running **2** : OVERCOME 〈difficulties to be *hurdled*〉

hur·dy–gur·dy \,hərd-ē-'gərd-ē\ *n, pl* **hur·dy–gur·dies** : HAND ORGAN

hurl \'hərl\ *vb* : to throw with force **synonyms** see THROW

hur·rah \hù-'rò, -'rä\ *or* **hoo·ray** *also* **hur·ray** \hù-'rā\ *interj* — used to express joy, approval, or encouragement

hur·ri·cane \'hər-ə-,kān, 'hər-i-kən\ *n* : a tropical cyclone with winds of thirty-three meters per second or greater usually accompanied by rain, thunder, and lightning

hur·ried \'hər-ēd\ *adj* **1** : going or working with speed : FAST 〈the *hurried* life of the city〉 **2** : done in a hurry — **hur·ried·ly** *adv*

¹hur·ry \'hər-ē\ *vb* **hur·ried; hur·ry·ing** **1** : to carry or cause to go with haste **2** : to move or act with haste **3** : to speed up 〈*hurried* the repair job〉

²hurry *n* : a state of eagerness or urgent need : extreme haste

¹hurt \'hərt\ *vb* **hurt; hurt·ing** **1** : to feel or cause pain **2** : to do harm to : DAMAGE **3** : ²DISTRESS, OFFEND **4** : to make poorer or more difficult 〈the fumble *hurt* our team's chance of winning〉

²hurt *n* **1** : an injury or wound to the body

2 : SUFFERING 1, ANGUISH 〈sympathy eases the *hurt*〉 **3** : ¹WRONG 〈you cannot undo the *hurt*〉

hurt·ful \'hərt-fəl\ *adj* : causing injury or suffering

hur·tle \'hərt-l\ *vb* **hur·tled; hur·tling** **1** : to rush suddenly or violently 〈rocks *hurtled* down the hill〉 **2** : to drive or throw violently

¹hus·band \'həz-bənd\ *n* : a married man

²husband *vb* : to manage with thrift : use carefully 〈*husbanding* my money〉

hus·band·ry \'həz-bən-drē\ *n* **1** : the management or wise use of resources : THRIFT **2** : the business and activities of a farmer

¹hush \'həsh\ *vb* : to make or become quiet, calm, or still : SOOTHE 〈*hush* a baby〉

²hush *n* : ¹QUIET

hush–hush \'həsh-,həsh\ *adj* : ¹SECRET 1, CONFIDENTIAL

¹husk \'həsk\ *n* : the outer covering of a fruit or seed

²husk *vb* : to strip the husk from — **husk·er** *n*

¹husky \'həs-kē\ *adj* **husk·i·er; husk·i·est** : HOARSE — **husk·i·ly** \-kə-lē\ *adv* — **husk·i·ness** \-kē-nəs\ *n*

²husky *adj* **husk·i·er; husk·i·est** : STRONG 1, burly — **husk·i·ness** *n*

³husky *n, pl* **husk·ies** : a husky person or thing

⁴hus·ky \'həs-kē\ *n, pl* **hus·kies** : a strong dog with a thick coat used to pull sleds in the arctic

¹hus·tle \'həs-əl\ *vb* **hus·tled; hus·tling** **1** : to push, crowd, or force forward roughly 〈*hustled* the prisoner to jail〉 **2** : HURRY

²hustle *n* : energetic activity

hus·tler \'həs-lər\ *n* : an energetic person who works fast

hut \'hət\ *n* : a small roughly made and often temporary dwelling

hutch \'həch\ *n* **1** : a low cupboard usually having open shelves on top **2** : a pen or coop for an animal

hy·a·cinth \'hī-ə-

hyacinth

sinth\ *n* : a plant of the lily family with stalks of fragrant flowers shaped like bells

¹hy·brid \'hī-brəd\ *n* **1** : an animal or plant whose parents differ in some hereditary characteristic or belong to different groups (as breeds, races, or species) **2** : something that is of mixed origin or composition

²hybrid *adj* : of or relating to a hybrid : of mixed origin

hydr- *or* **hydro-** *prefix* **1** : water ⟨*hydro*electric⟩ **2** : hydrogen ⟨*hydro*carbon⟩

hy·drant \'hī-drənt\ *n* : a pipe with a spout through which water may be drawn from the main pipes ⟨a fire *hydrant*⟩

hy·drau·lic \hī-'drȯ-lik\ *adj* **1** : operated, moved, or brought about by means of water **2** : operated by liquid forced through a small hole or through a tube ⟨*hydraulic* brakes⟩ — **hy·drau·li·cal·ly** \-li-kə-lē\ *adv*

hy·dro·car·bon \ˌhī-drə-'kär-bən\ *n* : a substance containing only carbon and hydrogen

hy·dro·chlo·ric acid \ˌhī-drə-ˌklōr-ik-\ *n* : a strong acid formed by dissolving in water a gas made up of hydrogen and chlorine

hy·dro·elec·tric \ˌhī-drō-i-'lek-trik\ *adj* : relating to or used in the making of electricity by waterpower

hy·dro·gen \'hī-drə-jən\ *n* : a colorless, odorless, and tasteless flammable gas that is the lightest of the chemical elements

Word History When hydrogen is burned it combines with oxygen to make water. That fact accounts for the name of this gas. The word *hydrogen* was formed from two Greek elements. The first meant "water," and the second meant "born."

hydrogen bomb *n* : a bomb whose great power is due to the sudden release of energy when the central portions of hydrogen atoms unite

hydrogen per·ox·ide \ˌhī-drə-jən-pə-'räk-ˌsīd\ *n* : a liquid chemical containing hydrogen and oxygen and used for bleaching and as an antiseptic

hy·dro·pho·bia \ˌhī-drə-'fō-bē-ə\ *n* : a deadly disease of dogs and some other animals that may be passed on to a person by the bite of an infected animal

hy·dro·plane \'hī-drə-ˌplān\ *n* **1** : a speedboat whose hull is completely or partly raised as it glides over the water **2** : SEAPLANE

hy·e·na \hī-'ē-nə\ *n* : a large mammal of Asia and Africa that lives on flesh

hyena

hy·giene \'hī-ˌjēn\ *n* **1** : a science that deals with the bringing about and keeping up of good health in the individual and the group **2** : conditions or practices necessary for health

hy·gien·ic \ˌhī-jē-'en-ik, hī-'jen-ik\ *adj* : of, relating to, or leading toward health or hygiene — **hy·gien·i·cal·ly** \-i-kə-lē\ *adv*

hy·gien·ist \hī-'jē-nəst\ *n* : a person skilled in hygiene and especially in a specified branch of hygiene ⟨a dental *hygienist*⟩

hy·grom·e·ter \hī-'gräm-ət-ər\ *n* : an instrument for measuring the humidity of the air

hymn \'him\ *n* : a song of praise especially to God

hym·nal \'him-nəl\ *n* : a book of hymns

hyper- *prefix* : excessively ⟨*hyper*sensitive⟩

hy·per·sen·si·tive \ˌhī-pər-'sen-sət-iv\ *adj* : very sensitive ⟨*hypersensitive* to cold⟩

hy·pha \'hī-fə\ *n, pl* **hy·phae** \-ˌfē\ : one of the fine threads that make up the body of a fungus

¹hy·phen \'hī-fən\ *n* : a mark - used to divide or to compound words or word elements

²hyphen *vb* : HYPHENATE

hy·phen·ate \'hī-fə-ˌnāt\ *vb* **hy·phen·at·ed; hy·phen·at·ing** : to connect or mark with a hyphen

\ə\ abut	\aů\ out	\i\ tip	\ȯ\ saw	\ů\ foot
\ər\ further	\ch\ chin	\ī\ life	\ȯi\ coin	\y\ yet
\a\ mat	\e\ pet	\j\ job	\th\ thin	\yü\ few
\ā\ take	\ē\ easy	\ng\ sing	\th\ this	\yů\ cure
\ä\ cot, cart	\g\ go	\ō\ bone	\ü\ food	\zh\ vision

hyp·no·tism \'hip-nə-ˌtiz-əm\ *n* : the act of putting a person or animal into a state like sleep in which he or she responds to suggestions of the hypnotizer

hyp·no·tist \'hip-nə-təst\ *n* : a person who practices hypnotism

hyp·no·tize \'hip-nə-ˌtīz\ *vb* **hyp·no·tized; hyp·no·tiz·ing** : to affect by or as if by hypnotism — **hyp·no·tiz·er** *n*

hy·poc·ri·sy \hi-'päk-rə-sē\ *n, pl* **hy·poc·ri·sies** : a pretending to be what one is not or to believe or feel what one does not

hyp·o·crite \'hip-ə-ˌkrit\ *n* : a person who practices hypocrisy

hy·pot·e·nuse \hī-'pät-n-ˌüs, -ˌyüs\ *n* : the side of a right triangle that is opposite the right angle

hy·poth·e·sis \hī-'päth-ə-səs\ *n, pl* **hy·poth·e·ses** \-ə-ˌsēz\ : something not proved but assumed to be true for purposes of argument or further study or investigation

hy·po·thet·i·cal \ˌhī-pə-'thet-i-kəl\ *adj* **1** : involving or based on a hypothesis **2** : being merely supposed ⟨a *hypothetical* situation⟩ — **hy·po·thet·i·cal·ly** *adv*

hys·ter·ia \his-'ter-ē-ə\ *n* **1** : a nervous disorder in which one loses control over the emotions **2** : a wild uncontrolled outburst of emotion — **hys·ter·i·cal** \-'ter-i-kəl\ *adj* — **hys·ter·i·cal·ly** *adv*

hys·ter·ics \his-'ter-iks\ *n sing or pl* : a fit of uncontrollable laughing or crying : HYSTERIA

hypotenuse

---

i \'ī\ *n, pl* **i's** *or* **is** \'īz\ *often cap* **1** : the ninth letter of the English alphabet **2** : one in Roman numerals

I \ī, 'ī\ *pron* : the person speaking or writing

-ial \ē-əl, yəl, əl\ *adj suffix* : ¹-AL ⟨aer*ial*⟩

-ian — see -AN

ibex \'ī-ˌbeks\ *n, pl* **ibex** *or* **ibex·es** : a wild goat of the Old World with horns that curve backward

-ibility — see -ABILITY

ibis \'ī-bəs\ *n, pl* **ibis** *or* **ibis·es** : a bird related to the herons but having a slender bill that curves down

-ible — see -ABLE

-ic \ik\ *adj suffix* **1** : of, relating to, or having the form of : being **2** : coming from, consisting of, or containing ⟨alcohol*ic*⟩ **3** : in the manner of **4** : associated or dealing with : using ⟨electron*ic*⟩ **5** : characterized by : exhibiting : affected with ⟨allerg*ic*⟩

-i·cal \i-kəl\ *adj suffix* : -IC ⟨symmetr*ical*⟩

¹ice \'īs\ *n* **1** : frozen water **2** : a substance like ice **3** : a frozen dessert usually made with sweetened fruit juice

²ice *vb* **iced; ic·ing** **1** : to coat or become coated with ice **2** : to chill with ice : supply with ice **3** : to cover with icing

ice·berg \'īs-ˌbərg\ *n* : a large floating mass of ice that has broken away from a glacier

ice·boat \'īs-ˌbōt\ *n* : a boatlike frame driven by sails and gliding over ice on runners

ice·bound \'īs-ˌbaúnd\ *adj* : surrounded or blocked by ice ⟨an *icebound* river⟩

ice·box \'īs-ˌbäks\ *n* : REFRIGERATOR

ice·break·er \'īs-ˌbrā-kər\ *n* : a ship equipped to make and keep open a channel through ice

ibis

ice cap *n* : a large more or less level glacier flowing outward in all directions from its center

ice–cold \ˈī-ˈskōld\ *adj* : very cold

ice cream *n* : a frozen food containing sweetened and flavored cream or butterfat

ice–skate \ˈīs-ˌskāt\ *vb* : to skate on ice — **ice skat·er** *n*

ici·cle \ˈī-ˌsik-əl\ *n* : a hanging mass of ice formed from dripping water

ic·ing \ˈī-sing\ *n* : a sweet coating for baked goods

-ics \iks\ *n sing or pl suffix* **1** : study : knowledge : skill : practice ⟨electron*ics*⟩ **2** : characteristic actions or qualities ⟨acrobat*ics*⟩

icy \ˈī-sē\ *adj* **ic·i·er; ic·i·est** **1** : covered with, full of, or being ice ⟨*icy* roads⟩ **2** : very cold **3** : UNFRIENDLY ⟨an *icy* look⟩ — **ic·i·ly** \ˈī-sə-lē\ *adv* — **ic·i·ness** \ˈī-sē-nəs\ *n*

I'd \ˈīd\ : I had : I should : I would

idea \ī-ˈdē-ə\ *n* **1** : a plan of action : INTENTION ⟨my *idea* is to study law⟩ **2** : something imagined or pictured in the mind : NOTION **3** : a central meaning or purpose ⟨do you get the *idea*⟩

¹ide·al \ī-ˈdē-əl\ *adj* **1** : existing only in the mind **2** : having no flaw : PERFECT ⟨*ideal* weather⟩ — **ide·al·ly** *adv*

²ideal *n* **1** : a standard of perfection, beauty, or excellence **2** : a perfect type **synonyms** see MODEL

iden·ti·cal \ī-ˈdent-i-kəl\ *adj* **1** : being one and the same **2** : being exactly alike or equal **synonyms** see SAME

iden·ti·fi·ca·tion \ī-ˌdent-ə-fə-ˈkā-shən\ *n* **1** : an act of identifying : the state of being identified **2** : something that shows or proves identity

iden·ti·fy \ī-ˈdent-ə-ˌfī\ *vb* **iden·ti·fied; iden·ti·fy·ing** **1** : to think of as identical **2** : ¹ASSOCIATE 2 **3** : to find out or show the identity of

iden·ti·ty \ī-ˈdent-ət-ē\ *n, pl* **iden·ti·ties** **1** : the fact or condition of being exactly alike : SAMENESS **2** : INDIVIDUALITY 1 **3** : the fact of being the same person or thing as claimed ⟨prove one's *identity*⟩

id·i·o·cy \ˈid-ə-ə-sē\ *n, pl* **id·i·o·cies** **1** : great lack of intelligence **2** : something very stupid or foolish

id·i·om \ˈid-ē-əm\ *n* : an expression that cannot be understood from the meanings of its separate words but must be learned as a whole ⟨the expression "give way," meaning "retreat," is an *idiom*⟩

id·i·ot \ˈid-ē-ət\ *n* **1** : a person of very low intelligence **2** : a silly or foolish person

id·i·ot·ic \ˌid-ē-ˈät-ik\ *adj* : showing idiocy : FOOLISH, STUPID ⟨*idiotic* behavior⟩ — **id·i·ot·i·cal·ly** \-i-kə-lē\ *adv*

¹idle \ˈīd-l\ *adj* **idler** \ˈīd-lər\; **idlest** \ˈīd-ləst\ **1** : not based on facts ⟨*idle* gossip⟩ **2** : not working or in use ⟨*idle* workers⟩ ⟨an *idle* factory⟩ **3** : LAZY 1 — **idle·ness** \ˈīd-l-nəs\ *n* — **idly** \ˈīd-lē\ *adv*

²idle *vb* **idled** \ˈīd-ld\; **idling** \ˈīd-ling\ **1** : to spend time doing nothing **2** : to run without being connected for doing useful work ⟨the engine is *idling*⟩ — **idler** \ˈīd-lər\ *n*

idol \ˈīd-l\ *n* **1** : an image worshiped as a god **2** : a much loved person or thing

idol·ize \ˈīd-l-ˌīz\ *vb* **idol·ized; idol·iz·ing** : to make an idol of : love or admire too much

-ie *also* **-y** \ē\ *n suffix, pl* **-ies** : little one ⟨lass*ie*⟩

-ier — see ²-ER

if \if\ *conj* **1** : in the event that ⟨*if* it rains we'll stay home⟩ **2** : WHETHER 1 ⟨see *if* they have left⟩

-i·fy \ə-ˌfī\ *vb suffix* **-i·fied; -i·fy·ing** : -FY

ig·loo \ˈig-lü\ *n, pl* **ig·loos** : an Eskimo house often made of blocks of snow and shaped like a dome

igloo

ig·ne·ous \ˈig-nē-əs\ *adj* : formed by hardening of melted mineral material ⟨*igneous* rock⟩

ig·nite \ig-ˈnīt\ *vb* **ig·nit·ed; ig·nit·ing** **1** : to set on fire : LIGHT **2** : to catch fire

\ə\ **abut**	\aů\ **out**	\i\ **tip**	\ȯ\ **saw**	\ů\ **foot**
\ər\ **further**	\ch\ **chin**	\ī\ **life**	\ȯi\ **coin**	\y\ **yet**
\a\ **mat**	\e\ **pet**	\j\ **job**	\th\ **thin**	\yü\ **few**
\ā\ **take**	\ē\ **easy**	\ng\ **sing**	\t͟h\ **this**	\yů\ **cure**
\ä\ **cot, cart**	\g\ **go**	\ō\ **bone**	\ü\ **food**	\zh\ **vision**

ig·ni·tion \ig-'nish-ən\ *n* **1** : the act or action of igniting **2** : the process or means (as an electric spark) of igniting a fuel mixture

ig·no·ble \ig-'nō-bəl\ *adj* : DISHONORABLE ⟨an *ignoble* act⟩ — **ig·no·bly** \-blē\ *adv*

ig·no·rance \'ig-nə-rəns\ *n* : the state of being ignorant

ig·no·rant \'ig-nə-rənt\ *adj* **1** : having little or no knowledge : not educated **2** : not knowing : UNAWARE ⟨*ignorant* of the plot⟩ **3** : resulting from or showing lack of knowledge — **ig·no·rant·ly** *adv*

ig·nore \ig-'nōr\ *vb* **ig·nored; ig·nor·ing** : to pay no attention to ⟨*ignore* a rude remark⟩

igua·na \i-'gwän-ə\ *n* : a very large tropical American lizard with a ridge of tall scales along its back

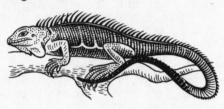

iguana

il- — see IN-

¹ill \'il\ *adj* **worse** \'wərs\; **worst** \'wərst\ **1** : ¹EVIL 2 ⟨*ill* deeds⟩ **2** : causing suffering or distress ⟨*ill* weather⟩ **3** : not normal or sound ⟨*ill* health⟩ **4** : not in good health ⟨an *ill* person⟩ **5** : ¹UNFORTUNATE 1, UNLUCKY ⟨an *ill* omen⟩ **6** : UNKIND, UNFRIENDLY ⟨*ill* feeling⟩ **7** : not right or proper

²ill *adv* **worse; worst 1** : with displeasure ⟨the remark was *ill* received⟩ **2** : in a harsh way ⟨*ill* treated⟩ **3** : SCARCELY 1, HARDLY ⟨can *ill* afford it⟩ **4** : in a faulty way ⟨*ill*-prepared to face the winter⟩

³ill *n* **1** : the opposite of good ⟨for good or *ill*⟩ **2** : SICKNESS 2 ⟨childhood *ills*⟩ **3** : ²TROUBLE 2 ⟨society's *ills*⟩

I'll \'īl\ : I shall : I will

il·le·gal \il-'ē-gəl\ *adj* : contrary to law : UNLAWFUL — **il·le·gal·ly** \il-'ē-gə-lē\ *adv*

il·leg·i·ble \il-'ej-ə-bəl\ *adj* : impossible to read — **il·leg·i·bly** \-blē\ *adv*

il·le·git·i·mate \,il-i-'jit-ə-mət\ *adj* : not legitimate — **il·le·git·i·mate·ly** *adv*

il·lic·it \il-'is-ət\ *adj* : not permitted : UNLAWFUL — **il·lic·it·ly** *adv*

il·lit·er·a·cy \il-'it-ə-rə-sē\ *n* : the quality or state of being illiterate

¹il·lit·er·ate \il-'it-ə-rət\ *adj* **1** : unable to read or write **2** : showing lack of education — **il·lit·er·ate·ly** *adv*

²illiterate *n* : an illiterate person

ill—man·nered \'il-'man-ərd\ *adj* : not polite

ill—na·tured \'il-'nā-chərd\ *adj* : having a bad disposition — **ill—na·tured·ly** *adv*

ill·ness \'il-nəs\ *n* : SICKNESS 1, 2

il·log·i·cal \il-'äj-i-kəl\ *adj* : not using or following good reasoning — **il·log·i·cal·ly** *adv*

ill—tem·pered \'il-'tem-pərd\ *adj* : ILL-NATURED

ill—treat \'il-'trēt\ *vb* : to treat in a cruel or improper way — **ill—treat·ment** \-'trēt-mənt\ *n*

il·lu·mi·nate \il-'ü-mə-,nāt\ *vb* **il·lu·mi·nat·ed; il·lu·mi·nat·ing 1** : to supply with light : light up **2** : to make clear : EXPLAIN

il·lu·mi·na·tion \il-,ü-mə-'nā-shən\ *n* **1** : the action of illuminating : the state of being illuminated **2** : the amount of light

ill—use \'il-'yüz\ *vb* : ILL-TREAT

il·lu·sion \il-'ü-zhən\ *n* **1** : a misleading image presented to the eye **2** : the state or fact of being led to accept as true something unreal or imagined **3** : a mistaken idea

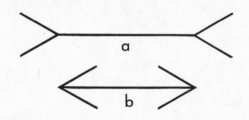

illusion 1: *a* is equal to *b* but *a* seems longer

il·lu·sive \il-'ü-siv\ *adj* : ILLUSORY

il·lu·so·ry \il-'ü-sə-rē\ *adj* : based on or producing illusion : DECEPTIVE

il·lus·trate \'il-əs-,trāt\ *vb* **il·lus·trat·ed; il·lus·trat·ing 1** : to make clear by using examples **2** : to supply with pictures or diagrams meant to explain or decorate **3** : to serve as an example

il·lus·tra·tion \,il-əs-'trā-shən\ *n* **1** : the action of illustrating : the condition of being illustrated **2** : an example or instance used to make something clear **3** : a picture or diagram that explains or decorates ⟨a dictionary with color *illustrations*⟩

il·lus·tra·tive \il-'əs-trət-iv\ *adj* : serving or meant to illustrate ⟨*illustrative* examples⟩

il·lus·tra·tor \'il-əs-,trāt-ər\ *n* : an artist who makes illustrations (as for books)

il·lus·tri·ous \il-'əs-trē-əs\ *adj* : EMINENT

ill will *n* : unfriendly feeling

im- — see IN-

I'm \īm\ : I am

¹im·age \'im-ij\ *n* **1** : something (as a statue) made to look like a person or thing **2** : a picture of an object formed by a device (as a mirror or lens) **3** : a mental picture of something not present : IMPRESSION **4** : a person very much like another

²image *vb* **im·aged; im·ag·ing 1** : to describe in words or pictures **2** : REFLECT 2

imag·in·able \im-'aj-ə-nə-bəl\ *adj* : possible to imagine

imag·i·nary \im-'aj-ə-,ner-ē\ *adj* : existing only in the imagination : not real

imag·i·na·tion \im-,aj-ə-'nā-shən\ *n* **1** : the act, process, or power of forming a mental picture of something not present and especially of something one has not known or experienced **2** : creative ability **3** : a creation of the mind

imag·i·na·tive \im-'aj-ə-nət-iv\ *adj* **1** : of or relating to imagination **2** : having a lively imagination — **imag·i·na·tive·ly** *adv*

imag·ine \im-'aj-ən\ *vb* **imag·ined; imag·in·ing 1** : to form a mental picture of **2** : THINK 2

¹im·be·cile \'im-bə-səl\ *n* : a person of such low intelligence as to need help in simple personal care

²imbecile *or* **im·be·cil·ic** \ə-'sil-ik\ *adj* : of very low intelligence : very stupid

im·be·cil·i·ty \,im-bə-'sil-ət-ē\ *n, pl* **im·be·cil·i·ties 1** : the quality or state of being imbecile **2** : something very foolish

imbed *variant of* EMBED

im·i·tate \'im-ə-,tāt\ *vb* **im·i·tat·ed; im·i·tat·ing 1** : to follow as a pattern, model, or example **2** : to be or appear like : RESEMBLE **3** : to copy exactly : MIMIC **synonyms** see COPY

¹im·i·ta·tion \,im-ə-'tā-shən\ *n* **1** : an act of imitating **2** : ¹COPY 1

²imitation *adj* : like something else and especially something better ⟨*imitation* leather⟩

im·i·ta·tive \'im-ə-,tāt-iv\ *adj* **1** : involving imitation **2** : given to imitating

im·mac·u·late \im-'ak-yə-lət\ *adj* **1** : having no stain or blemish : PURE **2** : perfectly clean — **im·mac·u·late·ly** *adv*

im·ma·te·ri·al \,im-ə-'tir-ē-əl\ *adj* : not important : INSIGNIFICANT

im·ma·ture \,im-ə-'tùr, -'tyùr\ *adj* : not yet fully grown or ripe — **im·ma·ture·ly** *adv*

im·mea·sur·able \im-'ezh-ə-rə-bəl\ *adj* : impossible to measure — **im·mea·sur·ably** \-blē\ *adv*

im·me·di·ate \im-'ēd-ē-ət\ *adj* **1** : acting or being without anything else between ⟨the *immediate* cause of death⟩ **2** : being next in line or nearest in relationship ⟨my *immediate* family⟩ **3** : closest in importance ⟨our *immediate* needs⟩ **4** : acting or being without any delay **5** : not far away in time or space ⟨in the *immediate* future⟩

im·me·di·ate·ly \im-'ēd-ē-ət-lē\ *adv* **1** : with nothing between **2** : right away

im·mense \im-'ens\ *adj* : very great in size or amount : HUGE — **im·mense·ly** *adv*

im·men·si·ty \im-'en-sət-ē\ *n, pl* **im·men·si·ties** : the quality or state of being immense

im·merse \im-'ərs\ *vb* **im·mersed; im·mers·ing 1** : to plunge into something (as a fluid) that surrounds or covers **2** : to become completely involved with

im·mi·grant \'im-i-grənt\ *n* : a person who comes to a country to live there

im·mi·grate \'im-ə-,grāt\ *vb* **im·mi·grat·ed; im·mi·grat·ing** : to come into a foreign country to live

im·mi·gra·tion \,im-ə-'grā-shən\ *n* : an act or instance of immigrating

im·mi·nent \'im-ə-nənt\ *adj* : being about to happen — **im·mi·nent·ly** *adv*

im·mo·bile \im-'ō-bəl\ *adj* : unable to move or be moved

im·mo·bi·lize \im-'ō-bə-,līz\ *vb* **im·mo·bi·lized; im·mo·bi·liz·ing** : to fix in place : make immovable

im·mod·est \im-'äd-əst\ *adj* : not modest ⟨*immodest* conduct⟩ — **im·mod·est·ly** *adv*

im·mod·es·ty \im-'äd-ə-stē\ *n* : lack of modesty

im·mor·al \im-'òr-əl\ *adj* : not moral : BAD 4 — **im·mor·al·ly** *adv*

im·mo·ral·i·ty \,im-ò-'ral-ət-ē\ *n, pl* **im·mo·ral·i·ties 1** : the quality or state of being immoral **2** : an immoral act or custom

¹im·mor·tal \im-'òrt-l\ *adj* : living or lasting forever — **im·mor·tal·ly** *adv*

²immortal *n* **1** : an immortal being **2** : a person of lasting fame

im·mor·tal·i·ty \,im-òr-'tal-ət-ē\ *n* **1** : the quality or state of being immortal : endless life **2** : lasting fame or glory

im·mov·able \im-'ü-və-bəl\ *adj* : impossible to move : firmly fixed — **im·mov·ably** \-blē\ *adv*

im·mune \im-'yün\ *adj* **1** : ¹EXEMPT ⟨*immune* from punishment⟩ **2** : having a strong or special power to resist

\ə\ abut	\aú\ out	\i\ tip	\ò\ saw	\ù\ foot
\ər\ further	\ch\ chin	\ī\ life	\òi\ coin	\y\ yet
\a\ mat	\e\ pet	\j\ job	\th\ thin	\yü\ few
\ā\ take	\ē\ easy	\ng\ sing	\th̲\ this	\yù\ cure
\ä\ cot, cart	\g\ go	\ō\ bone	\ü\ food	\zh\ vision

immune system *n* : the system of the body that fights infection and disease and that includes especially the white blood cells and antibodies and the organs that produce them

im·mu·ni·ty \im-'yü-nət-ē\ *n, pl* **im·mu·ni·ties 1** : EXEMPTION 1 ⟨*immunity* from a tax⟩ **2** : power to resist infection whether natural or acquired (as by vaccination)

im·mu·ni·za·tion \ˌim-yə-nə-'zā-shən\ *n* : treatment (as with a vaccine) to produce immunity to a disease

im·mu·nize \'im-yə-ˌnīz\ *vb* **im·mu·nized; im·mu·niz·ing** : to make immune

imp \'imp\ *n* **1** : a small demon **2** : a mischievous child

im·pact \'im-ˌpakt\ *n* **1** : a striking together of two bodies **2** : a strong effect

im·pair \im-'paər, -'peər\ *vb* : to make less (as in quantity, value, or strength) or worse : DAMAGE

im·pale \im-'pāl\ *vb* **im·paled; im·pal·ing** : to pierce with something pointed

im·part \im-'pärt\ *vb* **1** : to give or grant from a supply ⟨the sun *imparts* warmth⟩ **2** : to make known

im·par·tial \im-'pär-shəl\ *adj* : not partial or biased : FAIR, JUST — **im·par·tial·ly** *adv*

im·par·ti·al·i·ty \im-ˌpär-shē-'al-ət-ē\ *n* : the quality or state of being impartial

im·pass·able \im-'pas-ə-bəl\ *adj* : impossible to pass, cross, or travel

im·pas·sioned \im-'pash-ənd\ *adj* : showing very strong feeling

im·pas·sive \im-'pas-iv\ *adj* : not feeling or showing emotion — **im·pas·sive·ly** *adv*

im·pa·tience \im-'pā-shəns\ *n* **1** : lack of patience **2** : restless or eager desire

im·pa·tient \im-'pā-shənt\ *adj* **1** : not patient **2** : showing or coming from impatience ⟨an *impatient* reply⟩ **3** : restless and eager ⟨*impatient* to leave⟩ — **im·pa·tient·ly** *adv*

im·peach \im-'pēch\ *vb* : to charge a public official formally with misconduct in office

Word History The English word *impeach* originally meant "to hinder." It came from an early French word that had the same meaning. This early French word came from a Latin word that meant "to put shackles on the feet." This word was derived from two Latin words. The first meant "in" or "on" and the second meant "foot."

im·pede \im-'pēd\ *vb* **im·ped·ed; im·ped·ing** : to disturb the movement or progress of

im·ped·i·ment \im-'ped-ə-mənt\ *n* **1** : something that impedes **2** : a defect in speech

im·pel \im-'pel\ *vb* **im·pelled; im·pel·ling** : to urge or drive forward or into action : FORCE

im·pend \im-'pend\ *vb* : to threaten to occur very soon ⟨an *impending* storm⟩

im·pen·e·tra·ble \im-'pen-ə-trə-bəl\ *adj* **1** : impossible to penetrate ⟨*impenetrable* walls⟩ **2** : impossible to understand ⟨an *impenetrable* mystery⟩ — **im·pen·e·tra·bly** \-blē\ *adv*

im·pen·i·tent \im-'pen-ə-tənt\ *adj* : not penitent

im·per·a·tive \im-'per-ət-iv\ *adj* **1** : expressing a command, request, or strong encouragement ⟨"Come here" is an *imperative* sentence⟩ **2** : impossible to avoid or ignore : URGENT

im·per·cep·ti·ble \ˌim-pər-'sep-tə-bəl\ *adj* **1** : not perceptible by the senses or by the mind **2** : very small or gradual — **im·per·cep·ti·bly** \-blē\ *adv*

im·per·fect \im-'pər-fikt\ *adj* : not perfect : FAULTY — **im·per·fect·ly** *adv*

im·per·fec·tion \ˌim-pər-'fek-shən\ *n* **1** : the quality or state of being imperfect **2** : FLAW, FAULT

im·pe·ri·al \im-'pir-ē-əl\ *adj* : of or relating to an empire or its ruler ⟨an *imperial* decree⟩ — **im·pe·ri·al·ly** *adv*

im·per·il \im-'per-əl\ *vb* **im·per·iled** *or* **im·per·illed; im·per·il·ing** *or* **im·per·il·ling** : to place in great danger : ENDANGER

im·per·ish·able \im-'per-ish-ə-bəl\ *adj* : INDESTRUCTIBLE — **im·per·ish·ably** \-blē\ *adv*

im·per·son·al \im-'pərs-n-əl\ *adj* : not referring or belonging to a specific person — **im·per·son·al·ly** *adv*

im·per·son·ate \im-'pərs-n-ˌāt\ *vb* **im·per·son·at·ed; im·per·son·at·ing** : pretend to be another person ⟨*impersonate* a police officer⟩

synonyms IMPERSONATE, PLAY, and ACT mean to pretend to be somebody else. IMPERSONATE suggests that one tries to make oneself look and sound like some other person as much as possible ⟨you are very good at *impersonating* famous people⟩ PLAY suggests that one takes a part in a play, movie, or TV show ⟨you can *play* the part of the spy⟩ act may be used in situations other than performing in a drama or pretending to be a person ⟨*act* like you're a dog begging for a bone⟩

im·per·son·a·tion \im-ˌpərs-n-'ā-shən\ *n* : the act of impersonating

im·per·ti·nence \im-'pərt-n-əns\ *n* **1** : the

quality or state of being impertinent **2** : a rude act or remark

im·per·ti·nent \im-'pərt-n-ənt\ *adj* : INSOLENT, RUDE — **im·per·ti·nent·ly** *adv*

im·per·turb·able \ˌim-pər-'tər-bə-bəl\ *adj* : hard to disturb or upset — **im·per·turb·ably** \-blē\ *adv*

im·per·vi·ous \im-'pər-vē-əs\ *adj* : not letting something enter or pass through ⟨a coat *impervious* to rain⟩

im·pet·u·ous \im-'pech-ə-wəs\ *adj* : IMPULSIVE, RASH — **im·pet·u·ous·ly** *adv*

im·pi·ous \'im-pē-əs\ *adj* : not pious : IRREVERENT — **im·pi·ous·ly** *adv*

imp·ish \'im-pish\ *adj* : MISCHIEVOUS 3 ⟨an *impish* glance⟩ — **imp·ish·ly** *adv*

im·pla·ca·ble \im-'plak-ə-bəl, -'plā-kə-\ *adj* : impossible to please, satisfy, or change ⟨*implacable* enemies⟩ — **im·pla·ca·bly** \-blē\ *adv*

im·plant \im-'plant\ *vb* : to fix or set securely or deeply

im·ple·ment \'im-plə-mənt\ *n* : an article (as a tool) intended for a certain use ⟨farm *implements*⟩

im·pli·cate \'im-plə-ˌkāt\ *vb* **im·pli·cat·ed; im·pli·cat·ing** : to show to be connected or involved

im·pli·ca·tion \ˌim-plə-'kā-shən\ *n* **1** : the act of implicating : the state of being implicated **2** : the act of implying **3** : something implied

im·plic·it \im-'plis-ət\ *adj* **1** : understood though not put clearly into words **2** : ABSOLUTE 2 ⟨*implicit* trust⟩ — **im·plic·it·ly** *adv*

im·plore \im-'plōr\ *vb* **im·plored; im·plor·ing** : to call upon with a humble request : BESEECH

im·ply \im-'plī\ *vb* **im·plied; im·ply·ing** : to express indirectly : suggest rather than say plainly

im·po·lite \ˌim-pə-'līt\ *adj* : not polite — **im·po·lite·ly** *adv* — **im·po·lite·ness** *n*

¹im·port \im-'pōrt\ *vb* **1** : ²MEAN 3 **2** : to bring (as goods) into a country usually for selling ⟨*import* coffee⟩

²im·port \'im-ˌpōrt\ *n* **1** : MEANING 1 **2** : IMPORTANCE **3** : something brought into a country

im·por·tance \im-'pȯrt-ns\ *n* : the quality or state of being important : SIGNIFICANCE

im·por·tant \im-'pȯrt-nt\ *adj* **1** : SIGNIFICANT ⟨graduation is an *important* day in your lives⟩ **2** : having power or authority ⟨an *important* leader⟩ — **im·por·tant·ly** *adv*

im·por·ta·tion \ˌim-ˌpōr-'tā-shən\ *n* **1** : the act or practice of importing **2** : something imported

im·por·tu·nate \im-'pȯr-chə-nət\ *adj*

: making a nuisance of oneself with requests and demands — **im·por·tu·nate·ly** *adv*

im·por·tune \ˌim-pər-'tün, -'tyün\ *vb* **im·por·tuned; im·por·tun·ing** : to beg or urge so much as to be a nuisance

im·pose \im-'pōz\ *vb* **im·posed; im·pos·ing** **1** : to establish or apply as a charge or penalty ⟨*impose* a tax⟩ **2** : to force someone to accept or put up with ⟨*impose* one's will on another⟩ **3** : to take unfair advantage ⟨*impose* on a friend's good nature⟩

im·pos·ing \im-'pō-zing\ *adj* : impressive because of size, dignity, or magnificence

im·pos·si·bil·i·ty \im-ˌpäs-ə-'bil-ət-ē\ *n, pl* **im·pos·si·bil·i·ties** **1** : the quality or state of being impossible **2** : something impossible

im·pos·si·ble \im-'päs-ə-bəl\ *adj* **1** : incapable of being or of occurring **2** : HOPELESS 2 ⟨an *impossible* situation⟩ **3** : very bad or unpleasant — **im·pos·si·bly** \-blē\ *adv*

im·pos·tor \im-'päs-tər\ *n* : a person who pretends to be someone else in order to deceive

im·pos·ture \im-'päs-chər\ *n* : the act or conduct of an impostor

im·po·tence \'im-pə-təns\ *n* : the quality or state of being impotent

im·po·tent \'im-pə-tənt\ *adj* : lacking in power or strength — **im·po·tent·ly** *adv*

im·pound \im-'paund\ *vb* : to shut up in or as if in an enclosed place ⟨*impound* cattle⟩

im·pov·er·ish \im-'päv-ə-rish\ *vb* **1** : to make poor **2** : to use up the strength or richness of ⟨*impoverished* soil⟩

im·prac·ti·cal \im-'prak-ti-kəl\ *adj* : not practical ⟨an *impractical* plan⟩ — **im·prac·ti·cal·ly** *adv*

im·pre·cise \ˌim-pri-'sīs\ *adj* : not clear or exact — **im·pre·cise·ly** *adv*

im·preg·nate \im-'preg-ˌnāt\ *vb* **im·preg·nat·ed; im·preg·nat·ing** **1** : to make fertile or fruitful **2** : to cause (a material) to be filled with something

im·press \im-'pres\ *vb* **1** : to fix in or on one's mind ⟨*impress* these rules in your minds⟩ **2** : to move or affect strongly ⟨greatly *impressed* by the beauty of the city⟩

im·pres·sion \im-'presh-ən\ *n* **1** : the act or process of impressing **2** : something (as a design) made by pressing or stamp-

\ə\ **abut**	\au̇\ **out**	\i\ **tip**	\ȯ\ **saw**	\u̇\ **foot**
\ər\ **further**	\ch\ **chin**	\ī\ **life**	\ȯi\ **coin**	\y\ **yet**
\a\ **mat**	\e\ **pet**	\j\ **job**	\th\ **thin**	\yü\ **few**
\ā\ **take**	\ē\ **easy**	\ng\ **sing**	\th\ **this**	\yu̇\ **cure**
\ä\ **cot, cart**	\g\ **go**	\ō\ **bone**	\ü\ **food**	\zh\ **vision**

ing **3** : something that impresses or is impressed on one's mind ⟨these words made a strong *impression*⟩ **4** : a memory or belief that is vague or uncertain

im·pres·sion·able \im-'presh-ə-nə-bəl\ *adj* : easy to impress or influence

im·pres·sive \im-'pres-iv\ *adj* : having the power to impress the mind or feelings ⟨an *impressive* speech⟩ — **im·pres·sive·ly** *adv*

¹**im·print** \im-'print\ *vb* **1** : to mark by pressure : STAMP **2** : to fix firmly

²**im·print** \'im-,print\ *n* : something imprinted or printed : IMPRESSION

im·pris·on \im-'priz-n\ *vb* : to put in prison

im·pris·on·ment \im-'priz-n-mənt\ *n* : the act of imprisoning : the state of being imprisoned

im·prob·a·bil·i·ty \im-,präb-ə-'bil-ət-ē\ *n* : the quality or state of being improbable

im·prob·a·ble \im-'präb-ə-bəl\ *adj* : not probable — **im·prob·a·bly** \-blē\ *adv*

im·prop·er \im-'präp-ər\ *adj* : not proper, right, or suitable — **im·prop·er·ly** *adv*

improper fraction *n* : a fraction whose numerator is equal to or larger than the denominator ⟨¹³⁄₄ is an *improper fraction*⟩

im·prove \im-'prüv\ *vb* **im·proved; im·prov·ing** : to make or become better — **im·prov·er** *n*

im·prove·ment \im-'prüv-mənt\ *n* **1** : the act or process of improving **2** : increased value or excellence **3** : something that adds to the value or appearance (as of a house)

im·prov·i·sa·tion \im-,präv-ə-'zā-shən\ *n* **1** : the act or art of improvising **2** : something that is improvised

im·pro·vise \'im-prə-,vīz\ *vb* **im·pro·vised; im·pro·vis·ing 1** : to compose, recite, or sing without studying or practicing ahead of time **2** : to make, invent, or arrange with whatever is at hand

im·pu·dence \'im-pyəd-əns\ *n* : impudent behavior or speech : INSOLENCE, DISRESPECT

im·pu·dent \'im-pyə-dənt\ *adj* : being bold and disrespectful : INSOLENT — **im·pu·dent·ly** *adv*

im·pulse \'im-,pəls\ *n* **1** : a force that starts a body into motion **2** : the motion produced by a starting force **3** : a sudden stirring up of the mind and spirit to do something **4** : the wave of change that passes along a stimulated nerve and carries information to the brain

im·pul·sive \im-'pəl-siv\ *adj* **1** : acting or tending to act on impulse **2** : resulting from a sudden impulse — **im·pul·sive·ly** *adv*

im·pure \im-'pyùr\ *adj* **1** : not pure : UNCLEAN, dirty **2** : mixed with something else that is usually not as good — **im·pure·ly** *adv*

im·pu·ri·ty \im-'pyùr-ət-ē\ *n, pl* **im·pu·ri·ties 1** : the quality or state of being impure **2** : something that is or makes impure

¹**in** \in\ *prep* **1** : enclosed or surrounded by : WITHIN ⟨swim *in* the lake⟩ **2** : INTO 1 ⟨ran in the house⟩ **3** : DURING ⟨*in* the summer⟩ **4** : WITH 7 ⟨wrote *in* pencil⟩ **5** — used to show a state or condition ⟨you're *in* luck⟩ ⟨we're *in* trouble⟩ **6** — used to show manner or purpose ⟨*in* a hurry⟩ ⟨said *in* reply⟩ **7** : INTO 2 ⟨broke *in* pieces⟩

²**in** \'in\ *adv* **1** : to or toward the inside ⟨went *in* and closed the door⟩ **2** : to or toward some particular place ⟨flew *in* yesterday⟩ **3** : ¹NEAR 1 ⟨play close *in*⟩ **4** : into the midst of something ⟨mix *in* the flour⟩ **5** : to or at its proper place ⟨fit a piece *in*⟩ **6** : on the inner side : WITHIN ⟨everyone is *in*⟩ **7** : at hand or on hand ⟨the evidence is *in*⟩

³**in** \'in\ *adj* **1** : being inside or within ⟨the *in* part⟩ **2** : headed or bound inward ⟨the *in* train⟩

¹**in-** *or* **il-** *or* **im-** *or* **ir-** *prefix* : not : NON-, UN- — usually *il-*before *l* ⟨*il*logical⟩ and *im-* before *b*, *m*, or *p* ⟨*im*moral⟩ ⟨*im*practical⟩ and *ir-* before *r* ⟨*ir*reducible⟩ and *in-* before other sounds ⟨*in*complete⟩

²**in-** *or* **il-** *or* **im-** *or* **ir-** *prefix* **1** : in : within : into : toward : on ⟨*in*set⟩ — usually *il-* before *l*, *im-* before *b*, *m*, or *p*, *ir-* before *r* and *in-* before other sounds **2** : EN- ⟨*im*peril⟩

in·abil·i·ty \,in-ə-'bil-ət-ē\ *n* : the condition of being unable to do something : lack of ability

in·ac·ces·si·bil·i·ty \,in-ak-,ses-ə-'bil-ət-ē\ *n* : the quality or state of being inaccessible

in·ac·ces·si·ble \,in-ak-'ses-ə-bəl\ *adj* : hard or impossible to get to or at

in·ac·cu·ra·cy \in-'ak-yə-rə-sē\ *n, pl* **in·ac·cu·ra·cies 1** : lack of accuracy **2** : ERROR, MISTAKE

in·ac·cu·rate \in-'ak-yə-rət\ *adj* : not right or correct : not exact — **in·ac·cu·rate·ly** *adv*

in·ac·tive \in-'ak-tiv\ *adj* : not active : IDLE

in·ac·tiv·i·ty \,in-ak-'tiv-ət-ē\ *n* : the state of being inactive

in·ad·e·qua·cy \in-'ad-i-kwə-sē\ *n, pl* **in·ad·e·qua·cies** : the condition of being not enough or not good enough

in·ad·e·quate \in-'ad-i-kwət\ *adj* : not enough or not good enough

in·ad·vis·able \,in-əd-'vī-zə-bəl\ *adj* : not wise to do : UNWISE

in·alien·able \in-'āl-yə-nə-bəl\ *adj* : impossible to take away or give up ⟨*inalienable* rights⟩

inane \i-'nān\ *adj* : silly and pointless ⟨*inane* remarks⟩ — **inane·ly** *adv*

in·an·i·mate \in-'an-ə-mət\ *adj* : not living : LIFELESS

in·ap·pro·pri·ate \,in-ə-'prō-prē-ət\ *adj* : not appropriate — **in·ap·pro·pri·ate·ly** *adv*

in·as·much as \,in-əz-,məch-əz\ *conj* : considering that : ³SINCE 2

in·at·ten·tion \,in-ə-'ten-chən\ *n* : failure to pay attention

in·at·ten·tive \,in-ə-'tent-iv\ *adj* : not paying attention — **in·at·ten·tive·ly** *adv*

in·au·di·ble \in-'od-ə-bəl\ *adj* : impossible to hear — **in·au·di·bly** \-blē\ *adv*

in·au·gu·ral \in-'o-gyə-rəl\ *adj* : of or relating to an inauguration ⟨an *inaugural* ball⟩

in·au·gu·rate \in-'o-gyə-,rāt\ *vb* **in·au·gu·rat·ed; in·au·gu·rat·ing** **1** : to introduce into office with suitable ceremonies : INSTALL **2** : to celebrate the opening of **3** : to bring into being or action ⟨*inaugurate* a new plan⟩

in·au·gu·ra·tion \in-,o-gyə-'rā-shən\ *n* : an act or ceremony of inaugurating

in·born \'in-'bòrn\ *adj* : INSTINCTIVE

in·breed \'in-'brēd\ *vb* **in·bred** \-'bred\; **in·breed·ing** : to breed with closely related individuals

in·can·des·cent \,in-kən-'des-nt\ *adj* : white or glowing with great heat

incandescent lamp *n* : a lamp whose light is produced by the glow of a wire heated by an electric current

in·ca·pa·ble \in-'kā-pə-bəl\ *adj* : not able to do something

¹in·cense \'in-,sens\ *n* **1** : material used to produce a perfume when burned **2** : the perfume given off by burning incense

²in·cense \in-'sens\ *vb* **in·censed; in·cens·ing** : to make very angry

in·cen·tive \in-'sent-iv\ *n* : something that makes a person try or work hard or harder

in·ces·sant \in-'ses-nt\ *adj* : going on and on : not stopping or letting up — **in·ces·sant·ly** *adv*

¹inch \'inch\ *n* : a unit of length equal to ¹⁄₃₆ yard or 2.54 centimeters

²inch *vb* : to move a little bit at a time

in·ci·dent \'in-sə-dənt\ *n* : an often unimportant happening that may form a part of a larger event

synonyms INCIDENT, OCCURRENCE, and EVENT mean something that happens. INCIDENT suggests something that is brief and not very important ⟨although there were a few unpleasant *incidents*, the trip was a success⟩ OCCURRENCE may suggest something that is not planned or expected ⟨those *occurrences* could not have been predicted⟩ EVENT is often used of something that is important ⟨the big *events* of last year⟩

¹in·ci·den·tal \,in-sə-'dent-l\ *adj* **1** : happening by chance **2** : of minor importance ⟨*incidental* expenses⟩

²incidental *n* : something incidental

in·ci·den·tal·ly \,in-sə-'dent-l-ē\ *adv* : as a matter of less interest or importance

in·cin·er·ate \in-'sin-ə-,rāt\ *vb* **in·cin·er·at·ed; in·cin·er·at·ing** : to burn to ashes

in·cin·er·a·tor \in-'sin-ə-,rāt-ər\ *n* : a furnace or a container for burning waste materials

in·cise \in-'sīz\ *vb* **in·cised; in·cis·ing** : to cut into : CARVE, ENGRAVE

in·ci·sion \in-'sizh-ən\ *n* : a cutting into something or the cut or wound that results

in·ci·sor \in-'sī-zər\ *n* : a tooth (as any of the four front teeth of the human upper or lower jaw) for cutting

in·cite \in-'sīt\ *vb* **in·cit·ed; in·cit·ing** : to move to action : stir up : ROUSE

in·clem·ent \in-'klem-ənt\ *adj* : STORMY 1 ⟨*inclement* weather⟩

in·cli·na·tion \,in-klə-'nā-shən\ *n* **1** : an act or the action of bending or leaning **2** : a usually favorable feeling toward something ⟨had an *inclination* to laugh⟩ **3** : ²SLANT 1, TILT

¹in·cline \in-'klīn\ *vb* **in·clined; in·clin·ing** **1** : to cause to bend or lean **2** : to be drawn to an opinion or course of action **3** : ¹SLOPE, LEAN

²in·cline \'in-,klīn\ *n* : ²SLOPE 2

in·clined \in-'klīnd\ *adj* **1** : having an inclination ⟨not *inclined* to answer⟩ **2** : having a slope

inclose, inclosure *variant of* ENCLOSE, ENCLOSURE

in·clude \in-'klüd\ *vb* **in·clud·ed; in·clud·ing** : to take in or have as part of a whole

in·clu·sion \in-'klü-zhən\ *n* **1** : an act of including : the state of being included **2** : something included

in·clu·sive \in-'klü-siv, -ziv\ *adj* **1** : cover-

\ə\ abut	\aủ\ out	\i\ tip	\ȯ\ saw	\ủ\ foot	
\ər\ further	\ch\ chin	\ī\ life	\ȯi\ coin	\y\ yet	
\a\ mat	\e\ pet	\j\ job	\th\ thin	\yü\ few	
\ā\ take	\ē\ easy	\ng\ sing	\th\ this	\yủ\ cure	
\ä\ cot, cart	\g\ go	\ō\ bone	\ü\ food	\zh\ vision	

ing everything or all important points ⟨an *inclusive* fee⟩ ⟨an *inclusive* tour⟩ **2** : including the stated limits and all in between ⟨from ages three to ten *inclusive*⟩

in·cog·ni·to \ˌin-ˌkäg-'nēt-ō, in-'käg-nə-ˌtō\ *adv or adj* : with one's identity kept secret

in·co·her·ence \ˌin-kō-'hir-əns\ *n* : the quality or state of being incoherent

in·co·her·ent \ˌin-kō-'hir-ənt\ *adj* : not connected in a clear or logical way — **in·co·her·ent·ly** *adv*

in·come \'in-ˌkəm\ *n* : a gain usually measured in money that comes in from labor, business, or property

income tax *n* : a tax on the income of a person or business

in·com·pa·ra·ble \in-'käm-pə-rə-bəl\ *adj* : MATCHLESS — **in·com·pa·ra·bly** \-blē\ *adv*

in·com·pat·i·ble \ˌin-kəm-'pat-ə-bəl\ *adj* : not able to live or work together in harmony — **in·com·pat·i·bly** \-blē\ *adv*

in·com·pe·tence \in-'käm-pət-əns\ *n* : the state or fact of being incompetent

in·com·pe·tent \in-'käm-pət-ənt\ *adj* : not able to do a good job — **in·com·pe·tent·ly** *adv*

in·com·plete \ˌin-kəm-'plēt\ *adj* : not complete : not finished — **in·com·plete·ly** *adv*

in·com·pre·hen·si·ble \ˌin-ˌkäm-pri-'hen-sə-bəl\ *adj* : impossible to understand — **in·com·pre·hen·si·bly** \-blē\ *adv*

in·con·ceiv·able \ˌin-kən-'sē-və-bəl\ *adj* **1** : impossible to imagine or put up with **2** : hard to believe — **in·con·ceiv·ably** \-blē\ *adv*

in·con·gru·ous \in-'käng-grə-wəs\ *adj* : not harmonious, suitable, or proper ⟨*incongruous* colors⟩ — **in·con·gru·ous·ly** *adv*

in·con·sid·er·ate \ˌin-kən-'sid-ə-rət\ *adj* : careless of the rights or feelings of others

in·con·sis·tent \ˌin-kən-'sis-tənt\ *adj* **1** : not being in agreement **2** : not keeping to the same thoughts or practices : CHANGEABLE

in·con·spic·u·ous \ˌin-kən-'spik-yə-wəs\ *adj* : not easily seen or noticed — **in·con·spic·u·ous·ly** *adv*

¹in·con·ve·nience \ˌin-kən-'vē-nyəns\ *n* **1** : the quality or state of being inconvenient **2** : something inconvenient

²inconvenience *vb* **in·con·ve·nienced; in·con·ve·nienc·ing** : to cause inconvenience to

in·con·ve·nient \ˌin-kən-'vē-nyənt\ *adj* : not convenient — **in·con·ve·nient·ly** *adv*

in·cor·po·rate \in-'kȯr-pə-ˌrāt\ *vb* **in·cor·po·rat·ed; in·cor·po·rat·ing** **1** : to join or unite closely into a single mass or body **2**

: to make a corporation of ⟨decided to *incorporate* the family business⟩

in·cor·po·ra·tion \in-ˌkȯr-pə-'rā-shən\ *n* : an act of incorporating : the state of being incorporated

in·cor·rect \ˌin-kə-'rekt\ *adj* **1** : not correct : not accurate or true : WRONG **2** : showing no care for duty or for moral or social standards — **in·cor·rect·ly** *adv* — **in·cor·rect·ness** *n*

¹in·crease \in-'krēs\ *vb* **in·creased; in·creas·ing** : to make or become greater (as in size)

²in·crease \'in-ˌkrēs\ *n* **1** : the act of increasing **2** : something added (as by growth)

in·creas·ing·ly \in-'krē-sing-lē\ *adv* : more and more ⟨the path was *increasingly* rough⟩

in·cred·i·ble \in-'kred-ə-bəl\ *adj* : too strange or unlikely to be believed ⟨an *incredible* tale of adventure⟩— **in·cred·i·bly** \-blē\ *adv*

in·cre·du·li·ty \ˌin-kri-'dü-lət-ē, -'dyü-\ *n* : the quality or state of being incredulous

in·cred·u·lous \in-'krej-ə-ləs\ *adj* : feeling or showing disbelief : SKEPTICAL — **in·cred·u·lous·ly** *adv*

in·crim·i·nate \in-'krim-ə-ˌnāt\ *vb* **in·crim·i·nat·ed; in·crim·i·nat·ing** : to charge with or involve in a crime or fault : ACCUSE

incrust *variant of* ENCRUST

in·cu·bate \'ing-kyə-ˌbāt\ *vb* **in·cu·bat·ed; in·cu·bat·ing** **1** : to sit upon eggs to hatch them by warmth **2** : to keep under conditions good for hatching or development

in·cu·ba·tion \ˌing-kyə-'bā-shən\ *n* **1** : an act of incubating : the state of being incubated **2** : the time between infection with germs and the appearance of disease symptoms

in·cu·ba·tor \'ing-kyə-ˌbāt-ər\ *n* **1** : an apparatus that provides enough heat to hatch eggs artificially **2** : an apparatus to help the growth of tiny newborn babies

in·cum·bent \in-'kəm-bənt\ *n* : the holder of an office or position

in·cur \in-'kər\ *vb* **in·curred; in·cur·ring** : to bring upon oneself ⟨*incur* suspicion⟩

in·cur·able \in-'kyür-ə-bəl\ *adj* : impossible to cure — **in·cur·ably** \-blē\ *adv*

in·debt·ed \in-'det-əd\ *adj* : being in debt : owing something — **in·debt·ed·ness** *n*

in·de·cen·cy \in-'dēs-n-sē\ *n, pl* **in·de·cen·cies** **1** : lack of decency **2** : an indecent act or word

in·de·cent \in-'dēs-nt\ *adj* : not decent : COARSE, VULGAR

in·de·ci·sion \ˌin-di-'sizh-ən\ *n* : a swaying between two or more courses of action

in·de·ci·sive \ˌin-di-ˈsī-siv\ *adj* **1** : not decisive or final ⟨an *indecisive* battle⟩ **2** : finding it hard to make decisions ⟨an *indecisive* person⟩ — **in·de·ci·sive·ly** *adv* — **in·de·ci·sive·ness** *n*

in·deed \in-ˈdēd\ *adv* : in fact : TRULY

in·de·fen·si·ble \ˌin-di-ˈfen-sə-bəl\ *adj* : impossible to defend

in·def·i·nite \in-ˈdef-ə-nət\ *adj* **1** : not clear or fixed in meaning or details **2** : not limited (as in amount or length) — **in·def·i·nite·ly** *adv*

indefinite article *n* : either of the articles *a* or *an* used to show that the following noun refers to any person or thing of the kind named

in·del·i·ble \in-ˈdel-ə-bəl\ *adj* **1** : impossible to erase, remove, or blot out ⟨an *indelible* impression⟩ **2** : making marks not easily removed — **in·del·i·bly** \-blē\ *adv*

in·del·i·cate \in-ˈdel-i-kət\ *adj* : not polite or proper : COARSE — **in·del·i·cate·ly** *adv*

in·dent \in-ˈdent\ *vb* : to set (as the first line of a paragraph) in from the margin

in·den·ta·tion \ˌin-ˌden-ˈtā-shən\ *n* **1** : a cut or dent in something **2** : the action of indenting or the state of being indented

in·de·pen·dence \ˌin-də-ˈpen-dəns\ *n* : the quality or state of being independent

Independence Day *n* : July 4 observed as a legal holiday in honor of the adoption of the Declaration of Independence in 1776

¹in·de·pen·dent \ˌin-də-ˈpen-dənt\ *adj* **1** : not under the control or rule of another **2** : not connected with something else : SEPARATE **3** : not depending on anyone else for money to live on **4** : able to make up one's own mind — **in·de·pen·dent·ly** *adv*

²independent *n* : an independent person (as a voter who belongs to no political party)

in·de·scrib·able \ˌin-di-ˈskrī-bə-bəl\ *adj* : impossible to describe — **in·de·scrib·ably** \-blē\ *adv*

in·de·struc·ti·ble \ˌin-di-ˈstrək-tə-bəl\ *adj* : impossible to destroy — **in·de·struc·ti·bly** \-blē\ *adv*

¹in·dex \ˈin-ˌdeks\ *n, pl* **in·dex·es** *or* **in·di·ces** \ˈin-də-ˌsēz\ **1** : a list of names or topics (as in a book) given in alphabetical order and showing where each is to be found ⟨a card *index*⟩ **2** : POINTER 1 ⟨the *index* on a scale⟩ **3** : ¹SIGN 5, INDICATION ⟨the price of goods is an *index* of business conditions⟩

²index *vb* **1** : to provide with an index **2** : to list in an index

index finger *n* : the finger next to the thumb

¹In·di·an \ˈin-dē-ən\ *n* **1** : a person born or living in India **2** : a member of any of the first people to live in North and South America except the Eskimos

Word History Once the name *India* was not used just for the land that we now call *India*. The whole of the distant East was often called *India*. Columbus went west hoping to sail to the far East. When he reached the West Indies, he thought that he had come to the outer islands of "India," the far East. That is why the people that he found there were given the name *Indian*.

²Indian *adj* **1** : of or relating to India or its peoples **2** : of or relating to the American Indians or their languages

Indian club *n* : a wooden club swung for exercise

Indian corn *n* : a tall American cereal grass widely grown for its large ears of grain which are used as food or for feeding livestock

Indian pipe *n* : a waxy white leafless woodland herb with nodding flowers

Indian summer *n* : a period of mild weather in late autumn or early winter

in·di·cate \ˈin-də-ˌkāt\ *vb* **in·di·cat·ed; in·di·cat·ing** **1** : to point out or point to **2** : to state or express briefly

Indian pipe

in·di·ca·tion \ˌin-də-ˈkā-shən\ *n* **1** : the act of indicating **2** : something that indicates

in·dic·a·tive \in-ˈdik-ət-iv\ *adj* **1** : representing an act or state as a fact that can be known or proved ⟨in "I am here," the verb "am" is in the *indicative* mood⟩ **2** : pointing out

in·di·ca·tor \ˈin-də-ˌkāt-ər\ *n* **1** : one that indicates **2** : a pointer on a dial or scale **3** : ¹DIAL 3, GAUGE 3

indices *pl of* INDEX

\ə\ **abut**	\au̇\ **out**	\i\ **tip**	\ȯ\ **saw**	\u̇\ **foot**
\ər\ **further**	\ch\ **chin**	\ī\ **life**	\ȯi\ **coin**	\y\ **yet**
\a\ **mat**	\e\ **pet**	\j\ **job**	\th\ **thin**	\yü\ **few**
\ā\ **take**	\ē\ **easy**	\ng\ **sing**	\t̲h̲\ **this**	\yu̇\ **cure**
\ä\ **cot, cart**	\g\ **go**	\ō\ **bone**	\ü\ **food**	\zh\ **vision**

in·dict \in-'dīt\ *vb* : to charge with an offense or crime : ACCUSE — **in·dict·ment** \-'dīt-mənt\ *n*

in·dif·fer·ence \in-'dif-ə-rəns, -'dif-rəns\ *n* 1 : the condition or fact of being indifferent 2 : lack of interest

in·dif·fer·ent \in-'dif-ə-rənt, -'dif-rənt\ *adj* 1 : having no choice : showing neither interest nor dislike 2 : neither good nor bad — **in·dif·fer·ent·ly** *adv*

in·di·gest·ible \,in-dī-'jes-tə-bəl, -də-\ *adj* : not digestible : not easy to digest

in·di·ges·tion \,in-dī-'jes-chən, -də-\ *n* : discomfort caused by slow or painful digestion

in·dig·nant \in-'dig-nənt\ *adj* : filled with or expressing indignation — **in·dig·nant·ly** *adv*

in·dig·na·tion \,in-dig-'nā-shən\ *n* : anger caused by something unjust or unworthy

in·dig·ni·ty \in-'dig-nət-ē\ *n, pl* **in·dig·ni·ties** 1 : an act that injures one's dignity or self-respect 2 : treatment that shows a lack of respect

in·di·go \'in-di-,gō\ *n, pl* **in·di·gos** *or* **in·di·goes** 1 : a blue dye made artificially and formerly obtained from plants (**indigo plants**) 2 : a dark grayish blue

in·di·rect \,in-də-'rekt, -dī-\ *adj* 1 : not straight or direct ⟨an *indirect* route⟩ 2 : not straightforward ⟨*indirect* methods⟩ 3 : not having a plainly seen connection ⟨an *indirect* cause⟩ — **in·di·rect·ly** *adv* — **in·di·rect·ness** *n*

indirect object *n* : an object that represents the secondary goal of the action of its verb ⟨"me" in "you gave me the book" is an *indirect object*⟩

in·dis·creet \,in-dis-'krēt\ *adj* : not discreet — **in·dis·creet·ly** *adv*

in·dis·cre·tion \,in-dis-'kresh-ən\ *n* 1 : lack of discretion 2 : an indiscreet act or remark

in·dis·crim·i·nate \,in-dis-'krim-ə-nət\ *adj* : showing lack of discrimination

in·dis·pens·able \,in-dis-'pen-sə-bəl\ *adj* : ¹ESSENTIAL 2 ⟨an *indispensable* employee⟩ — **in·dis·pens·ably** \-blē\ *adv*

in·dis·posed \,in-dis-'pōzd\ *adj* 1 : somewhat unwell 2 : not willing

in·dis·po·si·tion \,in-,dis-pə-'zish-ən\ *n* : the condition of being indisposed : a slight illness

in·dis·put·able \,in-dis-'pyüt-ə-bəl, in-'dis-pyət-\ *adj* : not disputable : UNQUESTIONABLE — **in·dis·put·ably** \-blē\ *adv*

in·dis·tinct \,in-dis-'tingkt\ *adj* : not distinct — **in·dis·tinct·ly** *adv* — **in·dis·tinct·ness** *n*

in·dis·tin·guish·able \,in-dis-'ting-gwish-ə-bəl\ *adj* : impossible to distinguish clearly — **in·dis·tin·guish·ably** \-blē\ *adv*

¹in·di·vid·u·al \,in-də-'vij-ə-wəl\ *adj* 1 : of or relating to an individual 2 : intended for one person 3 : ¹PARTICULAR 1, SEPARATE 4 : having a special quality : DISTINCTIVE 1 ⟨an *individual* style⟩ — **in·di·vid·u·al·ly** *adv*

²individual *n* 1 : a single member of a class 2 : a single human being

in·di·vid·u·al·i·ty \,in-də-,vij-ə-'wal-ət-ē\ *n, pl* **in·di·vid·u·al·i·ties** 1 : the qualities that set one person or thing off from all others 2 : the quality or state of being an individual

in·di·vis·i·ble \,in-də-'viz-ə-bəl\ *adj* : impossible to divide or separate — **in·di·vis·i·bly** \-blē\ *adv*

in·doc·tri·nate \in-'däk-trə-,nāt\ *vb* **in·doc·tri·nat·ed; in·doc·tri·nat·ing** 1 : INSTRUCT 1, TEACH 2 : to teach the ideas, opinions, or beliefs of a certain group

in·doc·tri·na·tion \in-,däk-trə-'nā-shən\ *n* : the act or process of indoctrinating

in·do·lence \'in-də-ləns\ *n* : LAZINESS

in·do·lent \'in-də-lənt\ *adj* : LAZY, IDLE

in·dom·i·ta·ble \in-'däm-ət-ə-bəl\ *adj* : UNCONQUERABLE — **in·dom·i·ta·bly** \-blē\ *adv*

in·door \,in-'dōr\ *adj* 1 : of or relating to the inside of a building 2 : done, used, or belonging within a building ⟨an *indoor* job⟩ ⟨*indoor* clothes⟩

in·doors \'in-'dōrz\ *adv* : in or into a building ⟨games to be played *indoors*⟩

indorse *variant of* ENDORSE

in·du·bi·ta·ble \in-'dü-bət-ə-bəl, -'dyü-\ *adj* : being beyond question or doubt — **in·du·bi·ta·bly** \-blē\ *adv*

in·duce \in-'düs, -'dyüs\ *vb* **in·duced; in·duc·ing** 1 : to lead on to do something 2 : to bring about : CAUSE 3 : to produce (as an electric current) by induction

in·duce·ment \in-'düs-mənt, -'dyüs-\ *n* 1 : the act of inducing 2 : something that induces

in·duct \in-'dəkt\ *vb* 1 : to place in office : INSTALL 2 : to take in as a member of a military service

in·duc·tion \in-'dək-shən\ *n* 1 : the act or process of inducting 2 : the production of an electrical or magnetic effect through the influence of a nearby magnet, electrical current, or electrically charged body

in·dulge \in-'dəlj\ *vb* **in·dulged; in·dulg·ing** 1 : to give in to one's own or another's desires : HUMOR 2 : to allow oneself the pleasure of having or doing something

in·dul·gence \in-'dəl-jəns\ *n* **1** : the act of indulging : the state of being indulgent **2** : an indulgent act **3** : something indulged in

in·dul·gent \in-'dəl-jənt\ *adj* : characterized by indulgence : LENIENT — **in·dul·gent·ly** *adv*

in·dus·tri·al \in-'dəs-trē-əl\ *adj* **1** : of, relating to, or engaged in industry ⟨*industrial* work⟩ **2** : having highly developed industries ⟨*industrial* nations⟩ — **in·dus·tri·al·ly** *adv*

in·dus·tri·al·ist \in-'dəs-trē-ə-ləst\ *n* : a person owning or engaged in the management of an industry

in·dus·tri·al·iza·tion \in-,dəs-trē-ə-lə-'zā-shən\ *n* : the process of industrializing : the state of being industrialized

in·dus·tri·al·ize \in-'dəs-trē-ə-,līz\ *vb* **in·dus·tri·al·ized; in·dus·tri·al·iz·ing** : to make or become industrial

in·dus·tri·ous \in-'dəs-trē-əs\ *adj* : working hard and steadily : DILIGENT — **in·dus·tri·ous·ly** *adv*

in·dus·try \'in-dəs-trē\ *n, pl* **in·dus·tries** **1** : the habit of working hard and steadily **2** : businesses that provide a certain product or service ⟨the oil *industry*⟩ ⟨the shipping *industry*⟩ **3** : manufacturing activity ⟨*industry* was slowing down⟩

-ine \,īn, ən, ,ēn\ *adj suffix* : of, relating to, or like ⟨alkal*ine*⟩

in·ed·i·ble \in-'ed-ə-bəl\ *adj* : not fit for food

in·ef·fec·tive \,in-ə-'fek-tiv\ *adj* : not producing the desired effect — **in·ef·fec·tive·ly** *adv*

in·ef·fec·tu·al \,in-ə-'fek-chə-wəl\ *adj* : not producing the proper or usual effect — **in·ef·fec·tu·al·ly** *adv*

in·ef·fi·cien·cy \,in-ə-'fish-ən-sē\ *n, pl* **in·ef·fi·cien·cies** : the state or an instance of being inefficient

in·ef·fi·cient \,in-ə-'fish-ənt\ *adj* **1** : not effective : INEFFECTUAL **2** : not able or willing to do something well ⟨*inefficient* workers⟩ — **in·ef·fi·cient·ly** *adv*

in·elas·tic \,in-ə-'las-tik\ *adj* : not elastic

in·el·i·gi·bil·i·ty \in-,el-ə-jə-'bil-ət-ē\ *n* : the condition or fact of being ineligible

in·el·i·gi·ble \in-'el-ə-jə-bəl\ *adj* : not eligible

in·ept \in-'ept\ *adj* **1** : not suited to the occasion ⟨an *inept* remark⟩ **2** : lacking in skill or ability — **in·ept·ly** *adv* — **in·ept·ness** *n*

in·equal·i·ty \,in-i-'kwäl-ət-ē\ *n, pl* **in·equal·i·ties** **1** : the quality of being unequal or uneven **2** : an instance of being uneven

in·ert \in-'ərt\ *adj* : unable or slow to move or react ⟨*inert* gas⟩ — **in·ert·ly** *adv* — **in·ert·ness** *n*

in·er·tia \in-'ər-shə\ *n* **1** : a property of matter by which it remains at rest or in motion in the same straight line unless acted upon by some external force **2** : a tendency not to move or change

in·er·tial \in-'ər-shəl\ *adj* : of or relating to inertia

in·es·cap·able \,in-ə-'skā-pə-bəl\ *adj* : INEVITABLE — **in·es·cap·ably** \-blē\ *adv*

in·ev·i·ta·bil·i·ty \in-,ev-ət-ə-'bil-ət-ē\ *n* : the quality or state of being inevitable

in·ev·i·ta·ble \in-'ev-ət-ə-bəl\ *adj* : sure to happen : CERTAIN — **in·ev·i·ta·bly** \-blē\ *adv*

in·ex·act \,in-ig-'zakt\ *adj* : INACCURATE — **in·ex·act·ly** *adv* — **in·ex·act·ness** *n*

in·ex·cus·able \,in-ik-'skyü-zə-bəl\ *adj* : not to be excused — **in·ex·cus·ably** \-blē\ *adv*

in·ex·haust·ible \,in-ig-'zȯs-tə-bəl\ *adj* : plentiful enough not to give out or be used up — **in·ex·haust·ibly** \-blē\ *adv*

in·ex·o·ra·ble \in-'ek-sə-rə-bəl\ *adj* : RELENTLESS — **in·ex·o·ra·bly** \-blē\ *adv*

in·ex·pe·di·ent \,in-ik-'spēd-ē-ənt\ *adj* : not suitable or advisable

in·ex·pen·sive \,in-ik-'spen-siv\ *adj* : ¹CHEAP **1** — **in·ex·pen·sive·ly** *adv* — **in·ex·pen·sive·ness** *n*

in·ex·pe·ri·ence \,in-ik-'spir-ē-əns\ *n* : lack of experience

in·ex·pe·ri·enced \,in-ik-'spir-ē-ənst\ *adj* : having little or no experience

in·ex·pli·ca·ble \,in-ik-'splik-ə-bəl, in-'ek-splik-\ *adj* : impossible to explain or account for ⟨an *inexplicable* mystery⟩ — **in·ex·pli·ca·bly** \-blē\ *adv*

in·ex·press·ible \,in-ik-'spres-ə-bəl\ *adj* : being beyond one's power to express : INDESCRIBABLE — **in·ex·press·ibly** \-blē\ *adv*

in·fal·li·ble \in-'fal-ə-bəl\ *adj* **1** : not capable of being wrong **2** : not likely to fail : SURE ⟨an *infallible* remedy⟩ — **in·fal·li·bly** \-blē\ *adv*

in·fa·mous \'in-fə-məs\ *adj* **1** : having an evil reputation ⟨an *infamous* person⟩ **2** : DETESTABLE ⟨an *infamous* crime⟩ — **in·fa·mous·ly** *adv*

in·fa·my \'in-fə-mē\ *n, pl* **in·fa·mies** **1** : an evil reputation **2** : an infamous act

in·fan·cy \'in-fən-sē\ *n, pl* **in·fan·cies** **1**

\ə\ **a**bout	\au̇\ **ou**t	\i\ **ti**p	\ȯ\ **saw**	\u̇\ **foo**t
\ər\ **fur**ther	\ch\ **ch**in	\ī\ **li**fe	\ȯi\ **coi**n	\y\ **yet**
\a\ **mat**	\e\ **pet**	\j\ **job**	\th\ **thin**	\yü\ **few**
\ā\ **take**	\ē\ **easy**	\ng\ **sing**	\th\ **this**	\yu̇\ **cure**
\ä\ **cot, cart**	\g\ **go**	\ō\ **bone**	\ü\ **food**	\zh\ **vision**

: early childhood **2** : a beginning or early period of existence ⟨the *infancy* of our country⟩

¹**in·fant** \'in-fənt\ *n* **1** : a child in the first period of life **2** : ²MINOR

Word History The word *infant* came from a Latin word. The basic meaning of this Latin word was "not talking." This Latin word was used to refer to children who were too young to talk. In time the Latin word came to be used for older children as well. The English word *infant* is most often used for a very young child.

²**infant** *adj* **1** : of or relating to infancy **2** : intended for young children ⟨*infant* food⟩

in·fan·tile \'in-fən-ˌtīl\ *adj* : CHILDISH

infantile paralysis *n* : POLIO

in·fan·try \'in-fən-trē\ *n*, *pl* **in·fan·tries** : a branch of an army composed of soldiers trained to fight on foot

in·fat·u·at·ed \in-'fach-ə-ˌwāt-əd\ *adj* : having a foolish or very strong love or admiration

in·fat·u·a·tion \in-ˌfach-ə-'wā-shən\ *n* : the state of being infatuated

in·fect \in-'fekt\ *vb* **1** : to cause disease germs to be present in or on ⟨*infected* bedding⟩ **2** : to pass on a germ or disease to **3** : to enter and cause disease in ⟨bacteria that *infect* wounds⟩ **4** : to cause to share one's feelings

in·fec·tion \in-'fek-shən\ *n* **1** : the act or process of infecting : the state of being infected **2** : any disease caused by germs

in·fec·tious \in-'fek-shəs\ *adj* **1** : passing from one to another in the form of a germ **2** : capable of being easily spread ⟨an *infectious* laugh⟩

in·fer \in-'fər\ *vb* **in·ferred; in·fer·ring** **1** : to arrive at as a conclusion **2** : ¹SURMISE **3** : to point out **4** : HINT, SUGGEST

in·fer·ence \'in-fə-rəns\ *n* **1** : the act or process of inferring **2** : something inferred

¹**in·fe·ri·or** \in-'fir-ē-ər\ *adj* **1** : situated lower down (as in place or importance) **2** : of little or less importance, value, or merit

²**inferior** *n* : an inferior person or thing

in·fe·ri·or·i·ty \in-ˌfir-ē-'òr-ət-ē\ *n* **1** : the state of being inferior **2** : a sense of being inferior

in·fer·nal \in-'fərn-l\ *adj* **1** : of or relating to hell ⟨the *infernal* regions⟩ **2** : very bad or unpleasant : DAMNABLE ⟨stop that *infernal* noise⟩ — **in·fer·nal·ly** *adv*

in·fer·tile \in-'fərt-l\ *adj* : not fertile

in·fest \in-'fest\ *vb* : to spread or swarm in or over in a troublesome manner

in·fi·del \'in-fəd-l, -fə-ˌdel\ *n* : a person who does not believe in a certain religion

in·fi·del·i·ty \ˌin-fə-'del-ət-ē\ *n*, *pl* **in·fi·del·i·ties** **1** : lack of belief in a certain religion **2** : DISLOYALTY

in·field \'in-ˌfēld\ *n* **1** : the diamond-shaped part of a baseball field inside the bases and home plate **2** : the players in the infield

in·field·er \'in-ˌfēl-dər\ *n* : a baseball player who plays in the infield

in·fi·nite \'in-fə-nət\ *adj* **1** : having no limits of any kind **2** : seeming to be without limits ⟨took *infinite* care⟩ — **in·fi·nite·ly** *adv*

in·fin·i·tive \in-'fin-ət-iv\ *n* : a verb form serving as a noun or as a modifier and at the same time taking objects and adverbial modifiers ⟨"to do" in "I have nothing to do" is an *infinitive*⟩

in·fin·i·ty \in-'fin-ət-ē\ *n*, *pl* **in·fin·i·ties** **1** : the quality of being infinite **2** : a space, quantity, or period of time that is without limit

in·firm \in-'fərm\ *adj* : weak or frail in body (as from age or disease)

in·fir·ma·ry \in-'fər-mə-rē\ *n*, *pl* **in·fir·ma·ries** : a place for the care and housing of infirm or sick people

in·fir·mi·ty \in-'fər-mət-ē\ *n*, *pl* **in·fir·mi·ties** : the condition of being infirm

in·flame \in-'flām\ *vb* **in·flamed; in·flam·ing** **1** : to excite to too much action or feeling **2** : to cause to redden or grow hot (as from anger) **3** : to make or become sore, red, and swollen

in·flam·ma·ble \in-'flam-ə-bəl\ *adj* **1** : FLAMMABLE **2** : easily inflamed : EXCITABLE

in·flam·ma·tion \ˌin-flə-'mā-shən\ *n* **1** : the act of inflaming : the state of being inflamed **2** : a bodily response to injury in which heat, redness, and swelling are present

in·flam·ma·to·ry \in-'flam-ə-ˌtōr-ē\ *adj* **1** : tending to excite anger or disorder ⟨an *inflammatory* speech⟩ **2** : causing or having inflammation ⟨an *inflammatory* disease⟩

in·flat·able \in-'flāt-ə-bəl\ *adj* : possible to inflate ⟨an *inflatable* toy⟩

in·flate \in-'flāt\ *vb* **in·flat·ed; in·flat·ing** **1** : to swell or fill with air or gas ⟨*inflate* a balloon⟩ **2** : to cause to increase beyond proper limits ⟨*inflated* prices⟩

in·fla·tion \in-'flā-shən\ *n* **1** : an act of inflating : the state of being inflated **2** : a continual rise in the price of goods and services

in·flect \in-'flekt\ *vb* **1** : to change a word

by inflection **2** : to change the pitch of a person's voice

in·flec·tion \in-'flek-shən\ *n* **1** : a change in the pitch of a person's voice **2** : a change in a word that shows a grammatical difference (as of number, person, or tense)

in·flec·tion·al \in-'flek-shən-l\ *adj* : of or relating to inflection ⟨"darkened" and "darkening" are *inflectional* forms of the verb "darken"⟩

in·flex·i·ble \in-'flek-sə-bəl\ *adj* **1** : not easily bent or twisted : RIGID **2** : not easily influenced or persuaded : FIRM

in·flict \in-'flikt\ *vb* **1** : to give by or as if by striking ⟨*inflict* a wound⟩ **2** : to cause to be put up with ⟨*inflict* punishment⟩

in·flo·res·cence \,in-flə-'res-ns\ *n* : the arrangement of flowers on a stalk

¹**in·flu·ence** \'in-,flü-əns\ *n* **1** : the act or power of producing an effect without apparent force or direct authority **2** : a person or thing that influences

²**influence** *vb* **in·flu·enced; in·flu·enc·ing** : to have an influence on

in·flu·en·tial \,in-flü-'en-chəl\ *adj* : having influence

in·flu·en·za \,in-flü-'en-zə\ *n* : a very contagious virus disease like a severe cold with fever

Word History Once people blamed the stars for things that happened on earth. They even thought that some diseases were caused by the influence of the stars. An Italian word that meant "influence" came to be used for a disease as well. This disease broke out in Rome and spread through much of Europe. It was then that the word *influenza* came into the English language. It came from the Italian word that meant "influence."

in·form \in-'form\ *vb* **1** : to let a person know something **2** : to give information so as to accuse or cause suspicion — **in·form·er** *n*

in·for·mal \in-'for-məl\ *adj* **1** : not formal ⟨an *informal* party⟩ **2** : suitable for ordinary or everyday use ⟨*informal* clothes⟩ — **in·for·mal·ly** *adv*

in·for·mal·i·ty \,in-for-'mal-ət-ē\ *n, pl* **in·for·mal·i·ties** **1** : the quality or state of being informal **2** : an informal act

in·form·ant \in-'for-mənt\ *n* : a person who informs

in·for·ma·tion \,in-fər-'mā-shən\ *n* **1** : the giving or getting of knowledge **2** : knowledge obtained from investigation, study, or instruction **3** : NEWS 3

synonyms INFORMATION, KNOWLEDGE, and LEARNING mean what is or can be known. INFORMATION may suggest a collection of facts gathered from many places ⟨a book with much *information* about baseball⟩ KNOWLEDGE suggests a body of known facts and a set of ideas that are the product of study, observation, or experience ⟨a *knowledge* of birds⟩ LEARNING suggests knowledge acquired by long and careful study ⟨the *learning* of a lifetime went into that book⟩

in·for·ma·tive \in-'for-mət-iv\ *adj* : giving information : INSTRUCTIVE

in·frac·tion \in-'frak-shən\ *n* : VIOLATION

in·fra·red \,in-frə-'red\ *adj* : being, relating to, or producing rays like light but lying outside the visible spectrum at its red end

in·fre·quent \in-'frē-kwənt\ *adj* **1** : seldom happening : RARE **2** : not placed, made, or done at frequent intervals ⟨made *infrequent* stops⟩ — **in·fre·quent·ly** *adv*

in·fringe \in-'frinj\ *vb* **in·fringed; in·fring·ing** **1** : to fail to obey or act in agreement with : VIOLATE ⟨*infringe* a law⟩ **2** : to go further than is right or fair to another : ENCROACH — **in·fringe·ment** \-mənt\ *n*

in·fu·ri·ate \in-'fyur-ē-,āt\ *vb* **in·fu·ri·at·ed; in·fu·ri·at·ing** : to make furious : ENRAGE

in·fuse \in-'fyüz\ *vb* **in·fused; in·fus·ing** **1** : to put in as if by pouring ⟨*infused* a spirit of cooperation into the group⟩ **2** : to steep without boiling ⟨*infuse* tea⟩ — **in·fu·sion** \in-'fyü-zhən\ *n*

¹**-ing** \ing\ *vb suffix or adj suffix* — used to form the present participle ⟨sail*ing*⟩ and sometimes to form adjectives that do not come from a verb ⟨hulk*ing*⟩

²**-ing** *n suffix* **1** : action or process ⟨meet*ing*⟩ **2** : product or result of an action or process ⟨engrav*ing*⟩ ⟨earn*ings*⟩ **3** : something used in or connected with making or doing ⟨bedd*ing*⟩ ⟨roof*ing*⟩

in·ge·nious \in-'jēn-yəs\ *adj* : showing ingenuity : CLEVER ⟨an *ingenious* idea⟩ — **in·ge·nious·ly** *adv*

in·ge·nu·ity \,in-jə-'nü-ət-ē, -'nyü-\ *n, pl* **in·ge·nu·ities** : skill or cleverness in discovering, inventing, or planning

in·gen·u·ous \in-'jen-yə-wəs\ *adj* **1** : FRANK, STRAIGHTFORWARD **2** : NAIVE 1 — **in·gen·u·ous·ly** *adv* — **in·gen·u·ous·ness** *n*

\ə\ abut	\aů\ out	\i\ tip	\ȯ\ saw	\ů\ foot
\ər\ further	\ch\ chin	\ī\ life	\ȯi\ coin	\y\ yet
\a\ mat	\e\ pet	\j\ job	\th\ thin	\yü\ few
\ā\ take	\ē\ easy	\ng\ sing	\th\ this	\yů\ cure
\ä\ cot, cart	\g\ go	\ō\ bone	\ü\ food	\zh\ vision

in·got \'ing-gət\ *n* : a mass of metal cast into a shape that is easy to handle or store

in·gra·ti·ate \in-'grā-shē-,āt\ *vb* **in·gra·ti·at·ed; in·gra·ti·at·ing** : to gain favor for by effort

in·gra·ti·at·ing \in-'grā-shē-,āt-ing\ *adj* **1** : PLEASING ⟨an *ingratiating* smile⟩ **2** : intended to gain someone's favor ⟨*ingratiating* behavior⟩ — **in·gra·ti·at·ing·ly** *adv*

in·grat·i·tude \in-'grat-ə-,tüd, -,tyüd\ *n* : lack of gratitude

in·gre·di·ent \in-'grēd-ē-ənt\ *n* : one of the substances that make up a mixture

in·hab·it \in-'hab-ət\ *vb* : to live or dwell in

in·hab·it·ant \in-'hab-ət-ənt\ *n* : one who lives in a place permanently

in·ha·la·tion \,in-ə-'lā-shən, -hə-\ *n* : the act or an instance of inhaling

in·hale \in-'hāl\ *vb* **in·haled; in·hal·ing 1** : to draw in by breathing **2** : to breathe in

in·her·ent \in-'hir-ənt\ *adj* : belonging to or being a part of the nature of a person or thing — **in·her·ent·ly** *adv*

in·her·it \in-'her-ət\ *vb* **1** : to get by legal right from a person at his or her death **2** : to get by heredity ⟨*inherit* a strong body⟩

in·her·i·tance \in-'her-ət-əns\ *n* **1** : the act of inheriting **2** : something inherited

in·hib·it \in-'hib-ət\ *vb* : to prevent or hold back from doing something

in·hos·pi·ta·ble \,in-,häs-'pit-ə-bəl, in-'häs-pit-\ *adj* : not friendly or generous : not showing hospitality — **in·hos·pi·ta·bly** \-blē\ *adv*

in·hu·man \in-'hyü-mən, -'yü-\ *adj* **1** : lacking pity or kindness **2** : unlike what might be expected by a human ⟨an *inhuman* scream⟩ — **in·hu·man·ly** *adv*

in·hu·mane \,in-hyü-'mān, -yü-\ *adj* : not humane ⟨*inhumane* treatment⟩

in·hu·man·i·ty \,in-hyü-'man-ət-ē\ *n, pl* **in·hu·man·i·ties** : a cruel act or attitude

in·iq·ui·tous \in-'ik-wət-əs\ *adj* : WICKED 1

in·iq·ui·ty \in-'ik-wət-ē\ *n, pl* **in·iq·ui·ties** : ¹SIN 1

¹ini·tial \in-'ish-əl\ *adj* **1** : of, relating to, or being a beginning ⟨an *initial* effort⟩ **2** : placed or standing at the beginning : FIRST

²initial *n* **1** : the first letter of a name **2** : a large letter beginning a text or a paragraph

³initial *vb* **ini·tialed** *or* **ini·tialled; ini·tial·ing** *or* **ini·tial·ling** : to mark with an initial or with one's initials

ini·ti·ate \in-'ish-ē-,āt\ *vb* **ini·ti·at·ed; ini·ti·at·ing 1** : to set going **2** : to admit into a club by special ceremonies

ini·ti·a·tion \in-,ish-ē-'ā-shən\ *n* **1** : the act or an instance of initiating : the process of being initiated **2** : the ceremonies with which a person is made a member of a club

ini·tia·tive \in-'ish-ət-iv\ *n* **1** : a first step or movement ⟨take the *initiative*⟩ **2** : energy shown in initiating action : ENTERPRISE ⟨a person of great *initiative*⟩

in·ject \in-'jekt\ *vb* **1** : to throw or drive into something **2** : to force a fluid into (as a part of the body) for medical reasons

in·jec·tion \in-'jek-shən\ *n* **1** : an act or instance of injecting **2** : something injected

in·junc·tion \in-'jəngk-shən\ *n* : a court order commanding or forbidding the doing of some act

in·jure \'in-jər\ *vb* **in·jured; in·jur·ing 1** : to do an injustice to : WRONG **2** : to cause pain or harm to

in·ju·ri·ous \in-'jùr-ē-əs\ *adj* : causing injury

in·ju·ry \'in-jə-rē\ *n, pl* **in·ju·ries 1** : an act that damages or hurts **2** : hurt, damage, or loss suffered **synonyms** see HARM

in·jus·tice \in-'jəs-təs\ *n* **1** : violation of a person's rights **2** : an unjust act

¹ink \'ingk\ *n* : a usually liquid material for writing or printing

²ink *vb* : to put ink on

in·kling \'ing-kling\ *n* : a vague notion : HINT

ink·stand \'ingk-,stand\ *n* : a small stand for holding ink and pens

ink·well \'ing-,kwel\ *n* : a container for ink

inky \'ing-kē\ *adj* **ink·i·er; ink·i·est 1** : consisting of or like ink ⟨*inky* darkness⟩ **2** : soiled with or as if with ink ⟨*inky* hands⟩

in·laid \'in-'lād\ *adj* **1** : set into a surface in a decorative design **2** : decorated with a design or material set into a surface

¹in·land \'in-,land, -lənd\ *n* : the part of a country away from the coast or boundaries

²inland *adj* : of or relating to the part of a country away from the coast

³inland *adv* : into or toward the area away from a coast

in–law \'in-,lo\ *n* : a relative by marriage

¹in·lay \'in-'lā\ *vb* **in·laid** \-'lād\; **in·lay·ing** : to set into a surface for decoration or strengthening

²in·lay \'in-,lā\ *n* : inlaid work : material used in inlaying

in·let \'in-,let\ *n* **1** : a small or narrow bay **2** : an opening for intake

in·mate \'in-,māt\ *n* **1** : one of a group living in a single residence **2** : a person confined in an institution (as an asylum or prison)

in·most \'in-ˌmōst\ *adj* : INNERMOST

inn \'in\ *n* : a place that provides a place to sleep and food for travelers

in·ner \'in-ər\ *adj* **1** : located farther in **2** : of or relating to the mind or spirit

inner ear *n* : the inner hollow part of the ear that contains sense organs which perceive sound and help keep the body properly balanced

in·ner·most \'in-ər-ˌmōst\ *adj* : farthest inward

in·ning \'in-ing\ *n* : a division of a baseball game that consists of a turn at bat for each team

inn·keep·er \'in-ˌkē-pər\ *n* : the person who runs an inn

in·no·cence \'in-ə-səns\ *n* : the quality or state of being innocent

in·no·cent \'in-ə-sənt\ *adj* **1** : free from sin : PURE **2** : free from guilt or blame **3** : free from evil influence or effect : HARMLESS ⟨*innocent* fun⟩ — **in·no·cent·ly** *adv*

in·noc·u·ous \in-'äk-yə-wəs\ *adj* : not harmful

in·no·va·tion \ˌin-ə-'vā-shən\ *n* **1** : the introduction of something new **2** : a new idea, method, or device : NOVELTY

in·nu·mer·a·ble \in-'ü-mə-rə-bəl, -'yü-\ *adj* : too many to be counted

in·oc·u·late \in-'äk-yə-ˌlāt\ *vb* **in·oc·u·lat·ed; in·oc·u·lat·ing** : to inject a serum, vaccine, or weakened germ into to protect against or treat a disease

Word History You can insert a bud from one plant in another plant. If you are skillful and lucky, the bud will grow. The English word *inoculate* at first meant "to insert a bud in a plant." It came from a Latin word. This Latin word was formed from two Latin words. One meant "in." The other meant "eye" or "bud."

in·oc·u·la·tion \in-ˌäk-yə-'lā-shən\ *n* **1** : the act or an instance of inoculating **2** : material used in inoculating

in·of·fen·sive \ˌin-ə-'fen-siv\ *adj* **1** : not harmful **2** : PEACEFUL 1 **3** : not offensive

in·op·por·tune \in-ˌäp-ər-'tün, -'tyün\ *adj* : INCONVENIENT ⟨an *inopportune* time⟩

in·quest \'in-ˌkwest\ *n* : an official investigation especially into the cause of a death

in·quire \in-'kwīr\ *vb* **in·quired; in·quir·ing** **1** : to ask about ⟨*inquired* the way to the station⟩ **2** : to make an investigation **3** : to ask a question ⟨*inquired* about the weather⟩ — **in·quir·er** *n* — **in·quir·ing·ly** *adv*

in·qui·ry \'in-ˌkwī-rē, -kwə-\ *n, pl* **in·qui-**

ries **1** : the act of inquiring **2** : a request for information **3** : a thorough examination

in·quis·i·tive \in-'kwiz-ət-iv\ *adj* **1** : given to seeking information **2** : tending to ask questions — **in·quis·i·tive·ly** *adv* — **in·quis·i·tive·ness** *n*

in·sane \in-'sān\ *adj* **1** : not normal or healthy in mind **2** : used by or for people who are insane — **in·sane·ly** *adv*

in·san·i·ty \in-'san-ət-ē\ *n* : the condition of being insane : mental illness

in·sa·tia·ble \in-'sā-shə-bəl\ *adj* : impossible to satisfy ⟨*insatiable* thirst⟩

in·scribe \in-'skrīb\ *vb* **in·scribed; in·scrib·ing** **1** : to write, engrave, or print as a lasting record **2** : to write, engrave, or print something on or in ⟨*inscribe* a book⟩

in·scrip·tion \in-'skrip-shən\ *n* : something that is inscribed

in·sect \'in-ˌsekt\ *n* **1** : a small and often winged animal that has six jointed legs and a body formed of three parts ⟨flies, bees, and lice are true *insects*⟩ **2** : an animal (as a spider or a centipede) similar to the true insects

Word History The bodies of most insects are divided into parts. They look as if someone might have cut into them. The ancient Greeks gave insects a name that meant "cut up." The Latin word for an insect was a translation of the Greek name. This Latin word was formed from two Latin words. One meant "in" and the other meant "to cut." The English word *insect* came from the Latin word for an insect.

in·sec·ti·cide \in-'sek-tə-ˌsīd\ *n* : a chemical used to kill insects

in·se·cure \ˌin-si-'kyur\ *adj* : not safe or secure — **in·se·cure·ly** *adv*

in·se·cu·ri·ty \ˌin-si-'kyur-ət-ē\ *n* : the quality or state of being insecure

in·sen·si·ble \in-'sen-sə-bəl\ *adj* **1** : UNCONSCIOUS 1 **2** : not able to feel ⟨*insensible* to pain⟩ **3** : not aware of or caring about something ⟨*insensible* to fear⟩

in·sen·si·tive \in-'sen-sət-iv\ *adj* : not sensitive : lacking feeling — **in·sen·si·tive·ly** *adv*

in·sen·si·tiv·i·ty \in-ˌsen-sə-'tiv-ət-ē\ *n* : lack of sensitivity

in·sep·a·ra·bil·i·ty \in-ˌsep-ə-rə-'bil-ət-ē\ *n* : the quality or state of being inseparable

in·sep·a·ra·ble \in-'sep-ə-rə-bəl\ *adj* : im-

\ə\ abut	\au̇\ out	\i\ tip	\o\ saw	\u̇\ foot
\ər\ further	\ch\ chin	\ī\ life	\oi\ coin	\y\ yet
\a\ mat	\e\ pet	\j\ job	\th\ thin	\yü\ few
\ā\ take	\ē\ easy	\ng\ sing	\th\ this	\yu̇\ cure
\ä\ cot, cart	\g\ go	\ō\ bone	\ü\ food	\zh\ vision

possible to separate — **in·sep·a·ra·bly** \-blē\ *adv*

¹in·sert \in-'sərt\ *vb* **1** : to put in ⟨*insert* one's hands in one's pockets⟩ **2** : to set in and make fast ⟨*insert* a patch in the sleeve⟩

²in·sert \'in-,sərt\ *n* : something that is or is meant to be inserted

in·ser·tion \in-'sər-shən\ *n* **1** : the act or process of inserting **2** : ²INSERT

¹in·set \'in-,set\ *n* : ²INSERT

²inset *vb* **in·set** *or* **in·set·ted; in·set·ting** : ¹INSERT 2

¹in·side \in-'sīd, 'in-,sīd\ *n* **1** : an inner side, surface, or space : INTERIOR ⟨the *inside* of a box⟩ **2** : ENTRAILS — usually used in pl.

²inside *adj* **1** : of, relating to, or being on or near the inside ⟨an *inside* wall⟩ **2** : relating or known to a certain few people ⟨*inside* information⟩

³inside *prep* **1** : to or on the inside of ⟨they are *inside* the house⟩ **2** : before the end of : WITHIN ⟨I'll finish *inside* an hour⟩

⁴inside *adv* **1** : on the inner side ⟨cleaned my car *inside* and out⟩ **2** : in or into the interior ⟨go *inside*⟩

in·sid·er \in-'sīd-ər\ *n* : a person having information not generally available

in·sight \'in-,sīt\ *n* : the power or act of seeing what's really important about a situation

in·sig·nia \in-'sig-nē-ə\ *or* **in·sig·ne** \-nē\ *n, pl* **insignia** *or* **in·sig·ni·as** : an emblem of a certain office, authority, or honor

in·sig·nif·i·cance \,in-sig-'nif-i-kəns\ *n* : the quality or state of being insignificant

in·sig·nif·i·cant \,in-sig-'nif-i-kənt\ *adj* : not significant : UNIMPORTANT — **in·sig·nif·i·cant·ly** *adv*

in·sin·cere \,in-sin-'siər\ *adj* : not sincere — **in·sin·cere·ly** *adv*

in·sin·cer·i·ty \,in-sin-'ser-ət-ē\ *n* : lack of sincerity

in·sin·u·ate \in-'sin-yə-,wāt\ *vb* **in·sin·u·at·ed; in·sin·u·at·ing** **1** : to bring or get in little by little or in a secret way **2** : ²HINT, IMPLY ⟨*insinuated* that I had cheated⟩

in·sip·id \in-'sip-əd\ *adj* **1** : having little taste or flavor : TASTELESS **2** : not interesting or challenging : DULL

in·sist \in-'sist\ *vb* **1** : to place special stress or great importance ⟨*insists* on accuracy⟩ **2** : to make a demand

in·sis·tence \in-'sis-təns\ *n* : the quality or state of being insistent

in·sis·tent \in-'sis-tənt\ *adj* : demanding attention : PERSISTENT — **in·sis·tent·ly** *adv*

in·so·lence \'in-sə-ləns\ *n* : lack of respect for rank or authority

in·so·lent \'in-sə-lənt\ *adj* : showing insolence — **in·so·lent·ly** *adv*

in·sol·u·bil·i·ty \in-,säl-yə-'bil-ət-ē\ *n* : the quality or state of being insoluble

in·sol·u·ble \in-'säl-yə-bəl\ *adj* **1** : having no solution or explanation ⟨an *insoluble* problem⟩ **2** : difficult or impossible to dissolve ⟨*insoluble* in water⟩ — **in·sol·u·bly** \-blē\ *adv*

in·spect \in-'spekt\ *vb* **1** : to examine closely **2** : to view and examine in an official way ⟨*inspected* the troops⟩

in·spec·tion \in-'spek-shən\ *n* : the act of inspecting

in·spec·tor \in-'spek-tər\ *n* : a person who makes inspections

in·spi·ra·tion \,in-spə-'rā-shən\ *n* **1** : the act of breathing in **2** : the act or power of arousing the mind or the emotions ⟨the *inspiration* of music⟩ **3** : the state of being inspired **4** : something that is or seems inspired **5** : an inspiring agent or influence

in·spire \in-'spīr\ *vb* **in·spired; in·spir·ing** **1** : to move or guide by divine influence **2** : to give inspiration to : ENCOURAGE **3** : AROUSE 2 **4** : to bring about : CAUSE **5** : INHALE

in·sta·bil·i·ty \,in-stə-'bil-ət-ē\ *n* : the quality or state of being unstable

in·stall \in-'stȯl\ *vb* **1** : to put in office with ceremony **2** : to set up for use or service ⟨*install* the plumbing⟩

in·stal·la·tion \,in-stə-'lā-shən\ *n* **1** : the act of installing : the state of being installed **2** : something installed for use

¹in·stall·ment *or* **in·stal·ment** \in-'stȯl-mənt\ *n* : INSTALLATION 1

²installment *n* : one of the parts of a series

in·stance \'in-stəns\ *n* **1** : EXAMPLE 1 **2** : a certain point in an action or process

¹in·stant \'in-stənt\ *n* : MOMENT 1

²instant *adj* **1** : happening or done at once ⟨an *instant* success⟩ **2** : partially prepared by the manufacturer so that only final mixing is needed ⟨*instant* cake mix⟩ **3** : made to dissolve quickly in a liquid ⟨*instant* coffee⟩

in·stan·ta·ne·ous \,in-stən-'tā-nē-əs\ *adj* **1** : happening in an instant **2** : done without delay — **in·stan·ta·ne·ous·ly** *adv*

in·stant·ly \'in-stənt-lē\ *adv* : IMMEDIATELY 2

in·stead \in-'sted\ *adv* : as a substitute

instead of \in-,sted-əv\ *prep* : as a substitute for : rather than ⟨had milk *instead of* juice⟩

in·step \'in-,step\ *n* : the arched middle part of the human foot in front of the ankle joint

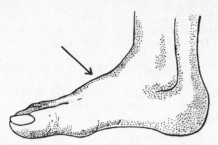

instep

in·sti·gate \'in-stə-,gāt\ *vb* **in·sti·gat·ed; in·sti·gat·ing** : PROVOKE 2, INCITE

in·still \in-'stil\ *vb* : to put into the mind little by little

in·stinct \'in-,stingkt\ *n* **1** : a natural ability **2** : an act or course of action in response to a stimulus that is automatic rather than learned **3** : behavior based on automatic reactions

in·stinc·tive \in-'stingk-tiv\ *adj* : of or relating to instinct : resulting from instinct — **in·stinc·tive·ly** *adv*

¹**in·sti·tute** \'in-stə-,tüt, -,tyüt\ *vb* **in·sti·tut·ed; in·sti·tut·ing** **1** : ESTABLISH 1 **2** : to set going : INAUGURATE

²**institute** *n* **1** : an organization for the promotion of a cause ⟨an *institute* for mental health⟩ **2** : a place for study usually in a special field ⟨the new art *institute*⟩

in·sti·tu·tion \,in-stə-'tü-shən, -'tyü-\ *n* **1** : the act of instituting : ESTABLISHMENT **2** : an established custom, practice, or law **3** : an established organization ⟨business *institutions*⟩

in·sti·tu·tion·al \,in-stə-'tü-shən-l, -'tyü-\ *adj* : of or relating to an institution

in·struct \in-'strəkt\ *vb* **1** : to help to get knowledge to : TEACH **2** : to give information to **3** : to give commands to : DIRECT **synonyms** see TEACH

in·struc·tion \in-'strək-shən\ *n* **1** : LESSON 3 **2 instructions** *pl* : DIRECTION 2, ORDER ⟨I left *instructions* that I was not to be disturbed⟩ **3 instructions** *pl* : an outline of how something is to be done ⟨follow the *instructions* on the blackboard⟩ **4** : the practice or method used by a teacher

in·struc·tive \in-'strək-tiv\ *adj* : helping to give knowledge — **in·struc·tive·ly** *adv*

in·struc·tor \in-'strək-tər\ *n* : TEACHER

in·stru·ment \'in-strə-mənt\ *n* **1** : a way of getting something done **2** : a device for doing a particular kind of work **3** : a device

used to produce music **4** : a legal document (as a deed) **5** : a measuring device

synonyms INSTRUMENT, TOOL, and UTENSIL mean a device for doing work. INSTRUMENT suggests a device that can be used to do complicated work ⟨the heart surgeon's *instruments*⟩ TOOL suggests a device used for a particular job and often suggests that a special skill is needed to use it ⟨a carpenter's *tools* such as hammers and saws⟩ UTENSIL may suggest a simple device used in jobs around the house ⟨kitchen *utensils* such as spoons and knives⟩

in·stru·men·tal \,in-strə-'ment-l\ *adj* **1** : acting to get something done ⟨was *instrumental* in organizing the club⟩ **2** : of or relating to an instrument **3** : being music played on an instrument rather than sung — **in·stru·men·tal·ly** \-l-ē\ *adv*

in·sub·or·di·nate \,in-sə-'bȯrd-n-ət\ *adj* : unwilling to obey authority : DISOBEDIENT

in·sub·or·di·na·tion \,in-sə-,bȯrd-n-'ā-shən\ *n* : failure to obey authority

in·sub·stan·tial \,in-səb-'stan-chəl\ *adj* **1** : not real : IMAGINARY **2** : not firm or solid — **in·sub·stan·tial·ly** *adv*

in·suf·fer·able \in-'səf-ə-rə-bəl\ *adj* : impossible to endure : INTOLERABLE ⟨*insufferable* behavior⟩ — **in·suf·fer·ably** \-blē\ *adv*

in·suf·fi·cien·cy \,in-sə-'fish-ən-sē\ *n, pl* **in·suf·fi·cien·cies** **1** : the quality or state of being insufficient **2** : a shortage of something

in·suf·fi·cient \,in-sə-'fish-ənt\ *adj* : not sufficient : INADEQUATE — **in·suf·fi·cient·ly** *adv*

in·su·late \'in-sə-,lāt\ *vb* **in·su·lat·ed; in·su·lat·ing** **1** : to separate from others : ISOLATE **2** : to separate a conductor of electricity, heat, or sound from other conducting bodies by means of something that will not conduct electricity, heat, or sound

in·su·la·tion \,in-sə-'lā-shən\ *n* **1** : the act of insulating : the state of being insulated **2** : material used in insulating

in·su·la·tor \'in-sə-,lāt-ər\ *n* **1** : one that insulates **2** : a material (as rubber or glass) that is a poor conductor of electricity or a device made of such material

in·su·lin \'in-sə-lən\ *n* : a hormone from

\ə\ abut	\au̇\ out	\i\ tip	\ȯ\ saw	\u̇\ foot	
\ər\ further	\ch\ chin	\ī\ life	\ȯi\ coin	\y\ yet	
\a\ mat	\e\ pet	\j\ job	\th\ thin	\yü\ few	
\ā\ take	\ē\ easy	\ng\ sing	\th\ this	\yu̇\ cure	
\ä\ cot, cart	\g\ go	\ō\ bone	\ü\ food	\zh\ vision	

the pancreas that prevents or controls diabetes

¹in·sult \in-'səlt\ *vb* : to treat with disrespect or scorn

²in·sult \'in-,səlt\ *n* : an act or expression showing disrespect or scorn

in·sur·ance \in-'shùr-əns\ *n* **1** : the act of insuring : the state of being insured **2** : the business of insuring persons or property **3** : a contract by which someone guarantees for a fee to pay someone else for the value of property lost or damaged (as through theft or fire) or usually a specified amount for injury or death **4** : the amount for which something is insured

in·sure \in-'shùr\ *vb* **in·sured; in·sur·ing 1** : to give or get insurance on or for **2** : ENSURE ⟨*insure* the comfort of a guest⟩ — **in·sur·er** *n*

in·sured \in-'shùrd\ *n* : a person whose life or property is insured

¹in·sur·gent \in-'sər-jənt\ *n* : ²REBEL

²insurgent *adj* : REBELLIOUS 1

in·sur·rec·tion \,in-sə-'rek-shən\ *n* : an act or instance of rebelling against a government

in·tact \in-'takt\ *adj* : not touched especially by anything that harms

in·take \'in-,tāk\ *n* **1** : a place where liquid or air is taken into something (as a pump) **2** : the act of taking in **3** : something taken in

¹in·tan·gi·ble \in-'tan-jə-bəl\ *adj* **1** : not possible to touch ⟨light is *intangible*⟩ **2** : not possible to think of as matter or substance ⟨goodwill is an *intangible* asset⟩

²intangible *n* : something intangible

in·te·ger \'int-i-jər\ *n* : a number that is a natural number (as 1, 2, or 3), the negative of a natural number (as −1, −2, −3), or 0

in·te·gral \'int-i-grəl\ *adj* : needed to make something complete ⟨an *integral* part⟩

in·te·grate \'int-ə-,grāt\ *vb* **in·te·grat·ed; in·te·grat·ing 1** : to form into a whole : UNITE **2** : to make a part of a larger unit **3** : to make open to all races ⟨*integrate* the schools⟩

in·te·gra·tion \,int-ə-'grā-shən\ *n* : an act, process, or instance of integrating

in·teg·ri·ty \in-'teg-rət-ē\ *n* **1** : the condition of being free from damage or defect **2** : total honesty and sincerity

in·tel·lect \'int-l-,ekt\ *n* **1** : the power of knowing **2** : the capacity for thought especially when highly developed **3** : a person with great powers of thinking and reasoning

¹in·tel·lec·tu·al \,int-l-'ek-chə-wəl\ *adj* **1** : of or relating to the intellect or understanding ⟨*intellectual* processes⟩ **2**

: having or showing greater than usual intellect **3** : requiring study and thought ⟨*intellectual* work⟩ — **in·tel·lec·tu·al·ly** \-wə-lē\ *adv*

²intellectual *n* : an intellectual person

in·tel·li·gence \in-'tel-ə-jəns\ *n* **1** : the ability to learn and understand **2** : NEWS 3, INFORMATION **3** : an agency that obtains information about an enemy or a possible enemy

in·tel·li·gent \in-'tel-ə-jənt\ *adj* : having or showing intelligence or intellect — **in·tel·li·gent·ly** *adv*

synonyms INTELLIGENT, CLEVER, and BRILLIANT mean having a good amount of mental ability. INTELLIGENT suggests that one can handle new situations and solve problems ⟨an *intelligent* person who knew what to do in an emergency⟩ CLEVER suggests that one learns very quickly ⟨the *clever* youngster learned how to do the trick in a few minutes⟩ BRILLIANT suggests that one's mental ability is much higher than normal ⟨a *brilliant* doctor discovered the cure for that disease⟩

in·tel·li·gi·ble \in-'tel-ə-jə-bəl\ *adj* : possible to understand — **in·tel·li·gi·bly** \-blē\ *adv*

in·tem·per·ance \in-'tem-pə-rəns\ *n* : lack of self-control (as in satisfying an appetite)

in·tem·per·ate \in-'tem-pə-rət\ *adj* **1** : not moderate or mild ⟨*intemperate* weather⟩ **2** : lacking or showing a lack of self-control (as in the use of alcoholic drinks) — **in·tem·per·ate·ly** *adv*

in·tend \in-'tend\ *vb* : to have in mind as a purpose or aim : PLAN ⟨*intend* to do better⟩

in·tense \in-'tens\ *adj* **1** : ¹EXTREME 1 ⟨*intense* heat⟩ **2** : done with great energy, enthusiasm, or effort ⟨*intense* concentration⟩ **3** : having very strong feelings ⟨an *intense* person⟩ — **in·tense·ly** *adv*

in·ten·si·fi·ca·tion \in-,ten-sə-fə-'kā-shən\ *n* : the act or process of intensifying

in·ten·si·fy \in-'ten-sə-,fī\ *vb* **in·ten·si·fied; in·ten·si·fy·ing** : to make or become intense or more intensive : HEIGHTEN

in·ten·si·ty \in-'ten-sət-ē\ *n, pl* **in·ten·si·ties 1** : extreme strength or force **2** : the degree or amount of a quality or condition

¹in·ten·sive \in-'ten-siv\ *adj* **1** : involving special effort or concentration : THOROUGH **2** — used to stress something ⟨the *intensive* pronoun "myself" in "I myself did it"⟩

²intensive *n* : an intensive word

¹in·tent \in-'tent\ *n* **1** : ¹PURPOSE, INTENTION ⟨with *intent* to kill⟩ **2** : MEANING 1 ⟨the *intent* of a letter⟩

²**intent** *adj* **1** : showing concentration or great attention ⟨an *intent* gaze⟩ **2** : showing great determination ⟨were *intent* on going⟩ — **in·tent·ly** *adv* — **in·tent·ness** *n*

in·ten·tion \in-'ten-chən\ *n* **1** : a determination to act in a particular way **2** : ¹PURPOSE, AIM **3** : MEANING 1, INTENT

in·ten·tion·al \in-'ten-chən-l\ *adj* : done by intention : not accidental **synonyms** see VOLUNTARY — **in·ten·tion·al·ly** *adv*

in·ter \in-'tər\ *vb* **in·terred; in·ter·ring** : BURY 1

inter- *prefix* **1** : between : among : together ⟨*inter*mingle⟩ ⟨*inter*twine⟩ **2** : mutual : mutually : reciprocal : reciprocally ⟨*inter*relation⟩ **3** : located, occurring, or carried on between ⟨*inter*national⟩

in·ter·act \int-ə-'rakt\ *vb* : to act upon one another

in·ter·ac·tion \int-ə-'rak-shən\ *n* : the action or influence of people, groups, or things on one another

in·ter·cede \int-ər-'sēd\ *vb* **in·ter·ced·ed; in·ter·ced·ing** **1** : to try to help settle differences between unfriendly individuals or groups **2** : to plead for the needs of someone else

in·ter·cept \int-ər-'sept\ *vb* : to take, seize, or stop before reaching an intended destination ⟨*intercept* a letter⟩ — **in·ter·cep·tor** \-'sep-tər\ *n*

in·ter·ces·sion \int-ər-'sesh-ən\ *n* : the act of interceding

in·ter·ces·sor \int-ər-'ses-ər\ *n* : a person who intercedes

¹**in·ter·change** \int-ər-'chānj\ *vb* **in·ter·changed; in·ter·chang·ing** : to put each in the place of the other : EXCHANGE

²**in·ter·change** \'int-ər-,chānj\ *n* **1** : an act or instance of interchanging **2** : a joining of highways that permits moving from one to the other without crossing traffic lanes

in·ter·change·able \int-ər-'chān-jə-bəl\ *adj* : possible to interchange — **in·ter·change·ably** \-blē\ *adv*

in·ter·com \'int-ər-,käm\ *n* : a communication system with a microphone and loudspeaker at each end

in·ter·course \'int-ər-,kōrs\ *n* : dealings between persons or groups

in·ter·de·pen·dence \int-ər-di-'pen-dəns\ *n* : the quality or state of being interdependent

in·ter·de·pen·dent \int-ər-di-'pen-dənt\ *adj* : depending on one another — **in·ter·de·pen·dent·ly** *adv*

¹**in·ter·est** \'in-trəst, 'int-ə-rəst\ *n* **1** : a right, title, or legal share in something ⟨have an *interest* in the business⟩ **2** : WELFARE 1, BENEFIT ⟨have only your *interest* in mind⟩

3 : the money paid by a borrower for the use of borrowed money **4 interests** *pl* : a group financially interested in an industry or business ⟨mining *interests*⟩ **5** : a feeling of concern, curiosity, or desire to be involved with something ⟨an *interest* in music⟩ **6** : the quality of attracting special attention or arousing curiosity **7** : something in which one is interested

²**interest** *vb* **1** : to persuade to become involved in **2** : to arouse and hold the interest of

in·ter·est·ed \'in-trəs-təd, 'int-ə-rəs-\ *adj* : having or showing interest

in·ter·est·ing \'in-trəs-ting, 'int-ə-rəs-\ *adj* : holding the attention : arousing interest — **in·ter·est·ing·ly** *adv*

in·ter·fere \int-ər-'fiər\ *vb* **in·ter·fered; in·ter·fer·ing** **1** : to be in opposition : CLASH **2** : to take a part in the concerns of others **synonyms** see MEDDLE

in·ter·fer·ence \int-ər-'fir-əns\ *n* **1** : the act or process of interfering **2** : something that interferes

in·ter·im \'in-tə-rəm\ *n* : INTERVAL 1

¹**in·te·ri·or** \in-'tir-ē-ər\ *adj* **1** : being or occurring within the limits : INNER **2** : far from the border or shore : INLAND

²**interior** *n* : the inner part of something

in·ter·ject \int-ər-'jekt\ *vb* : to put between or among other things ⟨*interject* a remark⟩

in·ter·jec·tion \int-ər-'jek-shən\ *n* **1** : an interjecting of something **2** : something interjected **3** : a word or cry (as "ouch") expressing sudden or strong feeling

in·ter·lace \int-ər-'lās\ *vb* **in·ter·laced; in·ter·lac·ing** : to unite by or as if by lacing together

in·ter·lock \int-ər-'läk\ *vb* : to lock together

in·ter·lop·er \int-ər-'lō-pər\ *n* : INTRUDER

in·ter·lude \'int-ər-,lüd\ *n* **1** : an entertainment between the acts of a play **2** : a period or event that comes between others **3** : a musical composition between parts of a longer composition or of a drama

in·ter·mar·riage \int-ər-'mar-ij\ *n* : marriage between members of different groups

in·ter·mar·ry \int-ər-'mar-ē\ *vb* **in·ter·mar·ried; in·ter·mar·ry·ing** : to become connected by intermarriage

\ə\ **abut**	\au̇\ **out**	\i\ **tip**	\ȯ\ **saw**	\u̇\ **foot**
\ər\ **further**	\ch\ **chin**	\ī\ **life**	\ȯi\ **coin**	\y\ **yet**
\a\ **mat**	\e\ **pet**	\j\ **job**	\th\ **thin**	\yü\ **few**
\ā\ **take**	\ē\ **easy**	\ng\ **sing**	\th\ **this**	\yu̇\ **cure**
\ä\ **cot, cart**	\g\ **go**	\ō\ **bone**	\ü\ **food**	\zh\ **vision**

in·ter·me·di·ary \,int-ər-'mēd-ē-,er-ē\ *n, pl* **in·ter·me·di·ar·ies** : GO-BETWEEN

¹in·ter·me·di·ate \,int-ər-'mēd-ē-ət\ *adj* : being or occurring in the middle or between — **in·ter·me·di·ate·ly** *adv*

²intermediate *n* : someone or something that is intermediate

in·ter·ment \in-'tər-mənt\ *n* : BURIAL

in·ter·mi·na·ble \in-'tər-mə-nə-bəl\ *adj* : ENDLESS 1 — **in·ter·mi·na·bly** \-blē\ *adv*

in·ter·min·gle \,int-ər-'ming-gəl\ *vb* **in·ter·min·gled; in·ter·min·gling** : to mix together

in·ter·mis·sion \,int-ər-'mish-ən\ *n* **1** : ¹PAUSE 1, INTERRUPTION ⟨continuing without *intermission*⟩ **2** : a temporary halt (as between acts of a play)

in·ter·mit·tent \,int-ər-'mit-nt\ *adj* : starting, stopping, and starting again — **in·ter·mit·tent·ly** *adv*

¹in·tern \'in-,tərn\ *vb* : to force to stay within certain limits especially during a war — **in·tern·ment** \in-'tərn-mənt\ *n*

²in·tern *or* **in·terne** \'in-,tərn\ *n* : a medical school graduate getting practical experience in a hospital — **in·tern·ship** \-,ship\ *n*

³in·tern \'in-,tərn\ *vb* : to work as an intern

in·ter·nal \in-'tərn-l\ *adj* **1** : being within something : INTERIOR, INNER **2** : having to do with the inside of the body **3** : of or relating to the domestic affairs of a country — **in·ter·nal·ly** *adv*

in·ter·na·tion·al \,int-ər-'nash-ən-l\ *adj* : of, relating to, or affecting two or more nations — **in·ter·na·tion·al·ly** *adv*

in·ter·plan·e·tary \,int-ər-'plan-ə-,ter-ē\ *adj* : existing, carried on, or operating between planets ⟨*interplanetary* travel⟩

in·ter·play \'int-ər-,plā\ *n* : INTERACTION

in·ter·pose \,int-ər-'pōz\ *vb* **in·ter·posed; in·ter·pos·ing** **1** : to put between **2** : to introduce between parts of a conversation ⟨*interpose* a question⟩ **3** : to be or come between

in·ter·po·si·tion \,int-ər-pə-'zish-ən\ *n* **1** : the act of interposing : the state of being interposed **2** : something that interposes or is interposed

in·ter·pret \in-'tər-prət\ *vb* **1** : to tell the meaning of : EXPLAIN, TRANSLATE **2** : to understand according to one's own belief, judgment, or interest **3** : to bring out the meaning of ⟨an actor *interprets* a role⟩ — **in·ter·pret·er** *n*

in·ter·pre·ta·tion \in-,tər-prə-'tā-shən\ *n* : the act or the result of interpreting

in·ter·pre·ta·tive \in-'tər-prə-,tāt-iv\ *adj* : designed or serving to interpret

in·ter·pre·tive \in-'tər-prət-iv\ *adj* : INTERPRETATIVE

in·ter·ra·cial \,int-ər-'rā-shəl\ *adj* : of or involving members of different races

in·ter·re·late \,int-ər-ri-'lāt\ *vb* **in·ter·re·lat·ed; in·ter·re·lat·ing** : to bring into or have a relationship with each other

in·ter·re·la·tion \,int-ər-ri-'lā-shən\ *n* : relation with each other — **in·ter·re·la·tion·ship** \-,ship\ *n*

in·ter·ro·gate \in-'ter-ə-,gāt\ *vb* **in·ter·ro·gat·ed; in·ter·ro·gat·ing** : to question thoroughly ⟨*interrogate* a prisoner⟩

in·ter·ro·ga·tion \in-,ter-ə-'gā-shən\ *n* : the act of interrogating

interrogation point *n* : QUESTION MARK

in·ter·rog·a·tive \,int-ə-'räg-ət-iv\ *adj* : asking a question ⟨an *interrogative* sentence⟩

in·ter·rog·a·to·ry \,int-ə-'räg-ə-,tōr-ē\ *adj* : containing or expressing a question

in·ter·rupt \,int-ə-'rəpt\ *vb* **1** : to stop or hinder by breaking in **2** : to put or bring a difference into

in·ter·rup·tion \,int-ə-'rəp-shən\ *n* : an act of interrupting : a state of being interrupted

in·ter·scho·las·tic \,int-ər-skə-'las-tik\ *adj* : existing or carried on between schools

in·ter·sect \,int-ər-'sekt\ *vb* : to cut or divide by passing through or across : CROSS

in·ter·sec·tion \,int-ər-'sek-shən\ *n* **1** : the act or process of intersecting **2** : the place or point where two or more things (as streets) intersect : CROSSING **3** : the set of mathematical elements common to two or more sets

in·ter·sperse \,int-ər-'spərs\ *vb* **in·ter·spersed; in·ter·spers·ing** **1** : to insert here and there **2** : to insert something at various places in or among

in·ter·state \,int-ər-'stāt\ *adj* : existing between or including two or more states

in·ter·stel·lar \,int-ər-'stel-ər\ *adj* : existing or taking place among the stars

in·ter·twine \,int-ər-'twīn\ *vb* **in·ter·twined; in·ter·twin·ing** : to twine or cause to twine about one another

in·ter·val \'int-ər-vəl\ *n* **1** : a space of time between events or states **2** : a space between things **3** : the difference in pitch between two tones

in·ter·vene \,int-ər-'vēn\ *vb* **in·ter·vened; in·ter·ven·ing** **1** : to come between events, places, or points of time **2** : to interfere with something so as to stop, settle, or change ⟨*intervene* in a quarrel⟩

in·ter·ven·tion \,int-ər-'ven-chən\ *n* : the act or fact of intervening

¹in·ter·view \'int-ər-,vyü\ *n* **1** : a meeting face to face to give or get information or advice **2** : a written report of an interview for publication

²in·ter·view *vb* : to meet and question in an interview ⟨*interview* people for a job⟩ — **in·ter·view·er** *n*

in·ter·weave \ˌint-ər-ˈwēv\ *vb* **in·ter·wove** \-ˈwōv\; **in·ter·wo·ven** \-ˈwō-vən\; **in·ter·weav·ing** 1 : to weave together 2 : INTER-MINGLE

in·tes·ti·nal \in-ˈtes-tən-l\ *adj* : of or relating to the intestine

in·tes·tine \in-ˈtes-tən\ *n* : the lower narrower part of the digestive canal in which most of the digestion and absorption of food occurs and through which waste material passes to be discharged

in·ti·ma·cy \ˈint-ə-mə-sē\ *n, pl* **in·ti·ma·cies** : the state or an instance of being intimate

¹in·ti·mate \ˈint-ə-ˌmāt\ *vb* **in·ti·mat·ed; in·ti·mat·ing** : to express (as an idea) indirectly : HINT

²in·ti·mate \ˈint-ə-mət\ *adj* 1 : most private : PERSONAL ⟨one's *intimate* thoughts⟩ 2 : marked by very close association ⟨*intimate* friends⟩ 3 : suggesting comfortable warmth or privacy : COZY ⟨*intimate* clubs⟩ — **in·ti·mate·ly** *adv*

³in·ti·mate \ˈint-ə-mət\ *n* : a very close friend

in·ti·ma·tion \ˌint-ə-ˈmā-shən\ *n* 1 : the act of intimating 2 : ¹HINT 1

in·tim·i·date \in-ˈtim-ə-ˌdāt\ *vb* **in·tim·i·dat·ed; in·tim·i·dat·ing** : to frighten especially by threats

in·tim·i·da·tion \in-ˌtim-ə-ˈdā-shən\ *n* : the act of intimidating : the state of being intimidated

in·to \ˈin-tə, -tü\ *prep* 1 : to the inside of ⟨ran *into* the house⟩ 2 : to the state, condition, or form of ⟨got *into* mischief⟩ ⟨cut the cake *into* eight pieces⟩ 3 : so as to hit : AGAINST ⟨ran *into* the wall⟩

in·tol·er·a·ble \in-ˈtäl-ə-rə-bəl\ *adj* : UN-BEARABLE — **in·tol·er·a·bly** \-blē\ *adv*

in·tol·er·ance \in-ˈtäl-ə-rəns\ *n* : the quality or state of being intolerant

in·tol·er·ant \in-ˈtäl-ə-rənt\ *adj* : not tolerant — **in·tol·er·ant·ly** \-rənt-lē\ *adv*

in·to·na·tion \ˌin-tə-ˈnā-shən\ *n* : the rise and fall in pitch of the voice in speech

in·tox·i·cate \in-ˈtäk-sə-ˌkāt\ *vb* **in·tox·i·cat·ed; in·tox·i·cat·ing** 1 : to make drunk 2 : to make wildly excited or enthusiastic

in·tox·i·ca·tion \in-ˌtäk-sə-ˈkā-shən\ *n* 1 : an unhealthy state that is or is like a poisoning ⟨intestinal *intoxication*⟩ 2 : the state of one who has drunk too much liquor : DRUNKENNESS

in·tra·mu·ral \ˌin-trə-ˈmyur-əl\ *adj* : being or occurring within the limits usually of a school ⟨*intramural* sports⟩

in·tran·si·tive \in-ˈtrans-ət-iv, -ˈtranz-\ *adj* : not having or containing a direct object ⟨an *intransitive* verb⟩

in·trep·id \in-ˈtrep-əd\ *adj* : feeling no fear : BOLD — **in·trep·id·ly** *adv*

in·tri·ca·cy \ˈin-tri-kə-sē\ *n, pl* **in·tri·ca·cies** 1 : the quality or state of being intricate 2 : something intricate

in·tri·cate \ˈin-tri-kət\ *adj* : very difficult to follow or understand — **in·tri·cate·ly** *adv*

¹in·trigue \in-ˈtrēg\ *vb* **in·trigued; in·trigu·ing** 1 : ²PLOT 2, SCHEME 2 : to arouse the interest or curiosity of

²in·trigue \ˈin-ˌtrēg, in-ˈtrēg\ *n* : a secret or sly scheme often for selfish purposes

in·tro·duce \ˌin-trə-ˈdüs, -ˈdyüs\ *vb* **in·tro·duced; in·tro·duc·ing** 1 : to bring into practice or use 2 : to lead or bring in especially for the first time 3 : to cause to be acquainted : make known 4 : to bring forward for discussion 5 : to put in : INSERT — **in·tro·duc·er** *n*

in·tro·duc·tion \ˌin-trə-ˈdək-shən\ *n* 1 : the action of introducing 2 : something introduced 3 : the part of a book that leads up to and explains what will be found in the main part 4 : the act of making persons known to each other

in·tro·duc·to·ry \ˌin-trə-ˈdək-tə-rē\ *adj* : serving to introduce : PRELIMINARY

in·trude \in-ˈtrüd\ *vb* **in·trud·ed; in·trud·ing** 1 : to force in, into, or on especially where not right or proper ⟨*intruded* an unwanted opinion⟩ 2 : to come or go in without an invitation or right — **in·trud·er** *n*

in·tru·sion \in-ˈtrü-zhən\ *n* : the act of intruding

intrust *variant of* ENTRUST

in·tu·ition \ˌin-tü-ˈish-ən, -tyü-\ *n* : a knowing or something known without mental effort

in·un·date \ˈin-ən-ˌdāt\ *vb* **in·un·dat·ed; in·un·dat·ing** : to cover with a flood : OVER-FLOW

in·un·da·tion \ˌin-ən-ˈdā-shən\ *n* : ¹FLOOD 1

in·vade \in-ˈvād\ *vb* **in·vad·ed; in·vad·ing** 1 : to enter by force to conquer or plunder 2 : to show lack of respect for ⟨*invaded* their privacy⟩ — **in·vad·er** *n*

¹in·val·id \in-ˈval-əd\ *adj* : not valid

²in·va·lid \ˈin-və-ləd\ *adj* 1 : SICKLY 1 2 : of or relating to a sick person ⟨*invalid* diet⟩

³in·va·lid \ˈin-və-ləd\ *n* : a sick or disabled person — **in·va·lid·ism** \-ˌiz-əm\ *n*

in·val·i·date \in-ˈval-ə-ˌdāt\ *vb* **in·val·i-**

\ə\ abut	\au̇\ out	\i\ tip	\ȯ\ saw	\u̇\ foot	
\ər\ further	\ch\ chin	\ī\ life	\ȯi\ coin	\y\ yet	
\a\ mat	\e\ pet	\j\ job	\th\ thin	\yü\ few	
\ā\ take	\ē\ easy	\ng\ sing	\th\ this	\yu̇\ cure	
\ä\ cot, cart	\g\ go	\ō\ bone	\ü\ food	\zh\ vision	

dat·ed; in·val·i·dat·ing : to weaken or destroy the effect of

in·valu·able \in-'val-yə-wə-bəl\ *adj* : having value too great to be estimated **:** PRICELESS

in·var·i·a·bil·i·ty \in-ˌver-ē-ə-'bil-ət-ē\ : the quality or state of being invariable

in·vari·able \in-'ver-ē-ə-bəl\ *adj* : not changing or capable of change — **in·vari·ably** \-'ver-ē-ə-blē\ *adv*

in·va·sion \in-'vā-zhən\ *n* : an act of invading

in·vei·gle \in-'vā-gəl, -'vē-\ *vb* **in·vei·gled; in·vei·gling :** to win over or obtain by flattery ⟨I *inveigled* an invitation to the party⟩

in·vent \in-'vent\ *vb* **1 :** to think up : make up **2 :** to create or produce for the first time — **in·ven·tor** \-'vent-ər\ *n*

synonyms INVENT, CREATE, and DISCOVER mean to bring something new into existence. INVENT suggests making something new for the first time and usually after some thinking and experimenting ⟨*invented* the first camera⟩ CREATE suggests making something out of nothing ⟨God *created* the world⟩ or producing something for its own sake ⟨*creates* unusual toys out of odds and ends⟩ DISCOVER is used when one finds and makes known something that already exists but is not known to others ⟨*discovered* an unknown planet⟩

in·ven·tion \in-'ven-chən\ *n* **1 :** an original device or process **2 :** ³LIE **3 :** the act or process of inventing

in·ven·tive \in-'vent-iv\ *adj* : CREATIVE

¹in·ven·to·ry \'in-vən-ˌtōr-ē\ *n, pl* **in·ven·to·ries 1 :** a list of items (as goods on hand) **2 :** the act or process of making an inventory

²inventory *vb* **in·ven·to·ried; in·ven·to·ry·ing :** to make an inventory of

¹in·verse \in-'vərs\ *adj* **1 :** opposite in order, nature, or effect **2 :** being a mathematical operation that is opposite in effect to another operation — **in·verse·ly** *adv*

²inverse *n* : something inverse

in·vert \in-'vərt\ *vb* **1 :** to turn inside out or upside down **2 :** to reverse the order or position of

¹in·ver·te·brate \in-'vərt-ə-brət\ *adj* : having no backbone

²invertebrate *n* : an invertebrate animal

¹in·vest \in-'vest\ *vb* **1 :** to give power or authority to **2 :** BESIEGE 1

²invest *vb* **1 :** to put out money in order to gain a financial return ⟨*invest* in a business⟩ **2 :** to put out (as effort) in support of

a usually worthy cause — **in·ves·tor** \-'ves-tər\ *n*

in·ves·ti·gate \in-'ves-tə-ˌgāt\ *vb* **in·ves·ti·gat·ed; in·ves·ti·gat·ing :** to study by close and careful observation — **in·ves·ti·ga·tor** \-ər\ *n*

in·ves·ti·ga·tion \in-ˌves-tə-'gā-shən\ *n* : the act or process of investigating

in·ves·ti·ture \in-'ves-tə-ˌchùr\ *n* : the act of placing in office

in·vest·ment \in-'vest-mənt\ *n* **1 :** the investing of money **2 :** a sum of money invested **3 :** a property in which money is invested

in·vig·o·rate \in-'vig-ə-ˌrāt\ *vb* **in·vig·o·rat·ed; in·vig·o·rat·ing :** to give life and energy to

in·vin·ci·bil·i·ty \in-ˌvin-sə-'bil-ət-ē\ *n* : the quality or state of being invincible

in·vin·ci·ble \in-'vin-sə-bəl\ *adj* : impossible to defeat — **in·vin·ci·bly** \-'vin-sə-blē\ *adv*

in·vi·o·la·ble \in-'vī-ə-lə-bəl\ *adj* **1 :** too sacred to be treated with disrespect **2 :** impossible to harm or destroy by violence

in·vi·o·late \in-'vī-ə-lət\ *adj* : not violated

in·vis·i·bil·i·ty \in-ˌviz-ə-'bil-ət-ē\ *n* : the quality or state of being invisible

in·vis·i·ble \in-'viz-ə-bəl\ *adj* **1 :** impossible to see ⟨the *invisible* wind⟩ **2 :** being out of sight **3 :** IMPERCEPTIBLE 1 — **in·vis·i·ble·ness** \-'viz-ə-bəl-nəs\ *n* — **in·vis·i·bly** \-blē\ *adv*

in·vi·ta·tion \ˌin-və-'tā-shən\ *n* **1 :** the act of inviting **2 :** the written or spoken expression by which a person is invited

in·vite \in-'vīt\ *vb* **in·vit·ed; in·vit·ing 1 :** to tend to bring on ⟨behavior that *invites* criticism⟩ **2 :** to request the presence or company of **3 :** ¹WELCOME 2 ⟨*invite* suggestions⟩

in·vit·ing \in-'vīt-ing\ *adj* : ATTRACTIVE — **in·vit·ing·ly** *adv*

in·vo·ca·tion \ˌin-və-'kā-shən\ *n* : a prayer for blessing or guidance at the beginning of a meeting or a service

¹in·voice \'in-ˌvòis\ *n* : a list of goods shipped usually showing the price and the terms of sale

²invoice *vb* **in·voiced; in·voic·ing :** to make an invoice of

in·voke \in-'vōk\ *vb* **in·voked; in·vok·ing 1 :** to call on for aid or protection (as in prayer) **2 :** to call forth by magic ⟨*invoke* spirits⟩ **3 :** to appeal to as an authority or for support

in·vol·un·tary \in-'väl-ən-ˌter-ē\ *adj* **1 :** not made or done willingly or from choice **2**

: not under the control of the will — **in·vol·un·tari·ly** \,in-,väl-ən-'ter-ə-lē\ *adv*

in·volve \in-'välv, -'vȯlv\ *vb* **in·volved; in·volv·ing 1 :** to draw into a situation : EN-GAGE **2 :** INCLUDE ⟨one problem *involves* others⟩ **3 :** to be sure to or need to be accompanied by ⟨the plan *involves* some risk⟩ ⟨success *involves* hard work⟩ — **in·volve·ment** \-mənt\ *n*

in·volved \in-'välvd, -'vȯlvd\ *adj* : COM-PLEX 2

in·vul·ner·a·bil·i·ty \in-,vəl-nə-rə-'bil-ət-ē\ *n* : the quality or state of being invulnera-ble

in·vul·ner·a·ble \in-'vəl-nə-rə-bəl\ *adj* **1** : impossible to injure or damage **2 :** safe from attack — **in·vul·ner·a·bly** \-'vəl-nə-rə-blē\ *adv*

¹in·ward \'in-wərd\ *adj* **1 :** situated on the inside : INNER **2 :** of or relating to the mind or spirit **3 :** directed toward the interior ⟨an *inward* flow⟩

²inward *or* **in·wards** \-wərdz\ *adv* **1 :** to-ward the inside or center ⟨slope *inward*⟩ **2 :** toward the mind or spirit ⟨turned my thoughts *inward*⟩

in·ward·ly \'in-wərd-lē\ *adv* **1 :** in the mind or spirit **2 :** beneath the surface **3 :** to oneself : PRIVATELY **4 :** toward the inside

io·dine \'ī-ə-,dīn, -əd-n\ *n* **1 :** a chemical element found in seawater and seaweeds and used especially in medicine and pho-tography **2 :** a solution of iodine in alcohol used to kill germs

io·dize \'ī-ə-,dīz\ *vb* **io·dized; io·diz·ing** : to add iodine to ⟨*iodized* salt⟩

ion \'ī-ən, 'ī-,än\ *n* : an atom or group of atoms that carries an electric charge

-ion *n suffix* **1 :** act or process ⟨con-struc*tion*⟩ **2 :** result of an act or process ⟨regula*tion*⟩ ⟨erup*tion*⟩ **3 :** state or con-dition ⟨perfec*tion*⟩

ion·ize \'ī-ə-,nīz\ *vb* **ion·ized; ion·iz·ing** : to change into ions

ion·o·sphere \ī-'än-ə-,sfiər\ *n* : the part of the earth's atmosphere beginning at an altitude of about 40 kilometers, extending outward 400 kilometers or more, and con-taining electrically charged particles

io·ta \ī-'ōt-ə\ *n* : a tiny amount : JOT

IOU \,ī-ō-'yü\ *n* : a written promise to pay a debt

-ious *adj suffix* : -OUS ⟨capac*ious*⟩

ir- — see IN-

iras·ci·ble \ir-'as-ə-bəl, ī-\ *adj* : easily an-gered

irate \ī-'rāt\ *adj* : ANGRY — **irate·ly** *adv* — **irate·ness** *n*

ire \'īr\ *n* : ¹ANGER, WRATH

ir·i·des·cence \,ir-ə-'des-ns\ *n* : a shifting and constant change of colors producing rainbow effects

ir·i·des·cent \,ir-ə-'des-nt\ *adj* : having iri-descence — **ir·i·des·cent·ly** *adv*

irid·i·um \i-'rid-ē-əm\ *n* : a hard brittle heavy metallic chemical element

iris \'ī-rəs\ *n* **1 :** the colored part around the pupil of an eye **2** : a plant with long pointed leaves and large usually brightly colored flowers

¹Irish \'īr-ish\ *adj* : of or relating to Ireland, its people, or the Irish language

²Irish *n* **1 Irish** *pl* : the people of Ire-land **2 :** a language of Ireland

irk \'ərk\ *vb* : to make weary, irritated, or bored

irk·some \'ərk-səm\ *adj* : causing bore-dom : TIRESOME — **irk·some·ness** *n*

iris 2

¹iron \'ī-ərn\ *n* **1 :** a heavy silvery white metallic chemical element that rusts eas-ily, is strongly attracted by magnets, oc-curs in meteorites and combined in minerals, and is necessary in biological processes **2 :** something made of iron **3 irons** *pl* **:** handcuffs or chains used to bind or to hinder movement **4 :** a device that is heated and used for pressing cloth

²iron *adj* **1 :** made of or relating to iron **2** : like iron

³iron *vb* : to press with a heated iron — **iron·er** *n*

iron·ic \ī-'rän-ik\ *or* **iron·i·cal** \-i-kəl\ *adj* : relating to, containing, or showing irony — **iron·i·cal·ly** \-i-kə-lē\ *adv*

iron lung *n* : an apparatus in which a person whose breathing is damaged (as by polio) can be placed to help the breathing

iron·work \'ī-ərn-,wərk\ *n* **1 :** work in iron **2 ironworks** *pl* **:** a mill where iron or steel is smelted or heavy iron or steel products are made

iro·ny \'ī-rə-nē\ *n, pl* **iro·nies 1 :** the use of words that mean the opposite of what one

\ə\ **abut**	\au̇\ **out**	\i\ **tip**	\ȯ\ **saw**	\u̇\ **foot**
\ər\ **further**	\ch\ **chin**	\ī\ **life**	\ȯi\ **coin**	\y\ **yet**
\a\ **mat**	\e\ **pet**	\j\ **job**	\th\ **thin**	\yü\ **few**
\ā\ **take**	\ē\ **easy**	\ng\ **sing**	\th\ **this**	\yu̇\ **cure**
\ä\ **cot, cart**	\g\ **go**	\ō\ **bone**	\ü\ **food**	\zh\ **vision**

really intends **2** : a result opposite to what was expected

ir·ra·di·ate \ir-'ād-ē-ˌāt\ *vb* **ir·ra·di·at·ed; ir·ra·di·at·ing 1** : to cast rays of light on **2** : to affect or treat with radiations (as X rays)

ir·ra·di·a·tion \ir-ˌād-ē-'ā-shən\ *n* **1** : the giving off of radiant energy (as heat) **2** : exposure to irradiation (as of X rays)

ir·ra·tio·nal \ir-'ash-ən-l\ *adj* **1** : not able to reason **2** : not based on reason ⟨*irrational* fears⟩ — **ir·ra·tio·nal·ly** *adv*

ir·rec·on·cil·able \ir-ˌek-ən-'sī-lə-bəl\ *adj* : impossible to bring into harmony

ir·re·cov·er·able \ˌir-i-'kəv-ə-rə-bəl\ *adj* : impossible to recover or set right

ir·re·deem·able \ˌir-i-'dē-mə-bəl\ *adj* : impossible to redeem

ir·re·duc·ible \ˌir-i-'düs-ə-bəl, -'dyüs-\ *adj* : not possible to reduce

ir·re·fut·able \ˌir-i-'fyüt-ə-bəl, ir-'ef-yət-\ *adj* : impossible to refute : INDISPUTABLE

ir·reg·u·lar \ir-'eg-yə-lər\ *adj* **1** : not following custom or rule **2** : not following the usual manner of inflection ⟨the *irregular* verb "sell"⟩ **3** : not even or having the same shape on both sides ⟨*irregular* flowers⟩ **4** : not continuous or coming at set times — **ir·reg·u·lar·ly** *adv*

ir·reg·u·lar·i·ty \ir-ˌeg-yə-'lar-ət-ē\ *n, pl* **ir·reg·u·lar·i·ties 1** : the quality or state of being irregular **2** : something irregular

ir·rel·e·vance \ir-'el-ə-vəns\ *n* **1** : the quality or state of being irrelevant **2** : something irrelevant

ir·rel·e·vant \ir-'el-ə-vənt\ *adj* : not relevant — **ir·rel·e·vant·ly** \-vənt-lē\ *adv*

ir·re·li·gious \ˌir-i-'lij-əs\ *adj* : not having or acting as if one has religious emotions or beliefs

ir·rep·a·ra·ble \ir-'ep-ə-rə-bəl\ *adj* : impossible to get back or to make right — **ir·rep·a·ra·bly** \-blē\ *adv*

ir·re·place·able \ˌir-i-'plā-sə-bəl\ *adj* : impossible to replace

ir·re·press·ible \ˌir-i-'pres-ə-bəl\ *adj* : impossible to repress or control

ir·re·proach·able \ˌir-i-'prō-chə-bəl\ *adj* : being beyond reproach

ir·re·sist·ible \ˌir-i-'zis-tə-bəl\ *adj* : impossible to resist — **ir·re·sist·ibly** \-blē\ *adv*

ir·res·o·lute \ir-'ez-ə-ˌlüt\ *adj* : uncertain how to act or proceed — **ir·res·o·lute·ly** *adv*

ir·re·spec·tive of \ˌir-i-'spek-tiv-əv\ *prep* : without regard to ⟨open to anyone *irrespective of* age⟩

ir·re·spon·si·bil·i·ty \ˌir-i-ˌspän-sə-'bil-ət-ē\ *n* : the quality or state of being irresponsible

ir·re·spon·si·ble \ˌir-i-'spän-sə-bəl\ *adj* : having or showing little or no sense of responsibility — **ir·re·spon·si·bly** \-'spän-sə-blē\ *adv*

ir·re·triev·able \ˌir-i-'trē-və-bəl\ *adj* : impossible to get back — **ir·re·triev·ably** \-blē\ *adv*

ir·rev·er·ence \ir-'ev-ə-rəns\ *n* **1** : lack of reverence **2** : something said or done that is irreverent

ir·rev·er·ent \ir-'ev-ə-rənt\ *adj* : not reverent : DISRESPECTFUL — **ir·rev·er·ent·ly** *adv*

ir·re·vers·i·ble \ˌir-i-'vər-sə-bəl\ *adj* : impossible to reverse

ir·rev·o·ca·ble \ir-'ev-ə-kə-bəl\ *adj* : impossible to take away or undo — **ir·rev·o·ca·bly** \-blē\ *adv*

ir·ri·gate \'ir-ə-ˌgāt\ *vb* **ir·ri·gat·ed; ir·ri·gat·ing 1** : to supply (as land) with water by artificial means **2** : to flush with a liquid

ir·ri·ga·tion \ˌir-ə-'gā-shən\ *n* : an act or process of irrigating

ir·ri·ta·bil·i·ty \ˌir-ət-ə-'bil-ət-ē\ *n* : the quality or state of being irritable

ir·ri·ta·ble \'ir-ət-ə-bəl\ *adj* : easily irritated — **ir·ri·ta·bly** \-blē\ *adv*

¹ir·ri·tant \'ir-ə-tənt\ *adj* : tending to cause irritation

²irritant *n* : something that irritates

ir·ri·tate \'ir-ə-ˌtāt\ *vb* **ir·ri·tat·ed; ir·ri·tat·ing 1** : to cause anger or impatience in : ANNOY **2** : to make sensitive or sore

ir·ri·ta·tion \ˌir-ə-'tā-shən\ *n* **1** : the act of irritating : the state of being irritated **2** : ²IRRITANT

is \iz\ *present 3d sing of* BE

-ish \ish\ *adj suffix* **1** : of, relating to, or being ⟨Finn*ish*⟩ **2** : characteristic of ⟨boy*ish*⟩ ⟨mul*ish*⟩ **3** : somewhat ⟨purpl*ish*⟩ **4** : about ⟨forty*ish*⟩

isin·glass \'īz-n-ˌglas, 'ī-zing-ˌglas\ *n* : mica in thin sheets

Is·lam \is-'läm, iz-\ *n* : a religion based on belief in Allah as the only God, in Muhammad as his prophet, and in the Koran

is·land \'ī-lənd\ *n* **1** : an area of land surrounded by water and smaller than a continent **2** : something suggesting an island in its isolation

is·land·er \'ī-lən-dər\ *n* : a person who lives on an island

isle \'īl\ *n* : a usually small island

is·let \'ī-lət\ *n* : a small island

-ism \ˌiz-əm\ *n suffix* **1** : act : practice : process ⟨baptism⟩ ⟨criticism⟩ **2** : manner of action or behavior like that of a specified person or thing ⟨heroism⟩ **3** : state : condition ⟨alcoholism⟩ **4** : teachings : theory : cult : system

isn't \'iz-nt\ : is not

iso·bar \'ī-sə-ˌbär\ *n* : a line on a map to

indicate areas having the same atmospheric pressure

iso·late \'ī-sə-ˌlāt\ *vb* **iso·lat·ed; iso·lat·ing** : to place or keep apart from others

iso·la·tion \ˌī-sə-ˈlā-shən\ *n* : the act of isolating : the condition of being isolated

isos·ce·les triangle \ī-ˌsäs-ə-ˌlēz-\ *n* : a triangle having two sides of equal length

¹Is·rae·li \iz-ˈrā-lē\ *adj* : of or relating to the Republic of Israel or the Israelis

²Israeli *n* : a person born or living in the Republic of Israel

Is·ra·el·ite \ˈiz-rē-ə-ˌlīt\ *n* : a member of the Hebrew people having Jacob as an ancestor

is·su·ance \ˈish-ü-əns\ *n* : the act of issuing

¹is·sue \ˈish-ü\ *n* **1** : the action of going, coming, or flowing out **2** : OFFSPRING, PROGENY **3** : what finally happens : RESULT **4** : something that is disputed **5** : a giving off (as of blood) from the body **6** : the act of bringing out, offering, or making available **7** : something (as a new stamp or a copy of a magazine) issued or the whole quantity issued

²issue *vb* **is·sued; is·su·ing 1** : to go, come, or flow out **2** : ¹RESULT 1 **3** : to distribute officially **4** : to send out for sale or circulation

-ist \əst\ *n suffix* **1** : performer of a specified action ⟨cyclist⟩ : maker : producer ⟨novelist⟩ **2** : one who plays a specified musical instrument or operates a specified mechanical device ⟨pianist⟩ **3** : one who specializes in a specified art or science or skill ⟨geologist⟩ **4** : one who follows or favors a specified teaching, practice, system, or code of behavior

isth·mus \ˈis-məs\ *n* : a neck of land separating two bodies of water and connecting two larger areas of land

¹it \it, ət\ *pron* **1** : the thing, act or matter about which these words are spoken or written **2** : the whole situation ⟨how's *it* going⟩ **3** — used with little meaning of its own in certain kinds of sentences ⟨*it*'s cold⟩

²it \ˈit\ *n* : the player who has to do something special in a children's game

¹Ital·ian \i-ˈtal-yən\ *n* **1** : a person born or living in Italy **2** : the language of the Italians

²Italian *adj* : of or relating to Italy, its people, or the Italian language

¹ital·ic \i-ˈtal-ik\ *adj* : of or relating to a type style with letters that slant to the right (as in "*these characters are italic*")

²italic *n* : an italic letter or italic type

ital·i·cize \i-ˈtal-ə-ˌsīz\ *vb* **ital·i·cized; ital·i·ciz·ing 1** : to print in italics **2** : UNDERLINE 1

¹itch \ˈich\ *vb* : to have or cause an itch

²itch *n* **1** : an uneasy irritating sensation in the skin **2** : a skin disorder in which an itch is present **3** : a restless usually constant desire

itchy \ˈich-ē\ *adj* **itch·i·er; itch·i·est** : that itches

it'd \ˌit-əd\ : it had : it would

-ite \ˌīt\ *n suffix* **1** : native : resident **2** : descendant ⟨Adam*ite*⟩ **3** : adherent : follower

item \ˈīt-əm\ *n* **1** : a single thing in a list, account, or series **2** : a brief piece of news

item·ize \ˈīt-ə-ˌmīz\ *vb* **item·ized; item·iz·ing** : to set down one by one : LIST

¹itin·er·ant \ī-ˈtin-ə-rənt\ *adj* : traveling from place to place

²itinerant *n* : a person who travels about

-i·tis \ˈīt-əs\ *n suffix* : inflammation of ⟨tonsill*itis*⟩ ⟨appendic*itis*⟩

it'll \ˌit-l\ : it shall : it will

its \its\ *adj* : of or relating to it or itself

it's \its\ **1** : it is **2** : it has

it·self \it-ˈself\ *pron* : its own self ⟨the cat gave *itself* a bath⟩ ⟨this *itself* is a good enough reason⟩

-i·ty \ət-ē\ *n suffix, pl* **-i·ties** : quality : state : degree ⟨similar*ity*⟩

I've \ˈīv\ : I have

-ive \iv\ *adj suffix* : that does or tends to do a specified action

ivo·ry \ˈī-və-rē, ˈīv-rē\ *n, pl* **ivo·ries 1** : the hard creamy-white material of which the tusks of a tusked mammal (as an elephant) are made **2** : a very pale yellow

ivy \ˈī-vē\ *n, pl* **ivies 1** : a woody vine with evergreen leaves, small yellowish flowers, and black berries often found growing on buildings **2** : a plant like ivy

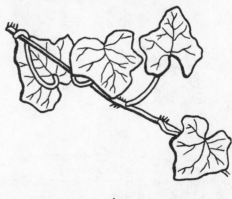

ivy

-iza·tion \ə-ˈzā-shən, ī-; *the second is to be understood at entries\ n suffix* : action : process : state

-ize \ˌīz\ *vb suffix* **-ized; -iz·ing 1** : cause to be or be like : form or cause to be formed into ⟨crystall*ize*⟩ **2** : cause to experience a specified action **3** : saturate, treat, or combine with **4** : treat like ⟨idol*ize*⟩ **5** : engage in a specified activity

j \ˈjā\ *n, pl* **j's** *or* **js** \ˈjāz\ *often cap* : the tenth letter of the English alphabet

¹jab \ˈjab\ *vb* **jabbed; jab·bing** : to poke quickly or suddenly with or as if with something sharp

²jab *n* : a quick or sudden poke

¹jab·ber \ˈjab-ər\ *vb* : to talk too fast or not clearly enough to be understood

²jabber *n* : confused talk : GIBBERISH

¹jack \ˈjak\ *n* **1** : a playing card marked with the figure of a man **2** : a device for lifting something heavy a short distance **3** : JACKASS 1 **4** : a small six-pointed metal object used in a children's game (**jacks**) **5** : a small national flag flown by a ship **6** : a socket used with a plug to connect one electric circuit with another

²jack *vb* : to move or lift by or as if by a jack

jack·al \ˈjak-əl, -ˌȯl\ *n* : any of several Old World wild dogs like but smaller than wolves

jackal

jack·ass \ˈjak-ˌas\ *n* **1** : a male donkey **2** : DONKEY 1 **3** : a stupid person

jack·daw \ˈjak-ˌdȯ\ *n* : a European bird somewhat like a crow

jack·et \ˈjak-ət\ *n* **1** : a short coat or coatlike garment **2** : an outer cover or casing ⟨a book *jacket*⟩

Jack Frost \ˈjak-ˈfrȯst\ *n* : frost or frosty weather thought of as a person

jack–in–the–box \ˈjak-ən-thə-ˌbäks\ *n, pl*

jack–in–the–box·es *or* **jacks–in–the–box** \ˈjak-sən-\ : a small box out of which a comical toy figure springs when the lid is raised

jack–in–the–pul·pit \ˌjak-ən-thə-ˈpu̇l-ˌpit\ *n, pl* **jack–in–the–pul·pits** *or* **jacks–in–the–pul·pit** \ˌjak-sən-\ : a plant that grows in moist shady woods and has a stalk of tiny yellowish flowers protected by a leaf bent over like a hood

jack-in-the-pulpit

¹jack·knife \ˈjak-ˌnīf\ *n, pl* **jack·knives** \-ˌnīvz\ : a knife with folding blade or blades that can be carried in one's pocket

²jackknife *vb* **jack·knifed; jack·knif·ing** : to double up like a jackknife

jack–of–all–trades \ˌjak-ə-ˈvȯl-ˌtrādz\ *n, pl* **jacks–of–all–trades** \ˌjak-səv-\ : a person who can do several kinds of work fairly well

jack–o'–lan·tern \ˈjak-ə-ˌlant-ərn\ *n* : a lantern made of a pumpkin cut to look like a human face

jack·pot \ˈjak-ˌpät\ *n* : a large and often unexpected success or reward

jack·rab·bit \'jak-ˌrab-ət\ *n* : a large North American hare with very long ears and long hind legs

jade \'jād\ *n* : a hard usually green stone used in making jewelry

jag·ged \'jag-əd\ *adj* : having a sharply uneven edge or surface ⟨a *jagged* tear in the sleeve⟩ — **jag·ged·ly** *adv*

jag·uar \'jag-ˌwär\ *n* : a large yellowish brown black-spotted animal of the cat family found from Texas to Paraguay

jaguar

¹jail \'jāl\ *n* : PRISON

²jail *vb* : to shut up in or as if in a prison

jail·bird \'jāl-ˌbərd\ *n* : a person who is or has been locked up in prison

jail·break \'jāl-ˌbrāk\ *n* : escape from prison by the use of force

jail·er *or* **jail·or** \'jā-lər\ *n* : a keeper of a prison

ja·lopy \jə-'läp-ē\ *n, pl* **ja·lop·ies** : a worn shabby old automobile or airplane

¹jam \'jam\ *vb* **jammed; jam·ming 1** : to crowd, squeeze, or wedge into a tight position **2** : to put into action hard or suddenly ⟨*jammed* the brake on⟩ ⟨*jammed* my foot on the brake⟩ **3** : to hurt by pressure ⟨*jammed* a finger in the car door⟩ **4** : to be or cause to be stuck or unable to work because a part is wedged tight ⟨*jam* a machine by overheating it⟩ **5** : to cause interference in (radio or television signals)

²jam *n* **1** : a crowded mass of people or things that blocks something ⟨a log *jam* in the river⟩ **2** : a difficult state of affairs

³jam *n* : a food made by boiling fruit with sugar until it is thick

jamb \'jam\ *n* : a vertical piece forming the side of an opening (as for a doorway)

jam·bo·ree \ˌjam-bə-'rē\ *n* **1** : a large jolly get-together **2** : a national or international camping assembly of boy scouts

¹jan·gle \'jang-gəl\ *vb* **jan·gled; jan·gling** : to make or cause to make a harsh sound

²jangle *n* : a harsh often ringing sound

jan·i·tor \'jan-ət-ər\ *n* : a person who takes care of a building (as a school)

Jan·u·ary \'jan-yə-ˌwer-ē\ *n* : the first month of the year

Word History The ancient Romans believed in many gods. One of these named Janus was the god of doors and gates and of beginnings. He had two faces, one that looked forward and one that looked back. The Latin name of the first month of the year came from the name of this god. The English word *January* came from the Latin name of the month.

¹Jap·a·nese \ˌjap-ə-'nēz\ *adj* : of or relating to Japan, its people, or the Japanese language

²Japanese *n, pl* **Japanese 1** : a person born or living in Japan **2** : the language of the Japanese

Japanese beetle *n* : a small glossy green or brown Asian beetle that has gotten into the United States where it is a harmful pest whose larvae feed on roots and whose adults eat leaves and fruits

¹jar \'jär\ *vb* **jarred; jar·ring 1** : to make a harsh unpleasant sound **2** : to have a disagreeable effect **3** : to shake or cause to shake hard ⟨the bolt *jarred* loose⟩

²jar *n* **1** : a harsh sound **2** : ²JOLT 1 **3** : ²SHOCK 3

³jar *n* : a usually glass or pottery container with a wide mouth

jar·gon \'jär-gən, -ˌgän\ *n* **1** : the special vocabulary of an activity or group ⟨sports *jargon*⟩ **2** : language that is not clear and is full of long words

jas·mine \'jaz-mən\ *n* : any of various mostly climbing plants of warm regions with fragrant flowers

jas·per \'jas-pər\ *n* : an opaque usually red, green, brown, or yellow stone used for making ornamental objects (as vases)

¹jaunt \'jȯnt\ *vb* : to make a short trip for pleasure

²jaunt *n* : a short pleasure trip

jaun·ty \'jȯnt-ē\ *adj* **jaun·ti·er; jaun·ti·est** : lively in manner or appearance ⟨wearing my hat at a *jaunty* angle⟩ — **jaun·ti·ly** \'jȯnt-l-ē\ *adv* — **jaun·ti·ness** \'jȯnt-ē-nəs\ *n*

Ja·va man \ˌjä-və-\ *n* : a small-brained prehistoric human known from skulls found in Java

jav·e·lin \'jav-lən, 'jav-ə-lən\ *n* **1** : a light spear **2** : a slender rod thrown for dis-

\ə\ abut	\au̇\ out	\i\ tip	\ȯ\ saw	\u̇\ foot
\ər\ further	\ch\ chin	\ī\ life	\ȯi\ coin	\y\ yet
\a\ mat	\e\ pet	\j\ job	\th\ thin	\yu̇\ few
\ā\ take	\ē\ easy	\ng\ sing	\th\ this	\yu̇\ cure
\ä\ cot, cart	\g\ go	\ō\ bone	\ü\ food	\zh\ vision

tance in a track-and-field contest (**javelin throw**)

jaw \'jȯ\ *n* **1** : either of the bony structures that support the soft parts of the mouth and usually bear teeth on their edge **2** : a part of an invertebrate animal (as an insect) that resembles or does the work of a jaw **3** : one of a pair of moving parts that open and close for holding or crushing something ⟨*jaws* of a vise⟩

jaw·bone \'jȯ-ˌbōn\ *n* : JAW 1

jay \'jā\ *n* : a noisy bird related to the crow but with brighter colors

jay·walk \'jā-ˌwȯk\ *vb* : to cross a street in a place or in a way that is against traffic regulations — **jay·walk·er** *n*

jazz \'jaz\ *n* : lively American music that developed from ragtime

jeal·ous \'jel-əs\ *adj* **1** : demanding complete faithfulness **2** : feeling a mean resentment toward someone more successful than oneself **3** : CAREFUL 1, WATCHFUL ⟨*jealous* of our rights⟩ — **jeal·ous·ly** *adv*

jeal·ou·sy \'jel-ə-sē\ *n, pl* **jeal·ou·sies** : a jealous attitude or feeling

jeans \'jēnz\ *n pl* : pants made of a heavy cotton cloth

> **Word History** *Jeans*, a word for a kind of pants, came from *jean*, a word for a kind of cloth. At first the word *jean* was an adjective. It was used to describe a kind of sturdy cotton cloth. This word *jean* came from *Gene*, an early English name for the city of Genoa, Italy, where the cloth was made.

¹**jeer** \'jiər\ *vb* **1** : to speak or cry out in scorn **2** : to scorn or mock with jeers

²**jeer** *n* : a scornful remark or sound : TAUNT

Je·ho·vah \ji-'hō-və\ *n* : GOD 1

jell \'jel\ *vb* **1** : to become as firm as jelly : SET **2** : to take shape ⟨an idea *jelled*⟩

¹**jel·ly** \'jel-ē\ *n, pl* **jel·lies** : a soft springy food made from fruit juice boiled with sugar, from meat juices, or from gelatin — **jel·ly·like** \-ˌlīk\ *adj*

²**jelly** *vb* **jel·lied; jel·ly·ing** **1** : JELL 1 **2** : to make jelly

jel·ly·fish \'jel-ē-ˌfish\ *n* : a free-swimming sea animal related to the corals that has a jellylike body shaped like a saucer

jen·net \'jen-ət\ *n* : a female donkey

jeop·ar·dize \'jep-ər-ˌdīz\ *vb* **jeop·ar·dized; jeop·ar·diz·ing** : to expose to danger

jeop·ar·dy \'jep-ər-dē\ *n* : DANGER 1

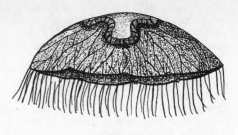

jellyfish

> **Word History** In French there is a phrase that means "divided game." This phrase was used for a situation in a game of chess where one could not be sure which of two plays would be better. With either play one would risk losing the game. The English word *jeopardy* came from the French phrase. At first the word was used for the risky situation in chess. Later it came to mean "risk" or "danger."

¹**jerk** \'jərk\ *vb* **1** : to give a quick sharp pull or twist to **2** : to move with jerks

²**jerk** *n* **1** : a short quick pull or jolt **2** : a foolish person

jer·kin \'jər-kən\ *n* : a close-fitting sleeveless jacket that extends to or just over the hips

jerky \'jər-kē\ *adj* **jerk·i·er; jerk·i·est** : moving with sudden starts and stops — **jerk·i·ly** \-kə-lē\ *adv* — **jerk·i·ness** \-kē-nəs\ *n*

jer·sey \'jər-zē\ *n, pl* **jer·seys** **1** : a knitted cloth (as of wool or cotton) used mostly for clothing **2** : a close-fitting knitted garment (as a shirt)

¹**jest** \'jest\ *n* **1** : a comic act or remark **2** : a playful mood or manner ⟨many a true word is spoken in *jest*⟩

²**jest** *vb* : to make jests : JOKE

jest·er \'jes-tər\ *n* **1** : a person formerly kept in royal courts to amuse people **2** : a person who often jests

Je·sus \'jē-zəs\ *n* : the founder of the Christian religion

¹**jet** \'jet\ *n* **1** : a black mineral that is often used for jewelry **2** : a very dark black

²**jet** *vb* **jet·ted; jet·ting** : ³SPURT 1

³**jet** *n* **1** : a rush of liquid, gas, or vapor through a narrow opening or a nozzle **2** : a nozzle for a jet of gas or liquid **3** : JET ENGINE **4** : JET AIRPLANE

jet airplane *n* : an airplane powered by a jet engine

jet engine *n* : an engine in which fuel burns to produce a jet of heated air and gases that shoot out from the rear and drive the engine forward

jet plane *n* : JET AIRPLANE

jet–pro•pelled \,jet-prə-'peld\ *adj* : driven forward or onward by a jet engine

jet•sam \'jet-səm\ *n* : goods thrown overboard to lighten a ship in danger of sinking

jet stream *n* : high-speed winds blowing from a westerly direction several kilometers above the earth's surface

jet•ti•son \'jet-ə-sən\ *vb* : to throw out especially from a ship or an airplane

jet•ty \'jet-ē\ *n, pl* **jet•ties 1** : a pier built to change the path of the current or tide or to protect a harbor **2** : a landing wharf

Jew \'jü\ *n* : a person who is a descendant of the ancient Hebrews or whose religion is Judaism

jew•el \'jü-əl\ *n* **1** : an ornament of precious metal often set with precious stones and worn on the person **2** : a person who is greatly admired **3** : GEM **4** : a bearing in a watch made of crystal or a precious stone

Word History The English word *jewel* came from an Old French word that meant "jewel." This Old French word was formed from another Old French word that meant "game" or "play." The basic meaning of the earlier Old French word for a jewel, then, was "little game" or "little plaything."

jew•el•er *or* **jew•el•ler** \'jü-ə-lər\ *n* : a person who makes or deals in jewelry and related articles (as silverware)

jew•el•ry \'jü-əl-rē\ *n* : ornamental pieces (as rings or necklaces) worn on the person

Jew•ish \'jü-ish\ *adj* : of or relating to Jews or Judaism

Jew's harp *or* **Jews' harp** \'jüz-,härp\ *n* : a small musical instrument that is held in the mouth and struck with the finger to give off a tone

Jew's harp

jib \'jib\ *n* : a three-cornered sail extending forward from the foremast

¹jibe \'jīb\ *vb* **jibed; jib•ing 1** : to shift suddenly from side to side **2** : to change the course of a boat so that the sail jibes

²jibe *variant of* GIBE

³jibe *vb* **jibed; jib•ing** : to be in agreement

jif•fy \'jif-ē\ *n, pl* **jif•fies** : MOMENT 1

¹jig \'jig\ *n* : a lively dance

²jig *vb* **jigged; jig•ging** : to dance a jig

¹jig•gle \'jig-əl\ *vb* **jig•gled; jig•gling** : to move or cause to move with quick little jerks

²jiggle *n* : a quick little jerk

jig•saw \'jig-,sȯ\ *n* : a machine saw used to cut curved and irregular lines or openwork patterns

jigsaw puzzle *n* : a puzzle made by cutting a picture into small pieces that must be fitted together again

jim•son•weed \'jim-sən-,wēd\ *n* : a coarse poisonous weedy plant related to the potato that is sometimes grown for its showy white or purple flowers

¹jin•gle \'jing-gəl\ *vb* **jin•gled; jin•gling** : to make or cause to make a light clinking sound

²jingle *n* **1** : a light clinking sound **2** : a short verse or song that repeats bits in a catchy way — **jin•gly** \'jing-glē\ *adj*

jinx \'jingks\ *n* : a bringer of bad luck

jit•ters \'jit-ərz\ *n pl* : extreme nervousness

jit•tery \'jit-ə-rē\ *adj* : very nervous

job \'jäb\ *n* **1** : a piece of work usually done on order at an agreed rate **2** : something produced by or as if by work ⟨can do a better *job*⟩ **3** : a regular paying employment ⟨has a good *job*⟩ **4** : a special duty or function **synonyms** see TASK — **job•less** \-ləs\ *adj*

jock•ey \'jäk-ē\ *n, pl* **jock•eys 1** : a professional rider in a horse race **2** : OPERATOR 1

¹jog \'jäg\ *vb* **jogged; jog•ging 1** : to give a slight shake or push to : NUDGE **2** : to rouse to alertness ⟨*jog* one's memory⟩ **3** : to move or cause to move at a jog **4** : to run slowly (as for exercise) ⟨*jogs* two miles every day⟩ — **jog•ger** *n*

²jog *n* **1** : a slight shake or push **2** : a slow jolting gait (as of a horse) **3** : a slow run

³jog *n* : a short change in direction ⟨a *jog* in a road⟩

jog•gle \'jäg-əl\ *vb* **jog•gled; jog•gling** : to shake or cause to shake slightly

john•ny•cake \'jän-ē-,kāk\ *n* : a bread made of cornmeal, water or milk, and leavening with or without flour, shortening, and eggs

join \'jȯin\ *vb* **1** : to come, bring, or fasten together **2** : ADJOIN **3** : to come or bring into close association **4** : to come into the company of **5** : to become a member of **6** : to take part in a group activity ⟨we all

\ə\ **abut**	\au̇\ **out**	\i\ **tip**	\ȯ\ **saw**	\u̇\ **foot**
\ər\ **further**	\ch\ **chin**	\ī\ **life**	\ȯi\ **coin**	\y\ **yet**
\a\ **mat**	\e\ **pet**	\j\ **job**	\th\ **thin**	\yü\ **few**
\ā\ **take**	\ē\ **easy**	\ng\ **sing**	\th\ **this**	\yu̇\ **cure**
\ä\ **cot, cart**	\g\ **go**	\ō\ **bone**	\ü\ **food**	\zh\ **vision**

joined in the chorus⟩ **7** : to combine the elements of ⟨*join* two sets⟩

¹joint \'jȯint\ *n* **1** : a part of an animal's body where two pieces (as bones) of the skeleton come together usually in a way that allows motion **2** : the part between two joints **3** : a place where two things or parts are joined — **joint·ed** \-əd\ *adj*

²joint *adj* **1** : joined together ⟨the *joint* effect of sun and rain⟩ **2** : done by or shared by two or more ⟨a *joint* bank account⟩ — **joint·ly** *adv*

joist \'jȯist\ *n* : any of the small timbers or metal beams laid crosswise in a building to support a floor or ceiling

¹joke \'jōk\ *n* **1** : something said or done to cause laughter **2** : a very short story with a humorous twist **3** : something not to be taken seriously ⟨the exam was a *joke*⟩

²joke *vb* **joked**; **jok·ing** **1** : to say or do something as a joke **2** : to make jokes

jok·er \'jō-kər\ *n* **1** : a person who jokes **2** : an extra card used in some card games

jok·ing·ly \'jō-king-lē\ *adv* : in a joking manner

jol·li·ty \'jäl-ət-ē\ *n* : the state of being jolly

¹jol·ly \'jäl-ē\ *adj* **jol·li·er**; **jol·li·est** : full of fun or high spirits

²jolly *adv* : ²VERY 1 ⟨a *jolly* good time⟩

¹jolt \'jōlt\ *vb* **1** : to move or cause to move with a sudden jerky motion **2** : to cause to be upset ⟨bad news *jolts* people⟩

²jolt *n* **1** : an abrupt jerky blow or movement **2** : a sudden shock or disappointment

jon·quil \'jän-kwəl, 'jäng-\ *n* : a plant related to the daffodil but with fragrant yellow or white flowers with a short central tube

josh \'jäsh\ *vb* **1** : ²KID 1 **2** : ²JOKE

jos·tle \'jäs-əl\ *vb* **jos·tled**; **jos·tling** : to knock against so as to jar : push roughly ⟨*jostled* by a crowd⟩

¹jot \'jät\ *n* : the least bit

²jot *vb* **jot·ted**; **jot·ting** : to write briefly or in a hurry : make a note of

jounce \'jaúns\ *vb* **jounced**; **jounc·ing** : to move, fall, or bounce so as to shake

jour·nal \'jern-l\ *n* **1** : a brief record (as in a diary) of daily happenings **2** : a daily record (as of business dealings) **3** : a daily newspaper **4** : a magazine that reports on things of special interest to a particular group

jour·nal·ism \'jərn-l-,iz-əm\ *n* **1** : the business of collecting and editing news (as for newspapers, radio, or television) **2** : writing of general or popular interest

jour·nal·ist \'jərn-l-əst\ *n* : an editor or reporter of the news

¹jour·ney \'jər-nē\ *n*, *pl* **jour·neys** : a traveling from one place to another

synonyms JOURNEY, TRIP, and TOUR mean travel from one place to another. JOURNEY usually suggests traveling a long distance and often that the traveling may be dangerous or difficult ⟨the long *journey* across the desert⟩ TRIP suggests that the traveling is brief, swift, or ordinary ⟨our weekly *trip* to the supermarket⟩ TOUR suggests a circular journey with several stopping places and an end at the place where one began ⟨the sightseers took a *tour* of the city⟩

²journey *vb* **jour·neyed**; **jour·ney·ing** : to go on a journey : TRAVEL — **jour·ney·er** *n*

jour·ney·man \'jər-nē-mən\ *n*, *pl* **jour·ney·men** \-mən\ : a worker who has learned a trade and usually works for another person by the day

¹joust \'jaúst, 'jəst\ *n* : a combat on horseback between two knights with lances

²joust *vb* : to take part in a joust : TILT

jo·vi·al \'jō-vē-əl\ *adj* : ¹JOLLY — **jo·vi·al·ly** *adv*

¹jowl \'jaúl\ *n* **1** : an animal's jaw and especially the lower jaw **2** : CHEEK 1

²jowl *n* : loose flesh (as a double chin) hanging from the lower jaw and throat

joy \'jȯi\ *n* **1** : a feeling of pleasure or happiness that comes from success, good fortune, or a sense of well-being **2** : something that gives pleasure or happiness **synonyms** see PLEASURE

joy·ful \'jȯi-fəl\ *adj* : feeling, causing, or showing joy — **joy·ful·ly** \-fə-lē\ *adv* — **joy·ful·ness** *n*

joy·ous \'jȯi-əs\ *adj* : JOYFUL ⟨a *joyous* occasion⟩ — **joy·ous·ly** *adv* — **joy·ous·ness** *n*

ju·bi·lant \'jü-bə-lənt\ *adj* : expressing great joy especially with shouting : noisily happy

ju·bi·lee \'jü-bə-,lē, ,jü-bə-'lē\ *n* **1** : a fiftieth anniversary **2** : time of celebration

Word History In ancient Hebrew law every fiftieth year was a special year. At the beginning of the special year trumpets made of rams' horns were blown. The Hebrew name for the year came from a Hebrew word that meant "ram's horn." The English word *jubilee* came from this Hebrew name.

Ju·da·ism \'jüd-ə-,iz-əm, 'jüd-ē-\ *n* : a religion developed among the ancient Hebrews that stresses belief in one God and faithfulness to the moral laws of the Old Testament

¹judge \'jəj\ *vb* **judged; judg·ing 1** : to form an opinion after careful consideration **2** : to act as a judge (as in a trial) **3** : THINK 2

²judge *n* **1** : a public official whose duty is to decide questions brought before a court **2** : a person appointed to decide in a contest or competition **3** : a person with the experience to give a meaningful opinion : CRITIC

judg·ment *or* **judge·ment** \'jəj-mənt\ *n* **1** : a decision or opinion (as of a court) given after judging **2** : an opinion or estimate formed by examining and comparing **3** : the ability for judging

ju·di·cial \jü-'dish-əl\ *adj* : of or relating to the providing of justice — **ju·di·cial·ly** *adv*

ju·di·cious \jü-'dish-əs\ *adj* : having, using, or showing good judgment : WISE — **ju·di·cious·ly** *adv* — **ju·di·ciousness** *n*

ju·do \'jü-dō\ *n* : a Japanese form of wrestling in which each person tries to throw or pin the opponent

jug \'jəg\ *n* : a large deep usually earthenware or glass container with a narrow mouth and a handle

jug·gle \'jəg-əl\ *vb* **jug·gled; jug·gling 1** : to keep several things moving in the air at the same time **2** : to mix things up in order to deceive **3** : to hold or balance insecurely — **jug·gler** \'jəg-lər\ *n*

juice \'jüs\ *n* : liquid that can be pressed out of cells and tissues of a plant or animal : a natural fluid of a living body

juicy \'jü-sē\ *adj* **juic·i·er; juic·i·est** : having much juice — **juic·i·ness** *n*

Ju·ly \jü-'lī\ *n* : the seventh month of the year

Word History The first Roman calendar began the year with March. The fifth month was the one we now know as *July*. The first Latin name given to this month came from the Latin word that meant "fifth." The Roman senate wanted to honor a Roman statesman named Julius Caesar so it decided to name this month after him. The English name *July* came from the Latin name *Julius*.

¹jum·ble \'jəm-bəl\ *vb* **jum·bled; jumbling** : to mix in a confused mass

²jumble *n* : a disorderly mass or pile

jum·bo \'jəm-bō\ *n, pl* **jum·bos** : something very large of its kind

Word History *Jumbo* was a famous circus elephant. The name *Jumbo* probably came from a word that meant "elephant" in a language of Africa. Our word *jumbo* came from the name of the famous elephant.

¹jump \'jəmp\ *vb* **1** : to spring into the air : LEAP **2** : to make a sudden movement : START **3** : to have or cause a sudden sharp increase ⟨prices *jumped*⟩ **4** : to make a hasty judgement **5** : to make a sudden attack ⟨*jumped* on me for being late⟩ **6** : to pass over or cause to pass over with or as if with a leap ⟨*jump* the fence⟩ — **jump the gun 1** : to start in a race before the starting signal **2** : to do something before the proper time

²jump *n* **1** : an act or instance of jumping : LEAP **2** : a sudden involuntary movement : START **3** : a sharp sudden increase **4** : an initial advantage ⟨we got the *jump* on the other team⟩

jump·er \'jəm-pər\ *n* **1** : a loose blouse or jacket often worn by workmen **2** : a sleeveless dress worn usually with a blouse

jumpy \'jəm-pē\ *adj* **jump·i·er; jump·i·est** : NERVOUS 3

jun·co \'jəng-kō\ *n, pl* **jun·cos** *or* **juncoes** : a small mostly gray American finch usually having a pink bill

junc·tion \'jəngk-shən\ *n* **1** : an act of joining **2** : a place or point of meeting

June \'jün\ *n* : the sixth month of the year

Word History The word *June* came from the Latin name of the month. It is most likely that this name came from an ancient Roman family name.

jun·gle \'jəng-gəl\ *n* **1** : a thick or tangled growth of plants **2** : a large area of land usually in a tropical region covered with a thick tangled growth of plants

¹ju·nior \'jün-yər\ *n* **1** : a person who is younger or lower in rank than another **2** : a student in the next-to-last year (as at high school)

²junior *adj* **1** : being younger — used to distinguish a son from a father with the same name ⟨John Doe, *Junior*⟩ **2** : lower in rank **3** : of or relating to juniors ⟨*junior* class⟩

ju·ni·per \'jü-nə-pər\ *n* : any of various evergreen trees and shrubs related to the pines but having tiny berrylike cones

¹junk \'jəngk\ *n* **1** : old iron, glass, paper, or waste : RUBBISH **2** : a poorly made product

\ə\ abut	\aů\ out	\i\ tip	\ȯ\ saw	\ů\ foot
\ər\ further	\ch\ chin	\ī\ life	\ȯi\ coin	\y\ yet
\a\ mat	\e\ pet	\j\ job	\th\ thin	\yü\ few
\ā\ take	\ē\ easy	\ng\ sing	\th\ this	\yů\ cure
\ä\ cot, cart	\g\ go	\ō\ bone	\ü\ food	\zh\ vision

²**junk** *vb* : to get rid of as worthless : SCRAP

³**junk** *n* : a sailing ship of Chinese waters

junk

Ju·pi·ter \'jü-pət-ər\ *n* : the planet that is fifth in order of distance from the sun and is the largest of the planets with a diameter of about 140,000 kilometers

ju·ror \'jür-ər\ *n* : a member of a jury

ju·ry \'jür-ē\ *n, pl* **ju·ries** **1** : a body of persons sworn to seek for and try to learn the truth about a matter put before them for decision **2** : a committee that judges and awards prizes (as at an exhibition)

¹**just** \'jəst\ *adj* **1** : having a foundation in fact or reason : REASONABLE **2** : agreeing with a standard of correctness **3** : morally right or good **4** : legally right **synonyms** see UPRIGHT — **just·ly** *adv*

²**just** *adv* **1** : exactly as wanted ⟨*just* right⟩ **2** : very recently ⟨*just* got here⟩ **3** : by a very small amount ⟨*just* enough⟩ **4** : by a very short distance ⟨*just* east of here⟩ **5** : nothing more than ⟨*just* a child⟩ **6** : ²VERY 2 ⟨*just* wonderful⟩

jus·tice \'jəs-təs\ *n* **1** : just or right action or treatment **2** : ²JUDGE 1 **3** : the carrying out of law ⟨a court of *justice*⟩ **4** : the quality of being fair or just

jus·ti·fi·able \'jəs-tə-,fī-ə-bəl\ *adj* : possible to justify — **jus·ti·fi·ably** \-blē\ *adv*

jus·ti·fi·ca·tion \,jəs-tə-fə-'kā-shən\ *n* **1** : the act or an instance of justifying **2** : something that justifies

jus·ti·fy \'jəs-tə-,fī\ *vb* **jus·ti·fied; jus·ti·fy·ing** : to prove or show to be just, right, or reasonable

jut \'jət\ *vb* **jut·ted; jut·ting** : to extend or cause to extend above or beyond a surrounding area

jute \'jüt\ *n* : a strong glossy fiber from a tropical plant used chiefly for making sacks and twine

¹**ju·ve·nile** \'jü-və-,nīl, -vən-l\ *adj* **1** : incompletely developed : IMMATURE **2** : of, relating to, or characteristic of children or young people

²**juvenile** *n* : a young person : YOUTH

k \'kā\ *n, pl* **k's** *or* **ks** \'kāz\ *often cap* : the eleventh letter of the English alphabet

kale \'kāl\ *n* : a hardy cabbage with wrinkled leaves that do not form a head

ka·lei·do·scope \kə-'līd-ə-skōp\ *n* **1** : a tube containing bits of colored glass or plastic and two mirrors at one end that shows many different patterns as it is turned **2** : a changing pattern or scene

Word History If you look into a kaleidoscope you will see changing shapes and pretty colors. The name of the device may seem strange, but it will make sense to a person who knows Greek. *Kaleidoscope* was made up out of three Greek words. The first means "beautiful," the second "shape," and the third "to look at."

kan·ga·roo \,kang-gə-'rü\ *n, pl* **kan·ga·roos** : any of numerous leaping mammals of Australia and nearby islands that feed on plants and have long powerful hind legs, a thick tail used as a support in standing or walking, and in the female a pouch on the abdomen in which the young are carried

kangaroo

ka·olin \'kā-ə-lən\ *n* : a very pure white clay used in making porcelain

kar·a·o·ke \,kar-ē-'ō-kē, kə-'rō-kē\ *n* : a device that plays music to which the user sings along and that records the user's singing with the music

kar·at \'kar-ət\ *n* : a unit of fineness for gold ⟨14-*karat* gold contains fourteen parts of gold mixed with ten parts of other metal to make it harder⟩

ka·ty·did \'kāt-ē-,did\ *n* : any of several large green American grasshoppers with males that make shrill noises

Word History Some people like to pretend that the sounds insects make are words. When a male katydid rubs his front wings together, it makes a shrill noise. Some think it sounds as if he says, "Katy did, Katy didn't," over and over. That is how the katydid got its name.

kay·ak \'kī-,ak\ *n* **1** : an Eskimo canoe made of a frame covered with skins except for a small opening in the center **2** : a small canvas-covered canoe

ka·zoo \kə-'zü\ *n, pl* **ka·zoos** : a toy musical instrument containing a membrane which produces a buzzing tone when one hums into the mouth hole

¹keel \'kēl\ *n* : a timber or plate running lengthwise along the center of the bottom of a ship and usually sticking out from the bottom

²keel *vb* : to turn over

keel over *vb* : to fall suddenly (as in a faint)

keen \'kēn\ *adj* **1** : having a fine edge or point : SHARP ⟨a *keen* knife⟩ **2** : seeming to cut or sting ⟨a *keen* wind⟩ ⟨a *keen* wit⟩ **3** : full of enthusiasm : EAGER **4** : having or showing mental sharpness **5** : very sensitive (as in seeing or hearing) ⟨*keen* eyesight⟩ **synonyms** see EAGER — **keen·ly** *adv* — **keen·ness** *n*

¹keep \'kēp\ *vb* **kept** \'kept\; **keep·ing** **1** : to be faithful to : FULFILL ⟨*keep* a promise⟩ **2** : to act properly in relation to ⟨*keep* the Sabbath⟩ **3** : PROTECT ⟨*keep* us from harm⟩ **4** : to take care of : TEND **5** : to continue doing something **6** : to have in one's service or at one's disposal ⟨*keep* a car⟩ **7** : to preserve a record in ⟨*keep* a diary⟩ **8** : to have on hand regularly for sale ⟨*keep* neckties⟩ **9** : to continue to have in one's possession or power **10** : to prevent from leaving : DETAIN ⟨*keep* a person in jail⟩ **11** : to hold back ⟨*keep* a secret⟩ **12** : to remain or cause to remain in a given place, situation, or condition ⟨*keep* off the grass⟩ ⟨*kept* us waiting⟩ **13** : to

continue in an unspoiled condition ⟨food that *keeps* well⟩ **14** : ¹REFRAIN ⟨unable to *keep* from talking⟩

²keep *n* **1** : the strongest part of a castle in the Middle Ages **2** : the necessities of life ⟨could not earn the family's *keep*⟩ — **for keeps** **1** : with the understanding that one may keep what is won ⟨we'll play marbles *for keeps*⟩ **2** : for a long time : PERMANENTLY

keep·er \'kē-pər\ *n* : a person who watches, guards, or takes care of something

keep·ing \'kē-ping\ *n* **1** : watchful attention : CARE **2** : a proper or fitting relationship : HARMONY ⟨a report in *keeping* with the facts⟩

keep·sake \'kēp-,sāk\ *n* : something kept or given to be kept in memory of a person, place, or happening

keep up *vb* **1** : MAINTAIN 1 ⟨*keep* standards *up*⟩ **2** : to stay well informed about something ⟨*keep up* with the news⟩ **3** : to continue without interruption ⟨the rain *kept up* all night⟩ **4** : to stay even with others (as in a race)

keg \'keg\ *n* **1** : a small barrel holding about 114 liters **2** : the contents of a keg

kelp \'kelp\ *n* : a large coarse brown seaweed

ken \'ken\ *n* **1** : range of vision : SIGHT **2** : range of understanding

ken·nel \'ken-l\ *n* **1** : a shelter for a dog **2** : a place where dogs are bred or housed

kept *past of* KEEP

ker·chief \'kər-chəf\ *n, pl* **ker·chiefs** **1** : a square of cloth worn as a head covering or as a scarf **2** : HANDKERCHIEF

Word History Look at the history of the word *kerchief* and you will see that it is a fine word for something that covers the head. The English word comes from an Old French word formed from two words. The first of these two French words was a verb that meant "to cover." The second was a noun that meant "head."

ker·nel \'kərn-l\ *n* **1** : the inner softer part of a seed, fruit stone, or nut **2** : the whole grain or seed of a cereal

ker·o·sene *or* **ker·o·sine** \'ker-ə-,sēn\ *n* : a thin oil obtained from petroleum and used as a fuel and solvent

ketch \'kech\ *n* : a fore-and-aft rigged ship with two masts

\ə\ abut	\au\ out	\i\ tip	\o\ saw	\u\ foot
\ər\ further	\ch\ chin	\ī\ life	\oi\ coin	\y\ yet
\a\ mat	\e\ pet	\j\ job	\th\ thin	\yü\ few
\ā\ take	\ē\ easy	\ng\ sing	\th\ this	\yu\ cure
\ä\ cot, cart	\g\ go	\ō\ bone	\ü\ food	\zh\ vision

ketchup *variant of* CATSUP

ket·tle \'ket-l\ *n* **1** : a pot for boiling liquids **2** : TEAKETTLE

ket·tle·drum \'ket-l-,drəm\ *n* : a large brass or copper drum that has a rounded bottom and can be varied in pitch

kettledrum

¹key \'kē\ *n* **1** : an instrument by which the bolt of a lock (as on a door) is turned **2** : a device having the form or function of a key ⟨a *key* for opening a can of meat⟩ **3** : a means of gaining or preventing entrance, possession, or control **4** : something (as a map legend) that gives an explanation : SOLUTION **5** : one of the levers with a flat surface that is pressed with a finger to activate a mechanism of a machine or instrument **6** : a system of seven musical tones arranged in relation to a keynote from which the system is named ⟨the *key* of C⟩ **7** : a characteristic way (as of thought) **8** : a small switch for opening or closing an electric circuit

²key *vb* **keyed; key·ing** **1** : to regulate the musical pitch of **2** : to bring into harmony

³key *adj* : of great importance : most important ⟨the *key* question is "Can we afford it?"⟩ ⟨the *key* people in the organization⟩

⁴key *n* : a low island or reef ⟨the Florida *keys*⟩

key·board \'kē-,bōrd\ *n* **1** : a row of keys by which a musical instrument (as a piano) is played **2** : the whole arrangement of keys (as on a typewriter)

key·hole \'kē-,hōl\ *n* : a hole for receiving a key

key·note \'kē-,nōt\ *n* **1** : the first and harmonically fundamental tone of a scale **2** : the fundamental fact, idea, or mood

key·stone \'kē-,stōn\ *n* **1** : the wedge-shaped piece at the top of an arch that locks the other pieces in place **2** : something on which other things depend for support

key up *vb* : to make nervous or tense ⟨was *keyed up* about the big game⟩

khaki \'kak-ē, 'kä-kē\ *n* **1** : a light yellowish brown **2** : a light yellowish brown cloth used especially for military uniforms

khan \'kän, 'kan\ *n* **1** : a Mongolian leader **2** : a local chieftain or man of rank in some countries of central Asia

kib·itz·er \'kib-ət-sər\ *n* : a person who looks on and often offers unwanted advice especially at a card game

¹kick \'kik\ *vb* **1** : to strike out or hit with the foot **2** : to object strongly : PROTEST ⟨*kicked* about their low grades⟩ **3** : to spring back when fired

²kick *n* **1** : a blow with the foot **2** : a sudden moving (as of a ball) with the foot **3** : the sudden move backward of a gun when fired **4** : a feeling of or cause for objection **5** : a feeling or source of pleasure

kick·ball \'kik-,bȯl\ *n* : a form of baseball played with a large rubber ball that is kicked instead of hit with a bat

kick·off \'kik-,ȯf\ *n* : a kick that puts the ball into play (as in football or soccer)

kick off \kik-'ȯf, 'kik-\ *vb* **1** : to make a kickoff **2** : BEGIN 1

¹kid \'kid\ *n* **1** : the young of a goat or a related animal **2** : the flesh, fur, or skin of a kid or something (as leather) made from one of these **3** : CHILD — **kid·dish** \'kid-ish\ *adj*

²kid *vb* **kid·ded; kid·ding** **1** : to deceive or trick as a joke **2** : ¹TEASE — **kid·der** *n*

kid·nap \'kid-,nap\ *vb* **kid·napped** *or* **kid·naped** \-,napt\; **kid·nap·ping** *or* **kid·nap·ing** : to carry away a person by force or by fraud and against his or her will — **kid·nap·per** *or* **kid·nap·er** *n*

kid·ney \'kid-nē\ *n, pl* **kid·neys** : either of a pair of organs near the backbone that give off waste from the body in the form of urine

kidney bean *n* : a common garden bean and especially one having large dark red seeds

¹kill \'kil\ *vb* **1** : to end the life of : SLAY **2**

keystone 1

: to put an end to ⟨*kill* all chance of success⟩ **3** : to use up ⟨*kill* time⟩ **4** : ¹DEFEAT 1 ⟨*kill* a proposed law⟩

synonyms KILL, MURDER and ASSASSINATE mean to take the life of. KILL suggests nothing about the manner of death and can apply to the death of anything ⟨the early frost *killed* the crops⟩ ⟨a person *killed* in an accident⟩ MURDER applies to the deliberate and unlawful killing of a person ⟨planned to *murder* the old merchant⟩ ASSASSINATE usually suggests the murder of an important person often for political reasons ⟨a secret plan to *assassinate* the President⟩

²kill *n* **1** : an act of killing **2** : an animal killed ⟨a lion devouring its *kill*⟩

kill·deer \'kil-ˌdiər\ *n* : a grayish brown North American plover that has a shrill mournful call

killdeer

Word History Killdeers are not vicious birds. They have no particular hatred for deer, nor do they eat venison, but to some people the cry of these birds sounds like "Kill deer! Kill deer! Kill deer!" That is why the killdeers got their unusual name.

¹kill·er \'kil-ər\ *n* : one that kills

²killer *adj* **1** : very impressive or effective ⟨a *killer* smile⟩ **2** very difficult ⟨a *killer* exam⟩ **3** : causing death or ruin ⟨a *killer* tornado⟩

kill·joy \'kil-ˌjȯi\ *n* : a person who spoils the pleasure of others

kiln \'kiln, 'kil\ *n* : a furnace or oven in which something (as pottery) is hardened, burned, or dried

ki·lo \'kē-lō, 'kē-ˌlō\ *n, pl* **ki·los 1** : KILOGRAM **2** : KILOMETER

kilo- *prefix* : thousand ⟨kilometer⟩

ki·lo·gram \'kē-lə-ˌgram, 'kil-ə-\ *n* : a metric unit of weight equal to 1000 grams

ki·lo·me·ter \kil-'äm-ət-ər, 'kil-ə-ˌmēt-ər\ *n* : a metric unit of length equal to 1000 meters

kilo·watt \'kil-ə-ˌwät\ *n* : a unit of electrical power equal to 1000 watts

kilt \'kilt\ *n* : a knee-length pleated skirt usually of tartan worn by men in Scotland

kil·ter \'kil-tər\ *n* : proper condition ⟨the TV is out of *kilter*⟩

ki·mo·no \kə-'mō-nə\ *n, pl* **ki·mo·nos 1** : a loose robe with wide sleeves that is traditionally worn with a broad sash as an outer garment by the Japanese **2** : a loose dressing gown worn chiefly by women

kimono 1

kin \'kin\ *n* **1** : a person's relatives **2** : KINSMAN

-kin \kən\ *also* **-kins** \kənz\ *n suffix* : little ⟨lamb*kin*⟩

¹kind \'kīnd\ *n* **1** : a natural group ⟨a bird of the hawk *kind*⟩ **2** : VARIETY **3** ⟨all *kinds* of people⟩ ⟨a hard *kind* of bread⟩

²kind *adj* **1** : wanting or liking to do good and to bring happiness to others : CONSIDERATE **2** : showing or growing out of gentleness or goodness of heart ⟨a *kind* act⟩

kin·der·gar·ten \'kin-dər-ˌgärt-n\ *n* : a school or a class for very young children

kind·heart·ed \'kīnd-'härt-əd\ *adj* : having or showing a kind and sympathetic nature — **kind·heart·ed·ly** *adv* — **kind·heart·ed·ness** *n*

kin·dle \'kin-dəl\ *vb* **kin·dled; kin·dling 1** : to set on fire : LIGHT **2** : to stir up : EXCITE ⟨the unfairness of the answer *kindled* our anger⟩

kin·dling \'kin-dling\ *n* : material that burns easily and is used for starting a fire

¹kind·ly \'kīn-dlē\ *adj* **kind·li·er; kind·li·est 1** : pleasant or wholesome in nature ⟨a *kindly* climate⟩ **2** : sympathetic or generous in nature ⟨*kindly* people⟩ — **kind·li·ness** *n*

²kindly *adv* **1** : in a willing manner ⟨take

\ə\ abut	\aù\ out	\i\ tip	\ȯ\ saw	\ù\ foot	
\ər\ further	\ch\ chin	\ī\ life	\ȯi\ coin	\y\ yet	
\a\ mat	\e\ pet	\j\ job	\th\ thin	\yü\ few	
\ā\ take	\ē\ easy	\ng\ sing	\th\ this	\yù\ cure	
\ä\ cot, cart	\g\ go	\ō\ bone	\ü\ food	\zh\ vision	

kindly to a change⟩ **2** : in a kind manner **3** : in an appreciative manner **4** : in an obliging manner

kind·ness \'kīnd-nəs\ *n* **1** : a kind deed : FAVOR **2** : the quality or state of being kind

kind of \ˌkīn-dəv, -də\ *adv* : to a moderate degree : SOMEWHAT ⟨it's *kind of* dark in here⟩

¹**kin·dred** \'kin-drəd\ *n* **1** : a group of related individuals **2** : a person's relatives

²**kindred** *adj* : alike in nature or character

kin·folk \'kin-ˌfōk\ *n* : ¹KINDRED 2

king \'king\ *n* **1** : a male ruler of a country who usually inherits his position and rules for life **2** : a chief among competitors ⟨an oil *king*⟩ **3** : the chief piece in the game of chess **4** : a playing card bearing the figure of a king **5** : a piece in checkers that has reached the opponent's back row — **king·ly** *adj*

king·dom \'king-dəm\ *n* **1** : a country whose ruler is a king or queen **2** : one of the three great divisions (**animal kingdom, plant kingdom, mineral kingdom**) into which all natural objects are grouped

king·fish·er \'king-ˌfish-ər\ *n* : any of a group of usually crested birds with a short tail, long sharp bill, and bright feathers

king·let \'king-lət\ *n* : a small bird resembling a warbler

king–size \'king-ˌsīz\ *or* **king–sized** \-ˌsīzd\ *adj* : unusually long or large

¹**kink** \'kingk\ *n* **1** : a short tight twist or curl (as in a thread or rope) **2** : ¹CRAMP 1 ⟨a *kink* in my back⟩ **3** : an imperfection that makes something hard to use or work — **kinky** \'kingk-ē\ *adj*

²**kink** *vb* : to form or cause to form a kink in

-kins — see -KIN

kin·ship \'kin-ˌship\ *n* : the quality or state of being kin

kins·man \'kinz-mən\ *n, pl* **kins·men** \-mən\ : a relative usually by birth

kins·wom·an \'kinz-ˌwum-ən\ *n, pl* **kins·wom·en** \-ˌwim-ən\ : a woman who is a relative usually by birth

¹**kiss** \'kis\ *vb* **1** : to touch with the lips as a mark of love or greeting **2** : to touch gently or lightly ⟨wind *kissing* the trees⟩

²**kiss** *n* **1** : a loving touch with the lips **2** : a gentle touch or contact **3** : a bite-size candy often wrapped in paper or foil

kit \'kit\ *n* **1** : a set of articles for personal use ⟨a travel *kit*⟩ **2** : a set of tools or supplies **3** : a set of parts to be put together ⟨a model-airplane *kit*⟩ **4** : a container (as a bag or case) for a kit

kitch·en \'kich-ən\ *n* : a room in which cooking is done

kitch·en·ette \ˌkich-ə-'net\ *n* : a small kitchen

kitchen garden *n* : a piece of land where vegetables are grown for household use

kite \'kīt\ *n* **1** : a hawk with long narrow wings and deeply forked tail that feeds mostly on insects and small reptiles **2** : a light covered frame for flying in the air at the end of a long string

kith \'kith\ *n* : familiar friends and neighbors or relatives ⟨our *kith* and kin⟩

kit·ten \'kit-n\ *n* : a young cat — **kit·ten·ish** \'kit-n-ish\ *adj*

kit·ty \'kit-ē\ *n, pl* **kit·ties** : CAT, KITTEN

ki·wi \'kē-wē\ *n* : a New Zealand bird that is unable to fly

kiwi

knack \'nak\ *n* **1** : a clever or skillful way of doing something : TRICK **2** : a natural ability : TALENT ⟨a *knack* for making friends⟩

knap·sack \'nap-ˌsak\ *n* : a carrying case or pouch slung from the shoulders over the back

knave \'nāv\ *n* **1** : RASCAL 1 **2** : ¹JACK 1

knead \'nēd\ *vb* **1** : to work and press into a mass with or as if with the hands ⟨*knead* dough⟩ **2** : ²MASSAGE — **knead·er** *n*

knee \'nē\ *n* **1** : the joint or region in which the thigh and lower leg come together **2** : something resembling a knee **3** : the part of a garment covering the knee

knee·cap \'nē-ˌkap\ *n* : a thick flat movable bone forming the front part of the knee

kneel \'nēl\ *vb* **knelt** \'nelt\ *or* **kneeled** \'nēld\; **kneel·ing** : to bend the knee : support oneself on one's knees

¹**knell** \'nel\ *vb* **1** : to ring slowly and solemnly : TOLL **2** : to summon, announce, or warn by a knell

²**knell** *n* **1** : a stroke or sound of a bell especially when rung slowly for a death, funeral, or disaster **2** : an indication (as a sound) of the end or failure of something

knew *past of* KNOW

knick·ers \'nik-ərz\ *n pl* : loose-fitting short pants gathered just below the knee

knick·knack \'nik-ˌnak\ *n* : a small ornamental object

¹**knife** \'nīf\ *n, pl* **knives** \'nīvz\ **1** : a cutting instrument consisting of a sharp blade fastened to a handle **2** : a cutting blade in a machine

²**knife** *vb* **knifed; knif·ing** : to stab, slash, or wound with a knife

¹**knight** \'nīt\ *n* **1** : a warrior of olden times who fought on horseback, served a king, held a special military rank, and swore to behave in a noble way **2** : a man honored by a sovereign for merit and in Great Britain ranking below a baronet **3** : one of the pieces in the game of chess — **knight·ly** *adj*

²**knight** *vb* : to make a knight of

knight·hood \'nīt-ˌhud\ *n* **1** : the rank, dignity, or profession of a knight **2** : the qualities that a knight should have **3** : knights as a class or body

knit \'nit\ *vb* **knit** *or* **knit·ted; knit·ting 1** : to form a fabric or garment by interlacing yarn or thread in connected loops with needles (**knitting needles**) ⟨*knit* a sweater⟩ **2** : to draw or come together closely as if knitted : unite firmly ⟨wait for a broken bone to *knit*⟩ **3** : ²WRINKLE ⟨*knit* one's brow⟩ — **knit·ter** *n*

knob \'näb\ *n* **1** : a rounded lump **2** : a small rounded handle **3** : a rounded hill

¹**knock** \'näk\ *vb* **1** : to strike with a sharp blow **2** : to bump against something **3** : to make a pounding noise **4** : to find fault with

²**knock** *n* **1** : a sharp blow **2** : a severe misfortune or hardship **3** : a pounding noise ⟨a *knock* in an automobile engine⟩

knock·er \'näk-ər\ *n* : a device made like a hinge and fastened to a door for use in knocking

knock–kneed \'näk-ˌnēd\ *adj* : having the legs bowed inward

knoll \'nōl\ *n* : a small round hill

¹**knot** \'nät\ *n* **1** : an interlacing (as of string or ribbon) that forms a lump or knob **2** : PROBLEM 2 **3** : a bond of union ⟨the marriage *knot*⟩ **4** : the inner end of a branch enclosed in a plant stem or a section of this in sawed lumber **5** : a cluster of persons or things **6** : an ornamental bow of ribbon **7** : one nautical mile per hour (about two kilometers per hour)

²**knot** *vb* **knot·ted; knot·ting 1** : to tie in or with a knot **2** : to unite closely

knot·hole \'nät-ˌhōl\ *n* : a hole in wood where a knot has come out

knot·ty \'nät-ē\ *adj* **knot·ti·er; knot·ti·est**

1 : full of knots **2** : DIFFICULT **3** ⟨a *knotty* problem⟩

know \'nō\ *vb* **knew** \'nü, 'nyü\; **known** \'nōn\; **know·ing 1** : to have understanding of ⟨*know* yourself⟩ **2** : to recognize the nature of ⟨*knew* them to be honest⟩ **3** : to recognize the identity of ⟨*knew* me by my walk⟩ **4** : to be acquainted or familiar with ⟨*knows* the city well⟩ **5** : to be aware of the truth of ⟨*know* that the earth is round⟩ **6** : to have a practical understanding of ⟨*knows* how to write⟩ **7** : to have information or knowledge ⟨ask someone who *knows*⟩ **8** : to be or become aware ⟨*knew* about the problem⟩

know·ing \'nō-ing\ *adj* **1** : having or showing special knowledge, information, or intelligence **2** : shrewdly and keenly alert **3** : INTENTIONAL — **know·ing·ly** *adv*

know–it–all \'nō-ət-ˌol\ *n* : a person who always claims to know everything

knowl·edge \'näl-ij\ *n* **1** : understanding and skill gained by experience ⟨a *knowledge* of carpentry⟩ **2** : the state of being aware of something or of having information **3** : range of information or awareness **4** : something learned and kept in the mind : LEARNING ⟨a vast *knowledge* of history⟩ **synonyms** see INFORMATION

knuck·le \'nək-əl\ *n* : the rounded lump formed by the ends of two bones (as of a finger) where they come together in a joint

ko·ala \kō-'ä-lə\ *n* : a tailless Australian animal with thick fur and big hairy ears, sharp claws for climbing, and a pouch like the kangaroo's for carrying its young

kohl·ra·bi \kōl-'rä-bē\ *n* : a cabbage that forms no head but has a fleshy edible stem

koala

Word History Kohlrabi is a kind of cabbage. Its large stem looks a bit like the root of a turnip. The Italians gave this plant a name made up of two Italian words. The first means "cabbage" and the second means "turnip." The Germans took the Italian name but changed it to fit their own way of speaking. The English word *kohlrabi* comes from the plant's German name.

\ə\ **abut**	\au̇\ **out**	\i\ **tip**	\o̅\ **saw**	\u̇\ **foot**
\ər\ **further**	\ch\ **chin**	\ī\ **life**	\oi\ **coin**	\y\ **yet**
\a\ **mat**	\e\ **pet**	\j\ **job**	\th\ **thin**	\yü\ **few**
\ā\ **take**	\ē\ **easy**	\ng\ **sing**	\th\ **this**	\yu̇\ **cure**
\ä\ **cot, cart**	\g\ **go**	\ō\ **bone**	\ü\ **food**	\zh\ **vision**

kook·a·bur·ra \'kůk-ə-ˌbər-ə\ *n* : an Australian kingfisher that has a call resembling loud laughter

Ko·ran \kə-'ran, -'rän\ *n* : a book of sacred writings accepted by Muslims as revealed to Muhammad by Allah

¹**Ko·re·an** \kə-'rē-ən\ *n* **1** : a person born or living in North Korea or South Korea **2** : the language of the Koreans

²**Korean** *adj* : of or relating to North Korea or South Korea, the Korean people, or their language

krill \'kril\ *n* : tiny floating sea creatures that are a chief food of whales

krim·mer \'krim-ər\ *n* : a gray curly fur from the pelt of young lambs

Word History There is a peninsula in southern Russia that juts out into the Black Sea. This piece of land is called the *Crimea.* Sheep are raised in the Crimea. The young lambs of these sheep have very fine wool. A gray curly fur called *krimmer* is made from the pelts of these lambs. The English word *krimmer* comes from the German word for this fur. This word was formed from the German name of the Crimea, where krimmer comes from.

kud·zu \'kůd-zü\ *n* : an Asian vine of the pea family widely grown for hay and for use in erosion control

kum·quat \'kəm-ˌkwät\ *n* : a small citrus fruit with sweet rind and sour pulp that is used mostly in preserves

Word History Kumquats first grew in China and Japan. The English got the fruit and its name from China. The word *kumquat* comes from a word in a variety of Chinese spoken in and near the city of Canton. The Chinese name for the kumquat is made up of two Chinese words. The first means "gold." The second is the word for the fruit we call *orange.*

L

l \'el\ *n, pl* **l's** *or* **ls** \'elz\ *often cap* **1** : the twelfth letter of the English alphabet **2** : fifty in Roman numerals

la \'lä\ *n* : the sixth note of the musical scale

lab \'lab\ *n* : LABORATORY

¹**la·bel** \'lā-bəl\ *n* **1** : a slip (as of paper or cloth) attached to something to identify or describe it **2** : a word or phrase that describes or names something ⟨a part-of-speech *label*⟩

²**label** *vb* **la·beled** *or* **la·belled; la·bel·ing** *or* **la·bel·ling** **1** : to attach a label to **2** : to name or describe with or as if with a label

la·bi·al \'lā-bē-əl\ *adj* : of or relating to the lips

¹**la·bor** \'lā-bər\ *n* **1** : effort that is hard and usually physical ⟨rest from *labor*⟩ **2** : the effort involved in giving birth **3** : something that has to be done : TASK **4** : workers as a body or class

synonyms LABOR and WORK mean action involving effort or exertion. WORK can apply to either mental or bodily effort and may involve something that is enjoyable but tiring ⟨decorating the gym was hard *work*⟩ LABOR suggests great or unpleasant exertion, especially of the body, and indicates that the work is done of necessity ⟨the dull *labor* of cleaning the stove⟩

²**labor** *vb* **1** : to work hard : TOIL **2** : to move slowly or heavily ⟨a truck *laboring* up the hill⟩

lab·o·ra·to·ry \'lab-rə-ˌtōr-ē, 'lab-ə-rə-\ *n, pl* **lab·o·ra·to·ries** : a room or building in which experiments and tests are done

Labor Day *n* : the first Monday in September observed as a legal holiday to honor the worker

la·bored \'lā-bərd\ *adj* : produced or done with effort or difficulty ⟨*labored* breathing⟩

la·bor·er \'lā-bər-ər\ *n* : a person who works on jobs that require strength rather than skill

la·bo·ri·ous \lə-'bōr-ē-əs\ *adj* : requiring much effort ⟨a *laborious* climb up the mountain⟩ — **la·bo·ri·ous·ly** *adv*

labor union *n* : an organization of workers designed to help them get better pay and working conditions

¹**lace** \'lās\ *n* **1** : a cord or string for pulling and holding together opposite edges (as of a shoe) **2** : an ornamental net of thread or cord usually with a design

Word History We usually try to avoid knotting our shoelaces. It might seem strange, then, that the English word *lace*

comes from an Old French word that meant "a knotted cord," but that is true. This Old French word came, in turn, from a Latin word that meant "snare" or "noose."

²lace *vb* **laced; lac·ing** : to fasten with a lace

lac·er·ate \'las-ə-ˌrāt\ *vb* **lac·er·at·ed; lac·er·at·ing** : to injure by tearing ⟨a *lacerated* knee⟩

lac·er·a·tion \ˌlas-ə-'rā-shən\ *n* : a lacerated place or wound

¹lack \'lak\ *vb* **1** : to be missing ⟨something is *lacking*⟩ **2** : to need or be without something ⟨you will never *lack* for friends⟩ ⟨I *lack* the necessary money⟩

²lack *n* **1** : the fact or state of being absent or needed ⟨a *lack* of time⟩ **2** : something that is absent or needed

¹lac·quer \'lak-ər\ *n* : a material like varnish that dries quickly into a shiny layer (as on wood or metal)

²lacquer *vb* : to coat with lacquer

la·crosse \lə-'krȯs\ *n* : a ball game played outdoors using a long-handled stick with a shallow net for catching, throwing, and carrying the ball

lacy \'lā-sē\ *adj* **lac·i·er; lac·i·est** : like or made of lace

lad \'lad\ *n* : BOY 1, YOUTH

lad·der \'lad-ər\ *n* : a device used for climbing usually consisting of two long pieces of wood, rope, or metal joined at short distances by horizontal pieces

lad·die \'lad-ē\ *n* : BOY 1, LAD

lad·en \'lād-n\ *adj* : heavily loaded ⟨a truck *laden* with gravel⟩

¹la·dle \'lād-l\ *n* : a spoon with a long handle and a deep bowl that is used for dipping

²ladle *vb* **la·dled; la·dling** : to take up and carry in a ladle

la·dy \'lād-ē\ *n, pl* **la·dies** **1** : a woman of high social position **2** : a pleasant well-bred woman or girl **3** : a woman of any kind or class — often used in speaking to a stranger ⟨*lady*, you dropped something⟩ **4** : WIFE **5** : a British noblewoman — used as a title ⟨*Lady* Jane Grey⟩

Word History There was in Old English a word *hlāf* that meant "bread" or "loaf." The modern English word *loaf* comes from this Old English word. A suffix -*dige* meaning "kneader" was long ago added to the old word for bread. The modern word *dough* is related to that Old English suffix. Together *hlāf* and -*dige* made a word *hlǣfdige* that meant "one who kneads bread." This word was used for a woman who was the head of a household.

The modern English word *lady* comes from this old word.

la·dy·bird \'lād-ē-ˌbərd\ *n* : LADYBUG

la·dy·bug \'lād-ē-ˌbəg\ *n* : a small rounded beetle that feeds mostly on plant lice

la·dy·like \'lād-ē-ˌlīk\ *adj* : WELL-BRED

la·dy·ship \'lād-ē-ˌship\ *n* : the rank of a lady — used as a title ⟨her *Ladyship* is not at home⟩

lady's slipper *or* **lady slipper** *n* : any of several North American wild orchids whose flowers suggest a slipper in shape

¹lag \'lag\ *vb* **lagged; lag·ging** : to move or advance slowly ⟨pupils who *lag* behind the rest of the class⟩

²lag *n* : the act or the amount of lagging

¹lag·gard \'lag-ərd\ *adj* : lagging behind : SLOW

²laggard *n* : a person who lags

la·goon \lə-'gün\ *n* : a shallow channel or pond near or connected to a larger body of water

lady's slipper

laid *past of* LAY

lain *past participle of* LIE

lair \'laər, 'leər\ *n* : the den or resting place of a wild animal

lake \'lāk\ *n* : a large inland body of still water

¹lamb \'lam\ *n* : a young sheep usually less than one year old

²lamb *vb* : to give birth to a lamb

lamb·kin \'lam-kən\ *n* : a young lamb

¹lame \'lām\ *adj* **lam·er; lam·est** **1** : not able to get around without pain or difficulty **2** : being stiff and sore ⟨a *lame* shoulder⟩ **3** : not very convincing : WEAK ⟨a *lame* excuse⟩ — **lame·ly** *adv* — **lame·ness** *n*

²lame *vb* **lamed; lam·ing** : to make or become lame ⟨*lamed* in a fall⟩

¹la·ment \lə-'ment\ *vb* **1** : to mourn aloud : WAIL **2** : to show sorrow for

\ə\ abut	\au̇\ out	\i\ tip	\ȯ\ saw	\u̇\ foot
\ər\ further	\ch\ chin	\ī\ life	\ȯi\ coin	\y\ yet
\a\ mat	\e\ pet	\j\ job	\th\ thin	\yü\ few
\ā\ take	\ē\ easy	\ng\ sing	\th\ this	\yu̇\ cure
\ä\ cot, cart	\g\ go	\ō\ bone	\ü\ food	\zh\ vision

²**lament** *n* **1** : a crying out in sorrow **2** : a sad song or poem

lam·en·ta·ble \'lam-ən-tə-bəl\ *adj* : RE-GRETTABLE ⟨a *lamentable* accident⟩

lam·en·ta·tion \ˌlam-ən-'tā-shən\ *n* : the act of lamenting

lam·i·nat·ed \'lam-ə-ˌnāt-əd\ *adj* : made of layers of material firmly joined together

lamp \'lamp\ *n* : a device for producing light ⟨a kerosene *lamp*⟩ ⟨an electric *lamp*⟩

lamp·black \'lamp-ˌblak\ *n* : a fine black soot made by burning material incompletely and used especially to color things black

lam·prey \'lam-prē\ *n, pl* **lam·preys** : a water animal that looks like an eel but has a sucking mouth with no jaws

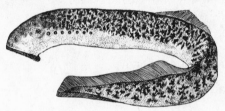

lamprey

¹**lance** \'lans\ *n* : a weapon with a long handle and a sharp steel head used in olden times by knights on horseback

²**lance** *vb* : to cut open with a small sharp instrument ⟨the doctor *lanced* the boil⟩

lance corporal *n* : an enlisted person in the Marine Corps ranking above a private first class

¹**land** \'land\ *n* **1** : the solid part of the surface of the earth **2** : a part of the earth's surface (as a country or a farm) marked off by boundaries **3** : the people of a country — **land·less** \-ləs\ *adj*

²**land** *vb* **1** : to go ashore or cause to go ashore from a ship **2** : to cause to reach or come to rest where planned ⟨*land* an arrow in the target⟩ **3** : to catch and bring in ⟨*land* a fish⟩ **4** : to get for oneself by trying ⟨*land* a job⟩ **5** : to come down or bring down and settle on a surface ⟨*landed* on the moon⟩ ⟨*land* an airplane⟩

land breeze *n* : a breeze blowing toward the sea

land·hold·er \'land-ˌhōl-dər\ *n* : an owner of land

land·ing \'lan-ding\ *n* **1** : the act of one that lands **2** : a place for unloading or taking on passengers and cargo **3** : the level part of a staircase (as between flights of stairs)

landing field *n* : a field where aircraft land and take off

landing strip *n* : AIRSTRIP

land·la·dy \'land-ˌlād-ē\ *n, pl* **land·la·dies** **1** : a woman who owns land or houses that she rents **2** : a woman who runs an inn or rooming house

land·locked \'land-ˌläkt\ *adj* **1** : shut in or nearly shut in by land ⟨a *landlocked* harbor⟩ **2** : kept from leaving fresh water by some barrier ⟨*landlocked* salmon⟩

land·lord \'land-ˌlord\ *n* **1** : a man who owns land or houses that he rents **2** : a man who runs an inn or rooming house

land·lub·ber \'land-ˌləb-ər\ *n* : a person who lives on land and knows little or nothing about the sea

land·mark \'land-ˌmärk\ *n* **1** : something (as a building, a large tree, or a statue) that is easy to see and can help a person find the way to a place near it **2** : a very important event **3** : a building of historical importance

land·own·er \'lan-ˌdō-nər\ *n* : a person who owns land

¹**land·scape** \'land-ˌskāp\ *n* **1** : a picture of natural scenery **2** : the land that can be seen in one glance

²**landscape** *vb* **land·scaped; land·scap·ing** : to improve the natural beauty of a piece of land

land·slide \'land-ˌslīd\ *n* **1** : the slipping down of a mass of rocks or earth on a steep slope **2** : the material that moves in a landslide **3** : the winning of an election by a very large number of votes

lane \'lān\ *n* **1** : a narrow path or road (as between fences or hedges) that is not used as a highway **2** : a special route (as for ships) **3** : a strip of road used for a single line of traffic

lan·guage \'lang-gwij\ *n* **1** : the words and expressions used and understood by a large group of people ⟨the English *language*⟩ **2** : the speech of human beings **3** : a means of expressing ideas or feelings ⟨sign *language*⟩ **4** : the way in which words are used ⟨forceful *language*⟩ **5** : the special words used by a certain group or in a certain field ⟨the *language* of science⟩ **6** : the study of languages

lan·guid \'lang-gwəd\ *adj* : having very little strength or energy — **lan·guid·ly** *adv* — **lan·guid·ness** *n*

lan·guish \'lang-gwish\ *vb* : to become weak especially from a lack of something needed or wanted — **lan·guish·er** *n* — **lan·guish·ing** *adj* — **lan·guish·ing·ly** *adv*

lan·guor \'lang-gər\ *n* **1** : weakness or

weariness of body or mind **2** : a state of dreamy idleness — **lan·guor·ous** *adj* — **lan·guor·ous·ly** *adv*

lank \'langk\ *adj* **1** : not well filled out : THIN ⟨*lank* cattle⟩ **2** : hanging straight and limp without spring or curl ⟨*lank* hair⟩ — **lank·ly** *adv* — **lank·ness** *n*

lanky \'lang-kē\ *adj* **lank·i·er; lank·i·est** : being very tall and thin — **lank·i·ly** \-kə-lē\ *adv* — **lank·i·ness** \-kē-nəs\ *n*

lan·tern \'lant-ərn\ *n* : a usually portable lamp with a protective covering

lan·yard \'lan-yərd\ *n* **1** : a short rope or cord used as a fastening on ships **2** : a cord worn around the neck to hold a knife or whistle **3** : a strong cord with a hook at one end used in firing cannon

¹lap \'lap\ *n* : the front part of a person between the waist and the knees when seated

²lap *vb* **lapped; lap·ping** : OVERLAP

³lap *n* **1** : a part of something that overlaps another part **2** : one time around a race-track **3** : a stage in a trip

⁴lap *vb* **lapped; lap·ping** **1** : to scoop up food or drink with the tip of the tongue **2** : to splash gently

⁵lap *n* : the act or sound of lapping

lap·dog \'lap-ˌdȯg\ *n* : a dog small enough to be held in the lap

la·pel \lə-'pel\ *n* : the part of the front of a collar that is turned back ⟨coat *lapels*⟩

lap·ful \'lap-ˌfu̇l\ *n, pl* **lap·fuls** \-fu̇lz\ *or* **laps·ful** \'laps-ˌfu̇l\ : as much as the lap can hold

¹lapse \'laps\ *n* **1** : a slight error or slip ⟨a *lapse* of memory⟩ **2** : a gradual falling away from a higher to a lower condition **3** : a gradual passing of time

²lapse *vb* **lapsed; laps·ing** **1** : to slip, pass, or fall gradually ⟨*lapse* into silence⟩ **2** : to become little used ⟨a custom that had *lapsed*⟩ **3** : to come to an end ⟨the car insurance *lapsed*⟩ — **laps·er** *n*

lar·board \'lär-bərd\ *n* : ³PORT

lar·ce·ny \'lärs-n-ē\ *n, pl* **lar·ce·nies** : the unlawful taking of personal property without the owner's consent : THEFT

larch \'lärch\ *n* : a tree related to the pine that sheds its needles each fall

¹lard \'lärd\ *vb* : to smear or soil with grease

²lard *n* : a white soft fat from fatty tissue of the hog

lar·der \'lärd-ər\ *n* : a place where food is kept

large \'lärj\ *adj* **larg·er; larg·est** : more than most others of a similar kind in amount or size : BIG — **large·ness** *n* — **at large 1** : not locked up : FREE ⟨the bank robbers are still *at large*⟩ **2** : as a whole ⟨the public *at large*⟩ **3** : representing a whole state or district ⟨a delegate-*at-large*⟩

large-heart·ed \'lärj-'härt-əd\ *adj* : GENEROUS 1

large intestine *n* : the wide lower part of the intestine from which water is absorbed and in which feces are made ready for passage

large·ly \'lärj-lē\ *adv* : MOSTLY, CHIEFLY

lar·i·at \'lar-ē-ət, 'ler-\ *n* : a long light rope used to catch livestock or tie up grazing animals

¹lark \'lärk\ *n* **1** : a small mostly brownish European songbird **2** : any of various birds that are mostly dull-colored and live on the ground

²lark *n* : something done for fun : PRANK

lark·spur \'lärk-ˌspər\ *n* : a tall branching plant related to the buttercups that is often grown for its stalks of showy blue, pink, or white flowers

lar·va \'lär-və\ *n, pl* **lar·vae** \-vē\ **1** : a wingless form (as a grub or caterpillar) in which many insects hatch from the egg **2** : an early form of any animal that at birth or hatching is very different from its parents

larkspur

Word History The ancient Romans had a word for a soldier who served merely for pay and not for the love of a country or a cause. Many people did not think highly of such soldiers. They thought that a soldier like that was not much better than a thief. So the Romans made a new word that meant "theft." This word was based on the word for a hired soldier. The English word *larceny* comes from that old word in Latin, the language of the ancient Romans.

Word History Many insects have different forms at different times in their lives. A young moth, for instance, looks a bit like a worm. We may think of the different forms as different disguises or masks of the in-

\ə\ **abut**	\au̇\ **out**	\i\ **tip**	\ȯ\ **saw**	\u̇\ **foot**
\ər\ **further**	\ch\ **chin**	\ī\ **life**	\ȯi\ **coin**	\y\ **yet**
\a\ **mat**	\e\ **pet**	\j\ **job**	\th\ **thin**	\yü\ **few**
\ā\ **take**	\ē\ **easy**	\ng\ **sing**	\th\ **this**	\yu̇\ **cure**
\ä\ **cot, cart**	\g\ **go**	\ō\ **bone**	\ü\ **food**	\zh\ **vision**

sect. Scientists who thought this way gave the young form the name *larva*. This word comes from a Latin word which looked like English *larva*. This Latin word meant "mask" or "ghost."

lar·yn·gi·tis \ˌlar-ən-ˈjīt-əs\ *n* : inflammation of the larynx : a sore throat

lar·ynx \ˈlar-ingks\ *n, pl* **la·ryn·ges** \lə-ˈrin-ˌjēz\ *or* **lar·ynx·es** : the upper part of the windpipe that contains the vocal cords

la·ser \ˈlā-zər\ *n* : a device that produces a very powerful beam of light

¹lash \ˈlash\ *vb* **1** : to move violently or suddenly **2** : to hit with a whip — **lash·er** *n*

²lash *n* **1** : a blow with a whip or switch **2** : the flexible part of a whip **3** : a sudden swinging blow **4** : EYELASH

³lash *vb* : to tie down with a rope or chain

lash·ing \ˈlash-ing\ *n* : something used for tying, wrapping, or fastening

lass \ˈlas\ *n* : GIRL 1

lass·ie \ˈlas-ē\ *n* : GIRL 1, LASS

¹las·so \ˈlas-ō, la-ˈsü\ *n, pl* **las·sos** *or* **las·soes** : a rope or long leather thong with a slipknot for catching animals

²lasso *vb* : to catch with a lasso

¹last \ˈlast\ *vb* **1** : to go on ⟨the game *lasted* till dark⟩ **2** : to stay in good condition ⟨the flowers *lasted* well⟩ — **last·er** *n*

lasso

²last *adj* **1** : following all the rest : FINAL **2** : most recent ⟨*last* week⟩ **3** : lowest in rank or position **4** : most unlikely

synonyms LAST and FINAL mean following all the others. LAST suggests being at the end of a series but it does not always suggest that the series is complete or permanently ended ⟨spent my *last* dollar on a ticket⟩ FINAL applies to something that positively closes a series and forever settles the matter ⟨the *final* game of the tennis championship⟩

³last *adv* **1** : at the end **2** : most recently

⁴last *n* : a person or thing that is last

⁵last *n* : a block shaped like a foot on which shoes are made

last·ing \ˈlas-ting\ *adj* : continuing for a long while — **last·ing·ly** *adv* — **last·ing·ness** *n*

last·ly \ˈlast-lē\ *adv* : at or as the end

¹latch \ˈlach\ *n* : a movable piece that holds a door or gate closed

²latch *vb* : to fasten with a latch

¹late \ˈlāt\ *adj* **lat·er; lat·est 1** : coming or remaining after the usual or proper time **2** : coming toward the end (as of the day or night) ⟨a *late* hour⟩ **3** : having died or recently left a certain position ⟨the *late* president⟩ **4** : RECENT 2 — **late·ness** *n*

²late *adv* **lat·er; lat·est 1** : after the usual or proper time **2** : LATELY

late·com·er \ˈlāt-ˌkəm-ər\ *n* : a person who arrives late

late·ly \ˈlāt-lē\ *adv* : not long ago : RECENTLY

la·tent \ˈlāt-nt\ *adj* : present but not visible or active ⟨*latent* fingerprints⟩ ⟨*latent* infection⟩ — **la·tent·ly** *adv*

lat·er·al \ˈlat-ə-rəl\ *adj* : being on or directed toward the side — **lat·er·al·ly** *adv*

la·tex \ˈlā-ˌteks\ *n* **1** : a milky plant juice **2** : a liquid made of small bits of rubber or plastic mixed with water and used especially in paints

lath \ˈlath\ *n, pl* **laths** \ˈlathz, ˈlaths\ : a thin strip of wood used (as in a wall or ceiling) as a base for plaster

lathe \ˈlāth\ *n* : a machine in which a piece of material is held and turned while being shaped by a tool

¹lath·er \ˈlath-ər\ *n* **1** : the foam made by stirring soap and water together **2** : foam from sweating

²lather *vb* **1** : to spread lather over **2** : to form a lather ⟨this soap *lathers* well⟩

¹Lat·in \ˈlat-n\ *adj* **1** : of or relating to the language of the ancient Romans ⟨*Latin* courses⟩ **2** : of or relating to Latin America or the Latin Americans

²Latin *n* **1** : the language of the ancient Romans **2** : a member of a people whose language and customs have descended from the ancient Romans **3** : a person born or living in Latin America

Lat·in–Amer·i·can \ˌlat-n-ə-ˈmer-ə-kən\ *adj* : of or relating to Latin America or its people

Latin American *n* : a person born or living in Latin America

lat·i·tude \ˈlat-ə-ˌtüd, -ˌtyüd\ *n* **1** : the distance north or south of the equator measured in degrees **2** : REGION **3** ⟨cold *latitudes*⟩ **3** : freedom to act or speak as one wishes

lat·ter \ˈlat-ər\ *adj* **1** : relating to or coming near the end ⟨we are in the *latter* stages of the work⟩ **2** : of, relating to, or being the second of two things referred to

lat·tice \ˈlat-əs\ *n* **1** : a structure made of thin strips of wood or metal that cross each other to form a network **2** : a window or gate having a lattice

¹laud \'lȯd\ *n* : ²PRAISE 1, ACCLAIM

²laud *vb* : ¹PRAISE 1, ACCLAIM

¹laugh \'laf, 'lȧf\ *vb* : to show amusement, joy, or scorn by smiling and making sounds (as chuckling) in the throat

²laugh *n* : the act or sound of laughing

laugh·able \'laf-ə-bəl, 'lȧf-\ *adj* : causing or likely to cause laughter — **laugh·able·ness** *n* — **laugh·ably** \-blē\ *adv*

laugh·ing·stock \'laf-ing-,stäk, 'lȧf-\ *n* : a person or thing that is made fun of

laugh·ter \'laf-tər, 'lȧf-\ *n* : the action or sound of laughing

¹launch \'lȯnch\ *vb* **1** : ¹THROW 1, 2, HURL ⟨*launch* a spear⟩ **2** : to set afloat ⟨*launch* a ship⟩ **3** : to send off especially with force ⟨*launch* an aircraft⟩ ⟨*launch* a spacecraft⟩ **4** : to give a start to ⟨*launch* a plan⟩

²launch *n* : an act of launching

³launch *n* : MOTORBOAT

launch·pad \'lȯnch-,pad\ *n* : a nonflammable platform from which a rocket can be launched

laun·der \'lȯn-dər\ *vb* : to wash or wash and iron clothes — **laun·der·er** *n*

laun·dress \'lȯn-drəs\ *n* : a woman whose work is washing clothes

laun·dry \'lȯn-drē\ *n, pl* **laun·dries** **1** : clothes or linens that have been laundered or are to be laundered **2** : a place where laundering is done

laun·dry·man \'lȯn-drē-mən\ *n, pl* **laun·dry·men** \-mən\ : a man who works in or for a laundry

lau·rel \'lȯr-əl\ *n* **1** : a small evergreen European tree with shiny pointed leaves used in ancient times to crown victors (as in sports) **2** : any of various plants (as the American **mountain laurel**) that resemble the European laurel **3** : a crown of laurel used as a mark of honor

laurel 2

la·va \'läv-ə, 'lav-ə\ *n* **1** : melted rock coming from a volcano **2** : lava that has cooled and hardened

lav·a·to·ry \'lav-ə-,tōr-ē\ *n, pl* **lav·a·to·ries** **1** : a small sink (as in a bathroom) **2** : a room for washing that usually has a toilet **3** : TOILET 3

lav·en·der \'lav-ən-dər\ *n* **1** : a European mint with narrow somewhat woolly leaves and stalks of small sweet-smelling pale violet flowers **2** : a pale purple

¹lav·ish \'lav-ish\ *adj* **1** : spending or giving more than is necessary : EXTRAVAGANT ⟨*lavish* with money⟩ **2** : spent, produced, or given freely ⟨*lavish* gifts⟩ — **lav·ish·ly** *adv* — **lav·ish·ness** *n*

lavender 1

Word History *Lavish* comes from an early English noun *lavish* that meant "plenty." This noun came from a French word that meant "a heavy rain." This French word can be traced back to a Latin verb that meant "to wash." Other English words that come from this Latin verb are *deluge, launder, laundry,* and *lavatory.*

²lavish *vb* : to spend, use, or give freely

law \'lȯ\ *n* **1** : a rule of conduct or action that a nation or a group of people agrees to follow **2** : a whole collection of established rules ⟨the *law* of the land⟩ **3** : a rule or principle that always works the same way under the same conditions ⟨the *law* of gravity⟩ **4** : a bill passed by a legislative group **5** : ¹POLICE **6** *cap* : the first part of the Jewish scriptures **7** : trial in court ⟨go to *law*⟩ **8** : the profession of a lawyer

law–abid·ing \'lȯ-ə-,bīd-ing\ *adj* : obeying the law

law·break·er \'lȯ-,brā-kər\ *n* : a person who breaks the law

law·ful \'lȯ-fəl\ *adj* **1** : permitted by law **2** : approved by law — **law·ful·ly** \-fə-lē\ *adv* — **law·ful·ness** *n*

\ə\ abut	\au̇\ out	\i\ tip	\ȯ\ saw	\u̇\ foot
\ər\ further	\ch\ chin	\ī\ life	\ȯi\ coin	\y\ yet
\a\ mat	\e\ pet	\j\ job	\th\ thin	\yü\ few
\ā\ take	\ē\ easy	\ng\ sing	\th\ this	\yu̇\ cure
\ä\ cot, cart	\g\ go	\ō\ bone	\ü\ food	\zh\ vision

law·less \'lo-ləs\ *adj* **1** : having no laws : not based on or controlled by law ⟨a *lawless* frontier society⟩ **2** : uncontrolled by law : UNRULY ⟨a *lawless* mob⟩ — **law·less·ly** *adv* — **law·less·ness** *n*

law·mak·er \'lo-ˌmā-kər\ *n* : one who takes part in writing and passing laws : LEGISLATOR — **law·mak·ing** \-ˌmā-king\ *adj or n*

lawn \'lon, 'län\ *n* : ground (as around a house) covered with grass that is kept mowed

lawn mower *n* : a machine used to mow the grass on lawns

lawn tennis *n* : TENNIS

law·suit \'lo-ˌsüt\ *n* : a complaint brought before a court of law for decision

law·yer \'lo-yər, 'loi-ər\ *n* : a person whose profession is to handle lawsuits for people or to give advice about legal rights and duties

lax \'laks\ *adj* **1** : not firm or tight : LOOSE **2** : not stern or strict ⟨*lax* discipline⟩ — **lax·ly** *adv* — **lax·ness** *n*

¹lax·a·tive \'lak-sət-iv\ *adj* : helpful against constipation

²laxative *n* : a laxative medicine that is nearly always mild

¹lay \'lā\ *vb* **laid** \'lād\; **lay·ing** **1** : to bring down (as with force) ⟨crops *laid* flat by the gale⟩ **2** : to put down ⟨*laid* my hat on the table⟩ **3** : to produce an egg **4** : to cause to disappear ⟨*laid* my fears⟩ **5** : to spread over a surface ⟨*lay* a pavement⟩ **6** : PREPARE 1, ARRANGE ⟨*lay* plans⟩ **7** : to put to : APPLY ⟨*laid* the watch to my ear⟩

²lay *n* : the way a thing lies in relation to something else ⟨the *lay* of the land⟩

³lay *past of* LIE

lay·away \'lā-ə-ˌwā\ *n* : something held for a customer until the price is paid

lay away *vb* : to put aside for later use or delivery

lay·er \'lā-ər\ *n* **1** : one that lays something **2** : one thickness of something laid over another

lay in *vb* : to store for later use

lay·man \'lā-mən\ *n, pl* **lay·men** \-mən\ **1** : a person who is not a member of the clergy **2** : a person who is not a member of a certain profession

lay off *vb* **1** : to stop employing (a person) usually temporarily **2** : to let alone

lay·out \'lā-ˌaut\ *n* : ¹PLAN 1, ARRANGEMENT

lay out \lā-'aut\ *vb* **1** : to plan in detail **2** : ARRANGE 1, DESIGN

lay up *vb* **1** : to store up **2** : to be confined by illness or injury

la·zy \'lā-zē\ *adj* **la·zi·er; la·zi·est** **1** : not willing to act or work **2** : ¹SLOW 3, SLUG-

GISH ⟨a *lazy* stream⟩ — **la·zi·ly** \-zə-lē\ *adv* — **la·zi·ness** \-zē-nəs\ *n*

leach \'lēch\ *vb* **1** : to treat (as earth) with a liquid (as water) to remove something soluble **2** : to remove (as a soluble salt) by leaching

¹lead \'lēd\ *vb* **led** \'led\; **lead·ing** **1** : to guide on a way often by going ahead **2** : to be at the head of ⟨*lead* the class⟩ **3** : to go through : LIVE ⟨*lead* a happy life⟩ **4** : to reach or go in a certain direction ⟨this road *leads* to town⟩

²lead *n* **1** : position at the front ⟨take the *lead*⟩ **2** : the distance that a person or thing is ahead **3** : the first part of a news story

³lead \'led\ *n* **1** : a heavy soft gray metallic element that is easily bent and shaped **2** : AMMUNITION 1 ⟨a shower of *lead*⟩ **3** : a long thin piece of graphite used in pencils

lead·en \'led-n\ *adj* **1** : made of lead **2** : heavy as lead **3** : dull gray — **lead·en·ly** *adv* — **lead·en·ness** *n*

lead·er \'lēd-ər\ *n* : one that leads or is able to lead — **lead·er·ship** \-ˌship\ *n*

¹leaf \'lēf\ *n, pl* **leaves** \'lēvz\ **1** : one of the green usually flat parts that grow from a stem or twig of a plant and together make up the foliage **2** : a specialized leaf (as of a flower petal) **3** : a single sheet of a book making two pages **4** : the movable part of the top of a table — **leaf·less** \'lē-fləs\ *adj* — **leaf·like** \'lē-ˌflīk\ *adj*

²leaf *vb* **1** : to grow leaves ⟨trees *leafing* out in spring⟩ **2** : to turn the leaves of a book

leaf·let \'lē-flət\ *n* **1** : a young or small leaf **2** : a division of a compound leaf **3** : PAMPHLET

leaf·stalk \'lēf-ˌstok\ *n* : PETIOLE

leafy \'lē-fē\ *adj* **leaf·i·er; leaf·i·est** : having, covered with, or like leaves

¹league \'lēg\ *n* **1** : a group of nations working together for a common purpose **2** : an association of persons or groups with common interests or goals **3** : ¹CLASS 7 ⟨out of one's *league*⟩

²league *vb* **leagued; leagu·ing** : to form a league

¹leak \'lēk\ *vb* **1** : to enter or escape or let enter or escape usually by accident ⟨fumes *leaking* in⟩ **2** : to make or become known

²leak *n* **1** : a crack or hole that accidentally lets fluid in or out **2** : something that accidentally or secretly causes or permits loss **3** : the act of leaking : LEAKAGE

leak·age \'lē-kij\ *n* **1** : the act or process of leaking **2** : the thing or amount that leaks

leaky \'lē-kē\ *adj* **leak·i·er; leak·i·est** : letting fluid leak in or out — **leak·i·ness** *n*

¹**lean** \'lēn\ *vb* **1** : to bend or tilt from a straight position ⟨a tree that *leans* badly⟩ ⟨*lean* the ladder against the wall⟩ **2** : to bend and rest one's weight on ⟨*lean* on me⟩ **3** : DEPEND 1, RELY **4** : to tend or move toward in opinion, taste, or desire

²**lean** *adj* **1** : having too little flesh : SKINNY ⟨*lean* cattle⟩ **2** : containing very little fat ⟨*lean* meat⟩ **3** : not large or plentiful ⟨a *lean* harvest⟩ — **lean·ness** *n*

synonyms LEAN, THIN, SKINNY mean not having a great amount of flesh. LEAN suggests a lack of unnecessary flesh and may also suggest the tough, muscular frame of an athlete ⟨the hard, *lean* body of a runner⟩ THIN applies to a person having not much flesh or fat and often having an amount less than is desirable for good health ⟨a *thin* and sickly child⟩ SKINNY suggests a bony, noticeably thin appearance that may indicate a lack of proper nourishment ⟨*skinny* children living in city slums⟩

lean–to \'lēn-,tü\ *n, pl* **lean–tos 1** : a building that has a roof with only one slope and is usually joined to another building **2** : a rough shelter held up by posts, rocks, or trees

¹**leap** \'lēp\ *vb* **leaped** *or* **leapt** \'lēpt, 'lept\; **leap·ing** \'lē-ping\ **1** : to jump or cause to jump from a surface ⟨*leaped* from the chair⟩ **2** : to move, act, or pass quickly — **leap·er** \'lē-pər\ *n*

²**leap** *n* **1** : an act of leaping : JUMP **2** : a place leaped over **3** : a distance leaped

leap·frog \'lēp-,fròg, -,fräg\ *n* : a game in which one player bends down and another leaps over the first player

leap year *n* : a year of 366 days with February 29 as the extra day

learn \'lərn\ *vb* **learned** \'lərnd\ *also* **learnt** \'lərnt\; **learn·ing 1** : to get knowledge of or skill in (by studying or practicing) ⟨*learn* algebra⟩ **2** : MEMORIZE **3** : to become able through practice ⟨a baby *learning* to walk⟩ **4** : to find out ⟨*learned* what had happened⟩ **5** : to gain knowledge ⟨children eager to *learn*⟩

learn·ed \'lər-nəd\ *adj* : having or showing knowledge or learning

learn·ing \'lər-ning\ *n* **1** : the act of a person who learns **2** : knowledge or skill gained from teaching or study **synonyms** see INFORMATION

¹**lease** \'lēs\ *n* **1** : an agreement by which a person exchanges property (as real estate) for a period of time for rent or services **2** : the period of time for which property is leased **3** : a piece of property that is leased

²**lease** *vb* **leased; leas·ing** : to give or get the use of (property) in return for services or rent

¹**leash** \'lēsh\ *n* : a line for leading or holding an animal

²**leash** *vb* : to put on a leash

¹**least** \'lēst\ *adj* : smallest in size or degree

²**least** *n* : the smallest or lowest amount or degree ⟨doesn't mind in the *least*⟩

³**least** *adv* : in or to the smallest degree

leath·er \'leth-ər\ *n* **1** : the tanned skin of an animal **2** : something made of leather

leath·ery \'leth-ə-rē\ *adj* : like leather

¹**leave** \'lēv\ *vb* **left** \'left\; **leav·ing 1** : to fail to include or take along ⟨*left* my books at home⟩ **2** : to have remaining ⟨a wound that *left* a scar⟩ ⟨taking 7 from 10 *leaves* 3⟩ **3** : to give by will ⟨*left* property to the children⟩ **4** : to let stay without interference ⟨*leave* them alone⟩ **5** : to go away from ⟨*leave* the house⟩ **6** : to give up **7** : DELIVER 2 ⟨agreed to *leave* the package on the way home⟩

²**leave** *n* **1** : PERMISSION ⟨ask *leave* to be absent⟩ **2** : permitted absence from one's duty or work **3** : the act of leaving and saying good-bye ⟨take *leave* of a friend⟩ **4** : a period of time during which a person is allowed to be absent from duties

leaved \'lēvd\ *adj* : having leaves

leaves *pl of* LEAF

leav·ings \'lē-vingz\ *n pl* : something left over ⟨the *leavings* of dinner⟩

¹**lec·ture** \'lek-chər\ *n* **1** : a talk that teaches something **2** : a severe scolding

²**lecture** *vb* **lec·tured; lec·tur·ing 1** : to give a lecture **2** : ²SCOLD — **lec·tur·er** *n*

led *past of* LEAD

ledge \'lej\ *n* **1** : a piece projecting from a top or an edge like a shelf ⟨the outer *ledge* of a window⟩ **2** : SHELF 2

¹**lee** \'lē\ *n* **1** : a protecting shelter **2** : the side (as of a ship) sheltered from the wind

²**lee** *adj* : of or relating to the lee

leech \'lēch\ *n* **1** : a bloodsucking worm related to the earthworm **2** : a person who clings like a leech to another person for what can be gained

Word History At first the English word *leech* meant "doctor." Many years ago

\ə\ **abut**		\aů\ **out**	\i\ **tip**	\ò\ **saw**	\ů\ **foot**
\ər\ **further**		\ch\ **chin**	\ī\ **life**	\òi\ **coin**	\y\ **yet**
\a\ **mat**		\e\ **pet**	\j\ **job**	\th\ **thin**	\yü\ **few**
\ā\ **take**		\ē\ **easy**	\ng\ **sing**	\th\ **this**	\yů\ **cure**
\ä\ **cot, cart**		\g\ **go**	\ō\ **bone**	\ü\ **food**	\zh\ **vision**

doctors thought that a good way to cure sick people was to make them bleed. They thought that the blood of a sick person had harmful things in it that would flow away with the blood. To take bad blood out of sick people, early doctors often used little worms that suck blood. Soon *leech*, the word for a doctor, was used for these worms as well.

leek \'lēk\ *n* : a garden plant grown for its thick stems which taste like a mild onion

¹leer \'liər\ *vb* : to look with a leer

²leer *n* : a mean or nasty glance

leery \'liər-ē\ *adj* : SUSPICIOUS 2, WARY

¹lee·ward \'lē-wərd\ *adj* : located away from the wind ⟨the *leeward* side of the house⟩

²leeward *n* : the lee side ⟨sail to the *leeward* of the buoy⟩

¹left \'left\ *adj* **1** : on the same side of the body as the heart ⟨the *left* leg⟩ **2** : located nearer to the left side of the body than to the right ⟨the *left* side of the road⟩

²left *n* : the left side or the part on the left side

³left *past of* LEAVE

left–hand \'left-,hand\ *adj* **1** : located on the left **2** : LEFT–HANDED

left–hand·ed \'left-'han-dəd\ *adj* **1** : using the left hand better or more easily than the right **2** : done or made with or for the left hand

left·over \'lef-,tō-vər\ *n* : something left over ⟨we had *leftovers* for supper⟩

lefty \'lef-tē\ *n, pl* **left·ies** : a left-handed person

leg \'leg\ *n* **1** : one of the limbs of an animal or person that support the body and are used in walking and running **2** : the part of the leg between the knee and the foot **3** : something like a leg in shape or use ⟨the *legs* of a table⟩ **4** : the part of a garment that covers the leg **5** : a stage or part of a journey ⟨the first *leg* of a trip⟩

leg·a·cy \'leg-ə-sē\ *n, pl* **leg·a·cies** : something left to a person by or as if by a will

le·gal \'lē-gəl\ *adj* **1** : of or relating to law or lawyers ⟨*legal* books⟩ **2** : based on law ⟨a *legal* right⟩ **3** : allowed by law or rules ⟨*legal* conduct⟩ ⟨a *legal* play in a game⟩ — **le·gal·ly** *adv*

le·gal·i·ty \li-'gal-ət-ē\ *n, pl* **le·gal·i·ties** : the quality or state of being legal

le·gal·ize \'lē-gə-,līz\ *vb* **le·gal·ized; le·gal·iz·ing** : to make legal ⟨*legalized* gambling⟩ — **le·gal·iza·tion** \,lē-gə-lə-'zā-shən\ *n*

leg·end \'lej-ənd\ *n* **1** : an old story that is widely believed but cannot be proved to be true **2** : writing or a title on an object **3** : a list of symbols used (as on a map)

leg·end·ary \'lej-ən-,der-ē\ *adj* : of, relating to, or like a legend

legged \'leg-əd, 'legd\ *adj* : having legs

leg·ging \'leg-ən, 'leg-ing\ *n* : an outer covering for the leg usually of cloth or leather ⟨a pair of *leggings*⟩

leg·i·ble \'lej-ə-bəl\ *adj* : clear enough to be read — **leg·i·bly** \-blē\ *adv*

le·gion \'lē-jən\ *n* **1** : a group of from 3000 to 6000 soldiers that made up the chief army unit in ancient Rome **2** : ARMY 1 **3** : a very great number ⟨has a *legion* of admirers⟩

leg·is·late \'lej-ə-,slāt\ *vb* **leg·is·lat·ed; leg·is·lat·ing** : to make laws — **leg·is·la·tor** \-ər\ *n*

leg·is·la·tion \,lej-ə-'slā-shən\ *n* **1** : the action of making laws **2** : the laws that are made

leg·is·la·tive \'lej-ə-,slāt-iv\ *adj* **1** : having the power or authority to make laws **2** : of or relating to legislation — **leg·is·la·tive·ly** *adv*

leg·is·la·ture \'lej-ə-,slā-chər\ *n* : a body of persons having the power to make, change, or cancel laws

le·git·i·ma·cy \li-'jit-ə-mə-sē\ *n* : the quality or state of being legitimate

le·git·i·mate \li-'jit-ə-mət\ *adj* **1** : accepted by the law as rightful : LAWFUL ⟨a *legitimate* heir⟩ **2** : being right or acceptable ⟨a *legitimate* excuse⟩ — **le·git·i·mate·ly** *adv*

leg·less \'leg-ləs\ *adj* : having no legs

leg·ume \'leg-,yüm\ *n* : any of a large group of plants (as peas, beans, and clover) with fruits that are pods and root nodules containing bacteria that fix nitrogen

lei·sure \'lē-zhər\ *n* **1** : freedom from work ⟨a time of *leisure*⟩ **2** : time that is free for use as one wishes

lei·sure·ly \'lē-zhər-lē\ *adj* : UNHURRIED ⟨a *leisurely* walk⟩

lem·on \'lem-ən\ *n* **1** : an oval yellow fruit with a sour juice that is related to the orange and grows on a small spiny tree **2** : something unsatisfactory : DUD

lem·on·ade \,lem-ə-'nād\ *n* : a drink made of lemon juice, sugar, and water

lemon 1

le·mur \ˌlē-mər\ *n* : a mammal related to monkeys that is active at night, lives in trees, and has large eyes and a long tail

Word History When scientists first discovered the lemur on an island near Africa, they must have thought its large eyes and nighttime activities reminded them of ghosts. The animal was given a name derived from a Latin word that means "ghost."

lend \ˈlend\ *vb* **lent** \ˈlent\; **lend·ing 1** : ²LOAN 1 **2** : to give usually for a time ⟨*lend* help to flood victims⟩ **3** : to make a loan or loans — **lend·er** *n*

length \ˈlength\ *n* **1** : the longest or the longer side of an object **2** : the distance from end to end ⟨a *length* of two meters⟩ **3** : amount of time something takes ⟨the *length* of a visit⟩ **4** : a long piece of something ⟨three *lengths* of pipe⟩ **5** : the sound of a vowel or syllable as it is affected by the time needed to pronounce it — **at length 1** : very fully ⟨tell a story *at length*⟩ **2** : at the end

length·en \ˈleng-thən\ *vb* : to make or become longer ⟨*lengthen* a dress⟩

length·ways \ˈlength-ˌwāz\ *adv* : LENGTHWISE

length·wise \ˈlength-ˌwīz\ *adv or adj* : in the direction of the length ⟨fold the paper *lengthwise*⟩ ⟨a *lengthwise* fold⟩

lengthy \ˈleng-thē\ *adj* **length·i·er; length·i·est** : very long ⟨a *lengthy* argument⟩ — **length·i·ly** \-thə-lē\ *adv* — **length·i·ness** \-thē-nəs\ *n*

le·nient \ˈlē-nē-ənt, ˈlēn-yənt\ *adj* : being kind and patient ⟨a *lenient* teacher⟩ — **le·ni·ent·ly** *adv*

lens \ˈlenz\ *n* **1** : a clear curved piece of material (as glass) used to bend the rays of light to form an image **2** : a part of the eye that focuses rays of light so as to form clear images

lent *past of* LEND

Lent \ˈlent\ *n* : a period of fasting and regret for one's sins that is observed on the forty weekdays from Ash Wednesday to Easter by many churches

len·til \ˈlent-l\ *n* : the flattened round edible seed of a plant related to the pea

Leo \ˈlē-ō\ *n* **1** : a constellation between Cancer and Virgo imagined as a lion **2** : the fifth sign of the zodiac or a person born under this sign

leop·ard \ˈlep-ərd\ *n* : a large cat of Asia and Africa that has a brownish buff coat with black spots

leopard

leop·ard·ess \ˈlep-ərd-əs\ *n* : a female leopard

le·o·tard \ˈlē-ə-ˌtärd\ *n* : a tight one-piece garment worn by dancers or acrobats

le·sion \ˈlē-zhən\ *n* : an abnormal spot or area of the body caused by sickness or injury

¹less \ˈles\ *adj* **1** : being fewer ⟨*less* than ten people showed up⟩ **2** : of lower rank, degree, or importance **3** : not so much : a smaller amount of ⟨we need *less* talk and more work⟩

²less *adv* : not so much or so well ⟨*less* difficult⟩

³less *prep* : ¹MINUS 1 ⟨the regular price *less* a discount⟩

⁴less *n* **1** : a smaller number or amount **2** : a thing that is poorer than another ⟨of two evils choose the *less*⟩

-less \ləs\ *adj suffix* **1** : not having ⟨friend*less*⟩ **2** : not able to be acted on or to act in a specified way ⟨cease*less*⟩

less·en \ˈles-n\ *vb* : to make or become less

¹less·er \ˈles-ər\ *adj* : of smaller size or importance

²lesser *adv* : ²LESS ⟨*lesser*-known writers⟩

les·son \ˈles-n\ *n* **1** : a part of the Scripture read in a church service **2** : a reading or exercise assigned for study **3** : something learned or taught

lest \ˌlest\ *conj* : for fear that ⟨tied the dog *lest* it should escape⟩

let \ˈlet\ *vb* **let; let·ting 1** : to cause to : MAKE ⟨*let* it be known⟩ **2** : to give use of in return for payment ⟨rooms to *let*⟩ **3** : to allow or permit to ⟨*let* them go⟩ **4** : to allow to go or pass ⟨*let* me through⟩ **syn·onyms** *see* HIRE

\ə\ abut	\au̇\ out	\i\ tip	\ȯ\ saw	\u̇\ foot
\ər\ further	\ch\ chin	\ī\ life	\ȯi\ coin	\y\ yet
\a\ mat	\e\ pet	\j\ job	\th\ thin	\yü\ few
\ā\ take	\ē\ easy	\ng\ sing	\th\ this	\yu̇\ cure
\ä\ cot, cart	\g\ go	\ō\ bone	\ü\ food	\zh\ vision

-let \lət\ *n suffix* **1** : small one ⟨book*let*⟩ **2** : something worn on ⟨ank*let*⟩

let-down \'let-,daùn\ *n* : DISAPPOINTMENT 2

let down \let-'daùn\ *vb* **1** : DISAPPOINT ⟨don't *let* me *down*⟩ **2** : RELAX 3

let on *vb* **1** : ADMIT 3 **2** : PRETEND 1

let's \lets\ : let us

¹let·ter \'let-ər\ *n* **1** : one of the marks that are symbols for speech sounds in writing or print and that make up the alphabet **2** : a written or printed communication (as one sent through the mail) **3 letters** *pl* : LITERATURE 2 **4** : the strict or outward meaning ⟨the *letter* of the law⟩ **5** : the initial of a school awarded to a student usually for athletic achievement

²letter *vb* : to mark with letters

letter carrier *n* : a person who delivers mail

let·ter·head \'let-ər-,hed\ *n* **1** : stationery having a printed or engraved heading **2** : the heading of a letterhead

let·ter·ing \'let-ə-ring\ *n* : letters used in an inscription

let·tuce \'let-əs\ *n* : a garden plant related to the daisies that has large crisp leaves eaten in salad

Word History Many kinds of lettuce have a milky white juice. Lettuce owes its name to this fact. The Latin name for lettuce, from which we get English *lettuce*, came from the Latin word for milk.

let up \let-'əp\ *vb* **1** : to slow down **2** : ¹STOP 4, CEASE ⟨the rain *let up*⟩

leu·ke·mia \lü-'kē-mē-ə\ *n* : a dangerous disease in which too many white blood cells are formed

lev·ee \'lev-ē\ *n* **1** : a bank built along a river to prevent flooding **2** : a landing place along a river

¹lev·el \'lev-əl\ *n* **1** : a device used (as by a carpenter) to find a horizontal line or surface **2** : a horizontal line or surface usually at a named height ⟨hold it at eye *level*⟩ **3** : a step or stage in height, position, or rank ⟨rose to the *level* of manager⟩

²level *vb* **lev·eled** *or* **lev·elled; lev·el·ing** *or* **lev·el·ling** : to make or become level, flat, or even — **lev·el·er** *or* **lev·el·ler** *n*

³level *adj* **1** : having a flat even surface ⟨a *level* lawn⟩ **2** : HORIZONTAL ⟨in a *level* position⟩ **3** : of the same height or rank : EVEN **4** : steady and cool in judgment ⟨people with *level* heads⟩ — **lev·el·ly** *adv* — **lev·el·ness** *n*

synonyms LEVEL, FLAT, EVEN mean having a surface without bends, curves, or interruptions. LEVEL applies especially to a surface or a line that does not slant up or down ⟨a *level* road between two hills⟩ FLAT applies to a surface that is free from curves or bumps or hollows but may not be parallel to the ground ⟨a room with *flat* walls⟩ EVEN stresses the lack of breaks or bumps in a line or surface but need not suggest that the object is level or straight ⟨trimmed the top of the hedge to make it *even*⟩

¹le·ver \'lev-ər, 'lē-vər\ *n* **1** : a bar used to pry or move something **2** : a stiff bar for lifting a weight at one point of its length by pressing or pulling at a second point while the bar turns on a support **3** : a bar or rod used to run or adjust something ⟨a gearshift *lever*⟩

²lever *vb* : to raise or move with a lever

¹levy \'lev-ē\ *n, pl* **lev·ies** **1** : a collection (as of taxes) by authority of the law **2** : the calling of troops into service **3** : something (as taxes) collected by authority of the law

²levy *vb* **lev·ied; levy·ing** **1** : to collect legally (as taxes) **2** : to raise or collect troops for service

li·a·ble \'lī-ə-bəl\ *adj* **1** : forced by law or by what is right to make good ⟨we are *liable* for damage that we do⟩ **2** : not sheltered or protected (as from danger or accident) **3** : LIKELY 1 ⟨it's *liable* to rain soon⟩

li·ar \'lī-ər\ *n* : a person who tells lies

¹li·bel \'lī-bəl\ *n* : something spoken or written that hurts a person's good name

²libel *vb* **li·beled** *or* **li·belled; li·bel·ing** *or* **li·bel·ling** : to hurt by a libel — **li·bel·er** *or* **li·bel·ler** *n*

lib·er·al \'lib-ə-rəl, 'lib-rəl\ *adj* **1** : not stingy : GENEROUS ⟨a *liberal* giver⟩ **2** : being more than enough ⟨a *liberal* spending allowance⟩ **3** : not strict **4** : BROAD 4 ⟨a *liberal* education⟩ — **lib·er·al·ly** *adv*

lib·er·ate \'lib-ə-,rāt\ *vb* **lib·er·at·ed; lib·er·at·ing** : to set free

lib·er·ty \'lib-ərt-ē\ *n, pl* **lib·er·ties** **1** : the state of those who are free and independent : FREEDOM **2** : freedom to do what one pleases ⟨give a child some *liberty*⟩ **3** : the state of not being busy : LEISURE **4** : behavior or an act that is too free ⟨take *liberties* with the truth⟩

Li·bra \'lē-brə, 'lī-\ *n* **1** : a constellation between Virgo and Scorpio imagined as a pair of scales **2** : the seventh sign of the zodiac or a person born under this sign

li·brar·i·an \lī-'brer-ē-ən\ *n* : a person in charge of a library

li·brary \'lī-,brer-ē\ *n, pl* **li·brar·ies** **1** : a place where books and magazines are kept for use and not for sale ⟨went to the city *library*⟩ **2** : a collection of books ⟨your family has a large *library*⟩

lice *pl of* LOUSE

¹**li·cense** *or* **li·cence** \'līs-ns\ *n* **1** : permission granted by qualified authority to do something **2** : a paper showing legal permission ⟨a driver's *license*⟩ **3** : liberty of action that is carried too far

²**license** *or* **licence** *vb* **li·censed** *or* **li·cenced; li·cens·ing** *or* **li·cenc·ing** : to permit or authorize by license

li·chen \'lī-kən\ *n* : a plant made up of an alga and a fungus growing together

¹**lick** \'lik\ *vb* **1** : to pass the tongue over ⟨*lick* a spoon⟩ **2** : to touch or pass over like a tongue ⟨flames *licking* a wall⟩ **3** : to hit again and again : BEAT **4** : to get the better of : DEFEAT — **lick·ing** *n*

²**lick** *n* **1** : the act of licking **2** : a small amount ⟨never did a *lick* of work⟩ **3** : a place (**salt lick**) where salt is found on the top of the ground and animals come to lick it up

lick·e·ty–split \,lik-ət-ē-'split\ *adv* : at top speed

lic·o·rice \'lik-ə-rish, -rəs\ *n* **1** : the dried root of a European plant related to the peas or a juice from it used in medicine and in candy **2** : candy flavored with licorice

lid \'lid\ *n* **1** : a movable cover ⟨the *lid* of a box⟩ **2** : EYELID — **lid·ded** \'lid-əd\ *adj* — **lid·less** \'lid-ləs\ *adj*

¹**lie** \'lī\ *vb* **lay** \'lā\; **lain** \'lān\; **ly·ing** \'lī-ing\ **1** : to stretch out or be stretched out (as on a bed or on the ground) **2** : to be spread flat so as to cover ⟨snow *lying* on the fields⟩ **3** : to be located or placed ⟨Ohio *lies* east of Indiana⟩ **4** : to be or stay ⟨the book *lies* on the table⟩

²**lie** *vb* **lied; ly·ing** : to make a statement that one knows to be untrue

³**lie** *n* : something said or done in the hope of deceiving : an untrue statement

¹**liege** \'lēj\ *adj* **1** : having the right to receive service and loyalty ⟨*liege* lord⟩ **2** : owing or giving service to a lord

²**liege** *n* **1** : VASSAL 1 **2** : a feudal lord

lieu·ten·ant \lü-'ten-ənt\ *n* **1** : an official who acts for a higher official **2** : a first lieutenant or second lieutenant (as in the Army) **3** : a commissioned officer in the Navy or Coast Guard ranking above a lieutenant junior grade

lieutenant colonel *n* : a commissioned officer in the Army, Air Force, or Marine Corps ranking above a major

lieutenant commander *n* : a commis-

sioned officer in the Navy or Coast Guard ranking above a lieutenant

lieutenant general *n* : a commissioned officer in the Army, Air Force, or Marine Corps ranking above a major general

lieutenant junior grade *n* : a commissioned officer in the Navy or Coast Guard ranking above an ensign

life \'līf\ *n, pl* **lives** \'līvz\ **1** : the quality that separates plants and animals from such things as water or rock : the quality that plants and animals lose when they die **2** : all the experiences that make up the existence of a person : the course of existence ⟨I never heard of such a thing in my *life*⟩ **3** : BIOGRAPHY **4** : the period during which a person or thing is alive or exists **5** : a way of living ⟨the *life* of the ant⟩ **6** : a living being ⟨many *lives* being saved by quick action⟩ **7** : ¹SPIRIT 5 ⟨put a lot of *life* into the dance⟩

life belt *n* : a life preserver worn like a belt

life·boat \'līf-,bōt\ *n* : a strong boat intended for use in saving lives at sea

life buoy *n* : a float consisting of a ring of very light material to hold up a person who has fallen into the water

life·guard \'līf-,gärd\ *n* : a guard employed at a beach or swimming pool to protect swimmers from drowning

life·less \'lī-fləs\ *adj* : having no life

life·like \'lī-,flīk\ *adj* : very like something that is alive

life·long \'lī-,flóng\ *adj* : continuing through life ⟨a *lifelong* friendship⟩

life preserver *n* : something (as a jacket lined with cork) used to keep a person from drowning

life raft *n* : a raft for use by people forced into the water

life·sav·er \'līf-,sā-vər\ *n* : a person trained in lifesaving

life·sav·ing \'līf-,sā-ving\ *n* : the methods that can be used to save lives especially of drowning persons ⟨took a course in *lifesaving*⟩

life–size \'līf-'sīz\ *or* **life–sized** \-'sīzd\ *adj* : of natural size : having the same size as the original ⟨a *life-size* portrait⟩

life·time \'līf-,tīm\ *n* : LIFE 4

¹**lift** \'lift\ *vb* **1** : to raise from a lower to a higher position, rate, or amount **2** : to rise from the ground ⟨planes *lifting* from the runway⟩ **3** : to move upward and disap-

\ə\ **abut**	\aú\ **out**	\i\ **tip**	\ó\ **saw**	\ú\ **foot**	
\ər\ **further**	\ch\ **chin**	\ī\ **life**	\ói\ **coin**	\y\ **yet**	
\a\ **mat**	\e\ **pet**	\j\ **job**	\th\ **thin**	\yü\ **few**	
\ā\ **take**	\ē\ **easy**	\ng\ **sing**	\th\ **this**	\yú\ **cure**	
\ä\ **cot, cart**	\g\ **go**	\ō\ **bone**	\ü\ **food**	\zh\ **vision**	

pear or become scattered ⟨the haze *lifted* when the sun rose⟩ — **lift·er** *n*

synonyms LIFT, RAISE, HOIST mean to move from a lower to a higher place or position. LIFT suggests a bringing up especially from the ground and also the need for exertion in order to pick up something heavy ⟨*lift* those boxes onto the table⟩ RAISE often suggests a suitable or intended higher position to which something is brought ⟨*raise* the flag a little higher⟩ HOIST often suggests the use of pulleys to increase the force applied in raising something very heavy ⟨*hoist* the crates onto the ship⟩

²lift *n* **1** : the amount that may be lifted at one time : LOAD **2** : the action or an instance of lifting **3** : help especially in the form of a ride ⟨give a person a *lift*⟩ **4** *chiefly British* : ELEVATOR 2 **5** : an upward force (as on an airplane wing) that opposes the pull of gravity

lift–off \'lif-ˌtȯf\ *n* : a vertical takeoff (as by a rocket)

lig·a·ment \'lig-ə-mənt\ *n* : a tough band of tissue or fibers that holds bones together or keeps an organ in place in the body

¹light \'līt\ *n* **1** : the bright form of energy given off by something (as the sun) that lets one see objects **2** : a source (as a lamp) of light **3** : DAYLIGHT 1 **4** : public knowledge ⟨facts brought to *light*⟩ **5** : something that helps one to know or understand ⟨the teacher's explanation threw *light* on the problem⟩

²light *adj* **1** : having light : BRIGHT ⟨a *light* room⟩ **2** : not dark or deep in color

³light *vb* **light·ed** *or* **lit** \'lit\; **light·ing** **1** : to make or become bright **2** : to burn or cause to burn ⟨*light* the gas⟩ **3** : to lead with a light ⟨*light* a guest up the stairs⟩

⁴light *adj* **1** : having little weight : not heavy **2** : not strong or violent ⟨a *light* breeze⟩ **3** : not hard to bear, do, pay, or digest ⟨*light* punishment⟩ **4** : active in motion ⟨*light* on my feet⟩ **5** : not severe ⟨a *light* case of measles⟩ **6** : free from care : HAPPY ⟨a *light* heart⟩ **7** : intended mainly to entertain ⟨*light* verse⟩ — **light·ly** *adv* — **light·ness** *n*

⁵light *adv* : with little baggage ⟨travel *light*⟩

⁶light *vb* **light·ed** *or* **lit** \'lit\; **light·ing** **1** : ²PERCH, SETTLE ⟨a bird *lighting* on a twig⟩ **2** : to come by chance ⟨*light* on a solution⟩

light bulb *n* : INCANDESCENT LAMP

¹light·en \'līt-n\ *vb* **1** : to make or become

light or lighter : BRIGHTEN **2** : to grow bright with lightning — **light·en·er** *n*

²lighten *vb* : to make or become less heavy — **lighten·er** *n*

light·face \'līt-ˌfās\ *n* : a type having light thin lines — **light·faced** \-ˌfāst\ *adj*

light·heart·ed \'līt-'härt-əd\ *adj* : free from worry — **light·heart·ed·ly** *adv* — **light·heart·ed·ness** *n*

light·house \'līt-ˌhaůs\ *n* : a tower with a powerful light at the top that is built on the shore to guide sailors at night

lighthouse

light·ing \'līt-ing\ *n* : supply of light or of lights ⟨the only *lighting* came through a small window⟩

light·ning \'līt-ning\ *n* : the flashing of light caused by the passing of electricity from one cloud to another or between a cloud and the earth

lightning bug *n* : FIREFLY

light·proof \'līt-'prüf\ *adj* : not letting in light ⟨*lightproof* box⟩

light·weight \'līt-ˌwāt\ *adj* : having less than the usual or expected weight

light–year \'līt-ˌyiər\ *n* : a unit of length in astronomy equal to the distance that light travels in one year or 9,458,000,000,000 kilometers

lik·able *or* **like·able** \'lī-kə-bəl\ *adj* : easily liked — **lik·able·ness** *n*

¹like \'līk\ *vb* **liked**; **lik·ing** **1** : to have a liking for : ENJOY ⟨*likes* games⟩ **2** : to feel toward : REGARD ⟨how do you *like* snow⟩ **3** : CHOOSE 3, PREFER ⟨did as they *liked*⟩

²like *n* : LIKING, PREFERENCE ⟨*likes* and dislikes are very personal things⟩

³like *adj* **1** : SIMILAR, ALIKE ⟨the twins are very *like*⟩ **2** : similar to or to that of — used after the word modified ⟨wolves are dog*like* animals⟩ ⟨dog*like* devotion⟩

⁴like *prep* **1** : similar or similarly to ⟨you're not *like* the rest of them⟩ ⟨they act *like* fools⟩ **2** : typical of ⟨it is just *like* them to leave without paying⟩ **3** : likely to ⟨looks *like* rain⟩ **4** : such as ⟨a subject *like* arithmetic⟩

⁵like *n* : ²EQUAL, COUNTERPART ⟨never saw their *like* before⟩

⁶like *conj* **1** : AS IF ⟨it looks *like* it might rain⟩ **2** : in the same way that : ¹AS 2 ⟨sounds just *like* I do⟩

like·li·hood \'līk-lē-,hùd\ *n* : PROBABILITY 1 ⟨in all *likelihood* we will go⟩

¹like·ly \'lī-klē\ *adj* **1** : very possibly going to happen ⟨that bomb is *likely* to explode⟩ **2** : seeming to be the truth : BELIEVABLE ⟨a *likely* story⟩ **3** : giving hope of turning out well : PROMISING ⟨a *likely* spot for a picnic⟩ **synonyms** see POSSIBLE — **like·li·ness** *n*

²likely *adv* : without great doubt

lik·en \'lī-kən\ *vb* : COMPARE 1

like·ness \'līk-nəs\ *n* **1** : the state of being like : RESEMBLANCE **2** : a picture of a person : PORTRAIT

like·wise \'lī-,kwīz\ *adv* **1** : in like manner ⟨do *likewise*⟩ **2** : ALSO ⟨you *likewise*⟩

lik·ing \'lī-king\ *n* : a being pleased with someone or something

li·lac \'lī-lək, -,lak, -,läk\ *n* **1** : a bush having clusters of fragrant grayish pink, purple, or white flowers **2** : a medium purple

lilt \'lilt\ *vb* : to sing or play in a lively cheerful manner — **lilt·ing·ly** *adv*

lily \'lil-ē\ *n, pl* **lil·ies** : a plant (as the white **Easter lily** or the orange **tiger lily**) with a leafy stem that grows from a bulb and has funnel-shaped flowers

lily of the valley : a low plant related to the lilies that has usually two leaves and a stalk of fragrant flowers shaped like bells

li·ma bean \,lī-mə-\ *n* : a bean with flat pale green or white seeds

limb \'lim\ *n* **1** : any of the paired parts (as an arm, wing, or leg) of an animal that stick out from the body and are used mostly in moving or grasping **2** : a large branch of a tree — **limbed** \'limd\ *adj* — **limb·less** \'lim-ləs\ *adj*

¹lim·ber \'lim-bər\ *adj* : bending easily — **lim·ber·ly** *adv* — **lim·ber·ness** *n*

²limber *vb* : to make or become limber ⟨*limber* up with exercises⟩

¹lime \'līm\ *n* : a white substance made by heating limestone or shells that is used in making plaster and cement and in farming

²lime *vb* **limed; lim·ing** : to treat or cover with lime ⟨*lime* a garden⟩

³lime *n* : a small greenish yellow fruit that is related to the lemon and orange

lim·er·ick \'lim-ə-rik\ *n* : a humorous poem five lines long

lily of the valley

lime·stone \'līm-,stōn\ *n* : a rock formed chiefly from animal remains (as shells or coral) that is used in building and gives lime when burned

lime·wa·ter \'līm-,wòt-ər, -,wät-\ *n* : a colorless water solution that contains calcium and turns white when carbon dioxide is blown through it

¹lim·it \'lim-ət\ *n* **1** : a boundary line ⟨the city *limits*⟩ **2** : a point beyond which a person or thing cannot go

²limit *vb* : to set limits to ⟨*limit* expenses⟩

lim·i·ta·tion \,lim-ə-'tā-shən\ *n* **1** : an act or instance of limiting **2** : the quality or state of being limited

lim·it·less \'lim-ət-ləs\ *adj* : having no limits

¹limp \'limp\ *vb* : to walk lamely

²limp *n* : a limping movement or gait

³limp *adj* : not firm or stiff — **limp·ly** *adv* — **limpness** *n*

limy \'lī-mē\ *adj* **lim·i·er; lim·i·est** : containing lime or limestone

lin·den \'lin-dən\ *n* : a shade tree with heart-shaped toothed leaves, drooping clusters of yellowish white flowers, and hard fruits like peas

LINDEN

¹line \'līn\ *vb* **lined; lin·ing** : to cover the inner surface of ⟨*line* a coat⟩

²line *n* **1** : a long thin cord ⟨fishing *lines*⟩ **2** : a pipe carrying a fluid (as steam, water, or oil) **3** : an outdoor wire carrying electricity for a telephone or power company **4** : a row of letters or words across a page or column **5 lines** *pl* : the words of a part in a play **6** : the direction followed by something in motion ⟨the *line* of flight of an arrow⟩ **7** : the boundary or limit of a place or lot ⟨the town *line*⟩ **8** : the track of a railway **9** : AGREEMENT 1, HARMONY ⟨bring their ideas into *line*⟩ **10** : a course of behavior or thought ⟨a liberal political *line*⟩ **11** : FAMILY 1 ⟨born of a royal *line*⟩ **12** : a system of transportation ⟨a bus *line*⟩ **13** : a long narrow mark (as one drawn by a pencil) **14** : the football players whose positions are along the line of scrimmage **15** : a geometric element produced by moving a point : a set of points **16** : ¹OUT-

\ə\ **abut**	\aú\ **out**	\i\ **tip**	\ó\ **saw**	\ú\ **foot**
\ər\ **further**	\ch\ **chin**	\ī\ **life**	\ói\ **coin**	\y\ **yet**
\a\ **mat**	\e\ **pet**	\j\ **job**	\th\ **thin**	\yü\ **few**
\ā\ **take**	\ē\ **easy**	\ng\ **sing**	\th\ **this**	\yù\ **cure**
\ä\ **cot, cart**	\g\ **go**	\ō\ **bone**	\ü\ **food**	\zh\ **vision**

line 1, CONTOUR ⟨a ship's *lines*⟩ **17** : a plan for making or doing something ⟨a story along these *lines*⟩

³line *vb* **lined; lin•ing 1** : to mark with a line or lines **2** : to place or be placed in a line along **3** : to form a line : form into lines

lin•eage \'lin-ē-ij\ *n* **1** : the ancestors from whom a person is descended **2** : people descended from the same ancestor

lin•ear \'lin-ē-ər\ *adj* **1** : of, relating to, or like a line : STRAIGHT **2** : involving a single dimension

lin•en \'lin-ən\ *n* **1** : smooth strong cloth or yarn made from flax **2** : household articles (as tablecloths or sheets) or clothing (as shirts or underwear) once often made of linen

line of scrimmage : an imaginary line in football parallel to the goal lines and running through the place where the ball is laid before each play begins

¹lin•er \'lī-nər\ *n* : a ship or airplane of a regular transportation line ⟨an ocean *liner*⟩

²liner *n* : one that lines or is used to line something

line segment *n* : SEGMENT 3

line•up \'lī-,nəp\ *n* **1** : a line of persons arranged especially for police identification **2** : a list of players taking part in a game (as baseball)

-ling \ling\ *n suffix* **1** : one associated with ⟨nest*ling*⟩ **2** : young, small, or minor one ⟨duck*ling*⟩

lin•ger \'ling-gər\ *vb* : to be slow in leaving : DELAY

lin•guist \'ling-gwəst\ *n* **1** : a person skilled in languages **2** : a person who specializes in linguistics

lin•guis•tics \ling-'gwis-tiks\ *n* : the study of human speech including the units, nature, structure, and development of language, languages, or a language

lin•i•ment \'lin-ə-mənt\ *n* : a liquid medicine rubbed on the skin (as to ease pain)

lin•ing \'lī-ning\ *n* : material that lines an inner surface ⟨a coat *lining*⟩

¹link \'lingk\ *n* **1** : a single ring of a chain **2** : ¹BOND 2, TIE ⟨the *link* of friendship⟩

²link *vb* : to join with or as if with links ⟨towns *linked* by a road⟩

linking verb *n* : an intransitive verb that links a subject with a word or words in the predicate ⟨"look" in "you look tired" and "are" in "my favorite fruits are apples and oranges" are *linking verbs*⟩

lin•net \'lin-ət\ *n* : a common small European finch often kept as a cage bird

Word History Linnets eat seeds, and they are especially fond of the seeds of flax plants. This liking for flax seeds has given the birds their name. The word *linnet* comes from the Latin word for flax. *Linen*, the English name for a cloth made from flax, comes from the same Latin word.

li•no•leum \lə-'nō-lē-əm, -'nōl-yəm\ *n* : a floor covering with a canvas back and a surface of hardened linseed oil and usually cork dust

lin•seed \'lin-,sēd\ *n* : FLAXSEED

linseed oil *n* : a yellowish oil obtained from flaxseed

lint \'lint\ *n* **1** : loose bits of thread **2** : ¹COTTON 1

lin•tel \'lint-l\ *n* : a horizontal piece or part across the top of an opening (as of a door) to carry the weight of the structure above it

li•on \'lī-ən\ *n* : a large flesh-eating animal of the cat family that has a brownish buff coat, a tufted tail, and in the male a shaggy mane and that lives in Africa and southern Asia

li•on•ess \'lī-ə-nəs\ *n* : a female lion

lip \'lip\ *n* **1** : either of the two folds of flesh that surround the mouth **2** : an edge (as of a flower or a wound) like or of flesh **3** : the edge of a hollow container especially where it is slightly spread out — **lip•less** \-ləs\ *adj* — **lip•like** \-,līk\ *adj* — **lipped** \'lipt\ *adj*

lip•stick \'lip-,stik\ *n* : a waxy solid colored cosmetic for the lips usually in stick form

liq•ue•fy \'lik-wə-,fī\ *vb* **liq•ue•fied; liq•ue•fy•ing** : to make or become liquid

¹liq•uid \'lik-wəd\ *adj* **1** : flowing freely like water **2** : neither solid nor gaseous **3** : like liquid in clearness or smoothness ⟨large *liquid* eyes⟩ **4** : made up of or easily changed into cash — **liq•uid•ly** *adv* — **liq•uid•ness** *n*

²liquid *n* : a liquid substance

liq•uor \'lik-ər\ *n* **1** : a liquid substance or solution ⟨*liquor* from boiled meat⟩ **2** : a strong alcoholic beverage (as whiskey)

¹lisp \'lisp\ *vb* : to pronounce the sounds \s\ and \z\ as \th\ and \th̲\

²lisp *n* : the act or habit of lisping

¹list \'list\ *n* : a record or catalog of names or items

²list *vb* : to put into a list

³list *vb* : to lean to one side ⟨a *listing* ship⟩

⁴list *n* : a leaning over to one side

lis•ten \'lis-n\ *vb* **1** : to pay attention in order to hear **2** : to give heed : follow advice — **lis•ten•er** \'lis-nər, -n-ər\ *n*

list•less \'list-ləs\ *adj* : too tired or too little

interested to want to do things — **list·less·ly** *adv* — **list·less·ness** *n*

lit *past of* LIGHT

li·ter \'lēt-ər\ *n* : a metric unit of liquid capacity equal to 1.057 quarts

lit·er·al \'lit-ə-rəl\ *adj* **1** : following the ordinary or usual meaning of the words ⟨the *literal* meaning of a passage⟩ **2** : true to fact ⟨a *literal* account⟩ — **lit·er·al·ly** *adv* — **lit·er·al·ness** *n*

lit·er·ary \'lit-ə-,rer-ē\ *adj* : of or relating to literature

lit·er·ate \'lit-ə-rət\ *adj* **1** : well educated : WELL-BRED **2** : able to read and write

lit·er·a·ture \'lit-ə-rə-,chür\ *n* **1** : written works having excellence of form or expression and ideas of lasting and widespread interest **2** : written material (as of a period or on a subject)

lithe \'līth, 'līth\ *adj* : ¹LIMBER, SUPPLE — **lithe·ly** *adv* — **lithe·ness** *n*

litho·sphere \'lith-ə-,sfiər\ *n* : the outer part of the solid earth

lit·mus paper \'lit-məs-\ *n* : paper treated with coloring matter that turns red in acid solutions and blue in alkaline solutions

¹lit·ter \'lit-ər\ *n* **1** : a covered and curtained couch having poles and used for carrying a single passenger **2** : a stretcher for carrying a sick or wounded person **3** : material spread out like a bed in places where farm animals (as cows or chickens) are kept to soak up their urine and feces **4** : the young born to an animal at a single time ⟨a *litter* of pigs⟩ **5** : a messy collection of things scattered about : RUBBISH

litter 1

Word History At first the English word *litter* meant "bed." It came from a Latin word that meant "bed." English *litter* does not mean "bed" any longer, but the different meanings of *litter* all come from the meaning "bed." A covered couch that a person is carried on is rather like a bed. So is a stretcher. Straw spread out as a bed for an animal is called *litter*. So are the young animals born at one time on such a bed. And trash scattered about might remind someone of the scattered straw of an animal's bed. This is called *litter* too.

²litter *vb* **1** : to cover with litter ⟨*litter* a road⟩ **2** : to scatter about in disorder

lit·ter·bug \'lit-ər-,bəg\ *n* : one that litters a public area

¹lit·tle \'lit-l\ *adj* **lit·tler** \'lit-lər\ *or* **less** \'ləs\; **lit·tlest** \'lit-ləst\ *or* **least** \'lēst\ **1** : small in size ⟨*little* feet⟩ **2** : small in quantity ⟨*little* food to eat⟩ **3** : small in importance ⟨concerned with *little* matters⟩ **4** : NARROW-MINDED, MEAN ⟨people with *little* minds⟩ **5** : short in duration or extent ⟨had *little* time left⟩ — **lit·tle·ness** *n*

²little *adv* **less** \'les\; **least** \'lēst\ : in a very small quantity or degree

³little *n* : a small amount or quantity

Little Dipper *n* : DIPPER 4

li·tur·gi·cal \lə-'tər-ji-kəl\ *adj* : of, relating to, or like liturgy

lit·ur·gy *n, pl* **lit·ur·gies** : a religious rite or body of rites

¹live \'liv\ *vb* **lived; liv·ing** **1** : to be alive **2** : to continue in life ⟨*live* to a great age⟩ **3** : DWELL 2 **4** : to pass one's life ⟨*live* peacefully⟩ — **live it up** : to live with great enthusiasm and excitement

²live \'līv\ *adj* **1** : not dead : ALIVE **2** : burning usually without flame ⟨*live* coals⟩ **3** : not exploded ⟨a *live* cartridge⟩ **4** : of present and continuing interest **5** : charged with an electric current **6** : broadcast at the time of production ⟨a *live* television program⟩

live·li·hood \'līv-lē-,hüd\ *n* : ²LIVING 3 ⟨an honest *livelihood*⟩

live·long \,liv-,long\ *adj* : during all of ⟨we worked the *livelong* day⟩

live·ly \'līv-lē\ *adj* **live·li·er; live·li·est** **1** : full of life : ACTIVE ⟨a *lively* puppy⟩ **2** : KEEN 4 ⟨a *lively* interest⟩ **3** : full of spirit or feeling : ANIMATED ⟨*lively* music⟩ — **live·li·ness** *n*

liv·en \'lī-vən\ *vb* : to make or become lively

live oak \'lī-,vōk\ *n* : any of several American oaks that have evergreen leaves

liv·er \'liv-ər\ *n* : a large gland of vertebrates (as fishes and humans) that has a

\ə\ **abut**	\au̇\ **out**	\i\ **tip**	\ȯ\ **saw**	\u̇\ **foot**
\ər\ **further**	\ch\ **chin**	\ī\ **life**	\ȯi\ **coin**	\y\ **yet**
\a\ **mat**	\e\ **pet**	\j\ **job**	\th\ **thin**	\yü\ **few**
\ā\ **take**	\ē\ **easy**	\ng\ **sing**	\th\ **this**	\yu̇\ **cure**
\ä\ **cot, cart**	\g\ **go**	\ō\ **bone**	\ü\ **food**	\zh\ **vision**

rich blood supply, secretes bile, and helps in storing some nutrients and in forming some body wastes

liv·er·ied \'liv-ə-rēd\ *adj* : wearing a livery

liv·er·wort \'liv-ər-ˌwərt, -ˌwȯrt\ *n* : any of a group of flowerless plants that are somewhat like mosses

liv·ery \'liv-ə-rē, 'liv-rē\ *n, pl* **liv·er·ies 1** : a special uniform worn by the servants of a wealthy household ⟨a footman in *livery*⟩ **2** : the clothing worn to distinguish an association of persons ⟨the *livery* of a school⟩ **3** : the care and stabling of horses for pay **4** : the keeping of horses and vehicles for hire or a place (**livery stable**) engaged in this

lives *pl of* LIFE

live·stock \'līv-ˌstäk\ *n* : animals kept or raised especially on a farm and for profit

live wire *n* : an alert active forceful person

liv·id \'liv-əd\ *adj* **1** : discolored by bruising **2** : pale as ashes ⟨*livid* with rage⟩ — **liv·id·ly** *adv* — **liv·id·ness** *n*

¹liv·ing \'liv-ing\ *adj* **1** : not dead : ALIVE ⟨*living* authors⟩ **2** : ACTIVE **4** ⟨*living* faith⟩ **3** : true to life ⟨the *living* image of your parents⟩

²living *n* **1** : the condition of being alive **2** : conduct or manner of life **3** : what one has to have to meet one's needs ⟨made a *living* as a cook⟩

living room *n* : a room in a house for general family use

liz·ard \'liz-ərd\ *n* : a usually harmless, four-legged, and small or medium-sized reptile with a scaly skin, movable eyelids, and a long slender tail

lla·ma \'lä-mə\ *n* : a South American hoofed animal that chews the cud

lo \'lō\ *interj* — used to call attention or to show wonder or surprise

¹load \'lōd\ *n* **1** : something taken up and carried : BURDEN **2** : a mass or weight supported by something **3** : something that depresses the mind or spirits **4** : a charge for a firearm **5** : the quantity of material loaded into a device at one time

²load *vb* **1** : to put a load in or on ⟨*load* a truck⟩ **2** : to supply abundantly ⟨*load* a person with honors⟩ **3** : to put a load into ⟨*load* film into a camera⟩ — **load·er** *n*

loadstar *variant of* LODESTAR

loadstone *variant of* LODESTONE

¹loaf \'lōf\ *n, pl* **loaves** \'lōvz\ **1** : a usually oblong mass of bread **2** : a dish (as of meat) baked in the form of a loaf

²loaf *vb* : to spend time idly or lazily ⟨*loaf* on the beach⟩ — **loaf·er** *n*

loam \'lōm\ *n* : a soil having the right amount of silt, clay, and sand for good plant growth

loamy \'lō-mē\ *adj* : made up of or like loam

¹loan \'lōn\ *n* **1** : money loaned at interest **2** : something loaned for a time to a borrower **3** : permission to use something for a time

²loan *vb* **1** : to give to another for temporary use with the understanding that the same or a like thing will be returned ⟨*loan* a book⟩ ⟨*loan* money⟩ **2** : LEND **3**

loath *or* **loth** \'lōth, 'lōth\ *adj* : not willing

loathe \'lōth\ *vb* **loathed; loath·ing** : to dislike greatly

loath·ing \'lō-thing\ *n* : very great dislike

loath·some \'lōth-səm, 'lōth-\ *adj* : very unpleasant : OFFENSIVE ⟨a *loathsome* sight⟩ — **loath·some·ly** *adv* — **loath·some·ness** *n*

loaves *pl of* LOAF

¹lob \'läb\ *vb* **lobbed; lob·bing** : to drive (as a ball) by hitting or throwing easily in a high arc

²lob *n* : a lobbed throw or shot (as in tennis)

lob·by \'läb-ē\ *n, pl* **lob·bies** : a hall or entry especially when large enough to serve as a waiting room ⟨a hotel *lobby*⟩

lobe \'lōb\ *n* : a rounded part ⟨a *lobe* of a leaf⟩ ⟨the *lobe* of the ear⟩ — **lobed** \'lōbd\ *adj*

lob·ster \'läb-stər\ *n* : a large edible sea crustacean with five pairs of legs of which the first pair usually has large claws

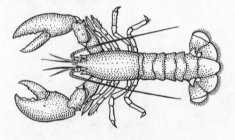

lobster

¹lo·cal \'lō-kəl\ *adj* **1** : of or relating to position in space **2** : relating to a particular place ⟨*local* news⟩ — **lo·cal·ly** *adv*

²local *n* **1** : a public vehicle (as a bus or train) that makes all or most stops on its run **2** : a local branch (as of a lodge or labor union)

lo·cal·i·ty \lō-'kal-ət-ē\ *n, pl* **lo·cal·i·ties** : a place and its surroundings

lo·cal·ize \'lō-kə-ˌlīz\ *vb* **lo·cal·ized; lo·cal·iz·ing** : to make or become local

lo·cate \'lō-ˌkāt\ *vb* **lo·cat·ed; lo·cat·ing 1** : to state and fix exactly the place or limits of ⟨*locate* a mining claim⟩ **2** : to settle or establish in a locality **3** : to look and find the position of ⟨*locate* a city on the map⟩

lo·ca·tion \lō-'kā-shən\ *n* **1** : the act or process of locating **2** : a place fit for some use (as a building)

¹lock \'läk\ *n* : a small bunch of hair or of fiber (as cotton or wool)

²lock *n* **1** : a fastening (as for a door) in which a bolt is operated (as by a key) **2** : the device for exploding the charge or cartridge of a firearm **3** : an enclosure (as in a canal) with gates at each end used in raising or lowering boats as they pass from level to level

³lock *vb* **1** : to fasten with or as if with a lock **2** : to shut in or out by or as if by means of a lock **3** : to make fast by the linking of parts together

lock·er \'läk-ər\ *n* : a cabinet, compartment, or chest for personal use or for storing frozen food at a low temperature

lock·et \'läk-ət\ *n* : a small ornamental case usually worn on a chain

lock·jaw \'läk-ˌjò\ *n* : TETANUS

lock·smith \'läk-ˌsmith\ *n* : a worker who makes or repairs locks

lock·up \'läk-ˌəp\ *n* : PRISON

lo·co \'lō-kō\ *adj* : not sane : CRAZY

lo·co·mo·tion \ˌlō-kə-'mō-shən\ *n* : the act or power of moving from place to place

lo·co·mo·tive \ˌlō-kə-'mōt-iv\ *n* : a vehicle that moves under its own power and is used to haul cars on a railroad

lo·cust \'lō-kəst\ *n* **1** : a grasshopper that moves in huge swarms and eats up the plants in its course **2** : CICADA **3** : a hardwood tree with feathery leaves and drooping flower clusters

lode·star *or* **load·star** \'lōd-ˌstär\ *n* : a guiding star

lode·stone *or* **load·stone** \'lōd-ˌstōn\ *n* : a rocky substance having magnetic properties **2** : something that attracts strongly

¹lodge \'läj\ *vb* **lodged; lodg·ing 1** : to provide temporary quarters for ⟨*lodge* guests for the night⟩ **2** : to use a place for living or sleeping ⟨we *lodged* in motels⟩ ⟨one of us had to *lodge* on a cot⟩ **3** : to come to rest ⟨the bullet *lodged* in a tree⟩ **4** : ³FILE 2 ⟨*lodge* a complaint⟩

²lodge *n* **1** : a house set apart for residence in a special season or by an employee on an estate ⟨a hunting *lodge*⟩ ⟨the caretaker's *lodge*⟩ **2** : the meeting place of a branch of a secret society

lodg·er \'läj-ər\ *n* : a person who lives in a rented room in another's house

lodg·ing \'läj-ing\ *n* **1** : a temporary living or sleeping place **2 lodgings** *pl* : a room or rooms in the house of another person rented as a place to live

loft \'lòft\ *n* **1** : an upper room or upper story of a building **2** : a balcony in a church **3** : an upper part of a barn

lofty \'lòf-tē\ *adj* **loft·i·er; loft·i·est 1** : PROUD 1 ⟨a *lofty* air⟩ **2** : of high rank or fine quality ⟨*lofty* lineage⟩ **3** : rising to a great height ⟨*lofty* trees⟩ **synonyms** see HIGH — **loft·i·ly** \-tə-lē\ *adv* — **loft·i·ness** \-tē-nəs\ *n*

¹log \'lòg, 'läg\ *n* **1** : a large piece of rough timber : a long piece of a tree trunk trimmed and ready for sawing **2** : a device for measuring the speed of a ship **3** : the daily record of a ship's speed and progress **4** : the record of a ship's voyage or of an aircraft's flight **5** : a record of how something (as a piece of equipment) works in actual use

²log *vb* **logged; log·ging 1** : to engage in cutting and hauling logs for timber **2** : to put details of or about in a log

log·ger·head \'lòg-ər-ˌhed, 'läg-\ *n* : a very large sea turtle found in the warmer parts of the Atlantic ocean

log·ic \'läj-ik\ *n* **1** : a science that deals with the rules and tests of sound thinking and reasoning **2** : sound reasoning

log·i·cal \'läj-i-kəl\ *adj* **1** : having to do with logic **2** : according to the rules of logic ⟨a *logical* argument⟩ **3** : according to what is reasonably expected ⟨the *logical* result⟩ — **log·i·cal·ly** *adv* — **log·i·cal·ness** *n*

-l·o·gy \l-ə-jē\ *n suffix* : area of knowledge : science

loin \'lòin\ *n* **1** : the part of the body between the hip and the lower ribs **2** : a piece of meat (as beef) from the loin of an animal

loi·ter \'lòit-ər\ *vb* **1** : to linger on one's way **2** : to hang around idly ⟨*loitering* in the hallway⟩ — **loi·ter·er** *n*

loll \'läl\ *vb* **1** : to hang loosely : DANGLE **2** : to lie around lazily

lol·li·pop *or* **lol·ly·pop** \'läl-ē-ˌpäp\ *n* : a lump of hard candy on the end of a stick

lone \'lōn\ *adj* **1** : having no companion ⟨a *lone* sentinel⟩ **2** : being by itself ⟨a *lone* outpost⟩

\ə\ **abut**	\aú\ **out**	\i\ **tip**	\ò\ **saw**	\ú\ **foot**
\ər\ **further**	\ch\ **chin**	\ī\ **life**	\òi\ **coin**	\y\ **yet**
\a\ **mat**	\e\ **pet**	\j\ **job**	\th\ **thin**	\yü\ **few**
\ā\ **take**	\ē\ **easy**	\ng\ **sing**	\th\ **this**	\yú\ **cure**
\ä\ **cot, cart**	\g\ **go**	\ō\ **bone**	\ü\ **food**	\zh\ **vision**

lone•ly \ˈlōn-lē\ *adj* **lone•li•er; lone•li•est**
1 : LONE 1 **2** : not often visited **3** : longing
for companions **synonyms** see ALONE —
lone•li•ness *n*

lone•some \ˈlōn-səm\ *adj* **1** : saddened
by a lack of companions **2** : not often
visited or traveled over — **lone•some•ly**
adv — **lone•some•ness** *n*

¹long \ˈlóng\ *adj* **long•er** \ˈlóng-gər\; **longest** \ˈlóng-gəst\ **1** : of great length from
end to end : not short **2** : having a greater
length than breadth **3** : lasting for some
time : not brief ⟨a *long* program at assem-
bly⟩ **4** : having a stated length (as in distance or time) ⟨a meter *long*⟩ ⟨an hour
long⟩ **5** : of, relating to, or being one of the
vowel sounds \ā, ȧ, ē, ī, ō, ü\ and sometimes \ä\ and \ȯ\

²long *adv* **1** : for or during a long time
⟨were you away *long*⟩ **2** : for the whole
length of ⟨slept all night *long*⟩ **3** : at a
distant point of time ⟨*long* ago⟩

³long *n* : a long time ⟨they'll be here before *long*⟩

⁴long *vb* : to wish for something very
much **synonyms** see YEARN — **long•ing-
ly** *adv*

long•hand \ˈlóng-ˌhand\ *n* : HANDWRITING

long•horn \ˈlóng-ˌhórn\ *n* : any of the half-
wild cattle with very long horns that were
once common in the southwestern United
States

longhorn

long–horned \ˈlóng-ˈhórnd\ *adj* : having
long horns or antennae ⟨a *long-horned*
grasshopper⟩

long•ing \ˈlóng-ing\ *n* : an eager desire

long•ish \ˈlóng-ish\ *adj* : somewhat long

lon•gi•tude \ˈlän-jə-ˌtüd, -ˌtyüd\ *n* : distance
measured in degrees east or west of a line
drawn (as through Greenwich, England)
between the north and south poles ⟨the
longitude of New York is 74 degrees west
of Greenwich⟩

lon•gi•tu•di•nal \ˌlän-jə-ˈtüd-n-əl, -ˈtyüd-\
adj : placed or running lengthwise — **lon-
gi•tu•di•nal•ly** *adv*

long–lived \ˈlóng-ˈlīvd, -ˈlivd\ *adj* : living
or lasting for a long time

long–range \ˈlóng-ˈrānj\ *adj* **1** : capable
of traveling or shooting great distances **2**
: lasting over or providing for a long period

long•sight•ed \ˈlóng-ˈsīt-əd\ *adj* : FAR-
SIGHTED — **long•sight•ed•ness** *n*

long–suf•fer•ing \ˈlóng-ˈsəf-ə-ring, -ˈsəf-
ring\ *adj* : very patient and forgiving

long–wind•ed \ˈlóng-ˈwin-dəd\ *adj* **1** : too
long ⟨a *long-winded* speech⟩ **2** : given to
talking too long ⟨a *long-winded* speaker⟩

¹look \ˈlùk\ *vb* **1** : to use the power of vision : SEE **2** : to appear suitable to ⟨*looks*
the part⟩ **3** : SEEM 1 ⟨*looks* thin⟩ **4** : to turn
one's attention or eyes ⟨*look* in the mir-
ror⟩ **5** : ²FACE 2 ⟨the house *looks* east⟩ —
look after : to take care of — **look down
on** : to regard with contempt — **look up to**
: RESPECT 1

²look *n* **1** : an act of looking ⟨we took a
look around⟩ **2** : the way one appears to
others ⟨I liked their *looks*⟩ ⟨the child had
an innocent *look*⟩ **3** : appearance that
suggests what something is or means
⟨the cloth has a *look* of linen⟩ ⟨black
clouds with a *look* of rain⟩

looking glass *n* : ¹MIRROR 1

look•out \ˈlùk-ˌaût\ *n* **1** : a careful watch
for something expected or feared ⟨on the
lookout for trouble⟩ **2** : a high place from
which a wide view is possible **3** : a person
who keeps watch

¹loom \ˈlüm\ *n* : a device for weaving cloth

²loom *vb* : to come into sight suddenly
and often with a dim or strange appearance

loon \ˈlün\ *n* : a large diving bird that lives
on fish and has webbed feet, a black
head, and a black back spotted with white

¹loop \ˈlüp\ *n* **1** : an almost oval form produced when something flexible and thin
(as a wire or a rope) crosses itself **2**
: something (as a figure or bend) suggesting a flexible loop ⟨make letters with large
loops⟩

²loop *vb* : to make a loop or loops in

loop•hole \ˈlüp-ˌhōl\ *n* : a way of escaping
something ⟨a *loophole* in the law⟩

¹loose \ˈlüs\ *adj* **loos•er; loos•est 1** : not
tightly fixed or fastened ⟨a *loose* board⟩ **2**
: not pulled tight ⟨a *loose* belt⟩ **3** : not tied
up or shut in ⟨a *loose* horse⟩ **4** : not
brought together in a package or binding
⟨*loose* sheets of paper⟩ **5** : not respectable ⟨*loose* conduct⟩ **6** : having parts that
are not squeezed tightly together ⟨*loose*

gravel⟩ ⟨cloth of *loose* weave⟩ **7** : not exact or careful ⟨*loose* thinking⟩ — **loose·ly** *adv* — **loose·ness** *n*

²**loose** *vb* **loosed; loos·ing 1** : to make loose : UNTIE **2** : to set free

loose–leaf \'lü-'slēf\ *adj* : arranged so that pages can be put in or taken out ⟨a *loose-leaf* notebook⟩

loos·en \'lüs-n\ *vb* : to make or become loose

¹**loot** \'lüt\ *n* : something stolen or taken by force

²**loot** *vb* : ¹PLUNDER — **loot·er** *n*

¹**lope** \'lōp\ *n* : a gait with long smooth steps

²**lope** *vb* **loped; lop·ing** : to go or ride at a lope

lop–eared \'läp-'iərd\ *adj* : having ears that droop

lop·sid·ed \'läp-'sīd-əd\ *adj* : UNBALANCED **1** — **lop·sid·ed·ly** *adv* — **lop·sid·ed·ness** *n*

¹**lord** \'lȯrd\ *n* **1** : a person having power and authority over others **2** *cap* : GOD 1 **3** *cap* : JESUS **4** : a British nobleman or a bishop of the Church of England entitled to sit in the House of Lords — used as a title ⟨*Lord* Cornwallis⟩ ⟨my *Lord* Archbishop⟩

Word History There was in Old English a word *hlāf* that meant "bread" or "loaf." The modern English word *loaf* comes from this Old English word. Another Old English word *weard* meant "keeper" or "guard." The modern English word *ward* is related to that Old English word. *Hlāf* and *weard* were put together to make a word *hlāford* that meant "one who guards or keeps bread." This word was used for a man who was the head of a household. The modern English word *lord* comes from this old word.

²**lord** *vb* : to act in a proud or bossy way toward others ⟨always tried to *lord* it over us⟩

lord·ship \'lȯrd-,ship\ *n* : the rank or dignity of a lord — used as a title ⟨his *Lordship* is not home⟩

lore \'lōr\ *n* : common knowledge or belief

lose \'lüz\ *vb* **lost** \'lȯst\; **los·ing** \'lü-zing\ **1** : to be unable to find or have at hand : MISLAY ⟨I *lost* my keys⟩ **2** : to be deprived of ⟨*lose* money on a deal⟩ **3** : ²WASTE 2 ⟨*lost* a morning daydreaming⟩ **4** : to be defeated in ⟨*lost* the game⟩ **5** : to fail to keep ⟨*lost* my temper⟩ — **los·er** *n* — **lose one's way** : to stray from the right path

loss \'lȯs\ *n* **1** : the act or fact of losing something ⟨the *loss* of a ship⟩ ⟨anger may cause a *loss* of self-control⟩ **2** : harm or distress that comes from losing something ⟨it was a real *loss* when our teacher retired⟩ **3** : something that is lost ⟨heat *loss* from bad insulation⟩ **4** : failure to win ⟨the team's first *loss* after two wins⟩

¹**lost** \'lȯst\ *past of* LOSE

²**lost** *adj* **1** : not used, won, or claimed ⟨a *lost* opportunity⟩ **2** : unable to find the way ⟨a *lost* puppy⟩ **3** : come or brought to a bad end ⟨a *lost* sinner⟩ **4** : no longer possessed or known ⟨a *lost* art⟩ ⟨long *lost* cousins⟩ **5** : fully occupied ⟨*lost* in thought⟩

lot \'lät\ *n* **1** : an object used in deciding something by chance or the use of such an object to decide something ⟨draw *lots*⟩ ⟨choose by *lot*⟩ **2** : FATE 2 ⟨it was their *lot* to do the hard work⟩ **3** : a piece or plot of land **4** : a large number or amount ⟨*lots* of books⟩ ⟨a *lot* of help⟩

loth \'lōth, 'lōth\ *variant of* LOATH

lo·tion \'lō-shən\ *n* : a liquid preparation used on the skin for healing or as a cosmetic

lot·tery \'lät-ə-rē\ *n, pl* **lot·ter·ies** : a way of raising money in which many tickets are sold and a few of these are drawn to win prizes

lo·tus \'lōt-əs\ *n* : any of various water lilies

lotus

¹**loud** \'laúd\ *adj* **1** : not low, soft, or quiet in sound : NOISY ⟨a *loud* cry⟩ **2** : not quiet or calm in expression ⟨a *loud* complaint⟩ **3** : too bright or showy to be pleasing ⟨*loud* clothes⟩ — **loud·ly** *adv* — **loud·ness** *n*

²**loud** *adv* : in a loud manner

loud·speak·er \'laúd-spē-kər\ *n* : an electronic device that makes sound louder

¹**lounge** \'laúnj\ *vb* **lounged; loung·ing 1** : to move or act in a slow, tired, or lazy way **2** : to stand, sit, or lie in a relaxed manner

²**lounge** *n* **1** : a comfortable room where one can relax or lounge **2** : SOFA

louse \'laús\ *n, pl* **lice** \'līs\ **1** : a small, wingless, and usually flat insect that lives on the bodies of warm-blooded animals **2** : PLANT LOUSE

\ə\ **abut**	\aú\ **out**	\i\ **tip**	\ȯ\ **saw**	\ú\ **foot**
\ər\ **further**	\ch\ **chin**	\ī\ **life**	\ȯi\ **coin**	\y\ **yet**
\a\ **mat**	\e\ **pet**	\j\ **job**	\th\ **thin**	\yü\ **few**
\ā\ **take**	\ē\ **easy**	\ng\ **sing**	\th\ **this**	\yú\ **cure**
\ä\ **cot, cart**	\g\ **go**	\ō\ **bone**	\ü\ **food**	\zh\ **vision**

lov·able \'ləv-ə-bəl\ *adj* : deserving to be loved or admired ⟨a *lovable* child⟩ — **lov·able·ness** *n* — **lov·ably** \-blē\ *adv*

¹**love** \'ləv\ *n* **1** : great and warm affection (as of a child for a parent) **2** : a great liking ⟨children with a *love* for reading⟩ **3** : a beloved person

²**love** *vb* **loved; lov·ing 1** : to feel warm affection for **2** : to like very much ⟨*loves* to ski⟩ — **lov·er** *n*

love·ly \'ləv-lē\ *adj* **love·li·er; love·li·est 1** : very beautiful **2** : very pleasing ⟨had a *lovely* time⟩ — **love·li·ness** *n*

lov·ing \'ləv-ing\ *adj* : feeling or showing love : AFFECTIONATE — **lov·ing·ly** *adv*

¹**low** \'lō\ *vb* : to make the calling sound of a COW : MOO

²**low** *n* : the mooing of a cow : MOO

³**low** *adj* **1** : not high : not tall ⟨a *low* building⟩ **2** : lying or going below the usual level ⟨*low* ground⟩ ⟨a *low* bow⟩ **3** : not loud : SOFT ⟨a *low* whisper⟩ **4** : deep in pitch ⟨a *low* note⟩ **5** : ¹PROSTRATE 3 **6** : SAD 1 ⟨in *low* spirits⟩ **7** : less than usual (as in quantity or value) ⟨*low* prices⟩ ⟨*low* pressure⟩ **8** : COARSE 4, VULGAR ⟨*low* talk⟩ **9** : not favorable : POOR ⟨a *low* opinion of someone⟩ — **low·ness** *n*

⁴**low** *n* **1** : something that is low **2** : a region of low barometric pressure **3** : the arrangement of gears in an automobile that gives the lowest speed of travel

⁵**low** *adv* : so as to be low ⟨fly *low*⟩ ⟨sing *low*⟩

¹**low·er** \'lō-ər\ *adj* **1** : being below the other of two similar persons or things ⟨the *lower* floor⟩ **2** : less advanced ⟨pupils in the *lower* grades⟩

²**lower** *vb* **1** : to move to a lower level : SINK ⟨the sun *lowered* in the west⟩ ⟨water *lowered* in the well⟩ **2** : to let or pull down ⟨*lower* a flag⟩ ⟨*lowered* the window shade⟩ **3** : to make or become less (as in value or amount) ⟨*lower* the price of food⟩ **4** : to make or become lower ⟨*lower* a fence⟩ ⟨their voices *lowered*⟩

low·land \'lō-lənd\ *n* : low flat country

¹**low·ly** \'lō-lē\ *adv* : in a humble way

²**lowly** *adj* **low·li·er; low·li·est** : of low rank or condition : HUMBLE — **low·li·ness** *n*

loy·al \'lói-əl\ *adj* **1** : faithful to one's country **2** : faithful to a person or thing one likes or believes in ⟨*loyal* to the home team⟩ **synonyms** see FAITHFUL — **loyal·ly** *adv*

loy·al·ty \'lói-əl-tē\ *n, pl* **loy·al·ties** : the quality or state of being loyal

synonyms LOYALTY and ALLEGIANCE mean faithfulness to whatever one is tied to by duty or by a pledge or promise. LOYALTY suggests a very personal or powerful kind of faithfulness and also often suggests a fighting of an urge to desert or betray ⟨I felt great *loyalty* to my teammates⟩ ALLEGIANCE stresses a duty to something other than a person, especially to a government or idea ⟨pledge *allegiance* to the flag⟩

loz·enge \'läz-nj\ *n* : a small candy often containing medicine

LSD \,el-,es-'dē\ *n* : a dangerous drug that causes hallucinations

lu·bri·cant \'lü-bri-kənt\ *n* : something (as oil or grease) that makes a surface smooth or slippery

lu·bri·cate \'lü-brə-,kāt\ *vb* **lu·bri·cat·ed; lu·bri·cat·ing 1** : to make smooth or slippery **2** : to apply oil or grease to ⟨*lubricate* a car⟩

lu·bri·ca·tion \,lü-brə-'kā-shən\ *n* : the act or process of lubricating or the state of being lubricated

lu·cid \'lü-səd\ *adj* **1** : showing a normal state of mind ⟨*lucid* behavior⟩ **2** : easily understood ⟨*lucid* writing⟩ — **lu·cid·ly** *adv* — **lu·cid·ness** *n*

luck \'lək\ *n* **1** : something that happens to a person by or as if by chance **2** : the accidental way events occur **3** : good fortune

lucky \'lək-ē\ *adj* **luck·i·er; luck·i·est 1** : helped by luck : FORTUNATE ⟨a *lucky* person⟩ **2** : happening because of good luck ⟨a *lucky* hit⟩ **3** : thought of as bringing good luck ⟨a *lucky* charm⟩ — **luck·i·ly** \'lək-ə-lē\ *adv*

lu·di·crous \'lü-də-krəs\ *adj* : funny because of being ridiculous : ABSURD — **lu·di·crous·ly** *adv* — **lu·di·crous·ness** *n*

lug \'ləg\ *vb* **lugged; lug·ging** : to find hard to carry or haul

lug·gage \'ləg-ij\ *n* : BAGGAGE

luke·warm \'lü-'kwòrm\ *adj* **1** : neither hot nor cold **2** : not very interested or eager ⟨*lukewarm* toward our plan⟩

¹**lull** \'ləl\ *vb* : to make or become quiet or less watchful

²**lull** *n* : a period of calm (as in a storm)

lul·la·by \'ləl-ə-,bī\ *n, pl* **lul·la·bies** : a song for helping babies to sleep

¹**lum·ber** \'ləm-bər\ *n* : timber especially when sawed into boards

²**lumber** *vb* : to cut logs : saw logs into lumber

³**lumber** *vb* : to move in an awkward way

lum·ber·jack \'ləm-bər-,jak\ *n* : a person who works at lumbering

lum·ber·man \'ləm-bər-mən\ *n, pl* **lum-ber·men** \-mən\ : a boss lumberjack

lum·ber·yard \'ləm-bər-ˌyärd\ *n* : a place where a stock of lumber is kept for sale

lu·mi·nous \'lü-mə-nəs\ *adj* : shining brightly — **lu·mi·nous·ly** *adv*

¹**lump** \'ləmp\ *n* : a small uneven mass (as a chunk or a swelling)

²**lump** *vb* **1** : to form into a lump **2** : to group together ⟨*lumped* our change to buy some candy⟩

lu·nar \'lü-nər\ *adj* **1** : of or relating to the moon **2** : measured by the revolutions of the moon ⟨a *lunar* month⟩

¹**lu·na·tic** \'lü-nə-ˌtik\ *adj* **1** : INSANE 1, CRAZY ⟨*lunatic* behavior⟩ **2** : INSANE 2 ⟨a *lunatic* asylum⟩

Word History In the past many people thought that insanity was affected by the moon. Someone who was insane, they thought, would be at his or her worst when the moon was full. But when there was a new moon he or she might act just like a normal person. We owe the word *lunatic* to the belief that the moon had an effect on madness. *Lunatic* comes from a Latin word that mant "insane." This word was formed from the Latin word for moon.

²**lunatic** *n* : an insane person

¹**lunch** \'lənch\ *n* **1** : a light meal especially when eaten in the middle of the day **2** : food prepared for lunch ⟨a picnic *lunch*⟩

²**lunch** *vb* : to eat lunch

lun·cheon \'lən-chən\ *n* **1** : ¹LUNCH 1 **2** : a formal lunch

lung \'ləng\ *n* : either of two organs in the chest that are like bags and are the main breathing structure in animals that breathe air

¹**lunge** \'lənj\ *vb* **lunged; lung·ing** : to push or drive with force ⟨we *lunged* through the crowd⟩ ⟨*lunge* a sword⟩

²**lunge** *n* : a sudden movement forward ⟨the horse started with a *lunge*⟩

lung·fish \'ləng-ˌfish\ *n* : any of several fishes that breathe with structures like lungs as well as with gills

lu·pine \'lü-pən\ *n* : a plant related to the clovers that has tall spikes of showy flowers like those of sweet peas

¹**lurch** \'lərch\ *n* **1** : a sudden roll of a ship to one side **2** : a swaying staggering movement or gait

²**lurch** *vb* : to move with a lurch

¹**lure** \'lu̇r\ *n* **1** : something that attracts or draws one on : TEMPTATION **2** : an artificial bait for catching fish

²**lure** *vb* **lured; lur·ing** : to tempt or lead away by offering some pleasure or advantage : ENTICE ⟨*lured* by gold⟩

lu·rid \'lu̇r-əd\ *adj* **1** : looking like glowing fire seen through smoke ⟨*lurid* flames⟩ **2** : SENSATIONAL 2 ⟨a *lurid* story⟩ — **lu·rid·ly** *adv* — **lu·rid·ness** *n*

lurk \'lərk\ *vb* : to hide in or about a place

lus·cious \'ləsh-əs\ *adj* **1** : very sweet and pleasing to taste and smell **2** : delightful to hear, see, or feel — **lus·cious·ly** *adv* — **lus·cious·ness** *n*

lush \'ləsh\ *adj* **1** : very juicy and fresh ⟨*lush* grass⟩ **2** : covered with a thick growth ⟨*lush* pastures⟩ — **lush·ly** *adv* — **lush·ness** *n*

lus·ter *or* **lus·tre** \'ləs-tər\ *n* : a glow of reflected light : SHEEN ⟨the *luster* of a pearl⟩

lus·trous \'ləs-trəs\ *adj* : having luster

lute \'lüt\ *n* : an old stringed instrument with a body shaped like a pear and usually paired strings played with the fingers

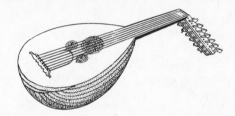

lute

lux·u·ri·ant \ˌləg-'zhu̇r-ē-ənt, ˌlək-'shu̇r-\ *adj* : growing freely and well ⟨a *luxuriant* growth of plants⟩ — **lux·u·ri·ant·ly** *adv*

lux·u·ri·ous \ˌləg-'zhu̇r-ē-əs, ˌlək-'shu̇r-\ *adj* **1** : loving pleasure and luxury **2** : very fine and comfortable ⟨a *luxurious* home⟩ — **lux·u·ri·ous·ly** *adv* — **lux·u·ri·ous·ness** *n*

lux·u·ry \'lək-shə-rē, 'ləg-zhə-\ *n, pl* **lux·u·ries** **1** : very rich, pleasant, and comfortable surroundings ⟨live in *luxury*⟩ **2** : something desirable but expensive or hard to get ⟨fresh strawberries are a *luxury* in winter⟩ **3** : something pleasant but not really needed for one's pleasure or comfort

¹**-ly** \lē\ *adj suffix* **1** : like : similar to ⟨queen*ly*⟩ ⟨father*ly*⟩ **2** : happening in each specified period of time : every ⟨hour*ly*⟩

²**-ly** *adv suffix* **1** : in a specified manner

\ə\ **abut**	\au̇\ **out**	\i\ **tip**	\ȯ\ **saw**	\u̇\ **foot**
\ər\ **further**	\ch\ **chin**	\ī\ **life**	\ȯi\ **coin**	\y\ **yet**
\a\ **mat**	\e\ **pet**	\j\ **job**	\th\ **thin**	\yü\ **few**
\ā\ **take**	\ē\ **easy**	\ng\ **sing**	\th\ **this**	\yu̇\ **cure**
\ä\ **cot, cart**	\g\ **go**	\ō\ **bone**	\ü\ **food**	\zh\ **vision**

⟨slow*ly*⟩ **2** : from a specified point of view

lye \'lī\ *n* : a dangerous compound containing sodium that dissolves in water and is used in cleaning

lying *present participle of* LIE

lymph \'limf\ *n* : a clear liquid like blood without the red cells that nourishes the tissues and carries off wastes

lym·phat·ic \lim-'fat-ik\ *adj* : of or relating to lymph ⟨a *lymphatic* duct⟩

lynx \'lingks\ *n, pl* **lynx** *or* **lynx·es** : any of several wildcats with rather long legs, a short tail, and often ears with small bunches of long hairs at the tip

lyre \'līr\ *n* : a stringed instrument like a harp used by the ancient Greeks

¹lyr·ic \'lir-ik\ *adj* **1** : suitable for singing : MUSICAL **2** : expressing personal emotion ⟨*lyric* poetry⟩

²lyric *n* **1** : a lyric poem **2 lyrics** *pl* : the words of a popular song

lyr·i·cal \'lir-i-kəl\ *adj* : ¹LYRIC

lynx

m \'em\ *n, pl* **m's** *or* **ms** \'emz\ *often cap* **1** : the thirteenth letter of the English alphabet **2** : 1000 in Roman numerals

ma \'mä, 'mȯ\ *n, often cap* : ¹MOTHER 1

ma'am \'mam\ *n* : MADAM

mac·ad·am \mə-'kad-əm\ *n* : a road surface made of small closely packed broken stone

ma·caque \mə-'kak, -'käk\ *n* : any of several mostly Asian monkeys with short tails

mac·a·ro·ni \ˌmak-ə-'rō-nē\ *n, pl* **mac·a·ro·nis** *or* **mac·a·ro·nies** : a food that is made of a mixture of flour and water formed into tubes and dried

mac·a·roon \ˌmak-ə-'rün\ *n* : a cookie made of the white of eggs, sugar, and ground almonds or coconut

ma·caw \mə-'kȯ\ *n* : a large parrot of Central and South America with a long tail, a harsh voice, and bright feathers

¹mace \'mās\ *n* : a fancy club carried before certain officials as a sign of authority

²mace *n* : a spice made from the dried outer covering of the nutmeg

ma·chete \mə-'shet-ē\ *n* : a large heavy knife used for cutting sugarcane and underbrush and as a weapon

¹ma·chine \mə-'shēn\ *n* **1** : VEHICLE **2** ⟨a flying *machine*⟩ **2** : a device that combines forces, motion, and energy in a way that does some desired work ⟨a sewing *machine*⟩

²machine *vb* **ma·chined; ma·chin·ing** : to shape or finish by tools run by machines

machine gun *n* : an automatic gun for continuous firing

ma·chin·ery \mə-'shē-nə-rē, -'shēn-rē\ *n* **1** : a group of machines ⟨the *machinery* in a factory⟩ **2** : the working parts of a machine **3** : the people and equipment by which something is done ⟨the *machinery* of government⟩

machine shop *n* : a workshop in which metal articles are machined and put together

ma·chin·ist \mə-'shē-nəst\ *n* : a person who makes or works on machines

mack·er·el \'mak-ə-rəl, 'mak-rəl\ *n, pl* **mackerel** *or* **mack·er·els** : a food fish of the North Atlantic that is green with blue bars above and silvery below

mace

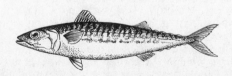

mackerel

mack·i·naw \'mak-ə-ˌnȯ\ *n* : a short heavy woolen coat

mac·ra·mé *also* **mac·ra·me** \'mak-rə-ˌmā\ *n* **1** : a coarse lace or fringe made by knotting threads or cords **2** : the art of tying knots in patterns

ma·cron \'mā-ˌkrän\ *n* : a mark ⁻ placed over a vowel to show that the vowel is long

mad \'mad\ *adj* **mad·der; mad·dest 1** : INSANE 1 **2** : done or made without thinking ⟨a *mad* promise⟩ **3** : very angry ⟨make the bull *mad*⟩ **4** : full of enthusiasm ⟨*mad* about dancing⟩ **5** : wildly gay ⟨in a *mad* mood⟩ **6** : having hydrophobia ⟨a *mad* dog⟩ — **mad·ly** *adv* — **mad·ness** *n*

mad·am \'mad-əm\ *n, pl* **mes·dames** \mā-'däm, -'dam\ — used as a form of polite address to a woman ⟨may I help you, *madam?*⟩

¹mad·cap \'mad-ˌkap\ *adj* : likely to do something mad or reckless : done for fun without thinking ⟨a *madcap* adventure⟩

²madcap *n* : a madcap person

mad·den \'mad-n\ *vb* : to make mad

made *past of* MAKE

made–up \'mā-'dəp\ *adj* : showing more imagination than concern with fact ⟨a *made-up* excuse⟩

mad·house \'mad-ˌhaus\ *n* : a place or scene of complete confusion

mag·a·zine \'mag-ə-ˌzēn\ *n* **1** : a storehouse or warehouse for military supplies **2** : a place for keeping explosives in a fort or ship **3** : a container in a gun for holding cartridges **4** : a publication issued at regular intervals (as weekly or monthly)

Word History The English word *magazine* came from a French word which in turn came from an Arabic word. Both the French and the Arabic words meant "a place where things are stored." At first the English word had the same meaning, and it is still used in this sense. However, a later sense is now more common—that of a collection of written pieces printed at set times. A magazine can be thought of as a storehouse for the written pieces.

mag·got \'mag-ət\ *n* : a legless grub that is the larva of a two-winged fly

¹mag·ic \'maj-ik\ *n* **1** : the power to control natural forces possessed by certain persons (as wizards and witches) in folk tales and fiction **2** : a power that seems mysterious ⟨the *magic* of a great name⟩ **3** : something that charms ⟨the *magic* of their singing⟩ **4** : the art or skill of performing tricks or illusions as if by magic for entertainment

²magic *adj* **1** : of or relating to magic **2** : having effects that seem to be caused by magic **3** : giving a feeling of enchantment

mag·i·cal \'maj-i-kəl\ *adj* : ²MAGIC 1, 2

ma·gi·cian \mə-'jish-ən\ *n* : a person skilled in magic

magic lantern *n* : an early kind of slide projector

mag·is·trate \'maj-ə-ˌstrāt\ *n* **1** : a chief officer of government **2** : a local official with some judicial power

mag·ma \'mag-mə\ *n* : molten rock within the earth

mag·na·nim·i·ty \ˌmag-nə-'nim-ət-ē\ *n* : the quality of being magnanimous

mag·nan·i·mous \mag-'nan-ə-məs\ *adj* **1** : having a noble and courageous spirit **2** : being generous and forgiving — **mag·nan·i·mous·ly** *adv*

mag·ne·sium \mag-'nē-zē-əm, -'nē-zhəm\ *n* : a silvery white metallic chemical element that is lighter than aluminum and is used in lightweight alloys

mag·net \'mag-nət\ *n* : a piece of material (as of iron, steel, or alloy) that is able to attract iron

mag·net·ic \mag-'net-ik\ *adj* **1** : acting like a magnet **2** : of or relating to the earth's magnetism **3** : having a great power to attract people

magnetic field *n* : the portion of space near a magnetic body within which magnetic forces can be detected

magnetic needle *n* : a narrow strip of magnetized steel that is free to swing around to show the direction of the earth's magnetism

magnetic pole *n* **1** : either of the poles of a magnet **2** : either of two small regions of the earth which are located near the North and South Poles and toward which a compass needle points

magnetic tape *n* : a thin ribbon of plastic coated with a magnetic material on which information (as sound) may be stored

mag·ne·tism \'mag-nə-ˌtiz-əm\ *n* **1** : the power to attract that a magnet has **2** : the power to attract others : personal charm

mag·ne·tize \'mag-nə-ˌtīz\ *vb* **mag·ne·tized; mag·ne·tiz·ing** : to cause to be magnetic

mag·ne·to \mag-'nēt-ō\ *n, pl* **mag·ne·tos** : a small generator used especially to produce the spark in some gasoline engines

mag·nif·i·cent \mag-'nif-ə-sənt\ *adj* : having impressive beauty : very grand

\ə\ **abut**	\aú\ **out**	\i\ **tip**	\ó\ **saw**	\ú\ **foot**	
\ər\ **further**	\ch\ **chin**	\ī\ **life**	\ói\ **coin**	\y\ **yet**	
\a\ **mat**	\e\ **pet**	\j\ **job**	\th\ **thin**	\yü\ **few**	
\ā\ **take**	\ē\ **easy**	\ng\ **sing**	\th\ **this**	\yú\ **cure**	
\ä\ **cot, cart**	\g\ **go**	\ō\ **bone**	\ü\ **food**	\zh\ **vision**	

⟨*magnificent* palaces⟩ — **mag·nif·i·cent·ly** *adv*

mag·ni·fy \'mag-nə-ˌfī\ *vb* **mag·ni·fied; mag·ni·fy·ing 1** : to enlarge in fact or appearance ⟨a microscope *magnifies* an object seen through it⟩ **2** : to cause to seem greater or more important : EXAGGERATE ⟨*magnify* a fault⟩

magnifying glass *n* : a lens that magnifies something seen through it

mag·ni·tude \'mag-nə-ˌtüd, -ˌtyüd\ *n* : greatness of size

mag·no·lia \mag-'nōl-yə\ *n* : a tree or tall shrub having showy white, pink, yellow, or purple flowers that appear before or sometimes with the leaves

magnolia

mag·pie \'mag-ˌpī\ *n* : a noisy black-and-white bird related to the jays

ma·hog·a·ny \mə-'häg-ə-nē\ *n, pl* **mahog·a·nies** : a strong reddish brown wood that is used especially for furniture and is obtained from several tropical trees

maid \'mād\ *n* **1** : an unmarried girl or woman **2** : a female servant

¹maid·en \'mād-n\ *n* : an unmarried girl or woman

²maiden *adj* **1** : UNMARRIED **2** : ¹FIRST 2 ⟨a *maiden* voyage⟩

maid·en·hair fern \'mād-n-ˌhaər, -ˌheər\ *n* : a fern with slender stems and delicate feathery leaves

maid·en·hood \'mād-n-ˌhu̇d\ *n* : the state or time of being a maiden

maiden name *n* : a woman's family name before she is married

maid of honor : an unmarried woman who stands with the bride at a wedding

maidenhair fern

¹mail \'māl\ *n* **1** : letters, parcels, and papers sent from one person to another through the post office **2** : the whole system used in the public sending and delivering of mail ⟨do business by *mail*⟩ **3** : something that comes in the mail

²mail *vb* : to send by mail

³mail *n* : a fabric made of metal rings linked together and used as armor

mail·box \'māl-ˌbäks\ *n* **1** : a public box in which to place outgoing mail **2** : a private box (as on a house) for the delivery of incoming mail

mail carrier *n* : LETTER CARRIER

mail·man \'māl-ˌman\ *n, pl* **mail·men** \-ˌmen\ : LETTER CARRIER

maim \'mām\ *vb* : to injure badly or cripple by violence

¹main \'mān\ *n* **1** : physical strength : FORCE ⟨with might and *main*⟩ **2** : HIGH SEAS ⟨over the bounding *main*⟩ **3** : the chief part : essential point ⟨the new workers are in the *main* well trained⟩ **4** : a principal line, tube, or pipe of a utility system ⟨water *main*⟩ ⟨gas *main*⟩

²main *adj* **1** : first in size, rank, or importance : CHIEF ⟨*main* part⟩ ⟨*main* street⟩ **2** : PURE **3**, SHEER ⟨by *main* force⟩ — **main·ly** *adv*

main·land \'mān-ˌland\ *n* : a continent or the main part of a continent as distinguished from an offshore island or sometimes from a cape or peninsula

main·mast \'mān-ˌmast, -məst\ *n* : the principal mast of a sailing ship

main·sail \'mān-ˌsāl, -səl\ *n* : the principal sail on the mainmast

main·spring \'mān-ˌspring\ *n* : the principal spring in a mechanical device (as a watch or clock)

main·stay \'mān-ˌstā\ *n* **1** : the large strong rope from the maintop of a ship usually to the foot of the foremast **2** : a chief support ⟨the *mainstay* of the family⟩

main·tain \mān-'tān\ *vb* **1** : to keep in a particular or desired state ⟨*maintain* one's health⟩ **2** : to defend by argument ⟨*maintain* a position⟩ **3** : CARRY ON 3, CONTINUE ⟨*maintain* a correspondence⟩ **4** : to provide for : SUPPORT ⟨*maintained* my family by working⟩ **5** : to insist to be true ⟨*maintained* that we were cheated⟩

main·te·nance \'mānt-n-əns\ *n* **1** : the act of maintaining : the state of being maintained ⟨*maintenance* of law and order⟩ ⟨money for the family's *maintenance*⟩ **2** : UPKEEP ⟨workers in charge of *maintenance*⟩

main·top \'mān-ˌtäp\ *n* : a platform around the head of a mainmast

maize \'māz\ *n* : INDIAN CORN

ma·jes·tic \mə-'jes-tik\ *adj* : very impressive and dignified : NOBLE — **ma·jes·ti·cal·ly** \-ti-kə-lē\ *adv*

maj·es·ty \'maj-ə-stē\ *n, pl* **maj·es·ties 1** : royal dignity or authority **2** : the quality or state of being majestic **3** — used as a title for a king, queen, emperor, or empress ⟨Your *Majesty*⟩

¹ma·jor \'mā-jər\ *adj* **1** : greater in number, quantity, rank, or importance ⟨the *major* part of the cost⟩ ⟨the *major* leagues⟩ **2** : of or relating to a musical scale of eight notes with half steps between the third and fourth and between the seventh and eighth notes and with whole steps between all the others

²major *n* : a commissioned officer in the Army, Air Force, or Marine Corps ranking above a captain

major general *n* : a commissioned officer in the Army, Air Force, or Marine Corps ranking above a brigadier general

ma·jor·i·ty \mə-'jȯr-ət-ē\ *n, pl* **ma·jor·i·ties** **1** : the age at which one is allowed to vote **2** : a number greater than half of a total **3** : the amount by which a majority is more than a minority ⟨winning by fifty-one to forty-nine, a *majority* of two⟩ **4** : a group or party that makes up the greater part of a whole body of persons ⟨the *majority* chose a leader⟩

¹make \'māk\ *vb* **made** \'mād\; **mak·ing** **1** : to cause to occur ⟨*make* trouble⟩ **2** : to form or put together out of material or parts ⟨*make* a dress⟩ ⟨*make* a chair⟩ **3** : to combine to produce ⟨two and two *make* four⟩ **4** : to set in order : PREPARE ⟨*make* a bed⟩ **5** : to cause to be or become ⟨*made* them happy⟩ **6** : ¹DO 1, PERFORM ⟨*make* a bow⟩ ⟨*make* war⟩ **7** : to produce by action ⟨*make* a mess of a job⟩ **8** : COMPEL ⟨*make* them go to bed⟩ **9** : GET 1, GAIN ⟨*make* money⟩ ⟨*make* friends⟩ **10** : to act so as to be ⟨*make* merry⟩ ⟨*make* sure⟩

synonyms MAKE, FORM, and MANUFACTURE mean to cause to come into being. MAKE is a word that can be used of many kinds of creation ⟨*make* a chair⟩ ⟨*made* many friends⟩ FORM suggests that the thing brought into being has a design or structure ⟨the colonies *formed* a new nation⟩ MANUFACTURE suggests making something in a fixed way and usually nowadays by machinery ⟨*manufactures* cars⟩

— **make believe** : to act as if something known to be imaginary is real or true —
make good 1 : FULFILL, COMPLETE ⟨*made* my promise *good*⟩ ⟨*made good* their escape⟩ **2** : SUCCEED **3** ⟨*made good* in the job⟩

²make *n* **1** : the way in which a thing is made : STRUCTURE **2** : ¹BRAND **4** ⟨a *make* of car⟩

¹make–be·lieve \'māk-bə-ˌlēv\ *n* : a pretending to believe (as in children's play)

²make–believe *adj* : not real : IMAGINARY

make out *vb* **1** : to write out ⟨*make out* a list⟩ ⟨*make out* a check⟩ **2** : UNDERSTAND 1 ⟨I can't *make out* what this letter means⟩ **3** : IDENTIFY 3 ⟨couldn't *make out* who it was⟩ **4** : ¹DO 4 ⟨how did you *make out*?⟩

¹make·shift \'māk-ˌshift\ *n* : a thing used as a temporary substitute for another

²makeshift *adj* : serving as a temporary substitute ⟨used a folded coat as a *makeshift* pillow⟩

make·up \'mā-ˌkəp\ *n* **1** : the way the parts or elements of something are put together or joined **2** : materials used in changing one's appearance for a part on the stage **3** : any of various cosmetics (as lipstick or powder)

make up *vb* **1** : to create from the imagination ⟨*made up* a story⟩ **2** : ²FORM 3, COMPOSE ⟨eleven players *make up* the team⟩ **3** : ¹RECOMPENSE, ATONE ⟨this will *make up* for your loss⟩ **4** : to become friendly again ⟨they quarreled but later *made up*⟩ **5** : to put on makeup — **make up one's mind** : to reach a decision

mal- *prefix* **1** : bad : badly ⟨*mal*treat⟩ **2** : abnormal : abnormally ⟨*mal*formation⟩

mal·ad·just·ed \ˌmal-ə-'jəs-təd\ *adj* : not properly adjusted ⟨a *maladjusted* student⟩

mal·a·dy \'mal-ə-dē\ *n, pl* **mal·a·dies** : a disease or ailment of body or mind

ma·lar·ia \mə-'ler-ē-ə\ *n* : a serious disease with chills and fever that is spread by the bite of one kind of mosquito

Word History The English word *malaria* came from two Italian words that together meant "bad air." The sickness that we call *malaria* is spread by mosquitoes. However, people once thought it was caused by bad air. That is why it was called *malaria*.

¹male \'māl\ *adj* **1** : of, relating to, or being the sex that fathers young **2** : bearing stamens but no pistil ⟨a *male* flower⟩ **3** : of, relating to, or like that of males — **male·ness** *n*

²male *n* : a male individual

mal·for·ma·tion \ˌmal-fȯr-'mā-shən\ *n*

\ə\ abut	\au̇\ out	\i\ tip	\ȯ\ saw	\u̇\ foot
\ər\ further	\ch\ chin	\ī\ life	\ȯi\ coin	\y\ yet
\a\ mat	\e\ pet	\j\ job	\th\ thin	\yü\ few
\ā\ take	\ē\ easy	\ng\ sing	\th\ this	\yu̇\ cure
\ä\ cot, cart	\g\ go	\ō\ bone	\ü\ food	\zh\ vision

: something that is badly or wrongly formed

mal·ice \'mal-əs\ *n* : ILL WILL

ma·li·cious \mə-'lish-əs\ *adj* **1** : doing mean things for pleasure **2** : done just to be mean ⟨*malicious* gossip⟩ — **ma·li·cious·ly** *adv*

¹ma·lign \mə-'līn\ *adj* : MALIGNANT 1

²malign *vb* : to say evil things about : SLANDER

ma·lig·nant \mə-'lig-nənt\ *adj* **1** : evil in influence or result : INJURIOUS **2** : MALICIOUS 1 **3** : likely to cause death : DEADLY — **ma·lig·nant·ly** *adv*

mal·lard \'mal-ərd\ *n* : a common wild duck of the northern hemisphere that is the ancestor of the domestic ducks

mallard

mal·lea·ble \'mal-ē-ə-bəl, 'mal-yə-bəl\ *adj* : capable of being beaten out, extended, or shaped by hammer blows

mal·let \'mal-ət\ *n* **1** : a hammer with a short handle and a barrel-shaped head of wood or soft material used for driving a tool (as a chisel) or for striking a surface without denting it **2** : a club with a short thick rod for a head and a long thin rod for a handle ⟨croquet *mallet*⟩

mal·low \'mal-ō\ *n* : a tall plant related to the hollyhock that has usually lobed leaves and white, rose, or purplish flowers with five petals

mal·nu·tri·tion \,mal-nú-'trish-ən, -nyú-\ *n* : faulty nourishment

malt \'mólt\ *n* **1** : grain and especially barley soaked in water until it has sprouted **2** : MALTED MILK

malt·ed milk \,mól-təd-\ *n* : a beverage made by dissolving a powder made from dried milk and cereals in a liquid (as milk)

mal·treat \mal-'trēt\ *vb* : to treat in a rough or unkind way : ABUSE

ma·ma *or* **mam·ma** \'mäm-ə\ *n, often cap* : ¹MOTHER 1

mam·mal \'mam-əl\ *n* : a warm-blooded animal that feeds its young with milk and has a backbone, two pairs of limbs, and a more or less complete covering of hair

¹mam·moth \'mam-əth\ *n* : a very large

hairy extinct elephant with tusks that curve upward

mammoth

²mammoth *adj* : very large : HUGE

mam·my \'mam-ē\ *n, pl* **mam·mies 1** *often cap* : ¹MOTHER 1 **2** : a black woman serving as a nurse to white children especially in the past in the southern states of the United States

¹man \'man\ *n, pl* **men** \'men\ **1** : a human being : PERSON **2** : an adult male human being **3** : the human race : MANKIND **4** : a member of the natural family to which human beings belong including both modern humans and extinct related forms **5** : HUSBAND ⟨*man* and wife⟩ **6** : an adult male servant or employee **7** : one of the pieces with which various games (as chess or checkers) are played

²man *vb* **manned; man·ning 1** : to station crew members at ⟨*man* the lifeboats⟩ **2** : to do the work of operating ⟨*man* the pumps⟩

man·age \'man-ij\ *vb* **man·aged; man·ag·ing 1** : to look after and make decisions about : be the boss of ⟨*manage* a factory⟩ **2** : to achieve what one wants to do ⟨I'll *manage* somehow⟩ ⟨they always *manage* to win⟩ **synonyms** see CONDUCT

man·age·ment \'man-ij-mənt\ *n* **1** : the managing of something **2** : the people who manage ⟨*management* and labor could not agree⟩

man·ag·er \'man-ij-ər\ *n* : a person who manages — **man·ag·er·ship** \-,ship\ *n*

man·da·rin \'man-də-rən\ *n* : a high public official of the Chinese Empire

man·date \'man-,dāt\ *n* **1** : an order from a higher court to a lower court **2** : the instruction given by voters to their elected representatives

man·di·ble \'man-də-bəl\ *n* **1** : a lower jaw often with its soft parts **2** : either the upper or lower part of the bill of a bird **3** : either of the first pair of mouth parts of some invertebrates (as an insect or crustacean) that often form biting organs

man·do·lin \,man-də-'lin, 'man-dl-ən\ *n* : a small stringed instrument with four pairs of strings played by plucking

mane \'mān\ *n* : long heavy hair growing from the neck or shoulders of an animal (as a horse or lion) — **maned** \'mānd\ *adj*

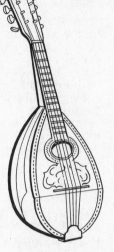

mandolin

¹**ma·neu·ver** \mə-'nü-vər, -'nyü-\ *n* **1** : a planned movement of troops or ships **2** : a training exercise by armed forces **3** : skillful action or management 〈avoided an accident by a quick *maneuver*〉

²**maneuver** *vb* **1** : to move in a maneuver **2** : to perform a maneuver **3** : to guide skillfully — **ma·neu·ver·able** \-'nü-və-rə-bəl, -'nyü-\ *adj*

ma·neu·ver·abil·i·ty \mə-,nü-və-rə-'bil-ət-ē, -,nyü-\ *n* : the quality or state of being maneuverable

man·ga·nese \'mang-gə-,nēz\ *n* : a grayish white brittle metallic chemical element that resembles iron

mange \'mānj\ *n* : a contagious skin disease usually of domestic animals in which there is itching and loss of hair

man·ger \'mān-jər\ *n* : an open box in which food for farm animals is placed

man·gle \'mang-gəl\ *vb* **man·gled; man·gling** **1** : to cut or bruise with repeated blows **2** : to spoil while making or performing 〈*mangle* a speech〉

man·go \'mang-gō\ *n, pl* **man·goes** *or* **man·gos** : a juicy somewhat acid tropical fruit that is yellow or reddish and is borne by an evergreen tree related to the sumac

mangy \'mān-jē\ *adj* **mang·i·er; mang·i·est** **1** : having mange or resulting from mange 〈a *mangy* dog〉 **2** : SHABBY 1 〈a *mangy* old rug〉 **3** : SEEDY 2 〈a *mangy* restaurant〉

man·hole \'man-,hōl\ *n* : a covered hole (as in a street or tank) large enough to let a person pass through

man·hood \'man-,hud\ *n* **1** : COURAGE **2** : the state of being an adult human male **3** : adult human males 〈the *manhood* of a nation〉

ma·nia \'mā-nē-ə, -nyə\ *n* **1** : often violent or excited insanity **2** : unreasonable enthusiasm

ma·ni·ac \'mā-nē-,ak\ *n* : a violently insane person

¹**man·i·cure** \'man-ə-,kyur\ *n* **1** : MANICURIST **2** : a treatment for the care of the hands and nails

²**manicure** *vb* **man·i·cured; man·i·cur·ing** : to give a manicure to

man·i·cur·ist \'man-ə-,kyur-əst\ *n* : a person who gives manicures

¹**man·i·fest** \'man-ə-,fest\ *adj* : clear to the senses or to the mind : easy to recognize : OBVIOUS 〈their relief was *manifest*〉

²**manifest** *vb* : to show plainly

man·i·fes·ta·tion \,man-ə-fəs-'tā-shən\ *n* **1** : the act of manifesting **2** : something that makes clear : EVIDENCE 〈the first *manifestations* of spring〉

man·i·fold \'man-ə-,fōld\ *adj* : of many and various kinds 〈*manifold* activities〉

ma·nip·u·late \mə-'nip-yə-,lāt\ *vb* **ma·nip·u·lat·ed; ma·nip·u·lat·ing** **1** : to work with the hands or by mechanical means and especially with skill 〈*manipulate* the levers of a machine〉 **2** : to manage skillfully and especially with intent to deceive 〈*manipulate* public opinion〉

man·kind *n* **1** \'man-'kīnd\ : human beings **2** \-,kīnd\ : men as distinguished from women

man·ly \'man-lē\ *adj* **man·li·er; man·li·est** : having qualities (as courage) often felt to be proper for a man — **man·li·ness** *n*

man–made \'man-'mād\ *adj* : made by people rather than nature 〈*man-made* fibers〉

man·na \'man-ə\ *n* : food supplied by a miracle to the Israelites in the wilderness

man·ne·quin \'man-i-kən\ *n* : a form representing the human figure used especially for displaying clothes

man·ner \'man-ər\ *n* **1** : ¹SORT 1 **2** : a way of acting 〈worked in a brisk *manner*〉 **3** **manners** *pl* : behavior toward or in the presence of other people 〈they have good *manners*〉

man·ner·ism \'man-ə-,riz-əm\ *n* : a habit (as of looking or moving in a certain way) that one notices in a person's behavior

man·ner·ly \'man-ər-lē\ *adj* : showing good manners : POLITE

\ə\ abut	\au\ out	\i\ tip	\ò\ saw	\u̇\ foot
\ər\ further	\ch\ chin	\ī\ life	\òi\ coin	\y\ yet
\a\ mat	\e\ pet	\j\ job	\th\ thin	\yü\ few
\ā\ take	\ē\ easy	\ng\ sing	\th\ this	\yu̇\ cure
\ä\ cot, cart	\g\ go	\ō\ bone	\ü\ food	\zh\ vision

man-of-war \ˌman-əv-'wȯr\ *n, pl* **men-of-war** \men-\ : WARSHIP

man·or \'man-ər\ *n* : a large estate

man·sion \'man-chən\ *n* : a large fine house

man·slaugh·ter \'man-ˌslȯt-ər\ *n* : the unintentional but unlawful killing of a person

man·tel \'mant-l\ *n* : a shelf above a fireplace

man·tel·piece \'mant-l-ˌpēs\ *n* **1** : a shelf above a fireplace along with side pieces **2** : MANTEL

man·tis \'mant-əs\ *n, pl* **man·tis·es** *or* **man·tes** \'man-ˌtēz\ : an insect related to the grasshoppers and roaches that feeds on other insects which are clasped in the raised front legs

mantis

man·tle \'mant-l\ *n* **1** : a loose sleeveless outer garment **2** : something that covers or wraps ⟨a *mantle* of snow⟩ **3** : a fold of the body wall of a mollusk that produces the shell material **4** : the part of the earth's interior beneath the crust and above the central core

¹**man·u·al** \'man-yə-wəl\ *adj* **1** : of or relating to the hands ⟨*manual* skill⟩ **2** : done or operated by the hands ⟨*manual* labor⟩ ⟨a *manual* gearshift⟩ — **man·u·al·ly** *adv*

²**manual** *n* : HANDBOOK ⟨a scout *manual*⟩

manual training *n* : training in work done with the hands and in useful arts ⟨woodworking is usually part of *manual training*⟩

¹**man·u·fac·ture** \ˌman-yə-'fak-chər\ *n* **1** : the making of products by hand or machinery **2** : PRODUCTION 1 ⟨the *manufacture* of blood in the body⟩

²**manufacture** *vb* **man·u·fac·tured; man·u·fac·turing** : to make from raw materials by hand or machin-ery **synonyms** see MAKE — **man·u·fac·tur·er** *n*

ma·nure \mə-'nu̇r, -'nyu̇r\ *n* : material (as animal wastes) used to fertilize land

Word History Long before we had modern machinery people had to grow food. It was not easy then, for all the work had to be done by hand. Back in those days the French had a verb that meant "to do work by hand" and it came to refer especially to the hard work of making the land grow crops. The English word *manure* came from this Old French verb and at first was used in just the same way. Later, perhaps because keeping the land fertile was such an important part of growing crops, the verb began to be used as a noun meaning "material used to make land fertile."

man·u·script \'man-yə-ˌskript\ *n* **1** : something written by hand or typewritten ⟨the *manuscript* of a book⟩ **2** : HANDWRITING

¹**many** \'men-ē\ *adj* **more** \'mȯr\; **most** \'mōst\ **1** : amounting to a large number **2** : being one of a large but not fixed number ⟨*many* a day⟩

²**many** *pron* : a large number ⟨*many* of the students were late⟩

³**many** *n* : a large number ⟨a good *many* left early⟩

¹**map** \'map\ *n* **1** : a picture or chart showing features of an area (as the surface of the earth or the moon) **2** : a picture or chart of the sky showing the position of stars and planets

Word History The English word *map* came from a Latin word that in the time of the ancient Romans meant "napkin." Some years later, people began to use the Latin word that meant "napkin" in a new way. They used it for a piece of parchment that had drawn on it a picture or chart of the world or of a part of the world. The shape of the parchment must have reminded these people of the shape of a napkin.

²**map** *vb* **mapped; map·ping 1** : to make a map of ⟨*map* the heavens⟩ **2** : to plan in detail ⟨*map* out a campaign⟩

ma·ple \'mā-pəl\ *n* : any of a group of trees having deeply notched leaves, fruits with two wings, and hard pale wood and including some whose sap is evaporated to a sweet syrup (**maple syrup**) and a brownish sugar (**maple sugar**)

mar \'mär\ *vb* **marred; mar·ring** : to make a blemish on : SPOIL

ma·ra·ca \mə-'räk-ə, -'rak-\ *n* : a musical rhythm instrument made of a dried gourd with seeds or pebbles inside that is usually played in pairs by shaking

mar·a·thon \'mar-ə-ˌthän\ *n* **1** : a long-distance running race **2** : a long hard contest

¹**mar·ble** \'mär-bəl\ *n* **1** : limestone that is capable of taking a high polish and is used in architecture and sculpture **2** : a little ball (as of glass) used in a children's game (marbles)

²**marble** *adj* : made of or like marble

¹**march** \'märch\ *vb* **1** : to move or cause to

move along steadily usually with long even steps and in step with others ⟨*march* in a parade⟩ **2** : to make steady progress ⟨science *marches* on⟩ — **march·er** *n*

²**march** *n* **1** : the action of marching **2** : the distance covered in marching ⟨a long day's *march*⟩ **3** : a regular step used in marching **4** : a musical piece in a lively rhythm with a strong beat that is suitable to march to

March \'märch\ *n* : the third month of the year

Word History The English word *March* came from the Latin name for the same month. The Latin name came from *Mars*, the name of the Roman god of war and farming. The planet Mars also got its name from this god.

mar·chio·ness \'mär-shə-nəs\ *n* **1** : the wife or widow of a marquess **2** : a woman who holds the rank of a marquess in her own right

mare \'maər, 'meər\ *n* : an adult female of the horse or a related animal (as a zebra or donkey)

mar·ga·rine \'mär-jə-rən\ *n* : a food product made usually from vegetable oils and skim milk and used as a spread or for cooking

mar·gin \'mär-jən\ *n* **1** : the part of a page outside the main body of print or writing **2** : ¹BORDER 1 **3** : an extra amount (as of time or money) allowed for use if needed ⟨we have a *margin* of five minutes⟩

mar·i·gold \'mar-ə-,gōld\ *n* : any of several plants related to the daisies that are grown for their yellow or brownish red and yellow flower heads

mar·i·jua·na \,mar-ə-'wä-nə\ *n* : dried leaves and flowers of the hemp plant smoked as a drug

ma·ri·na \mə-'rē-nə\ *n* : a dock or basin providing a place to anchor motorboats and yachts

¹**ma·rine** \mə-'rēn\ *adj* **1** : of or relating to the sea ⟨*marine* paintings⟩ ⟨fish and other *marine* animals⟩ **2** : of or relating to the navigation of the sea : NAUTICAL ⟨*marine* charts⟩ **3** : of or relating to marines ⟨*marine* barracks⟩

²**marine** *n* **1** : the ships of a country ⟨the merchant *marine*⟩ **2** : one of a class of soldiers serving on board a ship or in close cooperation with a naval force

mar·i·ner \'mar-ə-nər\ *n* : SEAMAN 1, SAILOR

mar·i·o·nette \,mar-ē-ə-'net, ,mer-\ *n* : a doll that can be made to move by means of strings : PUPPET

mar·i·tal \'mar-ət-l\ *adj* : of or relating to marriage

mar·i·time \'mar-ə-,tīm\ *adj* **1** : of or relating to ocean navigation or trade ⟨*maritime* law⟩ **2** : bordering on or living near the sea ⟨*maritime* nations⟩

¹**mark** \'märk\ *n* **1** : something designed or serving to record position ⟨high-water *mark*⟩ **2** : something aimed at : TARGET **3** : the starting line of a race **4** : INDICATION 2 ⟨a *mark* of friendship⟩ **5** : a blemish (as a scratch or stain) made on a surface ⟨the blow left a *mark*⟩ **6** : a written or printed symbol ⟨punctuation *mark*⟩ **7** : a grade or score showing the quality of work or conduct ⟨good *marks* in school⟩

²**mark** *vb* **1** : to set apart by a line or boundary ⟨*mark* off a tennis court⟩ **2** : to make a mark on ⟨*mark* the top with a cross⟩ **3** : to decide and show the value or quality of by marks : GRADE ⟨*mark* the tests⟩ **4** : to be an important characteristic of ⟨a disease *marked* by fever⟩ **5** : to take notice of ⟨*mark* my words⟩ — **mark·er** *n*

³**mark** *n* : a German coin or bill

marked \'märkt\ *adj* **1** : having a mark or marks **2** : NOTICEABLE ⟨speaks with a *marked* accent⟩

¹**mar·ket** \'mär-kət\ *n* **1** : a meeting of people at a fixed time and place to buy and sell things **2** : a public place where a market is held **3** : a store where foods are sold to the public ⟨a meat *market*⟩ **4** : the region in which something can be sold ⟨*markets* for American cotton⟩

²**market** *vb* : to buy or sell in a market

mar·ket·place \'mär-kət-,plās\ *n* : an open square or place in a town where markets or public sales are held

mark·ing \'mär-king\ *n* : a mark made

marionette

marks·man \'märk-smən\ *n, pl* **marks-men-** \ smən \ : a person who shoots well — **marks·man·ship** \-,ship\ *n*

mar·ma·lade \'mär-mə-,lād\ *n* : a jam containing pieces of fruit and fruit rind ⟨orange *marmalade*⟩

mar·mo·set \'mär-mə-,set\ *n* : a small monkey of South and Central America with soft fur and a bushy tail

mar·mot \'mär-mət\ *n* : a stocky animal with short legs, coarse fur, and bushy tail that is related to the squirrels

marmot

¹ma·roon \mə-'rün\ *vb* : to put ashore and abandon on a lonely island or coast

²maroon *n* : a dark red

mar·quess \'mär-kwəs\ *n* : a British nobleman ranking below a duke and above an earl

mar·quis \'mär-kwəs\ *n* : MARQUESS

mar·quise \mär-'kēz\ *n* : MARCHIONESS

mar·riage \'mar-ij\ *n* **1** : the legal relationship into which a man and a woman enter with the purpose of making a home and raising a family **2** : the act of getting married

mar·row \'mar-ō\ *n* : a soft tissue rich in fat and blood vessels that fills the cavities of most bones

mar·ry \'mar-ē\ *vb* **mar·ried; mar·ry·ing** **1** : to join in marriage as husband and wife ⟨they were *married* by a priest⟩ **2** : to give (as one's child) in marriage **3** : to take for husband or wife ⟨*married* a high school sweetheart⟩ **4** : to enter into a marriage relationship ⟨decide to *marry*⟩

Mars \'märz\ *n* : the planet that is fourth in order of distance from the sun, is known for its redness, and has a diameter of about 6800 kilometers

marsh \'märsh\ *n* : an area of soft wet land usually overgrown with grasses and related plants

¹mar·shal \'mär-shəl\ *n* **1** : a person who arranges and directs ceremonies ⟨*marshal* of the parade⟩ **2** : an officer of the highest rank in some military forces **3** : a federal official having duties similar to those of a sheriff **4** : the head of a division of a city government ⟨fire *marshal*⟩

²marshal *vb* **mar·shaled** *or* **mar·shalled; mar·shaling** *or* **mar·shal·ling** : to arrange in order ⟨*marshal* troops⟩

marsh·mal·low \'märsh-,mel-ō, -,mal-\ *n* : a soft spongy sweet made from corn syrup, sugar, and gelatin

marsh marigold *n* : a swamp plant with shiny leaves and bright yellow flowers like buttercups

marshy \'mär-shē\ *adj* **marsh·i·er; marsh·i·est** : like or being a marsh

mar·su·pi·al \mär-'sü-pē-əl\ *n* : a mammal (as a kangaroo or opossum) that carries its young in a pouch on the mother's abdomen

mart \'märt\ *n* : a trading place : MARKET

mar·ten \'märt-n\ *n* : a slender animal larger than the related weasels that eats flesh and is sought for its soft gray or brown fur

mar·tial \'mär-shəl\ *adj* : having to do with or suitable for war

mar·tin \'märt-n\ *n* **1** : a European swallow with a forked tail **2** : any of several birds (as the American **purple martin**) resembling or related to the true martin

marten

¹mar·tyr \'märt-ər\ *n* : a person who suffers greatly or dies rather than give up his or her religion or principles

²martyr *vb* : to put to death for refusing to give up a belief

¹mar·vel \'mär-vəl\ *n* : something that causes wonder or astonishment

²marvel *vb* **mar·veled** *or* **mar·velled; mar·vel·ing** *or* **mar·vel·ling** : to be struck with astonishment or wonder ⟨I *marvel* at your skill⟩

mar·vel·ous *or* **mar·vel·lous** \'mär-və-ləs\ *adj* **1** : causing wonder or astonishment **2** : of the finest kind or quality ⟨we had a *marvelous* time⟩ — **marvel·ous·ly** *adv*

mas·cot \'mas-,kät, -kət\ *n* : a person, animal, or object adopted by a group and believed to bring good luck

mas·cu·line \'mas-kyə-lən\ *adj* **1** : of the male sex **2** : ¹MALE 3

¹mash \'mash\ *n* **1** : a mixture of ground feeds used for feeding livestock **2** : a mass of something made soft and pulpy by beating or crushing

²mash *vb* : to make into a soft pulpy mass ⟨*mashed* potatoes⟩

¹mask \'mask\ *n* **1** : a cover for the face used for disguise or protection ⟨a Halloween *mask*⟩ ⟨a catcher's *mask*⟩ **2** : something that disguises or conceals ⟨under a *mask* of friendship⟩ **3** : a copy of a face molded in wax or plaster ⟨a death *mask*⟩

²mask *vb* : CONCEAL, DISGUISE ⟨*mask* one's anger behind a smile⟩

ma·son \'mās-n\ *n* : a person who builds or works with stone, brick, or cement

ma·son·ry \'mās-n-rē\ *n, pl* **ma·son·ries** **1** : the art, trade, or occupation of a mason **2** : the work done by a mason **3** : something built of stone, brick, or concrete

masque \'mask\ *n* **1** : ¹MASQUERADE 1 **2** : an old form of dramatic entertainment in which the actors wore masks

¹mas·quer·ade \ˌmas-kə-'rād\ *n* **1** : a party (as a dance) at which people wear masks and costumes **2** : a pretending to be something one is not

²masquerade *vb* **mas·quer·ad·ed; mas·quer·ad·ing** **1** : to disguise oneself **2** : to pass oneself off as something one is not : POSE ⟨*masquerade* as an expert⟩ — **mas·quer·ad·er** *n*

¹mass \'mas\ *n* **1** : an amount of something that holds or clings together ⟨a *mass* of iron ore⟩ **2** : BULK 1, SIZE ⟨an elephant's huge *mass*⟩ **3** : the principal part : main body ⟨the great *mass* of voters⟩ **4** : a large quantity or number ⟨a *mass* of figures⟩ **5 masses** *pl* : the body of ordinary or common people

²mass *vb* : to collect into a mass

Mass \'mas\ *n* : a religious service in celebration of the Eucharist

¹mas·sa·cre \'mas-ə-kər\ *vb* **mas·sa·cred; massa·cring** : to kill in a massacre : SLAUGHTER

²massacre *n* : the violent and cruel killing of a large number of persons

¹mas·sage \mə-'säzh\ *n* : treatment of the body by rubbing, kneading, and tapping

²massage *vb* **mas·saged; mas·sag·ing** : to give massage to

mas·sive \'mas-iv\ *adj* : very large, heavy, and solid

mast \'mast\ *n* **1** : a long pole that rises from the bottom of a ship and supports the sails and rigging **2** : a vertical or nearly vertical tall pole ⟨a *mast* on a derrick⟩ — **mast·ed** \'mas-təd\ *adj*

¹mas·ter \'mas-tər\ *n* **1** : a male teacher **2** : an artist or performer of great skill **3** : one having authority over another person or thing ⟨the slave's *master*⟩ ⟨*master* of a ship⟩ **4** : EMPLOYER **5** — used as a title for a young boy too young to be called *mister* ⟨*Master* Timothy Roe⟩

²master *vb* **1** : to get control of ⟨*master* your temper⟩ **2** : to become skillful at ⟨*master* arithmetic⟩

master chief petty officer *n* : a petty officer in the Navy or Coast Guard ranking above a senior chief petty officer

mas·ter·ful \'mas-tər-fəl\ *adj* **1** : tending to take control : BOSSY **2** : having or showing great skill

mas·ter·ly \'mas-tər-lē\ *adj* : showing the knowledge or skill of a master ⟨a *masterly* performance⟩

mas·ter·piece \'mas-tər-ˌpēs\ *n* : a work done or made with supreme skill

master sergeant *n* : a noncommissioned officer in the Army ranking above a sergeant first class or in the Air Force ranking above a technical sergeant or in the Marine Corps ranking above a gunnery sergeant

mas·tery \'mas-tə-rē\ *n, pl* **mas·ter·ies** **1** : the position or authority of a master **2** : VICTORY 1 ⟨gained the *mastery* over their opponents⟩ **3** : skill that makes one master of something

mast·head \'mast-ˌhed\ *n* : the top of a mast

mas·ti·cate \ˌmas-tə-ˌkāt\ *vb* **mas·ti·cat·ed; masti·cat·ing** : ¹CHEW

mas·tiff \'mas-təf\ *n* : a very large powerful dog with a smooth coat

mastiff

¹mat \'mat\ *n* **1** : a piece of coarse woven or braided fabric used as a floor or seat covering **2** : a piece of material in front of a door to wipe the shoes on **3** : a piece of material (as cloth or woven straw) used under dishes or vases or as an ornament **4** : a pad or

\ə\ abut	\au̇\ out	\i\ tip	\ȯ\ saw	\u̇\ foot
\ər\ further	\ch\ chin	\ī\ life	\ȯi\ coin	\y\ yet
\a\ mat	\e\ pet	\j\ job	\th\ thin	\yü\ few
\ā\ take	\ē\ easy	\ng\ sing	\th\ this	\yu̇\ cure
\ä\ cot, cart	\g\ go	\ō\ bone	\ü\ food	\zh\ vision

cushion for gymnastics or wrestling **5** : something made up of many tangled strands ⟨a *mat* of weeds⟩

²mat *vb* **mat·ted; mat·ting** : to form into a tangled mass

mat·a·dor \'mat-ə-ˌdȯr\ *n* : a bullfighter who plays the chief human part in a bullfight

¹match \'mach\ *n* **1** : a person or thing that is equal to or as good as another ⟨we are a *match* for the enemy⟩ **2** : a thing that is exactly like another thing ⟨this cloth is a *match* for that⟩ **3** : two people or things that go well together ⟨the curtains and carpet are a good *match*⟩ **4** : MARRIAGE 1 ⟨made a good *match*⟩ **5** : a contest between two individuals or teams ⟨a tennis *match*⟩ ⟨a boxing *match*⟩ ⟨a soccer *match*⟩

²match *vb* **1** : to place in competition ⟨*matched* my strength with my rival's⟩ **2** : to choose something that is the same as another or goes with it ⟨try to *match* this material⟩ **3** : to be the same or suitable to one another ⟨the colors *match*⟩

³match *n* **1** : a wick or cord that is made to burn evenly and is used for lighting a charge of powder **2** : a short slender piece of material tipped with a mixture that produces fire when scratched

match·book \'mach-ˌbu̇k\ *n* : a small folder containing rows of paper matches

match·less \'mach-ləs\ *adj* : having no equal : better than any other of the same kind — **match·less·ly** *adv*

match·lock \'mach-ˌläk\ *n* : a musket with a hole at the rear of the barrel into which a slowly burning cord is lowered to ignite the charge

¹mate \'māt\ *n* **1** : COMPANION 1, COMRADE **2** : an officer on a ship used to carry passengers or freight who ranks below the captain **3** : either member of a married couple **4** : either member of a breeding pair of animals **5** : either of two matched objects ⟨lost the *mate* to the glove⟩

²mate *vb* **mat·ed; mat·ing** : to join as mates : MARRY

¹ma·te·ri·al \mə-'tir-ē-əl\ *adj* **1** : of, relating to, or made of matter : PHYSICAL ⟨the *material* world⟩ **2** : of or relating to a person's bodily needs or wants ⟨money buys *material* comforts⟩ **3** : having real importance ⟨facts *material* to the case⟩ — **ma·teri·al·ly** *adv*

²material *n* **1** : the elements, substance, or parts of which something is made or can be made ⟨bricks and other building *material*⟩ **2 materials** *pl* : equipment needed for doing something ⟨writing *materials*⟩

ma·te·ri·al·ize \mə-'tir-ē-ə-ˌlīz\ *vb* **ma·te·ri·al·ized; ma·te·ri·al·iz·ing 1** : to cause to take on a physical form ⟨the medium claimed to *materialize* the spirits of the dead⟩ **2** : to become actual fact ⟨their hopes never *materialized*⟩

ma·ter·nal \mə-'tərn-l\ *adj* **1** : of or relating to a mother ⟨*maternal* love⟩ **2** : related through one's mother ⟨*maternal* grandparents⟩ — **ma·ter·nal·ly** *adv*

ma·ter·ni·ty \mə-'tər-nət-ē\ *n* : the state of being a mother

math \'math\ *n* : MATHEMATICS

math·e·mat·i·cal \ˌmath-ə-'mat-i-kəl\ *adj* **1** : of or relating to mathematics **2** : ²EXACT ⟨*mathematical* precision⟩ — **math·e·mat·i·cal·ly** *adv*

math·e·ma·ti·cian \ˌmath-ə-mə-'tish-ən\ *n* : a specialist in mathematics

math·e·mat·ics \ˌmath-ə-'mat-iks\ *n* : the science that studies and explains numbers, quantities, measurements, and the relations between them

mat·i·nee *or* **mat·i·née** \ˌmat-n-'ā\ *n* : a musical or dramatic performance in the afternoon

mat·ri·mo·ni·al \ˌma-trə-'mō-nē-əl\ *adj* : of or relating to marriage

mat·ri·mo·ny \'ma-trə-ˌmō-nē\ *n, pl* **mat·ri·mo·nies** : MARRIAGE 1

ma·tron \'mā-trən\ *n* **1** : a married woman **2** : a woman who is in charge of the household affairs of an institution **3** : a woman who looks after women prisoners in a police station or prison

¹mat·ter \'mat-ər\ *n* **1** : something to be dealt with or considered ⟨a serious *matter*⟩ **2** : PROBLEM 2, DIFFICULTY ⟨what's the *matter*⟩ **3** : the substance things are made of : something that takes up space and has weight **4** : material substance of a certain kind or function ⟨coloring *matter*⟩ ⟨gray *matter* of the brain⟩ **5** : PUS **6** : a more or less definite quantity or amount ⟨a *matter* of ten cents⟩ **7** : ¹MAIL 1 ⟨third class *matter*⟩ — **no matter** : it makes no difference

²matter *vb* : to be of importance ⟨it does not *matter*⟩

mat·ter–of–fact \ˌmat-ər-ə-'fakt\ *adj* : sticking to or concerned with fact ⟨a *matter-of-fact* answer⟩

mat·ting \'mat-ing\ *n* : material for mats

mat·tress \'ma-trəs\ *n* **1** : a springy pad for use as a resting place usually over springs on a bedstead **2** : a sack that can be filled with air or water and used as a mattress

¹ma·ture \mə-'tu̇r, -'tyu̇r\ *adj* **1** : fully grown or developed : ADULT, RIPE **2** : like that of a mature person ⟨a *mature* outlook⟩

²**mature** *vb* **ma·tured; ma·tur·ing** : to reach maturity

ma·tu·ri·ty \mə-'tùr-ət-ē, -'tyùr-\ *n* : the condition of being mature : full development

¹**maul** \'mòl\ *n* : a heavy hammer used especially for driving wedges or posts

²**maul** *vb* **1** : to beat and bruise severely **2** : to handle roughly

mauve \'mōv\ *n* : a medium purple, violet, or lilac

maxi- *prefix* : very long or large

max·il·la \mak-'sil-ə\ *n, pl* **max·il·lae** \-'sil-ē\ **1** : an upper jaw especially of a mammal **2** : either of the pair of mouth parts next behind the mandibles of an arthropod (as an insect or a crustacean)

max·im \'mak-səm\ *n* : a short saying expressing a general truth or rule of conduct

¹**max·i·mum** \'mak-sə-məm\ *n, pl* **max·i·mums** *or* **max·i·ma** \-sə-mə\ : the highest value : greatest amount ⟨we had to pay the *maximum*⟩

²**maximum** *adj* : as great as possible in amount or degree ⟨*maximum* efficiency⟩

may \'mā\ *helping verb, past* **might** \'mīt\ *present sing & pl* **may 1** : have permission to ⟨you *may* go now⟩ **2** : be in some degree likely to ⟨you *may* be right⟩ **3** — used to express a wish ⟨*may* you be happy⟩ **4** — used to express purpose ⟨we exercise so that we *may* be strong⟩

May \'mā\ *n* : the fifth month of the year

Word History The English word *May* came from the Latin name for the same month. The Latin name came from *Maia*, the name of a Roman goddess. Every year on the first of May, the ancient Romans made offerings to this goddess.

may·be \'mā-bē\ *adv* : possibly but not certainly

mayn't \'mā-ənt, mānt\ : may not

may·on·naise \'mā-ə-,nāz\ *n* : a creamy dressing usually made of egg yolk, oil, and vinegar or lemon juice

may·or \'mā-ər\ *n* : an official elected to serve as head of a city or borough

maze \'māz\ *n* : a confusing arrangement of paths or passages

me \mē\ *pron objective case of* ı

mead·ow \'med-ō\ *n* : usually moist and low grassland

mead·ow·lark \'med-ō-,lärk\ *n* : a bird that has brownish upper

meadowlark

parts and a yellow breast and is about as large as a robin

mea·ger *or* **mea·gre** \'mē-gər\ *adj* **1** : having little flesh : THIN **2** : INSUFFICIENT ⟨a *meager* income⟩

¹**meal** \'mēl\ *n* **1** : the food eaten or prepared for eating at one time **2** : the act or time of eating

²**meal** *n* **1** : usually coarsely ground seeds of a cereal grass and especially of Indian corn **2** : something like meal in texture ⟨fish *meal*⟩

mealy \'mē-lē\ *adj* **meal·i·er; meal·i·est** : like meal ⟨a *mealy* powder⟩ — **meal·i·ness** *n*

¹**mean** \'mēn\ *adj* **1** : low in quality, worth, or dignity ⟨*mean* houses⟩ ⟨that was no *mean* achievement⟩ **2** : lacking in honor or dignity ⟨your reasons are *mean*⟩ **3** : STINGY 1 **4** : deliberately unkind ⟨that was a *mean* trick to play⟩ **5** : ASHAMED 1 ⟨it made me feel *mean* and unhappy⟩ — **mean·ly** *adv* — **mean·ness** *n*

²**mean** *vb* **meant** \'ment\; **mean·ing** \'mē-ning\ **1** : to have in mind as a purpose : INTEND ⟨I *mean* to go⟩ **2** : to intend for a particular use ⟨a book *meant* for children⟩ **3** : to have as a meaning : SIGNIFY ⟨what does this word *mean*⟩ ⟨those clouds *mean* rain⟩

³**mean** *n* **1** : a middle point or something (as a place, time, number, or rate) that falls at or near a middle point : MODERATION **2** : ARITHMETIC MEAN **3 means** *pl* : something that helps a person to get what he or she wants ⟨use every *means* you can think of⟩ **4 means** *pl* : WEALTH 1 ⟨a person of *means*⟩ — **by all means** : CERTAINLY 1 — **by any means** : in any way — **by means of** : through the use of — **by no means** : certainly not

⁴**mean** *adj* : occurring or being in a middle position : AVERAGE ⟨*mean* temperature⟩

me·an·der \mē-'an-dər\ *vb* **1** : to follow a winding course ⟨a brook *meandering* through the fields⟩ **2** : to wander without a goal or purpose ⟨*meander* around town⟩

mean·ing \'mē-ning\ *n* **1** : the idea a person intends to express by something said or done ⟨what is the *meaning* of this⟩ **2** : the quality of communicating something or of being important ⟨a look full of *meaning*⟩

mean·ing·ful \'mē-ning-fəl\ *adj* : having a

\ə\ **abut**	\aú\ **out**	\i\ **tip**	\ò\ **saw**	\ú\ **foot**
\ər\ **further**	\ch\ **chin**	\ī\ **life**	\òi\ **coin**	\y\ **yet**
\a\ **mat**	\e\ **pet**	\j\ **job**	\th\ **thin**	\yü\ **few**
\ā\ **take**	\ē\ **easy**	\ng\ **sing**	\th\ **this**	\yú\ **cure**
\ä\ **cot, cart**	\g\ **go**	\ō\ **bone**	\ü\ **food**	\zh\ **vision**

meaning or purpose — **mean·ing·ful·ly** \-fə-lē\ *adv*

mean·ing·less \'mē-ning-ləs\ *adj* : having no meaning or importance

¹**mean·time** \'mēn-ˌtīm\ *n* : the time between two events

²**meantime** *adv* : in the meantime

¹**mean·while** \'mēn-ˌhwīl, -ˌwīl\ *n* : ¹meantime

²**meanwhile** *adv* **1** : ²MEANTIME **2** : at the same time

mea·sles \'mē-zəlz\ *n sing or pl* **1** : a contagious disease in which there are fever and red spots on the skin **2** : any of several diseases (as **German measles**) resembling true measles

mea·sly \'mēz-lē\ *adj* **mea·sli·er; mea·sli·est** : so small or unimportant as to be rejected with scorn

mea·sur·able \'mezh-ə-rə-bəl\ *adj* : capable of being measured

¹**mea·sure** \'mezh-ər\ *n* **1** : EXTENT 2, DEGREE, AMOUNT ⟨succeed in large *measure*⟩ **2** : the size, capacity, or quantity of something as fixed by measuring ⟨made to *measure*⟩ **3** : something (as a yardstick or cup) used in measuring **4** : a unit used in measuring **5** : a system of measuring ⟨liquid *measure*⟩ **6** : the notes and rests between bar lines on a musical staff **7** : a way of accomplishing something ⟨take *measures* to stop it⟩ ⟨a safety *measure*⟩ **8** : a legislative bill or act

²**measure** *vb* **mea·sured; mea·sur·ing** **1** : to find out the size, extent, or amount of ⟨*measure* the cloth with the tape measure⟩ **2** : ¹ESTIMATE 1 ⟨*measure* the distance with the eye⟩ **3** : to bring into comparison ⟨*measure* your skill against an opponent's⟩ **4** : to give a measure of : INDICATE ⟨a thermometer *measures* temperature⟩ **5** : to have as its measurement ⟨the cloth *measures* ten meters⟩

mea·sure·ment \'mezh-ər-mənt\ *n* **1** : the act of measuring **2** : the extent, size, capacity, or amount of something as fixed by measuring **3** : a system of measures

measure up *vb* : to satisfy needs or requirements ⟨they did not *measure up* to expectations⟩

meat \'mēt\ *n* **1** : solid food ⟨*meat* and drink⟩ **2** : the part of something that can be eaten ⟨nut *meats*⟩ **3** : animal and especially mammal tissue for use as food **4** : the most important part : SUBSTANCE ⟨the *meat* of the story⟩ — **meat·less** \-ləs\ *adj*

me·chan·ic \mi-'kan-ik\ *n* : a person who makes or repairs machines

me·chan·i·cal \mi-'kan-i-kəl\ *adj* **1** : of or relating to machinery ⟨*mechanical* engi-

neering⟩ **2** : made or operated by a machine ⟨a *mechanical* toy⟩ **3** : done or produced as if by a machine : lacking freshness and individuality ⟨sing in a *mechanical* way⟩ — **me·chan·i·cal·ly** *adv*

me·chan·ics \mi-'kan-iks\ *n sing or pl* **1** : a science dealing with the action of forces on bodies **2** : the way something works or things are done ⟨the *mechanics* of a watch⟩ ⟨the *mechanics* of writing plays⟩

mech·a·nism \'mek-ə-ˌniz-əm\ *n* **1** : a mechanical device **2** : the parts by which a machine operates ⟨the *mechanism* of a watch⟩ **3** : the parts or steps that make up a process or activity ⟨the *mechanism* of government⟩

mech·a·nize \'mek-ə-ˌnīz\ *vb* **mech·a·nized; mech·a·niz·ing** **1** : to make mechanical or automatic **2** : to equip with machinery

med·al \'med-l\ *n* : a piece of metal often in the form of a coin with design and words in honor of a special event, a person, or an achievement

Word History The English word *medal* came from a French word meaning "medal." The French word, however, came from an Italian word that was at first the name for a coin worth half as much as another coin. The name for this coin came from a Latin word that meant "middle" or "half." The Italian word came to mean "medal" before finding its way into French and from French into English.

me·dal·lion \mə-'dal-yən\ *n* **1** : a large medal **2** : something like a large medal (as in shape) ⟨a doily with a lace *medallion* in the center⟩

med·dle \'med-l\ *vb* **med·dled; med·dling** : to interest oneself in what is not one's concern

synonyms MEDDLE, INTERFERE, TAMPER mean to concern oneself with something that is not one's own business. MEDDLE stresses intruding in an inconsiderate and annoying fashion ⟨*meddling* in a friend's personal problems⟩ INTERFERE suggests getting in the way of or disturbing someone or something whether intentionally or not ⟨building the dam *interfered* with nature⟩ ⟨a bossy child always *interfering* with the others' play⟩ TAMPER implies intruding or experimenting that is wrong or uncalled-for and likely to be harmful ⟨*tampered* with the members of the jury⟩

med·dle·some \'med-l-səm\ *adj* : given to meddling

media *pl of* MEDIUM

med·i·cal \'med-i-kəl\ *adj* : of or relating to the science or practice of medicine or to the treatment of disease — **med·i·cal·ly** *adv*

med·i·cate \'med-ə-ˌkāt\ *vb* **med·i·cat·ed; med·i·cat·ing** **1** : to use medicine on or for ⟨*medicate* a sore throat⟩ **2** : to add medicinal material to ⟨*medicated* soap⟩

med·i·ca·tion \ˌmed-ə-'kā-shən\ *n* **1** : the act or process of medicating **2** : medicinal material

me·dic·i·nal \mə-'dis-n-əl\ *adj* : used or likely to relieve or cure disease — **me·dic·i·nal·ly** *adv*

med·i·cine \'med-ə-sən\ *n* **1** : something used to cure or relieve a disease **2** : a science or art dealing with the prevention, cure, or relief of disease

medicine dropper *n* : DROPPER 2

medicine man *n* : a member of a primitive tribe believed to have magic powers and called on to cure illnesses and keep away evil spirits

me·di·eval *or* **me·di·ae·val** \ˌmēd-ē-'ē-vəl, ˌmed-\ *adj* : of or relating to the Middle Ages

me·di·o·cre \ˌmēd-ē-'ō-kər\ *adj* : neither good nor bad : ORDINARY

med·i·tate \'med-ə-ˌtāt\ *vb* **med·i·tat·ed; med·i·tat·ing** **1** : to consider carefully : PLAN ⟨*meditate* a trip⟩ **2** : to spend time in quiet thinking : REFLECT

med·i·ta·tion \ˌmed-ə-'tā-shən\ *n* : the act or an instance of meditating

Med·i·ter·ra·nean \ˌmed-ə-tə-'rā-nē-ən, -'rān-yən\ *adj* : of or relating to the Mediterranean sea or to the lands or peoples surrounding it

¹me·di·um \'mēd-ē-əm\ *n, pl* **me·di·ums** *or* **me·dia** \-ē-ə\ **1** : something that is between or in the middle **2** : the thing by which or through which something is done ⟨money is a *medium* of exchange⟩ **3** : the substance in which something lives or acts ⟨the *medium* of air⟩ **4** : a person through whom other persons try to communicate with the spirits of the dead

²medium *adj* : intermediate in amount, quality, position, or degree ⟨*medium* size⟩

med·ley \'med-lē\ *n, pl* **med·leys** **1** : MIXTURE 2, JUMBLE ⟨a *medley* of tastes⟩ **2** : a musical selection made up of a series of different songs or parts of different compositions

me·dul·la ob·lon·ga·ta \mə-'dəl-ə-ˌäb-ˌlòng-'gät-ə\ *n* : the last part of the brain that joins the spinal cord and is concerned especially with control of involuntary activ-

ities (as breathing and beating of the heart)

meed \'mēd\ *n* : something deserved or earned : REWARD ⟨received their *meed* of praise⟩

meek \'mēk\ *adj* **1** : putting up with injury or abuse with patience **2** : lacking spirit or self-confidence — **meek·ly** *adv* — **meek·ness** *n*

¹meet \'mēt\ *vb* **met** \'met\; **meet·ing** **1** : to come upon or across ⟨*met* a friend while shopping⟩ **2** : to be at a place to greet or keep an appointment ⟨*meet* me at the airport⟩ ⟨*met* in the park for lunch⟩ **3** : to approach from the opposite direction ⟨when you *meet* another car, keep to the right⟩ **4** : to come together : JOIN, MERGE ⟨where the two rivers *meet*⟩ **5** : to be sensed by ⟨sounds that *meet* the ears⟩ **6** : to deal with ⟨*meet* problems as they appear⟩ **7** : to fulfill the requirements of : SATISFY ⟨unable to *meet* your demands⟩ **8** : to become acquainted ⟨they *met* at a party⟩ **9** : to hold a meeting

²meet *n* : a meeting for sports competition ⟨track *meet*⟩

meet·ing \'mēt-ing\ *n* **1** : the act of persons or things that meet **2** : ASSEMBLY 1 ⟨the club holds *meetings* once a month⟩

meet·ing·house \'mēt-ing-ˌhaus\ *n* : a building used for public assembly and especially for Protestant worship

mega·phone \'meg-ə-ˌfōn\ *n* : a device

megaphone

\ə\ abut	\au\ out	\i\ tip	\o\ saw	\u\ foot
\ər\ further	\ch\ chin	\ī\ life	\oi\ coin	\y\ yet
\a\ mat	\e\ pet	\j\ job	\th\ thin	\yu\ few
\ā\ take	\ē\ easy	\ng\ sing	\th\ this	\yu\ cure
\ä\ cot, cart	\g\ go	\ō\ bone	\ü\ food	\zh\ vision

shaped like a cone that is used to direct the voice and increase its loudness

¹mel·an·choly \'mel-ən-ˌkäl-ē\ *n* : a sad or gloomy mood

²melancholy *adj* : SAD 1

¹mel·low \'mel-ō\ *adj* **1** : tender and sweet because of ripeness ⟨a *mellow* peach⟩ **2** : made mild by age ⟨*mellow* wines⟩ ⟨a *mellow* character⟩ **3** : being clear, full, and pure : not coarse ⟨a *mellow* sound⟩ ⟨a *mellow* color⟩ — **mel·low·ness** *n*

²mellow *vb* : to make or become mellow

me·lo·di·ous \mə-'lōd-ē-əs\ *adj* : agreeable to the ear because of its melody — **me·lo·di·ous·ly** *adv* — **me·lo·di·ous·ness** *n*

mel·o·dy \'mel-əd-ē\ *n, pl* **mel·o·dies 1** : pleasing arrangement of sounds **2** : a series of musical notes or tones arranged in a definite pattern of pitch and rhythm **3** : the leading part in a musical composition

mel·on \'mel-ən\ *n* : a fruit (as a watermelon) having juicy and usually sweet flesh and growing on a vine related to the gourds

melt \'melt\ *vb* **1** : to change from a solid to a liquid usually through the action of heat ⟨*melt* sugar⟩ ⟨snow *melts*⟩ **2** : to grow less : DISAPPEAR ⟨clouds *melting* away⟩ **3** : to make or become gentle : SOFTEN ⟨kindness that *melts* the heart⟩ **4** : to lose clear outline ⟨sky *melting* into sea⟩

melting point *n* : the temperature at which a solid melts

mem·ber \'mem-bər\ *n* **1** : a part (as an arm, leg, leaf, or branch) of a person, animal, or plant **2** : one of the individuals (as persons) or units (as species) making up a group **3** : a part of a structure ⟨a horizontal *member* of a bridge⟩

mem·ber·ship \'mem-bər-ˌship\ *n* **1** : the state or fact of being a member **2** : the whole number of members

mem·brane \'mem-ˌbrān\ *n* : a thin soft flexible layer especially of animal or plant tissue

mem·bra·nous \'mem-brə-nəs\ *adj* : made of or like membrane

me·men·to \mi-'ment-ō\ *n, pl* **me·men·tos** *or* **me·men·toes** : something that serves as a reminder ⟨*mementos* of a trip to Europe⟩

mem·o·ra·ble \'mem-ə-rə-bəl, 'mem-rə-bəl\ *adj* : worth remembering : not easily forgotten — **mem·o·ra·bly** \-blē\ *adv*

mem·o·ran·dum \ˌmem-ə-'ran-dəm\ *n, pl* **mem·o·ran·dums** *or* **mem·o·ran·da** \-də\ **1** : an informal record or message **2** : a written reminder

¹me·mo·ri·al \mə-'mōr-ē-əl\ *adj* : serving to preserve the memory of a person or event ⟨a *memorial* service⟩

²memorial *n* : something by which the memory of a person or an event is kept alive : MONUMENT ⟨the Lincoln *Memorial*⟩

Memorial Day *n* **1** : May 30 once observed as a legal holiday in honor of dead servicemen **2** : the last Monday in May observed as a legal holiday in most states of the United States

mem·o·rize \'mem-ə-ˌrīz\ *vb* **mem·o·rized; mem·o·riz·ing** : to learn by heart

mem·o·ry \'mem-ə-rē, 'mem-rē\ *n, pl* **mem·o·ries 1** : the power or process of remembering **2** : the store of things learned and kept in the mind ⟨recite from *memory*⟩ **3** : the act of remembering and honoring ⟨in *memory* of a great soldier⟩ **4** : something remembered ⟨a pleasant *memory*⟩ **5** : the time within which past events are remembered ⟨within the *memory* of anyone living today⟩

men *pl of* MAN

¹men·ace \'men-əs\ *n* **1** : DANGER **2** ⟨the *menace* of disease⟩ **2** : an annoying person ⟨that child is a *menace*⟩

²menace *vb* **men·aced; men·ac·ing** : THREATEN 1

me·nag·er·ie \mə-'naj-ə-rē\ *n* : a collection of confined wild animals

¹mend \'mend\ *vb* **1** : IMPROVE, CORRECT ⟨*mend* your ways⟩ **2** : to restore to a whole condition **3** : to improve in health — **mend·er** *n*

synonyms MEND, PATCH, REPAIR mean to take something that has been damaged and make it usable again. MEND suggests making something that has been broken or damaged once again whole or fit for use ⟨*mend* a piece of china⟩ PATCH refers to mending a hole or tear by using the same or similar material ⟨*patched* my pants with scraps of cloth⟩ PATCH may also suggest a hurried, careless job ⟨just *patch* the roof for now⟩ REPAIR suggests a skillful mending of a complicated thing that has been damaged very much ⟨*repaired* our car⟩

²mend *n* **1** : the process of improving ⟨a broken leg on the *mend*⟩ **2** : a mended place

men·folk \'men-ˌfōk\ *or* **men·folks** \-ˌfōks\ *n pl* : the men of a family or community

men·ha·den \men-'hād-n\ *n, pl* **menhaden** : a fish of the Atlantic coast of the United States that is related to the herrings and is a source of oil and fertilizer

¹me·ni·al \'mē-nē-əl\ *adj* : of, relating to,

or suitable for servants : not needing skill ⟨*menial* tasks⟩

²menial *n* : a household servant

men–of–war *pl of* MAN-OF-WAR

men·stru·a·tion \ˌmen-strə-'wā-shən, men-'strā-shən\ *n* : a periodic discharge of bloody fluid from the uterus

-ment \mənt\ *n suffix* **1** : result, goal, or method of a specified action ⟨entangle*ment*⟩ ⟨entertain*ment*⟩ **2** : action : process ⟨develop*ment*⟩ **3** : place of a specified action ⟨encamp*ment*⟩ **4** : state : condition ⟨amaze*ment*⟩

men·tal \'ment-l\ *adj* **1** : of or relating to the mind **2** : done in the mind ⟨*mental* arithmetic⟩ — **men·tal·ly** *adv*

men·tal·i·ty \men-'tal-ət-ē\ *n* : mental power : ability to learn

men·thol \'men-ˌthȯl\ *n* : a white crystalline soothing substance from oils of mint

¹men·tion \'men-chən\ *n* : a brief reference to something

²mention *vb* : to refer to : speak about briefly

menu \'men-yü\ *n* **1** : a list of dishes served at or available for a meal **2** : the dishes or kinds of food served at a meal

Word History The English word *menu* came from a French word with the same spelling and meaning. The French noun that means "menu" came from an adjective that means "small," "slender," or "detailed." Since a menu is a detailed list, this last meaning must have given English and French the noun *menu*.

¹me·ow \mē-'au̇\ *n* : the cry of a cat

²meow *vb* : to utter a meow

mer·can·tile \'mər-kən-ˌtēl, -ˌtīl\ *adj* : of or relating to merchants or trade

¹mer·ce·nary \'mərs-n-ˌer-ē\ *n, pl* **mer·ce·nar·ies** : a soldier from a foreign country hired to fight in an army

²mercenary *adj* **1** : doing something only for the pay or reward **2** : greedy for money

mer·chan·dise \'mər-chən-ˌdīz, -ˌdīs\ *n* : goods that are bought and sold in trade

mer·chant \'mər-chənt\ *n* **1** : a person who carries on trade especially on a large scale or with foreign countries **2** : STOREKEEPER 1

mer·chant·man \'mər-chənt-mən\ *n, pl* **mer·chant·men** \-mən\ : a ship used in trading

merchant marine *n* **1** : the trading ships of a nation **2** : the persons who work in a merchant marine

mer·ci·ful \'mər-si-fəl\ *adj* : having or showing mercy or compassion — **mer·ci·ful·ly** \-fə-lē\ *adv*

mer·ci·less \'mər-si-ləs\ *adj* : having no mercy : PITILESS — **mer·ci·less·ly** *adv*

mer·cu·ric \ˌmər-'kyu̇r-ik\ *adj* : of, relating to, or containing mercury

mer·cu·ry \'mər-kyə-rē\ *n* **1** : a heavy silvery white metallic chemical element that is liquid at ordinary temperatures **2** : the column of mercury in a thermometer or barometer **3** *cap* : the planet that is nearest the sun and has a diameter of about 4700 kilometers

mer·cy \'mər-sē\ *n, pl* **mer·cies** **1** : kind and gentle treatment of a wrongdoer, an opponent, or some unfortunate person **2** : a kind sympathetic disposition : willingness to forgive, spare, or help **3** : a blessing as an act of divine love ⟨the *mercies* of God⟩ **4** : a fortunate happening ⟨it's a *mercy* that we arrived in time⟩

mere \'miər\ *adj, superlative* **mer·est** : nothing more than : SIMPLE ⟨*mere* rumors⟩

mere·ly \'miər-lē\ *adv* : nothing else than : JUST

merge \'mərj\ *vb* **merged; merg·ing** : to be or cause to be combined or blended into a single unit

merg·er \'mər-jər\ *n* : a combination of two or more businesses into one

me·rid·i·an \mə-'rid-ē-ən\ *n* **1** : the highest point reached **2** : any imaginary semicircle on the earth reaching from the north to the south pole **3** : a representation of a meridian on a map or globe numbered according to degrees of longitude

me·ringue \mə-'rang\ *n* **1** : a mixture of beaten white of egg and sugar put on pies or cakes and browned **2** : a shell made of baked meringue and filled with fruit or ice cream

me·ri·no \mə-'rē-nō\ *n, pl* **me·ri·nos** **1** : a

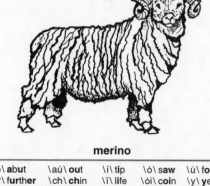

merino

\ə\ abut	\au̇\ out	\i\ tip	\ȯ\ saw	\u̇\ foot
\ər\ further	\ch\ chin	\ī\ life	\ȯi\ coin	\y\ yet
\a\ mat	\e\ pet	\j\ job	\th\ thin	\yü\ few
\ā\ take	\ē\ easy	\ng\ sing	\th\ this	\yu̇\ cure
\ä\ cot, cart	\g\ go	\ō\ bone	\ü\ food	\zh\ vision

sheep of a breed that produces a heavy fleece of white fine wool **2** : a fine soft fabric like cashmere

¹mer·it \'mer-ət\ *n* **1** : the condition or fact of deserving well or ill ⟨students are graded according to *merit*⟩ **2** : ²WORTH 1, VALUE ⟨a suggestion having great *merit*⟩ **3** : a quality worthy of praise : VIRTUE ⟨the *merit* of honesty⟩

²merit *vb* : to be worthy of or have a right to ⟨I think I *merit* a higher mark⟩ **synonyms** see DESERVE

mer·i·to·ri·ous \,mer-ə-'tōr-ē-əs\ *adj* : deserving reward or honor : PRAISEWORTHY — **mer·i·to·ri·ous·ly** *adv*

mer·maid \'mər-,mād\ *n* : an imaginary sea creature usually shown with a woman's body and a fish's tail

mer·man \'mər-,man\ *n, pl* **mer·men** \-,men\ : an imaginary sea creature usually shown with a man's body and a fish's tail

mer·ri·ment \'mer-i-mənt\ *n* : GAIETY, MIRTH

mer·ry \'mer-ē\ *adj* **mer·ri·er; mer·ri·est 1** : full of good humor and good spirits : JOY-OUS **2** : full of gaiety or festivity ⟨a *merry* Christmas⟩ — **mer·ri·ly** \'mer-ə-lē\ *adv*

mer·ry–go–round \'mer-ē-gō-,raund\ *n* : a circular revolving platform fitted with seats and figures of animals on which people sit for a ride

mer·ry·mak·er \'mer-ē-,mā-kər\ *n* : one taking part in merrymaking

mer·ry·mak·ing \'mer-ē-,mā-king\ *n* **1** : merry activity **2** : a festive occasion : PARTY

me·sa \'mā-sə\ *n* : a hill with a flat top and steep sides

mesdames *pl of* MADAM *or of* MRS.

¹mesh \'mesh\ *n* **1** : one of the spaces enclosed by the threads of a net or the wires of a sieve or screen **2** : NETWORK 1, 2 **3** : the coming or fitting together of the teeth of two sets of gears

²mesh *vb* : to fit together : INTERLOCK ⟨gear teeth that *mesh*⟩

Mes·o·zo·ic \,mez-ə-'zō-ik, ,mes-\ *n* : an era of geological history which extends from the Paleozoic to the Cenozoic and in which dinosaurs are present and the first birds and mammals and flowering plants appear

mes·quite \mə-'skēt\ *n* : a spiny shrub or small tree of the southwestern United States and Mexico that is related to the clovers

¹mess \'mes\ *n* **1** : a group of people (as military personnel) who regularly eat together **2** : the meal eaten by a mess **3** : a state of confusion or disorder ⟨left things in a *mess*⟩

²mess *vb* **1** : to take meals with a mess **2** : to make dirty or untidy ⟨*messed* the place up⟩ **3** : to mix up : BUNGLE ⟨*messed* up the schedule⟩ **4** : to work without serious goal : PUTTER **5** : ²FOOL 2, INTERFERE ⟨you'd better not *mess* with them⟩

mes·sage \'mes-ij\ *n* : a communication in writing, in speech, or by signals

mes·sen·ger \'mes-n-jər\ *n* : a person who carries a message or does an errand

Messrs. *pl of* MR.

messy \'mes-ē\ *adj* **mess·i·er; mess·i·est** : UNTIDY — **mess·i·ly** \'mes-ə-lē\ *adv* — **mess·i·ness** \'mes-ē-nəs\ *n*

met *past of* MEET

met·a·bol·ic \,met-ə-'bäl-ik\ *adj* : of or relating to metabolism — **met·a·bol·i·cal·ly** \-i-kə-lē\ *adv*

me·tab·o·lism \mə-'tab-ə-,liz-əm\ *n* : the processes by which a living being uses food to obtain energy and build tissue and disposes of waste material

¹met·al \'met-l\ *n* **1** : a substance (as gold, tin, copper, or bronze) that has a more or less shiny appearance, is a good conduc-tor of electricity and heat, and usually can be made into a wire or hammered into a thin sheet **2** : METTLE ⟨the soldiers showed their *metal*⟩

²metal *adj* : made of metal

me·tal·lic \mə-'tal-ik\ *adj* **1** : of, relating to, or being a metal **2** : containing or made of metal

met·al·lur·gi·cal \,met-l-'ər-ji-kəl\ *adj* : of or relating to metallurgy

met·al·lur·gy \'met-l-,ər-jē\ *n* : the science of obtaining metals from their ores and preparing them for use

meta·mor·phic \,met-ə-'mȯr-fik\ *adj* : formed by the action of pressure, heat, and water that results in a more compact form ⟨a *metamorphic* rock⟩

meta·mor·pho·sis \,met-ə-'mȯr-fə-səs\ *n, pl* **meta·mor·pho·ses** \-fə-,sēz\ : a sud-den and very great change especially in appearance or structure ⟨*metamor-phosis* of a caterpillar into a butterfly⟩

met·a·phor \'met-ə-,fȯr\ *n* : a figure of speech comparing two unlike things with-out using *like* or *as* ⟨"their cheeks were roses" is a *metaphor;* "their cheeks were like roses" is a simile⟩

mete \'mēt\ *vb* **met·ed; met·ing** : ALLOT ⟨*mete* out punishment⟩

me·te·or \'mēt-ē-ər\ *n* : one of the small pieces of matter in the solar system that enter the earth's atmosphere where fric-tion may cause them to glow and form a streak of light

me·te·or·ic \,mēt-ē-'ȯr-ik\ *adj* **1** : of or re-lating to a meteor or group of meteors **2**

: like a meteor in speed or in sudden and temporary brilliance ⟨a *meteoric* career⟩

me·te·or·ite \'mēt-ē-ə-ˌrīt\ *n* : a meteor that reaches the surface of the earth

me·te·o·rol·o·gist \ˌmēt-ē-ə-'räl-ə-jəst\ *n* : a specialist in meteorology

me·te·o·rol·o·gy \ˌmēt-ē-ə-'räl-ə-jē\ *n* : a science that deals with the atmosphere, weather, and weather forecasting

¹me·ter \'mēt-ər\ *n* **1** : a planned rhythm in poetry that is usually repeated **2** : the repeated pattern of musical beats in a measure

²meter *n* : a measure of length on which the metric system is based and which is equal to about 39.37 inches

³meter *n* : an instrument for measuring and sometimes recording the amount of something ⟨light *meter*⟩ ⟨gas *meter*⟩

-m·et·er \m-ət-ər\ *n suffix* : instrument for measuring

meth·od \'meth-əd\ *n* **1** : a certain way of doing something ⟨a *method* of teaching⟩ **2** : careful arrangement : PLAN ⟨work that lacks *method*⟩

me·thod·i·cal \mə-'thäd-i-kəl\ *adj* **1** : showing or done or arranged by method ⟨a *methodical* search⟩ **2** : following a method out of habit : SYSTEMATIC ⟨*methodical* teachers⟩ — **me·thod·i·cal·ly** *adv*

met·ric \'me-trik\ *adj* **1** : of or relating to measurement **2** : of or relating to the metric system

met·ri·cal \'me-tri-kəl\ *adj* : of or relating to meter (as in poetry or music)

metric system *n* : a system of weights and measures in which the meter is the unit of length and the kilogram is the unit of weight

metric ton *n* : a unit of weight equal to 1000 kilograms

met·ro·nome \'me-trə-ˌnōm\ *n* : an instrument that gives repeated ticks to help a music pupil play in exact time

me·trop·o·lis \mə-'träp-ə-ləs\ *n* **1** : the chief or capital city of a country, state, or region **2** : a large or important city

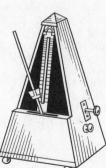

metronome

met·ro·pol·i·tan \ˌme-trə-'päl-ət-n\ *adj* : of, relating to, or like that of a metropolis ⟨in the *metropolitan* area⟩

met·tle \'met-l\ *n* : strength of spirit : COURAGE — **on one's mettle** : aroused to do one's best

¹mew \'myü\ *vb* : to make a meow or a similar sound ⟨*mewing* sea gulls⟩

²mew *n* : MEOW

¹Mex·i·can \'mek-si-kən\ *adj* : of or relating to Mexico or the Mexicans

²Mexican *n* : a person born or living in Mexico

mi \'mē\ *n* : the third note of the musical scale

mi·ca \'mī-kə\ *n* : a mineral that easily breaks into very thin transparent sheets

mice *pl of* MOUSE

micr- *or* **micro-** *prefix* **1** : small : tiny ⟨*microfilm*⟩ **2** : millionth

mi·crobe \'mī-ˌkrōb\ *n* : a very tiny and often harmful plant or animal : MICROORGANISM

mi·cro·film \'mī-krə-ˌfilm\ *n* : a film on which something (as printing or a drawing) is recorded in very much smaller size

mi·crom·e·ter \mī-'kräm-ət-ər\ *n* **1** : an instrument used with a telescope or microscope for measuring very small distances **2** : MICROMETER CALIPER

micrometer caliper *n* : an instrument having a rod moved by fine screw threads and used for making exact measurements

mi·cro·or·gan·ism \ˌmī-krō-'òr-gə-ˌniz-əm\ *n* : an organism (as a bacterium) of microscopic or less than microscopic size

mi·cro·phone \'mī-krə-ˌfōn\ *n* : an instrument in which sound is changed into an electrical effect for transmitting or recording (as in radio or television)

mi·cro·scope \'mī-krə-ˌskōp\ *n* : an instrument with one or more lenses used to help a person to see something very small by making it appear larger

mi·cro·scop·ic \ˌmī-krə-'skäp-ik\ *adj* **1** : of, relating to, or conducted with the microscope ⟨a *microscopic* examination⟩ **2** : so small as to be visible only through a microscope : very tiny — **mi·cro·scop·i·cal·ly** \-i-kə-lē\ *adv*

¹mi·cro·wave \'mī-krō-ˌwāv\ *n* **1** : a radio wave between one millimeter and one meter in wavelength **2** : MICROWAVE OVEN

²microwave *vb* : to cook or heat in a microwave oven

microwave oven *n* : an oven in which food is cooked by the heat produced as a result of penetration of the food by microwaves

\ə\ **abut**	\aů\ **out**	\i\ **tip**	\ò\ **saw**	\ů\ **foot**
\ər\ **further**	\ch\ **chin**	\ī\ **life**	\òi\ **coin**	\y\ **yet**
\a\ **mat**	\e\ **pet**	\j\ **job**	\th\ **thin**	\yü\ **few**
\ā\ **take**	\ē\ **easy**	\ng\ **sing**	\th\ **this**	\yů\ **cure**
\ä\ **cot, cart**	\g\ **go**	\ō\ **bone**	\ü\ **food**	\zh\ **vision**

¹mid \'mid\ *adj* : being the part in the middle

²mid *prep* : AMID

mid·air \'mid-'aər, -'eər\ *n* : a region in the air some distance above the ground ⟨planes crashed in *midair*⟩

mid·day \'mid-,dā\ *n* : NOON

¹mid·dle \'mid-l\ *adj* **1** : equally distant from the ends : CENTRAL ⟨the *middle* house in the row⟩ **2** : being at neither extreme ⟨of *middle* size⟩

²middle *n* : the middle part, point, or position : CENTER ⟨in the *middle* of the room⟩

middle age *n* : the period of life from about forty to about sixty years of age — **mid·dle–aged** \,mid-l-'ājd\ *adj*

Middle Ages *n pl* : the period of European history from about A.D. 500 to about 1500

middle class *n* : a social class between that of the wealthy and the poor

mid·dy \'mid-ē\ *n, pl* **mid·dies** **1** : MIDSHIPMAN **2** : a loose blouse with a collar cut wide and square in the back

midge \'mij\ *n* : a very small fly or gnat

midg·et \'mij-ət\ *n* : one (as a person) that is much smaller than usual or normal

middy 2

mid·night \'mid-,nīt\ *n* : twelve o'clock at night

mid·rib \'mid-,rib\ *n* : the central vein of a leaf

mid·riff \'mid-,rif\ *n* **1** : the middle part of the surface of the human body **2** : a part of a garment that covers the midriff

mid·ship·man \'mid-,ship-mən\ *n, pl* **mid·ship·men** \-mən\ : a student naval officer

¹midst \'midst\ *n* **1** : the inside or central part ⟨in the *midst* of the forest⟩ **2** : a position among the members of a group ⟨a stranger in our *midst*⟩ **3** : the condition of being surrounded ⟨in the *midst* of dangers⟩

²midst *prep* : in the midst of

mid·stream \'mid-'strēm\ *n* : the part of a stream away from both sides

mid·sum·mer \'mid-'səm-ər\ *n* **1** : the middle of summer **2** : the summer solstice

mid·way \'mid-,wā, -'wā\ *adv or adj* : in the middle of the way or distance : HALFWAY

mid·win·ter \'mid-'wint-ər\ *n* **1** : the middle of winter **2** : the winter solstice

mid·year \'mid-,yiər\ *n* : the middle of a year

mien \'mēn\ *n* : a person's appearance or way of acting that shows mood or personality

¹might \'mīt\ *past of* MAY — used as a helping verb to show that something is possible but not likely ⟨we *might* arrive before it rains⟩

²might \'mīt\ *n* : power that can be used (as by a person or group) ⟨our army's *might*⟩

mightn't \'mīt-nt\ : might not

¹mighty \'mīt-ē\ *adj* **might·i·er; might·i·est** **1** : having great power or strength ⟨a *mighty* nation⟩ **2** : done by might : showing great power ⟨*mighty* deeds⟩ **3** : great in influence, size, or effect ⟨a *mighty* famine⟩ — **might·i·ly** \'mīt-l-ē\ *adv*

²mighty *adv* : ²VERY 1 ⟨a *mighty* good friend⟩

mi·grant \'mī-grənt\ *n* : one that migrates

mi·grate \'mī-,grāt\ *vb* **mi·grat·ed; mi·grat·ing** **1** : to move from one country or region to another **2** : to pass from one region to another on a regular schedule ⟨birds *migrating* south for the winter⟩

mi·gra·tion \mī-'grā-shən\ *n* **1** : the act or an instance of migrating **2** : a group of individuals that are migrating

mi·gra·to·ry \'mī-grə-,tōr-ē\ *adj* **1** : having a way of life that includes making migrations ⟨*migratory* workers⟩ **2** : of or relating to migration

mike \'mīk\ *n* : MICROPHONE

milch \'milk, 'milch\ *adj* : giving milk : kept for milking ⟨a *milch* cow⟩

mild \'mīld\ *adj* **1** : gentle in personality or behavior **2** : not strong or harsh in action or effect ⟨*mild* weather⟩ — **mild·ly** *adv* — **mild·ness** *n*

¹mil·dew \'mil-,dü, -,dyü\ *n* **1** : a thin whitish growth of fungus on decaying material or on living plants **2** : a fungus that grows as a mildew

²mildew *vb* : to become affected with mildew

mile \'mīl\ *n* **1** : a measure of distance (**statute mile**) equal to 5280 feet (1609 meters) **2** : a measure of distance (**geographical mile** or **nautical mile**) equal to about 6076 feet (1852 meters)

Word History In English we use the word *mile* for two different lengths. The ancient Roman mile was not the same as either of these. But the English word *mile* comes from the Latin name for the Roman mile. This Latin word came from a phrase that meant "a thousand steps." From the Latin word for "thousand" we also get the words *mill* (a thousandth of a dollar) and *million* (a thousand thousands).

mile·age \'mī-lij\ *n* **1** : an amount of money given for traveling expenses at a certain rate per mile **2** : distance or distance covered in miles **3** : the number of miles that something (as a car or tire) will travel before wearing out **4** : the average number of miles a car or truck will travel on a gallon of fuel

mile·stone \'mīl-,stōn\ *n* **1** : a stone showing the distance in miles to a stated place **2** : an important point in progress or development

¹mil·i·tary \'mil-ə-,ter-ē\ *adj* **1** : of or relating to soldiers, the army, or war ⟨*military* drill⟩ **2** : carried on by soldiers : supported by armed force ⟨a *military* government⟩

²military *n, pl* **military** : members of the armed forces

mi·li·tia \mə-'lish-ə\ *n* : a body of citizens having some military training but called into service only in emergencies

¹milk \'milk\ *n* **1** : a whitish liquid secreted by the breasts or udder of a female mammal as food for her young **2** : a liquid (as a plant juice) like milk

²milk *vb* : to draw off the milk of (as by pressing or sucking) ⟨*milk* a cow⟩

milk·maid \'milk-,mād\ *n* : DAIRYMAID

milk·man \'milk-,man\ *n, pl* **milk·men** \-,men\ : a person who sells or delivers milk

milk of mag·ne·sia \-mag-'nē-shə, -'nē-zhə\ : a white liquid containing an oxide of magnesium in water and used as a laxative

milk shake *n* : a drink made of milk, a flavoring syrup, and ice cream shaken or mixed thoroughly

milk tooth *n* : one of the first and temporary teeth that in humans number twenty

milk·weed \'mil-,kwēd\ *n* : any of a group of plants with milky juice and flowers in dense clusters

milky \'mil-kē\ *adj* **milk·i·er; milk·i·est 1** : like milk in color or thickness **2** : full of or containing milk — **milk·i·ness** *n*

Milky Way *n* **1** : a broad band of light that stretches across the sky and is caused by the light of a very great number of faint stars **2** : MILKY WAY GALAXY

Milky Way galaxy *n* : the galaxy of which the sun and the solar system are a part and which contains the stars that make up the Milky Way

¹mill \'mil\ *n* **1** : a building in which grain is ground into flour **2** : a machine used in processing (as by grinding, crushing, stamping, cutting, or finishing) raw material **3** : a factory using machines ⟨a steel *mill*⟩

²mill *vb* **1** : to grind into flour or powder **2** : to shape or finish by means of a rotating cutter **3** : to give a raised rim to (a coin) **4** : to move about in a circle or in disorder ⟨cattle *milling* about⟩

³mill *n* : one tenth of a cent

mill·er \'mil-ər\ *n* **1** : a person who works in or runs a flour mill **2** : a moth whose wings seem to be covered with flour or dust

mil·let \'mil-ət\ *n* : an annual grass with clusters of small usually white seeds that is grown as a cereal and for animals to graze

milli- *prefix* : thousandth ⟨*milli*meter⟩

mil·li·gram \'mil-ə-,gram\ *n* : a unit of weight equal to ¹⁄₁₀₀₀ gram

mil·li·li·ter \'mil-ə-,lēt-ər\ *n* : a unit of capacity equal to ¹⁄₁₀₀₀ liter

mil·li·me·ter \'mil-ə-,mēt-ər\ *n* : a unit of length equal to ¹⁄₁₀₀₀ meter

mil·li·ner \'mil-ə-nər\ *n* : a person who makes, trims, or sells women's hats

¹mil·lion \'mil-yən\ *n* **1** : one thousand thousands : 1,000,000 **2** : a very large number ⟨*millions* of mosquitoes⟩

²million *adj* : being 1,000,000

mil·lion·aire \,mil-yə-'naər, -'neər\ *n* : a person having a million dollars or more

¹mil·lionth \'mil-yənth\ *adj* : being last in a series of a million

²millionth *n* : number 1,000,000 in a series

mil·li·pede \'mil-ə-,pēd\ *n* : an animal that is an arthropod with a long body somewhat like that of a centipede but with two pairs of legs on most of its many body sections

mill·stone \'mil-,stōn\ *n* : either of two circular stones used for grinding grain

mill wheel *n* : a waterwheel that drives a mill

mim·eo·graph \'mim-ē-ə-,graf\ *n* : a machine for making copies of typewritten, written, or drawn matter by means of stencils

¹mim·ic \'mim-ik\ *adj* : ²IMITATION ⟨a *mimic* war⟩

²mimic *n* : one that mimics another

³mimic *vb* **mim·icked; mim·ick·ing 1** : to imitate very closely **2** : to make fun of by

\ə\ abut	\au̇\ out	\i\ tip	\ȯ\ saw	\u̇\ foot
\ər\ further	\ch\ chin	\ī\ life	\ȯi\ coin	\y\ yet
\a\ mat	\e\ pet	\j\ job	\th\ thin	\yü\ few
\ā\ take	\ē\ easy	\ng\ sing	\th\ this	\yu̇\ cure
\ä\ cot, cart	\g\ go	\ō\ bone	\ü\ food	\zh\ vision

imitating ⟨*mimic* a person's speech⟩ **syn·onyms** see COPY

min·a·ret \,min-ə-'ret\ *n* : a tall slender tower of a mosque with a balcony from which the people are called to prayer

minaret

mince \'mins\ *vb* **minced; minc·ing 1** : to cut or chop very fine ⟨*minced* ham⟩ **2** : to act or speak in an unnaturally dainty way **3** : to keep (what one says) within the bounds of politeness ⟨I'll not *mince* words with you; you know you lied⟩

mince·meat \'min-,smēt\ *n* : a mixture of finely chopped and cooked raisins, apples, suet, spices, and sometimes meat that is used chiefly as a filling for pie (**mince pie**)

¹**mind** \'mīnd\ *n* **1** : MEMORY 1 ⟨keep my advice in *mind*⟩ **2** : the part of a person that feels, understands, thinks, wills, and especially reasons ⟨has a fine *mind*⟩ **3** : INTENTION 1 ⟨I changed my *mind*⟩ **4** : OPINION 1 ⟨speak your *mind*⟩

²**mind** *vb* **1** : to pay attention to : HEED ⟨*mind* what you're doing⟩ **2** : to pay careful attention to and obey ⟨*mind* the teacher⟩ **3** : to be bothered about ⟨never *mind* that mistake⟩ **4** : to object to : DISLIKE ⟨I don't *mind* the cold⟩ **5** : to take charge of ⟨*mind* the children⟩ **synonyms** see OBEY

mind·ed \'mīn-dəd\ *adj* **1** : having a specified kind of mind ⟨small-*minded*⟩ **2** : greatly interested in one thing ⟨safety-*minded*⟩

mind·ful \'mīnd-fəl\ *adj* : keeping in mind

¹**mine** \'mīn\ *pron* : that which belongs to me ⟨that glove is *mine*⟩ ⟨those gloves are *mine*⟩

²**mine** *n* **1** : a pit or tunnel from which minerals (as coal, gold, or diamonds) are taken **2** : an explosive buried in the ground and set to explode when disturbed (as by an enemy soldier or vehicle) **3** : an explosive placed in a case and sunk in the water to sink enemy ships **4** : a rich source of supply ⟨a *mine* of information⟩

³**mine** *vb* **mined; min·ing 1** : to dig a mine **2** : to obtain from a mine ⟨*mine* coal⟩ **3** : to work in a mine **4** : to dig or form mines under a place **5** : to lay military mines in or under ⟨*mine* a field⟩ ⟨*mine* a harbor⟩ — **min·er** *n*

¹**min·er·al** \'min-ə-rəl, 'min-rəl\ *n* **1** : a naturally occurring substance (as diamond or quartz) that results from processes other than those of plants and animals **2** : a naturally occurring substance (as ore, coal, petroleum, natural gas, or water) obtained for humans to use usually from the ground

²**mineral** *adj* **1** : of or relating to minerals **2** : containing gases or mineral salts ⟨*mineral* water⟩

min·gle \'ming-gəl\ *vb* **min·gled; min·gling 1** : to mix or be mixed so that the original parts can still be recognized **2** : to move among others within a group ⟨*mingle* with the crowd⟩

mini- *prefix* : very short or small

¹**min·ia·ture** \'min-ē-ə-,chùr, 'min-i-,chùr\ *n* **1** : a copy on a much reduced scale **2** : a very small portrait especially on ivory or metal

Word History A long time ago books were written by hand. Often titles were done in red to make them stand out against the black ink of the text. The red pigment used for titles was also used for pictures and had a Latin name. The Italians made a word from the Latin name of the red pigment. This Italian word was used for the pictures in books made by hand. The English word *miniature* comes from this Italian word. Since pictures in books done by hand are often quite small, the word *miniature* is used to mean anything that is small.

²**miniature** *adj* : very small : represented on a small scale

min·i·mize \'min-ə-,mīz\ *vb* **min·i·mized; min·i·miz·ing** : to make as small as possible ⟨*minimize* the risks of a dangerous situation⟩

¹**min·i·mum** \'min-ə-məm\ *n, pl* **min·i·ma** \-mə\ *or* **min·i·mums** : the lowest amount

²**minimum** *adj* : being the least possible ⟨a *minimum* loss of time⟩

min·ing \'mī-ning\ *n* : the process or business of working mines

¹**min·is·ter** \'min-əs-tər\ *n* **1** : a Protestant clergyman **2** : a government official at the head of a section of government activities ⟨*minister* of war⟩ **3** : a person who represents his or her government in a foreign country

²**minister** *vb* : to give aid or service ⟨*minister* to the sick⟩

min·is·try \'min-əs-trē\ *n, pl* **min·is·tries 1** : the act of ministering **2** : the office or duties of a minister **3** : a body of ministers

4 : a section of a government headed by a minister

mink \'mingk\ *n* : the soft usually brown fur of a slender animal that looks like the related weasels and has partly webbed feet and a bushy tail

mink

min·now \'min-ō\ *n* **1** : any of various small freshwater fishes (as a shiner) related to the carps **2** : a fish that looks like a true minnow

¹**mi·nor** \'mī-nər\ *adj* **1** : less in size, importance, or value **2** : of or relating to a musical scale having the third tone lowered a half step

²**minor** *n* : a person too young to have full civil rights

mi·nor·i·ty \mə-'nòr-ət-ē\ *n, pl* **mi·nor·i·ties** **1** : the state of being a minor **2** : a number less than half of a total **3** : a part of a population that is in some ways different from others and that is sometimes disliked or given unfair treatment

min·strel \'min-strəl\ *n* **1** : an entertainer in the Middle Ages who sang verses and played a harp **2** : one of a group of entertainers with blackened faces who sing, dance, and tell jokes

¹**mint** \'mint\ *n* **1** : a place where metals are made into coins **2** : a great amount especially of money

²**mint** *vb* **1** : ²COIN 1 ⟨*mint* silver dollars⟩ **2** : to make into coin ⟨*mint* silver⟩

³**mint** *n* **1** : any of a group of fragrant herbs and shrubs (as catnip or peppermint) with square stems **2** : a piece of candy flavored with mint

min·u·end \'min-yə-ˌwend\ *n* : a number from which another number is to be subtracted

min·u·et \ˌmin-yə-'wet\ *n* : a slow stately dance

¹**mi·nus** \'mī-nəs\ *prep* **1** : with the subtraction of : LESS ⟨7 *minus* 4 is 3⟩ **2** : ¹WITHOUT 2 ⟨went outside *minus* my hat⟩

²**minus** *adj* : located in the lower part of a range ⟨a grade of C *minus*⟩

minus sign *n* : a sign − used especially in mathematics to indicate subtraction (as in 8−6=2) or a quantity less than zero (as in −10°)

¹**min·ute** \'min-ət\ *n* **1** : the sixtieth part of an hour or of a degree : sixty seconds **2** : MOMENT 1 ⟨wait a *minute*⟩ **3 minutes** *pl* : a brief record of what happened during a meeting

²**mi·nute** \mī-'nüt, mə-, -'nyüt\ *adj* **mi·nut·er; mi·nut·est** **1** : very small : TINY **2** : paying attention to small details ⟨a *minute* description⟩ — **mi·nute·ly** *adv*

min·ute·man \'min-ət-ˌman\ *n, pl* **min·ute·men** \-ˌmen\ : a member of a group of armed men ready to fight at a minute's notice immediately before and during the American Revolution

mir·a·cle \'mir-i-kəl\ *n* **1** : an extraordinary event taken as a sign of the power of God **2** : something very rare, unusual, or wonderful

mi·rac·u·lous \mə-'rak-yə-ləs\ *adj* : being or being like a miracle — **mi·rac·u·lous·ly** *adv*

mi·rage \mə-'räzh\ *n* : an illusion sometimes seen at sea, in the desert, or over hot pavement that looks like a pool of water or a mirror in which distant objects are glimpsed

¹**mire** \'mīr\ *n* : heavy deep mud

²**mire** *vb* **mired; mir·ing** : to stick or cause to stick fast in mire

¹**mir·ror** \'mir-ər\ *n* **1** : a glass coated on the back with a reflecting substance **2** : something that gives a true likeness or description

²**mirror** *vb* : to reflect in or as if in a mirror

mirth \'mərth\ *n* : the state of being happy or merry as shown by laughter

mirth·ful \'mərth-fəl\ *adj* : full of or showing mirth — **mirth·ful·ly** \-fə-lē\ *adv*

mis- *prefix* **1** : in a way that is bad or wrong ⟨*mis*judge⟩ **2** : bad : wrong ⟨*mis*fortune⟩ **3** : opposite or lack of ⟨*mis*trust⟩

mis·ad·ven·ture \ˌmis-əd-'ven-chər\ *n* : an unfortunate or unpleasant event

mis·be·have \ˌmis-bi-'hāv\ *vb* **mis·be·haved; mis·be·hav·ing** : to behave badly

mis·car·ry \mis-'kar-ē\ *vb* **mis·car·ried; mis·car·ry·ing** : to go wrong : FAIL ⟨the plan *miscarried*⟩

mis·cel·la·neous \ˌmis-ə-'lā-nē-əs, -nyəs\ *adj* : consisting of many things of different sorts

\ə\ **abut**	\aú\ **out**	\i\ **tip**	\ò\ **saw**	\ú\ **foot**
\ər\ **further**	\ch\ **chin**	\ī\ **life**	\òi\ **coin**	\y\ **yet**
\a\ **mat**	\e\ **pet**	\j\ **job**	\th\ **thin**	\yü\ **few**
\ā\ **take**	\ē\ **easy**	\ng\ **sing**	\th\ **this**	\yú\ **cure**
\ä\ **cot, cart**	\g\ **go**	\ō\ **bone**	\ü\ **food**	\zh\ **vision**

mis·chance \mis-'chans\ *n* **1** : bad luck **2** : a piece of bad luck : MISHAP

mis·chief \'mis-chəf\ *n* **1** : injury or damage caused by a person **2** : conduct that annoys or bothers ⟨keep out of *mischief*⟩

mis·chie·vous \'mis-chə-vəs\ *adj* **1** : harming or intended to do harm ⟨*mischievous* gossip⟩ **2** : causing or likely to cause minor injury or harm ⟨a *mischievous* puppy⟩ **3** : showing a spirit of irresponsible fun or playfulness ⟨*mischievous* behavior⟩ — **mis·chie·vous·ly** *adv* — **mis·chie·vous·ness** *n*

¹mis·con·duct \mis-'kän-,dəkt\ *n* : wrong conduct : bad behavior

²mis·con·duct \,mis-kən-'dəkt\ *vb* : to manage badly

mis·count \mis-'kaúnt\ *vb* : to count incorrectly

mis·cre·ant \'mis-krē-ənt\ *n* : VILLAIN, RASCAL

mis·cue \mis-'kyü\ *n* : ²MISTAKE 2

mis·deal \mis-'dēl\ *vb* **mis·dealt** \-'delt\; **mis·deal·ing** \-'dē-ling\ : to deal in an incorrect way ⟨*misdeal* cards⟩

mis·deed \mis-'dēd\ *n* : a bad action

mis·di·rect \,mis-də-'rekt\ *vb* : to direct incorrectly

mi·ser \'mī-zər\ *n* : a stingy person who lives poorly in order to store away money

mis·er·a·ble \'miz-ə-rə-bəl, 'miz-ər-bəl\ *adj* **1** : very unsatisfactory ⟨a *miserable* dinner⟩ **2** : causing great discomfort ⟨a *miserable* cold⟩ **3** : very unhappy or distressed : WRETCHED — **mis·er·a·bly** \-blē\ *adv*

mi·ser·ly \'mī-zər-lē\ *adj* : of, relating to, or like a miser

mis·ery \'miz-ə-rē, 'miz-rē\ *n, pl* **mis·er·ies** : suffering or distress due to being poor, in pain, or unhappy

mis·fit \mis-'fit, 'mis-,fit\ *n* **1** : something that fits badly **2** : a person who cannot adjust to an environment

mis·for·tune \mis-'fȯr-chən\ *n* **1** : bad luck **2** : an unfortunate situation or event

mis·giv·ing \mis-'giv-ing\ *n* : a feeling of distrust or doubt especially about what is going to happen

mis·guid·ed \mis-'gīd-əd\ *adj* : having mistaken ideas or rules of conduct

mis·hap \'mis-,hap\ *n* : an unfortunate accident

mis·judge \mis-'jəj\ *vb* **mis·judged; mis·judg·ing** : to judge incorrectly or unjustly

mis·lay \mis-'lā\ *vb* **mis·laid** \-'lād\; **mis·lay·ing** : to put in a place later forgotten : LOSE **synonyms** see MISPLACE

mis·lead \mis-'lēd\ *vb* **mis·led** \-'led\;

mis·lead·ing : to lead in a wrong direction or into error

mis·place \mis-'plās\ *vb* **mis·placed; mis·plac·ing** **1** : to put in a wrong place ⟨*misplace* a comma⟩ **2** : MISLAY

synonyms MISPLACE and MISLAY mean to put in the wrong place. MISPLACE may mean to put something in a place that is not its usual location ⟨someone seems to have *misplaced* the crayons⟩ MISPLACE may also suggest putting something where it should not have been at all ⟨I *misplaced* my confidence in them⟩ MISLAY stresses not only placing something in the wrong location but also forgetting that location ⟨I *mislaid* my keys⟩

mis·print \'mis-,print\ *n* : a mistake in printing

mis·pro·nounce \,mis-prə-'naúns\ *vb* **mis·pro·nounced; mis·pro·nounc·ing** : to pronounce in a way considered incorrect

mis·pro·nun·ci·a·tion \,mis-prə-,nən-sē-'ā-shən\ *n* : incorrect pronunciation

mis·read \mis-'rēd\ *vb* **mis·read** \-'red\; **mis·read·ing** \-'rēd-ing\ **1** : to read incorrectly **2** : MISUNDERSTAND 2

mis·rep·re·sent \,mis-,rep-ri-'zent\ *vb* : to give a false or misleading idea of

¹miss \'mis\ *vb* **1** : to fail to hit, catch, reach, or get ⟨*miss* the target⟩ ⟨*miss* the ball⟩ **2** : ¹ESCAPE 2 ⟨just *missed* being hit by the falling rock⟩ **3** : to fail to have or go to ⟨were late and *missed* their lunch⟩ ⟨*miss* the bus⟩ **4** : to be aware of the absence of : want to be with ⟨*miss* an absent friend⟩

²miss *n* : failure to hit or catch

³miss *n* **1** — used as a title before the name of an unmarried woman ⟨*Miss* Doe⟩ **2** : a young woman or girl ⟨styles for *misses* and women⟩

mis·shap·en \mis-'shā-pən\ *adj* : badly shaped

mis·sile \'mis-əl\ *n* : an object (as a stone, arrow, bullet, or rocket) that is dropped, thrown, shot, or launched usually so as to strike something at a distance

miss·ing \'mis-ing\ *adj* **1** : ¹ABSENT 1 ⟨*missing* persons⟩ **2** : ²LOST 4 ⟨a *missing* book⟩

mis·sion \'mish-ən\ *n* **1** : a group of missionaries **2** : a place where the work of missionaries is carried on **3** : a group of persons sent by a government to represent it in a foreign country **4** : a task that is assigned or begun

¹mis·sion·ary \'mish-ə-,ner-ē\ *adj* : of or relating to religious missions ⟨a *missionary* society⟩

²mis·sion·ary *n, pl* **mis·sion·ar·ies** : a person sent (as to a foreign country) to spread a religious faith

mis·sive \'mis-iv\ *n* : ¹LETTER 2

mis·spell \mis-'spel\ *vb* : to spell in an incorrect way

mis·spend \mis-'spend\ *vb* **mis·spent** \-'spent\; **mis·spend·ing** : ²WASTE 2

mis·step \mis-'step\ *n* **1** : a wrong step **2** : ²MISTAKE 2, SLIP

¹mist \'mist\ *n* **1** : particles of water floating in the air or falling as fine rain **2** : something that keeps one from seeing or understanding clearly ⟨the meaning is lost in the *mist* of time⟩

²mist *vb* **1** : to be or become misty **2** : to become or cause to become dim or blurred ⟨eyes *misted* with tears⟩ **3** : to cover with mist ⟨the windshield was *misted* over⟩

¹mis·take \mə-'stāk\ *vb* **mis·took** \mə-'stük\; **mis·tak·en** \mə-'stā-kən\; **mis·tak·ing 1** : MISUNDERSTAND 2 **2** : to fail to recognize correctly ⟨*mistook* me for someone else⟩

²mistake *n* **1** : a wrong judgment **2** : a wrong action or statement **synonyms** see ERROR

mis·tak·en \mə-'stā-kən\ *adj* **1** : being in error : judging wrongly ⟨*mistaken* about the time⟩ **2** : ²WRONG 2, INCORRECT ⟨a *mistaken* idea⟩ — **mis·tak·en·ly** *adv*

mis·ter \'mis-tər\ *n* **1** — used sometimes in writing instead of the usual *Mr.* **2** : SIR 2 ⟨do you want a paper, *Mister*⟩

mis·tle·toe \'mis-əl-ˌtō\ *n* : a green plant with waxy white berries that grows on the branches and trunks of trees

mis·treat \mis-'trēt\ *vb* : to treat badly : ABUSE

mis·tress \'mis-trəs\ *n* : a woman who has control or authority ⟨the *mistress* of the household⟩

mistletoe

¹mis·trust \mis-'trəst\ *n* : ²DISTRUST

²mistrust *vb* **1** : ¹DISTRUST, SUSPECT **2** : to lack confidence in ⟨they *mistrust* your abilities⟩

misty \'mis-tē\ *adj* **mist·i·er; mist·i·est 1** : full of mist ⟨a *misty* valley⟩ **2** : clouded by or as if by mist ⟨through *misty* eyes⟩ **3** : VAGUE 3, indistinct ⟨a *misty* memory⟩ — **mist·i·ly** \-tə-lē\ *adv* — **mist·i·ness** \-tē-nəs\ *n*

mis·un·der·stand \ˌmis-ˌən-dər-'stand\ *vb* **mis·un·der·stood** \-'stüd\; **mis·un·der·stand·ing 1** : to fail to understand **2** : to take in a wrong meaning or way

mis·un·der·stand·ing \ˌmis-ˌən-dər-'stan-ding\ *n* **1** : a failure to understand **2** : DISAGREEMENT 3, QUARREL

¹mis·use \mis-'yüz\ *vb* **mis·used; mis·us·ing 1** : to use in a wrong way **2** : ¹ABUSE 3, MISTREAT

²mis·use \mis-'yüs\ *n* : incorrect or improper use ⟨*misuse* of public funds⟩

mite \'mīt\ *n* **1** : any of various tiny spiderlike animals often living on plants, animals, and stored foods **2** : a very small coin or amount of money **3** : a very small object or creature

mi·to·sis \mī-'tō-səs\ *n, pl* **mi·to·ses** \-'tō-ˌsēz\ : a process of cell division in which two new nuclei are formed each containing the original number of chromosomes

mitt \'mit\ *n* **1** : MITTEN **2** : a baseball catcher's or first baseman's glove

mit·ten \'mit-n\ *n* : a covering for the hand and wrist having a separate division for the thumb only

¹mix \'miks\ *vb* **1** : to make into one mass by stirring together : BLEND **2** : to make by combining different things **3** : to become one mass through blending ⟨oil will not *mix* with water⟩ **4** : CONFUSE 1 — **mixer** *n*

> **synonyms** MIX and BLEND mean to combine into a whole that is more or less the same all over. MIX suggests a fairly complete combining in which the elements may or may not lose their individual identity ⟨*mix* several vegetables for a salad⟩ ⟨*mix* wine and water⟩ BLEND suggests a complete uniting of similar things so that the original parts cannot be separated or recognized ⟨*blend* milk and syrup⟩

²mix *n* : MIXTURE 2

mixed \'mikst\ *adj* **1** : made up of two or more kinds ⟨*mixed* candy⟩ **2** : made up of persons of both sexes ⟨*mixed* company⟩

mixed number *or* **mixed numeral** *n* : a number (as 1⅔) made up of a whole number and a fraction

mix·ture \'miks-chər\ *n* **1** : the act of mixing **2** : something mixed or being mixed **3** : two or more substances mixed together in such a way that each remains un-

\ə\ abut	\au̇\ out	\i\ tip	\ȯ\ saw	\u̇\ foot
\ər\ further	\ch\ chin	\ī\ life	\ȯi\ coin	\y\ yet
\a\ mat	\e\ pet	\j\ job	\th\ thin	\yü\ few
\ā\ take	\ē\ easy	\ng\ sing	\th\ this	\yu̇\ cure
\ä\ cot, cart	\g\ go	\ō\ bone	\ü\ food	\zh\ vision

changed ⟨sand and sugar form a *mix-ture*⟩

mix-up \'mik-ˌsəp\ *n* : an instance of confusion ⟨a *mix-up* about the date⟩

miz·zen \'miz-n\ *n* **1** : a fore-and-aft sail set on the mizzenmast **2** : MIZZENMAST

miz·zen·mast \'miz-n-ˌmast, -məst\ *n* : the mast behind or next behind the mainmast

¹moan \'mōn\ *n* **1** : a long low sound showing pain or grief **2** : a mournful sound

²moan *vb* **1** : COMPLAIN 1 **2** : to utter a moan

moat \'mōt\ *n* : a deep wide ditch around the walls of a castle or fort that is usually filled with water

¹mob \'mäb\ *n* **1** : the common masses of people **2** : a rowdy excited crowd

²mob *vb* **mobbed; mob·bing** : to crowd about and attack or annoy

¹mo·bile \'mō-bəl, -ˌbēl, -ˌbīl\ *adj* **1** : easily moved : MOVABLE ⟨*mobile* television cameras⟩ **2** : changing quickly in expression ⟨a *mobile* face⟩

²mo·bile \'mō-ˌbēl\ *n* : an artistic structure whose parts can be moved especially by air currents

mo·bi·lize \'mō-bə-ˌlīz\ *vb* **mo·bi·lized; mo·bi·liz·ing** : to assemble (as military forces) and make ready for action

moc·ca·sin \'mäk-ə-sən\ *n* **1** : a soft shoe with no heel and the sole and sides made of one piece **2** : a poisonous snake of the southern United States

moccasin flower *n* : LADY'S SLIPPER

¹mock \'mäk\ *vb* **1** : to treat with scorn : RIDICULE **2** : ³MIMIC 2

²mock *adj* : not real : MAKE-BELIEVE ⟨a *mock* battle⟩

mock·ery \'mäk-ə-rē\ *n, pl* **mock·er·ies 1** : the act of mocking **2** : a bad imitation : FAKE ⟨a *mockery* of justice⟩

mock·ing·bird \'mäk-ing-ˌbərd\ *n* : a songbird of the southern United States noted for its sweet song and imitations of other birds

mock orange *n* : SYRINGA

¹mode \'mōd\ *n* **1** : a particular form or variety of something **2** : a form or manner of expressing or acting : WAY ⟨a *mode* of travel⟩

²mode *n* : a popular fashion or style

¹mod·el \'mäd-l\ *n* **1** : a small but exact copy of a thing **2** : a pattern or figure of something to be made **3** : a person who sets a good example ⟨a *model* of politeness⟩ **4** : a person who poses for an artist or photographer **5** : a person who wears and displays garments that are for sale **6** : a special type of a product ⟨our car is a recent *model*⟩

synonyms MODEL, EXAMPLE, and IDEAL mean something that is set before one for guidance or imitation. MODEL suggests that the thing or person is very worthy of imitation ⟨a saint who can be a *model* for all children⟩ EXAMPLE usually suggests that the person, act, or conduct is likely to be copied, even though this may not always be a good thing ⟨parents are *examples* for their children⟩ IDEAL suggests something, either real or imagined, to be the best of its kind that can exist ⟨the *ideal* of beauty⟩

²model *vb* **mod·eled** *or* **mod·elled; mod·el·ing** *or* **mod·el·ling 1** : to plan or shape after a pattern ⟨a sports car *modeled* on a racing car⟩ **2** : to make a model of ⟨*model* a dog in clay⟩ **3** : to act or serve as a model ⟨*model* for an artist⟩

³model *adj* **1** : worthy of being imitated ⟨a *model* student⟩ **2** : being a miniature copy ⟨a *model* airplane⟩

¹mod·er·ate \'mäd-ə-rət\ *adj* **1** : neither too much nor too little ⟨*moderate* heat⟩ **2** : neither very good nor very bad ⟨*moderate* success⟩ **3** : not expensive : REASONABLE ⟨*moderate* rates⟩ — **mod·er·ate·ly** *adv*

²mod·er·ate \'mäd-ə-ˌrāt\ *vb* **mod·er·at·ed; mod·er·at·ing** : to make or become less violent or severe

mod·er·a·tion \ˌmäd-ə-'rā-shən\ *n* **1** : the act of moderating **2** : the condition of being moderate

mod·ern \'mäd-ərn\ *adj* **1** : of, relating to, or characteristic of the present time or times not long past ⟨*modern* machinery⟩ **2** : of the period from about 1500 ⟨*modern* history⟩

mod·ern·ize \'mäd-ər-ˌnīz\ *vb* **mod·ern·ized; mod·ern·iz·ing** : to make or become modern

mod·est \'mäd-əst\ *adj* **1** : having a limited and not too high opinion of oneself and one's abilities : not boastful ⟨a *modest* winner⟩ **2** : limited in size or amount ⟨*modest* wealth⟩ **3** : clean and proper in thought, conduct, and dress — **mod·est·ly** *adv*

mod·es·ty \'mäd-ə-stē\ *n* : the quality of being modest

mod·i·fi·ca·tion \ˌmäd-ə-fə-'kā-shən\ *n* **1** : the act of modifying **2** : the result of modifying : a slightly changed form

mod·i·fi·er \'mäd-ə-ˌfi-ər\ *n* : a word (as an adjective or adverb) used with another word to limit its meaning

mod·i·fy \'mäd-ə-ˌfi\ *vb* **mod·i·fied; mod·i·fy·ing 1** : to make changes in ⟨*modify* a plan⟩ **2** : to lower or reduce in amount or scale ⟨*modify* a punishment⟩ **3** : to limit in meaning : QUALIFY ⟨"green" in the phrase "green gloves" *modifies* the word "gloves"⟩

mod·u·late \'mäj-ə-ˌlāt\ *vb* **mod·u·lat·ed; mod·u·lat·ing** **1** : to bring into proper proportion **2** : to tone down : SOFTEN ⟨*modulate* your voice⟩

mod·ule \'mäj-ˌül\ *n* : an independent unit of a spacecraft ⟨a command *module*⟩

mo·hair \'mō-ˌhaər, -ˌheər\ *n* : a fabric or yarn made from the long silky hair of an Asian goat

Mohammedan, Mohammedanism *variant of* MUHAMMADAN, MUHAMMADANISM

moist \'mȯist\ *adj* : slightly wet : DAMP — **moist·ness** *n*

moist·en \'mȯis-n\ *vb* : to make moist

mois·ture \'mȯis-chər\ *n* : a small amount of liquid that causes moistness

mo·lar \'mō-lər\ *n* : a tooth with a broad surface used for grinding : a back tooth

Word History A millstone is a large stone used for grinding grain. We have teeth, called *molars*, that are also used for grinding. The English word *molar* comes from a Latin word that means "mill" or "millstone." The English word *mill* also comes from this Latin word.

mo·las·ses \mə-'las-əz\ *n* : a thick brown syrup that drains from sugar as it is being made

¹mold *or* **mould** \'mōld\ *n* : light rich crumbly earth that contains decaying material

²mold *or* **mould** *n* **1** : a hollow form in which something is shaped ⟨a jelly *mold*⟩ **2** : something shaped in a mold ⟨a *mold* of jelly⟩

³mold *or* **mould** *vb* **1** : to work and press into shape ⟨*mold* loaves of bread⟩ **2** : to form in or as if in a mold

⁴mold *n* **1** : an often woolly surface growth of fungus on damp or decaying material **2** : a fungus that forms mold

⁵mold *vb* : to become moldy

mol·der \'mōl-dər\ *vb* : to crumble to bits by slow decay

mold·ing \'mōl-ding\ *n* **1** : the act or work of a person who molds **2** : a strip of material having a shaped surface and used as a decoration (as on a wall or the edge of a table)

moldy \'mōl-dē\ *adj* **mold·i·er; mold·i·est** : covered with or containing mold

¹mole \'mōl\ *n* : a small usually brown spot on the skin

²mole *n* : a small burrowing animal with very soft fur and very tiny eyes

mo·lec·u·lar \mə-'lek-yə-lər\ *adj* : of or relating to a molecule

mol·e·cule \'mäl-i-ˌkyül\ *n* **1** : the smallest portion of a substance having the properties of the substance ⟨a *molecule* of water⟩ **2** : a very small particle

mole·hill \'mōl-ˌhil\ *n* : a little ridge of earth pushed up by moles as they burrow underground

mo·lest \mə-'lest\ *vb* : to disturb or injure by interfering

mol·li·fy \'mäl-ə-ˌfi\ *vb* **mol·li·fied; mol·li·fy·ing** : to soothe in temper or disposition

mol·lusk \'mäl-əsk\ *n* : any of a large group of animals (as clams, snails, and octopuses) most of which live in water and have the body protected by a limy shell

molt *or* **moult** \'mōlt\ *vb* : to shed outer material (as hair, shell, or horns) that will be replaced by a new growth

mol·ten \'mōlt-n\ *adj* : melted especially by very great heat ⟨*molten* metal⟩

mo·lyb·de·num \mə-'lib-də-nəm\ *n* : a white metallic chemical element used in some steel to give greater strength and hardness

mom \'mäm, 'məm\ *n, often cap* : ¹MOTHER 1

mo·ment \'mō-mənt\ *n* **1** : a very brief time ⟨it disappeared in a *moment*⟩ **2** : IMPORTANCE ⟨a subject of great *moment*⟩

mo·men·tary \'mō-mən-ˌter-ē\ *adj* : lasting only a moment ⟨a *momentary* fright⟩ — **mo·men·tari·ly** \ˌmō-mən-'ter-ə-lē\ *adv*

mo·men·tous \mō-'ment-əs\ *adj* : very important ⟨a *momentous* decision⟩ — **mo·men·tous·ness** *n*

mo·men·tum \mō-'ment-əm\ *n* : the force that a moving body has because of its weight and motion

mon- *or* **mono-** *prefix* : one : single : alone ⟨*mono*syllable⟩

mon·arch \'män-ərk, -ˌärk\ *n* **1** : a person

monarch 2

\ə\ abut	\au̇\ out	\i\ tip	\ȯ\ saw	\u̇\ foot
\ər\ further	\ch\ chin	\ī\ life	\ȯi\ coin	\y\ yet
\a\ mat	\e\ pet	\j\ job	\th\ thin	\yü\ few
\ā\ take	\ē\ easy	\ng\ sing	\t͟h\ this	\yu̇\ cure
\ä\ cot, cart	\g\ go	\ō\ bone	\ü\ food	\zh\ vision

who reigns over a kingdom or empire **2** : a large orange and black American butterfly

mon·ar·chy \'män-ər-kē\ *n*, *pl* **mon·ar·chies 1** : a state or country having a monarch **2** : the system of government by a monarch

mon·as·tery \'män-əs-ˌter-ē\ *n*, *pl* **mon·as·ter·ies** : a place where a community of monks live and work

mo·nas·tic \mə-'nas-tik\ *adj* : of or relating to monks or monasteries ⟨took *monastic* vows⟩ ⟨*monastic* life⟩

Mon·day \'mən-dē\ *n* : the second day of the week

mon·e·tary \'män-ə-ˌter-ē\ *adj* : of or relating to money

mon·ey \'mən-ē\ *n*, *pl* **mon·eys** *or* **mon·ies** \-ēz\ **1** : metal (as gold, silver, or copper) coined or stamped and issued for use in buying and selling **2** : a printed or engraved certificate (**paper money**) legal for use in place of metal money **3** : wealth figured in terms of money

money order *n* : a piece of paper like a check that can be bought (as at a post office) and that tells another office to pay the sum of money printed on it to the one named

¹Mon·go·lian \män-'gōl-yən\ *adj* : of or relating to Mongolia or the Mongolians

²Mongolian *n* : a person born or living in Mongolia

mon·goose \'män-ˌgüs, 'mäng-ˌgüs\ *n*, *pl* **mon·goos·es** : a long thin furry animal that eats snakes, eggs, and rodents

mongoose

¹mon·grel \'məng-grəl, 'mäng-\ *n* : one (as a plant, person, or thing) of mixed or uncertain kind or origin

²mongrel *adj* : of mixed or uncertain kind or origin

¹mon·i·tor \'män-ət-ər\ *n* **1** : a pupil in a school picked for a special duty (as keeping order) **2** : a person or thing that monitors something

²monitor *vb* : to watch or check for a special reason ⟨*monitor* an enemy's radio broadcast⟩

monk \'məngk\ *n* : a member of a religious group of men who form a community and promise to stay poor, obey all the laws of their community, and not get married

¹mon·key \'məng-kē\ *n*, *pl* **mon·keys 1** : any of a group of mostly tropical furry animals that are like humans in many ways and are the nearest to humans in the animal kingdom — used especially of the smaller ones with long tails rather than the apes **2** : a mischievous child

²monkey *vb* **mon·keyed; mon·key·ing 1** : to act in a mischievous way ⟨just *monkeying* around⟩ **2** : ²TRIFLE **3**, FOOL ⟨don't *monkey* with the lawn mower⟩

mon·key·shine \'məng-kē-ˌshīn\ *n* : PRANK

monkey wrench *n* : a wrench with one fixed and one adjustable jaw

monks·hood \'məngks-ˌhüd\ *n* : a tall poisonous Old World plant related to the buttercups that is grown for its white or purplish flowers that are shaped like hoods or as a source of drugs

mono- — see MON-

mono·gram \'män-ə-ˌgram\ *n* : a design usually made by combining two or more of a person's initials

monkshood

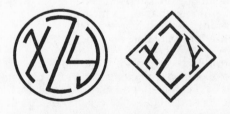

monograms

mono·plane \'män-ə-ˌplān\ *n* : an airplane with only one set of wings

mo·nop·o·lize \mə-'näp-ə-ˌlīz\ *vb* **mo·nop·o·lized; mo·nop·o·liz·ing** : to get or have complete control over ⟨*monopolized* the conversation⟩

mo·nop·o·ly \mə-'näp-ə-lē\ *n, pl* **mo·nop·o·lies** **1** : complete control of the entire supply of goods or a service in a certain market **2** : complete possession ⟨has no *monopoly* on bad manners⟩ **3** : a person or group having a monopoly

mono·syl·la·ble \'män-ə-ˌsil-ə-bəl\ *n* : a word of one syllable

mo·not·o·nous \mə-'nät-n-əs\ *adj* : boring from being always the same — **mo·not·o·nous·ly** *adv*

mo·not·o·ny \mə-'nät-n-ē\ *n, pl* **mo·not·o·nies** : a boring lack of change

mon·soon \män-'sün\ *n* **1** : a wind in the Indian ocean and southern Asia that blows from the southwest from April to October and from the northeast from October to April **2** : the rainy season that comes with the southwest monsoon

mon·ster \'män-stər\ *n* **1** : an animal or plant that is very unlike the usual type **2** : a strange or horrible creature **3** : something unusually large **4** : an extremely wicked or cruel person

mon·strous \'män-strəs\ *adj* **1** : unusually large : ENORMOUS **2** : very bad or wrong ⟨a *monstrous* error⟩ **3** : very different from the usual form : ABNORMAL — **mon·strous·ly** *adv*

month \'mənth\ *n* : one of the twelve parts into which the year is divided

¹month·ly \'mənth-lē\ *adj* **1** : happening, done, or published every month **2** : figured in terms of one month ⟨*monthly* salary⟩ **3** : lasting a month

²monthly *n, pl* **month·lies** : a magazine published every month

mon·u·ment \'män-yə-mənt\ *n* **1** : a structure (as a building, stone, or statue) made to keep alive the memory of a person or event **2** : a work, saying, or deed that lasts or is worth keeping or remembering

¹moo \'mü\ *vb* **mooed; moo·ing** : to make a moo : LOW

²moo *n, pl* **moos** : the low sound made by a cow

¹mood \'müd\ *n* : a state or frame of mind : DISPOSITION ⟨in a good *mood*⟩

²mood *n* : a set of forms of a verb that show whether the action or state expressed is to be thought of as a fact, a command, or a wish or possibility

moody \'müd-ē\ *adj* **mood·i·er; mood·i·est** : often feeling gloomy or in a bad mood — **mood·i·ly** \'müd-l-ē\ *adv* — **mood·i·ness** \'müd-ē-nəs\ *n*

¹moon \'mün\ *n* **1** : the natural celestial body that shines by reflecting light from the sun and revolves about the earth in about 29½ days **2** : SATELLITE 1 **3** : MONTH

²moon *vb* : to waste time by daydreaming

moon·beam \'mün-ˌbēm\ *n* : a ray of light from the moon

moon·light \'mün-ˌlīt\ *n* : the light of the moon

moon·stone \'mün-ˌstōn\ *n* : a partly transparent shining stone used as a gem

¹moor \'mùr\ *n* : an area of open land that is too wet or too poor for farming

²moor *vb* : to fasten in place with cables, lines, or anchors ⟨*moor* a boat⟩

moor·ing \'mùr-ing\ *n* **1** : a place where or an object to which a boat can be fastened **2** : a chain or line by which an object is moored

moor·land \'mùr-lənd\ *n* : land consisting of moors

moose \'müs\ *n* : a large deerlike animal with broad flattened antlers and humped shoulders that lives in forests of Canada and the northern United States

¹mop \'mäp\ *n* **1** : a tool for cleaning made of a bundle of cloth or yarn or a sponge fastened to a handle **2** : something that looks like a cloth or yarn mop ⟨a *mop* of hair⟩

²mop *vb* **mopped; mop·ping** : to wipe or clean with or as if with a mop

¹mope \'mōp\ *vb* **moped; mop·ing** : to be in a dull and sad state of mind

²mope *n* : a person without any energy or enthusiasm

mo·raine \mə-'rān\ *n* : a pile of earth and stones left by a glacier

¹mor·al \'mòr-əl\ *adj* **1** : concerned with or relating to what is right and wrong in human behavior ⟨*moral* problems⟩ ⟨a *moral* code⟩ **2** : able or fit to teach a lesson ⟨a *moral* story⟩ **3** : ¹GOOD 7, VIRTUOUS ⟨lead a *moral* life⟩ **4** : able to tell right from wrong ⟨humans are *moral* beings⟩ — **mor·al·ly** *adv*

²moral *n* **1** : the lesson to be learned from a story or experience **2 morals** *pl* : moral conduct ⟨people of bad *morals*⟩ **3 morals** *pl* : moral teachings or rules of behavior

mo·rale \mə-'ral\ *n* : the condition of the mind or feelings (as in relation to enthusiasm, spirit, or hope) of an individual or group

mo·ral·i·ty \mə-'ral-ət-ē\ *n, pl* **mo·ral·i-**

\ə\ abut	\aù\ out	\i\ tip	\ò\ saw	\ù\ foot
\ər\ further	\ch\ chin	\ī\ life	\òi\ coin	\y\ yet
\a\ mat	\e\ pet	\j\ job	\th\ thin	\yü\ few
\ā\ take	\ē\ easy	\ng\ sing	\th\ this	\yù\ cure
\ä\ cot, cart	\g\ go	\ō\ bone	\ü\ food	\zh\ vision

ties **1** : moral quality : VIRTUE ⟨judge the *morality* of an action⟩ **2** : moral conduct

mo·rass \mə-'ras\ *n* : MARSH, SWAMP

mor·bid \'mȯr-bəd\ *adj* : not healthy or normal ⟨*morbid* ideas⟩

¹more \'mōr\ *adj* **1** : greater in amount, number, or size ⟨you like *more* sugar in your tea than I do⟩ **2** : ¹EXTRA, ADDITIONAL ⟨take *more* time⟩

²more *adv* **1** : in addition ⟨wait one day *more*⟩ **2** : to a greater extent — often used with an adjective or adverb to form the comparative ⟨*more* active⟩ ⟨*more* actively⟩

³more *n* **1** : a greater amount or number ⟨got *more* than I expected⟩ **2** : an additional amount ⟨too full to eat any *more*⟩

more·over \mōr-'ō-vər\ *adv* : in addition to what has been said : BESIDES

morn \'mȯrn\ *n* : MORNING

morn·ing \'mȯr-ning\ *n* : the early part of the day : the time from sunrise to noon

morning glory *n* : a vine that climbs by twisting around something and has large bright flowers that close in the sunshine

morning glory

morning star *n* : any of the planets Venus, Jupiter, Mars, Mercury, or Saturn when rising before the sun

mo·ron \'mōr-ˌän\ *n* : a person with less than ordinary mental ability but able to do simple routine work

mor·phine \'mȯr-ˌfēn\ *n* : a habit-forming drug made from opium and used often to relieve pain

mor·row \'mär-ō\ *n* : the next following day

mor·sel \'mȯr-səl\ *n* **1** : a small piece of food : BITE **2** : a small amount : a little piece

¹mor·tal \'mȯrt-l\ *adj* **1** : capable of causing death : FATAL ⟨a *mortal* wound⟩ **2** : certain to die ⟨we all are *mortal*⟩ **3** : very unfriendly ⟨a *mortal* enemy⟩ **4** : very great or overpowering ⟨*mortal*

fear⟩ **5** : ¹HUMAN 1 ⟨*mortal* power⟩ **synonyms** see DEADLY — **mor·tal·ly** *adv*

²mortal *n* : a human being

¹mor·tar \'mȯrt-ər\ *n* **1** : a strong deep bowl in which substances are pounded or crushed with a pestle **2** : a short light cannon used to shoot shells high into the air

²mortar *n* : a building material made of lime and cement mixed with sand and water that is spread between bricks or stones so as to hold them together when it hardens

mor·ti·fy \'mȯrt-ə-ˌfi\ *vb* **mor·ti·fied; mor·ti·fy·ing** : to embarrass greatly : SHAME ⟨your bad behavior *mortifies* me⟩

mo·sa·ic \mō-'zā-ik\ *n* : a decoration on a surface made by setting small pieces of glass or stone of different colors into another material so as to make patterns or pictures

Moslem *variant of* MUSLIM

mosque \'mäsk\ *n* : a Muslim place of worship

mos·qui·to \mə-'skēt-ō\ *n, pl* **mos·qui·toes** : a small two-winged fly the female of which punctures the skin of people and animals to suck their blood

moss \'mȯs\ *n* **1** : any of a class of plants that have no flowers and grow as small leafy stems in cushion-like patches clinging to rocks, bark, or damp ground **2** : any of various plants (as lichens) resembling moss

mossy \'mȯs-ē\ *adj* **moss·i·er; moss·i·est** : like or covered with moss

¹most \'mōst\ *adj* **1** : the majority of ⟨*most* people believe this⟩ **2** : greatest in amount or extent ⟨the youngest of the group had the *most* courage⟩

²most *adv* **1** : to the greatest or highest level or extent — often used with an adjective or adverb to form the superlative ⟨*most* active⟩⟨ *most* actively⟩ **2** : to a very great extent ⟨a *most* careful driver⟩

³most *n* : the greatest amount, number, or part

most·ly \'mōst-lē\ *adv* : for the greatest part

mote \'mōt\ *n* : a small particle : SPECK

mo·tel \mō-'tel\ *n* : a building or group of buildings which provide lodgings and in which the rooms are usually reached directly from an outdoor parking area

moth \'mȯth\ *n, pl* **moths** \'mȯthz, 'mȯths\ **1** : CLOTHES MOTH **2** : an insect that usually flies at night and has mostly feathery antennae and stouter body, duller coloring, and smaller wings than the related butterflies

¹moth·er \'məth-ər\ *n* **1** *often cap* : a female parent **2** *often cap* : a nun in charge of a convent **3** : ¹CAUSE 1, ORIGIN ⟨necessity is the *mother* of invention⟩ — **mother·hood** \-ˌhȯd\ *n* — **moth·er·less** \-ləs\ *adj*

²mother *adj* **1** : of or having to do with a mother ⟨*mother* love⟩ **2** : being in the relation of a mother to others ⟨a *mother* church⟩ ⟨our *mother* country⟩ **3** : gotten from or as if from one's mother

³mother *vb* : to be or act as a mother to

moth·er–in–law \'məth-ər-ən-ˌlȯ\ *n, pl* **mothers–in–law** : the mother of one's husband or wife

moth·er·ly \'məth-ər-lē\ *adj* **1** : of, relating to, or characteristic of a mother ⟨*motherly* affection⟩ **2** : like a mother : MATERNAL

moth·er–of–pearl \ˌməth-ər-əv-'pərl\ *n* : a hard pearly material that lines the shell of some mollusks (as mussels) and is often used for ornamental objects and buttons

¹mo·tion \'mō-shən\ *n* **1** : a formal plan or suggestion for action offered according to the rules of a meeting ⟨a *motion* to adjourn⟩ **2** : the act or process of changing place or position : MOVEMENT — **mo·tion·less** \-ləs\ *adj* — **mo·tion·less·ness** *n*

²motion *vb* : to direct or signal by a movement or sign ⟨*motioned* them to come forward⟩

motion picture *n* **1** : a series of pictures projected on a screen rapidly one after another so as to give the appearance of a continuous picture in which the objects move **2** : MOVIE 1

mo·ti·vate \'mōt-ə-ˌvāt\ *vb* **mo·ti·vat·ed; mo·ti·vat·ing** : to provide with a reason for doing something ⟨ideas that *motivate* youth⟩

¹mo·tive \'mōt-iv\ *n* : a reason for doing something

²motive *adj* : causing motion ⟨*motive* power⟩

mot·ley \'mät-lē\ *adj* **1** : having various colors **2** : composed of various often unlike kinds or parts ⟨a *motley* collection of junk⟩

¹mo·tor \'mōt-ər\ *n* **1** : a machine that produces motion or power for doing work ⟨an electric *motor*⟩ ⟨a *motor* run by gasoline⟩ **2** : ²AUTOMOBILE — **mo·tored** \'mōt-ərd\ *adj*

²motor *adj* **1** : causing or controlling activity (as motion) ⟨*motor* nerves⟩ **2** : equipped with or driven by a motor **3** : of

or relating to an automobile **4** : designed for motor vehicles or motorists

³motor *vb* : ¹DRIVE 3

mo·tor·bike \'mōt-ər-ˌbīk\ *n* : a light motorcycle

mo·tor·boat \'mōt-ər-ˌbōt\ *n* : an often small boat driven by a motor

mo·tor·car \'mōt-ər-ˌkär\ *n* : ²AUTOMOBILE

mo·tor·cy·cle \'mōt-ər-ˌsī-kəl\ *n* : a vehicle for one or two passengers that has two wheels and is driven by a motor

mo·tor·ist \'mōt-ə-rəst\ *n* : a person who travels by automobile

mo·tor·ize \'mōt-ə-ˌrīz\ *vb* **mo·tor·ized; mo·tor·iz·ing** : to equip with a motor or with motor-driven vehicles

motor scooter *n* : a motorized vehicle having two or three wheels like a child's scooter but having a seat

motor vehicle *n* : a motorized vehicle (as an automobile or motorcycle) not operated on rails

mot·tled \'mät-ld\ *adj* : having spots or blotches of different colors

mot·to \'mät-ō\ *n, pl* **mot·toes** **1** : a phrase or word inscribed on something (as a coin or public building) to suggest its use or nature **2** : a short expression of a guiding rule of conduct

mould *variant of* MOLD

moult *variant of* MOLT

mound \'maund\ *n* : a small hill or heap of dirt (as one made to mark a grave)

¹mount \'maunt\ *n* : a high hill : MOUNTAIN — used especially before a proper name- ⟨*Mount* Everest⟩

²mount *vb* **1** : ASCEND, CLIMB ⟨*mount* a ladder⟩ **2** : to get up onto something ⟨*mount* a platform⟩ ⟨*mount* a horse⟩ **3** : to increase rapidly in amount ⟨*mounting* debts⟩ **4** : to prepare for use or display by fastening in position on a support ⟨*mount* a picture on cardboard⟩ **synonyms** see ASCEND

³mount *n* : that on which a person or thing is or can be mounted ⟨the horse was an excellent *mount*⟩

moun·tain \'maunt-n\ *n* **1** : an elevation higher than a hill **2** : a great mass or huge number ⟨a *mountain* of mail⟩

moun·tain·eer \ˌmaunt-n-'iər\ *n* **1** : a person who lives in the mountains **2** : a mountain climber

mountain goat *n* : a goatlike animal of the mountains of western North America with

\ə\ **abut**	\au̇\ **out**	\i\ **tip**	\ȯ\ **saw**	\u̇\ **foot**
\ər\ **further**	\ch\ **chin**	\ī\ **life**	\ȯi\ **coin**	\y\ **yet**
\a\ **mat**	\e\ **pet**	\j\ **job**	\th\ **thin**	\yü\ **few**
\ā\ **take**	\ē\ **easy**	\ng\ **sing**	\th\ **this**	\yu̇\ **cure**
\ä\ **cot, cart**	\g\ **go**	\ō\ **bone**	\ü\ **food**	\zh\ **vision**

thick white coat and slightly curved black horns

mountain goat

mountain lion *n* : COUGAR

moun·tain·ous \'maunt-n-əs\ *adj* **1** : having many mountains ⟨*mountainous* country⟩ **2** : like a mountain in size : HUGE

moun·tain·side \'maunt-n-ˌsīd\ *n* : the side of a mountain

mount·ing \'maunt-ing\ *n* : something that serves as a mount : SUPPORT ⟨a *mounting* for an engine⟩

mourn \'mōrn\ *vb* : to feel or show grief or sorrow especially over someone's death — **mourn·er** *n*

mourn·ful \'mōrn-fəl\ *adj* **1** : full of sorrow or sadness ⟨a *mournful* face⟩ **2** : causing sorrow ⟨*mournful* news⟩ — **mourn·ful·ly** \-fə-lē\ *adv* — **mourn·ful·ness** *n*

mourn·ing \'mōr-ning\ *n* **1** : the act of sorrowing **2** : an outward sign (as black clothes or an arm band) of grief for a person's death

mourning dove *n* : a wild dove of the United States named from its mournful cry

mouse \'maus\ *n*, *pl* **mice** \'mīs\ **1** : a furry gnawing animal like the larger related rats **2** : a person without spirit or courage — **mouse·like** \'maus-ˌslīk\ *adj*

mous·er \'mau-zər\ *n* : a cat good at catching mice

moustache *variant of* MUSTACHE

¹mouth \'mauth\ *n*, *pl* **mouths** \'mauthz, 'mauths\ **1** : the opening through which food passes into the body : the space containing the tongue and teeth **2** : an opening that is like a mouth ⟨the *mouth* of a cave⟩ **3** : the place where a stream enters a larger body of water

²mouth \'mauth\ *vb* : to repeat without being sincere or without understanding

mouth·ful \'mauth-ˌful\ *n* **1** : as much as the mouth will hold **2** : the amount put into the mouth at one time

mouth organ *n* : HARMONICA

mouth·piece \'mauth-ˌpēs\ *n* : the part put to, between, or near the lips ⟨the *mouthpiece* of a trumpet⟩ ⟨the *mouthpiece* of a telephone⟩

mov·able *or* **move·able** \'mü-və-bəl\ *adj* **1** : possible to move ⟨*movable* desks⟩ **2** : changing from one date to another ⟨Easter is a *movable* religious holiday⟩

¹move \'müv\ *vb* **moved; mov·ing** **1** : to go from one place to another ⟨*move* into the shade⟩ **2** : to change the place or position of : SHIFT **3** : to set in motion : STIR ⟨*move* the head⟩ **4** : to cause to act : INFLUENCE ⟨*moved* me to change my mind⟩ **5** : to stir the feelings of ⟨the sad story *moved* the children to tears⟩ **6** : to change position ⟨*moved* in my chair⟩ **7** : to suggest according to the rules in a meeting ⟨*move* to adjourn⟩ **8** : to change residence

²move *n* **1** : the act of moving a piece in a game **2** : the turn of a player to move ⟨it's your *move*⟩ **3** : an action taken to accomplish something : MANEUVER ⟨a *move* to end the dispute⟩ **4** : the action of moving : MOVEMENT

move·ment \'müv-mənt\ *n* **1** : the act or process of moving : an instance of moving **2** : a program or series of acts working toward a desired end ⟨a *movement* for political action⟩ **3** : a mechanical arrangement (as of wheels) for causing a particular motion (as in a clock or watch) **4** : RHYTHM 2, METER **5** : a section of a longer piece of music ⟨a *movement* in a symphony⟩ **6** : an emptying of the bowels : the material emptied from the bowels

mov·er \'mü-vər\ *n* : a person or company that moves the belongings of others (as from one home to another)

mov·ie \'mü-vē\ *n* **1** : a story represented in motion pictures **2** : a showing of a movie ⟨let's go to a *movie*⟩

mov·ing \'mü-ving\ *adj* **1** : changing place or position ⟨a *moving* target⟩ **2** : having the power to stir the feelings or sympathies ⟨a *moving* song⟩ — **mov·ing·ly** *adv*

moving picture *n* : MOTION PICTURE 1

¹mow \'mau\ *n* : the part of a barn where hay or straw is stored

²mow \'mō\ *vb* **mowed; mowed** *or* **mown** \'mōn\; **mow·ing** **1** : to cut down with a scythe or machine ⟨*mow* grass⟩ **2** : to cut the standing plant cover from ⟨*mow* the lawn⟩ **3** : to cause to fall in great numbers ⟨machine guns *mowed* down the attackers⟩ — **mow·er** \'mō-ər\ *n*

Mr. \ˌmis-tər\ *n, pl* **Messrs.** \ˌmes-ərz\ — used as a title before a man's name ⟨*Mr.* Doe⟩

Mrs. \ˌmis-əz, ˌmiz-\ *n, pl* **mes·dames** \mā-'däm, -'dam\ — used as a title before a married woman's name ⟨*Mrs.* Doe⟩

Ms. \ˌmiz\ *n* — often used instead of *Miss* or *Mrs.* ⟨*Ms.* Jane Doe⟩

¹much \'məch\ *adj* **more** \'mōr\; **most** \'mōst\ : great in amount or extent ⟨*much* money⟩

²much *adv* **more; most 1** : to a great or high level or extent ⟨*much* happier⟩ **2** : just about : NEARLY ⟨looks *much* as it did years ago⟩

³much *n* : a great amount or part ⟨*much* that was said is true⟩

mu·ci·lage \'myü-sə-lij\ *n* : a water solution of a gum or similar substance used especially to stick things together

muck \'mək\ *n* **1** : soft wet soil or barnyard manure **2** : DIRT 1, FILTH

mu·cous \'myü-kəs\ *adj* **1** : of, relating to, or like mucus **2** : containing or producing mucus ⟨a *mucous* membrane⟩

mu·cus \'myü-kəs\ *n* : a slippery sticky substance produced especially by mucous membranes (as of the nose and throat) which it moistens and protects

mud \'məd\ *n* : soft wet earth or dirt

¹mud·dle \'məd-l\ *vb* **mud·dled; mud·dling 1** : to be or cause to be confused or bewildered ⟨*muddled* by too much advice⟩ **2** : to mix up in a confused manner ⟨*muddle* the business accounts⟩ **3** : to make a mess of : BUNGLE

²muddle *n* : a state of confusion

¹mud·dy \'məd-ē\ *adj* **mud·di·er; mud·di·est 1** : filled or covered with mud **2** : looking like mud ⟨a *muddy* color⟩ **3** : not clear or bright : DULL ⟨a *muddy* skin⟩ **4** : being mixed up ⟨*muddy* thinking⟩ — **mud·di·ly** \'məd-l-ē\ *adv* — **mud·di·ness** \'məd-ē-nəs\ *n*

²muddy *vb* **mud·died; mud·dy·ing 1** : to soil or stain with or as if with mud **2** : to make cloudy or dull

¹muff \'məf\ *n* : a soft thick cover into which both hands can be shoved to protect them from cold

muff

²muff *vb* : to handle awkwardly : BUNGLE

muf·fin \'məf-ən\ *n* : a bread made of batter containing eggs and baked in a small container

muf·fle \'məf-əl\ *vb* **muf·fled; muf·fling 1** : to wrap up so as to hide or protect **2** : to deaden the sound of

muf·fler \'məf-lər\ *n* **1** : a scarf for the neck **2** : a device to deaden noise

mug \'məg\ *n* : a large drinking cup

mug·gy \'məg-ē\ *adj* **mug·gi·er; mug·gi·est** : being very warm and humid ⟨*muggy* weather⟩ — **mug·gi·ness** *n*

Mu·ham·mad·an *or* **Mo·ham·med·an** \mō-'ham-əd-ən, mü-, -'häm-\ *n* : MUSLIM

Mu·ham·mad·an·ism *or* **Mo·ham·med·an·ism** \mō-'ham-əd-ən-ˌiz-əm, mü-, -'häm-\ *n* : ISLAM

mul·ber·ry \'məl-ˌber-ē\ *n, pl* **mul·ber·ries** : a tree that bears edible usually purple fruit like berries and has leaves on which silkworms can be fed

¹mulch \'məlch\ *n* : a material (as straw or sawdust) spread over the ground to protect the roots of plants from heat, cold, or drying of the soil or to keep fruit clean

²mulch *vb* : to cover with mulch

mule \'myül\ *n* **1** : an animal that is an offspring of a donkey and a horse **2** : a stubborn person

mule 1

mule skinner *n* : a driver of mules

mu·le·teer \ˌmyü-lə-'tiər\ *n* : a driver of mules

mul·ish \'myü-lish\ *adj* : stubborn like a mule — **mul·ish·ly** *adv* — **mul·ish·ness** *n*

mul·let \'məl-ət\ *n* : any of various freshwater or saltwater food fishes some mostly gray (**gray mullets**) and others red or golden (**red mullets**)

mul·ti- \,məl-ti\ *prefix* **1** : many : much **2** : more than two **3** : many times over

mul·ti·cul·tur·al \'məl-,tī-'kəl-chə-rəl\ *adj* : of, relating to, or made up of several different cultures together ⟨a *multicultural* society⟩

¹**mul·ti·ple** \'məl-tə-pəl\ *adj* : being more than one ⟨*multiple* copies of a document⟩

²**multiple** *n* : the number found by multiplying one number by another ⟨35 is a *multiple* of 7⟩

mul·ti·pli·cand \,məl-tə-plə-'kand\ *n* : a number that is to be multiplied by another number

mul·ti·pli·ca·tion \,məl-tə-plə-'kā-shən\ *n* : a short way of finding out what would be the result of adding a figure the number of times indicated by another figure ⟨the *multiplication* of 7 by 3 gives 21⟩

mul·ti·pli·er \'məl-tə-,plī-ər\ *n* : a number by which another number is multiplied

mul·ti·ply \'məl-tə-,plī\ *vb* **mul·ti·plied;** **mul·ti·ply·ing 1** : to increase in number : make or become more numerous **2** : to find the product of by means of multiplication ⟨*multiply* 7 by 8⟩

mul·ti·tude \'məl-tə-,tüd, -,tyüd\ *n* : a great number of persons or things

mum \'məm\ *adj* : SILENT 1, 4 ⟨keep *mum*⟩

¹**mum·ble** \'məm-bəl\ *vb* **mum·bled;** **mum·bling** : to speak so that words are not clear

²**mumble** *n* : speech that is not clear enough to be understood

mum·my \'məm-ē\ *n, pl* **mum·mies** : a dead body preserved in the manner of the ancient Egyptians

mumps \'məmps\ *n sing or pl* : an infectious disease in which there is fever and soreness and swelling of glands and especially of those around the jaw

munch \'mənch\ *vb* : to chew with a crunching sound ⟨*munch* crackers⟩

mu·nic·i·pal \myü-'nis-ə-pəl\ *adj* : having to do with the government of a town or city

mu·nic·i·pal·i·ty \myü-,nis-ə-'pal-ət-ē\ *n, pl* **mu·nic·i·pal·i·ties** : a town or city having its own local government

mu·ni·tions \myü-'nish-ənz\ *n* : military equipment and supplies for fighting : AMMUNITION

¹**mu·ral** \'myür-əl\ *adj* : having to do with a wall

²**mural** *n* : a painting on a wall

¹**mur·der** \'mərd-ər\ *n* : the intentional and unlawful killing of a human being

²**murder** *vb* **1** : to commit murder **2** : to spoil by performing or using badly ⟨*murder* a song⟩ ⟨*murder* English⟩ **synonyms** see KILL — **mur·der·er** *n*

mur·der·ous \'mərd-ə-rəs\ *adj* **1** : intending or capable of murder : DEADLY **2** : very hard to bear or withstand ⟨*murderous* heat⟩ — **mur·der·ous·ly** *adv*

murk \'mərk\ *n* : GLOOM 1, DARKNESS

murky \'mər-kē\ *adj* **murk·i·er; murk·i·est 1** : very dark or gloomy **2** : FOGGY 1, MISTY — **murk·i·ness** *n*

¹**mur·mur** \'mər-mər\ *n* : a low faint sound ⟨the *murmur* of voices⟩

²**murmur** *vb* **1** : to make a murmur **2** : to say in a voice too low to be heard clearly

mus·ca·dine \'məs-kə-,dīn\ *n* : a grape of the southern United States

mus·cle \'məs-əl\ *n* **1** : an animal body tissue consisting of long cells (**muscle cells**) that can contract and produce motion **2** : a bodily organ that is a mass of muscle tissue attached at either end (as to bones) so that it can make a body part (as an arm) move **3** : strength or development of the muscles

Word History The English word *muscle* came from a Latin word that meant "small mouse." The movement of the muscles under the skin probably made someone think of a lively mouse.

mus·cle–bound \'məs-əl-,baůnd\ *adj* : having large muscles that do not move and stretch easily

mus·cu·lar \'məs-kyə-lər\ *adj* **1** : of, relating to, or being muscle **2** : done by the muscles **3** : STRONG 1

muse \'myüz\ *vb* **mused; mus·ing** : PONDER

mu·se·um \myů-'zē-əm\ *n* : a building in which are displayed objects of interest in one or more of the arts or sciences

¹**mush** \'məsh\ *n* : cornmeal boiled in water

²**mush** *vb* : to travel across snow with a sled drawn by dogs

¹**mush·room** \'məsh-,rüm, -,rům\ *n* **1** : a part of a fungus that bears spores, grows above ground, and suggests an umbrella in shape **2** : a fungus that produces mushrooms **3** : something shaped like a mushroom

²**mushroom** *vb* : to come into being suddenly or grow and develop rapidly

mushy \'məsh-ē\ *adj* **mush·i·er; mush·i·est** : soft like mush

mu·sic \'myü-zik\ *n* **1** : the art of producing pleasing or expressive combinations of tones especially with melody, rhythm, and usually harmony **2** : compositions made according to the rules of music **3** : pleasing sounds **4** : a musical composition set down on paper ⟨bring your *music*⟩

¹mu·si·cal \'myü-zi-kəl\ *adj* **1** : having to do with music or the writing or performing of music ⟨*musical* instruments⟩ **2** : pleasing like music ⟨a *musical* voice⟩ **3** : fond of or talented in music ⟨a *musical* family⟩ **4** : set to music — **mu·si·cal·ly** *adv*

²musical *n* : a movie or play that tells a story with both speaking and singing

music box *n* : a box that contains a mechanical device which uses gears like those of a clock to play a tune

mu·si·cian \myü-'zish-ən\ *n* : a person who writes, sings, or plays music with skill and especially as a profession

musk \'məsk\ *n* **1** : a strong-smelling material from a gland of an Asian deer (**musk deer**) used in perfumes **2** : any of several plants with musky odors

mus·ket \'məs-kət\ *n* : a firearm that is loaded through the muzzle and that was once used by infantry soldiers

Word History The musket was first used in Spain. When the Italians saw the new weapon, they named it after a weapon they already knew—a kind of arrow that sounded a bit like a fly when it whizzed through the air. The arrow got its name from the Italian word that meant "fly." This word in turn came from the Latin word for a fly. The French took their word for the musket from the Italians. The English word *musket* came from this French word.

mus·ke·teer \,məs-kə-'tiər\ *n* : a soldier armed with a musket

musk·mel·on \'məsk-,mel-ən\ *n* : a small round to oval melon with sweet usually green or orange flesh

musk–ox \'məs-,käks\ *n* : a shaggy ani-

mal like an ox found in Greenland and northern North America

musk·rat \'məs-,krat\ *n* : a North American water animal related to the rats that has webbed hind feet and a long scaly tail and is valued for its glossy usually dark brown fur

musky \'məs-kē\ *adj* **musk·i·er; musk·i·est** : suggesting musk in odor — **musk·i·ness** *n*

Mus·lim \'məz-ləm\ *or* **Mos·lem** \'mäz-\ *n* : a person whose religion is Islam

mus·lin \'məz-lən\ *n* : a cotton fabric of plain weave

¹muss \'məs\ *n* : ²DISORDER 1, CONFUSION

²muss *vb* : to make untidy

mus·sel \'məs-əl\ *n* **1** : a sea mollusk that has a long dark shell in two parts and is sometimes used as food **2** : any of various American freshwater clams with shells from which mother-of-pearl is obtained

must \'məst\ *helping verb, present and past all persons* **must 1** : to be required to ⟨a person *must* eat to live⟩ **2** : to be very likely to ⟨it *must* be time⟩ ⟨*must* have lost it⟩

mus·tache *or* **mous·tache** \'məs-,tash, məs-'tash\ *n* : the hair growing on the human upper lip

mus·tang \'məs-,tang\ *n* : a small hardy horse of western North America that is half wild

Word History Long ago in Spain, stray cattle were rounded up each year and sold. The Spanish word for this roundup of strays came from a Latin phrase that meant "mixed animals." From their word that meant "roundup of strays," the Spanish made another word that meant "a stray animal." In Mexico, this word was used for a kind of wild horse. That is where English *mustang* came from.

mus·tard \'məs-tərd\ *n* : a yellow powder that is prepared from the seeds of a plant related to the turnips, has a sharp taste, and is used in medicine and as a seasoning for foods

¹mus·ter \'məs-tər\ *vb* **1** : to call together (as troops) for roll call or inspection **2** : to bring into being or action ⟨*mustering* courage⟩

²muster *n* **1** : a formal military inspection **2** : an assembled group : COLLECTION

musk-ox

\ə\ abut	\au̇\ out	\i\ tip	\ȯ\ saw	\u̇\ foot
\ər\ further	\ch\ chin	\ī\ life	\ȯi\ coin	\y\ yet
\a\ mat	\e\ pet	\j\ job	\th\ thin	\yü\ few
\ā\ take	\ē\ easy	\ng\ sing	\th\ this	\yu̇\ cure
\ä\ cot, cart	\g\ go	\ō\ bone	\ü\ food	\zh\ vision

mustn't \'məs-nt\ : must not

musty \'məs-tē\ *adj* **must·i·er; must·i·est** : bad in odor or taste from the effects of dampness or mildew — **must·i·ness** *n*

¹mu·tant \'myüt-nt\ *adj* : of, relating to, or resulting from mutation

²mutant *n* : a mutant individual

mu·tate \'myü-,tāt\ *vb* **mu·tat·ed; mu·tat·ing** **1** : to undergo great changes **2** : to undergo mutation

mu·ta·tion \myü-'tā-shən\ *n* : a change in a gene or a resulting new trait inherited by an individual

¹mute \'myüt\ *adj* **mut·er; mut·est** **1** : unable to speak **2** : not speaking : SILENT

²mute *n* **1** : a person who cannot or does not speak **2** : a device on a musical instrument that deadens, softens, or muffles its tone

³mute *vb* **mut·ed; mut·ing** : to muffle or reduce the sound of

mu·ti·late \'myüt-l-,āt\ *vb* **mu·ti·lat·ed; mu·ti·lat·ing** **1** : to cut off or destroy a necessary part (as a limb) : MAIM **2** : to make imperfect by cutting or changing 〈*multilate* a book〉

mu·ti·neer \,myüt-n-'iər\ *n* : a person who is guilty of mutiny

mu·ti·nous \'myüt-n-əs\ *adj* : being inclined to or in a state of mutiny — **mu·ti·nous·ly** *adv*

¹mu·ti·ny \'myüt-n-ē\ *n, pl* **mu·ti·nies** **1** : refusal to obey authority **2** : a turning of a group (as of sailors) against an officer in authority

²mutiny *vb* **mu·ti·nied; mu·ti·ny·ing** : to refuse to obey authority

mutt \'mət\ *n* : a mongrel dog

mut·ter \'mət-ər\ *vb* **1** : to speak in a low voice with lips partly closed **2** : ¹GRUMBLE 1

mut·ton \'mət-n\ *n* : the flesh of a mature sheep

mu·tu·al \'myü-chə-wəl\ *adj* **1** : given and received in equal amount 〈*mutual* favors〉 **2** : having the same relation to one another 〈*mutual* enemies〉 **3** : shared by two or more at the same time 〈a *mutual* friend〉 — **mu·tu·al·ly** *adv*

¹muz·zle \'məz-əl\ *n* **1** : the nose and jaws of an animal **2** : a fastening or covering for the mouth of an animal to prevent it from biting or eating **3** : the open end of a gun from which the bullet comes out when the gun is fired

²muzzle *vb* **muz·zled; muz·zling** **1** : to put a muzzle on 〈*muzzle* your dog〉 **2** : to keep from free expression of ideas or opinions 〈the dictator *muzzled* the press〉

muzzle 2

my \'mī, mə\ *adj* : of or relating to me or myself 〈*my* head〉〈*my* injuries〉

my·nah *or* **my·na** \'mī-nə\ *n* : an Asian starling that can be trained to pronounce words and is sometimes kept as a cage bird

¹myr·i·ad \'mir-ē-əd\ *n* : a large but not specified or counted number 〈*myriads* of stars visible〉

²myriad *adj* : extremely numerous 〈the *myriad* grains of sand on the beach〉

myrrh \'mər\ *n* : a brown slightly bitter fragrant material obtained from African and Arabian trees and used especially in perfumes or formerly in incense

myr·tle \'mərt-l\ *n* **1** : an evergreen shrub of southern Europe **2** : ¹PERIWINKLE

my·self \mī-'self, mə-\ *pron* : my own self 〈I hurt *myself*〉〈I *myself* did it〉

mys·te·ri·ous \mis-'tir-ē-əs\ *adj* : containing a mystery : hard to understand : SECRET — **mys·te·ri·ous·ly** *adv* — **mys·te·ri·ous·ness** *n*

mys·tery \'mis-tə-rē\ *n, pl* **mys·ter·ies** **1** : something that is beyond human power to understand **2** : something that has not been explained **3** : a piece of fiction about a mysterious crime

mys·ti·fy \'mis-tə-,fī\ *vb* **mys·ti·fied; mys·ti·fy·ing** : CONFUSE 1

myth \'mith\ *n* **1** : a legend that tells about a being with more than human powers or an event which cannot be explained or that explains a religious belief or practice **2** : a person or thing existing only in the imagination

myth·i·cal \'mith-i-kəl\ *adj* **1** : based on or told of in a myth **2** : IMAGINARY

my·thol·o·gy \mi-'thäl-ə-jē\ *n, pl* **my·thol·o·gies** : a collection of myths

n \'en\ *n, pl* **n's** *or* **ns** \'enz\ *often cap* : the fourteenth letter of the English alphabet

-n — see -EN

nab \'nab\ *vb* **nabbed; nab·bing** : ¹ARREST 2

¹nag \'nag\ *n* : a usually old or worn-out horse

²nag *vb* **nagged; nag·ging** 1 : to find fault continually : COMPLAIN 2 : to annoy continually or again and again ⟨a *nagging* toothache⟩

na·iad \'nā-əd\ *n, pl* **na·iads** *or* **na·ia·des** \'nā-ə-‚dēz\ 1 : a nymph believed in ancient times to be living in lakes, rivers, and springs 2 : the larva of an insect (as a dragonfly) that lives in water

¹nail \'nāl\ *n* 1 : the horny scale at the end of each finger and toe 2 : a slender pointed piece of metal driven into or through something for fastening

²nail *vb* : to fasten with or as if with a nail

nail·brush \'nāl-‚brəsh\ *n* : a brush for cleaning the hands and fingernails

na·ive *or* **na·ïve** \nä-'ēv\ *adj* 1 : being simple and sincere 2 : showing lack of experience or knowledge ⟨a child's *naive* belief in fairies⟩ — **na·ive·ly** *adv*

na·ive·té *or* **na·ïve·té** \nä-‚ē-və-'tā\ *n* : the quality or state of being naive

na·ked \'nā-kəd\ *adj* 1 : having no clothes on : NUDE 2 : lacking a usual or natural covering ⟨*naked* trees⟩ 3 : not in its case or covering ⟨a *naked* sword⟩ 4 : stripped of anything misleading : PLAIN ⟨the *naked* truth⟩ 5 : not aided by an artificial device ⟨seen by the *naked* eye⟩ — **na·ked·ly** *adv* — **na·ked·ness** *n*

synonyms NAKED and BARE mean being without a natural or usual covering. NAKED suggests that there is neither protective nor ornamental covering ⟨a *naked* baby⟩ BARE stresses that there is no unnecessary covering or that all covering has been removed ⟨*bare* walls⟩

¹name \'nām\ *n* 1 : a word or combination of words by which a person or thing is known 2 : REPUTATION 2 ⟨only you can make a *name* for yourself⟩

²name *vb* **named; nam·ing** 1 : to give a name to : CALL ⟨*name* the baby⟩ 2 : to refer to by name ⟨can you *name* all the state capitals⟩ 3 : to nominate for a job of authority : APPOINT ⟨was *named* to the cabinet⟩ 4 : to decide on : CHOOSE ⟨*name* the date for a wedding⟩ 5 : ²MENTION ⟨*name* a price⟩

³name *adj* : well known because of wide distribution ⟨*name* brands⟩

name·less \'nām-ləs\ *adj* 1 : having no name 2 : not marked with a name ⟨a *nameless* grave⟩ 3 : ¹UNKNOWN, ANONYMOUS ⟨a *nameless* writer⟩ 4 : not to be described ⟨*nameless* fears⟩ — **name·less·ness** *n*

name·ly \'nām-lē\ *adv* : that is to say ⟨the cat family, *namely*, lions, tigers, and related animals⟩

name·sake \'nām-‚sāk\ *n* : a person who has the same name as another and especially one named for another

nan·ny \'nan-ē\ *n, pl* **nan·nies** : a female goat

¹nap \'nap\ *vb* **napped; nap·ping** 1 : to sleep briefly especially during the day 2 : to be unprepared ⟨was caught *napping*⟩

²nap *n* : a short sleep especially during the day

³nap *n* : a hairy or fluffy surface (as on cloth)

nape \'nāp\ *n* : the back of the neck

naph·tha \'naf-thə, 'nap-thə\ *n* : any of various usually flammable liquids prepared from coal or petroleum and used to dissolve substances or to thin paint

nap·kin \'nap-kən\ *n* : a small square of cloth or paper used at table to wipe the lips or fingers and protect the clothes

nar·cis·sus \när-'sis-əs\ *n, pl* **narcissus** *or* **nar·cis·sus·es** *or* **nar·cis·si** \-'sis-‚ī, -ē\ : a daffodil with flowers that have short tubes, grow separately on the stalk, and come in white, yellow, or a combination of both

¹nar·cot·ic \när-'kät-ik\ *n* : a drug (as opium) that in small doses dulls the senses, relieves pain, and brings on sleep but in larger doses is a dangerous poison

\ə\ **abut**	\aù\ **out**	\i\ **tip**	\ò\ **saw**	\ù\ **foot**
\ər\ **further**	\ch\ **chin**	\ī\ **life**	\òi\ **coin**	\y\ **yet**
\a\ **mat**	\e\ **pet**	\j\ **job**	\th\ **thin**	\yü\ **few**
\ā\ **take**	\ē\ **easy**	\ng\ **sing**	\th\ **this**	\yù\ **cure**
\ä\ **cot, cart**	\g\ **go**	\ō\ **bone**	\ü\ **food**	\zh\ **vision**

²**narcotic** *adj* **1** : acting as or being the source of a narcotic ⟨*narcotic* drugs⟩ ⟨the opium poppy is a *narcotic* plant⟩ **2** : of or relating to narcotics or their use or control ⟨*narcotic* laws⟩

nar·rate \'nar-ˌāt, na-'rāt\ *vb* **nar·rat·ed; nar·rat·ing** : to tell in full detail ⟨*narrate* the story of one's adventure⟩ **synonyms** see REPORT — **nar·ra·tor** \-ər\ *n*

nar·ra·tion \na-'rā-shən\ *n* **1** : the act or process or an instance of narrating **2** : ¹NARRATIVE 1

¹**nar·ra·tive** \'nar-ət-iv\ *n* **1** : something (as a story) that is narrated **2** : the art or practice of narrating

²**narrative** *adj* : of or relating to narration : having the form of a story

¹**nar·row** \'nar-ō\ *adj* **1** : of slender or less than usual width **2** : limited in size or extent **3** : not broad or open in mind or views **4** : barely successful : CLOSE ⟨a *narrow* escape⟩ — **nar·row·ly** *adv* — **nar·row·ness** *n*

²**narrow** *n* : a narrow passage connecting two bodies of water — usually used in pl.

³**narrow** *vb* : to make or become narrow

nar·row–mind·ed \ˌnar-ō-'mīn-dəd\ *adj* : ¹NARROW 3, INTOLERANT — **nar·row–mind·ed·ly** *adv* — **nar·row–mind·ed·ness** *n*

nar·whal \'när-ˌhwäl, -ˌwäl\ *n* : an arctic marine animal about twenty feet long that is related to the dolphin and in the male has a long twisted ivory tusk

narwhal

¹**na·sal** \'nā-zəl\ *n* : a nasal sound

²**nasal** *adj* **1** : of or relating to the nose **2** : uttered with the nose passage open ⟨the *nasal* consonants \m\, \n\, and \ng\⟩ — **na·sal·ly** *adv*

nas·tur·tium \nəs-'tər-shəm, nas-\ *n* : an herb with a juicy stem, roundish leaves, red, yellow, or white flowers, and seeds with a sharp taste

nasturtium

nas·ty \'nas-tē\ *adj* **nas·ti·er; nas·ti·est** **1** : very dirty : FILTHY **2** : INDECENT **3** : ¹MEAN **4** ⟨a *nasty* disposition⟩ **4** : HARMFUL, DANGEROUS ⟨a *nasty* fall⟩ **5** : very unpleasant ⟨*nasty* weather⟩ ⟨a *nasty* trick⟩ — **nas·ti·ly** \'nas-tə-lē\ *adv* — **nas·ti·ness** \'nas-tē-nəs\ *n*

na·tal \'nāt-l\ *adj* : of, relating to, or associated with birth ⟨*natal* day⟩

na·tion \'nā-shən\ *n* **1** : NATIONALITY 3 **2** : a community of people made up of one or more nationalities usually with its own territory and government **3** : a usually large independent division of territory : COUNTRY

¹**na·tion·al** \'nash-ən-l\ *adj* : of or relating to a nation ⟨our *national* parks⟩ — **na·tion·al·ly** *adv*

²**national** *n* : a citizen of a nation

na·tion·al·ism \'nash-ən-l-ˌiz-əm\ *n* : devotion to the interests of a certain country

na·tion·al·ist \'nash-ən-l-əst\ *n* : a person who believes in nationalism

na·tion·al·is·tic \ˌnash-ən-l-'is-tik\ *adj* **1** : of, relating to, or favoring nationalism **2** : ¹NATIONAL — **na·tion·al·is·ti·cal·ly** \-ti-kə-lē\ *adv*

na·tion·al·i·ty \ˌnash-ə-'nal-ət-ē\ *n, pl* **na·tion·al·i·ties** **1** : the fact or state of belonging to a nation **2** : the state of being a separate nation **3** : a group of people having a common history, tradition, culture, or language

na·tion·al·ize \'nash-ən-l-ˌīz\ *vb* **na·tion·al·ized; na·tion·al·iz·ing** : to place under government control

na·tion·wide \ˌnā-shən-'wīd\ *adj* : extending throughout a nation

¹**na·tive** \'nāt-iv\ *adj* **1** : NATURAL 1 ⟨*native* ability⟩ **2** : born in a certain place or country **3** : belonging to one because of one's place of birth ⟨*native* language⟩ **4** : grown, produced, or coming from a certain place ⟨*native* art⟩

²**native** *n* : one that is native

Native American *n* : AMERICAN INDIAN

na·tiv·i·ty \nə-'tiv-ət-ē\ *n, pl* **na·tiv·i·ties** **1** : BIRTH 1 **2** *cap* : the birth of Christ : CHRISTMAS

nat·ty \'nat-ē\ *adj* **nat·ti·er; nat·ti·est** : very neat, trim, and stylish — **nat·ti·ly** \'nat-l-ē\ *adv* — **nat·ti·ness** \'nat-ē-nəs\ *n*

nat·u·ral \'nach-ə-rəl, 'nach-rəl\ *adj* **1** : born in or with one ⟨*natural* abilities⟩ **2** : being such by nature : BORN ⟨a *natural* musician⟩ **3** : found in or produced by nature ⟨*natural* woodland⟩ **4** : of or relating to nature ⟨*natural* causes⟩ **5** : not made by humans ⟨*natural* rubber⟩ **6** : being simple and sincere ⟨*natural* manners⟩ **7** : LIFELIKE **8** : being neither sharp nor flat : having neither sharps nor flats — **nat·u·ral·ly** *adv* — **nat·u·ral·ness** *n*

nat·u·ral·ist \'nach-ə-rə-ləst, 'nach-rə-\ *n* : a student of nature and especially of plants and animals as they live in nature

nat·u·ral·iza·tion \,nach-ə-rə-lə-'zā-shən, ,nach-rə-\ *n* : the act or process of naturalizing : the state of being naturalized

nat·u·ral·ize \'nach-ə-rə-,līz, 'nach-rə-\ *vb* **nat·u·ral·ized; nat·u·ral·iz·ing 1** : to become or cause to become established as if native ⟨*naturalize* a plant⟩ **2** : to admit to citizenship

natural number *n* : the number 1 or any number (as 3, 12, 432) obtained by repeatedly adding 1 to 1

natural resource *n* : something (as a mineral, forest, or kind of animal) that is found in nature and is valuable to humans

na·ture \'nā-chər\ *n* **1** : the basic character of a person or thing **2** : ¹SORT 1, VARIETY **3** : natural feelings : DISPOSITION, TEMPERAMENT ⟨a generous *nature*⟩ **4** : the material universe ⟨the study of *nature*⟩ **5** : the working of a living body ⟨leave a cure to *nature*⟩ **6** : natural scenery

¹naught *or* **nought** \'not\ *pron* : ¹NOTHING 1 ⟨our efforts came to *naught* in the end⟩

²naught *or* **nought** *n* : ZERO 1, CIPHER

naugh·ty \'not-e\ *adj* **naugh·ti·er; naugh·ti·est** : behaving in a bad or improper way **synonyms** see BAD — **naugh·ti·ly** \'not-l-ē\ *adv* — **naugh·ti·ness** \'not-ē-nəs\ *n*

nau·sea \'no-zē-ə, 'no-shə\ *n* **1** : a disturbed condition of the stomach in which one feels like vomiting **2** : deep disgust : LOATHING

Word History The English word *nausea* came from a Latin word that meant "seasickness." The Latin word in turn came from a Greek word with the same meaning. This Greek word was formed from another Greek word meaning "sailor" which came from an earlier Greek word that meant "ship." Our word *nausea* has a more general meaning than either the Latin or Greek words.

nau·se·ate \'no-zē-,āt, 'no-shē-\ *vb* **nau·se·at·ed; nau·se·at·ing** : to affect or become affected with nausea — **nau·se·at·ing** *adj* — **nau·se·at·ing·ly** *adv*

nau·seous \'no-shəs, 'no-zē-əs\ *adj* **1** : suffering from nausea **2** : causing nausea

nau·ti·cal \'not-i-kəl\ *adj* : of or relating to sailors, navigation, or ships — **nau·ti·cal·ly** *adv*

na·val \'nā-vəl\ *adj* : of or relating to a navy or warships ⟨*naval* vessels⟩

nave \'nāv\ *n* : the long central main part of a church

na·vel \'nā-vəl\ *n* : a hollow in the middle of the abdominal wall

nav·i·ga·bil·i·ty \,nav-i-gə-'bil-ət-ē\ *n* : the quality or state of being navigable

nav·i·ga·ble \'nav-i-gə-bəl\ *adj* **1** : deep enough and wide enough to permit passage of ships ⟨a *navigable* river⟩ **2** : possible to steer ⟨a *navigable* balloon⟩

nav·i·gate \'nav-ə-,gāt\ *vb* **nav·i·gat·ed; nav·i·gat·ing 1** : to travel by water **2** : to sail over, on, or through **3** : to steer a course in a ship or aircraft **4** : to steer or direct the course of (as a boat)

nav·i·ga·tion \,nav-ə-'gā-shən\ *n* **1** : the act or practice of navigating **2** : the science of figuring out the position and course of a ship or aircraft

nav·i·ga·tor \'nav-ə-,gāt-ər\ *n* : an officer on a ship or aircraft responsible for its navigation

na·vy \'nā-vē\ *n, pl* **na·vies 1** : a nation's ships of war **2** : the complete naval equipment and organization of a nation **3** : a dark blue

¹nay \'nā\ *adv* : ¹NO 2

²nay *n* : ³NO 2

Na·zi \'nät-sē\ *n* : a member of a political party controlling Germany from 1933 to 1945

Ne·an·der·thal man \nē-,an-dər-,thȯl-\ *n* : a long gone ancient human who made tools of stone and lived by hunting

¹near \'niər\ *adv* **1** : at, within, or to a short distance or time **2** : ALMOST, NEARLY

²near *prep* : close to ⟨the table *near* the window⟩

³near *adj* **1** : closely related or associated ⟨a *near* relative⟩ **2** : not far away **3** : coming close : NARROW ⟨a *near* miss⟩ **4** : being the closer of two ⟨the *near* side⟩ — **near·ly** *adv* — **near·ness** *n*

⁴near *vb* : to come near : APPROACH

near·by \niər-'bī\ *adv or adj* : close at hand

near·sight·ed \'niər-'sīt-əd\ *adj* : able to see near things more clearly than distant ones — **near·sight·ed·ly** *adv* — **near·sight·ed·ness** *n*

neat \'nēt\ *adj* **1** : being simple and in

\ə\ abut	\aú\ out	\i\ tip	\ȯ\ saw	\ú\ foot
\ər\ further	\ch\ chin	\ī\ life	\ȯi\ coin	\y\ yet
\a\ mat	\e\ pet	\j\ job	\th\ thin	\yü\ few
\ā\ take	\ē\ easy	\ng\ sing	\th\ this	\yu̇\ cure
\ä\ cot, cart	\g\ go	\ō\ bone	\ü\ food	\zh\ vision

good taste 〈a *neat* suit〉 **2** : SKILLFUL 2 〈a *neat* trick〉 **3** : showing care and a concern for order 〈a *neat* room〉 — **neat·ly** *adv* — **neat·ness** *n*

synonyms NEAT, TIDY, and TRIM mean showing care and a concern for order. NEAT stresses that something is clean in addition to being orderly 〈your clothes should always be *neat*〉 TIDY suggests that something is continually kept orderly and neat 〈I work hard to keep my room *tidy*〉 TRIM stresses that something is orderly and compact 〈*trim*, comfortable houses〉

Word History The English word *neat* can be traced back to a Latin verb that meant "to shine." From this verb, the ancient Romans formed an adjective that meant "shining," "bright," or "clear." The French word that came from this Latin word had the same meanings and came into English as *neat*. English *neat* at first meant "shining," "bright," or "clear." Later it was used to mean "simple and in good taste," "skillful," and "tidy."

neb·u·la \'neb-yə-lə\ *n, pl* **neb·u·las** *or* **neb·u·lae** \-,lē\ : any of many clouds of gas or dust seen in the sky among the stars

neb·u·lous \'neb-yə-ləs\ *adj* : not clear : VAGUE — **neb·u·lous·ly** *adv* — **neb·u·lous·ness** *n*

¹**nec·es·sary** \'nes-ə-,ser-ē\ *n, pl* **nec·es·sar·ies** : something that is needed

²**necessary** *adj* : needing to be had or done : ESSENTIAL 〈food is *necessary* to life〉〈got the *necessary* work done first〉 — **nec·es·sar·i·ly** \,nes-ə-'ser-ə-lē\ *adv*

ne·ces·si·tate \ni-'ses-ə-,tāt\ *vb* **ne·ces·si·tat·ed; ne·ces·si·tat·ing** : to make necessary : REQUIRE

ne·ces·si·ty \ni-'ses-ət-ē\ *n, pl* **ne·ces·si·ties 1** : the state of things that forces certain actions 〈the *necessity* of eating〉 **2** : very great need 〈call us for help in case of *necessity*〉 **3** : the state of being without or unable to get necessary things : POVERTY 〈forced by *necessity* to beg〉 **4** : something that is badly needed 〈bought a few *necessities*〉

neck \'nek\ *n* **1** : the part connecting the head and the main part of the body **2** : the part of a garment covering or nearest to the neck **3** : something like a neck in shape or position 〈the *neck* of a bottle〉 — **necked** \'nekt\ *adj* — **neck and neck** : so nearly equal (as in a race) that one cannot be said to be ahead of the other

neck·er·chief \'nek-ər-chif\ *n, pl* **neck·er-**

chiefs \-chifs, -,chēvz\ : a square of cloth worn folded around the neck like a scarf

neck·lace \'nek-ləs\ : an ornament (as a string of beads) worn around the neck

neck·line \'nek-,līn\ *n* : the outline of the neck opening of a garment

neck·tie \'nek-,tī\ *n* : a narrow length of material worn around the neck and tied in front

nec·tar \'nek-tər\ *n* **1** : the drink of the Greek and Roman gods **2** : a sweet liquid given off by plants and used by bees in making honey

nec·tar·ine \,nek-tə-'rēn\ *n* : a peach with a smooth skin

née *or* **nee** \'nā\ *adj* : BORN 1 — used to identify a woman by her maiden name 〈Mrs. Jane Doe, *née* Roe〉

¹**need** \'nēd\ *n* **1** : something that must be done : OBLIGATION 〈the *need* to be careful〉 **2** : a lack of something necessary, useful, or desired 〈in great *need*〉 **3** : something necessary or desired 〈our daily *needs*〉

²**need** *vb* **1** : to suffer from the lack of something important to life or health 〈give to those who *need*〉 **2** : to be necessary 〈something *needs* to be done〉 **3** : to be without : REQUIRE 〈*need* advice〉

need·ful \'nēd-fəl\ *adj* : ²NECESSARY — **need·ful·ly** \-fə-lē\ *adv* — **need·ful·ness** *n*

¹**nee·dle** \'nēd-l\ *n* **1** : a slender pointed usually steel device used to make a hole and pull thread through in sewing **2** : a slender pointed piece of metal or plastic (used for knitting) **3** : a leaf (as of a pine) shaped like a needle **4** : a pointer on a dial **5** : a slender hollow instrument by which material is put into or taken from the body through the skin — **nee·dle·like** \'nēd-l-,līk\ *adj*

²**needle** *vb* **nee·dled; nee·dling** : ¹TEASE, TAUNT

nee·dle·point \'nēd-l-,pȯint\ *n* : embroidery done on canvas usually in simple even stitches across counted threads

need·less \'nēd-ləs\ *adj* : UNNECESSARY — **need·less·ly** *adv* — **need·less·ness** *n*

nee·dle·work \'nēd-l-,wərk\ *n* : work (as sewing or embroidery) done with a needle

needn't \'nēd-nt\ : need not

needs \'nēdz\ *adv* : because of necessity 〈must *needs* be recognized〉

needy \'nēd-ē\ *adj* **need·i·er; need·i·est** : very poor 〈*needy* people〉 — **need·i·ness** *n*

ne'er \'neər, naər\ *adv* : NEVER

ne'er–do–well \'neər-dù-,wel, 'naər-\ *n* : a worthless person who will not work

ne·gate \ni-'gāt\ *vb* **ne·gat·ed; ne·gat·ing 1** : to deny the existence or truth of **2** : to cause to be ineffective

ne·ga·tion \ni-'gā-shən\ *n* : the action of negating : DENIAL

¹**neg·a·tive** \'neg-ət-iv\ *adj* **1** : making a denial ⟨a *negative* reply⟩ **2** : not positive ⟨a *negative* test⟩ **3** : not helpful ⟨a *negative* attitude⟩ **4** : less than zero and shown by a minus sign ⟨−2 is a *negative* number⟩ **5** : of, being, or relating to electricity of which the electron is the unit and which is produced in a hard rubber rod that has been rubbed with wool ⟨a *negative* charge⟩ **6** : having more electrons than protons ⟨a *negative* particle⟩ **7** : being the part toward which the electric current flows from the outside circuit ⟨the *negative* pole of a storage battery⟩ — **neg·a·tive·ly** *adv* — **neg·a·tiv·i·ty** \,neg-ə-'tiv-ət-ē\ *n*

²**negative** *n* **1** : something that is the opposite of something else **2** : a negative number **3** : an expression (as the word *no*) that denies or says the opposite **4** : the side that argues or votes against something **5** : a photographic image on film from which a final picture is made

¹**ne·glect** \ni-'glekt\ *vb* **1** : to fail to give the right amount of attention to **2** : to fail to do or look after especially because of carelessness

synonyms NEGLECT and DISREGARD mean to pass over something without giving it any or enough attention. NEGLECT suggests that one has not given, whether deliberately or not, enough attention to something that deserves or requires attention ⟨you have been *neglecting* your homework⟩ DISREGARD suggests deliberately overlooking something usually because one feels that it is not worth noticing ⟨*disregarded* the "no smoking" sign⟩

²**neglect** *n* **1** : an act or instance of neglecting something **2** : the state of being neglected

ne·glect·ful \ni-'glekt-fəl\ *adj* : tending to neglect : NEGLIGENT — **neg·lect·ful·ly** \-fə-lē\ *adv* — **ne·glect·ful·ness** *n*

neg·li·gee \,neg-lə-'zhā\ *n* : a woman's loose robe worn especially while dressing or resting

neg·li·gence \'neg-lə-jəns\ *n* **1** : the state of being negligent **2** : an act or instance of being negligent

neg·li·gent \'neg-lə-jənt\ *adj* : likely to neglect things : CARELESS — **neg·li·gent·ly** *adv*

neg·li·gi·ble \'neg-lə-jə-bəl\ *adj* : so small

or unimportant as to deserve little or no attention — **neg·li·gi·bly** \-blē\ *adv*

ne·go·tia·ble \ni-'gō-shə-bəl\ *adj* : possible to negotiate — **ne·go·tia·bil·i·ty** \ni-,gō-shə-'bil-ət-ē\ *n*

ne·go·ti·ate \ni-'gō-shē-,āt\ *vb* **ne·go·ti·at·ed; ne·go·ti·at·ing 1** : to have a discussion with another in order to settle something ⟨*negotiate* with the enemy for peace⟩ **2** : to arrange for by discussing ⟨*negotiate* a loan⟩ **3** : to give to someone in exchange for cash or something of equal value ⟨*negotiate* a check⟩ **4** : to be successful in getting around, through, or over ⟨*negotiate* a turn⟩ — **ne·go·ti·a·tor** \-,āt-ər\ *n*

ne·go·ti·a·tion \ni-,gō-shē-'ā-shən\ *n* : the act or process of negotiating or being negotiated

Ne·gro \'nē-,grō\ *n, pl* **Ne·groes 1** : a member of any of the original peoples of Africa south of the Sahara **2** : a person with Negro ancestors — **Negro** *adj*

¹**neigh** \'nā\ *vb* : to make a neigh

²**neigh** *n* : the long loud cry of a horse

¹**neigh·bor** \'nā-bər\ *n* **1** : a person living or a thing located near another **2** : a fellow human being

²**neighbor** *vb* : to be near or next to — **neigh·bor·ing** *adj*

neigh·bor·hood \'nā-bər-,hůd\ *n* **1** : a place or region near : VICINITY **2** : an amount, size, or range that is close to ⟨cost in the *neighborhood* of ten dollars⟩ **3** : the people living near one another **4** : a section lived in by neighbors ⟨they are building a new house in our *neighborhood*⟩

neigh·bor·ly \'nā-bər-lē\ *adj* : of, relating to, or like neighbors : FRIENDLY — **neigh·bor·li·ness** *n*

¹**nei·ther** \'nē-thər, 'nī-\ *pron* : not the one and not the other ⟨*neither* of the bottles is full⟩

²**neither** *conj* **1** : not either ⟨*neither* good nor bad⟩ **2** : also not ⟨our parents did not want to go and *neither* did we⟩

³**neither** *adj* : not either ⟨*neither* hand⟩

ne·on \'nē-,än\ *n* : a colorless gaseous chemical element found in very small amounts in the air and used in electric lamps for signs

neo·phyte \'nē-ə-,fīt\ *n* **1** : a new convert **2** : BEGINNER, NOVICE

\ə\ abut	\aů\ out	\i\ tip	\ȯ\ saw	\ů\ foot
\ər\ further	\ch\ chin	\ī\ life	\ȯi\ coin	\y\ yet
\a\ mat	\e\ pet	\j\ job	\th\ thin	\yü\ few
\ā\ take	\ē\ easy	\ng\ sing	\th\ this	\yů\ cure
\ä\ cot, cart	\g\ go	\ō\ bone	\ü\ food	\zh\ vision

neph·ew \'nef-yü\ *n* : a son of one's brother or sister

Nep·tune \'nep-,tün, -,tyün\ *n* : the planet that is eighth in order of distance from the sun and has a diameter of about 45,000 kilometers

nep·tu·ni·um \nep-'tü-nē-əm, -'tyü-\ *n* : a radioactive chemical element similar to uranium

¹nerve \'nərv\ *n* **1** : one of the bands of nerve fibers that join centers (as the brain) of the nervous system with other parts of the body and carry nerve impulses **2** : FORTITUDE, DARING ⟨a test of *nerve*⟩ **3** : IMPUDENCE ⟨you've got a lot of *nerve* asking me that⟩ **4 nerves** *pl* : JITTERS **5** : the sensitive soft inner part of a tooth — **nerve·less** \-ləs\ *adj*

²nerve *vb* **nerved; nerv·ing** : to give strength or courage to

nerve cell *n* : a cell of the nervous system with fibers that conduct nerve impulses

nerve fiber *n* : any of the slender extensions of a nerve cell that carry nerve impulses

nerve impulse *n* : a progressive change of a nerve fiber by which information is brought to or orders sent from the central nervous system

ner·vous \'nər-vəs\ *adj* **1** : of or relating to nerve cells ⟨*nervous* tissue⟩ **2** : of, relating to, or made up of nerves or nervous tissue ⟨the *nervous* system⟩ **3** : easily excited or upset ⟨a *nervous* person⟩ **4** : TIMID ⟨*nervous* about answering in class⟩ — **ner·vous·ly** *adv* — **ner·vous·ness** *n*

nervy \'nər-vē\ *adj* **nerv·i·er; nerv·i·est 1** : showing calm courage : BOLD **2** : ¹FORWARD 2 **3** : NERVOUS 3 — **nerv·i·ness** *n*

-ness \nəs\ *n suffix* : state : condition ⟨good*ness*⟩ ⟨sick*ness*⟩

¹nest \'nest\ *n* **1** : a shelter made by a bird for its eggs and young **2** : a place where the eggs of some animals other than birds are laid and hatched ⟨a snake's *nest*⟩ **3** : a cozy home : a snug shelter **4** : those living in a nest ⟨a *nest* of robins⟩

²nest *vb* : to build or live in a nest ⟨*nesting* birds⟩

nes·tle \'nes-əl\ *vb* **nes·tled; nes·tling** \'nes-ling, -ə-ling\ **1** : to lie close and snug : CUDDLE **2** : to settle as if in a nest

nest·ling \'nest-ling\ *n* : a young bird not yet able to leave the nest

¹net \'net\ *n* **1** : a fabric made of threads, cords, ropes, or wires that weave in and out with much open space **2** : something made of net ⟨a *net* for catching fish⟩ **3** : something that traps one as if in a net ⟨a *net* of lies⟩ **4** : NETWORK 2

²net *vb* **net·ted; net·ting 1** : to cover with or as if with a net **2** : to catch in or as if in a net

³net *adj* : remaining after all charges or expenses have been subtracted ⟨*net* profit⟩

⁴net *vb* **net·ted; net·ting** : to gain or produce as profit : CLEAR ⟨each sale *nets* ten cents⟩

net·ting \'net-ing\ *n* : NETWORK 1, 2

net·tle \'net-l\ *n* : any of several tall coarse herbs with stinging hairs

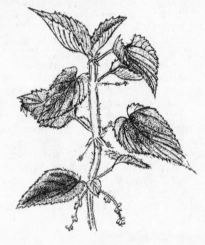

nettle

net·work \'net-,wərk\ *n* **1** : a net fabric or structure **2** : an arrangement of lines or channels crossing as in a net **3** : a group of connected radio or television stations

neu·ron \'nü-,rän, 'nyü-\ *n* : NERVE CELL

neu·ter \'nüt-ər, 'nyüt-\ *adj* : lacking sex organs : having sex organs that are not fully developed

¹neu·tral \'nü-trəl, 'nyü-\ *adj* **1** : not favoring either side in a quarrel, contest, or war **2** : of or relating to a neutral country **3** : being neither one thing nor the other **4** : having no color that stands out : GRAYISH **5** : neither acid nor basic **6** : not electrically charged

²neutral *n* **1** : one that is neutral **2** : a state in which the gears that pass on motion are not touching ⟨put the automobile into *neutral*⟩

neu·tral·i·ty \nü-'tral-ət-ē, nyü-\ *n* : the quality or state of being neutral

neu·tral·ize \'nü-trə-,līz, 'nyü-\ *vb* **neu·tral·ized; neu·tral·iz·ing 1** : to make chemically neutral ⟨*neutralize* an acid with lime⟩ **2** : to make ineffective — **neu-**

tral·iza·tion \,nü-trə-lə-'zā-shən, ,nyü-\ *n* — **neu·tral·iz·er** *n*

neu·tron \'nü-,trän, 'nyü-\ *n* : a particle that has a mass nearly equal to that of the proton but no electrical charge and that is present in all atomic nuclei except those of hydrogen

nev·er \'nev-ər\ *adv* **1** : not ever : at no time **2** : not to any extent or in any way ⟨*never* fear⟩

nev·er·more \,nev-ər-'mōr\ *adv* : never again

nev·er·the·less \,nev-ər-thə-'les\ *adv* : even so : HOWEVER

¹**new** \'nü, 'nyü\ *adj* **1** : not old : RECENT **2** : taking the place of one that came before ⟨a *new* teacher⟩ **3** : recently discovered or learned about ⟨*new* lands⟩ **4** : not known or experienced before ⟨*new* feelings⟩ **5** : not accustomed ⟨a person *new* to the job⟩ **6** : beginning as a repeating of a previous act or thing ⟨a *new* year⟩ **7** : being in a position, place, or state the first time ⟨*new* member⟩ — **new·ness** *n*

²**new** *adv* : NEWLY, RECENTLY ⟨*new*-mown hay⟩

new·born \'nü-'bȯrn, 'nyü-\ *adj* **1** : recently born **2** : made new or strong again ⟨*newborn* hopes⟩

new·com·er \'nü-,kəm-ər, 'nyü-\ *n* **1** : one recently arrived **2** : BEGINNER

new·el \'nü-əl, 'nyü-\ *n* : a post at the bottom or at a turn of a stairway

new·fan·gled \'nü-'fang-gəld, 'nyü-\ *adj* : of the newest style : NOVEL ⟨*newfangled* ideas⟩

new·ly \'nü-lē, 'nyü-\ *adv* : not long ago : RECENTLY ⟨a *newly* married couple⟩

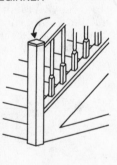

newel

new moon *n* **1** : the moon's phase when its dark side is toward the earth **2** : the thin curved outline of the moon seen shortly after sunset for a few days after the new moon

news \'nüz, 'nyüz\ *n* **1** : a report of recent events ⟨family *news*⟩ **2** : material reported in a newspaper or news magazine or on a newscast **3** : an event that is interesting enough to be reported

news·boy \'nüz-,bȯi, 'nyüz-\ *n* : a person who delivers or sells newspapers

news·cast \'nüz-,kast, 'nyüz-\ *n* : a radio or television broadcast of news

news·girl \'nüz-,gərl, 'nyüz-\ *n* : a girl who delivers or sells newspapers

news·man \'nüz-mən, 'nyüz-\ *n, pl* **news·men** \-mən\ : a person who gathers or reports news

news·pa·per \'nüz-,pā-pər, 'nyüz-\ *n* : a paper that is printed and sold usually every day or often several times a day and contains news, articles, and advertising

news·pa·per·man \'nüz-,pā-pər-,man, 'nyüz-\ *n, pl* **news·pa·per·men** \-,men\ : a man who owns or works on a newspaper

news·pa·per·wom·an \'nüz-,pā-pər-,wu̇m-ən, 'nyüz-\ *n, pl* **news·pa·per·wom·en** \-,wim-ən\ : a woman who owns or works on a newspaper

news·reel \'nüz-,rēl, 'nyüz-\ *n* : a short motion picture about current events

news·stand \'nüz-,stand, 'nyüz-\ *n* : a place where newspapers and magazines are sold

news·wom·an \'nüz-,wu̇m-ən, 'nyüz-\ *n, pl* **news·wom·en** \-,wim-ən\ : a woman who gathers or reports news

newsy \'nü-zē, 'nyü-\ *adj* **news·i·er**; **news·i·est** : filled with news ⟨a *newsy* letter⟩

newt \'nüt, 'nyüt\ *n* : a small salamander that lives mostly in water

New Year's Day *n* : January 1 observed as a legal holiday in many countries

¹**next** \'nekst\ *adj* : coming just before or after ⟨the *next* page⟩ ⟨we were *next* in line⟩

²**next** *adv* **1** : in the nearest place, time, or order following ⟨do that *next*⟩ **2** : at the first time after this ⟨when *next* we meet⟩

³**next** *prep* : NEXT TO

next–door \,neks-'dōr\ *adj* : located in the next building, apartment, or room

¹**next to** *prep* **1** : BESIDE 1 ⟨sat *next to* my friend⟩ **2** : following right after ⟨*next to* chocolate, strawberry ice cream is my favorite⟩

²**next to** *adv* : very nearly : ALMOST ⟨it was *next to* impossible⟩

nib \'nib\ *n* **1** : a pointed object (as the bill of a bird) **2** : the point of a pen

¹**nib·ble** \'nib-əl\ *vb* **nib·bled**; **nib·bling** : to bite or chew gently or bit by bit — **nib·bler** \'nib-lər\ *n*

²**nibble** *n* **1** : an act of nibbling **2** : a very small amount

nice \'nīs\ *adj* **nic·er**; **nic·est** **1** : very fussy (as about appearance, manners, or food)

\ə\ **abut**	\au̇\ **out**	\i\ **tip**	\ȯ\ **saw**	\u̇\ **foot**
\ər\ **further**	\ch\ **chin**	\ī\ **life**	\ȯi\ **coin**	\y\ **yet**
\a\ **mat**	\e\ **pet**	\j\ **job**	\th\ **thin**	\yü\ **few**
\ā\ **take**	\ē\ **easy**	\ng\ **sing**	\th\ **this**	\yu̇\ **cure**
\ä\ **cot, cart**	\g\ **go**	\ō\ **bone**	\ü\ **food**	\zh\ **vision**

2 : able to recognize small differences between things ⟨has a *nice* ear for music⟩ **3** : PLEASING, PLEASANT ⟨a *nice* time⟩ **4** : well behaved ⟨*nice* people⟩ — **nice·ly** *adv* — **nice·ness** *n*

Word History The English word *nice* came from an Old French word that meant "stupid." This Old French word came in turn from a Latin word that meant "ignorant." At first, English *nice* meant "stupid" or "foolish." Later it came to mean "finicky" or "fussy." From these later meanings came the meanings that *nice* has today.

ni·ce·ty \'nī-sət-ē\ *n, pl* **ni·ce·ties 1** : something dainty, delicate, or especially nice ⟨the *niceties* of life⟩ **2** : a fine detail ⟨*niceties* of workmanship⟩

niche \'nich\ *n* **1** : an open hollow in a wall (as for a statue) **2** : a place, job, or use for which a person or a thing is best fitted ⟨you've found your *niche*⟩

¹nick \'nik\ *n* **1** : a small cut or chip in a surface **2** : the last moment ⟨in the *nick* of time⟩

²nick *vb* : to make a nick in

¹nick·el \'nik-əl\ *n* **1** : a hard silvery white metallic chemical element that can be highly polished, resists weathering, and is used in alloys **2** : a United States coin worth five cents

Word History The coin that is called a *nickel* got its name from the metal called *nickel*. The name of the metal comes from a German word, which is the name of an ore that has nickel in it. This ore has a color like copper, but it has no copper in it. This misleading color must have given the ore its German name, made by putting together two German words. One means "copper" and the other means "goblin."

²nickel *vb* **nick·eled** *or* **nick·elled; nick·el·ing** *or* **nick·el·ling** : to plate with nickel

¹nick·er \'nik-ər\ *vb* : ¹NEIGH, WHINNY

²nicker *n* : ²NEIGH

¹nick·name \'nik-ˌnām\ *n* **1** : a usually descriptive name given in addition to the one belonging to an individual ⟨had the *nickname* "Nosy"⟩ **2** : a familiar form of a proper name ⟨"Bill" and "Willie" are *nicknames* for "William"⟩

Word History Many years ago there was an English word *ekename* that meant "an extra name." It was made of a word that meant "also" added to the word *name*. It started with a vowel, so *an* was used with this word instead of *a*. When *an ekename*

was said fast, it sounded a bit like *a nekename*. As a result, some people thought the word started with *n* and began to spell it *nekename*. They did not know they were taking *n* away from *an*, adding it to *ekename*, and so making a new word. From this new word came the word *nickname* that we use now.

²nickname *vb* **nick·named; nick·nam·ing** : to give a nickname to

nic·o·tine \'nik-ə-ˌtēn\ *n* : a poisonous substance found in small amounts in tobacco and used especially to kill insects

niece \'nēs\ *n* : a daughter of one's brother or sister

nig·gling \'nig-ling\ *adj* : PETTY 1

¹nigh \'nī\ *adv* **1** : near in time or place **2** : ALMOST, NEARLY

²nigh *adj* : ³CLOSE 5, NEAR

night \'nīt\ *n* **1** : the time between dusk and dawn when there is no sunlight **2** : NIGHTFALL **3** : the darkness of night

night·club \'nīt-ˌkləb\ *n* : a place of entertainment open at night usually serving food and liquor and having music for dancing

night crawl·er \'nīt-ˌkrȯ-lər\ *n* : EARTHWORM

night·fall \'nīt-ˌfȯl\ *n* : the coming of night

night·gown \'nīt-ˌgaun\ *n* : a loose garment worn in bed

night·hawk \'nīt-ˌhȯk\ *n* **1** : a bird that is related to the whippoorwill, flies mostly at twilight, and eats insects **2** : a person who stays up late at night

nighthawk 1

night·in·gale \'nīt-n-ˌgāl\ *n* : a reddish brown Old World thrush noted for the sweet song of the male

¹night·ly \'nīt-lē\ *adj* **1** : of or relating to the night or every night **2** : happening or done at night or every night

²nightly *adv* **1** : every night **2** : at or by night

night·mare \'nīt-ˌmaər, -ˌmeər\ *n* **1** : a frightening dream **2** : a horrible experience — **night·mar·ish** \'nīt-ˌmaər-ish, -ˌmeər-\ *adj*

Word History The *-mare* in *nightmare* comes from an Old English word for a kind of evil spirit. Such spirits were believed to bother people who were sleeping.

night·shirt \'nīt-ˌshərt\ *n* : a nightgown like a very long shirt

night·stick \'nīt-ˌstik\ *n* : a police officer's club

night·time \'nīt-ˌtīm\ *n* : NIGHT 1

nil \'nil\ *n* : ZERO 4, NOTHING

nim·ble \'nim-bəl\ *adj* **nim·bler; nim·blest 1** : quick and light in motion : AGILE ⟨a *nimble* dancer⟩ **2** : quick in understanding and learning : CLEVER ⟨a *nimble* mind⟩ — **nim·ble·ness** *n* — **nim·bly** \-blē\ *adv*

nim·bus \'nim-bəs\ *n, pl* **nim·bi** \-ˌbī\ *or* **nim·bus·es** : a rain cloud that is evenly gray and that covers the whole sky

nin·com·poop \'nin-kəm-ˌpüp, 'niŋ-\ *n* : ¹FOOL 1

¹nine \'nīn\ *adj* : being one more than eight

²nine *n* **1** : one more than eight : three times three : 9 **2** : the ninth in a set or series

¹nine·teen \nīn-'tēn, nīnt-\ *adj* : being one more than eighteen

²nineteen *n* : one more than eighteen : 19

¹nine·teenth \nīn-'tēnth, nīnt-\ *adj* : coming right after eighteenth

²nineteenth *n* : number nineteen in a series

¹nine·ti·eth \'nīnt-ē-əth\ *adj* : coming right after eighty-ninth

²ninetieth *n* : number ninety in a series

¹nine·ty \'nīnt-ē\ *adj* : being nine times ten

²ninety *n* : nine times ten : 90

nin·ja \'nin-jə\ *n* : a person trained in ancient Japanese arts of fighting and defending oneself and employed especially for espionage and assassinations

nin·ny \'nin-ē\ *n, pl* **nin·nies** : ¹FOOL 1

¹ninth \'nīnth\ *adj* : coming right after eighth

²ninth *n* **1** : number nine in a series **2** : one of nine equal parts

¹nip \'nip\ *vb* **nipped; nip·ping 1** : to catch hold of (as with teeth) and squeeze sharply though not very hard **2** : to cut off by or as if by pinching sharply **3** : to stop the growth or progress of ⟨*nip* plans in the bud⟩ **4** : to injure or make numb with cold

²nip *n* **1** : something that nips **2** : the act of nipping **3** : a small portion : BIT

³nip *n* : a small amount of liquor

nip and tuck \ˌnip-ən-'tək\ *adj or adv* : so close that the lead shifts rapidly from one contestant to another

nip·ple \'nip-əl\ *n* **1** : the part of the breast from which a baby or young animal sucks milk **2** : something (as the mouthpiece of a baby's bottle) like a nipple

nip·py \'nip-ē\ *adj* **nip·pi·er; nip·pi·est** : CHILLY ⟨a *nippy* day⟩

nit \'nit\ *n* : the egg of a louse

ni·trate \'nī-ˌtrāt\ *n* : a substance that is made from or has a composition as if made from nitric acid ⟨*nitrates* are used as fertilizers and explosives⟩

ni·tric acid \ˌnī-trik-\ *n* : a strong liquid acid that contains hydrogen, nitrogen, and oxygen and is used in making fertilizers, explosives, and dyes

ni·tro·gen \'nī-trə-jən\ *n* : a colorless odorless gaseous chemical element that makes up 78 percent of the atmosphere and forms a part of all living tissues

nitrogen cycle *n* : a continuous series of natural processes by which nitrogen passes from air to soil to organisms and back into the air

nitrogen fix·a·tion \-fik-'sā-shən\ *n* : the changing of free nitrogen into combined forms especially by bacteria (**nitrogen-fixing bacteria**)

ni·tro·glyc·er·in *or* **ni·tro·glyc·er·ine** \ˌnī-trō-'glis-ə-rən\ *n* : a heavy oily liquid explosive from which dynamite is made

nit·wit \'nit-ˌwit\ *n* : a very silly or stupid person

¹no \nō\ *adv* **1** : not at all : not any ⟨they are *no* better than they should be⟩ **2** : not so — used to express disagreement or refusal ⟨*no*, I'm not hungry⟩ **3** — used to express surprise, doubt, or disbelief ⟨*no*—you don't say⟩

²no *adj* **1** : not any ⟨has *no* money⟩ **2** : hardly any : very little ⟨finished in *no* time⟩ **3** : not a ⟨I'm *no* liar⟩

³no *n, pl* **noes** *or* **nos 1** : an act or instance of refusing or denying by the use of the word *no* : DENIAL **2** : a negative vote or decision **3** *noes or nos pl* : persons voting in the negative

no·bil·i·ty \nō-'bil-ət-ē\ *n, pl* **no·bil·i·ties 1** : the quality or state of being noble **2** : noble rank **3** : the class or a group of nobles

¹no·ble \'nō-bəl\ *adj* **no·bler; no·blest 1** : EMINENT, ILLUSTRIOUS **2** : of very high birth or rank **3** : having very fine qualities **4** : grand in appearance — **no·ble·ness** *n* — **no·bly** \-blē\ *adv*

²noble *n* : a person of noble birth or rank

\ə\ **abut**	\aů\ **out**	\i\ **tip**	\ȯ\ **saw**	\ů\ **foot**
\ər\ **further**	\ch\ **chin**	\ī\ **life**	\ȯi\ **coin**	\y\ **yet**
\a\ **mat**	\e\ **pet**	\j\ **job**	\th\ **thin**	\yü\ **few**
\ā\ **take**	\ē\ **easy**	\ng\ **sing**	\th\ **this**	\yů\ **cure**
\ä\ **cot, cart**	\g\ **go**	\ō\ **bone**	\ü\ **food**	\zh\ **vision**

no·ble·man \'nō-bəl-mən\ *n, pl* **no·ble·men** \-mən\ : a man of noble rank

no·ble·wom·an \'nō-bəl-,wum-ən\ *n, pl* **no·ble·wom·en** \-,wim-ən\ : a woman of noble rank

¹**no·body** \'nō-,bäd-ē, -bəd-ē\ *pron* : no person : not anybody ⟨*nobody* lives in that house⟩

²**nobody** *n, pl* **no·bod·ies** : a person of no importance

noc·tur·nal \näk-'tərn-l\ *adj* **1** : of, relating to, or happening at night : NIGHTLY **2** : active at night ⟨*nocturnal* insects⟩ — **noc·tur·nal·ly** *adv*

¹**nod** \'näd\ *vb* **nod·ded; nod·ding** **1** : to bend the head downward or forward (as in bowing, going to sleep, or indicating "yes") **2** : to move up and down ⟨daisies *nodded* in the breeze⟩ **3** : to show by a nod of the head ⟨*nod* agreement⟩

²**nod** *n* : the action of bending the head downward and forward

node \'nōd\ *n* : a thickened spot or part (as of a plant stem where a leaf develops)

nod·ule \'näj-ül\ *n* : a small node (as of a clover root)

no·el \nō-'el\ *n* **1** : a Christmas carol **2** *cap* : the Christmas season

noes *pl of* NO

¹**noise** \'noiz\ *n* **1** : a loud unpleasant sound **2** : ³SOUND 1 ⟨the *noise* of the wind⟩ — **noise·less** \-ləs\ *adj* — **noise·less·ly** *adv* — **noise·less·ness** *n*

Word History When we are seasick our stomachs quarrel with us. We are likely to quarrel and complain, too. An Old French word that meant "quarrel" or "loud confused sound" came from a Latin word that meant "seasickness." The English word *noise* came from this Old French word. The word *noise* is related to the word *nausea.*

²**noise** *vb* **noised; nois·ing** : to spread by rumor or report ⟨the story was *noised* about⟩

noise·mak·er \'noiz-,mā-kər\ *n* : a device used to make noise especially at parties

noisy \'noi-zē\ *adj* **nois·i·er; nois·i·est** **1** : making noise **2** : full of noise ⟨a *noisy* street⟩ — **nois·i·ly** \-zə-lē\ *adv* — **nois·i·ness** \-zē-nəs\ *n*

¹**no·mad** \'nō-,mad\ *n* **1** : a member of a people having no fixed home but wandering from place to place **2** : WANDERER

²**nomad** *adj* : NOMADIC 2

no·mad·ic \nō-'mad-ik\ *adj* **1** : of or relating to nomads **2** : roaming about with no special end in mind

nom·i·nal \'näm-ən-l\ *adj* **1** : being such

in name only ⟨the *nominal* president⟩ **2** : very small : TRIFLING ⟨a *nominal* price⟩ — **nom·i·nal·ly** *adv*

nom·i·nate \'näm-ə-,nāt\ *vb* **nom·i·nat·ed; nom·i·nat·ing** : to choose as a candidate for election, appointment, or honor ⟨*nominate* a candidate for president⟩ — **nom·i·na·tor** \-,nāt-ər\ *n*

nom·i·na·tion \,näm-ə-'nā-shən\ *n* **1** : the act or an instance of nominating **2** : the state of being nominated

nom·i·na·tive \'näm-ə-nət-iv\ *adj* : being or belonging to the case of a noun or pronoun that is usually the subject of a verb

nom·i·nee \,näm-ə-'nē\ *n* : a person nominated for an office, duty, or position

non- *prefix* : not ⟨*nonresident*⟩ ⟨*nonstop*⟩

non·al·co·hol·ic \,nän-,al-kə-'hol-ik, -'häl-\ *adj* : containing no alcohol

non·cha·lance \,nän-shə-'läns\ *n* : the state of being nonchalant

non·cha·lant \,nän-shə-'länt\ *adj* : having a confident and easy manner — **non·cha·lant·ly** \-'länt-lē\ *adv*

non·com·ba·tant \,nän-kəm-'bat-nt, 'nän-'käm-bət-ənt\ *n* **1** : a member (as a chaplain) of the armed forces whose duties do not include fighting **2** : ¹CIVILIAN

non·com·mis·sioned officer \,nän-kə-,mish-ənd-\ *n* : an officer in the Army, Air Force, or Marine Corps appointed from among the enlisted persons

non·com·mit·tal \,nän-kə-'mit-l\ *adj* : not telling or showing what one thinks or has decided ⟨a *noncommittal* answer⟩ — **non·com·mit·tal·ly** *adv*

non·com·mu·ni·ca·ble \,nän-kə-'myü-nə-kə-bəl\ *adj* : not spread from one individual to another ⟨*noncommunicable* diseases⟩

non·con·duc·tor \,nän-kən-'dək-tər\ *n* : a substance that conducts heat, electricity, or sound at a very low rate

non·con·form·ist \,nän-kən-'for-məst\ *n* : a person who does not conform to generally accepted standards or customs

non·de·script \,nän-di-'skript\ *adj* : of no certain class or kind : not easily described

¹**none** \'nən\ *pron* : not any : not one ⟨*none* of the trouble can be blamed on you⟩

²**none** *adv* **1** : not at all ⟨arrived *none* too soon⟩ **2** : in no way ⟨*none* the worse for wear⟩

non·en·ti·ty \nä-'nent-ət-ē\ *n, pl* **non·en·ti·ties** : someone or something of no importance

¹**non·es·sen·tial** \,nän-ə-'sen-chəl\ *adj* : not essential

²nonessential *n* : something that is not essential

none·the·less \ˌnən-thə-'les\ *adv* : NEVERTHELESS

non·fic·tion \'nän-'fik-shən\ *n* : writings that are not fiction

non·flam·ma·ble \'nän-'flam-ə-bəl\ *adj* : not flammable

non·green \'nän-'grēn\ *adj* : having no chlorophyll ⟨*nongreen* plants⟩

non·liv·ing \'nän-'liv-ing\ *adj* : not living

non·par·ti·san \'nän-'pärt-ə-zən\ *adj* : not partisan : not committed to one party or side

non·plus \'nän-'pləs\ *vb* **non·plussed; non·plus·sing** : to cause to be at a loss as to what to say, think, or do : PERPLEX

non·poi·son·ous \'nän-'póiz-n-əs\ *adj* : not poisonous ⟨*nonpoisonous* snakes⟩

non·prof·it \'nän-'präf-ət\ *adj* : not existing or carried on to make a profit ⟨*nonprofit* organizations⟩

¹non·res·i·dent \'nän-'rez-ə-dənt\ *adj* : not living in a certain place ⟨a *nonresident* student⟩

²nonresident *n* : a nonresident person

non·sched·uled \'nän-'skej-üld\ *adj* : licensed to carry pasengers or freight by air whenever demand requires ⟨*nonscheduled* airlines⟩

non·sec·tar·i·an \ˌnän-sek-'ter-ē-ən\ *adj* : not limited to a particular religious group

non·sense \'nän-ˌsens, -səns\ *n* **1** : foolish or meaningless words or actions **2** : things of no importance or value

non·sen·si·cal \nän-'sen-si-kəl\ *adj* : making no sense : ABSURD — **non·sen·si·cal·ly** *adv*

non·stan·dard \'nän-'stan-dərd\ *adj* : not standard

non·stop \'nän-'stäp\ *adv or adj* : without a stop ⟨will fly there *nonstop*⟩ ⟨a *nonstop* flight⟩

noo·dle \'nüd-l\ *n* : a food like macaroni made with egg and shaped into flat strips — usually used in pl.

nook \'núk\ *n* **1** : an inner corner ⟨a chimney *nook*⟩ **2** : a sheltered or hidden place ⟨a shady *nook*⟩

noon \'nün\ *n* : the middle of the day : twelve o'clock in the daytime

noon·day \'nün-ˌdā\ *n* : NOON, MIDDAY

no one *pron* : ¹NOBODY ⟨*no one* was home when I called⟩

noon·tide \'nün-ˌtīd\ *n* : NOON

noon·time \'nün-ˌtīm\ *n* : NOON

noose \'nüs\ *n* : a loop that passes through a knot at the end of a line so that it gets smaller when the other end of the line is pulled

nor \nər, nòr\ *conj* : and not ⟨neither young *nor* old⟩

norm \'nòrm\ *n* : ¹AVERAGE 2

¹nor·mal \'nòr-məl\ *adj* **1** : of the regular or usual kind : REGULAR **2** : of average intelligence **3** : sound in body or mind **synonyms** see REGULAR — **nor·mal·ly** *adv*

> **Word History** People who work with wood use something called a *square* to make and test right angles. The English word *normal* came from the Latin word for this kind of square which also meant "rule" or "pattern." *Normal* at first meant "forming a right angle." Later *normal* came to mean "by a rule or pattern" or "regular."

²normal *n* **1** : one that is normal **2** : ¹AVERAGE 2

nor·mal·cy \'nòr-məl-sē\ *n* : NORMALITY

nor·mal·i·ty \nòr-'mal-ət-ē\ *n* : the quality or state of being normal

Nor·man \'nòr-mən\ *n* **1** : one of the Scandinavians who conquered Normandy in the tenth century **2** : one of the people of mixed Norman and French blood who conquered England in 1066

Norse \'nòrs\ *n pl* **1** : people of Scandinavia **2** : people of Norway

¹north \'nòrth\ *adv* : to or toward the north

²north *adj* : placed toward, facing, or coming from the north

³north *n* **1** : the direction to the left of one facing east : the compass point opposite to south **2** *cap* : regions or countries north of a point that is mentioned or understood

¹North American *n* : a person born or living in North America

²North American *adj* : of or relating to North America or the North Americans

north·bound \'nòrth-ˌbaúnd\ *adj* : going north

¹north·east \nòr-'thēst\ *adj* : to or toward the northeast

²northeast *n* **1** : the direction between north and east **2** *cap* : regions or countries northeast of a point that is mentioned or understood

³northeast *adj* : placed toward, facing, or coming from the northeast

north·east·er·ly \nòr-'thē-stər-lē\ *adv or adj* **1** : from the northeast **2** : toward the northeast

north·east·ern \nòr-'thē-stərn\ *adj* **1** *of-*

\ə\ abut	\aú\ out	\i\ tip	\ò\ saw	\ú\ foot
\ər\ further	\ch\ chin	\ī\ life	\ói\ coin	\y\ yet
\a\ mat	\e\ pet	\j\ job	\th\ thin	\yü\ few
\ā\ take	\ē\ easy	\ng\ sing	\th\ this	\yú\ cure
\ä\ cot, cart	\g\ go	\ō\ bone	\ü\ food	\zh\ vision

ten cap : of, relating to, or like that of the Northeast **2** : lying toward or coming from the northeast

north•er•ly \'nȯr-thər-lē\ *adj or adv* **1** : toward the north **2** : from the north ⟨a *northerly* wind⟩

north•ern \'nȯr-thərn\ *adj* **1** *often cap* : of, relating to, or like that of the North **2** : lying toward or coming from the north

northern lights *n pl* : AURORA BOREALIS

north•land \'nȯrth-,land\ *n, often cap* : land in the north : the north of a country or region

north pole *n* **1** *often cap N&P* : the most northern point of the earth : the northern end of the earth's axis **2** : the end of a magnet that points toward the north when the magnet is free to swing

North Star *n* : the star toward which the northern end of the earth's axis very nearly points

¹**north•ward** \'nȯrth-wərd\ *adv or adj* : toward the north

²**northward** *n* : a northward direction or part

¹**north•west** \nȯrth-'west\ *adv* : to or toward the northwest

²**northwest** *n* **1** : the direction between north and west **2** *cap* : regions or countries northwest of a point that is mentioned or understood

³**northwest** *adj* : placed toward, facing, or coming from the northwest

north•west•er•ly \nȯrth-'wes-tər-lē\ *adv or adj* **1** : from the northwest **2** : toward the northwest

north•west•ern \nȯrth-'wes-tərn\ *adj* **1** *often cap* : of, relating to, or like that of the Northwest **2** : lying toward or coming from the northwest

¹**Nor•we•gian** \nȯr-'wē-jən\ *adj* : of or relating to Norway, its people, or the Norwegian language

²**Norwegian** *n* **1** : a person who is born or lives in Norway **2** : the language of the Norwegians

nos *pl of* NO

¹**nose** \'nōz\ *n* **1** : the part of a person's face or an animal's head that contains the nostrils **2** : the sense or organ of smell ⟨a dog with a good *nose*⟩ **3** : something (as a point, edge, or the front of an object) that suggests a nose ⟨the *nose* of an airplane⟩ **4** : an ability to discover ⟨a *nose* for news⟩ — **nosed** \'nōzd\ *adj*

²**nose** *vb* **nosed; nos•ing** **1** : to detect by or as if by smell : SCENT **2** : to touch or rub with the nose : NUZZLE **3** : to search in a nosy way : PRY ⟨you're always *nosing* around in someone else's business⟩ **4** : to

move ahead slowly or carefully ⟨the ship *nosed* into its berth⟩

nose•bleed \'nōz-,blēd\ *n* : a bleeding at the nose

nose cone *n* : a protective cone forming the forward end of a rocket or missile

nose–dive \'nōz-,dīv\ *vb* **nose–dived; nose–div•ing** : to plunge suddenly or sharply

nose dive *n* **1** : a downward plunge (as of an airplane) **2** : a sudden sharp drop (as in prices)

nos•tal•gia \nä-'stal-jə\ *n* : a wishing for something past

nos•tril \'näs-trəl\ *n* : either of the outer openings of the nose through which one breathes

nos•trum \'näs-trəm\ *n* : a medicine of secret formula and doubtful worth : a questionable remedy

nosy *or* **nos•ey** \'nō-zē\ *adj* **nos•i•er; nos•i•est** : tending to pry into someone else's business

not \'nät\ *adv* **1** — used to make a word or group of words negative ⟨the books are *not* here⟩ **2** — used to stand for the negative of a group of words that comes before ⟨sometimes hard to see and sometimes *not*⟩

¹**no•ta•ble** \'nōt-ə-bəl\ *adj* **1** : deserving special notice : REMARKABLE ⟨a *notable* sight⟩ **2** : DISTINGUISHED, PROMINENT ⟨a *notable* writer⟩ — **no•ta•bly** \-blē\ *adv*

²**notable** *n* : a famous person

no•ta•rize \'nōt-ə-,rīz\ *vb* **no•ta•rized; no•ta•riz•ing** : to sign as a notary public to show that a document is authentic

no•ta•ry public \,nōt-ə-rē-\ *n, pl* **no•ta•ries public** *or* **notary publics** : a public officer who witnesses the making of a document (as a deed) and signs it to show that it is authentic

no•ta•tion \nō-'tā-shən\ *n* **1** : the act of noting **2** : ²NOTE 5 ⟨make *notations* on a paper⟩ **3** : a system of signs, marks, or figures used to give specified information ⟨musical *notation*⟩ ⟨scientific *notation*⟩

¹**notch** \'näch\ *n* **1** : a cut in the shape of a V in an edge or surface **2** : a narrow pass between mountains **3** : DEGREE 1, STEP ⟨turn the radio up a *notch*⟩

²**notch** *vb* : to cut or make notches in

¹**note** \'nōt\ *vb* **not•ed; not•ing** **1** : to notice or observe with care **2** : to record in writing **3** : to call attention to in speech or writing

²**note** *n* **1** : a musical sound : TONE **2** : a symbol in music that by its shape and position on the staff shows the pitch of a tone and the length of time it is to be held

3 : the musical call or song of a bird **4** : a quality that shows a feeling ⟨a *note* of sadness in your voice⟩ **5** : something written down often to aid the memory ⟨I'll make a *note* of the appointment⟩ **6** : a printed comment in a book that helps explain part of the text **7** : DISTINCTION 3 ⟨artists of *note*⟩ **8** : a short written message or letter **9** : careful notice ⟨take *note* of the time⟩ **10** : a promise to pay a debt **11** : a piano key **12** : frame of mind : MOOD ⟨began the day on a happy *note*⟩

note·book \'nōt-ˌbuk\ *n* : a book of blank pages for writing in

not·ed \'nōt-əd\ *adj* : well-known and highly regarded

note·wor·thy \'nōt-ˌwər-thē\ *adj* : worthy of note : REMARKABLE — **note·wor·thi·ness** *n*

¹noth·ing \'nəth-ing\ *pron* **1** : not anything : no thing ⟨there's *nothing* in the box⟩ **2** : one of no interest, value, or importance ⟨your opinion is *nothing* to me⟩

²nothing *adv* : not at all : in no way

³nothing *n* **1** : something that does not exist **2** : ZERO 1, 4 **3** : something of little or no worth or importance — **noth·ing·ness** *n*

¹no·tice \'nōt-əs\ *n* **1** : WARNING ⟨on short *notice*⟩ **2** : an indication that an agreement will end at a specified time ⟨gave my employer *notice*⟩ **3** : ATTENTION 1, HEED ⟨take no *notice* of them⟩ **4** : a written or printed announcement **5** : a brief published criticism (as of a book or play)

²notice *vb* **no·ticed; no·tic·ing** : to take notice of : pay attention to ⟨given to *noticing* details⟩

no·tice·able \'nōt-ə-sə-bəl\ *adj* : deserving notice : likely to be noticed — **no·tice·ably** \-blē\ *adv*

no·ti·fi·ca·tion \ˌnōt-ə-fə-'kā-shən\ *n* **1** : the act or an instance of notifying **2** : something written or printed that gives notice

no·ti·fy \'nōt-ə-ˌfī\ *vb* **no·ti·fied; no·ti·fy·ing** : to give notice to : INFORM ⟨*notify* the police⟩

no·tion \'nō-shən\ *n* **1** : IDEA 2 ⟨haven't the faintest *notion* what to do⟩ **2** : WHIM ⟨a sudden *notion* to go home⟩ **3 notions** *pl* : small useful articles (as buttons, needles, and thread)

no·to·ri·ety \ˌnōt-ə-'rī-ət-ē\ *n* : the state of being notorious

no·to·ri·ous \nō-'tōr-ē-əs\ *adj* : widely known for some bad characteristic ⟨a *notorious* thief⟩ — **no·to·ri·ous·ly** *adv*

¹not·with·stand·ing \ˌnät-with-'stan-ding, -with-\ *prep* : in spite of ⟨we went ahead with our plan *notwithstanding* their objections⟩

²notwithstanding *adv* : NEVERTHELESS

nou·gat \'nü-gət\ *n* : a candy consisting of a sugar paste with nuts or fruit pieces

nought *variant of* NAUGHT

noun \'naun\ *n* : a word or phrase that is the name of something (as a person, place, or thing) and that is used in a sentence especially as subject or object of a verb or as object of a preposition

nour·ish \'nər-ish\ *vb* : to cause to grow or live in a healthy state especially by providing with enough good food — **nour·ish·ing** *adj*

nour·ish·ment \'nər-ish-mənt\ *n* **1** : something (as food) that nourishes **2** : the act of nourishing : the state of being nourished

¹nov·el \'näv-əl\ *adj* **1** : new and different from what is already known **2** : original or striking in design or appearance

²novel *n* : a long made-up story that usually fills a book

nov·el·ist \'näv-ə-ləst\ *n* : a writer of novels

nov·el·ty \'näv-əl-tē\ *n, pl* **nov·el·ties 1** : something new or unusual **2** : the quality or state of being novel **3** : a small article of unusual design intended mainly for decoration or adornment

No·vem·ber \nō-'vem-bər\ *n* : the eleventh month of the year

nov·ice \'näv-əs\ *n* **1** : a new member of a religious community who is preparing to take the vows of religion **2** : a person who has no previous experience with something : BEGINNER

¹now \nau\ *adv* **1** : at this time **2** : imme-

\ə\ abut		\au\ out	\i\ tip	\o\ saw	\u\ foot
\ər\ further		\ch\ chin	\ī\ life	\oi\ coin	\y\ yet
\a\ mat		\e\ pet	\j\ job	\th\ thin	\yu\ few
\ā\ take		\ē\ easy	\ng\ sing	\th\ this	\yu\ cure
\ä\ cot, cart		\g\ go	\ō\ bone	\ü\ food	\zh\ vision

diately before the present time ⟨left just *now*⟩ **3** : in the time immediately to follow ⟨will leave *now*⟩ **4** — used to express command or introduce an important point ⟨*now* this story is interesting⟩ **5** : SOMETIMES ⟨*now* one and *now* another⟩ **6** : in the present state ⟨*now* what can we do⟩ **7** : at the time referred to ⟨*now* the trouble began⟩

²**now** *conj* : in view of the fact that : ³SINCE **2** ⟨*now* you've come, we can begin⟩

³**now** \'naú\ *n* : the present time ⟨up till *now*⟩

now·a·days \'naú-ə-,dāz\ *adv* : at the present time

¹**no·where** \'nō-,hwear, -,wear, -,hwaər, -,waər\ *adv* **1** : not in or at any place **2** : to no place

²**nowhere** *n* : a place that does not exist

nox·ious \'näk-shəs\ *adj* : causing harm ⟨*noxious* fumes⟩

noz·zle \'näz-əl\ *n* : a short tube with a taper or constriction often used on a hose or pipe to direct or speed up a flow of fluid

-n't \nt, -nt, ənt\ *adv suffix* : not ⟨isn*'t*⟩

nu·cle·ar \'nü-klē-ər, 'nyü-\ *adj* **1** : of, relating to, or being a nucleus (as of a cell) **2** : of, relating to, or using the atomic nucleus, atomic energy, the atom bomb, or atomic power

nuclear energy *n* : ATOMIC ENERGY

nu·cle·us \'nü-klē-əs, 'nyü-\ *n, pl* **nu·clei** \-klē-,ī\ **1** : a central point, group, or mass **2** : a part of cell protoplasm enclosed in a nuclear membrane, containing chromosomes and genes, and concerned especially with the control of vital functions and heredity **3** : the central part of an atom that comprises nearly all of the atomic mass and that consists of protons and neutrons except in hydrogen in which it consists of one proton only

nude \'nüd, 'nyüd\ *adj* **nud·er; nud·est** : not wearing clothes : NAKED — **nude·ness** *n*

¹**nudge** \'nəj\ *vb* **nudged; nudg·ing** : to touch or push gently (as with the elbow) especially in order to attract attention

²**nudge** *n* : a slight push

nu·di·ty \'nüd-ət-ē, 'nyüd-\ *n* : the quality or state of being nude

nug·get \'nəg-ət\ *n* : a solid lump especially of precious metal

nui·sance \'nüs-ns, 'nyüs-\ *n* : an annoying person or thing

null \'nəl\ *adj* : having no legal force : not binding : VOID

null and void *adj* : NULL

¹**numb** \'nəm\ *adj* **1** : lacking in sensation especially from cold **2** : lacking feelings

: INDIFFERENT — **numb·ly** *adv* — **numbness** *n*

²**numb** *vb* : to make or become numb

¹**num·ber** \'nəm-bər\ *n* **1** : the total of persons, things, or units taken together : AMOUNT ⟨the *number* of people in a room⟩ **2** : a total that is not specified ⟨I got a *number* of presents on my birthday⟩ **3** : a quality of a word form that shows whether the word is singular or plural ⟨a verb agrees in *number* with its subject⟩ **4** : NUMERAL ⟨the *number* 5⟩ **5** : a certain numeral for telling one person or thing from another or from others ⟨a house *number*⟩ **6** : one of a series ⟨the March *number* of a magazine⟩

²**number** *vb* **1** : ¹COUNT 1 **2** : INCLUDE ⟨was *numbered* among the guests⟩ **3** : to limit to a certain number ⟨vacation days are *numbered* now⟩ **4** : to give a number to ⟨*number* the pages of a scrapbook⟩ **5** : to add up to or have a total of ⟨our group *numbered* ten in all⟩

num·ber·less \'nəm-bər-ləs\ *adj* : too many to count ⟨the *numberless* stars in the sky⟩

number line *n* : a line in which points are matched to numbers

nu·mer·al \'nü-mə-rəl, 'nyü-\ *n* : a symbol or group of symbols representing a number

nu·mer·a·tion \,nü-mə-'rā-shən, ,nyü-\ *n* : a system of counting

nu·mer·a·tor \'nü-mə-,rāt-ər, 'nyü-\ *n* : the part of a fraction that is above the line ⟨3 is the *numerator* of the fraction ⅗⟩

nu·mer·i·cal \nú-'mer-i-kəl, nyú-\ *adj* : of or relating to number : stated in numbers — **nu·mer·i·cal·ly** *adv*

nu·mer·ous \'nü-mə-rəs, 'nyü-\ *adj* : consisting of a large number ⟨*numerous* friends⟩ ⟨a *numerous* family⟩ — **nu·mer·ous·ly** *adv*

num·skull \'nəm-,skəl\ *n* : a stupid person

nun \'nən\ *n* : a woman belonging to a religious community and living by vows

nun·cio \'nən-sē-,ō, 'nún-\ *n, pl* **nun·ci·os** : a person who is the pope's representative to a civil government

nup·tial \'nəp-shəl\ *adj* : of or relating to marriage or a wedding

nup·tials \'nəp-shəlz\ *n pl* : WEDDING

¹**nurse** \'nərs\ *n* **1** : a woman employed for the care of a young child **2** : a person skilled or trained in the care of the sick

Word History The English word *nurse* can be traced back to a Latin word that meant "nourishing" or "feeding." In the past some mothers did not feed their babies at their own breasts but hired someone else to do so. The English word *nurse* was first used for such a woman. Later it came to be used for any woman hired to take care of a young child. The word *nurse* is also used now for a person who takes care of sick people.

²nurse *vb* **nursed; nurs·ing 1** : to feed at the breast **2** : to take care of (as a young child or a sick person) **3** : to treat with special care ⟨*nurse* a plant⟩

nurse·maid \'nər-ˌsmād\ *n* : ¹NURSE 1

nurs·ery \'nər-sə-rē, 'nərs-rē\ *n, pl* **nurs·er·ies 1** : a place set aside for small children or for the care of small children **2** : a place where young trees, vines, and plants are grown and usually sold

nurs·ery·man \'nər-sə-rē-mən, 'nərs-rē-\ *n, pl* **nurs·ery·men** \-mən\ : a person whose occupation is the growing of trees, shrubs, and plants

¹nur·ture \'nər-chər\ *n* **1** : UPBRINGING **2** : something (as food) that nourishes

²nurture *vb* **nur·tured; nur·tur·ing 1** : to supply with food **2** : EDUCATE 2 **3** : to provide for growth of

¹nut \'nət\ *n* **1** : a dry fruit or seed with a firm inner kernel and a hard shell **2** : the often edible kernel of a nut **3** : a piece of metal with a hole in it that is fastened to a bolt by means of a screw thread **4** : a foolish or crazy person — **nut·like** \-ˌlīk\ *adj*

²nut *vb* **nut·ted; nut·ting** : to gather or seek nuts

nut·crack·er \'nət-ˌkrak-ər\ *n* **1** : a device used for cracking the shells of nuts **2** : a bird related to the crows that lives mostly on the seeds of pine trees

nut·hatch \'nət-ˌhach\ *n* : a small bird that creeps on tree trunks and branches and eats insects

nut·let \'nət-lət\ *n* **1** : a small nut **2** : a small fruit like a nut

nut·meg \'nət-ˌmeg\ *n* : a spice that is the ground seeds of a small evergreen tropical tree

nuthatch

nu·tri·ent \'nü-trē-ənt, 'nyü-\ *n* : a substance used in nutrition ⟨green plants make their food from simple *nutrients* such as carbon dioxide and water⟩

nu·tri·ment \'nü-trə-mənt, 'nyü-\ *n* : something that nourishes

nu·tri·tion \nü-'trish-ən, nyü-\ *n* : the act or process of nourishing or being nourished : the processes by which a living being takes in and uses nutrients

nu·tri·tion·al \nü-'trish-ən-l, nyü-\ *adj* : of or relating to nutrition

nu·tri·tious \nü-'trish-əs, nyü-\ *adj* : providing nutrients : NOURISHING

nu·tri·tive \'nü-trət-iv, 'nyü-\ *adj* **1** : NUTRITIONAL **2** : NUTRITIOUS

nut·ty \'nət-ē\ *adj* **nut·ti·er; nut·ti·est 1** : not showing good sense **2** : having a flavor like that of nuts

nuz·zle \'nəz-əl\ *vb* **nuz·zled; nuz·zling 1** : to push or rub with the nose **2** : to lie close : NESTLE

ny·lon \'nī-ˌlän\ *n* : a synthetic material used in the making of textiles and plastics

nymph \'nimf\ *n* **1** : one of many goddesses in old legends represented as beautiful young girls living in the mountains, forests, and waters **2** : an immature insect that differs from the adult chiefly in the size and proportions of the body

o \'ō\ *n, pl* **o's** *or* **os** \'ōz\ *often cap* **1** : the fifteenth letter of the English alphabet **2** : ZERO 1

O *variant of* OH

oaf \'ōf\ *n* : a stupid or awkward person — **oaf·ish** \'ō-fish\ *adj*

oak \'ōk\ *n* : any of various trees and

shrubs related to the beech and chestnut whose fruits are acorns and whose tough

\ə\ **abut**	\au̇\ **out**	\i\ **tip**	\ȯ\ **saw**	\u̇\ **foot**
\ər\ **further**	\ch\ **chin**	\ī\ **life**	\ȯi\ **coin**	\y\ **yet**
\a\ **mat**	\e\ **pet**	\j\ **job**	\th\ **thin**	\yü\ **few**
\ā\ **take**	\ē\ **easy**	\ng\ **sing**	\th\ **this**	\yu̇\ **cure**
\ä\ **cot, cart**	\g\ **go**	\ō\ **bone**	\ü\ **food**	\zh\ **vision**

wood is much used for furniture and flooring

oak·en \'ō-kən\ *adj* : made of or like oak

oar \'ōr\ *n* : a long pole with a broad blade at one end used for rowing or steering a boat

oar·lock \'ōr-,läk\ *n* : a usually U-shaped device for holding an oar in place

oars·man \'ōrz-mən\ *n, pl* **oars·men** \-mən\ : a person who rows a boat

oa·sis \ō-'ā-səs\ *n, pl* **oa·ses** \-,sēz\ : a fertile or green spot in a desert

oat \'ōt\ *n* **1** : a cereal grass grown for its loose clusters of seeds that are used for human food and animal feed **2 oats** *pl* : a crop or the grain of the oat

oath \'ōth\ *n, pl* **oaths** \'ōthz, 'ōths\ **1** : a solemn appeal to God or to some deeply respected person or thing to witness to the truth of one's word or the sacredness of a promise ⟨under *oath* to tell the truth⟩ **2** : a careless or improper use of a sacred name

oat·meal \'ōt-,mēl\ *n* **1** : oats husked and

oat 1

ground into meal or flattened into flakes **2** : a hot cereal made from meal or flakes of oats

obe·di·ence \ō-'bēd-ē-əns\ *n* : the act of obeying : willingness to obey

obe·di·ent \ō-'bēd-ē-ənt\ *adj* : willing to obey : likely to mind — **obe·di·ent·ly** *adv*

obe·lisk \'äb-ə-,lisk, 'ōb-\ *n* : a four-sided pillar that becomes narrower toward the top and ends in a pyramid

obese \ō-'bēs\ *adj* : very fat

obey \ō-'bā\ *vb* **obeyed; obey·ing 1** : to follow the commands or guidance

obelisk

of **2** : to comply with : carry out ⟨*obey* an order⟩ ⟨*obey* the rules⟩

synonyms OBEY and MIND mean to do what another person says. OBEY suggests that one quickly yields to the authority of another or follows a rule or law ⟨*obey* your parents⟩ ⟨*obey* all traffic laws⟩ MIND is used like *obey* especially when speaking to children but it often stresses paying attention to the wishes or commands of another ⟨*mind* what I said about talking⟩

obit·u·ary \ō-'bich-ə-,wer-ē\ *n, pl* **obit·u·ar·ies** : a notice of a person's death (as in a newspaper)

¹ob·ject \'äb-jikt\ *n* **1** : something that may be seen or felt ⟨tables and chairs are *objects*⟩ **2** : something that arouses feelings in an observer ⟨the *object* of their envy⟩ **3** : ¹PURPOSE, AIM ⟨the *object* is to raise money⟩ **4** : a noun or a term behaving like a noun that receives the action of a verb or completes the meaning of a preposition

²ob·ject \əb-'jekt\ *vb* **1** : to offer or mention as an objection ⟨the treasurer *objected* that the funds were too low⟩ **2** : to oppose something firmly and usually with words ⟨*object* to a plan⟩

synonyms OBJECT and PROTEST mean to oppose something by arguing against it. OBJECT stresses one's great dislike or hatred ⟨I *object* to being called a liar⟩ PROTEST suggests the presenting of objections in speech, writing, or in an organized, public demonstration ⟨groups *protesting* the building of the airport⟩

ob·jec·tion \əb-'jek-shən\ *n* **1** : an act of objecting **2** : a reason for or a feeling of disapproval

ob·jec·tion·able \əb-'jek-shə-nə-bəl\ *adj* : arousing objection : OFFENSIVE

¹ob·jec·tive \əb-'jek-tiv\ *adj* **1** : being outside of the mind and independent of it **2** : dealing with facts without allowing one's feelings to confuse them ⟨an *objective* report⟩ **3** : being or belonging to the case of a noun or pronoun that is an object of a transitive verb or a preposition ⟨a noun in the *objective* case⟩ — **ob·jec·tive·ly** *adv*

²objective *n* : ¹PURPOSE, GOAL

ob·jec·tiv·i·ty \,äb-,jek-'tiv-ət-ē\ *n* : the quality or state of being objective

ob·li·gate \'äb-lə-,gāt\ *vb* **ob·li·gat·ed; ob·li·gat·ing 1** : to make (someone) do something by law or because it is right **2** : OBLIGE 2

ob·li·ga·tion \,äb-lə-'gā-shən\ *n* **1** : an act of making oneself responsible for doing something **2** : something (as the demands of a promise or contract) that requires one to do something **3** : something one must do : DUTY **4** : a feeling of being indebted for an act of kindness

oblige \ə-'blīj\ *vb* **obliged; oblig·ing 1** : ²FORCE 1, COMPEL ⟨the soldiers were *obliged* to retreat⟩ **2** : to earn the gratitude of ⟨you will *oblige* me by coming early⟩ **3** : to do a favor for or do something as a favor ⟨I'll be glad to *oblige*⟩

oblig·ing \ə-'blī-jing\ *adj* : willing to do favors — **oblig·ing·ly** *adv*

oblique \ō-'blēk, ə-\ *adj* : neither perpendicular nor parallel — **oblique·ly** *adv*

oblit·er·ate \ə-'blit-ə-,rāt\ *vb* **oblit·er·at·ed; oblit·er·at·ing** : to remove or destroy completely

obliv·i·on \ə-'bliv-ē-ən\ *n* **1** : an act of forgetting or the fact of having forgotten **2** : the quality or state of being forgotten

obliv·i·ous \ə-'bliv-ē-əs\ *adj* : ²UNAWARE, FORGETFUL ⟨*oblivious* of the crowd⟩ ⟨*oblivious* to the danger⟩

¹ob·long \'äb-,lóng\ *adj* : longer in one direction than the other with opposite sides parallel : RECTANGULAR

²oblong *n* : an oblong figure or object

ob·nox·ious \äb-'näk-shəs, əb-\ *adj* : very disagreeable : HATEFUL

oboe \'ō-bō\ *n* : a woodwind instrument in the form of a slender tube with holes and keys that is played by blowing into a reed mouthpiece

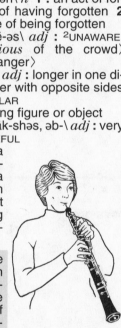

oboe

Word History The oboe, the English horn, and the bassoon belong to the same group of woodwind instruments. Of the three the oboe has the highest pitch. The English word *oboe* comes from the Italian name of the instrument. This Italian name comes from the oboe's French name. The French name is made up of two French words. The first means "high" and the second means "wood."

ob·scene \äb-'sēn, əb-\ *adj* : very shocking to one's sense of what is moral or decent

ob·scen·i·ty \äb-'sen-ət-ē, əb-\ *n, pl* **ob·scen·i·ties 1** : the quality or state of being obscene **2** : something that is obscene

¹ob·scure \äb-'skyur, əb-\ *adj* **1** : ¹DARK 1,

GLOOMY **2** : SECLUDED ⟨an *obscure* village in the country⟩ **3** : not easily understood or clearly expressed ⟨an *obscure* chapter in a book⟩ **4** : not outstanding or famous ⟨an *obscure* poet⟩

²obscure *vb* **ob·scured; ob·scur·ing** : to make obscure

ob·scu·ri·ty \äb-'skyur-ət-ē, əb-\ *n, pl* **ob·scu·ri·ties 1** : the quality or state of being obscure ⟨lived in *obscurity*⟩ **2** : something that is obscure ⟨the poems are filled with *obscurities*⟩

ob·serv·able \əb-'zər-və-bəl\ *adj* : NOTICEABLE — **ob·serv·ably** \-blē\ *adv*

ob·ser·vance \əb-'zər-vəns\ *n* **1** : an established practice or ceremony ⟨religious *observances*⟩ **2** : an act of following a custom, rule, or law ⟨careful *observance* of the speed laws⟩

ob·ser·vant \əb-'zər-vənt\ *adj* : quick to take notice : WATCHFUL, ALERT — **ob·ser·vant·ly** *adv*

ob·ser·va·tion \,äb-sər-'vā-shən, -zər-\ *n* **1** : an act or the power of seeing or of fixing the mind upon something **2** : the gathering of information by noting facts or occurrences ⟨weather *observations*⟩ **3** : an opinion formed or expressed after observing **4** : the fact of being observed

ob·ser·va·to·ry \əb-'zər-və-,tōr-ē\ *n, pl* **ob·ser·va·to·ries** : a place that has instruments for making observations (as of the stars)

ob·serve \əb-'zərv\ *vb* **ob·served; ob·serv·ing 1** : to act in agreement with : OBEY ⟨*observe* the law⟩ **2** : CELEBRATE 2 ⟨*observe* a religious holiday⟩ **3** : ¹WATCH 5 ⟨*observed* their actions carefully⟩ **4** : ¹REMARK 2, SAY ⟨*observed* that it was a fine day⟩ — **ob·serv·er** *n*

ob·sess \əb-'ses\ *vb* : to occupy the mind of completely or abnormally ⟨*obsessed* with a new scheme⟩

ob·ses·sion \äb-'sesh-ən\ *n* : a disturbing and often unreasonable idea or feeling that cannot be put out of the mind

ob·sid·i·an \əb-'sid-ē-ən\ *n* : a smooth dark rock formed by the cooling of lava

ob·so·lete \,äb-sə-'lēt\ *adj* : no longer in use : OUT-OF-DATE ⟨*obsolete* words⟩

ob·sta·cle \'äb-stə-kəl\ *n* : something that stands in the way or opposes : HINDRANCE

ob·sti·na·cy \'äb-stə-nə-sē\ *n* : the quality or state of being obstinate

\ə\ **abut**	\au̇\ **out**	\i\ **tip**	\ȯ\ **saw**	\u̇\ **foot**
\ər\ **further**	\ch\ **chin**	\ī\ **life**	\ȯi\ **coin**	\y\ **yet**
\a\ **mat**	\e\ **pet**	\j\ **job**	\th\ **thin**	\yü\ **few**
\ā\ **take**	\ē\ **easy**	\ng\ **sing**	\t͟h\ **this**	\yu̇\ **cure**
\ä\ **cot, cart**	\g\ **go**	\ō\ **bone**	\ü\ **food**	\zh\ **vision**

ob·sti·nate \'äb-stə-nət\ *adj* **1** : sticking stubbornly to an opinion or purpose **2** : not easily overcome or removed ⟨an *obstinate* fever⟩ — **ob·sti·nate·ly** *adv*

ob·struct \əb-'strəkt\ *vb* **1** : to stop up by an obstacle : BLOCK **2** : to be or come in the way of : HINDER

ob·struc·tion \əb-'strək-shən\ *n* **1** : an act of obstructing : the state of being obstructed **2** : something that gets in the way : OBSTACLE

ob·tain \əb-'tān\ *vb* : to gain or get hold of with effort ⟨*obtain* a ticket⟩ ⟨*obtained* the prisoner's release⟩

ob·tain·able \əb-'tā-nə-bəl\ *adj* : possible to obtain ⟨tickets were not *obtainable*⟩

ob·tuse \äb-'tüs, -'tyüs\ *adj* **1** : not quick or keen of understanding or feeling **2** : not pointed or sharp : BLUNT

obtuse angle *n* : an angle that is greater than a right angle

ob·vi·ous \'äb-vē-əs\ *adj* : easily found, seen, or understood — **ob·vi·ous·ly** *adv* — **ob·vi·ous·ness** *n*

oc·ca·sion \ə-'kā-zhən\ *n* **1** : a suitable opportunity : a good chance ⟨take the first *occasion* to write⟩ **2** : the time of an event ⟨on the *occasion* of the wedding⟩ **3** : a special event ⟨a great *occasion*⟩

oc·ca·sion·al \ə-'kā-zhən-l\ *adj* : happening or met with now and then ⟨went to an *occasional* movie⟩ — **oc·ca·sion·al·ly** *adv*

oc·cu·pan·cy \'äk-yə-pən-sē\ *n, pl* **oc·cu·pan·cies** : the act of occupying or taking possession

oc·cu·pant \'äk-yə-pənt\ *n* : a person who occupies or takes possession

oc·cu·pa·tion \,äk-yə-'pā-shən\ *n* **1** : one's business or profession ⟨a tailor by *occupation*⟩ **2** : the taking possession and control of an area ⟨*occupation* of a conquered country⟩

oc·cu·pa·tion·al \,äk-yə-'pā-shən-l\ *adj* : of or relating to one's occupation — **oc·cu·pa·tion·al·ly** *adv*

oc·cu·py \'äk-yə-,pī\ *vb* **oc·cu·pied; oc·cu·py·ing 1** : to take up the attention or energies of ⟨reading *occupied* me most of the summer⟩ **2** : to fill up (an extent of time or space) ⟨sports *occupy* our spare time⟩ ⟨a liter of water *occupies* 1000 cubic centimeters of space⟩ **3** : to take or hold possession of ⟨enemy troops *occupied* the town⟩ **4** : to live in as an owner or tenant ⟨*occupied* the house three years⟩

oc·cur \ə-'kər\ *vb* **oc·curred; oc·cur·ring 1** : to be found or met with : APPEAR ⟨a disease that *occurs* among animals⟩ **2** : to present itself : come by or as if by chance ⟨an accident *occurred* on the way to school⟩ ⟨success doesn't just *occur*, it is earned⟩ **3** : to come into the mind ⟨it just *occurred* to me⟩

oc·cur·rence \ə-'kər-əns\ *n* **1** : something that occurs **2** : the action or process of occurring **synonyms** see INCIDENT

ocean \'ō-shən\ *n* **1** : the whole body of salt water that covers nearly three fourths of the earth **2** : one of the large bodies of water into which the great ocean is divided

oce·an·ic \,ō-shē-'an-ik\ *adj* : of or relating to the ocean

ocean·og·ra·phy \,ō-shə-'näg-rə-fē\ *n* : a science that deals with the ocean

oce·lot \'äs-ə-,lät, 'ō-sə-\ *n* : a medium-sized American wildcat that is tawny or grayish and blotched with black

ocelot

o'clock \ə-'kläk\ *adv* : according to the clock ⟨the time is one *o'clock*⟩

octa- *or* **octo-** *also* **oct-** *prefix* : eight

oc·ta·gon \'äk-tə-,gän\ *n* : a flat figure with eight angles and eight sides

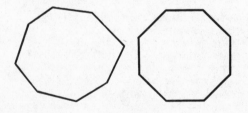

octagon

oc·tag·o·nal \äk-'tag-ən-l\ *adj* : having eight sides

oc·tave \'äk-tiv\ *n* **1** : a space of eight steps between musical notes **2** : a tone or note that is eight steps above or below another note or tone

oc·tet \äk-'tet\ *n* : a group or set of eight

Oc·to·ber \äk-'tō-bər\ *n* : the tenth month of the year

Word History The calendar first used in ancient Rome started the year with the month of March. October was the eighth month of the year. The Latin name for this month came from the Latin word that meant "eight." The English name *October* comes from the Latin name of the month.

oc·to·pus \'äk-tə-pəs\ *n, pl* **oc·to·pus·es** *or* **oc·to·pi** \-tə-ˌpī\ : a marine animal with no shell that has a rounded body with eight long flexible arms about its base which have sucking disks able to seize and hold things (as prey)

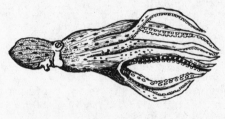

octopus

oc·u·lar \'äk-yə-lər\ *adj* : of or relating to the eye or eyesight

odd \'äd\ *adj* **1** : not one of a pair or a set ⟨an *odd* glove⟩ **2** : not capable of being divided by two without leaving a remainder ⟨the *odd* numbers 1, 3, 5, 7, etc.⟩ **3** : numbered with an odd number ⟨an *odd* year⟩ **4** : some more than the number mentioned ⟨fifty *odd* years ago⟩ **5** : not usual, expected, or planned ⟨*odd* jobs⟩ ⟨an *odd* stroke of luck⟩ **6** : not usual or traditional ⟨an *odd* thing to do⟩ — **odd·ly** *adv* — **odd·ness** *n*

odd·ball \'äd-ˌbȯl\ *n* : a person who behaves strangely

odd·i·ty \'äd-ət-ē\ *n, pl* **odd·i·ties** **1** : something odd **2** : the quality or state of being odd

odds \'ädz\ *n pl* **1** : a difference in favor of one thing over another ⟨the *odds* are in our favor⟩ **2** : DISAGREEMENT 1 ⟨friends who are at *odds*⟩

odds and ends *n pl* : things left over : miscellaneous things

ode \'ōd\ *n* : a lyric poem that expresses a noble feeling with dignity

odi·ous \'ōd-ē-əs\ *adj* : causing hatred or strong dislike : worthy of hatred

odom·e·ter \ō-'däm-ət-ər\ *n* : an instrument for measuring the distance traveled (as by a vehicle)

odor \'ōd-ər\ *n* **1** : a quality of something that one becomes aware of through the sense of smell **2** : a smell whether pleasant or unpleasant — **odored** \'ōd-ərd\ *adj* — **odor·less** \'ōd-ər-ləs\ *adj*

odor·ous \'ōd-ə-rəs\ *adj* : having or giving off an odor

o'er \ȯr\ *adv or prep* : OVER

of \əv, 'əv, 'äv\ *prep* **1** : proceeding from : belonging to ⟨*of* royal blood⟩ **2** : CONCERNING ⟨boast *of* success⟩ **3** — used to show what has been taken away or what one has been freed from ⟨a tree bare *of* leaves⟩ ⟨cured *of* a cold⟩ **4** : on account of ⟨afraid *of* the dark⟩ ⟨died *of* the flu⟩ **5** : made from ⟨a house *of* bricks⟩ **6** — used to join an amount or a part with the whole which includes it ⟨most *of* the children⟩ ⟨a pound *of* cheese⟩ **7** : that is ⟨the city *of* Rome⟩ **8** : that has : WITH 8 ⟨a person *of* courage⟩ ⟨a thing *of* no importance⟩

¹off \'ȯf\ *adv* **1** : from a place or position ⟨marched *off*⟩ **2** : from a course : ASIDE ⟨turned *off* onto a side street⟩ **3** : into sleep ⟨dozed *off* and dropped the book⟩ **4** : so as not to be supported, covering or enclosing, or attached ⟨rolled to the edge of the table and *off*⟩ ⟨the lid blew *off*⟩ ⟨the handle fell *off*⟩ **5** : so as to be discontinued or finished ⟨turn the radio *off*⟩ ⟨paid *off* their debts⟩ **6** : away from work ⟨took the day *off*⟩

²off \'ȯf\ *prep* **1** : away from the surface or top of ⟨*off* the table⟩ **2** : at the expense of ⟨lived *off* my parents⟩ **3** : released or freed from ⟨*off* duty⟩ **4** : below the usual level of ⟨a dollar *off* the price⟩ **5** : away from ⟨just *off* the highway⟩

³off \'ȯf\ *adj* **1** : more removed or distant ⟨the *off* side⟩ **2** : started on the way ⟨*off* on a trip⟩ **3** : not taking place ⟨the game is *off*⟩ **4** : not operating ⟨the radio is *off*⟩ **5** : not correct : WRONG ⟨your guess is way *off*⟩ **6** : not entirely sane **7** : small in degree : SLIGHT ⟨an *off* chance⟩ **8** : provided for ⟨well *off*⟩

of·fend \ə-'fend\ *vb* **1** : to do wrong : SIN ⟨*offend* against the law⟩ **2** : to hurt the feelings of : DISTRESS ⟨language that *offends* decent people⟩

of·fend·er \ə-'fen-dər\ *n* : a person who offends

of·fense *or* **of·fence** \ə-'fens\ *n* **1** : an act of attacking : ASSAULT **2** : an offensive team **3** : the act of offending : the state of being offended **4** : WRONGDOING, SIN

¹of·fen·sive \ə-'fen-siv\ *adj* **1** : relating to or made for or suited to attack ⟨*offensive* weapons⟩ **2** : of or relating to the attempt to score in a game or contest ⟨the *offen-*

\ə\ **abut**	\au̇\ **out**	\i\ **tip**	\ȯ\ **saw**	\u̇\ **foot**
\ər\ **further**	\ch\ **chin**	\ī\ **life**	\ȯi\ **coin**	\y\ **yet**
\a\ **mat**	\e\ **pet**	\j\ **job**	\th\ **thin**	\yü\ **few**
\ā\ **take**	\ē\ **easy**	\ng\ **sing**	\th\ **this**	\yu̇\ **cure**
\ä\ **cot, cart**	\g\ **go**	\ō\ **bone**	\ü\ **food**	\zh\ **vision**

sive team⟩ **3 :** causing displeasure or resentment ⟨an *offensive* smell⟩ ⟨an *offensive* question⟩ — **of·fen·sive·ly** *adv* — **of·fen·sive·ness** *n*

²**offensive** *n* **1 :** the state or attitude of one who is making an attack ⟨on the *offensive*⟩ **2 :** ²ATTACK 1

¹**of·fer** \ˈȯf-ər\ *vb* **1 :** to present as an act of worship : SACRIFICE **2 :** to present (something) to be accepted or rejected **3 :** to present for consideration : SUGGEST ⟨*offer* a suggestion⟩ **4 :** to declare one's willingness ⟨*offered* to help⟩ **5 :** PUT UP 5 ⟨*offered* no resistance to the invaders⟩

synonyms OFFER and PRESENT mean to put before another for acceptance. OFFER suggests that the thing may be accepted or refused ⟨*offered* more coffee to the guests⟩ PRESENT suggests that something is offered with the hope or expectation of its being accepted ⟨peddlers *presented* their goods for our inspection⟩ ⟨the principal *presented* the diplomas⟩

²**offer** *n* **1 :** an act of offering **2 :** a price suggested by one prepared to buy : BID

of·fer·ing \ˈȯf-ə-ring, ˈȯf-ring\ *n* **1 :** the act of one who offers **2 :** something offered **3 :** a sacrifice offered as part of worship **4 :** a contribution to the support of a church

off·hand \ˈȯf-ˈhand\ *adv or adj* **:** without previous thought or preparation ⟨can't say *offhand* how many there are⟩ ⟨*offhand* remarks⟩

of·fice \ˈȯf-əs\ *n* **1 :** a special duty or post and especially one of authority in government ⟨run for *office*⟩ **2 :** a place where business is done or a service is supplied ⟨ticket *office*⟩ ⟨a doctor's *office*⟩

of·fice·hold·er \ˈȯf-əs-ˌhōl-dər\ *n* **:** a person who holds public office

of·fi·cer \ˈȯf-ə-sər\ *n* **1 :** a person given the responsibility of enforcing the law ⟨police *officer*⟩ **2 :** a person who holds an office ⟨an *officer* of the company⟩ **3 :** a person who holds a commission in the armed forces ⟨an *officer* of the Navy⟩

¹**of·fi·cial** \ə-ˈfish-əl\ *n* **:** OFFICER 2

²**official** *adj* **1 :** of or relating to an office ⟨*official* duties⟩ **2 :** having authority to perform a duty ⟨the *official* referee⟩ **3 :** coming from or meeting the requirements of an authority ⟨an *official* American League baseball⟩ **4 :** proper for a person in office ⟨an *official* greeting⟩ — **of·fi·cial·ly** *adv*

of·fi·ci·ate \ə-ˈfish-ē-ˌāt\ *vb* **of·fi·ci·at·ed; of·fi·ci·at·ing** **1 :** to perform a ceremony or duty ⟨a bishop *officiated* at the wed-

ding⟩ **2 :** to act as an officer : PRESIDE ⟨*officiated* at the annual meeting⟩

off·ing \ˈȯf-ing\ *n* **:** the near future or distance ⟨see trouble in the *offing*⟩

¹**off·set** \ˈȯf-ˌset\ *n* **1 :** a new stalk from the base of a plant often able to produce a new plant **2 :** something that serves to make up for something else

²**offset** *vb* **offset; off·set·ting** **:** to make up for ⟨gains in one state *offset* losses in another⟩

off·shoot \ˈȯf-ˌshüt\ *n* **:** a branch of a main stem of a plant

¹**off·shore** \ˈȯf-ˈshōr\ *adv* **:** from the shore **:** at a distance from the shore

²**off·shore** \ˈȯf-ˌshōr\ *adj* **1 :** coming or moving away from the shore ⟨an *offshore* breeze⟩ **2 :** located off the shore ⟨*offshore* oil⟩

off·spring \ˈȯf-ˌspring\ *n, pl* **offspring** *also* **off·springs** **:** the young of a person, animal, or plant

off·stage \ˈȯf-ˈstāj\ *adv or adj* **:** off or away from the stage

off–the–rec·ord \ˌȯf-thə-ˈrek-ərd\ *adj* **:** given or made in confidence and not for publication ⟨the candidate's *off-the-record* remarks⟩

oft \ˈȯft\ *adv* **:** OFTEN

of·ten \ˈȯf-ən, -tən\ *adv* **:** many times

of·ten·times \ˈȯf-ən-ˌtīmz, ˈȯf-tən-\ *adv* **:** OFTEN

ogle \ˈō-gəl\ *vb* **ogled; ogling** **:** to look at (as a person) in a flirting way or with unusual attention or desire

ogre \ˈō-gər\ *n* **1 :** an ugly giant of fairy tales and folklore who eats people **2 :** a dreaded person or object

oh *or* **O** \ˈō, ō\ *interj* **1 —** used to express an emotion (as surprise or pain) **2 —** used in direct address ⟨*Oh*, children, stop that noise⟩

¹**-oid** \ˌȯid\ *n suffix* **:** something resembling a specified object or having a specified quality

²**-oid** *adj suffix* **:** resembling **:** having the form or appearance of

¹**oil** \ˈȯil\ *n* **1 :** any of numerous greasy usually liquid substances from plant, animal, or mineral sources that do not dissolve in water and are used especially as lubricants, fuels, and food **2 :** PETROLEUM **3 :** artists' paints made of pigments and oil **4 :** a painting in oils

²**oil** *vb* **:** to put oil on or in

oil·cloth \ˈȯil-ˌklȯth\ *n* **:** cloth treated with oil or paint so as to be waterproof and used for shelf and table coverings

oily \ˈȯi-lē\ *adj* **oil·i·er; oil·i·est** **1 :** of, relating to, or containing oil **2 :** covered or soaked with oil ⟨*oily* rags⟩ — **oil·i·ness** *n*

oint·ment \'óint-mənt\ *n* : a semisolid usually greasy medicine for use on the skin

¹**OK** *or* **okay** \ō-'kā\ *adv or adj* : all right

Word History More than a hundred years ago Boston newspapers were full of abbreviations. Just about anything might be abbreviated. *R.T.B.S.* stood for "remains to be seen." *S.P.* stood for "small potatoes." *N.G.* stood for "no go." *A.R.* stood for "all right." Soon some phrases were spelled wrong on purpose and then abbreviated. *K.G.*, for "know go," was used instead of *N.G. O.W.*, "oll wright," was used instead of *A.R. O.K.*, "oll korrect," was used instead of *A.C.* The fad faded, but the one abbreviation *O.K.* caught on and is still widely used.

²**OK** *or* **okay** *vb* **OK'd** *or* **okayed; OK'ing** *or* **okay·ing** : APPROVE 2, AUTHORIZE

³**OK** *or* **okay** *n* : APPROVAL

oka·pi \ō-'kä-pē\ *n* : an animal of the African forests related to the giraffe

okapi

okra \'ō-krə\ *n* : a plant related to the hollyhocks and grown for its edible green pods which are used in soups and stews

¹**old** \'ōld\ *adj* **1** : dating from the distant past : ANCIENT ⟨an *old* custom⟩ **2** : having lasted or been such for a long time ⟨an *old* friend⟩ ⟨*old* friendships⟩ **3** : having existed for a specified length of time ⟨a child three years *old*⟩ **4** : having lived a long time ⟨*old* people⟩ **5** : FORMER ⟨my *old* students⟩ **6** : showing the effects of time or use ⟨wore an *old* coat⟩

²**old** *n* : old or earlier time ⟨in days of *old*⟩

old·en \'ōl-dən\ *adj* : of or relating to earlier days

Old English *n* : the language of the English people from the earliest documents in the seventh century to about 1100

old–fash·ioned \'ōld-'fash-ənd\ *adj* **1** : of, relating to, or like that of an earlier time **2** : holding fast to old ways : CONSERVATIVE

Old French *n* : the French language from the ninth to the thirteenth century

Old Glory *n* : the flag of the United States

old maid *n* **1** : an elderly unmarried woman **2** : a very neat fussy person **3** : a card game in which cards are matched in pairs and the player holding the extra queen at the end loses

old·ster \'ōld-stər\ *n* : an old person

old–time \ˌōld-ˈtīm\ *adj* : ¹OLD 1

old–tim·er \'ōld-'tī-mər\ *n* **1** : ¹VETERAN 1 **2** : OLDSTER

old–world \'ōl-'dwərld\ *adj* : having old-fashioned charm

oleo·mar·ga·rine \ˌō-lē-ō-'mär-jə-rən\ *n* : MARGARINE

ol·fac·to·ry \äl-'fak-tə-rē, ōl-\ *adj* : of or relating to smelling or the sense of smell

ol·ive \'äl-iv\ *n* **1** : an oily fruit that is eaten both ripe and unripe, is the source of an edible oil (**olive oil**), and grows on an evergreen tree with hard smooth shining wood (**olive wood**) **2** : a yellowish green

Olym·pic Games \ə-ˌlim-pik-\ *n pl* : a series of international athletic contests held in a different country once every four years

om·elet *or* **om·elette** \'äm-ə-lət, 'äm-lət\ *n* : eggs beaten with milk or water, cooked without stirring until firm, and folded over or around a filling

Word History An Old French word that meant "the blade of a sword or knife" came from a Latin word meaning "a thin plate." An omelet, when folded over, looks something like a blade. That is why the French made a word meaning "omelet" from the earlier French word that meant "blade." English *omelet* came from the French word that means "omelet."

omen \'ō-mən\ *n* : a happening believed to be a sign or warning of a future event

om·i·nous \'äm-ə-nəs\ *adj* : being a sign of evil or trouble to come ⟨*ominous* clouds⟩ — **om·i·nous·ly** *adv* — **om·i·nous·ness** *n*

omis·sion \ō-'mish-ən\ *n* **1** : something

omitted **2** : the act of omitting : the state of being omitted

omit \ō-'mit\ *vb* **omit·ted; omit·ting 1** : to leave out : fail to include ⟨*omit* a name from a list⟩ **2** : to leave undone : NEGLECT ⟨they *omitted* to tell us how to do it⟩

om·ni·bus \'äm-ni-,bəs\ *n* : BUS

om·nip·o·tent \äm-'nip-ət-ənt\ *adj* : having power or authority without limit : ALMIGHTY

¹on \òn, än\ *prep* **1** : over and in contact with ⟨put the books *on* the table⟩ **2** : AGAINST **3** ⟨shadows *on* the wall⟩ **3** : near or connected with ⟨a town *on* the river⟩ **4** : ¹TO 1 ⟨the first house *on* the left⟩ **5** : sometime during ⟨*on* Monday⟩ **6** : in the state or process of ⟨*on* fire⟩ ⟨*on* sale⟩ **7** : ²ABOUT 3 ⟨a book *on* minerals⟩ **8** : by means of ⟨talk *on* the phone⟩

²on \'òn, 'än\ *adv* **1** : in or into contact with a surface ⟨put the kettle *on*⟩ ⟨has new shoes *on*⟩ **2** : forward in time, space, or action ⟨went *on* home⟩ ⟨the argument went *on* for weeks⟩ **3** : from one to another ⟨pass the word *on*⟩ ⟨and so *on*⟩ **4** : into operation or a position allowing operation ⟨turn the light *on*⟩

³on \'òn, 'än\ *adj* **1** : being in operation ⟨the radio is *on*⟩ **2** : placed so as to allow operation ⟨the switch is *on*⟩ **3** : taking place ⟨the game is *on*⟩ **4** : having been planned ⟨has nothing *on* for tonight⟩

¹once \'wəns\ *adv* **1** : one time only ⟨it happened just *once*⟩ **2** : at any one time : EVER ⟨if we hesitate *once*, all will be lost⟩ **3** : at some time in the past : FORMERLY ⟨it was *once* done that way⟩

²once *n* : one single time ⟨just this *once*⟩ **— at once 1** : at the same time ⟨two people talking *at once*⟩ **2** : IMMEDIATELY 2 ⟨leave *at once*⟩

³once *conj* : as soon as : WHEN ⟨*once* you've finished your homework, you may watch television⟩

once–over \'wən-,sō-vər\ *n* : a quick glance or examination

on·com·ing \'òn-,kəm-ing, 'än-\ *adj* : coming nearer ⟨an *oncoming* car⟩

¹one \'wən\ *adj* **1** : being a single unit or thing **2** : being a certain unit or thing ⟨early *one* morning⟩ **3** : being the same in kind or quality ⟨members of *one* class⟩ **4** : not specified ⟨at *one* time or another⟩

²one *pron* **1** : a single member or individual ⟨*one* of your friends⟩ **2** : any person ⟨*one* never knows⟩

³one *n* **1** : the number denoting a single unit : 1 **2** : the first in a set or series **3** : a single person or thing

one another *pron* : EACH OTHER

one·self \,wən-'self\ *pron* : one's own self ⟨one may feel proud of *oneself*⟩

one–sid·ed \'wən-'sīd-əd\ *adj* **1** : having or happening on one side only **2** : having one side more developed **3** : favoring one side ⟨a *one-sided* view of the case⟩

one·time \'wən-,tīm\ *adj* : FORMER

one–way \'wən-'wā\ *adj* : moving or allowing movement in one direction only

on·go·ing \'òn-,gō-ing, 'än-\ *adj* : being in progress or movement

on·ion \'ən-yən\ *n* : the edible bulb of a plant related to the lilies that has a sharp odor and taste and is used as a vegetable and to season foods

on·look·er \'òn-,lùk-ər, 'än-\ *n* : SPECTATOR

¹on·ly \'ōn-lē\ *adj* **1** : best without doubt ⟨the *only* person for me⟩ **2** : alone in or of a class or kind : SOLE ⟨the *only* survivor⟩

²only *adv* **1** : as a single fact or instance and nothing more or different ⟨worked *only* in the mornings⟩ **2** : no one or nothing other than ⟨*only* you know⟩ ⟨*only* this will do⟩ **3** : in the end ⟨it will *only* make you sick⟩ **4** : as recently as ⟨*only* last week⟩

³only *conj* : except that ⟨I'd like to play, *only* I'm too tired⟩

on·o·mato·poe·ia \,än-ə-,mat-ə-'pē-ə\ *n* : the forming of a word (as "buzz" or "hiss") in imitation of a natural sound

on·rush \'òn-,rəsh, 'än-\ *n* : a rushing forward

on·set \'òn-,set, 'än-\ *n* **1** : ²ATTACK 1 **2** : BEGINNING

on·slaught \'än-,slòt, 'òn-\ *n* : a violent attack

on·to \,òn-tə, ,än-\ *prep* : to a position on or against ⟨leaped *onto* the horse⟩

¹on·ward \'òn-wərd, 'än-\ *adv* : toward or at a point lying ahead in space or time : FORWARD

²onward *adj* : directed or moving onward ⟨the *onward* march of time⟩

oo·dles \'üd-lz\ *n pl* : a great quantity

¹ooze \'üz\ *n* : soft mud : SLIME

²ooze *vb* **oozed; ooz·ing** : to flow or leak out slowly

opal \'ō-pəl\ *n* : a mineral with soft changeable colors that is used as a gem

opaque \ō-'pāk\ *adj* **1** : not letting light through : not transparent **2** : not reflecting light : DULL ⟨an *opaque* paint⟩

¹open \'ō-pən\ *adj* **1** : not shut or blocked : not closed ⟨an *open* window⟩ ⟨*open* books⟩ **2** : not enclosed or covered ⟨an *open* boat⟩ ⟨an *open* fire⟩ **3** : not secret : PUBLIC ⟨an *open* dislike⟩ **4** : to be used, entered, or taken part in by all ⟨an *open* golf tournament⟩ ⟨an *open* meeting⟩ **5**

: easy to enter, get through, or see ⟨*open* country⟩ **6** : not drawn together : spread out ⟨an *open* flower⟩ ⟨*open* umbrellas⟩ **7** : not decided or settled ⟨an *open* question⟩ **8** : ready to consider appeals or ideas ⟨an *open* mind⟩ — **open·ly** *adv* — **open·ness** *n*

²open *vb* **1** : to change or move from a shut condition ⟨*open* a book⟩ ⟨the door *opened*⟩ **2** : to clear by or as if by removing something in the way ⟨*open* a road blocked with snow⟩ **3** : to make or become ready for use ⟨*open* a store⟩ ⟨the office *opens* at eight⟩ **4** : to have an opening ⟨the rooms *open* onto a hall⟩ **5** : BEGIN 1, START ⟨*open* talks⟩ ⟨*open* fire on an enemy⟩ — **open·er** \'ōp-ə-nər, 'ōp-nər\ *n*

³open *n* : open space : OUTDOORS

open–air \,ō-pən-'aər, -'eər\ *adj* : OUTDOOR

open–and–shut \,ō-pən-ən-'shət\ *adj* : ¹PLAIN 3, OBVIOUS ⟨an *open-and-shut* case⟩

open·heart·ed \,ō-pən-'härt-əd\ *adj* **1** : FRANK **2** : GENEROUS 1

open·ing \'ōp-ə-ning, 'ōp-ning\ *n* **1** : an act of opening ⟨the *opening* of a new store⟩ **2** : an open place : CLEARING **3** : BEGINNING ⟨the *opening* of the speech⟩ **4** : OCCASION 1 ⟨waiting for an *opening* to tell the joke⟩ **5** : a job opportunity ⟨an *opening* in the legal department⟩

open letter *n* : a letter (as one addressed to an official) for the public to see and printed in a newspaper or magazine

open·work \'ō-pən-,wərk\ *n* : something made or work done so as to show openings through the fabric or material

op·era \'äp-ə-rə, 'äp-rə\ *n* : a play in which the entire text is sung with orchestral accompaniment

opera glasses *n* : small binoculars or field glasses of low power for use in a theater

op·er·ate \'äp-ə-,rāt\ *vb* **op·er·at·ed; op·er·at·ing** **1** : to work or cause to work in a proper way ⟨a machine *operating* smoothly⟩ ⟨learn to *operate* a car⟩ **2** : to take effect ⟨a drug that *operates* quickly⟩ **3** : MANAGE 1 ⟨*operate* a farm⟩ ⟨*operates* a business⟩ **4** : to perform surgery : do an operation on (as a person)

op·er·a·tion \,äp-ə-'rā-shən\ *n* **1** : the act, process, method, or result of operating ⟨does the whole *operation* without thinking⟩ ⟨the *operation* of a drug⟩ **2** : the quality or state of being able to work ⟨the factory is now in *operation*⟩ **3** : a certain piece or kind of surgery ⟨an *operation* for appendicitis⟩ **4** : a process (as addition or multiplication) of getting one mathemati-

cal expression from others according to a rule **5** : the process of putting military or naval forces into action ⟨naval *operations*⟩

op·er·a·tion·al \,äp-ə-'rā-shən-l\ *adj* **1** : of or relating to operation or an operation **2** : ready for operation ⟨the new plant will be *operational* next week⟩

op·er·a·tor \'äp-ə-,rāt-ər\ *n* **1** : a person who operates something (as a business) **2** : a person in charge of a telephone switchboard ⟨dial the *operator*⟩

op·er·et·ta \,äp-ə-'ret-ə\ *n* : a light play set to music with speaking, singing, and dancing scenes

opin·ion \ə-'pin-yən\ *n* **1** : a belief based on experience and on seeing certain facts but not amounting to sure knowledge ⟨in my *opinion*⟩ **2** : a judgment about a person or thing ⟨a high *opinion* of themselves⟩ **3** : a statement by an expert after careful study ⟨get an *opinion* from a lawyer⟩

synonyms OPINION and BELIEF mean a judgment that one thinks is true. OPINION suggests that the judgment is not yet final or certain but is founded on some facts ⟨I soon changed my *opinion* of the plan⟩ BELIEF stresses that the judgment is certain and firm in one's own mind but says nothing about the amount or kind of evidence ⟨it's my *belief* that war is sure to come⟩

opin·ion·at·ed \ə-'pin-yə-,nāt-əd\ *adj* : holding to one's opinions too strongly

opi·um \'ō-pē-əm\ *n* : a bitter brownish narcotic drug that is the dried juice of one kind of poppy

opos·sum \ə-'päs-əm\ *n* : a common American animal related to the kangaroos

opossum

\ə\ abut	\aů\ out	\i\ tip	\ȯ\ saw	\ů\ foot
\ər\ further	\ch\ chin	\ī\ life	\ȯi\ coin	\y\ yet
\a\ mat	\e\ pet	\j\ job	\th\ thin	\yü\ few
\ā\ take	\ē\ easy	\ng\ sing	\th\ this	\yů\ cure
\ä\ cot, cart	\g\ go	\ō\ bone	\ü\ food	\zh\ vision

that lives mostly in trees and is active at night

op·po·nent \ə-'pō-nənt\ *n* : a person or thing that opposes another

op·por·tu·ni·ty \ˌäp-ər-'tü-nət-ē, -'tyü-\ *n*, *pl* **op·por·tu·ni·ties 1** : a favorable combination of circumstances, time, and place ⟨write when you have an *opportunity*⟩ **2** : a chance to better oneself ⟨felt the new job was a real *opportunity*⟩

op·pose \ə-'pōz\ *vb* **op·posed; op·pos·ing 1** : to be or place opposite to something ⟨*oppose* lies with the truth⟩ ⟨good *opposes* evil⟩ **2** : to offer resistance to : stand against : RESIST ⟨*oppose* a plan⟩

¹op·po·site \'äp-ə-zət\ *n* : either of two persons or things that are as different as possible

²opposite *adj* **1** : being at the other end, side, or corner ⟨live on *opposite* sides of the street⟩ **2** : being in a position to oppose or cancel out ⟨the *opposite* side of the question⟩ **3** : being as different as possible : CONTRARY ⟨came to *opposite* conclusions⟩

³opposite *adv* : on the opposite side

⁴opposite *prep* : across from and usually facing or on the same level with ⟨the park *opposite* our house⟩

op·po·si·tion \ˌäp-ə-'zish-ən\ *n* **1** : the state of being opposite **2** : the action of resisting ⟨offered *opposition* to the plan⟩ **3** : a group of persons that oppose someone or something ⟨defeated our *opposition* easily⟩ **4** *often cap* : a political party opposed to the party in power

op·press \ə-'pres\ *vb* **1** : to cause to feel burdened in spirit ⟨*oppressed* by grief⟩ **2** : to control or rule in a harsh or cruel way ⟨a country *oppressed* by a dictator⟩

op·pres·sion \ə-'presh-ən\ *n* **1** : cruel or unjust use of power or authority **2** : a feeling of low spirits

op·pres·sive \ə-'pres-iv\ *adj* **1** : cruel or harsh without just cause ⟨*oppressive* taxes⟩ **2** : causing a feeling of oppression ⟨*oppressive* heat⟩ — **op·pres·sive·ly** *adv*

op·tic \'äp-tik\ *adj* : of or relating to seeing or the eye ⟨the *optic* nerve⟩

op·ti·cal \'äp-ti-kəl\ *adj* : OPTIC

op·ti·cian \äp-'tish-ən\ *n* : a person who prepares eyeglass lenses and sells glasses

op·ti·mism \'äp-tə-ˌmiz-əm\ *n* : a habit of expecting things to turn out for the best

op·ti·mist \'äp-tə-məst\ *n* : an optimistic person

op·ti·mis·tic \ˌäp-tə-'mis-tik\ *adj* : showing optimism : expecting everything to come

out all right : HOPEFUL ⟨we are *optimistic* about the progress of the peace talks⟩

op·ti·mum \'äp-tə-məm\ *adj* : most desirable or satisfactory ⟨under *optimum* conditions⟩

op·tion \'äp-shən\ *n* **1** : the power or right to choose ⟨have an *option* between milk or juice⟩ **2** : a right to buy or sell something at a specified price during a specified period ⟨took an *option* on the house⟩

op·tion·al \'äp-shən-l\ *adj* : left to one's choice : not required

op·tom·e·trist \äp-'täm-ə-trəst\ *n* : a person who prescribes glasses or exercise to improve the eyesight

op·u·lent \'äp-yə-lənt\ *adj* : having or showing much wealth ⟨*opulent* homes⟩

or \ər, ȯr\ *conj* — used between words or phrases that are choices ⟨juice *or* milk⟩ ⟨pay *or* get out⟩

¹-or \ər\ *n suffix* : one that does a specified thing ⟨act*or*⟩ ⟨elevat*or*⟩

²-or *n suffix* : condition : activity ⟨demean*or*⟩

or·a·cle \'ȯr-ə-kəl\ *n* **1** : a person (as a priestess in ancient Greece) through whom a god is believed to speak **2** : the place where a god speaks through an oracle **3** : an answer given by an oracle

orac·u·lar \ȯ-'rak-yə-lər\ *adj* : of, relating to, or serving as an oracle

oral \'ōr-əl\ *adj* **1** : ²SPOKEN **1** ⟨an *oral* agreement⟩ **2** : of, relating to, given by, or near the mouth ⟨medicine for *oral* use⟩ — **oral·ly** *adv*

or·ange \'ȯr-inj\ *n* **1** : a sweet juicy fruit with a reddish yellow rind that grows on an evergreen citrus tree with shining leaves and fragrant white flowers **2** : a color between red and yellow

or·ange·ade \ˌȯr-in-'jād\ *n* : a drink made of orange juice, sugar, and water

orang·utan *or* **orang·ou·tan** \ə-'rang-ə-ˌtang, -ˌtan\ *n* : a large ape of Borneo and Sumatra that eats plants, lives in trees, and has very long arms and hairless face, feet, and hands

Word History Orangutans are found on islands off the southeast coast of Asia. They live among the trees, and—like most apes—they look a bit like people. The people of the islands gave these apes a name that means "man of the forest." The English word *orangutan* comes from the name the apes were given in the language of the islands where they live.

ora·tion \ə-'rā-shən\ *n* : an important speech given on a special occasion

or·a·tor \'òr-ət-ər\ *n* : a public speaker noted for skill and power in speaking

or·a·tor·i·cal \ˌòr-ə-'tòr-i-kəl\ *adj* : of, relating to, or like an orator or oratory — **or·a·tor·i·cal·ly** *adv*

or·a·to·ry \'òr-ə-ˌtōr-ē\ *n* **1** : the art of an orator **2** : the style of language used in an oration

orb \'òrb\ *n* : something in the shape of a ball (as a planet or the eye)

¹or·bit \'òr-bət\ *n* **1** : the bony socket of the eye **2** : the path taken by one body circling around another body ⟨the *orbit* of the earth around the sun⟩

²orbit *vb* **1** : to move in an orbit around : CIRCLE ⟨the moon *orbits* the earth⟩ **2** : to send up so as to move in an orbit ⟨*orbit* a man-made satellite around the earth⟩

or·bit·al \'òr-bət-l\ *adj* : of or relating to an orbit ⟨the orbital speed of a satellite⟩

or·chard \'òr-chərd\ *n* **1** : a place where fruit trees are grown **2** : the trees in an orchard

or·ches·tra \'òr-kə-strə\ *n* **1** : a group of musicians who perform instrumental music using mostly stringed instruments **2** : the front part of the main floor in a theater

Word History In ancient Greek plays the chorus danced and sang in a space in front of the stage. The Greek name for this space came from the Greek word that meant "to dance." The English word *orchestra* came from the Greek word for the space in front of a stage. At first the English word was used to refer to such a space but is now used to mean "the front part of the main floor." In today's theaters a group of musicians often sits in the space in front of the stage. Such a group, too, came to be called an *orchestra*.

or·ches·tral \òr-'kes-trəl\ *adj* : of, relating to, or written for an orchestra

or·chid \'òr-kəd\ *n* : any of a large group of plants with usually showy flowers with three petals of which the middle petal is enlarged into a lip and differs from the others in shape and color

or·dain \òr-'dān\ *vb* **1** : to make a person a Christian minister or priest by a special ceremony **2** : ²DECREE ⟨it was *ordained* by law⟩ **3** : DESTINE 1, FATE ⟨we seemed *ordained* to fail⟩

or·deal \òr-'dēl\ *n* : a severe test or experience

¹or·der \'òrd-ər\ *n* **1** : a group of people united (as by living under the same religious rules or by loyalty to common needs or duties) ⟨an *order* of monks⟩ **2 orders** *pl* : the office of a person in the Christian ministry ⟨holy *orders*⟩ **3** : a group of related plants or animals that comes below a class and above a family in a classification **4** : the arrangement of objects or events in space or time ⟨the *order* of the seasons⟩ ⟨a list of names in alphabetical *order*⟩ **5** : the way something should be ⟨kept the room in *order*⟩ **6** : the state of things when law or authority is obeyed ⟨restored *order* after the riot⟩ **7** : a certain rule or regulation : COMMAND ⟨an executive *order*⟩ **8** : good working condition ⟨the telephone is out of *order*⟩ **9** : a written direction to pay a sum of money **10** : a an *order* for groceries **11** : goods or items bought or sold — **in order to** : for the purpose of

²order *vb* **1** : to put in order : ARRANGE **2** : to give an order to or for ⟨*order* troops into battle⟩ ⟨*order* a hamburger and a milkshake⟩

¹or·der·ly \'òrd-ər-lē\ *adj* **1** : being in good order : NEAT, TIDY ⟨an *orderly* room⟩ **2** : obeying orders or rules : well-behaved ⟨an *orderly* meeting⟩ ⟨*orderly* children⟩ — **or·der·li·ness** *n*

²orderly *n, pl* **or·der·lies 1** : a soldier who works for an officer especially to carry messages **2** : a person who does cleaning and general work in a hospital

or·di·nal \'òrd-n-əl\ *n* : ORDINAL NUMBER

orangutan

\ə\ abut	\aú\ out	\i\ tip	\ò\ saw	\ú\ foot
\ər\ further	\ch\ chin	\ī\ life	\òi\ coin	\y\ yet
\a\ mat	\e\ pet	\j\ job	\th\ thin	\yü\ few
\ā\ take	\ē\ easy	\ng\ sing	\th\ this	\yú\ cure
\ä\ cot, cart	\g\ go	\ō\ bone	\ü\ food	\zh\ vision

ordinal number *n* : a number that is used to show the place (as first, fifth, twenty-second) taken by an element in a series

or·di·nance \'ord-n-əns\ *n* : a law or regulation especially of a city or town

or·di·nar·i·ly \ˌȯrd-n-'er-ə-lē\ *adv* : in the usual course of events : USUALLY ⟨*ordinarily* goes to bed at nine o'clock⟩

¹**or·di·nary** \'ȯrd-n-ˌer-ē\ *n* : the conditions or events that are usual or normal ⟨nothing out of the *ordinary* about that⟩

²**ordinary** *adj* 1 : to be expected : NORMAL, USUAL ⟨an *ordinary* day⟩ 2 : neither good nor bad : AVERAGE ⟨an *ordinary* student⟩ ⟨just *ordinary* people⟩ 3 : not very good : MEDIOCRE ⟨a very *ordinary* speech⟩ **synonyms** see COMMON — **or·di·nar·i·ness** *n*

ord·nance \'ȯrd-nəns\ *n* 1 : military supplies (as guns, ammunition, trucks, and tanks) 2 : ARTILLERY 1

ore \'ōr\ *n* : a mineral mined to obtain a substance (as gold) that it contains

or·gan \'ȯr-gən\ *n* 1 : a musical instrument played by means of one or more keyboards and having pipes sounded by compressed air 2 : a part of a person, plant, or animal that is specialized to do a particular task ⟨the eye is an *organ* of sight⟩ 3 : a way of getting something done ⟨courts are *organs* of government⟩

or·gan·ic \ȯr-'gan-ik\ *adj* 1 : relating to an organ of the body 2 : having parts that fit or work together ⟨an *organic* whole⟩ 3 : relating to or obtained from living things 4 : relating to carbon compounds : containing carbon

or·gan·ism \'ȯr-gə-ˌniz-əm\ *n* 1 : something having many related parts and functioning as a whole 2 : a living being made up of organs and able to carry on the activities of life : a living person, animal, or plant

or·gan·ist \'ȯr-gə-nəst\ *n* : a person who plays an organ

or·ga·ni·za·tion \ˌȯr-gə-nə-'zā-shən\ *n* 1 : the act or process of organizing ⟨the *organization* of a new club⟩ 2 : the state or way of being organized ⟨study the *organization* of city government⟩ 3 : a group of persons united for a common purpose ⟨a business *organization*⟩

or·ga·nize \'ȯr-gə-ˌnīz\ *vb* **or·ga·nized; or·ga·niz·ing** 1 : to make separate parts into one united whole 2 : to arrange in a certain order — **or·ga·niz·er** *n*

ori·ent \'ōr-ē-ˌent\ *vb* 1 : to set or arrange in a position especially so as to be lined up with certain points of the compass ⟨*oriented* the house to face east⟩ 2 : to ac-quaint with an existing situation or environment ⟨*orient* new students⟩ — **ori·en·ta·tion** \ˌōr-ē-ən-'tā-shən\ *n*

ori·en·tal \ˌōr-ē-'ent-l\ *adj, often cap* : of or relating to the Orient

Oriental *n* : a member of any of the native peoples of the Orient

or·i·gin \'ȯr-ə-jən\ *n* 1 : a person's ancestry ⟨people of humble *origin*⟩ 2 : the rise, beginning, or coming from a source ⟨the story has its *origin* in fact⟩ 3 : basic source or cause ⟨the *origin* of their quarrel is not known⟩

¹**orig·i·nal** \ə-'rij-ən-l\ *n* : something from which a copy or translation can be made ⟨the paintings are *originals*⟩ ⟨read the Russian novel in the *original*⟩

²**original** *adj* 1 : of or relating to the origin or beginning : FIRST ⟨the *original* part of an old house⟩ 2 : not copied from anything else : not translated : NEW ⟨an *original* painting⟩ ⟨an *original* idea⟩ 3 : able to think up new things : INVENTIVE ⟨an *original* mind⟩ — **orig·i·nal·ly** *adv*

orig·i·nal·i·ty \ə-ˌrij-ə-'nal-ət-ē\ *n* 1 : the quality or state of being original ⟨the *originality* of an idea⟩ 2 : the power or ability to think, act, or do something in ways that are new ⟨an artist of great *originality*⟩

orig·i·nate \ə-'rij-ə-ˌnāt\ *vb* **orig·i·nat·ed; orig·i·nat·ing** 1 : to bring into being : cause to be : INVENT, INITIATE ⟨*originate* a new game⟩ 2 : to come into being ⟨the custom *originated* in ancient times⟩ — **orig·i·na·tor** \-ˌnāt-ər\ *n*

ori·ole \'ōr-ē-ˌōl\ *n* 1 : an Old World yellow and black bird related to the crow 2 : an American songbird related to the blackbird and bobolink that has a bright orange and black male

¹**or·na·ment** \'ȯr-nə-mənt\ *n* 1 : something that adds beauty : DECORATION ⟨a Christmas-tree *ornament*⟩ 2 : the act of beautifying

²**or·na·ment** \'ȯr-nə-ˌment\ *vb* : DECORATE 1

¹**or·na·men·tal** \ˌȯr-nə-'ment-l\ *adj* : serving to ornament : DECORATIVE

²**ornamental** *n* : a plant grown for its beauty

or·na·men·ta·tion \ˌȯr-nə-mən-'tā-shən\ *n* 1 : the act or process of ornamenting : the state of being ornamented 2 : something that ornaments

or·nate \ȯr-'nāt\ *adj* : decorated in a fancy way — **or·nate·ly** *adv* — **or·nate·ness** *n*

or·nery \'ȯr-nə-rē, 'än-ə-\ *adj* **or·ner·i·er; or·ner·i·est** : having a bad disposition

¹**or·phan** \'ȯr-fən\ *n* : a child whose parents are dead

²orphan *vb* : to cause to become an orphan ⟨*orphaned* as a baby⟩

or·phan·age \'or-fə-nij\ *n* : an institution for the care of orphans

or·ris \'or-əs\ *n* : a European iris with a fragrant root (**orris root**) used especially in perfume and powder

orth·odon·tist \,or-thə-'dänt-əst\ *n* : a dentist who adjusts badly placed or irregular teeth

or·tho·dox \'or-thə-,däks\ *adj* **1** : holding established beliefs especially in religion ⟨an *orthodox* Christian⟩ **2** : approved as measuring up to some standard : CONVENTIONAL ⟨take an *orthodox* approach to a problem⟩

¹-o·ry \,or-ē, ə-rē\ *n suffix, pl* **-o·ries** : place of or for ⟨observat*ory*⟩

²-ory *adj suffix* : of, relating to, or associated with ⟨sens*ory*⟩

os·cil·late \'äs-ə-,lāt\ *vb* **os·cil·lat·ed; os·cil·lat·ing** : to swing back and forth like a pendulum

os·mo·sis \äs-'mō-səs, äz-\ *n* : a passing of material and especially water through a membrane (as of a living cell) that will not allow all kinds of molecules to pass

os·prey \'äs-prē\ *n, pl* **os·preys** : a large hawk that feeds chiefly on fish

os·ten·si·ble \ä-'sten-sə-bəl\ *adj* : shown in an outward way : APPARENT ⟨the *ostensible* reason⟩ — **os·ten·si·bly** \-blē\ *adv*

os·ten·ta·tious \,äs-tən-'tā-shəs\ *adj* : having or fond of unnecessary show

os·tra·cize \'äs-trə-,sīz\ *vb* **os·tra·cized; os·tra·ciz·ing** : to shut out of a group by the agreement of all ⟨was *ostracized* by my friends⟩

os·trich \'äs-trich\ *n* : a very large bird of Africa and the Arabian Peninsula that often weighs 300 pounds and runs very swiftly but cannot fly

¹oth·er \'əth-ər\ *adj* **1** : being the one (as of two or more) left ⟨broke my *other* arm⟩ **2** : ¹SECOND 1 ⟨every *other* page⟩ **3** : ¹EXTRA, ADDITIONAL ⟨some *other* guests are coming⟩

²other *n* : a remaining or different one ⟨lift one foot and then the *other*⟩ ⟨the *others* will follow us later⟩

³other *pron* : another thing ⟨there's always something or *other* going on⟩

oth·er·wise \'əth-ər-,wīz\ *adv* **1** : in another way ⟨could not do *otherwise*⟩ **2** : in different circumstances ⟨*otherwise* they might have won⟩ **3** : in other ways ⟨an *otherwise* busy street⟩

ot·ter \'ät-ər\ *n* : a web-footed animal related to the minks that feeds on fish

otter

ouch \'auch\ *interj* — used especially to express sudden pain

ought \'ot\ *helping verb* **1** — used to show duty ⟨you *ought* to obey your parents⟩ **2** — used to show what it would be wise to do ⟨you *ought* to take care of that cough⟩ **3** — used to show what is naturally expected ⟨they *ought* to be here by now⟩ **4** — used to show what is correct ⟨you *ought* to get nine for the answer⟩

oughtn't \'ot-nt\ : ought not

ounce \'auns\ *n* **1** : a unit of weight equal to 1/16 pound (about 28 grams) **2** : a unit of liquid capacity equal to 1/16 pint (about 30 milliliters)

ostrich

our \aǔr, är\ *adj* : of or relating to us : done, given, or felt by us ⟨*our* house⟩ ⟨*our* fault⟩

ours \aǔrz, 'aǔrz, ärz\ *pron* : that which belongs to us ⟨this classroom is *ours*⟩ ⟨these desks are *ours*⟩

our·selves \aǔr-'selvz, är-\ *pron* : our own selves ⟨we amused *ourselves*⟩ ⟨we did it *ourselves*⟩

-ous \əs\ *adj suffix* : full of : having : resembling ⟨clamor*ous*⟩ ⟨poison*ous*⟩

oust \'aǔst\ *vb* : to force or drive out (as from office or from possession of something)

oust·er \'aǔs-tər\ *n* : the act or an instance of ousting or being ousted

¹out \'aǔt\ *adv* **1** : in a direction away from the inside, center, or surface ⟨looked *out* at the snow⟩ **2** : away from home, business, or the usual or proper place ⟨went *out* for lunch⟩ **3** : beyond control or possession ⟨let a secret *out*⟩ **4** : so as to be used up, completed, or discontinued ⟨food supply ran *out*⟩ ⟨filled the form *out*⟩ ⟨blew the candle *out*⟩ **5** : in or into the open ⟨the sun came *out*⟩ **6** : ALOUD ⟨cried *out* in pain⟩ **7** : so as to put out or be put out in baseball ⟨threw the runner *out*⟩

²out *adj* **1** : located outside or at a distance **2** : no longer in power or use ⟨the *out* party⟩ ⟨lights are *out*⟩ **3** : not confined : not concealed or covered ⟨the secret is *out*⟩ ⟨the sun is *out*⟩ **4** : ¹ABSENT 1 ⟨a basket with its bottom *out*⟩ ⟨the barber is *out* today⟩ **5** : being no longer at bat and not successful in reaching base **6** : no longer in fashion

³out *prep* **1** : outward through ⟨looked *out* the window⟩ **2** : outward on or along ⟨drove *out* the road by the river⟩

⁴out *n* : PUTOUT

out- *prefix* : in a manner that goes beyond ⟨*out*number⟩ ⟨*out*run⟩

out–and–out \aǔt-n-aǔt\ *adj* : THOROUGH 1 ⟨an *out-and-out* crook⟩

out·board motor \aǔt-bōrd-\ *n* : a small gasoline engine with an attached propeller that can be fastened to the back end of a small boat

out·break \'aǔt-brāk\ *n* : something (as an epidemic of measles) that breaks out

out·build·ing \'aǔt-bil-ding\ *n* : a building (as a shed or stable) separate from a main building

out·burst \'aǔt-bərst\ *n* **1** : a sudden violent expression of strong feeling **2** : a sudden increase of activity or growth

¹out·cast \'aǔt-kast\ *adj* : rejected or cast out

²outcast *n* : a person who is cast out by society

out·class \aǔt-'klas\ *vb* : EXCEL, SURPASS

out·come \'aǔt-kəm\ *n* : ²RESULT 1

out·cry \'aǔt-krī\ *n, pl* **out·cries** **1** : a loud and excited cry **2** : a strong protest ⟨raised an *outcry* against the new rules⟩

out·dat·ed \aǔt-'dāt-əd\ *adj* : OBSOLETE, OUTMODED ⟨*outdated* methods of farming⟩

out·dis·tance \aǔt-'dis-təns\ *vb* **out·distanced; out·dis·tanc·ing** : to go far ahead of (as in a race)

out·do \aǔt-'dü\ *vb* **out·did** \-'did\; **out·done** \-'dən\; **out·do·ing** \-'dü-ing\; **out·does** \-'dəz\ : to do better than : SURPASS

out·door \,aǔt-,dōr\ *adj* **1** : of or relating to the outdoors ⟨an *outdoor* person⟩ **2** : used, being, or done outdoors ⟨*outdoor* sports⟩

¹out·doors \aǔt-'dōrz\ *adv* : outside a building : in or into the open air ⟨play *outdoors*⟩

²outdoors *n* **1** : the open air **2** : the world away from human dwellings

out·er \'aǔt-ər\ *adj* **1** : located on the outside or farther out ⟨an *outer* wall⟩ **2** : being beyond the earth's atmosphere or beyond the solar system ⟨*outer* space⟩

out·er·most \'aǔt-ər-,mōst\ *adj* : farthest out

out·field \'aǔt-,fēld\ *n* : the part of a baseball field beyond the infield and between the foul lines

out·field·er \'aǔt-,fēl-dər\ *n* : a baseball player who plays in the outfield

¹out·fit \'aǔt-,fit\ *n* **1** : the equipment or clothing for a special use ⟨a camping *outfit*⟩ ⟨a sports *outfit*⟩ **2** : a group of persons working together or associated in the same activity ⟨soldiers from the same *outfit*⟩

²outfit *vb* **out·fit·ted; out·fit·ting** : to supply with an outfit : EQUIP ⟨*outfit* children for school⟩ — **out·fit·ter** *n*

out·go \'aǔt-,gō\ *n, pl* **out·goes** : EXPENDITURE 2 ⟨income must be greater than *outgo*⟩

out·go·ing \'aǔt-,gō-ing\ *adj* **1** : going out ⟨an *outgoing* ship⟩ **2** : retiring from a place or position ⟨the *outgoing* president⟩ **3** : FRIENDLY 1 ⟨an *outgoing* person⟩

out·grow \aǔt-'grō\ *vb* **out·grew** \-'grü\; **out·grown** \-'grōn\; **out·grow·ing** **1** : to grow faster than ⟨one plant *outgrew* all the others⟩ **2** : to grow too large for ⟨*outgrew* my clothes⟩

out·growth \'aǔt-,grōth\ *n* : something

that grows out of or develops from something else

out·ing \'aút-ing\ *n* : a brief usually outdoor trip for pleasure ⟨an *outing* to the beach⟩

out·land·ish \aút-'lan-dish\ *adj* : very strange or unusual : BIZARRE ⟨*outlandish* behavior⟩ ⟨*outlandish* clothes⟩

out·last \aút-'last\ *vb* : to last longer than

¹out·law \'aút-,ló\ *n* : a lawless person or one who is running away from the law

²outlaw *vb* : to make illegal ⟨dueling was *outlawed*⟩

out·lay \'aút-,lā\ *n* : EXPENDITURE

out·let \'aút-,let\ *n* **1** : a place or opening for letting something out ⟨a lake with several *outlets*⟩ **2** : a way of releasing or satisfying a feeling or impulse ⟨needed an *outlet* for my anger⟩ **3** : a device (as in a wall) into which the prongs of an electrical plug are inserted for making connection with an electrical circuit

¹out·line \'aút-,līn\ *n* **1** : a line that traces or forms the outer limits of an object or figure and shows its shape **2** : a drawing or picture giving only the outlines of a thing : this method of drawing **3** : a short treatment of a subject : SUMMARY ⟨an *outline* of a composition⟩

²outline *vb* **out·lined; out·lin·ing** : to make or prepare an outline of

out·live \aút-'liv\ *vb* **out·lived; out·liv·ing** : to live longer than : OUTLAST ⟨a rule that has *outlived* its usefulness⟩

out·look \'aút-,lúk\ *n* **1** : a view from a certain place ⟨the *outlook* through a window⟩ **2** : a way of thinking about or looking at things ⟨a person with a cheerful *outlook*⟩ **3** : conditions that seem to lie ahead ⟨the *outlook* for business⟩

out·ly·ing \'aút-,lī-ing\ *adj* : being far from a central point : REMOTE

out·mod·ed \aút-'mōd-əd\ *adj* : no longer in style or in use ⟨an *outmoded* dress⟩ ⟨*outmoded* equipment⟩

out·num·ber \aút-'nəm-bər\ *vb* : to be more than in number

out of *prep* **1** : from the inside to the outside of : not in ⟨I walked *out of* the room⟩ ⟨they are *out of* town⟩ **2** : beyond the limits of ⟨the bird flew *out of* sight⟩ ⟨the patient is *out of* danger⟩ **3** : BECAUSE OF ⟨they obeyed *out of* fear⟩ **4** : in a group of ⟨I got only one answer right *out of* five⟩ **5** : ¹WITHOUT 2 ⟨the store is *out of* bread⟩ **6** : FROM 3 ⟨made a table *out of* some boxes and the legs of a chair⟩

out-of-bounds \,aút-əv-'baúndz\ *adv or adj* : outside the limits of the playing field

out-of-date \,aút-əv-'dāt\ *adj* : OUTMODED

out-of-door \,aút-əv-'dōr\ *or* **out-of-doors** \-'dōrz\ *adj* : OUTDOOR 2

out-of-doors \,aút-əv-'dōrz\ *n* : ²OUTDOORS

out·pa·tient \'aút-,pā-shənt\ *n* : a person who visits a hospital for examination or treatment but who does not stay overnight at the hospital

out·post \'aút-,pōst\ *n* **1** : a guard placed at a distance from a military force or camp **2** : the position taken by an outpost **3** : a settlement on a frontier or in a faraway place

¹out·rage \'aút-,rāj\ *n* **1** : an act of violence or cruelty **2** : an act that hurts someone or shows disrespect for a person's feelings **3** : angry feelings caused by injury or insult

²outrage *vb* **out·raged; out·rag·ing** **1** : to cause to suffer violent injury or great insult **2** : to cause to feel anger or strong resentment ⟨*outraged* by the way we were treated⟩

out·ra·geous \aút-'rā-jəs\ *adj* : going far beyond what is right, decent, or just

¹out·right \aút-'rīt\ *adv* **1** : COMPLETELY ⟨sold the business *outright*⟩ **2** : without holding back ⟨laughed *outright* at the story⟩ **3** : on the spot : INSTANTLY ⟨was killed *outright*⟩

²out·right \'aút-,rīt\ *adj* **1** : being exactly what is said ⟨an *outright* lie⟩ **2** : given without restriction ⟨an *outright* gift⟩

out·run \aút-'rən\ *vb* **out·ran** \-'ran\; **out·run; out·run·ning** : to run faster than

out·sell \aút-'sel\ *vb* **out·sold** \-'sōld\; **out·sell·ing** : to sell or be sold more than

out·set \'aút-,set\ *n* : BEGINNING 1, START

out·shine \aút-'shīn\ *vb* **out·shone** \-'shōn\; **out·shin·ing** **1** : to shine brighter than **2** : OUTDO, SURPASS

¹out·side \aút-'sīd\ *n* **1** : a place or region beyond an enclosure or boundary **2** : an outer side or surface ⟨painted white on the *outside*⟩ **3** : the greatest amount or limit : ³MOST ⟨will take a week at the *outside*⟩

²outside *adj* **1** : of, relating to, or being on the outside ⟨the *outside* edge⟩ **2** : coming from outside : not belonging to a place or group ⟨*outside* influences⟩

³outside *adv* : on or to the outside : OUTDOORS ⟨took the dog *outside*⟩

⁴outside *prep* : on or to the outside of

\ə\ **abut**	\aú\ **out**	\i\ **tip**	\ó\ **saw**	\ú\ **foot**
\ər\ **further**	\ch\ **chin**	\ī\ **life**	\ói\ **coin**	\y\ **yet**
\a\ **mat**	\e\ **pet**	\j\ **job**	\th\ **thin**	\yü\ **few**
\ā\ **take**	\ē\ **easy**	\ng\ **sing**	\th\ **this**	\yú\ **cure**
\ä\ **cot, cart**	\g\ **go**	\ō\ **bone**	\ü\ **food**	\zh\ **vision**

: beyond the limits of ⟨*outside* the door⟩ ⟨*outside* the law⟩

out·sid·er \aut-'sīd-ər\ *n* : a person who does not belong to a certain party or group

out·size \'aut-ˌsīz\ *adj* : unusually large or heavy

out·skirts \'aut-ˌskərts\ *n pl* : the area that lies away from the center of a place

out·smart \aut-'smärt\ *vb* : OUTWIT

out·spo·ken \aut-'spō-kən\ *adj* : direct or open in expression : BLUNT ⟨*outspoken* criticism⟩ ⟨an *outspoken* critic⟩ — **out·spo·ken·ly** *adv* — **out·spo·ken·ness** *n*

out·spread \aut-'spred\ *adj* : spread out

out·stand·ing \aut-'stan-ding\ *adj* **1** : UN- PAID ⟨several bills *outstanding*⟩ **2** : stand- ing out especially because of excellence ⟨a most *outstanding* musician⟩ **syn- onyms** see NOTICEABLE — **out·stand- ing·ly** *adv*

out·stay \aut-'stā\ *vb* : to stay beyond or longer than ⟨*outstayed* our welcome⟩

out·stretched \aut-'strecht\ *adj* : stretched out ⟨*outstretched* arms⟩

out·strip \aut-'strip\ *vb* **out·stripped; out- strip·ping 1** : to go faster or farther than ⟨*outstripped* the other runners⟩ **2** : to do better than : EXCEL

¹out·ward \'aut-wərd\ *adj* **1** : moving or turned toward the outside or away from a center ⟨an *outward* journey⟩ **2** : showing on the outside ⟨gave no *outward* signs of fear⟩

²outward *or* **out·wards** \'aut-wərdz\ *adv* : toward the outside : away from a center ⟨the city stretches *outward* for miles⟩

out·ward·ly \'aut-wərd-lē\ *adv* : on the outside : in outward appearance ⟨*out- wardly* calm⟩

out·weigh \aut-'wā\ *vb* : to be greater than in weight or importance

out·wit \aut-'wit\ *vb* **out·wit·ted; out·wit- ting** : to get ahead of by cleverness : BEST

out·worn \aut-'wōrn\ *adj* : no longer use- ful or accepted ⟨*outworn* ideas⟩

¹oval \'ō-vəl\ *adj* : having the shape of an egg : ELLIPTIC

²oval *n* : an oval fig- ure or object

ova·ry \'ō-və-rē\ *n, pl* **ova·ries 1** : an or- gan of the body in female animals in which eggs are pro- duced **2** : the larger lower part of the pistil of a flower in which the seeds are formed

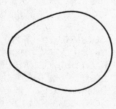

oval

ova·tion \ō-'vā-shən\ *n* : a making of a loud noise by many people (as by cheer- ing or clapping) to show great liking or respect

ov·en \'əv-ən\ *n* : a heated chamber (as in a stove) for baking, heating, or drying

¹over \'ō-vər\ *adv* **1** : across a barrier or space ⟨flew *over* to London⟩ **2** : in a di- rection down or forward and down ⟨fell *over*⟩ **3** : across the brim ⟨soup boiled *over*⟩ **4** : so as to bring the underside up ⟨turned the cards *over*⟩ **5** : beyond a limit ⟨the show ran a minute *over*⟩ **6** : more than needed ⟨has two cards left *over*⟩ **7** : once more : AGAIN ⟨please do it *over*⟩

²over *prep* **1** : above in place : higher than ⟨clouds *over* our heads⟩ **2** : above in power or value ⟨respected those *over* me⟩ **3** : on or along the surface of ⟨glide *over* the ice⟩ **4** : on or to the other side of : ACROSS ⟨jump *over* a puddle⟩ **5** : down from the top or edge of ⟨fell *over* a cliff⟩

³over *adj* **1** : being more than needed : SURPLUS **2** : brought or come to an end ⟨those days are *over*⟩

¹over·all \ˌō-vər-'ól\ *adv* : as a whole : in most ways ⟨did a nice job *overall*⟩

²overall *adj* : including everything ⟨*over- all* expenses⟩

over·alls \'ō-vər-ˌólz\ *n pl* : loose pants usually with shoulder straps and a piece in front to cover the chest

over·anx·ious \ˌō-vər-'angk-shəs\ *adj* : much too anxious

over·bear·ing \ˌō-vər-'baər-ing, -'beər-\ *adj* : acting in a proud or bossy way to- ward other people

over·board \'ō-vər-ˌbōrd\ *adv* **1** : over the side of a ship into the water ⟨fall *over- board*⟩ **2** : to extremes of enthusiasm ⟨go *overboard* about a popular singer⟩

over·bur·den \ˌō-vər-'bərd-n\ *vb* : to bur- den too heavily

over·cast \'ō-vər-ˌkast\ *adj* : clouded over

over·charge \ˌō-vər-'chärj\ *vb* **over- charged; over·charg·ing** : to charge too much

over·coat \'ō-vər-ˌkōt\ *n* : a heavy coat worn over indoor clothing

over·come \ˌō-vər-'kəm\ *vb* **over·came** \-'kām\; **overcome; over·com·ing 1** : to win a victory over : CONQUER ⟨*overcome* the enemy⟩ **2** : to make helpless ⟨*over- come* by gas⟩

over·con·fi·dent \ˌō-vər-'kän-fə-dənt\ *adj* : too sure of oneself

over·cooked \ˌō-vər-'kukt\ *adj* : cooked too long

over·crowd \ˌō-vər-'kraud\ *vb* : to cause to be too crowded ⟨schools were *over- crowded*⟩

over·do \ˌō-vər-'dü\ *vb* **over·did** \-'did\;

over·done \-'dən\; **over·do·ing** \-'dü-ing\ **1** : to do too much ⟨*overdoes* it getting ready for a party⟩ **2** : EXAGGERATE ⟨*overdo* praise⟩ **3** : to cook too long

over·dose \'ō-vər-ˌdōs\ *n* : too large a dose (as of a drug)

over·dress \ˌō-vər-'dres\ *vb* : to dress too well for the occasion

over·due \ˌō-vər-'dü, -'dyü\ *adj* **1** : not paid when due ⟨*overdue* bills⟩ **2** : delayed beyond an expected time ⟨the plane was an hour *overdue*⟩

over·eat \ˌō-vər-'ēt\ *vb* **over·ate** \-'āt\; **over·eat·en** \-'ēt-n\; **over·eat·ing** : to eat too much

over·es·ti·mate \ˌō-vər-'es-tə-ˌmāt\ *vb* **over·es·ti·mat·ed; over·es·ti·mat·ing** : to estimate too highly ⟨*overestimated* the amount of paper needed⟩

over·flight \'ō-vər-ˌflīt\ *n* : a passage over an area in an airplane

¹over·flow \ˌō-vər-'flō\ *vb* **1** : to cover with or as if with water ⟨visitors *overflowed* the town⟩ **2** : to flow over the top of ⟨the river *overflowed* its banks⟩ **3** : to flow over bounds ⟨the creek *overflows* every spring⟩

²over·flow \'ō-vər-ˌflō\ *n* **1** : a flowing over : FLOOD **2** : something that flows over : SURPLUS

over·grown \ˌō-vər-'grōn\ *adj* : grown too big ⟨just an *overgrown* puppy⟩

¹over·hand \'ō-vər-ˌhand\ *adj* : made with a downward movement of the hand or arm

²overhand *adv* : with an overhand movement ⟨throw the ball *overhand*⟩

overhand knot *n* : a simple knot often used to prevent the end of a cord from pulling apart

overhand knot

¹over·hang \'ō-vər-ˌhang\ *vb* **over·hung** \-ˌhəng\; **over·hang·ing** : to stick out or hang over ⟨an *overhanging* cliff⟩

²overhang *n* : a part that overhangs ⟨the *overhang* of a roof⟩

¹over·haul \ˌō-vər-'hȯl\ *vb* **1** : to make a thorough examination of and make necessary repairs and adjustments on ⟨*overhaul* an automobile engine⟩ **2** : to catch up with : OVERTAKE ⟨*overhauled* by a police car⟩

²over·haul \'ō-vər-ˌhȯl\ *n* : an instance of overhauling

¹over·head \ˌō-vər-'hed\ *adv* **1** : above one's head **2** : in the sky ⟨a plane flying *overhead*⟩

²over·head \'ō-vər-ˌhed\ *adj* : placed or passing overhead ⟨*overhead* garage doors⟩

³over·head \'ō-vər-ˌhed\ *n* : the general expenses (as for rent or heat) of a business

over·hear \ˌō-vər-'hiər\ *vb* **over·heard** \-'hərd\; **over·hear·ing** \-'hiər-ing\ : to hear something said to someone else and not meant for one's own ears

over·heat \ˌō-vər-'hēt\ *vb* : to heat too much : become too hot ⟨the engine *overheated*⟩

over·joy \ˌō-vər-'jȯi\ *vb* : to make very joyful

¹over·land \'ō-vər-ˌland\ *adv* : by land rather than by water ⟨travel *overland*⟩

²over·land *adj* : going overland ⟨an *overland* route⟩

over·lap \ˌō-vər-'lap\ *vb* **over·lapped; over·lap·ping** : to place or be placed so that a part of one covers a part of another : lap over

¹over·lay \ˌō-vər-'lā\ *vb* **over·laid** \-'lād\; **over·lay·ing** : to lay or spread over or across or over or across something ⟨*overlay* silver on copper⟩ ⟨*overlay* copper with silver⟩

²over·lay \'ō-vər-ˌlā\ *n* : something (as a veneer on wood) that is overlaid

over·load \ˌō-vər-'lōd\ *vb* : to put too great a load on ⟨*overload* a truck⟩ ⟨*overload* an electrical circuit⟩

over·look \ˌō-vər-'lùk\ *vb* **1** : to look over : INSPECT **2** : to look down upon from a higher position ⟨a house that *overlooks* a valley⟩ **3** : to fail to see : MISS ⟨*overlook* a name on the list⟩ **4** : to pass over without notice or blame : EXCUSE ⟨*overlook* a beginner's mistake⟩

over·lord \'ō-vər-ˌlȯrd\ *n* : a lord over other lords

over·ly \'ō-vər-lē\ *adv* : by too much ⟨*overly* worried⟩ ⟨an *overly* short skirt⟩

¹over·night \ˌō-vər-'nīt\ *adv* **1** : during or through the night ⟨stay *overnight*⟩ **2** : ²FAST 3, QUICKLY ⟨became famous *overnight*⟩

²overnight *adj* **1** : done or lasting through the night ⟨an *overnight* journey⟩ **2** : staying for the night ⟨an *overnight* guest⟩ **3** : for use on short trips ⟨an *overnight* bag⟩

over·pass \'ō-vər-ˌpas\ *n* : a crossing (as of two highways or a highway and a rail-

\ə\ abut	\aú\ out	\i\ tip	\ȯ\ saw	\ù\ foot
\ər\ further	\ch\ chin	\ī\ life	\ȯi\ coin	\y\ yet
\a\ mat	\e\ pet	\j\ job	\th\ thin	\yü\ few
\ā\ take	\ē\ easy	\ng\ sing	\th\ this	\yù\ cure
\ä\ cot, cart	\g\ go	\ō\ bone	\ü\ food	\zh\ vision

road) at different levels usually by means of a bridge

over·pow·er \,ō-vər-'paú-ər\ *vb* **1** : to overcome by greater force : DEFEAT **2** : to affect by being too strong ⟨an *overpowering* personality⟩

over·rate \,ō-vər-'rāt\ *vb* **over·rat·ed; over·rat·ing** : to value or praise too highly

over·ride \,ō-vər-'rīd\ *vb* **over·rode** \-'rōd\; **over·rid·den** \-'rid-n\; **over·rid·ing** \-'rīd-ing\ : to push aside as less important ⟨our hunger *overrode* our manners as we grabbed the food⟩

over·ripe \,ō-vər-'rīp\ *adj* : passed beyond ripeness toward decay ⟨*overripe* fruit⟩

over·rule \,ō-vər-'rül\ *vb* **over·ruled; over·rul·ing 1** : to decide against ⟨the chairman *overruled* the suggestion⟩ **2** : to set aside a decision or ruling made by someone having less authority ⟨mother *overruled* our plans⟩

over·run \,ō-vər-'rən\ *vb* **over·ran** \-'ran\; **overrun; over·run·ning 1** : to take over and occupy by force ⟨the outpost was *overrun* by the enemy⟩ **2** : to run past ⟨*overran* second base⟩ **3** : to spread over so as to cover ⟨a garden *overrun* by weeds⟩

¹**over·seas** \,ō-vər-'sēz\ *adv* : beyond or across the sea ⟨soldiers sent *overseas*⟩

²**overseas** *adj* : of, relating to, or intended for lands across the sea ⟨*overseas* trade⟩ ⟨*overseas* shipments⟩

over·see \,ō-vər-'sē\ *vb* **over·saw** \-'só\; **over·seen** \-'sēn\; **over·see·ing 1** : INSPECT 1, EXAMINE **2** : SUPERINTEND

over·seer \'ō-vər-,siər\ *n* : a person whose business it is to oversee something

over·shad·ow \,ō-vər-'shad-ō\ *vb* **1** : to cast a shadow over : DARKEN **2** : to be more important than

over·shoe \'ō-vər-,shü\ *n* : a shoe (as of rubber) worn over another for protection

over·shoot \,ō-vər-'shüt\ *vb* **over·shot** \-'shät\; **over·shoot·ing** : to miss by going beyond

over·sight \'ō-vər-,sīt\ *n* **1** : the act or duty of overseeing : watchful care **2** : an error or a leaving something out through carelessness or haste

over·sim·pli·fy \,ō-vər-'sim-plə-,fī\ *vb* **over·sim·pli·fied; over·sim·pli·fy·ing** : to make incorrect or misleading by simplifying too much ⟨*oversimplify* a complicated problem⟩

over·size \,ō-vər-'sīz\ *or* **over·sized** \-'sīzd\ *adj* : larger than the usual or normal size

over·sleep \,ō-vər-'slēp\ *vb* **over·slept** \-'slept\; **over·sleep·ing** : to sleep beyond the usual time or beyond the time set for getting up

over·spread \,ō-vər-'spred\ *vb* **over·spread; over·spread·ing** : to spread over or above

over·state \,ō-vər-'stāt\ *vb* **over·stat·ed; over·stat·ing** : to put in too strong terms : EXAGGERATE ⟨*overstated* the case⟩

over·step \,ō-vər-'step\ *vb* **over·stepped; over·step·ping** : to step over or beyond : EXCEED ⟨*overstepped* my authority⟩

over·stuffed \,ō-vər-'stəft\ *adj* : covered completely and deeply with upholstery ⟨an *overstuffed* chair⟩

over·sup·ply \,ō-vər-sə-'plī\ *n, pl* **over·sup·plies** : a supply that is too large

overt \o-'vərt, 'ō-,vərt\ *adj* : that can be seen or known : not secret — **overt·ly** *adj*

over·take \,ō-vər-'tāk\ *vb* **over·took** \-'túk\; **over·tak·en** \-'tā-kən\; **over·tak·ing 1** : to catch up with and often pass ⟨*overtook* the car ahead⟩ **2** : to come upon suddenly or without warning ⟨*overtaken* by rain⟩

¹**over·throw** \,ō-vər-'thrō\ *vb* **over·threw** \-'thrü\; **over·thrown** \-'thrōn\; **over·throw·ing 1** : OVERTURN 1 **2** : to cause the fall or end of : DEFEAT, DESTROY ⟨a government *overthrown* by rebels⟩

²**over·throw** \'ō-vər-,thrō\ *n* : an act of overthrowing : the state of being overthrown : DEFEAT, RUIN

over·time \'ō-vər-,tīm\ *n* : time spent working that is more than one usually works in a day or a week

over·ture \'ō-vər-,chúr\ *n* **1** : something first offered or suggested with the hope of reaching an agreement ⟨made *overtures* of peace⟩ **2** : a musical composition played by the orchestra at the beginning of an opera or musical play

over·turn \,ō-vər-'tərn\ *vb* **1** : to turn over : UPSET **2** : ¹OVERTHROW 2

¹**over·weight** *n* **1** \'ō-vər-,wāt\ : weight that is more than is required or allowed **2** \,ō-vər-'wāt\ : bodily weight that is greater than what is considered normal or healthy

²**over·weight** \,ō-vər-'wāt\ *adj* : weighing more than is right, necessary, or allowed

over·whelm \,ō-vər-'hwelm, -'welm\ *vb* **1** : to cover over completely : SUBMERGE ⟨a boat *overwhelmed* by a wave⟩ **2** : to overcome completely ⟨were *overwhelmed* by the larger army⟩ ⟨*overwhelmed* with grief⟩

¹**over·work** \,ō-vər-'wərk\ *vb* **1** : to work or cause to work too much or too hard **2** : to make too much use of ⟨*overworked* phrases⟩

²**overwork** *n* : too much work

ovip·a·rous \ō-'vip-ə-rəs\ *adj* : reproducing by eggs that hatch outside the parent's body ⟨birds are *oviparous* animals⟩

ovule \'äv-yül, 'ōv-\ *n* : any of the tiny egglike structures in a plant ovary that can develop into seeds

ovum \'ō-vəm\ *n, pl* **ova** \'ō-və\ : EGG CELL

owe \'ō\ *vb* **owed; ow·ing 1** : to be obligated to pay, give, or return ⟨*owe* money⟩ **2** : to be in debt to ⟨*owe* the grocer for food⟩ **3** : to have as a result ⟨*owe* success to hard work⟩

ow·ing \'ō-ing\ *adj* : due to be paid ⟨have bills *owing*⟩

owing to *prep* : BECAUSE OF ⟨absent *owing to* illness⟩

owl \'au̇l\ *n* : a bird with large head and eyes, hooked bill, and strong claws that is active at night and lives on rats and mice, insects, and small birds — **owl·ish** *adj*

owl·et \'au̇-lət\ *n* : a young or small owl

¹own \'ōn\ *adj* : belonging to oneself or itself ⟨have one's *own* room⟩

²own *vb* **1** : to have or hold as property : POSSESS **2** : ADMIT **3**, CONFESS **1** ⟨*own* a mistake⟩

own·er \'ō-nər\ *n* : a person who owns something

own·er·ship \'ō-nər-,ship\ *n* : the state or fact of being an owner

ox \'äks\ *n, pl* **ox·en** \'äk-sən\ *also* **ox 1** : one of our common domestic cattle or a closely related animal **2** : the adult castrated male of domestic cattle used especially for meat or for hauling loads : STEER

ox·bow \'äks-,bō\ *n* : a bend in a river in the shape of a U

ox·cart \'äk-,skärt\ *n* : a cart pulled by oxen

ox·ford \'äks-fərd\ *n* : a low shoe laced and tied over the instep

ox·i·da·tion \,äk-sə-'dā-shən\ *n* : the process of oxidizing

ox·ide \'äk-,sīd\ *n* : a compound of oxygen with another element or with a group of elements

ox·i·dize \'äk-sə-,dīz\ *vb* **ox·i·dized; ox·i·diz·ing** : to combine with oxygen : add oxygen to

ox·y·gen \'äk-si-jən\ *n* : a chemical element found in the air as a colorless odorless tasteless gas that is necessary for life

Word History People once thought that all acids were formed by adding oxygen to some other substance. This belief turned out not to be true. However, it did give oxygen its name. The first part of the word, *oxy-*, came from a Greek word that meant "acid" or "sharp." The second part, *-gen*, came from a Greek suffix that meant "born."

oys·ter \'ȯis-tər\ *n* : a soft gray shellfish that lives on stony bottoms (**oyster beds**) in shallow seawater, has a shell made up of two hinged parts, and is used as food

ozone \'ō-,zōn\ *n* **1** : a faintly blue form of oxygen that is present in the air in small quantities **2** : pure and refreshing air

ozone layer *n* : a layer of the upper atmosphere that is characterized by high ozone content which blocks most of the sun's radiation from entering the lower atmosphere

p \'pē\ *n, pl* **p's** *or* **ps** \'pēz\ *often cap* : the sixteenth letter of the English alphabet

pa \'pä, 'pȯ\ *n, often cap* : ¹FATHER 1

¹pace \'pās\ *n* **1** : rate of moving forward or ahead **2** : a manner of walking **3** : a horse's gait in which the legs on the same side move at the same time **4** : a single step or its length

²pace *vb* **paced; pac·ing 1** : to walk with slow steps **2** : to move at a pace ⟨a *pacing* horse⟩ **3** : to measure by steps ⟨*pace* off 300 meters⟩ **4** : to walk back and forth across ⟨*pacing* the floor⟩ **5** : to set or regulate the pace of

pa·cif·ic \pə-'sif-ik\ *adj* **1** : making peace : PEACEABLE **2** : ²CALM, PEACEFUL **3** *cap* : relating to the Pacific ocean

pac·i·fy \'pas-ə-,fī\ *vb* **pac·i·fied; pac·i·fy·ing** : to make peaceful or quiet : CALM, SOOTHE ⟨*pacify* a crying baby⟩

¹pack \'pak\ *n* **1** : a bundle arranged for carrying especially on the back of a person or animal **2** : a group of like persons

\ə\ abut	\au̇\ out	\i\ tip	\ȯ\ saw	\u̇\ foot
\ər\ further	\ch\ chin	\ī\ life	\ȯi\ coin	\y\ yet
\a\ mat	\e\ pet	\j\ job	\th\ thin	\yü\ few
\ā\ take	\ē\ easy	\ng\ sing	\th\ this	\yu̇\ cure
\ä\ cot, cart	\g\ go	\ō\ bone	\ü\ food	\zh\ vision

or things : BAND, SET ⟨a cub scout *pack*⟩ ⟨a wolf *pack*⟩

²**pack** *vb* **1** : to put into a container or bundle ⟨*pack* your clothes⟩ **2** : to put things into ⟨*pack* a suitcase⟩ **3** : to crowd into so as to fill full : CRAM ⟨a *packed* auditorium⟩ **4** : to send away ⟨*pack* children off to school⟩ — **pack·er** *n*

synonyms PACK, CRAM, and STUFF mean to fill something to its limit or beyond. PACK may suggest a tight filling up in an orderly way ⟨*pack* a trunk⟩ or it may suggest filling up something too much ⟨people were *packed* into the room like sardines⟩ CRAM usually suggests that something has been filled in a forceful, careless, or disorderly way ⟨*crammed* everything into one small box⟩ STUFF suggests filling something as much as it will hold and often to the point of bulging ⟨I *stuffed* my pockets with apples⟩

pack·age \'pak-ij\ *n* **1** : a bundle made up for shipping **2** : a box or case in which goods are shipped or delivered

pack·et \'pak-ət\ *n* : a small package

pack·ing·house \'pak-ing-,haus\ *n* : a building for preparing and packing food and especially meat

pact \'pakt\ *n* : AGREEMENT 2, TREATY

¹**pad** \'pad\ *n* **1** : something soft used for protection or comfort : CUSHION **2** : a piece of material that holds ink used in inking rubber stamps **3** : the hairy foot of some animals (as a fox or hare) **4** : a floating leaf of a water plant **5** : a tablet of writing or drawing paper

²**pad** *vb* **pad·ded; pad·ding 1** : to stuff or cover with soft material **2** : to make longer by adding words ⟨*pad* a speech⟩

³**pad** *vb* **pad·ded; pad·ding** : to walk or run with quiet steps ⟨a lion *padding* about its cage⟩

pad·ding \'pad-ing\ *n* : material used to pad something

¹**pad·dle** \'pad-l\ *n* **1** : an instrument like an oar used in moving and steering a small boat (as a canoe) **2** : one of the broad boards at the outer edge of a waterwheel or a paddle wheel **3** : an instrument for beating, mixing, or hitting

²**paddle** *vb* **pad·dled; pad·dling 1** : to move or drive forward with or as if with a paddle **2** : to stir or mix with a paddle **3** : to beat with or as if with a paddle

³**paddle** *vb* **pad·dled; pad·dling** : to move or splash about in the water with the hands or feet : WADE

paddle wheel *n* : a wheel with paddles near its outer edge used to drive a boat

pad·dock \'pad-ək\ *n* **1** : an enclosed area where animals are put to eat grass or to exercise **2** : an enclosed area where racehorses are saddled and paraded

pad·dy \'pad-ē\ *n, pl* **pad·dies** : wet land in which rice is grown

¹**pad·lock** \'pad-,läk\ *n* : a removable lock that has a curved piece that snaps into a catch

²**padlock** *vb* : to fasten with a padlock

¹**pa·gan** \'pā-gən\ *n* : ²HEATHEN 1

²**pagan** *adj* : of or relating to pagans or their worship : HEATHEN ⟨a *pagan* temple⟩

¹**page** \'pāj\ *n* **1** : a boy being trained to be a knight in the Middle Ages **2** : a person employed (as by a hotel or the United States congress) to carry messages or run errands

²**page** *vb* **paged; pag·ing** : to call out the name of (a person) in a public place

³**page** *n* : one side of a printed or written sheet of paper

pag·eant \'paj-ənt\ *n* **1** : a grand and fancy public ceremony and display **2** : an entertainment made up of scenes based on history or legend ⟨a Christmas *pageant*⟩

pa·go·da \pə-'gōd-ə\ *n* : a tower of several stories built as a temple or memorial in the Far East

paid *past of* PAY

pail \'pāl\ *n* **1** : a round container that usually has a curved handle and is used mainly for holding or carrying liquids : BUCKET ⟨a water *pail*⟩ **2** : PAILFUL ⟨poured a *pail* of water down the drain⟩

pail·ful \'pāl-,fùl\ *n, pl* **pail·fuls** \-,fùlz\ *or* **pails·ful** \'pālz-,fùl\ : the amount a pail holds

pagoda

¹**pain** \'pān\ *n* **1** : suffering that accompanies a bodily disorder (as a disease or an injury) ⟨*pain* in the chest⟩ **2** : a feeling (as a prick or an ache) that is caused by something harmful and usually makes one try to escape its source **3** : suffering of the mind or emotions : GRIEF **4 pains** *pl* : great care or effort ⟨took *pains* with the garden⟩ — **pain·ful** \'pān-fəl\ *adj* — **pain·ful·ly** \-fə-lē\ *adv* — **pain·less** \-ləs\ *adj*

²pain *vb* **1** : to cause pain in or to **2** : to give or feel pain

pains·tak·ing \'pān-ˌstā-king\ *adj* : taking pains : showing care ⟨a *painstaking* worker⟩ — **pains·tak·ing·ly** *adv*

¹paint \'pānt\ *vb* **1** : to cover a surface with or as if with paint ⟨*paint* a wall⟩ **2** : to make a picture or design by using paints ⟨*paint* a dog on the sign⟩ **3** : to describe clearly — **paint·er** *n*

²paint *n* : a mixture of coloring matter with a liquid that forms a dry coating when spread on a surface

¹pair \'paər, 'peər\ *n, pl* **pairs** *also* **pair** **1** : two things that match or are meant to be used together ⟨a *pair* of gloves⟩ ⟨a *pair* of draft horses⟩ **2** : a thing having two similar parts that are connected ⟨a *pair* of scissors⟩ **3** : a mated couple ⟨a *pair* of robins⟩

²pair *vb* **1** : to arrange or join in pairs ⟨the guests *paired* off for dancing⟩ **2** : to form a pair : MATCH ⟨this glove doesn't *pair* with that⟩

pa·ja·mas \pə-'jäm-əz, -'jam-əz\ *n pl* : loose clothes usually consisting of pants and top that match and that are worn for relaxing or sleeping

---

Word History When the English went to India they saw many people wearing light, loose trousers. The English called these trousers *pajamas*. The English word came from a word in a language of India. That word was made up of two words in a language of Iran. The first word meant "leg." The second meant "garment." The English began to use these trousers in place of nightshirts. Later the word *pajamas* came to be used for a two-piece sleeping suit.

---

¹Pak·i·stani \ˌpak-i-'stan-ē, ˌpäk-i-'stän-ē\ *n* : a person born or living in Pakistan

²Pakistani *adj* : of or relating to Pakistan or the Pakistanis

pal \'pal\ *n* : a close friend

pal·ace \'pal-əs\ *n* **1** : the home of a ruler **2** : a large or splendid house

pal·at·able \'pal-ət-ə-bəl\ *adj* : pleasant to the taste

pal·ate \'pal-ət\ *n* **1** : the roof of the mouth made up of a bony front part (**hard palate**) and a soft flexible back part (**soft palate**) **2** : the sense of taste

¹pale \'pāl\ *adj* **pal·er; pal·est** **1** : not having the warm color of a healthy person **2** : not bright or brilliant ⟨a *pale* star⟩ **3** : light in color or shade ⟨*pale* pink⟩ — **pale·ness** *n*

²pale *vb* **paled; pal·ing** : to make or become pale

Pa·leo·zo·ic \ˌpā-lē-ə-'zō-ik\ *n* : an era of geological history ending about 230,000,000 years ago which came before the Mesozoic and in which vertebrates and land plants first appeared

pal·ette \'pal-ət\ *n* **1** : a thin board or tablet on which a painter puts and mixes colors **2** : the set of colors that a painter puts on a palette

pal·i·sade \ˌpal-ə-'sād\ *n* **1** : a fence made of poles to protect against attack **2** : a line of steep cliffs

¹pall \'pol\ *n* **1** : a heavy cloth covering for a coffin, hearse, or tomb **2** : something that makes things dark and gloomy ⟨a *pall* of smoke⟩

²pall *vb* : to become dull or uninteresting : lose the ability to give pleasure

pall·bear·er \'pol-ˌbar-ər, -ˌber-\ *n* : a person who helps to carry or follows a coffin at a funeral

pal·let \'pal-ət\ *n* **1** : a mattress of straw **2** : a temporary bed on the floor

pal·lid \'pal-əd\ *adj* : ¹PALE 1

pal·lor \'pal-ər\ *n* : paleness of face

¹palm \'päm, 'pälm\ *n* : any of a group of mostly tropical trees, shrubs, and vines with a simple but often tall stem topped with leaves that are shaped like feathers or fans

palm

Word History *Palm*, the name of a tree, is related to *palm*, the word for the under part of the hand. Both English words come from the same Latin word. This Latin word first meant "palm of the hand." It came to mean "palm tree" as well because the leaves of a palm look something like large outstretched hands.

²palm *n* **1** : the under part of the hand between the fingers and the wrist **2** : a measure of length of about seven to ten centimeters

³palm *vb* : to hide in the hand ⟨*palm* a coin⟩

\ə\ **abut**	\aů\ **out**	\i\ **tip**	\ȯ\ **saw**	\ů\ **foot**
\ər\ **further**	\ch\ **chin**	\ī\ **life**	\ȯi\ **coin**	\y\ **yet**
\a\ **mat**	\e\ **pet**	\j\ **job**	\th\ **thin**	\yü\ **few**
\ā\ **take**	\ē\ **easy**	\ng\ **sing**	\th\ **this**	\yů\ **cure**
\ä\ **cot, cart**	\g\ **go**	\ō\ **bone**	\ü\ **food**	\zh\ **vision**

pal·met·to \pal-'met-ō\ *n*, *pl* **pal·met·tos** *or* **pal·met·toes** : a low palm with leaves shaped like fans

palm off *vb* : to get rid of or pass on in a dishonest way ⟨tried to *palm off* plastic as real leather⟩

Palm Sunday *n* : the Sunday before Easter celebrated in memory of Christ's entry into Jerusalem

pal·o·mi·no \ˌpal-ə-'mē-nō\ *n*, *pl* **pal·o·mi·nos** : a small strong horse that is light tan or cream in color with a lighter mane and tail

pal·pi·tate \'pal-pə-ˌtāt\ *vb* **pal·pi·tat·ed; pal·pi·tat·ing** : ¹THROB 1

pal·sy \'pȯl-zē\ *n* **1** : PARALYSIS **2** : a trembling of the head or hands that cannot be controlled

pal·try \'pȯl-trē\ *adj* **pal·tri·er; pal·tri·est** : of little importance : PETTY

pam·pas \'pam-pəz\ *n pl* : wide treeless plains of South America

pam·per \'pam-pər\ *vb* : to give someone or someone's desires too much care and attention : INDULGE

pam·phlet \'pam-flət\ *n* : a short publication without a binding : BOOKLET

> **Word History** A long time ago someone whose name we do not know wrote a Latin love poem called *Pamphilus* that became very popular. Many copies of the poem were made. The English formed a word from the name of this poem which they used for any written work too short to be called a book. The modern word *pamphlet* comes from this early English word.

¹**pan** \'pan\ *n* **1** : a shallow open container used for cooking **2** : a container somewhat like a cooking pan ⟨the *pans* of a pair of scales⟩

²**pan** *vb* **panned; pan·ning** : to wash earthy material so as to collect bits of metal (as gold)

pan·cake \'pan-ˌkāk\ *n* : a flat cake made of thin batter and cooked on both sides on a griddle

pan·cre·as \'pang-krē-əs\ *n* : a large gland in the abdomen that produces insulin and a fluid (**pancreatic juice**) that aids digestion

pan·cre·at·ic \ˌpang-krē-'at-ik\ *adj* : of or relating to the pancreas

pan·da \'pan-də\ *n* : either of two animals of western China which are related to the raccoon and of which the smaller is reddish with black feet and a bushy ringed tail and the larger (**giant panda**) is black and white and looks like a bear

pan·de·mo·ni·um \ˌpan-də-'mō-nē-əm\ *n*

: wild uproar ⟨*pandemonium* broke loose when the winning run scored⟩

pane \'pān\ *n* : a sheet of glass (as in a window)

¹**pan·el** \'pan-l\ *n* **1** : a group of persons appointed for some service ⟨a jury *panel*⟩ **2** : a group of persons taking part in a discussion or quiz program **3** : a part of something (as a door or a wall) often sunk below the level of the frame **4** : a piece of material (as plywood) made to form part of a surface (as of a wall) **5** : a board into which instruments or controls are set

²**panel** *vb* **pan·eled** *or* **pan·elled; pan·el·ing** *or* **pan·el·ling** : to supply or decorate with panels ⟨*panel* a wall⟩ ⟨a *paneled* ceiling⟩

pan·el·ing \'pan-l-ing\ *n* : panels joined in a continuous surface

pang \'pang\ *n* : a sudden sharp attack or feeling (as of hunger or regret)

¹**pan·ic** \'pan-ik\ *n* : a sudden overpowering fear especially without reasonable cause

> **Word History** The ancient Greeks had very many gods. One of these, named Pan, was the god of shepherds and hunters. Sometimes he wandered peacefully through the woods, playing a pipe. Sometimes he could also cause sudden fear that seemed to have no reason. People thought that he could make even giants afraid. The Greeks made a word that meant "sudden fright" from the name of this god. The English word *panic* comes from this Greek word.

pandas

²panic *vb* **pan·icked; pan·ick·ing** : to affect or be affected by panic

pan·icky \'pan-i-kē\ *adj* **1** : like or caused by panic ⟨*panicky* fear⟩ **2** : feeling or likely to feel panic

pan·ora·ma \,pan-ə-'ram-ə, -'räm-\ *n* : a clear complete view in every direction

pan out *vb* : to give a good result : SUCCEED

pan·sy \'pan-zē\ *n*, *pl* **pan·sies** : a garden plant related to the violets that has large velvety flowers with five petals usually in shades of yellow, purple, or brownish red

PANSY

¹pant \'pant\ *vb* : to breathe hard or quickly ⟨*pant* from running⟩

²pant *n* : a panting breath

pan·ta·loons \,pant-l-'ünz\ *n pl* : PANTS

pan·ther \'pan-thər\ *n* **1** : LEOPARD **2** : COUGAR **3** : JAGUAR

pant·ie *or* **panty** \'pant-ē\ *n*, *pl* **pant·ies** : a woman's or child's undergarment with short legs or no legs

¹pan·to·mime \'pant-ə-,mīm\ *n* **1** : a show in which a story is told by using expressions on the face and movements of the body instead of words **2** : a showing or explaining of something through movements of the body and face alone

²pantomime *vb* **pan·to·mimed; pan·to·mim·ing** : to tell through pantomime

pan·try \'pan-trē\ *n*, *pl* **pan·tries** : a small room where food and dishes are kept

pants \'pants\ *n pl* : an outer garment reaching from the waist to the ankle or only to the knee and covering each leg separately

pa·pa \'pä-pə\ *n*, *often cap* : ¹FATHER 1

pa·pal \'pā-pəl\ *adj* : of or relating to the pope

pa·paw *n* **1** \pə-'pȯ\ : PAPAYA **2** \'päp-ȯ, 'pȯp-\ : the greenish or yellow edible fruit of a North American tree with shiny leaves and purple flowers

pa·pa·ya \pə-'pī-ə\ *n* : a yellow edible fruit that looks like a melon and grows on a tropical American tree

¹pa·per \'pā-pər\ *n* **1** : a material made in thin sheets from fibers (as of wood or cloth) **2** : a sheet or piece of paper **3** : a piece of paper having something written or printed on it : DOCUMENT **4** : NEWS-

paper **5** : WALLPAPER **6** : a piece of written schoolwork

²paper *vb* : to cover or line with paper (as wallpaper) ⟨*paper* a room⟩

³paper *adj* **1** : made of paper ⟨*paper* carton⟩ **2** : like paper in thinness or weakness

pa·per·back \'pā-pər-,bak\ *n* : a book with a flexible paper binding

paper clip *n* : a clip of bent wire used to hold sheets of paper together

pa·pery \'pā-pə-rē\ *adj* : like paper

pa·poose \pa-'püs\ *n* : a baby of North American Indian parents

pa·pri·ka \pə-'prē-kə\ *n* : a mild red spice made from the fruit of some sweet peppers

pa·py·rus \pə-'pī-rəs\ *n*, *pl* **pa·py·rus·es** *or* **pa·py·ri** \-rē, -,rī\ **1** : a tall African plant related to the grasses that grows especially in Egypt **2** : a material like paper made from papyrus by ancient people and used by them to write on

papyrus 1

par \'pär\ *n* **1** : a fixed or stated value (as of money or a security) **2** : an equal level ⟨two people with talents on a *par*⟩ **3** : the score set for each hole of a golf course

par·a·ble \'par-ə-bəl\ *n* : a simple story that teaches a moral truth

¹par·a·chute \'par-ə-,shüt\ *n* : a folding device of light material shaped like an umbrella and used for making a safe jump from an airplane

²parachute *vb* **par·a·chut·ed; par·a·chut·ing** : to transport or come down by parachute

¹pa·rade \pə-'rād\ *n* **1** : great show or display ⟨the exhibition was a *parade* of American history⟩ **2** : the formation of troops before an officer for inspection **3** : a public procession ⟨a circus *parade*⟩ **4** : a crowd of people walking at an easy pace ⟨the Easter *parade*⟩

\ə\ abut	\au\ out	\i\ tip	\ȯ\ saw	\u̇\ foot
\ər\ further	\ch\ chin	\ī\ life	\ȯi\ coin	\y\ yet
\a\ mat	\e\ pet	\j\ job	\th\ thin	\yü\ few
\ā\ take	\ē\ easy	\ng\ sing	\th\ this	\yu̇\ cure
\ä\ cot, cart	\g\ go	\ō\ bone	\ü\ food	\zh\ vision

²**parade** *vb* **pa·rad·ed; pa·rad·ing 1 :** to march in an orderly group **2 :** SHOW OFF
synonyms see SHOW

par·a·dise \'par-ə-ˌdīs, -ˌdīz\ *n* **1 :** the garden of Eden **2 :** HEAVEN 2 **3 :** a place or state of great happiness

par·a·dox \'par-ə-ˌdäks\ *n* **:** a statement that seems to be the opposite of the truth or of common sense and yet is perhaps true

par·af·fin \'par-ə-fən\ *n* **:** a white odorless tasteless substance obtained from wood, coal, or petroleum and used in coating and sealing and in candles

¹**para·graph** \'par-ə-ˌgraf\ *n* **:** a part of a piece of writing that is made up of one or more sentences and has to do with one topic or gives the words of one speaker

²**paragraph** *vb* **:** to divide into paragraphs

par·a·keet *or* **par·ra·keet** \'par-ə-ˌkēt\ *n* **:** a small parrot with a long tail

¹**par·al·lel** \'par-ə-ˌlel\ *adj* **:** lying or moving in the same direction but always the same distance apart ⟨*parallel* lines⟩ ⟨*train tracks* are *parallel*⟩

parakeet

²**parallel** *n* **1 :** a parallel line or surface **2 :** one of the imaginary circles on the earth's surface parallel to the equator that mark latitude **3 :** agreement in many or most details ⟨the *parallel* between their lives⟩ **4 :** COUNTERPART, EQUAL

³**parallel** *vb* **1 :** to be like or equal to **2 :** to move, run, or extend in a direction parallel with ⟨the road *parallels* the river⟩

par·al·lel·o·gram \ˌpar-ə-'lel-ə-ˌgram\ *n* **:** a plane figure with four sides whose opposite sides are parallel and equal

pa·ral·y·sis \pə-'ral-ə-səs\ *n, pl* **pa·ral·y·ses** \-ˌsēz\ **:** partial or complete loss of one's ability to move or feel

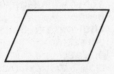

parallelogram

par·a·lyze \'par-ə-ˌlīz\ *vb* **par·a·lyzed; par·a·lyz·ing 1 :** to affect with paralysis **2 :** to destroy or decrease something's energy or ability to act ⟨the city was *paralyzed* by the heavy snowstorm⟩

par·a·me·cium \ˌpar-ə-'mē-shē-əm, -shəm\ *n, pl* **par·a·me·cia** \-shē-ə\ *also* **par·a-**
me·ciums : a tiny water animal that is a single cell shaped like a slipper

par·a·mount \'par-ə-ˌmaunt\ *adj* **:** highest in importance or greatness

par·a·pet \'par-ə-pət, -ˌpet\ *n* **1 :** a wall of earth or stone to protect soldiers **2 :** a low wall or fence at the edge of a platform, roof, or bridge

¹**para·phrase** \'par-ə-ˌfrāz\ *n* **:** a way of stating something again by giving the meaning in different words

²**paraphrase** *vb* **para·phrased; para·phras·ing :** to give the meaning of in different words

par·a·site \'par-ə-ˌsīt\ *n* **1 :** a person who lives at the expense of another **2 :** a plant or animal that lives in or on some other living thing and gets food and sometimes shelter from it

par·a·sit·ic \ˌpar-ə-'sit-ik\ *adj* **:** of or relating to parasites or their way of life **:** being a parasite — **par·a·sit·i·cal·ly** \-i-kə-lē\ *adv*

par·a·sol \'par-ə-ˌsòl\ *n* **:** a light umbrella used as a protection against the sun

par·a·troop·er \'par-ə-ˌtrü-pər\ *n* **:** a soldier trained and equipped to parachute from an airplane

¹**par·cel** \'pär-səl\ *n* **1 :** a plot of land **2 :** PACKAGE 1

²**parcel** *vb* **par·celed** *or* **par·celled; par·cel·ing** *or* **par·cel·ling 1 :** to divide and give out by parts **2 :** to wrap up into a package

parcel post *n* **:** a mail service that handles packages

parch \'pärch\ *vb* **:** to dry up from heat and lack of moisture

parch·ment \'pärch-mənt\ *n* **1 :** the skin of a sheep or goat prepared so that it can be written on **2 :** a paper similar to parchment

¹**par·don** \'pärd-n\ *n* **1 :** forgiveness for wrong or rude behavior **2 :** a setting free from legal punishment

²**pardon** *vb* **1 :** to free from penalty for a fault or crime **2 :** to allow (a wrong act) to pass without punishment **:** FORGIVE

pare \'paər, 'peər\ *vb* **pared; par·ing 1 :** to cut or shave off the outside or the ends of **2 :** to reduce as if by cutting ⟨*pare* the cost of a trip⟩

par·ent \'par-ənt, 'per-\ *n* **1 :** a father or mother of a child **2 :** an animal or plant that produces offspring or seed

par·ent·age \'par-ənt-ij, 'per-\ *n* **:** a line of ancestors **:** ANCESTRY

pa·ren·tal \pə-'rent-l\ *adj* **:** of or relating to parents ⟨*parental* love⟩

pa·ren·the·sis \pə-'ren-thə-səs\ *n, pl* **pa·ren·the·ses** \-ˌsēz\ **1 :** a word, phrase, or sentence inserted in a passage to explain or comment on it **2** : one of a pair of marks ( ) used to enclose a word or group of words or to group mathematical terms to be dealt with as a unit — **par·en·thet·ic** \,par-ən-'thet-ik\ *or* **par·en·thet·i·cal** \ -i-kəl\ *adj*

par·fait \pär-'fā\ *n* : a dessert made usually of layers of fruit, syrup, ice cream, and whipped cream

par·ish \'par-ish\ *n* **1** : a section of a church district under the care of a priest or minister **2** : the persons who live in a parish and attend the parish church **3** : the members of a church **4** : a division in the state of Louisiana that is similar to a county in other states

parish house *n* : a building for the educational and social activities of a church

pa·rish·io·ner \pə-'rish-ə-nər\ *n* : a member or resident of a parish

¹park \'pärk\ *n* **1** : an area of land set aside for recreation or for its beauty **2** : an enclosed field for ball games

²park *vb* : to stop (as an auto or truck) and leave it for a while ⟨never *park* in front of a hydrant⟩

par·ka \'pär-kə\ *n* : a warm windproof jacket with a hood

park·way \'pär-,kwā\ *n* : a broad landscaped highway

¹par·ley \'pär-lē\ *vb* **par·leyed; par·ley·ing** : to hold a discussion of terms with an enemy

²parley *n, pl* **par·leys** : a discussion with an enemy ⟨a truce *parley*⟩

par·lia·ment \'pär-lə-mənt\ *n* : an assembly that is the highest legislative body of a country (as the United Kingdom)

par·lor \'pär-lər\ *n* **1** : a room for receiving guests and for conversation **2** : a usually small place of business ⟨beauty *parlor*⟩ ⟨ice cream *parlor*⟩

pa·ro·chi·al \pə-'rō-kē-əl\ *adj* : of, relating to, or supported by a religious body (as a church) ⟨a *parochial* school⟩ ⟨*parochial* duties⟩

pa·role \pə-'rōl\ *n* : an early release of a prisoner

parrakeet *variant of* PARAKEET

par·rot \'par-ət\ *n* : a brightly colored tropical bird with a strong hooked bill sometimes trained to imitate human speech

¹par·ry \'par-ē\ *vb* **par·ried; par·ry·ing 1** : to turn aside an opponent's weapon or blow **2** : to avoid by a skillful answer ⟨*parry* an embarrassing question⟩

²parry *n, pl* **par·ries** : an act or instance of parrying

pars·ley \'pär-slē\ *n, pl* **pars·leys** : a garden plant related to the carrot that has finely divided leaves and is used to season or decorate various foods

pars·nip \'pär-snəp\ *n* : a vegetable that is the long white root of a plant related to the carrot

par·son \'pärs-n\ *n* : ¹MINISTER 1

par·son·age \'pärs-n-ij\ *n* : a house provided by a church for its pastor to live in

¹part \'pärt\ *n* **1** : one of the sections into which something is divided : something less than a whole **2** : a voice or instrument ⟨four-*part* harmony⟩ **3** : the music for a voice or instrument ⟨the soprano *part*⟩ **4** : a piece of a plant or animal body **5** : a piece of a machine **6** : a person's share or duty ⟨did my *part*⟩ **7** : one of the sides in a disagreement ⟨took my *part* in the quarrel⟩ **8** : the role of a character in a play **9** : a line along which the hair is divided

synonyms PART, PORTION, and SECTION mean something less than the whole to which it belongs. PART suggests only that something is taken away from the whole or thought of as being separate from the rest ⟨a *part* of the room is used for storage⟩ PORTION suggests that a whole has been divided into assigned parts ⟨cut the pie into six *portions*⟩ SECTION suggests that the parts of the whole are recognizable and have been separated by or as if by cutting ⟨this newspaper has four *sections*⟩

²part *vb* **1** : to leave someone : go away ⟨*part* from a friend⟩ **2** : to divide into parts **3** : to hold apart ⟨the fighters were *parted* by friends⟩ **4** : to come apart ⟨the rope *parted* under the strain⟩ **synonyms** see SEPARATE

par·take \pär-'tāk\ *vb* **par·took** \-'tůk\; **par·tak·en** \-'tā-kən\; **par·tak·ing** : to take a share or part ⟨*partake* of a dinner⟩ ⟨*partake* in a ceremony⟩

parrot

\ə\ **abut**	\aů\ **out**	\i\ **tip**	\ȯ\ **saw**	\ů\ **foot**	
\ər\ **further**	\ch\ **chin**	\ī\ **life**	\ȯi\ **coin**	\y\ **yet**	
\a\ **mat**	\e\ **pet**	\j\ **job**	\th\ **thin**	\yü\ **few**	
\ā\ **take**	\ē\ **easy**	\ng\ **sing**	\th\ **this**	\yů\ **cure**	
\ä\ **cot, cart**	\g\ **go**	\ō\ **bone**	\ü\ **food**	\zh\ **vision**	

part·ed \'pärt-əd\ *adj* : divided into parts

par·tial \'pär-shəl\ *adj* **1** : favoring one side of a question over another ⟨a *partial* judge⟩ **2** : fond or too fond of someone or something ⟨*partial* to ice cream sodas⟩ **3** : of one part only ⟨a *partial* eclipse⟩ **4** : not complete ⟨*partial* deafness⟩ — **par·tial·ly** \'pär-shə-lē\ *adv*

par·ti·al·i·ty \,pär-shē-'al-ət-ē\ *n, pl* **par·ti·al·i·ties** : the quality or state of being partial

par·tic·i·pant \pər-'tis-ə-pənt, pär-\ *n* : a person who takes part in something ⟨*participants* in a fight⟩

par·tic·i·pate \pər-'tis-ə-,pāt, pär-\ *vb* **par·tic·i·pat·ed; par·tic·i·pat·ing** : to join with others in doing something

par·tic·i·pa·tion \pär-,tis-ə-'pā-shən\ *n* : the act of participating

par·ti·ci·ple \'pärt-ə-,sip-əl\ *n* : a word formed from a verb but often used like an adjective while keeping some verb characteristics (as tense and the ability to take an object) ⟨"crying" in "the crying child ran home" is a *participle*⟩

par·ti·cle \'pärt-i-kəl\ *n* : a very small bit of something ⟨not a *particle* of sense⟩ ⟨a *particle* of sand⟩

¹par·tic·u·lar \pər-'tik-yə-lər\ *adj* **1** : relating to one person or thing ⟨each city has its *particular* problems⟩ **2** : not usual : SPECIAL ⟨a wind of *particular* force⟩ **3** : being one of several ⟨consider each *particular* item⟩ **4** : concerned about details ⟨our teacher is very *particular*⟩ — **par·tic·u·lar·ly** *adv*

²particular *n* : a single fact or detail ⟨the account was correct in every *particular*⟩

part·ing \'pärt-ing\ *n* : a place or point where a division or separation occurs

par·ti·san \'pärt-ə-zən, -sən\ *n* **1** : a person who aids or approves something (as a party or a point of view) or someone ⟨a *partisan* of the governor⟩ **2** : a soldier who lives and fights behind enemy lines — **par·ti·san·ship** \-,ship\ *n*

¹par·ti·tion \pər-'tish-ən, pär-\ *n* **1** : an act of dividing into parts ⟨the *partition* of a defeated country⟩ **2** : something that divides ⟨a *partition* between two rooms⟩

²partition *vb* **1** : to divide into shares ⟨*partition* an estate⟩ **2** : to divide into separate parts or areas ⟨*partitioned* the basement into three rooms⟩

part·ly \'pärt-lē\ *adv* : somewhat but not completely ⟨I was *partly* to blame⟩

part·ner \'pärt-nər\ *n* **1** : a person who does or shares something with another ⟨my favorite dancing *partner*⟩ **2** : either one of a married pair **3** : one who plays with another person on the same side in a game **4** : one of two or more persons who run a business together

part·ner·ship \'pärt-nər-,ship\ *n* **1** : the state of being a partner **2** : a group of people in business together

part of speech : a class of words (as adjectives, adverbs, conjunctions, interjections, nouns, prepositions, pronouns, or verbs) identified according to the kinds of ideas they express and the work they do in a sentence

partook *past of* PARTAKE

par·tridge \'pär-trij\ *n, pl* **partridge** *or* **par·tridg·es** : any of several plump game birds related to the chicken

partridge

part-time \'pärt-'tīm\ *adj* : involving fewer than the usual hours ⟨*part-time* work⟩

par·ty \'pärt-ē\ *n, pl* **par·ties** **1** : a group of persons who take one side of a question or share a set of beliefs ⟨a political *party*⟩ **2** : a social gathering or the entertainment provided for it **3** : a person or group concerned in some action ⟨a *party* to a lawsuit⟩

¹pass \'pas\ *vb* **1** : ¹MOVE 1, PROCEED **2** : to go away ⟨the pain will soon *pass*⟩ **3** : ¹DIE 1 ⟨*pass* on⟩ **4** : to go by or move past ⟨*pass* that car⟩ **5** : to go or allow to go across, over, or through ⟨they let me *pass*⟩ **6** : to move from one place or condition to another ⟨the business has *passed* into other hands⟩ **7** : HAPPEN 2 **8** : to be or cause to be approved ⟨the senate *passed* the bill⟩ **9** : to go successfully through an examination or inspection **10** : to be or cause to be identified or recognized ⟨*pass* for an expert⟩ **11** : to transfer or throw to another person ⟨*pass* the salt⟩ ⟨*pass* a football⟩ — **pass•er** *n*

²pass *n* **1** : an opening or way for passing along or through **2** : a gap in a mountain range

³pass *n* **1** : SITUATION 4 ⟨things have come to a strange *pass*⟩ **2** : a written permit to go or come **3** : the act or an instance of passing (as a ball) in a game

pass•able \'pas-ə-bəl\ *adj* **1** : fit to be traveled on ⟨*passable* roads⟩ **2** : barely good enough ⟨a *passable* imitation⟩ — **pass•ably** \-blē\ *adv*

pas•sage \'pas-ij\ *n* **1** : the act or process of passing from one place or condition to another ⟨a smooth *passage* over the sea⟩ **2** : a means (as a hall) of passing or reaching **3** : the passing of a law **4** : a right or permission to go as a passenger ⟨*passage* at a reduced rate⟩ **5** : a brief part of a speech or written work

pas•sage•way \'pas-ij-,wā\ *n* : a road or way by which a person or thing may pass

pas•sen•ger \'pas-n-jər\ *n* : someone riding on or in a vehicle

passenger pigeon *n* : a North American wild pigeon once common but now extinct

pass•er•by \,pas-ər-'bī\ *n, pl* **pass•ers•by** \-ərz-'bī\ : someone who passes by

¹pass•ing \'pas-ing\ *n* **1** : the act of passing ⟨the *passing* of winter⟩ **2** : DEATH 1

²passing *adj* **1** : going by or past **2** : lasting only for a short time ⟨a *passing* fad⟩ **3** : showing haste or lack of attention ⟨a *passing* glance⟩ **4** : used for passing ⟨*passing* lanes⟩ **5** : showing satisfactory work in a test or course of study ⟨a *passing* mark⟩

pas•sion \'pash-ən\ *n* **1** *cap* : the suffering of Christ between the night of the Last Supper and his death **2** : a strong feeling or emotion **3** : strong liking or desire : LOVE ⟨a *passion* for music⟩ **4** : an object of one's love, liking, or desire

pas•sion•ate \'pash-ə-nət\ *adj* **1** : easily angered **2** : showing or affected by strong feeling — **pas•sion•ate•ly** *adv*

pas•sive \'pas-iv\ *adj* **1** : not acting but acted upon ⟨*passive* spectators⟩ **2** : showing that the person or thing represented by the subject is acted on by the verb ⟨"were met" in "we were met by our friends" is *passive*⟩ **3** : offering no resistance ⟨*passive* obedience⟩ — **pas•sive•ly** *adv*

pass out *vb* : to become unconscious : FAINT

Pass•over \'pas-,ō-vər\ *n* : a Jewish holiday celebrated in March or April in honor of the freeing of the Hebrews from slavery in Egypt

pass•port \'pas-,pōrt\ *n* : a government document that allows a citizen to leave his or her country

pass up *vb* : to let go by : REFUSE

pass•word \'pas-,wərd\ *n* : a secret word or phrase that must be spoken by a person before being allowed to pass a guard

¹past \'past\ *adj* **1** : of or relating to a time that has gone by ⟨for the *past* month⟩ **2** : expressing a time gone by ⟨the *past* tense of the verb "run" is "ran"⟩ **3** : no longer serving ⟨a *past* president⟩

²past *prep* **1** : ²BEYOND ⟨twenty minutes *past* five⟩ **2** : going close to and then beyond ⟨walked *past* my house⟩

³past *n* **1** : a former time **2** : past life or history ⟨the nation's *past*⟩

⁴past *adv* : so as to pass by or beyond ⟨a deer ran *past*⟩

¹paste \'pāst\ *n* **1** : dough for pies or tarts **2** : a soft smooth mixture ⟨tomato *paste*⟩ ⟨mix cement and water into a *paste*⟩ **3** : a mixture of flour or starch and water used for sticking things together

²paste *vb* **past•ed; past•ing** : to stick on or together with paste

paste•board \'pāst-,bōrd\ *n* : a stiff material made of sheets of paper pasted together or of pulp pressed and dried

¹pas•tel \pas-'tel\ *n* **1** : a crayon made by mixing ground coloring matter with a watery solution of a gum **2** : a drawing made with pastel crayons **3** : a soft pale color

²pastel *adj* **1** : made with pastels **2** : light and pale in color

pas•teur•iza•tion \,pas-chə-rə-'zā-shən, ,pas-tə-\ *n* : the process or an instance of pasteurizing

pas•teur•ize \'pas-chə-,rīz, 'pas-tə-\ *vb* **pas•teur•ized; pas•teur•iz•ing** : to keep a liquid (as milk) for a time at a temperature high enough to kill many harmful germs and then cool it rapidly — **pas•teur•iz•er** *n*

pas•time \'pas-,tīm\ *n* : something (as a hobby) that helps to make time pass pleasantly

pas•tor \'pas-tər\ *n* : a minister or priest in charge of a church

pas•to•ral \'pas-tə-rəl\ *adj* **1** : of or relating to shepherds or peaceful rural scenes ⟨*pastoral* poetry⟩ **2** : of or relating to the pastor of a church ⟨*pastoral* duties⟩

past•ry \'pā-strē\ *n, pl* **past•ries 1** : sweet

\ə\ abut	\au̇\ out	\i\ tip	\ȯ\ saw	\u̇\ foot
\ər\ further	\ch\ chin	\ī\ life	\ȯi\ coin	\y\ yet
\a\ mat	\e\ pet	\j\ job	\th\ thin	\yü\ few
\ā\ take	\ē\ easy	\ng\ sing	\th\ this	\yu̇\ cure
\ä\ cot, cart	\g\ go	\ō\ bone	\ü\ food	\zh\ vision

baked goods (as pies) made mainly of flour and fat **2** : a piece of pastry

¹pas·ture \'pas-chər\ *n* **1** : plants (as grass) for feeding grazing animals **2** : land on which animals graze

²pasture *vb* **pas·tured; pas·tur·ing 1** : ¹GRAZE 1 **2** : to supply (as cattle) with pasture

¹pat \'pat\ *n* **1** : a light tap with the open hand or a flat instrument **2** : the sound of a pat or tap **3** : a small flat piece (as of butter)

²pat *vb* **pat·ted; pat·ting** : to tap or stroke gently with the open hand ⟨*pat* the dog⟩

³pat *adj* **pat·ter; pat·test 1** : exactly suitable ⟨a *pat* answer⟩ **2** : learned perfectly ⟨had my lines in the play down *pat*⟩ **3** : not changing ⟨stood *pat* against all arguments⟩

¹patch \'pach\ *n* **1** : a piece of cloth used to mend or cover a torn or worn place **2** : a small piece or area different from what is around it ⟨a *patch* of snow⟩ ⟨a *patch* of white on a dog's head⟩

²patch *vb* : to mend or cover with a patch **synonyms** see MEND

patch up *vb* : ADJUST 1 ⟨*patch up* a quarrel⟩

patch·work \'pach-,wərk\ *n* : pieces of cloth of different colors and shapes sewed together

¹pa·tent *for 1* 'pat-nt, *for 2* 'pat- *or* 'pāt-\ *adj* **1** : protected by a patent **2** : OBVIOUS, EVIDENT ⟨a *patent* lie⟩

²pat·ent \'pat-nt\ *n* : a document that gives the inventor of something the only right to make, use, and sell the invention for a certain number of years

³pat·ent \'pat-nt\ *vb* : to get a patent for ⟨*patented* their invention⟩

pa·ter·nal \pə-'tərn-l\ *adj* **1** : of or relating to a father : FATHERLY **2** : received or inherited from a father **3** : related through the father ⟨my *paternal* grandparents⟩

path \'path, 'pȧth\ *n, pl* **paths** \'pathz, 'pȧthz\ **1** : a track made by traveling on foot ⟨a *path* through the woods⟩ **2** : the way or track in which something moves ⟨the *path* of a planet⟩ **3** : a way of life or thought — **path·less** \-ləs\ *adj*

pa·thet·ic \pə-'thet-ik\ *adj* : making one feel pity, tenderness, or sorrow

path·way \'path-,wā, 'pȧth-\ *n* : PATH 1

pa·tience \'pā-shəns\ *n* : the ability to be patient or the fact of being patient ⟨need *patience* to do this work⟩

¹pa·tient \'pā-shənt\ *adj* **1** : putting up with pain or troubles without complaint **2** : showing or involving calm self-control

⟨a *patient* teacher⟩ ⟨made a *patient* effort to answer calmly⟩ — **pa·tient·ly** *adv*

²patient *n* : a person under medical care and treatment

pa·tio \'pat-ē-,ō, 'pät-\ *n, pl* **pa·ti·os 1** : an inner part of a house that is open to the sky **2** : an open area next to a house that is usually paved

pa·tri·arch \'pā-trē-,ärk\ *n* **1** : the father and ruler of a family or tribe **2** : a respected old man

pa·tri·ot \'pā-trē-ət\ *n* : a person who loves his or her country and enthusiastically supports it

pa·tri·ot·ic \,pā-trē-'ät-ik\ *adj* : having or showing patriotism

pa·tri·o·tism \'pā-trē-ə-,tiz-əm\ *n* : love of one's country

¹pa·trol \pə-'trōl\ *n* **1** : the action of going around an area for observation or guard **2** : a person or group doing the act of patrolling **3** : a part of a troop of boy scouts that consists of two or more boys **4** : a part of a troop of girl scouts that usually consists of six or eight girls

²patrol *vb* **pa·trolled; pa·trol·ling** : to go around an area for the purpose of watching or protecting

pa·trol·man \pə-'trōl-mən\ *n, pl* **pa·trol·men** \-mən\ : a police officer who has a regular beat

pa·tron \'pā-trən\ *n* **1** : a person who gives generous support or approval **2** : CUSTOMER **3** : a saint to whom a church or society is dedicated

pa·tron·age \'pa-trə-nij, 'pā-trə-\ *n* **1** : the help or encouragement given by a patron **2** : a group of patrons (as of a shop or theater) **3** : the control by officials of giving out jobs, contracts, and favors

pa·tron·ize \'pā-trə-,nīz, 'pa-trə-\ *vb* **pa·tron·ized; pa·tron·iz·ing 1** : to act as a patron to or of : SUPPORT ⟨*patronize* the arts⟩ **2** : to be a customer of ⟨*patronize* a neighborhood store⟩ **3** : to treat (a person) as if one were better or more important

¹pat·ter \'pat-ər\ *vb* **1** : to strike again and again with light blows ⟨rain *pattering* on a roof⟩ **2** : to run with quick light steps

²patter *n* : a series of quick light sounds ⟨the *patter* of little feet⟩

¹pat·tern \'pat-ərn\ *n* **1** : something worth copying ⟨a *pattern* of good behavior⟩ **2** : a model or guide for making something ⟨a dressmaker's *pattern*⟩ **3** : a form or figure used in decoration : DESIGN ⟨a rug with a fancy *pattern*⟩ — **pat·terned** \-ərnd\ *adj*

Word History In early English a person who served as a model to be copied was called a *patron*. Some people began to say *patron* in such a way that the sound of the *r* changed its place. *Patron* soon became *pattern*. After a time *pattern*, the new way of saying the word, was used just for the meaning "a model to be copied." The older *patron* lost that meaning. In this way we got a new word, *pattern*, from the old word, *patron*.

²pattern *vb* : to make or design by following a pattern

pat•ty \'pat-ē\ *n*, *pl* **pat•ties** : a small flat cake of chopped food ⟨a hamburger *patty*⟩

pau•per \'pȯ-pər\ *n* : a very poor person

¹pause \'pȯz\ *n* **1** : a temporary stop **2** : a sign ⌢ above a musical note or rest to show that the note or rest is to be held longer

²pause *vb* **paused; paus•ing** : to stop for a time : make a pause

pave \'pāv\ *vb* **paved; pav•ing** : to make a hard surface on (as with concrete or asphalt) ⟨*pave* a street⟩

pave•ment \'pāv-mənt\ *n* **1** : a paved surface (as of a street) **2** : material used in paving

pa•vil•ion \pə-'vil-yən\ *n* **1** : a very large tent **2** : a building usually with open sides that is used as a place for entertainment or shelter in a park or garden

pav•ing \'pā-ving\ *n* : PAVEMENT

¹paw \'pȯ\ *n* : the foot of a four-footed animal (as the lion, dog, or cat) that has claws

²paw *vb* **1** : to touch in a clumsy or rude way **2** : to touch or scrape with a paw ⟨the dog *pawed* the door⟩ **3** : to beat or scrape with a hoof

¹pawn \'pȯn\ *n* **1** : something of value given as a guarantee (as of payment of a debt) **2** : the condition of being given as a guarantee ⟨have a watch in *pawn*⟩

²pawn *vb* : to leave as a guarantee for a loan : PLEDGE ⟨*pawn* a watch⟩

³pawn *n* : the piece of least value in the game of chess

pawn•bro•ker \'pȯn-ˌbrō-kər\ *n* : a person who makes a business of lending money and keeping personal property as a guarantee

pawn•shop \'pȯn-ˌshäp\ *n* : a pawnbroker's shop

¹pay \'pā\ *vb* **paid** \'pād\; **pay•ing 1** : to give (as money) in return for services received or for something bought ⟨*pay* the taxi driver⟩ ⟨*pay* for a ticket⟩ **2** : to give what is owed ⟨*pay* a tax⟩ **3** : to get re-

venge on : get even with ⟨*pay* someone back for an injury⟩ **4** : to give or offer freely ⟨*pay* a compliment⟩ ⟨*pay* attention⟩ **5** : to get a suitable return for cost or trouble : be worth the effort or pains required ⟨it *pays* to drive carefully⟩ — **pay•er** *n*

²pay *n* **1** : the act of paying : PAYMENT **2** : the state of being paid or employed for money ⟨in the *pay* of the company⟩ **3** : SALARY

pay•able \'pā-ə-bəl\ *adj* : that may, can, or must be paid

pay•check \'pā-ˌchek\ *n* : a check or money received as wages or salary

pay•ment \'pā-mənt\ *n* **1** : the act of paying **2** : money given to pay a debt ⟨make *payments* on a car⟩

pay off *vb* **1** : to pay in full ⟨*pay off* a debt⟩ **2** : to have a good result ⟨hours of practice *paid off* in a successful show⟩

pay•roll \'pā-ˌrōl\ *n* **1** : a list of persons who receive pay **2** : the amount of money necessary to pay the employees of a business

pay up *vb* : to pay in full especially debts that are overdue

pea \'pē\ *n*, *pl* **peas** also **pease** \'pēz\ **1** : a vegetable that is the round seed found in the pods of a garden plant (**pea vine**) related to the clovers **2** : a plant (as the sweet pea) resembling or related to the garden pea

peace \'pēs\ *n* **1** : freedom from public disturbance or war **2** : freedom from upsetting thoughts or feelings **3** : agreement and harmony among persons **4** : an agreement to end a war

peace•able \'pē-sə-bəl\ *adj* : PEACEFUL 1, 3

peace•ful \'pēs-fəl\ *adj* **1** : liking peace : not easily moved to argue or fight ⟨a *peaceful* people⟩ **2** : full of or enjoying peace, quiet, or calm **3** : not involving fighting ⟨settle a dispute by *peaceful* means⟩ **synonyms** see CALM — **peace•ful•ly** \-fə-lē\ *adv* — **peace•ful•ness** *n*

peace•mak•er \'pēs-ˌmā-kər\ *n* : a person who settles an argument or stops a fight

peace pipe *n* : a decorated pipe of the American Indians used for certain ceremonies

peach \'pēch\ *n* **1** : a fruit that is related to the plum and has a sweet juicy pulp, hairy skin, and a large rough stone **2** : a pale yellowish pink color

\ə\ abut	\au̇\ out	\i\ tip	\ȯ\ saw	\u̇\ foot	
\ər\ further	\ch\ chin	\ī\ life	\ȯi\ coin	\y\ yet	
\a\ mat	\e\ pet	\j\ job	\th\ thin	\yü\ few	
\ā\ take	\ē\ easy	\ng\ sing	\th\ this	\yu̇\ cure	
\ä\ cot, cart	\g\ go	\ō\ bone	\ü\ food	\zh\ vision	

Word History The ancient Romans used the Latin word that meant "of Iran" as a handy term for anything from the East. They knew, for example, that peaches came from the East and gave the peach a name that meant "apple of Iran." In time, the phrase meaning "apple of Iran" was shortened and the word meaning "of Iran" was used by itself to mean "peach." The English word *peach* comes from the Latin word that meant "of Iran."

pea·cock \'pē-ˌkäk\ *n* : the male of a very large Asian pheasant with a very long brightly colored tail that can be spread or raised at will, a small crest, and in most forms brilliant blue or green feathers on the neck and shoulders

peacock

peak \'pēk\ *n* **1** : the top of a hill or mountain ⟨the *peak* of a hill⟩ **2** : a mountain all by itself ⟨a snow-capped *peak* rising from the plain⟩ **3** : the part of a cap that sticks out in front **4** : the highest point of development ⟨at the *peak* of one's career⟩

¹peal \'pēl\ *n* **1** : the sound of bells **2** : a loud sound : a series of loud sounds ⟨a *peal* of thunder⟩

²peal *vb* : to give out peals ⟨bells *pealing* in the distance⟩

pea·nut \'pē-ˌnət\ *n* : a plant related to the peas that has yellow flowers and is grown for its underground pods of oily nutlike edible seeds which yield a valuable oil (**peanut oil**) or are crushed to form a spread (**peanut butter**)

peanut

pear \'paər, 'peər\ *n* : the fleshy fruit that grows on a tree related to the apple and is commonly larger at the end opposite the stem

pearl \'pərl\ *n* **1** : a smooth body with a rich luster that is formed within the shell of some mollusks (as the **pearl oyster** of tropical seas) usually around something irritating (as a grain of sand) which has gotten into the shell **2** : MOTHER-OF-PEARL **3** : something like a pearl in shape, color, or value **4** : a pale bluish gray color

pearly \'pər-lē\ *adj* **pearl·i·er; pearl·i·est** : like a pearl especially in having a shining surface

peas·ant \'pez-nt\ *n* : a farmer owning a small amount of land or a farm worker in European countries

pease *pl of* PEA

peat \'pēt\ *n* : a blackish or dark brown material that is the remains of plants partly decayed in water and is dug and dried for use as fuel

peat moss *n* : a spongy brownish moss of wet areas that is often the chief plant making up peat

peb·ble \'peb-əl\ *n* : a small rounded stone

pe·can \pi-'kän, -'kan\ *n* : an oval edible nut that usually has a thin shell and is the fruit of a tall tree of the central and southern United States related to the walnuts

pec·ca·ry \'pek-ə-rē\ *n, pl* **pec·ca·ries** : either of two mostly tropical American animals that gather in herds, are active at night, and look like but are much smaller than the related pigs

peccary

¹peck \'pek\ *n* **1** : a unit of capacity equal to one quarter of a bushel **2** : a great deal : a large quantity ⟨a *peck* of trouble⟩

²peck *vb* **1** : to strike or pick up with the bill ⟨birds *pecking* cherries⟩ **2** : to strike with a sharp instrument (as a pick)

³peck *n* **1** : the act of pecking **2** : a mark made by pecking

pecking order *n* : a basic pattern of social organization within a flock of poultry in which each bird can peck another which is lower in the social rank without fear of being pecked in return but submits to being pecked by any bird of higher rank

pe·cu·liar \pi-'kyül-yər\ *adj* **1** : one's own : of or limited to some one person, thing, or place ⟨a custom *peculiar* to England⟩ **2** : different from the usual : ODD

Word History The word *peculiar* first meant "one's own." You may have some quality that is just your own. No one else has it. That surely makes it unusual. This is how *peculiar* came to mean "unusual" or "odd."

pe·cu·li·ar·i·ty \pi-ˌkyü-lē-'ar-ət-ē\ *n*, *pl* **pe·cu·li·ar·i·ties** **1** : the quality or state of being peculiar **2** : something peculiar or individual ⟨all of us have some *peculiarities*⟩

¹ped·al \'ped-l\ *n* : a lever worked by the foot or feet

²pedal *vb* **ped·aled** *or* **ped·alled; ped·al·ing** *or* **ped·al·ling** : to use or work the pedals of something ⟨*pedal* a bicycle⟩

ped·dle \'ped-l\ *vb* **ped·dled; ped·dling** : to go about especially from house to house with goods for sale

ped·dler *or* **ped·lar** \'ped-lər\ *n* : someone who peddles

ped·es·tal \'ped-əst-l\ *n* **1** : a support or foot of an upright structure (as a column, statue, or lamp) **2** : a position of high regard ⟨placed their teacher on a *pedestal*⟩

pe·des·tri·an \pə-'des-trē-ən\ *n* : a person who is walking

pe·di·a·tri·cian \ˌpēd-ē-ə-'trish-ən\ *n* : a doctor who specializes in the care of babies and children

ped·i·gree \'ped-ə-ˌgrē\ *n* **1** : a table or list showing the line of ancestors of a person or animal **2** : a line of ancestors

pe·dom·e·ter \pi-'däm-ət-ər\ *n* : an instrument that measures the distance one covers in walking

¹peek \'pēk\ *vb* **1** : to look slyly or cautiously **2** : to take a quick glance — **peeker** *n*

²peek *n* : a short or sly look

¹peel \'pēl\ *vb* **1** : to strip off the skin or bark of **2** : to strip or tear off **3** : to come off smoothly or in bits

²peel *n* : an outer covering and especially the skin of a fruit

¹peep \'pēp\ *vb* : to make a weak shrill sound such as a young bird makes — **peep·er** *n*

²peep *n* : a weak shrill sound

³peep *vb* **1** : to look through or as if through a small hole or a crack : PEEK **2** : to show slightly ⟨crocuses *peeping* through the grass⟩

⁴peep *n* **1** : a brief or sly look **2** : the first appearance ⟨the *peep* of dawn⟩

¹peer \'piər\ *n* **1** : a person of the same rank or kind : EQUAL **2** : a member of one of the five ranks (duke, marquis, earl, viscount, and baron) of the British nobility

²peer *vb* **1** : to look curiously or carefully **2** : to come slightly into view : peep out

peer·less \'piər-ləs\ *adj* : having no equal

pee·vish \'pē-vish\ *adj* **1** : complaining a lot : IRRITABLE — **pee·vish·ly** *adv* — **peevish·ness** *n*

pee·wee \'pē-ˌwē\ *n* : one that is small

¹peg \'peg\ *n* **1** : a slender piece (as of wood or metal) used especially to fasten things together or to hang things on ⟨a clothes *peg*⟩ **2** : a piece of wood to be driven into the ground to mark a boundary or to hold something ⟨a *peg* for a tent rope⟩ **3** : ¹STEP 11 ⟨took them down a *peg*⟩

²peg *vb* **pegged; peg·ging** **1** : to mark, plug, or fasten with pegs **2** : to work hard ⟨*pegging* away at my job⟩

pel·i·can \'pel-i-kən\ *n* : a bird with a large bill, webbed feet, and a great pouch on the lower jaw that is used to scoop in fish for food

pelican

pel·la·gra \pə-'lag-rə, -'lāg-\ *n* : a disease caused by a diet containing too little protein and too little of a necessary vitamin

\ə\ abut	\au̇\ out	\i\ tip	\ȯ\ saw	\u̇\ foot
\ər\ further	\ch\ chin	\ī\ life	\ȯi\ coin	\y\ yet
\a\ mat	\e\ pet	\j\ job	\th\ thin	\yü\ few
\ā\ take	\ē\ easy	\ng\ sing	\th\ this	\yu̇\ cure
\ä\ cot, cart	\g\ go	\ō\ bone	\ü\ food	\zh\ vision

pel·let \'pel-ət\ *n* **1** : a little ball (as of food or medicine) **2** : a piece of small shot

pell-mell \'pel-'mel\ *adv* **1** : in crowded confusion **2** : in a big hurry

¹pelt \'pelt\ *n* : a skin of an animal especially with its fur or wool

²pelt *vb* **1** : to strike with repeated blows **2** : HURL, THROW **3** : to beat or pound against something again and again ⟨rain *pelting* on the roof⟩

¹pen \'pen\ *n* : a small enclosure especially for animals ⟨a chicken *pen*⟩

²pen *vb* **penned; pen·ning** : to shut in or as if in a pen

³pen *n* : an instrument for writing with ink

⁴pen *vb* **penned; pen·ning** : to write with a pen

pe·nal \'pēn-l\ *adj* : of or relating to punishment

pe·nal·ize \'pēn-l-ˌīz, 'pen-\ *vb* **pe·nal·ized; pe·nal·iz·ing** : to give a penalty to ⟨*penalize* an athlete for a foul⟩

pen·al·ty \'pen-l-tē\ *n, pl* **pen·al·ties 1** : punishment for doing something wrong **2** : a loss or handicap given for breaking a rule in a sport or game

pence *pl of* PENNY

¹pen·cil \'pen-səl\ *n* : a device for writing or drawing consisting of a stick of black or colored material enclosed in wood, plastic, or metal

²pencil *vb* **pen·ciled** *or* **pen·cilled; pen·cil·ing** *or* **pen·cil·ling** : to write, mark, or draw with a pencil

pen·dant \'pen-dənt\ *n* : a hanging ornament (as an earring)

¹pend·ing \'pen-ding\ *prep* **1** : DURING 1 **2** : while waiting for ⟨will make no statement *pending* further information⟩

²pending *adj* : not yet decided ⟨*pending* questions⟩

pen·du·lum \'pen-jə-ləm, -dyə-\ *n* : an object hung from a fixed point so as to swing freely back and forth under the action of gravity ⟨the *pendulum* of a clock⟩

pen·e·trate \'pen-ə-ˌtrāt\ *vb* **pen·e·trat·ed; pen·e·trat·ing 1** : to pass into or through : PIERCE **2** : to see into or understand

pen·e·tra·tion \ˌpen-ə-'trā-shən\ *n* **1** : the act or process of penetrating **2** : keen understanding

pen·guin \'pen-gwən, 'peng-\ *n* : a seabird that cannot fly, has very short legs, and is found in the cold regions of the southern hemisphere

pen·i·cil·lin \ˌpen-ə-'sil-ən\ *n* : an antibiotic that is produced by a mold and is used especially against disease-causing round bacteria

pen·in·su·la \pə-'nin-sə-lə, -chə-lə\ *n* : a piece of land extending out into a body of water

pe·nis \'pē-nəs\ *n, pl* **pe·nes** \-,nēz\ *or* **pe·nis·es** : a male organ used in sexual intercourse

pen·i·tence \'pen-ə-təns\ *n* : sorrow for one's sins or faults

¹pen·i·tent \'pen-ə-tənt\ *adj* : feeling or showing penitence

²penitent *n* : a penitent person

pen·i·ten·tia·ry \ˌpen-ə-'ten-chə-rē\ *n, pl* **pen·i·ten·tia·ries** : a prison for criminals

pen·knife \'pen-ˌnīf\ *n, pl* **pen·knives** \-ˌnīvz\ : a small jackknife

pen·man \'pen-mən\ *n, pl* **pen·men** \-mən\ : a person who uses a pen : WRITER

pen·man·ship \'pen-mən-ˌship\ *n* : writing with a pen : style or quality of handwriting

pen name *n* : a false name that an author uses on his or her work ⟨a professor who wrote novels under a *pen name*⟩

pen·nant \'pen-ənt\ *n* **1** : a narrow pointed flag used for identification, signaling, or decoration **2** : a flag that serves as the emblem of a championship

pen·ni·less \'pen-i-ləs\ *adj* : very poor : having no money

pen·ny \'pen-ē\ *n, pl* **pen·nies** \'pen-ēz\ **1** *or pl* **pence** \'pens\ : a coin of the United Kingdom equal to ¹⁄₁₀₀ pound **2** : CENT

¹pen·sion \'pen-chən\ *n* : a sum paid regularly to a person who has retired from work

²pension *vb* : to grant or give a pension to

pen·sive \'pen-siv\ *adj* : lost in sober or sad thought ⟨a *pensive* mood⟩ — **pen·sive·ly** *adv* — **pen·sive·ness** *n*

pent \'pent\ *adj* : penned up : shut up ⟨*pent*-up feelings⟩

penta- *or* **pent-** *prefix* : five

penguin

pen·ta·gon \'pent-ə-ˌgän\ *n* : a flat figure having five angles and five sides

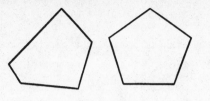

pentagons

pen·tag·o·nal \pen-'tag-ən-l\ *adj* : having five sides

pen·tath·lon \pen-'tath-lən, -ˌlän\ *n* : an athletic contest made up of five different track-and-field events

pent·house \'pent-ˌhaús\ *n* : an apartment built on the roof of a building

pe·on \'pē-ˌän\ *n* : a member of the landless laboring class in Spanish America

pe·o·ny \'pē-ə-nē\ *n, pl* **pe·o·nies** : a plant related to the buttercup that lives for years and is widely grown for its very large usually double white, pink, or red flowers

¹**peo·ple** \'pē-pəl\ *n, pl* **people** *or* **peo·ples 1** : a body of persons making up a race, tribe, or nation ⟨the *peoples* of Asia⟩ **2** : human beings — often used in compounds instead of *persons* ⟨sales*people*⟩ **3** : the persons of a certain group or place ⟨the *people* of this state⟩

²**people** *vb* **peo·pled; peo·pling 1** : to supply or fill with people **2** : to dwell on or in

¹**pep** \'pep\ *n* : brisk energy or liveliness

²**pep** *vb* **pepped; pep·ping** : to put pep into ⟨cool weather *peps* us up⟩

¹**pep·per** \'pep-ər\ *n* **1** : a product from the fruit of an East Indian climbing shrub that is sharp in flavor, is used as a seasoning or in medicine, and consists of the whole ground dried berry (**black pepper**) or of the ground seeds alone (**white pepper**) **2** : a plant related to the tomato that is grown for its fruits which may be very sharp in flavor (**hot peppers**) and are used mostly in pickles or dried and ground as a seasoning or may be mild and sweet (**sweet peppers**) and are used mostly as a vegetable

²**pepper** *vb* **1** : to season with or as if with pepper **2** : to hit with a shower of blows or objects ⟨hail *peppered* the hikers⟩

pep·per·mint \'pep-ər-ˌmint\ *n* : a mint with stalks of small usually purple flowers that yields an oil (**peppermint oil**) which is sharp in flavor and is used especially to flavor candies

pep·py \'pep-ē\ *adj* **pep·pi·er; pep·pi·est** : full of pep

pep·sin \'pep-sən\ *n* : an enzyme that starts the digestion of proteins in the stomach

per \pər\ *prep* **1** : to or for each ⟨ten dollars *per* day⟩ **2** : ACCORDING TO 1 ⟨was done *per* instructions⟩

per an·num \pər-'an-əm\ *adv* : by the year : in or for each year : ANNUALLY

per cap·i·ta \pər-'kap-ət-ə\ *adv or adj* : by or for each person ⟨the *per capita* wealth of a country⟩

per·ceive \pər-'sēv\ *vb* **per·ceived; per·ceiv·ing 1** : to become aware of through the senses and especially through sight **2** : UNDERSTAND 1

¹**per·cent** \pər-'sent\ *adv or adj* : out of every hundred : measured by the number of units as compared with one hundred

²**percent** *n, pl* **percent** : a part or fraction of a whole expressed in hundredths ⟨thirty *percent* of the class failed the test⟩

per·cent·age \pər-'sent-ij\ *n* **1** : a part of a whole expressed in hundredths **2** : a share of profits

per·cep·ti·ble \pər-'sep-tə-bəl\ *adj* : possible to detect ⟨a *perceptible* change⟩

per·cep·tion \pər-'sep-shən\ *n* **1** : an act or the result of grasping with one's mind **2** : the ability to grasp (as meanings and ideas) with one's mind **3** : a judgment formed from information grasped

¹**perch** \'pərch\ *n* **1** : a place where birds roost **2** : a raised seat or position

²**perch** *vb* : to sit or rest on or as if on a perch

³**perch** *n, pl* **perch** *or* **perch·es 1** : a European freshwater food fish that is mostly olive green and yellow **2** : any of numerous fishes related to or resembling the European perch

per·chance \pər-'chans\ *adv* : PERHAPS

per·co·late \'pər-kə-ˌlāt\ *vb* **per·co·lat·ed; per·co·lat·ing 1** : to trickle or cause to trickle through something porous : OOZE ⟨water *percolating* through sand⟩ **2** : to prepare (coffee) by passing hot water through ground coffee beans again and again — **per·co·la·tor** \-ˌlāt-ər\ *n*

per·co·la·tion \ˌpər-kə-'lā-shən\ *n* : the act or process of percolating

per·cus·sion \pər-'kəsh-ən\ *n* **1** : a sharp tapping **2** : the striking of an explosive cap to set off the charge in a gun **3** : the musi-

\ə\ **abut**	\aú\ **out**	\i\ **tip**	\ó\ **saw**	\ú\ **foot**
\ər\ **further**	\ch\ **chin**	\ī\ **life**	\ói\ **coin**	\y\ **yet**
\a\ **mat**	\e\ **pet**	\j\ **job**	\th\ **thin**	\yü\ **few**
\ā\ **take**	\ē\ **easy**	\ng\ **sing**	\th\ **this**	\yú\ **cure**
\ä\ **cot, cart**	\g\ **go**	\ō\ **bone**	\ü\ **food**	\zh\ **vision**

cal instruments of a band or orchestra that are played by striking or shaking

percussion instrument *n* : a musical instrument (as a drum, cymbal, or maraca) sounded by striking or shaking

¹**pe·ren·ni·al** \pə-'ren-ē-əl\ *adj* **1** : present all through the year ⟨a *perennial* stream⟩ **2** : never ending : CONTINUOUS ⟨*perennial* joy⟩ **3** : living from year to year ⟨a *perennial* plant⟩

²**perennial** *n* : a perennial plant

¹**per·fect** \'pər-fikt\ *adj* **1** : lacking nothing : COMPLETE ⟨a *perfect* set of teeth⟩ **2** : thoroughly skilled or trained : meeting the highest standards ⟨a *perfect* performance⟩ **3** : having no mistake, error, or flaw ⟨a *perfect* diamond⟩ — **per·fect·ly** *adv*

²**per·fect** \pər-'fekt\ *vb* : to make perfect

per·fec·tion \pər-'fek-shən\ *n* **1** : completeness in all parts or details **2** : the highest excellence or skill **3** : a quality or thing that cannot be improved

per·fo·rate \'pər-fə-ˌrāt\ *vb* **per·fo·rat·ed; per·fo·rat·ing** **1** : to make a hole through : PIERCE **2** : to make many small holes in

per·form \pər-'fórm\ *vb* **1** : to carry out : ACCOMPLISH, DO **2** : to do something needing special skill ⟨*perform* on the piano⟩ — **per·form·er** *n*

per·for·mance \pər-'fór-məns\ *n* **1** : the carrying out of an action ⟨the *performance* of daily chores⟩ **2** : a public entertainment

¹**per·fume** \'pər-ˌfyüm\ *n* **1** : a pleasant smell : FRAGRANCE **2** : a liquid used to make things smell nice

²**per·fume** \pər-'fyüm\ *vb* **per·fumed; per·fum·ing** : to make smell nice : add a pleasant scent to

per·haps \pər-'haps\ *adv* : possibly but not certainly : MAYBE

per·il \'per-əl\ *n* **1** : the state of being in great danger ⟨in *peril* of death⟩ **2** : a cause or source of danger

per·il·ous \'per-ə-ləs\ *adj* : DANGEROUS 1 ⟨sailing along a *perilous* coast⟩ — **per·il·ous·ly** *adv*

pe·rim·e·ter \pə-'rim-ət-ər\ *n* **1** : the whole outer boundary of a figure or area **2** : the length of the boundary of a figure

pe·ri·od \'pir-ē-əd\ *n* **1** : a punctuation mark . used chiefly to mark the end of a declarative sentence or an abbreviation **2** : a portion of time set apart by some quality ⟨a *period* of cool weather⟩ **3** : a portion of time that forms a stage in the history of something ⟨the colonial *period*⟩ **4** : one of the divisions of a school day

synonyms PERIOD and AGE mean a portion of time. PERIOD can be used of any portion of time, no matter how long or short ⟨a *period* of five minutes⟩ ⟨a new *period* of space exploration⟩ AGE suggests a longer period of time that is associated with an important person ⟨the *age* of Thomas Jefferson⟩ or some outstanding thing ⟨the ice *age*⟩

pe·ri·od·ic \ˌpir-ē-'äd-ik\ *adj* : occurring at regular intervals

¹**pe·ri·od·i·cal** \ˌpir-ē-'äd-i-kəl\ *adj* **1** : PERIODIC **2** : published at regular intervals — **pe·ri·od·i·cal·ly** *adv*

²**periodical** *n* : a periodical publication (as a magazine)

peri·scope \'per-ə-ˌskōp\ *n* : an instrument containing lenses and mirrors by which a person (as on a submarine) can get a view that would otherwise be blocked

per·ish \'per-ish\ *vb* : to become destroyed : DIE ⟨nations that have *perished* from the earth⟩

per·ish·able \'per-ish-ə-bəl\ *adj* : likely to spoil or decay ⟨*perishable* foods such as milk and eggs⟩

¹**per·i·win·kle** \'per-i-ˌwing-kəl\ *n* : an evergreen plant that spreads along the ground and has shining leaves and blue or white flowers

²**periwinkle** *n* : a small snail that lives along rocky seashores

perk \'pərk\ *vb* **1** : to lift in a quick, alert, or bold way ⟨a dog *perking* its ears⟩ **2** : to make fresher in appearance ⟨*perk* a room up with fresh paint⟩ **3** : to become more lively or cheerful ⟨I *perked* up when I heard the good news⟩

periwinkle

perky \'pər-kē\ *adj* **perk·i·er; perk·i·est** : being lively and cheerful

per·ma·nence \'pər-mə-nəns\ *n* : the quality or state of being permanent

per·ma·nent \'pər-mə-nənt\ *adj* : lasting or meant to last for a long time : not temporary — **per·ma·nent·ly** *adv*

per·me·able \'pər-mē-ə-bəl\ *adj* : having pores or openings that let liquids or gases pass through

per·me·ate \'per-mē-ˌāt\ *vb* **per·me·at·ed; per·me·at·ing** **1** : to pass through something that has pores or small openings or is in a loose form ⟨water *permeates* sand⟩ **2** : to spread throughout ⟨a room *permeated* with the smell of smoke⟩

per·mis·sion \pər-'mish-ən\ *n* : the consent of a person in authority

¹per·mit \pər-'mit\ *vb* **per·mit·ted; per·mit·ting 1** : to give permission : ALLOW **2** : to make possible : give an opportunity ⟨if time *permits*⟩

²per·mit \'pər-ˌmit\ *n* : a statement of permission (as a license or pass)

per·ni·cious \pər-'nish-əs\ *adj* : causing great damage or harm ⟨a *pernicious* disease⟩ ⟨a *pernicious* habit⟩

per·ox·ide \pə-'räk-ˌsīd\ *n* : an oxide containing much oxygen (as one of hydrogen used as an antiseptic)

¹per·pen·dic·u·lar \ˌpər-pən-'dik-yə-lər\ *adj* **1** : exactly vertical **2** : being at right angles to a line or surface — **per·pen·dic·u·lar·ly** *adv*

²perpendicular *n* : a perpendicular line, surface, or position

perpendicular

per·pe·trate \'pər-pə-ˌtrāt\ *vb* **per·pe·trat·ed; per·pe·trat·ing** : to bring about or carry out : COMMIT ⟨*perpetrate* a crime⟩ — **per·pe·tra·tor** \'pər-pə-ˌtrāt-ər\ *n*

per·pet·u·al \pər-'pech-ə-wəl\ *adj* **1** : lasting forever : ETERNAL **2** : occurring continually : CONSTANT ⟨*perpetual* arguments⟩ — **per·pet·u·al·ly** *adv*

per·pet·u·ate \pər-'pech-ə-ˌwāt\ *vb* **per·pet·u·at·ed; per·pet·u·at·ing** : to cause to last a long time

per·plex \pər-'pleks\ *vb* : to confuse the mind of : BEWILDER

per·plex·i·ty \pər-'plek-sət-ē\ *n, pl* **per·plex·i·ties 1** : a puzzled or anxious state of mind **2** : something that perplexes

per·se·cute \'pər-si-ˌkyüt\ *vb* **per·se·cut·ed; per·se·cut·ing** : to treat continually in a way meant to be cruel and harmful

per·se·cu·tion \ˌpər-si-'kyü-shən\ *n* **1** : the act of persecuting **2** : the state of being persecuted

per·se·ver·ance \ˌpər-sə-'vir-əns\ *n* : the act or power of persevering

per·se·vere \ˌpər-sə-'viər\ *vb* **per·se·vered; per·se·ver·ing** : to keep trying to do something in spite of difficulties ⟨*persevered* in learning to speak French⟩

per·sim·mon \pər-'sim-ən\ *n* : a fruit of or-

ange color that looks like a plum and grows on a tree related to the ebonies

per·sist \pər-'sist\ *vb* **1** : to keep on doing or saying something : continue stubbornly **2** : to last on and on : continue to exist or occur ⟨rain *persisting* for days⟩

per·sist·ence \pər-'sis-təns\ *n* **1** : the act or fact of persisting **2** : the quality of being persistent : PERSEVERANCE

persimmon

per·sist·ent \pər-'sis-tənt\ *adj* : continuing to act or exist longer than usual ⟨a *persistent* cold⟩ — **per·sist·ent·ly** *adv*

per·son \'pərs-n\ *n* **1** : a human being — used in compounds especially by those who prefer to avoid *man* in words that apply to both sexes ⟨chair*person*⟩ **2** : the body of a human being ⟨keep your *person* neat⟩ **3** : bodily presence ⟨appear in *person*⟩ **4** : reference to the speaker, to the one spoken to, or to one spoken of as shown especially by means of certain pronouns

per·son·age \'pərs-n-ij\ *n* : an important or famous person

per·son·al \'pərs-n-əl\ *adj* **1** : of, relating to, or belonging to a person : not public : not general ⟨*personal* property⟩ **2** : made or done in person ⟨*personal* attention⟩ **3** : of the person or body ⟨*personal* appearance⟩ **4** : relating to a particular person or his or her qualities ⟨make *personal* remarks⟩ **5** : intended for one particular person ⟨a *personal* letter⟩ **6** : relating to oneself ⟨*personal* pride⟩ — **per·son·al·ly** *adv*

per·son·al·i·ty \ˌpərs-n-'al-ət-ē\ *n, pl* **per·son·al·i·ties 1** : the qualities (as moods or habits) that make one person different from others ⟨your sparkling *personality*⟩ **2** : a person's pleasing qualities ⟨is pleasant but doesn't have much *personality*⟩ **3** : a person of importance or fame ⟨a dinner attended by movie and television *personalities*⟩

personal pronoun *n* : a pronoun (as *I*, *you*, *it*, or *they*) used as a substitute for a noun that names a definite person or thing

\ə\ abut	\aù\ out	\i\ tip	\ò\ saw	\ù\ foot
\ər\ further	\ch\ chin	\ī\ life	\òi\ coin	\y\ yet
\a\ mat	\e\ pet	\j\ job	\th\ thin	\yü\ few
\ā\ take	\ē\ easy	\ng\ sing	\th\ this	\yù\ cure
\ä\ cot, cart	\g\ go	\ō\ bone	\ü\ food	\zh\ vision

per·son·i·fy \pər-'sän-ə-ˌfī\ *vb* **per·son·i·fied; per·son·i·fy·ing** : to think of or represent as a person

per·son·nel \ˌpərs-n-'el\ *n* : a group of people employed in a business or an organization

per·spec·tive \pər-'spek-tiv\ *n* 1 : the art of painting or drawing a scene so that objects in it seem to have their right shape and to be the right distance apart 2 : the power to understand things in their true relationship to each other 3 : the true relationship of objects or events to one another

per·spi·ra·tion \ˌpər-spə-'rā-shən\ *n* 1 : the act or process of perspiring 2 : salty liquid given off from skin glands

per·spire \pər-'spīr\ *vb* **per·spired; per·spir·ing** : to give off salty liquid through the skin

per·suade \pər-'swād\ *vb* **per·suad·ed; per·suad·ing** : to win over to a belief or way of acting by argument or earnest request : CONVINCE

per·sua·sion \pər-'swā-zhən\ *n* 1 : the act of persuading 2 : the power to persuade ⟨you have the gift of *persuasion*⟩ 3 : a way of believing : BELIEF ⟨two persons of the same *persuasion*⟩

per·sua·sive \pər-'swā-siv\ *adj* : able or likely to persuade ⟨a *persuasive* voice⟩ — **per·sua·sive·ly** *adv* — **per·sua·sive·ness** *n*

pert \'pərt\ *adj* 1 : SAUCY 1 2 : PERKY

per·tain \pər-'tān\ *vb* 1 : to belong to as a part, quality, or function ⟨duties *pertaining* to the office of sheriff⟩ 2 : to relate to a person or thing ⟨laws *pertaining* to hunting⟩

per·ti·nent \'pərt-n-ənt\ *adj* : relating to the subject that is being thought about or discussed : RELEVANT ⟨a *pertinent* question⟩

per·turb \pər-'tərb\ *vb* : to disturb in mind : trouble greatly

pe·ruse \pə-'rüz\ *vb* **pe·rused; pe·rus·ing** 1 : READ 1 2 : to read through carefully

per·vade \pər-'vād\ *vb* **per·vad·ed; per·vad·ing** : to spread through all parts of : PERMEATE ⟨spicy smells *pervaded* the whole house⟩

per·verse \pər-'vərs\ *adj* : stubborn in being against what is right or sensible

pe·se·ta \pə-'sāt-ə\ *n* : a Spanish coin or bill

pe·so \'pā-sō\ *n, pl* **pe·sos** 1 : an old silver coin of Spain and Spanish America 2 : a coin of the Philippines or of any of various Latin American countries

pes·si·mist \'pes-ə-məst\ *n* : a pessimistic person

pes·si·mis·tic \ˌpes-ə-'mis-tik\ *adj* 1 : having no hope that one's troubles will end or that success or happiness will come : GLOOMY 2 : having the belief that evil is more common or powerful than good

pest \'pest\ *n* 1 : PESTILENCE 2 : a plant or animal that damages humans or their goods 3 : NUISANCE

pes·ter \'pes-tər\ *vb* : to bother again and again **synonyms** see ANNOY

pes·ti·cide \'pes-tə-ˌsīd\ *n* : a substance used to destroy pests

pes·ti·lence \'pes-tə-ləns\ *n* : a contagious often fatal disease that spreads quickly

pes·tle \'pes-əl\ *n* : a tool shaped like a small club for crushing substances in a mortar

¹pet \'pet\ *n* 1 : a tame animal kept for pleasure rather than for use 2 : a person who is treated with special kindness or consideration ⟨teacher's *pet*⟩

pestle in a mortar

²pet *adj* 1 : kept or treated as a pet 2 : showing fondness ⟨a *pet* name⟩ 3 : ²FAVORITE ⟨my *pet* project⟩

³pet *vb* **pet·ted; pet·ting** 1 : to stroke or pat gently or lovingly 2 : to kiss and caress

pet·al \'pet-l\ *n* : one of the often brightly colored modified leaves that make up the corolla of a flower — **pet·aled** *or* **pet·alled** \-ld\ *adj* — **pet·al·less** \-l-ləs\ *adj*

pet·i·ole \'pet-ē-ˌōl\ *n* : the stalk of a leaf

pe·tite \pə-'tēt\ *adj* : having a small trim figure

¹pe·ti·tion \pə-'tish-ən\ *n* 1 : an earnest appeal 2 : a document asking for something

²petition *vb* : to make a petition to or for — **pe·ti·tion·er** *n*

pe·trel \'pe-trəl, 'pē-\ *n* : a small seabird with long wings that flies far from land

pet·ri·fy \'pe-trə-ˌfī\ *vb* **pet·ri·fied; pet·ri·fy·ing** 1 : to change plant or animal matter into stone or something like stone ⟨*petrified* trees⟩ 2 : to frighten very much

pe·tro·leum \pə-'trō-lē-əm, -'trōl-yəm\ *n* : a raw oil that is obtained from wells drilled in the ground and that is the source of gasoline, kerosene, and fuel oils

pet·ti·coat \'pet-ē-ˌkōt\ *n* : a skirt worn under a dress or outer skirt

pet·ty \'pet-ē\ *adj* **pet·ti·er; pet·ti·est 1** : small and of no importance ⟨*petty* details⟩ **2** : showing or having a mean narrow-minded attitude — **pet·ti·ly** \'pet-l-lē\ *adv* — **pet·ti·ness** \'pet-ē-nəs\ *n*

petty officer *n* : an officer in the Navy or Coast Guard appointed from among the enlisted people

petty officer first class *n* : a petty officer in the Navy or Coast Guard ranking above a petty officer second class

petty officer second class *n* : a petty officer in the Navy or Coast Guard ranking above a petty officer third class

petty officer third class *n* : a petty officer in the Navy or Coast Guard ranking above a seaman

pet·u·lant \'pech-ə-lənt\ *adj* : easily put in a bad humor : CROSS

pe·tu·nia \pə-'tü-nyə, -'tyü-\ *n* : a plant related to the potato grown for its velvety brightly colored flowers that are shaped like funnels

petunia

pew \'pyü\ *n* : one of the benches with backs and sometimes doors set in rows in a church

pe·wee \'pē-,wē\ *n* : a small grayish or greenish brown bird (as a phoebe) that eats flying insects

pe·wit \'pē-,wit\ *n* : any of several birds (as a small gull or a pewee)

pew·ter \'pyüt-ər\ *n* **1** : a metallic substance made mostly of tin sometimes mixed with copper or antimony that is used in making utensils (as pitchers and bowls) **2** : utensils made of pewter

phantasy *variant of* FANTASY

phan·tom \'fant-əm\ *n* : an image or figure that can be sensed (as with the eyes or ears) but that is not real

phar·aoh \'feər-ō, 'faər-ō\ *n* : a ruler of ancient Egypt

phar·ma·cist \'fär-mə-səst\ *n* : a person skilled or engaged in pharmacy

phar·ma·cy \'fär-mə-sē\ *n, pl* **phar·ma·cies 1** : the art, practice, or profession of mixing and preparing medicines usually according to a doctor's prescription **2** : the place of business of a pharmacist : DRUGSTORE

phar·ynx \'far-ingks\ *n, pl* **pha·ryn·ges** \fə-'rin-,jēz\ *also* **phar·ynx·es** : the space behind the mouth into which the nostrils, gullet, and windpipe open — **pha·ryn·geal** \,far-ən-'jē-əl, fə-'rin-jē-əl\ *adj*

phase \'fāz\ *n* **1** : the way that the moon or a planet looks to the eye at any time in its series of changes with respect to how it shines ⟨the new moon and the full moon are two *phases* of the moon⟩ **2** : a step or part in a series of events or actions : STAGE **3** : a particular part or feature : ASPECT

pheas·ant \'fez-nt\ *n* : a large brightly colored game bird with a long tail that is related to the chicken

pheasant

phe·nom·e·nal \fi-'näm-ən-l\ *adj* : very remarkable : EXTRAORDINARY ⟨a *phenomenal* memory⟩

phe·nom·e·non \fi-'näm-ə-,nän\ *n, pl* **phe·nom·e·na** \-nə\ *or* **phe·nom·e·nons 1** *pl* **phenomena** : an observable fact or event **2** : a rare or important fact or event **3** *pl* **phenomenons** : an extraordinary or exceptional person or thing

¹-phil \,fil\ *or* **-phile** \,fīl\ *n suffix* : lover : one having a strong attraction to

²-phil *or* **-phile** *adj suffix* : having a fondness for or strong attraction to

phil·an·throp·ic \,fil-ən-'thräp-ik\ *adj* : of, relating to, or devoted to philanthropy : CHARITABLE — **phil·an·throp·i·cal·ly** \-i-kə-lē\ *adv*

phi·lan·thro·pist \fə-'lan-thrə-pəst\ *n* : a person who gives generously to help other people

phi·lan·thro·py \fə-'lan-thrə-pē\ *n, pl* **phi·lan·thro·pies 1** : active effort to help other people **2** : a philanthropic gift **3** : an organization giving or supported by charitable gifts

phil·o·den·dron \,fil-ə-'den-drən\ *n* : any of several plants that can stand shade and are often grown for their showy leaves

\ə\ abut	\au̇\ out	\i\ tip	\ȯ\ saw	\u̇\ foot	
\ər\ further	\ch\ chin	\ī\ life	\ȯi\ coin	\y\ yet	
\a\ mat	\e\ pet	\j\ job	\th\ thin	\yü\ few	
\ā\ take	\ē\ easy	\ng\ sing	\th\ this	\yu̇\ cure	
\ä\ cot, cart	\g\ go	\ō\ bone	\ü\ food	\zh\ vision	

phi·los·o·pher \fə-'läs-ə-fər\ *n* **1** : a student of philosophy **2** : a person who takes misfortunes with calmness and courage

phil·o·soph·i·cal \,fil-ə-'säf-i-kəl\ *or* **phil·o·soph·ic** \-'säf-ik\ *adj* **1** : of or relating to philosophy **2** : showing the wisdom and calm of a philosopher — **phil·o·soph·i·cal·ly** *adv*

phi·los·o·phy \fə-'läs-ə-fē\ *n, pl* **phi·los·o·phies** **1** : the study of the basic ideas about knowledge, right and wrong, reasoning, and the value of things **2** : the philosophical teachings or principles of a person or a group **3** : calmness of temper and judgment

phlox \'fläks\ *n, pl* **phlox** *or* **phlox·es** : any of a group of plants grown for their showy clusters of usually white, pink, or purplish flowers

phlox

pho·bia \'fō-bē-ə\ *n* : an unreasonable, abnormal, and lasting fear of something

phoe·be \'fē-bē\ *n* : a common American bird that is grayish brown above and yellowish white below and that eats flying insects

phon- *or* **phono-** *prefix* : sound : voice : speech ⟨*phonograph*⟩

¹phone \'fōn\ *n* : ¹TELEPHONE

²phone *vb* **phoned; phon·ing** : ²TELEPHONE

pho·neme \'fō-,nēm\ *n* : one of the smallest units of speech that distinguish one utterance from another

pho·net·ic \fə-'net-ik\ *adj* : of or relating to spoken language or speech sounds

phon·ics \'fän-iks\ *n* : a method of teaching beginners to read and pronounce words by learning the sound value of letters, letter groups, and syllables

pho·no·graph \'fō-nə-,graf\ *n* : an instrument that reproduces sounds recorded on a grooved disk (**phonograph record**)

phos·pho·rus \'fäs-fə-rəs\ *n* : a white or yellowish waxlike chemical element that gives a faint glow in moist air and is necessary in some form to plant and animal life

¹pho·to \'fōt-ō\ *n, pl* **pho·tos** : ¹PHOTOGRAPH

²photo *vb* : ²PHOTOGRAPH

¹pho·to·copy \'fōt-ō-,käp-ē\ *n* : a copy of usually printed material made using a process in which an image is formed by the action of light on an electrically charged surface

²photocopy *vb* : to make a photocopy of — **pho·to·cop·i·er** *n*

¹pho·to·graph \'fōt-ə-,graf\ *n* : a picture made by photography

²photograph *vb* : to take a picture of with a camera — **pho·tog·ra·pher** \fə-'täg-rə-fər\ *n*

pho·to·graph·ic \,fōt-ə-'graf-ik\ *adj* : obtained by or used in photography

pho·tog·ra·phy \fə-'täg-rə-fē\ *n* : the making of pictures by means of a camera that directs the image of an object onto a film made sensitive to light

pho·to·syn·the·sis \,fōt-ə-'sin-thə-səs\ *n* : the process by which green plants form carbohydrates from carbon dioxide and water in the presence of light — **pho·to·syn·thet·ic** \-sin-'thet-ik\ *adj*

¹phrase \'frāz\ *n* **1** : a brief expression **2** : a group of two or more words that express a single idea but do not form a complete sentence ⟨"out the door" in "they ran out the door" is a *phrase*⟩

²phrase *vb* **phrased; phras·ing** : to express in words

phy·lum \'fī-ləm\ *n, pl* **phy·la** \-lə\ : a group (as one of the primary divisions of the animal kingdom) set apart by features that suggest its members come from a common ancestor

phys·i·cal \'fiz-i-kəl\ *adj* **1** : of or relating to nature or the world as we see it : material and not mental, spiritual, or imaginary **2** : of the body : BODILY **3** : of or relating to physics — **phys·i·cal·ly** *adv*

phy·si·cian \fə-'zish-ən\ *n* : a specialist in healing human disease : a doctor of medicine

phys·i·cist \'fiz-ə-səst\ *n* : a specialist in physics

phys·ics \'fiz-iks\ *n* : a science that deals with the facts about matter and motion and includes the subjects of mechanics, heat, light, electricity, sound, and the atomic nucleus

phys·i·o·log·i·cal \,fiz-ē-ə-'läj-i-kəl\ *or* **phys·i·o·log·ic** \-'läj-ik\ *adj* : of or relating to physiology

phys·i·ol·o·gist \,fiz-ē-'äl-ə-jəst\ *n* : a specialist in physiology

phys·i·ol·o·gy \,fiz-ē-'äl-ə-jē\ *n* **1** : a branch of biology that deals with the working of the living body and its parts (as organs and cells) **2** : the processes and activities by which a living being or any of its parts functions

phy·sique \fə-'zēk\ *n* : the build of a person's body

pi \'pī\ *n, pl* **pis** \'pīz\ : the symbol π representing the ratio of the circumference of a circle to its diameter or about 3.1416

pi·an·ist \pē-'an-əst, 'pē-ə-nəst\ *n* : a person who plays the piano

pi·ano \pē-'an-ō\ *n, pl* **pi·an·os** : a keyboard instrument having steel wire strings that sound when struck by hammers covered with felt

Word History The English word *piano* comes from an Italian word spelled like English *piano*. This Italian word comes from another Italian word which comes from a phrase that means "soft and loud." When pianos were first made, people noticed that their softness and loudness could be controlled by the player. That is why the phrase for "soft and loud" was used to refer to this instrument.

pi·az·za \pē-'at-sə, -'az-ə\ *n* **1** : a large open square in an Italian town **2** : PORCH, VERANDA

pic·co·lo \'pik-ə-ˌlō\ *n, pl* **pic·co·los** : a small flute whose tones are an octave higher than those of the ordinary flute

piccolo

¹pick \'pik\ *vb* **1** : to strike or work on with a pointed tool **2** : to remove bit by bit ⟨*pick* meat from bones⟩ **3** : to gather one by one ⟨*pick* cherries⟩ **4** : CHOOSE 1, SELECT **5** : to eat sparingly or daintily **6** : to steal from ⟨*pick* a pocket⟩ **7** : to start (a fight) with someone else deliberately **8** : to unlock without a key **9** : to pluck with the fingers or with a pick ⟨*pick* a banjo⟩ — **pick·er** *n* — **pick on** : ¹TEASE

²pick *n* **1** : PICKAX **2** : a slender pointed instrument ⟨ice *pick*⟩ **3** : a thin piece of metal or plastic used to pluck the strings of a musical instrument **4** : the act or opportunity of choosing **5** : the best ones ⟨bought only the *pick* of the crop⟩

pick·ax \'pik-ˌaks\ *n* : a heavy tool with a wooden handle and a blade pointed at one or both ends for loosening or breaking up soil or rock

pick·er·el \'pik-ə-rəl, 'pik-rəl\ *n* : any of

pickerel

several fairly small fishes that look like the pike

¹pick·et \'pik-ət\ *n* **1** : a pointed stake or slender post (as for making a fence) **2** : a soldier or a group of soldiers assigned to stand guard **3** : a person stationed before a place of work where there is a strike

²picket *vb* **1** : ²TETHER ⟨*picket* a horse⟩ **2** : to walk or stand in front of as a picket ⟨*picket* a factory⟩

¹pick·le \'pik-əl\ *n* **1** : a mixture of salt and water or vinegar for keeping foods : BRINE **2** : a difficult or very unpleasant condition **3** : something (as a cucumber) that has been kept in a pickle of salty water or vinegar

²pickle *vb* **pick·led; pick·ling** : to soak or keep in a pickle

pick·pock·et \'pik-ˌpäk-ət\ *n* : a thief who steals from pockets and purses

pick·up \'pik-ˌəp\ *n* : a light truck with an open body and low sides

pick up \pik-'əp\ *vb* **1** : to take hold of and lift ⟨*picked* the book *up*⟩ **2** : to stop for and take along ⟨the bus *picked up* passengers⟩ **3** : to gain by study or experience : LEARN ⟨good readers *pick up* new words from their reading⟩ **4** : to get by buying : BUY ⟨*pick up* a bargain⟩ **5** : to come to and follow ⟨*picked up* the outlaw's trail⟩ **6** : to bring within range of hearing ⟨my radio *picks up* foreign broadcasts⟩ **7** : to get back speed or strength ⟨business *picked up*⟩

¹pic·nic \'pik-ˌnik\ *n* **1** : an outdoor party with food taken along and eaten in the open **2** : a nice experience ⟨a broken leg is no *picnic*⟩

²picnic *vb* **pic·nicked; pic·nick·ing** : to go on a picnic

pic·to·graph \'pik-tə-ˌgraf\ *n* : a diagram showing information by means of pictures

pic·to·ri·al \pik-'tōr-ē-əl\ *adj* **1** : of or relating to pictures ⟨*pictorial* art⟩ **2** : using pictures ⟨a *pictorial* magazine⟩

¹pic·ture \'pik-chər\ *n* **1** : an image of something formed on a surface (as by drawing, painting, printing, or photography) **2** : a very clear description ⟨a word *picture*⟩ **3** : an exact likeness : COPY **4** : MOVIE **5** : an image on the screen of a television set

²picture *vb* **pic·tured; pic·tur·ing; 1** : to draw or paint a picture of **2** : to describe

\ə\ abut	\au̇\ out	\i\ tip	\ȯ\ saw	\u̇\ foot
\ər\ further	\ch\ chin	\ī\ life	\ȯi\ coin	\y\ yet
\a\ mat	\e\ pet	\j\ job	\th\ thin	\yü\ few
\ā\ take	\ē\ easy	\ng\ sing	\th\ this	\yu̇\ cure
\ä\ cot, cart	\g\ go	\ō\ bone	\ü\ food	\zh\ vision

very clearly in words **3** : to form a mental image of : IMAGINE

picture graph *n* : PICTOGRAPH

pic·tur·esque \,pik-chə-'resk\ *adj* : like a picture : suggesting a painted scene ⟨a *picturesque* mountain view⟩

pie \'pī\ *n* : a food consisting of a crust and a filling (as of fruit or meat)

pie·bald \'pī-,bȯld\ *adj* : spotted or blotched with two colors and especially black and white ⟨a *piebald* horse⟩

¹piece \'pēs\ *n* **1** : a part cut, torn, or broken from a thing ⟨a *piece* of string⟩ **2** : one of a group, set, or mass of things ⟨a *piece* of mail⟩ ⟨a chess *piece*⟩ **3** : a portion marked off ⟨a *piece* of land⟩ **4** : a single item or example ⟨a *piece* of news⟩ **5** : a definite amount or size in which articles are made for sale or use ⟨buy lumber by the *piece*⟩ **6** : something made or written ⟨a *piece* of music⟩ **7** : ¹COIN 1 ⟨a fifty-cent *piece*⟩

²piece *vb* **pieced; piec·ing 1** : to repair or complete by adding a piece or pieces **2** : to make out of pieces ⟨*piece* a puzzle together⟩

piece·meal \'pē-,smēl\ *adv* : one piece at a time : little by little

pied \'pīd\ *adj* : having blotches of two or more colors

pier \'piər\ *n* **1** : a support for a bridge **2** : a structure built out into the water for use as a place to land or walk or to protect or form a harbor

pierce \'piərs\ *vb* **pierced; pierc·ing 1** : to run into or through : STAB **2** : to make a hole in or through ⟨have one's ears *pierced*⟩ **3** : to force into or through ⟨*pierce* the enemy's line⟩ **4** : to penetrate with the eye or mind : see through — **pierc·ing·ly** *adv*

pi·ety \'pī-ət-ē\ *n, pl* **pi·eties** : the state or fact of being pious : devotion to one's God

pig \'pig\ *n* **1** : a swine especially when not yet mature **2** : a person who lives or acts like a pig **3** : a metal cast (as of iron) poured directly from the smelting furnace into a mold

pi·geon \'pij-ən\ *n* : a bird with a stout body, short legs, and smooth feathers

pi·geon-toed \,pij-ən-'tōd\ *adj* : having the toes turned in

pig·gish \'pig-ish\ *adj* : like a pig especially in greed or dirtiness

pig·gy·back \'pig-ē-,bak\ *adv or adj* : on the back or shoulders

pig·gy bank \'pig-ē-\ *n* : a bank for coins often in the shape of a pig

pig·head·ed \'pig-'hed-əd\ *adj* : STUBBORN 1, 2

pig·ment \'pig-mənt\ *n* **1** : a substance that gives color to other substances **2** : coloring matter in persons, animals, and plants

pigmy *variant of* PYGMY

pig·pen \'pig-,pen\ *n* **1** : a place where pigs are kept **2** : a dirty place

pig·tail \'pig-,tāl\ *n* : a tight braid of hair

¹pike \'pīk\ *n, pl* **pike** *or* **pikes** : a long slender freshwater fish with a large mouth

²pike *n* : a long wooden pole with a steel point used long ago as a weapon by soldiers

³pike *n* : TURNPIKE, ROAD

¹pile \'pīl\ *n* : a large wooden or metal stake or pointed post driven into the ground to support a foundation

²pile *n* **1** : a mass of things heaped together : HEAP ⟨a *pile* of stones⟩ **2** : REACTOR 2

³pile *vb* **piled; pil·ing 1** : to lay or place in a pile : STACK ⟨*pile* firewood⟩ **2** : to heap in large amounts ⟨*pile* a table with food⟩ **3** : to move or push forward in a crowd or group ⟨they *piled* into the car⟩

⁴pile *n* : a velvety surface of fine short raised fibers ⟨a rug with a thick *pile*⟩

pil·fer \'pil-fər\ *vb* : to steal small amounts or articles of small value

pil·grim \'pil-grəm\ *n* **1** : a person who travels to a holy place as an act of religious devotion **2** *cap* : one of the English colonists who founded the first permanent settlement in New England at Plymouth in 1620

pil·grim·age \'pil-grə-mij\ *n* : a journey made by a pilgrim

pil·ing \'pī-ling\ *n* : a structure made of piles

pill \'pil\ *n* : a medicine in the form of a little ball to be swallowed whole

¹pil·lage \'pil-ij\ *n* : the act of robbing by force especially in war

²pillage *vb* **pillaged; pil·lag·ing** : to take goods and possessions by force

pil·lar \'pil-ər\ *n* **1** : a large post that supports something (as a roof) **2** : a column standing alone (as for a monument) **3** : something like a pillar : a main support ⟨a *pillar* of society⟩

pil·lo·ry \'pil-ə-rē\ *n, pl* **pil·lo·ries** : a device once used for

pillory

punishing someone in public consisting of a wooden frame with holes in which the head and hands can be locked

¹pil·low \'pil-ō\ *n* : a bag filled with soft or springy material used as a cushion usually for the head of a person lying down

²pillow *vb* **1** : to lay on or as if on a pillow **2** : to serve as a pillow for

pil·low·case \'pil-ō-ˌkās\ *n* : a removable covering for a pillow

¹pi·lot \'pī-lət\ *n* **1** : a person who steers a ship **2** : a person especially qualified to guide ships into and out of a port or in dangerous waters **3** : a person who flies or is qualified to fly an aircraft

²pilot *vb* : to act as pilot of

pi·mien·to \pə-'ment-ō, pəm-'yent-\ *also* **pi·men·to** \pə-'ment-ō\ *n, pl* **pi·mien·tos** *also* **pi·men·tos** : a sweet pepper with a mild thick flesh

pim·ple \'pim-pəl\ *n* : a small swelling of the skin often containing pus — **pim·pled** \-pəld\ *adj* — **pim·ply** \-plē\ *adj*

¹pin \'pin\ *n* **1** : a slender pointed piece (as of wood or metal) usually having the shape of a cylinder used to fasten articles together or in place **2** : a small pointed piece of wire with a head used for fastening cloth or paper **3** : something (as an ornament or badge) fastened to the clothing by a pin **4** : one of ten pieces set up as the target in bowling

²pin *vb* **pinned; pin·ning** **1** : to fasten or join with a pin **2** : to hold as if with a pin ⟨*pinned* the snake to the ground with a stick⟩

pin·a·fore \'pin-ə-ˌfōr\ *n* : a sleeveless garment with a low neck worn as an apron or a dress

pin·cer \'pin-chər, 'pin-sər\ *n* **1 pincers** *pl* : an instrument with two handles and two jaws for gripping something **2** : a claw (as of a lobster) like pincers

¹pinch \'pinch\ *vb* **1** : to squeeze between the finger and thumb or between the jaws of an instrument **2** : to squeeze painfully ⟨get a finger *pinched* in a door⟩ **3** : to cause to look thin or shrunken ⟨a face *pinched* with cold⟩ **4** : to be thrifty or stingy

²pinch *n* **1** : a time of emergency ⟨help out in a *pinch*⟩ **2** : a painful pressure or stress ⟨felt the *pinch* of hunger⟩ **3** : an act of pinching : SQUEEZE **4** : as much as may be picked up between the finger and the thumb ⟨a *pinch* of salt⟩

pinch hitter *n* **1** : a baseball player who is sent in to bat for another **2** : a person who does another's work in an emergency

pin·cush·ion \'pin-ˌkush-ən\ *n* : a small cushion in which pins may be stuck when not in use

¹pine \'pīn\ *vb* **pined; pin·ing** **1** : to lose energy, health, or weight through sorrow or worry **2** : to long for very much ⟨*pining* for home⟩ **synonyms** see YEARN

²pine *n* : an evergreen tree that has narrow needles for leaves, cones, and a wood that ranges from very soft to hard

pine·ap·ple \'pī-ˌnap-əl\ *n* : a tropical plant with long stiff leaves that is widely grown for its large juicy fruit

pin·feath·er \'pin-ˌfeth-ər\ *n* : a new feather just breaking through the skin of a bird

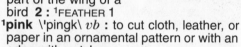

pin·ion \'pin-yən\ *n* **1** : the wing or the end part of the wing of a bird **2** : ¹FEATHER 1

pineapple

¹pink \'pingk\ *vb* : to cut cloth, leather, or paper in an ornamental pattern or with an edge with notches

²pink *n* **1** : any of a group of plants with thick stem joints and narrow leaves that are grown for their showy often fragrant flowers **2** : the highest degree ⟨athletes in the *pink* of condition⟩

³pink *n* : a pale red

⁴pink *adj* : of the color pink

pink·eye \'ping-ˌkī\ *n* : a very contagious disease of the eyes in which the inner part of the eyelids becomes sore and red

pink·ish \'ping-kish\ *adj* : somewhat pink

pin·na·cle \'pin-ə-kəl\ *n* **1** : a slender tower generally coming to a narrow point at the top **2** : a high pointed peak **3** : the highest point of development or achievement

pin·point \'pin-ˌpoint\ *vb* : to locate or find out exactly

pins and needles *n pl* : a prickling tingling sensation in an arm or leg which is regaining feeling after numbness — **on pins and needles** : in a nervous or jumpy state of expectation

pint \'pīnt\ *n* : a unit of capacity equal to one half quart or sixteen ounces (about .47 liter)

pint–size \'pīnt-ˌsīz\ *or* **pint–sized** \-ˌsīzd\ *adj* : TINY, SMALL

\ə\ **abut**	\au̇\ **out**	\i\ **tip**	\ȯ\ **saw**	\u̇\ **foot**
\ər\ **further**	\ch\ **chin**	\ī\ **life**	\ȯi\ **coin**	\y\ **yet**
\a\ **mat**	\e\ **pet**	\j\ **job**	\th\ **thin**	\yü\ **few**
\ā\ **take**	\ē\ **easy**	\ng\ **sing**	\th\ **this**	\yu̇\ **cure**
\ä\ **cot, cart**	\g\ **go**	\ō\ **bone**	\ü\ **food**	\zh\ **vision**

pin·to \'pin-tō\ *n, pl* **pin·tos** : a spotted horse or pony

pinto

pin·wheel \'pin-,hwēl, -,wēl\ *n* : a toy with fanlike blades at the end of a stick that spin in the wind

piny *or* **pin·ey** \'pī-nē\ *adj* : of, relating to, or like that of pine ⟨a *piny* odor⟩

¹**pi·o·neer** \,pī-ə-'niər\ *n* **1** : a person who goes before and prepares the way for others to follow **2** : an early settler

Word History Long ago there were special foot soldiers who marched ahead of the rest of the French army. They prepared the way by digging ditches and building bridges. The French word that had been used for any foot soldier came to be used only for these special foot soldiers. Later the word was used for anyone who prepared a way for others. The English word *pioneer* came from this French word.

²**pioneer** *vb* **1** : to explore or open up ways or regions for others to follow **2** : to start up something new or take part in the early development of something

pi·ous \'pī-əs\ *adj* **1** : showing respect and honor toward God **2** : making a show of being very honest or good

pip \'pip\ *n* : a small fruit seed

¹**pipe** \'pīp\ *n* **1** : a musical instrument or part of a musical instrument consisting of a tube (as of wood) played by blowing **2** : one of the tubes in a pipe organ that makes sound when air passes through it **3** : BAGPIPE — usually used in pl. **4** : a long tube or hollow body for transporting a substance (as water, steam, or gas) **5** : a tube with a small bowl at one end for smoking tobacco or for blowing bubbles

²**pipe** *vb* **piped; pip·ing** **1** : to play on a pipe **2** : to have or utter in a shrill tone **3** : to equip with pipes **4** : to move by means of pipes ⟨*pipe* water from a spring⟩ — **pip·er** *n*

pipe·line \'pī-,plīn\ *n* : a line of pipe with pumps and control devices (as for carrying liquids or gases)

¹**pip·ing** \'pī-ping\ *n* **1** : the music or sound of a person or thing that pipes ⟨the *piping* of frogs⟩ **2** : a quantity or system of pipes **3** : a narrow fold of material used to decorate edges or seams

²**piping** *adj* : having a high shrill sound

pip·it \'pip-ət\ *n* : a small bird like a lark

pi·ra·cy \'pī-rə-sē\ *n, pl* **pi·ra·cies** **1** : robbery on the high seas **2** : the using of another's work or invention without permission

pi·rate \'pī-rət\ *n* : a robber on the high seas : a person who commits piracy

pis *pl of* PI

Pi·sces \'pī-sēz, 'pis-,ēz\ *n* **1** : a constellation between Aquarius and Aries imagined as two fish **2** : the twelfth sign of the zodiac or a person born under this sign

pis·ta·chio \pə-'stash-ē-,ō\ *n, pl* **pis·ta·chios** : the green edible seed of a small tree related to the sumacs

pis·til \'pist-l\ *n* : the central organ in a flower that contains the ovary and produces the seed

pis·tol \'pist-l\ *n* : a short gun made to be aimed and fired with one hand

pis·ton \'pis-tən\ *n* : a disk or short cylinder that slides back and forth inside a larger cylinder and is moved by steam in steam engines and by the explosion of fuel in automobiles

¹**pit** \'pit\ *n* **1** : a cavity or hole in the ground **2** : an area set off from and often sunken below neighboring areas **3** : a hollow area usually of the surface of the body ⟨the *pit* of the stomach⟩ **4** : an indented scar (as from a boil) — **pit·ted** \'pit-əd\ *adj*

²**pit** *vb* **pit·ted; pit·ting** **1** : to make pits in **2** : to set against another in a contest

³**pit** *n* : a hard seed or stone (as of a cherry)

⁴**pit** *vb* **pit·ted; pit·ting** : to remove the pits from

¹**pitch** \'pich\ *n* **1** : a dark sticky substance left over from distilling tar and used in making roofing paper, in waterproofing seams, and in paving **2** : resin from pine trees

²**pitch** *vb* **1** : to set up and fix firmly in place ⟨*pitched* a tent⟩ **2** : to throw (as hay) usually upward or away from oneself **3** : to throw a baseball to a batter **4** : to plunge or fall forward ⟨*pitch* from a cliff⟩ **5** : ¹SLOPE **6** : to fix or set at a certain pitch or level **7** : to move in such a way that one end falls while the other end rises ⟨a ship *pitching* in a rough sea⟩

³**pitch** *n* **1** : the action or manner of pitch-

ing **2** : highness or lowness of sound **3** : amount of slope 〈*pitch* of a roof〉 **4** : the amount or level of something (as a feeling) — **pitched** \'picht\ *adj*

pitch·blende \'pich-ˌblend\ *n* : a dark mineral that is a source of radium and uranium

¹pitch·er \'pich-ər\ *n* : a container usually with a handle and a lip used for holding and pouring out liquids

²pitcher *n* : a baseball player who pitches

pitch·fork \'pich-ˌfȯrk\ *n* : a fork with a long handle used in pitching hay or straw

pit·e·ous \'pit-ē-əs\ *adj* : seeking or deserving pity 〈*piteous* cries for help〉 — **pit·e·ous·ly** *adv*

pit·fall \'pit-ˌfȯl\ *n* **1** : a covered or camouflaged pit used to capture animals or people : TRAP **2** : a danger or difficulty that is hidden or is not easily recognized

pith \'pith\ *n* **1** : the loose spongy tissue forming the center of the stem in some plants **2** : the important part

pith·ec·an·thro·pus \ˌpith-i-'kan-thrə-pəs\ *n* : a primitive and long gone type of human known from bones found in Java

piti·able \'pit-ē-ə-bəl\ *adj* : PITIFUL

piti·ful \'pit-i-fəl\ *adj* **1** : causing a feeling of pity or sympathy 〈a *pitiful* sight〉 **2** : deserving pitying scorn 〈a *pitiful* excuse〉

piti·less \'pit-i-ləs\ *adj* : having no pity : MERCILESS

pi·tu·itary \pə-'tü-ə-ˌter-ē, -'tyü-\ *n* : an endocrine gland at the base of the brain producing several hormones of which one affects growth

¹pity \'pit-ē\ *n, pl* **pi·ties** **1** : a sympathetic feeling for the distress of others **2** : a reason or cause of pity or regret

²pity *vb* **pit·ied; pity·ing** : to feel pity for

¹piv·ot \'piv-ət\ *n* **1** : a point or a fixed pin on the end of which something turns **2** : something on which something else turns or depends : a central member, part, or point

²pivot *vb* **1** : to turn on or as if on a pivot **2** : to provide with, mount on, or attach by a pivot

pix·ie *or* **pixy** \'pik-sē\ *n, pl* **pix·ies** : a mischievous elf or fairy

piz·za \'pēt-sə\ *n* : an open pie made usually of thinly rolled bread dough spread with a spiced mixture (as of tomatoes, cheese, and ground meat) and baked

plac·ard \'plak-ərd, -ˌärd\ *n* : a large card for announcing or advertising something : POSTER

pla·cate \'plāk-ˌāt, 'plak-\ *vb* **pla·cat·ed; pla·cat·ing** : to calm the anger of : SOOTHE

¹place \'plās\ *n* **1** : a short street **2** : an available space : ROOM 〈make a *place* for the newcomer〉 **3** : a building or spot set apart for a special purpose 〈a *place* of worship〉 **4** : a certain region or center of population 〈a *place* on the map〉 **5** : a piece of land with a house on it 〈a *place* in the country〉 **6** : position in a scale or series **7** : position in the order of taking up matters 〈in the first *place*〉 **8** : a space (as a seat in a theater) set aside for one's use **9** : usual space or use 〈paper towels take the *place* of linen〉 **10** : the position of a figure in a numeral **11** : a public square

²place *vb* **placed; plac·ing** **1** : to put or arrange in a certain place or position **2** : to appoint to a job or find a job for **3** : to identify by connecting with a certain time, place, or happening

place·hold·er \'plās-ˌhōl-dər\ *n* : a symbol (as x, Δ, *) used in mathematics in the place of a numeral

place-kick \'plā-ˌskik\ *n* : a kick in football made with the ball held in place on the ground

pla·cen·ta \plə-'sent-ə\ *n* : an organ that has a large blood supply and joins the fetus of a mammal to its mother's uterus

pla·gia·rism \'plā-jə-ˌriz-əm\ *n* : an act of stealing and passing off as one's own the ideas or words of another

¹plague \'plāg\ *n* **1** : something that causes much distress 〈a *plague* of locusts〉 **2** : a cause of irritation : NUISANCE **3** : a destructive epidemic disease

²plague *vb* **plagued; plagu·ing** **1** : to strike or afflict with disease or distress **2** : ¹TEASE, TORMENT

plaid \'plad\ *n* **1** : TARTAN **2** : a pattern consisting of rectangles formed by crossed lines of various widths

¹plain \'plān\ *adj* **1** : having no pattern or decoration 〈a *plain* cloth〉 **2** : open and clear to the sight 〈in *plain* view〉 **3** : clear to the mind 〈explained in *plain* words〉 **4** : FRANK 〈*plain* speaking〉 **5** : of common or average accomplishments or position : ORDINARY 〈*plain* people〉 **6** : not hard to do : not complicated 〈*plain* sewing〉 **7** : not handsome or beautiful

²plain *n* : a large area of level or rolling treeless land 〈the *plains* of the West〉

³plain *adv* : in a plain manner

plain·tive \'plānt-iv\ *adj* : showing or sug-

\ə\ **abut**	\au̇\ **out**	\i\ **tip**	\ȯ\ **saw**	\u̇\ **foot**
\ər\ **further**	\ch\ **chin**	\ī\ **life**	\ȯi\ **coin**	\y\ **yet**
\a\ **mat**	\e\ **pet**	\j\ **job**	\th\ **thin**	\yü\ **few**
\ā\ **take**	\ē\ **easy**	\ng\ **sing**	\th\ **this**	\yu̇\ **cure**
\ä\ **cot, cart**	\g\ **go**	\ō\ **bone**	\ü\ **food**	\zh\ **vision**

gesting sorrow : MOURNFUL, SAD ⟨a *plaintive* sigh⟩

¹plait \'plāt, 'plat\ *n* **1** : a flat fold : PLEAT **2** : a flat braid (as of hair)

²plait *vb* **1** : ²PLEAT **2** : ¹BRAID **3** : to make by braiding ⟨*plaiting* a basket⟩

¹plan \'plan\ *n* **1** : a drawing or diagram showing the parts or outline of something **2** : a method or scheme of acting, doing, or arranging ⟨vacation *plans*⟩

synonyms PLAN, PLOT, and SCHEME mean a method of making or doing something or achieving an end. PLAN suggests that some thinking was done beforehand and often that there is something written down or pictured ⟨a *plan* for a new school⟩ PLOT suggests a complicated, carefully shaped plan of several parts. It can be used as the plan of a story ⟨a mystery story with a good *plot*⟩ or it can be used of a secret, usually evil plan ⟨a *plot* to take over the government⟩ SCHEME suggests a sly plan often for evil reasons ⟨a *scheme* to cheat the old people⟩

²plan *vb* **planned; plan·ning 1** : to form a plan of or for : arrange the parts of ahead of time ⟨*plan* a bridge⟩ ⟨*plan* a picnic⟩ **2** : to have in mind : INTEND

¹plane \'plān\ *vb* **planed; plan·ing 1** : to smooth or level off with a plane **2** : to remove with or as if with a plane

²plane *n* : a tool for smoothing wood

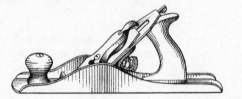

plane

³plane *adj* : HORIZONTAL, FLAT ⟨*plane* surface⟩

⁴plane *n* **1** : a surface any two points of which can be joined by a straight line lying wholly within it **2** : a level or flat surface **3** : a level of development ⟨exists on a low *plane*⟩ **4** : AIRPLANE

plan·et \'plan-ət\ *n* : a celestial body other than a comet or meteor that travels in orbit about the sun

Word History Most stars seem to have fixed positions when they are compared with other stars. You may look at the sky one night and see three stars in a row. Every night that you can see these three

stars at all they will still be in a row. There are certain heavenly bodies that look very much like stars but are not. They seem to wander about among the fixed stars. These heavenly bodies are the planets. The ancient Greeks gave them a name that meant "wanderer." The English word *planet* comes from this Greek name.

plan·e·tar·i·um \ˌplan-ə-'ter-ē-əm\ *n* : a building in which there is a device for projecting the images of celestial bodies on a ceiling shaped like a dome

plan·e·tary \'plan-ə-ˌter-ē\ *adj* **1** : of or relating to a planet **2** : having a motion like that of a planet

plank \'plangk\ *n* : a heavy thick board

plank·ton \'plangk-tən\ *n* : the tiny floating plants and animals of a body of water

¹plant \'plant\ *vb* **1** : to place in the ground to grow ⟨*plant* seeds in the spring⟩ **2** : to set firmly in or as if in the ground : FIX ⟨*plant* posts for a fence⟩ **3** : to introduce as a habit **4** : to cause to become established : SETTLE ⟨*plant* colonies⟩ **5** : to stock with something ⟨*plant* a stream with trout⟩

²plant *n* **1** : any member of the natural kingdom that includes living things (as grasses, trees, seaweeds, or fungi) with cellulose cell walls, without obvious nervous system or sense organs, and usually without ability to move about **2** : the buildings and equipment of an industrial business or an institution ⟨a power *plant*⟩ — **plant·like** \'plant-ˌlīk\ *adj*

¹plan·tain \'plant-n\ *n* : any of several common weeds having little or no stem, leaves with parallel veins, and a long stalk of tiny greenish flowers

²plantain *n* : a banana plant having greenish fruit that is larger, less sweet, and more starchy than the ordinary banana

plan·ta·tion \plan-'tā-shən\ *n* **1** : a group of plants and especially trees planted and cared for **2** : a planted area (as an estate) cultivated by laborers **3** : COLONY 1

plant·er \'plant-ər\ *n* **1** : one (as a farmer or a machine) that plants crops **2** : a person who owns or runs a plantation **3** : a container in which ornamental plants are grown

plant louse *n* : any of various small insects that are related to the true bugs and suck the juices of plants

plaque \'plak\ *n* **1** : a flat thin piece (as of metal) used for decoration or having writing cut in it **2** : a thin film containing bacteria and bits of food that forms on the teeth

plas·ma \'plaz-mə\ *n* : the watery part of blood, lymph, or milk

¹plas·ter \'plas-tər\ *n* **1** : an often medicated substance stiffer than ointment, spread on cloth or plastic, and applied to the body ⟨a mustard *plaster*⟩ **2** : a paste (as of lime, sand, and water) that hardens on drying and is used for coating walls and ceilings

²plaster *vb* **1** : to cover or smear with or as if with plaster **2** : to paste or fasten on especially so as to cover ⟨*plaster* a wall with posters⟩ — **plas·ter·er** *n*

plaster of par·is \-'par-əs\ *often cap 2d P* : a white powder that mixes with water to form a white paste that hardens quickly and is used for casts and molds

¹plas·tic \'plas-tik\ *adj* **1** : capable of being molded or modeled ⟨*plastic* clay⟩ **2** : made of plastic ⟨a *plastic* radio cabinet⟩ ⟨a *plastic* raincoat⟩

²plastic *n* : any of various manufactured materials that can be molded into objects or formed into films or fibers

¹plate \'plāt\ *n* **1** : a thin flat piece of material **2** : metal in sheets ⟨steel *plate*⟩ **3** : a piece of metal on which something is engraved or molded ⟨a license *plate*⟩ **4** : an illustration often covering a full page of a book **5** : household utensils made of or plated with gold or silver **6** : a shallow usually round dish **7** : a main course of a meal ⟨a vegetable *plate*⟩ ⟨two dollars a *plate*⟩ **8** : HOME PLATE **9** : a sheet of glass coated with a chemical sensitive to light for use in a camera

²plate *vb* **plat·ed; plat·ing** : to cover with a thin layer of metal (as gold or silver)

pla·teau \pla-'tō\ *n, pl* **pla·teaus** *or* **pla·teaux** \-'tōz\ : a broad flat area of high land

plat·form \'plat-,fȯrm\ *n* **1** : a statement of the beliefs and rules of conduct for which a group stands **2** : a level usually raised surface (as in a railroad station) **3** : a raised floor or stage for performers or speakers

plat·i·num \'plat-n-əm\ *n* : a heavy grayish white metallic chemical element

pla·toon \plə-'tün\ *n* : a part of a military company usually made up of two or more squads

platoon sergeant *n* : a noncommissioned officer in the Army ranking above a staff sergeant

plat·ter \'plat-ər\ *n* : a large plate especially for serving meat

platy·pus \'plat-i-pəs\ *n* : DUCKBILL

plau·si·ble \'plȯ-zə-bəl\ *adj* : seeming to be reasonable ⟨a *plausible* excuse⟩ — **plau·si·bly** \-blē\ *adv*

¹play \'plā\ *n* **1** : exercise or activity for amusement ⟨children at *play*⟩ **2** : the action of or a particular action in a game ⟨a great *play* by the shortstop⟩ **3** : one's turn to take part in a game ⟨it's your *play*⟩ **4** : absence of any bad intention ⟨said it in *play*⟩ **5** : quick or light movement ⟨the light *play* of a breeze through the room⟩ **6** : freedom of motion ⟨too much *play* in the steering wheel⟩ **7** : a story presented on stage

²play *vb* **1** : to produce music or sound ⟨*play* the piano⟩ ⟨*play* a record⟩ **2** : to take part in a game of ⟨*play* cards⟩ **3** : to take part in sport or recreation : amuse oneself **4** : to handle something idly : TOY ⟨*play* with a watch⟩ **5** : to act on or as if on the stage ⟨*play* a part⟩ **6** : PRETEND 1 ⟨*play* school⟩ **7** : to perform (as a trick) for fun **8** : to play in a game against ⟨*playing* the Dodgers today⟩ **9** : ²ACT 2, BEHAVE ⟨*play* fair⟩ **10** : to move swiftly or lightly ⟨leaves *playing* in the wind⟩ **11** : to put or keep in action ⟨*played* the water hose over the car⟩ **synonyms** see IMPERSONATE — **play hooky** \-'hu̇k-ē\ : to stay out of school without permission

play·act·ing \'plā-,ak-ting\ *n* : an acting out of make-believe roles

play·er \'plā-ər\ *n* **1** : a person who plays a game **2** : a person who plays a musical instrument **3** : a device that reproduces sounds or video images that have been recorded (as on magnetic tape)

player piano *n* : a piano containing a mechanical device by which it may be played automatically

play·ful \'plā-fəl\ *adj* **1** : full of play : MERRY **2** : HUMOROUS — **play·ful·ly** \-fə-lē\ *adv* — **play·ful·ness** *n*

play·ground \'plā-,grȧund\ *n* : an area used for games and playing

play·house \'plā-,hȧus\ *n* **1** : THEATER 1 **2** : a small house for children to play in

playing card *n* : any of a set of cards marked to show rank and suit (**spades, hearts, diamonds,** or **clubs**) and used in playing various games

play·mate \'plā-,māt\ *n* : a companion in play

play·pen \'plā-,pen\ *n* : a small enclosure in which a baby is placed to play

play·thing \'plā-,thing\ *n* : ¹TOY 2

play·wright \'plā-,rīt\ *n* : a writer of plays

\ə\ abut	\au̇\ out	\i\ tip	\ȯ\ saw	\u̇\ foot
\ər\ further	\ch\ chin	\ī\ life	\ȯi\ coin	\y\ yet
\a\ mat	\e\ pet	\j\ job	\th\ thin	\yü\ few
\ā\ take	\ē\ easy	\ng\ sing	\th\ this	\yu̇\ cure
\ä\ cot, cart	\g\ go	\ō\ bone	\ü\ food	\zh\ vision

pla·za \'plaz-ə, 'pläz-\ *n* : a public square in a city or town

plea \'plē\ *n* **1** : an argument in defense : EXCUSE **2** : an earnest appeal ⟨a *plea* for mercy⟩

plead \'plēd\ *vb* **plead·ed** *or* **pled** \'pled\; **plead·ing** **1** : to argue for or against : argue in court ⟨*plead* a case before a jury⟩ **2** : to answer to a charge ⟨*plead* guilty⟩ **3** : to offer as a defense, an excuse, or an apology ⟨*plead* illness⟩ **4** : to make an earnest appeal : BEG

pleas·ant \'plez-nt\ *adj* **1** : giving pleasure : AGREEABLE ⟨a *pleasant* day⟩ **2** : having pleasing manners, behavior, or appearance — **pleas·ant·ly** *adv* — **pleas·ant·ness** *n*

¹please \'plēz\ *vb* **pleased; pleas·ing 1** : to give pleasure or enjoyment to **2** : to be willing : LIKE, CHOOSE ⟨if you *please*⟩

²please *adv* — used to show politeness in asking or accepting

pleas·ing \'plē-zing\ *adj* : giving pleasure : AGREEABLE — **pleas·ing·ly** *adv*

plea·sur·able \'plezh-ə-rə-bəl\ *adj* : PLEASANT

plea·sure \'plezh-ər\ *n* **1** : a feeling of enjoyment ⟨reading for *pleasure*⟩ **2** : ²WISH 2 ⟨await the royal *pleasure*⟩ **3** : something that pleases or delights ⟨it is a *pleasure* to see you again⟩

synonyms PLEASURE, JOY, and ENJOYMENT mean the agreeable feeling that accompanies getting something good or much wanted. PLEASURE suggests an inner satisfaction rather than an open display of feeling ⟨the *pleasure* felt after helping others⟩ JOY suggests a radiant feeling that is very strong ⟨a life filled with *joy*⟩ ENJOYMENT suggests a conscious reaction to something intended to make one happy ⟨the songs added to our *enjoyment* of the movie⟩

¹pleat \'plēt\ *n* : a fold (as in cloth) made by doubling material over on itself

²pleat *vb* : to fold or arrange in pleats

pled *past of* PLEAD

¹pledge \'plej\ *n* **1** : something handed over to another to ensure that the giver will keep his or her promise or agreement **2** : something that is a symbol of something else ⟨the ring is a *pledge* of love⟩ **3** : a promise or agreement that must be kept

²pledge *vb* **pledged; pledg·ing 1** : to give as a pledge **2** : to hold by a pledge : PROMISE ⟨they *pledged* themselves to secrecy⟩ ⟨I *pledge* allegiance⟩

plen·te·ous \'plent-ē-əs\ *adj* : PLENTIFUL 2

plen·ti·ful \'plent-i-fəl\ *adj* **1** : giving or containing plenty : FRUITFUL **2** : present in large numbers or amount : ABUNDANT ⟨*plentiful* rain⟩ — **plen·ti·ful·ly** \-fə-lē\ *adv*

plen·ty \'plent-ē\ *n* : a full supply : more than enough

pleu·ri·sy \'plur-ə-sē\ *n* : a sore swollen state of the membrane that lines the chest often with fever, painful breathing, and coughing

plex·us \'plek-səs\ *n, pl* **plex·us·es** *or* **plex·us** \-səs, -,süs\ : a network usually of nerves or blood vessels

pli·able \'plī-ə-bəl\ *adj* **1** : possible to bend without breaking **2** : easily influenced

pli·ant \'plī-ənt\ *adj* : PLIABLE

pli·ers \'plī-ərz\ *n pl* : small pincers with long jaws used for bending or cutting wire or handling small things

plight \'plīt\ *n* : a usually bad condition or state : PREDICAMENT

plod \'pläd\ *vb* **plod·ded; plod·ding** : to move or travel slowly but steadily

¹plot \'plät\ *n* **1** : a small area of ground ⟨a cemetery *plot*⟩ **2** : the plan or main story of a play or novel **3** : a secret usually evil scheme **synonyms** see PLAN

²plot *vb* **plot·ted; plot·ting 1** : to make a map or plan of **2** : to plan or scheme secretly — **plot·ter** *n*

plo·ver \'pləv-ər, 'plō-vər\ *n* : any one of several shorebirds having shorter and stouter bills than the related sandpipers

¹plow *or* **plough** \'plaù\ *n* **1** : a farm machine used to cut, lift, and turn over soil **2** : a device (as a snowplow) used to spread or clear away matter on the ground

²plow *or* **plough** *vb* **1** : to open, break up, or work with a plow ⟨*plow* a furrow⟩ ⟨*plow* the soil⟩ **2** : to move through or cut as a plow does

plow·share \'plaù-,sheər, -,shaər\ *n* : the part of a plow that cuts the earth

¹pluck \'plək\ *vb* **1** : to pull off : PICK ⟨*pluck* grapes⟩ **2** : to remove something (as feathers) from by or as if by plucking ⟨*pluck* a chicken⟩ **3** : to seize and remove quickly : SNATCH **4** : to pull at (a string) and let go

²pluck *n* **1** : a sharp pull : TUG, TWITCH **2** : COURAGE, SPIRIT

plucky \'plək-ē\ *adj* **pluck·i·er; pluck·i·est** : showing courage : BRAVE

¹plug \'pləg\ *n* **1** : a piece (as of wood or metal) used to stop up or fill a hole **2** : a device usually on a cord used to make an electrical connection by putting it into another part (as a socket)

²plug *vb* **plugged; plug·ging 1 :** to stop or make tight with a plug **2 :** to keep steadily at work or in action ⟨*plugged* away at my homework⟩ **3 :** to connect to an electric circuit ⟨*plug* in a lamp⟩

plum \'pləm\ *n* **1 :** a roundish smooth-skinned edible fruit that has an oblong stone and grows on a tree related to the peaches and cherries **2 :** a dark reddish purple **3 :** a choice or desirable thing **:** PRIZE

plum·age \'plü-mij\ *n* **:** the feathers of a bird

¹plumb \'pləm\ *n* **:** a small weight (as of lead) attached to a line and used to show depth or an exactly straight up-and-down line

²plumb *vb* **:** to measure or test with a plumb ⟨*plumb* the depth of a well⟩ ⟨*plumb* a wall⟩

plumber \'pləm-ər\ *n* **:** a person who puts in or repairs plumbing

Word History The word *plumber* comes from a Latin word that meant "plumber." The Latin word for a plumber came from a Latin word that meant "lead." In the past water pipes in buildings were often made of lead. The plumbers who put in these pipes and took care of them were workers in lead.

plumb·ing \'pləm-ing\ *n* **1 :** a plumber's work **2 :** a system of pipes for supplying and carrying off water in a building

plume \'plüm\ *n* **1 :** a large or showy feather of a bird **2 :** an ornamental feather or tuft of feathers (as on a hat) — **plumed** \'plümd\ *adj*

plum·met \'pləm-ət\ *vb* **:** to fall straight down⟨the plane *plummeted* to earth⟩

¹plump \'pləmp\ *vb* **1 :** to drop or fall heavily or suddenly ⟨*plumped* down on the couch⟩ **2 :** to come out in favor of something ⟨*plumping* for my favorite candidate⟩

²plump *adv* **1 :** with a sudden or heavy drop **2 :** DIRECTLY 1 ⟨ran *plump* into the wall⟩

³plump *adj* **:** having a pleasingly rounded form **:** well filled out **synonyms** see FAT — **plump·ness** *n*

⁴plump *vb* **:** to make or become plump ⟨*plump* up the pillows⟩

¹plun·der \'plən-dər\ *vb* **:** to rob or steal especially openly and by force (as during war)

²plunder *n* **:** something taken by plundering **:** LOOT

¹plunge \'plənj\ *vb* **plunged; plung·ing 1 :** to thrust or force quickly ⟨*plunged* my

arm into the pipe⟩ **2 :** to leap or dive suddenly ⟨*plunged* into the water⟩ **3 :** to rush, move, or force with reckless haste ⟨*plunged* the family into debt⟩ **4 :** to dip or move suddenly downward or forward and downward

²plunge *n* **:** a sudden dive, rush, or leap

¹plu·ral \'plur-əl\ *adj* **:** of, relating to, or being a word form used to show more than one ⟨*plural* nouns⟩

²plural *n* **:** a form of a word used to show that more than one person or thing is meant

plu·ral·ize \'plur-əl-,īz\ *vb* **plu·ral·ized; plu·ral·iz·ing :** to make plural or express in the plural form

¹plus \'pləs\ *prep* **:** increased by **:** with the addition of ⟨4 *plus* 5 is 9⟩

²plus *adj* **:** falling high in a certain range ⟨a grade of C *plus*⟩

¹plush \'pləsh\ *n* **:** a cloth like a very thick soft velvet

²plush *adj* **:** very rich and fine ⟨a *plush* hotel⟩

plus sign *n* **:** a sign + used in mathematics to show addition (as in 8+6=14) or a quantity greater than zero (as in +10°)

Plu·to \'plüt-ō\ *n* **:** the planet that is farthest away from the sun and has a diameter of about 5800 kilometers

plu·to·ni·um \plü-'tō-nē-əm\ *n* **:** a radioactive metallic chemical element formed from neptunium and used for releasing atomic energy

¹ply \'plī\ *n, pl* **plies :** one of the folds, layers, or threads of which something (as yarn or plywood) is made up

²ply *vb* **plied; ply·ing 1 :** to use something steadily or forcefully ⟨*ply* an ax⟩ **2 :** to keep supplying ⟨*ply* a guest with food⟩ **3 :** to work hard and steadily at ⟨*ply* a trade⟩

ply·wood \'plī-,wud\ *n* **:** a strong board made by gluing together thin sheets of wood under heat and pressure

pneu·mat·ic \nu-'mat-ik, nyu-\ *adj* **1 :** of, relating to, or using air, gas, or wind **2 :** moved or worked by the pressure of air ⟨a *pneumatic* drill⟩ **3 :** made to hold or be inflated with compressed air ⟨a *pneumatic* tire⟩

pneu·mo·nia \nu-'mō-nyə, nyu-'mō-\ *n* **:** a serious disease in which the lungs are inflamed

\ə\ **abut**	\au̇\ **out**	\i\ **tip**	\ȯ\ **saw**	\u̇\ **foot**
\ər\ **further**	\ch\ **chin**	\ī\ **life**	\ȯi\ **coin**	\y\ **yet**
\a\ **mat**	\e\ **pet**	\j\ **job**	\th\ **thin**	\yü\ **few**
\ā\ **take**	\ē\ **easy**	\ng\ **sing**	\t͟h\ **this**	\yu̇\ **cure**
\ä\ **cot, cart**	\g\ **go**	\ō\ **bone**	\ü\ **food**	\zh\ **vision**

¹poach \'pōch\ *vb* : to cook slowly in liquid ⟨*poached* eggs⟩

²poach *vb* : to hunt or fish unlawfully on private property

pock \'päk\ *n* : a small swelling like a pimple on the skin (as in smallpox) or the mark it leaves

¹pock·et \'päk-ət\ *n* **1** : a small bag fastened into a garment for carrying small articles **2** : a place or thing like a pocket ⟨a *pocket* of gold in a mine⟩ **3** : a condition of the air (as a down current) that causes an airplane to drop suddenly ⟨an air *pocket*⟩

²pocket *vb* **1** : to put something in a pocket **2** : to take for oneself especially dishonestly ⟨*pocket* the profits⟩

³pocket *adj* : POCKET-SIZE ⟨a *pocket* dictionary⟩

pock·et·book \'päk-ət-ˌbuk\ *n* **1** : a case for carrying money or papers in the pocket **2** : HANDBAG **3** : amount of income ⟨a price suited to your *pocketbook*⟩

pock·et·knife \'päk-ət-ˌnīf\ *n*, *pl* **pock·et·knives** \-ˌnīvz\ : ¹JACKKNIFE

pock·et–size \'päk-ət-ˌsīz\ *adj* : small enough to fit in a pocket

pock·mark \'päk-ˌmärk\ *n* : the mark left by a pock — **pock·marked** \-ˌmärkt\ *adj*

pod \'päd\ *n* : a fruit (as of the pea or bean) that is dry when ripe and then splits open to free its seeds

po·em \'pō-əm\ *n* : a piece of writing often having rhyme or rhythm which tells a story or describes a feeling

po·et \'pō-ət\ *n* : a writer of poems

po·et·ic \pō-'et-ik\ *or* **po·et·i·cal** \-i-kəl\ *adj* **1** : of, relating to, or like that of poets or poetry **2** : written in verse

po·et·ry \'pō-ə-trē\ *n* **1** : writing usually with a rhythm that repeats : VERSE **2** : the writings of a poet

po·go stick \'pō-gō-\ *n* : a pole with a strong spring at the bottom and two rests for the feet on which a person stands and bounces along

poin·set·tia \ˌpoin-'set-ē-ə, -'set-ə\ *n* : a tropical plant much used at Christmas with showy usually red leaves that grow like petals around its small greenish flowers

¹point \'point\ *n* **1** : a separate or particular detail : ITEM ⟨explained the main *points* of the plan⟩ **2** : an individual quality ⟨has many good *points*⟩ **3** : the chief idea or meaning (as of a story or a speech) **4** : ¹PURPOSE, AIM ⟨keep to the *point*⟩ ⟨no *point* in trying any more⟩ **5** : a geometric element that has position but no dimensions and is pictured as a small dot **6** : a particular place or position ⟨*points* of interest in the city⟩ **7** : a particular stage or

moment ⟨the boiling *point*⟩ ⟨at the *point* of death⟩ **8** : the sharp end (as of a sword, pin, or pencil) **9** : a piece of land that sticks out **10** : a dot in writing or printing **11** : one of the thirty-two marks indicating direction on a compass **12** : a unit of scoring in a game ⟨scored fifteen *points*⟩ — **point·ed** \-əd\ *adj* — **point·less** \-ləs\ *adj*

²point *vb* **1** : to put a point on ⟨*point* a pencil⟩ **2** : to show the position or direction of something by the finger or by standing in a fixed position ⟨*pointed* to the door⟩ ⟨the dog was *pointing* a pheasant⟩ **3** : ¹AIM 1, DIRECT ⟨*point* a gun⟩ **4** : to separate figures into groups by placing decimal points ⟨*pointed* off three decimal places⟩

¹point–blank \'point-'blangk\ *adj* **1** : aimed at a target from a short distance away ⟨a *point-blank* shot⟩ **2** : ¹BLUNT 2 ⟨a *point-blank* refusal⟩

²point–blank *adv* : in a point-blank manner

point·er \'point-ər\ *n* **1** : something that points or is used for pointing **2** : a large hunting dog with long ears and short hair that is usually white with colored spots, hunts by scent, and points game **3** : a helpful hint ⟨get a few *pointers* on diving⟩

pointer 2

point of view : a way of looking at or thinking about something

point out *vb* **1** : to show the place or position of especially by pointing with the finger ⟨*point* it *out* to me⟩ **2** : to direct one's attention to ⟨*point out* the mistakes⟩

¹poise \'poiz\ *vb* **poised**; **pois·ing** : to hold or make steady by balancing

²poise *n* **1** : the state of being balanced **2** : a natural self-confident manner ⟨a speaker of great *poise*⟩ **3** : BEARING 1

¹poi·son \'poiz-n\ *n* : a substance that by its chemical action can injure or kill a living thing

²poison *vb* **1** : to injure or kill with poison **2** : to put poison on or in ⟨gas fumes *poisoned* the air⟩

poison ivy *n* : a common woody plant related to the sumacs and having leaves with three leaflets that can cause an itchy rash when touched

poison ivy

poison oak *n* : a poison ivy that grows as a bush

poi·son·ous \'póiz-n-əs\ *adj* : containing poison : having or causing an effect of poison

poison sumac *n* : a poison oak that grows in wet places

¹poke \'pōk\ *vb* **poked; pok·ing** **1** : JAB ⟨*poked* it with a stick⟩ **2** : to make by stabbing or piercing ⟨*poked* a hole in the bag⟩ **3** : to stick out, or cause to stick out ⟨*poked* my head out of the window⟩ **4** : to search over or through usually without purpose : RUMMAGE ⟨*poking* around in the attic⟩ **5** : to move slowly or lazily ⟨they were just *poking* along home⟩

²poke *n* : a quick thrust : JAB

¹pok·er \'pō-kər\ *n* : a metal rod used for stirring a fire

²po·ker \'pō-kər\ *n* : a card game in which each player bets on the value of his or her hand

poky \'pō-kē\ *adj* **pok·i·er; pok·i·est** : so slow as to be annoying

po·lar \'pō-lər\ *adj* **1** : of or relating to a pole of the earth or the region around it **2** : coming from or being like a polar region **3** : of or relating to a pole of a magnet

polar bear *n* : a large creamy-white bear of arctic regions

polar bear

Po·lar·is \pə-'lar-əs, -'lär-\ *n* : NORTH STAR

¹pole \'pōl\ *n* : a long slender piece (as of wood or metal)

²pole *vb* **poled; pol·ing** : to push or move with a pole ⟨*pole* a boat⟩

³pole *n* **1** : either end of an axis and especially of the earth's axis **2** : either of the two ends of a magnet **3** : either of the terminals of an electric battery

Pole \'pōl\ *n* : a person born or living in Poland

pole·cat \'pōl-,kat\ *n* **1** : a small dark European animal that eats flesh and is related to the weasel **2** : SKUNK

pole·star \'pōl-,stär\ *n* : NORTH STAR

pole vault *n* : a track-and-field contest in which each athlete uses a pole to jump over a high bar

¹po·lice \pə-'lēs\ *n, pl* **police** **1** : the department of government that keeps order and enforces law, investigates crimes, and makes arrests **2** **police** *pl* : members of a police force

²police *vb* **po·liced; po·lic·ing** : to keep order in or among ⟨*police* a city⟩

police dog *n* : a dog trained to help police

po·lice·man \pə-'lē-smən\ *n, pl* **po·lice·men** \-smən\ : a man who is a police officer

police officer *n* : a member of a police force

po·lice·wom·an \pə-'lē-,swúm-ən\ *n, pl* **po·lice·wom·en** \-,swim-ən\ : a woman who is a police officer

¹pol·i·cy \'päl-ə-sē\ *n, pl* **pol·i·cies** : a course of action chosen to guide people in making decisions ⟨a country's foreign *policy*⟩

²policy *n, pl* **pol·i·cies** : a document that contains the agreement made by an insurance company with a person whose life or property is insured

po·lio \'pō-lē-,ō\ *n* : a once common virus disease often affecting children and sometimes causing paralysis

po·lio·my·eli·tis \,pō-lē-,ō-,mī-ə-'līt-əs\ *n* : POLIO

¹pol·ish \'päl-ish\ *vb* **1** : to make smooth and glossy usually by rubbing ⟨*polish* silver⟩ **2** : to smooth or improve in manners, condition, or style ⟨took a few hours to *polish* the speech⟩ — **pol·ish·er** *n*

²polish *n* **1** : a smooth glossy surface **2** : good manners : REFINEMENT **3** : a substance prepared for use in polishing ⟨shoe *polish*⟩ ⟨metal *polish*⟩

¹Pol·ish \'pō-lish\ *adj* : of or relating to Poland, the Poles, or Polish

\ə\ abut	\aú\ out	\i\ tip	\ó\ saw	\ú\ foot
\ər\ further	\ch\ chin	\ī\ life	\ói\ coin	\y\ yet
\a\ mat	\e\ pet	\j\ job	\th\ thin	\yü\ few
\ā\ take	\ē\ easy	\ng\ sing	\th\ this	\yú\ cure
\ä\ cot, cart	\g\ go	\ō\ bone	\ü\ food	\zh\ vision

²Polish *n* : the language of the Poles

po·lite \pə-'līt\ *adj* **po·lit·er; po·lit·est** : showing courtesy or good manners **synonyms** see CIVIL — **po·lite·ly** *adv* — **po·lite·ness** *n*

po·lit·i·cal \pə-'lit-i-kəl\ *adj* : of or relating to politics, government, or the way government is carried on — **po·lit·i·cal·ly** *adv*

pol·i·ti·cian \ˌpäl-ə-'tish-ən\ *n* : a person who is actively taking part in party politics or in conducting government business

pol·i·tics \'päl-ə-ˌtiks\ *n sing or pl* **1** : the science and art of government : the management of public affairs **2** : activity in or management of the business of political parties

pol·ka \'pōl-kə\ *n* : a lively dance that originated in Bohemia or the music for it

¹poll \'pōl\ *n* **1** : the casting or recording of the votes or opinions of a number of persons ⟨a *poll* of the persons in the room⟩ **2** : the place where votes are cast — usually used in pl. ⟨go to the *polls*⟩

²poll *vb* **1** : to receive and record the votes of **2** : to receive (votes) in an election **3** : to cast a vote or ballot at a poll

pol·lack *or* **pol·lock** \'päl-ək\ *n, pl* **pollack** *or* **pollock** : an Atlantic food fish that looks like the related cod

pol·len \'päl-ən\ *n* : the fine usually yellow dust in the anthers of a flower that fertilizes the seeds

pol·li·nate \'päl-ə-ˌnāt\ *vb* **pol·li·nat·ed; pol·li·nat·ing** : to place pollen on the stigma of ⟨bees *pollinating* clover⟩

pol·li·na·tion \ˌpäl-ə-'nā-shən\ *n* : the act or process of pollinating

pol·li·wog *or* **pol·ly·wog** \'päl-ē-ˌwäg\ *n* : TADPOLE

pol·lut·ant \pə-'lüt-nt\ *n* : something that causes pollution

pol·lute \pə-'lüt\ *vb* **pol·lut·ed; pol·lut·ing** : to make impure ⟨*pollute* a water supply⟩ — **pol·lut·er** *n*

pol·lu·tion \pə-'lü-shən\ *n* : the action of polluting or the state of being polluted

po·lo \'pō-lō\ *n* : a game played by teams of players on horseback who drive a wooden ball with long-handled mallets

poly- *prefix* : many : much : MULTI-

poly·gon \'päl-i-ˌgän\ *n* : a plane figure having three or more straight sides

pol·yp \'päl-əp\ *n* : a small sea animal (as a coral) having a tubelike body closed

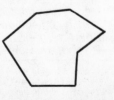

polygon

and attached to something (as a rock) at one end and opening at the other with a mouth surrounded by tentacles

pome·gran·ate \'päm-ˌgran-ət, 'päm-ə-\ *n* : a reddish fruit about the size of an orange that has a thick skin and many seeds in a pulp of acid flavor and grows on a tropical Old World tree

pomegranate

¹pom·mel \'pəm-əl\ *n* : a rounded knob on the handle of a sword or at the front and top of a saddle

²pommel *vb* **pom·meled** *or* **pom·melled; pom·mel·ing** *or* **pom·mel·ling** : PUMMEL

pomp \'pämp\ *n* : a show of wealth and splendor

pom-pom \'päm-ˌpäm\ *or* **pom·pon** \-ˌpän\ *n* : a fluffy ball used as trimming on clothing

pomp·ous \'päm-pəs\ *adj* **1** : making an appearance of importance or dignity **2** : SELF-IMPORTANT — **pomp·ous·ly** *adv* — **pomp·ous·ness** *n*

pon·cho \'pän-chō\ *n, pl* **pon·chos** **1** : a Spanish-American cloak like a blanket with a slit in the middle for the head **2** : a waterproof garment like a poncho worn as a raincoat

pond \'pänd\ *n* : a body of water usually smaller than a lake

pon·der \'pän-dər\ *vb* : to think over carefully

pon·der·ous \'pän-də-rəs\ *adj* **1** : very heavy **2** : unpleasantly dull ⟨a *ponderous* speech⟩

pond scum *n* : a mass of algae in still water or an alga that grows in such masses

pon·iard \'pän-yərd\ *n* : a slender dagger

pon·toon \pän-'tün\ *n* **1** : a small boat with a flat bottom **2** : a light watertight float used as one of the supports for a floating bridge **3** : a float attached to the bottom of an airplane for landing on water

po·ny \'pō-nē\ *n, pl* **po·nies** : a small horse

pony express *n* : a rapid postal system that operated across the western United States in 1860-61 by changing horses and riders along the way

poo·dle \'püd-l\ *n* : one of an old breed of active intelligent dogs with heavy coats of solid color

pooh \'pü, 'pu\ *interj* — used to express contempt or disapproval

¹pool \'pül\ *n* **1** : a small deep body of water ⟨the *pool* below the rock⟩ ⟨a swimming *pool*⟩ **2** : a small body of standing liquid : PUDDLE

²pool *n* **1** : a game of billiards played on a table with six pockets **2** : people, money, or things come together or put together for some purpose ⟨a car *pool*⟩

³pool *vb* : to contribute to a common fund or effort

poor \'pur\ *adj* **1** : not having riches or possessions **2** : less than enough ⟨a *poor* crop⟩ **3** : worthy of pity ⟨the *poor* dog was killed⟩ **4** : low in quality or value ⟨*poor* health⟩ — **poor·ly** *adv* — **poor·ness** *n*

¹pop \'päp\ *vb* **popped; pop·ping 1** : to burst or cause to burst with a sharp sound **2** : to move suddenly ⟨*pop* into bed⟩ **3** : to fire a gun : SHOOT ⟨*popping* at tin cans⟩ **4** : to stick out ⟨their eyes *popping* with surprise⟩

²pop *n* **1** : a short explosive sound **2** : SODA POP

pop·corn \'päp-,korn\ *n* : corn that bursts open into a white mass when heated

pope \'pōp\ *n, often cap* : the head of the Roman Catholic Church

pop·lar \'päp-lər\ *n* : a tree that has rough bark, catkins for flowers, and a white cottonlike substance around its seeds

pop·py \'päp-ē\ *n, pl* **pop·pies** : a plant with a hairy stem and showy usually red, yellow, or white flowers

pop·u·lace \'päp-yə-ləs\ *n* **1** : the common people **2** : POPULATION 1

pop·u·lar \'päp-yə-lər\ *adj* **1** : of, relating to, or coming from the whole body of people ⟨*popular* government⟩ **2** : enjoyed or approved by many people ⟨a *popular* game⟩ — **pop·u·lar·ly** *adv*

pop·u·lar·i·ty \,päp-yə-'lar-ət-ē\ *n* : the quality or state of being popular

pop·u·late \'päp-yə-,lāt\ *vb* **pop·u·lat·ed; pop·u·lat·ing** : to provide with inhabitants

pop·u·la·tion \,päp-yə-'lā-shən\ *n* **1** : the whole number of people in a country, city, or area **2** : the people or things living in a certain place

pop·u·lous \'päp-yə-ləs\ *adj* : having a large population

por·ce·lain \'pōr-sə-lən\ *n* : a hard white ceramic ware used especially for dishes and chemical utensils

porch \'pōrch\ *n* : a covered entrance to a building usually with a separate roof

por·cu·pine \'pōr-kyə-,pīn\ *n* : a gnawing animal having stiff sharp quills among its hairs

porcupine

Word History The word *porcupine* is related to the word *pork*. The word *pork* comes from a Latin word that meant "pig." A porcupine looks a little like a spiny pig. The English word *porcupine* comes from two Latin words. The first meant "pig" and the second meant "spine" or "thorn."

¹pore \'pōr\ *vb* **pored; por·ing** : to read with great attention : STUDY ⟨*pore* over a book⟩

²pore *n* : a tiny opening (as in the skin or in the soil)

por·gy \'pōr-gē\ *n, pl* **por·gies** : any of several food fishes of the Mediterranean sea and the Atlantic ocean

pork \'pōrk\ *n* : the fresh or salted flesh of a pig

po·rous \'pōr-əs\ *adj* **1** : full of pores ⟨*porous* wood⟩ **2** : capable of absorbing liquids ⟨*porous* blotting paper⟩

por·poise \'pōr-pəs\ *n* **1** : a sea animal somewhat like a small whale with a blunt rounded snout **2** : DOLPHIN 1

Word History The word *porpoise* is related to the word *pork*. The word *pork* comes from a Latin word that meant "pig." The snout of the porpoise must have reminded the ancient Romans of a pig's snout. They gave the porpoise a Latin name that meant "pig of the sea." The English word *porpoise* comes from two

\ə\ **abut**	\au\ **out**	\i\ **tip**	\o\ **saw**	\u\ **foot**
\ər\ **further**	\ch\ **chin**	\ī\ **life**	\oi\ **coin**	\y\ **yet**
\a\ **mat**	\e\ **pet**	\j\ **job**	\th\ **thin**	\yu\ **few**
\ā\ **take**	\ē\ **easy**	\ng\ **sing**	\th\ **this**	\yu\ **cure**
\ä\ **cot, cart**	\g\ **go**	\ō\ **bone**	\ü\ **food**	\zh\ **vision**

Latin words. The first meant "pig" and the second meant "fish."

por·ridge \\'pȯr-ij\\ *n* : a food made by boiling meal of a grain or a vegetable (as peas) in water or milk until it thickens

¹port \\'pōrt\\ *n* **1** : a place where ships may ride safe from storms **2** : a harbor where ships load or unload cargo **3** : AIRPORT

²port *n* **1** : an opening (as in machinery) for gas, steam, or water to go in or out **2** : PORTHOLE

³port *n* : the left side of a ship or airplane looking forward

por·ta·ble \\'pōrt-ə-bəl\\ *adj* : possible to carry or move about

por·tage \\'pōrt-ij\\ *n* : the carrying of boats or goods overland from one body of water to another

por·tal \\'pōrt-l\\ *n* : a grand or fancy door or gate

port·cul·lis \\pōrt-'kəl-əs\\ *n* : a heavy iron gate which can be let down to prevent entrance (as to a castle)

por·tend \\pȯr-'tend\\ *vb* : to give a sign or warning of beforehand

por·tent \\'pȯr-,tent\\ *n* : a sign or warning that something is going to happen

portcullis

por·ter \\'pōrt-ər\\ *n* **1** : a person who carries baggage (as at a terminal) **2** : an attendant on a train

port·fo·lio \\pōrt-'fō-lē-,ō\\ *n, pl* **port·fo·li·os** : a flat case for carrying papers or drawings

port·hole \\'pōrt-,hōl\\ *n* : an opening in the side of a ship or airplane

por·ti·co \\'pōrt-i-,kō\\ *n, pl* **por·ti·coes** *or* **por·ti·cos** : a row of columns supporting a roof around or at the entrance of a building

¹por·tion \\'pōr-shən\\ *n* : a part or share of a whole **synonyms** see PART

²portion *vb* : to divide into portions : DISTRIBUTE

por·trait \\'pōr-trət, -,trāt\\ *n* : a picture of a person usually showing the face

por·tray \\pōr-'trā\\ *vb* **1** : to make a portrait of **2** : to picture in words : DESCRIBE **3** : to play the role of ⟨*portray* the villain in a movie⟩

por·tray·al \\pōr-'trā-əl\\ *n* : the act or result of portraying

¹Por·tu·guese \\'pōr-chə-,gēz\\ *adj* : of or relating to Portugal, its people, or the Portuguese language

²Portuguese *n, pl* **Portuguese 1** : a person born or living in Portugal **2** : the language of Portugal and Brazil

¹pose \\'pōz\\ *vb* **posed; pos·ing 1** : to hold or cause to hold a special position of the body ⟨*pose* for a painting⟩ **2** : to set forth ⟨*pose* a problem⟩ **3** : to pretend to be what one is not ⟨*pose* as a police officer⟩

²pose *n* **1** : a position of the body held for a special purpose ⟨photographed in different *poses*⟩ **2** : a pretended attitude ⟨a *pose* of innocence⟩

po·si·tion \\pə-'zish-ən\\ *n* **1** : the way in which something is placed or arranged **2** : a way of looking at or considering things **3** : the place where a person or thing is ⟨took their *positions* at the head of the line⟩ **4** : the rank a person has in an organization or in society **5** : JOB 3

¹pos·i·tive \\'päz-ət-iv\\ *adj* **1** : definitely and clearly stated ⟨the police had *positive* orders⟩ **2** : fully confident : CERTAIN ⟨*positive* that I would win⟩ **3** : of, relating to, or having the form of an adjective or adverb that shows no degree of comparison **4** : having a real position or effect ⟨a *positive* change⟩ **5** : having the light and shade the same as in the original subject ⟨a *positive* photograph⟩ **6** : being greater than zero and often shown by a plus sign ⟨2 or +2 is a *positive* number⟩ **7** : of, being, or relating to electricity of a kind that is produced in a glass rod rubbed with silk ⟨a *positive* charge⟩ **8** : having a deficiency of electrons ⟨a *positive* particle⟩ **9** : being the part from which the electric current flows to the external circuit ⟨the *positive* pole of a storage battery⟩ **10** : showing acceptance or approval ⟨a *positive* answer⟩ **11** : showing the presence of what is looked for or suspected to be present ⟨the test for tuberculosis was *positive*⟩ — **pos·i·tive·ly** *adv*

²positive *n* : the positive degree or a positive form of an adjective or adverb

pos·sess \\pə-'zes\\ *vb* **1** : to have and hold as property : OWN **2** : to enter into and control firmly ⟨acted as if *possessed* by a devil⟩ — **pos·sess·or** \\-ər\\ *n*

pos·ses·sion \\pə-'zesh-ən\\ *n* **1** : the act of possessing or holding as one's own : OWNERSHIP ⟨charged with the *possession* of stolen goods⟩ **2** : something that is held as one's own property

¹pos·ses·sive \\pə-'zes-iv\\ *adj* **1** : being or belonging to the case of a noun or pronoun that shows possession **2** : showing the desire to possess or control

²**possessive** *n* : a noun or pronoun in the possessive case

pos·si·bil·i·ty \‚päs-ə-'bil-ət-ē\ *n, pl* **pos·si·bil·i·ties 1** : the state or fact of being possible ⟨face the *possibility* of failure⟩ **2** : something that may happen

pos·si·ble \'päs-ə-bəl\ *adj* **1** : being within the limits of one's ability ⟨a task *possible* to the youngest children⟩ **2** : being something that may or may not happen ⟨*possible* dangers⟩ **3** : able or fitted to be or to become ⟨a *possible* site for a camp⟩

synonyms POSSIBLE and LIKELY mean being such as may become true or actual. POSSIBLE suggests that something is within the limit of what may happen or of what a person or thing may do regardless of the chances for or against it actually happening ⟨it is *possible* that you may get rich⟩ LIKELY suggests that the chances are good that something will actually happen but there is no proof it will ⟨it is *likely* that you will get married⟩

pos·si·bly \'päs-ə-blē\ *adv* **1** : by any possibility ⟨that cannot *possibly* be true⟩ **2** : PERHAPS ⟨*possibly* it will rain⟩

pos·sum \'päs-əm\ *n* : OPOSSUM

¹**post** \'pōst\ *n* : a piece of solid substance (as metal or timber) placed firmly in an upright position and used especially as a support

²**post** *vb* **1** : to fasten on a post, wall, or bulletin board ⟨*post* examination results⟩ **2** : to make known publicly as if by posting a notice **3** : to forbid persons from entering or using by putting up warning notices ⟨*post* a trout stream⟩

³**post** *vb* **1** : to ride or travel with haste **2** : to send by mail : MAIL **3** : to make familiar with a subject ⟨keep me *posted*⟩

⁴**post** *n* **1** : the place at which a soldier or guard is stationed **2** : a place where a body of troops is stationed **3** : a place or office to which a person is appointed **4** : a trading settlement

⁵**post** *vb* : to station at a post ⟨*post* a guard⟩

post- *prefix* : after : later : following : behind

post·age \'pō-stij\ *n* : a fee for postal service

post·al \'pōst-l\ *adj* : of or relating to the post office or the handling of mail

postal card *n* **1** : a blank card with a postage stamp printed on it **2** : POSTCARD 1

post·card \'pōst-‚kärd\ *n* **1** : a card on which a message may be sent by mail without an envelope **2** : POSTAL CARD 1

post·er \'pō-stər\ *n* : a usually large sheet with writing or pictures on it that is displayed as a notice, advertisement, or for decoration

pos·ter·i·ty \pä-'ster-ət-ē\ *n* **1** : the line of individuals descended from one ancestor **2** : all future generations ⟨leave a record for *posterity*⟩

post·man \'pōst-mən\ *n, pl* **post·men** \-mən\ : LETTER CARRIER

post·mark \'pōst-‚märk\ *n* : a mark put on a piece of mail especially for canceling the postage stamp

post·mas·ter \'pōst-‚mas-tər\ *n* : a person in charge of a post office

post·mis·tress \'pōst-‚mis-trəs\ *n* : a woman in charge of a post office

post office *n* **1** : a government agency in charge of the mail **2** : a place where mail is received, handled, and sent out

post·paid \'pōst-'pād\ *adv* : with postage paid by the sender

post·pone \pōst-'pōn\ *vb* **post·poned; post·pon·ing** : to put off till some later time — **post·pone·ment** \-mənt\ *n*

post·script \'pōst-‚skript\ *n* : a note added at the end of a finished letter or book

¹**pos·ture** \'päs-chər\ *n* : the position of one part of the body with relation to other parts : the general way of holding the body

²**posture** *vb* **pos·tured; pos·tur·ing** : to take on a particular posture : POSE

po·sy \'pō-zē\ *n, pl* **po·sies 1** : ¹FLOWER 1, 2 **2** : BOUQUET

¹**pot** \'pät\ *n* **1** : a deep rounded container for household purposes **2** : the amount a pot will hold ⟨a *pot* of soup⟩

²**pot** *vb* **pot·ted; pot·ting 1** : to put or pack in a pot **2** : to plant (as a flower) in a pot to grow — often used with *up* ⟨*pot* up begonias⟩

pot·ash \'pät-‚ash\ *n* : potassium or a compound of potassium

po·tas·si·um \pə-'tas-ē-əm\ *n* : a silvery soft light metallic chemical element found especially in minerals

po·ta·to \pə-'tät-ō\ *n, pl* **po·ta·toes** : the thick edible under-

potato

\ə\ abut	\au̇\ out	\i\ tip	\ȯ\ saw	\u̇\ foot
\ər\ further	\ch\ chin	\ī\ life	\ȯi\ coin	\y\ yet
\a\ mat	\e\ pet	\j\ job	\th\ thin	\yü\ few
\ā\ take	\ē\ easy	\ng\ sing	\th\ this	\yu̇\ cure
\ä\ cot, cart	\g\ go	\ō\ bone	\ü\ food	\zh\ vision

ground tuber of a widely grown American plant related to the tomato

potato chip *n* : a very thin slice of white potato fried crisp and salted

po·tent \'pōt-nt\ *adj* **1** : having power or authority ⟨a *potent* ruler⟩ **2** : very effective : STRONG ⟨*potent* medicine⟩

po·ten·tial \pə-'ten-chəl\ *adj* : existing as a possibility — **po·ten·tial·ly** *adv*

pot·hole \'pät-ˌhōl\ *n* : a deep round hole (as in a stream bed or a road)

po·tion \'pō-shən\ *n* : a drink especially of a medicine or of a poison

pot·shot \'pät-ˌshät\ *n* : a shot taken in a casual manner or at an easy target

¹**pot·ter** \'pät-ər\ *n* : a person who makes pottery

²**potter** *vb* : PUTTER

pot·tery \'pät-ə-rē\ *n, pl* **pot·ter·ies 1** : a place where clay articles (as pots, dishes, and vases) are made **2** : the art of making clay articles **3** : articles made from clay that is shaped while moist and hardened by heat

pouch \'paùch\ *n* **1** : a small bag with a drawstring **2** : a bag often with a lock for carrying goods or valuables ⟨mail *pouch*⟩ **3** : a bag of folded skin and flesh especially for carrying the young (as on the abdomen of a kangaroo) or for carrying food (as in the cheek of many animals of the rat family)

poul·tice \'pōl-təs\ *n* : a soft and heated mass usually containing medicine and spread on the body surface to relieve pain, inflammation, or congestion

poul·try \'pōl-trē\ *n* : birds (as chickens, turkeys, ducks, and geese) grown to furnish meat or eggs for human food

¹**pounce** \'paùns\ *vb* **pounced; pounc·ing 1** : to swoop on and seize something with or as if with claws ⟨the cat *pounced* on a mouse⟩ **2** : to leap or attack very quickly

²**pounce** *n* : an act of pouncing : a sudden swooping or springing on something

¹**pound** \'paùnd\ *n* **1** : a measure of weight equal to sixteen ounces (about .45 kilogram) **2** : a coin or bill used in the United Kingdom and several other countries

²**pound** *vb* **1** : to crush to a powder or pulp by beating ⟨*pound* almonds into a paste⟩ **2** : to strike heavily again and again ⟨*pound* a piano⟩ **3** : to move along heavily ⟨*pounding* through mud⟩

³**pound** *n* : a public enclosure where stray animals are kept ⟨a dog *pound*⟩

pour \'pōr\ *vb* **1** : to flow or cause to flow in a stream **2** : to let loose something without holding back ⟨*poured* out my troubles⟩ **3** : to rain hard ⟨it *poured* all day long⟩

¹**pout** \'paùt\ *vb* : to show displeasure by pushing out one's lips

²**pout** *n* : an act of pouting

pov·er·ty \'päv-ərt-ē\ *n* **1** : the condition of being poor : lack of money or possessions **2** : a lack of something desirable ⟨*poverty* of the soil⟩

¹**pow·der** \'paùd-ər\ *n* **1** : the fine particles made (as by pounding or crushing) from a dry substance **2** : something (as a food, medicine, or cosmetic) made in or changed to the form of a powder **3** : an explosive used in shooting and in blasting

²**powder** *vb* **1** : to sprinkle with or as if with powder **2** : to reduce to powder **3** : to use face powder

powder horn *n* : a cow or ox horn made into a flask for carrying gunpowder

pow·dery \'paùd-ə-rē\ *adj* **1** : made of or like powder **2** : easily crumbled **3** : sprinkled with powder

¹**pow·er** \'paù-ər\ *n* **1** : possession of control, authority, or influence over others **2** : a nation that has influence among other nations **3** : the ability to act or to do ⟨lose the *power* to walk⟩ **4** : physical might : STRENGTH **5** : the number of times as shown by an exponent a number is used as a factor to obtain a product ⟨10^3 is the third *power* of 10 and means $10 \times 10 \times 10$⟩ **6** : force or energy used to do work ⟨electric *power*⟩ **7** : the rate of speed at which work is done **8** : the number of times an optical instrument magnifies the apparent size of the object viewed — **pow·er·less** \-ləs\ *adj*

powderhorn

synonyms POWER, ENERGY, and STRENGTH mean the ability to put out effort or force. POWER applies to the ability to act, whether only possible or actually used ⟨the king had the *power* to execute criminals⟩ ENERGY applies to stored-up power that can be used to do work ⟨the sun could be a great source of *energy*⟩ STRENGTH applies to that quality which gives a person or thing the ability to put out force or to oppose another's force or attack ⟨test the *strength* of this rope⟩

²**power** *adj* : relating to, supplying, or

using mechanical or electrical power ⟨*power* sources⟩ ⟨*power* drill⟩

³**power** *vb* : to supply with power

pow·er·ful \'paù-ər-fəl\ *adj* : full of or having power, strength, or influence — **pow·er·ful·ly** \-fə-lē\ *adv*

pow·er·house \'paù-ər-ˌhaùs\ *n* **1** : POWER PLANT **2** : a person or thing having unusual strength or energy

power plant *n* : a building in which electric power is generated

pow·wow \'paù-ˌwaù\ *n* **1** : a North American Indian ceremony or conference **2** : a meeting for discussion

prac·ti·ca·ble \'prak-ti-kə-bəl\ *adj* : possible to do or put into practice

prac·ti·cal \'prak-ti-kəl\ *adj* **1** : engaged in some work ⟨a *practical* farmer⟩ **2** : of or relating to action and practice rather than ideas or thought **3** : capable of being made use of ⟨a *practical* knowledge of carpentry⟩ **4** : ready to do things rather than just plan or think about them ⟨a *practical* mind⟩

practical joke *n* : a joke made up of something done rather than said : a trick played on someone

prac·ti·cal·ly \'prak-ti-kə-lē\ *adv* **1** : ACTUALLY ⟨a clever but *practically* worthless plan⟩ **2** : ALMOST ⟨*practically* friendless⟩

¹**prac·tice** *or* **prac·tise** \'prak-təs\ *vb* **prac·ticed** *or* **prac·tised; prac·tic·ing** *or* **prac·tis·ing 1** : to work at often so as to learn well ⟨*practice* music⟩ **2** : to engage in often or usually ⟨*practice* politeness⟩ **3** : to follow or work at as a profession ⟨*practice* medicine⟩

²**practice** *also* **practise** *n* **1** : actual performance : USE ⟨put into *practice*⟩ **2** : a usual way of doing ⟨follow the local *practice*⟩ **3** : repeated action for gaining skill ⟨*practice* makes perfect⟩

prai·rie \'preər-ē\ *n* : a large area of level or rolling grassland

prairie chicken *n* : a grouse of the Mississippi valley

prairie dog *n* : a burrowing animal related to the woodchuck but about the size of a large squirrel that lives in large colonies

prairie schooner *n* : a long covered wagon used by pioneers to cross the prairies

¹**praise** \'prāz\ *vb* **praised; prais·ing**

prairie dog

1 : to express approval of **2** : to glorify God or a saint especially in song **synonyms** see COMPLIMENT

²**praise** *n* **1** : an expression of approval **2** : ¹WORSHIP 1

praise·wor·thy \'prāz-ˌwər-_thē_\ *adj* : worthy of praise

prance \'prans\ *vb* **pranced; pranc·ing 1** : to rise onto or move on the hind legs **2** : to ride on a prancing horse **3** : ¹STRUT

prank \'prangk\ *n* : a mischievous act : PRACTICAL JOKE

prat·tle \'prat-l\ *vb* **prat·tled; prat·tling** : to talk a great deal without much meaning

prawn \'pròn\ *n* : an edible shellfish that looks like a shrimp

pray \'prā\ *vb* **1** : to ask earnestly : BEG **2** : to address God with adoration, pleading, or thanksgiving

prayer \'praər, 'preər\ *n* **1** : a request addressed to God ⟨a *prayer* for peace⟩ **2** : the act of praying to God ⟨kneel in *prayer*⟩ **3** : a set form of words used in praying ⟨the Lord's *prayer*⟩ **4** : a religious service that is mostly prayers ⟨evening *prayer*⟩

pray·ing mantis \ˌprā-ing-\ *n* : MANTIS

pre- *prefix* **1** : earlier than : before ⟨*prehistoric*⟩ **2** : beforehand ⟨*prepay*⟩ **3** : in front of : front ⟨*premolar*⟩

preach \'prēch\ *vb* **1** : to give a sermon **2** : to urge publicly : ADVOCATE ⟨*preach* patience⟩

preach·er \'prē-chər\ *n* **1** : a person who preaches **2** : ¹MINISTER 1

pre·am·ble \'prē-ˌam-bəl\ *n* : an introduction (as to a law) that often gives the reasons for the parts that follow

pre·car·i·ous \pri-'kar-ē-əs, -'ker-\ *adj* **1** : depending on chance or unknown conditions : UNCERTAIN **2** : lacking steadiness or security ⟨*precarious* balance⟩ ⟨*precarious* state of health⟩ — **pre·car·i·ous·ly** *adv* — **pre·car·i·ous·ness** *n*

pre·cau·tion \pri-'kò-shən\ *n* **1** : care taken beforehand **2** : something done beforehand to prevent evil or bring about good results ⟨take all possible *precautions* against fire⟩

pre·cede \pri-'sēd\ *vb* **pre·ced·ed; pre·ced·ing** : to be or go before in importance, position, or time

prec·e·dent \'pres-ə-dənt\ *n* : something that can be used as a rule or as a model to be followed in the future

\ə\ abut	\aù\ out	\i\ tip	\ò\ saw	\ù\ foot
\ər\ further	\ch\ chin	\ī\ life	\òi\ coin	\y\ yet
\a\ mat	\e\ pet	\j\ job	\th\ thin	\yü\ few
\ā\ take	\ē\ easy	\ng\ sing	_th_\ this	\yù\ cure
\ä\ cot, cart	\g\ go	\ō\ bone	\ü\ food	\zh\ vision

pre·ced·ing \pri-'sēd-ing\ *adj* : going before : PREVIOUS

pre·cious \'presh-əs\ *adj* **1** : very valuable ⟨diamonds, emeralds, and other *precious* stones⟩ **2** : greatly loved : DEAR

prec·i·pice \'pres-ə-pəs\ *n* : a very steep and high face of rock or mountain : CLIFF

pre·cip·i·tate \pri-'sip-ə-,tāt\ *vb* **pre·cip·i·tat·ed; pre·cip·i·tat·ing** **1** : to cause to happen suddenly or unexpectedly ⟨the misunderstanding *precipitated* a quarrel⟩ **2** : to change from a vapor to a liquid or solid and fall as rain or snow **3** : to separate from a solution ⟨*precipitate* salt from seawater⟩

pre·cip·i·ta·tion \pri-,sip-ə-'tā-shən\ *n* **1** : unwise haste **2** : water or the amount of water that falls to the earth as hail, mist, rain, sleet, or snow

pre·cise \pri-'sīs\ *adj* **1** : exactly stated or explained ⟨follow *precise* rules⟩ **2** : very clear ⟨a *precise* voice⟩ **3** : very exact : ACCURATE — **pre·cise·ly** *adv* — **pre·cise·ness** *n*

pre·ci·sion \pri-'sizh-ən\ *n* : the quality or state of being precise

pre·co·cious \pri-'kō-shəs\ *adj* : showing qualities or abilities of an adult at an unusually early age — **pre·co·cious·ly** *adv* — **pre·co·cious·ness** *n*

pred·a·tor \'pred-ət-ər\ *n* : an animal that lives mostly by killing and eating other animals

pred·a·to·ry \'pred-ə-,tōr-ē\ *adj* : living by preying upon other animals

pre·de·ces·sor \'pred-ə-,ses-ər, 'prēd-\ *n* : a person who has held a position or office before another

pre·dic·a·ment \pri-'dik-ə-mənt\ *n* : a bad or difficult situation : FIX

pred·i·cate \'pred-i-kət\ *n* : the part of a sentence or clause that tells what is said about the subject ⟨"rang" in "the doorbell rang" is the *predicate*⟩

predicate adjective *n* : an adjective that occurs in the predicate after a linking verb and describes the subject ⟨"sweet" in "sugar is sweet" is a *predicate adjective*⟩

predicate noun *n* : a noun that occurs in the predicate after a linking verb and refers to the same person or thing as the subject ⟨"parent" in "that person is my parent" is a *predicate noun*⟩

pre·dict \pri-'dikt\ *vb* : to figure out and tell beforehand ⟨*predict* the weather⟩ **synonyms** see FORETELL

pre·dic·tion \pri-'dik-shən\ *n* **1** : an act of predicting **2** : something that is predicted

pre·dom·i·nance \pri-'däm-ə-nəns\ *n* : the quality or state of being predominant

pre·dom·i·nant \pri-'däm-ə-nənt\ *adj* : greater than others in number, strength, influence, or authority

pre·dom·i·nate \pri-'däm-ə-,nāt\ *vb* **pre·dom·i·nat·ed; pre·dom·i·nat·ing** : to be predominant

preen \'prēn\ *vb* **1** : to smooth with or as if with the bill ⟨the sparrow *preened* its feathers⟩ **2** : to make one's appearance neat and tidy

pre·fab·ri·cate \prē-'fab-ri-,kāt\ *vb* **pre·fab·ri·cat·ed; pre·fab·ri·cat·ing** : to manufacture the parts of something beforehand so that it can be built by putting the parts together ⟨*prefabricate* houses⟩

pref·ace \'pref-əs\ *n* : a section at the beginning that introduces a book or a speech

pre·fer \pri-'fər\ *vb* **pre·ferred; pre·fer·ring** : to like better ⟨*prefer* chocolate ice cream⟩

pref·er·a·ble \'pref-ə-rə-bəl\ *adj* : deserving to be preferred : more desirable — **pref·er·a·bly** \-blē\ *adv*

pref·er·ence \'pref-ə-rəns, 'pref-rəns\ *n* **1** : a choosing of or special liking for one person or thing rather than another **2** : the power or chance to choose : CHOICE **3** : a person or thing that is preferred

¹pre·fix \'prē-,fiks\ *vb* : to put or attach at the beginning of a word : add as a prefix

²prefix *n* : a letter or group of letters that comes at the beginning of a word and has a meaning of its own

preg·nan·cy \'preg-nən-sē\ *n, pl* **preg·nan·cies** : the state of being pregnant

preg·nant \'preg-nənt\ *adj* **1** : carrying unborn offspring **2** : full of meaning

pre·hen·sile \prē-'hen-səl\ *adj* : able to grasp things ⟨a monkey's *prehensile* tail⟩

pre—His·pan·ic \'prē-his-,pan-ik\ *adj* : of, relating to, or being the time before the Spanish conquests in the western hemisphere

pre·his·tor·ic \,prē-his-'tȯr-ik\ *adj* : of, relating to, or being in existence in the period before written history began ⟨*prehistoric* animals⟩

¹prej·u·dice \'prej-ə-dəs\ *n* **1** : injury or damage to a case at law or to one's rights **2** : a liking or dislike for one rather than another without good reason

²prejudice *vb* **prej·u·diced; prej·u·dic·ing** **1** : to cause damage to (as a case at law) **2** : to cause prejudice in

prel·ate \'prel-ət\ *n* : a clergyman (as a bishop) of high rank

¹pre·lim·i·nary \pri-'lim-ə-,ner-ē\ *n, pl* **pre·lim·i·nar·ies** : something that is preliminary

²preliminary *adj* : coming before the main part : INTRODUCTORY

prel·ude \'prel-ˌyüd, 'prā-ˌlüd\ *n* **1** : something that comes before and prepares for the main or more important parts **2** : a short musical introduction (as for an opera) **3** : a piece (as an organ solo) played at the beginning of a church service

pre·ma·ture \ˌprē-mə-'tùr, -'tyùr\ *adj* : happening, coming, or done before the usual or proper time : too early — **pre·ma·ture·ly** *adv*

pre·med·i·tate \pri-'med-ə-ˌtāt\ *vb* **pre·med·i·tat·ed; pre·med·i·tat·ing** : to think about and plan beforehand

¹pre·mier \pri-'miər, 'prē-mē-ər\ *adj* : first in position or importance : CHIEF

²premier *n* : PRIME MINISTER

¹pre·miere \pri-'myeər, -'miər\ *n* : a first showing or performance ⟨*premiere* of a movie⟩

²premiere *adj* : ²CHIEF 2 ⟨the *premiere* dancer of a group⟩

prem·ise \'prem-əs\ *n* **1** : a statement taken to be true and on which an argument or reasoning may be based **2 premises** *pl* : a piece of land with the buildings on it

pre·mi·um \'prē-mē-əm\ *n* **1** : a prize to be gained by some special act **2** : a sum over and above the stated value ⟨sell stock at a *premium*⟩ **3** : the amount paid for a contract of insurance

pre·mo·lar \'prē-'mō-lər\ *n* : any of the teeth that come between the canines and the molars and in humans are normally two in each side of each jaw

pre·mo·ni·tion \ˌprē-mə-'nish-ən, 'prem-ə-\ *n* : a feeling that something is going to happen ⟨a *premonition* of danger⟩

pre·oc·cu·pied \prē-'äk-yə-ˌpīd\ *adj* : lost in thought

prepaid *past of* PREPAY

prep·a·ra·tion \ˌprep-ə-'rā-shən\ *n* **1** : the act of making ready beforehand for some special reason **2** : something that prepares ⟨finish *preparations* for a trip⟩ **3** : something prepared for a particular purpose ⟨a *preparation* for burns⟩

pre·par·a·to·ry \pri-'par-ə-ˌtōr-ē\ *adj* : preparing or serving to prepare for something ⟨a *preparatory* school⟩

pre·pare \pri-'paər, -'peər\ *vb* **pre·pared; pre·par·ing** **1** : to make ready beforehand for some particular reason ⟨*prepare* for college⟩ **2** : to put together the elements of ⟨*prepare* dinner⟩ ⟨*prepare* a vaccine⟩

pre·pay \'prē-'pā\ *vb* **pre·paid** \-'pād\; **pre·pay·ing** : to pay or pay for beforehand ⟨*prepay* the shipping charges⟩

prep·o·si·tion \ˌprep-ə-'zish-ən\ *n* : a word or group of words that combines with a noun or pronoun to form a phrase that usually acts as an adverb, adjective, or noun

prep·o·si·tion·al \ˌprep-ə-'zish-ən-l\ *adj* : of, relating to, or containing a preposition

pre·pos·ter·ous \pri-'päs-tə-rəs\ *adj* : making little or no sense : FOOLISH ⟨a *preposterous* excuse⟩

pre·req·ui·site \prē-'rek-wə-zət\ *n* : something that is needed beforehand or is necessary to prepare for something else

pre·scribe \pri-'skrīb\ *vb* **pre·scribed; pre·scrib·ing** **1** : to lay down as a rule of action : ORDER ⟨*prescribe* longer hours of rest⟩ **2** : to order or direct the use of as a remedy ⟨the doctor *prescribed* this cough medicine⟩

pre·scrip·tion \pri-'skrip-shən\ *n* **1** : a written direction or order for the preparing and use of a medicine **2** : a medicine that is prescribed

pres·ence \'prez-ns\ *n* **1** : the fact or condition of being present ⟨no one noticed the stranger's *presence*⟩ **2** : position close to a person ⟨on their best behavior in the *presence* of a guest⟩ **3** : a person's appearance

presence of mind : ability to think clearly and act quickly in an emergency

¹pres·ent \'prez-nt\ *n* : something presented or given : GIFT

²pre·sent \pri-'zent\ *vb* **1** : to introduce one person to another **2** : to take (oneself) into another's presence **3** : to bring before the public ⟨*present* a play⟩ **4** : to make a gift to **5** : to give as a gift **6** : to offer to view : SHOW, DISPLAY ⟨*presents* a fine appearance⟩ **synonyms** see GIVE, OFFER

³pres·ent \'prez-nt\ *adj* **1** : not past or future : now going on **2** : being before or near a person or in sight : being at a certain place and not elsewhere **3** : pointing out or relating to time that is not past or future ⟨the *present* tense of a verb⟩

⁴pres·ent \'prez-nt\ *n* : the present time : right now

pres·ent·able \pri-'zent-ə-bəl\ *adj* : having a satisfactory or pleasing appearance

pre·sen·ta·tion \ˌprē-ˌzen-'tā-shən, ˌprez-n-\ *n* **1** : an introduction of one person to another **2** : an act of presenting **3** : something offered or given

pres·ent·ly \'prez-nt-lē\ *adv* **1** : before

\ə\ abut	\aù\ out	\i\ tip	\ò\ saw	\ù\ foot
\ər\ further	\ch\ chin	\ī\ life	\òi\ coin	\y\ yet
\a\ mat	\e\ pet	\j\ job	\th\ thin	\yü\ few
\ā\ take	\ē\ easy	\ng\ sing	\t̲h̲\ this	\yù\ cure
\ä\ cot, cart	\g\ go	\ō\ bone	\ü\ food	\zh\ vision

long : SOON **2** : at the present time : NOW ⟨*presently* at work on a new novel⟩

pres·er·va·tion \,prez-ər-'vā-shən\ *n* : a keeping from injury, loss, or decay

¹**pre·serve** \pri-'zərv\ *vb* **pre·served; pre·serv·ing 1** : to keep or save from injury or ruin : PROTECT **2** : to prepare (as by canning or pickling) fruits or vegetables for keeping ⟨*preserved* peaches⟩ **3** : MAINTAIN 1, CONTINUE ⟨*preserve* silence⟩ — **pre·serv·er** *n*

²**preserve** *n* **1** : fruit cooked in sugar or made into jam or jelly — often used in pl. ⟨strawberry *preserves*⟩ **2** : an area where game or fish are protected

pre·side \pri-'zīd\ *vb* **pre·sid·ed; pre·sid·ing 1** : to act as chairperson of a meeting **2** : to be in charge

pres·i·den·cy \'prez-ə-dən-sē\ *n, pl* **pres·i·den·cies 1** : the office of president **2** : the term during which a president holds office

pres·i·dent \'prez-əd-ənt\ *n* **1** : a person who presides over a meeting **2** : the chief officer of a company or society **3** : the head of the government and chief executive officer of a modern republic

pres·i·den·tial \,prez-ə-'den-chəl\ *adj* : of or relating to a president or the presidency

Pres·i·dents' Day \'prez-əd-ənts-\ *n* : WASHINGTON'S BIRTHDAY

¹**press** \'pres\ *n* **1** : ²CROWD 1, THRONG **2** : a machine that uses pressure to shape, flatten, squeeze,or stamp **3** : a closet for clothing **4** : the act of pressing : PRESSURE **5** : a printing or publishing business **6** : the newspapers and magazines of a country

²**press** *vb* **1** : to bear down upon : push steadily against **2** : to squeeze so as to force out the juice or contents ⟨*press* oranges⟩ **3** : to flatten out or smooth by bearing down upon especially by ironing ⟨*press* clothes⟩ **4** : to ask or urge strongly ⟨*press* someone to go along⟩ **5** : to force or push one's way

press·ing \'pres-ing\ *adj* : needing one's immediate attention ⟨*pressing* business⟩

pres·sure \'presh-ər\ *n* **1** : the action of pressing or bearing down upon **2** : a force or influence that cannot be avoided ⟨social *pressure*⟩ **3** : the force with which one body presses against another **4** : the need to get things done ⟨works well under *pressure*⟩

pres·tige \pre-'stēzh\ *n* : importance in the eyes of people : REPUTE

pres·to \'pres-tō\ *adv or adj* : suddenly as if by magic

pre·sume \pri-'züm\ *vb* **pre·sumed; pre-**

sum·ing 1 : to undertake without permission or good reason : DARE ⟨*presume* to question a judge's decision⟩ **2** : to suppose to be true without proof ⟨*presume* a person innocent until proved guilty⟩

pre·sump·tion \pri-'zəmp-shən\ *n* **1** : presumptuous behavior or attitude **2** : a strong reason for believing something to be so **3** : something believed to be so but not proved

pre·sump·tu·ous \pri-'zəmp-chə-wəs\ *adj* : going beyond what is proper ⟨punished for *presumptuous* pride⟩ — **pre·sump·tu·ous·ly** *adv* — **pre·sump·tu·ous·ness** *n*

pre·tend \pri-'tend\ *vb* **1** : to make believe : SHAM **2** : to put forward as true something that is not true ⟨*pretend* friendship⟩ — **pre·tend·er** *n*

pre·tense *or* **pre·tence** \'prē-,tens, pri-'tens\ *n* **1** : a claim usually not supported by facts **2** : an effort to reach a certain condition or quality ⟨makes no *pretense* at completeness⟩

pre·ten·tious \pri-'ten-chəs\ *adj* : having or showing pretenses : SHOWY ⟨a *pretentious* house⟩ — **pre·ten·tious·ly** *adv* — **pre·ten·tious·ness** *n*

¹**pret·ty** \'prit-ē\ *adj* **pret·ti·er; pret·ti·est** : pleasing to the eye or ear especially because of being graceful or delicate ⟨a *pretty* face⟩ ⟨a *pretty* tune⟩ **synonyms** see BEAUTIFUL — **pret·ti·ly** \'prit-l-ē\ *adv* — **pret·ti·ness** \'prit-ē-nəs\ *n*

²**pret·ty** \,prit-ē, pərt-ē\ *adv* : in some degree : FAIRLY ⟨*pretty* good⟩

pret·zel \'pret-səl\ *n* : a brown cracker that is salted and is usually hard and shaped like a loose knot

Word History The English word *pretzel* comes from a German word. The German word for a pretzel came from a Latin word that meant "having branches like arms." This Latin word was formed from a Latin word that meant "arm." The most common shape for a pretzel is like a knot. This knot shape must have reminded someone of a pair of folded arms.

pre·vail \pri-'vāl\ *vb* **1** : to win a victory ⟨*prevailed* over their enemies⟩ **2** : to succeed in convincing ⟨we *prevailed* upon them to sing⟩ **3** : to be or become usual, common, or widespread ⟨west winds *prevail* in that region⟩

prev·a·lence \'prev-ə-ləns\ *n* : the state of being prevalent

prev·a·lent \'prev-ə-lənt\ *adj* : accepted, practiced, or happening often or over a wide area

pre·vent \pri-'vent\ vb **1** : to keep from happening ⟨help to *prevent* accidents⟩ **2** : to hold or keep back ⟨bad weather *prevented* us from leaving⟩ — **pre·vent·able** \-ə-bəl\ *adj*

pre·ven·tion \pri-'ven-chən\ *n* : the act or practice of preventing something ⟨study about the *prevention* of fires⟩

pre·ven·tive \prē-'vent-iv\ *adj* : used for prevention

pre·view \'prē-ˌvyü\ *n* : a showing of something (as a movie) before regular showings

pre·vi·ous \'prē-vē-əs\ *adj* : going before in time or order : PRECEDING — **pre·vi·ous·ly** *adv*

¹prey \'prā\ *n* **1** : an animal hunted or killed by another animal for food **2** : a person that is helpless and unable to escape attack : VICTIM **3** : the act or habit of seizing or pouncing upon ⟨birds of *prey*⟩

²prey *vb* **1** : to seize and eat something as prey ⟨dogs *preying* on small game⟩ **2** : to have a harmful effect ⟨fears *preying* on the mind⟩

¹price \'prīs\ *n* **1** : the quantity of one thing given or asked for something else : the amount of money paid or to be paid **2** : ²REWARD ⟨a *price* on one's head⟩ **3** : the cost at which something is gotten or done ⟨win a victory at the *price* of many lives⟩

synonyms PRICE, CHARGE, and COST mean the amount asked or given in payment for something. PRICE usually refers to what is asked for goods ⟨the *price* of a new car⟩ CHARGE usually refers to the amount asked for services ⟨the doctor's *charge* for an office visit⟩ COST is usually used to state what is paid for something by the buyer rather than what is asked by the seller ⟨the *cost* of our dinner seemed very high⟩

²price *vb* **priced; pric·ing 1** : to set a price on **2** : to ask the price of

price·less \'prī-sləs\ *adj* : too valuable to have a price : not to be bought at any price

¹prick \'prik\ *n* **1** : a mark or small wound made by a pointed instrument ⟨the *prick* of a pin⟩ **2** : something sharp or pointed **3** : a sensation of being pricked

²prick *vb* **1** : to pierce slightly with a sharp point **2** : to have or to cause a feeling of or as if of being pricked **3** : to point upward ⟨the horse *pricked* up its ears⟩

prick·er \'prik-ər\ *n* : ¹PRICKLE 1

¹prick·le \'prik-əl\ *n* **1** : a small sharp point (as a thorn) **2** : a slight stinging pain

²prickle *vb* **prick·led; prick·ling** : ²PRICK 2

prick·ly \'prik-lē\ *adj* **prick·li·er; prick·li-**

est **1** : having prickles ⟨a *prickly* cactus⟩ **2** : being or having a pricking ⟨a *prickly* sensation⟩ ⟨a *prickly* thumb⟩

prickly pear *n* : a usually spiny cactus with flat branching joints and a sweet pulpy fruit shaped like a pear

prickly pear

¹pride \'prīd\ *n* **1** : too high an opinion of one's own ability or worth : a feeling of being better than others **2** : a reasonable and justifiable sense of one's own worth : SELF-RESPECT ⟨*pride* in doing good work⟩ **3** : a sense of pleasure that comes from some act or possession ⟨take *pride* in their children's high marks⟩ **4** : something of which one is proud ⟨that car is my *pride* and joy⟩

²pride *vb* **prid·ed; prid·ing** : to think highly of (oneself) ⟨I *pride* myself on my spelling⟩

priest \'prēst\ *n* : a person who has the authority to lead or perform religious ceremonies

priest·ess \'prē-stəs\ *n* : a woman who is a priest

prim \'prim\ *adj* **prim·mer; prim·mest** : very fussy about one's appearance or behavior — **prim·ly** *adv*

pri·mar·i·ly \prī-'mer-ə-lē\ *adv* : in the first place

¹pri·ma·ry \'prī-ˌmer-ē, -mə-rē\ *adj* **1** : first in time or development ⟨the *primary* grades⟩ **2** : most important : PRINCIPAL ⟨*primary* duties⟩ **3** : not made or coming from something else : BASIC ⟨the *primary* source of trouble⟩ **4** : of, relating to, or being the heaviest of three levels of stress in pronunciation

²primary *n, pl* **pri·ma·ries** : an election in which members of a political party nominate candidates for office

primary color *n* : any of a set of colors from which all other colors may be made with the colors for light being red, green, and blue and for pigments or paint being red, yellow, and blue

\ə\ abut	\au̇\ out	\i\ tip
\ər\ further	\ch\ chin	\ī\ life
\a\ mat	\e\ pet	\j\ job
\ā\ take	\ē\ easy	\ng\ sing
\ä\ cot, cart	\g\ go	\ō\ bone
\ȯ\ saw	\u̇\ foot	
\ȯi\ coin	\y\ yet	
\th\ thin	\yü\ few	
\th\ this	\yu̇\ cure	
\ü\ food	\zh\ vision	

pri·mate \\'prī-ˌmāt\\ *n* : any of a group of mammals that includes humans together with the apes and monkeys and a few related forms

¹prime \\'prīm\\ *n* **1** : the first part : the earliest stage **2** : the period in life when a person is best in health, looks, or strength **3** : the best individual or part

²prime *adj* **1** : first in time : ORIGINAL ⟨*prime* cost⟩ **2** : having no factor except itself and one ⟨3 is a *prime* number⟩ **3** : first in importance, rank, or quality

³prime *vb* **primed; prim·ing 1** : to put a first color or coating on (an unpainted surface) **2** : to put into working order by filling ⟨*prime* a pump⟩ **3** : to tell what to say beforehand : COACH ⟨*prime* a witness⟩

prime minister *n* : the chief officer of the government in some countries

¹prim·er \\'prim-ər\\ *n* **1** : a small book for teaching children to read **2** : a book of first instructions on a subject

²prim·er \\'prī-mər\\ *n* **1** : a device (as a cap) for setting off an explosive **2** : material used to prime a surface

pri·me·val \\prī-'mē-vəl\\ *adj* : belonging to the earliest time : PRIMITIVE

prim·i·tive \\'prim-ət-iv\\ *adj* **1** : of or belonging to very early times ⟨*primitive* people⟩ **2** : of or belonging to an early stage of development ⟨*primitive* tools⟩

primp \\'primp\\ *vb* : to dress or arrange in a careful or fussy manner

prim·rose \\'prim-ˌrōz\\ *n* : a low perennial plant with large leaves growing from the base of the stem and showy often yellow or pink flowers

prince \\'prins\\ *n* **1** : MONARCH 1 **2** : the son of a monarch **3** : a nobleman of very high or the highest rank

prin·cess \\'prin-səs, -ˌses\\ *n* : a daughter or granddaughter of a monarch : a female member of a royal family

¹prin·ci·pal \\'prin-sə-pəl\\ *adj* : highest in rank or importance : CHIEF ⟨had the *principal* part in the school play⟩ — **prin·ci·pal·ly** *adv*

²principal *n* **1** : a leading or most important person or thing **2** : the head of a school **3** : a sum of money that is placed to earn interest, is owed as a debt, or is used as a fund

prin·ci·pal·i·ty \\ˌprin-sə-'pal-ət-ē\\ *n, pl* **prin·ci·pal·i·ties** : a small territory that is ruled by a prince ⟨the *principality* of Monaco⟩

principal parts *n pl* : the infinitive, the past tense, and the past and present participles of an English verb

prin·ci·ple \\'prin-sə-pəl\\ *n* **1** : a general or basic truth on which other truths or theories can be based ⟨scientific *principles*⟩ **2** : a rule of conduct ⟨a person of high *principles*⟩ **3** : a law or fact of nature which makes possible the working of a machine or device ⟨the *principle* of magnetism⟩ ⟨the *principle* of the lever⟩

¹print \\'print\\ *n* **1** : a mark made by pressure **2** : something which has been stamped with an impression or formed in a mold ⟨a *print* of butter⟩ **3** : printed matter **4** : printed letters ⟨clear *print*⟩ **5** : a picture, copy, or design taken from an engraving or photographic negative **6** : cloth upon which a design is stamped ⟨a cotton *print*⟩

²print *vb* **1** : to put or stamp in or on **2** : to make a copy of by pressing paper against an inked surface (as type or an engraving) **3** : PUBLISH 2 ⟨*print* a newspaper⟩ **4** : to stamp with a design by pressure ⟨*print* wallpaper⟩ **5** : to write in separate letters like those made by a typewriter **6** : to make (a picture) from a photographic negative

print·er \\'print-ər\\ *n* : a person whose business is printing

print·ing \\'print-ing\\ *n* **1** : the process of putting something in printed form **2** : the art, practice, or business of a printer

printing press *n* : a machine that makes printed copies

¹pri·or \\'prī-ər\\ *n* : a monk that is head of a priory

²prior *adj* **1** : being or happening before something else **2** : being more important than something else

pri·or·ess \\'prī-ə-rəs\\ *n* : a nun who is head of a priory

pri·or·i·ty \\prī-'ȯr-ət-ē\\ *n, pl* **pri·or·i·ties** : the quality or state of coming before another in time or importance

prior to *prep* : in advance of : BEFORE ⟨must be finished *prior to* July⟩

pri·o·ry \\'prī-ə-rē\\ *n, pl* **pri·o·ries** : a religious house under a prior or prioress

prism \\'priz-əm\\ *n* : a transparent object that usually has three sides and bends light so that it breaks up into rainbow colors

pris·on \\'priz-n\\ *n* : a place where criminals are locked up

pris·on·er \\'priz-n-ər, 'priz-nər\\ *n* : a person who has been captured or locked up

pri·va·cy \\'prī-və-sē\\ *n* **1** : the state of being out of the sight and hearing of other people **2** : SECRECY 2 ⟨talk together in *privacy*⟩

¹pri·vate \\'prī-vət\\ *adj* **1** : having to do with or for the use of a single person or group

: not public ⟨*private* property⟩ **2** : not holding any public office ⟨a *private* citizen⟩ **3** : ¹SECRET 1 ⟨*private* meetings⟩ — **pri·vate·ly** *adv* — **pri·vate·ness** *n*

²**private** *n* : an enlisted person of the lowest rank in the Marine Corps or of either of the two lowest ranks in the Army

pri·va·teer \ˌprī-və-'tiər\ *n* **1** : an armed private ship permitted by its government to make war on ships of an enemy country **2** : a sailor on a privateer

private first class *n* : an enlisted person in the Army or Marine Corps ranking above a private

priv·et \'priv-ət\ *n* : a shrub with white flowers that is related to the lilac and is often used for hedges

priv·i·lege \'priv-ə-lij\ *n* : a right or liberty granted as a favor or benefit especially to some and not others

priv·i·leged \'priv-ə-lijd\ *adj* : having more things and a better chance in life than most people ⟨*privileged* classes of society⟩

¹**prize** \'prīz\ *n* **1** : something won or to be won in a contest **2** : something unusually valuable or eagerly sought

²**prize** *adj* **1** : awarded a prize ⟨a *prize* essay⟩ **2** : awarded as a prize ⟨*prize* money⟩ **3** : outstanding of its kind ⟨a *prize* fool⟩ ⟨a *prize* student⟩

³**prize** *vb* **prized; priz·ing** **1** : to estimate the value of **2** : to value highly : TREASURE ⟨*prize* a picture⟩

⁴**prize** *n* : something taken (as in war) by force especially at sea

prize·fight·er \'prīz-ˌfit-ər\ *n* : a professional boxer

¹**pro** \'prō\ *n, pl* **pros** : an argument or evidence in favor of something ⟨discussed the *pros* and cons⟩

²**pro** *adv* : in favor of something ⟨argue *pro* and con⟩

³**pro** *n or adj* : PROFESSIONAL

pro- *prefix* : approving : in favor of

prob·a·bil·i·ty \ˌpräb-ə-'bil-ət-ē\ *n, pl* **prob·a·bil·i·ties** **1** : the quality or state of being probable **2** : something probable

prob·a·ble \'präb-ə-bəl\ *adj* : reasonably sure but not certain of happening or being true : LIKELY

prob·a·bly \'präb-ə-blē\ *adv* : very likely ⟨the clouds are dark and *probably* it will rain⟩

pro·ba·tion \prō-'bā-shən\ *n* : a period of trial for finding out or testing a person's fitness (as for a job)

¹**probe** \'prōb\ *n* **1** : a slender instrument for examining a cavity (as a deep wound) **2** : a careful investigation

²**probe** *vb* **probed; prob·ing** **1** : to examine with or as if with a probe **2** : to investigate thoroughly

prob·lem \'präb-ləm\ *n* **1** : something to be worked out or solved ⟨a *problem* in arithmetic⟩ **2** : a person or thing that is hard to understand or deal with

pro·bos·cis \prə-'bäs-əs, -kəs\ *n* : a long flexible hollow bodily structure (as the trunk of an elephant or the beak of a mosquito)

pro·ce·dure \prə-'sē-jər\ *n* **1** : the manner or method in which a business or action is carried on **2** : an action or series of actions ⟨the *procedure* of swearing in a club member⟩

pro·ceed \prō-'sēd\ *vb* **1** : to go forward or onward : ADVANCE **2** : to come from a source ⟨light *proceeds* from the sun⟩ **3** : to go or act by an orderly method ⟨*proceed* according to plan⟩

pro·ceed·ing \prō-'sēd-ing\ *n* **1** : PROCEDURE 2 **2 proceedings** *pl* : things that happen

pro·ceeds \'prō-ˌsēdz\ *n pl* : the money or profit that comes from a business deal

¹**pro·cess** \'präs-ˌes, 'prōs-\ *n* **1** : ²ADVANCE 1 ⟨the *process* of time⟩ **2** : a series of actions, motions, or operations leading to some result ⟨a *process* of manufacture⟩ **3** : the carrying on of a legal action ⟨due *process*⟩

²**process** *vb* : to change by a special treatment ⟨*process* cheese⟩

pro·ces·sion \prə-'sesh-ən\ *n* **1** : continuous forward movement : PROGRESSION **2** : a group of individuals moving along in an orderly often ceremonial way ⟨a funeral *procession*⟩

pro·claim \prō-'klām\ *vb* : to announce publicly : DECLARE ⟨*proclaim* a holiday⟩

proc·la·ma·tion \ˌpräk-lə-'mā-shən\ *n* **1** : the act of proclaiming **2** : something proclaimed

pro·cure \prə-'kyur\ *vb* **pro·cured; pro·cur·ing** **1** : OBTAIN ⟨*procure* a ticket to the game⟩ **2** : to bring about or cause to be done ⟨*procured* my friend's release from jail⟩

¹**prod** \'präd\ *vb* **prod·ded; prod·ding** **1** : to poke with something **2** : to stir a person or animal to action

²**prod** *n* **1** : something used for prodding ⟨a cattle *prod*⟩ **2** : an act of prodding **3** : a sharp urging or reminder

\ə\ **abut**	\au̇\ **out**	\i\ **tip**	\ȯ\ **saw**	\u̇\ **foot**
\ər\ **further**	\ch\ **chin**	\ī\ **life**	\ȯi\ **coin**	\y\ **yet**
\a\ **mat**	\e\ **pet**	\j\ **job**	\th\ **thin**	\yü\ **few**
\ā\ **take**	\ē\ **easy**	\ng\ **sing**	\th\ **this**	\yu̇\ **cure**
\ä\ **cot, cart**	\g\ **go**	\ō\ **bone**	\ü\ **food**	\zh\ **vision**

¹prod·i·gal \'präd-i-gəl\ *adj* : carelessly wasteful ⟨a *prodigal* spender⟩

²prodigal *n* : somebody who wastes money carelessly

prod·i·gy \'präd-ə-jē\ *n, pl* **prod·i·gies** **1** : an amazing event or action : WONDER **2** : an unusually talented child

¹pro·duce \prə-'düs, -'dyüs\ *vb* **pro·duced; pro·duc·ing** **1** : to bring to view : EXHIBIT ⟨*produce* evidence⟩ **2** : to bring forth : YIELD ⟨this tree *produces* good fruit⟩ **3** : ¹MAKE 2, MANUFACTURE ⟨a city that *produces* steel⟩ **4** : to prepare (as a play) for public presentation — **pro·duc·er** *n*

²pro·duce \'präd-,üs, 'prōd-, -,yüs\ *n* **1** : something produced **2** : fresh fruits and vegetables

prod·uct \'präd-əkt\ *n* **1** : something produced by manufacture, labor, thought, or growth **2** : the number resulting from the multiplication of two or more numbers ⟨the *product* of 3 and 5 is 15⟩

pro·duc·tion \prə-'dək-shən\ *n* **1** : the act of producing ⟨*production* of cars⟩ **2** : something produced ⟨a television *production* of a play⟩ **3** : the amount produced ⟨annual *production* of coal⟩

pro·duc·tive \prə-'dək-tiv\ *adj* **1** : having the power to produce plentifully ⟨*productive* soil⟩ **2** : producing something

¹pro·fane \prō-'fān\ *vb* **pro·faned; pro·fan·ing** : to treat with great disrespect — **pro·fan·er** *n*

²profane *adj* : showing no respect for God or holy things — **pro·fane·ly** *adv* — **pro·fane·ness** *n*

pro·fan·i·ty \prō-'fan-ət-ē\ *n, pl* **pro·fan·i·ties** : profane language

pro·fess \prə-'fes\ *vb* **1** : to declare openly ⟨*profess* confidence in a person⟩ **2** : PRETEND 2 ⟨*professed* to be my friend⟩

pro·fes·sion \prə-'fesh-ən\ *n* **1** : a public declaring or claiming ⟨a *profession* of religious faith⟩ **2** : an occupation (as medicine, law, or teaching) that is not mechanical or agricultural and that requires special education **3** : the people working in a profession **synonyms** see TRADE

¹pro·fes·sion·al \prə-'fesh-ən-l\ *adj* **1** : of, relating to, or like that of a profession **2** : taking part in an activity (as a sport) that others do for pleasure in order to make money — **pro·fes·sion·al·ly** *adv*

²professional *n* : a person whose work is professional

pro·fes·sor \prə-'fes-ər\ *n* : a teacher especially of the highest rank at a college or university

prof·fer \'präf-ər\ *vb* : ¹OFFER 2

pro·fi·cient \prə-'fish-ənt\ *adj* : very good at doing something : EXPERT ⟨a *proficient* reader⟩ — **pro·fi·cient·ly** *adv*

pro·file \'prō-,fil\ *n* : something (as a head) seen or drawn from the side

¹prof·it \'präf-ət\ *n* **1** : the gain or benefit from something ⟨it was to our *profit* to study hard⟩ **2** : the gain after all the expenses are subtracted from the total amount received ⟨a business that shows a *profit* of $100 a week⟩ — **prof·it·less** \-ləs\ *adj*

²profit *vb* **1** : to get some good out of something : GAIN ⟨*profit* by experience⟩ **2** : to be of use to (someone) ⟨an agreement that *profited* us all⟩

prof·it·able \'präf-ət-ə-bəl\ *adj* : producing profit ⟨a *profitable* business⟩ — **prof·it·ably** \-blē\ *adv*

pro·found \prə-'faùnd\ *adj* **1** : having or showing great knowledge and understanding ⟨a *profound* thinker⟩ **2** : very deeply felt ⟨*profound* sorrow⟩ — **pro·found·ly** *adv* — **pro·found·ness** *n*

pro·fuse \prə-'fyüs\ *adj* : very plentiful — **pro·fuse·ly** *adv* — **pro·fuse·ness** *n*

pro·fu·sion \prə-'fyü-zhən\ *n* : a plentiful supply : PLENTY

prog·e·ny \'präj-ə-nē\ *n, pl* **prog·e·nies** : human descendants or animal offspring

pro·gram \'prō-,gram, -grəm\ *n* **1** : a brief statement or written outline (as of a concert or play) **2** : PERFORMANCE 2 ⟨a television *program*⟩ **3** : a plan of action

¹prog·ress \'präg-rəs, -,res\ *n* **1** : a moving toward a goal ⟨a ship's *progress*⟩ **2** : gradual improvement

²pro·gress \prə-'gres\ *vb* **1** : to move forward : ADVANCE ⟨the story *progresses*⟩ **2** : to move toward a higher, better, or more advanced stage

pro·gres·sion \prə-'gresh-ən\ *n* **1** : the act of progressing or moving forward **2** : a continuous and connected series (as of acts, events, or steps)

pro·gres·sive \prə-'gres-iv\ *adj* **1** : of, relating to, or showing progress ⟨a *progressive* city⟩ **2** : taking place gradually or step by step ⟨*progressive* wearing away of the soil⟩ **3** : favoring or working for gradual political change and social improvement by action of the government — **pro·gres·sive·ly** *adv* — **pro·gres·sive·ness** *n*

pro·hib·it \prō-'hib-ət\ *vb* **1** : to forbid by authority ⟨parking *prohibited*⟩ **2** : to make impossible ⟨the high walls *prohibit* escape⟩

pro·hi·bi·tion \,prō-ə-'bish-ən\ *n* **1** : the act of prohibiting something **2** : the forbidding by law of the sale or manufacture of alcoholic liquids for use as beverages

¹proj·ect \'präj-,ekt, -ikt\ *n* **1** : a plan or scheme to do something **2** : a task or problem in school **3** : a group of houses or apartment buildings built according to a single plan

²pro·ject \prə-'jekt\ *vb* **1** : to cause to fall on a surface ⟨*project* motion pictures on a screen⟩ ⟨*project* a shadow on the wall⟩ **2** : to stick out ⟨a rock that *projects* above the ground⟩

pro·jec·tile \prə-'jek-təl\ *n* : something (as a bullet or rocket) that is thrown or driven forward especially from a weapon

pro·jec·tion \prə-'jek-shən\ *n* **1** : something that sticks out **2** : the act or process of projecting on a surface (as by means of motion pictures or slides)

pro·jec·tor \prə-'jek-tər\ *n* : a machine for projecting images on a screen

pro·lif·ic \prə-'lif-ik\ *adj* : producing young or fruit in large numbers

pro·long \prə-'lȯng\ *vb* : to make longer than usual or expected ⟨*prolong* a person's life⟩

prom \'präm\ *n* : a usually formal dance given by a high school or college class

prom·e·nade \,präm-ə-'nād, -'näd\ *n* **1** : a walk or ride for pleasure or to be seen **2** : a place for walking

prom·i·nence \'präm-ə-nəns\ *n* **1** : the quality, condition, or fact of being prominent : DISTINCTION ⟨a person of *prominence*⟩ **2** : something (as a mountain) that is prominent

prom·i·nent \'präm-ə-nənt\ *adj* **1** : sticking out beyond the surface **2** : attracting attention (as by size or position) : CONSPICUOUS **3** : DISTINGUISHED, EMINENT ⟨our town's most *prominent* resident⟩ — **prom·i·nent·ly** *adv*

¹prom·ise \'präm-əs\ *n* **1** : a statement by a person that he or she will do or not do something ⟨a *promise* to pay within a month⟩ **2** : a cause or ground for hope ⟨these plans give *promise* of success⟩

²promise *vb* **prom·ised; prom·is·ing** **1** : to give a promise about one's own actions ⟨I *promise* to clean my room this afternoon⟩ **2** : to give reason to expect ⟨the clouds *promise* rain⟩

prom·is·ing \'präm-ə-sing\ *adj* : likely to turn out well ⟨a very *promising* pupil⟩

prom·on·to·ry \'präm-ən-,tōr-ē\ *n, pl* **prom·on·to·ries** : a high point of land sticking out into the sea

pro·mote \prə-'mōt\ *vb* **pro·mot·ed; pro·mot·ing** **1** : to move up in position or rank ⟨was *promoted* to the next grade⟩ **2** : to help (something) to grow or develop ⟨good soil *promotes* plant growth⟩

pro·mo·tion \prə-'mō-shən\ *n* **1** : a moving up in position or rank ⟨*promotion* to a higher grade in school⟩ **2** : the promoting of something (as growth of health)

¹prompt \'prämpt\ *vb* **1** : to lead to do something ⟨curiosity *prompted* me to ask the question⟩ **2** : to remind of something forgotten or poorly learned ⟨*prompt* an actor⟩ **3** : to be the cause of : INSPIRE ⟨pride *prompted* the act⟩ — **prompt·er** *n*

²prompt *adj* **1** : quick and ready to act ⟨*prompt* to answer⟩ **2** : being on time : PUNCTUAL ⟨*prompt* in arriving⟩ **3** : done at once : given without delay ⟨*prompt* assistance⟩ **synonyms** see QUICK — **prompt·ly** *adv* — **prompt·ness** *n*

prone \'prōn\ *adj* **1** : likely to be or act a certain way ⟨*prone* to laziness⟩ **2** : having the front surface downward ⟨lying *prone* on the floor⟩ **3** : flattened out on a surface ⟨the wind blew the trees *prone*⟩ — **prone·ness** *n*

prong \'prȯng\ *n* **1** : one of the sharp points of a fork **2** : a slender part that sticks out (as a point of an antler)

prong·horn \'prȯng-,hȯrn\ *n* : an animal like an antelope that lives in the treeless parts of the western United States and Mexico

pronghorn

pro·noun \'prō-,naun\ *n* : a word used as a substitute for a noun

pro·nounce \prə-'nauns\ *vb* **pro·nounced; pro·nounc·ing** **1** : to state in

\ə\ **abut**	\au\ **out**	\i\ **tip**	\ȯ\ **saw**	\u̇\ **foot**
\ər\ **further**	\ch\ **chin**	\ī\ **life**	\ȯi\ **coin**	\y\ **yet**
\a\ **mat**	\e\ **pet**	\j\ **job**	\th\ **thin**	\yü\ **few**
\ā\ **take**	\ē\ **easy**	\ng\ **sing**	\th\ **this**	\yu̇\ **cure**
\ä\ **cot, cart**	\g\ **go**	\ō\ **bone**	\ü\ **food**	\zh\ **vision**

an official or solemn way ⟨the judge *pronounced* sentence⟩ **2** : to use the voice to make the sounds of ⟨*pronounce* these words⟩ **3** : to say correctly ⟨I can't *pronounce* your name⟩

pro·nounced \prə-'naúnst\ *adj* : very noticeable ⟨was walking with a *pronounced* limp⟩

pro·nun·ci·a·tion \prə-ˌnən-sē-'ā-shən\ *n* : the act or way of pronouncing a word or words

¹proof \'prüf\ *n* **1** : evidence of truth or correctness ⟨find *proof* of a statement⟩ **2** : ¹TEST 1 ⟨put a theory to the *proof*⟩ **3** : a printing (as from type) prepared for study and correction **4** : a test print made from a photographic negative

²proof *adj* : able to keep out something that could be harmful ⟨*proof* against tampering⟩ — usually used in compounds ⟨water*proof*⟩

proof·read \'prü-ˌfred\ *vb* **proof·read** \-ˌfred\; **proof·read·ing** \-ˌfred-ing\ : to read over and fix mistakes in (written or printed matter) ⟨*proofread* your paper before you hand it in⟩ — **proof·read·er** *n*

¹prop \'präp\ *n* : something that props or supports

²prop *vb* **propped; prop·ping 1** : to keep from falling or slipping by providing a support under or against **2** : to give help, encouragement, or support to

³prop *n* : PROPERTY 3

prop·a·gan·da \ˌpräp-ə-'gan-də\ *n* : an organized spreading of certain ideas or the ideas spread in such a way

prop·a·gate \'präp-ə-ˌgāt\ *vb* **prop·a·gat·ed; prop·a·gat·ing 1** : to have or cause to have offspring ⟨*propagate* a fine apple by grafting⟩ **2** : to cause (as an idea or belief) to spread out and affect a greater number or wider area ⟨*propagate* a faith⟩

prop·a·ga·tion \ˌpräp-ə-'gā-shən\ *n* : an act or process of propagating

pro·pel \prə-'pel\ *vb* **pro·pelled; pro·pel·ling** : to push or drive usually forward or onward ⟨*propel* a bicycle⟩

pro·pel·ler \prə-'pel-ər\ *n* : a device having a hub fitted with blades that is made to turn rapidly by an engine and that drives a ship, power boat, or airplane

prop·er \'präp-ər\ *adj* **1** : belonging naturally to something : SPECIAL ⟨every animal has its *proper* instincts⟩ **2** : considered without surrounding places, things, or events ⟨lived outside the city *proper*⟩ **3** : ¹RIGHT 1 ⟨the *proper* pay for the job⟩ **4** : obeying the social rules ⟨*proper* conduct⟩

proper fraction *n* : a fraction in which the numerator is smaller than the denominator

prop·er·ly \'präp-ər-lē\ *adv* **1** : in a fit or suitable way **2** : according to fact ⟨*properly* speaking, whales are not fish⟩

proper noun *n* : a noun that names a particular person, place, or thing ⟨"Tom," "Chicago," and "Friday" are *proper nouns*⟩

prop·er·ty \'präp-ərt-ē\ *n, pl* **prop·er·ties 1** : a special quality of a thing ⟨sweetness is a *property* of sugar⟩ **2** : something (as land or money) that is owned ⟨that chair is my aunt's *property*⟩ **3** : something other than scenery or costumes that is used in a play or movie

proph·e·cy \'präf-ə-sē\ *n, pl* **proph·e·cies 1** : the sayings of a prophet **2** : something foretold : PREDICTION

proph·e·sy \'präf-ə-ˌsī\ *vb* **proph·e·sied; proph·e·sy·ing 1** : to speak or write as a prophet **2** : FORETELL, PREDICT

proph·et \'präf-ət\ *n* **1** : one who declares publicly a message that one believes has come from God or a god **2** : a person who predicts the future

pro·phet·ic \prə-'fet-ik\ *adj* : of or relating to a prophet or prophecy

¹pro·por·tion \prə-'pōr-shən\ *n* **1** : the size, number, or amount of one thing or group of things as compared to that of another thing or group of things ⟨the *proportion* of boys to girls in our class is three to one⟩ **2** : a balanced or pleasing arrangement ⟨out of *proportion*⟩ **3** : a statement of the equality of two ratios (as ½ = ¹⁰⁄₂₀) **4** : a fair or just share ⟨did my *proportion* of the work⟩ **5** : DIMENSION ⟨a crisis of large *proportions*⟩

²proportion *vb* **1** : to adjust something to fit with something else **2** : to make the parts of fit well with each other

pro·por·tion·ate \prə-'pōr-shə-nət\ *adj* : being in proportion to something else — **pro·por·tion·ate·ly** *adv*

pro·pos·al \prə-'pō-zəl\ *n* **1** : a stating or putting forward of something for consideration **2** : something proposed : PLAN **3** : an offer of marriage

pro·pose \prə-'pōz\ *vb* **pro·posed; pro·pos·ing 1** : to make a suggestion to be thought over and talked about : SUGGEST **2** : to make plans : INTEND ⟨*propose* to buy a new house⟩ **3** : to suggest for filling a place or office ⟨*propose* someone for membership in the club⟩ **4** : to make an offer of marriage

prop·o·si·tion \ˌpräp-ə-'zish-ən\ *n* **1** : something proposed **2** : a statement to be proved, explained, or discussed

pro·pri·e·tor \prə-ˈprī-ət-ər\ *n* : a person who owns something : OWNER

pro·pri·ety \prə-ˈprī-ət-ē\ *n, pl* **pro·pri·eties** **1** : the quality or state of being proper **2** : correctness in manners or behavior ⟨behave with *propriety*⟩ **3 propri·eties** *pl* : the rules and customs of behavior followed by nice people

pro·pul·sion \prə-ˈpəl-shən\ *n* **1** : the act or process of propelling **2** : something that propels

pros *pl of* PRO

prose \ˈprōz\ *n* **1** : the ordinary language that people use in speaking or writing **2** : writing without the repeating rhythm that is used in verse

pros·e·cute \ˈpräs-i-ˌkyüt\ *vb* **pros·e·cut·ed; pros·e·cut·ing** **1** : to follow up to the end : keep at ⟨*prosecute* a war⟩ **2** : to carry on a legal action against an accused person to prove his or her guilt

pros·e·cu·tion \ˌpräs-i-ˈkyü-shən\ *n* **1** : the act of prosecuting especially a criminal case in court **2** : the one bringing charges of crime against a person being tried **3** : the state's lawyers in a criminal case ⟨the *prosecution* will try to prove it was murder⟩

pros·e·cu·tor \ˈpräs-i-ˌkyüt-ər\ *n* : a person who prosecutes especially a criminal case as lawyer for the state

¹pros·pect \ˈpräs-ˌpekt\ *n* **1** : a wide view ⟨a *prospect* of sea and land⟩ **2** : an imagining of something to come ⟨the *prospect* of a good time⟩ **3** : something that is waited for or expected : POSSIBILITY ⟨not much *prospect* of seeing them again⟩ **4** : a possible buyer or customer **5** : a likely candidate ⟨a presidential *prospect*⟩

²prospect *vb* : to explore especially for mineral deposits

pro·spec·tive \prə-ˈspek-tiv, ˈpräs-ˌpek-\ *adj* **1** : likely to come about ⟨*prospective* benefits⟩ **2** : likely to become ⟨a *prospective* buyer⟩ — **pro·spec·tive·ly** *adv*

pros·pec·tor \ˈpräs-ˌpek-tər\ *n* : a person who explores a region in search of valuable minerals (as metals or oil)

pros·per \ˈpräs-pər\ *vb* **1** : to succeed or make money in something one is doing **2** : ¹FLOURISH 1, THRIVE

pros·per·i·ty \präs-ˈper-ət-ē\ *n* : the state of being prosperous or successful

pros·per·ous \ˈpräs-pə-rəs\ *adj* **1** : having or showing success or financial good fortune **2** : strong and healthy in growth ⟨a *prosperous* crop⟩ — **pros·per·ous·ly** *adv*

¹pros·trate \ˈpräs-ˌtrāt\ *adj* **1** : stretched out with face on the ground **2** : spread out parallel to the ground ⟨a *prostrate* shrub⟩ **3** : lacking strength or energy ⟨*prostrate* with a cold⟩

²prostrate *vb* **pros·trat·ed; pros·trat·ing** **1** : to throw or put into a prostrate position **2** : to bring to a weak and powerless condition ⟨*prostrated* with grief⟩

pro·tect \prə-ˈtekt\ *vb* : to cover or shield from something that would destroy or injure : GUARD **synonyms** see DEFEND

pro·tec·tion \prə-ˈtek-shən\ *n* **1** : the act of protecting : the state of being protected **2** : a protecting person or thing

pro·tec·tive \prə-ˈtek-tiv\ *adj* : giving or meant to give protection — **pro·tec·tive·ly** *adv* — **pro·tec·tive·ness** *n*

pro·tec·tor \prə-ˈtek-tər\ *n* : a person or thing that protects or is intended to protect

pro·tein \ˈprō-ˌtēn\ *n* : a nutrient containing nitrogen that is found in all living plant or animal cells, is a necessary part of the diet, and is supplied especially by such foods as meat, milk, and eggs

¹pro·test \ˈprō-ˌtest\ *n* **1** : the act of protesting **2** : a complaint or objection against an idea, an act, or a way of doing things

²pro·test \prə-ˈtest\ *vb* **1** : to declare positively : ASSERT ⟨*protest* one's innocence⟩ **2** : to complain strongly about ⟨the fans *protested* the umpire's decision⟩ **synonyms** see OBJECT

¹Prot·es·tant \ˈprät-əs-tənt\ *n* : a member of a Christian church other than the Eastern Orthodox Church and the Roman Catholic Church

²Protestant *adj* : of or relating to Protestants

pro·ton \ˈprō-ˌtän\ *n* : a very small particle that occurs in the nucleus of every atom and has a positive charge of electricity

pro·to·plasm \ˈprōt-ə-ˌplaz-əm\ *n* : the usually colorless and jellylike living part of cells

pro·to·zo·an \ˌprōt-ə-ˈzō-ən\ *n* : any of a large group of mostly microscopic animals whose body is a single cell

pro·tract \prō-ˈtrakt\ *vb* : to make longer : draw out in time or space

pro·trac·tor \prō-ˈtrak-tər\ *n* : an instrument used for drawing and measuring angles

pro·trude \prō-ˈtrüd\ *vb* **pro·trud·ed; pro·trud·ing** : to stick out or cause to stick out

proud \ˈpraud\ *adj* **1** : having or showing

\ə\ abut	\au\ out	\i\ tip	\o\ saw	\u\ foot
\ər\ further	\ch\ chin	\ī\ life	\oi\ coin	\y\ yet
\a\ mat	\e\ pet	\j\ job	\th\ thin	\yü\ few
\ā\ take	\ē\ easy	\ng\ sing	\th\ this	\yu\ cure
\ä\ cot, cart	\g\ go	\ō\ bone	\ü\ food	\zh\ vision

a feeling that one is better than others : HAUGHTY **2** : having a feeling of pleasure or satisfaction : very pleased ⟨they were *proud* of their clever child⟩ **3** : having proper self-respect ⟨too *proud* to beg⟩ — **proud·ly** *adv*

prove \'prüv\ *vb* **proved; proved** *or* **prov·en** \'prü-vən\; **prov·ing 1** : to test by experiment or by a standard **2** : to convince others of the truth of something by showing the facts **3** : to test the answer to and check the way of solving an arithmetic problem

prov·erb \'präv-,ərb\ *n* : a short well-known saying containing a wise thought : MAXIM, ADAGE ⟨"haste makes waste" is a *proverb*⟩

pro·ver·bi·al \prə-'vər-bē-əl\ *adj* : of, relating to, or being a proverb — **pro·ver·bi·al·ly** *adv*

pro·vide \prə-'vīd\ *vb* **pro·vid·ed; pro·vid·ing 1** : to look out for or take care of beforehand ⟨*provide* for a rainy day⟩ **2** : to make as a condition ⟨the rules *provide* that all players must do good work in school⟩ **3** : to give something that is needed ⟨*provide* books⟩

pro·vid·ed \prə-'vīd-əd\ *conj* : IF **1** ⟨we'll start now *provided* you agree⟩

prov·i·dence \'präv-ə-dəns\ *n* **1** *often cap* : help or care from God or heaven **2** *cap* : God as the guide and protector of all human beings **3** : PRUDENCE, THRIFT

prov·ince \'präv-əns\ *n* **1** : a part of a country having a government of its own (as one of the divisions of the Dominion of Canada) **2 provinces** *pl* : the part or parts of a country far from the capital or chief city **3** : an area of activity or authority ⟨the *province* of science⟩

pro·vin·cial \prə-'vin-chəl\ *adj* **1** : of, relating to, or coming from a province **2** : lacking the social graces and sophistication of the city

¹pro·vi·sion \prə-'vizh-ən\ *n* **1** : the act of providing **2** : something done beforehand **3** : a stock or store of food — usually used in pl. ⟨lay in *provisions* for a holiday⟩ **4** : ¹CONDITION 1 ⟨the *provisions* of the contract⟩

²provision *vb* : to supply with provisions

prov·o·ca·tion \,präv-ə-'kā-shən\ *n* **1** : the act of provoking **2** : something that provokes

pro·voc·a·tive \prə-'väk-ət-iv\ *adj* : serving or likely to cause a reaction (as interest, curiosity, or anger) — **pro·voc·a·tive·ly** *adv*

pro·voke \prə-'vōk\ *vb* **pro·voked; pro·vok·ing 1** : to cause to become angry

⟨don't *provoke* the dog⟩ **2** : to bring about ⟨*provoke* a smile⟩

pro·vok·ing \prə-'vō-king\ *adj* : causing mild anger — **pro·vok·ing·ly** *adv*

prow \'praů\ *n* : the bow of a ship

prow·ess \'praů-əs\ *n* **1** : great bravery especially in battle **2** : very great ability

prowl \'praůl\ *vb* : to move about quietly and secretly like a wild animal hunting prey — **prowl·er** *n*

proxy \'präk-sē\ *n, pl* **prox·ies 1** : authority to act for another or a paper giving such authority **2** : a person with authority to act for another

prude \'prüd\ *n* : a person who cares too much about proper speech and conduct — **prud·ish** \-ish\ *adj*

pru·dence \'prüd-ns\ *n* : skill and good sense in taking care of oneself or of one's doings

pru·dent \'prüd-nt\ *adj* **1** : clever and careful in action or judgment **2** : careful in trying to avoid mistakes — **pru·dent·ly** *adv*

¹prune \'prün\ *n* : a dried plum

²prune *vb* **pruned; prun·ing 1** : to cut off dead or unwanted parts of a bush or tree **2** : to cut out useless or unwanted parts (as unnecessary words or phrases in a composition)

¹pry \'prī\ *vb* **pried; pry·ing** : to be nosy about something

²pry *vb* **pried; pry·ing 1** : to raise or open or try to do so with a lever **2** : to get at with great difficulty ⟨*pry* a secret out of a person⟩

pry·ing \'prī-ing\ *adj* : rudely nosy ⟨*prying* questions⟩

psalm \'säm, 'sälm\ *n* **1** : a sacred song or poem **2** *cap* : one of the hymns that make up the Old Testament Book of Psalms

psy·chi·a·trist \sə-'kī-ə-trəst, sī-\ *n* : a specialist in psychiatry

psy·chi·a·try \sə-'kī-ə-trē, sī-\ *n* : a branch of medicine dealing with problems of the mind, emotions, or behavior

psy·cho·log·i·cal \,sī-kə-'läj-i-kəl\ *adj* **1** : of or relating to psychology **2** : directed toward or meant to influence the mind ⟨*psychological* warfare⟩

psy·chol·o·gist \sī-'käl-ə-jəst\ *n* : a specialist in psychology

psy·chol·o·gy \sī-'käl-ə-jē\ *n* : the science that studies facts about the mind and its activities especially in human beings

pu·ber·ty \'pyü-bərt-ē\ *n* : the age at or period during which a person becomes able to reproduce sexually

¹pub·lic \'pəb-lik\ *adj* **1** : of or relating to the people as a whole ⟨*public* opinion⟩ **2**

: of, relating to, or working for a government or community ⟨*public* prosecutor⟩ ⟨holds *public* office⟩ **3** : open to all ⟨a *public* library⟩ **4** : known to many people : not kept secret ⟨the story became *public*⟩ **5** : WELL-KNOWN, PROMINENT ⟨*public* figures⟩ — **pub·lic·ly** *adv*

²**public** *n* **1** : the people as a whole ⟨open to the *public*⟩ **2** : a group of people having common interests ⟨a novelist's *public*⟩

pub·li·ca·tion \ˌpəb-lə-ˈkā-shən\ *n* **1** : the act or process of publishing **2** : a printed work (as a book or magazine) made for sale or distribution

pub·lic·i·ty \ˌpəb-ˈlis-ət-ē\ *n* **1** : public interest and approval **2** : something (as favorable news) used to attract public interest and approval

pub·li·cize \ˈpəb-lə-ˌsīz\ *vb* **pub·li·cized; pub·li·ciz·ing** : to give publicity to

public school *n* : a free school paid for by taxes and run by a local government

pub·lish \ˈpəb-lish\ *vb* **1** : to make widely known **2** : to bring printed works (as books) before the public usually for sale — **pub·lish·er** *n*

puck \ˈpək\ *n* : a rubber disk used in hockey

¹**puck·er** \ˈpək-ər\ *vb* : to draw or cause to draw up into folds or wrinkles ⟨*pucker* one's lips⟩

²**pucker** *n* : a fold or wrinkle in a normally even surface

pud·ding \ˈpu̇d-ing\ *n* : a soft spongy or creamy dessert

pud·dle \ˈpəd-l\ *n* : a very small pool (as of dirty or muddy water)

pudgy \ˈpəj-ē\ *adj* **pudg·i·er; pudg·i·est** : being short and plump : CHUBBY

pueb·lo \ˈpweb-lō\ *n, pl* **pueb·los** : an Indian village of Arizona or New Mexico made up of groups of stone or adobe houses with flat roofs

¹**Puer·to Ri·can** \ˌpwert-ə-ˈrē-kən, ˌpōrt-\ *adj* : of or relating to Puerto Rico or the Puerto Ricans

²**Puerto Rican** *n* : a person born or living in Puerto Rico

¹**puff** \ˈpəf\ *vb* **1** : to blow in short gusts **2** : to breathe hard : PANT **3** : to send out small whiffs or clouds (as of smoke) **4** : to swell up or become swollen with or as if with air ⟨the injured eye *puffed* up⟩ ⟨*puffed* out my cheeks⟩

²**puff** *n* **1** : a quick short sending or letting out of air, smoke, or steam ⟨*puffs* from a locomotive⟩ **2** : a slight swelling **3** : a soft pad for putting powder on the skin

puf·fin \ˈpəf-ən\ *n* : a seabird related to the auks that has a short thick neck and a deep grooved bill marked with several colors

puffin

puffy \ˈpəf-ē\ *adj* **puff·i·er; puff·i·est** **1** : blowing in puffs ⟨a *puffy* locomotive⟩ **2** : BREATHLESS 1 ⟨was still *puffy* after the long run⟩ **3** : somewhat swollen ⟨a *puffy* face⟩ **4** : like a puff : FLUFFY ⟨a *puffy* marshmallow pie⟩

pug \ˈpəg\ *n* **1** : a small dog having a thick body, a large round head, a square snout, a curled tail, and usually short hair **2** : a nose turning up at the tip and usually short and thick

pug

¹**pull** \ˈpu̇l\ *vb* **1** : to separate from a firm or a natural attachment ⟨*pull* a tooth⟩ ⟨*pull* up carrots⟩ **2** : to use force on so as to

\ə\ abut	\au̇\ out	\i\ tip	\ȯ\ saw	\u̇\ foot
\ər\ further	\ch\ chin	\ī\ life	\ȯi\ coin	\y\ yet
\a\ mat	\e\ pet	\j\ job	\th\ thin	\yü\ few
\ā\ take	\ē\ easy	\ng\ sing	\th\ this	\yu̇\ cure
\ä\ cot, cart	\g\ go	\ō\ bone	\ü\ food	\zh\ vision

cause or tend to cause movement toward the force ⟨*pulled* the rope⟩ ⟨*pulling* a wagon⟩ **3** : to stretch repeatedly ⟨*pull* taffy⟩ **4** : ¹MOVE 1 ⟨a train *pulling* out of the station⟩ **5** : to draw apart : TEAR, REND ⟨*pull* a flower to pieces⟩

²pull *n* **1** : the act or an instance of pulling ⟨two *pulls* on the cord⟩ **2** : the effort put forth in moving ⟨a long *pull* up the hill⟩ **3** : a device for pulling something **4** : a force that pulls ⟨the *pull* of gravity⟩

pul·let \'pul̇-ət\ *n* : a young hen

pul·ley \'pul̇-ē\ *n, pl* **pul·leys** : a wheel that has a grooved rim in which a belt, rope, or chain runs and that is used to change the direction of a pulling force and in combination to increase the force applied for lifting

pulley

pull·over \'pul̇-ˌō-vər\ *n* : a garment (as a sweater) that is put on by being pulled over the head

pull through *vb* : to survive a very difficult or dangerous period ⟨was seriously ill but *pulled through*⟩

pul·mo·nary \'pul̇-mə-ˌner-ē, 'pəl-\ *adj* : of or relating to the lungs

¹pulp \'pəlp\ *n* **1** : the soft juicy part of a fruit or vegetable ⟨the *pulp* of an orange⟩ **2** : a mass of vegetable matter from which the moisture has been squeezed **3** : the soft sensitive tissue inside a tooth **4** : a material prepared usually from wood or rags and used in making paper

²pulp *vb* : to make into a pulp

pul·pit \'pul̇-ˌpit\ *n* **1** : a raised place in which a clergyman stands while preaching or conducting a religious service **2** : preachers in general

pulp·wood \'pəlp-ˌwuḋ\ *n* : wood (as of aspen or spruce) from which wood pulp is made

pulpy \'pəl-pē\ *adj* **pulp·i·er; pulp·i·est** : like or made of pulp

pul·sate \'pəl-ˌsāt\ *vb* **pul·sat·ed; pul·sat·ing** : to have or show a pulse or beats

pul·sa·tion \ˌpəl-'sā-shən\ *n* : pulsating movement or action

pulse \'pəls\ *n* **1** : a regular beating or throbbing (as of the arteries) **2** : one complete beat of a pulse or the number of these in a given period (as a minute) ⟨exercise increases the *pulse*⟩

pul·ver·ize \'pəl-və-ˌrīz\ *vb* **pul·ver·ized; pul·ver·iz·ing** : to beat or grind into a powder or dust

pu·ma \'pyü-mə, 'pü-\ *n* : COUGAR

pum·ice \'pəm-əs\ *n* : a very light porous volcanic glass that is used in powder form for smoothing and polishing

pum·mel \'pəm-əl\ *vb* **pum·meled** *or* **pum·melled; pum·mel·ing** *or* **pum·mel·ling** : to strike again and again

¹pump \'pəmp\ *n* : a device for raising, moving, or compressing fluids

²pump *vb* **1** : to raise, move, or compress by using a pump ⟨*pump* water⟩ **2** : to free (as from water or air) by the use of a pump ⟨*pump* a boat dry⟩ **3** : to fill by using a pump ⟨*pump* up tires⟩ **4** : to draw, force, or drive onward in the manner of a pump ⟨heart *pumping* blood into the arteries⟩ **5** : to question again and again to find out something — **pump·er** *n*

pum·per·nick·el \'pəm-pər-ˌnik-əl\ *n* : a dark rye bread

pump·kin \'pəng-kən, 'pəmp-kən\ *n* : a large round orange or yellow fruit of a vine related to the squash vine that is used as a vegetable or as feed for farm animals

¹pun \'pən\ *n* : a form of joking in which a person uses a word in two senses

²pun *vb* **punned; pun·ning** : to make a pun

¹punch \'pənch\ *vb* **1** : to care for (range cattle) **2** : to strike with the fist **3** : to press or strike by or as if by punching ⟨*punch* a typewriter⟩ **4** : to pierce or stamp with a punch

²punch *n* : a blow with or as if with the fist

³punch *n* : a tool for piercing, stamping, or cutting

⁴punch *n* : a drink containing several things and often including wine or liquor

punc·tu·al \'pəngk-chə-wəl\ *adj* : acting at the right time : not late

punc·tu·ate \'pəngk-chə-ˌwāt\ *vb* **punc·tu·at·ed; punc·tu·at·ing** : to mark or divide with punctuation marks

punc·tu·a·tion \ˌpəngk-chə-'wā-shən\ *n* **1** : the act of punctuating **2** : a system of using marks (punctuation marks) such as commas and periods to make clear the meaning of written matter

¹punc·ture \'pəngk-chər\ *n* **1** : an act of puncturing **2** : a hole or wound made by puncturing

²puncture *vb* **punc·tured; punc·tur·ing** **1** : to pierce with something pointed **2** : to make useless or destroy as if by a puncture ⟨*puncture* an argument⟩

pun·gent \'pən-jənt\ *adj* : giving a sharp or biting sensation — **pun·gent·ly** *adv*

pun·ish \'pən-ish\ *vb* **1** : to make suffer for a fault or crime ⟨*punish* a child for lying⟩ **2**

: to make someone suffer for (as a crime) ⟨*punish* theft with prison⟩

synonyms PUNISH and DISCIPLINE mean to put a penalty on someone for doing wrong. PUNISH stresses the giving of some kind of pain or suffering to the wrongdoer rather than trying to reform the person ⟨*punished* the killers by ordering their deaths⟩ DISCIPLINE suggests penalizing the wrongdoer but stresses the effort to bring the person under control ⟨parents must *discipline* their children⟩

pun·ish·able \'pən-ish-ə-bəl\ *adj* : deserving to be punished ⟨a *punishable* offense⟩

pun·ish·ment \'pən-ish-mənt\ *n* **1** : the act of punishing : the state or fact of being punished **2** : the penalty for a fault or crime

¹punk \'pəngk\ *n* : a petty gangster or hoodlum

²punk *adj* **1** : poor in quality **2** : UNWELL, SICK ⟨feeling *punk* today⟩

¹punt \'pənt\ *vb* : to kick a ball dropped from the hands before it hits the ground — **punt·er** *n*

²punt *n* : an act or instance of punting a ball

pu·ny \'pyü-nē\ *adj* **pu·ni·er**; **pu·ni·est** : small and weak in size or power

Word History The English word *puny* first meant "younger" or "lower in rank" and came from an early French word that meant "younger." Someone who is younger than another person was, of course, born later. The French word meaning "younger" was made up of two words. The first of these two French words meant "afterward." The second meant "born."

pup \'pəp\ *n* **1** : PUPPY **2** : one of the young of any of several animals (as a seal)

pu·pa \'pyü-pə\ *n, pl* **pu·pae** \-,pē\ *or* **pu·pas** : an insect (as a bee, moth, or beetle) in an intermediate inactive stage of its growth in which it is enclosed in a cocoon or case

pu·pal \'pyü-pəl\ *adj* : of, relating to, or being a pupa

¹pu·pil \'pyü-pəl\ *n* : a child in school or under the care of a teacher

Word History The Latin word *pupilla* meant "girl." The English word *pupil* that means "a girl or boy in school" comes from that Latin word and a similar word that meant "boy." *Pupilla* is also the ancestor of our word for a pupil of the eye. In Latin this word meant "doll" as well as "girl." If you look in another person's eyes from close up, you can see yourself reflected. You will look like a little doll. That is why a word for a part of the eye was formed from a word meaning "doll" or "girl."

²pupil *n* : the opening in the iris through which light enters the eye

pup·pet \'pəp-ət\ *n* **1** : a doll moved by hand or by strings or wires **2** : one (as a person or government) whose acts are controlled by another

pup·py \'pəp-ē\ *n, pl* **pup·pies** : a young dog

¹pur·chase \'pər-chəs\ *vb* **pur·chased**; **pur·chas·ing** : to get by paying money

²purchase *n* **1** : an act of purchasing ⟨the *purchase* of supplies⟩ **2** : something purchased **3** : a firm hold or grasp or a safe place to stand ⟨could not get a *purchase* on the ledge⟩

pure \'pyùr\ *adj* **pur·er**; **pur·est** **1** : not mixed with anything else : free from everything that might injure or lower the quality ⟨*pure* water⟩ ⟨*pure* French⟩ **2** : free from sin : INNOCENT, CHASTE **3** : nothing other than : ABSOLUTE ⟨*pure* nonsense⟩ — **pure·ly** *adv* — **pure·ness** *n*

pure·bred \'pyùr-'bred\ *adj* : bred from ancestors of a single breed for many generations

¹purge \'pərj\ *vb* **purged**; **purg·ing** **1** : to make clean **2** : to have or cause frequent passage of loose or watery feces ⟨*purge* a person with castor oil⟩ **3** : to get rid of by a purge ⟨*purged* traitors from the party⟩

²purge *n* **1** : an act or instance of purging **2** : a getting rid of persons felt to be treacherous or disloyal **3** : something that purges

pu·ri·fi·ca·tion \,pyùr-ə-fə-'kā-shən\ *n* : an act or instance of purifying or of being purified

pu·ri·fy \'pyùr-ə-,fi\ *vb* **pu·ri·fied**; **pu·ri·fy·ing** : to make pure : free from impurities

pu·ri·tan \'pyùr-ət-n\ *n* **1** *cap* : a member of a sixteenth and seventeenth century Protestant group in England and New England opposing formal customs of the Church of England **2** : a person who practices or preaches or follows a stricter moral code than most people

\ə\ **abut**	\aù\ **out**	\i\ **tip**	\ò\ **saw**	\ù\ **foot**	
\ər\ **further**	\ch\ **chin**	\ī\ **life**	\òi\ **coin**	\y\ **yet**	
\a\ **mat**	\e\ **pet**	\j\ **job**	\th\ **thin**	\yü\ **few**	
\ā\ **take**	\ē\ **easy**	\ng\ **sing**	\th\ **this**	\yù\ **cure**	
\ä\ **cot, cart**	\g\ **go**	\ō\ **bone**	\ü\ **food**	\zh\ **vision**	

pu·ri·ty \'pyùr-ət-ē\ *n* **1** : freedom from dirt or impurities **2** : freedom from sin or guilt

pur·ple \'pər-pəl\ *n* : a color between red and blue

pur·plish \'pər-plish\ *adj* : somewhat purple

¹**pur·pose** \'pər-pəs\ *n* : something set up as a goal to be achieved : INTENTION, AIM — **on purpose** : PURPOSELY

²**purpose** *vb* **pur·posed; pur·pos·ing** : to have as one's intention : INTEND

pur·pose·ful \'pər-pəs-fəl\ *adj* : having a clear purpose or aim — **pur·pose·ful·ly** \-fə-lē\ *adv* — **pur·pose·ful·ness** *n*

pur·pose·ly \'pər-pəs-lē\ *adv* : with a clear or known purpose

purr \'pər\ *vb* : to make the low murmuring sound of a contented cat or a similar sound

¹**purse** \'pərs\ *n* **1** : a bag or pouch for money **2** : HANDBAG **3** : the contents of a purse : MONEY 1 **4** : a sum of money offered as a prize or collected as a present

²**purse** *vb* **pursed; purs·ing** : to draw into folds ⟨*purse* one's lips⟩

pur·sue \pər-'sü\ *vb* **pur·sued; pur·su·ing** **1** : to follow after in order to catch or destroy : CHASE ⟨*pursued* the retreating enemy⟩ **2** : to follow with an end in view ⟨*pursue* a wise course⟩ **3** : to go on with : FOLLOW ⟨*pursue* medical studies⟩ **syn·onyms** see CHASE — **pur·su·er** *n*

pur·suit \pər-'süt\ *n* **1** : the act of pursuing **2** : ACTIVITY 2, OCCUPATION

pus \'pəs\ *n* : thick yellowish matter (as in an abscess or a boil)

¹**push** \'pùsh\ *vb* **1** : to press against with force so as to drive or move away ⟨*push* a car to get it started⟩ **2** : to force forward, downward, or outward ⟨a tree *pushing* its roots deep in the soil⟩ **3** : to go or make go ahead ⟨*push* a task to completion⟩

²**push** *n* **1** : a sudden thrust : SHOVE ⟨gave it a *push* and it fell over⟩ **2** : a steady applying of force in a direction away from the body from which it comes ⟨gave the car a *push* up the hill⟩

push button *n* : a small button or knob that when pushed operates something usually by closing an electric circuit

push·cart \'pùsh-,kärt\ *n* : a cart pushed by hand

push·over \'pùsh-,ō-vər\ *n* **1** : an opponent that is easy to defeat ⟨thought the first team they played would be a *pushover*⟩ **2** : something easily done ⟨the exam was a *pushover*⟩

pushy \'pùsh-ē\ *adj* **push·i·er; push·i·est** : too aggressive : FORWARD

puss \'pùs\ *n* : CAT 1

pussy \'pùs-ē\ *n, pl* **puss·ies** : CAT 1

pussy willow \,pùs-ē-\ *n* : a willow with large silky catkins

put \'pùt\ *vb* **put; put·ting** **1** : to place in or move into a particular position ⟨*put* the book on the table⟩ ⟨*put* your hand up⟩ **2** : to bring into a specified state or condition ⟨*puts* the money to good use⟩ ⟨*put* the room in order⟩ **3** : to cause to stand for or suffer something ⟨was *put* to death⟩ ⟨*puts* them to shame⟩ **4** : to give expression to ⟨*put* my fear into words⟩ ⟨*puts* the idea clearly⟩ **5** : to give up to or urge to an activity ⟨if they *put* their minds to it⟩ ⟨*putting* us to work⟩ **6** : to think something to have : ATTRIBUTE ⟨*puts* a high value on peace⟩ **7** : to begin a voyage ⟨the ship *put* to sea⟩ — **put forward** : PROPOSE 1 ⟨*put forward* a new plan⟩

put away *vb* **1** : to give up : DISCARD ⟨*put away* foolish habits⟩ **2** : to take in food and drink ⟨*put away* a big dinner⟩

put by *vb* : to lay aside : SAVE ⟨*put by* money for fuel⟩

put down *vb* **1** : to bring to an end by force ⟨*put down* a riot⟩ **2** : to consider to belong to a particular class or to be due to a particular cause ⟨*put* them *down* as lazy⟩ ⟨we *put* our trouble *down* to carelessness⟩

put in *vb* **1** : to ask for ⟨*put in* for a job at the school⟩ **2** : to spend time in a place or activity ⟨*put in* six hours at school⟩

put off *vb* : DEFER ⟨*put off* an appointment⟩

put on *vb* **1** : to dress oneself in ⟨*put* a new jacket *on*⟩ **2** : PRETEND 2, SHAM ⟨*put on* a show of anger⟩ **3** : ¹PRODUCE 4 ⟨*put on* the senior play⟩

put·out \'pùt-,aùt\ *n* : the causing of a batter or runner to be out in baseball

put out \'pùt-'aùt\ *vb* **1** : to make use of ⟨*put out* a real effort to succeed⟩ **2** : EXTINGUISH 1 ⟨be sure to *put out* the light⟩ **3** : ¹MAKE 2 ⟨the factory *puts out* fine cloth⟩ **4** : IRRITATE 1, ANNOY ⟨I was very *put out* by the sharp answer⟩ **5** : to cause to be out (as in baseball) ⟨was *put out* at third base⟩

pussy willow

pu·trid \'pyü-trəd\ *adj* **1** : ROTTEN 1 ⟨*putrid* meat⟩ **2** : coming from or suggesting something rotten ⟨a *putrid* smell⟩

put·ter \'pət-ər\ *vb* : to act or work without much purpose ⟨*puttering* around the garden⟩

put through *vb* : to conclude with success ⟨*put through* a needed reform⟩

¹put·ty \'pət-ē\ *n, pl* **put·ties** : a soft cement (as for holding glass in a window frame)

²putty *vb* **put·tied; put·ty·ing** : to cement or seal up with putty

put up *vb* **1** : to make (as food) ready or safe for later use ⟨*put up* a lunch⟩ ⟨*put* vegetables *up* for winter⟩ **2** : NOMINATE ⟨*put* a candidate *up*⟩ **3** : to give or get shelter and often food ⟨*put* tourists *up*⟩ ⟨we *put up* at a motel⟩ **4** : ¹BUILD 1 ⟨*put up* a new school⟩ **5** : to make by action or effort ⟨*put up* a good fight⟩ — **put up to** : to urge or cause to do something wrong or unexpected ⟨we were the ones who *put* the others *up to* mischief⟩ — **put up with** : to stand for : TOLERATE ⟨the coach won't *put up with* any nonsense⟩

¹puz·zle \'pəz-əl\ *vb* **puz·zled; puz·zling** **1** : CONFUSE 1, PERPLEX ⟨*puzzled* by the answer⟩ **2** : to solve by thought or by clever guessing ⟨*puzzle* out a mystery⟩

²puzzle *n* **1** : something that puzzles : MYSTERY **2** : a question, problem, or device intended to test one's skill or cleverness

¹pyg·my *also* **pig·my** \'pig-mē\ *n, pl* **pyg·mies** *also* **pig·mies** : a person or thing very small for its kind : DWARF

²pygmy *adj* : very small

¹pyr·a·mid \'pir-ə-ˌmid\ *n* **1** : a large structure built especially in ancient Egypt that usually has a square base and four triangular sides meeting at a point and that contains tombs **2** : something that has the shape of a pyramid **3** : a solid with a polygon for its base and three or more triangles for its sides which meet to form the top

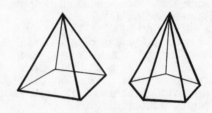

pyramids

²pyramid *vb* : to build up in the form of a pyramid

pyre \'pīr\ *n* : a heap of wood for burning a dead body

py·thon \'pī-ˌthän\ *n* : any of various large snakes of the Old World tropics that are related to the boas

q \'kyü\ *n, pl* **q's** *or* **qs** \'kyüz\ *often cap* : the seventeenth letter of the English alphabet

¹quack \'kwak\ *vb* : to make the cry of a duck

²quack *n* : a cry made by or as if by quacking

³quack *n* : an ignorant person who pretends to have medical knowledge and skill

⁴quack *adj* **1** : of, relating to, or like that of a quack **2** : pretending to cure disease ⟨*quack* remedies⟩

quad·ri- \'kwäd-rə\ *or* **quadr-** *or* **quad·ru-** \'kwäd-rə\ *prefix* **1** : four **2** : fourth

quad·ri·lat·er·al \ˌkwäd-rə-'lat-ə-rəl\ *n* : a figure of four sides and four angles

quad·ru·ped \'kwäd-rə-ˌped\ *n* : an animal having four feet

qua·dru·plet \kwä-'drüp-lət, -'drəp-\ *n* **1** : one of four offspring born at one birth **2** : a combination of four of a kind

¹quail \'kwāl\ *n, pl* **quail** *or* **quails** : any of

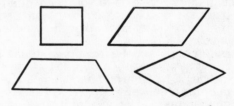

quadrilateral

various mostly small plump game birds (as the bobwhite) that are related to the chicken

²quail *vb* : to lose courage : shrink in fear

quaint \'kwānt\ *adj* **1** : being or looking unusual or different **2** : pleasingly old-fashioned or unfamiliar — **quaint·ly** *adv* — **quaint·ness** *n*

¹quake \'kwāk\ *vb* **quaked; quak·ing 1** : to shake usually from shock or lack of stability **2** : to tremble or shudder usually from cold or fear

²quake *n* : an instance (as an earthquake) of shaking or trembling

qual·i·fi·ca·tion \,kwäl-ə-fə-'kā-shən\ *n* **1** : the act or an instance of qualifying **2** : the state of being qualified **3** : a special skill, knowledge, or ability that fits a person for a particular work or position ⟨lacks the *qualifications* for teaching⟩ **4** : LIMITATION 1 ⟨agree without *qualification*⟩

qual·i·fy \'kwäl-ə-,fī\ *vb* **qual·i·fied; qual·i·fy·ing 1** : to narrow down or make less general in meaning : LIMIT ⟨*qualify* a statement⟩ ⟨adjectives *qualify* nouns⟩ **2** : to make less harsh or strict : SOFTEN ⟨*qualify* a punishment⟩ **3** : to fit by training, skill, or ability for a special purpose **4** : to show the skill or ability needed to be on a team or take part in a contest

qual·i·ty \'kwäl-ət-ē\ *n, pl* **qual·i·ties 1** : basic and individual nature ⟨know the *quality* of one's actions⟩ **2** : how good or bad something is ⟨food of excellent *quality*⟩ **3** : high social rank ⟨a person of *quality*⟩ **4** : what sets a person or thing apart : CHARACTERISTIC ⟨the salty *quality* of the water⟩

qualm \'kwäm, 'kwälm\ *n* **1** : a sudden attack of illness, faintness, or nausea **2** : a sudden fear **3** : a feeling of doubt or uncertainty that one's behavior is honest or right — **qualm·ish** \-ish\ *adj*

quan·da·ry \'kwän-də-rē, -drē\ *n, pl* **quan·da·ries** : a state of doubt or puzzled confusion ⟨in a *quandary* about what to do⟩

quan·ti·ty \'kwänt-ət-ē\ *n, pl* **quan·ti·ties 1** : ²AMOUNT, NUMBER ⟨a *quantity* of information⟩ **2** : a large number or amount ⟨a *quantity* of shoes⟩ ⟨*quantities* of money⟩

¹quar·an·tine \'kwȯr-ən-,tēn\ *n* **1** : a halting or forbidding of the moving of people or things out of a certain area to prevent the spread of disease or pests **2** : a period during which a person with a contagious disease is under quarantine **3** : a place (as a hospital) where persons are kept in quarantine

Word History Sometimes a ship comes to a port from another place where there is disease or pests. The ship is often kept apart for a time. No one may go ashore and no goods may be taken off until it is certain that the ship is not carrying the disease or pests. The time for keeping the ship apart was once forty days. This period was called *quarantine*, a word that came from an Italian word. The Italian word came from a French word that meant "a period of forty days."

²quarantine *vb* **quar·an·tined; quar·an·tin·ing** : to put or hold in quarantine

¹quar·rel \'kwȯr-əl\ *n* **1** : a cause of disagreement or complaint **2** : an angry difference of opinion

²quarrel *vb* **quar·reled** *or* **quar·relled; quar·rel·ing** *or* **quar·rel·ling 1** : to find fault **2** : to argue actively : SQUABBLE

quar·rel·some \'kwȯr-əl-səm\ *adj* : usually ready to quarrel

¹quar·ry \'kwȯr-ē\ *n, pl* **quar·ries** : an animal or bird hunted as game or prey

Word History There were hunters long ago, just as there are today. They rewarded their dogs each time they made a kill. The dogs' reward was a part of the slain beast's intestines. The French had a word for this portion fed to the dogs. This French word was taken into English. In time the word for the intestines was used for the hunted beast itself. This early word became our modern English *quarry*.

²quarry *n, pl* **quar·ries** : an open pit usually for obtaining building stone, slate, or limestone

Word History This word is not related to the word *quarry* that means "game" or "prey." Quarries provide stones for building. Such stones are usually squared. The English word *quarry* comes from a French word meaning "quarry" that came from a word meaning "squared stone." The source of this word was a Latin word that meant "square."

³quarry *vb* **quar·ried; quar·ry·ing 1** : to dig or take from or as if from a quarry **2** : to make a quarry in — **quar·ri·er** *n*

quart \'kwȯrt\ *n* : a measure of capacity that equals two pints (about .95 liter)

¹quar·ter \'kwȯrt-ər\ *n* **1** : one of four equal parts into which something can be divided **2** : a United States coin worth twenty-five cents **3** : someone or something (as a place, direction, or group) not clearly identified ⟨expects trouble from another *quarter*⟩ **4** : a particular division or district of a city **5 quarters** *pl* : a dwelling place ⟨winter *quarters*⟩ **6** : MERCY 1 ⟨show no *quarter* to the enemy⟩

²**quarter** *vb* **1** : to divide into four usually equal parts **2** : to provide with lodgings or shelter

³**quarter** *adj* : consisting of or equal to a quarter ⟨give it a *quarter* turn⟩

quar·ter·deck \'kwȯrt-ər-ˌdek\ *n* : the part of the upper deck that is located toward the rear of a ship

quarter horse *n* : a stocky muscular saddle horse capable of high speed over short distances

quarter horse

¹**quar·ter·ly** \'kwȯrt-ər-lē\ *adv* : four times a year ⟨interest compounded *quarterly*⟩

²**quarterly** *adj* : coming or happening every three months ⟨a *quarterly* meeting⟩

³**quarterly** *n, pl* **quar·ter·lies** : a magazine published four times a year

quar·ter·mas·ter \'kwȯrt-ər-ˌmas-tər\ *n* : an army officer who provides clothing and supplies for troops

quar·tet *also* **quar·tette** \kwȯr-'tet\ *n* : a group or set of four

quartz \'kwȯrts\ *n* : a common mineral often found in the form of colorless transparent crystals but sometimes (as in amethysts, agates, and jaspers) brightly colored

qua·ver \'kwā-vər\ *vb* **1** : ¹TREMBLE 1, SHAKE ⟨*quavering* inwardly⟩ **2** : to sound in shaky tones ⟨my voice *quavered*⟩

quay \'kē, 'kwā\ *n* : a paved bank or a solid artificial landing for loading and unloading ships

quea·sy \'kwē-zē\ *adj* **quea·si·er; quea·si·est 1** : somewhat nauseated **2** : full of doubt

queen \'kwēn\ *n* **1** : the wife or widow of a king **2** : a woman who rules a kingdom in her own right **3** : a woman of high rank, power, or attractiveness ⟨a society

queen⟩ **4** : the most powerful piece in the game of chess **5** : a playing card bearing the figure of a queen **6** : a fully developed adult female of social bees, ants, or termites — **queen·ly** *adj*

queer \'kwiər\ *adj* : oddly unlike the usual or normal ⟨a *queer* smell⟩ — **queer·ly** *adv*

quell \'kwel\ *vb* **1** : to put down by force ⟨*quell* a riot⟩ **2** : ⁴QUIET 1, CALM ⟨*quelled* their fears⟩

quench \'kwench\ *vb* **1** : to put out (as a fire) **2** : to end by satisfying ⟨*quenched* my thirst⟩

¹**que·ry** \'kwiər-ē, 'kweər-ē\ *n, pl* **que·ries 1** : ¹QUESTION 1 **2** : a question in the mind : DOUBT

²**query** *vb* **que·ried; que·ry·ing 1** : to put as a question ⟨*queried* it to their teacher⟩ **2** : to ask questions about especially in order to clear up a doubt ⟨*queried* the proceeding⟩ **3** : to ask questions of especially to obtain official or expert information ⟨*query* the professor⟩

¹**quest** \'kwest\ *n* : an act or instance of seeking : SEARCH ⟨in *quest* of fame⟩

²**quest** *vb* : to search for

¹**ques·tion** \'kwes-chən\ *n* **1** : something asked ⟨try to make your *questions* short⟩ **2** : a topic discussed or argued about ⟨an important *question* of the day⟩ **3** : a suggestion to be voted on ⟨put the *question* to the members⟩ **4** : an act or instance of asking **5** : OBJECTION 1, DISPUTE ⟨obey without *question*⟩

²**question** *vb* **1** : to ask questions of or about **2** : to doubt the correctness of ⟨*question* a decision⟩

ques·tion·able \'kwes-chə-nə-bəl\ *adj* **1** : not certain or exact : DOUBTFUL **2** : not believed to be true, sound, or proper ⟨*questionable* motives⟩

question mark *n* : a punctuation mark ? used chiefly at the end of a sentence to indicate a direct question

ques·tion·naire \ˌkwes-chə-'naər, -'neər\ *n* : a set of questions to be asked of a number of persons to collect facts about knowledge or opinions

¹**queue** \'kyü\ *n* **1** : PIGTAIL **2** : a waiting line ⟨a *queue* at a ticket window⟩

Word History The English word *queue* comes from a French word that means "tail." A long braid of hair worn at the back

\ə\ abut	\au̇\ out	\i\ tip	\ȯ\ saw	\u̇\ foot
\ər\ further	\ch\ chin	\ī\ life	\ȯi\ coin	\y\ yet
\a\ mat	\e\ pet	\j\ job	\th\ thin	\yü\ few
\ā\ take	\ē\ easy	\ng\ sing	\th\ this	\yu̇\ cure
\ä\ cot, cart	\g\ go	\ō\ bone	\ü\ food	\zh\ vision

of the head looks rather like a tail. A long line of people waiting for something must also have reminded someone of a tail. The French word meaning "tail" came to be used for a pigtail and a waiting line as well. The English word *queue* that comes from this French word does not mean "tail." It does mean "pigtail" or "waiting line."

²queue *vb* **queued; queu·ing** *or* **queue·ing** : to form or line up in a queue ⟨*queuing* up for tickets⟩

quib·ble \'kwib-əl\ *vb* **quib·bled; quib·bling 1** : to talk about unimportant things rather than the main point **2** : to find fault especially over unimportant points — **quib·bler** \'kwib-lər\ *n*

¹quick \'kwik\ *adj* **1** : very swift : SPEEDY ⟨*quick* steps⟩ **2** : mentally alert **3** : easily stirred up ⟨*quick* temper⟩ — **quick·ly** *adv* — **quick·ness** *n*

synonyms QUICK, PROMPT, and READY mean able to respond right away. QUICK stresses that the response is immediate and often suggests the ability is part of one's nature ⟨always had a *quick* mind⟩ PROMPT suggests that the ability to respond quickly is the product of training and discipline ⟨the store gives *prompt* service⟩ READY suggests ease or smoothness in response ⟨always had a *ready* answer to every question⟩

Word History The word *quick* first meant "alive." Most animals that are alive can move and run, so *quick* came to mean "moving" or "running." From this sense came the sense of *quick* that is most familiar today: "fast." New senses have come from this common sense. *Quick* means "alert," which is "fast in understanding." *Quick* means "sensitive," "reacting fast." *Quick* means "aroused fast or easily."

²quick *adv* : in a quick manner : FAST

³quick *n* **1** : a very tender area of flesh (as under a fingernail) **2** : one's innermost feelings ⟨hurt to the *quick* by the remark⟩

quick·en \'kwik-ən\ *vb* **1** : REVIVE 1 2 : AROUSE 2 ⟨curiosity *quickened* my interest⟩ **3** : to make or become quicker : HASTEN ⟨*quickened* their steps⟩ **4** : to begin or show active growth

quick·sand \'kwik-,sand\ *n* : a deep mass of loose sand mixed with water into which heavy objects sink

quick·sil·ver \'kwik-,sil-vər\ *n* : MERCURY 1

Word History The metal mercury has a color like silver. Most metals are solid but this one is not. Mercury moves and flows and acts almost as if it were alive. The word *quick* once meant "alive" or "moving." This is why mercury was given the name *quicksilver*.

quick–tem·pered \'kwik-'tem-pərd\ *adj* : easily made angry

quick–wit·ted \'kwik-'wit-əd\ *adj* : mentally alert

¹qui·et \'kwī-ət\ *n* : the quality or state of being quiet

²quiet *adj* **1** : marked by little or no motion or activity : CALM **2** : GENTLE 2, MILD ⟨a *quiet* disposition⟩ **3** : not disturbed : PEACEFUL ⟨a *quiet* lunch⟩ **4** : free from noise or uproar : STILL ⟨a *quiet* day⟩ **5** : not showy (as in color or style) **6** : SECLUDED ⟨a *quiet* nook⟩ — **qui·et·ly** *adv* — **qui·et·ness** *n*

³quiet *adv* : in a quiet manner : QUIETLY

⁴quiet *vb* **1** : to cause to be quiet : CALM ⟨*quieted* the crowd⟩ **2** : to become quiet ⟨*quieted* down after an exciting day⟩

qui·e·tude \'kwī-ə-,tüd, -,tyüd\ *n* : the state of being quiet : REST

quill \'kwil\ *n* **1** : a large stiff feather **2** : the hollow tubelike part of a feather **3** : a spine of a hedgehog or porcupine **4** : a pen made from a feather

¹quilt \'kwilt\ *n* : a bed cover made of two pieces of cloth with a filling of wool, cotton, or down held together by patterned stitching

²quilt *vb* : to stitch or sew together as in making a quilt

quince \'kwins\ *n* : a hard yellow fruit that grows on a shrubby tree related to the apple and is used especially in preserves

qui·nine \'kwī-,nīn\ *n* : a bitter drug obtained from cinchona bark and used to treat malaria

quin·tet \kwin-'tet\ *n* : a group or set of five

quince

quin·tup·let \kwin-'təp-lət, -'tüp-\ *n* **1** : a combination of five of a kind **2** : one of five offspring born at one birth

quirk \'kwərk\ *n* : a sudden turn, twist, or curve

quit \'kwit\ *vb* **quit; quit·ting** : to finish doing, using, dealing with, working on, or handling : LEAVE ⟨*quit* a job⟩

quite \'kwīt\ *adv* **1** : beyond question or doubt : COMPLETELY ⟨*quite* alone⟩ ⟨*quite* sure⟩ **2** : more or less : RATHER ⟨we live *quite* near the school⟩

quit·ter \'kwit-ər\ *n* : a person who gives up too easily

¹**quiv·er** \'kwiv-ər\ *n* : a case for carrying arrows

²**quiver** *vb* : to move with a slight trembling motion ⟨leaves *quivering* in the breeze⟩

³**quiver** *n* : the act or action of quivering ⟨the *quiver* of a leaf⟩

¹**quiz** \'kwiz\ *n, pl* **quiz·zes** : a short oral or written test ⟨a *quiz* in history⟩

²**quiz** *vb* **quizzed; quiz·zing** : to ask a lot of questions of

quoit \'kwāt, 'kwȯit\ *n* : a ring (as of rope) tossed at a peg in a game (**quoits**)

quo·rum \'kwȯr-əm\ *n* : the number of members of a group needed at a meeting in order for business to be legally carried on

quo·ta \'kwōt-ə\ *n* : a share assigned to each member of a group ⟨the *quota* of delegates from each state⟩

quo·ta·tion \kwō-'tā-shən\ *n* **1** : material (as a passage from a book) that is quoted **2** : the act or process of quoting

quotation mark *n* : one of a pair of punctuation marks " " or ' ' used chiefly to indicate the beginning and end of a direct quotation

quote \'kwōt\ *vb* **quot·ed; quot·ing** : to repeat (someone else's words) exactly ⟨*quote* a favorite poem⟩ ⟨*quote* the president's speech⟩

Word History Sometimes passages in books are numbered. The English word *quote* came from a Latin word that meant "to refer to a passage by number." The meaning of the English word is not quite the same. English *quote* means "to repeat the words of a passage exactly." The idea of number has been lost.

quo·tient \'kwō-shənt\ *n* : the number obtained by dividing one number by another

quiver

r \'är\ *n, pl* **r's** *or* **rs** \'ärz\ *often cap* : the eighteenth letter of the English alphabet

rab·bi \'rab-ˌī\ *n, pl* **rab·bis** **1** : ¹MASTER 1, TEACHER — used as a term of address for Jewish religious leaders **2** : a professionally trained leader of a Jewish congregation

rab·bit \'rab-ət\ *n* : a gnawing mammal that burrows and is smaller and has shorter ears than the related hare

rab·ble \'rab-əl\ *n* **1** : a crowd that is noisy and hard to control : MOB **2** : a group of people looked down upon as ignorant and hard to handle

ra·bid \'rab-əd, 'rā-bəd\ *adj* **1** : very angry : FURIOUS **2** : going to extreme lengths (as in interest or opinion) **3** : affected with rabies ⟨a *rabid* dog⟩ — **ra·bid·ly** *adv* — **ra·bid·ness** *n*

ra·bies \'rā-bēz\ *n* : HYDROPHOBIA

rac·coon \ra-'kün\ *n* : a small North American animal that lives in trees, eats flesh, is active mostly at night, and is sometimes hunted for sport, for its edible flesh, or for its coat of long fluffy fur

raccoon

\ə\ abut	\au̇\ out	\i\ tip	\ȯ\ saw	\u̇\ foot
\ər\ further	\ch\ chin	\ī\ life	\ȯi\ coin	\y\ yet
\a\ mat	\e\ pet	\j\ job	\th\ thin	\yü\ few
\ā\ take	\ē\ easy	\ng\ sing	\t̲h\ this	\yu̇\ cure
\ä\ cot, cart	\g\ go	\ō\ bone	\ü\ food	\zh\ vision

¹race \'rās\ *n* **1** : a strong or rapid current of water **2** : a contest of speed **3** : a contest involving progress toward a goal ⟨the *race* for the presidency⟩

²race *vb* **raced; rac·ing** **1** : to take part in a race **2** : to go, move, or drive at top speed **3** : to cause an engine of a motor vehicle in neutral to run fast

³race *n* **1** : a group of individuals with the same ancestors **2** : one of the three, four, or five great divisions based on easily seen things (as skin color) into which human beings are usually divided ⟨the black *race*⟩

race·course \'rā-,skórs\ *n* : a place for racing

race·horse \'rās-,hórs\ *n* : a horse bred or kept for racing

rac·er \'rā-sər\ *n* **1** : one that races or is used for racing **2** : any of several long slender active snakes (as a common American blacksnake)

race·track \'rā-,strak\ *n* : a usually oval course on which races are run

ra·cial \'rā-shəl\ *adj* : of, relating to, or based on race — **ra·cial·ly** *adv*

¹rack \'rak\ *n* **1** : an instrument of torture for stretching the body **2** : a frame or stand for storing or displaying things ⟨a magazine *rack*⟩ ⟨a hat *rack*⟩

²rack *vb* **1** : to cause to suffer torture, pain, or sorrow **2** : to stretch or strain violently

¹rack·et \'rak-ət\ *n* : a light bat consisting of a handle and a frame with a netting stretched tight across it

²racket *n* **1** : a loud confused noise **2** : a dishonest scheme for obtaining money (as by cheating or threats)

rack·e·teer \,rak-ə-'tiər\ *n* : a person who gets money or advantages by using force or threats

racy \'rā-sē\ *adj* **rac·i·er; rac·i·est** : full of energy or keen enjoyment

ra·dar \'rā-,där\ *n* : a radio device for detecting the position of things in the distance and the direction of moving objects (as distant airplanes or ships)

ra·di·ance \'rād-ē-əns\ *n* : the quality or state of being radiant : SPLENDOR

ra·di·ant \'rād-ē-ənt\ *adj* **1** : giving out or reflecting rays of light ⟨the *radiant* sun⟩ **2** : glowing with love, confidence, or joy ⟨a *radiant* smile⟩ **3** : transmitted by radiation **synonyms** see BRIGHT

radiant energy *n* : energy sent out in the form of electromagnetic waves ⟨heat, light, radio waves are forms of *radiant energy*⟩

ra·di·ate \'rād-ē-,āt\ *vb* **ra·di·at·ed; ra·di·at·ing** **1** : to send out rays : SHINE **2** : to come forth in the form of rays ⟨light *radi-*

ates from shining bodies⟩ **3** : to spread around from or as if from a center ⟨the news *radiated* through the crowd⟩

ra·di·a·tion \,rād-ē-'ā-shən\ *n* **1** : the process of radiating and especially of giving off radiant energy in the form of waves or particles **2** : something that is radiated

ra·di·a·tor \'rād-ē-,āt-ər\ *n* : a device to heat air (as in a room) or to cool an object (as an automobile engine)

¹rad·i·cal \'rad-i-kəl\ *adj* **1** : departing sharply from the usual or ordinary : EXTREME ⟨a *radical* change⟩ **2** : of or relating to radicals in politics — **rad·i·cal·ly** *adv*

Word History The English word *radical* which first meant "of a root" comes from a Latin word meaning "root." Since we can speak of the source or origin of something as its root, *radical* came to mean "of the origin." Later, since an extreme change can be said to go to the root of something, *radical* also came to mean "extreme."

²radical *n* : a person who favors rapid and sweeping changes especially in laws and methods of government

radii *pl of* RADIUS

¹ra·dio \'rād-ē-,ō\ *n, pl* **ra·di·os** **1** : the sending or receiving of signals by means of electromagnetic waves without a connecting wire **2** : a radio receiving set **3** : a radio message **4** : the radio broadcasting industry

²radio *adj* **1** : of or relating to radiant energy **2** : of, relating to, or used in radio

³radio *vb* : to communicate or send a message to by radio

ra·dio·ac·tive \,rād-ē-ō-'ak-tiv\ *adj* : of, caused by, or exhibiting radioactivity

ra·dio·ac·tiv·i·ty \,rād-ē-ō-ak-'tiv-ət-ē\ *n* : the giving off of rays of energy or particles by the breaking apart of atoms of certain elements (as uranium)

radio astronomy *n* : astronomy dealing with electromagnetic waves of radio frequency received from outside the earth's atmosphere — **radio astronomer** *n*

radio wave *n* : an electromagnetic wave used in radio, television, or radar communication

rad·ish \'rad-ish\ *n* : the fleshy edible root of a plant related to the mustards

ra·di·um \'rād-ē-əm\ *n* : a strongly radioactive element found in very small quantities in various minerals (as pitchblende) and used in the treatment of cancer

ra·di·us \'rād-ē-əs\ *n, pl* **ra·dii** \-ē-,ī\ **1** : the bone on the thumb side of the human forearm or a corresponding bone in lower forms **2** : a straight line extending from the center of a circle to the circumference or from the center of a sphere to the surface **3** : a nearly circular area defined by a radius ⟨within a *radius* of one kilometer from the school⟩

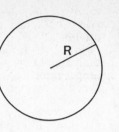

radius 2

raf·fle \'raf-əl\ *n* : the sale of chances for a prize whose winner is the one whose ticket is picked at a drawing

¹**raft** \'raft\ *n* : a flat structure (as a group of logs fastened together) for support or transportation on water

²**raft** *n* : a large amount or number

raf·ter \'raf-tər\ *n* : one of the usually sloping timbers that support a roof

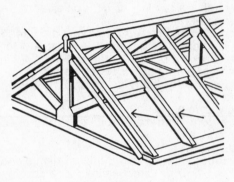

rafter

rag \'rag\ *n* **1** : a waste or worn piece of cloth **2 rags** *pl* : shabby clothing

rag·a·muf·fin \'rag-ə-ˌməf-ən\ *n* : a poorly clothed and often dirty child

¹**rage** \'rāj\ *n* **1** : very strong and uncontrolled anger : FURY **2** : violent action (as of wind or sea) **3** : FAD ⟨the current *rage*⟩ **synonyms** see ANGER

²**rage** *vb* **raged; rag·ing** **1** : to be in a rage **2** : to continue out of control ⟨the fire *raged* for hours⟩

rag·ged \'rag-əd\ *adj* **1** : having a rough or uneven edge or outline ⟨*ragged* cliffs⟩ **2** : very worn : TATTERED ⟨*ragged* clothes⟩ **3** : wearing tattered clothes **4** : done in an uneven way ⟨a *ragged* performance⟩ — **rag·ged·ly** *adv* — **rag·ged·ness** *n*

rag·gedy \'rag-əd-ē\ *adj* : RAGGED 2, 3

rag·time \'rag-ˌtīm\ *n* : jazz music that has a lively melody and a march-like rhythm

rag·weed \'rag-ˌwēd\ *n* : a common coarse weed with pollen that irritates the eyes and noses of some persons

¹**raid** \'rād\ *n* : a sudden attack or invasion

²**raid** *vb* : to make a raid on — **raid·er** *n*

¹**rail** \'rāl\ *n* **1** : a bar extending from one support to another and serving as a guard or barrier **2** : a bar of steel forming a track for wheeled vehicles **3** : RAILROAD ⟨travel by *rail*⟩

²**rail** *vb* : to provide with a railing

³**rail** *n* : any of a family of wading birds related to the cranes and hunted as game birds

⁴**rail** *vb* : to scold or complain in harsh or bitter language

rail·ing \'rā-ling\ *n* **1** : a barrier (as a fence) made up of rails and their supports **2** : material for making rails

rail·lery \'rā-lə-rē\ *n*, *pl* **rail·ler·ies** : an act or instance of making fun of someone in a good-natured way

¹**rail·road** \'rāl-ˌrōd\ *n* **1** : a permanent road that has parallel steel rails that make a track for cars **2** : a railroad together with the lands, buildings, locomotives, cars, and other equipment that belong to it

²**railroad** *vb* : to work on a railroad

rail·way \'rāl-ˌwā\ *n* : ¹RAILROAD 1

rai·ment \'rā-mənt\ *n* : CLOTHING 1

¹**rain** \'rān\ *n* **1** : water falling in drops from the clouds **2** : a fall of rain **3** : rainy weather **4** : a heavy fall of objects

²**rain** *vb* **1** : to fall as water in drops from the clouds **2** : to send down rain **3** : to fall like rain ⟨ashes *rained* from the volcano⟩ **4** : to give in large amounts ⟨*rain* advice on a friend⟩ — **rain cats and dogs** : to rain very hard

rain·bow \'rān-ˌbō\ *n* : an arc of colors that appears in the sky opposite the sun and is caused by the sun shining through rain, mist, or spray

rain·coat \'rān-ˌkōt\ *n* : a coat of waterproof or water-resistant material

rain·drop \'rān-ˌdräp\ *n* : a drop of rain

rain·fall \'rān-ˌfol\ *n* **1** : ¹RAIN 2 **2** : amount of precipitation ⟨annual *rainfall*⟩

rain·proof \'rān-'prüf\ *adj* : not letting in rain

rain·storm \'rān-ˌstȯrm\ *n* : a storm of or with rain

rain·wa·ter \'rān-ˌwȯt-ər, -ˌwät-\ *n* : water falling or fallen as rain

rainy \'rā-nē\ *adj* **rain·i·er; rain·i·est** : having much rain ⟨a *rainy* season⟩

\ə\ **abut**	\au̇\ **out**	\i\ **tip**	\ȯ\ **saw**	\u̇\ **foot**	
\ər\ **further**	\ch\ **chin**	\ī\ **life**	\ȯi\ **coin**	\y\ **yet**	
\a\ **mat**	\e\ **pet**	\j\ **job**	\th\ **thin**	\yü\ **few**	
\ā\ **take**	\ē\ **easy**	\ng\ **sing**	\th\ **this**	\yu̇\ **cure**	
\ä\ **cot, cart**	\g\ **go**	\ō\ **bone**	\ü\ **food**	\zh\ **vision**	

¹raise \'rāz\ *vb* **raised; rais·ing 1 :** to cause to rise : LIFT ⟨*raise* a window⟩ **2 :** to give life to : AROUSE ⟨enough noise to *raise* the dead⟩ **3 :** to set upright by lifting or building ⟨*raise* a monument⟩ **4 :** PROMOTE 1, ELEVATE ⟨was *raised* to captain⟩ **5 :** ²END **6 :** COLLECT 2 ⟨*raise* money for a party⟩ **7 :** to look after the growth and development of : GROW ⟨*raise* hogs for market⟩ **8 :** to bring up a child : REAR **9 :** to give rise to : PROVOKE ⟨*raise* a laugh⟩ **10 :** to bring to notice ⟨*raise* an objection⟩ **11 :** ¹INCREASE ⟨*raise* the rent⟩ **12 :** to make light and airy ⟨*raise* dough⟩ **13 :** to cause to form on the skin ⟨*raise* a blister⟩ **synonyms** see LIFT — **rais·er** *n*

²raise *n* **:** an increase in amount (as of pay)

rai·sin \'rāz-n\ *n* **:** a sweet grape dried for food

ra·ja *or* **ra·jah** \'räj-ə\ *n* **:** an Indian prince

¹rake \'rāk\ *n* **:** a garden tool with a long handle and a bar with teeth or prongs at the end

²rake *vb* **raked; rak·ing 1 :** to gather, loosen, or smooth with a rake ⟨*rake* leaves⟩ **2 :** to search through : RANSACK **3 :** to sweep the length of with gunfire

³rake *n* **:** a person with bad morals and conduct

¹ral·ly \'ral-ē\ *vb* **ral·lied; ral·ly·ing 1 :** to bring or come together for a common purpose **2 :** to bring back to order **3 :** to rouse from low spirits or weakness ⟨the patient *rallied*⟩ **4 :** ¹REBOUND 2

²rally *n, pl* **ral·lies 1 :** the act of rallying **2 :** a big meeting held to arouse enthusiasm

¹ram \'ram\ *n* **1 :** a male sheep **2 :** BATTERING RAM

²ram *vb* **rammed; ram·ming 1 :** to strike or strike against with violence **2 :** to force in, down, or together by driving or pressing ⟨*ram* clothes into a suitcase⟩ **3 :** ²FORCE 2 ⟨*ram* a bill through congress⟩

¹ram·ble \'ram-bəl\ *vb* **ram·bled; rambling 1 :** to go aimlessly from place to place : WANDER ⟨spent a year *rambling* around the country⟩ **2 :** to talk or write without a clear purpose or point **3 :** to grow or extend irregularly ⟨a *rambling* vine⟩ **synonyms** see WANDER

²ramble *n* **:** a long stroll with no particular destination

ram·bler \'ram-blər\ *n* **:** a hardy climbing rose with large clusters of small flowers

ram·bunc·tious \ram-'bəngk-shəs\ *adj* **:** UNRULY — **ram·bunc·tious·ly** *adv* — **ram·bunc·tious·ness** *n*

ram·i·fi·ca·tion \,ram-ə-fə-'kā-shən\ *n* **1 :** a branching out **2 :** one thing that comes from another like a branch ⟨study the *ramifications* of a problem⟩

ram·i·fy \'ram-ə-,fī\ *vb* **ram·i·fied; ram·i·fy·ing :** to spread out or split up into branches or divisions

ramp \'ramp\ *n* **:** a sloping passage or roadway connecting different levels

ram·page \'ram-,pāj\ *n* **:** a course of violent or reckless action or behavior

ram·pant \'ram-pənt\ *adj* **:** not checked in growth or spread ⟨fear was *rampant* in the town⟩ — **ram·pant·ly** *adv*

ram·part \'ram-,pärt\ *n* **:** a broad bank or wall raised as a protective barrier

ram·rod \'ram-,räd\ *n* **:** a cleaning rod for firearms

ram·shack·le \'ram-,shak-əl\ *adj* **:** ready to fall down ⟨a *ramshackle* barn⟩

ran *past of* RUN

¹ranch \'ranch\ *n* **1 :** a place for the raising of livestock (as cattle) on range **2 :** a farm devoted to a special crop ⟨a fruit *ranch*⟩

²ranch *vb* **:** to live or work on a ranch — **ranch·er** *n*

ran·cid \'ran-səd\ *adj* **:** having the strong disagreeable smell or taste of stale oil or fat ⟨*rancid* butter⟩ — **ran·cid·ness** *n*

ran·cor \'rang-kər\ *n* **:** deep hatred

ran·cor·ous \'rang-kə-rəs\ *adj* **:** showing rancor ⟨a *rancorous* answer⟩ — **ran·cor·ous·ly** *adv*

ran·dom \'ran-dəm\ *adj* **:** lacking a clear plan

rang *past of* RING

¹range \'rānj\ *n* **1 :** a series of things in a line ⟨a *range* of mountains⟩ **2 :** a cooking stove **3 :** open land over which livestock may roam and feed **4 :** the distance a gun will shoot **5 :** a place where shooting is practiced ⟨a rifle *range*⟩ **6 :** the distance or amount included or gone over : SCOPE ⟨the *range* of one's knowledge⟩ **7 :** a variety of choices within a scale ⟨new cars with a wide *range* of prices⟩

²range *vb* **ranged; rang·ing 1 :** to set in a row or in proper order **2 :** to set in place among others of the same kind **3 :** to roam over or through **4 :** to come within an upper and a lower limit ⟨prices *range* from three to ten dollars⟩

rang·er \'rān-jər\ *n* **1 :** a person who watches over and patrols forest lands **2 :** a member of a body of troops who range over a region **3 :** COMMANDO 2

rangy \'rān-jē\ *adj* **rang·i·er; rang·i·est :** tall and slender in body build — **rang·i·ness** *n*

¹rank \'rangk\ *adj* **1 :** strong and active in growth ⟨*rank* weeds⟩ **2 :** ¹EXTREME 1 ⟨a *rank* beginner⟩ **3 :** having an unpleasant smell ⟨the room was *rank* with cigarette smoke⟩ — **rank·ly** *adv* — **rank·ness** *n*

²**rank** *n* **1** : ³ROW 1, SERIES ⟨*ranks* of houses⟩ **2** : a line of soldiers standing side by side **3 ranks** *pl* : the body of enlisted persons in an army ⟨rose from the *ranks*⟩ **4** : position within a group ⟨a poet of the first *rank*⟩ **5** : high social position **6** : official grade or position ⟨the *rank* of major⟩

³**rank** *vb* **1** : to arrange in lines or in a formation **2** : to arrange in a classification **3** : to take or have a certain position in a group ⟨*ranks* near the top of the class⟩

ran·kle \'rang-kəl\ *vb* **ran·kled; ran·kling** : to cause anger, irritation, or bitterness

Word History The words *rankle* and *dragon* are related. *Dragon* came from a Latin word that meant "snake" or "dragon." Certain sores must have looked to people like little snakes. A Latin word that meant "little snake" was used to mean "inflamed sore." This word came from the Latin word that meant "snake" or "dragon." The English word *rankle* came from the Latin word that first meant "little snake" or "inflamed sore." *Rankle* was first used to refer to sores. It meant "to become inflamed." Later it came to be used more often of hurt or bitter feelings.

ran·sack \'ran-ˌsak\ *vb* **1** : to search thoroughly **2** : to search through in order to rob ⟨a burglar *ransacked* the house⟩

¹**ran·som** \'ran-səm\ *n* **1** : something paid or demanded for the freedom of a captured person **2** : the act of ransoming

²**ransom** *vb* : to free from captivity or punishment by paying a price — **ran·som·er** *n*

rant \'rant\ *vb* : to talk loudly and wildly — **rant·er** *n*

¹**rap** \'rap\ *n* : a sharp blow or knock

²**rap** *vb* **rapped; rap·ping** : to give a quick sharp blow : ¹KNOCK 1

³**rap** *vb* **rapped; rap·ping 1** : to talk freely and informally **2** : to perform rap music

⁴**rap** *n* **1** : an informal talk : CHAT **2** : a rhythmic chanting often in unison of rhymed verses to a musical accompaniment

ra·pa·cious \rə-'pā-shəs\ *adj* **1** : very greedy **2** : PREDATORY — **ra·pa·cious·ly** *adv* — **ra·pa·cious·ness** *n*

¹**rape** \'rāp\ *n* : a plant related to the mustards that is grown for animals to graze on and for its seeds used as birdseed and as a source of oil

²**rape** *vb* **raped; rap·ing** : to have sexual intercourse with by force

³**rape** *n* : an act of raping

rap·id \'rap-əd\ *adj* : very fast **synonyms** see FAST — **rap·id·ly** *adv*

ra·pid·i·ty \rə-'pid-ət-ē\ *n* : the quality or state of being rapid

rap·ids \'rap-ədz\ *n pl* : a part of a river where the current flows very fast usually over rocks

ra·pi·er \'rā-pē-ər\ *n* : a straight sword with a narrow blade having two sharp edges

rap·port \ra-'pōr\ : friendly relationship : ACCORD

rapt \'rapt\ *adj* : showing complete delight or interest ⟨were listening with *rapt* attention⟩

rap·ture \'rap-chər\ *n* : a strong feeling of joy, delight, or love

¹**rare** \'raər, 'reər\ *adj* **rar·er; rar·est 1** : not thick or compact : THIN ⟨the atmosphere is *rare* at high altitudes⟩ **2** : very fine : EXCELLENT ⟨a *rare* June day⟩ **3** : very uncommon ⟨collect *rare* coins⟩

rapier

synonyms RARE, SCARCE, and UNCOMMON mean being in short supply. RARE usually applies to an object or quality of which only a few examples are to be found and which is therefore especially appreciated ⟨a *rare* gem⟩ ⟨*rare* beauty⟩ SCARCE applies to something that for a while is in too short supply to meet the demand for it ⟨food was *scarce* that winter⟩ UNCOMMON can be used of anything which is not often found, but usually there is no suggestion that more would be desirable or needed ⟨identical twins are *uncommon*⟩

²**rare** *adj* **rar·er; rar·est** : cooked so that the inside is still red ⟨*rare* roast beef⟩

rar·efy \'rar-ə-ˌfi, 'rer-\ *vb* **rar·efied; rar·efy·ing** : to make or become less dense or solid

rare·ly \'raər-lē, 'reər-\ *adv* : not often : SELDOM

rar·i·ty \'rar-ət-ē, 'rer-\ *n, pl* **rar·i·ties 1** : the quality, state, or fact of being rare **2** : something that is uncommon

ras·cal \'ras-kəl\ *n* **1** : a mean or dishonest person **2** : a mischievous person

¹**rash** \'rash\ *adj* : too hasty in decision,

\ə\ abut	\au̇\ out	\i\ tip	\ȯ\ saw	\u̇\ foot
\ər\ further	\ch\ chin	\ī\ life	\ȯi\ coin	\y\ yet
\a\ mat	\e\ pet	\th\ thin	\yü\ few
\ā\ take	\ē\ easy	\ng\ sing	\th\ this	\yu̇\ cure
\ä\ cot, cart	\g\ go	\ō\ bone	\ü\ food	\zh\ vision

action, or speech — **rash·ly** *adv* — **rash-ness** *n*

²rash *n* : a breaking out of the skin with red spots (as in measles)

¹rasp \'rasp\ *vb* **1** : to rub with or as if with a rough file ⟨*rasp* off the rough edges⟩ **2** : IRRITATE 1 ⟨their remarks *rasped* my nerves⟩ **3** : to make a harsh sound ⟨a *rasping* voice⟩

²rasp *n* **1** : a coarse file with cutting points instead of lines **2** : a rasping sound or sensation

rasp·ber·ry \'raz-,ber-ē\ *n, pl* **rasp·berries** : a sweet edible red, black, or purple berry

¹rat \'rat\ *n* **1** : a gnawing animal with brown, black, white, or grayish fur that looks like but is larger than the mouse **2** : a person who betrays friends

²rat *vb* **rat·ted; rat·ting** **1** : to betray one's friends **2** : to hunt or catch rats

¹rate \'rāt\ *n* **1** : a price or charge set according to a scale or standard ⟨hotel *rates*⟩ **2** : amount of something measured in units of something else ⟨walk at a *rate* of four miles per hour⟩ — **at any rate** : in any case

²rate *vb* **rat·ed; rat·ing** **1** : CONSIDER 3, REGARD ⟨you are *rated* an expert⟩ **2** : to have a rating : RANK ⟨our school *rates* high in math⟩ **3** : to have a right to : DESERVE ⟨*rates* a promotion⟩

rath·er \'rath-ər\ *adv* **1** : more willingly ⟨would *rather* stay home⟩ **2** : more correctly or truly ⟨ten minutes away, or *rather* nine and a half⟩ **3** : INSTEAD ⟨not for better but *rather* for worse⟩ **4** : ²SOMEWHAT ⟨a *rather* cold day⟩

rat·i·fi·ca·tion \,rat-ə-fə-'kā-shən\ *n* : the act or process of ratifying

rat·i·fy \'rat-ə-fi\ *vb* **rat·i·fied; rat·i·fy·ing** : to give legal approval to (as by a vote) ⟨*ratify* the treaty⟩

rat·ing \'rāt-ing\ *n* : a position within a grading system ⟨credit *rating*⟩

ra·tio \'rā-shō, -shē-,ō\ *n, pl* **ra·tios** : the relationship in number or quantity between two or more things ⟨the *ratio* of births to deaths⟩

¹ra·tion \'rash-ən, 'rā-shən\ *n* **1** : a food allowance for one day **2 rations** *pl* : ¹PROVISION 3 **3** : the amount one is allowed by authority ⟨gas *ration*⟩

²ration *vb* **1** : to control the amount one can use ⟨the government *rationed* gas⟩ **2** : to use sparingly ⟨a diet means *rationing* your food⟩

ra·tio·nal \'rash-ən-l\ *adj* **1** : having the ability to reason ⟨humans are *rational* creatures⟩ **2** : relating to, based on, or showing reason ⟨*rational* thinking⟩ — **ra·tio·nal·ly** *adv*

ra·tio·nale \,rash-ə-'nal\ *n* : a basic explanation or reason for something

ra·tio·nal·ize \'rash-ən-l-,īz\ *vb* **ra·tio·nal·ized; ra·tio·nal·iz·ing** : to find believable but untrue reasons for (one's conduct)

rat·ter \'rat-ər\ *n* : a dog or cat that catches rats

¹rat·tle \'rat-l\ *vb* **rat·tled; rat·tling** **1** : to make or cause to make a rapid series of short sharp sounds **2** : to move with a clatter ⟨the wagon *rattled* down the road⟩ **3** : to say or do in a brisk lively way ⟨*rattle* off the answers⟩ **4** : to disturb the calmness of : UPSET ⟨*rattle* the speaker⟩

²rattle *n* **1** : a series of short sharp sounds **2** : a device (as a toy) for making a rattling sound **3** : a rattling organ at the end of a rattlesnake's tail

rat·tler \'rat-lər\ *n* : RATTLESNAKE

rat·tle·snake \'rat-l-,snāk\ *n* : a poisonous American snake with a rattle at the end of its tail

rattlesnake

rat·tle·trap \'rat-l-,trap\ *n* : something (as an old car) rickety and full of rattles

rau·cous \'rȯ-kəs\ *adj* **1** : being harsh and unpleasant ⟨a *raucous* voice⟩ **2** : behaving in a rough and noisy way ⟨a *raucous* crowd⟩ — **rau·cous·ly** *adv* — **rau·cous·ness** *n*

¹rav·age \'rav-ij\ *n* : violently destructive action or effect ⟨repair the *ravages* of war⟩

²ravage *vb* **rav·aged; rav·ag·ing** : to attack or act upon with great violence ⟨a forest *ravaged* by fire⟩ — **rav·ag·er** *n*

rave \'rāv\ *vb* **raved; rav·ing** **1** : to talk wildly or as if crazy **2** : to talk with great enthusiasm ⟨*raved* about the new play⟩

rav·el \'rav-əl\ *vb* **rav·eled** *or* **rav·elled; rav·el·ing** *or* **rav·el·ling** : UNRAVEL 1 ⟨*ravel* out a sweater and use the wool again⟩

¹ra·ven \'rā-vən\ *n* : a large shiny black bird like a crow that is found in northern regions

²**raven** *adj* : shiny and black like a raven's feathers

rav·en·ous \'rav-ə-nəs\ *adj* : very hungry — **rav·en·ous·ly** *adv*

ra·vine \rə-'vēn\ *n* : a small narrow valley with steep sides that is larger than a gully and smaller than a canyon

rav·ish \'rav-ish\ *vb* **1** : to seize and take away by force **2** : to overcome with a feeling and especially one of joy or delight

raw \'ro\ *adj* **1** : not cooked **2** : being in or nearly in the natural state ⟨*raw* materials⟩ **3** : lacking a normal or usual finish ⟨*raw* edge of a seam⟩ **4** : having the skin rubbed off **5** : not trained or experienced ⟨*raw* recruits⟩ **6** : unpleasantly damp or cold ⟨a *raw* day⟩ — **raw·ly** *adv* — **raw·ness** *n*

raw·hide \'ro-,hīd\ *n* **1** : a whip of untanned hide **2** : untanned cattle skin

¹**ray** \'rā\ *n* : a flat broad fish related to the sharks that has its eyes on the top of its head

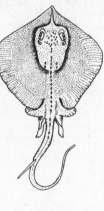

ray

²**ray** *n* **1** : one of the lines of light that appear to be given off by a bright object ⟨*rays* of sunlight⟩ **2** : a thin beam of radiant energy (as light) **3** : light cast in rays **4** : any of a group of lines that spread out from the same center **5** : a straight line extending from a point in one direction only **6** : a plant or animal structure like a ray **7** : a tiny bit : PARTICLE ⟨a *ray* of hope⟩

ray·on \'rā-,än\ *n* : a cloth made from fibers produced chemically from cellulose

raze \'rāz\ *vb* **razed; raz·ing** : to destroy completely by knocking down or breaking to pieces : DEMOLISH

ra·zor \'rā-zər\ *n* : a sharp cutting instrument used to shave off hair

razz \'raz\ *vb* : to make fun of : TEASE

re \'rā\ *n* : the second note of the musical scale

re- *prefix* **1** : again ⟨*refill*⟩ **2** : back : backward ⟨*recall*⟩

¹**reach** \'rēch\ *vb* **1** : to stretch out : EXTEND **2** : to touch or move to touch or take by sticking out a part of the body (as the hand) or something held in the hand **3** : to extend or stretch to ⟨their land *reaches* the river⟩ **4** : to arrive at : COME ⟨*reached*

home late⟩ **5** : to communicate with ⟨tried to *reach* them on the phone⟩

synonyms REACH, GAIN, and ACHIEVE mean to arrive at a point or end by work or effort. REACH may apply to anything arrived at by any amount of effort ⟨they *reached* the city after many days⟩ ⟨we have *reached* our goal of a million dollars⟩ GAIN suggests a struggle to arrive at a goal ⟨the slaves *gained* their freedom⟩ ACHIEVE suggests that skill or courage is involved ⟨*achieved* the confidence of the people⟩.

²**reach** *n* **1** : an unbroken stretch (as of a river) **2** : the act of reaching especially to take hold of something **3** : ability to stretch (as an arm) so as to touch something ⟨a person with a long *reach*⟩

re·act \rē-'akt\ *vb* **1** : to act or behave in response (as to stimulation or an influence) ⟨*reacted* violently to this suggestion⟩ **2** : to oppose a force or influence — usually used with against ⟨*react* against unfair treatment⟩ **3** : to go through a chemical reaction

re·ac·tion \rē-'ak-shən\ *n* **1** : an instance of reacting ⟨our *reaction* to the news⟩ **2** : a response (as of body or mind) to a stimulus (as a treatment, situation, or stress) ⟨studied the patient's *reaction* to the drug⟩ **3** : a chemical change that is brought about by the action of one substance on another and results in a new substance being formed

re·ac·tion·ary \rē-'ak-shə-,ner-ē\ *adj* : of, relating to, or favoring old-fashioned political or social ideas

re·ac·tor \rē-'ak-tər\ *n* **1** : one that reacts **2** : a device using atomic energy to produce heat

read \'rēd\ *vb* **read** \'red\; **read·ing** \'rēd-ing\ **1** : to understand language through written symbols for speech sounds **2** : to speak aloud written or printed words ⟨*read* a poem to the class⟩ **3** : to learn from what one has seen in writing or printing ⟨*read* about the fire⟩ **4** : to discover or figure out the meaning of ⟨*read* palms⟩ **5** : to give meaning to ⟨*read* guilt in the child's manner⟩ **6** : to show by letters or numbers ⟨the thermometer *reads* zero⟩ — **read between the lines** : to understand more than is directly stated

\ə\ abut	\au̇\ out	\i\ tip	\ȯ\ saw	\u̇\ foot
\ər\ further	\ch\ chin	\ī\ life	\oi\ coin	\y\ yet
\a\ mat	\e\ pet	\j\ job	\th\ thin	\yü\ few
\ā\ take	\ē\ easy	\ng\ sing	\th\ this	\yu̇\ cure
\ä\ cot, cart	\g\ go	\ō\ bone	\ü\ food	\zh\ vision

read·able \'rēd-ə-bəl\ *adj* : able to be read easily

read·er \'rēd-ər\ *n* **1** : one that reads **2** : a book for learning or practicing reading

read·ing \'rēd-ing\ *n* **1** : something read or for reading **2** : the form in which something is written : VERSION **3** : the number or fact shown on an instrument ⟨take a *reading* from the thermometer⟩

¹**ready** \'red-ē\ *adj* **read·i·er; read·i·est 1** : prepared for use or action ⟨dinner is *ready*⟩ **2** : likely to do something ⟨*ready* to cry⟩ **3** : WILLING 1 ⟨*ready* to help⟩ **4** : showing ease and promptness **5** : available right away : HANDY ⟨*ready* money⟩ **synonyms** see QUICK — **read·i·ly** \'red-l-ē\ *adv* — **read·i·ness** \'red-ē-nəs\ *n*

²**ready** *vb* **read·ied; ready·ing** : to make ready : PREPARE

ready–made \,red-ē-'mād\ *adj* : made beforehand in large numbers ⟨*ready-made* clothes⟩

re·al \'rē-əl, 'rēl\ *adj* **1** : of, relating to, or made up of land and buildings ⟨*real* property⟩ **2** : not artificial : GENUINE ⟨*real* leather⟩ **3** : not imaginary : ACTUAL ⟨*real* life⟩ — **re·al·ness** *n*

synonyms REAL, ACTUAL, and TRUE mean agreeing with known facts. REAL suggests that a thing is what it appears to be ⟨this is a *real* diamond⟩ ACTUAL stresses that someone or something does or did occur or exist ⟨is Santa Claus an *actual* person?⟩ TRUE may apply to something that is real or actual ⟨a *true* story⟩ or to something that agrees with a standard ⟨a whale is not a *true* fish⟩

real estate *n* : property consisting of buildings and land

re·al·ism \'rē-ə-,liz-əm\ *n* : willingness to face facts or to give in to what is necessary

re·al·is·tic \,rē-ə-'lis-tik\ *adj* **1** : true to life or nature ⟨a *realistic* painting⟩ **2** : ready to see things as they really are and to deal with them sensibly — **re·al·is·ti·cal·ly** \-ti-kə-lē\ *adv*

re·al·i·ty \rē-'al-ət-ē\ *n, pl* **re·al·i·ties 1** : actual existence **2** : someone or something real or actual ⟨the *realities* of life⟩

re·al·iza·tion \,rē-ə-lə-'zā-shən\ *n* : the action of realizing : the state of being realized

re·al·ize \'rē-ə-,līz\ *vb* **re·al·ized; re·al·iz·ing 1** : to bring into being : ACCOMPLISH ⟨*realize* a lifelong ambition⟩ **2** : to get as a result of effort : GAIN ⟨*realize* a large profit⟩ **3** : to be aware of : UNDERSTAND ⟨*realized* their danger⟩

re·al·ly \'rē-ə-lē, 'rē-lē\ *adv* **1** : in fact ⟨didn't *really* mean it⟩ **2** : without question ⟨a *really* fine day⟩

realm \'relm\ *n* **1** : KINGDOM 1 **2** : field of activity or influence ⟨the *realm* of fancy⟩

re·al·ty \'rē-əl-tē\ *n* : REAL ESTATE

¹**ream** \'rēm\ *n* **1** : a quantity of paper that may equal 480, 500, or 516 sheets **2 reams** *pl* : a great amount ⟨*reams* of notes⟩

²**ream** *vb* **1** : to shape or make larger with a reamer **2** : to clean or clear with a reamer

ream·er \'rē-mər\ *n* : a tool with cutting edges for shaping or enlarging a hole

reap \'rēp\ *vb* **1** : to cut (as grain) or clear (as a field) with a sickle, scythe, or machine **2** : HARVEST ⟨*reap* a crop⟩

reap·er \'rē-pər\ *n* **1** : a worker who harvests crops **2** : a machine for reaping grain

re·ap·pear \,rē-ə-'piər\ *vb* : to appear again

¹**rear** \'riər\ *vb* **1** : to put up by building : CONSTRUCT **2** : to raise or set on end **3** : to take care of the breeding and raising of ⟨*rear* cattle⟩ **4** : BRING UP ⟨*rear* children⟩ **5** : to rise high **6** : to rise up on the hind legs ⟨the horse *reared* in fright⟩

²**rear** *n* **1** : the part (as of an army) or area farthest from the enemy **2** : the space or position at the back

³**rear** *adj* : being at the back

rear admiral *n* : a commissioned officer in the Navy or Coast Guard ranking above a captain

re·ar·range \,rē-ə-'rānj\ *vb* **re·ar·ranged; re·ar·rang·ing** : to arrange again usually in a different way

¹**rea·son** \'rēz-n\ *n* **1** : a statement given to explain a belief or an act ⟨gave a *reason* for my absence⟩ **2** : a good basis ⟨have *reasons* for what I did⟩ **3** : ¹CAUSE 1 ⟨wanted to know the *reason* for rain⟩ **4** : the power to think **5** : a sound mind

²**reason** *vb* **1** : to talk with another so as to influence his or her actions or opinions **2** : to use the power of reason

rea·son·able \'rēz-nə-bəl, -n-ə-bəl\ *adj* **1** : not beyond what is usual or expected : MODERATE **2** : ¹CHEAP 1, INEXPENSIVE **3** : able to reason — **rea·son·able·ness** *n* — **rea·son·ably** \-blē\ *adv*

re·as·sure \,rē-ə-'shur\ *vb* **re·as·sured; re·as·sur·ing 1** : to assure again **2** : to give fresh confidence to : free from fear

¹**re·bate** \'rē-,bāt\ *vb* **re·bat·ed; re·bat·ing** : to make a rebate to or give as a rebate ⟨*rebate* the interest on the bill⟩

²**rebate** *n* : a returning of part of a payment or of an amount owed

¹**reb·el** \'reb-əl\ *adj* **1** : being or fighting

against one's government or ruler **2** : not obeying

²**rebel** *n* : a person who refuses to give in to authority

³**re·bel** \ri-'bel\ *vb* **re·belled; re·bel·ling 1** : to be or fight against authority and especially the authority of one's government **2** : to feel or show anger or strong dislike

re·bel·lion \ri-'bel-yən\ *n* **1** : open opposition to authority ⟨the strict rules caused *rebellion* in the class⟩ **2** : an open fight against one's government

re·bel·lious \ri-'bel-yəs\ *adj* **1** : taking part in rebellion ⟨*rebellious* troops⟩ **2** : tending to fight against or disobey authority — **re·bel·lious·ly** *adv* — **re·bel·lious·ness** *n*

re·birth \'rē-'bərth\ *n* **1** : a new or second birth **2** : a return to importance ⟨a *rebirth* of democratic ideas⟩

re·born \'rē-'bȯrn\ *adj* : born again

¹**re·bound** \'rē-'baund, ri-\ *vb* **1** : to spring back on hitting something **2** : to get over a disappointment

²**re·bound** \'rē-ˌbaund\ *n* **1** : the action of rebounding : RECOIL **2** : an immediate reaction to a disappointment

¹**re·buff** \ri-'bəf\ *vb* : to refuse or criticize sharply ⟨the suggestion was *rebuffed*⟩

²**rebuff** *n* : a refusal to meet an advance or offer

re·build \'rē-'bild\ *vb* **re·built** \-'bilt\; **re·build·ing 1** : to make many or important repairs to or changes in ⟨*rebuild* an old house⟩ **2** : to build again ⟨planned to *rebuild* after the fire⟩

¹**re·buke** \ri-'byük\ *vb* **re·buked; re·buk·ing** : to criticize severely

²**rebuke** *n* : an expression of strong disapproval

re·but \ri-'bət\ *vb* **re·but·ted; re·but·ting** : to prove to be wrong especially by argument or by proof that the opposite is right

¹**re·call** \ri-'kȯl\ *vb* **1** : to ask or order to come back **2** : to bring back to mind ⟨*recall* an address⟩ **3** : CANCEL 2, REVOKE ⟨*recall* an order⟩

²**re·call** \ri-'kȯl, 'rē-ˌkȯl\ *n* **1** : a command to return **2** : remembrance of what has been learned or experienced

re·cap·ture \'rē-'kap-chər\ *vb* **re·captured; re·cap·tur·ing 1** : to capture again **2** : to experience again ⟨*recapture* one's youth⟩

re·cede \ri-'sēd\ *vb* **re·ced·ed; re·ced·ing 1** : to move back or away **2** : to slant backward

¹**re·ceipt** \ri-'sēt\ *n* **1** : RECIPE **2** : the act of receiving **3 receipts** *pl* : something re-

ceived ⟨the *receipts* from the sale⟩ **4** : a written statement saying that money or goods have been received

²**receipt** *vb* **1** : to give a receipt for **2** : to mark as paid

re·ceive \ri-'sēv\ *vb* **re·ceived; re·ceiv·ing 1** : to take or get something that is given, paid, or sent ⟨*receive* the money⟩ ⟨*receive* a letter⟩ **2** : to let enter one's household or company : WELCOME ⟨*receive* friends⟩ **3** : to be at home to visitors **4** : ²EXPERIENCE ⟨*receive* a shock⟩ **5** : to change incoming radio waves into sounds or pictures

re·ceiv·er \ri-'sē-vər\ *n* **1** : one that receives **2** : a device for changing electricity or radio waves into light or sound ⟨a telephone *receiver*⟩ ⟨a radio *receiver*⟩

re·cent \'rēs-nt\ *adj* **1** : of or relating to a time not long past ⟨*recent* history⟩ **2** : having lately appeared to come into being : NEW, FRESH ⟨*recent* events⟩ — **re·cent·ly** *adv* — **re·cent·ness** *n*

re·cep·ta·cle \ri-'sep-tə-kəl\ *n* : something used to receive and contain smaller objects

re·cep·tion \ri-'sep-shən\ *n* **1** : the act or manner of receiving ⟨a warm *reception*⟩ **2** : a social gathering at which someone is often formally introduced or welcomed **3** : the receiving of a radio or television broadcast

re·cep·tion·ist \ri-'sep-shə-nəst\ *n* : an office employee who greets callers

re·cep·tive \ri-'sep-tiv\ *adj* : able or willing to receive ideas — **re·cep·tive·ly** *adv* — **re·cep·tive·ness** *n*

re·cep·tor \ri-'sep-tər\ *n* : a cell or group of cells that receives stimuli : SENSE ORGAN

¹**re·cess** \'rē-ˌses, ri-'ses\ *n* **1** : an inward curve or hollowed-out place in a line or surface **2** : a secret or hidden-away place **3** : a brief period for relaxation between work periods

²**recess** *vb* **1** : to put into a recess ⟨*recessed* lighting⟩ **2** : to interrupt for or take a recess

re·ces·sion \ri-'sesh-ən\ *n* : a period of reduced business activity

re·ces·sive \ri-'ses-iv\ *adj* : not dominant ⟨*recessive* genes⟩ ⟨a *recessive* trait⟩

rec·i·pe \'res-ə-pē\ *n* : a set of instructions for making something (as a food dish) by combining various things

\ə\ abut	\au\ out	\i\ tip	\ȯ\ saw	\u̇\ foot
\ər\ further	\ch\ chin	\ī\ life	\ȯi\ coin	\y\ yet
\a\ mat	\e\ pet	\j\ job	\th\ thin	\yü\ few
\ā\ take	\ē\ easy	\ng\ sing	\th\ this	\yu̇\ cure
\ä\ cot, cart	\g\ go	\ō\ bone	\ü\ food	\zh\ vision

re·cip·i·ent \ri-'sip-ē-ənt\ *n* : one that receives

re·cip·ro·cal \ri-'sip-rə-kəl\ *n* : one of a pair of numbers (as 9 and ⅑, ⅔ and ³⁄₂) whose product is one

re·cit·al \ri-'sīt-l\ *n* 1 : a reciting of something ⟨the *recital* of their troubles⟩ 2 : a public performance given by one musician ⟨piano *recital*⟩ 3 : a public performance by pupils (as dancing pupils)

rec·i·ta·tion \,res-ə-'tā-shən\ *n* 1 : a complete telling or listing of something 2 : the reciting before an audience of something memorized 3 : a student's oral reply to questions

re·cite \ri-'sīt\ *vb* **re·cit·ed; re·cit·ing** 1 : to repeat from memory ⟨*recite* a poem⟩ 2 : to tell about in detail 3 : to answer questions about a lesson

reck·less \'rek-ləs\ *adj* : being or given to wild careless behavior — **reck·less·ly** *adv* — **reck·less·ness** *n*

reck·on \'rek-ən\ *vb* 1 : ¹COUNT 1, COMPUTE ⟨*reckon* the days till vacation⟩ 2 : to regard or think of as : CONSIDER ⟨was *reckoned* among the leaders⟩

re·claim \ri-'klām\ *vb* 1 : to make better in behavior or character : REFORM 2 : to change to a desirable condition or state ⟨*reclaim* a swamp⟩ 3 : to obtain from a waste product or by-product ⟨*reclaimed* rubber⟩

rec·la·ma·tion \,rek-lə-'mā-shən\ *n* : the act or process of reclaiming : the state of being reclaimed

re·cline \ri-'klīn\ *vb* **re·clined; re·clin·ing** 1 : to lean backward 2 : to lie down

rec·og·ni·tion \,rek-ig-'nish-ən\ *n* 1 : the act of recognizing 2 : special attention or notice ⟨a writer whose work was slow to win *recognition*⟩

rec·og·nize \'rek-ig-,nīz\ *vb* **rec·og·nized; rec·og·niz·ing** 1 : to know and remember upon seeing ⟨*recognize* an old friend⟩ 2 : to be willing to acknowledge ⟨*recognized* my own faults⟩ 3 : to take approving notice of ⟨*recognize* an act of bravery by the award of a medal⟩ 4 : to show one is acquainted with ⟨*recognize* someone with a nod⟩

¹re·coil \ri-'kȯil\ *vb* 1 : to draw back ⟨*recoil* in horror⟩ 2 : to spring back to a former position ⟨the gun *recoiled* upon firing⟩

²recoil *n* 1 : the act or action of recoiling 2 : a springing back (as of a gun just fired) 3 : the distance through which something (as a spring) recoils

rec·ol·lect \,rek-ə-'lekt\ *vb* : to call to mind : REMEMBER ⟨*recollect* what happened⟩

rec·ol·lec·tion \,rek-ə-'lek-shən\ *n* 1 : the act or power of recalling to mind : MEMORY ⟨a good *recollection*⟩ 2 : something remembered ⟨my earliest *recollections*⟩

rec·om·mend \,rek-ə-'mend\ *vb* 1 : to make a statement in praise of ⟨*recommend* a person for a promotion⟩ 2 : to put forward as one's advice, as one's choice, or as having one's support ⟨*recommend* that the matter be dropped⟩ 3 : to cause to receive favorable attention ⟨children *recommended* by their good manners⟩

rec·om·men·da·tion \,rek-ə-mən-'dā-shən\ *n* 1 : the act of recommending 2 : something that recommends ⟨a written *recommendation*⟩ 3 : a thing or course of action recommended

¹rec·om·pense \'rek-əm-,pens\ *vb* **rec·om·pensed; rec·om·pens·ing** : to pay for or pay back

²recompense *n* : a return for something done, suffered, or given : PAYMENT

rec·on·cile \'rek-ən-,sīl\ *vb* **rec·on·ciled; rec·on·cil·ing** 1 : to make friendly again ⟨*reconcile* friends who have quarreled⟩ 2 : ²SETTLE 7, ADJUST ⟨*reconcile* differences of opinion⟩ 3 : to make agree ⟨a story that cannot be *reconciled* with the facts⟩ 4 : to cause to give in or accept ⟨*reconcile* oneself to a loss⟩

re·con·di·tion \,rē-kən-'dish-ən\ *vb* : to restore to good condition (as by repairing or replacing parts)

re·con·nais·sance \ri-'kän-ə-zəns\ *n* : a survey (as of enemy territory) to get information

re·con·noi·ter \,rē-kə-'nȯit-ər, ,rek-ə-\ *vb* : to make a reconnaissance (as in preparation for military action)

re·con·sid·er \,rē-kən-'sid-ər\ *vb* : to consider again especially with a view to change

re·con·sid·er·a·tion \,rē-kən-,sid-ə-'rā-shən\ *n* : the act of reconsidering : the state of being reconsidered

re·con·struct \,rē-kən-'strəkt\ *vb* : to construct again : REBUILD, REMODEL

¹re·cord \ri-'kȯrd\ *vb* 1 : to set down in writing 2 : to register permanently 3 : to change sound or visual images into a form (as on magnetic tape) that can be listened to or watched at a later time

²rec·ord \'rek-ərd\ *n* 1 : the state or fact of being recorded ⟨a matter of *record*⟩ 2 : something written to preserve an account 3 : the known or recorded facts about a person or thing ⟨has a good school *record*⟩ 4 : a recorded top performance ⟨broke the scoring *record*⟩ 5 : something on which sound or visual images have been recorded

³**rec·ord** \'rek-ərd\ *adj* : outstanding among other like things ⟨a *record* crop⟩

re·cord·er \ri-'kȯrd-ər\ *n* **1** : a person or device that records **2** : a musical instrument like a long hollow whistle with eight finger holes

¹**re·count** \ri-'kaunt\ *vb* : to tell all about : NARRATE ⟨*recount* an adventure⟩

²**re·count** \'rē-'kaunt\ *vb* : to count again ⟨*recount* the votes⟩

³**re·count** \'rē-ˌkaunt, -'kaunt\ *n* : a counting again (as of election votes)

re·course \'rē-ˌkōrs\ *n* **1** : a turning for help or protection **2** : a source of help or strength

re·cov·er \ri-'kəv-ər\ *vb* **1** : to get back : REGAIN ⟨*recover* a lost wallet⟩ **2** : to regain normal health, self-confidence, or position **3** : RECLAIM 2 ⟨*recover* land from the sea⟩ **4** : to make up for ⟨*recover* lost time⟩

re–cov·er \'rē-'kəv-ər\ *vb* : to cover again

re·cov·ery \ri-'kəv-ə-rē, -'kəv-rē\ *n, pl* **re·cov·er·ies** : the act, process, or an instance of recovering

rec·re·ation \ˌrek-rē-'ā-shən\ *n* **1** : a refreshing of mind or body after work or worry **2** : a means of refreshing mind or body ⟨exercise is healthful *recreation*⟩

¹**re·cruit** \ri-'krüt\ *n* : a newcomer to a field of activity

Word History An early French verb with the meaning "to grow up again" came from a Latin verb meaning "to grow." The French made a noun meaning "fresh growth" from the verb meaning "to grow up again." Someone apparently compared new troops of soldiers to a fresh growth of plants. The noun that meant "fresh growth" came to mean "a new group of soldiers called into service." The English noun *recruit* came from this French noun.

²**recruit** *vb* **1** : to form or strengthen with new members ⟨*recruit* an army⟩ **2** : to get the services of ⟨*recruit* engineers⟩ **3** : to restore or increase the health or vigor of

rect·an·gle \'rek-ˌtang-gəl\ *n* : a four-sided figure with right angles and with opposite sides parallel

rect·an·gu·lar \rek-'tang-gyə-lər\ *adj* : shaped like a rectangle

rec·ti·fy \'rek-tə-ˌfī\

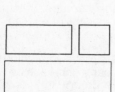

rectangles

vb **rec·ti·fied; rec·ti·fy·ing** : to set or make right

rec·tor \'rek-tər\ *n* : PASTOR

rec·tum \'rek-təm\ *n, pl* **rec·tums** *or* **rec·ta** \-tə\ : the last part of the large intestine

re·cu·per·ate \ri-'kü-pə-ˌrāt, -'kyü-\ *vb* **re·cu·per·at·ed; re·cu·per·at·ing** : to regain health or strength

re·cu·per·a·tion \ri-ˌkü-pə-'rā-shən, -ˌkyü-\ *n* : a getting back to health or strength

re·cur \ri-'kər\ *vb* **re·curred; re·cur·ring** : to occur or appear again ⟨the fever *re·curred*⟩

re·cur·rence \ri-'kər-əns\ *n* : the state of occurring again and again

re·cy·cle \'rē-'sī-kəl\ *vb* **re·cy·cled; re·cy·cling** : to process (as waste, glass, or cans) in order to regain materials for human use

¹**red** \'red\ *adj* **red·der; red·dest 1** : of the color red **2** : of or relating to Communism or Communists — **red·ness** *n*

²**red** *n* **1** : the color of fresh blood or of the ruby **2** : something red in color **3** : a person who seeks or favors revolution **4** : COMMUNIST 2

red·bird \'red-ˌbərd\ *n* : any of several birds (as a cardinal) with mostly red feathers

red blood cell *n* : one of the tiny reddish cells of the blood that have no nuclei and carry oxygen from the lungs to the tissues

red·breast \'red-ˌbrest\ *n* : a bird (as a robin) with a reddish breast

red·cap \'red-ˌkap\ *n* : PORTER 1

red cell *n* : RED BLOOD CELL

red·coat \'red-ˌkōt\ *n* : a British soldier especially during the Revolutionary War

red corpuscle *n* : RED BLOOD CELL

red·den \'red-n\ *vb* : to make or become red

red·dish \'red-ish\ *adj* : somewhat red

re·deem \ri-'dēm\ *vb* **1** : to buy back ⟨*redeem* a watch from the pawnshop⟩ **2** : to ransom, free, or rescue through payment or effort **3** : to make up for ⟨*redeem* a mistake⟩ **4** : to make good : FULFILL ⟨*redeem* a promise⟩ **5** : to free from sin — **re·deem·er** *n*

re·demp·tion \ri-'demp-shən\ *n* : the act or process or an instance of redeeming

red–hand·ed \'red-'han-dəd\ *adv or adj* : in the act of doing something wrong ⟨was caught *red-handed*⟩

\ə\ abut	\aú\ out	\i\ tip	\ȯ\ saw	\ú\ foot
\ər\ further	\ch\ chin	\ī\ life	\ȯi\ coin	\y\ yet
\a\ mat	\e\ pet	\j\ job	\th\ thin	\yü\ few
\ā\ take	\ē\ easy	\ng\ sing	\th\ this	\yú\ cure
\ä\ cot, cart	\g\ go	\ō\ bone	\ü\ food	\zh\ vision

red·head \'red-ˌhed\ *n* : a person having reddish hair

red–hot \'red-'hät\ *adj* **1** : glowing red with heat **2** : very active and emotional ⟨*red-hot* anger⟩ ⟨a *red-hot* campaign⟩

re·di·rect \ˌrē-də-'rekt, -dī-\ *vb* : to change the course or direction of

re·dis·cov·er \ˌrē-dis-'kəv-ər\ *vb* : to discover again

red–let·ter \'red-'let-ər\ *adj* : of special importance : MEMORABLE ⟨a *red-letter* day in my life⟩

re·do \'rē-'dü\ *vb* **re·did** \-'did\; **re·done** \-'dən\; **re·do·ing** \-'dü-ing\ : to do over or again

re·dress \ri-'dres\ *vb* : to set right : REMEDY

red tape *n* : usually official rules and regulations that waste people's time

re·duce \ri-'düs, -'dyüs\ *vb* **re·duced; re·duc·ing** **1** : to make smaller or less ⟨*reduce* expenses⟩ **2** : to force to surrender ⟨*reduce* a fort⟩ **3** : to lower in grade or rank **4** : to change from one form into another ⟨*reduce* fractions to lowest terms⟩ **5** : to lose weight by dieting

re·duc·tion \ri-'dək-shən\ *n* **1** : the act of reducing : the state of being reduced **2** : the amount by which something is reduced ⟨a ten-cent *reduction* in price⟩ **3** : something made by reducing ⟨a *reduction* of a picture⟩

red·wood \'red-ˌwùd\ *n* : a tall timber tree of California that bears cones and has a light long-lasting brownish red wood

reed \'rēd\ *n* **1** : a tall slender grass of wet areas that has stems with large joints **2** : a stem or a growth or mass of reeds **3** : a thin flexible piece of cane, plastic, or metal fastened to the mouthpiece or over an air opening in a musical instrument (as a clarinet or accordion) and set in vibration by an air current (as the breath)

reef \'rēf\ *n* : a chain of rocks or ridge of sand at or near the surface of water

¹reek \'rēk\ *n* : a strong or unpleasant smell

²reek *vb* : to have a strong or unpleasant smell

¹reel \'rēl\ *n* **1** : a device that can be turned round and round and on which something flexible may be wound **2** : a quantity of something wound on a reel ⟨two *reels* of wire⟩

²reel *vb* **1** : to wind on a reel **2** : to pull by the use of a reel ⟨*reel* in a fish⟩

³reel *vb* **1** : to whirl around **2** : to be in a confused state ⟨heads *reeling* with excitement⟩ **3** : to fall back (as from a blow) **4** : to walk or move unsteadily : STAGGER

⁴reel *n* : a reeling motion

⁵reel *n* : a lively folk dance

re·elect \ˌrē-ə-'lekt\ *vb* : to elect for another term

reel off *vb* : to tell or recite rapidly or easily ⟨*reeled off* the right answers⟩

re·en·ter \'rē-'ent-ər\ *vb* : to enter again

re·es·tab·lish \ˌrē-əs-'tab-lish\ *vb* : to establish again

re·fer \ri-'fər\ *vb* **re·ferred; re·fer·ring** **1** : to send or direct to some person or place for treatment, aid, information, or decision ⟨*refer* a patient to a specialist⟩ ⟨*refer* a student to the dictionary⟩ **2** : to call attention ⟨the teacher *referred* to a story in the newspaper⟩

¹ref·er·ee \ˌref-ə-'rē\ *n* **1** : a person to whom something that is to be investigated or decided is referred **2** : a sports official with final authority for conducting a game or match

²referee *vb* **ref·er·eed; ref·er·ee·ing** : to act or be in charge of as referee

ref·er·ence \'ref-ə-rəns, 'ref-rəns\ *n* **1** : the act of referring **2** : a relation to or concern with something ⟨with *reference* to what was said⟩ **3** : something that refers a reader to another source of information **4** : a person of whom questions can be asked about the honesty or ability of another person **5** : a written statement about someone's honesty or ability **6** : a work (as a dictionary) that contains useful information

ref·er·en·dum \ˌref-ə-'ren-dəm\ *n, pl* **ref·er·en·da** \-də\ *or* **ref·er·en·dums** : the idea or practice of letting the voters approve or disapprove laws

¹re·fill \'rē-'fil\ *vb* : to fill or become filled again

²re·fill \'rē-ˌfil\ *n* : a new or fresh supply of something

re·fine \ri-'fin\ *vb* **re·fined; re·fin·ing** **1** : to bring to a pure state ⟨*refine* sugar⟩ **2** : to make better : IMPROVE ⟨*refined* their methods of forecasting the weather⟩

re·fined \ri-'find\ *adj* **1** : freed from impurities : PURE ⟨*refined* gold⟩ **2** : having or showing good taste or training ⟨*refined* manners⟩

re·fine·ment \ri-'fin-mənt\ *n* **1** : the act or process of refining **2** : excellence of manners, feelings, or tastes ⟨a person of *refinement*⟩ **3** : something meant to improve something else ⟨*refinements* in a car to increase its efficiency⟩

re·fin·ery \ri-'fi-nə-rē\ *n, pl* **re·fin·er·ies** : a building and equipment for refining metals, oil, or sugar

re·fin·ish \'rē-'fin-ish\ *vb* : to give (as furniture) a new surface

re·fit \'rē-'fit\ *vb* **re·fit·ted; re·fit·ting** : to get ready for use again ⟨*refit* a ship⟩

re·flect \ri-'flekt\ *vb* **1** : to bend or throw back (waves of light, sound, or heat) ⟨a polished surface *reflects* light⟩ **2** : to give back an image or likeness of in the manner of a mirror **3** : to bring as a result ⟨your achievement *reflects* credit on your school⟩ **4** : to bring disapproval or blame ⟨our bad conduct *reflects* upon our training⟩ **5** : to think seriously ⟨*reflected* on the problem⟩

re·flec·tion \ri-'flek-shən\ *n* **1** : the return of light or sound waves from a surface **2** : an image produced by or as if by a mirror **3** : something that brings blame or disgrace ⟨it's a *reflection* on my honesty⟩ **4** : an opinion formed or a remark made after careful thought **5** : careful thought ⟨much *reflection* upon the problem⟩

re·flec·tor \ri-'flek-tər\ *n* : a shiny surface for reflecting light or heat

re·flex \'rē-,fleks\ *n* : an action that occurs automatically when a sense organ is stimulated

reflex act *n* : REFLEX

re·for·est \'rē-'fȯr-əst\ *vb* : to renew forest growth by planting seeds or young trees

re·for·es·ta·tion \,rē-,fȯr-ə-'stā-shən\ *n* : the act of reforesting

¹re·form \ri-'fȯrm\ *vb* **1** : to make better or improve by removal of faults ⟨*reform* a criminal⟩ ⟨wants to *reform* spelling⟩ **2** : to correct or improve one's own behavior or habits

²reform *n* **1** : improvement of what is bad **2** : a removal or correction of a wrong or an error

ref·or·ma·tion \,ref-ər-'mā-shən\ *n* : the act of reforming : the state of being reformed

re·for·ma·to·ry \ri-'fȯr-mə-,tōr-ē\ *n, pl* **re·for·ma·to·ries** : an institution for reforming usually young or first offenders

re·form·er \ri-'fȯr-mər\ *n* : a person who works for reform

re·fract \ri-'frakt\ *vb* : to subject to refraction

re·frac·tion \ri-'frak-shən\ *n* : the bending of a ray when it passes at an angle from one medium into another in which its speed is different (as when light passes from air into water)

re·frac·to·ry \ri-'frak-tə-rē\ *adj* **1** : STUBBORN 3 **2** : capable of enduring very high temperatures ⟨*refractory* clays⟩

¹re·frain \ri-'frān\ *vb* : to hold oneself back

²refrain *n* : a phrase or verse repeated regularly in a poem or song

re·fresh \ri-'fresh\ *vb* : to make fresh or fresher : REVIVE ⟨sleep *refreshes* the body⟩ — **re·fresh·er** *n*

re·fresh·ment \ri-'fresh-mənt\ *n* **1** : the act of refreshing : the state of being refreshed **2** : something (as food or drink) that refreshes — often used in pl.

re·frig·er·ate \ri-'frij-ə-,rāt\ *vb* **re·frig·er·at·ed; re·frig·er·at·ing** : to make or keep cold or cool

re·frig·er·a·tor \ri-'frij-ə-,rāt-ər\ *n* : a device or room for keeping articles (as food) cool

re·fu·el \'rē-'fyü-əl\ *vb* : to provide with or take on more fuel

ref·uge \'ref-yüj\ *n* **1** : shelter or protection from danger or distress **2** : a place that provides shelter or protection ⟨wildlife *refuge*⟩

ref·u·gee \,ref-yu-'jē\ *n* : a person who flees for safety usually to a foreign country

¹re·fund \ri-'fənd\ *vb* : to give back : REPAY ⟨*refund* the cost⟩

²re·fund \'rē-,fənd\ *n* : a sum of money refunded

re·fus·al \ri-'fyü-zəl\ *n* : the act of refusing

¹re·fuse \ri-'fyüz\ *vb* **re·fused; re·fus·ing** **1** : to say one will not accept ⟨*refuse* a job⟩ **2** : to say one will not do, give, or allow something ⟨*refused* to help⟩

²ref·use \'ref-,yüs\ *n* : TRASH 1, RUBBISH

re·fute \ri-'fyüt\ *vb* **re·fut·ed; re·fut·ing** : to prove wrong by argument or evidence — **re·fut·er** *n*

re·gain \ri-'gān\ *vb* **1** : to gain or get again : get back ⟨*regained* my health⟩ **2** : to get back to : reach again ⟨*regain* the shore⟩

re·gal \'rē-gəl\ *adj* : of, relating to, or suitable for a monarch : ROYAL — **re·gal·ly** *adv*

re·gale \ri-'gāl\ *vb* **re·galed; re·gal·ing** **1** : to entertain richly **2** : to give pleasure or amusement to

¹re·gard \ri-'gärd\ *n* **1** : ²LOOK 1 ⟨a tender *regard*⟩ **2** : CONSIDERATION 2 ⟨*regard* for others⟩ **3** : a feeling of respect ⟨held in high *regard*⟩ **4** **regards** *pl* : friendly greetings ⟨give them my *regards*⟩ **5** : a point to be considered ⟨be careful in this *regard*⟩

²regard *vb* **1** : to pay attention to **2** : to show respect or consideration for **3** : to have a high opinion of **4** : to look at **5** : to think of : CONSIDER ⟨*regarded* them as friends⟩

re·gard·ing \ri-,gärd-ing\ *prep* : relating to : ABOUT ⟨talked with them *regarding* their behavior⟩

\ə\ abut	\au̇\ out	\i\ tip	\ȯ\ saw	\u̇\ foot	
\ər\ further	\ch\ chin	\ī\ life	\ȯi\ coin	\y\ yet	
\a\ mat	\e\ pet	\j\ job	\th\ thin	\yü\ few	
\ā\ take	\ē\ easy	\ng\ sing	\th\ this	\yu̇\ cure	
\ä\ cot, cart	\g\ go	\ō\ bone	\ü\ food	\zh\ vision	

re·gard·less \ri-'gärd-ləs\ *adv* : come what may ⟨I will go *regardless*⟩

regardless of *prep* : in spite of ⟨*regardless of* race⟩

re·gat·ta \ri-'gät-ə, -'gat-\ *n* : a rowing, speedboat, or sailing race or a series of such races

re·gen·er·ate \ri-'jen-ə-,rāt\ *vb* **re·gen·er·at·ed; re·gen·er·at·ing** : to form (as a lost part) once more ⟨the lizard *regenerated* its lost tail⟩

re·gent \'rē-jənt\ *n* **1** : a person who governs a kingdom (as during the childhood of the monarch) **2** : a member of a governing board (as of a state university)

re·gime \rā-'zhēm, ri-\ *n* : a form or system of government or management

reg·i·men \'rej-ə-mən\ *n* : a systematic course of treatment

reg·i·ment \'rej-ə-mənt\ *n* : a military unit made up usually of a number of battalions

re·gion \'rē-jən\ *n* **1** : an area having no definite boundaries **2** : VICINITY 2 ⟨a pain in the *region* of the heart⟩ **3** : a broad geographical area

re·gion·al \'rē-jən-l\ *adj* : of, relating to, or characteristic of a certain region

¹reg·is·ter \'rej-əs-tər\ *n* **1** : a written record or list containing regular entries of items or details **2** : a book or system of public records ⟨a *register* of deeds⟩ **3** : a device for regulating ventilation or the flow of heated air from a furnace **4** : a mechanical device (as a **cash register**) that records items

²register *vb* **1** : to enter or enroll in a register (as a list of voters, students, or guests) **2** : to record automatically ⟨the thermometer *registered* zero⟩ **3** : to get special protection for by paying extra postage ⟨*register* a letter⟩ **4** : to show by expression and bodily movements ⟨*register* surprise⟩

reg·is·tra·tion \,rej-ə-'strā-shən\ *n* **1** : the act of registering **2** : an entry in a register **3** : the number of persons registered **4** : a document showing that something is registered ⟨a car *registration*⟩

reg·is·try \'rej-ə-strē\ *n, pl* **reg·is·tries** : a place where registration takes place

¹re·gret \ri-'gret\ *vb* **re·gret·ted; re·gret·ting** **1** : to mourn the loss or death of **2** : to be sorry for ⟨*regret* one's faults⟩

²regret *n* **1** : sorrow aroused by events beyond one's control **2** : an expression of sorrow **3** **regrets** *pl* : a note politely refusing to accept an invitation ⟨send *regrets*⟩

re·gret·ful \ri-'gret-fəl\ *adj* : full of regret — **re·gret·ful·ly** \-fə-lē\ *adv*

re·gret·ta·ble \ri-'gret-ə-bəl\ *adj* : deserving regret — **re·gret·ta·bly** \-blē\ *adv*

re·group \'rē-'grüp\ *vb* : to form into a new grouping ⟨to subtract 129 from 531 *regroup* 531 into 5 hundreds, 2 tens, and 11 ones⟩

reg·u·lar \'reg-yə-lər\ *adj* **1** : formed, built, or arranged according to an established rule, law, principle, or type **2** : even or balanced in form or structure **3** : steady in practice or occurrence ⟨*regular* habits⟩ **4** : following established usages or rules **5** : ¹NORMAL 1 **6** : of, relating to, or being a permanent army — **reg·u·lar·ly** *adv*

synonyms REGULAR, NORMAL, and TYPICAL mean being of the sort that is considered to be usual, ordinary, or average. REGULAR stresses that something follows a rule, standard, or pattern ⟨a *regular* school holiday⟩ NORMAL stresses that something does not vary from what is the most usual or expected ⟨*normal* behavior for a child of that age⟩ TYPICAL suggests that all the important characteristics of a type, class, or group are shown ⟨a *typical* small American town⟩

reg·u·lar·i·ty \,reg-yə-'lar-ət-ē\ *n* : the quality or state of being regular

reg·u·late \'reg-yə-,lāt\ *vb* **reg·u·lat·ed; reg·u·lat·ing** **1** : to govern or direct by rule **2** : to bring under the control of authority ⟨*regulate* prices⟩ **3** : to bring order or method to ⟨*regulated* my habits⟩ **4** : to fix or adjust the time, amount, degree, or rate of — **reg·u·la·tor** \-,lāt-ər\ *n*

reg·u·la·tion \,reg-yə-'lā-shən\ *n* **1** : the act of regulating : the state of being regulated **2** : a rule or order telling how something is to be done or having the force of law

re·hears·al \ri-'hər-səl\ *n* : a private performance or practice session in preparation for a public appearance

re·hearse \ri-'hərs\ *vb* **re·hearsed; re·hears·ing** : to practice in private in preparation for a public performance ⟨*rehearse* a play⟩

Word History A device called a *harrow* is used to break up and smooth soil. Sometimes the first run with the harrow does not break up all the lumps of earth. The farmer then has to take the harrow over the ground more than once. An early French verb meant "to go over again with a harrow." The English verb *rehearse* comes from this early French verb. When we rehearse something we are, so to speak, going over the same ground again and again.

¹reign \\'rān\\ *n* **1 :** the authority or rule of a monarch **2 :** the time during which a monarch rules

²reign *vb* **1 :** to rule as a monarch **2 :** to be usual or widespread

re·im·burse \\,rē-əm-'bərs\\ *vb* **re·im·bursed; re·im·burs·ing :** to pay back **:** REPAY — **re·im·burse·ment** \\-mənt\\ *n*

¹rein \\'rān\\ *n* **1 :** a line or strap attached at either end of the bit of a bridle to control an animal — usually used in pl. **2 :** an influence that slows, limits, or holds back ⟨kept the child under a tight *rein*⟩ **3 :** controlling or guiding power ⟨seized the *reins* of government⟩

²rein *vb* **:** to check, control, or stop by or as if by reins

re·in·car·na·tion \\,rē-,in-,kär-'nā-shən\\ *n* **:** rebirth of the soul in a new body

rein·deer \\'rān-,diər\\ *n, pl* **reindeer :** a large deer that has antlers in both the male and the female and is found in northern regions

reindeer

re·in·force \\,rē-ən-'fōrs\\ *vb* **re·in·forced; re·in·forc·ing 1 :** to strengthen with new force, assistance, material, or support ⟨*reinforce* a wall⟩ **2 :** to strengthen with extra troops or ships

re·in·force·ment \\,rē-ən-'fōr-smənt\\ *n* **1 :** the act of reinforcing **:** the state of being reinforced **2 :** something that reinforces

re·in·state \\,rē-ən-'stāt\\ *vb* **re·in·stat·ed; re·in·stat·ing :** to place again in a former position or condition — **re·in·state·ment** \\-mənt\\ *n*

re·it·er·ate \\rē-'it-ə-,rāt\\ *vb* **re·it·er·at·ed; re·it·er·at·ing :** to say or do over again or repeatedly

¹re·ject \\ri-'jekt\\ *vb* **1 :** to refuse to admit, believe, or receive **2 :** to throw away as useless or unsatisfactory **3 :** to refuse to consider ⟨*reject* a request⟩

²re·ject \\'rē-,jekt\\ *n* **:** a rejected person or thing

re·jec·tion \\ri-'jek-shən\\ *n* **1 :** the act of rejecting **:** the state of being rejected **2 :** something rejected

re·joice \\ri-'jȯis\\ *vb* **re·joiced; re·joic·ing 1 :** to give joy to **:** GLADDEN ⟨news that *rejoices* the heart⟩ **2 :** to feel joy ⟨*rejoiced* over their good luck⟩

re·join \\ri-'jȯin\\ *vb* **1 :** to join again **:** return to ⟨*rejoined* my family after the trip⟩ **2 :** to reply sharply

re·join·der \\ri-'jȯin-dər\\ *n* **:** ²REPLY

¹re·lapse \\ri-'laps, 'rē-,laps\\ *n* **:** a fresh period of an illness after an improvement

²re·lapse \\ri-'laps\\ *vb* **re·lapsed; re·laps·ing :** to slip or fall back into a former condition after a change for the better

re·late \\ri-'lāt\\ *vb* **re·lat·ed; re·lat·ing 1 :** to give an account of **:** NARRATE ⟨*related* their experiences⟩ **2 :** to show or have a relationship to or between **:** CONNECT ⟨the events are *related*⟩ ⟨the lesson *relates* to history⟩

re·lat·ed \\ri-'lāt-əd\\ *adj* **:** connected by common ancestry or by marriage

re·la·tion \\ri-'lā-shən\\ *n* **1 :** the act of telling or describing **2 :** CONNECTION 2 ⟨the *relation* between sleep and death⟩ ⟨the *relation* between teacher and pupils⟩ **3 :** a related person **:** RELATIVE **4 :** RELATIONSHIP 2 **5 :** REFERENCE 2, RESPECT ⟨in *relation* to this matter⟩ **6 relations** *pl* **:** business or public affairs ⟨foreign *relations*⟩

re·la·tion·ship \\ri-'lā-shən-,ship\\ *n* **1 :** the state of being related or connected **2 :** connection by blood or marriage

¹rel·a·tive \\'rel-ət-iv\\ *n* **:** a person connected with another by blood or marriage

²relative *adj* **1 :** RELEVANT ⟨questions *relative* to world peace⟩ **2 :** existing in comparison to something else ⟨the *relative* value of two houses⟩ — **rel·a·tive·ly** *adv*

re·lax \\ri-'laks\\ *vb* **1 :** to make or become loose or less tense ⟨*relaxed* my attention⟩ **2 :** to make or become less severe or strict ⟨*relax* discipline⟩ **3 :** to rest or enjoy oneself away from one's usual duties

re·lax·ation \\,rē-,lak-'sā-shən\\ *n* **1 :** the act or fact of relaxing or of being relaxed **2 :** a relaxing activity or pastime

\\ə\\ abut	\\au̇\\ out	\\i\\ tip	\\ȯ\\ saw	\\u̇\\ foot
\\ər\\ further	\\ch\\ chin	\\ī\\ life	\\ȯi\\ coin	\\y\\ yet
\\a\\ mat	\\e\\ pet	\\j\\ job	\\th\\ thin	\\yü\\ few
\\ā\\ take	\\ē\\ easy	\\ng\\ sing	\\th\\ this	\\yu̇\\ cure
\\ä\\ cot, cart	\\g\\ go	\\ō\\ bone	\\ü\\ food	\\zh\\ vision

¹re·lay \'rē-ˌlā\ *n* **1** : a fresh supply (as of horses or people) arranged to relieve others **2** : a race between teams in which each team member covers a certain part of the course

²re·lay \'rē-ˌlā, ri-'lā\ *vb* **re·layed; re·lay·ing** : to pass along by stages ⟨*relay* a message from person to person⟩

¹re·lease \ri-'lēs\ *vb* **re·leased; re·leas·ing 1** : to set free (as from prison) **2** : to relieve from something that holds or burdens **3** : to give up in favor of another ⟨*release* a claim to property⟩ **4** : to permit to be published, sold, or shown ⟨*release* a news story⟩ — **re·leas·er** *n*

²release *n* **1** : relief or rescue from sorrow, suffering, or trouble **2** : a discharge from an obligation **3** : a giving up of a right or claim **4** : a setting free : the state of being freed **5** : a device for holding or releasing a mechanism **6** : the act of permitting publication or performance **7** : matter released for publication or performance

re·lent \ri-'lent\ *vb* : to become less severe, harsh, or strict

re·lent·less \ri-'lent-ləs\ *adj* : very stern or harsh — **re·lent·less·ly** *adv* — **re·lent·less·ness** *n*

rel·e·vance \'rel-ə-vəns\ *n* : relation to the matter at hand

rel·e·vant \'rel-ə-vənt\ *adj* : having something to do with the matter at hand ⟨a *relevant* question⟩ — **rel·e·vant·ly** *adv*

re·li·abil·i·ty \ri-ˌlī-ə-'bil-ət-ē\ *n* : the quality or state of being reliable

re·li·able \ri-'lī-ə-bəl\ *adj* : fit to be trusted : DEPENDABLE — **re·li·ably** \-blē\ *adv*

re·li·ance \ri-'lī-əns\ *n* **1** : the act of relying **2** : the condition or attitude of one who relies

rel·ic \'rel-ik\ *n* **1** : an object treated with great respect because of its connection with a saint or martyr **2** : something left behind after decay or disappearance ⟨*relics* of an ancient civilization⟩

re·lief \ri-'lēf\ *n* **1** : removal or lightening of something painful or troubling **2** : WELFARE **3** : military assistance in or rescue from a position of difficulty **4** : release from a post or from performance of a duty **5** : elevation of figures or designs from the background (as in sculpture) **6** : elevations of a land surface ⟨a map showing *relief*⟩

re·lieve \ri-'lēv\ *vb* **re·lieved; re·liev·ing 1** : to free partly or wholly from a burden or from distress **2** : to release from a post or duty ⟨*relieve* a sentry⟩ **3** : to break the sameness of ⟨a dark red house *relieved* by white trim⟩ — **re·liev·er** *n*

re·li·gion \ri-'lij-ən\ *n* **1** : the service and worship of God or the supernatural **2** : a system of religious beliefs and practices

re·li·gious \ri-'lij-əs\ *adj* **1** : relating to or showing devotion to God or to the powers or forces believed to govern life ⟨a *religious* person⟩ **2** : of or relating to religion ⟨*religious* books⟩ **3** : very devoted and faithful ⟨pay *religious* attention to one's teacher⟩ — **re·li·gious·ly** *adv* — **re·li·gious·ness** *n*

re·lin·quish \ri-'ling-kwish\ *vb* : GIVE UP 1 : let go of

¹rel·ish \'rel-ish\ *n* **1** : a pleasing taste **2** : great enjoyment ⟨eats with *relish*⟩ **3** : a highly seasoned food eaten with other food to add flavor

²relish *vb* **1** : to be pleased by : ENJOY **2** : to like the taste of

re·live \'rē-'liv\ *vb* **re·lived; re·liv·ing** : to experience again (as in the imagination)

re·luc·tance \ri-'lək-təns\ *n* : the quality or state of being reluctant

re·luc·tant \ri-'lək-tənt\ *adj* : showing doubt or unwillingness ⟨*reluctant* to answer⟩ — **re·luc·tant·ly** *adv*

re·ly \ri-'lī\ *vb* **re·lied; re·ly·ing** : to place faith or confidence : DEPEND

re·main \ri-'mān\ *vb* **1** : to be left after others have been removed, subtracted, or destroyed ⟨little *remained* after the fire⟩ **2** : to be something yet to be done or considered ⟨a fact that *remains* to be proved⟩ **3** : to stay after others have gone **4** : to continue unchanged ⟨the weather *remained* cold⟩

re·main·der \ri-'mān-dər\ *n* **1** : a remaining group or part **2** : the number left after a subtraction **3** : the number left over from the dividend after division that is less than the divisor

remains \ri-'mānz\ *n pl* **1** : whatever is left over or behind ⟨ the *remains* of a meal⟩ **2** : a dead body

re·make \'rē-'māk\ *vb* **re·made** \-'mād\; **re·mak·ing** : to make again or in a different form

¹re·mark \ri-'märk\ *vb* **1** : to take note of : OBSERVE **2** : to make a comment

²remark *n* **1** : a telling of something in speech or writing **2** : a brief comment

re·mark·able \ri-'mär-kə-bəl\ *adj* : worth noticing : UNUSUAL — **re·mark·able·ness** *n* — **re·mark·ably** \-blē\ *adv*

re·match \'rē-'mach\ *n* : a second meeting between the same contestants

re·me·di·al \ri-'mēd-ē-əl\ *adj* : intended to make something better ⟨classes in *remedial* reading⟩ — **re·me·di·al·ly** *adv*

¹rem·e·dy \'rem-ə-dē\ *n, pl* **rem·e·dies 1**

: a medicine or treatment that cures or relieves **2** : something that corrects an evil

²remedy *vb* **rem·e·died; rem·e·dy·ing** : to provide or serve as a remedy for

re·mem·ber \ri-'mem-bər\ *vb* **1** : to bring to mind or think of again **2** : to keep in mind ⟨*remember* your promise⟩ **3** : to pass along greetings from ⟨*remember* us to your family⟩

re·mem·brance \ri-'mem-brəns\ *n* **1** : the act of remembering **2** : something remembered ⟨a vivid *remembrance*⟩ **3** : something (as a souvenir) that brings to mind a past experience

re·mind \ri-'mīnd\ *vb* : to cause to remember — **re·mind·er** *n*

rem·i·nisce \,rem-ə-'nis\ *vb* **rem·i·nisced; rem·i·nisc·ing** : to talk or think about things in the past

rem·i·nis·cence \,rem-ə-'nis-ns\ *n* **1** : a recalling or telling of a past experience **2 reminiscences** *pl* : a story of one's memorable experiences

rem·i·nis·cent \,rem-ə-'nis-nt\ *adj* **1** : of, relating to, or engaging in reminiscence **2** : reminding one of something else

re·miss \ri-'mis\ *adj* : careless in the performance of work or duty — **re·miss·ly** *adv* — **re·miss·ness** *n*

re·mit \ri-'mit\ *vb* **re·mit·ted; re·mit·ting 1** : ²PARDON 2 **2** : to send money (as in payment) — **re·mit·ter** *n*

re·mit·tance \ri-'mit-ns\ *n* : money sent in payment

rem·nant \'rem-nənt\ *n* : something that remains or is left over ⟨a *remnant* of cloth⟩

re·mod·el \'rē-'mäd-l\ *vb* **re·mod·eled** *or* **re·mod·elled; re·mod·el·ing** *or* **re·mod·el·ling** : to change the structure of

re·mon·strate \ri-'män-,strāt\ *vb* **re·mon·strat·ed; re·mon·strat·ing** : ²PROTEST 2

re·morse \ri-'mȯrs\ *n* : deep regret for one's sins or for acts that wrong others — **re·morse·ful** \-fəl\ *adj* — **re·morse·less** \-ləs\ *adj*

re·mote \ri-'mōt\ *adj* **re·mot·er; re·mot·est 1** : far off in place or time ⟨*remote* countries⟩ ⟨*remote* ages⟩ **2** : SECLUDED ⟨a *remote* valley⟩ **3** : not closely connected or related ⟨a *remote* relative⟩ **4** : small in degree ⟨a *remote* possibility⟩ **5** : distant in manner : ALOOF — **re·mote·ly** *adv* — **re·mote·ness** *n*

re·mov·able \ri-'mü-və-bəl\ *adj* : possible to remove

re·mov·al \ri-'mü-vəl\ *n* : the act of removing : the fact of being removed

re·move \ri-'müv\ *vb* **re·moved; re·mov-**

ing **1** : to move by lifting or taking off or away ⟨please *remove* your hat⟩ ⟨*removed* a book from the shelf⟩ **2** : to dismiss from office ⟨the treasurer was *removed* after a year⟩ **3** : to get rid of ⟨*remove* the causes of poverty⟩ — **re·mov·er** *n*

Re·nais·sance \,ren-ə-'säns\ *n* **1** : the period of European history between the fourteenth and seventeenth centuries marked by a fresh interest in ancient art and literature and by the beginnings of modern science **2** *often not cap* : a movement or period of great activity in literature, science, and the arts

re·name \rē-'nām\ *vb* **re·named; re·nam·ing** : to give a new name to ⟨*rename* a street⟩

rend \'rend\ *vb* **rent** \'rent\; **rend·ing** : to tear apart by force

ren·der \'ren-dər\ *vb* **1** : to obtain by heating ⟨*render* lard from fat⟩ **2** : to furnish or give to another ⟨*render* a report⟩ ⟨*render* aid⟩ **3** : to cause to be or become ⟨*rendered* helpless by the blow⟩ **4** : PERFORM 2 ⟨*render* a song⟩

ren·dez·vous \'rän-di-,vü, -dā-\ *n, pl* **ren·dez·vous** \-,vüz\ **1** : a place agreed on for a meeting **2** : a planned meeting

ren·di·tion \ren-'dish-ən\ *n* : an act or a result of rendering

ren·e·gade \'ren-i-,gād\ *n* : a person who deserts a faith, cause, or party

re·nege \ri-'nig, -'neg\ *vb* **re·neged; re·neg·ing** : to go back on a promise or agreement

re·new \ri-'nü, -'nyü\ *vb* **1** : to make or become new, fresh, or strong again **2** : to make, do, or begin again ⟨*renew* a complaint⟩ **3** : to put in a fresh supply of ⟨*renew* the water in a tank⟩ **4** : to continue in force for a new period ⟨*renew* a lease⟩

re·new·al \ri-'nü-əl, -'nyü-\ *n* **1** : the act of renewing : the state of being renewed **2** : something renewed

re·nounce \ri-'naúns\ *vb* **re·nounced; re·nounc·ing 1** : to give up, abandon, or resign usually by a public declaration ⟨*renounced* the throne⟩ **2** : REPUDIATE 1, DISCLAIM ⟨*renounce* one's religion⟩

ren·o·vate \'ren-ə-,vāt\ *vb* **ren·o·vat·ed; ren·o·vat·ing** : to put in good condition again — **ren·o·va·tor** \-,vāt-ər\ *n*

\ə\ abut	\aú\ out	\i\ tip	\ȯ\ saw	\ú\ foot
\ər\ further	\ch\ chin	\ī\ life	\ȯi\ coin	\y\ yet
\a\ mat	\e\ pet	\j\ job	\th\ thin	\yü\ few
\ā\ take	\ē\ easy	\ng\ sing	\t͟h\ this	\yú\ cure
\ä\ cot, cart	\g\ go	\ō\ bone	\ü\ food	\zh\ vision

re·nown \ri-'naun\ *n* : the state of being widely and favorably known

re·nowned \ri-'naund\ *adj* : having renown

¹rent \'rent\ *n* : money paid for the use of another's property — **for rent** : available for use at a price

²rent *vb* **1** : to take and hold property under an agreement to pay rent **2** : to give the possession and use of in return for rent ⟨*rented* a cottage to friends⟩ **3** : to be for rent ⟨the house *rents* for $200 a month⟩ **synonyms** see HIRE

³rent *past of* REND

⁴rent *n* : an opening (as in cloth) made by tearing

¹rent·al \'rent-l\ *n* : an amount paid or collected as rent

²rental *adj* : of, relating to, or available for rent

rent·er \'rent-ər\ *n* : a person who pays rent for something (as a place to live)

re·open \'rē-'ō-pən\ *vb* : to open again

re·or·ga·nize \'rē-'ȯr-gə-ˌnīz\ *vb* **re·or·ga·nized**; **re·or·ga·niz·ing** : to organize again

¹re·pair \ri-'paər, -'peər\ *vb* **1** : to put back in good condition ⟨*repair* a broken toy⟩ **2** : to make up for⟨*repair* a wrong⟩ **synonyms** see MEND

²repair *n* **1** : the act or process of repairing **2** : ¹CONDITION 3 ⟨a house in bad *repair*⟩

rep·a·ra·tion \ˌrep-ə-'rā-shən\ *n* **1** : the act of making up for a wrong **2** : something paid by a country losing a war to the winner to make up for damages done in the war

re·past \ri-'past\ *n* : ¹MEAL

re·pay \rē-'pā\ *vb* **re·paid** \-'pād\; **re·pay·ing** **1** : to pay back ⟨*repay* a loan⟩ **2** : to make a return payment to ⟨*repay* a creditor⟩

re·pay·ment \rē-'pā-mənt\ *n* : the act or an instance of paying back

re·peal \ri-'pēl\ *vb* : to do away with especially by legislative action ⟨*repeal* a law⟩

¹re·peat \ri-'pēt\ *vb* **1** : to state or tell again ⟨*repeat* a question⟩⟨*repeat* gossip⟩ **2** : to say from memory : RECITE ⟨*repeat* a poem⟩ **3** : to make or do again ⟨*repeat* a mistake⟩ — **re·peat·er** *n*

²repeat *n* **1** : the act of repeating **2** : something repeated

re·peat·ed \ri-'pēt-əd\ *adj* : done or happening again and again — **re·peat·ed·ly** *adv*

re·pel \ri-'pel\ *vb* **re·pelled**; **re·pel·ling** **1** : to drive back ⟨*repel* the enemy⟩ **2** : to turn away : REJECT ⟨*repel* a suggestion⟩ **3** : to keep out : RESIST ⟨cloth treated to

repel water⟩ **4** : ²DISGUST ⟨a sight that *repelled* everyone⟩

re·pel·lent \ri-'pel-ənt\ *n* : a substance used to keep off pests (as insects)

re·pent \ri-'pent\ *vb* **1** : to feel sorrow for one's sin and make up one's mind to do what is right **2** : to feel sorry for something done : REGRET ⟨*repent* a rash decision⟩

re·pen·tance \ri-'pent-ns\ *n* : the action or process of repenting

re·pen·tant \ri-'pent-nt\ *adj* : feeling or showing regret for something one has done — **re·pen·tant·ly** *adv*

re·per·cus·sion \ˌrē-pər-'kəsh-ən\ *n* **1** : a return action or effect **2** : a widespread, indirect, or unexpected effect of something said or done

rep·er·toire \'rep-ər-ˌtwär\ *n* : a list or supply of plays, operas, or pieces that a company or person is prepared to perform

rep·er·to·ry \'rep-ər-ˌtōr-ē\ *n*, *pl* **rep·er·to·ries** : REPERTOIRE

rep·e·ti·tion \ˌrep-ə-'tish-ən\ *n* **1** : the act or an instance of repeating **2** : something repeated

re·place \ri-'plās\ *vb* **re·placed**; **replac·ing** **1** : to put back in a former or proper place ⟨*replace* a card in a file⟩ **2** : to take the place of ⟨paper money has *replaced* gold coins⟩ **3** : to put something new in the place of ⟨*replace* a broken dish⟩

re·place·ment \ri-'plās-mənt\ *n* **1** : the act of replacing : the state of being replaced **2** : ¹SUBSTITUTE

re·plen·ish \ri-'plen-ish\ *vb* : to make full or complete once more ⟨*replenish* a supply of fuel⟩ — **re·plen·ish·er** *n* — **re·plen·ish·ment** \-mənt\ *n*

re·plete \ri-'plēt\ *adj* : well supplied ⟨the game was *replete* with thrills⟩ — **re·plete·ness** *n*

rep·li·ca \'rep-li-kə\ *n* : a very exact copy

¹re·ply \ri-'plī\ *vb* **re·plied**; **re·ply·ing** : to say or do in answer : RESPOND

²reply *n*, *pl* **re·plies** : something said, written, or done in answer

¹re·port \ri-'pȯrt\ *n* **1** : ¹RUMOR **2** : REPUTATION 1 ⟨people of evil *report*⟩ **3** : a usually complete description or statement ⟨a weather *report*⟩ **4** : an explosive noise ⟨the *report* of a gun⟩

²report *vb* **1** : to make a statement about or description of : RELATE **2** : to describe or discuss in a newspaper article ⟨*report* a baseball game⟩ **3** : to present oneself ⟨*report* for duty⟩ **4** : to make known to the proper authorities ⟨*report* a fire⟩ **5** : to make a charge of misconduct against — **re·port·er** *n*

synonyms REPORT, DESCRIBE, and NAR-RATE mean to talk or write about something. REPORT suggests the giving of information to others often after one has done some investigation ⟨newspapers *report* important events⟩ DESCRIBE stresses the giving to the hearers or readers a clear mental picture of an event or situation ⟨*describe* a day at school⟩ NARRATE suggests the telling of a story with a beginning and an end ⟨*narrated* a tale about pirates and sailors⟩

report card *n* : a report on a student's grades that is regularly sent by a school to the student's parents or guardian

¹**re·pose** \ri-'pōz\ *vb* **re·posed; re·pos·ing 1** : to lay at rest **2** : to lie at rest ⟨*reposing* on the couch⟩

²**repose** *n* **1** : a state of resting and especially sleep after effort or strain **2** : freedom from disturbance or excitement : CALM

rep·re·sent \,rep-ri-'zent\ *vb* **1** : to present a picture, image, or likeness of : PORTRAY ⟨this picture *represents* a scene at King Arthur's court⟩ **2** : to be a sign or symbol of ⟨the flag *represents* our country⟩ **3** : to act for or in place of ⟨we elect men and women to *represent* us in Congress⟩

rep·re·sen·ta·tion \,rep-ri-,zen-'tā-shən\ *n* **1** : one (as a picture or symbol) that represents something else **2** : the act of representing : the state of being represented (as in a legislative body)

¹**rep·re·sen·ta·tive** \,rep-ri-'zent-ət-iv\ *adj* **1** : serving to represent ⟨a painting *representative* of a battle⟩ **2** : standing or acting for another **3** : carried on by elected representatives ⟨a *representative* government⟩ **4** : being a typical example of the thing mentioned ⟨chosen by the class as a *representative* athlete⟩

²**representative** *n* **1** : a typical example (as of a group or class) **2** : a person who represents another (as in a legislature)

re·press \ri-'pres\ *vb* : to hold in check by or as if by pressure

¹**re·prieve** \ri-'prēv\ *vb* **re·prieved; re·priev·ing** : to delay the punishment of (as a prisoner sentenced to die)

²**reprieve** *n* **1** : a postponing of a prison or death sentence **2** : a temporary relief

¹**rep·ri·mand** \'rep-rə-,mand\ *n* : a severe or formal criticism : CENSURE

²**reprimand** *vb* : to criticize (a person) severely or formally

re·pri·sal \ri-'prī-zəl\ *n* : an act in return for harm done by another

¹**re·proach** \ri-'prōch\ *n* **1** : something that calls for blame or disgrace ⟨their dirty yard is a *reproach* to the whole street⟩ **2** : an expression of disapproval

²**reproach** *vb* : to find fault with : BLAME

re·pro·duce \,rē-prə-'düs, -'dyüs\ *vb* **re·pro·duced; re·pro·duc·ing 1** : to produce again ⟨the cooling of steam *reproduces* water⟩ **2** : to produce another living thing of the same kind ⟨many plants *reproduce* by means of seeds⟩ — **re·pro·duc·er** *n*

re·pro·duc·tion \,rē-prə-'dək-shən\ *n* **1** : the act or process of reproducing **2** : ¹COPY 1

re·pro·duc·tive \,rē-prə-'dək-tiv\ *adj* : of, relating to, capable of, or concerned with reproduction ⟨*reproductive* cells⟩

re·proof \ri-'prüf\ *n* : blame or criticism for a fault

re·prove \ri-'prüv\ *vb* **re·proved; re·prov·ing** : to express blame or disapproval of : SCOLD ⟨*reprove* a child⟩

rep·tile \'rep-təl, -,tīl\ *n* : any of a group of vertebrates (as snakes, lizards, turtles, and alligators) that are cold-blooded, breathe air, and usually have the skin covered with scales or bony plates

Word History Most of the animals we call *reptiles* creep or crawl about. Some, like snakes, crawl about on their bellies. Some, like lizards, creep about on little, short legs. The English word *reptile* came from a Latin word that meant "creeping." This Latin word came from a Latin verb meaning "to creep."

re·pub·lic \ri-'pəb-lik\ *n* **1** : a government having a chief of state who is not a monarch and who is usually a president **2** : a government in which supreme power lies in the citizens through their right to vote **3** : a state or country having a republican government

¹**re·pub·li·can** \ri-'pəb-li-kən\ *adj* : of, relating to, or like a republic ⟨a *republican* form of government⟩

²**republican** *n* : a person who favors a republican form of government

re·pu·di·ate \ri-'pyüd-ē-,āt\ *vb* **re·pu·di·at·ed; re·pu·di·at·ing 1** : to refuse to have anything to do with **2** : to refuse to accept, admit, or pay ⟨*repudiate* a debt⟩

¹**re·pulse** \ri-'pəls\ *vb* **re·pulsed; re·puls·ing 1** : to drive or beat back : REPEL **2** : to treat with discourtesy : SNUB

\ə\ abut	\au̇\ out	\i\ tip	\ȯ\ saw	\u̇\ foot
\ər\ further	\ch\ chin	\ī\ life	\ȯi\ coin	\y\ yet
\a\ mat	\e\ pet	\j\ job	\th\ thin	\yü\ few
\ā\ take	\ē\ easy	\ng\ sing	\th\ this	\yu̇\ cure
\ä\ cot, cart	\g\ go	\ō\ bone	\ü\ food	\zh\ vision

²repulse *n* **1** : ²REBUFF, SNUB **2** : the action of driving back an attacker

re·pul·sive \ri-'pəl-siv\ *adj* : causing disgust ⟨a *repulsive* sight⟩ — **re·pul·sive·ly** *adv* — **re·pul·sive·ness** *n*

rep·u·ta·ble \'rep-yət-ə-bəl\ *adj* : having a good reputation ⟨*reputable* citizens⟩ — **rep·u·ta·bly** \-blē\ *adv*

rep·u·ta·tion \,rep-yə-'tā-shən\ *n* **1** : overall quality or character as seen or judged by people in general ⟨this car has a good *reputation*⟩ **2** : notice by other people of some quality or ability ⟨have the *reputation* of being a good tennis player⟩

¹re·pute \ri-'pyüt\ *vb* **re·put·ed; re·put·ing** : CONSIDER 3 ⟨a person *reputed* to be a millionaire⟩

²repute *n* **1** : REPUTATION 1 **2** : good reputation : HONOR

¹re·quest \ri-'kwest\ *n* **1** : an asking for something **2** : something asked for ⟨grant every *request*⟩ **3** : the condition of being requested ⟨tickets are available on *request*⟩

²request *vb* **1** : to make a request to or of ⟨*request* them to sing⟩ **2** : to ask for ⟨*request* a loan⟩

req·ui·em \'rek-wē-əm\ *n* **1** : a mass for a dead person **2** : a musical service or hymn in honor of the dead

re·quire \ri-'kwīr\ *vb* **re·quired; re·quir·ing** **1** : to have a need for ⟨a trick that *requires* skill⟩ **2** : ²ORDER 2, COMMAND ⟨the law *requires* drivers to obey traffic signals⟩

re·quire·ment \ri-'kwīr-mənt\ *n* : something that is required or necessary ⟨complete all *requirements*⟩ ⟨sleep is a *requirement* for health⟩

¹req·ui·site \'rek-wə-zət\ *adj* : needed for reaching a goal or achieving a purpose

²requisite *n* : REQUIREMENT

re·read \'rē-'rēd\ *vb* **re·read** \-'red\; **re·read·ing** : to read again

¹res·cue \'res-kyü\ *vb* **res·cued; res·cu·ing** : to free from danger or evil : SAVE — **res·cu·er** *n*

²rescue *n* : an act of rescuing

re·search \ri-'sərch, 'rē-,sərch\ *n* : careful study and investigation for the purpose of discovering and explaining new knowledge — **re·search·er** *n*

re·sem·blance \ri-'zem-bləns\ *n* : the quality or state of resembling something else

re·sem·ble \ri-'zem-bəl\ *vb* **re·sem·bled; re·sem·bling** : to be like or similar to

re·sent \ri-'zent\ *vb* : to feel annoyance or anger at ⟨*resent* criticism⟩

re·sent·ment \ri-'zent-mənt\ *n* : a feeling of angry displeasure at a real or imagined wrong, insult, or injury

res·er·va·tion \,rez-ər-'vā-shən\ *n* **1** : an act of reserving **2** : an arrangement to have something (as a hotel room) held for one's use **3** : something (as land) reserved for a special use ⟨an Indian *reservation*⟩ **4** : something that limits ⟨agree without *reservations*⟩

¹re·serve \ri-'zərv\ *vb* **re·served; re·serv·ing** **1** : to keep in store for future or special use **2** : to hold over to a future time or place ⟨*reserve* judgment⟩ **3** : to arrange to have set aside and held for one's use ⟨*reserve* a hotel room⟩

²reserve *n* **1** : something stored or available for future use ⟨oil *reserves*⟩ **2** **reserves** *pl* : military forces held back or available for later use **3** : an area of land set apart ⟨wild game *reserve*⟩ **4** : an act of reserving **5** : caution in one's words and behavior

re·served \ri-'zərvd\ *adj* **1** : cautious in words and actions **2** : kept or set apart for future or special use

res·er·voir \'rez-ərv-,wär\ *n* : a place where something (as water) is kept in store for future use

re·set \'rē-'set\ *vb* **re·set; re·set·ting** : to set again

re·ship·ment \'rē-'ship-mənt\ *n* : an act of shipping again

re·side \ri-'zīd\ *vb* **re·sid·ed; re·sid·ing** **1** : to live permanently and continuously : DWELL **2** : to have its place : EXIST ⟨the right to decide *resides* in the voters⟩

res·i·dence \'rez-ə-dəns\ *n* **1** : the act or fact of residing **2** : the place where one actually lives **3** : a building used for a home **4** : the time during which a person lives in a place ⟨a *residence* of ten years⟩

¹res·i·dent \'rez-ə-dənt\ *adj* **1** : living in a place for some length of time **2** : serving in a full-time position at a certain place ⟨the hospital's *resident* doctors⟩

²resident *n* : a person who lives in a place

res·i·den·tial \,rez-ə-'den-chəl\ *adj* **1** : used as a residence or by residents ⟨a *residential* hotel⟩ **2** : suitable for or containing residences ⟨a *residential* section of the city⟩

res·i·due \'rez-ə-,dü, -,dyü\ *n* : whatever remains after a part is taken, set apart, or lost

re·sign \ri-'zīn\ *vb* **1** : to give up by a formal or official act ⟨*resign* an office⟩ **2** : to prepare to accept something usually unpleasant ⟨*resigned* myself to the loss⟩

res·ig·na·tion \,rez-ig-'nā-shən\ *n* **1** : an act of resigning **2** : a letter or written statement that gives notice of resignation **3** : the feeling of a person who is resigned

re·signed \ri-'zīnd\ *adj* : giving in patiently (as to loss or sorrow) — **re·sign·ed·ly** \-'zī-nəd-lē\ *adv*

res·in \'rez-n\ *n* **1** : a yellowish or brownish substance obtained from the gum or sap of some trees (as the pine) and used in varnishes and medicine **2** : any of various manufactured products that are similar to natural resins in properties and are used especially as plastics

re·sist \ri-'zist\ *vb* **1** : to withstand the force or effect of ⟨*resist* disease⟩ **2** : to fight against : OPPOSE ⟨*resist* arrest⟩

re·sis·tance \ri-'zis-təns\ *n* **1** : an act or instance of resisting **2** : the ability to resist ⟨the body's *resistance* to disease⟩ **3** : an opposing or slowing force ⟨the *resistance* of air to an airplane in motion⟩ **4** : the opposition offered by a substance to the passage through it of an electric current

re·sis·tant \ri-'zis-tənt\ *adj* : giving or capable of resistance

res·o·lute \'rez-ə-ˌlüt\ *adj* : firmly determined — **res·o·lute·ly** *adv* — **res·o·lute·ness** *n*

res·o·lu·tion \ˌrez-ə-'lü-shən\ *n* **1** : the act of resolving **2** : the act of solving : SOLUTION ⟨the *resolution* of a problem⟩ **3** : something decided on ⟨New Year *resolutions*⟩ **4** : firmness of purpose **5** : a statement expressing the feelings, wishes, or decisions of a group

¹re·solve \ri-'zälv\ *vb* **re·solved; re·solv·ing** **1** : to find an answer to : SOLVE ⟨*resolve* a difficulty⟩ **2** : to reach a firm decision about something ⟨*resolve* to work hard⟩ **3** : to declare or decide by a formal resolution and vote

²resolve *n* **1** : something resolved **2** : firmness of purpose

res·o·nance \'rez-n-əns\ *n* : the quality or state of being resonant

res·o·nant \'rez-n-ənt\ *adj* : being or making sound with a rich vibrating quality ⟨a *resonant* voice⟩ — **res·o·nant·ly** *adv*

¹re·sort \ri-'zȯrt\ *n* **1** : one that is looked to for help **2** : HANGOUT **3** : a place where people go for pleasure, sport, or a change ⟨a ski *resort*⟩ ⟨vacation *resorts*⟩

²resort *vb* **1** : to go often or again and again **2** : to seek aid, relief, or advantage ⟨*resorted* to force in order to check the mob⟩

re·sound \ri-'zaúnd\ *vb* **1** : to become filled with sound : REVERBERATE ⟨the hall *resounded* with cheers⟩ **2** : to sound loudly ⟨the organ *resounds* through the hall⟩

re·source \'rē-ˌsȯrs\ *n* **1** : a new or a reserve source of supply or support **2** **resources** *pl* : a usable stock or supply (as of money or products) ⟨America has great natural *resources*⟩ **3** : the ability to meet and deal with situations

re·source·ful \ri-'sȯrs-fəl\ *adj* : clever in dealing with problems — **re·source·ful·ly** \-fə-lē\ *adv* — **re·source·ful·ness** *n*

¹re·spect \ri-'spekt\ *n* **1** : relation to or concern with something specified ⟨with *respect* to your last letter⟩ **2** : high or special regard : ESTEEM **3 respects** *pl* : an expression of regard or courtesy ⟨pay my *respects*⟩ **4** : ¹DETAIL 2 ⟨perfect in all *respects*⟩

²respect *vb* **1** : to consider worthy of high regard : ESTEEM **2** : to pay attention to ⟨*respected* their wishes⟩ — **re·spect·er** *n*

re·spect·able \ri-'spek-tə-bəl\ *adj* **1** : deserving respect ⟨acted in a *respectable* manner⟩ **2** : decent or correct in conduct : PROPER ⟨*respectable* people⟩ **3** : fair in size or quantity ⟨a *respectable* amount⟩ **4** : fit to be seen : PRESENTABLE ⟨*respectable* clothes⟩ — **re·spect·ably** \-blē\ *adv*

re·spect·ful \ri-'spekt-fəl\ *adj* : showing respect ⟨a *respectful* manner⟩ — **re·spect·ful·ly** \-fə-lē\ *adv* — **re·spect·ful·ness** *n*

re·spect·ing \ri-ˌspek-ting\ *prep* : CONCERNING ⟨information *respecting* stolen goods⟩

re·spec·tive \ri-'spek-tiv\ *adj* : not the same or shared : SEPARATE ⟨they hurried to their *respective* homes⟩ — **re·spec·tive·ly** *adv*

re·spell \'rē-'spel\ *vb* : to spell again or in another way ⟨*respelled* pronunciations⟩

res·pi·ra·tion \ˌres-pə-'rā-shən\ *n* **1** : the act or process of breathing **2** : the physical and chemical processes (as breathing and oxidation) by which a living being gets the oxygen it needs to live

res·pi·ra·tor \'res-pə-ˌrāt-ər\ *n* **1** : a device covering the mouth or nose especially to prevent the breathing in of something harmful **2** : a device used for aiding one to breathe

res·pi·ra·to·ry \'res-pə-rə-ˌtōr-ē\ *adj* : of, relating to, or concerned with respiration ⟨the *respiratory* system⟩

re·spire \ri-'spīr\ *vb* **re·spired; re·spir·ing** : BREATHE 1

\ə\ **abut**	\aú\ **out**	\i\ **tip**	\ȯ\ **saw**	\ú\ **foot**
\ər\ **further**	\ch\ **chin**	\ī\ **life**	\ȯi\ **coin**	\y\ **yet**
\a\ **mat**	\e\ **pet**	\j\ **job**	\th\ **thin**	\yü\ **few**
\ā\ **take**	\ē\ **easy**	\ng\ **sing**	\th\ **this**	\yú\ **cure**
\ä\ **cot, cart**	\g\ **go**	\ō\ **bone**	\ü\ **food**	\zh\ **vision**

res·pite \'res-pət\ *n* **1** : a short delay **2** : a period of rest or relief

re·splen·dent \ri-'splen-dənt\ *adj* : shining brightly : SPLENDID — **re·splen·dent·ly** *adv*

re·spond \ri-'spänd\ *vb* **1** : to say something in return : REPLY **2** : to act in response : REACT ⟨*respond* to surgery⟩

re·sponse \ri-'späns\ *n* **1** : an act or instance of replying : ANSWER ⟨there was no *response* to my question⟩ **2** : words said or sung by the people or choir in a religious service **3** : a reaction of a living being (as to a drug)

re·spon·si·bil·i·ty \ri-ˌspän-sə-'bil-ət-ē\ *n*, *pl* **re·spon·si·bil·i·ties** **1** : the quality or state of being responsible **2** : the quality of being dependable ⟨show *responsibility* by always doing your homework⟩ **3** : something for which one is responsible

re·spon·si·ble \ri-'spän-sə-bəl\ *adj* **1** : getting the credit or blame for one's acts or decisions ⟨*responsible* for the damage⟩ **2** : RELIABLE ⟨*responsible* persons⟩ **3** : needing a person to take charge of or be trusted with things of importance ⟨a *responsible* job⟩ — **re·spon·si·bly** \-blē\ *adv*

re·spon·sive \ri-'spän-siv\ *adj* **1** : giving response ⟨a *responsive* glance⟩ **2** : quick to respond or react in a sympathetic way — **re·spon·sive·ly** *adv* — **re·spon·sive·ness** *n*

¹rest \'rest\ *n* **1** : ¹SLEEP 1 **2** : freedom from activity or work **3** : a state of not moving or not doing anything **4** : a place for resting or stopping **5** : a silence in music **6** : a symbol in music that stands for a certain period of silence in a measure **7** : something used for support ⟨a head *rest*⟩

rest 6

²rest *vb* **1** : to get rest by lying down : SLEEP **2** : to give rest to ⟨*rest* your eyes now and then⟩ **3** : to lie dead **4** : to not take part in work or activity **5** : to sit or lie fixed or supported ⟨a house *rests* on its foundation⟩ **6** : DEPEND 2 ⟨the success of the flight *rests* on the wind⟩ **7** : to fix or be fixed in trust or confidence ⟨*rested* their hopes on their children⟩

³rest *n* : something that is left over : REMAINDER

re·state·ment \'rē-'stāt-mənt\ *n* : a saying again or in another way

res·tau·rant \'res-tə-rənt\ *n* : a public eating place

rest·ful \'rest-fəl\ *adj* **1** : giving rest ⟨a *restful* chair⟩ **2** : giving a feeling of rest : QUIET ⟨a *restful* scene⟩ — **rest·ful·ly** \-fə-lē\ *adv* — **rest·ful·ness** *n*

rest·ing \'res-ting\ *adj* : DORMANT ⟨a *resting* spore⟩

res·tive \'res-tiv\ *adj* **1** : resisting control **2** : not being at ease — **res·tive·ly** *adv* — **res·tive·ness** *n*

rest·less \'rest-ləs\ *adj* **1** : having or giving no rest ⟨a *restless* night⟩ **2** : not quiet or calm ⟨the *restless* sea⟩ — **rest·less·ly** *adv* — **rest·less·ness** *n*

res·to·ra·tion \ˌres-tə-'rā-shən\ *n* **1** : an act of restoring : the condition of being restored **2** : something (as a building) that has been restored

re·store \ri-'stōr\ *vb* **re·stored; re·stor·ing** **1** : to give back : RETURN ⟨*restore* a purse to its owner⟩ **2** : to put back into use or service **3** : to put or bring back to an earlier or original state ⟨*restore* an old house⟩

re·strain \ri-'strān\ *vb* **1** : to keep from doing something ⟨*restrain* a crowd⟩ **2** : to keep back : CURB ⟨*restrain* anger⟩ — **re·strain·er** *n*

re·straint \ri-'strānt\ *n* **1** : the act of restraining : the state of being restrained **2** : a restraining force or influence **3** : control over one's thoughts or feelings

re·strict \ri-'strikt\ *vb* : to keep within bounds : set limits to

re·stric·tion \ri-'strik-shən\ *n* **1** : something (as a law or rule) that restricts **2** : an act of restricting : the condition of being restricted

re·stric·tive \ri-'strik-tiv\ *adj* : serving or likely to restrict — **re·stric·tive·ly** *adv* — **re·stric·tive·ness** *n*

¹re·sult \ri-'zəlt\ *vb* **1** : to come about as an effect ⟨disease *results* from infection⟩ **2** : to end as an effect ⟨the disease *results* in death⟩

²result *n* **1** : something that comes about as an effect or end ⟨the *results* of war⟩ **2** : a good effect ⟨this method gets *results*⟩

re·sume \ri-'züm\ *vb* **re·sumed; re·sum·ing** **1** : to take or occupy again ⟨*resume* your seats⟩ **2** : to begin again ⟨*resume* play⟩

re·sump·tion \ri-'zəmp-shən\ *n* : the act of resuming ⟨*resumption* of work⟩

res·ur·rect \ˌrez-ə-'rekt\ *vb* **1** : to raise from the dead : bring back to life **2** : to bring to view or into use again ⟨*resurrect* an old song⟩

res·ur·rec·tion \,rez-ə-'rek-shən\ *n* **1** *cap* : the rising of Christ from the dead **2** *often cap* : the rising again to life of all human dead before the final judgment **3** : a coming back into use or importance

re·sus·ci·tate \ri-'səs-ə-,tāt\ *vb* **re·sus·ci·tat·ed; re·sus·ci·tat·ing** : to bring back from apparent death or unconsciousness — **re·sus·ci·ta·tor** \-,tāt-ər\ *n*

¹re·tail \'rē-,tāl\ *vb* : to sell in small amounts to people for their own use — **re·tail·er** *n*

²retail *n* : the sale of products or goods in small amounts to people for their own use

³retail *adj* : of, relating to, or engaged in selling by retail ⟨*retail* stores⟩ ⟨*retail* prices⟩

re·tain \ri-'tān\ *vb* **1** : to keep in one's possession or control ⟨*retain* knowledge⟩ **2** : to hold safe or unchanged ⟨lead *retains* heat⟩

re·tal·i·ate \ri-'tal-ē-,āt\ *vb* **re·tal·i·at·ed; re·tal·i·at·ing** : to get revenge by returning like for like

re·tal·i·a·tion \ri-,tal-ē-'ā-shən\ *n* : the act or an instance of retaliating

re·tard \ri-'tärd\ *vb* : to slow up : keep back : DELAY — **re·tard·er** *n*

re·tard·ed \ri-'tärd-əd\ *adj* : very slow especially in mind

retch \'rech\ *vb* : to vomit or try to vomit

re·ten·tion \ri-'ten-chən\ *n* **1** : the act of retaining : the state of being retained **2** : the power of retaining

ret·i·na \'ret-n-ə\ *n, pl* **ret·i·nas** *or* **ret·i·nae** \-n-,ē\ : the membrane that lines the back part of the eyeball and is the sensitive part for seeing

re·tire \ri-'tīr\ *vb* **re·tired; re·tir·ing** **1** : to get away from action or danger : RETREAT **2** : to go away especially to be alone **3** : to give up one's job permanently : quit working **4** : to go to bed **5** : to take out of circulation — **re·tire·ment** \-mənt\ *n*

re·tired \ri-'tīrd\ *adj* : not working at active duties or business

re·tir·ing \ri-'tīr-ing\ *adj* : ¹SHY 2, RESERVED

¹re·tort \ri-'tort\ *vb* **1** : to answer back : reply angrily or sharply **2** : to reply with an argument against

²retort *n* : a quick, clever, or angry reply

re·trace \rē-'trās\ *vb* **re·traced; re·trac·ing** : to go over once more ⟨*retrace* one's steps⟩

re·tract \ri-'trakt\ *vb* **1** : to pull back or in ⟨a cat can *retract* its claws⟩ **2** : to take back (as an offer or statement) : WITHDRAW

¹re·tread \'rē-'tred\ *vb* **re·tread·ed; re·tread·ing** : to put a new tread on the cord fabric of (a tire)

²re·tread \'rē-,tred\ *n* : a retreaded tire

¹re·treat \ri-'trēt\ *n* **1** : an act of going away from something dangerous, difficult, or disagreeable **2** : a military signal for turning away from the enemy **3** : a place of privacy or safety : REFUGE **4** : a period in which a person goes away to pray, think quietly, and study

²retreat *vb* : to make a retreat

re·trieve \ri-'trēv\ *vb* **re·trieved; re·triev·ing** **1** : to find and bring in killed or wounded game ⟨a dog that *retrieves* well⟩ **2** : to make good a loss or damage : RECOVER — **re·triev·er** *n*

ret·ro–rock·et \'re-trō-,räk-ət\ *n* : a rocket (as on a space vehicle) used to slow forward motion

ret·ro·spect \'re-trə-,spekt\ *n* : a looking back on things past

¹re·turn \ri-'tərn\ *vb* **1** : to come or go back **2** : ¹ANSWER 1, REPLY **3** : to make an official report of ⟨the jury *returned* a verdict⟩ **4** : to bring, carry, send, or put back : RESTORE ⟨*return* a book to the library⟩ **5** : ¹YIELD 4, PRODUCE ⟨the loan *returned* good interest⟩ **6** : REPAY 1 ⟨*return* borrowed money⟩

²return *n* **1** : the act of coming back to or from a place or condition **2** : RECURRENCE ⟨the *return* of spring⟩ **3** : a report of the results of voting ⟨election *returns*⟩ **4** : a statement of income to be taxed **5** : the profit from labor, investment, or business **6** : the act of returning something (as to an earlier place or condition) **7** : something given (as in payment)

³return *adj* **1** : played or given in return ⟨a *return* game⟩ **2** : used for returning ⟨*return* ticket⟩

re·union \rē-'yün-yən\ *n* **1** : the act of reuniting : the state of being reunited **2** : a reuniting of persons after being apart ⟨class *reunion*⟩

re·unite \,rē-yü-'nīt\ *vb* **re·unit·ed; re·unit·ing** : to come or bring together again after being apart

rev \'rev\ *vb* **revved; rev·ving** : to increase the number of revolutions per minute of (a motor)

re·veal \ri-'vēl\ *vb* **1** : to make known ⟨*reveal* a secret⟩ **2** : to show clearly ⟨the way you work *reveals* what you really are⟩

\ə\ abut	\au̇\ out	\i\ tip	\ȯ\ saw	\u̇\ foot
\ər\ further	\ch\ chin	\ī\ life	\ȯi\ coin	\y\ yet
\a\ mat	\e\ pet	\j\ job	\th\ thin	\yü\ few
\ā\ take	\ē\ easy	\ng\ sing	\th\ this	\yu̇\ cure
\ä\ cot, cart	\g\ go	\ō\ bone	\ü\ food	\zh\ vision

rev·eil·le \'rev-ə-lē\ *n* : a signal sounded at about sunrise on a bugle or drum to call soldiers or sailors to duty

¹rev·el \'rev-əl\ *vb* **rev·eled** *or* **rev·elled**; **rev·el·ing** *or* **rev·el·ling** 1 : to be social in a wild noisy way 2 : to take great pleasure ⟨*reveling* in success⟩

²revel *n* : a noisy or merry celebration

rev·e·la·tion \,rev-ə-'lā-shən\ *n* 1 : an act of revealing 2 : something revealed

rev·el·ry \'rev-əl-rē\ *n, pl* **rev·el·ries** : rough and noisy merrymaking

¹re·venge \ri-'venj\ *vb* **re·venged**; **re·veng·ing** : to cause harm or injury in return for ⟨*revenge* a wrong⟩

²revenge *n* 1 : an act or instance of revenging 2 : a desire to repay injury for injury 3 : a chance for getting satisfaction

re·venge·ful \ri-'venj-fəl\ *adj* : given to or seeking revenge

rev·e·nue \'rev-ə-,nü, -,nyü\ *n* 1 : the income from an investment 2 : money collected by a government (as through taxes)

re·ver·ber·ate \ri-'vər-bə-,rāt\ *vb* **re·ver·ber·at·ed**; **re·ver·ber·at·ing** : to continue in or as if in a series of echoes

re·vere \ri-'viər\ *vb* **re·vered**; **re·ver·ing** : to think of with reverence

¹rev·er·ence \'rev-ə-rəns, 'rev-rəns\ *n* : honor and respect mixed with love and awe

²reverence *vb* **rev·er·enced**; **rev·er·enc·ing** : to show reverence to or toward

rev·er·end \'rev-ə-rənd, 'rev-rənd\ *adj* 1 : worthy of honor and respect 2 — used as a title for a member of the clergy ⟨the *Reverend* John Doe⟩ ⟨the *Reverend* Jane Doe⟩

rev·er·ent \'rev-ə-rənt, 'rev-rənt\ *adj* : very respectful — **rev·er·ent·ly** *adv*

rev·er·ie *or* **rev·ery** \'rev-ə-rē\ *n, pl* **rev·er·ies** 1 : ¹DAYDREAM 2 : the condition of being lost in thought

re·ver·sal \ri-'vər-səl\ *n* : an act or the process of reversing

¹re·verse \ri-'vərs\ *adj* 1 : opposite to a previous or normal condition 2 : acting or working in a manner opposite to the usual — **re·verse·ly** *adv*

²reverse *vb* **re·versed**; **re·vers·ing** 1 : to turn completely around or upside down or inside out 2 : ANNUL ⟨*reverse* a legal decision⟩ 3 : to go or cause to go in the opposite direction

³reverse *n* 1 : something opposite to something else : CONTRARY 2 : an act or instance of reversing 3 : the back part of something 4 : a gear that reverses something

re·vert \ri-'vərt\ *vb* : to come or go back ⟨*reverted* to savagery⟩

¹re·view \ri-'vyü\ *n* 1 : a military parade put on for high officers 2 : a general survey 3 : a piece of writing about the quality of a book, performance, or show 4 : a fresh study of material studied before

²review *vb* 1 : to look at a thing again : study or examine again ⟨*review* a lesson⟩ 2 : to make an inspection of (as troops) 3 : to write a review about (as a book) 4 : to look back on ⟨*review* accomplishments⟩ — **re·view·er** *n*

re·vile \ri-'vīl\ *vb* **re·viled**; **re·vil·ing** : to speak to or yell at in an insulting way — **re·vil·er** *n*

re·vise \ri-'vīz\ *vb* **re·vised**; **re·vis·ing** 1 : to look over again to correct or improve ⟨*revise* an essay⟩ 2 : to make a new version of ⟨*revise* a dictionary⟩

re·viv·al \ri-'vī-vəl\ *n* 1 : a reviving of interest (as in art) 2 : a new presentation of a play or movie 3 : a gaining back of strength or importance ⟨a *revival* of business⟩ 4 : a meeting or series of meetings led by a preacher to stir up religious feelings or to make converts

re·vive \ri-'vīv\ *vb* **re·vived**; **re·viv·ing** 1 : to bring back or come back to life, consciousness, freshness, or activity 2 : to bring back into use ⟨*revive* an old custom⟩

re·voke \ri-'vōk\ *vb* **re·voked**; **re·vok·ing** : to take away or cancel ⟨*revoke* a driver's license⟩

¹re·volt \ri-'vōlt\ *vb* 1 : to rebel against the authority of a ruler or government 2 : to be or cause to be disgusted or shocked

²revolt *n* : REBELLION, INSURRECTION

rev·o·lu·tion \,rev-ə-'lü-shən\ *n* 1 : the action by a celestial body of going round in a fixed course 2 : completion of a course (as of years) : CYCLE 3 : a turning round a center or axis : ROTATION 4 : a single complete turn (as of a wheel) 5 : a sudden, extreme, or complete change (as in manner of living or working) 6 : the overthrow of one government and the substitution of another by the governed

rev·o·lu·tion·ary \,rev-ə-'lü-shə-,ner-ē\ *adj* 1 : of, relating to, or involving revolution ⟨a *revolutionary* war⟩ ⟨*revolutionary* improvements⟩ 2 : ¹RADICAL 2 ⟨*revolutionary* ideas⟩

rev·o·lu·tion·ist \,rev-ə-'lü-shə-nəst\ *n* : a person taking part in or supporting a revolution

rev·o·lu·tion·ize \,rev-ə-'lü-shə-,nīz\ *vb* **rev·o·lu·tion·ized**; **rev·o·lu·tion·iz·ing**

: to change greatly or completely ⟨*revolutionize* an industry by new methods⟩

re·volve \ri-'välv, -'vȯlv\ *vb* **re·volved; re·volv·ing 1** : to think over carefully **2** : to move in an orbit ⟨planets *revolving* around the sun⟩ **3** : ROTATE 1

re·volv·er \ri-'väl-vər, -'vȯl-\ *n* : a pistol having a revolving cylinder holding several bullets all of which may be shot without loading again

re·vue \ri-'vyü\ *n* : a theatrical entertainment consisting usually of short and often funny sketches and songs

¹re·ward \ri-'wȯrd\ *vb* : to give a reward to or for

²reward *n* : something (as money) given or offered in return for a service (as the return of something lost)

re·word \'rē-'wərd\ *vb* : to state in different words ⟨*reword* a question⟩

re·write \'rē-'rīt\ *vb* **re·wrote** \-'rōt\; **re·writ·ten** \-'rit-n\; **re·writ·ing** \-'rīt-ing\ : to write over again especially in a different form

rhap·so·dy \'rap-səd-ē\ *n, pl* **rhap·so·dies** : a written or spoken expression of extreme praise or delight

rhea \'rē-ə\ *n* : a tall flightless South American bird that has three toes on each foot and is like but smaller than the ostrich

rheu·mat·ic \rú-'mat-ik\ *adj* : of, relating to, or suffering from rheumatism —**rheu·mat·i·cal·ly** \-i-kə-lē\ *adv*

rhea

rheu·ma·tism \'rü-mə-ˌtiz-əm\ *n* : any of several disorders in which muscles or joints are red, hot, and painful

rhi·no \'rī-nō\ *n, pl* **rhino** *or* **rhi·nos** : RHINOCEROS

rhi·noc·er·os \rī-'näs-ə-rəs\ *n, pl* **rhi·noc·er·os·es** *or* **rhinoceros** : a large mammal of Africa and Asia with a thick skin, three toes on each foot, and one or two heavy upright horns on the snout

rho·do·den·dron \ˌrōd-ə-'den-drən\ *n* : a shrub or tree with long usually shiny and evergreen leaves and showy clusters of white, pink, red, or purple flowers

rhom·bus \'räm-bəs\ *n* : a parallelogram whose sides are equal

rhu·barb \'rü-ˌbärb\ *n* : a plant with broad green leaves and thick juicy pink or red stems that are used for food

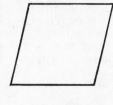

rhombus

¹rhyme *or* **rime** \'rīm\ *n* **1** : close similarity in the final sounds of two or more words or lines of verse **2** : a verse composition that rhymes

²rhyme *or* **rime** *vb* **rhymed** *or* **rimed; rhym·ing** *or* **rim·ing 1** : to make rhymes **2** : to end with the same sound **3** : to cause lines or words to end with a similar sound

rhythm \'rith-əm\ *n* **1** : a flow of rising and falling sounds produced in poetry by a regular repeating of stressed and unstressed syllables **2** : a flow of sound in music having regular accented beats **3** : a movement or activity in which some action repeats regularly ⟨the *rhythm* of breathing⟩

rhyth·mic \'rith-mik\ *or* **rhyth·mi·cal** \-mi-kəl\ *adj* : having rhythm — **rhyth·mi·cal·ly** *adv*

¹rib \'rib\ *n* **1** : one of the series of curved bones that are joined in pairs to the backbone of humans and other vertebrates and help to stiffen the body wall **2** : something (as a piece of wire supporting the fabric of an umbrella) that is like a rib in shape or use **3** : one of the parallel ridges in a knitted or woven fabric — **ribbed** \'ribd\ *adj*

²rib *vb* **ribbed; rib·bing 1** : to provide or enclose with ribs **2** : to form ribs in (a fabric) in knitting or weaving

rib·bon \'rib-ən\ *n* **1** : a narrow strip of fabric (as silk) used for trimming or for tying or decorating packages **2** : a long narrow strip like a ribbon ⟨typewriter *ribbon*⟩ **3** : TATTER 1, SHRED ⟨torn to *ribbons*⟩

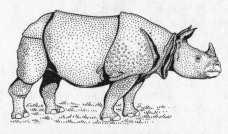

rhinoceros

\ə\ abut	\aú\ out	\i\ tip	\ȯ\ saw	\ú\ foot
\ər\ further	\ch\ chin	\ī\ life	\ȯi\ coin	\y\ yet
\a\ mat	\e\ pet	\j\ job	\th\ thin	\yü\ cure
\ā\ take	\ē\ easy	\ng\ sing	\th\ this	\yú\ few
\ä\ cot, cart	\g\ go	\ō\ bone	\ü\ food	\zh\ vision

rice \'rīs\ *n* : an annual cereal grass widely grown in warm wet regions for its grain that is a chief food in many parts of the world

rich \'rich\ *adj* **1** : having great wealth ⟨*rich* people⟩ **2** : ¹VALUABLE 1, EXPENSIVE ⟨*rich* robes⟩ **3** : containing much sugar, fat, or seasoning ⟨*rich* food⟩ **4** : high in fuel content ⟨a *rich* mixture⟩ **5** : deep and pleasing in color or tone **6** : ABUNDANT ⟨a *rich* harvest⟩ **7** : FERTILE 1 ⟨*rich* soil⟩ — **rich·ly** *adv* — **rich·ness** *n*

rich·es \'rich-əz\ *n pl* : things that make one rich : WEALTH

rick·ets \'rik-əts\ *n* : a disease in which the bones are soft and deformed and which usually attacks the young and is caused by lack of the vitamin that controls the use of calcium and phosphorus

rick·ety \'rik-ət-ē\ *adj* : SHAKY, UNSOUND ⟨*rickety* stairs⟩

rick·sha *or* **rick·shaw** \'rik-,shȯ\ *n* : a small hooded carriage with two wheels that is pulled by one person and was used originally in Japan

ricksha

¹**ric·o·chet** \'rik-ə-,shā\ *n* : a bouncing off at an angle (as of a bullet off a wall)

²**ricochet** *vb* **ric·o·cheted; ric·o·chet·ing** : to bounce off at an angle

rid \'rid\ *vb* **rid** *also* **rid·ded; rid·ding** : to free from something : RELIEVE ⟨*rid* a dog of fleas⟩

rid·dance \'rid-ns\ *n* : the act of ridding : the state of being rid of something

¹**rid·dle** \'rid-l\ *n* : a puzzling question to be solved or answered by guessing

²**riddle** *vb* **rid·dled; rid·dling** : to pierce with many holes

¹**ride** \'rīd\ *vb* **rode** \'rōd\; **rid·den** \'rid-n\; **rid·ing** \'rīd-ing\ **1** : to go on an animal's back or in a vehicle (as a car) **2** : to sit on and control so as to be carried along ⟨*ride* a bicycle⟩ **3** : to float or move on water **4** : to travel over a surface **5** : CARRY 1 ⟨*rode* the child on my shoulders⟩ — **rid·er** \'rīd-ər\ *n*

²**ride** *n* **1** : a trip on horseback or by vehicle **2** : a mechanical device (as a merry-go-round) that one rides for fun **3** : a means of transportation ⟨wants a *ride* to school⟩

ridge \'rij\ *n* **1** : a range of hills or mountains **2** : a raised strip **3** : the line made where two sloping surfaces come together ⟨the *ridge* of a roof⟩ — **ridged** \'rijd\ *adj*

ridge·pole \'rij-,pōl\ *n* : the highest horizontal timber in a sloping roof to which the upper ends of the rafters are fastened

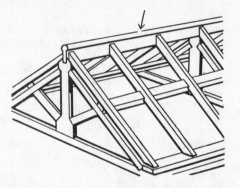

ridgepole

¹**rid·i·cule** \'rid-ə-,kyül\ *n* : the act of making fun of someone

²**ridicule** *vb* **rid·i·culed; rid·i·cul·ing** : to make fun of : DERIDE

ri·dic·u·lous \rə-'dik-yə-ləs\ *adj* : causing or deserving ridicule : ABSURD — **ri·dic·u·lous·ly** *adv* — **ri·dic·u·lous·ness** *n*

riff·raff \'rif-,raf\ *n* : RABBLE 2

¹**ri·fle** \'rī-fəl\ *vb* **ri·fled; ri·fling** **1** : to search through fast and roughly especially in order to steal **2** : ¹STEAL 2

Word History There was an early French verb that meant "to scratch or file." This verb was also used to mean "to plunder." The English verb *rifle* came from this early French verb. The English noun *rifle* also came from the early French verb meaning "to scratch or file." The noun *rifle* first meant "a spiral groove cut or filed into the barrel of a gun." Later the word *rifle* came to be used for guns with such spiral grooves in their barrels.

²**rifle** *n* : a gun having a long barrel with spiral grooves on its inside

rift \'rift\ *n* **1** : an opening made by splitting or separation : CLEFT **2** : a break in friendly relations

¹**rig** \'rig\ *vb* **rigged; rig·ging** **1** : to fit out (as a ship) with rigging **2** : CLOTHE 1, 2,

DRESS **3** : EQUIP **4** : to set up usually for temporary use ⟨*rigged* a shelter of branches⟩

²rig *n* **1** : the shape, number, and arrangement of sails on a ship of one class or type that sets it apart from ships of other classes or types **2** : apparatus for a certain purpose ⟨oil-drilling *rig*⟩

rig·ging \'rig-ing\ *n* : the ropes and chains that hold and move the masts, sails, and spars of a ship

¹right \'rīt\ *adj* **1** : being just or good : UPRIGHT **2** : ACCURATE, CORRECT ⟨the *right* answer⟩ **3** : SUITABLE, APPROPRIATE ⟨the *right* person for the job⟩ **4** : STRAIGHT 1 ⟨a *right* line⟩ **5** : of, relating to, located on, or being the side of the body away from the heart ⟨the *right* hand is stronger in most persons⟩ **6** : located nearer to the right hand ⟨the *right* arm of my chair⟩ **7** : made to be placed or worn outward ⟨*right* side out⟩ **8** : healthy in mind or body — **right·ly** *adv* — **right·ness** *n*

²right *n* **1** : the ideal of what is right and good ⟨loyalty, honesty, and faithfulness are elements of the *right*⟩ **2** : something to which one has a just claim ⟨the *right* to freedom⟩ **3** : the cause of truth or justice **4** : the right side or a part that is on or toward the right side

³right *adv* **1** : according to what is right ⟨live *right*⟩ **2** : in the exact location or position : PRECISELY ⟨it's *right* where you left it⟩ **3** : in a direct line or course : STRAIGHT ⟨went *right* home⟩ **4** : according to truth or fact ⟨guessed *right*⟩ **5** : in the right way : CORRECTLY ⟨you're not doing it *right*⟩ **6** : all the way ⟨*right* to the end⟩ **7** : without delay : IMMEDIATELY ⟨*right* after lunch⟩ **8** : on or to the right ⟨turn *right*⟩

⁴right *vb* **1** : to make right (something wrong or unjust) **2** : to adjust or restore to a proper state or condition **3** : to bring or bring back to a vertical position **4** : to become vertical

right angle *n* : an angle formed by two lines that are perpendicular to each other — **right-an·gled** \'rīt-'ang-gəld\ *adj*

righ·teous \'rī-chəs\ *adj* : doing or being what is right ⟨*righteous* people⟩ ⟨a *righteous* action⟩ — **righ·teous·ly** *adv* — **righ·teous·ness** *n*

right·ful \'rīt-fəl\ *adj* : LAWFUL 2, PROPER ⟨the *rightful* owner⟩— **right·ful·ly** \-fə-lē\ *adv* — **right·ful·ness** *n*

right–hand \,rīt-,hand\ *adj* **1** : located on the right **2** : RIGHT-HANDED **3** : relied on most of all

right–hand·ed \'rīt-'han-dəd\ *adj* **1** : us-ing the right hand more easily than the left ⟨a *right–handed* pitcher⟩ **2** : done or made with or for the right hand **3** : CLOCKWISE

right–of–way \,rīt-əv-'wā\ *n, pl* **rights–of–way** \,rīt-səv-\ **1** : the right to pass over someone else's land **2** : the right of some traffic to go before other traffic

right triangle *n* : a triangle having a right angle

rig·id \'rij-əd\ *adj* **1** : not flexible : STIFF **2** : STRICT 1, SEVERE ⟨*rigid* discipline⟩ — **rigid·ly** *adv* — **rig·id·ness** *n*

rig·ma·role \'rig-mə-,rōl\ *n* : NONSENSE 1

rig·or \'rig-ər\ *n* : a harsh severe condition (as of discipline or weather)

rig·or·ous \'rig-ə-rəs\ *adj* **1** : very strict **2** : hard to put up with : HARSH — **rig·or·ous·ly** *adv* — **rig·or·ous·ness** *n*

rill \'ril\ *n* : a very small brook

rim \'rim\ *n* **1** : an outer edge especially of something curved **2** : the outer part of a wheel **synonyms** see BORDER — **rimmed** \'rimd\ *adj*

¹rime \'rīm\ *n* : ¹FROST 2

²rime *variant of* RHYME

rind \'rīnd\ *n* : a usually hard or tough outer layer ⟨bacon *rind*⟩

¹ring \'ring\ *n* **1** : a circular band worn as an ornament or used for holding or fastening **2** : something circular in shape ⟨smoke *ring*⟩ **3** : a place for exhibitions (as at a circus) or contests (as in boxing) **4** : a group of persons who work together for selfish or dishonest purposes — **ringed** \'ringd\ *adj* — **ring·like** \'ring-,līk\ *adj*

²ring *vb* **ringed; ring·ing** **1** : to place or form a ring around : to throw a ring over (a peg or hook) in a game (as quoits)

³ring *vb* **rang** \'rang\; **rung** \'rəng\; **ring·ing** **1** : to make or cause to make a rich vibrating sound when struck ⟨the bell *rang* clearly⟩ ⟨*ring* the school bell⟩ **2** : to sound a bell ⟨*ring* for the waiter⟩ **3** : to announce by or as if by striking a bell ⟨*ring* in the New Year⟩ **4** : to sound loudly ⟨their cheers *rang* out⟩ **5** : to be filled with talk or report ⟨the whole school *rang* with the news⟩ **6** : to repeat loudly **7** : to seem to be a certain way ⟨their story *rings* true⟩ **8** : to call on the telephone

⁴ring *n* **1** : a clear ringing sound made by vibrating metal **2** : a tone suggesting that of a bell **3** : a loud or continuing noise **4** : something that suggests a certain quality

\ə\ **abut**	\au̇\ **out**	\i\ **tip**	\ȯ\ **saw**	\u̇\ **foot**	
\ər\ **further**	\ch\ **chin**	\ī\ **life**	\ȯi\ **coin**	\y\ **yet**	
\a\ **mat**	\e\ **pet**	\j\ **job**	\th\ **thin**	\yü\ **few**	
\ā\ **take**	\ē\ **easy**	\ng\ **sing**	\th\ **this**	\yu̇\ **cure**	
\ä\ **cot, cart**	\g\ **go**	\ō\ **bone**	\ü\ **food**	\zh\ **vision**	

⟨their story had the *ring* of truth⟩ **5** : a telephone call

ring·lead·er \'ring-ˌlēd-ər\ *n* : a leader especially of a group of persons who cause trouble

ring·let \'ring-lət\ *n* : a long curl

ring·worm \'ring-ˌwərm\ *n* : a contagious skin disease with discolored rings on the skin

rink \'ringk\ *n* : a place for skating

¹rinse \'rins\ *vb* **rinsed; rins·ing 1** : to wash lightly with water ⟨*rinse* one's mouth⟩ **2** : to cleanse (as of soap) with clear water ⟨*rinse* the dishes⟩ **3** : to treat (hair) with a rinse

²rinse *n* **1** : an act of rinsing **2** : a liquid used for rinsing **3** : a solution that temporarily tints hair

¹ri·ot \'rī-ət\ *n* **1** : public violence, disturbance, or disorder **2** : a colorful display

²riot *vb* : to create or take part in a riot

¹rip \'rip\ *vb* **ripped; rip·ping** : to cut or tear open — **rip·per** *n*

²rip *n* : ³TEAR 2

ripe \'rīp\ *adj* **rip·er; rip·est 1** : fully grown and developed ⟨*ripe* fruit⟩ **2** : having mature knowledge, understanding, or judgment **3** : ¹READY 1 ⟨*ripe* for action⟩ — **ripe·ness** *n*

rip·en \'rī-pən\ *vb* : to make or become ripe

¹rip·ple \'rip-əl\ *vb* **rip·pled; rip·pling 1** : to become or cause to become covered with small waves **2** : to make a sound like that of water flowing in small waves

²ripple *n* **1** : the disturbing of the surface of water **2** : a sound like that of rippling water

¹rise \'rīz\ *vb* **rose** \'rōz\; **ris·en** \'riz-n\; **ris·ing** \'rī-zing\ **1** : to get up from lying, kneeling, or sitting **2** : to get up from sleep or from one's bed **3** : to return from death **4** : to take up arms **5** : to appear above the horizon **6** : to go up : ASCEND ⟨smoke *rises*⟩ **7** : to swell in size or volume ⟨their voices *rose* as they argued⟩ **8** : to become encouraged ⟨their spirits *rose*⟩ **9** : to gain a higher rank or position **10** : to increase in amount or number ⟨*rising* prices⟩ **11** : ARISE 3 **12** : to come into being : ORIGINATE **13** : to show oneself equal to a demand or test ⟨*rise* to the occasion⟩ — **ris·er** \'rī-zər\ *n*

²rise *n* **1** : an act of rising : a state of being risen **2** : BEGINNING 1, ORIGIN **3** : an increase in amount, number, or volume **4** : an upward slope **5** : a spot higher than surrounding ground **6** : an angry reaction

¹risk \'risk\ *n* : possibility of loss or injury **synonyms** see DANGER

²risk *vb* **1** : to expose to danger **2** : to take the risk or danger of

risky \'ris-kē\ *adj* **risk·i·er; risk·i·est** : DANGEROUS 1

rite \'rīt\ *n* **1** : a set form of conducting a ceremony **2** : a ceremonial act or action

rit·u·al \'rich-ə-wəl\ *n* **1** : an established form for a ceremony **2** : a system of rites

¹ri·val \'rī-vəl\ *n* : one of two or more trying to get what only one can have

Word History We can trace the English word *rival* back to a Latin word that meant "stream." Another Latin word was formed from the word that meant "stream." This word meant "one who uses the same stream as another." Those who must share a stream may fight about who has the better right to the water. There will often be disputes like that when two people want the same thing. The Latin word for people who share streams was used for others who are likely to fight, too. It meant "a man in love with the same woman some other man loves." The word *rival* came from this Latin word.

²rival *adj* : having the same worth ⟨*rival* claims⟩

³rival *vb* **ri·valed** *or* **ri·valled; ri·val·ing** *or* **ri·val·ling 1** : to be in competition with **2** : ³EQUAL

ri·val·ry \'rī-vəl-rē\ *n*, *pl* **ri·val·ries** : the act of rivaling : the state of being a rival : COMPETITION

riv·er \'riv-ər\ *n* **1** : a natural stream of water larger than a brook or creek **2** : a large stream ⟨a *river* of oil⟩

riv·et \'riv-ət\ *n* : a bolt with a head at one end used for uniting two or more pieces by passing the shank through a hole in each piece and then beating or pressing down the plain end so as to make a second head

riv·u·let \'riv-yə-lət\ *n* : a small stream

roach \'rōch\ *n* : COCKROACH

road \'rōd\ *n* **1** : an open way for vehicles, persons, and animals **2** : PATH 3, ROUTE ⟨the *road* to prosperity⟩

road·bed \'rōd-ˌbed\ *n* **1** : the foundation of a road or railroad **2** : the traveled surface of a road

road·side \'rōd-ˌsīd\ *n* : the strip of land along a road : the side of a road

road·way \'rōd-ˌwā\ *n* **1** : the strip of land over which a road passes **2** : the part of the surface of a road traveled by vehicles

roam \'rōm\ *vb* : to go from place to place with no fixed purpose or direction **synonyms** see WANDER — **roam·er** *n*

¹roan \'rōn\ *adj* : of a dark color (as black

or brown) sprinkled with white ⟨a *roan* horse⟩

²roan *n* : an animal (as a horse) with a roan coat

¹roar \'rōr\ *vb* **1** : to utter a long full loud sound **2** : to laugh loudly — **roar·er** *n*

²roar *n* : a long shout, bellow, or loud confused noise

¹roast \'rōst\ *vb* **1** : to cook with dry heat (as in an oven) **2** : to be or make very hot — **roast·er** *n*

²roast *n* **1** : a piece of meat roasted or suitable for roasting **2** : an outing at which food is roasted

³roast *adj* : cooked by roasting ⟨*roast* beef⟩

rob \'räb\ *vb* **robbed; rob·bing** **1** : to take something away from a person or place in secrecy or by force, threat, or trickery **2** : to keep from getting something due, expected, or desired — **rob·ber** *n*

rob·bery \'räb-ə-rē, 'räb-rē\ *n, pl* **rob·ber·ies** : the act or practice of robbing

¹robe \'rōb\ *n* **1** : a long loose or flowing garment ⟨a judge's *robe*⟩ **2** : a covering for the lower part of the body ⟨snuggled under the lap *robe*⟩

²robe *vb* **robed; rob·ing** **1** : to put on a robe **2** : ¹DRESS 2 ⟨*robed* in white⟩

rob·in \'räb-ən\ *n* **1** : a small European thrush with a yellowish red throat and breast **2** : a large North American thrush with a grayish back and dull reddish breast

ro·bot \'rō-,bät\ *n* **1** : a machine that looks and acts like a human being **2** : a capable but unfeeling person

Word History A man in Czechoslovakia wrote a play about machines that looked like people. The machines were meant to work like slaves. The name given to these machines came from a word that meant "forced work" in the language of Czechoslovakia. The English word *robot* comes from the name of the machines in the play.

ro·bust \rō-'bəst\ *adj* : strong and vigorously healthy — **ro·bust·ly** *adv* — **ro·bust·ness** *n*

¹rock \'räk\ *vb* **1** : to move back and forth as in a cradle **2** : to sway or cause to sway back and forth ⟨an earthquake *rocked* the town⟩

²rock *n* **1** : a rocking movement **2** : popular music played on instruments that are amplified electronically

³rock *n* **1** : a large mass of stone **2** : solid mineral deposits **3** : something like a rock in firmness : SUPPORT

rock·er \'räk-ər\ *n* **1** : a curving piece of wood or metal on which an object (as a

rocking chair) rocks **2** : a structure or device that rocks on rockers **3** : a mechanism that works with a rocking motion

¹rock·et \'räk-ət\ *n* **1** : a firework that is driven through the air by the gases produced by a burning substance **2** : a jet engine that operates like a firework rocket but carries the oxygen needed for burning its fuel **3** : a bomb, missile, or vehicle that is moved by a rocket

²rocket *vb* **1** : to rise swiftly **2** : to travel rapidly in or as if in a rocket

rock·ing horse \'räk-ing-\ *n* : a toy horse mounted on rockers

rock 'n' roll *or* **rock and roll** *n* : ²ROCK 2

rock salt *n* : common salt in large crystals

rocky \'räk-ē\ *adj* **rock·i·er; rock·i·est** : full of or consisting of rocks — **rock·i·ness** *n*

rod \'räd\ *n* **1** : a straight slender stick or bar **2** : a stick or bundle of twigs used in whipping a person **3** : a measure of length equal to 16½ feet (about 5 meters) **4** : any of the sensory bodies shaped like rods in the retina that respond to faint light **5** : a light flexible pole often with line and a reel attached used in fishing — **rod·like** \-,līk\ *adj*

rode *past of* RIDE

ro·dent \'rōd-nt\ *n* : any of a group of mammals (as squirrels, rats, mice, and beavers) with sharp front teeth used in gnawing

ro·deo \'rōd-ē-,ō, rə-'dā-ō\ *n, pl* **ro·de·os** **1** : a roundup of cattle **2** : an exhibition that features cowboy skills (as riding and roping)

¹roe \'rō\ *n, pl* **roe** *or* **roes** **1** : ROE DEER **2** : DOE

²roe *n* : the eggs of a fish especially while still held together in a membrane

roe·buck \'rō-,bək\ *n* : a male roe deer

roe deer *n* : a small deer of Europe and Asia with erect antlers forked at the tip

rogue \'rōg\ *n* **1** : a dishonest or wicked person **2** : a pleasantly mischievous person

rogu·ish \'rō-gish\ *adj* : being or like a rogue — **rogu·ish·ly** *adv* — **rogu·ish·ness** *n*

role \'rōl\ *n* **1** : a character assigned or taken on **2** : a part played by an actor or singer **3** : ¹FUNCTION 1 ⟨the *role* of the teacher in education⟩

¹roll \'rōl\ *n* **1** : a writing that may be rolled

\ə\ abut	\au̇\ out	\i\ tip	\ȯ\ saw	\u̇\ foot
\ər\ further	\ch\ chin	\ī\ life	\ȯi\ coin	\y\ yet
\a\ mat	\e\ pet	\j\ job	\th\ thin	\yü\ few
\ā\ take	\ē\ easy	\ng\ sing	\th\ this	\yu̇\ cure
\ä\ cot, cart	\g\ go	\ō\ bone	\ü\ food	\zh\ vision

up : SCROLL **2** : an official list of names **3** : something or a quantity of something that is rolled up or rounded as if rolled **4** : a small piece of baked bread dough

²roll *vb* **1** : to move by turning over and over on a surface without sliding **2** : to shape or become shaped in rounded form **3** : to make smooth, even, or firm with a roller **4** : to move on rollers or wheels **5** : to sound with a full echoing tone or with a continuous beating sound **6** : to go by : PASS ⟨time *rolled* by⟩ **7** : to flow in a continuous stream ⟨the money was *rolling* in⟩ **8** : to move with a side-to-side sway ⟨the ship *rolled*⟩

³roll *n* **1** : a sound produced by rapid strokes on a drum **2** : a heavy echoing sound ⟨the *roll* of thunder⟩ **3** : a rolling movement or action

roll·er \'rō-lər\ *n* **1** : a turning cylinder over or on which something is moved or which is used to press, shape, or smooth something **2** : a rod on which something (as a map) is rolled up **3** : a small wheel **4** : a long heavy wave on the sea

roll·er coast·er \'rō-lər-ˌkō-stər\ *n* : an elevated railway (as in an amusement park) with sharp curves and steep slopes on which cars roll

roller skate *n* : a skate that has wheels instead of a runner

roll·ing pin *n* : a cylinder (as of wood) used to roll out dough

¹Ro·man \'rō-mən\ *n* **1** : a person born or living in Rome **2** : a citizen of the Roman Empire **3** *not cap* : roman letters or type

²Roman *adj* **1** : of or relating to Rome or the Romans **2** *not cap* : of or relating to a type style with upright characters (as in "these definitions")

¹ro·mance \rō-'mans\ *n* **1** : an old tale of knights and noble ladies **2** : an adventure story **3** : a love story **4** : a love affair **5** : an attraction or appeal to one's feelings ⟨the *romance* of the sea⟩

²romance *vb* **ro·manced; ro·manc·ing** : to have romantic thoughts or ideas

Roman numeral *n* : a numeral in a system of figures based on the ancient Roman system ⟨some *Roman numerals* with corresponding Arabic numerals are I = 1; IV = 4; V = 5; IX = 9; X = 10; XI = 11; L = 50; C = 100; D = 500; M = 1000⟩

ro·man·tic \rō-'mant-ik\ *adj* **1** : not founded on fact : IMAGINARY **2** : IMPRACTI-CAL ⟨a *romantic* scheme⟩ **3** : stressing or appealing to the emotions or imagination **4** : of, relating to, or associated with love — **ro·man·ti·cal·ly** \-i-kə-lē\ *adv*

¹romp \'rämp\ *n* : rough and noisy play : FROLIC

²romp *vb* : to play in a rough and noisy way

romp·ers \'räm-pərz\ *n pl* : a child's one-piece garment with the lower part shaped like bloomers

¹roof \'rüf, 'rùf\ *n, pl* **roofs** **1** : the upper covering part of a building **2** : something like a roof in form, position, or purpose — **roofed** \'rüft, 'rùft\ *adj*

²roof *vb* : to cover with a roof

roof·ing \'rüf-ing, 'rùf-\ *n* : material for a roof

roof·tree \'rüf-ˌtrē, 'rùf-\ *n* : RIDGEPOLE

¹rook \'rùk\ *n* : an Old World bird similar to the related crows

²rook *vb* : ²CHEAT 1, SWINDLE

³rook *n* : one of the pieces in the game of chess

rook·ie \'rùk-ē\ *n* : BEGINNER, RECRUIT

¹room \'rüm, 'rùm\ *n* **1** : available space ⟨had barely *room* to move⟩ **2** : a divided part of the inside of a building **3** : the people in a room **4 rooms** *pl* : LODGING 2 **5** : a suitable opportunity ⟨you have *room* to improve your work⟩

²room *vb* : to provide with or live in lodgings

room·er \'rüm-ər, 'rùm-\ *n* : LODGER

rooming house *n* : a house for renting furnished rooms to lodgers

room·mate \'rüm-ˌmāt, 'rùm-\ *n* : one of two or more persons sharing a room or dwelling

roomy \'rüm-ē, 'rùm-\ *adj* **room·i·er; room·i·est** : SPACIOUS — **room·i·ness** *n*

¹roost \'rüst\ *n* : a support on which birds perch

²roost *vb* : to settle on a roost

roost·er \'rüs-tər\ *n* : an adult male chicken

¹root \'rüt, 'rùt\ *n* **1** : a leafless underground part of a plant that stores food and holds the plant in place **2** : the part of something by which it is attached **3** : something like a root especially in being a source of support or growth **4** : SOURCE 2 ⟨the *root* of evil⟩ **5** : ¹CORE 2 ⟨get to the *root* of the matter⟩ **6** : a word or part of a word from which other words are obtained by adding a prefix or suffix ⟨"hold" is the *root* of "holder"⟩ — **root·ed** \-əd\ *adj*

²root *vb* **1** : to form or cause to form roots **2** : to attach by or as if by roots **3** : UPROOT 1 ⟨*root* crime from our cities⟩

³root *vb* : to turn up or dig with the snout

⁴root \'rüt\ *vb* : ²CHEER 2 — **root·er** *n*

root beer *n* : a sweet drink flavored with extracts of roots and herbs

¹rope \'rōp\ *n* **1** : a large stout cord of strands (as of fiber or wire) twisted or braided together **2** : a noose used for hanging **3** : a row or string (as of beads) made by braiding, twining, or threading

²rope *vb* **roped; rop•ing 1** : to bind, fasten, or tie with a rope **2** : to set off or divide by a rope ⟨*rope* off a street⟩ **3** : ²LASSO — **rop•er** *n*

ro•sa•ry \'rō-zə-rē\ *n, pl* **ro•sa•ries** : a string of beads used in counting prayers

¹rose *past of* RISE

²rose \'rōz\ *n* **1** : a showy and often fragrant white, yellow, pink, or red flower that grows on a prickly shrub (**rosebush**) with compound leaves **2** : a moderate purplish red

rose•mary \'rōz-,mer-ē\ *n* : a fragrant mint that has branching woody stems and is used in cooking and in perfumes

ro•sette \rō-'zet\ *n* : a badge or ornament of ribbon gathered in the shape of a rose

rose•wood \'rōz-,wùd\ *n* : a reddish or purplish wood streaked with black and that is valued for making furniture

Rosh Ha•sha•nah \,rōsh-hə-'shō-nə\ *n* : the Jewish New Year observed as a religious holiday in September or October

ros•in \'räz-n\ *n* : a hard brittle yellow to dark red substance obtained especially from pine trees and used in varnishes and on violin bows

ros•ter \'räs-tər\ *n* : an orderly list usually of people belonging to some group

ros•trum \'räs-trəm\ *n, pl* **ros•trums** *or* **ros•tra** \-trə\ : a stage or platform for public speaking

rosy \'rō-zē\ *adj* **ros•i•er; ros•i•est 1** : of the color rose **2** : PROMISING, HOPEFUL ⟨*rosy* prospects⟩

¹rot \'rät\ *vb* **rot•ted; rot•ting 1** : to undergo decay : SPOIL **2** : to go to ruin

²rot *n* **1** : the process of rotting : the state of being rotten **2** : a disease of plants or of animals in which tissue decays

ro•ta•ry \'rōt-ə-rē\ *adj* **1** : turning on an axis like a wheel **2** : having a rotating part

ro•tate \'rō-,tāt\ *vb* **ro•tat•ed; ro•tat•ing 1** : to turn about an axis or a center **2** : to do or cause to do something in turn **3** : to pass in a series

ro•ta•tion \rō-'tā-shən\ *n* **1** : the act of rotating especially on an axis **2** : the growing of different crops in the same field usually in a regular order

rote \'rōt\ *n* : repeating from memory of forms or phrases with little or no attention to meaning ⟨learn by *rote*⟩

ro•tor \'rōt-ər\ *n* **1** : the part of an electrical machine that turns **2** : a system of spinning horizontal blades that support a helicopter in the air

rot•ten \'rät-n\ *adj* **1** : having rotted **2** : morally bad **3** : very unpleasant or worthless ⟨a *rotten* game⟩ — **rot•ten•ly** *adv* — **rot•ten•ness** *n*

ro•tund \rō-'tənd\ *adj* **1** : somewhat round **2** : ³PLUMP — **ro•tund•ly** *adv* — **ro•tund•ness** *n*

rouge \'rüzh\ *n* : a cosmetic used to give a red color to cheeks or lips

¹rough \'rəf\ *adj* **1** : uneven in surface **2** : not calm ⟨*rough* seas⟩ **3** : being harsh or violent ⟨*rough* treatment⟩ **4** : coarse or rugged in nature or look **5** : not complete or exact ⟨a *rough* estimate⟩ **synonyms** see HARSH — **rough•ly** *adv* — **rough•ness** *n*

²rough *n* **1** : uneven ground covered with high grass, brush, and stones **2** : something in a crude or unfinished state

³rough *vb* **1** : ROUGHEN **2** : to handle roughly : BEAT ⟨*roughed* up by hoodlums⟩ **3** : to make or shape roughly — **rough it** : to live without ordinary comforts

rough•age \'rəf-ij\ *n* : coarse food (as bran) whose bulk increases the activity of the bowel

rough•en \'rəf-ən\ *vb* : to make or become rough

rough•neck \'rəf-,nek\ *n* : a rough person : ROWDY

¹round \'raùnd\ *adj* **1** : having every part of the surface or circumference the same distance from the center **2** : shaped like a cylinder **3** : ³PLUMP **4** : ¹COMPLETE 1, FULL ⟨a *round* dozen⟩ **5** : nearly correct or exact ⟨in *round* numbers⟩ **6** : LARGE ⟨a good *round* sum⟩ **7** : moving in or forming a circle **8** : having curves rather than angles — **round•ish** \'raùn-dish\ *adj* — **round•ly** *adv* — **round•ness** *n*

²round *adv* : ¹AROUND

³round *prep* : ²AROUND 1, 2, 3 ⟨travel *round* the world⟩

⁴round *n* **1** : something (as a circle or globe) that is round **2** : a song in which three or four singers sing the same melody and words one after another at intervals **3** : a round or curved part (as a rung of a ladder) **4** : an indirect path **5** : a regularly covered route **6** : a series or cycle of repeated actions or events **7** : one shot fired by a soldier or a gun **8**

\ə\ abut	\aù\ out	\i\ tip	\ò\ saw	\ù\ foot
\ər\ further	\ch\ chin	\ī\ life	\òi\ coin	\y\ yet
\a\ mat	\e\ pet	\j\ job	\th\ thin	\yü\ few
\ā\ take	\ē\ easy	\ng\ sing	\th\ this	\yù\ cure
\ä\ cot, cart	\g\ go	\ō\ bone	\ü\ food	\zh\ vision

: ammunition for one shot **9** : a unit of play in a contest or game **10** : a cut of beef especially between the rump and the lower leg

⁵**round** *vb* **1** : to make or become round **2** : to go or pass around **3** : to bring to completion ⟨*round* out a career⟩ **4** : to express as a round number **5** : to follow a winding course

round·about \'raùn-də-,baùt\ *adj* : not direct ⟨took a *roundabout* route

round·house \'raùnd-,haùs\ *n, pl* **round·hous·es** \-,haù-zəz\ : a circular building where locomotives are kept or repaired

round trip *n* : a trip to a place and back usually over the same route

round·up \'raùn-,dəp\ *n* **1** : the gathering together of animals on the range by riding around them and driving them in **2** : a gathering together of scattered persons or things **3** : ²SUMMARY ⟨a *roundup* of the day's news⟩

round up *vb* **1** : to collect (as cattle) by circling on horseback and driving **2** : to gather in or bring together

round·worm \'raùn-,dwərm\ *n* : any of a group of worms with long round bodies that are not segmented and that include serious parasites of people and animals

rouse \'raùz\ *vb* **roused; rous·ing 1** : ¹AWAKE **1 2** : to stir up : EXCITE

¹**rout** \'raùt\ *n* **1** : a state of wild confusion or disorderly retreat **2** : a disastrous defeat ⟨we lost 44–0 — it was a *rout*⟩

²**rout** *vb* **1** : to put to flight **2** : to defeat completely

¹**route** \'rüt, 'raùt\ *n* : a regular, chosen, or assigned course of travel

²**route** *vb* **rout·ed; rout·ing 1** : to send or transport by a selected route **2** : to arrange and direct the order of (as a series of factory operations)

¹**rou·tine** \rü-'tēn\ *n* : a standard or usual way of doing

²**routine** *adj* **1** : ²COMMONPLACE, ORDINARY **2** : done or happening in a standard or usual way — **rou·tine·ly** *adv*

rove \'rōv\ *vb* **roved; rov·ing** : to wander without definite plan or direction — **rov·er** *n*

¹**row** \'rō\ *vb* **1** : to move a boat by means of oars **2** : to travel or carry in a rowboat

²**row** *n* : an act or instance of rowing

³**row** *n* **1** : a series of persons or things in an orderly sequence **2** : ¹WAY **1**, STREET

⁴**row** \'raù\ *n* : a noisy disturbance or quarrel

row·boat \'rō-,bōt\ *n* : a boat made to be rowed

¹**row·dy** \'raùd-ē\ *adj* **row·di·er; row·**

di·est : coarse or rough in behavior ⟨don't bring your *rowdy* friends⟩ — **row·di·ness** *n*

²**rowdy** *n, pl* **row·dies** : a rowdy person

roy·al \'rói-əl\ *adj* **1** : of or relating to a sovereign : REGAL **2** : fit for a king or queen ⟨gave the team a *royal* welcome⟩ — **roy·al·ly** *adv*

roy·al·ty \'rói-əl-tē\ *n, pl* **roy·al·ties 1** : royal status or power **2** : royal character or conduct **3** : members of a royal family **4** : a share of a product or profit (as of a mine) claimed by the owner for allowing another to use the property **5** : payment made to the owner of a patent or copyright for the use of it

¹**rub** \'rəb\ *vb* **rubbed; rub·bing 1** : to move along the surface of a body with pressure **2** : to wear away or chafe with friction **3** : to cause discontent, irritation, or anger **4** : to scour, polish, erase, or smear by pressure and friction

²**rub** *n* **1** : something that gets in the way : DIFFICULTY **2** : something that is annoying **3** : the act of rubbing

rub·ber \'rəb-ər\ *n* **1** : something used in rubbing **2** : an elastic substance obtained from the milky juice of some tropical plants **3** : a synthetic substance like rubber **4** : something (as an overshoe) made of rubber

rubber band *n* : a continuous band made of rubber for holding things together : ELASTIC

rubber stamp *n* : a stamp with a printing face of rubber

rub·bish \'rəb-ish\ *n* : TRASH

rub·ble \'rəb-əl\ *n* : a confused mass of broken or worthless things

ru·ble \'rü-bəl\ *n* : a Russian coin or bill

ru·by \'rü-bē\ *n, pl* **ru·bies 1** : a precious stone of a deep red color **2** : a deep purplish red

ruck·us \'rək-əs\ *n* : ⁴ROW

rud·der \'rəd-ər\ *n* : a movable flat piece attached at the rear of a ship or aircraft for steering

rud·dy \'rəd-ē\ *adj* **rud·di·er; rud·di·est**

rowboat

: having a healthy reddish color — **rud·di·ness** *n*

rude \'rüd\ *adj* **rud·er; rud·est 1** : roughly made **2** : not refined or cultured : UN-COUTH **3** : IMPOLITE — **rude·ly** *adv* — **rude·ness** *n*

ru·di·ment \'rüd-ə-mənt\ *n* : a basic principle

ru·di·men·ta·ry \,rüd-ə-'ment-ə-rē\ *adj* **1** : ELEMENTARY, SIMPLE **2** : not fully developed

rue \'rü\ *vb* **rued; ru·ing** : to feel sorrow or regret for

rue·ful \'rü-fəl\ *adj* **1** : exciting pity or sympathy **2** : MOURNFUL 1, REGRETFUL

ruff \'rəf\ *n* **1** : a collar of pleated muslin or linen worn by men and women in the sixteenth and seventeenth centuries **2** : a fringe of long hair or feathers on the neck of an animal or bird

ruff 1

ruf·fi·an \'rəf-ē-ən\ *n* : a brutal cruel person

¹**ruf·fle** \'rəf-əl\ *vb* **ruf·fled; ruf·fling 1** : to disturb the smoothness of **2** : ¹TROUBLE 1, VEX **3** : to erect (as feathers) in or like a ruff **4** : to make into or provide with a ruffle

²**ruffle** *n* : a strip of fabric gathered or pleated on one edge

rug \'rəg\ *n* : a piece of thick heavy fabric usually with a nap or pile used especially as a floor covering

rug·ged \'rəg-əd\ *adj* **1** : having a rough uneven surface **2** : involving hardship ⟨*rugged* training⟩ **3** : STRONG 9, TOUGH **synonyms** see HARSH — **rug·ged·ly** *adv* — **rug·ged·ness** *n*

¹**ru·in** \'rü-ən\ *n* **1** : complete collapse or destruction **2 ruins** *pl* : the remains of something destroyed **3** : a cause of destruction

²**ruin** *vb* **1** : to reduce to ruins **2** : to damage beyond repair **3** : ²BANKRUPT

ru·in·ous \'rü-ə-nəs\ *adj* : causing or likely to cause ruin : DESTRUCTIVE — **ru·in·ous·ly** *adv*

¹**rule** \'rül\ *n* **1** : a guide or principle for conduct or action **2** : an accepted method, custom, or habit **3** : the exercise of authority or control : GOVERNMENT **4** : the time of a particular sovereign's reign **5** : a straight strip of material (as wood or metal) marked off in units and used for measuring or as a guide in drawing straight lines

²**rule** *vb* **ruled; rul·ing 1** : ¹CONTROL 2, DIRECT **2** : to exercise authority over : GOVERN **3** : to be supreme or outstanding in **4** : to give or state as a considered decision **5** : to mark with lines drawn along the straight edge of a rule

rul·er \'rü-lər\ *n* **1** : ¹SOVEREIGN 1 **2** : ¹RULE 5

rum \'rəm\ *n* : an alcoholic liquor made from sugarcane or molasses

¹**rum·ble** \'rəm-bəl\ *vb* **rum·bled; rum·bling** : to make or move with a low heavy rolling sound

²**rumble** *n* : a low heavy rolling sound

¹**ru·mi·nant** \'rü-mə-nənt\ *n* : an animal (as a cow) that chews the cud

²**ruminant** *adj* **1** : chewing the cud **2** : of or relating to the group of hoofed mammals that chew the cud

ru·mi·nate \'rü-mə-,nāt\ *vb* **ru·mi·nat·ed; ru·mi·nat·ing 1** : to engage in thought : MEDITATE **2** : to bring up and chew again what has been previously swallowed

¹**rum·mage** \'rəm-ij\ *vb* **rum·maged; rum·mag·ing** : to make an active search especially by moving about, turning over, or looking through the contents of a place or container ⟨*rummaging* through the attic for old toys⟩

²**rummage** *n* : a confused collection of different articles

rum·my \'rəm-ē\ *n* : a card game in which each player tries to lay down cards in groups of three or more

¹**ru·mor** \'rü-mər\ *n* **1** : widely held opinion having no known source : HEARSAY **2** : a statement or story that is in circulation but has not been proven to be true

²**rumor** *vb* : to tell by rumor : spread a rumor

rump \'rəmp\ *n* **1** : the back part of an animal's body where the hips and thighs join **2** : a cut of beef between the loin and the round

rum·ple \'rəm-pəl\ *vb* **rum·pled; rum·pling** : ²WRINKLE, MUSS

rum·pus \'rəm-pəs\ *n* : ⁴ROW, FRACAS

¹**run** \'rən\ *vb* **ran** \'ran\; **run; run·ning 1** : to go at a pace faster than a walk **2** : to take to flight **3** : to move freely about as one wishes **4** : to go rapidly or hurriedly **5** : to do something by or as if by running ⟨*run* errands⟩ **6** : to take part in a race **7** : to move on or as if on wheels **8** : to go back and forth often according to a fixed schedule **9** : to migrate or move in schools ⟨the salmon are *running* early this year⟩

\ə\ abut	\au̇\ out	\i\ tip	\ȯ\ saw	\u̇\ foot
\ər\ further	\ch\ chin	\ī\ life	\ȯi\ coin	\y\ yet
\a\ mat	\e\ pet	\j\ job	\th\ thin	\yü\ few
\ā\ take	\ē\ easy	\ng\ sing	\th\ this	\yu̇\ cure
\ä\ cot, cart	\g\ go	\ō\ bone	\ü\ food	\zh\ vision

10 : ²FUNCTION, OPERATE **11** : to continue in force **12** : to pass into a specified condition **13** : ¹FLOW 1 **14** : DISSOLVE 1 ⟨dyes guaranteed not to *run*⟩ **15** : to give off liquid ⟨a *running* sore⟩ **16** : to tend to develop a specified feature or quality **17** : ¹STRETCH 2 **18** : to be in circulation ⟨the story *runs* that our principal is going to resign⟩ **19** : ²TRACE 4 **20** : to pass over, across, or through **21** : to slip through or past ⟨*run* a blockade⟩ **22** : to cause to penetrate **23** : to cause to go ⟨*ran* them out of town⟩ ⟨*ran* my car off the road⟩ **24** : INCUR — **run into** : to meet by chance

²run *n* **1** : an act or the action of running **2** : a continuous series especially of similar things ⟨had a long *run* of cloudy days⟩ **3** : sudden heavy demands from depositors, creditors, or customers ⟨a *run* on a bank⟩ **4** : the quantity of work turned out in a continuous operation **5** : the usual or normal kind ⟨people of the common *run*⟩ **6** : the distance covered in a period of continuous traveling **7** : a regular course or trip **8** : freedom of movement ⟨had the *run* of the house⟩ **9** : a way, track, or path frequented by animals ⟨a deer *run*⟩ **10** : an enclosure for animals where they may feed and exercise **11** : a score made in baseball by a base runner reaching home plate **12** : ²SLOPE 1 ⟨a ski *run*⟩ **13** : a ravel in a knitted fabric

¹run·away \'rən-ə-ˌwā\ *n* **1** : ²FUGITIVE **2** : a horse that is running out of control

²runaway *adj* : running away : escaping from control ⟨a *runaway* horse⟩

run–down \'rən-'daün\ *adj* **1** : being in poor condition ⟨a *run-down* farm⟩ **2** : being in poor health

¹rung \'rəng\ *past participle of* RING

²rung *n* **1** : a rounded part placed as a crosspiece between the legs of a chair **2** : one of the crosspieces of a ladder

run-in \'rən-ˌin\ *n* : an angry dispute : QUARREL

run·ner \'rən-ər\ *n* **1** : one that runs **2** : MESSENGER **3** : a thin piece or part on or in which something slides **4** : a slender creeping branch of a plant that roots at the end or at the joints to form new plants **5** : a plant that forms or spreads by runners **6** : a long narrow carpet (as for a hall)

run·ner–up \'rən-ə-ˌrəp\ *n*, *pl* **run·ners–up** \'rən-ər-ˌzəp\ : the competitor in a contest who finishes next to the winner

run·ny \'rən-ē\ *adj* : running or likely to run ⟨a *runny* nose⟩

run over *vb* : ¹OVERFLOW 2

runt \'rənt\ *n* : an unusually small person or animal

run·way \'rən-ˌwā\ *n* **1** : a path beaten by animals in going to and from feeding grounds **2** : a surfaced strip of ground for the landing and takeoff of aircraft

ru·pee \rü-'pē\ *n* : any of various coins (as of India or Pakistan)

¹rup·ture \'rəp-chər\ *n* **1** : a break in peaceful or friendly relations **2** : a breaking or tearing apart (as of body tissue) **3** : a condition in which a body part (as a loop of intestine) bulges through the weakened wall of the cavity that contains it

²rupture *vb* **rup·tured; rup·tur·ing 1** : to part by violence : BREAK **2** : to produce a rupture in **3** : to have a rupture

ru·ral \'rür-əl\ *adj* : of or relating to the country, country people or life, or agriculture

rural free delivery *n* : the free delivery of mail on routes in country districts

ruse \'rüs, 'rüz\ *n* : ¹TRICK 4, ARTIFICE

¹rush \'rəsh\ *n* : a grasslike marsh plant with hollow stems used in chair seats and mats

²rush *vb* **1** : to move forward or act with great haste or eagerness **2** : to perform in a short time or at high speed **3** : ¹ATTACK 1, CHARGE — **rush·er** *n*

³rush *n* **1** : a violent forward motion **2** : a burst of activity or speed **3** : a crowding together of people usually at a new place and in search of wealth ⟨gold *rush*⟩

⁴rush *adj* : demanding special speed ⟨a *rush* order⟩

¹Rus·sian \'rəsh-ən\ *adj* : of or relating to Russia, its people, or the Russian language

²Russian *n* **1** : a person born or living in Russia **2** : a language of the Russians

¹rust \'rəst\ *n* **1** : a reddish coating formed on metal (as iron) when it is exposed especially to moist air **2** : a plant disease caused by fungi that makes spots on plants **3** : a fungus that causes a rust — **rust·like** \-ˌlīk\ *adj*

²rust *vb* : to make or become rusty

¹rus·tic \'rəs-tik\ *adj* **1** : of, relating to, or suitable for the country **2** : ¹PLAIN 5, SIMPLE

²rustic *n* : a person living or raised in the country

¹rus·tle \'rəs-əl\ *vb* **rus·tled; rus·tling 1** : to make or cause to make a rustle **2** : to steal (as cattle) from the range — **rus·tler** \'rəs-lər\ *n*

²rustle *n* : a quick series of small sounds

rusty \'rəs-tē\ *adj* **rust·i·er; rust·i·est 1** : affected by rust ⟨a *rusty* nail⟩ **2** : less skilled and slow through lack of practice or old age — **rust·i·ness** *n*

¹rut \'rət\ *n* **1** : a track worn by a wheel or by habitual passage **2** : ¹ROUTINE

²rut *vb* **rut·ted; rut·ting** : to make a rut in

ru·ta·ba·ga \'rüt-ə-,bā-gə\ *n* : a turnip with a large yellow root

ruth·less \'rüth-ləs\ *adj* : having no pity : CRUEL — **ruth·less·ly** *adv* — **ruth·less·ness** *n*

-ry \rē\ *n suffix, pl* **-ries** : -ERY ⟨citizen*ry*⟩

rye \'rī\ *n* : a hardy cereal grass grown especially for its edible seeds that are used in flour and animal feeds and in making whiskey

s \'es\ *n, pl* **s's** *or* **ss** \'es-əz\ *often cap* **1** : the nineteenth letter of the English alphabet **2** : a grade rating a student's work as satisfactory

¹-s \s *after sounds* f, k, p, t, th; əz *after sounds* ch, j, s, sh, z, zh; z *after other sounds*\ *n pl suffix* **1** — used to form the plural of most nouns that do not end in *s, z, sh, ch,* or *y* following a consonant ⟨head*s*⟩ ⟨book*s*⟩ ⟨belief*s*⟩ and with or without an apostrophe to form the plural of abbreviations, numbers, letters, and symbols used as nouns ⟨4*s*⟩ ⟨num*s*⟩ ⟨B'*s*⟩ **2** — used to form adverbs showing usual or repeated action or state ⟨always at home Sunday*s*⟩

²-s *vb suffix* — used to form the third person singular present of most verbs that do not end in *s, z, sh, ch,* or *y* following a consonant ⟨fall*s*⟩ ⟨take*s*⟩ ⟨play*s*⟩

-'s *n suffix or pron suffix* — used to form the possessive of singular nouns ⟨elephant'*s*⟩, of plural nouns not ending in *s* ⟨children'*s*⟩, and of some pronouns ⟨anyone'*s*⟩

Sab·bath \'sab-əth\ *n* **1** : the seventh day of the week in the Jewish calendar beginning at sundown on Friday and lasting until sundown on Saturday **2** : the first day of the week (as Sunday) kept for rest and worship

sa·ber *or* **sa·bre** \'sā-bər\ *n* : a cavalry sword with a curved blade

sa·ber–toothed tiger \,sā-bər-,tütht-\ *n* : a very large prehistoric cat with long sharp curved eyeteeth

Sa·bin vaccine \'sā-bən-\ *n* : a material that is taken by mouth to prevent polio

sa·ble \'sā-bəl\ *n* **1** : the color black **2** : a meat-eating animal of northern Europe and Asia that is related to the marten and prized for its soft rich brown fur

¹sab·o·tage \'sab-ə-,täzh\ *n* : deliberate destruction of or damage to property or machinery (as by enemy agents) to block production or a nation's war effort

²sabotage *vb* **sab·o·taged; sab·o·tag·ing** : to damage or block by sabotage

sac \'sak\ *n* : a baglike part of a plant or animal often containing a liquid — **sac·like** \-,līk\ *adj*

sa·chem \'sā-chəm\ *n* : a North American Indian chief

¹sack \'sak\ *n* **1** : ¹BAG 1 **2** : a sack and its contents ⟨a *sack* of potatoes⟩

²sack *vb* : to put into a sack

³sack *n* : the looting of a city by its conquerors

⁴sack *vb* : to loot after capture

sack·ing \'sak-ing\ *n* : a strong rough cloth (as burlap) from which sacks are made

sac·ra·ment \'sak-rə-mənt\ *n* : a religious act or ceremony that is considered especially sacred ⟨baptism is a Christian *sacrament*⟩

sa·cred \'sā-krəd\ *adj* **1** : HOLY 1 ⟨the *sacred* name of God⟩ **2** : RELIGIOUS 2 ⟨*sacred* songs⟩ **3** : deserving to be respected and honored ⟨a *sacred* right⟩ — **sa·cred·ness** *n*

¹sac·ri·fice \'sak-rə-,fis\ *n* **1** : the act or ceremony of making an offering to God or a god especially on an altar **2** : something offered as a religious act **3** : an unselfish giving ⟨a *sacrifice* of our time to help others⟩ **4** : a loss of profit

²sacrifice *vb* **sac·ri·ficed; sac·ri·fic·ing** **1** : to offer or kill as a sacrifice **2** : to give for the sake of something else ⟨*sacrificed* their lives for their country⟩ **3** : to sell at a loss

sad \'sad\ *adj* **sad·der; sad·dest** **1** : filled with sorrow or unhappiness **2** : causing or showing sorrow or gloom — **sad·ly** *adv* — **sad·ness** *n*

\ə\ abut	\aú\ out	\i\ tip	\ò\ saw	\ú\ foot
\ər\ further	\ch\ chin	\ī\ life	\òi\ coin	\y\ yet
\a\ mat	\e\ pet	\j\ job	\th\ thin	\yü\ few
\ā\ take	\ē\ easy	\ng\ sing	\th\ this	\yú\ cure
\ä\ cot, cart	\g\ go	\ō\ bone	\ü\ food	\zh\ vision

sad·den \'sad-n\ *vb* : to make or become sad

¹sad·dle \'sad-l\ *n* **1** : a seat (as for a rider on horseback) that is padded and usually covered with leather **2** : something like a saddle in shape, position, or use

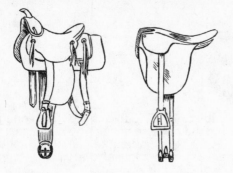

saddle 1

²saddle *vb* **sad·dled; sad·dling 1** : to put a saddle on ⟨*saddle* a horse⟩ **2** : to put a load on : BURDEN ⟨*saddles* with the hardest job⟩

saddle horse *n* : a horse suited for or trained for riding

sa·fa·ri \sə-'fär-ē\ *n* : a hunting trip especially in Africa

¹safe \'sāf\ *adj* **saf·er; saf·est 1** : free or secure from harm or danger **2** : successful in reaching base in baseball **3** : giving protection or security against danger ⟨a *safe* harbor⟩ **4** : HARMLESS **5** : unlikely to be wrong : SOUND ⟨a *safe* answer⟩ **6** : not likely to take risks : CAREFUL ⟨a *safe* driver⟩ — **safe·ly** *adv* — **safe·ness** *n*

synonyms SAFE and SECURE mean free from danger. SAFE suggests freedom from a present danger ⟨felt *safe* as soon as I crossed the street⟩ SECURE suggests freedom from a possible future danger or risk ⟨the locks on the door made us feel *secure*⟩

²safe *n* : a metal chest for keeping something (as money) safe

¹safe·guard \'sāf-,gärd\ *n* : something that protects and gives safety

²safeguard *vb* : to keep safe **synonyms** see DEFEND

safe·keep·ing \'sāf-'kē-ping\ *n* : the act of keeping safe : protection from danger or loss

safe·ty \'sāf-tē\ *n* : freedom from danger : SECURITY

safety belt *n* : a belt for holding a person to something (as a car seat)

safety pin *n* : a pin that is bent back on itself to form a spring and has a guard that covers the point

saf·fron \'saf-rən\ *n* **1** : an orange powder used especially to color or flavor foods that consists of the dried stigmas of a crocus with purple flowers **2** : an orange to orange yellow

¹sag \'sag\ *vb* **sagged; sag·ging 1** : to sink, settle, or hang below the natural or right level ⟨the roof *sags*⟩ **2** : to become less firm or strong ⟨our *sagging* spirits⟩

²sag *n* : a sagging part or area

sa·ga \'sä-gə\ *n* : a story of heroic deeds

sa·ga·cious \sə-'gā-shəs\ *adj* : quick and wise in understanding and judging — **sa·ga·cious·ly** *adv* — **sa·ga·cious·ness** *n*

¹sage \'sāj\ *adj* : ²WISE 1 — **sage·ly** *adv*

²sage *n* : a very wise person

³sage *n* **1** : a mint that grows as a low shrub and has grayish green leaves used to flavor foods **2** : a mint grown for its showy usually scarlet flowers **3** : SAGEBRUSH

sage·brush \'sāj-,brəsh\ *n* : a western American plant related to the daisies that grows as a low shrub and has a bitter juice and sharp smell

Sag·it·tar·i·us \,saj-ə-'ter-ē-əs\ *n* **1** : a constellation between Scorpio and Capricorn imagined as a centaur **2** : the ninth sign of the zodiac or a person born under this sign

sa·gua·ro \sə-'gwä-rō\ *n, pl* **sa·gua·ros** : a giant cactus of the southwestern United States

said *past of* SAY

¹sail \'sāl\ *n* **1** : a sheet of fabric (as canvas) used to catch enough wind to move boats through the water or over ice **2** : the sails of a ship **3** : a sailing ship **4** : a voyage or trip on a sailing ship

²sail *vb* **1** : to travel on a boat moved by the wind **2** : to travel by water **3** : to move or pass over by ship **4** : to manage or direct the motion of (a boat or ship moved by the wind) **5** : to move or glide along

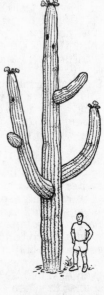

saguaro

sail·boat \'sāl-,bōt\ *n* : a boat equipped with sails

sail·fish \'sāl-ˌfish\ *n* : a fish related to the swordfish but with a large sail-like fin on its back

sail·or \'sā-lər\ *n* : a person who sails

saint \'sānt\ *n* **1** : a good and holy person and especially one who is declared to be worthy of special honor **2** : a person who is very good especially about helping others

Saint Ber·nard \ˌsānt-bər-'närd\ *n* : a very large powerful dog bred originally in the Swiss Alps

Saint Bernard

saint·ly \'sānt-lē\ *adj* : like a saint or like that of a saint ⟨a *saintly* smile⟩ — **saint·li·ness** *n*

sake \'sāk\ *n* **1** : ¹PURPOSE ⟨for the *sake* of argument⟩ **2** : WELFARE 1, BENEFIT ⟨for the *sake* of the country⟩

sal·able *or* **sale·able** \'sā-lə-bəl\ *adj* : good enough to sell : likely to be bought

sal·ad \'sal-əd\ *n* **1** : a dish of raw usually mixed vegetables served with a dressing **2** : a cold dish of meat, shellfish, fruit, or vegetables served with a dressing

sal·a·man·der \'sal-ə-ˌman-dər\ *n* : any of a group of animals that are related to the frogs but look like lizards

sal·a·ry \'sal-ə-rē, 'sal-rē\ *n, pl* **sal·a·ries** : a fixed amount of money paid at regular times for work done

Word History In ancient times, salt was used not only to make food taste better but to keep it from spoiling. Because salt was not always easy to get, Roman soldiers were given money to buy salt. The Latin word for salt money came to be used for any money paid to soldiers. Later the same word was used for money paid to public officials. The English word *salary* comes from this Latin word

sale \'sāl\ *n* **1** : an exchange of goods or property for money **2** : the state of being available for purchase ⟨a house offered for *sale*⟩ **3** : ¹AUCTION **4** : a selling of goods at lowered prices

sales·clerk \'sālz-ˌklərk\ *n* : a person who sells in a store

sales·man \'sālz-mən\ *n, pl* **sales·men** \-mən\ : a person who sells either in a territory or in a store

sales·per·son \'sālz-ˌpərs-n\ *n* : one who sells especially in a store

sales tax *n* : a tax paid by the buyer on goods bought

sales·wom·an \'sālz-ˌwùm-ən\ *n, pl* **sales·wom·en** \-ˌwim-ən\ : a woman who sells either in a territory or in a store

sa·li·va \sə-'lī-və\ *n* : a watery fluid that contains enzymes which break down starch and is secreted into the mouth from glands in the neck

sal·i·vary \'sal-ə-ˌver-ē\ *adj* : of, relating to, or producing saliva ⟨*salivary* glands⟩

Salk vaccine \'sòk-\ *n* : a material given by injection to prevent polio

sal·low \'sal-ō\ *adj* : of a grayish greenish yellow color ⟨*sallow* skin⟩

¹sal·ly \'sal-ē\ *n, pl* **sal·lies** **1** : a rushing out to attack especially by besieged soldiers **2** : a funny remark

²sally *vb* **sal·lied; sal·ly·ing** : to rush out

salm·on \'sam-ən\ *n* : a large food fish with pinkish or reddish flesh

sa·loon \sə-'lün\ *n* **1** : a large public hall (as on a passenger ship) **2** : a place where liquors are sold and drunk : BAR

sal·sa \'sòl-sə, 'säl-\ *n* **1** : a spicy sauce of tomatoes, onions, and hot peppers **2** : popular music of Latin American origin with characteristics of jazz and rock

¹salt \'sòlt\ *n* **1** : a colorless or white substance that consists of sodium and chlorine and is used in seasoning foods, preserving meats and fish, and in making soap and glass **2** : a compound formed by replacement of hydrogen in an acid by a metal or group of elements that act like a metal

²salt *vb* : to add salt to

³salt *adj* : containing salt : SALTY

salt·wa·ter \ˌsòlt-ˌwòt-ər, -ˌwät-\ *adj* : of, relating to, or living in salt water

salty \'sòl-tē\ *adj* **salt·i·er; salt·i·est** : of, tasting of, or containing salt

sal·u·ta·tion \ˌsal-yə-'tā-shən\ *n* **1** : an act or action of greeting **2** : a word or phrase

\ə\ abut	\aú\ out	\i\ tip	\ò\ saw	\ú\ foot
\ər\ further	\ch\ chin	\ī\ life	\òi\ coin	\y\ yet
\a\ mat	\e\ pet	\j\ job	\th\ thin	\yú\ few
\ā\ take	\ē\ easy	\ng\ sing	\th\ this	\yü\ cure
\ä\ cot, cart	\g\ go	\ō\ bone	\ü\ food	\zh\ vision

used as a greeting at the beginning of a letter

¹sa·lute \sə-'lüt\ *vb* **sa·lut·ed; sa·lut·ing 1** : to address with expressions of kind wishes, courtesy, or honor **2** : to honor by a standard military ceremony **3** : to give a sign of respect to (as a military officer) especially by a smart movement of the right hand to the forehead

²salute *n* **1** : GREETING 1, SALUTATION **2** : a military show of respect or honor ⟨a twenty-one-gun *salute*⟩ **3** : the position taken or the movement made to salute a military officer

¹sal·vage \'sal-vij\ *n* **1** : money paid for saving a wrecked or endangered ship or its cargo or passengers **2** : the act of saving a ship **3** : the saving of possessions in danger of being lost **4** : something that is saved (as from a wreck)

²salvage *vb* **sal·vaged; sal·vag·ing** : to recover (something usable) especially from wreckage

sal·va·tion \sal-'vā-shən\ *n* **1** : the saving of a person from the power and the results of sin **2** : something that saves

¹salve \'sav, 'sàv\ *n* : a healing or soothing ointment

²salve *vb* **salved; salv·ing** : to quiet or soothe with or as if with a salve

¹same \'sām\ *adj* **1** : not another : IDENTICAL ⟨lived in the *same* house all their lives⟩ **2** : UNCHANGED ⟨is always the *same* no matter what happens⟩ **3** : very much alike ⟨eat the *same* breakfast every day⟩

synonyms SAME, IDENTICAL, and EQUAL mean not different or not differing from one another. SAME suggests that the things being compared are really one thing and not two or more things ⟨we saw the *same* person⟩ IDENTICAL usually suggests that two or more things are just like each other in every way ⟨these glasses are *identical*⟩ EQUAL suggests that the things being compared are like each other in some particular way ⟨two baseball players of *equal* ability⟩

²same *pron* : something identical with or like another ⟨you had an ice cream cone and I had the *same*⟩

same·ness \'sām-nəs\ *n* **1** : the quality or state of being the same **2** : MONOTONY

sam·pan \'sam-,pan\ *n* : a Chinese boat with a flat bottom that is usually moved with oars

¹sam·ple \'sam-pəl\ *n* : a part or piece that shows the quality of the whole

²sample *vb* **sam·pled; sam·pling** : to judge the quality of by samples : TEST

sam·pler \'sam-plər\ *n* : a piece of cloth with letters or verses embroidered on it

san·a·to·ri·um \,san-ə-'tōr-ē-əm\ *n* : a place for the care and treatment usually of people recovering from illness or having a disease likely to last a long time

sanc·tion \'sangk-shən\ *n* **1** : approval by someone in charge **2** : an action short of war taken by several nations to make another nation behave

sanc·tu·ary \'sangk-chə-,wer-ē\ *n, pl* **sanc·tu·ar·ies 1** : a holy or sacred place **2** : a building for worship **3** : the most sacred part (as near the altar) of a place of worship **4** : a place of safety ⟨a wildlife *sanctuary*⟩ **5** : the state of being protected

¹sand \'sand\ *n* **1** : loose material in grains produced by the natural breaking up of rocks **2** : a soil made up mostly of sand

²sand *vb* **1** : to sprinkle with sand **2** : to smooth or clean with sand or sandpaper — **sand·er** *n*

san·dal \'san-dəl\ *n* : a shoe that is a sole held in place by straps

san·dal·wood \'san-dəl-,wùd\ *n* : the fragrant yellowish heartwood of an Asian tree

sand·bag \'sand-,bag\ *n* : a bag filled with sand and used as a weight (as on a balloon) or as part of a wall or dam

sand·bar \'sand-,bär\ *n* : a ridge of sand formed in water by tides or currents

sand dollar *n* : a flat round sea urchin

sand·man \'sand-,man\ *n, pl* **sand·men** \-,men\ : a genie said to make children sleepy by sprinkling sand in their eyes

¹sand·pa·per \'sand-,pā-pər\ *n* : paper that has rough material (as sand) glued on one side and is used for smoothing and polishing

²sandpaper *vb* : to rub with sandpaper

sand·pip·er \'sand-,pī-pər\ *n* : a small shorebird related to the plovers

sand·stone \'sand-,stōn\ *n* : rock made of sand held together by a natural cement

sand·storm \'sand-,stòrm\ *n* : a storm of wind (as in a desert) that drives clouds of sand

sampan

¹**sand·wich** \'sand-,wich\ *n* : two pieces of bread with something (as meat or cheese) between them

²**sandwich** *vb* : to fit in between things

sandy \'san-dē\ *adj* **sand·i·er; sand·i·est 1** : full of or covered with sand **2** : of a yellowish gray color

sane \'sān\ *adj* **san·er; san·est 1** : having a healthy and sound mind **2** : very sensible — **sane·ness** \-nəs\ *n*

sang *past of* SING

san·i·tar·i·um \,san-ə-'ter-ē-əm\ *n* : SANATORIUM

san·i·tary \'san-ə-,ter-ē\ *adj* **1** : of or relating to health or hygiene **2** : free from filth, infection, or other dangers to health

san·i·ta·tion \,san-ə-'tā-shən\ *n* **1** : the act or process of making sanitary **2** : the act of keeping things sanitary

san·i·ty \'san-ət-ē\ *n* : the state of being sane

sank *past of* SINK

San·ta Claus \'sant-ə-,klòz\ *n* : the spirit of Christmas as represented by a jolly old man in a red suit

¹**sap** \'sap\ *n* : a watery juice that circulates through a higher plant and carries food and nutrients

²**sap** *vb* **sapped; sap·ping** : to weaken or exhaust little by little ⟨it *saps* your strength⟩

sap·ling \'sap-ling\ *n* : a young tree

sap·phire \'saf-,īr\ *n* : a clear bright blue precious stone

Word History People in ancient India believed that each planet had its own god. They thought of the god of the planet Saturn as a dark man with dark clothes who was very fond of a certain dark gem. It is likely that this gem was the sapphire. The Indians gave this gem a name that meant "dear to Saturn." The English word *sapphire* comes from this old Indian word.

sap·wood \'sap-,wùd\ *n* : young wood found just beneath the bark of a tree and usually lighter in color than the heartwood

sar·casm \'sär-,kaz-əm\ *n* : the use of words that normally mean one thing to mean just the opposite usually to hurt someone's feelings or show scorn ⟨to say to someone who has just lost some money "You are a careful person, aren't you?" is to use *sarcasm*⟩

sar·cas·tic \sär-'kas-tik\ *adj* **1** : having the habit of sarcasm **2** : showing or related to sarcasm — **sar·cas·ti·cal·ly** \-ti-kə-lē\ *adv*

sar·dine \sär-'dēn\ *n* : a young or very small fish often preserved in oil and used for food

sa·ri \'sä-rē\ *n* : a piece of clothing worn mainly by women of India that is a long light cloth wrapped around the body

sar·sa·pa·ril·la \,sas-ə-pə-'ril-ə, ,sär-sə-\ *n* : the dried root of a tropical American plant used especially as a flavoring

¹**sash** \'sash\ *n* : a broad band of cloth worn around the waist or over the shoulder

²**sash** *n* **1** : a frame for a pane of glass in a door or window **2** : the movable part of a window

sari

¹**sass** \'sas\ *n* : a rude fresh reply

²**sass** *vb* : to reply to in a rude fresh way

sas·sa·fras \'sas-ə-,fras\ *n* : a tall tree of eastern North America whose dried root bark is used in medicine or as a flavoring

sassy \'sas-ē\ *adj* **sass·i·er; sass·i·est** : given to or made up of sass ⟨*sassy* children⟩ ⟨a *sassy* answer⟩

sat *past of* SIT

Sa·tan \'sāt-n\ *n* : ¹DEVIL 1

satch·el \'sach-əl\ *n* : a small bag for carrying clothes or books

sat·el·lite \'sat-l-,īt\ *n* **1** : a smaller body that revolves around a planet **2** : a vehicle sent out from the earth to revolve around the earth, moon, sun, or a planet **3** : a country controlled by another more powerful country

sat·in \'sat-n\ *n* : a cloth (as of silk) with a shiny surface

sat·ire \'sa-,tīr\ *n* : writing or cartoons meant to make fun of and often show the weaknesses of someone or something ⟨a *satire* on television commercials⟩

sa·tir·i·cal \sə-'tir-i-kəl\ *adj* : of, relating to, or showing satire

sat·is·fac·tion \,sat-əs-'fak-shən\ *n* **1** : the act of satisfying : the condition of being satisfied **2** : something that satisfies

sat·is·fac·to·ry \,sat-əs-'fak-tə-rē\ *adj* : causing satisfaction — **sat·is·fac·to·ri·ly**

\ə\ **abut**	\aù\ **out**	\i\ **tip**
\ər\ **further**	\ch\ **chin**	\ī\ **life**
\a\ **mat**	\e\ **pet**	\j\ **job**
\ā\ **take**	\ē\ **easy**	\ng\ **sing**
\ä\ **cot, cart**	\g\ **go**	\ō\ **bone**

\ò\ **saw**	\ù\ **foot**
\òi\ **coin**	\y\ **yet**
\th\ **thin**	\yü\ **few**
\th\ **this**	\yù\ **cure**
\ü\ **food**	\zh\ **vision**

\-rə-lē\ *adv* — **sat·is·fac·to·ri·ness** \-rē-nəs\ *n*

sat·is·fy \'sat-əs-ˌfī\ *vb* **sat·is·fied; sat·is·fy·ing 1** : to carry out the terms of (as a contract) **2** : to make contented ⟨was *satisfied* with the job⟩ **3** : to meet the needs of ⟨it *satisfied* our hunger⟩ **4** : CONVINCE ⟨*satisfied* the story is true⟩

sat·u·rate \'sach-ə-ˌrāt\ *vb* **sat·u·rat·ed; sat·u·rat·ing** : to soak full or fill to the limit

Sat·ur·day \'sat-ər-dē\ *n* : the seventh day of the week

Sat·urn \'sat-ərn\ *n* : the planet that is sixth in distance from the sun and has a diameter of about 115,000 kilometers

sa·tyr \'sāt-ər, 'sat-\ *n* : a forest god of the ancient Greeks believed to have the ears and the tail of a horse or goat

sauce \'sȯs\ *n* **1** : a tasty liquid poured over food **2** : stewed fruit ⟨cranberry *sauce*⟩

sauce·pan \'sȯs-ˌspan\ *n* : a small deep cooking pan with a handle

sau·cer \'sȯ-sər\ *n* : a small shallow dish often with a slightly lower center for holding a cup

saucy \'sas-ē, 'sȯs-\ *adj* **sauc·i·er; sauc·i·est 1** : being rude usually in a lively and playful way **2** : ²TRIM — **sauc·i·ly** \-ə-lē\ *adv* — **sauc·i·ness** \-ē-nəs\ *n*

sau·er·kraut \'saù-ər-ˌkraùt\ *n* : finely cut cabbage soaked in a salty mixture

saun·ter \'sȯnt-ər\ *vb* : to walk in a slow relaxed way : STROLL

sau·sage \'sȯ-sij\ *n* **1** : spicy ground meat (as pork) usually stuffed in casings **2** : a roll of sausage in a casing

¹sav·age \'sav-ij\ *adj* **1** : not tamed : WILD ⟨*savage* beasts⟩ **2** : being cruel and brutal : FIERCE ⟨a *savage* attack⟩ — **sav·age·ly** *adv* — **sav·age·ness** *n*

Word History A good place to look for wild animals is in the woods. The English word *savage* at first meant "wild." It comes from a Latin word that meant "woods."

²savage *n* **1** : a person belonging to a group with a low level of civilization **2** : a cruel person

sav·age·ry \'sav-ij-rē\ *n, pl* **sav·age·ries 1** : an uncivilized condition ⟨ancient tribes living in *savagery*⟩ **2** : savage behavior

¹save \'sāv\ *vb* **saved; sav·ing 1** : to free from danger **2** : to keep from being ruined : PRESERVE ⟨*save* fruits from spoiling⟩ ⟨*save* the company's good name⟩ **3** : to put aside for later use ⟨*save* a snack for bedtime⟩ **4** : to keep from being spent, wasted, or lost ⟨*save* energy⟩ **5** : to make unnecessary ⟨*saves* a long detour⟩

²save \'sāv\ *prep* : ²EXCEPT ⟨it rained every day this week *save* one⟩

sav·ing \'sā-ving\ *n* **1** : the act of rescuing **2** : something saved ⟨a *saving* in labor⟩ **3**

savings *pl* : money put aside (as in a bank)

sav·ior *or* **sav·iour** \'sāv-yər\ *n* **1** : a person who saves from ruin or danger **2** *cap* : JESUS

sa·vory \'sā-və-rē\ *adj* : pleasing to the taste or smell ⟨*savory* sausages⟩

¹saw *past of* SEE

²saw \'sȯ\ *n* **1** : a tool with a tooth-edged blade for cutting hard material **2** : a machine that operates a toothed blade

³saw *vb* **sawed; sawed** *or* **sawn** \'sȯn\; **saw·ing** : to cut or shape with a saw

⁴saw *n* : a common saying : PROVERB

saw·dust \'sȯ-ˌdəst\ *n* : tiny bits (as of wood) which fall from something being sawed

saw·horse \'sȯ-ˌhȯrs\ *n* : a frame or rack on which wood is rested while being sawed

sawhorses

saw·mill \'sȯ-ˌmil\ *n* : a mill or factory having machinery for sawing logs

saw–toothed \'sȯ-'tütht\ *adj* : having an edge or outline like the teeth of a saw

sax·o·phone \'sak-sə-ˌfōn\ *n* : a musical wind instrument with a reed mouthpiece and a bent tubelike metal body with keys

¹say \'sā\ *vb* **said** \'sed\; **say·ing** \'sā-ing\ **1** : to express in words **2** : to give as one's opinion or decision : DECLARE ⟨I *say* you are wrong⟩ **3** : ¹REPEAT 2, RECITE ⟨*say* one's prayers⟩

saxophone

²say *n* **1** : an expression of opinion ⟨everybody had a *say* at the meeting⟩ **2** : the power to decide or help decide

say·ing \'sā-ing\ *n* : PROVERB

scab \'skab\ *n* **1** : SCABIES **2** : a plant disease in which crusted spots form on stems or leaves **3** : a crust that forms over and protects a sore or wound

scab·bard \'skab-ərd\ *n* : a protective case or sheath for the blade of a sword or dagger

scab·by \'skab-ē\ *adj* **scab·bi·er; scab·bi·est 1** : having scabs **2** : diseased with scab

sca·bies \'skā-bēz\ *n, pl* **scabies** : an itch or mange caused by mites living as parasites in the skin

scaf·fold \'skaf-əld\ *n* **1** : a raised platform built as a support for workers and their tools and materials **2** : a platform on which a criminal is executed

¹scald \'skold\ *vb* **1** : to burn with or as if with hot liquid or steam **2** : to pour very hot water over **3** : to bring to a heat just below the boiling point

²scald *n* : an injury caused by scalding

¹scale \'skāl\ *n* **1** : either pan of a balance or the balance itself **2** : an instrument or machine for weighing

²scale *vb* **scaled; scal·ing 1** : to weigh on scales **2** : to have a weight of

³scale *n* **1** : one of the small stiff plates that cover much of the body of some animals (as fish and snakes) **2** : a thin layer or part (as a special leaf that protects a plant bud) suggesting a fish scale — **scaled** \'skāld\ *adj* — **scale·less** \'skāl-ləs\ *adj* — **scale·like** \-,līk\ *adj*

⁴scale *vb* **scaled; scal·ing 1** : to remove the scales of **2** : ²FLAKE

⁵scale *n* **1** : a series of spaces marked off by lines and used for measuring distances or amounts **2** : a number of like things arranged in order from the highest to the lowest **3** : the size of a picture, plan, or model of a thing compared to the size of the thing itself **4** : a standard for measuring or judging **5** : a series of tones going up or down in pitch in fixed steps

⁶scale *vb* **scaled; scal·ing 1** : to climb by or as if by a ladder **2** : to arrange according to a scale

scale insect *n* : any of a group of insects that are related to the plant lice, suck the juices of plants, and have winged males and wingless females which look like scales attached to the plant

¹scal·lop \'skäl-əp\ *n* **1** : an edible shellfish that is a mollusk with a ribbed shell in two parts **2** : any of a series of rounded half-circles that form a border on an edge (as of lace)

²scallop *vb* **1** : to bake with crumbs, butter, and milk **2** : to embroider, cut, or edge with scallops

¹scallop 1

¹scalp \'skalp\ *n* : the part of the skin and flesh of the head usually covered with hair

²scalp *vb* : to remove the scalp from

scaly \'skā-lē\ *adj* **scal·i·er; scal·i·est** : covered with or like scales ⟨a *scaly* skin⟩

scamp \'skamp\ *n* : RASCAL

¹scam·per \'skam-pər\ *vb* : to run or move lightly

²scamper *n* : a playful scampering or scurrying

scan \'skan\ *vb* **scanned; scan·ning 1** : to read or mark verses so as to show stress and rhythm **2** : to look over

scan·dal \'skan-dəl\ *n* **1** : something that causes a general feeling of shame : DISGRACE **2** : talk that injures a person's good name

scan·dal·ous \'skan-də-ləs\ *adj* **1** : being or containing scandal **2** : very bad or objectionable ⟨*scandalous* behavior⟩

Scan·di·na·vian \,skan-də-'nā-vē-ən, -vyən\ *n* : a person born or living in Scandinavia

¹scant \'skant\ *adj* **1** : barely enough ⟨a *scant* lunch⟩ **2** : not quite full ⟨a *scant* quart of milk⟩ **3** : having only a small supply ⟨*scant* of money⟩

²scant *vb* : to give or use less than needed : be stingy with

scanty \'skant-ē\ *adj* **scant·i·er; scant·i·est** : barely enough

¹scar \'skär\ *n* **1** : a mark left after injured tissue has healed **2** : an ugly mark (as on furniture) **3** : the lasting effect of some unhappy experience

²scar *vb* **scarred; scar·ring** : to mark or become marked with a scar

scar·ab \'skar-əb\ *n* : a large dark beetle used in ancient Egypt as a symbol of eternal life

scarab

\ə\ **abut**	\au̇\ **out**	\i\ **tip**	\ȯ\ **saw**	\u̇\ **foot**
\ər\ **further**	\ch\ **chin**	\ī\ **life**	\ȯi\ **coin**	\y\ **yet**
\a\ **mat**	\e\ **pet**	\j\ **job**	\th\ **thin**	\yü\ **few**
\ā\ **take**	\ē\ **easy**	\ng\ **sing**	\th\ **this**	\yu̇\ **cure**
\ä\ **cot, cart**	\g\ **go**	\ō\ **bone**	\ü\ **food**	\zh\ **vision**

scarce \'skeərs, 'skaərs\ *adj* **scarc·er; scarc·est 1** : not plentiful **2** : hard to find : RARE **synonyms** see RARE — **scarce-ness** *n*

scarce·ly \'skeər-slē, 'skaər-\ *adv* **1** : only just ⟨*scarcely* enough to eat⟩ **2** : certainly not

scar·ci·ty \'sker-sət-ē, 'skar-\ *n, pl* **scar-ci·ties** : the condition of being scarce

¹scare \'skeər, 'skaər\ *vb* **scared; scar-ing** : to be or become frightened suddenly

²scare *n* **1** : a sudden fright **2** : a wide-spread state of alarm

scare·crow \'skeər-ˌkrō, 'skaər-\ *n* : a crude human figure set up to scare away birds and animals from crops

scarf \'skärf\ *n, pl* **scarves** \'skärvz\ *or* **scarfs 1** : a piece of cloth worn loosely around the neck or on the head **2** : a long narrow strip of cloth used as a cover (as on a bureau)

scar·la·ti·na \ˌskär-lə-'tē-nə\ *n* : a mild scarlet fever

¹scar·let \'skär-lət\ *n* : a bright red

²scarlet *adj* : of the color scarlet

scarlet fever *n* : a contagious disease in which there is a sore throat, a high fever, and a rash

scary \'skeər-ē, 'skaər-\ *adj* **scar·i·er; scar·i·est** : causing fright ⟨a *scary* movie⟩

scat \'skat\ *vb* **scat·ted; scat·ting** : to go away quickly

scat·ter \'skat-ər\ *vb* **1** : to toss, sow, or place here and there **2** : to separate and go in different ways ⟨the crowd *scattered*⟩

scat·ter·brain \'skat-ər-ˌbrān\ *n* : a flighty thoughtless person — **scat·ter·brained** \-ˌbrānd\ *adj*

scav·en·ger \'skav-ən-jər\ *n* **1** : a person who picks over junk or garbage for useful items **2** : an animal that lives on decayed material

scene \'sēn\ *n* **1** : a division of an act in a play **2** : a single interesting or important happening in a play or story **3** : the place and time of the action in a play or story **4** : the painted screens and slides used as backgrounds on the stage : SCENERY **5** : something that attracts or holds one's gaze : VIEW **6** : a display of anger or mis-conduct

scen·ery \'sē-nə-rē, 'sēn-rē\ *n* **1** : the painted scenes used on a stage and the furnishings that go with them **2** : outdoor scenes or views

sce·nic \'sē-nik\ *adj* **1** : of or relating to stage scenery **2** : giving views of natural scenery ⟨a *scenic* drive⟩

¹scent \'sent\ *vb* **1** : to become aware of or follow through the sense of smell **2** : to

get a hint of **3** : to fill with an odor : PER-FUME

²scent *n* **1** : an odor left by some animal or person no longer in a place or given off (as by flowers) at a distance **2** : a usual or particular and often agreeable odor **3** : power or sense of smell **4** : a course followed by someone in search or pursuit of something **5** : ¹PERFUME 2

scep·ter *or* **scep·tre** \'sep-tər\ *n* : a rod carried by a ruler as a sign of authority

¹sched·ule \'skej-ül, -əl\ *n* **1** : a written or printed list **2** : a list of the times set for certain events : TIMETABLE **3** : AGENDA, PROGRAM

²schedule *vb* **sched·uled; sched·ul·ing** : to form into or add to a schedule

¹scheme \'skēm\ *n* **1** : a plan or program of something to be done : PROJECT **2** : a secret plan : PLOT **3** : an organized design ⟨color *scheme* of a room⟩ **syn-onyms** see PLAN

²scheme *vb* **schemed; schem·ing** : to form a scheme — **schem·er** *n*

Schick test \'shik-\ *n* : a test to find out whether a person might easily catch diph-theria

schol·ar \'skäl-ər\ *n* **1** : a student in a school : PUPIL **2** : a person who knows a great deal about one or more subjects

schol·ar·ly \'skäl-ər-lē\ *adj* : like that of or suitable to learned persons

schol·ar·ship \'skäl-ər-ˌship\ *n* **1** : the qualities of a scholar : LEARNING **2** : money given a student to help pay for further education

scho·las·tic \skə-'las-tik\ *adj* : of or relat-ing to schools, pupils, or education

¹school \'skül\ *n* **1** : a place for teaching and learning **2** : the teachers and pupils of a school **3** : a session of school **4** : SCHOOLHOUSE **5** : a group of persons who share the same opinions and beliefs

Word History You may not think of school as a form of leisure. The English word *school*, however, can be traced back to a Greek word meaning "leisure." To the an-cient Greeks it seemed only natural to spend leisure time in learning. The Greek word that meant "leisure" came to mean "time spent in learning." Later the word came to mean "a place for learning." En-glish *school* comes from this Greek word.

²school *vb* : TEACH 2, TRAIN

³school *n* : a large number of one kind of fish or water animals swimming to-gether

school·bag \'skül-ˌbag\ *n* : a bag for carry-ing schoolbooks

school·book \'skül-,bùk\ *n* : a book used in schools

school·boy \'skül-,bòi\ *n* : a boy who goes to school

school·girl \'skül-,gərl\ *n* : a girl who goes to school

school·house \'skül-,haùs\ *n, pl* **school·hous·es** \-,haù-zəz\ : a building used as a place for teaching and learning

school·ing \'skü-ling\ *n* : EDUCATION 1

school·mas·ter \'skül-,mas-tər\ *n* : a man who has charge of a school or teaches in a school

school·mate \'skül-,māt\ *n* : a fellow pupil

school·mis·tress \'skül-,mis-trəs\ *n* : a woman who has charge of a school or teaches in a school

school·room \'skül-,rüm, -,rùm\ *n* : CLASSROOM

school·teach·er \'skül-,tē-chər\ *n* : a person who teaches in a school

school·work \'skül-,wərk\ *n* : lessons done at school or assigned to be done at home

school·yard \'skül-,yärd\ *n* : the playground of a school

schoo·ner \'skü-nər\ *n* : a ship usually having two masts with the mainmast located toward the center and the shorter mast toward the front

schooner

schwa \'shwä\ *n* 1 : an unstressed vowel that is the usual sound of the first and last vowels of the English word *America* 2 : the symbol ə commonly used for a schwa and sometimes also for a similarly pronounced stressed vowel (as in *cut*)

sci·ence \'sī-əns\ *n* 1 : a branch of knowledge in which what is known is presented in an orderly way 2 : a branch of study that is concerned with collecting facts and forming laws to explain them

sci·en·tif·ic \,sī-ən-'tif-ik\ *adj* 1 : of or relating to science or scientists 2 : using or applying the methods of science — **sci·en·tif·i·cal·ly** \-'tif-i-kə-lē\ *adv*

sci·en·tist \'sī-ən-təst\ *n* : a person who knows much about science or does scientific work

scis·sors \'siz-ərz\ *n sing or pl* : a cutting instrument with two blades fastened together so that the sharp edges slide against each other

scoff \'skäf, 'skòf\ *vb* : to show great disrespect with mocking laughter or behavior

¹scold \'skōld\ *n* : a person given to criticizing and blaming others

²scold *vb* : to find fault with or criticize in an angry way — **scold·ing** *n*

¹scoop \'sküp\ *n* 1 : a large shovel (as for shoveling coal) 2 : a shovellike tool or utensil for digging into a soft substance and lifting out some of it 3 : a motion made with or as if with a scoop 4 : the amount held by a scoop

²scoop *vb* 1 : to take out or up with or as if with a scoop 2 : to make by scooping

scoot \'sküt\ *vb* : to go suddenly and fast

scoot·er \'skü-tər\ *n* 1 : a vehicle consisting of a narrow base mounted between a front and a back wheel and guided by a handle attached to the front wheel 2 : MOTOR SCOOTER

scope \'skōp\ *n* 1 : space or opportunity for action or thought 2 : the area or amount covered, reached, or viewed

scorch \'skòrch\ *vb* 1 : to burn on the surface 2 : to burn so as to brown or dry out

¹score \'skōr\ *n* 1 : a group of twenty things : TWENTY 2 : a line (as a scratch) made with or as if with something sharp 3 : a record of points made or lost (as in a game) 4 : DEBT 2 5 : a duty or an injury kept in mind for later action ⟨have a *score* to settle with you⟩ 6 : ¹GROUND 3, REASON ⟨we were tired but wouldn't leave on that *score*⟩ 7 : the written or printed form of a musical composition — **score·less** \-ləs\ *adj*

²score *vb* **scored; scor·ing** 1 : to set down in an account : RECORD 2 : to keep the score in a game 3 : to cut or mark with a line, scratch, or notch 4 : to make or cause to make a point in a game 5 : ACHIEVE 2, WIN 6 : ²GRADE 3, MARK

¹scorn \'skòrn\ *n* 1 : an emotion involving both anger and disgust 2 : a person or thing very much disliked

\ə\ abut	\aù\ out	\i\ tip	\ò\ saw	\ù\ foot
\ər\ further	\ch\ chin	\ī\ life	\òi\ coin	\y\ yet
\a\ mat	\e\ pet	\j\ job	\th\ thin	\yü\ few
\ā\ take	\ē\ easy	\ng\ sing	\th\ this	\yù\ cure
\ä\ cot, cart	\g\ go	\ō\ bone	\ü\ food	\zh\ vision

²scorn *vb* : to show scorn for **synonyms** see DESPISE

scorn·ful \'skòrn-fəl\ *adj* : feeling or showing scorn — **scorn·ful·ly** \-fə-lē\ *adv*

Scor·pio \'skòr-pē-ō\ *n* **1** : a constellation between Libra and Sagittarius imagined as a scorpion **2** : the eighth sign of the zodiac or a person born under this sign

scor·pi·on \'skòr-pē-ən\ *n* : an animal related to the spiders that has a long jointed body ending in a slender tail with a poisonous stinger at the end

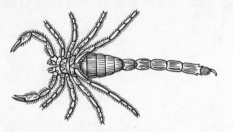

scorpion

Scot \'skät\ *n* : a person born or living in Scotland

¹Scotch \'skäch\ *adj* : ¹SCOTTISH

²Scotch *n pl* : ²SCOTTISH

scot–free \'skät-'frē\ *adj* : completely free from duty, harm, or punishment

¹Scot·tish \'skät-ish\ *adj* : of or relating to Scotland or the Scottish

²Scottish *n pl* : the people of Scotland

scoun·drel \'skaún-drəl\ *n* : a mean or wicked person : VILLAIN

¹scour \'skaúr\ *vb* : to go or move swiftly about, over, or through in search of something ⟨*scoured* the records for a clue⟩

²scour *vb* **1** : to rub hard with a rough substance in order to clean **2** : to free or clear from impurities by or as if by rubbing

³scour *n* : an action or result of scouring

¹scourge \'skərj\ *n* **1** : ²WHIP 1 **2** : a cause of widespread or great suffering

²scourge *vb* **scourged; scourg·ing 1** : to whip severely : FLOG **2** : to cause severe suffering to : AFFLICT

¹scout \'skaút\ *vb* **1** : to go about in search of information **2** : to make a search

²scout *n* **1** : a person, group, boat, or plane that scouts **2** : the act of scouting **3** *often cap* : BOY SCOUT **4** *often cap* : GIRL SCOUT

scout·ing \'skaút-ing\ *n* **1** : the act of one that scouts **2** *often cap* : the general activities of Boy Scout and Girl Scout groups

scout·mas·ter \'skaút-,mas-tər\ *n* : the leader of a troop of Boy Scouts

scow \'skaú\ *n* : a large boat with a flat bottom and square ends that is used chiefly for loading and unloading ships and for carrying rubbish

¹scowl \'skaúl\ *vb* : ¹FROWN 1

²scowl *n* : an angry look

scram \'skram\ *vb* **scrammed; scram·ming** : to go away at once

¹scram·ble \'skram-bəl\ *vb* **scram·bled; scram·bling 1** : to move or climb quickly on hands and knees **2** : to work hard to win or escape something ⟨had to *scramble* to earn a living⟩ **3** : to mix together in disorder ⟨don't *scramble* up those papers⟩ **4** : to cook the mixed whites and yolks of eggs by stirring them while frying

²scramble *n* : the act or result of scrambling

¹scrap \'skrap\ *n* **1** *scraps pl* : pieces of leftover food **2** : a small bit **3** : waste material (as metal) that can be made fit to use again

²scrap *vb* **scrapped; scrap·ping 1** : to break up (as a ship) into scrap **2** : to throw away as worthless

³scrap *n* : ¹QUARREL 2, FIGHT

scrap·book \'skrap-,búk\ *n* : a blank book in which clippings or pictures are kept

¹scrape \'skrāp\ *vb* **scraped; scrap·ing 1** : to remove by repeated strokes of a sharp or rough tool **2** : to clean or smooth by rubbing **3** : to rub or cause to rub so as to make a harsh noise : SCUFF **4** : to hurt or roughen by dragging against a rough surface **5** : to get with difficulty and a little at a time ⟨*scrape* together money for a vacation⟩ — **scrap·er** *n*

²scrape *n* **1** : the act of scraping **2** : a sound, mark, or injury made by scraping **3** : a disagreeable or trying situation

¹scratch \'skrach\ *vb* **1** : to scrape or injure with claws, nails, or an instrument **2** : to make a scraping noise **3** : to erase by scraping

²scratch *n* : a mark or injury made by scratching ⟨received a *scratch* while playing with the kitten⟩

scratchy \'skrach-ē\ *adj* **scratch·i·er; scratch·i·est** : likely to scratch or make sore or raw

¹scrawl \'skròl\ *vb* : to write quickly and carelessly : SCRIBBLE

²scrawl *n* : something written carelessly or without skill

scraw·ny \'skrò-nē\ *adj* **scraw·ni·er; scraw·ni·est** : poorly nourished : SKINNY

¹scream \'skrēm\ *vb* : to cry out (as in fright) with a loud and shrill sound

²scream *n* : a long cry that is loud and shrill

¹screech \'skrēch\ *n* : a shrill harsh cry usually expressing terror or pain

²screech *vb* : to cry out usually in terror or pain **synonyms** see SHOUT

¹screen \'skrēn\ *n* **1** : a curtain or wall used to hide or to protect **2** : a network of wire set in a frame for separating finer parts from coarser parts (as of sand) **3** : the curtain or wall on which movies are projected **4** : the movie industry **5** : a frame that holds a usually wire netting and is used to keep out pests (as insects) **6** : the part of a television set on which the picture appears

²screen *vb* **1** : to hide or protect with or as if with a screen **2** : to separate or sift with a screen

¹screw \'skrü\ *n* **1** : a nail-shaped or rod-shaped piece of metal with a winding ridge around its length used for fastening and holding pieces together **2** : the act of screwing tight : TWIST **3** : PROPELLER

²screw *vb* **1** : to attach or fasten with a screw **2** : to operate, tighten, or adjust with a screw **3** : to turn or twist on a thread on or like that on a screw

screw•driv•er \'skrü-ˌdrī-vər\ *n* : a tool for turning screws

¹scrib•ble \'skrib-əl\ *vb* **scrib•bled; scrib•bling** : to write quickly or carelessly — **scrib•bler** \'skrib-lər\ *n*

²scribble *n* : something scribbled

scribe \'skrīb\ *n* **1** : a teacher of Jewish law **2** : a person who copies writing (as in a book)

scrim•mage \'skrim-ij\ *n* **1** : a confused struggle **2** : the action between two football teams when one attempts to move the ball down the field

script \'skript\ *n* **1** : HANDWRITING **2** : a type used in printing that resembles handwriting **3** : the written form of a play or movie or the lines to be said by a radio or television performer

scrip•ture \'skrip-chər\ *n* **1** *cap* : BIBLE 1 **2** : writings sacred to a religious group

scroll \'skrōl\ *n* **1** : a roll of paper or parchment on which something is written or engraved **2** : an ornament resembling a length of paper usually rolled at both ends

scroll 1

¹scrub \'skrəb\ *n* **1** : a thick growth of small or stunted shrubs or trees **2** : one of poor size or quality

²scrub *vb* **scrubbed; scrub•bing** : to rub hard in washing

³scrub *n* : the act or an instance or a period of scrubbing

scrub•by \'skrəb-ē\ *adj* **scrub•bi•er; scrub•bi•est** **1** : of poor size or quality **2** : covered with scrub

scruff \'skrəf\ *n* : the loose skin on the back of the neck

scruffy \'skrəf-ē\ *adj* **scruff•i•er; scruff•i•est** : dirty or shabby in appearance

scru•ple \'skrü-pəl\ *n* **1** : a sense of right and wrong that keeps one from doing as one pleases **2** : a feeling of guilt when one does wrong : QUALM

scru•pu•lous \'skrü-pyə-ləs\ *adj* : having or showing very careful and strict regard for what is right and proper : CONSCIENTIOUS — **scru•pu•lous•ly** *adv*

scuff \'skəf\ *vb* **1** : to scrape the feet while walking **2** : to become rough or scratched through wear

¹scuf•fle \'skəf-əl\ *vb* **scuf•fled; scuffling** **1** : to struggle in a confused way at close quarters **2** : to shuffle one's feet

²scuffle *n* : a rough confused struggle

scull \'skəl\ *n* **1** : an oar used at the rear of a boat to drive it forward **2** : one of a pair of short oars **3** : a boat driven by one or more pairs of sculls

sculp•tor \'skəlp-tər\ *n* : one that sculptures

¹sculp•ture \'skəlp-chər\ *n* **1** : the action or art of making statues by carving or chiseling (as in wood or stone), by modeling (as in clay), or by casting (as in melted metal) **2** : work produced by sculpture ⟨put a new piece of *sculpture* in the park⟩

²sculpture *vb* **sculp•tured; sculp•tur•ing** : to make sculptures

scum \'skəm\ *n* **1** : a film of matter that rises to the top of a boiling or fermenting liquid **2** : a coating on the surface of still water

scurf \'skərf\ *n* : thin dry scales or a coating of these (as on a leaf or the skin)

¹scur•ry \'skər-ē\ *vb* **scur•ried; scur•ry•ing** : to move in a brisk way

²scurry *n, pl* **scur•ries** : the act or an instance of scurrying

¹scur•vy \'skər-vē\ *adj* **scur•vi•er; scur•vi•est** : ¹MEAN 4, CONTEMPTIBLE

²scurvy *n* : a disease caused by lack of

\ə\ abut	\au̇\ out	\i\ tip	\ȯ\ saw	\u̇\ foot
\ər\ further	\ch\ chin	\ī\ life	\ȯi\ coin	\y\ yet
\a\ mat	\e\ pet	\j\ job	\th\ thin	\yü\ few
\ā\ take	\ē\ easy	\ng\ sing	\th\ this	\yu̇\ cure
\ä\ cot, cart	\g\ go	\ō\ bone	\ü\ food	\zh\ vision

vitamin C in which the teeth loosen, the gums soften, and there is bleeding under the skin

¹scut·tle \'skət-l\ *n* : a pail or bucket for carrying coal

²scuttle *n* : a small opening with a lid or cover (as in the deck of a ship)

³scuttle *vb* **scut·tled; scut·tling** : to sink by cutting holes through the bottom or sides

⁴scuttle *vb* **scut·tled; scut·tling** : to run rapidly from view

scythe \'sīth\ *n* : a tool with a curved blade on a long curved handle that is used to mow grass or grain by hand

scythe

sea \'sē\ *n* **1** : a body of salt water not as large as an ocean and often nearly surrounded by land **2** : OCEAN 1 **3** : rough water **4** : something suggesting a sea's great size or depth

sea anemone *n* : a hollow sea animal with a flowerlike cluster of tentacles about its mouth

sea·bird \'əsē,bərd\ *n* : a bird (as a gull) that lives about the open ocean

sea·coast \'sē-,kōst\ *n* : the shore of the sea

sea cucumber *n* : a sea animal related to the starfishes and sea urchins that has a long flexible muscular body shaped like a cucumber

sea dog *n* : an experienced sailor

sea·far·er \'sē-,far-ər, -,fer-\ *n* : a person who travels over the ocean : MARINER

¹sea·far·ing \'sē-,far-ing, -,fer-\ *adj* : of, given to, or employed in seafaring

²seafaring *n* : a traveling over the sea as work or as recreation

sea·food \'sē-,füd\ *n* : edible saltwater fish and shellfish

sea·go·ing \'sē-,gō-ing\ *adj* : suitable or used for sea travel

sea gull *n* : a gull that lives near the sea

sea horse *n* : a small fish with a head which looks like that of a horse

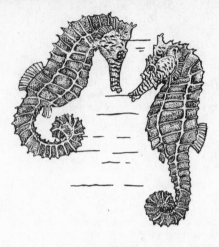

sea horses

¹seal \'sēl\ *n* **1** : a sea mammal that swims with flippers, lives mostly in cold regions, mates and bears young on land, eats flesh, and is hunted for fur, hides, or oil **2** : the soft dense fur of a northern seal

²seal *n* **1** : something (as a pledge) that makes safe or secure **2** : a device with a cut or raised design or figure that can be stamped or pressed into wax or paper **3** : a piece of wax stamped with a design and used to seal a letter or package **4** : a stamp that may be used to close a letter or package ⟨Christmas *seals*⟩ **5** : something that closes tightly **6** : a closing that is tight and perfect

³seal *vb* **1** : to mark with a seal **2** : to close or make fast with or as if with a seal — **seal·er** *n*

sea level *n* : the surface of the sea midway between the average high and low tides

sea lion *n* : a very large seal of the Pacific ocean

seal·skin \'sēl-,skin\ *n* : ¹SEAL 2

¹seam \'sēm\ *n* **1** : the fold, line, or groove made by sewing together or joining two edges or two pieces of material **2** : a layer of a mineral or metal ⟨a *seam* of coal⟩

²seam *vb* **1** : to join with a seam **2** : to mark with a line, scar, or wrinkle ⟨a face *seamed* with age⟩

sea·man \'sē-mən\ *n, pl* **sea·men** \-mən\ **1** : a person who helps in the handling of a ship at sea : SAILOR **2** : an enlisted person in the Navy or Coast Guard ranking above a seaman apprentice

seaman apprentice *n* : an enlisted person in the Navy or Coast Guard ranking above a seaman recruit

seaman recruit *n* : an enlisted person of the lowest rank in the Navy or Coast Guard

seam·stress \'sēm-strəs\ *n* : a woman who earns her living by sewing

sea·plane \'sē-,plān\ *n* : an airplane that can rise from and land on water

sea·port \'sē-,pōrt\ *n* : a port, harbor, or town within reach of seagoing ships

sear \'siər\ *vb* **1** : to dry by or as if by heat : PARCH **2** : to scorch or make brown on the surface by heat

¹search \'sərch\ *vb* **1** : to go through carefully and thoroughly in an effort to find something ⟨*search* the house⟩ **2** : to look in the pockets or the clothing of for something hidden ⟨all of us were *searched*⟩ **synonyms** see SEEK — **search·ing·ly** *adv*

²search *n* : an act or instance of searching

search·light \'sərch-,līt\ *n* : a lamp for sending a beam of bright light

sea·shell \'sē-,shel\ *n* : the shell of a sea creature

sea·shore \'sē-,shōr\ *n* : the shore of a sea

sea·sick \'sē-,sik\ *adj* : sick at the stomach from the pitching or rolling of a ship — **sea·sick·ness** *n*

sea·side \'sē-,sīd\ *n* : SEACOAST

¹sea·son \'sēz-n\ *n* **1** : one of the four quarters into which a year is commonly divided **2** : a period of time associated with something special ⟨the Christmas *season*⟩ ⟨the strawberry *season*⟩

²season *vb* **1** : to make pleasant to the taste by use of seasoning **2** : to make suitable for use (as by aging or drying) ⟨*seasoned* lumber⟩

sea·son·al \'sēz-n-əl\ *adj* : of, relating to, or coming only at a certain season ⟨*seasonal* foods⟩

sea·son·ing \'sēz-n-ing\ *n* : something added to food to give it more flavor

¹seat \'sēt\ *n* **1** : something (as a chair) used to sit in or on **2** : the part of something on which one rests in sitting ⟨chair *seat*⟩ ⟨*seat* of my pants⟩ **3** : the place on or at which a person sits ⟨take your *seat*⟩ **4** : a place that serves as a capital or center ⟨a *seat* of learning⟩ — **seat·ed** \'sēt-əd\ *adj*

²seat *vb* **1** : to place in or on a seat **2** : to provide seats for ⟨the hall *seats* 500 persons⟩

seat belt *n* : a strap (as in an automobile or airplane) designed to hold a person in a seat

sea urchin *n* : a rounded shellfish related to the starfishes that lives on or burrows in the sea bottom and is covered with spines

sea·wall \'sē-,wȯl\ *n* : a bank or a wall to prevent sea waves from cutting away the shore

sea·wa·ter \'sē-,wȯt-ər, -,wät-\ *n* : water in or from the sea

sea·weed \'sē-,wēd\ *n* : an alga (as a kelp) that grows in the sea

se·clud·ed \si-'klüd-əd\ *adj* : hidden from sight

se·clu·sion \si-'klü-zhən\ *n* : the condition of being secluded

¹sec·ond \'sek-ənd\ *adj* **1** : being next after the first ⟨the *second* time⟩ **2** : next lower in rank, value, or importance than the first ⟨*second* prize⟩

²second *adv* : in the second place or rank

³second *n* : one that is second

⁴second *n* **1** : a sixtieth part of a minute of time or of a degree **2** : MOMENT 1, INSTANT

⁵second *vb* : to support a motion or nomination so that it may be debated or voted on

sec·ond·ary \'sek-ən-,der-ē\ *adj* **1** : second in rank, value, or importance **2** : of, relating to, or being the second of three levels of stress in pronunciation **3** : derived from or coming after something original or primary ⟨*secondary* schools⟩

sec·ond·hand \,sek-ənd-'hand\ *adj* **1** : not new : having had a previous owner ⟨a *secondhand* automobile⟩ **2** : selling used goods

second lieutenant *n* : a commissioned officer of the lowest rank in the Army, Air Force, or Marine Corps

sec·ond·ly \'sek-ənd-lē\ *adv* : in the second place

sec·ond–rate \,sek-ən-'drāt\ *adj* : of ordinary quality or value

se·cre·cy \'sē-krə-sē\ *n, pl* **se·cre·cies** **1** : the habit of keeping things secret **2** : the quality or state of being secret or hidden

¹se·cret \'sē-krət\ *adj* **1** : hidden from the knowledge of others ⟨keep your plans *secret*⟩ **2** : done or working in secrecy ⟨a *secret* agent⟩ — **se·cret·ly** *adv*

²secret *n* : something kept or planned to be kept from others' knowledge

\ə\ **abut**	\au̇\ **out**	\i\ **tip**	\ȯ\ **saw**	\u̇\ **foot**
\ər\ **further**	\ch\ **chin**	\ī\ **life**	\ȯi\ **coin**	\y\ **yet**
\a\ **mat**	\e\ **pet**	\j\ **job**	\th\ **thin**	\yü\ **few**
\ā\ **take**	\ē\ **easy**	\ng\ **sing**	\th\ **this**	\yu̇\ **cure**
\ä\ **cot, cart**	\g\ **go**	\ō\ **bone**	\ü\ **food**	\zh\ **vision**

sec·re·tary \'sek-rə-ˌter-ē\ *n, pl* **sec·re·tar·ies** **1** : a person who is employed to take care of records and letters for another person **2** : an officer of a business corporation or society who has charge of the letters and records and who keeps minutes of meetings **3** : a government official in charge of the affairs of a department **4** : a writing desk with a top section for books

secretary 4

¹se·crete \si-'krēt\ *vb* **se·cret·ed; se·cret·ing** : to produce and give off as a secretion ⟨glands that *secrete* mucus⟩

²secrete *vb* **se·cret·ed; se·cret·ing** : to put in a hiding place

se·cre·tion \si-'krē-shən\ *n* **1** : the act or process of secreting some substance **2** : a substance formed in and given off by a gland that usually performs a useful function in the body ⟨digestive *secretions* contain enzymes⟩ **3** : a concealing or hiding of something

se·cre·tive \'sē-krət-iv, si-'krēt-\ *adj* : not open or frank

sect \'sekt\ *n* : a group within a religion which has a special set of teachings or ways of doing things

¹sec·tion \'sek-shən\ *n* **1** : a part cut off or separated ⟨a *section* of an orange⟩ **2** : a part of a written work ⟨the sports *section* of a newspaper⟩ **3** : the appearance that a thing has or would have if cut straight through ⟨a drawing of a gun in *section*⟩ **4** : a part of a country, group of people, or community ⟨the business *section* of town⟩ **synonyms** see PART

²section *vb* : to cut into sections

sec·tor \'sek-tər\ *n* : a part of an area or of a sphere of activity

sec·u·lar \'sek-yə-lər\ *adj* **1** : not concerned with religion or the church ⟨*secular* affairs⟩ ⟨*secular* music⟩ **2** : not bound by a monk's vows : not belonging to a religious order ⟨a *secular* priest⟩

¹se·cure \si-'kyùr\ *adj* **se·cur·er; se·cur·est** **1** : free from danger or risk **2** : strong or firm enough to ensure safety ⟨a *secure* lock⟩ **3** : ¹SURE 5, ASSURED ⟨the victory was *secure*⟩ **synonyms** see SAFE

²secure *vb* **se·cured; se·cur·ing** **1** : to make safe ⟨*secure* troops against attack⟩ **2** : to fasten tightly ⟨*secure* a door⟩ **3** : to get hold of : ACQUIRE ⟨*secure* information⟩ ⟨*secured* a job⟩

se·cu·ri·ty \si-'kyùr-ət-ē\ *n, pl* **se·cu·ri·ties** **1** : the state of being secure : SAFETY **2** : something given as a pledge of payment ⟨*security* for a loan⟩ **3** : something (as a stock certificate) that is evidence of debt or ownership

se·dan \si-'dan\ *n* **1** : SEDAN CHAIR **2** : a closed automobile seating four or more persons that has two or four doors and a permanent top

sedan chair *n* : a portable and often covered chair made to hold one person and to be carried on two poles by two men

sedan chair

se·date \si-'dāt\ *adj* : quiet and steady in manner or conduct — **se·date·ly** *adv* — **se·date·ness** *n*

¹sed·a·tive \'sed-ət-iv\ *adj* : tending to calm or to relieve tension

²sedative *n* : a sedative medicine

sedge \'sej\ *n* : a plant that is like grass but has solid stems and grows in tufts in marshes

sed·i·ment \'sed-ə-mənt\ *n* **1** : the material from a liquid that settles to the bottom **2** : material (as stones and sand) carried onto land or into water by water, wind, or a glacier

sed·i·men·ta·ry \ˌsed-ə-'ment-ə-rē\ *adj* : of, relating to, or formed from sediment ⟨sandstone is a *sedimentary* rock⟩

se·duce \si-'düs, -'dyüs\ *vb* **se·duced; se·duc·ing** : to persuade to do wrong ⟨was *seduced* into crime⟩

¹see \'sē\ *vb* **saw** \'sò\; **seen** \'sēn\; **see·ing** **1** : to have the power of sight : view with the eyes **2** : to have experience of : UNDERGO ⟨*saw* some action during the war⟩ **3** : to understand the meaning or importance of **4** : to make sure ⟨*see* that the job gets done⟩ **5** : to attend to ⟨I'll *see* to your order at once⟩ **6** : to meet with ⟨the doctor will *see* you now⟩ **7** : ACCOMPANY 1, ESCORT ⟨I'll *see* you home⟩

²see *n* **1** : the city in which a bishop's church is located **2** : DIOCESE

¹seed \'sēd\ *n* **1** : a tiny resting plant closed in a protective coat and able to develop under suitable conditions into a plant like the one that produced it **2** : a small structure (as a spore or a tiny dry fruit) other than a true seed by which a plant reproduces itself **3** : the descendants of one individual ⟨the *seed* of David⟩ **4** : a source of development or growth : GERM 2 — **seed·ed** \-əd\ *adj* — **seed·less** \-ləs\ *adj*

²seed *vb* **1** : ²SOW 2, PLANT **2** : to produce or shed seeds ⟨a plant that *seeds* early⟩ **3** : to take the seeds out of ⟨*seed* raisins⟩

seed·case \'sēd-,kās\ *n* : a dry hollow fruit (as a pod) that contains seeds

seed·ling \'sēd-ling\ *n* **1** : a plant grown from seed **2** : a young plant (as a tree younger than a sapling)

seed plant *n* : a plant that reproduces by true seeds

seed·pod \'sēd-,päd\ *n* : POD

seedy \'sēd-ē\ *adj* **seed·i·er; seed·i·est 1** : having or full of seeds ⟨a *seedy* fruit⟩ **2** : poor in condition or quality

seek \'sēk\ *vb* **sought** \'sȯt\; **seek·ing 1** : to try to find ⟨*seek* help⟩ **2** : to try to win or get ⟨*seek* fame⟩ **3** : to make an attempt ⟨*seek* to end a war⟩

synonyms SEEK, SEARCH, and HUNT mean to look for something. SEEK may be used in looking for either material or mental things ⟨*seeking* new friends⟩ ⟨*seek* the truth⟩ SEARCH suggests looking for something in a very careful, thorough way ⟨we *searched* all over the house for the letter⟩ HUNT suggests a long pursuit, as if one were going after game ⟨I *hunted* all day for the right present⟩

seem \'sēm\ *vb* **1** : to give the impression of being : APPEAR ⟨they certainly *seemed* pleased⟩ **2** : to suggest to one's own mind ⟨I *seem* to have lost my key⟩

seem·ing \'sē-ming\ *adj* : APPARENT 3 ⟨suspicious of our *seeming* enthusiasm⟩ — **seem·ing·ly** *adv*

seen *past participle of* SEE

seep \'sēp\ *vb* : to flow slowly through small openings ⟨water *seeped* into the basement⟩

seer \'siər\ *n* : a person who predicts events

¹see·saw \'sē-,sȯ\ *n* **1** : a children's game of riding on the ends of a plank balanced in the middle with one end going up while the other goes down **2** : the plank used in seesaw **3** : an action or motion like that of a seesaw

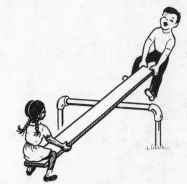

seesaw 2

²seesaw *vb* **1** : to ride on a seesaw **2** : to move like a seesaw

seethe \'sēth\ *vb* **seethed; seeth·ing 1** : to move without order as if boiling ⟨flies *seething* around garbage⟩ **2** : to be in a state of great excitement ⟨*seethe* with rage⟩

seg·ment \'seg-mənt\ *n* **1** : any of the parts into which a thing is divided or naturally separates **2** : a part cut off from a figure (as a circle) by means of a line or plane **3** : a part of a straight line included between two points — **seg·ment·ed** \-,ment-əd\ *adj*

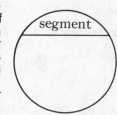

segment 2

seg·re·gate \'seg-ri-,gāt\ *vb* **seg·re·gat·ed; seg·re·gat·ing** : to set apart from others

seg·re·ga·tion \,seg-ri-'gā-shən\ *n* **1** : an act, process, or instance of segregating **2** : enforced separation of a race, class, or group from the rest of society

seize \'sēz\ *vb* **seized; seiz·ing 1** : to take possession of by force ⟨*seize* a fortress⟩ **2** : to take hold of suddenly or with force

synonyms see TAKE

sei·zure \'sē-zhər\ *n* : an act of seizing : the state of being seized

sel·dom \'sel-dəm\ *adv* : not often : RARELY

¹**se·lect** \sə-'lekt\ *adj* 1 : chosen to include the best or most suitable individuals ⟨*select* committees⟩ ⟨a *select* library⟩ 2 : of special value or excellence ⟨a *select* hotel⟩

²**select** *vb* : to pick out from a number or group : CHOOSE ⟨*select* a ripe peach⟩ **synonyms** see CHOOSE

se·lec·tion \sə-'lek-shən\ *n* 1 : the act or process of selecting 2 : something that is chosen

se·lec·tive \sə-'lek-tiv\ *adj* : involving or based on selection

se·le·ni·um \sə-'lē-nē-əm\ *n* : a gray powdery chemical element used chiefly in electronic devices

self \'self\ *n, pl* **selves** \'selvz\ 1 : a person regarded as an individual apart from everyone else 2 : a special side of a person's character ⟨your better *self*⟩

self- *prefix* 1 : oneself or itself ⟨*self*-governing⟩ 2 : of or by oneself or itself ⟨*self*-control⟩ 3 : to, with, for, or toward oneself or itself ⟨*self*-respect⟩

self–ad·dressed \,sel-fə-'drest, 'sel-'fad-,rest\ *adj* : addressed for return to the sender

self–cen·tered \'self-'sent-ərd\ *adj* : SELFISH

self–con·fi·dence \'self-'kän-fə-dəns\ *n* : confidence in oneself and one's abilities

self–con·scious \'self-'kän-chəs\ *adj* : too much aware of one's feelings or appearance when in the presence of other people — **self–con·scious·ly** *adv* — **self–con·scious·ness** *n*

self–con·trol \,self-kən-'trōl\ *n* : control over one's own impulses, emotions, or actions

self–ev·i·dent \'sel-'fev-ə-dənt\ *adj* : having no need of proof ⟨*self-evident* truths⟩

self–gov·ern·ing \'self-'gəv-ər-ning\ *adj* : having self-government

self–gov·ern·ment \'self-'gəv-ərn-mənt, -ər-mənt\ *n* : government by action of the people making up a community : democratic government

self–im·por·tant \,sel-fim-'pórt-nt\ *adj* : believing or acting as if one's importance is greater than it really is

self·ish \'sel-fish\ *adj* : taking care of oneself without thought for others — **self·ish·ness** *n*

self·less \'sel-fləs\ *adj* : not selfish — **self·less·ly** *adv* — **self·less·ness** *n*

self–pro·pelled \,self-prə-'peld\ *adj* : containing within itself the means for its own movement

self–re·li·ance \,sel-fri-'lī-əns\ *n* : trust in one's own efforts and abilities

self–re·spect \,sel-fri-'spekt\ *n* 1 : a proper regard for oneself as a human being 2 : regard for one's standing or position

self–re·straint \,sel-fri-'strānt\ *n* : proper control over one's actions or emotions

self–righ·teous \'sel-'frī-chəs\ *adj* : strongly convinced of the rightness of one's actions or beliefs

self·same \'self-,sām\ *adj* : exactly the same

self–serv·ice \'self-'sər-vəs\ *n* : the serving of oneself with things to be paid for to a cashier usually upon leaving

sell \'sel\ *vb* **sold** \'sōld\; **sell·ing** 1 : to betray a person or duty ⟨the traitors *sold* their ruler to the enemy⟩ 2 : to exchange in return for money or something else of value ⟨*sell* groceries⟩ 3 : to be sold or priced ⟨these *sell* for a dollar apiece⟩ — **sell·er** *n*

selves *pl of* SELF

sem·a·phore \'sem-ə-,fōr\ *n* 1 : a device for sending signals that can be seen by the receiver 2 : a system of sending signals with two flags held one in each hand

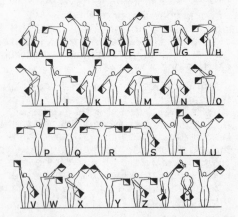

semaphore–alphabet; 3 positions following Z: error, end of word, numerals follow; numeral: 1, 2, 3, 4, 5, 6, 7, 8, 9, 0 same as A through J

sem·blance \'sem-bləns\ *n* : outward appearance

se·mes·ter \sə-'mes-tər\ *n* : either of two terms that make up a school year

Word History The English word *semester* that means "half a school year" came from a Latin word that meant "every half year." This word in turn came from two Latin words. The first meant "six" and the second meant "month." A half year is, after all, six months.

semi- *prefix* **1** : half ⟨*semi*circle⟩ **2** : partly : not completely **3** : partial

semi·cir·cle \'sem-i-ˌsər-kəl\ *n* : half of a circle

semi·cir·cu·lar \ˌsem-i-'sər-kyə-lər\ *adj* : having the form of a semicircle

semicircle

semi·co·lon \'sem-i-ˌkō-lən\ *n* : a punctuation mark ; that can be used to separate parts of a sentence which need clearer separation than would be shown by a comma, to separate main clauses which have no conjunction between, and to separate phrases and clauses containing commas

semi·con·duc·tor \ˌsem-i-kən-'dək-tər\ *n* : a device (as a transistor) which is used to control the flow of electricity (as in a television set) and which has an ability to conduct electricity between that of a conductor and an insulator

¹semi·fi·nal \ˌsem-i-'fin-l\ *adj* : coming before the final round in a tournament

²semi·fi·nal \'sem-i-ˌfin-l\ *n* : a semifinal match or game

sem·i·nary \'sem-ə-ˌner-ē\ *n, pl* **sem·i·nar·ies** **1** : a private school at or above the high school level **2** : a school for the training of priests, ministers, or rabbis

semi·sol·id \ˌsem-i-'säl-əd\ *adj* : having the qualities of both a solid and a liquid

sen·ate \'sen-ət\ *n* **1** : the upper and smaller branch of a legislature in a country or state **2** : a governing body

sen·a·tor \'sen-ət-ər\ *n* : a member of a senate — **sen·a·tor·ship** \-ˌship\ *n*

send \'send\ *vb* **sent** \'sent\; **send·ing** **1** : to cause to go ⟨*sent* the pupil home⟩ **2** : to set in motion by physical force ⟨*sent* the ball into right field⟩ **3** : to cause to happen ⟨asked the Lord to *send* some rain⟩ **4** : to cause someone to pass a message on or do an errand ⟨*send* out for coffee⟩ **5** : to give an order or request to come or go ⟨the principal *sent* for the child⟩ **6** : to bring into a certain condition ⟨*sent* me into a rage⟩ — **send·er** *n*

¹se·nior \'sēn-yər\ *n* **1** : a person older or higher in rank than someone else **2** : a student in the final year of high school or college

²senior *adj* **1** : being older — used to dis-

tinguish a father from a son with the same name ⟨John Doe, *Senior*⟩ **2** : higher in rank or office ⟨the *senior* partner of the law firm⟩ **3** : of or relating to seniors in a high school or college

senior airman *n* : an enlisted person in the Air Force who ranks above airman first class but who has not been made sergeant

senior chief petty officer *n* : a petty officer in the Navy or Coast Guard ranking above a chief petty officer

senior master sergeant *n* : a noncommissioned officer in the Air Force ranking above a master sergeant

sen·sa·tion \sen-'sā-shən\ *n* **1** : awareness (as of noise or heat) or a mental process (as seeing or smelling) resulting from stimulation of a sense organ **2** : an indefinite bodily feeling ⟨a *sensation* of flying⟩ **3** : a state of excited interest or feeling ⟨the rumor caused a *sensation*⟩ **4** : a cause or object of excited interest ⟨the play was a *sensation*⟩

sen·sa·tion·al \sen-'sā-shən-l\ *adj* : causing or meant to cause great interest

¹sense \'sens\ *n* **1** : a meaning or one of a set of meanings a word, phrase, or story may have **2** : a specialized function or mechanism (as sight, taste, or touch) of the body that involves the action and effect of a stimulus on a sense organ ⟨the pain *sense*⟩ **3** : a particular sensation or kind of sensation ⟨a good *sense* of balance⟩ **4** : awareness arrived at through or as if through the senses ⟨a vague *sense* of danger⟩ **5** : an awareness or understanding of something ⟨a *sense* of humor⟩ **6** : the ability to make wise decisions **7** : good reason or excuse ⟨no *sense* in waiting⟩

²sense *vb* **sensed; sens·ing** : to be or become conscious of ⟨*sense* the approach of a storm⟩

sense·less \'sen-sləs\ *adj* **1** : UNCONSCIOUS **1** ⟨was knocked *senseless*⟩ **2** : STUPID **2** — **sense·less·ly** *adv* — **sense·less·ness** *n*

sense organ *n* : a bodily structure (as the retina of the eye) that reacts to a stimulus (as light) and activates associated nerves so that they carry impulses to the brain

sen·si·bil·i·ty \ˌsen-sə-'bil-ət-ē\ *n, pl* **sen·si·bil·i·ties** **1** : the ability to receive or feel sensations **2** : the emotion or feeling of which a person is capable ⟨a person of keen *sensibility*⟩

\ə\ abut	\aü\ out	\i\ tip	\ȯ\ saw	\u̇\ foot
\ər\ further	\ch\ chin	\ī\ life	\ȯi\ coin	\y\ yet
\a\ mat	\e\ pet	\j\ job	\th\ thin	\yü\ cure
\ā\ take	\ē\ easy	\ng\ sing	\th\ this	\yu̇\ few
\ä\ cot, cart	\g\ go	\ō\ bone	\ü\ food	\zh\ vision

sen·si·ble \'sen-sə-bəl\ *adj* **1** : possible to take in by the senses or mind ⟨*sensible* impressions⟩ **2** : capable of feeling or perceiving ⟨*sensible* to pain⟩ **3** : showing or containing good sense or reason ⟨a *sensible* argument⟩ — **sen·si·ble·ness** *n* — **sen·si·bly** \-blē\ *adv*

sen·si·tive \'sen-sət-iv\ *adj* **1** : capable of responding to stimulation ⟨*sensitive* structures of the ear⟩ **2** : easily or strongly affected, impressed, or hurt ⟨a *sensitive* child⟩ **3** : readily changed or affected by the action of a certain thing ⟨plants *sensitive* to light⟩ — **sen·si·tive·ly** *adv* — **sen·si·tive·ness** *n*

sen·si·tiv·i·ty \,sen-sə-'tiv-ət-ē\ *n* : the quality or state of being sensitive

sen·so·ry \'sen-sə-rē\ *adj* : of or relating to sensation or the senses ⟨*sensory* nerves⟩

sen·su·al \'sen-chə-wəl\ *adj* : relating to the pleasing of the senses

sen·su·ous \'sench-ə-wəs, 'sench-wəs\ *adj* : relating to the senses or to things that affect the senses

sent *past of* SEND

¹sen·tence \'sent-ns\ *n* **1** : JUDGMENT 1 **2** : punishment set by a court ⟨served a *sentence* for robbery⟩ **3** : a group of words that makes a statement, asks a question, or expresses a command, wish, or exclamation **4** : a mathematical statement (as an equation) in words or symbols

²sentence *vb* **sen·tenced; sen·tenc·ing** : to give a sentence to ⟨the judge *sentenced* the prisoner⟩

sen·ti·ment \'sent-ə-mənt\ *n* **1** : a thought or attitude influenced by feeling ⟨a strong religious *sentiment*⟩ **2** : OPINION 1 **3** : tender feelings of affection or yearning

sen·ti·men·tal \,sent-ə-'ment-l\ *adj* **1** : influenced strongly by sentiment **2** : primarily affecting the emotions ⟨*sentimental* music⟩

sen·ti·nel \'sent-n-əl\ *n* : SENTRY

sen·try \'sen-trē\ *n, pl* **sen·tries** : a person (as a soldier) on duty as a guard

se·pal \'sē-pəl, 'sep-əl\ *n* : one of the specialized leaves that form the calyx of a flower

¹sep·a·rate \'sep-ə-,rāt\ *vb* **sep·a·rat·ed; sep·a·rat·ing** **1** : to set or keep apart ⟨*separate* an egg yolk from the white⟩ **2** : to make a distinction between ⟨*separate* fact from fiction⟩ **3** : to cease to be together : PART

²sep·a·rate \'sep-ə-rət, 'sep-rət\ *adj* **1** : set or kept apart ⟨the motel contains fifty *separate* units⟩ **2** : divided from each other ⟨where church and state are *separate*⟩ **3** : not shared : INDIVIDUAL ⟨we were each busy with our *separate* concerns⟩ **4** : having independent existence ⟨the *separate* pieces of a puzzle⟩

sep·a·rate·ly \'sep-ə-rət-lē\ *adv* : apart from others

sep·a·ra·tion \,sep-ə-'rā-shən\ *n* **1** : the act of separating : the state of being separated **2** : a point or line at which something is divided

sep·a·ra·tor \'sep-ə-,rāt-ər\ *n* : a machine for separating cream from milk

Sep·tem·ber \sep-'tem-bər\ *n* : the ninth month of the year

Word History The first Roman calendar had only ten months. The first month was March. The seventh month was September. The Latin name for this month came from the Latin word that meant "seven." When January and February were later added September kept its name, even though it became the ninth month. English *September* comes from the Latin name of the month.

sep·tet \sep-'tet\ *n* : a group or set of seven

sep·ul·cher *or* **sep·ul·chre** \'sep-əl-kər\ *n* : ¹GRAVE, TOMB

se·quel \'sē-kwəl\ *n* **1** : an event that follows or comes afterward : RESULT **2** : a book that continues a story begun in another

se·quence \'sē-kwəns\ *n* **1** : the condition or fact of following or coming after something else **2** : ²RESULT 1, SEQUEL **3** : the order in which things are or should be connected, related, or dated

se·quin \'sē-kwən\ *n* : a bit of shiny metal or plastic used as an ornament usually on clothing

se·quoia \si-'kwȯi-ə\ *n* **1** : a California tree that grows almost 100 meters tall and has needles as leaves and small egg-shaped cones **2** : REDWOOD

se·ra·pe \sə-'räp-ē, -'rap-\ *n* : a colorful woolen shawl or blanket

ser·e·nade \,ser-ə-'nād\ *n* : music sung or played at night under the window of a lady

se·rene \sə-'rēn\ *adj* **1** : ¹CLEAR **2** **2** : being calm and quiet ⟨a *serene* manner⟩ — **se·rene·ly** *adv* — **se·rene·ness** *n*

se·ren·i·ty \sə-'ren-ət-ē\ *n* : the quality or state of being serene

serf \'serf\ *n* : a servant or laborer of olden times who was treated as part of the land worked on and went along with the land if it was sold

serge \'sərj\ *n* : a woolen cloth that wears well

ser·geant \'sär-jənt\ *n* **1** : a noncommissioned officer in the Army or Marine Corps ranking above a corporal or in the Air Force ranking above an airman first class **2** : an officer in a police force

sergeant first class *n* : a noncommissioned officer in the Army ranking above a staff sergeant

sergeant major *n* **1** : the chief noncommissioned officer at a military headquarters **2** : a noncommissioned officer in the Marine Corps ranking above a first sergeant **3** : a staff sergeant major or command sergeant major in the Army

¹se·ri·al \'sir-ē-əl\ *adj* : arranged in or appearing in parts or numbers that follow a regular order — **se·ri·al·ly** *adv*

²serial *n* : a story appearing (as in a magazine or on television) in parts at regular intervals

se·ries \'siər-ēz\ *n, pl* **series** : a number of things or events arranged in order and connected by being alike in some way

se·ri·ous \'sir-ē-əs\ *adj* **1** : thoughtful or quiet in appearance or manner **2** : requiring much thought or work ⟨a *serious* task⟩ **3** : being in earnest : not light or casual ⟨give a *serious* answer to a *serious* question⟩ **4** : IMPORTANT **1** ⟨*serious* responsibilities⟩ **5** : being such as to cause distress or harm ⟨a *serious* accident⟩ — **se·ri·ous·ly** *adv* — **se·ri·ous·ness** *n*

serape

ser·mon \'sər-mən\ *n* **1** : a speech usually by a priest, minister, or rabbi for the purpose of giving religious instruction **2** : a serious talk to a person about his or her conduct

ser·pent \'sər-pənt\ *n* : a usually large snake

se·rum \'sir-əm\ *n* : the liquid part that can be separated from coagulated blood, contains antibodies, and is sometimes used to prevent or cure disease

ser·vant \'sər-vənt\ *n* : a person hired to perform household or personal services

¹serve \'sərv\ *vb* **served; serv·ing** **1** : to be a servant **2** : to give the service and respect due **3** : ²WORSHIP **1** ⟨*serve* God⟩ **4** : to put in : SPEND ⟨*served* three years in the army⟩ **5** : to be of use : answer some purpose ⟨the tree *served* as shelter⟩ **6** : to provide helpful services **7** : to be enough for ⟨a pie that will *serve* eight people⟩ **8** : to hold an office : perform a duty ⟨*serve* on a jury⟩ **9** : to help persons to food or set out helpings of food or drink **10** : to furnish with something needed or desired **11** : to make a serve (as in tennis)

²serve *n* : an act of putting the ball or shuttlecock in play (as in tennis or badminton)

¹ser·vice \'sər-vəs\ *n* **1** : the occupation or function of serving or working as a servant **2** : the work or action of one that serves ⟨gives quick *service*⟩ **3** : ²HELP **1**, USE ⟨be of *service* to them⟩ **4** : a religious ceremony ⟨the Sunday *service*⟩ **5** : a helpful or useful act : good turn ⟨did me a *service*⟩ **6** : ²SERVE **7** : a set of dishes or silverware ⟨a silver tea *service*⟩ **8** : a branch of public employment or the people working in it **9** : a nation's armed forces ⟨called into the *service*⟩ **10** : an organization for supplying some public demand or keeping up and repairing

\ə\ abut	\au̇\ out	\i\ tip	\ȯ\ saw	\u̇\ foot	
\ər\ further	\ch\ chin	\ī\ life	\ȯi\ coin	\y\ yet	
\a\ mat	\e\ pet	\j\ job	\th\ thin	\yü\ few	
\ā\ take	\ē\ easy	\ng\ sing	\th\ this	\yu̇\ cure	
\ä\ cot, cart	\g\ go	\ō\ bone	\ü\ food	\zh\ vision	

something ⟨bus *service*⟩ ⟨television sales and *service*⟩

²service *vb* **ser·viced; ser·vic·ing** : to work at taking care of or repairing

ser·vice·able \'sər-və-sə-bəl\ *adj* **1** : fit for or suited to some use **2** : lasting or wearing well in use ⟨*serviceable* shoes⟩ — **ser·vice·able·ness** *n*

ser·vice·man \'sər-vəs-,man\ *n, pl* **ser·vice·men** \-,men\ : a male member of the armed forces

service station *n* : a place for servicing motor vehicles especially with gasoline and oil

ser·vile \'sər-vəl\ *adj* **1** : of or suitable to a slave ⟨*servile* work⟩ **2** : lacking spirit or independence

serv·ing \'sər-ving\ *n* : a helping of food

ser·vi·tude \'sər-və-,tüd, -,tyüd\ *n* : the condition of a slave

ses·sion \'sesh-ən\ *n* **1** : a single meeting (as of a court, lawmaking body, or school) **2** : a whole series of meetings ⟨congress was in *session* for six months⟩ **3** : the time during which a court, congress, or school meets

¹set \'set\ *vb* **set; set·ting** **1** : to cause to sit **2** : to cover and warm eggs to hatch them ⟨*setting* hens⟩ **3** : to put or fix in a place or condition ⟨*set* the box on the table⟩ **4** : to arrange in a desired and especially a normal position ⟨*set* a broken bone⟩ **5** : ¹START 5 ⟨*set* a fire⟩ **6** : to cause to be, become, or do ⟨*set* the prisoner free⟩ **7** : to fix at a certain amount : SETTLE ⟨*set* a price⟩ **8** : to furnish as a model ⟨*set* an example for others⟩ **9** : to put in order for immediate use ⟨*set* the table⟩ **10** : to provide (as words or verses) with music **11** : to fix firmly **12** : to become or cause to become firm or solid ⟨wait for the cement to *set*⟩ **13** : to form and bring to maturity ⟨the old tree still *sets* a good crop of apples⟩ **14** : to pass below the horizon : go down ⟨the sun is *setting*⟩ — **set about** : to begin to do — **set forth** : to start out ⟨*set forth* on a journey⟩

²set *adj* **1** : fixed by authority ⟨a *set* rule⟩ **2** : not very willing to change ⟨*set* in their ways⟩ **3** : ¹READY 1 ⟨are you all *set*⟩

³set *n* **1** : the act or action of setting : the condition of being set **2** : a number of persons or things of the same kind that belong or are used together **3** : the form or movement of the body or of its parts ⟨the *set* of the shoulders⟩ **4** : an artificial setting for a scene of a play or motion picture **5** : a group of tennis games that make up a match **6** : a collection of mathematical elements **7** : an electronic apparatus ⟨a television *set*⟩

set·back \'set-,bak\ *n* : a slowing of progress : a temporary defeat

set down *vb* **1** : to place at rest on a surface **2** : to land an aircraft

set in *vb* : to make its appearance : BEGIN ⟨winter *set in* early⟩

set off *vb* **1** : to cause to stand out ⟨dark eyes *set off* by a pale face⟩ **2** : to set apart ⟨words *set off* by commas⟩ **3** : to cause to start ⟨the story *set* them *off* laughing⟩ **4** : EXPLODE 1 ⟨*set* the bomb *off*⟩ **5** : to start a journey ⟨*set off* for home⟩

set on *vb* : to urge to attack or chase ⟨threatened to *set* the dogs *on* me⟩

set out *vb* **1** : UNDERTAKE 1 **2** : to begin on a course or journey

set·tee \se-'tē\ *n* : a long seat with a back

set·ter \'set-ər\ *n* **1** : one that sets **2** : a large dog that has long hair and is used in hunting birds

setter 2

set·ting \'set-ing\ *n* **1** : the act of one that sets ⟨*setting* of type⟩ **2** : that in which something is set or mounted ⟨a gold *setting* for a ruby⟩ **3** : the background (as time and place) of the action of a story or play **4** : a batch of eggs for hatching

¹set·tle \'set-l\ *n* : a long wooden bench with arms and a high solid back

settle

²settle *vb* **set·tled; set·tling 1 :** to place so as to stay ⟨*settle* oneself in a chair⟩ **2 :** to come to rest ⟨birds *settling* on a branch⟩ ⟨dust *settled* on the table⟩ **3 :** to sink gradually to a lower level ⟨the foundations of the house *settled*⟩ **4 :** to sink in a liquid **5 :** to make one's home ⟨*settle* in the country⟩ **6 :** to apply oneself ⟨*settle* down to work⟩ **7 :** to fix by agreement **8 :** to put in order ⟨*settled* their affairs⟩ **9 :** to make quiet : CALM ⟨*settled* my nerves⟩ **10 :** DECIDE 1 ⟨*settle* a question⟩ **11 :** to complete payment on ⟨*settle* a bill⟩ **12 :** AD-JUST 1 ⟨*settle* a quarrel⟩

set·tle·ment \'set-l-mənt\ *n* **1 :** the act of settling : the condition of being settled **2 :** final payment (as of a bill) **3 :** the act or fact of establishing colonies ⟨the *settlement* of New England⟩ **4 :** a place or region newly settled **5 :** a small village **6 :** an institution that gives help to people in a crowded part of a city

set·tler \'set-lər\ *n* : a person who settles in a new region : COLONIST

set up *vb* **1 :** to place or secure in position **2 :** to put in operation : FOUND, ESTABLISH

¹sev·en \'sev-ən\ *adj* : being one more than six

²seven *n* : one more than six : 7

¹sev·en·teen \ˌsev-ən-'tēn\ *adj* : being one more than sixteen

²seventeen *n* : one more than sixteen : 17

¹sev·en·teenth \ˌsev-ən-'tēnth\ *adj* : coming right after sixteenth

²seventeenth *n* : number seventeen in a series

¹sev·enth \'sev-ənth\ *adj* : coming right after sixth

²seventh *n* **1 :** number seven in a series **2 :** one of seven equal parts

¹sev·en·ti·eth \'sev-ən-tē-əth\ *adj* : coming right after sixty-ninth

²seventieth *n* : number seventy in a series

¹sev·en·ty \'sev-ən-tē, -dē\ *adj* : being seven times ten

²seventy *n* : seven times ten : 70

sev·er \'sev-ər\ *vb* **1 :** to put or keep apart : DIVIDE **2 :** to come or break apart

¹sev·er·al \'sev-ə-rəl, 'sev-rəl\ *adj* **1 :** separate or distinct from others : DIFFERENT ⟨federal union of the *several* states⟩ **2 :** consisting of more than two but not very many ⟨*several* persons⟩

²several *pron* : a small number : more than two but not many

se·vere \sə-'viər\ *adj* **se·ver·er; se·ver-est 1 :** serious in feeling or manner : GRAVE **2 :** very strict : HARSH ⟨a *severe* ruler⟩ **3 :** not using unnecessary orna-ment : PLAIN ⟨a *severe* style⟩ **4 :** hard to bear or deal with ⟨*severe* suffering⟩ ⟨a *severe* test⟩ — **se·vere·ly** *adv* — **se·vere-ness** *n*

se·ver·i·ty \sə-'ver-ət-ē\ *n* : the quality or state of being severe

sew \'sō\ *vb* **sewed; sewed** *or* **sewn** \'sōn\; **sew·ing 1 :** to join or fasten by stitches **2 :** to work with needle and thread

sew·age \'sü-ij\ *n* : waste materials carried off by sewers

¹sew·er \'sō-ər\ *n* : one that sews

²sew·er \'sü-ər\ *n* : a usually covered drain to carry off water and waste

sew·er·age \'sü-ə-rij\ *n* **1 :** SEWAGE **2 :** the removal and disposal of sewage by sewers **3 :** a system of sewers

sew·ing \'sō-ing\ *n* **1 :** the act, method, or occupation of one that sews **2 :** material being sewed or to be sewed

sex \'seks\ *n* **1 :** either of two divisions of living things and especially humans, one made up of males, the other of females **2 :** the things that make males and females different from each other **3 :** sexual activity

sex·tet \sek-'stet\ *n* : a group or set of six

sex·ton \'sek-stən\ *n* : an official of a church who takes care of church buildings and property

sex·u·al \'sek-shə-wəl\ *adj* **1 :** of or relating to sex or the sexes **2 :** of, relating to, or being the form of reproduction in which germ cells from two parents combine in fertilization to form a new individual — **sex·u·al·ly** *adv*

shab·by \'shab-ē\ *adj* **shab·bi·er; shab-bi·est 1 :** faded and worn from use or wear **2 :** dressed in worn clothes **3 :** not fair or generous ⟨*shabby* treatment⟩ — **shab·bi·ly** \'shab-ə-lē\ *adv* — **shab·bi-ness** \'shab-ē-nəs\ *n*

shack \'shak\ *n* : HUT, SHANTY

¹shack·le \'shak-əl\ *n* **1 :** a ring or band that prevents free use of the legs or arms **2 :** something that prevents free action ⟨the *shackles* of superstition⟩ **3 :** a U-shaped metal device for joining or fastening something

²shackle *vb* **shack·led; shack·ling 1 :** to bind or fasten with a shackle **2 :** HINDER

shad \'shad\ *n, pl* **shad** : any of several sea fishes related to the herrings that have deep bodies, swim up rivers to spawn, and are important food fish

\ə\ abut	\au̇\ out	\i\ tip	\ȯ\ saw	\u̇\ foot
\ər\ further	\ch\ chin	\ī\ life	\ȯi\ coin	\y\ yet
\a\ mat	\e\ pet	\j\ job	\th\ thin	\yü\ few
\ā\ take	\ē\ easy	\ng\ sing	\th\ this	\yu̇\ cure
\ä\ cot, cart	\g\ go	\ō\ bone	\ü\ food	\zh\ vision

¹shade \'shād\ *n* **1** : partial darkness ⟨the trees cast *shade*⟩ **2** : space sheltered from light or heat and especially from the sun ⟨sit in the *shade* of a tree⟩ **3 shades** *pl* : the shadows that gather as darkness falls ⟨the *shades* of night⟩ **4** : GHOST, SPIRIT **5** : something that blocks off or cuts down light ⟨a lamp *shade*⟩ ⟨a window *shade*⟩ **6** : the darkening of some objects in a painting or drawing to suggest that they are in shade **7** : the darkness or lightness of a color ⟨four *shades* of brown⟩ **8** : a very small difference or amount ⟨just a *shade* taller⟩ ⟨*shades* of meaning⟩

²shade *vb* **shad·ed; shad·ing 1** : to shelter from light or heat **2** : to mark with shades of light or color ⟨*shade* a drawing⟩ **3** : to show or begin to have slight differences of color, value, or meaning

¹shad·ow \'shad-ō\ *n* **1** : ¹SHADE 1 ⟨the valley was in *shadow*⟩ **2** : a reflected image **3** : shelter from danger or view **4** : the dark figure cast on a surface by a body that is between the surface and the light ⟨my *shadow* stays with me⟩ **5** : PHANTOM **6 shadows** *pl* : darkness caused by the setting of the sun **7** : a very little bit : TRACE ⟨beyond a *shadow* of doubt⟩

²shadow *vb* **1** : to cast a shadow upon **2** : to cast gloom over **3** : to follow and watch closely especially in a secret way

shad·owy \'shad-ə-wē\ *adj* **1** : not realistic ⟨*shadowy* dreams of glory⟩ **2** : full of shadow ⟨a *shadowy* lane⟩

shady \'shād-ē\ *adj* **shad·i·er; shad·i·est 1** : sheltered from the sun's rays **2** : not right or honest ⟨*shady* business deals⟩ — **shad·i·ness** *n*

shaft \'shaft\ *n* **1** : the long handle of a weapon (as a spear) **2** : one of two poles between which a horse is hitched to pull a wagon or carriage **3** : an arrow or its narrow stem **4** : a narrow beam of light **5** : a long narrow part especially when round ⟨the *shaft* of a feather⟩ **6** : the handle of a tool or instrument **7** : a bar to support rotating pieces of machinery or to give them motion **8** : a tall monument (as a column) **9** : a mine opening made for finding or mining ore **10** : an opening or passage straight down through the floors of a building ⟨an air *shaft*⟩

shag·gy \'shag-ē\ *adj* **shag·gi·er; shag·gi·est 1** : covered with or made up of a long, coarse, and tangled growth (as of hair or vegetation) ⟨a dog with a *shaggy* coat⟩ **2** : having a rough or hairy surface ⟨a *shaggy* tweed⟩ — **shag·gi·ly** \'shag-ə-lē\ *adv* — **shag·gi·ness** \'shag-ē-nəs\ *n*

¹shake \'shāk\ *vb* **shook** \'shuk\; **shak·en** \'shā-kən\; **shak·ing 1** : to tremble or make tremble : QUIVER **2** : to make less firm : WEAKEN ⟨had their confidence *shaken*⟩ **3** : to move back and forth or to and fro ⟨*shake* your head⟩ **4** : to cause to be, become, go, or move by or as if by a shake ⟨*shake* apples from a tree⟩

²shake *n* : the act or motion of shaking

shak·er \'shā-kər\ *n* : one that shakes or is used in shaking ⟨salt *shaker*⟩

shaky \'shā-kē\ *adj* **shak·i·er; shak·i·est** : easily shaken : UNSOUND ⟨*shaky* arguments⟩ — **shak·i·ly** \-kə-lē\ *adv* — **shak·i·ness** \-kē-nəs\ *n*

shale \'shāl\ *n* : a rock with a fine grain formed from clay, mud, or silt

shall \shəl, 'shal\ *helping verb, past* **should** \shəd, 'shud\ *present sing & pl* **shall 1** : am or are going to or expecting to : WILL ⟨I *shall* never mention it again⟩ **2** : is or are forced to : MUST ⟨they *shall* not pass⟩

¹shal·low \'shal-ō\ *adj* **1** : not deep **2** : showing little knowledge, thought, or feeling — **shal·low·ness** *n*

²shallow *n* : a shallow place in a body of water — usually used in pl.

¹sham \'sham\ *n* : ³COUNTERFEIT, imitation

²sham *vb* **shammed; sham·ming** : to act in a deceiving way

³sham *adj* : not real : FALSE ⟨*sham* battle⟩

sham·ble \'sham-bəl\ *vb* **sham·bled; sham·bling** : to walk in an awkward unsteady way

sham·bles \'sham-bəlz\ *n sing or pl* : a place or scene of disorder or destruction

¹shame \'shām\ *n* **1** : a painful emotion caused by having done something wrong or improper **2** : ability to feel shame ⟨have you no *shame*⟩ **3** : ¹DISHONOR 1, DISGRACE **4** : something that brings disgrace or causes shame or strong regret

²shame *vb* **shamed; sham·ing 1** : to make ashamed **2** : ²DISHONOR **3** : to force by causing to feel shame ⟨they were *shamed* into confessing⟩

shame·faced \'shām-'fāst\ *adj* : seeming ashamed — **shame·faced·ly** \-'fā-səd-lē\ *adv* — **shame·faced·ness** \-səd-nəs\ *n*

shame·ful \'shām-fəl\ *adj* : bringing shame : DISGRACEFUL ⟨*shameful* behavior⟩ — **shame·ful·ly** \-fə-lē\ *adv* — **shame·ful·ness** *n*

shame·less \'shām-ləs\ *adj* : having no shame ⟨a *shameless* liar⟩ — **shame·less·ly** *adv* — **shame·less·ness** *n*

¹sham·poo \sham-'pü\ *vb* : to wash the hair and scalp

²**shampoo** *n, pl* **sham·poos** **1** : a washing of the hair **2** : a cleaner made for washing the hair

sham·rock \'sham-ˌräk\ *n* : a plant (as some clovers) that has leaves with three leaflets and is used as an emblem by the Irish

shamrock

shank \'shangk\ *n* **1** : the lower part of the human leg : the equivalent part of a lower animal **2** : the part of a tool that connects the working part with a part by which it is held or moved ⟨the *shank* of a drill bit⟩

shan't \shant\ : shall not

shan·ty \'shant-ē\ *n, pl* **shan·ties** : a small roughly built shelter or dwelling

¹**shape** \'shāp\ *vb* **shaped; shap·ing** **1** : to give a certain form or shape to ⟨*shape* the dough into loaves⟩ **2** : DEVISE ⟨*shaped* a secret plan⟩ **3** : to make fit especially for some purpose : ADAPT ⟨*shaping* the minds of future leaders⟩ **4** : to take on a definite form or quality : DEVELOP ⟨plans were *shaping* up⟩ — **shap·er** *n*

²**shape** *n* **1** : outward appearance : FORM ⟨the *shape* of a pear⟩ **2** : the outline of a body : FIGURE ⟨a square *shape*⟩ **3** : definite arrangement and form ⟨a plan is taking *shape*⟩ **4** : ¹CONDITION 3 ⟨the car is in poor *shape*⟩ — **shaped** \ˌshāpt\ *adj*

shape·less \'shā-pləs\ *adj* **1** : having no fixed or regular shape **2** : not shapely — **shape·less·ly** *adv* — **shape·less·ness** *n*

shape·ly \'shā-plē\ *adj* **shape·li·er; shape·li·est** : having a pleasing shape — **shape·li·ness** *n*

¹**share** \'sheər, 'shaər\ *n* **1** : a portion belonging to one person **2** : the part given or belonging to one of a number of persons owning something together ⟨sold my *share* of the business⟩ **3** : any of the equal portions into which a property or corporation is divided ⟨100 *shares* of stock⟩

²**share** *vb* **shared; shar·ing** **1** : to divide and distribute in portions ⟨*shared* the lunch⟩ **2** : to use, experience, or enjoy with others ⟨*share* a room⟩ **3** : to take a part ⟨*share* in planning the program⟩

³**share** *n* : the cutting blade of a plow

share·crop \'sheər-ˌkräp, 'shaər-\ *vb* **share·cropped; share·crop·ping** : to farm another's land for a share of the crop or profit — **share·crop·per** *n*

¹**shark** \'shärk\ *n* : any of a group of fierce sea fishes that are typically gray, have skeletons of cartilage, and include some large forms that may attack humans

²**shark** *n* : a sly greedy person who takes advantage of others

¹**sharp** \'shärp\ *adj* **1** : having a thin edge or fine point ⟨a *sharp* knife⟩ **2** : brisk and cold ⟨a *sharp* wind⟩ **3** : QUICK-WITTED, SMART ⟨a *sharp* student⟩ **4** : ATTENTIVE 1 ⟨keep a *sharp* watch⟩ **5** : having very good ability to see or hear ⟨you have *sharp* eyes⟩ **6** : ENERGETIC, BRISK ⟨keep up a *sharp* pace⟩ **7** : SEVERE 2, ANGRY ⟨a *sharp* reply⟩ **8** : very trying to the feelings : causing distress ⟨a *sharp* pain⟩ ⟨*sharp* criticism⟩ **9** : strongly affecting the senses ⟨a *sharp* taste⟩ **10** : ending in a point or edge ⟨a *sharp* peak⟩ **11** : involving an abrupt change ⟨a *sharp* drop in the temperature⟩ ⟨a *sharp* turn to the right⟩ **12** : DISTINCT 2 ⟨a *sharp* image⟩ **13** : raised in pitch by a half step **14** : higher than true pitch — **sharp·ly** *adv* — **sharp·ness** *n*

²**sharp** *adv* **1** : in a sharp manner ⟨sang *sharp*⟩ **2** : at an exact time ⟨four o'clock *sharp*⟩

³**sharp** *n* **1** : a note or tone that is a half step higher than the note named **2** : a sign ♯ that tells that a note is to be made higher by a half step

sharp·en \'shär-pən\ *vb* : to make or become sharp or sharper — **sharp·en·er** *n*

shat·ter \'shat-ər\ *vb* **1** : to break or fall to pieces **2** : to damage badly : RUIN, WRECK ⟨*shattered* hopes⟩

¹**shave** \'shāv\ *vb* **shaved; shaved** *or* **shav·en** \'shā-vən\; **shav·ing** **1** : to cut or trim off with a sharp blade ⟨*shaved* the hair off my arm⟩ **2** : to make bare or smooth by cutting the hair from ⟨the doctor *shaved* my arm⟩ **3** : to trim closely ⟨a lawn *shaven* close⟩

²**shave** *n* **1** : an operation of shaving **2** : a narrow escape ⟨a close *shave*⟩

shav·ing \'shā-ving\ *n* : a thin slice or strip sliced off with a cutting tool ⟨wood *shavings*⟩

shawl

shawl \'shol\ *n* : a square or oblong piece of cloth used

\ə\ abut	\au̇\ out	\i\ tip	\o̊\ saw	\u̇\ foot
\ər\ further	\ch\ chin	\ī\ life	\o̊i\ coin	\y\ yet
\a\ mat	\e\ pet	\j\ job	\th\ thin	\yü\ few
\ā\ take	\ē\ easy	\ng\ sing	\th\ this	\yu̇\ cure
\ä\ cot, cart	\g\ go	\ō\ bone	\ü\ food	\zh\ vision

especially by women as a loose covering for the head or shoulders

she \shē\ *pron* : that female one

sheaf \'shēf\ *n, pl* **sheaves** \'shēvz\ **1** : a bundle of stalks and ears of grain **2** : a group of things fastened together ⟨a *sheaf* of arrows⟩ — **sheaf·like** \'shē-,flīk\ *adj*

shear \'shiər\ *vb* **sheared; sheared** *or* **shorn** \'shōrn\; **shear·ing 1** : to cut the hair or wool from : CLIP ⟨*shear* sheep⟩ **2** : to strip of as if by cutting ⟨*shorn* of their power⟩ **3** : to cut or break sharply ⟨a telephone pole *sheared* off by a car⟩ — **shear·er** *n*

sheaf 1

shears \'shiərz\ *n pl* : a cutting tool like a pair of large scissors

sheath \'shēth\ *n, pl* **sheaths** \'shēthz\ **1** : a case for a blade (as of a knife) **2** : a covering (as the outer wings of a beetle) suggesting a sheath in form or use

sheathe \'shēth\ *vb* **sheathed; sheath·ing 1** : to put into a sheath ⟨*sheathe* your sword⟩ **2** : to cover with something that protects

sheath·ing \'shē-thing\ *n* : the first covering of boards or of waterproof material on the outside wall of a frame house or on a timber roof

sheaves *pl of* SHEAF

¹**shed** \'shed\ *vb* **shed; shed·ding 1** : to give off in drops ⟨*shed* tears⟩ **2** : to cause (blood) to flow from a cut or wound **3** : to spread abroad ⟨the sun *sheds* light and heat⟩ **4** : REPEL 3 ⟨raincoats *shed* water⟩ **5** : to cast (as a natural covering) aside ⟨a snake *sheds* its skin⟩

²**shed** *n* : a structure built for shelter or storage ⟨a tool *shed*⟩

she'd \shēd\ : she had : she would

sheen \'shēn\ *n* : a bright or shining condition : LUSTER

sheep \'shēp\ *n, pl* **sheep 1** : an animal related to the goat that is raised for meat or for its wool and skin **2** : a weak helpless person who is easily led

sheep·fold \'shēp-,fōld\ *n* : a pen or shelter for sheep

sheep·herd·er \'shēp-,hərd-ər\ *n* : a worker in charge of a flock of sheep

sheep·ish \'shē-pish\ *adj* **1** : like a sheep **2** : embarrassed especially over being found out in a fault ⟨a *sheepish* look⟩ — **sheep·ish·ly** *adv* — **sheep·ish·ness** *n*

sheep·skin \'shēp-,skin\ *n* : the skin of a sheep or leather prepared from it

¹**sheer** \'shiər\ *adj* **1** : very thin or transparent ⟨*sheer* stockings⟩ **2** : THOROUGH 1, ABSOLUTE ⟨*sheer* nonsense⟩ **3** : very steep ⟨a *sheer* cliff⟩ — **sheer·ly** *adv* — **sheer·ness** *n*

²**sheer** *adv* **1** : COMPLETELY **2** : straight up or down

¹**sheet** \'shēt\ *n* **1** : a broad piece of cloth (as an article of bedding used next to the body) **2** : a broad piece of paper (as for writing or printing) **3** : a broad surface ⟨a *sheet* of water⟩ **4** : something that is very thin as compared with its length and width ⟨a *sheet* of iron⟩ — **sheet·like** \-,līk\ *adj*

²**sheet** *n* : a rope or chain used to adjust the angle at which the sail of a boat is set to catch the wind

sheikh *or* **sheik** \shēk, 'shāk\ *n* : an Arab chief

shek·el \'shek-əl\ *n* **1** : any of various ancient units of weight (as of the Hebrews) **2** : a coin weighing one shekel

shelf \'shelf\ *n, pl* **shelves** \'shelvz\ **1** : a flat piece (as of board or metal) set above a floor (as on a wall or in a bookcase) to hold things **2** : something (as a sandbar or ledge of rock) that suggests a shelf

¹**shell** \'shel\ *n* **1** : a stiff hard covering of an animal (as a turtle, oyster, or beetle) **2** : the tough outer covering of an egg **3** : the outer covering of a nut, fruit, or seed especially when hard or tough and fibrous **4** : something like a shell (as in shape, function, or material) ⟨a pastry *shell*⟩ **5** : a narrow light racing boat rowed by one or more persons **6** : a metal or paper case holding the explosive charge and the shot or object to be fired from a gun or cannon — **shelled** \'sheld\ *adj*

²**shell** *vb* **1** : to take out of the shell or husk ⟨*shell* peas⟩ **2** : to remove the kernels of grain from (as a cob of Indian corn) **3** : to shoot shells at or upon

she'll \shēl\ : she shall : she will

¹**shel·lac** \shə-'lak\ *n* : a varnish made from a material given off by an Asian insect dissolved usually in alcohol

²**shellac** *vb* **shel·lacked; shel·lack·ing** : to coat with shellac

shell·fish \'shel-,fish\ *n, pl* **shellfish** : an invertebrate animal that lives in water and has a shell — used mostly of edible forms (as oysters or crabs)

¹shel·ter \'shel-tər\ *n* **1** : something that covers or protects **2** : the condition of being protected ⟨find *shelter* with friends⟩

²shelter *vb* **1** : to be a shelter for : provide with shelter **2** : to find and use a shelter

shelve \'shelv\ *vb* **shelved; shelv·ing 1** : to place or store on shelves **2** : ¹DEFER ⟨*shelve* a plan⟩

shelves *pl of* SHELF

¹shep·herd \'shep-ərd\ *n* : a person who takes care of sheep

²shepherd *vb* : to care for as or as if a shepherd

shep·herd·ess \'shep-ərd-əs\ *n* : a woman who takes care of sheep

sher·bet \'shər-bət\ *n* : a frozen dessert of fruit juice to which milk, the white of egg, or gelatin is added before freezing

sher·iff \'sher-əf\ *n* : the officer of a county who is in charge of enforcing the law

she's \shēz\ : she is : she has

Shet·land pony \,shet-lənd-\ *n* : any of a breed of small stocky horses with shaggy coats

Shetland pony

¹shield \'shēld\ *n* **1** : a broad piece of armor carried on the arm to protect oneself in battle **2** : something that serves as a defense or protection

²shield *vb* : to cover or screen with or as if with a shield

¹shift \'shift\ *vb* **1** : to exchange for another of the same kind **2** : to change or remove from one person or place to another ⟨*shift* a bag to the other shoulder⟩ **3** : to change the arrangement of gears transmitting power (as in an automobile) **4** : to get along without help : FEND ⟨can *shift* for myself⟩

²shift *n* **1** : the act of shifting : TRANSFER **2** : a group of workers who work together during a scheduled period of time **3** : the period during which one group of workers is working **4** : GEARSHIFT

shift·less \'shift-ləs\ *adj* : lacking in ambition and energy : LAZY — **shift·less·ly** *adv* — **shift·less·ness** *n*

shifty \'shif-tē\ *adj* **shift·i·er; shift·i·est** : not worthy of trust : TRICKY — **shift·i·ly** \-tə-lē\ *adv* — **shift·i·ness** \-tē-nəs\ *n*

shil·ling \'shil-ing\ *n* : an old British coin equal to ¹⁄₂₀ pound

shim·mer \'shim-ər\ *vb* : to shine with a wavering light : GLIMMER ⟨*shimmering* silks⟩

¹shin \'shin\ *n* : the front part of the leg below the knee

²shin *vb* **shinned; shin·ning** : to climb (as a pole) by grasping with arms and legs and moving oneself upward by repeated jerks

¹shine \'shīn\ *vb* **shone** \'shōn\ *or* **shined; shin·ing 1** : to give light ⟨the sun *shone*⟩ **2** : to be glossy : GLEAM **3** : to be outstanding ⟨*shines* in sports⟩ **4** : to make bright by polishing ⟨*shined* my shoes⟩

²shine *n* **1** : brightness from light given off or reflected **2** : fair weather : SUNSHINE ⟨rain or *shine*⟩ **3** : ²POLISH 1

shin·er \'shī-nər\ *n* **1** : a small silvery American freshwater fish related to the carp **2** : an eye discolored by injury : a black eye

¹shin·gle \'shing-gəl\ *n* **1** : a small thin piece of building material (as wood or an asbestos composition) for laying in overlapping rows as a covering for the roof or sides of a building **2** : a small sign

²shingle *vb* **shin·gled; shin·gling** : to cover with shingles

shin·ny \'shin-ē\ *vb* **shin·nied; shin·ny·ing** : ²SHIN

shiny \'shī-nē\ *adj* **shin·i·er; shin·i·est** : bright in appearance

¹ship \'ship\ *n* **1** : a large seagoing boat **2** : a ship's crew **3** : AIRSHIP, AIRPLANE **4** : a vehicle for traveling beyond the earth's atmosphere ⟨a rocket *ship*⟩

²ship *vb* **shipped; ship·ping 1** : to put or receive on board for transportation by water **2** : to cause to be transported ⟨*ship* grain by rail⟩ **3** : to take into a ship or boat ⟨*ship* oars⟩ **4** : to sign on as a crew member on a ship

-ship \,ship\ *n suffix* **1** : state : condition : quality ⟨friend*ship*⟩ **2** : office : rank

\ə\ abut	\aů\ out	\i\ tip	\ȯ\ saw	\ů\ foot
\ər\ further	\ch\ chin	\ī\ life	\ȯi\ coin	\y\ yet
\a\ mat	\e\ pet	\j\ job	\th\ thin	\yü\ few
\ā\ take	\ē\ easy	\ng\ sing	\th\ this	\yů\ cure
\ä\ cot, cart	\g\ go	\ō\ bone	\ü\ food	\zh\ vision

: profession ⟨lord*ship*⟩ ⟨author*ship*⟩ **3** : skill ⟨horseman*ship*⟩ **4** : something showing a quality or state of being ⟨champion*ship*⟩ ⟨town*ship*⟩ **5** : one having a specified rank ⟨your Lord*ship*⟩

ship·board \'ship-ˌbōrd\ *n* **1** : a ship's side **2** : ¹SHIP 1 ⟨met on *shipboard*⟩

ship·ment \'ship-mənt\ *n* **1** : the act of shipping **2** : the goods shipped

ship·ping \'ship-ing\ *n* **1** : the body of ships in one place or belonging to one port or country **2** : the act or business of a person who ships goods

ship·shape \'ship-'shāp\ *adj* : being neat and orderly : TIDY

¹ship·wreck \'ship-ˌrek\ *n* **1** : a wrecked ship **2** : the loss or destruction of a ship

²shipwreck *vb* **1** : to destroy (a ship) by driving ashore or sinking **2** : to cause to experience shipwreck

ship·yard \'ship-ˌyärd\ *n* : a place where ships are built or repaired

shirk \'shərk\ *vb* **1** : to get out of doing what one ought to do **2** : AVOID

shirt \'shərt\ *n* **1** : a garment for the upper part of the body usually with a collar, sleeves, a front opening, and a tail long enough to be tucked inside pants or a skirt **2** : UNDERSHIRT

¹shiv·er \'shiv-ər\ *vb* : to be made to shake (as by cold or fear) : QUIVER

²shiver *n* : an instance of shivering

¹shoal \'shōl\ *adj* : ¹SHALLOW 1 ⟨*shoal* water⟩

²shoal *n* **1** : a place where a sea, lake, or river is shallow **2** : a bank or bar of sand just below the surface of the water

³shoal *n* : ³SCHOOL ⟨a *shoal* of mackerel⟩

¹shock \'shäk\ *n* : a bunch of sheaves of grain or stalks of corn set on end in the field

²shock *n* **1** : the sudden violent collision of bodies in a fight ⟨the *shock* of battle⟩ **2** : a violent shake or jerk ⟨an earthquake *shock*⟩ **3** : a sudden and violent disturbance of mind or feelings ⟨a *shock* of surprise⟩ **4** : the effect of a charge of electricity passing through the body of a person or animal **5** : a state of bodily collapse that usually follows severe crushing injuries, burns, or hemorrhage

³shock *vb* **1** : to strike with surprise, horror, or disgust ⟨their behavior *shocked* us⟩ **2** : to affect by electrical shock **3** : to drive into or out of by or as if by a shock ⟨*shocked* the public into action⟩

⁴shock *n* : a thick bushy mass (as of hair)

shock·ing \'shäk-ing\ *adj* : causing horror or disgust ⟨a *shocking* crime⟩ — **shock·ing·ly** *adv*

shod·dy \'shäd-ē\ *adj* **shod·di·er; shod·di·est** : poorly done or made ⟨*shoddy* work⟩ — **shod·di·ly** \'shäd-l-ē\ *adv* — **shod·di·ness** \'shäd-ē-nəs\ *n*

¹shoe \'shü\ *n* **1** : an outer covering for the human foot usually having a thick and somewhat stiff sole and heel and a lighter upper part **2** : something (as a horseshoe) like a shoe in appearance or use

²shoe *vb* **shod** \'shäd\ *also* **shoed** \'shüd\; **shoe·ing** : to put a shoe on : furnish with shoes

shoe·horn \'shü-ˌhȯrn\ *n* : a curved piece (as of metal) to help in putting on a shoe

shoe·lace \'shü-ˌlās\ *n* : a lace or string for fastening a shoe

shoe·mak·er \'shü-ˌmā-kər\ *n* : a person who makes or repairs shoes

shoe·string \'shü-ˌstring\ *n* : SHOELACE

shone *past of* SHINE

shoo \'shü\ *vb* : to wave, scare, or send away by or as if by crying *shoo*

shook *past of* SHAKE

¹shoot \'shüt\ *vb* **shot** \'shät\; **shoot·ing** **1** : to let fly or cause to be driven forward with force ⟨*shoot* an arrow⟩ **2** : to cause a missile to be driven out of ⟨*shoot* a gun⟩ **3** : to cause a weapon to discharge a missile ⟨*shoot* at a target⟩ **4** : to force (a marble) forward by snapping the thumb **5** : to hit or throw (as a ball or puck) toward a goal **6** : to score by shooting ⟨*shoot* a basket⟩ **7** : ²PLAY 2 ⟨*shot* a round of golf⟩ **8** : to strike with a missile from a bow or gun ⟨*shot* a deer⟩ **9** : to push or slide into or out of a fastening ⟨*shoot* the door bolt⟩ **10** : to thrust forward swiftly ⟨lizards *shooting* out their tongues⟩ **11** : to grow rapidly ⟨the corn is *shooting* up⟩ **12** : to go, move, or pass rapidly ⟨they *shot* past on skis⟩ **13** : to pass swiftly along or through ⟨*shot* the rapids in a canoe⟩ **14** : to stream out suddenly : SPURT — **shoot·er** *n*

²shoot *n* **1** : the part of a plant that grows above ground or as much of this as comes from a single bud **2** : a hunting party or trip ⟨a duck *shoot*⟩

shooting star *n* : a meteor appearing as a temporary streak of light in the night sky

¹shop \'shäp\ *n* **1** : a worker's place of business **2** : a building or room where goods are sold at retail : STORE **3** : a place in which workers are doing a particular kind of work ⟨a repair *shop*⟩

²shop *vb* **shopped; shop·ping** : to visit shops for the purpose of looking over and buying goods — **shop·per** *n*

shop·keep·er \'shäp-ˌkē-pər\ *n* : STOREKEEPER 1

shop·lift·er \'shäp-ˌlif-tər\ *n* : a person

who steals merchandise on display in stores

¹shore \'shōr\ *n* : the land along the edge of a body of water (as the sea)

²shore *vb* **shored; shor·ing** : to support with one or more bracing timbers

shore·bird \'shōr-ˌbərd\ *n* : any of various birds (as the plovers) that frequent the seashore

shore·line \'shōr-ˌlīn\ *n* : the line where a body of water touches the shore

shorn *past participle of* SHEAR

¹short \'shȯrt\ *adj* **1** : not long or tall ⟨a *short* coat⟩ **2** : not great in distance ⟨a *short* trip⟩ **3** : brief in time ⟨a *short* delay⟩ **4** : cut down to a brief length **5** : not coming up to the regular standard ⟨give *short* measure⟩ **6** : less in amount than expected or called for ⟨three dollars *short*⟩ **7** : less than : not equal to ⟨a little *short* of perfect⟩ **8** : not having enough ⟨*short* of money⟩ **9** : FLAKY, CRUMBLY ⟨a *short* biscuit⟩ **10** : of, relating to, or being one of the vowel sounds \ə,a, e,i, u̇\ and sometimes \ä\ and \ȯ\ — **short·ness** *n*

²short *adv* **1** : with suddenness ⟨stop *short*⟩ **2** : so as not to reach as far as expected ⟨fall *short* of the mark⟩

³short *n* **1** : something shorter than the usual or regular length **2 shorts** *pl* : pants that reach to or almost to the knees **3 shorts** *pl* : short underpants **4** : SHORT CIRCUIT

short·age \'shȯrt-ij\ *n* : a lack in the amount needed : DEFICIT ⟨a *shortage* in the accounts⟩

short·cake \'shȯrt-ˌkāk\ *n* : a dessert made usually of rich biscuit dough baked and served with sweetened fruit

short circuit *n* : an electric connection made between points in an electric circuit between which current does not normally flow

short·com·ing \'shȯrt-ˌkəm-ing\ *n* : FAULT 1

short·cut \'shȯrt-ˌkət\ *n* : a shorter, quicker, or easier way

short·en \'shȯrt-n\ *vb* : to make or become short or shorter

short·en·ing \'shȯrt-n-ing, 'shȯrt-ning\ *n* : a fatty substance (as lard) used to make pastry flaky

short·hand \'shȯrt-ˌhand\ *n* : a method of rapid writing by using symbols for sounds or words

short·horn \'shȯrt-ˌhȯrn\ *n* : any of a breed of beef cattle developed in England and including good producers of milk from which a separate dairy breed (**milking shorthorn**) has come

short–lived \'shȯrt-'līvd, -'livd\ *adj* : living or lasting only a short time

short·ly \'shȯrt-lē\ *adv* **1** : in a few words : BRIEFLY **2** : in or within a short time : SOON

short–sight·ed \'shȯrt-'sīt-əd\ *adj* : NEARSIGHTED

short·stop \'shȯrt-ˌstäp\ *n* : a baseball infielder whose position is between second and third base

¹shot \'shät\ *n* **1** : the act of shooting **2** *pl* **shot** : a bullet, ball, or pellet for a gun or cannon **3** : something thrown, cast forth, or let fly with force **4** : ²ATTEMPT, TRY ⟨take another *shot* at the puzzle⟩ **5** : the flight of a missile or the distance it travels : RANGE ⟨within rifle *shot*⟩ **6** : a person who shoots ⟨that hunter is a good *shot*⟩ **7** : a heavy metal ball thrown for distance in a track-and-field contest (**shot put**) **8** : a stroke or throw at a goal ⟨a long *shot* in basketball⟩ **9** : an injection of something (as medicine) into the body

²shot *past of* SHOOT

shot·gun \'shät-ˌgən\ *n* : a gun with a long barrel used to fire shot at short range

should \shəd, shu̇d\ *past of* SHALL **1** : ought to ⟨you *should* study harder⟩ ⟨they *should* be here soon⟩ **2** : happen to ⟨if you *should* see them, say hello for me⟩ **3** — used as a politer or less assured form of *shall* ⟨*should* I turn the light out⟩

¹shoul·der \'shōl-dər\ *n* **1** : the part of the body of a person or animal where the arm or foreleg joins the body **2** : the part of a garment at the wearer's shoulder **3** : a part that resembles a person's shoulder ⟨the *shoulder* of a bottle⟩ **4** : the edge of a road

²shoulder *vb* **1** : to push with one's shoul-

shorthorn

\ə\ **abut**	\au̇\ **out**	\i\ **tip**	\ȯ\ **saw**	\u̇\ **foot**
\ər\ **further**	\ch\ **chin**	\ī\ **life**	\ȯi\ **coin**	\y\ **yet**
\a\ **mat**	\e\ **pet**	\j\ **job**	\th\ **thin**	\yü\ **few**
\ā\ **take**	\ē\ **easy**	\ng\ **sing**	\th\ **this**	\yu̇\ **cure**
\ä\ **cot, cart**	\g\ **go**	\ō\ **bone**	\ü\ **food**	\zh\ **vision**

der **2** : to accept as one's burden or duty ⟨*shoulder* the blame for a mistake⟩

shoulder blade *n* : the flat triangular bone in a person's or animal's shoulder

shouldn't \'shùd-nt\ : should not

¹**shout** \'shaut\ *vb* : to make a sudden loud cry (as of joy, pain, or sorrow)

synonyms SHOUT, SHRIEK, and SCREECH mean to utter a loud cry. SHOUT suggests any kind of loud cry that is uttered in order to be heard either far away or above other noise ⟨we *shouted* to them across the river⟩ SHRIEK suggests a high-pitched shrill cry that is a sign of strong feeling (as fear or anger) ⟨the children *shrieked* upon seeing the stranger⟩ SCREECH suggests an extended shriek that is usually without words and very harsh and unpleasant ⟨the cats fought and *screeched*⟩

²**shout** *n* : a sudden loud cry

¹**shove** \'shəv\ *vb* **shoved; shov·ing 1** : to push with steady force **2** : to push along or away carelessly or rudely ⟨*shove* a person out of the way⟩

²**shove** *n* : the act or an instance of shoving

¹**shov·el** \'shəv-əl\ *n* **1** : a broad scoop used to lift and throw loose material (as snow) **2** : as much as a shovel will hold

²**shovel** *vb* **shov·eled** *or* **shov·elled; shov·el·ing** *or* **shov·el·ling 1** : to lift or throw with a shovel **2** : to dig or clean out with a shovel ⟨*shovel* a ditch⟩ **3** : to throw or carry roughly or in a mass as if with a shovel ⟨*shoveled* food into my mouth⟩

¹**show** \'shō\ *vb* **showed; shown** \'shōn\ *or* **showed; show·ing 1** : to place in sight : DISPLAY **2** : REVEAL 2 ⟨*showed* themselves to be cowards⟩ **3** : to give from or as if from a position of authority ⟨*show* them no mercy⟩ **4** : TEACH 1, INSTRUCT ⟨*showed* them how to play⟩ **5** : PROVE 2 ⟨that *shows* we're right⟩ **6** : ¹DIRECT 3, USHER ⟨*showed* them to the door⟩ **7** : APPEAR ⟨anger *showed* in their faces⟩ **8** : to be noticeable ⟨the patch hardly *shows*⟩

synonyms SHOW, EXHIBIT, and PARADE mean to display something so that it will attract attention. SHOW suggests letting another see or examine ⟨*show* me a picture of your family⟩ EXHIBIT suggests putting something out in public ⟨the children *exhibited* their drawings at the fair⟩ PARADE suggests making a great show of something ⟨look at them *parading* their new bikes⟩

²**show** *n* **1** : a display made for effect ⟨a *show* of strength⟩ **2** : a false outward

appearance ⟨made a *show* of friendship⟩ **3** : a true indication : SIGN ⟨a *show* of reason⟩ **4** : a display meant to impress others **5** : a ridiculous spectacle **6** : an entertainment or exhibition especially by performers (as on TV or the stage)

show·boat \'shō-ˌbōt\ *n* : a river steamboat used as a traveling theater

show·case \'shō-ˌkās\ *n* : a protective glass case in which things are displayed

¹**show·er** \'shaù-ər\ *n* **1** : a short fall of rain over a small area **2** : something like a shower ⟨a *shower* of sparks⟩ **3** : a party where gifts are given especially to a bride or a pregnant woman **4** : a bath in which water is showered on a person or a device for providing such a bath

²**shower** *vb* **1** : to wet with fine spray or drops **2** : to fall in or as if in a shower **3** : to provide in great quantity ⟨*showered* them with presents⟩ **4** : to bathe in a shower

show·man \'shō-mən\ *n, pl* **show·men** \-mən\ **1** : the producer of a theatrical show **2** : a person having a special skill for presenting something in a dramatic way

shown *past participle of* SHOW

show off *vb* : to make an obvious display of one's abilities or possessions

show up *vb* **1** : to reveal the true nature of : EXPOSE ⟨*shown up* for what they really were⟩ **2** : APPEAR 2 ⟨didn't *show up* for work today⟩

showy \'shō-ē\ *adj* **show·i·er; show·i·est 1** : attracting attention : STRIKING **2** : given to or being too much outward display : GAUDY **— show·i·ly** \'shō-ə-lē\ *adv* **— show·i·ness** \'shō-ē-nəs\ *n*

shrank *past of* SHRINK

shrap·nel \'shrap-nl\ *n* **1** : a shell designed to burst and scatter the metal balls with which it is filled along with jagged fragments of the case **2** : metal pieces from an exploded bomb, shell, or mine

¹**shred** \'shred\ *n* **1** : a long narrow piece torn or cut off : STRIP **2** : ²BIT 1, PARTICLE ⟨not a *shred* of evidence⟩

²**shred** *vb* **shred·ded; shred·ding** : to cut or tear into shreds

shrew \'shrü\ *n* **1** : a small mouselike ani-

shrew 1

mal with a long pointed snout and tiny eyes that lives on insects and worms **2** : an unpleasant quarrelsome woman

shrewd \'shrüd\ *adj* : showing quick practical cleverness : ASTUTE — **shrewd·ly** *adv* — **shrewd·ness** *n*

¹shriek \'shrēk\ *vb* : to utter a sharp shrill cry **synonyms** see SHOUT

²shriek *n* : a sharp shrill cry

shrike \'shrīk\ *n* : a grayish or brownish bird with a hooked bill that feeds mostly on insects and often sticks them on thorns before eating them

shrike

¹shrill \'shril\ *vb* : to make a high sharp piercing sound : SCREAM

²shrill *adj* : having a sharp high sound ⟨a *shrill* whistle⟩ — **shrill·ness** *n* — **shril·ly** \'shril-lē\ *adv*

shrimp \'shrimp\ *n* **1** : a small shellfish related to the crabs and lobsters **2** : a small or unimportant person or thing — **shrimp·like** \'shrim-ˌplīk\ *adj*

shrine \'shrīn\ *n* **1** : a case or box for sacred relics (as the bones of saints) **2** : the tomb of a holy person (as a saint) **3** : a place that is considered sacred ⟨the Lincoln Memorial is a *shrine* to all lovers of freedom⟩

shrink \'shringk\ *vb* **shrank** \'shrangk\ *also* **shrunk** \'shrəngk\; **shrunk; shrink·ing** **1** : to curl up or withdraw in or as if in fear or pain ⟨*shrink* in horror⟩ **2** : to make or become smaller ⟨the sweater *shrank* when it got wet⟩

shrink·age \'shring-kij\ *n* : the amount by which something shrinks or becomes less

shriv·el \'shriv-əl\ *vb* **shriv·eled** *or* **shriv·elled; shriv·el·ing** *or* **shriv·el·ling** : to shrink and become dry and wrinkled

¹shroud \'shraùd\ *n* **1** : the cloth placed over or around a dead body **2** : something that covers or shelters like a shroud **3**

: one of the ropes that go from the masthead of a boat to the sides to support the mast

²shroud *vb* : to cover with or as if with a shroud

shrub \'shrəb\ *n* : a woody plant having several stems and smaller than most trees

shrub·bery \'shrəb-ə-rē\ *n, pl* **shrub·ber·ies** : a group or planting of shrubs

shrug \'shrəg\ *vb* **shrugged; shrug·ging** : to draw or hunch up the shoulders usually to express doubt, uncertainty, or lack of interest

shrunk *past & past participle of* SHRINK

shrunk·en \'shrəng-kən\ *adj* : made or grown smaller (as in size or value)

¹shuck \'shək\ *n* : a covering shell or husk

²shuck *vb* : to free (as an ear of corn) from the shuck

¹shud·der \'shəd-ər\ *vb* : to tremble with fear or horror or from cold

²shudder *n* : an act of shuddering : SHIVER

¹shuf·fle \'shəf-əl\ *vb* **shuf·fled; shuf·fling** **1** : to push out of sight or mix in a disorderly mass ⟨odds and ends *shuffled* in a drawer⟩ **2** : to mix cards to change their order in the pack **3** : to move from place to place ⟨*shuffle* chairs⟩ **4** : to move in a clumsy dragging way ⟨*shuffled* their feet⟩

²shuffle *n* **1** : an act of shuffling **2** : ²JUMBLE **3** : a clumsy dragging walk

shun \'shən\ *vb* **shunned; shun·ning** : to avoid purposely or by habit

shunt \'shənt\ *vb* **1** : to turn off to one side or out of the way : SHIFT ⟨*shunt* cattle into a corral⟩ **2** : to switch (as a train) from one track to another

shut \'shət\ *vb* **shut; shut·ting** **1** : to close or become closed ⟨*shut* the door⟩ ⟨the door *shut* slowly⟩ **2** : to close so as to prevent entrance or leaving : BAR ⟨*shut* the cottage for the winter⟩ **3** : to keep in a place by enclosing or by blocking the way out : IMPRISON ⟨*shut* them in a jail cell⟩ **4** : to close by bringing parts together ⟨*shut* your eyes⟩

shut–in \'shət-ˌin\ *n* : a sick person kept indoors

shut·out \'shət-ˌaùt\ *n* : a game in which one side fails to score

shut·ter \'shət-ər\ *n* **1** : a movable cover for a window **2** : a device in a camera that opens to let in light when a picture is taken

¹shut·tle \'shət-l\ *n* **1** : an instrument used

in weaving to carry the thread back and forth from side to side through the threads that run lengthwise **2** : a vehicle (as a bus or train) that goes back and forth over a short route **3** : SPACE SHUTTLE

²**shuttle** *vb* **shut·tled; shut·tling** : to move back and forth rapidly or often

shut·tle·cock \'shət-l-,käk\ *n* : a light object (as a piece of cork with feathers stuck in it) used in badminton

shuttlecock

¹**shy** \'shī\ *adj* **shi·er** *or* **shy·er; shi·est** *or* **shy·est 1** : easily frightened : TIMID **2** : not feeling comfortable around people : not wanting or able to call attention to oneself : BASHFUL **3** : having less than a full or an expected amount or number ⟨we were *shy* about ten dollars⟩ — **shy·ly** *adv* — **shy·ness** *n*

synonyms SHY and BASHFUL mean feeling awkward with others. SHY suggests not wanting to meet or talk with people either by habit or for special reasons ⟨at the new school I was *shy* at first⟩ BASHFUL suggests being shy and afraid like a very young child ⟨the toddler was *bashful* and would hide when company came⟩

²**shy** *vb* **shied; shy·ing 1** : to draw back in dislike or distaste ⟨*shied* from publicity⟩ **2** : to move quickly to one side in fright ⟨the horse *shied*⟩

sick \'sik\ *adj* **1** : affected with disease or ill health : not well **2** : of, relating to, or intended for use in or during illness ⟨*sick* pay⟩ **3** : affected with or accompanied by nausea ⟨a *sick* headache⟩ **4** : badly upset by strong emotion (as shame or fear) **5** : tired of something from having too much of it ⟨*sick* of flattery⟩ **6** : filled with disgust ⟨such gossip makes me *sick*⟩

sick·bed \'sik-,bed\ *n* : a bed on which a sick person lies

sick·en \'sik-ən\ *vb* : to make or become sick

sick·en·ing \'sik-ə-ning\ *adj* : causing sickness or disgust ⟨a *sickening* smell⟩ — **sick·en·ing·ly** *adv*

sick·le \'sik-əl\ *n* : a

sickle

tool with a sharp curved metal blade and a short handle used to cut grass

sick·ly \'sik-lē\ *adj* **sick·li·er; sick·li·est 1** : somewhat sick : often ailing ⟨I was *sickly* as a child⟩ **2** : caused by or associated with ill health ⟨a *sickly* complexion⟩ **3** : not growing well : SPINDLING ⟨*sickly* plants⟩

sick·ness \'sik-nəs\ *n* **1** : ill health : ILLNESS **2** : a specific disease : MALADY **3** : NAUSEA 1

¹**side** \'sīd\ *n* **1** : the right or left part of the trunk of the body **2** : a place, space, or direction away from or beyond a central point or line ⟨set something to one *side*⟩ **3** : a surface or line forming a border or face of an object **4** : an outer part of a thing considered as facing in a certain direction ⟨the upper *side*⟩ **5** : a position viewed as opposite to another ⟨can see both *sides* of the question⟩ **6** : a body of contestants ⟨our *side* won⟩ **7** : a line of ancestors traced back from either parent ⟨French on my mother's *side*⟩

²**side** *adj* **1** : of, relating to, or being on the side ⟨*side* pockets⟩ **2** : aimed toward or from the side ⟨a *side* thrust⟩ **3** : related to something in a minor or unimportant way ⟨a *side* remark⟩ **4** : being in addition to a main portion ⟨a *side* order of French fries⟩

³**side** *vb* **sid·ed; sid·ing** : to take the same side ⟨*sided* with our friend in the argument⟩

side·arm \'sīd-,ärm\ *adv* : with the arm moving out to the side ⟨threw the ball *sidearm*⟩

side·board \'sīd-,bōrd\ *n* : a piece of furniture for holding dishes, silverware, and table linen

sid·ed \'sīd-əd\ *adj* : having sides often of a stated number or kind ⟨a four-*sided* figure⟩

side·line \'sīd-,līn\ *n* **1** : a line marking the side of a playing field or court **2** : a business or a job done in addition to one's regular occupation

¹**side·long** \'sīd-,lȯng\ *adv* : out of the corner of one's eye ⟨glanced *sidelong* at the pie on the table⟩

²**sidelong** *adj* **1** : made to one side or out of the corner of one's eye ⟨a *sidelong* look⟩ **2** : INDIRECT 2

side·show \'sīd-,shō\ *n* : a small show off to the side of a main show or exhibition (as of a circus)

side·step \'sīd-,step\ *vb* **side·stepped; side·step·ping 1** : to take a step to the side **2** : to avoid by a step to the side **3** : to avoid answering or dealing with ⟨*sidestep* a question⟩

side·track \'sīd-ˌtrak\ *vb* **1** : to transfer from a main railroad line to a side line **2** : to turn aside from a main purpose or direction ⟨*sidetrack* the conversation⟩

side·walk \'sīd-ˌwȯk\ *n* : a usually paved walk at the side of a street or road

side·ways \'sīd-ˌwāz\ *adv or adj* **1** : from one side ⟨look at it *sideways*⟩ **2** : with one side forward ⟨sliding *sideways* down the hill⟩ **3** : to one side ⟨moved *sideways* to let them through⟩

side·wise \'sīd-ˌwīz\ *adv or adj* : SIDE-WAYS

sid·ing \'sīd-ing\ *n* **1** : a short railroad track connected with the main track **2** : material (as boards or metal pieces) used to cover the outside walls of frame buildings

si·dle \'sīd-l\ *vb* **si·dled; si·dling** : to go or move with one side forward ⟨the crab *sidled* away⟩

siege \'sēj\ *n* **1** : the moving of an army around a fortified place to capture it **2** : a lasting attack (as of illness)

si·er·ra \sē-'er-ə\ *n* : a range of mountains especially with jagged peaks

si·es·ta \sē-'es-tə\ *n* : a nap or rest especially at midday

Word History The ancient Romans counted the hours of the day from sunrise to sunset, an average of about twelve hours. The sixth hour in the Roman day was noon. The Latin name for noon came from the Latin word that meant "sixth." A Spanish word for a nap taken about noon came from the Latin word that meant "noon." English *siesta* comes from the Spanish word.

sieve \'siv\ *n* : a utensil with meshes or holes to separate finer particles from coarser ones or solids from liquids

sift \'sift\ *vb* **1** : to pass or cause to pass through a sieve ⟨*sift* flour⟩ **2** : to separate or separate out by or as if by passing through a sieve **3** : to test or examine carefully ⟨*sift* evidence⟩ — **sift·er** *n*

¹sigh \'sī\ *vb* **1** : to take or let out a long loud breath often as an expression of sadness or weariness **2** : to make a sound like sighing ⟨wind *sighing* in the branches⟩ **3** : YEARN ⟨*sighing* for the days of youth⟩

²sigh *n* : the act or a sound of sighing

¹sight \'sīt\ *n* **1** : something that is seen : SPECTACLE **2** : something that is worth seeing ⟨showed us the *sights* of the city⟩ **3** : something that is peculiar, funny, or messy ⟨you're a *sight*⟩ **4** : the function, process, or power of seeing : the sense by which one becomes aware of the position, form, and color of objects **5** : the act of seeing **6** : the presence of an object within the field of vision ⟨can't bear the *sight* of it⟩ **7** : the distance a person can see ⟨a ship came into *sight*⟩ **8** : a device (as a small metal bead on a gun barrel) that aids the eye in aiming or in finding the direction of an object

²sight *vb* **1** : to get sight of : SEE ⟨*sighted* the ship⟩ **2** : to look at through or as if through a sight

sight·less \'sīt-ləs\ *adj* : lacking sight : BLIND

sight·se·er \'sīt-ˌsē-ər\ *n* : a person who goes about to see places and things of interest

¹sign \'sīn\ *n* **1** : a motion, action, or movement of the hand that means something ⟨made a *sign* for them to be quiet⟩ **2** : one of the twelve parts of the zodiac **3** : a symbol (as + or ÷) indicating a mathematical operation **4** : a public notice that advertises something or gives information **5** : something that indicates what is to come ⟨the first *signs* of spring⟩ **6** : ¹TRACE 2 ⟨no *sign* of life⟩

²sign *vb* **1** : to make or place a sign on **2** : to represent or show by a sign or signs **3** : to write one's name on to show that one accepts, agrees with, or will be responsible for ⟨*signed* the order form⟩

¹sig·nal \'sig-nl\ *n* **1** : a sign, event, or word that serves to start some action ⟨a *signal* to light the fires⟩ **2** : a sound, a movement of part of the body, or an object that gives warning or a command ⟨make a *signal* with one's hand⟩ ⟨a traffic *signal*⟩ **3** : a radio wave that transmits a message or effect (as in radio or television)

²signal *vb* **sig·naled** *or* **sig·nalled; sig·nal·ing** *or* **sig·nal·ling 1** : to notify by a signal **2** : to communicate by signals

³signal *adj* **1** : unusually great ⟨a *signal* honor⟩ **2** : used for signaling ⟨a *signal* light⟩

sig·na·ture \'sig-nə-ˌchu̇r\ *n* **1** : the name of a person written by that person **2** : a sign or group of signs placed at the beginning of a staff in music to show the key (**key signature**) or the meter (**time signature**)

\ə\ abut	\au̇\ out	\i\ tip	\ȯ\ saw	\u̇\ foot
\ər\ further	\ch\ chin	\ī\ life	\ȯi\ coin	\y\ yet
\a\ mat	\e\ pet	\j\ job	\th\ thin	\yü\ few
\ā\ take	\ē\ easy	\ng\ sing	\th\ this	\yu̇\ cure
\ä\ cot, cart	\g\ go	\ō\ bone	\ü\ food	\zh\ vision

sign·board \'sīn-,bōrd\ *n* : a board with a sign or notice on it

sig·nif·i·cance \sig-'nif-i-kəns\ *n* **1** : MEANING 1 **2** : IMPORTANCE ⟨it's a subject of some *significance*⟩

sig·nif·i·cant \sig-'nif-i-kənt\ *adj* **1** : having meaning and especially a special or hidden meaning ⟨gave them a *significant* smile⟩ **2** : IMPORTANT 1

sig·ni·fy \'sig-nə-,fī\ *vb* **sig·ni·fied; sig·ni·fy·ing 1** : ²MEAN 3, DENOTE **2** : to show especially by a sign : make known ⟨*signified* their pleasure⟩ **3** : to have importance

sign language *n* : a system of hand movments used for communications (as by people who are deaf)

sign·post \'sīn-,pōst\ *n* : a post with a sign (as for directing travelers)

si·lage \'sī-lij\ *n* : fodder fermented (as in a silo) to produce a good juicy feed for livestock

¹si·lence \'sī-ləns\ *n* **1** : the state of keeping or being silent ⟨the teacher motioned for *silence*⟩ **2** : the state of there being no sound or noise : STILLNESS

²silence *vb* **si·lenced; si·lenc·ing 1** : to stop the noise or speech of : cause to be silent **2** : SUPPRESS 1 ⟨*silence* objections⟩

si·lent \'sī-lənt\ *adj* **1** : not speaking : not talkative ⟨a *silent* person⟩ **2** : free from noise or sound : STILL **3** : done or felt without being spoken ⟨*silent* reading⟩ ⟨*silent* prayer⟩ **4** : making no mention ⟨they were *silent* about their plan⟩ **5** : not active in running a business ⟨a *silent* partner⟩ **6** : not pronounced ⟨the *e* in "came" is *silent*⟩

¹sil·hou·ette \,sil-ə-'wet\ *n* **1** : a drawing or picture of the outline of an object filled in with a solid usually black color **2** : a profile portrait done in silhouette **3** : ¹OUTLINE 1

silhouette 2

²silhouette *vb* **sil·hou·ett·ed; sil·hou·ett·ing** : to represent by a silhouette : show against a light background ⟨an airplane *silhouetted* against the sky⟩

sil·i·con \'sil-i-kən, 'sil-ə-,kän\ *n* : a chemical element that is found combined as the most common element next to oxygen in the earth's crust

silk \'silk\ *n* **1** : a fine fiber that is spun by many insect larvae usually to form their cocoon or by spiders to make their webs and that includes some kinds used for weaving cloth **2** : thread, yarn, or fabric made from silk **3** : something suggesting silk ⟨the *silk* of an ear of corn⟩

silk·en \'sil-kən\ *adj* **1** : made of or with silk **2** : like silk especially in its soft and smooth feel ⟨*silken* hair⟩

silk·worm \'sil-,kwərm\ *n* : a yellowish hairless caterpillar that is the larva of an Asian moth (**silk moth** or **silkworm moth**), is raised in captivity on mulberry leaves, and produces a strong silk that is the silk most used for thread or cloth

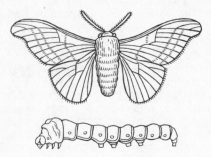

silkworm and silk moth

silky \'sil-kē\ *adj* **silk·i·er; silk·i·est** : soft and smooth as silk

sill \'sil\ *n* **1** : a horizontal supporting piece at the base of a structure **2** : a heavy horizontal piece (as of wood) that forms the bottom part of a window frame or a doorway

sil·ly \'sil-ē\ *adj* **sil·li·er; sil·li·est 1** : not very intelligent **2** : showing a lack of common sense ⟨a *silly* mistake⟩ **3** : not serious or important ⟨a *silly* reason⟩ **synonyms** see ABSURD — **sil·li·ness** *n*

si·lo \'sī-lō\ *n, pl* **si·los** : a covered trench, pit, or especially a tall round building in which silage is made and stored

¹silt \'silt\ *n* **1** : particles of small size left as sediment from water **2** : a soil made up mostly of silt and containing little clay

²silt *vb* : to choke, fill, cover, or block with silt

¹sil·ver \'sil-vər\ *n* **1** : a soft white metallic chemical element that takes a high polish and is used for money, jewelry and ornaments, and table utensils **2** : coin made of silver **3** : SILVERWARE ⟨table *silver*⟩ **4** : a medium gray

²silver *adj* **1** : made of, coated with, or yielding silver **2** : having the color of silver

³silver *vb* : to coat with or as if with silver

sil·ver·smith \'sil-vər-ˌsmith\ *n* : a person who makes objects of silver

sil·ver·ware \'sil-vər-ˌwaər, -ˌweər\ *n* : things (as knives, forks, and spoons) made of silver, silver-plated metal, or stainless steel

sil·very \'sil-və-rē\ *adj* : having a shine like silver

sim·i·lar \'sim-ə-lər\ *adj* : having qualities in common ⟨houses *similar* in design⟩ — **sim·i·lar·ly** *adv*

sim·i·lar·i·ty \ˌsim-ə-'lar-ət-ē\ *n, pl* **sim·i·lar·i·ties** : the quality or state of being similar : RESEMBLANCE

sim·i·le \'sim-ə-ˌlē\ *n* : a figure of speech comparing two unlike things using *like* or *as* ⟨"their cheeks are like roses" is a *simile*, "their cheeks are roses" is a metaphor⟩

sim·mer \'sim-ər\ *vb* **1** : to cook gently at or just below the boiling point **2** : to be on the point of bursting out with violence or anger

sim·ple \'sim-pəl\ *adj* **sim·pler; simplest 1** : INNOCENT 1, MODEST **2** : not rich or important ⟨*simple* folk⟩ **3** : lacking in education, experience, or intelligence **4** : not fancy ⟨neat *simple* clothing⟩ **5** : having few parts : not complicated ⟨a *simple* machine⟩ **6** : ABSOLUTE 2 ⟨the *simple* truth⟩ **7** : not hard to understand or solve **8** : EASY 1, STRAIGHTFORWARD ⟨a *simple* explanation⟩

silo

sim·ple·ton \'sim-pəl-tən\ *n* : a foolish or stupid person

sim·plic·i·ty \sim-'plis-ət-ē\ *n, pl* **sim-plic·i·ties 1** : the quality or state of being simple or plain and not complicated or difficult **2** : SINCERITY **3** : directness or clearness in speaking or writing

sim·pli·fy \'sim-plə-ˌfi\ *vb* **sim·pli·fied; sim·pli·fy·ing** : to make simple or simpler : make easier

sim·ply \'sim-plē\ *adv* **1** : in a clear way ⟨explain *simply*⟩ **2** : in a plain way ⟨dressed *simply*⟩ **3** : DIRECTLY 1, CANDIDLY ⟨told the story as *simply* as a child would⟩ **4** : ²ONLY 1, MERELY ⟨ask a question *simply* out of curiosity⟩ **5** : in actual fact : REALLY, TRULY ⟨*simply* marvelous⟩

si·mul·ta·ne·ous \ˌsī-məl-'tā-nē-əs\ *adj* : existing or taking place at the same time — **si·mul·ta·ne·ous·ly** *adv*

¹sin \'sin\ *n* **1** : an action that breaks a religious law **2** : an action that is or is felt to be bad

²sin *vb* **sinned; sin·ning** : to be guilty of a sin

¹since \sins\ *adv* **1** : from a definite past time until now ⟨has stayed there ever *since*⟩ **2** : before the present time : AGO ⟨long *since* dead⟩ **3** : after a time in the past ⟨has *since* become rich⟩

²since *prep* **1** : in the period after ⟨haven't seen them *since* last week⟩ **2** : continuously from ⟨have lived here *since* 1976⟩

³since *conj* **1** : in the period after ⟨we've played better *since* you joined the team⟩ **2** : BECAUSE ⟨*since* you have finished your work, you may go⟩

sin·cere \sin-'siər\ *adj* **1** : HONEST 2, STRAIGHTFORWARD ⟨a *sincere* person⟩ **2** : being what it seems to be : GENUINE ⟨*sincere* good wishes⟩ — **sin·cere·ly** *adv*

sin·cer·i·ty \sin-'ser-ət-ē\ *n* : freedom from fraud or deception : HONESTY

sin·ew \'sin-yü\ *n* : TENDON

sin·ewy \'sin-yə-wē\ *adj* **1** : full of tendons : TOUGH, STRINGY ⟨a *sinewy* piece of meat⟩ **2** : STRONG 1, POWERFUL ⟨*sinewy* arms⟩

sin·ful \'sin-fəl\ *adj* : being or full of sin : WICKED ⟨a *sinful* act⟩ ⟨*sinful* people⟩

sing \'sing\ *vb* **sang** \'sang\ *or* **sung** \'səng\; **sung; sing·ing 1** : to produce musical sounds with the voice ⟨*sing* for joy⟩ **2** : to express in musical tones ⟨*sing* a song⟩ **3** : ¹CHANT 2 ⟨*sing* mass⟩ **4** : to make musical sounds ⟨birds *singing* at dawn⟩ **5** : to make a small shrill sound ⟨arrows *singing* through the air⟩ **6** : to

\ə\ **abut**	\aú\ **out**	\i\ **tip**	\ȯ\ **saw**	\ú\ **foot**
\ər\ **further**	\ch\ **chin**	\ī\ **life**	\ȯi\ **coin**	\y\ **yet**
\a\ **mat**	\e\ **pet**	\j\ **job**	\th\ **thin**	\yü\ **few**
\ā\ **take**	\ē\ **easy**	\ng\ **sing**	\th\ **this**	\yú\ **cure**
\ä\ **cot, cart**	\g\ **go**	\ō\ **bone**	\ü\ **food**	\zh\ **vision**

speak with enthusiasm ⟨*sing* their praises⟩ **7** : to do something with song ⟨*sing* a baby to sleep⟩ — **sing·er** *n*

¹singe \'sinj\ *vb* **singed; singe·ing 1** : to burn lightly or on the surface : SCORCH **2** : to remove the hair, down, or fuzz from by passing briefly over a flame ⟨*singe* a plucked chicken⟩

²singe *n* : a slight burn

¹sin·gle \'sing-gəl\ *adj* **1** : not married **2** : being alone : being the only one **3** : made up of or having only one **4** : having but one row of petals or rays ⟨a *single* rose⟩ **5** : being a separate whole : INDIVIDUAL ⟨a *single* thread⟩ **6** : of, relating to, or involving only one person

²single *n* **1** : a separate individual person or thing **2** : a hit in baseball that enables the batter to reach first base

³single *vb* **sin·gled; sin·gling** : to select or distinguish (as one person or thing) from a number or group ⟨*singled* out for praise⟩

sin·gle–hand·ed \,sing-gəl-'han-dəd\ *adj* **1** : done or managed by one person or with one hand **2** : working alone : lacking help

sin·gly \'sing-gə-lē, 'sing-glē\ *adv* : one by one : INDIVIDUALLY

¹sin·gu·lar \'sing-gyə-lər\ *adj* **1** : of, relating to, or being a word form used to show not more than one ⟨a *singular* noun⟩ **2** : ¹SUPERIOR 2, EXCEPTIONAL **3** : of unusual quality : UNIQUE **4** : STRANGE 2, ODD ⟨*singular* habits⟩

²singular *n* : a form of a word used to show that only one person or thing is meant

sin·is·ter \'sin-əs-tər\ *adj* **1** : ¹EVIL 1, CORRUPT **2** : threatening evil, harm, or danger ⟨*sinister* rumors⟩

¹sink \'singk\ *vb* **sank** \'sangk\ *or* **sunk** \'səngk\; **sunk; sink·ing 1** : to move or cause to move downward so as to be swallowed up ⟨the ship *sank*⟩ **2** : to fall or drop to a lower level ⟨the lake *sank* during the drought⟩ **3** : to lessen in amount ⟨the temperature *sank*⟩ **4** : to cause to penetrate ⟨*sank* an ax into the tree⟩ **5** : to go into or become absorbed ⟨the water *sank* into the ground⟩ **6** : to form by digging or boring ⟨*sink* a well⟩ **7** : to spend (money) unwisely

²sink *n* : a basin usually with water faucets and a drain fixed to a wall or floor

sin·ner \'sin-ər\ *n* : a sinful person

si·nus \'sī-nəs\ *n* : any of several spaces in the skull mostly connected with the nostrils

¹sip \'sip\ *vb* **sipped; sip·ping** : to take small drinks of

²sip *n* **1** : the act of sipping **2** : a small amount taken by sipping

¹si·phon \'sī-fən\ *n* **1** : a bent pipe or tube through which a liquid can be drawn by air pressure up and over the edge of a container **2** : a tubelike organ in an animal and especially a mollusk or arthropod used to draw in or squirt out a fluid

siphon 1

²siphon *vb* : to draw off by a siphon

sir \'sər, sər\ *n* **1** — used as a title before the given name of a knight or a baronet ⟨*Sir* Walter Raleigh⟩ **2** — used as a form of polite address to a man ⟨may I help you, *sir?*⟩

¹sire \'sīr\ *n* **1** *often cap* : ¹FATHER 1 **2** : ANCESTOR **3** : the male parent of an animal

²sire *vb* **sired; sir·ing** : to become the father of

si·ren \'sī-rən\ *n* : a device that makes a loud shrill warning sound and is often operated by electricity ⟨an ambulance *siren*⟩

sir·loin \'sər-,lȯin\ *n* : a cut of beef taken from the part just in front of the rump

sirup *variant of* SYRUP

si·sal \'sī-səl, -zəl\ *n* **1** : a long strong white fiber used to make rope and twine **2** : a West Indian agave that yields sisal

sis·ter \'sis-tər\ *n* **1** : a female person or animal related to another person or animal by having one or both parents in common **2** : a member of a religious society of women : NUN **3** : a woman related to another by a common tie or interest — **sister·ly** *adj*

sis·ter·hood \'sis-tər-,hu̇d\ *n* **1** : the state of being a sister **2** : women joined in a group

sis·ter–in–law \'sis-tər-ən-,lȯ\ *n, pl* **sisters–in–law 1** : the sister of one's husband or wife **2** : the wife of one's brother

sit \'sit\ *vb* **sat** \'sat\; **sit·ting 1** : to rest upon the part of the body where the hips and legs join **2** : to cause (as oneself) to be seated ⟨*sat* myself down to write a letter⟩ **3** : ²PERCH **4** : to hold a place as a member of an official group ⟨*sit* in congress⟩ **5** : to hold a session ⟨the court *sat* last month⟩ **6** : to pose for a portrait or photograph **7** : to be located ⟨the vase *sits* on the table⟩ **8** : to remain quiet or still ⟨the car *sits* in the garage⟩

site \'sīt\ *n* **1** : the space of ground a building rests upon **2** : the place where something (as a town or event) is found or took place ⟨a famous battle *site*⟩

sit·ting \'sit-ing\ *n* **1** : an act of one that sits : the time taken in such a sitting **2** : SESSION 1 ⟨a *sitting* of the legislature⟩

sitting room *n* : LIVING ROOM

sit·u·at·ed \'sich-ə-ˌwāt-əd\ *adj* **1** : having its place ⟨a town *situated* on a hill⟩ **2** : being in such financial circumstances ⟨not rich but comfortably *situated*⟩

sit·u·a·tion \ˌsich-ə-'wā-shən\ *n* **1** : LOCATION 2, PLACE **2** : position or place of employment : JOB **3** : position in life : STATUS **4** : the combination of surrounding conditions ⟨a bad *situation*⟩

¹six \'siks\ *adj* : being one more than five

²six *n* : one more than five : two times three : 6

six–gun \'siks-ˌgən\ *n* : a revolver having six chambers

six·pence \'sik-spens\ *n* **1** : the sum of six pence **2** : an old British coin worth six pence

six–shoot·er \'sik-ˌshüt-ər, 'siks-\ *n* : SIX-GUN

¹six·teen \sik-'stēn\ *adj* : being one more than fifteen

²sixteen *n* : one more than fifteen : four times four : 16

¹six·teenth \sik-'stēnth\ *adj* : coming right after fifteenth

²sixteenth *n* : number sixteen in a series

¹sixth \'siksth\ *adj* : coming right after fifth

²sixth *n* **1** : number six in a series **2** : one of six equal parts

¹six·ti·eth \'sik-stē-əth\ *adj* : coming right after fifty-ninth

²sixtieth *n* : number sixty in a series

¹six·ty \'sik-stē\ *adj* : being six times ten

²sixty *n* : six times ten : 60

siz·able *or* **size·able** \'sī-zə-bəl\ *adj* : fairly large

size \'sīz\ *n* **1** : amount of space occupied : BULK **2** : the measurements of a thing ⟨the *size* of a book⟩ **3** : one of a series of measures especially of manufactured articles (as clothing) ⟨a *size* 8 shoe⟩ — **sized** \'sīzd\ *adj*

siz·zle \'siz-əl\ *vb* **siz·zled; siz·zling** : to make a hissing or sputtering noise in or as if in frying or burning

¹skate \'skāt\ *n* : a very flat fish related to

the sharks that has large and nearly triangular fins

²skate *n* **1** : a metal runner fitting the sole of the shoe or a shoe with a permanently attached metal runner used for gliding on ice **2** : ROLLER SKATE

³skate *vb* **skat·ed; skat·ing** **1** : to glide along on skates **2** : to slide or move as if on skates — **skat·er** *n*

skate·board \'skāt-ˌbōrd\ *n* : a narrow board about two feet long mounted on roller-skate wheels

skein \'skān\ *n* : a quantity of yarn or thread arranged in a loose coil

skel·e·tal \'skel-ət-l\ *adj* : of, relating or attached to, forming, or like a skeleton ⟨*skeletal* muscles⟩

skel·e·ton \'skel-ət-n\ *n* **1** : a firm supporting or protecting structure or framework of a living being : the usually bony framework of a vertebrate (as a fish, bird, or human) **2** : FRAMEWORK ⟨the steel *skeleton* of a building⟩

skep·ti·cal \'skep-ti-kəl\ *adj* : having or showing doubt

¹sketch \'skech\ *n* **1** : a rough outline or drawing showing the main features of something to be written, painted, or built **2** : a short written composition (as a story or essay)

²sketch *vb* **1** : to make a sketch, rough draft, or outline of **2** : to draw or paint sketches

sketchy \'skech-ē\ *adj* **sketch·i·er; sketch·i·est** **1** : like a sketch : roughly outlined **2** : lacking completeness or clearness ⟨a *sketchy* description⟩

¹ski \'skē\ *n, pl* **skis** : one of a pair of narrow wooden, metal, or plastic strips bound one on each foot and used in gliding over snow or water

²ski *vb* **skied; ski·ing** : to glide on skis — **ski·er** *n*

¹skid \'skid\ *n* **1** : a support (as a plank) used to raise and hold an object ⟨put a boat on *skids*⟩ **2** : one of the logs, planks, or rails along or on which something heavy is rolled or slid **3** : the act of skidding : SLIDE

²skid *vb* **skid·ded; skid·ding** **1** : to roll or slide on skids **2** : to slide sideways **3** : ¹SLIDE 1, SLIP ⟨*skid* across the ice⟩

skiff \'skif\ *n* **1** : a small light rowboat **2** : a sailboat light enough to be rowed

\ə\ **abut**		\aů\ **out**	\i\ **tip**	\ò\ **saw**	\ů\ **foot**
\ər\ **further**		\ch\ **chin**	\ī\ **life**	\òi\ **coin**	\y\ **yet**
\a\ **mat**		\e\ **pet**	\j\ **job**	\th\ **thin**	\yü\ **few**
\ā\ **take**		\ē\ **easy**	\ng\ **sing**	\th\ **this**	\yů\ **cure**
\ä\ **cot, cart**		\g\ **go**	\ō\ **bone**	\ü\ **food**	\zh\ **vision**

ski·ing \'skē-ing\ *n* : the art or sport of gliding and jumping on skis

skill \'skil\ *n* **1** : ability that comes from training or practice **2** : a developed or acquired ability ⟨*skills* of swimming and diving⟩

skilled \'skild\ *adj* **1** : having skill ⟨a *skilled* mason⟩ **2.** : requiring skill and training ⟨a *skilled* trade⟩

skil·let \'skil-ət\ *n* : a frying pan

skill·ful *or* **skil·ful** \'skil-fəl\ *adj* **1** : having or showing skill : EXPERT **2** : done or made with skill — **skill·ful·ly** \-fə-lē\ *adv*

synonyms SKILLFUL and EXPERT mean having the knowledge and experience needed to succeed at what one does. SKILLFUL suggests being very skilled at doing a particular job ⟨a *skillful* truck driver⟩ EXPERT suggests having a thorough knowledge of a subject as well as being very skillful at working in it ⟨an *expert* surgeon⟩

skim \'skim\ *vb* **skimmed; skim·ming 1** : to clean a liquid of scum or floating substance : remove (as cream or film) from the top part of a liquid **2** : to read or examine quickly and not thoroughly **3** : to throw so as to skip along the surface of water **4** : to pass swiftly or lightly over

skim milk *n* : milk from which the cream has been taken

skimp \'skimp\ *vb* : to give too little or just enough attention or effort to or funds for

skimpy \'skim-pē\ *adj* **skimp·i·er; skimp·i·est** : not enough especially because of skimping : SCANTY

¹skin \'skin\ *n* **1** : the hide especially of a small animal or one that has fur **2** : the outer limiting layer of an animal body that in vertebrate animals (as humans) is made up of two layers of cells forming an inner dermis and an outer epidermis **3** : an outer or surface layer (as of a fruit) — **skin·less** \-ləs\ *adj* — **skinned** \'skind\ *adj*

²skin *vb* **skinned; skin·ning 1** : to strip, scrape, or rub off the skin of ⟨*skin* one's knee⟩ **2** : to remove an outer layer from (as by peeling)

skin dive *vb* : to swim below the surface of water with a face mask and sometimes a portable breathing device — **skin diver** *n*

skin·ny \'skin-ē\ *adj* **skin·ni·er; skin·ni·est** : very thin **synonyms** see LEAN

¹skip \'skip\ *vb* **skipped; skip·ping 1** : to move lightly with leaps and bounds **2** : to bound or cause to bound off one point after another : SKIM **3** : to leap over lightly and nimbly **4** : to pass over : OMIT ⟨*skip* a page⟩ **5** : to pass to the grade beyond the next higher ⟨*skip* third grade⟩ **6** : to fail to attend ⟨*skipped* the meeting⟩

²skip *n* **1** : a light bounding step **2** : a way of moving by hops and steps

skip·per \'skip-ər\ *n* : the master of a ship and especially of a fishing, trading, or pleasure boat

¹skir·mish \'skər-mish\ *n* **1** : a minor fight in war **2** : a minor dispute or contest

²skirmish *vb* : to take part in a skirmish

¹skirt \'skərt\ *n* **1** : a woman's or girl's garment or part of a garment that hangs from the waist down **2** : either of two flaps on a saddle covering the bars on which the stirrups are hung **3** : a part or attachment serving as a rim, border, or edging

²skirt *vb* **1** : ²BORDER **2** : to go or pass around or about the outer edge of

skit \'skit\ *n* : a brief sketch in play form

skit·tish \'skit-ish\ *adj* : easily frightened ⟨a *skittish* horse⟩

skulk \'skəlk\ *vb* : to hide or move in a sly or sneaking way ⟨*skulked* behind a fence⟩

skull \'skəl\ *n* : the case of bone or cartilage that forms most of the skeleton of the head and face, encloses the brain, and supports the jaws

skunk \'skəngk\ *n* **1** : a North American animal related to the weasels and minks that has coarse black and white fur and can squirt out a fluid with a very unpleasant smell **2** : a mean person who deserves to be scorned

skunk 1

sky \'skī\ *n, pl* **skies 1** : the upper air : the vast arch or dome that seems to spread over the earth **2** : WEATHER, CLIMATE ⟨sunny *skies* are predicted⟩

sky·lark \'skī-,lärk\ *n* : a European lark noted for its song

sky·light \'skī-,līt\ *n* : a window or group of windows in a roof or ceiling

sky·line \'skī-,līn\ *n* **1** : the line where earth and sky seem to meet : HORIZON **2** : an outline against the sky ⟨buildings forming the *skyline* of a city⟩

sky·rock·et \'skī-ˌräk-ət\ *n* : ¹ROCKET 1

sky·scrap·er \'skī-ˌskrā-pər\ *n* : a very tall building

sky·writ·ing \'skī-ˌrīt-ing\ *n* : writing formed in the sky by means of smoke or vapor released from an airplane

slab \'slab\ *n* : a flat thick piece or slice (as of stone, wood, or bread)

¹slack \'slak\ *adj* **1** : CARELESS 2, NEGLIGENT **2** : not energetic : SLOW ⟨a *slack* pace⟩ **3** : not tight or firm ⟨a *slack* rope⟩ **4** : not busy or active ⟨business is *slack*⟩

²slack *vb* : to make or become looser, slower, or less energetic : LOOSEN, SLACKEN

³slack *n* **1** : a stopping of movement or flow **2** : a part (as of a rope or sail) that hangs loose without strain **3 slacks** *pl* : pants especially for informal wear

slack·en \'slak-ən\ *vb* **1** : to make slower or less energetic : slow up ⟨*slacken* speed at a crossing⟩ **2** : to make less tight or firm : LOOSEN ⟨*slacken* the reins⟩

slag \'slag\ *n* : the waste left after the melting of ores and the separation of the metal from them

slain *past participle of* SLAY

slake \'slāk\ *vb* **slaked; slak·ing 1** : QUENCH 2 ⟨*slaked* my thirst⟩ **2** : to cause solid lime to heat and crumble by treating it with water

¹slam \'slam\ *vb* **slammed; slam·ming 1** : to strike or beat hard **2** : to shut with noisy force : BANG ⟨*slam* the door⟩ **3** : to put or place with force ⟨*slam* down the money⟩ **4** : to criticize harshly

²slam *n* **1** : a severe blow **2** : a noisy violent closing : BANG

¹slan·der \'slan-dər\ *n* : a false and spiteful statement that damages another person's reputation

²slander *vb* : to utter slander against : DEFAME

slang \'slang\ *n* : an informal nonstandard vocabulary composed mostly of invented words, changed words, and exaggerated or humorous figures of speech

¹slant \'slant\ *vb* : to turn or incline from a straight line or level : SLOPE

²slant *n* **1** : a slanting direction, line, or surface : SLOPE **2** : something that slants

³slant *adj* : not level or straight up and down

slant·wise \'slant-ˌwīz\ *adv or adj* : so as to slant : at a slant : in a slanting position

¹slap \'slap\ *n* **1** : a quick sharp blow especially with the open hand **2** : a noise like that of a slap

²slap *vb* **slapped; slap·ping 1** : to strike with or as if with the open hand **2** : to make a sound like that of slapping **3** : to put, place, or throw with careless haste or force

¹slash \'slash\ *vb* **1** : to cut by sweeping blows : GASH **2** : to whip or strike with or as if with a cane **3** : to reduce sharply ⟨*slash* prices⟩

²slash *n* **1** : an act of slashing **2** : a long cut or slit made by slashing **3** : a sharp reduction ⟨a *slash* in prices⟩

slat \'slat\ *n* : a thin narrow strip of wood, plastic, or metal

slate \'slāt\ *n* **1** : a fine-grained usually bluish gray rock that splits into thin layers or plates and is used mostly for roofing and blackboards **2** : a framed piece of slate used to write on

¹slaugh·ter \'slȯt-ər\ *n* **1** : the act of killing **2** : the killing and dressing of animals for food **3** : destruction of many lives especially in battle

²slaughter *vb* **1** : ²BUTCHER 1 **2** : ¹MASSACRE

slaugh·ter·house \'slȯt-ər-ˌhaús\ *n, pl* **slaugh·ter·hous·es** \-ˌhaú-zəz\ : an establishment where animals are killed and dressed for food

Slav \'släv, 'slav\ *n* : a person speaking a Slavic language as a native tongue

¹slave \'slāv\ *n* **1** : a person who is owned by another person and can be sold at the owner's will **2** : one who is like a slave in not being his or her own master ⟨a *slave* to alcohol⟩ **3** : DRUDGE

Word History A long time ago the people of western Europe conquered most of the Slavic people of eastern Europe. The Slavs became slaves. The Latin word that meant "Slav" came to be used for all slaves, even if they were not Slavic. The English word *slave* came from the Latin word that meant "Slav." The word *Slav* did, too.

²slave *vb* **slaved; slav·ing** : to work like a slave

slave·hold·er \'slāv-ˌhōl-dər\ *n* : an owner of slaves

slav·ery \'slā-və-rē, 'släv-rē\ *n* **1** : hard tiring labor : DRUDGERY **2** : the state of being a slave : BONDAGE **3** : the custom or practice of owning slaves

Slav·ic \'slav-ik, 'släv-\ *adj* : of, relating to,

or characteristic of the Slavs or their languages

slav·ish \'slā-vish\ *adj* **1** : of or characteristic of slaves ⟨*slavish* tasks⟩ **2** : following or copying something or someone without questioning ⟨*slavish* imitators⟩

slay \'slā\ *vb* **slew** \'slü\; **slain** \'slān\; **slay·ing** : ¹KILL 1 — **slay·er** *n*

¹sled \'sled\ *n* **1** : a vehicle on runners for carrying loads especially over snow **2** : a small vehicle with runners used mostly by children for sliding on snow and ice

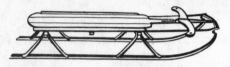

sled 2

²sled *vb* **sled·ded; sled·ding** : to ride or carry on a sled

¹sledge \'slej\ *n* : SLEDGEHAMMER

²sledge *n* : a strong heavy sledlike vehicle for heavy loads

sledge·ham·mer \'slej-,ham-ər\ *n* : a large heavy hammer usually used with both hands

¹sleek \'slēk\ *vb* : ¹SLICK

²sleek *adj* **1** : smooth and glossy as if polished ⟨*sleek* dark hair⟩ **2** : having a plump healthy look ⟨*sleek* cattle⟩

¹sleep \'slēp\ *n* **1** : a natural periodic loss of consciousness during which the body rests and refreshes itself **2** : an inactive state (as hibernation or trance) like true sleep **3** : DEATH ⟨have an animal put to *sleep*⟩ — **sleep·less** \-ləs\ *adj* — **sleep·less·ness** *n*

²sleep *vb* **slept** \'slept\; **sleep·ing** : to take rest in sleep : be or lie asleep

sleep·er \'slē-pər\ *n* **1** : one that sleeps **2** : a horizontal beam to support something on or near ground level **3** : a railroad car with berths for sleeping

sleep·walk·er \'slēp-,wò-kər\ *n* : a person who walks about while asleep — **sleep·walk·ing** \-,wò-king\ *n*

sleepy \'slē-pē\ *adj* **sleep·i·er; sleep·i·est** **1** : ready to fall asleep : DROWSY ⟨is *sleepy* and wants to go to bed⟩ **2** : not active, noisy, or busy ⟨a *sleepy* town⟩ — **sleep·i·ness** *n*

¹sleet \'slēt\ *n* : frozen or partly frozen rain

²sleet *vb* : to shower sleet

sleeve \'slēv\ *n* **1** : the part of a garment covering the arm **2** : a part that fits over or around something like a sleeve —

sleeved \'slēvd\ *adj* — **sleeve·less** \'slēv-ləs\ *adj*

¹sleigh \'slā\ *n* : an open usually horse-drawn vehicle with runners for use on snow or ice

sleigh

²sleigh *vb* : to drive or ride in a sleigh

sleight of hand \,slīt-əv-'hand\ : skill and quickness in the use of the hands especially in doing magic tricks

slen·der \'slen-dər\ *adj* **1** : gracefully thin **2** : narrow for its height ⟨a *slender* pole⟩ **3** : very little ⟨a *slender* income⟩

slept *past of* SLEEP

slew *past of* SLAY

¹slice \'slīs\ *n* : a thin flat piece cut from something ⟨a *slice* of bread⟩

²slice *vb* **sliced; slic·ing** **1** : to cut with or as if with a knife **2** : to cut into slices

¹slick \'slik\ *vb* : to make sleek or smooth

²slick *adj* **1** : having a smooth surface : SLIPPERY **2** : CRAFTY, CLEVER ⟨*slick* sales tricks⟩

slick·er \'slik-ər\ *n* : a long loose raincoat

¹slide \'slīd\ *vb* **slid** \'slid\; **slid·ing** \'slīd-ing\ **1** : to move or cause to move smoothly over a surface : GLIDE ⟨*slide* over the ice⟩ **2** : to move or pass smoothly and without much effort ⟨*slid* into the seat⟩

²slide *n* **1** : the act or motion of sliding **2** : a loosened mass that slides : AVALANCHE **3** : a surface down which a person or thing slides **4** : something that operates or adjusts by sliding **5** : a transparent picture that can be projected on a screen **6** : a glass plate for holding an object to be examined under a microscope

¹slight \'slīt\ *adj* **1** : not large or stout ⟨a trim *slight* figure⟩ **2** : FLIMSY, FRAIL **3** : not important : TRIVIAL ⟨a *slight* wound⟩ **4** : small of its kind or in amount ⟨a *slight* smell of gas⟩ — **slight·ly** *adv*

²slight *vb* : to treat without proper care, respect, or courtesy ⟨felt we had been *slighted* by their actions⟩ ⟨don't *slight* your work⟩

³slight *n* **1** : an act or an instance of slighting **2** : the state or an instance of being slighted

slight·ing \'slīt-ing\ *adj* : showing a lack of respect or caring ⟨a *slighting* remark⟩

¹slim \'slim\ *adj* **slim·mer; slim·mest 1** : SLENDER 1 **2** : very small ⟨a *slim* chance⟩

²slim *vb* **slimmed; slim·ming** : to make or become slender

slime \'slīm\ *n* **1** : soft slippery mud **2** : a soft slippery material (as on the skin of a slug or catfish)

slimy \'slī-mē\ *adj* **slim·i·er; slim·i·est 1** : having the feel or look of slime **2** : covered with slime

¹sling \'sling\ *vb* **slung** \'sləng\; **sling·ing 1** : to throw with a sudden sweeping motion : FLING **2** : to hurl with a sling

²sling *n* **1** : a device (as a short strap with a string attached at each end) for hurling stones **2** : SLINGSHOT **3** : a device (as a rope or chain) by which something is lifted or carried **4** : a hanging bandage put around the neck to hold up the arm or hand

³sling *vb* **slung** \'sləng\; **sling·ing 1** : to put in or move or support with a sling **2** : to hang from two points ⟨*sling* a hammock⟩

sling·shot \'sling-,shät\ *n* : a forked stick with an elastic band attached for shooting small stones

slink \'slingk\ *vb* **slunk** \'sləngk\; **slinking** : to move or go by or as if by creeping especially so as not to be noticed (as in fear or shame)

¹slip \'slip\ *vb* **slipped; slip·ping 1** : to move easily and smoothly ⟨*slipped* the knife into the sheath⟩ **2** : to move quietly : STEAL ⟨*slipped* from the room⟩ **3** : to pass or let pass or escape without being noted, used, or done ⟨time *slipped* by⟩ **4** : to get away from ⟨*slipped* the pursuers⟩ **5** : to escape the attention of ⟨it just *slipped* my mind⟩ **6** : to slide into or out of place or away from a support ⟨*slip* the bolt⟩ ⟨the book *slipped* out of my hand⟩ **7** : to slide on a slippery surface so as to lose one's balance ⟨*slipped* on the wet floor⟩ **8** : to put on or take off a garment quickly and carelessly ⟨*slipped* out of the coat⟩

²slip *n* **1** : a ramp where ships can be landed or repaired **2** : a place for a ship between two piers **3** : a secret or quick departure or escape ⟨gave them the *slip*⟩ **4** : a small mistake : BLUNDER **5** : the act or an instance of slipping down or out of place ⟨a *slip* on the ice⟩ **6** : a sudden mishap **7** : a fall from some level or standard : DECLINE ⟨a *slip* in stock prices⟩ **8**

: an undergarment made in dress length with straps over the shoulders **9** : PILLOWCASE

³slip *n* **1** : a piece of a plant cut for planting or grafting **2** : a long narrow piece of material **3** : a piece of paper used for some record ⟨a sales *slip*⟩ **4** : a young and slender person

⁴slip *vb* **slipped; slip·ping** : to take slips from (a plant)

slip·cov·er \'slip-,kəv-ər\ *n* : a cover (as for a sofa or chair) that may be slipped off and on

slip·knot \'slip-,nät\ *n* : a knot made by tying the end of a line around the line itself to form a loop so that the size of the loop may be changed by slipping the knot

slipknot

slip·per \'slip-ər\ *n* : a light low shoe that is easily slipped on the foot

slip·pery \'slip-ə-rē\ *adj* **slip·per·i·er; slip·per·i·est 1** : having a surface smooth or wet enough to make something slide or make one lose one's footing or hold ⟨fell on the *slippery* walk⟩ **2** : not to be trusted : TRICKY

slip·shod \'slip-'shäd\ *adj* : very careless : SLOVENLY ⟨their work was *slipshod*⟩

slip up *vb* : to make a mistake

¹slit \'slit\ *vb* **slit; slit·ting** : to make a long narrow cut in : SLASH

²slit *n* : a long narrow cut or opening

slith·er \'slith-ər\ *vb* : ¹GLIDE ⟨a snake *slithering* along⟩

¹sliv·er \'sliv-ər\ *n* : a long slender piece cut or torn off : SPLINTER

²sliver *vb* : to cut or form into slivers

¹slob·ber \'släb-ər\ *vb* : to let saliva or liquid dribble from the mouth

²slobber *n* : dripping saliva

slo·gan \'slō-gən\ *n* : a word or phrase used by a party, a group, or a business to attract attention (as to its goal, worth, or beliefs)

sloop \'slüp\ *n* : a sailing boat with one mast and a fore-and-aft mainsail and jib

¹slop \'släp\ *n* **1** : thin tasteless drink or liquid food ⟨prison *slops*⟩ **2** : liquid spilled

\ə\ abut	\aù\ out	\i\ tip	\ò\ saw	\ù\ foot
\ər\ further	\ch\ chin	\ī\ life	\òi\ coin	\y\ yet
\a\ mat	\e\ pet	\j\ job	\th\ thin	\yü\ few
\ā\ take	\ē\ easy	\ng\ sing	\th\ this	\yù\ cure
\ä\ cot, cart	\g\ go	\ō\ bone	\ü\ food	\zh\ vision

or splashed **3** : food waste or gruel fed to animals **4** : body waste

²slop *vb* **slopped; slop·ping 1** : to spill or spill something on or over ⟨*slopped* my shirt with gravy⟩ ⟨*slopped* gravy on the table⟩ **2** : to feed slop to ⟨*slop* the pigs⟩

¹slope \'slōp\ *vb* **sloped; slop·ing** : to take a slanting direction ⟨the bank *slopes* down to the river⟩

²slope *n* **1** : a piece of slanting ground (as a hillside) **2** : upward or downward slant ⟨the *slope* of a roof⟩

slop·py \'släp-ē\ *adj* **slop·pi·er; slop·pi·est 1** : wet enough to spatter easily ⟨*sloppy* mud⟩ **2** : careless in work or in appearance

slosh \'släsh\ *vb* **1** : to walk with trouble through water, mud, or slush **2** : ¹SPLASH 1, 2, 3

¹slot \'slät\ *n* : a narrow opening, groove, or passage

²slot *vb* **slot·ted; slot·ting** : to cut a slot in

sloth \'slòth, 'slōth\ *n* **1** : the state of being lazy **2** : an animal of Central and South America that hangs back downward and moves slowly along the branches of trees on whose leaves, twigs, and fruits it feeds

sloth 2

¹slouch \'slaùch\ *n* **1** : a lazy worthless person **2** : a lazy drooping way of standing, sitting, or walking

²slouch *vb* : to walk, stand, or sit with a slouch

slough \'slü, 'slaù\ *n* : a wet marshy or muddy place

slov·en·ly \'sləv-ən-lē\ *adj* : personally untidy

¹slow \'slō\ *adj* **1** : not as smart or as quick to understand as most people **2** : not easily aroused or excited ⟨*slow* to anger⟩ **3**

: moving, flowing, or going at less than the usual speed ⟨a *slow* stream⟩ ⟨*slow* music⟩ **4** : indicating less than is correct ⟨my watch is five minutes *slow*⟩ **5** : not lively or active ⟨business was *slow*⟩ ⟨a very *slow* party⟩ — **slow·ly** *adv* — **slow·ness** *n*

²slow *adv* : in a slow way

³slow *vb* : to make or go slow or slower

slow·poke \'slō-ˌpōk\ *n* : a very slow person

sludge \'sləj\ *n* : a soft muddy mass resulting from sewage treatment

¹slug \'sləg\ *n* : a long wormlike land mollusk that is related to the snails but has an undeveloped shell or none at all

²slug *n* **1** : a small piece of shaped metal **2** : BULLET **3** : a metal disk often used in place of a coin

slug

³slug *n* : a hard blow especially with the fist

⁴slug *vb* **slugged; slug·ging** : to hit hard with the fist or with a bat

slug·gard \'sləg-ərd\ *n* : a lazy person

slug·ger \'sləg-ər\ *n* : a boxer or baseball batter who hits hard

slug·gish \'sləg-ish\ *adj* : slow in movement or reaction — **slug·gish·ly** *adv* — **slug·gish·ness** *n*

¹sluice \'slüs\ *n* **1** : an artificial passage for water with a gate for controlling its flow or changing its direction **2** : a device for controlling the flow of water **3** : a sloping trough for washing ore or for floating logs

²sluice *vb* **sluiced; sluic·ing 1** : to wash in a stream of water running through a sluice **2** : ³FLUSH 2, DRENCH

slum \'sləm\ *n* : a very poor crowded dirty section especially of a city

¹slum·ber \'sləm-bər\ *vb* : to be asleep

²slumber *n* : ¹SLEEP

¹slump \'sləmp\ *vb* **1** : to drop or slide down suddenly : COLLAPSE ⟨*slumped* into a chair⟩ **2** : ²SLOUCH ⟨don't *slump* when you walk⟩ **3** : to drop sharply ⟨prices *slumped*⟩

²slump *n* : a big or continued drop especially in prices, business, or performance

slung *past of* SLING

slunk *past of* SLINK

¹slur \'slər\ *vb* **slurred; slur·ring 1** : to pass over without proper mention or stress **2** : to run one's speech together so that it is hard to understand

²slur *n* : a slurred way of talking

³**slur** *n* **1** : an insulting remark **2** : STIGMA 1, STAIN

slush \'sləsh\ *n* : partly melted snow

sly \'slī\ *adj* **sli•er** *or* **sly•er; sli•est** *or* **sly•est 1** : both clever and tricky **2** : being sneaky and dishonest **3** : MISCHIEVOUS 3 — **sly•ly** *adv* — **sly•ness** *n*

synonyms SLY, CUNNING, and TRICKY mean tending to use crooked methods to get what one wants. SLY suggests secrecy and dishonesty as well as skill in hiding one's goals and methods ⟨a *sly* trader of horses⟩ CUNNING suggests using one's intelligence in order to achieve one's ends ⟨the *cunning* lawyer tried every trick⟩ TRICKY, unlike *cunning*, suggests having more plain dishonesty than skill ⟨the *tricky* politicians in this town⟩

— **on the sly** : so as not to be seen or caught : SECRETLY

¹**smack** \'smak\ *n* : a slight taste, trace, or touch of something

²**smack** *vb* : to have a flavor, trace, or suggestion ⟨it *smacks* of garlic⟩

³**smack** *vb* **1** : to close and open the lips noisily especially in eating **2** : to kiss usually loudly or hard **3** : to make or give a smack : SLAP

⁴**smack** *n* **1** : a quick sharp noise made by the lips (as in enjoyment of some taste) **2** : a loud kiss **3** : a noisy slap or blow

¹**small** \'smȯl\ *adj* **1** : little in size **2** : few in numbers or members ⟨a *small* crowd⟩ **3** : little in amount ⟨a *small* supply⟩ **4** : not very much ⟨*small* success⟩ **5** : UNIMPORTANT **6** : operating on a limited scale ⟨*small* dealers⟩ **7** : lacking in strength ⟨a *small* voice⟩ ⟨*small* beer⟩ **8** : not generous : MEAN **9** : made up of units of little worth ⟨*small* change⟩ **10** : ¹HUMBLE 3, MODEST ⟨a *small* beginning⟩ **11** : lowered in pride **12** : being letters that are not capitals — **small•ness** *n*

²**small** *n* : a part smaller and usually narrower than the rest ⟨the *small* of the back⟩

small intestine *n* : the long narrow upper part of the intestine in which food is mostly digested and from which digested food is absorbed into the body

small•pox \'smȯl-ˌpäks\ *n* : an acute disease which is caused by a virus and in which fever and skin eruptions occur

¹**smart** \'smärt\ *vb* **1** : to cause or feel a sharp stinging pain **2** : to feel distress ⟨*smart* under criticism⟩

²**smart** *adj* **1** : BRISK, SPIRITED ⟨walking at a *smart* pace⟩ **2** : quick to learn or do : BRIGHT **3** : SAUCY 1 **4** : stylish in appearance ⟨a *smart* dresser⟩ — **smart•ly** *adv* — **smart•ness** *n*

³**smart** *n* : a stinging pain usually in one spot

smart al•eck \'smärt-ˌal-ik\ *n* : a person who likes to show off

¹**smash** \'smash\ *vb* **1** : to break in pieces : SHATTER **2** : to drive or move violently ⟨the ball *smashed* through the window⟩ **3** : to destroy completely : WRECK **4** : to go to pieces : COLLAPSE

²**smash** *n* **1** : a smashing blow or attack **2** : the condition of being smashed : RUIN, COLLAPSE **3** : the action or sound of smashing

¹**smear** \'smiər\ *n* : a spot or streak made by or as if by an oily or sticky substance : SMUDGE

²**smear** *vb* **1** : to spread or soil with something oily or sticky : DAUB **2** : to spread over a surface **3** : to blacken the good name of

¹**smell** \'smel\ *vb* **smelled** \'smeld\ *or* **smelt** \'smelt\; **smell•ing 1** : to become aware of the odor of by means of sense organs located in the nose **2** : to detect by means or use of the sense of smell **3** : to have or give off an odor

²**smell** *n* **1** : the sense by which a person or animal becomes aware of an odor **2** : the sensation one gets through the sense of smell : ODOR, SCENT

¹**smelt** \'smelt\ *n, pl* **smelts** *or* **smelt** : a small food fish that looks like the related trouts, lives in coastal sea waters, and swims up rivers to spawn

²**smelt** *vb* : to melt (as ore) in order to separate the metal : REFINE

smelt•er \'smel-tər\ *n* **1** : a person whose work or business is smelting **2** : a place where ores or metals are smelted

¹**smile** \'smīl\ *vb* **smiled; smil•ing 1** : to have, produce, or show a smile **2** : to look with amusement or scorn **3** : to express by a smile ⟨*smile* approval⟩

²**smile** *n* : an expression on the face in which the lips curve upward especially to show amusement or pleasure

smite \'smīt\ *vb* **smote** \'smōt\; **smitten** \'smit-n\; **smit•ing** \'smīt-ing\ : to strike hard especially with the hand or a weapon

smith \'smith\ *n* **1** : a worker in metals **2** : BLACKSMITH

smithy \'smith-ē\ *n, pl* **smith•ies** : the

\ə\ abut	\aù\ out	\i\ tip	\ȯ\ saw	\ù\ foot
\ər\ further	\ch\ chin	\ī\ life	\ȯi\ coin	\y\ yet
\a\ mat	\e\ pet	\j\ job	\th\ thin	\yü\ few
\ā\ take	\ē\ easy	\ng\ sing	\th\ this	\yù\ cure
\ä\ cot, cart	\g\ go	\ō\ bone	\ü\ food	\zh\ vision

workshop of a smith and especially of a blacksmith

smock \'smäk\ *n* : a loose outer garment worn especially for protection of clothing

smog \'smäg\ *n* : a fog made heavier and thicker by the action of sunlight on air polluted by smoke and automobile fumes

¹smoke \'smōk\ *n* **1** : the gas of burning materials (as coal, wood, or tobacco) made visible by particles of carbon floating in it **2** : a mass or column of smoke : SMUDGE **3** : the act of smoking tobacco

²smoke *vb* **smoked; smok·ing 1** : to give out smoke **2** : to draw in and breathe out the fumes of burning tobacco **3** : to drive (as mosquitoes) away by smoke **4** : to expose (as meat) to smoke to give flavor and keep from spoiling — **smok·er** *n*

smoke·house \'smōk-ˌhau̇s\ *n, pl* **smoke·hous·es** \-ˌhau̇-zəz\ : a building where meat or fish is cured with smoke

smoke·stack \'smōk-ˌstak\ *n* : a large chimney or a pipe for carrying away smoke (as on a factory or ship)

smoky \'smō-kē\ *adj* **smok·i·er; smok·i·est 1** : giving off smoke especially in large amounts ⟨*smoky* stoves⟩ **2** : like that of smoke ⟨a *smoky* flavor⟩ **3** : filled with or darkened by smoke ⟨a *smoky* room⟩

¹smol·der *or* **smoul·der** \'smōl-dər\ *n* : a slow often smoky fire

²smolder *or* **smoulder** *vb* **1** : to burn slowly usually with smoke and without flame ⟨a fire *smoldering* in the grate⟩ **2** : to burn inwardly ⟨anger *smoldered* in my heart⟩

¹smooth \'smüth\ *adj* **1** : not rough or uneven in surface ⟨a *smooth* board⟩ **2** : not hairy **3** : free from difficulties or things in the way ⟨a *smooth* path⟩ **4** : moving or progressing without breaks, sudden changes, or shifts ⟨a *smooth* stream⟩ ⟨*smooth* speech⟩ **5** : able to make things seem right or easy or good : GLIB ⟨a *smooth* excuse⟩ — **smooth·ly** *adv* — **smooth·ness** *n*

²smooth *vb* **1** : to make smooth **2** : ¹POLISH 2, REFINE ⟨*smooth* one's style in writing⟩ **3** : to free from trouble or difficulty ⟨*smoothed* the way for us⟩

smote *past of* SMITE

smoth·er \'sməth-ər\ *vb* **1** : to overcome by depriving of air or exposing to smoke or fumes : SUFFOCATE **2** : to become suffocated **3** : to cover up : SUPPRESS ⟨*smother* a yawn⟩ **4** : to cover thickly ⟨steak *smothered* with onions⟩

¹smudge \'sməj\ *vb* **smudged; smudg·ing** : to soil or blur by rubbing or smearing

²smudge *n* **1** : a blurred spot or streak : SMEAR **2** : a smoky fire (as to drive away mosquitoes or protect fruit from frost)

smug \'sməg\ *adj* **smug·ger; smug·gest** : very satisfied with oneself — **smug·ly** *adv*

smug·gle \'sməg-əl\ *vb* **smug·gled; smug·gling 1** : to export or import secretly and unlawfully especially to avoid paying taxes ⟨*smuggle* jewels⟩ **2** : to take or bring secretly — **smug·gler** \'sməg-lər\ *n*

smut \'smət\ *n* **1** : something (as a particle of soot) that soils or blackens **2** : a destructive disease of plants (as cereal grasses) in which plant parts (as seeds) are replaced by masses of dark spores of the fungus that causes the disease **3** : a fungus that causes smut

snack \'snak\ *n* : a light meal : LUNCH

¹snag \'snag\ *n* **1** : a stump or stub of a tree branch especially when hidden under water **2** : a rough or broken part sticking out from something **3** : an unexpected difficulty

²snag *vb* **snagged; snag·ging** : to catch or damage on or as if on a snag ⟨*snag* one's clothes⟩

snail \'snāl\ *n* **1** : a small slow-moving mollusk with a spiral shell into which it can draw itself for safety **2** : a person who moves slowly

¹snake \'snāk\ *n* **1** : a limbless crawling reptile that has a long body and lives usually on large insects or small animals and birds **2** : a horrid or treacherous person

²snake *vb* **snaked; snak·ing** : to crawl, wind, or move like a snake

snaky \'snā-kē\ *adj* **snak·i·er; snak·i·est 1** : of or like a snake **2** : full of snakes

¹snap \'snap\ *vb* **snapped; snap·ping 1** : to grasp or grasp at something suddenly with the mouth or teeth ⟨fish *snapping* at the bait⟩ **2** : to grasp at something eagerly ⟨*snapped* at the chance to go⟩ **3** : to get, take, or buy at once ⟨*snap* up a bargain⟩ **4** : to speak or utter sharply or irritably ⟨*snap* out a command⟩ **5** : to break or break apart suddenly and often with a cracking noise ⟨the branch *snapped*⟩ **6** : to make or cause to make a sharp or crackling sound ⟨*snap* a whip⟩ **7** : to close or fit in place with a quick movement ⟨the lid *snapped* shut⟩ **8** : to put into or remove from a position suddenly or with a snapping sound ⟨*snap* off a switch⟩ **9** : to close by means of snaps or fasteners **10** : to act or be acted on with snap ⟨*snapped* to attention⟩ **11** : to take a snapshot of

²snap *n* **1** : the act or sound of snapping **2**

: something that is easy and presents no problems ⟨that job is a *snap*⟩ **3** : a small amount : BIT ⟨doesn't care a *snap*⟩ **4** : a sudden spell of harsh weather ⟨a cold *snap*⟩ **5** : a catch or fastening that closes or locks with a click ⟨the *snap* on a purse⟩ **6** : a thin brittle cookie **7** : SNAPSHOT **8** : smartness of movement or speech : ENERGY

³snap *adj* **1** : made suddenly or without careful thought ⟨a *snap* judgment⟩ **2** : closing with a click or by means of a device that snaps ⟨a *snap* lock⟩ **3** : very easy ⟨a *snap* course⟩

snap·drag·on \'snap-,drag-ən\ *n* : a garden plant with stalks of mostly white, pink, crimson, or yellow flowers with two lips

snap·per \'snap-ər\ *n* **1** : one that snaps **2** : SNAPPING TURTLE **3** : an active sea fish important for sport and food

snap·ping tur·tle \,snap-ing-'tərt-l\ *n* : a large American turtle that catches its prey with a snap of the powerful jaws

snap·py \'snap-ē\ *adj* **snap·pi·er; snap·pi·est** **1** : full of life : LIVELY **2** : briskly cold : CHILLY **3** : STYLISH, SMART ⟨a *snappy* suit⟩

snapdragon

snap·shot \'snap-,shät\ *n* : a photograph taken usually with an inexpensive hand-held camera

¹snare \'snaər, 'sneər\ *n* **1** : a trap (as a noose) for catching small animals and birds **2** : something by which one is entangled, trapped, or deceived

²snare *vb* **snared; snar·ing** : to catch or entangle by or as if by use of a snare

snare drum *n* : a small drum with two heads that has strings stretched across its lower head to produce a rattling sound

¹snarl \'snärl\ *n* **1** : a tangle usually of hairs or thread : KNOT **2** : a tangled situation ⟨a traffic *snarl*⟩

²snarl *vb* : to get into a tangle

³snarl *vb* **1** : to growl with a showing of teeth **2** : to speak in an angry way **3** : to utter with a growl

⁴snarl *n* : an angry growl

¹snatch \'snach\ *vb* : to take hold of or try to take hold of something quickly or suddenly

²snatch *n* **1** : an act of snatching **2** : a brief period ⟨slept in *snatches*⟩ **3** : something brief, hurried, or in small bits ⟨*snatches* of old songs⟩

snaz·zy \'snaz-ē\ *adj* **snaz·zi·er; snaz·zi·est** : FANCY ⟨a *snazzy* sports car⟩

¹sneak \'snēk\ *vb* : to move, act, bring, or put in a sly or secret way

²sneak *n* **1** : a person who acts in a sly or secret way **2** : the act or an instance of sneaking

sneak·er \'snē-kər\ *n* : a canvas or leather shoe with a rubber sole

sneak·ing \'snē-king\ *adj* **1** : being secretive and dishonest **2** : not openly expressed or recognized ⟨a *sneaking* admiration for a rival⟩

sneaky \'snē-kē\ *adj* **sneak·i·er; sneak·i·est** : behaving in a sly or secret way or showing that kind of behavior ⟨a *sneaky* person⟩ ⟨a *sneaky* trick⟩

¹sneer \'sniər\ *vb* **1** : to smile or laugh while making a face that shows scorn **2** : to speak or write in a scorning way

²sneer *n* : a sneering expression or remark

¹sneeze \'snēz\ *vb* **sneezed; sneez·ing** : to force out the breath in a sudden loud violent action

²sneeze *n* : an act or instance of sneezing

¹snick·er \'snik-ər\ *vb* : to give a small and often mean or sly laugh

²snicker *n* : an act or sound of snickering

snide \'snīd\ *adj* : slyly insulting ⟨a *snide* remark⟩

¹sniff \'snif\ *vb* **1** : to draw air into the nose in short breaths loud enough to be heard **2** : to show scorn ⟨*sniffed* at simple jobs⟩ **3** : to smell by taking short breaths ⟨*sniff* perfume⟩

²sniff *n* **1** : the act or sound of sniffing **2** : an odor or amount sniffed

snif·fle \'snif-əl\ *vb* **snif·fled; snif·fling** **1** : to sniff repeatedly **2** : to speak with sniffs

snif·fles \'snif-əlz\ *n pl* : a common cold in which the main symptom is a runny nose

¹snig·ger \'snig-ər\ *vb* : ¹SNICKER

²snigger *n* : ²SNICKER

¹snip \'snip\ *n* **1** : a small piece that is snipped off **2** : an act or sound of snipping

²snip *vb* **snipped; snip·ping** : to cut or cut off with or as if with shears or scissors

\ə\ **abut**	\aú\ **out**	\i\ **tip**	\ò\ **saw**	\ú\ **foot**	
\ər\ **further**	\ch\ **chin**	\ī\ **life**	\òi\ **coin**	\y\ **yet**	
\a\ **mat**	\e\ **pet**	\j\ **job**	\th\ **thin**	\yü\ **few**	
\ā\ **take**	\ē\ **easy**	\ng\ **sing**	\th\ **this**	\yú\ **cure**	
\ä\ **cot, cart**	\g\ **go**	\ō\ **bone**	\ü\ **food**	\zh\ **vision**	

¹snipe \'snīp\ *n, pl* **snipes** *or* **snipe** : a game bird that lives in marshes and has a long straight bill

snipe

²snipe *vb* **sniped; snip·ing** : to shoot from a hiding place (as at individual enemy soldiers) — **snip·er** *n*

snob \'snäb\ *n* : a person who imitates, admires, or wants to be friends with people of higher position and looks down on or avoids those felt to be less important

Word History The word *snob* first meant "cobbler" in England. Since most cobblers belonged to the lower classes *snob* came to mean "a common person of low rank in society." However some people of low rank longed to be part of the upper classes. These people considered themselves better than others of their class and looked down on them. Such people came to be called *snobs*. Today a snob is thought of as any person who puts on airs and looks down on other people.

snob·bish \'snäb-ish\ *adj* : of, relating to, or being a snob

¹snoop \'snüp\ *vb* : to look or search especially in a sneaking or nosy way — **snoop·er** \'snö-pər\ *n*

²snoop *n* : a person who snoops

snoot \'snüt\ *n* : ¹NOSE 1

¹snooze \'snüz\ *vb* **snoozed; snooz·ing** : to take a nap

²snooze *n* : a short sleep : NAP

¹snore \'snōr\ *vb* **snored; snor·ing** : to breathe with a rough hoarse noise while sleeping

²snore *n* : an act or sound of snoring

¹snort \'snȯrt\ *vb* : to force air through the nose with a rough harsh sound

²snort *n* : an act or sound of snorting

snout \'snaut\ *n* **1** : a long projecting nose (as of a pig) **2** : the front part of a head (as of a weevil) that sticks out like the snout of a pig **3** : a usually large and ugly nose

¹snow \'snō\ *n* **1** : small white crystals of ice formed directly from the water vapor of the air **2** : a fall of snowflakes : a mass of snowflakes fallen to earth

²snow *vb* **1** : to fall or cause to fall in or as snow ⟨it's *snowing*⟩ **2** : to cover or shut in with snow

snow·ball \'snō-ˌbȯl\ *n* : a round mass of snow pressed or rolled together

snow·bird \'snō-ˌbərd\ *n* : a small bird (as a junco) seen mostly in winter

snow–blind \'snō-ˌblīnd\ *or* **snow–blind-ed** \-ˌblīn-dəd\ *adj* : having the eyes red and swollen and unable to see from the effect of glare reflected from snow — **snow blindness** *n*

snow·bound \'snō-ˈbaund\ *adj* : shut in by snow

snow·drift \'snō-ˌdrift\ *n* : a bank of drifted snow

snow·fall \'snō-ˌfȯl\ *n* **1** : a fall of snow **2** : the amount of snow that falls in a single storm or in a certain period

snow·flake \'snō-ˌflāk\ *n* : a snow crystal : a small mass of snow crystals

snow·man \'snō-ˌman\ *n, pl* **snow·men** \-ˌmen\ : snow shaped to look like a person

snow·mo·bile \'snō-mō-ˌbēl\ *n* : a motor vehicle designed for travel on snow

snow·plow \'snō-ˌplau\ *n* : any of various devices used for clearing away snow

¹snow·shoe \'snō-ˌshü\ *n* : a light frame of wood strung with a net (as of rawhide) and worn under one's shoe to prevent sinking into soft snow

²snowshoe *vb* **snow·shoed; snow-shoe·ing** : to go on snowshoes

snow·storm \'snō-ˌstȯrm\ *n* : a storm of falling snow

snowy \'snō-ē\ *adj* **snow·i·er; snow·i-est** **1** : having or covered with snow **2** : white like snow

¹snub \'snəb\ *vb* **snubbed; snub·bing** : to ignore or treat rudely on purpose

²snub *n* : an instance of snubbing

snub–nosed \'snəb-ˈnōzd\ *adj* : having a stubby and usually slightly turned-up nose

¹snuff \'snəf\ *vb* **1** : to cut or pinch off the burned end of the wick of a candle **2** : EXTINGUISH 1

²snuff *vb* : to draw through or into the nose with force

³snuff *n* : powdered tobacco that is chewed, placed against the gums, or drawn in through the nostrils

¹snuf·fle \'snəf-əl\ *vb* **snuf·fled; snuf-fling** : to breathe noisily through a nose that is partly blocked

²snuffle *n* : the sound made in snuffling

snug \'snəg\ *adj* **snug·ger; snug·gest 1** : fitting closely and comfortably ⟨a *snug* coat⟩ **2** : COMFORTABLE 1, COZY ⟨a *snug* corner⟩ **3** : offering protection or a hiding place ⟨a *snug* harbor⟩ — **snugly** *adv*

snug·gle \'snəg-əl\ *vb* **snug·gled; snug·gling 1** : to curl up comfortably or cozily : CUDDLE **2** : to pull in close to one

¹so \'sō\ *adv* **1** : in the way indicated ⟨said I'd go and did *so*⟩ **2** : in the same way : ALSO ⟨they wrote well and *so* did you⟩ **3** : ¹THEN 2 ⟨and *so* to bed⟩ **4** : to an indicated extent or way ⟨had never felt *so* well⟩ **5** : to a great degree : VERY, EXTREMELY ⟨loved them *so*⟩ **6** : to a definite but not specified amount ⟨can do only *so* much in a day⟩ **7** : most certainly : INDEED ⟨you did *so* say it⟩ **8** : THEREFORE ⟨is honest and *so* returned the wallet⟩

²so *conj* **1** : in order that ⟨be quiet *so* I can sleep⟩ **2** : and therefore ⟨we were hungry, *so* we ate⟩

³so \'sō\ *pron* **1** : the same : THAT ⟨they told me *so*⟩ **2** : approximately that ⟨I'd been there a month or *so*⟩

¹soak \'sōk\ *vb* **1** : to lie covered with liquid **2** : to place in a liquid to wet or as if to wet thoroughly **3** : to enter or pass through something by or as if by tiny holes : PERMEATE **4** : to draw out by or as if by soaking in a liquid ⟨*soak* the dirt from clothes⟩ **5** : to draw in by or as if by absorption ⟨*soaked* up the sunshine⟩

²soak *n* : the act or process of soaking : the state of being soaked

¹soap \'sōp\ *n* : a substance that is usually made by the action of alkali on fat, dissolves in water, and is used for washing

²soap *vb* : to rub soap over or into something

soap·stone \'sōp-ˌstōn\ *n* : a soft stone having a soapy or greasy feeling

soap·suds \'sōp-ˌsədz\ *n pl* : SUDS

soapy \'sō-pē\ *adj* **soap·i·er; soap·i·est 1** : smeared with or full of soap **2** : containing or combined with soap **3** : like soap

soar \'sōr\ *vb* : to fly or sail through the air often at a great height

¹sob \'säb\ *vb* **sobbed; sob·bing** : to cry or express with gasps and catching in the throat ⟨*sobbed* out the story⟩

²sob *n* **1** : an act of sobbing **2** : a sound of or like that of sobbing

¹so·ber \'sō-bər\ *adj* **1** : not drinking too much : TEMPERATE **2** : not drunk **3** : having a serious attitude : SOLEMN ⟨a *sober* child⟩ **4** : having a quiet color ⟨*sober* clothes⟩ **5** : not fanciful or imagined ⟨a matter of *sober* fact⟩

²sober *vb* : to make or become sober

so–called \'sō-'kóld\ *adj* : usually but often wrongly so named ⟨my *so-called* friend⟩

soc·cer \'säk-ər\ *n* : a game played between two teams of eleven players in which a round inflated ball is moved toward a goal usually by kicking

so·cia·ble \'sō-shə-bəl\ *adj* **1** : liking to be around other people : FRIENDLY **2** : involving pleasant social relations ⟨enjoyed a *sociable* evening⟩

¹so·cial \'sō-shəl\ *adj* **1** : FRIENDLY 1, SOCIABLE ⟨a *social* evening⟩ **2** : living or growing naturally in groups or communities ⟨bees are *social* insects⟩ **3** : of or relating to human beings as a group ⟨*social* institutions⟩ **4** : of, relating to, or based on rank in a particular society ⟨*social* classes⟩ **5** : of or relating to fashionable society ⟨a *social* leader⟩ — **so·cial·ly** *adv*

²social *n* : a friendly gathering usually for a special reason ⟨a church *social*⟩

so·cial·ism \'sō-shə-ˌliz-əm\ *n* : a theory or system of government based on public ownership and control of the means of production and distribution of goods

so·cial·ist \'sō-shə-ləst\ *n* : a person who believes in socialism

social studies *n pl* : the studies (as civics, history, and geography) that deal with human relationships and how society works

so·ci·ety \sə-'sī-ət-ē\ *n, pl* **so·ci·et·ies 1** : friendly association with others **2** : human beings viewed as a system within which the individual lives : all of the people ⟨urban *society*⟩ **3** : a group of persons with a common interest or purpose ⟨the school French *society*⟩ **4** : a part of a community thought of as different in some way ⟨literary *society*⟩ **5** : the group or set of fashionable persons

¹sock \'säk\ *n, pl* **socks** *or* **sox** \'säks\ : a knitted or woven covering for the foot usually reaching past the ankle and sometimes to the knee

²sock *vb* : ¹HIT 1, PUNCH

³sock *n* : ²PUNCH

sock·et \'säk-ət\ *n* : a hollow thing or place that receives or holds something ⟨an electric light *socket*⟩ ⟨eye *socket*⟩

sock·eye \'säk-ˌī\ *n* : a small Pacific salmon that is the source of most of the salmon with red flesh that we eat

\ə\ **abut**	\aú\ **out**	\i\ **tip**	\ó\ **saw**	\ú\ **foot**
\ər\ **further**	\ch\ **chin**	\ī\ **life**	\ói\ **coin**	\y\ **yet**
\a\ **mat**	\e\ **pet**	\j\ **job**	\th\ **thin**	\yü\ **few**
\ā\ **take**	\ē\ **easy**	\ng\ **sing**	\t͟h\ **this**	\yú\ **cure**
\ä\ **cot, cart**	\g\ **go**	\ō\ **bone**	\ü\ **food**	\zh\ **vision**

¹sod \'säd\ *n* : the layer of the soil filled with roots (as of grass)

²sod *vb* **sod·ded; sod·ding** : to cover with sod

so·da \'sōd-ə\ *n* **1** : a powdery substance like salt used in washing and in making glass or soap **2** : SODIUM BICARBONATE **3** : SODA WATER **4** : SODA POP **5** : a sweet drink made of soda water, flavoring, and ice cream ⟨a chocolate *soda*⟩

soda fountain *n* : a counter where soft drinks and ice cream are served

soda pop *n* : a flavored beverage containing carbon dioxide

soda water *n* : water with carbon dioxide added

sod·den \'säd-n\ *adj* : SOGGY 1

so·di·um \'sōd-ē-əm\ *n* : a soft waxy silver-white chemical element occurring in nature in combined form (as in salt)

sodium bicarbonate *n* : a white powder used in cooking and medicine

sodium chlo·ride \-'klōr-,īd\ *n* : ¹SALT 1

so·fa \'sō-fə\ *n* : a long upholstered seat usually with a back and arms

¹soft \'sȯft\ *adj* **1** : having a pleasing or comfortable effect **2** : not bright or glaring ⟨*soft* lights⟩ **3** : quiet in pitch or volume ⟨*soft* voices⟩ **4** : smooth or delicate in appearance or feel ⟨a *soft* silk⟩ **5** : not violent ⟨*soft* breezes⟩ **6** : EASY 1 ⟨a *soft* job⟩ **7** : sounding as in *ace* and *gem* — used of *c* and *g* **8** : easily affected by emotions ⟨a *soft* heart⟩ **9** : lacking in strength ⟨*soft* from good living⟩ **10** : not hard, solid, or firm ⟨a *soft* mattress⟩ **11** : free from substances that prevent lathering of soap ⟨*soft* water⟩ **12** : not containing alcohol ⟨*soft* drinks⟩ — **soft·ness** *n*

²soft *adv* : SOFTLY

soft·ball \'sȯft-,bȯl\ *n* **1** : a game like baseball played with a larger ball **2** : the ball used in softball

soft·en \'sȯf-ən\ *vb* : to make or become soft or softer — **soft·en·er** *n*

soft·ly \'sȯft-lē\ *adv* : in a soft way : QUIETLY, GENTLY ⟨speak *softly*⟩ ⟨walked *softly* across the room⟩

soft·wood \'sȯf-,twu̇d\ *n* : the wood of a cone-bearing tree (as a pine or spruce)

sog·gy \'säg-ē, 'sȯg-\ *adj* **sog·gi·er; sog·gi·est** **1** : heavy with water or moisture ⟨*soggy* ground⟩ **2** : heavy or doughy because of poor cooking

¹soil \'sȯil\ *vb* : to make or become dirty

²soil *n* **1** : the loose finely divided surface material of the earth in which plants have their roots **2** : COUNTRY 2, LAND ⟨my native *soil*⟩ — **soil·less** \'sȯil-ləs\ *adj*

¹so·journ \'sō-,jərn\ *n* : a temporary stay

²sojourn *vb* : to stay as a temporary resident

sol \'sōl\ *n* : the fifth note of the musical scale

so·lar \'sō-lər\ *adj* **1** : of or relating to the sun **2** : measured by the earth's course around the sun ⟨a *solar* year⟩ **3** : produced or made to work by the action of the sun's light or heat ⟨a *solar* furnace⟩

solar system *n* : the sun and the planets, asteroids, comets, and meteors that revolve around it

sold *past of* SELL

¹sol·der \'säd-ər\ *n* : a metal or a mixture of metals used when melted to join or mend surfaces of metal

²solder *vb* : to join together or repair with solder

sol·dier \'sōl-jər\ *n* : a person in military service : an enlisted person who is not a commissioned officer

¹sole \'sōl\ *n* **1** : the bottom of the foot **2** : the bottom of a shoe, slipper, or boot

²sole *vb* **soled; sol·ing** : to furnish with a sole ⟨*sole* shoes⟩

³sole *n* : a flatfish that has a small mouth and small eyes set close together and is a popular food fish

⁴sole *adj* **1** : ¹SINGLE 2, ONLY ⟨the *sole* heir⟩ **2** : limited or belonging only to the one mentioned ⟨gave me *sole* authority⟩

sole·ly \'sōl-lē\ *adv* **1** : without another : ALONE **2** : ²ONLY 2 ⟨done *solely* for money⟩

sol·emn \'säl-əm\ *adj* **1** : celebrated with religious ceremony : SACRED **2** : ¹FORMAL ⟨a *solemn* procession⟩ **3** : done or made seriously and thoughtfully ⟨a *solemn* promise⟩ **4** : very serious ⟨a *solemn* moment⟩ **5** : being dark and gloomy : SOMBER ⟨a robe of *solemn* black⟩ **synonyms** see SERIOUS — **sol·emn·ly** *adv*

so·lem·ni·ty \sə-'lem-nət-ē\ *n*, *pl* **so·lem·ni·ties** **1** : a solemn ceremony, event, day, or speech **2** : formal dignity

so·lic·it \sə-'lis-ət\ *vb* **1** : to come to with a request or plea **2** : to try to get ⟨*solicited* the help of their neighbors⟩

¹sol·id \'säl-əd\ *adj* **1** : not hollow **2** : not loose or spongy : COMPACT ⟨a *solid* mass of rock⟩ **3** : neither liquid nor gaseous **4** : made firmly and well ⟨a *solid* chair⟩ **5** : being without a break, interruption, or change ⟨practiced for three *solid* hours⟩ **6** : UNANIMOUS ⟨had the *solid* support of her party⟩ **7** : RELIABLE, DEPENDABLE ⟨a *solid* citizen⟩ **8** : of one material, kind, or color ⟨*solid* gold⟩ **synonyms** see HARD — **sol·id·ly** *adv* — **sol·id·ness** *n*

²solid *n* **1** : something that has length,

width, and thickness **2** : a solid substance : a substance that keeps its size and shape

so·lid·i·fy \sə-'lid-ə-ˌfi\ *vb* **so·lid·i·fied; so·lid·i·fy·ing** : to make or become solid

so·lid·i·ty \sə-'lid-ət-ē\ *n, pl* **so·lid·i·ties** : the quality or state of being solid

sol·i·taire \'säl-ə-ˌtaər, -ˌteər\ *n* : a card game played by one person alone

sol·i·tary \'säl-ə-ˌter-ē\ *adj* **1** : all alone ⟨a *solitary* traveler⟩ **2** : seldom visited : LONELY **3** : growing or living alone : not one of a group or cluster ⟨*solitary* insects⟩ **synonyms** see ALONE

sol·i·tude \'säl-ə-ˌtüd, -ˌtyüd\ *n* **1** : the quality or state of being alone or away from others : SECLUSION **2** : a lonely place

¹so·lo \'sō-lō\ *n, pl* **so·los 1** : music played or sung by one person either alone or with accompaniment **2** : an action (as in a dance) in which there is only one performer

²solo *adv or adj* : ²ALONE 2 ⟨fly *solo*⟩ ⟨a *solo* dancer⟩

³solo *vb* : to fly solo in an airplane

so·lo·ist \'sō-lə-wəst\ *n* : a person who performs a solo

sol·stice \'säl-stəs, 'sōl-, 'sȯl-\ *n* : the time of the year when the sun is farthest north (**summer solstice,** about June 22) or south (**winter solstice,** about December 22) of the equator

sol·u·ble \'säl-yə-bəl\ *adj* **1** : capable of being dissolved in liquid ⟨sugar is *soluble* in water⟩ **2** : capable of being solved or explained ⟨a *soluble* mystery⟩ ⟨a *soluble* problem⟩

so·lu·tion \sə-'lü-shən\ *n* **1** : the act or process of solving **2** : the result of solving a problem ⟨a correct *solution*⟩ **3** : the act or process by which a solid, liquid, or gas is dissolved in a liquid **4** : a liquid in which something has been dissolved

solve \'sälv, 'sȯlv\ *vb* **solved; solv·ing** : to find the answer to or a solution for

sol·vent \'säl-vənt, 'sȯl-\ *n* : a usually liquid substance in which another substance can dissolve ⟨water is a *solvent* for sugar⟩

som·ber *or* **som·bre** \'säm-bər\ *adj* **1** : being dark and gloomy : DULL ⟨*somber* colors⟩ **2** : showing or causing low spirits ⟨a *somber* mood⟩

som·bre·ro \səm-'breər-ō\ *n, pl* **som·bre·ros** : a tall hat of felt or straw with a very wide brim worn especially in the Southwest and Mexico

¹some \'səm *or; for 2 and 3,* səm\ *adj* **1** : being one unknown or not specified ⟨*some* person called⟩ **2** : being one, a part, or an unspecified number of some-

thing ⟨*some* gems are hard⟩ **3** : being of an amount or number that is not mentioned ⟨buy *some* flour⟩ **4** : being at least one and sometimes all of ⟨*some* years ago⟩

²some \'səm\ *pron* : a certain number or amount ⟨*some* of the milk has spilled⟩ ⟨*some* of the puppies are for sale⟩

¹-some \səm\ *adj suffix* : distinguished by a specified thing, quality, state, or action ⟨trouble*some*⟩

²-some *n suffix* : group of so many members ⟨four*some*⟩

¹some·body \'səm-ˌbäd-ē, -bəd-ē\ *pron* : some person ⟨*somebody* was looking for you⟩

²somebody *n, pl* **some·bod·ies** : a person of importance ⟨wanted to be a *somebody*⟩

some·day \'səm-ˌdā\ *adv* : at some future time

some·how \'səm-ˌhau̇\ *adv* : in one way or another

some·one \'səm-wən, -ˌwən\ *pron* : some person ⟨*someone* has to do the job⟩

¹som·er·sault \'səm-ər-ˌsȯlt\ *n* : a moving of the body through one complete turn in which the feet move up and over the head

²somersault *vb* : to turn a somersault

some·thing \'səm-thing\ *pron* **1** : a thing that is not surely known or understood ⟨we'll have to do *something* about it soon⟩ **2** : a thing or amount that is clearly known but not named ⟨I have *something* here for you⟩ **3** : SOMEWHAT ⟨is *something* of an expert⟩

some·time \'səm-ˌtīm\ *adv* **1** : at a future time ⟨will pay *sometime*⟩ **2** : at a time not known or not specified

sombrero

\ə\ **abut**	\au̇\ **out**	\i\ **tip**	\ȯ\ **saw**	\u̇\ **foot**
\ər\ **further**	\ch\ **chin**	\ī\ **life**	\ȯi\ **coin**	\y\ **yet**
\a\ **mat**	\e\ **pet**	\j\ **job**	\th\ **thin**	\yü\ **few**
\ā\ **take**	\ē\ **easy**	\ng\ **sing**	\ṯh\ **this**	\yu̇\ **cure**
\ä\ **cot, cart**	\g\ **go**	\ō\ **bone**	\ü\ **food**	\zh\ **vision**

some·times \'səm-ˌtīmz\ *adv* : now and then : OCCASIONALLY

some·way \'səm-ˌwā\ *adv* : SOMEHOW

¹**some·what** \'səm-ˌhwät, -ˌwät, -ˌhwət, -ˌwət\ *pron* : some amount or extent ⟨came as *somewhat* of a surprise⟩

²**somewhat** *adv* : to some extent ⟨*somewhat* more comfortable⟩

some·where \'səm-ˌhweər, -ˌweər, -ˌhwaər, -ˌwaər\ *adv* **1** : in, at, or to a place not known or named **2** : at some time not specified ⟨*somewhere* around two o'clock⟩

son \'sən\ *n* **1** : a male child or offspring **2** *cap* : the second person of the Trinity **3** : a man or boy closely associated with or thought of as a child of something (as a country, race, or religion) ⟨*sons* of liberty⟩

so·na·ta \sə-'nät-ə\ *n* : a musical composition usually for a single instrument consisting of three or four separate sections in different forms and keys

song \'sȯng\ *n* **1** : vocal music **2** : poetic composition : POETRY **3** : a short musical composition of words and music **4** : a small amount ⟨can be bought for a *song*⟩

song·bird \'sȯng-ˌbərd\ *n* : a bird that sings

song·ster \'sȯng-stər\ *n* : a person or a bird that sings

son·ic \'sän-ik\ *adj* : using, produced by, or relating to sound waves

sonic boom *n* : a sound like an explosion made by an aircraft traveling at supersonic speed

son–in–law \'sən-ən-ˌlȯ\ *n, pl* **sons–in–law** : the husband of one's daughter

son·ny \'sən-ē\ *n, pl* **son·nies** : a young boy — used mostly to address a stranger

so·no·rous \sə-'nōr-əs, 'sän-ə-rəs\ *adj* **1** : producing sound (as when struck) **2** : loud, deep, or rich in sound : RESONANT

soon \'sün\ *adv* **1** : without delay : before long **2** : in a prompt way : QUICKLY **3** : ¹EARLY 2 ⟨arrived too *soon*⟩ **4** : by choice : WILLINGLY ⟨would *sooner* walk than ride⟩

soot \'sut, 'sət\ *n* : a black powder formed when something is burned : the very fine powder that colors smoke

soothe \'süth\ *vb* **soothed; sooth·ing 1** : to please by praise or attention **2** : RELIEVE 1 **3** : to calm down : COMFORT

sooth·say·er \'süth-ˌsā-ər\ *n* : a person who claims to foretell events

sooty \'sut-ē, 'sət-\ *adj* **soot·i·er; soot·i·est 1** : soiled with soot **2** : like soot especially in color

sop \'säp\ *vb* **sopped; sop·ping 1** : to soak or dip in or as if in liquid **2** : to mop up (as water)

soph·o·more \'säf-ˌmōr, 'säf-ə-ˌmōr\ *n* : a student in his or her second year at a high school or college

so·pra·no \sə-'pran-ō, -'prän-\ *n, pl* **so·pra·nos 1** : the highest part in harmony having four parts **2** : the highest singing voice of women or boys **3** : a person having a soprano voice **4** : an instrument having a soprano range or part

sor·cer·er \'sȯr-sər-ər\ *n* : a person who practices sorcery or witchcraft : WIZARD

sor·cer·ess \'sȯr-sə-rəs\ *n* : a woman who practices sorcery or witchcraft : WITCH

sor·cery \'sȯr-sə-rē\ *n, pl* **sor·cer·ies** : the use of magic : WITCHCRAFT

sor·did \'sȯrd-əd\ *adj* **1** : very dirty : FOUL ⟨*sordid* surroundings⟩ **2** : of low moral quality : VILE ⟨a *sordid* life⟩

¹**sore** \'sōr\ *adj* **sor·er; sor·est 1** : causing distress ⟨*sore* news⟩ **2** : very painful or sensitive : TENDER ⟨muscles *sore* from exercise⟩ **3** : hurt or red and swollen so as to be or seem painful **4** : ANGRY — **sore·ly** *adv* — **sore·ness** *n*

²**sore** *n* : a sore spot (as an ulcer) on the body usually with the skin broken or bruised and often with infection

sor·ghum \'sȯr-gəm\ *n* **1** : a tall grass that looks like Indian corn and includes sorgo and other forms used for forage and grain **2** : syrup from sorgo juice

sor·go \'sȯr-gō\ *n, pl* **sor·gos** : a sorghum grown mostly for its sweet juice from which syrup is made and for fodder and silage

so·ror·i·ty \sə-'rȯr-ət-ē\ *n, pl* **so·ror·i·ties** : a club of girls or women especially at a college

¹**sor·rel** \'sȯr-əl\ *n* **1** : an animal (as a horse) of a sorrel color **2** : a brownish orange to light brown

sorghum

²**sorrel** *n* : any of several plants with sour juice

¹**sor·row** \'sär-ō\ *n* **1** : sadness or grief caused by loss (as of something loved) **2** : a cause of grief or sadness **3** : a feeling of regret

synonyms SORROW, GRIEF, and WOE mean distress of mind. SORROW suggests a feeling that something has been lost and often feelings of guilt and regret ⟨expressed *sorrow* for having caused the accident⟩ GRIEF stresses feeling great sorrow usually for a particular reason ⟨the *grief* of the parents when their only child died⟩ WOE suggests feeling hopeless and miserable ⟨all my troubles left me in a state of *woe*⟩

²sorrow *vb* : to feel or express sorrow : GRIEVE

sor·row·ful \'sär-ō-fəl, -ə-fəl\ *adj* **1** : full of or showing sorrow ⟨a *sorrowful* face⟩ **2** : causing sorrow

sor·ry \'sär-ē\ *adj* **sor·ri·er; sor·ri·est 1** : feeling sorrow or regret ⟨*sorry* for the mistake⟩ **2** : causing sorrow, pity, or scorn : WRETCHED ⟨a *sorry* sight⟩

¹sort \'sȯrt\ *n* **1** : a group of persons or things that have something in common : CLASS ⟨all *sorts* of people⟩ **2** : PERSON 1, INDIVIDUAL ⟨not a bad *sort*⟩ **3** : general disposition : NATURE ⟨people of an evil *sort*⟩ — **out of sorts 1** : not feeling well **2** : easily angered : IRRITABLE

²sort *vb* : to separate and arrange according to kind or class : CLASSIFY ⟨*sort* mail⟩

SOS \ˌes-ō-'es\ *n* **1** : an international radio code distress signal used especially by ships and airplanes calling for help **2** : a call for help

¹so-so \'sō-'sō\ *adv* : fairly well ⟨did *so-so* on the test⟩

²so-so *adj* : neither very good nor very bad

sought *past of* SEEK

soul \'sōl\ *n* **1** : the spiritual part of a person believed to give life to the body **2** : the essential part of something **3** : a person who leads or stirs others to action : LEADER ⟨the *soul* of the campaign⟩ **4** : a person's moral and emotional nature **5** : human being : PERSON ⟨a kind *soul*⟩

¹sound \'saȯnd\ *adj* **1** : free from flaw or decay ⟨*sound* timbers⟩ **2** : free from disease or weakness ⟨a *sound* body⟩ **3** : ¹SOLID 4, FIRM ⟨a building of *sound* construction⟩ **4** : free from error ⟨a *sound* argument⟩ **5** : showing good sense : WISE ⟨*sound* advice⟩ **6** : based on the truth ⟨*sound* beliefs⟩ **7** : THOROUGH 1 ⟨a *sound* beating⟩ **8** : ¹DEEP 5, UNDISTURBED ⟨a *sound* sleep⟩ — **sound·ly** *adv* — **sound·ness** *n*

²sound *adv* : to the full extent ⟨*sound* asleep⟩

³sound *n* **1** : the sensation experienced through the sense of hearing : an instance or occurrence of this **2** : one of the noises that together make up human speech ⟨the *sound* \s\ in "sit"⟩ **3** : the suggestion carried or given by something heard or read ⟨this excuse has a suspicious *sound*⟩ **4** : hearing distance : EARSHOT — **sound·less** \'saȯnd-ləs\ *adj* — **sound·less·ly** *adv*

⁴sound *vb* **1** : to make or cause to make a sound or noise ⟨*sound* the trumpet⟩ **2** : PRONOUNCE 2 ⟨*sound* each word clearly⟩ **3** : to make known : PROCLAIM ⟨*sound* the alarm⟩ **4** : to order, signal, or indicate by a sound ⟨the clock *sounded* noon⟩ **5** : to make or give an impression : SEEM ⟨the story *sounds* false⟩

⁵sound *n* : a long stretch of water that is wider than a strait and often connects two larger bodies of water or forms a channel between the mainland and an island

⁶sound *vb* **1** : to measure the depth of (as by a weighted line dropped down from the surface) **2** : to find or try to find the thoughts or feelings of a person ⟨*sounded* them out on the idea⟩

sound·proof \'saȯnd-'prüf\ *adj* : capable of keeping sound from entering or escaping ⟨a *soundproof* room⟩

sound wave *n* : a wave that is produced when a sound is made and is responsible for carrying the sound to the ear

soup \'süp\ *n* : a liquid food made from the liquid in which vegetables, meat, or fish have been cooked and often containing pieces of solid food

¹sour \'saȯr\ *adj* **1** : having an acid taste **2** : having become acid through spoiling ⟨*sour* milk⟩ **3** : suggesting decay ⟨a *sour* smell⟩ **4** : not pleasant or friendly ⟨a *sour* look⟩ **5** : acid in reaction ⟨*sour* soil⟩ — **sour·ish** \-ish\ *adj* — **sour·ly** *adv* — **sour·ness** *n*

²sour *vb* : to make or become sour

source \'sōrs\ *n* **1** : the beginning of a stream of water **2** : the cause or starting point of something ⟨nobody knows the *source* of the rumor⟩ **3** : one that supplies information

sou·sa·phone \'sü-zə-

sousaphone

fōn, -sə-\ *n* : a large circular tuba designed to rest on the player's shoulder and used chiefly in marching bands

¹south \'saůth\ *adv* : to or toward the south

²south *adj* : placed toward, facing, or coming from the south

³south *n* **1** : the direction to the right of one facing east : the compass point opposite to north **2** *cap* : regions or countries south of a point that is mentioned or understood

¹South American *adj* : of or relating to South America or the South Americans

²South American *n* : a person born or living in South America

south·bound \'saůth-,baůnd\ *adj* : going south

¹south·east \saů-'thēst\ *adv* : to or toward the southeast

²southeast *n* **1** : the direction between south and east **2** *cap* : regions or countries southeast of a point that is mentioned or understood

³southeast *adj* : placed toward, facing, or coming from the southeast

south·east·er·ly \saů-'thē-stər-lē\ *adv or adj* **1** : from the southeast **2** : toward the southeast

south·east·ern \saů-'thē-stərn\ *adj* **1** *often cap* : of, relating to, or like that of the Southeast **2** : lying toward or coming from the southeast

south·er·ly \'səth-ər-lē\ *adv or adj* **1** : toward the south **2** : from the south ⟨a *southerly* wind⟩

south·ern \'səth-ərn\ *adj* **1** *often cap* : of, relating to, or like that of the South **2** : lying toward or coming from the south

South·ern·er \'səth-ər-nər\ *n* : a person who is born or lives in the South

south·paw \'saůth-,pȯ\ *n* : a person (as a baseball pitcher) who is left-handed

south pole *n, often cap S&P* **1** : the most southern point of the earth : the southern end of the earth's axis **2** : the end of a magnet that points toward the south when the magnet is free to swing

¹south·ward \'saůth-wərd\ *adv or adj* : toward the south

²southward *n* : a southward direction or part

¹south·west \saůth-'west\ *adv* : to or toward the southwest

²southwest *n* **1** : the direction between south and west **2** *cap* : regions or countries southwest of a point that is mentioned or understood

³southwest *adj* : placed toward, facing, or coming from the southwest

south·west·er·ly \saůth-'wes-tər-lē\ *adv*

or adj **1** : from the southwest **2** : toward the southwest

south·west·ern \saůth-'wes-tərn\ *adj* **1** *often cap* : of, relating to, or like that of the Southwest **2** : lying toward or coming from the southwest

sou·ve·nir \'sü-və-,niər\ *n* : something that serves as a reminder

sou'·west·er \saů-'wes-tər\ *n* : a waterproof hat with wide slanting brim that is longer in back than in front

sou'wester

¹sov·er·eign \'säv-ə-rən, 'säv-rən\ *n* **1** : a person (as a king or queen) or body of persons having the highest power and authority in a state **2** : an old British gold coin

²sovereign *adj* **1** : highest in power or authority ⟨a *sovereign* ruler⟩ **2** : having independent authority ⟨a *sovereign* state⟩

sov·er·eign·ty \'säv-ə-rən-tē, 'säv-rən-\ *n, pl* **sov·er·eign·ties** **1** : supreme power especially over a political unit **2** : freedom from outside control **3** : one (as a country) that is sovereign

¹sow \'saů\ *n* : an adult female hog

²sow \'sō\ *vb* **sowed; sown** \'sōn\ *or* **sowed; sow·ing** **1** : to plant or scatter (as seed) for growing **2** : to cover with or as if with scattered seed for growing ⟨*sow* a field to oats⟩ **3** : to set in motion : cause to exist ⟨*sow* discontent⟩ — **sow·er** *n*

sow bug \'saů-\ *n* : WOOD LOUSE

sox *pl of* SOCK

soy·bean \'sȯi-,bēn\ *n* : an annual Asian plant related to the clovers that is widely grown especially for its edible seeds which yield a valuable oil (**soybean oil**) and a residue (**soybean oil meal** or **soybean meal**) containing much protein and used in animal feeds and in the chemical industry

¹space \'spās\ *n* **1** : a period of time **2** : a part of a distance, area, or volume that can be measured **3** : a certain place set apart or available ⟨a parking *space*⟩ **4** : the area without limits in which all things exist and move **5** : the region beyond the earth's atmosphere **6** : an empty place

²space *vb* **spaced; spac·ing** : to place with space between

space·craft \'spā-,skraft\ *n, pl* **spacecraft** : a vehicle for travel beyond the earth's atmosphere

space·man \'spā-,sman, -smən\ *n, pl*
space·men \'spā-,smen, -smən\ : a person who travels outside the earth's atmosphere

space·ship \'spās-,ship\ *n* : SPACECRAFT

space shuttle *n* : a spacecraft designed to transport people and cargo between earth and space that can be used repeatedly

space station *n* : an artificial satellite designed to stay in orbit permanently and to be occupied by humans for long periods

space suit *n* : a suit equipped to keep its wearer alive in space

spa·cious \'spā-shəs\ *adj* : having ample space

¹**spade** \'spād\ *n* : a kind of shovel made so that it can be pushed into the ground with the foot

²**spade** *vb* **spad·ed; spad·ing** : to dig with a spade

spa·ghet·ti \spə-'get-ē\ *n* : a food made of a mixture of flour and water and dried in the form of strings that are prepared for eating by boiling

¹**span** \'span\ *n* **1** : the distance from the end of the thumb to the end of the little finger when the hand is stretched wide open **2** : a limited portion of time ⟨*span* of life⟩ **3** : the spread (as of an arch) from one support to another

²**span** *vb* **spanned; span·ning 1** : to measure by or as if by the hand stretched wide open **2** : to reach or extend across ⟨a bridge *spans* the river⟩ **3** : to place or construct a span over

³**span** *n* : two animals (as mules) worked or driven as a pair

span·gle \'spang-gəl\ *n* : SEQUIN

Span·iard \'span-yərd\ *n* : a person born or living in Spain

span·iel \'span-yəl\ *n* : a small or medium-sized dog with a thick wavy coat, long drooping ears, and usually short legs

Word History There are many kinds of spaniels today that come from different places in Europe. The ancestors of all spaniels, however, came from Spain. The English word *spaniel* came from an early French word that meant "Spaniard."

¹**Span·ish** \'span-ish\ *adj* : of or relating to Spain, its people, or the Spanish language

²**Spanish** *n* **1** : the language of Spain and the countries colonized by Spaniards **2 Spanish** *pl* : the people of Spain

spank \'spangk\ *vb* : to strike on the buttocks with the open hand

spank·ing \'spang-king\ *adj* : BRISK 1, LIVELY ⟨a *spanking* breeze⟩

¹**spar** \'spär\ *n* : a long rounded piece of wood or metal (as a mast, yard, or boom) to which a sail is fastened

²**spar** *vb* **sparred; spar·ring 1** : to box or make boxing movements with the fists for practice or in fun **2** : ²SKIRMISH

¹**spare** \'spaər, 'speər\ *vb* **spared; spar·ing 1** : to keep from being punished or harmed : show mercy to ⟨will *spare* the prisoners⟩ **2** : to free of the need to do something ⟨was *spared* the work⟩ **3** : to keep from using or spending ⟨more pancakes, please, and don't *spare* the syrup⟩ **4** : to give up especially as not really needed ⟨can you *spare* me a few minutes?⟩⟨couldn't *spare* a dime⟩ **5** : to have left over ⟨got there with time to *spare*⟩

²**spare** *adj* **spar·er; spar·est 1** : held in reserve ⟨a *spare* tire⟩ **2** : being over what is needed ⟨*spare* time⟩ **3** : somewhat thin **4** : SCANTY

³**spare** *n* **1** : a spare or duplicate piece or part **2** : the knocking down of all ten bowling pins with the first two balls

spare·ribs \'spaər-,ribz, 'speər-\ *n pl* : a cut of pork ribs separated from the bacon strips

spar·ing \'spaər-ing, 'speər-\ *adj* : careful in the use of money or supplies **synonyms** see ECONOMICAL — **spar·ing·ly** *adv*

¹**spark** \'spärk\ *n* **1** : a small bit of burning material **2** : a hot glowing bit struck from a mass (as by steel on flint) **3** : a short bright flash of electricity between two points **4** : ²SPARKLE 1 **5** : ¹TRACE 2 ⟨showed a *spark* of interest⟩

spaniel

\ə\ **abut**	\au̇\ **out**	\i\ **tip**	\ȯ\ **saw**	\u̇\ **foot**
\ər\ **further**	\ch\ **chin**	\ī\ **life**	\oi̇\ **coin**	\y\ **yet**
\a\ **mat**	\e\ **pet**	\j\ **job**	\th\ **thin**	\yü\ **few**
\ā\ **take**	\ē\ **easy**	\ng\ **sing**	\th̲\ **this**	\yu̇\ **cure**
\ä\ **cot, cart**	\g\ **go**	\ō\ **bone**	\ü\ **food**	\zh\ **vision**

²**spark** *vb* **1** : to give off or cause to give off sparks **2** : to set off ⟨*spark* a discussion⟩

¹**spar·kle** \'spär-kəl\ *vb* **spar·kled; spar·kling** **1** : to throw off sparks **2** : to give off small flashes of light ⟨the diamond *sparkled*⟩ **3** : to be lively or active ⟨the conversation *sparkled*⟩ **synonyms** *see* GLEAM

²**sparkle** *n* **1** : a little flash of light **2** : the quality of sparkling ⟨the *sparkle* of a diamond⟩

spar·kler \'spär-klər\ *n* : a firework that throws off very bright sparks as it burns

spark plug *n* : a device used in an engine to produce a spark that ignites a fuel mixture

spar·row \'spar-ō\ *n* : a small brownish bird related to the finches

sparrow hawk *n* : a small hawk or falcon

sparse \'spärs\ *adj* **spars·er; spars·est** : not thickly grown or settled — **sparse·ly** *adv*

spasm \'spaz-əm\ *n* **1** : a sudden involuntary and usually violent contracting of muscles ⟨back *spasms*⟩ **2** : a sudden, violent, and temporary effort, emotion, or outburst ⟨a *spasm* of coughing⟩

spas·mod·ic \spaz-'mäd-ik\ *adj* : relating to or affected by spasm : involving spasms ⟨*spasmodic* breathing⟩ — **spas·mod·i·cal·ly** \-i-kə-lē\ *adv*

¹**spat** \'spat\ *past of* SPIT

²**spat** *n* : a cloth or leather covering for the instep and ankle

³**spat** *n* : a brief unimportant quarrel

spa·tial \'spā-shəl\ *adj* : of or relating to space

²**spat**

¹**spat·ter** \'spat-ər\ *vb* **1** : to splash with drops or small bits of something wet **2** : to scatter by splashing

²**spatter** *n* **1** : the act or sound of spattering **2** : a drop or splash spattered on something : a spot or stain due to spattering

spat·u·la \'spach-ə-lə\ *n* : a knifelike instrument with a broad flexible blade that is used mostly for spreading or mixing soft substances

¹**spawn** \'spȯn\ *vb* : to produce or deposit eggs or spawn ⟨salmon go up rivers to *spawn*⟩

²**spawn** *n* : the eggs of a water animal (as an oyster or fish) that produces many small eggs

spay \'spā\ *vb* : to remove the ovaries of (a female animal) ⟨a *spayed* cat⟩

speak \'spēk\ *vb* **spoke** \'spōk\; **spo·ken** \'spō-kən\; **speak·ing** **1** : to utter words : TALK **2** : to utter in words ⟨*speak* the truth⟩ **3** : to mention in speech or writing ⟨*spoke* of being ill⟩ **4** : to use or be able to use in talking ⟨*speak* French⟩

synonyms SPEAK, TALK, and CONVERSE mean to express oneself in words. SPEAK applies to anything said, whether it is understood or not and whether it is heard or not ⟨we didn't know what language they were *speaking*⟩ TALK suggests there is a listener who understands what is said and often that both people do some speaking ⟨we *talked* about school⟩ CONVERSE suggests an exchange of thoughts and opinions ⟨the scientists *conversed* about traveling in space⟩

speak·er \'spē-kər\ *n* **1** : a person who speaks **2** : a person who conducts a meeting **3** : LOUDSPEAKER

¹**spear** \'spiər\ *n* **1** : a weapon with a long straight handle and sharp head or blade used for throwing or jabbing **2** : an instrument with a sharp point and curved hooks used in spearing fish

²**spear** *vb* : to strike or pierce with or as if with a spear

³**spear** *n* : a usually young blade or sprout (as of grass)

¹**spear·head** \'spiər-ˌhed\ *n* **1** : the head or point of a spear **2** : the person, thing, or group that is the leading force (as in a development or an attack)

²**spearhead** *vb* : to serve as leader of ⟨*spearhead* a campaign for better schools⟩

spear·mint \'spiər-ˌmint\ *n* : a common mint used for flavoring

spe·cial \'spesh-əl\ *adj* **1** : UNUSUAL, EXTRAORDINARY ⟨a *special* occasion⟩ **2** : liked very well ⟨a *special* friend⟩ **3** : UNIQUE 2 ⟨a *special* case⟩ **4** : ¹EXTRA ⟨a *special* edition⟩ **5** : meant for a particular purpose or occasion ⟨a *special* diet⟩ — **spe·cial·ly** *adv*

spe·cial·ist \'spesh-ə-ləst\ *n* **1** : a person who studies or works at a special occupation or branch of learning ⟨an eye *specialist*⟩ **2** : a person working in a special skill in the Army in any of the four ranks equal to the ranks of corporal through sergeant first class

spe·cial·ize \'spesh-ə-ˌlīz\ *vb* **spe·cial·ized; spe·cial·iz·ing** **1** : to limit one's attention or energy to one business, subject, or study ⟨*specialize* in jet airplanes⟩ **2** : to change and develop so as to be suited for some particular use or living conditions ⟨*specialized* sense organs⟩

spe·cial·ty \'spesh-əl-tē\ *n, pl* **spe·cial·ties** **1** : a product of a special kind or of special excellence ⟨pancakes were the cook's *specialty*⟩ **2** : something a person specializes in

spe·cies \'spē-shēz, -sēz\ *n, pl* **species** **1** : a class of things of the same kind and with the same name : KIND, SORT **2** : a group of plants or animals that forms a distinct part of a genus and that is made up of related individuals producing or able to produce young one with another

spe·cif·ic \spi-'sif-ik\ *adj* **1** : being an actual example of a certain kind of thing ⟨a *specific* case⟩ **2** : clearly and exactly presented or stated ⟨*specific* directions⟩ **3** : of, relating to, or being a species

spec·i·fi·ca·tion \,spes-ə-fə-'kā-shən\ *n* **1** : the act or process of specifying **2** : a single specified item **3** : a description of work to be done or materials to be used — often used in pl. ⟨the architect's *specifications* for a new building⟩

spec·i·fy \'spes-ə-,fi\ *vb* **spec·i·fied; spec·i·fy·ing** **1** : to mention or name exactly and clearly ⟨*specify* the cause⟩ **2** : to include in a specification ⟨*specify* oak flooring⟩

spec·i·men \'spes-ə-mən\ *n* : a part or a single thing that shows what the whole thing or group is like : SAMPLE

speck \'spek\ *n* **1** : a small spot or blemish **2** : a very small amount : BIT

¹speck·le \'spek-əl\ *n* : a small mark (as of color)

²speckle *vb* **speck·led; speck·ling** : to mark with speckles

spec·ta·cle \'spek-ti-kəl\ *n* **1** : an unusual or impressive public display (as a big parade) **2 spectacles** *pl* : a pair of glasses held in place by parts passing over the ears

spec·tac·u·lar \spek-'tak-yə-lər\ *adj* : STRIKING, SHOWY ⟨a *spectacular* sunset⟩

spec·ta·tor \'spek-,tāt-ər\ *n* : a person who looks on (as at a sports event)

spec·ter *or* **spec·tre** \'spek-tər\ *n* : GHOST

spec·trum \'spek-trəm\ *n, pl* **spec·tra** \-trə\ *or* **spec·trums** : the group of different colors including red, orange, yellow, green, blue, indigo, and violet seen when light passes through a prism and falls on a surface or when sunlight is affected by drops of water (as in a rainbow)

spec·u·late \'spek-yə-,lāt\ *vb* **spec·u·lat·ed; spec·u·lat·ing** **1** : MEDITATE **2 2** : to engage in a business deal in which much profit may be made although at a big risk

spec·u·la·tion \,spek-yə-'lā-shən\ *n* **1** : ²GUESS **2** : the taking of a big risk in business in hopes of making a big profit

speech \'spēch\ *n* **1** : the communication or expression of thoughts in spoken words **2** : something that is spoken **3** : a public talk **4** : a form of communication (as a language or dialect) used by a particular group **5** : the power of expressing or communicating thoughts by speaking

speech·less \'spēch-ləs\ *adj* **1** : unable to speak **2** : not speaking for a time : SILENT ⟨*speechless* with surprise⟩

¹speed \'spēd\ *n* **1** : quickness in movement or action **2** : rate of moving or doing

²speed *vb* **sped** \'sped\ *or* **speed·ed; speed·ing** **1** : to move or cause to move fast : HURRY **2** : to go or drive at too high a speed **3** : to increase the speed of : ACCELERATE

speed·boat \'spēd-,bōt\ *n* : a fast motorboat

speed bump *n* : a low raised ridge across a roadway (as in a parking lot) to limit vehicle speed

speed·om·e·ter \spi-'däm-ət-ər\ *n* **1** : an instrument that measures speed **2** : an instrument that measures speed and records distance traveled

speedy \'spēd-ē\ *adj* **speed·i·er; speed·i·est** : moving or taking place fast ⟨made a *speedy* recovery⟩ — **speed·i·ly** \'spēd-l-ē\ *adv*

¹spell \'spel\ *n* **1** : a spoken word or group of words believed to have magic power : CHARM **2** : a very strong influence

²spell *vb* **1** : to name, write, or print in order the letters of a word **2** : to make up the letters of ⟨"c-a-t" *spells* the word "cat"⟩ **3** : to amount to : MEAN ⟨another drought would *spell* famine⟩

³spell *vb* : to take the place of for a time : RELIEVE ⟨*spell* a person at shoveling⟩

⁴spell *n* **1** : one's turn at work or duty **2** : a period spent in a job or occupation **3** : a short period of time **4** : a stretch of a specified kind of weather **5** : a period of bodily or mental distress or disorder

spell·bound \'spel-,baund\ *adj* : held by or as if by a spell

spell·er \'spel-ər\ *n* **1** : a person who spells words **2** : a book with exercises for teaching spelling

spell·ing \'spel-ing\ *n* **1** : the forming of words from letters **2** : the letters composing a word

\ə\ abut	\aù\ out	\i\ tip	\o\ saw	\ù\ foot
\ər\ further	\ch\ chin	\ī\ life	\oi\ coin	\y\ yet
\a\ mat	\e\ pet	\j\ job	\th\ thin	\yü\ few
\ā\ take	\ē\ easy	\ng\ sing	\th\ this	\yù\ cure
\ä\ cot, cart	\g\ go	\ō\ bone	\ü\ food	\zh\ vision

spend \'spend\ *vb* **spent** \'spent\; **spend-ing 1 :** to use up : pay out **2 :** to wear out : EXHAUST **3 :** to use wastefully : SQUAN-DER **4 :** to cause or allow (as time) to pass

spend·thrift \'spend-,thrift\ *n* : one who spends wastefully

spent \'spent\ *adj* **1 :** used up **2 :** drained of energy

sperm \'spərm\ *n* : SPERM CELL

sperm cell *n* : a male germ cell

sperm whale *n* : a large whale of warm seas hunted mostly for its oil (**sperm oil**)

sperm whale

spew \'spyü\ *vb* : to pour out ⟨a volcano *spewing* lava⟩

sphere \'sfiər\ *n* **1 :** a body (as the moon) shaped like a ball **2 :** a figure so shaped that every point on its surface is an equal distance from the center of the figure **3 :** a field of influence or activity ⟨a subject out-side one's *sphere*⟩

spher·i·cal \'sfir-i-kəl, 'sfer-\ *adj* : relating to or having the form of a sphere

sphinx \'sfingks\ *n* : an Egyptian figure having the body of a lion and the head of a man, a ram, or a hawk

sphinx

¹spice \'spīs\ *n* **1 :** a plant product (as pepper or nutmeg) that has a strong pleasant smell and is used to flavor food **2 :** something that adds interest ⟨variety is the *spice* of life⟩

²spice *vb* **spiced; spic·ing :** to season with or as if with spices

spick–and–span *or* **spic–and–span** \,spik-ən-'span\ *adj* **1 :** quite new and un-used **2 :** very clean and neat

spicy \'spī-sē\ *adj* **spic·i·er; spic·i·est 1 :** flavored with or containing spice **2 :** somewhat shocking or indecent ⟨a *spicy* story⟩

spi·der \'spīd-ər\ *n* **1 :** a wingless animal somewhat like an insect but having eight legs instead of six and a body divided into two parts instead of three **2 :** a cast-iron frying pan

spi·der·web \'spīd-ər-,web\ *n* : the silken web spun by most spiders and used as a resting place and a trap for prey

spig·ot \'spig-ət, 'spik-\ *n* **1 :** a plug used to stop the vent in a barrel **2 :** FAUCET

¹spike \'spīk\ *n* **1 :** a very large nail **2 :** one of the metal objects attached to the heel and sole of a shoe (as a baseball shoe) to prevent slipping

²spike *vb* **spiked; spik·ing 1 :** to fasten with spikes **2 :** to pierce or cut with or on a spike

³spike *n* **1 :** an ear of grain ⟨*spikes* of wheat⟩ **2 :** a long usually rather narrow flower cluster in which the blossoms grow very close to a central stem

¹spill \'spil\ *vb* **spilled** \'spild\ *also* **spilt** \'spilt\; **spill·ing 1 :** to cause (blood) to flow by wounding or killing **2 :** to let (liquid) fall, flow, or run out by accident **3 :** to fall or run out and be lost or wasted ⟨the milk *spilled*⟩ **4 :** to let out : make known ⟨*spill* a secret⟩

²spill *n* **1 :** an act of spilling **2 :** a fall especially from a horse or vehicle **3 :** something spilled ⟨mop up a *spill* on the floor⟩

¹spin \'spin\ *vb* **spun** \'spən\; **spin·ning 1 :** to make yarn or thread from (fibers) ⟨*spin* flax⟩ **2 :** to make (yarn or thread) from fibers ⟨*spin* thread⟩ **3 :** to form threads or a web or cocoon by giving off a sticky fluid that quickly hardens into silk **4 :** to turn or cause to turn round and round rapidly : TWIRL ⟨*spin* a top⟩ **5 :** to feel as if in a whirl ⟨my head was *spinning*⟩ **6 :** to make up and tell using the imagination ⟨*spin* a yarn⟩ **7 :** to move swiftly on wheels or in a vehicle **8 :** to make, shape, or produce by or as if by whirling ⟨*spun* sugar⟩

²spin *n* **1 :** a rapid whirling motion **2 :** a short trip in or on a wheeled vehicle ⟨let's take a *spin* on our bikes⟩

spin·ach \'spin-ich\ *n* : a leafy plant that is grown for use as food

spi·nal \'spīn-l\ *adj* : of, relating to, or lo-cated near the backbone or the spinal cord — **spi·nal·ly** *adv*

spinal column *n* : BACKBONE 1

spinal cord *n* : the thick cord of nervous tissue that extends from the brain down the back, fills the cavity of the backbone, and is concerned especially with reflex action

spin·dle \'spin-dəl\ *n* **1** : a slender round rod or stick with narrowed ends by which thread is twisted in spinning and on which it is wound **2** : something (as an axle or shaft) which is shaped or turned like a spindle or on which something turns

spin·dling \'spin-dling\ *adj* : being long or tall and thin and usually feeble or weak

spin·dly \'spin-dlē\ *adj* **spin·dli·er; spin·dli·est** : SPINDLING

spine \'spīn\ *n* **1** : BACKBONE 1 **2** : a stiff pointed part growing from the surface of a plant or animal

spine·less \'spīn-ləs\ *adj* **1** : lacking spines **2** : having no backbone **3** : lacking spirit, courage, or determination

spin·et \'spin-ət\ *n* : a low piano built with the strings running up and down

spin·ning jen·ny \'spin-ing-ˌjen-ē\ *n, pl* **spin·ning jen·nies** : an early machine for spinning wool or cotton by means of many spindles

spinning wheel *n* : a small machine driven by the hand or foot that is used to spin yarn or thread

spin·ster \'spin-stər\ *n* : an unmarried woman past the usual age for marrying

spiny \'spī-nē\ *adj* **spin·i·er; spin·i·est** : covered with spines

spinning wheel

spir·a·cle \'spir-ə-kəl\ *n* : an opening (as in the head of a whale or the abdomen of an insect) for breathing

¹spi·ral \'spī-rəl\ *adj* **1** : circling around a center like the thread of a screw ⟨a *spiral* staircase⟩ **2** : winding or circling around a center and gradually getting closer to or farther away from it ⟨the *spiral* curve of a watch spring⟩ — **spi·ral·ly** *adv*

²spiral *n* **1** : a single turn or coil in a spiral object **2** : something that has a spiral form

³spiral *vb* **spi·raled** *or* **spi·ralled; spi·ral·ing** *or* **spi·ral·ling** : to move in a spiral path

spire \'spīr\ *n* **1** : a pointed roof especially of a tower **2** : STEEPLE

spi·rea *or* **spi·raea** \spī-'rē-ə\ *n* : a shrub related to the roses that bears clusters of small white or pink flowers

¹spir·it \'spir-ət\ *n* **1** : a force within a human being thought to give the body life, energy, and power : SOUL **2** *cap* : the active presence of God in human life **3** : a being (as a ghost) whose existence cannot be explained by the known laws of nature **4** : ¹MOOD ⟨in good *spirits*⟩ **5** : a lively or brisk quality **6** : an attitude governing one's actions ⟨said in a *spirit* of fun⟩ **7** : PERSON 1 ⟨a bold *spirit*⟩ **8** : an alcoholic liquor — usually used in pl. **9 spirits** *pl* : a solution in alcohol ⟨*spirits* of camphor⟩ **10** : real meaning or intention ⟨the *spirit* of the law⟩ — **spir·it·less** \-ləs\ *adj*

²spirit *vb* : to carry off secretly or mysteriously

spir·it·ed \'spir-ət-əd\ *adj* : full of courage or energy

¹spir·i·tu·al \'spir-i-chə-wəl\ *adj* **1** : of, relating to, or consisting of spirit : not bodily or material **2** : of or relating to sacred or religious matters — **spir·i·tu·al·ly** *adv*

²spiritual *n* : a religious folk song developed especially among Negroes of the southern United States

¹spit \'spit\ *n* **1** : a thin pointed rod for holding meat over a fire **2** : a small point of land that runs out into a body of water

²spit *vb* **spit** *or* **spat** \'spat\; **spit·ting 1** : to cause (as saliva) to spurt from the mouth **2** : to express by or as if by spitting ⟨*spitting* an angry answer⟩ **3** : to give off usually briskly : EMIT ⟨the fire is *spitting* sparks⟩ **4** : to rain lightly or snow in flurries

³spit *n* **1** : SALIVA **2** : the act of spitting **3** : a foamy material given out by some insects **4** : perfect likeness ⟨the child was the *spit* and image of the parent⟩

¹spite \'spīt\ *n* : dislike or hatred for another person with a wish to torment, anger, or defeat — **in spite of** : without being stopped by ⟨succeeded *in spite of* many difficulties⟩

²spite *vb* **spit·ed; spit·ing** : ANNOY, ANGER ⟨did it to *spite* me⟩

spite·ful \'spīt-fəl\ *adj* : filled with or showing spite : MALICIOUS — **spite·ful·ly** \-fə-lē\ *adv*

spit·tle \'spit-l\ *n* **1** : SALIVA **2** : ³SPIT 3

¹splash \'splash\ *vb* **1** : to hit (something liquid or sloppy) and cause to move and scatter roughly ⟨*splash* water⟩ **2** : to wet or soil by spattering with water or mud ⟨*splashed* by a passing car⟩ **3** : to move or strike with a splashing sound ⟨*splash* through a puddle⟩ **4** : to spread or scatter

\ə\ abut	\au̇\ out	\i\ tip	\o̅\ saw	\u̇\ foot
\ər\ further	\ch\ chin	\ī\ life	\o̅i\ coin	\y\ yet
\a\ mat	\e\ pet	\j\ job	\th\ thin	\yü\ few
\ā\ take	\ē\ easy	\ng\ sing	\th\ this	\yu̇\ cure
\ä\ cot, cart	\g\ go	\o̅\ bone	\ü\ food	\zh\ vision

like a splashed liquid ⟨the sunset *splashed* the sky with red⟩

²splash *n* **1** : splashed material **2** : a spot or smear from or as if from splashed liquid **3** : the sound or action of splashing

¹splat•ter \'splat-ər\ *vb* : ¹SPLASH, SPATTER

²splatter *n* : ²SPLASH

spleen \'splēn\ *n* : an organ near the stomach that destroys worn-out red blood cells and produces some of the white blood cells

splen•did \'splen-dəd\ *adj* **1** : having or showing splendor : BRILLIANT **2** : impressive in beauty, excellence, or magnificence ⟨did a *splendid* job⟩ ⟨a *splendid* palace⟩ **3** : GRAND **4** — **splen•did•ly** *adv*

synonyms SPLENDID, GLORIOUS, and SUPERB mean very impressive. SPLENDID suggests that something is far above the ordinary in excellence or magnificence ⟨what a *splendid* idea⟩ ⟨a *splendid* jewel⟩ GLORIOUS suggests that something is radiant with light or beauty ⟨a *glorious* sunset⟩ SUPERB suggests the highest possible point of magnificence or excellence ⟨a *superb* museum⟩ ⟨the food was *superb*⟩

splen•dor \'splen-dər\ *n* **1** : great brightness ⟨the *splendor* of the sun⟩ **2** : POMP, GLORY ⟨the *splendors* of ancient Rome⟩

¹splice \'splīs\ *vb* **spliced; splic•ing 1** : to unite (as two ropes) by weaving together **2** : to unite (as rails or pieces of film) by connecting the ends together

splice

²splice *n* : a joining or joint made by splicing

splint \'splint\ *n* **1** : a thin flexible strip of wood woven together with others in making a chair seat or basket **2** : a device for keeping a broken or displaced bone in place

¹splin•ter \'splint-ər\ *n* : a thin piece split or torn off lengthwise : SLIVER

²splinter *vb* : to break into splinters

¹split \'split\ *vb* **split; split•ting 1** : to divide lengthwise or by layers ⟨*split* a log⟩ **2** : to separate the parts of by putting something between ⟨a river *split* the town⟩ **3** : to burst or break apart or in pieces ⟨the melon fell and *split* open⟩ **4**

: to divide into shares or sections ⟨we *split* the profit⟩

²split *n* **1** : a product or result of splitting : CRACK **2** : the act or process of splitting : DIVISION ⟨a *split* in a political party⟩ **3** : the feat of lowering oneself to the floor or leaping into the air with the legs extended in a straight line and in opposite directions

³split *adj* : divided by or as if by splitting

¹spoil \'spȯil\ *n* : stolen goods : PLUNDER

²spoil *vb* **spoiled** \'spȯild\ *or* **spoilt** \'spȯilt\; **spoil•ing 1** : ¹PLUNDER, ROB **2** : to damage badly : RUIN **3** : to damage the quality or effect of ⟨a quarrel *spoiled* the celebration⟩ **4** : to decay or lose freshness, value, or usefulness by being kept too long ⟨the milk *spoiled*⟩ **5** : to damage the disposition of by letting get away with too much ⟨*spoil* a child⟩

spoil•age \'spȯi-lij\ *n* : the action of spoiling or condition of being spoiled ⟨food *spoilage*⟩

¹spoke *past of* SPEAK

²spoke \'spōk\ *n* : one of the bars or rods extending from the hub of a wheel to the rim

¹spoken *past participle of* SPEAK

²spo•ken \'spō-kən\ *adj* **1** : expressed in speech : ORAL ⟨a *spoken* message⟩ **2** : used in speaking ⟨the *spoken* language⟩ **3** : speaking in a specified manner ⟨soft-*spoken*⟩

spoke

spokes•man \'spōk-smən\ *n, pl* **spokes-men** \'spōk-smən\ : SPOKESPERSON

spokes•per•son \'spōk-ˌspərs-n\ *n* : a person who speaks for another or for a group

spokes•wom•an \'spōk-ˌswu̇m-ən\ *n, pl* **spokes•wom•en** \-ˌswim-ən\ : a woman who is a spokesperson

¹sponge \'spənj\ *n* **1** : a springy mass of horny fibers that forms the skeleton of a group of sea animals, is able to absorb water freely, and is used for cleaning **2** : any of a group of water animals that have the form of hollow cell colonies made up of two layers and that include those whose skeletons are sponges **3** : a manufactured product (as of rubber or plastic) having the springy absorbent quality of natural sponge **4** : a pad of folded gauze used in surgery and medicine — **sponge-like** \-ˌlīk\ *adj*

²sponge *vb* **sponged; spong•ing 1** : to clean or wipe with a sponge **2** : to absorb with or like a sponge **3** : to get something or live at the expense of another

spongy \'spən-jē\ *adj* **spong·i·er; spong·i·est** : like a sponge in appearance or in ability to absorb : soft and full of holes or moisture

¹spon·sor \'spän-sər\ *n* **1** : a person who takes the responsibility for some other person or thing ⟨agreed to be our *sponsor* at the club⟩ **2** : GODPARENT **3** : a person or an organization that pays for or plans and carries out a project or activity **4** : a person or an organization that pays the cost of a radio or television program — **spon·sor·ship** \-,ship\ *n*

²sponsor *vb* : to act as sponsor for

spon·ta·ne·ous \spän-'tā-nē-əs\ *adj* **1** : done, said, or produced freely and naturally ⟨*spontaneous* laughter⟩ **2** : acting or taking place without outside force or cause — **spon·ta·ne·ous·ly** *adv*

spontaneous combustion *n* : a bursting of material into flame from the heat produced within itself through chemical action

spook \'spük\ *n* : GHOST, SPECTER

spooky \'spü-kē\ *adj* **spook·i·er; spook·i·est** **1** : like a ghost ⟨a *spooky* figure⟩ **2** : suggesting the presence of ghosts ⟨a *spooky* place⟩

¹spool \'spül\ *n* : a small cylinder which has rims at each end and on which thread or wire is wound

²spool *vb* : to wind on a spool

¹spoon \'spün\ *n* : a utensil with a shallow bowl and a handle used especially in cooking and eating

²spoon *vb* : to take up in or as if in a spoon

spoon·bill \'spün-,bil\ *n* : a wading bird

spoonbill

related to the ibises and having a bill which widens and flattens at the tip

spoon·ful \'spün-,ful\ *n, pl* **spoon·fuls** \-,fulz\ *or* **spoons·ful** \'spünz-,ful\ : as much as a spoon can hold

spore \'spōr\ *n* : a reproductive body of various plants and some lower animals that consists of a single cell and is able to produce a new individual — **spored** \'spōrd\ *adj*

¹sport \'spōrt\ *vb* **1** : to amuse oneself : FROLIC **2** : to speak or act in fun **3** : SHOW OFF ⟨*sport* new shoes⟩

²sport *n* **1** : PASTIME, RECREATION **2** : physical activity (as hunting or an athletic game) engaged in for pleasure **3** : ¹JEST 2 **4** : a person who shows good sportsmanship

sports·man \'spōrt-smən\ *n, pl* **sports·men** \'spōrt-smən\ : a person who engages in or is interested in sports and especially outdoor sports (as hunting and fishing)

sports·man·ship \'spōrt-smən-,ship\ *n* : fair play, respect for opponents, and gracious behavior in winning or losing

sports·wom·an \'spōrt-,swum-ən\ *n, pl* **sports·wom·en** \-,swim-ən\ : a woman who engages in or is interested in sports and especially outdoor sports

¹spot \'spät\ *n* **1** : something bad that others know about one : FAULT **2** : a small part that is different (as in color) from the main part **3** : an area soiled or marked (as by dirt) **4** : a particular place ⟨a good *spot* for a picnic⟩ — **spot·ted** \'spät-əd\ *adj* — **on the spot** **1** : right away : IMMEDIATELY **2** : at the place of action **3** : in difficulty or danger

²spot *vb* **spot·ted; spot·ting** **1** : to mark or be marked with spots **2** : to single out : IDENTIFY

spot·less \'spät-ləs\ *adj* : free from spot or blemish : perfectly clean or pure — **spot·less·ly** *adv* — **spot·less·ness** *n*

¹spot·light \'spät-,līt\ *n* **1** : a spot of light used to show up a particular area, person, or thing (as on a stage) **2** : public notice **3** : a light to direct a narrow strong beam of light on a small area

²spotlight *vb* **spot·light·ed** *or* **spot·lit** \-,lit\; **spot·light·ing** **1** : to light up with a spotlight **2** : to bring to public attention

spotted owl *n* : a rare brown owl with white spots and dark stripes that is found

\ə\ abut	\au̇\ out	\i\ tip	\ȯ\ saw	\u̇\ foot
\ər\ further	\ch\ chin	\ī\ life	\ȯi\ coin	\y\ yet
\a\ mat	\e\ pet	\j\ job	\th\ thin	\yü\ few
\ā\ take	\ē\ easy	\ng\ sing	\th\ this	\yu̇\ cure
\ä\ cot, cart	\g\ go	\ō\ bone	\ü\ food	\zh\ vision

from British Columbia to southern California and central Mexico

spot·ty \'spät-ē\ *adj* **spot·ti·er; spot·ti·est 1** : having spots **2** : not always the same especially in quality ⟨your work has been *spotty*⟩

spouse \'spaús\ *n* : a married person : HUSBAND, WIFE

¹spout \'spaút\ *vb* **1** : to shoot out (liquid) with force ⟨wells *spouting* oil⟩ **2** : to speak with a long and quick flow of words so as to sound important **3** : to flow out with force : SPURT

²spout *n* **1** : a tube, pipe, or hole through which something (as rainwater) spouts **2** : a sudden strong stream of fluid

¹sprain \'sprān\ *n* **1** : a sudden or severe twisting of a joint with stretching or tearing of ligaments **2** : a sprained condition

²sprain *vb* : to injure by a sudden or severe twist

sprang *past of* SPRING

¹sprawl \'spról\ *vb* **1** : to lie or sit with arms and legs spread out **2** : to spread out in an uneven or awkward way ⟨a *sprawling* city⟩

²sprawl *n* : the act or posture of sprawling

¹spray \'sprā\ *n* : a green or flowering branch or a usually flat arrangement of these

²spray *n* **1** : liquid flying in fine drops like water blown from a wave **2** : a burst of fine mist (as from an atomizer) **3** : a device (as an atomizer) for scattering a spray of liquid or mist

³spray *vb* **1** : to scatter or let fall in a spray ⟨*spray* paint⟩ **2** : to scatter spray on or into ⟨*spray* an orchard⟩ — **spray·er** *n*

spray gun *n* : a device for spraying paints, varnishes, or insect poisons

¹spread \'spred\ *vb* **spread; spread·ing 1** : to open over a larger area ⟨*spread* out a map⟩ **2** : to stretch out : EXTEND ⟨*spread* my arms wide⟩ **3** : SCATTER 1, STREW ⟨*spread* fertilizer⟩ **4** : to give out over a period of time or among a group ⟨*spread* work to make it last⟩ **5** : to put a layer of on a surface ⟨*spread* butter on bread⟩ **6** : to cover something with ⟨*spread* a cloth on the table⟩ **7** : to prepare for a meal : SET ⟨*spread* a table⟩ **8** : to pass from person to person ⟨the news *spread* rapidly⟩ ⟨flies *spread* disease⟩ **9** : to stretch or move apart ⟨*spreading* my fingers⟩

²spread *n* **1** : the act or process of spreading ⟨the *spread* of education⟩ **2** : extent of spreading ⟨the *spread* of a bird's wings⟩ **3** : a noticeable display in a magazine or newspaper **4** : a food to be spread on bread or crackers **5** : a very fine meal : FEAST **6** : a cloth cover for a table or bed **7** : distance between two points

spree \'sprē\ *n* : an outburst of activity ⟨went on a buying *spree*⟩

sprig \'sprig\ *n* : a small shoot or twig

spright·ly \'sprīt-lē\ *adj* **spright·li·er; spright·li·est** : full of spirit : LIVELY

¹spring \'spring\ *vb* **sprang** \'sprang\ *or* **sprung** \'sprəng\; **sprung; spring·ing 1** : to appear or grow quickly ⟨weeds *sprang* up overnight⟩ **2** : to come from by birth or descent ⟨*sprang* from poor parents⟩ **3** : to come into being : ARISE ⟨hope *springs* eternal⟩ **4** : to move suddenly upward or forward : LEAP **5** : to have (a leak) appear **6** : to move quickly by elastic force ⟨the lid *sprang* shut⟩ **7** : ²WARP 1 **8** : to cause to operate suddenly ⟨*spring* a trap⟩

²spring *n* **1** : a source of supply (as of water coming up from the ground) **2** : the season between winter and summer including in the northern hemisphere usually the months of March, April, and May **3** : a time or season of growth or development **4** : an elastic body or device that recovers its original shape when it is released after being squeezed or stretched **5** : the act or an instance of leaping up or forward **6** : elastic power or force ⟨a *spring* in your step⟩

spring·board \'spring-,bōrd\ *n* : a flexible board usually fastened at one end and used for jumping high in the air in gymnastics or diving

spring peep·er \-'pē-pər\ *n* : a small animal that is related to the toads and frogs, lives in trees, and makes a shrill call mostly in early spring

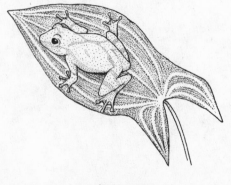

spring peeper

spring·time \'spring-,tīm\ *n* : the season of spring

springy \'spring-ē\ *adj* **spring·i·er; spring·i·est 1** : ¹ELASTIC **2** : having or showing a lively and energetic movement ⟨walks with a *springy* step⟩

¹**sprin·kle** \'spring-kəl\ *vb* **sprin·kled; sprin·kling 1** : to scatter in drops ⟨*sprinkle* water⟩ **2** : to scatter over or in or among **3** : to rain lightly — **sprin·kler** \-klər\ *n*

²**sprinkle** *n* **1** : a light rain **2** : SPRINKLING

sprin·kling \'spring-kling\ *n* : a very small number or amount

¹**sprint** \'sprint\ *vb* : to run at top speed especially for a short distance — **sprint·er** *n*

²**sprint** *n* **1** : a short run at top speed **2** : a race over a short distance

sprite \'sprīt\ *n* : ELF, FAIRY

sprock·et \'spräk-ət\ *n* : one of many points that stick up on the rim of a wheel (**sprocket wheel**) shaped so as to fit into the links of a chain

¹**sprout** \'spraủt\ *vb* : to produce or cause to produce fresh young growth ⟨new twigs *sprouting* from an old tree⟩ ⟨we need rain to *sprout* the seeds⟩

²**sprout** *n* : a young stem of a plant especially when coming directly from a seed or root

¹**spruce** \'sprüs\ *n* : an evergreen tree shaped like a cone with a thick growth of short needles, drooping cones, and light soft wood

²**spruce** *adj* **spruc·er; spruc·est** : neat or stylish in appearance

³**spruce** *vb* **spruced; spruc·ing** : to make or make oneself spruce ⟨*spruce* up a room⟩ ⟨*spruce* up a bit before a meeting⟩

sprung *past of* SPRING

spry \'sprī\ *adj* **spri·er** *or* **spry·er; spri·est** *or* **spry·est** : LIVELY 1, ACTIVE ⟨busy *spry* old people⟩

spun *past of* SPIN

spunk \'spəngk\ *n* : COURAGE, SPIRIT

Word History The English word *spunk* comes from a word in a language of Scotland that meant "tinder" or "sponge." This word, in turn, came from a Latin word that meant "sponge." The English word at first meant "tinder," which is a spongy material that catches fire easily. Since the human spirit can also be thought of as catching fire, *spunk* came to mean "spirit" or "pluck."

¹**spur** \'spər\ *n* **1** : a

pointed device fastened to the back of a rider's boot and used to urge a horse on **2** : something that makes one want to do something : INCENTIVE **3** : a stiff sharp point (as a horny spine on the leg of a rooster) **4** : a mass of jagged rock coming out from the side of a mountain **5** : a short section of railway track coming away from the main line — **spurred** \'spərd\ *adj*

²**spur** *vb* **spurred; spur·ring 1** : to urge a horse on with spurs **2** : INCITE

spurn \'spərn\ *vb* : to reject with scorn ⟨*spurn* an offer⟩

¹**spurt** \'spərt\ *n* : a brief burst of increased effort

²**spurt** *vb* : to make a spurt

³**spurt** *vb* **1** : to pour out suddenly : SPOUT **2** : ¹SQUIRT

⁴**spurt** *n* : a sudden pouring out : JET

¹**sput·ter** \'spət-ər\ *vb* **1** : to spit or squirt bits of food or saliva noisily from the mouth **2** : to speak in a hasty or explosive way in confusion or excitement ⟨*sputtered* out protests⟩ **3** : to make explosive popping sounds ⟨the motor *sputtered* and died⟩

²**sputter** *n* : the act or sound of sputtering

¹**spy** \'spī\ *vb* **spied; spy·ing 1** : to watch secretly ⟨*spy* on an enemy⟩ **2** : to catch sight of : SEE ⟨*spy* land from a ship⟩

²**spy** *n, pl* **spies 1** : a person who watches the movement or actions of others especially in secret **2** : a person who tries secretly to get information especially about an unfriendly country or its plans and actions

spy·glass \'spī-,glas\ *n* : a small telescope

squab \'skwäb\ *n* : a young pigeon especially when about four weeks old and ready for use as food

¹**squab·ble** \'skwäb-əl\ *n* : a noisy quarrel usually over unimportant things

²**squabble** *vb* **squab·bled; squab·bling** : to quarrel noisily for little or no reason

squad \'skwäd\ *n* **1** : a small group of soldiers **2** : a small group working or playing together ⟨a football *squad*⟩

squad car *n* : CRUISER 2

squad·ron \'skwäd-rən\ *n* : a group especially of cavalry riders, military airplanes, or naval ships moving and working together

squal·id \'skwäl-əd\ *adj* : filthy or degraded from a lack of care or money

¹**squall** \'skwȯl\ *vb* : to let out a harsh cry or scream

spur

\ə\ abut	\aủ\ out	\i\ tip	\ȯ\ saw	\ủ\ foot
\ər\ further	\ch\ chin	\ī\ life	\ȯi\ coin	\y\ yet
\a\ mat	\e\ pet	\j\ job	\th\ thin	\yü\ few
\ā\ take	\ē\ easy	\ng\ sing	\th\ this	\yủ\ cure
\ä\ cot, cart	\g\ go	\ō\ bone	\ü\ food	\zh\ vision

²squall *n* : a sudden strong gust of wind often with rain or snow

squal·or \'skwäl-ər\ *n* : the quality or state of being squalid ⟨live in *squalor*⟩

squan·der \'skwän-dər\ *vb* : to spend foolishly : WASTE

¹square \'skwaər, 'skweər\ *n* **1** : an instrument having at least one right angle and two or more straight edges used to mark or test right angles ⟨a carpenter's *square*⟩ **2** : a flat figure that has four equal sides and four right angles **3** : something formed like a square ⟨the *squares* of a checkerboard⟩ **4** : the product of a number or amount multiplied by itself **5** : an open place or area where two or more streets meet **6** : ¹BLOCK 6, 7

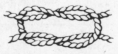

square 1

²square *adj* **squar·er; squar·est 1** : having four equal sides and four right angles **2** : forming a right angle ⟨a *square* corner⟩ **3** : multiplied by itself **4** : having outlines that suggest sharp corners rather than curves ⟨a *square* jaw⟩ **5** : being a unit of area consisting of a square whose sides have a given length ⟨a *square* meter⟩ **6** : having a specified length in each of two equal dimensions ⟨ten meters *square*⟩ **7** : exactly adjusted **8** : ¹JUST 3, FAIR ⟨a *square* deal⟩ **9** : leaving no balance : EVEN ⟨make accounts *square*⟩ **10** : large enough to satisfy ⟨three *square* meals a day⟩ — **square·ly** *adv*

³square *vb* **squared; squar·ing 1** : to make square : form with right angles, straight edges, and flat surfaces ⟨*square* a timber⟩ **2** : to make straight ⟨*squared* my shoulders⟩ **3** : to multiply a number by itself **4** : AGREE 4 ⟨your story does not *square* with the facts⟩ **5** : ²BALANCE 1, SETTLE ⟨*square* an account⟩

square knot *n* : a knot made of two

square knot

half-knots tied in opposite directions and typically used to join the ends of two cords

square–rigged \'skwaər-'rigd, 'skweər-\ *adj* : having the principal sails extended on yards fastened in a horizontal position to the masts at their center

square root *n* : a factor of a number that when multiplied by itself gives the number ⟨the *square root* of 9 is 3⟩

¹squash \'skwäsh\ *vb* : to beat or press into a soft or flat mass : CRUSH

²squash *n* : the fruit of any of several plants related to the gourds that is cooked as a vegetable or used for animal feed

¹squat \'skwät\ *vb* **squat·ted; squat·ting 1** : to crouch by bending the knees fully so as to sit on or close to the heels **2** : to settle without any right on land that one does not own **3** : to settle on government land in order to become the owner of the land

²squat *n* **1** : the act of squatting **2** : a squatting posture

³squat *adj* **squat·ter; squat·test 1** : bent in a deep crouch **2** : low to the ground **3** : having a short thick body

squaw \'skwȯ\ *n* : an American Indian woman

¹squawk \'skwȯk\ *vb* **1** : to make a harsh short scream **2** : to complain or protest loudly or with strong feeling

²squawk *n* **1** : a harsh short scream **2** : a noisy complaint

¹squeak \'skwēk\ *vb* **1** : to make a short shrill cry **2** : to get, win, or pass with trouble : barely succeed ⟨just *squeaked* by⟩

²squeak *n* : a sharp shrill cry or sound

squeaky \'skwē-kē\ *adj* **squeak·i·er; squeak·i·est** : likely to squeak ⟨a *squeaky* door⟩

¹squeal \'skwēl\ *vb* **1** : to make a sharp long shrill cry or noise **2** : INFORM 2

²squeal *n* : a shrill sharp cry or noise

¹squeeze \'skwēz\ *vb* **squeezed; squeez·ing 1** : to press together from the opposite sides or parts of : COMPRESS **2** : to get by squeezing ⟨*squeeze* juice from a lemon⟩ **3** : to force or crowd in by compressing ⟨*squeeze* into a box⟩

²squeeze *n* : an act or instance of squeezing

squid \'skwid\ *n* : a sea mollusk that is

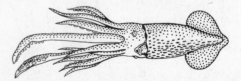

squid

related to the octopus but has a long body and ten arms

¹squint \'skwint\ *adj* : not able to look in the same direction — used of the two eyes

²squint *vb* **1** : to have squint eyes **2** : to look or peer with the eyes partly closed

³squint *n* **1** : the condition of being cross-eyed **2** : the action or an instance of squinting

¹squire \'skwīr\ *n* **1** : a person who carries the shield or armor of a knight **2** : ¹ESCORT 1 **3** : an owner of a country estate

²squire *vb* **squired; squir·ing** : to act as a squire or escort for

squirm \'skwərm\ *vb* **1** : to twist about like an eel or a worm **2** : to feel very embarrassed

squir·rel \'skwər-əl\ *n* : a small gnawing animal (as the common American red squirrel and gray squirrel) usually with a bushy tail and soft fur and strong hind legs for leaping

Word History When a squirrel sits up, its long tail curves up and over its head and sometimes casts a shadow. The English word *squirrel* comes from the Greek word for a squirrel, which was made up of two words. The first meant "shadow." The second meant "tail."

¹squirt \'skwərt\ *vb* : to shoot out liquid in a thin stream : SPURT

²squirt *n* **1** : an instrument for squirting liquid **2** : a small powerful stream of liquid : JET **3** : the action of squirting

¹stab \'stab\ *n* **1** : a wound produced by or as if by a pointed weapon **2** : ²THRUST 1 **3** : ³TRY, EFFORT ⟨make a *stab* at it⟩

²stab *vb* **stabbed; stab·bing** **1** : to wound or pierce with a stab **2** : ¹DRIVE 2, THRUST ⟨*stab* a fork into meat⟩

sta·bil·i·ty \stə-'bil-ət-ē\ *n, pl* **sta·bil·i·ties** : the condition of being stable

sta·bi·lize \'stā-bə-ˌlīz\ *vb* **sta·bi·lized; sta·bi·liz·ing** : to make or become stable — **sta·bi·liz·er** *n*

¹sta·ble \'stā-bəl\ *n* : a building in which domestic animals are housed and cared for

²stable *vb* **sta·bled; sta·bling** : to put or keep in a stable

³stable *adj* **sta·bler; sta·blest** **1** : not easily changed or affected ⟨a *stable* government⟩ **2** : not likely to change suddenly or greatly ⟨a *stable* income⟩ **3** : LASTING ⟨a *stable* peace⟩ **4** : RELIABLE

stac·ca·to \stə-'kät-ō\ *adj* **1** : cut short so as not to sound connected ⟨*staccato* notes⟩ **2** : played or sung with breaks between notes ⟨a *staccato* passage⟩

¹stack \'stak\ *n* **1** : a large pile (as of hay) usually shaped like a cone **2** : a neat pile of objects usually one on top of the other **3** : a large number or amount **4** : CHIMNEY 1, SMOKESTACK **5** : a structure with shelves for storing books

²stack *vb* : to arrange in or form a stack : PILE

sta·di·um \'stād-ē-əm\ *n, pl* **sta·di·ums** *or* **sta·dia** \'stād-ē-ə\ : a large outdoor structure with rows of seats for spectators at sports events

staff \'staf\ *n, pl* **staffs** *or* **staves** \'stavz\ **1** : a pole, stick, rod, or bar used as a support or as a sign of authority ⟨the *staff* of a flag⟩ ⟨a bishop's *staff*⟩ **2** : something that is a source of strength ⟨bread is the *staff* of life⟩ **3** : the five parallel lines with their four spaces on which music is written **4** *pl* **staffs** : a group of persons serving as assistants to or employees under a chief ⟨a hospital *staff*⟩ **5** *pl* **staffs** : a group of military officers who plan and manage for a commanding officer

staff sergeant *n* : a noncommissioned officer in the Army, Air Force, or Marine Corps ranking above a sergeant

staff sergeant major *n* : a noncommissioned officer in the Army ranking above a master sergeant

¹stag \'stag\ *n* **1** : an adult male deer especially of the larger kind **2** : a man who goes to a social gathering without escorting a woman

²stag *adj* : intended or thought suitable for men only ⟨a *stag* party⟩

¹stage \'stāj\ *n* **1** : a raised floor (as for speaking or giving plays) **2** : a place where something important happens **3** : the theatrical profession or art **4** : a step forward in a journey, a task, a process, or a development : PHASE **5** : STAGECOACH

²stage *vb* **staged; stag·ing** : to produce or show to the public on or as if on the stage ⟨*stages* two plays each year⟩

stage·coach \'stāj-ˌkōch\ *n* : a coach pulled by horses that runs on a schedule from place to place carrying passengers and mail

¹stag·ger \'stag-ər\ *vb* **1** : to move unsteadily from side to side as if about to fall : REEL **2** : to cause to move unsteadily **3** : to cause great surprise or shock in **4** : to place or arrange in a zigzag but balanced

\ə\ abut	\aú\ out	\i\ tip	\ȯ\ saw	\ú\ foot
\ər\ further	\ch\ chin	\ī\ life	\ȯi\ coin	\y\ yet
\a\ mat	\e\ pet	\j\ job	\th\ thin	\yü\ few
\ā\ take	\ē\ easy	\ng\ sing	\th\ this	\yu̇\ cure
\ä\ cot, cart	\g\ go	\ō\ bone	\ü\ food	\zh\ vision

way ⟨*stagger* the nails along either edge of the board⟩

²stagger *n* : a reeling or unsteady walk

stag·nant \'stag-nənt\ *adj* **1** : not flowing ⟨a *stagnant* pool⟩ **2** : not active or brisk : DULL ⟨*stagnant* business⟩

stag·nate \'stag-ˌnāt\ *vb* **stag·nat·ed; stag·nat·ing** : to be or become stagnant

¹stain \'stān\ *vb* **1** : to soil or discolor especially in spots **2** : ²COLOR 2, TINGE **3** : ¹CORRUPT 1 **4** : ¹DISGRACE

²stain *n* **1** : ¹SPOT 3, DISCOLORATION **2** : a mark of guilt or disgrace : STIGMA **3** : something (as a dye) used in staining — **stain·less** \-ləs\ *adj*

stainless steel *n* : an alloy of steel and chromium that is resistant to stain, rust, and corrosion

stair \'staər, 'steər\ *n* **1** : a series of steps or flights of steps for going from one level to another — often used in pl. ⟨ran down the *stairs*⟩ **2** : one step of a stairway

stair·case \'staər-ˌkās, 'steər-\ *n* : a flight of stairs with their supporting structure and railings

stair·way \'staər-ˌwā, 'steər-\ *n* : one or more flights of stairs usually with connecting landings

¹stake \'stāk\ *n* **1** : a pointed piece (as of wood) driven or to be driven into the ground as a marker or to support something **2** : a post to which a person is tied to be put to death by burning **3** : something that is put up to be won or lost in gambling ⟨play cards for high *stakes*⟩ **4** : the prize in a contest **5** : ¹SHARE 1, INTEREST ⟨a *stake* in the business⟩ — **at stake** : in a position to be lost if something goes wrong ⟨your job is *at stake*⟩

²stake *vb* **staked; stak·ing 1** : to mark the limits of by stakes ⟨*stake* out a mining claim⟩ **2** : to fasten or support (as plants) with stakes **3** : ²BET 1 **4** : to give money to to help (as with a project)

sta·lac·tite \stə-'lak-ˌtīt\ *n* : a deposit hanging from the roof or side of a cave in the shape of an icicle formed by the partial evaporating of dripping water containing lime

sta·lag·mite \stə-'lag-ˌmīt\ *n* : a deposit like an upside

stalactites and stalagmites

down stalactite formed by the dripping of water containing lime onto the floor of a cave

¹stale \'stāl\ *adj* **stal·er; stal·est 1** : having lost a good taste or quality through age ⟨*stale* bread⟩ **2** : used or heard so often as to be dull ⟨*stale* jokes⟩ **3** : not so strong, energetic, or effective as before ⟨felt *stale* from lack of exercise⟩ — **stale·ly** *adv* — **stale·ness** *n*

²stale *vb* **staled; stal·ing** : to make or become stale

¹stalk \'stok\ *vb* **1** : to hunt slowly and quietly ⟨a cat *stalking* a bird⟩ **2** : to walk in a stiff or proud manner **3** : to move through or follow as if stalking prey ⟨famine *stalked* the land⟩ — **stalk·er** *n*

²stalk *n* **1** : the act of stalking **2** : a stalking way of walking

³stalk *n* **1** : a plant stem especially when not woody ⟨*stalks* of asparagus⟩ **2** : a slender supporting structure ⟨the *stalk* of a goblet⟩ — **stalked** \'stokt\ *adj* — **stalk·less** \'stok-ləs\ *adj*

¹stall \'stol\ *n* **1** : a compartment for one animal in a stable **2** : a space set off (as for parking an automobile) **3** : a seat in a church choir : a church pew **4** : a booth, stand, or counter where business may be carried on or articles may be displayed for sale

²stall *vb* **1** : to put or keep in a stall **2** : to stop or cause to stop usually by accident ⟨*stall* an engine⟩

³stall *n* : a trick to deceive or delay

⁴stall *vb* : to distract attention or make excuses to gain time ⟨quit *stalling* and answer the question⟩ ⟨try to *stall* them until I get the place cleaned up⟩

stal·lion \'stal-yən\ *n* : a male horse

stal·wart \'stol-wərt\ *adj* : STURDY, RESOLUTE ⟨a *stalwart* body⟩ ⟨*stalwart* spirits⟩

sta·men \'stā-mən\ *n* : any of a row of organs at the center of a flower that bear the anthers which produce the pollen

stamen

stam·i·na \'stam-ə-nə\ *n* : VIGOR 1, ENDURANCE

¹stam·mer \'stam-ər\ *vb* : to speak with involuntary stops and much repeating — **stam·mer·er** *n*

²stammer *n* : an act or instance of stammering

¹stamp \'stamp\ *vb* **1** : to bring the foot down hard and with noise ⟨don't *stamp* around in the house⟩ **2** : to put an end to by or as if by hitting with the bottom of the foot ⟨*stamp* out the fire⟩ ⟨*stamp* out crime⟩ **3** : to mark or cut out with a tool or device having a design ⟨*stamp* the bill paid⟩ ⟨*stamping* out coins⟩ **4** : to attach a postage stamp to **5** : CHARACTERIZE 1 ⟨*stamped* them as cowards⟩

²stamp *n* **1** : a device or instrument for stamping **2** : the mark made by stamping **3** : a sign of a special quality ⟨the *stamp* of genius⟩ **4** : the act of stamping **5** : a small piece of paper or a mark attached to something to show that a tax or fee has been paid ⟨a postage *stamp*⟩

¹stam·pede \stam-'pēd\ *n* **1** : a wild dash or flight of frightened animals ⟨a cattle *stampede*⟩ **2** : a sudden foolish action or movement of a crowd of people ⟨the rumor started a *stampede* of buying⟩

²stampede *vb* **stam·ped·ed; stam·ped·ing 1** : to run or cause (as cattle) to run away in panic **2** : to act or cause to act together suddenly and without thought ⟨refused to be *stampeded* by threats⟩

stance \'stans\ *n* : way of standing : POS-TURE

stanch \'stȯnch\ *vb* : to stop or check the flow of (as blood)

¹stand \'stand\ *vb* **stood** \'stůd\; **stand·ing 1** : to be in or take a vertical position on one's feet **2** : to take up or stay in a specified position or condition ⟨*stands* first in the class⟩ ⟨*stands* accused⟩ ⟨machines *standing* idle⟩ **3** : to have an opinion ⟨how do you *stand* on taxes?⟩ **4** : to rest, remain, or set in a usually vertical position ⟨*stand* the box in the corner⟩ **5** : to stay on the hill⟩ **6** : to stay in effect ⟨the order still *stands*⟩ **7** : to put up with : ENDURE ⟨can't *stand* pain⟩ **8** : UNDERGO ⟨*stand* trial⟩ **9** : to perform the duty of ⟨*stand* guard⟩ — **stand by** : to be or remain loyal or true to ⟨*stand by* a promise⟩ — **stand for 1** : to be a symbol for : REPRE-SENT **2** : to put up with : PERMIT ⟨won't *stand for* any nonsense⟩

²stand *n* **1** : an act of standing **2** : a halt for defense or resistance ⟨made a *stand* against the enemy⟩ **3** : a place or post especially where one stands : STATION ⟨took the witness *stand*⟩ **4** : a structure containing rows of seats for spectators of a sport or spectacle **5** : a raised area (as for speakers or performers) **6** : a stall or booth often outdoors for a small business **7** : a small structure (as a rack or table) on or in which something may be placed ⟨an umbrella *stand*⟩ **8** : POSITION 2 ⟨they took a strong *stand* on the question⟩

¹stan·dard \'stan-dərd\ *n* **1** : a figure used as a symbol by an organized body of people **2** : the personal flag of the ruler of a state **3** : something set up as a rule for measuring or as a model ⟨a *stan-dard* of weight⟩ ⟨*standards* of good manners⟩ **4** : an upright support ⟨a lamp *standard*⟩

²standard *adj* **1** : used as or matching a standard ⟨*standard* weight⟩ **2** : regularly and widely used ⟨a *standard* practice in the trade⟩ **3** : widely known and accepted to be of good and permanent value ⟨*standard* reference works⟩

stan·dard·ize \'stan-dər-,dīz\ *vb* **stan-dard·ized; stan·dard·iz·ing** : to make standard or alike

standard time *n* : the time established by law or by common usage over a region or country

stand by *vb* **1** : to be present ⟨we *stood by* and watched the fight⟩ **2** : to be or get ready to act ⟨*stand by* to help⟩

¹stand·ing \'stan-ding\ *adj* **1** : ¹ERECT ⟨*standing* grain⟩ **2** : not flowing : STAG-NANT ⟨a *standing* pool⟩ **3** : remaining at the same level or amount until canceled ⟨a *standing* offer⟩ **4** : PERMANENT ⟨a *standing* army⟩

²standing *n* **1** : the action or position of one that stands **2** : length of existence or service ⟨a custom of long *standing*⟩ **3** : POSITION 4, STATUS ⟨had the highest *standing* in the class⟩

stand out *vb* : to be easily seen or recognized

stand·point \'stand-,pȯint\ *n* : a way in which things are thought about : POINT OF VIEW

stand·still \'stand-,stil\ *n* : the condition of not being active or busy : STOP ⟨business was at a *standstill*⟩

stand up *vb* **1** : to stay in good condition ⟨*stands up* well under hard use⟩ **2** : to fail to keep an appointment with ⟨you *stood* me *up* yesterday⟩ — **stand up for** : DE-FEND 2 — **stand up to** : to face boldly

stank *past of* STINK

stan·za \'stan-zə\ *n* : a group of lines forming a division of a poem

¹sta·ple \'stā-pəl\ *n* **1** : a piece of metal shaped like a U with sharp points to be driven into a surface to hold something (as a hook, rope, or wire) **2** : a short thin wire with bent ends that is driven through papers and clinched to hold them together or driven through thin material to fasten it to a

\ə\ **abut**	\aů\ **out**	\i\ **tip**	\ȯ\ **saw**	\ů\ **foot**
\ər\ **further**	\ch\ **chin**	\ī\ **life**	\ȯi\ **coin**	\y\ **yet**
\a\ **mat**	\e\ **pet**	\j\ **job**	\th\ **thin**	\yü\ **few**
\ā\ **take**	\ē\ **easy**	\ng\ **sing**	\t̲h̲\ **this**	\yů\ **cure**
\ä\ **cot, cart**	\g\ **go**	\ō\ **bone**	\ü\ **food**	\zh\ **vision**

surface ⟨fasten cardboard to wood with *staples*⟩

²staple *vb* **sta·pled; sta·pling** : to fasten with staples

³staple *n* **1** : a chief product of business or farming of a place **2** : something that is used widely and often **3** : the chief part of something ⟨potatoes are the *staple* of their diet⟩ **4** : fiber (as cotton or wool) suitable for spinning into yarn

⁴staple *adj* **1** : much used, needed, or enjoyed usually by many people ⟨a *staple* plot in mystery novels⟩ **2** : ¹PRINCIPAL, CHIEF ⟨*staple* foods⟩

sta·pler \'stā-plər\ *n* : a device that staples

¹star \'stär\ *n* **1** : any of those celestial bodies except planets which are visible at night and look like fixed points of light **2** : a star or especially a planet that is believed in astrology to influence one's life ⟨born under a lucky *star*⟩ **3** : a figure or thing (as a medal) with five or more points that represents or suggests a star **4** : the principal member of a theater or opera company **5** : a very talented or popular performer

²star *vb* **starred; star·ring** **1** : to sprinkle or decorate with or as if with stars **2** : to mark with a star as being special or very good **3** : to mark with an asterisk **4** : to present in the role of a star **5** : to play the most important role ⟨*star* in a new play⟩ **6** : to perform in an outstanding manner

star·board \'stär-bərd\ *n* : the right side of a ship or airplane looking forward

¹starch \'stärch\ *vb* : to stiffen with starch

²starch *n* : a white odorless tasteless substance that is the chief storage form of carbohydrates in plants, is an important food, and has also various household and business uses (as for stiffening clothes)

starchy \'stär-chē\ *adj* **starch·i·er; starch·i·est** : like or containing starch

¹stare \'staər, 'steər\ *vb* **stared; star·ing** : to look at hard and long often with wide-open eyes **synonyms** see GAZE

²stare *n* : the act or an instance of staring

star·fish \'stär-ˌfish\ *n* : any of a group of sea animals mostly having five arms that spread out from a central disk and feeding mostly on mollusks

¹stark \'stärk\ *adj* **1** : ¹BARREN **2**, DESOLATE ⟨a *stark* landscape⟩ **2** : ¹UTTER, ABSOLUTE ⟨*stark* folly⟩

²stark *adv* : COMPLETELY ⟨*stark* mad⟩

star·light \'stär-ˌlīt\ *n* : the light given by the stars

star·ling \'stär-ling\ *n* : a dark brown or in summer greenish black European bird

about the size of a robin that is now common and often a pest in the United States

star·lit \'stär-ˌlit\ *adj* : lighted by the stars

star·ry \'stär-ē\ *adj* **star·ri·er; star·ri·est** **1** : full of stars ⟨*starry* heavens⟩ **2** : of, relating to, or consisting of stars ⟨*starry* light⟩ **3** : shining like stars ⟨*starry* eyes⟩

Stars and Stripes *n sing or pl* : the flag of the United States

¹start \'stärt\ *vb* **1** : to move suddenly and quickly : give a sudden twitch or jerk (as in surprise) **2** : to come or bring into being or action ⟨*start* a rumor⟩ ⟨rain is likely to *start* soon⟩ **3** : to stick out or seem to stick out ⟨their eyes *started* from the sockets⟩ **4** : SET OUT 2 ⟨*start* for home⟩ **5** : to set going ⟨*start* the motor⟩

²start *n* **1** : a sudden movement ⟨a *start* of surprise⟩ **2** : a brief act, movement, or effort ⟨work by fits and *starts*⟩ **3** : a beginning of movement, action, or development ⟨got an early *start*⟩ **4** : a place of beginning (as of a race)

start·er \'stärt-ər\ *n* : someone or something that starts something or causes something else to start ⟨there were seven *starters* in the race⟩ ⟨the *starter* of a motor⟩

star·tle \'stärt-l\ *vb* **star·tled; star·tling** **1** : to cause to move or jump (as in surprise or fear) **2** : to frighten suddenly but slightly

star·tling *adj* : causing a moment of fright or surprise

star·va·tion \stär-'vā-shən\ *n* : the act or an instance of starving : the condition of being starved

starve \'stärv\ *vb* **starved; starv·ing** **1** : to suffer or die or cause to suffer or die from lack of food **2** : to suffer or cause to suffer from a lack of something other than food ⟨a child *starving* for affection⟩

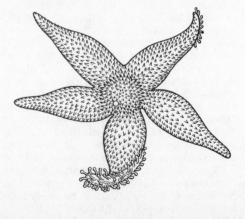

starfish

¹state \'stāt\ *n* **1** : manner or condition of being ⟨water in the gaseous *state*⟩⟨a nervous *state*⟩ **2** : a body of people living in a certain territory under one government : the government of such a body of people **3** : one of the divisions of a nation having a federal government ⟨the United *States* of America⟩

²state *vb* **stat·ed; stat·ing 1** : to set by rule, law, or authority : FIX ⟨at *stated* times⟩ **2** : to express especially in words ⟨*state* an opinion⟩

state·house \'stāt-ˌhau̇s\ *n* : the building where the legislature of a state meets

state·ly \'stāt-lē\ *adj* **state·li·er; state·li·est 1** : having great dignity ⟨*stately* language⟩ **2** : impressive especially in size : IMPOSING ⟨a *stately* building⟩ — **state·li·ness** *n*

state·ment \'stāt-mənt\ *n* **1** : something that is stated : REPORT, ACCOUNT **2** : a brief record of a business account ⟨a monthly bank *statement*⟩

state·room \'stāt-ˌrüm, -ˌru̇m\ *n* : a private room on a ship or a train

states·man \'stāt-smən\ *n, pl* **states·men** \'stāt-smən\ : a person who is active in government and who gives wise leadership in making policies

¹stat·ic \'stat-ik\ *adj* **1** : showing little change or action ⟨a *static* population⟩ **2** : of or relating to charges of electricity (as one produced by friction) that do not flow

²static *n* : noise produced in a radio or television receiver by atmospheric or electrical disturbances

¹sta·tion \'stā-shən\ *n* **1** : the place or position where a person or thing stands or is assigned to stand or remain **2** : a regular stopping place (as on a bus line) : DEPOT **3** : a post or area of duty ⟨military *station*⟩ **4** : POSITION 4, RANK ⟨a person of high *station*⟩ **5** : a place for specialized observation or for a public service ⟨weather *station*⟩ ⟨police *station*⟩ **6** : a collection of radio or television equipment for transmitting or receiving **7** : the place where a radio or television station is

²station *vb* : to assign to or set in a station or position : POST

sta·tion·ary \'stā-shə-ˌner-ē\ *adj* **1** : having been set in a certain place or post : IMMOBILE ⟨a *stationary* laundry tub⟩ **2** : not changing : STABLE ⟨their weekly income remained *stationary*⟩

sta·tion·ery \'stā-shə-ˌner-ē\ *n* : writing paper and envelopes

station wagon *n* : an automobile that is longer on the inside than a sedan and has one or more folding or removable seats but no separate luggage compartment

stat·ue \'stach-ü\ *n* : an image or likeness (as of a person or animal) sculptured, modeled, or cast in a solid substance (as marble or bronze)

stat·ure \'stach-ər\ *n* **1** : natural height (as of a person) **2** : quality or fame one has gained (as by growth or development) ⟨artists of *stature*⟩

sta·tus \'stāt-əs, 'stat-\ *n* **1** : position or rank of a person or thing ⟨lost my *status* as an amateur⟩ **2** : state of affairs : SITUATION ⟨the economic *status* of a country⟩

stat·ute \'stach-üt\ *n* : LAW 4 ⟨the *statutes* of our state⟩

staunch \'stȯnch, 'stänch\ *adj* **1** : strongly built : SUBSTANTIAL ⟨*staunch* foundations⟩ **2** : LOYAL 2, STEADFAST ⟨they were *staunch* friends for many years⟩ — **staunch·ly** *adv*

¹stave \'stāv\ *n* **1** : a wooden stick : STAFF **2** : one of a number of narrow strips of wood or iron plates placed edge to edge to form the sides, covering, or lining of something (as a barrel or keg)

²stave *vb* **staved** *or* **stove** \'stōv\; **stav·ing 1** : to break in the staves of ⟨*stave* in a boat⟩ **2** : to smash a hole in : crush or break inward ⟨*staved* in several ribs⟩

stave off *vb* : to keep away : ward off ⟨*stave off* trouble⟩

staves *pl of* STAFF

¹stay \'stā\ *n* : a strong rope or wire used to steady or brace something (as a mast)

²stay *vb* : to fasten (as a smokestack) with stays

³stay *vb* **1** : to stop going forward : PAUSE **2** : ¹REMAIN 3, 4 ⟨*stayed* after the party to help⟩ ⟨we *stayed* friends for many years⟩ **3** : to stand firm **4** : to live for a while ⟨*staying* with friends⟩ **5** : ²CHECK 1, HALT ⟨*stay* an execution⟩

⁴stay *n* **1** : the action of bringing to a stop : the state of being stopped **2** : a period of living in a place ⟨made a long *stay* in the country⟩

⁵stay *n* **1** : ¹PROP, SUPPORT **2** : a thin firm strip (as of steel or plastic) used to stiffen a garment (as a corset) or part of a garment (as a shirt collar)

⁶stay *vb* : to hold up ⟨*stay* a person who is about to fall⟩

stead \'sted\ *n* **1** : ²AVAIL — used mostly in the phrase *stand one in good stead* **2**

\ə\ **abut**	\au̇\ **out**	\i\ **tip**	\ȯ\ **saw**	\u̇\ **foot**
\ər\ **further**	\ch\ **chin**	\ī\ **life**	\ȯi\ **coin**	\y\ **yet**
\a\ **mat**	\e\ **pet**	\j\ **job**	\th\ **thin**	\yü\ **few**
\ā\ **take**	\ē\ **easy**	\ng\ **sing**	\th\ **this**	\yu̇\ **cure**
\ä\ **cot, cart**	\g\ **go**	\ō\ **bone**	\ü\ **food**	\zh\ **vision**

: the place usually taken or duty carried out by the one mentioned ⟨try to get someone to work in your *stead*⟩

stead·fast \'sted-,fast\ *adj* **1** : not changing : RESOLUTE ⟨a *steadfast* aim⟩ **2** : LOYAL **2** ⟨*steadfast* friends⟩ — **stead·fast·ly** *adv* — **stead·fast·ness** *n*

¹steady \'sted-ē\ *adj* **stead·i·er; stead·i·est 1** : firmly fixed in position **2** : direct or sure in action ⟨worked with *steady* hands⟩ ⟨took *steady* aim⟩ **3** : showing little change ⟨*steady* prices⟩ ⟨a *steady* flow of water⟩ **4** : not easily upset ⟨*steady* nerves⟩ **5** : RELIABLE — **stead·i·ly** \'sted-l-ē\ *adv* — **stead·i·ness** \'sted-ē-nəs\ *n*

²steady *vb* **stead·ied; steady·ing** : to make, keep, or become steady

steak \'stāk\ *n* **1** : a slice of meat and especially beef **2** : a slice of a large fish (as salmon)

¹steal \'stēl\ *vb* **stole** \'stōl\; **sto·len** \'stō-lən\; **steal·ing 1** : to come or go quietly or secretly ⟨*stole* out of the room⟩ **2** : to take and carry away (something that belongs to another person) without right and with the intention of keeping **3** : to get more than one's share of attention during ⟨*stole* the show⟩ **4** : to take or get for oneself secretly or without permission ⟨*stole* a nap⟩

²steal *n* **1** : the act or an instance of stealing **2** : ¹BARGAIN **2**

stealth \'stelth\ *n* : sly or secret action

stealthy \'stel-thē\ *adj* **stealth·i·er; stealth·i·est** : done in a sly or secret manner — **stealth·i·ly** \-thə-lē\ *adv*

¹steam \'stēm\ *n* **1** : the vapor into which water is changed when heated to the boiling point **2** : steam when kept under pressure so that it supplies heat and power ⟨houses heated by *steam*⟩ **3** : the mist formed when water vapor cools **4** : driving force : POWER ⟨arrived under their own *steam*⟩

²steam *vb* **1** : to rise or pass off as steam **2** : to give off steam or vapor **3** : to move or travel by or as if by the power of steam ⟨the ship *steamed* out of the harbor⟩ **4** : to expose to steam (as for cooking)

steam·boat \'stēm-,bōt\ *n* : a boat driven by steam

steam engine *n* : an engine driven by steam

steam·er \'stē-mər\ *n* **1** : a container in which something is steamed **2** : a ship driven by steam **3** : an engine, machine, or vehicle run by steam

steam·roll·er \'stēm-'rō-lər\ *n* : a machine formerly driven by steam that has wide heavy rollers for pressing down and smoothing roads

steam·ship \'stēm-,ship\ *n* : STEAMER **2**

steam shovel *n* : a power machine for digging that was formerly operated by steam

steed \'stēd\ *n* : a usually lively horse

¹steel \'stēl\ *n* **1** : a hard and tough metal made by treating iron with great heat and mixing carbon with it **2** : an article (as a sword) made of steel

²steel *adj* : made of or like steel

³steel *vb* : to fill with courage or determination ⟨I *steeled* myself for the struggle⟩

steely \'stē-lē\ *adj* **steel·i·er; steel·i·est 1** : made of steel **2** : like steel (as in hardness or color)

¹steep \'stēp\ *adj* **1** : having a very sharp slope : almost straight up and down **2** : too great or high ⟨*steep* prices⟩ — **steep·ly** *adv* — **steep·ness** *n*

²steep *vb* **1** : to soak in a liquid ⟨*steep* tea⟩ **2** : to fill with or involve deeply ⟨*steeped* in learning⟩ ⟨a story *steeped* with legend⟩

stee·ple \'stē-pəl\ *n* **1** : a tall pointed structure usually built on top of a church tower **2** : a church tower

stee·ple·chase \'stē-pəl-,chās\ *n* **1** : a horse race across country **2** : a race on a course that has hedges, walls, and ditches to be crossed

¹steer \'stiər\ *n* : a castrated bull usually raised for beef

²steer *vb* **1** : to control a course or the course of : GUIDE ⟨*steer* by the stars⟩ ⟨*steer* a boat⟩ **2** : to follow a course of action **3** : to be guided ⟨this car *steers* well⟩

steering wheel *n* : a wheel for steering something by hand

¹stem \'stem\ *n* **1** : the main stalk of a plant that develops buds and sprouts and usually grows above ground **2** : a plant part (as a leafstalk or flower stalk) that supports some other part **3** : the bow of a ship **4** : a line of ancestors : STOCK **5** : the basic part of a word to which prefixes or suffixes may be added **6** : something like a stalk or shaft ⟨the *stem* of a goblet⟩ — **stem·less** \-ləs\ *adj*

²stem *vb* **stemmed; stem·ming 1** : to come from a certain source ⟨illness that *stems* from an accident⟩ **2** : to remove the stem from ⟨*stem* cherries⟩

³stem *vb* **stemmed; stem·ming 1** : to make progress against **2** : to check or hold back the progress of

⁴stem *vb* **stemmed; stem·ming** : to stop or check by or as if by damming ⟨*stem* the flow of blood⟩

stemmed \'stemd\ *adj* : having a stem

¹sten·cil \'sten-səl\ *n* **1** : a material (as a sheet of paper, thin wax, or woven fabric) with cut out lettering or a design through which ink, paint, or metallic powder is forced onto a surface to be printed **2** : a pattern, design, or print produced with a stencil

²stencil *vb* **sten·ciled** *or* **sten·cilled**; **sten·cil·ing** *or* **sten·cil·ling** **1** : to mark or paint with a stencil ⟨*stencil* a box with designs⟩ **2** : to produce with a stencil ⟨*stencil* a number⟩

ste·nog·ra·pher \stə-'näg-rə-fər\ *n* : one employed chiefly to take and make a copy of dictation

¹step \'step\ *n* **1** : a rest or place for the foot in going up or down : STAIR 2 **2** : a movement made by raising one foot and putting it down in another spot **3** : a combination of foot and body movements in a repeated pattern ⟨a waltz *step*⟩ **4** : manner of walking **5** : FOOTPRINT **6** : the sound of a footstep **7** : the space passed over in one step **8** : a short distance ⟨the house is only a *step* away⟩ **9** : the height of one stair **10** **steps** *pl* : ¹COURSE 3 ⟨directed our *steps* toward home⟩ **11** : a level, grade, or rank in a scale or series : a stage in a process **12** : ¹MEASURE 7 ⟨took *steps* to correct the condition⟩ **13** : a space in music between two notes of a scale or staff that may be a single degree of the scale (**half step**) or two degrees (**whole step**) — **in step** : with one's foot or feet moving in time with other feet or in time to music ⟨march *in step*⟩

²step *vb* **stepped**; **step·ping** **1** : to move by taking a step or steps ⟨*stepped* into the bus⟩ **2** : ¹DANCE 1 **3** : to go on foot : WALK ⟨*stepped* slowly along the path⟩ **4** : to move at a good speed ⟨the car was really *stepping*⟩ **5** : to press down with the foot ⟨*step* on the pedal⟩ **6** : to come as if at a single step ⟨*step* into a good job⟩ **7** : to measure by steps ⟨*step* off ten yards⟩

step·fa·ther \'step-ˌfäth-ər, -ˌfáth-\ *n* : the husband of one's mother after the death or divorce of one's real father

step·lad·der \'step-ˌlad-ər\ *n* : a light portable set of steps with a hinged frame for steadying

step·moth·er \'step-ˌməth-ər\ *n* : the wife of one's father after the death or divorce of one's real mother

steppe \'step\ *n* : land that is dry, usually rather level, and covered with grass in regions (as much of southeastern Europe and parts of Asia) of wide temperature range

step·ping–stone \'step-ing-ˌstōn\ *n* **1** : a stone on which to step (as in crossing a stream) **2** : a means of progress or advancement ⟨a *stepping-stone* to success⟩

step up *vb* : to increase especially by a series of steps ⟨*step up* production⟩

-ster \stər\ *n suffix* **1** : one that does or handles or operates **2** : one that makes or uses ⟨song*ster*⟩ **3** : one that is associated with or takes part in ⟨gang*ster*⟩ **4** : one that is ⟨young*ster*⟩

ste·reo \'ster-ē-ˌō, 'stir-\ *n*, *pl* **ste·re·os** **1** : stereophonic reproduction **2** : a stereophonic sound system

ste·reo·phon·ic \ˌster-ē-ə-'fän-ik, ˌstir-\ *adj* : of or relating to sound reproduction designed to create the effect of listening to the original

ste·reo·scope \'ster-ē-ə-ˌskōp, 'stir-\ *n* : an optical instrument that blends two slightly different pictures of the same subject to make it look real

ster·ile \'ster-əl\ *adj* **1** : not able to produce fruit, crops, or offspring : not fertile ⟨*sterile* soil⟩ **2** : free from living germs

ster·il·ize \'ster-ə-ˌlīz\ *vb* **ster·il·ized**; **ster·il·iz·ing** : to make sterile and especially free from harmful germs

¹ster·ling \'stər-ling\ *n* **1** : British money **2** : sterling silver : articles made from sterling silver

²sterling *adj* **1** : of or relating to British sterling **2** : being or made of an alloy of 925 parts of silver with 75 parts of copper **3** : EXCELLENT ⟨had a *sterling* voice⟩

¹stern \'stərn\ *adj* **1** : hard and severe in nature or manner ⟨a *stern* judge⟩ **2** : firm and not changeable ⟨*stern* determination to succeed⟩ — **stern·ly** *adv* — **stern·ness** *n*

²stern *n* : the rear end of a boat

ster·num \'stər-nəm\ *n*, *pl* **ster·nums** *or* **ster·na** \-nə\ : BREASTBONE

stetho·scope \'steth-ə-ˌskōp\ *n* : an instrument used by doctors for listening to sounds produced in the body and especially in the chest

¹stew \'stü, 'styü\ *n* **1** : food (as meat with vegetables) prepared by slow boiling **2** : a state of excitement, worry, or confusion

²stew *vb* **1** : to boil slowly : SIMMER **2** : to become excited or worried

stew·ard \'stü-ərd, 'styü-\ *n* **1** : a manager of a very large home, an estate, or an organization **2** : a person employed to

\ə\ abut	\aú\ out	\i\ tip	\ó\ saw	\ú\ foot
\ər\ further	\ch\ chin	\ī\ life	\ói\ coin	\y\ yet
\a\ mat	\e\ pet	\j\ job	\th\ thin	\yü\ few
\ā\ take	\ē\ easy	\ng\ sing	\th\ this	\yú\ cure
\ä\ cot, cart	\g\ go	\ō\ bone	\ü\ food	\zh\ vision

manage the supply and distribution of food (as on a ship) **3** : a worker who serves and looks after the needs of passengers (as on an airplane or ship)

stew•ard•ess \'stü-ərd-əs, 'styü-\ *n* : a woman who looks after passengers (as on an airplane or ship)

¹stick \'stik\ *n* **1** : a cut or broken branch or twig **2** : a long thin piece of wood **3** : WALKING STICK 1 **4** : something like a stick in shape or use ⟨a *stick* of dynamite⟩

²stick *vb* **stuck** \'stək\; **stick•ing 1** : to stab with something pointed **2** : to cause to penetrate ⟨*stuck* a needle in my finger⟩ **3** : to put in place by or as if by pushing ⟨*stick* cloves in a ham⟩ **4** : to push out, up, into, or under ⟨*stuck* out my hand⟩ **5** : to put in a specified place or position ⟨*stuck* a cap on my head⟩ **6** : to cling or cause to cling ⟨the jam *stuck* to the knife⟩ ⟨*stick* a stamp on a letter⟩ **7** : to halt the movement or action of ⟨the car was *stuck* in the mud⟩ **8** : BAFFLE **9** : to burden with something unpleasant ⟨*stuck* with the job of washing the dishes⟩ **10** : to remain in a place, situation, or environment ⟨decided to *stick* where we were⟩ **11** : to become blocked or jammed ⟨the door is *stuck*⟩

stick•er \'stik-ər\ *n* : something (as a slip of paper with gum or glue on its back) that can be stuck to a surface

stick•le•back \'stik-əl-ˌbak\ *n* : a small scaleless fish with sharp spines on its back

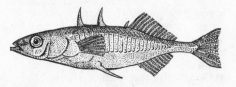

stickleback

sticky \'stik-ē\ *adj* **stick•i•er; stick•i•est 1** : ADHESIVE 1 **2** : coated with a sticky substance **3** : MUGGY, HUMID ⟨a *sticky* day⟩ **4** : tending to stick ⟨*sticky* windows⟩ — **stick•i•ness** *n*

stiff \'stif\ *adj* **1** : not easily bent ⟨*stiff* leather⟩ **2** : not easily moved ⟨*stiff* muscles⟩ **3** : not flowing easily : being thick and heavy ⟨*stiff* glue⟩ **4** : FIRM 5 **5** : hard fought : STUBBORN ⟨a *stiff* fight⟩ **6** : not easy or graceful in manner : FORMAL **7** : POWERFUL, STRONG ⟨a *stiff* wind⟩ **8** : SEVERE 2 ⟨a *stiff* penalty⟩ **9** : DIFFICULT 1 ⟨a *stiff* test⟩ — **stiff•ly** *adv* — **stiff•ness** *n*

stiff•en \'stif-ən\ *vb* : to make or become stiff or stiffer — **stiff•en•er** *n*

sti•fle \'stī-fəl\ *vb* **sti•fled; sti•fling 1** : to kill by depriving of or die from lack of oxygen or air : SMOTHER **2** : to keep in check by deliberate effort ⟨*stifle* one's anger⟩

stig•ma \'stig-mə\ *n, pl* **stig•ma•ta** \stig-'mät-ə, 'stig-mət-ə\ *or* **stig•mas 1** : a mark of disgrace or discredit **2** : the upper part of the pistil of a flower which receives the pollen grains and on which they complete their development

stile \'stīl\ *n* **1** : a step or set of steps for crossing a fence or wall **2** : TURNSTILE

sti•let•to \stə-'let-ō\ *n, pl* **sti•let•tos** *or* **sti•let•toes** : a slender pointed dagger

¹still \'stil\ *adj* **1** : having no motion **2** : making no sound **3** : free from noise and confusion : QUIET — **still•ness** *n*

²still *vb* : to make or become still : QUIET

³still *adv* **1** : without motion ⟨sit *still*⟩ **2** : up to this or that time ⟨we *still* live there⟩ **3** : NEVERTHELESS ⟨they know it's not true, but they *still* believe it⟩ **4** : ²EVEN 4 ⟨ran *still* faster⟩

⁴still *n* : ¹QUIET, SILENCE

⁵still *n* **1** : a place where alcoholic liquors are made **2** : a device used in distillation

still•born \'stil-'bȯrn\ *adj* : born dead

stilt \'stilt\ *n* **1** : one of a pair of tall poles each with a high step or loop for the support of a foot used to lift the person wearing them above the ground in walking **2** : a stake or post used to support a structure above ground or water level

stilt•ed \'stil-təd\ *adj* : not easy and natural ⟨a *stilted* speech⟩

¹stim•u•lant \'stim-yə-lənt\ *n* **1** : something (as a drug) that makes the body or one of its parts more active for a while ⟨a heart *stimulant*⟩ **2** : STIMULUS 1

²stimulant *adj* : stimulating or tending to stimulate

stiletto

stilts

stim·u·late \'stim-yə-ˌlāt\ *vb* **stim·u·lat-ed; stim·u·lat·ing 1 :** to make active or more active : ANIMATE, AROUSE **2 :** to act toward as a bodily stimulus or stimulant

stim·u·la·tion \ˌstim-yə-'lā-shən\ *n* : an act or result of stimulating

stim·u·lus \'stim-yə-ləs\ *n, pl* **stim·u·li** \-ˌlī, -ˌlē\ **1 :** something that stirs or urges to action **2 :** an influence that acts usually from outside the body to partly change bodily activity (as by exciting a sense organ) ⟨light, heat, and sound are common *stimuli*⟩

¹sting \'sting\ *vb* **stung** \'stəng\; **sting·ing 1 :** to prick painfully usually with a sharp or poisonous stinger ⟨a bee *stung* my hand⟩ **2 :** to suffer or affect with sharp quick burning pain ⟨hail *stung* their faces⟩ **3 :** to cause to suffer severely ⟨*stung* with regret⟩

²sting *n* **1 :** an act of stinging **2 :** a wound or pain caused by or as if by stinging **3 :** STINGER

sting·er \'sting-ər\ *n* : a sharp organ by which an animal (as a wasp or scorpion) wounds and often poisons an enemy

sting·ray \'sting-ˌrā\ *n* : a very flat fish with a stinging spine on its whiplike tail

stin·gy \'stin-jē\ *adj* **stin·gi·er; stin·gi·est 1 :** not generous : giving or spending as little as possible **2 :** very small in amount ⟨a *stingy* portion⟩ — **stin·gi·ly** \-jə-lē\ *adv* — **stin·gi·ness** \-jē-nəs\ *n*

¹stink \'stingk\ *vb* **stank** \'stangk\ *or* **stunk** \'stəngk\; **stunk; stink·ing 1 :** to give off or cause to have a strong unpleasant smell **2 :** to be of very bad quality

²stink *n* : a strong unpleasant smell

stink·bug \'stingk-ˌbəg\ *n* : a bug that gives off a bad smell

¹stint \'stint\ *vb* : to be stingy or saving ⟨don't *stint* when health is concerned⟩

²stint *n* : an amount of work given to be done

¹stir \'stər\ *vb* **stirred; stir·ring 1 :** to make or cause to make a usually slight movement or change of position **2 :** to make active (as by pushing, beating, or prodding) ⟨*stir* up the fire⟩ **3 :** to mix, dissolve, or make by a continued circular movement ⟨*stir* sugar into coffee⟩ **4 :** AROUSE 2 ⟨*stir* up trouble⟩

²stir *n* **1 :** a state of upset or activity ⟨the whole town is in a *stir*⟩ **2 :** a slight movement **3 :** the act of stirring

stir·ring \'stər-ing\ *adj* : LIVELY 3, MOVING ⟨a *stirring* song⟩

stir·rup \'stər-əp\ *n* : either of a pair of small light frames often of metal hung by

straps from a saddle and used as a support for the foot of a horseback rider

¹stitch \'stich\ *n* **1 :** a sudden sharp pain especially in the side **2 :** one in-and-out movement of a threaded needle in sewing : a portion of thread left in the material after one such movement **3 :** a single loop of thread or yarn around a tool (as a knitting needle or crochet hook) **4 :** a method of stitching

²stitch *vb* **1 :** to fasten or join with stitches **2 :** to make, mend, or decorate with or as if with stitches **3 :** SEW 2

¹stock \'stäk\ *n* **1 :** a stump of a tree : a block of wood **2 :** the wooden part by which a rifle or shotgun is held during firing **3 stocks** *pl* : a wooden frame with holes for the feet or the feet and hands once used to punish a wrongdoer publicly **4 :** an original (as a person, race, or language) from which others descend **5 :** the whole supply or amount on hand **6 :** farm animals : LIVESTOCK, CATTLE **7 :** the ownership element in a business which is divided into shares that can be traded independently **8 :** liquid in which meat, fish, or vegetables have been simmered — **in stock :** on hand : in the store and available for purchase

stocks

²stock *vb* **1 :** to provide with or get stock or a stock ⟨*stock* a farm⟩ ⟨*stock* up on groceries⟩ **2 :** to get or keep a stock of ⟨that store *stocks* only the best goods⟩

³stock *adj* **1 :** kept regularly in stock ⟨comes in *stock* sizes⟩ **2 :** commonly used : STANDARD ⟨gave a *stock* answer⟩

stock·ade \stä-'kād\ *n* **1 :** a line of strong

\ə\ **abut**	\au̇\ **out**	\i\ **tip**	\ȯ\ **saw**	\u̇\ **foot**
\ər\ **further**	\ch\ **chin**	\ī\ **life**	\ȯi\ **coin**	\y\ **yet**
\a\ **mat**	\e\ **pet**	\j\ **job**	\th\ **thin**	\yü\ **few**
\ā\ **take**	\ē\ **easy**	\ng\ **sing**	\t̲h\ **this**	\yu̇\ **cure**
\ä\ **cot, cart**	\g\ **go**	\ō\ **bone**	\ü\ **food**	\zh\ **vision**

posts set in the ground to form a defense **2** : an enclosure formed by stakes driven into the ground

stock·bro·ker \'stäk-ˌbrō-kər\ *n* : a person who handles orders to buy and sell stocks

stock·hold·er \'stäk-ˌhōl-dər\ *n* : an owner of stock

stock·ing \'stäk-ing\ *n* : a close-fitting usually knit covering for the foot and leg

stock market *n* : a place where shares of stock are bought and sold

stocky \'stäk-ē\ *adj* **stock·i·er; stock·i·est** : compact, sturdy, and relatively thick in build : THICKSET

stock·yard \'stäk-ˌyärd\ *n* : a yard for stock and especially for keeping livestock about to be slaughtered or shipped

¹stole \'stōl\ *past of* STEAL

²stole *n* : a long wide scarf worn about the shoulders

stolen *past participle of* STEAL

¹stom·ach \'stəm-ək\ *n* **1** : the pouch into which food goes after it leaves the mouth and has passed down the throat **2** : ABDOMEN 1 **3** : ²DESIRE 1, LIKING ⟨had no *stomach* for trouble⟩

²stomach *vb* : to bear patiently : put up with ⟨I couldn't *stomach* their rude behavior⟩

stomp \'stämp, 'stȯmp\ *vb* : to walk heavily or noisily : STAMP ⟨*stomped* angrily out of the room⟩

¹stone \'stōn\ *n* **1** : earth or mineral matter hardened in a mass : ROCK **2** : a piece of rock coarser than gravel ⟨throw *stones*⟩ **3** : GEM **4** : a stony mass sometimes present in a diseased organ **5** : the kernel of a fruit in its hard case **6** *pl usually* **stone** : an English measure of weight equaling fourteen pounds (about 6.5 kilograms)

²stone *vb* **stoned; ston·ing 1** : to throw stones at **2** : to remove the stones of ⟨*stone* cherries⟩

³stone *adj* : of, relating to, or made of stone

Stone Age *n* : the oldest period in which human beings are known to have existed : the age during which stone tools were used

stone–blind \'stōn-'blīnd\ *adj* : completely blind

stone–deaf \'stōn-'def\ *adj* : completely deaf

stony \'stō-nē\ *adj* **ston·i·er; ston·i·est 1** : full of stones ⟨*stony* soil⟩ **2** : insensitive as stone : UNFEELING ⟨a *stony* stare⟩ **3** : hard as stone

stood *past of* STAND

stool \'stül\ *n* **1** : a seat without back or arms supported by three or four legs or by a central post **2** : FOOTSTOOL **3** : a mass of material discharged from the intestine

¹stoop \'stüp\ *vb* **1** : to bend down or over **2** : to carry the head and shoulders or the upper part of the body bent forward **3** : to do something that is beneath one ⟨*stoop* to lying⟩

²stoop *n* : a forward bend of the head and shoulders ⟨walks with a *stoop*⟩

³stoop *n* : a porch, platform, or stairway at the entrance of a house or building

¹stop \'stäp\ *vb* **stopped; stop·ping 1** : to close an opening by filling or blocking it : PLUG ⟨*stopped* my ears with cotton⟩ **2** : to hold back : RESTRAIN ⟨*stop* a person from going⟩ **3** : to halt the movement or progress of ⟨*stop* the car⟩ **4** : to come to an end : CEASE **5** : to make a visit : STAY ⟨*stop* with friends⟩

²stop *n* **1** : ¹END 2, FINISH **2** : a set of organ pipes of one tone quality : a control knob for such a set **3** : something that delays, blocks, or brings to a halt **4** : STOPPER, PLUG **5** : the act of stopping : the state of being stopped **6** : a halt in a journey : STAY ⟨made a *stop* in the mountains⟩ **7** : a stopping place ⟨a bus *stop*⟩

stop·light \'stäp-ˌlīt\ *n* **1** : a light on the rear of a motor vehicle that goes on when the driver presses the brake pedal **2** : a signal light used in controlling traffic

stop·over \'stäp-ˌō-vər\ *n* : a stop made during a journey

stop·page \'stäp-ij\ *n* : the act of stopping : the state of being stopped

stop·per \'stäp-ər\ *n* : something (as a cork or plug) used to stop openings

stop·watch \'stäp-ˌwäch\ *n* : a watch having a hand that can be started and stopped for exact timing (as of a race)

stor·age \'stōr-ij\ *n* **1** : space or a place for storing **2** : an amount stored **3** : the act of storing : the state of being stored **4** : the price charged for storing something

storage battery *n* : a battery that can be renewed by passing an electric current through it

¹store \'stōr\ *vb* **stored; stor·ing 1** : to provide with what is needed : SUPPLY ⟨*store* a ship with goods⟩ **2** : to put away for future use ⟨*store* food in the freezer⟩ **3** : to put somewhere for safekeeping ⟨*store* the jewels in a safe⟩

²store *n* **1** **stores** *pl* : something collected and kept for future use ⟨a ship's *stores*⟩ **2** : a large quantity, supply, or number ⟨a *store* of natural resources⟩ **3** : a place where goods are sold : SHOP ⟨a candy *store*⟩ — **in store** : ¹READY 1 ⟨we have a big surprise *in store* for you⟩

store·house \'stŏr-ˌhaús\ *n, pl* **store·hous·es** \-ˌhaú-zəz\ **1 :** a building for storing goods **2 :** a large supply or source

store·keep·er \'stŏr-ˌkē-pər\ *n* **1 :** an owner or manager of a store or shop **2 :** a person in charge of supplies (as in a factory)

store·room \'stŏr-ˌrüm, -ˌrúm\ *n* **:** a room for storing things not in use

stork \'stŏrk\ *n* **:** a large Old World wading bird that looks like the related herons and includes one European form (the **white stork**) that often nests on roofs and chimneys

stork

¹storm \'stŏrm\ *n* **1 :** a heavy fall of rain, snow, or sleet often with strong wind **2 :** a violent outburst ⟨a *storm* of protest⟩ **3 :** a violent attack on a defended position ⟨took the fort by *storm*⟩

²storm *vb* **1 :** to blow hard and rain or snow heavily **2 :** to make a mass attack against **3 :** to be very angry : RAGE **4 :** to rush about violently ⟨the mob *stormed* through the streets⟩

stormy \'stŏr-mē\ *adj* **storm·i·er; storm·i·est 1 :** relating to or affected by a storm ⟨a *stormy* sea⟩ **2 :** displaying anger and excitement ⟨a *stormy* meeting⟩ — **storm·i·ness** *n*

¹sto·ry \'stŏr-ē\ *n, pl* **sto·ries 1 :** a report about incidents or events : ACCOUNT **2 :** a short often amusing tale **3 :** a tale shorter than a novel **4 :** a widely told rumor **5 :** ³LIE, FALSEHOOD

²sto·ry *or* **sto·rey** \'stŏr-ē\ *n, pl* **sto·ries** *or* **sto·reys :** a set of rooms or an area making up one floor level of a building

stout \'staút\ *adj* **1 :** of strong character : BRAVE, FIRM **2 :** of a strong or lasting sort : STURDY, TOUGH **3 :** bulky in body : FLESHY **synonyms** see FAT — **stout·ly** *adv* — **stout·ness** *n*

¹stove \'stōv\ *n* **:** a structure usually of iron or steel that burns fuel or uses electricity to provide heat (as for cooking or heating)

²stove *past of* STAVE

stove·pipe \'stōv-ˌpīp\ *n* **:** a metal pipe to carry away smoke from a stove

stow \'stō\ *vb* **1 :** to put away : STORE **2 :** to arrange in an orderly way : PACK **3 :** ²LOAD 1

stow·away \'stō-ə-ˌwā\ *n* **:** a person who hides (as in a ship or airplane) to travel free

strad·dle \'strad-l\ *vb* **strad·dled; strad·dling 1 :** to stand, sit, or walk with the legs spread wide apart **2 :** to stand, sit, or ride with a leg on either side of ⟨*straddle* a horse⟩ **3 :** to favor or seem to favor two opposite sides of ⟨*straddle* a question⟩

strag·gle \'strag-əl\ *vb* **strag·gled; strag·gling 1 :** to wander from a straight course or way : STRAY **2 :** to trail off from others of its kind — **strag·gler** \'strag-lər\ *n*

¹straight \'strāt\ *adj* **1 :** following the same direction throughout its length : not having curves, bends, or angles ⟨a *straight* line⟩ **2 :** not straying from the main point or proper course ⟨*straight* thinking⟩ **3 :** not straying from what is right or honest ⟨a *straight* answer⟩ **4 :** correctly ordered or arranged ⟨keep accounts *straight*⟩ — **straight·ness** *n*

²straight *adv* **:** in a straight manner, course, or line

straight·en \'strāt-n\ *vb* **1 :** to make or become straight **2 :** to put in order ⟨*straighten* up a room⟩

straight·for·ward \strāt-'fŏr-wərd\ *adj* **:** being plain and honest : FRANK ⟨gave a *straightforward* reply⟩ — **straight·for·ward·ly** *adv* — **straight·for·ward·ness** *n*

straight·way \'strāt-ˌwā\ *adv* **:** IMMEDIATELY 2

¹strain \'strān\ *n* **1 :** a line of ancestors to whom a person is related **2 :** a group of individuals that cannot be told from related kinds by appearance alone ⟨a new *strain* of wheat⟩ **3 :** a quality or disposition that runs through a family or race **4 :** a small amount : TRACE ⟨a *strain* of sadness⟩ **5 :** MELODY 2, AIR

²strain *vb* **1 :** to stretch or be stretched, pulled, or used to the limit ⟨muscles *straining* under a load⟩ **2 :** to stretch beyond a proper limit ⟨*strain* the truth⟩ **3 :** to try one's hardest ⟨*strain* to lift a heavy box⟩ **4 :** to injure or be injured by too much or too hard use or effort ⟨*strain* one's heart⟩ **5 :** to press or pass through a strainer : FILTER

³strain *n* **1 :** the act of straining **2 :** the state of being strained **3 :** ²OVERWORK, WORRY **4 :** bodily injury resulting from strain or from a wrench or twist that stretches muscles and ligaments

strained \'strānd\ *adj* **1 :** not easy or natu-

\ə\ **abut**	\aú\ **out**	\i\ **tip**	\ó\ **saw**	\ú\ **foot**
\ər\ **further**	\ch\ **chin**	\ī\ **life**	\ói\ **coin**	\y\ **yet**
\a\ **mat**	\e\ **pet**	\j\ **job**	\th\ **thin**	\yü\ **few**
\ā\ **take**	\ē\ **easy**	\ng\ **sing**	\th\ **this**	\yú\ **cure**
\ä\ **cot, cart**	\g\ **go**	\ō\ **bone**	\ü\ **food**	\zh\ **vision**

ral ⟨a *strained* smile⟩ **2** : brought close to war ⟨*strained* relations between countries⟩

strain·er \'strā-nər\ *n* : a device (as a screen, sieve, or filter) to hold back solid pieces while a liquid passes through

strait \'strāt\ *n* **1** : a narrow channel connecting two bodies of water **2** : ¹DISTRESS 1, NEED — often used in pl. ⟨in difficult *straits*⟩

¹strand \'strand\ *n* : the land bordering a body of water : SHORE, BEACH

²strand *vb* **1** : to run, drive, or cause to drift onto a strand : run aground **2** : to leave in a strange or unfavorable place especially without any chance to get away ⟨*stranded* in a strange city⟩

³strand *n* **1** : one of the fibers, threads, strings, or wires twisted or braided to make a cord, rope, or cable **2** : something long or twisted like a rope ⟨a *strand* of pearls⟩ ⟨a *strand* of hair⟩

strange \'strānj\ *adj* **strang·er; strang·est** **1** : of or relating to some other person, place, or thing ⟨the cuckoo lays its eggs in a *strange* nest⟩ **2** : exciting curiosity, surprise, or wonder because of not being usual or ordinary ⟨a *strange* sight⟩ **3** : UNFAMILIAR 1 ⟨*strange* surroundings⟩ **4** : ill at ease : SHY ⟨felt *strange* on the first day at school⟩ — **strange·ly** *adv* — **strange·ness** *n*

strang·er \'strān-jər\ *n* **1** : one who is not in the place where one's home is : FOREIGNER **2** : GUEST 1, VISITOR **3** : a person whom one does not know or has not met

stran·gle \'strang-gəl\ *vb* **stran·gled; stran·gling** **1** : to choke to death by squeezing the throat **2** : to choke in any way — **stran·gler** \-glər\ *n*

¹strap \'strap\ *n* : a narrow strip of flexible material (as leather) used especially for fastening, binding, or wrapping

²strap *vb* **strapped; strap·ping** **1** : to fasten with or attach by means of a strap **2** : BIND 1, 2, CONSTRICT **3** : to whip with a strap

strap·ping \'strap-ing\ *adj* : LARGE, STRONG

strat·a·gem \'strat-ə-jəm\ *n* : a trick in war to deceive or outwit the enemy

stra·te·gic \strə-'tē-jik\ *adj* **1** : of, relating to, or showing the use of strategy ⟨a *strategic* retreat⟩ **2** : useful or important in strategy ⟨*strategic* weapons⟩

strat·e·gy \'strat-ə-jē\ *n, pl* **strat·e·gies** **1** : the skill of using military, naval, and air forces to win a war **2** : a clever plan or method

strat·o·sphere \'strat-ə-ˌsfiər\ *n* : an upper portion of the atmosphere more than eleven kilometers above the earth where temperature changes little and clouds rarely form

stra·tum \'strāt-əm, 'strat-\ *n, pl* **stra·ta** \-ə\ : LAYER 2 ⟨a *stratum* of rock⟩

stra·tus \'strāt-əs, 'strat-\ *n, pl* **stra·ti** \'strāt-ˌī, 'strat-\ : a cloud extending over a large area at an altitude of from 600 to 2000 meters

straw \'strȯ\ *n* **1** : stalks especially of grain after threshing **2** : a single dry coarse plant stalk : a piece of straw **3** : a slender tube for sucking up a beverage

straw·ber·ry \'strȯ-ˌber-ē\ *n, pl* **straw·ber·ries** : the juicy edible usually red fruit of a low herb (**strawberry vine**) with white flowers and long slender runners

strawberry

¹stray \'strā\ *vb* **1** : to wander from a group or from the proper place : ROAM ⟨the gate was left open and the cattle *strayed*⟩ **2** : to go off from a straight or the right course ⟨your story *strays* from the truth⟩

²stray *n* : a person or animal that strays

³stray *adj* **1** : having strayed or been lost ⟨a *stray* dog⟩ ⟨found a few *stray* mittens⟩ **2** : occurring here and there : CHANCE ⟨a few *stray* comments⟩

¹streak \'strēk\ *n* **1** : a line or mark of a different color or composition from its background **2** : a narrow band of light ⟨a *streak* of lightning⟩ **3** : a small amount : TRACE, STRAIN ⟨a *streak* of humor⟩ **4** : a short series of something ⟨a *streak* of luck⟩ ⟨a winning *streak*⟩ — **streaked** \'strēkt, 'strē-kəd\ *adj*

²streak *vb* **1** : to make streaks in or on ⟨hair *streaked* with gray⟩ **2** : to move swiftly : RUSH ⟨a jet *streaking* across the sky⟩

¹stream \'strēm\ *n* **1** : a body of water (as a brook or river) flowing on the earth **2** : a flow of liquid ⟨a *stream* of tears⟩ **3** : a steady flow ⟨a *stream* of words⟩

²stream *vb* **1** : to flow or cause to flow in or as if in a stream ⟨tears *streaming* down their faces⟩ **2** : to pour out streams of liquid ⟨a face *streaming* with sweat⟩ **3** : to trail out at full length ⟨hair *streaming* in the wind⟩ **4** : to move forward in a steady stream ⟨passengers *streamed* off the ship⟩

stream·er \'strē-mər\ *n* **1** : a flag that streams in the wind : PENNANT **2** : a long narrow wavy strip (as of ribbon on a hat) suggesting a banner floating in the wind **3 streamers** *pl* : AURORA BOREALIS

stream·lined \strēm-'līnd\ *adj* **1** : designed or constructed to make motion through water or air easier or as if for this purpose ⟨a *streamlined* automobile⟩ **2** : made shorter, simpler, or more efficient ⟨a *streamlined* course of study⟩

street \'strēt\ *n* **1** : a public way especially in a city, town, or village **2** : the people living along a street ⟨the whole *street* was excited⟩

street·car \'strēt-,kär\ *n* : a passenger vehicle that runs on rails and operates mostly on city streets

strength \'strength\ *n* **1** : the quality of being strong **2** : power to resist force ⟨the *strength* of a rope⟩ **3** : power to resist attack **4** : intensity of light, color, sound, or odor **5** : force as measured in numbers ⟨the full *strength* of an army⟩ **synonyms** see POWER

strength·en \'streng-thən\ *vb* : to make, grow, or become stronger

stren·u·ous \'stren-yə-wəs\ *adj* **1** : very active : ENERGETIC ⟨a *strenuous* supporter of the president⟩ **2** : showing or requiring much energy ⟨*strenuous* exercise⟩ — **stren·u·ous·ly** *adv*

strep·to·my·cin \,strep-tə-'mīs-n\ *n* : a substance produced by a soil bacterium and used especially in treating tuberculosis

¹stress \'stres\ *n* **1** : a force that tends to change the shape of a body **2** : something that causes bodily or mental tension : a state of tension resulting from a stress **3** : special importance given to something **4** : relative prominence of sound : a syllable carrying this stress : ACCENT

²stress *vb* **1** : ²ACCENT 1 ⟨*stress* the first syllable⟩ **2** : to expose to stress : STRAIN **3** : to give special importance to ⟨*stressed* the need to save energy⟩

stress mark *n* : a mark used with a written syllable in the respelling of a word to show that this syllable is to be stressed when spoken

¹stretch \'strech\ *vb* **1** : to reach out : EXTEND, SPREAD ⟨*stretched* out a hand for the apple⟩ **2** : to draw out in length or width or both : EXPAND, ENLARGE **3** : to draw up from a cramped, stooping, or relaxed position ⟨awoke and *stretched* myself⟩ **4** : to pull tight ⟨canvas *stretched* over a frame⟩ **5** : to cause to reach or continue ⟨*stretch* a wire between two

posts⟩ **6** : EXAGGERATE **7** : to become extended without breaking ⟨rubber *stretches* easily⟩

²stretch *n* **1** : the act of extending or drawing out beyond ordinary or normal limits ⟨a *stretch* of the imagination⟩ **2** : the extent to which something may be stretched **3** : a continuous extent in length, area, or time ⟨a fine *stretch* of country⟩ **4** : the act or an instance of stretching the body or one of its parts

stretch·er \'strech-ər\ *n* **1** : one that stretches ⟨a curtain *stretcher*⟩ **2** : a light bedlike device for carrying sick or injured persons

strew \'strü\ *vb* **strewed; strewed** *or* **strewn** \'strün\; **strew·ing** **1** : to spread by scattering ⟨*strew* crumbs for the birds⟩ **2** : to cover by or as if by scattering something

strick·en \'strik-ən\ *adj* **1** : hit or wounded by or as if by a missile **2** : troubled with disease, misfortune, or sorrow

strict \'strikt\ *adj* **1** : permitting no avoidance or escape ⟨*strict* discipline⟩ **2** : kept with great care : ABSOLUTE ⟨*strict* secrecy⟩ **3** : carefully observing something (as a rule or principle) : EXACT, PRECISE ⟨a *strict* Catholic⟩ — **strict·ly** *adv* — **strict·ness** *n*

¹stride \'strīd\ *vb* **strode** \'strōd\; **strid·den** \'strid-n\; **strid·ing** \'strīd-ing\ **1** : to walk or run with long even steps **2** : to step over : STRADDLE

²stride *n* **1** : a long step : the distance covered by such a step **2** : a step forward : ADVANCE ⟨made great *strides* in their studies⟩ **3** : a way of striding

strife \'strīf\ *n* **1** : bitter and sometimes violent disagreement **2** : ²STRUGGLE 1, CONTENTION

¹strike \'strīk\ *vb* **struck** \'strək\; **struck** *or* **strick·en** \'strik-ən\; **strik·ing** \'strī-king\ **1** : GO 1, PROCEED ⟨*strike* off into the woods⟩ **2** : to touch or hit with force ⟨*struck* me with a whip⟩ ⟨lightning never *strikes* twice⟩ **3** : to lower (as a flag or sail) usually in salute or surrender **4** : to come into contact or collision with ⟨the ship *struck* a rock⟩ **5** : to make a military attack : FIGHT ⟨*strike* for freedom⟩ **6** : to remove or cancel with or as if with the stroke of a pen ⟨*strike* a name from the list⟩ **7** : to make known by sounding or cause to sound ⟨the clock *struck* one⟩

\ə\ **abut**	\aů\ **out**	\i\ **tip**	\ȯ\ **saw**	\ů\ **foot**	
\ər\ **further**	\ch\ **chin**	\ī\ **life**	\ȯi\ **coin**	\y\ **yet**	
\a\ **mat**	\e\ **pet**	\j\ **job**	\th\ **thin**	\yü\ **few**	
\ā\ **take**	\ē\ **easy**	\ng\ **sing**	\th\ **this**	\yů\ **cure**	
\ä\ **cot, cart**	\g\ **go**	\ō\ **bone**	\ü\ **food**	\zh\ **vision**	

⟨*strike* a bell⟩ **8** : to affect usually suddenly ⟨*stricken* with a high fever⟩ **9** : to produce by stamping with a die or punch ⟨*strike* a medal⟩ **10** : to produce by or as if by a blow ⟨*strike* fear into the enemy⟩ **11** : to cause to ignite by scratching ⟨*strike* a match⟩ **12** : to agree on the arrangements of ⟨*strike* a bargain⟩ **13** : to make an impression on ⟨it *struck* me as funny⟩ **14** : to come upon : DISCOVER ⟨*strike* oil⟩ **15** : to stop work in order to obtain a change in conditions of work

²strike *n* **1** : an act or instance of striking **2** : a stopping of work by workers to force an employer to agree to demands **3** : a discovery of a valuable mineral deposit **4** : a baseball pitch that is swung at or that passes through a certain area over home plate (**strike zone**) and that counts against the batter **5** : DISADVANTAGE, HANDICAP **6** : the knocking down of all ten bowling pins with the first ball **7** : a military attack

strike•out \'strī-ˌkau̇t\ *n* : an out in baseball that results from a batter's striking out

strike out \strī-'kau̇t\ *vb* : to be out in baseball by getting three strikes as a batter

strik•ing \'strī-kiŋ\ *adj* : attracting attention : REMARKABLE ⟨a *striking* resemblance⟩ — **strik•ing•ly** *adv*

¹string \'striŋ\ *n* **1** : a small cord used to bind, fasten, or tie **2** : a thin tough plant structure (as the fiber connecting the halves of a bean pod) **3** : the gut, wire, or plastic cord of a musical instrument that vibrates to produce a tone **4 strings** *pl* : the stringed instruments of an orchestra **5** : a group, series, or line of objects threaded on a string or arranged as if strung together ⟨a *string* of automobiles⟩

²string *vb* **strung** \'strəŋ\; **string•ing 1** : to provide with strings ⟨*string* a violin⟩ **2** : to make tense ⟨my nerves were *strung* up⟩ **3** : ²THREAD **4** ⟨*string* beads⟩ **4** : to tie, hang, or fasten with string **5** : to remove the strings of ⟨*string* beans⟩ **6** : to set or stretch out in a line ⟨*string* wires from tree to tree⟩

string bass *n* : DOUBLE BASS

string bean *n* : a bean grown primarily for its pods which are eaten before the seeds are full grown

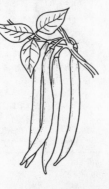

string bean

stringed instrument \'striŋd-\ *n* : a musical instrument (as a violin, guitar, or piano) sounded by plucking or striking or by drawing a bow across tight strings

string•er \'striŋ-ər\ *n* : a long strong piece of wood or metal used for support or strengthening in building (as under a floor)

stringy \'striŋ-ē\ *adj* **string•i•er; string•i•est** : containing, consisting of, or like string ⟨*stringy* meat⟩ ⟨*stringy* hair⟩

¹strip \'strip\ *vb* **stripped; strip•ping 1** : to remove clothes : UNDRESS **2** : to take away all duties, honors, or special rights ⟨they were *stripped* of their rank⟩ **3** : to remove a covering layer ⟨*strip* bark from a tree⟩ **4** : to take away everything of value ⟨thieves *stripped* the car⟩

²strip *n* : a long narrow piece or area

strip–crop•ping \'strip-ˌkräp-iŋ\ *n* : the growing of a food crop (as potatoes) in alternate strips with a crop (as grass) that forms sod and helps keep the soil from being worn away

¹stripe \'strīp\ *n* **1** : a line or long narrow division or section of something different in color or appearance from the background **2** : a piece of material often with a special design worn (as on a sleeve) to show military rank or length of service

²stripe *vb* **striped; strip•ing** : to make stripes on

striped \'strīpt, 'strī-pəd\ *adj* : having stripes

strive \'strīv\ *vb* **strove** \'strōv\; **striv•en** \'striv-ən\ *or* **strived; striv•ing** \'strī-viŋ\ **1** : to carry on a conflict or effort : CONTEND ⟨*strive* against fate⟩ **2** : to try hard ⟨*strive* to win⟩

strode *past of* STRIDE

¹stroke \'strōk\ *vb* **stroked; strok•ing** : to rub gently in one direction

²stroke *n* **1** : the act of striking : BLOW **2** : a single unbroken movement especially in one direction : one of a series of repeated movements (as in swimming or rowing a boat) **3** : the hitting of a ball in a game (as golf or tennis) **4** : a sudden action or process that results in something being struck ⟨a *stroke* of lightning⟩ **5** : a sudden or unexpected example ⟨a *stroke* of luck⟩ **6** : a sudden weakening or loss of consciousness and powers of voluntary movement that results from the breaking or blocking of an artery in the brain **7** : effort by which something is done or the results of such effort ⟨it was a *stroke* of genius⟩ **8** : the sound of striking (as of a clock or bell) ⟨at the *stroke* of midnight⟩ **9** : a mark made by a single movement of a brush, pen, or tool

¹stroll \'strōl\ *vb* : to walk in a leisurely manner : RAMBLE

²stroll *n* : a leisurely walk : RAMBLE

stroll·er \'strō-lər\ *n* : a small carriage in which a baby can sit and be pushed around

strong \'stróng\ *adj* **strong·er** \'stróng-gər\; **strong·est** \'stróng-gəst\ **1** : having great power in the muscles **2** : HEALTHY 1, 2, ROBUST **3** : having great resources ⟨a *strong* nation⟩ **4** : of a specified number ⟨an army 10,000 *strong*⟩ **5** : PERSUASIVE ⟨*strong* arguments⟩ **6** : having much of some quality ⟨*strong* coffee⟩ ⟨*strong* light⟩ **7** : moving with speed and force ⟨a *strong* wind⟩ **8** : ENTHUSIASTIC, ZEALOUS **9** : not easily injured or overcome ⟨a *strong* bridge⟩ ⟨a *strong* opponent⟩ **10** : well established : FIRM ⟨*strong* beliefs⟩ — **strong·ly** \'stróng-lē\ *adv*

synonyms STRONG, STURDY, and TOUGH mean showing the power to endure opposing force. STRONG suggests great bodily or material power ⟨a *strong* person is needed to lift that⟩ ⟨a *strong* army⟩ STURDY suggests the ability to endure pressure or hard use ⟨a *sturdy* table⟩ TOUGH suggests that something is very firm and elastic ⟨this meat is *tough*⟩ ⟨a *tough* fabric that will last many years⟩

strong·hold \'stróng-‚hōld\ *n* : FORTRESS

strove *past of* STRIVE

struck *past of* STRIKE

struc·tur·al \'strək-chə-rəl\ *adj* **1** : of, relating to, or affecting structure ⟨*structural* weaknesses⟩ **2** : used or formed for use in construction ⟨*structural* steel⟩

struc·ture \'strək-chər\ *n* **1** : something built (as a house or dam) **2** : the manner in which something is built : CONSTRUCTION **3** : the arrangement or relationship of parts or organs ⟨the *structure* of the body⟩

¹strug·gle \'strəg-əl\ *vb* **strug·gled; strug·gling 1** : to make a great effort to overcome someone or something : STRIVE ⟨*struggled* with the burglar⟩ ⟨*struggling* with money problems⟩ **2** : to move with difficulty or with great effort ⟨*struggled* through the snow⟩

²struggle *n* **1** : a violent effort **2** : ²FIGHT 1, CONTEST

strum \'strəm\ *vb* **strummed; strumming** : to play on a stringed instrument by brushing the strings with the fingers ⟨*strum* a guitar⟩

strung *past of* STRING

¹strut \'strət\ *vb* **strut·ted; strut·ting** : to walk in a stiff proud way

²strut *n* **1** : a bar or brace used to resist lengthwise pressure **2** : a strutting step or walk

¹stub \'stəb\ *n* **1** : a short part remaining after the rest has been removed or used up ⟨a pencil *stub*⟩ **2** : a small part of a check kept as a record of what was on the detached check

²stub *vb* **stubbed; stub·bing** : to strike (as the toe) against an object

stub·ble \'stəb-əl\ *n* **1** : the stem ends of herbs and especially cereal grasses left in the ground after harvest **2** : a rough growth or surface like stubble in a field : a short growth of beard

stub·born \'stəb-ərn\ *adj* **1** : refusing to change an opinion or course of action in spite of difficulty or urging ⟨*stubborn* as a mule⟩ **2** : PERSISTENT ⟨a *stubborn* cough⟩ **3** : difficult to handle, manage, or treat ⟨*stubborn* hair⟩ — **stub·born·ly** *adv* — **stub·born·ness** *n*

stub·by \'stəb-ē\ *adj* **stub·bi·er; stub·bi·est** : short and thick like a stub ⟨*stubby* fingers⟩

¹stuc·co \'stək-ō\ *n, pl* **stuc·cos** *or* **stuc·coes** : a plaster for coating walls

²stucco *vb* : to coat or decorate with stucco

stuck *past of* STICK

stuck–up \'stək-'əp\ *adj* : VAIN 2, CONCEITED ⟨they're awfully *stuck-up*⟩

¹stud \'stəd\ *n* **1** : one of the smaller vertical braces of the walls of a building to which the wall materials are fastened **2** : a removable device like a button used to fasten something or as an ornament ⟨shirt *studs*⟩ **3** : one of the metal cleats used on a snow tire to provide a better grip

²stud *vb* **stud·ded; stud·ding 1** : to supply or cover with or as if with studs **2** : to set thickly together ⟨water *studded* with islands⟩

stu·dent \'stüd-nt, 'styüd-\ *n* : a person who studies especially in school : PUPIL

stu·dio \'stüd-ē-‚ō, 'styüd-\ *n, pl* **stu·di·os 1** : the place where an artist works **2** : a place for the study of an art **3** : a place where movies are made **4** : a place from which radio or television programs are broadcast

stu·di·ous \'stüd-ē-əs, 'styüd-\ *adj* : devoted to and fond of study ⟨a *studious* child⟩

\ə\ abut	\aú\ out	\i\ tip	\ó\ saw	\ú\ foot
\ər\ further	\ch\ chin	\ī\ life	\ói\ coin	\y\ yet
\a\ mat	\e\ pet	\j\ job	\th\ thin	\yü\ few
\ā\ take	\ē\ easy	\ng\ sing	\th\ this	\yü\ cure
\ä\ cot, cart	\g\ go	\ō\ bone	\ü\ food	\zh\ vision

¹**study** \'stəd-ē\ *n, pl* **stud·ies** **1** : use of the mind to get knowledge **2** : a careful investigation or examination of something ⟨the *study* of a disease⟩ **3** : a room especially for study, reading, or writing

²**study** *vb* **stud·ied; study·ing** **1** : to use the mind to learn about something by reading, investigating, or memorizing **2** : to give close attention to ⟨*studied* the request carefully⟩

¹**stuff** \'stəf\ *n* **1** : materials, supplies, or equipment that people need or use **2** : something mentioned or understood but not named ⟨wipe that *stuff* off your face⟩ **3** : writing, speech, or ideas of little value ⟨it's just *stuff* and nonsense⟩ **4** : basic part of something : SUBSTANCE ⟨shows the *stuff* of greatness⟩

²**stuff** *vb* **1** : to fill by packing or crowding things in : CRAM ⟨*stuffed* the suitcases⟩ **2** : OVEREAT, GORGE ⟨*stuffed* themselves on candy⟩ **3** : to fill with a stuffing ⟨*stuff* a turkey⟩ **4** : to stop up : CONGEST ⟨a *stuffed* nose⟩ **5** : to force into something : THRUST ⟨*stuffed* the clothes into the drawer⟩ **synonyms** see PACK

stuff·ing \'stəf-ing\ *n* **1** : material used in filling up or stuffing something **2** : a mixture (as of bread crumbs and seasonings) used to stuff meat, vegetables, eggs, or poultry

stuffy \'stəf-ē\ *adj* **stuff·i·er; stuff·i·est** **1** : needing fresh air ⟨a *stuffy* room⟩ **2** : stuffed or choked up ⟨a *stuffy* nose⟩ **3** : ¹DULL 8

¹**stum·ble** \'stəm-bəl\ *vb* **stum·bled; stum·bling** **1** : to trip in walking or running **2** : to walk unsteadily **3** : to speak or act in a clumsy manner ⟨*stumbled* through the recitation⟩ **4** : to come unexpectedly or accidentally ⟨*stumbled* onto a clue⟩

²**stumble** *n* : an act or instance of stumbling

¹**stump** \'stəmp\ *n* **1** : the part of something (as an arm, a tooth, or a pencil) that remains after the rest has been removed, lost, or worn away : STUB **2** : the part of a tree that remains in the ground after the tree is cut down

²**stump** *vb* **1** : to walk or walk over heavily, stiffly, or clumsily as if with a wooden leg **2** : PERPLEX, BAFFLE ⟨the question *stumped* the experts⟩ **3** : ²STUB

stun \'stən\ *vb* **stunned; stun·ning** **1** : to make dizzy or senseless by or as if by a blow **2** : to affect with shock or confusion : fill with disbelief ⟨*stunned* by the news⟩

stung *past of* STING

stunk *past of* STINK

stun·ning \'stən-ing\ *adj* **1** : able or likely to make a person senseless or confused ⟨a *stunning* blow⟩ **2** : unusually lovely or attractive : STRIKING

¹**stunt** \'stənt\ *vb* : to hold back the normal growth of ⟨*stunt* a tree⟩

²**stunt** *n* : an unusual or difficult performance or act ⟨acrobatic *stunts*⟩

stu·pe·fy \'stü-pə-,fī, 'styü-\ *vb* **stu·pe·fied; stu·pe·fy·ing** **1** : to make stupid, dull, or numb by or as if by drugs **2** : ASTONISH, BEWILDER

stu·pen·dous \stü-'pen-dəs, styü-\ *adj* : amazing especially because of great size or height

stu·pid \'stü-pəd, 'styü-\ *adj* **1** : slow or dull of mind **2** : showing or resulting from a dull mind or a lack of proper attention ⟨a *stupid* mistake⟩ **3** : not interesting or worthwhile ⟨a *stupid* plot⟩ — **stu·pid·ly** *adv*

stu·pid·i·ty \stü-'pid-ət-ē, styü-\ *n, pl* **stu·pid·i·ties** **1** : the quality or state of being stupid **2** : a stupid thought, action, or remark

stu·por \'stü-pər, 'styü-\ *n* : a condition in which the senses or feelings become dull ⟨in a drunken *stupor*⟩

stur·dy \'stərd-ē\ *adj* **stur·di·er; stur·di·est** **1** : firmly built or made **2** : strong and healthy in body : ROBUST **3** : RESOLUTE **synonyms** see STRONG — **stur·di·ly** \'stərd-l-ē\ *adv* — **sturd·i·ness** \'stərd-ē-nəs\ *n*

stur·geon \'stər-jən\ *n* : a large food fish with tough skin and rows of bony plates

sturgeon

¹**stut·ter** \'stət-ər\ *vb* : to speak or say in a jerky way with involuntary repeating or interruption of sounds

²**stutter** *n* : the act or an instance of stuttering

¹**sty** \'stī\ *n, pl* **sties** : a pen for swine

²**sty** *or* **stye** \'stī\ *n, pl* **sties** *or* **styes** : a painful red swelling on the edge of an eyelid

¹**style** \'stīl\ *n* **1** : the narrow middle part of the pistil of a flower **2** : a way of speaking or writing **3** : an individual way of doing something ⟨a batter's *style* of holding the bat⟩ **4** : a method or manner that is felt to be very respectable, fashionable, or proper : FASHION ⟨dine in *style*⟩ ⟨clothes

that are out of *style*⟩ **synonyms** see FASHION

²style *vb* **styled; styl·ing** 1 : to identify by some descriptive term : CALL 2 : to design and make in agreement with an accepted or a new style ⟨well-*styled* hats⟩

styl·ish \'stī-lish\ *adj* : having style : FASHIONABLE — **styl·ish·ly** *adv* — **styl·ish·ness** *n*

sty·lus \'stī-ləs\ *n, pl* **sty·li** \-,lī\ *or* **sty·lus·es** : a pointed instrument used in ancient times for writing on wax tablets

¹sub \'səb\ *n* : ¹SUBSTITUTE

²sub *vb* **subbed; sub·bing** : to act as a substitute

³sub *n* : ²SUBMARINE

sub- *prefix* 1 : under : beneath : below ⟨*sub*marine⟩ 2 : lower in importance or rank : lesser 3 : division or part of ⟨*sub*set⟩ 4 : so as to form, stress, or deal with lesser parts or relations

sub·di·vide \,səb-də-'vīd\ *vb* **sub·di·vid·ed; sub·di·vid·ing** 1 : to divide the parts of into more parts 2 : to divide into several parts ⟨*subdivide* a farm into building lots⟩

sub·di·vi·sion \,səb-də-'vizh-ən\ *n* 1 : the act of subdividing 2 : one of the parts into which something is subdivided

sub·due \səb-'dü, -'dyü\ *vb* **sub·dued; sub·du·ing** 1 : to overcome in battle ⟨*subdued* the enemy⟩ 2 : to bring under control ⟨*subduing* one's fears⟩ 3 : to reduce the brightness or strength of : SOFTEN ⟨*subdued* light⟩

sub·head \'səb-,hed\ *or* **sub·head·ing** \-,hed-ing\ *n* : a heading under which one of the divisions of a subject is listed

¹sub·ject \'səb-jikt\ *n* 1 : a person under the authority or control of another 2 : a person who owes loyalty to a monarch or state 3 : a course of study 4 : an individual that is studied or experimented on 5 : the person or thing discussed : TOPIC 6 : the word or group of words about which the predicate makes a statement

²subject *adj* 1 : owing obedience or loyalty to another 2 : likely to be affected by ⟨*subject* to temptation⟩ ⟨*subject* to colds⟩ 3 : depending on ⟨*subject* to your approval⟩

³sub·ject \səb-'jekt\ *vb* 1 : to bring under control or rule 2 : to cause to put up with ⟨unwilling to *subject* us to embarrassment⟩

sub·lime \sə-'blīm\ *adj* 1 : grand or noble in thought, expression, or manner ⟨*sublime* truths⟩ 2 : having beauty enough or being impressive enough to arouse a mixed feeling of admiration and wonder ⟨*sublime* scenery⟩

¹sub·ma·rine \'səb-mə-,rēn\ *adj* : being, acting, growing, or used under water especially in the sea

²submarine *n* : a naval ship designed to operate underwater

sub·merge \səb-'mərj\ *vb* **sub·merged; sub·merg·ing** 1 : to put under or plunge into water 2 : to cover or become covered with or as if with water ⟨floods *submerged* the town⟩

sub·mis·sion \səb-'mish-ən\ *n* 1 : the act of submitting something (as for consideration or comment) 2 : the condition of being humble or obedient 3 : the act of submitting to power or authority

sub·mis·sive \səb-'mis-iv\ *adj* : willing to submit to others

sub·mit \səb-'mit\ *vb* **sub·mit·ted; sub·mit·ting** 1 : to leave to the judgment or approval of someone else ⟨*submit* a plan for consideration⟩ 2 : to put forward as an opinion, reason, or idea 3 : to yield to the authority, control, or choice of another

¹sub·or·di·nate \sə-'bórd-n-ət\ *adj* 1 : being in a lower class or rank : INFERIOR 2 : yielding to or controlled by authority

²subordinate *n* : one that is subordinate

³sub·or·di·nate \sə-'bórd-n-,āt\ *vb* **sub·or·di·nat·ed; sub·or·di·nat·ing** : to make subordinate

sub·scribe \səb-'skrīb\ *vb* **sub·scribed; sub·scrib·ing** 1 : to make known one's approval by or as if by signing ⟨we *subscribe* to your plan⟩ 2 : to agree to give or contribute by signing one's name with the amount promised ⟨*subscribe* fifty dollars to the building fund⟩ 3 : to place an order (as for a newspaper) with payment or a promise to pay — **sub·scrib·er** *n*

sub·scrip·tion \səb-'skrip-shən\ *n* 1 : an act or instance of subscribing 2 : a thing or amount subscribed ⟨a *subscription* of ten dollars⟩

sub·se·quent \'səb-si-kwənt\ *adj* : following in time, order, or place ⟨*subsequent* events⟩ — **sub·se·quent·ly** *adv*

sub·set \'səb-,set\ *n* : a mathematical set each of whose members is also a member of a larger set

sub·side \səb-'sīd\ *vb* **sub·sid·ed; sub·sid·ing** 1 : to become lower : SINK ⟨the flood *subsided*⟩ 2 : to become quiet or less ⟨the pain *subsided*⟩

sub·sist \səb-'sist\ *vb* : to continue living or being ⟨*subsisting* on bread and water⟩

\ə\ **abut**	\au̇\ **out**	\i\ **tip**	\ȯ\ **saw**	\u̇\ **foot**
\ər\ **further**	\ch\ **chin**	\ī\ **life**	\ȯi\ **coin**	\y\ **yet**
\a\ **mat**	\e\ **pet**	\j\ **job**	\th\ **thin**	\yü\ **few**
\ā\ **take**	\ē\ **easy**	\ng\ **sing**	\th\ **this**	\yu̇\ **cure**
\ä\ **cot, cart**	\g\ **go**	\ō\ **bone**	\ü\ **food**	\zh\ **vision**

sub·sis·tence \səb-'sis-təns\ *n* : the smallest amount (as of food and clothing) necessary to support life

sub·soil \'səb-ˌsȯil\ *n* : a layer of soil lying just under the topsoil

sub·stance \'səb-stəns\ *n* **1** : ESSENCE 1 **2** : the most important part ⟨the *substance* of a speech⟩ **3** : material of a certain kind ⟨an oily *substance*⟩ **4** : material belongings : WEALTH ⟨a person of *substance*⟩

sub·stan·dard \ˌsəb-'stan-dərd\ *adj* : being below what is standard

sub·stan·tial \səb-'stan-chəl\ *adj* **1** : made up of or relating to substance ⟨dreams are not *substantial*⟩ **2** : ABUNDANT ⟨a *substantial* meal⟩ **3** : PROSPEROUS 1 **4** : firmly constructed **5** : large in amount ⟨a *substantial* improvement⟩

¹sub·sti·tute \'səb-stə-ˌtüt, -ˌtyüt\ *n* : a person or thing that takes the place of another

²substitute *vb* **sub·sti·tut·ed; sub·sti·tut·ing** **1** : to put in the place of another **2** : to serve as a substitute

sub·sti·tu·tion \ˌsəb-stə-'tü-shən, -'tyü-\ *n* : the act or process of substituting

sub·tle \'sət-l\ *adj* **sub·tler** \'sət-lər\; **sub·tlest** \'sət-ləst\ **1** : DELICATE 1 ⟨a *subtle* fragrance⟩ **2** : SHREWD, KEEN ⟨*subtle* questions⟩ **3** : CLEVER 2, SLY — **sub·tly** \'sət-lē\ *adv*

sub·top·ic \'səb-ˌtäp-ik\ *n* : a topic (as in a composition) that is a division of a main topic

sub·tract \səb-'trakt\ *vb* : to take away (as one part or number from another) : DEDUCT

sub·trac·tion \səb-'trak-shən\ *n* : the subtracting of one number from another

sub·tra·hend \'səb-trə-ˌhend\ *n* : a number that is to be subtracted from another number

sub·urb \'səb-ˌərb\ *n* **1** : a part of a city or town near its outer edge **2** : a smaller community close to a city **3 suburbs** *pl* : the area of homes close to or surrounding a city — **sub·ur·ban** \sə-'bər-bən\ *adj or n*

sub·way \'səb-ˌwā\ *n* **1** : an underground tunnel **2** : a usually electric underground railway

suc·ceed \sək-'sēd\ *vb* **1** : to come after : FOLLOW **2** : to take the place of a ruler or leader who has died, resigned, or been removed **3** : to be successful

suc·cess \sək-'ses\ *n* **1** : satisfactory completion of something **2** : the gaining of wealth, respect, or fame **3** : a person or thing that succeeds

suc·cess·ful \sək-'ses-fəl\ *adj* **1** : resulting or ending well or in success **2** : gaining or having gained success — **suc·cess·ful·ly** \-fə-lē\ *adv*

suc·ces·sion \sək-'sesh-ən\ *n* **1** : the order, act, or right of succeeding to a throne, title, or property **2** : a series of persons or things that follow one after another

suc·ces·sive \sək-'ses-iv\ *adj* : following in order and without interruption — **suc·ces·sive·ly** *adv*

suc·ces·sor \sək-'ses-ər\ *n* : a person who succeeds to a throne, title, property, or office

suc·cor \'sək-ər\ *n* : ²HELP 1, RELIEF

suc·cu·lent \'sək-yə-lənt\ *adj* : JUICY

suc·cumb \sə-'kəm\ *vb* **1** : to yield to force or pressure ⟨*succumb* to temptation⟩ **2** : ¹DIE 1

¹such \'səch, səch\ *adj* **1** : of a kind just specified or to be specified ⟨a bag *such* as a doctor carries⟩ **2** : of the same class, type, or sort : SIMILAR ⟨opened three *such* stores⟩ **3** : so great : so remarkable ⟨*such* courage⟩

²such *pron* : that sort of person, thing, or group ⟨has a plan, if it may be called *such*⟩ ⟨*such* were the Romans⟩ ⟨boards and nails and *such*⟩

suck \'sək\ *vb* **1** : to draw in liquid and especially mother's milk with the mouth **2** : to draw liquid from by action of the mouth ⟨*suck* an orange⟩ **3** : to allow to dissolve gradually in the mouth ⟨*suck* a lollipop⟩ **4** : to put (as a thumb) into the mouth and draw on as if sucking **5** : ABSORB 1 ⟨plants *suck* moisture from the soil⟩

suck·er \'sək-ər\ *n* **1** : one that sucks : SUCKLING **2** : a freshwater fish related to the carps that has thick soft lips for sucking in food **3** : a new stem from the roots or lower part of a plant **4** : LOLLIPOP **5** : a person easily fooled or cheated

suck·le \'sək-əl\ *vb* **suck·led; suck·ling** : to feed from the breast or udder

suck·ling \'sək-ling\ *n* : a young mammal still sucking milk from its mother

suc·tion \'sək-shən\ *n* **1** : the act or process of sucking **2** : the process of drawing something into a space (as in a pump) by removing air from the space **3** : the force caused by suction

sud·den \'səd-n\ *adj* **1** : happening or coming quickly and unexpectedly ⟨a *sudden* shower⟩ **2** : met with unexpectedly ⟨a *sudden* turn in the road⟩ **3** : ¹STEEP 1 **4** : HASTY 2 ⟨a *sudden* decision⟩ — **sud·den·ly** *adv* — **sud·den·ness** *n*

suds \'sədz\ *n pl* **1** : soapy water especially when foamy **2** : the foam on soapy water

sue \'sü\ *vb* **sued; su•ing** : to seek justice or right by bringing legal action

suede \'swād\ *n* : leather tanned and rubbed so that it is soft and has a nap

su•et \'sü-ət\ *n* : the hard fat about the kidneys in beef and mutton from which tallow is made

suf•fer \'səf-ər\ *vb* **1** : to feel pain **2** : to experience something unpleasant ⟨*suffer* a defeat⟩ **3** : to bear loss or damage ⟨the business *suffered* during the storm⟩ **4** : [1]PERMIT — **suf•fer•er** \'səf-ər-ər\ *n*

suf•fer•ing \'səf-ə-ring, 'səf-ring\ *n* **1** : the state or experience of one that suffers **2** : a cause of distress : HARDSHIP

suf•fice \sə-'fis\ *vb* **suf•ficed; suf•fic•ing** **1** : to satisfy a need **2** : to be enough for

suf•fi•cient \sə-'fish-ənt\ *adj* : enough to achieve a goal or fill a need — **suf•fi•cient•ly** *adv*

suf•fix \'səf-,iks\ *n* : a letter or group of letters that comes at the end of a word and has a meaning of its own

suf•fo•cate \'səf-ə-,kāt\ *vb* **suf•fo•cat•ed; suf•fo•cat•ing** **1** : to kill by stopping the breath or depriving of oxygen to breathe **2** : to be or become choked or smothered **3** : to have or cause to have a feeling of smothering

suf•fo•ca•tion \,səf-ə-'kā-shən\ *n* : the act of suffocating or state of being suffocated

suf•frage \'səf-rij\ *n* : the right to vote

[1]sug•ar \'shug-ər\ *n* **1** : a sweet substance obtained from sugarcane, sugar beets, or maple syrup **2** : any of numerous soluble and usually sweet carbohydrates

[2]sugar *vb* **1** : to mix, cover, or sprinkle with sugar **2** : to make something less hard to take or put up with ⟨*sugar* advice with praise⟩ **3** : to change to crystals of sugar

sugar beet *n* : a large beet with white roots that is grown as a source of sugar

sug•ar•cane \'shug-ər-,kān\ *n* : a tall strong grass with jointed stems widely raised in tropical regions for the sugar it yields

sugar maple *n* : an American maple tree with hard strong wood and a sweet

sugarcane

sap that yields maple syrup and maple sugar

sug•gest \səg-'jest, sə-'jest\ *vb* **1** : to put (as a thought or desire) into a person's mind **2** : to offer as an idea ⟨*suggest* going for a walk⟩ **3** : to bring into one's mind through close connection or association ⟨smoke *suggests* fire⟩

sug•ges•tion \səg-'jes-chən, sə-'jes-\ *n* **1** : the act or process of suggesting **2** : a thought or plan that is suggested **3** : [1]HINT **2** ⟨gray with a *suggestion* of blue⟩

sug•ges•tive \səg-'jes-tiv, sə-'jes-\ *adj* **1** : giving a suggestion **2** : full of suggestions : PROVOCATIVE **3** : suggesting something improper or indecent

su•i•cide \'sü-ə-,sīd\ *n* **1** : the act of killing oneself purposely **2** : a person who commits suicide

[1]suit \'süt\ *n* **1** : an action in court for enforcing a right or claim **2** : an earnest request **3** : COURTSHIP **4** : a number of things used together : SET ⟨a *suit* of clothes⟩ **5** : all the playing cards of one kind (as spades) in a pack

[2]suit *vb* **1** : to be suitable or satisfactory **2** : to make suitable : ADAPT ⟨*suit* the action to the word⟩ **3** : to be proper for or pleasing with ⟨the scarf does not *suit* the dress⟩ **4** : to meet the needs or desires of

suit•abil•i•ty \,süt-ə-'bil-ət-ē\ *n* : the quality or state of being suitable

suit•able \'süt-ə-bəl\ *adj* : being fit or right for a use or group ⟨a movie *suitable* for children⟩ — **suit•ably** \-blē\ *adv*

suit•case \'süt-,kās\ *n* : a flat rectangular traveling bag

suite \'swēt, 'süt\ *n* **1** : a number of connected rooms (as in a hotel) **2** : a set of matched furniture for a room

suit•or \'süt-ər\ *n* : a man who courts a woman

sul•fur *or* **sul•phur** \'səl-fər\ *n* : a yellow chemical element that is found widely in nature and is used in making chemicals and paper

sul•fu•rous *or* **sul•phu•rous** \'səl-fə-rəs\ *adj* : containing or suggesting sulfur ⟨a *sulfurous* odor⟩

[1]sulk \'səlk\ *vb* : to be sullenly silent or irritable

[2]sulk *n* **1** : the state of one sulking **2** : a sulky mood or spell

[1]sulky \'səl-kē\ *adj* **sulk•i•er; sulk•i•est** : sulking or given to sulking

\ə\ abut	\au̇\ out	\i\ tip	\o̊\ saw	\u̇\ foot
\ər\ **further**	\ch\ **chin**	\ī\ **life**	\o̊i\ **coin**	\y\ **yet**
\a\ **mat**	\e\ **pet**	\j\ **job**	\th\ **thin**	\yü\ **few**
\ā\ **take**	\ē\ **easy**	\ng\ **sing**	\th̲\ **this**	\yu̇\ **cure**
\ä\ **cot, cart**	\g\ **go**	\ō\ **bone**	\ü\ **food**	\zh\ **vision**

²**sulky** *n, pl* **sulk·ies** : a light vehicle with two wheels, a seat for the driver only, and usually no body

sulky

sul·len \'səl-ən\ *adj* 1 : not sociable 2 : DREARY — **sul·len·ly** *adv*

sul·tan \'səlt-n\ *n* : a ruler especially of a Muslim state

sul·tana \,səl-'tan-ə\ *n* : the wife, mother, sister, or daughter of a sultan

sul·try \'səl-trē\ *adj* **sul·tri·er; sul·tri·est** : very hot and humid

¹**sum** \'səm\ *n* 1 : a quantity of money 2 : the whole amount ⟨the *sum* of your experience⟩ 3 : the result obtained by adding numbers ⟨the *sum* of 4 and 5 is 9⟩ 4 : a problem in arithmetic

²**sum** *vb* **summed; sum·ming** : to find the sum of by adding or counting

su·mac *or* **su·mach** \'shü-,mak, 'sü-\ *n* : any of a group of trees, shrubs, or woody vines having leaves with many leaflets and loose clusters of red or white berries

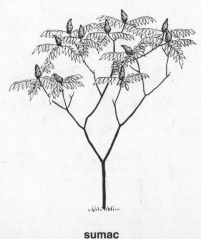

sumac

sum·ma·rize \'səm-ə-,rīz\ *vb* **sum·ma·rized; sum·ma·riz·ing** : to tell in or reduce to a summary

¹**sum·ma·ry** \'səm-ə-rē\ *adj* 1 : expressing or covering the main points briefly : CONCISE ⟨a *summary* account⟩ 2 : done without delay ⟨*summary* punishment⟩

²**summary** *n, pl* **sum·ma·ries** : a short statement of the main points (as in a book or report)

¹**sum·mer** \'səm-ər\ *n* 1 : the season between spring and autumn which is in the northern hemisphere usually the months of June, July, and August 2 : YEAR 2 ⟨a youth of sixteen *summers*⟩

²**summer** *vb* : to pass the summer

sum·mer·time \'səm-ər-,tīm\ *n* : the summer season

sum·mery \'səm-ə-rē\ *adj* : of, relating to, or typical of summer

sum·mit \'səm-ət\ *n* : the highest point (as of a mountain) : TOP

sum·mon \'səm-ən\ *vb* 1 : to call or send for : CONVENE 2 : to order to appear before a court of law 3 : to call into being : AROUSE ⟨*summon* up courage⟩ — **sum·mon·er** *n*

sum·mons \'səm-ənz\ *n, pl* **sum·mons·es** 1 : the act of summoning 2 : a call by authority to appear at a place named or to attend to some duty 3 : a written order to appear in court

sump·tu·ous \'səmp-chə-wəs\ *adj* : very expensive or luxurious

sum up *vb* : SUMMARIZE

¹**sun** \'sən\ *n* 1 : the celestial body whose light makes our day : the member of the solar system round which the planets revolve 2 : a celestial body like our sun 3 : SUNSHINE 1

²**sun** *vb* **sunned; sun·ning** 1 : to expose to or as if to the rays of the sun 2 : to sun oneself

sun·bathe \'sən-,bā<u>th</u>\ *vb* **sun·bathed; sun·bath·ing** : ²SUN 2

sun·beam \'sən-,bēm\ *n* : a ray of sunlight

sun·block \'sən-,bläk\ *n* : a strong sunscreen

sun·bon·net \'sən-,bän-ət\ *n* : a bonnet with a wide curving brim that shades the face and usually a ruffle at the back that protects the neck from the sun

sunbonnet

¹sun·burn \'sən-ˌbərn\ *vb* **sun·burned** \-ˌbərnd\ *or* **sun·burnt** \-ˌbərnt\; **sun·burn·ing** : to burn or discolor by the sun

²sunburn *n* : a sore red state of the skin caused by too much sunlight

sun·dae \'sən-dē\ *n* : a serving of ice cream topped with fruit, syrup, or nuts

Sun·day \'sən-dē\ *n* : the first day of the week : the Christian Sabbath

Sunday school *n* : a school held on Sunday in a church for religious education

sun·di·al \'sən-ˌdī-əl\ *n* : a device to show the time of day by the position of the shadow cast onto a marked plate by an object with a straight edge

sundial

sun·down \'sən-ˌdaun\ *n* : SUNSET

sun·dries \'sən-drēz\ *n pl* : various small articles or items

sun·dry \'sən-drē\ *adj* : more than one or two : VARIOUS ⟨we disagreed for *sundry* reasons⟩

sun·fish \'sən-ˌfish\ *n, pl* **sunfish** *or* **sun·fish·es** : any of numerous mostly small and brightly colored American freshwater fishes related to the perches

sun·flow·er \'sən-ˌflau-ər\ *n* : a tall plant often grown for its large flower heads with brown center and yellow petals or for its edible oily seeds

sung *past of* SING

sun·glass·es \'sən-ˌglas-əz\ *n pl* : glasses to protect the eyes from the sun

sunk *past of* SINK

sunk·en \'səng-kən\ *adj* 1 : lying at the bottom of a body of water ⟨*sunken* ships⟩ 2 : fallen in : HOLLOW ⟨*sunken* cheeks⟩ 3 : built or settled below the surrounding or normal level ⟨a *sunken* garden⟩

sun·lamp \'sən-ˌlamp\ *n* : an electric lamp that gives off radiation in the ultraviolet to infrared range

sun·less \'sən-ləs\ *adj* : being without sunlight : DARK

sun·light \'sən-ˌlīt\ *n* : SUNSHINE

sun·lit \'sən-ˌlit\ *adj* : lighted by the sun

sun·ny \'sən-ē\ *adj* **sun·ni·er; sun·ni·est** 1 : bright with sunshine ⟨a *sunny* day⟩ 2 : MERRY 1, CHEERFUL ⟨a *sunny* smile⟩

sun·rise \'sən-ˌrīz\ *n* 1 : the apparent rise of the sun above the horizon : the light and color that go with this 2 : the time at which the sun rises

sun·screen \'sən-ˌskrēn\ *n* : a substance used on the skin to help protect it from the sun's ultraviolet radiation

sun·set \'sən-ˌset\ *n* 1 : the apparent passing of the sun below the horizon : the light and color that go with this 2 : the time at which the sun sets

sun·shade \'sən-ˌshād\ *n* : something (as a parasol) used to protect from the sun's rays

sun·shine \'sən-ˌshīn\ *n* 1 : the sun's light or direct rays : the warmth and light given by the sun's rays 2 : something that spreads warmth or happiness

sun·stroke \'sən-ˌstrōk\ *n* : a disorder marked by high fever and collapse and caused by too much sun

sun·tan \'sən-ˌtan\ *n* : a browning of skin exposed to the sun

sun·up \'sən-ˌəp\ *n* : SUNRISE

sun·ward \'sən-wərd\ *adv or adj* : toward or facing the sun

su·per \'sü-pər\ *adj* 1 : very great 2 : very good

super- *prefix* 1 : more than ⟨*super*human⟩ 2 : extremely : very

su·perb \su̇-'pərb\ *adj* : outstandingly excellent, impressive, or beautiful **synonyms** see SPLENDID

su·per·fi·cial \ˌsü-pər-'fish-əl\ *adj* 1 : of or relating to the surface or appearance only ⟨a *superficial* cut⟩ 2 : not thorough : SHALLOW ⟨a *superficial* piece of work⟩ — **su·per·fi·cial·ly** *adv*

su·per·flu·ous \su̇-'pər-flə-wəs\ *adj* : going beyond what is enough or necessary : EXTRA

su·per·high·way \ˌsü-pər-'hī-ˌwā\ *n* : an expressway for high-speed traffic

su·per·hu·man \ˌsü-pər-'hyü-mən\ *adj* : going beyond normal human power, size, or ability

su·per·in·tend \ˌsü-pər-in-'tend\ *vb* : to have or exercise the charge of

su·per·in·tend·ent \ˌsü-pər-in-'ten-dənt\ *n* : a person who looks after or manages something (as schools or a building)

¹su·pe·ri·or \su̇-'pir-ē-ər\ *adj* 1 : situated higher up : higher in rank, importance, numbers, or quality 2 : excellent of its kind : BETTER 3 : feeling that one is better or more important than others : ARROGANT

²superior *n* 1 : one that is higher than another in rank, importance, or quality 2 : the head of a religious house or order

su·pe·ri·or·i·ty \su̇-ˌpir-ē-'ȯr-ət-ē\ *n* : the state or fact of being superior

¹su·per·la·tive \su̇-'pər-lət-iv\ *adj* 1 : of,

\ə\ abut	\au̇\ out	\i\ tip	\ȯ\ saw	\u̇\ foot	
\ər\ further	\ch\ chin	\ī\ life	\ȯi\ coin	\y\ yet	
\a\ mat	\e\ pet	\j\ job	\th\ thin	\yü\ few	
\ā\ take	\ē\ easy	\ng\ sing	\th\ this	\yu̇\ cure	
\ä\ cot, cart	\g\ go	\ō\ bone	\ü\ food	\zh\ vision	

relating to, or being the form of an adjective or adverb that shows the highest or lowest degree of comparison **2** : better than all others : SUPREME

²superlative *n* : the superlative degree or a superlative form in a language

su·per·mar·ket \'sü-pər-ˌmär-kət\ *n* : a self-service market selling foods and household items

su·per·nat·u·ral \ˌsü-pər-'nach-ə-rəl, -'nach-rəl\ *adj* : of or relating to something beyond or outside of nature or the visible universe

su·per·sede \ˌsü-pər-'sēd\ *vb* **su·per·sed·ed; su·per·sed·ing** : to take the place or position of

su·per·son·ic \ˌsü-pər-'sän-ik\ *adj* **1** : relating to or being vibrations too rapid to be heard **2** : having a speed from one to five times that of sound ⟨a *supersonic* airplane⟩

su·per·sti·tion \ˌsü-pər-'stish-ən\ *n* : beliefs or practices resulting from ignorance, fear of the unknown, or trust in magic or chance

su·per·sti·tious \ˌsü-pər-'stish-əs\ *adj* : of, relating to, showing, or influenced by superstition

su·per·vise \'sü-pər-ˌvīz\ *vb* **su·per·vised; su·per·vis·ing** : SUPERINTEND, OVERSEE

su·per·vi·sion \ˌsü-pər-'vizh-ən\ *n* : the act of supervising : MANAGEMENT

su·per·vi·sor \'sü-pər-ˌvī-zər\ *n* **1** : a person who supervises **2** : an officer in charge of a unit or an operation of a business, government, or school

sup·per \'səp-ər\ *n* **1** : the evening meal especially when dinner is eaten at midday **2** : refreshments served late in the evening especially at a social gathering

sup·plant \sə-'plant\ *vb* : to take the place of another usually unfairly

sup·ple \'səp-əl\ *adj* **sup·pler** \'səp-lər\; **sup·plest** \'səp-ləst\ **1** : ADAPTABLE ⟨a *supple* mind⟩ **2** : capable of bending or of being bent easily without stiffness, creases, or damage ⟨a *supple* body⟩ ⟨*supple* leather⟩

¹sup·ple·ment \'səp-lə-mənt\ *n* : something that supplies what is needed or adds to something else ⟨a food *supplement*⟩ ⟨the *supplement* at the back of the book⟩

²sup·ple·ment \'səp-lə-ˌment\ *vb* : to add to : COMPLETE ⟨*supplement* their incomes by doing odd jobs⟩

sup·ple·men·ta·ry \ˌsəp-lə-'ment-ə-rē\ *adj* : added as a supplement : ADDITIONAL

sup·pli·cate \'səp-lə-ˌkāt\ *vb* **sup·pli·cat-**ed; **sup·pli·cat·ing** : to ask or beg in a humble way : BESEECH

sup·pli·ca·tion \ˌsəp-lə-'kā-shən\ *n* : the act of supplicating

¹sup·ply \sə-'plī\ *vb* **sup·plied; sup·ply·ing** **1** : to provide for : SATISFY ⟨enough to *supply* the demand⟩ **2** : to make available : FURNISH ⟨the trees *supplied* us with shelter⟩ ⟨*supplied* sandwiches for a picnic⟩

²supply *n, pl* **sup·plies** **1** : the amount of something that is needed or can be gotten ⟨the nation's oil *supply*⟩ **2** : ²STORE 1 ⟨keep a *supply* of pencils in my desk drawer⟩ **3** : the act or process of supplying something ⟨engaged in the *supply* of raw materials⟩

¹sup·port \sə-'pōrt\ *vb* **1** : to take sides with : FAVOR ⟨*support* a candidate⟩ **2** : to provide evidence for : VERIFY ⟨they cannot *support* this claim⟩ **3** : to pay the costs of : MAINTAIN ⟨*supports* a large family⟩ **4** : to hold up or in position : serve as a foundation or prop for ⟨posts *support* the porch roof⟩ **5** : to keep going : SUSTAIN ⟨not enough air to *support* life⟩ — **sup·port·er** *n*

²support *n* **1** : the act of supporting : the condition of being supported **2** : one that supports

sup·pose \sə-'pōz\ *vb* **sup·posed; sup·pos·ing** **1** : to think of as true or as a fact for the sake of argument ⟨*suppose* you had to leave⟩ **2** : BELIEVE 2, THINK ⟨I *suppose* they are honest⟩ **3** : ¹GUESS 1 ⟨who do you *suppose* won⟩

sup·posed \sə-'pōzd\ *adj* **1** : believed to be true or real ⟨the *supposed* murderer⟩ **2** : forced or required to do something ⟨I am *supposed* to be home early⟩ — **sup·pos·ed·ly** \-'pō-zəd-lē\ *adv*

sup·press \sə-'pres\ *vb* **1** : to put down (as by authority or force) : SUBDUE ⟨*suppress* a riot⟩ **2** : to hold back : REPRESS ⟨could hardly *suppress* a smile⟩

sup·pres·sion \sə-'presh-ən\ *n* : an act or instance of suppressing : the state of being suppressed

su·prem·a·cy \sù-'prem-ə-sē\ *n, pl* **su·prem·a·cies** : the highest rank, power, or authority

su·preme \sù-'prēm\ *adj* **1** : highest in rank, power, or authority **2** : highest in degree or quality : UTMOST ⟨*supreme* confidence⟩ **3** : ¹EXTREME 1, FINAL ⟨the *supreme* sacrifice⟩ — **su·preme·ly** *adv*

Supreme Being *n* : GOD 1

Supreme Court *n* : the highest court of the United States consisting of a chief justice and eight associate justices

¹sure \'shùr\ *adj* **sur·er; sur·est** **1** : firmly

established : STEADFAST ⟨a *sure* grip⟩ ⟨*sure* foundation⟩ **2** : RELIABLE, TRUST-WORTHY ⟨a *sure* remedy⟩ **3** : having no doubt : CONFIDENT ⟨I'm *sure* of it⟩ **4** : not to be doubted : CERTAIN ⟨speaks from *sure* knowledge⟩ **5** : bound to happen ⟨*sure* disaster⟩ **6** : bound as if by fate ⟨you are *sure* to win⟩

²sure *adv* : SURELY 2, 3 ⟨*sure*, we'll be there⟩

sure·ly \'shur-lē\ *adv* **1** : with confidence : CONFIDENTLY ⟨answered their questions *surely*⟩ **2** : without doubt ⟨a book you will *surely* enjoy⟩ **3** : beyond question : REALLY ⟨I *surely* do miss them⟩

surf \'sərf\ *n* **1** : the waves of the sea that splash on the shore **2** : the sound, splash, and foam of breaking waves

¹sur·face \'sər-fəs\ *n* **1** : the outside or any one side of an object **2** : the outside appearance ⟨on the *surface* the plan seems good⟩

²surface *vb* **sur·faced; sur·fac·ing 1** : to give a surface to : make smooth (as by sanding or paving) **2** : to come to the surface ⟨the submarine *surfaced*⟩

³surface *adj* **1** : of or relating to a surface : acting on a surface **2** : not deep or real ⟨*surface* friendship⟩

surf·board \'sərf-,bōrd\ *n* : a long narrow board that floats and is ridden in surfing

surf·ing \'sər-fing\ *n* : the act or sport of riding waves in to shore usually while standing on a surfboard

¹surge \'sərj\ *vb* **surged; surg·ing 1** : to rise and fall with much action **2** : to move in or as if in waves ⟨crowds *surging* through the streets⟩

²surge *n* **1** : an onward rush like that of a wave ⟨a *surge* of anger⟩ **2** : a large wave ⟨*surges* of water⟩

sur·geon \'sər-jən\ *n* : a doctor who specializes in surgery

sur·gery \'sər-jə-rē\ *n*, *pl* **sur·ger·ies 1** : a branch of medicine concerned with the correction of defects, the repair and healing of injuries, and the treatment of diseased conditions by operation **2** : the work done by a surgeon

sur·gi·cal \'sər-ji-kəl\ *adj* : of, relating to, or associated with surgery or surgeons ⟨*surgical* dressings⟩

sur·ly \'sər-lē\ *adj* **sur·li·er; sur·li·est** : having a mean rude disposition : UN-FRIENDLY

Word History The word *surly* comes from the word *sir*. Long ago, some Englishmen who had the title *Sir* became too proud of it. Such men were called *sirly*, a word that

meant "overbearing" and "arrogant." Over the years the spelling changed to *surly* and came to be used of anyone who is rude and unfriendly.

¹sur·mise \sər-'mīz\ *vb* **sur·mised; sur·mis·ing** : to form an idea on very little evidence : ¹GUESS 1

²surmise *n* : a thought or idea based on very little evidence : ²GUESS

sur·mount \sər-'maunt\ *vb* **1** : OVERCOME 1 ⟨*surmount* difficulties⟩ **2** : to get to the top of **3** : to be at the top of ⟨a castle *surmounts* the cliff⟩

sur·name \'sər-,nām\ *n* : a family name : a last name

sur·pass \sər-'pas\ *vb* **1** : to be greater, better, or stronger than : EXCEED **2** : to go beyond the reach or powers of ⟨a task that *surpassed* their strength⟩

¹sur·plus \'sər-pləs\ *n* : an amount left over : EXCESS

²surplus *adj* : left over : EXTRA ⟨*surplus* wheat⟩

¹sur·prise \sər-'prīz, sə-'prīz\ *n* **1** : an act or instance of coming upon without warning ⟨they were taken by *surprise*⟩ **2** : something that surprises ⟨I have a *surprise* for you⟩ **3** : ASTONISHMENT, AMAZEMENT

²surprise *vb* **sur·prised; sur·pris·ing 1** : to attack without warning : capture by an unexpected attack **2** : to come upon without warning **3** : to cause to feel wonder or amazement because of being unexpected

synonyms SURPRISE, ASTONISH, and AMAZE mean to impress forcibly by being unexpected, startling, or unusual. SURPRISE stresses that something is unexpected even though it by itself is not startling ⟨the sudden storm *surprised* the people at the picnic⟩ ASTONISH means to surprise very much with something that is hard or impossible to believe ⟨the first airplanes *astonished* people⟩ AMAZE stresses that something causes one to wonder and puzzle over it ⟨the magician *amazed* the children by making the rabbit disappear⟩

sur·pris·ing \sər-'prī-zing\ *adj* : causing surprise : UNEXPECTED — **sur·pris·ing·ly** *adv*

¹sur·ren·der \sə-'ren-dər\ *vb* **1** : to give oneself or something over to the power,

\ə\ abut	\au\ out	\i\ tip	\o\ saw	\u\ foot
\ər\ further	\ch\ chin	\ī\ life	\oi\ coin	\y\ yet
\a\ mat	\e\ pet	\j\ job	\th\ thin	\yü\ few
\ā\ take	\ē\ easy	\ng\ sing	\th\ this	\yu\ cure
\ä\ cot, cart	\g\ go	\ō\ bone	\ü\ food	\zh\ vision

control, or possession of another especially under force : YIELD ⟨*surrender* the fort⟩ **2** : RELINQUISH ⟨*surrendered* our place in line⟩

²surrender *n* : the act of giving up or yielding oneself or something into the possession or control of someone else

sur·rey \'sər-ē\ *n, pl* **sur·reys** : a pleasure carriage that has two wide seats and four wheels and is drawn by horses

surrey

sur·round \sə-'raund\ *vb* : to enclose on all sides : ENCIRCLE

sur·round·ings \sə-'raun-dingz\ *n pl* : the circumstances, conditions, or things around an individual : ENVIRONMENT

¹sur·vey \sər-'vā\ *vb* **sur·veyed; sur·vey·ing 1** : to look over : EXAMINE ⟨the governor *surveyed* the damage caused by the flood⟩ **2** : to find out the size, shape, or position of (as an area of land) **3** : to gather information from : make a survey of ⟨*surveyed* the students to find out who was the most popular teacher⟩

²sur·vey \'sər-ˌvā\ *n, pl* **sur·veys 1** : the action or an instance of surveying **2** : something that is surveyed **3** : a careful examination to learn facts ⟨a *survey* of the school system⟩ **4** : a history or description that covers a large subject briefly ⟨a *survey* of English literature⟩

sur·vey·ing \sər-'vā-ing\ *n* **1** : the act or occupation of a person who makes surveys **2** : a branch of mathematics that teaches how to measure the earth's surface and record these measurements accurately

sur·vey·or \sər-'vā-ər\ *n* : a person who surveys or whose occupation is surveying

sur·viv·al \sər-'vī-vəl\ *n* **1** : a living or continuing longer than another person or thing **2** : one that survives

sur·vive \sər-'vīv\ *vb* **sur·vived; sur·viv·ing 1** : to remain alive : continue to exist **2** : to live longer than or past the end of

⟨*survived* their children⟩ ⟨at least we *survived* the flood⟩ — **sur·vi·vor** \sər-'vī-vər\ *n*

sus·cep·ti·ble \sə-'sep-tə-bəl\ *adj* **1** : of such a nature as to permit ⟨words *susceptible* of being misunderstood⟩ **2** : having little resistance ⟨*susceptible* to colds⟩ **3** : easily affected or impressed by ⟨*susceptible* to flattery⟩

¹sus·pect \'səs-ˌpekt, sə-'spekt\ *adj* : thought of with suspicion ⟨a person whose honesty is *suspect*⟩

²sus·pect \'səs-ˌpekt\ *n* : a person who is suspected

³sus·pect \sə-'spekt\ *vb* **1** : to have doubts of : DISTRUST **2** : to imagine to be guilty without proof **3** : to suppose to be true or likely

sus·pend \sə-'spend\ *vb* **1** : to force to give up some right or office for a time ⟨*suspended* from school⟩ **2** : to stop or do away with for a time ⟨*suspend* a rule⟩ **3** : to stop operation or action for a time ⟨all business *suspended* during the storm⟩ **4** : to hang especially so as to be free except at one point ⟨*suspend* a ball by a thread⟩

sus·pend·er \sə-'spen-dər\ *n* : one of a pair of supporting straps that fasten to trousers or a skirt and pass over the shoulders

sus·pense \sə-'spens\ *n* : uncertainty or worry about the result of something

sus·pen·sion \sə-'spen-chən\ *n* **1** : the act or an instance of suspending **2** : the state of being suspended **3** : the period during which someone or something is suspended

sus·pi·cion \sə-'spish-ən\ *n* **1** : an act or instance of suspecting or the state of being suspected ⟨was above *suspicion*⟩ **2** : a feeling that something is wrong : DOUBT

sus·pi·cious \sə-'spish-əs\ *adj* **1** : likely to arouse suspicion ⟨*suspicious* actions⟩ **2** : likely to suspect or distrust ⟨*suspicious* of everything new⟩ **3** : showing distrust ⟨a *suspicious* glance⟩

sus·tain \sə-'stān\ *vb* **1** : to give support or relief to : HELP ⟨*sustained* by their faith⟩ **2** : to provide with what is needed ⟨machines that *sustain* our economy⟩ ⟨food *sustains* life⟩ **3** : to keep up : PROLONG ⟨books that *sustain* our interest⟩ **4** : to hold up the weight of : PROP **5** : to keep up the spirits of ⟨hope *sustained* us⟩ **6** : to put up with without giving in ⟨*sustaining* the burdens of life⟩ **7** : ²EXPERIENCE ⟨the army *sustained* heavy losses⟩ **8** : to allow or uphold as true, legal, or fair ⟨the judge *sustained* the plea⟩ **9** : CONFIRM 1, PROVE ⟨this report *sustains* our story⟩

sus·te·nance \'səs-tə-nəns\ *n* **1** : ²LIVING 3, SUBSISTENCE **2** : the act of sustaining : the state of being sustained **3** : ²SUPPORT 2 ⟨God is our *sustenance* in time of trouble⟩

¹swab \'swäb\ *n* **1** : ¹MOP 1 **2** : a small piece of gauze or absorbent cotton usually on the end of a small stick that is used to apply medicine or to clean a sore or wound

²swab *vb* **swabbed; swab·bing** : to use a swab on : clean or wash with a swab

¹swag·ger \'swag-ər\ *vb* : to walk with a proud strut

²swagger *n* : an act or instance of swaggering

¹swal·low \'swäl-ō\ *n* : any of a group of small migratory birds with long wings, forked tails, and a graceful flight

²swallow *vb* **1** : to take into the stomach through the mouth and throat **2** : to perform the actions used in swallowing something ⟨clear your throat and *swallow* before answering⟩ **3** : to take in as if by swallowing : ENGULF ⟨a ship *swallowed* by the waves⟩ **4** : to accept or believe without question, protest, or anger ⟨you *swallow* every story you hear⟩ ⟨*swallow* an insult⟩ **5** : to keep from expressing or showing : REPRESS ⟨*swallowed* my disgust⟩

³swallow *n* **1** : an act of swallowing **2** : an amount that can be swallowed at one time

swam *past of* SWIM

¹swamp \'swämp\ *n* : wet spongy land often partly covered with water

²swamp *vb* **1** : to fill or cause to fill with water : sink after filling with water ⟨high waves *swamped* the boat⟩ ⟨the boat *swamped* and we had to swim to shore⟩ **2** : OVERWHELM 2 ⟨was *swamped* with work⟩

swampy \'swäm-pē\ *adj* **swamp·i·er; swamp·i·est** : of, relating to, or like a swamp

swan \'swän\ *n* : a usually white water bird with a long neck and a heavy body that is related to but larger than the geese

swan

¹swap \'swäp\ *vb* **swapped; swapping** : to give in exchange : make an exchange : TRADE

²swap *n* : ¹EXCHANGE 1, TRADE

¹swarm \'swȯrm\ *n* **1** : a large number of bees that leave a hive together to form a new colony elsewhere **2** : a large moving crowd (as of people or insects)

²swarm *vb* **1** : to form a swarm and leave the hive ⟨*swarming* bees⟩ **2** : to move or gather in a swarm or large crowd ⟨shoppers *swarmed* into the stores⟩ **3** : to be filled with a great number : TEEM ⟨the floor is *swarming* with ants⟩

swar·thy \'swȯr-the, -thē\ *adj* **swar·thi·er; swar·thi·est** : having a dark complexion

¹swat \'swät\ *vb* **swat·ted; swat·ting** : to hit with a quick hard blow

²swat *n* : a hard blow

swath \'swäth\ *or* **swathe** \'swäth\ *n* **1** : a sweep of a scythe or machine in mowing or the path cut in one course **2** : a row of cut grass (as grain)

¹sway \'swā\ *vb* **1** : to swing slowly back and forth or from side to side ⟨tree branches *swaying* in the breeze⟩ **2** : to change often between one point, position, or opinion and another **3** : ²INFLUENCE ⟨we were *swayed* by their arguments⟩

²sway *n* **1** : the action or an instance of swaying or of being swayed **2** : a controlling influence or force : RULE

swear \'swaər, 'sweər\ *vb* **swore** \'swōr\; **sworn** \'swōrn\; **swear·ing 1** : to make a statement or promise under oath : VOW ⟨*swear* to tell the truth⟩ **2** : to give an oath to ⟨*swear* a witness⟩ **3** : to bind by an oath ⟨*swore* them to secrecy⟩ **4** : to take an oath **5** : to use bad or vulgar language : CURSE

¹sweat \'swet\ *vb* **sweat** *or* **sweat·ed; sweat·ing 1** : to give off salty moisture through the pores of the skin : PERSPIRE **2** : to collect moisture on the surface ⟨a pitcher of ice water *sweats* on a hot day⟩ **3** : to work hard enough to perspire ⟨*sweat* over a lesson⟩

²sweat *n* **1** : PERSPIRATION 2 **2** : moisture coming from or collecting in drops on a surface **3** : the condition of one sweating

sweat·er \'swet-ər\ *n* : a knitted or crocheted jacket or pullover

sweat gland *n* : any of numerous small skin glands that give off perspiration

Swede \'swēd\ *n* : a person born or living in Sweden

¹Swed·ish \'swēd-ish\ *adj* : of or relating to Sweden, the Swedes, or Swedish

²Swedish *n* : the language of the Swedes

¹sweep \'swēp\ *vb* **swept** \'swept\; **sweep·ing 1** : to remove with a broom or

\ə\ abut	\au̇\ out	\i\ tip	\ȯ\ saw	\u̇\ foot
\ər\ further	\ch\ chin	\ī\ life	\ȯi\ coin	\y\ yet
\a\ mat	\e\ pet	\j\ job	\th\ thin	\yu̇\ few
\ā\ take	\ē\ easy	\ng\ sing	\th\ this	\yü\ cure
\ä\ cot, cart	\g\ go	\ō\ bone	\ü\ food	\zh\ vision

brush ⟨*sweep* up the dirt⟩ **2** : to clean by removing loose dirt or small trash with a broom or brush ⟨*sweep* the floor⟩ **3** : to move over or across swiftly with force or destruction ⟨fire *swept* the village⟩ **4** : to move or gather as if with a broom or brush ⟨*swept* the money from the table⟩ **5** : to touch a surface as if with a brush ⟨the musician's fingers *swept* the piano keys⟩ **6** : to drive along with steady force ⟨was *swept* away by the tide⟩ **7** : to move the eyes or an instrument through a wide curve ⟨they *swept* the hill for some sign of the enemy⟩ — **sweep·er** *n*

²sweep *n* **1** : something that sweeps or works with a sweeping motion **2** : an act or instance of sweeping **3** : a complete or easy victory **4** : a curving movement, course, or line ⟨brushed it away with a *sweep* of my hand⟩ **5** : ¹RANGE 6, SCOPE ⟨outside the *sweep* of our vision⟩ **6** : CHIMNEY SWEEP

¹sweep·ing \'swē-ping\ *n* **1** : the act or action of one that sweeps **2 sweepings** *pl* : things collected by sweeping

²sweeping *adj* **1** : moving or extending in a wide curve or over a wide area ⟨gave the audience a *sweeping* glance⟩ **2** : EXTENSIVE ⟨*sweeping* changes in teaching methods⟩

sweep·stakes *n sing or pl* : a contest in which money or prizes are given to winners picked by chance (as by drawing names from a box)

¹sweet \'swēt\ *adj* **1** : pleasing to the taste **2** : containing or tasting of sugar **3** : pleasing to the mind or feelings : AGREEABLE ⟨*sweet* memories⟩ **4** : ¹KINDLY 2, MILD ⟨a *sweet* disposition⟩ **5** : FRAGRANT ⟨a *sweet* smell⟩ **6** : pleasing to the ear or eye ⟨the *sweet* sounds of a violin⟩ **7** : much loved : DEAR **8** : not sour, stale, or spoiled ⟨*sweet* milk⟩ **9** : FRESH 1 ⟨*sweet* butter⟩ — **sweet·ish** \'swēt-ish\ *adj* — **sweet·ly** *adv* — **sweet·ness** *n*

²sweet *n* **1** : something (as candy) that is sweet to the taste **2** : ¹DARLING 1, DEAR

sweet corn *n* : an Indian corn with kernels rich in sugar that is cooked as a vegetable while young

sweet·en \'swēt-n\ *vb* : to make or become sweet or sweeter

sweet·en·ing \'swēt-n-ing\ *n* **1** : the act or process of making sweet **2** : something that sweetens

sweet·heart \'swēt-,härt\ *n* : a person whom one loves

sweet·meat \'swēt-,mēt\ *n* : a food (as a piece of candy or candied fruit) rich in sugar

sweet pea *n* : a climbing plant related to the peas that is grown for its fragrant flowers of many colors

sweet potato *n* : the large sweet edible root of a tropical vine somewhat like a morning glory

sweet wil·liam \-'wil-yəm\ *n, often cap W* : a European pink grown for its thick flat clusters of many-colored flowers

sweet william

¹swell \'swel\ *vb* **swelled; swelled** *or* **swol·len** \'swō-lən\; **swell·ing 1** : to enlarge in an abnormal way usually by pressure from within or by growth ⟨a *swollen* ankle⟩ **2** : to grow or make bigger (as in size or value) **3** : to stretch upward or outward : BULGE ⟨a breeze *swelled* the sails⟩ **4** : to fill or become filled with emotion ⟨a heart *swelling* with gratitude⟩

²swell *n* **1** : a becoming larger (as in size or value) **2** : a long rolling wave or series of waves in the open sea **3** : a very fashionably dressed person

³swell *adj* **1** : STYLISH, FASHIONABLE ⟨*swell* clothes⟩ **2** : EXCELLENT, FIRST-RATE ⟨we had a *swell* time⟩

swell·ing \'swel-ing\ *n* : a swollen lump or part

swel·ter \'swel-tər\ *vb* : to suffer, sweat, or be faint from heat

swept *past of* SWEEP

¹swerve \'swərv\ *vb* **swerved; swerv·ing** : to turn aside suddenly from a straight line or course ⟨*swerved* to avoid an oncoming car⟩

²swerve *n* : an act or instance of swerving

¹swift \'swift\ *adj* **1** : moving or capable of moving with great speed **2** : occurring suddenly **3** : ¹READY 3, ALERT **synonyms** see FAST — **swift·ly** *adv* — **swift·ness** *n*

²swift *adv* : SWIFTLY ⟨a *swift*-flowing stream⟩

³swift *n* : a small usually sooty black bird that is related to the hummingbirds but looks like a swallow

swig \'swig\ *n* : the amount drunk at one time : GULP

¹swill \'swil\ *vb* : to eat or drink greedily

²swill *n* **1** : ¹SLOP 3 **2** : GARBAGE, REFUSE

¹swim \'swim\ *vb* **swam** \'swam\; **swum** \'swəm\; **swim·ming 1** : to move through or in water by moving arms, legs, fins, or tail **2** : to glide smoothly and quietly **3** : to float on or in or be covered with or as if with a liquid ⟨meat *swimming* in gravy⟩ **4** : to be dizzy : move or seem to move dizzily ⟨my head *swam* in the smoky room⟩ **5** : to cross by swimming ⟨*swim* the river⟩ — **swim·mer** *n*

²swim *n* **1** : an act or period of swimming ⟨enjoyed a good *swim*⟩ **2** : the main current of activity ⟨in the social *swim*⟩

swim·ming \ˈswim-ing\ *adj* **1** : capable of or used to swimming ⟨*swimming* birds⟩ **2** : used in or for swimming

¹swin·dle \ˈswin-dəl\ *vb* **swin·dled; swin·dling** : to get money or property from by dishonest means : CHEAT

²swindle *n* : an act or instance of swindling

swin·dler \ˈswin-dlər\ *n* : a person who swindles

Word History A German noun that means "a dizzy person" came to mean "a person who has fantastic schemes." The English word *swindler* came from the German word that means "one who has fantastic schemes." Swindlers often use fantastic schemes to cheat people.

swine \ˈswīn\ *n, pl* **swine** : a hoofed domestic animal that comes from the wild boar, has a long snout and bristly skin, and is widely raised for meat

swine·herd \ˈswīn-ˌhərd\ *n* : a person who tends swine

¹swing \ˈswing\ *vb* **swung** \ˈswəng\; **swing·ing** **1** : to move rapidly in a sweeping curve ⟨*swing* a bat⟩ **2** : to throw or toss in a circle or back and forth ⟨*swing* a lasso⟩ **3** : to sway to and fro ⟨sheets *swung* on the clothes line⟩ **4** : to hang or be hung so as to move freely back and forth or in a curve ⟨*swing* a hammock between two trees⟩ **5** : to turn on a hinge or pivot ⟨the door *swung* open⟩ **6** : to manage or handle successfully ⟨able to *swing* the job⟩ **7** : to march or walk with free swaying movements

²swing *n* **1** : an act of swinging **2** : a swinging movement, blow, or rhythm **3** : the distance through which something swings ⟨measured the *swing* of the pendulum⟩ **4** : a swinging seat usually hung by overhead ropes **5** : a style of jazz marked by lively rhythm and played mostly for dancing

¹swipe \ˈswīp\ *n* : a strong sweeping blow

²swipe *vb* **swiped; swip·ing** : ¹STEAL 2

¹swirl \ˈswərl\ *n* **1** : a whirling mass or motion : EDDY **2** : whirling confusion **3** : a twisting shape or mark ⟨hair worn in a *swirl*⟩

²swirl *vb* : to move with a whirling or twisting motion

¹swish \ˈswish\ *vb* : to make, move, or strike with a soft rubbing or hissing sound

²swish *n* **1** : a hissing sound (as of a whip cutting the air) or a light sweeping or rubbing sound (as of a silk skirt) **2** : a swishing movement

¹Swiss \ˈswis\ *n, pl* **Swiss** : a person born or living in Switzerland

²Swiss *adj* : of or relating to Switzerland or the Swiss

¹switch \ˈswich\ *n* **1** : a narrow flexible whip, rod, or twig **2** : an act of switching **3** : a blow with a switch or whip **4** : a change from one thing to another ⟨a *switch* in plans⟩ **5** : a device for adjusting the rails of a track so that a train or streetcar may be turned from one track to another **6** : SIDING 1 **7** : a device for making, breaking, or changing the connections in an electrical circuit

²switch *vb* **1** : to strike or whip with or as if with a switch **2** : to lash from side to side ⟨a cow *switching* its tail⟩ **3** : to turn, shift, or change by operating a switch ⟨*switch* off the light⟩ **4** : to make a shift or change ⟨*switched* to a new barber⟩

switch·board \ˈswich-ˌbōrd\ *n* : an apparatus consisting of a panel on which are mounted electric switches so arranged that a number of circuits may be connected, combined, and controlled ⟨the *switchboards* of a telephone exchange⟩

¹swiv·el \ˈswiv-əl\ *n* : a device joining two parts so that one or both can turn freely (as on a bolt or pin)

²swivel *vb* **swiv·eled** *or* **swiv·elled; swiv·el·ing** *or* **swiv·el·ling** : to turn on or as if on a swivel

swollen *past participle of* SWELL

¹swoon \ˈswün\ *vb* : ²FAINT

²swoon *n* : ³FAINT

¹swoop \ˈswüp\ *vb* : to rush down or pounce suddenly like a hawk attacking its prey

²swoop *n* : an act or instance of swooping

sword \ˈsōrd\ *n* : a weapon

swivel

having a long blade usually with a sharp point and edge

sword·fish \'sōrd-ˌfish\ *n, pl* **swordfish** *or* **sword·fish·es** : a very large ocean food fish having a long swordlike beak formed by the bones of the upper jaw

swordfish

swords·man \'sōrdz-mən\ *n, pl* **swords-men** \-mən\ : a person who fights with a sword

swore *past of* SWEAR

sworn *past participle of* SWEAR

swum *past participle of* SWIM

swung *past of* SWING

syc·a·more \'sik-ə-ˌmōr\ *n* **1** : the common fig tree of Egypt and Asia Minor **2** : an American tree with round fruits and bark that forms flakes

syl·lab·ic \sə-'lab-ik\ *adj* **1** : of, relating to, or being syllables **2** : not accompanied by a vowel sound in the same syllable ⟨\l\ is a *syllabic* consonant in \'bat-l\ *battle*⟩

syl·lab·i·cate \sə-'lab-ə-ˌkāt\ *vb* **syl·lab·i·cat·ed; syl·lab·i·cat·ing** : SYLLABIFY

syl·lab·i·ca·tion \sə-ˌlab-ə-'kā-shən\ *n* : the forming of syllables : the dividing of words into syllables

syl·lab·i·fi·ca·tion \sə-ˌlab-ə-fə-'kā-shən\ *n* : SYLLABICATION

syl·lab·i·fy \sə-'lab-ə-ˌfi\ *vb* **syl·lab·i·fied; syl·lab·i·fy·ing** : to form or divide into syllables

syl·la·ble \'sil-ə-bəl\ *n* **1** : a unit of spoken language that consists of one or more vowel sounds alone or of a syllabic consonant alone or of either of these preceded or followed by one or more consonant sounds **2** : one or more letters (as *syl, la,* and *ble*) in a written word (as *syl·la·ble*) usually separated from the rest of the word by a centered dot or a hyphen and used as guides to the division of the word at the end of a line

sym·bi·o·sis \ˌsim-ˌbī-'ō-səs, -bē-\ *n* : a living together in close association of two different kinds of organisms in a relationship that is beneficial to both — **sym·bi·ot·ic** \-ät-ik\ *adj*

sym·bol \'sim-bəl\ *n* **1** : something that stands for something else : EMBLEM ⟨the cross is the *symbol* of Christianity⟩ **2** : a letter, character, or sign used instead of a word to represent a quantity, position, relationship, direction, or something to be done ⟨the sign + is the *symbol* for addition⟩ **synonyms** see EMBLEM

sym·bol·ic \sim-'bäl-ik\ *or* **sym·bol·i·cal** \-i-kəl\ *adj* : of, relating to, or using symbols or symbolism ⟨a *symbolic* meaning⟩

sym·bol·ize \'sim-bə-ˌlīz\ *vb* **sym·bol·ized; sym·bol·iz·ing** : to serve as a symbol of ⟨a lion *symbolizes* courage⟩

sym·met·ri·cal \sə-'me-tri-kəl\ *or* **sym·met·ric** \-rik\ *adj* : having or showing symmetry

sym·me·try \'sim-ə-trē\ *n, pl* **sym·me·tries** : close agreement in size, shape, and position of parts that are on opposite sides of a dividing line or center : an arrangement involving regular and balanced proportions ⟨the *symmetry* of the human body⟩

sym·pa·thet·ic \ˌsim-pə-'thet-ik\ *adj* **1** : fitting one's mood or disposition ⟨a *sympathetic* atmosphere⟩ **2** : feeling sympathy ⟨received much help from *sympathetic* friends⟩ **3** : feeling favorable ⟨*sympathetic* to their ambitions⟩ — **sym·pa·thet·i·cal·ly** \-i-kə-lē\ *adv*

sym·pa·thize \'sim-pə-ˌthīz\ *vb* **sym·pa·thized; sym·pa·thiz·ing** **1** : to feel or show sympathy ⟨*sympathize* with a family in its sorrow⟩ **2** : to be in favor of something ⟨*sympathize* with a friend's ambitions⟩

sym·pa·thy \'sim-pə-thē\ *n, pl* **sym·pa·thies** **1** : a relationship between persons or things in which whatever affects one similarly affects the other **2** : readiness to think or feel alike : similarity of likes, interest, or aims that makes a bond of goodwill ⟨*sympathy* between friends⟩ **3** : readiness to favor or support ⟨political *sympathies*⟩ **4** : the act of or capacity for entering into the feelings or interests of another **5** : sorrow or pity for another **6** : a showing of sorrow for another's loss, grief, or misfortune

sym·phon·ic \sim-'fän-ik\ *adj* : of or relating to a symphony or symphony orchestra

sym·pho·ny \'sim-fə-nē\ *n, pl* **sym·pho·nies** **1** : harmonious arrangement (as of sound or color) **2** : a usually long musical composition for a full orchestra **3** : a large orchestra of wind, string, and percussion instruments

symp·tom \'simp-təm\ *n* **1** : a noticeable change in the body or its functions typical of a disease **2** : INDICATION 2, SIGN ⟨*symptoms* of fear⟩

syn·a·gogue *or* **syn·a·gog** \'sin-ə-ˌgäg\ *n* : a Jewish house of worship

syn·apse \'sin-ˌaps\ *n* : the point at which a nerve impulse passes from one nerve cell to another

syn·co·pa·tion \ˌsing-kə-'pā-shən\ *n* : a temporary accenting of a normally weak beat in music to vary the rhythm

syn·o·nym \'sin-ə-ˌnim\ *n* : a word having the same or almost the same meaning as another word in the same language

syn·on·y·mous \sə-'nän-ə-məs\ *adj* : alike in meaning

syn·tax \'sin-ˌtaks\ *n* : the way in which words are put together to form phrases, clauses, or sentences

syn·the·size \'sin-thə-ˌsīz\ *vb* **syn·the·sized; syn·the·siz·ing** : to build up from simpler materials ⟨glands *synthesizing* enzymes⟩

syn·thet·ic \sin-'thet-ik\ *adj* : produced artificially especially by chemical means : produced by human beings

sy·rin·ga \sə-'ring-gə\ *n* : a garden shrub with often fragrant flowers of a white or cream color

sy·ringe \sə-'rinj\ *n* : a device used to force fluid into or withdraw it from the body or its cavities

syr·up *or* **sir·up** \'sər-əp, 'sir-\ *n* **1** : a thick sticky solution of sugar and water often containing flavoring or a medicine **2** : the juice of a fruit or plant with some of the water removed

sys·tem \'sis-təm\ *n* **1** : a group of parts combined to form a whole that works or moves as a unit ⟨a heating *system*⟩ **2** : a body that functions as a whole ⟨the disease affected the entire *system*⟩ **3** : a group of bodily organs that together carry on some vital function ⟨the nervous *system*⟩ **4** : an orderly plan or method of governing or arranging ⟨a democratic *system* of government⟩ **5** : regular method or order : ORDERLINESS

sys·tem·at·ic \ˌsis-tə-'mat-ik\ *adj* **1** : having, using, or acting on a system **2** : carrying out a plan with thoroughness or regularity ⟨*systematic* efforts⟩ — **sys·tem·at·i·cal·ly** \-i-kə-lē\ *adv*

sys·tem·ic \sis-'tem-ik\ *adj* : of or relating to the body as a whole ⟨*systemic* disease⟩

T

t \'tē\ *n, pl* **t's** *or* **ts** \'tēz\ *often cap* : the twentieth letter of the English alphabet —
to a T : just fine : EXACTLY

tab \'tab\ *n* **1** : a short flap or tag attached to something for filing, pulling, or hanging **2** : a careful watch ⟨keep *tabs* on the weather⟩

tab·by \'tab-ē\ *n, pl* **tab·bies** **1** : a domestic cat with a gray or tawny coat striped and spotted with black **2** : a female domestic cat

Word History A kind of silk cloth was once made in a district of the city of Baghdad. The Arabic name for this cloth was taken from the name of the district where it was made. The English word *tabby* was first used for this silk cloth and came from the cloth's Arabic name. The cloth called *tabby* had a striped finish and was marked with spots of several colors or shades. That is why striped and mottled cats came to be called *tabbies*.

tab·er·na·cle \'tab-ər-ˌnak-əl\ *n* **1** *often cap* : a structure of wood hung with curtains used in worship by the Israelites during their wanderings in the wilderness with Moses **2** : a house of worship

¹ta·ble \'tā-bəl\ *n* **1** : a piece of furniture having a smooth flat top on legs **2** : food to eat ⟨sets a good *table*⟩ **3** : the people around a table **4** : short list ⟨a *table* of contents⟩ **5** : an arrangement in rows or columns for reference ⟨multiplication *tables*⟩

²table *vb* **ta·bled; ta·bling** **1** : TABULATE **2** : to put on a table

tab·leau \'tab-ˌlō\ *n, pl* **tab·leaus** *or* **tab·leaux** \-ˌlōz\ : a scene or event shown by a group of persons who remain still and silent

ta·ble·cloth \'tā-bəl-ˌkloth\ *n* : a covering spread over a dining table before the places are set

ta·ble·land \'tā-bəl-ˌland\ *n* : PLATEAU

\ə\ abut	\au̇\ out	\i\ tip	\o̅\ saw	\u̇\ foot
\ər\ further	\ch\ chin	\ī\ life	\oi\ coin	\y\ yet
\a\ mat	\e\ pet	\j\ job	\th\ thin	\yü\ few
\ā\ take	\ē\ easy	\ng\ sing	\th\ this	\yu̇\ cure
\ä\ cot, cart	\g\ go	\ō\ bone	\ü\ food	\zh\ vision

ta·ble·spoon \'tā-bəl-ˌspün\ *n* **1** : a large spoon used mostly for dishing up food **2** : TABLESPOONFUL

ta·ble·spoon·ful \ˌtā-bəl-'spün-ˌful\ *n, pl* **ta·ble·spoon·fuls** \-ˌfulz\ *or* **ta·ble·spoons·ful** \-'spünz-ˌful\ **1** : as much as a tablespoon will hold **2** : a unit of measure used in cooking equal to three teaspoonfuls (about fifteen milliliters)

tab·let \'tab-lət\ *n* **1** : a thin flat slab used for writing, painting, or drawing **2** : a number of sheets of writing paper glued together at one edge **3** : a flat and usually round mass of material containing medicine ⟨aspirin *tablets*⟩

table tennis *n* : a game played on a table by two or four players who use paddles to hit a small hollow plastic ball back and forth over a net

ta·ble·ware \'tā-bəl-ˌwaər, -ˌweər\ *n* : utensils (as of china, glass, or silver) for use at the table

tab·u·late \'tab-yə-ˌlāt\ *vb* **tab·u·lat·ed; tab·u·lat·ing** : to put in the form of a table

tac·it \'tas-ət\ *adj* : understood or made known without being put into words — **tac·it·ly** *adv*

¹tack \'tak\ *n* **1** : a small nail with a sharp point and usually a broad flat head for fastening a light object or material to a solid surface **2** : the direction a ship is sailing as shown by the position the sails are set in or the movement of a ship with the sails set in a certain position **3** : a change of course from one tack to another **4** : a zigzag movement or course **5** : a course of action **6** : a temporary stitch used in sewing

²tack *vb* **1** : to fasten with tacks **2** : to attach or join loosely **3** : to change from one course to another in sailing **4** : to follow a zigzag course

¹tack·le \'tak-əl\ *n* **1** : a set of special equipment ⟨fishing *tackle*⟩ **2** : an arrangement of ropes and wheels for hoisting or pulling something heavy **3** : an act of tackling

tackle 2

²tackle *vb* **tack·led; tack·ling** **1** : to seize and throw (a person) to the ground **2** : to begin working on ⟨*tackle* a job⟩

ta·co \'täk-ō\ *n, pl* **ta·cos** \'täk-ōz, -ōs\ : a flat round cake of cornmeal rolled up with or folded over a filling

tact \'takt\ *n* : a keen understanding of how to get along with other people

tact·ful \'takt-fəl\ *adj* : having or showing tact — **tact·ful·ly** \-fə-lē\ *adv* — **tact·ful·ness** *n*

tac·tic \'tak-tik\ *n* : a planned action for some purpose

tac·tics \'tak-tiks\ *n sing or pl* **1** : the science and art of arranging and moving troops or warships for best use **2** : a system or method for reaching a goal

tac·tile \'tak-təl\ *adj* : of or relating to the sense of touch

tact·less \'takt-ləs\ *adj* : having or showing no tact — **tact·less·ly** *adv* — **tact·less·ness** *n*

tad·pole \'tad-ˌpōl\ *n* : the larva of a frog or toad that has a long tail, breathes with gills, and lives in water

Word History A young tadpole, which looks like a large head with a tail, will in time become a toad or a frog. The English word *tadpole* comes from an early English word that was made up of two words. The first of these was a word that meant "toad." The second was a word that meant "head."

taf·fy \'taf-ē\ *n, pl* **taf·fies** : a candy made usually of molasses or brown sugar boiled and pulled until soft

¹tag \'tag\ *n* **1** : a small flap or tab fixed or hanging on something ⟨a price *tag*⟩ **2** : an often quoted saying

²tag *vb* **tagged; tag·ging** **1** : to put a tag on **2** : to follow closely and continually

³tag *n* : a game in which one player who is it chases the others and tries to touch one of them to make that person it

⁴tag *vb* **tagged; tag·ging** **1** : to touch in or as if in a game of tag **2** : to touch a runner in baseball with the ball and cause the runner to be out

¹tail \'tāl\ *n* **1** : the rear part of an animal or a usually slender flexible extension of this part **2** : something that in shape, appearance, or position is like an animal's tail ⟨the *tail* of a coat⟩ **3** : the back, last, or lower part of something ⟨the *tail* of an airplane⟩ **4** : the side or end opposite the head — **tailed** \'tāld\ *adj* — **tail·less** \'tāl-ləs\ *adj* — **tail·like** \'tāl-ˌlīk\ *adj*

²tail *adj* : being at or coming from the rear

³tail *vb* : to follow closely to keep watch on

tail·gate \'tāl-,gāt\ *n* : a panel at the back end of a vehicle that can be let down for loading and unloading

tail·light \'tāl-,līt\ *n* : a red warning light at the rear of a vehicle

¹**tai·lor** \'tā-lər\ *n* : a person whose business is making or making adjustments in men's or women's clothes

²**tailor** *vb* **1** : to make or make adjustments in (clothes) **2** : to change to fit a special need ⟨*tailored* their plans to suit the weather⟩

tail pipe *n* : the pipe carrying off the exhaust gases from the muffler of an engine in a car or truck

tail·spin \'tāl-,spin\ *n* : a dive by an airplane turning in a circle

¹**taint** \'tānt\ *vb* **1** : to affect slightly with something bad **2** : to rot slightly ⟨*tainted* meat⟩

²**taint** *n* : a trace of decay

¹**take** \'tāk\ *vb* **took** \'tủk\ **tak·en** \'tā-kən\ **tak·ing** **1** : to get control of : CAPTURE ⟨*took* the fort⟩ **2** : ¹GRASP 1 ⟨*take* it by the handle⟩ **3** : to come upon ⟨they were *taken* by suprise⟩ **4** : CAPTIVATE ⟨were *taken* with its beauty⟩ **5** : to receive into the body ⟨*take* your medicine⟩ **6** : to get possession or use of ⟨*took* the book from the table ⟩ ⟨will *take* a cottage by the shore for the summer⟩ **7** : ASSUME 1 ⟨*take* office⟩ **8** : to be formed or used with ⟨prepositions *take* objects⟩ **9** : to adopt as one's own or for oneself ⟨*took* my side in the argument⟩ ⟨*took* all the credit⟩ **10** : WIN 3 ⟨*took* second prize⟩ **11** : CHOOSE 1, SELECT ⟨I'll *take* the red one⟩ **12** : to sit in or on ⟨*take* a chair⟩ **13** : to use as a way of going from one place to another ⟨ *take* the bus⟩ ⟨we'll *take* the highway⟩ **14** : REQUIRE ⟨it will *take* a long time⟩⟨I *take* a size ten⟩ **15** : to find out by special methods ⟨*take* your temperature⟩ **16** : to save in some permanent form ⟨*took* down every word of the speech⟩ ⟨*take* a picture⟩ **17** : to put up with : ENDURE ⟨I don't have to *take* that from you⟩ **18** : BELIEVE 2, 3 ⟨I *took* it to be the truth⟩ ⟨ *take* my word for it⟩ **19** : to be guided by : FOLLOW ⟨*take* my advice⟩ **20** : to become affected suddenly ⟨*took* sick⟩ **21** : UNDERSTAND 4, INTERPRET ⟨I *took* it to mean something different⟩ **22** : to react in a certain way ⟨*take* pleasure in music⟩ ⟨don't *take* offense⟩ **23** : to carry or go with from one place to another ⟨I'll *take* you home⟩ ⟨this bus will *take* us there⟩ **24** : REMOVE 3, SUBTRACT ⟨*take* 2 from 4 ⟩ **25** : to do the action of ⟨*take* a walk⟩ **26** : to have effect : be successful ⟨ the vaccination *took*⟩ — **tak·er** *n*

synonyms TAKE, SEIZE, and GRASP mean to get a hold on with or as if with the hand. TAKE can be used of any way of getting something into one's possession or control ⟨*take* this gift⟩ ⟨you *took* more food than you can use⟩ SEIZE suggests the taking of something suddenly and by force ⟨the police officer *seized* the thief in the act of escaping⟩ GRASP stresses taking something in the hand and keeping it there firmly ⟨*grasp* my arm and walk slowly⟩

— **take advantage of** **1** : to make good use of **2** : to treat (someone) unfairly — **take after** : RESEMBLE ⟨*take after* their parents⟩ — **take care** : to be careful — **take care of** : to do what is needed : look after — **take effect** **1** : to go into effect ⟨the new rate *takes effect* Monday⟩ **2** : to have an intended or expected effect — **take hold** : to become attached or established — **take part** : to do or join in something together with others ⟨*take part* in the fun⟩ — **take place** : to come into being and last for a time — used of events or actions ⟨the meeting *took place* yesterday⟩

²**take** *n* **1** : the act of taking **2** : something that is taken **3** : a bodily reaction that shows a smallpox vaccination to be successful

take back *vb* : to try to cancel (as something said) ⟨*take back* a mean remark⟩

take in *vb* **1** : to make smaller ⟨*took* the dress *in*⟩ **2** : to receive as a guest ⟨*took in* the travelers for the night⟩ **3** : to allow to join ⟨the club is not *taking in* new members⟩ **4** : to receive (work) to be done in one's home for pay ⟨*taking in* washing⟩ **5** : to have within its limits ⟨the tour *takes in* both museums⟩ **6** : to go to ⟨*take in* a movie⟩ **7** : to get the meaning of ⟨*took in* the situation at a glance⟩ **8** : ²CHEAT 2 ⟨they were *taken in* by an old trick⟩

take·off \'tā-,kȯf\ *n* **1** : an imitation especially to mock the original **2** : an act or instance of taking off from the ground (as by an airplane) **3** : a spot at which one takes off

take off \'tā-'kȯf\ *vb* **1** : to take away (a covering) : REMOVE ⟨*take* your shoes *off*⟩ **2** : DEDUCT ⟨*take off* ten percent⟩ **3** : to leave a surface in beginning a flight or leap ⟨the plane is *taking off* now⟩

take on *vb* **1** : to begin (a task) or struggle

\ə\ abut	\aủ\ out	\i\ tip	\ȯ\ saw	\ủ\ foot
\ər\ further	\ch\ chin	\ī\ life	\ȯi\ coin	\y\ yet
\a\ mat	\e\ pet	\j\ job	\th\ thin	\yü\ few
\ā\ take	\ē\ easy	\ng\ sing	\th\ this	\yủ\ cure
\ä\ cot, cart	\g\ go	\ō\ bone	\ü\ food	\zh\ vision

against (an opponent) ⟨*took on* the champion⟩ **2** : to gain or show as or as if a part of oneself ⟨the city *took on* a carnival mood⟩ **3** : ¹EMPLOY 2 ⟨*take on* more workers⟩ **4** : to make an unusual show of one's grief or anger ⟨don't *take on* so⟩

take over *vb* : to get control of ⟨military leaders *took over* the government⟩

take up *vb* **1** : to get together from many sources ⟨*take up* a collection⟩ **2** : to start something for the first time or after a pause ⟨*take up* painting⟩ ⟨*took up* the lesson where we left off⟩ **3** : to change by making tighter or shorter ⟨*take up* the dress in the back⟩

tak·ing \'tā-king\ *adj* **1** : ATTRACTIVE ⟨*taking* ways⟩ **2** : INFECTIOUS 1

talc \'talk\ *n* : a soft mineral that has a soapy feel and is used in making talcum powder and for coloring

tal·cum powder \'tal-kəm-\ *n* : a usually perfumed powder for the body made of talc

tale \'tāl\ *n* **1** : something told ⟨a *tale* of woe⟩ **2** : a story about an imaginary event **3** : ³LIE **4** : a piece of harmful gossip

tal·ent \'tal-ənt\ *n* **1** : unusual natural ability **2** : a special often creative or artistic ability **3** : persons having special ability **synonyms** see ability — **tal·ent·ed** \'tal-ən-təd\ *adj*

Word History *Talent* is the name of a unit of value of old Palestine. There is in the Bible a story about such talents. A man gave each of three servants a certain number of talents. After a time he asked what they had done with the money. The first two had invested it and made more, and their master praised them. The third had buried his talents and could give back no more than he had received. Him the master scolded. In the same way, says the Bible, God gives us natural gifts. We should make good use of them. From this story came a new meaning of *talent*: "natural gift."

tal·is·man \'tal-ə-smən\ *n, pl* **tal·is·mans** : a ring or stone carved with symbols and believed to have magical powers : CHARM

¹talk \'tok\ *vb* **1** : to express in speech : SPEAK **2** : to speak about : DISCUSS ⟨*talk* business⟩ **3** : to cause or influence by talking ⟨*talked* them into agreeing⟩ **4** : to use a certain language ⟨*talk* Spanish⟩ **5** : to exchange ideas by means of spoken words : CONVERSE ⟨let's sit and *talk*⟩ **6** : to pass on information other than by speaking ⟨*talk* with one's hands⟩ **7** : ²GOSSIP **8** : to reveal secret information

⟨forced the spy to *talk*⟩ **synonyms** see SPEAK — **talk·er** *n*

²talk *n* **1** : the act of talking : SPEECH **2** : a way of speaking : LANGUAGE **3** : CONFERENCE **4** : ¹RUMOR 2, GOSSIP **5** : the topic of comment or gossip ⟨it's the *talk* of the town⟩ **6** : an informal address

talk·ative \'tok-ət-iv\ *adj* : fond of talking — **talk·ative·ness** *n*

talk·ing-to \'to-king-ˌtü\ *n* : an often wordy scolding

¹tall \'tol\ *adj* **1** : having unusually great height **2** : of a stated height ⟨two meters *tall*⟩ **3** : made up ⟨a *tall* tale⟩ **synonyms** see HIGH — **tall·ness** *n*

²tall *adv* : so as to be or look tall ⟨stand *tall*⟩

tal·low \'tal-ō\ *n* : a white solid fat obtained by heating fatty tissues of cattle and sheep

¹tal·ly \'tal-ē\ *n, pl* **tal·lies** **1** : a device for keeping a count **2** : a recorded count **3** : a score or point made (as in a game)

²tally *vb* **tal·lied; tal·ly·ing** **1** : to keep a count of **2** : to make a tally : SCORE **3** : CORRESPOND 1

tal·on \'tal-ən\ *n* : the claw of a bird of prey — **tal·oned** \-ənd\ *adj*

ta·ma·le \tə-'mä-lē\ *n* : seasoned ground meat rolled in cornmeal, wrapped in corn husks, and steamed

tam·bou·rine \ˌtam-bə-'rēn\ *n* : a small shallow drum with only one head and loose metal disks around the rim that is played by shaking or hitting with the hand

tambourine

¹tame \'tām\ *adj* **tam·er; tam·est** **1** : made useful and obedient to humans : DOMESTIC 3 **2** : not afraid of people **3** : not interesting : DULL — **tame·ly** *adv* — **tame·ness** *n*

²tame *vb* **tamed; tam·ing** **1** : to make or become gentle or obedient **2** : ²HUMBLE — **tam·able** *or* **tame·able** \'tā-mə-bəl\ *adj* — **tam·er** *n*

tamp \'tamp\ *vb* : to drive down or in with several light blows

tam·per \'tam-pər\ *vb* : to interfere in a secret or incorrect way **synonyms** see MEDDLE

¹tan \'tan\ *vb* **tanned; tan·ning** **1** : to change hide into leather by soaking in a tannin solution **2** : to make or become brown or tan in color **3** : ¹BEAT 1, THRASH

²**tan** *n* **1** : a brown color given to the skin by the sun or wind **2** : a light yellowish brown color

³**tan** *adj* **tan·ner; tan·nest** : of the color tan

tan·a·ger \'tan-i-jər\ *n* : a very brightly colored bird related to the finches

¹**tan·dem** \'tan-dəm\ *n* **1** : a carriage pulled by horses hitched one behind the other **2** : a bicycle for two people sitting one behind the other

²**tandem** *adv* : one behind another

tang \'tang\ *n* : a sharp flavor or smell ⟨the *tang* of salt air⟩

tan·ger·ine \'tan-jə-,rēn\ *n* : a Chinese orange with a loose skin and sweet pulp

tan·gi·ble \'tan-jə-bəl\ *adj* **1** : possible to touch or handle **2** : actually real : MATERIAL — **tan·gi·bly** \-blē\ *adv*

¹**tan·gle** \'tang-gəl\ *vb* **tan·gled; tan·gling** : to twist or become twisted together into a mass hard to straighten out again ⟨the dog *tangled* its leash around the bushes⟩

²**tangle** *n* **1** : a tangled twisted mass (as of yarn) **2** : a complicated or confused state

¹**tank** \'tangk\ *n* **1** : an often large container for a liquid ⟨water *tank*⟩ ⟨fish *tank*⟩ **2** : an enclosed combat vehicle that has heavy armor and guns and a tread which is an endless belt

²**tank** *vb* : to put, keep, or treat in a tank

tan·kard \'tang-kərd\ *n* : a tall cup with one handle and often a lid

tank·er \'tang-kər\ *n* : a vehicle or ship with tanks for carrying a liquid ⟨oil *tankers*⟩

tan·ner \'tan-ər\ *n* : a person who tans hides into leather

tan·nery \'tan-ə-rē\ *n, pl* **tan·ner·ies** : a place where hides are tanned

tankard

tan·nin \'tan-ən\ *n* : a substance often made from oak bark or sumac and used in tanning, dyeing, and making ink

tan·ta·lize \'tant-l-,īz\ *vb* **tan·ta·lized; tan·ta·liz·ing** : to make miserable by or as if by showing something desirable but keeping it out of reach — **tan·ta·liz·er** *n*

tan·trum \'tan-trəm\ *n* : an outburst of bad temper

¹**tap** \'tap\ *n* : FAUCET, SPIGOT — **on tap** : on hand : AVAILABLE

²**tap** *vb* **tapped; tap·ping** **1** : to let out or cause to flow by making a hole or by pulling out a plug ⟨*tap* wine from a barrel⟩ **2** : to make a hole in to draw off a liquid ⟨*tap* maple trees for sap⟩ **3** : to draw from or upon ⟨*tapped* my bank to go to the movies⟩ **4** : to connect into (a telephone wire) to listen secretly — **tap·per** *n*

³**tap** *vb* **tapped; tap·ping** **1** : to hit lightly **2** : to make by striking something lightly again and again ⟨*tap* out a note on the typewriter⟩ — **tap·per** *n*

⁴**tap** *n* : a light blow or its sound

¹**tape** \'tāp\ *n* **1** : a narrow band of cloth **2** : a narrow strip or band of material (as paper, steel, or plastic) **3** : MAGNETIC TAPE

²**tape** *vb* **taped; tap·ing** **1** : to fasten, cover, or hold up with tape **2** : to measure with a tape measure **3** : to make a record of on tape

tape deck *n* : a device used to play back and often to record on magnetic tapes

tape·line \'tā-,plīn\ *n* : TAPE MEASURE

tape measure *n* : a tape marked off for measuring

¹**ta·per** \'tā-pər\ *n* **1** : a slender candle **2** : a gradual lessening in thickness or width in a long object

²**taper** *vb* **1** : to make or become gradually smaller toward one end **2** : to grow gradually less and less

tape recorder *n* : a device for recording on and playing back magnetic tapes

tap·es·try \'tap-ə-strē\ *n, pl* **tap·es·tries** : a heavy cloth that has designs or pictures woven into it and is used especially as a wall hanging — **tap·es·tried** \-strēd\ *adj*

tape·worm \'tāp-,wərm\ *n* : a worm with a long flat body that lives in human or animal intestines

tap·i·o·ca \,tap-ē-'ō-kə\ *n* : small pieces of starch from roots of a tropical plant used especially in puddings

ta·pir \'tā-pər\ *n* : a large hoofed mammal of tropical America, Malaya, and Sumatra that has thick legs, a short tail, and a long flexible snout

tapir

tap·root \'tap-,rüt, -,rüt\ *n* : a main root of a plant that grows straight down and gives off smaller side roots

taps \'taps\ *n sing or pl* : the last bugle call at night blown as a signal to put out the lights

¹**tar** \'tär\ *n* : a thick dark sticky liquid made from wood, coal, or peat

²**tar** *vb* **tarred; tar·ring** : to cover with or as if with tar

³**tar** *n* : SAILOR

ta·ran·tu·la \tə-'ran-chə-lə\ *n* **1** : a large European spider whose bite was once believed to cause a wild desire to dance **2** : any of several large hairy American spiders mistakenly believed to be dangerous

tarantula 2

tar·dy \'tärd-ē\ *adj* **tar·di·er; tar·di·est** : not on time : LATE — **tar·di·ly** \'tärd-l-ē\ *adv* — **tar·di·ness** \'tärd-ē-nəs\ *n*

tar·get \'tär-gət\ *n* **1** : a mark or object to shoot at **2** : a person or thing that is talked about, criticized, or laughed at **3** : a goal to be reached

tar·iff \'tar-əf\ *n* **1** : a list of taxes placed by a government on goods coming into a country **2** : the tax or the rate of taxation set up in a tariff list

¹**tar·nish** \'tär-nish\ *vb* : to make or become dull, dim, or discolored

²**tarnish** *n* : a surface coating formed during tarnishing

tar·pau·lin \tär-'pȯ-lən\ *n* : a sheet of waterproof canvas

¹**tar·ry** \'tar-ē\ *vb* **tar·ried; tar·ry·ing** **1** : to be slow in coming or going **2** : to stay in or at a place

²**tar·ry** \'tär-ē\ *adj* : of, like, or covered with tar

¹**tart** \'tärt\ *adj* **1** : pleasantly sharp to the taste **2** : BITING ⟨a *tart* manner⟩ — **tart·ly** *adv* — **tart·ness** *n*

²**tart** *n* : a small pie often with no top crust

tar·tan \'tärt-n\ *n* : a woolen cloth with a plaid design first made in Scotland

tar·tar \'tärt-ər\ *n* **1** : a substance found in the juices of grapes that forms a reddish crust on the inside of wine barrels **2** : a crust that forms on the teeth made up of deposits of saliva, food, and calcium

task \'task\ *n* : a piece of assigned work

synonyms TASK, DUTY, and JOB mean a piece of work assigned or to be done. TASK suggests work given by a person in a position of authority ⟨the boss used to give me every difficult *task*⟩ DUTY stresses that one has responsibility to do the work ⟨the *duty* of the police is to protect the people⟩ JOB may suggest that the work is necessary, hard, or important ⟨we all have to do our *job*⟩

tas·sel \'tas-əl\ *n* **1** : a hanging ornament made of a bunch of cords of the same length fastened at one end **2** : something like a tassel ⟨the *tassel* of Indian corn⟩

¹**taste** \'tāst\ *vb* **tast·ed; tast·ing** **1** : ²EXPERIENCE **2** : to find out the flavor of something by taking a little into the

tassel 1

mouth **3 :** to eat or drink usually in small amounts **4 :** to recognize by the sense of taste ⟨can *taste* salt in the soup⟩ **5 :** to have a certain flavor ⟨the milk *tastes* sour⟩ — **tast•er** *n*

²taste *n* **1 :** a small amount tasted **2 :** the one of the special senses that recognizes sweet, sour, bitter, or salty flavors and that acts through sense organs (**taste buds**) in the tongue **3 :** the quality of something recognized by the sense of taste or by this together with smell and touch : FLAVOR **4 :** a personal liking ⟨children with a *taste* for reading⟩ ⟨has very expensive *tastes*⟩ **5 :** the ability to choose and enjoy what is good or beautiful

taste•ful \'tāst-fəl\ *adj* **:** having or showing good taste — **taste•ful•ly** \-fə-lē\ *adv* — **taste•ful•ness** *n*

taste•less \'tāst-ləs\ *adj* **1 :** having little flavor **2 :** not having or showing good taste — **taste•less•ly** *adv* — **taste•less-ness** *n*

tasty \'tās-tē\ *adj* **tast•i•er; tast•i•est** **:** pleasing to the taste ⟨a *tasty* dessert⟩ — **tast•i•ness** *n*

tat•ter \'tat-ər\ *n* **1 :** a part torn and left hanging : SHRED **2 tatters** *pl* **:** ragged clothing

tat•tered \'tat-ərd\ *adj* **1 :** torn in or worn to shreds **2 :** dressed in ragged clothes

tat•tle \'tat-l\ *vb* **tat•tled; tat•tling** **1 :** PRAT-TLE **2 :** to give away secrets : tell on some-one — **tat•tler** \'tat-lər\ *n*

tat•tle•tale \'tat-l-ˌtāl\ *n* **:** a person who lets secrets out

¹tat•too \ta-'tü\ *n, pl* **tat•toos :** a picture or design made by tattooing

²tattoo *vb* **tat•tooed; tat•too•ing :** to mark the body with a picture or pattern by using a needle to put color under the skin — **tat-too•er** *n*

taught *past of* TEACH

¹taunt \'tȯnt\ *vb* **:** to make fun of or say mean insulting things to

²taunt *n* **:** a mean insulting remark

Tau•rus \'tȯr-əs\ *n* **1 :** a constellation be-tween Aries and Gemini imagined as a bull **2 :** the second sign of the zodiac or a person born under this sign

taut \'tȯt\ *adj* **1 :** tightly stretched ⟨make a rope *taut*⟩ **2 :** HIGH-STRUNG, TENSE **3 :** kept in good order — **taut•ly** *adv* — **taut-ness** *n*

tav•ern \'tav-ərn\ *n* **1 :** a place where beer and liquor are sold and drunk **2 :** INN

taw•ny \'tȯ-nē\ *adj* **:** of a brownish orange color

¹tax \'taks\ *vb* **1 :** to require to pay a tax **2 :** to accuse of something ⟨*taxed* them with

carelessness⟩ **3 :** to cause a strain on ⟨*taxed* their strength⟩ — **tax•er** *n*

²tax *n* **1 :** money collected by the govern-ment from people or businesses for public use **2 :** a difficult task

tax•able \'tak-sə-bəl\ *adj* **:** subject to tax ⟨*taxable* property⟩

tax•a•tion \tak-'sā-shən\ *n* **1 :** the action of taxing **2 :** money gotten from taxes

¹taxi \'tak-sē\ *n, pl* **tax•is** \-sēz\ **:** TAXICAB

²taxi *vb* **tax•ied; taxi•ing** *or* **taxy•ing** **1 :** to go by taxicab **2 :** to run an airplane slowly along the ground under its own power

taxi•cab \'tak-sē-ˌkab\ *n* **:** a car that carries passengers for money often recorded by a meter

taxi•der•my \'tak-sə-ˌdər-mē\ *n* **:** the art of stuffing and mounting the skins of animals

tax•on•o•my \tak-'sän-ə-mē\ *n* **1 :** the study of classification **2 :** a classification (as of animals) using a system that is usu-ally based on relationship

tax•pay•er \'tak-ˌspā-ər\ *n* **:** a person who pays or is responsible for paying a tax

TB \tē-'bē\ *n* **:** TUBERCULOSIS

tea \'tē\ *n* **1 :** the dried leaves and leaf buds of a shrub widely grown in eastern and southern Asia **2 :** a drink made by soaking tea in boiling water **3 :** a drink or medicine made by soaking plant parts (as dried roots) ⟨ginger *tea*⟩ **4 :** refreshments often including tea served in late after-noon **5 :** a party at which tea is served

teach \'tēch\ *vb* **taught** \'tȯt\; **teach•ing** **1 :** to show how ⟨*teach* a child to swim⟩ **2 :** to guide the studies of **3 :** to cause to know the unpleasant results of something ⟨that will *teach* you to talk back⟩ **4 :** to give lessons in ⟨*teach* math⟩

synonyms TEACH, INSTRUCT, and TRAIN mean to cause to gain knowledge or skill. TEACH can be used of any method of pass-ing on information or skill so that others may learn ⟨*teach* me how to swim⟩ ⟨*teach* children to read⟩ INSTRUCT stresses that the teaching is done in a formal or orderly manner ⟨teachers will *instruct* all stu-dents in the sciences⟩ TRAIN stresses in-struction with a particular purpose in mind ⟨*trained* workers to operate the new ma-chines⟩

teach•er \'tē-chər\ *n* **:** a person who teaches

\ə\ abut	\au̇\ out	\i\ tip	\ȯ\ saw	\u̇\ foot
\ər\ further	\ch\ chin	\ī\ life	\ȯi\ coin	\y\ yet
\a\ mat	\e\ pet	\j\ job	\th\ thin	\yü\ few
\ā\ take	\ē\ easy	\ng\ sing	\th\ this	\yu̇\ cure
\ä\ cot, cart	\g\ go	\ō\ bone	\ü\ food	\zh\ vision

teach·ing \'tē-ching\ *n* **1** : the duties or profession of a teacher **2** : something taught

tea·cup \'tē-ˌkəp\ *n* : a cup used with a saucer for hot drinks

teak \'tēk\ *n* : the hard wood of a tall tree which grows in the East Indies and resists decay

tea·ket·tle \'tē-ˌket-l\ *n* : a covered kettle that is used for boiling water and has a handle and spout

teal \'tēl\ *n* : a small wild duck that is very swift in flight

¹team \'tēm\ *n* **1** : two or more animals used to pull the same vehicle or piece of machinery **2** : a group of persons who work or play together

²team *vb* **1** : to haul with or drive a team **2** : to form a team

team·mate \'tēm-ˌmāt\ *n* : a person who belongs to the same team as someone else

team·ster \'tēm-stər\ *n* : a worker who drives a team or a truck

team·work \'tēm-ˌwərk\ *n* : the work of a group of persons acting together

tea·pot \'tē-ˌpät\ *n* : a pot for making and serving tea

¹tear \'tiər\ *n* : a drop of the salty liquid that keeps the eyeballs and inside of the eyelids moist

²tear \'taər, 'teər\ *vb* **tore** \'tōr\; **torn** \'tōrn\; **tear·ing** **1** : to pull into two or more pieces by force **2** : LACERATE ⟨fell and *tore* my knee⟩ **3** : to remove by force ⟨children *torn* from their parents⟩ **4** : to move powerfully or swiftly ⟨*tore* up the street⟩

³tear \'taər, 'teər\ *n* **1** : the act of tearing **2** : damage from being torn

tear·drop \'tiər-ˌdräp\ *n* : ¹TEAR

tear·ful \'tiər-fəl\ *adj* : flowing with, accompanied by, or causing tears — **tear·ful·ly** \-fə-lē\ *adv*

¹tease \'tēz\ *vb* **teased; teas·ing** : to annoy again and again **synonyms** see AN-NOY — **teas·er** *n*

²tease *n* **1** : the act of teasing : the state of being teased **2** : a person who teases

tea·spoon \'tē-ˌspün\ *n* **1** : a small spoon used especially for stirring drinks **2** : TEA-SPOONFUL

tea·spoon·ful \'tē-ˌspün-ˌfúl\ *n, pl* **tea-spoon·fuls** \-ˌfúlz\ *or* **tea·spoons·ful** \-ˌspünz-ˌfúl\ **1** : as much as a teaspoon can hold **2** : a unit of measure used especially in cooking and pharmacy equal to about five milliliters

teat \'tit, 'tēt\ *n* : NIPPLE 1 — used mostly of domestic animals

tech·ni·cal \'tek-ni-kəl\ *adj* **1** : having spe-
cial knowledge especially of a mechanical or scientific subject **2** : of or relating to a single and especially a practical or scientific subject **3** : according to a strict explanation of the rules — **tech·ni·cal·ly** *adv*

tech·ni·cal·i·ty \ˌtek-nə-'kal-ət-ē\ *n, pl* **tech·ni·cal·i·ties** : something having meaning only to a person with special training

technical sergeant *n* : a noncommissioned officer in the Air Force ranking above a staff sergeant

tech·ni·cian \tek-'nish-ən\ *n* : a person skilled in the details or techniques of a subject, art, or job ⟨a dental *technician* helps the dentist⟩

tech·nique \tek-'nēk\ *n* **1** : the manner in which technical details are used in reaching a goal **2** : technical methods

tech·no·log·i·cal \ˌtek-nə-'läj-i-kəl\ *adj* : of or relating to technology

tech·nol·o·gist \tek-'näl-ə-jəst\ *n* : a specialist in technology

tech·nol·o·gy \tek-'näl-ə-jē\ *n, pl* **tech-nol·o·gies** **1** : the use of science in solving problems (as in industry or engineering) **2** : a technical method of doing something

ted·dy bear \'ted-ē-\ *n* : a stuffed toy bear

te·di·ous \'tēd-ē-əs, 'tē-jəs\ *adj* : tiring because of length or dullness — **te·di·ous·ly** *adv* — **te·di·ous·ness** *n*

tee \'tē\ *n* : a peg on which a golf ball is placed to be hit

teem \'tēm\ *vb* : to be full of something ⟨the streams *teemed* with fish⟩

teen·age \'tēn-ˌāj\ *or* **teen·aged** \-ˌājd\ *adj* : of, being, or relating to teenagers ⟨*teenage* styles⟩

teen·ag·er \'tēn-ˌā-jər\ *n* : a person in his or her teens

teens \'tēnz\ *n pl* : the years thirteen through nineteen in a person's life

tee·ny \'tē-nē\ *adj* **tee·ni·er; tee·ni·est** : TINY

tee shirt *variant of* T-SHIRT

tee·ter \'tēt-ər\ *vb* **1** : to move unsteadily **2** : ²SEESAW

tee·ter–tot·ter \'tēt-ər-ˌtät-ər\ *n* : ¹SEESAW

teeth *pl of* TOOTH

teethe \'tēth\ *vb* **teethed; teeth·ing** : to cut one's teeth : grow teeth

tele- *or* **tel-** *prefix* **1** : at a distance ⟨*tele*gram⟩ **2** : television ⟨*tele*cast⟩

¹tele·cast \'tel-i-ˌkast\ *n* : a program broadcast by television

²telecast *vb* **telecast** *also* **tele·cast·ed; tele·cast·ing** : to broadcast by television — **tele·cast·er** *n*

tele·gram \'tel-ə-ˌgram\ *n* : a message sent by telegraph

¹tele·graph \'tel-ə-ˌgraf\ *n* : an electric device or system for sending messages by a code over connecting wires

²telegraph *vb* 1 : to send by telegraph 2 : to send a telegram to

te·leg·ra·phy \tə-'leg-rə-fē\ *n* : the use of a telegraph

te·lep·a·thy \tə-'lep-ə-thē\ *n* : communication which appears to take place from one mind to another without speech or signs

¹tele·phone \'tel-ə-ˌfōn\ *n* : an instrument for transmitting and receiving sounds over long distances by electricity

²telephone *vb* **tele·phoned; tele·phon·ing** : to speak to by telephone

¹tele·scope \'tel-ə-ˌskōp\ *n* : an instrument shaped like a long tube that has lenses for viewing objects at a distance and especially for observing objects in outer space

²telescope *vb* **tele·scoped; tele·scop·ing** : to slide or force one part into another like the sections of a small telescope

tele·vise \'tel-ə-ˌvīz\ *vb* **tele·vised; tele·vis·ing** : to send (a program) by television

tele·vi·sion \'tel-ə-ˌvizh-ən\ *n* 1 : an electronic system of sending images together with sound over a wire or through space by devices that change light and sound into electrical waves and then change these back into light and sound 2 : a television receiving set 3 : television as a way of communicating

tell \'tel\ *vb* **told** \'tōld\; **tell·ing** 1 : ¹COUNT 1 ⟨all *told* there were 27 of us⟩ 2 : to describe item by item ⟨*tell* a story⟩ 3 : ¹SAY 1 ⟨*tell* a lie⟩ 4 : to make known ⟨*tell* a secret⟩ 5 : to report to ⟨I'll *tell* them when they get here⟩ 6 : ²ORDER 2 ⟨*told* us to wait⟩ 7 : to find out by observing ⟨learned to *tell* time⟩ 8 : to act as a tattletale ⟨don't *tell* on me⟩ 9 : to have a noticeable result ⟨the pressure began to *tell* on them⟩ 10 : to act as evidence ⟨smiles *telling* of success⟩

tell·er \'tel-ər\ *n* 1 : NARRATOR 2 : a person who counts votes 3 : a bank employee who receives and pays out money

¹tem·per \'tem-pər\ *vb* 1 : SOFTEN ⟨the mountains *temper* the wind⟩ 2 : to make a substance as thick, firm, or tough as is wanted 3 : to heat and cool a substance (as steel) until it is as hard, tough, or flexible as is wanted

²temper *n* 1 : the hardness or toughness of a substance (as metal) 2 : characteristic state of feeling 3 : calmness of mind ⟨lost my *temper*⟩ 4 : an angry mood ⟨control your *temper*⟩

tem·per·a·ment \'tem-pə-rə-mənt, -prə-mənt\ *n* : a person's attitude as it affects what he or she says or does ⟨nervous *temperament*⟩

tem·per·a·men·tal \ˌtem-pə-rə-'ment-l, -prə-'ment-l\ *adj* : having or showing a nervous sensitive temperament — **tem·per·a·men·tal·ly** *adv*

tem·per·ance \'tem-pə-rəns, -prəns\ *n* 1 : control over one's actions, thoughts, or feelings 2 : the use of little or no alcoholic drink

tem·per·ate \'tem-pə-rət, -prət\ *adj* 1 : keeping or held within limits : MILD 2 : not drinking much liquor 3 : showing self-control 4 : not too hot or too cold

tem·per·a·ture \'tem-pə-rə-ˌchùr, -prə-ˌchùr, -pə-ˌchùr, -chər\ *n* 1 : degree of hotness or coldness as shown by a thermometer 2 : level of heat above what is normal for the human body : FEVER

tem·pest \'tem-pəst\ *n* 1 : a strong wind often accompanied by rain, hail, or snow 2 : UPROAR

tem·pes·tu·ous \tem-'pes-chə-wəs\ *adj* : very stormy — **tem·pes·tu·ous·ly** *adv*

¹tem·ple \'tem-pəl\ *n* : a building for worship

²temple *n* : the space between the eye and forehead and the upper part of the ear

tem·po \'tem-pō\ *n, pl* **tem·pi** \-ˌpē\ *or* **tem·pos** : the rate of speed at which a musical composition is played or sung

tem·po·ral \'tem-pə-rəl\ *adj* : of, relating to, or limited by time

tem·po·rary \'tem-pə-ˌrer-ē\ *adj* : not permanent — **tem·po·rar·i·ly** \ˌtem-pə-'rer-ə-lē\ *adv*

tempt \'tempt\ *vb* 1 : to make someone think of doing wrong (as by promise of gain) 2 : to risk the dangers of ⟨*tempt* one's luck⟩ — **tempt·er** *n*

temp·ta·tion \temp-'tā-shən\ *n* 1 : the act of tempting or the state of being tempted 2 : something that tempts

¹ten \'ten\ *adj* : being one more than nine

²ten *n* : one more than nine : two times five : 10

te·na·cious \tə-'nā-shəs\ *adj* 1 : not easily pulled apart 2 : PERSISTENT

te·nac·i·ty \tə-'nas-ət-ē\ *n* : the quality or state of being tenacious

¹ten·ant \'ten-ənt\ *n* 1 : a person who rents property (as a house) from the owner 2 : OCCUPANT, DWELLER

\ə\ abut	\aù\ out	\i\ tip	\ò\ saw	\ù\ foot
\ər\ further	\ch\ chin	\ī\ life	\òi\ coin	\y\ yet
\a\ mat	\e\ pet	\j\ job	\th\ thin	\yü\ few
\ā\ take	\ē\ easy	\ng\ sing	\th\ this	\yù\ cure
\ä\ cot, cart	\g\ go	\ō\ bone	\ü\ food	\zh\ vision

²tenant *vb* : to hold or live in as a tenant

¹tend \'tend\ *vb* **1** : to pay attention ⟨*tend* strictly to business⟩ **2** : to take care of **3** : to manage the operation of ⟨*tend* a machine⟩

²tend *vb* **1** : to move or turn in a certain direction : LEAD **2** : to be likely

ten·den·cy \'ten-dən-sē\ *n, pl* **ten·den·cies 1** : the direction or course toward something **2** : a leaning toward a particular kind of thought or action

¹ten·der \'ten-dər\ *adj* **1** : not tough ⟨a *tender* steak⟩ **2** : DELICATE 4 ⟨*tender* plants⟩ **3** : YOUTHFUL 1 ⟨children of *tender* years⟩ **4** : feeling or showing love ⟨a *tender* look⟩ **5** : very easily hurt ⟨a *tender* scar⟩ — **ten·der·ly** *adv* — **ten·der·ness** *n*

²tend·er \'ten-dər\ *n* **1** : one that tends or takes care of something **2** : a car attached to a locomotive for carrying fuel or water **3** : a ship used to attend other ships (as to supply food) **4** : a boat that carries passengers or freight to a larger ship

³ten·der \'ten-dər\ *n* **1** : ²OFFER **2** : something (as money) that may be offered in payment

⁴ten·der *vb* **1** : to offer in payment **2** : to present for acceptance

ten·der·foot \'ten-dər-ˌfut\ *n, pl* **ten·der·feet** \-ˌfēt\ *also* **ten·der·foots** : a person who is not used to a rough outdoor life

ten·der·heart·ed \ˌten-dər-'härt-əd\ *adj* : easily affected with feelings of love, pity, or sorrow

ten·don \'ten-dən\ *n* : a strip or band of tough white fiber connecting a muscle to another part (as a bone)

ten·dril \'ten-drəl\ *n* **1** : a slender leafless winding stem by which some climbing plants fasten themselves to a support **2** : something that winds like a plant's tendril ⟨*tendrils* of hair⟩

tendril 1

ten·e·ment \'ten-ə-mənt\ *n* **1** : a house used as a dwelling **2** : APARTMENT 1 **3** : a building divided into separate apartments for rent

ten·nis \'ten-əs\ *n* : a game played on a level court by two or four players who use rackets to hit a ball back and forth across a low net dividing the court

ten·or \'ten-ər\ *n* **1** : the next to the lowest part in harmony having four parts **2** : the highest male singing voice **3** : a singer or an instrument having a tenor range or part

ten·pins \'ten-ˌpinz\ *n* : a bowling game played with ten pins

¹tense \'tens\ *n* : a form of a verb used to show the time of the action or state

²tense *adj* **tens·er; tens·est 1** : stretched tight **2** : feeling or showing nervous tension **3** : marked by strain or uncertainty ⟨a *tense* moment⟩ — **tense·ly** *adv* — **tense·ness** *n*

³tense *vb* **tensed; tens·ing** : to make or become tense

ten·sion \'ten-chən\ *n* **1** : the act of straining or stretching : the condition of being strained or stretched **2** : a state of mental unrest **3** : a state of unfriendliness

¹tent \'tent\ *n* : a portable shelter (as of canvas) stretched and supported by poles

²tent *vb* : to live in a tent — **tent·er** *n*

ten·ta·cle \'tent-ə-kəl\ *n* : one of the long thin flexible structures that stick out about the head or the mouth of an animal (as an insect or fish) and are used especially for feeling or grasping

tentacle

ten·ta·tive \'tent-ət-iv\ *adj* : not final ⟨*tentative* plans⟩ — **ten·ta·tive·ly** *adv*

tent caterpillar *n* : any of several caterpillars that spin tent-like webs in which they live in groups

¹tenth \'tenth\ *adj* : coming right after ninth

²tenth *n* **1** : number ten in a series **2** : one of ten equal parts

te·pee \'tē-ˌpē\ *n* : a tent shaped like a cone and used as a home by some American Indians

tep·id \'tep-əd\ *adj* : LUKEWARM 1 ⟨*tepid* water⟩

¹term \'tərm\ *n* **1** : a period of time fixed especially by law or custom ⟨a school *term*⟩ **2 terms** *pl* : conditions that limit the nature and scope of something (as a treaty or a will) **3** : a word or expression that has an exact meaning in some uses or is limited to a subject or field ⟨legal *terms*⟩ **4** : the numerator or denominator

tepee

of a fraction **5** : any one of the numbers in a series **6 terms** *pl* : relationship between people ⟨was on good *terms* with the neighbors⟩

²term *vb* : to apply a term to ⟨*termed* them liars⟩

¹ter·mi·nal \'tər-mən-l\ *adj* : of, relating to, or forming an end

²terminal *n* **1** : a part that forms the end : EXTREMITY **2** : a device at the end of a wire or on a machine for making an electrical connection **3** : either end of a transportation line or a passenger or freight station located at it

ter·mi·nate \'tər-mə-ˌnāt\ *vb* **ter·mi·nat·ed; ter·mi·nat·ing** : END, CLOSE

ter·mi·na·tion \ˌtər-mə-'nā-shən\ *n* **1** : the end of something **2** : the act of ending something

ter·mi·nus \'tər-mə-nəs\ *n*, *pl* **ter·mi·ni** \-ˌnī, -ˌnē\ *or* **ter·mi·nus·es 1** : final goal : END **2** : either end of a transportation line or travel route

ter·mite \'tər-ˌmīt\ *n* : a chewing antlike insect of a light color that lives in large colonies and feeds on wood

tern \'tərn\ *n* : any of numerous small slender sea gulls with black cap, white body, and narrow wings

¹ter·race \'ter-əs\ *n* **1** : a flat roof or open platform **2** : a level area next to a building **3** : a raised piece of land with the top leveled **4** : a row of houses on raised ground or a slope

²terrace *vb* **ter·raced; ter·rac·ing** : to form into a terrace or supply with terraces

ter·rain \tə-'rān\ *n* : the features of the surface of a piece of land

ter·ra·pin \'ter-ə-pən\ *n* : a North American turtle that eats flesh and lives in water

ter·rar·i·um \tə-'rar-ē-əm, -'rer-\ *n*, *pl* **ter·rar·ia** \-ē-ə\ *or* **ter·rar·i·ums** : a box usually made of glass that is used for keeping and observing small animals or plants

ter·res·tri·al \tə-'res-trē-əl\ *adj* **1** : of or relating to the earth or its people **2** : living or growing on land

ter·ri·ble \'ter-ə-bəl\ *adj* **1** : causing great fear ⟨*terrible* weapons⟩ **2** : very great in degree : INTENSE ⟨a *terrible* fright⟩ **3** : very bad ⟨*terrible* writing⟩ — **ter·ri·bly** \-blē\ *adv*

ter·ri·er \'ter-ē-ər\ *n* : any of various usually small dogs originally used by hunters to drive animals from their holes

Word History Terriers were first used in hunting small game. Their job was to dig for the animals and drive them from their holes. Terriers got their name because

they dug in the earth. The English word *terrier* came from a Latin word that meant "earth."

ter·rif·ic \tə-'rif-ik\ *adj* **1** : causing terror : TERRIBLE ⟨the *terrific* damage from the earthquake⟩ **2** : very unusual : EXTRAORDINARY ⟨going at *terrific* speed⟩ **3** : very good : EXCELLENT ⟨had a *terrific* time at the party⟩ — **ter·rif·i·cal·ly** \-i-kə-lē\ *adv*

ter·ri·fy \'ter-ə-ˌfi\ *vb* **ter·ri·fied; ter·ri·fy·ing** : to frighten greatly

ter·ri·to·ri·al \ˌter-ə-'tōr-ē-əl\ *adj* : of or relating to a territory

ter·ri·to·ry \'ter-ə-ˌtōr-ē\ *n*, *pl* **ter·ri·to·ries 1** : a geographical area belonging to or under the rule of a government **2** : a part of the United States not included within any state but organized with a separate governing body **3** : REGION 1, DISTRICT

ter·ror \'ter-ər\ *n* **1** : a state of great fear **2** : a cause of great fear

ter·ror·ism \'ter-ər-ˌiz-əm\ *n* : the use of threat or violence especially as a means of forcing others to do what one wishes

ter·ror·ize \'ter-ər-ˌīz\ *vb* **ter·ror·ized; ter·ror·iz·ing 1** : to fill with terror **2** : to use terrorism against

terse \'tərs\ *adj* **ters·er; ters·est** : being brief and to the point : CONCISE — **terse·ly** *adv* — **terse·ness** *n*

¹test \'test\ *n* **1** : a means of finding out the nature, quality, or value of something **2** : a set of questions or problems by which a person's knowledge, intelligence, or skills are measured

Word History The English word *test* first meant "a small bowl used in analyzing metals." It came from a Latin word that meant "a bowl or pot made of clay." The bowl called a *test* was used to examine things. That is why the word *test* came to mean "examination."

²test *vb* : to put to a test : EXAMINE ⟨*test* pupils in arithmetic⟩ ⟨*test* milk for germs⟩

tes·ta·ment \'tes-tə-mənt\ *n* **1** : either of two main parts (**Old Testament** and **New Testament**) of the Bible **2** : ²WILL 3

tes·ti·fy \'tes-tə-ˌfi\ *vb* **tes·ti·fied; tes·ti·fy·ing** : to make a formal statement of what one swears is true

\ə\ abut	\aú\ out	\i\ tip	\ó\ saw	\ú\ foot
\ər\ further	\ch\ chin	\ī\ life	\ói\ coin	\y\ yet
\a\ mat	\e\ pet	\j\ job	\th\ thin	\yü\ few
\ā\ take	\ē\ easy	\ng\ sing	\th\ this	\yú\ cure
\ä\ cot, cart	\g\ go	\ō\ bone	\ü\ food	\zh\ vision

tes·ti·mo·ny \'tes-tə-ˌmō-nē\ *n, pl* **tes·ti·mo·nies** : a statement made by a witness under oath especially in a court

tes·tis \'tes-təs\ *n, pl* **tes·tes** \'tes-ˌtēz\ : a male reproductive gland

test tube *n* : a plain tube of thin glass closed at one end

tet·a·nus \'tet-n-əs, 'tet-nəs\ *n* : a dangerous disease in which spasms of the muscles occur often with locking of the jaws and which is caused by poison from a germ that enters wounds and grows in damaged tissue

¹**teth·er** \'teth-ər\ *n* : a line by which an animal is fastened so as to limit where it can go

²**tether** *vb* : to fasten by a tether

text \'tekst\ *n* **1** : the actual words of an author's work **2** : the main body of printed or written matter on a page **3** : a passage from the Bible chosen as the subject of a sermon **4** : TEXTBOOK

text·book \'tekst-ˌbuk\ *n* : a book that presents important information about a subject and is used as a basis of instruction

tex·tile \'tek-ˌstīl, 'teks-təl\ *n* : a woven or knit cloth

tex·ture \'teks-chər\ *n* : the structure, feel, and appearance of something (as cloth)

-th \th\ *or* **-eth** \əth\ *adj suffix* — used to form numbers that show the place of something in a series ⟨hundred*th*⟩ ⟨forti*eth*⟩

than \thən, than\ *conj* : when compared to the way in which, the extent to which, or the degree to which ⟨you are older *than* I am⟩

thank \'thangk\ *vb* **1** : to express gratitude to **2** : to hold responsible

thank·ful \'thangk-fəl\ *adj* : feeling or showing thanks : GRATEFUL — **thank·ful·ly** \-fə-lē\ *adv* — **thank·ful·ness** *n*

thank·less \'thangk-ləs\ *adj* **1** : UNGRATEFUL **2** : not appreciated ⟨a necessary but *thankless* job⟩

thanks \'thangks\ *n* **1** : GRATITUDE **2** : an expression of gratitude (as for something received) — **thanks to** **1** : with the help of **2** : BECAUSE OF

thanks·giv·ing \thangks-'giv-ing\ *n* **1** : the act of giving thanks **2** : a prayer expressing gratitude **3** *cap* : THANKSGIVING DAY

Thanksgiving Day *n* : the fourth Thursday in November observed as a legal holiday for public thanksgiving to God

¹**that** \that\ *pron, pl* **those** \thōz\ **1** : the one seen, mentioned, or understood ⟨*that* is my book⟩ ⟨*those* are my shoes⟩ **2** : the one farther away ⟨this is an elm, *that* is a

hickory⟩ **3** : the one : the kind ⟨the richest ore is *that* found higher up⟩

²**that** *adj, pl* **those** **1** : being the one mentioned, indicated, or understood ⟨*that* boy⟩ **2** : being the one farther away ⟨this book or *that* one⟩

³**that** \thət, that\ *conj* **1** : the following, namely ⟨said *that* we'd go⟩ **2** : which is, namely ⟨a chance *that* it might rain⟩ **3** : ²SO 1 ⟨shouted *that* all might hear⟩ **4** : as to result in the following, namely ⟨so hungry *that* I fainted⟩ **5** : BECAUSE ⟨glad *that* you came⟩

⁴**that** \thət, that\ *pron* **1** : WHO 3, WHOM, ²WHICH 2 ⟨the person *that* won the race⟩ ⟨the people *that* you saw⟩ ⟨the food *that* I like⟩ **2** : in, on, or at which ⟨the year *that* I joined the army⟩

⁵**that** \'that\ *adv* : to such an extent or degree ⟨need a nail about *that* long⟩

¹**thatch** \'thach\ *vb* : to cover with thatch

²**thatch** *n* : a plant material (as straw) for use as roofing

¹**thaw** \'tho\ *vb* **1** : to melt or cause to melt **2** : to grow less unfriendly or quiet in manner

²**thaw** *n* **1** : the action, fact, or process of thawing **2** : a period of weather warm enough to thaw ice and snow

¹**the** *especially before consonant sounds* thə, *before vowel sounds* the, *4 is often* 'thē\ *definite article* **1** : that or those mentioned, seen, or clearly understood ⟨put *the* cat out⟩ ⟨I'll take *the* red one⟩ **2** : that or those near in space, time, or thought ⟨news of *the* day⟩ **3** : ¹EACH ⟨forty cookies to *the* box⟩ **4** : that or those considered best, most typical, or most worth singling out ⟨is *the* person for this job⟩ **5** : any one typical of or standing for the entire class named ⟨useful tips for *the* beginner⟩ **6** : all those that are ⟨*the* British⟩

²**the** *adv* **1** : than before ⟨none *the* wiser⟩ **2** : to what extent ⟨*the* sooner the better⟩ **3** : to that extent ⟨the sooner *the* better⟩

the·ater *or* **the·atre** \'thē-ət-ər\ *n* **1** : a building in which plays or motion pictures are presented **2** : a place like a theater in form or use **3** : a place or area where some important action is carried on ⟨a *theater* of war⟩ **4** : plays or the performance of plays

the·at·ri·cal \thē-'at-ri-kəl\ *adj* : of or relating to the theater or the presentation of plays

thee \thē\ *pron, objective case of* THOU

theft \'theft\ *n* : the act of stealing

their \thər, theər, thaər\ *adj* : of or relating to them or themselves especially as owners or as agents or objects of an action ⟨*their* clothes⟩ ⟨*their* deeds⟩ ⟨*their* pain⟩

theirs \'theərz, 'thaərz\ *pron* : that which belongs to them ⟨the red house is *theirs*⟩ ⟨the toys are *theirs*⟩

them \thəm, them\ *pron, objective case of* THEY

theme \'thēm\ *n* 1 : a subject on which one writes or speaks 2 : a written exercise 3 : a main melody in a piece of music

them·selves \thəm-'selvz\ *pron* : their own selves ⟨they enjoyed *themselves*⟩ ⟨they did the whole job *themselves*⟩

¹**then** \then\ *adv* 1 : at that time 2 : soon after that : NEXT 3 : in addition : BESIDES 4 : in that case 5 : as an expected result

²**then** \'then\ *n* : that time ⟨wait until *then*⟩

³**then** \'then\ *adj* : existing or acting at that time ⟨the *then* president⟩

thence \'thens\ *adv* 1 : from that place 2 : from that fact

thence·forth \'thens-,fōrth\ *adv* : from that time on

thence·for·ward \thens-'fȯr-wərd\ *adv* : onward from that place or time

the·ol·o·gy \thē-'äl-ə-jē\ *n, pl* **the·ol·o·gies** : the study and explanation of religious faith, practice, and experience

the·o·ry \'thē-ə-rē, 'thir-ē\ *n, pl* **the·o·ries** 1 : the general rules followed in a science or an art ⟨music *theory*⟩ 2 : a general rule offered to explain experiences or facts ⟨wave *theory* of light⟩ 3 : an idea used for discussion or as a starting point for an investigation

ther·a·peu·tic \,ther-ə-'pyüt-ik\ *adj* : MEDICINAL

ther·a·pist \'ther-ə-pəst\ *n* : a specialist in therapy and especially in methods of treatment other than drugs and surgery

ther·a·py \'ther-ə-pē\ *n, pl* **ther·a·pies** : treatment of an abnormal state in the body or mind

¹**there** \'thaər, 'theər\ *adv* 1 : in or at that place ⟨stand over *there*⟩ 2 : to or into that place ⟨take the basket *there* and leave it⟩ 3 : in that situation or way ⟨*there* you have a choice⟩

²**there** \thaər, theər\ *pron* — used to introduce a sentence in which the subject comes after the verb ⟨*there* is a person outside⟩

³**there** \'thaər, 'theər\ *n* : that place ⟨get away from *there*⟩

there·abouts \,thar-ə-'baůts, ,ther-\ *or* **there·about** \-'baůt\ *adv* 1 : near that place or time 2 : near that number, degree, or amount

there·af·ter \tha-'raf-tər, the-\ *adv* : after that

there·at \tha-'rat, the-\ *adv* 1 : at that place 2 : because of that

there·by \thaər-'bī, theər-\ *adv* 1 : by that 2 : related to that

there·fore \'thaər-,fōr, 'theər-\ *adv* : for that reason

there·in \tha-'rin, the-\ *adv* : in or into that place, time, or thing ⟨the world and all that is *therein*⟩

there·of \tha-'rəv, the-, -'räv\ *adv* 1 : of that or it 2 : from that cause

there·on \tha-'rȯn, the-, -'rän\ *adv* : on that

there·to \thaər-'tü, theər-\ *adv* : to that

there·up·on \'thar-ə-,pȯn, 'ther-, -,pän\ *adv* 1 : on that thing 2 : for that reason 3 : immediately after that : at once

there·with \thaər-'with, theər-, -'with\ *adv* : with that

ther·mal \'thər-məl\ *adj* : of, relating to, caused by, or saving heat

ther·mom·e·ter \thər-'mäm-ət-ər, thə-'mäm-\ *n* : an instrument for measuring temperature usually in the form of a glass tube with mercury or alcohol sealed inside and with a scale marked in degrees on the outside

ther·mos \'thər-məs\ *n* : VACUUM BOTTLE

ther·mo·stat \'thər-mə-,stat\ *n* : a device that automatically controls temperature

these *pl of* THIS

the·sis \'thē-səs\ *n, pl* **the·ses** \-,sēz\ 1 : a statement that a person wants to discuss or prove 2 : an essay presenting results of original research

they \thā\ *pron* : those individuals : those ones

they'd \thād\ : they had : they would

they'll \thāl\ : they shall : they will

they're \thər, theər\ : they are

they've \thāv\ : they have

thi·a·min \'thī-ə-mən\ *n* : a member of the vitamin B complex whose lack causes beriberi

¹**thick** \'thik\ *adj* 1 : having great size from one surface to its opposite 2 : heavily built 3 : closely packed together 4 : occurring in large numbers : NUMEROUS ⟨mosquitos were *thick* in the shade⟩ 5 : not flowing easily ⟨a *thick* milk shake⟩ 6 : having haze, fog, or mist 7 : measuring a certain amount in the smallest of three dimensions ⟨two millimeters *thick*⟩ 8

\ə\ abut	\aů\ out	\i\ tip	\ȯ\ saw	\ů\ foot
\ər\ further	\ch\ chin	\ī\ life	\ȯi\ coin	\y\ yet
\a\ mat	\e\ pet	\j\ job	\th\ thin	\yü\ few
\ā\ take	\ē\ easy	\ng\ sing	\th\ this	\yů\ cure
\ä\ cot, cart	\g\ go	\ō\ bone	\ü\ food	\zh\ vision

: not clearly spoken ⟨*thick* speech⟩ **9** : STUPID **1** **synonyms** see DENSE — **thick·ly** *adv*

²thick *n* **1** : the most crowded or active part ⟨in the *thick* of the battle⟩ **2** : the part of greatest thickness

thick·en \'thik-ən\ *vb* : to make or become thick — **thick·en·er** *n*

thick·et \'thik-ət\ *n* : a thick usually small patch of bushes or low trees

thick·ness \'thik-nəs\ *n* **1** : the quality or state of being thick **2** : the smallest of three dimensions ⟨length, width, and *thickness*⟩

thick·set \'thik-'set\ *adj* **1** : closely placed or planted **2** : STOCKY

thief \'thēf\ *n, pl* **thieves** \'thēvz\ : a person who steals : ROBBER

thieve \'thēv\ *vb* **thieved; thiev·ing** : ¹STEAL 2, ROB

thiev·ery \'thē-və-rē\ *n, pl* **thiev·er·ies** : THEFT

thiev·ish \'thē-vish\ *adj* **1** : likely to steal **2** : of, relating to, or like a thief

thigh \'thī\ *n* : the part of a leg between the knee and the main part of the body

thim·ble \'thim-bəl\ *n* : a cap or cover used in sewing to protect the finger that pushes the nee-dle

thimble

¹thin \'thin\ *adj* **thin-ner; thin·nest 1** : having little size from one surface to its opposite : not thick ⟨*thin* paper⟩ **2** : having the parts not close together ⟨*thin* hair⟩ **3** : hav-ing little body fat **4** : having less than the usual number ⟨attendance was *thin*⟩ **5** : not very convincing ⟨a *thin* excuse⟩ **6** : somewhat weak or shrill ⟨a *thin* voice⟩ **synonyms** see LEAN — **thin-ly** *adv* — **thin·ness** *n*

²thin *vb* **thinned; thin·ning** : to make or become thin

thine \thīn\ *pron, archaic* : that which be-longs to thee

thing \'thing\ *n* **1** : AFFAIR 2, MATTER ⟨have a *thing* or two to take care of⟩ **2 things** *pl* : state of affairs ⟨*things* are improving⟩ **3** : EVENT 1 ⟨the accident was a terrible *thing*⟩ **4** : ¹DEED 1, ACHIEVEMENT ⟨expect great *things* from them⟩ **5** : something that exists and can be talked about ⟨all *things* bright and beautiful⟩ ⟨say the first *thing* that pops into your mind⟩ ⟨how do

you work this *thing?*⟩ **6 things** *pl* : per-sonal possessions ⟨pack your *things,* we're leaving⟩ **7** : a piece of clothing ⟨not a *thing* to wear⟩ **8** : ¹DETAIL 2 ⟨checks every little *thing*⟩ **9** : what is needed or wanted ⟨it's just the *thing* for a cold⟩ **10** : an action or interest that one very much enjoys ⟨music is my *thing*⟩

think \'thingk\ *vb* **thought** \'thȯt\; **think-ing 1** : to form or have in the mind ⟨afraid to even *think* what had happened⟩ **2** : to have as an opinion or belief ⟨I *think* you can do it⟩ **3** : REMEMBER 1 ⟨I didn't *think* to ask⟩ **4** : to use the power of reason ⟨you're just not *thinking*⟩ **5** : to invent something by thinking ⟨*think* up an ex-cuse⟩ **6** : to hold a strong feeling ⟨they *think* highly of you⟩ **7** : to care about ⟨I must *think* first of my family⟩ — **think·er** *n*

thin·ner \'thin-ər\ *n* : a liquid used to thin paint

¹third \'thərd\ *adj* : coming right after sec-ond

²third *n* **1** : number three in a series **2** : one of three equal parts

¹thirst \'thərst\ *n* **1** : a feeling of dryness in the mouth and throat that accompanies a need for liquids **2** : the bodily condition that produces thirst ⟨die of *thirst*⟩ **3** : a strong desire

²thirst *vb* **1** : to feel thirsty **2** : to have a strong desire

thirsty \'thər-stē\ *adj* **thirst·i·er; thirst·i·est 1** : feeling thirst **2** : needing moisture ⟨*thirsty* crops⟩ **3** : having a strong desire : EAGER — **thirst·i·ly** \'thər-stə-lē\ *adv*

¹thir·teen \,thər-'tēn\ *adj* : being one more than twelve

²thirteen *n* : one more than twelve : 13

¹thir·teenth \,thər-'tēnth\ *adj* : coming right after twelfth

²thirteenth *n* : number thirteen in a series

¹thir·ti·eth \'thərt-ē-əth\ *adj* : coming right after twenty-ninth

²thirtieth *n* : number thirty in a series

¹thir·ty \'thərt-ē\ *adj* : being three times ten

²thirty *n* : three times ten : 30

¹this \this\ *pron, pl* **these** \thēz\ **1** : the one close or closest in time or space ⟨*this* is your book⟩ ⟨*these* are my friends⟩ **2** : what is in the present or is being seen or talked about ⟨*this* is where it hap-pened⟩

²this *adj, pl* **these 1** : being the one pre-sent, near, or just mentioned ⟨*this* morn-ing⟩ ⟨friends all *these* years⟩ **2** : being the one nearer or last mentioned ⟨*this* book or that one⟩

³this \'this\ *adv* : to the degree suggested

by something in the present situation ⟨didn't expect to wait *this* long⟩

this·tle \'this-əl\ *n* : a prickly plant related to the daisies that has usually purplish often showy heads of mostly tubular flowers

thith·er \'thith-ər\ *adv* : to that place : THERE

tho *variant of* THOUGH

thong \'thóŋ\ *n* : a strip of leather used especially for fastening something

tho·rax \'thōr-,aks\ *n*, *pl* **tho·rax·es** *or* **tho·ra·ces** \'thōr-ə-,sēz\ **1** : the part of

thistle

the body of a mammal that lies between the neck and the abdomen and contains the heart and lungs **2** : the middle of the three main divisions of the body of an insect

thorn \'thórn\ *n* **1** : a woody plant (as hawthorn) with sharp briers, prickles, or spines **2** : a short hard sharp-pointed leafless branch on a woody plant

thorny \'thór-nē\ *adj* **thorn·i·er; thorn·i·est 1** : full of or covered with thorns **2** : full of difficulties

thor·ough \'thər-ō\ *adj* **1** : being such to the fullest degree : COMPLETE ⟨a *thorough* search⟩ **2** : careful about little things ⟨a *thorough* worker⟩ — **thor·ough·ly** *adv* — **thor·ough·ness** *n*

¹thor·ough·bred \'thər-ō-,bred\ *adj* **1** : bred from the best blood through a long line **2** *cap* : of, relating to, or being a member of the Thoroughbred breed of horses

²thoroughbred *n* **1** *cap* : any of an English breed of light speedy horses kept mainly for racing **2** : a purebred or pedigreed animal **3** : a very fine person

thor·ough·fare \'thər-ō-,faər, -,feər\ *n* **1** : a street or road open at both ends **2** : a main road

thor·ough·go·ing \,thər-ə-'gō-iŋ\ *adj* : THOROUGH 1

those *pl of* THAT

thou \thaù\ *pron, archaic* : the one these words are spoken or written to

¹though *also* **tho** \'thō\ *adv* : HOWEVER 3, NEVERTHELESS ⟨not for long, *though*⟩

²though \thō\ *conj* : ALTHOUGH ⟨*though* it was raining, we went out⟩

¹thought \'thót\ *past of* THINK

²thought *n* **1** : the act or process of thinking and especially of trying to decide about something ⟨give *thought* to the future⟩ **2** : power of reasoning and judging **3** : power of imagining **4** : something (as an idea or fancy) formed in the mind

thought·ful \'thót-fəl\ *adj* **1** : deep in thought **2** : showing careful thinking ⟨a *thoughtful* essay⟩ **3** : considerate of others — **thought·ful·ly** \-fə-lē\ *adv* — **thought·ful·ness** *n*

thought·less \'thót-ləs\ *adj* **1** : not careful and alert **2** : NEGLIGENT ⟨a *thoughtless* mistake⟩ **3** : not considerate of others — **thought·less·ly** *adv* — **thought·less·ness** *n*

¹thou·sand \'thaùz-nd\ *n* **1** : ten times one hundred : 1000 **2** : a very large number ⟨*thousands* of things to do⟩

²thousand *adj* : being 1000

¹thou·sandth \'thaùz-nth\ *adj* : coming right after 999th

²thousandth *n* : number 1000 in a series

thrash \'thrash\ *vb* **1** : THRESH 1 **2** : to beat very hard **3** : to move about violently ⟨something was *thrashing* wildly in the brush⟩

¹thrash·er \'thrash-ər\ *n* : one that thrashes

²thrasher *n* : an American bird (as the common reddish brown **brown thrasher**) related to the thrushes and noted for its song

²thoroughbred 1

¹thread \'thred\ *n* **1** : a thin fine cord formed by spinning and twisting short fibers into a continuous strand **2** : some-

\ə\ abut	\aù\ out	\i\ tip	\ó\ saw	\ù\ foot
\ər\ further	\ch\ chin	\ī\ life	\ói\ coin	\y\ yet
\a\ mat	\e\ pet	\j\ job	\th\ thin	\yü\ few
\ā\ take	\ē\ easy	\ŋ\ sing	\th\ this	\yù\ cure
\ä\ cot, cart	\g\ go	\ō\ bone	\ü\ food	\zh\ vision

thing suggesting a thread ⟨a *thread* of light⟩ **3 :** the ridge or groove that winds around a screw **4 :** a line of reasoning or train of thought that connects the parts of an argument or story — **thread·like** \-₁līk\ *adj*

²**thread** *vb* **1 :** to put a thread in working position (as in a needle) **2 :** to pass through like a thread ⟨*thread* a pipe with wire⟩ **3 :** to make one's way through or between **4 :** to put together on a thread : STRING

thread·bare \'thred-₁baər, -₁beər\ *adj* **1 :** worn so much that the thread shows : SHABBY **2 :** TRITE

threat \'thret\ *n* **1 :** a showing of an intention to do harm **2 :** something that threatens ⟨the *threat* of punishment⟩

threat·en \'thret-n\ *vb* **1 :** to make threats against **2 :** to give warning of by a threat or sign ⟨clouds that *threatened* rain⟩ — **threat·en·ing·ly** *adv*

¹**three** \'thrē\ *adj* **:** being one more than two

²**three** *n* **1 :** one more than two **:** 3 **2 :** the third in a set or series

three·fold \'thrē-₁fōld\ *adj* **:** being three times as great or as many

three·score \'thrē-₁skōr\ *adj* **:** SIXTY

thresh \'thrash, 'thresh\ *vb* **1 :** to separate (as grain from straw) by beating **2 :** THRASH 3

thresh·er \'thrash-ər, 'thresh-\ *n* **:** one (as a machine for separating grain from straw) that threshes

thresh·old \'thresh-₁ōld\ *n* **1 :** the sill of a door **2 :** a point or place of beginning or entering ⟨at the *threshold* of an adventure⟩

threw *past of* THROW

thrice \'thrīs\ *adv* **:** three times

thrift \'thrift\ *n* **:** careful management especially of money

thrifty \'thrif-tē\ *adj* **thrift·i·er; thrift·i·est** **1 :** tending to save money **2 :** doing well in health and growth ⟨*thrifty* cattle⟩ **syn·onyms** *see* ECONOMICAL

¹**thrill** \'thril\ *vb* **1 :** to have or cause to have a sudden feeling of excitement or pleasure **2 :** ¹TREMBLE 2, VIBRATE — **thrill·er** *n*

Word History The English word *thrill* is related to the English word *through*. Modern English *through* comes from an Old English word that meant "through." An Old English word meaning "hole" was formed from the word meaning "through." An Old English word meaning "to pierce" was formed from the word meaning "hole." The modern word *thrill* comes from the Old English word meaning "to pierce." When you are thrilled you are not really pierced, of course. You do feel, however, as if something has gone through you.

²**thrill** *n* **1 :** a feeling of being thrilled **2** **:** VIBRATION 3

thrive \'thrīv\ *vb* **throve** \'thrōv\ *or* **thrived; thriv·en** \'thriv-ən\ *also* **thrived; thriv·ing** \'thrī-ving\ **1 :** to grow very well **:** FLOURISH **2 :** to gain in wealth or possessions

throat \'thrōt\ *n* **1 :** the part of the neck in front of the backbone **2 :** the passage from the mouth to the stomach and lungs ⟨a sore *throat*⟩ **3 :** something like the throat especially in being an entrance or a narrowed part

¹**throb** \'thräb\ *vb* **throbbed; throb·bing** **1 :** to beat hard or fast ⟨our hearts *throbbed* from fright⟩ **2 :** to beat or rotate in a normal way ⟨the motor *throbbed* quietly⟩

²**throb** *n* **:** ²BEAT 2, PULSE

throne \'thrōn\ *n* **1 :** the chair of state especially of a monarch or bishop **2 :** royal power and dignity

¹**throng** \'thröng\ *n* **:** a large group of assembled persons **:** CROWD

²**throng** *vb* **:** ¹CROWD 4

¹**throt·tle** \'thrät-l\ *vb* **throt·tled; throt·tling** **1 :** STRANGLE 1, CHOKE **2 :** to reduce the speed of (an engine) by closing the throttle

²**throttle** *n* **1 :** a valve for regulating the flow of steam or fuel in an engine **2** **:** a lever that controls the throttle valve

¹**through** \'thrü\ *prep* **1 :** into at one side and out at the other side of ⟨drove a nail *through* the wood⟩ **2 :** by way of ⟨got in *through* the window⟩ **3 :** AMONG 1 ⟨a path *through* the trees⟩ **4 :** by means of ⟨succeeded *through* hard work⟩ **5 :** over the whole of ⟨the rumor swept *through* school⟩ **6 :** during the whole of ⟨slept *through* the night⟩

²**through** \'thrü\ *adv* **1 :** from one end or side to the other ⟨the arm was pierced *through*⟩ **2 :** from beginning to end ⟨read the book *through* in one evening⟩ **3 :** to completion ⟨see the job *through*⟩ **4 :** in or to every part ⟨was wet *through*⟩ **5 :** into the open ⟨break *through*⟩

³**through** \'thrü\ *adj* **1 :** allowing free or continuous passage **:** DIRECT ⟨a *through* road⟩ **2 :** going from point of origin to destination without changes or transfers ⟨*through* trains⟩ **3 :** coming from and

going to points outside a local zone ⟨*through* traffic⟩ **4** : having reached an end ⟨we're *through* with the job⟩

¹through·out \thrü-'aut\ *adv* **1** : EVERY-WHERE ⟨of one color *throughout*⟩ **2** : from beginning to end ⟨remained loyal *throughout*⟩

²throughout *prep* **1** : in or to every part of ⟨traveling *throughout* the country⟩ **2** : during the whole period of ⟨rained *throughout* the day⟩

throughway *variant of* THRUWAY

throve *past of* THRIVE

¹throw \'thrō\ *vb* **threw** \'thrü\; **thrown** \'thrōn\; **throw·ing** **1** : to send through the air with a quick forward motion of the arm ⟨*throw* a ball⟩ **2** : to send through the air in any way **3** : to cause to fall ⟨the horse *threw* the rider⟩ **4** : to put suddenly in a certain position or condition ⟨was *thrown* out of work⟩ **5** : to put on or take off in a hurry ⟨*throw* on a coat⟩ **6** : to move quickly ⟨*throw* in reinforcements⟩ **7** : to move (as a switch) to an open or closed position **8** : to give by way of entertainment ⟨*throw* a party⟩ — **throw·er** *n*

synonyms THROW, TOSS, and HURL mean to drive something swiftly through space often by a movement of the arm. THROW is the broadest word and can be used of almost any motion and driving force ⟨*throw* a ball⟩⟨the crash *threw* the driver from the car⟩ TOSS suggests a light or careless throwing ⟨*toss* a coin to see which side comes up⟩ ⟨*tossed* the paper into the wastebasket⟩ HURL suggests a throwing with strong force ⟨the angry mob *hurled* rocks at the police⟩

²throw *n* **1** : an act of throwing **2** : the distance something is or may be thrown

throw up *vb* : ²VOMIT

thrum \'thrəm\ *vb* **thrummed; thrum·ming** : to play a stringed instrument idly : STRUM

thrush \'thrəsh\ *n* : any of numerous song-birds that eat insects and are usually of a plain color but sometimes spotted below

¹thrust \'thrəst\ *vb* **thrust; thrust·ing** **1** : to push or drive with force : SHOVE **2** : PIERCE 1, STAB **3** : to push forth : EXTEND **4** : to press the acceptance of on someone ⟨always *thrusting* new jobs on me⟩

²thrust *n* **1** : a lunge with a pointed weapon **2** : a military attack **3** : a forward or upward push

thru·way *or* **through·way** \'thrü-ˌwā\ *n* : EXPRESSWAY

¹thud \'thəd\ *vb* **thud·ded; thud·ding** : to move or strike so as to make a dull sound

²thud *n* : a dull sound : THUMP

thug \'thəg\ *n* : RUFFIAN

Word History In a language of India there is a word that means "thief." This word was used for the members of a certain gang of thieves who strangled the people they robbed. The English word *thug* was taken from the Indian word meaning "thief" and was first used for these vicious Indian thieves.

¹thumb \'thəm\ *n* **1** : the short thick finger next to the forefinger **2** : the part of a glove covering the thumb

²thumb *vb* **1** : to turn the pages of quickly with the thumb **2** : to seek or get (a ride) in a passing automobile by signaling with the thumb

thumb·tack \'thəm-ˌtak\ *n* : a tack with a broad flat head for pressing into a board or wall with the thumb

¹thump \'thəmp\ *vb* **1** : to strike or beat with something thick or heavy so as to cause a dull sound **2** : ²POUND 2, KNOCK

²thump *n* **1** : a blow with something blunt or heavy **2** : the sound made by a thump

¹thun·der \'thən-dər\ *n* **1** : the loud sound that follows a flash of lightning **2** : a noise like thunder

²thunder *vb* **1** : to produce thunder **2** : to make a sound like thunder **3** : ¹ROAR 1, SHOUT ⟨*thundered* their approval⟩

thun·der·bolt \'thən-dər-ˌbōlt\ *n* : a flash of lightning and the thunder that follows it

thun·der·cloud \'thən-dər-ˌklaud\ *n* : a dark storm cloud that produces light-ning and thunder

thun·der·head \'thən-dər-ˌhed\ *n* : a rounded mass of dark cloud with white edges often appearing before a thunder-storm

thun·der·show·er \'thən-dər-ˌshau-ər\ *n* : a shower with thunder and light-ning

thun·der·storm \'thən-dər-ˌstorm\ *n* : a storm with thunder and lightning

thun·der·struck \'thən-dər-ˌstrək\ *adj* : stunned as if struck by a thunder-bolt

Thurs·day \'thərz-dē\ *n* : the fifth day of the week

thus \'thəs\ *adv* **1** : in this or that way **2** : to this degree or extent : SO ⟨a mild winter *thus* far⟩ **3** : because of this or that : THEREFORE

\ə\ abut	\au\ out	\i\ tip	\o\ saw	\u\ foot
\ər\ further	\ch\ chin	\ī\ life	\oi\ coin	\y\ yet
\a\ mat	\e\ pet	\j\ job	\th\ thin	\yü\ few
\ā\ take	\ē\ easy	\ng\ sing	\th\ this	\yu\ cure
\ä\ cot, cart	\g\ go	\ō\ bone	\ü\ food	\zh\ vision

thwart \'thwȯrt\ *vb* : to oppose successfully

thy \thī\ *adj, archaic* : of, relating to, or done by or to thee or thyself

thyme \'tīm\ *n* : a mint with tiny fragrant leaves used to season foods or formerly in medicine

thy·roid \'thī-ˌroid\ *n* : an endocrine gland at the base of the neck that produces a secretion which affects growth, development, and metabolism

thy·self \thī-'self\ *pron, archaic* : thy own self

ti \'tē\ *n* : the seventh note of the musical scale

¹tick \'tik\ *n* **1** : an animal with eight legs that is related to the spiders and attaches itself to humans and animals from which it sucks blood **2** : a wingless fly that sucks blood from sheep

tick 1

²tick *n* **1** : a light rhythmic tap or beat (as of a clock) **2** : a small mark used chiefly to draw attention to something or to check an item on a list

³tick *vb* **1** : to make a tick or a series of ticks ⟨a *ticking* clock⟩ **2** : to mark, count, or announce by or as if by ticks ⟨a meter *ticking* off the cab fare⟩ **3** : OPERATE 1, RUN ⟨tried to understand what makes them *tick*⟩ **4** : ²CHECK 4 ⟨*ticked* off each item in the list⟩

¹tick·et \'tik-ət\ *n* **1** : a summons or warning issued to a person who breaks a traffic law **2** : a document or token showing that a fare or an admission fee has been paid **3** : a list of candidates for nomination or election **4** : a slip or card recording a sale or giving information

²ticket *vb* **1** : to attach a ticket to : LABEL **2** : to give a traffic ticket to

¹tick·le \'tik-əl\ *vb* **tick·led; tick·ling 1** : to have a tingling or prickling sensation ⟨my foot *tickles*⟩ **2** : to excite or stir up agreeably **3** : AMUSE 2 **4** : to touch (a body part) lightly so as to excite the surface nerves and cause uneasiness, laughter, or jerky movements

²tickle *n* : a tickling sensation

tick·lish \'tik-lish\ *adj* **1** : sensitive to tickling **2** : calling for careful handling ⟨a *ticklish* situation⟩

tid·al \'tīd-l\ *adj* : of or relating to tides : flowing and ebbing like tides

tidal wave *n* **1** : a great wave of the sea that sometimes follows an earthquake **2** : an unusual rise of water along a shore due to strong winds

tid·bit \'tid-ˌbit\ *n* **1** : a small tasty piece of food **2** : a pleasing bit (as of news)

¹tide \'tīd\ *n* **1** : the rising and falling of the surface of the ocean caused twice daily by the attraction of the sun and the moon ⟨carried away by the *tide*⟩ **2** : something that rises and falls like the tides of the sea

Word History The English word *tide* at first meant "time" or "a space of time." Later the word was used for the space of time between the rising and falling of the sea's surface. Then *tide* came to mean "the rising and falling of the sea." This is the most common meaning of the word today.

²tide *vb* **tid·ed; tid·ing** : to help to overcome or put up with a difficulty ⟨a loan to *tide* them over⟩

tid·ings \'tīd-ingz\ *n pl* : NEWS 3

¹ti·dy \'tīd-ē\ *adj* **ti·di·er; ti·di·est 1** : well ordered and cared for : NEAT **2** : LARGE, SUBSTANTIAL ⟨a *tidy* sum⟩ **synonyms** see NEAT — **ti·di·ness** *n*

Word History The English word *tidy* comes from the English word *tide*. *Tide* first meant "time," and *tidy* first meant "timely, at the proper time." Soon *tidy* came to mean "in good condition." The current meaning "neat" developed from this sense.

²tidy *vb* **ti·died; ti·dy·ing 1** : to put in order **2** : to make things tidy ⟨*tidied* up after supper⟩

¹tie \'tī\ *n* **1** : a line, ribbon, or cord used for fastening, joining, or closing **2** : a part (as a beam or rod) holding two pieces together **3** : one of the cross supports to which railroad rails are fastened **4** : a connecting link : BOND ⟨family *ties*⟩ **5** : an equality in number (as of votes or scores) **6** : a contest that ends with an equal score **7** : NECKTIE

²tie *vb* **tied; ty·ing** \'tī-ing\ *or* **tie·ing 1** : to fasten, attach, or close by means of a tie **2** : to form a knot or bow in ⟨*tie* your necktie⟩ **3** : to bring together firmly : UNITE **4** : to hold back from freedom of action **5** : to make or have an equal score with in a contest

tier \'tiər\ *n* : a row, rank, or layer usually arranged in a series one above the other

ti·ger \'tī-gər\ *n* : a large Asian flesh-eating

animal of the cat family that is light brown with black stripes

tiger

¹tight \'tīt\ *adj* **1** : so close in structure as not to allow a liquid or gas to pass through ⟨a *tight* roof⟩ **2** : fixed or held very firmly in place ⟨a *tight* jar cover⟩ **3** : firmly stretched or drawn : TAUT ⟨a *tight* rope⟩ **4** : fitting too closely ⟨*tight* shoes⟩ **5** : difficult to get through or out of ⟨in a *tight* spot⟩ **6** : firm in control ⟨keeps a *tight* hand on affairs⟩ **7** : STINGY 1 **8** : very closely packed or compressed ⟨a *tight* bundle⟩ **9** : low in supply : SCARCE ⟨money is *tight*⟩ — **tight·ly** *adv* — **tight·ness** *n*

²tight *adv* **1** : in a firm, secure, or close manner ⟨shut the door *tight*⟩ ⟨hold on *tight*⟩ **2** : in a deep and uninterrupted manner : SOUNDLY ⟨sleep *tight*⟩

tight·en \'tīt-n\ *vb* : to make or become tight

tight·rope \'tīt-,rōp\ *n* : a rope or wire stretched tight on which an acrobat performs

tights \'tīts\ *n pl* : a garment closely fitted to the body and covering it usually from the waist down

tight squeeze *n* : a difficult situation that one can barely get through

tight·wad \'tīt-,wäd\ *n* : a stingy person

ti·gress \'tī-grəs\ *n* : a female tiger

¹tile \'tīl\ *n* **1** : a thin piece of material (as plastic, stone, concrete, or rubber) used especially for roofs, walls, floors, or drains **2** : a pipe of earthenware used for a drain

²tile *vb* **tiled; til·ing** : to cover with tiles

¹till \til\ *prep or conj* : UNTIL ⟨won't finish *till* next week⟩

²till \'til\ *vb* : to work by plowing, sowing, and raising crops on ⟨*till* the fields⟩

³till \'til\ *n* : a drawer for money

till·age \'til-ij\ *n* : cultivated land

til·ler \'til-ər\ *n* : a lever used to turn the rudder of a boat from side to side

¹tilt \'tilt\ *vb* **1** : to move or shift so as to slant or tip ⟨*tilt* a ladder against a wall⟩ **2**

: to take part in a contest with lances : JOUST

²tilt *n* **1** : a contest on horseback in which two opponents charging with lances try to unhorse one another : JOUST **2** : ¹SPEED 2 ⟨going at full *tilt*⟩ **3** : ²SLANT 1, TIP

tim·ber \'tim-bər\ *n* **1** : wood for use in making something **2** : a usually large or thick piece of lumber squared or finished for use **3** : wooded land or growing trees forming a source of lumber

tim·ber·land \'tim-bər-,land\ *n* : wooded land

tim·ber·line \'tim-bər-,līn\ *n* : the upper limit beyond which trees do not grow (as on mountains)

¹time \'tīm\ *n* **1** : a period during which an action, process, or condition exists or continues **2** : part of the day when one is free to do as one pleases ⟨found *time* to read⟩ **3** : a point or period when something occurs : OCCASION **4** : a set or usual moment or hour for something to occur ⟨arrived on *time*⟩ **5** : an historical period : AGE **6** : conditions of a period — usually used in pl. ⟨hard *times*⟩ **7** : rate of speed : TEMPO **8** : RHYTHM 2 **9** : a moment, hour, day, or year as shown by a clock or calendar ⟨what *time* is it⟩ **10** : a system of determining time ⟨solar *time*⟩ **11** : one of a series of repeated instances or actions ⟨told them many *times*⟩ **12** *times pl* : multiplied instances ⟨five *times* greater⟩ — **at times** : SOMETIMES — **for the time being** : for the present — **from time to time** : once in a while — **in time** **1** : soon enough **2** : as time goes by **3** : at the correct speed in music — **time after time** : over and over again — **time and time again** : over and over again

²time *vb* **timed; tim·ing** **1** : to arrange or set the time or rate at which something happens **2** : to measure or record the time, length of time, or rate of ⟨*time* a performance⟩ — **tim·er** *n*

time·keep·er \'tīm-,kē-pər\ *n* **1** : a clerk who keeps records of the time worked by employees **2** : an official who keeps track of the playing time in a sports contest

time·ly \'tīm-lē\ *adj* **time·li·er; time·li·est** **1** : coming early or at the right time **2** : especially suitable to the time ⟨a *timely* book⟩

time·piece \'tīm-,pēs\ *n* : a device (as a

\ə\ abut	\au̇\ out	\i\ tip	\ȯ\ saw	\u̇\ foot
\ər\ further	\ch\ chin	\ī\ life	\ȯi\ coin	\y\ yet
\a\ mat	\e\ pet	\j\ job	\th\ thin	\yü\ few
\ā\ take	\ē\ easy	\ng\ sing	\th\ this	\yu̇\ cure
\ä\ cot, cart	\g\ go	\ō\ bone	\ü\ food	\zh\ vision

clock or watch) to measure the passing of time

times \tīmz\ *prep* : multiplied by ⟨2 *times* 4 is 8⟩

time·ta·ble \'tīm-,tā-bəl\ *n* : a table telling when something (as a bus or train) leaves or arrives

tim·id \'tim-əd\ *adj* : feeling or showing a lack of courage or self-confidence : SHY — **tim·id·ly** *adv* — **tim·id·ness** *n*

tim·o·rous \'tim-ə-rəs\ *adj* : easily frightened — FEARFUL — **tim·o·rous·ly** *adv*

tin \'tin\ *n* **1** : a soft bluish white metallic chemical element used chiefly in combination with other metals or as a coating to protect other metals **2** : something (as a can or sheet) made from tinplate

tin·der \'tin-dər\ *n* : material that burns easily and can be used as kindling

tin·foil \'tin-,fȯil\ *n* : a thin metal sheeting usually of aluminum or an alloy of tin and lead

¹tin·gle \'ting-gəl\ *vb* **tin·gled; tin·gling** : to feel or cause a prickling or thrilling sensation

²tingle *n* : a tingling sensation or condition

tin·ker \'ting-kər\ *vb* : to repair or adjust something in an unskilled or experimental manner

¹tin·kle \'ting-kəl\ *vb* **tin·kled; tin·kling** : to make or cause to make a series of short high ringing or clinking sounds

²tinkle *n* : a sound of tinkling

tin·plate \'tin-'plāt\ *n* : thin steel sheets covered with tin

tin·sel \'tin-səl\ *n* **1** : a thread, strip, or sheet of metal, paper, or plastic used to produce a glittering effect **2** : something that seems attractive but is of little worth

tin·smith \'tin-,smith\ *n* : a worker in tin or sometimes other metals

¹tint \'tint\ *n* **1** : a slight or pale coloring **2** : a shade of color

²tint *vb* : to give a tint to : COLOR

tin·ware \'tin-,waer, -,wear\ *n* : objects made of tinplate

ti·ny \'tī-nē\ *adj* **ti·ni·er; ti·ni·est** : very small

¹tip \'tip\ *n* **1** : the pointed or rounded end of something **2** : a small piece or part serving as an end, cap, or point

²tip *vb* **tipped; tip·ping** **1** : to attach a tip to **2** : to cover or decorate the tip of

³tip *vb* **tipped; tip·ping** **1** : to turn over **2** : to bend from a straight position : SLANT **3** : to raise and tilt forward

⁴tip *n* : a small sum of money given for a service

⁵tip *n* : a piece of useful or secret information

⁶tip *vb* **tipped; tip·ping** : to give a tip to

¹tip·toe \'tip-,tō\ *n* : the ends of the toes

²tiptoe *adv or adj* : on or as if on tiptoe

³tiptoe *vb* **tip·toed; tip·toe·ing** : to walk tiptoe

¹tip·top \'tip-'täp\ *n* : the highest point

²tiptop *adj* : EXCELLENT, FIRST-RATE

¹tire \'tīr\ *vb* **tired; tir·ing** **1** : to make or become weary **2** : to wear out the patience or attention of : BORE

²tire *n* **1** : a metal band that forms the tread of a wheel **2** : a rubber cushion that usually contains compressed air and fits around a wheel (as of an automobile)

tired \'tīrd\ *adj* : ¹WEARY 1

tire·less \'tīr-ləs\ *adj* : able to work a long time without becoming tired — **tire·less·ly** *adv* — **tire·less·ness** *n*

tire·some \'tīr-səm\ *adj* : likely to tire one because of length or dullness : BORING — **tire·some·ly** *adv*

'tis \'tiz\ : it is

tis·sue \'tish-ü\ *n* **1** : a fine lightweight fabric **2** : a piece of soft absorbent paper **3** : a mass or layer of cells usually of one kind that together with their supporting structures form a basic structural material of an animal or plant body ⟨muscular *tissue*⟩

tit \'tit\ *n* : NIPPLE 1, TEAT

ti·tan·ic \tī-'tan-ik\ *adj* : enormous in size, force, or power : GIGANTIC

ti·tle \'tīt-l\ *n* **1** : a legal right to the ownership of property **2** : the name given to something (as a book, song, or job) to identify or describe it **3** : a word or group of words attached to a person's name to show an honor, rank, or office ⟨mayor and senator are *titles* of office⟩ **4** : CHAMPIONSHIP ⟨won the batting *title*⟩

tit·mouse \'tit-,maùs\ *n, pl* **tit·mice** \-,mīs\ : any of several small birds that have long tails and are related to the nuthatches

TNT \,tē-,en-'tē\ *n* : an explosive used in artillery shells and bombs and in blasting

¹to \tə, tü\ *prep* **1** : in the direction of ⟨walking *to* school⟩ **2** : AGAINST 3, ON ⟨apply salve *to* a burn⟩ **3** : as far as ⟨from the top *to* the bottom⟩ **4** : so as to become or bring about ⟨broken *to* pieces⟩ **5** : ²BEFORE 3 ⟨it's ten *to* six⟩ **6** : ¹UNTIL ⟨from May *to* December⟩ **7** : fitting or being a part of ⟨a key *to* the lock⟩ **8** : along with ⟨skip *to* the music⟩ **9** : in relation to or comparison with ⟨similar *to* that one⟩ ⟨won ten *to* six⟩ **10** : in agreement with ⟨made *to* order⟩ **11** : within the limits of ⟨*to* my knowledge⟩ **12** : contained, occurring, or included in ⟨two pints *to* a quart⟩ **13** : TOWARD 3 ⟨our attitude *to* our friends⟩ **14** — used to show the one or ones that an action is directed toward ⟨spoke *to* my parents⟩ ⟨gave it *to* them⟩ **15** : for no one except ⟨had the room *to* ourselves⟩ **16** : into the action of ⟨we got *to* talking⟩ **17** — used to mark an infinitive ⟨I like *to* swim⟩

²**to** \'tü\ *adv* **1** : in a direction toward ⟨run *to* and fro⟩ **2** : to a conscious state ⟨came *to* an hour after the accident⟩

toad \'tōd\ *n* : a tailless leaping amphibian that has rough skin and usually lives on land

toad

toad·stool \'tōd-ˌstül\ *n* : a mushroom especially when poisonous or unfit for food

¹**toast** \'tōst\ *vb* **1** : to make (as bread) crisp, hot, and brown by heat **2** : to warm completely — **toast·er** *n*

²**toast** *n* **1** : sliced toasted bread **2** : a person in whose honor other people drink **3** : a highly admired person ⟨the *toast* of the town⟩ **4** : an act of drinking in honor of a person

³**toast** *vb* : to suggest or drink to as a toast

to·bac·co \tə-'bak-ō\ *n*, *pl* **to·bac·cos** : a tall plant related to the tomato and potato that has pink or white flowers and broad sticky leaves which are dried and prepared for use in smoking or chewing or as snuff

¹**to·bog·gan** \tə-'bäg-ən\ *n* : a long light sled made without runners and curved up at the front

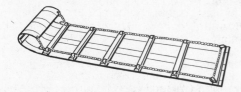

toboggan

²**toboggan** *vb* : to slide on a toboggan

¹**to·day** \tə-'dā\ *adv* **1** : on or for this day **2** : at the present time

²**today** *n* : the present day, time, or age

tod·dler \'täd-lər\ *n* : a small child

¹**toe** \'tō\ *n* **1** : one of the separate parts of the front end of a foot **2** : the front end or part of a foot or hoof — **toed** \'tōd\ *adj*

²**toe** *vb* **toed**; **toe·ing** : to touch, reach, or kick with the toes

toe·nail \'tō-ˌnāl\ *n* : the hard covering at the end of a toe

to·ga \'tō-gə\ *n* : the loose outer garment worn in public by citizens of ancient Rome

to·geth·er \tə-'geth-ər\ *adv* **1** : in or into one group, body, or place ⟨gathered *together*⟩ **2** : in touch or in partnership with ⟨in business *together*⟩ **3** : at one time ⟨they all cheered *together*⟩ **4** : one after the other : in order ⟨for days *together*⟩ **5** : in or by combined effort ⟨worked *together* to clear the road⟩ **6** : in or into agreement ⟨get *together* on a plan⟩ **7** : considered as a whole ⟨gave more than all the others *together*⟩

toga

¹**toil** \'tȯil\ *n* : long hard labor

Word History To get olive oil you must crush olives. Even in ancient times there were machines for crushing olives. The Latin word for such a machine came from a Latin word that meant "hammer." The Romans made a verb from the word for a machine that crushed olives. This Latin verb meant "to crush." From this Latin verb came an Old French verb that meant "to disturb" or "to argue." The French formed a noun from this verb. This Old French noun meant "confusion" or "battle." An early English noun meaning "battle" or "struggle" came from this Old French noun. Our modern English noun *toil* developed from this early English noun.

²**toil** *vb* **1** : to work hard and long **2** : to go on with effort ⟨*toiling* up a steep hill⟩

\ə\ abut	\au̇\ out	\i\ tip	\ȯ\ saw	\u̇\ foot
\ər\ further	\ch\ chin	\ī\ life	\ȯi\ coin	\y\ yet
\a\ mat	\e\ pet	\j\ job	\th\ thin	\yü\ few
\ā\ take	\ē\ easy	\ng\ sing	\th\ this	\yu̇\ cure
\ä\ cot, cart	\g\ go	\ō\ bone	\ü\ food	\zh\ vision

toi·let \'tȯi-lət\ *n* **1** : the act or process of dressing and making oneself neat **2** : BATHROOM **3** : a device for removing body wastes consisting essentially of a bowl that is flushed with water

to·ken \'tō-kən\ *n* **1** : an outer sign : PROOF ⟨a *token* of friendship⟩ **2** : an object used to suggest something that cannot be pictured **3** : SOUVENIR **4** : INDICATION 2 **5** : a piece like a coin that has a special use ⟨a bus *token*⟩ **synonyms** see EMBLEM

told *past of* TELL

tol·er·a·ble \'täl-ə-rə-bəl\ *adj* **1** : capable of being put up with **2** : fairly good ⟨*tolerable* weather⟩ — **tol·er·a·bly** \-blē\ *adv*

tol·er·ance \'täl-ə-rəns\ *n* **1** : ability to put up with something harmful or bad **2** : sympathy for or acceptance of feelings or habits which are different from one's own

tol·er·ant \'täl-ə-rənt\ *adj* : showing tolerance — **tol·er·ant·ly** *adv*

tol·er·ate \'täl-ə-ˌrāt\ *vb* **tol·er·at·ed; tol·er·at·ing** **1** : to allow something to be or to be done without making a move to stop it **2** : to stand the action of ⟨*tolerate* a drug⟩

¹toll \'tōl\ *n* **1** : a tax paid for a privilege (as the use of a highway or bridge) **2** : a charge paid for a service **3** : the cost in life or health

²toll *vb* **1** : to announce or call by the sounding of a bell **2** : to sound with slow strokes

³toll *n* : the sound of a bell ringing slowly

¹tom·a·hawk \'täm-i-ˌhȯk\ *n* : a light ax used as a weapon by North American Indians

tomahawk

²tomahawk *vb* : to cut, strike, or kill with a tomahawk

to·ma·to \tə-'māt-ō, -'mät-\ *n, pl* **to·ma·toes** : a red or yellow juicy fruit that is used as a vegetable or in salads and is produced by a hairy plant related to the potato

tomb \'tüm\ *n* **1** : ¹GRAVE **2** : a house or burial chamber for dead people

tom·boy \'täm-ˌbȯi\ *n* : a girl who enjoys things that some people think are more suited to boys

tomb·stone \'tüm-ˌstōn\ *n* : GRAVESTONE

tom·cat \'täm-ˌkat\ *n* : a male cat

¹to·mor·row \tə-'mär-ō\ *adv* : on or for the day after today

²tomorrow *n* : the day after today

tom–tom \'täm-ˌtäm\ *n* : a usually long and narrow drum beaten with the hands

ton \'tən\ *n* : a measure of weight equal either to 2000 pounds (about 907 kilograms) (**short ton**) or 2240 pounds (about 1016 kilograms) (**long ton**) with the short ton being more frequently used in the United States and Canada

¹tone \'tōn\ *n* **1** : quality of spoken or musical sound **2** : a sound on one pitch **3** : an individual way of speaking or writing ⟨reply in a friendly *tone*⟩ **4** : common character or quality **5** : a shade of color ⟨decorated in soft *tones*⟩ **6** : a color that changes another ⟨gray with a blue *tone*⟩ **7** : a healthy state of the body or any of its parts **8** : power to function under pressure

²tone *vb* **toned; ton·ing** **1** : to give tone to : STRENGTHEN ⟨medicine to *tone* up the system⟩ **2** : to soften or blend in color, appearance, or sound

tongs \'tängz\ *n pl* : a device for taking hold of something that consists usually of two movable pieces joined at one end

tongs

tongue \'təng\ *n* **1** : an organ of the mouth used in tasting, in taking and swallowing food, and by human beings in speaking **2** : the power of communication : SPEECH **3** : LANGUAGE 1 ⟨a foreign *tongue*⟩ **4** : something like an animal's tongue in being long and fastened at one end

tongue–tied \'təng-ˌtīd\ *adj* : unable to speak clearly or freely (as from shyness)

¹ton·ic \'tän-ik\ *adj* : making (as the mind or body) stronger or healthier

²tonic *n* **1** : a tonic medicine **2** : the first note of a scale

¹to·night \tə-'nīt\ *adv* : on this present night or the night following this present day

²tonight *n* : the present or the coming night

ton·nage \'tən-ij\ *n* **1** : a tax on ships based on tons carried **2** : ships in terms of the total number of tons that are or can be carried **3** : total weight in tons shipped, carried, or mined

ton·sil \'tän-səl\ *n* : either of a pair of masses of spongy tissue at the back of the mouth

ton·sil·li·tis \,tän-sə-'līt-əs\ *n* : a sore reddened state of the tonsils

too \tü\ *adv* **1** : in addition : ALSO **2** : to a greater than wanted or needed degree ⟨the load was *too* heavy⟩ **3** : [2]VERY 1 ⟨the climb was not *too* hard though the hill was steep⟩

took *past of* TAKE

[1]**tool** \'tül\ *n* **1** : an instrument (as a saw, file, knife, or wrench) used or worked by hand or machine **2** : something that helps to gain an end **3** : a person used by another : DUPE **synonyms** see INSTRUMENT

[2]**tool** *vb* **1** : to shape, form, or finish with a tool **2** : to equip a plant or industry with machines and tools for production

tool·box \'tül-,bäks\ *n* : a box for storing or carrying tools

[1]**toot** \'tüt\ *vb* **1** : to sound a short blast **2** : to blow or sound an instrument (as a horn) especially in short blasts

[2]**toot** *n* : a short blast (as on a horn)

tooth \'tüth\ *n, pl* **teeth** \'tēth\ **1** : one of the hard bony structures set in sockets on the jaws of most vertebrates and used in taking hold of and chewing food and in fighting **2** : something like or suggesting an animal's tooth in shape, arrangement, or action ⟨the *teeth* of a comb⟩ **3** : one of the projections around the rim of a wheel that fit between the projections on another part causing the wheel or the other part to move along — **tooth·less** \'tüth-ləs\ *adj*

tooth·ache \'tü-,thāk\ *n* : pain in or near a tooth

tooth·brush \'tüth-,brəsh\ *n* : a brush for cleaning the teeth — **tooth·brush·ing** \-ing\ *n*

toothed \'tütht\ *adj* **1** : having teeth or such or so many teeth **2** : JAGGED

tooth·paste \'tüth-,pāst\ *n* : a paste for cleaning the teeth

tooth·pick \'tüth-,pik\ *n* : a pointed instrument for removing substances caught between the teeth

[1]**top** \'täp\ *n* **1** : the highest point, level, or part of something **2** : the upper end, edge, or surface **3** : the stalk and leaves of a plant and especially of one with roots that are used for food ⟨beet *tops*⟩ **4** : an upper piece, lid, or covering ⟨put the *top* on the jar⟩ **5** : the highest position

[2]**top** *vb* **topped; top·ping 1** : to remove or cut the top of ⟨*top* a tree⟩ **2** : to cover with a top or on the top **3** : to be better than **4** : to go over the top of

[3]**top** *adj* : of, relating to, or at the top

[4]**top** *n* : a child's toy with a tapering point on which it can be made to spin

to·paz \'tō-,paz\ *n* : a mineral that when occurring as perfect yellow crystals is valued as a gem

top·coat \'täp-,kōt\ *n* : a lightweight overcoat

top·ic \'täp-ik\ *n* **1** : a heading in an outline of a subject or explanation **2** : the subject or a section of the subject of a speech or writing

topic sentence *n* : a sentence that states the main thought of a paragraph

top·knot \'täp-,nät\ *n* : a tuft of feathers or hair on the top of the head

top·mast \'täp-,mast, -məst\ *n* : the second mast above a ship's deck

top·most \'täp-,mōst\ *adj* : highest of all

top·ple \'täp-əl\ *vb* **top·pled; top·pling 1** : to fall from being too heavy at the top **2** : to push over

top·sail \'täp-,sāl, -səl\ *n* **1** : the sail next above the lowest sail on a mast in a square-rigged ship **2** : the sail above the large sail on a mast in a ship with a fore-and-aft rig

top·soil \'täp-,sȯil\ *n* : the rich upper layer of soil in which plants have most of their roots

top·sy–tur·vy \,täp-sē-'tər-vē\ *adv or adj* **1** : upside down **2** : in complete disorder

torch \'tȯrch\ *n* **1** : a flaming light that is made of something which burns brightly and that is usually carried in the hand **2** : something that guides or gives light or heat like a torch **3** : a portable device for producing a hot flame

tore *past of* TEAR

[1]**tor·ment** \'tȯr-,ment\ *n* **1** : extreme pain or distress of body or mind **2** : a cause of suffering in mind or body

[2]**tor·ment** \tȯr-'ment\ *vb* **1** : to cause severe suffering of body or mind to **2** : VEX 1, HARASS

torn *past participle of* TEAR

tor·na·do \tȯr-'nād-ō\ *n, pl* **tor·na·does** *or* **tor·na·dos** : a violent whirling wind accompanied by a cloud that is shaped like a funnel and moves overland in a narrow path

[1]**tor·pe·do** \tȯr-'pēd-ō\ *n, pl* **tor·pe·does 1** : a fish related to the rays that has a pair of organs near the head that can give its prey an electric shock **2** : a metal case which is shaped like a cigar, filled with an explosive charge, and so made that it directs and moves itself underwater

\ə\ **abut**	\au̇\ **out**	\i\ **tip**	\ȯ\ **saw**	\u̇\ **foot**
\ər\ **further**	\ch\ **chin**	\ī\ **life**	\ȯi\ **coin**	\y\ **yet**
\a\ **mat**	\e\ **pet**	\j\ **job**	\th\ **thin**	\yü\ **few**
\ā\ **take**	\ē\ **easy**	\ng\ **sing**	\th\ **this**	\yu̇\ **cure**
\ä\ **cot, cart**	\g\ **go**	\ō\ **bone**	\ü\ **food**	\zh\ **vision**

Word History The English word *torpedo* came from a Latin word that meant "numbness." This Latin word was formed from a Latin word that meant "to be numb." English *torpedo* was first used for a fish that gives an electric shock which can make its victim numb. That is why the fish was named *torpedo*. The explosive device called a *torpedo* was named after the fish. Like a fish, it belongs in water. It also gives quite a shock to anything it hits. The word *torpid* is related to the word *torpedo*.

²**torpedo** *vb* **tor·pe·doed; tor·pe·do·ing** : to hit with or destroy by a torpedo

tor·pid \'tor-pəd\ *adj* **1** : having lost motion or the power of exertion or feeling ⟨a bear *torpid* in winter sleep⟩ **2** : having too little energy or strength : DULL ⟨a *torpid* mind⟩

tor·rent \'tor-ənt\ *n* **1** : a rushing stream of liquid **2** : ³RUSH 1, 2

tor·rid \'tor-əd\ *adj* : very hot and usually dry

tor·so \'tor-sō\ *n, pl* **tor·sos** *or* **tor·si** \-ˌsē\ : the human body except for the head, arms, and legs

tor·ti·lla \tor-'tē-ə\ *n* : a round flat cake of cornmeal baked on a heated stone or iron

tor·toise \'tort-əs\ *n* : any of various turtles (as a land turtle or large sea turtle)

tor·toise·shell \'tort-əs-ˌshel\ *n* **1** : the hornlike covering of the shell of a sea tortoise that is mottled brown and yellow and is used for ornamental objects **2** : any of several brightly colored butterflies

tor·tu·ous \'tor-chə-wəs\ *adj* : having many twists and turns ⟨a *tortuous* path⟩

¹**tor·ture** \'tor-chər\ *n* **1** : the causing of great pain especially to punish or to obtain a confession **2** : distress of body or mind

²**torture** *vb* **tor·tured; tor·tur·ing** **1** : to punish or force someone to do or say something by causing great pain **2** : to cause great suffering to — **tor·tur·er** *n*

¹**toss** \'tos\ *vb* **1** : to throw or swing to and fro or up and down ⟨waves *tossed* the ship about⟩ **2** : to throw with a quick light motion **3** : to lift with a sudden motion ⟨the horse *tossed* its head⟩ **4** : to be thrown about rapidly ⟨a canoe *tossing* on the waves⟩ **5** : to move about restlessly **6** : to stir or mix lightly ⟨*tossed* salad⟩ **synonyms** see THROW

²**toss** *n* : an act or instance of tossing

tot \'tät\ *n* : a young child

¹**to·tal** \'tōt-l\ *adj* **1** : of or relating to the whole of something ⟨a *total* eclipse of the sun⟩ **2** : making up the whole ⟨collected the *total* amount⟩ **3** : being such to the fullest degree ⟨*total* ruin⟩ **4** : making use of every means to do something ⟨*total* war⟩ — **to·tal·ly** *adv*

²**total** *n* **1** : a result of addition : SUM **2** : an entire amount

³**total** *vb* **to·taled** *or* **to·talled; to·tal·ing** *or* **to·tal·ling** **1** : to add up **2** : to amount to : NUMBER

tote \'tōt\ *vb* **tot·ed; tot·ing** : CARRY 1, HAUL

to·tem \'tōt-əm\ *n* **1** : an object (as an animal or plant) serving as the emblem of a family or clan **2** : something usually carved or painted to represent a totem (as on a **totem pole**)

tot·ter \'tät-ər\ *vb* **1** : to sway or rock as if about to fall **2** : to move unsteadily : STAGGER

totem 2

tou·can \'tü-ˌkan\ *n* : a brightly colored tropical bird that has a very large beak and feeds on fruit

¹**touch** \'təch\ *vb* **1** : to feel or handle (as with the fingers) especially so as to be aware of with the sense of touch **2** : to be or cause to be in contact with something **3** : to be or come next to **4** : to hit lightly **5** : ²HARM ⟨no one will dare to *touch* you⟩ **6** : to make use of ⟨never *touches* meat⟩ **7** : to refer to in passing **8** : to affect the interest of **9** : to move emotionally ⟨*touched* by your kindness⟩

²**touch** *n* **1** : a light stroke or tap **2** : the act or fact of touching or being touched **3** : the special sense by which one is aware of light pressure ⟨soft to the *touch*⟩ **4** : an impression gotten through the sense of touch ⟨the soft *touch* of silk⟩ **5** : a state of contact or communication ⟨keep in *touch* with friends⟩ **6** : a small amount : TRACE ⟨a *touch* of humor⟩

toucan

touch·down \'təch-ˌdaůn\ *n* : a score made in football by carrying or catching the ball over the opponent's goal line

touch·ing \'təch-ing\ *adj* : causing a feeling of tenderness or pity

touch pad *n* : a flat surface on an electronic device (as a microwave oven) divided into several differently marked areas that are touched to make choices in controlling the device

touch up *vb* : to improve by or as if by small changes

touchy \'təch-ē\ *adj* **touch·i·er; touch·i·est 1** : easily hurt or insulted **2** : calling for tact or careful handling ⟨a *touchy* subject⟩

¹tough \'təf\ *adj* **1** : strong or firm but flexible and not brittle ⟨*tough* fibers⟩ **2** : not easily chewed ⟨*tough* meat⟩ **3** : able to put up with strain or hardship **4** : STUBBORN 1 **5** : very difficult ⟨a *tough* problem⟩ **6** : LAWLESS 2 ⟨a *tough* neighborhood⟩ **synonyms** see STRONG — **tough·ness** *n*

²tough *n* : ²ROWDY, RUFFIAN

tough·en \'təf-ən\ *vb* : to make or become tough

¹tour \'tůr\ *n* **1** : a fixed period of duty **2** : a trip usually ending at the point where it started ⟨a *tour* of the city⟩ **synonyms** see JOURNEY

²tour *vb* : to make a tour of : travel as a tourist

tour·ist \'tůr-əst\ *n* : a person who travels for pleasure

tour·na·ment \'tůr-nə-mənt\ *n* **1** : a contest of skill and courage between knights wearing armor and fighting with blunted lances or swords **2** : a series of contests played for a championship

tour·ni·quet \'tůr-ni-kət\ *n* : a device (as a bandage twisted tight) for stopping bleeding or blood flow

tou·sle \'taů-zəl\ *vb* **tou·sled; tou·sling** : to put into disorder by rough handling ⟨*tousled* my hair⟩

¹tow \'tō\ *vb* : to draw or pull along behind

²tow *n* **1** : a rope or chain for towing **2** : an act or instance of towing : the fact or state of being towed **3** : something (as a barge) that is towed

³tow *n* : short broken fiber of flax, hemp, or jute used for yarn, twine, or stuffing

to·ward \'tō-ərd, tə-'wȯrd\ *or* **to·wards** \'tō-ərdz, tə-'wȯrdz\ *prep* **1** : in the direction of ⟨heading *toward* town⟩ **2** : along a course leading to ⟨efforts *toward* peace⟩ **3** : in regard to ⟨attitude *toward* life⟩ **4** : so as to face ⟨their backs were *toward* me⟩ **5** : ²NEAR ⟨awoke *toward* morning⟩

6 : as part of the payment for ⟨$100 *toward* a new car⟩

tow·el \'taů-əl\ *n* : a cloth or piece of absorbent paper for wiping or drying

¹tow·er \'taů-ər\ *n* **1** : a building or structure that is higher than its length or width, is high with respect to its surroundings, and may stand by itself or be attached to a larger structure **2** : CITADEL 1

²tower *vb* : to reach or rise to a great height

tow·er·ing \'taů-ə-ring\ *adj* **1** : rising high : TALL **2** : reaching a high point of strength or force ⟨*towering* rage⟩ **3** : going beyond proper bounds ⟨*towering* ambition⟩

tow·head \'tō-ˌhed\ *n* : a person having soft whitish hair

town \'taůn\ *n* **1** : a compactly settled area that is usually larger than a village but smaller than a city **2** : CITY 1 **3** : the people of a town

town·ship \'taůn-ˌship\ *n* **1** : a unit of local government in some northeastern and north central states **2** : a division of territory in surveys of United States public lands containing thirty-six square miles (about ninety-three square kilometers)

tow·path \'tō-ˌpath, -ˌpȧth\ *n* : a path traveled by people or animals towing boats

tox·ic \'täk-sik\ *adj* : of, relating to, or caused by a poison ⟨*toxic* effects⟩

Word History Sometimes people put poison on the points of arrows. Even a slight wound from such an arrow can be fatal. The ancient Greeks had a word for the poison used on arrows. A Latin word that meant "poison" came from the Greek word that meant "arrow poison." The English word *toxic* comes from this Latin word.

tox·in \'täk-sən\ *n* : a poison produced by an animal, a plant, or germs

¹toy \'tȯi\ *n* **1** : something of little or no value **2** : something for a child to play with **3** : something small of its kind

²toy *vb* : to amuse oneself as if with a toy

¹trace \'trās\ *n* **1** : a mark left by something that has passed or is past **2** : a very small amount

²trace *vb* **traced; trac·ing 1** : ²SKETCH 1 **2** : to form (as letters) carefully **3** : to copy (as a drawing) by following the lines or letters as seen through a transparent sheet placed over the thing copied **4** : to

\ə\ **abut**	\aů\ **out**	\i\ **tip**	\ȯ\ **saw**	\ů\ **foot**
\ər\ **further**	\ch\ **chin**	\ī\ **life**	\ȯi\ **coin**	\y\ **yet**
\a\ **mat**	\e\ **pet**	\j\ **job**	\th\ **thin**	\yü\ **few**
\ā\ **take**	\ē\ **easy**	\ng\ **sing**	\th\ **this**	\yů\ **cure**
\ä\ **cot, cart**	\g\ **go**	\ō\ **bone**	\ü\ **food**	\zh\ **vision**

follow the footprints, track, or trail of **5 :** to study or follow the development and progress of in detail — **trac·er** *n*

³trace *n* **:** either of the two straps, chains, or ropes of a harness that fasten a horse to a vehicle

trace·able \'trā-sə-bəl\ *adj* **:** capable of being traced

tra·chea \'trā-kē-ə\ *n, pl* **tra·che·ae** \-kē-,ē\ **1 :** WINDPIPE **2 :** a breathing tube of an insect

trac·ing \'trā-sing\ *n* **1 :** the act of a person that traces **2 :** something that is traced

¹track \'trak\ *n* **1 :** a mark left by something that has gone by ⟨rabbit *tracks*⟩ **2 :** PATH 1, TRAIL **3 :** a course laid out for racing **4 :** a way for a vehicle with wheels ⟨railroad *track*⟩ **5 :** awareness of things or of the order in which things happen or ideas come ⟨lose *track* of time⟩ ⟨keep *track* of expenses⟩ **6 :** either of two endless metal belts on which a vehicle (as a tank) travels **7 :** track-and-field sports

²track *vb* **1 :** to follow the tracks or traces of **2 :** to make tracks on or with

track–and–field *adj* **:** relating to or being sports events (as racing, throwing, and jumping contests) held on an oval running track and on an enclosed field

¹tract \'trakt\ *n* **:** a pamphlet of political or religious ideas and beliefs

²tract *n* **1 :** an indefinite stretch of land ⟨a large *tract* of forest⟩ **2 :** a defined area of land ⟨sold off several 40 acre *tracts*⟩ **3 :** a system of body parts or organs that serve some special purpose ⟨the digestive *tract*⟩

trac·tor \'trak-tər\ *n* **1 :** a vehicle that has large rear wheels or moves on endless belts and is used especially for pulling farm implements **2 :** a short truck for hauling a trailer

¹trade \'trād\ *n* **1 :** the business or work in which a person takes part regularly : OCCUPATION **2 :** an occupation requiring manual or mechanical skill : CRAFT **3 :** the persons working in a business or industry **4 :** the business of buying and selling items : COMMERCE **5 :** an act of trading : TRANSACTION **6 :** a firm's customers

synonyms TRADE, BUSINESS, and PROFESSION mean an occupation requiring skill or training by which one earns a living. TRADE applies chiefly to occupations requiring skilled labor and usually the handling of tools or machines ⟨the *trade* of a carpenter⟩ BUSINESS is used mainly of occupations concerned with the buying or selling of goods and services or of similar occupations such as transportation and finance ⟨the hotel and restaurant *business*⟩ PROFESSION is used of occupations that require a college or university education and much training ⟨the medical *profession*⟩

²trade *vb* **trad·ed; trad·ing 1 :** to give in exchange for something else **2 :** to take part in the exchange, purchase, or sale of goods **3 :** to deal regularly as a customer

trade·mark \'trād-,märk\ *n* **:** a device (as a word) that points clearly to the origin or ownership of merchandise to which it is applied and that is legally reserved for use only by the owner

trad·er \'trād-ər\ *n* **1 :** a person who trades **2 :** a ship engaged in trade

trades·man \'trādz-mən\ *n, pl* **trades·men** \-mən\ **1 :** a person who runs a retail store **2 :** CRAFTSMAN 1

trades·peo·ple \'trādz-,pē-pəl\ *n pl* **:** people engaged in trade

trade wind *n* **:** a wind blowing steadily toward the equator from an easterly direction

trad·ing post \'trād-ing-\ *n* **:** a station or store of a trader or trading company set up in a thinly settled region

tra·di·tion \trə-'dish-ən\ *n* **1 :** the handing down of information, beliefs, or customs from one generation to another **2 :** a belief or custom handed down by tradition

tra·di·tion·al \trə-'dish-ən-l\ *adj* **1 :** handed down from age to age ⟨a *traditional* explanation⟩ **2 :** based on custom : CONVENTIONAL ⟨the *traditional* Thanksgiving dinner⟩ — **tra·di·tion·al·ly** *adv*

¹traf·fic \'traf-ik\ *n* **1 :** the business of carrying passengers or goods ⟨the tourist *traffic*⟩ **2 :** the business of buying and selling : COMMERCE **3 :** exchange of information ⟨*traffic* with the enemy⟩ **4 :** the persons or goods carried by train, boat, or airplane or passing along a road, river, or air route **5 :** the movement (as of vehicles) along a route

²traffic *vb* **traf·ficked; traf·fick·ing :** ²TRADE 2

trag·e·dy \'traj-ə-dē\ *n, pl* **trag·e·dies 1 :** a serious play that has a sorrowful or disastrous ending **2 :** a disastrous event

trag·ic \'traj-ik\ *adj* **1 :** of or relating to tragedy ⟨a *tragic* actress⟩ **2 :** very unfortunate ⟨came to a *tragic* end⟩

¹trail \'trāl\ *vb* **1 :** to drag or draw along behind ⟨the horse *trailed* its reins⟩ **2 :** to lag behind **3 :** to follow in the tracks of : PURSUE **4 :** to hang or let hang so as to touch the ground or float out behind **5 :** to become weak, soft, or less ⟨the sound *trailed* off⟩

²trail *n* **1** : something that trails or is trailed ⟨a *trail* of smoke⟩ **2** : a trace or mark left by something that has passed or been drawn along **3** : a beaten path **4** : a path marked through a forest or mountainous region

trail·er \'trā-lər\ *n* **1** : a vehicle designed to be hauled (as by a tractor) **2** : a vehicle designed to serve wherever parked as a dwelling or a place of business

¹train \'trān\ *n* **1** : a part of a gown that trails behind the wearer **2** : the followers of an important person **3** : a moving line of persons, vehicles, or animals ⟨a wagon *train*⟩ **4** : a connected series ⟨*train* of thought⟩ **5** : a connected series of railway cars usually hauled by a locomotive

train 1

²train *vb* **1** : to direct the growth of (a plant) usually by bending, pruning, and tying **2** : to give or receive instruction, discipline, or drill **3** : to teach in an art, profession, or trade ⟨*train* radio operators⟩ **4** : to make ready (as by exercise) for a sport or test of skill **5** : to aim (as a gun) at a target **synonyms** see TEACH — **train·er** *n*

train·ing \'trā-ning\ *n* **1** : the course followed by one who trains or is being trained **2** : the condition of one who has trained for a test or contest ⟨in perfect *training*⟩

trait \'trāt\ *n* : a quality that sets one person or thing off from another

trai·tor \'trāt-ər\ *n* **1** : a person who betrays another's trust or is false to a personal duty **2** : a person who commits treason

trai·tor·ous \'trāt-ə-rəs\ *adj* **1** : guilty or capable of treason **2** : amounting to treason ⟨*traitorous* acts⟩ **synonyms** see FAITHLESS — **trai·tor·ous·ly** *adv*

¹tramp \'tramp\ *vb* **1** : to walk heavily **2** : to tread on forcibly and repeatedly **3** : to travel or wander through on foot ⟨*tramp* the woods⟩

²tramp *n* **1** : a person who wanders from place to place, has no home or job, and often lives by begging or stealing **2** : ²HIKE **3** : the sounds made by the beat of marching feet

tram·ple \'tram-pəl\ *vb* **tram·pled; tram·pling** **1** : to tramp or tread heavily so as to bruise, crush, or injure something ⟨*trampled* on the flowers⟩ **2** : to crush under the feet ⟨don't *trample* the flowers⟩ **3** : to injure or harm by treating harshly and without mercy

tram·po·line \,tram-pə-'lēn\ *n* : a canvas sheet or web supported by springs in a metal frame used for springing and landing in acrobatic tumbling

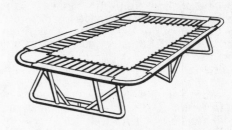

trampoline

trance \'trans\ *n* **1** : STUPOR **2** : a condition like sleep (as deep hypnosis) **3** : a state of being so deeply absorbed in something as not to be aware of one's surroundings

tran·quil \'trang-kwəl\ *adj* : very calm and quiet : PEACEFUL ⟨a *tranquil* life⟩ **synonyms** see CALM

tran·quil·iz·er \'trang-kwə-,lī-zər\ *n* : a drug used to ease worry and nervous tension

tran·quil·li·ty *or* **tran·quil·i·ty** \tran-'kwil-ət-ē\ *n* : the state of being calm : QUIET

trans- *prefix* **1** : on or to the other side of : across : beyond ⟨*trans*atlantic⟩ **2** : so as to change or transfer

trans·act \trans-'akt\ *vb* : to carry on : MANAGE, CONDUCT

trans·ac·tion \trans-'ak-shən\ *n* **1** : a business deal **2 transactions** *pl* : the record of the meeting of a club or organization

trans·at·lan·tic \,trans-ət-'lant-ik\ *adj* : crossing or being beyond the Atlantic ocean

tran·scend \tran-'send\ *vb* **1** : to rise above the limits of **2** : to do better or more than

trans·con·ti·nen·tal \,trans-,känt-n-'ent-l\ *adj* : crossing, extending across, or being on the farther side of a continent

tran·scribe \tran-'skrīb\ *vb* **tran·scribed;**

\ə\ abut	\au̇\ out	\i\ tip	\ȯ\ saw	\u̇\ foot
\ər\ further	\ch\ chin	\ī\ life	\ȯi\ coin	\y\ yet
\a\ mat	\e\ pet	\j\ job	\th\ thin	\yü\ few
\ā\ take	\ē\ easy	\ng\ sing	\t͟h\ this	\yu̇\ cure
\ä\ cot, cart	\g\ go	\ō\ bone	\ü\ food	\zh\ vision

tran·scrib·ing 1 : to make a copy of **2** : to record for a later broadcast

tran·script \'tran-,skript\ *n* **1** : ¹COPY 1 **2** : an official copy of a student's school record

¹**trans·fer** \trans-'fər\ *vb* **trans·ferred; trans·fer·ring 1** : to pass or cause to pass from one person, place, or condition to another **2** : to give over the possession or ownership of ⟨*transfer* title to the house to the new owners⟩ **3** : to copy (as by printing) from one surface to another by contact **4** : to move to a different place, region, or job **5** : to change from one vehicle or transportation line to another

²**trans·fer** \'trans-,fər\ *n* **1** : a giving over of right, title, or interest in property by one person to another **2** : an act or process of transferring **3** : someone or something that transfers or is transferred **4** : a ticket allowing a passenger on a bus or train to continue the journey on another route without paying more fare

trans·fix \trans-'fiks\ *vb* : to pierce through with or as if with a pointed weapon

trans·form \trans-'fȯrm\ *vb* : to change completely ⟨*transform* waterpower into electric power⟩ — **trans·form·er** *n*

trans·for·ma·tion \,trans-fər-'mā-shən\ *n* : the act or process of transforming : a complete change

trans·fu·sion \trans-'fyü-zhən\ *n* **1** : a passing of one thing into another **2** : a transferring (as of blood or salt solution) into a vein of a person or animal

¹**tran·sient** \'tran-chənt\ *adj* : not lasting or staying long ⟨a *transient* illness⟩

²**transient** *n* : a person who is not staying long in a place

tran·sis·tor \tran-'zis-tər\ *n* : a small solid electronic device used especially in radios for controlling the flow of electricity

tran·sit \'trans-ət, 'tranz-\ *n* **1** : a passing through or across **2** : the act or method of carrying things from one place to another **3** : local transportation of people in public vehicles **4** : a surveyor's instrument for measuring angles

tran·si·tion \trans-'ish-ən, tranz-\ *n* : a passing from one state, stage, place, or subject to another : CHANGE

tran·si·tive \'trans-ət-iv, 'tranz-\ *adj* : having or containing a direct object ⟨*transitive* verbs⟩

trans·late \trans-'lāt\ *vb* **trans·lat·ed; trans·lat·ing 1** : to change from one state or form to another ⟨*translate* words into action⟩ **2** : to turn from one language into another

trans·la·tion \trans-'lā-shən\ *n* : the act, process, or result of translating

trans·lu·cent \trans-'lüs-nt\ *adj* : not transparent but clear enough to allow rays of light to pass through — **trans·lu·cent·ly** *adv*

trans·mis·sion \trans-'mish-ən\ *n* **1** : an act or process of transmitting ⟨the *transmission* of a disease⟩ **2** : the gears by which the power is transmitted from the engine to the axle that gives motion to a motor vehicle

trans·mit \trans-'mit\ *vb* **trans·mit·ted; trans·mit·ting 1** : to transfer from one person or place to another **2** : to pass on by or as if by inheritance **3** : to pass or cause to pass through space or through a material ⟨glass *transmits* light⟩ **4** : to send out by means of radio waves

trans·mit·ter \trans-'mit-ər\ *n* **1** : one that transmits **2** : the instrument in a telegraph system that sends out messages **3** : the part of a telephone that includes the mouthpiece and a device that picks up sound waves and sends them over the wire **4** : the device that sends out radio or television signals

tran·som \'tran-səm\ *n* **1** : a piece that lies crosswise in a structure (as in the frame of a window or of a door that has a window above it) **2** : a window above a door or another window

trans·par·en·cy \trans-'par-ən-sē, -'per-\ *n* : the quality or state of being transparent

trans·par·ent \trans-'par-ənt, -'per-\ *adj* **1** : clear enough or thin enough to be seen through **2** : easily detected ⟨a *transparent* lie⟩ — **trans·par·ent·ly** *adv*

trans·pi·ra·tion \,trans-pə-'rā-shən\ *n* : an act or instance of transpiring

trans·pire \trans-'pīr\ *vb* **trans·pired; trans·pir·ing 1** : to give off or pass off in the form of a vapor usually through pores **2** : to become known or apparent **3** : to come to pass : HAPPEN

¹**trans·plant** \trans-'plant\ *vb* **1** : to dig up and plant again in another soil or location ⟨*transplant* seedlings⟩ **2** : to remove from one place and settle or introduce elsewhere

²**trans·plant** \'trans-,plant\ *n* **1** : something transplanted **2** : the process of transplanting

¹**trans·port** \trans-'pōrt\ *vb* **1** : to carry from one place to another **2** : to fill with delight

²**trans·port** \'trans-,pōrt\ *n* **1** : the act of transporting : TRANSPORTATION **2** : a state of great joy or pleasure **3** : a ship for carrying soldiers or military equipment **4**

: a vehicle used to transport persons or goods

trans·por·ta·tion \,trans-pər-'tā-shən\ *n* **1** : an act, instance, or means of transporting or being transported **2** : public transporting of passengers or goods especially as a business

trans·pose \trans-'pōz\ *vb* **trans·posed; trans·pos·ing 1** : to change the position or order of ⟨*transpose* the letters in a word⟩ **2** : to write or perform in a different musical key

trans·verse \trans-'vərs\ *adj* : lying or being across : placed crosswise — **trans·verse·ly** *adv*

¹trap \'trap\ *n* **1** : a device for catching animals **2** : something by which one is caught or stopped unawares ⟨set a *trap* for the criminal⟩ **3** : a light one-horse carriage with springs **4** : a device that allows something to pass through but keeps other things out ⟨a *trap* in a drain⟩

²trap *vb* **trapped; trap·ping 1** : to catch in a trap ⟨*trap* game⟩ **2** : to provide (a place) with traps ⟨*trap* a stream⟩ **3** : to set traps for animals especially as a business **synonyms** see CATCH — **trap·per** *n*

trap·door \'trap-'dōr\ *n* : a lifting or sliding door covering an opening in a floor or roof

tra·peze \tra-'pēz\ *n* : a short horizontal bar hung from two parallel ropes and used by acrobats

trap·e·zoid \'trap-ə-,zȯid\ *n* : a figure with four sides but with only two sides parallel

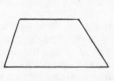

trapezoid

trap·pings \'trap-ingz\ *n pl* **1** : ornamental covering especially for a horse **2** : outward decoration or dress

trash \'trash\ *n* **1** : something of little or no worth **2** : low worthless persons

¹trav·el \'trav-əl\ *vb* **trav·eled** *or* **trav·elled; trav·el·ing** *or* **trav·el·ling 1** : to journey from place to place or to a distant place **2** : to get around : pass from one place to another ⟨the news *traveled* fast⟩ **3** : to journey through or over ⟨*travel* the countryside⟩ — **trav·el·er** *or* **trav·el·ler** *n*

Word History An Old French word that meant "to torture" came from the Latin name of an instrument of torture. In time this Old French word developed milder meanings and came to mean "to trouble" and "to work." Long ago taking a trip was not easy. A journey cost a great deal of work and trouble. The English word *travel* came from the Old French word that meant "to trouble" or "to work."

²travel *n* **1** : the act or a means of traveling ⟨air *travel* is fast⟩ **2** : ¹JOURNEY, TRIP — often used in pl. **3** : the number traveling : TRAFFIC

traveling bag *n* : a bag carried by hand and designed to hold a traveler's clothing and personal articles

tra·verse \tra-'vərs\ *vb* **tra·versed; tra·vers·ing** : to pass through, across, or over

¹trawl \'trȯl\ *vb* : to fish or catch with a trawl

²trawl *n* : a large net in the shape of a cone dragged along the sea bottom in fishing

trawl·er \'trȯ-ler\ *n* : a boat used for trawling

tray \'trā\ *n* : an open container with a flat bottom and low rim for holding, carrying, or showing articles ⟨a waiter's tray⟩

treach·er·ous \'trech-ə-rəs\ *adj* **1** : guilty of or likely to commit treachery **2** : not to be trusted ⟨a *treacherous* memory⟩ **3** : not safe because of hidden dangers — **treach·er·ous·ly** *adv*

treach·ery \'trech-ə-rē\ *n, pl* **treach·er·ies 1** : a betraying of trust or faith **2** : an act or instance of betraying trust

¹tread \'tred\ *vb* **trod** \'träd\; **trod·den** \'träd-n\ *or* **trod; tread·ing 1** : to step or walk on or over **2** : to move on foot : WALK **3** : to beat or press with the feet — **tread water** : to keep the body in an up and down position in the water and the head above water by a walking or running motion of the legs helped by moving the hands

²tread *n* **1** : a mark made by or as if by treading **2** : the action, manner, or sound of treading **3** : the part of something (as a shoe or tire) that touches a surface **4** : the horizontal part of a step

trea·dle \'tred-l\ *n* : a device worked by the foot to drive a machine

tread·mill \'tred-,mil\ *n* **1** : a device moved by persons treading on steps around the rim of a wheel or by animals walking on an endless belt **2** : a tiresome routine

trea·son \'trēz-n\ *n* **1** : the betraying of a trust **2** : the crime of trying or helping to overthrow the government of one's country or cause its defeat in war

¹trea·sure \'trezh-ər\ *n* **1** : wealth (as money or jewels) stored up or held

\ə\ abut	\au̇\ out	\i\ tip	\ȯ\ saw	\u̇\ foot
\ər\ further	\ch\ chin	\ī\ life	\ȯi\ coin	\y\ yet
\a\ mat	\e\ pet	\j\ job	\th\ thin	\yü\ few
\ā\ take	\ē\ easy	\ng\ sing	\th\ this	\yu̇\ cure
\ä\ cot, cart	\g\ go	\ō\ bone	\ü\ food	\zh\ vision

in reserve **2** : something of great value

²treasure *vb* **trea·sured; trea·sur·ing** : to treat as precious : value highly : CHERISH
synonyms see APPRECIATE

trea·sur·er \'trezh-ər-ər\ *n* : a person (as an officer of a club) who has charge of the money

trea·sury \'trezh-ə-rē\ *n, pl* **trea·sur·ies 1** : a place in which stores of wealth are kept **2** : a place where money collected is kept and paid out **3** *cap* : a government department in charge of finances

¹treat \'trēt\ *vb* **1** : to have as a subject especially in writing **2** : to handle, use, or act toward in a usually stated way ⟨*treat* these flowers gently⟩ ⟨*treat* this as secret⟩ **3** : to pay for the food or entertainment of **4** : to give medical or surgical care to : to use a certain medical care on ⟨*treat* a patient for fever⟩ ⟨*treat* cancer with drugs⟩ **5** : to expose to some action (as of a chemical) ⟨*treat* soil with lime⟩

²treat *n* **1** : an entertainment given without expense to those invited **2** : an often unexpected or unusual source of pleasure or amusement

treat·ment \'trēt-mənt\ *n* **1** : the act or manner of treating someone or something **2** : a substance or method used in treating

trea·ty \'trēt-ē\ *n, pl* **trea·ties** : an agreement between two or more states or sovereigns

¹tre·ble \'treb-əl\ *n* **1** : the highest part in harmony having four parts : SOPRANO 1 **2** : an instrument having the highest range or part **3** : a voice or sound that has a high pitch **4** : the upper half of the musical pitch range

²treble *adj* **1** : being three times the number or amount **2** : relating to or having the range of a musical treble

³treble *vb* **tre·bled; tre·bling** : to make or become three times as much

¹tree \'trē\ *n* **1** : a woody plant that lives for years and has a single usually tall main stem with few or no branches on its lower part **2** : a plant of treelike form ⟨a banana *tree*⟩ **3** : something suggesting a tree ⟨a clothes *tree*⟩ — **tree·less** \-ləs\ *adj* — **tree·like** \-,līk\ *adj*

²tree *vb* **treed; tree·ing** : to drive to or up a tree

tree fern *n* : a tropical fern with a tall woody stalk and a crown of often feathery leaves

tre·foil \'trē-,fȯil\ *n* **1** : a clover or related plant having leaves with three leaf

lets **2** : a fancy design with three leaflike parts

trefoil 2

¹trek \'trek\ *n* : a slow or difficult journey

²trek *vb* **trekked; trek·king** : to make one's way with difficulty

trel·lis \'trel-əs\ *n* : a frame of lattice used especially as a screen or a support for climbing plants

¹trem·ble \'trem-bəl\ *vb* **trem·bled; trem·bling 1** : to shake without control (as from fear or cold) : SHIVER **2** : to move, sound, or happen as if shaken ⟨the building *trembled*⟩ ⟨my voice *trembled*⟩ **3** : to have strong fear or doubt ⟨I *tremble* to think of what might happen⟩

²tremble *n* : the act or a period of trembling

tre·men·dous \tri-'men-dəs\ *adj* **1** : causing fear or terror : DREADFUL **2** : astonishingly large, strong, or great — **tre·men·dous·ly** *adv*

trem·or \'trem-ər\ *n* **1** : a trembling or shaking especially from weakness or disease **2** : a shaking motion of the earth (as during an earthquake)

trem·u·lous \'trem-yə-ləs\ *adj* **1** : marked by trembling or shaking ⟨a *tremulous* voice⟩ **2** : FEARFUL 2, TIMID

trench \'trench\ *n* : a long narrow ditch

¹trend \'trend\ *vb* : to have or take a general direction

²trend *n* : general direction taken in movement or change ⟨a down *trend* in the stock market⟩ ⟨new *trends* in fashion⟩

¹tres·pass \'tres-pəs\ *n* **1** : ¹SIN, OFFENSE **2** : unlawful entry upon someone's land

²trespass *vb* **1** : to do wrong : SIN **2** : to enter upon someone's land unlawfully — **tres·pass·er** *n*

tress \'tres\ *n* : a long lock of hair

tres·tle \'tres-əl\ *n* **1** : a braced frame consisting usually of a horizontal piece with spreading legs at each end that supports something (as the top of a table) **2** : a structure of timbers or steel for supPorting a road or railroad over a low place

tri- *prefix* **1** : three **2** : thrice : every third

tri·ad \'trī-,ad\ *n* : a chord made up usually of the first, third, and fifth notes of a scale

tri·al \'trī-əl\ *n* **1** : the action or process of trying or testing **2** : the hearing and judgment of something in court **3** : a test of faith or of one's ability to continue or stick with something **4** : an experiment to test quality, value, or usefulness **5** : ²ATTEMPT

tri·an·gle \'trī-,ang-gəl\ *n* **1** : a figure that has three sides and three angles **2** : an object that has three sides and three angles ⟨a *triangle* of land⟩ **3** : a musical instrument made of a steel rod bent in the shape of a triangle with one open angle

triangle 1

tri·an·gu·lar \trī-'ang-gyə-lər\ *adj* **1** : of, relating to, or having the form of a triangle **2** : having three angles, sides, or corners ⟨a *triangular* sign⟩ **3** : of, relating to, or involving three parts or persons

trib·al \'trī-bəl\ *adj* : of, relating to, or like that of a tribe ⟨a *tribal* custom⟩

tribe \'trīb\ *n* **1** : a group of people including many families, clans, or generations ⟨an Indian *tribe*⟩ **2** : a group of people who are of the same kind or have the same occupation or interest **3** : a group of related plants or animals ⟨the cat *tribe*⟩

tribes·man \'trībz-mən\ *n, pl* **tribes·men** \-mən\ : a member of a tribe

trib·u·la·tion \,trib-yə-'lā-shən\ *n* **1** : distress or suffering resulting from cruel and unjust rule of a leader, persecution, or misfortune **2** : an experience that is hard to bear

tri·bu·nal \trī-'byün-l\ *n* : a court of justice

¹trib·u·tary \'trib-yə-,ter-ē\ *adj* : flowing into a larger stream or a lake

²tributary *n, pl* **trib·u·tar·ies** : a stream flowing into a larger stream or a lake

trib·ute \'trib-yüt\ *n* **1** : a payment made by one ruler or state to another especially to gain peace **2** : a tax put on the people to raise money for tribute **3** : something given to show respect, gratitude, or affection

tri·chi·na \trə-'kī-nə\ *n, pl* **tri·chi·nae** \-nē\

: a small roundworm which enters the body when infected meat is eaten and whose larvae form cysts in the muscles and cause a painful and dangerous disease (**trichinosis**)

¹trick \'trik\ *n* **1** : an action intended to deceive or cheat **2** : a mischievous act : PRANK **3** : an unwise or childish action **4** : an action designed to puzzle or amuse **5** : a quick or clever way of doing something **6** : the cards played in one round of a game

²trick *vb* : to deceive with tricks : CHEAT

trick·ery \'trik-ə-rē\ *n, pl* **trick·er·ies** : the use of tricks to deceive or cheat

¹trick·le \'trik-əl\ *vb* **trick·led; trick·ling 1** : to run or fall in drops **2** : to flow in a thin slow stream

²trickle *n* : a thin slow stream

trick or treat *n* : a children's Halloween practice of asking for treats from door to door and threatening to play tricks on those who refuse

trick·ster \'trik-stər\ *n* : a person who uses tricks

tricky \'trik-ē\ *adj* **trick·i·er; trick·i·est 1** : likely to use tricks **2** : requiring special care and skill **synonyms** see SLY

tri·cy·cle \'trī-,sik-əl\ *n* : a vehicle with three wheels that is moved usually by pedals

tri·dent \'trīd-nt\ *n* : a spear with three prongs

¹tried \'trīd\ *past of* TRY

²tried *adj* : found good or trustworthy through experience or testing ⟨a *tried* and true remedy⟩

¹tri·fle \'trī-fəl\ *n* **1** : something of little importance **2** : a small amount (as of money)

²trifle *vb* **tri·fled; tri·fling 1** : to talk in a joking way **2** : to act in a playful way **3** : to handle something in an absentminded way : TOY

tri·fling \'trī-fling\ *adj* **1** : not serious : FRIVOLOUS **2** : of little value

trig·ger \'trig-ər\ *n* : the part of the lock of a gun that is pressed to release the hammer so that it will fire

¹trill \'tril\ *n* **1** : a quick movement back and forth between two musical tones one step apart **2** : ¹WARBLE 1 **3** : the rapid vibration of one speech organ against another ⟨pronounce *r*'s with a *trill*⟩

²trill *vb* : to utter as or with a trill

tril·lion \'tril-yən\ *n* : a thousand billions

\ə\ **abut**	\au̇\ **out**	\i\ **tip**	\ȯ\ **saw**	\u̇\ **foot**
\ər\ **further**	\ch\ **chin**	\ī\ **life**	\ȯi\ **coin**	\y\ **yet**
\a\ **mat**	\e\ **pet**	\j\ **job**	\th\ **thin**	\yü\ **few**
\ā\ **take**	\ē\ **easy**	\ng\ **sing**	\th\ **this**	\yu̇\ **cure**
\ä\ **cot, cart**	\g\ **go**	\ō\ **bone**	\ü\ **food**	\zh\ **vision**

tril·li·um \\'tril-ē-əm\ *n* : a plant related to the lilies that has three leaves and a single flower with three petals and that blooms in the spring

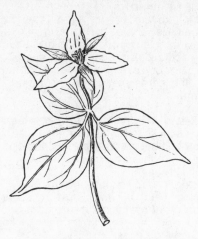

trillium

¹trim \\'trim\ *vb* **trimmed; trim·ming** **1** : to put ornaments on : ADORN ⟨*trim* a Christmas tree⟩ **2** : to make neat especially by cutting or clipping ⟨*trim* a hedge⟩ **3** : to free of unnecessary matter ⟨*trim* a budget⟩ ⟨*trim* a steak⟩ **4** : to cause (as a ship) to take the right position in the water by balancing the load carried **5** : to adjust (as an airplane or submarine) for horizontal movement or for motion upward or downward **6** : to adjust (as a sail) to a desired position — **trim·mer** *n*

²trim *adj* **trim·mer; trim·mest** : neat and compact in line or structure **synonyms** see NEAT — **trim·ly** *adv*

³trim *n* **1** : the state of a ship as being ready for sailing **2** : good condition : FITNESS **3** : material used for ornament or trimming **4** : the woodwork in the finish of a building especially around doors and windows

trim·ming \\'trim-ing\ *n* **1** : the action of one that trims **2** : something that trims, ornaments, or completes **3 trimmings** *pl* : parts removed by trimming

Trin·i·ty \\'trin-ət-ē\ *n* : the unity of Father, Son, and Holy Spirit in some Christian doctrines

trin·ket \\'tring-kət\ *n* : a small ornament (as a jewel)

trio \\'trē-ō\ *n, pl* **tri·os 1** : a musical composition for three instruments or voices **2** : a group or set of three

¹trip \\'trip\ *vb* **tripped; trip·ping 1** : to move (as in dancing) with light quick steps

⟨*tripped* lightly around the room⟩ **2** : to catch the foot against something so as to stumble : cause to stumble **3** : to make or cause to make a mistake ⟨their tricky questions *tripped* us up⟩ **4** : to release (as a spring) by moving a catch

²trip *n* **1** : a traveling from one place to another : VOYAGE ⟨a *trip* to Europe⟩ **2** : a brief errand having a certain aim or being more or less regular ⟨a *trip* to the dentist⟩ **3** : the action of releasing something mechanically **4** : a device for releasing something by tripping a mechanism **synonyms** see JOURNEY

tripe \\'trīp\ *n* : a part of the stomach of a cow used for food

¹tri·ple \\'trip-əl\ *vb* **tri·pled; tri·pling** : to make or become three times as great or as many

²triple *n* **1** : a sum, amount, or number that is three times as great **2** : a combination, group, or series of three **3** : a hit in baseball that lets the batter reach third base

³triple *adj* **1** : having three units or parts **2** : being three times as great or as many **3** : repeated three times

tri·plet \\'trip-lət\ *n* **1** : a combination, set, or group of three **2** : one of three offspring born at one birth

tri·pod \\'trī-,päd\ *n* **1** : something (as a container or stool) resting on three legs **2** : a stand (as for a camera) having three legs

trite \\'trīt\ *adj* **trit·er; trit·est** : so common that the newness and cleverness have worn off : STALE ⟨*trite* remarks⟩ — **trite·ness** *n*

¹tri·umph \\'trī-əmf\ *n* **1** : the joy of victory or success **2** : an outstanding victory **synonyms** see VICTORY

²triumph *vb* **1** : to celebrate victory or success in high spirits and often with boasting **2** : to gain victory : WIN

tri·um·phal \trī-'əm-fəl\ *adj* : of or relating to a triumph

tri·um·phant \trī-'əm-fənt\ *adj* **1** : VICTORIOUS, SUCCESSFUL **2** : rejoicing for or celebrating victory — **tri·um·phant·ly** *adv*

triv·i·al \\'triv-ē-əl\ *adj* : of little worth or importance

trod *past of* TREAD

trod·den *past participle of* TREAD

¹troll \\'trōl\ *vb* **1** : to sing the parts of (a song) in succession **2** : to fish with a hook and line drawn through the water

²troll *n* : a lure or a line with its lure and hook used in trolling

³troll *n* : a dwarf or giant of folklore living in caves or hills

trol·ley *or* **trol·ly** \'träl-ē\ *n, pl* **trol·leys** *or* **trol·lies** **1 :** a device (as a grooved wheel on the end of a pole) to carry current from a wire to an electrically driven vehicle **2 :** a passenger car that runs on tracks and gets its power through a trolley **3 :** a wheeled carriage running on an overhead track

trom·bone \träm-'bōn\ *n* : a brass musical instrument made of a long bent tube that has a wide opening at one end and one section that slides in and out to make different tones

trombone

¹troop \'trüp\ *n* **1 :** a cavalry unit **2 troops** *pl* : armed forces : MILITARY **3 :** a group of beings or things **4 :** a unit of boy or girl scouts under a leader

²troop *vb* : to move or gather in groups

troop·er \'trü-pər\ *n* **1 :** a soldier in a cavalry unit **2 :** a mounted police officer **3 :** a state police officer

tro·phy \'trō-fē\ *n, pl* **tro·phies** **1 :** something taken in battle or conquest especially as a memorial **2 :** something given to celebrate a victory or as an award for achievement

trop·ic \'träp-ik\ *n* **1 :** either of two parallels of the earth's latitude of which one is about 23½ degrees north of the equator and the other about 23½ degrees south of the equator **2 tropics** *pl, often cap* : the region lying between the two tropics

trop·i·cal \'träp-i-kəl\ *adj* : of, relating to, or occurring in the tropics

tropical fish *n* : any of various small often brightly colored fishes kept in aquariums

¹trot \'trät\ *n* **1 :** a moderately fast gait of an animal with four feet in which a front foot and the opposite hind foot move as a pair **2 :** a human jogging pace between a walk and a run

²trot *vb* **trot·ted; trot·ting** **1 :** to ride, drive, or go at a trot **2 :** to cause to go at a trot **3 :** to go along quickly : HURRY

¹trou·ble \'trəb-əl\ *vb* **trou·bled; trou·bling** **1 :** to disturb or become disturbed mentally or spiritually : WORRY **2 :** to produce physical disorder in : AFFLICT **3 :** to put to inconvenience **4 :** to make an effort ⟨do not *trouble* to write⟩

²trouble *n* **1 :** the quality or state of being troubled : MISFORTUNE ⟨people in *trouble*⟩ **2 :** an instance of distress or distur-

bance **3 :** a cause of disturbance or distress **4 :** extra work or effort ⟨took the *trouble* to write⟩ **5 :** ill health : AILMENT **6 :** failure to work normally ⟨had *trouble* with the engine⟩

trou·ble·some \'trəb-əl-səm\ *adj* **1 :** giving trouble or anxiety ⟨a *troublesome* infection⟩ **2 :** difficult to deal with — **trou·ble·some·ly** *adv* — **trou·ble·some·ness** *n*

trough \'trof\ *n* **1 :** a long shallow open container especially for water or feed for livestock **2 :** a channel for water : GUTTER **3 :** a long channel or hollow

trounce \'trauns\ *vb* **trounced; trounc·ing** **1 :** to beat severely : FLOG **2 :** to defeat thoroughly

troupe \'trüp\ *n* : a group especially of performers on the stage

trou·sers \'trau-zərz\ *n pl* : PANTS — used chiefly of such a garment for men and boys

trout \'traut\ *n, pl* **trout** **1 :** any of various fishes (as the eastern **brook trout** or the European **brown trout**) mostly smaller than the related salmon and often speckled with dark colors **2 :** any of various fishes (as a **rock trout** or greenling or a **sea trout** or weakfish) that look somewhat like the true trouts

trout 1

trow·el \'trau-əl\ *n* **1 :** a small hand tool with a flat blade used for spreading and smoothing mortar or plaster **2 :** a small hand tool with a curved blade used by gardeners

tru·ant \'trü-ənt\ *n* **1 :** a person who neglects his or her duty **2 :** a student who stays out of school without permission

truce \'trüs\ *n* **1 :** ARMISTICE **2 :** a short rest especially from something unpleasant

¹truck \'trək\ *n* **1 :** ²BARTER **2 :** goods for barter or for small trade **3 :** close association ⟨wanted no *truck* with criminals⟩

²truck *n* : a vehicle (as a strong heavy wagon or motor vehicle) for carrying heavy articles or hauling a trailer

³truck *vb* : to transport on a truck

trudge \'trəj\ *vb* **trudged; trudg·ing** : to walk or march steadily and usually with much effort

¹true \'trü\ *adj* **tru·er; tru·est** **1 :** com-

\ə\ abut	\au\ out	\i\ tip	\o\ saw	\u\ foot
\ər\ further	\ch\ chin	\ī\ life	\oi\ coin	\y\ yet
\a\ mat	\e\ pet	\j\ job	\th\ thin	\yü\ few
\ā\ take	\ē\ easy	\ng\ sing	\th\ this	\yu\ cure
\ä\ cot, cart	\g\ go	\ō\ bone	\ü\ food	\zh\ vision

pletely loyal : FAITHFUL **2** : that can be relied on : CERTAIN **3** : agreeing with the facts : ACCURATE ⟨a *true* story⟩ **4** : HONEST 1, SINCERE ⟨*true* friendship⟩ **5** : properly so called : GENUINE ⟨mosses have no *true* seeds⟩ **6** : placed or formed accurately : EXACT ⟨*true* pitch⟩ **7** : being or holding by right : LEGITIMATE ⟨the *true* owner⟩ **synonyms** see FAITHFUL, REAL

2true *n* : the quality or state of being accurate (as in alignment) ⟨out of *true*⟩

3true *vb* **trued; true·ing** *also* **tru·ing** : to bring to exactly correct condition as to place, position, or shape

4true *adv* **1** : in agreement with fact : TRUTHFULLY **2** : in an accurate manner : ACCURATELY ⟨the bullet flew straight and *true*⟩ **3** : without variation from type ⟨breed *true*⟩

true–blue \'trü-'blü\ *adj* : very faithful

truf·fle \'trəf-əl\ *n* : the edible usually dark and wrinkled fruiting body of a European fungus that grows in the ground

tru·ly \'trü-lē\ *adv* : in a true manner

1trum·pet \'trəm-pət\ *n* **1** : a brass musical instrument that consists of a tube formed into a long loop with a wide opening at one end and that has valves by which different tones are produced **2** : something that is shaped like a trumpet **3** : a sound like that of a trumpet

2trumpet *vb* **1** : to blow a trumpet **2** : to make a sound like that of a trumpet — **trum·pet·er** *n*

trumpet creeper *or* **trumpet vine** *n* : a North American woody vine having red flowers shaped like trumpets

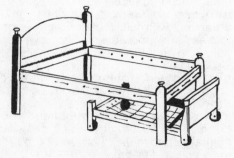

trumpet creeper

1trun·dle \'trən-dəl\ *n* **1** : a small wheel or roller **2** : a cart or truck with low wheels

2trundle *vb* **trun·dled; trun·dling** : to roll along : WHEEL

trundle bed *n* : a low bed on small wheels that can be rolled under a higher bed

trunk \'trəngk\ *n* **1** : the main stem of a tree apart from branches and roots **2** : the body of a person or animal apart from the head, arms, and legs **3** : a box or chest for holding clothes or other articles especially for traveling **4** : the enclosed space usually in the rear of an automobile for carrying articles **5** : the long round muscular

nose of an elephant **6 trunks** *pl* : men's shorts worn chiefly for sports

1truss \'trəs\ *vb* **1** : to bind or tie firmly **2** : to support, strengthen, or stiffen by a truss

2truss *n* **1** : a framework of beams or bars used in building and engineering **2** : a device worn to hold a ruptured body part in place

1trust \'trəst\ *n* **1** : firm belief in the character, strength, or truth of someone or something **2** : a person or thing in which confidence is placed **3** : confident hope **4** : financial credit **5** : a property interest held by one person or organization (as a bank) for the benefit of another **6** : a combination of firms or corporations formed by a legal agreement and often held to reduce competition **7** : something (as a public office) held or managed by someone for the benefit of another **8** : responsibility for safety and well-being

2trust *vb* **1** : to place confidence : DEPEND **2** : to be confident : HOPE **3** : to place in one's care or keeping : ENTRUST **4** : to rely on or on the truth of : BELIEVE **5** : to give financial credit to

trust·ee \ˌtrəs-'tē\ *n* : a person who has been given legal responsibility for someone else's property

trust·ful \'trəst-fəl\ *adj* : full of trust — **trust·ful·ly** \-fə-lē\ *adv* — **trust·ful·ness** *n*

trust·ing \'trəs-ting\ *adj* : having trust, faith, or confidence

trust·wor·thy \'trəst-ˌwər-ᵺē\ *adj* : deserving trust and confidence — **trust·wor·thi·ness** *n*

1trusty \'trəs-tē\ *adj* **trust·i·er; trust·i·est** : TRUSTWORTHY, RELIABLE

2trusty *n, pl* **trust·ies** : a convict considered trustworthy and allowed special privileges

trundle bed

truth \'trüth\ *n, pl* **truths** \'trüᵺz\ **1** : the quality or state of being true **2** : the body of real events or facts **3** : a true or accepted statement **4** : agreement with fact or reality

truth·ful \'trüth-fəl\ *adj* : telling or being in the habit of telling the truth — **truth·ful·ly** \-fə-lē\ *adv* — **truth·ful·ness** *n*

¹try \'trī\ *vb* **tried** \'trīd\; **try·ing** **1** : to examine or investigate in a court of law **2** : to conduct the trial of **3** : to put to a test **4** : to test to the limit **5** : to melt down (as tallow) and obtain in a pure state **6** : to make an effort to do

²try *n, pl* **tries** : an effort to do something : ATTEMPT

try·ing \'trī-ing\ *adj* : hard to bear or put up with

try on *vb* : to put on (a garment) in order to test the fit

try·out \'trī-,aut\ *n* : a test of the ability (as of an athlete or an actor) to fill a part or meet standards

T–shirt *also* **tee shirt** \'tē-,shərt\ *n* **1** : a cotton undershirt with short sleeves and no collar **2** : a cotton or wool jersey outer shirt designed like a T-shirt

¹tub \'təb\ *n* **1** : a wide low container **2** : an old or slow boat **3** : BATHTUB **4** : BATH 1 **5** : the amount that a tub will hold

²tub *vb* **tubbed; tub·bing** : to wash or bathe in a tub

tu·ba \'tü-bə, 'tyü-\ *n* : a brass musical instrument of lowest pitch with an oval shape and valves for producing different tones

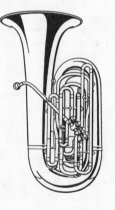

tuba

tube \'tüb, 'tyüb\ *n* **1** : a long hollow cylinder used especially to carry fluids **2** : a slender channel within a plant or animal body : DUCT **3** : a soft container shaped something like a tube whose contents (as toothpaste or glue) can be removed by squeezing **4** : a hollow cylinder of rubber inside a tire to hold air **5** : ELECTRONIC TUBE **6** : TELEVISION — always used with *the* — **tubed** \'tü-bd, 'tyübd\ *adj* — **tube·less** \'tü-bləs, 'tyü-\ *adj* — **tube·like** \'tü-,blīk, 'tyü-\ *adj*

tu·ber \'tü-bər, 'tyü-\ *n* : a short fleshy usually underground stem (as of a potato plant) bearing tiny leaves like scales each with a bud at its base

tu·ber·cu·lo·sis \tu-,bər-kyə-'lō-səs, tyu-\ *n* : a disease (as of humans or cattle) which is caused by a bacillus and in which fever, wasting, and formation of cheesy nodules especially in the lungs occur

tu·ber·ous \'tü-bə-rəs, 'tyü-\ *adj* : of, relating to, or like a tuber

tu·bu·lar \'tü-byə-lər, 'tyü-\ *adj* **1** : having the form of or made up of a tube **2** : made with tubes

¹tuck \'tək\ *vb* **1** : to pull up into a fold **2** : to make stitched folds in **3** : to put or fit into a snug or safe place ⟨*tucked* their money away in the bank⟩ **4** : to push in the edges of ⟨*tuck* in your shirt⟩ **5** : to cover by tucking in bedclothes ⟨*tucked* the children in for the night⟩

²tuck *n* : a fold stitched into cloth usually to alter it

Tues·day \'tüz-dē, 'tyüz-\ *n* : the third day of the week

¹tuft \'təft\ *n* **1** : a small bunch of long flexible things (as hairs) growing out **2** : a bunch of soft fluffy threads used for ornament **3** : ¹CLUMP 1, CLUSTER

²tuft *vb* **1** : to provide or decorate with a tuft **2** : to grow in tufts **3** : to make (as upholstery) firm by stitching through the stuffing here and there

¹tug \'təg\ *vb* **tugged; tug·ging** **1** : to pull hard ⟨*tug* at a rope⟩ **2** : to move by pulling hard : DRAG **3** : to tow with a tugboat

²tug *n* **1** : an act of tugging : PULL **2** : a strong pulling force ⟨the *tug* of gravity⟩ **3** : a struggle between two people or forces **4** : TUGBOAT

tug·boat \'təg-,bōt\ *n* : a small powerful boat used for towing ships

tug–of–war \,təg-əv-'wor\ *n, pl* **tugs–of–war** **1** : a struggle to win **2** : a contest in which two teams pull against each other at opposite ends of a rope

tu·i·tion \tu-'ish-ən, tyu-\ *n* : money paid for instruction (as at a college)

tu·lip \'tü-ləp, 'tyü-\ *n* : a plant related to the lilies that grows from a bulb and has a large cup-shaped flower in early spring

tulip

\ə\ **abut**	\au̇\ **out**	\i\ **tip**	\o̅\ **saw**	\u̇\ **foot**
\ər\ **further**	\ch\ **chin**	\ī\ **life**	\o̅i\ **coin**	\y\ **yet**
\a\ **mat**	\e\ **pet**	\j\ **job**	\th\ **thin**	\yü\ **few**
\ā\ **take**	\ē\ **easy**	\ng\ **sing**	\th\ **this**	\yu̇\ **cure**
\ä\ **cot, cart**	\g\ **go**	\ō\ **bone**	\ü\ **food**	\zh\ **vision**

Word History We often think of the tulip as a Dutch flower. The Dutch do grow tulips, but they first got the flower from Turkey. The tulip's Latin name came from a Turkish word that meant "turban." A tulip looks just a bit like a turban. The English word *tulip* comes from the Latin name.

¹tum·ble \'təm-bəl\ *vb* **tum·bled; tum·bling** **1** : to perform gymnastic feats of rolling and turning **2** : to fall suddenly and helplessly **3** : to suffer a sudden downward turn or defeat **4** : to move or go in a hurried or confused way **5** : to come to understand **6** : to toss together into a confused mass

²tumble *n* **1** : a messy state or collection **2** : an act or instance of tumbling and especially of falling down

tum·ble·down \'təm-bəl-ˌdaun\ *adj* : DILAPIDATED ⟨a *tumbledown* old house⟩

tum·bler \'təm-blər\ *n* **1** : a person (as an acrobat) who tumbles **2** : a drinking glass **3** : a movable part of a lock that must be adjusted (as by a key) before the lock will open

tum·ble·weed \'təm-bəl-ˌwēd\ *n* : a plant that breaks away from its roots in autumn and is tumbled about by the wind

tum·my \'təm-ē\ *n, pl* **tum·mies** : ¹STOMACH 1, 2

tu·mor \'tü-mər, 'tyü-\ *n* : an abnormal growth of body tissue

tu·mult \'tü-ˌməlt, 'tyü-\ *n* **1** : UPROAR ⟨the *tumult* raised by the rioters⟩ **2** : great confusion of mind

tu·mul·tu·ous \tu-'məl-chə-wəs, tyü-\ *adj* : being or suggesting tumult

tu·na \'tü-nə, 'tyü-\ *n* : any of several large sea fishes related to the mackerels and valued for food and sport

tun·dra \'tən-drə\ *n* : a treeless plain of arctic regions

¹tune \'tün, 'tyün\ *n* **1** : a series of pleasing musical tones : MELODY **2** : the main melody of a song **3** : correct musical pitch or key ⟨were singing out of *tune*⟩ **4** : AGREEMENT 1, HARMONY ⟨your feelings are in *tune* with mine⟩ **5** : general attitude ⟨changed their *tune* when they knew all the facts⟩ — **tune·ful** \-fəl\ *adj*

²tune *vb* **tuned tun·ing** **1** : to adjust in musical pitch ⟨*tuned* my guitar⟩ **2** : to come or bring into harmony **3** : to adjust a radio or television set so that it receives clearly — often used with *in* **4** : to put (as an engine) in good working order — often used with *up* — **tun·er** *n*

tung·sten \'təng-stən\ *n* : a grayish-white hard metallic chemical element used especially for electrical purposes (as for the fine wire in an electric light bulb) and to make alloys (as steel) harder

tu·nic \'tü-nik, 'tyü-\ *n* **1** : a usually knee-length belted garment worn by ancient Greeks and Romans **2** : a shirt or jacket reaching to or just below the hips

tuning fork *n* : a metal instrument that gives a fixed tone when struck and is useful for tuning musical instruments

¹tun·nel \'tən-l\ *n* : a passage under the ground

²tunnel *vb* **tun·neled** *or* **tun·nelled; tun·nel·ing** *or* **tun·nel·ling** : to make a tunnel

tun·ny \'tən-ē\ *n, pl* **tun·nies** : TUNA

tur·ban \'tər-bən\ *n* **1** : a head covering worn especially by Muslims and made of a long cloth wrapped around the head or around a cap **2** : a woman's small soft hat with no brim

tur·bid \'tər-bəd\ *adj* : dark or discolored with sediment ⟨a *turbid* stream⟩

tur·bine \'tər-bən\ *n* : an engine whose central driving shaft is fitted with a series of winglike parts that are whirled around by the pressure of water, steam, or gas

turban 1

tur·bot \'tər-bət\ *n, pl* **turbot** : a large brownish flatfish

tur·bu·lent \'tər-byə-lənt\ *adj* : causing or being in a state of unrest, violence, or disturbance

tu·reen \tə-'rēn\ *n* : a deep bowl from which food (as soup) is served

turf \'tərf\ *n* : the upper layer of soil bound into a thick mat by roots of grass and other plants

Turk \'tərk\ *n* : a person born or living in Turkey

tur·key \'tər-kē\ *n, pl* **tur·keys** : a large American bird related to the chicken and widely raised for food

turkey

Word History Guinea fowl were once called *turkeycocks*. They came from Africa, but some people thought they came from Turkey. The birds we call *turkeys* are American. When the English first saw them, some confused them with guinea fowl. That is why the new birds were called *turkey-cocks,* too. The word *turkey* is short for *turkey-cock.*

¹Turk·ish \'tər-kish\ *adj* : of or relating to Turkey, the Turks, or Turkish

²Turkish *n* : the language of the Turks

tur·moil \'tər-ˌmȯil\ *n* : a very confused or disturbed state or condition

¹turn \'tərn\ *vb* **1** : to move or cause to move around a center : ROTATE **2** : to twist so as to bring about a desired end ⟨*turn* the key to unlock the door⟩ **3** : ²WRENCH 2 ⟨*turn* an ankle⟩ **4** : to change in position usually by moving through an arc of a circle ⟨they *turned* and walked away⟩ ⟨*turn* the child over in bed⟩ ⟨*turn* pancakes⟩ **5** : to think over : PONDER **6** : to become dizzy : REEL **7** : ¹UPSET 3 ⟨*turn* one's stomach⟩ **8** : to set in another and especially an opposite direction **9** : to change course or direction ⟨the road *turns* to the left⟩ **10** : to go around **11** : to reach or pass beyond **12** : to move or direct toward or away from something ⟨we *turned* toward home⟩ **13** : to make an appeal ⟨*turned* to an agency for help⟩ **14** : to become or make very unfriendly **15** : to make or become spoiled ⟨the milk *turned*⟩ **16** : to cause to be or look a certain way ⟨the weather *turned* the leaves red⟩ **17** : to pass from one state to another ⟨the weather *turned* cold⟩ **18** : ¹CHANGE 1, TRANSFORM ⟨*turn* lead into gold⟩ **19** : TRANSLATE 2 **20** : to give a rounded form to (as on a lathe) — **turn a hair** : to be or become upset or frightened — **turn tail** : to turn so as to run away — **turn the trick** : to bring about the desired result — **turn turtle** : OVERTURN 1

²turn *n* **1** : a turning about a center **2** : a change or changing of direction, course, or position **3** : a change or changing of the general state or condition ⟨business took a *turn* for the better⟩ **4** : a place at which something turns ⟨a *turn* in the road⟩ **5** : a short walk or ride **6** : an act affecting another ⟨do a friend a good *turn*⟩ **7** : proper place in a waiting line or time in a schedule ⟨take your *turn*⟩ **8** : a period of action or activity : SPELL **9** : a special purpose or need ⟨that will serve the *turn*⟩ **10** : special quality **11** : the shape or form in which something is molded : CAST **12** : a single circle or loop (as of rope passed around an object) **13** : natural or special skill ⟨has

a *turn* for writing⟩ — **at every turn** : all the time : CONSTANTLY, CONTINUOUSLY — **to a turn** : precisely right

turn·about \'tər-nə-ˌbaut\ *n* : a change from one direction or one way of thinking or acting to the opposite

turn down *vb* **1** : to fold back or down ⟨*turn down* the bedclothes⟩ **2** : to lower by using a control ⟨*turn down* the heat⟩ **3** : ¹REFUSE 1, REJECT ⟨*turn down* a job⟩

tur·nip \'tər-nəp\ *n* : the thick white or yellow edible root of a plant related to the cabbage

turn off *vb* **1** : to turn aside ⟨*turned off* onto another road⟩ **2** : to stop by using a control ⟨*turn off* the alarm⟩

turn on *vb* : to make work by using a control ⟨*turn on* the light⟩

turn·out \'tər-ˌnaut\ *n* : a gathering of people for a special reason ⟨a good *turnout* for the meeting⟩

turn out *vb* **1** : TURN OFF 2 ⟨who *turned out* the light⟩ **2** : to prove to be ⟨it *turned out* to be the cat⟩

turn·pike \'tərn-ˌpīk\ *n* **1** : a road that one must pay to use **2** : a main road

turn·stile \'tərn-ˌstīl\ *n* : a post having arms that turn around set in an entrance or exit so that persons can pass through only on foot one by one

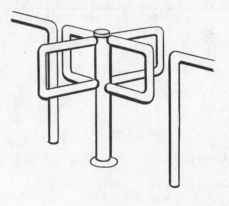

turnstile

turn·ta·ble \'tərn-ˌtā-bəl\ *n* : a round flat plate that turns a phonograph record

tur·pen·tine \'tər-pən-ˌtīn\ *n* **1** : a mixture of oil and resin obtained mostly from pine trees **2** : an oil made from turpentine and used as a solvent and as a paint thinner

\ə\ abut	\au̇\ out	\i\ tip	\ȯ\ saw	\u̇\ foot
\ər\ further	\ch\ chin	\ī\ life	\ȯi\ coin	\y\ yet
\a\ mat	\e\ pet	\j\ job	\th\ thin	\yü\ few
\ā\ take	\ē\ easy	\ng\ sing	\th\ this	\yu̇\ cure
\ä\ cot, cart	\g\ go	\ō\ bone	\ü\ food	\zh\ vision

tur·quoise \'tər-ˌkȯiz, -ˌkwȯiz\ *n* : a blue to greenish gray mineral used in jewelry

tur·ret \'tər-ət\ *n* **1** : a little tower often at a corner of a building **2** : a low usually rotating structure (as in a tank, warship, or airplane) in which guns are mounted

tur·tle \'tərt-l\ *n* : a reptile having a horny beak and a bony shell that covers the body

turtle

tur·tle·dove \'tərt-l-ˌdəv\ *n* : any of several small wild pigeons

tur·tle·neck \'tərt-l-ˌnek\ *n* : a high turned-over collar (as of a sweater)

tusk \'təsk\ *n* : a very long large tooth (as of an elephant) usually growing in pairs and used in digging and fighting — **tusked** \'təskt\ *adj*

¹tus·sle \'təs-əl\ *vb* **tus·sled; tus·sling** : to struggle roughly : SCUFFLE

²tussle *n* **1** : a physical contest or struggle **2** : a rough argument or a struggle against difficult odds

tus·sock \'təs-ək\ *n* : a compact tuft or clump (as of grass)

¹tu·tor \'tüt-ər, 'tyüt-\ *n* : a person who has the responsibility of instructing and guiding another

²tutor *vb* : to teach usually individually

TV \'tē-'vē\ *n* : TELEVISION

twad·dle \'twäd-l\ *n* : silly idle talk

twain \'twān\ *n* : ²TWO 1

¹twang \'twang\ *n* **1** : a harsh quick ringing sound **2** : nasal speech

²twang *vb* **1** : to sound or cause to sound with a twang **2** : to speak with a nasal twang

'twas \twəz, 'twäz\ : it was

¹tweak \'twēk\ *vb* : to pinch and pull with a sudden jerk and twist

²tweak *n* : an act of tweaking

tweed \'twēd\ *n* **1** : a rough woolen cloth **2** **tweeds** *pl* : tweed clothing (as a suit)

¹tweet \'twēt\ *n* : a chirping sound

²tweet *vb* : ²CHIRP

tweez·ers \'twē-zərz\ *n pl* : a small instrument that is used like pincers in grasping or pulling something

¹twelfth \'twelfth\ *adj* : coming right after eleventh

²twelfth *n* : number twelve in a series

¹twelve \'twelv\ *adj* : being one more than eleven

²twelve *n* : one more than eleven : three times four : 12

twelve·month \'twelv-ˌmənth\ *n* : YEAR

¹twen·ti·eth \'twent-ē-əth\ *adj* : coming right after nineteenth

²twentieth *n* : number twenty in a series

¹twen·ty \'twent-ē\ *adj* : being one more than nineteen

²twenty *n* : one more than nineteen : four times five : 20

twen·ty–first \ˌtwent-ē-'fərst\ *adj* : coming right after twentieth

¹twen·ty–one \ˌtwent-ē-'wən\ *adj* : being one more than twenty

²twenty–one *n* : one more than twenty : 21

twice \'twīs\ *adv* : two times

twid·dle \'twid-l\ *vb* **twid·dled; twid·dling** : ¹TWIRL ⟨*twiddle* one's thumbs⟩

twig \'twig\ *n* : a small shoot or branch

twi·light \'twī-ˌlīt\ *n* : the period or the light from the sky between full night and sunrise or between sunset and full night

twill \'twil\ *n* : a way of weaving cloth that produces a pattern of diagonal lines

¹twin \'twin\ *adj* **1** : born with one other or as a pair at one birth ⟨*twin* calves⟩ **2** : made up of two similar, related, or connected members or parts **3** : being one of a pair

²twin *n* **1** : either of two offspring produced at one birth **2** : one of two persons or things closely related to or very like each other

¹twine \'twīn\ *n* : a strong string of two or more strands twisted together

²twine *vb* **twined; twin·ing** **1** : to twist together **2** : to coil around a support **3** : ⁴WIND 1

¹twinge \'twinj\ *vb* **twinged; twing·ing** *or* **twinge·ing** : to affect with or feel a sudden sharp pain

²twinge *n* : a sudden sharp stab (as of pain)

¹twin·kle \'twing-kəl\ *vb* **twin·kled; twin·kling** **1** : to shine or cause to shine with a flickering or sparkling light ⟨stars *twinkling* in the sky⟩ **2** : to appear bright with amusement ⟨eyes *twinkled* at the joke⟩ **3** : to move or flutter rapidly

²twinkle *n* **1** : a very short time **2** : ²SPARKLE 1, FLICKER

twin·kling \'twing-kling\ *n* : ²TWINKLE 1

¹twirl \'twərl\ *vb* : to turn or cause to turn rapidly ⟨a *twirling* windmill⟩ — **twirl·er** *n*

²twirl *n* : an act of twirling

¹twist \'twist\ *vb* **1** : to unite by winding

one thread, strand, or wire around another **2** : ²TWINE 2 **3** : to turn so as to sprain or hurt ⟨*twist* one's ankle⟩ **4** : to change the meaning of ⟨you're *twisting* my words; that's not what I meant⟩ **5** : to pull off, rotate, or break by a turning force ⟨*twist* a flower from its stem⟩ **6** : to follow a winding course ⟨the path *twisted* between the trees⟩

²twist *n* **1** : something that is twisted **2** : an act of twisting : the state of being twisted **3** : a spiral turn or curve **4** : a strong personal tendency : BENT **5** : a changing of meaning **6** : something (as a plan of action) that is both surprising and strange **7** : a lively dance in which the hips are twisted

twist·er \'twis-tər\ *n* **1** : TORNADO **2** : WATERSPOUT 2

¹twitch \'twich\ *vb* **1** : to move or pull with a sudden motion : JERK **2** : ¹PLUCK 1 **3** : ²QUIVER

²twitch *n* **1** : an act of twitching **2** : a short sharp contracting of muscle fibers

¹twit·ter \'twit-ər\ *vb* **1** : to make a series of chirping noises **2** : to talk in a chattering fashion **3** : to make or become very nervous and upset

²twitter *n* **1** : a nervous upset state ⟨we were all of a *twitter*⟩ **2** : the chirping of birds **3** : a light chattering

¹two \'tü\ *adj* : being one more than one

²two *n* **1** : one more than one : 2 **2** : the second in a set or series

two·fold \'tü-,föld\ *adj* : being twice as great or as many

two–winged fly \,tü-,wingd-\ *n* : an insect belonging to the same group as the housefly

ty·coon \tī-'kün\ *n* : a very powerful and wealthy business person

tying *present participle of* TIE

¹type \'tīp\ *n* **1** : a set of letters or figures that are used for printing or the letters or figures printed by them **2** : the special things by which members of a group are set apart from other groups ⟨horses of draft *type*⟩ **3** : a particular kind, class, or group ⟨a seedless *type* of orange⟩ ⟨I don't like people of that *type*⟩

²type *vb* **typed; typ·ing 1** : TYPEWRITE **2** : to identify as belonging to a type

type·write \'tī-,prīt\ *vb* **type·wrote** \-,prōt\;

type·writ·ten \-,prit-n\; **type·writ·ing** \-,prīt-ing\ : to write with a typewriter

type·writ·er \'tī-,prīt-ər\ *n* : a machine that prints letters or figures when a person pushes its keys down

type·writ·ing \'tī-,prīt-ing\ *n* **1** : the use of a typewriter **2** : writing done with a typewriter

¹ty·phoid \'tī-,foid\ *adj* **1** : of, relating to, or like typhus **2** : of, relating to, or being typhoid

²typhoid *n* : a disease in which a person has fever, diarrhea, an inflamed intestine, and great weakness and which is caused by a bacterium (**typhoid bacillus**) that passes from one person to another in dirty food or water

ty·phoon \tī-'fün\ *n* : a tropical cyclone in the region of the Philippines or the China Sea

ty·phus \'tī-fəs\ *n* : a disease carried to people especially by body lice and marked by high fever, stupor and delirium, severe headache, and a dark red rash

typ·i·cal \'tip-i-kəl\ *adj* : combining or showing the special characteristics of a group or kind ⟨a *typical* Sunday dinner⟩ **synonyms** see REGULAR — **typ·i·cal·ly** *adv*

typ·i·fy \'tip-ə-,fi\ *vb* **typ·i·fied; typ·i·fy·ing 1** : REPRESENT 2 **2** : to have or include the special or main characteristics of

typ·ist \'tī-pəst\ *n* : a person who uses a typewriter

ty·ran·ni·cal \tə-'ran-i-kəl\ *adj* : of, relating to, or like that of tyranny or a tyrant ⟨*tyrannical* acts⟩

tyr·an·ny \'tir-ə-nē\ *n, pl* **tyr·an·nies 1** : a government in which all power is in the hands of a single ruler **2** : harsh, cruel, and severe government or conduct **3** : a tyrannical act

ty·rant \'tī-rənt\ *n* **1** : a ruler who has no legal limits on his or her power **2** : a ruler who exercises total power harshly and cruelly **3** : a person who uses authority or power harshly ⟨my boss is a real *tyrant*⟩

\ə\ abut	\aú\ out	\i\ tip	\ó\ saw	\ú\ foot
\ər\ further	\ch\ chin	\ī\ life	\ói\ coin	\y\ yet
\a\ mat	\e\ pet	\j\ job	\th\ thin	\yü\ few
\ā\ take	\ē\ easy	\ng\ sing	\th\ this	\yú\ cure
\ä\ cot, cart	\g\ go	\ō\ bone	\ü\ food	\zh\ vision

U

u \'yü\ *n, pl* **u's** *or* **us** \'yüz\ *often cap* **1** : the twenty-first letter of the English alphabet **2** : a grade rating a student's work as unsatisfactory

ud·der \'əd-ər\ *n* : an organ (as of a cow) made up of two or more milk glands enclosed in a common pouch but opening by separate nipples

ugh \'əg\ *interj* — used to indicate the sound of a cough or to express disgust or horror

ug·ly \'əg-lē\ *adj* **ug·li·er; ug·li·est 1** : unpleasant to look at : not attractive ⟨an *ugly* color⟩ **2** : ¹OFFENSIVE 3 ⟨*ugly* smells⟩ ⟨*ugly* habits⟩ **3** : not pleasant : TROUBLESOME ⟨an *ugly* situation⟩ ⟨*ugly* weather⟩ **4** : showing a mean or quarrelsome disposition ⟨an *ugly* temper⟩ — **ug·li·ness** *n*

uku·le·le \,yü-kə-'lā-lē\ *n* : a musical instrument like a small guitar with four strings

ukulele

ul·cer \'əl-sər\ *n* : an open sore in which tissue is eaten away and which may discharge pus

ul·cer·ate \'əl-sə-,rāt\ *vb* **ul·cer·at·ed; ul·cer·at·ing** : to cause or have an ulcer ⟨an *ulcerated* leg⟩

ul·cer·ation \,əl-sə-'rā-shən\ *n* **1** : the process of forming or state of having an ulcer **2** : ULCER

ul·cer·ous \'əl-sə-rəs\ *adj* : being or accompanied by ulceration

ul·na \'əl-nə\ *n, pl* **ul·nas** *or* **ul·nae** \-nē\ : the bone on the side of the forearm opposite the thumb

ul·te·ri·or \,əl-'tir-ē-ər\ *adj* : not seen or made known ⟨*ulterior* motives⟩

ul·ti·mate \'əl-tə-mət\ *adj* **1** : last in a series : FINAL **2** : ¹EXTREME 1 ⟨the *ultimate* sacrifice⟩ **3** : FUNDAMENTAL, ABSOLUTE ⟨*ultimate* reality⟩ — **ul·ti·mate·ly** *adv*

ul·ti·ma·tum \,əl-tə-'māt-əm\ *n, pl* **ul·ti·ma·tums** *or* **ul·ti·ma·ta** \-'māt-ə\ : a final condition or demand that if rejected could end peaceful talks and lead to forceful action

ul·tra \'əl-trə\ *adj* : ¹EXTREME 1, EXCESSIVE

ultra- *prefix* **1** : beyond in space : on the other side ⟨*ultra*violet⟩ **2** : beyond the limits of : SUPER- **3** : beyond what is ordinary or proper : too

ul·tra·vi·o·let \,əl-trə-'vī-ə-lət\ *adj* : relating to or producing ultraviolet light

ultraviolet light *n* : waves that are like light but cannot be seen, that lie beyond the violet end of the spectrum, and that are found especially along with light from the sun

um·bil·i·cal cord \,əm-,bil-i-kəl-\ *n* : a cord joining a fetus to its placenta

um·brel·la \,əm-'brel-ə\ *n* : a fabric covering stretched over folding ribs attached to a rod or pole and used as a protection against rain or sun

It was formed from a Latin word that meant "shade" or "shadow."

umi·ak \'ü-mē-,ak\ *n* : an open Eskimo boat made of a wooden frame covered with hide

umiak

um·pire \'əm-,pīr\ *n* : a sports official who rules on plays

¹**un-** \-,ən, 'ən\ *prefix* : not : IN-, NON- ⟨*un*-skilled⟩

²**un-** *prefix* **1** : do the opposite of : DE- 1, DIS- 1 ⟨*un*dress⟩ ⟨*un*fold⟩ **2** : deprive of, remove a specified thing from, or free or release from ⟨*un*leash⟩ ⟨*un*hand⟩ **3** : completely ⟨*un*loose⟩

un·able \,ən-'ā-bəl\ *adj* : not able

un·ac·count·able \,ən-ə-'kaunt-ə-bəl\ *adj* : not accountable : not to be explained : STRANGE — **un·ac·count·ably** \-blē\ *adv*

un·ac·cus·tomed \,ən-ə-'kəs-təmd\ *adj* : not accustomed : not customary

un·af·fect·ed \,ən-ə-'fek-təd\ *adj* **1** : not influenced or changed **2** : free from false behavior intended to impress others : GENUINE — **un·af·fect·ed·ly** *adv*

un·afraid \,ən-ə-'frād\ *adj* : not afraid

un·aid·ed \,ən-'ād-əd\ *adj* : not aided

un·al·loyed \,ən-l-'oid\ *adj* : PURE 1, 3

unan·i·mous \yu̇-'nan-ə-məs\ *adj* **1** : having the same opinion ⟨they were *unanimous* in their choice for club president⟩ **2** : showing total agreement ⟨a *unanimous* vote⟩

un·armed \,ən-'ärmd\ *adj* : having no weapons or armor

un·asked \,ən-'askt\ *adj* : not asked or asked for

un·as·sum·ing \,ən-ə-'sü-ming\ *adj* : MODEST 1

un·avoid·able \,ən-ə-'void-ə-bəl\ *adj* : IN-EVITABLE — **un·avoid·ably** \-blē\ *adv*

¹**un·aware** \,ən-ə-'waər, -'weər\ *adv* : UN-AWARES

²**unaware** *adj* : not aware : IGNORANT ⟨*un*aware of danger⟩ — **un·aware·ness** *n*

un·awares \,ən-ə-'waərz, -'weərz\ *adv* **1** : without warning : by surprise ⟨taken *un*awares⟩ **2** : without knowing : UNINTEN-TIONALLY

un·bal·anced \,ən-'bal-ənst\ *adj* **1** : not balanced **2** : not completely sane

un·bear·able \,ən-'bar-ə-bəl, -'ber-\ *adj* : seeming too great or too bad to put up with ⟨*unbearable* pain⟩ — **un·bear·ably** \-blē\ *adv*

un·be·com·ing \,ən-bi-'kəm-ing\ *adj* : not becoming : not suitable or proper ⟨*unbe-coming* clothes⟩ ⟨*unbecoming* behavior⟩ — **un·be·com·ing·ly** *adv*

un·be·lief \,ən-bə-'lēf\ *n* : lack of belief

un·be·liev·able \,ən-bə-'lē-və-bəl\ *adj* : too unlikely to be believed — **un·be·liev·ably** \-blē\ *adv*

un·be·liev·er \,ən-bə-'lē-vər\ *n* **1** : a person who doubts what is said **2** : a person who has no religious beliefs

un·bend \,ən-'bend\ *vb* **un·bent** \-'bent\; **un·bend·ing** : RELAX 3

un·bend·ing \,ən-'ben-ding\ *adj* : not re-laxed and easy in manner

un·bi·ased \,ən-'bī-əst\ *adj* : free from bias

un·bind \,ən-'bīnd\ *vb* **un·bound** \-'baund\; **un·bind·ing** **1** : to remove a band from : UNTIE **2** : to set free

un·born \,ən-'bȯrn\ *adj* : not yet born

un·bos·om \,ən-'buz-əm\ *vb* : to tell some-one one's own thoughts or feelings

un·bound·ed \,ən-'baun-dəd\ *adj* : having no limits ⟨*unbounded* enthusiasm⟩

un·break·able \,ən-'brā-kə-bəl\ *adj* : not easily broken

un·bro·ken \,ən-'brō-kən\ *adj* **1** : not dam-aged : WHOLE **2** : not tamed for use ⟨an *unbroken* colt⟩ **3** : not interrupted

un·buck·le \,ən-'bək-əl\ *vb* **un·buck·led; un·buck·ling** : to unfasten the buckle of (as a belt)

un·bur·den \,ən-'bərd-n\ *vb* **1** : to free from a burden **2** : to free oneself from (as cares)

un·but·ton \,ən-'bət-n\ *vb* : to unfasten the buttons of (as a garment)

un·called–for \,ən-'kȯld-,fȯr\ *adj* : not needed or wanted : not proper ⟨*uncalled-for* remarks⟩

un·can·ny \,ən-'kan-ē\ *adj* **1** : MYSTE-RIOUS, EERIE **2** : suggesting powers or abilities greater than normal for humans ⟨an *uncanny* sense of direction⟩ — **un·can·ni·ly** \-'kan-l-ē\ *adv*

un·ceas·ing \,ən-'sē-sing\ *adj* : never stopping : CONTINUOUS — **un·ceas·ing·ly** *adv*

un·cer·tain \,ən-'sərt-n\ *adj* **1** : not exactly known or decided on ⟨an *uncertain* amount⟩ **2** : likely to change : not depend-

\ə\ abut	\au̇\ out	\i\ tip	\ȯ\ saw	\u̇\ foot
\ər\ further	\ch\ chin	\ī\ life	\ȯi\ coin	\y\ yet
\a\ mat	\e\ pet	\j\ job	\th\ thin	\yü\ few
\ā\ take	\ē\ easy	\ng\ sing	\th\ this	\yu̇\ cure
\ä\ cot, cart	\g\ go	\ō\ bone	\ü\ food	\zh\ vision

able ⟨*uncertain* weather⟩ **3** : not sure **4** : not known for sure — **un·cer·tain·ly** *adv*

un·cer·tain·ty \ˌən-'sərt-n-tē\ *n, pl* **un·cer·tain·ties 1** : lack of certainty : DOUBT **2** : something uncertain

un·change·able \ˌən-'chān-jə-bəl\ *adj* : not changing or capable of being changed

un·changed \ˌən-'chānjd\ *adj* : not changed

un·chang·ing \ˌən-'chān-jing\ *adj* : not changing or able to change

un·charged \ˌən-'chärjd\ *adj* : having no electric charge

un·civ·il \ˌən-'siv-əl\ *adj* : IMPOLITE — **un·civ·il·ly** *adv*

un·civ·i·lized \ˌən-'siv-ə-ˌlīzd\ *adj* **1** : not civilized : BARBAROUS **2** : far away from civilization : WILD

un·cle \'əng-kəl\ *n* **1** : the brother of one's father or mother **2** : the husband of one's aunt

un·clean \ˌən-'klēn\ *adj* **1** : not pure and innocent : WICKED **2** : not allowed for use by religious law **3** : DIRTY 1, FILTHY — **un·clean·ness** *n*

¹un·clean·ly \ˌən-'klen-lē\ *adj* : UNCLEAN 1, 3 — **un·clean·li·ness** *n*

²un·clean·ly \ˌən-'klēn-lē\ *adv* : in an unclean manner

un·cleared \ˌən-'kliərd\ *adj* : not cleared especially of trees or brush

Un·cle Sam \ˌəng-kəl-'sam\ *n* : the American government, nation, or people pictured or thought of as a person

un·clothed \ˌən-'klōthd\ *adj* : NAKED 1, 2

un·com·fort·able \ˌən-'kəm-fərt-ə-bəl, -'kəmf-tər-bəl\ *adj* **1** : causing discomfort ⟨an *uncomfortable* chair⟩ **2** : feeling discomfort : UNEASY — **un·com·fort·ably** \-blē\ *adv*

un·com·mon \ˌən-'käm-ən\ *adj* **1** : not often found or seen : UNUSUAL **2** : not ordinary : REMARKABLE **synonyms** see RARE — **un·com·mon·ly** *adv* — **un·com·mon·ness** *n*

un·com·pro·mis·ing \ˌən-'käm-prə-ˌmī-zing\ *adj* : not willing to give in even a little — **un·com·pro·mis·ing·ly** *adv*

un·con·cern \ˌən-kən-'sərn\ *n* : lack of care or interest : INDIFFERENCE

un·con·cerned \ˌən-kən-'sərnd\ *adj* **1** : not involved or interested ⟨*unconcerned* with winning if the game is fun⟩ **2** : free of worry ⟨an *unconcerned* smile⟩ ⟨*unconcerned* about the test⟩ — **un·con·cern·ed·ly** \-'sər-nəd-lē\ *adv*

un·con·di·tion·al \ˌən-kən-'dish-ən-l\ *adj* : without any special exceptions ⟨*unconditional* surrender⟩ — **un·con·di·tion·al·ly** *adv*

un·con·quer·able \ˌən-'käng-kə-rə-bəl\ *adj* : not capable of being beaten or overcome

un·con·scious \ˌən-'kän-chəs\ *adj* **1** : having lost consciousness ⟨knocked *unconscious* by a fall⟩ **2** : not aware ⟨*unconscious* of being watched⟩ **3** : not intentional or planned ⟨an *unconscious* error⟩ — **un·con·scious·ly** *adv* — **un·con·scious·ness** *n*

un·con·sti·tu·tion·al \'ən-ˌkän-stə-'tü-shən-l, -'tyü-\ *adj* : not according to the constitution (as of a government)

un·con·trol·la·ble \ˌən-kən-'trō-lə-bəl\ *adj* : hard or impossible to control — **un·con·trol·la·bly** \-blē\ *adv*

un·con·trolled \ˌən-kən-'trōld\ *adj* : not being controlled

un·couth \ˌən-'küth\ *adj* : vulgar in conduct or speech : CRUDE ⟨*uncouth* manners⟩ ⟨*uncouth* people⟩ — **un·couth·ly** *adv*

Word History The word *uncouth* first meant "unknown" or "strange." It was made up of the prefix *un-* and an Old English word that meant "known." The modern English words *can* and *know* are relatives of this Old English word.

un·cov·er \ˌən-'kəv-ər\ *vb* **1** : to make known ⟨*uncover* a crime⟩ **2** : to make visible by removing some covering

un·cul·ti·vat·ed \ˌən-'kəl-tə-ˌvāt-əd\ *adj* : not cultivated ⟨*uncultivated* fields⟩

un·curl \ˌən-'kərl\ *vb* : to make or become straightened out from a curled position

un·daunt·ed \ˌən-'dont-əd\ *adj* : not discouraged or frightened : FEARLESS

un·de·cid·ed \ˌən-di-'sīd-əd\ *adj* **1** : not settled ⟨the date for the picnic is still *undecided*⟩ **2** : not having decided ⟨we are still *undecided* about the date⟩

un·de·clared \ˌən-di-'klaərd, -'kleərd\ *adj* : not announced or openly confessed ⟨an *undeclared* war⟩

un·de·fined \ˌən-di-'find\ *adj* : not defined

un·de·ni·able \ˌən-di-'nī-ə-bəl\ *adj* : plainly true — **un·de·ni·ably** \-blē\ *adv*

¹un·der \'ən-dər\ *adv* **1** : in or into a position below or beneath something ⟨the diver went *under* again⟩ **2** : below some quantity or level ⟨ten dollars or *under*⟩ **3** : so as to be covered or hidden ⟨turned *under* by the plow⟩

²under *prep* **1** : lower than and topped or sheltered by ⟨*under* a tree⟩ **2** : below the surface of ⟨*under* the sea⟩ **3** : in or into such a position as to be covered or hidden by ⟨a vest *under* my jacket⟩ **4** : commanded or guided by ⟨the soldiers who served *under* George Washington⟩ **5**

: controlled or limited by ⟨*under* lock and key⟩ **6** : affected or influenced by the action or effect of ⟨the disease is *under* treatment⟩ **7** : within the division or grouping of ⟨*under* this heading⟩ **8** : less or lower than (as in size, amount, or rank) ⟨paid *under* a dollar⟩ ⟨weighs *under* two pounds⟩

³under *adj* **1** : lying or placed below or beneath **2** : ¹SUBORDINATE 1 ⟨the *under* secretary⟩

un·der·brush \'ən-dər-ˌbrəsh\ *n* : shrubs and small trees growing among large trees

un·der·clothes \'ən-dər-ˌklōz, -ˌklōthz\ *n pl* : UNDERWEAR

un·der·cloth·ing \'ən-dər-ˌklō-thing\ *n* : UNDERWEAR

un·der·dog \'ən-dər-ˌdog\ *n* : a person or team thought to have little chance of winning (as an election or a game)

un·der·foot \ˌən-dər-'fut\ *adv* **1** : under the feet ⟨flowers trampled *underfoot*⟩ **2** : close about one's feet : in one's way ⟨a puppy always *underfoot*⟩

un·der·gar·ment \'ən-dər-ˌgär-mənt\ *n* : a garment to be worn under another

un·der·go \ˌən-dər-'gō\ *vb* **un·der·went** \-'went\; **un·der·gone** \-'gon\; **un·der·go·ing** \-'gō-ing\ : to have (something) done or happen to oneself : EXPERIENCE ⟨*undergo* an operation⟩

¹un·der·ground \ˌən-dər-'graund\ *adv* **1** : beneath the surface of the earth **2** : in or into hiding or secret operation

²un·der·ground \'ən-dər-ˌgraund\ *adj* **1** : being or growing under the surface of the ground **2** : done or happening secretly

³un·der·ground \'ən-dər-ˌgraund\ *n* **1** : SUBWAY 2 **2** : a secret political movement or group

un·der·growth \'ən-dər-ˌgrōth\ *n* : UNDERBRUSH

¹un·der·hand \'ən-dər-ˌhand\ *adv* : in a secret or dishonest manner

²underhand *adj* **1** : done in secret or so as to deceive **2** : made with an upward movement of the hand or arm ⟨an *underhand* throw⟩

un·der·hand·ed \ˌən-dər-'han-dəd\ *adj* : ²UNDERHAND 1 — **un·der·hand·ed·ly** *adv* — **un·der·hand·ed·ness** *n*

un·der·lie \ˌən-dər-'lī\ *vb* **un·der·lay** \-'lā\; **un·der·lain** \-'lān\; **un·der·ly·ing** \-'lī-ing\ **1** : to be under **2** : to form the foundation of : SUPPORT ⟨the ideas that *underlie* democracy⟩

un·der·line \'ən-dər-ˌlīn\ *vb* **un·der·lined**; **un·der·lin·ing 1** : to draw a line under **2** : EMPHASIZE

un·der·lip \ˌən-dər-'lip\ *n* : the lower lip

un·der·mine \ˌən-dər-'mīn\ *vb* **un·der·mined**; **un·der·min·ing 1** : to dig out or wear away the supporting earth beneath ⟨*undermine* a wall⟩ **2** : to weaken secretly or little by little ⟨*undermining* their confidence⟩

¹un·der·neath \ˌən-dər-'nēth\ *prep* : directly under ⟨wore their bathing suits *underneath* their clothes⟩

²underneath *adv* **1** : below a surface or object : BENEATH ⟨soaked through to the shirt *underneath*⟩ **2** : on the lower side ⟨the bread was scorched *underneath*⟩

un·der·nour·ished \ˌən-dər-'nər-isht\ *adj* : given too little nourishment — **un·der·nour·ish·ment** \-ish-mənt\ *n*

un·der·pants \'ən-dər-ˌpants\ *n pl* : pants worn under an outer garment

un·der·part \'ən-dər-ˌpärt\ *n* : a part lying on the lower side especially of a bird or mammal

un·der·pass \'ən-dər-ˌpas\ *n* : a passage underneath something (as for a road passing under a railroad or another road)

un·der·priv·i·leged \ˌən-dər-'priv-ə-lijd\ *adj* : having fewer advantages than others especially because of being poor

un·der·rate \ˌən-dər-'rāt\ *vb* **un·der·rat·ed**; **un·der·rat·ing** : to rate too low : UNDERVALUE

un·der·score \'ən-dər-ˌskōr\ *vb* **un·der·scored**; **un·der·scor·ing** : UNDERLINE

¹un·der·sea \ˌən-dər-ˌsē\ *adj* **1** : being or done under the sea or under the surface of the sea **2** : used under the surface of the sea ⟨an *undersea* fleet⟩

²un·der·sea \ˌən-dər-'sē\ *or* **un·der·seas** \-'sēz\ *adv* : under the surface of the sea

un·der·sell \ˌən-dər-'sel\ *vb* **un·der·sold** \-'sōld\; **un·der·sell·ing** : to sell articles cheaper than ⟨*undersell* a competitor⟩

un·der·shirt \'ən-dər-ˌshərt\ *n* : a collarless garment with or without sleeves that is worn next to the body

un·der·side \'ən-dər-ˌsīd\ *n* : the side or surface lying underneath

un·der·skirt \'ən-dər-ˌskərt\ *n* : PETTICOAT

un·der·stand \ˌən-dər-'stand\ *vb* **un·der·stood** \-'stud\; **un·der·stand·ing 1** : to get the meaning of **2** : to know thoroughly ⟨I *understand* Spanish⟩ **3** : to have reason to believe ⟨I *understand* that they will come today⟩ **4** : to take as meaning something not openly made known ⟨I un

\ə\ **abut**	\au\ **out**	\i\ **tip**	\o\ **saw**	\u\ **foot**
\ər\ **further**	\ch\ **chin**	\ī\ **life**	\oi\ **coin**	\y\ **yet**
\a\ **mat**	\e\ **pet**	\j\ **job**	\th\ **thin**	\yü\ **few**
\ā\ **take**	\ē\ **easy**	\ng\ **sing**	\th\ **this**	\yu\ **cure**
\ä\ **cot, cart**	\g\ **go**	\ō\ **bone**	\ü\ **food**	\zh\ **vision**

derstand the letter to be a refusal⟩ **5** : to have a sympathetic attitude **6** : to accept as settled ⟨it is *understood* that I will pay⟩

un·der·stand·able \ˌən-dər-'stan-də-bəl\ *adj* : possible or easy to understand — **un·der·stand·ably** \-blē\ *adv*

¹**un·der·stand·ing** \ˌən-dər-'stan-ding\ *n* **1** : ability to get the meaning of and judge **2** : AGREEMENT 2 ⟨we've come to an *understanding* about how to decorate the room⟩

²**understanding** *adj* : having or showing kind or favorable feelings toward others : SYMPATHETIC

un·der·study \'ən-dər-ˌstəd-ē\ *n, pl* **un·der·stud·ies** : an actor who is prepared to take over another actor's part if necessary

un·der·take \ˌən-dər-'tāk\ *vb* **un·der·took** \-'tuk\; **un·der·tak·en** \-'tā-kən\; **un·der·tak·ing 1** : to plan or try to accomplish ⟨*undertook* a trip around the world⟩ **2** : to take on as a duty : AGREE ⟨I *undertake* to pay you ten percent interest⟩

un·der·tak·er \'ən-dər-ˌtā-kər\ *n* : a person whose business is to prepare the dead for burial and to take charge of funerals

un·der·tak·ing \'ən-dər-ˌtā-king\ *n* **1** : the act of a person who undertakes something **2** : the business of an undertaker **3** : something undertaken ⟨learning a language is a serious *undertaking*⟩

un·der·tone \'ən-dər-ˌtōn\ *n* **1** : a low or quiet tone ⟨spoke in *undertones*⟩ **2** : a partly hidden feeling ⟨an *undertone* of anger in the answer⟩

un·der·tow \'ən-dər-ˌtō\ *n* : a current beneath the surface of the water that moves away from or along the shore while the surface water above it moves toward the shore

un·der·val·ue \ˌən-dər-'val-yü\ *vb* **un·der·val·ued; un·der·valu·ing** : to value below the real worth

¹**un·der·wa·ter** \ˌən-dər-ˌwȯt-ər, -ˌwät-\ *adj* : lying, growing, worn, or operating below the surface of the water

²**un·der·wa·ter** \ˌən-dər-'wȯt-ər, -'wät-\ *adv* : under the surface of the water ⟨liked to swim *underwater*⟩

un·der·wear \'ən-dər-ˌwaər, -ˌweər\ *n* : clothing worn next to the skin and under other clothing

un·der·weight \ˌən-dər-'wāt\ *adj* : weighing less than what is normal, average, or necessary

underwent *past of* UNDERGO

un·der·world \'ən-dər-ˌwərld\ *n* : the world of organized crime

¹**un·de·sir·able** \ˌən-di-'zī-rə-bəl\ *adj* : not desirable — **un·de·sir·ably** \-blē\ *adv*

²**undesirable** *n* : an undesirable person

un·de·vel·oped \ˌən-di-'vel-əpt\ *adj* : not developed

un·di·gest·ed \ˌən-dī-'jest-əd, -də-\ *adj* : not digested

un·dig·ni·fied \ˌən-'dig-nə-ˌfid\ *adj* : not dignified

un·dis·cov·ered \ˌən-dis-'kəv-ərd\ *adj* : not discovered

un·dis·put·ed \ˌən-dis-'pyüt-əd\ *adj* : not disputed : UNQUESTIONABLE ⟨the *undisputed* leader⟩

un·dis·turbed \ˌən-dis-'tərbd\ *adj* : not disturbed

un·do \ˌən-'dü\ *vb* **un·did** \-'did\; **un·done** \-'dən\; **un·do·ing** \-'dü-ing\; **un·does** \-'dəz\ **1** : UNTIE, unfasten ⟨*undo* a knot⟩ ⟨*undo* a boat from its mooring⟩ **2** : UNWRAP, OPEN ⟨*undo* a package⟩ **3** : to destroy the effect of **4** : to cause the ruin of

un·do·ing \ˌən-'dü-ing\ *n* **1** : an act or instance of unfastening **2** : a cause of ruin or destruction ⟨my quick temper was my *undoing*⟩

un·done \ˌən-'dən\ *adj* : not done or finished

un·doubt·ed \ˌən-'daut-əd\ *adj* : not doubted

un·doubt·ed·ly \ˌən-'daut-əd-lē\ *adv* : without doubt : SURELY

un·dress \ˌən-'dres\ *vb* : to remove the clothes or covering of

un·dy·ing \ˌən-'dī-ing\ *adj* : living or lasting forever : IMMORTAL ⟨*undying* devotion⟩

un·earth \ˌən-'ərth\ *vb* **1** : to drive or draw from the earth : dig up ⟨*unearth* a fox from its den⟩ **2** : to bring to light : UNCOVER ⟨*unearthed* a plot to cheat the government⟩

un·easy \ˌən-'ē-zē\ *adj* **un·eas·i·er; un·eas·i·est 1** : not easy in manner : AWKWARD **2** : disturbed by pain or worry : RESTLESS — **un·eas·i·ly** \-zə-lē\ *adv* — **un·eas·i·ness** \-zē-nəs\ *n*

un·ed·u·cat·ed \ˌən-'ej-ə-ˌkāt-əd\ *adj* : not educated

un·em·ployed \ˌən-im-'plȯid\ *adj* : not employed : having no job

un·em·ploy·ment \ˌən-im-'plȯi-mənt\ *n* : the state of being unemployed

un·end·ing \ˌən-'en-ding\ *adj* : having no ending : ENDLESS — **un·end·ing·ly** *adv*

un·equal \ˌən-'ē-kwəl\ *adj* **1** : not alike (as in size or value) **2** : badly balanced or matched ⟨an *unequal* fight⟩ **3** : not having the needed abilities ⟨proved *unequal* to the task⟩ — **un·equal·ly** *adv*

un·equaled \ˌən-'ē-kwəld\ *adj* : not equaled

un·even \ˌən-'ē-vən\ *adj* **1** : ODD **2** ⟨*uneven* numbers⟩ **2** : not level or smooth ⟨an *uneven* surface⟩ **3** : IRREGULAR 3 ⟨*uneven* teeth⟩ **4** : varying in quality ⟨an *uneven* performance⟩ **5** : UNEQUAL 2 — **un·even·ly** *adv* — **un·even·ness** *n*

un·event·ful \ˌən-i-'vent-fəl\ *adj* : noteventful : including no interesting or important happenings ⟨an *uneventful* vacation⟩ — **un·event·ful·ly** \-fə-lē\ *adv*

un·ex·pect·ed \ˌən-ik-'spek-təd\ *adj* : not expected ⟨an *unexpected* visit⟩ — **un·expect·ed·ly** *adv* — **un·ex·pect·ed·ness** *n*

un·fail·ing \ˌən-'fā-ling\ *adj* : not failing or likely to fail — **un·fail·ing·ly** *adv*

un·fair \ˌən-'faər, -'feər\ *adj* : not fair, honest, or just — **un·fair·ly** *adv* — **un·fair·ness** *n*

un·faith·ful \ˌən-'fāth-fəl\ *adj* : not faithful : DISLOYAL — **un·faith·ful·ly** \-fə-lē\ *adv* — **un·faith·ful·ness** *n*

un·fa·mil·iar \ˌən-fə-'mil-yər\ *adj* **1** : not well known : STRANGE ⟨look up *unfamiliar* words in your dictionary⟩ **2** : not well acquainted ⟨I'm *unfamiliar* with this word⟩

un·fa·mil·iar·i·ty \ˌən-fə-ˌmil-'yar-ət-ē\ *n* : the quality or state of being unfamiliar

un·fas·ten \ˌən-'fas-n\ *vb* : to make or become loose : UNDO

un·fa·vor·able \ˌən-'fā-və-rə-bəl\ *adj* **1** : not approving **2** : likely to make difficult or unpleasant ⟨*unfavorable* weather for a camping trip⟩ — **un·fa·vor·ably** \-blē\ *adv*

un·feel·ing \ˌən-'fē-ling\ *adj* **1** : not able to feel ⟨the *unfeeling* sky⟩ **2** : having no kindness or sympathy : CRUEL — **un·feel·ing·ly** *adv*

un·fin·ished \ˌən-'fin-isht\ *adj* : not finished

un·fit \ˌən-'fit\ *adj* **1** : not suitable ⟨*unfit* to eat⟩ **2** : not qualified **3** : UNSOUND 1, 2 ⟨feeling very *unfit*⟩ — **un·fit·ness** *n*

un·fledged \ˌən-'flejd\ *adj* : not feathered or ready for flight ⟨a nest of *unfledged* robins⟩

un·fold \ˌən-'fōld\ *vb* **1** : to open the folds of : open up **2** : to lay open to view : REVEAL ⟨*unfold* a plan⟩ **3** : to develop gradually

un·fore·seen \ˌən-fōr-'sēn\ *adj* : not known beforehand

un·for·get·ta·ble \ˌən-fər-'get-ə-bəl\ *adj* : not likely to be forgotten ⟨an *unforgettable* experience⟩ — **un·for·get·ta·bly** \-blē\ *adv*

un·for·giv·able \ˌən-fər-'giv-ə-bəl\ *adj* : not to be forgiven or pardoned — **un·forgiv·ably** \-blē\ *adv*

¹un·for·tu·nate \ˌən-'fȯr-chə-nət\ *adj* **1** : not fortunate : UNLUCKY **2** : not proper or suitable ⟨an *unfortunate* remark⟩ **synonyms** see UNLUCKY — **un·for·tu·nate·ly** *adv*

²unfortunate *n* : an unfortunate person

un·found·ed \ˌən-'faun-dəd\ *adj* : being without a sound basis

un·friend·ly \ˌən-'frend-lē\ *adj* **un·friend·li·er; un·friend·li·est** : not friendly or favorable : HOSTILE — **un·friend·li·ness** *n*

un·fruit·ful \ˌən-'früt-fəl\ *adj* **1** : not bearing fruit or offspring **2** : not producing a desired result ⟨*unfruitful* efforts⟩

un·furl \ˌən-'fərl\ *vb* : to open out from a rolled or folded state ⟨*unfurl* a flag⟩

un·fur·nished \ˌən-'fər-nisht\ *adj* : not supplied with furniture ⟨an *unfurnished* apartment⟩

un·gain·ly \ˌən-'gān-lē\ *adj* **un·gain·li·er; un·gain·li·est** : CLUMSY 1, AWKWARD ⟨an *ungainly* walk⟩ — **un·gain·li·ness** *n*

un·god·ly \ˌən-'gäd-lē\ *adj* **un·god·li·er; un·god·li·est 1** : disobedient to or denying God : IMPIOUS **2** : SINFUL, WICKED **3** : not normal or bearable ⟨got up at an *ungodly* hour⟩

un·gra·cious \ˌən-'grā-shəs\ *adj* : not gracious or polite — **un·gra·cious·ly** *adv*

un·grate·ful \ˌən-'grāt-fəl\ *adj* : not grateful — **un·grate·ful·ly** \-fə-lē\ *adv* — **un·grate·ful·ness** *n*

¹un·gu·late \'əng-gyə-lət\ *adj* : having hooves ⟨horses and cows are *ungulate* animals⟩

²ungulate *n* : a hoofed animal

un·hand \ˌən-'hand\ *vb* : to remove the hand from : let go

un·hap·py \ˌən-'hap-ē\ *adj* **un·hap·pi·er; un·hap·pi·est 1** : not fortunate : UNLUCKY **2** : not cheerful : SAD **3** : not suitable — **un·hap·pi·ly** \-'hap-ə-lē\ *adv* — **un·hap·pi·ness** \-'hap-ē-nəs\ *n*

un·health·ful \ˌən-'helth-fəl\ *adj* : not healthful

un·healthy \ˌən-'hel-thē\ *adj* **un·health·i·er; un·health·i·est 1** : not good for one's health ⟨an *unhealthy* climate⟩ **2** : not in good health : SICKLY **3** : HARMFUL, BAD ⟨an *unhealthy* situation⟩ — **un·health·i·ly** \-thə-lē\ *adv*

un·heard \ˌən-'hərd\ *adj* : not heard

un·heard–of \ˌən-'hərd-ˌəv, -ˌäv\ *adj* : not known before

un·hin·dered \ˌən-'hin-dərd\ *adj* : not hindered : not kept back ⟨*unhindered* progress⟩

un·hitch \ˌən-'hich\ *vb* : to free from being hitched

un·ho·ly \ˌən-'hō-lē\ *adj* **un·ho·li·er; un·ho·li·est 1** : not holy : WICKED **2** : UNGODLY **3** ⟨stop that *unholy* racket⟩ — **un·ho·li·ness** *n*

un·hook \ˌən-'hùk\ *vb* **1** : to remove from a hook **2** : to unfasten the hooks of

un·horse \ˌən-'hòrs\ *vb* **un·horsed; un·hors·ing** : to cause to fall from or as if from a horse

un·hur·ried \ˌən-'hər-ēd\ *adj* : not hurried

uni- \'yü-ni\ *prefix* : one : single

uni·corn \'yü-nə-ˌkȯrn\ *n* : an imaginary animal that looks like a horse with one horn in the middle of the forehead

unicorn

un·iden·ti·fied \ˌən-ī-'dent-ə-ˌfīd\ *adj* : not identified

uni·fi·ca·tion \ˌyü-nə-fə-'kā-shən\ *n* : the act, process, or result of unifying : the state of being unified

¹uni·form \'yü-nə-ˌfòrm\ *adj* **1** : having always the same form, manner, or degree : not changing **2** : of the same form with others ⟨hats of *uniform* style⟩ — **uni·form·ly** *adv*

²uniform *n* : special clothing worn by members of a particular group (as an army)

uni·formed \'yü-nə-ˌfòrmd\ *adj* : dressed in uniform

uni·for·mi·ty \ˌyü-nə-'fòr-mət-ē\ *n, pl* **uni·for·mi·ties** : the quality or state or an instance of being uniform

uni·fy \'yü-nə-ˌfī\ *vb* **uni·fied; uni·fy·ing** : to make into or become a unit : UNITE

un·im·por·tant \ˌən-im-'pòrt-nt\ *adj* : not important

un·in·hab·it·ed \ˌən-in-'hab-ət-əd\ *adj* : not lived in or on ⟨an *uninhabited* island⟩

un·in·tel·li·gi·ble \ˌən-in-'tel-ə-jə-bəl\ *adj* : impossible to understand

un·in·ten·tion·al \ˌən-in-'ten-chən-l\ *adj* : not intentional — **un·in·ten·tion·al·ly** *adv*

un·in·ter·est·ed \ˌən-'in-trəs-təd, -'int-ə-rəs-\ *adj* : not interested

un·in·ter·est·ing \ˌən-'in-trəs-ting, -'int-ə-rəs-\ *adj* : not attracting interest or attention

un·in·ter·rupt·ed \'ən-ˌint-ə-'rəp-təd\ *adj* : not interrupted : CONTINUOUS

union \'yün-yən\ *n* **1** : an act or instance of uniting two or more things into one **2** : something (as a nation) formed by a combining of parts or members **3** : a device for connecting parts (as of a machine) **4** : LABOR UNION

Union *adj* : of or relating to the side favoring the federal union in the American Civil War

unique \yu-'nēk\ *adj* **1** : being the only one of its kind **2** : very unusual — **unique·ly** *adv* — **unique·ness** *n*

uni·son \'yü-nə-sən\ *n* **1** : sameness of musical pitch **2** : the state of being tuned or sounded at the same pitch or at an octave **3** : exact agreement

unit \'yü-nət\ *n* **1** : the least whole number : ONE **2** : a fixed quantity (as of length, time, or value) used as a standard of measurement **3** : a single thing, person, or group forming part of a whole **4** : a part of a school course with a central theme

unite \yu-'nīt\ *vb* **unit·ed; unit·ing 1** : to put or come together to form a single unit **2** : to bind by legal or moral ties ⟨nations *united* by a treaty⟩ **3** : to join in action ⟨the two groups *united* to fight for better schools⟩

unit·ed \yu-'nīt-əd\ *adj* **1** : made one ⟨*United* States of America⟩ **2** : being in agreement

uni·ty \'yü-nət-ē\ *n* **1** : the quality or state of being one **2** : the state of those who are in full agreement : HARMONY ⟨live in *unity* with one another⟩

uni·ver·sal \ˌyü-nə-'vər-səl\ *adj* **1** : including, covering, or taking in all or everything **2** : present or happening everywhere — **uni·ver·sal·ly** *adv*

uni·verse \'yü-nə-ˌvərs\ *n* : all created things including the earth and celestial bodies viewed as making up one system

uni·ver·si·ty \ˌyü-nə-'vər-sət-ē\ *n, pl* **uni·ver·si·ties** : an institution of higher learning that gives degrees in special fields (as law and medicine) as well as in the arts and sciences

un·just \ˌən-'jəst\ *adj* : not just : UNFAIR ⟨an *unjust* decision⟩ — **un·just·ly** *adv*

un·kempt \ˌən-'kempt\ *adj* **1** : not combed ⟨*unkempt* hair⟩ **2** : not neat and orderly : UNTIDY

un·kind \ˌən-ˈkīnd\ *adj* : not kind or sympathetic ⟨an *unkind* remark⟩ — **un·kind·ly** *adv* — **un·kind·ness** *n*

¹un·known \ˌən-ˈnōn\ *adj* : not known ⟨*unknown* lands⟩

²unknown *n* : one (as a quantity) that is unknown

un·lace \ˌən-ˈlās\ *vb* **un·laced; un·lac·ing** : to untie the laces of ⟨*unlace* a shoe⟩

un·latch \ˌən-ˈlach\ *vb* : to open by lifting a latch

un·law·ful \ˌən-ˈlò-fəl\ *adj* : not lawful : ILLEGAL — **un·law·ful·ly** \-fə-lē\ *adv*

un·learned *adj* **1** \ˌən-ˈlər-nəd\ : not educated **2** \-ˈlərnd\ : not based on experience : INSTINCTIVE

un·leash \ˌən-ˈlēsh\ *vb* : to free from or as if from a leash ⟨a storm *unleashed* its fury⟩

un·less \ən-ˌles\ *conj* : except on the condition that ⟨you can't have dessert *unless* you finish your dinner⟩

¹un·like \ˌən-ˈlīk\ *prep* **1** : different from ⟨you are *unlike* the rest⟩ **2** : unusual for ⟨it's *unlike* them to be so late⟩ **3** : differently from ⟨I behave *unlike* the others⟩

²unlike *adj* : DIFFERENT, UNEQUAL — **un·like·ness** *n*

un·like·ly \ən-ˈlī-klē\ *adj* **un·like·li·er; un·like·li·est 1** : not likely ⟨an *unlikely* story⟩ **2** : not promising ⟨an *unlikely* place for fishing⟩ — **un·like·li·ness** *n*

un·lim·it·ed \ˌən-ˈlim-ət-əd\ *adj* **1** : having no restrictions or controls ⟨*unlimited* freedom⟩ **2** : BOUNDLESS, INFINITE

un·load \ˌən-ˈlōd\ *vb* **1** : to take away or off : REMOVE ⟨*unload* cargo⟩ **2** : to take a load from ⟨*unload* a ship⟩ **3** : to get rid of or be freed from a load or burden ⟨the ship is *unloading*⟩

un·lock \ˌən-ˈläk\ *vb* **1** : to unfasten the lock of **2** : to make known ⟨scientists *unlocking* the secrets of nature⟩

un·looked–for \ˌən-ˈlükt-ˌfór\ *adj* : not expected ⟨an *unlooked-for* treat⟩

un·loose \ˌən-ˈlüs\ *vb* **un·loosed; un·loos·ing 1** : to make looser : RELAX ⟨*unloose* one's grip on a rope⟩ **2** : to set free

un·lucky \ˌən-ˈlək-ē\ *adj* **un·luck·i·er; un·luck·i·est 1** : not fortunate **2** : likely to bring misfortune **3** : causing distress or regret — **un·luck·i·ly** \-ˈlək-ə-lē\ *adv* — **un·luck·i·ness** \-ˈlək-ē-nəs\ *n*

un·man·age·able \ˌən-ˈman-ij-ə-bəl\ *adj* : hard or impossible to manage

un·man·ner·ly \ˌən-ˈman-ər-lē\ *adj* : not having or showing good manners

un·mar·ried \ˌən-ˈmar-ēd\ *adj* : not married

un·mis·tak·able \ˌən-mə-ˈstā-kə-bəl\ *adj* : impossible to mistake for anything else — **un·mis·tak·ably** \-blē\ *adv*

un·moved \ˌən-ˈmüvd\ *adj* **1** : not moved by deep feelings or excitement : CALM **2** : staying in the same place or position

un·nat·u·ral \ˌən-ˈnach-ə-rəl, -ˈnach-rəl\ *adj* **1** : not natural or normal **2** : ARTIFICIAL **3** — **un·nat·u·ral·ly** *adv* — **un·nat·u·ral·ness** *n*

un·nec·es·sary \ˌən-ˈnes-ə-ˌser-ē\ *adj* : not necessary — **un·nec·es·sar·i·ly** \ˈən-ˌnes-ə-ˈser-ə-lē\ *adv*

un·nerve \ˌən-ˈnərv\ *vb* **un·nerved; un·nerv·ing** : to cause to lose confidence, courage, or self-control

un·no·tice·able \ˌən-ˈnōt-ə-sə-bəl\ *adj* : not easily noticed

un·num·bered \ˌən-ˈnəm-bərd\ *adj* **1** : not numbered ⟨an *unnumbered* page⟩ **2** : INNUMERABLE

un·ob·served \ˌən-əb-ˈzərvd\ *adj* : not observed

un·oc·cu·pied \ˌən-ˈäk-yə-ˌpīd\ *adj* **1** : not busy **2** : not occupied : EMPTY

un·of·fi·cial \ˌən-ə-ˈfish-əl\ *adj* : not official — **un·of·fi·cial·ly** *adv*

un·pack \ˌən-ˈpak\ *vb* **1** : to separate and remove things that are packed **2** : to open and remove the contents of ⟨*unpack* a suitcase⟩

un·paid \ˌən-ˈpād\ *adj* : not paid

un·paint·ed \ˌən-ˈpānt-əd\ *adj* : not painted

un·par·al·leled \ˌən-ˈpar-ə-ˌleld\ *adj* : having no parallel or equal

un·pleas·ant \ˌən-ˈplez-nt\ *adj* : not pleasant — **un·pleas·ant·ly** *adv* — **un·pleas·ant·ness** *n*

un·pop·u·lar \ˌən-ˈpäp-yə-lər\ *adj* : not popular

un·pre·dict·able \ˌən-pri-ˈdik-tə-bəl\ *adj* : impossible to predict ⟨*unpredictable* hazards of travel⟩

\ə\ **abut**	\aú\ **out**	\i\ **tip**	\ò\ **saw**	\ú\ **foot**
\ər\ **further**	\ch\ **chin**	\ī\ **life**	\òi\ **coin**	\y\ **yet**
\a\ **mat**	\e\ **pet**	\j\ **job**	\th\ **thin**	\yü\ **few**
\ā\ **take**	\ē\ **easy**	\ng\ **sing**	\th\ **this**	\yú\ **cure**
\ä\ **cot, cart**	\g\ **go**	\ō\ **bone**	\ü\ **food**	\zh\ **vision**

un·prej·u·diced \ˌən-ˈprej-ə-dəst\ *adj* : not prejudiced

un·pre·pared \ˌən-pri-ˈpaərd, -ˈpeərd\ *adj* : not prepared

un·prin·ci·pled \ˌən-ˈprin-sə-pəld\ *adj* : not having or showing high moral principles ⟨*unprincipled* behavior⟩

un·ques·tion·able \ˌən-ˈkwes-chə-nə-bəl\ *adj* : being beyond question or doubt — **un·ques·tion·ably** \-blē\ *adv*

un·rav·el \ˌən-ˈrav-əl\ *vb* **un·rav·eled** *or* **un·rav·elled; un·rav·el·ing** *or* **un·rav·el·ling** 1 : to separate the threads of : UNTANGLE 2 : SOLVE ⟨*unravel* a mystery⟩

un·re·al \ˌən-ˈrē-əl\ *adj* : not real

un·rea·son·able \ˌən-ˈrēz-n-ə-bəl\ *adj* : not reasonable ⟨*unreasonable* behavior⟩ ⟨*unreasonable* prices⟩ — **un·rea·son·able·ness** *n* — **un·rea·son·ably** \-blē\ *adv*

un·re·lent·ing \ˌən-ri-ˈlent-ing\ *adj* 1 : not giving in or softening in determination : STERN 2 : not letting up or weakening in energy or pace — **un·re·lent·ing·ly** *adv*

un·re·li·able \ˌən-ri-ˈlī-ə-bəl\ *adj* : not reliable

un·rest \ˌən-ˈrest\ *n* : a disturbed or uneasy state ⟨political *unrest*⟩

un·righ·teous \ˌən-ˈrī-chəs\ *adj* : not righteous — **un·righ·teous·ly** *adv* — **un·righ·teous·ness** *n*

un·ripe \ˌən-ˈrīp\ *adj* : not ripe or mature

un·ri·valed *or* **un·ri·valled** \ˌən-ˈrī-vəld\ *adj* : having no rival

un·roll \ˌən-ˈrōl\ *vb* 1 : to unwind a roll of 2 : to become unrolled

un·ruf·fled \ˌən-ˈrəf-əld\ *adj* 1 : not upset or disturbed 2 : ¹SMOOTH 4 ⟨*unruffled* water⟩

un·ruly \ˌən-ˈrü-lē\ *adj* **un·rul·i·er; un·rul·i·est** : not yielding easily to rule or restriction — **un·rul·i·ness** *n*

un·safe \ˌən-ˈsāf\ *adj* : exposed or exposing to danger ⟨people are *unsafe* on the streets⟩ ⟨the bridge is *unsafe* for heavy trucks⟩

un·san·i·tary \ˌən-ˈsan-ə-ˌter-ē\ *adj* : not sanitary

un·sat·is·fac·to·ry \ˈən-ˌsat-əs-ˈfak-tə-rē\ *adj* : not satisfactory — **un·sat·is·fac·to·ri·ly** \-rə-lē\ *adv*

un·sat·is·fied \ˌən-ˈsat-əs-ˌfid\ *adj* : not satisfied

un·say \ˌən-ˈsā\ *vb* **un·said** \-ˈsed\; **un·say·ing** \-ˈsā-ing\ : to take back (something said)

un·schooled \ˌən-ˈsküld\ *adj* : not trained or taught

un·sci·en·tif·ic \ˈən-ˌsī-ən-ˈtif-ik\ *adj* : not scientific — **un·sci·en·tif·i·cal·ly** \-i-kə-lē\ *adv*

un·scram·ble \ˌən-ˈskram-bəl\ *vb* **un·scram·bled; un·scram·bling** : to make orderly or clear again ⟨*unscramble* a mix-up about seating⟩ ⟨*unscramble* a radio message⟩

un·screw \ˌən-ˈskrü\ *vb* 1 : to remove the screws from 2 : to loosen or withdraw by turning ⟨*unscrew* a light bulb⟩

un·scru·pu·lous \ˌən-ˈskrü-pyə-ləs\ *adj* : not scrupulous — **un·scru·pu·lous·ly** *adv*

un·seal \ˌən-ˈsēl\ *vb* : to break or remove the seal of : OPEN

un·sea·son·able \ˌən-ˈsēz-n-ə-bəl\ *adj* : happening or coming at the wrong time ⟨*unseasonable* weather⟩ — **un·sea·son·ably** \-blē\ *adv*

un·sea·soned \ˌən-ˈsēz-nd\ *adj* : not made ready or fit for use (as by the passage of time) ⟨*unseasoned* lumber⟩

un·seat \ˌən-ˈsēt\ *vb* 1 : to throw from one's seat 2 : to remove from a position of authority

un·seem·ly \ˌən-ˈsēm-lē\ *adj* **un·seem·li·er; un·seem·li·est** : not polite or proper

un·seen \ˌən-ˈsēn\ *adj* : not seen : INVISIBLE

un·self·ish \ˌən-ˈsel-fish\ *adj* : not selfish — **un·self·ish·ly** *adv* — **un·self·ish·ness** *n*

un·set·tle \ˌən-ˈset-l\ *vb* **un·set·tled; un·set·tling** : to disturb the quiet or order of : UPSET ⟨heavy food *unsettles* my stomach⟩ ⟨social changes that *unsettle* old beliefs⟩

un·set·tled \ˌən-ˈset-ld\ *adj* 1 : not staying the same ⟨*unsettled* weather⟩ 2 : not calm ⟨*unsettled* waters⟩ 3 : not able to make up one's mind : DOUBTFUL 4 : not paid ⟨an *unsettled* account⟩ 5 : not taken over and lived in by settlers

un·shaped \ˌən-ˈshāpt\ *adj* : imperfect especially in form ⟨*unshaped* ideas⟩

un·sheathe \ˌən-ˈshēth\ *vb* **un·sheathed; un·sheath·ing** : to draw from or as if from a sheath

un·sight·ly \ˌən-ˈsīt-lē\ *adj* : not pleasant to look at : UGLY — **un·sight·li·ness** *n*

un·skilled \ˌən-ˈskild\ *adj* 1 : not skilled 2 : not needing skill ⟨*unskilled* jobs⟩

un·skill·ful \ˌən-ˈskil-fəl\ *adj* : not skillful : not having skill — **un·skill·ful·ly** \-fə-lē\ *adv*

un·sound \ˌən-ˈsaúnd\ *adj* 1 : not healthy or in good condition 2 : being or having a mind that is not normal 3 : not firmly made or placed 4 : not fitting or true ⟨*unsound* argument⟩ — **un·sound·ly** *adv* — **un·sound·ness** *n*

un·speak·able \ˌən-'spē-kə-bəl\ *adj* **1** : impossible to express in words ⟨*unspeakable* beauty⟩ **2** : extremely bad ⟨*unspeakable* conduct⟩ — **un·speak·ably** \-blē\ *adv*

un·spec·i·fied \ˌən-'spes-ə-ˌfīd\ *adj* : not specified

un·spoiled \ˌən-'spȯild\ *adj* : not spoiled

un·sta·ble \ˌən-'stā-bəl\ *adj* : not stable ⟨an *unstable* boat⟩ ⟨*unstable* prices⟩

un·steady \ˌən-'sted-ē\ *adj* **un·stead·i·er; un·stead·i·est** : not steady : UNSTABLE — **un·stead·i·ly** \-'sted-l-ē\ *adv*

un·stressed \ˌən-'strest\ *adj* : not stressed ⟨*unstressed* syllables⟩

un·suc·cess·ful \ˌən-sək-'ses-fəl\ *adj* : not successful — **un·suc·cess·ful·ly** \-fə-lē\ *adv*

un·sup·port·ed \ˌən-sə-'pōrt-əd\ *adj* **1** : not supported or proved ⟨*unsupported* claims⟩ **2** : not held up ⟨the roof is *unsupported* in places⟩

un·sur·passed \ˌən-sər-'past\ *adj* : not surpassed (as in excellence)

un·sus·pect·ing \ˌən-sə-'spek-ting\ *adj* : having no suspicion : TRUSTING

un·tan·gle \ˌən-'tang-gəl\ *vb* **un·tan·gled; un·tan·gling** **1** : to remove a tangle from **2** : to straighten out ⟨*untangle* a problem⟩

un·tanned \ˌən-'tand\ *adj* : not put through a tanning process

un·think·able \ˌən-'thing-kə-bəl\ *adj* : not to be thought of or considered as possible

un·think·ing \ˌən-'thing-king\ *adj* : not taking thought : HEEDLESS ⟨*unthinking* neglect⟩

un·ti·dy \ˌən-'tīd-ē\ *adj* **un·ti·di·er; un·ti·di·est** : not neat — **un·ti·di·ly** \-'tīd-l-ē\ *adv* — **un·ti·di·ness** \-'tīd-ē-nəs\ *n*

un·tie \ˌən-'tī\ *vb* **un·tied; un·ty·ing** *or* **un·tie·ing** : to free from something that ties, fastens, or holds back ⟨*untie* a package⟩

¹**un·til** \ən-ˌtil\ *prep* : up to the time of ⟨worked *until* noon⟩

²**until** *conj* : up to the time that ⟨wait *until* I call⟩

¹**un·time·ly** \ˌən-'tīm-lē\ *adv* : before a good or proper time

²**untimely** *adj* **1** : happening or done before the expected, natural, or proper time ⟨came to an *untimely* end⟩ **2** : coming at the wrong time ⟨an *untimely* joke⟩ — **un·time·li·ness** *n*

un·tir·ing \ˌən-'tī-ring\ *adj* : not making or becoming tired : TIRELESS — **un·tir·ing·ly** *adv*

un·to \ˌən-tə, 'ən-tü\ *prep* : ¹TO

un·told \ˌən-'tōld\ *adj* **1** : not told or made

public ⟨*untold* secrets⟩ **2** : not counted : VAST ⟨*untold* resources⟩

un·to·ward \ˌən-'tō-ərd\ *adj* : causing trouble or unhappiness : UNLUCKY ⟨an *untoward* accident⟩

un·trou·bled \ˌən-'trəb-əld\ *adj* : not troubled : free from worry

un·true \ˌən-'trü\ *adj* **1** : not faithful : DISLOYAL **2** : not correct : FALSE — **un·tru·ly** *adv*

un·truth \ˌən-'trüth\ *n* **1** : the state of being false **2** : ³LIE

un·truth·ful \ˌən-'trüth-fəl\ *adj* : not containing or telling the truth : FALSE — **un·truth·ful·ly** \-fə-lē\ *adv* — **un·truth·ful·ness** *n*

un·used \ˌən-'yüzd, *1 often* -'yüst *before* "to"\ *adj* **1** : not accustomed **2** : not having been used before ⟨fresh *unused* linen⟩ **3** : not being used ⟨an *unused* chair⟩

un·usu·al \ˌən-'yü-zhə-wəl\ *adj* : not usual — **un·usu·al·ly** *adv*

un·ut·ter·able \ˌən-'ət-ə-rə-bəl\ *adj* : being beyond one's powers of description ⟨*unutterable* horrors⟩

un·veil \ˌən-'vāl\ *vb* : to show or make known to the public for the first time ⟨*unveil* a statue⟩ ⟨*unveiled* a new plan for the city⟩

un·voiced \ˌən-'vȯist\ *adj* : VOICELESS

un·want·ed \ˌən-'wȯnt-əd\ *adj* : not wanted

un·wary \ˌən-'waər-ē, -'weər-ē\ *adj* **un·war·i·er; un·war·i·est** : easily fooled or surprised — **un·war·i·ness** *n*

un·washed \ˌən-'wȯsht, -'wäsht\ *adj* : not having been washed : DIRTY

un·wea·ried \ˌən-'wiər-ēd\ *adj* : not tired

un·well \ˌən-'wel\ *adj* : being in poor health

un·whole·some \ˌən-'hōl-səm\ *adj* : not good for bodily, mental, or moral health

un·wieldy \ˌən-'wēl-dē\ *adj* : hard to handle or control because of size or weight — **un·wield·i·ness** *n*

un·will·ing \ˌən-'wil-ing\ *adj* : not willing — **un·will·ing·ly** *adv* — **un·will·ing·ness** *n*

un·wind \ˌən-'wīnd\ *vb* **un·wound** \-'waünd\; **un·wind·ing** **1** : UNROLL ⟨*unwind* yarn from a ball⟩ ⟨the fishing line *unwound* from the reel⟩ **2** : RELAX **3** ⟨*unwind* after a hard day at the office⟩

un·wise \ˌən-'wīz\ *adj* : not wise : FOOLISH — **un·wise·ly** *adv*

un·wor·thy \ˌən-'wər-thē\ *adj* **un·wor·thi·er; un·wor·thi·est** : not worthy — **un-**

\ə\ abut	\aü\ out	\i\ tip	\ȯ\ saw	\ü\ foot
\ər\ further	\ch\ chin	\ī\ life	\ȯi\ coin	\y\ yet
\a\ mat	\e\ pet	\j\ job	\th\ thin	\yü\ few
\ā\ take	\ē\ easy	\ng\ sing	\th\ this	\yü\ cure
\ä\ cot, cart	\g\ go	\ō\ bone	\ü\ food	\zh\ vision

wor·thi·ly \-thə-lē\ *adv* — **un·wor·thi·ness** \-thē-nəs\ *n*

un·wrap \ˌən-'rap\ *vb* **un·wrapped; un·wrap·ping** : to remove the wrapping from

un·writ·ten \ˌən-'rit-n\ *adj* : not in writing : followed by custom 〈*unwritten* law〉

un·yield·ing \ˌən-'yēl-ding\ *adj* **1** : not soft or flexible : HARD **2** : showing or having firmness or determination

¹up \'əp\ *adv* **1** : in or to a higher position : away from the center of the earth **2** : from beneath a surface (as ground or water) 〈come *up* for air〉 **3** : from below the horizon 〈the sun came *up*〉 **4** : in or into a vertical position 〈stand *up*〉 **5** : out of bed **6** : with greater force 〈speak *up*〉 **7** : in or into a better or more advanced state 〈bring *up* a child〉 **8** : so as to make more active 〈stir *up* a fire〉 **9** : into being or knowledge 〈the missing ring turned *up*〉 **10** : for discussion 〈brought *up* the matter of taxes〉 **11** : into the hands of another 〈gave myself *up*〉 **12** : COMPLETELY 〈use it *up*〉 **13** — used to show completeness 〈fill *up* the gas tank〉 **14** : into storage 〈lay *up* supplies〉 **15** : so as to be closed 〈seal *up* the package〉 **16** : so as to approach or arrive 〈walked *up* and said "hello"〉 **17** : in or into pieces 〈tore it *up*〉 **18** : to a stop 〈pull *up* at the curb〉

²up *adj* **1** : risen above the horizon or ground 〈the sun is *up*〉 **2** : being out of bed **3** : unusually high 〈prices are *up*〉 **4** : having been raised or built 〈the windows are *up*〉 〈the house is *up*〉 **5** : moving or going upward 〈an *up* elevator〉 **6** : being on one's feet and busy 〈likes to be *up* and doing〉 **7** : well prepared 〈the team was *up* for the game〉 〈we were all *up* for the test〉 **8** : going on 〈find out what's *up*〉 **9** : at an end 〈time is *up*〉 **10** : well informed 〈*up* on the latest news〉

³up *vb* **upped; up·ping 1** : to act suddenly or surprisingly 〈*upped* and left home〉 **2** : to make or become higher 〈*upped* prices by 10 percent〉

⁴up *prep* **1** : to, toward, or at a higher point of 〈*up* a ladder〉 **2** : to or toward the beginning of 〈*up* a river〉 **3** : ¹ALONG 1 〈walk *up* the street〉

⁵up *n* : a period or state of doing well 〈you've had your *ups* and downs〉

up·beat \'əp-ˌbēt\ *n* : a beat in music that is not accented and especially one just before a downbeat

up·braid \ˌəp-'brād\ *vb* : to criticize or scold severely

up·bring·ing \'əp-ˌbring-ing\ *n* : the process of raising and training

up·com·ing \ˌəp-ˌkəm-ing\ *adj* : coming soon

up·draft \'əp-ˌdraft\ *n* : an upward movement of gas (as air)

up·end \ˌəp-'end\ *vb* : to set, stand, or rise on end

up·grade \'əp-ˌgrād\ *vb* **up·grad·ed; up·grad·ing** : to raise to a higher grade or position

up·heav·al \ˌəp-'hē-vəl\ *n* : a period of great change or violent disorder

¹up·hill \'əp-'hil\ *adv* **1** : in an upward direction **2** : against difficulties

²up·hill \'əp-'hil\ *adj* **1** : going up 〈an *uphill* trail〉 **2** : DIFFICULT 1 〈an *uphill* battle〉

up·hold \ˌəp-'hōld\ *vb* **up·held** \-'held\; **up·hold·ing 1** : to give support to 〈*upholds* the ideals of the nation〉 **2** : to lift up

up·hol·ster \ˌəp-'hōl-stər\ *vb* : to provide with or as if with upholstery — **up·hol·ster·er** *n*

up·hol·stery \ˌəp-'hōl-stə-rē\ *n, pl* **up·hol·ster·ies** : materials used to make a soft covering for a seat

Word History The word *upholstery* comes from the word *uphold*. *Uphold* means "to hold up or support." It once meant "to repair" as well. In early English a new word was formed from the word *uphold*. This word was used for a person who sold or repaired small and used goods. Such people often repaired and recovered furniture. The word for a person who sold used goods was later used for people who covered chairs, too. The word *upholstery* comes from this early English word.

up·keep \'əp-ˌkēp\ *n* : the act or cost of keeping something in good condition

up·land \'əp-lənd, -ˌland\ *n* : high land usually far from a coast or sea

¹up·lift \ˌəp-'lift\ *vb* **1** : to lift up **2** : to improve the moral, mental, or bodily condition of

²up·lift \'əp-ˌlift\ *n* : an act, process, or result of uplifting

up·on \ə-'pȯn, ə-'pän\ *prep* : ¹ON 1, 2, 3, 4, 8 〈the plate *upon* the table〉

¹up·per \'əp-ər\ *adj* **1** : higher in position or rank 〈the *upper* classes〉 **2** : farther inland 〈the *upper* Mississippi〉

²upper *n* : something (as the parts of a shoe above the sole) that is upper

upper hand *n* : ADVANTAGE 1

up·per·most \'əp-ər-ˌmōst\ *adj* **1** : farthest up **2** : being in the most important position 〈the thought is *uppermost* in my mind〉

up·raise \ˌəp-'rāz\ *vb* **up·raised; up·rais·ing** : to raise or lift up

¹up·right \'əp-ˌrīt\ *adj* **1** : VERTICAL **2** ⟨an *upright* post⟩ **2** : straight in posture **3** : having or showing high moral standards — **up·right·ly** *adv* — **up·right·ness** *n*

synonyms UPRIGHT, HONEST, and JUST mean having or showing a great concern for what is right. UPRIGHT suggests having high moral standards in all areas of life ⟨an *upright* person whose life was an example to the whole community⟩ HONEST suggests dealing with others in a fair and truthful way ⟨an *honest* merchant who wouldn't cheat anyone⟩ JUST stresses that one's fairness comes from both conscious choice and habit ⟨a *just* principal who treats all students alike⟩

²upright *n* **1** : the state of being upright **2** : something that is upright

up·rise \ˌəp-'rīz\ *vb* **up·rose** \-'rōz\; **up·ris·en** \-'riz-n\; **up·ris·ing** \-'rī-zing\ : ¹RISE 1, 2, 7

up·ris·ing \'əp-ˌrī-zing\ *n* : REBELLION

up·roar \'əp-ˌrōr\ *n* : a state of commotion, excitement, or violent disturbance

Word History The word *uproar* appears to be made up of the words *up* and *roar,* but it is not. English *uproar* first meant "revolt." It came from a Dutch word meaning "revolt." This Dutch word was formed from a word meaning "up" and a word meaning "motion." The Dutch word meaning "up" is a relative of English *up.* The Dutch word meaning "motion" is not related to English *roar.*

up·root \ˌəp-'rüt, -'rut\ *vb* **1** : to take out by or as if by pulling up by the roots **2** : to take, send, or force away from a country or a traditional home ⟨the war *uprooted* many families⟩

¹up·set \ˌəp-'set\ *vb* **up·set; up·set·ting** **1** : to force or be forced out of the usual position : OVERTURN **2** : to worry or make unhappy ⟨the bad news *upset* us all⟩ **3** : to make somewhat ill ⟨pizza *upsets* my stomach⟩ **4** : to cause confusion in ⟨rain *upset* our plans⟩ **5** : to defeat unexpectedly

²up·set \'əp-ˌset\ *n* : an act or result of upsetting : a state of being upset

up·shot \'əp-ˌshät\ *n* : the final result

up·side \'əp-ˌsīd\ *n* : the upper side or part

up·side–down \ˌəp-ˌsīd-'daun\ *adj* **1** : having the upper part underneath and the lower part on top **2** : showing great confusion

up·side down \ˌəp-ˌsīd-'daun\ *adv* **1** : with the upper part underneath and the

lower part on top **2** : in or into great confusion

¹up·stairs \'əp-'staərz, -'steərz\ *adv* : up the stairs : on or to an upper floor

²up·stairs \ˌəp-ˌstaərz, -ˌsteərz\ *adj* : being on or relating to an upper floor ⟨*upstairs* bedrooms⟩

³up·stairs \'əp-'staərz, -'steərz\ *n* : the part of a building above the ground floor

up·stand·ing \ˌəp-'stan-ding\ *adj* : HONEST 2

up·start \'əp-ˌstärt\ *n* : a person who gains quick or unexpected success and who makes a great show of pride in that success

up·stream \'əp-'strēm\ *adv* : at or toward the beginning of a stream ⟨rowed *upstream*⟩

up·swing \'əp-ˌswing\ *n* : a great increase or rise ⟨an *upswing* in business⟩

up to *prep* **1** : as far as ⟨in mud *up to* our ankles⟩ **2** : in accordance with ⟨the game was not *up to* our standards⟩ **3** : to the limit of ⟨the car holds *up to* six people⟩

up–to–date \ˌəp-tə-'dāt\ *adj* **1** : lasting up to the present time **2** : knowing, being, or making use of what is new or recent ⟨*up-to-date* information⟩

up·town \'əp-'taun\ *adv* : to, toward, or in what is thought of as the upper part of a town or city

¹up·turn \'əp-ˌtərn, ˌəp-'tərn\ *vb* : to turn upward or up or over

²up·turn \'əp-ˌtərn\ *n* : an upward turning

¹up·ward \'əp-wərd\ *or* **up·wards** \-wərdz\ *adv* **1** : in a direction from lower to higher **2** : toward a higher or better state **3** : toward a greater amount or a higher number or rate

²upward *adj* : turned toward or being in a higher place or level ⟨an *upward* gaze⟩ ⟨an *upward* movement of prices⟩ — **up·ward·ly** *adv*

up·wind \'əp-'wind\ *adv or adj* : in the direction from which the wind is blowing

ura·ni·um \yu̇-'rā-nē-əm\ *n* : a radioactive metallic chemical element used as a source of atomic energy

Ura·nus \'yu̇r-ə-nəs, yu̇-'rā-nəs\ *n* : the planet that is seventh in order of distance from the sun and has a diameter of about 47,000 kilometers

ur·ban \'ər-bən\ *adj* : of, relating to, or being a city ⟨*urban* life⟩

\ə\ **abut**	\au̇\ **out**	\i\ **tip**	\ȯ\ **saw**	\u̇\ **foot**
\ər\ **further**	\ch\ **chin**	\ī\ **life**	\ȯi\ **coin**	\y\ **yet**
\a\ **mat**	\e\ **pet**	\j\ **job**	\th\ **thin**	\yü\ **few**
\ā\ **take**	\ē\ **easy**	\ng\ **sing**	\th\ **this**	\yu̇\ **cure**
\ä\ **cot, cart**	\g\ **go**	\ō\ **bone**	\ü\ **food**	\zh\ **vision**

ur·chin \'ər-chən\ *n* **1** : a mischievous or disrespectful youngster **2** : SEA URCHIN

Word History The English word *urchin* first meant "hedgehog." Many years ago some people compared mischievous children to hedgehogs and began calling them *urchins*. The sea urchin got its name because it has spines like a hedgehog.

-ure *suffix* **1** : act : process ⟨expos*ure*⟩ **2** : office : duty **3** : body performing an office or duty ⟨legislat*ure*⟩

urea \yu̇-'rē-ə\ *n* : a compound of nitrogen that is the chief solid substance dissolved in the urine of a mammal and is formed by the breaking down of protein

¹urge \'ərj\ *vb* **urged**; **urg·ing** **1** : to try to get (something) accepted : argue in favor of ⟨*urge* a plan⟩ **2** : to try to convince ⟨*urge* a guest to stay⟩ **3** : ²FORCE 1, DRIVE ⟨the dog *urged* the sheep onward⟩

²urge *n* : a strong desire

ur·gen·cy \'ər-jən-sē\ *n* : the quality or state of being urgent

ur·gent \'ər-jənt\ *adj* **1** : calling for immediate action ⟨an *urgent* need⟩ **2** : having or showing a sense of urgency ⟨an *urgent* manner⟩ — **ur·gent·ly** *adv*

uri·nal \'yu̇r-ən-l\ *n* **1** : a container for urine **2** : a place for urinating

uri·nary \'yu̇r-ə-ˌner-ē\ *adj* : of or relating to urine or the organs producing it ⟨the *urinary* bladder⟩

uri·nate \'yu̇r-ə-ˌnāt\ *vb* **uri·nat·ed**; **uri·nat·ing** : to discharge urine

uri·na·tion \ˌyu̇r-ə-'nā-shən\ *n* : the act of urinating

urine \'yu̇r-ən\ *n* : the yellowish liquid produced by the kidneys and given off from the body as waste

urn \'ərn\ *n* **1** : a container usually in the form of a vase resting on a stand **2** : a closed container with a faucet used for serving a hot beverage ⟨coffee *urn*⟩

us \əs, 'əs\ *pron, objective case of* WE

us·able \'yü-zə-bəl\ *adj* : suitable or fit for use

us·age \'yü-sij, -zij\ *n* **1** : usual way of doing things **2** : the way in which words and phrases are actually used **3** : the action of using : USE

urn 1

¹use \'yüs\ *n* **1** : the act of using something ⟨put knowledge to *use*⟩ **2** : the fact or state of being used ⟨a book in daily *use*⟩ **3** : way of using ⟨the proper *use* of tools⟩ **4** : the ability or power to use something ⟨have the *use* of one's legs⟩ **5** : the quality or state of being useful **6** : a reason or need to use ⟨I've no *use* for it⟩ **7** : LIKING ⟨we have no *use* for such people⟩

²use \'yüz\ *vb* **used** \'yüzd, *in the phrase* "used to" *usually* 'yüst\; **us·ing** \'yü-zing\ **1** : to put into action or service : make use of ⟨*use* tools⟩ ⟨*use* good English⟩ **2** : to take into the body ⟨people who *use* drugs⟩ ⟨I don't *use* sugar in tea⟩ **3** : to do something by means of ⟨*use* care⟩ **4** : to behave toward : TREAT ⟨*used* the children kindly⟩ **5** — used with *to* to show a former custom, fact, or state ⟨said winters *used* to be harder⟩ — **us·er** *n*

used \'yüzd, *2 often* 'yüst *before* "to"\ *adj* **1** : SECONDHAND 1 ⟨bought a *used* car⟩ **2** : having the habit of doing or putting up with something ⟨*used* to flying⟩ ⟨*used* to criticism⟩

use·ful \'yüs-fəl\ *adj* : that can be put to use : USABLE ⟨*useful* scraps of material⟩ — **use·ful·ly** \-fə-lē\ *adv* — **use·ful·ness** *n*

use·less \'yü-sləs\ *adj* : being of or having no use — **use·less·ly** *adv* — **use·less·ness** *n*

¹ush·er \'əsh-ər\ *n* : a person who shows people to seats (as in a theater)

²usher *vb* **1** : to show to a place as an usher **2** : to come before as if to lead in or announce ⟨a party to *usher* in the new year⟩

usu·al \'yü-zhə-wəl\ *adj* : done, found, used or existing most of the time ⟨this is the *usual* state of the house⟩ — **usu·al·ly** *adv*

usurp \yu̇-'sərp, -'zərp\ *vb* : to take and hold unfairly or by force ⟨*usurp* power from the king⟩ — **usurp·er** *n*

uten·sil \yu̇-'ten-səl\ *n* **1** : a tool or container used in a home and especially a kitchen **2** : a useful tool **synonyms** see INSTRUMENT

uter·us \'yüt-ə-rəs\ *n, pl* **uteri** \'yüt-ə-ˌrī\ : the organ of a female mammal in which the young develop before birth

util·i·ty \yu̇-'til-ət-ē\ *n, pl* **util·i·ties** **1** : the quality or state of being useful **2** : a business that supplies a public service (as electricity or gas) under special regulation by the government

uti·li·za·tion \ˌyüt-l-ə-'zā-shən\ *n* : the action of utilizing : the state of being utilized

uti·lize \'yüt-l-ˌīz\ *vb* **uti·lized; uti·liz-ing** : to make use of especially for a certain job

¹ut·most \'ət-ˌmōst\ *adj* : of the greatest or highest degree or amount ⟨the *utmost* importance⟩

²utmost *n* : the most possible

¹ut·ter \'ət-ər\ *adj* : in every way : TOTAL

⟨*utter* nonsense⟩ ⟨*utter* strangers⟩ — **ut·ter·ly** *adv*

²utter *vb* **1** : to send forth as a sound ⟨*uttered* a short cry⟩ **2** : to express in usually spoken words ⟨*utter* an angry protest⟩

ut·ter·ance \'ət-ə-rəns\ *n* : something uttered

v \'vē\ *n, pl* **v's** *or* **vs** \'vēz\ *often cap* **1** : the twenty-second letter of the English alphabet **2** : five in Roman numerals

va·can·cy \'vā-kən-sē\ *n, pl* **va·can·cies 1** : something (as an office or hotel room) that is vacant **2** : empty space **3** : the state of being vacant

va·cant \'vā-kənt\ *adj* **1** : not filled, used, or lived in ⟨a *vacant* house⟩ **2** : free from duties or care **3** : showing a lack of thought : FOOLISH **synonyms** see EMPTY

va·cate \'vā-ˌkāt\ *vb* **va·cat·ed; va·cat·ing** : to leave vacant

¹va·ca·tion \vā-'kā-shən\ *n* **1** : a period during which activity (as of a school) is stopped for a time **2** : a period spent away from home or business in travel or amusement

²vacation *vb* : to take or spend a vacation — **va·ca·tion·er** *n*

vac·ci·nate \'vak-sə-ˌnāt\ *vb* **vac·ci·nat·ed; vac·ci·nat·ing** : to inoculate with weak germs in order to protect against a disease

vac·ci·na·tion \ˌvak-sə-'nā-shən\ *n* **1** : the act of vaccinating **2** : the scar left by vaccinating

vac·cine \vak-'sēn, 'vak-ˌsēn\ *n* : a material (as one containing killed or weakened bacteria or virus) used in vaccinating

Word History Cowpox is a disease that cows get. It is something like smallpox but much less serious. People can get cowpox, too, and if they do they will never get smallpox. An English doctor gave people shots of a substance that came from cows with cowpox. He found that this made the people immune to smallpox. The substance was named *vaccine*. This word came from a Latin word that meant "of cows." This Latin word was formed from the Latin word that meant "cow."

vac·il·late \'vas-ə-ˌlāt\ *vb* **vac·il·lat·ed; vac·il·lat·ing** : to hesitate between courses or opinions : be unable to choose

¹vac·u·um \'vak-yə-wəm, -ˌyüm\ *n, pl* **vac·u·ums** *or* **vac·ua** \-yə-wə\ **1** : a space completely empty of matter **2** : a space from which most of the air has been removed (as by a pump) **3** : VACUUM CLEANER

²vacuum *adj* : of, containing, producing, or using a partial vacuum

³vacuum *vb* : to use a vacuum cleaner on

vacuum bottle *n* : a container shaped like a cylinder that has a vacuum between an inner and an outer wall and is used to keep liquids hot or cold

vacuum cleaner *n* : an electrical appliance for cleaning (as floors or rugs) by suction

vacuum tube *n* : an electron tube having a high vacuum

¹vag·a·bond \'vag-ə-ˌbänd\ *adj* : moving from place to place without a fixed home

²vagabond *n* : a person who leads a vagabond life

va·gi·na \və-'jī-nə\ *n* : a canal leading out from the uterus

¹va·grant \'vā-grənt\ *n* : a person who has no steady job and wanders from place to place

²vagrant *adj* **1** : wandering about from place to place **2** : having no fixed course ⟨*vagrant* breezes⟩

vague \'vāg\ *adj* **vagu·er; vagu·est 1** : not clearly expressed ⟨a *vague* answer⟩ **2** : not clearly understood ⟨they knew in a *vague* way what they wanted⟩ **3** : not

\ə\ abut	\au̇\ out	\i\ tip	\ȯ\ saw	\u̇\ foot
\ər\ further	\ch\ chin	\ī\ life	\ȯi\ coin	\y\ yet
\a\ mat	\e\ pet	\j\ job	\th\ thin	\yü\ few
\ā\ take	\ē\ easy	\ng\ sing	\th\ this	\yu̇\ cure
\ä\ cot, cart	\g\ go	\ō\ bone	\ü\ food	\zh\ vision

clearly outlined : SHADOWY — **vague·ly** *adv* — **vague·ness** *n*

vain \'vān\ *adj* **1** : having no success ⟨made a *vain* effort to escape⟩ **2** : proud of one's looks or abilities — **vain·ly** *adv* — **in vain 1** : without success **2** : in an unholy way

vain·glo·ri·ous \vān-'glōr-ēəs\ *adj* : being vain and boastful — **vain·glo·ri·ous·ly** *adv* — **vain·glo·ri·ous·ness** *n*

vain·glo·ry \'vān-ˌglōr-ē\ *n* : too much pride especially in what one has done

vale \'vāl\ *n* : VALLEY

vale·dic·to·ri·an \ˌval-ə-dik-'tōr-ē-ən\ *n* : a student usually of the highest standing in a class who gives the farewell speech at the graduation ceremonies

val·en·tine \'val-ən-ˌtīn\ *n* **1** : a sweetheart given something as a sign of affection on Saint Valentine's Day **2** : a gift or greeting sent or given on Saint Valentine's Day

val·et \'val-ət, 'val-ā, va-'lā\ *n* : a male servant or hotel employee who takes care of a man's clothes and does personal services

val·iant \'val-yənt\ *adj* **1** : boldly brave **2** : done with courage : HEROIC — **val·iant·ly** *adv*

val·id \'val-əd\ *adj* **1** : legally binding **2** : based on truth or fact — **val·id·ly** *adv*

val·i·date \'val-ə-ˌdāt\ *vb* **val·i·dat·ed; val·i·dat·ing** : to make valid

va·lid·i·ty \və-'lid-ət-ē\ *n* : the quality or state of being valid

va·lise \və-'lēs\ *n* : TRAVELING BAG

val·ley \'val-ē\ *n, pl* **val·leys** : an area of lowland between ranges of hills or mountains

val·or \'val-ər\ *n* : COURAGE

val·or·ous \'val-ə-rəs\ *adj* : having or showing valor : BRAVE ⟨*valorous* knights⟩ — **val·or·ous·ly** *adv*

¹valu·able \'val-yə-wə-bəl, 'val-yə-bəl\ *adj* **1** : worth a large amount of money **2** : of great use or service

²valuable *n* : a personal possession (as a jewel) of great value

¹val·ue \'val-yü\ *n* **1** : a fair return in goods, services, or money for something exchanged **2** : worth in money **3** : worth, usefulness, or importance in comparison with something else ⟨the changing *value* of the dollar⟩ **4** : something valuable — **val·ue·less** \-ləs\ *adj*

²value *vb* **val·ued; valu·ing 1** : to estimate the worth of ⟨*valued* at two hundred dollars⟩ **2** : to think highly of ⟨I *value* your friendship⟩

valve \'valv\ *n* **1** : a structure in a tube of the body (as a vein) that closes tempo-

rarily to prevent passage of material or allows movement of a fluid in one direction only **2** : a mechanical device by which the flow of liquid, gas, or loose material may be controlled by a movable part **3** : a device on a brass musical instrument that changes the pitch of the tone **4** : one of the separate pieces that make up the shell of some animals (as clams) and are often hinged — **valve·less** \-ləs\ *adj*

vam·pire \'vam-ˌpīr\ *n* **1** : the body of a dead person believed to come from the grave at night and suck the blood of sleeping persons **2** : a bat that feeds or is said to feed on blood

¹van \'van\ *n* : VANGUARD

²van *n* : a usually closed wagon or truck for moving goods or animals

va·na·di·um \və-'nād-ē-əm\ *n* : a metallic chemical element used in making a strong alloy of steel

van·dal \'van-dəl\ *n* : a person who destroys or damages property on purpose

van·dal·ism \'van-dəl-ˌiz-əm\ *n* : intentional destruction of or damage to property

vane \'vān\ *n* **1** : a movable device attached to something high to show which way the wind blows **2** : a flat or curved surface that turns around a center when moved by wind or water

van·guard \'van-ˌgärd\ *n* **1** : the troops moving at the front of an army **2** : FOREFRONT

va·nil·la \və-'nil-ə, -'nel-\ *n* : a flavoring made from the long beanlike pods of a tropical American climbing orchid (**vanilla orchid**)

van·ish \'van-ish\ *vb* : to pass from sight or existence : DISAPPEAR

van·i·ty \'van-ət-ē\ *n, pl* **van·i·ties 1** : something that is vain **2** : the quality or fact of being vain **3** : a small box for cosmetics

van·quish \'vang-kwish\ *vb* : OVERCOME 1

va·por \'vā-pər\ *n* **1** : fine bits (as of fog or smoke) floating in the air and clouding it **2** : a substance in the form of a gas ⟨water *vapor*⟩

va·por·ize \'vā-pə-ˌrīz\ *vb* **va·por·ized; va·por·iz·ing** : to turn from a liquid or solid into vapor — **va·por·iz·er** \-ˌrī-zər\ *n*

¹vari·able \'ver-ē-ə-bəl, 'var-\ *adj* **1** : able to change : likely to be changed : CHANGEABLE **2** : having differences **3** : not true to type — **vari·able·ness** *n* — **vari·ably** \-blē\ *adv*

²variable *n* **1** : something that is variable **2** : PLACEHOLDER

vari·ant \'ver-ē-ənt, 'var-\ *n* **1** : an individual that shows variation from a type **2**

: one of two or more different spellings or pronunciations of a word

vari·a·tion \,ver-ē-'ā-shən, ,var-\ *n* **1** : a change in form, position, or condition **2** : amount of change or difference **3** : departure from what is usual to a group

var·ied \'veər-ēd, 'vaər-\ *adj* **1** : having many forms or types **2** : VARIEGATED 2

var·ie·gat·ed \'ver-ē-ə-,gāt-əd, 'ver-i-,gāt-, 'var-\ *adj* **1** : having patches, stripes, or marks of different colors **2** : full of variety

va·ri·ety \və-'rī-ət-ē\ *n, pl* **va·ri·et·ies** **1** : the quality or state of having different forms or types **2** : a collection of different things : ASSORTMENT **3** : something differing from others of the class to which it belongs **4** : entertainment made up of performances (as dances and songs) that follow one another and are not related

var·i·ous \'ver-ē-əs, 'var-\ *adj* **1** : of different kinds **2** : different one from another : UNLIKE **3** : made up of an indefinite number greater than one ⟨played *various* sports⟩

¹var·nish \'vär-nish\ *n* : a liquid that is spread on a surface and dries into a hard coating

²varnish *vb* : to cover with or as if with varnish

var·si·ty \'vär-sət-ē\ *n, pl* **var·si·ties** : the main team that represents a college, school, or club in contests

vary \'veər-ē, 'vaər-ē\ *vb* **var·ied; vary·ing** **1** : to make a partial change in **2** : to make or be of different kinds **3** : DEVIATE **4** : to differ from the usual members of a group **synonyms** see CHANGE

vas·cu·lar \'vas-kyə-lər\ *adj* : of, relating to, containing, or being bodily vessels

vase \'vās, 'vāz\ *n* : an often round container of greater depth than width used chiefly for ornament or for flowers

vas·sal \'vas-əl\ *n* : a person in the Middle Ages who received protection and land from a lord in return for loyalty and service

vast \'vast\ *adj* : very great in size or amount — **vast·ly** *adv* — **vast·ness** *n*

vat \'vat\ *n* : a large container (as a tub) especially for holding liquids in manufacturing processes

vaude·ville \'vȯd-ə-vəl, 'vȯd-vəl\ *n* : theatrical entertainment made up of songs, dances, and comic acts

¹vault \'vȯlt\ *n* **1** : an arched structure of stone or concrete forming a ceiling or roof **2** : an arch suggesting a vault **3** : a room or compartment for storage or safekeeping **4** : a burial chamber

vault 1

²vault *vb* : to leap with the aid of the hands or a pole

³vault *n* : ²LEAP

VCR \,vē-,sē-'är\ *n* : a device for recording (as television programs) on videocassettes and playing them back

veal \'vēl\ *n* : a young calf or its flesh for use as meat

vec·tor \'vek-tər\ *n* : a creature (as a fly) that carries disease germs

vee·jay \'vē-,jā\ *n* : an announcer of a program (as on television) that features music videos

veer \'viər\ *vb* : to change direction or course

vee·ry \'viər-ē\ *n, pl* **vee·ries** : a common brownish woodland thrush of the eastern United States

¹veg·e·ta·ble \'vej-tə-bəl, 'vej-ət-ə-\ *adj* **1** : of, relating to, or made up of plants **2** : gotten from plants ⟨*vegetable* dyes⟩

²vegetable *n* **1** : ²PLANT 1 **2** : a plant or plant part grown for use as human food and usually eaten with the main part of a meal

veg·e·tar·i·an \,vej-ə-'ter-ē-ən\ *n* : a person who lives on plants and their products

veg·e·ta·tion \,vej-ə-'tā-shən\ *n* : plant life or cover (as of an area)

veg·e·ta·tive \'vej-ə-,tāt-iv\ *adj* **1** : of, relating to, or functioning in nutrition and growth rather than reproduction **2** : of, relating to, or involving reproduction by other than sexual means

ve·he·mence \'vē-ə-məns\ *n* : the quality or state of being vehement

ve·he·ment \'vē-ə-mənt\ *adj* **1** : showing great force or energy **2** : highly emotional — **ve·he·ment·ly** *adv*

ve·hi·cle \'vē-,ik-əl, -,hik-\ *n* **1** : a means by which something is expressed, achieved, or shown **2** : something used to transport persons or goods

\ə\ **abut**	\au̇\ **out**	\i\ **tip**	\ȯ\ **saw**	\u̇\ **foot**
\ər\ **further**	\ch\ **chin**	\ī\ **life**	\ȯi\ **coin**	\y\ **yet**
\a\ **mat**	\e\ **pet**	\j\ **job**	\th\ **thin**	\yü\ **few**
\ā\ **take**	\ē\ **easy**	\ng\ **sing**	\th\ **this**	\yu̇\ **cure**
\ä\ **cot, cart**	\g\ **go**	\ō\ **bone**	\ü\ **food**	\zh\ **vision**

¹veil \'vāl\ *n* **1** : a piece of cloth or net worn usually by women over the head and shoulders and sometimes over the face **2** : something that covers or hides like a veil ⟨a *veil* of secrecy⟩

²veil *vb* : to cover or provide with a veil

vein \'vān\ *n* **1** : a long narrow opening in rock filled with mineral matter ⟨a *vein* of gold⟩ **2** : one of the blood vessels that carry the blood back to the heart **3** : one of the bundles of fine tubes that make up the framework of a leaf and carry food, water, and nutrients in the plant **4** : one of the thickened parts that support the wing of an insect **5** : a streak of different color or texture (as in marble) **6** : a style of expression ⟨in a witty *vein*⟩ — **veined** \'vānd\ *adj*

veld *or* **veldt** \'felt, 'velt\ *n* : an area of grassy land especially in southern Africa

ve·loc·i·ty \və-'läs-ət-ē\ *n, pl* **ve·loc·i·ties** : quickness of motion : SPEED

¹vel·vet \'vel-vət\ *n* : a fabric with short soft raised fibers

²velvet *adj* **1** : made of or covered with velvet **2** : VELVETY

vel·vety \'vel-vət-ē\ *adj* : soft and smooth like velvet

ve·na·tion \vā-'nā-shən, vē-\ *n* : an arrangement or system of veins

vend \'vend\ *vb* : to sell or offer for sale — **vend·er** *or* **ven·dor** \'ven-dər\ *n*

¹ve·neer \və-'niər\ *n* **1** : a thin layer of wood bonded to other wood usually to provide a finer surface or a stronger structure **2** : a protective or ornamental facing (as of brick)

²veneer *vb* : to cover with a veneer

ven·er·a·ble \'ven-ə-rə-bəl\ *adj* **1** : deserving to be venerated — often used as a religious title **2** : deserving honor or respect

ven·er·ate \'ven-ə-ˌrāt\ *vb* **ven·er·at·ed; ven·er·at·ing** : to show deep respect for

ven·er·a·tion \ˌven-ə-'rā-shən\ *n* **1** : the act of venerating : the state of being venerated **2** : a feeling of deep respect

ve·ne·re·al \və-'nir-ē-əl\ *adj* : of or relating to sexual intercourse or to diseases that pass from person to person by it

ve·ne·tian blind \və-ˌnē-shən-\ *n* : a blind having thin horizontal slats that can be adjusted to keep out light or to let light come in between them

ven·geance \'ven-jəns\ *n* : punishment given in return for an injury or offense

ven·i·son \'ven-ə-sən, -ə-zən\ *n* : the flesh of a deer used as food

ven·om \'ven-əm\ *n* : poisonous matter produced by an animal (as a snake) and passed to a victim usually by a bite or sting

ven·om·ous \'ven-ə-məs\ *adj* : having or producing venom : POISONOUS

ve·nous \'vē-nəs\ *adj* : of, relating to, or full of veins ⟨*venous* blood⟩

¹vent \'vent\ *vb* **1** : to provide with an outlet **2** : to serve as an outlet for **3** : ³EXPRESS 1 ⟨*vent* one's anger⟩

²vent *n* **1** : OUTLET 1, 2 **2** : an opening for the escape of a gas or liquid

ven·ti·late \'vent-l-ˌāt\ *vb* **ven·ti·lat·ed; ven·ti·lat·ing** **1** : to discuss freely and openly **2** : to let in air and especially a current of fresh air **3** : to provide with ventilation

ven·ti·la·tion \ˌvent-l-'ā-shən\ *n* **1** : the act or process of ventilating **2** : a system or means of providing fresh air

ven·ti·la·tor \'vent-l-ˌāt-ər\ *n* : a device for letting in fresh air or driving out bad or stale air

ven·tral \'ven-trəl\ *adj* : of, relating to, or being on or near the surface of the body that in man is the front but in most animals is the lower surface ⟨a fish's *ventral* fins⟩

ven·tri·cle \'ven-tri-kəl\ *n* : the part of the heart from which blood passes into the arteries

ven·tril·o·quist \ven-'tril-ə-kwəst\ *n* : a person skilled in speaking in such a way that the voice seems to come from a source other than the speaker

¹ven·ture \'ven-chər\ *vb* **ven·tured; ven·tur·ing** **1** : to expose to risk **2** : to face the risks and dangers of **3** : to offer at the risk of being criticized ⟨*venture* an opinion⟩ **4** : to go ahead in spite of danger

²venture *n* : a task or an act involving chance, risk, or danger

ven·ture·some \'ven-chər-səm\ *adj* **1** : tending to take risks **2** : involving risk **synonyms** see ADVENTUROUS — **ven·ture·some·ly** *adv* — **ven·ture·some·ness** *n*

ven·tur·ous \'ven-chə-rəs\ *adj* : VENTURESOME — **ven·tur·ous·ly** *adv* — **ven·tur·ous·ness** *n*

Ve·nus \'vē-nəs\ *n* : the planet that is second in order of distance from the sun and has a diameter of about 12,200 kilometers

ve·ran·da *or* **ve·ran·dah** \və-'ran-də\ *n* : a long porch extending along one or more sides of a building

verb \'vərb\ *n* : a word that expresses an act, occurrence, or state of being

¹ver·bal \'vər-bəl\ *adj* **1** : of, relating to, or consisting of words **2** : of, relating to, or formed from a verb ⟨a *verbal* adjective⟩ **3**

: spoken rather than written — **ver·bal·ly** *adv*

²**verbal** *n* : a word that combines characteristics of a verb with those of a noun or adjective

ver·be·na \vər-'bē-nə\ *n* : a garden plant with fragrant leaves and heads of white, pink, red, blue, or purple flowers with five petals

verbena

ver·dant \'vərd-nt\ *adj* : green with growing plants — **ver·dant·ly** *adv*

ver·dict \'vər-dikt\ *n* **1** : the decision reached by a jury **2** : JUDGMENT 2, OPINION

ver·dure \'vər-jər\ *n* : green vegetation

¹**verge** \'vərj\ *n* **1** : something that borders, limits, or bounds : EDGE **2** : THRESHOLD 2, BRINK ⟨on the *verge* of bankruptcy⟩

²**verge** *vb* **verged; verg·ing** : to come near to being ⟨this *verges* on madness⟩

ver·i·fi·ca·tion \,ver-ə-fə-'kā-shən\ *n* : the act or process of verifying : the state of being verified

ver·i·fy \'ver-ə-,fi\ *vb* **ver·i·fied; ver·i·fy·ing** **1** : to prove to be true or correct : CONFIRM **2** : to check or test the accuracy of

ver·mi·cel·li \,vər-mə-'chel-ē\ *n* : a food similar to but thinner than spaghetti

ver·min \'vər-mən\ *n, pl* **vermin** : small common harmful or objectionable animals (as fleas or mice) that are difficult to get rid of

Word History Today we use the term *vermin* for any small common animals that are harmful. Fleas and mice are likely to be called vermin. Even rabbits are called vermin when they invade our gardens. The English word *vermin* came from an early French word that meant much the same thing as today's English word. This French word came from a Latin word that was a bit more specific. The Latin word meant "worm."

ver·sa·tile \'vər-sət-l\ *adj* **1** : able to do many different kinds of things **2** : having many uses ⟨a *versatile* tool⟩

ver·sa·til·i·ty \,vər-sə-'til-ət-ē\ *n* : the quality or state of being versatile

verse \'vərs\ *n* **1** : a line of writing in which words are arranged in a rhythmic pattern **2** : writing in which words are arranged in a rhythmic pattern **3** : STANZA **4** : one of the short parts of a chapter in the Bible

versed \'vərst\ *adj* : having knowledge or skill as a result of experience, study, or practice

ver·sion \'vər-zhən\ *n* **1** : a translation especially of the Bible **2** : an account or description from a certain point of view

ver·sus \'vər-səs\ *prep* : AGAINST 1 ⟨our football team *versus* theirs⟩

ver·te·bra \'vərt-ə-brə\ *n, pl* **ver·te·brae** \-,brā, -brē\ : one of the bony sections making up the backbone

¹**ver·te·brate** \'vərt-ə-brət\ *adj* **1** : having vertebrae or a backbone **2** : of or relating to the vertebrates

²**vertebrate** *n* : any of a large group of animals that includes the fishes, amphibians, reptiles, birds, and mammals all of which have a backbone extending down the back of the body

ver·tex \'vər-,teks\ *n, pl* **ver·ti·ces** \'vərt-ə-,sēz\ *or* **ver·tex·es** **1** : the point opposite to and farthest from the base of a geometrical figure **2** : the common endpoint of the sides of an angle

vertex 2

¹**ver·ti·cal** \'vərt-i-kəl\ *adj* **1** : directly overhead **2** : rising straight up and down from a level surface — **ver·ti·cal·ly** *adv*

²**vertical** *n* : something (as a line or plane) that is vertical

ver·ti·go \'vərt-i-,gō\ *n, pl* **ver·ti·goes** *or* **ver·ti·gos** : a dizzy state

¹**very** \'ver-ē\ *adj* **1** : ²EXACT, PRECISE ⟨the *very* heart of the city⟩ **2** : exactly suitable or necessary ⟨that's the *very* thing for this job⟩ **3** : MERE, BARE ⟨the *very* thought frightened them⟩ **4** : exactly the same

²**very** *adv* **1** : to a great degree : EXTREMELY **2** : in actual fact : TRULY

ves·pers \'ves-pərz\ *n pl, often cap* : a late afternoon or evening church service

ves·sel \'ves-əl\ *n* **1** : a hollow utensil (as a cup or bowl) for holding something **2** : a craft larger than a rowboat for navigation of the water **3** : a tube (as an artery) in

\ə\ abut	\au̇\ out	\i\ tip	\ȯ\ saw	\u̇\ foot
\ər\ further	\ch\ chin	\ī\ life	\ȯi\ coin	\y\ yet
\a\ mat	\e\ pet	\j\ job	\th\ thin	\yü\ few
\ā\ take	\ē\ easy	\ng\ sing	\th\ this	\yu̇\ cure
\ä\ cot, cart	\g\ go	\ō\ bone	\ü\ food	\zh\ vision

which a body fluid is contained and carried or circulated

¹vest \'vest\ *vb* **1** : to place or give into the possession or control of some person or authority **2** : to clothe in vestments

²vest *n* : a sleeveless garment usually worn under a suit coat

ves·ti·bule \'ves-tə-,byül\ *n* : a hall or room between the outer door and the inside part of a building

ves·tige \'ves-tij\ *n* : a tiny amount or visible sign of something lost or vanished : TRACE

ves·tig·i·al \ves-'tij-ē-əl\ *adj* : of, relating to, or being a vestige

vest·ment \'vest-mənt\ *n* : an outer garment especially for wear during ceremonies or by an official

¹vet \'vet\ *n* : VETERINARIAN

²vet *n* : ¹VETERAN 2

¹vet·er·an \'vet-ə-rən, 've-trən\ *n* **1** : a person who has had long experience **2** : a former member of the armed forces especially in war

²veteran *adj* : having gained skill through experience

Veterans Day *n* : November 11 observed as a legal holiday in memory of the end of war in 1918 and 1945

vet·er·i·nar·i·an \,vet-ə-rə-'ner-ē-ən\ *n* : a doctor who treats diseases and injuries of animals

¹vet·er·i·nary \'vet-ə-rə-,ner-ē\ *adj* : of, relating to, or being the medical care of animals and especially domestic animals

²veterinary *n, pl* **vet·er·i·nar·ies** : VETERINARIAN

¹ve·to \'vēt-ō\ *n, pl* **ve·toes** **1** : a forbidding of something by a person in authority **2** : the power of a president, governor, or mayor to prevent something from becoming law

²veto *vb* **1** : FORBID, PROHIBIT **2** : to prevent from becoming law by use of a veto

vex \'veks\ *vb* **1** : to bring trouble, distress, or worry to **2** : to annoy by small irritations

vex·a·tion \vek-'sā-shən\ *n* **1** : the quality or state of being vexed **2** : the act of vexing **3** : a cause of trouble or worry

via \'vī-ə, 'vē-ə\ *prep* : by way of ⟨went *via* the northern route⟩

vi·a·ble \'vī-ə-bəl\ *adj* **1** : capable of living or growing **2** : possible to use or apply ⟨a *viable* plan⟩

via·duct \'vī-ə-,dəkt\ *n* : a bridge for carrying a road or railroad over something (as a gorge or highway)

vi·al \'vī-əl\ *n* : a small container (as for medicines) that is usually made of glass or plastic

vi·brant \'vī-brənt\ *adj* : having or giving the sense of life, vigor, or action ⟨a *vibrant* personality⟩ — **vi·brant·ly** *adv*

vi·brate \'vī-,brāt\ *vb* **vi·brat·ed; vi·brat·ing** : to swing or cause to swing back and forth

vi·bra·tion \vī-'brā-shən\ *n* **1** : a rapid motion (as of a stretched cord) back and forth **2** : the action of vibrating : the state of being vibrated **3** : a trembling motion

vi·bur·num \vī-'bər-nəm\ *n* : any of a group of shrubs often grown for their broad clusters of usually white flowers

vic·ar \'vik-ər\ *n* **1** : a minister in charge of a church who serves under the authority of another minister **2** : a church official who takes the place of or represents a higher official

vi·car·i·ous \vī-'ker-ē-əs, -'kar-\ *adj* : experienced or understood though actually happening to someone else especially through the imagination or a closeness with the other person — **vi·car·i·ous·ly** *adv* — **vi·car·i·ous·ness** *n*

vice \'vīs\ *n* **1** : evil conduct or habits **2** : a moral fault or weakness

vice- \'vīs\ *prefix* : one that takes the place of ⟨*vice*-president⟩

vice admiral *n* : a commissioned officer in the Navy or Coast Guard ranking above a rear admiral

vice–pres·i·dent \'vīs-'prez-ə-dənt\ *n* : an official (as of a government) whose rank is next below that of the president and who takes the place of the president when necessary

vice·roy \'vīs-,roi\ *n* : the governor of a country who rules as the representative of a king or queen

vice ver·sa \,vī-si-'vər-sə, 'vīs-'vər-\ *adv* : with the order turned around

vi·cin·i·ty \və-'sin-ət-ē\ *n, pl* **vi·cin·i·ties** **1** : the state of being close **2** : a surrounding area : NEIGHBORHOOD ⟨there is a school in the *vicinity*⟩

vi·cious \'vish-əs\ *adj* **1** : doing evil things : WICKED **2** : very dangerous ⟨a *vicious* dog⟩ **3** : filled with or showing unkind feelings ⟨*vicious* gossip⟩ — **vi·cious·ly** *adv* — **vi·cious·ness** *n*

vic·tim \'vik-təm\ *n* **1** : a living being offered as a religious sacrifice **2** : an individual injured or killed (as by disease) **3** : a person who is cheated, fooled, or hurt by another

vic·tim·ize \'vik-tə-,mīz\ *vb* **vic·tim·ized; vic·tim·iz·ing** : to make a victim of

vic·tor \'vik-tər\ *n* : WINNER, CONQUEROR

vic·to·ri·ous \vik-'tōr-ē-əs\ *adj* : having won a victory — **vic·to·ri·ous·ly** *adv*

vic·to·ry \'vik-tə-rē\ *n, pl* **vic·to·ries 1** : the defeating of an enemy or opponent **2** : success in a struggle against difficulties

synonyms VICTORY, CONQUEST, and TRI-UMPH mean a successful result in a competition or struggle. VICTORY stresses the fact of winning, either against an opponent or over difficult problems ⟨modern medicine can claim many *victories*⟩ CONQUEST stresses the overcoming of someone or something and then bringing the defeated under one's control ⟨the Vikings' *conquests* in Britain⟩ TRIUMPH suggests an especially great victory that brings honor and glory to the victor ⟨a battle that was a *triumph* for the general⟩

vict·ual \'vit-l\ *n* **1** : food fit for humans **2 victuals** *pl* : supplies of food

vi·cu·ña *or* **vi·cu·na** \vi-'kün-yə, vī-'kü-nə\ *n* : a wild animal of the Andes that is related to the llama and produces a fine wool

vicuña

¹vid·eo \'vid-ē-ˌō\ *n* **1** : TELEVISION **2** : the visual part of television **3** : ²VIDEOTAPE 1 **4** : a videotaped performance of a song ⟨a rock *video*⟩

²video *adj* **1** : relating to or used in the sending or receiving of television images **2** : being, relating to, or involving images on a television screen or computer display

vid·eo·cas·sette \ˌvid-ē-ō-kə-'set\ *n* **1** : a case containing videotape for use with a VCR **2** : a recording (as of a movie) on a videocassette

videocassette recorder *n* : VCR

video game *n* : a game played with images on a video screen

¹vid·eo·tape \'vid-ē-ō-ˌtāp\ *n* **1** : a recording of visual images and sound (as of a television production) mode on magnetic tape **2** : the magnetic tape used for such a recording

²videotape *vb* : to make a videotape of

vie \'vī\ *vb* **vied; vy·ing** : COMPETE ⟨*vied* for first place⟩

¹view \'vyü\ *n* **1** : the act of seeing or examining **2** : OPINION 1, 2, JUDGMENT **3** : all that can be seen from a certain place : SCENE ⟨the *view* of the mountains⟩ **4** : range of vision ⟨there is no one in *view*⟩ **5** : ¹PURPOSE ⟨studied hard with a *view* to getting a scholarship⟩ **6** : a picture that represents something that can be seen ⟨several *views* of the old building⟩

²view *vb* **1** : to look at carefully ⟨*view* an exhibit⟩ **2** : ¹SEE 1 — **view·er** *n*

view·point \'vyü-ˌpoint\ *n* : the angle from which something is considered

vig·il \'vij-əl\ *n* **1** : the day before a religious feast **2** : a staying awake to keep watch when one normally would be sleeping

vig·i·lance \'vij-ə-ləns\ *n* : a staying alert especially to possible danger

vig·i·lant \'vij-ə-lənt\ *adj* : alert especially to avoid danger — **vig·i·lant·ly** *adv*

vig·i·lan·te \ˌvij-ə-'lant-ē\ *n* : a member of a group of volunteers organized to stop crime and punish criminals especially when the proper officials are not doing so

vig·or \'vig-ər\ *n* **1** : strength or energy of body or mind **2** : active strength or force

vig·or·ous \'vig-ə-rəs\ *adj* **1** : having vigor **2** : done with vigor — **vig·or·ous·ly** *adv*

Vi·king \'vī-king\ *n* : a member of the Scandinavian invaders of the coasts of Europe in the eighth to tenth centuries

vile \'vīl\ *adj* **vil·er; vil·est 1** : of little worth **2** : WICKED 1 **3** : very objectionable — **vile·ly** \'vīl-lē\ *adv* — **vile·ness** *n*

vil·i·fy \'vil-ə-ˌfi\ *vb* **vil·i·fied; vil·i·fy·ing** : to speak of as worthless or wicked

vil·la \'vil-ə\ *n* **1** : an estate in the country **2** : a large expensive home especially in the country or suburbs

vil·lage \'vil-ij\ *n* : a place where people live that is usually smaller than a town

vil·lag·er \'vil-ij-ər\ *n* : a person who lives in a village

vil·lain \'vil-ən\ *n* : a wicked person

vil·lain·ous \'vil-ə-nəs\ *adj* : WICKED

vil·lainy \'vil-ə-nē\ *n, pl* **vil·lain·ies** : conduct or actions of or like those of a villain

vil·lus \'vil-əs\ *n, pl* **vil·li** \'vil-ˌī, -ē\ : one of

\ə\ abut	\au̇\ out	\i\ tip	\ȯ\ saw	\u̇\ foot
\ər\ further	\ch\ chin	\ī\ life	\ȯi\ coin	\y\ yet
\a\ mat	\e\ pet	\j\ job	\th\ thin	\yü\ few
\ā\ take	\ē\ easy	\ng\ sing	\th\ this	\yu̇\ cure
\ä\ cot, cart	\g\ go	\ō\ bone	\ü\ food	\zh\ vision

the tiny extensions that are shaped like fingers, line the small intestine, and are active in absorbing nutrients

vim \\'vim\ *n* : ENERGY 1, VIGOR

vin·di·cate \\'vin-də-ˌkāt\ *vb* **vin·di·cat·ed; vin·di·cat·ing 1** : to free from blame or guilt **2** : to show to be true or correct : JUSTIFY

vin·dic·tive \vin-'dik-tiv\ *adj* : likely to seek revenge : meant to be harmful

vine \\'vīn\ *n* : a plant whose stem requires support and which climbs by tendrils or twining or creeps along the ground — **vine·like** \-ˌlīk\ *adj*

vin·e·gar \\'vin-i-gər\ *n* : a sour liquid made from cider, wine, or malt and used to flavor or preserve foods

violet

Word History The English word *vinegar* came from an Old French word that had the same meaning. Vinegar was thought of as sour wine. The Old French word was made by combining two words. The first meant "wine" and the second meant "sharp" or "sour."

vin·e·gary \\'vin-i-gə-rē\ *adj* : like vinegar

vine·yard \\'vin-yərd\ *n* : a field of grapevines

vin·tage \\'vint-ij\ *n* **1** : the grapes grown or wine made during one season **2** : a usually excellent wine of a certain type, region, and year **3** : the time when something started or was made ⟨slang of recent *vintage*⟩

¹vi·o·la \vē-'ō-lə\ *n* : an instrument of the violin family slightly larger and having a lower pitch than a violin

²viola \vī-'ō-lə, vē-\ *n* : a hybrid garden flower that looks like but is smaller than a pansy

vi·o·late \\'vī-ə-ˌlāt\ *vb* **vi·o·lat·ed; vi·o·lat·ing 1** : to fail to keep : BREAK ⟨*violate* the rules⟩ **2** : to do harm or damage to **3** : to treat in a very disrespectful way **4** : DISTURB 1 ⟨*violate* their privacy⟩ — **vi·o·la·tor** \-ˌlāt-ər\ *n*

vi·o·la·tion \ˌvī-ə-'lā-shən\ *n* : an act or instance of violating : the state of being violated

vi·o·lence \\'vī-ə-ləns\ *n* **1** : the use of force to harm a person or damage property **2**

: great force or strength ⟨the *violence* of the storm⟩

vi·o·lent \\'vī-ə-lənt\ *adj* **1** : showing very strong force ⟨a *violent* storm⟩ **2** : ¹EXTREME 1, INTENSE ⟨*violent* pain⟩ **3** : caused by force ⟨a *violent* death⟩ — **vi·o·lent·ly** *adv*

vi·o·let \\'vī-ə-lət\ *n* **1** : a wild or garden plant related to the pansies that has small often fragrant white, blue, purple, or yellow flowers **2** : a reddish blue

vi·o·lin \ˌvī-ə-'lin\ *n* : a stringed musical instrument with four strings that is usually held against the shoulder under the chin and played with a bow

vi·o·lon·cel·lo \ˌvī-ə-lən-'chel-ō, ˌvē-\ *n*, *pl* **vi·o·lon·cel·los** : CELLO

vi·per \\'vī-pər\ *n* : a snake that is or is believed to be poisonous

vi·reo \\'vir-ē-ˌō\ *n*, *pl* **vir·e·os** : a small songbird that eats insects and is olive-green or grayish in color

violin

¹vir·gin \\'vər-jən\ *n* **1** : an unmarried woman devoted to religion **2** : a girl or woman who has not had sexual intercourse

²virgin *adj* **1** : not soiled ⟨*virgin* snow⟩ **2** : being a virgin **3** : not changed by human actions ⟨*virgin* forests⟩

Vir·go \\'vər-gō, 'viər-\ *n* **1** : a constellation between Leo and Libra imagined as a woman **2** : the sixth sign of the zodiac or a person born under this sign

vir·ile \\'vir-əl, 'viər-ˌīl\ *adj* **1** : having qualities generally associated with a man **2** : ENERGETIC, VIGOROUS

vir·tu·al \\'vər-chə-wəl\ *adj* : being almost but not quite complete ⟨the *virtual* ruler of the country⟩ ⟨rain is a *virtual* certainty for the weekend⟩ — **vir·tu·al·ly** *adv*

vir·tue \\'vər-chü\ *n* **1** : moral excellence : knowing what is right and acting in a right way **2** : a desirable quality ⟨truth is a *virtue*⟩

Word History From the Latin word that meant "man," the Romans formed another word. The second word was used to describe such so-called "manly" qualities as strength and courage. Gradually this word was used for any good qualities in males or females. The English word *virtue* came from this second Latin word.

vir·tu·o·so \,vər-chə-'wō-sō, -zō\ *n, pl* **vir·tu·o·sos** *or* **vir·tu·o·si** \-sē, -zē\ : a person who is an outstanding performer especially in music

vir·tu·ous \'vər-chə-wəs\ *adj* : having or showing virtue — **vir·tu·ous·ly** *adv*

vir·u·lent \'vir-ə-lənt\ *adj* : very infectious or poisonous : DEADLY

vi·rus \'vī-rəs\ *n* **1** : an agent too tiny to be seen by the ordinary microscope that causes disease and that may be a living organism or may be a very special kind of protein molecule **2** : a disease caused by a virus

vis·count \'vī-,kaunt\ *n* : a British nobleman ranking below an earl and above a baron

vis·count·ess \'vī-,kaunt-əs\ *n* **1** : the wife or widow of a viscount **2** : a woman who holds the rank of a viscount in her own right

vise \'vīs\ *n* : a device with two jaws that works by a screw or lever for holding or clamping work

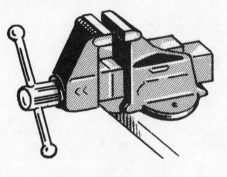

vise

vis·i·bil·i·ty \,viz-ə-'bil-ət-ē\ *n* **1** : the quality or state of being visible **2** : the degree of clearness of the atmosphere

vis·i·ble \'viz-ə-bəl\ *adj* **1** : capable of being seen **2** : easily seen or understood : OBVIOUS — **vis·i·bly** \-blē\ *adv*

vi·sion \'vizh-ən\ *n* **1** : something seen in the mind (as in a dream) **2** : a vivid picture created by the imagination **3** : the act or power of imagination **4** : unusual ability to think or plan ahead **5** : the act or power of seeing : SIGHT **6** : the special sense by which the qualities of an object (as color) that make up its appearance are perceived

vi·sion·ary \'vizh-ə-,ner-ē\ *n, pl* **vision·ar·ies** : a person whose ideas or plans are impractical

¹vis·it \'viz-ət\ *vb* **1** : to go to see in order to comfort or help **2** : to call on as an act of friendship or courtesy or as or for a professional service **3** : to stay with for a time as a guest **4** : to go to for pleasure ⟨*visit* a theater⟩ **5** : to come to or upon ⟨we were *visited* by many troubles⟩

²visit *n* **1** : a brief stay : CALL **2** : a stay as a guest **3** : a professional call

vis·i·tor \'viz-ət-ər\ *n* : a person who visits

synonyms VISITOR, GUEST, and CALLER mean someone who visits a person or place. VISITOR is usually used of a person who comes for a reason other than business ⟨I had several surprise *visitors* while at the hospital⟩ GUEST is usually used of an invited visitor who is staying for more than a short time ⟨we had five *guests* over the weekend⟩ CALLER is used of anyone who comes to a home or place of business and may come for personal or business reasons ⟨we had a *caller* from a local charity⟩

vi·sor \'vī-zər\ *n* **1** : the movable front upper piece of a helmet **2** : a part that sticks out to protect or shade the eyes

vis·ta \'vis-tə\ *n* : a distant view through an opening or along an avenue

vi·su·al \'vizh-ə-wəl\ *adj* **1** : of, relating to, or used in vision **2** : obtained by the use of sight ⟨a *visual* impression⟩ **3** : appealing to the sense of sight ⟨*visual* aids⟩ — **vi·su·al·ly** *adv*

vi·su·al·ize \'vizh-ə-wə-,līz\ *vb* **vi·su·al·ized; vi·su·al·iz·ing** : to see or form a mental image

vi·tal \'vīt-l\ *adj* **1** : of or relating to life **2** : concerned with or necessary to the continuation of life ⟨*vital* organs⟩ **3** : full of life and energy **4** : very important — **vi·tal·ly** *adv*

vi·tal·i·ty \vī-'tal-ət-ē\ *n, pl* **vi·tal·i·ties 1** : capacity to live and develop **2** : ENERGY 1

vi·tals \'vīt-lz\ *n pl* : the vital organs (as heart, lungs, and liver) of the body

vi·ta·min \'vīt-ə-mən\ *n* : any of a group of organic substances that are found in natural foods, are necessary in small quantities to health, and include one (**vitamin A** found mostly in animal products and needed for good vision, several (**vitamin**

\ə\ **abut**	\au̇\ **out**	\i\ **tip**	\ȯ\ **saw**	\u̇\ **foot**
\ər\ **further**	\ch\ **chin**	\ī\ **life**	\ȯi\ **coin**	\y\ **yet**
\a\ **mat**	\e\ **pet**	\j\ **job**	\th\ **thin**	\yü\ **few**
\ā\ **take**	\ē\ **easy**	\ng\ **sing**	\th\ **this**	\yu̇\ **cure**
\ä\ **cot, cart**	\g\ **go**	\ō\ **bone**	\ü\ **food**	\zh\ **vision**

B **complex**) found in many foods and needed especially for growth, one (**vitamin C**) found in fruits and leafy vegetables and used as an enzyme and to prevent scurvy, and another (**vitamin D**) found in fish-liver oils, eggs, and milk and needed for healthy bone development

vi·va·cious \və-'vā-shəs, vī-\ *adj* : full of life : LIVELY — **vi·va·cious·ly** *adv*

vi·vac·i·ty \və-'vas-ət-ē, vī-\ *n* : the quality or state of being vivacious

vi·var·i·um \vī-'var-ē-əm, -'ver-\ *n, pl* **vi·var·ia** \-ē-ə\ *or* **vi·var·i·ums** : an enclosure for keeping or studying plants or animals indoors

viv·id \'viv-əd\ *adj* **1** : seeming full of life and freshness 〈a *vivid* sketch of the children〉 **2** : very strong or bright 〈*vivid* red〉 **3** : producing strong mental images 〈a *vivid* description〉 **4** : acting clearly and powerfully 〈a *vivid* imagination〉 — **viv·id·ly** *adv* — **viv·id·ness** *n*

vi·vip·a·rous \vī-'vip-ə-rəs\ *adj* : giving birth to living young rather than laying eggs

vivi·sec·tion \ˌviv-ə-'sek-shən\ *n* : the operating or experimenting on a living animal usually for scientific study

vix·en \'vik-sən\ *n* : a female fox

vo·cab·u·lary \vō-'kab-yə-ˌler-ē\ *n, pl* **vo·cab·u·lar·ies** **1** : a list or collection of words defined or explained **2** : a stock of words used in a language, by a group or individual, or in relation to a subject

vo·cal \'vō-kəl\ *adj* **1** : uttered by the voice : ORAL **2** : composed or arranged for or sung by the human voice **3** : of, relating to, or having the power of producing voice — **vo·cal·ly** *adv*

vocal cords *n pl* : membranes at the top of the windpipe that produce vocal sounds when drawn tight and vibrated by the outgoing breath

vo·cal·ist \'vō-kə-ləst\ *n* : SINGER

vo·ca·tion \vō-'kā-shən\ *n* **1** : a strong desire for a certain career or course of action **2** : the work in which a person is regularly employed : OCCUPATION

vo·ca·tion·al \vō-'kā-shən-l\ *adj* **1** : of, relating to, or concerned with a vocation **2** : concerned with choice of or training in a vocation — **vo·ca·tion·al·ly** *adv*

vod·ka \'väd-kə\ *n* : a colorless alcoholic liquor

vogue \'vōg\ *n* **1** : the quality or state of being popular at a certain time **2** : a period in which something is in fashion **3** : something that is in fashion at a certain time

¹voice \'vȯis\ *n* **1** : sound produced through the mouth by vertebrates and es-

pecially by human beings in speaking or shouting **2** : musical sound produced by the vocal cords **3** : SPEECH **5** **4** : a sound similar to vocal sound **5** : a means of expression **6** : the right to express a wish, choice, or opinion

²voice *vb* **voiced; voic·ing** : to express in words 〈*voice* a complaint〉

voice box *n* : LARYNX

voiced \'vȯist\ *adj* : spoken with vibration of the vocal cords 〈the *voiced* consonants \b\, \d\, and \th\〉

voice·less \'vȯi-sləs\ *adj* : spoken without vibration of the vocal cords 〈the *voiceless* consonants \p\, \t\, and \th\〉

¹void \'vȯid\ *adj* : containing nothing : EMPTY

²void *n* : empty space

vol·a·tile \'väl-ət-l\ *adj* **1** : easily becoming a vapor at a fairly low temperature **2** : likely to change suddenly 〈a *volatile* disposition〉 〈*volatile* markets〉

vol·can·ic \väl-'kan-ik, vȯl-\ *adj* **1** : of or relating to a volcano **2** : likely to explode 〈a *volcanic* temper〉

vol·ca·no \väl-'kā-nō, vȯl-\ *n, pl* **vol·ca·noes** *or* **vol·ca·nos** **1** : a hole in the earth's crust from which hot or melted rock and steam come **2** : a hill or mountain composed of material thrown out in a volcanic eruption

Word History The Romans believed that Vulcanus, the god of fire, had his forge in a fiery mountain on an island off the coast of Italy. The English word *volcano* came (by way of Italian) from the Latin name for the Roman god of fire.

vole \'vōl\ *n* : any of various small rodents that look like fat mice or rats with short tails and are sometimes harmful to crops

vole

vo·li·tion \vō-'lish-ən\ *n* : the act or power of making one's own choices or decisions : WILL

¹vol·ley \'väl-ē\ *n, pl* **vol·leys** **1** : a group of missiles (as arrows or bullets) passing through the air **2** : a firing of a number of weapons (as rifles) at the same time **3** : a bursting forth of many things at once **4** : the act of volleying

²volley *vb* **vol·leyed; vol·ley·ing 1** : to shoot in a volley **2** : to hit an object (as a ball) while it is in the air before it touches the ground

vol·ley·ball \'väl-ē-,bȯl\ *n* : a game played by volleying a large ball filled with air across a net

volt \'vōlt\ *n* : a unit for measuring the force that moves an electric current

volt·age \'vōl-tij\ *n* : electric force measured in volts ⟨the *voltage* of a current⟩

vol·u·ble \'väl-yə-bəl\ *adj* : having a smooth and fast flow of words in speaking — **vol·u·bly** \-blē\ *adv*

vol·ume \'väl-yəm, -yüm\ *n* **1** : ¹BOOK 1 **2** : any one of a series of books that together form a complete work or collection **3** : space included within limits as measured in cubic units ⟨the *volume* of a cylinder⟩ **4** : ²AMOUNT **5** : the degree of loudness of a sound

Word History The earliest books were not like the books we read today. Instead of having pages that could be turned, they were written on rolls of a material something like paper. The Latin word for such a book came from a Latin verb that meant "to roll." The English word *volume* came from this Latin word. At first *volume* meant "scroll" or "book," but later it came to mean "the size of a book" as well. The later meaning led to the more general meaning of "size" or "amount"—as in the volume of a jar or the volume of sales. From this sense came still another meaning: "loudness or intensity of sound."

vo·lu·mi·nous \və-'lü-mə-nəs\ *adj* **1** : of great volume or bulk **2** : filling or capable of filling a large volume or several volumes

vol·un·tary \'väl-ən-,ter-ē\ *adj* **1** : done, given, or made of one's own free will or choice **2** : not accidental : INTENTIONAL **3** : of, relating to, or controlled by the will — **vol·un·tari·ly** \,väl-ən-'ter-ə-lē\ *adv*

synonyms VOLUNTARY, INTENTIONAL, and DELIBERATE mean done or brought about of one's own will. VOLUNTARY suggests free choice ⟨joining the club is *voluntary*⟩ or control by the will ⟨*voluntary* blinking of the eyes⟩ INTENTIONAL suggests that something is done for a reason and only after some thinking about it ⟨*intentional* neglect of a task⟩ DELIBERATE suggests that one is fully aware of what one is doing and of the likely results of the action ⟨*deliberate* insult⟩

¹vol·un·teer \,väl-ən-'tiər\ *n* **1** : a person who volunteers for a service **2** : a plant growing without direct human care especially from seeds lost from a previous crop

²volunteer *adj* : of, relating to, or done by volunteers ⟨a *volunteer* fire department⟩

³volunteer *vb* **1** : to offer or give without being asked **2** : to offer oneself for a service of one's own free will

¹vom·it \'väm-ət\ *n* : material from the stomach gotten rid of through the mouth

²vomit *vb* : to rid oneself of the contents of the stomach through the mouth

vo·ra·cious \vȯ-'rā-shəs, və-\ *adj* **1** : greedy in eating **2** : very eager ⟨a *voracious* reader⟩ — **vo·ra·cious·ly** *adv*

¹vote \'vōt\ *n* **1** : a formal expression of opinion or will (as by ballot) **2** : the decision reached by voting **3** : the right to vote **4** : the act or process of voting **5** : a group of voters with some common interest or quality ⟨the farm *vote*⟩

²vote *vb* **vot·ed; vot·ing 1** : to express one's wish or choice by or as if by a vote **2** : to elect, decide, pass, defeat, grant, or make legal by a vote **3** : to declare by general agreement

vot·er \'vōt-ər\ *n* : a person who votes or who has the legal right to vote

vouch \'vaúch\ *vb* : to give a guarantee ⟨the teacher *vouched* for their honesty⟩

vouch·safe \vaúch-'sāf\ *vb* **vouch·safed; vouch·saf·ing** : to grant as a special favor

¹vow \'vaú\ *n* : a solemn promise or statement

²vow *vb* : to make a vow : SWEAR

vow·el \'vaú-əl\ *n* **1** : a speech sound (as \ə\, \ā\, or \ȯ\) produced without obstruction or audible friction in the mouth **2** : a letter (as *a, e, i, o, u*) representing a vowel

¹voy·age \'vȯi-ij\ *n* : a journey especially by water from one place or country to another

²voyage *vb* **voy·aged; voy·ag·ing** : to take a trip — **voy·ag·er** *n*

vul·can·ize \'vəl-kə-,nīz\ *vb* **vul·can·ized; vul·can·iz·ing** : to treat rubber with chemicals in order to give it useful properties (as strength)

vul·gar \'vəl-gər\ *adj* **1** : of or relating to the common people **2** : having poor taste or manners : COARSE **3** : offensive in language

vul·gar·i·ty \,vəl-'gar-ət-ē\ *n, pl* **vul·gar·i·ties 1** : the quality or state of being

\ə\ **abut**	\aú\ **out**	\i\ **tip**	\ȯ\ **saw**	\ú\ **foot**
\ər\ **further**	\ch\ **chin**	\ī\ **life**	\ȯi\ **coin**	\y\ **yet**
\a\ **mat**	\e\ **pet**	\j\ **job**	\th\ **thin**	\yü\ **few**
\ā\ **take**	\ē\ **easy**	\ng\ **sing**	\th\ **this**	\yú\ **cure**
\ä\ **cot, cart**	\g\ **go**	\ō\ **bone**	\ü\ **food**	\zh\ **vision**

vulgar **2 :** a vulgar expression or action

vul·ner·a·ble \'vəl-nə-rə-bəl\ *adj* **1 :** possible to wound or hurt **2 :** open to attack or damage — **vul·ner·a·bly** \-blē\ *adv*

vul·ture \'vəl-chər\ *n* **:** a large bird related to the hawks and eagles that has a naked head and feeds mostly on animals found dead

vying *present participle of* VIE

w \'dəb-əl-yü\ *n, pl* **w's** *or* **ws** \-yüz\ *often cap* **:** the twenty-third letter of the English alphabet

wacky \'wak-ē\ *or* **whacky** \'hwak-ē, 'wak-\ *adj* **wacki·er** *or* **whacki·er; wacki·est** *or* **whacki·est :** CRAZY 2, INSANE

¹wad \'wäd\ *n* **1 :** a small mass or lump **2 :** a soft plug or stopper to hold a charge of powder (as in cartridges) **3 :** a soft mass of cotton, cloth, or fibers used as a plug or pad

²wad *vb* **wad·ded; wad·ding :** to form into a wad

¹wad·dle \'wäd-l\ *vb* **wad·dled; wad·dling :** to walk with short steps swaying like a duck

²waddle *n* **:** a waddling walk

wade \'wād\ *vb* **wad·ed; wad·ing 1 :** to walk or step through something (as water, mud, or snow) that makes it hard to move **2 :** to proceed with difficulty ⟨trying to *wade* through a dull assignment⟩ **3 :** to pass or cross by stepping through water ⟨*wade* the stream⟩

wading bird *n* **:** a shorebird or water bird with long legs that wades in water in search of food

wa·fer \'wā-fər\ *n* **:** a thin crisp cake or cracker

waf·fle \'wäf-əl\ *n* **:** a crisp cake of batter baked in a waffle iron

waffle iron *n* **:** a cooking utensil with two hinged metal parts that come together for making waffles

waft \'wäft, 'waft\ *vb* **:** to move or be moved lightly by or as if by the action of waves or wind

¹wag \'wag\ *vb* **wagged; wag·ging :** to swing to and fro or from side to side ⟨the dog *wagged* its tail⟩

²wag *n* **1 :** a wagging movement **2 :** a person full of jokes and humor

¹wage \'wāj\ *vb* **waged; wag·ing :** to engage in **:** CARRY ON ⟨*wage* a fight against crime⟩

²wage *n* **1 :** payment for work done especially when figured by the hour or day **2**

wages *sing or pl* **:** something given or received in return **:** REWARD ⟨the *wages* of sin is death⟩

¹wa·ger \'wā-jər\ *n* **1 :** ¹BET 1 **2 :** the act of betting

²wager *vb* **:** to bet on the result of a contest or question — **wa·ger·er** *n*

wag·gish \'wag-ish\ *adj* **:** showing or done in a spirit of harmless mischief

wag·gle \'wag-əl\ *vb* **wag·gled; waggling :** to move backward and forward or from side to side

wag·on \'wag-ən\ *n* **:** a vehicle having four wheels and used for carrying goods

waif \'wāf\ *n* **:** a stray person or animal

¹wail \'wāl\ *vb* **:** to utter a mournful cry

²wail *n* **:** a long cry of grief or pain

wain·scot \'wān-skət, -,skōt, -,skät\ *n* **:** the bottom part of an inside wall especially when made of material different from the rest

wain·scot·ing \'wān-,skōt-ing\ *or* **wainscot·ting** \-,skät-\ *n* **:** WAINSCOT

waist \'wāst\ *n* **1 :** the part of the body between the chest and the hips **2 :** the central part of a thing when it is narrower or thinner than the rest **3 :** a garment or part of a garment covering the body from the neck to the waist

¹wait \'wāt\ *vb* **1 :** to stay in a place looking forward to something that is expected to happen **2 :** to serve food as a waiter or waitress **3 :** ²DELAY 1 ⟨*wait* until we're through⟩

²wait *n* **1 :** ²AMBUSH — used chiefly in the expression *lie in wait* **2 :** an act or period of waiting

wait·er \'wāt-ər\ *n* **:** a man who serves food to people at tables (as in a restaurant)

waiting room *n* **:** a room for the use of persons waiting (as for a train)

wait·ress \'wā-trəs\ *n* **:** a girl or woman who serves food to people at tables

waive \'wāv\ *vb* **waived; waiv·ing** : to give up claim to

¹wake \'wāk\ *vb* **waked** *or* **woke** \'wōk\; **waked** *or* **wo·ken** \'wō-kən\; **wak·ing 1** : to be or stay awake **2** : to stay awake on watch especially over a corpse **3** : ¹AWAKE 1 ⟨*wake* us at six⟩

²wake *n* : a watch held over the body of a dead person before burial

³wake *n* : a track or mark left by something moving especially in the water

wake·ful \'wāk-fəl\ *adj* **1** : VIGILANT **2** : not sleeping or able to sleep — **wake·ful·ness** *n*

wak·en \'wā-kən\ *vb* : ¹AWAKE 1

¹walk \'wok\ *vb* **1** : to move or cause to move along on foot at a natural slow pace **2** : to cover or pass over at a walk ⟨*walked* twenty miles⟩ **3** : to go or cause to go to first base after four balls in baseball — **walk·er** *n*

²walk *n* **1** : a going on foot **2** : a place or path for walking **3** : distance to be walked often measured in time required by a walker to cover **4** : position in life or the community **5** : way of walking **6** : an opportunity to go to first base after four balls in baseball

walking stick *n* **1** : a stick used in walking **2** : a sticklike insect with a long round body and long thin legs

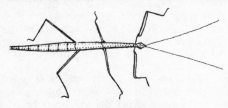

walking stick 2

walk·out \'wo-ˌkaut\ *n* **1** : a labor strike **2** : the leaving of a meeting or organization as a way of showing disapproval

walk·over \'wo-ˌkō-vər\ *n* : an easy victory

¹wall \'wol\ *n* **1** : a solid structure (as of stone) built to enclose or shut off a space **2** : something like a wall that separates one thing from another ⟨a *wall* of mountains⟩ **3** : a layer of material enclosing space ⟨the heart *wall*⟩ ⟨the *wall* of a pipe⟩ — **walled** \'wold\ *adj*

²wall *vb* : to build a wall in or around

wall·board \'wol-ˌbord\ *n* : a building material (as of wood pulp) made in large stiff sheets and used especially for inside walls and ceilings

wal·let \'wäl-ət\ *n* : a small flat case for carrying paper money and personal papers

wall·eye \'wo-ˌlī\ *n* : a large strong American freshwater sport and food fish that is related to the perches but looks like a pike

¹wal·lop \'wäl-əp\ *n* : a hard blow

²wallop *vb* : to hit hard

¹wal·low \'wäl-ō\ *vb* **1** : to roll about in or as if in deep mud **2** : to be too much interested or concerned with ⟨*wallowing* in misery⟩

²wallow *n* : a muddy or dust-filled hollow where animals wallow

wall·pa·per \'wol-ˌpā-pər\ *n* : decorative paper for covering the walls of a room

wal·nut \'wol-ˌnət\ *n* : the edible nut (as the American **black walnut** with a rough shell or the Old World **English walnut** with a smoother shell) that comes from trees related to the hickories and including some valued also for their wood

Word History Walnut trees grew in southern Europe for a long time before they were grown in England. As a result the English gave the walnut a name which showed plainly that it was not an English nut. The Old English name for this southern nut meant "a foreign nut." It was formed from two Old English words. The first meant "foreigner." The second meant "nut." The modern English word *walnut* comes from the Old English name.

wal·rus \'wol-rəs\ *n* : a large animal of northern seas related to the seals and hunted for its hide, for the ivory tusks of the males, and for oil

walrus

¹waltz \'wolts\ *n* : a dance in which couples glide to music having three beats to a measure

\ə\ **abut**	\au\ **out**	\i\ **tip**	\o\ **saw**	\ú\ **foot**
\ər\ **further**	\ch\ **chin**	\ī\ **life**	\oi\ **coin**	\y\ **yet**
\a\ **mat**	\e\ **pet**	\j\ **job**	\th\ **thin**	\yü\ **few**
\ā\ **take**	\ē\ **easy**	\ng\ **sing**	\th\ **this**	\yü\ **cure**
\ä\ **cot, cart**	\g\ **go**	\ō\ **bone**	\ü\ **food**	\zh\ **vision**

²**waltz** *vb* : to dance a waltz — **waltz·er** *n*

wam·pum \'wäm-pəm\ *n* : beads made of shells and once used for money or ornament by North American Indians

wan \'wän\ *adj* **wan·ner; wan·nest** : having a pale or sickly color — **wan·ly** *adv* — **wan·ness** *n*

wand \'wänd\ *n* : a slender rod (as one carried by a fairy or one used by a magician in doing tricks)

wan·der \'wän-dər\ *vb* **1** : to move about without a goal or purpose : RAMBLE **2** : to follow a winding course **3** : to get off the right path : STRAY — **wan·der·er** *n*

synonyms WANDER, ROAM, and RAMBLE mean to move about from place to place without a reason or plan. WANDER suggests that one does not follow a fixed course while moving about ⟨the tribes *wandered* in the desert for forty years⟩ ROAM suggests a carefree wandering over a wide area often for the sake of enjoyment ⟨I *roamed* over the hills and through the meadows⟩ RAMBLE suggests that one wanders in a careless way and without concern for where one goes ⟨horses *rambling* over the open range⟩

wan·der·lust \'wän-dər-,ləst\ *n* : a strong wish or urge to travel

wane \'wān\ *vb* **waned; wan·ing 1** : to grow smaller or less **2** : to lose power or importance : DECLINE

¹**want** \'wȯnt, 'wänt\ *vb* **1** : to be without : LACK **2** : to feel or suffer the need of something **3** : to desire, wish, or long for something

²**want** *n* **1** : ²LACK 2, SHORTAGE ⟨a *want* of common sense⟩ **2** : the state of being very poor ⟨they died in *want*⟩ **3** : a wish for something : DESIRE

want·ing \'wȯnt-ing, 'wänt-\ *adj* : falling below a standard, hope, or need ⟨the plan was found *wanting*⟩

wan·ton \'wȯnt-n\ *adj* **1** : PLAYFUL 1 ⟨a *wanton* breeze⟩ **2** : not modest or proper : INDECENT **3** : showing no thought or care for the rights, feelings, or safety of others ⟨*wanton* cruelty⟩ — **wan·ton·ly** *adv* — **wan·ton·ness** *n*

¹**war** \'wȯr\ *n* **1** : a state or period of fighting between states or nations **2** : the art or science of warfare **3** : a struggle between opposing forces

²**war** *vb* **warred; war·ring** : to make war : FIGHT

¹**war·ble** \'wȯr-bəl\ *n* **1** : low pleasing sounds that form a melody (as of a bird) **2** : the action of warbling

²**warble** *vb* **war·bled; war·bling** : to sing with a warble

war·bler \'wȯr-blər\ *n* **1** : any of a group of Old World birds related to the thrushes and noted for their musical song **2** : any of a group of brightly colored American migratory songbirds that eat insects and have a weak call

¹**ward** \'wȯrd\ *n* **1** : a part of a hospital **2** : one of the parts into which a town or city is divided for management **3** : a person under the protection of a guardian

²**ward** *vb* **1** : to keep watch over : GUARD **2** : to turn aside ⟨*ward* off a blow⟩

¹**-ward** \wərd\ *also* **-wards** \wərdz\ *adj suffix* **1** : that moves, faces, or is pointed toward ⟨wind*ward*⟩ **2** : that is found in the direction of

²**-ward** *or* **-wards** *adv suffix* **1** : in a specified direction ⟨up*ward*⟩ **2** : toward a specified place

war·den \'wȯrd-n\ *n* **1** : a person who sees that certain laws are followed ⟨game *warden*⟩ **2** : the chief official of a prison

ward·robe \'wȯr-,drōb\ *n* **1** : a room or closet where clothes are kept **2** : the clothes a person owns

ware \'waər, 'weər\ *n* **1** : manufactured articles or products of art or craft **2** : items (as dishes) of baked clay : POTTERY

ware·house \'waər-,haüs, 'weər-\ *n, pl* **ware·hous·es** \-,haü-zəz\ : a building for storing goods and merchandise

war·fare \'wȯr-,faər, -,feər\ *n* **1** : military fighting between enemies **2** : strong continued effort : STRUGGLE ⟨our *warfare* against crime⟩

war·like \'wȯr-,līk\ *adj* **1** : fond of war **2** : of or relating to war **3** : threatening war

¹**warm** \'wȯrm\ *adj* **1** : somewhat hot ⟨*warm* milk⟩ **2** : giving off heat **3** : making a person feel heat or experience no loss of bodily heat ⟨*warm* clothing⟩ **4** : having a feeling of warmth **5** : showing strong feeling ⟨a *warm* welcome⟩ **6** : newly made : FRESH **7** : near the object sought ⟨keep going, you're getting *warm*⟩ **8** : of a color in the range yellow through orange to red — **warm·ly** *adv*

²**warm** *vb* **1** : to make or become warm **2** : to give a feeling of warmth **3** : to become more interested than at first ⟨begin to *warm* to an idea⟩

warm–blood·ed \'wȯrm-'bləd-əd\ *adj* **1** : able to keep up a body temperature that is independent of that of the surroundings **2** : warm in feeling — **warm–blood·ed·ness** *n*

warmth \'wȯrmth\ *n* **1** : gentle heat **2** : strong feeling

warm–up \'wȯr-ˌməp\ *n* : a practice or period of exercise before a game

warm up \wȯr-'məp\ *vb* **1** : to exercise or practice before a game or sports contest **2** : to run (as a motor) at slow speed before using

warn \'wȯrn\ *vb* **1** : to put on guard : CAUTION **2** : to notify especially in advance

warn•ing \'wȯr-ning\ *n* : something that warns ⟨storm *warnings*⟩

¹warp \'wȯrp\ *n* **1** : the threads that go lengthwise in a loom and are crossed by the woof **2** : a twist or curve that has developed in something once flat or straight

²warp *vb* **1** : to curve or twist out of shape **2** : to cause to judge, choose, or act wrongly ⟨their thinking is *warped* by greed⟩

war•path \wȯr-ˌpath, -ˌpȧth\ *n* : the route taken by a group of American Indians going off to fight — **on the warpath** : ready to fight or argue

war•plane \'wȯr-ˌplān\ *n* : a military or naval airplane

¹war•rant \'wȯr-ənt\ *n* **1** : a reason or cause for an opinion or action **2** : a document giving legal power

²warrant *vb* **1** : to be sure of or that ⟨I'll *warrant* they know the answer⟩ **2** : ²GUARANTEE 2 ⟨a toaster *warranted* for ninety days⟩ **3** : to call for : JUSTIFY ⟨the report *warrants* careful study⟩

warrant officer *n* **1** : an officer in the armed forces in one of the grades between commissioned officers and enlisted persons **2** : a warrant officer of the lowest rank

war•ren \'wȯr-ən\ *n* : a place for keeping or raising small game (as rabbits)

war•rior \'wȯr-yər, 'wȯr-ē-ər\ *n* : SOLDIER

war•ship \'wȯr-ˌship\ *n* : a ship armed for combat

wart \'wȯrt\ *n* : a small hard lump of thickened skin

warty \'wȯr-tē\ *adj* **wart•i•er; wart•i•est 1** : covered with or as if with warts **2** : like a wart

wary \'waər-ē, 'weər-ē\ *adj* **wari•er; wari•est** : very cautious — **wari•ly** \'war-ə-lē, 'wer-\ *adv* — **wari•ness** \'war-ē-nəs, 'wer-\ *n*

was *past 1st & 3d sing of* BE

¹wash \'wȯsh, 'wäsh\ *vb* **1** : to cleanse with water and usually a cleaning agent (as soap) **2** : to wet completely with liquid **3** : to flow along or overflow against ⟨waves *washing* the shore⟩ **4** : to remove by the action of water **5** : to stand washing without injury ⟨linen *washes* well⟩

²wash *n* **1** : articles (as of clothing) in the laundry **2** : the flow, sound, or action of water **3** : a backward flow of water (as made by the motion of a boat) **4** : material carried or set down by water

wash•board \'wȯsh-ˌbōrd, 'wäsh-\ *n* : a grooved board to scrub clothes on

wash•bowl \'wȯsh-ˌbōl, 'wäsh-\ *n* : a large bowl for water to wash one's hands and face

wash•er \'wȯsh-ər, 'wäsh-\ *n* **1** : WASHING MACHINE **2** : a ring (as of metal) used to make something fit tightly or to prevent rubbing

wash•ing \'wȯsh-ing, 'wäsh-\ *n* : ²WASH 1

washing machine *n* : a machine used especially for washing clothes and household linen

Wash•ing•ton's Birthday \ˌwȯsh-ing-tənz-, ˌwäsh-\ *n* : the third Monday in February observed as a legal holiday in most of the United States

wash•out \'wȯsh-ˌaut, 'wäsh-\ *n* **1** : the washing away of earth (as from a road) **2** : a place where earth is washed away **3** : a complete failure

wash•tub \'wȯsh-ˌtəb, 'wäsh-\ *n* : a tub for washing clothes or for soaking them before washing

wasn't \'wəz-nt, 'wäz-\ : was not

wasp \'wäsp, 'wȯsp\ *n* : a winged insect related to the bees and ants that has a slender body with the abdomen attached by a narrow stalk and that in females and

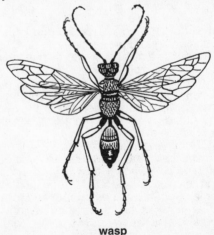

wasp

workers is capable of giving a very painful sting

wasp·ish \'wäs-pish, 'wos-\ *adj* : [3]CROSS 3, IRRITABLE — **wasp·ish·ly** *adv* — **wasp·ish·ness** *n*

[1]**waste** \'wāst\ *n* **1** : [1]DESERT, WILDERNESS **2** : WASTELAND **3** : the action of wasting : the state of being wasted **4** : material left over or thrown away **5** : material produced in and of no further use to the living body

[2]**waste** *vb* **wast·ed; wast·ing** **1** : to bring to ruin **2** : to spend or use carelessly or uselessly **3** : to lose or cause to lose weight, strength, or energy

[3]**waste** *adj* **1** : being wild and not lived in or planted to crops : BARREN **2** : of no further use

waste·bas·ket \'wāst-,bas-kət\ *n* : an open container for odds and ends to be thrown away

waste·ful \'wāst-fəl\ *adj* **1** : wasting or causing waste **2** : spending or using in a careless or foolish way — **waste·ful·ly** \-fə-lē\ *adv* — **waste·ful·ness** *n*

waste·land \'wāst-,land\ *n* : land that is barren or not fit for crops

[1]**watch** \'wäch\ *vb* **1** : to stay awake **2** : to be on one's guard **3** : to take care of : TEND ⟨*watch* the house until I get back⟩ **4** : to be on the lookout ⟨*watching* for a signal⟩ **5** : to keep one's eyes on ⟨*watch* a game⟩ — **watch·er** *n*

[2]**watch** *n* **1** : an act of keeping awake to guard or protect **2** : close observation **3** : [1]GUARD 2 **4** : the time during which one is on duty to watch **5** : a small timepiece to be worn or carried

watch·dog \'wäch-,dog\ *n* : a dog kept to watch and guard property

watch·ful \'wäch-fəl\ *adj* : ATTENTIVE 1, VIGILANT — **watch·ful·ly** \-fə-lē\ *adv* — **watch·ful·ness** *n*

watch·man \'wäch-mən\ *n, pl* **watch·men** \-mən\ : a person whose job is to watch and guard property at night or when the owners are away

watch·tow·er \'wäch-,taù-ər\ *n* : a tower on which a guard or watchman is placed

watch·word \'wäch-,wərd\ *n* : PASSWORD

[1]**wa·ter** \'wot-ər, 'wät-\ *n* **1** : the liquid that comes from the clouds as rain and forms streams, lakes, and seas **2** : a liquid that contains or is like water **3** : a body of water or a part of a body of water

[2]**water** *vb* **1** : to wet or supply with water ⟨*water* horses⟩ **2** : to add water to **3** : to fill with liquid (as tears)

wa·ter·bird \'wot-ər-,bərd, 'wät-\ *n* : a swimming or wading bird

water buffalo *n* : a common oxlike work animal of Asia

water buffalo

water clock *n* : a device or machine for measuring time by the fall or flow of water

wa·ter·col·or \'wot-ər-,kəl-ər, 'wät-\ *n* **1** : a paint whose liquid part is water **2** : a picture painted with watercolor **3** : the art of painting with watercolor

wa·ter·course \'wot-ər-,kōrs, 'wät-\ *n* **1** : a channel in which water flows **2** : a stream of water (as a river or brook)

wa·ter·cress \'wot-ər-,kres, 'wät-\ *n* : a plant related to the mustards that grows in cold flowing waters and is used especially in salads

wa·ter·fall \'wot-ər-,fol, 'wät-\ *n* : a fall of water from a height

water flea *n* : a small active often brightly colored freshwater animal related to the crabs and lobsters

watercress

wa·ter·fowl \'wot-ər-,faùl, 'wät-\ *n, pl* **waterfowl** **1** : a bird that is found or lives near water **2** *waterfowl pl* : swimming game birds that are neither shorebirds nor upland game birds

wa·ter·front \'wot-ər-,frənt, 'wät-\ *n* : land or a section of a town that borders on a body of water

water hyacinth *n* : a floating water plant that often blocks streams in the southern United States

water lily *n* : any of a group of water plants with rounded floating leaves and showy often fragrant flowers with many petals

water lily

wa·ter·line \'wȯt-ər-ˌlīn, 'wät-\ *n* : any of several lines marked on the outside of a ship that match the surface of the water when the ship floats evenly

wa·ter·logged \'wȯt-ər-ˌlȯgd, 'wät-, -ˌlägd\ *adj* : so filled or soaked with water as to be heavy or hard to manage

wa·ter·mark \'wȯt-ər-ˌmärk, 'wät-\ *n* **1** : a mark that shows a level to which water has risen **2** : a mark made in paper during manufacture and visible when the paper is held up to the light

wa·ter·mel·on \'wȯt-ər-ˌmel-ən, 'wät-\ *n* : a large edible fruit with a hard outer layer and a sweet red juicy pulp

water moccasin *n* : MOCCASIN 2

water polo *n* : a ball game played in water by teams of swimmers

wa·ter·pow·er \'wȯt-ər-ˌpau̇-ər, 'wät-\ *n* : the power of moving water used to run machinery

¹wa·ter·proof \ˌwȯt-ər-'prüf, ˌwät-\ *adj* : not letting water through ⟨a *waterproof* tent⟩

²waterproof *vb* : to make waterproof

wa·ter·shed \'wȯt-ər-ˌshed, 'wät-\ *n* **1** : a dividing ridge (as a mountain range) separating one drainage area from others **2** : the whole area that drains into a lake or river

wa·ter·spout \'wȯt-ər-ˌspau̇t, 'wät-\ *n* **1** : a pipe for carrying off water from a roof **2** : a slender cloud that is shaped like a funnel and extends down to a cloud of spray torn up from the surface of a body of water by a whirlwind

water strid·er \-'strīd-ər\ *n* : a bug with long legs that skims over the surface of water

water strider

wa·ter·tight \ˌwȯt-ər-'tīt, ˌwät-\ *adj* : so tight as to be waterproof ⟨a *watertight* joint in a pipe⟩

wa·ter·way \'wȯt-ər-ˌwā, 'wät-\ *n* : a channel or a body of water by which ships can travel

wa·ter·wheel \'wȯt-ər-ˌhwēl, 'wät-, -ˌwēl\ *n* : a wheel turned by a flow of water against it

wa·ter·works \'wȯt-ər-ˌwərks, 'wät-\ *n pl* : a system of dams, reservoirs, pumps, and pipes for supplying water (as to a city)

wa·tery \'wȯt-ə-rē, 'wät-\ *adj* **1** : of or relating to water **2** : full of or giving out liquid ⟨*watery* eyes⟩ **3** : being like water **4** : being soft and soggy

watt \'wät\ *n* : a unit for measuring electric power

wat·tle \'wät-l\ *n* : a fleshy flap of skin that hangs from the throat (as of a bird)

¹wave \'wāv\ *vb* **waved; wav·ing 1** : to move like a wave **2** : to move (as one's hand) to and fro as a signal or in greeting **3** : to curve like a wave or series of waves

²wave *n* **1** : a moving ridge on the surface of water **2** : a shape like a wave or series of waves ⟨the *wave* in your hair⟩ **3** : a waving motion **4** : ²FLOW 3 **5** : a rapid increase ⟨a *wave* of buying⟩ **6** : a motion that is somewhat like a wave in water and transfers energy ⟨sound *waves*⟩

wave·length \'wāv-ˌlength\ *n* : the distance in the line of advance of a wave from any one point to the next similar point

wave·let \'wāv-lət\ *n* : a little wave

wa·ver \'wā-vər\ *vb* **1** : to sway one way and the other **2** : to be uncertain in opinion **3** : to move unsteadily

wavy \'wā-vē\ *adj* **wav·i·er; wav·i·est** : like, having, or moving in waves ⟨*wavy* hair⟩ — **wav·i·ness** *n*

¹wax \'waks\ *n* **1** : a dull yellow sticky substance made by bees and used in building honeycomb : BEESWAX **2** : a substance like beeswax

²wax *vb* : to treat with wax

³wax *vb* **1** : to grow larger or stronger **2** : BECOME 1, GROW ⟨*waxed* angry as the rumor spread⟩

wax bean *n* : a string bean with yellow waxy pods

waxed paper *or* **wax paper** *n* : paper treated with wax to make it resistant to water and grease and used especially as a wrapping

wax·en \'wak-sən\ *adj* : of or like wax

wax myrtle *n* : the bayberry shrub

\ə\ **abut**	\au̇\ **out**	\i\ **tip**	\ȯ\ **saw**	\u̇\ **foot**
\ər\ **further**	\ch\ **chin**	\ī\ **life**	\ȯi\ **coin**	\y\ **yet**
\a\ **mat**	\e\ **pet**	\j\ **job**	\th\ **thin**	\yü\ **few**
\ā\ **take**	\ē\ **easy**	\ng\ **sing**	\th\ **this**	\yu̇\ **cure**
\ä\ **cot, cart**	\g\ **go**	\ō\ **bone**	\ü\ **food**	\zh\ **vision**

wax·wing \'wak,swing\ *n* : a crested mostly brown bird having smooth feathers (as the American **cedar waxwing** with yellowish belly)

waxy \'wak-sē\ *adj* **wax·i·er; wax·i·est** **1** : being like wax **2** : made of or covered with wax

¹**way** \'wā\ *n* **1** : a track for travel : PATH, STREET **2** : the course traveled from one place to another : ROUTE **3** : a course of action ⟨chose the easy *way*⟩ **4** : personal choice as to situation or behavior : WISH **5** : the manner in which something is done or happens **6** : a noticeable point **7** : ¹STATE 1 **8** : ¹DISTANCE 1 ⟨a short *way*⟩ **9** : progress along a course ⟨working my *way* through college⟩ **10** : a special or personal manner of behaving **11** : NEIGHBORHOOD 1, DISTRICT **12** : room to advance or pass ⟨make *way*⟩ **13** : CATEGORY, KIND ⟨had little in the *way* of help⟩

waxwing

²**way** *adv* : ¹FAR 1 ⟨the sleeves hung *way* down⟩

way·far·er \'wā-,far-ər, -,fer-\ *n* : a traveler especially on foot

way·lay \'wā-,lā\ *vb* **way·laid** \-,lād\; **way·lay·ing** : to attack from hiding

-ways \,wāz\ *adv suffix* : in such a way, direction, or manner ⟨side*ways*⟩

way·side \'wā-,sīd\ *n* : the edge of a road

way·ward \'wā-wərd\ *adj* **1** : DISOBEDIENT **2** : opposite to what is wished or hoped for

we \wē\ *pron* : I and at least one other

weak \'wēk\ *adj* **1** : lacking strength of body, mind, or spirit **2** : not able to stand much strain or force ⟨a *weak* rope⟩ **3** : easily overcome ⟨a *weak* argument⟩ **4** : not able to function well ⟨*weak* eyes⟩ **5** : not rich in some usual or important element ⟨*weak* tea⟩ ⟨*weak* colors⟩ **6** : lacking experience or skill **7** : of, relating to, or being the lightest of three levels of stress in pronunciation

synonyms WEAK, FEEBLE, and FRAIL mean not strong enough to stand pressure or hard effort. WEAK can be used of either a temporary or permanent loss of strength or power ⟨felt *weak* after the operation⟩ ⟨I have *weak* lungs⟩ FEEBLE stresses very great and pitiful weakness ⟨a *feeble* old beggar wandering in the streets⟩ FRAIL can be used of a person who since birth has had a delicate body ⟨a *frail* child always getting sick⟩ or of any kind of flimsy construction ⟨the *frail* boat was wrecked in the first storm⟩

weak·en \'wē-kən\ *vb* : to make or become weak or weaker

weak·fish \'wēk-,fish\ *n* : any of several sea fishes related to the perches (as a common sport and market fish of the eastern coast of the United States)

weak·ling \'wē-kling\ *n* : a person or animal that is weak

¹**weak·ly** \'wē-klē\ *adv* : in a weak manner

²**weakly** *adj* **weak·li·er; weak·li·est** : not strong or healthy

weak·ness \'wēk-nəs\ *n* **1** : lack of strength **2** : a weak point : FLAW

wealth \'welth\ *n* **1** : a large amount of money or possessions **2** : a great amount or number ⟨a *wealth* of ideas⟩

wealthy \'wel-thē\ *adj* **wealth·i·er; wealth·i·est** : having wealth : RICH

wean \'wēn\ *vb* **1** : to get a child or young animal used to food other than its mother's milk **2** : to turn one away from desiring a thing one has been fond of

weap·on \'wep-ən\ *n* : something (as a gun, knife, or club) to fight with

¹**wear** \'waər, 'weər\ *vb* **wore** \'wōr\; **worn** \'wōrn\; **wear·ing** **1** : to use as an article of clothing or decoration **2** : to carry on the body ⟨*wearing* a watch⟩ **3** : ¹SHOW 1 ⟨*wear* a smile⟩ **4** : to damage, waste, or make less by use or by scraping or rubbing **5** : to make tired **6** : to cause or make by rubbing ⟨*wear* a hole in a coat⟩ **7** : to last through long use ⟨cloth that *wears* well⟩ — **wear·er** *n*

²**wear** *n* **1** : the act of wearing : the state of being worn **2** : things worn or meant to be worn ⟨children's *wear*⟩ **3** : the result of wearing or use ⟨showing signs of *wear*⟩

wea·ri·some \'wir-ē-səm\ *adj* : TEDIOUS, DULL

wear and tear *n* : the loss or damage that occurs to something in the course of normal use

wear out *vb* **1** : to make useless by long or hard use **2** : ¹TIRE 1

¹**wea·ry** \'wiər-ē\ *adj* **wea·ri·er; wea·ri·est** **1** : made tired usually from work **2** : having one's patience, pleasure, or interest worn out **3** : causing a loss of strength or interest — **wea·ri·ly** \'wiər-ə-lē\ *adv* — **wea·ri·ness** \'wiər-ē-nəs\ *n*

²**weary** *vb* **wea·ried; wea·ry·ing** : to make or become weary

wea·sel \'wē-zəl\ *n* : a small slender active animal related to the minks that feeds on small birds and animals (as mice)

weasel

¹weath·er \'weth-ər\ *n* : the state of the air and atmosphere in regard to how warm or cold, wet or dry, or clear or stormy it is

²weather *adj* : ¹WINDWARD

³weather *vb* **1** : to expose to the weather **2** : to change (as in color or structure) by the action of the weather **3** : to be able to last or come safely through ⟨*weather* a storm⟩

weath·er·cock \'weth-ər-ˌkäk\ *n* : a weather vane shaped like a rooster

weath·er·man \'weth-ər-ˌman\ *n*, *pl* **weath·er·men** \-ˌmen\ : a person who reports and forecasts the weather

weather vane *n* : VANE 1

¹weave \'wēv\ *vb* **wove** \'wōv\; **wo·ven** \'wō-vən\; **weav·ing** **1** : to form (as cloth) by lacing together strands of material **2** : ¹SPIN 3 **3** : to make by or as if by lacing parts together ⟨*weave* a tale of adventure⟩ **4** : to move back and forth, up and down, or in and out ⟨*weaving* through traffic⟩ — **weav·er** \'wē-vər\ *n*

²weave *n* : a method or pattern of weaving

¹web \'web\ *n* **1** : a woven fabric on a loom or coming from a loom **2** : COBWEB 1 **3** : something like a cobweb **4** : a membrane especially when joining toes (as of a duck)

²web *vb* **webbed**; **web·bing** : to join or surround with a web

¹web 4

web·foot \'web-ˌfut\ *n*, *pl* **web·feet** \-ˌfēt\ : a foot (as of a duck) with toes joined by webs — **web–foot·ed** \-'fut-əd\ *adj*

wed \'wed\ *vb* **wed·ded** *also* **wed**; **wed·ding** **1** : MARRY **2** : to attach firmly

we'd \wēd\ : we had : we should : we would

wed·ding \'wed-ing\ *n* : a marriage ceremony

¹wedge \'wej\ *n* **1** : a piece of wood or metal that tapers to a thin edge and is used for splitting (as logs) or for raising something heavy **2** : something (as a piece of cake or a formation of wild geese flying) with a triangular shape

²wedge *vb* **wedged**; **wedg·ing** **1** : to fasten or tighten with a wedge **2** : to crowd or squeeze in tight

wed·lock \'wed-ˌläk\ *n* : MARRIAGE 1

Wednes·day \'wenz-dē\ *n* : the fourth day of the week

wee \'wē\ *adj* : very small : TINY

¹weed \'wēd\ *n* : a plant that tends to grow thickly where not wanted

²weed *vb* **1** : to remove weeds from ⟨*weed* the garden⟩ **2** : to get rid of what is not wanted ⟨*weed* out the poor performers⟩

weedy \'wēd-ē\ *adj* **weed·i·er**; **weed·i·est** **1** : full of or consisting of weeds **2** : like a weed especially in coarse strong rapid growth **3** : very skinny

week \'wēk\ *n* **1** : seven days in a row especially beginning with Sunday and ending with Saturday **2** : the working or school days that come between Sunday and Saturday

week·day \'wēk-ˌdā\ *n* : a day of the week except Sunday or sometimes except Saturday and Sunday

week·end \'wē-ˌkend\ *n* : the period between the close of one work or school week and the beginning of the next

¹week·ly \'wē-klē\ *adj* **1** : happening, done, produced, or published every week **2** : figured by the week ⟨*weekly* wages⟩

²weekly *n*, *pl* **week·lies** : a newspaper or magazine published every week

weep \'wēp\ *vb* **wept** \'wept\; **weep·ing** : to shed tears : CRY

weep·ing \'wē-ping\ *adj* : having slender drooping branches ⟨a *weeping* willow⟩

wee·vil \'wē-vəl\ *n* : any of various small beetles with a hard shell and a long snout many of which are harmful to fruits, nuts, grain, or trees

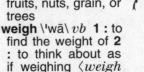

weevil

weigh \'wā\ *vb* **1** : to find the weight of **2** : to think about as if weighing ⟨*weigh* their chances of winning⟩ **3** : to measure

\ə\ **abut**	\au̇\ **out**	\i\ **tip**	\ȯ\ **saw**	\u̇\ **foot**
\ər\ **further**	\ch\ **chin**	\ī\ **life**	\ȯi\ **coin**	\y\ **yet**
\a\ **mat**	\e\ **pet**	\j\ **job**	\th\ **thin**	\yü\ **few**
\ā\ **take**	\ē\ **easy**	\ng\ **sing**	\th\ **this**	\yu̇\ **cure**
\ä\ **cot, cart**	\g\ **go**	\ō\ **bone**	\ü\ **food**	\zh\ **vision**

out on or as if on scales **4** : to lift an anchor before sailing **5** : to have weight or a specified weight ⟨*weigh* one kilogram⟩

weigh down *vb* : to cause to bend down

¹**weight** \'wāt\ *n* **1** : the amount that something weighs ⟨sold by *weight*⟩ **2** : the force with which a body is pulled toward the earth **3** : a unit (as a kilogram) for measuring weight **4** : an object (as a piece of metal) of known weight for balancing a scale in weighing other objects **5** : a heavy object used to hold or press down something **6** : ¹BURDEN 2 ⟨a *weight* on one's mind⟩ **7** : strong influence : IMPORTANCE

²**weight** *vb* **1** : to load or make heavy with a weight **2** : to trouble with a burden

weighty \'wāt-ē\ *adj* **weight·i·er; weight·i·est** **1** : having much weight : HEAVY **2** : very important

weird \'wiərd\ *adj* **1** : of or relating to witchcraft or magic ⟨the *weird* happenings in the haunted castle⟩ **2** : very unusual : STRANGE, FANTASTIC

Word History The adjective *weird* came from an earlier noun *weird*, which meant "fate." A long time ago people started to use the noun *weird* as an adjective in a phrase "the Weird Sisters." The Weird Sisters were three goddesses who determined the fates of men and women. At first the adjective *weird* meant "having to do with fate." Later it came to mean "magical," "fantastic," or "strange."

weirdo \'wiərd-ō\ *n, pl* **weird·os** : a very strange person

¹**wel·come** \'wel-kəm\ *vb* **wel·comed; wel·com·ing** **1** : to greet with courtesy **2** : to receive or accept with pleasure

Word History When you welcome people to your house you are greeting them as desirable guests. The word *welcome* comes from an Old English word that meant "a desirable guest." It was formed from two words. The first meant "desire" or "wish." The second meant "guest." The word that meant "desire" is related to the modern English word *will*. The word that meant "guest" is related to the modern English word *come*.

²**welcome** *adj* **1** : greeted or received gladly ⟨visitors are *welcome*⟩⟨a *welcome* rain⟩ **2** : giving pleasure : PLEASING ⟨a *welcome* sight⟩ **3** : willingly permitted to do, have, or enjoy something **4** — used in the phrase "You're welcome" as a reply to an expression of thanks

³**welcome** *n* : a friendly greeting

¹**weld** \'weld\ *vb* **1** : to join two pieces of metal or plastic by heating and allowing the edges to flow together **2** : to join closely **3** : to become or be capable of being welded — **weld·er** *n*

²**weld** *n* : a welded joint

wel·fare \'wel-,faər, -,feər\ *n* **1** : the state of being or doing well **2** : aid in the form of money or necessities for people who are poor, aged, or disabled

¹**well** \'wel\ *n* **1** : a source of supply **2** : a hole made in the earth to reach a natural deposit (as of water, oil, or gas) **3** : something suggesting a well

²**well** *vb* : to rise to the surface and flow out

³**well** *adv* **bet·ter** \'bet-ər\; **best** \'best\ **1** : so as to be right : in a satisfactory way ⟨do your work *well*⟩ **2** : in a good-hearted or generous way ⟨they always speak *well* of you⟩ **3** : in a skillful or expert manner ⟨plays the guitar *well*⟩ **4** : by as much as possible : COMPLETELY ⟨we are *well* aware of the problem⟩ **5** : with reason or courtesy ⟨I cannot *well* refuse⟩ **6** : in such a way as to be pleasing : as one would wish ⟨everything has gone *well* this week⟩ **7** : without trouble ⟨we could *well* afford the extra cost⟩ **8** : in a thorough manner ⟨shake *well* before using⟩ **9** : in a familiar manner ⟨I knew them *well*⟩ **10** : by quite a lot ⟨*well* over a million⟩

⁴**well** *interj* **1** — used to express surprise or doubt **2** — used to begin a conversation or to continue one that was interrupted

⁵**well** *adj* **1** : being in a satisfactory or good state ⟨all is *well*⟩ **2** : free or recovered from ill health : HEALTHY **3** : FORTUNATE 1 ⟨it was *well* that we left⟩

we'll \wēl\ : we shall : we will

well—be·ing \'wel-'bē-ing\ *n* : WELFARE 1

well—bred \'wel-'bred\ *adj* : having or showing good manners : POLITE

well—known \'wel-'nōn\ *adj* : known by many people

well—nigh \'wel-'nī\ *adv* : ALMOST

well—to—do \,wel-tə-'dü\ *adj* : having plenty of money and possessions

¹**Welsh** \'welsh\ *adj* : of or relating to Wales or the people of Wales

²**Welsh** *n* : the people of Wales

welt \'welt\ *n* : a ridge raised on the skin by a blow

¹**wel·ter** \'wel-tər\ *vb* **1** : to twist or roll one's body about **2** : to rise and fall or toss about in or with waves

²**welter** *n* : a confused jumble

wend \'wend\ *vb* : to go one's way : PROCEED

went *past of* GO

wept *past of* WEEP

were *past 2d sing, past pl, or past subjunctive of* BE

we're \wiər, wər\ : we are

weren't \wərnt\ : were not

were·wolf \wiər-,wu̇lf, wər-\ *n, pl* **werewolves** \-,wu̇lvz\ : a person in folklore who is changed or is able to change into a wolf

Word History The modern English word *werewolf* came from an Old English word that was formed from two other words. The first meant "man" and the second meant "wolf."

¹**west** \west\ *adv* : to or toward the west

²**west** *adj* : placed toward, facing, or coming from the west

³**west** *n* **1** : the direction of sunset : the compass point opposite to east **2** *cap* : regions or countries west of a point that is mentioned or understood

west·bound \west-,bau̇nd\ *adj* : going west

west·er·ly \wes-tər-lē\ *adv or adj* **1** : toward the west **2** : from the west ⟨a *westerly* wind⟩

¹**west·ern** \wes-tərn\ *adj* **1** *often cap* : of, relating to, or like that of the West **2** : lying toward or coming from the west

²**western** *n, often cap* : a story, film, or radio or television show about life in the western United States especially in the last part of the nineteenth century

¹**west·ward** \west-wərd\ *adv or adj* : toward the west

²**westward** *n* : a westward direction or part

¹**wet** \wet\ *adj* **wet·ter; wet·test** **1** : containing, covered with, or soaked with liquid (as water) ⟨a *wet* cloth⟩ **2** : RAINY ⟨*wet* weather⟩ **3** : not yet dry ⟨*wet* paint⟩ — **wet·ness** *n*

²**wet** *n* **1** : ¹WATER **2** : MOISTURE **3** : rainy weather : RAIN

³**wet** *vb* **wet** *or* **wet·ted; wet·ting** : to make wet

we've \wēv\ : we have

¹**whack** \hwak, wak\ *vb* : to hit with a hard noisy blow

²**whack** *n* **1** : a hard noisy blow **2** : the sound of a whack

whacky *variant of* WACKY

¹**whale** \hwāl, wāl\ *n* : a warm-blooded sea animal that looks like a huge fish but breathes air and feeds its young with its milk

²**whale** *vb* **whaled; whal·ing** : to hunt whales

whale·boat \hwāl-,bōt, wāl-\ *n* : a long rowboat once used by whalers

whale·bone \hwāl-,bōn, wāl-\ *n* : a substance like horn from the upper jaw of some whales

whal·er \hwā-lər, wā-\ *n* : a person or ship that hunts whales

wharf \hwȯrf, wȯrf\ *n, pl* **wharves** \hwȯrvz, wȯrvz\ *or* **wharfs** : a structure built on the shore for loading and unloading ships

¹**what** \hwät, hwət, wät, wət\ *pron* **1** : which thing or things ⟨*what* happened⟩ **2** : which sort of thing or person ⟨*what* is this⟩ ⟨*what* are they, doctors?⟩ **3** : that which ⟨do *what* you're told⟩ — **what for** : ¹WHY — **what if 1** : what would happen if ⟨*what if* they find out?⟩ **2** : what does it matter if ⟨so *what if* they do? I don't care⟩

²**what** *adv* **1** : in what way : HOW ⟨*what* does it matter⟩ **2** — used before one or more phrases that tell a cause ⟨*what* with the cold and the hunger, they nearly died⟩

³**what** *adj* **1** — used to ask about the identity of a person, object, or matter ⟨*what* books do you read⟩ **2** : how remarkable or surprising ⟨*what* an idea⟩ **3** : ²WHATEVER 1

¹**what·ev·er** \hwät-'ev-ər, hwət-, wät-, wət-\ *pron* **1** : anything that ⟨take *whatever* you need⟩ **2** : no matter what ⟨*whatever* you do, don't cheat⟩ **3** : what in the world ⟨*whatever* made you do something as stupid as that⟩

²**whatever** *adj* **1** : any and all : any . . . that ⟨take *whatever* money you need⟩ **2** : of any kind at all ⟨there's no food *whatever*⟩

wheat \hwēt, wēt\ *n* : a cereal grain that grows in tight clusters on the tall stalks of a widely cultivated grass, yields a fine white flour, is the chief source of bread in temperate regions, and is also important in animal feeds

wheat·en \hwēt-n, wēt-n\ *adj* : containing or made from wheat ⟨*wheaten* bread⟩

whee·dle \hwēd-l, wēd-l\ *vb* **whee·dled; whee·dling** **1** : to get (someone) to think or act a certain way by flattering : COAX **2** : to gain or get by coaxing or flattering ⟨trying to *wheedle* money out of them⟩

¹**wheel** \hwēl, wēl\ *n* **1** : a disk or circular frame that can turn on a central point **2** : something like a wheel (as in being round or in turning) ⟨a *wheel* of cheese⟩ **3** : something having a wheel as its main part ⟨a spinning *wheel*⟩ **4** **wheels** *pl*

\ə\ **abut**	\au̇\ **out**	\i\ **tip**	\ȯ\ **saw**	\u̇\ **foot**
\ər\ **further**	\ch\ **chin**	\ī\ **life**	\ȯi\ **coin**	\y\ **yet**
\a\ **mat**	\e\ **pet**	\j\ **job**	\th\ **thin**	\yü\ **few**
\ā\ **take**	\ē\ **easy**	\ng\ **sing**	\th\ **this**	\yu̇\ **cure**
\ä\ **cot, cart**	\g\ **go**	\ō\ **bone**	\ü\ **food**	\zh\ **vision**

: moving power : necessary parts ⟨the *wheels* of government⟩ — **wheeled** \'hwēld, wēld\ *adj*

²**wheel** *vb* **1** : to carry or move on wheels or in a vehicle with wheels **2** : ROTATE 1 **3** : to change direction as if turning on a central point ⟨I *wheeled* and faced them⟩

wheel·bar·row \'hwēl-ˌbar-ō, 'wēl-\ *n* : a small vehicle with two handles and usually one wheel for carrying small loads

wheel·chair \'hwēl-ˌcheər, 'wēl-, -ˌchaər\ *n* : a chair with wheels in which a crippled or sick person can get about

wheel·house \'hwēl-ˌhaůs, 'wēl-\ *n, pl* **wheel·hous·es** \-ˌhaů-zəz\ : a small house containing a ship's steering wheel that is built on or above the top deck

¹**wheeze** \'hwēz, 'wēz\ *vb* **wheezed; wheez·ing** **1** : to breathe with difficulty and usually with a whistling sound **2** : to make a sound like wheezing

²**wheeze** *n* : a wheezing sound

whelk \'hwelk, 'welk\ *n* : a large sea snail that has a spiral shell and is used in Europe for food

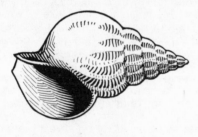

whelk

¹**whelp** \'hwelp, 'welp\ *n* : one of the young of an animal that eats flesh and especially of a dog

²**whelp** *vb* : to give birth to whelps

¹**when** \hwen, wen, hwən, wən\ *adv* **1** : at what time ⟨*when* did you leave⟩ **2** : the time at which ⟨not sure of *when* they'd come⟩ **3** : at, in, or during which ⟨came at a time *when* things were upset⟩

²**when** *conj* **1** : at, during, or just after the time that ⟨leave *when* I do⟩ **2** : in the event that : IF ⟨*when* you have no family, you're really on your own⟩ **3** : ALTHOUGH ⟨why do you tease, *when* you know it's wrong⟩

³**when** \ˌhwen, ˌwen\ *pron* : what or which time ⟨since *when* have you been an expert⟩

whence \hwens, wens\ *adv* **1** : from what place, source, or cause ⟨*whence* come all these questions⟩ **2** : from or out of which ⟨the land *whence* they came⟩

when·ev·er \hwen-'ev-ər, wen-, hwən-, wən-\ *conj or adv* : at whatever time ⟨you may leave *whenever* you are ready⟩

¹**where** \hweər, hwaər, weər, waər, hwər, wər\ *adv* **1** : at, in, or to what place ⟨*where* are they⟩ **2** : at or in what way or direction ⟨*where* does this plan lead⟩ ⟨*where* am I wrong⟩

²**where** *conj* **1** : at, in, or to the place indicated ⟨sit *where* the light's better⟩ **2** : every place that ⟨they go *where* they want to⟩

³**where** \'hweər, 'hwaər, 'weər, 'waər\ *pron* : what place ⟨*where* are you from⟩

¹**where·abouts** \'hwer-ə-ˌbaůts, 'hwar-, 'wer-, 'war-\ *adv* : near what place ⟨*whereabouts* did you lose it⟩

²**whereabouts** *n sing or pl* : the place where someone or something is

where·as \hwer-'az, hwar-, wer-, war-\ *conj* **1** : since it is true that **2** : while just the opposite ⟨water quenches fire, *whereas* gasoline feeds it⟩

where·by \hweər-'bī, hwaər-, weər-, waər-\ *adv* : by or through which

where·fore \'hweər-ˌfōr, 'hwaər-, 'weər-, 'waər-\ *adv* : ¹WHY

where·in \hwer-'in, hwar-, wer-, war-\ *adv* **1** : in what way **2** : in which

where·of \hwer-'əv, hwar-, wer-, war-, -'äv\ *conj* : of what : that of which ⟨I know *whereof* I speak⟩

where·on \hwer-'ȯn, hwar-, wer-, war-, -'än\ *adv* : on which

where·up·on \'hwer-ə-ˌpȯn, 'hwar-, 'wer-, 'war-, -ˌpän\ *conj* : and then : at which time ⟨the first attempt failed, *whereupon* they tried even harder⟩

¹**wher·ev·er** \hwer-'ev-ər, hwar-, wer-, war-\ *adv* : where in the world ⟨*wherever* have you been⟩

²**wherever** *conj* **1** : at, in, or to whatever place ⟨we can have lunch *wherever* you like⟩ **2** : in any situation in which : at any time that ⟨*wherever* it is possible, they try to help out⟩

whet \'hwet, 'wet\ *vb* **whet·ted; whet·ting** **1** : to sharpen the edge of by rubbing on or with a stone **2** : to make (as the appetite) stronger

wheth·er \'hweth-ər, 'weth-\ *conj* **1** : if it is or was true that ⟨see *whether* they've left⟩ **2** : if it is or was better ⟨wondered *whether* to stay or go home⟩ **3** — used to introduce two or more situations of which only one can occur ⟨the game will be played *whether* it rains or shines⟩

whet·stone \'hwet-ˌstōn, 'wet-\ *n* : a stone on which blades are sharpened

whew *often read as* 'hwü, 'wü, 'hyü\ *n* : a sound almost like a whistle made as an exclamation chiefly to show amazement, discomfort, or relief

whey \'hwā, 'wā\ *n* : the watery part of milk that separates after the milk sours and thickens

¹**which** \hwich, wich\ *adj* : what certain one or ones ⟨*which* hat should I wear⟩

²**which** *pron* **1** : which one or ones ⟨*which* is the right answer⟩ **2** — used in place of the name of something other than people at the beginning of a clause ⟨we caught the dog *which* got loose⟩ ⟨the suggestion *which* you made was a good one⟩

¹**which·ev·er** \hwich-'ev-ər, wich-\ *pron* : whatever one or ones ⟨buy the sweater or the coat, *whichever* you like better⟩

²**whichever** *adj* : being whatever one or ones : no matter which ⟨take *whichever* book you want⟩

¹**whiff** \'hwif, 'wif\ *n* **1** : a small gust **2** : a small amount (as of a scent or a gas) that is breathed in **3** : a very small amount : HINT

²**whiff** *vb* : to puff, blow out, or blow away in very small amounts

¹**while** \'hwīl, 'wīl\ *n* **1** : a period of time ⟨let's rest a *while*⟩ **2** : time and effort used in doing something ⟨I'll make it worth your *while* to help out⟩

²**while** *conj* **1** : during the time that ⟨someone called *while* you were out⟩ **2** : ALTHOUGH ⟨*while* the book is famous, it is seldom read⟩

³**while** *vb* **whiled; whil·ing** : to cause to pass especially in a pleasant way ⟨*while* away time⟩

whim \'hwim, 'wim\ *n* : a sudden wish or desire : a sudden change of mind

¹**whim·per** \'hwim-pər, 'wim-\ *vb* : to cry in low broken sounds : WHINE

²**whimper** *n* : a whining cry

whim·si·cal \'hwim-zi-kəl, 'wim-\ *adj* **1** : full of whims **2** : DROLL

¹**whine** \'hwīn, 'wīn\ *vb* **whined; whin·ing** **1** : to make a shrill troubled cry or a similar sound ⟨a saw *whining* through knots⟩ **2** : to complain by or as if by whining ⟨*whine* about one's troubles⟩

²**whine** *n* : a whining cry or sound

¹**whin·ny** \'hwin-ē, 'win-ē\ *vb* **whin·nied; whin·ny·ing** : to neigh usually in a low gentle way

²**whinny** *n, pl* **whin·nies** : a low gentle neigh

¹**whip** \'hwip, 'wip\ *vb* **whipped; whip·ping** **1** : to move, snatch, or jerk quickly or with force ⟨*whipped* the cloth off the table⟩ **2** : to hit with something slender and flexible : LASH **3** : to punish with blows **4** : to beat into foam ⟨*whip* cream⟩ **5** : to move back and forth in a lively way ⟨a flag whipping in the breeze⟩

²**whip** *n* **1** : something used in whipping **2** : a light dessert made with whipped cream or whipped whites of eggs

whip·pet \'hwip-ət, 'wip-\ *n* : a small swift dog that is like a greyhound and is often used for racing

whippet

whip·poor·will \' hwip-ər-,wil, 'wip-\ *n* : a bird of eastern North America that flies at night and eats insects and is named from its peculiar call

whippoorwill

¹**whir** \'hwər, 'wər\ *vb* **whirred; whir·ring** : to fly, move, or turn rapidly with a buzzing sound

²**whir** *n* : a whirring sound

¹**whirl** \'hwərl, 'wərl\ *vb* **1** : to turn or move in circles rapidly **2** : to feel dizzy ⟨my head *whirls*⟩ **3** : to move or carry around or about very rapidly

²**whirl** *n* **1** : a whirling movement **2** : something that is or seems to be whirling **3** : a state of busy movement : BUSTLE

\ə\ abut	\au̇\ out	\i\ tip	\ȯ\ saw	\u̇\ foot
\ər\ further	\ch\ chin	\ī\ life	\ȯi\ coin	\y\ yet
\a\ mat	\e\ pet	\j\ job	\th\ thin	\yü\ few
\ā\ take	\ē\ easy	\ng\ sing	\th\ this	\yu̇\ cure
\ä\ cot, cart	\g\ go	\ō\ bone	\ü\ food	\zh\ vision

whirl·pool \'hwərl-,pül, 'wərl-\ *n* : a rapid swirl of water with a low place in the center into which floating objects are drawn

whirl·wind \'hwərl-,wind, 'wərl-\ *n* : a small windstorm in which the air turns rapidly in circles

¹**whisk** \'hwisk, 'wisk\ *n* **1** : a quick sweeping or brushing motion **2** : a kitchen utensil of wire used for whipping eggs or cream

whisk²

²**whisk** *vb* **1** : to move suddenly and quickly ⟨*whisk* around the corner⟩ **2** : to beat into foam **3** : to brush with or as if with a whisk broom ⟨*whisked* dust off the coat⟩

whisk broom *n* : a small broom with a short handle used especially as a clothes brush

whis·ker \'hwis-kər, 'wis-\ *n* **1** **whiskers** *pl* : the part of the beard that grows on the sides of the face and on the chin **2** : one hair of the beard **3** : a long bristle or hair growing near the mouth of an animal

whis·key *or* **whis·ky** \'hwis-kē, 'wis-\ *n, pl* **whis·keys** *or* **whis·kies** : a strong drink containing alcohol and usually made from grain

Word History Most of the people of Ireland and Scotland speak English. Each of these countries has a language of its own as well. The Irish language is a close relative of the Scottish language. The two are only distant relatives of English. The English word *whiskey* has two sources. One is an Irish word. The other is a Scottish word. These words are very much alike. Both mean "water of life."

¹**whis·per** \'hwis-pər, 'wis-\ *vb* **1** : to speak very low **2** : to tell by whispering **3** : to make a low rustling sound ⟨the wind *whispered* in the trees⟩

²**whisper** *n* **1** : a low soft way of speaking that can be heard only by persons who are near **2** : the act of whispering **3** : something said in a whisper **4** : ¹HINT 1

¹**whis·tle** \'hwis-əl, 'wis-\ *n* **1** : a device by which a shrill sound is produced **2** : a shrill sound of or like whistling

²**whistle** *vb* **whis·tled; whis·tling** **1** : to make a shrill sound by forcing the breath through the teeth or lips **2** : to move, pass, or go with a shrill sound ⟨the arrow *whistled* past⟩ **3** : to sound a whistle **4** : to

express by whistling ⟨*whistled* my surprise⟩

whit \'hwit, 'wit\ *n* : a very small amount ⟨had not a *whit* of sense⟩

¹**white** \'hwīt, 'wit\ *adj* **whit·er; whit·est** **1** : of the color white **2** : light or pale in color ⟨*white* wine⟩ **3** : pale gray : SILVERY **4** : having a light skin ⟨the *white* races⟩ **5** : ¹BLANK 2 ⟨*white* spaces on the page⟩ **6** : not intended to cause harm ⟨*white* lies⟩ **7** : SNOWY 1 ⟨a *white* Christmas⟩ — **white·ness** *n*

²**white** *n* **1** : the color of fresh snow : the opposite of black **2** : the white part of something (as an egg) **3** : white clothing **4** : a person belonging to a white race

white blood cell *n* : one of the tiny whitish cells of the blood that help fight infection

white·cap \'hwīt-,kap, 'wit-\ *n* : the top of a wave breaking into foam

white cell *n* : WHITE BLOOD CELL

white·fish \'hwīt-,fish, 'wit-\ *n* : a freshwater fish related to the trouts that is greenish above and silvery below and is used for food

white flag *n* : a flag of plain white raised in asking for a truce or as a sign of surrender

whit·en \'hwīt-n, 'wit-n\ *vb* : to make or become white : BLEACH ⟨*whiten* sheets⟩

white oak *n* : a large oak tree known for its hard strong wood that lasts well and is not easily rotted by water

white·tail \'hwīt-,tāl, 'wit-\ *n* : the common deer of eastern North America with the underside of the tail white

whitetail

¹**white·wash** \'hwīt-,wȯsh, 'wit-, -,wäsh\ *vb* **1** : to cover with whitewash **2** : to try to

hide the wrongdoing of ⟨*whitewash* a politician caught lying⟩

²**whitewash** *n* : a mixture (as of lime and water) for making a surface (as a wall) white

whith·er \'hwith-ər, 'with-\ *adv* 1 : to what place 2 : to which place

whit·ish \'hwīt-ish, 'wīt-\ *adj* : somewhat white

whit·tle \'hwit-l, 'wit-l\ *vb* **whit·tled; whit·tling** 1 : to cut or shave off chips from wood : shape by such cutting or shaving 2 : to reduce little by little ⟨*whittle* down their spending⟩

¹**whiz** *or* **whizz** \'hwiz, 'wiz\ *vb* **whizzed; whiz·zing** : to move, pass, or fly rapidly with a buzzing sound

²**whiz** *n* : a buzzing sound ⟨the *whiz* of passing traffic⟩

who \'hü\ *pron* 1 : what person or people ⟨*who* is that⟩ 2 : the person or people that ⟨we know *who* did it⟩ 3 — used to stand for a person or people at the beginning of a clause ⟨students *who* need help should ask for it⟩

whoa \'wō, 'hō, 'hwō\ *vb* — used as a command to an animal pulling a load to stop

who·ev·er \hü-'ev-ər\ *pron* : whatever person ⟨*whoever* wants a snack must tell me now⟩

¹**whole** \'hōl\ *adj* 1 : completely healthy or sound in condition 2 : not cut up or ground ⟨a *whole* onion⟩ 3 : keeping all its necessary elements in being made ready for the market ⟨*whole* milk⟩ 4 : made up of all its parts : TOTAL ⟨the *whole* family⟩ 5 : not scattered or divided ⟨give it my *whole* attention⟩ 6 : each one of the ⟨the *whole* ten days⟩ — **wholeness** *n*

²**whole** *n* 1 : something that is whole 2 : a sum of all the parts and elements — **on the whole** 1 : all things considered 2 : in most cases

whole·heart·ed \'hōl-'härt-əd\ *adj* : not holding back ⟨a *wholehearted* effort⟩

whole number *n* : a number that is zero or any of the natural numbers

¹**whole·sale** \'hōl-,sāl\ *n* : the sale of goods in large quantities to dealers

²**wholesale** *adj* 1 : of, relating to, or working at wholesaling 2 : done on a large scale

³**wholesale** *vb* **whole·saled; whole·saling** : to sell to dealers usually in large lots — **whole·sal·er** *n*

whole·some \'hōl-səm\ *adj* 1 : helping to improve or keep the body, mind, or spirit in good condition ⟨*wholesome* food⟩ 2

: sound in body, mind, or morals — **whole·some·ness** *n*

whol·ly \'hō-lē\ *adv* : to the limit : COMPLETELY ⟨a *wholly* honest person⟩

whom \'hüm\ *pron, objective case of* WHO

whom·ev·er \hü-'mev-ər\ *pron, objective case of* WHOEVER

¹**whoop** \'hüp, 'hup\ *vb* 1 : to shout or cheer loudly and strongly 2 : to make the shrill gasping sound that follows a coughing attack in whooping cough

²**whoop** *n* : a whooping sound

whooping cough *n* : a bacterial disease especially of children in which severe attacks of coughing are often followed by a shrill gasping intake of breath

whooping crane *n* : a large white nearly extinct North American crane that has a loud whooping call

whop·per \'hwäp-ər, 'wäp-\ 1 : something huge of its kind 2 : a monstrous lie

whorl \'hwȯrl, 'wȯrl, 'hwərl, 'wərl\ *n* 1 : a row of parts (as leaves or petals) encircling a stem 2 : something that whirls or winds ⟨a *whorl* of smoke hung over the chimney⟩

¹**whose** \'hüz\ *adj* : of or relating to whom or which ⟨*whose* bag is it⟩ ⟨the book *whose* cover is torn⟩

²**whose** *pron* : whose one : whose ones

¹**why** \'hwī, 'wī\ *adv* : for what cause or reason ⟨*why* did you do it⟩

²**why** *conj* 1 : the cause or reason for which ⟨we know *why* you did it⟩ 2 : for which ⟨here's the reason *why* I did it⟩

³**why** *n, pl* **whys** : the cause of or reason for something

⁴**why** \wī, hwī\ *interj* — used to express surprise, uncertainty, approval, disapproval, or impatience ⟨*why*, how did you know that⟩

wick \'wik\ *n* : a cord, strip, or ring of loosely woven material through which a liquid (as oil) is drawn to the top in a candle, lamp, or oil stove for burning

wick·ed \'wik-əd\ *adj* 1 : bad in behavior, moral state, or effect : EVIL 2 : DANGEROUS 2 ⟨a *wicked* storm⟩ **synonyms** see BAD — **wick·ed·ly** *adv* — **wick·ed·ness** *n*

¹**wick·er** \'wik-ər\ *n* 1 : a flexible twig (as of willow) used in basketry 2 : WICKERWORK

²**wicker** *adj* : made of wicker ⟨*wicker* furniture⟩

wick·er·work \'wik-ər-,wərk\ *n* : basketry made of wicker

\ə\ **abut**	\aú\ **out**	\i\ **tip**	\ȯ\ **saw**	\ú\ **foot**
\ər\ **further**	\ch\ **chin**	\ī\ **life**	\ȯi\ **coin**	\y\ **yet**
\a\ **mat**	\e\ **pet**	\j\ **job**	\th\ **thin**	\yü\ **few**
\ā\ **take**	\ē\ **easy**	\ng\ **sing**	\th\ **this**	\yú\ **cure**
\ä\ **cot, cart**	\g\ **go**	\ō\ **bone**	\ü\ **food**	\zh\ **vision**

wick·et \'wik-ət\ *n* **1** : a small gate or door in or near a larger gate or door **2** : a small window (as in a bank or ticket office) through which business is conducted **3** : either of the two sets of three rods topped by two crosspieces at which the ball is bowled in cricket **4** : an arch (as of wire) through which the ball is hit in the game of croquet

¹wide \'wīd\ *adj* **wid·er; wid·est 1** : covering a very large area **2** : measured across or at right angles to length ⟨cloth 100 centimeters *wide*⟩ **3** : having a large measure across : BROAD ⟨a *wide* street⟩ **4** : opened as far as possible ⟨eyes *wide* with wonder⟩ **5** : not limited ⟨*wide* reading⟩ **6** : far from the goal or truth ⟨the shot was *wide*⟩ — **wide·ly** *adv* — **wide·ness** *n*

²wide *adv* **wid·er; wid·est 1** : over a wide area ⟨travel far and *wide*⟩ **2** : to the limit : COMPLETELY ⟨*wide* open⟩

wide–awake \ˌwīd-ə-'wāk\ *adj* : not sleepy, dull, or without energy : ALERT

wid·en \'wīd-n\ *vb* : to make or become wide or wider

wide·spread \'wīd-'spred\ *adj* **1** : widely stretched out ⟨*widespread* wings⟩ **2** : widely scattered ⟨*widespread* public interest⟩

¹wid·ow \'wid-ō\ *n* : a woman who has lost her husband by death

²widow *vb* : to make a widow or widower of

wid·ow·er \'wid-ə-wər\ *n* : a man who has lost his wife by death

width \'width\ *n* **1** : the shortest or shorter side of an object **2** : BREADTH 1

wield \'wēld\ *vb* **1** : to use (as a tool) in an effective way ⟨*wield* a broom⟩ **2** : ²EXERCISE 1 ⟨*wield* influence⟩

wie·ner \'wē-nər\ *n* : FRANKFURTER

wife \'wīf\ *n, pl* **wives** \'wīvz\ : a married woman — **wife·ly** *adj*

wig \'wig\ *n* : a manufactured covering of natural or artificial hair for the head

¹wig·gle \'wig-əl\ *vb* **wig·gled; wig·gling 1** : to move to and fro in a jerky way **2** : to proceed with twisting and turning movements

²wiggle *n* : a wiggling motion

wig·gler \'wig-lər\ *n* : WRIGGLER

wig·gly \'wig-lē\ *adj* **wig·gli·er; wig·gli·est 1** : given to wiggling ⟨a *wiggly* worm⟩ **2** : WAVY ⟨*wiggly* lines⟩

wig·wag \'wig-ˌwag\ *vb* **wig·wagged; wig·wag·ging** : to signal by movement of a flag or light

wig·wam \'wig-ˌwäm\ *n* : an Indian hut made of poles spread over with bark, rush mats, or hides

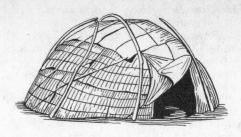

wigwam

¹wild \'wīld\ *adj* **1** : living in a state of nature and not under human control and care : not tame ⟨*wild* game animals⟩ **2** : growing or produced in nature : not cultivated by people ⟨*wild* honey⟩ ⟨*wild* grapes⟩ **3** : not civilized : SAVAGE **4** : not kept under control ⟨*wild* rage⟩ **5** : wide of the intended goal or course ⟨a *wild* guess⟩ ⟨a *wild* throw⟩ — **wild·ly** *adv* — **wild·ness** *n*

²wild *n* : WILDERNESS

wild boar *n* : an Old World wild hog from which most domestic swine derive

wild boar

wild·cat \'wīld-ˌkat\ *n* : any of various cats (as an ocelot or bobcat) of small or medium size

wil·der·ness \'wil-dər-nəs\ *n* : a wild region which is not used for farming and in which few people live

wild·fire \'wīld-ˌfir\ *n* : a fire that destroys a wide area

wild flower *n* : a wild plant with showy flowers

wild·fowl \'wīld-ˌfaúl\ *n, pl* **wildfowl** : a bird and especially a waterfowl hunted as game

wild·life \'wīld-ˌlīf\ *n* : creatures that are neither human nor domesticated : the wild animals of field and forest

¹wile \'wīl\ *n* : a trick meant to trap or deceive

²wile *vb* **wiled; wil·ing** : ²LURE

¹will \wəl, wil\ *helping verb, past* **would** \wəd, wu̇d\ *present sing & pl* **will** **1** : wish to ⟨they *will* have hamburgers⟩ **2** : am, is, or are willing to ⟨I *will* go if you ask me⟩ **3** : am, is, or are determined to ⟨we *will* go in spite of the storm⟩ **4** : am, is, or are going to ⟨everyone *will* be there⟩ **5** : is or are commanded to ⟨you *will* come here at once⟩

²will \'wil\ *n* **1** : a firm wish or desire ⟨the *will* to win⟩ **2** : the power to decide or control what one will do or how one will act **3** : a legal paper in which a person states to whom the things which he or she owns are to be given after death

³will \'wil\ *vb* **1** : ²ORDER 2, DECREE ⟨it will happen if God *wills* it⟩ **2** : to bring to a certain condition by the power of the will ⟨*will* yourself to sleep⟩ **3** : to leave by will ⟨*willed* their property to the children⟩

will·ful *or* **wil·ful** \'wil-fəl\ *adj* **1** : STUBBORN 1 ⟨*willful* children⟩ **2** : INTENTIONAL ⟨*willful* murder⟩ — **will·ful·ly** \-fə-lē\ *adv* — **will·ful·ness** *n*

will·ing \'wil-ing\ *adj* **1** : feeling no objection ⟨*willing* to go⟩ **2** : not slow or lazy ⟨a *willing* worker⟩ **3** : made, done, or given of one's own choice : VOLUNTARY — **will·ing·ly** *adv* — **will·ing·ness** *n*

wil·low \'wil-ō\ *n* **1** : a tree or bush with narrow leaves, catkins for flowers, and tough flexible stems used in making baskets **2** : the wood of the willow tree

¹wilt \'wilt\ *vb* **1** : to lose freshness and become limp ⟨*wilting* roses⟩ **2** : to lose strength

²wilt *n* : a plant disease (as of tomatoes) in which wilting and browning of leaves leads to death of the plant

wily \'wī-lē\ *adj* **wil·i·er; wil·i·est** : full of tricks : CRAFTY

win \'win\ *vb* **won** \'wən\; **win·ning** **1** : to achieve the victory in a contest **2** : to get by effort or skill : GAIN ⟨*win* praise⟩ **3** : to obtain by victory ⟨*win* a prize in a contest⟩ **4** : to be the victor in ⟨*win* a race⟩ **5** : to ask and get the favor of

wince \'wins\ *vb* **winced; winc·ing** : to draw back (as from pain)

winch \'winch\ *n* : a machine that has a roller on which rope is wound for pulling or lifting

¹wind \'wind\ *n* **1** : a movement of the air : BREEZE **2** : power to breathe ⟨the fall knocked the *wind* out of the child⟩ **3** : air carrying a scent (as of game) **4** : limited knowledge especially about something secret : HINT ⟨they got *wind* of our plans⟩ **5 winds** *pl* : wind instruments of a band or orchestra

²wind *vb* **1** : to get a scent of ⟨the dogs *winded* game⟩ **2** : to cause to be out of breath

³wind \'wīnd, 'wind\ *vb* **wound** \'wau̇nd\; **wind·ing** : to sound by blowing ⟨*wind* a horn⟩

⁴wind \'wīnd\ *vb* **wound** \'wau̇nd\; **wind·ing** **1** : to twist around ⟨*wind* thread on a spool⟩ **2** : to cover with something twisted around : WRAP ⟨*wind* an arm with a bandage⟩ **3** : to make the spring of tight ⟨*wound* my watch⟩ **4** : to move in a series of twists and turns ⟨the trail *wound* between the trees⟩

⁵wind \'wīnd\ *n* : ²BEND

wind·break \'wind-ˌbrāk\ *n* : something (as a growth of trees and shrubs) that breaks the force of the wind

wind·fall \'wind-ˌfȯl\ *n* **1** : something (as fruit from a tree) blown down by the wind **2** : an unexpected gift or gain

wind instrument *n* : a musical instrument (as a clarinet, harmonica, or trumpet) sounded by the vibration of a stream of air and especially by the player's breath

wind·lass \'wind-ləs\ *n* : a winch used especially on ships for pulling and lifting

wind·mill \'wind-ˌmil\ *n* : a mill or a machine (as for pumping water) worked by the wind turning sails or vanes at the top of a tower

win·dow \'win-dō\ *n* **1** : an opening in a wall to admit light and air **2** : the glass and frame that fill a window opening

windmill

Word History The English word *window* came from a word in an old Scandinavian language. This word was formed from two words. One meant "wind" or "air." The other meant "eye." A window can be thought of as an eye, or hole, through which the wind enters.

window box *n* : a box for growing plants in or by a window

win·dow·pane \'win-dō-,pān\ *n* : a pane in a window

wind·pipe \'wind-,pīp\ *n* : a tube with a firm wall that connects the pharynx with the lungs and is used in breathing

wind·proof \'wind-'prüf\ *adj* : protecting from the wind

wind·shield \'wind-,shēld\ *n* : a clear screen (as of glass) attached to the body of a vehicle (as a car) in front of the riders to protect them from the wind

wind·storm \'wind-,stȯrm\ *n* : a storm with strong wind and little or no rain

wind·up \'wīn-,dəp\ *n* 1 : the last part of something : FINISH 2 : a swing of a baseball pitcher's arm before the pitch is thrown

wind up *vb* 1 : to bring to an end : CONCLUDE 2 : to swing the arm before pitching a baseball

¹**wind·ward** \'win-dwərd\ *adj* : moving or placed toward the direction from which the wind is blowing

²**windward** *n* : the side or direction from which the wind is blowing ⟨sail to the *windward*⟩

windy \'win-dē\ *adj* **wind·i·er; wind·i·est** : having much wind ⟨a *windy* day⟩

wine \'wīn\ *n* 1 : fermented grape juice containing various amounts of alcohol 2 : the usually fermented juice of a plant product (as a fruit) used as a drink

win·ery \'wīn-ə-rē\ *n, pl* **win·er·ies** : a place where wine is made

¹**wing** \'wing\ *n* 1 : one of the paired limbs or limblike parts with which a bird, bat, or insect flies 2 : something like a wing in appearance, use, or motion ⟨the *wings* of an airplane⟩ 3 : a part (as of a building) that sticks out from the main part 4 : a division of an organization 5 **wings** *pl* : an area just off the stage of a theater — **wing·like** \-,līk\ *adj* — **on the wing** : in flight

²**wing** *vb* : to go with wings : FLY

winged \'wingd, 'wing-əd\ *adj* : having wings or winglike parts ⟨*winged* insects⟩

wing·less \'wing-ləs\ *adj* : having no wings

wing·spread \'wing-,spred\ *n* : the distance between the tips of the spread wings

¹**wink** \'wingk\ *vb* 1 : to close and open the eyelids quickly 2 : to close and open one eye quickly as a signal or hint

²**wink** *n* 1 : a brief period of sleep 2 : a hint or sign given by winking 3 : an act of winking 4 : a very short time

win·ner \'win-ər\ *n* : one that wins

¹**win·ning** \'win-ing\ *n* 1 : the act of one that wins 2 : something won especially in gambling — often used in pl.

²**winning** *adj* 1 : being one that wins ⟨a *winning* team⟩ 2 : tending to please or delight ⟨a *winning* smile⟩

win·now \'win-ō\ *vb* : to remove (as waste from grain) by a current of air

win·some \'win-səm\ *adj* : ²WINNING 2

¹**win·ter** \'wint-ər\ *n* 1 : the season between autumn and spring (as the months of December, January, and February in the northern half of the earth) 2 : YEAR 2 ⟨a person of seventy *winters*⟩

²**winter** *vb* 1 : to pass the winter ⟨*wintered* in Florida⟩ 2 : to keep, feed, or manage during the winter ⟨*winter* livestock on silage⟩

win·ter·green \'wint-ər-,grēn\ *n* : a low evergreen plant with white flowers that look like little bells and are followed by red berries which produce an oil (**oil of wintergreen**) used in medicine and flavoring

win·ter·time \'wint-ər-,tīm\ *n* : the winter season

win·try \'win-trē\ *adj* **win·tri·er; win·tri·est** 1 : of, relating to, or characteristic of winter 2 : not friendly : COLD ⟨a *wintry* welcome⟩

¹**wipe** \'wīp\ *vb* **wiped; wip·ing** 1 : to clean or dry by rubbing ⟨*wipe* dishes⟩ 2 : to remove by or as if by rubbing ⟨*wipe* away tears⟩ — **wip·er** *n*

²**wipe** *n* : an act of wiping : RUB

wipe out *vb* : to destroy completely

¹**wire** \'wīr\ *n* 1 : metal in the form of a thread or slender rod 2 : a telephone or telegraph wire or system 3 : TELEGRAM, CABLEGRAM

²**wire** *vb* **wired; wir·ing** 1 : to provide or equip with wire 2 : to bind, string, or mount with wire 3 : to send or send word to by telegraph

¹**wire·less** \'wīr-ləs\ *adj* 1 : having no wire 2 : relating to communication by electric waves but without connecting wires : RADIO 2

²**wireless** *n* 1 : wireless telegraphy 2 : ¹RADIO

wiry \'wīr-ē\ *adj* **wir·i·er; wir·i·est** 1 : of or like wire 2 : being slender yet strong and active

wis·dom \'wiz-dəm\ *n* : knowledge and the ability to use it to help oneself or others

wisdom tooth *n* : the last tooth of the full set on each half of each jaw of an adult

¹**wise** \'wīz\ *n* : MANNER 2, WAY — used in such phrases as *in any wise, in no wise, in this wise*

²**wise** *adj* **wis·er; wis·est** 1 : having or showing good sense or good judgment : SENSIBLE 2 : having knowledge or information — **wise·ly** *adv*

-wise \,wīz\ *adv suffix* 1 : in the manner

of **2** : in the position or direction of ⟨clock*wise*⟩ **3** : with regard to

wise•crack \'wīz-,krak\ *n* : a clever and often insulting statement usually made in joking

¹wish \'wish\ *vb* **1** : to have a desire for : WANT **2** : to form or express a desire concerning ⟨the teacher *wished* that we would be quiet⟩ **synonyms** see DESIRE

²wish *n* **1** : an act or instance of wishing **2** : something wished ⟨got my *wish*⟩ **3** : a desire for happiness or good fortune ⟨send them my best *wishes*⟩

wish•bone \'wish-,bōn\ *n* : a bone in front of a bird's breastbone that is shaped like a V

wishbone

wish•ful \'wish-fəl\ *adj* : having, showing, or based on a wish

wishy–washy \'wish-ē-,wȯsh-ē, -,wäsh-\ *adj* : lacking spirit, courage, or determination : WEAK

wisp \'wisp\ *n* **1** : a small bunch of hay or straw **2** : a thin piece or strand ⟨*wisps* of hair⟩ **3** : a thin streak ⟨*wisps* of smoke⟩

wispy \'wis-pē\ *adj* **wisp•i•er; wisp•i•est** : being thin and flimsy

wis•tar•ia \wis-'tir-ē-ə, -'ter-\ *n* : WISTERIA

wis•te•ria \wis-'tir-ē-ə\ *n* : a woody vine related to the beans that is grown for its long clusters of violet, white or pink flowers

wisteria

wist•ful \'wist-fəl\ *adj* : feeling or showing a timid longing ⟨a *wistful* expression⟩ — **wist•ful•ly** \-fə-lē\ *adv* — **wist•ful•ness** *n*

wit \'wit\ *n* **1** : power to think, reason, or decide ⟨a person of little *wit*⟩ **2** : normal mental state — usually used in pl. ⟨scared me out of my *wits*⟩ **3** : cleverness in making sharp and usually amusing comments **4** : witty comments, expressions, or talk **5** : a witty person

witch \'wich\ *n* **1** : a woman believed to have magic powers **2** : an ugly or mean old woman

witch•craft \'wich-,kraft\ *n* : the power or doings of a witch

witch doctor *n* : a person who uses magic to cure illness and fight off evil spirits

witch•ery \'wich-ə-rē\ *n, pl* **witch•er•ies 1** : WITCHCRAFT **2** : power to charm or fascinate

witch ha•zel \'wich-,hā-zəl\ *n* **1** : a shrub with small yellow flowers in late fall or very early spring **2** : a soothing alcoholic lotion made from witch hazel bark

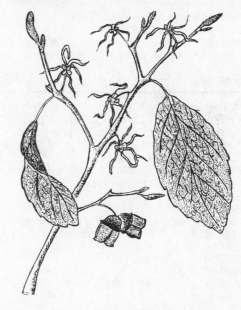

witch hazel 1

with \'with, 'with\ *prep* **1** : AGAINST 2 ⟨argued *with* the child's parents⟩ **2** : in shared relation to ⟨talk *with* friends⟩ **3** : having in or as part of it ⟨coffee *with*

\ə\ **abut**	\au̇\ **out**	\i\ **tip**	\ȯ\ **saw**	\u̇\ **foot**
\ər\ **further**	\ch\ **chin**	\ī\ **life**	\ȯi\ **coin**	\y\ **yet**
\a\ **mat**	\e\ **pet**	\j\ **job**	\th\ **thin**	\yü\ **few**
\ā\ **take**	\ē\ **easy**	\ng\ **sing**	\th\ **this**	\yu̇\ **cure**
\ä\ **cot, cart**	\g\ **go**	\ō\ **bone**	\ü\ **food**	\zh\ **vision**

cream⟩ **4** : in regard to ⟨patient *with* children⟩ **5** : compared to ⟨identical *with* the rest⟩ **6** : in the opinion or judgment of ⟨is the party all right *with* your parents⟩ **7** : by the use of ⟨hit me *with* a ruler⟩ **8** : so as to show ⟨spoke *with* pride⟩ **9** : in the company of ⟨went to the show *with* a friend⟩ **10** : in possession of ⟨arrived *with* good news⟩⟨animals *with* horns⟩ **11** : as well as ⟨hits the ball *with* the best of them⟩ **12** : FROM 2 ⟨parting *with* friends⟩ **13** : BECAUSE OF ⟨pale *with* anger⟩ **14** : DESPITE ⟨*with* all your tricks you failed⟩ **15** : if given ⟨*with* your permission, I'll leave⟩ **16** : at the time of or shortly after ⟨get up *with* the dawn⟩⟨*with* that, I paused⟩ **17** : in support of ⟨I'm *with* you all the way⟩ **18** : in the direction of ⟨sail *with* the tide⟩

with·draw \with-'drȯ, with-\ *vb* **with·drew** \-'drü\; **with·drawn** \-'drȯn\; **with·drawing** **1** : to draw back : take away ⟨*withdraw* money from the bank⟩ **2** : to take back (as something said or suggested) **3** : to go away especially for privacy or safety

with·draw·al \with-'drȯ-əl, with-\ *n* : an act or instance of withdrawing

with·er \'with-ər\ *vb* : to shrink up from or as if from loss of natural body moisture : WILT

with·ers \'with-ərz\ *n pl* : the ridge between the shoulder bones of a horse

with·hold \with-'hōld, with-\ *vb* **with·held** \-'held\; **with·hold·ing** : to refuse to give, grant, or allow ⟨*withhold* permission⟩

¹with·in \with-'in, with-\ *adv* : ⁴INSIDE ⟨a bomb exploded *within*⟩

²within *prep* **1** : ³INSIDE 1 ⟨stay *within* the house⟩ **2** : not beyond the limits of ⟨live *within* your income⟩

¹with·out \with-'au̇t, with-\ *prep* **1** : ⁴OUTSIDE **2** : completely lacking ⟨they're *without* hope⟩ **3** : not accompanied by or showing ⟨spoke *without* thinking⟩

²without *adv* : ³OUTSIDE

with·stand \with-'stand, with-\ *vb* **with·stood** \-'stu̇d\; **with·stand·ing** **1** : to hold out against ⟨able to *withstand* the worst weather⟩ **2** : to oppose (as an attack) successfully

wit·less \'wit-ləs\ *adj* : lacking in wit or intelligence : FOOLISH

¹wit·ness \'wit-nəs\ *n* **1** : TESTIMONY ⟨give false *witness*⟩ **2** : a person who sees or otherwise has personal knowledge of something ⟨*witnesses* of an accident⟩ **3** : a person who gives testimony in court **4** : a person who is present at an action (as the signing of a will) so as to be able to say who did it

²witness *vb* **1** : to be a witness to **2** : to give testimony to : testify as a witness **3** : to be or give proof of ⟨their actions *witness* their guilt⟩

wit·ted \'wit-əd\ *adj* : having wit or understanding — used in combination ⟨quick-*witted*⟩ ⟨slow-*witted*⟩

wit·ty \'wit-ē\ *adj* **wit·ti·er; wit·ti·est** : having or showing wit ⟨a *witty* person⟩

wives *pl of* WIFE

wiz·ard \'wiz-ərd\ *n* **1** : SORCERER, MAGICIAN **2** : a very clever or skillful person

¹wob·ble \'wäb-əl\ *vb* **wob·bled; wobbling** : to move from side to side in a shaky manner — **wob·bly** \'wäb-lē\ *adj*

²wobble *n* : a rocking motion from side to side

woe \'wō\ *n* : great sorrow, grief, or misfortune : TROUBLE ⟨a tale of *woe*⟩ **synonyms** see SORROW

woe·ful \'wō-fəl\ *adj* **1** : full of grief or misery ⟨a *woeful* heart⟩ **2** : bringing woe or misery ⟨a *woeful* day⟩

woke *past of* WAKE

woken *past participle of* WAKE

¹wolf \'wu̇lf\ *n, pl* **wolves** \'wu̇lvz\ **1** : a large intelligent doglike wild animal that eats flesh and has ears which stand up and a bushy tail **2** : a person felt to resemble a wolf (as in craftiness or fierceness) — **wolf·ish** \'wu̇l-fish\ *adj*

²wolf *vb* : to eat greedily

wolf dog *n* **1** : WOLFHOUND **2** : the hybrid offspring of a wolf and a domestic dog **3** : a dog that looks like a wolf

wolf·hound \'wu̇lf-,hau̇nd\ *n* : any of several large dogs used in hunting large animals

wol·fram \'wu̇l-frəm\ *n* : TUNGSTEN

wol·ver·ine \,wu̇l-və-'rēn\ *n* : a blackish wild animal with shaggy fur that is related to the martens and sables, eats flesh, and is found chiefly in the northern parts of North America

wolverine

wolves *pl of* WOLF

wom·an \'wùm-ən\ *n, pl* **wom·en** \'wim-ən\ **1** : an adult female person **2** : women considered as a group

wom·an·hood \'wùm-ən-ˌhùd\ *n* **1** : the state of being a woman **2** : womanly characteristics **3** : WOMAN 2

wom·an·kind \'wùm-ən-ˌkīnd\ *n* : WOMAN 2

wom·an·ly \'wùm-ən-lē\ *adj* : having the characteristics of a woman

womb \'wüm\ *n* : UTERUS

wom·en·folk \'wim-ən-ˌfōk\ *or* **wom·en·folks** \-ˌfōks\ *n pl* : women especially of one family or group

won *past of* WIN

¹**won·der** \'wən-dər\ *n* **1** : something extraordinary : MARVEL **2** : a feeling (as of astonishment) caused by something extraordinary

²**wonder** *vb* **1** : to feel surprise or amazement **2** : to be curious or have doubt

won·der·ful \'wən-dər-fəl\ *adj* **1** : causing wonder : MARVELOUS **2** : very good or fine ⟨had a *wonderful* time⟩ — **won·der·ful·ly** \-fə-lē\ *adv*

won·der·ing·ly \'wən-də-ring-lē\ *adv* : in or as if in wonder ⟨looked at them *wonderingly*⟩

won·der·land \'wən-dər-ˌland\ *n* : a place of wonders or surprises

won·der·ment \'wən-dər-mənt\ *n* : AMAZEMENT

won·drous \'wən-drəs\ *adj* : WONDERFUL 1

¹**wont** \'wónt, 'wōnt\ *adj* : being in the habit of doing ⟨slept longer than I was *wont*⟩

²**wont** *n* : usual custom : HABIT ⟨slept longer than was my *wont*⟩

won't \wōnt\ : will not

woo \'wü\ *vb* **wooed; woo·ing** **1** : to try to gain the love of **2** : to try to gain ⟨*woo* public favor⟩

¹**wood** \'wùd\ *n* **1** : a thick growth of trees **2** : a hard fibrous material that makes up most of the substance of a tree or shrub within the bark and is often used as a building material or fuel

²**wood** *adj* **1** : WOODEN 1 **2** : used for or on wood ⟨a *wood* chisel⟩ **3** *or* **woods** \'ùdz\ : living or growing in woodland ⟨*woods* herbs⟩

wood·bine \'wùd-ˌbīn\ *n* : any of several climbing vines of Europe and America (as honeysuckle)

wood·carv·er \'wùd-ˌkär-vər\ *n* : a person who carves useful or ornamental things from wood

wood·chuck \'wùd-ˌchək\ *n* : a reddish brown rodent that hibernates : GROUNDHOG

wood·cock \'wùd-ˌkäk\ *n* : a brown game bird that has a long bill and is related to the snipe

woodcock

wood·craft \'wùd-ˌkraft\ *n* : knowledge about the woods and how to take care of oneself in them

wood·cut·ter \'wùd-ˌkət-ər\ *n* : a person who cuts wood especially as an occupation

wood·ed \'wùd-əd\ *adj* : covered with trees

wood·en \'wùd-n\ *adj* **1** : made of wood **2** : stiff like wood : AWKWARD ⟨a *wooden* posture⟩ **3** : lacking spirit, ease, or charm ⟨a *wooden* manner⟩

wood·land \'wùd-lənd, -ˌland\ *n* : land covered with trees and shrubs : FOREST

wood·lot \'wùd-ˌlät\ *n* : a small wooded section (as of a farm) kept to meet fuel and timber needs

wood louse *n* : a small flat gray crustacean that lives usually under stones or bark

wood·peck·er \'wùd-ˌpek-ər\ *n* : a bird that climbs trees and drills holes in them with its bill in search of insects

wood·pile \'wùd-ˌpīl\ *n* : a pile of wood especially for use as fuel

wood·shed \'wùd-ˌshed\ *n* : a shed for storing wood and especially firewood

woods·man \'wùdz-mən\ *n, pl* **woods·men** \-mən\ **1** : a person who cuts down trees as an occupation **2** : a person skilled in woodcraft

woodpecker

woodsy \'wùd-zē\ *adj* : of, relating to, or suggestive of woodland

wood thrush *n* : a large thrush of eastern North America noted for its loud clear song

\ə\ **abut**	\au̇\ **out**	\i\ **tip**	\ȯ\ **saw**	\u̇\ **foot**
\ər\ **further**	\ch\ **chin**	\ī\ **life**	\ȯi\ **coin**	\y\ **yet**
\a\ **mat**	\e\ **pet**	\j\ **job**	\th\ **thin**	\yü\ **few**
\ā\ **take**	\ē\ **easy**	\ng\ **sing**	\th\ **this**	\yu̇\ **cure**
\ä\ **cot, cart**	\g\ **go**	\ō\ **bone**	\ü\ **food**	\zh\ **vision**

wood•wind \'wu̇d-,wind\ *n* : one of the group of wind instruments consisting of the flutes, oboes, clarinets, bassoons, and sometimes saxophones

wood•work \'wu̇d-,wərk\ *n* : work (as the edge around doorways) made of wood

wood•work•ing \'wu̇d-,wər-king\ *n* : the art or process of shaping or working with wood

woody \'wu̇d-ē\ *adj* **wood•i•er; wood•i•est 1** : being mostly woods ⟨*woody* land⟩ **2** : of or containing wood or wood fibers ⟨a *woody* stem⟩ **3** : very much like wood ⟨*woody* texture⟩

woof \'wu̇f, 'wüf\ *n* **1** : the threads that cross the warp in weaving a fabric **2** : a woven fabric or its texture

wool \'wu̇l\ *n* **1** : soft heavy wavy or curly hair especially of the sheep **2** : a substance that looks like a mass of wool ⟨glass *wool*⟩ **3** : a material (as yarn) made from wool

wool•en *or* **wool•len** \'wu̇l-ən\ *adj* **1** : made of wool **2** : of or relating to wool or cloth made of wool ⟨a *woolen* mill⟩

wool•ly \'wu̇l-ē\ *adj* **wool•li•er; wool•li•est** : made of or like wool

¹word \'wərd\ *n* **1** : a sound or combination of sounds that has meaning and is spoken by a human being **2** : a written or printed letter or letters standing for a spoken word **3** : a brief remark or conversation **4** : ²COMMAND 2, ORDER **5** : NEWS ⟨any *word* on how they are⟩ **6** : ¹PROMISE 1 ⟨I give you my *word*⟩ **7 words** *pl* : remarks said in anger or in a quarrel

²word *vb* : to express in words : PHRASE

word•ing \'wərd-ing\ *n* : the way something is put into words

wordy \'wərd-ē\ *adj* **word•i•er; word•i•est** : using or containing many words or more words than are needed — **word•i•ness** *n*

wore *past of* WEAR

¹work \'wərk\ *n* **1** : the use of a person's strength or ability in order to get something done or get some desired result : LABOR ⟨the *work* of a carpenter⟩ **2** : OCCUPATION 1, EMPLOYMENT **3** : something that needs to be done : TASK, JOB ⟨have *work* to do⟩ **4** : DEED 1, ACHIEVEMENT ⟨honor the club for its good *works*⟩ **5** : something produced by effort or hard work ⟨an author's latest *work*⟩ **6 works** *pl* : a place where industrial labor is done : PLANT, FACTORY ⟨a locomotive *works*⟩ **7 works** *pl* : the working or moving parts of a mechanical device ⟨the *works* of a watch⟩ **8** : the way one works : WORKMANSHIP ⟨a job spoiled by careless *work*⟩ **synonyms** see LABOR

²work *vb* **worked** *or* **wrought** \'rȯt\;

work•ing 1 : to do work especially for money or because of a need instead of for pleasure : labor or cause to labor **2** : to perform or act or to cause to act as planned : OPERATE ⟨a plan that *worked* well⟩ ⟨*work* a machine⟩ **3** : to move or cause to move slowly or with effort ⟨*work* the liquid into a cloth⟩ ⟨the screw *worked* loose⟩ **4** : to cause to happen ⟨*work* miracles⟩ **5** : ¹MAKE 2, SHAPE ⟨a vase beautifully *wrought*⟩ **6** : to carry on one's occupation in, through, or along ⟨two agents *worked* the city⟩ **7** : EXCITE 2, PROVOKE ⟨*work* yourself into a rage⟩

work•able \'wər-kə-bəl\ *adj* : capable of being worked or done

work•bench \'wərk-,bench\ *n* : a bench on which work is done (as by mechanics)

work•book \'wərk-,bu̇k\ *n* : a book made up of a series of problems or practice examples for a student to use as part of a course of study

work•er \'wər-kər\ *n* **1** : a person who works **2** : one of the members of a colony of bees, ants, wasps, or termites that are only partially developed sexually and that do most of the labor and protective work of the colony

work•ing \'wər-king\ *adj* **1** : doing work especially for a living ⟨*working* people⟩ **2** : relating to work ⟨*working* hours⟩ **3** : good enough to allow work or further work to be done ⟨a *working* agreement⟩

work•ing•man \'wər-king-,man\ *n, pl* **work•ing•men** \-,men\ : a person who works for wages usually at common labor or in industry : a member of the working class

work•man \'wərk-mən\ *n, pl* **work•men** \-mən\ **1** : WORKINGMAN **2** : a skilled worker (as an electrician or carpenter)

work•man•ship \'wərk-mən-,ship\ *n* **1** : the art or skill of a workman **2** : the quality of a piece of work ⟨take pride in good *workmanship*⟩

work•out \'wər-,kau̇t\ *n* : an exercise or practice to test or increase ability or performance ⟨the team had a good *workout*⟩

work out \,wər-'kau̇t\ *vb* : to invent or solve by effort ⟨*work out* a new kind of machine⟩ ⟨*work* it *out* for yourself⟩

work•shop \'wərk-,shäp\ *n* : a shop where work and especially skilled work is carried on

world \'wərld\ *n* **1** : EARTH 3 **2** : people in general : HUMANITY **3** : a state of existence ⟨a future *world*⟩ **4** : a great number or amount ⟨a *world* of troubles⟩ **5** : a part or section of the earth and the people living there

Word History The word *world* came from an Old English word that meant "this world" or "lifetime." It was used to refer to the life of human beings on earth as contrasted with life after death. The Old English word that meant "this world" or "lifetime" was formed from two words. The first meant "man." The second meant "old."

world·ly \'wərld-lē\ *adj* **world·li·er; world·li·est** : of or relating to this world

¹**worm** \'wərm\ *n* **1** : any of various long creeping or crawling animals that usually have soft bodies **2** : a person hated or pitied **3 worms** *pl* : the presence of or disease caused by worms living in the body ⟨a dog with *worms*⟩

²**worm** *vb* **1** : to move slowly by creeping or wriggling ⟨*worm* through thick brush⟩ **2** : to get hold of or escape from by trickery ⟨*worm* a secret from a friend⟩ ⟨*worm* one's way out of trouble⟩ **3** : to free from worms ⟨*worm* a puppy⟩

wormy \'wər-mē\ *adj* **worm·i·er; worm·i·est** : containing worms

worn *past participle of* WEAR

worn–out \'wōr-'naủt\ *adj* **1** : useless from long or hard wear **2** : very weary

wor·ri·some \'wər-ē-səm\ *adj* **1** : given to worrying **2** : causing worry

¹**wor·ry** \'wər-ē\ *vb* **wor·ried; wor·ry·ing 1** : to shake and tear or mangle with the teeth **2** : to make anxious or upset : DISTURB ⟨the child's illness *worried* the parents⟩ **3** : to feel or express great concern

²**worry** *n, pl* **wor·ries 1** : ANXIETY **2** : a cause of great concern

¹**worse** \'wərs\ *adj, comparative of* BAD *or of* ILL **1** : more bad or evil : poorer in quality or worth **2** : being in poorer health

²**worse** *n* : something worse ⟨a turn for the *worse*⟩

³**worse** *adv, comparative of* BADLY *or of* ILL : not as well : in a worse way

wors·en \'wərs-n\ *vb* : to get worse

¹**wor·ship** \'wər-shəp\ *n* **1** : deep respect toward God, a god, or a sacred object **2** : too much respect or admiration

²**worship** *vb* **wor·shiped** *or* **wor·shipped; wor·ship·ing** *or* **wor·ship·ping 1** : to honor or respect as a divine being **2** : to regard with respect, honor, or devotion **3** : to take part in worship or an act of worship — **wor·ship·er** *or* **wor·ship·per** *n*

¹**worst** \'wərst\ *adj, superlative of* BAD *or of* ILL : most bad, ill or evil : POOREST

²**worst** *n* : a person or thing that is worst

³**worst** *adv, superlative of* BADLY *or of* ILL : in the worst way possible ⟨treated you *worst* of all⟩

⁴**worst** *vb* : to get the better of : DEFEAT

wor·sted \'wủs-təd, 'wərs-\ *n* **1** : a smooth yarn spun from pure wool **2** : a fabric woven from a worsted yarn

¹**worth** \'wərth\ *prep* **1** : equal in value to ⟨a painting *worth* thousands⟩ **2** : having possessions or income equal to ⟨a singer *worth* millions⟩ **3** : deserving of ⟨well *worth* the effort⟩ **4** : capable of ⟨ran for all I was *worth*⟩

²**worth** *n* **1** : the quality or qualities of a thing making it valuable or useful **2** : value as expressed in money **3** : EXCELLENCE 1

worth·less \'wərth-ləs\ *adj* **1** : lacking worth **2** : USELESS

worth·while \'wərth-'hwīl, -'wīl\ *adj* : being worth the time spent or effort used

wor·thy \'wər-thē\ *adj* **wor·thi·er; wor·thi·est 1** : having worth or excellence ⟨a *worthy* goal⟩ **2** : having enough value or excellence ⟨students *worthy* of promotion⟩ — **wor·thi·ness** *n*

would \wəd, wủd\ *past of* WILL **1** : strongly desire : WISH ⟨I *would* that I were gone⟩ **2** — used as a helping verb to show that something might be likely or meant to happen under certain conditions ⟨I *would* have won except I fell⟩ ⟨they *would* be here by now if they were coming at all⟩ ⟨if I were you, I *would* save my money⟩ **3** : prefers or prefer to ⟨they *would* die rather than surrender⟩ **4** : was or were going to ⟨we wish that you *would* go⟩ **5** : is or are able to : COULD ⟨no stone *would* break that window⟩ **6** — used as a politer form of *will* ⟨*would* you please turn the radio down⟩

wouldn't \'wủd-nt\ : would not

¹**wound** \'wünd\ *n* **1** : an injury that involves cutting or breaking of bodily tissue (as by violence, accident, or surgery) **2** : an injury or hurt to a person's feelings or reputation

²**wound** *vb* **1** : to hurt by cutting or breaking tissue **2** : to hurt the feelings or pride of

³**wound** \'waủnd\ *past of* WIND

wove *past of* WEAVE

woven *past participle of* WEAVE

¹**wran·gle** \'rang-gəl\ *vb* **wran·gled; wran·gling** : to have an angry quarrel : BICKER **2** : ARGUE 2, DEBATE

²**wrangle** *n* : ¹QUARREL 2

wran·gler \'rang-glər\ *n* **1** : a person who

\ə\ abut	\aủ\ out	\i\ tip	\ȯ\ saw	\ủ\ foot
\ər\ further	\ch\ chin	\ī\ life	\ȯi\ coin	\y\ yet
\a\ mat	\e\ pet	\j\ job	\th\ thin	\yü\ few
\ā\ take	\ē\ easy	\ng\ sing	\th\ this	\yủ\ cure
\ä\ cot, cart	\g\ go	\ō\ bone	\ü\ food	\zh\ vision

wrangles **2** : a worker on a ranch who tends the saddle horses

¹wrap \'rap\ *vb* **wrapped; wrap·ping 1** : to cover by winding or folding **2** : to enclose in a package **3** : to wind or roll together : FOLD **4** : to involve completely ⟨*wrapped* in thought⟩

²wrap *n* : a warm loose outer garment (as a shawl, cape, or coat)

wrap·per \'rap-ər\ *n* **1** : what something is wrapped in **2** : a person who wraps merchandise **3** : a garment that is worn wrapped about the body

wrap·ping \'rap-ing\ *n* : something used to wrap something else : WRAPPER

wrap up *vb* **1** : to bring to an end ⟨that *wraps up* the meeting⟩ **2** : to put on warm clothing ⟨*wrap up* warm, it's cold outside⟩

wrath \'rath\ *n* : violent anger : RAGE

wrath·ful \'rath-fəl\ *adj* **1** : full of wrath **2** : showing wrath

wreak \'rēk\ *vb* : to bring down as or as if punishment ⟨*wreak* revenge on an enemy⟩ ⟨the storm *wreaked* destruction⟩

wreath \'rēth\ *n, pl* **wreaths** \'rēthz, 'rēths\ : something twisted or woven into a circular shape ⟨a *wreath* of flowers⟩

wreathe \'rēth\ *vb* **wreathed; wreath·ing 1** : to form into wreaths **2** : to crown, decorate, or cover with or as if with a wreath ⟨the poet's head was *wreathed* with laurel⟩ ⟨the hill was *wreathed* with mist⟩

¹wreck \'rek\ *n* **1** : the remains (as of a ship or vehicle) after heavy damage usually by storm, collision, or fire **2** : a person or animal in poor health or without strength **3** : the action of breaking up or destroying something

²wreck *vb* **1** : ²SHIPWRECK 1 **2** : to damage or destroy by breaking up ⟨*wreck* a car⟩ ⟨*wreck* an old building⟩ **3** : to bring to ruin or an end ⟨the fire *wrecked* the business⟩ ⟨our picnic was *wrecked* by the storm⟩

wreck·age \'rek-ij\ *n* **1** : a wrecking or being wrecked **2** : the remains of a wreck

wreck·er \'rek-ər\ *n* **1** : a person who wrecks something or deals in wreckage **2** : a ship used in salvaging wrecks **3** : a truck for removing wrecked or broken-down cars

wren \'ren\ *n* : any of a group of small brown songbirds (as the **house wren**) with short rounded wings and short erect tail

¹wrench \'rench\ *n* **1** : a violent twist to one side or out of shape **2** : an injury caused by twisting or straining : SPRAIN **3** : a tool used in turning nuts or bolts

²wrench *vb* **1** : to pull or twist with sudden sharp force ⟨*wrenched* a branch from the tree⟩ **2** : to injure or cripple by a sudden

sharp twisting or straining ⟨*wrenched* my knee⟩

wrest \'rest\ *vb* **1** : to pull away by twisting or wringing **2** : to obtain only by great and steady effort

¹wres·tle \'res-əl\ *vb* **wres·tled; wres·tling 1** : to grasp and attempt to turn, trip, or throw down an opponent or to prevent the opponent from being able to move **2** : to struggle to deal with ⟨*wrestle* with a problem⟩

²wrestle *n* : ²STRUGGLE 1

wres·tling \'res-ling\ *n* : a sport in which two opponents wrestle each other

wretch \'rech\ *n* **1** : a miserable unhappy person **2** : a very bad person : WRONGDOER

wretch·ed \'rech-əd\ *adj* **1** : very unhappy or unfortunate : suffering greatly **2** : causing misery or distress ⟨*wretched* living conditions⟩ **3** : of very poor quality : INFERIOR ⟨*wretched* food⟩ ⟨I have a *wretched* memory⟩

wrig·gle \'rig-əl\ *vb* **wrig·gled; wrig·gling 1** : to twist or move like a worm : SQUIRM, WIGGLE **2** : to advance by twisting and turning

wrig·gler \'rig-lər\ *n* **1** : one that wriggles **2** : a mosquito larva or pupa

wring \'ring\ *vb* **wrung** \'rəng\; **wring·ing 1** : to twist or press so as to squeeze out moisture ⟨*wring* out the clothes⟩ **2** : to get by or as if by twisting or pressing ⟨*wring* water from the clothes⟩ ⟨*wrung* a confession from the criminal⟩ **3** : to twist so as to strangle ⟨*wrung* its neck⟩ **4** : to affect as if by wringing ⟨the bad news *wrung* our hearts⟩

wring·er \'ring-ər\ *n* : a machine or device for squeezing liquid out of something (as laundry)

¹wrin·kle \'ring-kəl\ *n* **1** : a crease or small fold (as in the skin or in cloth) **2** : a clever notion or trick ⟨thought up a new *wrinkle*⟩

²wrinkle *vb* **wrin·kled; wrin·kling** : to mark or become marked with wrinkles

wrist \'rist\ *n* : the joint or the region of the joint between the hand and arm

wrist·band \'rist-,band\ *n* **1** : the part of a sleeve that goes around the wrist **2** : a band that goes around the wrist (as for support or warmth)

wrist·watch \'rist-,wäch\ *n* : a watch attached to a bracelet or strap and worn on the wrist

writ \'rit\ *n* : an order in writing signed by an officer of a court ordering someone to do or not to do something

write \'rīt\ *vb* **wrote** \'rōt\; **writ·ten** \'rit-n\; **writ·ing** \'rīt-ing\ **1** : to form letters or words with pen or pencil **2 :** to form the letters or the words of (as on paper) **3 :** to put down on paper **4 :** to make up and set down for others to read ⟨*write* a novel⟩ **5 :** to write a letter to

writ·er \'rīt-ər\ *n* : a person who writes especially as a business or occupation

writhe \'rīth\ *vb* **writhed; writh·ing 1 :** to twist and turn this way and that ⟨*writhing* in pain⟩ **2 :** to suffer from shame or confusion : SQUIRM

writ·ing \'rīt-ing\ *n* **1 :** the act of a person who writes **2 :** HANDWRITING **3 :** something (as a letter or book) that is written

¹wrong \'rȯng\ *n* : something (as an idea, rule, or action) that is wrong

²wrong *adj* **1 :** not right : SINFUL, EVIL ⟨it is *wrong* to lie⟩ **2 :** not correct or true : FALSE ⟨your addition is *wrong*⟩ **3 :** not the one wanted or intended ⟨took the *wrong* train⟩ **4 :** not suitable ⟨what is *wrong* with this coat⟩ **5 :** made so as to be placed down or under and not to be

seen ⟨the *wrong* side of cloth⟩ **6 :** not proper ⟨swallowed something the *wrong* way⟩ — **wrong·ly** *adv* — **wrong·ness** *n*

³wrong *adv* : in the wrong direction, manner, or way ⟨answer *wrong*⟩

⁴wrong *vb* : to do wrong to

wrong·do·er \'rȯng-'dü-ər\ *n* : a person who does wrong and especially a moral wrong

wrong·do·ing \'rȯng-'dü-ing\ *n* : bad behavior or action ⟨guilty of *wrongdoing*⟩

wrong·ful \'rȯng-fəl\ *adj* **1 :** ²WRONG 1, UNJUST **2 :** UNLAWFUL

wrote *past of* WRITE

¹wrought \'rȯt\ *past of* WORK

²wrought *adj* **1 :** beaten into shape by tools ⟨*wrought* metals⟩ **2 :** much too excited ⟨don't get all *wrought* up over the test⟩

wrung *past of* WRING

wry \'rī\ *adj* **wry·er; wry·est 1 :** turned abnormally to one side ⟨a *wry* neck⟩ **2 :** made by twisting the features ⟨a *wry* smile⟩

x \'eks\ *n, pl* **x's** *or* **xs** \'ek-səz\ *often cap* **1 :** the twenty-fourth letter of the English alphabet **2 :** ten in Roman numerals **3 :** an unknown quantity

Xmas \'kris-məs\ *n* : CHRISTMAS

Word History Some people dislike the use of *Xmas* for *Christmas*, saying it is wrong to take *Christ* out of *Christmas*. Really, they are the ones who are wrong, for the *X* in *Xmas* stands for a Greek letter that looks just like our *X* and is the first letter of *Christ* in Greek. For many centuries this letter has been used as an abbreviation and a holy symbol for Christ.

x–ray \'eks-ˌrā\ *vb, often cap X* : to examine, treat, or photograph with X rays

X ray \'eks-ˌrā\ *n* **1 :** a powerful invisible ray made up of very short waves that is somewhat similar to light and that is able to pass through various thicknesses of solids and act on photographic film like light **2 :** a photograph taken by the use of X rays

Word History English *X ray* came from the German name of a ray that passes through some solid objects that light cannot pass through. The German scientist

who discovered this strange ray did not know why it behaves the way it does. In naming his discovery, he therefore used the letter *x* (the scientific symbol for something unknown) plus the German word for "ray."

xy·lo·phone \'zī-lə-ˌfōn\ *n* : a musical instrument consisting of a series of wooden

xylophone

\ə\ **abut**	\aú\ **out**	\i\ **tip**	\ȯ\ **saw**	\ú\ **foot**
\ər\ **further**	\ch\ **chin**	\ī\ **life**	\ȯi\ **coin**	\y\ **yet**
\a\ **mat**	\e\ **pet**	\j\ **job**	\th\ **thin**	\yü\ **few**
\ā\ **take**	\ē\ **easy**	\ng\ **sing**	\th\ **this**	\yú\ **cure**
\ä\ **cot, cart**	\g\ **go**	\ō\ **bone**	\ü\ **food**	\zh\ **vision**

bars of different lengths made to sound the musical scale and played with two wooden hammers

Word History The English word *xylo-* *phone* came from two Greek words. The first meant "wood." The second meant "sound." The musical sound of a xylophone is made by striking wooden bars.

y \'wī\ *n, pl* **y's** *or* **ys** \'wīz\ *often cap* : the twenty-fifth letter of the English alphabet

¹**-y** *also* **-ey** \ē\ *adj suffix* **-i•er; -i•est 1** : showing, full of, or made of ⟨dirt*y*⟩ ⟨mudd*y*⟩ ⟨ic*y*⟩ **2** : like ⟨wintr*y*⟩ **3** : devoted to : enthusiastic about **4** : tending to ⟨sleep*y*⟩ **5** : somewhat : rather ⟨chill*y*⟩

²**-y** \ē\ *n suffix, pl* **-ies 1** : state : condition : quality ⟨jealous*y*⟩ **2** : occupation, place of business, or goods dealt with ⟨laundr*y*⟩ **3** : whole body or group

³**-y** *n suffix, pl* **-ies** : occasion or example of a specified action ⟨entreat*y*⟩ ⟨inquir*y*⟩

⁴**-y** — see -IE

¹**yacht** \'yät\ *n* : a small ship used for pleasure cruising or racing

Word History Long ago the Dutch built sailing ships designed to chase pirates and smugglers. The Dutch word for such a ship came from a German word that meant "hunting ship." The Dutch gave one of their hunting ships to an English king who used it for pleasure. Other English people made ships like the king's and called them *yachts,* their spelling of the Dutch word. That is how the word *yacht* came into the English language.

²**yacht** *vb* : to race or cruise in a yacht

yacht•ing \'yät-ing\ *n* : the action, fact, or recreation of racing or cruising in a yacht

yachts•man \'yät-smən\ *n, pl* **yachts-men** \-smən\ : a person who owns or sails a yacht

yak \'yak\ *n* : a wild or domestic ox of the uplands of Asia that has very long hair

yam \'yam\ *n* **1** : the starchy root of a plant related to the lilies that is an important food in much of the tropics **2** : a sweet potato with a moist and usually orange flesh

¹**yank** \'yangk\ *n* : a strong sudden pull : JERK

²**yank** *vb* : ¹JERK 1 ⟨*yanked* the drawer open⟩

Yan•kee \'yang-kē\ *n* **1** : a person born or living in New England **2** : a person born or living in the northern United States **3** : a person born or living in the United States

¹**yap** \'yap\ *vb* **yapped; yap•ping 1** : to bark in yaps **2** : ²SCOLD, CHATTER

²**yap** *n* : a quick shrill bark

¹**yard** \'yärd\ *n* **1** : a measure of length equal to three feet or thirty-six inches (about .91 meter) **2** : a long pole pointed toward the ends that holds up and spreads the top of a sail

²**yard** *n* **1** : a small and often fenced area open to the sky and next to a building **2** : the grounds of a building **3** : a fenced area for livestock **4** : an area set aside for a business or activity ⟨a navy *yard*⟩ **5** : a system of railroad tracks especially for keeping and repairing cars

yard•age \'yärd-ij\ *n* **1** : a total number of yards **2** : the length or size of something measured in yards

yard•arm \'yärd-,ärm\ *n* : either end of the yard of a square-rigged ship

yard•mas•ter \'yärd-,mas-tər\ *n* : the person in charge of operations in a railroad yard

yard•stick \'yärd-,stik\ *n* **1** : a measuring stick a yard long **2** : a rule or standard by which something is measured or judged

¹**yarn** \'yärn\ *n* **1** : natural or manufactured fiber (as cotton, wool, or rayon) formed as

yak

a continuous thread for use in knitting or weaving **2** : an interesting or exciting story

²yarn *vb* : to tell a yarn

yawl \'yȯl\ *n* : a sailboat having two masts with the shorter one behind the point where the stern enters the water

yawl

¹yawn \'yȯn\ *vb* **1** : to open wide ⟨a *yawning* cavern⟩ **2** : to open the mouth wide usually as a reaction to being tired or bored

²yawn *n* : a deep drawing in of breath through the wide-open mouth

ye \yē\ *pron, archaic* : YOU 1

¹yea \'yā\ *adv* : ¹YES 1 — used in spoken voting

²yea *n* **1** : a vote in favor of something **2** : a person casting a yea vote

year \'yiər\ *n* **1** : the period of about 365¼ days required for the earth to make one complete trip around the sun **2** : a period of 365 days or in leap year 366 days beginning January 1 **3** : a fixed period of time ⟨the school *year*⟩

year·book \'yiər-,bùk\ *n* **1** : a book published yearly especially as a report **2** : a school publication recording the history and activities of a graduating class

year·ling \'yiər-ling\ *n* : a person or animal that is or is treated as if a year old

year·ly \'yiər-lē\ *adj* : ¹ANNUAL 1

yearn \'yərn\ *vb* : to feel an eager desire

synonyms YEARN, LONG, and PINE mean to desire something very much. YEARN suggests a very eager desiring along with restless, painful feelings ⟨*yearning* for the day when they would be free⟩ LONG suggests wanting something with one's whole heart and often actually striving to get it ⟨*longing* to become a successful writer⟩

PINE suggests that one grows weak as one continues to desire something that one is not ever going to have ⟨*pining* away for a long lost friend⟩

yearn·ing \'yər-ning\ *n* : an eager desire ⟨a *yearning* for friends⟩

year–round \'yiər-'raùnd\ *adj* : being in operation for the full year

yeast \'yēst\ *n* **1** : material that may be found on the surface or at the bottom of sweet liquids, is made up mostly of the cells of a tiny fungus, and causes a reaction in which alcohol is produced **2** : a commercial product containing living yeast plants and used especially to make bread dough rise **3** : any of the group of tiny fungi that form alcohol or raise bread dough

¹yell \'yel\ *vb* : to cry or scream loudly

²yell *n* **1** : ²SCREAM, SHOUT **2** : a cheer used especially in schools or colleges to encourage athletic teams

¹yel·low \'yel-ō\ *adj* **1** : of the color yellow **2** : having a yellow or light brown complexion or skin ⟨the *yellow* races⟩ **3** : COWARDLY

²yellow *vb* : to turn yellow

³yellow *n* **1** : the color in the rainbow between green and orange **2** : something yellow in color

yellow fever *n* : a disease carried by mosquitoes in hot countries

yel·low·ish \'yel-ə-wish\ *adj* : somewhat yellow

yellow jacket *n* : a small colonial wasp with yellow markings that usually nests in the ground

¹yelp \'yelp\ *vb* : to make a quick shrill bark or cry ⟨a dog *yelping* in pain⟩

²yelp *n* : a quick shrill bark or cry

yen \'yen\ *n* : a strong desire : LONGING

yellow jacket

yeo·man \'yō-mən\ *n, pl* **yeo·men** \-mən\ **1** : a naval petty officer who works as a clerk **2** : a small farmer who cultivates his or her own land

-yer — see ²-ER

¹yes \'yes\ *adv* **1** — used to express

\ə\ **abut**	\aù\ **out**	\i\ **tip**	\ȯ\ **saw**	\ù\ **foot**
\ər\ **further**	\ch\ **chin**	\ī\ **life**	\ȯi\ **coin**	\y\ **yet**
\a\ **mat**	\e\ **pet**	\j\ **job**	\th\ **thin**	\yü\ **few**
\ā\ **take**	\ē\ **easy**	\ng\ **sing**	\th\ **this**	\yù\ **cure**
\ä\ **cot, cart**	\g\ **go**	\ō\ **bone**	\ü\ **food**	\zh\ **vision**

agreement ⟨are you ready? *Yes*, I am⟩ **2** — used to introduce a phrase with greater emphasis or clearness ⟨we are glad, *yes*, very glad to see you⟩ **3** — used to show interest or attention ⟨*yes*, what can I do for you⟩

²yes *n* : a positive reply

¹yes·ter·day \'yes-tər-dē\ *adv* : on the day next before today

²yesterday *n* **1** : the day next before this day **2** : time not long past ⟨fashions of *yesterday*⟩

yes·ter·year \'yes-tər-,yiər\ *n* : the recent past

¹yet \'yet\ *adv* **1** : ¹BESIDES ⟨gives *yet* another reason⟩ **2** : ²EVEN 4 ⟨a *yet* higher speed⟩ **3** : up to now : so far ⟨hasn't done much *yet*⟩ **4** : at this or that time ⟨not time to go *yet*⟩ **5** : up to the present ⟨is *yet* a new country⟩ **6** : at some later time ⟨may *yet* decide to go⟩ **7** : NEVERTHELESS

²yet *conj* : but nevertheless ⟨I was sick *yet* I went to school⟩

yew \'yü\ *n* : a tree or shrub with stiff poisonous evergreen leaves, a fleshy fruit, and tough wood used especially for bows and small articles

Yid·dish \'yid-ish\ *n* : a language that comes from German and is used by some Jews

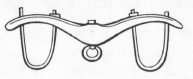

yew

Word History The language called Yiddish is based on German. The Jews who first spoke this language had a phrase to describe it. This phrase meant "Jewish German." In time this Yiddish phrase was shortened and the first word, which meant "Jewish," was used alone to mean "the language Yiddish." The English word *Yiddish* came from this Yiddish word.

¹yield \'yēld\ *vb* **1** : to give up possession of on claim or demand **2** : to give (oneself) up to a liking, temptation, or habit **3** : to bear as a natural product ⟨the tree *yielded* its first crop last year⟩ **4** : to return as income or profit ⟨an investment that *yields* a steady eight percent⟩ **5** : to be productive : bring good results ⟨the garden did not *yield* well⟩ **6** : to stop opposing or objecting to something ⟨*yielded* to a friend's plea⟩ **7** : to give way under physical force so as to bend, stretch, or break ⟨the rope *yielded* under the strain⟩

8 : to admit that someone else is better

²yield *n* : the amount produced or returned ⟨a good *yield* of wheat per acre⟩

¹yip \'yip\ *vb* **yipped; yip·ping** : ¹YELP — used chiefly of a dog

²yip *n* : a noise made by or as if by yelping

¹yo·del \'yōd-l\ *vb* **yo·deled** *or* **yo·delled; yo·del·ing** *or* **yo·del·ling 1** : to sing with frequent sudden changes from the natural voice range to a higher range and back **2** : to call or shout in the manner of yodeling — **yo·del·er** *n*

²yodel *n* : a yodeled shout

¹yoke \'yōk\ *n* **1** : a wooden bar or frame by which two work animals (as oxen) are harnessed at the heads or necks for drawing a plow or load **2** : a frame fitted to a person's shoulders to carry a load in two equal parts **3** : a clamp that joins two parts to hold or connect them in position **4** *pl usually* **yoke** : two animals yoked together **5** : something that brings to a state of hardship, humiliation, or slavery **6** : SLAVERY 2 **7** : ¹TIE 4, BOND **8** : a fitted or shaped piece at the shoulder of a garment or at the top of a skirt

yoke 1

²yoke *vb* **yoked; yok·ing 1** : to put a yoke on **2** : to attach a work animal to ⟨*yoke* a plow⟩

yo·kel \'yō-kəl\ *n* : a country person with little education or experience

yolk \'yōk\ *n* : the yellow inner part of the egg of a bird or reptile containing stored food material for the developing young — **yolked** \'yōkt\ *adj*

Word History The modern English word *yolk* came from an Old English word that meant "the yellow part of an egg." This Old English word came in turn from an Old English word that meant "yellow." The modern English word *yellow* came from this Old English word, too.

Yom Kip·pur \,yōm-ki-'pùr, ,yòm-, -'kip-ər\ *n* : a Jewish holiday observed in September or October with fasting and prayer

¹yon \'yän\ *adj* : ²YONDER 2

²yon *adv* **1** : ¹YONDER **2** : THITHER ⟨ran hither and *yon*⟩

¹**yon·der** \'yän-dər\ *adv* : at or in that place ⟨look *yonder* down the hill⟩

²**yonder** *adj* **1** : more distant ⟨the *yonder* side of the hill⟩ **2** : being at a distance within view ⟨*yonder* hills⟩

yore \'yōr\ *n* : time long past ⟨stories of *yore*⟩

you \yü, yə\ *pron* **1** : the one or ones these words are spoken or written to **2** : ²ONE 2 ⟨*you* never know what will happen⟩

you'd \yüd, yəd\ : you had : you would

you'll \yül, yəl\ : you shall : you will

¹**young** \'yəng\ *adj* **young·er** \'yəng-gər\; **young·est** \'yəng-gəst\ **1** : being in the first or an early stage of life or growth **2** : INEXPERIENCED **3** : recently come into being : NEW **4** : YOUTHFUL 1

²**young** *n, pl* **young 1** *young pl* : young persons **2** *young pl* : immature offspring ⟨a cat and her *young*⟩ **3** : a single recently born or hatched animal

young·est \'yəng-gəst\ *n, pl* **youngest** : one that is the least old especially of a family

young·ster \'yəng-stər\ *n* **1** : a young person : YOUTH **2** : CHILD

your \yər, yür\ *adj* **1** : of or belonging to you ⟨*your* book⟩ **2** : by or from you ⟨*your* gifts⟩ **3** : affecting you ⟨*your* enemies⟩ **4** : of or relating to one ⟨when you face the north, east is at *your* right⟩ **5** — used before a title of honor in addressing a person ⟨*your* Majesty⟩ ⟨*your* Holiness⟩

you're \yər, yür\ : you are

yours \yürz\ *pron* : that which belongs to you ⟨the bike is *yours*⟩ ⟨the boots are *yours*⟩

your·self \yər-'self\ *pron, pl* **your·selves** \-'selvz\ : your own self ⟨you might hurt *yourself* if you're not careful⟩ ⟨you are responsible *yourselves* for the problem⟩

youth \'yüth\ *n, pl* **youths** \'yüthz, 'yüths\ **1** : the period of life between being a child and an adult **2** : a young man **3** : young people ⟨the *youth* of today⟩ **4** : the quality or state of being young

youth·ful \'yüth-fəl\ *adj* **1** : of or relating to youth **2** : being young and not yet fully grown **3** : having the freshness of youth — **youth·ful·ly** \-fə-lē\ *adv* — **youth·ful·ness** *n*

you've \yüv, yəv\ : you have

¹**yowl** \'yaùl\ *vb* : ¹WAIL

²**yowl** *n* : a loud long moaning cry (as of a cat)

yo–yo \'yō-yō\ *n, pl* **yo–yos** *also* **yo–yoes** : a thick divided disk that is made to fall and rise to the hand by unwinding and winding again on a string

yuc·ca \'yək-ə\ *n* : a plant related to the lilies that grows in dry regions and has stiff pointed leaves at the base of a tall stiff stalk of usually whitish flowers

yule \'yül\ *n, often cap* : CHRISTMAS

yule log *n, often cap Y* : a large log once put in the fireplace on Christmas Eve as the foundation of the fire

yule·tide \'yül-ˌtīd\ *n, often cap* : the Christmas season

yucca

Z

z \'zē\ *n, pl* **z's** *or* **zs** \'zēz\ *often cap* : the twenty-sixth letter of the English alphabet

¹**za·ny** \'zā-nē\ *n, pl* **za·nies 1** : ¹CLOWN 2 **2** : a silly or foolish person

Word History In early Italian plays, there was usually a clown who copied the actions of the chief actor in a comical way. The English word *zany*, which at first meant "clown," came from the Italian name for the stage clown.

²**zany** *adj* **za·ni·er; za·ni·est 1** : being or like a zany **2** : FOOLISH, SILLY ⟨a *zany* plan⟩

zeal \'zēl\ *n* : eager desire to get something done or see something succeed

\ə\ abut	\aù\ out	\i\ tip	\ȯ\ saw	\ù\ foot
\ər\ further	\ch\ chin	\ī\ life	\ȯi\ coin	\y\ yet
\a\ mat	\e\ pet	\j\ job	\th\ thin	\yü\ few
\ā\ take	\ē\ easy	\ng\ sing	\t̶h̶\ this	\yù\ cure
\ä\ cot, cart	\g\ go	\ō\ bone	\ü\ food	\zh\ vision

zeal·ous \'zel-əs\ *adj* : filled with or showing zeal — **zeal·ous·ly** *adv* — **zeal·ous·ness** *n*

ze·bra \'zē-brə\ *n* : an African wild animal related to the horses that has a hide striped in black and white or black and buff

ze·bu \'zē-byü\ *n* : an Asian domestic ox that differs from the related European cattle in having a large hump over the shoulders and a loose skin with hanging folds

zebu

ze·nith \'zē-nəth\ *n* **1** : the point in the heavens directly overhead **2** : the highest point

zeph·yr \'zef-ər\ *n* **1** : a breeze from the west **2** : a gentle breeze

zep·pe·lin \'zep-ə-lən\ *n* : a huge long balloon that has a metal frame and is driven through the air by engines carried on its underside

ze·ro \'zē-rō, 'ziər-ō\ *n, pl* **ze·ros** *or* **ze·roes** **1** : the numerical symbol 0 meaning the absence of all size or quantity **2** : the point on a scale (as on a thermometer) from which measurements are made **3** : the temperature shown by the zero mark on a thermometer **4** : a total lack of anything : NOTHING **5** : the lowest point

zest \'zest\ *n* **1** : an enjoyable or exciting quality **2** : keen enjoyment ⟨eat with *zest*⟩ — **zest·ful** \-fəl\ *adj* — **zest·ful·ly** \-fə-lē\ *adv* — **zest·ful·ness** *n*

Word History The English word *zest* came from a French word that meant "the peel of an orange or a lemon." Because their flavor made food more tasty and enjoyable, lemon and orange peels were used to season food. In time the word *zest* came to mean any quality that made life more enjoyable.

¹zig·zag \'zig-,zag\ *n* **1** : one of a series of short sharp turns or angles in a course **2** : a line, path, or pattern that bends sharply this way and that

²zigzag *adv* : in or by a zigzag path or course ⟨ran *zigzag* across the field⟩

³zigzag *adj* : having short sharp turns or angles ⟨a *zigzag* road⟩

⁴zigzag *vb* **zig·zagged; zig·zag·ging** : to form into or move along a zigzag

zinc \'zingk\ *n* : a bluish white metal that tarnishes only slightly in moist air and is used mostly to make alloys and to give iron a protective coating

zing \'zing\ *n* **1** : a shrill humming sound **2** : a lively or energetic quality

zin·nia \'zin-ē-ə, 'zin-yə\ *n* : a tropical American herb related to the daisies that is widely grown for its bright flower heads that last a long time

zinnia

¹zip \'zip\ *vb* **zipped; zip·ping** **1** : to move or act with speed and force **2** : to move or pass with a shrill hissing or humming sound

²zip *n* **1** : a sudden shrill hissing sound **2** : ENERGY 1

³zip *vb* **zipped; zip·ping** : to close or open with a zipper

zip code *or* **ZIP Code** *n* : a number consisting of five digits that identifies each postal area in the United States

zip·per \'zip-ər\ *n* : a fastener (as for a jacket) consisting of two rows of metal or plastic teeth on strips of tape and a sliding piece that closes an opening by drawing the teeth together — **zip·pered** \-ərd\ *adj*

zip·py \'zip-ē\ *adj* **zip·pi·er; zip·pi·est** : full of energy : LIVELY

zith·er \'zith-ər, 'zith-\ *n* : a stringed instrument with thirty to forty tuned strings that are plucked with the fingers or with a pick

zo·di·ac \'zōd-ē-,ak\ *n* : an imaginary belt in the heavens that includes the paths of most of the planets and is divided into twelve constellations or signs

zom·bie *or* **zom·bi** \'zäm-bē\ *n* : a person who is believed to have died and been brought back to life

Word History The word *zombie* developed from the name of a snake god of western Africa. Africans believed that the snake god could bring the dead back to life. People who were thought to have been brought back from the dead in this way were also called *zombies*. The word *zombie* came into the English language through southern slaves whose roots go back to western Africa.

¹zone \'zōn\ *n* **1** : any of the five great parts that the earth's surface is divided into according to latitude and temperature ⟨two frigid *zones*, two temperate *zones*, and one torrid *zone*⟩ **2** : a band or belt that surrounds ⟨a *zone* of trees⟩ **3** : a section set off or marked as different in some way ⟨a war *zone*⟩ ⟨a business *zone*⟩

Word History The ancient Greeks had a word that meant "belt." From that word, the ancient Romans made a Latin word that also meant "belt." The Romans thought of the world as being divided into five regions or five great belts that circled the world. That is why the Latin word that meant "belt" was used to refer to the five divisions. The English word *zone* came from this Latin word.

²zone *vb* **zoned; zon•ing** : to divide into zones for different uses

zoo \'zü\ *n, pl* **zoos** : a collection of living animals for display

zoo•log•i•cal \ˌzō-ə-'läj-i-kəl\ *adj* : of or relating to zoology

zoological garden *n* : a garden or park where wild animals are kept for exhibition

zo•ol•o•gist \zō-'äl-ə-jəst\ *n* : a specialist in zoology

zo•ol•o•gy \zō-'äl-ə-jē\ *n* **1** : a branch of biology dealing with animals and animal life **2** : animal life (as of a region)

¹zoom \'züm\ *vb* **1** : to speed along with a loud hum or buzz **2** : to move upward quickly at a sharp angle ⟨the airplane *zoomed* into the sky⟩

²zoom *n* **1** : an act or process of zooming **2** : a zooming sound

zwie•back \'swē-ˌbak, 'swī-\ *n* : a usually sweetened bread made with eggs that is baked and then sliced and toasted until dry and crisp

zy•gote \'zī-ˌgōt\ *n* : the new cell produced when a sperm cell joins with an egg

ABBREVIATIONS

Most of these abbreviations are shown in one form only. Variation in use of periods, in kind of type, and in capitalization is frequent and widespread (as *mph, MPH, m.p.h., Mph*)

abbr abbreviation
AD in the year of our Lord
adj adjective
adv adverb, advertisement
AK Alaska
AL, Ala Alabama
alt alternate, altitude
a.m., AM before noon
Am, Amer America, American
amt amount
anon anonymous
ans answer
Apr April
AR Arkansas
Ariz Arizona
Ark Arkansas
assn association
asst assistant
atty attorney
Aug August
ave avenue
AZ Arizona

BC before Christ
bet between
bldg building
blvd boulevard
Br, Brit Britain, British
bro brother
bros brothers
bu bushel

c carat, cent, centimeter, century, chapter, cup
C Celsius, centigrade
CA, Cal, Calif California
Can, Canad Canada, Canadian
cap capital, capitalize, capitalized
Capt captain
ch chapter, church
cm centimeter
co company, county
CO Colorado
COD cash on delivery, collect on delivery
col column

Col colonel, Colorado
Colo Colorado
conj conjunction
Conn Connecticut
ct cent, court
CT Connecticut
cu cubic
CZ Canal Zone

d penny
DC District of Columbia
DDS doctor of dental surgery
DE Delaware
Dec December
Del Delaware
dept department
DMD doctor of dental medicine
doz dozen
Dr doctor
DST daylight saving time

E east, eastern, excellent
ea each
e.g. for example
Eng England, English
esp especially
etc et cetera

f false, female, forte
F Fahrenheit
FBI Federal Bureau of Investigation
Feb February
fem feminine
FL, Fla Florida
fr father, from
Fri Friday
ft feet, foot, fort

g gram
G good
Ga, GA Georgia
gal gallon
gen general
geog geographic, geographical, geography
gm gram

gov governor
govt government
gt great
GU Guam

HI Hawaii
hr hour
HS high school
ht height

Ia, IA Iowa
ID Idaho
i.e. that is
IL, Ill Illinois
in inch
IN Indiana
inc incorporated
Ind Indian, Indiana
interj interjection
intrans intransitive

Jan January
jr, jun junior

Kans Kansas
kg kilogram
km kilometer
KS Kansas
Ky, KY Kentucky

l left, liter
La, LA Louisiana
lb pound
Lt lieutenant
ltd limited

m male, meter, mile
MA Massachusetts
Maj major
Mar March
masc masculine
Mass Massachusetts
Md Maryland
MD doctor of medicine, Maryland
Me, ME Maine
Mex Mexican, Mexico
mg milligram
mi mile

MI, Mich Michigan
min minute
Minn Minnesota
Miss Mississippi
ml milliliter
mm millimeter
MN Minnesota
mo month
Mo, MO Missouri
Mon Monday
Mont Montana
mpg miles per gallon
mph miles per hour
MS Mississippi
mt mount, mountain
MT Montana
mtn mountain

n noun
N north, northern
NC North Carolina
ND, N Dak North Dakota
NE Nebraska, northeast
Neb, Nebr Nebraska
Nev Nevada
NH New Hampshire
NJ New Jersey
NM, N Mex New Mexico
no north, number
Nov November
NV Nevada
NW northwest
NY New York

O Ohio
obj object, objective
Oct October
off office
OH Ohio
OK, Okla Oklahoma
OR, Ore, Oreg Oregon
oz ounce, ounces

p page, piano
Pa, PA Pennsylvania
part participle
pat patent
Penn, Penna Pennsylvania
pg page
pk park, peck
pkg package

pl plural
p.m., PM afternoon
PO post office
poss possessive
pp pages
pr pair
PR Puerto Rico
prep preposition
pres present, president
prof professor
pron pronoun
PS postscript, public
   school
pt pint, point
PTA Parent-Teacher
   Association
PTO Parent-Teacher
   Organization

qt quart

r right
rd road, rod, round
recd received
reg region, register,
   registered, regular
res residence
Rev reverend
RFD rural free delivery
RI Rhode Island
rpm revolutions per minute
RR railroad
RSVP please reply
rt right
rte route

S south, southern
Sat Saturday
SC South Carolina
sci science
Scot Scotland, Scottish
SD, S Dak South Dakota
SE southeast
sec second
Sept September
SI International System of
   Units
sing singular
so south
sq square
sr senior
Sr sister

SS steamship
st state, street
St saint
Sun Sunday
SW southwest

t true
tbsp tablespoon
TD touchdown
Tenn Tennessee
Tex Texas
Thurs, Thur, Thu Thursday
TN Tennessee
trans transitive
tsp teaspoon
Tues, Tue Tuesday
TX Texas

UN United Nations
US United States
USA United States of
   America
USSR Union of Soviet
   Socialist Republics
usu usual, usually
UT Utah

v verb
Va, VA Virginia
var variant
vb verb
VG very good
vi verb intransitive
VI Virgin Islands
vol volume
VP vice president
vs versus
vt verb transitive
Vt, VT Vermont
W west, western
WA, Wash Washington
Wed Wednesday
WI, Wis, Wisc Wisconsin
wk week
wt weight
WV, W Va West Virginia
WY, Wyo Wyoming
yd yard
yr year

PRESIDENTS OF THE U.S.

No.	Name (pronunciation)	Life dates	Birthplace	Term dates
1	George Washington \'wȯsh-ing-tən, 'wäsh-\	1732–1799	Va.	1789–1797
2	John Adams \'ad-əmz\	1735–1826	Mass.	1797–1801
3	Thomas Jefferson\'jef-ər-sən\	1743–1826	Va.	1801–1809
4	James Madison \'mad-ə-sən\	1751–1836	Va.	1809–1817
5	James Monroe \mən-'rō\	1758–1831	Va.	1817–1825
6	John Quincy Adams \'ad-əmz\	1767–1848	Mass.	1825–1829
7	Andrew Jackson \'jak-sən\	1767–1845	S. C.	1829–1837
8	Martin Van Buren \van-'byur-ən\	1782–1862	N. Y.	1837–1841
9	William Henry Harrison \'har-ə-sən\	1773–1841	Va.	1841
10	John Tyler \'tī-lər\	1790–1862	Va.	1841–1845
11	James Knox Polk \'pōk\	1795–1849	N. C.	1845–1849
12	Zachary Taylor \'tā-lər\	1784–1850	Va.	1849–1850
13	Millard Fillmore \'fil-ˌmōr\	1800–1874	N. Y.	1850–1853
14	Franklin Pierce \'piərs\	1804–1869	N. H.	1853–1857
15	James Buchanan \byü-'kan-ən\	1791–1868	Penn.	1857–1861
16	Abraham Lincoln \'ling-kən\	1809–1865	Ky.	1861–1865
17	Andrew Johnson \'jän-sən\	1808–1875	N. C.	1865–1869
18	Ulysses S. Grant \'grant\	1822–1885	Ohio	1869–1877
19	Rutherford B. Hayes \'hāz\	1822–1893	Ohio	1877–1881
20	James A. Garfield \'gär-ˌfēld\	1831–1881	Ohio	1881
21	Chester A. Arthur \'är-thər\	1830–1886	Vt.	1881–1885
22	Grover Cleveland \'klēv-lənd\	1837–1908	N. J.	1885–1889
23	Benjamin Harrison \'har-ə-sən\	1833–1901	Ohio	1889–1893
24	Grover Cleveland \'klēv-lənd\	1837–1908	N. J.	1893–1897
25	William McKinley \mə-'kin-lē\	1843–1901	Ohio	1897–1901
26	Theodore Roosevelt \'rō-zə-ˌvelt\	1858–1919	N. Y.	1901–1909
27	William Howard Taft \'taft\	1857–1930	Ohio	1909–1913
28	Woodrow Wilson \'wil-sən\	1856–1924	Va.	1913–1921
29	Warren G. Harding \'härd-ing\	1865–1923	Ohio	1921–1923
30	Calvin Coolidge \'kü-lij\	1872–1933	Vt.	1923–1929
31	Herbert C. Hoover \'hü-vər\	1874–1964	Iowa	1929–1933
32	Franklin D. Roosevelt \'rō-zə-ˌvelt\	1882–1945	N. Y.	1933–1945
33	Harry S Truman \'trü-mən\	1884–1972	Miss.	1945–1953
34	Dwight D. Eisenhower \'īz-n-ˌhaủ-ər\	1890–1969	Texas	1953–1961
35	John F. Kennedy \'ken-ə-dē\	1917–1963	Mass.	1961–1963
36	Lyndon B. Johnson \'jän-sən\	1908–1973	Texas	1963–1969
37	Richard M. Nixon \'nik-sən\	1913–1994	Calif.	1969–1974
38	Gerald R. Ford \'fōrd\	1913–	Neb.	1974–1977
39	Jimmy Carter \'kärt-ər\	1924–	Ga.	1977–1981
40	Ronald W. Reagan \'rā-gən\	1911–	Ill.	1981–1989
41	George H. W. Bush \'bủsh\	1924–	Mass.	1989–1993
42	William J. Clinton \'klin-tən\	1946–	Ark.	1993–

VICE PRESIDENTS OF THE U.S.

No.	Name (pronunciation)	Life dates	Birthplace	Term dates
1	John Adams \'ad-əmz\	1735–1826	Mass.	1789–1797
2	Thomas Jefferson \'jef-ər-sən\	1743–1826	Va.	1797–1801
3	Aaron Burr \'bər\	1756–1836	N. J.	1801–1805
4	George Clinton \'klint-n\	1739–1812	N. Y.	1805–1812
5	Elbridge Gerry \'ger-ē\	1744–1814	Mass.	1813–1814
6	Daniel D. Tompkins \'tämp-kənz\	1774–1825	N. Y.	1817–1825
7	John C. Calhoun \kal-'hün\	1782–1850	S. C.	1825–1832
8	Martin Van Buren \van-'byùr-ən\	1782–1862	N. Y.	1833–1837
9	Richard M. Johnson \'jän-sən\	1780–1850	Ky.	1837–1841
10	John Tyler \'tī-lər\	1790–1862	Va.	1841
11	George M. Dallas \'dal-əs\	1792–1864	Penn.	1845–1849
12	Millard Fillmore \'fil-ˌmōr\	1800–1874	N. Y.	1849–1850
13	William R. King \'king\	1786–1853	N. C.	1853
14	John C. Breckinridge \'brek-ən-rij\	1821–1875	Ky.	1857–1861
15	Hannibal Hamlin \'ham-lən\	1809–1891	Maine	1861–1865
16	Andrew Johnson \'jän-sən\	1808–1875	N. C.	1865
17	Schuyler Colfax \'kōl-ˌfaks\	1823–1885	N. Y.	1869–1873
18	Henry Wilson \'wil-sən\	1812–1875	N. H.	1873–1875
19	William A. Wheeler \'hwē-lər, 'wē\	1819–1887	N. Y.	1877–1881
20	Chester A. Arthur \'är-thər\	1830–1886	Vt.	1881
21	Thomas A. Hendricks \'hen-driks\	1819–1885	Ohio	1885
22	Levi P. Morton \'mòrt-n\	1824–1920	Vt.	1889–1893
23	Adlai E. Stevenson \'stē-vən-sən\	1835–1914	Ky.	1893–1897
24	Garret A. Hobart \'hō-ˌbärt\	1844–1899	N. J.	1897–1899
25	Theodore Roosevelt \'rō-zə-ˌvelt\	1858–1919	N. Y.	1901
26	Charles W. Fairbanks \'faər-ˌbangks, 'feər-\	1852–1918	Ohio	1905–1909
27	James S. Sherman \'shər-mən\	1855–1912	N. Y.	1909–1912
28	Thomas R. Marshall \'mär-shəl\	1854–1925	Ind.	1913–1921
29	Calvin Coolidge \'kü-lij\	1872–1933	Vt.	1921–1923
30	Charles G. Dawes \'dòz\	1865–1951	Ohio	1925–1929
31	Charles Curtis \'kərt-əs\	1860–1936	Kan.	1929–1933
32	John N. Garner \'gär-nər\	1868–1967	Texas	1933–1941
33	Henry A. Wallace \'wäl-əs\	1888–1965	Iowa	1941–1945
34	Harry S Truman \'trü-mən\	1884–1972	Mo.	1945
35	Alben W. Barkley \'bär-klē\	1877–1956	Ky.	1949–1953
36	Richard M. Nixon \'nik-sən\	1913–1994	Calif.	1953–1961
37	Lyndon B. Johnson \'jän-sən\	1908–1973	Texas	1961–1963
38	Hubert H. Humphrey \'həm-frē\	1911–1978	S. D.	1965–1969
39	Spiro T. Agnew \'ag-nü, -nyü\	1918–	Md.	1969–1973
40	Gerald R. Ford \'fòrd\	1913–	Neb.	1973–1974
41	Nelson A. Rockefeller \'räk-i-ˌfel-ər\	1908–1979	Maine	1974–1977
42	Walter F. Mondale \'män-ˌdāl\	1928–	Minn.	1977–1981
43	George H. W. Bush \'bùsh\	1924–	Mass.	1981–1989
44	James Danforth Quayle \'kwāl\	1947–	Ind.	1989–1993
45	Albert Gore, Jr. \'gōr\	1948–	Wash., D.C.	1993–

BRANCHES OF GOVERNMENT

EXECUTIVE

President, elected (by vote of the Electoral College after a popular vote) for a four-year term; serves as chief executive, head of state, and commander-in-chief of the armed forces; responsible for administering the laws, proposing new legislation to Congress, and for meeting with foreign heads of state and making treaties.

Vice President, elected with the President; serves as a stand-in for the President; presides over the Senate but does not vote as a member except when a tie-breaking vote is needed.

Cabinet, appointed by the President with approval of the Senate; acts as advisors to the President; includes the secretaries of State, the Treasury, Defense, Interior, Agriculture, Commerce, Labor, Health and Human Services, Housing and Urban Development, Transportation, Energy, Education, Veterans Affairs, and the Attorney General.

Principal agencies under authority of the Executive Branch include the Office of Budget and Management, the National Security Council, and the Council of Economic Advisors.

LEGISLATIVE

Congress, made up of the Senate and the House of Representatives, has the power to levy taxes, borrow money, declare war, and regulate commerce between states. Bills must be approved by both houses and signed by the President to become law.

Senate, consists of 100 members (two members elected at large from each state) with each elected for a term of six years; presided over by the Vice President; special responsibility for approving or rejecting Cabinet and Supreme Court appointees and treaties made by the President.

House of Representatives, consists of 435 members (the number of representatives for each state based on population) with each elected for a term of two years; presided over by the Speaker of the House chosen by the majority vote in the House; special responsibility for initiating all bills involving taxation.

Principal agencies under authority of the Legislative Branch include the General Accounting Office, the Government Printing Office, and the Library of Congress.

JUDICIAL

Supreme Court, consists of a Chief Justice and eight Associate Justices, each appointed for life terms after nomination by the President and approval by the Senate; has original jurisdiction for all cases affecting ambassadors to the United States and public ministers (including the President), and all matters between individual states; has responsibility for hearing appeals of cases from the federal and state court system.

Other courts in the federal Judicial Branch include the U.S. Tax Court, the U.S. Court of Customs and Patent Appeals, and the twelve circuit Courts of Appeals.

GEOGRAPHICAL NAMES

THE STATES OF THE U.S.A.

State	Capital
Alabama \ˌal-ə-ˈbam-ə\	Montgomery \mənt-ˈgəm-ə-rē, mänt-\
Alaska \ə-ˈlas-kə\	Juneau \ˈjü-nō, jù-ˈnō\
Arizona \ˌar-ə-ˈzō-nə\	Phoenix \ˈfē-niks\
Arkansas \ˈär-kən-ˌsȯ\	Little Rock \ˈlit-l-ˌräk\
California \ˌkal-ə-ˈfȯr-nyə\	Sacramento \ˌsak-rə-ˈment-ō\
Colorado \ˌkäl-ə-ˈrad-ō, -ˈräd-\	Denver \ˈden-vər\
Connecticut \kə-ˈnet-i-kət\	Hartford \ˈhärt-fərd\
Delaware \ˈdel-ə-ˌwaər, -ˌweər\	Dover \ˈdō-vər\
Florida \ˈflȯr-əd-ə\	Tallahassee \ˌtal-ə-ˈhas-ē\
Georgia \ˈjȯr-jə\	Atlanta \ət-ˈlant-ə, at-\
Hawaii \hə-ˈwä-ē, -ˈwȯ-ē\	Honolulu \ˌhän-l-ˈü-ˌlü, ˌhōn-\
Idaho \ˈīd-ə-ˌhō\	Boise \ˈbȯi-sē, -zē\
Illinois \ˌil-ə-ˈnȯi\	Springfield \ˈspring-ˌfēld\
Indiana \ˌin-dē-ˈan-ə\	Indianapolis \ˌin-dē-ə-ˈnap-ə-ləs\
Iowa \ˈī-ə-wə\	Des Moines \di-ˈmȯin\
Kansas \ˈkan-zəs\	Topeka \tə-ˈpē-kə\
Kentucky \kən-ˈtək-ē\	Frankfort \ˈfrangk-fərt\
Louisiana \lù-ˌē-zē-ˈan-ə, ˌlü-ə-zē-\	Baton Rouge \ˌbat-n-ˈrüzh\
Maine \ˈmān\	Augusta \ȯ-ˈgəs-tə, ə-\
Maryland \ˈmer-ə-lənd\	Annapolis \ə-ˈnap-ə-ləs\
Massachusetts \ˌmas-ə-ˈchü-səts, -zəts\	Boston \ˈbȯ-stən\
Michigan \ˈmish-i-gən\	Lansing \ˈlan-sing\
Minnesota \ˌmin-ə-ˈsōt-ə\	Saint Paul \ˌsānt-ˈpȯl, sənt-\
Mississippi \ˌmis-ə-ˈsip-ē\	Jackson \ˈjak-sən\
Missouri \mə-ˈzùr-ē, -ˈzùr-ə\	Jefferson City \ˌjef-ər-sən-\
Montana \män-ˈtan-ə\	Helena \ˈhel-ə-nə\
Nebraska \nə-ˈbras-kə\	Lincoln \ˈling-kən\
Nevada \nə-vad-ə, -ˈväd-\	Carson City \ˌkärs-n-\
New Hampshire \-ˈhamp-shər, -ˌshiər\	Concord \ˈkäng-kərd\
New Jersey \-ˈjər-zē\	Trenton \ˈtrent-n\
New Mexico \-ˈmek-si-ˌkō\	Santa Fe \ˌsant-ə-ˈfā\
New York \-ˈyȯrk\	Albany \ˈȯl-bə-nē\
North Carolina \-ˌkar-ə-ˈlī-nə\	Raleigh \ˈrȯ-lē, ˈräl-ē\
North Dakota \-də-ˈkōt-ə\	Bismarck \ˈbiz-ˌmärk\
Ohio \ō-ˈhī-ō\	Columbus \kə-ˈləm-bəs\
Oklahoma \ō-klə-ˈhō-mə\	Oklahoma City
Oregon \ˈȯr-i-gən, ˈär-\	Salem \ˈsā-ləm\
Pennsylvania \ˌpen-səl-ˈvān-yə\	Harrisburg \ˈhar-əs-ˌbərg\
Rhode Island \rō-ˈdī-lənd\	Providence \ˈpräv-ə-dəns, -ˌdens\
South Carolina \-ˌkar-ə-ˈlī-nə\	Columbia \kə-ˈləm-bē-ə\
South Dakota \-də-ˈkōt-ə\	Pierre \ˈpiər\
Tennessee \ˌten-ə-ˈsē\	Nashville \nash-ˌvil, -vəl\
Texas \ˈtek-səs, -siz\	Austin \ˈȯ-stən\
Utah \ˈyü-tȯ, -ˌtä\	Salt Lake City
Vermont \vər-ˈmänt\	Montpelier \mänt-ˈpēl-yər, -ˈpil-\
Virginia \vər-ˈjin-yə\	Richmond \ˈrich-mənd\
Washington \ˈwȯsh-ing-tən, ˈwäsh-\	Olympia \ə-ˈlim-pē-ə\
West Virginia \-vər-ˈjin-yə\	Charleston \ˈchärl-stən\
Wisconsin \wis-ˈkän-sən\	Madison \ˈmad-ə-sən\
Wyoming \wī-ˈō-ming\	Cheyenne \shī-ˈan, -ˈen\

THE PROVINCES AND TERRITORIES OF CANADA

Province or Territory	Capital
Alberta \al-'bərt-ə\	Edmonton \'ed-mən-tən\
British Columbia \-kə-'ləm-bē-ə\	Victoria \vik-'tōr-ē-ə\
Manitoba \ˌman-ə-'tō-bə\	Winnipeg \'win-ə-ˌpeg\
New Brunswick \-'brənz-wik\	Fredericton \'fred-rik-tən\
Newfoundland \'nü-fən-lənd, 'nyü-, -ˌland\	Saint John's \sānt-'jänz, sənt-\
Northwest Territories	Yellowknife \'yel-ə-ˌnīf\
Nova Scotia \ˌnō-və-'skō-shə\	Halifax \'hal-ə-ˌfaks\
Ontario \än-'ter-ē-ō, -'tar-\	Toronto \tə-'ränt-ō\
Prince Edward Island \-ˌed-wərd-\	Charlottetown \'shär-lət-ˌtaùn\
Quebec \kwi-'bek, ki-\	Quebec
Saskatchewan \se-'skach-ə-wən, -ˌwän\	Regina \ri-'jī-nə\
Yukon Territory \'yü-ˌkän-\	Whitehorse \'hwīt-ˌhòrs, 'wīt-\

CONTINENTS AND OCEANS OF THE WORLD

Continent	Ocean
Africa \'af-ri-kə\	Arctic \'ärk-tik, 'ärt-ik\
Antarctica \ant-'ärk-ti-kə, -'är-ti-\	Atlantic \ət-'lant-ik, at-\
Asia \'ā-zhə, -shə\	Indian \'in-dē-ən\
Australia \ò-'strāl-yə\	Pacific \pə-'sif-ik\
Europe \'yùr-əp\	
North America \-ə-'mer-ə-kə\	
South America	

NATIONS OF THE WORLD

AFRICA

Nation	Capital
Algeria \al-'jir-ē-ə\	Algiers \al-'jiərz\
Angola \ang-'gō-lə, an-\	Luanda \lù-'an-də\
Benin \be-'nin, -'nēn\	Porto-Novo \ˌpōrt-ə-'nō-vō\
Botswana \bät-'swän-ə\	Gaborone \ˌgäb-ə-'rōn\
Burkina Faso \bùr-'kē-nə-'fäs-ō\	Ouagadougou \ˌwä-gä-'dü-(ˌ)gü\
Burundi \bù-'rün-dē\	Bujumbura \ˌbü-jəm-'bùr-ə\
Cameroon \ˌkam-ə-'rün\	Yaoundé \yaùn-'dā\
Cape Verde Islands \-ˌvərd-\	Praia \'prī-ə\
Central African Republic	Bangui \bäng-'gē\
Chad \'chad\	Ndjamena \ən-'jäm-ə-nə\
Comoro Islands \käm-ə-ˌrō-\	Moroni \mò-'rō-nē\
Congo \'käng-gō\	Brazzaville \'braz-ə-ˌvil\
Djibouti \jə-'büt-ē\	Djibouti
Egypt \'ē-jəpt\	Cairo \'kī-rō\
Equatorial Guinea \-'gin-ē\	Malabo \mä-'lä-bō\
Eritrea \ˌer-i-'trē-ə, -'trā-\	Asmara \az-'mär-ə, -'mar-\
Ethiopia \ˌē-thē-'ō-pē-ə\	Addis Ababa \ˌad-ə-'sab-ə-bə\
Gabon \ga-'bōn\	Libreville \ˌlē-brə-ˌvil, -ˌvēl\
Gambia \'gam-bē-ə\	Banjul \'bän-jül\
Ghana \'gän-ə, 'gan-ə\	Accra \ə-'krä\
Guinea \'gin-ē\	Conakry \'kän-ə-krē\
Guinea-Bissau \ˌgin-ē-bis-'aù\	Bissau \bis-'aù\

Ivory Coast	Abidjan \,ab-i-'jän\
Kenya \'ken-yə, 'kēn-\	Nairobi \nī-'rō-bē\
Lesotho \lə-'sō-tō\	Maseru \'maz-ə-,rü\
Liberia \lī-'bir-ē-ə\	Monrovia \mən-'rō-vē-ə\
Libya \'lib-ē-ə\	Tripoli \'trip-ə-lē\
Madagascar \,mad-ə-'gas-kər\	Antananarivo \,an-tə-,nan-ə-'rē-vō\
Malawi \mə-'lä-wē\	Lilongwe \li-'lóng-wā\
Mali \'mäl-ē, 'mal-\	Bamako \,bäm-ə-'kō\
Mauritania \,mór-ə-'tā-nē-ə\	Nouakchott \nù-'äk-,shät\
Mauritius \mò-'rish-ē-əs\	Port Louis \-'lü-əs, -'lü-ē, -lù-'ē\
Morocco \mə-'räk-ō\	Rabat \rə-'bät\
Mozambique \,mō-zəm-'bēk\	Maputo \mä-'pü-tō\
Namibia \nə-'mib-ē-ə\	Windhoek \'vint-,hùk\
Niger \'nī-jər\	Niamey \nē-'ä-ā
Nigeria \nī-'jir-ē-ə\	Abuja \ä-'bü-jä\
Rwanda \rù-,än-də\	Kigali \ki-'gäl-ē\
São Tomé and Principe \,saùt-ə-'mā-ən-'prin-sə-pə\	São Tomé
Senegal \,sen-i-'gól\	Dakar \'dak-,är\
Seychelles \sā-'shelz, -'shel\	Victoria \vik-'tōr-ē-ə\
Sierra Leone \sē-,er-ə-lē-'ōn\	Freetown \'frē-,taùn\
Somalia \sō-'mäl-ē-ə\	Mogadishu \,mäg-ə-'dish-ü, -'dēsh-\
South Africa, Republic of \-'af-ri-kə\	Pretoria \pri-'tōr-ē-ə; Cape Town \'kāp-,taùn\; Bloemfontein \'blüm-fən-,tān, -,fän-\
Sudan \sü-'dan, -'dän\	Khartoum \kär-'tüm\
Swaziland \'swäz-ē-,land\	Mbabane \,em-bə-'bän\
Tanzania \,tan-zə-'nē-ə\	Dar es Salaam \,där-,es-sə-'läm\
Togo \'tō-gō\	Lomé \lō-mā\
Tunisia \tü-'nē-zhə, tyü-\	Tunis \'tü-nəs, 'tyü-\
Uganda \yü-'gan-də, -'gän-\	Kampala \käm-'päl-ə\
Zaire \'zīr, zä-'iər\	Kinshasa \kin-'shäs-ə\
Zambia \'zam-bē-ə\	Lusaka \lü-'säk-ə\
Zimbabwe \zim-'bäb-wē\	Harare \hə-'rä-,rā\

ASIA

Nation	Capital
Afghanistan \af-'gan-ə-,stan\	Kabul \'käb-əl, kə-'bül\
Bahrain \bä-'rān\	Manama \mə-'nam-ə\
Bangladesh \,bän-glə-'desh, ,bang-\	Dacca \'dak-ə, 'däk-\
Bhutan \bü-'tan, -'tän\	Thimbu \'thim-bü\
Cambodia \kam-'bō-dē-ə\	Phnom Penh \'nóm-'pen, pə-'näm-\
China \'chī-nə\	Peking \'pē-'king\
Cyprus \'sī-prəs\	Nicosia \,nik-ə-'sē-ə\
India \'in-dē-ə\	New Delhi \-'del-ē\
Indonesia \,in-də-'nē-zhə, -shə\	Djakarta \jə-'kär-tə\
Iran \i-'ran, i-'rän, ī-'ran\	Tehran \,tā-ə-'ran, -'rän\
Iraq \i-'räk, i-rak\	Baghdad \'bag-,dad\
Israel \'iz-rē-əl\	Jerusalem \je-'rü-sə-ləm, -zə-\
Japan \jə-'pan, ji-, ja-\	Tokyo \'tō-kē-ō\
Jordan \'jòrd-n\	Amman \a-'män, -'man\
Kazakhstan \,ka-zak-'stan, ,kä-zäk-'stän\	Alma-Ata \,al-mə-ə-'tä, äl-\
Korea, North \kə-'rē-ə\	Pyongyang \pē-'óng-'yäng\
Korea, South	Seoul \'sōl\
Kuwait \kə-'wāt\	Kuwait
Kyrgyzstan \,kir-gi-'stan, -'stän\	Bishkek \bish-'kek\

Laos \'laus, 'lā-ˌäs, 'lä-ōs\	Vientiane \vyen-'tyän\
Lebanon \'leb-ə-nən, -ˌnän\	Beirut \bā-'rüt\
Malaysia \mə-'lā-zhə, -shə\	Kuala Lumpur \ˌkwäl-ə-'lùm-ˌpùr, -'ləm-\
Maldive Islands \'mòl-ˌdēv-, -ˌdīv-\	Male \'mäl-ē\
Mongolia \män-'gōl-yə, mäng-\	Ulan Bator \ˌü-ˌlän-'bä-ˌtòr\
Myanmar \'myän-ˌmär\	Yangon \ˌyän-'gōn\
Nepal \ne-'pòl, -'päl, -'pal\	Kathmandu \ˌkat-ˌman-'dü\
Oman \ō-'män, -'man\	Muscat \'məs-ˌkat, -kət\
Pakistan \ˌpak-i-'stan, ˌpäk-i-'stän\	Islamabad \is-'läm-ə-ˌbad\
Philippines \ˌfil-ə-'pēnz\	Manila \mə-'nil-ə\
Qatar \'kät-ər, 'gät-, 'gət-\	Doha \'dō-hä\
Saudia Arabia \ˌsaùd-ē-ə-'rä-bē-ə, ˌsòd-, sä-ˌüd-\	Riyadh \rē-ˌäd\
Singapore \ˌsing-ə-ˌpōr, -gə-\	Singapore
Sri Lanka \srē-'läng-kə\	Colombo \kə-'ləm-bō\
Syria \'sir-ē-ə\	Damascus \də-'mas-kəs\
Taiwan \ˌtī-'wän\	Taipei \'tī-'pā\
Tajikistan \tä-ˌjē-ki-'stan, -'stän\	Dushanbe \dü-'sham-bə, -'shäm-\
Thailand \'tī-ˌland, -lənd\	Bangkok \'bang-ˌkäk\
Turkey \'tər-kē\	Ankara \'ang-kə-rə\
Turkmenistan \tərk-ˌmen-i-'stan, -'stän\	Ashkhabad \'ask-kə-ˌbad, -ˌbäd\
United Arab Emirates \-i-'mir-əts, -i-'miər-ˌāts\	Abu Dhabi \ˌäb-ˌü-'däb-ē\
Uzbekistan \ùz-ˌbek-i-'stan, -'stän\	Tashkent \tash-'kent, 'täsh-\
Vietnam \vē-'et-'näm, ˌvē-ət-, -'nam\	Hanoi \ha-'nòi, hə-\
Yemen \'yem-ən\	San'a \'san-ˌä, san-'ä\

EUROPE

Nation   **Capital**

Albania \al-'bā-nē-ə\	Tirane \ti-'rän-ə\
Andorra \an-'dòr-ə\	Andorra la Vella \-lä-'vel-ə\
Armenia \är-'mē-nē-ə\	Yerevan \ˌyer-ə-'vän\
Austria \'òs-trē-ə\	Vienna \vē-'en-ə\
Azerbaijan \ˌaz-ər-ˌbī-'jän\	Baku \bä-'kü\
Belarus \ˌbē-lə-'rüs, byel-ə-\	Minsk \'minsk\
Belgium \'bel-jəm\	Brussels \'brəs-əlz\
Bosnia and Herzegovina \'bäz-nē-ə-ənd-ˌhert-sə-gō-'vē-nə, -'gō-vin-ə\	Sarajevo \ˌsar-ə-'yā-vō\
Bulgaria \ˌbəl-'gar-ē-ə, -'ger-\	Sofia \'sō-fē-ə, 'sò-\
Croatia \krō-'ā-shə\	Zagreb \'zä-ˌgreb\
Czech Republic \'chek-\	Prague \'präg\
Denmark \'den-ˌmärk\	Copenhagen \ˌkō-pən-'hā-gən, -'hä-\
Estonia \es-'tō-nē-ə\	Tallinn \'tal-ən, 'täl-\
Finland \'fin-lənd\	Helsinki \'hel-ˌsing-kē\
France \'frans\	Paris \'par-əs\
Georgia, Republic of \-'jòr-jə\	Tbilisi \tə-'blē-sē\
Germany \'jər-mə-nē\	Berlin \bər-'lin\
Greece \'grēs\	Athens \'ath-ənz\
Hungary \'həng-gə-rē\	Budapest \'büd-ə-ˌpest\
Iceland \'īs-lənd, -ˌland\	Reykjavik \'rā-kyə-ˌvik, -ˌvēk\
Ireland \'īr-lənd\	Dublin \'dəb-lən\
Italy \'it-l-ē\	Rome \'rōm\
Latvia \'lat-vē-ə\	Riga \'rē-gə\
Liechtenstein \'lik-tən-ˌstīn\	Vaduz \vä-'düts\
Lithuania \ˌlith-ə-'wā-nē-ə\	Vilnius \'vil-nē-əs\

Luxembourg \'lək-səm-,bərg\	Luxembourg
Macedonia, Former Yugoslav Republic of \-,mas-ə-'dō-nē-ə\	Skopje \'skóp-,yä, -yə\
Malta \'mól-tə\	Valletta \və-'let-ə\
Moldova \mól-'dō-və\	Kishinev \'kish-i-,nef\
Monaco \'män-ə-,kō\	Monaco
Netherlands \'neth-ər-ləndz\	Amsterdam \'am-stər-,dam\
	The Hague \thə-'häg\
Norway \'nór-,wä\	Oslo \'äz-lō, 'äs-\
Poland \'pō-lənd\	Warsaw \'wór-,só\
Portugal \'pór-chi-gəl\	Lisbon \'liz-bən\
Romania \rù-'mä-nē-ə, rō-\	Bucharest \'bü-kə-,rest\
Russia \'rəsh-ə\	Moscow \'mäs-,kō, -,kaú\
San Marino \,san-mə-'rē-nō\	San Marino
Slovakia \slō-'väk-ē-ə\	Bratislava \,brät-ə-'släv-ə\
Slovenia \slō-'vē-nē-ə\	Ljubljana \lē-,ü-blē-'än-ə\
Spain \'spän\	Madrid \mə-'drid\
Sweden \'swēd-n\	Stockholm \'stäk-,hōm, -,hōlm\
Switzerland \'swit-sər-lənd\	Bern \'bərn, 'bern\
Ukraine \yü-'krän, -'krīn\	Kiev \'kē-,ef, -,ev\
United Kingdom	London \'lən-dən\
Vatican City \'vat-i-kən-\	
Yugoslavia \,yü-gō-'slä-vē-ə\	Belgrade \'bel-,gräd, -,gräd\

NORTH AMERICA

Nation	Capital
Antigua and Barbuda \an-'tē-gə-ənd-bär-'bü-də\	Saint John's \sänt-'jänz, sənt-\
Bahamas \bə-'häm-əz\	Nassau \'nas-,ó\
Barbados \bär-'bäd-əs, -ōz\	Bridgetown \'brij-,taún\
Bermuda \bər-'myüd-ə\	Hamilton \'ham-əl-tən\
Canada \'kan-ə-də\	Ottawa \'ät-ə-,wä, -wə\
Costa Rica \,käs-tə-'rē-kə, ,kòs-\	San Jose \,san-ə-'zä, -hō-'zä\
Cuba \'kyü-bə\	Havana \hə-'van-ə\
Dominica \däm-ə-'nē-kə, də-'min-ə-kə\	Roseau \rō-'zō\
Dominican Republic \də-,min-i-kən-\	Santo Domingo \,sant-ə-də-'ming-gō\
El Salvador \el-'sal-və-,dor\	San Salvador \san-'sal-və-,dór\
Grenada \grə-'näd-ə\	Saint George's \sänt-'jór-jəz, sənt-\
Guatemala \,gwät-ə-'mäl-ə\	Guatemala City
Haiti \'hät-ē\	Port-au-Prince \,pōrt-ō-'prins, -'prans\
Honduras \hän-'dùr-əs, -'dyùr-\	Tegucigalpa \tə-,gü-sə-'gal-pə\
Jamaica \jə-'mā-kə\	Kingston \'king-stən\
Mexico \'mek-si-,kō\	Mexico City
Nicaragua \,nik-ə-'räg-wə\	Managua \mə-'näg-wə\
Panama \'pan-ə-,mä, -,mó\	Panama City
Saint Kitts-Nevis \sänt-'kits-'nē-vəs, sənt-\	Basseterre \bas-'ter, bäs-\
Saint Lucia \sänt-'lü-shə, sənt-\	Castries \'kas-,trēz, -,trēs\
Saint Vincent and the Grenadines \sänt-'vin-sənt-ənd- ulineə-,grən-ə-'dēnz, sənt-	Kingstown \'kingz-,taún\
Trinidad and Tobago \'trin-ə-,dad-n-tə-'bā-gō\	Port of Spain \-'spän\
United States of America \-ə-'mer-ə-kə\	Washington \'wósh-ing-tən, 'wäsh-\

OCEANIA \ˌō-shē-ˈan-ē-ə, -ˈän-\
(group of island nations in the Pacific)

Nation	Capital
Australia \ȯ-ˈstrāl-yə\	Canberra \ˈkan-bə-rə, -ˌber-ə\
Fiji \ˈfē-ˌjē\	Suva \ˈsü-və\
Kiribati \ˈkir-ə-ˌbas\	Tarawa \tə-ˈrä-wə\
Marshall Islands \ˈmär-shəl-\	Majuro \mə-ˈjur-ō\
Nauru \nä-ˈü-rü\	
New Zealand \-ˈzē-lənd\	Wellington \ˈwel-ing-tən\
Papua New Guinea \ˈpap-yə-wə-nü-ˈgin-ē, ˈpäp-ə-wə-, -nyü-\	Port Moresby \-ˈmȯrz-bē\
Solomon Islands \ˈsäl-ə-mən-\	Honiara \ˌhō-nē-ˈär-ə\
Tonga \ˈtäng-gə\	Nuku'alofa \ˌnü-kü-ä-ˈlō-fə\
Tuvalu \tü-ˈväl-ü\	Funafuti \ˌfü-nə-ˈfüt-ē\
Vanuatu \ˌvan-wä-ˈtü\	Vila \ˈvē-lə\
Western Samoa \-sə-ˈmō-ə\	Apia \ə-ˈpē-ə\

SOUTH AMERICA

Nation	Capital
Argentina \ˌär-jən-ˈtē-nə\	Buenos Aires \ˌbwā-nə-ˌsaər-ēz, -ˈseər-, -ˈsīr-\
Bolivia \bə-ˈliv-ē-ə\	La Paz \lə-ˈpaz, -ˈpäz; Sucre \ˈsü-krā\
Brazil \brə-ˈzil\	Brasília \brə-ˈzil-yə\
Chile \ˈchil-ē\	Santiago \ˌsant-ē-ˈäg-ō, ˌsänt-\
Colombia \kə-ləm-bē-ə\	Bogotá \ˌbō-gə-ˈtȯ, -ˈtä\
Ecuador \ˈek-wə-ˌdȯr\	Quito \ˈkē-tō\
Guyana \gī-ˈan-ə\	Georgetown \ˈjȯrj-ˌtaůn\
Paraguay \ˈpar-ə-ˌgwī, -ˌgwä\	Asunción \ə-ˌsün-sē-ˈōn\
Peru \pə-ˈrü\	Lima \ˈlē-mə\
Suriname \ˈsůr-ə-ˌnäm-ə\	Paramaribo \ˌpar-ə-ˈmar-ə-ˌbō\
Uruguay \ˈyůr-ə-ˌgwī, -ˌgwä\	Montevideo \ˌmänt-ə-və-ˈdā-ō, -ˈvid-ē-ō\
Venezuela \ˌven-ə-zə-ˈwā-lə\	Caracas \kə-ˈrak-əs, -ˈräk-\

WEIGHTS AND MEASURES

Length

UNIT (abbreviation)	EQUIVALENTS (same system)	METRIC EQUIVALENT
mile (mi)	5280 feet, 1760 yards	1.609 kilometers
rod (rd)	5.50 yards, 16.5 feet	5.029 meters
yard (yd)	3 feet, 36 inches	0.9144 meter
foot (ft or ')	12 inches, 1/3 yard	30.48 centimeters
inch (in or ")		2.54 centimeters

Area

UNIT (abbreviation)	EQUIVALENTS (same system)	METRIC EQUIVALENT
square mile (sq mi, mi^2)	640 acres	2.590 square kilometers
acre	4840 square yards, 43,560 square feet	4047 square meters
square rod (sq rd, rd^2)	30.25 square yards	25.293 square meters
square yard (sq yd, yd^2)	1296 square inches, 9 square feet	0.836 square meter
square foot (sq ft, ft^2)	144 square inches	0.093 square meter
square inch (sq in, in^2)		6.452 square centimeters

Volume

UNIT (abbreviation)	EQUIVALENTS (same system)	METRIC EQUIVALENT
cubic yard (cu yd, yd^3)	27 cubic feet, 46,656 cubic inches	0.765 cubic meter
cubic foot (cu ft, ft^3)	1728 cubic inches	0.028 cubic meter
cubic inch (cu in, in^3)		16.387 cubic centimeters

Weight

UNIT (abbreviation)	EQUIVALENTS (same system)	METRIC EQUIVALENT
avoirdupois		
ton		
short ton	20 short cwt, 2000 pounds	0.907 metric ton
long ton	20 long cwt, 2240 pounds	1.016 metric tons
hundredweight (cwt)		
short cwt	100 pounds	45.359 kilograms
long cwt	112 pounds	50.802 kilograms
pound (lb, #)	16 ounces, 7000 grains	0.454 kilogram
ounce (oz)	16 drams, 437.5 grains	28.350 grams
dram (dr)	27.344 grains	1.772 grams
grain (gr)		0.0648 gram
troy		
pound (lb t)	12 ounces, 5760 grains	0.373 kilogram
ounce (oz t)	20 pennyweight, 480 grains	31.103 grams
pennyweight (dwt, pwt)	24 grains, 1/20 ounce	1.555 grams
grain (gr)		0.0648 gram
apothecaries'		
pound (lb ap)	12 ounces, 5760 grains	0.373 kilogram
ounce (oz ap)	8 drams, 480 grains	31.103 grams
dram (dr ap)	3 scruples, 60 grains	3.888 grams
scruple (s ap)	20 grains, 1/3 dram	1.296 grams
grain (gr)		0.0648 gram

Capacity

UNIT (abbreviation)	EQUIVALENTS (same system)	METRIC EQUIVALENT
U. S. liquid measure		
gallon (gal)	4 quarts	3.785 liters
quart (qt)	2 pints	0.946 liter
pint (pt)	4 gills	0.473 liter
gill (gi)	4 fluidounces	118.294 milliliters
fluidounce (fl oz)	8 fluidrams	29.573 milliliters
fluidram (fl dr)	60 minims	3.697 milliliters
minim (min)	1/60 fluidram	0.061 milliliter
U. S. dry measure		
bushel (bu)	4 pecks	35.239 liters
peck (pk)	8 quarts	8.810 liters
quart (qt)	2 pints	1.101 liters
pint (pt)	1/2 quart	0.551 liter

METRIC SYSTEM

Length

UNIT (abbreviation)	METERS	U.S. EQUIVALENT
kilometer (km)	1,000	0.62 mile
hectometer (hm)	100	109.36 yards
dekameter (dam)	10	32.81 feet
meter (m)	1	39.37 inches
decimeter (dm)	1/10	3.94 inches
centimeter (cm)	1/100	0.39 inch
millimeter (mm)	1/1000	0.039 inch

Area

UNIT (abbreviation)	SQUARE METERS	U.S. EQUIVALENT
square kilometer (sq km, km²)	1,000,000	0.3861 square mile
hectare (ha)	10,000	2.47 acres
are (a)	100	119.60 square yards
square centimeter (sq cm, cm²)	1/10000	0.155 square inch

Volume

UNIT (abbreviation)	CUBIC CENTIMETERS	U.S. EQUIVALENT
cubic meter (m³)	1,000,000	1.307 cubic yards
cubic decimeter (dm³)	1,000	61.023 cubic inches
cubic centimeter (cm³, cc)	1	0.061 cubic inch

Capacity

UNIT (abbreviation)	LITERS	U.S. EQUIVALENT	
		dry	liquid
kiloliter (kl)	1,000		
hectoliter (hl)	100	2.84 bushels	
dekaliter (dal)	10	1.14 pecks	2.64 gallons
liter (l)	1	0.908 quart	1.057 quarts
deciliter (dl)	1/10	0.18 pint	0.21 pint
centiliter (cl)	1/100	0.338 fluidounce	
milliliter (ml)	1/1000		0.27 fluidram

Mass and Weight

UNIT (abbreviation)	GRAMS	U.S. EQUIVALENT
metric ton (t)	1,000,000	1.102 short tons
kilogram (kg)	1,000	2.2046 pounds
hectogram (hg)	100	3.527 ounces
dekagram (dag)	10	0.353 ounce
gram (g)	1	0.035 ounce
decigram (dg)	1/10	1.543 grains
centigram (cg)	1/100	0.154 grain
milligram (mg)	1/1000	0.015 grain

PLANETS OF THE SOLAR SYSTEM

SYMBOL	NAME	MEAN DISTANCE FROM THE SUN (million miles)	PERIOD OF REVOLUTION	EQUATORIAL DIAMETER (in miles)
☿	Mercury	36.0	87.97 days	3,032
♀	Venus	67.2	224.70 days	7,523
☉	Earth	92.9	365.26 days	7,928
♂	Mars	141.5	686.98 days	4,218
♃	Jupiter	483.4	11.86 years	88,900
♄	Saturn	884.6	29.46 years	74,900
♅	Uranus	1783.8	84.01 years	31,800
♆	Neptune	2793.9	164.79 years	30,800
♇	Pluto	3690.5	247.69 years	1,400

©1995, Encyclopædia Britannica, Inc.